. . .

# THE NATIVE
# NORTH AMERICAN
# ALMANAC

SECOND EDITION

• • •

# THE NATIVE
# NORTH AMERICAN
# ALMANAC

**SECOND EDITION**

A Reference

Work on Native

North Americans

in the United

States and

Canada

**Duane Champagne,**
editor

**GALE GROUP**

★ ™

**THOMSON LEARNING**

Detroit • New York • San Diego • San Francisco
Boston • New Haven, Conn. • Waterville, Maine
London • Munich

Rebecca Parks, *Editor*
Shelly Dickey, *Managing Editor*
William Harmer, *Contributing Editor*
Laura L. Brandau, *Associate Editor*
Brian J. Koski, *Associate Editor*
Jeffrey Wilson, *Associate Editor*
Mark Springer, *Technical Training Specialist*

Mary Beth Trimper, *Composition and Electronic Prepress Manager*
Evi Seoud, *Assistant Composition and Electronic Prepress Manager*

Kenn Zorn, *Product Design Manager*
Jennifer Wahi, *Art Director*
Barbara Yarrow, *Manager, Imaging and Multimedia Content*
Randy Bassett, *Imaging Supervisor*
Pamela A. Reed, *Imaging Coordinator*
Leitha Etheridge-Sims, Mary K. Grimes, David G. Oblender, *Image Catalogers*

*The Native North American Almanac/* edited by Duane Champagne
Cover artwork: *The Veteran,* courtesy of Richard Glazer-Danay. *White Hopi Clown Child,*
courtesy of Owen Seumptewa.

ISBN 0–7876-1655–9
ISSN 1070–8014

Printed in the United States of America
10 9 8 7 6 5 4 3 2 1

## Board of Advisors

John Aubrey, *Librarian, The Newberry Library, Chicago, Illinois*
Cheryl Metoyer-Duran, *Librarian, Mashantucket Pequot Research Center and Museum, Mashantucket, Connecticut*
G. Edward Evans, *University Librarian, Loyola Marymount University, Los Angeles*
Hanay Geiogamah, *Professor of Theater, University of California, Los Angeles*
Carole Goldberg-Ambrose, *Professor of Law, University of California, Los Angeles*

## Editorial Team at the American Indian Studies Center, University of California, Los Angeles

Editor: Duane Champagne, *Director, American Indian Studies Center, and Professor of Sociology, University of California, Los Angeles*
Assistant Editors: Amy Ware, Alexandra Harris, Tim Petete, Elton Naswood, Jacob Goff, Demelza Champagne, and Garrett Saracho.
Photographic Editor: Roselle Kipp
Bibliographic Editor: Ken Wade
Graphic Artist: James Perkins

## Biographers

Angela Aleiss, *American Indian Studies Center, University of California, Los Angeles*
Paola Carini, *English Department, University of California, Los Angeles*
Duane Champagne, *American Indian Studies Center, University of California, Los Angeles*
James Coulon, *Coulon, Ink., San Diego, California*
Troy Johnson, *American Indian Studies Department, California State University, Long Beach*
Richard Keeling, *Ethnomusicology Department, University of California, Los Angeles*
Patrick Macklem, *Faculty of Law, University of Toronto, Toronto, Ontario, Canada*
Tim Petete, *American Indian Studies Center, University of California, Los Angeles*
Amy Kathleen Simmons, *American Indian Studies Center, University of California, Los Angeles*
Amy Ware, *American Indian Studies Center, University of California, Los Angeles*

## Contributing Authors

Frances Abele, *School of Public Administration, Carleton University, Ottawa, Ontario, Canada*
Gerald Alfred, *School of Public Administration, The University of Victoria, Victoria, Canada*
Karen Baird-Olson, *Department of Sociology and Anthropology, University of Central Florida, Orlando, Florida*
Russel Lawrence Barsh, *Native Studies, University of Lethbridge, Lethbridge, Alberta, Canada*
Janet Berlo, *Department of Art History, University of Rochester, New York*
Peggy Berryhill, *Native Media Resource Center (NMRC), Bodega Bay, California*
Ted Binnema, *History Department, The University of Northern British Columbia, Prince George, British Columbia, Canada*
Nancy Bonvillain, *Simon's Rock College of Bard, Great Barrington, Massachusetts*
Daniel Boxberger, *Department of Anthropology, Western Washington University, Bellingham, Washington*
Simon Brascoupe, *Department of Sociology and Anthropology, Carleton University, Ottawa, Ontario, Canada*
William Bright, *Department of Linguistics, University of Colorado, Boulder, Colorado*
Tara Browner, *Department of Ethnomusicology, University of California, Los Angeles, California*
Gregory Cajete, *Center for Research and Cultural Exchange, University of New Mexico, Albuquerque, New Mexico*
Edward Castillo, *Native American Studies, Sonoma State University, Rohnert Park, California*
Katherine Beatty Chiste, *Department of Social Sciences, University of Lethbridge, Lethbridge, Alberta, Canada*

Anthony Clark, *Department of Sociology, University of Kansas, Lawrence, Kansas*

Richmond Clow, *Native American Studies, University of Montana, Missoula, Montana*

Heather Coleman, *Faculty of Social Work, University of Calgary, Calgary, Alberta, Canada*

David de Jong, *Prescott High School, Arizona*

Henry Dobyns, *Independent Consultant, Tucson, Arizona*

Leroy Eid, *Department of History, University of Dayton, Dayton, Ohio*

Jo-Anne Fiske, *Anthropology Department, The University of Northern British Columbia, Prince George, British Columbia, Canada*

Donald Fixico, *Department of History, The University of Kansas, Lawrence, Kansas*

Hanay Geiogamah, *Theater Department, University of California, Los Angeles, California*

Douglas George-Kanentiio, *Journalist, Oneida Iroquois Territory, Oneida, New York*

Ian Getty, *Research Director, Stoney Tribe, Nakota Institute, Calgary, Alberta, Canada*

Carole Goldberg-Ambrose, *School of Law, University of California, Los Angeles, California*

Charlotte Heth, *Department of Ethnomusicology, University of California, Los Angeles, California*

Ann Marie Hodes, *Health Services Center, University of Alberta, Edmonton, Alberta, Canada*

Felicia Schanche Hodge, *University of California, San Francisco, and University of Minnesota, Minneapolis*

Cornelius Jaenen, *Department of History, University of Ottawa, Ottawa, Ontario, Canada*

Jennie Joe, *Native American Research and Training Center, University of Arizona, Tucson, Arizona*

Clara Sue Kidwell, *Native American Studies, University of Oklahoma, Norman, Oklahoma*

Rita Ledesma, *Department of Social Welfare, California State University, Los Angeles*

John D. Loftin, *Loftin & Loftin, Hillsborough, North Carolina*

Carol Lujan, *American Indian Studies Program, Arizona State University, Tempe, Arizona*

John A. (Ian) Mackenzie, *Centre for Indian Scholars, Terrace, British Columbia, Canada*

David C. Mass, *Department of Political Science, University of Alaska, Anchorage, Alaska*

Donald McCaskill, *Department of Native Studies, Trent University, Peterborough, Ontario, Canada*

Alan McMillan, *Department of Archaeology, Simon Fraser College, Burnaby, British Columbia, Canada*

Dorothy Lonewolf Miller, *Native American Studies, University of California, Berkeley, California*

C. Patrick Morris, *Department of Native American Studies, Salish Kootenai College, Pablo, Montana*

Ken Morrison, *Religious Studies, Arizona State University, Tempe, Arizona*

Bradford Morse, *Faculty of Law, University of Ottawa, Ottawa, Ontario, Canada*

Joane Nagel, *Department of Sociology, University of Kansas, Lawrence, Kansas*

Elton Naswood, *American Indian Studies Center, University of California, Los Angeles*

David Newhouse, *Department of Native Studies, Trent University, Peterborough, Ontario, Canada*

Brigid O'Donnell, *Department of Ecology and Evolutionary Biology, University of Connecticut*

James H. O'Donnell III, *Department of History, Marietta College, Marietta, Ohio*

Michael O'Donnell, *Director of Distance Education, Salish Kootenai Community College, Pablo, Montana*

Darren Ranco, *Department of Ethnic Studies, University of California, Berkeley*

Audry Jane Roy, *School of Public Administration, The University of Victoria, Victoria, Canada*

Kathryn W. Shanley, *Department of English, Cornell University, Ithaca, New York*

Leanne Simpson, *Department of Native Studies, University of Manitoba, Winnipeg, Manitoba, Canada*

Gerald Slater, *Vice President of Academic Affairs, Salish Kootenai Community College, Pablo, Montana*

Dean Smith, *College of Business Administration, Northern Arizona University, Flagstaff, Arizona*

C. Matthew Snipp, *Department of Sociology, Stanford University, Stanford, California*

Rennard Strickland, *School of Law, University of Oklahoma, Norman, Oklahoma*

Paul Stuart, *School of Social Welfare, University of Alabama, Tuscaloosa, Alabama*

Imre Sutton, *Professor Emeritus, Department of Geography, California State University, Fullerton, California*

Karen Swisher, *College of Education, Arizona State University, Tempe, Arizona*

Steve Talbot, *Department of Sociology and Anthropology, San Joaquin College, Stockton, California*

Wesley Thomas, *Department of Anthropology, Idaho State University, Pocatello, Idaho*

Loretta Todd, *Film Maker, Vancouver, British Columbia, Canada*

Clifford Trafzer, *Department of Ethnic Studies, University of California, Riverside, California*

Ronald Trosper, *Department of Forestry, Northern Arizona University, Flagstaff, Arizona*

Daniel Usner, *History Department, Cornell University, Ithaca, New York*

Joan Vastokas, *Department of Anthropology, Trent University, Peterborough, Ontario, Canada*

Tarajean Yazzie, *School of Education, Harvard University, Cambridge, Massachusetts*

Brother,

When you first came to this island

you were as children, in need of food and shelter,

and we, a great and mighty nation.

But we took you by the hand

and we planted you and watered you

and you grew to be a great oak,

we a mere sapling in comparison.

Now we are the children

(in need of food and shelter).

*An opening speech often used by Northeastern Indian leaders at conferences with Europeans during the early colonial period.*

## Highlights

Persons interested in a comprehensive reference providing information on all aspects of the Native American and Canadian experience can turn to one accurate source: *The Native North American Almanac*. The first seventeen chapters are composed of signed essays, annotated directory information, and documentary excerpts; the final chapter presents more than 500 concise biographies of prominent Native North Americans. The Native North American Almanac covers a broad scope of topics, including:

- History and historical landmarks
- Health
- Law and legislation
- Major culture areas
- Activism
- Environment
- Urbanization and non-reservation populations
- Administration
- Education
- Economy
- Languages
- Demography
- Religion
- Arts
- Literature
- Media
- Women
- Gender Relations

## Arrangement Allows for Quick Information Access

*The Native North American Almanac* provides a wealth of information, and its logical format makes it easy to use. The chapters contain subject-specific bibliographies and are enlivened by close to 350 photographs, maps, and charts. Other value-added features include:

- Contents section details each chapter's coverage, including directories and bibliographies
- Alphabetical and geographical lists of tribes
- Multimedia bibliography of sources for further reading and research
- Glossary of Native terms
- Comprehensive keyword index listing tribe and band names (with alternate spellings), personal names, important events, and geographic locations
- Detailed occupational index giving insight into Natives who have excelled in their field of endeavor

# Contents

# Acknowledgments

The undertaking of the update and revision of this volume was a far greater task than originally anticipated, and a great many people contributed to its compilation, writing, editing, and production. I am greatly honored to express thanks to my numerous colleagues who contributed their updated and revised manuscripts, and provided the inspiration for a reference book about contemporary Native North American peoples. The contributors were enthusiastic about updating the Almanac; most thought that over the past seven years many events and changes occurred in Indian Country that required new interpretations and additional material. The book benefits greatly from these many contributors who bring their expertise and understanding into one volume. We all share the same vision and the understanding of having put forth our best efforts for a worthy cause.

Great credit and thanks are due to people at the Gale Group for their vision and support. Chris Nasso deserves special recognition for developing the idea and groundwork for the volume; our readers and the Native peoples are indebted to her for her sympathetic foresight. The Gale editors made workable a long and difficult project. Rebecca Parks deserves special and heartfelt recognition for taking on a difficult and complicated project. With her patience, guidance, and perseverance, the second edition is made possible.

Special mention must also be made of our advisory board. I fondly remember the two days in early summer 1991 when we hammered out the outline and basic entry assignments for the entire volume. These sessions are a testament that hard work and engaging company need not be separate events. G. Edward Evans, in particular, provided many insights and a guiding hand, and for this we are grateful. Since the first edition, board member Vee Salabiye passed away, and we miss her insight, knowledge and understanding. She made many comments and contributions that shaped the philosophy and direction of the Almanac.

Many of my friends and associates provided valuable contributions, and I take this opportunity to give them thanks. Roselle Kipp provided greatly needed help in securing photographs and producing digital images; Kenneth Wade worked diligently on the bibliographies, glossaries and some directories; Amy Ware worked cheerfully and tirelessly throughout the entire project in copyediting the manuscript, and we all give thanks for her care, understanding, and concern in creating a quality product. Many students had an opportunity to contribute on parts of the Almanac, and I thank them for their help and effort. In particular I wish to thank Jacob Goff, Demelza Champagne, and Alexandra Harris for their hard work on difficult tasks. Too numerous to thank are the people who helped collect the many illustrations and photographs, but special mention must be made to Ilka Hartmann, Sara Wiles, Carole Lujan, Mary Wentz, Sara Loe, and Mike McClure who all generously made available their artistic and informative photographs and images. Special thanks to Gurrett Saracho whose help was indispensable for bringing the entire project to a happy conclusion.

*Duane Champagne*
*March 2001*

# *Preface*

The *Native North American Almanac* (*NNAA*) provides historical and contemporary information about the Native peoples of North America. Too often reference books about Native North Americans stop providing information after the 1890s. Consequently, many people cannot find accurate, accessible, and systematic information about contemporary Native culture, art, communities, life, and legal relations. Furthermore, many reference works have given little attention to Canadian Natives, even though Canadian Natives often play a more central role in Canadian constitutional issues and politics than do Native peoples in the United States. In this volume, special efforts were made to gather together experts on many aspects of U.S. and Canadian Native life, as well as to include as many U.S. and Canadian Native authors as possible. This effort paid off greatly, since these authors provided many points of view and information that could only come from individuals continually engaged in Native life and issues. In this way, the book represents an overview of the history of Native peoples in North America and provides new and probing perspectives not found in comparable reference works.

At the beginning of the twentieth century, many people believed that Native Americans would disappear and assimilate into Canadian or U.S. society. The experience of the twentieth century, however, has shown that Native communities have survived, and are strongly entrenched in their traditions and institutions. At the beginning of the twenty-first century Native Nations continue to struggle to protect their land, political rights, religions, and cultures. The *NNAA* informs the reader about the struggle of contemporary Native North Americans and gives considerable insight into their present conditions regarding health, education, economy, politics, art, and other areas. This work is devoted to the student who has had little background or knowledge about Native Americans, and we hope it will inspire, inform, and educate students and the general public about Native peoples. If this book creates greater understanding and appreciation between the peoples of North America and peoples around the world it will have served one of its primary purposes.

## Terminology: Is Indian the Right Name?

Throughout the *NNAA*, a variety of terms are used interchangeably for Native North Americans, such as Indian, American Indian, Native, aborigine, First Nations, First Peoples, and others. The Native peoples of the Americas have the unfortunate distinction of having been given the wrong name, Indians, since the Native people of the Americas were not from the country or civilization of India, the subcontinent in southern Asia. The search for a single name, however, has not been entirely successful. In the United States, Native American has been used but has recently fallen out of favor, and American Indian is now preferred. Nevertheless, American Indian still retains the unfortunate Indian terminology and consequently is not an entirely satisfactory term. Native American also has serious difficulties since anyone born in North or South America may claim to be a "native American."

The Canadians have wrestled with this question of names, and many Native Canadians reject the appellation of Indian. Métis (mixed bloods) and Inuit (often called Eskimos) in Canada will not answer to the name Indian. Similarly, in Alaska the Inuit, Yupik, and Aleut peoples consider themselves distinct from Indian peoples, and do not wish to be called Indian. The Canadians have developed a range of terms such as Native, aboriginal, First Nations, and First Peoples, which in many ways more accurately describes the Native peoples. Throughout the text, we have tried to respect the Canadian preference for avoiding the inclusive term "Indian" for denoting all Native peoples. Many Native people in Canada are called "Indian," and it is appropriate for most Native peoples below the subarctic region, except for the Métis, who consider themselves a distinct ethnic group from Native as well as non-Native Canadians.

The ultimate problem in these terminological difficulties is that Native peoples in North America do not form a single ethnic group but are better understood as thousands of distinct communities and cultures. Many Native peoples have distinct languages, religious beliefs, ceremonies, and sociopolitical organization. Characterizing this diverse array of cultures and peoples with one inclusive name presents serious difficulties from the start, and no one word can characterize such diversity. The inclusive word "Indian" must be seen as something akin to "European," where there is clear recognition of peoples who occupy a contiguous geographic area but have a wide variety of language, culture, and sociopolitical organization. The same applies in Native North America: the term "Indian" or other generic terms can denote only the collection of people who occupied the North American continent, but it says little about the diversity and independence of the cultures.

The best way to characterize Native North Americans is by recognizing their specific tribal or community identities, such as Blackfeet, Cherokee, or Cree. Such identifications more accurately capture the unique and varied tribal and cultural distinctions found among Native North American peoples.

Every effort has been made to keep Native tribal and community identities distinct, but when broader tribal designations were appropriate we allowed the many authors to use their own terms. We do not wish to offend anyone, and we offer our apologies to anyone who is offended, but for ease of presentation and because our many authors used a variety of terms, we have decided not to favor one particular term but rather hoped to see that the various terms were used appropriately in all situations.

## The Native North American Peoples

Native North Americans occupied their continent for at least the last ten thousand years, if not for a considerably longer period. Unlike all other groups that live in North America, Natives do not have a recent immigrant experience but rather live in cultures that predate the present institutions and societies of Canada and the United States. Native peoples have legal, cultural, and political claims to priority over Canada and the United States for use of the land, for rights to self-government, and for the practice of their cultures and religions. Over the past five hundred years Native people have experienced considerable change and dislocation, yet most Native communities have survived and will continue as communities into the next centuries. Native North Americans live in thousands of small communities and exhibit considerable differences in culture, language, religion, and social organization. Perhaps the strongest unifying force among these diverse cultures and communities is the general insistence by U.S. and Canadian societies and governments to treat Natives as a homogeneous ethnic group. Nothing could be further from the truth, but since they are treated as homogeneous, there are many situations in which Natives can act collectively to pursue their economic and political goals. Consequently, Natives have operated in mass North American society in increasingly well-organized national organizations and interest groups. These trends will most likely continue and become a major force in contemporary Native affairs.

## Scope and Content

*The Native North American Almanac* covers the range of Native history and culture in the United States and Canada, providing a chronology, demographic and distribution descriptions and histories, and discussions of religion and religious change, art, music, theater, film, traditional arts, history, economy, administration, and law and legal issues.

Eighteen chapters were written by over sixty scholarly contributors while students worked to collect information for wide-ranging directories of Native North American communities, major Native cultural events and major writings, films, and videos produced by Native peoples. The range of topics provides an overview and introduction to the history and present-day life of Native North Americans. Each chapter has an ample bibliography for those users interested in further reading or who wish to conduct more specialized studies. Chapter 18 comprises biographical essays on significant Native North Americans, about one-third of whom are historical figures.

An extensive glossary provides definitions of words and concepts that are commonly used in Native affairs and history.

The index provides a quick means to find information on special topics that are discussed throughout the *Almanac.*

Close to four hundred illustrations—including photographs, line drawings, tables, maps, and figures—complement the text. Every effort was made to use Native photographers and to present views of everyday Native life and scenes.

## Suggestions Are Welcome

A work as large as *The Native North American Almanac* may contain oversights and errors, and we appreciate any suggestions for correction of factual material or additions that will make future editions more accurate, sympathetic, and useful. Please send comments to:

Editor
*The Native North American Almanac*
The Gale Group
27500 Drake Rd.
Farmington Hills, MI 48331
Toll Free: (800) 347–4253

*Duane Champagne*
*March 2001*

Duane Champagne has been teaching at the University of California, Los Angeles, since 1984. In 1986, he became editor of the *American Indian Culture and Research Journal* and went on to be named professor in 1997.

Dr. Champagne received a doctoral degree in sociology from Harvard University in 1982, and accepted a postdoctoral award from the Rockefeller Foundation in 1982–83. During this time, he completed fieldwork trips to the Tlingit of southeast Alaska and to the Northern Cheyenne in Montana.

Most of Dr. Champagne's writings focus on issues of social, cultural, and political change in American Indian societies as they adapted to European political, cultural, and economic incorporation. He has published in both the sociology and American Indian studies fields, including his two books *American Indian Societies: Strategies and Conditions of Political and Cultural Survival* (1989) and *Social Order and Political Change: Constitutional Governments Among the Cherokee, the Choctaw, the Chickasaw, and the Creek* (1992). He is an active writer and has produced over sixty papers and book publications.

Dr. Champagne is also the director of the UCLA American Indian Studies Center, which carries out research, conducts a master's degree program in American Indian studies, and publishes books for both academic and Indian communities.

**California–Northern and Central Federally Recognized Tribes (Not shown on map)**

| | | |
|---|---|---|
| Elem Pomo of Sulpher Bank Rancheria | Lytton Rancheria | Santa Rosa Rancheria |
| Elk Valley Rancheria | Manchester Rancheria Pomo | Scotts Valley Pomo |
| Enterprise Rancheria | Mechoopda Chico Rancheria | Sheep Ranch Rancheria Me-Wuk |
| Greenville Rancheria | Mooretown Rancheria Maidu | Sherwood Valley Rancheria Pomo |
| Grindstone Rancheria Wintun-Wailake | Paskenta Nomlaki | Shingle Springs Rancheria |
| Guidiville Rancheria | Picayune Rancheria Chunkchansi | Smith River Rancheria |
| Hopland Pomo Rancheria | Pinoleville Rancheria Pomo | Susanville Rancheria |
| Ione Miwok | Pit River | Table Bluff Rancheria |
| Jackson Rancheria Me-Wuk | Potter Valley Rancheria Pomo | United Auburn Rancheria |
| Karuk | Quartz Valley Reservation | Upper Lake Rancheria |
| Kashia Pomo Stewarts Point Rancheria | Redding Rancheria | Utu Utu Gwaitu Paiute |
| | Redwood Valley Rancheria Pomo | Yurok Reservation |
| | Resighini Rancheria Yurok | Coastal Miwok |
| | Robinson Rancheria Pomo | Middletown Rancheria |

(Alaska not to scale )

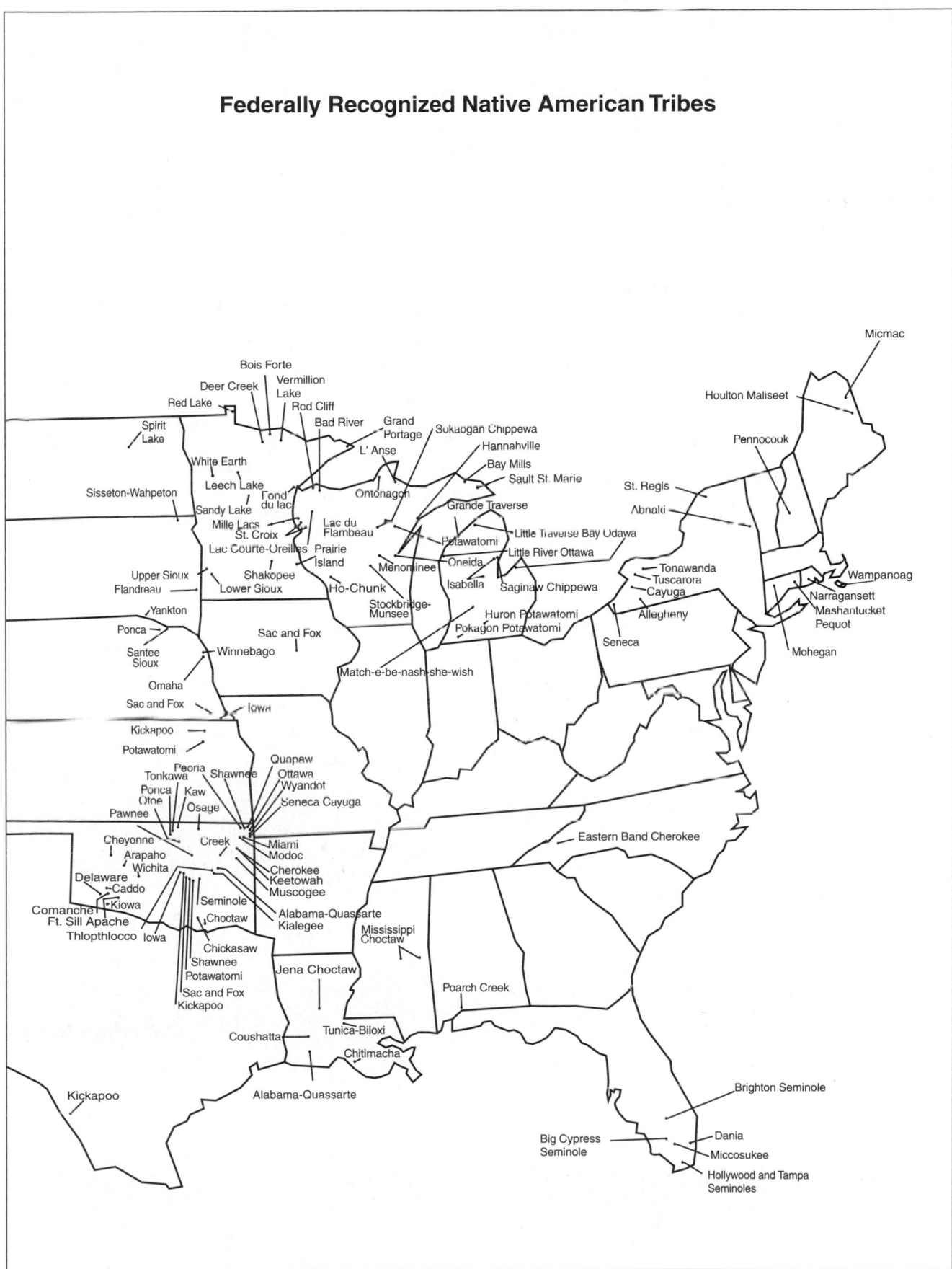

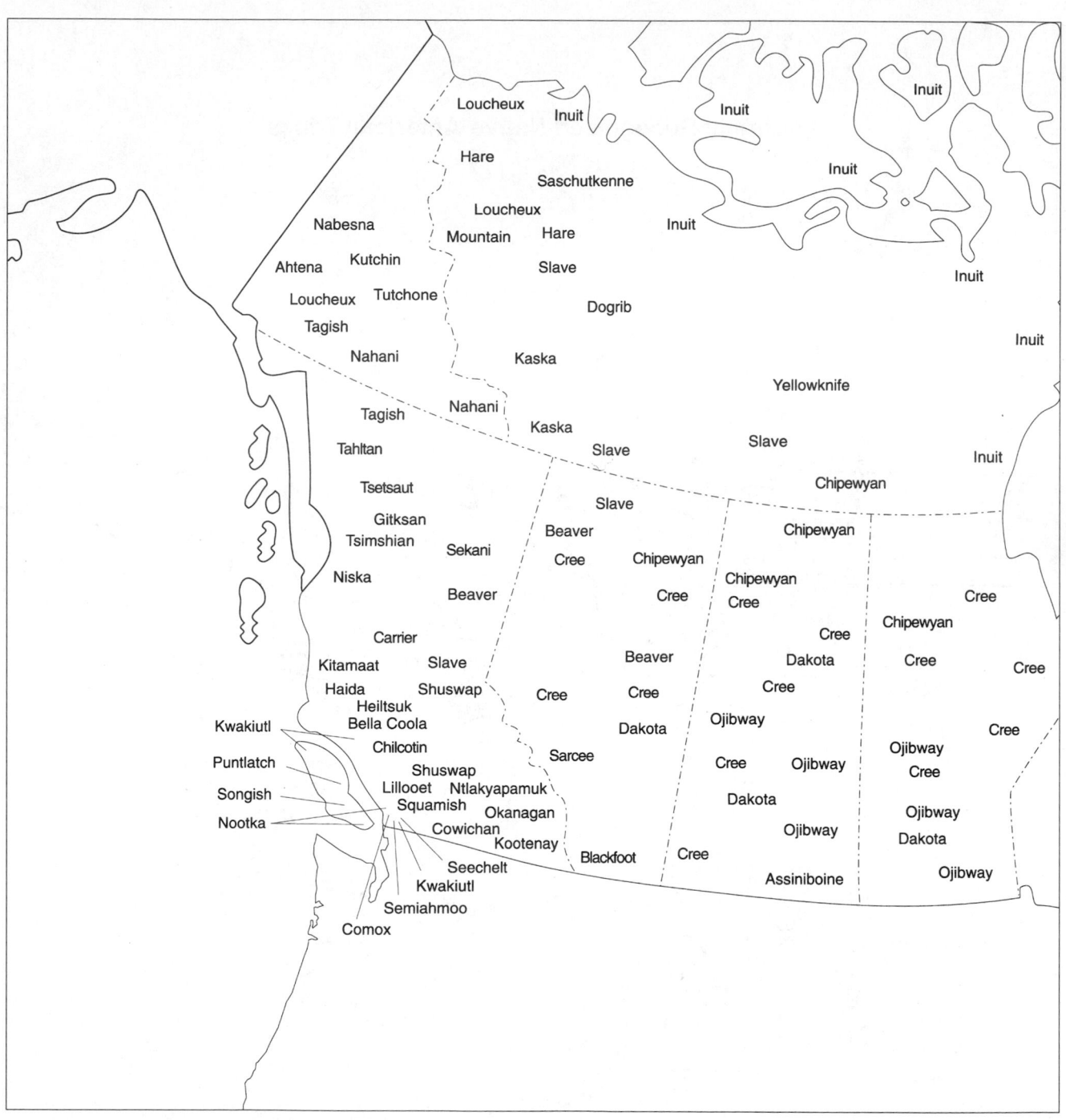

**Canadian Native**

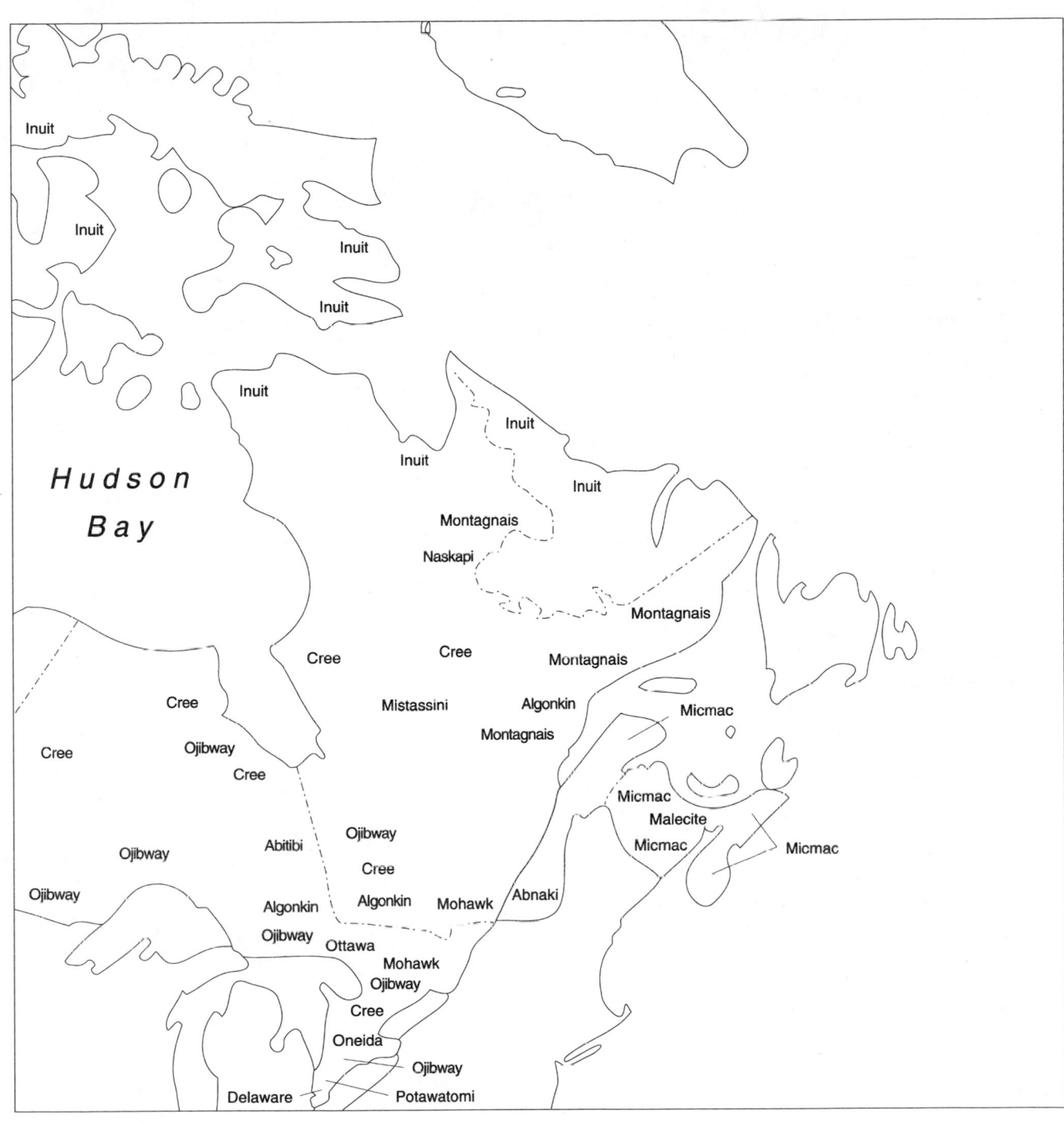

**Culture Groups**

# *Major Native Nations*

## UNITED STATES

### ♦ NORTHEAST

Abenaki
Brotherton
Cayuga
Chickahominy
Chippewa (Ojibway)
Fox
Huron
Maliseet
Mattaponi
Menominee
Miami
Mohawk
Mohegan
Montauk
Nanticoke
Narragansett
Nipmuc-Hassanamisco
Oneida
Onondaga
Ottawa
Pamunkey
Passamaquoddy
Paugusset
Penobscot
Pequot
Piscataway
Poosepatuck
Potawatomi
Rappahanock
Sauk
Schaghticoke
Seneca
Shawnee
Shinnecock
Sioux
Stockbridge-Munsee
Tuscarora
Wampanoag

Winnebago

### ♦ SOUTHEAST

Alabama
Biloxi
Catawba
Cherokee (Eastern)
Chitimacha
Choctaw (Mississippi)
Coharie
Coushatta
Creek
Edisto
Haliwa
Houma
Lumbee
Miccosukee
Santee
Saponi
Seminole
Texas Kickapoo
Tunica
Waccamaw

### ♦ OKLAHOMA

Apache
Caddo
Cherokee
Cheyenne-Arapaho
Chickasaw
Choctaw
Comanche
Creek
Delaware
Iowa
Kaw
Kickapoo

Kiowa
Miami
Modoc
Osage
Otoe-Missouri
Ottawa
Pawnee
Peoria
Ponca
Potawatomi
Quapaw
Sac and Fox
Seminole
Seneca-Cayuga
Shawnee
Tonkawa
Wichita
Wyandotte

### ♦ PLAINS

Arikara
Assiniboine
Blackfeet
Cheyenne
Chippewa
Crow
Delaware
Gros Ventre
Hidatsa
Iowa
Kickapoo
Mandan
Omaha
Plains Ojibwa
Potawatomi
Sac and Fox
Sioux
Winnebago
Wyandotte

### ◆ ROCKY MOUNTAIN AREA

Arapaho
Bannock
Cayuse
Coeur d'Alene
Confederated Tribes of
    Colville
Flathead
Gosiute
Kalispel
Klamath
Kootenai
Nespelem
Nez Percé
Paiute (Northern)
Sanpoil
Shoshoni (Northern)
Spokane
Umatilla
Ute
Walla Walla
Warm Springs
Wasco
Washo
Yakima

### ◆ SOUTHWEST

Apache
Chemehuevi
Havasupai
Hopi
Hualapai
Maricopa
Mohave
Navajo
Paiute
Pima
Pueblo
Tohono O'Odham (Papago)
Yaqui
Yavapai
Yuma
Zuni

### ◆ CALIFORNIA

Achumawi
Atsugewi
Cahuilla
Cupeño
Diegueño
Gabrielino
Hupa
Karok
Luiseño
Maidu
Miwok
Mohave
Mono
Ohlone
Paiute
Patwin
Pomo
Serrano
Shasta
Shoshoni (Western)
Tolowa
Washo
Wintu
Wiyot
Yana
Yokuts
Yuki
Yurok

### ◆ NORTHWEST COAST

Bella Bella
Bella Coola
Chehalis
Chinook
Clallam
Coos
Coquille
Gitksan
Haida
Heiltsuk
Hoh
Kalapuya

Kwakiutl
Lillooet
Lummi
Makah
Molala
Muckleshoot
Nisgha
Nisqually
Nooksack
Nootka
Puyallup
Quileute
Quinault
Rogue River
Sauk-Suiattle
Shasta
Siletz
Siuslaw
Skagit
Skokomish
Snohomish
Squaxin Island
Stillaguamish
Suquamish
Swinomish
Tillamook
Tlingit
Tsimshian
Tulalip
Twana
Umpqua
Wishram

### ◆ ALASKA

Ahtena
Aleut
Athapascan
Eyak
Haida
Inuit
Tlingit
Tsimshian
Yupik

# CANADA

Abenaki
Algonquin
Assiniboine
Beaver
Bella Bella
Bella Coola
Blackfoot
Blood
Carrier
Chilcotin
Chipewyan
Chippewa (Ojibway)
Comox
Cowichan
Cree
Dakota
Dogrib

Gitksan
Gros Ventre
Haida
Haisla
Hare
Heiltsuk
Huron
Inuit
Kootenay
Kutchin
Kwakiutl
Lillooet
Loucheux
Maliseet
Micmac
Mohawk
Montagnais

Nahani
Naskapi
Nisgha
Nootka
Ntlakyapamuk
Okanagon
Potawatomi
Sarsi
Sekani
Shuswap
Slave
Songhees
Squamish
Tagish
Tahltan
Tsimshian

# Chronology

## ♦ CHRONOLOGY OF NATIVE NORTH AMERICAN HISTORY, PRE-CONTACT TO 1500

**38,000** B.C.E. **Texas.** From initial human migration to North America until the end of the Ice Age, big-game hunting is the dominant way of life. Most hunting societies track large Pleistocene game such as woolly mammoths, mastodons, saber-toothed tigers, American lions, camels, bighorn bison, short-faced bears, and other mammals for sustenance. In Lewisville, Texas, the concentration of human and animal remains indicates the presence of early societies in the area. Fingerprints discovered in Pendejo Cave at Fort Bliss, Texas, date back 36,000 years before the present time. Evidence indicates that these societies rely on bone implements and wooden spears. The period from about 50,000 B.C.E. to 25,000 B.C.E. is often referred to as the Pre-Projectile Point Stage.

**circa 33,000 to 12,000** B.C.E. **Alaska.** Over a period of years small bands of hunters steadily make their way across the Bering Sea Land Bridge from Siberia. Anthropologists speculate that these people and their descendants spread throughout North and South America to become the ancestors of all subsequent generations of Native Americans. Some archaeologists believe the first people came across before 18,000 B.C.E. Although questionable, possible bone artifacts found along the Old Crow River in Canada's Yukon Territory were dated at 24,000 to 27,000 B.C.E. Linguistic evidence supports an even earlier appearance, 33,000 B.C.E., of North American peoples.

**25,000** B.C.E. **North America.** New technologies appear among the Paleo-Indian societies of North America. Workable stone—especially flint, chert, and obsidian—is crafted into functional tools such as knives, scrappers, choppers, and, most importantly, spear points. The introduction of stone spear points dramatically alters the subsistence patterns of Paleo-Indians. Different periods of Paleo-Indian history are classified by the types of spear points used and normally bear the name of the site at which a particular stone point has been found, such as Sandia, Clovis, Folsom, and Plano.

**25,000** B.C.E. **Sandia Mountains, New Mexico.** Paleo-Indian societies that develop in the Southwest use the Sandia stone point. From two to four inches long, the Sandia points have rounded bases with a bulge on one side for greater stability. The development of this point, first uncovered in the Sandia Mountains in New Mexico, is limited to the societies of the Southwest. The length and width of the point reveals a reliance on large game for sustenance.

**22,000** B.C.E. **Northern Pacific Rim.** Seafaring ancestors of today's American Indian people may have worked their way along the Northern Pacific Rim in small boats. These people make landfall and gradually migrate to the interior of present-day North and South America.

**15,000** B.C.E. **North America.** The Clovis culture, also referred to as Llano, becomes much more widespread than the Sandia. Although named after the original Clovis site in New Mexico, Clovis stone points

1

are used in every mainland state of the United States. Characterized by its slender point with lengthwise channels on both sides, Clovis points are crafted by pressure flaking, and are used to hunt numerous Pleistocene animals, especially mammoths and mastodons. Widespread use of Clovis stone points disappears around 9200 B.C.E..

**11,000 B.C.E. Lindenmeier Site, Colorado.** The Paleo-Indians are the first people to come to the Americas. They live a nomadic life based on hunting many types of animals and collecting wild plants. Located just south of the Wyoming border in Colorado, the Lindenmeier site is the first Paleo-Indian campsite studied. It helped verify the antiquity of humans in the Americas.

**10,500 B.C.E. Monte Verde, Chile.** Wood, bone, and stone tools indicate that people established a sophisticated village site at Monte Verde on the southernmost tip of South America. Evidence suggests that people were at the site as early as 28,000 B.C.E. and that their tools bear no resemblance to those of the vanished Clovis culture. The Monte Verde site is considered one of the oldest verifiable sites in the Americas and casts serious doubt on the Bering migration theory.

**10,200 B.C.E. North America.** Dogs have always been with people in North America. Dog remains found at the Jones-Miller site in Colorado and other Paleo-Indian sites in the western United States show animals closely related to wolves, but about three-fourths their size.

**10,000 B.C.E. North America.** Among the first people to come to the Americas are the Clovis hunters and gatherers. They hunt Pleistocene animals, such as mammoths, horses, camels, and bison, and collect a variety of plants. By this date, Clovis people are spread over most of North and South America. Evidence for their distinctive type of tools dies out about 9200 B.C.E.

**10,000 B.C.E. Southwest.** As big-game animals begin to die off, societal economies in the Southwest become more diversified. People begin to rely on wild plants and nomadic hunting, and use vegetable-grinding tools such as manos, milling stones, and, later, mortars and pestles. Human burial also appear in specific locations, suggesting a belief in an afterlife as well as the growing sedentary nature of many societies in this region. The atlatl becomes a primary tool for hunting. The atlatl is also called a spear-thrower and consists of a slender spear point fitted into a long shaft, secured with plant-fiber twine. A spear launched by an atlatl travels up to 300 feet with great accuracy and is effective against large animals such as deer, elk, horses, and camels.

**9200 B.C.E. North America.** Following Clovis, a new Paleo-Indian tradition called Folsom emerges across the continent. The Folsom people are hunters and gatherers like their Clovis ancestors, but they make smaller spear points and focus more attention on hunting the now-extinct giant bison called *Bison antiquus*. By the end of the Folsom tradition (8000 B.C.E.), many of the North American Ice Age mammals, such as the giant ground sloth, woolly mammoth, and dire wolf, are extinct.

**9000 B.C.E. Arctic.** In areas untouched by glaciers, people of the Paleoarctic tradition develop an effective hunting way of life and are the first people in the Americas to find ways of living in the harsh arctic environment. Their tools include scrapers, spear points, and very small, razor-sharp stone tools called microblades. They live in small, highly mobile groups that move over wide territories to take advantage of the best hunting conditions.

**9000 B.C.E. Great Basin.** Artifacts similar to those found in the San Dieguito complex in California also occur at Danger Cave, west of Salt Lake City, Utah. As defined for California, the San Dieguito complex is a distinctive tradition with a heavy reliance on hunting and no evidence for the use of grinding stones. Some typical San Dieguito artifacts include small, leaf-shaped projectile points and knives, scrapers, and engraving tools. The San Dieguito artifacts may represent a transitional period between the earlier Clovis Paleo-Indians and the later Archaic period cultures in this region.

**9000 B.C.E. Great Plains.** *Bison antiquus* becomes a major food source. Herds increase greatly following the extinction of predators like lions and short-faced bears, and after the climatic changes foster the expansion of shortgrass prairie.

**9000 B.C.E. Blackwater Draw, New Mexico.** Early campsites in present-day eastern New Mexico, used by Paleo-Indian groups for more than one thousand years, show that people took advantage of a local environment much wetter than today's. Remains recovered from the site include those of mammoth and other now-extinct species.

**8500 B.C.E. Marmes Rockshelter, Washington.** At Marmes Rockshelter on the lower Snake River in southeast Washington, some of the best early evidence for human habitation of the Plateau region documents the hunting of a wide variety of animals.

**8500 B.C.E. Agate Basin Site, Wyoming.** Located in extreme eastern Wyoming near the Cheyenne River, the Agate Basin site is one of a growing number of places that reveal the hunting strategies of the Paleo-Indians. In this location bison are driven into an arroyo, or gully, where they are surrounded and killed.

**8000 B.C.E. California.** Seagoing people are living in the Channel Islands off the coast of Southern California.

**8000 B.C.E. California.** Although few artifacts or remains indicate the development of major Paleo-Indian societies in this region, many postglacial societies emerge in southern California during this period. Findings from the Lake Mojave region in the southeast, as well as from the San Dieguito complex near the southern coast, reveal many similarities with the Desert culture of the Great Basin, such as small-game hunting tools.

**8000 B.C.E. Holcombe Site, Western Great Lakes.** At the Holcombe site, just north of Detroit, early Archaic period foraging peoples develop tools such as gravers, scrapers, and various projectile point forms, replacing earlier styles used by Paleo-Indian groups.

**8000 B.C.E. North America.** Across the continent people adapt to a new, more diverse, post-Ice Age environment, marking the end of the Paleo-Indian period in most regions.

**8000 B.C.E. Danger Cave, Utah.** Repeated use by early hunters and gatherers reveals a remarkable record of adaptation to a difficult desert environment.

**8000 B.C.E. Columbia River, Oregon.** From earliest times to the modern day, people have camped along the Columbia River in a stretch of rapids called the Dalles to take advantage of the rich salmon resources. At sites along the great rapids, on the middle portion of the Columbia River, thousands of salmon bones and a wide variety of tools have been discovered.

**8000 B.C.E. Colorado.** At the Olson-Chubbuck site, near the Kansas border in east-central Colorado, hunters stampede almost two hundred bison into an arroyo where they kill and butcher them. Bison kill sites like Olson-Chubbuck are known in several places on the Great Plains.

**8000 B.C.E. Bonfire Shelter, Texas.** At a bison jump site, in Val Verde County, western Texas, Paleo-Indians on at least two separate occasions drive herds of bison over a cliff.

**7500 B.C.E. Southeastern United States.** Near the end of the Paleo-Indian period a tool complex called Dalton is recognized from such places as the Brand site in Arkansas. The Dalton point style is often used as a projectile as well as a knife and is found in association with stone scrapers and woodworking tools.

**7300 B.C.E. Columbia River, Washington.** An unidentified male believed to be Native American and identified as Kennewick Man dies. Kennewick Man's skeletal remains are discovered in 1999 and spark a debate between the Umatilla Indians, who claim that he was one of their ancestors, and anthropologists, who say that the skeletal remains are more like those of the ancient Japanese Ainu than of today's American Indians. Kennewick Man's remains indicate that he led a difficult life and include multiple fractures, a crushed chest, a withered arm, evidence of a skull fracture, and a stone projectile buried in a hip bone.

**7000 B.C.E. Northwest Coast.** As the glaciers retreat, hunting-and-gathering peoples move into the coastal regions from the interior plateau.

**6500 B.C.E. Southeast.** Freshwater mussels and other river resources become a major part of the diet for Archaic-period peoples. Expanding use of these resources probably results from climate change and the beginnings of a lengthy period of river stabilization that increase their availability.

**6400 B.C.E. Hogup Cave, Utah.** People living along the edges of ancient lakes, in the region west of present-day Salt Lake City, collect pickleweed and hunt a variety of water fowl. The remains of nets and traps also indicate the hunting of rabbits and other small game.

**6000 B.C.E. North America.** In many regions, groups adapt to smaller ranges as populations begin to increase. Local cultural differences multiply due to decreased interaction.

**6000 B.C.E. Moorehead Cave, Texas.** At this cave in the Great Bend region of Texas, about 120 miles west of San Antonio, a long history of use associated with the Coahuiltecan cultural tradition verifies a hunting-and-gathering lifestyle that exists until European contact. The people of the Coahuiltecan culture live in small bands that hunt and collect over a vast region of southwest Texas and northern Mexico. They fish in the Pecos River and the Rio Grand and use throwing sticks to hunt rabbits. Because this region is so arid, the Coahuiltecan people never adopt agriculture.

**5500 B.C.E. North America.** Grinding stones called manos and metates used for processing seeds and other plant products are used in Archaic period sites.

**5500 B.C.E. Southern California.** Cultures of the Encinitas tradition develop along the California coast from Paleo-Indian ancestors. Grinding stones and remains of abundant shellfish provide evidence for an economy based on marine coastal resources. In the San Diego area, the Encinitas tradition lasts until C.E. 1000.

**5000 B.C.E. Arctic and Subarctic.** By this time hunting and foraging groups of the Northern Archaic tradition begin exploiting the increasingly ice-free environments. They live in small camps and hunt throughout the tundra and forests. On the northern forest fringes, caribou hunting is a primary occupation. In the dense woodlands slightly farther south, elk, deer, and moose are important.

**5000 B.C.E. Aberdeen Lake, Canadian Subarctic.** For the next 4,000 years, Northern Archaic tradition hunters camp on Aberdeen Lake, about three hundred miles west of Hudson Bay, to intercept the seasonal migrations of vast caribou herds.

**5000 B.C.E. Plateau Region.** For the next 2,000 years there is evidence of increased contact and sharing of ideas between peoples of the Plateau and Great Basin.

**5000 B.C.E. Southern Great Basin.** For the next 3,400 years, Pinto Basin cultures practice a hunting-and-gathering way of life. Some evidence of small circular houses indicates they may have been semisedentary.

**5000 B.C.E. Northwestern Great Plains.** For the next 2,500 years, a drier climate prevails, causing reduction in prairie grasses and a dwindling of the bison herds. Fewer archaeological sites for this period indicates that human populations also move out of the region.

**4500 B.C.E. Northeastern California.** People of the Menlo phase (4500–2500 B.C.E.) are the first to build sturdy, semisubterranean earth lodges in this region. From these relatively permanent hamlets they exploit environments ranging from the mountains to the river valleys. Later in time, the climate becomes drier and the people are forced to move more often to find food. They respond by shifting to lighter, easier-to-build dwellings made of brush.

**4000 B.C.E. Ocean Bay, Kodiak Island, Alaska.** Kodiak Island, about 215 miles south of present-day Anchorage, is one of the places where Arctic hunters begin adapting their skills to exploit marine resources.

**4000 B.C.E. Onion Portage, Alaska.** Some of the earliest Northern Archaic artifacts are found at Onion Portage on the Kobuk River in northeast Alaska. They give evidence for increasingly diverse subsistence strategies including a shift to caribou hunting.

**4000 B.C.E. Koster Site, Illinois.** At least by this date, throughout the Midwest, hunters and gatherers of the Archaic period begin building permanent shelters at base camps. Some of these camps were discovered in southern Illinois, about seventy miles north of St. Louis, at the Koster site.

**3000 B.C.E. Umnak Island, Alaska.** At Umnak and other islands in the Aleutian chain, people skilled at hunting seals, sea lions, and whales build villages with small oval houses three to five meters in diameter.

**3000 B.C.E. Southern California.** In some areas along the coast, the Encinitas tradition is replaced by the Campbell tradition, which has a greater orientation toward hunting deer and other game animals. Artifacts of the Campbell tradition include leaf-shaped points and stone mortars and pestles. The Campbell tradition is a precursor to the modern Chumash of the Santa Barbara area.

**3000 B.C.E. Southwest.** Beginning about this time, favorable conditions for widespread trade and interaction develop, permitting the eventual spread of important domesticated plants from Mexico, especially maize, beans, and squash.

**3000 B.C.E. Southwest.** Four regional Archaic period traditions of hunting-and-gathering peoples, known collectively as the Picosa culture, take shape. In the west is the little-known San Dieguito-Pinto tradition. The best-known artifact of this tradition is the small Pinto Basin projectile point, but there are a variety of other artifacts, including small grinding slabs and choppers. In the north, the Oshara tradition shows many connections in artifact styles with the western San

Dieguito-Pinto tradition. In the east, the Hueco and Coahuiltecan cultural complexes are known to include many wooden and other perishable objects, such as nets and sandals, recovered from dry caves. In the south, during the Chiricahua and San Pedro phases of the Cochise tradition, people use a wide variety of plant processing and hunting tools.

**2600 B.C.E. Southeast.** Throughout the region there is an expansion of long-distance trade. It is not clear why trade increases at this time, but there is evidence that expanding populations use trade to maintain good relations with a growing number of neighboring groups. It is also possible that exotic items are becoming important as markers of wealth and status.

**2500 B.C.E. Central California.** For the next 2000 years people of the Windmiller period (also called the Windmiller pattern) cultures live in permanent villages and practice a wide variety of hunting-and-gathering activities in California's Central Valley. They bury their dead in small mounds. Among the many objects made by Windmiller people are distinctive, large, obsidian (volcanic glass) projectile points, stone smoking pipes, alabaster charmstones, various types of baskets, and grinding stones.

**2500 B.C.E. Charles River, Massachusetts.** Several large fish traps, called weirs, are positioned at the mouth of the Charles and other rivers as they feed into the Atlantic Ocean. These types of traps are probably used well before 2500 B.C.E. and continue in use into the period of European contact.

**2500 B.C.E. Southeast.** The earliest pottery north of Mexico is made at sites in Georgia and Florida. The simple styles are constructed using plant fibers as tempering material to strengthen the vessels. This and later pottery represent a major technological advance in the preparation and storage of food and other resources.

**2000 B.C.E. Alaska.** The Arctic Small Tool tradition develops and spreads east as far as Greenland. These hunters and fishers are the first humans to live in the eastern Arctic, other than Antarctica, the last uninhabited region of the world. The people of the Arctic Small Tool tradition are the ancestors of the modern-day Inuit. They are responsible for developing some of the most remarkable technologies for surviving in the world's harshest environment. They develop special harpoons and techniques for hunting seals, walrus, and whales.

**2000 B.C.E. Northwest Coast.** Beginning as early as 2000 bc, archaeological remains, designated the Strait of Georgia tradition, point to coastal and interior adaptations that eventually lead to the development of complex societies like the present-day Coast Salish and Bella Bella. Initially, artifact styles are similar to those from Kodiak Island, Alaska, and include a wide variety of harpoons and fishing equipment. By C.E. 400 distinctive Strait of Georgia tradition artifacts include ground slate spear points, barbed points made of bone, and spindle whorls used to make cloth.

**2000 B.C.E. Labrador.** Ramah Chalcedony, a translucent type of stone easily worked into a variety of tools, becomes an important trade item after the arrival of Inuit peoples. This stone is traded from Labrador to New England.

**2000 B.C.E. Midwest.** From about this time into the period of European contact, people mine copper in the Lake Superior area. The copper is obtained in relatively pure chunks and is cold hammered into a variety of tools and ornaments. Over time, copper from this region is traded widely across the eastern woodlands.

**2000 B.C.E. Eastern United States.** By this date, four native plants are being domesticated in this region. Two of these plants, squash and sunflowers, are still commonly used today. The other two, marsh elder and chenopodium, are now thought of as only weeds.

**1500 B.C.E. Subarctic.** A period of increasing cold causes the southerly retreat of forests. Northern Archaic tradition hunters, who are adapted to forest environments, also move south. For these hunters the migratory caribou herds are a major food source. Not long after the Northern Archaic tradition hunters move south, Inuit (Eskimo) peoples fill the vacuum.

**1500 B.C.E. Central California.** Flexed burials, some cremation, coiled basketry, wooden mortars, barbed harpoons, and the bow and arrow appear. Village sties become larger and "shell mounds" and other burial sites are built. Evidence of concentrated, economically diversified, and culturally complex societies indicates the growth of unique and dynamic cultures with specialized modes of production and ideological systems.

**1500 B.C.E. Subarctic.** A period of increasing cold causes the southward retreat of forests. Northern Archaic tradition hunters who are accustomed to forest environments follow the migratory caribou herds. Shortly after the Archaic tradition hunters move south, Inuit (Eskimo) peoples begin living in these northern regions. Many of their communities exist today.

Dogs were domesticated by Native people as far back as 10,000 B.C.E. Paleo-Indians often trained dogs to pull loads during their seasonal migrations. (Photo by Lori Cooper. Courtesy of the UCLA American Indian Studies Center)

**1400 B.C.E. Louisiana.** By this date, people living along the lower Mississippi River and its tributaries are constructing large mounds and living in planned communities. The best-known example is the Poverty Point site, located fifty-five miles west of Vicksburg, Mississippi, where a massive semicircle of concentric mounds is constructed. Some archaeologists believe Poverty Point is the first chiefdom north of Mexico. There are approximately one hundred lesser sites with cultural connections to Poverty Point.

**1000 B.C.E. Southwest.** The first evidence of the use of maize in the Southwest is documented at Bat Cave and Jemez Cave in southwest New Mexico, north of Silver City.

**1000 B.C.E. Central California.** Cultures of the Cosumnes period grow out of the earlier Windmiller culture. Artifactual evidence suggests they rely more on harvesting acorns and fishing than their Windmiller culture ancestors, although hunting continues to be important.

**1000 B.C.E. Northeast.** Vessels carved from a stone called steatite are a common trade item from New England to the southern Appalachian Mountains.

**800 B.C.E. Choris Peninsula, Alaska.** The first pottery in Alaska appears in this area of Kotzebue Sound, about 160 miles north of Nome. Styles and methods of manufacture show recent contact with Asia.

**700 B.C.E. Foxe Basin and Baffin Island, Canada.** In this vast region north of Hudson Bay, Dorset Inuit culture develops, eventually spreading to many parts of the eastern Arctic. Excavations at the Kapuivik site, near Igloolik, reveal the oldest documented occurrence of Dorset culture. Dwellings used by the Dorset people include skin tents, sod houses, and pit houses.

**500 B.C.E. Eastern Great Plains.** Throughout the eastern border of the Plains for the next 1500 years people of the Plains Woodland tradition build many small mounds.

**500** B.C.E. **Southeast.**  The older practice of using plant fiber as a tempering agent in pottery is replaced by the use of sand and limestone. At about this time, there is a huge increase in the variety of decorations used on pottery throughout the region. This corresponds with expanding cultural diversity and the shift from a hunting-and-gathering way of life to the establishment of small permanent villages and the cultivation of native plants like sunflower, marsh elder, may grass, and squash. The seeds from the sunflower, marsh elder, and may grass could be collected and ground to produce flour.

**500** B.C.E. **Midwest.**  In the Ohio River Valley and surrounding regions, an Early Woodland cultural complex, called Adena, develops from late Archaic antecedents. The Adena people build burial mounds and live in small villages of circular semipermanent dwellings.

**500** B.C.E. **Southwest.**  Beans make their first appearance in the Southwest about this time, becoming more common after 300 C.E. Beans contain vital amino acids, which corn lacks. Beans also return nitrogen to the soil, which corn depletes. Consequently, by growing beans and corn in tandem, Southwestern farmers improve their health and increase the soil's longevity.

**400** B.C.E. **Ohio.**  People of the Adena Culture build a huge earthwork, today called Serpent Mound. The body of the serpent measures 382 meters long. Today its symbolism is unknown.

**350** B.C.E. **Southwest.**  Beans and squash, already widely cultivated in Mesoamerica, are introduced and eventually become important food sources.

**250** B.C.E. **Eastern United States.**  Peoples begin cultivation of locally domesticated plants.

**250** B.C.E. **Eastern Great Plains.**  A variety of cultures referred to as Plains Woodland develop in this region. They differ markedly from earlier cultures; especially noteworthy is their use of pottery, sedentary villages, and mounds as places for a variety of religious purposes, including burial of the dead.

**100** B.C.E. **Midwest.**  Centered in Ohio and Illinois, Hopewell societies develop from local roots. The Hopewell people are especially noted for constructing massive, geometric-shaped earthworks. Hopewell societies are also known for participating in trade networks extending from the Great Lakes to the Gulf of Mexico. Some of the items traded include conch shell, shark teeth, mica, lead, copper, and various kinds of stone.

C.E. **1 Eastern Kansas.**  For the next 500 years, Hopewellian communities with affinities to the east live in the area of present-day Kansas City. Their semipermanent villages provide evidence for the early cultivation of maize.

C.E. **1 Eastern Woodlands.**  In many parts of the present-day eastern United States, small-scale groups develop more complex social hierarchies with leaders whose authority is derived from group consensus.

C.E. **1 Southeast.**  Throughout the region small oval mounds are built for the burial of important members of society.

C.E. **1 Southwest.**  The roots of the Hohokam cultural tradition emerge in the Sonoran Desert of south-central Arizona and adjacent regions of Chihuahua and Sonora in Mexico. The earlier Hohokam people are hunters and gatherers, but later develop agriculture and build massive irrigation systems to water their fields. The central Hohokam area is in south-central Arizona around the modern city of Phoenix. The Hohokam tradition continues until after European arrival. The ancient Hohokam may be ancestral to the present-day Pima and Tohono O'Odham.

C.E. **100 Southwest.**  Maize becomes a significant food crop in the region.

C.E. **100 Louisiana.**  Sharing similarities with the Hopewellian peoples farther north, the Marksville culture becomes an important regional variant of the Woodland period. The Marksville people develop an economy based on hunting and cultivation of native plants. They also build mounds for ceremonial purposes, including the burial of important individuals.

C.E. **100 Alaska.**  Remains ancestral to modern Inuit peoples are identified in eastern Siberia and western Alaska. By about C.E. 1000 all northern Native Americans from Alaska to Greenland are part of this same cultural heritage, called the Thule or Northern Maritime tradition. Archaeologically, the Thule tradition is recognized for the use of polished slate and elaborately carved bone and ivory tools used for hunting sea mammals.

C.E. **200 Southwest.**  Small sedentary villages develop, marking the end of the nomadic hunting-and-gathering lifestyle in many parts of the region.

C.E. **200 New Mexico.** The first evidence for the Mogollon is found in the mountainous areas of southern New Mexico, eastern Arizona, and adjacent portions of Chihuahua and Sonora, Mexico. Like their neighbors to the north and south, the Mogollon people develop first small villages of earth-covered houses and later multistory pueblos and techniques for cultivating crops in a dry environment. Some people of the modern Western Pueblos are believed descended from the Mogollon.

C.E. **200 Southwest.** The Patayan tradition has its origins in southwestern Arizona, but is primarily associated with the Colorado River region. The Patayan tradition occupies a vast area extending from northern Baja California to northwest Arizona. The Patayan people are among the first pottery producers in the Southwest. Several sites excavated south of the Grand Canyon in Arizona give some information on dwellings and subsistence. Their early dwellings are small and made of wood or masonry, usually with an attached ramada or open-air porch. They probably grow corn and squash and hunt a variety of local animals.

C.E. **300 Central Arizona.** Construction of what will become massive irrigation systems begins in the earliest period of the Hohokam cultural tradition.

C.E. **300 Midwest.** Around this date Hopewellian societies give way to cultures of the Late Woodland period. The reason for the decline of Hopewell in the Midwest is not known, but it may be related to the breakup of long-distance trade connections, increased warfare, and climate change.

C.E. **400 Southwest.** Pottery, used for storage and cooking, comes into wide use. Most pottery in the Southwest is made by coiling strips of clay to build up the body of the vessel.

C.E. **400 Southwest.** The Anasazi tradition emerges in the Four Corners region of Arizona, New Mexico, Colorado, and Utah. The Anasazi practice agriculture and through time move from pit-house villages to the construction of large multiroom apartment buildings, some with more than 1,200 rooms. The pueblos in Chaco Canyon in western New Mexico are examples of Anasazi dwellings. The Anasazi produce many distinctive styles of pottery; especially recognizable are the black on white geometric designs. The people of the modern Pueblos of Arizona and New Mexico are descended from the Anasazi.

C.E. **400 North America.** By this date the bow and arrow are in use in several regions and spread rapidly through the continent as a major technological advance for hunting and warfare. Before the bow and arrow, spears and a weapon called the atlatl are used widely. The atlatl, also called a spear thrower, consists of a spear held on top of a long handle. By holding the handle and propelling the spear forward a lever effect is achieved to add throwing force. Although the bow and arrow become very popular, the spear and atlatl still receive some use.

C.E. **450 Lower Mississippi Valley.** The people of the Lower Mississippi Valley build conical burial mounds and some of the first flat-top platform mounds in North America. The flat-top platform mounds are probably used as substructures for temples or residences for important people. Platform mounds become a hallmark of the later Mississippian period.

C.E. **500 Eastern Great Basin.** The Fremont culture develops with a lifeway similar to that of the Puebloan agriculturists to the south. The Fremont culture includes a number of discernibly southwestern characteristics, including cultivation of maize, pottery, pit houses, and later stone architecture. By C.E. 1350, declining rainfall brings an end to widespread agriculture and the Fremont culture.

C.E. **500 Central California.** Hotchkiss period cultures develop out of the earlier Cosumnes period.

*Thunderbird.* A petroglyph in Jeffers National Park in southern Minnesota. (Photo by Sarah Loe. Courtesy of the UCLA American Indian Studies Center)

An early colonial drawing of an Indian town in the Southwest.

Hotchkiss-period economy is based heavily on acorn gathering, but also fishing, fowling, and hunting.

C.E. **500 Central Arizona.** A ball game is played in large oval courts, similar to those found in Mesoamerica at the famous Mayan ceremonial center of Chichén Itzá on the Yucatan Peninsula and the city of Teotihuacan in central Mexico near Mexico City.

C.E. **500 Florida and Georgia.** Hopewellian cultures along the Gulf Coast continue to thrive after those of the Midwest disintegrate. One of the largest sites is Kolomoki in southern Georgia, with numerous burial mounds and a large rectangular, flat-top mound. The site may have had a population of about one thousand people.

C.E. **500 Eastern United States.** Cultures of the Late Woodland period are widespread. Compared to earlier cultures in the eastern woodlands, Late Woodland peoples build very few mounds and do not often participate in long-distance trade. The Late Woodland groups are organized more simply than their Poverty Point, Adena, or Hopewell ancestors.

C.E. **700 Crenshaw Site, Arkansas.** This site, near Texarkana, Texas, is the earliest known ceremonial center linked to the modern Caddo people who once occupied the area of western Arkansas, eastern Louisiana, eastern Texas, and eastern Oklahoma, but were removed to lands in western Oklahoma, where many of them live today. Between c.e. 900 and 1100, at least six mounds were constructed at the Crenshaw site. One of the mounds contained the remains of more than two thousand deer antlers.

c.e. **750 Eastern United States.** The simple cultures of the Late Woodland period begin a process of transformation into the more complex societies of the Mississippian period. In some areas there is a dramatic shift in subsistence and social complexity. At about this time, many groups intensify agriculture based on maize cultivation. This is associated with the growth of elaborate status hierarchies and hereditary leadership.

c.e. **750 Range Site, Southern Illinois.** This site, near eastern St. Louis, provides some of the first tangible evidence for centralized, large-scale storage of food and settlements planned around a plaza. This may represent evidence for the further development of social hierarchies responsible for the distribution of shared resources.

c.e. **800 Toltec Site, Arkansas.** The Toltec site, near Little Rock, Arkansas, consists of ten mounds arranged around a plaza, enclosed by a two-meter-high earth embankment. This is the most complex settlement known in the Southeast at this time. Although named for the Toltec people of Mexico, the site is the outgrowth of local social developments and not the result of a migration of people from Mexico.

c.e. **800 Zebree Site, Arkansas.** At this site about fifty-five miles north of Memphis, Tennessee, some of the first evidence for larger storage pits corresponds to the increased importance of maize throughout the region as an easily stored food resource.

c.e. **850 Great Plains.** Throughout the region, cultures of the Plains Village tradition develop along major and minor river valleys. They practice agriculture in conjunction with bison hunting and wild plant gathering. In the northern and central Plains they build large, well-insulated earth lodges. In the south they construct houses with grass roofs.

c.e. **880 Spiro Site, Oklahoma.** On the uplands near the Arkansas River, twelve miles west of Fort Smith, Arkansas, Caddoans build a series of large, square ceremonial buildings around a plaza. Over the next two hundred years these buildings are periodically destroyed and rebuilt as part of an elaborate ceremonial cycle. By

c.e. 1100, Spiro becomes a major ceremonial center known for its extensive trade connections.

c.e. **900 Southwest.** By this date, agriculture is commonly practiced in most areas. Maize becomes a major crop. Although maize contains less nutritional value than some wild plants, it produces higher and more predictable yields. Southwestern farmers use a variety of irrigation canals, dams, and planting methods to conserve scarce rainfall.

c.e. **900 Alaska.** Thule Inuit (Eskimo) culture begins to spread east, replacing and acculturating existing Dorset groups.

c.e. **900 Eastern United States.** In many areas, cultures referred to as Mississippian take shape. These cultures are organized as chiefdoms, with an economy based on maize cultivation and locally domesticated crops. These societies participate in long-distance trade and a widespread religion termed the Southeastern Ceremonial Complex.

c.e. **900 Kincaid Site, Ohio.** One of the major regional mound centers of the Mississippian period, Kincaid is occupied for five hundred years. The Kincaid site is located at the confluence of the Ohio, Tennessee, and Cumberland rivers, near the town of Paducah, Kentucky. It contains two mound groups, a large village, and a palisade.

c.e. **900–1450 Snaketown, Casa Grande, and the Hohokam Climax.** During the Colonial and Classic periods, consolidation and expansion of many major Hohokam sites occurs. Above-ground adobe structures come into use, irrigation canal systems are greatly expanded, and, in several places, Mesoamerica-style platform mounds and ball courts are constructed. One of the largest Hohokam settlements, Snaketown, serves as an important trading center during this time, linking the Southwest with Mesoamerica groups such as the Toltec. During their Classic phase, the Hohokam build Casa Grande on the Gila River in the Phoenix Basin. The main structure at the Casa Grande site is four stories tall and made with caliche-adobe walls, reflecting pueblo-style architectural influences.

c.e. **950 South Dakota.** People of the Middle Missouri tradition migrate to the Great Plains from Minnesota and Iowa. They bring with them a heritage of farming, and settle along the fertile bottomlands of the Missouri River in present-day South Dakota where maize, squash, and other crops grow in spite of the cold winters and often dry summers. They are recognized as the ancestors of the modern-day Mandan and Hidatsa.

C.E. **985 Greenland.**   Thule Inuit encounter the first expedition of Norsemen to reach North America.

C.E. **1000 Owens, Panamint, and Death Valleys, Utah.**   By this time, archaeological remains linked with the history of the modern Paiute are identifiable.

C.E. **1000 Central and Southern New Mexico.**   Some of the earliest compact villages, later called pueblos by the Spanish, develop around central plazas in the region of the Mogollon cultural tradition.

C.E. **1000 Kansas and Nebraska.**   Along the major rivers in this region, cultures grouped as the Central Plains tradition develop a farming lifestyle focused on maize, beans, squash, tobacco, and sunflowers. They live in large, multifamily, earth-covered houses with extended entryways.

C.E. **1000 New York and St. Lawrence River Valley.**   During the Owasco period (ad 1000–1300), people build small villages throughout this region and the first clear evidence for cultivation of maize, beans, and squash occurs. By the end of the Owasco period, dwellings consist of multifamily longhouses, some more than two hundred feet long, and villages are surrounded by fortifications, indicating the prevalence of warfare. People of the Owasco period are the ancestors of the Iroquois.

C.E. **1040 Western New Mexico.**   Over a period of years, several pueblos with hundreds of rooms are constructed near each other. In Chaco Canyon, construction of the huge pueblos, like Pueblo Bonito and Chetro Ketl, reach their maximum extent between C.E. 1040 and 1150. Chaco Canyon is connected throughout a wide region by a road system stretching many miles across the desert.

C.E. **1060 Chihuahua, Mexico.**   At the Casas Grandes site (also called Paquime), 200 miles southwest of El Paso, a large settlement is built with connections probably derived from the west coast of Mexico. It is generally believed that traders from Mexico establish the site to improve trade between the civilizations of Mexico and those of the Southwest. About C.E. 1205 the settlement is destroyed, possibly by a revolt.

C.E. **1100 Casa Grande Site, Arizona.**   During the Classic period (ad 1100–1450), the Hohokam build a "big house" on the Gila River in the Phoenix Basin. The building is four stories high and made with caliche-adobe walls. The structure may serve as a chief's house.

C.E. **1100 Eastern United States.**   Heavy reliance on starchy foods, especially maize, is linked to the poorer health of Mississippian period populations, especially those living in larger villages.

C.E. **1100 New York Region.**   By this date, the archaeological remains linked to the cultural development of the modern Iroquois can be recognized.

C.E. **1100 Northeast.**   Beginning about this time many groups construct fortifications around their villages, indicating widespread warfare.

C.E. **1100 Cahokia Region, Southern Illinois.**   The Mississippian culture, centered at the Cahokia site near St. Louis, reaches its highest level of complexity. More than one hundred mounds are constructed at Cahokia. The principal mound, Monks Mound, is the largest ancient construction north of Mexico. The town surrounding the mounds hold a population of more than ten thousand people.

C.E. **1100–1300 Mesa Verde Climax.**   Inhabited continuously from C.E. 600 to 1300, the Mesa Verde site in southern Colorado reaches its height after 1100. At about this time, the Anasazi residents of Mesa Verde begin to move off the mesas and into sheltered areas in the cliffs below, apparently for defensive reasons. By the time the move is completed, the Fewkes Canyon settlements consist of more than thirty-three cliff dwelling sites, with more than 500 living and storage rooms and sixty kivas. The largest of these, Cliff Palace, contains some 220 rooms and twenty-three kivas, and houses up to 350 people. By about 1300 the entire San Juan drainage, including the Mesa Verde area, is abandoned by the Pueblo peoples, who migrate to the Hopi/Zuni and Rio Grande areas to the south and southeast.

C.E. **1100–1804 Southern California Coast Late Period.**   Use of shell money becomes widespread throughout the southern California area, indicating the growing complexity of cultures in this region. The people of this time are the Hokan-speaking Chumash and others, ancestors to the coastal groups that would later meet European explorers and missionaries. Studies of shell beads and other artifacts suggest that

Chumash society may have developed continuously for over 7,000 years in the area now known as the Santa Barbara Channel.

C.E. **1175 Awatovi Site, Arizona.** Located seventy-five miles north of Winslow, Arizona, the Hopi call this site "Place of the Bow Clan People." At one point the Pueblo consists of 1,300 ground-floor rooms with a population of more than 1,000. About C.E. 1450, a large two-story Pueblo is built. The Franciscans build a church there in the sixteenth century.

C.E. **1200 Oklahoma.** In central Oklahoma the people of the Washita River phase (C.E. 1200–1450) develop villages based on an economy of maize cultivation and the hunting of deer and bison.

C.E. **1220 Texas and Oklahoma Panhandles.** Groups move from New Mexico to take advantage of better agricultural conditions resulting from a moister climate.

**circa C.E. 1300 Deganawida, Huron Spiritual Leader Flourishes in the Eastern United States.** Deganawida is the founder of the Iroquois Confederacy. The confederacy's origin is unknown, but it is generally dated before the landing of Columbus in 1492. In Iroquois history, Deganawida lives in a time when there is little peace among the Iroquois-speaking nations, of which the Huron, Deganawida's tribe (then residing in Ontario) is one. Deganawida has a vision from the Great Spirit that instructs him to give the Great Law of Peace, a set of rules and procedures for working out differences and settling hostilities between nations. Hiawatha becomes the spokesperson for the message of Deganawida and the Great Spirit. Both Deganawida and Hiawatha travel among the Iroquois nations, and convince them to form a confederacy of forty-nine chiefs. Through ceremonies and agreements they settle their disputes and form the Iroquois League. The purpose of the league is to create peace and spread the Great Law of Peace to all nations of the world.

C.E. **1300 Eastern United States.** Common beans were present by at least C.E. 1070; however, they do not come into wide usage until C.E. 1300. Although beans are an important nutritional addition to maize-based diets, they are not adopted in all areas.

C.E. **1300–1600 Midwest.** Great Temple Mound (or Middle Mississippi) civilization flourishes in the river valleys of Arkansas, Mississippi, Alabama, Tennessee, Missouri, Kentucky, southern Illinois, southern Indiana, and Ohio. These societies are organized into republics dominated by a large city surrounded by smaller cities. Each city consists of a plaza, one or more pyramid-like temple mounds, temples, chief's houses, and other houses.

C.E. **1350 Eastern Great Basin.** Hunting-and-gathering peoples associated with the modern southern Paiute, Ute, and Shoshoni replace the earlier Fremont culture.

C.E. **1350 Moundville, Alabama.** One of the largest Mississippian-period ceremonial centers is located forty miles south of Tuscaloosa. By this date, the site consists of twenty mounds and an associated village. It is probably the center of a chiefdom that includes a

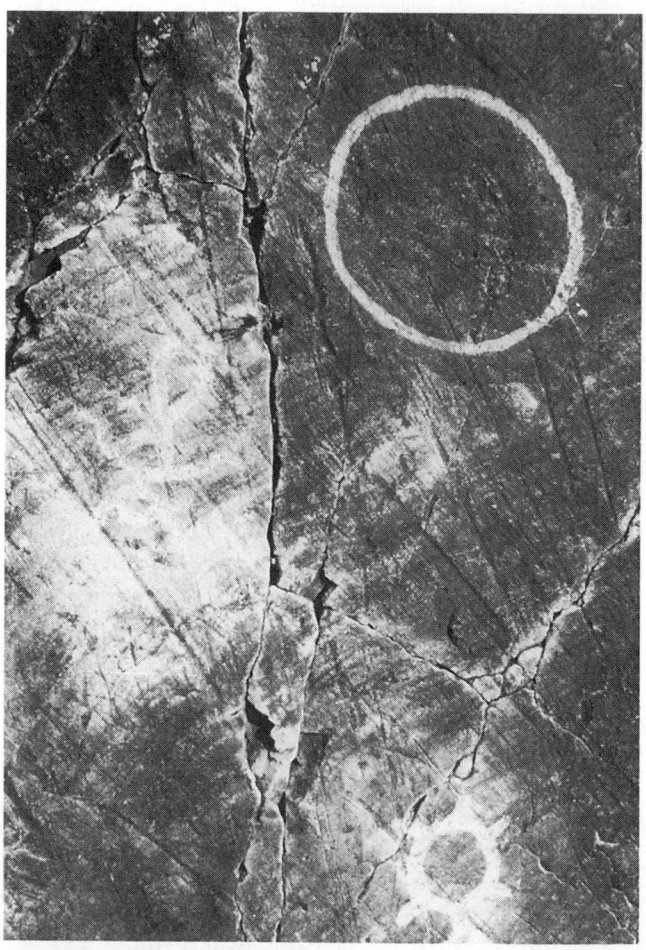

A circle petroglyph at Jeffers National Park in southern Minnesota. (Photo by Sarah Loe. Courtesy of the UCLA American Indian Studies Center)

Mesa Verde. (Photo by Manny Pedraza)

number of other sites situated along the Black Warrior River and adjacent areas in west-central Alabama.

**c.e. 1400 Southern California.** Archaeological remains of the Chumash, a tribe that lived in the vicinity of modern-day Santa Barbara, date through the period of European contact. The Chumash are known archaeologically by the term Canalino.

**c.e. 1400 Midwest.** Through a broad section of Missouri and Illinois, including the once densely populated Cahokia region, an "empty quarter" develops, possibly as a result of a poorer climate for agriculture.

**c.e. 1450 Nebraska.** Groups related to the Pawnee migrate north to the Missouri River in South Dakota. Their descendants are recognized as the present-day Arikara. Today, the Arikara live in North Dakota and are members of the Three Affiliated Tribes, along with their neighbors, the Mandan and Hidatsa.

**c.e. 1492 Caribbean.** The expedition led by Christopher Columbus touches ground on an island in the Bahamas called Guanahani by Natives and San Salvador by Europeans.

**c.e. 1500 Caribbean.** Columbus and his successors consolidate Spanish control of the Caribbean and begin a period of exploration and exploitation in North and Central America that has repercussions to the present day.

*Troy Johnson*
*California State University, Long Beach, California*

## ◆ CHRONOLOGY OF NATIVE NORTH AMERICAN HISTORY, 1500 TO 1964

**1500 Population Decline.** The sixteenth century marks the beginning of a widespread decline in Native population. Over the next four centuries, perhaps as many as sixty million people die primarily of European-imported diseases such as smallpox and scarlet fever.

In the United States, the population decline continues until about 1900, when Indian populations begin to recover.

**1502–1503 Early English Contact and Trade.** English fishermen begin making regular trips to the waters off Newfoundland and the East Coast of the United States. Various tribal groups begin occasional trade with European fishermen and whalers. They frequently exchange furs and food for metal goods and cloth. European disease is introduced through microbes contained on and in trade goods.

**1511 Priests Decry Spanish Treatment of Native Americans.** Antonio de Montesinos, a Catholic priest, gives a stirring sermon to the Spanish leaders of Hispaniola, condemning them for their treatment of Native Americans. Another priest, Bartolome de las Casas, writes *Destruction of the Indies*, in which he chronicles the Spanish conquistadors' cruelty against Native Americans. These gruesome cruelties include butchering men, women, and children like "sheep in the slaughter house."

**1512 Laws of Burgos and the Requerimiento.** De las Casas and others attempt to stop the atrocities and begin a reform movement to alter the Spanish Indian policies. The result is the Laws of Burgos, a series of reforms that outlaws Indian slavery and orders the owners of large tracts of land—taken from the Indians and known as *encomiendas*—to improve the treatment of their Indian laborers. The Spanish conquistadors cannot legally invade, enslave, or exploit Indians without first reading them the Requerimiento, a document outlining the Christian interpretation of creation and the hierarchy of the Catholic Church. Indians are told to surrender their hearts, souls, and bodies to the Church and Spanish Crown or face utter devastation. "We ask and require. . . that you acknowledge the Church," the document reads. If Indians did not obey, the Spanish promised to "make war against you. . . subject you to the yoke and obedience of the Church [and Crown]. . . take you, and your wives, and your children, and. . . make slaves of them. . . take away your goods and. . . do you all the harm and damage we can."

The Requerimiento is intended to offer Native Americans a chance to surrender and submit peacefully to Spanish rule. But as with the Laws of Burgos, the Spanish ignore the substance as well as the spirit of the Requerimiento. The Laws of Burgos fail to end Spanish abuses, for they continue throughout Latin America for four hundred more years.

Cliff dwellings at Bandelier National Monument near Los Alamos, New Mexico. (Photo by Alexandra Harris)

**1513–21 Ponce de Leon.** Juan Ponce de Leon, the governor of Puerto Rico, is given license by the Spanish king to explore and settle Florida, which the Spanish name Bimini, meaning "life source." Though one stated goal of de Leon's mission is to obtain slaves, it is his search for the Fountain of Youth for which he is best known. Ponce de Leon reaches Florida in 1513 and has extensive contact with the peoples of that region. The Saturiwa and Ai nations both greet the expedition with hostility, as do the Calusa, who, in eighty war canoes, drive de Leon's ships away from the coast. Ponce de Leon returns to Bimini in 1521 in an attempt to conquer the Indian Nations. De Leon is shot in the thigh by a Calusa arrow and later dies in Havana from the wound.

**1520 Hernando Cortes Defeats the Aztec.** The Spanish adventurer, Hernando Cortes, accompanied by a few hundred Spaniards and a large number of Tlaxcala and other Indian allies, defeat the Aztec at Mexico City. The Spanish thereafter substitute their control over the Indians once subject to Aztec rule. After defeating the Aztec Empire, which controlled most of southern Mexico, Cortes establishes himself as ruler of Mexico.

**1520–34 Guayocuya.** Within three decades of the establishment of the Spanish colony on Hispaniola, the population of the island drops from estimates of over one million people to only a few thousand. Rebelling against further labor exploitation and the rape of Native women, Guayocuya, a Taino Indian, leads a guerilla war against the Spanish. Guayocuya and his followers refuse to negotiate with the Spanish and after fourteen years of fighting the Spanish submit and Guayocuya and the other refugees are granted land upon which to live in freedom.

**1539 Marcos de Niza.** As reconnaissance for the impending Coronado expedition, a Franciscan friar named Marcos de Niza explores the region now known as the American Southwest, searching for the fabled Seven Cities of Cíbola. De Niza is accompanied by an escort of Mexican Indians from the Opata region as well as the slave Estevánico, who, as a survivor of the Narv'aez expedition, had traveled through the region several years earlier. Estevánico and the Opata contingent travel some distance ahead of de Niza. Near the six Pueblos of Zuni, de Niza meets fleeing members of the advance party who inform the Franciscan that the Zuni had killed Estevánico and many others. De Niza returns to Mexico falsely claiming that the Zuni Pueblos had wealth greater than the Aztecs or Incas.

**1539–43 Hernando de Soto.** A Spanish expedition led by Hernando de Soto travels through the present-day southeastern United States. De Soto and his company pillage and fight the Creek, Hitchiti, Chickasaw, Chakchiuma, Choctaw, Tunica, Alabama, and other indigenous nations. The Spanish find little gold and encounter strong resistance from the southeastern Indian nations.

**1540–42 Francisco Coronado.** Acting on the reports of wealth spread by Friar Marcos de Niza, the Spanish explorer Francisco Coronado travels into present-day Arizona and New Mexico, and perhaps as far east as present-day Oklahoma. The expedition meets with several Pueblo peoples, including the Zuni and Hopi. Hostilities develop because of Spanish atrocities; the Zuni and their Indian allies force the Spanish to retreat in 1542.

**1540–1600 Disease Decimates Mississippian Peoples.** De Soto and other Spaniards encounter the remnants of the southeastern Mississippian culture, which consists of politically and ceremonially centralized chiefdoms, or small city-states, often managed by priests or sacred chiefs. Diseases transmitted by European explorers, fishermen, and slave raiders decimate Mississippian culture populations. By 1600, most Mississippian ceremonial centers are abandoned and the formerly Mississippian culture groups move up and down the Mississippi Valley and into the present-day southeastern United States, dispersed into decentralized political alliances and confederacies of villages or local kinship groups. By the early 1700s much of the Mississippian culture has disappeared. Some of the remnant Mississippian culture nations are known today as the Creek, Cherokee, Natchez, Chickasaw, Caddo, Pawnee, and Choctaw.

**circa 1540–1600 Introduction of Wool.** The use of wool is introduced in the Southwest when Indians of that region begin raising sheep brought to North America by the Spanish. At about this time, Pueblo Indians begin weaving on flat looms. The Navajo begin weaving around 1700, learning the skill from their Pueblo neighbors.

**1542–1600 Early Displacement.** The Iroquoian-speaking nations (Wyandotte, Huron, Five Nations, and others) who live along the St. Lawrence River are invaded and displaced by Algonkian-speaking nations (Montagnais, Ottawa, Algonquin, and others) from the north and west. The Iroquoian-speaking nations retreat south and to the lower Great Lakes area.

**1563–65 Huguenots.** Protestants known as Huguenots flee Catholic France. They attempt to colonize an area from present-day South Carolina to St. Augustine, in present-day Florida. The colony does not survive because of internal dissension and Spanish attack. The French artist Jacques le Moyne draws some of the earliest known European representations of Native North Americans.

**1565–68 Settlement at St. Augustine.** The first permanent European settlement in North America is

Town of Secoton in present-day Beaufort County, North Carolina, was engraved by De Bry in the seventeenth century to illustrate the village life of peoples he met. This drawing and those of other settlements visited by early English observers give a visual idea of the lifeways that developed eight hundred years earlier throughout the Southeast and Midwest at the beginning of the Mississippian period. (Courtesy of American Heritage Press)

established at St. Augustine in present-day Florida. Small posts are established up the Atlantic coastline to present-day Georgia; the area is called Guale. Later, Catholic missions, built to Christianize the Natives, will be established throughout Guale.

**1578–1579 Sir Francis Drake.**  Sir Francis Drake of England explores the California coast and encounters such groups as the Coastal Miwok.

**1582–1606 The Spanish Begin Settlement of New Mexico.**  Spanish expeditions begin to enter the southern Plains and Pueblo territory by way of the Rio Grande Valley, in eastern New Mexico. In 1598, a Spanish colony is established at San Juan Pueblo, in present-day northern New Mexico. In 1598 and 1599, Indians at Acoma Pueblo revolt against the Spanish, but are put down a year later by a Spanish retaliatory expedition. The Spanish introduce sheep and trade to the Pueblo peoples.

**1585–1707 Roanoke Colony.**  Sir Walter Raleigh founds the first English colony in the New World on Roanoke Island, present-day North Carolina, but the settlement does not survive. What happens to the English settlers at the Roanoke colony remains a mystery. The Rappahannock people of present-day Virginia come into contact with Spanish and English fishermen, slave raiders, and explorers, although many contacts were probably not recorded.

**1598–99 Pueblo Colonization.**  Juan de O'nate, governor of New Mexico, leads an expedition through Pueblo territory with the primary mission of subduing the peoples of that region and establishing a Spanish colony. His initial contact with Acoma, a Pueblo situated on a 300-foot mesa, is peaceful, but when Juan de Zaldivar brings reinforcements, diplomacy turns to hostility. Zaldivar is killed. One month later, on 21 January 1599, Vincente de Zaldivar arrives with a force of seventy men to avenge his brother's death. Zaldivar and his men gain access to the village, burn building and slaughter people indiscriminately. By the end of the three-day battle, 800 Acoma are dead. Another 570 are put on trial. Women between the ages of twelve and twenty-five are indentured to twenty years' servitude at the Spanish capital of San Juan. Men are also condemned to servitude, but as an added punishment are publicly mutilated as well. In the plazas of other Pueblos, males over twelve years of age have one foot chopped off. Two Hopi visitors to Acoma are sent home with their right hands severed to show their people what resistance to the Spanish crown will bring.

**1606–14 New Mexico Turmoil.**  Continual warfare develops between the Spanish and Indians in New Mexico, especially the Navajo, Jeez, and Pueblo refugees. Indians capturing herds of horses are among some of the earliest reports of Native use of these animals in North America.

**1607 English Settlement in Virginia.**  The British Virginia Company, a monopoly granted by King James I, establishes a settlement at Jamestown (present-day Virginia) on the lands of the Pamunkey Indians, a subgroup of the Powhatan Confederacy. Like those from other European nations, English citizens come to America to exploit its resources and get rich. When the colonizers arrive, they spend much of their time exploring the James River and gathering rocks believed to contain gold. The gold turns out to be pyrite or fool's gold, and the English cast about for another resource.

Wahunsonacock, the leader of the Powhatan Confederacy (referred to simply as Powhatan by the English) warmly receives the colonizers. During the first winter, the Indians save the Englishmen from starvation. George Percy, one of the Jamestown settlers, writes that English rations are reduced to "but a small can of barley, sodden in water, to five men a day." Percy praises God who "put the terror into the sauvages' hearts" so that the "wild and cruel pagans" would not destroy the English. Percy proclaims that God sent "those people which were our mortal enemies, to relieve us with victuals, as bread, corn, fish, and flesh in great plenty." Without the help of Powhatan and his people, they would have all perished.

The English soon repay the Pamunkey by demanding their submission to English rule and the payment of an annual tribute of corn. John Smith, the leader of the Jamestown settlement, advocates an aggressive policy toward the Indians, which causes conflicts between the settlers and the Indians of Chesapeake Bay. At first, Powhatan aids the colonists, but after a few years he becomes disillusioned with the English. He asks, "Why will you destroy us who supply you with food? What can you get by war?" He cannot understand the English animosity toward the Indians and does not comprehend the full extent of European desire for material gain.

**1609 Henry Hudson and John Smith.**  Henry Hudson, sailing for the Netherlands, opens the lucrative

*Proceedings of the Floridians in deliberating on important affairs* (1591). Drawing by Le Moyne, from an engraving by T. De Bry, *America,* part 11, plate XXIX. (Courtesy of American Heritage Press)

fur trade with the Lenape, Wappinger, Manhattan, Hackensack, Munsee, and Mohican nations of New Netherlands (present-day New York).

John Smith, of Jamestown colony, is captured by members of the Powhatan Confederacy under suspicion that he participated in a raid on one of their villages. Smith is brought to Powhatan's village. Tradition has it that Pocahontas, Powhatan's young daughter, intercedes and prevents Smith's execution. Captain Smith is released and allowed to return to Jamestown.

**1613–14 Marriage of Pocahontas and John Rolfe.** Pocahontas is captured by English settlers and eventually converts to Christianity. In 1614, she marries John Rolfe, the Englishman credited with beginning the European tobacco industry. Pocahontas travels to England, but soon dies of an illness. The marriage further complicates the relationship between Powhatan and the English. Tobacco growing requires new acreage for cultivation every five to seven years; therefore, the colonists seek more land inland in Indian hunting areas

or lands that the Indians have already cleared and used for farming. The extension of the tobacco plantations further aggravates relations between colonists and Indians; Powhatan, however, seeks to keep the peace.

**1615 Continued Migration.** The confederacy of Algonkian-speaking nations (Ottawa, Potawatomi, Chippewa, and possibly Cree) continue a migration starting near the Atlantic Coast, then through the St. Lawrence River basin, and finally to the Lake Michigan and Lake Superior area. These nations have a tradition of political and ceremonial unity, although they begin to separate into small bands because of the demands of the fur trade economy. Indians trade furs for European manufactured goods such as rifles, metal hatchets and knives, cloth, beads, alcohol, and other items. The Indians quickly recognize the value of the manufactured goods and find that the Europeans are willing to trade for skins and furs, most often deerskins and beaver skins, which are made into leather and hats. Indians begin to hunt for fur-bearing animals more often, for

*Pocahontas saving the life of Captain John Smith.* From an engraving by T. De Bry, *America,* part XIII, 1634.

longer periods of time, and for the market, instead of for necessity. Consequently, some nations, like the Potawatomi, Ottawa, and Chippewa, migrate into the interior in search of territories that support fur-bearing animals. The fur trade defines the primary economic relation between Europeans and Indians until about 1800.

**1615–40s Establishment of Trade Networks.** The Wendat (Huron), an Iroquoian-speaking nation of thirty to thirty-five thousand people living near Lake Huron, in alliance with other Iroquoian-speakers—Tobacco, Attiwandaronk (Neutral Nation), and Erie of present-day Ohio—establish a vast trade network in the eastern interior of North America. Goods are exchanged through trade networks that extend into Mexico, the Gulf of Mexico, and as far west as present-day Minnesota. By the early 1600s these trade networks are distributing manufactured goods, metal knives, guns, tools, cloth, and others items, which are gained in trade with the French in New France (present-day southeastern Canada). By 1635, beaver supplies in the Huron homeland are depleted thanks to European fur demands. The Huron are forced to trade with other nations or hunt on the territories of other Native nations. In the late 1640s the Five Nations (Iroquois of upstate New York), with Dutch supplies of guns, ball, and powder, destroy the Huron and allied nations' trade empire. Under French influence, the Huron and their allies refuse to grant the

Five Nations trade access to the interior from the early 1620s to 1649.

**1616–20 Disease.**   A smallpox epidemic ravages the New England Indians who live along the coastline from present-day Massachusetts to Maine.

**1618–31 The First Powhatan War.**   Powhatan dies in 1618. His brother, Opechancanough, assumes leadership of the tribal confederation. Relations between the colonists and Indians grow more hostile until 1622 when Opechancanough moves against the English, who lose more than one-third of their colony and nearly leave Virginia. The English Crown takes over Jamestown and Virginia, providing aid and protection to the settlers.

Some English feel that the war of 1622 ultimately would be good for the colony. John Smith writes that the conflict "will be good for the Plantation, because we have just cause to destroy them by all meanes possible." Another Englishman writes that the English are "now set at liberty by the treacherous violence of Sauvages." By right of war, the English can now invade Indian lands and thereby "enjoy their cultivated places. . . and possessing the fruits of other labours. Now their cleared grounds in all their villages (which are situated in the fruitfullest places of the land) shall be inhabited by us, whereas heretofore the grubbing of woods was the greatest labour."

The first Virginia War intermittently lasts nearly ten years with many deaths among the Natives and colonists. The territory of the Chickahominy Nation, an ally nation within the Powhatan Confederacy, is ravaged by colonial attacks throughout the 1620s. The Native population in Virginia begins to decline significantly, mostly because of disease, warfare, and most likely migration. In 1608, about thirty thousand Natives live on Chesapeake Bay, but by 1669 only two thousand remain.

**1620 Arrival of the Pilgrims.**   The Pilgrims arrive aboard the Mayflower at Plymouth, Massachusetts. Before landing, they sign a compact calling for self-rule. The Pilgrims barely survive their first winter in Massachusetts, but are helped by several friendly Indians, one of whom was Tisquantum, more commonly known as Squanto. He is captured sometime between 1605 and 1614, when an English ship abducts several Indians and carries them off for sale in Europe. Tisquantum is brought to Malaga Island, Spain, and sold. He makes his way back home by way of England and Newfoundland, only to find that his home village has been wiped out by disease. Tisquantum lives with the Wampanoag and their chief, Massasoit, who enjoys influence over much of present-day Massachusetts and Rhode Island. During his travels, Tisquantum learns some English.

Tisquantum, like other Native Americans, aids the colonists, showing them where to hunt and fish, and how to grow and prepare native crops such as squash, corn, and beans. After the disastrous first winter, the Pilgrims learn quickly from the Indians' lessons. In the fall of 1621 they invite Massasoit to a feast to give thanks; he arrives with ninety people. When the Pilgrims do not have sufficient food, Massasoit asks his people to provide food as well.

**1626 Sale of Manhattan Island.**   Peter Minuit, governor of New Netherlands, the Dutch colony in the New World, trades sixty guilders of goods—legend says worth twenty-four dollars—for Manhattan Island, part of present-day New York City. Minuit buys the land from a band of Shinnecock Indians, but later has to buy it again from the Manhattan band, which claims hunting rights to the island.

Huron dancing ceremony to cure sickness, from Champlain, *Voyages et descouvertures,* Paris, 1620.

**1629–33 Establishment of Churches in the Southwest.** Spanish missionaries establish Catholic churches at Acoma, Hopi, and Zuni Pueblos.

**1630 Arrival of the Puritans.** Ten years after the Pilgrims' arrival, the Puritans (a Protestant religious sect) led by John Winthrop, arrive in Massachusetts. The Puritans believe that they are on a mission from God to establish a "City Upon the Hill," a perfect Christian society in which the Puritans form a covenant among themselves and with God to live a holy life. Outsiders are not invited into the covenant unless they agree to subjugate themselves to the rules of the religious community. Most Native Americans do not want to join this covenant and are considered outside of God's law. In fact, Puritan minister Cotton Mather maintains that Indians are the "accursed seed of Canaan" who have been dispatched by Satan "in hopes that the gospel of Jesus Christ would never come here to destroy or disturb his absolute empire over them." Reverend Mather points to the devastating disease that ravages Native populations to prove English superiority. He called the smallpox epidemic of 1633–1635, which kills thousands of Natives, a "remarkable and terrible stroke of God upon the natives." The Puritans argue that God sent the disease to kill Satan's children and to clear the land for his true flock.

**1636–37 Pequot Wars.** The Puritans attack the Pequot, who are living in present-day Connecticut. In 1634, Indians kill John Stone and eight companions who are hunting for Native slaves. Puritans use Stone's death to claim jurisdiction over the Pequot and to demand their surrender of land, valuable goods, and Stone's killers. The Narragansett, living to the east of the Pequot, are believed to have committed the murders, but the Pequot agree to the Puritan demands. However, they do not abide by the terms of the agreement, and relations with the English grow steadily worse. In 1636, several Narragansett kill an English trader and then flee into Pequot country. When the English demand the return of the Narragansett, the Pequot refuse and a fight ensues. In May 1637, the Massachusetts General Court, the colony's legislature, drafts articles of war, raises an army against the Pequot, and surrounds the Indian village and fort on the Mystic River. Puritans, pilgrims, Mohican, and Narragansett attack and set fire to the Pequot fort, killing as many as seven hundred men, women, and children.

**1637–41 Rise of the Ute.** Some Spaniards in search of slaves attack the peaceful Ute, who capture Spanish horses, escape, and introduce horses among their people. The Ute then become one of the most powerful people in the Great Basin region.

**1638 Early Reservations.** The Puritans establish what would now be called a "reservation" for the Quinnipiac Nation living near present-day New Haven, Connecticut. Under the terms of their agreement, the Quinnipiac retain only 1,200 acres of their original land on which they are subject to the jurisdiction of an English magistrate or agent. Under English rule, Quinnipiac people cannot sell or leave their lands or receive "foreign" Indians. They cannot buy guns, powder, or whiskey. They must accept Christianity and reject their traditional spiritual beliefs, which Puritans feel are the teachings of Satan.

**1638–84 The Beaver Wars.** After failing to gain a reliable trade agreement with the Huron and their trading allies, the Five Nations, with Dutch support and guns and powder, initiate a series of intermittent wars against the Susquehannock, Huron, Neutral Nation, Erie, Wyandotte, Ottawa, and other French trading nations. By 1650, the Huron trade empire is destroyed by the Five Nations. The Ottawa then assume the role of middlemen traders between the interior nations of the Great Lakes area and the French. Thereafter, the Five Nations carry their wars and diplomacy to the Indian nations of the interior, attacking the Chippewa, the Illinois Confederacy, and the Ottawa, and pushing these nations farther into the Great Lakes regions of present-day Michigan and Wisconsin. The Five Nations are generally successful in these wars and are able to supply the Dutch, until 1664, with trade goods. After 1664, the English capture New Netherlands and rename it New York. The English continue the policies of the Dutch traders by supplying the Five Nations with weapons to carry on their trade wars with the interior nations. The French are reluctant to supply their trading partners with guns, and therefore the interior nations are at a disadvantage against the better supplied Five Nations.

**1640 Five Nations Exhaust Local Beaver Supplies.** The Five Nations (Iroquois) are no longer able to supply their trade requirements by hunting and trapping on their home territory (present-day upstate New York). The Five Nations have come to depend on trade with the Dutch at Fort Orange (present-day Albany, New York) to supply knives, axes, cloth, beads, and guns and powder. After 1640, the Five Nations look to the interior nations to supply them with trade ties or allow them access to beaver territories. During the 1640s, the Five Nations try to negotiate trade and diplomatic agreements with the Huron, Neutral Nation,

Domed wigwam. (Photo by Sarah Loe. Courtesy of the UCLA American Indian Studies Center)

Erie, and Wyandotte, but the French move to prevent permanent trade agreements.

**1644–46 The Second Powhatan War.** The Powhatan Confederacy stages a second war against Virginia colony. After the war of 1622, the Indians try to live in peace with the settlers, but the English expand onto Indian lands. Some Indians are held as slaves or servants. By 1641, the English have settled in Maryland and south of the James River and covet the land of the Rappahannock, a major Powhatan ally. By 1642, the English are selecting land sites, even some that include Indian villages. The war of 1644–46 temporarily prevents English territorial expansion.

After two years of warfare, the Indians and colonists negotiate an agreement defining a boundary between the two. The Treaty of 1646 prohibits English land expansion; however, the Indians are left with only a portion of their former lands. The colonists agree to respect Native rights to these territories. Indians become subject to the rule of the colonial Virginia courts and must provide an annual tribute of beaver pelts.

Nevertheless, by 1649 English colonists are already disregarding the treaty and moving farther into Indian territory.

**1649 Iroquois Attack Huronia.** The Iroquois Confederacy initiates a concerted attack on Huronia that kills or scatters the entire Huron population. Some survivors are integrated into neighboring groups, including the tribes of the Iroquois Confederacy, others migrate throughout the Great Lakes area where they become known as the Wyandot. In 1652 the Iroquois also destroy the Petun and Neutral.

**1650 Cheyenne Migration Begins.** Because of the expanding Iroquois trade empire, the Cheyenne, probably living in present-day southern Ontario or Quebec, are forced to migrate westward. By 1775, they reach the Great Plains of present-day Montana and Dakotas, where they adopt Plains culture with buffalo hunting, an original Sun Dance ceremony, and sacred bundles, given to them by the prophetic figure Sweet Medicine.

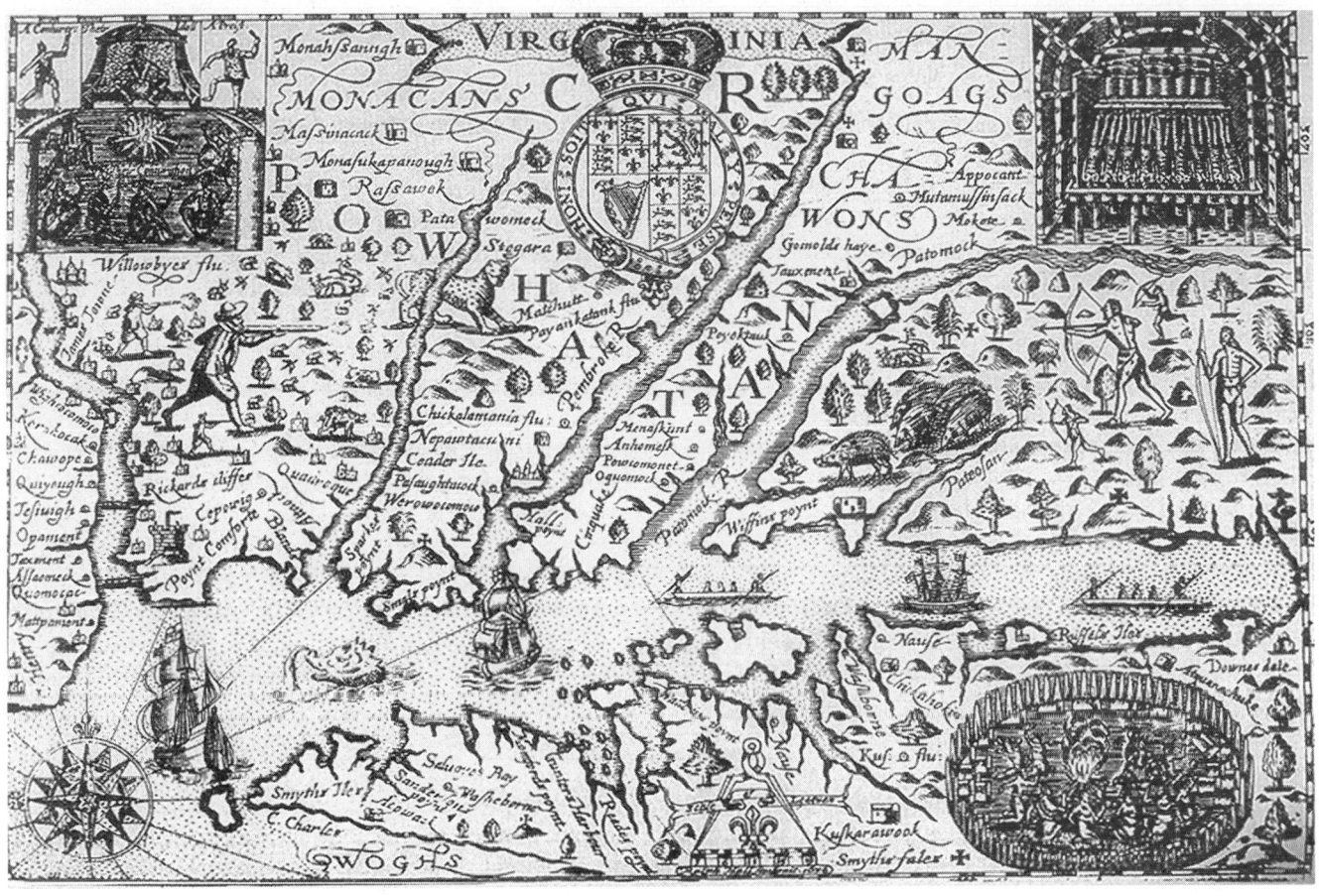

Map of Virginia, 1636, by Ralph Hall.

**1660 The Chippewa-Sioux Wars.** The Chippewa (Ojibway) living in the upper Great Lakes region start to move west, armed with guns and trade goods. Pushed by colonial and Five Nation expansion, the Chippewa move into Sioux territory in present-day Minnesota. After much fighting with the Chippewa, many Sioux migrate onto the Plains in the 1700s, where they adopt the buffalo-hunting horse culture, for which they are well known in U.S. history. Before this time, the Sioux were a settled horticultural people living in the woodlands east of the Plains area.

**1660 Western Apache in the Southwest.** Western Apache have control over the area from Sonora and Pima north to the lands of Coninas and to the Hopi area and are said to wage war on all other Indian groups in surrounding areas.

**1661 The Chickahominy Are Dispossessed.** The Chickahominy Nation, part of the Powhatan Confederacy, move from the Pamunkey River to the Mattaponi River. The Chickahominy sell 2,000 acres of land to an Englishman named Hammond. Phillip Mallory buys 743 acres from the Chickahominy, the beginning of the Mallory family's two-century effort to acquire Chickahominy lands in Virginia.

**1661 Spanish Suppression of Pueblo Religions.** The Spanish raid the sacred kivas of many Pueblo Indians, destroying hundreds of kachina masks and attempting to suppress Pueblo religions.

**1670–1710 Carolina Colony and Early Southern Indian Slave Trade.** Charles Town, in present-day South Carolina, is established. Early encounters lead to conflict with local tribal groups such as the Cusabo and Westo. The English attempt to enslave many Indians for plantation work and enlist other nations such as the Creek and Cherokee to raid interior nations like the Choctaw, living in present-day Mississippi and Louisiana, for slaves. During the 1680s and 1690s, the Choctaw are under considerable pressure and lose many

Native nations and confederacies of New England, 1640. (Drawing by John Kahionhes Fadden)

people to slave raids. In 1699, the French establish Louisiana colony, and supply the Choctaw with some weapons, which they use to protect themselves from the English, Creek, and Cherokee slave raids. Some Choctaw regions thereafter are strongly allied to the French in gratitude for their help in preserving the Choctaw Nation. By 1710, the Indian slave trade declines; Indians make poor slaves since they know the local area and escaped often. Thereafter, the fur trade becomes the primary economic relation of the southern Indians to the colonists.

**1671–80 Apache Migration.** Apaches begin migrating to the Southwest from the southern Plains. They

raid Spanish settlements and Indian Pueblos; sheep, horses, and trade goods are stolen. By this time, the Apache are well equipped with guns and horses and are able to elude and challenge Spanish armed forces.

**1675–76 King Philip's War.** The Puritans proceed to concentrate Indians on reservations and open former Indian lands to Puritan resettlement. By 1671, the Puritans have established fourteen reservations and many Indians have been forced from their homelands. Metacom, the Wampanoag son of Massasoit known to the English as King Philip, protests Puritan policies. He argues that the English set out to destroy Native American cultures and steal Indian lands. In 1671, Puritans arrest Metacom, but release him. He continues to move among the tribes, telling them that the settlers are destroying Indian culture and sovereignty. By 1675, Metacom has a sufficient following to launch a war against the English. Abenaki, Nipmuck, Narragansett, and Wampanoag Indians join forces and attack more than half of the ninety English settlements in New England. The Indians, however, do not stand long against the English. Upon conclusion of hostilities, the English General Court decreases the number of reservations from fourteen to five and places all Indians they can find upon these reserves. The Puritan government has Metacom executed and his wife, son, and hundreds of followers sold into slavery. Many of King Philip's allies, such as the Wampanoag, Nipmuck, and Narragansett, are enslaved or flee to the Mahican, a linguistically related group to the Mohican, in New York, or to the Abenaki Confederation in present-day Maine. The remnant northeastern Indian nations settle down to English rule in small communities, and over the next few centuries establish about fifteen "praying towns" of Christian Indians. These "praying" Indians become socially and economically marginalized in New England society.

**1675–77 Bacon's Rebellion.** In 1675 and 1676, a third major war erupts between Indians and Virginia settlers. This time Maryland settlers are involved. The Rappahannock flee their villages, and their land is taken by Virginia settlers. The colonists defeat the Susquehannock, who are pressed in the north by expanding Iroquois trade wars. Some Susquehannock move into Virginia territory only to be abused by Virginia traders. The colonists are led by Nathaniel Bacon, who seeks to free Virginia colony from English rule. The English restore order, but not before Bacon's army kills and enslaves many Susquehannock, Occnaneechi, Appomatuck, Manakin, and members of the Powhatan Confederacy. The Indians lose heavily in the war.

In 1677, a treaty of peace is signed between some Indian nations and Virginia colony. This treaty guarantees the signing Indians at least three miles of land in each direction from each of their villages. This leaves the rest of the land open to Virginia settlements and plantations. The Indians of Virginia are forced to acknowledge English law and courts, are subject to Virginian rule, and are left without significant land resources.

**1677–1731 Shawnee Migrations and Regroupings.** The Shawnee probably occupied present-day northern Kentucky and southern Ohio before European contact. During the late 1600s Chickasaw and Cherokee slave-raiding and fur-trading expeditions force the Shawnee to retreat from their homeland. Some Shawnee migrate south to Georgia to live on the Savannah River, which is named after them, while others move to present-day western Virginia and Pennsylvania. Others join the Creek Nation, in present-day Alabama, where they establish a permanent village within the Creek Nation. By the 1690s many Shawnee are congregating in present-day eastern Pennsylvania, where they are joined by remnant bands of Delaware, Munsee, and Susquehannock. Sometime before 1680 the Five Nations grant the Delaware, Susquehannock, Shawnee, and other remnant coastal nations the right to occupy territory in present-day eastern Pennsylvania, and many locate near what is now Philadelphia. Most of these nations are now landless, and the Iroquois use the landless Indian nations to create a buffer zone between themselves and the English colonies.

**1680 Fur Trade.** The Ottawa and Chippewa actively trade with the French. The Iroquois are unsuccessful in persuading or forcing the Algonkian-speaking Indian allies to trade with them or with the English in New York. The Iroquois, however, make greater inroads for hunting and trading south of the Great Lakes area, using both diplomacy and armed forces to attain their commercial ends.

**1680–1693 The Pueblo Revolt.** Popé, from San Juan Pueblo, leads an armed revolt against the Spanish. The Pueblo Revolt begins at Taos Pueblo in August 1680 and moves steadily southward, driving the Spanish to El Paso del Norte (El Paso, Texas). The Pueblos kill more than four hundred people and recover their homelands. Nine years later, a Spanish army returns. More than six hundred Indians are killed in the initial battle for the reconquest of New Mexico. In 1691, the Spanish military commander Diego de Vargas begins the bloody recovery in earnest, ending four years later. Rather than live under Spanish rule, many Pueblos flee to the small Navajo bands in the north, bringing much knowledge of the Pueblo cultural worldview and economic lifestyle to the Navajo, who until then live mostly by hunting and gathering fruits and nuts.

**1682 Pennsylvania Colony and Delaware Treaty.** William Penn purchases the present site of Philadelphia, Pennsylvania. The treaty is negotiated with a leading Delaware chief, sometimes called Tammany. An early period of peaceful relations begins between Quakers and the Indians, although relations are not always peaceful with Pennsylvania colony, especially after the 1730s.

Walpi, an ancient Hopi Pueblo village. (Courtesy of Owen Seumptewa)

**1683–1690s Shawnee Slave Trade.**  The Shawnee of the Savannah River dominate trade with South Carolina, getting guns in exchange for furs and slaves. The Shawnee capture their slaves by raiding the Winyah, Appomatuck, Cherokee, and Chatot peoples.

**1689–97 King William's War.**  King William's War initiates a series of colonial conflicts that last until the end of the War of 1812. During this time, there is an undeclared war on the frontier, first between the English and French and their respective Indian allies until 1763, or the end of the French and Indian War. Frontier warfare starts again with the Revolutionary War in 1776 and continues intermittently until 1795. The War of 1812 is the last war before the United States establishes military control over the eastern coastal frontiers. During this period of more than 125 years of intermittent warfare, Indian nations maintain trade relations with one or more European colonies and seek to retain their territory and political independence from colonial domination. Since Indian nations cannot produce metal goods or guns and powder, they depend on trade with European powers to supply these and other more domestic economic requirements. This dependency on trade forces the Indian nations to side with one or the other European power in order to have access to trade and weapons, which becomes increasingly important for defense within the climate of almost constant colonial struggle and warfare. Indian nations often sell themselves as mercenaries to one European power as a means of obtaining goods, other than by trapping furs and trading. In the north, the Algonkian-speaking nations often side with the French, until their defeat in 1760. After 1760, the western Algonkian-speaking nations (Ottawa, Chippewa, Potawatomi, Miami, and others) side with the British against the United States until the end of the War of 1812. Some nations, like the Five Nations and the Creek in the south, try to balance power diplomatically among the European colonies by not taking sides and by threatening an opponent with defection to gain political or trade concessions from the Europeans.

**1692 Reconquest of the Pueblos.**  On August 16, the governor of New Mexico, Diego de Vargas, leaves Guadelupe del Paso to begin preliminary military pacification of the Pueblos. He succeeds through diplomacy in restoring twenty-three Pueblo villages to the Spanish crown. On 13 October 1693, the recolonization of New Mexico begins. Only Santa Ana, Zia, San Felipe, and Pecos Pueblos demonstrate loyalty to the Spanish, while the Tewa, Tano, Picuris, Taos, Jemez, Acoma, and Hopi remain hostile. Considerable force is used to subjugate these groups and whole villages are destroyed and people scattered.

**1700 The Missions.**  Native Americans influenced the Spanish in many areas, particularly with their gifts of foods, natural resources, and architecture. In return, American Indians acquire horses, cattle, sheep, mules, and other livestock. In California and Texas, Indians become skilled cowboys and cowgirls. Some Indians learn the new religion and Christianity spreads widely among the American tribes. Spanish priests, generally of the Jesuit and Franciscan orders, establish missions from the Atlantic to the Pacific. The priests oversee Indian life at the missions where Indians supply the labor to build the beautiful structures so admired today.

The mission system is not a positive experience for most Native Americans. Indians often die from the meager diet and hard work, and sometimes go unattended following injuries or infection. When Indians refuse to work, priests or Christian Indians whip the people, including women and children, into submission. When families flee the missions, presidio soldiers hunt them down and force them to return. Native Americans die in large numbers at the missions from overwork, disease, and unsanitary conditions. Epidemics occur periodically in California under the Spanish occupation, the first recorded one in 1777 at Mission Santa Clara. An epidemic of diphtheria and pneumonia occurs in 1802, ravaging the young from Mission San Carlos to San Luis Obispo. Still another epidemic decimates Native Americans from San Francisco to Santa Barbara with more than 1,600 dead due to measles. Children under the age of ten are almost wiped out in this epidemic. The Native American population declines by as much as 45 percent under the Spanish occupation of California as the direct result of introduced sickness and disease.

**circa 1700–60 Early Migration onto the Great Plains.**  The Shoshone, buffalo hunters of the western plains between the Missouri and the Red Deer rivers, acquire horses for the first time. This gives them an important military advantage over their northern enemies. As a result, the Siksika, Kainai (Blood), Peigan (Blackfeet in Montana, but Blackfoot in Canada), and Atsina retreat toward the Northeast. Horse ownership spreads to most Plains groups by 1760, bringing important changes to Indian societies and to relations among Indian groups. For example, horses make buffalo hunting and transporting goods much easier. Thus, the size of residential bands grows, and horse ownership becomes a symbol of prestige and wealth in formerly egalitarian societies.

**1701–55 The Iroquois Adopt Neutrality.**  The Iroquois shift their policy from alliance with the English to

Iroquois conference, 1753. (Drawing by John Kahionhes Fadden)

neutrality between French (in New France, or present-day Canada) and the English colonies. Late in the 1690s the English begin to occupy Iroquois territory in the Mohawk Valley; this, along with the burden and losses of warfare with the French and their Indian allies, convinces the Iroquois that their English allies were as much a threat as the French. During the 1690s the Iroquois suffered from a series of military setbacks and the new English land threats. In response they developed a new policy of a united front against the Europeans by designating one speaker for the entire confederacy of Five Nations whereby one voice, rather than five chiefs, would speak for their nations.

After a treaty of peace with the French in 1701, the Iroquois Confederacy negotiates commercial agreements with the Ottawa, Chippewa, Illinois Confederacy, and other interior nations. In exchange for allowing the Iroquois to hunt and trade in the interior and Great Lakes area, the interior nations are allowed to travel to Albany, New York, to trade with the English, who had cheaper, better quality goods than the French. This agreement supports Iroquois influence in the region until the 1740s, when Pennsylvania traders follow the retreating Delaware and Shawnee into the Ohio Valley and beyond. The Iroquois restrict English trade to Albany, but the Pennsylvania traders go directly to the interior villages. Thus, the Iroquois lose their strong trade position, and their power and influence decline. The English continue to support the Iroquois Confederacy as a means to gain trade relations and diplomatic influence over the interior nations.

**1702–13 Queen Anne's War.** Queen Anne's War, pitting the English against the French and Spanish, starts in Europe, but is also fought in the American colonies. Between 1702 and 1704, the English and Indian allies (Creek and probably Cherokee) attack the Florida mission Indians of Guale (present-day Georgia) and nearly annihilate the entire population of Apalachee Indians, a remnant of which later joins the Creek. The area from the Savannah River (Georgia) to St. Augustine, Florida, is depopulated of Indian people and the Spanish missions are destroyed. Some Yamasee Indians, mission Indians in Guale, migrate to Spanish protection in Florida. The Spanish are unable or unwilling to protect them from English expansion into Florida.

**1711–22 Tuscarora War and Migration.** The Tuscarora, an Iroquoian-speaking nation living in present-day North Carolina, become involved in war with the English arising from trade disputes. Many Tuscarora become indebted to English traders, who give them credit in the form of goods in the fall of the year and collect the credit in the spring after the hunt. Many Tuscarora cannot pay back the credit, and some traders confiscate the hunters' children and wives to sell as slaves. This manner of collecting the debts leads to war in 1711, and the Tuscarora are defeated by 1713. Many Tuscarora migrate out of eastern North Carolina and travel north, where they find that the Tuscarora and the Iroquois (Five Nations) speak a language similar to their own. The Tuscarora are invited by the Oneida, one of the Five Nations of the Iroquois Confederacy, to live with them and join the confederacy. Between 1715 and 1722, many Tuscarora settle in New York with the Iroquois and are adopted into the confederacy. Nevertheless, the forty-nine chiefs do not wish to create new Tuscarora chiefs, which would violate the sacred constitution of the confederacy, and so the Oneida chiefs speak and represent the Tuscarora, at least until the 1800s, when the confederacy was disrupted. After 1715, the Iroquois Five Nations becomes known as the Six Nations.

**1715–17 The Yamasee War and Creek Neutrality.** The Yamasee of present-day Georgia, in alliance with the Creek and other smaller coastal nations such as the Hitchiti, Yuchi, and Mikasuki, rise up against the English because of a series of trade abuses and the like. The Yamasee and allies are defeated, and many tribes migrate south into Florida, ultimately forming part of the Seminole Nation, while others join the Creek Confederacy, then occupying what is now central Georgia and Alabama. This defeat convinces the Creek leaders that war against the English is not profitable, and the Creek embark on a policy of neutrality between the English colonies in the Carolinas, the Spanish in Florida and West Florida (now southern Alabama and Mississippi), and the French colony of Louisiana. The Creek balance power among rival European powers and attempt to maximize trade with and diplomatic concessions from the colonists.

**1716–27 The Creek and Cherokee War.** In the Yamasee War, the Cherokee side with the English against the Creek and their allies. This leads to bloodshed and several failed attempts to reestablish peace. In 1716, a pro-English faction of Cherokee kills a delegation of visiting Creek and Yamasee emissaries, which initiates the war. The Creek and Cherokee carry on a war of raiding parties and revenge attacks against one another.

**1720–60 The French Wars on the Chickasaw.** The Chickasaw are attracted to an English alliance because they are enticed by the low price and high quality of English trade goods. The English, in turn, seek a Chickasaw alliance because they wish to disrupt the French plan to control the Mississippi Valley by erecting a series of forts and making alliances with the Indian nations along the Mississippi River. In general, the Chickasaw favor the English, although there is a small pro-French faction. Between 1729 and 1752, the French launch four major military expeditions against the Chickasaw villages near the Mississippi in present-day western Kentucky and northwestern Mississippi. The Chickasaw survive all these attacks, although at times they are desperate for supplies and ammunition. In 1739, some Chickasaw migrate to South Carolina for English protection, while others, many of whom are survivors of the Natchez Nation that sought Chickasaw protection from the French in 1729, move to live among the western Creek. The Chickasaw are a major military obstacle to the French plan of enveloping the British colonies and restricting them to the Atlantic seaboard.

**1729 Destruction of the Natchez Nation.** The Natchez Nation, a Muskogean-speaking society with a centralized sacred chieftain, The Great Sun, and a remnant society of the Mississippian culture, rebels against French attempts to impose taxes and confiscate land in their central village, Natchez. The French at Natchez plantation, in the Louisiana colony, are wiped out. The French and their Choctaw allies counterattack and destroy the Natchez villages. The Great Sun is captured, along with several hundred other captives, and is sold into slavery in the Caribbean Islands. The Natchez descendants still live on the island of St. Helena. Other Natchez escape, some seeking refuge among the Chickasaw, who give them shelter, but this intensifies warring relations between the Natchez and the French and Choctaw.

**1739 Arikara Migrate North.** About this time, a group of Indians known now as the Arikara (a tribe closely related to the Pawnee) begin to migrate north from the Loup River in present-day Nebraska and travel up the Missouri River to settle eventually in present-day central North Dakota.

**1740–1805 Russians Explore the Northwest Coast.** The first Russian explorers sail over to Alaska and explore the entire Alaskan coastline and encounter many Pacific Northwest Coast tribal groups, like the Haida, Tlingit, Aleut, and others. In the 1740s and 1750s, following Vitus Bering who in 1741 sighted the North American continent and explored the Bering Sea and

Early colonists often observed Native societies. (Drawing by John Kahionhes Fadden)

Bering Strait, the Russians open trade with Natives for sea otter pelts. Russian fur traders expand their enterprises in the far Northwest and by 1805 reach San Francisco, California. French, Dutch, and Russians establish colonies primarily to exploit the rich resource in fur. They trade guns, powder, lead, pots and pans, knives, fishhooks, beads, and cloth for furs. Indians often alter their traditional lives to obtain furs to trade for these items; in doing so, their cultures change and many become dependent on the European supply of manufactured goods.

In the second half of the eighteenth century, the Russian government sends over many Russian Orthodox priests to convert and protect the Natives. Many of these early Russian Orthodox churches and their Native congregations, sometimes singing mass in archaic Russian, can still be found in several places in Alaska.

**1744–48 King George's War.** King George's War is initiated in Europe and is fought, in part, by the European colonies in North America. This war pits the French against the English, and each side persuades its Indian allies to fight. It is cheaper and more efficient for colonial governments to hire Indian fighters to engage in war than to import troops from Europe, where they are badly needed. In North America, the war is inconclusive; the Treaty of Aix-la-Chapelle, negotiated in Europe, restores all original boundaries.

**1748–51 The Choctaw Civil War.** The Choctaw Nation is divided during the 1730s and 1740s between loyalty to the French and cheap trade goods given by the English. One region, the central and northeast villages, favors English trade, while the western and southern villages favor French alliance. Civil war erupts between the regions when Red Shoes, the head warrior of the eastern allied towns, is assassinated for a bounty by a pro-French Indian. Both sides rely on their allies to supply weapons and ammunition, but the British fail to provide enough support and the pro-British eastern villages are defeated. After 1751, Choctaw political relations are organized into three autonomous political regions: the conservative Six Towns district (or *iksa*, a Choctaw term for a matrilineal descent group) in the south favor the French; the western villages, called "people of the long hair," also favor the French; and the northeastern villages, called the "potato people," favor the British. Each district has a chief and a council, and each decides its own internal matters, rarely meeting with the other two districts to discuss national business. The three-district political system lasts among the Choctaw until 1907, when the U.S. government abolishes the government of the Choctaw Nation.

**1749–63 French and Indian War.** The French and Indian War begins with the French construction of Fort Duquesne (present-day Pittsburgh, Pennsylvania) on land already claimed by Virginia. The European colonies go to war over lands along the Ohio River. Many Iroquois (primarily Mohawk) reluctantly side with the British, while Seneca favor the French for a time. Many Indians align themselves with the French, including the Wyandotte, Shawnee, Chippewa, Ottawa, Miami, Abenaki, and Lenape. At first the war goes well for the French and their Spanish and Indian allies, but in the end the French lose nearly all their claims in the Americas, including Canada and the Illinois-Mississippi River valleys. Indians who fought with the French now find themselves without their allies and without suppliers of arms and trade goods.

**1750–1850 The Chickahominy Nation Disperses.** The Chickahominy Nation of Virginia breaks into several smaller communities. Some join the Pamunkey, Mattaponi, and other remaining nations living near the Chesapeake Bay area, while others hang onto their lands, living by hunting and fishing. By the 1760s and later, the Chickahominy people are no longer mentioned in the Virginia records.

**1754 The Albany Plan.** Benjamin Franklin, a prominent citizen and statesman from Pennsylvania, proposes a plan of union for the British colonies. Franklin has several times visited the Iroquois Confederacy (Six Nations) and suggests their model for unifying the colonies. He remarks that it is strange that the Six Nations could form an apparently indissoluble union, while ten or twelve British colonies could not. The plan fails in 1754—for want of interest by more than a few colonists—but is revived later in the U.S. Articles of Confederation (1777–88), the first laws of U.S. government, and the U.S. Constitution (implemented in 1789).

**1760–75 The British in Sole Control of Eastern North America.** The French defeat by 1760 changes the situation of the eastern Native nations. Since about 1600, there were at least two or more major European powers fighting for control of trade and land. Now only the British remain, and only one nation controls trade relations and supplies of goods, weapons, and ammunition. The British try to regulate the distribution of trade and weapons, which makes the formerly French allied Indians suspicious of British intentions. Furthermore, the British intend to occupy the old French forts, such as Detroit and Chicago, in the Great Lakes area, which was territory the Indians claimed and did not grant British occupation. Ottawa, Wyandotte, Miami, Great Lakes nations, and Shawnee Indians living north of the Ohio River fear British political domination. In the 1760s and early 1770s, the British administration plans to regulate the Indians' trade and activities, but these plans are disrupted by the emergence of the revolutionary war in 1775.

**1760–63 The Delaware Prophet.** After the French defeat in 1760, and while the British threaten domination, several prophets emerge among the Delaware people. Two major figures teach very different messages. One brings a militant message, involving borrowed Christian concepts of personal salvation in heaven; the other "domestic" Delaware prophet teaches a message also borrowed from Christian ideas of heaven and a central god, but establishes a new religion designed only for the Delaware, not for any other Indian or European nations.

The more militant prophet emphasizes that the Europeans will have to be driven off the continent and the Indians return to the customs of their ancestors before they can be restored to their former prosperous and happy state. This message greatly influences the Ottawa leader Pontiac, who uses it to mobilize warriors from different nations to strike at the English in 1763. The "domestic" Delaware prophet creates a new national religion, reorganizes the Delawares' disrupted kinship system, and creates new and permanent chiefs for the three reorganized kinship-religious divisions of the religiously and politically unified Delaware Nation.

Hendrick, Abraham, and Franklin at the Albany Conference, 1754. (Drawing by John Kahionhes Fadden)

**1763 Pontiac's War.** Pontiac follows the militant Delaware prophet and, through this religious revitalization movement, forms a confederacy of the Ottawa, Lenape (Delaware), Wyandotte, Seneca, Potawatomi, Kickapoo, Shawnee, and Miami tribes. Pontiac leads the confederacy in a short-lived war, which does not prevent the British from occupying the old French forts of the Ohio and Great Lakes area.

**1763 The Proclamation of 1763.** The British government's proclamation results in a boundary, the Proclamation Line of 1763, running along the crest of the Appalachian Mountains. Indian country is west of the line from the Appalachian Mountains to the Mississippi River, while colonists can settle lands east of the line. This act recognizes Indian rights to land, but many colonists disregard the act and move across the Appalachians, causing conflict with the Indian nations that regard the colonists as intruders.

**1763–74 Pre-Revolutionary Policy.** Between 1763 and 1774, most of the nations in the eastern portion of North America reassess their relationship with the

British government and the colonists. Native Americans realize that a rift has developed between the British homeland and the colonists, and many seek positions of neutrality; however, as the British government and the colonists drift closer to war, some of the nations favor alliance with the British. Many Indians believe that in the event of war, the British will win. Many Indians also believe that the colonists, who are interested in acquiring more land, are a greater threat to the Indians than the British government.

**1765 Paxton Boys' Massacre.** Frustrated by the failure of Pennsylvania's Quaker-dominated assembly to take more aggressive action against the Indians of that state, a group of seventy-five Presbyterians from Paxton in Lancaster County take matters into their own hands. They attack a village of Conestoga Mission Indians (Christianized Susquehannock and others) and violently murder six people, scalping them all. The remaining Conestoga are moved to the Lancaster jail for their own protection. Governor John Penn issues a proclamation denouncing the incident and orders the violence to stop. In spite of his orders the Paxton Boys strike again, breaking into the jail on December 27 and murdering the remaining fourteen Conestoga.

**1768 Treaty of Fort Stanwix.**   Bowing to British insistence, the Six Nations cede land ranging from south of the Ohio River into present-day northern Kentucky. Most of this land comprises the traditional Shawnee homeland, and the Shawnee recognize no right of the Six Nations to sell it to the British. Thereafter, the Shawnee and their ally, the Delaware (both nations then residing in present-day Ohio) organize a pan-Indian confederacy without the leadership of the Six Nations, now seen as puppets of the British. The Six Nations, since about 1700, gain informal leadership of a broad coalition of Indian nations, once boasting that they could muster warriors from fifty nations. Now the influence of the Six Nations declines, and the loose confederacy of western Indian nations are led by the Shawnee, Delaware, and Miami. The Indian confederation tries to keep settlers out of the Old Northwest, the area west of the Ohio River, including the Great Lakes area. This confederacy defends the Old Northwest until the end of the War of 1812.

**1769 Missions Established in California.**   The San Diego Mission, the first in a series of twenty-one religious agrarian settlements to be built approximately a day's journey apart along El Camino Real, the Spanish land route from San Diego to San Francisco, is established. The missions support two Franciscan friars as overseers, a protective military garrison, and hundreds of "Christianized" Indians, who are impressed for mission work and religious conversion. Those who do not obey are subject to a number of punishments, including solitary confinement, lashing, branding, and execution. Mission Indians find life very difficult; the Spanish forbid any practice of traditional cultures and religions, and many Indians die of disease and hardship.

In response to this invasion of their territory, California Indian groups begin to resist almost immediately. The Ipai and Tipai Indians, on whose land the San Diego Mission is built, attack the Spanish camp within a month of its establishment. Six years later on 4 November 1775, under the leadership of two baptized village headmen, a force of 800 Ipai and Tipai destroy the mission there, killing the resident padre. Other acts of rebellion take place, most notably the 1824 revolt at Missions La Purisima and Santa Barbara, when mistreated neophytes capture both missions for a short time. In the end all these revolts are defeated.

**1773–74 Lord Dunmore's War.**   Angry about settlers from Virginia moving onto their lands and sometimes murdering Indians, the Shawnee and their allies move to protect territories in western Virginia and Pennsylvania. Lord Dunmore, governor of Virginia, musters an army and fights a series of skirmishes with the Indians along the Virginia and Pennsylvania frontier.

**1774–75 Formation of the Indian Departments.** During the First Continental Congress in 1774, the delegates, worried about Indian loyalties, commit £40,000 to Indian affairs and appoint a Committee on Indian Affairs to negotiate terms of neutrality or support from the Indians. In 1775, the First Continental Congress assumes control over Indian affairs, removing such power from the individual colonies. Northern, southern, and middle departments are created, with commissioners appointed to the head of each. Indian affairs are considered of such importance at this juncture in U.S. history that Benjamin Franklin, Patrick Henry, and James Wilson, all central leaders in the Revolution, are named the first commissioners of the Indian departments. The commissioners are authorized to make treaties and to arrest British agents. They open negotiations with the Six Nations in order to win their neutrality in the impending war, if not their alliance. The commissioners offer trade goods and blacksmith services as a part of a treaty of alliance, but the Six Nations decline the offer.

**1775 Cheyenne Receive the Sacred Law.**   According to their tradition, the Cheyenne are granted their sacred law and covenant with the Creator at this time through the prophet Sweet Medicine. Sweet Medicine receives the law directly from the Creator on a sacred mountain, present-day Bear Butte in South Dakota. Sweet Medicine then gives the Cheyenne instructions to form a council of forty-four chiefs—forty chiefs elected from the ten traditional Cheyenne bands and four chiefs appointed to represent the four sacred directions. The covenant relation obliges the Cheyenne people to uphold the sacred law and ceremonies; in return, the Creator preserves the Cheyenne Nation from physical and cultural destruction.

**1777–83 Iroquois Confederacy Is Dispersed.**   The Revolutionary War permanently disrupts the unity of the Iroquois Confederacy. At the beginning of the war, many Iroquois, especially the Seneca and Onondaga, prefer neutrality and do not wish to join with either warring party. Some Mohawk, led by Joseph Brant, a close family friend to the British agent William Johnson, prefer to fight with the British. The Oneida and Tuscarora, because of local trade and friendship ties with settlers, prefer to side with the United States. This absence of agreement about how to handle the war does not allow the Confederate Council to arrive at a

On 11 June 1776, an Onondaga sachem gave John Hancock an Iroquois name at Independence Hall. (Drawing by John Kahionhes Fadden)

common plan of action (all six nations of the confederacy must agree to all decisions, otherwise each nation acts independently). Since there is no agreement, the individual nations, villages, even families make their own decisions about alliance or neutrality. This causes a deep rift within the confederacy, which is not effectively restored, even after the Revolutionary War. The pro-British Iroquois move to Canada during and after the war and eventually form their own confederacy, and the Iroquois remaining in New York do likewise. Thus, by the early 1800s two independent Iroquois Confederacies emerge.

**1777–87 Articles of Confederation.**   Under the Articles of Confederation—the first U.S. laws of national government—Native Americans are treated as sovereign nations. Under the terms of the Peace of Paris (1783), the United States receives claim to all the land from the Atlantic to the Mississippi River, and from the Great Lakes to the Florida border. Congress has administrative authority over these lands, but most of them belong to Indians. The British long followed the precedent that Native Americans had a "natural right" to the land but that they could relinquish title to the lands through agreements. For the most part, the United States follows this principle, although the country will claim vast areas of land from the Indians by right of conquest. In 1779, the Continental Congress passes a law asserting that only the national government can transfer ownership of Indian lands, and, by the Ordinance of 1787, the United States promises that Native Americans' "land and property shall never be taken from them without their consent; and in their property, rights and liberty, they shall never be invaded or disturbed, unless in just and lawful wars authorized by Congress."

**17 September 1778 First U.S.-Indian Treaty Is Signed.**   At Fort Pitt (now Pittsburgh, Pennsylvania), the Delaware, primarily the Turtle, one of three Delaware divisions, sign a peace treaty with the United States. The treaty offers the Delawares the right to send representatives to Congress and become part of the U.S. nation. This clause, however, is never implemented. The Delaware Treaty is the first of 370 treaties signed with Indian nations between 1778 and 1871, when Congress passes a law forbidding the government to make treaties with Indians.

**1783–95 Intermittent Border Wars.**   After the end of the Revolutionary War in 1783, the political and military situation remains extremely unstable. Between 1783 and 1795 the British continue to occupy the forts of the Old Northwest, at Detroit and Chicago, although by treaty they are to be evacuated. The United States has neither the military strength nor the will to dislodge the British soldiers. The British occupy the forts and supply their Indian allies west of the Ohio River with goods and weapons, hoping that the Indian nations will create a buffer zone between the United States and Canada. The Indian nations (Delaware, Miami, Shawnee, Ottawa, and others) hope to use British support to keep U.S. settlers from streaming across the Ohio River and taking Indian land.

The U.S. government has little money with which to operate, but it claims all Indian land west to the Mississippi River. The new nation makes considerable money by selling western lands in Ohio, Indiana, Kentucky, and Tennessee. In the north, the Wyandotte, Delaware, Shawnee, Miami, Chippewa, Potawatomi, Kickapoo, Ottawa, and some Iroquois warriors join to defy the U.S. invasion of the Old Northwest, bringing war to the settlers in Ohio in their attempt to drive them out. Between 1783 and 1790 perhaps one thousand settlers lose their lives; there are no estimates regarding Indian deaths north of the Ohio River caused by war and disease.

In the 1780s, several unsuccessful treaties are signed between small Indian groups and the U.S. government. The U.S. commissioners negotiate these treaties at Fort Stanwix with the Six Nations (1784); at Fort McIntosh with the Wyandotte, Delaware, Chippewa, and Ottawa (1785); at Fort Finney with the Shawnee (1786); and at Fort Hopewell with the Cherokee, Choctaw, and Chickasaw (1786). The treaties typically contain several articles, including those that cede certain lands to the United States. Not all the Indian leaders of the various nations agree with or sign the treaties. Trouble results when settlers move onto western lands they purchase from land companies. In Ohio, Kentucky, and Tennessee, settlers often find Native Americans still residing on and laying claim to lands that the settlers have bought. Although some settlers and Indians live peacefully beside one another, there is continued conflict over land ownership.

Land disputes result in intermittent skirmishes along the frontier between 1790 and 1794. President George Washington answers the Indian challenge by directing General Josiah Harmer and 1,500 troops to engage the Indians. Kickapoo, Shawnee, and Miami snipers harass the soldiers as they march south of the Maumee River in Ohio. In September 1790 the Indian alliance launches a successful battle that defeats Harmer and provokes Washington into sending Governor Arthur St. Clair and 3,000 troops to the Maumee River, in present-day Indiana, to confront the Indians. Once again Native American forces strike hard, killing and wounding more than 900 soldiers. Still determined to destroy the Indian alliance in the Old Northwest, Washington orders General Anthony Wayne into Ohio. In August 1794, the confederated nations, led by Little Turtle of the Miami Nation, go into battle against Wayne, known to the Indians as Blacksnake, at the Battle of Fallen Timbers, near present-day Fort Wayne, Indiana. Partly because the British fail to come to the Indians' aid at the battle, the Indians are forced to retreat. The Indians' political position further erodes when, in late 1794, the United States and Britain sign Jay's Treaty; the English depart to Canada and withdraw their military support for their Indian allies. This forces the Indians of the Old Northwest to treat with the United States in 1795 at Fort Greenville, in present-day Indiana. The Indian nations recognize the United States as the primary non-Indian power in the area and cede most of Ohio to the United States for $20,000 worth of goods and an annuity of $10,000. The Indian nations of the Old Northwest— the Wyandotte, Shawnee, Delaware, Potawatomi, Miami, Kickapoo, Ottawa, and Chippewa—lose considerable land and power.

In the South, parts of the Cherokee, Creek, Choctaw, and Chickasaw nations side with the Spanish in order to curtail U.S.-settler expansion into their territories. Like the British in the North, the Spanish in Florida and West Florida (present-day Alabama and Mississippi)

On 2 May 1780, Cornplanter addressed Congress in New York City. (Drawing by John Kahionhes Fadden)

provide the southern Indians with trade and weapons. This leads to intermittent warfare between the westward-moving settlers and the Indian nations, who are intent on defending their territory.

Like the British, the Spanish hope to prevent the territorial expansion of the young United States. In 1795, when the Napoleonic Wars begin in Europe, the Spanish turn their attention to Europe and ignore their relatively unprofitable Florida colonies. Thus, the southern Indian nations, in a series of treaties in the middle 1790s, are forced to recognize the United States as the major non-Indian power in the South.

**7 August 1786 Federal Indian Reservation.** The first federal Indian reservation is established. Congress establishes two departments: the northern, with jurisdiction north of the Ohio River and west of the Hudson River, and the southern, which covers the area south of the Ohio River. A superintendent is appointed to head each department, reporting to the secretary of war. Each of these officials has the power to grant licenses to trade and live among the Indian people.

**1787–89 Indians and the U.S. Constitution.** In 1787, delegates come to Philadelphia to frame the Constitution. Some Native Americans and scholars argue that the delegates learned much about representative government from the Iroquois, and that the Constitution is patterned after the political ideas of the Iroquois and the political structure of their league. Furthermore, ideas of individual political freedom, free speech, political equality, and political community are recorded in sixteenth- and seventeenth-century encounters with Native societies. Many of these observations are incorporated into the Enlightenment philosophy of the 1700s by such men as Jean-Jacques Rousseau and Voltaire. The Enlightenment philosophy in turn influences contemporary political thought and the organization of democracy in Western nations.

After much debate, the states ratify the Constitution and it becomes the supreme law in the United States. The constitutional delegates want Indian policy to be centralized and determined by Congress. Article 1, Section 8 of the Constitution, often called the Commerce Clause, empowers Congress to make all laws pertaining to the Indian trade and diplomatic relations.

This clause prohibits the original thirteen colonies from negotiating treaties directly with Indian nations and leaves control over Indian land in federal hands, outside individual state's jurisdiction. Through treaty-making, which requires ratification by the Senate with a two-thirds vote and signature by the president, the Indian nations form a legal relationship with the U.S. government. Treaties end wars and cede to the government millions of acres of land.

**1787 The Northwest Ordinances.**  The Northwest Ordinance of 1787 calls for the division of lands north of the Ohio River into territories that can eventually become states. In this way, the Congress establishes the mechanism by which territories and states will be created. In order to open lands for settlement, Congress passes the Ordinance of 1785, which calls for the survey of so-called public land into townships of six miles square divided into thirty-six sections of 640 acres each, costing $640. This method favors land speculators with money to invest. Real estate companies emerge, buying large tracts of land and subdividing them to make purchases more affordable for smaller farmers. Yet, in order for the two ordinances to work, the United States must secure Indian title to the land. The government establishes this through treaties.

**1789 Indian Affairs Moved to War Department.** Since 1784, Congress has delegated negotiation of treaties to the War Department. In 1786, the secretary of war assumes management of Indian Affairs, and in 1789, with the creation of the new War Department, Indian Affairs are delegated to the first Secretary of War, Henry Knox. Because many Indian nations on the frontier are allied with the British or Spanish and resist U.S. settlement, the War Department is seen as the most appropriate agency to manage Indians relations.

**1799 Religious Revitalization and Handsome Lake.**  Handsome Lake, a Seneca clan leader, becomes so ill that his family and friends gather to pay their respects before he dies. Not long after his apparent death, Handsome Lake recovers and tells everyone that his soul left his body and met three Native angels. They told Handsome Lake to end his drinking, live a good life, and follow the teachings of the Creator who would reveal himself in the months ahead. In the fall of 1799, Handsome Lake has a second vision, in which he meets the Creator and learns lessons that become the hallmark of the revitalized Longhouse religion. By the late 1830s, the religion becomes the Handsome Lake Church. His visions and teachings are known as the Gaiwiio, the good word. He teaches that Native Americans should live in peace with the United States, but that they should spiritually or culturally be Iroquois.

His doctrines stress peace within the family and among all people.

**1803 The Louisiana Purchase.**  The United States buys from France a large portion of land west of the Mississippi River extending in the north to the Pacific Ocean. This land contains large numbers of Indian nations, many of whom have yet to have extended political relations with a European or U.S. government. With the purchase of these western lands, President Thomas Jefferson proposes that many of the Indian nations living east of the Mississippi River be removed west to lands where they would be out of the way of U.S. settlers, and the eastern land would be open to settlement.

**1805–1806 Sacajawea Aids Lewis and Clark Expedition.**  While wintering in present-day North Dakota, explorers William Clark and Meriwether Lewis meet Sacajawea, a Shoshone woman married to French trader Toussaint Charbonneau. Charbonneau is hired as an interpreter and guide. Sacajawea proves invaluable to the men's expedition because she can speak to Indians encountered along the way. Her female presence is seen as a peaceful symbol to them.

**1805 The Munsee Prophetess.**  In the early 1800s U.S. officials in present-day Indiana pressure leaders of the Delaware, Shawnee, and other Old Northwest Indian nations into selling significant tracts of land, resulting in considerable tension and dismay among most members of the Indian nations. Between 1803 and 1805, while the Delaware and Munsee are living in what is now the area between Indianapolis and Munsee, Indiana, several Delaware have visions. But in 1805, a female, now known only as the Munsee Prophetess, has a vision and consequently introduces modifications to the Delaware Big House Religion, the Delaware national religion since the Delaware prophet of the 1760s. The Munsee Prophetess teaches that the Indians must retain their traditions and reject farming, Christianity, trade, and European clothing, otherwise the Delaware Nation will continue to decline politically, economically, and spiritually. When Tenskwatawa, the Shawnee prophet who lives in the Delaware and Munsee villages, emerges in February 1806, the prophetess defers to him.

**1806–1809 Tecumseh and Tenskwatawa, the Shawnee Prophet.**  In February 1806, while living among the Delaware and Munsee, Tenskwatawa reportedly dies. While his family prepares him for burial, he regains consciousness, saying that he had died and visited the Master of Life. Tenskwatawa reports that through him, The Open Door, Native Americans can learn the Way.

Thousands of Indians gravitate toward Tenskwatawa and his teachings, flocking to hear him preach in a village called Prophetstown. So many Native peoples come to the village that resources are depleted, and the prophet is forced to move his town west, settling near the junction of the Tippecanoe and Wabash rivers in eastern Indiana. Through his religious revitalization movement, Tenskwatawa unites many tribes to stand against the United States. Using his brother's spiritual movement, Tecumseh forges a pan-Indian confederacy that is both political and military.

**1811 Battle of Tippecanoe.** With a Creek medicine man named Seekaboo, Tecumseh travels to the southern Indian nations, seeking support for his confederacy. Only a portion of the Creek, known as Red Sticks, join the movement. Tecumseh returns to the north to learn that against his instructions, his brother the prophet, entered into battle with U.S. troops. In November 1811, Governor William Henry Harrison, future U.S. president, leads 1,000 soldiers within a few miles of Prophetstown. Tenskwatawa, the prophet, provides ceremonial protection from bullets and encourages his followers to attack the soldier's camp. During the battle the Prophet's followers suffer casualties. Thereafter, most of the Indians abandon the his leadership and religion.

**1812–14 The War of 1812.** The War of 1812 devastates the land and populations of the Indians of the Old Northwest. At the Treaty of Ghent, which ends the war, the British agree that all the territory south of the Great Lakes belongs to the United States, and the British agree not to give aid to their ally Indians there. This leaves the Indian nations living east of the Mississippi River entirely within the sphere of the U.S. government's influence. The Indians no longer have the supplies or alliance of a rival European power to balance against the United States. By 1819, the Spanish sell Florida and West Florida to the United States, and U.S. claims to the land east of the Mississippi River are undisputed, except by the Indian nations still living there. After 1817 to 1819, however, the political and diplomatic position of the Indian nations rapidly deteriorates, and they are less able to retain territory and political independence.

**1813–14 The Red Stick War.** Angry over U.S. interference and control within the Creek government and influenced by Tecumseh's message of resistance to the United States, Creeks living in present-day Alabama called Red Sticks attack Creek villages allied with the United States. Sometime later the Red Sticks also attack Fort Mims, killing U.S. citizens there and providing an excuse for the United States to enter into the Creek civil war. General Andrew Jackson, with five thousand troops and Indian allies, marches against the Red Sticks at the village of Tohopeka at Horseshoe Bend on the Tallapoosa River. Surrounded and assaulted by cannon fire, the Red Sticks suffer losses of more than eight hundred men, women, and children. The Creek Nation, including the U.S.-allied Creek, is forced to accept the Treaty of Fort Jackson, which cedes 22 million acres of Creek land in Georgia and Alabama to the U.S. government.

**1817–18 The First Seminole War.** In Florida, a U.S. attack on Fowltown, home of the Seminole chief Neamathla, officially begins the war on 21 November 1817. Forces led by General Andrew Jackson destroy Seminole villages and farms in northern Florida, leading to the cession of Florida to the United States by Spain. Some Creek Red Sticks join the Seminole in Florida and continue resistance to the United States with the help of English trade companies.

**1817–1819 Cherokee Migration.** Because of continuing harassment from U.S. settlers, several thousand Cherokee emigrate beyond the Mississippi River into Arkansas, forming a Cherokee Nation West.

**1821 The Cherokee Syllabary.** Sequoyah, a Cherokee living in present-day Arkansas, develops the Cherokee syllabary, a writing code using symbols for syllables rather than for sounds. Many Cherokee quickly learn to read and write in the Cherokee syllabary. Translations of the Bible are made into Cherokee, and Cherokee spiritual leaders and healers record sacred and medicinal knowledge.

**1823 *Johnson v. M'Intosh*.** In *Johnson v. M'Intosh*, a case before the U.S. Supreme Court, Justice John Marshall recognizes that Indians have the right to land by their prior use, but rules that Indian tribes cannot sell land to private individuals and must sell only to the federal government. This case curtails Indian control over the use and sale of their own territory.

**1827–28 The Cherokee Republic.** The Cherokee watch the drift toward a policy of forced removal and decide upon a unique course of action in their attempt to prevent their own removal. In the early 1820s, the Cherokee establish a capital in New Echota, in present-day Georgia. In 1827, they write a constitution calling for three branches of government, in many ways similar to the U.S. federal constitution. In 1828, the Cherokee ratify the new constitution and elect John Ross, a wealthy Cherokee slaveholder, principal chief. The Cherokee wish to establish their government and right to preserve their homeland in present-day Georgia, Tennessee, and eastern Alabama. In January 1829 the Georgia legislature, wanting to remove the Cherokee from their chartered limits, pass a series of laws that abolish the Cherokee government and appropriate Cherokee territory.

**1828–35 *The Cherokee Phoenix.*** *The Cherokee Phoenix*, a weekly newspaper printed in English and Cherokee, is published. The newspaper's first editor is Elias Boudinot, who was educated in Cornwall, Connecticut, after attending primary school among the Moravian missionaries in Tennessee. The newspaper is discontinued when the U.S. government presses the Cherokee Nation to move west. Boudinot joins a minority group in signing the Treaty of New Echota in 1835, which, according to the U.S. government, obligates the Cherokee to move west to present-day Oklahoma.

**1830–60 The Removal Era.** In 1830, Congress votes in favor of the Indian Removal Act. The removal of Native Americans from their lands becomes an integral element of national Indian policy. During the 1830s and 1840s, the U.S. Army forces thousands of Indian families to leave their belongings and move to lands west of present-day Iowa, Missouri, Kansas, Nebraska, Arkansas, and Oklahoma. The United States forces the Cherokee onto the Trail of Tears, which directly results in the death of four thousand to eight thousand people. One soldier writes: "I fought through the Civil War and have seen men shot to pieces and slaughtered by thousands, but the Cherokee removal was the cruelest work I ever knew."

The Cherokee Nation is not the only Native nation to remove to Indian Territory. Other nations include the Choctaw, Chickasaw, Creek, Seminole, Wyandotte, Ottawa, Peoria, Miami, Potawatomi, Sac, Fox, Delaware, Seneca and many others. The government is ill prepared to handle so many Indians along the trails and in new homes. In 1841, Major Ethan Allan Hitchcock investigates Indian affairs in the West and concludes that the American Indian policy is filled with "bribery, perjury and forgery, short weights, issues of spoiled meat and grain, and every conceivable subterfuge."

**1830 Treaty at Dancing Rabbit Creek.** The Choctaw sign the Treaty at Dancing Rabbit Creek, ceding more than 10 million acres of land in Alabama and Mississippi. In exchange they are promised peace, friendship, and land in the West. They are not compensated, as promised, for farm buildings, schoolhouses, and livestock that they lose by giving up their homelands.

The move takes nearly three years, and hundreds of Choctaw die during the removal.

**1831 *Cherokee Nation v. Georgia.*** Against Georgia's efforts to remove the Cherokee from their homeland, the Cherokee counter with a lawsuit in the Supreme Court. *Cherokee Nation v. Georgia* is based on a clause in the Constitution that allows foreign nations to seek redress in the U.S. Supreme Court for damages caused by U.S. citizens. Chief Justice John Marshall rules that the Cherokee Nation is not a foreign republic, but a domestic dependent nation. Indians are not citizens of the United states but are wards of the government.

**1832 *Worcester v. Georgia.*** *Worcester v. Georgia* is brought by the Cherokee Nation with the help of two missionaries, Samuel Worcester and John Butterick. Since the Cherokee are not citizens and the court ruled they are not a foreign nation, the Cherokee must rely on U.S. citizens to make their case against Georgia. The missionaries defy Georgia law by carrying on Cherokee Nation business and refuse to swear allegiance to Georgia, for which they are arrested and sentenced to hard labor. In this case, the Court strikes down the Georgia law arguing that only the federal government has the right to regulate affairs in Indian country, while states cannot extend their laws over Indian governments. The Indian Nations sign treaties recognizing U.S. power, but do not cede rights to self government or territory. The Cherokee are forced to move between 1835 and 1839. *Worcester v. Georgia* now stands as a major precedent supporting Indian rights to self-government as long as they do not conflict with federal or constitutional law.

**1832 The Black Hawk War.** Remnant bands of the Sauk and Fox tribes attempt to reclaim land in Wisconsin and Illinois but are quickly repressed by U.S. troops. Black Hawk, a keeper of a major medicine bundle among the Sauk and Fox, is strongly opposed to ceding territory in present-day Illinois.

**1835–42 The Second U.S. and Seminole War.** U.S. troops battle in the swamps of Florida. The Seminole conduct a guerrilla-style warfare that costs the U.S. government more than $20 million and the lives of 1,500 troops. The Seminole leader Osceola is deceived and captured under a flag of truce and dies in prison in 1838.

**1837–53 Kenekuk, the Kickapoo Prophet.** After the end of the War of 1812, Kenekuk, a Kickapoo, assumes leadership of a segment of the Kickapoo Nation, then living along the Osage River in Illinois.

Based on Kenekuk's teachings, these Kickapoo form a community of 350 that turns to agriculture and adopts selected Protestant, Catholic, and traditional religious and moral teachings. While strongly resisting removal from their homeland, they are finally forced to migrate to Missouri in 1833 and to present-day Kansas by 1837. There, the prophet converts a group of Potawatomi, who join the prophet's community in 1851. This community survives to the present. Kenekuk dies in Kansas in 1853, but not before promising his faithful that he will rise again after three days.

**1837–70 Smallpox Epidemic on the Plains.** The once numerous Mandan and Hidatsa, living in present-day central North Dakota, are decimated. Both tribes lose as much as 90 percent of their population, leaving only a few hundred survivors. Other Plains nations are also hit hard, some left with only about 20 percent of their previous numbers. Between 1837 and 1870, at least four smallpox epidemics kill thousands of people among the Plains Indian nations.

**1840–60 Indian Territory and the Indian State.** During the 1840s and 1850s, U.S. officials adhere to a plan to ultimately move all Indians to Indian Territory, present-day Kansas and Oklahoma. U.S. officials believe that more land can be opened to settlers, and the Indians can be incorporated into the United States by means of their own state, with elected officials representing Indian interests in Congress. In the post–Civil War period, however, this plan is abandoned because many Indian nations do not want to move to Indian Territory, and most do not want to be incorporated under one Indian political government or be included in the U.S. Congress and government.

**1846–48 Mexican-American War.** Between 1846 and 1848 the United States fights Mexico in a war that ends with the Treaty of Guadelupe Hidalgo. Mexico cedes to the United States any and all claims to California and the Southwest. The U.S. government thus brings American Indian policy to that region of the country and to the Pacific Northwest. As in other parts of the nation, the government considers that Indians have a "natural right" to the land; however, the Indians can also relinquish their lands through treaties. Throughout the West, the United States commissions agents to extinguish Indian title to millions of acres. Nations such as the Navajo, Sioux, Kiowa, and Modoc fight back against the U.S. Army. Others such as the Crow, Caddo, Blackfeet, Hopi, and Nespelem do not. Regardless of the policies followed by the various nations, the ultimate results are the same: the United States asserts its authority through the army and the Indian administration. Lands are taken from the Indians through

treaties or by right of conquest. Western Indians secure for themselves only a minute portion of their former lands and live on lands ruled by Indian agents. Many Indians are relocated to lands controlled by their neighbors. Others are concentrated on reservations with other Indian nations, including former enemies.

**1846 Navajo Resistance.** At the end of the Mexican-American War, U.S. settlers move into California and New Mexico where the *Diné* (Navajo for "the people") face the U.S. Army. The Navajo are one of the first Indian nations in the American Southwest to deal with the United States. Between 1600 and 1846 the Navajo confront the Nakai, or Spanish, who moved into the Rio Grande Valley of New Mexico onto lands belonging to Pueblo Indians. The Europeans introduce cattle, sheep, and horses to the Natives, and the Navajo take advantage of the innovations by sweeping down on New Mexican villages to steal stock. Comanche, Kiowa, Apache, Ute, and others follow suit, giving rise to an economy based in part on raiding. By 1846, when the United States enters New Mexico, Navajo people already have extensive holdings of cattle, sheep, and horses.

When Colonel Stephen Watts Kearny enters New Mexico in 1846, he promises to end Navajo raids on New Mexican villages and, to this end, he dispatches Colonel Alexander W. Doniphan to Navajo country. Doniphan meets with a group of Navajo Naat'aani (headmen) at Bear Springs near present-day Gallup, New Mexico. He concludes the first treaty with the Navajo, which is ratified by the Senate and signed by the president.

During the 1850s, a number of Navajo leaders sign treaties with the United States intended to end hostilities and establish trade relations between Indian and non-Indian communities of New Mexico. The agreements fail because the Navajo continue to raid New Mexican villages and because New Mexicans enslave Navajo. The conflict centers on livestock and slaves, not land, since most non-Indians consider Navajo land beautiful but unproductive. In 1860, Colonel Edward R. S. Canby, who had fought the Seminole in Florida, leads a campaign against the Navajo. By sending out small raiding parties and striking purposefully at civilian populations, Canby brings the Navajo to the bargaining table. In the spring of 1861 several Navajo leaders, including Manuelito, Barboncito, Armijo, Herrero, and Ganada Mucho, agree to a peace treaty. Canby's campaign probably would have ended the Navajo wars had it not been for the U.S. Civil War.

**1848 The California Gold Rush.** In 1848, Maidu and other California Indians working for James Marshall, a miller, discover gold on the American River, near Sacramento, California. At first, Native Americans in California work in the gold mines, contributing significantly to their discovery and success. Between 1848 and 1850 California officials estimate that more than one-half of the miners in California were Natives. During the 1850s some California miners abuse and kill many Indian men, women, and children.

**1849 The Office of Indian Affairs.** The Office of Indian Affairs is transferred from the War Department to the newly created Department of the Interior. The new department is created to manage public land, Indian land, and Indian affairs.

**1850–60 Nonratification of California Indian Treaties.** In California, numerous treaties are signed by federal officials with the California Indian nations, but non-Indian Californians prevent their ratification in Congress. Many leading Californians believe that Indian lands contained gold. Consequently, most California Indians are not recognized by treaty, and many California Indian communities continue to seek official federal recognition.

**1850–80 Genocide of California Indians.** Fearing widespread Indian uprisings, non-Indian Californians kill and terrorize California Indians. California militia and self-appointed vigilantes indiscriminately hunt down and kill thousands of peaceful California Indian men, women, and children. Indian women are often kidnapped to be used as prostitutes, concubines, or, along with Indian children, sold into slavery. The Indian population in California declines from about 100,000 in 1850 to 16,000 in 1880.

**1850–1907 Religious Renewal in the Northwest.** Many Indian peoples turn to their old spiritual beliefs. Indians of the Northwest Plateau (present-day western Washington) join new religious movements like the Indian Shaker Church, or *Waptashi*, the Feather Religion. Some Indians follow the teachings of Smohalla, the Wanapum prophet, who is said to have died on two occasions and traveled to the Sky World to converse with the Creator. Smohalla was given the sacred dance and ceremony known as the Washat and told to return to his people and remember the ceremonies of thanks for first foods and other gifts of creation. Smohalla leads a fierce resistance to selling land, and provides a new religion that mixes both Christian and traditional northwestern Indian ideas. The new religion helps individual Indians and Indian communities better cope with the rapidly changing political, economic, and social conditions in their lives. His church becomes known as the Shaker Church and continues to gather congregations among several northwestern Indian nations such as the Nez Percé.

**1851–80 The "Final Solution" to the Indian Problem.** During these years federal bureaucrats gradually develop plans for "the final solution of the Indian problem." In essence, the plans call for the complete control of tribal affairs by colonial administrators through the Office of Indian Affairs, the complete destruction of the tribal structure, and rapid reduction of the size of the Indian land base. Commissioner Luke Lea sets forth the doctrine in 1851 when he calls for the Indians' "concentration, their domestication and their incorporation." In 1857, Commissioner Denver advocates small reservations that will force the Indians to become farmers and in which the land will be allotted individually. By the 1880s this policy is in full operation.

**1853–56 Treaties with Indians.** During this period many Indian nations are induced to sell most of their remaining land and accept small parcels of land, commonly called reservations. The Chippewa in the 1850s cede most of their lands in Wisconsin and Minnesota and are relegated to small and scattered reservations. The Indian nations of present-day Washington State cede most of their lands and reluctantly settle on small reservations. Between 1853 and 1856 more than fifty-two treaties are made with Indian groups, and the United States acquires 174 million acres of Indian land. In many cases, the Indian communities are economically destitute and Indians are forced to trade land for goods; in some cases, for example in Washington and Wisconsin, Indians retain the right to hunt and fish on their former lands. These hunting and fishing rights are disputed and ignored by U.S. citizens.

**1854 Indian Removal Policy.** Indian Commissioner George Manypenny calls for the abandonment of the Indian removal policy, saying: "By alternate persuasion and force, some of these tribes have been removed, step by step, from mountains to valley, and from river to plain until they have been pushed half-way across the continent. They can go no further. On the ground they now occupy, the crisis must be met, and their future determined." By 1854 virtually all Indian tribes, with the exception of small isolated groups, have been removed from their ancestral homelands east of the Mississippi and relocated west of the Mississippi to Indian Territory.

**1855–58 The Seminole Form New Government.** The Seminole in Florida again engage U.S. forces. The army cannot defeat the Seminole and allies, who retreat to the southern Florida swamps. Eventually, the

United States reconciles itself to leaving the Seminole in Florida. In previous years, in the 1830s, some Seminole were captured and moved to Indian Territory (present-day Oklahoma), where they were joined with the Creek Nation. Both nations speak Muskogean languages and have a history of kindred relations. By 1855, the Oklahoma Seminole withdraw from the Creek Nation and create their own government, one that very much resembles traditional Creek government, with about a dozen politically independent villages that meet together to form a national council. The government stays in effect until 1907, when the U.S. government dissolves the major Indian governments in Indian Territory.

**1855–1907 The Chickasaw Constitutional Government.** In 1856, the Chickasaw Nation adopts a constitution, modeled after the U.S. Constitution, with a "governor" as chief executive, a legislature, and a judiciary. In 1834, the Chickasaw sign a removal treaty, but cannot find a new location in the west. In 1838, the Chickasaw agree to join the Choctaw government, then already in Indian Territory (present-day Oklahoma). Between 1840 and 1855, however, most Chickasaw do not wish to live under Choctaw law, feeling they were discriminated against. The Chickasaw appeal to the United States for a return to a independent nationality, and in an 1855 treaty the Chickasaw are granted independence. In 1856, the Chickasaw form a constitutional government, which replaces an older form of government based on clan chiefs and priests. The constitutional government manages Chickasaw affairs until 1907, when the United States abolishes it.

**1860–1907 The Choctaw Constitutional Government.** In 1860, after twenty-five years of constitutional change and amendment, the Choctaw residing in Indian Territory (present-day eastern Oklahoma) adopt a centralized constitutional government, with a principal chief, three district chiefs (as was the Choctaw political tradition), a national legislature, and a court system. The government remains in power until 1907, when the U.S. government abolishes the Choctaw government and makes Indian Territory into the state of Oklahoma.

**1861–68 The Long Walk.** Colonel Christopher (Kit) Carson is appointed field commander over an army of volunteers in New Mexico. In weeks, this force captures a group of Mescalero Apache and relocates them to the Bosque Redondo of eastern New Mexico onto a bleak, windswept reservation on the Llano Estacado, or Staked Plains, near the Pecos River. It was the government's plan to gather the Mescalero and Navajo tribes together at Bosque Redondo to civilize and Christianize them. Under orders, Carson pursues Navajo men, women, and children throughout the summer, fall, and winter of 1863 and 1864, causing the deaths of many from hardship, hunger, and exposure. The U.S. government forcefully removes about 8,500 Navajo 350 miles to the Bosque Redondo, a place Navajo call Hweeldi (prison). This forced march is remember bitterly by the Navajo as the Long Walk. There they remain until 1868, when General William Tecumseh Sherman concludes a treaty with the Navajo permitting them to return to a reservation located on a portion of Dinetah.

**1862–64 The Minnesota Sioux Uprising.** Because of Indian agents' corruption and incompetence in their administration of relations with the Minnesota Sioux, the Sioux almost starve from lack of supplies. Under the leadership of Little Crow, they attack Minnesota settlements. The uprising quickly spreads to other Santee Sioux bands living in the eastern Dakotas. Thirty-eight Sioux are sentenced and hanged for their part in the uprising.

**1862–65 Kickapoo Migration to Mexico.** Two bands of Kickapoo, about 1,300 people, migrate to Mexico, believing their lands are unfairly treated by the U.S. government and people. Both bands fight battles with Texas troops, who strongly oppose Indians settling or traveling through Texas. Both groups settle in the province of Coahiula, in northern Mexico. Earlier in 1839, a band of Kickapoo had already migrated to Morelos, Mexico, and they were joined by Machemanet, a Kickapoo headman, and six hundred Kickapoo who left Kansas for Mexico, hoping for better treatment at the hands of the Mexican government. By 1865, all Kickapoo, except the band formerly led by the Prophet Kenekuk, leave Kansas because of corrupt handling by U.S. Indian agents and crooked dealings by U.S. citizens. In 1867, about one hundred Kickapoo return from the south and resettle near present-day Leavenworth, Kansas.

**1863 The Nez Percé and the Thief Treaty.** The Nez Percé Indians of Oregon and Idaho attempt to live in peace with the settlers and remain neutral during the Plateau Indian War of 1855–58. In 1855, the Nez Percé sign a treaty with the United States, securing nearly all their land, but in 1860 non-Indian "traders" discover gold while prospecting on the Nez Percé Reservation in

Idaho. Non-Indians flood onto Indian land. Nez Percé leaders complain to the Indian Service and the government responds in 1863 by writing a new treaty reducing the reservation to one-tenth its original size. When government officials disclose the plan to Nez Percé leaders, almost all the chiefs leave the council, refusing to accept the new treaty. Only Chief Lawyer, upon whose lands the council is held, agrees to its terms. Lawyer and fifty-one Nez Percé sign the document, and it is ratified by the Senate and signed by the president. According to tribal law, Lawyer could speak only for his band and not the tribe as a whole. Chief Joseph and the other Nez Percé leaders refuse to adhere to the Thief Treaty. Chief Joseph objects: "If we ever owned the land we own it still for we never sold it."

**1864 The Chivington Massacre.**    Colonel John M. Chivington and Governor John Evans of Colorado allow Chief Black Kettle and his peaceful Cheyenne followers to camp near Fort Lyon for the purpose of negotiating at treaty. By night, Chivington deploys his Third Colorado Cavalry around Sand Creek, including 700 men and four howitzers. On November 29, Chivington leads an unprovoked attack on the Indian camp killing up to 164 men, women, and children. The Sand Creek Massacre, as it becomes known, is one of the bloodiest and cruelest events of the Civil War. Although punishment of the parties responsible for the massacre is demanded by the public and by a U.S. congressional committee, no action is taken.

**1866 Post–Civil War Indian Reservations.**    In 1853, California Superintendent of Indian Affairs Edward Fitzgerald Beale places a number of Indians in the Tejon Valley to become ranchers and farmers. Although this and other reservations meet with only limited success, the system becomes national policy after the Civil War. The Peace Commission meets with many tribes, concluding treaties, and establishing reservations. Some of the tribes, or portions of them, agree to remain on reservations; others do not. In 1867, the commissioners conclude an agreement with some Kiowa and Comanche, creating a reservation in the southwest corner of present-day Oklahoma. At the same time, a portion of Cheyenne and Arapaho country is recognized as a reservation.

**1866–74 The Montana Gold Rush.**    By the summer of 1866, non-Indians are flooding into Montana to find gold. Many miners take the Bozeman Trail from Fort Laramie, Wyoming, to the new diggings around Virginia City, Montana. The trail, however, runs though the lands of the Oglala and Brule Sioux, who fight to keep the miners out of the region. The army establishes a series of forts along the trail for the miners' protection, but under attack by Sioux and Cheyenne, agrees to abandon them at the Treaty of Fort Laramie in 1868. Under this agreement, some Sioux and Cheyenne leaders agree to move to the reservations in Montana, Wyoming, and the Dakotas. Indians secure for themselves much of the hunting grounds along the Big Horn and Powder rivers (present-day Montana). The treaty does not end U.S. incursion into Indian land, and miners, buffalo hunters, and railroad men continue to trespass on Sioux and Cheyenne country.

In 1874, Colonel George Armstrong Custer leads an expedition to the Paha Sapa, the Sioux word for black hills, of South Dakota where geologists and journalists confirm the presence of gold. A new rush commences, and the Northern Pacific Railroad moves closer to Sioux land.

**1867 The United States Purchases Alaska.**    The U.S. government purchases Alaska from the Russian government. The purchase does not change the situation of the Aleuts, Eskimos, and Indians living in Alaska. The Russians do not claim Indian lands and the Indians are left undisturbed in possession of their territories.

**1867–1907 The Creek Constitutional Government.**    In 1867, the Creek Nation, now living in Indian Territory, adopts a constitutional government. The first elections in 1867 are controversial, and a small majority of conservatives demand a return to the traditional Creek government based on central villages and a council composed of village leaders. The United States supports the constitutional government and on various occasions uses marshals and troops to defend it against conservative Creek. Compared to the constitutional governments of the Cherokee, Choctaw, and Chickasaw, the Creek constitutional government is fraught with rebellion and political instability. In 1907, the Creek government is abolished over the protests of the conservative Creek who do not wish to join U.S. society or renounce their treaty and land rights.

**1869–71 The First Indian Commissioner of Indian Affairs Is Appointed.**    Brigadier General Ely Parker, a Seneca Indian and personal friend of President Ulysses S. Grant, is appointed commissioner of Indian affairs. Parker helps initiate a policy of providing Indians with

Hide-covered tipi, Pipestone National Park. (Photo by Sarah Loe)

food and clothing in exchange for reconciling themselves to life on small, economically marginal reservations of land.

**1870–90 The Peyote Road.**   For centuries Indians in northern Mexico have used the peyote plant in religious ceremonies. Peyote induces a mild hallucinatory state, which brings the user closer to the spirit world. In the late nineteenth century the Peyote religion spreads among the Kiowa, Comanche, Cheyenne, and Arapaho. Tribal members develop their own ceremonies, songs, symbolism, visions, and prayers, incorporating them into the Peyote religion. Peyote is ingested as a sacrament and followers vow to follow the Peyote Road. They promise to be trustworthy, honorable, and community-oriented. Family, children, and cultural survival become a major emphasis of this movement. Elements of Christianity become a part of the worship service, and in 1918 the membership organize themselves into the Native American church.

The Office of Indian Affairs attempts to extinguish the religion but does not succeed. In the twentieth century Indians introduce the church to Native peoples throughout the United States. The Native American Church has survived but continues to face legal attacks during the last decade of the twentieth century.

**1870 The First Ghost Dance Movement.**   Perhaps the best known of the Native American religious revitalization movements is the Ghost Dance. Wodziwob, a Paiute living on the California/Nevada border, is credited with beginning this religion in 1870. Wodziwob was informed by the Creator that non-Ghost Dancers would be swallowed up by a great earthquake. Indians would be spared or resurrected in three days so that they might live much as they had before European contact.

**3 March 1871 The End of Treaty Making.**   Congress passes an act that it will no longer negotiate treaties with Indian nations. All treaties signed between 1778 and 1871 are not invalidated, but are to be upheld by the federal government. After this act, agreements with Indian groups are made by congressional acts and executive orders, which are agreements made by the president or designated official, usually by the secretary of the interior.

**1871–90 Extermination of the Buffalo.**   As early as 1871 U.S. hunters and traders begin a systematic killing of buffalo on the Plains. Hundreds of thousands are killed for their tongue meat and hides. By the late 1880s there are only about one thousand buffalo left; not enough for the subsistence requirements of the Plains Indians. With their economic base destroyed, the Plains Indians are destitute and eventually forced onto small reservations, where they are dependent on the United States for food and supplies, and, consequently, fall under U.S. political and administrative control.

**1875–83 The Northern Cheyenne Flee Indian Territory.**   In 1875, the Northern Cheyenne, then living in present-day Montana and the western Dakotas, reluctantly agrees to migrate to Indian Territory. One band of Northern Cheyenne fight with the Sioux at Little Big Horn against Custer in 1876, but most Northern Cheyenne are induced to migrate to Indian Territory. In 1877, Chief Dull Knife, of the Northern Cheyenne, refuses to remain in Indian Territory and leads an escape of his people to return to their homeland in the northern plains. This dramatic escape captures the imagination of the American people through the press and convinces U.S. officials that it would be extremely difficult to detain unwilling Indian nations in Indian Territory. In 1883, the Northern Cheyenne are granted a reservation in eastern Montana. U.S. Indian policymakers abandon the attempt to relocate Indians nations in Indian Territory and allow them to take reservations within their home territories.

**1876–81 Custer and the End of Sioux Resistance.**
After gold miners start working in the Black Hills, which is sacred land to the Sioux, several bands of Sioux leave their reservations to protect the Black Hills from sacrilege. Led by Crazy Horse of the Oglala Sioux and Sitting Bull of the Hunkpapa band of Teton Sioux, the Indians gather to face the army, which is protecting the miners. Three columns converge on the Sioux and their Cheyenne and Arapaho allies. One of the columns, led by General Alfred Terry, includes the Seventh Cavalry commanded by Colonel George Armstrong Custer. Terry sent Custer to the southern end of Little Big Horn Valley (present-day eastern Montana) where the colonel and his Crow and Arikara scouts locate a large Indian encampment. On 25 June 1876, Custer divides his force for tactical purposes, and with a command of 225 men advances on the Indian camp. Sioux and Cheyenne meet his advance and kill every man, including Custer, and are only prevented from doing likewise to the other forces because the forces are rescued by General Terry's command. The army pursues the Sioux and in 1877 shoot down Crazy Horse in what the soldiers described as an escape attempt. Sitting Bull and remnants of the Sioux flee to Canada and do not return to the Dakotas until 1881.

**1877 The Nez Percé War.**   Between 1863 and 1876 the non-treaty Nez Percé continue to reject the Thief Treaty of 1763. After the defeat of Custer at Little Big Horn, the army orders that all nonreservation Nez Percé be placed on reservations. On the way to their assigned reservations, a skirmish breaks out and the Nez Percé and their Palouse allies fight several running battles with the army as they change directions and travel toward Montana. The Nez Percé move into Wyoming, hoping to settle with the Crow and live like buffalo-hunting Plains people. But they are rejected by the Crow and so move farther north heading for Canada. When they are but forty miles from the Canadian border, they are caught and attacked again by the army. After days of fighting, Chief Joseph concludes a conditional surrender whereby the Nez Percé will not be

punished for their resistance but will be allowed to settle on the reservation in Idaho. General Howard and Colonel Nelson A. Miles agree to these conditions, but they are reversed by General William Tecumseh Sherman. Sherman exiles the Nez Percé and Palouse to Fort Leavenworth, Kansas, as prisoners of war, before moving them to the Quapaw Agency in northeastern Indian Territory (present-day Oklahoma) and then to the Ponca Agency.

**1877–79 The Nez Percé Exiled and Returned.**
Throughout the exile, Joseph presses the government to live up to the terms of the conditional surrender. In 1879, he takes his case to Washington, D.C. More importantly, he gives an interview to the editor of the *North American Review*. The resulting essay clearly reflects his feelings about the injustice of the Nez Percé exile to *Eekish Pah*, the Hot Place, and stirs many people to demand the Nez Percé's return to the northwest. In 1885, the U.S. government agrees to permit the Nez Percé to return. Some Nez Percé relocate to the reservation in Idaho, but Joseph is forced to move to the Colville Reservation in north-central Washington. For years he tries to buy a portion of his homeland, the Wakllowa, the Place of Winding Waters, but settlers living there refuse to sell him any land and he dies on the Colville Reservation in 1904.

**1879–90 Civilization and Christianization.**   In 1879, the Carlisle Indian School in Pennsylvania is founded in an effort to show that Indians can be educated in the ways of American culture. Other schools are founded in California, Oregon, Oklahoma, New Mexico, and Arizona, as well as on the individual reservations. U.S. reformers take Indian children from their homes and communities in the belief that it would be in the interest of the children to destroy their Native culture. Government teachers force Indian children to learn English and punish them with whippings and food deprivation when they break the rules and use the Native language. Curricula are established for vocational education, since Indians are not considered intelligent enough to learn the professions, but children are taught some academic skills. When the children reach first grade, government agents routinely take them from their families and send them to Indian boarding schools.

**1881–84 *A Century of Dishonor* Published.**   Helen Hunt Jackson, in *A Century of Dishonor* (1881), writes an indictment of U.S. Indian policy and the treatment of American Indians in U.S. society. Because of her work

Congress forms a special commission to investigate and suggest reforms of Indian affairs. Jackson's research on the special commission provides her with material to write a biographical novel, *Ramona*, about the life of a California Indian woman. The romanticized biography stimulates considerable interest in the United States about the plight and life of Indians.

**1887 The General Allotment Act.** Congress passes the General Allotment Act, also known as the Dawes Act, dividing reservation land into individual parcels. The Act is intended to safeguard the Indians on the land and, to this end, allotments are to be protected for twenty-five years. The Burke Act (1906) amends the Allotment Act of 1887, extending the original twenty-five year trust period for another twenty-five years. Surplus land is purchased by the U.S. government and then opened to settlement, thus making thousands of acres available. Between 1887 and 1934, when the Allotment Act is repealed, the U.S. government divests Native Americans of about 90 million acres.

**1889–90 The Second Ghost Dance Religion and Wounded Knee.** Wovoka becomes the second Ghost Dance prophet. He is the son of Tavibo, a Paiute shaman in western Nevada. In 1889, Wovoka reportedly speaks with the Creator, who advises Native Americans to live peacefully with all peoples. The Creator instructs Indians to work hard in this life and pray for an apocalypse that will restore the world to its aboriginal state. If the Indians follow the Ghost Dance path, their dead relatives will rise up, and the game and plants will return.

The Ghost Dance religion spreads to many tribes throughout the West. Some Sioux, devastated by war, reservations, poverty, and disease, turn Wovoka's teachings into a movement advocating violence. Soldiers, settlers, government agents, and missionaries fear for their lives as rumors spread that the Ghost Dance will inspire the Sioux to fight again for their rights and freedom. In 1890, the Office of Indian Affairs outlaws the Ghost Dance, and the U.S. government agents and military strengthens its command on the northern Plains. A group of Sioux Ghost Dancers, led by Big Foot, retreats to a site known as Wounded Knee. They are pursued by the Seventh Cavalry, Custer's old unit. After some misunderstandings about the Ghost Dancers' intentions, the army fires on the Sioux and kills more than three hundred Indian men, women, and children. This incident is known as the Wounded Knee Massacre.

**1890–1900 "Vanishing Americans."**

At the turn of the twentieth century, most non-Indians believe that the Native peoples are "Vanishing Americans" and will not long survive. The American Indian population declines to a low point of 237,196 in the 1900 U.S. Census. After 1900, however, the Indian population slowly recovers. In 1920, the Census Bureau records 244,437 Native Americans. This number increases to 357,499 in 1950, 1,366,676 in 1980, and 1,959,234 in 1990.

**1890–1934 The Assimilationist Policy.** After 1890 most Indian nations are located on reservations or are not recognized by the federal government. Reservation Indians come under direct administrative control from U.S. Indian agents. Since most reservation economies cannot support their Indian populations, Indian reservation residents become economically and politically dependent on the Office of Indian Affairs and its field agents. Food, clothing, medicine, education, and ceremonial life come under strict regulations. Traditional tribal governments are inhibited from operating, and ceremonies, like the Plains Sun Dances, are prohibited. Children are sent to boarding schools, where they cannot speak their Native language. Federal policymakers hope to reeducate Indian children and incorporate them into U.S. society, and then abolish the reservations. This policy of assimilation is not successful. Traditional government, traditional ceremonial life, and Indian language and lifestyle persist, despite the efforts to force Indians into U.S. economic and social life.

**1900s Struggle and Change in the Twentieth Century.** The early years of the twentieth century are difficult times for Native Americans who continue to feel the disastrous effects of the General Allotment Act of 1887. Federal, state, and county officials often work together with the private sector to divest the American Indian of his estate. Railroad, cattle, mining, timber, and oil companies take every opportunity to liquidate Indian title to lands and resources.

Indians living on tribal lands are required to be versatile. Hunting, fishing, gathering, and farming continue and at times government rations are received, but these are not sufficient for survival. For this reason, many Native Americans become wage earners. Indians work as migrant workers, moving from one labor camp to the next during harvests. Indians also work on ranches, performing a variety of menial jobs, while others find employment on the reservations themselves. Sometimes the Office of Indian Affairs hires reservation Indians as police officers and judges. And some

Indians receive an income from leasing their allotments to non-Indian farmers and ranchers.

**1902 *Lone Wolf v. Hitchcock*.** In 1902, Lone Wolf, a Kiowa leader, files a lawsuit to prevent the Interior Department from allotting and selling surplus lands guaranteed by the Treaty of Medicine Lodge in 1869. The Supreme Court rules against him in *Lone Wolf v. Hitchcock*, giving Congress the authority to abrogate treaties and dispose of Indian lands. This decision creates the doctrine that Congress has plenary powers in Indian affairs, meaning that there is no higher authority in deciding issues in Indian affairs. *Lone Wolf* affirms the policy that it is within Congress's power to abrogate, or ignore or change, Indian treaties. This decision is a major blow to Indian treaty rights.

**16 November 1907 Indian Territory Is Formed into Oklahoma.** The state of Oklahoma is admitted to the Union. Most Indian governments in the former Indian Territory have been abolished, including the constitutional governments of the Cherokee, Choctaw, Chickasaw, Seminole, and Creek nations. Most Indian land is allotted to individuals, sometimes forcibly to conservative Indians who do not recognize U.S. rights to abolish their government or to take their land. In the late 1890s and early 1900s, the Creek Snake Indians under Chitto Harjo and Red Bird Smith among the Nighthawk Keetoowah society, as well as less well known movements among the Seminole, Choctaw, and Chickasaw, resist allotment and dissolution of their national governments and land. Oklahoma citizens urge that the remaining Indian lands be put on the market and that Indian landholdings be taxed. Over the next thirty years, many Indians lose their land allotments owing to debt, legal fraud, and inability to pay taxes. The tribal governments of the former Indian Territory nations are kept up informally, and some are revived starting in the late 1930s. The Choctaw, Cherokee, Chickasaw, Creek, and Seminole regain the right to elect their own governments in the early 1970s, but the governments are now under the jurisdiction of the Bureau of Indian Affairs.

**1908 Winter's Doctrine.** The Supreme Court decides that Indians on reservation lands retain the right to sufficient access to water to provide for agriculture. This doctrine is designed to preserve water and is a decision in favor of conservationists, who think Indians would not use as much water as free market users. The doctrine, however, guarantees Indian reservations rights to water for economic and agricultural use. This doctrine becomes very important after the 1960s, when Colorado, Arizona, New Mexico, and California divide scarce water resources. Indian reservations in the area are guaranteed access to water for reservation development, because the western states cannot entirely ignore the Winter's Doctrine.

**1911 Ishi, the Last Yahi Indian.** After years of hiding from California settlers, a Yahi Indian known as Ishi allows himself to be captured. He creates a sensation in the newspapers, which refer to him as the "last wild Indian in North America." Ishi survives for five years, living at a museum in San Francisco and providing much ethnographic and linguistic material to the famous anthropologist Alfred Kroeber.

**1911 Society of the American Indian Organized.** In April 1911 seven prominent American Indian leaders meet in Columbus, Ohio, and establish a pan-Indian organization known as the Society of American Indians (SAI). A national conference takes place in October 1911. Headquartered in Washington, D.C., SAI lobbies for better educational programs and improved reservation conditions. For about a decade SAI gives Indian people a new dimension of representation, providing a much-needed voice and calling for reforms in federal Indian policy.

**1912 Founding of the Alaska Native Brotherhood.** Modeled after religious organizations of the Russian Orthodox and Protestant churches, the Alaska Native Brotherhood is formed in 1912 in Juneau, Alaska, by eleven Tlingits and one Tsimshian, all strong Presbyterians, who attended the Presbyterian-administered boarding school at Sitka, Alaska, an old Tlingit village. In 1915, an auxiliary organization, the Alaska Native Sisterhood, follows the same path at the Brotherhood. The Brotherhood promotes civil rights issues such as the right to vote, access to public education for Native children, and civil rights in public places such as the right to attend movie theaters. It defends Native workers in the Alaskan canneries, defends the rights of Native fishermen, and fights a major land case for the taking of the Tongass Forest from the Tlingit and Haida tribes of panhandle Alaska. The Brotherhood wins the Tongass Forest case in the 1950s and receives payment of $7.5 million after a long legal struggle starting in 1929. The Brotherhood continues to the present day as an active political force in Alaska Native issues.

**1912 Jim Thorpe Wins Olympic Decathlon.** Jim Thorpe, from the Sauk and Fox Nation, wins the decathlon in the 1912 Olympic games held in Norway.

Henry Bond (Choctaw) was the first state tax assessor of Oklahoma, 1907. (Courtesy of James Perkins)

Thorpe's medal is taken away from him, however, because he played semiprofessional baseball; it is formally reinstated in 1978. Thorpe goes on to star in professional football during its early days.

**1918 Establishment of the Native American Church.** U.S. courts and law officers persecute Indian peyote users. Indians argue that the peyote is used to enhance religious experience, but they are denied the right to worship with peyote because the worshipers do not have a church organization. Consequently, the Native American Church is incorporated into the state of Oklahoma by members of several Oklahoma nations (Kiowa, Comanche, Apache, Cheyenne, Ponca, and Oto). Since the late 1800s the peyote religion has spread quickly across the Plains tribes and reservation communities, where the old forms of religion and culture no longer sustain the Indians under the new conditions of economic poverty and political and cultural suppression.

**1923 The Committee of One Hundred.** Reformers begin pressing the government to improve Indian living conditions, and in 1923 Secretary of Interior Hubert Work appoints the Committee of One Hundred to survey American Indian policies and to make recommendations. The committee recommends increasing funds for health care, public education, scholarships, claims courts, and a scientific investigation into the effects of peyote usage.

**2 June 1924 Indians Are Granted U.S. Citizenship.** Because of the services Indian soldiers performed during the World War I and lobbying by the Alaska Native Brotherhood, Congress grants all Indians the rights of U.S. citizenship. The act, however, does not take away rights that Indians have by treaty or by the Constitution. It allows Indians to vote in federal elections, but some states, such as New Mexico, prohibit Indians from voting in state elections.

**1928 The Meriam Report.** Secretary of Interior Hubert Work also asks the Board of Indian Commissioners to make a study of Indian living conditions, but they provide little help. With a grant from John D. Rockefeller Jr., the Brooking Institute hires Lewis Meriam and nine scholars to investigate the status of Indian economies, health, education, and the federal administration of Indian affairs.

In 1928, Meriam and his committee publish a significant volume, *The Problem of Indian Administration*, commonly known as the Meriam Report. The study describes the conditions of Indian people as "deplorable," particularly because of high infant mortality and deaths at all ages from tuberculosis, pneumonia, and measles. Navajo, Apache, Pima, and other Arizona nations have death rates from tuberculosis seventeen times the national average. The report details the educational failures and poor living conditions found at the boarding schools, and Meriam's committee recommends increased funding for Indian health and education. It also details the incidence of malnutrition, poverty, and marginal land tenure among American Indians. The Meriam Report urges Congress to appropriate money to fulfill its treaty obligations to the tribes in terms of health, education, and subsistence. It urges the president, secretary of the interior, and commissioner of Indian affairs to reform the Office of Indian Affairs.

## 1934 The Indian Reorganization Act.

The Great Depression slows the prospects for Indian reform during President Herbert Hoover's administration. Franklin Roosevelt's administration, however, implements a program of reform. Secretary of Interior Harold Ickes and Commissioner of Indian Affairs John Collier work closely to create an Indian New Deal. The Indian Reorganization Act, or the Wheeler-Howard Act, is passed to fulfill the recommendations of the Meriam Report and to promote the well-being of Native Americans by recognizing the value of their diverse cultures, religions, languages, and economies. Indian tribal governments are allowed to establish their own constitutions, laws, and memberships and are encouraged to form economic business corporations.

## 1934 The Johnson-O'Malley Act.

Congress adopts the Johnson-O'Malley Act, which allows the federal government to contract with states and territories to provide services for the Indians, including health, social welfare, and education. As another part of the Indian New Deal, the commissioner of Indian affairs orders the Indian Service to hire more Indians and to cease interference with Native American spiritual beliefs, ceremonies, and traditions. Indians join the Works Project Administration, the Public Works Administration, and the Civilian Conservation Corps (CCC). While

participating in such programs as the CCC, Indian families are introduced to modern farming, ranching, and forestry techniques and are taught English and basic mathematics. Opinions vary about the effect of the Indian New Deal, but the 1930s would prove to be a watershed in American Indian history and a step toward Native American self-determination.

## 1941–45 World War II.

On 7 December 1941 the United States enters World War II. More than 25,000 Indian men and women join the services, and those who remain home participate in the war effort through work, buying of war bonds, blood drives, and collecting rubber, paper, and metal. A group of Navajo serve as code talkers in the South Pacific, devising a code based on the Navajo language but constructed in such a way that even a Navajo speaker could not decipher it without the key. The Japanese were never able to break the code. The Navajo code talkers most likely saved the lives of thousands of U.S. soldiers. Members of several other tribes serve as code talkers during World War II, employing their Native languages.

## 1942 *Seminole Nation v. the United States.*

In *Seminole Nation v. the United States* the court addresses the issue of payment of trust fund monies and the fiduciary responsibility of the federal government to Indian tribes. In its decision the Supreme Court refers to the federal responsibility toward managing Indian land and assets as a "moral obligation of the highest responsibility and trust." Since then it has been called the "trust responsibility."

## 1944 The National Congress of American Indians.

The Second World War develops a new leadership of Native Americans who are not satisfied with the status quo. In 1944, tribal leaders meet in Denver, Colorado, to form the National Congress of American Indians, a group dedicated to guarding Indian rights and preserving Native culture, reservations, and tribal lands.

## 1946–49 Reorganization of the Bureau of Indian Affairs.

A special congressional commission investigates the Bureau of Indian Affairs (BIA) and recommends reform. For years, the BIA administration has suffered from overcentralization at the Washington, D.C. office. All local agency offices send their requests directly to the capitol, and it often takes months to get responses. The new BIA organization creates twelve

Native Americans, including Choctaw Chief Allen Wright (r.) and Henry J. Bond (far right), lay flowers on the monument to Choctaw Chief Pushmataha in Arlington National Cemetery in Washington, D.C. Pushmataha died in 1824 while visiting on government business. (Courtesy of James Perkins)

area offices among the ninety agency offices on the reservations and the Washington, D.C. office. Much of the day-to-day administrative power of the commissioner of Indian affairs is delegated to the twelve area offices.

**1946–78 The Indian Claims Commission.**  Even as Native Americans began to organize, a conservative movement is growing in the national capitol, calling for a renunciation of New Deal era politics. In 1946, Congress creates the Indian Claims Commission, enabling tribes to sue the federal government for past wrongs. This bill overcomes conservative opposition to become the last piece of Indian New Deal legislation. The claims cases take years to resolve and are a major cost. Although the commission makes several awards to Native Americans, no land is returned and very meager monetary rewards are given to Indian claimants.

**1949 The Hoover Commission.**  In 1949, the Hoover Commission, under former president Herbert Hoover,

recommends that Native Americans be "integrated, economically and politically, as well as culturally." Hoover's report suggests that "when the trust status of Indian lands has ended, thus permitting taxation, and surplus Indian families have established themselves off the reservations, special aid to the state and local governments for Indian programs should end." The commission recommends that the federal government remove itself from regulation of and responsibility for Indian affairs. This program gathers considerable support from congressional leaders. Many reservations contain timber, oil, gas, coal, uranium, water, and other natural resources coveted by non-Indians and major corporations.

**1952 Relocation.**  During the 1950s, the government begins the relocation program, which assists Indian families to move to urban areas. Administrators argue that with housing and employment in urban areas, Indians will find new lives away from their old lands and become integrated into mainstream America. In 1952, the Bureau of Indians Affairs establishes the Voluntary Relocation Program (also known as the Employment Assistance Program), which pays for training, travel, moving, and assistance in finding urban work. The BIA also provides a strong vocational and academic training program for Indians who relocate. By 1960, approximately 35,000 Native Americans have relocated, but one-third of these return home to the reservations.

**1953 The Termination Resolution.**   House Concurrent Resolution 108 is passed. It calls for the end of the special legal relation between Indian governments and the federal government. This legal relation is created by the commerce clause in the Constitution and recognized by a series of court decisions starting in the 1820s and 1830s. The House Resolution sets the tone of Indian Affairs policy by indicating its desire to end the reservation system and to assimilate Indians into U.S. society by terminating Indian treaty rights and legal status as historical nationalities and independent cultural communities.

In the same year, Congress passes Public Law 280, which empowers certain states (California, Wisconsin, Nebraska, Minnesota, Oregon, and, in 1959, Alaska) to assume management over criminal justice on Indian reservations. This law opens the possibility of state jurisdiction over reservation courts. Previously, federal law and courts had upheld the separation of state and Indian government relations because this separation is explicitly written out in the commerce clause of the Constitution.

**1954–62 Termination.**   Congress adopts the policy often termed *termination*, a plan to end tribal sovereignty, health care, and most federal obligations to Indians as specified in past treaties or acts of Congress. Responsive to the national conservative swing in the 1950s, Congress passes a series of laws implementing the termination of Indian reservations. Between 1954 and 1962 more than one hundred bands, communities, and rancherias are terminated or severed from direct relations with the federal government. As a result, the terminated Indian communities lose protections and services formerly provided by the national government. The National Congress of American Indians fights against termination and by the late 1950s the movement has lost its momentum. Termination ends during President John F. Kennedy's administration because of opposition by Indians and state governments, who think the policy will result in higher state service costs to Indians.

James King Overman (Oneida) as a cadet, 1953. During tours in the Korean and Vietnam wars, he earned three Distinguished Flying Crosses, eighteen Air Medals, and the Presidential Unit Citation for Extraordinary Heroism. He retired as a major in 1972. (Courtesy of James Overman)

**1959–71 Alaska Native Land Claims.**   Alaska becomes a state in 1959; the federal government grants the new state the right to select 102 million acres of land. Indian title in Alaska, however, has not been settled, and Alaska Native villages protest state land selections by making claims to land with the Bureau of Land Management. By 1964, Alaska Natives claim more than 300 million acres, and Secretary of the Interior Stewart Udall prohibits the state from selecting land until Indian title is clarified. Alaska Natives mobilize around the land claims issue and other issues like education, health, and jobs. They form local and regional associations of villages. In 1965 and 1966, Alaska Natives create the Alaska Federated Natives (AFN), a statewide organization empowered to pursue land claims and other community interests. The AFN leads Alaska Natives to a Congressional settlement in 1971, called the Alaska Native Claims Settlement Act (ANCSA), which gives control of land, resources, and a portion of the cash settlement to Native people. ANCSA also preserves for the Natives 44 million acres and $962 million for giving up claims to the rest of Alaska.

### 1961 The Chicago Indian Conference.

After mobilizing against the threat of termination in the late 1950s, representatives from ninety tribes meet in Chicago and set out a policy agenda. The new agenda emphasizes greater academic training for Indian children, increased job training, improved housing on reservations, better medical facilities, access to loans for economic development, and increased emphasis on industrial development and employment on the reservations.

### 1961 The National Indian Youth Council.

An activist organization, the National Indian Youth Council, is formed. This organization challenges the approaches of traditional advocate groups such as Christian churches, the National Congress of American Indians, and the Indian Rights Association. The National Indian Youth Council presents a more activist and nationalist orientation to solving Indian problems.

### 1962 Indian Voting Rights.

Indians became U.S. citizens in 1924, but many states refuse to allow Indians to vote in state and local elections (although Congress ensures Indians the right to vote in federal elections). This year, the federal government forces New Mexico to grant its large Indian population the right to vote in state and local elections.

### 1964 The American Indian Historical Society.

Rupert Costo and Jeanette Henry Costo organize the American Indian Historical Society, dedicated to historical research and teaching about Native Americans. The society begins publishing *The Indian Historian*, a journal that presents articles on Indian history primarily from an Indian perspective.

### 1964–66 Indian Community Action Programs.

President Lyndon B. Johnson's Great Society legislation for alleviating poverty is implemented by creation of the Office of Economic Opportunity (OEO). The OEO organizes an Indian Desk for managing antipoverty programs on Indian reservations. The Bureau of Indian Affairs (BIA) insists on administering Indian antipoverty funds, but the OEO, suspicious of paternalistic BIA management of Indian affairs, delivers antipoverty funds

directly to the tribal governments. For the first time, most Indian tribal governments gain direct access to federal funds that are not administered by BIA officials. Community Action Programs (CAP) become the primary funding source and administrative organization for managing Indian antipoverty funds. During the late 1960s and 1970s many tribal governments rapidly expand in personnel, budget, and programs administered. The method of granting funds directly to tribal government control becomes the model for the Self-Determination Policy starting in the early 1970s and for the Self-Determination and Education Assistance Act of 1975.

### 1964–74 Fishing Rights in Washington State.

Treaties dating from the 1850s give many Washington Indian tribes the right to fish at their traditional fishing places and rights to one-half of the fish in the rivers. Over the years, state laws and court decisions increasingly excluded Indians from fishing with traps and certain kinds of fishing nets. Washington Indians become increasingly active in asserting their treaty rights

Billy Mills wins the 10,000-meter event at the 1964 Olympics. (Courtesy of Billy Mills)

to take fish at their traditional fishing camps and with traditional fishing methods. Eventually, the issue is sent before state and federal courts and is partially settled in 1974 by a federal court ruling, often called the Boldt Decision. The decision affirms Indian treaty rights to at least half the fish in many western Washington State rivers.

*Troy Johnson*
*California State University, Long Beach, California*

## ◆ CHRONOLOGY OF NATIVE NORTH AMERICAN HISTORY, 1965 TO 2000

**1965 California Indian Land Claims.**   After many years of hearings, California Indians receive an award of more than $29 million for outstanding land claims. The settlement amounts to only 47¢ an acre for 64 million acres of land taken, nearly two-thirds the state's total area. Since the number of eligible descendants is about 33,000 most California Indians receive less than $900.

**7 April 1965 Reexamination of Termination Policy.**   American Indian National Congress executive director and tribal representatives testify before U.S. Senate subcommission against the termination of the Colville tribe of Washington, D.C. The congressional termination policy began in 1953 with the passage of House Concurrent Resolution 108, whose objective was to solve "the Indian problem" by assimilating Indian people into the American mainstream. This process was to be accomplished by ending the government's relationship with tribes and bands that were considered to have reached a satisfactory level of economic and social achievement. Among the first tribes whose relationship with the federal government were terminated were the Klamath of Oregon and the Menomonee of Wisconsin. Many other smaller groups around the nation were also terminated. By 1965, it becomes increasingly clear that the effect of the termination policy on Indian communities is disastrous.

**26 May 1965 Miami Tribe Receives Land Claims Award.**   The House of Representatives approves a $4.7 million award by the Indian Claims Commission to the Miami Indians of Indiana and Oklahoma for the loss of their lands in the nineteenth century.

**15 February 1966 Fish-Ins.**   Comedian Dick Gregory and his wife are arrested for illegal net fishing, which they engage in with members of the Nisqually tribe in a protest fish-in. The tribe, arguing that they reserve the right to fish according to their own laws in their 1856 treaty with the federal government, protests the application of state game laws that dictate hook-and-line fishing, thereby preventing the tribe from fishing according to their traditional ways.

**14–16 April 1966 Tribal Advisory Commission Established.**   Approximately eighty tribal leaders representing sixty-two tribes attend an "emergency conference" called by the National Congress of American Indians to protest their exclusion from a congressionally sponsored conference. The conference was called by the chairman of the House Commission on Interior and Insular Affairs, Morris Udall, to discuss the reorganization of the Bureau of Indian Affairs. Representative Udall announces the admittance of representatives to the BIA's conference and confirms that the House commission will establish a tribally comprised group to advise him on the BIA's reorganization.

**30 April 1966 Bennett Appointed BIA Commissioner.**   The Senate confirms the appointment of Robert LaFollette Bennett (Oneida) as the BIA commissioner, succeeding Phileo Nash. Bennett is only the second Indian appointed commissioner, following in the footsteps of Ely Parker, a Seneca, appointed by Ulysses S. Grant in 1869.

**30 April 1966 Havasupai Reject BIA's Modernization Proposals.**   The three hundred members of the Havasupai tribe,who live at the base of the Grand Canyon, reject a Bureau of Indian Affairs proposal to modernize their village, Supai. Each year, one to two thousand visitors make the rough eight-mile trek by horseback to the only village on the 518-acre reservation. The council votes against the BIA's goals to link the reservation by roads, chair lifts, and helicopters.

**Spring 1966 Rough Rock Demonstration School.**   The Navajo contract with the BIA to establish the Rough Rock Demonstration School. Impetus for the school's creation comes from the realization that more than one-half of all reservation school students fail to complete their high school education. Studies suggest that the high dropout rate results from the teachers' lack of knowledge about Indian culture and behavior and from discriminatory treatment. The Navajo hope that by running their own school, they will be able to reverse the dropout rate and improve the education of their children.

**October 1966 Alaska Federation of Natives.** The Alaska Federation of Natives (AFN) meets in Anchorage, Alaska. Originally organized by Emil Notti, president of the Cook Inlet Native Association, the three-hundred-member organization discusses resolutions and strategies for the preservation of their land base. Alaska Natives, who never signed treaties with the U.S. government, are recognized by the government as possessing an aboriginal title to their lands. The exact meaning of aboriginal title, beyond a recognition that Alaska Natives lived on their lands for thousands of years, however, is unclear. The Alaskan Statehood Act of 1958 guarantees the Natives' hunting and fishing rights, and gives the state of Alaska the right to appropriate 102 million acres of land for its own use. As economic development and tourism in Alaska increase, the Natives' subsistence living, based on hunting, fishing, and trapping, becomes increasingly endangered.

**November 1966 American Indian Education Conference.** The forty-four-year-old Association of American Indian Affairs holds a conference on the dismal record of educating American Indian youth. Attended by thirty-five specialists, including the recently appointed chief of education in the Bureau of Indian Affairs, the group hears grim statistics concerning the lack of educational success achieved by Indian children. Coming under particular attack are the eighty-one boarding schools operated by the Bureau of Indian Affairs for some 30,000 students. In many instances, very young children are forced to attend boarding schools 600 miles from their homes and families because there are no local schools available. Both the boarding school children and the 91,000 other Indian students who attend public, church, or private schools face serious problems of adjustment and discrimination, leading to a 50 percent dropout rate among Indian students.

**10 January 1967 President Johnson Addresses Indian Self-Determination.** President Lyndon B. Johnson, in his State of the Union message, urges, "We should embark upon a major effort to provide self-help assistance to the forgotten in our midst—the American Indians."

**16 January 1967 National Indian Education Advisory Committee Formed.** The Bureau of Indian Affairs announces the formation of a National Indian Education Advisory Committee to assist in the improvement of educational services to Indian students.

**5 February 1967 Iowa Repeals Discriminatory Law.** The Iowa Senate approves the repeal of one of the last examples of discriminatory legislation against Indians: a law that prohibits the sale of liquor to Indians. Congress repealed federal prohibitions against the sale of liquor to Indians in 1954.

**20–21 March 1967 Indian Claims Commission Tenure Prolonged.** The U.S. Senate and House of Representatives approve a bill to extend the life of the Indian Claims Commission to 1972 and to expand its membership to five. The commission, first established in 1946, still has 347 unadjudicated cases on its dockets.

**10 June 1967 Seminole Land Claims Upheld.** The U.S. Claims Court upholds a 1964 decision by the Indian Claims Commission finding that the Seminole of Florida and Oklahoma have claims to 32 million acres of Florida lands under the terms of the Seminole Nation's 1823 treaty with the federal government.

**6 August 1967 Fiscal Compensation for Sioux Lands.** The Indian Claims Commission awards $12.2 million to eight Sioux tribes for the compensation of 29 million acres taken in fraudulent treaties during the 1800s. The illegally taken lands include one-half of Minnesota and parts of Iowa, North and South Dakota, and Wisconsin.

**11 September 1967 NAACP Reports on American Indian Genocide.** The New York Division of National Association for the Advancement of Colored People (NAACP) announces the preparation of a report detailing the United States' genocide of American Indians. The report is to be submitted to the United Nations.

**1968 *Menominee Tribe of Indians v. United States*.** In the court case *Menominee Tribe of Indians v. United States*, the U.S. Supreme Court upholds the power of Congress to terminate the Menominee Tribe. The Court gives the 1954 legislation that terminated the Menominee Tribe a narrow interpretation, however. Treaty rights persist unless expressly legislated away, the court observes. Hunting and fishing rights reserved by the Menominee in their 1854 treaty are not mentioned specifically by Congress in 1954 and therefore are not terminated. The Menominee continue to fight for restoration of those tribal rights that were expressly extinguished by Congress in 1954, and finally succeed in obtaining congressional restoration of their legal status in 1973.

**6 March 1968 Johnson Sends Message of Self-Determination.**   Johnson delivers his "Special Message to Congress on the Problem of the American Indian: 'The Forgotten American.'" In announcing his request for a 10 percent increase in federal funding for Indian programs, Johnson outlines three goals in his message: (1) "A standard of living for the Indian equal to that of the country as a whole"; (2) "Freedom of choice: an opportunity to remain in their homelands, if they choose, without surrendering their dignity; and opportunity to move to towns and cities of America, if they choose, equipped with the skills to live in equality and dignity"; and (3) "Full participation in the life of modern America, with a full share of economic opportunity and social justice." The new federal objective, according to Johnson, is "a goal that ends the old debate about 'termination' of Indian programs and stresses self-determination."

The same day, President Johnson signs an executive order establishing the National Council on Indian Opportunity. Chaired by the vice-president and comprised of six Indian leaders and the heads of the departments of interior, agriculture, commerce, labor, health, education, and welfare, and housing and urban affairs and the Office of Economic Opportunity, the council is charged with coordinating efforts to improve programs for Indians.

**11 April 1968 American Indian Civil Rights Act Passes.**   Congress passes the American Indian Civil Rights Act, which guarantees reservation residents many of the same civil rights and liberties in relation to tribal authorities that the U.S. Constitution guarantees all persons in relation to federal and state authorities. The act is introduced by Senator Sam Ervin after seven years of investigations into rights denied to individual Indians by tribal, state, and federal governments.

The act is not fully supported by all tribes, especially the Pueblos, who fear that the act will alter their traditional forms of governments and culture. The act also limits the rights of tribes to levy penalties over crimes committed on their reservations to $1,000 in fines or six months in jail.

Tribal leaders support other provisions of the legislation. Title IV of the act, for example, amends Public Law 280, an act passed by Congress in 1953 that gives states the authority to extend criminal and civil jurisdiction over reservations. The act also allows states to retrocede, or give back, criminal and civil jurisdiction to the tribes. Other parts of the law direct the secretary of the interior to publish updated versions of Charles Kappler's *Indian Affairs: Laws and Treaties*, and Felix Cohen's *Handbook of Federal Indian Law*.

**8 May 1968 John Collier Dies.**   John Collier, U.S. commissioner of Indian affairs from 1935 until 1945, dies in Taos, New Mexico. Collier was responsible for the reaffirmation of tribal authority and the strengthening of tribal governments. He sincerely believed in the values of Indian cultures and that Indian problems were best solved by Indian people. He established the Indian Arts and Crafts Board, and oversaw the passage of the 1934 Indian Reorganization Act (IRA), which stopped the sale of Indian allotments.

**18 May 1968 Peace Treaty with Navajo Commemorated.**   President Lyndon Johnson signs a bill commemorating the centennial of the federal government's peace treaty with the Navajo. The Navajo Nation inhabits a 16-million-acre reservation located in Arizona, New Mexico, and Utah. In terms of population and acreage, the Navajo Nation is larger than twenty-six independent countries in the world.

**19 May 1968 Indian Leaders Tour Major Cities.**   The National Congress of American Indians sponsors a tour by forty-nine Indian leaders from fifteen western tribes. The group, which visits New York City and other cities, is designed to encourage companies to establish businesses on reservations.

**27 May 1968 *Puyallup Tribe v. Department of Game*.**   A unanimous Supreme Court in *Puyallup Tribe v. Department of Game* upholds the right of Washington State to prohibit Indian net fishing for salmon in the interest of conservation. The case is an important departure from previous holdings, because it allows state regulation of some treaty fishing rights. One-hundred-and-fifty Indians march outside the plaza of the Supreme Court building in protest of the Supreme Court's decision in the Puyallup case.

**July 1968 AIM Founded.**   The American Indian Movement (AIM) is founded by Dennis Banks, Clyde

Bellecourt, Eddie Benton-Bonai, George Mitchell, and Mary Wilson in Minneapolis, Minnesota. During a period of general civil unrest and protests by African-Americans and Mexican-Americans, the movement is organized to improve federal, state, and local social services to urban Indian neighborhoods and prevent the harassment of Indians by the local police. AIM members form patrols to monitor police activity and demonstrate against Indian mistreatment.

**16 July 1968 Dick Gregory Released from Jail.** Comedian Dick Gregory is released from jail in Olympia, Washington, after fasting for six weeks to call attention to the violation of Indian treaty rights.

**21 October 1968 Supplemental Appropriations Act.** Congress enacts the Supplemental Appropriations Act of 1969, which includes an appropriation for $100,000 to implement the National Council on Indian Opportunity, established by Executive Order 11399 on 6 March 1968. This act is an important piece of President Johnson's efforts to improve Indian socioeconomic conditions. The council is given the following charge: (1) to encourage the complete application of federal programs designed to aid Indians; (2) to encourage interagency cooperation in the implementation of federal programs; (3) to assess the effect of federal programs; and (4) to suggest ways in which government programs can be improved.

**24 October 1968 Yavapai Land Settlement.** The Yavapai of Arizona and the federal government agree to a $5 million settlement for the loss of over 9 million acres illegally taken from the tribe by the federal government in 1874.

**1969 First Native American Studies Program Created.** In the spring, the University of California, Berkeley campus chapter of United Native Americans joins the Third World student strike, spurring the creation of a Native American studies program. Leaders of the Indian effort include LaNada Boyer, Patty Silvas, and Jack Forbes. Plans are also being developed for Native American studies centers on other California college campuses. Forbes drafts a proposal for a College of Native American Studies to be created on one of the University of California campuses. The California State Legislature endorses the idea.

**21 January 1969 Navajo Community College Opens.** The Navajo Community College opens at Many Farms, Arizona. The college is the first tribally established and controlled community college.

**5 March 1969 Office of Minority Business Enterprise Established.** President Richard Nixon signs an executive order establishing the Office of Minority Business Enterprise. It is the office's function to ensure that a fair proportion of the total government purchases and contracts are awarded to businesses that are owned wholly or in part by minorities and women. Indian tribes, acting in their commercial capacity, are expressly included in the act's provisions. The act's objective is to assist tribes in the economic development of their reservations, where more than one-half of all families live below the poverty level and unemployment on some reservations is as high as 90 percent.

**23 March 1969 Life Expectancy Gap Closes.** The Indian Health Service reports that the life expectancy for Indians is sixty-four years of age, compared to an average life expectancy of 70.5 years for non-Indians. Despite the gap, the new statistics reveal a major improvement in Indian health care. Twenty years previous, the average life expectancy for an Indian male was only forty-four years.

**23 March 1969 Mohawk Trial Begins.** The trial of seven Mohawks begins on charges stemming from demonstrations on the International Bridge between the United States and Canada. The bridge is located on the Akwesasne Reservation that straddles Canada and the United States. Demonstrators were protesting the imposition of Canadian custom duties on their goods. The Indians argue that the 1794 Jay Treaty signed between the United States and Great Britain guaranteed tribes' free passage over the border and freedom from import and export taxes on goods traversing the border. Because of the failure of Canada and the United States to recognize the tribes' right to freely export and import goods, Indian families must pay taxes on goods that are only carried from one family member's house to another.

**5 May 1969 Momaday Receives Pulitzer Prize.** Kiowa author N. Scott Momaday is awarded the Pulitzer Prize for his book *House Made of Dawn*. The book details the life of a young Indian man who leaves the reservation and explores his subsequent difficulties adjusting to the outside world. Momaday is the first American Indian awarded a Pulitzer since the prize's inception in 1917.

**18 May 1969 Klamath Tribe Awarded Money for Land Loss.** The Klamath tribe of Oregon wins a judgment of $4.1 million from the Indian Claims Commission for the loss of lands resulting from faulty surveys conducted by the government of their reservation in 1871 and 1888.

**19 June 1969 NCAI Makes Effort to Bring Business to Reservations.** The National Congress of American Indians (NCAI) hosts an exhibition and briefing sessions in New York City in an effort to attract private businesses to reservations. NCAI president Wendall Chino announces that 159 new enterprises have been started on reservations in the previous five years, with a total investment of more than $100 million.

**7 August 1969 Bruce Appointed Commissioner of Indian Affairs.** President Richard Nixon appoints Louis R. Bruce, a Mohawk-Oglala Sioux and one of the founders of the National Congress of American Indians, the new commissioner of Indian affairs.

**23 August 1969 Tribal Representatives Call for New Interior Secretary.** Representatives of forty-six North American Indian nations meet at the Onondaga Reservation in New York. Representing traditional peoples, the conference passes a resolution calling for the immediate ousting of Interior Secretary Walter Hickel. They charge that Hickel has not protected Indian resources and is insensitive to the needs of Indian peoples.

**September 1969 Corporations Acquire Oil from Alaska Natives.** Multinational oil corporations offer hundreds of millions of dollars to acquire oil in Alaska belonging to the Inuit people. They plan the development of an oil pipeline across Inuit and Dene lands. Several Alaska Native villages prevent the construction of an oil pipeline over their land.

**7 October 1969 Kennedy Calls for Conference on Indian Problems.** U.S. Senator Edward Kennedy calls for a White House conference on Indian problems. Announcing that he will introduce a bill to authorize and finance such a project, Kennedy criticizes the Bureau of Indian Affair's handling of Native American affairs as "unsatisfactory even under the best of circumstances." He calls for the creation of a Select Committee on Human Needs of American Indians, saying, "The BIA is notorious for its resistance to reform, to innovation, and to discharging its responsibilities in a competent and sensitive fashion."

**November 1969 NIEA Organized.** The National Indian Education Association (NIEA) is organized in Minneapolis, Minnesota, to improve the quality of Indian education. The organization is established specifically to improve communications on Indian educational issues through national conventions and workshops; to advocate for increased funding and creative programs for the education of Indian children; and to provide technical assistance to educators in the field.

**3 November 1969 Final Report on Indian Education Issued.** The Senate Subcommittee on Indian Education issues its final report following a two-year investigation. Chaired by Senator Edward Kennedy, who took over following the death of his brother, Robert Kennedy, the committee spends two years reviewing all areas of Indian education. The report concludes that "our national policies for educating American Indians are a failure of major proportions." Their comparative analysis of statistics leaves the committee shocked at "the low quality of virtually every aspect of schooling available to Indian children." The report spells out sixty recommendations to improve Indian education and urges that Indian people be given greater control over the schooling of their children.

**20 November 1969 Alcatraz Island Occupied.** Indian activists occupy Alcatraz Island in San Francisco Bay and symbolically claim the island for Indian people. The protesters incorporate as Indians of All Tribes, Inc. and offer to purchase the island from the federal government for $24 worth of beads. The occupation of Alcatraz lasts until 11 June 1971. Inspired by the Alcatraz occupation, Indian activists, led by former participants in the protest, occupy over sixty government facilities across the United States, demanding that Indian rights be recognized. During the occupation, President Nixon signs legislation returning the sacred Blue Lake to the Taos people. Nixon formally announces an end to the termination era and the beginning of a government policy of self-determination for Indians.

**1970 Indian Demonstrations and Protests.** Concerned with Indians' abysmally low economic status in an otherwise healthy and vigorous national economy, Indian youth groups press for change and agitate for a "new look" for the "First Americans." Indian youth set

Members of the Iroquois League protest for their rights to cross the U.S.-Canadian border in accordance with the 1794 Jay Treaty, July 1969. (Courtesy of the Buffalo and Erie County Historical Society)

out to accomplish change through the use of political power and activism. Because of the formal nature of treaty relations with the federal government, activist protests and demonstrations are not considered acceptable by older and sometimes more conservative Indians. Consequently, youth strategies, influenced by the civil rights movements of the 1960s, begin to adopt an overtly proactive stance. Indian groups demonstrate throughout the United States to direct attention to current Indian concerns and inequities.

**17 January 1970.** A Senate and House of Representatives subcommittee publishes a two-volume report on economic conditions on reservations. Detailed in the report are charges by Bureau of Indian Affairs official William Veeder, a water resources expert, that the government has caused "irreparable damage" to the Indians and to the economic development of Indian reservations. Veeder asserts that the basic problem results from an inherent conflict of interest between the Interior and Justice departments, which are responsible for protecting public lands and streams as well

assuring Indian property rights. Veeder suggests that Congress create an independent governmental agency for the protection of Indian water rights.

**8 March 1970 Fonda and Indians Arrested.** Actress Jane Fonda and thirteen Indians are arrested following an attempt by a large group of Indians, organized as United Indians of All Tribes, to take over Fort Lawton, Washington, near Seattle. The group demands the base for use as an Indian cultural center. The military uses clubs to beat and forcibly remove the demonstrators. Jane Fonda is taken into custody and given a letter of expulsion banning her from the post.

**22–23 March 1970 Protests Lead to Arrests.** Nine Indians are arrested near Denver and twenty-three are arrested at the Bureau of Indian Affair's offices in Chicago for sit-in protests against the BIA's employment policies. Similar protests are held in Cleveland, Minneapolis, Sacramento, and Santa Fe.

**11 April 1970 Legislation Provides for Tribal Loans.** The government enacts legislation to provide for loans to federally recognized tribes or tribal corporations from the Farmers Home Administration for the purpose of acquiring lands or interest to lands within reservation boundaries. The act is an extension of the 1934 Indian Reorganization Act, which sought to prevent the further erosion of the tribal land base and to assist tribes in the consolidation of their lands.

**27 April 1970 *Choctaw Nation et al. v. Oklahoma et al.*** In the case of the *Choctaw Nation et al. v. Oklahoma et al.*, the Choctaw, Chickasaw, and Cherokee nations of Oklahoma win control of the lower Arkansas River by a vote of four to three. The Supreme Court finds that the government ceded the riverbed and oil and mineral resources beneath the land to the tribes in the 1830 Treaty of Dancing Rabbit Creek and the 1835 Treaty of New Echota.

**5 May 1970 Isleta Women Enfranchised.** A tribal election at the Isleta Pueblo, located outside Albuquerque, New Mexico, grants women the right to vote.

**14 May 1970 Seminole Land Claims Settlement.** The Indian Claims Commission awards $12.2 million to the Seminole tribe for the government's illegal taking of lands in Florida. The money is to be distributed among the 1,500 Seminole in Florida and the 3,500 Seminole living in Oklahoma. The Seminole, who fought three successive wars with the federal government resisting forced relocation to Oklahoma, successfully argued to the court that the government had taken title to their lands in Florida under duress.

**29 June 1970 Navajo Land Claims Settlement.** The Navajo win a decisive court victory to prove title to 40 million acres of western land. The Indians charge that they were inadequately compensated for the lands when put on an 8-million-acre reservation in 1868. The Indian Claims Commission agrees with the Navajo, but the federal government insists that the Navajo could not prove claim to more than 10 million acres. Under court procedures, the Navajo will not receive the land. Instead the precise acreage will be determined and a value affixed to the property; the Navajo are to receive a monetary settlement.

**8 July 1970 Nixon Sends Native-Focused Message to Congress.** President Richard Nixon delivers a special message to Congress dealing exclusively with American Indians and Alaska Natives, setting forth a legislative program that expresses the idea of self-determination without the threat of termination. "The time has come," Nixon states, "to break decisively with the past and to create the conditions for a new era in which the Indian future is determined by Indian acts and Indian decisions." Nixon proposes that the Termination Act (House Concurrent Resolution 108) be overturned; that tribes secure the means to administer programs now operated by the Bureau of Indian Affairs; that Native peoples gain greater control over Indian education; that Blue Lake be restored to the Taos Pueblo; that greater federal funds be allocated to improve Indian health and the status of urban Indians; that the position of assistant secretary of Indian affairs be created to elevate the status of the BIA within the Department of the Interior; and that an Indian Trust Counsel Authority be established to represent Indians in the protection of their lands and resources.

**12 July 1970 Iroquois Meeting.** Two hundred members of the Iroquois Confederacy meet in Geneva, New York, to discuss proposals for regaining political power lost to state and federal governments. The Iroquois Confederacy, or Haudenosaunee, established more than five hundred years ago, is comprised of the Onondaga, Mohawk, Seneca, Oneida, Cayuga, and Tuscarora.

**15 July 1970 Oglala Sioux Takeover.** Members of the Oglala Sioux seize an area on Sheep Mountain, South Dakota, demanding the return of a gunnery range that the military took from the tribe during World War II.

**1 August 1970 Puyallup Fish-in.** Puyallup Indians set up a camp on the Puyallup River in Washington State and begin fishing to reestablish their tribal fishing rights.

**September 1970 Mount Rushmore Takeover.** Approximately fifty Indians from different tribes climb to the top of Mount Rushmore and announce their takeover of the historic landmark. The occupiers intend to occupy Mount Rushmore until 123,000 acres of Indian land, unjustly taken for a gunnery range during World War II, is returned.

**20 September 1970 Osage Land Settlement.** The Justice Department announces a $13.2 million settlement with the Osage Indian Nation of Oklahoma for 28

Indians protesting discrimination in hiring at the Bureau of Indian Affairs office in Denver, Colorado, 1970. (Courtesy of the Denver Public Library, Western History Collection)

million acres of lands purchased by the federal government in Arkansas, Kansas, Missouri, and Oklahoma between 1803 and 1819.

**8 November 1970 Occupation of Army Communications Center.** Approximately seventy-five Indians seize an abandoned army communications center in Davis, California. The Indians demand that the center be turned over to them for use as an Indian cultural center.

**1970 *Mayflower II* Seized.** On Thanksgiving, members of the American Indian Movement (AIM) seize the

*Mayflower II* in Plymouth, Massachusetts. Proclaiming Thanksgiving day a national day of mourning, AIM protests the taking of Indian lands by European colonists. This is one of AIM's first national demonstrations. Previously AIM focused upon providing physical protection against police harassment of Indian people living in Minneapolis, Cleveland, and Washington, D.C.

**15 December 1970 Taos Land Bill.** President Richard Nixon signs the Taos Land Bill. The legislation returns forty-eight thousand acres of land, including Blue Lake, to the Taos Pueblo. This bill, the first legislation to restore a sizable piece of land to an Indian tribe, acknowledges that the Taos Pueblo Indians practiced their religion at this sacred site for over seven hundred years. The Pueblo lost the lands in 1906 when President Theodore Roosevelt added the area to the Carson National Forest. The Taos Pueblo lobbied sixty years for the return of their sacred lands.

On this date President Nixon also signs legislation authorizing the payment of $1.1 million to the Nez Percé tribe of Idaho and the Confederated Tribe of Colville of Washington State. The funds were awarded to the tribes by the Indian Claims Commission for the illegal loss of tribal lands to the federal government in the nineteenth century.

**1971 Tribal Sovereignty Efforts and the Creation of NARF.**　The Bureau of Indian Affairs establishes regulations allowing for the direct election of the chiefs of the Five Civilized Tribes. The Five Civilized Tribes—the Cherokee, Creek, Seminole, Choctaw, and Chickasaw—along with more than thirty other tribes, were relocated in the 1800s to Indian Territory, present-day Oklahoma. Despite their promise that the territory would always remain in Indian control, Congress allotted tribal lands in the 1890s and, for the most part, dissolved tribal governments. The BIA was given the authority to appoint a chief for each of the Five Civilized Tribes. Tribes view the return of control over their own electoral system as an important step in government revitalization.

The Native American Rights Fund (NARF) is created with its central office located in Boulder, Colorado, and a branch office in Washington, D.C. NARF was established as a special pilot project of the California Indian Legal Services. Funded by the Ford Foundation, the organization's objectives are to pursue the legal protection of Indian lands, treaty rights, individual rights, and the development of tribal law.

**13 January 1971 Report Charges Misuse of Indian Education Funds.**　The NAACP Legal Defense and Education Fund and Harvard University's Center for Law and Education release a 162-page report charging state and local officials with a gross misuse of funds appropriated under the Elementary and Secondary Education Act and the 1934 Johnson-O'Malley Act. Funds, the report charges, which are to be used for the benefit and education of Indian children, are frequently used for non-Indian educational purposes. Some 250 examples of alleged impropriety are provided, such as buying expensive equipment for non-Indian schools and

reducing non-Indian property taxes. "By every standard," the report emphasizes, "Indians receive the worst education of any children in the community."

**14 January 1971 Army Communications Center Given to Indians.**　The San Francisco regional office of the Health, Education, and Welfare Department gives custody of a 647-acre army communications center in Davis, California, to local Indians. The Indians who receive the "care, custody, protection and maintenance" of the base occupied the deserted building in November 1970. A spokesman for the group, Jack Forbes, announces plans to establish a college for American Indians and Mexican-Americans on the site. In April 1971 the federal government turns over land title to the trustees of Deganawida-Quetzelquatl University (DQU). The new university takes a hemispheric and indigenous approach to teaching and research.

**19–20 February 1971 National Tribal Chairmen's Association Formed.**　Tribal leaders from fifty reservations in twelve states meet in Billings, Montana, to discuss the establishment of a national association of tribal council leaders. The decision to establish the National Tribal Chairmen's Association stems from a concern by tribal reservation leaders that national Indian policy is being made in response to the actions of urban Indians and young militant reservation Indians.

**25 April 1971 Population Increase.**　The U.S. Census Bureau reports that the 1970 Census counted 791,839 Indians, an increase of more than 50 percent from the 1960 Census. The increase in population is primarily due to a declining death rate, high birth rate, and changing Native identities. More people with Native ancestry are willing to identify themselves as Indian.

**15 May 1971 Hopi File Suit to Stop Strip-Mining.**　The Native American Rights Fund files suit in federal court on behalf of sixty-two members of the Hopi tribe to stop strip-mining on one hundred square miles of the Hopi Reservation. The religious leaders contend that Black Mesa is sacred to Hopi religion and culture. The suit is part of a larger effort by other Indians and conservationists to stop the development of a major power grid in the Four Corners area. The Hopi traditionalists' objective is to prevent mining of the coal by the Peabody Company for use in six proposed power plants.

**21 May 1971 AIM Occupies Naval Air Station.**　Members of the American Indian Movement (AIM)

An exuberant occupier of Alcatraz Island flashes the peace sign. (Photo by Ilka Hartmann)

occupy a naval air station in Milwaukee, Wisconsin. The group argues that under the terms of the 1868 treaty between the federal government and the Lakota, all abandoned federal property should revert to Indians.

**26 May 1971 OEO Establishes Urban Indian Centers.** The director of the Office of Economic Opportunity (OEO) announces the provision of $880,000 in grants to establish a Model Urban Indian Center program. The funds are to be used to establish Indian centers in Los Angeles, Minneapolis, Gallup, and Fairbanks. The program's objective is to provide models for the improvements of services in the forty other existing urban Indian service centers.

According to the 1970 census, 44.5 percent of the Native population lives in urban areas, an increase of almost 15 percent during the previous ten years. Much of the urban migration is facilitated by the Bureau of Indian Affair's relocation program. In an effort to assimilate Indians into the mainstream, tribal members are encouraged to move to the urban areas to find work. Others move on their own, leaving their reservation homes in search of jobs.

**6–7 June 1971 Indians Occupy Mount Rushmore.** Forty Indians, demanding that the federal government honor its 1868 treaty with the Sioux Nation, which states that all lands west of the Missouri River would belong forever to the Sioux Nation, establish a camp on the top of the Mount Rushmore National Memorial. Police arrest twenty protesters for climbing the monument.

**11 June 1971 Alcatraz Occupation Ends.** The last fifteen Indians occupying Alcatraz Island are removed by federal marshals, ending the nineteen-month takeover of the island. The activists, approximately one hundred protesters from fifty Indian nations, hoped to turn Alcatraz into a center for Native American studies, an Indian center of ecology, an American Indian museum, and an Indian training school.

**14–17 June 1971 Indian Protesters Occupy Army Site.** Lakota leader John Trudell and fifty Indians occupy a deserted army missile site near Richmond,

California. One hundred police remove the protesters three days later.

**14 June–1 July 1971 Indian Protesters Occupy Missile Site.** One hundred Indians occupy an abandoned Nike missile site outside Chicago, protesting the lack of housing for Indians in Chicago.

**30 July 1971 Indian Protesters Occupy Missile Site.** Seventy-five Indians occupy a former Nike site on the grounds of the Argonne National Laboratories in Hinsdale, Illinois.

**14 August 1971 AIM Seizes Abandoned Coast Guard Station.** Members of the Milwaukee chapter of the American Indian Movement seize an abandoned Coast Guard station.

**26 August–1 September 1971 Report Indicates Low College Enrollment among Indians.** The Office of Civil Rights of the Health, Education, and Welfare Department reports that 29,000 American Indians are enrolled in colleges and universities.

**16 September 1971 Indian Polytechnic Institute Dedicated.** Assistant Secretary of the Interior Harrison Loesch participates in the dedication of the new $13 million Southwestern Indian Polytechnic Institute in Albuquerque, New Mexico. The school will serve seven hundred Indian students from sixty-four tribes. The 164-acre campus will offer training in business management, clerical work, drafting, radio, electronics, commercial food preparation, telecommunications, television, engineering, and optical technology.

**5 October 1971 Alaska Natives File Suit against Alaska.** The Arctic Slope Native Association files suit against the state of Alaska, claiming the 26,000-acre North Slope of Alaska. The suit claims that the state's selection of this oil-rich area in 1964 violated Native land rights in that the "Eskimo people have occupied, used and exercised dominion" over the area. The region is currently under lease to private oil companies for approximately $1 billion.

**9 October 1971 Indian Education Bill Passes.** The Senate passes a $390.3 million education bill designed to give greater control to tribes over the education of their children.

**13–15 October 1971 First National AIM Convention.** The American Indian Movement holds its first national convention. Approximately one hundred delegates representing eighteen chapters attend the conference at Camp Owendigo, Minnesota.

**15 December 1971 Navajo Community College Act.** The Navajo Community College Act provides $5.5 million for the construction and operation of a new facility for the Navajo Community College.

**18 December 1971 Alaska Native Claims Settlement Act.** President Richard Nixon signs the Alaska Native Claims Settlement Act (ANSCA) into law. The act extinguishes Alaska Native title to nine-tenths of Alaska in return for 44 million acres and $962.5 million. The House passed the bill on December 14 by a vote of 307 to sixty and the Senate by a voice vote. The legislation provides for the creation of villages and regional corporations under state law for the management of the lands and funds provided by the act.

Although the Alaska Federation of Natives approved the bill by a vote of 511 to fifty-six, the act remains controversial among Alaska Natives who fear that ANCSA will destroy their traditional lifestyle, which is centered on hunting and fishing.

**19 February 1972 Chippewa Subsistence Rights Upheld.** A federal court order takes effect protecting the Chippewa's right to hunt, fish, trap, and gather wild rice according to tribal laws on their Leech Lake Reservation. The Leech Lake Band of Chippewa Indians won a suit against the state of Minnesota in December 1971, upholding their 1855 treaty with the United States which guaranteed their right to hunt, fish, trap, and gather wild rice on the reservation.

**2 March 1972 Stanford Changes Mascot.** Bowing to pressures by Indian students on campus, Stanford University in Palo Alto, California, ends a forty-year tradition of using an American Indian symbol for its athletic teams.

**4 March 1972 Five Persons Convicted in Murder.** Five persons are charged in Gordon, Nebraska, with manslaughter and false imprisonment in the death of R. Yellow Thunder, a forty-one-year-old Oglala Sioux Indian.

**7 March 1972 National American Indian Council Formed.** Urban Indians hold a conference in Omaha, Nebraska, forming the National American Indian Council. The council is committed to working on behalf of urban Indians nationwide.

**23 April 1972 Peaceful AIM Sit-in.** Thirty Lakota and Chippewa American Indian Movement members stage a peaceful protest on the Fort Totten Indian Reservation in North Dakota. The sit-in's purpose is to call attention to police brutality on the reservation. According to the protesters, three Indians have died in jail in the last few months.

**20 May 1972 Indian Education Act.** Congress passes the Indian Education Act of 1972, creating a BIA-level Office of Indian Education as well as a National Advisory Council on Indian Education (NACIE) designed to improve the quality of public education for Indian students through grants and contracts for teachers of Indian students.

President Richard Nixon signs an order restoring 21,000 acres in Gifford Pinchot National Forest to the Yakima Indians of Washington.

**June 1972 Lumbee Struggle to Retain Historic Building.** Lumbee students at Pembroke State University strive to prevent the destruction of a historic Indian building on the campus. In 1885, the state of North Carolina permitted the Lumbees to operate their own school systems. The state's fifty-year-old constitution recognized the Lumbees as "free people of color,"

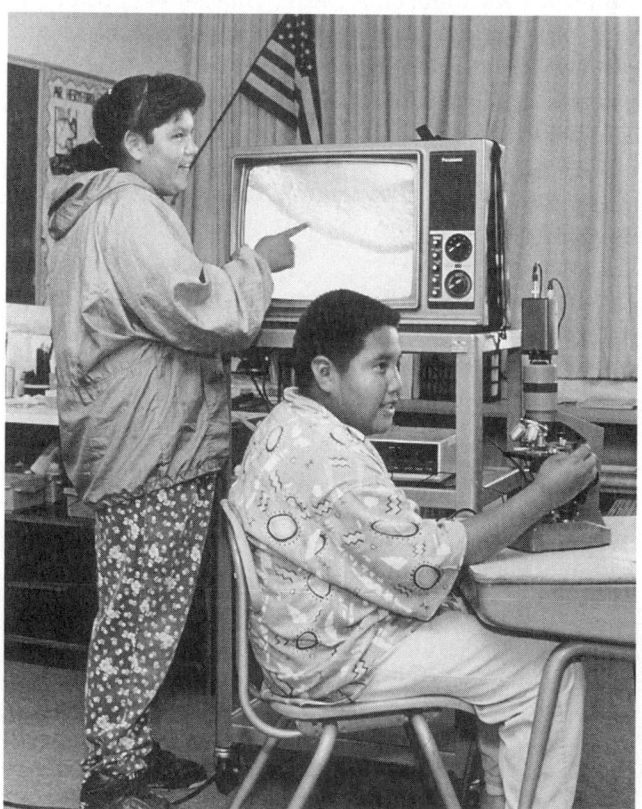

Title VII's (Indian Education) program for gifted and talented students provided this electronic video microscope for elementary classes. Patricia C'Hair and Franklin Martel show how the TV monitor can display microscopic views to large groups. (Photo by Mike McClure)

but barred them from attending white schools. Permitting them to operate their own schools proved an important step in Lumbee advancement. The school, started in 1887, became a four-year college in 1935. Old Main, as the building is known, served for many years as the only building on campus. With a current enrollment of 2,500, 92 percent of whom are white, the mostly white campus administration finds itself pitted against the Lumbee who are determined to save the historic building.

**24 August 1972 Interior Department Charged with Environmental Failure.** The General Accounting Office (GAO) issues a report charging that the Department of Interior has failed to enforce the Environmental Policy Act in its regulation of strip coal-mining on Indian and federal lands.

**13 September 1972 Natives Seize BIA Building.** Approximately forty Indians seize control of the Bureau of Indian Affairs building in Pawnee, Oklahoma, protesting the use of federal funds and presenting a list of demands to federal and state authorities.

**2–8 November 1972 Trail of Broken Treaties.** Five hundred Indians arrive in Washington, D.C., with the Trail of Broken Treaties to protest the government's policies toward Indians. The leaders, mostly members of the American Indian Movement, bring with them a twenty-point program, which they plan to present to the administration. Among their demands are that treaty relations be reestablished between the federal government and the Indian nations; that termination policies be repealed, including Public Law 280; that the Indian land base be doubled; that tribes be given criminal jurisdiction over non-Indians on reservations; and that cultural and economic conditions for Indians be improved.

The twenty-point program is quickly forgotten in the wake of a disagreement over housing and food provisions during the march in Washington, D.C. In protest, members of the Trail of Broken Treaties occupy the Bureau of Indian Affairs building in Washington, D.C.

After almost a week of occupation, during which time activists destroy files, furniture, and Indian art, the government agrees to pay for the protesters' return trip home and to consider the demands presented in the twenty-point program. On 9 June 1973 the federal government officially rejects the demands received from the leaders of the Trail of Broken Treaties.

**9 November 1972 Paiute Prevail in Case against Interior Department.** The Paiute tribe of Nevada wins its suit against the Department of Interior for the

Urban Indian children take care of a baby. (Photo by Ilka Hartmann)

department's management of Pyramid Lake. The court agrees that the Interior Department had violated its trust responsibility by allowing water diversion from the lake, thereby threatening the economic and spiritual existence of the tribe.

**14 November 1972 Natives Charge Commission with Inconsistency.**   The U.S. Commission on Civil Rights hears testimony from American Indian witnesses that the agency directs its attention to the needs of African- and Hispanic-Americans, overlooking the needs of American Indians.

**6–8 February 1973 AIM Protest Turns Violent.** Two hundred American Indian Movement protesters clash with police in Custer, South Dakota. Thirty-seven Indians are arrested during a melee with police over a judge's decision to grant bail to the white man charged with the stabbing death of Wesley Bad Heart.

**12 February 1973 Withhorn Released from Jail.** Two hundred-fifty Indians gather in Sturgis, South Dakota, to witness the setting of bond for Harold Withhorn, whom police have charged with the murder of a non-Indian.

**27 February–8 May 1973 Wounded Knee Occupied.**   Two hundred Indians under AIM leadership occupy Wounded Knee on the Pine Ridge Reservation in South Dakota. American Indian Movement leaders are asked to the reservation by traditionalists to assist them in their struggle against the elected chairman Richard Wilson, whose administration, they charge, is rife with corruption, nepotism, intimidation, and violence.

Federal marshals and Federal Bureau Investigation (FBI) officers immediately surround the hamlet, creating a standoff that draws national and world-wide media attention. The Indian militants, who are well armed, make clear their intention to fight rather than surrender to outside forces. The Indian occupiers are surrounded by 300 federal marshals and FBI agents equipped with guns and armored personnel carriers. The impasse ends after sixty-seven days with a negotiated settlement and the withdrawal of both sides.

**March 1973 Clashes between Hopi and Navajo.** Clashes occur between Hopi and Navajo over the disposition of the Joint Use Area.

**27 March 1973 *Mescalero Apache Tribe v. Jones*.** The Supreme Court rules in *Mescalero Apache Tribe v. Jones, Commissioner, Board of Revenue of New Mexico et al.* that Indians are exempt from state taxation on incomes earned within reservation boundaries.

**31 March 1973 Cheyenne Order BIA to End Strip-Mining.** The Northern Cheyenne Tribal Council of Montana votes to instruct the Bureau of Indian Affairs to cancel strip-mining leases worth millions of dollars negotiated by the BIA on reservation lands. Lawyers for the Cheyenne tribe found thirty-six illegal sections in the leases that the BIA had negotiated on behalf of the tribe.

**14 June 1973 BIA Charged with Unfair Trading Practices.** The Federal Trade Commission issues a report charging that a number of non-Indian traders, licensed by the Bureau of Indian Affairs, are engaged in unfair trading practices leading to poor economic conditions for the inhabitants of the Navajo Reservation. The report finds that prices charged by the trading posts exceeded off-reservation stores by 16.6 percent and exceeded the national average by 27 percent.

**16 July 1973 Census Report Findings.** The Census Bureau reports that the median income for Indian families in 1969 was $5,832, compared to a national average of $9,590. Forty percent of Indian families live below the poverty level, compared to 14 percent of all families and 32 percent of Black families. Education statistics indicate the greatest degree of increase since the last census. One-third of all Indians over twenty-five have completed high school, with a median number of 9.8 years of school for all Indians. The number of Indian students in college has doubled since 1960.

**13 August 1973 Office of Indian Rights Created.** An Office of Indian Rights is created within the Civil Rights Division of the Justice Department. The office is established to investigate and protect individual Indian rights guaranteed under the Indian Civil Rights Act.

**17 November 1973 Grand Jury Issues Indictments.** The grand jury in Sioux Falls, South Dakota, returns four indictments against Indians arrested following the Wounded Knee standoff.

**19 November 1973 *Department of Game of Washington v. Puyallup Tribe et al.*** The Supreme Court, in a unanimous decision in *Department of Game of Washington v. Puyallup Tribe et al.*, rules that Washington State had abrogated the Puyallup Indians' treaty rights by prohibiting the tribe from commercial fishing. State law restricted all available fish to sports fishing.

**22 November 1973 Arctic-Area Natives Meet.** Indigenous peoples of the Arctic area—Eskimos, Lapps, and Indians—meet in Copenhagen, Denmark, to formulate demands for self-government and for control over land and resources. Indigenous peoples from Alaska, Canada, Greenland, Norway, and Sweden attend the four-day meeting.

**22 December 1973 Public Law 93–197.** President Richard Nixon signs Public Law 93–197 restoring the Menominee Indian tribe of Wisconsin to full federally recognized status.

**28 December 1973 Comprehensive Employment and Training Act.** Congress enacts the Comprehensive Employment and Training Act of 1973 or CETA, as it is commonly known. Title III of the act, Special Federal Responsibilities, Indian Manpower Programs, is designed to assist unemployed and economically disadvantaged Indians.

**21 January 1974 Supreme Court Reversal.** The Supreme Court reverses a lower court decision that barred the Oneida Indian Nation from suing the State of New York for rental on 5 million acres of land the tribe claims was taken in illegal state treaties in 1788 and 1795.

**7 February 1974 Oglala Sioux Election Runoff.** Russell Means, leader of the American Indian Movement, is defeated by incumbent Richard Wilson in a runoff election for chairman of the Oglala Sioux Tribal Council. Means had led in a field of twelve nominees by a small margin in the initial vote on January 22. Means, who lost 1,709 to 1,530, vowed to destroy the "white man's tribal government" and to reestablish "a type of government where all Indians would have a voice." Wilson pledged to continue full cooperation with the federal government. Charges of corruption and illegal vote counting followed the final outcome of the election.

**12 February 1974 *United States v. State of Washington*.** U.S. District Court Judge Boldt rules in *United States v. State of Washington* that the 1854 and 1855 treaties signed by the tribes of northwestern Washington, in which they reserved "the right of taking fish, at all usual and accustomed grounds and stations. . . in common with all citizens of the Territory," entitle the tribes to 50 percent of the allowable salmon catch.

**16 February 1974 Wounded Knee Trial.** Russell Means and Dennis Banks, leaders in the American Indian Movement, are brought to trial for charges stemming from the 1973 occupation of Wounded Knee, South Dakota.

**20 February 1974 *Morton v. Ruiz*.** The Supreme Court, in *Morton v. Ruiz*, unanimously upholds the right of Indians living off-reservation to receive general welfare payments from the Bureau of Indian Affairs.

**12 April 1974 Indian Financing Act.** Congress passes the Indian Financing Act, making available $250 million in credits and grants up to $50,000 to facilitate financing the economic development of Indians and Indian organizations.

**17 June 1974 Supreme Court Refuses to Review Navajo Case.** The Supreme Court declines to review a lower court decision upholding the election of an Arizona county supervisor who is a member of the Navajo nation. Non-Indian voters had challenged his eligibility for office on the grounds that his status as a reservation Indian made him immune from state taxes and the normal legal process.

**17 June 1974 *Morton v. Mancari*.** The Supreme Court, in *Morton v. Mancari*, upholds the preferential hiring of American Indians within the Bureau of Indian Affairs. The suit, which was brought by non-Indian BIA employees, argued that preferential hiring of Indians violated the equal protection clause of the Constitution. The Court denies the claim, pointing out that the federal government has a special obligation to Indians. Special preferences are given to Indians in BIA employment, the Court said, not because of their membership in a racial group, but because of their membership in quasi-sovereign nations that have entered into a political relationship with the federal government.

**28–30 August 1974 Civil Rights Commission Hearings.** The New Mexico Advisory Committee of the U.S. Civil Rights Commission holds three days of hearings near Farmington, New Mexico. The hearings are prompted by the beating death of three Navajo men by three white teenagers who had found the men drunk. The teenagers, according to the terms of state juvenile laws, were sentenced to two to three years in a reformatory. Navajo leaders testified to a variety of abuses ranging from commercial cheating to murder suffered by Navajo in off reservation towns located in Colorado, Utah, and New Mexico. Several Navajo leaders request support closing nearby off-reservation taverns.

**22 December 1974 Hopi and Navajo Relocation Act.** Congress passes the Hopi and Navajo Relocation Act providing for negotiations between the two tribes over their dispute concerning the Joint Use Area. The bill provides for the partition of the 1.8-million-acre Joint Use Area between the Hopi and Navajo and for $16 million to compensate eight hundred Navajo families who will be required to relocate as a result of the partition.

This legislation is the latest attempt by Congress to deal with the long-standing Navajo-Hopi land dispute. The conflict between the Hopi and the Navajo is complex. The Hopi never signed a treaty with the United States. In contrast, the Navajo entered into a treaty with the United States in 1868, following years of hostility and relocations. The treaty established the Navajo Reservation in northwestern New Mexico and northeastern Arizona. Prior to the adoption of this treaty, a number of Navajo families already lived in areas claimed by the Hopi.

In 1882, in response to Hopi complaints about Navajo encroachment, the president issued an executive order establishing the Hopi Reservation. Hopi lands continued to be settled by Navajo and Mormon families.

In an effort to solve the growing conflict between the two tribes, Congress authorized the courts to make a determination as to the competing land claims. In response, the courts created the Joint Use area, composed of 1.8 million acres, while allotting 650,000 acres of the 1882 reservation for the exclusive use of the Hopi.

**1 January–4 February 1975 Indians Seize Catholic Novitiate.** Forty-five Indians of the Menominee Warrior Society seize a Catholic novitiate in Gresham, Wisconsin. The Warrior Society demands that the Alexian Brothers give the 225-acre complex to the tribe for use as a hospital. The compound, comprised of a twenty-room mansion and another sixty-four room building, is currently unused by the religious order.

**2 January 1975 Congress Reviews Tribal-Federal Relations.** Congress, pursuant to a joint resolution of both houses, agrees to review the government's historical and special legal relationship with the Indian people. The American Indian Policy Review Commission is chaired by Senator James Abourezk of South Dakota. The task force includes three senators, three representatives, and five tribal representatives.

**4 January 1975 Indian Self-Determination and Education Assistance Act.** Congress passes the Indian Self-Determination and Education Assistance Act, expanding tribal control over reservation programs and authorizing federal funds to build needed

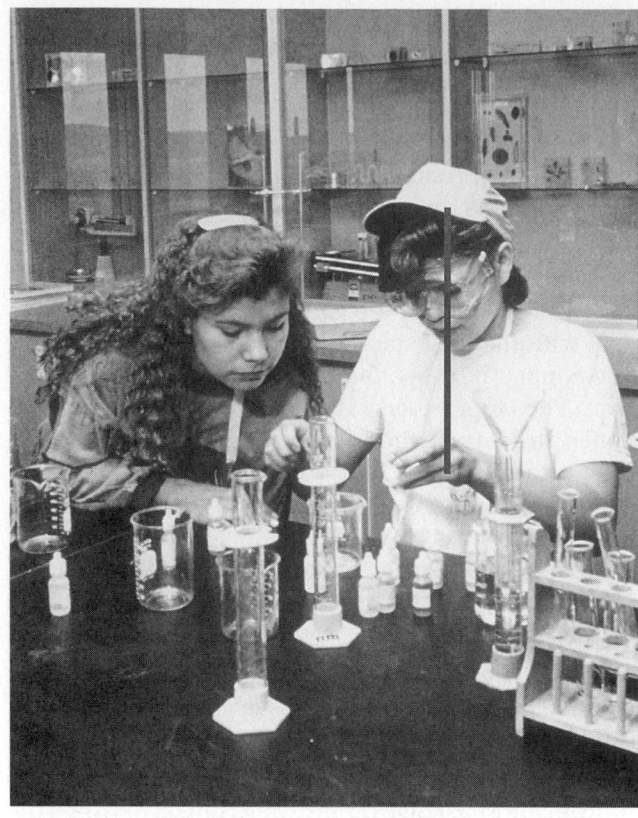

Wyoming Indian high school students Yvonda Hubbard and Marla Jimerson. (Photo by Mike McClure)

public school facilities on or near Indian reservations. Hailed as the most important piece of legislation passed since the 1934 Indian Reorganization Act, the Self-Determination Act's goal is to contract management of federal programs to tribal governments and other Indian organizations.

**8 January 1975 Pine Ridge Election Declared Invalid.**  A U.S. Commission on Civil Rights report on the tribal chairman's election at Pine Ridge Reservation is termed invalid and recommends a new election. The election race involves Richard Wilson and Russell Means. After reviewing the ballots, the commission reports, "almost one-third of all votes cast appear to have been in some manner improper. . . .  The procedures for ensuring the security of the election were so inadequate that actual fraud or wrongdoing could easily have gone undetected."

**13 March 1975 Navajo Plant Closes.**  The Fairchild Camera and Instrument Corporation announces that it will close its Shiprock, New Mexico, electronic plant on the Navajo Reservation. The plant was occupied by armed members of the American Indian Movement

(AIM) for eight days in protest of the plants layoff of 140 Indian employees. The company, which produces semiconductors and integrated circuits for computers, employed approximately 600 Navajos before the layoffs took effect in February. In assessing the damage of the takeover, which ended March 3, a Fairchild spokesperson stated, "Fairchild has concluded that it couldn't be reasonably assured that future disruptions wouldn't occur."

**22 April 1975 Violence Continues on Pine Ridge.**  A story in the *New York Times* reports that violence on the Pine Ridge Reservation has continued since the end of the Wounded Knee seizure. According to an FBI report, six people have been killed and sixty-seven assaulted since January 1. The violence, according to the story, is the legacy of the 1973 takeover, which divided the reservation into two opposing factions.

**16 June 1975 AIM National Convention.**  The American Indian Movement (AIM) ends its national convention in Farmington, New Mexico, with a statement declaring that the U.S. government, religion, and education are the most potent enemies of Indian people.

**26 June 1975 AIM-FBI Shootout.**  A shootout on the Pine Ridge Reservation in South Dakota between AIM members and the FBI results in the death of two agents. Leonard Peltier is charged and convicted for the murder of the FBI agents and is presently serving two life sentences in prison.

**10 July 1975 Alexian Brothers Rescind Offer.**  The Alexian Brothers Roman Catholic order rescinds its offer to deed to the Menominee tribe of Wisconsin its novitiate in Gresham, Wisconsin, for use as a tribal hospital.

**6 August 1975 Voting Rights Act Amendments.**  President Gerald Ford signs into law the Voting Rights Act Amendments of 1975. The act, which is designed to protect the voting rights of non-English speaking citizens by permitting voting in more than one language, specifically includes the rights of American Indians.

**13 August 1975 Report on Farmington, New Mexico, Released.**  The New Mexico advisory committee to the U.S. Civil Rights Commission issues "The Farmington Report: A Conflict of Cultures." The study concludes that Navajo in San Juan County, New Mexico, which includes Farmington, are subjected to a wide range of injustices and mistreatment. Discrimination, according to the report, is intensified by poverty, severe alcoholism, and substandard health care. The county, the committee points out, has no detoxification or rehabilitation centers, despite the fact that 85 percent of the 21,000 Navajo arrested between 1969 and 1973 were arrested on alcohol-related offenses. The report also takes note of the inadequately staffed and funded Indian Health Service Hospital in Shiprock, and the lack of cooperation and commitment evidenced by local doctors responsible for the care of the Navajo population.

**25 November 1975 Four Indians Indicted in South Dakota.**   A federal grand jury indicts four Indians, Leonard Peltier, Robert Eugene Robideau, Darrelle Dean Butler, and James Theodore Eagle, on charges of the premeditated death of two FBI officers. The officers were killed on July 26 in a gun battle on the Pine Ridge Reservation in South Dakota.

**23 December 1975 *Passamaquoddy Tribe v. Morton*.**   The U.S. Court of Appeals, First Circuit, upholds Judge Edward Gignoux's decision in *Passamaquoddy Tribe v. Morton*. The Passamaquoddy and Penobscot of Maine, two non-federally recognized tribes, argue that the 1790 Trade and Non-Intercourse Act established a trust relationship between them and the federal government. The 1790 act forbade the sale of Indian lands without the approval of the federal government. The colony of Massachusetts (which later divided into the states of Massachusetts and Maine) had purchased land from the Passamaquoddy and Penobscot tribes in treaty. The federal government argued that it was not obligated to represent the tribes in their suit against the state of Maine because the tribes were not federally recognized. Judge Gignoux's decision upholds the principle that the federal government has an obligation to protect the land rights of all tribes, whether recognized or not.

**2 March 1976 *Fisher v. District Court*.**   The Supreme Court rules in *Fisher v. District Court* that the Northern Cheyenne tribe of Montana has exclusive authority over adoption proceedings in which the participants are all tribal members and residents of the reservation.

**27 April 1976 *Moe v. Salish and Kootenai Tribes*.**   The Supreme Court, in *Moe v. Salish and Kootenai Tribes*, rules that the states may not tax either personal property on the reservation or cigarette sales by Indians to Indians on the reservation. The Court, however, rules that tribes must collect cigarette sales tax on the reservation on sales by Indians to non-Indians.

**29 May 1976 Indian Crimes Act of 1976.**   Congress passes the Indian Crimes Act of 1976. The act ensures that all individuals, Indian and non-Indian alike, receive equal treatment when violating crimes on federal lands, including Indian reservations, military installations, and national parks.

**8 June 1976 AIM Members Stand Trial.**   American Indian Movement members Robert Robideau and Darrelle Butler stand trial for the 25 June 1975 murder of two FBI agents on Pine Ridge Reservation.

**15 June 1976 *Bryan v. Itasca*.**   The U.S. Supreme Court rules in *Bryan v. Itasca* that Public Law 280, a statute giving six states criminal and civil jurisdiction over Indian reservations, does not give states the authority to levy state property tax on Indians living within reservation boundaries.

**1 September 1976 All Indian Pueblo Cultural Center Opens.**   The All Indian Pueblo Cultural Center opens in Albuquerque, New Mexico. The $2.3 million Indian Cultural Center is a joint effort of the nineteen Pueblos that lie along the Rio Grande. The center houses a museum, a restaurant, and a gift shop.

**16 September 1976 Indian Health Care Improvement Act.**   Congress passes the Indian Health Care Improvement Act, authorizing seven years of increased appropriations in an effort to improve Indian health care. The bill provides $480 million in funds for recruiting and training Indian health professionals; providing health services, including patient, dental, and alcoholism treatment; constructing and renovating health facilities; and providing services to urban Indians.

**8 October 1976 Indian Claims Commission Terminated.**   President Gerald Ford signs a bill to terminate the Indian Claims Commission on 31 December 1978. Unresolved cases are to be forwarded to the U.S. Court of Claims for final resolution. The bill provides an additional amount, not to exceed $1,650,000 for the dissolution of the Indian Claims Commission on 30 September 1978.

**13 October 1976 Mesquakie Land Claims Settlement.**   The federal government awards $6.6 million to the Mesquakie tribe for lands taken in Iowa, Missouri, Illinois, and Kansas in ten treaties signed between the federal government and the tribe between 1804 and 1867.

**31 October 1976 Puyallup Occupy.**   Approximately sixty members of the Puyallup tribe, including members of the tribal council, occupy the Cascadia Juvenile Diagnostic Center in Tacoma, Washington. After a weeklong occupation, during which time the tribe claimed

Dennis Banks and supporters. (Photo by Ilka Hartmann)

title to the building, the governor of Washington announces an agreement to give six acres of land to the tribe.

**13 December 1976 Navajo Radio Network.** The Navajo Radio Network broadcasts its first day of news and public interest programming on the reservation in the Navajo language.

**13 January 1977 Crow Coal Agreements Rescinded.** Secretary of Interior Thomas S. Kleppe rescinds a number of coal leases and lease options on coal reserves on the Crow reservations. The strip-mining agreements, which provided for a royalty payment of 17.5¢ per ton on subtracted coal, came under attack by Crow tribal members. Tribal members filed suits to have leases held by Shell Oil, AMAX Inc., Peabody, and Gulf revoked.

**4 April 1977 Catawba Ask Congress to Settle Claims.** The Catawba Indians of South Carolina vote 101 to two in a tribal council meeting to ask Congress to settle their claims to 144,000 acres in York and Lancaster counties. The tribe, which is requesting recognition of a reservation within their former lands, argues that their 1763 treaty with Great Britain guarantees their ownership of the land. Barring congressional relief, the tribe agrees to take their suit to court.

**5 April 1977 *Rosebud Sioux Tribe v. Kneip*.** The Supreme Court, in *Rosebud Sioux Tribe v. Kneip*, rules that the congressional legislation, which opened surplus reservation lands to American settlers in the nineteenth century, diminished the size of the reservation and thereby the tribe's jurisdictional authority over that area.

**18 April 1977 Peltier Found Guilty.** American Indian Movement member Leonard Peltier, thirty-two, is found guilty of two charges of first-degree murder in the 1975 shooting deaths of two FBI agents on the Pine Ridge Reservation. Two men, previously charged with Peltier, had been acquitted of the charges on 16 July 1976. Peltier is sentenced to two consecutive life terms by a Fargo, North Dakota, court on 2 June 1977.

**13 May 1977 Mohawks, State of New York Reach Agreement.** A group of Mohawks, who for three years occupy a 612-acre campsite in the Adirondack Mountains, reach an agreement with the state of New York. In return for a grant of two separate sites, the Mohawks agree to vacate within the next five months the site they have renamed Ganienkeh or "Land of the Flint." The larger area of land, consisting of 5,000 acres, is located within the Macomb State Park. A smaller parcel of seven hundred acres lies near the town of Altona, New York. The Mohawks claim the area as part of the land guaranteed to the tribe in an eighteenth century treaty.

**18 May 1977 American Indian Policy Review Report Released.** Congress releases its multivolume American Indian Policy Review Commission Report. Eleven study groups, comprised of thirty-three members, thirty-one of whom are Indian, worked for two years to produce the report. The commission recommends the formation of a separate Department of Indian Affairs with cabinet status and suggests that stronger self-governing powers be given to tribes, wherein they can levy taxes on their reservations, try reservation offenders in tribal courts, and control Native resources such as waterways, hunting, and fishing. Despite strong support, Indian affairs remain under the authority of the Department of Interior. The commission's final report reveals that more than one hundred tribes are not federally recognized and recommends procedures for their recognition.

**2 June 1977 Peltier Sentenced.** Leonard Peltier is sentenced by a Fargo, North Dakota, court to two consecutive life terms for the killings of two FBI agents.

**13–17 June 1977 First Inuit Conference Convenes.** Two hundred indigenous peoples from Alaska, Canada, and Greenland, convene the first Inuit Circumpolar Conference in Barrows, Alaska. The conference is the first attempt to organize the 100,000 Inuits who inhabit the North Pole region. Delegates adopt resolutions concerning the preservation of their cultures and the recognition of self-sufficiency. The delegates also decide on environmental protections and ban all weapons testing and disposal in the Arctic.

**17 June 1977 Council Provides List of Grievances to Soviet Union.** The *New York Times* reports that the International Indian Treaty Council, which represents ninety-seven tribes, announces its intention to provide the Soviet Union with a list of human rights abuses by the United States against tribes. The list, which includes treaty violations, the destruction of Native cultures and religions, and the interference in

tribal economic and social life, would be provided for Soviet use at the upcoming meetings on the Helsinki Accords in Belgrade, Yugoslavia. The Helsinki Accords, signed by thirty-five nations in 1975, pledge signatory states to respect the self-determination and human rights of all peoples.

**24 July 1977 Ute and Comanche End 200-Year Dispute.** The Ute and Comanche nations meet to formally end a 200-year-old dispute over hunting rights in jointly claimed territory. More than two thousand members from both tribes attend the traditional ceremony, which includes the exchange of buckskin scrolls, the smoking of a peace pipe, and the shaking of hands.

**1 August 1977 Seneca Opens Museum.** The Seneca Nation holds an opening ceremony for its new $265,000 museum in Salamanca, New York. The museum, designed and constructed by the tribe from federal grants, houses artifacts from the Seneca Nation and the Iroquois Confederacy, as well as art work.

**September 1977 Alaskan Eskimo Whaling Commission Founded.** The Alaskan Eskimo Whaling Commission is founded to fight the International Whaling Commission's ban against the hunting of all bowhead whale. Culturally and economically dependent on the hunting of bowhead, the Alaskan Eskimo Whaling Commission commits itself to ensure that all hunts are conducted in a traditional and non-wasteful manner to educate non-Native Alaskans about the cultural importance of whaling and to promote scientific research to ensure the bowhead's continued existence.

**13 October 1977 Assistant Secretary of Indian Affairs Appointed.** Forrest J. Gerard (Blackfeet) is appointed by President Jimmy Carter as the first assistant secretary of Indian affairs. First proposed by President Richard Nixon, the creation of the position elevates the Bureau of Indian Affairs administration to a level similar to other major agencies within the Interior Department.

**2 January 1978 Devils Lake Sioux Land Claims Settlement.** The Bureau of Indian Affairs reports that the federal government has reached an out-of-court settlement with the Devils Lake Sioux Indian tribe for the illegal taking of 100,000 acres of land between 1880 and 1890. The tribe will receive $8.5 million for land taken from the Fort Totten Indian Reservation.

**11 February–15 July 1978 The Longest Walk.** Indian participants begin the Longest Walk at Alcatraz Island, California, in protest of the government's ill

Members of AIM at a San Francisco anti-nuclear rally, c. 1977. (Photo by Ilka Hartmann)

treatment of Indians. The five-month trek begins on Alcatraz Island, the site of the 1969 occupation that lasted nineteen months and gave impetus to many subsequent occupation events. The walk concludes with 30,000 marchers in Washington, D.C. Religious and traditional Indian leaders meet for three hours with Vice President Walter Mondale and Secretary of the Interior Cecil Andrus.

**2 March 1978 Narragansett Land Settlement.** The Narragansett Indians of Rhode Island receive 1,800 acres in a negotiated settlement with state officials. The tribe filed suit against Rhode Island for the taking of 3,500 acres in violation of the 1790 Trade and Non-Intercourse Act.

**6 March 1978 *Oliphant v. Suquamish Indian Tribe.*** The Supreme Court rules in *Oliphant v. Suquamish Indian Tribe* that tribal courts do not possess jurisdiction over crimes committed by non-Indians on reservations. The case is brought by two U.S. citizens who were arrested by the Suquamish tribal police for disturbing the peace and resisting arrest during the tribe's annual Chief Seattle Days. The men argue that tribal governments do not have the inherent authority to exercise criminal jurisdiction over non-Indians. The decision inhibits tribes in the protection of their inherent sovereignty. The ruling also presents tribes with the practical problem of how to protect their lands and citizens from criminal actions by non-Indians. For the most part, state police officers do not have the authority to enforce law and order on Indian reservations.

**22 March 1978 *United States v. Wheeler.*** The Supreme Court rules unanimously in *United States v. Wheeler* that the United States did not violate a Navajo Indian man's protection against double jeopardy by trying him for rape in a federal court when he had been convicted on a lesser charge arising from the same incident in the Navajo tribal courts. The Court underscores that tribal governments are not creations of the federal government, but are separate sovereigns. As separate sovereigns, they have the authority to make and to adjudicate their own laws within limits established by Congress.

**24 March 1978 Mashpee Wampanoag Land Claim Dismissed.** The Mashpee Wampanoag land claim in the Cape Cod area of Massachusetts is dismissed by the U.S. District Court in Boston. The tribe, which had initiated its suit three years earlier, suffered a setback on January 6 when a jury ruled that although the Mashpee constituted a tribe in 1834 and 1842, they had lost their tribal status by 1869, when the land passed into non-Indian hands. Because of the tribe's failure to meet the definitions of a tribe after 1869, the court rejected Mashpee claims of more than 11,000 acres.

**17 April 1978 Navajo Nation Reaches Agreement with Oil Companies.** An agreement between four oil companies and the Navajo Nation is reached, ending a seventeen-day occupation of an Aneth, Utah, oil field. The four companies, Conoco, Phillips, Superior Oil, and Texaco, agree to institute a code of conduct for their oil workers and establish a hiring preference program for Indian employees. The protesters demanded the code of conduct because of the oil workers' use of alcohol on the reservation and their harassment of Navajo women.

**19 April 1978 Banks's Extradition Denied.** Governor Edmund G. Brown of California refuses an official request from Governor Richard F. Kneip of South Dakota to extradite Dennis Banks to stand trial in South Dakota. Banks, an Ojibway leader in the American Indian Movement, was convicted by a South Dakota court in 1975 of assault with a deadly weapon. The conviction arose out of the ninety-day seizure of Wounded Knee in 1973. Jumping bail, Banks, forty-five, fled to Oregon and then to California, where he has been teaching at a Deganawida-Quetzelquatl University (DQU) near Sacramento. In his letter to the South Dakota governor, Brown referred to "the strong hostility there against the American Indian Movement as well as its leaders." Brown's refusal to extradite Banks to South Dakota was upheld by the California Supreme Court on 20 March 1978.

**22 April 1978 Reservation Denies Access to Non-Indians.** The Fort Hall Indian Reservation's business council votes to deny access of non-Indians to the reservation for all purposes, including hunting and fishing in the Snake River basin. The action is taken in reaction to the Supreme Court's decision in the *Oliphant* case that tribal governments do not possess criminal jurisdiction over non-Indians.

**30 April 1978 Department of Education Established.** The Senate passes a bill to establish a new cabinet level agency, the Department of Education. A provision is included to transfer Indian education programs from the Department of the Interior to the newly established Department of Education.

**13 May 1978 Reservation Housing Decline.** The General Accounting Office reports that substandard housing for reservation families increased from 63,000 in June 1970 to 86,500 in a six-year period. New housing construction on reservations also dropped from 5,000 units to 3,500 units during the same time period.

**15 May 1978 *Santa Clara Pueblo v. Martinez.*** The Supreme Court rules in *Santa Clara Pueblo v. Martinez* that the Indian Civil Rights Act provides only for review of tribal habeas corpus cases. The case stems from a request by Mrs. Martinez of the Santa Clara Pueblo tribe that the Pueblo's tribal membership law be overturned to allow her children's enrollment. Current tribal law states that the children of enrolled women who marry outside the tribe are ineligible for membership. The ordinance extends membership to the children of men who married outside the tribe. Santa Clara Pueblo reckons descent by patrilineal clan and tribal membership is extended to members of clans, the clan of one's father. Mrs. Martinez charged that the tribal ordinance constituted a denial of equal protection under federal law. The Supreme Court held that Indian tribes have the power to determine membership according to their own rules, and that U.S. law is not applicable.

**21 May 1978 Chumash Protests Conclude.** Approximately twenty-five Chumash Indians agree to end their three-day protest at the site of an ancient burial ground at Little Cohu Bay, Pt. Conception, California, one of the proposed locations for a $1 billion coast site for the importation of liquefied natural gas. Under the terms of an agreement worked out between the tribe and the utility companies, the tribe will be allowed to have access to the area for religious practices, to protect all ruins and artifacts, and to have six tribal members monitor future excavations.

**24 May 1978 AIM Activists Acquitted in Taxi Driver's Death.** Two Indian activists, Paul Skyhorse and Richard Mohawk, are found innocent of murder and robbery in the death of a taxi driver. The driver's body had been found on 10 October 1974, near an American Indian Movement campsite north of Los Angeles. In the courts for three-and-a-half years, the case took thirteen months to try and cost $1.25 million to prosecute. Both men, whom supporters argued were framed for their AIM activities, remained in jail during the entire three-and-a-half years.

**8 June 1978 Council of Energy Resources Tribes Established.** Tribal leaders from twenty-five reservations containing energy resources agree to establish the Council of Energy Resources Tribes. The organization, to be known as CERT, will have its headquarters in Denver, Colorado. Its primary function will be to assist tribes in the development of their energy and mineral resources.

**21 June 1978 Aleut Land Claims Settlement.** The *Tundra Times* reports the award of $11.2 million by the Indian Claims Commission to the Aleut of Pribilof Islands for mistreatment by the federal government in the sale of seal fur from 1870 to 1946. The award settles a twenty-seven-year struggle by the Aleut to gain recompense from the federal government.

**13 August 1978 American Indian Religious Freedom Act.** President Jimmy Carter signs the American Indian Religious Freedom Act (AIRFA) in which Congress recognizes its obligation to "protect and preserve for American Indians their inherent right of freedom to believe, express and exercise their traditional religions." The act directs all federal agencies to examine their regulations and practices for any inherent conflict with the practice of Indian religious rights. The drafters of the legislation intend that the act will reverse a long history of governmental actions designed to suppress and destroy tribal religions. Until 1924, for example, the Bureau of Indian Affairs had regulations prohibiting the practice of Indian religion. Violators, if caught, could receive ten days in jail. In more recent times, Indians have been prohibited from entering sacred areas, from gathering and transporting sacred herbs, and from obtaining eagle feathers and meats necessary for ceremonies.

**5 September 1978 Federal Acknowledgment Program Established.** The Bureau of Indian Affairs publishes regulations for the newly organized Federal Acknowledgment Program. The BIA estimates that more than 250 tribes are unrecognized in thirty-eight states. The regulations create a Federal Acknowledgment Branch, comprised of a historian, an anthropologist, a sociologist, and a genealogist, who will be responsible for deciding if tribal petitions for recognition meet the stated requirements.

To gain recognition, tribes must prove the following: (1) continuous existence as an aboriginal tribe; (2) that they live in a geographically contiguous area; (3) that the group has been under the recognized authority of a governing body from historical times to the present; (4)

that they are currently governed by a constitution or other document; (5) that they have developed membership criteria; (6) that they possess a list of current members; and (7) that the federal government has not previously terminated its relationship with the tribe.

**11 September 1978 Andrus Mediates Salmon Dispute.** Secretary of Interior Cecil Andrus agrees to mediate a dispute between the Yurok Indians and federal officials over a two-week-old government ban on salmon fishing, imposed in response to a noticeable drop in salmon returning to the Klamath River to spawn. The ban resulted in a violent confrontation between the tribe and game wardens on the Klamath River in northern California, with the tribe arguing that the ban violates their religious rights given the spiritual importance placed upon fishing in Yurok culture. The reduction in the salmon runs is attributed to heavy fishing by all involved in the fishing industry and to the polluting effects of heavy logging in the area.

**17 October 1978 Tribally Controlled Community Colleges Act.** Congress enacts the Tribally Controlled Community Colleges Act. The legislation provides for grants to tribally controlled colleges, including Alaska Native villages and corporations.

**November 1978 Oglala Sioux Television Station Planned.** The Oglala Sioux tribe announces plans to construct the first Indian-owned and operated television station. The station will serve 14,000 people on the Pine Ridge Reservation in South Dakota.

**1 November 1978 Education Amendment Act.** Congress passes the Education Amendment Act of 1978, giving substantial control of education programs to local Indian communities.

**8 November 1978 Indian Child Welfare Act.** Congress passes the Indian Child Welfare Act (ICWA), establishing a federal policy to promote the stability and security of Indian tribes and families by giving tribal courts jurisdiction over foster care and the adoption of Indian children. Tribal leaders lobbied extensively for passage of the act. Surveys conducted by the Association on American Indian Affairs reported that 25 to 35 percent of all Indian children are raised in non-Indian foster and adoptive homes or institutions. The ICWA established standards for the placement of Indian children in foster homes and provides authority for the secretary of the interior to make grants to Indian tribes and organizations for establishment of Indian child and family service programs.

Indian maiden on the Northern Cheyenne Indian Reservation in Lame Deer, Montana. (Photo by Lori Cooper. Courtesy of the UCLA American Indian Studies Center)

Poster for the Indian Child Welfare Conference at the University of California, Los Angeles. (Courtesy of the UCLA American Indian Studies Center)

**29 May 1979 Mohawk Takeover.** A nine-hour takeover of the Akwesasne police station ends peacefully. The protest, which stemmed from the arrest of a traditionalist chief over a property dispute, is part of a longstanding issue between Mohawk traditionalists and those tribal members who support the elected form of government. The traditionalists do not recognize the authority of either the state police or the Franklin County Sheriff's Department, despite it being composed of sixteen Indian officers.

**13 June 1979 Lakota Nation Refuses Settlement for Black Hills.** The U.S. Court of Claims awards the Lakota Nation $122.5 million for the federal government's taking of the Black Hills in South Dakota. The Lakota Nation refuses to accept the award and demands the return of the Black Hills to Lakota jurisdiction. The federal government refuses to return land and holds $122 million, plus accumulating interest, in trust for the Lakota people.

**21 July 1979 Silverheels Receives Star on Walk of Fame.** Jay Silverheels, who played Tonto in the television series *The Lone Ranger* is the first Indian actor to have a star commemorated in the Hollywood Walk of Fame. Silverheels, a member of the Mohawk tribe and an actor for more than thirty-five years, is the founder of the Indian Actors Workshop.

**27 July 1979 Boldt Decision Affirmed.** The Supreme Court upholds the Boldt decision, affirming the right of Washington tribes to one-half the salmon catch.

**19 August 1979 Narragansett Land Claim Settlement.** The 800-member Narragansett Indian tribe of Rhode Island is the first of the eastern tribes to settle its land claim against federal and state governments. Filing suit in 1975 for ownership to 3,500 acres, the tribe will receive 1,800 acres. The tribe will purchase 900 acres with federal funds and receive the other 900 acres

Dennis Banks addresses participants in the 500-mile Indian Marathon from Los Angeles to D-Q University, 1979. (Photo by Ilka Hartmann)

from public state lands. While hailed as a victory by some tribal members, others express dissatisfaction with the agreement, frustrated that the agreement is inadequate for the loss of thousands of acres of land and 300 years of mistreatment.

**31 October 1979 Archaeological Resources Protection Act.** Congress enacts the Archaeological Resources Protection Act of 1979, which provides protection for all important archeological sites on federal public lands and Indian lands. It further requires that scientists or lay personnel must obtain a special permit before excavation will be allowed. Indians are exempt from obtaining federal permits for excavations on Indian lands.

**November 1979 Natives Subjected to Racism Over Fishing Rights.** Ottawa and Chippewa are subjected to racist and violent actions as they exercise their right to fish as guaranteed in their treaties with the United States. Indian fishers experience shootings, tire slashings, and the smashing of their boats. Bumper

stickers also begin to appear containing derogatory sayings, such as "Spear an Indian—Save a Fish."

**8 December 1979 Oneida File Class-Action Suit.** The Oneida Indian Nation files a class-action suit against New York State, local governments, farmers, and cooperatives in an effort to regain control of 3 million acres illegally taken by the state in violation of the 1790 Trade and Intercourse Act.

**9 December 1979 Navajo and Hopi Settlement.** The Navajo and Hopi tribes agree to a settlement of a one hundred-year-old dispute over control of the Joint Use Area. The dispute between the Navajo and Hopi involves the ownership and use of 1.8 million acres of land. The dispute between the two tribes arises from an 1882 executive order by President Arthur assigning the land to both tribes for their joint use.

**9 December 1979 Tribes, States Sign Energy Agreement.** Tribal leaders whose reservations contain energy resources and the governors of Alaska, Arizona,

Colorado, Montana, Nebraska, New Mexico, North Dakota, South Dakota, Utah, and Wyoming sign an agreement to ensure that tribal concerns are considered in any national effort to achieve energy independence. Fearing that the more populous eastern portion of the country will enact an energy policy to the detriment of the West, the agreement's objective is to protect western energy resources for the economic benefit of the areas in which they are located. Tribal and state lands in the West contain an estimated 50 percent of the nation's coal, 33 percent of the oil, 22 percent of the natural gas, 92 percent of the uranium, and 100 percent of the most easily developed oil shale.

**17 January 1980 Omaha Land Claim Upheld.**  The U.S. Court of Appeals upholds the Omaha tribe in their claim to 2,900 acres of land in Iowa. The land, originally on the Nebraska side of the Missouri River, initially belonged to the tribe, as recognized in their 1854 treaty with the federal government.

**23 January 1980 Peltier Sentenced to Seven More Years.**  Leonard Peltier, the American Indian Movement activist serving two life terms in prison, is sentenced to an additional seven years for escaping from a federal prison. Peltier, considered a political prisoner by many Indian supporters, was convicted of killing two FBI agents on the Pine Ridge Reservation in June 1975. Peltier escaped, with another inmate, from the Federal Correctional Institution in Lompoc, California, in July 1979.

**18 February 1980 European Parliament Members Meet with Iroquois.**  The Italian representative to the European Parliament, Mario Capanna, holds a meeting with the Grand Council of Six Nation Iroquois Confederation on the Onondaga Reservation. Capanna is one of twenty-two European Parliament members who introduced a resolution in January calling for the Parliament's condemnation of the state sending state troopers into the Mohawk Reservation.

**13 March 1980 Case Goes to European Parliament.**  Five members of the Iroquois and Lakota tribes take their case to the European Parliament, requesting support for their efforts at the international and national levels to gain recognition for their rights.

**April 1980 IHS Issues Report.**  The Indian Health Service issues a report stating that the most serious Indian health problems are no longer tuberculosis and gastroenteritis. Accidents, alcoholism, diabetes, mental health, suicides and homicides remain the greatest Indian health threats.

**3 April 1980 Congress Restores Relations with Paiute Bands.**  Congress passes legislation to restore a federal trust relationship with the 501 members of the Shvwits, Kanosh, Koosharem, and Indian Peaks bands and Cedar City bands of Paiute Indians of Utah. The tribes, whose relationship with Congress was terminated twenty-seven years earlier, will acquire the rights to approximately fifteen thousand acres in southwestern Utah and access to educational, employment training, and health benefits. An estimated 60 percent of the adults are unemployed, and 40 percent of the children do not attend school regularly.

**13 April 1980 Court Upholds Washoe Hunting Laws.**  The Washoe Nation wins a federal court decision that upholds the tribes right to enforce its own hunting laws on 60,000 acres of off-reservation land in the Pine Nut Mountains of Nevada.

**13 April 1980 Harris Selected as Citizen's Party VP.**  The Citizen's Party selects environmentalist Barry Commoner as its nominee for president and LaDonna Harris, a Comanche Indian activist from Oklahoma and former wife of Senator Fred Harris, as his vice-presidential running mate.

**15 April 1980 Eastern Cherokee Suit Dismissed.**  The U.S. Court of Appeals for the Sixth Circuit dismisses a suit brought by members of the Eastern Cherokee who are seeking to prevent the construction of the Tellico Dam in eastern Tennessee. Tribal members argue that the dam, a project of the Tennessee Valley Authority, would flood ancestral lands sacred to the Cherokee and thus violate their right to freely practice their religion as protected under the free exercise clause of the First Amendment. The appeals court, affirming a lower court decision, rules that the plaintiffs are unable to demonstrate that the land in question is indispensable to the practice of the tribe's religion.

**20 April 1980 Mohawk, Federal Government Reach Tentative Agreement.**  St. Regis Mohawk (in New York State) and the federal government reach a tentative agreement on the disposition of tribally claimed land near the St. Lawrence Seaway. According to the terms of the agreement, the Mohawk of Akwesasne will receive 9,750 acres south of the reservation and $6 million in federal funds.

**14 June 1980 Police Sent to Akewsasne.**  New York State sends seventy police to Akwesasne, the St. Regis Mohawk Indian Reservation that straddles the Canadian-United States border. For the previous ten months, in an effort to prevent the arrest of several traditional leaders involved in the 1979 takeover of the Akwesasne police station, approximately seventy Mohawk traditionalists maintained a camp on twenty acres along the St. Lawrence.

**17 June 1980 Congress Passes Commerce Legislation.** Congress passes legislation regulating and protecting Indian tribes in their commercial dealings with federally licensed Indian traders.

**22 June 1980 Tekakwitha Beatified.** The Vatican beatifies Kateri Tekakwitha, a Mohawk woman who died three hundred years ago at the age of twenty-four. The beatification process is the last step before achieving sainthood in the eyes of the Church. She is the first American Indian beatified by the Catholic Church. She was renamed Kateri at her baptism at the age of twenty (her Mohawk name was Ioragode, or Sunshine).

**30 June 1980 *U.S. v. Sioux Nation.*** The Supreme Court in *U.S. v. Sioux Nation* upholds the $122 million judgment against the United States by the Court of Claims for the taking of the Black Hills. The Fort Laramie Treaty of 1868 guaranteed the Lakota possession of the Black Hills, or *Paha Sapa*, an area of sacred significance to the tribe. The discovery of gold in 1874, however, brought a flood of prospectors, mining companies, and military units into the area. After enduring years of war and the intentional killing off of the buffalo, the tribe's staple food, the Sioux, or Lakota, signed an agreement in 1876 ceding the Black Hills to the United States.

**8 July 1980 Navajo-Hopi Relocation Act.** Congress enacts the Navajo-Hopi Relocation Act, which requires the relocation of some Navajo and Hopi families in an effort to settle the joint-use land dispute. The legislation provides for funds to assist in the purchase of additional lands for the Navajo tribe.

**18 July 1980 Oglala Sioux File Suit against Federal Government.** The Oglala Sioux file a class-action suit against the federal government and the state of South Dakota for $11 billion, seeking $10 billion for the loss of nonrenewable resources from the Black Hills and $1 billion for "hunger, malnutrition, disease and death" incurred by the Sioux resulting from the loss of their traditional lands.

**20 July 1980 Martinez Dies.** Maria Martinez, ninety-five, dies at San Ildefonso Pueblo, New Mexico. A world renowned potter, Martinez, working with her husband, revived the traditional black pottery of the Pueblos. Her pottery was perfectly crafted and shaped,

even though she worked without the use of a potter's wheel. Her pots appear in collections throughout the world.

**18 August 1980 Creek Nation Regains Ownership of Sacred Grounds.** The Creek Nation, or Alabama Creek as they are called locally, east of the Mississippi River regains ownership to a thirty-three-acre village site known as Hickory Grounds. The site was the location of one of the most sacred Creek villages before their removal from the Southeast in the 1830s, and was purchased with the proceeds of a $165,000 federal grant. In the 1830s, the village of Hickory Ground was relocated during removal to present-day Oklahoma and the sacred objects and stories were carried to the new location.

**4 September 1980 Congress Establishes Reservation for Siletz.** Congress establishes a reservation of 3,663 acres for the Confederated Tribes of Siletz Indians of Oregon. Congress terminated its relationship with the confederation of twenty-four tribes and bands in 1956. The Confederated Tribes, with approximately nine hundred members, were restored to federal recognition in 1977.

**12 October 1980 Maine Tribes Settle Land Dispute.** President Jimmy Carter, using a symbolic feather pen, signs legislation settling the claim of the Passamaquoddy, Penobscot, and Maliseet to two-thirds of Maine. The settlement provides for an $81.5 million settlement to the tribes. The money includes a $27 million trust fund and $54.5 million to purchase 300,000 acres of land. The agreement followed the tribes' claim that the state of Maine inappropriately treated for their homeland, the northern two-thirds of Maine, in violation of the 1790 Trade and Intercourse Act, which granted authority only to the federal government to purchase land from the Indian Nations.

**8 November 1980 Helsinki Conference.** The U.S. representatives provide the Helsinki Conference, meeting in Madrid, Spain, with a federal study on the United States' compliance with the 1975 Helsinki Accords in its treatment of American Indians. The report concludes that the United States' record is "neither as deplorable as sometimes alleged nor as successful as one might hope."

**23 November 1980 Cayuga File Suit against New York.** The Cayuga Indian Nation files suit against

New York State for taking former Cayuga lands located in the Finger Lakes region. The Cayuga Nation demands return of 100 square miles, payment of $350 million in damages, and the relocation of 7,000 property owners.

**2 December 1980 Russell Tribunal Finds U.S. Guilty of Genocide.**   The Russell Tribunal, an international human rights body located in the Netherlands, finds the United States, Canada, and several countries in Latin America guilty of cultural and physical genocide and of the unlawful seizure of land in their treatment of their Indian populations. The verdict comes following an eight-day hearing during which the human rights activists heard testimony from fourteen Indian communities. The "judges," many of whom are lawyers, base their decision, which has no legal authority, on the protections afforded to Indian people in the 1975 Helsinki Accords, the International Covenant on Civil and Political Rights, and the Universal Declaration of Human Rights.

**22 December 1980 Salmon and Steelhead Conservation Act.**   Congress passes the Salmon and Steelhead Conservation Act of 1980. The bill, designed in part to meet the guarantees promised by the federal government in treaties signed with the tribes in the mid-1800s, provides for the conservation and enhancement of the salmon and steelhead runs.

**3 March 1981 Navajo and Hopi Protest Ski Resort Construction.**   Navajo and Hopi religious leaders request a federal district court to halt ski resort construction in the San Francisco Peaks mountains. Arguing that the First Amendment protects their right to religious freedom, the tribal leaders' suit states that construction would destroy sacred sites and that the desecration would anger their gods.

**18 April 1981 Joint Use Area Divided Equally.**   A federal court partitions the 1.8 million-acre Joint Use Area equally between the Navajo and Hopi. The division forces the relocation of 3,000 to 6,000 Navajo and one hundred Hopi tribal members. Four days later, Bureau of Indian Affairs officials begin gathering Navajo livestock for removal.

**8 May 1981 Tribal Leaders Call for Watt's Resignation.**   One hundred fifty tribal leaders, attending the National Tribal Government Conference in Washington, D.C., send a letter to President Ronald Reagan demanding the immediate resignation of Secretary of Interior James G. Watt. Citing Watt's unwillingness to consult with tribes as dictated by law, the leaders write: "We find this callous disregard of his lawful function and responsibility as the Federal official with general statutory-delegated authority in Indian matters completely intolerable." Elmer Savilla, spokesperson for the group, called further attention to Reagan's proposal to cut Indian funds by consolidating the financing of ten Bureau of Indian Affairs programs into one block grant, and reducing the allocation of funds by 26 percent. Other administration proposals call for the reduction of adult and child education, housing, employment, assistance, and vocational training programs.

**24 May 1981 *Montana v. U.S.*.**   The Supreme Court rules in *Montana v. U.S.* that the state of Montana has the authority to regulate hunting and fishing on the Bighorn River flowing through the Crow Indian Rreservation. The Court rules that the state assumed title to the riverbed upon its entrance into the Union in 1889. The case is a blow to tribal authority and the tribe's efforts to regulate hunting and fishing within its own boundaries.

**11 June 1981 Civil Rights Commission Issues Report.**   The U.S. Civil Rights Commission issues a major report on the federal government's treatment of American Indians. Commission Chairman Arthur Flemming sums up the government's policy toward American Indians as one of "inaction and missed opportunities." The commission, after a decade of research, proposes several changes in federal policy toward tribes. One of its primary recommendations is that Congress apportion, as in the case of states, federal funds to tribes as block grants. The commission also recommends the establishment of an Office of Indian Rights within the Civil Rights Division of the Justice Department. The report urges the government to act expeditiously and fairly in the resolution of fishing rights disputes and eastern land claims, and impels Congress to pass legislation allowing tribal government the option to assume criminal jurisdiction over all peoples within their reservation boundaries.

**10 July 1981 Tribes Win Court Battle Over Fishing Rights.**   The Bay Mills and Sault Ste. Marie Chippewa and Grand Traverse tribe of Ottawa Indians win a nine-year court battle in the U.S. Court of Appeals for the

Sixth Circuit, recognizing their fishing rights in lakes Michigan, Superior, and Huron. The federal court lets stand a district court decision in which tribes successfully proved that the treaties of 1836 and 1855 guaranteed their right to fish in the Great Lakes. In addition to acknowledging their fishing rights, the courts rule that tribes may continue to use their traditional gill nets, an apparatus banned under state law. The next step is for the tribes to enter into negotiations with the federal government and the state of Michigan for the development of a fishing management plan.

**13 August 1981 Omnibus Budget Reconciliation Act.** Through the enactment of the Omnibus Budget Reconciliation Act of 1981, Congress allows the Secretary of Health and Human Services to make community block grants to Indian tribes. The legislation also provides for the establishment of Head Start programs on Indian reservations and for improvements in the loan process to small, tribe-owned businesses.

**20 August 1981 Montana Orders Crow to Open River to Fishing.** The state of Montana orders the Crow tribe to open access to fishing on the Bighorn River. In response, members of the Crow tribe barricade a highway bridge over the river near Hardin, Montana. The tribe, which claims ownership of the river, had closed the river to fishing by non-Indians in 1975. In March, the Supreme Court ruled that the state of Montana owned title to the fifty-mile section of the river under dispute. The blockade of both lanes of Highway 313, consisting of approximately fifteen cars, campers, and pick-ups, was lifted fourteen hours later when federal marshals served notice on the tribe that the blockade was illegal.

**14 October 1981 Amnesty International Calls Marshall, Pratt Political Prisoners.** Amnesty International, in a 144-page report, charges the U.S. government with retaining Richard Marshall of the American Indian Movement and Elmer Pratt of the Black Panther Movement as political prisoners. The report alleges official misconduct in the investigations and trials of both leaders.

**7 January 1982 Nuclear Waste Policy Act.** Congress passes the Nuclear Waste Policy Act of 1982. The act calls for the "development of repositories for the disposal of high-level radioactive waste and spent nuclear fuel, to establish a program of research, development, and demonstration regarding the disposal of

high-level radioactive waste and spent nuclear fuel." Section 2 of the act allows the administrator of the Environmental Protection Agency to authorize such repositories to be located within the boundaries of Indian reservations "upon the petition of the appropriate governmental officials of the tribe." Passage of this act draws considerable criticism from several tribes who interpret the act as a federal attempt to desecrate Indian lands.

**21 January 1982 Watt Revises Interior's Royalty Policy.** In response to a special commission's sharp criticisms of the Interior Department's collection of royalty money, Secretary of Interior James G. Watt announces a revision in the department's policy for obtaining royalties on oil and natural gas on federal lands.

**25 January 1982 *Merrion v. Jicarilla Apache Tribe.*** The Supreme Court rules in the *Merrion v. Jicarilla Apache Tribe* that Indian tribes have the authority to levy severance taxes on the extraction of minerals from tribal lands, even though the tax falls on nontribal members.

**11 June 1982 Tlingit Demand Apology.** Tlingit Indians arrive in Washington, D.C., seeking an official apology from the navy for its 1882 shelling of Angoon village in the Admiralty Islands. The navy's actions were undertaken as a means of forcing the Alaskan Indians to return to work for private whalers.

**14 August 1982 Reagan Declares Code Talkers Day.** President Ronald Reagan declares August 14 as National Navajo Code Talkers Day, commemorating the cadre of Navajo servicemen who sent messages in their tribal language during World War II. The system was never cracked by the Germans or Japanese.

**13 October 1982 Thorpe Family Receives Gold Medals.** The International Olympic Committee announces that it will restore to Jim Thorpe's family the two gold medals Thorpe won in the 1912 Olympic games for the decathlon and the pentathlon. Thorpe was stripped of his medals for having played minor league baseball for $2 a game. The two medals are returned in a ceremony to Thorpe's daughter Charlotte during the 1984 Olympics in Los Angeles.

**2 November 1982 Zah Elected Navajo Chairman.** The Navajo Nation elects a new tribal chairman, Peterson

Grace Thorpe, holding a picture of her dad, Jim, on the Oklahoma map, another of him with his baseball team, and one of his gold medals. Prague, Oklahoma, 1997. (Photo by Ilka Hartmann)

Zah, who defeats Peter MacDonald, Navajo chairman for the last twelve years, by a vote of 29,208 to 24,665. Zah, the founder of the reservation's legal aid organization, pledges to stop further exploitation of energy, minerals, timber, and water resources on reservation lands by non-Indians. Zah's platform also includes a proposal that the Navajo and Hopi seek to mediate their dispute over the Joint Use Area without the interference of the federal government.

**22 December 1982 Indian Mineral Development Act.**  Passage of the Indian Mineral Development Act of 1982 confirms and provides federal support for

tribes to enter into commercial ventures for the development of their tribal resources.

**30 December 1982 Reagan Recognizes 300 Umpqua.**  President Ronald Reagan signs legislation extending federal recognition to approximately three hundred members of the Cow Creek Band of Umpqua tribe in Oregon.

**8 January 1983 Congress Allows Texas Kickapoo to Apply for Citizenship.**  Congress passes legislation to allow the Texas Kickapoo to apply for U.S.

citizenship and for federal services. The Texas, or Mexican, Kickapoo, as they are called, were part of the larger Kickapoo Nation pushed out of their aboriginal homelands in northern Illinois and southern Wisconsin in the early 1800s. One band sought refuge in Mexico, settling near Nacimiento Kickapoo, eighty miles from the Texas border. Today, the six hundred members of the tribe spend their summers in or near Eagle Pass, Texas, working as migrant laborers. In the winters, they return to their home in Mexico for the tribe's sacred winter ceremonial.

**12 January 1983 Federal Oil and Gas Royalty Management Act.** Passage of the Federal Oil and Gas Royalty Management Act of 1982 provides for cooperative agreements among the secretary of the interior, Indian tribes, and states for the sharing of oil- and gas-royalty management information.

**12 January 1983 Indian Land Consolidation Act.** Congress passes the Indian Land Consolidation Act to assist tribes in consolidating fractional land interests in many reservation lands. Tribes whose reservation lands were allotted under the terms of the 1887 General Allotment Act now possess, in some cases, allotments owned by over two hundred individuals. The original allotments of eighty to 160 acres were, by federal regulations, divided equally among allottee heirs. Passage of this act allows for tribes to purchase and consolidate these lands in an effort to make them more economically productive.

**14 January 1983 Indian Tribal Tax Status Act.** Passage of the Indian Tribal Tax Status Act of 1982 confirms that tribes possess many of the federal tax advantages enjoyed by states. Like states, tribes are acknowledged to have the power to issue tax-exempt bonds to enable tribal governments to fund economic development projects.

**19 January 1983 Watt's Televised Comments Incite Indian Country.** Secretary of Interior James Watt states during a television interview: "If you want an example of the failures of socialism, don't go to Russia. Come to America, and see the American Indian reservations. . . . Socialism toward the American Indian," Watt said, "had led to alcoholism, unemployment, venereal disease, and drug addiction." Watt's remarks provoked an outcry across Indian Country demanding his resignation.

**24 January 1983 Reagan Issues Policy Statement.** President Reagan issues the first Indian policy statement since 1975. Emphasizing that "the Constitution, treaties, laws, and court decisions have consistently recognized a unique political relationship between Indian tribes and the United States," the president states his commitment to deal with Indian tribes on a "government-to-government" basis. The address, which promotes economic development on reservations, states the government's support for industrial development of resources on Indian lands. Tribes and the American society "stand to gain from the prudent development and management of the vast coal, oil, gas, uranium and other resources found on Indian lands." The address is met with skepticism by many Indian leaders who fear an underlying terminationist message.

**25 January 1983 *Lac Courte Oreilles Band of Lake Superior Chippewa Indians v. Voigt*.** The U.S. Court of Appeals for the Seventh Circuit affirms in *Lac Courte Oreilles Band of Lake Superior Chippewa Indians v. Voigt* that the Chippewa's treaties with the United States in 1837 and 1842 preserved the rights of six Chippewa bands to hunt, fish, and cut timber in lands they ceded to the federal government.

**31 January 1983 Reagan's Budget Calls for Cut in Indian Program Funding.** President Ronald Reagan sends his first budget to Congress. Proposals include a one-third cut in the total budget for Indian programs.

**15 March 1983 Pacific Salmon Treaty Act.** Congressional passage of the Pacific Salmon Treaty Act of 1984 clarifies and protects tribal fishing rights as provided in executive orders and Indian treaties as they relate to the United States treaty with Canada over Pacific salmon fishing.

**23 March 1983 Onondaga Grants Asylum to Banks.** The Onondaga Nation, located south of Syracuse, New York, agrees to grant asylum to American Indian Movement leader Dennis Banks, who is fleeing charges in South Dakota arising from the takeover of Wounded Knee.

**30 March 1983 *Arizona v. California*.** The Supreme Court rejects in *Arizona v. California* a federally appointed fact finder's report that five Indian reservations—the Cocopah, Ft. Mohave, Ft. Yuma, Colorado River, and the Chemehuevi—are entitled to receive a larger share of water allocation in the lower basin of the Colorado River. The five tribes requested larger water allocations on the basis of an increase in reservation populations.

**2 June 1983 Tribal Chairmen Criticize Reagan.** The National Indian Tribal Chairman's Association holds a news conference to criticize President Ronald Reagan for his failure to uphold his pledge to free tribes of federal regulations and to provide tribal governments with greater self-determination.

**13 June 1983 *New Mexico v. Mescalero Apache Tribe*.**  The Supreme Court rules in *New Mexico v. Mescalero Apache Tribe* that the state of New Mexico cannot enforce state laws against non-Indians hunting and fishing on tribal lands within reservation boundaries. The imposition of state laws in this instance, the Court stated, would interfere with "Congress' overriding objective of encouraging tribal self-government and economic development."

**24 June 1983 *Nevada v. U.S.***  The Supreme Court in *Nevada v. U.S.* unanimously upholds a lower court ruling affirming the allocation of water rights to the Pyramid Lake Reservation in western Nevada.

**1 July 1983 *Rice v. Rehner*.**  The Supreme Court rules six to three in *Rice v. Rehner* that states have the authority to enforce liquor laws on reservations. Tribes, according to the opinion written by Justice Sandra Day O'Connor, are required to obtain state licenses before selling liquor on the reservation.

**15 July 1983 *Arizona v. San Carlos Apache Tribe*.**  The Supreme Court rules in *Arizona v. San Carlos Apache Tribe* that state courts have the authority to decide water rights disputes involving Indians. The decision is another blow to tribes in their quest to preserve their water rights. Tribes attempted to prove that water rights disputes must be settled in the federal courts. Tribes feared that the state courts, under pressure to protect the progress and development of major cities and areas throughout the West, would not provide tribes with a fair hearing.

**30 July 1983 Seminole Agree to Establish Traditional Judicial System.**  Fifteen hundred Seminole tribal members, who occupy five reservations in southern Florida, approve a referendum to establish a judicial system reflecting traditional values and principles. Tribal leaders, who are in the process of developing the new judicial system, are giving careful examination to the neighboring system of the Miccousukee tribe, which operates with two judges, one schooled in modern law and the other in traditional law.

**13 September 1983 Banks Surrenders.**  American Indian Movement co-founder Dennis Banks surrenders to state authorities in Rapid City, South Dakota, following nine years as a fugitive. Banks's surrender allows the state to prosecute him for assault and rioting charges stemming from the 1973 Wounded Knee takeover and flight to avoid prosecution. Banks, who states

that he feared for his life, explains that he had given himself up for the sake of his family. Banks had spent six years in California, under the protection of Governor Jerry Brown, before fleeing to the Onondaga Reservation in New York when Brown's successor, Governor George Deukmejian, indicated his willingness to extradite Banks to South Dakota. New York governor Mario Cuomo agreed to return Banks to South Dakota but forbade marshals from entering the Onondaga Reservation.

**20 October 1983 Mashantucket Pequot Federally Recognized.**  President Ronald Reagan signs legislation acknowledging the Mashantucket Pequot Indians of Connecticut as a federally recognized tribe with all powers of self-government. The legislation also provides for a $900,000 appropriation to the Pequots for the purchase of land near their reservation. President Reagan vetoed a similar bill on 10 April 1983.

**25 March 1984 Cherokees Meet in Tennessee.**  Members of the Eastern Band of Cherokee and the Cherokee Nation of Oklahoma hold their first joint council meeting in 146 years. An estimated 10,000 tribal members attend the historic meeting held at the Cherokee's sacred ground in Red Clay, Tennessee. The two tribes, which confirmed their permanent split, agree to meet annually in the Council of Cherokees to discuss issues and needs of common concern.

**8 June 1984 Senate Select Committee on Indian Affairs Made Permanent.**  The U.S. Senate agrees to make the Senate Select Committee on Indian Affairs a permanent body. The body, which is responsible for the consideration of Indian affairs and oversight, was established on a temporary basis in 1977.

**5 July 1984 Cayuga, New York Reach Agreement.**  The Cayuga Indian Nation agrees to accept approximately 8,500 acres of land in Cayuga and Seneca counties of New York State in return for relinquishing claims to 64,000 acres.

**2 September 1984 Pequote Take Possession of Land.**  The Mashantucket Pequot Indians from eastern Connecticut take possession of 650 acres of land. Tribal title to the land ends an eight-year struggle by the tribe to regain former reservations lands.

**23 September 1984 Santa Fe Publication Apologizes to Santo Domingo.**  The Santa Fe *New Mexican* apologizes to the Santo Domingo Indian community for the publication of two photos of sacred dances.

Bolinas supports American Indian prisoner Leonard Peltier, San Francisco Federal Building, June 1984. (Photo by Ilka Hartmann)

The community has a posted policy of forbidding the taking of photographs at sacred ceremonies.

**8 October 1984 Banks Sentenced.**    Dennis Banks is sentenced in Custer, South Dakota, to three years in prison for his part in the Custer Courthouse Riot in 1975.

**30 November 1984 Reservation Economies Commission Presents Report.**    The Presidential Commission on Indian Reservation Economies presents its report to President Ronald Reagan. Characterizing the Bureau of Indian Affair's organization and administration as "byzantine," and "incompetent," the report called for the BIA's replacement with an Indian Trust Services Administration. As an illustration of the BIA's top-heavy administration and over-regulation, the report points out that two-thirds of the BIA's budget goes into administration; less than one-third of the federal funds reach the reservation.

Other recommendations in the report include the placement of tribal businesses in individual hands, the subordination of tribal courts to federal courts in interpreting law, the reduction of tribal immunity, and the allowance of tribal taxation only after the vote of all Indian and non-Indian residents on the reservation. The report further recommends that tribal leaders and federal officials tackle the issue of tribal self-determination through private economic development. The report draws a cool reception from many tribes.

**9 January 1985 Kickapoo Resettle in Texas.**    Charitable contributions provide for the purchase of a 125-acre parcel of land on the Rio Grande near Eagle Pass, Texas, for the resettlement of the Kickapoo tribe.

**11 January 1985 Tribal Leaders Reject Private-Enterprise Proposal.**    The National Tribal Council Association, a national group comprised of tribal political leaders, votes eighty-four to eighteen to reject a proposed program for the development of private enterprises on Indian reservations. As explained by Elmer Savilla, the association's executive director, the program's philosophy is in opposition to the "Indian way," which is "to go into business to provide income for tribal members, to provide employment for as many tribal members as you can."

**11 February 1985 Federal Government Settles with Wyandotte.** The federal government agrees to pay $5.5 million to Wyandotte Indians in Kansas and Oklahoma for forcing their ancestors to sell their aboriginal lands in 1842 for less than fair market value.

**20 February 1985 *Dann et al. v. United States*.** In *Dann et al. v. United States*, the Supreme Court rejects a suit by two Shoshone Indians claiming ownership of 5,100 acres of the tribe's aboriginal homeland. In 1951, the Shoshone tribe sought compensation for the loss of their aboriginal homeland and were awarded $26 million by the Indian Claims Commission. The tribe refused to accept payment of the funds, requesting instead the return of their lands. The courts ruled that once the funds were placed in an interest-bearing account, the tribe's claim to the lands were extinguished.

**4 March 1985 *County of Oneida v. Oneida Nation*.** The Supreme Court, in *County of Oneida v. Oneida Nation*, upholds the right of the Oneida Nation of New York State to sue for lands illegally taken in 1795.

**5 March 1985 Scientists Find that Natives Developed Calendars.** The *Journal of the Society for American Archeology* reports that scientists, through the analysis of Winnebago calendar sticks, have the first evidence that tribes, through systematic astronomical observations, had developed full-year calendars.

**15 March 1985 Pacific Salmon Treaty Act.** After a thirteen-year effort, Congress passes the Pacific Salmon Treaty Act of 1985. The act, which many legislators and biologists hail as the most important key to saving the salmon runs from extinction, was passed following the intervention and support of the northwestern tribes that depend on fishing for cultural and economic survival.

**16 April 1985 *Kerr-McGee Corp. v. Navajo Tribe*.** The Supreme Court, in *Kerr-McGee Corp. v. Navajo Tribe*, unanimously upholds the right of the Navajo Nation to tax business on the reservation without first obtaining federal approval. The decision allows for the Navajo to continue taxation of mineral leases on reservation lands.

**16 May 1985 Montana Governor, Tribes Reach Water Rights Agreement.** Montana Governor Ted

Schwinden signs an agreement with the Sioux and Assiniboine tribes guaranteeing water allocations between the tribes and their neighbors.

**3 June 1985 *Montana v. Blackfeet Tribe*.** The Supreme Court, in *Montana v. Blackfeet Tribe*, upholds a Court of Appeals ruling that Montana could not tax the royalty interests earned by the Blackfeet from leases issued in accordance with the Indian Mineral Leasing Act of 1938. At issue was the legal status of state taxation of oil, gas, and minerals from Indian lands.

**2 July 1985 Jicarilla Apache Offer Tax-Exempt Bonds.** The Jicarilla Apache tribe of New Mexico is the first tribe to offer tax-exempt municipal bonds to institutional investors, issuing $30.2 million in revenue bonds.

**2 October 1985 Wind River Suicide Rates Skyrocket.** News services report that nine young Arapaho and Shoshone Indians on the Wind River Reservation in Wyoming have hanged themselves in the last two months. The reservation, which has a population of six thousand people and an unemployment rate of 80 percent, reported forty-eight suicide attempts in 1985. The National Center of Health reported that the suicide rate at the Wind River Reservation, 233 suicides per 100,000, is almost twenty times higher than the national average, twelve per 100,000.

**22 November 1985 Kickapoo Issued Citizenship Cards.** One hundred forty-three members of the Kickapoo of Texas and Mexico are issued citizenship cards acknowledging their status as a "subgroup" of the Kickapoo tribe of Oklahoma.

**22 November 1985 Banks Granted Parole.** American Indian Movement leader Dennis Banks is granted parole from the South Dakota Penitentiary. He served approximately one year of a three-year prison term, which arose from a 1973 disturbance at Custer County Courthouse in South Dakota.

**13 December 1985 Swimmer Sworn In as Assistant Secretary of Indian Affairs.** Ross Swimmer, Cherokee and former principal chief of the Cherokee Nation of Oklahoma, is sworn in as assistant secretary of the interior for Indian affairs in Washington, D.C.

**14 December 1985 Mankiller Sworn in as Cherokee Principal Chief.** Wilma Mankiller is sworn in as

Activist Rigoberta Menchu (second from the left) with Ilka Hartmann (l.) and Dennis Jennings (r.) in the mid-1980s. Menchu accepted the Nobel Peace Prize for her work on behalf of indigenous peoples. (Photo by Ilka Hartmann)

Principal Chief of the Cherokee Nation of Oklahoma. The nation, the largest Indian tribe in the country after the Navajo, is headed by a fifteen-member council.

**14 February 1986 Smithsonian Agrees to Return Skeletal Remains to Tribes.** The Smithsonian's Museum of Natural History agrees to return skeletal remains to tribal leaders for reburial when a clear biological or cultural link can be established. Several Indian organizations, while applauding the museum's decision, request that all Indian remains be returned for reburial, as required by Indian spiritual beliefs. Studies estimate that more than one million Indian remains are in the hands of museums and universities.

**24 March 1986 White Earth Reservation Lands Settlement Act.** Congress signs the White Earth Reservation Lands Settlement Act of 1985, settling "unresolved claims relating to certain allotted Indian lands on the White Earth Reservation, to remove clouds from the titles to certain land," regarding checkerboard non-Chippewa land ownership.

**15 May 1986 Lummi Fight IRS Demands.** The Lummi Indian tribe of western Washington is fighting a demand from the Internal Revenue Service that Indian fishers pay an income tax on the sale of salmon caught by the tribe in Puget Sound. The tribe argues that their natural resources, as guaranteed to the tribe by treaty, are immune from taxation.

**3 June 1986 Supreme Court Denies Catawba Land Settlement.** The Catawba lose a major case before the Supreme Court in their quest to reclaim 144,000 acres of aboriginal lands now in private hands. The Court rules that the tribe lost the opportunity to bring a suit due to a statute of limitations.

**18 August 1986 Wampanoag Receive Land Claims Settlement.** Congress passes legislation to settle the land claims of the Wampanoag Tribal Council of Gay Head, Massachusetts. In exchange for relinquishing further land claims, the state of Massachusetts will pay

$225 million to the tribe for the purchase of tribal trust lands.

**27 August 1986 Bands Trust Relations Restored.** Congress restores federal trust relations to the Klamath, Modoc, and the Yahuskin band of Snake Indians of Oregon. The approximately 3,000-member tribe was one of the first terminated by Congress in the 1950s. The Klamaths, Modocs, and Snakes, along with the Menominees of Wisconsin, were the largest tribes to be terminated.

**17 October 1986 Institute of American Indian and Alaska Native Culture and Arts Development.** Legislative approval is granted for the establishment of an Institute of American Indian and Alaska Native Culture and Arts Development. The institute, to be administered by a board of trustees, is charged with acknowledging and promoting the contributions of Native arts to American society.

**27 October 1986 Indian Alcohol and Substance Abuse Prevention and Treatment Act.** Recognizing that alcoholism and alcohol and substance abuse is a severe social and health problem among Indian people, Congress passes the Indian Alcohol and Substance Abuse Prevention and Treatment Act of 1986. When adjusted for age, Indians are four times more likely to die from alcoholism than the general population. Four of the top ten causes of death among Indians are alcohol related. Indians between the ages of fifteen and twenty-four years are twice as likely to die from vehicular accidents, 75 percent of which are alcohol related.

**27 October 1986 Indian Civil Rights Act Amended.** Congress revises the Indian Civil Rights Act to allow tribal courts to impose fines of $5,000 and one year in jail for violating tribal criminal offenses.

**4 November 1986 MacDonald Elected Navajo Chairman.** Peter MacDonald regains his elected position as the tribal chairman of the Navajo Nation. MacDonald, chairman from 1970 to 1982, defeated the incumbent, Peterson Zah.

**6 November 1986 Campbell Elected to House.** Ben Nighthorse Campbell, a member of the Northern Cheyenne tribe of Montana, is elected to the U.S. House of Representatives from the third district of Colorado.

Campbell is only the second Indian elected to the U.S. House of Representative in recent times. Ben Reifel, a Sioux from South Dakota, served in the House from 1961 to 1971.

**19 November 1986 American Indian Vietnam Plaque Dedicated.** The Grandfather Plaque, or American Indian Vietnam Plaque, is dedicated at Arlington National Cemetery in Virginia. The plaque commemorates the service of approximately 43,000 indigenous combatants who served in Vietnam. An estimated one out of every four eligible Indian males served in Vietnam.

**1 January 1987 Woman Elected Isleta Governor.** Isleta Pueblo, located near Albuquerque, New Mexico, elects its first woman governor.

**25 February 1987 *California v. Cabazon Band of Mission Indians*.** In *California v. Cabazon Band of Mission Indians* the U.S. Supreme Court rules that the state of California may not regulate bingo and gaming on the Cabazon and Morongo Indian reservations. The Court rules that Public Law 280 nor the 1970 Organized Crime Control Act carry congressional approval for California state regulation of gaming on Indian land.

**23 August 1987 Reagan Cedes Land to Wampanoag.** President Ronald Reagan signs a bill ceding to the Wampanoag more than four hundred acres of undeveloped land located on Martha's Vineyard, Massachusetts. The Bureau of Indian Affairs extended federal recognition to the Wampanoag Indians of Gay Head, Massachusetts, on March 8.

**18 September 1987 Pope Speaks to Indian Leaders.** Pope John Paul II speaks to a group of 1,600 American Indian leaders in Phoenix, Arizona, urging them to forget the past and to focus on the church's current support of Indian rights. An American Indian Catholic attendee responds that the Church still has much to accomplish in the United States.

**9 October 1987 Charges Against Seminole Chief Dropped.** The U.S. Justice Department drops all charges against Seminole Indian Chief James E. Billie, who killed a rare species of Florida panther, and was arrested for violating the Endangered Species Act. Billie admitted killing the panther in December 1983, but argued that his right to hunt panthers was a religious act that was protected by the Seminole's treaty of

1842 with the United States. Billie's first trial ended in a mistrial on 27 August 1987, when the jury could not agree on how Billie could identify the panther when the hunting occurred at night. Billie's second trial ended in an acquittal October 8.

**2 December 1987 Bill Commemorating Cherokee Removal Passed.** The U.S. House of Representatives passes a bill commemorating the centennial anniversary of the army's forcible removal of the Cherokees from the southeastern portion of the United States to northeastern Oklahoma.

**11 January 1988 Cheyenne Tax BIA Contractors.** The Northern Cheyenne tribe in Montana proposes to exercise its inherent right to tax by levying a tax on BIA contractors operating within reservation boundaries.

**1 February 1988 Tuscarora Men Hold Newspaper Office, Employees Hostage.** Two Tuscarora Indian men seize the newspaper office of the *Robesonian* in Lumberton, North Carolina. They hold seventeen of the newspaper's employees hostage for ten hours, demanding that the paper investigate corruption and discrimination by the police against the African-Americans and Indians of the area. The standoff ends with an agreement by the governor of North Carolina to investigate the charges.

**6 February 1988 Reagan Signs Amendments to Alaska Native Claims Settlement Act.** President Ronald Reagan signs into law a set of amendments to the 1971 Alaska Native Claims Settlement Act, which extinguished the Natives' title to their lands in exchange for 44 million acres and $962.5 million. The lands and money were distributed among over two hundred village corporations and thirteen regional corporations. According to the 1971 act, individuals would have been free to sell their shares in the corporations, a move that many Alaska Natives feared would result in the loss of Native lands and rights in Alaska. According to the 1988 amendments, corporations may only sell their stock if a majority of the shareholders support the sale.

**17 March 1988 Conference on Suicide.** The Warm Springs tribe of Oregon hosts a conference on suicide among Indians. The conference follows a rash of suicides on the reservation inhabited by 2,800 members of the Wascoe, Paiute, and Warm Springs tribes. Six young people killed themselves and sixteen others tried in the last two months. Nationwide, young Indian men kill themselves at a rate more than twice the national average.

The conference, which is attended by Indian leaders and families as well as psychologists and social workers, seeks in part to find the answer to the recent epidemics by returning to traditional practices and methods of counseling for young people.

**19 April 1988 *Lyng v. Northwest Indian Cemetery Protective Association*.** The Supreme Court, in a five-to-three decision, rules in *Lyng v. Northwest Indian Cemetery Protective Association* that the Forest Service is free to build a five-mile logging road through the sacred lands of the Yurok, Karok, and Tolowa tribes of California. Three justices, William T. Brennan Jr., Thurgood Marshall, and Harry Blackmun, dissent, arguing against the majority's "surreal" logic that "governmental action that will virtually destroy a religion is nevertheless deemed not to 'burden' that religion."

**28 April 1988 Elementary and Secondary Education Act.** As part of the Elementary and Secondary Education Act, H.R. 5, Title V, Congress repeals the termination policy established by House Concurrent Resolution 108, passed in 1953. The act also prohibited the BIA from terminating, consolidating, or transferring BIA-administered schools without the consent of the affected tribes.

**2 June 1988 Mohawks Protest Smuggling Charges.** Mohawk Indians at Kahnawake', a reserve on the south shore of the St. Lawrence River, block two highways and the Mercier bridge for thirty hours to protest a June 1 police raid in which seventeen Mohawks are charged with smuggling cigarettes from the United States. The Mohawk claim that the Jay Treaty of 1794 gives them the right to bring goods across the border without paying duty.

**29 June 1988 U.S. Housing Act Amended to Include Natives.** Indians and Alaska Natives are included in the U.S. Housing Act of 1937 with an amendment establishing a separate program under the supervision of the Secretary of Housing and Urban Development.

**8 July 1988 *Oklahoma Tax Commission v. Muscogee (Creek) Nation*.** In *Oklahoma Tax Commission v. Muscogee (Creek) Nation*, the Supreme

Performance of the Pueblo Indian tale "Arrow to the Sun" at the Wyoming Indian Elementary School. (Photo by Mike McClure)

Court refuses to overturn a lower court ruling that exempted the Creek Nation from paying a state sales tax on their bingo operations. The gaming operation, located in Tulsa, is built on Creek tribal trust lands.

**10 August 1988 Reagan Includes Apology to Aleut in Internment Camp Bill.** In a White House ceremony, President Ronald Reagan signs into law a reparations bill for Japanese-Americans interned during World War II. Included in the bill are an apology and $12,000 in reparations for the survivors of the several hundred Aleut who were forcibly relocated from their villages on the island of Attu in 1942. Although they were removed for fear of a Japanese attack, the government

admitted that the relocation "resulted in widespread illness, disease and death among the residents of the camps."

**17 September 1988 Ceremony Commemorates Iroquois Origins.** A ceremony is held to commemorate the origin of the Iroquois Confederacy. The confederacy was organized by the Mohawk, Seneca, Oneida, Cayuga, and Onondaga tribes in the mid-1600s. Estimates of the origin of the Iroquois Confederacy vary from 500 to 1,000 years ago.

**17 October 1988 Indian Gaming Regulatory Act.** It is estimated that by the late 1980s close to one hundred tribes, acting on their inherent sovereignty and freedom from state laws, establish gaming facilities as a means of improving tribal economies and providing employment for tribal members. Pursuant to concerns expressed by non-Indian neighbors, federal officials, and some tribal officials, Congress passes the Indian Gaming Regulatory Act, Public Law 100–497. The legislation provides for the establishment of federal regulations and standards for the conduct of gaming on Indian lands. The act has two basic purposes: to strengthen tribal governments and promote economic self-sufficiency through gaming, and to provide regulation of tribal gaming thereby allaying fears of criminal influences in gaming operations. In order to ensure the effective regulation of gaming operations, the act establishes the National Indian Gaming Commission with the authority to monitor gaming on Indian lands.

**12 December 1988 Reagan Meets with Indian Leaders.** President Ronald Reagan holds a meeting at the White House with sixteen Indian leaders. Billed as a "meeting among friends," the meeting is an attempt to smooth over the controversy caused by the president's remarks to Russian students in the Soviet Union in May. While speaking at Moscow University, Reagan stated: "Maybe we made a mistake. Maybe we should not have humored them [the Indians] in wanting to stay in that kind of primitive lifestyle. Maybe we should have said: 'No come join us. Be citizens along with the rest of us.'" President Reagan also made reference to the fact that a large number of Indians had become very wealthy due to oil money. Both remarks, which Indians leaders quickly pointed out were incorrect, raised considerable concern in Indian Country as to the level of knowledge possessed by the administration regarding the current state of Indian affairs.

The twenty-minute meeting was viewed as successful by the participants. The vice chairman of the Navajo Nation, Johnny Thompson, stated that "there was a spirit of forgiveness by all of us."

**19 January 1989 Seneca, New York Settle Tax Dispute.** The Seneca Indians of New York agree to the settlement of a dispute over taxes with outside local governments and with the state of New York. The tribe, standing on its sovereign authority to levy taxes, established stores selling non-taxed goods on the reservation. In response to pressures by outside competitors, the tribe agrees to levy its own tribal tax on goods, thereby making products comparable in price. In return, the state agrees to allow the tribe to keep all tax revenues for tribal programs and to dismiss its suit against the tribe for $10 million in state sales tax for goods sold to non-Indians.

**3 March 1989 *Lac Courte Oreilles Band of Lake Superior Chippewa Indians et al. v. State of Wisconsin.*** In the case of the *Lac Courte Oreilles Band of Lake Superior Chippewa Indians et al. v. State of Wisconsin*, several Chippewa Indian tribes seek to clarify their rights, based on the treaties of 1837 and 1842, to hunt, fish, and gather on off-reservation lands. Judge Barbara Crabb, presiding over the U.S. District Court for the western district of Wisconsin, rules that the Chippewa are not obligated to negotiate with the state concerning the length of their spearfishing season, the number of lakes to be fished, or the size of the catch. Furthermore, the court rules that the usufructuary rights of the Chippewa Indians, their rights to use the resources of their lands, may only be regulated if it is shown that such regulation is both reasonable and necessary for public health or for the conservation of natural resources. Moreover, it must be shown that such regulation does not discriminate against the Chippewa.

**3 April 1989 *Mississippi Choctaw Band v. Holyfield.*** In *Mississippi Choctaw Band v. Holyfield*, the Supreme Court upholds the jurisdictional rights of tribal courts under the Indian Child Welfare Act of 1978. The Indian Child Welfare Act addresses issues that resulted from the separation of large numbers of Indian children from their families and their subsequent placement in non-Indian homes. The 1978 act gave sole jurisdiction in custody proceedings to tribal courts. This case involves an attempt by the Mississippi Choctaw band to negate an adoption decree that had been signed by the parents. The Supreme Court of Mississippi originally ruled that the adoption decree was binding in part because the twins were born off-reservation and had never been "domiciled" there and, thus, the decree did not come under the tribal court's jurisdiction. The Supreme Court overturns the lower court's decision and rules that the twins were domiciled on the Mississippi Choctaw Band's reservation and, therefore, that the tribal court has exclusive jurisdiction.

**23 April–7 May 1989 Fishing Protests Lead to Arrests.** More than one hundred people are arrested in protests against the rights of northern Wisconsin tribes to fish as guaranteed by their treaties of 1837 and 1842. Almost nine hundred individuals assembled to protest the Indian's fishing rights, while more than one hundred people gathered in support of the Indians.

**24 June 1989 Stanford Agrees to Repatriate Ohlone Remains.** Stanford University agrees to repatriate for reburial the remains of 550 Ohlone Indians to descendant tribes in northern California. Stanford is one of the first universities to agree to a repatriation request by tribal leaders.

**28 June 1989 Coquille Tribe of Indians Trust Relationship Act.** The Coquille Tribe of Indians Trust Relationship Act restores Congress' federal relationship with the Coquille Indians of Oregon, which was canceled by the Termination Act of 1954 in an attempt to facilitate the assimilation of the Coquille into American society. In light of the failure of this integration strategy, Congress began to reestablish federal recognition of Indian tribes in the 1970s.

**7 July 1989 Brown Sworn in as Assistant Secretary of Indian Affairs.** Eddie Brown, an enrolled member of the Pasqua Yaqui of Arizona, takes the oath of office as Assistant Secretary for Indian Affairs.

**21 July 1989 *Brendale v. Confederated Tribes and Bands of the Yakima Indian Council.*** The Supreme Court rules in *Brendale v. Confederated Tribes and Bands of the Yakima Indian Council* that tribal zoning laws do not apply to non-Indian-owned lands within reservation boundaries where that land is surrounded by other non-Indian-owned lands. Non-Indian-owned land surrounded by tribally owned lands is subject to tribal zoning laws.

**21 July 1989 State Troopers, FBI Agents Close Casinos, Make Arrests.** Approximately 225 state troopers and FBI agents sweep into the part of the St. Regis Reservation (Akwesasne) located in the United States around Hogansburg, New York, closing down seven suspected casinos and arresting eight people.

**22 July 1989 Navajo Nation Riots.** Two individuals are killed and nine injured in a clash in Window Rock, Arizona, between police and the supporters of ousted Navajo Chairman Peter MacDonald. The tribal council had voted on February 17 to place MacDonald on involuntary leave in the wake of bribery accusations.

**27 July 1989 New York Police Close Roads to Mohawk Reservation.** New York State police close all roads to the New York portion of the St. Regis Mohawk Reservation. Tribal factions dispute the legality of gambling on the reservation and whether the traditional Mohawk Sovereignty Security Force or the state police properly exercises jurisdiction over the reservation.

**4 August 1989 Tohono O'Odham Demand Return of Land.** Tohono O'Odham tribal leaders request Mexican government officials in Mexico City to return thousands of acres of indigenously owned lands to the tribe. The Tohono O'Odham Nation argues that the Gadsden Treaty of 1853 illegally divided its tribal lands by the establishment of the international boundary.

**10 August 1989 Mohawk Vote in Favor of Gaming.** State and federally recognized tribal officials report that the St. Regis Mohawk Reservation voted to allow gambling on the United States side within reservation boundaries.

**11 August 1989 Working Group on Indian Water Settlements.** Secretary of Interior Manuel Lujan announces the formation of the Working Group on Indian Water Settlements. The group, which will report to the Interior's Water Policy Council, is charged with establishing principles to guide Indian water settlements; assisting in negotiations with tribes; and reporting to the council on the progress of such negotiations.

**11 August 1989 Centennial Accord.** Washington Governor Booth Gardner and the state's twenty-six federally recognized tribes sign the Centennial Accord. In the historic agreement, the state recognizes the sovereignty of Washington tribes and agrees to a government-to-government process for solving problems of mutual concern between the two governmental entities.

**13 August 1989 New York Returns Wampum Belts to Onondaga.** New York State agrees to return twelve wampum belts to the Onondaga Nation of New York. The wampum belts, woven of shells and beads, signify important historical and cultural events in Onondaga and Iroquois Confederacy history. The New York Senate and Assembly had passed legislation in 1971 requiring the return of five wampum belts to the nation.

**21 August 1989 Harvard Museum Returns Sacred Pole.** The Peabody Museum at Harvard University returns the Sacred Pole of the Omaha tribe. The pole, estimated to be three hundred years old, is a symbol of unity to the tribe. The sacred object was placed in the museum's care 101 years ago by Yellow Smoke, the last keeper.

**8 October 1989 Inspector General Details BIA Fund Mismanagement.** The inspector general issues a report detailing the Bureau of Indian Affairs' irresponsible management of Indian trust funds. Trust funds totaling $1.8 billion are administered by the BIA under its obligation of trustee for Indian moneys. The report states that some $17 million is missing as a result of sloppy bookkeeping.

**17 November 1989 Senate Issues Report on Mismanagement of Indian Lands and Monies.** A specially convened Senate panel issues its report following a two-year investigation into the corruption and mismanagement of American Indian lands and money. The report, the first study of its kind in more than a decade, uncovers corruption in the administration of tribal governments and a failure of the federal trust responsibility. Specifically cited as a violation of the trust obligation is Bureau of Indian Affairs management that allowed oil companies to rob tribes of oil proceeds and inadequate monitoring of teachers in BIA boarding schools found guilty of sexually molesting Indian children. The report's major recommendation is that tribes be given greater control over federal funds and programs. In particular, the panel proposes that a new executive agency be given responsibility for providing the more than five hundred Indian tribes and Alaska Native groups with block grants to administer their own programs.

**28 November 1989 National Museum of the American Indian Established.** Congress approves a bill to establish a National Museum of the American Indian under the administration of the Smithsonian Institution. The museum, which will be devoted to Indian culture and history, will be located in Washington, D.C.

**27 February 1990 Tribal Leaders Agree to Defend Treaty Rights.** Leaders of several North American tribes enter into an agreement to collectively defend rights granted by their treaties with the government of the United States. In accordance with the agreement, several tribes from both the United States and Canada will assist each other with legal services and lobbying and law-enforcement aid. The tribes also agree to work together in attempting to educate the non-Indian public about federal treaties with Indians.

**25 March 1990 Puyallup Settles Land Dispute.** The Puyallup tribe of Washington ends a long-standing land dispute with the city of Tacoma and the state. In return for extinguishing its land claims, the tribe agrees to a $162 million package settlement comprised of money, jobs, and education guarantees, and title to a section of the Tacoma waterfront.

**17 April 1990 *Oregon v. Smith*.** The U.S. Supreme Court rules, six to three, in *Oregon v. Smith* that a state ban against the use of peyote by American Indians did not violate the plaintiffs' First Amendment rights. The decision represents another blow to tribes in their efforts to protect their religious freedoms. The case involved the firing of two Indian drug counselors after testing positive for drug use. As members of the Native American church, the two men had ingested peyote as part of the church's ritual. Formally established in 1918, but based on thousands of years of tradition, the church's beliefs are a mixture of Native traditions and Christianity. Members believe that the taking of peyote allows them to communicate more closely with God.

**30 April–3 May 1990 Akwesasne Gambling Dispute.** A factional dispute between those in favor of gambling and those opposed on the Akwesasne Reservation results in the killing of two men on the Canadian side of the reservation. Hundreds of New York and Canadian police are sent to seal off the reservation, while negotiators sent by Governor Mario Cuomo attempt to settle the dispute.

**22 May 1990 Seneca, Salamanca Reach Agreement.** The Seneca Nation, local leaders of Salamanca, New York, and state and federal officials reach an agreement on Seneca land rented by the city of Salamanca. Under the terms of the first lease, negotiated in 1892, the town paid the nation $17,000 annually. Ninety percent of the town of 6,600 lies within the boundaries of the Allegany Reservation. According to the terms of the new lease, the town, which is the only city in the United States built on leased Indian land, will pay the tribe $800,000 a year. In addition, state and federal officials will reimburse the tribe $60 million for the inequities of the previous lease.

**29 May 1990 *Duro v. Reina*.** The Supreme Court rules in *Duro v. Reina* that tribes do not possess the authority to exercise criminal jurisdiction over nonmember Indians on the reservation. The decision is a major legal and political blow to tribes in their struggle to regain and protect their inherent right of self-determination. The decision also creates a very difficult situation on reservations, where many nonenrolled tribal members have married within the tribe or are working on the reservation. According to the Court's decision, no governmental body currently possesses criminal jurisdiction over these individuals.

**2–3 July 1990 Brown Signs Agreements with Tribes.** Assistant Secretary of the Interior Eddie

Martin Gutierrez, 12, looks on as Baudelio Gutierrez, 13, shows their grandfather, Thomas Brown, Sr., 78, some of the textbooks during Grandparent's Day activities at Wyoming Indian Middle School. (Photo by Mike McClure)

Brown signs historic agreements with six tribes: the Quinault Indian Nation, Tahola, Washington; Lummi Indian Nation, Bellingham, Washington; Jamestown Klallam Indian tribe, Sequim, Washington; Hoopa Valley Indian tribe, Hoopa, California; Cherokee Nation, Tahlequah, Oklahoma; and Mille Lacs Band of Chippewa Indians, Onamia, Minnesota. The tribes are part of a Self-Governance Pilot Program that will ultimately allow up to twenty tribes the authority to administer and set priorities for federal funds received directly from the government.

**August 1990 White House Conference on Indian Education Legislation Passed.**  Congress passes legislation to convene the White House Conference on Indian Education. The conference is charged with examining the feasibility of establishing an independent Indian Board of Education that will oversee all federal programs directed at Indian education and recommend improvements to current educational programs.

The Bureau of Indian Affairs currently funds 182 schools, attended by 39,000 Indian children. Of these 18,270 are contracted by tribal education committees. Another 400,000 Indian children attend public schools operated by the states.

**3 August 1990 Heritage Month Declared.**  Congress declares November as American Indian Heritage Month.

**25 September 1990 Tribally Controlled Vocational Institutional Support Act.**  Congress enacts the Tribally Controlled Vocational Institutional Support Act of 1990. The legislation provides for grants to operate and improve tribally controlled post-secondary vocational institutions.

**28 September 1990 Lujan, Brown Call Tribal Leader Conference.**  Secretary of Interior Manuel Lujan and Assistant Secretary Eddie Brown call the Indian Tribal Leaders Conference in Albuquerque, New Mexico, to discuss proposals to reorganize the Bureau of Indian Affairs. More than 1,000 Indian tribal leaders attend the first such meeting since 1976.

**4 October 1990 Indian Environmental Regulatory Act.** Congress passes the Indian Environmental Regulatory Act, which reinforces and clarifies the authority of Interior officials to protect areas of environmental concern in Indian Country.

**30 October 1990 Native American Languages Act.** Congress enacts the Native American Languages Act which is designed to preserve, protect, and promote the practice and development of Indian languages. The act is important given the government's historic efforts, especially in the nineteenth century, to eradicate Indian languages. It is estimated that more than one-half of all Indian languages are now extinct. Approximately 250 Indian languages remain in existence, although some are spoken by only a few individuals.

**31 October 1990 Ponca Restoration Act.** Congress passes the Ponca Restoration Act to reestablish all formal ties and services to the Ponca tribe of Nebraska. Federal recognition of the tribe had been taken away in 1962. As with other Indian tribes, the termination policy had negative ramifications for the Ponca both economically and culturally.

**6 November 1990 Defense Bill Delays *Duro* Decision.** President George Bush signs a defense appropriations bill that includes an amendment to delay enforcement of the *Duro* decision until 30 September 1991. The amendment, according to the bill's authors, filled the vacuum created by "an emergency situation": "Throughout the history of this country, the Congress has never questioned the power of tribal governments to exercise misdemeanor jurisdiction over non-tribal member Indians in the same manner that such courts exercise misdemeanor jurisdiction over tribal members."

**16 November 1990 Native American Graves Protection and Repatriation Act.** Bowing to intense lobbying efforts by individual tribes and national and local Indian organizations, Congress enacts the Native American Graves Protection and Repatriation Act. The act provides for the protection of American Indian gravesites and the repatriation of Indian remains and cultural artifacts to tribes.

**20 November 1990 Zah Elected Navajo Nation President.** Peterson Zah is elected President of the Navajo Nation. Zah assumes leadership of the tribe from Peter MacDonald Sr., who was convicted of taking bribes by the Navajo tribal court in October.

**28 November 1990 Child Abuse Increase on Reservations.** Historically a rare problem, child abuse is being experienced increasingly on tribal reservations. Now, under the terms of the Indian Child Protection and Family Abuse Prevention Act, tribes are required to report abusive situations and to establish tribal programs to treat and prevent future abuse.

**28 November 1990 National Indian Forest Resources Management Act.** The passage of the National Indian Forest Resources Management Act provides for improved protection and coordination between the Department of Interior and Indian tribes in the management of Indian forest lands.

**29 November 1990 Indian Arts and Crafts Act.** With the increase in value of tribal art work and jewelry, tribal artists have faced competition from non-Indian, machine-manufactured art works. Now, under the terms of the Indian Arts and Crafts Act of 1990, Congress gives the Indian Arts and Crafts Board, first established by the 1935 Indian Arts and Crafts Act, expanded powers to bring civil and criminal jurisdiction over counterfeit Indian arts and crafts.

**December 1990 Lujan Forms BIA Reorganization Task Force.** Secretary of Interior Manuel Lujan announces the formation of a forty-three-member advisory task force to recommend reorganization plans for the Bureau of Indian Affairs. The task force is composed of thirty-six Indian tribal leaders and seven Department of Interior and Bureau of Interior representatives.

Although the BIA reports that tribes contracted administration of approximately one-third of all BIA programs, the secretary of the interior urges reorganization so that less funding be used for administering tribal programs. By contracting with the BIA, tribes are free to operate and manage federal programs, some $415 million annually.

**29 December 1990 Wounded Knee Centennial.** Approximately four hundred people attend the centennial of the Wounded Knee massacre. On October 19, the House of Representatives provided the final approval needed for a resolution expressing "deep regret" over the Seventh Cavalry's massacre on the Pine Ridge Reservation. The Seventh Cavalry rounded up and killed more than three hundred women, men, and children at Wounded Knee, South Dakota, in 1890.

**29 January 1991 MacDonald Convicted of Conspiracy.** Peter MacDonald Sr., the former Navajo Nation chairman, is convicted by a tribal court on charges of conspiracy, fraud, and ethics violations. The tribal court had previously convicted him and his son of

Indian students march during American Indian Heritage Month. (Photo by Mike McClure)

accepting bribes and violating the tribe's ethics code. At that time, the tribal court suspended MacDonald from tribal office and prohibited him from holding office for four years. In addition, he was sentenced to almost six years in prison and fined $11,000. His son was sentenced to eighteen months in prison and was fined $2,500.

**5 March 1991 National Museum of the American Indian Announces Repatriation Policy.** The new National Museum of the American Indian, under the auspices of the Smithsonian Institution, announces its policy for the return of Indian artifacts. Tribes may formally request the return of all sacred objects, funerary artifacts, communally owned tribal property, and illegally obtained objects

**4 April 1991 Census Bureau Report.** The Census Bureau announces that 1,959,234 American Indians and Alaska Natives live in the United States. Of these numbers, 1,878,285 are American Indian, 57,152 are Eskimo, and 23,797 are Aleut. These figures represent a total increase in population since 1980 of almost 40

percent. The increase is attributed to improved census taking and a greater willingness on the part of individuals to be identified as American Indian. Included in these numbers are 510 federally recognized tribes in the United States and approximately 200 Alaska Native villages and communities.

**20 May 1991 Chippewa Tribes Reach Fishing Rights Agreement.** Members of the Chippewa tribes of Wisconsin and the state of Wisconsin announce an agreement which ends a seventeen-year dispute over treaty fishing rights in Wisconsin. Based on previous court decisions, the tribes and the state agree to compromise on a number of issues that had divided them for more than a decade. Under the terms of the agreement, tribes will continue to spearfish in Wisconsin lakes, but only according to strictly held conservation limits. The Chippewa also agree not to appeal a ruling that prevents their harvesting timber from off-reservation lands.

**24 May 1991 Lujan Approves Pequot Gaming Plans.** Secretary of Interior Manuel Lujan approves a request from the Mashantucket Pequot to operate a

Edlore Quiver, Jr., the first Arapaho veteran to return from the Gulf War, is given a hero's welcome at the Riverton Airport in Riverton, Wyoming, by his family and the Arapaho Color Guard. (Photo by Sara Wiles)

gambling casino on tribal lands. Permission is granted under the terms of the 1988 Indian Gaming Regulatory Act, which permits Indian gaming if generally legal under state law. Connecticut state officials seek to block approval. The Pequot casino becomes the only casino on the East Coast besides the operations in Atlantic City, New Jersey.

**14 June 1991 Bush Reaffirms Indian Self-Determination.** President George Bush issues his policy statement on American Indians in which he reaffirms the government's commitment to the government-to-government relationship between the federal government and the Indian nations.

**26 November 1991 National Monument Renamed.** Congress passes a bill, after considerable debate, renaming the Custer Battlefield National Monument in eastern Montana as the Little Bighorn Battlefield Monument. At the Little Bighorn site in 1876, Colonel George Armstrong Custer and more than 250 soldiers of the Seventh Cavalry lost a battle against allied groups of Lakota, Cheyenne, and Shoshone. This well publicized battle is often known as Custer's Last Stand.

**December 1991 BIA Publication Reports Responsibilities.** According to *American Indians Today*, a publication by the Bureau of Indian Affairs issued in the winter of 1991, the BIA is responsible in its trusteeship capacity for 278 reservations, comprising some 56.2 million acres. (The term *reservation* includes reservations, pueblos, rancherias, communities, and the like.)

The federal government's trusteeship responsibility extends to 510 federally recognized tribes, including about 200 village groups in Alaska. Since the establishment of the Federal Acknowledgment Program in 1978, the BIA has received 126 petitions for federal recognition; it extended recognition to eight Native communities and denied recognition to twelve. The U.S. Congress during this time legislatively recognized twelve previously unrecognized Native communities.

The same publication reports that the Bureau of Indian Affairs currently provides grants for the operation of twenty-two tribally controlled community colleges, enrolling approximately seven thousand students. The BIA further estimates that more than seventy thousand Indian students are attending colleges and universities. More than four hundred Indian students are known to be pursuing graduate or law degrees.

**4 December 1991 Indian Self-Determination and Education Assistance Act Amended.** Congress passes legislation to amend the Indian Self-Determination and Education Assistance Act. Entitled the Tribal Self-Governance Demonstration Project, the act extends the number of tribes taking part in the tribal self-governance pilot project from twenty to thirty.

**1992 Native American Arts Council Hosts Indigenous Leaders Meeting.** The Native American Council of New York City hosts a meeting of indigenous leaders for the United Nations opening of the Year of Indigenous Peoples that will begin in 1993. More than 250 delegates attend, including representatives of the aboriginal peoples of Australia, the Saami of Norway, the Mapuche from Chile, and the Nanentz from Russia. Delegates from the Iroquois, Sioux, Navajo, and Cree nations represent the indigenous people of North America.

**Columbus Quincentennial.** The Columbus Quincentennial focuses the nation's attention on American Indian contributions to the world as well as the injustices of Spain during the period of conquest. A planned voyage of replicas of Columbus's three ships, the *Nina*, *Pinta*, and *Santa Maria*, ends in bankruptcy.

**Foxwoods Casino Opens.** The same year, Foxwoods Casino, built by the Mashantucket Pequot Tribe opens in Ledyard, Connecticut. It quickly becomes the most profitable casino in the United States.

**21 October 1992 PBS Broadcasts Documentary.** The Public Broadcasting System (PBS) airs *Surviving Columbus*, a documentary produced in cooperation with KNME television in Albuquerque, New Mexico, and the Institute of American Indian Arts in Santa Fe. The two-hour special represents the Native American response to the Columbus Quincentennial, and traces Pueblo history from European contact to the present. Production includes an all-Indian crew consisting of Edmund Ladd, producer (Zuni); George Burdeau, co-executive producer (Blackfeet); Diane Reyna, director (Taos Pueblo); and Simon Ortiz, writer (Acoma Pueblo.)

**November 1992 Campbell Elected to Senate.** Ben Nighthorse Campbell, Northern Cheyenne, is elected to the U.S. Senate as a member of the Democratic Party. Campbell is the first Native American to serve in the Senate.

**10 December 1992 UN Invites Indigenous Leaders to Headquarters.** The secretary general of the United Nations (UN) welcomes more than 200 representatives of indigenous peoples to the New York City, UN headquarters. The representatives gather to mark 1993 as the International Year of Indigenous Peoples. For the first time, indigenous people are invited to address the UN General Assembly. The proceedings begin with a prayer offered by Avrol Looking Horse, keeper of the Lakota sacred pipe.

**5 January 1993 Campbell Sworn in as Senator.** Representative Ben Nighthorse Campbell becomes Senator Campbell when he and thirty-eight colleagues are sworn in as U.S. senators by Vice President Dan Quayle. Campbell, a Democrat, is the first American Indian to serve in the Senate in more than sixty years. Campbell represented Colorado's third congressional district for three terms before deciding to run for the Senate.

**6 February 1993 First Annual Totem Awards.** The First Annual Totem Awards are presented to outstanding Native American artists in film, television, theater, and music. The event is organized by First Americans in the Arts, a nonprofit organization dedicated to encouraging the participation of Native Americans in the entertainment industry. The dinner and awards ceremony is held in Beverly Hills, California. Recipients include John Trudell (Santee Sioux), Graham Greene (Oneida), Sheila Tousey (Menominee), Wes Studi (Cherokee), and Hanay Geiogamah (Kiowa).

**27 February 1993 AIM Members Remember Wounded Knee II.** Members of the American Indian Movement return to Wounded Knee where they waged a seventy-one-day occupation and armed conflict with federal authorities in February 1973. Accompanied by traditional songs and ceremony, several hundred AIM members and their supporters gather around the burial site of the Lakota people killed at Wounded Knee Creek in 1890.

**March 1993 Apache Nation Attempts to Halt Telescope Project.** The Apache Nation urges the University of Pittsburgh not to involve the school in a $60 million telescope project in Arizona. Raleigh Thompson (San Carlos Apache) informs Chancellor J. Dennis O'Connor that the proposed Columbus Project is being built on land considered sacred to the Apache people. The University of Pittsburgh stated that they had made no commitment to the Mount Graham project and have spent no money on it. "Our involvement in the Project doesn't exist at this time," Vice Chancellor Ben Tuchi says.

**April 1993 American Indian Religious Freedom Act Amendments.** Over 1,000 Indian people from thirteen states attend hearings at Augsburg College in Minneapolis, Minnesota, to hear testimony concerning proposed amendments to the American Indian Religious Freedom Act (AIRFA). The United States Senate Select Committee conducts field hearings for strengthening AIRFA. Tribal delegates urge greater protection of the Pipestone quarries, Native American airspace, return of the Black Hills to the Lakota Nation, and the repatriation of Native American sacred objects. John Sun Child, a tribal leader, expresses sorrow that laws are required to protect the religion given to the first people. Senator Dan Inouye states that "Eight hundred treaties were entered into by the U.S. government. My predecessors examined and ratified 370. I'm sad to report EVERY treaty was violated."

**3 June 1993 First Native American Film Festival.** "Wind and Glacier Voices: The Native American Film and Media Celebration" opens at the Lincoln Center for the Performing Arts in New York City. It is the first film festival showcasing works produced solely by the American and Canadian Indian community. The five-day event includes an awards ceremony honoring Native filmmakers and performers, panel discussions on contemporary Indian issues, and daily screenings of independent films. The festival highlights key Indian filmmakers and their works.

**17 June 1993 Gabrielino Protest Building on Sacred Land.** The American Civil Liberties Union joins Native Americans in opposing California State University, Long Beach's plan to build a mini-mall and parking lot on a location considered sacred by many southern California Indians. Members of the Gabrielino Indians and other California tribes argue that that the university is built on the remains of Puvungna village, a spiritual center that was the birthplace of Chinigchinix, the founder of the Luiseño-Cahuilla religion. Cindi Alvitre, cultural educator of the Gabrielino-Tongva tribal youth council, said the Native Americans oppose the university's proposal for further study. "We want people to understand that we are not just 'malcontented ethnics' crying for public attention," she said. "Puvungna is where our creator. . . had his funeral. Our cry is the same you would hear if someone came to dig Jesus out of his tomb to assess his cultural significance."

**June–July 1993 Hanta Virus Takes Indian Lives.** During the months of June and July, the Hanta virus, a rodent-borne disease, is responsible for the deaths of sixteen Indian people, primarily Navajo, in the Four Corners region of the southwestern United States. Initially specialists from the Indian Health Service in Albuquerque, New Mexico, stated, "We don't know what causes it." Guided in part by Navajo medicine men, researchers soon traced the contagion to the deer mice, the cotton rat, the white-footed mice, and possibly the rice mice. While the disease is first thought to be concentrated in the southwestern United States, it is now known that it exists in over one-half of U.S. states.

**July 1993 Clinton Appoints Deer Secretary of Indian Affairs.** Following confirmation hearings, the U.S. Senate confirms Ada Elizabeth Deer (Menominee) as President William Jefferson Clinton's choice for Secretary of Indian Affairs in the U.S. Department of the Interior. She is the first woman, and the sixth Indian, to fill the post.

**9–10 July 1993 Ortiz Presented with Lifetime Achievement Award.** The Native Writers' Circle of the Americas presents a lifetime achievement award to Simon J. Ortiz at the 1993 international Returning the Gift conference, attended by nearly 400 Native American poets, fiction writers, and playwrights. His published works include *Fightin': New and Collected Stories* and *Woven Stone*.

**10 July 1993 Cheyenne Remains Buried.** The remains of eighteen Cheyenne people are buried at the Concho, Oklahoma Cemetery after more than 125 years in the collections of the Army Medical Museum and the Smithsonian's National Museum of Natural History. The remains were repatriated under the provisions of the Native American Graves Protection and Repatriation Act of 1990. Five sets of the remains were collected by the U.S. Army following the Sand Creek Massacre of 1864 led by Colonel John Chivington.

**7 August 1993 Deer Sworn in as BIA Head.** Ada Deer, a Menominee and alumna of the University of Wisconsin-Madison and Columbia University, is sworn in as the new head of the U.S. Bureau of Indian Affairs. During the inauguration ceremony, tribal leaders from across the country praise her and present her with gifts. At a news conference, Deer states that she wants Native American communities to have more autonomy in the use of BIA funding.

**28 August 1993 Sac and Fox Declare Nuclear Free Zone.** The Sac and Fox Nation becomes the first tribe in Oklahoma to declare a Nuclear Free Zone (NFZ) on their tribal lands. Mary Black Osborn, chairman of the Sac and Fox Nation's health commission and a registered nurse said, "As a nurse, I am probably more aware of the threats to our environment. If the environment is contaminated or polluted, we in the health field are treating symptoms instead of getting at the real problem." The Sac and Fox join several other tribes in North American that have declared their lands to be nuclear free. The Inuit of Alaska appealed to the United Nations to establish a NFZ in the arctic in 1981.

**15 October 1993 Senate Approves Study of Uranium Health Effects.** The United States Senate authorizes a study on how uranium milling and mining has affected the health of Navajo and others involved in such work over a thirty-year period. The study will focus on the health effects of uranium milling that took place primarily on or near the Navajo reservation from the late 1940s through 1971.

**15 October 1993 Cuomo Signs Gaming Compact with Mohawk.** New York Governor Mario Cuomo signs a gaming compact with the Mohawk Nation, clearing the way for the state's second legal casino. The Mohawk Casino will offer roulette and blackjack games, but not slot machines. Under the negotiated compact, New York State police will have unlimited access to the casino, as will officials from the state Racing and Wagering Board. No alcohol will be allowed in the facility.

**27 October 1993 Catawba Indian Land Claim Settlement Act.** President Clinton signs the Catawba Indian Land Claim Settlement Act of 1993, restoring the Catawba Tribe's government-to-government relationship with the United States and ending the 153 years of conflict with the state of South Carolina. The act provides a total of $30 to $40 million in benefits and contributions and a payment of $50 million over five years from federal, state, and local governments and private contributors. These funds will be placed in trust for land acquisition, economic development, education, and social services for the Catawba Tribe.

**28 October 1993 Lumbee Receive Federal Recognition.** The House of Representatives voted to recognize the Lumbee Tribe of Cheraw Indians of North Carolina, consisting of 40,000 members. After filing for federally recognized status with the Interior Department, Lumbee Indians can adopt a constitution and bylaws. However, the tribe is not entitled to federal services provided by the Bureau of Indian Affairs and the Indian Health Service until Congress appropriates funds for that purpose. Although the state of North Carolina recognized the Lumbee Indians as a tribe

in 1885, the Interior Department opposed numerous congressional bills for granting the Lumbee federal recognition.

**November 1993 Milk Creek Battle Memorial Erected.** Approximately 1,000 people gathered in Meeker, Colorado, to honor the Ute warriors who died at the Battle of Milk Creek in 1879. This is the nation's first memorial dedicated to Native Americans and erected by Native people. According to Clifford Duncan, an elder of the Uintah-Ouray Ute tribe of Utah, the Ute people have been invisible in U.S. history books. This memorial provides an opportunity for the Ute to voice their own version of the Milk Creek battle.

**22–23 November 1993 Spiritual Leaders Meet to Discuss Environmental Issues.** American Indian spiritual leaders from the four directions gather at the United Nations to share ancient Native prophecies warning of environmental destruction of the natural world at a historic conference called Cry of the Earth, the Legacy of First Nations. Religious leaders from the Algonquin, Lakota, Hopi, Iroquois, Micmac, Huichol, and Mayan nations deliver powerful messages handed down by oral tradition. Warning that the world is on the brink of self-destruction, Leon Shenandoah, Tadadaho of the Six Nations Iroquois Confederacy states, "Our instructions says that the end of the world will be near when the trees start dying from the tops down—that's what the maples are doing today." The conference was preceded by the Iroquois Confederacy's ceremonial planting of a Tree of Peace in New York's Central Park.

**27 November 1993 Black Kettle Descendants Honor Ancestors.** Descendants of Cheyenne Chief Black Kettle and approximately 100 tribal members who perished when George Armstrong Custer attacked their sleeping encampment 125 years ago, honored their ancestors with songs and chants during a memorial service. Tribal members in traditional dress sing as replicas of Cheyenne burial gifts are placed on a cottonwood burial scaffold. Most Cheyenne killed were women and children.

**30 November 1993 George Posthumously Awarded Medal of Honor.** Charles George is posthumously awarded the Congressional Medal of Honor. George was a rifleman in Company C of the 179th Infantry Regiment of the 45th Infantry Division during the Korean War. On 30 November 1952, George threw himself on an enemy hand grenade to save the lives of his comrades. A bronze bust of George is atop the center marker of the Tribal Veterans Monument in Cherokee, North Carolina. The citation that accompanies the Medal of Honor states that "While in the process of

Students at the Arapaho School play the traditional shinny game with willow sticks and leather balls during Heritage Day activities. (Photo by Sara Wiles)

leaving the trenches a hostile enemy soldier hurled a hand grenade into their midst. Private George shouted a warning to one comrade, pushed the other out of danger and with full knowledge of the consequences unhesitatingly threw himself upon the grenade absorbing the full blast of the explosion."

**December 1993 Mankiller Releases Autobiography.** Wilma Mankiller, Cherokee Nation Principal Chief, tours throughout American cities to promote her autobiography, *Mankiller: A Chief and Her People*, coauthored by Michael Wallis. Mankiller's autobiography recalls her early years as well as some contemporary history of Cherokee.

**9 December 1993 Dann Sisters Receive Right Livelihood Award.** Carrie and Mary Dann receive the 1993 Right Livelihood Award, known as the alternative Nobel Peace Prize. According to the Right Livelihood Foundation, the Dann sisters are honored for "their courage and perseverance in asserting the rights of indigenous people to their land." Accompanying

this honor is a $200,000 award that the sisters will share with three other women from Israel, Zimbabwe, and India.

**17–18 December 1993 AIM Chapters Meet to Restructure.** Several American Indian Movement chapters meet in New Mexico to discuss chapter autonomy, the restructuring of AIM, and schedule a tribunal to hear testimony on the alleged disruptive activities of AIM leadership.

**1994 Blackgoat Named America's Unsung Woman.** Roberta Blackgoat, Navajo, is named America's Unsung Woman by the National Women's History Project for her twenty-year leadership in the environmental and human rights struggle on Black Mesa and the relocation of 12,000 Navajo.

**14–24 January 1994 Natives Travel to Rome for Festival.** Native American performers and scholars

The Dann sisters, Carrie (l.) and Mary (r.) have fought a decades-long battle for grazing rights. (Photo by Ilka Hartmann)

travel to Rome to participate in the festival "The Feather, The Flute, The Drum," featuring music, dance, and storytelling performances; an art installation; video programs; a panel discussion of history and culture; and demonstrations of herb-use and cooking. The festival begins with a traditional procession and prayer led by Ken Ryan, Assiniboine spiritual leader. Other participants include Litefoot, a Cherokee musician; Kevin Locke, a renowned Lakota flutist and hoop dancer; Sharon Burch, a Navajo musician; and Sara Batges, a Cherokee visual artist.

**19 January 1994 Native American Studies Approved at University of Oklahoma.**   After months of negotiation and community pressure, the Oklahoma State Board of Regents approves a Native American Studies Program at the University of Oklahoma. As an interdisciplinary program it offers students a wide range of courses, including fine arts, anthropology, and sociology. Students may use the program to work with Native American community organizations or perform library and museum work.

**February 1994 Appeals Court Upholds MacDonald Conviction.**   A federal appeals court upholds the convictions of former Navajo tribal chairman Peter MacDonald on charges of taking bribes to steer a tribal loan to business associates. MacDonald was chairman of the Navajo Nation in 1971–1983 and 1987–1989. He was convicted in 1992 of racketeering, fraud, and related charges. MacDonald is serving a five-year prison sentence and an additional tribal jail term concurrently with a fourteen-year sentence for a conspiracy conviction in a 1989 riot at tribal headquarters that left two dead and five injured.

**1–4 February 1994 Mescalero Apache Sign Nuclear Waste Agreement.**   The Mescalero Apache, one of more than fifty tribes approached by the U.S. government, sign a multimillion-dollar nuclear-waste storage planning agreement with the federal government. They are the only tribe to do so and the agreement was reached despite a tribal referendum that defeated the proposed nuclear-storage dump. A second referendum passed by a narrow margin.

**7 February 1994 Clinton's Budget Plan Proposes BIA Cuts.** The Clinton administration's 1995 budget plan proposes significant cuts in three BIA economic development grant programs. The $2.5 million direct loan program, $4.3 million in technical assistance grants, and $1.4 million for special tribal courts funding are scheduled to be eliminated. According to BIA spokesman Carl Shaw, the direct loan program is a failure because it has experienced a 70 percent default rate. Ada Deer, assistant secretary for Indian affairs, says that the administration's budget proposal continues the transfer of resources from the BIA to tribal government and Indian trust relationship.

**11 February 1994 Wisconsin Winnebago Purchases Land.** With cash from casino profits, the Wisconsin Winnebago Nation purchases approximately 600 acres of land on the Wisconsin River for $1.2 million. Winnebago elders and others are convinced that the land was once the site of a Winnebago village and contained at least sixty-four sculptured earthen mounds that have spiritual significance in Winnebago culture. The Winnebago plan to locate and mark all sites of the original mounds. With the approval of Winnebago elders, some of the mounds may be restored to their original size and shape. The purchased land will also be used for the construction of a cultural center, a youth camp, prairie restoration, and a buffalo farm.

**11 February–3 April 1994 Teters Exhibits Stereotypes.** Charlene Teters, Spokane, creates a thought-provoking exhibit, "It was Only an Indian: Native American Stereotypes," that explores how Native Americans have been and continue to be objectified and dehumanized in popular culture. Teters exposes racism toward Native Americans by asking: What does it mean to be the brunt of stereotyping? How would you feel to be examined, probed, and mocked in this manner? Why does this continue to be acceptable? For several years Teters has collected and studied apparently innocuous objects such as Indian head cigarette ashtrays, toilet paper, and potbellied Indian planters, all of which promote stereotyping. Teters works as a placement and alumni director for the Institute of American Indian Arts in Santa Fe, while continuing to actively place racism under public scrutiny.

**11 February–15 July 1994 Walk for Justice.** AIM co-founders Dennis Banks and Mary Jan Wilson-Medrano lead a Walk for Justice from Alcatraz Island in California to Washington, D.C., bringing public attention to Native issues and collecting signatures requesting executive clemency for Leonard Peltier, who has served eighteen years in prison for allegedly shooting two FBI agents on the Pine Ridge Reservation in South Dakota

in 1975. Other issues brought to public attention by the walk are the James Bay Great Whale Project, where an expanding hydraulic dam threatens fishing and hunting rights of the Cree and Ojibwa tribes; the fishing treaty rights struggle in Wisconsin; continued nuclear testing which is destroying water, land, and health for the Western Shoshone in Nevada; the Dann family's (Shoshone) conflict over land and treaty rights with the Bureau of Land Management; the Big Mountain issue involving involuntary relocation of Navajo from disputed land with the Hopi; and the return of the Black Hills to the Lakota people.

**March 1994 NCAI Supports Black Caucus.** The National Congress of American Indians (NCAI), a confederation of 162 tribal governments and the nation's oldest and largest Indian organization, agrees to support the Black Caucus of State Legislators, a caucus of 540 African American state legislators from forty-two states in their struggles for African-American rights. In December 1993, the Black Caucus of State Legislators passed a similar resolution to support Native American tribal sovereignty. Both groups agree that since they share similar histories of economic and political oppression in the United States, they need to build coalition networks to fight for basic economic and human rights.

**9 March 1994 Indian Students Receive Scholarships, Internships.** Greg Powderface, a Gros Ventres graduate student at the Stanford University School of Business, and Wendy Wisdom, a Hopi, Choctaw, and Chickasaw third-year college student majoring in social welfare and Native American Studies, are winners of a scholarship and internship program sponsored by Columbia Pictures and Sony Pictures Entertainment in connection with Columbia Pictures' December 1993 release of *Geronimo: An American Legend.* They, along with several hundred American Indian college student applicants, submitted an essay addressing the question, "How can the media better highlight and honor American Indian culture and heritage?" The program provides summer 1994 internship employment in the Columbia Pictures marketing department and a $2,500 scholarship to each winner.

**11 March 1994 Roessel Appointed Deputy Assistant Secretary for Indian Affairs.** Faith Roessel, a member of the Navajo Nation and former staff attorney with the Native American Rights Fund (NARF), is appointed deputy assistant secretary for Indian affairs. In her new post, Roessel continues her work of assisting tribal governments in their efforts to protect Indian trust assets.

Tommy White and Baillie wait outside the Wind River Reservation Museum in Wyoming. (Photo by Sara Wiles)

**21 March 1994 Mole Lake Chippewa Lose Legal Battle.**  The Mole Lake Chippewa tribe loses its eight-year legal battle to regain rights to a 144-square-mile area in northeast Wisconsin. The U.S. Supreme Court refuses to consider their claims regarding nineteenth century treaties. The Mole Lake Chippewa state that they never surrendered the disputed land, most of which is now claimed by Exxon Corporation. The tribe sues Exxon in federal court contending that the tribe never surrendered rights received in the 1842 treaty.

**21 March 1994 Clinton Meets with Tribal Leaders.**  President Clinton invites leaders of all 545 federally recognized American Indian and Alaska Native tribes to the White House. President Clinton hosts the tribal leaders at the White House April 29. Attorney General Janet Reno and Interior Secretary Bruce Babbitt travel to Albuquerque, New Mexico, where they meet with tribal leaders on May 5 and 6. Tribal leaders are concerned because President Clinton had made promising statements to Indian people during his bid for the presidency but later said that he wanted to spend less money on Indian health care.

**29 April 1994 Clinton Signs Directives.**  President William Clinton welcomes more than 300 leaders of federally recognized Indian Nations to the White House. Clinton signs two directives before the tribal leaders, one of which was directed to every executive department instructing them to cooperate with tribal governments to accommodate "wherever possible" the need for eagle feathers in the practice of Native religions. The other document directed every executive department and agency of government to remove all barriers that inhibit cooperative relations with tribal governments and to make certain if they take action affecting tribal trust resources they consult with tribal governments before that decision.

**10 May 1994 Crazy Horse Malt Liquor Banned.**  Minnesota Governor Arne Carlson signed into law a bill banning the sale of Crazy Horse malt liquor in the state. This bill makes Minnesota the second state to ban the sale of Crazy Horse beer. A coalition of groups, including members of the American Indian Movement, Honor Our Neighbors Origins and Rights, and the National Coalition on Racism in Sports and the Media,

President Bill Clinton meets with BIA officials. (Photo by Carol Lujan)

spearheaded the passage of the bill. Seth Big Crow Sr., a distant relative of the Sioux leader Crazy Horse, said the "It's monumental to us that there's a group of people out there who believe in doing what is right."

**13 June 1994 *Department of Taxation and Finance of New York et al. v. Milhelm Attea & Brothers, Inc. et al.*** In *Department of Taxation and Finance of New York et al. v. Milhelm Attea & Brothers, Inc. et al.*, the United States Supreme Court holds that a state tax scheme to collect taxes on cigarettes sold on Indian reservations does not improperly burden Indian trading and does not violate the Indian Trader Statutes.

**15 July 1994 Walk for Justice Reaches Washington, D.C.** The Walk for Justice that began on Alcatraz Island on 11 February 1994 reaches its destination at the Lincoln Memorial in Washington, D.C. AIM cofounders Dennis Banks and Mary Jan Wilson-Medrano lead the walk. Hundreds of Native American people gather at Ladybird Johnson Park in Arlington, Virginia, to finish the last miles of the five month, 3,800-mile journey that began on Alcatraz Island. The purpose of the Walk for Justice was to bring public attention to Native issues including violation of treaty rights, grave desecration, nuclear waste dumping, and Native prisoner rights.

**15 July 1994 FBI Agents Run Ad in *Washington Post*.** A group representing 15,000 past and present FBI special agents run an advertisement in *The Washington Post* urging President Clinton to refuse the request for clemency for Leonard Peltier presented by organizers and supporters of The Walk For Justice, which ended in Washington, D.C. FBI Director Louis J. Freeh issues a statement stating that "Peltier's guilt has been firmly established." The advertisement in *The Washington Post* states that "Leonard Peltier is a vicious, violent and cowardly criminal who hides behind legitimate Native American issues."

**20 August 1994 White Buffalo Born in Northern Plains.** News of the birth of a rare white buffalo is spreading among American Indians, inspiring pilgrimages to the Wisconsin farm where it was born.

The buffalo calf, named Miracle is the first white buffalo born in more than fifty years. The white buffalo is particularly sacred to the Cheyenne, Sioux, and other Indian Nations of the Northern Plains that once relied on the buffalo for sustenance.

**5 September 1994 Tlingits Banished for Crime.** Andrian Guthrie and Simon Roberts, both Tlingits, are banished to separate uninhabited islands by a Tlingit tribal court for beating and robbing a pizza delivery man. Over the objection of prosecutors in a Washington State courtroom, the Tlingit rendered a decision for banishment. Tribal members made reparation payments to the victims of the crimes and their families, including building them a new home. Four elders accompanied the boys to the island to instruct them in subsistence hunting and fishing skills. A considerable amount of food was provided as well. Guthrie and Roberts were ultimately returned to the state court system for punishment. The boys arranged for others to bring them supplies, and they were seen leaving the islands. The boys disobeyed the tribal council and were returned to the state court, which sentenced them to three-and-a-half to five-and-a-half years in prison.

**21 September 1994 Clinton Recognizes Three Michigan Tribal Communities.** President Clinton signs legislation awarding federally recognized tribal status to three Michigan Indian communities. The two bills signed by the president recognize the Pokagon Band of the Potawatomi, the Little River Band of Ottawa, and the Little Traverse Bay Band of Ottawa. The legislation excluded all three bands from federal benefits and services. All three bands signed nineteenth-century treaties ceding Michigan land to the federal government.

**2 October 1994 Monument to American Indian Civil War Veterans Dedicated.** A monument honoring American Indian Civil War veterans is dedicated on the Iowa Reservation near White Cloud, Kansas. The names of forty-nine Indian soldiers serving with the Fourteenth Calvary of the Union Army are inscribed on the monument.

**5 October 1994 Tribal Colleges Awarded Land Grant Status.** In legislation passed by the House and the Senate, tribal colleges are awarded land grant status. Jack Briggs, president of the Fond du Lac Tribal and Community College, stated that "It's ironic that Indians were the first people of the land, and the last to receive land-grant status." Research conducted in support of land grant status revealed that tribal colleges receive approximately $3,000 per student through federal sources while the national average is $7,000 per student.

**24 October 1994 Tribal Self-Governance Act.** President Clinton signs the Tribal Self-Governance Act into law. The act gives permanent self-governance status to the twenty-eight Indian Nations participating in the Self-Governance Demonstration Project. The project was a tribal initiative intended to allow Indian nations greater flexibility and control in meeting the needs of their communities while preserving the trust responsibility of the federal government. The act permits the Department of the Interior to increase the number of tribes participating in self-governance by up to twenty each year.

**25 October 1994 National Museum of the American Indian Opens.** The National Museum of the American Indian (NMAI) opens an exhibition hall at the Customs House in lower Manhattan in New York City. The George W. Heye Museum, the first of three planned NMAI museum locations, opens to the general public starting on Sunday, October 30.

**31 October 1994 American Indian Radio Network Begins Programming.** An American Indian radio network linking twenty-five tribal radio stations begins regular programming. AIROS, American Indian Radio on Satellite, will offer a storytelling series as well as interviews with Native Americans, historical specials, and a multi-part series on breaking the cycle of child abuse. Network officials hope to eventually expand into a twenty-four-hour format. The twenty-five stations are located in ten states.

**December 1994 Ho Chunk Nation Receives BIA Approval.** The Wisconsin Winnebago Tribe has received final approval from the Bureau of Indian Affairs to change its name to Ho Chunk Nation. The name was chosen as part of the tribe's new constitution, which was given final approval by the BIA. The Ho Chunk Nation has 4,900 members, most living in Wisconsin, Illinois, and Minnesota.

**1995 Pequot Add Land to Reservation.** The U.S. Department of the Interior issues a decision to allow the Mashantucket Pequot to add 247 non-taxable acres to their reservation. Opponents of the decision argued that the Pequot were the "world's richest Indian tribe grossing nearly $1 billion a year." The tribe's highly successful Foxwoods Resorts Casino draws nearly 50,000 visitors a day. The tribe also pays the state of Connecticut millions of dollars a year from slot machine profits for exclusive gaming rights. This year the Pequot are expected to pay $130 million to the state.

Department of Interior officials and Pueblo officials. (Photo by Carol Lujan)

**15 January 1995 Global Peace Walk Begins.** The United Nations Fiftieth Anniversary Global Peace Walk begins in New York City. As the walkers pass through the Navajo Reservation, Albert Hale, president of the Navajo Nation, states, "World peace is a noble effort that everyone should aim for." Miss Navajo Nation Karen Leupp joins the small group of national and international walkers.

**31 January 1995 Mescalero Apache Reject Nuclear Waste Proposal.** The Mescalero Apache vote 490 to 362 to reject a planning grant of $10 million to consider hosting a nuclear waste disposal site on their reservation. Proponents argued the proposal ultimately promised about $250 million for schools and capital for diversifying Mescalero Apache businesses. Opponents argue that the site would endanger the environment and the people living on and around the 461,000-acre reservation.

**March 1995 Indians Protest Desecration of Sacred Devil's Tower.** American Indians petition the federal government to ban climbers on Devil's Tower located in the northeast corner of Wyoming. Indian leaders say that the 860-foot-high monolith is a sacred site where Indian people have traveled to seek religious visions and leave prayer bundles of tobacco and sage. Indians say that climbers are desecrating a sacred site by riveting its face with climbing bolts and urinating on its walls. They also state that increased climbing and tourism interferes with their ability to communicate with the Great Spirit. National park officials have created a task force of climbers, American Indians, and local officials to arrive at a management policy agreeable to all sides. Monument officials hope to have a joint plan implemented by 1996 that would allow a voluntary climbing ban each June when important Indian ceremonies are celebrated.

**3 June 1995 St. Regis Elects Smoke Chief.** The Mohawk of the St. Regis Reservation in northern New York elect Douglas Smoke as their chief. Smoke opposed gaming on the Akwesasne Reservation. A new written constitution is approved as well and the new chiefs replace a three-chief system. There is an executive branch which includes a chief executive officer and vice chief, a legislative branch consisting of a five-member council, and a judicial branch.

**5 June 1995 National Native-Focused Radio Show Begins.** "Native America Calling" is the first national call-in radio program devoted to American Indians and hosted by the Public Broadcasting Consortium and the Alaska Public Radio Network. The program informs people about Indian issues and is broadcast out of the University of New Mexico, which helps produce the program. The hour-long show is broadcast Monday through Friday and is distributed via the American Indian Radio on Satellite Network for play on twenty-nine Indian-owned stations in twelve states.

**July 1995 Kennedy Visits Menominee Nation.** Robert F. Kennedy, Jr., son of the former U.S. attorney general, visits the Menominee Nation to discuss forestry practices with members of the Canadian Nuu-chah-nulth and Menominee Tribal Enterprises delegation. Kennedy recognizes the Menominee Nation for its sustainable forestry practices. The Nuu-chah-nulth is a consortium of fourteen tribes in the Clayoquot Sound area of Canada and is interested in the Menominee program as a model for its own resource preservation program.

Also at this time, the Makah Tribe of Neah Bay, Washington, announces plans to resume their traditional whale harvest. The tribe seeks to harvest up to five whales for ceremonial and subsistence purposes starting in 1996.

**22 July 1995 Harjo Receives Lifetime Achievement Award.** Joy Harjo, Muscogee (Creek) poet, receives the fourth annual Lifetime Achievement Award from the Native Writer's Circle of the Americas. Harjo receives the award in person at the Oklahoma Memorial Union, University of Oklahoma. Harjo is a professor at the University of New Mexico and is the author of a number of volumes of poetry that have helped to inspire an entire generation of young Native poets.

**August 1995 Native American Prep School Opens.** The Native American Preparatory School (NAPS) located in the Pecos River Valley, east of Santa Fe, New Mexico, opens as a residential college-preparatory high school. NAPS is dedicated to nurturing the intellectual, ethical, and leadership potential of Indian students.

**9 August 1995 International Indigenous Day Honored at UN.** International Indigenous Day is honored at the UN. Delphine Red Shirt, Lakota, conducts the World Sacred Pipe Ceremony to honor the first observance of the World's Indigenous People on the grounds of the United Nations Building in New York City.

**12 September 1995 One Mind, One Voice Prayer Vigil Held.** Native Americans hold a One Mind, One Voice, One Prayer Vigil on the Mall near the Washington Monument in Washington, D.C. Indian representatives from tribes from across the nation gather on Capital Hill to protest proposed cuts in federal spending for the BIA, Indian education, and other Indian social programs. Vice President Al Gore states that President Clinton will veto the Department of Interior Bill because of the proposed cuts.

**November 1995 Construction Begins on Replacement Fishing Sites.** Ground is broken on the first of thirty-one sites intended to be replacements for fishing sites flooded by the Bonneville Dam. The initial 7.8-acre site on the Columbia River's north side will have a campground, drying sheds, water, and sanitation facilities. Treaties between the federal government and Columbia River Nations—Nez Percé, Umatilla, Warm Springs, and Yakama—guaranteed the right to fish at their usual places along the river. Many of these fishing sites were flooded when the massive dams were built.

**8 November 1995 Indian Dance Stamps Unveiled.** American Indian dance stamp series is announced. Arlin Humeyumptewa, Hopi, a Denver postal clerk, joins with the Denver Postmaster Michael Flores in unveiling the upcoming issue of the American Indian Dance stamp. The stamps, which depict five dance styles are slated to be available for purchase in 1996.

**13–15 November 1995 Tribal Leadership Summit.** More than 200 tribal and federal natural resource managers, tribal leaders, and representatives from national intertribal natural-resource oriented organizations attend the first Tribal Leadership Summit on Government Relationship and Management of Indian Trust/Natural Resources held in Denver, Colorado. The summit was organized by ten national intertribal natural resource oriented organizations in response to President Clinton's executive order to enhance intergovernmental partnerships. Tribal leaders expressed their views on treaties with the U.S. government and agreed that the government is ignoring treaty obligations. A follow-up meeting is planned in early 1996 to begin addressing the recommendations of the summit.

**1996 Native American Free Exercise of Religion Act.** Native American Free Exercise of Religion Act is introduced in Congress. The act is designed to negate the Supreme Court ruling that interferes with the free practice of religion by members of the Native American Church and to strengthen religious rights as set out in the earlier American Indian Religious Freedom Act.

**January 1996 *In re Bridget R.*** The California Second District Court of Appeals in the case *In re Bridget R.*, rules against Richard and Cindy Adams of Long Beach, California, who put their twin daughters Bridget and Lucy up for adoption in November 1993, shortly after they were born. The Adams claim descent from the California Dry Creek Pomo Indian tribe, and claim that the children are approximately one-eighth Pomo. When the children were four months old, the Adams changed their minds and petitioned to have their children returned under provisions of the Indian Child Welfare Act of 1978. Stating that the birth parents appeared to have "no connection, nor ties. . . and apparently no interest at all" in their tribes, the Court of Appeals rules that the Ohio couple who adopted the children could keep the children, thus applying a new interpretation of the ICWA. John Dodd, an attorney for the adoptive parents states that, "essentially, the court approved a new concept of law, what has now become known as the Existing Indian Family doctrine." This interpretation means that the biological parents have to have a meaningful social, cultural, or political relationship with the tribe in order for ICWA to hold any meaning. ICWA contains no such language or provision.

**27 March 1996 *Seminole Tribe of Florida v. Florida et al.*** In *Seminole Tribe of Florida v. Florida et al.*, the United States Supreme Court finds that states may not be sued by Indian nations even when the states does not negotiate gaming compacts in good faith according to the Indian Gaming Regulatory Act (IGRA). IGRA imposes upon the states an obligation to negotiate in good faith with an Indian tribe toward the formation of a compact and authorizes a tribe to bring suit in federal court against a state for failure to negotiate a compact. The Court holds that IGRA does not supersede a state's right to sovereign immunity, which protects states from lawsuits by their citizens.

**5 July 1996 NARF Files Suit against Federal Departments.** A class action suit representing 300,000 American Indians is filed in federal court today against the Bureau of Indian Affairs, the United States Treasury, and the Department of the Interior. The suit, filed by the Native American Rights Fund (NARF), alleges that the BIA has mishandled $450 million in revenues from mineral leases on lands held in trust for Indians. This amount is later raised to $2.5 billion. The suit further alleges that no accurate records were kept of the monies collected, and that funds were illegally diverted to other projects.

**14 July 1997 Documentary Awarded Golden Apple.** Jay Rosenstein's documentary *In Whose Honor?* is named a Golden Apple Award Winner by the National Educational Media Network, the leading organization for educational videos. *In Whose Honor?* highlights Charlene Teters' efforts to eliminate the Chief Illiniwek mascot used by the University of Illinois at Urbana-Champaign.

**10 November 1997 Wauneka Dies.** Annie Dodge Wauneka, the first woman elected to the Navajo Tribal Council, dies. Wauneka was born in the Navajo Nation near Sawmill, Arizona, and received a bachelor of science degree in public health from the University of Arizona. She was active in the Navajo Tribal Council Health Committee, and hosted a biweekly radio show on KGAK in Gallup. Wauneka also served as a board member of the National Tuberculosis Association and was appointed to the Surgeon General's Advisory Board.

**1998 Campbell Introduces Legislation to Identify Sand Creek Massacre Site.** Republican Senator Ben Nighthorse Campbell introduces legislation directing the National Park Service to identify the location of the 1864 Sand Creek Massacre. The legislation is signed into law on 6 October 1998.

**5 September 1998 Skeletal Remains Found at Oil Refinery.** California state officials search for the living descendants of several prehistoric skeletal remains found at the ARCO oil refinery in Carson, California, earlier this month. Workers stumbled across the human skeletal remains while draining water from a sixty-foot by sixty-foot trench. The water caused the sides of the four-foot-deep trench to slough off, exposing the remains. A forensic expert from the Los Angeles County coroner's office determined that the remains were over 1,000 years old and appeared to belong to five humans. A spokesperson from the coroner's office said that the site appeared to be a Native American burial ground.

**3 November 1998 Proposition 5 Passes.** California voters approve Proposition 5, the Tribal Government Gaming and Economic Self-Sufficiency Act of 1998 by a margin of 62.6 percent to 37.4 percent. Approximately $96 million is spent by both sides, $58 million by California Indian tribes supporting the initiative, and $30 million by Nevada casino interests. The initiative effort for Proposition 5 was organized and conducted

Schoolchildren visit the Assistant Secretary of Interior in Washington, D.C. (Courtesy of Carol Lujan)

by an Indian political coalition named Californians for Indian Self-Reliance, which seeks to obtain a gaming compact with the state of California by means of a state-wide referendum vote, since California state officials will not provide a satisfactory agreement to the California Indian nations.

**25 February 1999 Timbisha Shoshone, Federal Agencies Agree to Park Partnership.** The Timbisha Shoshone strike an agreement with the federal agencies to serve as partners in the management of a 3.2 million-acre national park. The Timbisha Shoshone have been largely exiled from their traditional homelands in Death Valley since 1933, when Death Valley was added to the National Park System.

**June 1999 Sand Creek Massacre Site Identified.** Historians and archeologists working with the National Park Service locate the site of the 1864 Sand Creek Massacre. Over 300 artifacts, including shell fragments from artillery used to bombard the Indians, are found. Other artifacts include cooking pot fragments, tin cups, eating utensils, arrowheads, and personal items. A special resource study that includes future management plans for the site is scheduled for release in October 1999.

**6 December 1999 Court Master Blames Treasury Department for Mismanagement of Documents.** A special court master blames senior Treasury Department officials for allowing the destruction of 162 boxes of documents that could have helped resolve the claims of thousands of Native Americans who say the government has mismanaged billions of dollars in trust funds it was holding for them in trust. The destruction of these documents is the latest development in a long-running class-action lawsuit against the government filed on behalf of 300,000 Native Americans.

**11 December 1999 Class-Action Suit Concludes.** U.S. District Judge Royce C. Lamberth calls the government's century-old mismanagement of Indian trust fund money inexcusable. Judge Lamberth pledges to oversee reform of a program that will pay thousands of Native Americans as much as $2.5 billion in royalties. This action caps the largest class-action lawsuit in history against the federal government. Judge Lamberth will require quarterly progress reports from the secretary of the interior and the Bureau of Indian Affairs for as long as five years for trust fund accounting. The trust fund, which affects Native Americans in every state west of the Mississippi River, was established in the 1830s during the administration of Andrew Jackson.

**2000 NARF Files Suit against Babbitt, Rubin.** The Native American Rights Fund files a class action lawsuit against Bruce Babbitt, secretary of the interior, and Robert Rubin, U.S. treasury secretary, for mismanagement of tribal trust funds. In an audit conducted by the Arthur Andersen accounting firm, the BIA is unable to account for over $2.4 billion in Indian trust fund accounts.

**27 January 2000 Clinton Honors Commitment to Native Americans.**   President Clinton honors America's commitments to Native Americans. In his State of the Union Address, President Clinton states that "I also... [want] to make special efforts to address the areas of our nation with the highest rates of poverty— our Native American reservations and the Mississippi Delta. My budget includes. . . a billion dollars to increase economic opportunity, health care, education and law enforcement for our Native American communities."

**8 February 2000 Campbell Calls for Hate-Crime Investigation.**   Senator Ben Campbell calls on the Department of Justice to launch a hate-crimes investigation into a newspaper advertisement announcing the start of "Indian Hunting Season." The advertisement, which ran in a South Dakota newspaper, is intended to look like a real hunting season announcement. The c.e. declares open season on the Sioux reservations, sets a limit of ten kills per day, and mentions other regulations for where and in what manner Indians may be killed.

**11 February 2000 Land Returned to Northern Ute.** Utah state, federal, and tribal officials sign an agreement that will return 84,000 acres to the Northern Ute tribe as part of an agreement to clean up tons of uranium waste leaking into the Colorado River. Called the biggest federal return of Indian land in U.S. history, the land was reclaimed by the Ute in 1882 but taken again in 1916 on the eve of the U.S. entry into World War I to create a reserve supply of oil for the U.S. Navy fleet. Under the agreement to return the land, one-half of the estimated $300 million cleanup cost will be absorbed by the federal government. The Ute will pay an estimated $80 million to $100 million toward the cleanup

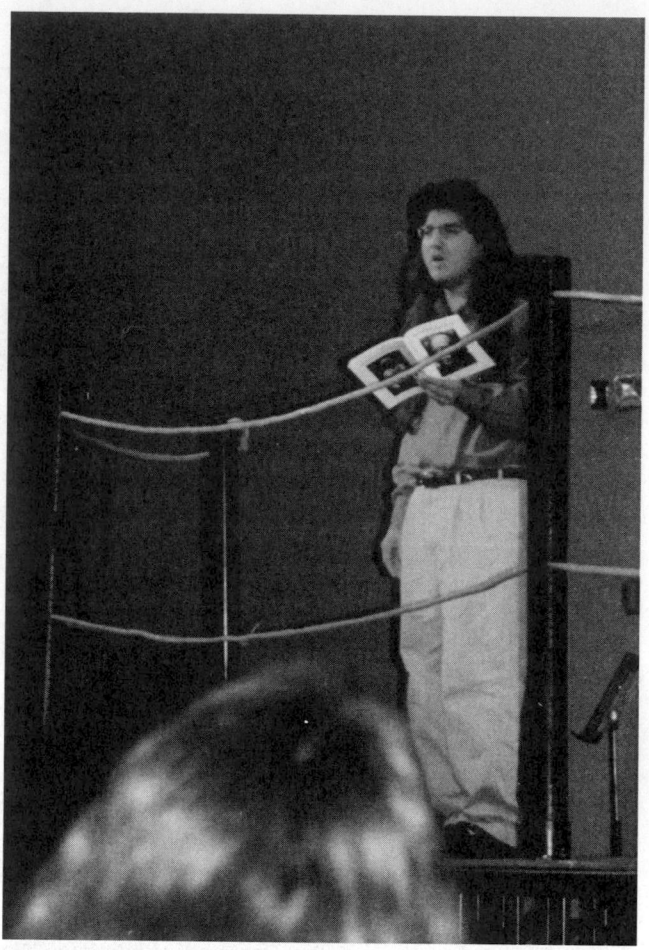

Sherman Alexie (Spokane/Coeur d'Alene) reading poetry. (Photo by Carol Lujan)

and provide added protection to the seventy-five miles of the Green River, which forms the reservation's western boundary.

**25 February 2000 Clinton Calls for Passage of Native American Initiative.**   President Clinton calls for passage of his historic Fiscal Year 2001 Native American Initiative. The president is joined by tribal and congressional leaders, who call for passage of his $9.4 billion Native American fiscal year 2001 budget initiative, an increase in funding of $1.2 billion from the last year, the largest increase ever. President Clinton's initiative recognizes that the entire federal government has a trust responsibility for Native American tribes. The initiative provides funding across many agencies, rather than to the Department of the Interior's BIA and Department of Health and Human Services only. The initiative makes critical investments in education, health care, law enforcement, infrastructure, and economic development in Indian Country.

California Indians campaign for a state constitutional amendment to allow casino gaming on Indian reservations. The referendum was listed as "1A" on the ballot. (Photo by Victor Rocha)

Pechanga Tribal Chair Mark Macarro celebrates victory in Proposition 1A. The California voters strongly supported a state and federal agreement to support Native-owned casino gaming. (Photo by Victor Rocha)

**28 February 2000 Appeals Court Rules on Indian Crime.** A federal appeals court rules that an Indian person who commits a crime on another tribe's land and is convicted in tribal court can be prosecuted again, with a longer sentence, in federal court. The Ninth U.S. Circuit Court of Appeals said the multiple prosecutions do not violate the Constitution's ban on double jeopardy, being prosecuted twice for the same crime. The court states that an Indian tribe and the federal government are separate sovereignties and can file separate charges for the same conduct, in the same way that a defendant can be charged in both state and federal court for the same acts.

**March 2000 Proposition 1A Passes.** California voters approve Proposition 1A, which provides a state constitutional amendment allowing California Indian tribes to operate slot machines and banked card games, such as black jack. Proposition 1A was introduced as the result of an earlier gaming initiative, Proposition 5, which was approved by California voters in 1998 but struck down by the California Supreme Court in 1999.

**May 2000 BIA No Longer Wants Involvement in Recognition.** Kevin Gover, the assistant interior secretary of Indian affairs, announces that the Bureau of Indian Affairs "no longer wants to be the agency that grants federal recognition to American Indian Tribes."

The Senate Committee on Indian Affairs is considering legislation by Senator Ben Nighthorse Campbell that would create a three-person commission appointed by the president to decide which tribes should be federally recognized.

**5 June 2000 Complaint Filed Over Alleged Finance Law Violation.** A California group titled California Common Cause files a complaint alleging more than 300 campaign finance law violations by gaming interests, primarily Indian tribes. The report accuses Governor Gray Davis of failing to disclose $169,000 in 1998 contributions, including $113,000 from the Cabazon Band of Mission Indians and $50,000 from the Twenty-nine Palms Band of Missions Indians, which both operate casinos outside Palm Springs. Governor Davis calls the report "garbage," and states that "This is a typical Common Cause political stunt."

**9 June 2000 Makah Whaling Issues Reviewed.** A federal appeals court rejects the environmental assessment that allowed the Makah Indian tribe to hunt gray whales off the coast of Washington, ruling that the government's review was "slanted" in favor of allowing the Makah to hunt. Attorneys for the Makah, a small tribe in northwestern Washington State, sought to revive a long-standing whaling tradition. The federal government conducted an environmental review after it backed the Makah's petition to the International Whaling Commission to engage in subsistence whale hunting. The government concluded that the gray whales' recovery from near extinction in the early part of the century was sufficient to assure the population would not be affected by the Makah's subsistence whale hunting needs.

**July 2000 BIA Proposes Changes to Indian Blood Certificate.** The Bureau of Indian Affairs publishes a notice in the Federal Register, proposing rules to establish the documentation requirements and standards for filing, processing, and issuing a Certificate of Degree of Indian Blood (CDIB). The proposed rule sets forth the policies and standards that will allow the bureau to issue, amend, or invalidate CDIBs. The Advocates for American Indian Children say that a preliminary analysis of the proposed rules indicate that the bureau will limit access to BIA programs and services by degree of Indian blood.

**8 July 2000 Court Sides with Alabama-Coushatta Tribe.** A federal court rules that U.S. settlers wrongfully took a 2.8 million-acre tract of Texas forest from the Alabama and Coushatta Indians, possibly entitling the tribe to millions of dollars in reimbursement. On June 19, a three-judge panel of the U.S. Claims Court sided with the 400 members of the Alabama-Coushatta tribe, which began the land rights fight in 1967, and ruled that the tribe has title to land in nine Texas counties, stretching from the Louisiana border to just north of Houston. Congress must ultimately approve any settlement, but tribal leaders hope that the Justice Department will resolve the issue quickly.

**13 July 2000 Democrats Criticize Republicans for Anti-Sovereignty Measures.** Democratic National Committee National Chair Joe Andrew criticizes the Washington State Republican party for passing a resolution calling for the abolition of tribal governments. "Trying to dissolve tribal sovereignty is an insult to Native Americans across the nation," Andrew says. "I call upon Governor George W. Bush and the Republican National Committees to publicly denounce these unjust and racist actions by the Washington State Republican Party." Tribal leaders call the GOP resolution "outrageous and an affront to their rights under treaties

signed by Congress." Ron Allen, chairman of the Jamestown Klallam Tribe states that "It's absolutely the reverse of what Republican principles stand for—to protect all rights and to uphold the integrity and honor of this nation and of all the commitments it makes."

**August 2000 Ishi's Brain Returned.** A delegation of Indians from the Pit River tribe of California travel to Washington, D.C. to reclaim the brain of Ishi, presumed to be the last of the Yahi Indians. The preserved brain was found in a Smithsonian Institution warehouse in February 1999. Ishi came to the attention of the American public when he came out of the California mountain country in 1911. Anthropologist Alfred Kroeber took Ishi to the University of California, Berkeley, where he lived and worked at the Phoebe Hearst Museum. Thousands of tourists visited the museum and Ishi became an internationally recognized symbol of the genocide of California Indian people. Ishi died in 1916. His body was cremated against his wishes and his brain was removed and sent to the Smithsonian Institution to join the remains of 18,000 other anonymous Native American people. The Pit River tribal members are descendants of the Yana, the parent tribe of the Yahi. Ishi's brain will be buried in an undisclosed site in the foothills of Mt. Lassen.

**3 August 2000 Bush Threatens Tribal Sovereignty.** Texas governor George W. Bush states during his acceptance speech of the Republican presidential candidacy that "Now is the time, not to defend outdated treaties but to defend the American people." Taken in light of Bush's 1999 statement when he said Indian affairs were best left to the individual states, Bush's statement is interpreted by many to mean that he will, as president, terminate all Indian treaties and suspend the U.S. Justice Department's role in resolving Indian land claims. Bush's pledge is frightening to Indians because it comes on the heels of a motion by the Washington State Republican Party to supplant Native governments, using force if necessary. Bush also states during a campaign stop in New York State that "Indian Tribes should be subject to state law. My view is that state law reigns supreme when it comes to the Indians, whether it be gambling or any other issue."

**7 August 2000 Washington Republicans Apologize.** The Washington State Republican Party, scrambling to undo some of the damage resulting from a recent resolution against tribal sovereignty, apologizes and offers a substitute statement that affirms Indian's rights to self-government. The new resolution is adopted by the GOP state executive board at the suggestion of party Chairman Don Benton and is the latest effort at damage control. Indian tribes, human rights groups, Democrats, and newspaper editorials denounced a resolution sponsored by John Fleming, a non-Indian, that called for the federal government to "take whatever steps necessary to terminate all such nonrepublican forms of government on Indian reservations."

**8 August 2000 California Gaming Tribes Support Non-Gaming Tribes.**  An accountant representing California Indian tribes that operate gaming casinos delivers a check for $34.5 million to California Attorney General Bill Lockyer under an agreement negotiated between California Indian tribes and Governor Gray Davis in 1999. Voters in a March 2000 election ratified the compact. Tribal officials state that part of the $34 million is the first payment by casino operators into a fund to benefit California tribes that have no gaming operations.

**15 August 2000 Indian Delegates Gather at Formal Political Caucus.**  For the first time in the history of the Democratic Party, American Indian delegates gather at a formal political caucus to plan their political future.

**8 September 2000 Cabazon, Firestone Make Deal.** The Cabazon Band of Mission Indians of California reaches a deal with the Bridgestone/Firestone tire company to accept almost 5,000 defective Firestone tires a day for the next year from dealers across the Southwest. Bridgestone/Firestone voluntarily recalled 6.5 millions tires in the United States and the number is estimated to grow to 275 million. The tribes will grind the tires into crumbs at a plant near Mecca, east of Palm Springs, California. The crumbs will be turned into asphalt playground surfaces and floor mats.

**9 September 2000 Gover Apologizes for BIA Injustices.**  Kevin Gover, Pawnee, assistant secretary of the interior, apologizes for the Bureau of Indian Affair's relocations and attempts to wipe out Native languages and cultures. Gover states that he is apologizing on behalf of the BIA, not the federal government as a whole. In his remarks Gover states that the federal Bureau of Indian Affairs apologized for the agency's "legacy of racism and inhumanity" that included massacres, forced relocations of tribes, and attempts to wipe out Indian languages and cultures. Gover said that "never again will we attack your religions, your languages, your rituals or any of your tribal ways…. Never again will we seize your children nor teach them to be ashamed of who they are. Never again."

Assistant Secretary of the Interior Kevin Gover. (Photo by Carol Lujan)

**15 September 2000 Resolution 185.**  The California Legislature unanimously passes a resolution that points to a genuine concern for American Indian people. The legislature passes Concurrent Resolution 185, written by Assemblyman Jim Battin, a summary of which states that "this measure will reaffirm state recognition of the sovereign status of federally recognized Indian tribes as separate and independent political communities within the United States, encourages all state agencies, when engaging in activities or developing policies affecting Native American tribal rights or trust resources, to do so in a knowledgeable, sensitive manner that is respectful of tribal sovereignty, and, in recognizing their tribal sovereignty, encourages all state agencies to continue to reevaluate and improve the implementation of laws affecting Native American tribal rights"

**October 2000 National Tribal Justice Resource Center Established.**  The National Tribal Justice Resource Center, a project of the National American Indian Court Judges Association (NAICJA) is established. The Center which is established with start-up

Mary Ann Andreas, chairwoman of the Morongo Band of Mission Indians, presents to the California lieutenant governor 59 handmade arrows, encased in a lucite box, representing the 59 tribal-state compacts signed by California tribes. (Photo by Victor Rocha)

funding from the U.S. Department of Justice's Bureau of Justice Assistance is setting up its offices at the Native American Rights Fund (NARF) at its National Indian Law Library in Boulder, Colorado.

**1 October 2000 Babbitt Announces Plans to Repatriate Kennewick Man.** Secretary of the Interior Department Bruce Babbitt announces that the department plans to repatriate the Kennewick Man to five claimant Indian tribes in the Pacific Northwest. Babbitt's decision is consistent with the Native American Graves Protection and Repatriation Act, passed in 1990 that allows for repatriation of human remains once a cultural affiliation is determined. Scientists from the Smithsonian Institution fought against the return of the human remains "without the prospect of learning what he [Kennewick Man] has to tell us." Displaying an ongoing insensitivity toward Native American people the scientist said "that there was a wealth of information locked inside those bones."

**23 October 2000 Campbell Introduces Bill Honoring Natives.** Senator Ben Nighthorse Campbell introduces a bill in Congress to establish a memorial honoring Native Americans killed by the U.S. Army in the 1864 Sand Creek Massacre. The legislation passed by voice vote in the House today and by the Senate earlier. President Clinton has indicated that he will sign the bill. Senator Campbell's ancestors were among the 164 Cheyenne and Arapaho Indians who died on 29 November 1864 when troops under the command of Colonel John Chivington slaughtered Cheyenne and Arapaho women, children, and elderly men. Captain Silas Soule, who rode with Colonel Chivington, later wrote "It was hard to see little children on their knees have their brains beat out by men professing to be civilized."

**December 2000 California Tribe Receives Federal Recognition.** The Coast Miwok of Northern California receive federal recognition. The 401-member tribe once numbered from 3,000 to 5,000 people, but were

Gila Crossing students. (Photo by Carol Lujan)

decimated by disease, slavery, and murder after European contact. They are one of many California tribes trying to gain federal recognition.

*Troy Johnson*
*California State University*
*Long Beach, California*
*Elton Naswood*
*Tribal Law and Policy Institute*

## ◆ CHRONOLOGY OF CANADIAN NATIVE HISTORY, 1500 TO 2000

Native history has unfolded differently in Canada and the United States. Except for the Native groups living in the St. Lawrence River and Great Lakes area, and along the Pacific Coast, Canadian Native groups were smaller and more decentralized than many U.S. Indian nations. In terms of Native-newcomer relations, Canada today roughly corresponds to the portion of North America where the fur trade dominated the economy for extended periods. Thus Natives in Canada

have a significant history of mutually beneficial economic relations with non-Native newcomers. Furthermore, Canadian Natives did not experience the protracted open conflict with the Canadian government that has marred the experiences of many U.S. Indian nations. In fact, many Native groups in Canada were allied with European powers. By 1867, however, governments in Canada had begun to exert considerable influence over Native life. Even when designed to protect Native interests, outside laws had the effect of undermining Native sovereignty. Between 1880 and 1920 government policy became increasingly coercive. After the 1920s the government became less coercive, but powerful law courts and political interests generally ruled against Canadian Native land claims and Native assertions of self-government. Nevertheless, the latter half of the twentieth century has seen a major revival among Canadian Natives. Arguably the most important turning point was the response of Natives to the Canadian government's White Paper in 1969. The 1970s saw the formation of many Native organizations and direct attempts by Canadian Natives to gain acceptance of Native rights to land and recognition of rights to

Native self-government. Native political influence may have peaked in the 1980s when Native organizations exerted considerable influence in the drafting of Canada's Constitution (1982) which entrenched various aboriginal rights. Since then, the influence of Native organizations has declined as government funding for these organizations dwindled, and as public pressure to include Natives in national discussions waned. However, in 1996, the report of the Royal Commission on Aboriginal People, the largest royal commission in Canadian history, recommended a wholesale change in the way the Canadian government interacts with Native communities. Still, the government has been reluctant to accept many of the recommendations. On the other hand, Native claimants celebrated major victories in the courts and in land claims. Most noteworthy were the Supreme Court's decisions in the *Delgamuukw* case in 1997 and the *Marshall* case in 1999. Also noteworthy was the establishment of the territory of Nunavut in 1999, which had been part of an Inuit land claim submitted in the 1970s, and the implementation of the Nisga'a agreement in 2000, which finally settled a land claim dating to the nineteenth century. Although Canadian Native history has taken some very different turns than U.S. Native history, Natives in both countries face many of the same challenges today. The similarities and differences between the two nations invite comparison.

**1503.** Various indigenous peoples along the east coast of Canada begin desultory trade with groups of European fishermen and whalers. The Natives trade furs for European manufactures.

**1535–36.** Villagers from the Iroquois village of Stadacona (Quebec City) trade with French explorer Jacques Cartier, but are annoyed when his party sails upriver to trade at Hochelaga (Montreal). Stadaconans claim the right to control traffic traveling up the St. Lawrence River.

**1541–43.** Hostility on the part of the villagers at Stadacona prevents the success of a French settlement nearby. The Iroquois resent the newcomers because they make little attempt to establish friendly relations.

**1543–88.** Instead of establishing permanent settlements, Europeans embark for important Indian coastal trade centers each year. The Montagnais, nomadic hunter-gatherers of the area north of the St. Lawrence River and other Indian traders, greatly improve their returns by trading only when at least two competing ships are on hand.

**1576–78.** A party of Inuit (aboriginal inhabitants of the Arctic) has a hostile encounter with English mariner Martin Frobisher on Baffin Island in the northeastern Arctic. Frobisher kidnaps one Inuk man, who causes a stir in London.

**1588.** King Henry III of France grants a fur trade monopoly to nephews of Jacques Cartier. During the following decades monopolies are granted and revoked as monopoly holders fail to force interlopers to honor the monopoly. Indians find increased demand for *castor gras* (greasy beaver), beaver skins that have shed their guard hairs and absorbed perspiration and body oils after being used as clothing for a season or two. Europeans seek *castor gras* to make felt.

**1604–1607.** French traders establish Port Royal, a year-round trading base on the Bay of Fundy, a large bay separating today's provinces of Nova Scotia and New Brunswick. Micmac chief Membertou concludes an agreement with the French that gives the Micmac access to European weapons in exchange for food and furs. The Micmac are the Native inhabitants of most of Acadia, France's possessions southeast of the St. Lawrence River. Port Royal is abandoned in 1607 because of its poor location.

**1608.** Samuel de Champlain establishes Quebec City (New France) as the new French trading base. Since 1544 the agricultural, Iroquoian inhabitants have been displaced by nomadic Algonkian-speaking peoples. The Algonkian language family is the largest in Canada. Algonkian languages are spoken by many Indian groups from the Atlantic Ocean to the Rocky Mountains. Iroquoian languages dominate only in the southern Great Lakes-St. Lawrence River region.

**1609.** A group of Huron led by Chief Ochasteguin and Algonquin led by Chief Iroquet visit Quebec to negotiate a trade alliance. The Huron are Iroquoian, agricultural peoples of the area just east of Lake Huron. The Algonquin are hunter-gatherers of the regions north of the St. Lawrence River. They induce Champlain to join them on a raid against the Iroquois Five Nations Confederacy (Cayuga, Mohawk, Oneida, Onondaga, and Seneca), located southeast of Quebec. The battle initiates almost two centuries of enmity between the Five Nations and the French. Following Indian customs, French and Indians intermarry and Indians accept French emissaries, including missionaries. Some of these emissaries provide valuable information to the French about the area around the Great Lakes.

**1610.** A lone Cree man trades with an English party led by Henry Hudson on the shores of Hudson Bay. The

In order to cement a trade alliance, Champlain joined a Huron and Algonquin raid on the Iroquois in 1609. This was the first and most successful of several raids that Champlain joined. (Courtesy of the National Library of Canada)

Cree are Algonkian-speaking Indians who today live in areas from Quebec to Alberta.

**1615–29.** Indian groups accept Roman Catholic Récollet missionaries as emissaries from their French trading partners. They also send some of their children to be educated by the missionaries. In 1615 the Ottawa, Algonkian hunters living east of Lake Huron's Georgian Bay, conduct Champlain as far as Lake Huron.

**1615–49.** Huron villagers host Champlain at their villages southeast of Lake Huron to conclude a trade and military alliance with the French. As the northernmost agriculturalists in the area, the Huron are central to a web of trade relations between agriculturalists and hunting and gathering societies to the north and west. Thus the Huron are able to distribute European goods widely to other Native groups to the north and west as far away as Hudson Bay and Lake Michigan. (By essentially demanding payment for delivery of goods, Indian intermediaries acquire European goods without having

to trap themselves.) In order to protect their intermediary role, the Huron prevent direct trade between the French and neighboring Indians. Increased wealth allows for increasingly elaborate celebrations of such Huron rituals as the Feast of the Dead, an important Huron burial ceremony held every ten to fifteen years.

**1623.** The French government grants its first *seigneury* (feudal land grant) in New France. Indians do not acknowledge French sovereignty to any land, just as the French do not recognize aboriginal rights to the land. Thus Indians and the French do not negotiate any land cession treaties (treaties in which one party surrenders its land rights to another).

**1635.** Jesuits establish residential schools for Indians in New France. The Jesuits arrived in New France in 1632 to begin an intensive missionary effort among the Huron and Algonquin. They replaced the Récollets.

**1635–40.** Smallpox reduces the Huron population from about twenty thousand to ten thousand.

**1639.** The Jesuits establish a mission settlement at Sainte-Marie-among-the-Huron (Midland, Ontario).

**1641.** The French begin selling guns to Huron who profess to be Christian. The Iroquois begin unlimited warfare on the French.

**1649–50.** In a concerted effort to seize the middleman role in the French fur trade, the Iroquois crush the Huron. Some Huron are integrated into the Five Nations and other peoples, some relocate to Lorette near Quebec City, and some scatter throughout the Great Lakes region where they become known as Wyandotte. The Ottawa assume the main middleman role. *Coureurs de bois* (traveling French fur traders who spend most of their time among the Indians) also assume an important role in trading with interior Indians. This increases Indian contact and intermarriage with the French.

**1666–67.** With the two thousand colonists of New France threatened by continual Iroquois attack, French troops attack Iroquois villages. The expedition kills few Indians but destroys Iroquois villages and crops. As a result, the Iroquois and French conclude a truce that lasts ten years.

**1667.** Iroquois converts move to La Prairie (Caughnawaga) near Montreal. They become allies of the French. Missionaries seek to isolate Indian settlements because they believe Europeans are a corrupting influence on the Indians.

**1668.** Three hundred Cree trade with men on a British ship at the mouth of the Rupert River along the coast of James Bay, a large bay in Hudson Bay. French fur traders Pierre Esprit Radisson and Médard Chouart des Grosseliers realized the value of the Hudson Bay as a fur-trading base after a foray to the James Bay hinterland earlier in the decade.

**1670.** Cree and Ojibwa (also referred to as Ojibway and Chippewa), Algonkian hunters centered along the eastern and northern shores of Lake Superior, begin traveling to the Hudson's Bay Company (HBC) posts at mouths of the Rupert, Moose, and Albany rivers on James Bay in present-day northern Quebec and Ontario. The HBC sends no missionaries to the Indians.

**1671–73.** The French establish forts on the Great Lakes as far northwest as Sault Ste. Marie, at the *sault* (falls) on the St. Marys River, which joins Lakes Superior and Huron, for the purpose of defense, trade, missions, and diplomacy. Competition with the Hudson's Bay Company induces the French to dramatically increase their trade in firearms. Ojibwa ceremonial life

becomes more elaborate as they become important traders around the Sault.

**1682–1774.** The Hudson's Bay Company establishes York Factory at the mouth of the Nelson and Hayes rivers on the western shores of Hudson Bay in present-day Manitoba. The rivers drain a vast territory as far west as the Rocky Mountains. Cree and Assiniboine become middlemen, trading European goods with Plains Indians as far west and south as the Rocky Mountains and the Missouri River Basin before 1750. Access to European goods, particularly weaponry, increases the wealth and power of Cree and Assiniboine bands. The Assiniboine are Siouan-speaking, a group that inhabited areas south and southeast of Lake Winnipeg (in today's Manitoba) at that time.

**1700–1750.** The Shoshoni in today's southwestern Alberta become the first Indians residing in present-day Canada to acquire horses. Horses spread to most Plains Indians by 1750, bringing significant changes in social and economic relations, balances of power, and diplomacy.

**1701.** The Iroquois and French conclude a peace agreement, ending a century of hostilities. Iroquois power and population has been significantly reduced by years of warfare. The Mississauga (Ojibwa) have expanded from the north to occupy most of the former Huron lands north of the Great Lakes.

**1713.** By the Treaty of Utrecht, France cedes Acadia (renamed Nova Scotia) to England and relinquishes claims to Newfoundland and Hudson Bay. France also recognizes the Iroquois as English subjects. The Micmac (Mi'kmaq) and the Maliseet (Malecite), who occupy lands west of the St. John River (in today's New Brunswick), begin opposing the English, and the Iroquois continue to see themselves as subject to no foreign power.

**1713–53.** French traders establish fur-trade posts as far west as Lake Winnipeg and the Saskatchewan River. Some of the Ojibwa, originally centered near Sault Ste. Marie, just east of Lake Superior, spread as far west as the prairies.

**1717.** The Hudson's Bay Company establishes Fort Prince of Wales (Churchill) on the western shores of Hudson Bay (in present-day Manitoba), allowing bands of Chipewyan to establish themselves as middlemen. The Chipewyan are Athapaskan-speaking hunter-gatherers centered in the region of today's northern Manitoba and Saskatchewan and southern Northwest Territories. They guard their role by preventing

Yellowknife and Dogrib, both Athapaskan hunters of the Great Bear Lake and Great Slave Lake area (in today's Northwest Territories) from reaching the post. Secure access to European goods allows them to expand against other Indians and Inuit, leading to acrimonious relations between the Chipewyan and these other Indians. Most Indians in the area that will become northwestern Canada speak an Athapaskan language.

**1729.**   Four hundred Iroquois of Caughnawaga settle at a mission at Lake of Two Mountains (Oka), just west of Montreal.

**1752.**   The Subenacadie band of Micmac sign the Halifax Treaty with the British, easing hostility between the Micmac and the British in Nova Scotia. The British deny that the Indians hold any rights to land in Nova Scotia.

**1755.**   Some Christian Iroquois settle at St. Regis (Akwesasne). Today Akwesasne straddles the Ontario-Quebec-New York State borders near Montreal.

**1760.**   New France falls to the British. The British agree to respect land granted to Indians by the French, but anger Indians by ending the French practice of giving gifts to Indians to cement alliances.

**1763–66.**   Pontiac, a chief of the Ottawa tribe, leads Indian resistance to the British. In 1763 Indian forces capture all British forts west of Niagara Falls except Fort Detroit and Fort Pitt (Pittsburgh). Detroit is besieged for five months.

**7 October 1763.**   The British Royal Proclamation of 1763 recognizes the right of North American Indians to possess all land in British territories outside established colonies (Hudson's Bay Company land is exempt), but claims underlying title for the king. The Crown claims the exclusive right to negotiate land surrender and peace treaties with the Indians and prohibits settlement in areas not covered by land cession treaties. The Indians see the proclamation as a major recognition of their rights. (The proclamation has since been enshrined in Canada's 1982 Constitution.)

**1767.**   Newly surveyed land in Prince Edward Island in the Gulf of St. Lawrence is granted to British proprietors. No land is set aside for indigenous peoples.

**1774.**   The Hudson's Bay Company establishes Cumberland House on the Saskatchewan River as its first inland trading post after learning that Cree and Assiniboine are trading many of their highest quality furs to Canadian traders who have infiltrated the area around Lake Winnipeg (in today's Manitoba).

**1774–1800.**   The Hudson's Bay Company and Canadian traders establish competing fur-trade posts throughout the northern prairies, dramatically reducing the cost of European goods to Plains Indians, who can now trade directly with Euro-Canadians. These Indians are able to displace Indian groups with poor access to trading posts. Former Cree and Assiniboine middlemen assume roles as Home Guard Indians and provisioners at North West Company and HBC posts. Intermarriage between Indians and fur traders produces a sizable mixed-blood population.

**1774.**   Nootka (Nuu-chah-nulth), coastal Indians of Vancouver Island, trade with Spanish explorer Juan Perez. West Coast Indians have already begun trading with Russians. The Indians of the Northwest Coast of North America live in substantial villages and rely heavily on abundant supplies of salmon. Coastal Indians' highly structured, hierarchical societies are unique among Native groups of northern North America.

**1775–83.**   Britain's Indian allies take a prominent role in the American War of Independence. They believe the British best represent their interests.

**1779–81.**   A smallpox epidemic originating in Mexico City spreads as far north as the Chipewyan, devastating Native societies along the way. Smallpox kills up to one-half of the Plains Indians and up to nine-tenths of the Chipewyan.

**1779–1821.**   The North West Company, operating from Montreal, becomes the dominant force in the fur trade and in exploration of the northwest, allowing many northern Indian groups to trade directly with Euro-Canadian traders. This alters interethnic relations in the region. Natives on the prairies supply large amounts of pemmican, a preserved meat usually produced from buffalo and used to feed traders in the north.

**1783.**   By the Treaty of Versailles, the British cede land south of the Great Lakes to the United States, angering their Indian allies who still control the area.

**1784.**   The British negotiate land purchases from Mississauga (Ojibwa) Indians and grant the land to loyalist Indians who had found their land turned over to the United States. Iroquois Captain Joseph Brant (Thyendanega) and more than 1,550 Iroquois are given a tract of land on the Grand River (Six Nations Reserve near Brantford, Ontario), and Captain John Deseronto's

Mohawk are given land near the Bay of Quinte on the north shore of Lake Ontario.

**1784.** New Brunswick is formed as a separate province as loyalists settle there. Maliseet and Micmac begin to suffer encroachment on their lands.

**1785.** The Indians of the West Coast begin regular trade with shipborne traders, increasing their returns by trading only when competing ships are at hand. Coastal middlemen trade with Indians well inland. Sea otter pelts and blankets become trade staples, with blankets forming a kind of currency.

**1794.** The Jay Treaty establishes the border between the United States and British North America beyond the Great Lakes. Britain agrees to withdraw troops and traders from land ceded to the United States in 1783. The British had kept troops posted there to appease

The eighteenth-century engraving, *Indians trading furs,* 1785, demonstrates the importance of the fur trade between Natives and Euro-Canadians. (C. W. Jefferys. Courtesy of the National Archives of Canada)

their Indian allies in the region. Indians are guaranteed unhindered travel across the border.

**1812.** The Hudson's Bay Company establishes the Red River Colony (Selkirk Settlement) near today's Winnipeg. Chief Peguis's band of Saulteaux (Ojibwa) provides important help to the settlers in their first difficult years.

**1812–14.** Tecumseh (Shawnee) leads Britain's Indian allies in their important role in the War of 1812. Many Indian groups ally with Britain in the hope that the British will able to create a buffer state for them.

**1814.** The Treaty of Ghent, ending the War of 1812, ends Indian hopes of a buffer state.

**1816.** At the Battle of Seven Oaks (Red River), twenty-one Red River settlers and one Métis die in a skirmish. The battle fosters an increased sense of nationhood among the Métis. The Métis, of mixed Indian-European descent, begin to develop a unique society and culture that will be based on trading between their Indian and European kin, small-scale farming, and buffalo hunting.

**1818.** The British government begins its practice of acquiring Indian land in exchange for annuities rather than lump-sum payments.

**1820.** John West of the Anglican Church Missionary Society (CMS) arrives to serve the English speaking, non-Catholic population at the Red River Colony. The CMS and the Roman Catholic Oblates of Mary Immaculate become the major missionary groups in the Northwest.

**1821.** The North West Company and the Hudson's Bay Company merge, retaining the name of the HBC. The HBC reduces employment and opportunities for Indians and mixed-blood inhabitants throughout the northwest. It also reduces trade in alcohol. Many mixed-blood move to the Red River settlement where a large Métis community develops.

**1827.** With the establishment of Fort Langley on the Fraser River (in the southwestern corner of today's British Columbia), land-based trade in the region begins. The region is the home of Coast Salish, who live in villages and depend heavily on salmon.

**1829.** Shanawdithit, the last Beothuk, dies. The reclusive Beothuk, the Native inhabitants of Newfoundland, gradually disappeared as a result of disease,

Interior of an Inuit house. (Public domain)

hostilities with Indian and non-Indian enemies, and the unforgiving environment of the island.

**1830.** Responsibility for Indian affairs in Upper Canada is transferred from military to civilian administrators, reflecting the waning importance of Indians as military allies and a growing emphasis on assimilation of Indians into non-Indian society. The government also adopts a policy of establishing reserves for Indians whenever they sign land surrenders.

**1835–40.** Smallpox kills up to one-third of some British Columbia coastal Indians.

**1836.** A plan to relocate Upper Canada's Indians to the Manitoulin Islands (in Lake Huron) is abandoned after humanitarian groups committed to the assimilation of Indians oppose the plan.

**1837–38.** Smallpox kills up to three-fourths of the Plains Indians. Hudson's Bay Company traders vaccinate the Cree, preventing the spread of the disease to the Cree and their northern neighbors.

**1840s.** Roman Catholic missionaries (Oblates of Mary Immaculate) arrive in British Columbia.

**1841.** Methodist missionary James Evans prints a hymnal using the Cree syllabics that he devised. The written Cree language, adapted to Athapaskan and Inuit languages, stimulates the growth of literacy among northern Natives.

**1842.** The first significant attempt to establish reserves for Indians in Nova Scotia begins.

**1844.** The New Brunswick government passes legislation restricting Indian reserves to twenty hectares per family.

**1844.** The Bagot Commission Report on Indian Affairs in the Province of Canada (present-day Ontario and Quebec) recommends an Indian affairs policy with the aim of the complete assimilation of Indians into Canadian society. The Bagot Commission was chosen in 1842 to make recommendations relating to Indian policy.

**1850.** In a law designed to protect Indian lands in Lower Canada, the government provides the first legal definition of an Indian.

**1850.** Ojibwa bands sign the Robinson Treaties covering land north of Lake Superior. These treaties, covering twice as much land as all earlier treaties in Upper Canada combined, are the first treaties signed to clear the way for mineral exploration rather than settlement.

**1851.** Coast Salish Indians of Vancouver Island and James Douglas, governor of the Hudson's Bay Company colony on Vancouver Island, conclude the first of fourteen land cession treaties covering small areas of the island.

**1857.** The government of the Province of Canada passes the Gradual Civilization Act, which creates a process by which Indians are expected to seek "enfranchisement," the acceptance of citizenship and renunciation of any legal distinction as an Indian. Adult male Indians seeking enfranchisement for themselves and their families will need to demonstrate that they are educated, debt free, capable of managing their own affairs, and of "good moral character." Enfranchised individuals will be granted their share of band funds and ownership of twenty hectares of reserve land and will lose their Indian status. In order to acquaint unenfranchised Indians with the Canadian political system, the act encourages the formation of elected band councils to replace traditional leaders by offering such councils limited powers over reserve affairs.

**1858.** Thousands of gold seekers come to the lower Fraser River Valley (in present-day British Columbia) and clash with resident Salish Indians.

**1860.** The Imperial government transfers control of Indian affairs to the Province of Canada.

**1862.** William Duncan of the Anglican's Church Missionary Society establishes an isolated missionary settlement for Tsimshian Indians at Metlakatla, near Port Simpson, British Columbia. Tsimshian are coastal Indians of the Skeena River Region of British Columbia's north coast. In British Columbia, Anglicans and Roman Catholics focus their efforts in separate regions. As a result, entire Indian communities there become either overwhelmingly Catholic or Protestant.

**1862.** Indians of the interior of British Columbia clash with thousands of gold seekers rushing to the Caribou region. Smallpox decimates Indians in the interior and coast of British Columbia.

**1864.** James Douglas retires as governor of Vancouver Island. Joseph Trutch, the new chief commissioner of lands and works in the colony, adopts a policy of refusing to negotiate land surrender agreements with Indians.

**1 July 1867.** The British North America Act, recognizing Canadian Confederation, grants legislative responsibility for Indian affairs to the new federal government, but gives control of land and natural resources to the provincial governments, thus giving both levels of government an interest in future land-claims negotiations. Land cession treaties have been negotiated only in Ontario, although reserves have been granted in the other provinces.

**1868.** The Canadian government's first Indian legislation adopts the pre-Confederation Indian policy of the Province of Canada.

**1869.** The Gradual Enfranchisement Act lays out Canada's Indian policy. Responding to Indian resistance to the establishment of elected band councils, agents are given power to depose traditional leaders for "dishonesty, intemperance and immorality," and to impose elected band councils. This act also stipulates that Indian women and their children will lose their Indian status when they marry non-Indians. It also introduces "location tickets," a means by which provisional individual title to reserve lands can be given to those seeking enfranchisement.

**1869–70.** Smallpox decimates Natives on the northern plains.

**1869–74.** After the whiskey trade is repressed in Montana, traders establish posts in the British possessions, bringing serious social problems to the Blackfoot (Blackfeet). The Blackfoot are composed of the Siksika (Blackfoot), Blood, and Peigan (Piegan), Plains Indians who inhabit the southwestern plains of Canada and the northwestern plains of the United States.

**1870.** Canada acquires Hudson's Bay Company lands from the British government with the provision that it will negotiate land cession treaties with the Indians. Most of the area becomes the North-West Territories, administered by the federal government. As a result of negotiations with a provisional government established by Métis leader Louis Riel, a small area becomes the province of Manitoba. The federal government recognizes Métis land title in the province.

**1871.** British Columbia (BC) enters the Confederation. It retains control of land and natural resources, but agrees to transfer land to the federal government for use as Indian reserves. The Canadian government is poorly informed about BC Indian policy.

**1871.** The first of eleven numbered treaties covering former Hudson's Bay Company lands is signed. Treaty 1, covering Manitoba (including the area of the Selkirk treaty of 1817) and areas of the Northwest Territories (today's southern Manitoba), is signed by the Saulteaux (Ojibwa) and Swampy Cree. Treaty 2, covering areas of the Northwest Territories (today's central and southwest Manitoba, and southeast Saskatchewan) is signed by the Ojibwa. Both treaties promise land and farm implements and seed, but make no mention of hunting, fishing, or trapping rights.

**1873.** The province of Prince Edward Island enters the Confederation having signed no land cession treaties with Indian groups. Responsibility for Indian affairs in the province is handed over to the federal government.

**1873.** Ten Americans and Canadians kill up to thirty Assiniboine in the Cypress Hills Massacre. The Cypress Hills are in Canada's southwestern prairies. The deaths induce the Canadian government to create a police force for the West.

**1873.** The Saulteaux sign Treaty 3 covering today's western Ontario and southeastern Manitoba. The treaty promises land and livestock, but also includes hunting, fishing, and trapping rights.

**1874.** The Plains Cree, Assiniboine, and Saulteaux tribes sign Treaty 4, covering areas of the Northwest Territories (now southern Saskatchewan).

**1874.** The North-West Mounted Police are sent to the Canadian prairies to stop the whisky trade, prevent such violence as the Cypress Hills Massacre (1873), and prepare the West for peaceful settlement. Not powerful enough to control the Indians by force, the police adopt a conciliatory policy toward the Indians.

**1875.** The Saulteaux and Swampy Cree sign Treaty 5 covering land in today's northern Manitoba and western Ontario. Treaties 1 and 2 are revised to increase land allotments.

**1876.** A new Indian Act makes elected band councils voluntary. It also gives such councils wider powers. Location tickets, reintroduced in eastern Canada, are part of a plan to lead Indians to abandon the practice of holding land in common. Location tickets give individuals rights to twenty hectares of reserve land. Indians who farm their allotment over a period of three years are to be enfranchised and receive absolute title to the land. Only one Indian was enfranchised between 1857 and 1876. The act forbids the sale of alcohol to Indians and bars non-Indians from reserves after nightfall.

**1876.** Plains Cree, Woodland Cree, and Assiniboine tribes sign Treaty 6, covering areas of the Northwest Territories (today's central Alberta and Saskatchewan). The treaty includes famine relief provisions and a "medicine chest" provision, which later becomes the basis of free health care for all Indians.

**1877.** The Blackfoot (Blackfeet), Sarcee, and Stoney (Assiniboine) sign Treaty 7, covering areas of the North-West Territories (today's southern Alberta).

**1879.** Buffalo disappear from the Canadian prairies, forcing Indian bands to follow herds into the United States or face famine. The government rejects a demand by Cree bands led by Piapot, Little Pine, and Big Bear for contiguous reserves in the Cypress Hills. Plains Indian groups gradually settle on reserves in western Canada.

**1883.** The Canadian government begins establishing residential schools for Indians in the west. Most Indians seek education for their children but resist the assimilative aims of government schools.

**1885.** Amendments to the Indian Act prohibit Indians from traveling off their reserves without a pass from an Indian Affairs agent, prohibit the reelection of deposed Indian leaders, and prohibit Sun Dances, annual midsummer Plains Indian ceremonies, and potlatches, elaborate ceremonies held among coastal Indians. Agricultural instructors are sent to Indian reserves in western Canada.

**1885.** At Batoche, North-West Territories (now in Saskatchewan), federal government forces crush a Métis uprising led by Louis Riel. After his execution for treason in November, Riel becomes a powerful symbol for the Métis.

**1885.** Members of Big Bear's Cree band kill nine people at Frog Lake and members of Cree chief Poundmaker's band raid homesteads near Duck Lake, North-West Territories (now in Saskatchewan). Big Bear, Poundmaker, and forty-two other Indians are jailed.

**1889.** In the case of *St. Catharine's Milling and Lumber Company v. The Queen* (the Indian Land Title Case), the Privy Council rules that aboriginal land rights were created by the Royal Proclamation of 1763 and can be abolished by unilateral legislative action.

## LOUIS RIEL,

### CHEF MÉTIS,

*Exécuté le 16 Novembre 1885,*

#### MARTYR POLITIQUE !

*Coupable d'avoir aimé ses compatriotes opprimés,*

Victime du fanatisme orangiste, auquel l'ont sacrifié des politiciens sans âme et sans cœur.

#### QUE LES VRAIS PATRIOTES S'EN SOUVIENNENT !!

Louis Riel's execution in 1885 vaulted him to the status of martyr for the Métis cause. He remains one of the most controversial figures in Canadian history. (Drawing by John Vereist. Courtesy of the National Archives of Canada)

**1897–99.** Thousands of gold seekers disrupt the lives of Indians in Yukon, in northwestern Canada. Yukon is created as a separate territory.

**1899.** The Cree of present-day northern Alberta; the Beaver, Athapaskan hunters of the Peace River region of today's northern Alberta; the Sekani, Athapaskan hunters of the Finlay and Parsnip River region of northeastern British Columbia; and the Chipewyan of today's northern Alberta and the North-West Territories south of Great Slave Lake, sign Treaty 8. The Indians demanded the treaty as the number of non-Indians in the area increased during the Yukon gold rush.

**1905.** The Cree and Ojibwa of northern Ontario sign Treaty 9.

**1906.** The Chipewyan and Cree of northern Ontario sign Treaty 10.

**1909.** The Indian Tribes of the Province of British Columbia, an alliance of twenty Indian nations, appeals to the British throne for help in settling their land claims.

**1911.** About this time, the Canadian Indian population reaches its nadir (under 110,000 persons).

**1912.** Quebec is granted territory as far north as Hudson Strait on the condition it will negotiate land surrender agreements with Natives.

**1912–16.** A Royal Commission on Indian Affairs in British Columbia (the McKenna-McBride Commission) meets to determine the appropriate size for each British Columbia Reserve. Its final report recommends adding land to some reserves and cutting off land (of considerably greater value) from others. The recommendations are rejected by the Allied Tribes of British Columbia.

**1914–18.** Up to four thousand Indians, approximately 35 percent of those eligible, fight for Canada in World War I.

**1915.** Opposition to the conduct of the McKenna-McBride Commission (1912–16) spurs Reverend Peter Kelly (Haida) and Andrew Paull (Squamish) to organize the Allied Tribes of British Columbia. It appeals to the federal government for help in settling Nishga and Salish land claims. British Columbia has the longest history of pan-tribal organization in Canada.

**1919–20.** Following recommendations of the McKenna-McBride Commission, the British Columbia government begins adjusting the size of reserves.

**1920.** The federal government amends the Indian Act to allow for compulsory enfranchisement. Only 250 Indians have opted for enfranchisement between 1857 and 1920. Provisions allowing for compulsory enfranchisement are repealed in 1922 but reenacted in 1933.

**1921.** The Slave, Dogrib, and Hare tribes, all Athapaskan hunters of western Northwest Territories, sign Treaty 11, covering land north and west of Great Slave Lake, Northwest Territories. The Canadian government sought the treaty after oil was discovered at Norman Wells, along the Mackenzie River in the Northwest Territories.

**1923.** Several disputed pre-confederation treaties in southern Ontario are resolved several decades after the government acknowledged that, because of missing papers, unclear agreements, or misunderstandings, the Indians had legitimate claims.

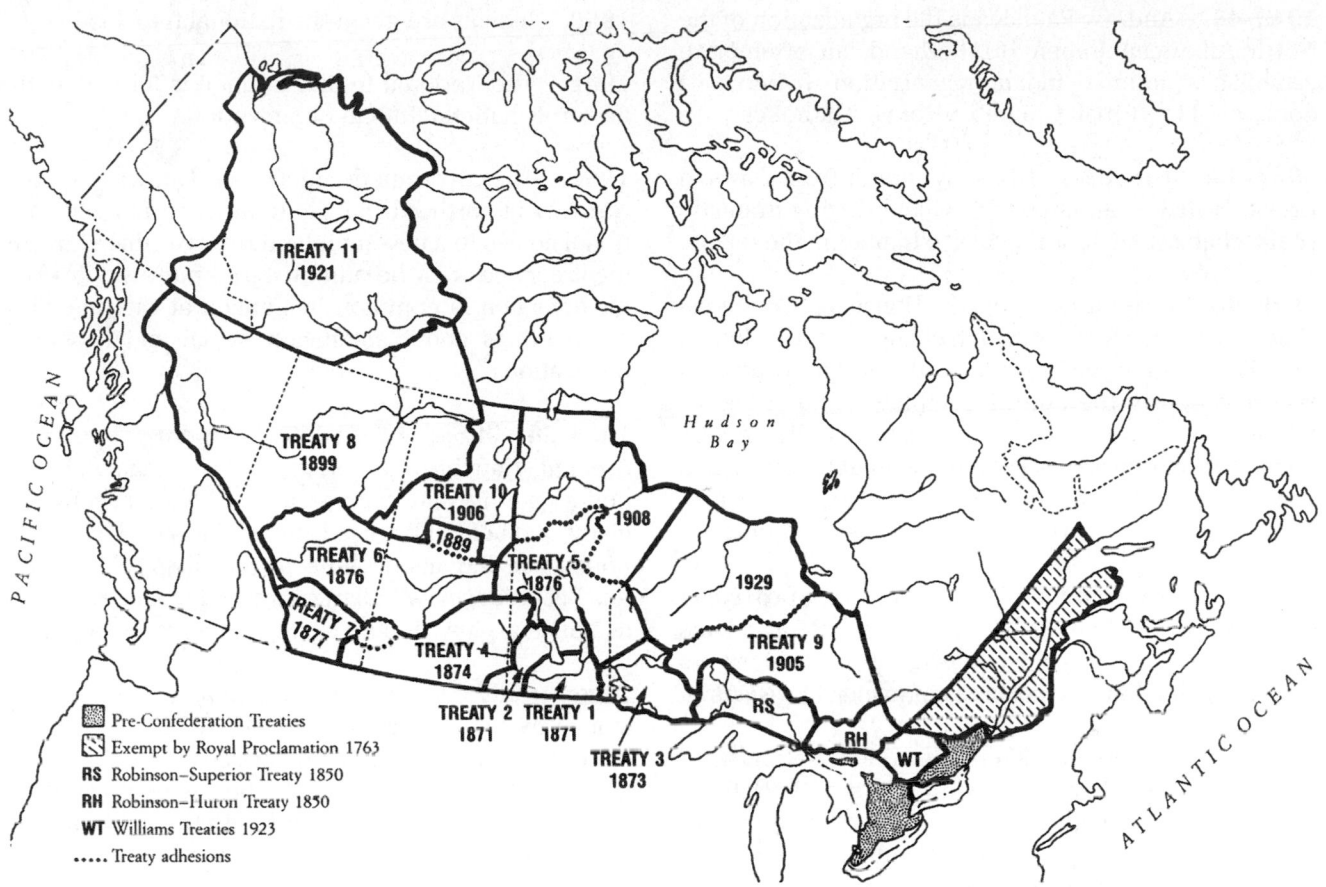

Indian treaty area in Canada. (Map by Brian McMillan from *Native Peoples and Cultures of Canada* by Alan D. McMillan, 1988, published by Douglas & McIntyre. Reprinted by permission)

**1927.** A joint Parliamentary Committee decides that British Columbia Indians have established no legal claim to land. In place of treaty money, British Columbia Indians will get $100,000 annually. The Allied Tribes of British Columbia collapses soon after the ruling.

**1927.** An amendment to the Indian Act makes it illegal to raise or donate funds for the prosecution of any Indian land claims. The law remains in force until 1951.

**1930–39.** The Great Depression brings great hardship to Natives in Canada. Plummeting fur prices affect those who live by trapping, while falling commodities prices affect those employed in resource industries. In parts of Canada, the depression halts a trend of increasing Native participation as wage earners in the Canadian economy.

**1931.** The Native Brotherhood of British Columbia is formed by Haida Alfred Adams.

**1938.** Alberta passes the Métis Population Betterment Act, establishing eight Métis settlements in the province.

**1939.** The Supreme Court of Canada rules that Inuit (Eskimo) are to be legally regarded as Indians. This makes them the responsibility of the federal government.

**1939–45.** Up to six thousand Indians volunteer for service in World War II. Their status as non-citizens makes them ineligible for conscription or for certain veterans' benefits.

**1941.** A census shows that the Indian population is growing steadily. Indian populations stopped their decline between 1911 and 1921.

**1942.** The Pacific Coast Native Fisherman's Association merges with the Native Brotherhood of British Columbia (NBBC), which consists of Protestant British Columbia Indians.

**1942–43.** Andrew Paull leads the organization of the North American Indian Brotherhood, an attempt to establish a national Indian organization. It becomes dominated by British Columbia Roman Catholics.

**1942–43.** The Alaska Highway is built from Dawson Creek, British Columbia, to Alaska, bringing dramatic social change and new diseases to Indians in the region.

**1946–48.** A Joint Senate and House of Commons Committee meets to consider changes to the Indian Act. This committee consults with Indian groups. Its report supports the aim of complete assimilation of Indian peoples but recommends that the Indian Act be revised to eliminate its coercive elements and that a commission be established to settle Indian land claims. Indian organizations reject the aim of assimilation.

**1949.** British Columbia Indians vote in a provincial election for the first time. Only Nova Scotia Indians already have the franchise. Nishga Frank Calder becomes the first Indian elected to a provincial legislature.

**1949.** Newfoundland enters the confederation without having negotiated land surrenders with Natives. Under the agreement, Natives in the province are not recognized as status Indians and remain the responsibility of the Newfoundland government.

**1951.** The federal government passes a new Indian Act, which adopts the main thrust of the Joint Senate and House of Commons Committee report of 1948, significantly reducing the powers of the Indian Affairs Department but retaining the assimilative aim of the Indian Act. The government rejects the establishment of a land claims commission. The new act makes it easier for Indians to be enfranchised and to acquire location tickets. It also makes provisions allowing Indian children to be placed in integrated provincial schools.

**1953.** Inuit families from Port Harrison, on the eastern shore of Hudson Bay, and Pond Inlet on Baffin Island, in Canada's Arctic, are moved north to new communities at Resolute Bay (Cornwallis Island) and Grise Fiord (Ellesmere Island), both in the high Arctic. Hundreds of Inuit were relocated in government-sponsored relocations beginning in the 1930s.

**1955.** The construction of the Distant Early Warning (DEW) line (a line of radar stations intended to warn of Soviet attack) in Canada's Arctic increases the presence of non-Natives in northern Canada and increases cross-cultural contact. Increased interest in the resources of the north also increases the non-aboriginal population of the north.

**1960.** Indians are given the national franchise.

**1961.** The National Indian Council is formed as the first truly national Indian organization.

**1964.** The government induces the Ojibwa of Grassy Narrows in northern Ontario to move from their traditional homes to a new mainland reserve where government services can be administered more easily. This phenomenon is common in Canada at the time. The move brings about significant social and economic dislocation.

**1966–68.** *A Survey of the Contemporary Indians of Canada* (Hawthorn Report) criticizes Canadian Indian policy, noting that Natives are an economically, socially, and politically disadvantaged group. The report, noting that Indians have been treated as "citizens minus," calls for a new Indian policy that would treat them as "citizens plus." Indian leaders endorse the report.

**August 1967.** *Indians and the Law*, a study commissioned by the Department of Indian Affairs and conducted by the Canadian Corrections Association, issues its report. The report, the first in-depth study of the extent of Natives' problems with the law, criticizes the impact of police and legal services on Indians.

**February 1968.** The National Indian Council separates into the National Indian Brotherhood (NIB) and the Canadian Métis Society. The NIB will seek to protect benefits status Indians enjoy under treaties and the Indian Act. The Canadian Métis Society will seek to protect the aboriginal rights of Métis and non-status Indians.

**25 July 1968.** The federal government begins consultations with Indian groups toward establishing a new Indian policy.

**March 1969.** Quebec Indians become the last Indians in Canada to be given the provincial franchise.

**25 June 1969.** Jean Chrétien, minister of Indian affairs, releases the federal government's White Paper (policy paper) *Statement of the Government of Canada on Indian Policy, 1969*. The discussion paper rejects the Hawthorn Report's recommendation that Indians be treated as "citizens plus," arguing instead that Indians' special legal status has hindered their social, economic, and political development. Thus the policy paper proposes legislation to end all legal and constitutional distinctions relating to Indians. The Indian Act and the Indian Affairs Department would be abolished in about five years, and reserves, held in trust by the government since before confederation, would pass to Indian ownership. The provinces would assume the same jurisdiction over Indians as they do over other Canadians. During a transition period, Indians would be given aid to alleviate social and economic problems on reserves. The policy paper dismisses aboriginal land claims as too general and vague to be remedied.

**June–December 1969.**   Indians and Indian organizations begin to unite in opposition to the government's White Paper. As early as June 26, Walter Deiter, leader of the National Indian Brotherhood rejects the White Paper, saying that it ignores both the views Indians expressed during the government's consultations and the special status for Indians as guaranteed by treaties. In the following months most aboriginal organizations fight the government's policy.

**September 1969.**   Trent University in Peterborough, Ontario, begins the first Native studies program in Canada.

**20 November 1969.**   In the case of *Regina v. Drybones*, the Supreme Court strikes down sections of the Indian Act that restrict liquor sales to Indians because they contravene sections of the 1960 Bill of Rights guaranteeing all Canadians equality before the law. This, the first ruling on the Bill of Rights, finds that the Bill of Rights prevails over other legislation.

**19 December 1969.**   Lloyd Barber, vice president of the University of Saskatchewan, is appointed land claims commissioner according to guidelines set out in June's White Paper.

**1970.**   The Canadian government begins funding various Indian organizations, thus marking the reversal of its 1927 law repressing Indian political organizations. Funding helps further strengthen organizations established or united by opposition to the White Paper.

**4 June 1970.**   Two hundred Indians from across Canada present *Citizens Plus* (the Red Paper) to Minister of Indian Affairs Jean Chrétien and Prime Minister Pierre Trudeau. The Red Paper was written as the Indian Association of Alberta's response to the government's White Paper. Following some revisions on June 3, Indian organizations from across Canada adopt it as the official Indian response to the White Paper. Taking its title from the Hawthorn Report of 1968, *Citizens Plus* condemns the government's proposal to remove Indians' special status and to transfer responsibility for Indians to the provinces. The Red Paper demands that

the special legal status of Indians be retained and that treaty obligations be kept. It also calls for a reorganization of the federal Indian Affairs Department in order to make it more responsive to the needs and desires of Indian peoples. The Red Paper also calls for the creation of an Indian Claims Commission with the power to settle the claims. Upon receiving the submission, Trudeau implies that the government is willing to withdraw the White Paper.

**1 September 1970.**   A Cree band in northeastern Alberta takes over control of the Blue Quills school from the federal government, thus becoming the first Indian band in Canada to control its own school.

**17 March 1971.**   Jean Chrétien, minister of Indian affairs, formally announces the retraction of the White Paper.

**30 June 1971.**   A House of Commons committee on Indian Affairs recommends that control of education be turned over to Indians rather than to the provinces. Since 1951 an increasing number of Indians are being educated in provincial schools.

**17 November 1971.**   The Union of British Columbia Indian Chiefs releases "A Declaration of Indian Rights—The British Columbia Indian Position Paper," usually known as the Brown Paper. It rejects the White Paper along similar lines as the Red Paper, but puts more emphasis on land claims issues. Since the Red Paper, other Indian groups have also submitted their position papers rejecting the proposed federal policy.

**3 May 1972.**   The Cree and Inuit of northern Quebec file for a permanent injunction to halt construction of the James Bay Hydroelectric Project. This is their first court action to stop the development announced by the Quebec government in April 1971. Phase one of the project would flood about 10,500 square kilometers (4000 square miles) and divert several rivers. The Cree and Inuit of the region, who view the project as a threat to their way of life, were not consulted before the project was announced. Quebec has not negotiated land surrender agreements with the Natives of the region despite a 1912 agreement to do so.

**December 1972.**   The National Indian Brotherhood (NIB) presents "Indian Control of Indian Education," which calls for greater band control of Indian education. The NIB statement calls attention to the fact that Indians do not enjoy parental or local control over education-rights taken for granted by most Canadians.

**31 January 1973.** The Supreme Court rules in the case of *Calder v. Attorney General* that aboriginal rights to land exist in law, but that the rights of British Columbia Indians and of Nishga claimants specifically have been extinguished by government legislation. On this basis the court rejects the claim of the Nishga of the Nass River Valley in West Central British Columbia but greatly strengthens the case for Indian land claims.

**14 February 1973.** The Yukon Indian Brotherhood presents the first northern land claim, *Together Today For Our Children Tomorrow*, on behalf of the twelve Indian bands of the Yukon Territory. Prime Minister Trudeau announces that a federal committee will negotiate the claim.

**8 August 1973.** The Canadian government announces that it will establish an Office of Native Claims, a branch of the Department of Indian Affairs and Northern Development. It will negotiate "comprehensive claims," claims for land not covered by treaty, and "specific claims," claims based on treaties, the Indian Act, or other legislation. The office will deal with only six comprehensive claims at a time. Indian Affairs Minister Jean Chrétien cites the *Calder* ruling as influencing this complete reversal of the White Paper's land claims proposals. Native leaders cautiously approve of the announcement.

**27 August 1973.** In the case of *Attorney General Canada v. Lavell*, the Supreme Court decides that provisions in the Indian Act that remove Indian status from Indian women who marry non-Indians are an excusable violation of the Bill of Right's equality guarantees. Most treaty Indian organizations welcome the ruling because they fear that the Bill of Rights could be used to strike down the entire Indian Act.

**6 September 1973.** In *Re Paulette et al. v. Registrar of Titles*, the Supreme Court of the Northwest Territories rules that Northwest Territories Indians have the right to file a caveat (notice of claim) on approximately one-third of the Northwest Territories, because there is significant doubt about whether treaties 8 and 11 are legitimate land cession treaties. The case is appealed to a higher court.

**November 1973.** The Quebec Superior Court grants the Cree and Inuit of northern Quebec an injunction halting development of the James Bay Hydroelectric Project in northern Quebec on the grounds that Quebec has not kept provisions of the Proclamation of 1763 or its 1912 agreement with the federal government. The Quebec Court of Appeal overturns the injunction a week later, but the Quebec government begins negotiating the Indian and Inuit claims immediately.

**July 1974.** The federal government establishes the Office of Native Claims to evaluate and negotiate Indian land claims.

**28 August 1974.** A group of Ojibwa end a five-week occupation of the Anicinibe Park in Kenora (in northwestern Ontario) after reaching a tentative agreement with authorities. The Ojibwa claim the fourteen-acre park occupies land taken from their reserve without their permission in 1959. The confrontation had become an armed siege on August 13.

**20 September 1974.** Five Indians are arrested for assaulting and obstructing police officers as two hundred Indians, trying to storm the Parliament buildings in Ottawa, battle with police and the military. The protest started September 15 when the Native Caravan began traveling from Vancouver to Ottawa to demand settlement of their land claims and to protest the poor housing conditions and social services on their reserves.

**1975.** The Union of British Columbia Indian Chiefs and the British Columbia Association of Non-Status Indians collapse (although both organizations are later revived). Both organizations were formed in 1969 to lead opposition to the White Paper. A trend of forming organizations to represent status and non-status Indians of specific tribes lines gains strength. This trend is unique to British Columbia.

**April 1975.** The federal government creates a Joint Cabinet-National Indian Brotherhood Committee and a Cabinet-Native Council of Canada Committee to improve communication between the government and Native organizations.

**24 June 1975.** The British Columbia government and the Indians of British Columbia agree to settle the issue of "cut-off" reserve lands. Following the recommendations of the McKenna-McBride Commission the British Columbia government "cut off" (removed) land from twenty-two British Columbia bands in 1919 and 1920, but they did not get the Indians' consent to do so.

**19 July 1975.** The Indian Brotherhood of the Northwest Territories and the Métis Association of the Northwest Territories issue the Dene Declaration, declaring that the aboriginal peoples of the Northwest Territories form a nation with the right to self-government. Dene means "people" in most Athapaskan dialects.

**27 October 1975.** Seven Indian bands, including the Lubicon Cree band, submit a caveat on land in northern Alberta. A ruling on a similar caveat filed in the Northwest Territories suggests that such a caveat would be accepted in an Alberta court.

**11 November 1975.** The East Main Cree, Montagnais, Naskapi (6,500 people), and Inuit (4,200 people) bands of northern Quebec sign the James Bay and Northern Quebec Agreement with the federal and Quebec governments and three Quebec Crown Corporations. In the agreement the Natives surrender their claims to 1,062,000 square kilometers (410,000 square miles) of land for a cash settlement ($225 million over twenty years) and surrender their aboriginal rights in exchange for rights granted them in the agreement. These rights include significant control over their political, economic, and social affairs. The agreement creates three land categories in northern Quebec-Natives will own 14,000 square kilometers (5,408 square miles) and will enjoy exclusive hunting, fishing, and trapping rights on an additional 62,160 square kilometers (24,000 square miles). The general public will have equal access to the rest of the land. The agreement also includes income security for Cree hunters and trappers. Some Natives criticize the deal, claiming it compares poorly with a land claims settlement in Alaska (the Alaska Native Claims Settlement Act) in 1971, which gave the Alaska Natives 44 million acres of land and $962.5 million. Cree Chief Billy Diamond and Inuit Charlie Watt have led the negotiations for the Natives.

**27 February 1976.** The Inuit Tapirisat of Canada presents its claim to an immense area in Canada's Arctic. The claim, on behalf of all the Inuit of the Northwest Territories, follows a unique federally funded study of Inuit land use and occupancy in the Northwest Territories. It proposes to establish Nunavut ("our land"), as a new territory covering most of Canada north of the treeline. The territory, which would be taken from the Northwest Territories, would be controlled by the Inuit who comprise over 80 percent of the population of that region.

**May 1976.** The Yukon Indians (status and non-status) reach an agreement-in-principle with the Canadian government to settle their land claim. Under the agreement the Indians would retain title to 52 hectares (128 acres) per person and exclusive hunting, trapping, and fishing rights on an additional 44,000 square kilometers (17,000 square miles). The agreement would have them

surrender subsurface rights to all the land. The membership of the organization rejects the deal because they believe it compares poorly to a settlement in Alaska in 1971.

**May 1976.** The Saskatchewan Indian Federated College, an independent college integrated with the University of Regina, is organized as the first college under Native control. Intended to encourage Native socioeconomic development and contribute to the general academic community, it will accept aboriginal and non-aboriginal students.

**22 June 1976.** A team of doctors recommends closing the English/Wabigoon river systems in northern Ontario to all fishing because of mercury pollution. The Ojibwa of Grassy Narrows have been told not to eat fish from the rivers, but they continue to eat them because the rivers remain open to sport fishermen. Experts have found evidence of mercury poisoning among the Indians.

**26 October 1976.** The Dene of the Northwest Territories present their claim to much of the land in the western Northwest Territories. The claim includes a proposal for an Indian government for the Northwest Territories with powers like that of a province. The Métis Association does not support this claim and instead is asking for separate funds from the federal government in order to fund their own claims research.

**20 December 1976.** On a technicality, the Supreme Court of Canada rules against the Indians of the Northwest Territories for the right to file a caveat. The ruling does not alter the lower court's finding, which casts doubt on the legality of Treaties 8 and 11 as land cession treaties. On this basis, the federal government has already accepted the Dene claim as a comprehensive claim. The proposed Mackenzie Valley Pipeline would pass through part of the area in question.

**1977.** The Labrador Inuit Association releases "Our Footprints are Everywhere," a land-use study similar to that done in the Northwest Territories. Later in the year, it presents the claim of the Labrador Inuit to land and sea-ice in northern Labrador.

**1977.** The Conseil Attikamek/Montagnais, an alliance of Attikamek (Téte-de-Boule) and Montagnais-Naskapi Indians of northern Quebec and Labrador, presents its claim to land in Quebec and Labrador.

**March 1977.** The Committee for Original People's Entitlement (COPE), established in 1969, presents

*Inuvialuit Nunangat*, a land claim on behalf of 2,500 Inuit in the western Arctic. COPE was originally part of the Inuit Tapirisat of Canada claim presented in February 1976 but, because of differences of opinion, withdrew in order to present its own claim.

**17 March 1977.** The Canadian government and the National Indian Brotherhood establish the Canadian Indian Rights Commission to replace the federal government's Indian Claims Commission established in 1969.

**15 April 1977.** The Mackenzie Valley Pipeline Inquiry (Berger Inquiry) calls for a ten-year moratorium on construction of any pipeline in the Mackenzie Valley to allow time for the Indians and Inuit to settle their land claims with the government and for the residents to prepare for changes the development would bring. Hearings of the inquiry ended in November 1976. The report points out that residents fear the development and that aboriginals have not benefitted from northern developments in the past. The Indian Brotherhood of the Northwest Territories, the Native Council of Canada and the National Indian Brotherhood endorse the report, but the Northwest Territories Métis Association, which supports the principle of the development, expresses disappointment with the report.

**May 1977.** The Alberta government passes a law that makes it impossible to file a caveat on unpatented Crown land. The law is to be applied retroactively, effectively killing an attempt by several Alberta Indian bands to file such a caveat. The provincial government has been fighting the caveat since October 1975.

**29 July 1977.** Kenneth Lysyk, the chair of the Alaska Highway Pipeline Inquiry, recommends approval-in-principle of the Alaska Highway Pipeline but recommends that construction be delayed by two years in order that Indian land claims can be settled before construction begins.

**3 August 1977.** The federal government rejects the proposals for separate Dene and Inuit governments in the Northwest Territories. These proposals are stalling negotiations on northern land claims.

**28 September 1977.** The Métis and non-status Indians of the Northwest Territories present their claim to land in the Mackenzie Valley in the Northwest Territories to the federal government. This group had been part of the Dene claim of October 1976, but withdrew to present its own claim.

**31 October 1977.** The James Bay Settlement Acts are passed by the Quebec and Canadian governments.

This gives the James Bay Agreement greater legal force than former Indian treaties.

**November 1977.** The Naskapi-Montagnais Innu Association of Labrador presents a claim on behalf of the Naskapi and Montagnais tribes in northern Labrador. The claim includes a declaration of sovereignty similar to the 1975 Dene Declaration.

**December 1977.** The Inuit Tapirisat of Canada presents a revised claim to land in the central and eastern Arctic. The revised claim was made necessary by the withdrawal of the Inuit of the western Arctic from the original ITC claim.

**8 December 1977.** A special Native commission created by the Native Council of Canada condemns the effects of the Canadian justice system on Natives. It associates the large number of Indians in jails with high unemployment, little education, pervasive poverty, and lack of opportunities among Natives.

**12 January 1978.** The Naskapi and Inuit of northeastern Quebec sign an agreement parallel to the James Bay and Northern Quebec Agreement of 1975.

**30 March 1978.** The Indian Brotherhood of the Northwest Territories changes its name to the Dene Nation and opens membership not only to treaty Indians, but also to all Native people, including Métis. The Dene and Métis have claims to the same regions of the Northwest Territories, and differences between the two have complicated negotiations with the federal government since 1976.

**13 April 1978.** The National Indian Brotherhood (NIB) pulls out of a joint Cabinet-National Indian Brotherhood Committee formed in 1975.

**June 1978.** The federal government's discussion paper *A Time For Action* calls for Native constitutional issues to be addressed and identified in the upcoming constitutional reform process. Constitutional reform became a prominent issue after Quebec elected a separatist government in 1976.

**31 October 1978.** The Committee for Original People's Entitlement signs an agreement-in-principle with the Canadian government to settle the Inuvialuit (Inuit of the western Arctic) land claim in the western Arctic.

**1979.** The Native Council of Canada issues its *Declaration of Métis and Indian Rights*. The document claims Natives have rights to self-determination, to representation in legislatures and in the constitutional reform process, and to recognition of special status in confederation.

**January 1979.** The Canadian Indian Rights Commission (a joint federal government-National Indian Brotherhood commission) is officially dissolved because of dissatisfaction on the part of the NIB.

**5–6 February 1979.** Canada's first ministers (prime minister and premiers) meet to discuss constitutional reform. Indian groups are offered observer status at the talks, but boycott the meeting to underscore their demands for direct participation in the talks.

**1 July 1979.** Three hundred Indian chiefs of the National Indian Brotherhood visit London to press British politicians to block any change to the British North America Act unless Indians are given a greater role in constitutional reform discussions. The Indians are fighting the government's proposed constitutional amendment that would recognize the existence of two founding nations (English and French) in Canada, but would give no special recognition to Aboriginals. Aboriginals demand direct participation in constitutional talks.

**1980.** The Tungavik Federation of Nunavut, formed by the Inuit Tapirisat of Canada in 1979 to negotiate its claim in the central and eastern Arctic, agrees to set aside demands for the Nunavut Territory in order to get negotiations on its land claim started.

**1980.** Negotiations resume between the Council of Yukon Indians and the federal and Yukon governments. Negotiations broke off after the Yukon Indians rejected a tentative agreement in May 1976.

**1980.** In the case of *Hamlet of Baker Lake et al. v. Minister of Indian Affairs and Northern Development*, the federal court rules that the aboriginal inhabitants of the Northwest Territories have hunting, trapping, and fishing rights to the land based on occupancy, not based on the Royal Proclamation of 1763. The court, however, also finds that governments can extinguish aboriginal title unilaterally. The ruling includes criteria by which the court can determine whether a group has proven to have aboriginal rights to land. According to these criteria, members of an organized society have a legitimate claim if they can prove that their ancestors belonged to an organized society that occupied the claimed land to the exclusion of other societies at the time the government asserted its sovereignty over the area. Notwithstanding the ruling, the Indians of Baker Lake lose this case because the court

Indians gather at the home of Grace McCarthy, Human Resources Minister, to protest the British Columbia government's child welfare policies. (Photo by Kate Bird. Courtesy of *Vancouver Sun*–Ken Oakes, October 1980)

finds that aboriginal rights do not allow them to prevent mining in the area.

**8–12 September 1980.** The first ministers (prime minister and provincial premiers) meet to discuss constitutional reform. Representatives of Native organizations are permitted to attend as observers.

**13 October 1980.** Seven hundred British Columbia Indians protest the number of Native children placed in non-Native foster homes in the 1960s and 1970s. As a result, the government begins to increase band control of child welfare services, a trend that also begins in other provinces.

**7 November 1980.** Indian leaders hold a press conference in London to explain why they feel threatened by Canada's constitutional proposals. Prime Minister Trudeau announces that he is willing to include a provision to protect aboriginal rights in the Constitution if such an amendment would be accepted by the premiers.

**17 December 1980.** National Indian Brotherhood president Del Riley, appearing before a Joint Parliamentary Committee on constitutional reform, protests the lack of Native involvement in the reform process. He says aboriginal peoples want a third level of government that would allow them to control their own land, resources, and people. He also calls for the entrenchment of the Proclamation of 1763 in the new Constitution.

**1981.** In the case of *R. v. Taylor and Williams*, the Supreme Court of Ontario finds that the terms of a cession treaty (a treaty in which Natives surrender their land rights in exchange for other rights) must be kept even if they do not appear in the treaty document.

**30 January 1981.** The federal government accepts a constitutional amendment that would entrench the provisions of the Proclamation of 1763. Another amendment would read: "The aboriginal and treaty rights of the aboriginal peoples of Canada are hereby recognized and affirmed." Del Riley, president of the National Indian Brotherhood, endorses the amendments.

**2 September 1981.** The United Nations Human Rights Commission rules that Canada's Indian Act violates international human rights because it discriminates on the basis of sex. The ruling was made in regard to Sandra Lovelace, a Maliseet, who had lost her Indian status and right to live on her tribal reserve because she married a non-Indian.

**2–5 November 1981.** Nine of ten provinces accept an amending formula for the Constitution and a Charter of Rights only after amendments guaranteeing aboriginal rights (30 January 1981) are deleted from the package. Several premiers oppose the provisions because they find them too poorly defined. The agreement meets with immediate angry denunciation by Indian leaders across Canada.

**26 November 1981.** The House of Commons reinstates a reworded version of a constitutional provision agreed upon on 30 January 1981. The new amendment recognized "existing aboriginal and treaty rights." Indian groups demanded the removal of the word "existing" despite assurances that the word would not alter the intended meaning of the section. The House of Commons also adds a provision that guarantees a federal-provincial conference, with Native participation, to define these existing rights.

**29 January 1982.** The British Court of Appeal rules that Britain no longer has any responsibility for the protection of Indian rights in Canada. Indian groups made the appeal to the British court in an attempt to convince the British government to block patriation (transfer to Canada) of the Constitution.

**17 April 1982.** Canada's new Constitution and Charter of Rights and Freedoms is proclaimed by the British government despite opposition by Canadian Indian groups. Section 25 of the Charter says that its equality guarantees do not affect aboriginal treaty rights or rights recognized by the Proclamation of 1763. Section 35 of the Constitution recognizes "existing aboriginal and treaty rights of the aboriginal peoples." (Indians, Inuit, and Métis are explicitly identified as aboriginal peoples.) The Constitution also guarantees aboriginal participation at a conference to define what these existing rights are. Indian groups boycott celebrations and denounce the new Constitution.

**21 April 1982.** David Ahenakew, a Cree from Saskatchewan, is elected to replace Del Riley as the new president of the National Indian Brotherhood. The National Indian Brotherhood announces its reorganization as the Assembly of First Nations (AFN), an association of chiefs rather than an alliance of bands.

**July 1982.** The federal government announces it will inject $61.4 million to deal with problems with the James Bay Agreement. The announcement follows reviews by the Indian Affairs Department and the Justice Department that found that the federal government is keeping the letter but not the spirit of the 1975 agreement.

**22 September 1982.** The Parliamentary Sub-Committee on Indian Women and the Indian Act releases its report calling for an end to sexual discrimination in the Indian Act.

**March 1983.** Alberta, Saskatchewan, and Manitoba associations of the Native Council of Canada withdraw to form the Métis National Council, over differences on the constitutional negotiation process.

**15–16 March 1983.** At a conference guaranteed by the 1982 Constitution, representatives of aboriginal peoples, the first ministers, and the elected governments of Yukon and Northwest Territories agree to alter Section 25 of the Charter of Rights to recognize all aboriginal rights acquired in past and future land claims settlements. Section 35 of the Constitution will be amended to guarantee gender equality in the enjoyment

Indian chiefs open the first ministers' conference on aboriginal issues, March 1983. This conference, guaranteed by the 1982 constitution, marked the first time that aboriginals were given full participation in constitutional conferences. (Courtesy of CP Pictures Archives)

of treaty rights. Native groups are also guaranteed participation at two more conferences to define the nature and extent of "existing" aboriginal and treaty rights enshrined in Section 35 of the Constitution. This is the first constitutional conference in which Native groups have full participation. Indian leaders endorse the amendments but express frustration at the slow progress being made on central issues.

**3 November 1983.**   The Report of the Special Parliamentary Committee on Indian Self-Government (the Penner Report) unanimously agrees that the aboriginal right to self-government should be entrenched in the

Constitution. The commission also recommends abolishing the Indian Act and the Indian Affairs Department. The report receives unanimous support in the House of Commons.

**1984.**   The Canadian Education Association reports that Indian bands that have taken over control of Indian education have witnessed marked improvement in student achievement. Since 1970 increasing numbers of Indian bands have taken over control of Indian education.

**8–9 March 1984.**   The second first ministers' constitutional conference on aboriginal issues ends with an agreement to amend the Indian Act to guarantee gender equality but without agreement on the major aim of defining aboriginal rights. Six premiers reject a proposed amendment that would recognize the right to aboriginal self-government, complaining that it was too vague.

**17 May 1984.** Alberta Indians walk out of an Assembly of First Nations (AFN) meeting because of disagreement over the gender equality amendment. The Indian Association of Alberta then withdraws from the AFN for a time.

**5 June 1984.** The final agreement is reached on the comprehensive claim of the Committee of Original People's Entitlement (COPE) on behalf of the 2,500 Inuvialuit of the Mackenzie Valley. This is the first comprehensive land claims settlement north of the 60th parallel. The agreement calls for the Inuvialuit to surrender their aboriginal rights in return for the rights and benefits provided in the agreement, which include a cash settlement and provisions regarding wildlife, the environment, and economic development. The agreement is unique in that it gives the Inuvialuit outright ownership of 82,880 square kilometers (32,000 square miles) including subsurface rights in 13,000 square kilometers (5,000 square miles). It also allows the Inuvialuit to participate in wildlife management decisions. The federal government also agrees to establish a 13,000 square-kilometer (5,000 square-mile) National Wilderness Area in which the Inuit will enjoy hunting, trapping, and fishing rights. Native leaders criticized the provisions that would have the Inuit give up their aboriginal rights in exchange for the rights specified by the agreement.

**12 June 1984.** The Micmac of Conne River, Newfoundland, are recognized as an Indian band under the Indian Act. They settled at Conne River in 1870.

**21 June 1984.** The first amendments to the Canadian Constitution are proclaimed. The two amendments are provisions agreed upon at the first ministers' conference in March 1983.

**3 July 1984.** The Canadian Government proclaims the Cree-Naskapi (of Quebec) Act according to a provision in the James Bay and Northern Quebec Agreement of 1975. The act gives the Natives of northern Quebec a type of self-government. The Indians no longer fall under the jurisdiction of the Indian Act.

**23 October 1984.** The Gitksan and Wet'suwet'en (Carrier) Indians of the Skeena and Bulkley River Valleys of northern British Columbia initiate a court action to claim over 57,000 square kilometers of northwestern and north central British Columbia.

**November 1984.** In the *Guerin* case, the Supreme Court rules that the Canadian government must pay the Musqueam band, in Vancouver, $10 million for violating its legal obligations to the band. The Court rules that aboriginal rights were not created by law.

**26 February 1985.** Inuit from Grise Fiord, Ellesmere Island, in Canada's high Arctic, meet with Indian Affairs Minister John Crosbie to seek help to move south. The Inuit were relocated from Port Harrison, Quebec, in 1953.

**2–3 April 1985.** At a constitutional conference on aboriginal issues, four premiers refuse to approve a constitutional amendment that would entrench the Indian right to self-government without a clear definition of such a right. The Assembly of First Nations refuses an amendment that would entrench the principle of self-rule for Aboriginals but would not guarantee a process for defining such powers. The participants agree to meet again in June.

**5–6 June 1985.** Constitutional talks with first ministers and aboriginal organizations fail to make progress in defining Indian rights to self-government. The federal government announces that it will begin negotiating self-government agreements with individual groups of Indians.

**28 June 1985.** Passage of Bill C-31 removes sections of the Indian Act that discriminate against women in order to harmonize the Indian Act with the Charter of Rights and Freedoms. Some Indians protest that the federal government has no right to define who is or is not an Indian. Many Indian bands are also concerned about the effect of a sudden influx of new status Indians on reserve life and band funds.

**29–31 July 1985.** The Prairie Treaty Nations Alliance (PTNA), accounting for approximately one-third of the membership of the Assembly of First Nations, walks out of an Assembly of First Nations convention in Vancouver over disagreements arising out of the AFN's negotiating strategy with the government. The defection follows earlier defections by Alberta and Atlantic organizations. Incumbent AFN leader, David Ahenakew from Saskatchewan, facing questions about the AFN's $3.6 million debt, becomes leader of the PTNA. Dene Georges Erasmus from the Northwest Territories is chosen president of the AFN. Under Erasmus, the Indian Association of Alberta and Atlantic Indians return, and the debt is eliminated.

**November 1985.** Seventy-two Haida and their supporters are arrested while trying to prevent logging on Lyell Island (Queen Charlotte Islands, British Columbia). The Haida, who have protested logging in the area since 1974, filed a claim in 1983 and set up a blockade on October 30 after the British Columbia government approved logging on the island.

**December 1985.** Minister of Indian Affairs David Crombie issues *Living Treaties: Lasting Agreements* (the Coolican Report), a revision of the government's comprehensive land claims policy. The new policy notes that little progress has been made in settling land claims. It announces the government's commitment to settling claims through negotiation rather than litigation. The new policy announces that land claims agreements would not necessarily require Natives to surrender their aboriginal rights and would be viewed as flexible over time. The policy also calls for agreements that will allow Native peoples to share in the financial rewards of development in their territories. Native organizations welcome the new policy as a breakthrough.

**December 1985.** The Ojibwa of the Grassy Narrows Band and nearby Whitedog Reserve in northwestern Ontario accept an offer of $16.7 million from the federal and Ontario governments for compensation for mercury poisoning on both reserves and for land on the Whitedog Reserve flooded by a hydroelectric project in 1958.

**9 October 1986.** Legislation giving the Sechelt band of Salish Indians in British Columbia self-government is passed. The band has agreed to a form of self-government akin to a municipal government.

**December 1986.** Indian Affairs Minister Bill McKnight unveils a new comprehensive land claims policy, which announces the government's intention to restrict land claims negotiations to land issues. The government will seek to make one-time settlements with Indians.

**26–27 March 1987.** The final constitutional conference on aboriginal issues guaranteed by amendments to the Constitution of 1982 ends with no agreement on how to define Indian rights to self-government, and no agreement to meet again. Differences center around the concept of the "inherent" aboriginal right to self-government.

**30 April 1987.** The prime minister and the premiers unanimously agree on a constitutional reform package, which becomes known as the Meech Lake Accord. The first ministers formulate the new package because Quebec refused to sign the Constitution of 1982. This reform package makes no reference to aboriginal issues.

**28 May 1987.** Native leaders hold a press conference to accuse the first ministers of holding a double standard in the Meech Lake Accord. They accuse the governments of being willing to enshrine an undefined recognition of Quebec as a distinct society after rejecting amendments guaranteeing aboriginal rights to self-government because they are undefined. They also protest that they were shut out of these constitutional talks.

**1 July 1987.** The federal government announces an agreement with the British Columbia government to establish a national park in the South Moresby region of the Queen Charlotte Islands. The Haida have been protesting logging operations in the area.

**11 September 1988.** The Innu of North West River in Labrador begin protesting low-altitude training at a NATO training base near Goose Bay, which began in 1980 by camping at the end of a runway at the base. The Innu claim that the flights are causing reduction of wildlife populations, particularly of the George River Caribou herd upon which they depend, and is causing distress to the Indians themselves.

**22 October 1988.** Chief Bernard Ominayak of the Lubicon Lake Cree band reaches a preliminary agreement with Alberta Premier Don Getty on terms to settle the band's long-standing land claim. The agreement would provide the band with a 250 square kilometer (95 square mile) reserve. On October 15, the Lubicon set up a blockade on the road leading to their community after negotiations with the federal government broke down. On October 20, twenty-seven Indians were arrested when the Royal Canadian Mounted Police removed the blockade. The Lubicon gained international attention by organizing a boycott of "The Spirit Sings," an exposition of Native artifacts held during the Calgary Olympics in February 1988. The Lubicon Lake band was missed when the government and northern Alberta Indians signed Treaty 8 in 1899. The band launched a claim in 1933 and was promised a reserve in 1940. However, no reserve was ever given to them. In 1980 an access road was built to their settlement area and about four hundred oil wells were drilled, seriously disrupting the band's traditional self-sufficient dependence on hunting and trapping. Most of the band turned to welfare.

**27 February 1989.** The Ontario Court of Appeal upholds a 1984 finding that the Teme-Augama Anishnabai (Bear Island People) band of Ojibway had lost title to its land in 1850 even though they had not signed the treaty. The federal government had granted the Indians a reserve at the south end of Lake Temagami, in east-central Ontario, in 1885, but the Ontario government refused to transfer the land in the agreement.

**March 1989.** The federal government announces a ceiling on funding for Indian students attending post-secondary institutions. Indians protest with sit-ins and hunger strikes in Thunder Bay (western Ontario), claiming that the funding is a treaty right. Special funding for Indians in post-secondary education began in 1968 with the number of Indians in post-secondary institutions increasing dramatically since then.

**10 May 1989.** Cree of northern Quebec file suit to stop construction of the $7.5 billion Great Whale Project (Phase II of the James Bay Hydroelectric Project) in northern Quebec. Studies by Hydro-Quebec confirmed that mercury levels in reservoirs created by the first phase of the James Bay project increased to up to nine times the federal government's guidelines for safety. The 1975 James Bay and Northern Quebec Agreement made provisions for this second phase, even bigger than the first, but the Quebec government elected to begin construction without the project undergoing the environmental review process established by the agreement.

**28 August 1989.** The federal government announces that it will settle with a band (the Woodland Cree) composed of Indians it claims have defected from the Lubicon Lake band in northern Alberta. This follows the federal government's rejection of an agreement reached between Chief Bernard Ominayak of the Lubicon Lake band and the Alberta premier in October 1988, and the Lubicon's rejection of the Government's offer of January 1989.

**September 1989.** The Nisga'a (Nishga) sign a framework agreement with the federal government toward resolving their claim to land in west central British Columbia, but the British Columbia government refuses to recognize the legitimacy of the claim.

**26 January 1990.** An inquiry in Nova Scotia finds that, because of racism and incompetence in the police force and legal community, Donald Marshall, a Micmac, had been wrongfully convicted of murder in 1972 and spent the next eleven years in prison. The report recommends that the government establish a cabinet committee on race relations and a Native criminal justice system.

**7 February 1990.** The Nova Scotia government issues an apology to Donald Marshall. The government announces that it will establish a cabinet committee on race relations and establish a Native criminal court as a pilot project.

**7 March 1990.** The Nova Scotia Court of Appeal rules that provisions in the Constitution Act of 1982 give Micmac Indians the constitutional right to fish for food and give them some immunity from government regulations.

**31 March 1990.** The Council of Yukon Indians, representing 6,500 Indians, and the federal government and Yukon governments reach an umbrella final agreement to settle their 1973 land claim. This agreement is designed to serve as the blueprint for negotiations between the government and the fourteen First Nations of the Council. It is unique in that it offers the Indians a share of federal royalties from mining and exemption from some forms of taxation, although the status Indians will give up their rights under the Indian Act in exchange for rights specified in the agreement. The Indians will retain title to 41,440 square kilometers (8.6 percent of the land in the Yukon) and will receive $242.7 million over fifteen years.

**4 April 1990.** The New York State legislature passes a law that will require an environmental assessment of the Great Whale Project before it signs a contract to buy the power from the project. The legislation followed lobbying by the Cree of northern Quebec who oppose the project. The Cree began fighting the project immediately after the government's 1989 announcement that it would begin construction.

**9 April 1990.** The thirteen thousand Dene and Métis of the Northwest Territories sign a land-claim agreement for the Mackenzie Valley in the western Arctic. The agreement would give the claimants title to 180,000 square kilometers of land. Issues of treaty rights and self-government remain to be negotiated.

**23 April 1990.** The Teme-Augama Anishnabai Indian band is granted a veto over logging on a tract of land, which they claim as theirs.

**24 May 1990.** In the case of *R. v. Sioui*, the Supreme Court rules that a 230-year-old treaty signed by the Huron Indians of Quebec supersedes later legislation that contradicts it. The ruling is based upon Section 35 of the Constitution of 1982, which guarantees aboriginal treaty rights.

**31 May 1990.** The Supreme Court of Canada orders a retrial for Ronald Sparrow, from the Musqueam band

(Vancouver), who had been convicted of violating federal fishing regulations. The Court rules that Section 35 of the Charter supersedes wildlife regulations.

**22 June 1990.** Elijah Harper, a Cree-Ojibwa member of the provincial legislature in Manitoba, is able to use procedural rules to prevent the passage of the Meech Lake Accord in the Manitoba legislature. This effectively kills the constitutional reform package that Aboriginals have been opposing since its inception in 1987.

**11 July 1990.** A police officer is killed after Quebec police storm a barricade on the Mohawk reserve at Kanesatake (Oka), near Montreal. The Mohawk set up the blockade in March to prevent construction of a golf course on land they claim. After their failed attempt to storm the barricades on July 11, police surround Kanesatake. In sympathy with the Mohawk at Kanesatake, members of the Mohawk Warrior Society at Kahnawake (Caughnawaga), south of Montreal, block access to the Mercier Bridge, a bridge linking the southern suburbs of Montreal with the city. The actions initiate a seventy-eight-day standoff between the police and military and the Mohawk Warriors of Kahnawake and Kanesatake, a conflict that draws worldwide attention.

**19 July 1990.** The Dene and Métis reject their comprehensive land claim settlement with the federal government because of concern over the provision that would have them surrender their aboriginal rights.

**9 August 1990.** The British Columbia government announces that it is willing to join Indians and the federal government in land claims negotiations based on the legitimacy of aboriginal title. The policy reverses the position held by every British Columbia government since 1864. The promise is made after Indians bands blocked rail lines and roads in the province.

**7 September 1990.** The Royal Canadian Mounted Police move in on the Peigan Lonefighters (a revived warrior society) camp, ending a month-long attempt by the Lonefighters to divert the Oldman River around the site of a partially completed dam. The leader of the Lonefighters, Milton Born With a Tooth, is arrested on weapons charges. The Lonefighters oppose the dam because it would flood land they consider sacred and because they fear its environmental effects.

**25 September 1990.** Prime Minister Brian Mulroney announces a new government agenda to meet aboriginal grievances. He commits the government to speeding up settlement of all land claims and meeting all its outstanding treaty obligations. For the first time, the government will begin negotiating more than six comprehensive claims at a time. He also announces a commitment to improve housing, sewage treatment, and water facilities on reserves, and to increase aboriginal control over their own affairs.

**26 September 1990.** The warriors at Kahnawake and Kanesatake surrender after an eleven-week standoff with police and soldiers. The seventy-eight day armed standoff attracted international attention and made Canadians more aware of the depth of frustration among many Native Canadians. The federal government refused to negotiate with the Indians as long as the standoff continued.

**11 October 1990.** The British Columbia government signs an agreement to join the federal government in land claims negotiations with the Nisga'a (Nishga) Tribal Council.

**7 November 1990.** The federal government announces that as a result of the rejection by the Dene and Métis of their land claims settlement in July, the government will begin negotiating with individual Indian groups in the western Arctic, saying that such groups had indicated their desire to negotiate separately. Indian leaders accuse the government of adopting a "divide and conquer" strategy.

**30 November 1990.** The Naskapi-Montagnais Innu Association signs a framework agreement with the federal and Labrador/Newfoundland governments toward settlement of its land claim in Labrador. The claim was submitted in 1977. Negotiations were slowed by the group's claim to sovereignty, acrimonious relations between the Quebec and Newfoundland governments, and Innu protests of low-level flights at a NATO base at Goose Bay in 1989.

**19 December 1990.** The federal and Alberta governments reach an agreement with a band known as the Woodland Cree, formed in 1989 as a breakaway band of the Lubicon Lake band, which has been seeking a settlement since the 1930s.

**8 March 1991.** The British Columbia Supreme Court rules in *Delgamuukw v. Attorney-General* that the Gitksan-Wet'suwet'ens of west central British Columbia do not hold aboriginal title to fifty-seven thousand square kilometers they claim, because such title was extinguished by British Columbia before it entered Confederation and because the Proclamation of 1763 does not apply to British Columbia. The Indians announce that they will appeal the decision. The British

Columbia government announces that the decision will not change its policy of negotiating with Indian claimants.

**12 June 1991.** Ovide Mercredi, a Cree lawyer from Manitoba, is elected as the new president of the Assembly of First Nations.

**26 June 1991.** Indian Affairs Minister Tom Siddon announces that the government will seek to ameliorate damage done to Indian societies by residential schools. Evidence of physical and sexual abuse at residential schools has been revealed in the past few years.

**6 July 1991.** The Woodland Cree band, a band created by the federal government in 1989, votes to accept the government's offer to settle its land claim.

**13 July 1991.** The Gwich'in (Kutchin), Athapaskan Indians of the Mackenzie delta, reach a land claims settlement with the federal government based on the agreement rejected by the Dene and Métis of Northwest Territories in April 1990. The agreement gives the Indians fifteen thousand square kilometers in the Northwest Territories and the Yukon.

**12 August 1991.** The report of the Manitoba Aboriginal Justice Inquiry finds that aboriginal peoples suffer discrimination in the justice system. It recommends the establishment of a separate aboriginal justice system that would give the aboriginal people the right to enact and enforce laws in their own communities. The inquiry finds that racism played an important part in the deaths of Helen Betty Osborne, a Cree woman murdered by non-Natives in The Pas, in northern Manitoba, and J. J. Harper, a Cree man killed by a Winnipeg police officer.

**27 August 1991.** The Quebec government announces that construction of the Great Whale Project (Phase II of the James Bay Hydroelectric Project) will be delayed one year. The announcement follows a negotiations between Quebec and New York State. The Quebec government hopes to sell most of the electricity to the northern states of the United States. The Cree of northern Quebec have lobbied New York legislators to refuse to buy the power.

**7 December 1991.** The Council of Yukon Indians votes to accept their umbrella final agreement on their land claim with the federal government. The agreement establishes guidelines for settlements with the each of Yukon's fourteen First Nations. The Indians will receive title to 41,440 square kilometers (8.6 percent of the Yukon) and $257 million. The agreement includes provisions for self-government for the Indians.

**16 December 1991.** Indian Affairs Minister Tom Siddon announces that the government has reached a final agreement with the Inuit (Tungavik Federation of Nunavut) of the eastern Arctic. The agreement follows fifteen years of negotiations. The agreement would create a new territory of Nunavut in the eastern Arctic. The new territory would be publicly governed although Inuit presently account for 80 percent of the area's population. The provision resembles part of the Inuit's original claim, but had been rejected earlier by the federal government. The agreement also calls for the Inuit to surrender their aboriginal rights. They would be given cash ($580 million over fourteen years) in exchange for title to most of the land, but would retain 350,000 square kilometers of land (approximately 17.5 percent of the territory).

**28 January 1992.** Responding to the report of the Manitoba Justice Inquiry, the Manitoba government announces that it will hire more Native judges and improve legal services to Indians in the provinces, but rejects the suggestion that a separate justice system be established in Manitoba.

**31 March 1992.** The Quebec government blames the Cree of northern Quebec for New York State's decision to cancel a contract to buy power from the Great Whale Project, putting the project in jeopardy. The Cree have lobbied against the project.

**April 1992.** Representatives of the federal government, nine provincial provinces, two territories, and four aboriginal groups unanimously agree that the Constitution should recognize the inherent aboriginal right to self-government. The exact powers of Indian governments that would form a third level of government has not been negotiated, but aboriginal leaders and governments hail the agreement as the beginning of a new era for Canada's Natives. The Assembly of First Nations announces the creation of a women's committee on constitutional matters to meet criticism that it is ignoring the concerns of Native women. The Native Women's Association of Canada has argued that Native governments must be bound by the Charter of Rights to protect aboriginal women.

**22 May 1992.** The federal government announces that it will build a healing lodge (federal prison) at Maple Creek, Saskatchewan. It will be designed to allow native women prisoners to be kept near their communities. Up to now all women in federal prisons have been kept in one prison in Kingston, Ontario. While only 3 percent of Canada's population is aboriginal, 15 percent of its female prison population is aboriginal.

**20 August 1992.** Prime Minister Brian Mulroney, Canada's ten premiers, and the leaders of the Assembly of First Nations, the Native Council of Canada, the Métis National Council and the Inuit Tapirisat of Canada reach unanimous agreement on provisions that would entrench aboriginal self-government in Canada's Constitution (The Charlottetown Accord). All agree that laws passed by aboriginal governments will have to be consistent with laws passed by the federal and provincial governments and with Canadian standards of peace, order and good government. While most Canadians and natives greet the agreement enthusiastically, there are also immediate voices of criticism.

**3 September 1992.** Prime Minister Brian Mulroney announces that a national referendum will be held on October 26 on the "Charlottetown Accord," a proposed new Constitution for Canada that includes provisions that would grant a form of self-government for Canada's aboriginal peoples.

**21 September 1992.** Prime Minister Brian Mulroney, British Columbia Premier Mike Harcourt, and British Columbia Indians agree to establish a British Columbia Treaty Commission to facilitate the settlement of land claims in British Columbia.

**26 October 1992.** In a nation-wide referendum, Canadians reject the Charlottetown Accord. Pollsters suggest that most Canadians did not reject the proposal because of its provisions regarding aboriginal self-government. Nevertheless, status Indians do not appear to have supported the proposal. Sixty-two percent of those on Indian reserves who voted, rejected the Accord. Many natives complained that the self-government provisions were not adequately spelled out. Seventy-five percent of the Inuit voted for the agreement.

**20 November 1992.** The Federal Court of Appeal rules the federal government of Canada does not have to do an environmental assessment of the Eastmain hydroelectric project because it is authorized by the 1975 James Bay and Northern Quebec Agreement.

**13 January 1993.** The Sahtu Tribal Council representing 2200 Sahtu (Bearlake) Dene and Métis reach a land claim agreement with the federal government. The agreement will give the Sahtu $75 million dollars over fifteen years. The agreement also grants the Sahtu ownership and subsurface rights to some land and a share of royalties for resources extracted from the region.

**19 January 1993.** Police seize unlicenced gambling equipment on five reserves in Manitoba. The Indians

and the provincial government have disputed the legality of the gambling establishments.

**26 January 1993.** Television news reports show six Innu children aged twelve to fourteen, at the remote village of Davis Inlet, in Labrador, sniffing gasoline in an apparent suicide attempt. The Innu at Davis Inlet say the level of substance abuse in the village reflects the community's despair. The story captures national and international attention.

**9 February 1993.** Tom Siddon, Canadian Minister of Indian Affairs announces that the government will pay for the relocation of the Innu village of Davis Inlet to the nearby mainland location at Sango Bay. The Department of Health and Welfare Canada is also paying ($1.7 million) for seventeen Innu children who are being treated for their substance abuse at Poundmaker's Lodge, a Native-run addictions treatment center near Edmonton.

**1 June 1993.** According to a Canadian census, 783,980 people in Canada identify themselves as Indian (626,000 are status Indians); 212,650 as Métis; and 49,255 Inuit. Sixty-five percent of Canadian natives live west of Ontario.

**25 June 1993.** The British Columbia Court of Appeal rules in the case of *Delgamuukw v. The Queen* that the 8000 Gitksan-Wet'suwet'en claimants do enjoy some rights to land which they are claiming in west-central British Columbia. The ruling overturns portions of a March 1991 British Columbia Supreme Court ruling which said that any land rights the Gitksan-Wet'suwet'en may have had were extinguished before British Columbia entered the Canadian Confederation. The claimants welcome the decision as a victory. The British Columbia government expresses its commitment to resolve the claim through negotiation.

**11 November 1993.** New Minister of Indian Affairs Ron Irwin meets with Indian chiefs in an effort to begin negotiations toward an agreement that would establish aboriginal self-government in Canada.

**3 February 1994.** The recipients of the first Canadian National Aboriginal Achievement Awards are announced. The founder of the award program is John Kim Bell. A special lifetime achievement award was granted to Bill Reid, Haida artist.

**22 February 1994.** Canadian finance minister Paul Martin announces that Camp Ipperwash, a military training base in southern Ontario, will be returned to the Ojibwa community at the Kettle and Stoney Point reserves. The land was originally taken from the band in 1942 under the War Measures Act. The band struggled ever since to have the land returned. In 1980 the federal government gave the band $2.5 million to compensate for the expropriation, but some members of the band had been occupying the base since last May in efforts to have the land returned.

**27 February 1994.** The Native Council of Canada is reorganized as the Congress of Aboriginal Peoples during its convention in Ottawa.

**16 March 1994.** For the sixth straight year, Max Yalden of the Canadian Human Rights Commission points to the discrimination faced by Natives as the most serious human rights problem in Canada.

**31 May 1994.** The Canadian government introduces legislation to enact its agreement with the Yukon Indians. The agreement is with four First Nations in the Yukon—the Vuntut Gwitchin First Nation, the Champagne and Aishihik First Nation, the Teslin Tlingit Council, and the Nacho Nyak Dunand First Nation. The agreement covers more than 41,000 square kilometers of the Yukon, and will pay the four First Nations $242.6 million over the next fifteen years. The First Nations communities will have control over hunting, fishing, and other land use on their own land. Ten other bands have not yet approved the agreement.

**1 September 1994.** Phil Fontaine, the grand chief of the Assembly of Manitoba Chiefs announces that his organization has approved a preliminary agreement aimed at dismantling the Department of Indian Affairs in Manitoba and handing over greater powers to Indian communities in Manitoba. Manitoba was chosen for this experiment because leaders like Fontaine are willing to move toward a form of self government without the passage of constitutional amendments or federal legislation.

**9 September 1994.** Milton Born With a Tooth is sentenced to sixteen months in prison after being convicted of weapons offenses committed during the 1990 standoff at the construction site of the Oldman River Dam in southern Alberta.

**5 December 1994.** The Ontario government announces that the Rama Ojibwa Reserve in southern Ontario will be the site of Ontario's first Native casino. The decision that the profits from the casino will be shared by the 131 Indian bands in the province sparks protest from nonstatus Native communities and organizations.

**6 February 1995.** About 150 Innu travel to Voisey's Bay in northern Labrador to protest drilling there. The International Nickel Company discovered a large nickel deposit at Voisey's Bay, near Nain, in 1994, but the Innu do not want the deposit exploited until their claims have been settled.

**10 February 1995.** The Saskatchewan government reaches a deal with the Saskatchewan Federation of Indian Nations to open four casinos on Indian reserves in the province. The Natives will get 75 percent of the profits of these casinos. Throughout Canada, Native communities have been attempting to assert a right to operate casinos on reserves, much like Indian communities in the United States. Twice, however, the Supreme Court has ruled that provinces have exclusive jurisdiction over gaming. Thus, these communities have found it necessary to work with provincial governments before they could legally establish such gaming operations. The Saskatchewan government shut down a casino operation on the White Bear Reserve in 1993, but chose to negotiate with its First Nations communities rather than fight a protracted battle with them.

**20 February 1995.** Nova Scotia Indians sign a deal that will see them get one-half of the government's share of profits from a casino planned for Sydney. Manitoba, Ontario, Nova Scotia, and New Brunswick are also working with First Nations communities to share gambling profits.

**6 September 1995.** Dudley George is shot to death during a protest at Ipperwash Provincial Park, about forty-five kilometers northeast of Sarnia, Ontario. Dissident members of the Kettle and Stoney Point Ojibwa band in southern Ontario took over Camp Ipperwash, an abandoned military base, in July. The 900-hectare parcel of land was taken from the Stoney Point Reserve in 1942 under the authority of the War Measures Act. They were given $50,000 at the time. In 1980 they were given $2.4 million more in compensation. A group of protestors began occupying the base on 5 May 1993, and in February 1994 the government agreed to turn the land over to the band after the military had a chance to clean up the base and dispose of unexploded ammunition. The continued occupation prevented the clean up, however. More recently, the camp has attracted a renegade group that includes Indians from other parts of Ontario and the United States. On July 30, with the protestors becoming more militant, the army abandoned the camp to avoid bloodshed. Then, on September 4, several dozen people including some from the United States, began occupying the adjoining Ipperwash Provincial Park as it was being closed for the season. They claim that the park includes a Native burial site.

**17 September 1995.** Rebels who have been occupying land near Gustafsen Lake, near 100 Mile House, British Columbia, since June, surrender after John Stevens, a spiritual leader from Alberta's Stoney Reserve advises them to do so. The owner of the ranch had allowed a group to hold a Sun Dance on his property every year since 1990. The standoff began in June when the owner discovered a group had remained on his property, and refused to abide by an eviction order. The Natives claim that the land is sacred to the Shuswap Indians. The standoff escalated on August 18 when a police officer was shot at. Ovide Mercredi, the leader of the Assembly of First Nations, then attempted to mediate on August 25 and 26, but failed. Mercredi called on the group to surrender, but he accused the police of undermining his mediation efforts, and criticized political leaders for refusing to get involved at all. Tensions rose again on August 27 when two police officers were hit by gunfire. They were uninjured because they were wearing bullet-proof jackets.

**26 October 1995.** In a referendum, the Inuit of northern Quebec vote 94 percent to stay in Canada. The vote comes in anticipation of a province-wide referendum sponsored by the Quebec government. The Inuit referendum result is similar to those of a referendum they held in 1980. Indian Affairs Minister Ron Irwin responds to the results by saying that the aboriginal people of Quebec have the right to secede from Quebec in the event of separation, a position that the Quebec government rejects.

**30 October 1995.** In a province-wide referendum, the people of Quebec narrowly defeat a proposal to separate from Canada. In that referendum, Quebeckers vote narrowly against separation, but the narrowness of the victory leads some separatist leaders to suggest that ethnic minorities are preventing French Quebeckers from realizing their political aspirations. The referendum and its aftermath lead many to fear reprisals. The 7,500 Inuit and 11,000 Cree of Quebec have been consistent opponents of Quebec separation, as have most of the Indian groups in the province. Approximately 62,000 Indians live in Quebec.

**February 1996.** British Columbia abandons land-claim talks with the Gitskan band of northern British Columbia, arguing that the band has been too rigid in its demands. Negotiations began after the British Columbia Court of Appeal ruled in favor of the Gitskan in the *Delgamuukw* case in 1993. Now, however, both sides seem willing to take on the risks and costs involved with an appeal of that decision to the Supreme Court, an appeal that had been suspended as long as the negotiations continued. Some argue that the British

Columbia government has taken a hard line because a provincial election is looming.

**26 February 1996.** The Supreme Court rules that Aboriginals do not have an inherent right to govern themselves. The decision will mean that Indian bands will continue to have to negotiate with provincial governments to gain access to gaming profits. Several provinces, including Ontario, have already signed agreements with Indian bands that would see governments share gambling profits with Indian bands, but the ruling that Aboriginals do not have the inherent right to govern themselves will have important implications.

**10 March 1996.** The Department of Indian Affairs releases reports that suggest that living conditions for aboriginal Canadians improved noticeably between 1980 and 1995. Still, the numbers study shows that more progress will be necessary before Indians have the same living standards as other Canadians.

**28 March 1996.** Quebec Inuit accept an offer from the Canadian government to compensate them for being relocated to the high Arctic in 1953. The government relocated about ninety Quebec Inuit from Inukjuak and Pond Inlet to Resolute Bay and Grise Fiord.

**21 August 1996.** The Supreme Court rules that Native people cannot claim an aboriginal right to sell fish unless they can prove that they sold fish historically. Specifically, the court upheld a conviction of Dorothy Van der Peet, a Sto:lo from British Columbia who sold salmon in 1987 without a commercial license.

**29 October 1996.** The residents of Davis Inlet vote 97 percent in favor of accepting an agreement reached with the Canadian government in July that would see them relocate to a mainland village at Sango Bay.

**21 November 1996.** The Royal Commission on Aboriginal People releases its six-volume, 3,537-page final report. The report includes 440 recommendations. The report calls on the government to commit itself to a comprehensive restructuring of its relationship with aboriginal people. Among its many specific recommendations, it calls on the government to provide new lands and resources for Native communities. It recommends increasing spending by $1.5 billion to $2 billion annually. It also recommends that the government concede Aboriginals the inherent right to self-government. It calls on the government to establish a new independent tribunal to monitor land claims, establish an aboriginal parliament, and apologize for its past mistakes. The commission recommends that the Department of Indian Affairs be replaced by two new departments, one of which would deal with Native governments, while the other would deal with communities not yet prepared for self-government. It urges the government to provide an adequate land and revenue base to all aboriginal communities, including Métis communities. The Royal Commission on Aboriginal Peoples was established during the aftermath of the Oka Crisis in 1990. It has been controversial because of its cost—at $58 million it is the most expensive royal commission in Canadian history—and because the report has been delayed—the commission was originally told to submit its final report in the fall of 1994. The five-volume report is accompanied by thousands of pages of supporting documents and reports. Ron Irwin, the minister of Indian Affairs, responds cautiously to the report, suggesting that it would be too expensive to implement the recommendations.

**18 December 1996.** The European Union agrees not to ban Canadian fur imports as scheduled in the beginning of January. The move comes after Canada agrees to phase out the leghold trap. The concession is very important for Native people, because more than one-half the trappers in Canada are Native.

**14 February 1997.** Nine Mi'kmaq bands in Nova Scotia become the first in Canada to take over jurisdiction of their children's education. The federal government hand over $140 million to help them establish their own school boards. The development is seen as a potential precedent for other parts of Canada.

**17 April 1997.** Natives hold a national day of protest to show their dissatisfaction with the lack of government action in implementing the recommendations of the Royal Commission on Aboriginal Peoples, and to protest proposed changes to the Indian Act. The protests slow traffic in Canada. Indian Affairs Minister Ron Irwin says some of the recommendations of the Royal Commission have already been implemented, but that it would be impossible to implement them all.

**May 1997.** The Association for the Survivors of the Subenacadie Indian Residential School file a class action lawsuit against the federal government and the Roman Catholic Diocese of Halifax. The claimants say that students at the school suffered as a result of racism and physical, emotional, and sexual abuse. The school, which closed in 1967, educated more than 2,000 students. It was one of seventy-four such schools built by the Canadian government since the 1880s. Former students in schools across the country have begun filing lawsuits to seek compensation for alleged abuse.

**20 May 1997.** The British Columbia Supreme Court convicts William Jones Ignace (Wolverine) of mischief endangering life for his role in the Gustafsen Lake standoff during the summer of 1995. Several others are convicted of lesser charges.

**31 July 1997.** Phil Fontaine is elected as the head of the Assembly of First Nations (AFN) at that group's annual meeting. Fontaine proposes to follow a more conciliatory approach than Ovide Mercredi, his predecessor. Fontaine promises to seek partnerships with governments, businesses, community agencies, and special interest groups. The former Minister of Indian Affairs, Ron Irwin, increasingly snubbed Mercredi and the AFN and dealt directly with individual First Nations communities.

**8 August 1997.** The Pe Sakastew Centre, the first prison built for Native male inmates opens officially at Hobbema, Alberta. The prison will house forty minimum security prisoners. Most of the staff are Aboriginal. Leaders on the Samson Reserve first suggested the idea for the prison six years ago.

**7 November 1997.** Native leaders in New Brunswick threaten to seek an injunction to stop all logging in New Brunswick unless the provincial government abandons it intention to appeal a recent court decision. On November 4, Justice John Turnbull of the New Brunswick Court of Queen's Bench ruled that the Dummer's Treaty of 1720 gives the aboriginal people of the province the unrestricted right to cut trees on Crown Land. Because of the implications of the decision for New Brunswick (forestry is the largest industry in New Brunswick), and other parts of Canada (especially Nova Scotia and British Columbia), the New Brunswick government has said it will appeal the decision.

**11 December 1997.** British Columbia Native leader Joe Mathias announces that "Aboriginal title is alive and well and living in the territories of First Nations in British Columbia" after the Supreme Court of Canada makes its landmark ruling in the case of *Delgamuukw v. The Queen*. The decision is one of the most important Supreme Court decisions of the century because it makes the first attempt to define aboriginal title. The court rules aboriginal title is protected by the Constitution, that no province has the power to extinguish that title, that aboriginal lands are communally owned, that Natives have exclusive rights to their lands, and that lands can be used for "modern" purposes as long as those modern uses do not conflict with aboriginal practices. The decision is also important because the court rules that the judge who decided the case in 1991 erred when he did not evaluate the claimants' oral histories correctly. The court rules that oral histories must be given due consideration by the courts. The decision is also of historical interest, because it is rooted in the longest-running land claim in Canada. This decision means that the case must be retried or negotiated. The judges recommend that the dispute be settled through negotiation. In response to this decision the British Columbia and Canadian governments renew their commitment to negotiation.

**7 January 1998.**   Native leaders give mixed reviews after Indian Affairs Minister Jane Stewart delivers the Canadian government's response to the Royal Commission on Aboriginal Peoples (RCAP) report. Stewart pledges to overhaul the government's relationship with aboriginal people. At the center of the response is an apology on behalf of the Canadian government for past mistreatment of Natives in Canada. Stewart explicitly mentions the residential school experience. She also announces the creation of a $350 million healing fund to help victims deal with the results of abuse suffered at the schools. A seventeen-member management board will administer the healing fund. Several churches involved in the residential schools have already apologized. Over the past year hundreds of lawsuits have been filed in connection with abuse at Native residential schools. Stewart also announces the creation of another $250 million fund to address other problems faced by aboriginal people. It will go to help pay for various programs ranging from improvements to Native housing, employment programs, and policing programs, to the establishment of an aboriginal health institute to help deal with the high rates of AIDS, tuberculosis, and suicide among Natives. Stewart also announces the creation of an independent claims commission to address the backlog of Native claims. These were recommendations of the RCAP.

**10 March 1998.**   Chiefs at an Assembly of First Nations policy meeting in Edmonton vote seventy-two to twelve to accept Jane Stewart's apology of January 7 and the $350 million healing fund, which will go toward counseling services, healing centers, preservation of Native languages, and job training. The vote is a victory for Phil Fontaine who was urging acceptance of the apology. He described the fund and apology as "the first step into the sunlight after generations of darkness." Many leaders have argued that Stewart's gesture does not go far enough to make up for past abuses. Marilyn Buffalo, the president of the Native Women's Association of Canada, who has been particularly vocal in her criticism of the deal, left the room after the vote. Both Fontaine and Buffalo are former students of residential schools.

**22 March 1998.**   Tsuu T'ina (Sarcee) woman Connie Jacobs and her son Ty are killed in an exchange of gunfire with police on the Tsuu T'ina Reserve near Calgary. The shooting occurred as authorities were attempting to remove six children from the home.

**18 June 1998.**   Leaders of the Kettle and Stoney Point First Nation sign an Agreement-in-Principle to return Camp Ipperwash to the Stoney Point Ojibwa. The deal will be worth $26.3 million to the band. The land was expropriated during World War II to establish a military base. In 1980 the government gave the band $2.4 million to compensate for the loss of the land since World War II. Negotiations toward this agreement began in March 1996.

**30 November 1998.**   Joseph Gosnell, the chief of the Nisga'a people, addresses the British Columbia legislature, an honor normally reserved for visiting heads of state. He is speaking as the legislature considers the historic Nisga'a Agreement. The treaty still requires approval of the Canadian and British Columbia governments, but the treaty is viewed as so significant because it is British Columbia's first comprehensive modern-day treaty. For over a century the British Columbia government refused to negotiate land-surrender agreements with Indians in the province. This deal would give the 6,000 Nisga'a title to 2,019 square kilometers of the lower Nass Valley, limited self-government, extensive fishing and logging rights, and $340 million. The Nisga'a approved the agreement in a referendum earlier this month. It still needs to be ratified by the British Columbia legislature and the House of Commons before it is implemented.

**February 1999.**   The Samson Cree of central Alberta file a legal claim of $40 billion for control of a 51,800-square-kilometer swath of central Alberta. The claim includes the rich Bonnie Glen and Leduc oilfields. This is the biggest cash claim in Canadian history. The Cree band's lawyer, James O'Reilly, said the band is claiming an 1876 treaty never surrendered Cree control of resource revenue in "traditional lands" around Hobbema, Leduc, and Pigeon Lake.

**17 February 1999.**   The Supreme Court of Canada rules that the custody of a young Indian boy should go to his non-Native grandparents in Connecticut, rather than his Native grandfather in Vancouver. The case is viewed as significant because the Court rules that the child's biological heritage should play no part in the court's decision regarding the child's best interests, and because it questions the legitimacy of a British Columbia law that encourages the placement of Native children in Native homes. Some Native groups denounce the decision.

**1 April 1999.** The Inuit in the north celebrate the creation of Nunavut with fireworks. The territory was carved out of the Northwest Territories and covers one-fifth of Canada's land area, from the sixtieth parallel to the northern tip of Ellsemere Island. The territory has a population of 27,000, of whom 85 percent are Inuit. Iqaluit, with a population of 4,500 is its largest community and the area's capital.

**10 May 1999.** The Labrador Inuit sign an Agreement-in-Principle with the federal and Newfoundland governments to settle their twenty-two-year old claim. The deal is worth $255 million. The deal would give the Inuit 15,800 square kilometers of land, and a settlement area of 72,520 square kilometers. The 5,000 Inuit will also get a central government which will control their education and health and social services. The Inuit will also get a $140 million trust fund and a portion of future mining revenues from their territory, including development of the Voisey Bay nickel deposit.

**20 May 1999.** In *Corbiere v. Canada (Minister of Indian and Northern Affairs)*, the Supreme Court rules that portions of the Indian Act denying voting privileges to members of reserve communities who are living off reserves contravene the equality provisions of the Canadian Constitution. The ruling has far-reaching implications partly because, since the addition of new band members as a result of Bill C-31, some bands have more non-resident than resident members.

**September 1999.** Trent University begins the first doctoral program in Native studies in Canada.

The flag of Nunavut. (Public Domain)

**1 September 1999.** The Aboriginal Peoples Television Network (APTN), Canada's (and the world's) first national aboriginal TV network, broadcasts for the first time. The opening lineup includes singer Susan Aglukark, a comedy duo from Whitehorse called Susie and Sara, and Go For Baroque and the Nikumoon Top Hat Choir singing Cree to Beethoven. The $15-million-a-year project is aimed at giving viewers a taste of the variety of Native life in Canada and around the world.

**17 September 1999.** In *R. v. Marshall*, the Supreme Court of Canada rules that a 1760 treaty between the Mi'kmaq (Micmac) and the British Crown still gives the Mi'kmaq the right to make a moderate living from commercial fishing. The case involved Donald Marshall Jr., a Cape Breton Mi'kmaq who was arrested in 1993 for catching and selling 210 kilograms of eels out of season and without a license. This is the same man who spent eleven years in prison for a murder he did not commit. In this case, Marshall argued that the Mi'kmaq-British treaty permitted him to catch and sell fish commercially. The Supreme Court agreed, ruling that the treaty allows all Nova Scotia natives covered by the treaty to hunt and fish without a licence at any time of year, although only to fish for their own needs, or to earn a "moderate livelihood." It does not give them the right to establish commercial fishing ventures. Justice Ian Binnie wrote that "The 1760 treaty does affirm the right of the Mi'kmaq people to continue to provide for their own sustenance by taking the products of their hunting, fishing and other gathering activities, and trading for what in 1760 was termed 'necessaries.'"

**4 October 1999.** The leaders of Quebec's Innu call on the federal government to stop work on a joint Quebec and Newfoundland government hydroelectric project on Churchill Falls. They say they are ready to go to court to stop further development on the $10-billion project unless the governments involved offer a treaty that spells out the Innu's ancestral rights to the land surrounding the proposed dam within sixty days.

**26 October 1999.** The New Brunswick government seizes a load of lumber harvested from Crown Land by Mi'kmaq loggers and brought to a sawmill at Belledune, near Bathurst. The issue of Native logging in New Brunswick has been simmering for more than two years, but the Supreme Court decision of September 17 has encouraged Mi'kmaq loggers on the Big Cove Reserve to force the issue over aboriginal cutting rights on Crown land. Maritime Natives argue that the decision in the Marshall case gives them a wide-ranging right to log, hunt, and fish.

**1 November 1999.**   A British Columbia court begins hearing evidence concerning how thirty former Nuu-chah-nulth students at the Alberni Indian residential schools should be compensated for physical and sexual abuse. With more than 3,000 claims having been filed for compensation for abuse in Indian residential schools, the decision will be potentially very significant. It is expected that victims across the country will eventually be awarded billions of dollars in compensation. Last June the British Columbia Supreme Court ruled that the United Church and Canadian government share "vicarious liability" for abuse at the school. There were more than eighty residential schools in Canada between 1880 and the 1980s. Approximately 105,000 children attended these schools. Claims are being filed at a rate of approximately fifteen to twenty per week.

**16 November 1999.**   Robert Levi, chief of the Big Cove Reserve on New Brunswick's east coast agrees to a deal that will give his band access to trees on Crown land. Access will be permitted according to the same formula that other bands in the province have already agreed to. Aboriginal loggers will be given 5 percent of the total annual allowable cut. The Mi'kmaq have been in a long struggle with the New Brunswick government over Native logging rights, and the recent Marshall decision has renewed the struggle. The Mi'kmaq insist that the Marshall decision gives them the unrestricted right to harvest trees on Crown land.

**17 November 1999.**   Mi'kmaq (Micmac) leaders in Atlantic Canada are disappointed after the Supreme Court rules that the Canadian government does have the power to regulate the Native fishery in Atlantic Canada. The ruling comes after the Supreme Court refuses to rehear the controversial ruling it handed down in the Marshall case on September 17, but agrees to issue a "clarification" of the decision. Since the decision of September 17 the maritime has witnessed violent confrontations between non-Native fishermen and Mi'kmaq fishermen.

**13 December 1999.**   The Nisga'a treaty overcomes its final political hurdle as the House of Commons votes 217 to forty-eight to pass the treaty into law. It must now pass the Senate, which is expected to happen in February. The bill passed despite the Reform Party's record-setting stalling tactics. The Reform Party conducted a forty-two-hour filibuster in the House of Commons beginning on December 7. The Reform Party opposes the treaty, arguing that because the treaty is based on race it sets a bad precedent for future treaties. It also argues that the treaty does not guarantee that average band members will benefit from the treaty. The party called for a referendum on the treaty in British Columbia.

**20 January 2000.**   The Ontario Superior Court of Justice rules that Métis people have the constitutional right to hunt without a license. The decision will be appealed.

**21 March 2000.**   Dissident members of the Nisga'a file a challenge to the constitutionality of the Nisga'a land claim in British Columbia's Supreme Court. The group from the village of Kincolith argues that the treaty violates sections 25 and 35 of the Constitution Act of 1982 by arguing that the Nisga'a Tribal Council and the government violated the rights of the Nisga'a by claiming that the Tribal Council has authority over the Nisga'a. The plaintiffs argue that the Tribal Council is not a valid aboriginal government.

**25 March 2000.**   Canadian, provincial, and Innu negotiators are nearly ready to sign a framework agreement toward an Agreement-in-Principle to settle the Innu land claim. When completed, the deal may be more extensive than the Nisga'a Agreement that has attracted much attention lately. Despite the optimism, some doubt that an agreement would do much to alleviate the troubled Innu communities in Labrador.

**5 April 2000.**   Indian Affairs Minister Robert Nault tells a parliamentary committee that Indians in Canada are filing court claims against the federal government related to abuse at residential schools at a rate of twenty cases a week. Since 1997 the number of claims has jumped from eighty-four to 3,152. The department expects to spend nearly $1.5 billion in the next three years in order settle all other kinds of Native claims. Meanwhile the department is also grappling with Supreme Court decisions that are undermining the Indian Act. In this context, Nault argues, there is a danger of conflict.

**11 April 2000.**   Two Saskatoon city police officers are charged with unlawful confinement and assault after Darrell Night, an aboriginal man, alleged that the officers drove him to the outskirts of the city in bitterly cold weather last January 28, took his jacket, and told him to find his own way back to the city. The allegations led to the appointment of an RCMP task force in February consisting of fifteen to twenty investigators who took four weeks to look into five suspicious deaths and allegations that the police (both the Saskatoon city police and the RCMP) routinely took Aboriginals to the edge of the city to find their own way back. Night made his allegation shortly after the partially clothed body of

Rodney Naistus, from Onion Lake, was discovered on January 29, and the frozen body of Lawrence Kim Wegner was found on February 3. In March the Federation of Saskatchewan Indian Nations (FSIN) announced that it has also hired investigators to look into the allegations because it does not trust the RCMP to investigate properly. The FSIN has also called for a public inquiry to look into the matter.

**13 April 2000.** Shortly after the Nisga'a agreement receives Royal Assent, Nisga'a Chief Joseph Gosnell stands on the steps of the Senate chambers and says "The Royal Assent of our treaty signifies the end of the colonial era for the Nisga'a people. It is a great and historic day for all Canadians, and this achievement is a beacon of hope for colonized people in our own country and throughout the world." Surrounded by politicians from the Nisga'a Nation and the Canadian parliament, Gosnell declares that "Today, the Nisga'a people become full-fledged Canadians as we step out from under the Indian Act—forever. Finally, after a struggle of more than 130 years, the government of this country clearly recognizes that the Nisga'a were a self-governing people since well before European contact. We remain self-governing today, and we are proud to say that this inherent right is now clearly recognized and protected in the Constitution of Canada."

**13 April 2000.** New Brunswick Provincial Court Judge Denis Lordon rules that two eighteenth-century treaties do not give the Mi'kmaq the right to cut trees on commercial land today. In his fifty-page ruling, the judge wrote that "to interpret the right to gather as a right to participate in the wholesale, uncontrolled exploitation of natural resources would alter the terms of the treaty and wholly transform the rights therein conferred." This is the first significant legal test since the Supreme Court's decision in the Marshall case last September. The case is likely to be appealed to the Supreme Court.

**13 April 2000.** A report by the six-member Indian Claims Commission tabled in Parliament argues that the claims process is not working. It notes that while about 450 claims await evaluation, only five to ten are resolved each year.

**17 April 2000.** The Manitoba government announces that it will hand over control of child and family services to the First Nations of the province. The announcement comes after the new government of the province established a committee to implement the recommendations of the 1991 Manitoba aboriginal justice inquiry. The committee was established soon after the election of the New Democratic Party last year.

**1 May 2000.** Hearings begin in the Samson Cree lawsuit against the federal government. The Samson Cree of Hobbema are suing the government for $1.3 billion alleging that the government has misspent and mismanaged the band's oil revenues. Observers predict that if the band is successful, many other bands in Canada could be expected to file their own claims. In February the Samson Cree filed a $40-billion lawsuit in which they argue that they have rights to much of the oil-producing region in Central Alberta.

**13 May 2000.** Nisga'a Chief Joe Gosnell announces that "we're no longer beggars in our own land," and hundreds of Nisga'a sing "O Canada" as they celebrate the implementation of their agreement with the Canadian government at an elaborate celebration at Gitwinksihlkw, British Columbia, in their homeland in the Nass Valley.

**15 May 2000.** The British Columbia Supreme Court begins hearing a court challenge of the validity of the Nisga'a Agreement. The British Columbia Liberal Party, which is leading the challenge, argues that the treaty is unconstitutional because it creates a third order of government. They argue that the agreement can stand only if the Constitution is amended—something that, according to British Columbia law, requires a province-wide referendum. If the Liberals win the case, it would very likely end up in the Supreme Court.

**16 May 2000.** Judge Thomas Goodson releases the result of his fatality inquiry into the death of Connie and Ty Jacobs on the Tsuu T'ina (Sarcee) Reserve on 22 March 1998. The report makes eighteen recommendations, many of which suggest that the tribal police force was understaffed and poorly prepared to deal with the very serious conditions that developed. The report says that the Jacobs may not have died if RCMP officers and paramedics had responded together when the domestic dispute first came to light. Goodson also called for better training for the child and family services workers and First Nations police officers. Band officials and members of the Jacobs' family welcome the recommendations.

**31 May 2000.** The Sechelt band announces that it is withdrawing from treaty negotiations with the British Columbia government, raising fears that the entire British Columbia Treaty Commission process may be threatened. Last year, the Sechelt became the first band to sign an Agreement-in-Principle after passing through the process. Representatives of the band suggest that recent court decisions suggest that the band should be offered far more than they were offered in the Agreement-in-Principle. More than one hundred First Nation

Nisga'a Chief Joe Gosnell shakes hands with Premier Ujjal Dosanjh to finalize the historic treaty. (Photo by Kate Bird. Courtesy of *Vancouver Sun* files)

communities in British Columbia are awaiting land claim settlements with the British Columbia Treaty Commission.

**1 June 2000.** Officers from the Department of Fisheries and Oceans seize forty-three lobster traps set by Mi'kmaq fishermen in Miramichi Bay, New Brunswick. This action is part of a simmering dispute set off by the Supreme Court's decision in the Marshall case in September. The Mi'kmaq claim the right to fish according to their own rules, while the federal government claims that the Mi'kmaq may fish only if they have federal licenses. Disputes and impasses in various parts of Canada have raised fears that the summer of 2000 will see violent confrontations between Native groups and Canadian authorities.

**12 June 2000.** The Supreme Court hears arguments from lawyers of the Musqueam band and lawyers of seventy-three leaseholders whose homes are on land owned by the band. The lawyers for the band say that a lower court has set the rents too low, while the lease-holders' lawyers will argue that the rent has been set too high.

**12 July 2000.** Matthew Coon Come, a Cree from northern Quebec, is elected the new head chief of the Assembly of First Nations, defeating the incumbent Phil Fontaine. Fontaine was accused of being too friendly with the federal government and of ignoring the priorities of most reserve Indians in Canada. During the week leading up to the vote, Coon Come promised to continue employing the openly confrontational approach that made him successful during his struggles with the Quebec government. Coon Come is known as a bold, confident, articulate leader with a sharp sense of practical politics.

**23 July 2000.** The 2,000 members of the Squamish band in Vancouver vote to accept the federal government's offer to settle their land claim. The federal government offered the band $92.5 million to settle their claim to 600 hectares of land in parcels in and near

Vancouver which was taken from their reserve during the last century. Today, much of the land is prime real estate in Vancouver. The money will go into a trust fund. The Squamish initiated litigation in this case in 1977.

**23 July 2000.** The Nisga'a of northern British Columbia, and the government of the province, celebrate after Justice Paul Williamson of the Supreme Court of British Columbia rules that the Nisga'a Agreement does not violate the Canadian Constitution. The case was brought to the court by Gordon Campbell, the leader of the British Columbia Liberal Party, who has vowed to appeal the decision.

*Theodore Binnema*
*University of Northern British Columbia*

# Sites and Landmarks

## UNITED STATES

### ◆ ALABAMA

MOUNDVILLE STATE MONUMENT
P.O. Box 66
Moundville, AL 35474
(205) 371–2572
www.ua.edu/mndvillle.htm

RUSSELL CAVE NATIONAL MONUMENT
3729 County Rd 98
Bridgeport, AL 35740
(256) 495–2672
www.nps.gov/ruca/
Archaic, Woodland, and Mississippian periods.

### ◆ ALASKA

SITKA NATIONAL HISTORIC PARK
106 Metlakatla P.O. Box 738
Sitka, AK 99835
(907) 747–6281

### ◆ ARIZONA

AWATOVI RUINS
Keams Canyon, AZ 86034
No phone number available.
(On the National Register of Historical
    Places, 1/30/92)

CANYON DE CHELLY NATIONAL MONUMENT
P.O. Box 588
Chinle, AZ 86503
(520) 674–5500
www.nps.gov/cach

CASA GRANDE RUINS NATIONAL
    MONUMENT
1100 Ruins Dr.
Coolidge, AZ 85228
(520) 723–3172
Hohokam village site, c.e. 500–1450.

CHIRICAHUA NATIONAL MONUMENT
    MUSEUM
H.R.C. 2, Box 6500
Wilcox, AZ 85643
(520) 824–3560

GUEVAVI MISSION RUINS
Nogales, AZ 85621
No phone number available.
(On the National Register of Historical
    Places, 1/30/92)

HUBBELL TRADING POST NATIONAL
    HISTORIC SITE
P.O. Box 150
Ganado, AZ 86505
(520) 755–3475
www.nps.gov/hutr/
Oldest continually operating Indian trading post.

MISSION SAN XAVIER DEL BAC
1950 West San Xavier
Tucson, AZ 85746
(520) 294–2624
Spanish colonial Indian mission.

MONTEZUMA CASTLE MUSEUM
P.O. Box 219
Camp Verde, AZ 86322
(520) 567–3322
www.nps.gov/moca

NAVAJO NATIONAL MONUMENT
HC 71, Box 3
Tonalea, AZ 86044–9704
(520) 672–2366
Site of three cliff villages, of the Kayenta, Anasazi,
and Navajo cultures.

OLD ORAIBI
Hopi Indian Reservation
Oraibi, AZ 86039
No phone number available.
(On the National Register of Historical
Places, 1/30/92)

PUEBLO GRANDE MUSEUM
4619 East Washington St.
Phoenix, AZ 85034
(602) 495–0901
Hohokam site, 300 B.C.E.–C.E.1450

TONTO NATIONAL MONUMENT MUSEUM
HC 02, Box 4602
Roosevelt, AZ 85545
(602) 467–2241
Prehistoric Salado Indian cliff dwellings.

TUMACACORI NATIONAL HISTORICAL PARK
P.O. Box 67
Tumacacori, AZ 85640
(520) 398–2341
www.nps.gov/tuma

TUZIGOOT NATIONAL MONUMENT
P.O. Box 68
Clarkdale, AZ 86324
(520) 634–5564

WALNUT CANYON NATIONAL MONUMENT
Walnut Canyon Rd.
Flagstaff, AZ 86004–9705
(520) 526–3367
www.npsgov/wacca
Sinagua Indian ruins site, C.E. 110–1270

WUPATKI AND SUNSET CRATER NATIONAL
MONUMENT
HC 33, Box 444A
Flagstaff, AZ 86001
(520) 556–7152
Ruins of the Lomaki, Nalakihum Citadel, Wuwoki,
and Wupatki.

♦ **ARKANSAS**

CADDO-HA INDIAN VILLAGE
P.O. Box 669
Murfreesboro, AR 71958
(870) 285–3736
www.caddotc.com
Caddo (mound builders) grounds, site excavation.

TOLTEC MOUNDS ARCHEOLOGICAL
STATE PARK
490 Toltec Mounds Rd.
Scotts, AR 72142
(501) 961–9221

♦ **CALIFORNIA**

DEATH VALLEY NATIONAL PARK
P.O. Box 579
Death Valley, CA 92328
(760) 786–2331
www.npsgov/deva
Exhibits of local basketry; archaeological artifacts.

LA PURISIMA MISSION STATE
HISTORIC PARK
2295 Purisima Rd.
Lompoc, CA 93436
(805) 733–3713
www.parks.ca.gov

LAVA BEDS NATIONAL MONUMENT
P.O. Box 867
Tulelake, CA 96134
(530) 667–2287
Modoc Indian war (1872–73) museum.

♦ **COLORADO**

BENT'S OLD FORT NATIONAL HISTORIC SITE
35110 Highway 194 E.
La Junta, CO 81050
(719) 384–2800
Adobe trading post built in 1833.

GREAT SAND DUNES NATIONAL
MONUMENT
11500 Highway 150
Mosca, CO 81146
(719) 378–2312

HOVENWEEP NATIONAL MONUMENT
McEmo RT.
Cortez, CO 81321
(970) 562–4282
www.nps.gov

MESA VERDE NATIONAL PARK MUSEUM
P.O. Box 38
Mesa Verde, CO 81330
(970) 529–4465
Prehistoric Pueblo dwellings, with museums of
Anasazi remains, c.e. 500–1330

#### ◆ FLORIDA

INDIAN TEMPLE MOUND
139 Miracle Strip Pkwy. SE
Fort Walton Beach, FL 32548
(850) 833–9595
www.fwb.org
The largest Mississippian temple mound on the
    Gulf Coast.

#### ◆ GEORGIA

CHIEF VANN HOUSE
82 HWY 225 NC
Chattsworth, GA 30705
(706) 517–4255

ETOWAH INDIAN MOUNDS STATE
    HISTORIC SITE
813 Indian Mounds Rd. S.E.
Cartersville, GA 30120
(770) 387–3747
Seven mounds; excavations.

KOLOMOKI MOUNDS MUSEUM
Rte. 1, Box 114
Blakely, GA 31723
(912) 724–2151
Indian burial mound and village, c. c.e. 1250.

NEW ECHOTA HISTORIC SITE
1211 Chatsworth Hwy. N.E.
Calhoun, GA 30701
(706) 624–1321
www.gastateprkff.org
1825 capital of the Cherokee Nation; a Preservation
    Project.

OCMULGEE NATIONAL MONUMENT
1207 Emery Hwy.
Macon, GA 31217
(912) 752–8257
www.npsgov/ocma
Seven mounds, about c.e. 900.

#### ◆ IDAHO

NEZ PERCÉ NATIONAL HISTORICAL
    PARK MUSEUM
P.O. Box 100
Spalding, ID 83540
(208) 843–2001
www.nps.gov
Early mission site.

#### ◆ ILLINOIS

CAHOKIA MOUNDS STATE HISTORIC SITE
INTERPRETIVE CENTER MUSEUM
30 Ramey 3
Collinsville, IL 62234
(618) 346–5160

DICKSON MOUNDS MUSEUM
Rtes. 97 and 78
Lewiston, IL 61542
(309) 547–3721

STARVED ROCK STATE PARK
P.O. Box 509
Utica, IL 61373
(815) 667–4726
dnr.state.il.us
Site of village occupied first by Illinois Indians, then
    Ottawa and Potawatomi.

#### ◆ INDIANA

ANGEL MOUNDS STATE HISTORIC SITE
8215 Pollack Ave.
Evansville, IN 47715
(812) 853–3956
Mississippian archaeological site; ten mounds, c.e.
1250–1450; reconstructed structures.

CHIEF RICHARDSVILLE HOUSE AND MIAMI
    TREATY GROUNDS
Huntington, IN 46750
No phone number available.
(On the National Registry of Historic Places, 1/30/92)

SONOTABAC PREHISTORIC INDIAN MOUND
AND MUSEUM
P.O. Box 941
2401 Wabash Ave.
Vincennes, IN 47591
(812) 885–4330
Largest ceremonial mound in Indiana.

### ◆ IOWA

CHIEF WAPELLO'S MEMORIAL PARK
Agency, IA 52530
No phone number available.
(On the National Register of Historic Places, 1/30/92)

EFFIGY MOUNDS NATIONAL MONUMENT
151 HWY 76
Harpers Ferry, IA 52146
(319) 873–3491
www.nps.gov/efmo
Burial mounds.

SPIRIT LAKE MASSACRE LOG CABIN
Arnolds Park, IA 51331
No phone number available.
(On the National Register of Historic Places, 1/30/92)

### ◆ KANSAS

CORONADO QUIVIRA MUSEUM
105 W. Lyon
Lyons, KS 67554
(316) 257–3941

FORT LARNED NATIONAL HISTORIC SITE
R.R. 3
Larned, KS 67550
(316) 285–6911
www.nps.gov/fols

KAW-INDIAN MISSION
500 North Mission
Council Groove, KS 66846
(316) 767–5410
www.kshs.org

NATIVE AMERICAN HERITAGE MUSEUM
Highland Mission State Historic Site
1737 Elgin Road
Highland, KS 66035
(785) 442–3304
kshs.org/places/highland.htm

PAWNEE INDIAN VILLAGE MUSEUM
R.R. 1 Box 475
Republic, KS 66964
(785) 361–2255
ww.kshs.org
Best preserved Pawnee earth lodge site on
the Plains.

PAWNEE ROCK
Pawnee Rock, KS 67567
No phone number available.
(On the National Register of Historic Places, 1/30/92)

SHAWNEE INDIAN MISSION
Mission Road
Fairway, KS 66205
(913) 262–0867

### ◆ KENTUCKY

WICKLIFFE MOUND RESEARCH CENTER
P.O. Box 155
Wickliffe, KY 42087
(270) 335–3681
http:campus.murraystate.edu.htm

### ◆ MASSACHUSETTS

WAMPANOAG INDIAN PROGRAM OF
PLYMOUTH PLANTATION
P.O. Box 1620
Plymouth, MA 02362
(508) 746–1622
Outdoor living history museum of colonial period.

### ◆ MINNESOTA

GRAND PORTAGE NATIONAL MONUMENT
P.O. Box 668
Grand Marais, MN 55064
(218) 387–2788

LOWER SIOUX AGENCY HISTORY CENTER
Minnesota Historical Society
32469 County Hwy.
Morton, MN 56270
(507) 697–6321, or (888) 727–8386
www.mnhs.org
1835 Indian mission.

PIPESTONE NATIONAL MONUMENT
36 Reservation Ave.
Pipestone, MN 56164–1269
(507) 825–5464
www.nps.gov/pipe
Original Dakota pipestone quarry for
    ceremonial pipes.

## ◆ MISSISSIPPI

EMERAL MOUND
Natchez Trace Parkway
2680 Natchez Trace Parkway
Tupclo, MS 38804
(662) 680–4025

THE GRAND VILLAGE OF THE NATCHEZ
    INDIANS
400 Jefferson Davis Blvd.
Natchez, MS 39120
(601) 446–6502
mdah.state ms.us
Ceremonial mound center for the Natchez Tribe,
    1250–1730.

WINTERVILLE MOUNDS
2415 Hwy 1 north
Greenville, MS 38701
(662) 334–4684
mdah.state ms.us
Ceremonial center for Prehistoric Tribes, C.E.
1000–1450.

## ◆ MONTANA

BIG HOLE NATIONAL BATTLEFIELD
P.O. Box 237
Wisdom, MT 59761
(406) 689–3156
Preserves scene of battle between Nez Percé and
    the Seventh U.S. Infantry, 1877.

CHIEF PLENTY COUPS STATE PARK
    AND MUSEUM
P.O. Box 100
Pryor, MT 59066
(406) 252–1289
Crow Indian Museum.

LITTLE BIGHORN BATTLEFIELD NATIONAL
    MONUMENT
P.O. Box 39
Crow Agency, MT 59022
(406) 638–2621
www.nps.gov/libi
National Cemetery and site where the Battle of the
    Little Bighorn took place on June 25th and
    26th, 1876.

MADISON BUFFALO JUMP STATE
    MONUMENT
Logan, MT 59741
No phone number available.
(On the National Register of Historic Places, 1/30/92)

## ◆ NEBRASKA

OREGON TRAIL MUSEUM
Scotts Bluff National Monument
P.O. Box 27
Gering, NB 69341–0027
(308) 436–5794

## ◆ NEVADA

GATECLIFF ROCKSHELTER
Austin, NV 89310
No phone number available.
(On the National Register of Historic Places, 1/30/92)

## ◆ NEW MEXICO

AZTEC RUINS NATIONAL MONUMENT
P.O. Box 640
Aztec, NM 87410
(505) 334–6174
www.nps.gov/azaru
Pueblo ruins at Chaco Canyon and Mesa Verde.

BANDELIER NATIONAL MONUMENT
HCR 1, Box 1, Suite 15
Los Alamos, NM 87544
(505) 672–3861
www.nps.gov/band
Anasazi ruins, C.E. 1200–1600.

CHACO CULTURE NATIONAL
   HISTORICAL PARK
P.O. Box 220
Nageezi, NM 87037
(505) 786–7014
www.nps.gov/chcu/
Thirteen major Anasazi sites; more than 400 smaller
   village sites.

CORONADO STATE MONUMENT
P.O. Box 95
Bernalillo, NM 87004
(505) 867–5351
Pueblo ruin, c.e. 1300–1600; reconstructed kiva.

EL MORRO NATIONAL MONUMENT
Rte. 2, Box 43
Ramah, NM 87321
(505) 783–4226
Archaeological site of Inscription Rock;
   Pueblo ruins.

PECOS NATIONAL HISTORICAL PARK
P.O. Drawer 418
Pecos, NM 87552
(505) 757–6414
www.nps.gov/peco
Pueblo ruins; Spanish church ruins.

SALINAS PUEBLO MISSION NATIONAL
   MONUMENT
P.O. Box 517
Mountainair, NM 87036–0517
(505) 847–2585
Prehistoric pit houses, c.e. 800, ruins, c.e. 1100–1670;
Spanish mission ruins, c.e. 1627–72.

SALMON RUIN
San Juan County Museum Association
975 U.S. Highway 64
Farmington, NM 87401
(505) 632–2013
Anasazi ruin.

#### ◆ NEW YORK

MOHAWK-CAUGHNAWAGA MUSEUM
Rte. 5, Box 55
Fonda, NY 12068
No phone number available.
Located near Tekakwitha Shrine (see next entry).
Excavated Caughnawaga Indian village.

TEKAKWITHA SHRINE
P.O. Box 6298
Fonda, NY 1206
(518) 853–3646
Mohawk Indian castle; residence of Kateri
   Tekakwitha.
Religious shrine and historic archaeological site,
   1666–93.

#### ◆ NORTH CAROLINA

MUSEUM OF THE CHEROKEE INDIAN
P.O. Box 1599
Cherokee, NC 28719
(828) 497–3481
www.cherokee.museum.org

OCONALUFTEE INDIAN VILLAGE
P.O. Box 398
Cherokee, NC 28719
(828) 497–2315
www.oconaluftee.com
A replica of a 1750 Cherokee village.

TOWN CREEK INDIAN MOUND STATE
   HISTORIC SITE
509 Town Mound Rd
Mt. Gilead, NC 27306
(910) 439–6802
www.ah.dcr.state.nc.us/section/hs/town
Reconstructed sixteenth-century Indian ceremonial
   center.

#### ◆ NORTH DAKOTA

BIG HIDATSA VILLAGE SITE
Stanton, ND 58571
No phone number available.
(On the National Register of Historic Places, 1/30/92)

#### ◆ OHIO

FORT ANCIENT MUSEUM
Fort Ancient State Memorial
6123 State Route 350
Oregonia, OH 45054
(513) 932–4421
www.ohiohistory.org

HOPEWELL CULTURE NATIONAL
   HISTORICAL PARK
16062 State Route 104
Chillecothe, OH 45601
(740) 774–1125
www.nps.gov/hocu
Twenty-three Hopewell culture burial mounds, 200
B.C.E.–500 C.E.

MOUND BUILDERS STATE MEMORIAL
   AND MUSEUM
99 Cooper Ave.
Newark, OH 43055
(740) 344–1920
www.ohiohistory.org.places.moundbld
The Great Circle Earthworks: Ceremonial grounds of
Hopewell culture, 200 B.C.E.–C.E. 600

PIQUA HISTORICAL MUSEUM
509 North Main
Piqua, OH 45356
(937) 773–2307
Collection of pre-contact tools and weapons from
   the Adena, Hopewell, and Fort Ancient cultures.

SERPENT MOUND MUSEUM
3850 Rte. 73, Box 234
Peebles, OH 45660
(513) 587–2796
(800) 653–6446
Adena culture.

#### ◆ OKLAHOMA

CREEK INDIAN COUNCIL HOUSE MUSEUM
106 W. 6th Street
Council House Square
Okmulgee, OK 74447
(918) 756–2324

SEQUOYAH'S CABIN
Rte. 1, Box 141
Sallisaw, OK 74955
(918) 775–2413
www.ok-history.mus.ok.us
1829 log cabin of Cherokee leader Sequoyah.

#### ◆ PENNSYLVANIA

BUSHY RUN BATTLEFIELD PARK
P.O. Box 468
Harrison City, PA 15636–0468
(724) 527–5584
Site of Chief Pontiac's rebellion, 1763.

#### ◆ SOUTH DAKOTA

BEAR BUTTE STATE PARK
P.O. Box 688
Sturgis, SD 57785
(605) 347–5240
Native American traditional religious site.

INDIAN MUSEUM OF NORTH AMERICA
Crazy Horse Memorial Foundation
Avenue of the Chiefs
Crazy Horse, SD 57730–9506
(605) 673–4681
www.crazyhorse.org
Crazy Horse Memorial project in the Black Hills.

THE HERITAGE CENTER
Red Cloud Indian School
P.O. Box 100
Pine Ridge, SD 57770
(605) 867–5491
www.basec.net/~rchertiage
Art museum near scene of Wounded Knee Massacre.

#### ◆ TENNESSEE

CHUCALISSA INDIAN VILLAGE
1987 Indian Village Dr.
Memphis, TN 38109
(901) 785–3160
Museum and rebuilt Indian village.

PINSON MOUNDS STATE
   ARCHAEOLOGICAL AREA
460 Ozier Rd.
Pinson, TN 38366
(901) 988–5614
Middle Woodland Period ceremonial site; mounds
   and earthworks.

RED CLAY STATE HISTORICAL PARK
1140 Red Clay Park Road S.W.
Cleveland, TN 37311
(423) 478–0339
www.state.tn.us/environment/parks/redclay
Cherokee government seat, 1832–38; Cherokee
   Council site.

## ◆ TEXAS

### CADDOAN MOUNDS STATE HISTORIC SITE

Rte. 2, Box 85C
Alto, TX 75925
(409) 858–3218
Caddoan village and ceremonial center with three
mounds, C.E. 750–1300.

## ◆ UTAH

### ANASAZI STATE HISTORICAL MONUMENT

P.O. Box 1429
Boulder, UT 84716
(435) 335–7308
Excavated Anasazi Indian village, C.E. 1050–1200.

### EDGE OF THE CEDARS STATE PARK AND MUSEUM

600 West, 400 North
Blanding, UT 84511
(435) 678–2238
Anasazi ruins, C.E. 700–1220.

### INDIAN CREEK STATE PARK

Monticello, UT 84535
No phone number available.
(On the National Register of Historic Places, 1/30/92)

## ◆ VIRGINIA

### PAMUNKEY CULTURAL CENTER MUSEUM

Rte. 1, Box 787
King William, VA 23086
(804) 843–4792

### WOODLAWN HISTORIC AND ARCHEOLOGICAL DISTRICT

Port Conway, VA
No phone number available.
On the National Register of Historic Places, 1/30/92)

## ◆ WEST VIRGINIA

### MOUND MUSEUM

801 Jefferson Ave.
Moundsville, WV 26041
(304) 845–2773

## ◆ WISCONSIN

### BARRON COUNTY PIPESTONE QUARRIES

Rice Lake, WI 54868
No phone number available.
(On the National Register of Historic Places, 1/30/92)

### OLD INDIAN AGENCY HOUSE

Portage, WI 53901
No phone number available.
(On the National Register of Historic Places, 1/30/92)

### RICE LAKE MOUNDS

Rice Lake, WI 54868
No phone number available.
(On the National Register of Historic Places, 1/30/92)

### WAUKESHA COUNTY HISTORICAL MUSEUM

101 West Main St.
Waukesha, WI 53186
(262) 521–2859
Located on prehistoric burial mound of the Turtle.

# CANADA

## ◆ ALBERTA

### WRITING-ON-STONE PROVISIONAL PARK

P.O. Box 297
Milk River, AL T0K 1M0
(403) 647–2364

## ◆ NEWFOUNDLAND

### CASTLE HILL NATIONAL HISTORIC PARK

P.O. Box 10
Jersey Side
Placentia Bay, NF A0B 2G0
(709) 227–2401

## ◆ ONTARIO

### CHAMPLAIN TRAIL MUSEUM

1035 Pembroke St. E.
Pembroke, ON K8A 6Z2
(613) 735–0517
Agricultural artifacts of the 1840s.

## LONDON MUSEUM OF ARCHAEOLOGY
1600 Attawandaron Rd.
London, ON N6G 3M6
(519) 473–1360
Archaeological site of a reconstructed 500-year-old
Iroquoian village; prehistory of Ontario.

## OLD FORT WILLIAM
Vickers Heights Post Office
Thunder Bay, ON P0T 2Z0
(807) 577–8461
Reconstruction of the nineteenth-century inland
headquarters of the North West Company,
including a living history program reenacting the
fur trade activities of Scottish partners, French-
Canadian voyeurs, and native Ojibwa.

## SERPENT MOUNDS PROVINCIAL PARK
R.R. 3
Keene, ON K0L 2G0
(705) 295–6879
Walking path to Indian burial mounds.

## SKA-NAH-DOHT INDIAN VILLAGE
Longwoods Rd. Conservation Area, R.R. 1
Mt. Brydges, ON N0L 1W0
(519) 264–2420
A recreated Iroquoian village of about one thousand
years ago. Ska-Nah-Doht means "A village stands
again" (Oneida).

# Native American Place Names

## UNITED STATES

### ◆ ALABAMA

**Alabama:** Name of state and river; meaning "clearers of thickets" (Choctaw)

**Autauga:** Name of county and creek; meaning "border" (Creek)

**Chickasaw:** Name of town; derived from tribal name (Chickasaw)

**Choctaw:** Name of city and county; derived from tribal name (Choctaw)

**Conecuh:** Name of county, river, and national forest; probably meaning "land of cane" (Creek)

**Eufaula:** Name of city and wildlife refuge; derived from former village name (Creek)

**Mobile:** Name of city, county, and river; derived from tribal name, probably meaning "the rowers" (Choctaw)

**Natchez:** Name of town; derived from tribal name, probably meaning "timber land" (Muskogean)

**Sipsey:** Name of town and river; meaning "poplar tree" (Chickasaw-Choctaw)

**Talladega:** Name of city, county, and national forest; derived from village name, meaning "town on the border" (Creek)

**Tuscaloosa:** Name of city and county; named after chief whose name means "Black warrior" (Choctaw)

**Tuscumbia:** Name of city; named after chief whose name means "warrior rain maker" (Cherokee)

**Tuskegee:** Name of town, institute, and national forest; derived from tribal name, meaning "warrior" (probably Creek)

### ◆ ALASKA

**Alaska:** Name of state, gulf, and peninsula; meaning "a great country or continent" (Aleut)

**Anaktuvuk:** Name of river and pass; meaning "dung everywhere" (Inupiat)

**Iditarod:** Name of river; derived from a former Indian village (Ingalik)

**Kenai:** Name of lake, mountains, and peninsula; derived from tribal name (Kenai)

**Ketchikan:** Name of city and lake; meaning "eagle wing river" or "city under the eagle" (probably Tlingit or Haida)

**Kodiak:** Name of town, island, and national wildlife refuge; meaning "island" (probably Eskimo)

**Metlakatla:** Name of town; derived from former village name (Tsimshian)

**Nunivak:** Name of island and national wildlife refuge; probably meaning "big land" (Eskimo)

**Sitka:** Name of town, national monument, and sound; probably meaning "by the sea" (Tlingit)

**Skagway:** Name of village and river; probably meaning "home of the north wind" (Tlingit)

**Stikine:** Name of river and strait; meaning "great river" (Tlingit)

**Tanana:** Name of village, river, and island; derived from tribal name, meaning "mountain river" (Athapascan)

**Unalaska:** Name of village, island, bay, and lake; meaning "dwelling together harmoniously" (Aleut)

**Yukon:** Name of river; meaning "big river" (Yupik Eskimo)

### ◆ ARIZONA

**Ajo:** Name of town and mountains; meaning "paint" (Tohono O'Odham, also known as Papago)

Apache: Name of town, county, lake, pass, and peak; derived from tribal name, meaning "enemy" (Yuma or Zuni)

Arizona: Name of state; meaning "small place of the spring" (Tohono O'Odham)

Chinle: Name of town and trading center; meaning "mouth of canyon" (Navajo)

Chiricahua: Name of mountains, peak, and national monument; derived from tribal name, meaning "great mountain" (Apache)

Chuska: Name of mountains; meaning "white spruce" (probably Navajo)

Cochise: Name of county; named after famous chief (Chiricahua Apache)

Coconino: Name of county, plateau, and national forest; derived from tribal name, meaning "pinyon people" (Zuni) or "little water" (Havasupai)

Hopi: Name of Indian reservation; derived from tribal name, meaning "the peaceful ones" (Hopi)

Kaibab: Name of town, plateau, and national forest; meaning "a mountain lying down" (Paiute)

Kayenta: Name of town; meaning "where they fell into a creek" (Navajo)

Maricopa: Name of town and county; derived from tribal name (Pima)

Mohave: Name of county, mountains, and lake; derived from tribal name, meaning "three mountains" (Mohave)

Navajo: Name of Indian reservation and county; derived from tribal name, probably meaning "large area of cultivated lands" (Spanish)

Paria: Name of river and plateau; meaning "elk water" (Paiute)

Pima: Name of town and county; derived from tribal name, meaning "no" (probably Spanish)

Yavapai: Name of county; derived from tribal name, meaning "people of the sun" (Yuman)

Yuma: Name of town, county, and desert; derived from tribal name, probably meaning "sons of the river" (Hokan)

## ◆ ARKANSAS

Ponca: Name of town; derived from tribal name, meaning "sacred head" (Siouan)

## ◆ CALIFORNIA

Azusa: Name of town; meaning "skunk hill" (Gabrieleno)

Cahuilla: Name of town and valley; derived from tribal name, probably meaning "master" (Cahuilla)

Chemehuevi: Name of valley; derived from tribal name (Chemehuevi)

Chowchilla: Name of town; derived from tribal name, meaning "to kill" (Yokuts)

Cucamonga: Name of town; meaning "sandy place" (probably Gabrieleno)

Gualala: Name of town; derived from village name, meaning "river mouth" (Kashaya Pomo)

Inyo: Name of mountains, county, and national forest; meaning "dwelling place of a great spirit" (probably Paiute)

Lompoc: Name of town; probably meaning "where the waters break through" (Chumash)

Malibu: Name of city; probably derived from former village name (Chumash)

Marin: Name of county and peninsula; named after a leader (Coast Miwok)

Napa: Name of town and county; meaning "house" or "fish" (probably Patwin)

Ojai: Name of town; meaning "moon" (Chumash)

Otay: Name of town; meaning "brushy" (Diegueo)

Pala: Name of town; probably meaning "water" (Luiseño)

Petaluma: Name of town; derived from village and tribal name, meaning "flat" (Coast Miwok)

Simi: Name of valley; probably meaning "valley of the wind" or "village" (Chumash)

Sonoma: Name of town and county; derived from village name (Coast Miwok)

Tahoe: Name of city, lake, and national forest; meaning "big water" (Washo)

## ◆ COLORADO

Apishapa: Name of river; meaning "standing water" (Ute)

Kiowa: Name of town and county; derived from tribal name, meaning "principal people" (Shoshonean and Tanoan)

Montezuma: Name of town and county; named after the ruler of Mexico (Aztec)

Uncompahgre: Name of mountains, peak, plateau, river, and national forest; meaning "red water canyon" (Ute)

Yampa: Name of town and river; derived from name of band and name of edible root (Ute)

## ◆ CONNECTICUT

Connecticut: Name of state and river; meaning "the long river" (Mohican)

Mystic: Name of town; meaning "great tidal river" (Algonkian)

Naugatuck: Name of town and river; meaning "long tree" (Algonkian)

Niantic: Name of town and river; derived from tribal name, meaning "at the point of land on a tidal river" (Algonkian)

Ouray: Name of town, county, and peak; named after chief, probably meaning "the arrow" (probably Algonkian)

Saugatuck: Name of town, river, and reservoir; meaning "tidal outlet" (Paugusett)

Taconic: Name of town and mountain; probably meaning "forest" (Algonkian)

Willimantic: Name of river and reservoir; meaning "good cedar swamp" (Nipmuc)

Yantic: Name of town and river; meaning "tidal limit" (Mohegan)

## ◆ DELAWARE

Minquadale: Name of town; derived from Iroquoian tribe also known as Susquehanna (Iroquois)

## ◆ FLORIDA

Alachua: Name of town and county; meaning "grassy, marshy plain" (probably Creek)

Apalachicola: Name of town, river, bay, and national forest; meaning "people on the other side" (Hitchiti)

Chokoloskee: Name of town; meaning "old house" (Seminole)

Chuluota: Name of town; meaning "fox den" (probably Seminole)

Loxahatchee: Name of town and river; meaning "turtle river" (Seminole)

Miami: Name of city; meaning "people of the peninsula" (Ojibway)

Micanopy: Name of town; meaning "head chief" (Seminole)

Miccosukee: Name of town and lake; derived from tribal name (probably Muskogean)

Myakka: Name of town and river; derived from former village name (Timucuan)

Ocala: Name of town and national forest; derived from former village name (Timucuan)

Ochlockonee: Name of river; meaning "yellow water" (Hitchiti)

Okaloosa: Name of county; meaning "black water" (Choctaw)

Okeechobee: Name of town, county, and lake; meaning "big water" (Hitchiti)

Pensacola: Name of town and river; derived from tribal name, meaning "long-haired people" (Choctaw)

Seminole: Name of town, county, and lake; derived from tribal name, meaning "runaway" or "pioneer" (Muskogean)

Steinhatchee: Name of town and river; meaning "manhisriver" (Seminole)

Suwannee: Name of town, county, sound, and river; meaning "echo" (probably Algonkian)

Tallahassee: Name of city and bay; derived from village name, meaning "old town" (Creek)

Tampa: Name of city and bay; derived from village name, meaning "near it" (probably Muskogean)

Wakulla: Name of town, county, river, and springs; meaning "loon" (Seminole)

## ◆ GEORGIA

Alapaha: Name of town; derived from former village name (Seminole)

Canoochee: Name of town and river; derived from name of an ancient Indian region (Creek)

Catoosa: Name of county; named after chief whose name means "high place" (probably Cherokee)

Chickamauga: Name of town and river; derived from tribal name, meaning "sluggish water" (Cherokee)

Coosa: Name of town; derived from tribal name, meaning "reed" (Creek)

Ellijay: Name of town; derived from former village name (Cherokee)

Hiawassee: Name of town; meaning "meadow" (Cherokee)

Muscogee: Name of county; derived from tribal name (Muskogean)

Ocmulgee: Name of river and national monument; derived from tribal name, meaning "where the water bubbles up" (Hitchiti)

Oconee: Name of town, county, river, and national forest; meaning "water" (Muskogean)

Okefenokee: Name of swamp and national wildlife refuge; meaning "trembling water" (Hitchiti)

Satolah: Name of town and battlefield; meaning "six" (Cherokee)

Savannah: Name of river; meaning "southerner" (Shawnee)

Withlacoochie: Name of river; meaning "little creek" (Creek)

## ◆ IDAHO

Bannock: Name of county, river, mountain and peak; derived from tribal name, meaning "hair in backward motion" (Shoshonean)

Blackfoot: Name of river and reservoir; derived from tribal name referring to their dyeing their moccasins black (Algonkian)

Kootenai: Name of county, river and national wildlife refuge; derived from tribal name, meaning "water people" (Algonkian)

Lochsa: Name of river; meaning "rough water" (Flathead)

Minidoka: Name of town, county, national wildlife refuge; meaning "broad expanse" (probably Shoshonean)

Nez Percé_: Name of town, county, and national forest; derived from tribal name, meaning "pierced nose" (French version of Indian word)

Pocatello: Name of city; named after Bannock chief, probably meaning "the wayward one" (Shoshonean)

Potlatch: Name of town; meaning "giveaway," a type of public event (Chinook)

Shoshone: Name of town, county, and falls; derived from tribal name (Shoshonean)

Targhee: Name of pass and national forest; probably named after Shoshoni chief (Bannock)

## ◆ ILLINOIS

Aptakisic: Name of town; named after chief whose name means "halfday" (Potawatomi)

Cahokia: Name of town; derived from tribal name (Cahokia)

Chicago: Name of city and river; meaning "onion place" (Algonkian)

Chillicothe: Name of town; derived from tribal name, meaning "village" (probably Shawnee)

Illinois: Name of state and river; derived from tribal name, meaning "men" (Algonkian)

Iroquois: Name of city, county, and river; derived from tribal name, meaning "real adders" (Algonkian, with French spelling)

Kankakee: Name of town, county, and river; meaning "wolf land" (Mohegan)

Kaskaskia: Name of river; derived from tribal name (Kaskaskia)

Macoupin: Name of county; meaning "potato" (Algonkian)

Ottawa: Name of city; derived from tribal name, meaning "to trade" (Algonkian)

Peoria: Name of town and county; derived from tribal name, meaning "carriers" (Peoria)

Prophetstown: Name of town; named after medicine man, White Cloud (English version of Winnebago word)

Sangamon: Name of county and river; probably meaning "outlet" (Ojibway)

Sauk: Name of town; derived from tribal name, meaning "people of the yellow earth" (Algonkian)

Skokie: Name of town and river; meaning "marsh" (Potawatomi)

Spoon: Name of river; meaning "mussel shell" (Algonkian)

Waukegan: Name of town; meaning "trading post" (Algonkian)

## ◆ INDIANA

Genesee: Name of city; meaning "beautiful valley" (Algonkian)

Indiana: Name of state and county; derived from the Latinized form of Indian

Kokomo: Name of city; named after chief whose name means "black walnut" (Miami)

Muncie: Name of city; derived from tribal name, meaning "people of the stone country" (Algonkian)

Muscatatuck: Name of river and national wildlife refuge; meaning "clear river" (Delaware)

Wabash: Name of county and river; meaning "white water" (Miami)

## ◆ IOWA

Black Hawk: Name of city, county, and lake; named after chief of Sauk and Fox tribes

Iowa: Name of state, county, river, and falls; derived from tribal name, meaning "sleepy ones" (Siouan)

Keokuk: Name of town and county; named after Fox chief whose name means "he who moves around alert" (Algonkian)

Lakota: Name of city; derived from tribal name (often called Sioux), meaning "allies" (Siouan)

Maquoketa: Name of town and river; meaning "bear river" (Algonkian)

Muscatine: Name of town, county, and island; derived from tribal name (Muscatine)

Oskaloosa: Name of town; named after one of Osceola's wives whose name means "black water" (Choctaw)

Oto: Name of town; derived from tribal name, meaning "lovers" or "lechers" (Siouan)

Pocahontas: Name of city and county; named after the Indian princess whose name means "radiant" or "playful" (Algonkian)

Poweshiek: Name of county; named after chief whose name means "he who shakes something off" (Fox)

Sac: Name of city and county; derived from tribal name (same as Sauk), meaning "people of the yellow earth" (Algonkian)

Sioux: Name of city, county, and river; derived from Ojibway word, meaning "snakes" or "enemies" (French version of Ojibway word for Dakota)

Wapello: Name of town and county; named after Fox chief whose name means "he, of the morning" (Algonkian)

Wapsipinicon: Name of river; meaning "white potato" (Algonkian)

Winneshiek: Name of county; named after chief (Winnebago)

## ◆ KANSAS

Comanche: Name of county; derived from tribal name, meaning "always ready to fight" (Shoshonean)

Kansas: Name of state, city, and river; derived from tribal name, meaning "people of the south wind" (Siouan)

Kiowa: Name of county; derived from tribal name, meaning "principal people" (Shoshonean and Tanoan)

Osage: Name of city, county, and river; derived from tribal name, probably meaning "people" (Siouan)

Potawatomi: Name of county; derived from tribal name, meaning "people of the place of fire" (Algonkian)

Satanta: Name of city; named after chief (Kiowa)

Shawnee: Name of city and county; derived from tribal name, meaning "southerner" (Algonkian)

Topeka: Name of city; meaning "good potato place" (Kansa)

Wabaunsee: Name of county; named after Potawatomi chief (Algonkian)

Wichita: Name of city and county; derived from tribal name, meaning "man" (Caddoan)

## ◆ KENTUCKY

Kentucky: Name of state, lake, and river; meaning "land of tomorrow" (Wyandotte) or "meadow land" (Iroquoian)

Paducah: Name of town; named after chief and derived from tribal name (Chickasaw)

## ◆ LOUISIANA

Atchafalaya: Name of bay and river; meaning "long river" (Choctaw)

Bogalusa: Name of town; meaning "large stream" (Choctaw)

Caddo: Name of parish and lake; derived from tribal name, meaning "chief" (Caddoan)

Coushatta: Name of town; derived from tribal name, meaning "white canebreak" (Choctaw)

Houma: Name of town; derived from tribal name, meaning "red" (Choctaw)

Kisatchie: Name of town and national forest; meaning "reed river" (Choctaw)

Natchez: Name of city; derived from tribal name, probably meaning "timber land" (Muskogean)

Natchitoches: Name of town and parish; derived from tribal name, meaning "chestnut eaters" (Caddoan)

Tichfaw: Name of town and river; probably meaning "pine rest" (Choctaw)

Tunica: Name of town; derived from tribal name, meaning "the people" (Tunican)

## ◆ MAINE

Allagash: Name of river; meaning "bark shelter" (Abnaki)

Androscoggin: Name of county, river, and lake; derived from tribal name, meaning "fish spearing" (probably Algonkian)

Aroostook: Name of county and river; meaning "good, beautiful, or clear river" (Algonkian)

Kennebec: Name of county and river; meaning "long lake" (Algonkian)

Kennebunk: Name of town and river; meaning "long cut bank" (Algonkian)

Passadumkeag: Name of town and mountains; meaning "rapids over sandy places" (Abnaki)

Penobscot: Name of county, bay, lake, and river; derived from tribal name, meaning "rocky place" (Algonkian)

Piscataquis: Name of county and river; meaning "at the fork of the river" (Abnaki)

Saco: Name of town and river (Algonkian)

Sagadahoc: Name of county; meaning "mouth of river" (Algonkian)

Sebec: Name of town and lake; meaning "big lake" (Algonkian)

Seboeis: Name of town, lake, and river; meaning "small lake" (Algonkian)

Tulamdie: Name of river; meaning "canoe sandbar" (Algonkian)

## ◆ MARYLAND

Nanticoke: Name of town and river; derived from tribal name, meaning "tidewater people" (Delaware)

Pocomoke: Name of town and sound; meaning "small field" (Algonkian)

Potomac: Name of city and river; derived from tribal name, meaning "where the goods are brought in" (probably Algonkian)

Wicomico: Name of county and river; derived from tribal name, meaning "pleasant village" (Delaware)

## ◆ MASSACHUSETTS

Chappaquiddick: Name of island; meaning "seplaceted island" (Wampanoag)

Chicopee: Name of town and river; meaning "swift water" (Algonkian)

Housatonic: Name of town and river; meaning "at the place beyond the mountain" (Mahican)

Massachusetts: Name of state and bay; meaning "great hill" (Algonkian)

Muskegel: Name of channel and island; meaning "grassy place" (Wampanoag)

Nantucket: Name of county, island, and sound; meaning "narrow tidal river at" (Algonkian)

Natick: Name of town; derived from tribal name, meaning "a place of hills" (Algonkian)

Weweantic: Name of river; meaning "crooked river" (Algonkian)

## ◆ MICHIGAN

Cheboygan: Name of town, county, and river; probably meaning "pipe" (Algonkian)

Chippewa: Name of county and river; derived from tribal name, meaning "voice" and "gathering up" (Ojibway)

Gogebic: Name of county and lake; meaning "high lake" (Ojibway)

Kalamazoo: Name of town and county; meaning "it smokes" (Algonkian)

Mackinaw: Name of town, county, island, and straits; meaning "island of the large turtle" (Ojibway)

Manistee: Name of town, county, river, and national forest; meaning "crooked river" (Ojibway)

Manitou: Name of islands; meaning "spirit" (Algonkian)

Mecosta: Name of county; named after chief whose name means "bear cub" (Potawatomi)

Menominee: Name of town, county, river, and mountains; derived from tribal name, meaning "wild rice people" (Algonkian)

Michigan: Name of state and one of the Great Lakes; meaning "big lake" (Ojibway)

Missaukee: Name of county and lake; after Ottawa chief whose name means "big outlet at" (probably Algonkian)

Munuscong: Name of lake and river; meaning "the place of the reeds" (Algonkian)

Muskegon: Name of town, county, and river; meaning "swampy" (Ojibway)

Ontonagon: Name of town, county, and river; meaning "a place where game was shot by luck" (Ojibway)

Otsego: Name of town, county, and lake; meaning "rock place" (Iroquoian)

Pontiac: Name of city; named after Ottawa chief (probably Algonkian)

Sanilac: Name of county; named after Wyandotte chief (probably Iroquoian)

Shiawassee: Name of county and national wildlife refuge; meaning "straight ahead water" (Algonkian)

Tahquamenon: Name of river and falls; meaning "dark-colored water" (Ojibway)

Tecumseh: Name of town; named after chief whose name means "a panther crouching for its prey" (Shawnee)

Tittabawassee: Name of river; probably meaning "river following the line of the shore" (Algonkian)

Washtenaw: Name of county; meaning "on the river" (Ojibway)

## ◆ MINNESOTA

Anoka: Name of town and county; meaning "on both sides" (Siouan)

Bemidji: Name of town and lake; named after chief whose name probably means "river crossing lake" (probably Algonkian)

Chanhassen: Name of town and river; meaning "tree with sweet juice" (Siouan)

Chaska: Name of town, lake, and creek; meaning "first-born son" (Siouan)

Chisago: Name of county; meaning "large and beautiful" (Ojibway)

Isanti: Name of town and county; derived from tribal name (probably Siouan)

Kanabec: Name of county; meaning "snake" (Ojibway)

Kandiyohi: Name of county; meaning "buffalo fish come" (Siouan)

Koochiching: Name of county; probably meaning "rainy lake" (Cree)

Mahnomen: Name of town and county; meaning "wild rice" (Ojibway)

Mesabi: Name of mountains; meaning "giant" (Ojibway)

Minneapolis: Name of city; meaning "waterfall" (Siouan) and "city" (Creek)

Minnesota: Name of state, lake, and river; probably meaning "land of many lakes" (Siouan)

Minnetonka: Name of town and lake; meaning "big water" (Siouan)

Wabasha: Name of town and county; a personal name for hereditary chiefs, meaning "red leaf" or "red battle-standard" (Siouan)

Wadena: Name of town and county; meaning "little round hill" (Ojibway)

Waseca: Name of town and county; meaning "fertile" (Siouan)

Watonwan: Name of county and river; meaning "where fish bait can be found" (probably Siouan)

## ◆ MISSISSIPPI

Biloxi: Name of town, bay, and river; derived from tribal name, meaning "broken pot" (probably Muskogean)

Chickasawhay: Name of river; derived from village name, meaning "potato" (Choctaw)

Escatawpa: Name of town and river; meaning "cane cut there" (Choctaw)

Hatchie: Name of river and natural wildlife refuge; meaning "stream" (Choctaw)

Homochitto: Name of river and national forest; meaning "red chief" (Choctaw)

Issaquena: Name of county; meaning "deer's head" (Choctaw)

Mississippi: Name of state and river; meaning "big river" (Algonkian)

Neshoba: Name of town and county; probably meaning "wolf" (Choctaw)

Noxubee: Name of county and river; meaning "stinking water" (Choctaw)

Oktibbeha: Name of county; meaning "pure water" (Choctaw)

Pascagoula: Name of town and river; derived from tribal name, meaning "bread people" (probably Muskogean)

Pontotoc: Name of town and county; meaning "cattails on the prairie" (Chickasaw)

Tallahatchie: Name of county and river; meaning "town" and "river" (Creek)

Tishomingo: Name of town and county; after chief whose name means "assistant chief" (Chickasaw)

Tombigbee: Name of river and national forest; meaning "coffin makers" (Choctaw)

Tougaloo: Name of city; meaning "fork of a stream" (Cherokee)

Tunica: Name of county; derived from tribal name, meaning "the people" (Tunica)

Yalobusha: Name of county and river; meaning "little tadpole" (Choctaw)

Yazoo: Name of town, county, and river; derived from tribal name, probably meaning "those who are the people" (Tunican)

## ◆ MISSOURI

Meramec: Name of river; derived from tribal name, meaning "catfish" (Meramec)

Missouri: Name of state and river; derived from tribal name, meaning "muddy water" (probably Siouan)

Neosho: Name of town; meaning "cold, clear water" (Osage)

Pemiscot: Name of county; meaning "place of the long rock" (possibly Fox)

Wyaconda: Name of town and river; meaning "spirit" (Siouan)

## ◆ MONTANA

Chinook: Name of town; derived from tribal name (Chinookan)

Flathead: Name of county, river, lake, and national forest; derived from tribal name (Flathead)

Kootenai: Name of river and mountains; derived from tribal name, meaning "water people" (Kootenai)

Mackinac: Name of town; meaning "island of the large turtle" (Ojibway)

Missoula: Name of town and county; meaning "feared water" (Flathead)

Tepee: Name of mountains and Indian tent (Siouan)

## ◆ NEBRASKA

Arapaho: Name of town; derived from tribal name, meaning "he who trades" (Pawnee)

Nebraska: Name of state and national forest; meaning "wide water" (probably Siouan)

Niobrara: Name of river; meaning "spreading water river" (unknown)

Ogallala: Name of city; derived from tribal name, meaning "to scatter one's own" (Siouan)

Omaha: Name of city; derived from tribal name, meaning "those who live upstream beyond others" (probably Siouan)

Pawnee: Name of county; derived from tribal name, meaning "horn," "hunter," or "braid" (Caddoan)

Red Cloud: Name of town; named after chief (Siouan)

Santee: Name of town; derived from tribal name, meaning "knife" (Dakota)

## ◆ NEVADA

Beowawe: Name of pass to canyon; meaning "an open gate" (Shoshonean)

Hiko: Name of mountain range; meaning "white people" (Southern Paiute)

Pahranagat: Name of valley and mountain range; derived from tribal name, meaning "people of the marshy spring" (Paiute)

Pequop: Name of mountain; derived from tribal name (Algonkian)

Timpahute: Name of mountain range; derived from tribal name, meaning "rock spring people" (Paiute)

Toana: Name of mountain range; meaning "black hill" (Shoshonean)

Toquima: Name of mountain range; derived from tribal name, meaning "black backs" (Shoshonean)

Washoe: Name of town, county, lake, valley, and mountain range; derived from tribal name, meaning "person" (Hokan)

Winnemucca: Name of lake; meaning "bread giver" (Paiute)

## ◆ NEW HAMPSHIRE

Coos: Name of county; meaning "pine tree" (Pennacook)

Merrimack: Name of town, county, and river; probably meaning "deep place" (Algonkian)

Nashua: Name of town and river; derived from tribal name, meaning "beautiful river with pebbly bottom" (probably Algonkian)

Ossipee: Name of town, lake, river, and mountains; meaning "beyond the water" (Abenaki)

Suncook: Name of town, river, and lakes; meaning "at the rocks" (Algonkian)

Winnisquam: Name of lake; meaning "salmon" (Algonkian)

## ◆ NEW JERSEY

Hackensack: Name of city and river; derived from tribal name, probably meaning "hook mouth" or "big snake land" (Algonkian)

Hoboken: Name of city; meaning "land of the tobacco pipe" (Delaware)

Hopatcong: Name of city and lake; probably meaning "hill above a body of still water having an outlet" (Algonkian)

Navesink: Name of town and river; meaning "point at" (Algonkian)

Parsippany: Name of town; probably derived from tribal name (probably Algonkian)

Passaic: Name of city, county, and river; probably meaning "valley" or "peace" (Delaware)

Pequannock: Name of city and river; meaning "open field" (Algonkian)

Raritan: Name of city, river, and bay; derived from tribal name, probably meaning "stream overflows" or "forked river" (Algonkian)

Wanaque: Name of city and reservoir; probably meaning "sassafras place" (Algonkian)

Whippany: Name of city and river; probably meaning "arrow stream" (Delaware)

## ◆ NEW MEXICO

Abiquiu: Name of city and reservoir; probably derived from village name, meaning "chokecherry" (Tewa)

Acomita: Name of city; named after Indian pueblo and people, meaning "whiterock people" (Pueblo)

Aztec: Name of town; derived from tribal name, meaning "place of the heron" or "land of flamingos" (Aztec)

Mescalero: Name of city; derived from a Spanish word for an Apache tribe, referring to their practice of preparing a food called mescal (Spanish)

Mexico: Name of state and gulf; meaning "place of the war god" (Aztec)

Taos: Name of city and county; probably meaning "red willow place" or "at the village" (Tewa)

Tucumcari: Name of city and mountain; meaning "to lie in ambush" (Comanche)

Ute: Name of city and park; derived from tribal name (Uto-Aztecan)

Zuni: Name of city, river, and mountains; derived from village and tribal names (Zuni)

## ◆ NEW YORK

Adirondacks: Name of town, park, and mountain range; derived from tribal name, meaning "bark eaters" (Iroquoian)

Allegheny: Name of plateau and reservoir; probably from the name for Allegheny and Ohio rivers (Delaware)

Canadaigua: Name of town and lake; meaning "town set off" (Iroquoian)

Cassadaga: Name of town, creek, and lakes; meaning "under the rocks" (Iroquoian)

Cattaraugus: Name of town, county, and creek; meaning "bad smelling shore" (Iroquoian)

Cayuga: Name of town, county, canal, and lake; derived from tribal name, meaning "where they take the boats out" (probably Iroquoian)

Chemung: Name of town, county, and river; meaning "big horn" (Seneca)

Chenango: Name of county and river; meaning "bull thistle" (Onondaga)

Manhasset: Name of town; derived from tribal name (Algonkian)

Manhattan: Name of island and borough; derived from tribal name, probably meaning "island-mountain" (Algonkian)

Mohawk: Name of town and river; derived from a name used by their Algonkian enemies, meaning "man eaters" (Algonkian)

Niagara: Name of town, county, river, and falls; meaning "point of land cut in two" (Iroquoian)

Oneida: Name of town, county, and lake; derived from tribal name, meaning "stone people" (Iroquoian)

Onondaga: Name of county; derived from tribal name, meaning "hill people" (Iroquoian)

Oswego: Name of town, county, river, and lake; probably meaning "the outpouring" or "the place where the valley widens" (Iroquoian)

Poughkeepsie: Name of town; meaning "little rock at water" (Algonkian)

Saratoga: Name of town, county, and lake; meaning "springs from the hillside" (probably Mohawk)

Seneca: Name of county, river, lake, and falls; derived from tribal name, probably meaning "people of the stone" (Mohegan)

Susquehanna: Name of river; derived from tribal name (Iroquoian)

Tuscarora: Name of town; derived from tribal name, meaning "hemp gatherers" (Iroquoian)

## ◆ NORTH CAROLINA

Alamance: Name of county and creek; meaning "noisy stream" (probably Siouan)

Catawba: Name of town, county, and river; derived from tribal name (probably Siouan)

Cherokee: Name of town, county, and national forest; derived from tribal name, meaning "people of a different speech" (probably Algonkian)

Chowan: Name of county and river; derived from tribal name (probably Algonkian)

Croatoan: Name of city and national forest; probably meaning "talk town" (probably Algonkian)

Currituck: Name of town, county, and sound; derived from tribal name, probably meaning "wild geese" (probably Algonkian)

Nantahala: Name of mountains, gorge, lake, river, and national forest; meaning "place of the middle sun" (Cherokee)

Pasquotank: Name of county; derived from tribal name, probably meaning "divided tidal river" (Weapemeoc)

Perquimans: Name of county and river; derived from tribal name (Weapemeoc)

Tuckaseigee: Name of river; derived from village name, probably meaning "crawling turtle" (Cherokee)

Waccamaw: Name of lake and river; derived from tribal name (probably Siouan)

## ◆ NORTH DAKOTA

Dakota: Name of states and river; derived from tribal name of people also known as Sioux, meaning "allies" (Siouan)

Mandan: Name of city; derived from tribal name, meaning "those who live along the bank of the river" (Dakota)

Minnewaukan: Name of city; meaning "water of the bad spirit" (Siouan)

Pembina: Name of town, county, and river; meaning "summer berry" (Ojibway)

Wahpeton: Name of town; derived from one of the seven divisions of the Dakotas, meaning "dwellers among the leaves" (Siouan)

## ◆ OHIO

Cuyahoga: Name of county, river, and falls; meaning "important river" (probably Iroquoian)

Mahoning: Name of county; meaning "salt lick" (Delaware)

Maumee: Name of town and river; derived from tribal name, meaning "people of the peninsula" (Ojibway)

Mississinewa: Name of river; meaning "river of big stones" (Algonkian)

Muskingum: Name of county and river; derived from village name, meaning "at the river" (Algonkian)

Newcomerstown: Name of town; named after chief Netawatwees, whose name means "beaver" (Delaware)

Ohio: Name of state and river; meaning "beautiful" (Iroquoian)

Sandusky: Name of town, county, bay, and river; meaning "source of pure water" (Wyandotte)

Tippecanoe: Name of city; meaning "buffalo fish" (Potawatomi)

Wyandotte: Name of county; derived from tribal name, meaning "islanders" or "peninsula dwellers" (Iroquoian)

## ◆ OKLAHOMA

Atoka: Name of town and county; named after the Choctaw athlete, Captain Atoka, whose name means "ball ground" (Choctaw)

Broken Arrow: Name of city; derived from a Creek village name (translated from Muskogean)

Cheyenne: Name of city; derived from tribal name, meaning "red talkers" (Algonkian)

Coweta: Name of town; derived from a Creek town name (Muskogean)

Creek: Name of county; derived from tribal name given by the English to the Muskogee tribe (English)

Kiamichi: Name of river; derived from village name (Caddoan)

Muskogee: Name of town and county; derived from tribal name (Muskogean)

Nowata: Name of town and county; meaning "welcome" (Delaware)

Okfuskee: Name of county; meaning "promontory" (Muskogean)

Oklahoma: Name of city, county, and state; meaning "red people" (Muskogean)

Okmulgee: Name of town and county; derived from tribal name, meaning "where water boils up" (Hitchiti)

Oologah: Name of town and reservoir; named after chief whose name means "dark cloud"

Pushmataha: Name of county; named after chief (Choctaw)

Sequoyah: Name of county; named after a Cherokee who devised a written language (Cherokee)

Tonkawa: Name of city; derived from tribal name, meaning "they all stay together" (probably Waco)

Tulsa: Name of city and county; derived from a Creek village name, meaning "old town" (Muskogean)

Wewoka: Name of town and creek; derived from a Creek village name, meaning "water roaring" (Muskogean)

Wichita: Name of mountains; derived from tribal name, meaning "man" (Caddoan)

#### ◆ OREGON

Clackamas: Name of county and river; derived from name of a subtribe (Chinookan)

Clatsop: Name of county; derived from name of a subtribe (Chinookan)

Klamath: Name of county, lake, and river; derived from a tribal name (Chinook)

Metolius: Name of town and river; meaning "light colored fish"

Multnomah: Name of county and falls; derived from tribal name (Multnomah)

Nehalem: Name of river; derived from a tribal name (Chinook)

Oregon: Name of state; probably meaning "place of plenty" or "river of the west" (Shoshonean)

Sacajawea: Name of peak; named after the Shoshoni woman who was part of the Lewis and Clark Expedition, meaning "bird woman" (Shoshonean)

Siskiyou: Name of town, national forest and mountains; meaning "bobtail horse" (probably Cree)

Siuslaw: Name of river and national forest; derived from tribal name, meaning "people of Nehalem" (Chinook)

Tillamook: Name of county, bay, and cape; derived from tribal name (Tillamook)

Umatilla: Name of town, county, river, and dam; derived from tribal name, probably meaning "water rippling over sand" (Umatilla)

Umpqua: Name of town and river; derived from tribal name, meaning "thunder" or "high and low water" (Athapascan)

Wallowa: Name of town, county, lake, river, national forest, and mountains; meaning "triangular stakes," a type of fish trap (Nez Percé_)

#### ◆ PENNSYLVANIA

Aliquippa: Name of borough; named after a Seneca matron (Iroquoian)

Lenape: Name of town; derived from tribal name, meaning "men of our nation" or "real people" (Delaware)

Lycoming: Name of county; meaning "sandy creek" (Delaware)

Monongahela: Name of town and river; meaning "river with the sliding banks" (Delaware)

Pocono: Name of lake, creek, and mountains; probably meaning "valley stream" (Delaware)

Shenango: Name of river and reservoir; derived from village name, meaning "beautiful one" (probably Algonkian)

Susquehanna: Name of county and river; derived from tribal name (Iroquoian)

Tioga: Name of town, county, and river; meaning "at the forks" (Iroquoian)

## ◆ RHODE ISLAND

Narragansett: Name of city and bay; derived from tribal name, meaning "people of the small point" (Algonkian)

Pascoag: Name of town and reservoir; meaning "forking place" (Algonkian)

Pawtucket: Name of city; meaning "at the falls in the river" (Algonkian)

Wallum: Name of town and lake; meaning "dog" (Nipmuc)

Woonsocket: Name of city; probably meaning "at a steep spot" (Algonkian)

## ◆ SOUTH CAROLINA

Congaree: Name of river; derived from tribal name (Congaree)

Coosawhatchie: Name of town and river; meaning "stream with cane" (Muskogean)

Edisto: Name of island and river; derived from tribal name (probably Muskogean)

Pacolet: Name of town and river; derived from tribal name (Pacolet)

Wateree: Name of river and lake; derived from a subtribe (Catawba)

## ◆ SOUTH DAKOTA

Dakota: Name of states; derived from tribal name of people also known as Sioux, meaning "allies" (Siouan)

Wakpala: Name of town; meaning "creek" (Siouan)

Waubay: Name of town and lake; meaning "nesting place for wild fowl" (Siouan)

Wetonka: Name of town; meaning "big" (probably Siouan)

Wewela: Name of town; meaning "small spring" (probably Siouan)

Yankton: Name of town and county; derived from tribal village, meaning "end village" (Siouan)

## ◆ TENNESSEE

Chattanooga: Name of city; meaning "rock rising to a point" (Creek)

Obion: Name of town, county and river; probably meaning "many forks" (unknown)

Sequatchie: Name of county and river; named after a chief whose name means "hog river" (Cherokee)

Telico: Name of town; derived from village name, probably meaning "place of refuge" (Cherokee)

Tennessee: Name of state and river; derived from village name (Cherokee)

Unicoi: Name of town, county, and pass; meaning "white" (Cherokee)

## ◆ TEXAS

Anahuac: Name of national wildlife refuge; meaning "plain near the water" (Aztec)

Miami: Name of town; derived from tribal name, meaning "people of the peninsula" (Ojibway)

Nacogdoches: Name of county; derived from tribal name (Caddoan)

Neches: Name of river; derived from tribal name, meaning "snow river" (Hasinai)

Pecos: Name of county and river; meaning "watering place" (Keresan)

Quanah: Name of town; named after chief, meaning "better flowers" (Comanche)

Tehuacana: Name of town; meaning "the three canes" (Wichita)

Waco: Name of lake; derived from tribal name, meaning "heron" (probably Caddoan)

Waxahachie: Name of town; meaning "cow stream" (Tonkawa)

## ◆ UTAH

Goshute: Name of town; derived from tribal name, meaning "dust people" (probably Shoshonean)

Juab: Name of county; meaning "valley" (Gosiute)

Paiute: Name of county; derived from tribal name, meaning "Ute of the water" (Paiute)

Panguitch: Name of town and lake; derived from tribal name, meaning "fish people" (Paiute)

Parowan: Name of town; derived from tribal name, meaning "marsh people" (Parowan)

Sanpete: Name of county; meaning "homelands" (Ute)

Uinta: Name of river, national forest, and mountains; de—rived from tribal name, meaning "pineland" (Shoshonean)

Utah: Name of state, county, and lake; derived from tribal name, meaning "high up" or "the land of the sun" (Ute)

Wah Wah: Name of mountains; probably meaning "juniper" (Paiute)

## ◆ VERMONT

Missisquoi: Name of river; meaning "much water fowl" (Algonkian)

Winooski: Name of town and river; meaning "onion land" (Abenaki)

## ◆ VIRGINIA

Accomac: Name of town and county; derived from tribal name, meaning "the other side" (probably Algonkian)

Alleghany: Name of town and county; named for Allegheny and Ohio Rivers (Delaware)

Appomattox: Name of town, county, and river; derived from tribal name, probably meaning "tobacco plant country" or "curving tidal estuary" (Algonkian)

Chesapeake: Name of city and bay; probably meaning "on the big bay" (Algonkian)

Nansemond: Name of county; derived from tribal name, meaning "whence we were driven off" (Nansemond)

Nottoway: Name of town, county, and river; derived from tribal name, meaning "rattlesnake" (Algonkian)

Powhatan: Name of city and county; named after chief, probably meaning "falls in a current of water" (Algonkian)

Rappahannock: Name of county and river; derived from tribal name, meaning "back-and-forth stream" (Algonkian)

Roanoke: Name of town, county, and river; probably meaning "white-shell place" (Algonkian)

## ◆ WASHINGTON

Chehalis: Name of city, county, river, and Indian reservation; derived from tribal name, meaning "shining sands" (Salishan)

Clallam: Name of county, river, and bay; derived from tribal name, meaning "big brave nation" (Clallam)

Cowlitz: Name of county and river; derived from tribal name, meaning "capturing the medicine spirit" (Cowlitz)

Duwamish: Name of river; derived from tribal name, meaning "the people living on the river" (Duwamish)

Hoh: Name of river and Indian reservation; derived from tribal name (Hoh)

Kitsap: Name of county and lake; named after chief, meaning "brave" (Kitsap)

Kittitas: Name of town and county; probably derived from tribal name, meaning "shoal people" (Kittitas)

Klickitat: Name of county and river; derived from tribal name, meaning "beyond" (Klickitat)

Lummi: Name of river, island, and Indian reservation; derived from tribal name (Lummi)

Nespelem: Name of town; derived from tribal name, meaning "large, open meadow" (Nespelem)

Okanogan: Name of county, river, and national forest; derived from tribal name, probably meaning "meeting place" (Okanogan)

Puyallup: Name of city and river; derived from tribal name, meaning "generous people" (Puyallup)

Seattle: Name of city; named after chief (Salishan)

Skagit: Name of county, river, and bay; derived from tribal name (Skagit)

Snoqualmie: Name of river, pass, and national forest; derived from tribal name, meaning "moon" (Snoqualmie)

Spokane: Name of city, county, river, and mountain; derived from tribal name, meaning "chief of the sun" (Spokane)

Tulalip: Name of bay and Indian reservation; meaning "bay with a small mouth" (Tulalip)

Walla Walla: Name of city, county, valley, and river; derived from tribal name, meaning "little swift river" (Walla Walla)

Wenatchee: Name of city, lake, national forest, and mountains; derived from tribal name, meaning "river issuing from canyon" (Wenatchee)

Yakima: Name of city, county, and river; derived from tribal name, probably meaning "runaway" (Yakima)

## ◆ WEST VIRGINIA

Chattaroy: Name of town; derived from tribal name (probably Algonkian)

Kanawha: Name of county and river; derived from tribal name, probably meaning "hurricane" (Kanawha)

Mingo: Name of county; meaning "stealthy" or "treacherous" (Algonkian)

## ◆ WISCONSIN

Horicon: Name of town and national wildlife refuge; derived from tribal name, probably meaning "silver water" (Horicon)

Kenosha: Name of town and county; meaning "pickerel" (Potawatomi)

Kickapoo: Name of river; derived from tribal name, meaning "he moves about" (Algonkian)

Manitowoc: Name of town and county; meaning "land of the spirit" (Algonkian)

Milwaukee: Name of city, county, river, and bay; probably meaning "good land" (Algonkian)

Monona: Name of town and lake; named after either an Indian divinity or a legendary Indian girl who jumped into the Mississippi River when she thought her lover had been killed (Algonkian)

Namekagon: Name of town, lake, and river; meaning "place for sturgeon" (Ojibway)

Necedah: Name of town and national wildlife refuge; meaning "yellow" (Winnebago)

Oconto: Name of town, county, river, and falls; meaning "pickerel place" (Menominee)

Ojibway: Name of town; derived from tribal name, meaning "puckered up," referring to a style of moccasin (Ojibway)

Ozaukee: Name of county; derived from tribal name, meaning "river mouth people" or "yellow earth" (Ozaukee)

Waukesha: Name of town and county; derived from tribal name (Potawatomi)

Winnebago: Name of town, county, and lake; derived from tribal name, probably meaning "people of the filthy waters" (Algonkian)

Wisconsin: Name of state, river, lake, and rapids; meaning "the gathering of the waters" or "grassy place" (French version of Ojibway word)

## ◆ WYOMING

Absaroka: Name of mountains; named after a bird, meaning "crow" (Siouan)

Sundance: Name of town and mountain; named after an-nual purification or world renewal ceremony (English)

Washakie: Name of town, county, lake, mountain, creek, and national forest; named after Snake chief (unknown)

Wyoming: Name of state, range, and peak; meaning "large meadows" (Delaware)

# CANADA

## ◆ ALBERTA

Athabaska: Name of river and mountain; meaning "where there are needs" (Cree)

Chipewyan: Name of lakes, river, and Hudson's Bay Company post; derived from tribal name, meaning "pointed skins" (Cree)

Okotoks: Name of town and mountains; meaning "big rock" (Blackfoot)

Ponoka: Name of town; meaning "black elk" (Blackfoot)

Wetaskiwin: Name of city; meaning "hills of peace" (Cree)

## ◆ BRITISH COLUMBIA

Chilliwack: Name of city; derived from tribal name, meaning "valley of many waters" (Halkomelem)

Coquitlam: Name of river and mountain; derived from tribal name, meaning "stinking of fish slime" (Halkomelem)

Cowichan: Name of village, river, and lake; derived from tribal name, meaning "warm country" (Halkomelem)

Illecillewaet: Name of river, glacier, and mining district; meaning "end of water" (Okanagan)

Kelowna: Name of city; meaning "female grizzly bear" (Okanagan)

Kootenay: Name of river and national park; derived from tribal name, meaning "water people" (Kootenai)

Lillooet: Name of town, district, and river; derived from tribal name, meaning "wild onion" (Lillooet)

Naas: Name of river and bay; meaning "satisfier of the stomach" (Tlingit)

Nanaimo: Name of city, river, and harbor; meaning "strong, strong water" (Halkomelem)

Okanagan: Name of town, valley, and lake; derived from tribal name, meaning "place of water" (Straits Salish)

Skeena: Name of river; meaning "out of the clouds" (Tsimshian)

Stikine: Name of river; meaning "great river" (Tlingit)

## ◆ MANITOBA

Manitoba: Name of province and lake; meaning "the strait of the spirit" (Cree)

Minnedosa: Name of town and river; meaning "swift water" (Siouan)

Pembina: Name of county, river, and mountains; meaning "summer berry" (Cree)

Tadoule: Name of lake; meaning "floating charcoal" (Chipewyan)

Winnipeg: Name of city, river, and lake; probably meaning "murky water" (Cree)

## ◆ NEW BRUNSWICK

Great Manan: Name of island; meaning "the island" (Malecite-Passamaquoddy)

Kennebecasis: Name of island, river, and bay; meaning "little, long bay place" (Malecite)

Miramichi: Name of river; meaning "the land of the Micmacs" (Algonkian)

Oromocto: Name of island, village, river, and lake; meaning "good river" (Micmac and Malecite)

Petitcodiac: Name of village and river; meaning "river that bends in a bow fitted to an arrow" (Micmac)

Shippigan: Name of island, village, and harbor; meaning "a small passage through which ducks fly" (Micmac)

## ◆ NORTHWEST TERRITORIES

Akimiski: Name of island; meaning "the land across" (Cree)

Aklavik: Name of town; meaning "place of the barren land grizzly" (Inuit)

Akpatok: Name of island; meaning "place of birds" (Inuit)

Auyuittuq: Name of national park; meaning "the place where ice does not melt" (Inuit)

Inuvik: Name of locality; meaning "the place of man" (Inuit)

Keewatin: Name of district; meaning "north wind" (Cree)

## ◆ NOVA SCOTIA

Antigonish: Name of county and harbor; meaning "broken branches" (Micmac)

Arichat: Name of island; meaning "the camping ground" (Micmac)

Chignecto: Name of bay; meaning "foot cloth" (Micmac)

Maccan: Name of settlement; meaning "fishing place" (Micmac)

Missinaibi: Name of lake and river; meaning "pictures on the water" (Micmac)

Pugwash: Name of river and bay; meaning "a bank of sand " or "shallow water" (Micmac)

Scubenacadie: Name of village, river, and lake; meaning "where nuts grow in abundance" (Micmac)

## ◆ ONTARIO

Abitibi: Name of lake and river; derived from tribal name, meaning "halfway water" (Algonkian)

Brant/Brantford: Name of city and county; named after chief Joseph Brant (Mohawk)

Cataraqui: Name of river; meaning "where river and lake meet" (Iroquoian)

Cayuga: Name of town and county; derived from tribal name, meaning "here they take the boats out" (Iroquoian)

Iroquois: Name of town; derived from tribal name, meaning "real adders" (Algonkian word with French spelling)

Muskota: Name of district, lake, river, and bay; probably named after a chief (Ojibway)

Niagara: Name of township, river, and falls; probably meaning "thunderer of waters" or "resounding with great noise" (Iroquoian)

Oneida: Name of township; derived from tribal name, meaning "people of the upright stone" (Iroquoian)

Ottawa: Name of city and river; derived from tribal name, probably meaning "to trade" (Algonkian)

Petawawa: Name of township, village, and river; meaning "where one hears the noise of water far away" (probably Algonkian)

Saugeen: Name of township and river; meaning "river mouth" (Huron)

Tecumseh: Name of township; named after chief whose name means "a panther crouching for its prey" (Shawnee)

Toronto: Name of city; probably meaning "fallen trees in the water" or "a place of meeting" (Huron)

## ◆ QUEBEC

Arthabaska: Name of county and cantons; meaning "a place obstructed by reeds and grass" (Cree)

Chibougamau: Name of settlement, river, and lake; meaning "the water is stopped" (Algonkian)

Chicoutimi: Name of city, county, and river; meaning "end of the deep water" (Montagnais)

Matane: Name of town, county, river, and lakes; meaning "beaver ponds" (Micmac)

Pontiac: Name of county; named after Ottawa chief (probably Algonkian)

Quebec: Name of city, county, and province; meaning "where the river narrows" (Algonkian)

Shawinigan: Name of lake, river, and falls; meaning "a portage shaped like a beech-nut" (probably Cree)

Temiscouata: Name of county and lake; meaning "deep lake" (Cree)

Ungava: Name of bay; meaning "an unknown, faraway land" (Inuit)

## ◆ SASKATCHEWAN

Assiniboine: Name of river; derived from a word for a Sioux tribe, meaning "he who cooks with stones" (Ojibway)

Saskatchewan: Name of province and river; meaning "swift-flowing river" (Cree)

Saskatoon: Name of city; named for edible red berry (Cree)

Wakaw: Name of lake; meaning "crooked lake" (Cree)

## ◆ YUKON TERRITORY

Dezadeash: Name of lake; meaning "a native fishing method" (Athapascan)

Itsi: Name of lake and mountains; meaning "wind" (Athapascan)

Klondike: Name of village and river; meaning "river full of fish"

Teslin: Name of town, lake, and river; meaning "long waters" (Athapascan)

Ulu: Name of mountain; named for a knife with a crescent-shaped blade and a handle of bone or wood (Inuit)

Yukon: Name of river and mountain; meaning "great river" (probably Athapascan)

# Tribal Collections

## UNITED STATES

### ◆ ALASKA

AKUTAN ALEUT MUSEUM
P.O. Box 89
Akutan, AK 99553

CHICKALOON NUKDIN ITNU TRIBAL
MUSEUM
Chickaloon Village, Box 1105
Chickaloon, AK 99674
(907) 745-0707

UNIVERSITY OF ALASKA MUSEUM
907 Youkon Dr.
Fairbanks, AK 99775
(907) 474-7505
www.uaf.edu/museum

NANA MUSEUM OF THE ARTIC
P.O. Box 49
Kotzebue, AK 99752
(907) 442-3441

### ◆ ARIZONA

AK-CHIN HIM DAK ECO MUSEUM
Ak-Chin Indian Community
47685 N. Eco Museum Rd.
Maricopa, AZ 85239
(520) 568-9480

COLORADO RIVER INDIAN TRIBES MUSEUM
Rte. 1, Box 23B
Parker, AZ 85344
(520) 669-1335
Mohave, Chemehuevi, Navajo, and Hopi.

COCOPAH TRIBAL MUSEUM
County 15 & Aveune G
Somerton, AZ 85350
(520) 627-1992

DINE MUSEUM
Navajo Community College
Box 35
Tsaile, AZ 86556
(520) 724-6653

NAVAJO NATION TRIBAL MUSEUM
P.O. Box 1840, Hwy. 264
Window Rock, AZ 86515
(520) 871-7941

### ◆ CALIFORNIA

HOOPA TRIBAL MUSEUM
P.O. Box 1348
Hoopa, CA 95546
(530) 625-4110
Hupa, Yurok, and Karuk.

MALKI MUSEUM
Morongo Reservation
P.O. Box 578
11-795 Fields Rd.
Banning, CA 92220
(909) 849-7289
www.the-pass.com/Malki/fallg.html
Cahuilla, Serrano, Luiseño, and other California
Tribal Groups.

### ◆ COLORADO

SOUTHERN UTE INDIAN MUSEUM
1482 Hwy. 172 N.
Ignacio, CO 81137
(970) 563-9583

UTE INDIAN MUSEUM
17253 Chiopeta Rd.
Montrose, CO 81401
(970) 249-3098

### ◆ CONNECTICUT

**TANTAQUIDGEON INDIAN MUSEUM**
Rte. 32, Norwich-New London Rd.
Uncasville, CT 06382
(860) 848–9145
Built and maintained by descendants of uncas, chief
　of the Mohegans.

### ◆ DELAWARE

**NANTICOKE INDIAN MUSEUM**
Rte. 4, Box 107A
Millsboro, DE 19966
(302) 945–7022

### ◆ FLORIDA

**AH-TAH-THI-KI MUSEUM**
HC 21, Box 21A
Clewiston, FL 33440
(863) 902–1113
www.seminoletribe.com/museum

**COO-TAUN CHOBE MUSEUM**
Bobby's Seminole Indian Village and Gift Shop
5221 North Orient Rd.
Tampa, FL 33610
(813) 620–3077

**SEMINOLE OKALEE INDIAN VILLAGE
　AND MUSEUM**
5845 South State Rd. 7
Fort Lauderdale, FL 33314
(954) 792–1213

### ◆ IDAHO

**SHOSHONE-BANNOCK TRIBAL MUSEUM**
P.O. Box 793
I-15, Exit 80
Fort Hall, ID 83203
(208) 237–9791

### ◆ KANSAS

**MID-AMERICA ALL INDIAN CENTER
　MUSEUM**
650 North Seneca
Wichita, KS 67203
(316) 262–5221

### ◆ MAINE

**MAINE TRIBAL UNITY MUSEUM**
Unity College
HC 78 Box 1
Quaker Hill Rd.
Unity, ME 04988
(207) 948–3131

**PENOBSCOT NATION MUSEUM**
5 Down Street
Indian Island, ME 04468
(207) 827–4153

### ◆ MICHIGAN

**MUSEUM OF OJBIWA CULTURE**
500 N. State St.
St. Ignaces, MI 49781
(906) 643–9161
www.stignace.com

### ◆ MINNESOTA

**MILLE LACS INDIAN MUSEUM**
43408 Oodena Dr.
Onamia, MN 56359
(320) 532–4181

### ◆ MISSISSIPPI

**THE CHOCTAW MUSEUM OF THE
　SOUTHERN INDIAN**
Mississippi Band of Choctaw Indians
P.O. Box 6010
Philadelphia, MS 39350
(601) 656–5251

### ◆ MONTANA

**CHEYENNE INDIAN MUSEUM**
Ashland, MT
(406) 784–2744

**FLATHEAD INDIAN MUSEUM**
Flathead Indian Reservation
P.O. Box 460 I
1 Museum Ln.
St. Ignatius, MT 59865
(406) 745–2951

FORT PECK TRIBAL MUSEUM
Assiniboine Sioux Tribes
Fort Peck Indian Reservation
P.O. Box 1027
Poplar, MT 59255
(406) 768–5155 ext. 328

## ◆ NEW MEXICO

PICURIS PUEBLO MUSEUM
P.O. Box 127
Penasco, NM 87553
(505) 587–2957

SAN ILDEFONSO PUEBLO MUSEUM
Rte. 5, Box 315-A
Santa Fe, NM 87501
(505) 455–2424

## ◆ NEW YORK

AKWESASNE MUSEUM
Rte. 37
Hogansburg, NY 13655
(518) 358–2461

IROQUOIS INDIAN MUSEUM
P.O. Box 7 Cavers Rd
Howes Cave, NY 12092
(518) 296–8949
www.iroquoismuseum.org

SENECA-IROQUOIS NATIONAL MUSEUM
Allegany Indian Reservation
794814 Broad St.
Salamanca, NY 14779
(716) 945–1738

## ◆ NORTH CAROLINA

MUSEUM OF THE CHEROKEE INDIAN
P.O. Box 1599
Drama Rd. Hwy. 44
Cherokee, NC 28719
(828) 497–3481
www.cherokeemuseum.org

## ◆ NORTH DAKOTA

THREE AFFILIATED TRIBES MUSEUM
P.O. Box 147
New Town, ND 58763
(701) 627–4477

## ◆ OKLAHOMA

CHEROKEE NATIONAL MUSEUM (TSALAGI)
Cherokee Heritage Center
P.O. Box 515
Tahlequah, OK 74465
(918) 456–6007

CHICKASAW COUNCIL HOUSE MUSEUM
200 N. Fisher P.O. Box 717
Tishomingo, OK 73460
(580) 371–3351

CHOCTAW NATION MUSEUM
Hc 64 Box 3270
Tuskahoma, OK 74574–9758
(918) 569–4465

CREEK COUNCIL HOUSE MUSEUM
Town Square
Okmulgee, OK 74447
(918) 756–2324

DELAWARE TRIBAL MUSEUM
c/o Delaware Executive Board
P.O. Box 825
Anadarko, OK 73005
(405) 247–2448

OSAGE TRIBAL MUSEUM
Osage Agency Reserve
P.O. Box 779
819 Grand View Ave.
Pawhuska, OK 74056
(918) 287–4622

POTAWATOMI INDIAN NATION ARCHIVES
    AND MUSEUM
1901 South Gordon Cooper Dr.
Shawnee, OK 74801
(405) 275–3121

SEMINOLE NATION MUSEUM
524 South Wewoka, Box 1532
Wewoka, OK 74884
(405) 257–5580

TONKAWA TRIBAL MUSEUM
P.O. Box 70
Tonkawa, OK 74653
(580) 628–2561

♦ **OREGON**

MUSEUM AT WARM SPRINGS
P.O. Box 753
Warm Springs, OR 97761–0753
(541) 553–3331

♦ **RHODE ISLAND**

TOMAQUAG INDIAN MEMORIAL MUSEUM
Box 386 Summit Rd.
Exeter, RI 02822
(401) 539–7213

♦ **SOUTH DAKOTA**

BUECHEL MEMORIAL LAKOTA MUSEUM
350 S. Oak St.
P.O. Box 499
St. Francis, SD 575572
(605) 747–5509

♦ **TENNESSEE**

SEQUOYAH BIRTHPLACE MUSEUM
576 Hwy 360 P.O. Box 69
Vonore, TN 37885
(423) 884–6246
www.sequoyahmuseum.org

♦ **TEXAS**

ALABAMA-COUSHATTA INDIAN MUSEUM
Rte. 3, Box 640, Hwy. 190
Livingston, TX 77351
(409) 563–4391

♦ **UTAH**

UTE TRIBAL MUSEUM
P.O. Box 190, Hwy. 40
Fort Duchesne, UT 84026
(801) 722–4992

♦ **VIRGINIA**

MATTAPONI INDIAN MUSEUM AND
    TRADING POST
Mattaponi Indian Reservation
Rte. 2, Box 255
West Point, VA 23181
(804) 769–2194

MONACAN INDIAN ANCESTRAL MUSEUM
2009 Kenmore Rd.
Amherst, VA 24521
(804) 946–5391

♦ **WASHINGTON**

COLVILLE CONFEDERATED TRIBES
    MUSEUM
P.O. Box 233
Coulee Dam, WA 99116
(509) 634–4711

PUYALLUP TRIBE MUSEUM
2215 East 22nd St.
Tacoma, WA 98404
(206) 597–6200

SUQUAMISH MUSEUM
15838 Sandy Hook N.E.
P.O. Box 498
Suquamish, WA 98392
(206) 598–3311

♦ **WISCONSIN**

ONEIDA NATION MUSEUM
Oneida Nation Cultural Center
P.O. Box 365
Oneida, WI 54155
(414) 869–2768

STOCKBRIDGE-MUNSEE HISTORICAL
    LIBRARY AND MUSEUM
Rte. 1, Box 300
Bowler, WI 54416
(715) 793–4270

WINNEBAGO INDIAN MUSEUM
3889 North River Rd.
P.O. Box 441
Wisconsin Dells, WI 53965
(608) 254–2268

♦ **WYOMING**

ARAPAHO CULTURAL MUSEUM
P.O. Box 8066
Ethete, WY 82520
(307) 332–2660

# CANADA

## ◆ ALBERTA

TSUT'INA K'OSA (SARCEE)
3700 Anderson Rd. S.W.
Box 67
Calgary, AB T2W 3T0
(403) 238–2677

## ◆ ONTARIO

CHIEFSWOOD MUSEUM
Hwy 54 Chiefswood Rd.
P.O. Box 640
Ohsweken, ON N0A 1M0
(519) 752–5005

NORTH AMERICAN TRAVELING
COLLEGE MUSEUM
Rt 3
Cornwall Island, ON K6H 5R7
(613) 932–9452

WOODLANDS MUSEUM
184 Mowhawk St.
Brantford,ON N3S 2X2
(519) 759–2650

## ◆ BRITISH COLUMBIA

KSAN HISTORICAL VILLAGE AND MUSEUM
P.O. Box 326
Hazelton, BC V0J 1Y0
(250) 842–5544

SECWEPEMC MUSEUM AND NATIVE
HERITAGE PARK
Kamloops Indian Reserve
345 Yellowhead Hwy.
Kamloops, BC V6H 1H1
(250) 828–9801
www.ohwy.com/bc/s/secwepem.htm

## ◆ QUEBEC

MUSEE DE ABENAKIS
108 Waban-Aki
Odanak, QB J0G 1H0
(450) 568–2600

MUSEE AMERINDIAN DE MASHTEWIATSH
1787 Amishk St
Mashteuiatsch, QB G0W 2H0
(418) 275–4842

# Major Museums

## United States

### ◆ ALABAMA

BIRMINGHAM MUSEUM OF ART
2000 Eighth Ave. N.
Birmingham, AL 35203–2278
(205) 254–2566
www.artsBMA.org
North, Central, and South American Indian art.

### ◆ ALASKA

ALASKA STATE MUSEUM
395 Whittier St.
Juneau, AK 99801–1718
(907) 465–2901
www.museums.state.ak.us/asmhome.html
Alaskan Native Gallery (companion museum to
    Sheldon Jackson Museum).

ANCHORAGE MUSEUM OF HISTORY
    AND ART
121 West Seventh Ave.
Anchorage, AK 99501
(907) 343–4326
www.ci.anchorage.ak.us/Services/Departments/
    Culture/Museum/index.html
Alaskan tribes, Plains; Cook Inlet Region, Inc.,
    Community Collection (CIRI).

SHELDON JACKSON MUSEUM
104 College Dr.
Sitka, AK 99835–7657
(907) 747–8981
www.museums.state.ak.us/sjhome.html
Alaskan Native Gallery (companion museum to
    Alaska State Museum).

### ◆ ARIZONA

THE AMERIND FOUNDATION MUSEUM
2100 N. Amerind Road
P.O. Box 400
Dragoon, AZ 85609
(520) 586–3666
www.amerind.org
North America; emphasis on regional prehistoric.

THE HEARD MUSEUM
22 East Monte Vista Rd.
Phoenix, AZ 85004
(602) 252–8840
www.heard.org
Southwestern Native American Artists Resource
    Collection contains documentation of individual
    artists' achievements.

### ◆ ARKANSAS

ARKANSAS STATE UNIVERSITY MUSEUM
P.O. Box 490
State University, AR 72467
(870) 972–2074
www.astate.edu/docs/admin/museum/index.html
Northeast Arkansas regional emphasis.

### ◆ CALIFORNIA

PHOEBE A. HEARST MUSEUM OF
    ANTHROPOLOGY
103 Kroeber Hall
University of California
Berkeley, CA 94720–3712
(510) 642–3682
www.qal.berkeley.edu/~hearst/
North America, especially California.

SAN DIEGO MUSEUM OF MAN
1350 El Prado
San Diego, CA 92101
(619) 239–2001
www.museumofman.org
Native cultures of the western Americas, especially
California and the Southwest.

SOUTHWEST MUSEUM
234 Museum Dr.
Los Angeles, CA 90065
(323) 221–2164
www.southwestmuseum.org
Native people of the Americas, especially California
and Southwest.

◆ **COLORADO**

DENVER MUSEUM OF NATURE AND
SCIENCE
2001 Colorado Blvd.
Denver, CO 80205
(303) 322–7009 (800) 925–2250
www.dmnh.org
Emphasis on regional, including the original Folsom
point (found at Folsom site, New Mexico,
between the ribs of an extinct buffalo).

UNIVERSITY OF COLORADO MUSEUM
Henderson Bldg., Campus Box 218
Boulder, CO 80309–0218
(303) 492–6892
www.Colorado.EDU/CUMUSEUM/index.html
North American prehistory, especially the Plains and
Southwest.

◆ **CONNECTICUT**

THE INSTITUTE FOR AMERICAN INDIAN
STUDIES
P.O. Box 1260
Off Route 199, 38 Curtis Rd.
Washington, CT 06793–0260
(860) 868–0518
Primarily Northeast Woodlands, including Indian
Village.

PEABODY MUSEUM OF NATURAL HISTORY
Yale University
170 Whitney Ave.
New Haven, CT 06511–8902
(203) 432–5050
www.peabody.yale.edu
Extensive archaeological collection, especially
regional.

◆ **DELAWARE**

DELAWARE STATE MUSEUMS
102 S. State Street
Dover, DE 19901
(302) 739–5316
www.destatemuseums.org
Regional emphasis.

◆ **DISTRICT OF COLUMBIA**

NATIONAL MUSEUM OF THE
AMERICAN INDIAN
National Mall
Washington, D.C.
Executive Offices:
470 L'Enfant Plaza S.W.
Suite 7103
Washington, D.C. 20560–0934
(202) 357–3164
www.si.edu/nmai
Currently under construction with completion
scheduled for 2002.

NATIONAL MUSEUM OF NATURAL HISTORY
Department of Anthropology
10th Street and Constitution Avenue N. W.
NHB 112, Smithsonian Institution
Washington, D.C. 20560–0112
(202) 357–2363
www.nmnh.si.edu/departments/anthro.html/
Indians of the Americas (over two million objects);
Human Studies Film Archives; American Indian
Program internships and fellowships; National
Anthropological Archives; Arctic Studies Center;
Handbook of North American Indians.

◆ **FLORIDA**

LOWE ART MUSEUM
University of Miami
1301 Stanford Dr.
Coral Gables, FL 33124–6310
(305) 284–3535
www.lowemuseum.org

The Americas, especially the Alfred I. Barton
Collection of Southwest Indian art.

### ◆ GEORGIA

**COLUMBUS MUSEUM**

1251 Wynnton Rd.
Columbus, GA 31906
(706) 649–0713
www.columbusmuseum.com
Artifacts from Paleo through Mississippian cultures,
especially Yuchi.

### ◆ IDAHO

**IDAHO STATE HISTORICAL MUSEUM**

610 North Julia Davis Dr.
Boise, ID 83702
(208) 334–2120
www.state.id.us/ishs/index.htm
Northwest Coast, Alaskan, and Plains, especially
Upper Great Basin.

### ◆ ILLINOIS

**FIELD MUSEUM OF NATURAL HISTORY**

1400 S. Lake Shore Dr.
Chicago, IL 60605–2496
(312) 922–9410
www.fmnh.org
North and South America, diverse and extensive;
Pawnee earth lodge.

**ILLINOIS STATE MUSEUM**

Corner of Spring and Edwards Streets
Springfield, IL 62706–5000
(217) 782–7387
www.museum.state.il.us
Paleo into historic. Archaeological site branch:
Dickson Mounds Museum, Lewistown, IL 61542;
phone: (309)547–3721.

### ◆ INDIANA

**EITELJORG MUSEUM OF AMERICAN INDIAN
AND WESTERN ART**

500 West Washington St.
Indianapolis, IN 46204
(317) 636–9378
www.eiteljorg.org
Primarily North American, especially Northeast
Woodlands, Great Plains, Southwest.

**WILLIAM HAMMOND MATHERS MUSEUM**

Indiana University
601 East Eighth St.
Bloomington, IN 47408
(812) 855–6873
www.indiana.edu/~mathers
North America, especially Plains and Alaskan
Eskimo; Wanamaker Collection of American
Indian Photographs.

### ◆ IOWA

**STATE HISTORICAL SOCIETY OF IOWA**

State of Iowa Historical Building
600 East Locust St.
Des Moines, IA 50319
(515) 281–5111
www.iowahistory.org/museum/index.html
Emphasis on Western Great Lakes and Plains.

### ◆ KANSAS

**MUSEUM OF ANTHROPOLOGY**

Spooner Hall
University of Kansas
Lawrence, KS 66045
(785) 864–4245
www.ukans.edu/~kuma/
North America, especially regional, Southwest, and
Northwest Coast.

### ◆ KENTUCKY

**THE SPEED ART MUSEUM**

2035 South Third St.
Louisville, KY 40208
(502) 634–2700
www.speedmuseum.org
Primarily Plains.

**WILLIAM S. WEBB MUSEUM OF
ANTHROPOLOGY**

Department of Anthropology
211 Lafferty Hall
University of Kentucky
Lexington, KY 40506–0024
(859) 257–8208
www.uky.edu/AS/Anthropology/Museum/
museum.htm

### ◆ LOUISIANA

MUSEUM OF NATURAL SCIENCE
119 Foster Hall
Louisiana State University
Baton Rouge, LA 70803
(225) 388–2855
www.museum.lsu.edu
North America; regional emphasis.

### ◆ MAINE

THE ABBE MUSEUM
Sieur de Monts Spring in Acadia National Park
P.O. Box 286
Bar Harbor, ME 04609
(207) 288–3519
www.acadia.net/abbemuseum
Primarily Maine and Maritime Provinces (Canada),
    prehistoric and historic.

THE PEARY-MACMILLAN ARCTIC MUSEUM
    AND ARCTIC STUDIES CENTER
Hubbard Hall
Bowdoin College
Brunswick, ME 04011
(207) 725–3416
www.bowdoin.edu/dept/arctic/
Labrador, Baffin, and Greenland Inuit and Indian.

### ◆ MARYLAND

NATIONAL MUSEUM OF THE AMERICAN
    INDIAN CULTURAL RESOURCES CENTER
4220 Silver Hill Road
Suitland, MD 20746
301–238-6624
Curatorial offices, conservation facilities and
    repository for the NMAI collections.

### ◆ MASSACHUSETTS

PEABODY MUSEUM OF ARCHAEOLOGY AND
    ETHNOLOGY
Harvard University
11 Divinity Ave.
Cambridge, MA 02138
(617) 496–1027
www.peabody.harvard.edu
North America, especially dynamics of interactions
    between Indians and whites over past 500 years.

### ◆ MICHIGAN

CRANBROOK INSTITUTE OF SCIENCE
39221 Woodward
Bloomfield Hills, MI 48303–0801
(877) 462–7262
www.cranbrook.edu/institute
North America, especially Woodlands and Plains.

UNIVERSITY OF MICHIGAN MUSEUM OF
    ANTHROPOLOGY
Natural Science Museum Building
1109 Geddes Ave.
Ann Arbor, MI 48109–1079
(734) 764–0485
www.umma.lsa.umich.edu/museum.html
North America.

### ◆ MINNESOTA

MINNESOTA HISTORICAL SOCIETY MUSEUM
345 Kellogg Blvd. West
St. Paul, MN 55102–1906
(651) 296–6126
www.mnhs.org/places/historycenter/index.html
Minnesota emphasis, especially Dakota (Sioux) and
    Ojibwa (Chippewa).

### ◆ MISSOURI

KANSAS CITY MUSEUM
3218 Gladstone Blvd.
Kansas City, MO 64123–1199
(816) 483–8300
www.kcmuseum.com
Southern and Central Plains, Eastern Woodlands,
    Southwest, Northwest Coast; extensive.

MUSEUM OF ANTHROPOLOGY
University of Missouri
104 Swallow Hall
University of Missouri
Columbia, MO
(573) 882–3573
www.missouri.edu/~anthmjo/
Missouri and regional emphasis.

ST. LOUIS SCIENCE CENTER
5050 Oakland Ave.
St. Louis, MO 63110
(314) 289–4400
www.slsc.org
Emphasis on midwestern cultures, especially
    Mississippian.

## ◆ MONTANA

### MUSEUM OF THE PLAINS INDIAN
Junction of U. S. Highways 2 and 89 West
Box 410
Browning, MT 59417
(406) 338–2230
www.doi.gov/iacb/museum/museum_plains.html
Northern Plains. Administered by the Indian Arts
and Crafts Board.

## ◆ NEBRASKA

### MUSEUM OF THE FUR TRADE
6321 Highway 20
Chadron, NE 69337
(308) 432–3843
www.furtrade.org
North American Indian cultures; influence of fur
trade on cultures.

### MUSEUM OF NEBRASKA HISTORY
131 Centennial Mall North
Lincoln, NE 68501–2554
P.O. Box 82554
(402) 471–4754
www.nebraskahistory.org/sites/mnh/index.htm
Emphasis on Nebraska and Central Plains.

## ◆ NEVADA

### NEVADA HISTORICAL SOCIETY MUSEUM
1650 North Virginia St.
Reno, NV 89503
(775) 688–1190
lahontan.clan.lib.nv.us/polpac/html_client/default.asp
(via State Library, Division of Museums and
History)
Emphasis on Washo, Northern Paiute, Southern
Paiute, Western Shoshone.

### NEVADA STATE MUSEUM
600 N. Carson Street
Carson City, NV 89701
(775) 687–4811
lahontan.clan.lib.nv.us/polpac/html_client/default.asp
(via State Library, Division of Museums and
History web site).
Emphasis on Nevada.

## ◆ NEW HAMPSHIRE

### HOOD MUSEUM OF ART
Dartmouth College
Wheelock Street
Hanover, NH 03755
(603) 646–2808
www.dartmouth.edu/acad-support/hood/Menu.html
North, Central, and South America, especially
Southwestern and New England.

## ◆ NEW JERSEY

### MORRIS MUSEUM OF ARTS AND SCIENCES
6 Normandy Heights Rd.
Morristown, NJ 07961
(973) 538–0454
www.morrismuseum.org
Woodlands, Northwest Coast, Southwest, Plains.

### NEW JERSEY STATE MUSEUM
205 West State St.
P.O. Box 530
Trenton, NJ 08625–0530
(609) 292–6464
www.state.nj.us/state/museum/musidx.html
Emphasis on New Jersey and the surrounding
region.

## ◆ NEW MEXICO

### INSTITUTE OF AMERICAN INDIAN ARTS MUSEUM
108 Cathedral Place
Santa Fe, NM 87501
(505) 983–1777
www.iaiancad.org/museum/
Paintings, graphics, sculpture, ceramics, textiles,
costumes, jewelry, and ethnographic material,
primarily by Native American students.

### MAXWELL MUSEUM OF ANTHROPOLOGY
University of New Mexico
Albuquerque, NM 87131–1201
(505) 277–4404
www.unm.edu/~maxwell/
Archaeology and ethnography, especially Southwest.

MUSEUM OF INDIAN ARTS AND CULTURE
Laboratory of Anthropology
Museum Plaza, Camino Lejo
P.O. Box 2087
Santa Fe, NM 87504–2087
(505) 476–1250
www.miaclab.org/
Primarily Southwest; emphasis on Pueblo,
Navajo, Apache.

WHEELWRIGHT MUSEUM OF THE
AMERICAN INDIAN
704 Camino Lejo
P.O. Box 5153
Santa Fe, NM 87502
(505) 982–4636
www.wheelwright.org/
North America, especially Southwest; emphasis
on Navajo.

#### ◆ NEW YORK

AMERICAN MUSEUM OF NATURAL HISTORY
79th St. and Central Park West
New York, NY 10024–5192
(212) 769–5100
www.amnh.org
Extensive and diverse.

GEORGE GUSTAV HEYE CENTER
National Museum of the American Indian
Alexander Hamilton U.S. Custom House
One Bowling Green
New York, N.Y. 10004
(212) 514–3700
www.si.edu/nmai/abmus/index.htm
Public exhibition spaces, photography collection,
film and video center, and resource center.

#### ◆ NORTH CAROLINA

INDIAN MUSEUM OF THE CAROLINAS
607 Turnpike Rd.
Laurinburg, NC 28352
(910) 276–5880
Southeast, primarily North and South Carolina.

MUSEUM OF THE NATIVE AMERICAN
RESOURCE CENTER
University of North Carolina, Pembroke
Old Main Bldg.
Pembroke, NC 28372
(910) 521–6282
www.uncp.edu/nativemuseum/
North and South America, especially Eastern
Woodlands.

SCHIELE MUSEUM OF NATURAL HISTORY
AND PLANETARIUM
1500 East Garrison Blvd.
Gastonia, NC 28056
(704) 866–6908
www.schielemuseum.org
Extensive collection from twelve cultural areas,
especially Southeast and North Carolina.

#### ◆ NORTH DAKOTA

BUFFALO TRAILS MUSEUM
Main Street
P.O. Box 22
Epping, ND 58843
(701) 859–4361
Upper Missouri area.

STATE HISTORICAL SOCIETY OF
NORTH DAKOTA
North Dakota Heritage Center
612 East Boulevard Ave.
Bismarck, ND 58505
(701) 328–2666
www.state.nd.us/hist
Primarily northern Great Plains.

#### ◆ OHIO

CLEVELAND MUSEUM OF NATURAL
HISTORY
1 Wade Oval Dr., University Circle
Cleveland, OH 44106–1767
(216) 231–4600
www.cmnh.org
North America, especially Ohio.

OHIO HISTORICAL CENTER
1982 Velma Ave.
Columbus, OH 43211
(614) 297–2300
www.ohiohistory.org
Emphasis on regional prehistory.

### ◆ OKLAHOMA

GILCREASE MUSEUM
1400 Gilcrease Museum Rd.
Tulsa, OK 74127–2100
(918) 596–2700
www.gilcrease.org/
North America, prehistory to present; extensive.
　World's largest collection of art of
　American West.

PHILBROOK MUSEUM OF ART
2727 South Rockford Road
Tulsa, OK 74114
(918) 749–7941
www.philbrook.org
North America, notable basketry and pottery
　collections.

SAM NOBLE OKLAHOMA MUSEUM OF
　NATURAL HISTORY
University of Oklahoma
2401 Chatauqua
Norman, OK 73072
(405) 325–4712
www.snomnh.ou.edu/
North America, especially Southern Plains,
　Southwest, Northwest Coast, Spiro Mounds.

SOUTHERN PLAINS INDIAN MUSEUM
715 East Central Boulevard
Anadarko, OK 73005
(405) 247–6221
www.doi.gov/iacb/museum/museum_s_plains.html
Tribes of western Oklahoma: Kiowa, Comanche,
　Kiowa–Apache, Southern Cheyenne, Southern
　Arapaho, Wichita, Caddo, Delaware, Fort Sill
　Apache. Administered by the Indian Arts and
　Crafts Board.

### ◆ OREGON

MUSEUM OF NATURAL HISTORY
University of Oregon
1680 East 15th Ave.
Eugene, OR 97403–1224
(541) 346–3024
natural-history.uoregon.edu/
North America, especially Northwest Coast and
　Pacific Rim.

PORTLAND ART MUSEUM
1219 SW Park Ave.
Portland, OR 97205
(503) 226–2811
www.pam.org
North and Middle America, especially
　Northwest Coast.

### ◆ PENNSYLVANIA

THE CARNEGIE MUSEUM OF NATURAL
　HISTORY
4400 Forbes Ave.
Pittsburgh, PA 15213–4080
(412) 622–3131
www.clpgh.org/cmnh/
North and South America, especially Upper Ohio
　Valley.

### ◆ RHODE ISLAND

THE HAFFENREFFER MUSEUM OF
　ANTHROPOLOGY
Brown University
300 Tower Street
Bristol, RI 02809
(401) 253–8388
www.brown.edu/Facilities/Haffenreffer/
The Americas, especially Arctic and Red Paint
　(Maine).

### ◆ SOUTH CAROLINA

CHESTER COUNTY HISTORICAL
　SOCIETY MUSEUM
107 McAiley Street
P.O. Box 811
Chester, SC 29706
(803) 385–2330
Regional; over 30,000 Catawba Indian artifacts.

### ◆ SOUTH DAKOTA

SIOUX INDIAN MUSEUM
222 New York Street
P.O. Box 1504
Rapid City, SD 57709
(605) 394–2381
www.doi.gov/iacb/museum/museum_sioux.html
North America, especially Sioux. Administered by
　the Indian Arts and Crafts Board.

THE W. H. OVER STATE MUSEUM
1110 Ratingen Street
Vermillion, SD 57069
(605) 677–5228
www.usd.edu/whover
Emphasis on South Dakota Sioux.

#### ◆ TENNESSEE

FRANK H. MCCLUNG MUSEUM
University of Tennessee, Knoxville
1327 Circle Park Dr.
Knoxville, TN 37996–3200
(865) 974–2144
mcclungmuseum.utk.edu
Regional emphasis.

THE TENNESSEE STATE MUSEUM
505 Deaderick St.
Nashville, TN 37243–1120
(615) 741–2692
Regional emphasis; prehistoric Mississippian.

#### ◆ TEXAS

PANHANDLE-PLAINS HISTORICAL MUSEUM
2401 Fourth Ave.
WTAMU Box 60967
Canyon, TX 79016
(806) 656–2244
www.wtamu.edu/museum/
Emphasis on Comanche, Kiowa.

TEXAS MEMORIAL MUSEUM
University of Texas, Austin
2400 Trinity
Austin,, TX 78705
(512) 471–1604
www.utexas.edu/depts/tmm
Emphasis on Texas, Southwest, Latin America.

WITTE MUSEUM
3801 Broadway
San Antonio, TX 78209
(210) 357–1900
www.wittemuseum.org
North America, emphasis on Texas and Southwest.

#### ◆ UTAH

MUSEUM OF PEOPLES AND CULTURES
Brigham Young University, Allen Hall
700 North 100 East
Provo, UT 84602
(801) 378–6112
fhss.byu.edu/mpc/
North America, emphasis on Maya, Anasazi,
    Fremont, Mogollon, Casas Grandes.

UTAH MUSEUM OF NATURAL HISTORY
University of Utah
1309 E. President's Circle
Salt Lake City, UT 84112–0050
(801) 581–6927
www.umnh.utah.edu/
Regional, Great Basin, Southwest.

#### ◆ VERMONT

ROBERT HULL FLEMING MUSEUM
University of Vermont
61 Colchester Ave.
Burlington, VT 05405
(802) 656–2090
www.uvm.edu/~fleming/
North America.

#### ◆ VIRGINIA

JAMESTOWN SETTLEMENT
P.O. Box 1607
Williamsburg, VA 23187
(888) 593–4682
www.historyisfun.org
Virginia Indian artifacts; reconstruction of
    Powhatan's lodge.

#### ◆ WASHINGTON

BURKE MUSEUM OF NATURAL HISTORY
    AND CULTURE
Box 353010
University of Washington
Seattle, WA 98195–3010
(206) 543–7907
www.washington.edu/burkemuseum/
Emphasis on Northwest Coast.

CHENEY COWLES MUSEUM
Eastern Washington State Historical Society
2316 West First Ave.
Spokane, WA 99204
(509) 456–3931
www.cheneycowles.org
Americas; emphasis on Plateau tribes.

#### ◆ WISCONSIN

LOGAN MUSEUM OF ANTHROPOLOGY
Beloit College
700 College St.
Beloit, WI 53511
(608) 363–2677
www.beloit.edu/~museum/logan/index.html
Regional emphasis; North and South America.

MILWAUKEE PUBLIC MUSEUM
800 West Wells St.
Milwaukee, WI 53233
(414) 278–2700
www.mpm.edu/
North America, especially Midwest archaeology.

#### ◆ WYOMING

PLAINS INDIAN MUSEUM
Buffalo Bill Historical Center
720 Sheridan Ave.
Cody, WY 82414
(307) 587–4771
www.bbhc.org
Primarily Northern Plains; recreation of 1890
    Sioux camp.

WYOMING STATE MUSEUM
Barrett Bldg.
2301 Central
Cheyenne, WY 82002
(307) 777–7022
spacr.state.wy.us/cr/wsm/index.htm
Primarily Northern Plains.

## CANADA

#### ◆ ALBERTA

GLENBOW MUSEUM
130 9th Ave. S.E.
Calgary, AB T2G 0P3
(403) 268–4100
www.glenbow.org/museum.htm

Primary focus Northern Plains; also Northwest
    Coast, Arctic and Subarctic.

PROVINCIAL MUSEUM OF ALBERTA
12845 102nd Ave.
Edmonton, AB T5N OM6
(780) 453–9100
www.pma.edmonton.ab.ca/
Emphasis on Alberta, Northern Plains, Inuit.

#### ◆ BRITISH COLUMBIA

MUSEUM OF ANTHROPOLOGY
University of British Columbia
6393 N.W. Marine Drive
Vancouver, BC V6T 1Z2
(604) 822–3825
www.moa.ubc.ca/menu.html

MUSEUM OF NORTHERN BRITISH
    COLUMBIA
P.O. Box 669
Prince Rupert, BC V8J 3S1
(250) 624–3207
Northwest Coast, especially Tsimshian, Haida,
    Tlingit.

ROYAL BRITISH COLUMBIA MUSEUM
P.O. Box 9815 Stn. Prov. Govt.
675 Belleville St.
Victoria, BC V8W 9W2
(250) 387–3701
rbcm1.rbcm.gov.bc.ca/
Regional archaeology; totem pole exhibit in
    Thunderbird Park.

#### ◆ MANITOBA

MANITOBA MUSEUM OF MAN AND NATURE
190 Rupert Ave.
Winnipeg, MB R3B ON2
(204) 956–2830
www.manitobamuseum.mb.ca
Regional; relationship between humans and
    environment.

#### ◆ NEWFOUNDLAND

NEWFOUNDLAND MUSEUM
285 Duckworth St.
St. Johns, NF A1C 1G9
(709) 729–2329
www.nfmuseum.com/
Regional, especially Beothuk and Naskapi.

## ◆ NORTHWEST TERRITORIES

DENE CULTURAL INSTITUTE
P.O. Box 207
Yellowknife, NT X1A 2N2
(403) 873–6617

NORTHERN LIFE MUSEUM AND NATIONAL
EXHIBITION CENTRE
110 King Street
P.O. Box 420
Fort Smith, NT X0E 0P0
(867) 872–2859
Regional, especially Athapascan and Inuit.

## ◆ NOVA SCOTIA

MUSEUM OF NATURAL HISTORY
Nova Scotia Museum
1747 Summer St.
Halifax, NS B3H 3A6
(902) 424–7353
museum.gov.ns.ca/
Regional Paleo-Indian through Woodland cultures,
especially Micmac.

## ◆ ONTARIO

THE NORTH AMERICAN INDIAN TRAVELING
COLLEGE
THE LIVING MUSEUM AND WOODLANDS INDIAN
VILLAGE
R.R. 3, Cornwall Island
Cornwall, ON K6H 5R7
(613) 932–9452
Eastern Woodlands cultural and educational center;
traditional structures, and crafts.

ROYAL ONTARIO MUSEUM
100 Queen's Park
Toronto, ON M5S 2C6
(416) 586–5549
www.rom.on.ca/
North America, especially Canada, Arctic, regional.

## ◆ PRINCE EDWARD ISLAND

PRINCE EDWARD ISLAND MUSEUM AND
HERITAGE FOUNDATION
2 Kent St.
Charlottetown, PEI C1A 1M6
(902) 368–6600

## ◆ QUEBEC

CANADIAN MUSEUM OF CIVILIZATION
100 Laurier St.
Box 3100, Station B
Hull, PQ J8X 4H2
(819) 776–7000
www.civilization.ca/
Extensive First Nations' collections.

## ◆ SASKATCHEWAN

ROYAL SASKATCHEWAN MUSEUM
2445 Albert Street
Wascana Park
Regina, SK S4P 3V7
(306) 787–2810
www.gov.sk.ca/rsm/
Regional, especially Cree, Assiniboine, Saulteaux,
Dakota, Dene.

## ◆ YUKON TERRITORY

MACBRIDE MUSEUM
1st Avenue and Wood Street
P.O. Box 4037
Whitehorse, YT Y1A 3S9
(867) 667–2709
Regional, especially Athapascan, Tlingit, Inuvialuit.

# Archives and Special Collections

## United States

### ◆ ALABAMA

ALABAMA DEPARTMENT OF ARCHIVES AND
   HISTORY
624 Washington Ave.
Montgomery, AL 36130–0100
(334) 242–4363
www.archives.state.al.usa

### ◆ ARIZONA

ARIZONA HISTORICAL SOCIETY
   RESEARCH LIBRARY
949 East Second St.
Tucson, AZ 85719
(520) 628–5774
Maps of Indian reservations; manuscripts of
   teachers, doctors, and agents on their
   observations of various reservations.

CAPITOL MUSEUM
1700 West Washington St.
Phoenix, AZ 85007–2896
(602) 542–4675
www.lib.az.us/museum/index.html

HEARD MUSEUM LIBRARY AND MUSEUM
NATIVE AMERICAN ARCHIVES
2301 N. Central Ave.
Phoenix, Az 85004–1323
(602) 251–0267
www.heard.org

MUSEUM OF NORTHERN ARIZONA
301 N. Fort Valley Rd.
Flagstaff, AZ 86001
(520) 774–5211
www.musnaz.org
Natural history and Native American museum;
   one of the largest collections in the country,

containing more than two million Native
American artifacts.

PUEBLO GRANDE MUSEUM AND
   ARCHEOLOGICAL PARK
4619 East Washington St.
Phoenix, AZ 85034
(602) 495–0901
www.pueblogrande.com

### ◆ ARKANSAS

ARKANSAS STATE UNIVERSITY MUSEUM
Arkansas State University
P.O. Box 490
State University, AR 72467
Quapaw, Osage, and Cherokee mound builders.

### ◆ CALIFORNIA

AMERICAN INDIAN RESOURCE CENTER
Los Angeles Public Library
6518 Miles Ave.
Huntington Park, CA 90255
(323) 583–1461

AMERICAN INDIAN STUDIES CENTER
   LIBRARY
University of California
3220 Campbell Hall
Los Angeles, CA 90024–1548
(310) 206–7510
www.sscnetucla.edu/indian/

BANCROFT LIBRARY AND THE HEARST
   MUSEUM OF ANTHROPLOGY LIBRARY
University of California
103 Kroeber Hall
Berkeley, CA 94720
(510) 642–3781
www.library.berkly.edu
California Indians.

HUNTINGTON LIBRARY
1151 Oxford Rd.
San Marino, CA 91108
(626) 405–2141

RANCHO LOS CERRITOS HISTORIC SITE
4600 Virginia Rd.
Long Beach, CA 90807
(565) 570–1755
www.ci.long-beach.ca.us/parks/ranchlc.htm
California and Western history.

#### ◆ COLORADO

CENTER FOR THE STUDY OF NATIVE
 LANGUAGES OF THE PLAINS AND
 SOUTHWEST
University of Colorado
Department of Linguistics CB 295
Boulder, CO 80309
(303) 492–2728

COLORADO HISTORICAL SOCIETY
Stephen H. Hart Library
1300 Broadway
Denver, CO 80203
(303) 866–2305

MUSEUM OF WESTERN STUDIES COLORADO
 ARCHIVES
248 S. 4th Street
Grand Junction, C0 81501
(303) 242–0971

NATIONAL INDIAN LAW LIBRARY
Native American Rights Fund
1522 Broadway
Boulder, CO 80302
(303) 447–8760
Collections exclusively on federal Indian law.

#### ◆ CONNECTICUT

THE INSTITUTE FOR AMERICAN INDIAN
 STUDIES AND RESEARCH
38 Curtis Rd. Box 1260
Washington Green, CT 06793
(203) 868–0518

MASHANTUCKET PEQUOT RESEARCH
 LIBRARY
ARCHIVES AND SPECIAL COLLECTIONS
CHILDREN'S RESEARCH LIBRARY
110 Pequot Trail, P.O. Box 3180
Mashantucket, CT 06339
(800) 411–9671

#### ◆ DISTRICT OF COLUMBIA

THE LIBRARY OF CONGRESS
101 Independence Ave. S. E.
Washington, DC 20540
(202) 707–5522
www.loc.gov
Records of tribal council minutes; manuscripts on
 the relations of tribes with the United States;
 prints and photographs.

NATIONAL ANTHROPOLOGICAL ARCHIVES
Natural History Museum
Smithsonian Institution
10 Street Constitution Ave.
Washington, DC 20560–0152
(202) 357–1976
www.nmhs.si.edu/naa

NATIONAL ARCHIVES AND RECORDS
 ADMINISTRATION
8th & Pennsylvania Ave. NW
Washington, DC 20408
(202) 501–5395
www.nara.gov

UNITED STATES DEPARTMENT OF THE
 INTERIOR LIBRARY
Mail Stop 1151
Washington, DC 20240
(202) 208–5815
library.doi.gov/ill.html
Manuscripts of treaties between the federal
 government and Indians; Indian Claims
 Commission annual reports.

#### ◆ FLORIDA

BILLY OSCEOLA MEMORIAL LIBRARY
Route 6, Box 668
Okeeochoee, FL 34974
(941) 763–4236

HISTORIC MUSEUM OF SOUTHERN FLORIDA
101 W. Flagella St.
Miami, FL 33130
(305) 375–1492

JOHN C. PACE LIBRARY
Special Collection Division
University Of West Florida
11000 University Parkway
Pensacola, FL 32514
(850) 474–2758

WILLIE FRANK MEMORIAL LIBRARY
HC 61 Box 46 A
Clewiston, FL 33440
(941) 983–6724

#### ◆ GEORGIA

HARGRETT RARE BOOKS AND
   MANUSCRIPT LIBRARY
University of Georgia
Athens, GA 30602
(706) 542–7123
www.libs.uga.edu/hargrett/speccoll.htlm
Rare manuscripts and photographs of the Cherokee
   and Creek; holdings of the Cherokee Phoenix
   (probably the first American Indian newspaper).

#### ◆ ILLINOIS

MADISON COUNTY HISTORICAL MUSEUM
715 North Main St.
Edwardsville, IL 62025
(618) 656–7562
John R. Sutter Collection: regional and
   Southwest items.

#### ◆ INDIANA

LILLY LIBRARY
Indiana University
Bloomington, IN 47405
(812) 855–2452
www.indiana.edu/~liblilly/text/lillyhome.html
Collection of folk tales of North American Western
   Indian groups; record of interviews of Indian
   survivors from Custer's Last Stand.

#### ◆ MAINE

THE PEARY MACMILLAN ARCTIC MUSEUM
Bowdoin College
9500 College Station
Brunswick, ME 04011
(207) 725–3416
www.bowdoin.edu/dept./Arctic

ROBERT ABBE MUSEUM
P.O. Box 286
Bar Harbor, ME 04609
(207) 288–3519
www.abbemuseum.org

#### ◆ MASSACHUSETTS

CHAPIN LIBRARY OF RARE BOOKS
Williams College
Williamston, MA 012267
(413) 597–2462
www.ohwy.com/ma/c/chaplirb.htm

FRUIT LANDS MUSEUM
102 Prospect Hill Rd.
Harvard, MA 01451
(978) 457–3924

TOSSER LIBRARY
Harvard University
21 Divinity Ave.
Cambridge, MA 02138
(617) 495–2248

#### ◆ MICHIGAN

FORT ST. JOSEPH MUSEUM
508 East Main St.
Niles, MI 49120
(616) 683–4702
Plym/Quimby Collection of Sioux Indian artifacts,
   1881–83, including drawings by Sitting Bull and
   Rain-in-the-Face.

WILLIAM CLEMENTS LIBRARY
HATCHER GRADUATE LIBRARY
University of Michigan
Ann Arbor, MI
(313) 764–2347
www. clements.umich.edu/clempage.html

## ◆ MINNESOTA

**MINNESOTA HISTORICAL SOCIETY LIBRARY**
Research Center
345 Kellogg Blvd. W.
St. Paul, MN 55102–1906
(651) 296–2143
www.mnhs.org
Print, sound, and visual collections of Plains Indians,
    especially the Ojibwa and Dakota.

## ◆ NEBRASKA

**LIBRARY AND STATE ARCHIVES**
Nebraska Historical Society
1500 R Street
Lincoln, NE 68501
(402) 471–3270
Central Plains Indians.

## ◆ NEW JERSEY

**FIRESTONE LIBRARY**
PRINCETON COLLECTIONS OF WESTERN
    AMERICANA
Princeton University
1 Washington
Princeton, NJ 08544
(609) 258–3222

## ◆ NEW MEXICO

**INDIAN PUEBLO CULTURAL CENTER**
2401 12th St. N.W.
Albuquerque, NM 87102
(505) 843–7270
Archival collection on the Southwest; owned and
    operated by nineteen pueblos of New Mexico.

**LABORATORY OF ANTHROPOLOGY LIBRARY**
Museum of Indian Arts & Culture
P.O. Box 2087
Santa Fe, NM 87504
(505) 476–1263
www.myaclab.org

**SAN JUAN COUNTY ARCHAEOLOGICAL**
    RESEARCH CENTER AND LIBRARY AT
    SALMON RUIN
P.O. Box 125
Broomfield, NM 87413
(505) 632–2013
Anasazi artifacts; oral history collection,
    especially Navajo.

**SCHOOL OF AMERICAN RESEARCH**
Indian Arts Research Center
P.O. Box 2188
Santa Fe, NM 87501
(505) 954–7204
www.sarweb.org
Southwestern American Indian art.

**ZUNI CULTURAL RESOURCE ENTERPRISE**
P.O. Box 1149
Zuni, NM 87327
(505) 782–4814
Archaeological site records, maps, air photos of Zuni
    Reservation; unpublished manuscripts on Zuni.

## ◆ NEW YORK

**HUNTINGTON FREE LIBRARY**
9 Westchester Sq.
Bronx, NY 10461
(718) 829–7770
Outstanding archival collections on American Indian
    languages and newspapers; field notes of
    prominent archaeologists.

**NEW YORK PUBLIC LIBRARY**
Humanities and Social Sciences Library
General Research Department
Fifth Ave. and 42nd St.
New York, NY 10018
(212) 930–0827

## ◆ NORTH CAROLINA

**HUNTER LIBRARY**
Special Collections Department
Western Carolina University
Cullowhee, NC 28723
(828) 227–7307
Collections on the Cherokee.

**NORTH CAROLINA STATE ARCHIVES**
Department of Cultural Research
109 East Jones St.
Raleigh, NC 27601–2807
(919) 733–3952
www.ah.dcr.state.nc.us
North Carolina Indian records.

## ◆ OHIO

THE HISTORY LIBRARY OF THE WESTERN
  RESERVE HISTORICAL SOCIETY
10825 East Blvd.
Cleveland, OH 44106
(216) 721–5722

OHIO HISTORICAL SOCIETY ARCHIVES AND
  LIBRARY DIVISION
1982 Velma Ave.
Columbus, OH 43211
(614) 297–2352
www.ohiohistory.org
Ohio Indians.

## ◆ OKLAHOMA

ARCHIVES AND MANUSCRIPTS DIVISION,
  OKLAHOMA HISTORICAL SOCIETY
2100 North Lincoln Blvd.
Oklahoma City, OK 73105
(405) 522–5209
www.ok-history.mus
Five Civilized Tribes in Oklahoma.

MUSEUM OF THE GREAT PLAINS
601 NW Farris Ave.
Lawton, OK 73502
(580) 581–3460
www.museumofthegreatplains.org
Photograph collections of the Great Plains.

WESTERN HISTORY COLLECTIONS
University of Oklahoma Libraries
630 Parrington Oval, Room 452
Norman, OK 73091
(405) 325–3641
One of the largest collections on North American
  Indians, especially on Southern Plains Indians.

## ◆ PENNSYLVANIA

AMERICAN PHILOSOPHICAL SOCIETY
  LIBRARY
105 South Fifth St.
Philadelphia, PA 19106–3386
(215) 440–3423
www.amphil/soc.org
Field notes of prominent anthropologists who
  worked closely with Indians.

READING PUBLIC MUSEUM AND ART
  GALLERY
500 Museum Rd.
Reading, PA 19611
(215) 371–5850
www.readingpublicmuseum.org
Special collection of southeastern Pennsylvania
  lithic objects; Speck Collection of Delaware
  material; mound pottery.

VAN PELT LIBRARY AND UNIVERSITY
  MUSEUM LIBRARY
University of Pennsylvania
3420 Walnut Street
Philadelphia, PA 19104
(215) 898–7091
www.library.upenn.edu

## ◆ RHODE ISLAND

JOHN CARTER BROWN LIBRARY
Brown University
P.O. Box 1894
Providence, RI 02912
(401) 863–2725
www.jcbl.org
Rare manuscripts; Americana collections from
  1492 to 1830.

## ◆ SOUTH DAKOTA

CENTER FOR WESTERN STUDIES
Augustana College
P.O. Box 727
Sioux Falls, SD 57197
(605) 336–4007
Native American Historical Research and
  Archival Agency.

I.D. WEEKS LIBRARY
University of South Dakota
414 East Clark St.
Vermillion, SD 57069
(605) 677–5371
www.usdedu/edulibrary/idweeks.htm
Upper Great Plains Sioux Indians.

MUSEUM OF SOUTH DAKOTA
Historical Society
900 Governors Dr.
Pierre, SD 57501
(605) 773–3458
www.state.sd.us/deca/
    culturalarchivesmanuscripts.collections
Special Plains Indian collection.

SIOUXLAND HERITAGE MUSEUM
200 West Sixth St.
Sioux Falls, SD 57102
(605) 367–4210
Pettigrew-Drady Indian Collection, primarily Dakota
    artifacts, 1870–1920; Photograph Collection,
    1870–1900.

## ◆ TEXAS

CROCKETT COUNTY MUSEUM
404 11th Street
Ozona, TX 76943
(915) 392–2837
Frank Mills Indian Collection.

SOUTHERN METHODIST UNIVERSITY
FIKES HALL OF SPECIAL COLLECTIONS
De Golyer Library
P.O. Box 750396, SMU Station
Dallas, TX 75275
(214) 692–2253
History and archaeology of the American West.

## ◆ UTAH

FAMILY HISTORY LIBRARY
35 North West Temple
Salt Lake City, UT 84150
(801) 240–4750
Genealogical information on American Indians.

## ◆ WASHINGTON

ALLEN LIBRARY
Manuscripts Special Collections and Archives
    Department
University of Washington
Box 352900
Seattle, WA 98195
(206) 543–1929
www.washington.edu/admin/ada/allenlib.htm
Pacific Northwest region.

## ◆ WEST VIRGINIA

WEST VIRGINIA STATE MUSEUM
Department of Culture and History
1900 Kanawha Blvd. E.
Charleston, WV 25305–0300
(304) 558–0220
Migration records of Indian groups.

## ◆ WISCONSIN

FAIRLAWN HISTORICAL MUSEUM
Harvard View Pkwy.
Superior, WI 54880
(715) 394–5712
David F. Barry Collection of Sioux Indian Portraits;
    Catlin Lithographs of Indians of the Plains.

THE RAHR PUBLIC MUSEUM
610 North Eighth St.
Manitowoc, WI 54220
(414) 683–4501
Manitowoc County Indian Artifacts Collection.

## ◆ WYOMING

AMERICAN HERITAGE CENTER
University of Wyoming
P.O. Box 3924
Laramie, WY 82071
(307) 766–4114
www.uwadmnweb.uwyo.edu/ahc/

# CANADA

## ◆ ALBERTA

PROVINCIAL MUSEUM OF ALBERTA
Archeological & Ethnological Research Division
12845–102 Ave.
Edmonton AB T5N 0M6
(780) 453–9147
www.gov.ab.ca/mcd/mhs/pma/pma.htm

## ◆ BRITISH COLUMBIA

KAMLOOPS MUSEUM AND ARCHIVES
207 Seymour St.
Kamloops BC V2C 2E7
(250) 828–3576
www.museumsassn.bc.ca/museums/kma.html

MUSEUM OF ANTHROPOLOGY AND LIBRARY
University of British Columbia
6353 N. W. Marian Dr.
Vancouver BC V6T 1W5
(250) 228–5087

### ◆ MANITOBA

DEPARTMENT OF CULTURAL AFFAIRS AND
   HISTORICAL RESOURCES PROVINCIAL
   ARCHIVES
200 Vaughn St.
Winnipeg, MB R3C 0V8

ESKIMO MUSEUM LIBRARY
242 La Verendrye St.
Churchill, MB R0B 0E0
(204) 675–2541

### ◆ NEWFOUNDLAND

MEMORIAL UNIVERSITY OF NEW
   FOUNDLAND
Centre For New Foundland Studies
Queen Elizabeth II Library
St. John's, NF A1B 3Y1
(709) 737–7476

### ◆ NORTHWEST TERRITORY

DENE MUSEUM AND ARCHIVES
c/o General Delivery
Fort Good Hope, NT X0E 0H0

### ◆ NOVA SCOTIA

SCHOOL OF SOCIAL WORK LIBRARY
Maritime School of Social Work
Dalhousie University
6420 Coburg RD
Halifax, NS B3H 3J5

### ◆ ONTARIO

MUSEUM OF INDIAN ARCHEOLOGY
University of Western Ontario
Lawson Jury Bdg
London, ON N6G 3M6
(519) 473–1360

NORTHERN DEVELOPMENTAL LIBRARY
Department of Indian Affairs
Ottawa, ON KIA OH4
(819) 997–0811

ROYAL ONTARIO MUSEUM
100 Queens Park
Toronto, ON M5S 2C6
(416) 586–5724
www.rom.on.ca/

### ◆ SASKATCHEWAN

NATIVE LAW LIBRARY
NATIVE LAW CENTRE
University Of Saskatchewan
101 Diefenbaker Centre
Saskatoon, SK S7N 5B8
(306) 966–6189
www.usask.ca/nativelaw/index.html

### ◆ QUEBEC

CANADIAN MUSEUM OF CIVILIZATION
P.O. Box 3100, Station "B"
Hull, PQ J8X 4H2
(819) 776 8430
www.civilization.ca/

# Historical Societies and Scholarly Organizations

## United States

### ◆ ARIZONA

ARIZONA HISTORICAL SOCIETY
Central Arizona Division
1300 N. College Ave.
Tempe, AZ 85281
(480) 929–0292
www.tempe.gov/ahs/

SOCIETY FOR HISTORICAL ARCHAEOLOGY
P.O. Box 30446
Tucson, AZ 85751
(520) 886–8006
sha.org/

### ◆ ARKANSAS

ARKANSAS HISTORY COMMISSION
One Capitol Mall
Little Rock, AR 72201
(501) 682–6900
www.state.ar.us/ahc/

ORDER OF THE INDIAN WARS
P.O. Box 7401
Little Rock, AR 72217
(501) 225–3996
lbha.org/oiw.html

### ◆ CALIFORNIA

CALIFORNIA HISTORICAL SOCIETY
2099 Pacific Ave.
San Francisco, CA 94109
(415) 567–1848
www.calhist.org/index.html

SOCIETY FOR THE STUDY OF THE
INDIGENOUS LANGUAGES OF THE
AMERICAS
P.O. Box 555
Arcata, CA 95518
www.ssila.org

### ◆ CONNECTICUT

CONNECTICUT HISTORICAL SOCIETY
1 Elizabeth St.
Hartford, CT 06105
(203) 236–5621
www.chs.org

### ◆ DISTRICT OF COLUMBIA

AMERICAN HISTORICAL ASSOCIATION
400 A St. SE
Washington, DC 20003–3889
(202) 544–2422
www.theaha.org/

NATIONAL GEOGRAPHIC SOCIETY
1145 17th Street N.W.
Washington, D.C. 20036–4688
(800) 647–5463
www.nationalgeographic.org/

SOCIETY FOR AMERICAN ARCHAEOLOGY
900 Second Street NE #12
Washington, D.C. 20002–3557
(202) 789–8200
www.saa.org

#### ◆ IDAHO

IDAHO STATE HISTORICAL SOCIETY
450 North 4th Street
Boise, ID 83702
(208) 334–5335
www.state.id.us/ishs/index.html

#### ◆ ILLINOIS

AMERICAN INDIAN LIBRARY
   ASSOCIATION (AILA)
American Library Association
Office of Library Outreach Services (OLOS)
50 East Huron St.
Chicago, IL 60611
(800) 545–2433 Ext. 4294
www.nativeculture.com/lisamitten/aila.html

AMERICAN SOCIETY FOR ETHNOHISTORY
For information about the Society contact:
Anne McMullen, Secretary-Treasurer
National Museum of the American Indian
Cultural Resources Center
4220 Silver Hill Street
Suitland, Maryland 20746
(301) 238–6624
www.ethnohistory.org/index.html

#### ◆ INDIANA

SOCIETY FOR ETHNOMUSICOLOGY
Indiana University
Morrison Hall 005
Bloomington, IN 47405–2501
(812) 855–6672
www.ethnomusicology.org/

#### ◆ KANSAS

KANSAS STATE HISTORICAL SOCIETY
6425 SW Sixth Avenue
Topeka, KS 66615–1099
(785) 272–8681
www.kshs.org/

#### ◆ MASSACHUSETTS

AMERICAN ANTIQUARIAN SOCIETY
185 Salisbury St.
Worcester, MA 01609
(508) 755–5221
www.americanantiquarian.org/

ARCHAEOLOGICAL INSTITUTE OF AMERICA
Boston University
656 Beacon Street, 4th floor
Boston, MA 02215–2006
(617) 353–9361
www.archaeological.org/

#### ◆ MICHIGAN

MICHIGAN HISTORICAL CENTER
717 West Allegan
Lansing, MI 48918–1800
(517) 373–3559
www.sos.state.mi.us/history/museum/explore/
   explore2.html

#### ◆ MINNESOTA

MINNESOTA HISTORICAL SOCIETY
345 Kellogg Blvd. West
St. Paul, MN 55102–1906
(651) 296–6126
www.mnhs.org/places/historycenter/index.html

#### ◆ MISSOURI

MISSOURI HISTORICAL SOCIETY
225 S. Skinker
P.O. Box 11940
St. Louis, MO 63112–0040
(314) 746–4500
www.mohistory.org/

◆ **MONTANA**

MONTANA HISTORICAL SOCIETY
225 North Roberts
Helena, MT 59620
(406) 444–2694
www.his.state.mt.us/

◆ **NEBRASKA**

NEBRASKA STATE HISTORICAL SOCIETY
P.O. Box 82554
1500 R Street
Lincoln, NE 68501
(402) 471–4746
www.nebraskahistory.org/index.html

◆ **NEVADA**

NEVADA HISTORICAL SOCIETY
1650 North Virginia St.
Reno, NV 89503
(775) 688–1190
lahontan.clan.lib.nv.us/polpac/html_client/default.asp
    (via State Library, Division of Museums and
    History)

◆ **NEW MEXICO**

THE ARCHAEOLOGICAL CONSERVANCY
5301 Central Avenue NE, Suite 1218
Albuquerque, NM 87108–1517
(505) 266–1540
www.americanarchaeology.com/aaabout.html

WESTERN HISTORY ASSOCIATION
University of New Mexico
1080 Mesa Vista Hall
Albuquerque, NM 87131–1181
(505) 277–5234
www.unm.edu/~wha/

◆ **NORTH CAROLINA**

CHEROKEE HISTORICAL ASSOCIATION
P.O. Box 398
Cherokee, NC 28719
(828) 497–2315
(828) 497–2111 [off season]
www.oconalufteevillage.com

◆ **NORTH DAKOTA**

STATE HISTORICAL SOCIETY OF
    NORTH DAKOTA
612 East Blvd. Avenue
Bismarck, ND 58505–0830
(701) 328–2666
www.state.nd.us/hist/index.html

◆ **OKLAHOMA**

CHEROKEE NATIONAL HISTORICAL SOCIETY
P.O. Box 515
Tahlequah, OK 74465
(918) 456–6007
www.powersource.com/heritage/

CHICKASAW HISTORICAL SOCIETY
P.O. Box 1548
Ada, OK 74820
(580) 332–8685
www.chickasaw.net/heritage/journal/

OKLAHOMA HISTORICAL SOCIETY
2100 North Lincoln Blvd.
Wiley Post Historical Blvd.
Oklahoma City, OK 73105–4997
(405) 521–2491
www.ok-history.mus.ok.us/#

◆ **OREGON**

OREGON HISTORICAL SOCIETY
1200 SW Park Avenue
Portland, OR 97205–2483
(503) 222–1741
www.ohs.org/

◆ **RHODE ISLAND**

RHODE ISLAND HISTORICAL SOCIETY
110 Benevolent St.
Providence, RI 02906
(401) 331–8575
www.rihs.org/

◆ **SOUTH CAROLINA**

SOUTH CAROLINA HISTORICAL SOCIETY
100 Meeting Street
Charleston, S.C. 29401
(843) 723–3225
www.schistory.org/

◆ **SOUTH DAKOTA**

SOUTH DAKOTA STATE HISTORICAL
   SOCIETY
Cultural Heritage Center
900 Governor's Drive
Pierre, SD 57501–2217
(605) 773–3458
www.state.sd.us/deca/cultural/sdshs.htm

◆ **VERMONT**

VERMONT HISTORICAL SOCIETY
109 State St.
Montpelier, VT 05609–0901
(802) 828–2291
www.state.vt.us/vhs/

◆ **VIRGINIA**

AMERICAN ANTHROPOLOGICAL
   ASSOCIATION
AMERICAN ETHNOLOGICAL SOCIETY
4350 North Fairfax Drive, Suite 640
Arlington, VA 22203–1620
(703) 528–1902
www.aaanet.org/

VIRGINIA HISTORICAL SOCIETY
428 North Blvd.
Richmond, VA 23220
(804) 358–4901
www.vahistorical.org/

◆ **WASHINGTON**

WASHINGTON STATE HISTORICAL SOCIETY
Research Center
315 North Stadium Way
Tacoma, WA 98403

(253) 798–5914
www.wshs.org/

◆ **WISCONSIN**

STATE HISTORICAL SOCIETY OF WISCONSIN
816 State St.
Madison, WI 53706
(608) 264–6400
www.shsw.wisc.edu/

# CANADA

CANADIAN ANTHROPOLOGICAL SOCIETY
Wilfrid Laurier University Press
75 University Avenue
Waterloo, ON N2L 3C5
socserv2.socsci.mcmaster.ca/~casca/

CANADIAN ARCHAEOLOGICAL ASSOCIATION
Executive Assistant
Department of Anthropology and Archaeology
University of Saskatchewan
55 Campus Drive
Saskatoon, Saskatchewan S7N 5B1
(306) 966–4188
www.canadianarchaeology.com

CANADIAN HISTORICAL ASSOCIATION
395 Wellington St.
Ottawa, ON K1A 0N3
(613) 233–7885
www.yorku.ca/research/cha

CANADA'S NATIONAL HISTORICAL SOCIETY
478—167 Lombard Ave
Winnipeg MB R3B OT6
(204) 988–9300
www.historysociety.ca/

# Cultural Centers

## UNITED STATES

### ◆ ALASKA

ALASKA NATIVE HERITAGE CENTER
8800 Heritage Center Dr.
Anchorage, AK 99506
(907) 330–8000
www.alaskanative.net

ALASKAN INDIAN ARTS, INC.
P.O. Box 271
23 Fort Sewards Dr.
Haines, AK 99827
(907) 766–2160
Tlingit and Chilkat.

INUPIAT HERITAGE CENTER
P.O. Box 749
Barrow, AK 99723
(907) 852–4594

SOUTHEAST ALASKA INDIAN CULTURAL
    CENTER, INC.
106 Metlakatla St.
Sitka, AK 99835
(907) 747–8061

### ◆ ARIZONA

APACHE CULTURAL CENTER AND MUSEUM
P.O. Box 507
Fort Apache, AZ 85926
(520) 338–1392

FORT MCDOWELL MOHAVE-APACHE
    CULTURAL CENTER
P.O. Box 7779
Fountain Hills, AZ 85269
(480) 733–8113

HOPI CULTURAL CENTER MUSEUM
P.O. Box 7
Second Mesa, AZ 86043
(520) 734–2401
www.psv.com/hopi.html

SAN CARLOS APACHE CULTURAL CENTER
P.O. Box 760
Peridot, AZ 85542
(520) 475–2894
www.carizona.com/super/attractions/san_carlos.html

### ◆ CALIFORNIA

AGUA CALIENTE CULTURAL CENTER
219 S. Palm Canyon Dr.
Palm Springs, CA 92262
(760) 323–0151
www.prinet.com/accmuseum

CUPA CULTURAL CENTER
PALA INDIAN RESERVATION MUSEUM
P.O. Box 445
Pala, CA 92059
(760) 742–1590
hometown.aol.com/lmir635563/

### ◆ COLORADO

SOUTHERN UTE INDIAN CULTURAL CENTER
3066 Country Rd. 311
Ignacio, Colorado 81137–9130
(970) 563–9583

### ◆ FLORIDA

MICCOUSUKEE TRIBE CULTURAL CENTER
P.O. Box 440021
Miami, FL 33144
(305) 894–2375

## ◆ LOUISIANA

TUNICA-BILOXI REGIONAL INDIAN CENTER
　AND MUSEUM
P.O. Box 1589
Marksville, LA 71351
(318) 253–8174
www.tunica.org

## ◆ MICHIGAN

CULTURAL HERITAGE CENTER
Bay Mills Community College
Brimly, MI 49715
(906) 248–5852

## ◆ MINNESOTA

LITTLE FEATHER INTERPRETIVE CENTER
317 4th St., NE
P.O. Box 334
Pipestone, MN 56164
(507) 825–3579
www.littlefeathercenter.com

MINNEAPOLIS AMERICAN INDIAN CENTER
1530 E. Franklin Ave.
Minneapolis, MN 55404
(612) 879–1755

UPPER MIDWEST INDIAN CULTURAL
　CENTER
PIPESTONE INDIAN SHRINE ASSOCIATION
P.O. Box 727
Pipestone, MN 56164
(507) 825–5463

## ◆ MONTANA

THE PEOPLE'S CENTER MUSEUM
P.O. Box 278
Pablo, MT 59855
(406) 675–0160
www.peoplescenter.org/museum.htm
Salish, Kootenai and Pend d'Orielle Tribal Nations.

## ◆ NEW JERSEY

POWHATAN RENAPE NATION
　CULTURAL CENTER
P.O. Box 225
Rancocas, NJ 08073
(609) 261–4747
www.powhatan.org/museum.html

## ◆ NEW MEXICO

ACOMA TOURIST AND VISITOR CENTER
P.O. Box 309
Pueblo of Acoma
Acomita, NM 87034
(800) 747–0181
www.acomazuni.com/acoma.cfm

A-SHIWI AWAN MUSEUM AND
　HERITAGE CENTER
122 Hwy. 53
Zuni, NM 87034
(505) 782–4403
www.nmculture.org/cgi-bin/showInst.pl?InstID=AISH

INDIAN PUEBLO CULTURAL CENTER
2401 12th St. NW
Albuquerque, NM
(505) 242–4943
www.indianpueblo.org

MESCALERO CULTURAL CENTER
P.O. Box 176
Mescalero, NM 88340
(505) 671–4494

WATATOWA VISITOR CENTER
7413 Hwy. 4 Box 100
Jemez Pueblo, NM
(505) 834–7235
www.jemezpueblo.org

## ◆ NEW YORK

AKWESASNE MUSEUM
AKWESASNE CULTURAL CENTER
RR1 Box 14C
Hogansburg, NY 13055
(518) 358–2240
library.usask.ca/native/directory/english/
　akwesasne.html

## ◆ NORTH CAROLINA

THE MUSEUM OF THE NATIVE AMERICAN
　RESOURCE CENTER
P.O. Box 1510 UNCP
Pembroke, NC 28372
(910) 521–6282
www.uncp.edu/nativemuseum

### ◆ NORTH DAKOTA

TURTLE MOUNTAIN CHIPPEWA
 HERITAGE CENTER
P.O. Box 257
Belcourt, ND 58316
(701) 477–6140
chippewa.utma.com/index2.html

### ◆ OKLAHOMA

CADDO CULTURAL CENTER
P.O. Box 487
Binger, OK 73009
(405) 656–2344

CHEYENNE CULTURAL CENTER
2250 NE Route 66
Clinton, OK 73601
(580) 323–6224

CHICKASAW CULTURAL CENTER
520 Arlington Rd.
P.O. Box 1548
Ada, OK 74820–1548
(580) 332–1990
www.chickasaw.net/museum/index.htm

WITCHITA TRIBAL CULTURAL CENTER
P.O. Box 726
Anadarko, OK 73005
(405) 247–2425

### ◆ SOUTH CAROLINA

CATAWBA CULTURAL CENTER
611 E. Main St.
Rock Hill, SC 29730
(803) 328–2427
www.ccppcrafts.com

### ◆ SOUTH DAKOTA

H.V. JOHNSTON AMERICAN INDIAN
 CULTURAL CENTER
Cheyenne River Reservation
P.O. Box 857
Eagle Butte, SD 57625
(605) 964–2542

### ◆ TEXAS

TIGUA PUEBLO CULTURAL CENTER
305 Yaya Ln.
El Paso, TX 79907
(915) 859–5287

### ◆ VERMONT

ABENAKI CULTURAL CENTER
HCR1 Box 110
Morrisville, VT 05661
(802) 868–2559

### ◆ WASHINGTON

MAKAH CULTURAL RESEARCH CENTER
Bayview Ave., Highway 112
P.O. Box 160
Neah Bay, WA 98357
(360) 645–2711
www.makah.com/museum.htm

STEILACOOM TRIBAL CULTURAL CENTER
1515 LaFayette St.
P.O. Box 88419
Steilacoom, WA 98388
(253) 584–6308
www.ohwy.com/wa/t/tribaccm.htm

WANAPUM DAM INTERPRETIVE CENTER
P.O. Box 878
Ephraita, WA 98823
(509) 932–3571 ext 2571

### ◆ WISCONSIN

LAC DU FLAMBEAU CHIPPEWA
 CULTURAL CENTER
P.O. Box 804
Lac du Flambeau, WI 54538
(715) 588–3333

### ◆ WYOMING

EASTERN SHOSHONE TRIBAL
 CULTURAL CENTER
P.O. Box 1008
Fort Washakie, WY 82514
(307) 332–9106

# CANADA

## ◆ ALBERTA

ANDERSON NATIVE HERITAGE AND
  CULTURAL CENTRE
13140 St. Albert Tr.
Edmonton, AB T5L 4R8
(401) 455–2200

NINASTAKO CULTURAL CENTRE
P.O. Box 1299
Standoff, AB T0K 0K0
(403) 737–3774

OLDMAN RIVER CULTURAL CENTER
P.O. Box 70
Brocket, AB P0K 0H0
(403) 965–3939

## ◆ BRITISH COLUMBIA

HEILTSUK CULTURAL EDUCATION CENTRE
Box 880
Waglisla, BC V0T 1Z0
(250) 957–2626

SHESHAHT CULTURAL CENTRE
5211 Wilkinson Rd.
Port Alberni, BC V9Y 7B2
(604) 723–5421

U'MISTA CULTURAL CENTRE
P.O. Box 253
Alert Bay, BC V0N 1A0
(604) 974–5403

## ◆ MANITOBA

BROKENHEAD OJIBWA NATION HISTORICAL
  VILLAGE
General Delivery
Scanterbury, MB R0E 1W0
(204) 766–2483

MANITOBA INDIAN CULTURAL
  EDUCATION CENTER
119 Sutherland Ave.
Winnipeg, MB R2W 3C9
(204) 942–0228

NORWAY HOUSE CREE NATION CULTURAL
  EDUCATION CENTER
Norway House, MB R0B 1B0
(204) 359–6296
www.schoolnet.ca/autochtone/norway/index-e.html

## ◆ ONTARIO

LAKE OF THE WOODS OJIBWA
  CULTURAL CENTER
P.O. Box 159
Kenora, ON P9N 3X3
(807) 548–5744
www.schoolnet.ca/aboriginal/kenora/index-e.html

OJIBWA AND CREE CULTURAL CENTRE
210 Spruce St. S., Suite 306
Timmins, ON P4N 2M5
(705) 267–7911
www.schoolnet.ca/aboriginal/occc/index-e.html

## ◆ QUEBEC

KANESATAKEHRO:NON TSI
  NIHATWEIENNO:TEN CULTURAL CENTRE
664 Ste. Philomene
Kansehsatake, PQ J0N 1E0
(514) 479–1783
www.schoolnet.ca/aboriginal/kanesata/index-e.html

KANIEN'KEHAKA RAOTITIOHKWA
  CULTURAL CENTER
P.O. Box 969
Kahnawake, PQ J0L 1B0
(450) 638–0880
library.usask.ca/native/directory/english/
  kanienkehaka.html

## ◆ SASKATCHEWAN

SASKATCHEWAN INDIAN CULTURAL
  CENTRE
120 33rd St. E.
Saskatoon, SK S7K 0S2
(360) 244–1146
www.schoolnet.ca/aboriginal/sicc-cat/

## References

### Before AD 1500

Cordell, Linda S. *Prehistory of the Southwest*. Orlando,
  Fla.: Academic Press, 1984.

Deetz, James. *Invitation to Archaeology*. Garden City, N.Y.: Published for the American Museum of Natural History by the Natural History Press, 1967.

Jelks, Edward B. and Juliet C. Jelks, eds. *Historical Dictionary of North American Archaeology*. New York: Greenwood Press, 1988.

Jennings, Jesse D., ed. *Ancient Native Americans*. San Francisco: W. H. Freeman, 1978.

Milanich, Jerald T. and Charles H. Fairbanks. *Florida Archaeology*. New York: Academic Press, 1980.

Moratto, Michael J. *California Archaeology*. Orlando, Fla.: Academic Press, 1984.

Morse, Dan F. and Phyliss A. Morse. *Archaeology of the Central Mississippi Valley*. New York: Academic Press, 1983.

Ritchie, William A. *The Archaeology of New York State*. Rev. edition. Garden City, NY: Published for the American Museum of Natural History by the Natural History Press, 1969.

Smith, Bruce D., ed. *Mississippian Settlement Patterns*. New York: Academic Press, 1978.

Snow, Dean R. *The Archaeology of New England*. New York: Academic Press, 1980.

Taylor, R. E. and Clement W. Meighan, eds. *Chronologies in New World Archaeology*. New York: Academic Press, 1978.

Wedel, Waldo R. *Prehistoric Man on the Great Plains*. Norman: University of Oklahoma Press, 1961.

## U.S. Indians, 1500–1965

Aberle, David. *The Peyote Religion among the Navaho*. Chicago: Aldine, 1966.

Baird, W. David. *Peter Pitchlynn: Chief of the Choctaws*. Norman: University of Oklahoma Press, 1972.

Bannon, John F. *The Mission Frontier in Sonora, 1620–1687*. Edited by James A. Reynolds. New York: U.S. Catholic Historical Society, 1955.

Berthrong, Donald J. *The Southern Cheyennes*. Norman: University of Oklahoma Press, 1963.

Casas, Bartolome de las. *A Short Account of the Destruction of the Indies*. New York: Penguin, 1992.

Cohen, Felix S. *Handbook of Federal Indian Law*. Albuquerque: University of New Mexico Press, 1971.

Corkran, David H. *The Cherokee Frontier: Conflict and Survival, 1740–62*. Norman: University of Oklahoma Press, 1962.

Debo, Angie. *A History of the Indians of the United States*. Norman: University of Oklahoma Press, 1971.

———. *And Still the Waters Run*. Princeton: Princeton University Press, 1940.

Edmunds, R. David. *The Shawnee Prophet*. Lincoln: University of Nebraska Press, 1983.

———. *Tecumseh and the Quest for Indian Leadership*. Boston: Little, Brown, 1984.

Foreman, Grant. *Indian Removal: The Emigration of the Five Civilized Tribes of Indians*. Norman: University of Oklahoma Press, 1932.

———. *Last Trek of the Indians*. Chicago: University of Chicago Press, 1946.

Gibson, Arrell M. *The American Indian: Prehistory to the Present*. Lexington, Mass.: D.C. Heath, 1980.

———, ed. *America's Exiles: Indian Colonization in Oklahoma*. Oklahoma City: Oklahoma Historical Society, 1976.

Grinde, Donald A. and Bruce E. Johansen. *Exemplar of Liberty: Native America and the Evolution of Democracy*. Los Angeles: American Indian Studies Center, UCLA, 1991.

Hagan, William T. *Indian Police and Judges: Experiments in Acculturation and Control*. Lincoln: University of Nebraska Press, 1980.

Heizer, Robert A., ed. *The Destruction of California Indians*. Santa Barbara, Calif.: Peregrine Smith, 1974.

Hertzberg, Hazel. *The Search for an American Indian Identity: Modern Pan-Indian Movements*. Syracuse, N.Y.: Syracuse University Press, 1971.

Hoig, Stan. *The Sand Creek Massacre*. Norman: University of Oklahoma Press, 1961.

*The Indian Historian*. San Francisco: American Indian Historical Society, 1967–1979.

Jackson, Helen Hunt. *A Century of Dishonor*. New York: Harper & Brothers, 1881.

Jahoda, Gloria. *The Trail of Tears*. New York: Holt, Rinehart and Winston, 1975.

Jane, Cecil, trans. *Select Documents Illustrating the Four Voyages of Columbus*. Vol. 1. London: Hakluyt Society, 1930.

Josephy, Alvin M., Jr. *The Indian Heritage of America*. New York: Knopf, 1968.

———. *Now That the Buffalo's Gone: A Study of Today's American Indians*. New York: Knopf, 1982.

La Barre, Weston. *The Ghost Dance: Origins of Religion*. Garden City, N.Y.: Doubleday, 1970.

Miner, Craig H. *The Corporation and the Indian: Tribal Sovereignty and Industrial Civilization in Indian Territory*. Columbia: University of Missouri Press, 1976.

Otis, Delos S. *The Dawes Act and the Allotment of Indian Lands*. Norman: University of Oklahoma Press, 1973.

Philp, Kenneth R. *John Collier's Crusade for Indian Reform, 1920–1954*. Tucson: University of Arizona Press, 1977.

Ruby, Robert H. and John A. Brown. *Indians of the Pacific Northwest: A History*. Norman: University of Oklahoma Press, 1981.

Satz, Ronald N. *American Indian Policy in the Jacksonian Era*. Lincoln: University of Nebraska Press, 1975.

Szasz, Margaret C. *Education and the American Indian: The Road to Self-Determination, 1928–1973*. Albuquerque: University of New Mexico Press, 1974.

Thompson, Gerald. *The Army and the Navajo: The Bosque Redondo Reservation Experiment, 1863–1868*. Tucson: University of Arizona Press, 1976.

Trafzer, Clifford E. *The Kit Carson Campaign: The Last Great Navajo War*. Norman: University of Oklahoma Press, 1982.

Trafzer, Clifford E. and Richard D. Scheuerman. *Renegade Tribe: The Palouse Indians and the Invasion of the Pacific Northwest*. Pullman: Washington State University Press, 1986.

Trennert, Robert A., Jr. *Alternative to Extinction: Federal Indian Policy and the Beginnings of the Reservation System, 1846–51*. Philadelphia: Temple University Press, 1975.

Tyler, S. Lyman. *A History of Indian Policy*. Washington, D.C.: U.S. Department of the Interior, Bureau of Indian Affairs, 1973.

Unrau, William E. *The Kansa Indians: A History of the Wind People*. Norman: University of Oklahoma Press, 1971.

Utley, Robert M. *Frontier Regulars: The United States Army and the Indian, 1866–1891*. New York: Macmillan, 1974.

Vaughan, Alden T. *New England Frontier: Puritans and Indians, 1620–1675*. Boston: Little, Brown, 1965.

Washburn, Wilcomb E., comp. *The American Indian and the United States: A Documentary History*. New York: Random House, 1973.

## U.S. Indians, 1965–2000

*American Antiquity*. Washington, D.C., 1935–present.

American Friends Service Committee. *Uncommon Controversy: Fishing Rights of the Muckleshoot, Puyallup and Nisqually Indians*. Seattle: University of Washington Press, 1970.

*American Indians Today: Answers to Your Questions*. Washington, D.C.: U.S. Department of the Interior, Bureau of Indian Affairs, 1991.

Cahn, Edgar, ed. *Our Brother's Keeper: The Indian in White America*. Washington, D.C.: New Community Press, 1969.

Castile, George P. and Robert L. Bee. *State and Reservation: New Perspectives in Federal Indian Policy*. Tucson: University of Arizona Press, 1992.

Cohen, Felix S. *Felix S. Cohen's Handbook of Federal Indian Law*. Charlottesville, Va.: Michie: Bobbs-Merrill, 1982.

Deloria, Vine, Jr. *Behind the Trail of Broken Treaties: An Indian Declaration of Independence*. New York: Delacorte Press, 1974.

———. *Custer Died for Your Sins: An Indian Manifesto*. New York: Macmillan, 1969.

———. *We Talk, You Listen: New Tribes, New Turf*. New York: Macmillan, 1970.

Dorris, Michael. *The Broken Cord*. New York: Harper & Row, 1989.

Fixico, Donald L. *The Urban Indian Experience in America*. Albuquerque: University of New Mexico Press, 2000.

———. *Urban Indians*. New York: Chelsea House, 1991.

Gibson, Arrell M. *The American Indian: Prehistory to Present*. Lexington, Mass.: D.C. Heath, 1980.

*Indian Country Today*. Rapid City, S.Dak. 1992–2000.

Iverson, Peter. *We Are Still Here: American Indians in the Twentieth Century*. Wheeling, Ill.: Harlan Davidson, 1998.

Johnson, Troy R. *The Occupation of Alcatraz Island: Indian Self-determination and the Rise of Indian Activism*. Urbana: University of Illinois Press, 1996.

Josephy, Alvin Jr. *Now That the Buffalo's Gone: A Study of Today's American Indians*. Norman: University of Oklahoma Press, 1984.

Josephy, Alvin Jr., Joane Nagel, and Troy Johnson, eds. *Red Power: The American Indians' Fight for Freedom*. Rev. ed. Lincoln: University of Nebraska Press, 1999.

Kappler, Charles J., comp. and ed. *Indian Affairs: Laws and Treaties*. Washington, D.C.: GPO, 1903–1941.

Messerschmidt, Jim. *The Trial of Leonard Peltier*. Boston: South End Press, 1983.

Momaday, N. Scott. *House Made of Dawn*. New York: Harper & Row, 1968.

*News From Indian Country*. Hayward, Wis. 1990–2000.

O'Brien, Sharon. *American Indian Tribal Governments*. Norman: University of Oklahoma Press, 1989.

Prucha, Francis P. *American Indian Policy*. Norman: University of Oklahoma Press, 1986.

———. *The Great Father: The United States Government and the American Indians*. 2 vols. Lincoln: University of Nebraska Press, 1984.

Smith, Paul Chaat, and Robert Allen Warrior. *Like a Hurricane: The Indian Movement from Alcatraz to Wounded Knee*. New York: New Press, 1996.

Steiner, Stan. *The New Indians*. New York: Harper & Row, 1968.

*Tundra Times*. Anchorage, Alaska, 1962–1982.

*Troy Johnson*
*Elton Naswood*

## Canadian Natives, 1500–2000

Abel, Kerry. *Drum Songs: Glimpses of Dene History*. Montreal: McGill-Queen's University Press, 1993.

Allen, Robert S. *His Majesty's Indian Allies: British Indian Policy in the Defence of Canada, 1774–1815.* Toronto: Dundurn Press, 1992.

Calloway, Colin G. *Crown and Calumet: British-Indian Relations, 1783–1815.* Norman: University of Oklahoma Press, 1987.

Carter, Sarah. *Lost Harvests: Prairie Indian Reserve Farmers and Government Policy.* Montreal: McGill-Queen's University Press, 1990.

Coates, Kenneth. *Best Left as Indians: Native-White Relations in the Yukon Territory, 1840–1950.* Montreal: McGill-Queen's University Press, 1991.

Coates, Ken S. & Robin Fisher, eds. *Out of the Background: Readings on Canadian Native History.* 2d ed. Toronto: Copp Clark, 1996.

Gibson, James R. *Otter Skins, Boston Ships, and China Goods: The Maritime Fur Trade of the Northwest Coast, 1785–1811.* Montreal: McGill-Queen's University Press; Seattle: University of Washington Press, 1992.

Jenness, Diamond. *The Indians of Canada.* 7th edition. Toronto: University of Toronto Press, 1977.

Miller, James Rodger. *Shingwauk's Vision: A History of Native Residential Schools.* Toronto: University of Toronto Press, 1996.

———. *Skyscrapers Hide the Heavens: A History of Indian-White Relations in Canada.* 3d ed. Toronto: University of Toronto Press, 2000.

———. *Sweet Promises: A Reader on Indian-White Relations in Canada.* Toronto: University of Toronto Press, 1991.

Nichols, Roger L. *Indians in the United States and Canada : A Comparative History.* Lincoln: University of Nebraska Press, 1998.

Ray, Arthur J. *I Have Lived Here Since the World Began: An Illustrated History of Canada's Native People.* Toronto: Lester Pub., 1996.

Titley, E. Brian. *A Narrow Vision: Duncan Campbell Scott and the Administration of Indian Affairs in Canada.* Vancouver: University of British Columbia Press, 1986.

Trigger, Bruce G. *Natives and Newcomers : Canada's "Heroic Age" Reconsidered.* Kingston: McGill-Queen's University Press, 1985.

*Ted Binnema*

# 2

# *Demography*

- ◆ Native Demography Before 1700
- ◆ Geographic and Demographic Change During the Eighteenth Century
- ◆ Indian Geographic Distribution, Habitat, and Demography During the Nineteenth Century
- ◆ Indian Land Tenure in the Twentieth Century
- ◆ Canadian Native Distribution, Habitat, and Demography

## ◆ NATIVE DEMOGRAPHY BEFORE 1700

Indian groups moved from place to place in search of adequate food sources, for protection, or to escape changing climatic conditions, such as long droughts in the region. Many Indian peoples tell stories of migrations, which sometimes send people on religious quests. For example, one Creek story claims that the people migrated east for many years in search of the home of the sun. Upon reaching the Atlantic Ocean, however, they gave up the quest and decided to settle. While there were some migrations prior to 1500, Indian migrations and population changes began to increase rapidly after the arrival of European colonists. The territorial expansion of the European colonies pushed many coastal Indian nations into the interior, where they were incorporated into other Indian nations or where they resettled, far from their original homelands. New trade relations with the Europeans, especially the fur trade, induced many Indian nations to seek new hunting territories, which often expanded into the other nations' lands. Perhaps the greatest change to Indian populations came with the introduction of several European diseases, such as smallpox and scarlet fever, previously unknown to Indians. These diseases caused many deaths among the Indians, and were possibly responsible for 60 million deaths in North and South America by 1900, when the U.S. Indian population declined to a low point of about 250,000. These events are often referred to as a demographic catastrophe. Native American demography is especially interesting because of the rapid decline and dispersion of the population after colonial contact.

### Paleo-Indians

Archeologists, students of ancient cultures, believe that the first human beings entered the Americas by way of a land bridge that connected Siberia and Alaska toward the end of the last glacial period, approximately 15,000 to 25,000 years ago. At this time, huge continental glaciers contained so much frozen water that sea level had fallen below the bottom of what is now the Bering Strait. After crossing, the first Americans spread rapidly beyond present-day Alaska, and by the end of glacial times, about 12,000 years ago, had settled throughout North and South America.

It is important to note that some Native Americans do not believe that their ancestors walked across the Bering Strait. Most Indian cultures have oral traditions recounting the origins of people on earth. Many of these stories are analogous to the stories of Adam and Eve in the Bible. Other Indians have traditions of eastward migrations. For example, the Lenape, or Delaware Indians, who are considered by many Indian nations to be the grandfather of the Algonkian-speaking nations, have a long epic tradition of migration from the northwest to the Atlantic coast in present-day New England. Other nations, such as the Cherokee, Choctaw, Chickasaw, and Creek, have similar migration stories in which their entire nation was led by the instructions of a sacred pole, which each day pointed in the direction of that day's journey, and finally indicated the end of the march and new homeland by remaining upright. The migration traditions are not inconsistent with archeologists' Bering Strait theory, and considering the age of many creation stories, it is possible that these ancient traditions have roots that predate a migration over the Bering Strait.

For a few thousands years after the glacial period, many large game animals, including woolly mammoths and large bison, roamed North America. These animals died out about 10,000 years ago, probably because of changing climatic conditions caused by the retreat of the glaciers north. Early Paleo-Indian cultures revolved around hunting these animals. Paleo-Indians were large game-hunting Indian peoples whose cultures predate the adoption of horticulture and the bow and arrow. Because of large game animals' extinction, Native Americans hunted smaller game, fished, and foraged for wild plant foods for the next seven or eight thousand years. Sometime around 1500 B.C.E. Indian groups began to plant crops such as corn, squash, and beans. Particularly in the present-day eastern and southwestern United States, Indian groups became increasingly dependent on horticulture, or farming with hand tools.

Native Americans slowly increased in numbers for several millennia. People acquired and transmitted specialized knowledge to their descendants about the natural resources in different regions and eventually regional culture areas formed. These cultural areas are now known as the Northeast, Southeast, Plains, Southwest, Great Basin, California, Plateau, Pacific Northwest, Subarctic, and Arctic (see the culture area sections of chapter 3).

By C.E. 1500, between seven and fifteen million people inhabited the present-day United States. Many people resided in the Southeast and Mississippi Valley where they dry-farmed or irrigated their crops. In the dry-farming Southeast, large towns grew on the natural levees flood waters formed along the edges of the major rivers. Levees rose high enough to keep settlements safe from most floods and to support a large assortment of plants that attracted game animals, making hunting easy and efficient near the towns. Townspeople depended significantly on fish caught from backwater lakes left by stream channel shifts. This cultural pattern is usually called *Mississippian*.

In the Southwest sometime after C.E. 1200, the Hohokam, ancestors of the present-day Piman-speaking tribes, began constructing multi-story, earthen-walled buildings. The Hohokam gardened using irrigation methods, and stored their crops within the earthen buildings. Ancestors of the present-day Pueblos began building similar multi-stories as early as C.E. 900. The Spanish word *pueblo* applies to these compact, multi-storied fortress towns. Pueblo peoples sharing a common culture, despite linguistic differences, occupied hundreds of *pueblos* by C.E. 1500.

The peoples of California, the Pacific Northwest, the Great Basin, and the Subarctic and Arctic by 1500 had not adopted horticulture and continued surviving as hunters and gatherers as they had for thousands of years.

## Sixteenth Century

Few records dating from 1500 to 1620 describe life in what is now the United States. Yet the available documents consistently attest that European diseases rapidly spread throughout the Native American groups. By the time of his second voyage in 1493, Christopher Columbus' crews and colonists had transmitted diseases to the Native Americans. The "Columbian Exchange" of microbes and viruses turned into a demographic catastrophe for the Indians.

**The Southeast.** In the early 1500s, the Indians of the Southeast met the Spanish. One disease of unknown type reached present-day Florida by 1514, and in 1528 Spanish castaways transmitted an undiagnosed ailment to their Galveston Island hosts on the modern Texas coast. Although it killed half the area's Natives, we do not know how far the disease spread. From 1539 to 1543, Fernando de Soto's Spanish army marauded through the Southeast, slaughtering warriors, kidnapping women, and transmitting diseases to the Natives. De Soto found several Indian villages that were already unoccupied owing to diseases that preceded his arrival. Natives probably contracted these diseases from unrecorded Spanish explorations or trading expeditions, and Native travelers and traders most likely transmitted the diseases from one village to another.

In 1559, a Spanish colonizing expedition carried epidemic influenza from Veracruz, Mexico, to Florida's Pensacola Bay. Colonists traveled inland seeking supplies from some of the populous towns de Soto had visited. The colonists stayed hungry because the populous and prosperous southeastern Indian nations that de Soto's marauders had seen dispersed into small village groups between 1543 and 1559. Malaria and stomach disorders probably caused most of the mortality, although the plague might have spread from the Spanish occupation of Mexico. In the Southeast, disease caused a significant loss of life as well as the reorganization of Native political and social structures. Many of the southeastern Indians were part of centralized Mississippian culture groups with hierarchical bodies of priests and chiefs. After the population declined, these Mississippian cultures collapsed and the Indians regrouped as egalitarian coalitions of villages. It was these egalitarian Indian nations that the colonists encountered in the 1700s. Known today as the Cherokee, Catawba, Creek, and Choctaw, these groups survived by constantly incorporating remnant peoples.

**The Northeast.** In 1535, Jacques Cartier, a French explorer, and his crews transmitted a lethal disease to the Iroquois who were living along the Saint Lawrence River. Before the century's end, the Iroquois would abandon their homeland because Algonkian-speaking

Drawing depicting the storing of crops by Southwest Natives in the public granary. Twice a year the crops are gathered, carried home in canoes, stored in low and roomy granaries built of stone and earth, and thickly roofed with palm branches and soft earth. (Drawing by John White and Jacques Le Moyne and engraved by Theodore de Bry)

nations—the Chippewa, Ottawa, and others—invaded the Saint Lawrence area. Some Iroquois probably migrated to join the Mohawk in present-day upstate New York. By the end of the 1500s, Chippewa, Ottawa, Potawatomi, and other Algonkian-speaking tribes were beginning to migrate from eastern Canada toward the Great Lakes. Iroquois and Algonkian communities dispersed and were forced to migrate inland because of rampant disease and new colonial occupation.

Southward, in the middle Atlantic area of present-day Virginia, Europeans reported outbreaks of smallpox in 1564 among Indian peoples ranging from the Timucuan in Florida to the Chesapeake Bay people, such as the Powhatan, Pamunkey, and Mattaponi. The virus apparently spread north up the Susquehanna River through present-day Pennsylvania, carried by Native traders and travelers. As a consequence, the Susquehannock lost so many people to disease that the entire nation was reduced to a single village by 1580.

English colonists carried lethal disease to Roanoke Island Natives in 1585. Viral diseases evidently killed

one-quarter of North Carolina's Indian population during that same year. In 1586, English explorer Francis Drake attacked the Spanish at Saint Augustine, Florida, and transmitted disease to the Timucuan, a major tribe of the region.

**The Southwest.** Because colonists often could not diagnose diseases that struck Natives, it is difficult to estimate how far the diseases spread. As the Native population declined, survivors abandoned some settlements and amalgamated in others. The sequence of abandonment of Hopi pueblos on the Little Colorado River in present-day Arizona provides clues to epidemic disease among all Pueblo peoples. About 1500, the Hopi, a western Pueblo nation, inhabited about ten riverine pueblos. When Spaniards arrived in 1540, seven were still inhabited, indicating that disease perhaps had spread from New Spain, or present-day Mexico.

In 1583, when the Spaniards next encountered the Hopi, only five riverine pueblos were occupied. This attrition indicates that one or more of the four major epidemics that afflicted Mexico during the interval had spread among the Pueblo, resulting in abandonment and amalgamation. Hopi inhabited four pueblos in 1598 and epidemics of smallpox or measles probably reached them sometime between 1592 and 1593. This epidemic caused significant mortality and abandonment of one pueblo. After the 1613 to 1620 plague epidemic, the Hopi abandoned the remaining pueblos on the Little Colorado River. The survivors migrated to join five Hopi pueblos at Black Mesa, sixty miles to the north, also in present-day Arizona. Thus, between 1519 and 1650, the ten formerly populous Hopi pueblos were decimated and abandoned.

Historic attrition among other Pueblo language groups shows that depopulation was typical among all Pueblos. By 1630 Franciscan missionaries had consolidated 6,000 Piro from fourteen pueblos in three missions and one village, a 71 percent reduction in the number of Piro Pueblo settlements. Southern-Tiwa speakers inhabited sixteen Rio Grande Valley pueblos in 1540; by 1641 only three Tiwa pueblos were left, an 81 percent reduction in settlements. Other Pueblo peoples, such as the Jemez and Towa speakers in the Rio Grande Valley, suffered similar declines in population.

Thanks to European records of the 1500s, we know more about the demography of the East and Southwest Indian groups than we do about the demography of the Native peoples of the Subarctic, Northeast Coast, California, Plateau, or Great Basin areas during this time. While we know virtually nothing about these groups during the 1500s, there is more information about these peoples from the following century.

## Seventeenth Century

As European colonies proliferated so did records of migrations and epidemics. In contrast to the 1500s, which were marked by severe demographic change due to disease, the 1600s were characterized more by the intensification of trade relations and the expansion of colonial empires. Indian nations came under great pressure to adapt to European trade and political pressures, and many Indian nations were forced to migrate into the interior for relief from colonial expansion, while some remained in their homelands and attempted to accommodate the new laws and political domination of the European colonists. Despite increased pressure to migrate and adapt, disease and death continued as a persistent feature of Indian life during the 1600s.

**The Northeast.** When English colonists came to what became Jamestown in present-day Virginia, they encountered the Powhatan, a confederacy of twenty-seven tribes on the James, York, and Potomac rivers, with a total population exceeding 10,000. Sixteen other Algonkian-speaking groups, numbering about 15,000

people, also lived in the same coastal area. In 1607 the English colonists invaded the Powhatan territory, causing some deaths among the Powhatan and their neighboring allies. Between 1613 and 1617 the Powhatan and allies suffered a plague epidemic that originated with Florida's Indian population. In an apparent response to the loss of life and continued colonial aggression, the Powhatan rose up against the colonists in 1622. The war lasted intermittently for about ten years, causing many deaths on both sides. The surviving Powhatan rose up against the colonists again in 1644 and 1646 but were defeated and forced to cede their lands between the York and Blackwater rivers. By the late 1600s, most of the Indians in the area were dispossessed and made subject to Virginia law.

In 1614, Dutch merchants on the Hudson River in present-day New York established a trading post in Mahican territory near present-day Albany, New York. The fur trade—the exchange of beaver, deer, and other skins for European manufactured goods (especially metal goods such as guns, hoes, and hatchets)—became the most significant exchange between the early colonists and Indian nations. Indians quickly realized the value of European goods over their own stone tools, and soon found the Europeans willing to trade for furs, which were sold as beaver hats, leather goods, and coats in Europe. After a few years, the Indians began to prefer trade goods and discontinued production of many traditional arts and crafts. Soon, many Indian nations were not willing or able to meet their own material or economic needs, and came to depend on the trade of furs to fill basic economic and manufacturing needs. Thereafter, the Indians were dependent on the Europeans to supply many basic needs; they could no longer live without trade with the colonists.

For three years, from 1614 to 1617, Algonkian-speaking Mahican collected tribute from the Mohawk, the easternmost nation of the Five Nations Iroquois Confederacy, for crossing their territory to trade with the Dutch. In 1624 the Dutch built Fort Orange, now Albany, and a Mahican village moved nearby. From 1624 to 1648, the Mohawk waged war on the Mahican and ousted them from the area around the new European outpost.

Death rates ran high among Natives on New England's frontier. For example, between 1613 and 1617, plague killed half of Florida's Native population. The plague spread northward along the Atlantic coast, weakening the Powhatan. It killed so many Massachusetts Indians that the Puritans who settled in the area during the 1630s believed that God had cleared the lands of infidel Natives, preparing it for Puritan arrival and settlement. In 1634 the Nipmuck lost 450 of 1,000

Taos Pueblo. (Photo by Manny Pedraza)

inhabitants of one town. Colonists compounded the impact of scarlet fever with the Pequot War in 1637, which started when the Pequot allowed Dutch traders to establish a post east of the Connecticut River at present-day East Hartford. The English raised an army, including Narragansett and Mohegan allies, and burned down a major Pequot village, killing at least 300 men, women, and children. Two hundred survivors were sold into slavery.

Because the Natives depended on trade, they began fighting over areas of access to European trading posts and to areas that were endowed with fur-bearing animals that could be traded to Europeans. In 1643 the Mahican conquered three Algonkian-speaking tribes and several hundred others fled to Manhattan and Pavoia where the Dutch massacred them, ensuring Mahican dominance. This conflict cost about 1,000 Native lives.

Because of a scarlet fever epidemic in 1638, 600 Wenro, an Iroquoian-speaking nation living along the lower Great Lakes, abandoned their territory and moved in with the Huron, another Iroquoian-speaking group

living nearby. Other Wenro found refuge among other Iroquoian-speaking nations.

Epidemics might have motivated the Mascouten, Kickapoo, Fox, Sauk, and Potawatomi to leave Michigan's lower peninsula in about 1641 to migrate to Winnebago territory at Green Bay. The once powerful Winnebago lost 1,500 men to an epidemic and lost another 500 men to war with the Fox, which greatly weakened the Winnebago's ability to prevent other Indian nations from moving into their territory.

By the 1640s, the Iroquois, or the Five Nations, had already over-exploited their fur-bearing territories and were looking westward to gain access to other trade or hunting areas. Most tribes in the Great Lakes region sided with the French, who wished to prevent Iroquois expansion into the interior, since the Iroquois were Dutch and English trading allies. In the late 1640s, unable to secure trade agreements with the interior nations (the Huron, the Erie, the Petun, the Neutral Nation, and others), the Iroquois initiated military action to secure access to fur-bearing territories. Dutch traders supported the Five Nations by supplying them with guns and powder, giving the Five Nations an advantage over the French-allied Indians, since the French were reluctant to trade weapons with the Indians. Between 1649 and 1700, the Iroquois waged a series of conflicts with interior nations such as the Illinois Confederacy, the Ottawa, the Huron, and others. These wars, called the Beaver Wars, represent a period of almost constant warfare in the northeast region among the Five Nations, the French, and their Indian trade allies.

During the winter of 1649 and 1650, an Iroquois army marched west and dispersed the Petun people, and a Seneca and Mohawk army, composed of two of the Five Nations of the Iroquois Confederacy, then attacked the Neutral Nation traders and its refugees, dispersing them. The campaign demonstrated that the Seneca and Mohawk were extremely dependent on European goods. In 1652 the Iroquois defeated the Susquehannock people, taking from 500 to 600 prisoners, reducing the Susquehannock's population to between 2,000 and 3,000. In 1653, the Iroquois waged war on the Erie people and dispersed them. Between 1649 and 1670, most of the Iroquoian-speaking nations of the lower Great Lakes, such as the Huron, the Petun, the Erie, and the Neutral Nation, were either destroyed, dispersed, or adopted by the Five Nations' military expansion.

At the time of the Iroquois expansion, New England's colonists openly waged a genocidal war of territorial conquest against Native peoples in 1675. The Wampanoag of Massachusetts bore the brunt of the assault. The colonists virtually exterminated the Wampanoag in a war the colonists called King Philip's War after a Wampanoag leader. By this time the Massachusetts Indians had been so reduced by disease that the colonists ignored them. Although the Narragansett people of Connecticut and Rhode Island did not participate early in King Philip's War, a colonial army invaded their territory and broke their power. The Narragansett either found refuge with the Niantic people or left New England altogether. The New England Indians were thereafter subject to English law and many lived on the outskirts of English settlements, eking out a marginal existence. About fifteen New England Indian villages adopted Christianity; they became known as Praying Towns and, to a certain extent, lived in the tradition of New England town government and Puritan religion.

By the late 1600s, the Indian nations of Virginia and Maryland were also subject to colonial law and were to a large extent dispossessed of their original coastal lands. Disease and war caused their populations to decline significantly, and the colonists already outnumbered them in the colonial territories. By 1700, the colonial governments largely ignored most Indians in the middle Atlantic colonies; the Indian communities persisted, however, and remained targets of land speculators, who often succeeded in purchasing the remnants of their land.

Not every Indian nation was dispossessed of its homeland by the colonists. During most of the 1600s, the Shawnee lived in northern Kentucky, southern Ohio, and western Virginia. By the late 1690s, however, the Chickasaw and Cherokee constantly raided the tribe for slaves, whom they sold to English colonists. The Shawnee abandoned their homeland in the 1690s. Some moved to present-day Georgia, others migrating to join the Creek Nation, while still others joined the Delaware in eastern Pennsylvania. There, on land granted by the Five Nations, and under obligation to pay tribute to the Iroquois Empire, the Shawnee joined in alliance with the Delaware, who themselves had retreated from the coastal areas of New York and New Jersey in search of fur-bearing territories and refuge from colonial expansion. Both the Shawnee and Delaware nations were buffeted throughout their history by colonial expansion, and were subjected to trade dependency, requiring them to work as hunters for European traders. Both nations were eventually forced to migrate into Ohio, Indiana, and by the early 1800s to Kansas or Indian Territory, present-day Oklahoma. Many nations of the Northeast were also forced to migrate further west, but the Delaware and Shawnee illustrate the fate of a people ultimately forced to migrate halfway across the North American continent to find refuge from colonial expansion.

The Susquehannock, who during the late 1600s lived in southern present-day Pennsylvania, virtually disappeared because of disease and colonial expansion. Although they held their native Susquehanna River against Iroquois assaults until 1675, mortality from epidemic influenza that spread among the Iroquois and New England's Native peoples in 1675 during King Philip's War might have been the decisive factor in the Susquehannock's decline and subjugation. Suffering calamitous losses during the Iroquois wars against the French beginning in 1677, many of the remaining Susquehannock joined the Shawnee and Delaware who were living near present-day Philadelphia between 1677 and 1700.

Further west, in the Great Lakes area, many of the Algonkian speakers and other nations were also affected by the Beaver Wars and colonial expansion. The Potawatomi who lived between Lake Michigan and Green Bay, Wisconsin, were by 1670, expanding south along the western shore of the lake, into Winnebago territory. The Winnebago entered the fur trade in 1665, abandoning their former warlike actions against the western migrating Indian nations. Indeed, Winnebago married Ojibwa, Potawatomi, Sauk, and Fox, all of whom were invaders into Winnebago territory.

New fur trade opportunities and rivalries among Indian nations motivated a shift in inter-group alliances and residence. For example, in 1667 traders reached the Menominee living northwest of Green Bay. After the Menominee entered the fur trade, they quickly abandoned their villages and scattered in small bands. In 1666 the Mascouten, Kickapoo, and Miami shared with some Peoria a large trading village upstream from Green Bay. The fur trade had become so economically important to Native Americans that several tribes that had never lived near each other before came together to live in one trading village.

The nations of the Illinois Confederacy—including the Kaskaskia, the Cahokia, the Peoria, and others— were also displaced as a result of the Beaver Wars and new trade opportunities. According to French reports, the Illinois Confederacy numbered about 100,000 people in the mid 1600s, inhabiting sixty villages in present-day Iowa, Illinois, and Wisconsin. Chequamegon Bay on Lake Superior became a trading center for Illinois trappers, and the Illinois began migrating further north from their original territories. In 1682 French traders built a post at Starved Rock in northern Illinois and attracted nearly 18,000 Illinois, Miami, and Shawnee. At about the same time, the nations of the Illinois Confederacy came under attack by the Iroquois interested in Illinois fur-trading lands. For example, the Espenimkia tribe of the Illinois Confederacy was virtually destroyed by an Iroquois attack. The Iroquois, in search of access to beaver producing areas, continued to invade and attack the Illinois Confederacy villages until the end of the 1600s. By 1700 there remained only about 6,500 members of the Illinois Confederacy.

Further west, in present-day Minnesota, the Chippewa, who were migrating from the east (in part, because of the Iroquois military expansion for fur-bearing territories), invaded Dakota (Sioux) lands. The Sioux and the Chippewa would fight over this land for the next century. In the end, the Chippewa forced many Sioux to migrate onto the Plains, where they adapted to the horse riding and buffalo hunting lifestyle for which they are now well known. The Chippewa ultimately moved into the Minnesota region, where they continued to hunt, trade, and harvest wild rice.

**The Southeast.** Unlike the Northeast, where permanent settlements began in the 1620s, the Southeast did not have permanent European settlements until after 1670. Spanish Florida, established at Saint Augustine in 1565, was the exception. The Spanish built a series of Catholic missions for the Indians throughout Florida and present-day Georgia. These missions soon failed because diseases killed the Indians, and English attacks destroyed the remaining missionary efforts in the 1690s. In spite of this initial Spanish settlement, scholars know less about southeastern Indian demography than about the Northeast for most of the 1600s.

In the mid-1660s, yellow fever and smallpox decimated Florida Natives. Measles killed more than 10,000 Florida Natives in 1658, and a smallpox epidemic between 1665 and 1667 affected Natives from Florida to Virginia, with unknown death tolls. As their numbers declined, Native peoples amalgamated despite traditional animosities and linguistic differences. For example, some Algonkian-speaking Weanock joined the Iroquoian-speaking Nottaway in the Virginia Piedmont region before 1700. The once powerful Natchez gave refuge to remnants of other nations that were abandoning their homelands near the coast of the Gulf of Mexico. By 1700 migrating Tunican tribes joined the Natchez villages on the Mississippi River in present-day west Mississippi.

After the 1670 settlement of Charles Town in South Carolina, many tribes, such as the Creek and Cherokee, started to trade with the English. During this period, the English were interested in acquiring slaves for their plantations; they traded guns and other manufactured goods to Indians who accompanied them on slave raids in the interior Indian nations. For example, the Shawnee in the 1680s and 1690s suffered severe losses as a result of English, Chickasaw, and Cherokee slave raids. In particular, the Choctaw, a populous nation that once lived in present-day Mississippi and Louisiana, were decimated during this period by such slave raids. Some traditional districts of the Choctaw Nation were so depleted by slave raids that it is now virtually impossible to reconstruct their original social and political organization. The beleaguered Choctaw found an ally in the French, who established the Louisiana Colony in 1699. The French supplied the Choctaw with guns, which they used to withstand the continuing English-supported slave raids.

Between 1670 and 1710, trade relations between the Indians and the English were dominated by the capture and sale of Indian slaves. Indians, however, did not make very good slaves. Enslaving people in their homeland was difficult because they knew the land and the people much better than their English captors. For this reason, the Indian slaves found it relatively easy to escape and hide. After 1700, the English began to transport Indian slaves to the Caribbean, where escape

*Construction of Fortified Towns among the Floridians.* Drawing by Le Moyne, engraving from Theodore de Bry, *America,* part II, 1591, plate XXX. (Courtesy of American Heritage Press)

was more difficult. Thereafter, the English imported slaves from Africa to work the plantations.

**The Plains.**   During the 1600s, the people living on the Plains began to be greatly affected by the north-ward migration of the horse, which the Spanish had brought to the Southeast and Mexico during the mid-1500s. The horse's ability to travel far and fast eventu-ally transformed the grassy Plains from a nearly vacant zone into an overpopulated area. Nearly constant inter-group strife and horse rustling characterized life on the Plains. As was true of the Northeastern tribes, the Plains peoples soon became dependent on trade goods. Plains tribes traded horses, mules, and tanned hides for firearms, axes, knives, and other tools. French and English demand for horses and mules drove the post-horse Plains economy. Because Plains Natives did not breed horses and mules, they rustled them from each other and from Spanish settlements.

By the late 1600s many formerly horticultural na-tions began migrating to the Plains area from places farther east. During the 1500s, many of the nations living in the Mississippi Valley had been part of the Mississippi Culture, which built elaborate mounds and ceremonial centers. Some, such as the Caddoan and Siouan nations, had large populations in small towns; they were decimated by the epidemics of the 1500s, however, and by the early 1600s, only small local groups without strong central organization remained. These small tribal groups began feeling the pressure of the expanding eastern trade networks and wars, and encountered the western-moving Indian nations that were forced westward by the colonists and the expan-sive Iroquois, or Five Nations.

Before 1600, most nations in the Plains area survived through horticultural means. By the late 1600s, the adoption of horses made it possible to raid corn-fields and put pressure on nations that preferred to grow corn and to remain in settled villages. As the horse raids became increasingly effective, more and more of the Indian peoples living on or near the Plains were forced to acquire horses for self-defense and retaliatory raids. This situation led to an intensification of economic raids and revenge attacks among the different nations; peoples with horses had clear advantages in these early skirmishes.

Nevertheless, many nations, such as the Hidatsa, Mandan, and Cheyenne, were reluctant to give up horticulture. While the Cheyenne gradually began to specialize in buffalo hunting and raiding, the Hidatsa and Mandan tried to maintain their villages and horticultural economy. Such tribes' efforts reflected the old Indian traditions more than did the new culture associated with raiding, buffalo hunting, the Sun Dance (an annual world renewal ceremony), warrior societies, and annual tribal hunts, all of which are considered representative of high Plains culture as it developed over the next two centuries. This Plains culture has become the most recognized image of American Indians, even though it does not have a long history and does not represent a long-standing tradition among any Indian nation.

Many Mississippi Valley Indian nations moved westward in the late 1600s. Native migrations from the Great Lakes forced several Siouan-speaking nations, including the Iowa and Chiwere, into the Minnesota and Iowa region. By the 1680s, some of the first Sioux, or Teton Dakota, moved onto the Plains, while most other Sioux remained and fought with the invading Chippewa. The Osage, Caddoan speakers living in present-day western Missouri, continued to grow corn, squash and pumpkins, but turned to replenishing their horses by raiding other Caddoan-speaking nations in present-day Oklahoma. The Hidatsa and Mandan, also Caddoan speakers from old Mississippian mound-building cultures, migrated up the Missouri River, where they began trading horticultural products for European goods by the late 1600s. The Crow, led by a religious leader who claimed he had visions of a new sacred land, left the Hidatsa to wander northward on the Plains. The religious leader took the Crow people on a pilgrimage into the Canadian plains and finally settled in the 1700s in the western and northern Plains, in what is approximately present-day Montana.

Many of the Indian nations that migrated to the southern Plains were Athapascan—Apache and Navajo—hunters and gatherers who had very different traditions from the horticultural peoples moving onto the Plains in the north. The southern Athapascan migrated south from northeastern Canada or Alaska during the thirteenth or fourteenth centuries, and remained big-game hunters and wild-food collectors. They fitted pack-dogs to travois, or small sleds, and carried trade goods between the Pueblo villages on the Rio Grande

and the Caddoan horticulturists along the Mississippi Valley.

Southern Athapascan acquired horses from the Spanish, who arrived in 1598. Beginning soon after 1600, Apache, with the aid of horses and Spanish-style lances, dominated the southern Plains. The Apache prospered, grew in number, and divided into several different bands. Jicarilla and Faraon Apache lived on the Canadian River in northeastern New Mexico and the Texas Panhandle. Carlana Apache lived on the Purgatoire River tributary of the Arkansas River in modern-day Colorado, and Cuartelejo Apache inhabited the upper Arkansas River Valley. Paloma Apache resided along the upper Republican River in present-day Nebraska and Lipan Apache migrated over much of what is now Texas. Although they rustled Pueblo and Spanish livestock, Apache peoples traded slaves for stock and other commodities at Taos and Pecos Pueblo, where periodic trading took place.

A few southern Athapascan acquired not only horses, but also sheep, which they learned to pasture and breed. By 1630 the Spanish recognized these Athapascan as "Navajo." With the increase in the standard of living associated with the permanent supply of domesticated mutton, the Navajo population began to increase steadily. The Navajo are now the largest U.S. Indian nation, with nearly 200,000 people.

**The Southwest.**   Although the Apache lived primarily on the southern Plains, by the second half of the 1600s they also traded with and raided Pueblo and Spanish settlements in the Southwest. In 1670 a disease killed many Apache horses. The Apache subsequently migrated into New Mexico, where they depended on hunting and fighting for their survival. By 1672 they began to rustle what they could not purchase. Almost overnight, traditional horse traders became horse raiders. When their traditional Apache trading partners turned into rustlers, residents of five Pueblos—Tajique, Chililí, Quarai, Abó, and Pueblo de los Jumanos—migrated to Pueblo villages along the Rio Grande.

In 1680 most Pueblo peoples used weapons to force Spanish colonists from Indian lands. The Spaniards, along with loyal Pueblos, retreated down the Rio Grande to present-day El Paso, Texas, where their descendants still live.

The collapse of the eastern Pueblo frontier, coupled with the Spanish retreat, removed a military barrier that in effect allowed the Apache to remain on the southern Plains. By 1698 an Apache vanguard migrated westward to the mountains on the present-day Arizona-New Mexico border and would later evolve into eight bands. Meanwhile, Spaniards re-colonized Pueblo territory in 1694, and in 1696, a smallpox epidemic triggered an abortive revolt. Tewa Pueblo people who refused to live under Spanish rule fled west to Hopi First Mesa. As a minority group, the Tewa Pueblo learned the Hopi language and served as interpreters and traders, and assisted in Hopi defense.

The Jemez people defended a mesa-top town until 1695, when they submitted to the Spanish by returning to their fields. In the 1696 growing season, the Jemez joined other Pueblo and rebelled against the Spaniards in the wake of a smallpox epidemic. After slaying resident Spaniards in Jemez pueblo, the Jemez retreated to their mesa-top fortification. After repelling a Spanish attack, they dispersed. Having established close relations with the Navajo between 1680 and 1694, many of the Jemez fled to them. Inasmuch as the Navajo reckon descent through the mother, the children of Jemez women created a new Navajo clan. The refugee Jemez people had great influence on Navajo ceremony, religion, crafts, and horticulture.

### Conclusion

Disease and military expansion greatly changed Indian demography and social and political order even before they had direct and sustained contact with Europeans.

During the 1600s the best, although fragmented, evidence of Native Americans is found among the nations of the Plains, Northeast, Southeast, and Southwest. We know very little about the demography of Indian peoples before 1700 in the Great Basin, California, the Pacific Northwest, the Plateau, the Subarctic, and the Arctic regions. In the East, by the late 1600s, very few Native Americans escaped the military turmoil of European expansion. European diseases continued to infect Native Americans and diminished their numbers. By 1700, two centuries of European diseases reduced Native American populations in the Northeast, Southeast, and Southwest to less than one-tenth of what their numbers had been in 1500. Many groups simply disappeared. Those who endured by amalgamating the survivors of villages, towns, and former tribes became much more egalitarian than the populous, socially stratified societies that thrived prior to 1500. The Mississippi Culture, with its full-time artists and priests, had mostly perished from disease and military turmoil. Between 1500 and 1700 so many Native Americans died that they lost a considerable amount of knowledge about their traditional cultures and political

Three Ojibwa grave houses on the Bad River Reservation in Odanah, northern Wisconsin. (Photo by Sarah Loe)

systems; most of what is known about Indian societies is based on documents and knowledge of the post-1700 societies. Because these societies were greatly changed during the period between 1500 and 1700, they only partially reflect the age-old traditions of thousands of years of culture that existed before European arrival.

*Henry Dobyns*

### ◆ GEOGRAPHIC AND DEMOGRAPHIC CHANGE DURING THE EIGHTEENTH CENTURY

The eighteenth century brought a wide variety of geographic and demographic changes to the many Native American societies across North America. Numerous diverse cultures had experienced close contact with European colonies since the sixteenth century.

Others were just entering into direct relationships with colonial societies, while many more remained distant from the expansion of European empires. The contest over Indian trade and territory among Spain, France, and England affected all Native American societies in some way before the end of the eighteenth century.

At the beginning of the 1700s the French implemented a strategic plan of encircling the English colonies on the Atlantic coast by creating a chain of Indian alliances and forts along the Mississippi River. In the late 1690s, the French created Louisiana Colony and struggled with the English until the end of the French and Indian War in 1760. The period between the 1690s and the end of the eighteenth century was marked by constant warfare in eastern North America with such campaigns as Queen Anne's War, King William's War, the French and Indian War, and the American War of Independence, as well as considerable intermittent border warfare during times of undeclared war. Warfare and trade relations greatly affected the location and political relations of the Native nations, which managed their affairs and interests within the context of increasingly powerful and competitive colonial governments.

Many changes in the location of Indian peoples were made on their own initiatives and for their own objectives. As the colonies grew more powerful, some Indians acted to protect their economic and trade interests by establishing neutrality and bargaining relations with the rival European colonists, as was the case with the Iroquois and Creek. Other Indian nations sought close trade and political relations with specific European colonies, as did the Cherokee who often sought trade and diplomatic ties with Carolina Colony, or the Ottawa who had long-standing trade ties with the French in New France. In order to develop greater capacities for managing trade and diplomatic relations with the colonists, some nations, such as the Creek and Iroquois, created confederacies and sought to strengthen political and trade relations among themselves. Sporadically throughout the 1700s, the Iroquois stated that they commanded the men of fifty nations, although this was a bluff intended to impress English and French diplomats and military officers. Nevertheless, the confederacy of western Indian nations that the Iroquois led was passed onto other nations, especially after the 1750s, when Iroquois power was declining and the British government openly supported the Iroquois in order to gain trade and indirect diplomatic control over the western Indian nations.

During the 1750s the Delaware and Shawnee increasingly took the initiative in forming a confederacy of Indian nations that fought to prevent westward colonial expansion. During the early 1760s, the Delaware Prophet emerged, preaching that God commanded the Indian nations to unite and drive the Europeans from the continent; only then would prosperity and happiness be restored to the Indian peoples. Pontiac, the Ottawa leader, used the teachings of the Delaware Prophet to muster attacks on the British forts in the Great Lakes area in 1763. Although Pontiac was not able to drive the British out of Indian land, he temporarily convened a military confederacy of western Indian nations. During the 1780s and early 1790s Little Turtle, a Miami war chief, led the western nations. The Indian confederacy resisted U.S. attempts to settle the Ohio and Great Lakes area. After Little Turtle's death, the Shawnee leader Tecumseh and his brother, the Shawnee Prophet, revived the confederacy of Indian nations from 1806 to 1813. After the War of 1812, the Indian confederacy of Ohio and Great Lakes Indians disbanded.

While the eighteenth century did not see major demographic movements among Indian nations, political and economic change greatly affected their economies and political relations. By the beginning of the century, most eastern Indian nations were engaged in trading furs for European manufactured goods, especially guns, powder, metal goods, and textiles. Most tribes became quickly dependent on trade in order to secure newly desired and needed goods, and hence trade became a new way of life. In the Southeast, Indian slaves were sought, but were found difficult to contain; thus, they were exported to the Caribbean Islands, while Black slaves from Africa were imported to the continent to work on tobacco and other plantations. Since interior Indians became victims of slave raids by coastal Indians and their English allies, guns and ammunition soon became necessary, and the eastern nations found that they had to develop trade and diplomatic relations with one or more European colonies to secure a steady supply of guns, powder, ball, and other trade goods.

Epidemics and wars had traumatically reduced Native American groups along the Atlantic seaboard by 1700, but through coalescence and adaptation many refugees from different tribes reorganized themselves into new communities. In the early eighteenth century, Wampanoag and Pequot in southern New England, Chickahominy and Nanticoke in the Chesapeake Bay region, and Catawba and Apalachee in the South managed to maintain a degree of political autonomy while securing stable social and economic relations with neighboring settlements and towns. However, in the Southeast, slave-raiding starting in the 1680s decimated many nations, such as the Shawnee in present-day Kentucky and the Choctaw in present-day Mississippi and Louisiana. The Shawnee Nation was dispersed. Some joined the Delaware near present-day Philadelphia, others joined the Creek Nation in present-day Alabama, and a third group settled for awhile in Georgia, but decided to rejoin the Shawnee in Pennsylvania. The raids on the Choctaw were so severe that the several major groups within their social order were permanently disrupted and Choctaw social and political relations gravitated toward secular, local, and regional organization. Choctaw society was so disrupted by slave raids that it might be impossible for historians to reconstruct the traditional relations of clans, villages, and government.

The Yamasee War of 1715 and the Natchez War of 1729 were the last major struggles of resistance waged by coastal tribes in the eastern woodlands. The Yamasee War started because many Indians incurred debts to English traders, and the traders employed harsh methods, such as taking and enslaving children, in order to satisfy the debts. The powerful Creek Confederacy sought to aid the coastal Yamasee in the war, but when the war ended badly, the Creek turned to a new strategy of balancing diplomatic and trade relations among the English colonies on the east coast, the Spanish in Florida, and the French in Louisiana Colony. The Natchez War (1729) started because the French wished to impose taxes on the Natchez fur trade. The Natchez were one of the few remaining Mississippian culture societies still intact in the early 1700s, and their leader was the sacred priest-leader called the Great Sun. The French, with their Choctaw allies, quickly destroyed the Natchez Nation and captured the Great Sun, who was deported into slavery to the Caribbean Islands with several thousand other Natchez. Some Natchez fled to live with the Chickasaw in present-day northern Louisiana and western Tennessee; others went to live among the Creek in present-day Alabama. The Natchez and Chickasaw thereafter fought a constant war, with several major campaigns waged against the French and Choctaw from 1729 to 1760, when the French were defeated by the English in the French and Indian War.

These wars and slave raids, together with English raids against mission Indians in Spanish Florida in the early 1700s, caused the death of thousands of Indian people and the exportation of thousands more, as slaves, to the West Indies. Some refugees from these southeastern conflicts migrated into the territory of larger Indian nations such as the Creek and Chickasaw. After fighting several battles with North Carolina militia in the early 1710s, the Tuscarora fled North Carolina and joined their Iroquoian brethren in New York, becoming the sixth nation of the Iroquois Confederacy.

In the mid-Atlantic region, discontent over settlers' encroachment and traders' abuses drove Delaware, Shawnee, Nanticoke, and smaller groups up the Susquehanna River during the 1720s and 1730s. Eventually, most of these Indian migrants resettled in the Ohio River Valley. The Great Lakes and Ohio River region already had become a dynamic world of pan-tribal migration and mixture. Under the influence of French trade, Wyandot, Miami, Potawatomi, Ottawa, and tribes farther west interacted across a vast and fluid network of villages and posts. Intermarriage with French traders created a Métis population, which grew in close association with Indian villagers. When the Seven Years' War erupted between Great Britain and France in 1754, Native American nations in the Great Lakes area entered a long and difficult period of military resistance against the English and, after 1783, against U.S. expansion, which lasted until the end of the War of 1812.

Most interior tribes of the Eastern woodlands experienced a measure of peace and stability during the first half of the eighteenth century. The Iroquois Nations in the Northeast and the Cherokee Nation in the Southeast developed strong trade ties to English colonies, but did not relinquish their avenues to French diplomacy and commerce. During the 1600s, the Iroquois allied themselves to the Dutch and English against the French, but by 1700 the expanding English colonies alerted the Iroquois, who thereafter embarked on policy-neutral diplomatic and trade relations with the French and English colonies. The populous and tribally diverse Creek Confederacy maintained an effective position of neutrality among British, Spanish, and French colonies along its borders. In the lower Mississippi Valley, the powerful Choctaw were highly regarded trade partners and military allies of French Louisiana. The Chickasaw allied themselves with the British and were consequently in continuous conflict with the French and their Indian allies. Even during times of stability and peace, all these large Native American groups suffered population decline from contagious diseases introduced by European settlers and traders. Their involvement in the Seven Years' War and in the American Revolution during the second half of the eighteenth century took an especially heavy toll on the Iroquois and Cherokee peoples.

Geographic and demographic changes occurred in various forms among Native Americans in the eighteenth-century Southwest. By 1696 the Spanish had completed their re-conquest of New Mexico, following

A bent framing for a wigwam at Itasca State Park in northern Minnesota. (Photo by Sarah Loe. Courtesy of the UCLA American Indian Studies Center)

the Pueblo Revolt of 1680. Pueblo communities worked out a stable social and economic relationship with Hispanic settlements. They accepted missionaries into their towns on the condition that they not meddle with traditional beliefs and rituals. The Hopi maintained the greatest degree of independence among Pueblo peoples, destroying the mission town of Awatowi in 1700. Depopulation slowed over the eighteenth century, but diseases continued to plague the Native American populations of the Southwest. The Pueblo and Hispano developed closer ties to the Navajo, Ute, and Apache occupying territory around New Mexico in scattered, mobile bands. The Navajo incorporated sheep-herding into their already diversified livelihood, setting themselves on a course of geographic and demographic expansion. The migration of Comanche onto the southern Plains during the eighteenth century circumscribed colonial expansion in the northern Rio Grande Valley until peace was established in 1786.

The migration of Native American groups to the Great Plains was perhaps the most significant demographic and geographic movement of the eighteenth century. From the eastern woodlands around Lake Superior, Cheyenne and Lakota Sioux migrated across the Missouri River to the northern Plains. The Sioux and Cheyenne were woodland people who farmed corn, collected wild plants, and hunted, but they soon took up the Sun Dance, buffalo hunting, horse riding, and migratory lifeways characteristic of the Plains culture. From the Rocky Mountains came the Kiowa and Comanche, who eventually populated the southern Plains. These emigrants combined uses of the gun and horse to develop a vibrant culture and economy based on buffalo hunting. Meanwhile, the townspeople who had occupied the lower Missouri River and its tributaries for centuries—Pawnee, Oto, and Mandan, among others—suffered a steady decline in population. The Hidatsa, Arikara, and Crow migrated up the Missouri River and eventually settled near present-day Bismarck, North Dakota. These sedentary horticultural peoples depended heavily on corn production and lived in houses that looked like earthen mounds. They represented the primary form of social and economic life found on the Plains before the introduction of the horse. The migrant Lakota began to raid the corn fields of the sedentary nations, putting considerable economic pressure on them. By the end of the century, the sedentary Indian nations were facing intensive trade pressures from Europeans along with competitive territorial pressures from Cheyenne and Sioux newcomers.

Throughout most of the eighteenth century, other trans-Mississippi Native Americans experienced little or no direct contact with Europeans. Trade goods from the Hudson's Bay Company's expansive Subarctic and northern Plains network began to reach Rocky Mountain and Great Basin societies. Through raiding and trading, these same people also acquired horses. Ute in the southern Rockies and Nez Percé in the Columbia Basin, for example, attained greater mobility in procuring food, fighting enemies, and trading with allies. Contagious diseases introduced by Europeans from different directions undoubtedly affected most Native Americans in the western interior, but migration and intertribal relations were still determined principally by their own design.

During the second half of the eighteenth century, external forces began to reach the Far West from the Pacific Coast. In 1769 Spain established its first mission among California Native Americans at San Diego. Poor living conditions and diseases rapidly took their toll on mission Indians along the California coast, from the Diegueo northward to the Miwok. Expeditions to replace them intimidated interior tribes like the Yokut and Wintun. Throughout the remainder of the eighteenth century, Spanish Franciscan missionaries established missions at locations farther north in California. Thousands of Indians were brought into the missions and induced to become Christians. They worked as laborers to support and build the California missions, and many died from overwork and disease, while many others no longer practiced their traditional cultures.

Russian explorers began sailing along the Alaska coast by 1741 and reported good prospects for trade in seal and sea otter skins. During the 1700s these skins were in high demand in China, where they were used to make clothing. By the 1760s Russian traders and Russian Orthodox priests were extending political and cultural control over the Aleutian Islands and along the southern coastal regions of Alaska. Russian forts and trading establishments extended as far south as present-day northern California. In particular, the Aleut suffered greatly from Russian colonization, and many were forced to hunt and secure furs. Aleutian culture significantly disintegrated under the force of Russian political and cultural domination. Nevertheless, the

Tlingit, living on the Alaska Panhandle, kept their political and cultural independence from the Russians, although the Russian-American Company located its center of operations at New Archangel, present-day Sitka, Alaska, which is near a long-standing Tlingit village. The Tlingit quickly joined in the fur trade with the Russians and added the newfound wealth to their traditional potlatches, where significant quantities of food, tools, art, sacred objects, and symbolic goods were exchanged in ceremonies designed to honor clan ancestors.

In the Pacific Northwest, British and American merchants began commerce with coastal Native Americans for sea otter pelts and other furs. By the 1790s the Chinook, Nootka, and Tlingit were trading regularly with ships from New England and Europe. The Russian-American Company's trade settlements along the Gulf of Alaska drew large quantities of seal and sea otter skins from Native American hunters. The vibrant life of this commercial frontier produced a growing number of people of mixed Native American and Russian descent. Many Alaska Natives converted to the Russian Orthodox religion, as missionaries and churches usually accompanied the establishment of major trade posts.

Meanwhile, in the Eastern Woodlands, Native American societies were facing the aftermath of the American Revolution. The Treaty of Paris (1783) rearranged the geopolitical map of North America more profoundly than any previous agreement made in Europe during the colonial period. The creation along the Atlantic seaboard of a new nation by rebellious English colonies set in motion forces that Native Americans had not experienced before. As the United States asserted power over much of eastern North America, and as European governments wound down their imperial contest over the continent, Indian nations lost their former allies and found themselves face-to-face with an ambitious new republic. Military resistance by Ohio Valley and Great Lakes tribes climaxed in costly defeat by 1794. Many of the Indian nations of the Ohio and Great Lakes area, already immigrants from eastern territories, tried to prevent U.S. expansion across the Ohio River, which the Indians considered a border between themselves and the United States. Several battles were fought in the Indiana and Ohio areas. Nevertheless, the signing of Jay's Treaty by the United States and England in late 1794 changed the diplomatic situation dramatically, and the Indian nations were forced to recognize the United States as the major power in the region. The British agreed not to support the Indian nations, who wished to prevent U.S. occupation of the forts and towns in the Ohio and Great Lakes region.

In the Southeast, the Creek Confederacy, especially the towns in present-day Alabama, allied itself to the Spanish colony in Florida and hoped to resist U.S. territorial expansion. A segment of the Cherokee Nation called the Chickamauga also waged a war of resistance against encroaching settlements and began to migrate west of the Mississippi River during the 1790s. As long as the Chickamauga and Creek had military support from the Spanish, they had access to military supplies that enabled them to resist U.S. efforts to occupy their territory. In 1795, however, the Spanish government turned its attention to the wars in Europe and decided to limit investment in Florida Colony. Like their northern Indian neighbors, the southern Indian nations were forced to sign treaties after 1795 that recognized the United States as the predominant power in the region.

Migration was selected by several Native American societies as a means of preserving their autonomy against U.S. aggression. Following the Revolutionary War, many Iroquois people decided to take permanent refuge in British Canada. Many had joined the British cause during the Revolutionary War and after the war the British offered their Iroquois allies a relatively small tract of land in southern Ontario, which constitutes the present-day Iroquois reserve. Other Iroquois who fought with the colonists during the war stayed on to live in New York within their traditional homeland. Nevertheless, because of increasing impoverishment and U.S. land pressures, by 1796, the Iroquois land base was reduced to a handful of small tracts of land. The once influential Iroquois Nation had to reconcile itself to life under the powerful shadow of the United States.

The movement of many Creek Indians into Florida during the late eighteenth century resulted in the formation of a new tribal group called the Seminole. As early as the 1750s, many Creek and Hitchiti Indians migrated into Florida and ceased to communicate with the Creek Nation. The Seminole, discontented with English colonial relations, formed a loose confederacy and created a new nation. Sizable groups of Shawnee, Delaware, Peoria, and Piankashaw sought social and economic security by migrating across the Mississippi River into Missouri and Arkansas country, on lands offered them by Spanish Louisiana. Southeastern Indian emigrants, especially Choctaw, Tunica, Biloxi, Apalachee, and Coushatta, began settling parts of Louisiana and east Texas in the 1790s.

Encroachment on Native Americans' territory and disruption of their livelihood escalated significantly in eastern North America by the end of the eighteenth century. Epidemic disease continued to besiege Indian societies at varying rates, and demographic and geographic change became increasingly determined by the expansionist policies of the United States. By 1800 the U.S. government began a policy of assimilating Indians into Christianity and farming culture. It was reasoned that if Indians turned to farming they would no longer need large areas of land to carry on their hunting and fur-trading practices. As farmers, Indians would be more willing to sell land to the United States and also enter into citizenship. Missionaries were hired to teach school, religion, farming, and homemaking to the Indians. Some of these first missions were to the Seneca reservations in western New York.

With the Louisiana Purchase of 1803, however, Native Americans across western North America began to face unprecedented challenges and threats. Early in the nineteenth century, the prospect of U.S. expansion across the continent changed early policies of quick assimilation and later focused on removal and reservations. Strategies of adaptation and resistance tested over the eighteenth century, especially migration and consolidation, would serve many of the Native American groups effectively in future struggles for cultural and political survival.

*Daniel H. Usner Jr.*
*Cornell University*

# ◆ INDIAN GEOGRAPHIC DISTRIBUTION, HABITAT, AND DEMOGRAPHY DURING THE NINETEENTH CENTURY

## Indian America after 1800

Indian America after 1800 was soon to become a place of constantly relocated displaced-persons camps under military surveillance, located primarily for the benefit of non-Indians. Most of the U.S.-Indian treaties negotiated between 1817 and 1849 dealt with tribal removals to the so-called vacant lands in the West. In 1800, most surviving tribes of the Northeast woodlands were already on their way to reservations west of the Mississippi River or to the extreme northern and western regions of the Great Lakes. Removing a large percentage of the estimated 100,000 Indians east of the Mississippi River did not take place all at once, but proceeded in an evolutionary manner that reflected the historical vagaries of the advancing European-American settlement frontier. The Delaware (or Lenni Lenape)

Indians, who led a seasonal hunting, fishing, and gathering life, met William Penn on the Atlantic Coast in the 1680s. In 1800, however, the tribe was tentatively living in Indiana. Some Delaware were already living in Missouri, from which they were moved successively to Arkansas, Texas, Kansas, and finally Oklahoma. Tribes regularly splintered during this period. In the 1840s some Kickapoo moved to Texas, some to Missouri, and some to Kansas. Very few Northeast groups, such as the remnants of the Five (Six) Nation Iroquois of upstate New York and the Chippewa (Ojibwa) of the lower Great Lakes, remained in part of their original tribal homelands. By 1812 Indian title had been lost in much of Ohio, Indiana, and Illinois. By 1840, Michigan, Wisconsin, Iowa, and Minnesota were largely left open to non-Indian exploitation. An 1842 congressional report listed 82,118 Indians on the frontier who had been "removed west by Government."

Most Indians wound up in John C. Calhoun's creation, the so-called Indian Territory, which originally included Nebraska and Kansas. When reduced in size to present-day Oklahoma, it came to possess the greatest number of Indians of any state. After the period of forced dislocations, Indian Territory had nine times as many tribes as before. Indians moving there encountered a variety of land forms that supported different lifestyles. In the east were the Ozark mountains and plateaus; in the southeast were level plains similar to those of Louisiana, Mississippi, and Alabama; and in the rest of the territory were the gradually rising plains from the Central Lowlands west to the Great Plains and the High Plains of the western half of the Oklahoma Panhandle.

The first tribes to be exiled to Oklahoma were the five nations of the Southeast: the Cherokee, Creek, Chickasaw, Choctaw, and Seminole. Their removal has become the symbol of American attitudes toward Indians in general. While the numerous southern coastal tribes had mostly disappeared by 1800, the large and adaptive tribes of the southern piedmont and mountainous areas approached the new century with some confidence. Nevertheless, an 1802 agreement between the new federal government and the state of Georgia would be used by an aggressive frontier culture as the club to force out these five "civilized" tribes by the late 1830s.

At the turn of the nineteenth century in Texas, California, and the Gila and Rio Grande River areas of Arizona and New Mexico, the Spanish continued to interact with quite disparate Indian societies in 1800. The ancient inhabitants of the Southwest had evolved characteristic cities and farm communities, or pueblos. On the outskirts of these stable communities lived the Navajo and the even more nomadic Apache and Comanche peoples. In Texas, the nomadic Plains Indians met the wandering gatherers of the deserts of southern Texas. Relying particularly on Pueblo Indian allies, Spanish officials tried to restrain the nomadic groups. The marauding nomadic tribes had, for their part, found the Spanish and their Indian allies to be unending sources of revenue. The Pueblo Indians paid lip service to Spanish rule and religion, and then did what they pleased.

This was certainly not the case in 1800 for the Indians of California whose lives had long centered on the dependable supply of acorns gathered from groves of oak trees. Starting in 1769, the Spanish were systematically assaulting the peaceful and sedentary California Native peoples along the coast through the founding of church missions and military presidios as far north as the San Francisco area. Friars and soldiers combined to impose a penitentiary-like existence on many California Indians. Some interior tribes moved east to avoid both the mission-induced epidemics and the near-slavery of mission life. In 1800 there were indications that their newly acquired equestrian skills and newly found love of horse meat would energize the interior tribes of California to resist further white aggression. However, the northern California gold strike of 1848 doomed the California Indians within a decade.

North of California, the fishing life of the Indians of the Pacific Northwest (Oregon and Washington) was hardly touched by any European menace in 1800. In 1805 the Lewis and Clark expedition would end Northwest Indian isolation, and by the 1850s survivors of epidemics and wars would already be relegated by the Americans to military supervision on small reservations.

The Lewis and Clark expedition also initiated U.S. claims to the Plains. For several decades before Americans could appear in force, however, Indian life on the Plains would be greatly enriched by European artifacts. With horses acquired from the Spanish borderlands in the Southwest and guns gained from Europeans and Americans through the fur trade, Plains Indians would revel for a full generation as lords of the lands between the Mississippi River and the Rockies. Many Indians, including the Flathead, Kutenai, or Nez Percé, living in the Plateau area between the Rocky Mountains and the California Mountains also participated in this Plains lifestyle. It must be stressed that most of the tribes enjoying this lifestyle were originally immigrants, and some, such as the Dakota and Cheyenne, had fled misery caused ultimately by the westward movement of the Americans. The early nineteenth century for these fugitive groups was simply a period of rest before they would again be uprooted. By the 1870s they would be subjected to American rule, often on reservations quite far from their Plains homelands.

A number of Indians had met very few Europeans by 1800. These were the ill-defined groups, such as the Paiute, who lived in the quite inhospitable Great Basin region. That harsh and stingy environment had long forced them to live the simplest of any Indian tribe as they moved constantly in search of food. Additionally, their lot had worsened by 1800 because Plains, Plateau, and Southwest marauding Indians all raided the Great Basin looking for captives to trade for Spanish and American goods. Nevertheless, in 1800 nobody desired their land, and they would not be elbowed aside by covetous Americans for another half a century.

In summary, Indian America circa 1800 witnessed flourishing Native American lifestyles in the Southeast, the Plains, the Northwest, and the Plateau areas. In the Southwest and the western part of the Northeast, Indian lifestyles were under attack but still so strong that Spanish and American leaders feared their power. In California, however, Indian lifestyles were under heavy assault, and very few Indians could be found east of Ohio.

## Population

The most important reason for the success of the continuing assault on Native America, most scholars agree, was the terrible number of deaths resulting from the introduction of European diseases. In 1837, the Mandan, who were agriculturists of the Missouri River, were dramatically reduced by smallpox from 1,600 to 31. The Blackfeet, Comanche, and Kiowa tribes of the Great Plains also suffered similar disastrous epidemics. Seventy-four percent of 220 Hopi who refused Western medicine in an 1898 smallpox epidemic died. Such high mortality rates have been verified by comparison with various epidemics striking the Amazon Indians in the twentieth century. This disease fueled depopulation, constituting the most important part of the seizure of Indian lands in what has been called the European and American conquest of Native America.

Scholars traditionally estimated that north of the Rio Grande the aboriginal Indian population never exceeded more than one million people. Today some important scholars argue that the population was many times larger than one million. Even so, by 1800 the "widowed"

Indian population seemed close to the older traditional figures. A conservative estimate by the Office of Indian Affairs (1943) projected an 1800 Indian population of around 600,000. Jedediah Morse, who was sent by the federal government on a fact-finding tour of Indian tribes, carefully collected information for his *Report on Indian Affairs* (1822) and estimated the Indian population to be slightly over 471,000, not counting California. The vast dislocation of Indians in the East and Plains, the extraordinary decline of California Indians, and the demoralization among all Indians forcibly relocated, initiated a sharp decline in the Indian population in the nineteenth century.

Many of the northeastern tribes moved west of the Mississippi, and Kansas, as part of the northern half of Indian Territory, was a temporary home for many displaced Eastern Indians. Although the western two-thirds of Kansas belongs to the Great Plains, the many hills and valleys of the eastern third was familiar to these exiles. Some of the most prominent of the nearly thirty tribes to settle there were the Wyandot and Shawnee from Ohio, Miami (with the Wea and Piankashaw) from Indiana, Kaskaskia and Peoria from Illinois, Ottawa and Potawatomi from Michigan, Kickapoo, Sauk, and Fox from Wisconsin, and some Cherokee from Tennessee. In the early 1850s both pro- and anti-slavery factions agreed that these Indians must be pushed out of Kansas and Nebraska. In punishing the Five Civilized Tribes for joining the Confederacy in the American Civil War, the United States acquired land in Oklahoma to relocate Kansas tribes. Some of these Indians (Shawnee, Wyandot, and Ottawa) were fortunate in 1867 in finally being placed in the extreme northeast part of Oklahoma where a scenic beauty combines with fertile soil. On the other hand, the numerous members of the Osage, Kansa, and Ottawa tribes were nearly halved as a result of difficulties suffered under this second Trail of Tears.

California Indian population declined from an estimated 300,000 to approximately 20,000—a decline of 90 percent—between 1770 when the Spanish missions started and 1900. Although the Catholic priests in charge of the California missions were often of good intent, living conditions in the missions caused lethal diseases to flourish. By the end of Mexican occupation (1846–1847), the Native California population was down to around 150,000. The Gold Rush decade quickly added to the death toll in a brutal (even genocidal) fashion as the number of Indians quickly dropped to 50,000.

By 1850 the nation's entire Indian population, according to the U.S. Census, dropped to around 400,000.

By 1900, the U.S. Census estimated a further drop in the Indian population to only 237,000 Indians, not counting those in Alaska. In short, there was a marked decline in the Indian population in the nineteenth century, and the end of the century marked the Indian population's nadir.

## Land Hunger and Racism

Just as disease and relocation accounted for the decline in Indian population, land hunger and racism were the major reasons for mistreatment of Indians. Americans and European immigrants wanted the land that Indians had lived on for millennia. Called the Westward Movement by historians and rationalized by participants as Manifest Destiny, the central thrust of nineteenth-century America was the acquisition of as much land as possible, by any means possible. The federal government revealed an array of techniques for acquiring Indian land: secretly paying and gifting leaders; feting Indian delegates; bringing Indian leaders to Washington, D.C.; establishing stores with liberal credit guaranteeing that Indians would become deeply in debt; dealing with minority chiefs; buying land from groups that did not actually control it; deliberately withholding annuity payments to force negotiations or compliance; allowing non-Indians to squat illegally on Indian land and to harass Indian farmers and cattlemen; permitting whites to acquire individually owned Indian land (allotments) by any method; and—behind every other technique—the use of naked power. In short, Indians may have delayed the inevitable, as Kenekuk did for the Indiana Kickapoo, but in the end they were forced off their land.

Frontier ruffians and entrepreneurs fueled the Jacksonian Indian removal policy. Few tribes were left unaffected by such a harsh policy. Even tribes such as the Wyandot (Huron), which included many white people through marriage, was noted for its long and sincere acceptance of Christianity, and individual land-allotments, and its inclusion of many American citizens, still suffered inequality, impoverishment, and settler depredations in Kansas. Some tribes driven out of Kansas by such mistreatment, such as the Kickapoo, Wea, and Piankashaw, had already undergone similar processes elsewhere.

By 1816, the defeats of Tecumseh, the Shawnee leader, and the Red Stick faction of the Creek Nation in the War of 1812 guaranteed that there would be no permanent Indian barrier to American expansion. American frontier pressures splintered tribes into conflicting factions. Some segments voluntarily moved west. Some entire Indian groups would be forced to move because of battle-hardened Indian enemies who were better equipped militarily. For example, the Chippewa (Ojibwa) continued successfully to push north, west, and south against Indian enemies in the first half of the nineteenth century. More generally, however, tribes were simply trying to get out of the way of lawless American frontiersmen.

Any national or individual guilt over how Indians lost their lands was partially assuaged by the fallacious arguments that Indians had wasteful ideas of land ownership and no concepts of personal property. It was almost universally accepted that Indians must stop roaming over vast territories and settle down on a reasonable number of acres that could be farmed. In fact many Indians did farm and, indeed, Indian farming before allotment was growing at a substantial rate. Such farming generally was carried out on individual plots with tribal recognition of each family's plot of ground. Americans assumed, nevertheless, that Indians had to substitute an individualistic concept of property for their ancient communal concept of ownership. In fact, many Indians, particularly with the passage of time, did possess concepts of personal property. The Yakima and Flathead Indians of the Plateau, for example, had a workable system of individual property in place before the arrival of the forced allotment period.

In any case, the argument that Indians could not understand the European concept of private property was a red herring. Mexico in the 1830s believed in private property in the European sense, but that did not keep America from coveting its Texas and California lands. President James Polk almost took all of Mexico. National and individual land hunger explains in great part the despoliation of Indian lands.

Racism joined with avarice to guarantee that Indians would not be able, in general, to live the lives of frontier farmers. What Chief Justice Taney in the *Dred Scott* decision declared of Blacks was true in practice for Indians: they possessed "no rights which the white man was bound to respect."

The history of many of the Sauk and Fox Indians in Kansas (originally part of the Indian Territory) is typical of Indians pushed out of an area even though they were making efforts to live like typical westerners (see maps of Indian Territory in Oklahoma section of Chapter 3). After the Indians accepted personal allotments of land, speculators defrauded hapless Indians of their property, and many of the successful Indians were coerced into selling and moving to an Indian Territory reservation.

The key legal consideration that forced most Indians to leave Kansas (as well as other states) were the difficulties involved in becoming state citizens. For example, tribal leaders could suddenly face state laws levying huge fines for anyone functioning as the leader of the tribe. President Andrew Jackson, who served as president from 1828 to 1836, knew what he was doing in 1829 when he gave Indians only two options: move west or become subject to the selective and discriminatory enforcement of state laws. Observers knew that Indians believed that no state would place them on an equal footing with U.S. citizens. Georgia, for example, forbade the Cherokee from mining their own gold, and many states refused to allow Indians to testify against non-Indians. As late as 1908, Oklahoma passed a law declaring that all adult Indians were incompetent to legally manage their farms. The federal government, for its part, refused to give treaty-guaranteed protection against exploitation and cheating. Indeed, President Jackson had earlier negotiated several questionable Indian treaties, and his refusal to enforce an 1832 ruling by the U.S. Supreme Court (*Worcester v. Georgia*) ensured Georgian domination over the Cherokee.

Inevitably, the American commissioner would appear to make an offer for land that could not be refused. By every method possible, tribes would be forced to cede—or appear to cede—their lands. Chief Spotted Tail of the Sioux is supposed to have tongue-in-cheeked the quip, "Why does not the Great Father put his red children on wheels, so he can move them as he will?" Indians were not just pushed off one parcel of land; they were forced to relocate on different assigned lands. These reserved lands in time would then be either totally eliminated or taken away piecemeal by new treaties (or by negotiation after 1871), unjust state laws, or individual acts of barbarism. Shortly after the end of the nineteenth century, most of the remaining lands were lost through a process called allotment, in which Indians were forced to live on small parcels of privately owned land. By 1900, most tribes had lost their communal lands, and most Indian people would soon lose the allotted land given them.

By the turn of the twentieth century, the continuing decline of the total Indian population and the continuous loss of most of the valuable Indian lands reinforced the idea that the Indian was disappearing. No one realized that the low point of Indian population figures had been reached and that Indians would multiply dramatically in the twentieth century. Certainly, no such renaissance was possible in land ownership—the Indian land heritage was forever gone, and oftentimes the old lifestyle tied to that land was only a memory among tribal elders. Of the nearly three billion acres of pre-Columbian Indian America, Indians owned only 48 million acres, a great deal of it located on unproductive land, in 1934.

## Representative Case Studies

The Abenaki (Penobscot and Passamaquoddy) of New England are an example of New England tribe members who barely maintained themselves on small parcels of their old land. In 1786 they refused to sign a treaty with Massachusetts, but in 1794 they ceded the state more than one million acres. By 1820, the Abenaki owned only a few thousand acres. By 1850, they were confined to two separate villages. Some were even forced out of villages in Vermont by whites and fled to relatives in Canada. It would be 130 years before the federal government paid them $81.5 million for land taken illegally.

The Miami-speaking Indians are an Eastern tribe, most of whose members were forcibly relocated in the West, although a significant number were allowed to stay on allotted land in Indiana. The Piankashaw, a small Miami-speaking tribe, had begun selling their Indian lands as early as 1804 and had been moved as prisoners of war in 1814 to Missouri. In 1832, the Piankashaw had to cede their lands in Missouri and go to Kansas. The tribe then was moved again to the Indian Territory. Another closely related Miami-speaking group, the Wea, ceded their lands in Indiana in 1820 and 1824. The Wea then moved to Missouri and like the Piankashaw were forced to emigrate to Kansas. Large groups of the Miami left Indiana at various times beginning in the early 1830s. After several treaties failed to convince the remaining Miami to emigrate (infuriating President Jackson), their head chief suddenly announced in 1838 that the last part of the tribe was ready to move. The rapid influx of hostile squatters into Miami areas seems to have been the final motivator. Another chief skillfully procrastinated until rather good terms had been negotiated for the removal of the tribe and for the sale of tribal lands. Families and relatives of the principal chiefs, and most of the mixed-bloods, were exempted from the movement west by the terms of the treaty. Although only the presence of the army insured the movement to Kansas of the less-influential Miami, the 1846 exodus was more humane in general than many such forced migrations. The reluctant Miami were also convinced by the fact that government annuities would now be paid only to Indians in the new western lands. A few years later they were forced to move again, this time to the Oklahoma Indian Territory.

The fate of the Catawbas, a Siouan-speaking tribe of the coastal Carolinas, illustrates how some minuscule Indian groups survived in the southern coastal region. Although in 1763 the British Crown had given them 144,000 fertile acres, by 1800 disease had so decimated the tribe that they could offer no resistance to white encroachment. After South Carolina purchased the 144,000 acres in 1840, a number of Catawbas moved to the Indian Territory. So many Catawbas would not leave the state, or returned after being unpleasantly rejected from North Carolina, that South Carolina started a 630-acre reservation in 1841. That miniature Catawba state lasted until 1962, when a billion-dollar court claim filed by the Catawbas kept the issue of the treatment of Indians in the Jacksonian Era alive.

The 1830s Trail of Tears that involved the Five Tribes of the Southeast is a rather well known example of the personal and communal tragedies that accompanied the many forced deportations of Indians during most of the nineteenth century. By the end of the 1830s, the Southeast had lost 60 to 90 percent of the estimated 150,000 Indians counted at the start of the decade. The history of the Southeastern Indians represents the most thoroughgoing application of the Jacksonian removal policy.

The Cherokee, whose unhappy relocation from Alabama, Georgia, and Tennessee to the West seems to have been the worst migratory experience in American history, saw the first group leave to present-day Arkansas after an 1808 treaty. Another Cherokee land cession and emigration took place between 1817 and 1819. The state of Georgia increasingly insisted that the federal government live up to the Compact of 1802 in which Georgia gave up the territory that became Alabama and Mississippi in return for the federal government's help in extinguishing Indian title to land within the state. At the same time, Andrew Jackson emphasized the "Indian must move west" policy, which had been enunciated in 1824 by President Monroe and accepted by his successor, John Quincy Adams, as the only solution to the Indian situation. Indeed, as early as 1804, at Thomas Jefferson's request, Congress gave the president the power to exchange lands west of the Mississippi River for ceded Indian lands east of the river.

Faced with this long history of antagonism, a small group of Cherokee signed the Treaty of New Echota in 1835, exchanging all Southeast Cherokee lands for land in southeast Oklahoma. Although 15,000 Cherokee signed a petition denouncing the treaty, the U.S. government proceeded to force the Cherokee out. In the summer of 1838, the U.S. Army rounded up and imprisoned in stockades individual Cherokee after burning their homes and crops. In the suddenness of the attack, parents and their children often became separated. Water and food were at a premium in the stockades. Leaving late in the fall, some detachments were delayed as much as six months on the 800-mile journey west. In traveling to their new homes in the winter of 1838–1839, between one-fourth and one-third of the 13,000 reluctant émigrés died. Meeting the survivors in Indian Territory were the "Old Settlers," or the 1808 Cherokee group, recently ejected by whites from their Arkansas homes.

Only about one thousand Cherokee in western North Carolina—most of whom descended from Cherokee who had accepted American citizenship and 640 acres of land in the 1819 treaty—were not forced west by General Winfield Scott. Along with some who escaped detection and some who returned over the years, this 1819 group became the present Eastern Cherokee of the Great Smoky Mountains.

All the other Southeast tribes suffered similar fates. The Choctaw Nation of southern Mississippi and Alabama was the first to go west, leaving over three years (1831–1834) in parties of 500 to 1,000. Hundreds died from exposure to winter blizzards, cholera epidemics, and lack of necessary supplies. The death rate in the new environment continued to be high for some years.

Two Southeast tribes fought back. In the Creek War of 1836, General Winfield Scott had to capture and shackle the Indian leaders. On the way to Oklahoma, the sinking of a steamboat cost 300 Creek lives. The usual diseases, hunger, and exposure also claimed a large number. Over 20 percent of the 15,000 Creek died within a short period as a result of exposure and the unhealthy conditions in the new homeland. Seminole in Florida fought the Second Seminole War (1835–1842) to protest migration. In the end, however, 90 to 95 percent of the Seminole were removed.

Historians consider the forced migration of the Chickasaw of northern Mississippi and Alabama as the least lethal among the Southeast tribes. The Chickasaw made the best financial arrangements concerning the sale of their ancient lands. Even so, they suffered the usual deprivations and epidemics on the journey. For several years, the Chickasaw lived in tents in immigrant camps. They found that hostile Plains tribes (Kiowa and Comanche) and marauding Shawnee and Kickapoo Indians had made the assigned area nearly uninhabitable for a decade.

Unlike the Five Tribes, the California Indians were often of marked pacifist tendencies. Miwok and Yokut carried on an effective hit-and-run guerrilla war in the 1830s against the Mexicans, but this military expertise was atypical. California Indians were pushed aside early. In addition, Indians in California lacked any legal control of land, for neither Spain nor Mexico acknowledged Indian land ownership. The secularization of the Catholic missions in 1834 benefited the Indians not a whit. When in 1851 and 1852 the Indians' negotiation with the federal government led to treaties promising 7 million acres of reservation lands, the Californians responded so violently that Congress rejected the treaties. Nevertheless, the lands ceded in those rejected treaties were considered valid cessions. One militarily adept tribe, the Hupa, did indeed gain land in their homeland. However, the participants in the 1870s Modoc War in northern California found themselves exiled to Oklahoma. The Yokayo Pomo found a new secure home only because they paid for it out of their own funds. When reservations began to appear in the 1880s in California, the Mission Indians found that their reservations in southern California were practically worthless because of an inadequate water supply. The Ohlone of the San Francisco Bay Area illustrate the severity of Indian decline in California. From a populous group possessing some thirty to forty permanent villages in the years before the Spanish arrival in 1768, the Ohlone could be found only as parts of small multi-Indian nation ghetto-like villages by the 1860s. By 1900 all communal Ohlone life had ceased (for more detail, see the California section of Chapter 3).

Almost all Great Plains Indians had a history different from such people as the Ohlone, who from time immemorial lived in just one fixed locale. In the late seventeenth century the Cheyenne, for example, were a farming people in the northeast and north-central parts of Minnesota. By the 1750s, they had moved (under Sioux pressure) both south to the Minnesota River area and west to the Sheyenne River of North Dakota. By 1780 they were buffalo hunters in South Dakota. At the beginning of the 1800s, they were on the Cheyenne River at the southwestern corner of South Dakota. Under constant pressure from Indian enemies they moved even farther west to the upper branches of the Platte River. There in the Rocky Mountains they became completely involved in the nomadic horse culture. By 1851, the Southern Cheyenne lived on the Arkansas River in southern Colorado and the Northern Cheyenne lived at the headwaters of the Platte and Yellowstone rivers. After the Medicine Lodge Council of 1867, the United States assigned them a reservation in western Oklahoma. A well-publicized desertion in 1878 of some 300 Northern Cheyenne under Dull Knife

and their continuing escape from some thirteen thousand pursuing U.S. troops caused an embarrassed U.S. government to allow the Northern Cheyenne to settle in Montana, while the Southern Cheyenne stayed in Oklahoma (see also the Plains section of Chapter 3).

Like the Plains Indians, the dramatically reduced number of Plateau Indians of western Oregon and Washington, Idaho, and Montana struggled in several wars to save their lands. By the 1850s, however, they began to be placed on reduced portions of their former lands. The Americans, by then, succeeded in building a wall between Indians in the eastern parts of Oregon and Washington and whites in the fertile valleys near the coast. The Cayuse Indians, one prominent Plateau tribe, had first brought on the wrath of the Americans in 1847 by killing a missionary (Marcus Whitman), his wife, and twelve others. A vigilante army wreaked havoc on the Cayuse. A year after the 1855 Walla Walla Treaty council, a general war broke out between most of the Plateau Indians and the United States. In essence, the Indians wanted their lands back, but the Cayuse were unable to keep their Walla Walla Valley and had to move to the Umatilla Reservation. Disease and drink continued to undermine the tribe. When settlers noticed the beautiful grazing land on the Umatilla Reservation, the reservation was reduced in 1886 by about one-fourth.

While relatively few readers may know about the Cayuse and their troubles, many among the reading public know about the 1864 Long Walk of the Navajo, the culmination of a long period of hostility between Navajo and U.S. society. Previously the Navajo had come into constant conflict with Spanish and then Mexican slave catchers. The Americans continued the hostile Hispanic approach when they arrived in the late 1840s. In 1858, the Bonneville Treaty drastically reduced the size of the area that the Navajo considered theirs. In 1860 one thousand Navajo unsuccessfully attacked Fort Defiance, located in the heart of their country. In 1862 General Carleton arrived with a column of troops from California, bringing with him the Californian Indian extermination policy. Carleton ordered Kit Carson and the New Mexico Volunteers to move against the Navajo, and in early 1864 Carleton's scorched earth policy led to the surrender of the Navajo bastion of Canyon de Chelly. The Navajo were walked under duress 800 miles to a forty-square-mile reserve at Fort Sumner (Bosque Redondo), New Mexico. Ten percent of 2,500 Navajo died in a March 1864 convoy to Fort Sumner. Whites enslaved stragglers and captured their livestock. Absolutely no mercy was shown the trekking Navajo.

Plains social dance, 1893. (Photo by J.A. Anderson. Courtesy of South Dakota State Historical Society)

Some 9,000 Navajo (and 500 Mescalero Apache) herders and hunters were to be made into farmers. At Fort Sumner crops failed because of lack of water, alkaline soil, and hordes of grasshoppers. Available wood was five to eighteen miles away; the local Comanche Indians were hostile; and inadequate government financial support led to starvation and suffering. Conditions were so bad that the Santa Fe, New Mexico newspaper publicized the fort's more inhumane shortcomings. For such reasons, the government in 1868 allowed the Navajo to return to a portion (10 percent) of the hills and mesa of their old homeland. Ten years later, more land was added to the reservation, the first of many additions made to a tribe whose population began to rise dramatically. While the Navajo were quite pleased with these additions, the neighboring Hopi reservation saw with chagrin that they had become completely surrounded by the Navajo and their herds.

Besides the Navajo Apache, most of the other Apache of the Southwest were militarily inclined Indians. Their homeland, Apacheria, was the last Indian area to lay down its arms. Because the Apachean-speaking tribes

of the Southwest were not a centralized group, their history is accordingly complex. The Mescalero Apache of southeastern New Mexico, Texas, and the Chihuahua and Coahuila areas of Mexico were placed first on two tiny reservations in Texas. When vigilante Texans vigorously objected, the Apache were moved to safety in Oklahoma. In 1862, some five hundred Mescalero complied with an order to join the Navajo on the Pecos River wasteland at Bosque Redondo. Most soon deserted. A decade later, they were moved to reservations in south central New Mexico near Fort Stanton. For a time, the Jicarilla Apache also lived there. In 1922, Congress finally did for the Mescalero Reservation what Spain never did: it confirmed the Indians' title to their land.

Through administrative indecision, the Jicarilla Apache of northeastern New Mexico were, in 1873, the only New Mexico tribe not living on a reservation. Only in 1887 did the Jicarilla finally get a reservation that annoyed neither Washington, D.C., local New Mexican whites, nor the Jicarilla. Of course, it was still a most wrenching move, since it was a bit west of the historic

Jicarilla home and most of the valuable lands were already owned by non-Indian farmers and ranchers.

The various groups comprising the Western Apache began to receive reservations in 1871 and 1872, although keeping them on the reservations to the east of Phoenix was a constant problem. Discovery of gold in their territory in 1863 began the troubles between the Americans and the Tonto Apache. However, the more northerly White Mountain and Cibecue Apache remained, rather uneasily, at peace.

Particularly hard to keep on any reservation were the Chiricahua Apache of southern New Mexico and Arizona, who lived just west of the Mescalero. The Chiricahua first had run into problems when tough silver and gold miners flooded their country in 1852. For a while, the Chiricahua had a reservation in the extreme southeastern corner of Arizona abutting the international line. Then the American government tried to move them into the quite different environment of the San Carlos Reservation on the Gila River in Arizona, where the Western Apaches were living. Discovery of coal brought intrusive miners, and whites seized water rights on the Gila River. Such difficulties led to more than two decades of war (1860–1886) against the Americans under leaders such as Mangas Coloradas, Cochise, and Geronimo. After a final sixteen-month flight (1885–1886), they were captured and treated as prisoners of war. They were punished by being sent to Florida, then to Alabama, and finally to Oklahoma. Later, in 1913, most surviving Chiricahua chose to go to the Mescalero Reservation rather than become allottees in Oklahoma.

The history of the Yuman (or Quechan) tribe also represents the treatment accorded a hostile military group of the Southwest. In 1884, a reservation (Fort Yuma) of 45,000 acres of land on the California side of the Colorado River was established. As usual, the tract included only a small portion of the territory the tribe had previously controlled, and contained a good portion of land unfit for farming. The reservation was allotted, or divided into individual portions, in 1893. The usual governmental mismanagement, Indian hostility to agricultural pursuits, and white cupidity led to many Indians not receiving the ten-acre allotment, at least not in the valuable irrigable area.

By the 1870s, there were no more places to exile Indians when whites wanted their lands. Some principle for concentrating Indians on smaller areas was needed to augment the reservation policy. As seen in the Yuman case, an old technique could be used to separate the Indians from most of their good land.

Many of the sixty treaties concluded between 1853 and 1857 called for the allotment of tribal lands. In 1887, after eight years of congressional debate, President Grover Cleveland signed the Dawes General Allotment Act into law. The president was given the authority to subdivide communal Indian land into private ownership of individual plots, a practice sometimes referred to in legal language as "fee simple ownership." The traditional plot of a homesteader (160 acres) was given to the head of a family and smaller plots were awarded to others. Acreage was doubled on reservations suited only for grazing. A group could be punished as were the recalcitrant Kickapoo in Indian Territory, who were only assigned eighty acres each. The land so awarded could not be sold for twenty-five years. In general, only some northern Plains and Southwest Indians escaped allotment.

Allotment was supposed to guarantee the assimilation of Indians into the American mainstream. Instead, it led to permanent underclass status as Indian real estate began to shrivel in three ways during the allotment era. Outside pressures and internal weaknesses combined to encourage tribes to lease out communal tribal lands. For example, in the early 1880s seven cattlemen had leases on the Cheyenne and Arapaho Reservation in Oklahoma ranging in size from 140,000 to 570,000 acres. More ominously, unallocated reservation lands were declared surplus and put up for sale to non-Indians. In addition, laws had been passed allowing many Indians to sell their land earlier than the original twenty-five year no-sale period. In 1891 alone, one-seventh (17.4 million acres) of all remaining Indian lands were lost. In 1881, 155 million acres were Indian owned; in 1900, this number dropped to about 78 million. Land ownership figures, however, are misleadingly high. When it was noticed that a large percentage of Indian land was held by women, orphans, children, and incapacitated males, a law was passed in 1891 allowing these groups to lease their allotted land. Thus, quite quickly reservations often had the majority of their acres leased to non-Indians. In the decades after the 1887 allotment law, Indians lost at least two-thirds of all their landholdings. Ninety percent of the acres originally allotted in Oklahoma are no longer owned by Oklahoma Indians.

Originally, intense opposition from the Five Tribes in Indian Territory left them exceptions to the Dawes Act. Nevertheless, between 1897 and 1902 the Dawes Commission forced them to accept allotment, and today Oklahoma has no reservations. Congress began to open up the Indian Territory (Oklahoma) to non-Indian settlers early. In fact, a number of trespassers were already "booming" the rich lands while waiting for the federal government to legalize their squatter actions. In 1889, President Benjamin Harrison opened up nearly two million acres of land in the "Oklahoma District" in central Oklahoma. On 22 April 1889, the army supervised people recklessly seeking homesteads in an area known for its fertility and which in time produced great petroleum wealth. One hundred thousand non-Indians participated in the 5.7-million-acre Cherokee (plus Pawnee and Tonkawa "surplus" land) Outlet Run on 16 September 1893. The model for these nearly instantaneous transfers of land from Indian to individual non-Indian settler was the earlier opening of the rich Iowa farm lands on 1 May 1843 (with a second run in 1845) of what had once been the domain of the Sauk and Fox. Similar Oklahoma "runs" opened up 868,000 acres of Iowa, Sauk and Fox, and Potawatomi-Shawnee lands on 22 September 1891; the 3.5-million-acre Cheyenne-Arapaho areas on 19 April 1892; and the 85,000-acre Kickapoo land in Oklahoma on 23 May 1895. In 1901, the 3.2 million acres of the Kiowa-Comanche and the Wichita-Caddo reservations were opened, and 170,000 persons registered for a drawing of 13,000 quarter-sections.

The imperative to force Indian cession of lands—which lay behind the allotment principle—also led Congress in 1889 to break up the Great Sioux Reservation of North and South Dakota into six smaller reservations: Pine Ridge, Rosebud, Cheyenne River, Standing Rock, Lower Brule, and Crow Creek. In 1851, at Fort Laramie, the Dakota Sioux signed a treaty defining the boundaries of their domain. In 1868, a new Fort Laramie treaty reduced the reservation to give U.S. miners access to Montana's gold. After Custer's defeat in 1876, the Sioux were punished by having the western part of their land, which includes the Black Hills, sliced off the reservation. In 1889, another eleven million acres were lost.

Another large group of Indians who had to accept the same allotment treatment in 1889 was the Chippewa of Minnesota. Through the years, the Chippewa of the Lake Superior region were forced to cede huge areas, including a large section of west central Wisconsin and east central Minnesota in 1837, most of northern Wisconsin in 1842, and the northeastern portion of Minnesota in 1854. Civil War era treaties limited the Chippewa of Minnesota to a number of large reservations where the land was to be allotted. In 1889, six Chippewa reservations had to cede land to the government, which in turn sold the land to non-Indians with the proceeds held in trust for the tribe. The individual Chippewa were given the choice of either accepting allotments on the original reservation or relocating to the White Earth Reservation and taking allotments there.

A similar rapid disappearance of land can be seen in the history of the Comanche, another Plains tribe. The Treaty of the Little Arkansas (1865) allowed these non-Apache Plains nomads to retain 30 million acres. Then, just two years later, in the Medicine Lodge Treaty, the United States bowed to Texan objections by cutting Comanche land back to 3 million acres. By 1901, other cessions had reduced the Comanche tribal estate to 1 percent of the 1865 area.

One Plains tribe landed on its feet, despite land cessions, frequent forced relocations, and allotment. Challenged by both eastern immigrant and Plains tribes, the once-powerful Osage had little ability to resist American pressure. In a series of treaties in 1808, 1818, 1825, and 1870, the Osage watched the ground disappear from under them. In 1872 they had to leave Kansas for Oklahoma, a removal so traumatic that nearly 50 percent of the tribe died between 1877 and 1884. Then it was discovered that the bluestem grass covering their new acres provided excellent grazing, and that the ground below contained oil. Just as important, Osage intransigence allowed them to reserve all mineral rights for the tribe as a whole, and this communal factor protected a great deal of the wealth flowing in. In forty years, the Osage received about $300 million in royalties. Finally, they were able to acquire individually 658 acres of land because they won the right to allot all their lands to the tribe. There was no Sooner-type or open run land grab.

It should be noted, also, that one large group of Indians neither was moved nor suffered a large amount of land loss. Possessing a relatively secure niche in Spanish New Mexican colonial society, the Pueblo Indians were divided into the Eastern Pueblo along the Rio Grande in New Mexico, and the Western Pueblo in western New Mexico and northeastern Arizona. A liberal interpretation by the Spanish governor of an 1812 Spanish constitution allowed the Pueblo by the late 1820s full citizenship and legal equality. In addition, the Pueblo Indian population not only stabilized, but also was steadily increasing. On the other hand, during the short-lived period of Mexican rule, the Pueblos received a great deal less protection from rapacious neighbors than they had been able to wring from Spanish officialdom. The later violent history of Indians in Mexico centered on the Mexican policy (particularly after 1857) of breaking up corporate Indian land holdings and placing land tenure on a completely individual basis. Fortunately for the Pueblo Indians in the

Omaha dance. (Courtesy of the South Dakota State Historical Society)

territory newly acquired by the Americans after the Treaty of Guadalupe Hidalgo in 1848, Congress confirmed thirty-five Spanish grants to the Pueblo, totaling 700,000 acres. This enlightened Indian land-ownership policy compares radically to the governmental philosophy in California and Texas after the Mexicans were ejected. Greedy settlers, of course, began to move in on much of the choice irrigable land. Since the Pueblos are not a single entity, their autonomous villages often lacked the funds and leadership to oppose interlopers on their lands. Only in 1924 did Congress assure the Pueblo the right to their prime agricultural land.

For the general history of American Indians, the Osage and Pueblo success stories represent exceptions to the rule. More generally, American Indians were clobbered during the nineteenth century by having most of their communally owned and individually allotted lands taken away, their people reduced by some 40 percent, and their frequent relocations anytime their homelands looked attractive to non-Indians. Understandably, even among the over 50 percent of Indians who were American citizens by 1900, there remained an abhorrence of the American way of life. Even without a land base, the Native American was not Americanized.

*Leroy Eid*
*University of Dayton (Ohio)*

Cheyenne Indians hunting buffalo near the newly laid tracks of the Union Pacific railroad and telegraph lines. (Courtesy of the Utah Historical Society)

## ◆ INDIAN LAND TENURE IN THE TWENTIETH CENTURY

By the beginning of the twentieth century, few tribes and Indian communities continued to hold land tenure as they did at the time of contact and well into the early national period. Most Indian groups and societies once had occupied and claimed territory in common as hunting bands, farming communities, and as larger political entities. The environment was revered and respected, and their utilization of natural resources depended upon need. Land was never treated as a commodity and, although examples of individual holdings existed, the practices of private property exhibited by Western culture were alien to most Indians. Land cessions by treaty and dispossession by other means, including armed force, reduced Indian occupation to reservations, representing fragments of indigenous geography and territoriality. Thus, a new order supplanted the traditional and evolving land institutions, reflected in the policies of the government as administered by the Office (later the Bureau) of Indian Affairs (BIA).

Subsequently, three major federal policies affected the way Indians lived. In the first three decades, Indians were still mostly isolated on reservations. Owing to laws enacted in the nineteenth century and still in force into the 1920s, Indians continued to lose considerable land through the process of allotment, which divided up the tribal estate. During this period, the government was too often more preoccupied with the management of Indian realty than with the sound planning and development of reservation-based economies. Simply keeping maps up to date and maintaining a cadastral office consumed much of their efforts. Yet the Bureau of Indian Affairs, the designated trustee, provided some aid and participated in construction—irrigation systems, for example—to abet subsistent land use.

A later policy, especially after World War II, saw the migration of Indians to urban areas stemming from a federally funded relocation program. In part, this program sought to alleviate economic and environmental conditions on many reservations by reducing the resident number living on the land. Ultimately, more than

75 percent of the Indian population ended up living in either urban settings or in rural areas adjacent to many reservations. The latest major policy came in 1975 with the enactment of the Indian Self-Determination and Education Assistance Act that gave the tribes increased autonomy over the management of their trust lands. This 'government-to-government' policy, which has continued into the twenty-first century, has liberated many tribes from the constraints of federal supervision and given Indians renewed options to pursue different environmental and economic goals. Yet the land tenure structure in place has not basically changed in more than one hundred years.

## The Geography of Reservations

Most Indian reservations and other trust lands for Native Americans (Indians, Aleuts, and Eskimos) are found in the Great Plains and in the West, including Alaska. A smaller number of reservations exist in the eastern United States. The larger land units are occupied by the Lakota, Oglala, and other Sioux tribes in the Dakota states, and by the Navajo, whose reservation in the Southwest is equivalent in area to West Virginia. But in upstate New York remnant lands of the Iroquois exist as trust holdings; and other reservations can be found in the Lake States and in the South. The majority of southern tribes were forcibly relocated in the Trail of Tears during the 1830s and ended up in what is today Oklahoma. In that state the majority of trust lands comprise non-contiguous, scattered parcels in a number of counties; only the Osage hold a single, identifiable reservation.

Reservations, to be sure, represent but a fraction of original tribal territory. For example, the Zuni Reservation in New Mexico comprises nearly 500,000 acres of an original 15,000,000. A few tribes—the Menominee (WI), the Quinault (WA), and the White Mountain Apache (AZ)—hold significant forest reserves. Many reservations contain arable lands but lack sufficient water to develop them and/or capital in order to compete in the marketplace. Fragmentation of individual holdings reduces the economic utilization of much cultivable acreage. Another group of reservations—including the Osage, the Uintah and Ouray, and the Navajo—contain important oil and mineral reserves. The most ubiquitous resource cutting across Indian Country is grazing land, some of which sustains favorable range condition for year-round or seasonal grazing. The vast majority of the acreage, however, is marginal and subject to erosion and loss of browsable vegetation.

As we move into a new century, what has become quite valued is location, specifically selective trust lands that lie within reach of major metropolitan areas. Examples of such sites include those occupied by the Agua Caliente Indians at Palm Springs (CA), located within one hundred miles of Los Angeles, and the Mashantucket Pequot, who occupy a reservation near Ledyard (CT), located within a two- to three-hour drive from New York, Boston, and other urban centers. Such locations have encouraged many tribes to establish casinos which will draw upon this vast urban population. But location alone does not govern the option to open a casino: trust status of the land is primal.

## Land Allotment

Prior to 1900 U.S. policymakers had already come to believe that the reservation system would pacify Indians and thereby stabilize land relations with settlers. As early as 1887 the government implemented policies to assimilate Indians into U.S. society. Part of the assimilation plan involved a major readjustment of Indian land tenure by allotting reservation lands. This land policy not only led to the breakup of tribal lands but also ultimately caused the fragmentation of holdings within reservations. Proponents of land allotment held that the ideal policy was to separate individual Indians from their tribe. They asserted that if Indians were granted private land, or an allotment, which is analogous to a homestead, they would soon become productive yeoman farmers. Thus Congress passed the General Allotment Act of 1887 (known also as the Dawes Act), which authorized the BIA to survey reservation lands in order to lay out individual farms. Under the act, farmer/teachers were assigned to work with Indians during an apprenticeship period. After twenty-five years, Indians would receive a fee title or a deed to their allotments; once obtained, this deed "liberated" an Indian from his trustee. So long as Indian land remained in trust, no property taxes could be assessed. This tax-free status has provided considerable security for individual Indians, although other aspects of allotment have continued to diminish this trust security.

Many Indians, whom BIA officials judged as "competent," received fee title well before the twenty-five-year period. Many of these Indians tended to sell their lands or just abandon them; others leased their allotments, moved to cities, or worked on non-Indian lands within or outside of reservation borders. Still others were forced to live with more prudent relatives or to live on surviving tribal holdings that had not been allotted to individuals. Congress, in amending the Allotment Act in 1906, required that if Indians did not exploit their lands in a manner acceptable to policy, the government could lease their lands. In the early twentieth century, at least 25 percent of allotted lands were so leased; today, that percentage is much greater.

Once the government surveyed and distributed allotted lands among living tribal members—even over their protests—it opened the remaining Indian lands to settlement by non-Indian homesteaders. One of many shortcomings of this policy was that the unborn would not receive an allotment at a later date. Besides locating non-Indians side by side on the land with Indians, opening the reservations encouraged the establishment of towns such as Toppenish on the Yakama Indian Reservation (WA), which contains far more non-Indian than Indian residents. Other towns include Parker on the Colorado River Indian Reservation (AZ), Browning on the Blackfoot Indian Reservation (MT), and, uniquely, Palm Springs, which occupies a checkerboard with the Agua Caliente Indian Reservation (CA). Nearly a half-century later, by 1934, Indians had lost ownership of about 90 million acres through allotment. Moreover, since many Indian allottees left no wills that designated their heirs, this land became subject to state inheritance laws as authorized in various allotment statutes. Thousands of allotments thus became encumbered by multiple joint heirship. Over time, the joint undivided shares have resulted in plots of land much too small to farm profitably and thousands of acres continue to stand idle and unmanaged.

## The New Deal and the Indian Reorganization Act

Land allotment disrupted tribal culture and fragmented reservation lands and resources. In *Red Man's Land/White Man's Law*, the late historian Wilcomb E. Washburn noted that Indians had been "forced to limit their life and their vision to an incomprehensible individual plot of 160 or so acres in a checkerboard of neighbors, hostile and friendly, rich and poor, white and red" (p. 75). In the 1920s, even conservative officials sought to modify what had become a destructive process. In 1934, as part of the New Deal administration, Congress stopped the process of land allotment by creating the Indian Reorganization Act (IRA). The IRA restored some surplus lands to tribal ownership, added some new lands, and authorized tribal restoration of allotted lands by purchase, provided it was fiscally possible. The IRA also encouraged tribal self-government and economic enterprises. New Deal planners contended that what many religious groups and national leaders had believed—that holding land in private property would lead to the acculturation and assimilation of Indians—simply was an untenable idea. In reality, speculative interests in Indian cropland, range, minerals, and timber successfully urged Congress to sustain and even step up the pace of granting title to Indians, because it too often meant the sale or lease of Indian land. Ultimately, many Indians were

dispossessed of their land and became dependent on government social services. Such destruction of tribal institutions could not be entirely reversed and tribal opposition to New Deal measures did not help the cause.

All reform efforts have their proponents and opponents, and New Deal measures for the tribes were no exception. For example, many tribal governments did not support the IRA; of 258 tribal communities at the time only seventy-seven accepted the measure. Many tribes voted against the IRA out of fear that treaties would be annulled. Despite the intent of the IRA, tribal governments did not gain appreciable authority over the expenditure of their funds or over signing leases, for the BIA continued to overrule tribal council decisions. In effect, the IRA allowed some tribal governments to form new constitutions but in the end did not grant them any new or considerable powers. In fact, a criticism then still persisted until into the 1980s: tribal government was nearly autonomous on paper, but in reality, much less in charge than the tribes expected. Public officials and academic scholars alike agreed that the onerous allotment practice had to be reversed but that the government needed to move more slowly and be sensitive to tribal concerns, among them the establishment of conservation programs. A number of such programs enlisted cooperation from other agencies, including the Forest Service and the Soil Conservation Service.

## Termination of Trust Status

Despite the efforts of Commissioner of Indian Affairs John Collier (1933–1945) to make the Indian Reorganization Act work, Congress in the post-World War II era elected to discontinue the trusteeship of Indian tribes. By House Resolution 108 (1953), Indians became subject to the same laws, privileges, and responsibilities of all U.S. citizens. This resolution aimed to end Indian wardship. Under this policy of termination, the U.S. government intended to sever all special legal ties and social service relations with Indian communities. In 1954, Congress terminated the Klamath Indians of southern Oregon; four Paiute bands, and the Uintah and Ouray of Utah; and the Alabama and Coushatta of Texas. Other terminations followed over the next few years, including the Menominee of Wisconsin and numerous rancherias (very small reservations) in central and northern California.

Most tribes affected by this policy could not survive outside the legal protections of trusteeship. The Menominee, terminated despite their appeals and fears of additional taxes, were obliged to sell valuable lakefront property to non-Indians. The former Menominee Reservation became a county under Wisconsin law. The

Menominee struggled to sustain their lumber operations, the tribe's major source of income, but many tribal members became impoverished. Because of their economic plight, the Menominee sought to be reinstated as an Indian nation; they appealed to Congress for restoration of their federal recognition. By the mid-1970s, the Menominee became the first Indian nation to regain federal recognition after termination. Several terminated Indian groups, including the Siletz of Oregon and more than a half-dozen California rancherias, later regained trust status.

## Land Restoration and Claims

At various times, Congress has enacted legislation returning some former "surplus" lands or adding acreage to reservations. Congress has restored some lands subsequent to land claims litigation as with the Havasupai, a recognized tribe, and has restored land subsequent to acknowledging an unrecognized tribe such as the Timbisha. Recognized tribes gain several benefits from services and federal funding, whereas unrecognized Indian communities neither receive these benefits nor hold trust lands. In the case of the Havasupai, whose ancestral home was reduced to a small parcel within the Grand Canyon, the tribe regained land that had become part of national forests and parks; similarly, a small portion of land within Death Valley National Park has been restored to the Timbisha.

During the last quarter of the century, other tribes continued to litigate claims to gain access and exclusive use of sites of Native cultural heritage, notably burial grounds and sacred places. The Yakama in Washington and the Taos and Zuni Pueblos in New Mexico succeeded in regaining limited sacred acreage. When restoration has not transpired, some tribes have turned to the provisions of the American Indian Religious Freedom Act (AIRFA) and the Native American Graves and Repatriation Act (NAGPRA) in order to secure access to land for the exclusive purpose of religious worship. Navajo and Hopi sued the U.S. Forest Service to stop the development of a ski resort located on the slopes of the San Francisco Peaks north of Flagstaff (AZ), arguing that the mountains, as part of a sacred place, should in part be restored to them. The tribes, however, did not convince the court that they made exclusive use of the sacred places. Unfortunately, tribes that have evoked the AIRFA or NAGPRA have not always found these laws supportive of their cause. In 1990 the Havasupai filed suit against the Forest Service, alleging that the agency failed to uphold requirements of an environmental impact statement (EIS) as they sought to determine if the Canyon Uranium Mine located within the Kaibab National Forest (AZ) should be established at a site declared to be sacred but lying outside lands restored to the tribe. The mine location lay near Red Butte, which is believed to be the locus of an "earth navel" through which ancestors climbed to the present world. The record shows that the Forest Service went to great lengths to determine if environmental constraints and religious concerns should prohibit mining operations and found none. Ultimately, the mineral market declined and the mine became inoperative.

Unlike the Havasupai, the Hopi Indians have chosen to enter a partnership with the Kaibab National Forest as a means to have a voice in the preservation of sacred shrines on ancestral lands, some of which were adjudicated by the Indian Claims Commission. The Hopi have established a Cultural Preservation Office that interacts with a tribal liaison officer of the forest.

In recent years, issues and litigation over the preservation of Indian cultural, historic, or sacred places on federal lands have also invoked the First Amendment, especially the Free Exercise Clause. In 1999 Devil's Tower, known as Bear Lodge and perceived as a sacred site by various Sioux tribes, the Crow, and other Indians, was the subject of litigation. The National Park Service (NPS), which administers the tower as a national monument, attempted some accommodation by denying permits for commercially guided climbs during June and asked the public to voluntarily refrain from climbing at that time. June is the month when Indians revere the tower. But the tower is also generally acknowledged to be a popular rock-climbing natural feature. While the court found the voluntary closure permissible, the ban against commercial use was declared unconstitutional. At issue is the comparative rights of (Native) religion versus rock climbing. For the claimant Indians, exclusive access was to be protected by the American Indian Religious Freedom Act (AIRFA), but the court did not contend that the establishment clause denied them a separate religious right. Instead, the court sustained the argument that rock-climbers had an equal right to exercise their outdoor activity. This is but one of several cases in which the Free Exercise Clause, rather than the Establishment Clause, has been the point of law defeating tribes that invoked the AIRFA.

Tribal hopes fell dramatically when land claims litigation did not result in land restoration. In 1946 Congress created the Indian Claims Commission (ICC) so that one tribunal would hear all land claims from Indian tribes. Congress empowered the ICC to establish ground rules and procedures for the research and adjudication of hundreds of tribal claims over wrongful taking of land. It is possible that Congress intended to

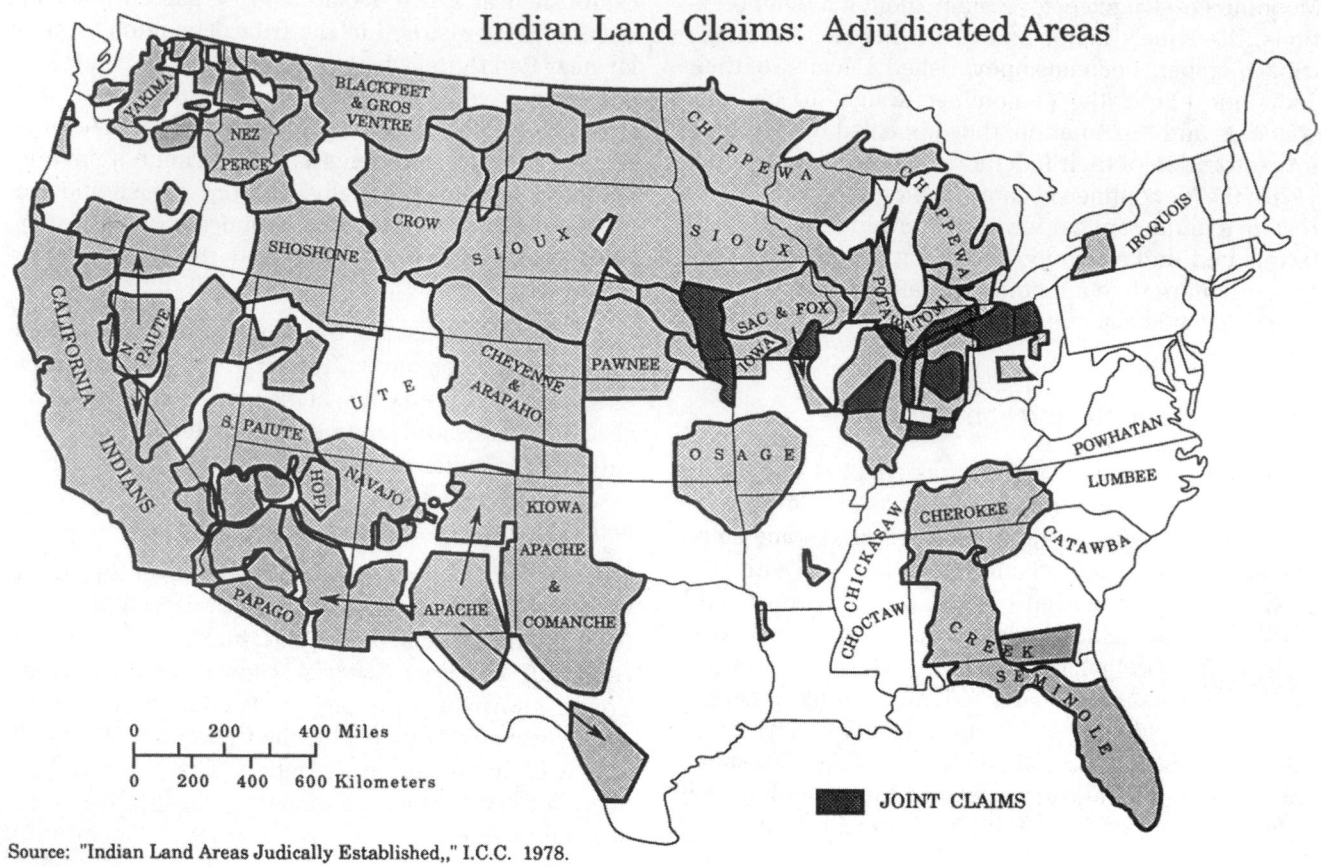

## Indian Land Claims: Adjudicated Areas

JOINT CLAIMS

Source: "Indian Land Areas Judically Established,," I.C.C. 1978.

This map is based on "Indian Land Areas Judicially Established," as published in the *Final Report,* Indian Claims Commission, 1978, and published by permission of the University of New Mexico Press. (Courtesy of Imre Sutton)

retire outstanding claims that clouded title to properties long held by non-Indians. Moreover, the claims process coincided in time with federal sentiments toward selective termination of trust responsibilities. Many tribes expected the ICC to award land, the title to which had passed out of Indian hands primarily in the nineteenth century. Unfortunately, the ICC chose early on to interpret its authority as limited to awarding money, not land. Many tribes, even those accepting money, have been disappointed or angered by this day in court, for the acceptance of a monetary award signaled the final quieting of all aboriginal claims to the territory litigated.

The claims process focused on the geographic extent of aboriginal territory—that is, recognized title lands or those ceded by treaties and original title lands based on historic and ethnographic reconstruction relying, in part, on Indian informants—as the basis for ascertaining the amount of money that tribes would net for their loss of land. Researchers for the plaintiff tribes and for the defendant U.S. government examined the historic documentary record and explored the

ethnographic past. While the tribes hoped for the largest geographic adjudication, the defendant government sought a much reduced acreage figure. The process based monetary awards on the market value of an acre at the time of taking, which was usually much less than $1.

Many Indians openly rejected the judicial process, condemning it as a means to exhaust Indian land claims. The noted legal scholar, Vine Deloria, Jr. (Standing Rock Sioux), observed that many Indians who accepted monetary awards suffered an irrevocable loss of land. Accepting the adjudication was an emotionally painful decision that few Indians made willingly. It meant that the tribes acquiesced in the decisions of the ICC and the courts and readily acknowledged the termination of their aboriginal land rights. This reasoning, in part, explains why the Oglala and Teton Sioux continue to reject an award of more than $100 million for the loss of the Black Hills in South Dakota. As recently as February 2000, the Western Shoshone continued to argue among themselves over the acceptance or rejection of an award of $116 million. It is anticipated that in the near future a resolution may be at hand to distribute this money for the loss of nearly 24 million acres in the heart of the Great Basin. While many tribal members willingly intend to accept the money, others will stand with those few tribes still holding out for land restoration. Although involving much less acreage in northern California forests, the Pit River Indians still refuse their award despite the fact that the bulk of the California Indians accepted a meager monetary award following the adjudication of their claims in the 1960s.

Even though the retirement in 1978 of the ICC presumably signaled the finality of claims litigation, the Federal Claims Court has continued to hear both unresolved cases and new ones. In 1991 the Zuni Indians won a $25 million award for the loss of 15 million acres. Other tribal claims have been resolved by a combination of litigation, negotiation, and congressional involvement. For example, the Catawba of South Carolina argued a claims case before several courts, but ultimately Congress passed a settlement act in 1993 that conveyed a sizable monetary grant which has led to the quieting of ancient titles but makes possible the purchase of land and development of tribal resources. Settlement acts result when Congress steps in to terminate long drawn-out litigation. Other recent acts include the Saddleback Mountain Settlement Act of 1995, which finally resolved a controversy between the city of Scottsdale (AZ) and the Salt River Pima-Maricopa Indians over lands abutting the northern boundary of their reservation. This act provides for joint purchase of land and the preservation of about half of it in a natural state for a public park and recreation grounds. Congress also funded other eastern tribes to help them purchase lands. The Penobscot and Passamaquoddy of Maine, for instance, will ultimately acquire about 300,000 acres of forest lands.

In a different way, some land restoration did take place in the later 1990s. A small group of Western Shoshone—the Timbisha—whose home territory always embraced parts of Death Valley (CA), pursued the restoration of some aboriginal acreage which today lies within Death Valley National Park. The Timbisha, acknowledged as a tribe by the BIA in 1982, and the NPS reached an agreement in 1999 that allows the Timbisha to own and develop 300 acres at Furnace Creek, enjoy exclusive use of an adjacent 1,000 acres, and share in the management of a 300,000 acre expanse of parkland to be known as the Timbisha preservation area. Another 6,000 acres lying outside the park, currently administered by the Bureau of Land Management, will be turned over to the tribe.

Even though few efforts to regain land have been successful, a group of Abenaki of New England holds some expectation of restoration of acreage and/or a financial settlement for a claim against Vermont. The Abenaki claim that their land title was extinguished by Vermont without consent of Congress, yet the Vermont Supreme Court ruled that the "increasing weight of history" supported a view that the longer time passed without federal protection of tribal lands, the assumption would be that the federal government intended to extinguish Indian title. Vermont contends that Abenaki title was extinguished when the Republic of Vermont severed from New York. Had the court acknowledged the Abenaki claim, then Congress would likely pass a settlement act, but perhaps one encumbered by Mohawk claims to lands within Vermont.

## Trust Lands and Economic Options

Today government programs seek to encourage individual and family farming or ranching and small business enterprises, in addition to tribally operated agriculture, ranching, lumbering, and tourism. Many Indians hope that the economic development of their reservations will sustain tribal lifeways, improve Indian income, and minimize interaction and confrontation with non-Indians. With the assistance of the BIA and other field agencies, the Apache, Arapaho, Blackfeet, Navajo, and other Indian nations have developed grazing programs. Many Indians—among them, the Arapaho and Shoshone of Wind River, and the Zuni—manage housing projects for resident families. Generally, such housing occupies tribal lands and if Indians purchase the homes, they hold only land occupancy rights. Several tribes have entered into short- and long-term contracts for lease developments of timber, minerals, and other resources; they have also established various forms of manufacturing in conjunction with the private sector. The White Mountain Apache in Arizona borrowed and repaid funds to develop a lumber industry to harvest pine and Douglas fir on the reservation and have employed more than three hundred Indians. The Blackfeet in Montana have established a pen-and-pencil factory, which employs mostly Indians. Crow Indians in Montana have entered into leases for the exploitation of coal and oil. Many reservations—such as the Yakama, the Acoma Pueblo, and Gila Bend—have established visitor centers, museums, and craft stores, while others, such as the Fort Hall Indian Reservation (ID), operate tribally run gas stations and other commercial ventures.

Because only a small percentage of Indians benefit from economic developments on reservations, many resident families receive welfare support and live at or below the poverty level. Indians are usually reported at the bottom of national income statistics and high unemployment characterizes most reservations. Among

Pit River land claims protests. (Photo by Ilka Hartmann)

the poorest of reservations is Pine Ridge in South Dakota, where, it is estimated, there is nearly 75 percent unemployment. Tribal enterprises such as resort developments—including the one found at Warm Springs Indian Reservation (OR)—as well as lumber operations—such as the business at Menominee, Warm Springs, and White Mountain Apache—have successfully employed a number of Indians on a regular basis. However, Indian enterprises are not immune to general market downturns, and there are inadequate numbers of enterprises on reservations. By and large, enterprises run by tribal governments as corporate entities fare better than those operated by individuals or families on allotments. However, not all tribes choose to invite non-Indian industry or business onto the reservation.

Heirship, as one unfortunate legacy of land allotment, continues to thwart economic growth of countless acres of allotted lands. The severity of the heirship problem is most critical among Sioux tribes in the northern Great Plains, but it persists on many reservations in the West. Some tribes have sought to consolidate encumbered allotments by invoking the Indian

Land Consolidation Act (1983), but this has led to litigation brought by heirs and relatives of deceased allottees, who contend that the escheat provision—whereby a tribe can unilaterally take back allotted lands—is unconstitutional. The act did intend to enable tribes to acquire marginal lands held in undivided interests. But in recent litigation the courts argued that tribal acquisitions under the act constituted a "taking," requiring just compensation; ultimately, the U.S. Supreme Court declared the act unconstitutional.

Certainly, individual Indians and families are entitled to equal protection under the law, yet tribal acquisition of allotments seems an appropriate option—laudable in terms of the better environmental management of reservation resources. Heirship problems so limit land use because too many heirs cannot agree on utilization or cannot be found in order to render appropriate land use decisions. The tribes are deemed the legitimate first claimants of such encumbered acreage. Congress even attempted to revise the act, yet the Supreme Court continued to rule against its constitutionality. Of course, tribes can continue to purchase inherited parcels, making them part of tribal holdings.

Tribal efforts at land consolidation, of course, predicate a more holistic planning concept, which countless tribes invoke.

When land does not directly support tribal members, many of them have turned to employment in administrative and supervisory roles in tribal government. They may work in the administration directly, as elected or appointed officials, or as staff personnel in tribal planning, housing, health services, or more recently in various environmental programs such as archaeology and water management. Some Indians, of course, work for the BIA, and today one finds qualified Indians employed in other field agencies. An increasing number of young Indians have successfully completed high school, and some have attended, if not completed, college. In general, better educated Indians are more likely to work off the reservation and many tribes may be desperate to hold onto their own by creating suitable positions. But few reservation communities have a sufficient number of college-educated Indians who might assume positions demanding professional skills. In response to this fact, the University of Oklahoma established a graduate program in American Indian Natural Resource Management, which is, to date, the nation's sole academic program aimed at educating professional Indians to manage or co-manage tribal resources. There are a number of Native American college programs, but few of them focus attention on indigenous planning and resource management. One exception is the Menominee of Wisconsin, who in 1997 began to develop, implement, and maintain a reservation and county-wide multipurpose land information system and subsequently has developed an advanced computer lab utilizing digitized maps that will enhance local capabilities and also provide on-reservation training. These efforts are part of a larger program of the tribal Sustainable Development Institute.

Reservation economies, in order to succeed, have followed the general trend toward increased mechanization and specialization, and both preclude the need for a large work force but do necessitate the employment of skilled and professional Indians. No better example of this need is the implementation of Geographic Information Systems (GIS), which provide cartographic and other technical data to help assess reservation resource bases and coordinate environmental planning. Until recently, the BIA's branch of natural resources assisted tribes in this endeavor. Tribal leaders and planners are realistic in recognizing that reservation resources are far too limited in order to support all resident members. Aside from some limited high quality farm or ranch lands and notable timber and mineral resources, most reservations offer few long-term economic options. Many Indians, however, do not willingly choose to be farmers and do not care to engage in rural economic enterprises. Some Indians have done reasonably well in ranching, despite the overgrazed status of much of the tribal range.

Another factor that is gradually being selectively overcome is the absence of investment capital and business experience and entrepreneurship. Tenure structure of many reservations encourages non-Indian enterprises, which outweigh Indian enterprises unless the tribe is well-capitalized and takes on the economic venture itself. Consequently, leasing offers a way out for many Indians. In fact, in recent decades 60 percent of irrigated lands and 75 percent of dry-farmed acreage have been leased. While approximately fourteen reservations receive the bulk of the lease income from timber sales, most of the saw-timber cut on reservations in the Pacific Northwest is milled outside the area by non-Indian companies. In 1975 some twenty-two tribes formed the Council of Energy Resource Tribes (CERT), which has since expanded to forty-nine tribes. The CERT members collectively hold about 60 percent of all Indian lands and represent about half of all reservation Indians. CERT has emphasized the prudent development of tribal energy resources and improved tribal managerial skills, and it advises tribes about leasing in order to avoid contracts that return too little. The Blackfeet, Navajo, Osage, and Uintah and Ouray earn substantial income from natural resource sales. The Northern Arapaho and Eastern Shoshone, who share the Wind River Indian Reservation (WY), earn modest incomes from the sale of oil, normally about $75 a month. In spring 2000 they demonstrated that fluctuations in oil prices related to the downturn in production of the OPEC nations led to minor increases in monthly income. For Indians at Wind River, there are potential royalties from 200 oil leases on a reservation that has little else to support its membership; fluctuations in the market can be both a blessing and a curse.

The BIA's administrative control over reservation resources continues to confound many tribes. While individuals and families freely engage in agriculture, ranching, and some forms of commerce, the BIA still supervises leasing for oil and other minerals. This and other inconsistencies in administrative practice rankle the tribes and contribute to skepticism over the purpose of government programs.

## Residence, Mobility, and Relocation

Membership in a tribe is a basic determinant of the right to reside on a reservation. Non-Indian spouses of members and their children usually enjoy most privileges akin to membership. They would sustain an ownership interest in allotted lands, but without the tribal member they may not retain tenure rights to tribal resources or land. At one time the BIA passed on all tribal rules regarding residence as well as membership. Today many tribes determine their own rules and may deny residence on the grounds that someone is less Indian due to intermarriage with a non-Indian. Countless Indians moved away in past generations and today their descendants may not be perceived as sufficiently Indian in culture and association. More critically, however, is a very different demographic fact: on many reservations, non-Indians have come to outnumber Indians living on the reservation. The presence of a large non-Indian population, sometimes the majority, makes it increasingly difficult for Indians to manage their own government and to control their economic institutions. Largely a result of the allotment process that led to the opening of reservations to non-Indians, the Native population on many reservations averages less than 50 percent. On reservations in Arizona, the Dakotas, and New Mexico, Indians generally represent more than 90 percent of the populations, whereas in California, in some Great Lakes states, and in Washington, Indians represent less than 30 percent of the reservation populations. Policy makers once envisioned that the mix of Indian and non-Indian neighbors on reservation lands would hasten the assimilation of the tribes. Nevertheless, recent history demonstrates that simply mixing populations does not dissolve Indian identity and community but does create an unfortunate arena for conflict and litigation.

Motivated by the expectation that Indians would find gainful employment in cities, the BIA also sought an alternative means to enable Indians to assimilate more readily. In the 1950s, the BIA instituted the Voluntary Relocation Program that sought to encourage Indians, especially younger ones, to leave reservations in order to live and work in larger urban centers such as Chicago, Dallas, Denver, Los Angeles, Oklahoma City, and Seattle. Reservation Indians understood that relocation would not normally diminish their tenure rights. Despite financial and social assistance, many Indians have had considerable difficulty securing employment and adjusting to urban life, and often seek out other Indians in a perceived hostile environment. Unfortunately, the longer some Indians remain away from their tribal homeland, their potential return may be hindered by political changes on the reservation, and individuals may suffer from a state of mind known as anomie in which Indians become alienated by being too imbued by non-Indian culture that they can not be readily accepted by tribal members. Simply stated, they no longer fit in.

Although the urbanization of Indians began well before the second World War, only 25 percent of all Indians were urbanized by 1960. According to the 1990 Census, 62 percent of all Indians lived in towns and cities. More than 20,000 Indians live in each of several metropolitan areas such as Los Angeles, Oklahoma City, Phoenix, and Tulsa, and at least 10,000 resided in some dozen smaller urban centers. Unfortunately, the living circumstances of urban Indians mirror those of most reservation Indians: urbanizing Indians too often exchange rural poverty for urban poverty—inadequate housing, unemployment, and discrimination in the city. An unaccountable number of urban Indians remain enrolled tribal members who still retain legal and cultural ties to a tribe. As such, they may occasionally benefit from per capita monetary distributions, such as have occurred with land claims awards and, most recently, owing to gaming income. Even though they live in urban areas, many tribally affiliated Indians continue to own or hold undivided interest in trust land; they may frequently return to reservations to visit relatives, to attend powwows and council meetings, to hunt and fish or generally recreate, and possibly to vote in elections. Non-residence on a reservation has not generally precluded the right to vote in tribal elections. Membership and tenure rights in tribal assets often outweigh on-reservation residence as for those Western Cherokee and Chickasaw who live in California and other states. For example, in election years, candidates from these tribes have campaigned in California. It is to be expected that some Indians would choose to be buried on tribal land. Conversely, reservation residents also frequent nearby towns and cities. They, too, may be visiting relatives, but usually they hold permanent or temporary jobs to which they commute. They also take advantage of nearby local commercial and public services. Many reservation Indian students attend schools in nearby non-Indian communities, while some non-Indian students living on or adjacent to reservations attend reservation schools and colleges. Since tribal Indians more often sustain a legal tie to the tribe and the land, reservation residence is non-obligatory. However, it is also safe to say that many generations of urbanized Indians no longer know of their birthright.

## Self-Determination

As the core concept of a redirected Indian policy, self-determination ideally recognizes tribal sovereignty. Tribal governments, for example, when they face no federal prohibitions, are autonomous within the borders of reservations. Sovereignty applies to the tribe, its membership, and the reservation but not to individual Indians living or even working away from the reservation. The policy of self-determination intends to shift more responsibility to the tribes, but this has not always been translated into a working reality. For example, although empowered by the Clean Water Act, few tribes have yet to assume regulatory authority over water quality standards on reservations. When Congress passed the Indian Self-Determination and Education Assistance Act in 1975, it granted tribes greater negotiating authority to "plan, conduct and administer programs" independent of the BIA but still dependent on federal funding. As early as 1980, 370 tribal communities contracted for millions of dollars of federal services, most often coming from Housing and Urban Development (HUD) and Health and Human Services (HHS). Many tribes now assume fuller responsibility for the management of their funds and for reservation programs such as housing and water development. Provisions of this act have both strengthened tribal government and encouraged tribes to take on functions of taxation, planning, and the regulation of reservation activities. While some tribes have embraced the goals of self-determination, others continue to fear that a show of too much independence or an assertion of inherent sovereignty might lead to the reinstatement of the dreaded termination policies of the 1950s. One example of this independence occurs whenever tribes attempt to tax non-Indian landholdings and enterprises.

Several tribal activities demonstrate how effective self-determination can be when Indians assume responsibilities for their own affairs. The Zuni provide a good example of what is possible under the policy: they wrested control of federal programs such as housing, decentralized authority to the community level, replaced many officials with tribal officers and staff, and even required other BIA personnel to move into the Indian community to foster closer interaction. The tribe, not Washington, D.C., supervises BIA staff. On an even grander scale, the Navajo expanded their functions, and even established a Washington office. Education is crucial to self-determination; many tribes assumed supervision of reservation schools and, following the Navajo lead, established community colleges. Health programs and tribally-run health centers increased. Many tribes quickly learned how to manipulate the federal system in order to achieve their goals and to gain the services they required.

Since the advent of the self-determination policy, several other agencies have assumed or have been assigned aspects of the trust responsibility by the tribes. Among the most notable is the Administration for Native Americans (ANA). This agency has worked closely with CERT, and has provided grant funds for priority projects encouraging economic growth and tribal governance. Since its establishment in 1974, ANA has directly aided such tribal enterprises as the 110-unit Best Western Hotel on the Tulalip Indian Reservation in

Washington. On the Yakama Indian Reservation, ANA helped fund a major wildlife resource management program that enhanced a public hunting program. This tribe markets its own hunting licenses and anticipates a multi-million-dollar revenue in the coming decades. When the ANA came up for renewal in 1991, Gregg Bourland, chair of the Cheyenne River Sioux (SD), expressed his tribe's support in these words: "[The ANA] has consistently increased the ability of many tribes to further their struggle for self-sufficiency... without imposing unnecessary and restrictive policies." Michael Pablo, chair of the Confederated Salish and Kootenai (MT), also spoke in laudatory terms: "The ANA is more than just a model of an effective government agency…. [I]t is also a key player in the renaissance of Indian Self-Determination." Such statements by Indians demonstrate that many tribes have increasingly relied upon support and assistance of a number of agencies exclusive of or in addition to the BIA.

In a different way, self-determination has encouraged tribes to seek out assistance or partnerships with other federal and state agencies. In the past, the U.S. Forest Service assisted in the management of tribal forests and the Soil Conservation Service (now the Natural Resources Conservation Service) established field projects in soil and water conservation. On reservations today, the Bureau of Reclamation assists some tribes with water development projects; and the National Park Service has guided Indian communities in the management of tribal parks. In fact, the NPS has been a supporter of the creation of a Wounded Knee National Tribal Park, which would include areas within both the Pine Ridge and Cheyenne River Indian reservations (SD). The park would be managed by Indians with the assistance of the NPS. Unfortunately, to date Congress has not established this park. The Army Corps of Engineers and the Environmental Protection Agency have also become more supportive of tribal goals. Pursuant to a Secretarial Order in 1997, the Departments of Commerce (National Marine Fisheries Service) and the Interior (Fish and Wildlife Service) have sat down with tribes over the designation of critical habitats that include tribal lands. Despite the wording of the Endangered Species Act (ESA), the government has withdrawn the designation of critical habitats on such reservations as the Nez Percé, Yakama, Umpqua/Siuslaw, Hoopa Valley, and others because of tribal protests that say the ESA unfairly encumbers economic development on reservations.

Off reservation, tribes have been encouraged to interact especially with public land agencies. For example, in the late 1990s the Forest Service, perhaps hoping to create a better image of an agency sensitive to tribal concerns, established the position of tribal liaison to be filled by a person who works with tribes toward the protection of Indian cultural heritage on former tribal lands. As such the Hopi, Havasupai, Yavapai, and other Indian communities have been working in partnership with the agency on the Kaibab National Forest in Arizona. In a similar way, a tribal liaison officer has been interacting with Indians who lay claim to territory that includes the Midewin Tallgrass Prairie, administered by the Forest Service, in Illinois.

In the 1990s, in response to a presidential memorandum on government-to-government relations, the Army Corps of Engineers began to conduct workshops and data-collecting to "assess the scope, extent and quality of Corps-tribal interactions." Long known to be insensitive to the tribes, the corps came to recognize that "a conflict exists between the Corps' multistage execution of its water resource missions and its obligations, as a Federal agency, to honor the commitments made to Federally Recognized Tribes. . . . " To the tribes, corps assistance in the protection of traditional cultural properties relative to provisions of NAGPRA was and continues to be central to their concerns.

It should be emphasized that, in the past, many agencies besides the BIA were often found to be involved in conflicts-of-interest with the tribes. Besides the aforementioned conflicts with agencies that protect wildlife, the Bureau of Reclamation comes to mind because its construction of dams have led to the inundation of tribal lands as in the Missouri River Valley and elsewhere in western watersheds. The Army Corps, of course, also has been identified with negative environmental impacts on tribal lands, not only on the Missouri River, but also on the Allegheny River, a tributary of the Ohio River in Pennsylvania and New York, where Allegheny Seneca have been displaced.

As changing policy follows the mandate for self-determination, tribes perforce remain furtive, not knowing just when new laws and court decisions will undermine the gains made under this policy. To be sure, tribes embrace the greater autonomy but do not want to see the erosion of funding and other benefits. Critics of the policy of self-determination note that the BIA and other agencies still make basic decisions, and the policy, as Philip Deloria (Standing Rock Sioux), a law professor at the University of New Mexico, noted, is a "tactical shift in the fundamental commitment of society to bring Indians into the mainstream, not a movement toward true recognition of permanent rights to exist." Moreover, historian Paul Francis Prucha suggests that Indians' drive for self-determination and sovereignty is contradicted by the "seeds of dependency." More than one critic contends that tribes cannot

have political self-determination without economic self-determination, yet most tribes continue to depend upon federal funds. The American Indian Policy Review Commission, also established in 1975, strongly endorsed tribal sovereignty and self-determination, yet demonstrated that almost all the demands of tribes included the request for federal funds. Policy makers and their critics often seem ambivalent about the role of self-determination: at one extreme it maintains dependence, while at the other extreme it implies independence, which is seen as one step closer to termination of the trust relationship.

## Trust Land as the Locus of Indian Gaming

Because Indian gaming is predicated on the unique land tenure structure that sustains Indian Country, it is germane to consider some of its long-term implications. Since tribes are sovereign and generally immune from state laws, gaming may flourish on trust lands; this is a political, not proprietal, role of the reservation. However, the Indian Gaming Regulation Act of 1988 invites state participation by requiring tribes to uphold state gaming laws. In order to establish a casino, the tribe must enter into a compact or agreement with the state. If estimates are correct, more than one hundred tribes have established casinos on trust lands since the passage of the act.

The development of tribal gaming has not arrived on the scene without controversy. Many states have sought ways to prevent Indian gaming, many have not negotiated in good faith, and others, having once signed agreements, no longer are so supportive of tribal casinos. Casino income has been lucrative; it has filled a critical void in on-reservation employment and funding, and it has become a major political force in some states. Because gambling nets well into the millions of dollars yearly, California gaming bands (equivalent to tribes but smaller in number) invested heavily in an election campaign that saw an initiative placed on the ballot in early 2000 that has led to a major change in the state constitution's provisos governing gambling. Encouraged by this gain, some Indians want to buy land in better locations, hoping to gain trust status for it in order to establish a casino. California casinos have generated so much revenue that gaming bands and tribes that are members of the California Indian Gaming Alliance are distributing funds to non-gaming Indian communities and absorbing nearly all funding that otherwise has come from the federal government. At the other end of the continent, Foxwoods Casino near Ledyard (CT), run by the Mashantucket Pequot, is perhaps the most well known. Indian casinos are found in nearly every state in which there are Indian reservations.

## Indian Country and Tribal Sovereignty

An Indian reservation is property and a political unit. It comprises real estate held by tribes, by their members as tenants-in-common, and by allottees or their heirs. Probably half of all reservations include non-Indian-owned former allotted lands, which constitute a part of reservations even though non-Indians are not part of the on-reservation body politic. Because of the existence of tribal governments, reservations are also political places. It is better to characterize reservations as one political entity in tripartite Indian Country: federal, tribal, and state (or its civil divisions such as cities and counties). While in legal usage, the term *Indian Country* normally applies only to trust lands, in its political/geographical reality, Indian Country also embraces civil divisions such as towns, cities, and counties. All non-Indian land lying within Indian Country predicates the existence of multiple governing units, which form the bases for continued conflicts. Although state laws rarely apply to trust lands or tribal governments, since the 1970s states and local governments have been asserting jurisdiction over environmental and other matters and tribes have resisted this intrusion through litigation. In this regard, for example, the EPA has come to their aid.

Historically, Congress established federal law-and-order jurisdiction on reservations while retaining exclusive authority to enforce the law. At various times, Congress has granted some measure of authority to the states. In 1952, for example, limited criminal and civil authority was transferred to several states: Iowa, Kansas, New York, and North Dakota. The following year, Congress, in Public Law 280, expanded this law-and-order authority onto reservations in California, Nebraska, Minnesota, Oregon, and Wisconsin, and offered other states the option to adopt similar laws. This jurisdiction, which excluded the authority to tax or encumber Indian lands, was misinterpreted and became the vehicle for state intervention into tribal affairs. Congress amended this policy in the Indian Civil Rights Act (1964) so that states could not assume law-and-order jurisdiction without tribal consent, and tribes could seek retrocession of any existing state law-and-order authority. This new legislation did not necessarily curtail state intervention or clear up the confusion over state and tribal jurisdictions.

Tribal assertions of sovereignty or autonomy resurfaced as early as the termination era. By 1968, the American Indian Movement (AIM) was organized and spread across the nation, drawing its membership from both reservation and urban Indians. Litigation and a new spirit of militancy overshadowed the efforts of older Indian advocacy organizations dominated by non-Indian supporters (the Indian Rights Association and the Association on American Indian Affairs). The takeover of Alcatraz Island in northern California in 1969 and the caravan of protesters who marched on Washington, D.C. in the fall of 1972 in the so-called Trail of Broken Treaties contributed to Indian agitation. The confrontation in 1973 between tribal members and local law enforcement and the FBI at Wounded Knee on the Pine Ridge Reservation in South Dakota demonstrated that Indians were increasingly demanding greater autonomy within Indian Country. Resolution of the controversial Native land claims in Alaska finally came about through the passage of the Native Alaska Land Settlement Act in 1971. Indians in the 1970s and since have been demanding that the government fully honor all treaties. Federal funding created the Legal Services Corporation and the Native American Rights Fund (NARF) which, together with other organizations, help to defend Indians and to mount successful lawsuits against non-Indians as well as public agencies (see Chapter 7 on Activism).

Conversely, toward the end of the last century, federal courts were becoming less supportive of tribal sovereignty even as the executive branch championed self-determination. For example, in a case argued by the Devils Lake Sioux, the U.S. Supreme Court decided in favor of a dichotomous jurisdiction on the Fort Totten Indian Reservation (ND). This decision has undermined tribal efforts to establish holistic environmental management. The plaintiff tribe contended that the Court must look at demographics in evaluating the Indian character of the reservation. Despite earlier declines in numbers up to the 1930s, and a commensurate increase in non-Indian numbers, today it is the reverse. However, the Court based its decision on the fact that non-Indian land ownership, concentrated in larger farms on the peripheries of the reservation, had diminished Indian character so that some state jurisdiction applied. As the Court put it, "tribal sovereignty is present where its exercise affects mainly tribal members and not present where its impact falls mainly on nontribal members."

In similar litigation, the Yakama lost holistic jurisdiction over land use where non-Indians formed the majority of owner/operators of lands within reservation borders. On the Yakama Indian Reservation, open and closed areas were designated, the former being mostly non-Indian and thus not subject to tribal authority, the latter constituting an exclusively Indian area. In the late 1990s, the Confederated Salish and Kootenai on the Flathead Indian Reservation (MT) failed to sustain tribal authority despite the provisos in the Clean Water Act that empower tribes to assume regulatory jurisdiction over non-Indians on reservations in terms of setting water standards. The EPA asserted that tribal authority had to fall within the scope of inherent sovereign powers. Such litigation causes tribes much anxiety, for case law points to a direction the courts seem to be taking to diminish tribal authority over non-Indians within reservation borders despite the congressional intent of self-determination.

### Retrospect and Prospect

Logically enough, trust lands have been the locus of experimentation in Indian affairs for the past century. The treatment of tribes as nations and later as self-governing entities, and the treatment of Indians as wards and then later as citizens, reflects efforts to modify the trust relationship. Ambivalently, policy makers have urged tribes to take control of reservation economic affairs and to assert tribal property rights. Some critics feel that the BIA lacks accountability in terms of abetting Indian economic growth and that tribes need grassroots entrepreneurial capital and employers. Moreover, today the tribes are equally concerned with protecting, preserving, and managing their environments according to their traditional beliefs. Lawmakers, administrators, and scholars alike recognize the need for multiple approaches in Indian affairs. Not all tribes are equally ready to go independent. Yet some Indians, such as the Navajo, White Mountain Apache, and Warm Springs are moving toward levels of autonomy that provide them with greater opportunities to pursue their own goals. One failing of policy has been the slow pace of acknowledging dozens of unrecognized Indian communities. They neither hold land in trust, nor benefit from services and funding unless they are among the recognized tribes that are the corpus of trust responsibility.

While more tribal Indians will likely move to cities or otherwise separate themselves from the land, there is some indication that a number of Indians have chosen to return to reservations where they may find employment in the casinos or otherwise receive tribal income. Despite the urbanizing trend, Indian residence on the land will continue to reflect a desire to sustain a way of life and ethnic identity, as well as a territorial link to the past, all of which helps to sustain tribal culture and society.

*Imre Sutton*
*California State University, Fullerton*

## ◆ CANADIAN NATIVE DISTRIBUTION, HABITAT, AND DEMOGRAPHY

### Aboriginal Peoples in Canada

Canada's constitution (Canada Act, 1982) specifies three categories of "aboriginal peoples": Indians, Inuit, and Métis. The term *Indian* is a historical misnomer. Although it is still required in various legal contexts (such as those referring to the Indian Act), the preferred term today is *First Nations*, with its implication of many separate and formerly sovereign entities. In total, aboriginal people today are estimated to form approximately 2.7 percent of Canada's population.

Indians (First Nations) form by far the largest and most diverse of these categories. Upon contact with Europeans, Indian people occupied all but the northernmost reaches of Canada. Great differences in language, culture, and history separate Canadian First Nations, impeding common political action. In all, 610 Indian bands exist as independent legal and administrative units. Land claims and similar issues tend to be negotiated at the local level, often involving tribal councils of neighboring and related bands. At the national level, the Assembly of First Nations acts as the political voice for Canadian Indians. As of 31 May 2000, a total of 666,335 people were legally recognized by the Canadian government as Indians.

The Inuit, once known as the Eskimo (a term that has now almost totally disappeared in Canada), are the aboriginal occupants of the Arctic. They are a distinct people who are culturally and biologically separate from other aboriginal Canadians. They form a much more homogeneous population in Canada than Indian groups, speaking dialects of a single language (Inuktitut) from the Mackenzie River delta in the west near the Alaska border to Labrador in the east on the Atlantic Ocean. They fall under several political jurisdictions, but are united in a national political body, the Inuit Tapirisat of Canada. Unlike Indians, individual Inuit are not registered by the federal government, so population figures are less exact, but estimates state that there are approximately 45,000 Inuit in Canada.

The Métis, unlike the previous two groups, emerged in Canada only in the historic period. They are a product of the unions between male fur traders, most commonly of French-Canadian origin, and Native women, particularly Cree. The resultant population of mixed ancestry forged a common identity on the Canadian Plains during the nineteenth century. Aspirations for a Métis Nation in the Canadian West ended with their suppression by military forces in Saskatchewan in 1885. After this time they were expected to blend in with the dominant population, and the federal government took no administrative responsibility for them. Only in recent years have the Métis reemerged into public consciousness. Despite being recognized as one of the aboriginal peoples of Canada when the constitution was enacted in 1982, it is still not clear how Métis should be defined today or how many people should be considered under this category.

Aboriginal peoples in Canada can be divided into eleven language families, with approximately fifty different languages. Algonkian is by far the largest and most widespread of the language families. Cree and Ojibwa, the two largest Algonkian languages, are spoken by Native people from Alberta to northern Quebec. The other large language family is Athapascan, with many closely related languages, spread across the northwestern portion of the country. Siouan, spoken by several groups on the Plains, and Iroquoian, around the eastern Great Lakes, are other major language families. Inuktitut, the language of the Canadian Inuit, belongs to the Eskimoan family. Six more families, some consisting of a single language, are restricted to the western portion of the country, in British Columbia.

The great majority of the aboriginal languages of Canada, however, are endangered. Colonial policies of suppressing indigenous languages, particularly through the residential school system, resulted in great language loss. In the Aboriginal Peoples Survey of 1991 only 36 percent of Native adults responded that they could carry on a conversation in an aboriginal language. Only three aboriginal languages—Cree, Ojibwa, and Inuktitut—are spoken over large areas today and are considered to have excellent chances of survival. Many aboriginal communities are making determined efforts to halt or reverse the gradual erosion of their languages. Language and cultural programs have been established in many schools, and a substantial percentage of aboriginal children now receive some form of Native language instruction.

### The Algonkians of Eastern Canada

Members of the far-flung Algonkian family occupy a vast area of eastern and central Canada. They include the Ojibwa and their relatives around the western Great Lakes, the Cree of northern Ontario and Quebec, the Innu (formerly known as the Naskapi and Montagnais) of Labrador and adjacent Quebec, and the Mi'kmaq and Maliseet of the Maritime Provinces of the east coast. All have traditional territories in the woodlands and northern forests. The Algonkians of the Plains will be covered in a later section.

The first aboriginal Canadians to come into continuous contact with Europeans were the Beothuk, the occupants of the island of Newfoundland. Their early extinction has left us too little evidence even to be certain that their language belongs to the Algonkian family. These were the original "Red Indians," a term that referred to their fondness for painting the body with red ochre and grease that was later commonly but erroneously applied to other North American First Nations. They were primarily a coastal people, collecting shellfish and hunting both land and sea mammals. Bark-covered canoes allowed them to travel out into the stormy north Atlantic to harpoon seals and collect bird eggs from offshore islands. During the late autumn and winter the Beothuk moved into the interior forests where they constructed long wooden barriers to channel the caribou herds to where the hunters waited with spears or bows and arrows. Enough meat had to be taken and preserved from these hunts to last through the severe winters.

The historic extinction of the Beothuk is one of the tragic chapters in Canada's history. Increasing European settlement along the coastline forced the Beothuk into the interior of the island. Introduced diseases and hostile encounters with the newcomers greatly reduced their population. By the early nineteenth century, they were reduced to a small group, plagued by tuberculosis and malnutrition, living near the center of the island. When Shanawdithit, a Beothuk captive who was the last known survivor, sucumbed to tuberculois in 1829, the Beothuk passed into extinction.

The Mi'kmaq (formerly written Micmac) occupied the east coast of the Canadian mainland, including all three Maritime Provinces (Nova Scotia, New Brunswick, and Prince Edward Island) and Atlantic Quebec. During the early historic period, the search for new sources of furs also led them to settle in southern Newfoundland. The closely related Maliseet were more inland, along the St. John River valley in western New Brunswick.

Like the Beothuk, the Mi'kmaq moved with the seasons between coast and interior. Fish played a major role in their diet, along with shellfish, other seafoods such as lobster, sea birds and their eggs, and seals. Land mammals such as beaver and moose were hunted inland. They carried out this seasonal round with the use of bark-covered canoes along the coast and with snowshoes, sleds, and toboggans (the latter taking its English name directly from the Mi'kmaq) for the deep snow of the interior.

The numerous groups collectively known today as Ojibwa (or Ojibway, or, particularly in the United States, Chippewa) were originally centered on the western Great Lakes area. During the fur trade they expanded rapidly, east as far as Saskatchewan, north into northern Ontario, and south into southern Ontario and such

American states as Michigan and Wisconsin. No collective identity was held across this vast area; they consisted of numerous small independent bands speaking a continuum of mutually intelligible dialects. Numerous separate groups, known in the historic records as Saulteaux, Ottawa, Nipissing, Mississauga, and others, are considered to be Ojibwa, based on a common language and shared traditions.

Ojibwa subsistence was based on an annual round of hunting, fishing, and plant collecting. Sizable populations congregated seasonally at particularly good fishing locales, such as the rapids at Sault Sainte Marie on Lake Superior. The shallow lakes of the area provided wild rice, which was an important part of the diet for many Ojibwa. Maple sugar was prepared from the sweet sap of the maple tree and used as a seasoning for a wide range of foods. Some of the southern groups, in contact with the Iroquoian-speaking Huron, practiced marginal agriculture or traded fish and furs for agricultural produce.

To the north were the Cree, who occupied the northern forests from Alberta to Quebec, along with the Innu (Naskapi and Montagnais) of Labrador and northeastern Quebec. As their environment provided fewer wild plant resources and good fishing locations, the northern groups relied more heavily on hunting. Moose, caribou, bear, and beaver were the major game species. This was a precarious lifestyle, particularly in winter when few resources were available, and winter starvation was an ever-present threat.

Numerous shared features characterize the Algonkian people of the woodlands. Social organization usually took the form of small, highly mobile bands, although southern groups were able to gather seasonally in larger numbers. Societies were essentially egalitarian, although status distinctions developed among some of the larger groups. To meet the needs of a mobile population, housing had to be simple and portable. Birchbark provided the ideal cover, although moose or caribou hide was used in the north. These could be rolled up and carried between camps, then quickly stretched over a framework of poles to form the dome-shaped structure known throughout eastern North America by the Algonkian term *wigwam*. Birchbark also provided lightweight cover for the canoes that were so important to summer travel throughout the region. Snowshoes were essential in winter.

A fundamental part of Algonkian religious belief was respect for the animals they hunted. The hunter's skill alone was not enough; the animal had to offer itself to the hunter. Only through proper ceremonial acts could humans wrest from nature what they needed to survive. Feasts were held after the kill of larger game to celebrate and honor the animal. Particular care had to be taken with the bones, so that the animals would not be offended and avoid the hunters on future occasions. Animal skulls were hung from trees, and special platforms were built to keep the bones out of reach of the camp's dogs. Divination rituals were also practiced to determine the location of the animals or to predict the outcome of the hunt. All the Algonkian groups had shamans, who used their ties to the supernatural world to cure diseases or to foretell the future. A widespread ritual was the shaking tent, where the violent movements of a small shelter announced the arrival of spirit visitors to assist the shaman in such endeavors.

European arrival and the subsequent fur trade caused major changes in Algonkian life. Trade relations may have begun even prior to the earliest recorded contact. When Jacques Cartier first encountered the Mi'kmaq off the east coast in 1534, they were waving furs and hailing the ship, signaling their desire to trade. Iron knives and hatchets, copper kettles, blankets, and other European goods soon replaced many objects of aboriginal manufacture. A French writer in the 1630s noted that the Indians of the St. Lawrence River, the major trade artery of the early historic period, had already forsaken their traditional garb for European clothing, and copper kettles had completely replaced traditional vessels of bark. Establishment of trading posts throughout Algonkian territory further tied Native groups to the fur trade and led many to relocate their villages around the posts. Alcohol was widely used in trade, with devastating effects on many Natives. Diseases also arrived with the traders, causing great loss of Native life. The search for new trapping lands for beaver and other fur-bearers led many Cree and Ojibwa groups to spread north and west; their far-flung distribution today is largely a result of the new opportunities offered by the historic fur trade.

Today the Algonkians are scattered in small reserves across a large part of the country. Hunting, fishing, and trapping are still important activities for many groups, particularly in the north. Environmental degradation, however, poses major problems. Massive hydroelectric projects in northern Quebec and in northern Manitoba have flooded large areas and threaten the Cree way of life. In northwestern Ontario, industrial wastes have resulted in mercury pollution of the waterways, making fish, the mainstay of the Ojibwa economy, unsafe to eat. In Labrador, the Innu maintain that low-level military training flights over their hunting grounds have scattered the caribou and destroyed traditional hunting activities.

Although many Algonkian groups signed historic treaties, no such land surrenders took place in Quebec and Labrador. The Cree and Naskapi of northern Quebec signed the first land claims agreements in modern

Canadian history in the 1970s. Other groups are still pressing for resolution of their claims.

## The Iroquoians of the Eastern Great Lakes

The Iroquoians were part of a large linguistic stock centered on the area around the eastern Great Lakes. At contact, the Canadian Iroquoians consisted of the Huron, Petun, and Neutral in southern Ontario, and the lesser-known St. Lawrence Iroquoians, primarily in southern Quebec. Most in Canada today, however, are Iroquois proper or Six Nations, whose arrival in Canada from upper New York State stems from the tumultuous events of the historic period.

An agricultural economy distinguished the Iroquoian groups from all other aboriginal Canadians. They grew corn, beans, and squash, supplementing this agricultural diet by fishing and hunting. The everyday meal was a thick corn soup, to which pieces of fish, meat, or squash might be added for variety. Tobacco was also grown in their fields; in fact, the Jesuits referred to the Petun as "the Tobacco Nation."

Villages were large collections of longhouses, some containing several thousand individuals. The bark-covered longhouses sheltered multiple families, and could easily be extended in length if populations grew. Raised benches or sleeping platforms ran the length of each side, leaving a central corridor for the cooking fires. Fish and corn, as well as personal belongings, hung from the roof of the house or were kept in covered pits. Many villages were surrounded with palisades of poles twisted into the ground, often in several rows. Exhaustion of nearby soils and firewood supplies meant that villages had to be moved every ten to fifteen years.

The first to be encountered by Europeans were the Iroquoians of the St. Lawrence River. Jacques Cartier sailed up the St. Lawrence in 1535 and wintered near the village of Stadacona (where modern Quebec City now stands). Cartier provides few details on the appearance of Stadacona but has left a fuller account of his brief visit to Hochelaga, a larger village upriver at the location of modern Montreal. Typical of Iroquoian villages, it was situated well back from the river for defensive reasons, requiring a walk through extensive fields of corn. Cartier describes about fifty bark-covered longhouses surrounded by a triple row of palisades, with ladders leading to platforms where defenders could stand during an attack.

The St. Lawrence Iroquoians were also the first casualties in a series of extinctions that were to overtake the northeastern groups early in the historic period. After Cartier's departure, no further historic records exist until the arrival of Samuel de Champlain on the St. Lawrence in 1603. By this time the Stadaconans and Hochelagans had vanished, leaving only Algonkian and Mohawk war parties locked in bitter conflict over control of this vital trade waterway.

The Ontario Iroquoians, consisting of the Huron, Petun, and Neutral, survived into the mid-seventeenth century. The closely related Huron and Petun had coalesced by the early historic period around Georgian Bay, at the eastern end of Lake Huron. The Huron had particularly close ties with the French, who were drawn into this area by a combination of colonial policy, a lucrative fur trade, and missionary zeal. The most important source of information on traditional Huron culture is the voluminous writings of the Jesuits, chronicling their missionizing activities among the Huron from 1634 to 1650. The Neutral were to the south, concentrated around the western end of Lake Ontario. Their rejection of the Jesuits' proselytizing efforts means that details of their traditional culture are less well known.

All three groups were confederacies of separate tribes, linked in a common council. Village affairs were conducted by local councils, one concerned with feasts, ceremonies, and other peaceful pursuits, and another dedicated to matters of war. Councils attempted to reach a consensus, and all present were able to express their views.

Warfare shaped much of Iroquoian life. Prior to the disruptions of the early historic period, it seems to have been primarily motivated by a desire to avenge previous deaths and acquire personal prestige. Later the Iroquoians became embroiled in bitter warfare over access to furs and fur trade routes. Captives and trophies of enemies killed were taken back to their villages. Some captives were tortured and killed, while others were adopted and incorporated into the society. The latter was an important historic method of replacing individuals lost in warfare.

Infectious diseases brought by Europeans greatly weakened the Ontario Iroquoian groups, but it was warfare that destroyed them as distinct political entities. Between 1648 and 1651 the Huron, Petun, and Neutral were overwhelmed by the military force of the League of the Iroquois, particularly the Seneca and Mohawk. Many perished at the hands of the Iroquois, others were driven out of their homelands to form refugee populations and eventually lose their distinct identity, and still others were taken captive and incorporated into Iroquois groups. When the Jesuits abandoned their base among the Huron and fled to Quebec City in 1650, they took with them several hundred Huron survivors. Known as the Huron of Lorette, or more recently as the Nation Huronne Wendat, this

French-speaking community of several thousand people in present-day Quebec is the only recognized vestige of Huron culture in Canada.

The great majority of Iroquoian people in Canada today are Iroquois proper, members of the famed League of the Iroquois, whose homeland was in New York State. From west to east these were the Seneca, Cayuga, Onondaga, Oneida, and Mohawk. Early in the eighteenth century, an additional Iroquoian group, the Tuscarora, joined the league. The term Six Nations is commonly applied to the league members after this time.

The first of the League Iroquois to move into Canada came as a result of the missionizing efforts of the Jesuits. Large numbers of converts to Catholicism, primarily Mohawk, settled along the St. Lawrence River during the late seventeenth century. Eventually these settlements became the modern Mohawk communities of Kahnawake and Kanesatake, near Montreal, and Akwesasne, straddling the international border with portions in Ontario, Quebec, and New York.

The largest wave of Iroquois arrived in Canada after the American Revolution. The Mohawk had been staunch British loyalists, and most of the Iroquois fought on the British side during the war. After the war, they were granted lands in Canada for their loyalty. One group of Mohawk moved to the Bay of Quinte on northern Lake Ontario. A larger group, under the famed Mohawk war leader Joseph Brant, settled along the Grand River in southern Ontario near modern Brantford. The several thousand individuals who arrived with Brant included members of all six Iroquois nations, plus a considerable number of Delaware (an Algonkian-speaking people) and others who had lost their homelands and sought refuge in the league. Each established separate tribal villages along the Grand River. Today this land grant, although greatly reduced in size, is home to the largest Native community in Canada, the Six Nations of the Grand River. Over 20,000 people, in thirteen separate "registry groups" (stemming from the original settlements), are members of this First Nation.

A final arrival came with several hundred Oneida in the 1840s. Loss of their traditional lands and a desire to reunite with other members of the league led to their movement into southern Ontario. Today they are a large community known as the Oneida Nation of the Thames.

The Canadian Iroquois now outnumber those who remain in their American homeland. Three of the four largest First Nations in Canada are Iroquois. The Mohawk predominate, and it is the Mohawk language that has the best chance of survival. Mohawk insistence on controlling their own educational programs, particularly at Kahnawake, helps safeguard the language.

The Iroquois are in a unique situation in Canada. They consider themselves to be a sovereign people, entering Canada as loyal allies. They have rejected the policies of the Canadian government, which treats them as dependents. For many traditionalists, the only valid government structures are the hereditary councils within the League of the Iroquois. This position has led to numerous clashes with the Canadian and U.S. governments.

This tension erupted in violence during the summer of 1990. The flashpoint was at Kanesatake, the Mohawk community at Oka, just west of Montreal. Expansion of a municipal golf course onto lands the Mohawk considered theirs led to resistance. When armed provincial police stormed the Mohawk barricades, the Mohawk responded with armed force. Mohawk from other communities rushed to join the defenders at the Oka barricades, and the people of Kahnawake forcefully closed the bridge that runs through their reserve, cutting off one of the major traffic arteries into Montreal. The Canadian government sent the army into what became a seventy-eight-day military standoff. Although the situation was eventually defused, the underlying issues have not been resolved. It did, however, focus the attention of the Canadian government and people on Native grievances across the country.

## First Nations of the Plains

The environment of the Canadian Plains is the flat, semi-arid grasslands extending across the southern portions of Alberta, Saskatchewan, and Manitoba. Vast herds of bison once roamed across this open land, providing the economic basis for all Plains Natives. Not only did the Plains hunters rely on the bison for meat but also for the hides, which provided shelter and clothing. The stereotyped image of Indians in the public imagination is the Plains bison hunter and warrior, on horseback and clad in buckskin and feathers.

Despite the common image of the warrior on horseback, horses were not always part of Plains culture. Throughout the millennia prior to European contact, Plains people traveled and hunted on foot, using dogs to help carry their goods. Horses arrived with the Spanish and were in common use among the southern Plains tribes by the mid-seventeenth century. It was a century later, however, before they were a significant feature in the lives of the Canadian Plains groups. Once horses were available in considerable numbers they transformed Plains societies, fostering greater mobility, increased trade and warfare, larger social groupings, and more elaborate material culture.

Speakers of Algonkian languages dominated the northern Plains. In the west were the members of the

Assiniboine Indian running a buffalo. Painting by Paul Kane from his travels in the 1840s. (Courtesy of Royal Ontario Museum)

powerful Blackfoot Confederacy, composed of the Siksika (formerly known as Blackfoot), Blood, and Peigan Nations. Their bitter foes throughout much of the historic period were the Plains Cree and Plains Ojibwa, recent arrivals from the woodlands to the east, along with their Assiniboine allies, who were members of the Siouan language family. Finally, a small Athapascan-speaking group, the Sarcee, arrived on the Plains from the north early in the historic period and became part of the Blackfoot Confederacy.

All Plains groups based their lives on the vast herds of bison. With the arrival of the horse, hunters could ride along with the stampeding herd, selecting the animal with care and dispatching it with the bow and arrow. Techniques that had been used for millennia continued throughout the historic period. Communal hunting methods, where large numbers of bison could be taken, include jumps, where bison were driven over a cliff edge, and pounds, where they were driven into a corral or natural trap. Both required considerable preparation, including construction of long drive lines to funnel the animals to the desired location. The cliffs at Head-Smashed-In in southern Alberta, perhaps the most

famous of such sites, were used repeatedly for nearly 6,000 years, most recently by the historic Blackfoot.

Essential to the nomadic lifestyle were the tipi and travois. A cover of sewn bison hides was supported on a framework of poles to form the conical tipi. Flaps at the top helped control smoke from the central fire. An inside liner protected the occupants from drafts. Sleeping robes laid around the walls served as couches during the day. When the camp was set to move, the tipi could be taken down quickly and the cover packed with other possessions on a travois, a framework of poles that was dragged behind the horse.

Warfare was a pervasive part of the culture and provided the major route to prestige for young men. Military excursions ranged from a few individuals setting out to steal horses to large parties of allied groups engaged in full-scale war against traditional enemies. Warrior societies kept order in camp and on the hunt and provided a common bond linking the various bands into larger political organizations.

Religion permeated everyday life. Supernatural power could reside in any unusual object or feature of the landscape. Young people sought supernatural assistance by fasting and praying in secluded locations, hoping for a vision. Medicine bundles, the most important ritual possessions, contained sacred objects, often those indicated through supernatural encounters. Opening the bundle required elaborate ceremonies, as did its transfer to a new owner, each object being reverently displayed while prayers and songs invoked its spiritual power. Important religious events, such as the Sun Dance, brought together large numbers of people to participate in the ceremonies. These tradional religious beliefs have survived the period of historic suppression; ceremonies such as the Sun Dance are again being held and medicine bundles are being repatriated from museums for ritual use.

Introduced diseases and destruction of the bison herds struck at the heart of Plains cultures. Smallpox epidemics swept the Plains at intervals during the eighteenth and nineteenth centuries, taking great tolls on Native life. Wanton slaughter of the bison and opening of the prairies for European agricultural settlement meant disappearance of the herds by the early 1880s.

The Natives of the Plains, with their populations reduced and the bison largely gone, were in no position to resist government offers of assistance in exchange for signing treaties. Between 1871 and 1877, the Canadian Plains tribes ceded by treaty all claims to their lands. The treaties allocated reserves and provided small payments of money and farm equipment. Instructors were sent to the reserves to supervise the transition to farming, which was frequently a failure. Widespread hunger and disease, along with suppression of traditional customs and beliefs, characterized this period.

Refugees from American battles also moved into Canada during this time. The Dakota (also known as the Sioux) arrived in two waves. The first were eastern (Santee) Dakota from Minnesota, fleeing their homeland after a disastrous uprising and defeat in 1862. Initially settling near Fort Garry in southern Manitoba, many followed the declining bison herds west and north. The second arrival involved the western (Teton) Dakota and their famed chief Sitting Bull, seeking sanctuary after their annihilation of George Custer's troops at the Battle of the Little Big Horn. Thousands of Dakota, including Sitting Bull, arrived in Saskatchewan during 1876 and 1877. By this time, however, the bison were nearly gone and the other Plains Natives were being confined to reserves. The Teton were denied land and rations, eventually forcing most to leave. Today the Dakota in Canada are primarily Santee, although one Teton community remains. All were eventually assigned reserves and are administered as Canadian Indians, although without treaty.

Despite miserable living conditions, outbreaks of violence were few. The only exception occurred in 1885 with the Métis resistence under Louis Riel in Saskatchewan (see Riel's biography in "Prominent Native North Americans"). Several groups of Plains Cree and Assiniboine, under chiefs Big Bear and Poundmaker (see their biographies in "Prominent Native North Americans"), took up arms in sympathy, but the members of the Blackfoot Confederacy refused to be drawn into the conflict. The rebellion was short-lived and failed to win any consideration of Native grievances.

Today many reserve communities, particularly in Manitoba and Saskatchewan, lack any real economic base. Movement to the cities is a common response, with Regina and Winnipeg having among the highest percentages of Native residents in the country. In Alberta, oil and gas revenues for some bands and ranching for others have offered higher levels of economic security.

## The Plateau

The high, generally arid Plateau lies between the Rocky Mountains on the east and the Coast Mountains on the west. The environment varies from sagebrush near-desert in the rainshadow of the Coast Mountains to heavily forested mountain slopes on the edge of the Rockies. Only the northern half of the Plateau is in Canada, in southern British Columbia.

Three Native language families can be found in this area. The largest is the interior branch of the Salish family, containing four languages: Lillooet, Thompson, Okanagan, and Shuswap. The Kutenai, in the mountainous southeast of British Columbia, are a linguistic isolate. The Plateau Athapascans consist of the now-extinct Nicola in the central Canadian Plateau and the Chilcotin and several groups of southern Carrier in the north.

The Interior Salish, along with neighboring Athapascans, practiced a way of life based on hunting, fishing, and gathering plant foods, moving with the seasons as resources became available. Salmon played the major role in the economies of most groups, and much of the late summer and fall was spent intercepting the spawning runs. Canyons provided particularly good fishing locations, where masses of fish teemed in the eddies and could be easily scooped out of the water in large dip-nets or could be harpooned or taken in traps. Large numbers of people congregated around such locations, resulting in very high population densities in favored parts of the Plateau, such as the territory of the Thompson and Upper Lillooet. Large quantities of salmon were cut into thin strips and dried in the warm canyon breezes, providing an assured supply of food for the long winter months and a valued trading commodity to groups lacking adequate supplies of this vital resource.

The dominant type of winter dwelling in the Plateau was the semi-subterranean pit house. A log superstructure over a circular pit was covered with bark and earth, providing effective insulation against the cold. Winter villages consisted of a small cluster of pit houses, each sheltering several families. Each of these villages was politically autonomous. A few groups did not use the pit house, instead banking earth and snow against their mat-covered lodges. In the warmer months people dispersed to their fishing, hunting, root-digging, or berry-picking camps, living in simple structures of bark or mats over a framework of poles.

The Kutenai (spelled Ktunaxa by the tribal council), on the mountainous eastern edge of the Plateau, differed considerably from other Plateau groups. They are a distinct people, speaking a unique language. Many of their culture traits resemble those of the Plains, where they were first encountered by European explorers. The Upper Kutenai, higher into the Rockies and closest to the Plains, had the strongest Plains cast to their culture. They hunted big game such as elk, deer, and mountain goats and sheep, and crossed the mountains several times a year to hunt bison on the Plains. Such excursions brought them into conflict with the Blackfoot, requiring the full military organization of Plains warriors. The Lower Kutenai, further down the Kootenay River and along Kootenay Lake, relied on more typical Plateau resources such as deer, ducks, and fish. The Plains-style, bison-hide-covered tipi was the year-round dwelling among the Upper Kutenai, while the Lower Kutenai resided in mat-covered tipis, with elongated mat-covered lodges as winter dwellings. Both groups wore the typical tanned hide clothing of the Plains and Plateau.

Initial contacts with Europeans came with Alexander Mackenzie's travel through Shuswap and Chilcotin lands to the Pacific in 1793 and with Simon Fraser's epic journey down the Fraser River in 1808. Fraser noticed copper kettles and other European goods traded in from the coast among the Plateau Salish. Extensive disruption of Native cultures, however, did not occur until 1858, with the gold rush in the Fraser Canyon. The sudden influx of thousands of gold-seekers resulted in Natives being displaced from their traditional lands. Smallpox and other diseases greatly diminished their numbers. During the 1870s and 1880s, they were assigned small, scattered reserves. The Plateau groups, however, never ceded their land through treaties. Today land claims are among the most contentious issues, along with such other grievances as legal restrictions on Native fisheries.

## The Northwest Coast

Rainforest blankets the rugged Pacific coastline of British Columbia. The mountainous terrain, with its myriad islands, bays, and inlets, provided a bountiful environment for cultures adapted to a maritime way of life. Large dugout cedar canoes once traversed these waterways, providing the only means of transportation along the coast. Villages of cedar-plank houses were nestled in locations sheltered from the winter storms. Coastal culture extended far up the major rivers—the Nass, the Skeena, and the Fraser—so that even groups lacking direct access to salt water shared the coastal lifestyle.

This is by far the most linguistically diverse area of aboriginal Canada. Sixteen mutually unintelligible languages, clustered into five separate language families, are spoken. In the north are the Haida of the Queen Charlotte Islands and the Tsimshian on the mainland, along with the Tlingit, who occupied southeastern Alaska and extended a short distance into Canada. Haida and Tlingit are linguistic isolates, but Tsimshian has three languages—Coast Tsimshian, Nisga'a (Nass River), and Gitksan (Skeena River). To the south are members of the large Wakashan family, divided into northern and southern branches. The northern Wakashans, from north to south, are the Haisla, Heiltsuk, and Kwakwaka'wakw or Kwagiulth (historically known as the "Southern Kwakiutl"). The southern Wakashans, on the west coast of Vancouver Island, are the Nuu-chah-nulth and the closely related Ditidaht (both formerly but erroneously referred to as the "Nootka"). The large Salish family includes the Nuxalk (formerly called the Bella Coola) on the central coast, and the Comox, Sechelt, Squamish, Halkomelem, and Straits languages on the southern coast. Four of these five language families occur only on the Northwest Coast, and all five are unique in Canada to British Columbia.

Everywhere along the coast people relied on the bounty of the sea, beach, and rivers. Salmon was the fundamental resource for almost all groups. Huge quantities were taken by hook and line, nets, traps, and harpoons, with much being dried and stored for winter use. Halibut, cod, and other fish were also important. Herring were valued for the spawn, and eulachon, a small greasy smelt, was rendered down for its oil, providing a sauce to enliven the taste of dried foods. Seals and sea lions were hunted by all groups, although only the Nuu-chah-nulth went out onto the open sea to harpoon whales. Digging clams, prying mussels off the rocks, and collecting other such beach foods were important tasks, as was collecting various plant foods such as berries, shoots, and roots. Effective exploitation of various resources frequently required shifting residence in a seasonal pattern of movement. Important resource locations, such as salmon streams or productive berry patches, were jealously guarded private property. The abundance and security of the food supply supported the densest aboriginal populations in Canada.

The western red cedar provided the basis for the technology of all Northwest Coast groups. The wood's long, straight grain allowed large planks to be split from a cedar log, using wedges of antler or hardwood tapped with a stone hammer. Most of the material culture items, from houses to canoes to storage and cooking boxes, were made of cedar. Architectural styles varied from north to south, but all shared a basic pattern. Massive cedar posts supported huge roof beams and a series of rafters, forming a framework covered with split-cedar planks. These were large structures, meant to shelter a number of related families. Inside support posts could be carved with crest animals, and at the front of the house might stand a number of carved cedar monuments, the famous totem poles of the Northwest Coast. These were primarily heraldic in function, as important chiefs commissioned artists to depict family-owned crest images. Regional art styles differed considerably, and not all groups carved free-standing poles, but all had some tradition of monumental artwork in wood.

While woodworking was a male task, responsibility for weaving fell to the women, who used the bark and roots of the cedar to craft beautiful basketry, matting, and clothing. Most everyday clothing on the coast was woven from strips of cedar bark, pounded until soft and supple. Wide-brimmed woven hats protected both sexes from the sun and rain. Men wrapped cedar-bark blankets around their bodies, often fastening them with a pin at the front. Women wore skirts of shredded cedar bark and blankets or capes. In colder weather fur robes were added. For special occasions, chiefs were wrapped in beautifully woven blankets of mountain goat wool. Most people went barefoot year-round; only the upriver and most northerly groups used footgear. The hide moccasins and tailored hide clothing worn across the rest of aboriginal Canada were poorly suited to the wet conditions of the Northwest Coast.

The primary social unit all along the coast was a group of kin who shared a name and a tradition of descent from a common ancestor. Among the northern groups, membership in this kin group was matrilineal (traced through the mother). Elsewhere on the coast, membership could be claimed through either the male or female lines. These kin groups held ownership to all important resource locations, as well as such intangibles as names, ritual dances, and rights to depict certain crest figures such as ravens or killer whales.

Northwest Coast people placed great emphasis on inherited rank and privileges. Chiefs and nobles held high-ranking names and controlled access to group-owned territories and rights. Management of the group's resources allowed chiefs to accumulate wealth, which could be publicly distributed at feasts and potlatches to enhance their status. High-ranking individuals sought marriage partners of equivalent rank in other social groups, providing an opportunity for political alliance and the transfer of wealth, including names and ceremonial prerogatives. Commoners, who lacked important inherited rights, were essential to provide the labor necessary to accumulate food and wealth. Slaves, obtained through purchase or warfare, performed the most menial tasks.

The major ceremony was the potlatch, which played an essential role in the ranking system. Any change in status required a chief and his kin to invite others to witness their claim. A high-status marriage, birth of an heir, the assumption of an inherited name, or the raising of a totem pole were examples of such occasions. An essential feature of the potlatch was the distribution of large quantities of gifts to all present. Performances of masked dancers also enlivened such events. As much theater as dance, the performances reenacted ancestral encounters with supernatural beings, when important rights were transferred to the human world. Some of the finest examples of Northwest Coast art are the masks, rattles, and other items used in these performances.

Contact with Europeans did not occur until the 1770s. Fleeting contact with several Spanish expeditions preceded the arrival of Captain James Cook among the Nuu-chah-nulth in 1778. These early expeditions set the stage for the period of intensive trade that followed. Vessels from several nations descended on the coast beginning in the mid-1780s in a quest for valuable furs, particularly those of the sea otter. In return the coastal people received metal tools and other European goods, which sparked new heights in potlatching and artistic production. Introduced diseases also arrived with the traders' ships. Destruction of the sea otter stocks brought this period to a close early in the nineteenth century.

The land-based fur trade period soon followed. Hudson's Bay Company trading posts were established at key locations along the coast. Many Native groups resettled around the posts, requiring extensive changes in their economic and social systems. Readily available European goods, such as the Hudson's Bay Company blanket, replaced many items of aboriginal manufacture. Firearms from the traders made inter-tribal warfare more deadly, and alcohol brought social problems and demoralization to many groups. The more settled conditions around the posts also fostered the spread of epidemic diseases, taking great tolls of Native life.

The arrival of settlers led to the establishment of colonial governments, first on Vancouver Island and later on mainland British Columbia. Fourteen colonial treaties were signed with individual Native groups on Vancouver Island between 1850 and 1854, allocating small reserves and payments of money. Reserves were based on traditional use of the land, resulting in each group receiving a number of small scattered locations corresponding to seasonal villages and fishing stations. After British Columbia entered the Canadian confederation in 1871, responsibility for Indian administration shifted to the federal government. The process of establishing numerous small reserves based on traditional use of the land continued, although no further treaties were signed. Native customs were attacked by government agents and missionaries, leading in 1884 to the outlawing of the potlatch through a provision in the Indian Act.

Land claims have continued to be the paramount political concern for the First Nations of British Columbia. The Nisga'a of the north coast were the first to form a tribal council to pursue their claims. Their legal suit against the Canadian government (the Calder case) reached a historic, although inconclusive, decision in the Supreme Court in 1973. Although the judgement was a technical defeat for the Nisga'a, it demonstrated the strength of their legal case and forced the federal government to reconsider its position. The resulting negotiations were prolonged, but an agreement among the Nisga'a, Canada, and British Columbia was finally reached in 1998. This agreement, after ratification by all three parties and the Senate, came into legal effect in 2000. It provides the Nisga'a with lands, financial compensation, and a wide range of self-governing powers. Other bands and tribal councils are now engaged in similar negotiations.

A cultural revival has occurred in recent decades. Northwest Coast art has been recognized as one of the world's great art forms, and a number of artists have achieved national and international acclaim. Dances and ceremonies are continuing or being reestablished in many Native communities. Local councils are taking control of their own educational programs, ensuring that their languages and histories are being taught to their children.

## The Athapascans of the Western Subarctic

Members of the large Athapascan language family occupy much of northwestern North America, from the west side of Hudson Bay to interior Alaska. More than twenty Athapascan languages, including those in Alaska, have been defined for the Subarctic. All are closely related and tend to grade into one another through a series of intermediate dialects. Athapascan languages in the Canadian Subarctic, in rough order of number of speakers today, are: Chipewyan, Carrier, Slavey, Gwich'in, Tutchone, Tahltan, Dogrib, Hare, Beaver, Kaska, Sekani, Han, and Tagish. The latter two hang on the brink of extinction. Many Athapascans, particularly those in the north, refer to themselves collectively as the Dene.

Northern boreal forest covers the land, which is crossed by numerous rivers and dotted with lakes. The region is physiographically diverse, with three broad divisions. In the east is the rocky country of the Canadian Shield. In the center are the Mackenzie Lowlands, sloping gradually to the Mackenzie River Delta. In the west are the mountains and valleys of the Cordillera, extending from the Yukon to central British Columbia.

Caribou and moose were the among the most important game animals for the Athapascan hunters. Bison herds were also available to some of the more southerly groups, and in the Cordillera mountain goats and sheep were hunted. Smaller mammals, especially the snowshoe hare, played an important role in the diet. Great numbers of migratory waterfowl could be taken for brief periods each year, and the lakes and rivers provided whitefish, lake trout, grayling, and other fish. Groups on the western edge of the Subarctic, where rivers flow to the Pacific, had access to bountiful runs of salmon.

Athapascan societies were small and highly mobile, following game across a large area. Snowshoes and sleds or toboggans were essential to winter transportation, while in summer people traveled along the lakes and rivers in bark-covered canoes. Housing differed by region, but most groups used simple hide-covered conical or domed structures. Group size and economy varied with available resources, but throughout the Subarctic population density was low. Groups lacked formal chiefs, but individuals could take leadership roles for specific tasks, such as hunting, trade, or war. The social organization was flexible, and cultures differed with the environment. The Chipewyan and the Tahltan provide good examples of differing local adaptations.

The Chipewyan, the most numerous and widespread of the Subarctic Athapascans, were an "edge-of-the-forest" people, wintering in the northern forest and following the caribou herds far out onto the tundra or barrenlands during the summer. Caribou were taken along their migration routes, often by driving the herds into large circular brush enclosures where they could be more easily killed. The meat was dried for winter use; the hides were made into clothing and lodge covers, and cut into strips for snares, nets, and snowshoe lacings; the antlers and bones were important raw materials for tools, and the sinew was essential for sewing clothing. Fishing also provided a major part of the diet.

In the mountains of the Cordillera to the west are the Tahltan of northwestern British Columbia. The Stikine River provided the salmon runs that formed the basis of their economy, although they also hunted caribou, mountain goats, and other game. Contact with the Tlingit downriver resulted in the adoption of many Northwest Coast traits, such as potlatching and matrilineal clans. Their location allowed the Tahltan to become intermediaries in trade between the Tlingit on the coast and the Athapascans further inland.

The historic fur trade brought major changes to the Western Subarctic. Posts were established on western Hudson Bay as early as 1682, although initially the trade was dominated by the Cree. Access to firearms and other goods gave the Cree an advantage in warfare, causing losses in lives and land among the Chipewyan. To bring the Chipewyan into direct trade, the Hudson's Bay Company constructed Fort Churchill in 1717, after negotiating a peace with the Cree. The Chipewyan did not embrace the fur-trade lifestyle as fully as the Cree had done, but some groups moved further south to get better access to fur-bearing animals, abandoning their northern caribou hunts.

Following the epic travels of Alexander Mackenzie to the mouth of the Mackenzie River in 1789 and to the Pacific in 1793, the North West Company established fur trade posts throughout Athapascan territory, forcing the Hudson's Bay Company to move inland and do likewise. This period of competition ended with the merger of the two companies in 1821. Many Athapascan groups settled around the trading posts, focusing their economies on trapping animals for furs and trading for European goods. Metal tools and European clothing replaced aboriginal counterparts, and firearms and ammunition became essential trade items.

Discovery of gold brought massive cultural disruptions to the Cordilleran Athapascans. The Caribou gold rush, which reached its height in 1862, brought large numbers of gold-seekers into Carrier territory. The 1898 Klondike gold rush profoundly affected the Yukon Athapascans, nearly destroying the Han whose lands were at the center.

Increased non-Indian settlement in the northwest led the Canadian government to negotiate treaties with the Athapascans. Much of the Western Subarctic is covered under large federal treaties, signed between 1899 and 1921. In other areas, modern political efforts have focused on land claims. Recent agreements have been reached with the Athapascans of the Yukon and Mackenzie Delta areas.

Athapascan communities in northern Canada today rely on some combination of trapping, government assistance, and wage labor. Continued encroachment of resource industries and non-Native settlement threatens local trapping and subsistence hunting. Native political organizations, such as the Dene Nation in the Northwest Territories, are fighting for recognition of Native land claims and right to self-determination.

## The Inuit

The Inuit are the aboriginal occupants of the Arctic, the lands lying north of the tree line. The Arctic is physiographically varied, ranging from the rugged mountains and fjords of the eastern islands, to the rocky rolling terrain of the interior barrenlands, to the flat plain of the Mackenzie Delta. Winters are long and extremely cold, with a midwinter period in the northern regions where sunlight is entirely absent. Summers are short and moderate in temperature, with long daylight hours.

Inuktitut, the Inuit language, was spoken across the entire Canadian Arctic. Population density across this vast area was low. Social groups were generally small, although certain seasonal tasks, such as winter sealing among the Central Inuit and whaling among the Mackenzie Delta Inuit, brought together larger numbers. Leadership was informal, with the opinion of the most experienced and respected elder carrying greatest weight.

All groups relied on some combination of hunting land and sea mammals, along with fishing. Caribou were by far the most important of the land mammals, while seals were the vital sea mammals, although walrus and whales were taken by some groups. Caribou were also essential for their hides, taken in fall when they were in best condition and used to make warm winter clothing. Sealskin boots were also essential for wetter conditions. Women's clothing was often more elaborate than men's, with extra space at the back of the coat to carry babies against the mother's skin. Regional differences in clothing style and decoration were evident.

The successful food quest also required strict observation of taboos. One of the most widespread was the belief that products of land and sea must not be mixed. As a result, seal and caribou meat could never be cooked together, and all sewing of caribou skins for winter clothing had to be completed before the people moved to their sealing camps on the sea ice. Shamans held supernatural power, which enabled them to cure the sick, prophesy the future, and locate the game animals.

In the west were the Inuit of the Mackenzie Delta region, who were closely related to Inuit groups in northern Alaska. Whaling was an important part of their economy. The large bowhead whale was hunted on the Beaufort Sea from umiaks (large, hide-covered open boats), and the small beluga whales were hunted in the shallows of the delta from kayaks. This economy allowed the densest concentration of Inuit people in Canada, living in large villages of semi-subterranean driftwood log houses along the delta. Infectious diseases nearly wiped out these people by the end of the nineteenth century, and the population has been replaced in subsequent years by more recent arrivals from Alaska. These people consider themselves distinct from other Canadian Inuit today, referring to themselves as the Inuvialuit.

In the central Arctic are the Copper, Netsilik, Iglulik, and Baffinland Inuit. In the winter most groups moved far out onto the sea ice, hunting seals through their breathing holes in the ice. During this time they lived in dome-shaped snow houses, or igloos, which were lit and heated by blubber lamps made of soapstone. In summer and fall people lived inland, fishing and hunting caribou while living in sealskin tents. The closely related Caribou Inuit occupied the interior barrenlands west of Hudson Bay. Theirs was a specialized way of life, relying almost totally on hunting caribou. Such reliance on a single resource is perilous, and periods of starvation did occur.

In the east were the various Inuit groups of northern Quebec and Labrador. They relied heavily on hunting sea mammals, including walrus and several species of seals and whales. These were harpooned from kayaks or umiaks in summer and from the ice edge in winter. Caribou and fish were also important.

Initial contact between Inuit and Europeans goes back to the Norse settlement of Greenland in the tenth century. The Inuit of the eastern Canadian Arctic were also in at least fleeting contact with the Norse. Shortly after 1500, European fishermen and whalers arrived in the waters off the Labrador coast and undoubtedly encountered Natives. The voyages of Martin Frobisher, beginning in 1576, began a new period of European exploration in the Arctic.

Moravian missionaries were active among the Inuit of Labrador by the 1770s. For the rest of the Canadian Arctic, however, sustained contact did not begin until the whalers arrived in the late nineteenth century. European whalers began to winter over in northern Hudson Bay, while American whalers established a base on the northern Yukon coast. European goods became commonplace, while diseases drastically reduced Inuit populations. The Sadlermiut of Southampton Island in Hudson Bay went extinct, and the Inuit of the Mackenzie Delta were reduced to a small remnant population.

After the collapse of the whaling industry around 1910, European presence was limited to a relatively small number of trading posts, police posts, and mission stations. This lasted until World War II brought large numbers of military personnel into the Arctic. Following the war, the Canadian government took a much more active role in Inuit administration. Schools and medical stations were built, and housing programs were established. The Inuit were encouraged to move out of their hunting camps and relocate in settlements.

The Inuit Tapirisat of Canada is the national political organization formed to promote Inuit culture and identity and to provide a common front on political and economic issues. Four regional branches represent the people of the western Arctic (the Inuvialuit), the central Arctic (Nunavut), northern Quebec (Nunavik), and Labrador. Canadian Inuit also participate in the Inuit Circumpolar Conference, an international organization bringing together Inuit from Greenland, Canada, Alaska, and Russia to strengthen pan-Inuit communication and cultural activities, as well as to provide international cooperation in protecting the Arctic environment.

Land claims have been a major part of modern Inuit political struggles. Settlements were finalized with the Inuit of northern Quebec in 1975 and the Inuvialuit of the western Arctic in 1984. The largest and most complex settlement, however, was the 1993 agreement with the Tungavik Federation of Nunavut, representing most Inuit in what was then the Northwest Territories. In addition to establishing Inuit lands and financial compensation, a major feature of this agreement involved a commitment to partition the Northwest Territories, creating a new self-governing homeland for the Inuit in the eastern portion. This new Canadian territory, known as Nunavut, which translates to "Our Land" in Inuktitut, came into being in 1999. It is the largest jurisdiction in Canada, covering one-fifth of the country's land mass. It is governed by an elected legislative assembly responsible for all residents. However, the Inuit majority (approximately 85 percent of the population) ensures that this will be a primarily Inuit government. Inuktitut, along with English and French, is an official language of the new territory and the primary language of administration.

### The Métis

The Métis, whose name derives from an old French word meaning "mixed," emerged during the historic fur trade as the product of unions between the European male traders and Native women. Racial mixture by itself, however, does not determine a person's social or political identity. The numerous offspring from casual encounters during the early years of contact on Canada's east coast were simply raised as Indians, without a separate social group developing. The term *Métis* is best applied to those who, during the nineteenth century, forged a common identity on the eastern Plains and their descendants.

As the fur trade moved westward from the St. Lawrence River, many French-speaking men followed, establishing stable unions with Cree and Ojibwa women. Kinship ties from such unions provided alliances that facilitated trade. Native wives served as interpreters and performed such skilled tasks as making snowshoes, drying meat, and dressing furs. Male children frequently also became traders, and a distinct group of mixed heritage individuals began to emerge.

To the north, the English and Scottish employees of the Hudson's Bay Company established unions with the surrounding Cree, despite company restrictions on racial mixture. In the early years of contact, such traders usually returned to Britain at the end of their service, leaving their "country-born" offspring at the forts. Only a few high-ranking officers sent their mixed-race sons to be educated in England.

By the mid-eighteenth century, a large mixed-blood population had settled around the Great Lakes. Substantial communities of log cabins emerged at such strategic locations as Sault Sainte Marie. Intermarriages contributed to a common identity, merging the separate elements of their heritage. Depleted fur stocks and increased settlement from the east, however, led many to move westward to the Plains, where the distinctive Métis culture finally emerged.

The Métis heartland was at the confluence of the Red and Assiniboine rivers (modern Winnipeg, Manitoba). There they established themselves as buffalo hunters and provisioners for the North West Company, serving as an essential link in the long trade chain from Montreal to the northwestern posts. Geographic and social isolation, as well as a shared lifestyle, promoted a group identity, although differences still remained between the predominant French-speaking Métis, who were Catholics, and the Protestants of partial English and Scottish descent. Years of bitter confrontation between the two great fur trade companies helped forge the concept of a Métis Nation in the Canadian West.

The Métis lifestyle was threatened when the Hudson's Bay Company granted lands along the Red River for an agricultural colony in 1811. The North West Company, along whose main trade route the new colony lay, fueled the sparks of emerging Métis nationalism. The Métis organized under Cuthbert Grant, and the subsequent clash in 1816, known as the Battle of Seven Oaks, left the colony's governor and twenty settlers dead and forcefully established Métis rights in the area. After merger of the two fur trade companies in 1821 the Métis community at Red River grew rapidly and flourished in virtual isolation for nearly half a century.

The communal bison hunt was crucial to the Métis economy and central to their self-identity. Large parties set out on the hunt in their two-wheeled Red River carts pulled by horses or oxen. Once the herds were located, the bison were killed from horseback. The meat was cut into strips, dried, pounded into coarse powder, mixed with melted fat, and sewn into hide bags. This pemmican was a vital part of the fur trade economy, meant as provisions to the trading posts of the distant northwest. By the 1850s, however, the bison herds were disappearing, forcing the hunters to move further and further afield. Many began to winter out on the Plains, shortly followed by more permanent Métis settlements.

A serious threat to the Métis of the Red River area came with the transfer of Hudson's Bay Company lands to the Canadian government in 1869. Government surveyors began laying out lots without regard to local residents' holdings. Métis resistance was led by Louis Riel. They seized Fort Garry, the center of the Red River settlement, and established a provisional government. Their demands led to the Manitoba Act of 1870, by which Manitoba became a province of Canada. Despite provision for Métis land grants in the act, the new settlers and troops usurped most Métis lands, and their open hostility led the majority of the Manitoba Métis to move west, establishing new communities in Saskatchewan. Despite his election to the Canadian Parliament, Louis Riel was forced into exile and was never able to take his seat.

The Métis communities in Saskatchewan soon faced encroachment from the east. Government failure to deal with Métis claims to the land led to the Northwest Rebellion of 1885. Led again by Louis Riel, along with Gabriel Dumont as military commander, the Métis declared a provisional government at their capital of Batoche. Several groups of Cree and Assiniboine to the west joined in the uprising. The Canadian military eventually overran the Métis at Batoche, and Riel was

Métis hunting buffalo. Painting by Paul Kane from his travels in the 1840s. (Courtesy of Royal Ontario Museum)

hanged at the Saskatchewan capital of Regina for his role in the rebellion.

The defeat at Batoche brought the end of aspirations for a Métis Nation. Some Métis drifted south to Montana, while others moved north into the boreal forest, reaching as far as the Mackenzie River, where they could live by hunting and trapping. Those who remained found themselves largely excluded from the new economic order. As the Métis were expected to disappear, they were ignored by the Canadian government. Sir John A. Macdonald, the prime minister, denied their existence as a people, stating, "If they are Indians, they go with the tribe; if they are half-breeds they are whites." Excluded from reserves and federal programs for Indians, many Métis existed in poverty.

In the 1930s, several prominent Métis leaders emerged, and the Métis Association of Alberta was formed. Political pressure on the Alberta government led to the passage of the Métis Betterment Act in 1938, which set aside lands for Métis settlements. The eight settlements that remain in Alberta, which are home to about 6,000 people, are the only major communal Métis lands in Canada today. In 1990, the province of Alberta transfered title to these lands to the Métis and allowed for limited self-government.

After nearly a century as Canada's forgotten people, the Métis are experiencing a cultural and political awakening. Part of the stimulus came from the 1982 constitutional recognition of the Métis as one of the "aboriginal peoples of Canada," although it is still uncertain what benefits have been obtained and who is entitled to share in them. The Native Council of Canada (now the Congress of Aboriginal Peoples), the national organization for aboriginal peoples not recognized by government, drew little distinction between Métis and non-status Indians. In 1983 the Métis of the Plains withdrew to form the Métis National Council, which has pressed for recognition of their distinct aboriginal identity and rights, including entitlement to a land base. Population estimates vary widely, but even a narrow definition of Métis would include over 100,000 people. The Métis today are primarily in the provinces of Manitoba, Saskatchewan, and Alberta, but substantial numbers are also in western Ontario, northeastern

British Columbia, and the Mackenzie Valley region of the Northwest Territories.

### Early Indian Administration

At confederation, the British North America Act, now known as the Constitution Act of 1867, assigned the federal government responsibility for "Indians and Lands reserved for Indians." This has meant that Indians are treated differently than all other Canadians, who receive most services, such as education, health, and welfare, from the provincial governments. In order to administer its charges, the federal government passed the first Indian Act in 1876. This again isolated Indian people, putting them under different legislation than other Canadians. The act provided government control over all aspects of Indian life, and served as a vehicle of assimilation by legally suppressing such Native ceremonies as the Sun Dance on the Plains and the potlatch on the Pacific coast. Although the act was extensively rewritten in 1951 and prohibitions on Native traditions were dropped, the act remains essentially a nineteenth-century colonial document.

Indian status comes from being registered on a list held by the federal government, which had the power to decide who was an Indian. Decisions were only partially based on race. Enfranchisement, the voluntary or involuntary loss of Indian status, was a peculiar provision of the Indian Act from its inception until 1985. It reflects the initial belief that Indian status was a transitional measure, providing protection only until a certain level of acculturation had occurred. The most infamous example is the provision that took away Indian status from all Indian women who married non-Indian men. As dependent children also lost status, a large population of non-status Indians emerged. The sexist nature of this provision is clear from the fact that Indian males did not lose status when they married non-Indians; instead, their wives became Indians under the Indian Act, regardless of their racial origins. In 1985 an amendment to the Indian Act (Bill C-31) removed the section on enfranchisement. Status now can neither be gained nor lost. People who had been enfranchised, plus their first generation descendants, can now reclaim status, a process that has swelled the number of legally recognized Indians.

Indian reserves were set aside for the "use and benefit" of specific Indian bands, the administrative units recognized by the federal government. The earliest reserves appear to have been established in New France by the Catholic church. Later, reserves were determined through treaties in many areas; in others, such as Quebec and most of British Columbia, reserves were allocated without treaties. The process remains incomplete, as few reserves have been established in the Yukon and Northwest Territories. Title to reserve land is held by the Crown, making the reserves pockets of federal jurisdiction within the provinces. Under the terms of the Indian Act, a band cannot sell or otherwise dispose of reserve lands without surrendering them to the Crown. As reserves are set apart physically and legally, they have served to isolate Indian communities and, at the same time, have helped maintain distinct ethnic identities. Many bands are now moving toward self-government, and federal control of reserve lands is increasingly being challenged.

Responsibility for education of Indian children was initially taken by Catholic religious orders in New France. Later, Protestant churches also became active in Indian education. By the nineteenth century, government policy involved the establishment of church-run residential schools. Such facilities supported government goals of acculturation by removing Indian children from their families, prohibiting their languages, and promoting a Christian Euro-Canadian lifestyle. The federal government continued to use the residential schools to meet their responsibilities for Indian education into the mid-twentieth century.

The Inuit are also considered a federal responsibility, although they are not subject to the provisions of the Indian Act and do not have reserves. Non-status Indians and Métis are not administered by the federal government. They fall under the jurisdiction of the provinces, as do all other Canadians, and receive no benefits or government recognition of Native status.

### Historic Treaties with Canada's First Nations

The earliest treaties between the British government and Indians were the "peace and friendship" treaties on the east coast, signed in the late seventeenth and eighteenth centuries. The British sought to forge alliances with First Nations to gain their assistance in wars with the French. These early treaties did not include purchase or surrender of the land. After the defeat of the French and with increased European settlement, the focus of the treaties shifted to land surrenders. Between about 1780 and 1850, small land conveyance treaties were negotiated with the Indians of what was to become southern Ontario. These treaties varied greatly but often involved only small, one-time payments for land.

In 1850, treaties with the Indians of the upper Great Lakes were negotiated by Commissioner W. B. Robinson. Known as the Robinson-Superior and Robinson-Huron treaties, they involved the surrender of large areas of land in exchange for reserves, lump-sum cash payments, annual payments to each member of the band, and promises of hunting and fishing rights over unoccupied Crown lands. These provided a model for later federal treaties.

The final pre-confederation treaties were negotiated on the Pacific coast between 1850 and 1854. Fourteen small treaties were signed on Vancouver Island, at that time a separate crown colony. In return for surrendering their land, the Indians were confirmed in possession of their village sites, assured that they would be "at liberty to hunt over the unoccupied lands, and to carry on fisheries as formerly," and given small payments.

After confederation, Canada sought to extinguish Native claims in the west, in order to open the land for settlement. The federal "numbered treaties" began in 1871 with Treaty Number 1, affecting the Ojibwa and Cree of southern Manitoba. By the time Treaty Number 7 was signed with the Indians of southern Alberta only six years later, the lands from western Lake Superior to the Rocky Mountains had been covered. Except for a northward addition to Treaty Number 6, treaty-making came to a halt for twenty-two years, until gold and oil discoveries in the north brought about new negotiations. Between Treaty Number 8 in 1899 and Treaty Number 11 in 1921, Native title was extinguished across much of northern Canada, from northern Ontario to the Mackenzie River in the Northwest Territories. Finally, the Williams treaties of 1923, which extinguished Native title to the last unsurrendered lands in southern Ontario, brought treaty-making in Canada to a halt (see the map of Canadian treaties in the Canadian Chronology section of chapter 1).

Only minor differences exist in the terms of the federal treaties. Indians agreed to "cede, release, surrender, and yield up" their rights to the land in exchange for reserves, small cash payments, ammunition, uniforms and medals for the chiefs, small annual payments to each band member, and promises of continued hunting and fishing rights. Lasting benefits have been few. Gifts such as flags and medals were meant to enhance the illusion that these were pacts of friendship, when they were primarily deeds of sale. Not all reserve lands or other benefits promised under treaty were allocated, leading to a number of modern specific claims. Hunting and fishing rights have been eroded by subsequent legislation. The 1982 constitution guarantees protection of existing treaty rights but cannot restore rights lost prior to that time.

### Land Claims and Modern Treaty-Making

Two types of land claims are recognized in government negotiations. Comprehensive claims are those based on aboriginal title, while specific claims are based on breach of lawful obligation. Specific claims frequently involve unfulfilled treaty promises. These include reserve lands which were never allocated or resources, such as cattle, which were never provided. Other specific claims allege mismanagement of Indian lands or assets. Numerous claims of this type have been made in recent years, and a considerable number have been settled.

Comprehensive claims apply to areas where aboriginal title has never been extinguished through treaty or other legal process. Aboriginal title derives from Native ownership of the land prior to European colonization. An important part of the legal argument stems from the Royal Proclamation of 1763. This decree by King George III states that any lands not ceded to the crown are reserved for Indians. Thus, it has been argued, treaties are legally mandatory to extinguish Native title, and any land not ceded by treaty is still Native land. The colonial and dominion practice of signing treaties with Indians clearly indicates some recognition of aboriginal rights to the land. Recent court cases have also clearly specified that aboriginal rights, including claims to the land, are still in effect unless explicitly extinguished through legal means, such as a treaty.

In the 1970s, federal government policy changed to allow recognition of Native land claims. In part this was a response to the legal claim of the Nisga'a of northern British Columbia and the failure of the Supreme Court of Canada to come to a conclusive decision in 1973. The Office of Native Claims was established in Ottawa in 1974 to receive proposals for negotiation and the Nisga'a were the first to present their claim.

Modern treaty-making has occurred primarily in Canada's north, where no historic treaties were signed. The first such settlement, the James Bay Agreement, was reached with the Cree and Inuit of northern Quebec in 1975. This was in response to provincial plans for massive hydroelectric development in the area. In 1978 the agreement was extended to include the Naskapi of northeastern Quebec. Then in 1984 the Inuvialuit of the western Arctic reached an agreement. Also in the Northwest Territories, agreements were signed with the Gwich'in of the lower Mackenzie River (1992) and Sahtu-Dene and Métis of Great Bear Lake (1993). All these settlements extinguished Native claim to the land in exchange for monetary compensation, ownership of some traditional lands, hunting and trapping rights, and control of social programs such as education and health. A tentative agreement with the Dene of the Mackenzie Valley, however, floundered over government insistence on extinguishment of aboriginal rights.

In the Yukon a 1993 agreement was signed with the Council for Yukon Indians, representing fourteen separate First Nations. Under the terms of the Umbrella Final Agreement, Yukon First Nations agree to "cede, release and surrender" their aboriginal claims in exchange for title to certain lands and financial compensation. Separate agreements with individual First Nations, only half of which have been completed as yet, are required to deal with specific issues. The Umbrella Agreement also allows each Yukon First Nation to negotiate separate self-government agreements, removing them from the jurisdiction of the Indian Act and providing them with authority over a wide range of local issues.

The largest of these northern agreements was the 1993 settlement with the Tungavik Federation of Nunavut, representing the Inuit of what was then the eastern portion of the Northwest Territories. The Inuit agreed to "cede, release and surrender" all aboriginal claims to the land in exchange for title to about 350,000 square kilometers, about 10 percent of which includes mineral rights. They retain their right to hunt, fish, and trap throughout their former territories and will have joint control with the federal government over land-use planning and wildlife management. The settlement also provides about $1.15 billion in financial compensation and resource royalty sharing. Integral to the agreement were parallel negotions that culminated in the 1999 splitting of the Northwest Territories to create Nunavut, a new political jurisdiction in which the Inuit majority ensures control of the legislative assembly.

Native groups in other non-treaty areas of Canada, such as Labrador and most of British Columbia, are also pursuing comprehensive claims. In British Columbia this is taking place at the level of individual bands or regional tribal councils. The only completed agreement is with the Nisga'a Tribal Council of the north coast. This 1998 agreement removes the Nisga'a from the jurisdiction of the Indian Act and allows them to establish their own government with authority over a wide range of local issues. Almost 2,000 square kilometers became Nisga'a lands, not Indian reserves, and a substantial financial settlement compensates for traditional lands which were not included. Similar combinations of financial compensation, lands, and self-government powers feature in negotiations currently underway with fifty-one different bands or tribal councils through the British Columbia Treaty Commission process.

Land claims represent one of the major areas of unfinished business between Canadian Natives and government. They are seen by many as a validation of their aboriginal rights and as a mechanism by which economic independence can be achieved. As many aboriginal groups are moving toward their goal of self-government, land claims are seen as vital to ensure an economic base.

## Modern First Nations Populations

First Nations and Inuit populations in Canada are young and rapidly growing (as the Métis are an undefined group, no demographic profile is available). The number of registered First Nations people has more than doubled in the past twenty years. This stems from both a natural rate of growth that is substantially higher than the Canadian average and from changes in the Indian Act (Bill C-31) that allowed additional enrollments. Almost half (48 percent) of the population is under twenty-five years of age, compared to about 34 percent in the Canadian population as a whole. Only 5 percent of the registered Indian population is over sixty-five, compared to about 12 percent in the general population. Ontario has the largest First Nations population, at about 23 percent of the total, followed by British Columbia, Manitoba, and Saskatchewan. Although absolute numbers are lower in the Yukon and Northwest Territories, First Nations people make up the largest percentage of the total population in those jurisdictions.

The registered Indian population is divided into 610 bands, now generally known as First Nations. Almost one-third of this total is in British Columbia, where bands tend to be small. The average band size in Canada is slightly over one thousand people, while in British Coumbia it is only half that number. The small and scattered nature of First Nations populations impedes effective economic development. In many areas, neighboring and related First Nations have formed tribal councils to provide greater political voice and more effective economic programs.

There are about 2,500 reserves in Canada. Most (about two-thirds) are in British Columbia, where the average size is very small. The majority of Canadian reserves are in rural or remote areas. Almost 20 percent of the on-reserve population is characterized as living in remote or "special assess" (no year-round road access) locations. The small, scattered, and isolated nature of most reserves hinders the provision of adequate facilities and any economic self-sufficiency.

Problems of poverty plague many modern reserve communities. Inadequate housing, which is often overcrowded and lacking running water, is a common feature of reserve life, particularly for those in remote locations. Poor economic conditions also affect Native health; despite considerable progress in recent decades, Native life expectancy is still about six years less than the national average.

A major concern for many band councils today is to initiate developments that will provide employment on their reserves. Native businesses, many aided by federal funding, have sprung up on reserves across Canada. Some fortunate bands hold valuable real estate near modern urban centers or have natural resources such as oil and gas on their land. For bands with small isolated reserves and few resources, opportunities for economic development are minimal, and conditions of poverty are widespread.

The search for employment and better economic conditions has led many Native people to relocate to the cities. About 42 percent of registered Canadian Indians now normally reside off-reserve, a figure nearly double that of two decades ago. The figures are highest for Ontario, Saskatchewan, and British Columbia, where nearly one-half of registered Indians do not live on reserves. A considerable proportion of this off-reserve population resides in urban centers. Métis and non-status Indians also swell the numbers of urban Natives. Substantial inner city Native populations now characterize such Canadian centers as Winnipeg, Manitoba, and Edmonton, Alberta. Reserve populations, however, also continue to increase.

Canadian First Nations are increasingly taking control of administering their own lands and finances. A government committee on Indian self-government released its findings in 1983, dismissing the Indian Act and the present system of administration as unacceptable for the future. The committee report supported the right of Indian people to self-government and recommended that this be explicitly stated and entrenched in the Constitution of Canada. First Nations governments would then be recognized as a distinct order of government within Canada. However, constitutional conferences with federal, provincial, and First Nations leaders collapsed in failure, largely due to provincial concerns over the undefined terms and costs of aboriginal self-government. The attempt to recognize self-government in the constitution has been abandoned, at least temporarily. Many First Nations are now looking to land claims agreements to achieve control of their own affairs.

Education plays a key role in Native plans for the future, both for the preservation of Native cultures and languages and in providing modern skills needed for self-government. Most Canadian First Nations now administer all or part of their educational programs. Three aboriginal groups, the Nisga'a of British Columbia and the Cree and Inuit of northern Quebec, operate

Larry Pierre of the Okanagan on the occasion of the First Nations constitutional conference, 1980, demanding native participation in constitutional tasks. (Courtesy of CP Pictures Archives)

their own school boards. At the post-secondary level, federal funding for Indian and Inuit students to attend colleges and universities is resulting in the appearance of many young, articulate, educated Native leaders.

The First Nations of Canada have rejected the assimilationist policies of the Canadian government since confederation. Despite government assumptions, evident in some of the provisions of the Indian Act, First Nations were not doomed to disappear as distinct cultures. Today, populations of Indian, Inuit, and Métis peoples are rapidly growing and determined steps are being taken to preserve their languages and cultures. Aboriginal self-governments are emerging as an opportunity to take control over their own lives and ensure the survival of their cultures.

*Alan D. McMillan*
*Simon Fraser University*

## References

### Native Demography Before 1700

Borah, Woodrow W. and Sherburne F. Cook. *The Aboriginal Population of Central Mexico on the Eve of the Spanish Conquest*. Ibero-Americana, 45. Berkeley: University of California Press, 1963.

Cook, Noble D. *Born to Die: Disease and New World Conquest, 1492–1650*. New York: Cambridge University Press, 1998.

Cook, Noble D. and W. George Lovell, eds. *Secret Judgments of God: Old World Disease in Colonial Spanish America*. Norman: University of Oklahoma Press, 1991.

Cook, Sherburne F. and Woodrow Borah. *Essays in Population History: Mexico and the Caribbean*. Berkeley: University of California Press, 1971 (vol. 1); 1974 (vol. 2).

——. *Essays in Population History: Mexico and California*, vol. 3. Berkeley: University of California Press, 1979.

——. *The Indian Population of Central Mexico, 1531–1610*. Ibero-Americana, 44. Berkeley: University of California Press, 1960.

Crosby, Jr., Alfred W. *The Columbian Exchange: Biological and Cultural Consequences of 1492*. Westport, Conn.: Greenwood Publishing Company, 1972.

——. *Ecological Imperialism: The Biological Expansion of Europe, 900–1900*. Cambridge: Cambridge University Press, 1986.

Daniels, John D. "The Indian Population of North America in 1492."*William and Mary Quarterly* 49:2 (April 1992): 298–320.

Denevan, William M., ed. *The Native Population of the Americas in 1492*. 2d ed. Madison: University of Wisconsin Press, 1992.

Dobyns, Henry F. "Estimating Aboriginal American Population: An Appraisal of Techniques with a New Hemispheric Estimate." *Current Anthropology* 7, no. 4 (1966): 395–416.

——. *Native American Historical Demography: A Critical Bibliography*. Bloomington: Indiana University Press in cooperation with the Newberry Library Center for the History of the American Indian, 1976.

——. *Their Number Become Thinned: Native American Population Dynamics in Eastern North America*. Knoxville: University of Tennessee Press in cooperation with the Newberry Library Center for the History of the American Indian, 1983.

Stearn, E. Wagner and Allen E. Stearn. *The Effect of Smallpox on the Destiny of the Amerindian*. Boston: B. Humphries, 1945.

Stiffarm, Lenore A. and Phil Lane, Jr. "The Demography of Native North America: A Question of American Indian Survival." In *The State of Native America: Genocide, Colonization, and Resistance*, edited by M. Annette Jaimes, 23–53. Boston: South End Press, 1992.

Thornton, Russell. *American Indian Holocaust and Survival: A Population History Since 1492*. Norman: University of Oklahoma Press, 1987.

Verano, John and Douglas H. Ubelaker, eds. *Disease and Demography in the Americas*. Washington: Smithsonian Institution Press, 1992.

*Henry Dobyns*

## Geographic and Demographic Change During the Eighteenth Century

Anderson, Gary C. *Kinsmen of Another Kind: Dakota-White Relations in the Upper Mississippi Valley, 1650–1862*. Lincoln: University of Nebraska Press, 1984.

Cook, Sherburne F. *The Conflict Between the California Indian and White Civilization*. Berkeley: University of California Press, 1976.

Edmunds, R. David. *The Potawatomis: Keepers of the Fire*. Norman: University of Oklahoma Press, 1978.

Gutierrez, Ramn A. *When Jesus Came, the Corn Mothers Went Away: Marriage, Sexuality, and Power in New Mexico, 1500–1846*. Stanford, Calif.: Stanford University Press, 1991.

Jackson, Robert H. *Indian Population Decline: the Missions of Northwestern New Spain, 1687–1840*. Albuquerque: University of New Mexico Press, 1994.

Jennings, Francis. *Empire of Fortune: Crowns, Colonies, and Tribes in the Seven Years War in America*. New York: Norton, 1988.

McConnell, Michael N. *A Country Between: The Upper Ohio Valley and Its Peoples, 1724–1774*. Lincoln: University of Nebraska Press, 1992.

Merrell, James H. *The Indians' New World: Catawbas and Their Neighbors from European Contact through the Era of Removal*. Chapel Hill: University of North Carolina Press in cooperation with the Institute of Early American History and Culture, 1989.

Ray, Arthur J. *Indians in the Fur Trade: Their Role as Trappers, Hunters, and Middlemen in the Lands Southwest of Hudson Bay, 1660–1870*. Toronto: University of Toronto Press, 1974.

Richter, Daniel K. *The Ordeal of the Longhouse: The Peoples of the Iroquois League in the Era of European Colonization*. Chapel Hill: University of North Carolina Press in cooperation with the Institute of Early American History and Culture, 1992.

Salisbury, Neal. "Native People and European Settlers in Eastern North America, 1600–1783." In *The Cambridge History of the Native Peoples of the Americas*. Vol. 1: *North America*, edited by Bruce G. Trigger and Wilcomb E. Washburn, pt. 1, 399–460. Cambridge: Cambridge University Press, 1996.

Usner, Jr., Daniel H. *Indians, Settlers, and Slaves in a Frontier Exchange Economy: The Lower Mississippi Valley before 1783*. Chapel Hill: University of North Carolina Press in cooperation with the Institute of Early American History and Culture, 1992.

White, Richard. *The Middle Ground: Indians, Empires, and Republics in the Great Lakes Region, 1650–1815*. New York: Cambridge University Press, 1991.

*Dan Usner*

## Indian Geographic Distribution, Habitat, and Demography During the Nineteenth Century

Bee, Robert L. *The Yuma*. New York: Chelsea House, 1989.

Boyd, Robert T. *The Coming Spirit of Pestilence: Introduced Infectious Diseases and Population Decline Among Northwest Coast Indians, 1774–1874*. Seattle: University of Washington Press, 1999.

Calloway, Colin G. *The Abenaki*. New York: Chelsea House, 1989.

Calloway, Colin G., ed. *Our Hearts Fell to the Ground: Plains Indian Views of How the West Was Lost*. Boston: Bedford Books of St. Martin's Press, 1996.

Carlson, Leonard A. *Indians, Bureaucrats, and Land: The Dawes Act and the Decline of Indian Farming*. Westport, Conn.: Greenwood Press, 1981.

Dobyns, Henry F. *The Pima-Maricopa*. New York: Chelsea House, 1989.

Fisher, Robin. "The Northwest From the Beginning of Trade with Europeans to the 1880s." In *The Cambridge History of the Native Peoples of the Americas*. Vol. 1: *North America*, edited by Bruce G. Trigger and Wilcomb E. Washburn, pt. 2, 117–182. Cambridge: Cambridge University Press, 1996.

Fowler, Loretta. "The Great Plains From the Arrival of the Horse to 1885." In *The Cambridge History of the Native Peoples of the Americas*. Vol. 1: *North America*, edited by Bruce G. Trigger and Wilcomb E. Washburn, pt. 2, 1–56. Cambridge: Cambridge University Press, 1996.

Gibson, Arrell M. *The American Indian: Prehistory to Present*. Lexington, Mass.: D. C. Heath, 1980.

Green, Michael D. "The Expansion of European Colonization to the Mississippi Valley, 1780–1880." In *The Cambridge History of the Native Peoples of the Americas*. Vol. 1: *North America*, edited by Bruce G.

Trigger and Wilcomb E. Washburn, pt. 1, 461–538. Cambridge: Cambridge University Press, 1996.

Lamar, Howard R. and Sam Truett. "The Greater Southwest and California From the Beginning of European Settlement to the 1880's." In *The Cambridge History of the Native Peoples of the Americas*. Vol. 1: *North America*, edited by Bruce G. Trigger and Wilcomb E. Washburn, pt. 2, 57–116. Cambridge: Cambridge University Press, 1996.

Maxwell, James A., ed. *America's Fascinating Indian Heritage*. Pleasantville, N.Y.: Reader's Digest Association, 1978.

Merrell, James H. *The Catawbas*. New York: Chelsea House, 1989.

Olson, James S. and Raymond Wilson. *Native Americans in the Twentieth Century*. Provo, Utah: Brigham Young University Press, 1984.

Prucha, Francis Paul. *Atlas of American Indian Affairs*. Lincoln: University of Nebraska Press, 1990.

Simmons, William S. *The Narragansett*. New York: Chelsea House, 1989.

Spicer, Edward H. *The American Indians*. Cambridge, Mass.: Belnap Press of Harvard University Press, 1980.

Tanner, Helen H., ed. *Atlas of Great Lakes Indian History*. Norman: University of Oklahoma Press in cooperation with the Newberry Library, 1987.

Trigger, Bruce, ed. *Northeast*. Vol. 15 of *Handbook of North American Indians*, edited by William C. Sturtevant. Washington, D.C.: Smithsonian Institution, 1978.

Washburn, Wilcomb, ed. *History of Indian-White Relations*. Vol. 4 of *Handbook of North American Indians*, edited by William C. Sturtevant. Washington, D.C.: Smithsonian Institution, 1988.

Wright, Muriel H. *A Guide to the Indian Tribes of Oklahoma*. Norman: University of Oklahoma Press, 1986.

*Leroy Eid*

## Indian Land Tenure in the Twentieth Century

Burt, Larry W. *Tribalism in Crisis: Federal Indian Policy, 1953–1961*. Albuquerque: University of New Mexico Press, 1982.

Carlson, Leonard A. *Indians, Bureaucrats, and Land: The Dawes Act and the Decline of Indian Farming*. Westport, Conn.: Greenwood Press, 1981

Castile, George P. and Robert L. Bee. *State and Reservation: New Perspectives on Federal Indian Policy*. Tucson: University of Arizona Press, 1992.

Champagne, Duane. *American Indian Societies: Strategies and Conditions of Political and Cultural Survival*. Cultural Survival Report 32. Cambridge, Mass.: Cultural Survival, 1989.

Cohen, Fay G. *Treaties on Trial: The Continuing Controversy over Northwest Indian Fishing Rights.* Seattle: University of Washington Press, 1986.

Deloria, Vine, Jr., ed. *American Indian Policy in the Twentieth Century.* Norman: University of Oklahoma Press, 1985.

Deloria, Vine, Jr. *Behind the Trail of Broken Treaties: An Indian Declaration of Independence.* New York: Delacorte, 1974.

Deloria, Vine, Jr., and Clifford Lytle. *American Indians, American Justice.* Austin: University of Texas Press, 1983.

Deloria, Vine, Jr., and David E. Wilkins. *Tribes, Treaties, & Constitutional Tribulations.* Austin: University of Texas Press, 1999.

Getches, David H., Charles F. Wilkinson, and Robert A. Williams, Jr. *Case and Materials on Federal Indian Law,* 4th Ed. St. Paul: West Pub., 1998.

McCool, Daniel. *Command of the Waters: Iron Triangles, Federal Water Development, and Indian Water.* Berkeley: University of California Press, 1987.

McDonnell, Janet A. *The Dispossession of the American Indian, 1887–1934.*, Bloomington: Indiana University Press, 1991.

Momaday, N. Scott. *House Made of Dawn.* New York: Harper & Row, 1968.

Philp, Kenneth R., ed. *Indian Self-Rule: First Hand Accounts of Indian-White Relations From Roosevelt to Reagan.* Salt Lake City: Howe Bros., 1986.

Prucha, Francis P. *American Indian Treaties: The History of a Political Anomaly.* Berkeley and Los Angeles: University of California Press, 1994.

———. *Atlas of American Indian Affairs.* Lincoln: University of Nebraska Press, 1990.

———. *The Indians in American Society: From the Revolutionary War to the Present.* Berkeley: University of California Press, 1985.

Shipek, Florence C. *Pushed Into the Rocks: Southern California Indian Land Tenure, 1769–1986.* Lincoln: University of Nebraska Press, 1988.

Snipp, C. Matthew. *American Indians: The First of This Land.* New York: Russell Sage Foundation, 1989.

Sutton, Imre. *Indian Land Tenure: Bibliographical Essays and a Guide to the Literature.* New York: Clearwater, 1975.

———., ed. *Irredeemable America: The Indians' Estate and Land Claims.* Albuquerque: University of New Mexico Press, 1985.

Vecsey, Christopher and William A. Starna, eds. *Iroquois Land Claims.* Syracuse, N.Y.: Syracuse University Press, 1988.

Vogel, Virgil J. *This Country Was Ours: A Documentary History of the American Indian.* New York: Harper & Row, 1972.

Washburn, Wilcomb E., ed. *History of Indian-White Relations.* Vol. 4 of *Handbook of North American Indians.* Washington, DC: Smithsonian Institution, 1988.

Washburn, Wilcomb E. *Red Man's Land/White Man's Law: A Study of the Past and Present Status of the American Indian.* New York: Scribner, 1971.

Wilkinson, Charles F. *American Indians, Time and the Law: Native Societies in a Modern Constitutional Democracy.* New Haven: Yale University Press, 1987.

*Imre Sutton*

## Canadian Native Distribution, Habitat, and Demography

Damas, David, ed. *Arctic.* Vol. 5 of *Handbook of North American Indians,* edited by William C. Sturtevant. Washington D.C.: Smithsonian Institution, 1984.

Dickason, Olive P. *Canada's First Nations: A History of Founding Peoples from Earliest Times.* 2nd ed. Toronto: Oxford University Press, 1997.

Fisher, Robin and Kenneth Coates, eds. *Out of the Background: Readings On Canadian Native History.* 2nd ed. Toronto: Copp Clarke, 1996.

Frideres, James S. *Aboriginal Peoples in Canada: Contemporary Conflicts.* 5th ed. Scarborough, Ont.: Prentice-Hall Canada, 1998.

Hedican, Edward J. *Applied Anthropology in Canada: Understanding Aboriginal Issues.* Toronto: University of Toronto Press, 1995.

Helm, June, ed. *Subarctic.* Vol. 6 of *Handbook of North American Indians,* edited by William C. Sturtevant. Washington, D.C.: Smithsonian Institution, 1981.

Long, David A. and Olive P. Dickason, eds. *Visions of the Heart: Canadian Aboriginal Issues.* Toronto: Harcourt Brace Canada, 1996.

McMillan, Alan D. *Native Peoples and Cultures of Canada: An Anthropological Overview.* 2nd ed. Vancouver: Douglas & McIntyre, 1995.

Miller, J.R. *Skyscrapers Hide the Heavens: A History of Indian-White Relations in Canada.* 3rd ed. Toronto: University of Toronto Press, 2000.

Morrison, R. Bruce and C. Roderick Wilson, eds. *Native Peoples: The Canadian Experience.* 2nd ed. Toronto: McClelland and Stewart, 1995.

Ponting, J. Rick., ed. *Arduous Journey: Canadian Indians and Decolonization.* Toronto: McClelland and Stewart, 1986.

Ponting, J. Rick. *First Nations in Canada: Perspectives on Opportunity, Empowerment, and Self-Determination.* Toronto: McGraw-Hill Ryerson, 1997.

Richardson, Boyce, ed. *Drum Beat: Anger and Renewal in Indian Country.* Toronto: Summerhill Press, 1989.

Suttles, Wayne, ed. *Northwest Coast.* Vol. 7 of *Handbook of North American Indians*, edited by William C. Sturtevant. Washington, D.C.: Smithsonian Institution, 1990.

Trigger, Bruce G. *Natives and Newcomers: Canada's "Heroic Age" Reconsidered.* Kingston, Ont.: McGill-Queen's University Press, 1985.

———, ed. *Northeast.* Vol. 15 of *Handbook of North American Indians*, edited by William C. Sturtevant. Washington, D.C.: Smithsonian Institution, 1978.

*Alan McMillan*

# 3

# Major Culture Areas

♦ Native Peoples of the Northeast  ♦ Southeastern Indians  ♦ Southwestern Indians
♦ Northern Plains Indians  ♦ Northwest Coast Indians  ♦ Alaska Natives
♦ Oklahoma Indians  ♦ Indians of the Plateau, Great Basin, and Rocky Mountains
♦ California Indians  ♦ Aboriginal Peoples in Canada
♦ Federally Recognized U.S. Indian Communities  ♦ Canadian Indian Bands

## ♦ NATIVE PEOPLES OF THE NORTHEAST

Survival and adaptation are themes unifying the diverse indigenous cultures that occupy the Northeast part of North America. From 1000 to 200 B.C.E., the Adena Culture, a variety of "mound-building" sites and cultures—so called by archaeologists because of the material culture they left behind in mounds of burial artifacts—were spread across the present-day Ohio Valley and extended east to sites in present-day western New York and western Pennsylvania. The Hopewell Culture, another mound-building culture stretching across the southern Great Lakes and the Mississippi and Ohio valleys, followed from 300 to 700 C.E.. Both the Hopewell and Adena peoples lived in villages, and corn was a staple part of their diet. The mounds of this period, often built as burial memorials, were cone-shaped. The Mississippian Culture, 800 to 1600 C.E., had influence only in the southern portion of the northeast coast, and here the mounds became temples for an aristocratic priesthood. When the earliest Europeans visited the Northeast in the 1500s, they did not find stratified societies with temples built on mounds, but fortified sedentary towns with houses organized according to clan and lineage group, as were found among the Iroquois along the St. Lawrence River. In the early 1500s, the peoples of the Northeast had hunting cultures, and horticulture (farming with hand implements) became more common to the south. During the latter part of the sixteenth century, Algonkian-speaking hunting nations, like the Ottawa and Ojibwa, migrated into the northeast area and started pushing sedentary Iroquoian people further west and south. Many Algonkian-speaking nations, such as the Lenape (or Delaware) and Wampanoag, occupied the coastal regions of present-day southern New England, and they

lived by hunting, fishing, and planting corn, beans, pumpkins, and other vegetables. Iroquoian peoples occupied present-day upstate New York and sites along the lower Great Lakes. It appears that during the 1500s, the Iroquoian peoples were already subject to territory disputes with the neighboring Algonkian tribes, and the arrival of the Europeans tended to intensify the struggle. By the 1700s, the land pressure of European arrival in the east forced many New England Algonkian nations to move further west into the Great Lakes region, where they then had to compete with other Natives for resources. Riding the wave of colonial expansion, the Ojibwa, Potawatomi, and Ottawa all migrated into the upper Great Lakes area and had a hand in displacing the peoples of the Illinois Confederacy, who moved from Wisconsin to present-day Illinois. During the 1700s, the Ojibwa moved into the Minnesota region and began to contest hunting, trapping, and wild rice resources. American Indians in the Northeast sustained almost continual contact with European explorers from about 1497 onward. Native American contact with Europeans was particularly prolonged and intense along the eastern seaboard of the Atlantic Ocean.

As in New England, the Indian nations of the Great Lakes had to compete with French and English colonists for resources and political control. The Great Lakes region was inhabited by Central Algonkian and Siouan-speaking groups such as the Shawnee, Fox, Sauk, Kickapoo, Winnebago, Menominee, Potawatomi, Chippewa, Ottawa and others who engaged in horticulture and hunting. Except for a few isolated examples, these groups did not come in contact with French traders until the latter part of the seventeenth century. Until the latter part of the eighteenth century, the French used the Iroquois as middlemen in the fur trade, or they had to use other, more indirect routes to overcome the economic and military control of the Iroquois. In 1763 Pontiac, an Ottawa chief, and from 1805 to 1812, Tecumseh, a Shawnee warrior, organized alliances among tribal groups and made political and military efforts to slow down European encroachment in the Great Lakes region. These military efforts represent just one of the ways Great Lakes and other Indian groups in the Northeast resisted European domination in the seventeenth and eighteenth centuries.

While some important groups in the Great Lakes—such as the Shawnee, Delaware, Potawatomi, and others—were overrun by settler land-greed and were removed to Oklahoma and other areas, many of today's indigenous groups along the Great Lakes live on reservation lands within their traditional homelands and hunting territories. Many of the Great Lakes tribes, such as the Ojibwa groups in Michigan, Wisconsin, and Minnesota, have maintained their rights to hunt and fish in their usual and accustomed places. These treaty rights, negotiated mostly in the 1850s, became a source of political and legal organization among Great Lakes Indian communities in the 1960s and remain a primary site of cultural assertions of Indian identity and political resistance to the current day.

## The Iroquoian Peoples

*Iroquoian* is a term used to identify several indigenous nations that share a similar language and culture. The major Iroquoian nations include the Mohawk, Seneca, Cayuga, Onondaga, Oneida, Susque-hannock, Erie, Huron, and others. The Iroquoian peoples share a similar way of life, usually based on intensive horticulture, fishing, and hunting. Their traditional villages were often organized according to clans, kinship groups reckoned through mothers.

At the time of European contact in the early 1500s, the Iroquoian peoples lived along the St. Lawrence River in upper New York State, along the lower Great Lakes, and in the Susquehanna River Valley in present-day Pennsylvania. Because of their inland location, they were relatively unaffected, compared to Native coastal peoples, by early European trade and settler expansion. Thus, we know more about the precolonial lifestyles of the Iroquoian nations than we know about cultures and histories of the indigenous coastal nations.

One of the most well-known Iroquoian groups was the Five Nations of the Haudenosaunee, which means *People of the Longhouse.* Sometime between 1000 and 1350 C.E., the Mohawk, Oneida, Onondaga, Cayuga, and Seneca formed a confederation consisting of their five nations, with chiefs drawn from forty-nine families, who were present at the origin of the confederacy. The origin story of the Iroquois confederacy holds that a Peacemaker, Deganawidah, and his spokesman, Hiawatha, planted a Great Tree of Peace at the Onondaga Nation near Syracuse, New York, to resolve the blood feuds that had been dividing the Haudenosaunee people. Through the symbolic tree planting, the Haudenosaunee Peacemaker instituted peace, unity, and clear thinking among the Haudenosaunee people. Deganawidah passed on the Great Law, which is the constitution of the Iroquois Confederacy.

During the colonial period, this structure enabled them to take advantage of their political, economic, and geographic position in the Northeast. By adopting members of other Iroquoian groups, such as the Huron and Tuscarora, the Haudenosaunee maintained their historically strategic position in the Northeast, between the colonies of New France and New York, in the fur trade, and during the diplomatic rivalries between England and France in the seventeenth and eighteenth centuries. At the height of their influence, from about 1650 to 1777, the Haudenosaunee heartland extended from Albany, New York, to Niagara Falls, with its outermost borders stretching to southeastern Ontario, New England, northern Pennsylvania, and northeastern Ohio.

The Iroquois played an important role in the birth of the United States. Even before the advent of the American Revolution, the Haudenosaunee had counseled American leaders on the virtues of Iroquois-style unity, democracy, and liberty. From the writing of the Albany Plan of Union, a 1755 plan to unite the colonies, to the creation of the United States Constitution, the Iroquois were present in body and spirit as Americans sought to create a democratic alternative to the British monarchy. At the request of the founding fathers, Iroquois chiefs were present at the debates on the Declaration of Independence in Philadelphia in May and June 1776. Over the course of several weeks, the Iroquois observed the new American nation emerging and gave the President, John Hancock, an Iroquois name, Karanduawn, which means "the Great Tree." Indeed, some Americans, such as Thomas Jefferson, believed that American governments were very similar to American Indian governments like that of the Iroquois; Jefferson stated in 1787 that the "only condition on earth to be compared to [our government]. . . is that of the Indians, where they still have less government than we." On the eve of the Constitutional Convention, John Adams admonished the delegates to the Constitutional

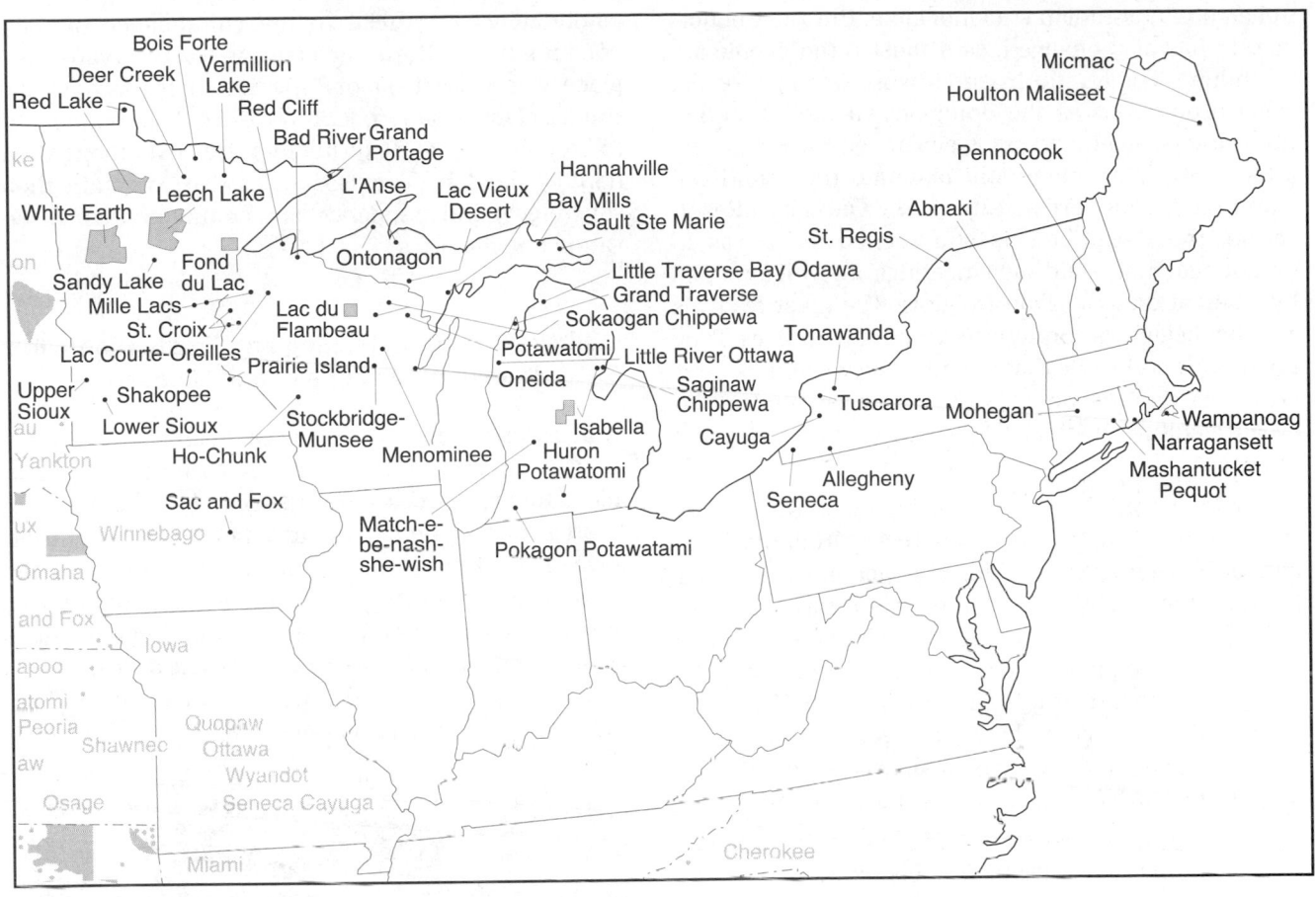

Northeastern federally recognized tribes' reservations. (Courtesy of the UCLA American Indian Studies Center)

Convention to conduct "an accurate investigation of the form of government of the. . . Indians" since the separation of powers in American Indian governments like the Iroquois is "marked with a precision that excludes all controversy." During the Constitutional Convention, delegates such as James Wilson of Pennsylvania clearly stated that the "British government cannot be our model." In 1790 Thomas Jefferson and others toasted the U.S. Constitution as a "tree of peace" that sheltered the Americans "with its branches of union." Thus, American Indian ideas associated with groups like the Iroquois of the Northeast had a decided impact on the development of American democracy.

Even though the Founding Fathers respected the Iroquois for their wisdom in governmental organization, between 1777 and 1800 the U.S. government allowed various land companies to buy virtually all Iroquois lands. By 1880 the Iroquois either left to live in Canada or were relegated to several small reservations in upper New York State. The remaining Iroquois lands and disputed territories were guaranteed by contract with the land companies and by treaties with the United States and New York State.

## Contemporary Haudenosaunee

The Haudenosaunee of the twentieth century saw the traditionalist Longhouse religion of the prophet, Handsome Lake, revived on the Caughnawaga and St. Regis Mohawk reservations. Handsome Lake was a Seneca prophet whose ministry extended from 1799 to 1815. His message urged accommodation to the presence of the white people while maintaining many of the important traditional ways of the Haudenosaunee. In the 1830s, Iroquois traditionalists and the followers of Handsome Lake formed a church and resurrected the traditional Iroquois chief system in opposition to the "elected" chief system that currently asserts power on their reservations. Today, the Iroquois traditional chieftainship system is present on three reservations in New York (Onondaga, Tuscarora, and Tonawanda Seneca). There, the clan mothers still nominate the chiefs of their clans, and the chiefs are brought into office through an ancient condolence ceremony.

The Iroquois have survived and they have struggled to maintain their ancient traditions. Various Iroquois languages are still spoken and they are being taught to

Indian and non-Indian students alike. But the Iroquois culture has also changed, as it must if the people are to endure. Today, the Iroquois work in many of the same professions as the dominant society. They are ironworkers, steel workers, teachers, businessmen, and artists. However, many still maintain the traditional culture in the modern setting. At the Onondaga Reservation, the Great Law is still recited as it was in precolonial times, and such meetings are well-attended by reservation and urban Iroquois. The great festivals and thanksgivings continue as a part of their lives. They are forging a lifestyle that includes the wisdom of their ancestors and the benefits of modern technology, to create a culture in which they can live comfortably and in peace.

Contemporary Iroquois are insisting on their treaty rights. For example, since the 1920s, Iroquois stage annual "border crossings" into Canada in the summer to assert their right, through the Jay's Treaty (1794), to uninhibited passage across the United States-Canadian border. The Iroquois have also filed claims against the U.S. government relating to fraudulent loss of land. The results of these claims have been uneven; many Iroquois believe that the only real settlement of land claims can come through some form of land restoration.

Recently, after a generation of struggle, the Iroquois were also able to repatriate, or reclaim, wampum belts that had been held in the New York State Museum. Wampum belts are diplomatic and ceremonial records made from shells and fastened into a string or chain of several rows. Symbols were embroidered into the belts as documents and historical records of diplomatic agreements, treaties, records of important historical events, and records of sacred and ceremonial law. The Iroquois wanted the wampum belts returned so that they could be used and cared for by people who can read and interpret these important documents. Today, as in the past, the Haudenosaunee use the wampum belts as a record of their laws, treaties, and other important events of the past. Wampum belts are analogous in importance to U.S. government documents, such as the Declaration of Independence and the United States Constitution.

Recently, Iroquois leaders have also been active in numerous international treaty forums relating to indigenous people's rights. Since the early 1900s, the Iroquois Confederacy has issued its own passports, which are recognized for travel purposes by many nations.

The Iroquois continue to have a strong affinity for their homeland. Their reservations are parcels of land that they have held on to for hundreds of years of settler pressure. Maintaining and preserving contemporary landholdings is crucial to the continuance of their communities, culture, and identity. The reservation is a place where the Iroquois practice their customs and rituals. Many urban Iroquois return to these homelands to be culturally and spiritually refreshed among their friends and kin. The Iroquois strive to retain their sovereignty, independence, and culture on their reservation communities.

## Ojibwa/Chippewa Fishing and Treaty Rights in Michigan, Wisconsin, and Minnesota

Many tribes in the Northeast maintain traditional lifeways by asserting their treaty rights to fish, hunt, and gather resources. Often, these rights, negotiated in treaties in the eighteenth and nineteenth centuries, have to be fought for politically and legally in the current day. A prominent example of how this is a critical struggle for contemporary Native communities in the Northeast involves the retention of fishing and hunting rights among the Ojibwa (also called Chippewa) of Wisconsin and Minnesota.

The men make their grand entrance at the Red Lake 4th of July Powwow on the Red Lake Reservation in northern Minnesota. (Photo by Sarah Loe. Courtesy of the UCLA American Indian Studies Center)

In the early 1980s, the Lake Superior Chippewa began to fish, hunt, and gather in areas specified in treaties negotiated in the nineteenth century with the U.S. Congress. These activities resulted in legal disputes. On 25 January 1983 a federal court, in what is called the Voight Decision, agreed with the Lake Superior Chippewa that the hunting, fishing, and gathering rights in treaties were still reserved and protected for the Chippewa. In later court decisions involving the Wisconsin and the Lake Superior Chippewa, the scope of these treaty rights were further defined to include:

1. the harvesting and selling of hunting, fishing, and gathering products
2. the exercise of these rights on private land if necessary to produce a modest living.

In addition, portions of game and forest products (excluding commercial timber) available to Chippewa through their treaty rights have been quantified in later decisions.

The fact that the Chippewa had to fight for rights guaranteed them in treaties, "the supreme law of the United States," shows the political, legal, and racial struggle that defines a great deal of the Native experience in the Northeast and the rest of the country. During the Indian spear-fishing seasons in the late 1980s, Chippewa were subjected to numerous episodes of violent harassment by non-Indians while attempting to exercise their treaty rights. They were also subject to numerous racial slurs; anti–spear-fishing slogans, found on bumper stickers and signs across Wisconsin included "Save a Walleye. Spear a squaw" and "Custer had the right idea." A suit filed by the American Civil Liberties Union on behalf of the Chippewa served to deter some of the more ardent anti-Indian violent protests by the 1990 fishing season.

In 1990 the Mille Lacs Band of Chippewa sued the state of Minnesota, asserting that an 1837 treaty with the U.S. government gave them the right to hunt, fish, and gather free of state regulation on land ceded in the treaty. In an attempt to avoid a lengthy court battle, the Minnesota Department of Natural Resources (DNR) proposed a negotiated settlement. That proposal would have required the band to withdraw their lawsuit, limit the Lake Mille Lacs walleye harvest to 24,000 pounds per year, and adhere to a band conservation code. In return, the state would give the band $8.6 million, 7,500 acres of land, and exclusive fishing rights on 4.5 percent of Lake Mille Lacs. The agreement also allowed traditional spear-fishing and netting practices.

During the 1993 session the Minnesota Legislature narrowly defeated the negotiated settlement. Legislators opposed to the settlement argued that the use of gill nets would decimate the walleye population and harm tourism. Treaty proponents argued that the use of gill nets and spears were important components of Indian culture and religion and that their use would be limited.

On 24 August 1994 U.S. District Court Judge Diana Murphy ruled that the Mille Lacs band retained the hunting, fishing, and gathering rights granted in the 1837 treaty. A second phase of the trial was ordered to determine the band's fish and game allocation and the extent of any state regulation. Phase II concluded on 29 January 1997 when District Court Judge Michael Davis ruled that the band's fishing and hunting activities in the twelve-county region were to be regulated by the band's Conservation Code, rather than by the state's fish and game rules.

The state of Minnesota filed an appeal with the Eighth U.S. Circuit Court of Appeals in March 1997. On 26 August 1997 a three-judge panel of the circuit court upheld the lower court decisions. In November 1997 the Eighth U.S. Circuit Court of Appeals denied a request to reconsider the ruling of the three-judge panel. An appeal was filed with the U.S. Supreme Court, which heard the case on 2 December 1998. On 24 March 1999, the U.S. Supreme Court upheld by a 5–4 vote that the Mille Lacs Band of Chippewa retain the hunting and fishing rights guaranteed to them under the 1837 treaty. In December 1999 U.S. District Court Judge Michael Davis ordered the state of Minnesota to pay the legal expenses of the Mille Lacs Band of Chippewa and six other bands. They were awarded a total of $3.95 million.

### Termination and the Menominee Nation of Wisconsin

In the 1950s the U.S. government embarked on a policy to "terminate" the treaties and reservations of American Indian nations. The Menominee, a Northeast Indian nation, was the first to be stripped of treaty rights and the protections offered by the federal government under this policy. Although they were one of the most self-sufficient Indian nations, the Menominee were not prepared to cope with the withdrawal of federal services and trust responsibilities by the time their termination became final in 1961. Although criticism of the termination policy was rapidly mounting in Congress from 1958 to 1960, the Menominee were unsuccessful in having their termination decision reevaluated.

Menominee Enterprises, Inc. (MEI) was set up to manage the tribe's forests, lumber mill, and other assets after termination, but it was forced to give too

Totem symbols at the Lac du Flambeau Museum and Cultural Center on the Lac du Flambeau Reservation in northern Wisconsin. (Photo by Sarah Loe. Courtesy of the UCLA American Indian Studies Center)

much power to non-Menominee individuals. While the Menominee were made shareholders in the new corporation, a Milwaukee trust company controlled a block vote of minors and incompetents (almost 50 percent of the shareholder votes). When the Menominee Reservation became Menominee County, taxes became unrealistically high, unemployment rose, medical care deteriorated, and a large part of the housing stock became substandard. In 1967 MEI contracted with a land developer to subdivide lakefront property for sale to vacationers so that the tax base could be broadened. This decision outraged most Menominee, leading to the creation of DRUMS (Determination of Rights and Unity for Menominee Shareholders), which filed suit against MEI. The group also protested land sales to outsiders and advocated the restoration of federal jurisdiction on Menominee lands. In 1975 congressional legislation was finally passed to restore the Menominee treaty rights and federal trust status.

Since then, the Menominee have fought the long road back to self-rule and sovereignty, and have once again become a flourishing tribal nation. They remain on the forefront of maintaining traditional Indian values within the colonial economic structure of the United States. For example, in 1993 Menominee community leaders organized the Sustainable Development Institute (SDI), part of the College of the Menominee Nation, to help articulate Menominee expertise in silviculture and forestry, and to advance the tenets of sustainability to other economic and social sectors. Menominee expertise in forest management has gained widespread attention, receiving commendation by the United Nations in 1995, and designation as the first awardee of the Presidential Award for Sustainable Development in 1996.

## New England Indian Survival, Resistance, and History

Conventional histories of New England American Indian groups have them decimated by disease, military aggression, land cessions, and political demands by the end of the war waged by followers of Metacomet—referred to as King Philip by the English—against colonial settlers between 1675 and 1676. Metacomet was a

Wampanoag chief who led the Wampanoags and other Indian peoples of southern and central (and later northern) New England in a war of resistance against the English colonial order. With the help of Governor Andros of New York, Captain Benjamin Church fought Metacomet with the help of Mohawk Indians from the west, first capturing his wife and nine-year-old son in July 1676, and finally capturing Metacomet himself in August 1676, duly cutting off his head and quartering his body and hanging the pieces from a tree for all to see.

The real story of Indian existence and resistance in New England does not end with Metacomet's demise. That is not to say that being Indian in New England after Metacomet was easy. Land pressure and colonial rule in southern New England meant that Indians worked as servants in white households, many forced into voluntary servitude for nonpayment of debts, caused by a new economy that did not adhere to traditional Native lifeways. Massachusetts and Connecticut imposed guardian systems that were supposed to protect Indian lands and resources, but guardians often abused the system and sold Indian lands. The Indian town of Mashpee on Cape Cod petitioned for relief from its guardians and won a measure of self-government under the British Crown in 1763, but Massachusetts reinstated the guardian system after the Revolution. Where Indians and whites shared the same town—as at Natick and Stockbridge—whites gained control of town offices and further disenfranchised Indians.

This disenfranchisement of Indians from control over their lands and resources forced them to live and confront life under colonial rule. Most profoundly, this meant Indians had to change the ways that they supported themselves in a new economy. After Metacomet's resistance movement, a diaspora of New England Indian peoples was created, looking for safety and work all over northeastern United States and southeastern Canada. Indians from New England migrated north and west, mingling with other tribes and building new communities. Refugees from King Philip's War joined Abenaki communities in Maine, Vermont, and New Hampshire, and many Abenakis retreated from the English war zone in the eighteenth century and relocated in the northern reaches of their homelands or around French mission villages in Quebec. There were Abenakis living in Indian communities around the Great Lakes by the early eighteenth century, and Spanish records contain references to people they identified as Abenakis as far west as Arkansas and Missouri in the decade after the American Revolution.

Like their non-Indian neighbors, many Native people had to change their ways of living and working in areas of New England that were becoming increasingly industrial and urban in the nineteenth century. Many young women left home to find work in textile mills in Lowell and Worcester, Massachusetts, or in Manchester, New Hampshire. Many men moved to Boston or New York City for work in heavier industry. A mobile Indian labor force developed, as people moved from job to job and city to city and home community to urban slum. Other Indians, especially in Northern New England, preferred occupations that more closely resembled traditional patterns of life, work, and movement. Men found employment as seasonal laborers, loggers, trappers, and guides. Women wove baskets, and peddled them door to door in white settlements. Later, they sold baskets to Victorian tourists at summer resorts in the White Mountains of New Hampshire and on the coast of Maine, and they crafted smaller, more elaborate and more colorful "fancy baskets" for the tourist trade. Such patterns of labor and community continued through the nineteenth and first half of the twentieth century, in which Indians in New England maintained their identities and (especially in southern New England) fragmenting communities, often in the shadow of white society and official histories of New England. Many individuals did not represent themselves as Indians in official circumstances to outsiders out of fear of discrimination, and so the "disappearance" of Indians in New England, a story created by the colonialists, became a self-fulfilling prophecy.

By the middle of the twentieth century, assimilation pressures remained, but Indians in New England began to form political alliances to preserve their lands and cultures. In 1923 the New England Indian Council formed, adopting the motto, "I still live." After World War II, this type of political organization was crucial in helping the tribes in New England gain federal recognition and settle land disputes stretching back as far as the eighteenth century.

### The Non-Intercourse Act and Northeastern Land Claims

In the winter of 1964 George Stevens, a Passamaquoddy from eastern Maine, discovered that a local landowner had decided to expand his tourist cabin business within Passamaquoddy lands at Indian Township. As a tribe recognized by the state of Maine, the attorney general of the state was supposed to prosecute such incursions, but did nothing. In the days following, the Passamaquoddy Tribal Council voted to take a public stand and five of the seventy-five Passamaquoddy who blocked the illegal development of their land were arrested. What followed from this basic incursion of tribal rights is perhaps one of the most important struggles for Indian tribes in the Northeast since Metacomet.

The 1964 land incursion eventually led to political pressure from the Passamaquoddy and Penobscot in Maine on Associate Solicitor for Indian Affairs in the Department of Interior William Gershuny to support the tribes in Maine against such incursions as they supported tribes in the western part of the United States. Gershuny did nothing to help the tribes, so a new legal strategy had to be developed to force the United States government to do something to protect the Maine tribes. Tom Tureen, who represented the Maine tribes at that time, went to a fairly obscure mechanism to argue that the federal government was not meeting its obligation to tribes in Maine: the Non-Intercourse Act of 1790. The Act stated, in part:

> No sale of lands made by Indians, or any nation or Tribe of Indians within the United States, shall be valid to any person or persons, or to any state, whether having the right of preemption to such lands or not, unless the same shall be made duly executed by some public treaty, held under the authority of the United States.

Tureen knew that in two treaties signed with the Commonwealth of Massachusetts in the mid–1790s (Maine was still then a part of Massachusetts), the Passamaquoddy and Penobscots had ceded most of their aboriginal lands in exchange for payment. However, these treaties were not ratified by Congress at the time of their signing—they were not "duly executed... under the authority of the United States." Therefore, beyond the official recognition of the Maine tribes as deserving federal protection from non-Indians on their lands, was the fact that two-thirds of the state of Maine, 12.5 million acres, was potentially Indian Country, because it had been acquired illegally.

Using the application of the Non-Intercourse Act as their legal mechanism, the Passamaquoddy filed suit against Secretary of Interior Rogers Morton on 2 June 1972 to file a claim against the states of Maine and Massachusetts for these lands. Judge Edward Gignoux, a widely respected judge at the United States District Court in Portland, heard the case over the course of 1973 and 1974. On 20 January 1975 he handed down his decision, finding that (1) the Passamaquoddy were an Indian tribe under the 1790 Non-Intercourse Act; (2) the Act applies to Passamaquoddy and other Indians within the original thirteen colonies; and (3) there is a trust relationship between the federal government and the tribes in Maine that was never severed because of illegal treaties with the states of Massachusetts and Maine. The case was appealed to the circuit court and it reaffirmed the rulings of the lower court.

## Maine Indian Claims

In the mid–1970s, the fallout of the Passamaquoddy case was palpable for Indians and non-Indians living in Maine, and interests in a speedy, out-of-court resolution mounted. Maine politicians, led by Governor Longley, started to put pressure on Washington, and began race-baiting, and Maine's Indians suffered. After a few years of squabbling over how best to resolve the case, the Carter Administration brought the state of Maine, the Maine Indians, and the Department of Interior together to hammer out a settlement. The settlement, finally reached in 1980, gave roughly $81.5 million to be shared equally by the Passamaquoddy and Penobscot—$54.5 million to purchase 300,000 acres of trust lands and $27 million to set up a trust fund for tribal members in exchange for the tribes giving up title to the 12.5 million acres of land in question from the illegal transfers. A much smaller amount of land and resources was provided for the Houlton Band of Maliseet Indians, with $900,000 for land acquisition and $200,000 for a trust fund. The settlement, like all such political projects, was a compromise, and the Maine Indian Claims Settlement Act, the federal law enforcing the settlement, has become a legal quagmire for Maine Indians—the precise contours of self-government in the Settlement Act were overly vague and are currently in suit in federal court. Despite these legal hang-ups, Maine Indians are intent, as they have been for thousands of years, on controlling their own destinies as sovereign governments.

The Passamaquoddy case, and the settlement that followed, paved the way for a series of Indian land claims in the Northeast, where states had acquired Indian lands without the consent of Congress in New York, Connecticut, Massachusetts, and Rhode Island.

## Contemporary Connecticut Indian Land Claims

Passed in 1983, the Connecticut Indian Claims Settlement Act originally only applied to the Western Pequot Tribe (known now as the Mashantucket Pequot Tribe). Granting them federal recognition at the time of its passage, the settlement act also gave money to the tribe to purchase back some of its land and rebuild its community, whose few remaining members, save one or two, had been forced out during the suburbanization of western Connecticut after World War II. The Mashantucket, a tribe of 383 members, have rebuilt their community in a profound way, and now control the largest gaming complex in the Western Hemisphere,

Menominee sweat lodge. (Courtesy of Southwest Museum)

the Foxwoods Casino and Resort, and have recently completed an Indian Museum and Cultural Center, which serves Indian nations across North America.

After a federal district court held that the Mohegans of Uncasville, Connecticut, were indeed an Indian tribe, the Connecticut Land Claims Settlement Act was amended to include them in 1994. A tribe of 1,185 people, they have also built an Indian gaming operation, which emphasizes sustainability in all of its operations, from reuse and recycling to green development and alternative energies. The Eastern Pequots and the Schaghticoke Nation are also pursuing recognition, and their cases are both pending.

### Claims by Massachusetts Indians in the Last Generation

While the Passamaquoddy case was being heard in federal court during the early 1970s, the Wampanoag Tribe of Gay Head (Aquinnah) used a similar legal argument to sue for 5,000 acres of land on Martha's

Vineyard in 1974. A series of negotiations and legal squabbles eventually led to the passage of the Massachusetts Indian Claims Settlement Act in 1987. Briefly, the settlement act (1) recognized the Wampanoag Tribe of Gay Head (Aquinnah) as having a government-to-government relationship with the United States; (2) authorized the conveyance of lands from the town of Gay Head to the secretary of interior to be held in trust for the Wampanoag Tribal Council; and (3) recognized the authority of the Wampanoag Council to regulate hunting by Indians on settlement lands that is conducted by means other than firearms or crossbow. A tribe of 801 members, they currently have recovered 531 acres of land, held in trust by the United States.

In 1976 the Mashpee Wampanoags on Cape Cod filed suit to recover 17,000 acres of land taken from them without the consent of Congress after 1790, therefore in violation of the Non-Intercourse Act. A federal court held that the tribe did not function as a tribe at certain points during the last two hundred years, and were therefore not able to lay claim to the lands in question. At the time, this decision sent shock waves through

Indian New England, opening a door to overturn the landmark Passamaquoddy decision. If nothing else, the decision made tribes wary of choosing legal routes to recover lands taken away from them, and assured that the endpoint for most land claims in New England were political compromises, passed by the United States Congress.

### Current Narragansett Indian Land Claims

During the negotiations of the Maine Settlement Act, the Narragansett Tribe, located in southeastern Rhode Island, started and completed their land claims settlement, passed in 1978 by the United States Congress. The Rhode Island Settlement Act is somewhat unique in that it did not give federal recognition to the Narragansett, as the settlement acts in Massachusetts and Connecticut did for tribes located in those states, but instead the settlement gave 900 acres of land (and another 900 acres to be purchased later) and $3.5 million to the nonprofit corporation known as the Narragansett Tribe of Indians. In 1983 the secretary of interior recognized the Narragansetts as an Indian Nation, thus ensuring that the lands held by the corporation cannot be sold, granted, or taken by anyone without the permission of the secretary of the interior. Currently, the Narragansetts have approximately 2,693 acres of trust lands and 2,150 tribal members, most of whom live on or adjacent to these lands.

### Conclusion

Land claims settlements and assertions of treaty rights are the battles tribes in the Northeast fight on a daily basis to assure the preservation of their peoples and cultures for future generations. Casinos and cash disbursements for past wrongs can hardly be considered justice, but tribal peoples in the Northeast are creative in asserting their rights and cultures in the wake of these partial victories. For these tribes, land issues remain cultural issues—the right to survive as peoples. Tribes in the Northeast, most notably the Penobscot Indian Nation in Maine, are engaged in regulating, monitoring, and protecting treaty fishing resources by using modern environmental management techniques and indigenous knowledge at the same time. The Mashantucket Pequot have rebuilt wetlands with casino profits. The Passamaquoddy and Wampanoag are studying the effects of acid rain on the liver of deer and other wildlife in their hunting territories. Menominee forestry, Mohegan green industry, the

list goes on and on—Northeastern peoples still live and lead as protectors of the earth for us all.

*Darren Ranco*
*University of California, Berkeley*

## ◆ SOUTHEASTERN INDIANS

When Europeans reached the southeastern United States, they encountered Native peoples who were the predecessors of tribes known today as the Catawba, Cherokee, Creek, Chickasaw, Choctaw, and Seminole. Some of these peoples were emerging from the decline of the once widespread culture identified as Mississippian, a term referring to practices associated with the construction of ceremonial mounds central to a village and its cultivated fields of corn, beans, and squash. Although the earthen mounds were passing into disuse, the lives of the succeeding Native peoples still were town-centered. In the sixteenth century the villages of the southeastern peoples were distributed across a territory bounded by the Atlantic Ocean, the Gulf of Mexico, the Trinity River in present-day Texas, and the Ohio River.

Central to the ritual life of these peoples was the Green Corn ceremony, an elaborate thanksgiving and renewal festival usually observed in midsummer. The occasion was significant because the maturation of new corn promised food for winter and seeds for spring; crop failures could result in immediate hunger and long-term famine.

The successful farming reflected in the Green Corn celebration was only part of the economy of the southeastern Indians. Hunting also provided important dietary ingredients. Like farming, hunting was interconnected with spiritual beliefs. Hunters prayed to the spirits of the game before they went hunting, lest offending the animal spirits meant no game for the next hunt. Likewise, once on the hunt the hunter killed no more than needed, since useless slaughter also might anger the spirits of the game.

Even as the Southeastern peoples shared common practices in farming, hunting, and spiritual beliefs, they also shared games. One of the most widely played was the ball game, vividly captured by the American painter George Catlin in his 1834 portrayals of a Choctaw ball play in Oklahoma. So great was Catlin's fascination that he depicted not only two scenes from a match, one with the ball in the air and the other with it on the ground,

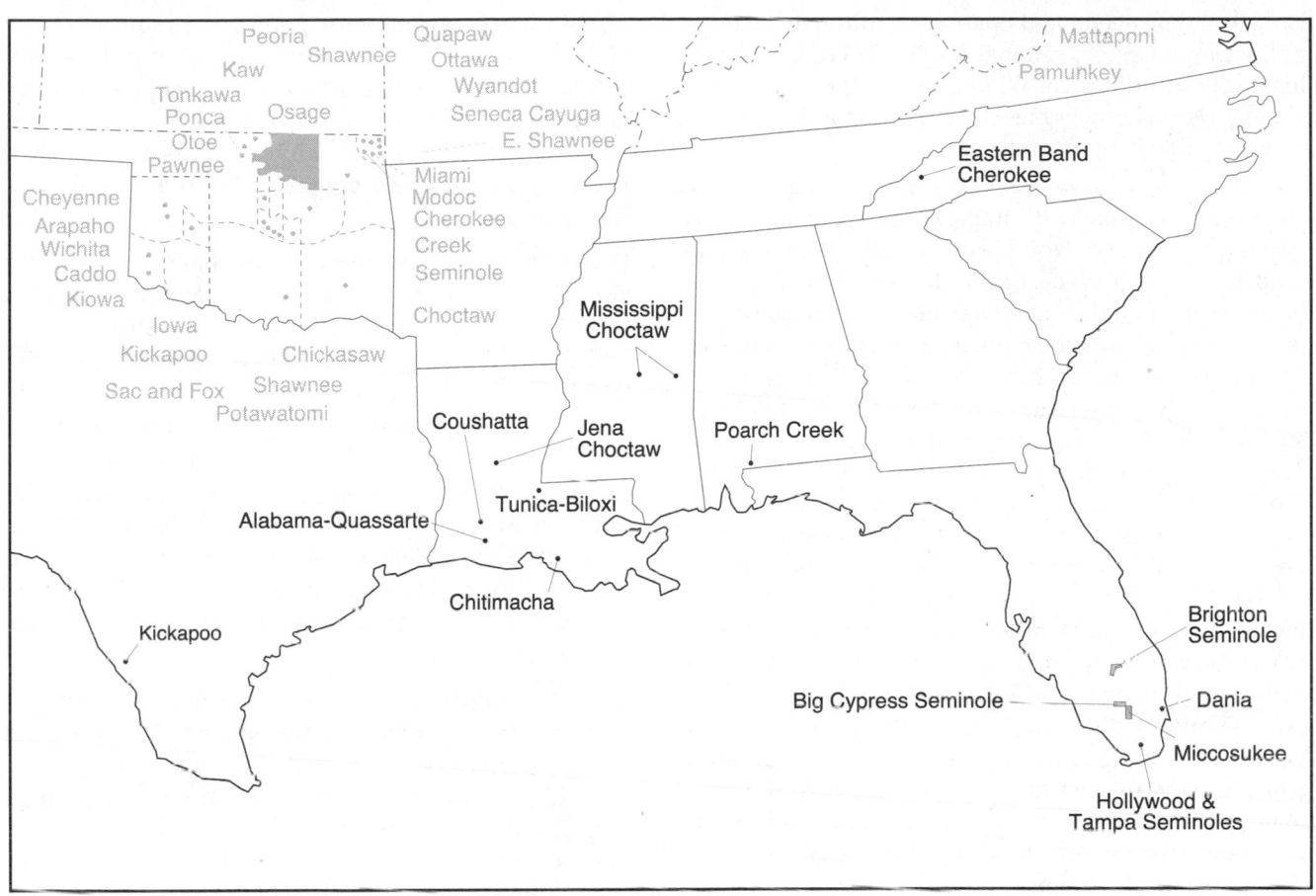

Map of Southeast tribes. (Courtesy of the UCLA American Indian Studies Center)

but also left a portrait of the Choctaw ball player named He-Who-Drinks-the-Juice-of-Stone. The contest was played by teams from competing villages on a level field perhaps 200 yards long. The object was for a team to throw a deerskin ball (stuffed with deer or squirrel hair) past the opposition's goal post at the other end of the field. In the southeastern versions of the game, the players carried two ball play sticks, which could be used to scoop up the ball and forward it. Given the intensity of the physical competition and accompanying gambling, modern attempts to revive the ball game pale in comparison.

Two other rituals common to the southeastern cultures were the use of sacred tobacco and the black drink. The black drink, as the Europeans called it, was a tea brewed from the roasted leaves of the yaupon holly, a shrub that contained caffeine like coffee. Because the Black Drink ceremony was often a preliminary to any major decision or celebration, the participants were left highly stimulated. So important was this shrub to ceremonial life that it was cultivated in small patches far outside its normal range.

A second plant-oriented ritual involved the use of tobacco smoked in a pipe, a ceremony associated with welcome and diplomacy. The sacred or so-called white tobacco was put in a pipe and passed around the circle of participants, a practice that nauseated English Lieutenant Henry Timberlake on his visit to the Cherokee villages in 1760s.

Another similarity for these southeastern peoples was their life in villages, often bound together by common practices and language into a tribe. Most villages were governed by a council of elders and warriors presided over by a chief, who usually came to power through a combination of talent, accomplishment, and membership in an influential family or clan. In most southeastern societies, descent was traced through the mother's line.

Beyond the family, clan membership was extremely important, since clans transcended village boundaries, thus affording the individual a social and political connection throughout the tribe. The mixed-blood Creek leader Alexander McGillivray, for example, had the advantages of bilinguality, basic education, service as a

British trading agent, and opportunity through the death of the Upper Creek principal warrior in 1782, but it was his mother's influential Wind Clan that provided him a Creek political power base from 1783 to 1793, when he was a primary Creek leader.

Tribes were loose associations of villages bound together by language, heritage, custom, and close geographic proximity. None were tightly structured by modern standards; the Creek, for example, more appropriately might be called a confederation, since they were formed as much by outside pressure as by powerful cultural bonds. Certain villages in a tribal grouping sometimes were more influential or sacred than others, such as the Cherokee town of Chota on the Little Tennessee River in present-day Tennessee; yet even the leader of a prominent town really had no more power than persuasion could provide. Efforts by European colonial powers to designate emperors for particular tribes were largely empty gestures. In most instances, if all tribal villages or a percentage of them voted for war or approved a treaty, that decision prevailed only while those villages continued their support. Withdrawal of any village's support freed its people from obligations, a practice that frustrated Europeans, who professed to operate in terms of permanent treaties, boundaries, and alliances. Native peoples, however, were more attuned to political flexibility, social harmony, and spiritual significance than to contractual agreements.

Indeed the religious values of the southeastern peoples might be expressed best in terms of balance or harmony among human beings and the natural and spiritual worlds in which they saw themselves. All things had spirits, either good or evil; success in life depended on the careful cultivation of these spirits by the proper behaviors or the appropriate remedy if you were guilty of an act of disharmony. Even so grave an act as murder might be compensated for if the proper remedies were taken.

The old harmonies were shattered forever when the Europeans arrived. The first visitation for which there is substantial historical evidence was led by the Spanish adventurer Hernando de Soto. During 1540 and 1541, de Soto led his expedition from Tampa Bay into Georgia and then to the Mississippi River. From these newcomers the southeastern peoples learned of a foreign culture, and, unfortunately, of fatal European diseases, against which Native peoples carried no inherited resistance; they died by the thousands. Continued Spanish exploration brought settlements along the Gulf and Atlantic borders from St. Augustine to Pensacola in present-day Florida.

Ultimately, European imperial rivalry brought French and English adventurers to the southeastern region.

By the early seventeenth century, Spain, England, and France expanded their global territories by establishing outposts, subjugating Native peoples, and developing an economic exchange. Although all three promoted conversion of Native peoples to Christianity, only the Spanish achieved limited and temporary success.

For the Native peoples, the exchange of furs and skins for European manufactures created a major alteration in the balance of their lives. Previously hunters had pursued the white-tailed deer only as need dictated. Because deer range only a five square mile area during their lifetimes, only careful avoidance of overhunting and controlled burning of forest underbrush, which renewed the vegetation, maintained the deer herds. The new trade changed the balance, as European market demands for leather enticed the hunters to kill more than they needed. By the 1730s, there was a noticeable decline in the Southeastern deerskin trade.

At the same time, the trade goods impacted cultural patterns. The attraction of finished cloth and clothing items persuaded villagers that bartering was far easier than tanning deerskins. Desirable luxury items also could be obtained in the trade, which provided mirrors, knives, awls, scissors, and Jew's harps. As a result, certain handicrafts disappeared, displaced by European weapons, tools, cloth, and decorative goods. Other dramatic trade-induced changes altered Native societies as alcohol was introduced, gender roles were realigned, and towns became more non-Indian. Alcohol quickly became a curse, as alcoholism and excessive drinking undermined village stability. Alcohol was used by unscrupulous colonials to influence the Native peoples into disadvantageous agreements.

Gender roles, too, were modified by the trade. Formerly these matrilineal, agricultural societies defined roles for males and females in relatively clear, yet balanced terms. Females were important because they bore the children, provided food from the fields, and transformed raw materials into usable products. The trade, however, gave a place of greater importance to the hunters, since commercial hunting brought both staples and luxury goods to the villages. Trading activities also ignored women, since the male-oriented Europeans sought to bargain with the hunters.

Still further social changes took place as traders took up residence in the villages. The households they developed were patterned after the male-dominated European families. The children of these unions adopted their fathers' entrepreneurial lifestyles, thus diluting traditional social practices and increasing the number of mixed-bloods. As a result many tribes became economically dominated by mixed-blood trader families toward the end of the eighteenth century.

The emergence of these trader-originated families intensified tribal divisions. The mixed-blood peoples often were among the first to adopt lifestyles similar to their neighbors who were U.S. citizens. Among the Cherokee, Choctaw, Chickasaw, and Creek, the new European cultural orientations were reflected in economic terms, as the mixed-bloods used their linguistic, educational, and political advantages to prosper. Ferries, inns, trading posts, and farms most often were owned or controlled by those of mixed ancestry. In the 1830s, when the U.S. government sought to relocate the southeastern peoples west of the Mississippi River, antagonism between conservatives and mixed-blood entrepreneurs heightened arguments over whether or not the tribes should move. After removal, even though they may have lost more both in quality and quantity of life, the mixed-bloods were better equipped to start again. Once relocated, they contended for political leadership and held economic control of mills, ferries, inns, stores, and ranching operations.

In the three centuries before their forced move westward, southeastern tribal governments underwent evolution and transformation. From the earliest contacts, European sought to impose their own governmental views on their new neighbors by designating Indian nations, kings, princesses, and emperors. Such titles had little meaning for the Native peoples, who continued their tribal associations until early in the nineteenth century. Only as their populations became more and more mixed and as their U.S. neighbors greedily eyed their lands and pressured for removal did villages and tribal councils seek more formally structured governments, modeled for practical diplomatic purposes after the government of the United States. In the decades just before the tribes were forced westward, they adopted constitutions and created governing bodies that were then transferred west. The Cherokee adopted a constitutional government in 1828, while the Choctaw constitution of 1826 to 1830 proved unstable but was revived again in 1834. The more conservative Creek and Chickasaw retained their traditional government with little change until after removal to Indian Territory, where they adopted constitutional governments in the 1850s and 1860s. Originally they hoped such nation building would help them resist pressure from the United States. However, both before removal and during the period of so-called detribalization in the years between 1880 and 1934, much of this structure was destroyed. In the last fifty years, however, some tribes have reconstituted their governments into the leadership that serves them today.

During the era of removal, because of the continued focus of basic power at the village level, not every individual tribal member, family, or village participated in the move west. The Native peoples living east of the Mississippi River today testify powerfully to the persistence and cultural tenacity of these peoples against overwhelming odds. Today's descendants of the southeastern tribal peoples proudly continue to claim the heritage of their ancestors, in most cases virtually indistinguishable from their non-Indian neighbors. In 1992 there were 222,000 persons of Native American descent living in the ten southeastern states (North Carolina, South Carolina, Georgia, Florida, Kentucky, Tennessee, Alabama, Mississippi, Arkansas, and Louisiana). The inclusion of Virginia and Texas would add another 17,000 and 77,000 respectively. In addition, Oklahoma has a Native American population of 252,000, many descended from southeastern peoples. A century-and-a-half after most of the Southeastern peoples were forced to move west, the Catawba, Cherokee, Creek, Seminole, Choctaw, and other smaller tribal remnants continue to live across the Southeast. Their numbers reflect a general upsurge across the nation between 1980 and 1998 of more than 40 percent in those claiming Native American descent.

## The Catawba

Today most Catawba live in the vicinity of Rock Hill, South Carolina; unlike many Native peoples, all live relatively close to their eighteenth-century homelands. Because they are few in number and lack a large land base or potentially profitable natural resource, in the past they were not well known. Their recent successful actions in securing settlement from the federal and state governments in 1992 has given them a somewhat higher profile. Their present status testifies powerfully to their persistence, resilience, creativity, and flexibility. Time after time observers predicted the end of the Catawba, yet they still survive.

As the British colonies emerged in the late seventeenth century, Indians settled along the upper Wateree River in South Carolina were identified as the Catawba Nation. From the outset of Catawba-South Carolina relations, the Catawba followed a policy of friendly cooperation. During the American Revolution they served as scouts for the South Carolinians. They paid dearly for this when British raiders destroyed their settlements. In the years after the revolution, however, the Catawba wrapped themselves in the flag of patriotism shared with other revolutionary veterans, thus making it difficult for South Carolina to ignore them. Because they could claim no ancestral homeland since time immemorial, and because of colonial South Carolina's rapid expansion, the Catawba sought and received a 144,000 acre reservation in 1763. For the next forty years they persisted by leasing their land, selling pottery and skins, practicing subsistence farming, and serving as slave catchers for tidewater slave owners. After 1800, the equation changed when slavery and upland cotton marched into the Piedmont, the region of rolling hills between the level coastal plain of the Atlantic Ocean and the rugged mountains of the southern Appalachians. At that point Catawba land became more valuable than tribal slave catching. Reduced in population to no more than thirty families and under unrelenting pressure to sell their land, the Catawba signed a treaty with South Carolina in 1840, exchanging their 144,000 acres for $5,000 and promises of assistance in relocation. Many moved to North Carolina in a fruitless attempt to live with the Cherokee. Within twelve years they returned to South Carolina, where they were given 630 acres of their old land.

After the Civil War, their survival faced another threat in the form of Jim Crow legislation; in 1879 South Carolina law forbade interracial marriage. Freedom to move back and forth socially and economically became further restricted. Consequently the Catawba either had to cling to the security of Indianness or face an insurmountable color barrier that placed them in the "black" category. The Catawba responded by asserting their Indianness through speaking Catawba and expanding the production and sale of Indian crafts. Then, in a departure from their traditional resistance toward converting to Christianity, they welcomed Mormon missionaries in 1883. Over time the Mormons assisted the Catawba in building community cohesion and gaining education through the establishment of Catawba schools, a necessity in South Carolina, where the only schools for non-whites were for blacks. In the last fifty years, however, a modified racial climate has eliminated the need for separate Catawba schools; there are none listed in the 1990 report of the National Advisory Council on Indian Education.

In 1943 they became legal citizens of South Carolina and federally recognized Indians, which means they were acknowledged as a tribe by the U.S. government and were eligible for governmental benefits accompanying such recognition. The next year an additional 3,400 acres of land were purchased for them. Although this step was intended to allow the Catawba to become small farmers, that option proved unprofitable. By 1959, consequently, they voted to terminate their tribal status and sell most of their lands. Under the plan, any tribal member could choose land from the reservation tract or a cash settlement from the sale of unclaimed portions of the reservation. On 2 July 1960, the final tribal roll listed 631 Catawba; termination came on 1 July 1962. Within a matter of years, observers assumed the people of the river would be no more.

Early in the 1980s, however, the Catawba underwent a resurgence, choosing to fight for restored status rather than capitulate and disappear. They not only sought federal recognition, but also instigated land recovery lawsuits that would have challenged the land titles of more than 60,000 defendants. They sought recovery of more than $2 billion worth of land plus trespass damages, attorneys' fees, and court costs. In 1993 federal legislation was signed eliminating their claim to 144,000 acres of prime real estate, but giving them a variety of federal and state benefits. Included was the right to build two high stakes bingo parlors in South Carolina, one on off-reservation lands. Analysts of this victory argue that the Catawba received high ratings in a "policy formula model" used to determine recognition.

All Catawba now may point with pride to their new status. In these modern Catawba still survive the spirits of ancestral heroes many decades after the predicted demise of the tribe.

## The Cherokee

The Cherokee Indians who once inhabited the southern Appalachian mountains live today in widely separated areas. Those of the Eastern Band live largely in western North Carolina on or near the Qualla Boundary, as the Eastern Reservation is called; those who claim membership in the Western Band generally live in Oklahoma. There are many from both bands who live and work as Cherokee Americans throughout the United States. Those who keep their language alive speak an Iroquoian language with some regional variations.

According to archaeological evidence, the Cherokee and their ancestors lived in the southern Appalachians for several hundred years before the Europeans arrived. Seventeenth-century visitors to the Cherokee villages found them located in mountain river valleys where there was adequate space for dwellings, council houses, and agricultural fields. Because the Cherokee were a matrilineal society, their fields were controlled by Cherokee women. Women of great influence became known as Beloved Women, often working behind the scenes in shaping decisions. A woman who had taken her husband's place in war might be awarded the title War Woman. That the role of women still has a powerful effect today is reflected in Wilma Mankiller's elections as tribal chair of the Western Cherokee in 1987 and 1991.

Assistant Secretary of the Interior Kevin Gover addresses southeast tribal leaders. (Photo by Carol Lujan)

In the late seventeenth century, there were approximately 30,000 Cherokee living in about sixty settlements. Within one hundred years, smallpox, other epidemics, and warfare had reduced their population to only 7,500. From the early seventeenth through the twentieth centuries, the major point of contention between the Cherokee and the Europeans was land. From 1783 to 1835 the Cherokee fought a losing battle in defense of their lands. After the revolution, land-hungry settlers crossed the mountains in search of homesteads; then came eager planters seeking new soil for upland cotton cultivation. By 1825 some Cherokee had relocated voluntarily to Arkansas and Texas, hoping to escape the encroaching Americans. Those still in the east were divided between the highly acculturated mixed-bloods and the more conservative, traditionalist full-bloods.

In 1835 a minority of the tribal leaders, primarily mixed-bloods, signed the controversial Treaty of New Echota, which led to the eviction of those Cherokee living in South Carolina, Georgia, Tennessee, and Alabama. In North Carolina, however, about 1,000 Cherokee managed to escape removal with the cooperation of sympathetic state officials. According to their understanding of the treaties in 1817, 1819, and 1835, the Cherokee claimed North Carolina citizenship. One North Carolinian, William H. Thomas (or Wil-Usdi, as the Cherokee called him) bought land in his name for the Cherokee, went to court in their defense, and visited Washington, D.C. on behalf of the Eastern Band's share in any general settlement with all Cherokee. When the majority of the Cherokee moved to the Indian Territory (present-day Oklahoma), the tribe's internal problems were not solved. Hatred deepened after the political murders on 22 June 1839 of John Ridge, Major Ridge, and Elias Boudinot, three Cherokee leaders who signed the despised removal agreement.

During the early years west of the Mississippi, the Cherokee sought to survive economically, establish a workable government acceptable to all, reduce tribal factionalism, avoid rivalries with traditional tribal enemies, and maintain relations with the federal bureaucracy. Even in the West the Cherokee could not escape demands on their land base. Ranchers desired the Cherokee Outlet, a sixty-mile-wide strip running west from the ninety-sixth to the one-hundredth meridians.

After the Civil War, the federal government demanded land as compensation because the Cherokee Nation officially joined the South; this action ignored the loyal Union service of several hundred non-slave owners. Then promoters of all stripes began eyeing the unused or unassigned Cherokee lands. Even after the Cherokee ceded their unassigned lands to the federal government in 1891, speculators schemed to divide the tribal land into individual allotments. Land interests ultimately prevailed with the passage of the Dawes Act (1887) and the Curtis Act (1898); the former divided the lands and the latter eliminated tribal governments. The Curtis Act, however, led to wholesale fraud. After Oklahoma statehood in 1907 almost every species of trickery imaginable was practiced; the Cherokee were bribed, threatened, cajoled, bought out, and generally manipulated. With few exceptions all the mineral rich or arable lands fell into the hands of non-Cherokee.

Today, the Western Cherokee number more than 175,000, many of whom live in northeastern Oklahoma. Despite the frequent assertions of some non-Indians that there are fewer Indians, the opposite is true. There are more numerically, and, of those, an increasing number are proud to identify themselves as such. In combination with their eastern counterparts the Cherokee are one of the four largest tribes in the United States.

During the 1980s and 1990s, the Western Cherokee reasserted themselves under the leadership of Principal Chief Wilma Mankiller. An inspirational leader who empowers people to independence, Mankiller was reelected with more than 83 percent of the vote. Community rebuilding since the early 1980s has resulted in tribally owned businesses, including defense subcontracting plants and horticultural operations. The annual budget for the tribe is $54 million. Whether the accomplishment is as basic as the men, women, and children of the tiny village of Bell laying sixteen miles of pipe for running water, or as venturesome as the construction of a hydroelectric facility worth millions of dollars, power is returning to these Western Cherokee peoples at every level. The key to their success, says Mankiller, is that Cherokee never give up.

During the first three decades of the twentieth century, the Eastern Band wrestled with the related difficulties of tribal membership, enrollment, and allotment. When a tribal roll was opened, more than 12,000 people applied to be included; tribal leaders protested that no more than 2,000 could possibly be eligible. The long disagreement over this matter delayed any action of dividing the land until the Indian Reorganization Act of 1934 ended allotment of Indian land. There was a further economic decline in the 1930s when a chestnut blight destroyed more than 60 percent of the timber on the tribal lands. After World War II some economic recovery came to the Eastern Cherokee in the form of highways, a national park, and a historical drama. The roads needed for modern automobile travel were developed by those seeking creation of the Great Smoky Mountains National Park, whose lands lay adjacent to the Cherokee homeland. If visitors who came to the park in search of natural splendor could be tempted to stay overnight, an income–producing tourist industry might develop. By the early 1950s the Cherokee Historical Association had commissioned and then produced *Unto These Hills*, an emotional drama based on the Cherokee experiences. Regardless of its historical accuracy, it attracts many visitors, as does Oconoluftee Village and the Museum of the Cherokee Indian. All are aimed at affording a glimpse of Cherokee culture, distinct from the trinket businesses, where a few Cherokee pose for tourists in Plains Indian costumes. Even this prosperity, however, has its problems, since much of the money and influence tends to be controlled by relatively few Cherokee.

A cross section of Eastern Cherokee society includes tribal members with relatively stable incomes as well as many living near or below the poverty level. The relative isolation of many tribal members plus the seasonal nature of the tourist industry continues to work to the economic disadvantage of many Cherokee. One unusual bright spot on the economic horizon has been the development of an enormous bingo parlor, where almost 4,000 people can play for prizes worth thousands of dollars.

Today, there are more than 9,500 Eastern Cherokee who share an abiding sense of place and kinship, as well as an egalitarianism that makes tribal politics both interesting and fractious. Most of those who live on the Qualla Boundary, as the reservation for the Eastern Band of Cherokee is known, work in Waynesville or Sylva, North Carolina, while those from the outlying conservative Cherokee village known as Snowbird work for the National Forest Service, the Tennessee Valley Authority, or the Stanley Furniture plant in nearby Robbinsville, North Carolina. In an attempt to guarantee employment for their children, the Eastern Cherokee paid $28.8 million for the Carolina Mirror Company in 1986; as the tribal council leader has indicated, there is no future without jobs. Jobs will mean the Cherokee can continue their tradition of mixed dependency on Indian economic culture and personal self-reliance that has allowed them to face the twenty-first century as both Cherokee and Americans.

## The Creek

At the end of the twentieth century, the Creek, like their former adversaries the Cherokee, lived in widely separated areas. Before the Civil War, the majority remained in Alabama. Today their descendants lived in Alabama, Oklahoma, and across the United States. After the arrival of the Europeans, the Muskogee peoples moved inland away from the expanding newcomers. Clustering on Ochese Creek as well as on the Chattahoochee River, the villagers were labeled Creek by British traders from Charleston, South Carolina. Those nearest Charleston were called the Lower Creek, those farther away the Upper Creek. Expansion of Georgia after 1733 pushed these peoples deeper into the interior, eventually into present-day Alabama. From their towns they attempted to play off the European powers seeking dominance in eastern North America. Wherever they located, Creek lands lay in the path of the westward expanding United States. Creek defensive actions brought repeated invasions until 1814, when forces under General Andrew Jackson defeated them at the Battle of Horseshoe Bend. In the minds of Jackson and his fellow expansionists, Creek resistance legitimized removal beyond the Mississippi River. Although the Creek ceded 20 million acres of southern Georgia and central Alabama lands at the Treaty of Fort Jackson, the Jacksonians would not be satisfied until all Native Americans east of the Mississippi had been relocated.

The Creek War provided a convenient excuse for Tennessee to demand the removal of the Creek, Cherokee, and Chickasaw. Georgia politicians, moreover, were eager to manipulate the Creek agency for purposes of profit and land speculation. When Georgia succeeded in expelling the Creek, her neighbor Alabama acted to keep the refugees moving west. First, Alabama extended her laws over all the Indian lands in the state. Then, under the Treaty of 1832, the Creek Nation in the east was no longer recognized by the federal or state governments. Creeks who wished to claim allotments and stay in the east were soon subjected to constant harassment, as their white neighbors sought to drive them away.

From 1820 to 1840, by one means or another, the Creek were forced to move to Indian Territory. They were exposed to a foreign climate, often without the barest of necessities, despite promised aid from the U.S. government. Dispossessed and abandoned, many died, yet others survived, intent on rebuilding the Creek Nation in the West. Those who remained behind in Alabama eked out a marginal existence, while resisting pressure to move. They insisted that according to the Treaty of Fort Jackson (1814) they could claim a section of land.

Despite the pressures against them, a few held on; land belonging to the McGhee family was reaffirmed in 1836. Lynn McGhee's 240–acre claim at the headwaters of Perdido Creek became the center for three nearby settlements that came to be known as the Poarch Band of Creek. In 1975 the Poarch Band of Creek petitioned the U.S. government for recognition and was acknowledged as a federally recognized tribe in 1984. Today these Poarch Creek peoples number more than 400; in 1990 their tribal chairman was Eddie L. Tullis, who was also chairperson of the National Advisory Council on Indian Education.

## The Seminole

During the years of Creek withdrawal westward, a number of Lower Creek migrated into present-day Florida. In order to distinguish them from their kinsmen, British officials called these separatists the Seminole Creek, or Seminole, a corruption of the Spanish *cimarrone*. Quickly adapting to their new environment, they became skillful herders, raising sleek ponies and fat cattle on the grassy savannas. So complete was their cultural adjustment that one of their leading chiefs was named Cowkeeper, who was vividly described in the prose of William Bartram, a Philadelphia botanist who visited the Seminole in the 1770s.

When Georgia frontiersmen expanded farther south, the Seminole retreated again. They continued their adaptation, adopting lighter dress and modifying the Creek cabin so that it became an open-sided dwelling, called a *chiki*, with a raised floor and thatched roof. Changes in agricultural patterns followed, since Florida soils differ from those to the north. Ultimately, the pressure of expanding plantations and farms pushed the Seminole so far south they had little land.

During the period that these former Creek were becoming Seminole, they attracted the attention of both the neighboring states and the national government. Officials in Georgia, Alabama, and Florida became unhappy because the Seminole would not agree to join the exodus westward by southeastern tribes. Their presence threatened Florida's claim to all the state's lands. At the same time, the Seminole were regarded as dangerous to peace and stability, because they harbored runaway slaves. As long as the Seminole camps remained in Florida, their camps were a refuge for runaways, and no slave-owning planter could feel secure. For the slaves captured by the Seminole, however, slavery was a much less rigorous institution. Several former slaves rose to positions of influence through their ability as interpreters and their familiarity with the plantation lifeways. In the 1830s the increasingly racist and xenophobic society in the southern United States denounced Seminole tolerance of

African Americans. Outside the South, ironically, courageous Seminole resistance attracted some public sympathy.

No amount of sympathy, however, changed the federal government's demand that the Seminole move. By force and by forced treaty, the Seminole were transported west. By 1842, there were 2,833 Seminole survivors in Indian Territory. The Oklahoma Seminole of today are the descendants of these refugee people.

While many Seminole moved west, small bands in Florida remained hidden deep in the Big Cypress Swamp, in the Everglades, and in other isolated areas. During the second half of the nineteenth century and the first decade of the next, these survivors lived by hunting, trapping, and fishing. The fashion industry's demand for bird feathers and animal skins offered them a means to trade for basic necessities unavailable in their local area. Most of their food came from subsistence farming of small patches.

Their fragile lifesystem began to collapse, however, early in the twentieth century. In 1908, Florida began to drain the Everglades in hopes of producing more agricultural land for commercial purposes; more people came to Florida via the ever expanding railroad system. Both federal and state laws outlawed the use of bird plumes.

In the 1890s, however, Florida officials began buying land as a place for the Seminole to locate. The greatest difficulty arose in trying to persuade these fiercely independent people that they should live on these reservations. By 1932 less than 20 percent of the 562 Florida Seminole had relocated. The spirit of resistance and self-reliance built from years of avoiding the federal government was unlikely to disappear overnight. Living in remote, self-sufficient camps, they supplied their basic needs, but needed cash to buy coffee, salt, sugar, rifles, ammunition, and the seemingly ever-present sewing machine. With the decline of the trade in plumes and hides, seasonal agricultural labor became a source of cash. A few families became part of the growing tourist industry by establishing commercial villages where they put on public displays of Seminole life.

During the 1930s, however, in response both to federal Indian policy and activities by tribal leaders and pro-tribal Florida interest groups, Seminole life patterns began to change. Tracts of land were obtained through purchase and exchange that resulted in the creation of several reservations, two of which were developed into cattle-raising operations. The success of the cattle ranches attracted some Seminole to abandon isolated settlements and relocate on the reservations. A new and more dependable economic base

likewise meant an improved quality of life for the Seminole. At the same time the creation of federal agencies for the Seminole increased the tribe's exposure to and cooperation with federal officials. Also during the 1930s and 1940s came the first major success in converting the Seminole to Christianity. All these changes went a long way toward forming the lives of the twentieth-century Seminole. Indeed the adaptability they have displayed since the seventeenth century has assisted them over and over again. Thereby they were able to deal with the termination policies of the 1950s as well as the creation and federal recognition in 1957 of the Seminole Tribe of Florida, Incorporated, followed in 1962 by the separation of a group who wished to be recognized as the Miccosukee Tribe of Indians.

Today, both the Seminole and the Miccosukee survive in heavily populated, non-Indian Florida. Beginning in 1979, the Seminole began operating a bingo parlor offering 1,700 seats and $10,000 jackpots. Since that time, more parlors have been opened, generating enough revenue to endow tribal scholarships, establish a credit union, and expand the tribal cattle herds. Despite this success, the tribe must be aware that they receive only 50 percent of the income and that organized crime is always ready to move in. On the environmental front, too, some difficulties may arise, as developers seek far and wide for new sources of natural resources, such as those in the Big Cypress area.

## The Choctaw

Before the majority of the Choctaw were forced west in the nineteenth century, their settlements were located in present–day central and southern Mississippi, as well as southwestern Alabama. During the seventeenth and eighteenth centuries, their lives were impacted by European newcomers. Although the French (and the Spanish after 1783) at New Orleans were the closest in proximity, enterprising English traders also reached their villages; the trade introduced cloth, firearms, tools, and alcohol. During the late seventeenth and early eighteenth centuries there was also traffic in Indian slaves, an exchange that intensified rivalries with the Chickasaw, the Creek, and other nearby peoples. Trade generated rivalries, as some villages supported the most generous provider of quality goods at the lowest prices, whether France, Spain or Great Britain. Included in the trade-induced stress were the resident traders, whose mixed-blood families later rose to positions of prominence in the tribe.

After the emergence of the United States, Choctaw lands became the stumbling block in Choctaw relations with the new country. Eager land developers paid little attention to Choctaw claims as they laid lines across the maps of the Mississippi Territory. So great was the demand for new acreage that the federal government pressured for rights of way to allow the construction of roads through the Choctaw homeland. Nothing seemed an obstacle to the settlers. From the time the Mississippi Territory was organized in 1798 until removal, politicians repeated their demands for the relocation of the tribes and the distribution of their lands. The cooperation of some Choctaw leaders was bought with cash and other gifts. Choctaw tribal integrity also was undermined by the efforts of missionaries to convert them into Christian farmers, who could practice a market agriculture.

In 1801, the Choctaw signed the Treaty of Fort Adams, hoping a definition of tribal boundaries would satisfy the demands of the United States. No treaty was ever enough, not even the combined results of Fort Adams, Mount Dexter (1805), and Doak's Stand (1820), the latter of which exchanged 8 million acres of Choctaw homelands for 13 million unfamiliar western acres. Although a few moved voluntarily, most wished to stay. Yet even loyal service as allies during the Creek War of 1813 and 1814 did not protect them, for the determined state of Mississippi moved to terminate all their rights. By the notorious Dancing Rabbit Creek Treaty in September 1830, the Choctaw signed over their homelands and agreed to emigrate; this was accomplished through a combination of threatened force and the bribery of certain chiefs.

The Choctaw movement west was as painful as those of their southeastern neighbors Fraud, mismanagement, and corruption marked those in charge of the move, while disease and death stalked the Choctaw each mile. The combined deaths from the journey's difficulties and subsequent cholera and smallpox outbreaks reduced the tribal population from 18,963 in 1830 to 13,666 by 1860.

Once in the West, the Choctaw tended to follow divisional lines between mixed-bloods and full-bloods, with the former following the market agricultural economy they had practiced in Mississippi and the latter retreating to subsistence agriculture. Despite privation, drought, and floods, the Choctaw rebuilt their government, towns, and farms. By the 1850s their economy had recovered sufficiently to allow them to market cotton, cattle, and timber.

When they moved west, the Choctaw took along their slaves. Because of their close proximity to the Confederate states of Arkansas and Texas, the tribe almost unanimously sided with the Confederacy in 1861. At war's end, however, the Choctaw were forced to abolish slavery and cede the western portion of their territory, for which they were compensated $300,000.

Yet even as they tried to rebuild once more, the U.S. government pressured the Choctaw to abandon tribal control in favor of private land ownership. Railroad expansionists clamored for rights-of-way and land grants, while coal developers pressured for mineral rights and access. The end of the Choctaw Nation was assured by the Curtis Act of 1898, under which the remaining tribal lands in Indian Territory were divided into individual private allotments. The process required the creation of a tribal roll listing 18,981 Oklahoma Choctaw, 5,994 freedmen and their descendants, and 1,639 Choctaw who had moved west from Mississippi after the Civil War. Approximately 1,000 Choctaw still lived in the east. After 1906 there was no tribal government, a status in effect until 1934 when the Indian Reorganization Act allowed a return to tribal governments; the Choctaw first formed an advisory council, but did not elect a tribal chief until 1948.

In Oklahoma today, the tribal government promotes programs aimed at improving the quality of life among the Choctaw people. There is a Choctaw Housing Authority in Hugo, an Indian Hospital in Tallahina, three Indian health clinics, five community centers, and ten Head Start centers. Several businesses are operated by the Choctaw, including a bingo parlor, a resort complex, and a travel center. Profits from these along with federal funds then can be directed toward projects needed by the tribe. With success comes responsibility, as the Choctaw discovered in 2000 when the Tenth Circuit Court held them responsible for certain gaming taxes from which the Choctaw believed themselves exempt.

During the early nineteenth century, those who remained behind in Mississippi were driven into the depths of poverty by the new landowners. Yet the Mississippi Choctaw persisted. After the passage of the Indian Reorganization Act, they moved slowly toward recognition as a separate entity; their cause was helped in 1944 by the creation of a land base, a 16,000–acre reservation. Under the provisions of federal recognition granted in 1978, the government also established the Mississippi Choctaw Agency, which assists the seven Choctaw settlements with education and general welfare. With their tribal headquarters at Philadelphia, Mississippi, they have established a development company and created an industrial park, which houses plants producing not only greeting cards but also wiring harnesses and radio speakers for automobiles.

The most dramatic results for the Mississippi Choctaw have come under the leadership of Chief Philip Martin, whose pursuit of Choctaw self-determination won him an unprecedented fourth-term election in 1991. Through the adroit application of economic development principles and skillful use of Washington,

D.C. lobbyists, the Choctaw in Mississippi have undergone an economic transformation in the past twenty years. Average household income has risen from $2500 to $24,100 and the unemployment rate has dropped from 75 percent to 2 percent. The Choctaw are now the third largest employer in Mississippi, employing 6,000 people at wages of more $123 million a year. In addition to the original automobile parts production facility and greeting card plant, there are two golf courses with two more underway, a casino in operation with another under construction, and a Chat Enterprise subsidiary in Mexico.

More than 8,000 Choctaw live in Mississippi today, with approximately 4,400 living on the reservation itself. The majority speak both Choctaw and English, but there are continuing adult education efforts aimed at improving language skills and educational attainment. According to the revised tribal constitution of 1975, the Mississippi Choctaw govern themselves under the protection of the federal government. Together with their Oklahoma kin and those living elsewhere, the Choctaw number more than 45,000. Many travel each year to the Choctaw Indian Fair each July at Pearl River, Mississippi, or to the Tuskahoma, Oklahoma, Labor Day festival to celebrate and preserve their Choctaw heritage.

### The Chickasaw

The Chickasaw, kinsmen of the Choctaw with whom they share the Muskogean language and a migration story, lived in extreme northwestern Alabama, northern Mississippi, western Tennessee, and western Kentucky. Although relatively few in number, the 3,500 to 4,500 Chickasaw gained wide respect for courageously defending their homelands. Their success in defeating French invaders on three different occasions attracted the attention of the British, who won the Chickasaw as allies by exploiting their trade advantage. However, this involved the Chickasaw in an almost unending series of wars against France and her Indian allies. As a result many Chickasaw lives were lost; some losses were replaced, however, by the Chickasaw practice of adoption and absorption of remnant tribes.

After the defeat of France in 1763, the Chickasaw lived in relative peace for more than twenty years under the leadership of Payamataha and Piomingo. Both these leaders tried to stem the tide of European influences, but pressure to accommodate came from increasing numbers of mixed-blood families, whose success in trade, agriculture, and slavery created a lifestyle different from the traditional Chickasaw way. During the American Revolution, Chickasaw service as British allies brought more outsiders when Loyalists sought refuge in the Chickasaw towns. After the Revolution, the Chickasaw signed a treaty with the United States at Hopewell, South Carolina, in January 1786. The treaty guaranteed the Chickasaw their lands, territories, and the right to manage their own affairs.

Initial U.S. relations with the Chickasaw were ineffective because the Spanish at New Orleans wooed the tribe. Consequently Chickasaw politics were complicated by rivalries among a Spanish–allied party, an American–allied party, those who vacillated, and the self-serving mixed-bloods. Pressure from the pro–Spanish Creek under Alexander McGillivray added to Chickasaw woes. McGillivray's death in 1793 and the signing of the Treaty of San Lorenzo (1798) reduced Chickasaw difficulties slightly.

Despite internal political rivalries, the Chickasaw became increasingly tied to the United States. After 1802 a government trading post operated at Chickasaw Bluffs (present-day Memphis) to trade for the skins and furs brought in by the still-successful Chickasaw hunters. The tribe supported the United States by rejecting Tecumseh's appeals in 1811 and aiding Jackson's forces against the Redstick Creek at Horseshoe Bend in 1814. Their loyalty, however, did not protect them when U.S. commissioners stripped them in 1818 of their Tennessee and Kentucky lands, leaving only their territory in northern Mississippi and northwestern Alabama.

Although political rivalries prevailed within the nation, all agreed in their opposition to removal. Under constant pressure from both federal and state governments, a few Chickasaw leaders were persuaded to look at a proposed western territory in 1828, but they returned to report they found nothing suitable. Despite their persistence, their resistance was undermined by the passage of the Indian Removal Act (1830) in 1830 and the impact of Mississippi and Alabama state laws, especially the statutes that abolished tribal law and forbade the functioning of tribal government.

In 1830 at Franklin, Tennessee, the Chickasaw finally agreed to exchange their eastern territory for suitable western lands. The new stumbling block was suitability, which delayed migration for another seven years. When no acceptable land was found, the treaty of Pontotoc Creek (1832) was forced on them to increase the pressure. By then most Chickasaw regarded removal as inevitable. Ultimately, the Chickasaw were permitted to buy land in Indian Territory from their former neighbors, the Choctaw. This arrangement was to be temporary, but after their migrations began in 1837, many Chickasaw preferred the security of Choctaw lands. They were persuaded to relocate only after the federal government had built Forts Washita and Arbuckle to protect them from the plains peoples.

By the 1850s, the beginnings of Chickasaw recovery were apparent in the farms, ferries, mills, gins, and mercantile establishments appearing in the Chickasaw District. Prosperity especially was obvious among the mixed-bloods; a Colbert family member operated a Red River ferry at an annual profit of $1,000. One promising development was in stock raising, a natural step for the well-known breeders of the Chickasaw horse. During the 1850s a tribal constitution and government were put in place and efforts undertaken to establish schools.

Much of their recovery was undermined, however, by the Civil War. Although the Chickasaw had little affection for the South, their location near the southern states of Arkansas and Texas prompted them to join the Confederacy. Tragedy came in the destruction and dislocation caused by the war, as once again they underwent economic decline and loss of land. A particularly thorny problem was the place of the Chickasaw freedmen, the former slaves of the Chickasaw who became free at the end of the Civil War. From 1866 to 1906, the Chickasaw resisted pressure to incorporate the freedmen into the tribe. Final settlement of the matter came only when the names of 4,670 Chickasaw freedmen were listed on the tribal rolls in 1906. Pressure for more land cessions after the war disturbed the Chickasaw even as it did their neighbors. Some Chickasaw favored allotment as a means of ending the ongoing disputes with the federal and state governments and to satisfy individuals and businesses clamoring for land. Under the stipulations of the Dawes Commission, the Chickasaw began enrollment and allotment. The Chickasaw list included the names of 1,538 full-bloods, 4,146 mixed-bloods, 635 intermarried whites, and 4,670 Chickasaw freedmen. The result of this procedure ultimately was the loss of most Chickasaw lands and mineral developments. Even the tribal leadership became a shadow.

Within the last three decades, there has been an attempt to reestablish a Chickasaw presence in Oklahoma. One of the obstacles in the path is the fractional number of those who can claim to be Chickasaw. Practically speaking the Chickasaw, never numerous to begin with, are perhaps the most intermarried of those who once lived in the Southeast. Nevertheless there are more than 8,000 persons today who identify themselves as Chickasaw. In recent years the governor and council of the Chickasaw Nation have worked to reawaken a sense of pride. Several local councils have been organized in Oklahoma counties and an annual gathering called at Byng, Oklahoma. The Chickasaw Housing Authority worked tirelessly in the 1970s to improve the quality of housing, especially for those living below the poverty level. Like many tribes in the late twentieth century, the Chickasaw have attempted to profit from federally approved Indian gaming (controlled by the Indian Gaming Regulatory Act). In addition, arts and crafts outlets, a motel owned by the tribe, and several educational programs have been pushed, all of which offer economic opportunities and encouragement to the people who proudly carry their Chickasaw heritage into the twenty-first century.

## Conclusion

For many Native peoples living in the Southeast today, the past twenty years have been a period of marked population growth, parallel to similar gains nationally. Those who reported their Indian heritage to the census questions in 1970 numbered nearly 70,000, while in 1990 the total had risen to more than 211,000. Included in this total are persons living as independent citizens in urban centers as well as those living as members of organized groups on or near reservations, such as the Eastern Cherokee, the Mississippi Choctaw, the Poarch Creek, the Seminole, the Miccosukee, the Catawba, the Coushatta, the Chitimacha, and the Tunica-Biloxi. There are others closely attached to tribal remnants, some of whom wish for federal recognition, while others have achieved it, such as the Catawba. Yet others, like the Lumbee of North Carolina and the Houma of Louisiana, have been unsuccessful in their applications for federal status. Analysts of these failures cite possible racism on the part of authorizing agencies, which could be one of the hidden factors in not achieving positive ratings on the "policy formulation model" for federal recognition.

In Virginia, those who may be called Pocahontas's people have adopted a strategy of state recognition. The Pamunkey and Mattaponi have state reservations along the upper tributaries of the York River, while nearby live other neighboring groups such as the Rappahannock, the Eastern Chickahominy, and the Western Chickahominy. Presently, their relatively small numbers and inability to cooperate effectively limit the programs undertaken.

Attempts to retain identity through practicing culture and language are difficult as well as painstakingly slow. For those who speak no Cherokee, for example, the learning process is a difficult one. Attending tribal gatherings, participating in attempts at intertribal cooperation, and pursuing recognition are all steps that may be taken. Many Southeastern peoples, however, face the twenty-first century with pride and expectation. The Seminole, the Eastern Cherokee, the Miccosukee, the Mississippi Choctaw, the Catawba, and the Poarch Creek enjoy the benefits of tribal organization and federal status. They anticipate continued economic opportunity and improvement. Their success, moreover, may encourage some of the smaller groups to press for federal recognition in hope of improving their situation.

*James H. O'Donnell III*
*Marietta College*

## ◆ SOUTHWESTERN INDIANS

Contrary to anthropological northern migration theory, many Southwestern American Indian nations believe that their people and cultures evolved from or near the Southwest. These beliefs are embedded in American Indian religions and cultural ceremonies and are passed from one generation to the next. Consequently, land is considered sacred and has important significance and meaning that is integrated into the American Indian cultures and religions. Mostly a desert and alpine semiarid region, there are numerous sacred sites located throughout the Southwest such as the four sacred mountains of the Navajo Nation and the sacred Blue Lake of Taos Pueblo.

The precolonized Southwest saw the gradual development of many agricultural communities, which by C.E. 900 consisted of multistory buildings and large ceremonial centers. These buildings resembled the round underground kiva ceremonial rooms found among the present-day Hopi in northern Arizona and the Pueblo villages in eastern New Mexico. First on the Colorado Plateau (Mesa Verde) in present-day Colorado, were the Anasazi, or Ancient Ones, who lived in multistoried cliff dwellings. Between C.E. 900 and 1200, many major trade and ceremonial societies emerged at places known today as Canyon de Chelly and Chaco Canyon, where archaeologists have been studying the ruins of these relatively large prehistoric cities. Some one to two hundred cities developed and were interconnected by walkways and trade relations. Large cities of the Southwest appear to have carried on trade with cities as far south as Central America and as far west as the Pacific Coast. Artifacts have been found to indicate that significant trade took place among these ancient civilizations located hundreds of miles apart.

An extreme drought between 1275 and 1300 caused the southwestern peoples to leave their cities and move closer to fresh water sources. The Hopi moved to villages along the Colorado River, while most others moved to present-day eastern New Mexico and constructed villages along the Rio Grande River and its tributaries. In 1540, on the eve of Spanish exploration of northern Mexico, the village-dwelling agriculturists numbered around 200,000. Other peoples, including many Hohokam speakers such as the Tohono O'Odham and Pima, previously lived by irrigation and farming but were forced to rely more and more on hunting and gathering in the desert area of the Southwest, and to live near major water sources such as the Colorado River.

Besides the Pueblo and Hohokam (present-day Pima and Tohono O'Odham), the other major people in the Southwest were the Athapascan-speaking Dine (Navajo) and Apache. The Athapascan traded and intermarried with the Pueblo peoples and also became involved in intersociety politics over such issues as water usage and territory. Navajo and Apaches allied with one or another of the villages. These alliances influenced both Athapascan and Pueblo cultures. Athapascans integrated some aspects of Pueblo worldview within their own cultural themes that enhanced further their already complex and powerful creation histories and pantheons of spirit beings.

When Spanish colonization began in the early 1600s, the village peoples were controlled strictly and their ceremonies and rituals suppressed. The Spanish authorities gave land grants to military officers for past service and granted the officers the right to command Indian labor. Many Pueblos were forced to perform work annually on the ranches and farms of the Spanish officers and upper class. Furthermore, by 1628 Spanish missionaries were establishing churches among the Pueblos and demanding conversion to Christianity and abandonment of traditional Indian religious views. Young Puebloans were forced into the Spanish military, which existed principally to make slave raids into areas peripheral to the New Mexico colony. For two centuries, the Navajo, Apache, and Ute people, who were in the present-day southern Colorado area, defended themselves from these attacks.

In 1682 the Pueblo spiritual leader Pope led a rebellion that forced the Spanish and allied Indians to retreat to present-day El Paso, Texas. By 1696 Spanish military forces again regained control of the Pueblo villages in the Rio Grande Valley, and some Pueblos left their villages to join the Navajo for protection from the Spanish invaders. During that period Navajos fought against the Spanish by raiding farms for horses, manufactured goods, cattle, and sheep. Navajo raids were in retaliation for kidnapping Navajo women and children or to gain material necessities for survival. Eventually, during the 1700s, many Navajo relied less on hunting and adopted ranching as a major form of subsistence. Sheep constitute an integral part of Navajo culture. Rug weaving became a major source of revenue exchange for Navajo families as they became more dependent on

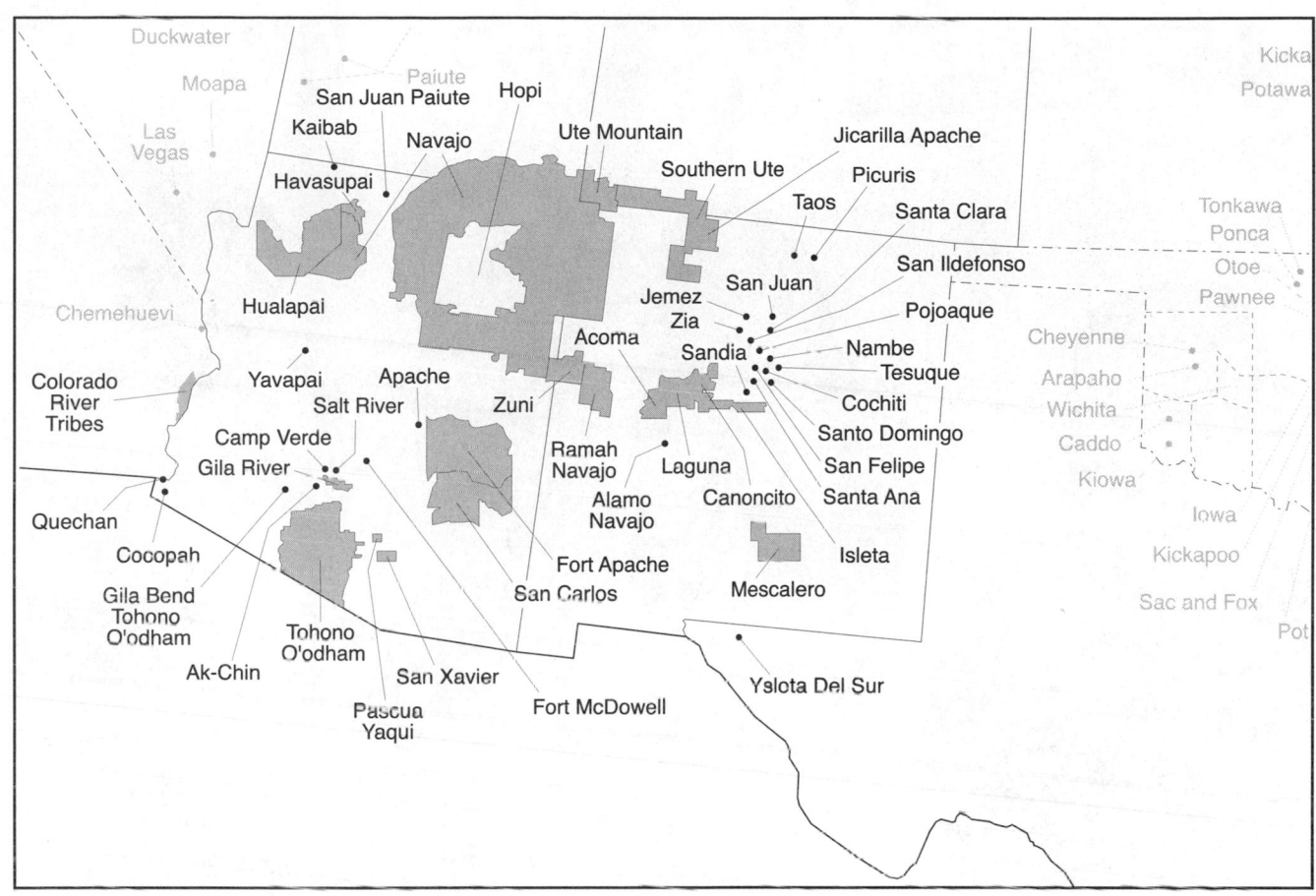

Map of Southwest tribes. (Courtesy of the UCLA American Indian Studies Center)

manufactured goods from the trading posts located throughout the vast Navajo Nation. Numerous Navajo women perfected their weaving skills and are known internationally for their expert rug-weaving techniques and use of natural dyes.

During the early eighteenth century, the Comanche emigrated from their Shoshone homeland in present-day Wyoming into the northern Spanish colony of New Mexico. They set out to control the horse trade on the southern Plains and, by the mid–eighteenth century, the Comanche were the dominant bison-hunting people of the southern Plains and the Southwest. Their trade dominance grew to the point that they controlled the horse and gun trade, selling even to the Spanish themselves. By the late 1700s there were 2,000 Comanche living east of the Rio Grande River and 4,000 living on the west side. Using war and bribery, the Spanish reached peace and trade agreements with a large number of Comanche who, with many Ute and Pueblos, fought as allies in Spanish campaigns against the Apache and Navajo. The raids and antagonism between the Athapascan southwestern Indians and the Mexicans did not entirely diminish during the period of rule by

the Mexican Republic (1820–1848). The U.S. military and traders entered the Southwest in full force in 1848 after the Mexican-American War. They met strong opposition from the Indian people, particularly the Apache.

## The Apache Nations

The Apache are Athapascan-speaking nations linguistically related to the Navajo. The Apache formed into two major groups with distinct languages or dialects: (1) the Jicarilla, Lipan and Kiowa (Apache) living in the southern Plains, and (2) the Chiricahua, Mescalero, and Western Apache. The Apache people once hunted in a vast land area in the Southwest that includes New Mexico and Arizona and extends into Chihuahua, Mexico. For example, the Jicarilla Apache utilized over 50 million acres that were bordered by four sacred rivers. The Apache lived by hunting and gathering wild plants and some farming. Their main shelter was a circular brush lodge with a fire in the center. Each Apachean group was composed of clans, basic social, economic, and political units, based on matrilineal inherited leadership.

Isleta school children. (Photo by Carol Lujan)

In the 1870s and 1880s, the U.S. military forced the Apache to live on federally designated reservations in Arizona and New Mexico. Geronimo, a Chiricahua Apache medicine man, is best known among the Apache leaders who resisted settlement onto reservations. Their resistance assured Apache survival and reservation land bases in Arizona and New Mexico.

Contemporary Apache nations are now making significant progress in economic development. The White Mountain Apache in Arizona manage a number of successful business enterprises including a ski resort, hotel and casino, and a lumber mill. Their Sunrise Resort Hotel is the reservation's third largest revenue generator in terms of tourism-related activities. The lumber company employs about 350 Apache residents and grosses about $5 million annually. The Mescalero Apache have a successful casino and hotel employing approximately 355 people on a seasonal basis. Ski Apache employs 350 people during the ski season. In addition, the Mescalero Apache Nation owns their own lumber mill. The Jicarilla Apache Nation's most important source of revenue stems from its mineral reserves. They have large amounts of oil, gas, coal, uranium, and

geothermal reserves. In the early 1990s the Jicarilla Apache purchased a 300–acre range. Other Apache reservations are investing in tourism by opening cultural centers and annual festivals to the public, and some reservation lands and lakes are open for public fishing and outdoor recreation such as elk hunting. The Apache people retain strong ties to their religion, culture, language, dances, and other traditions. Powwows are held each year, and many Indian people from other reservations attend.

### The Navajo Nation

The Navajo Nation is the largest Native nation in the United States geographically and numerically. With approximately 17 million acres, the Navajo Reservation in Arizona and New Mexico is comparable to the size of the state of West Virginia. In the year 2000 the Navajo population consisted of approximately 250,000 people. The youth population is increasing rapidly and some estimates project that the Navajo population will increase to approximately half-a-million within twenty-five years. The present-day Navajo territory is located

Kelsey Begay, president of the Navajo Nation. (Photo by Carol Lujan)

in the Four Corners region of Arizona, New Mexico, Utah, and Colorado, with land in all but the latter. The Navajo are a clan-based matrilineal society with approximately sixty clans. Some clans are part of the original clans created by the Holy People and other clans, such as the Mexican Clan and Zuni Clan, were added when new groups became part of Navajo Nation. According to the Dine way of life, the universe is a harmonious order of related elements that connect the land, the people, animals, plant life and the cosmos. Everything has its place in the universe and everything is interrelated.

Between 1820 and 1848 Navajo land was claimed by the Mexican Republic although the Navajo never submitted to Mexican authority. The United States annexed Navajo territory under the 1848 Treaty of Guadalupe Hidalgo, which ended the Mexican-American War. Unlike the Mexican government, however, the United States used warfare to subdue the Indians and control their land base. The Navajo successfully resisted U.S. control for seventeen years, until the U.S. Civil War (1861–1865), when the U.S. army and irregulars, including Kit Carson, launched expeditions to search out the Navajo and destroy their economic livelihood. Many

Navajo cornfields were burned, homes and communities demolished, fruit trees destroyed, and livestock slaughtered, until the Navajo faced starvation during 1863 and 1864 and finally surrendered.

Eight thousand Navajo were arrested and forced to walk, guarded by heavily armed soldiers, to a military-administered concentration camp at Fort Sumner in the barren area of Bosque Redondo in eastern New Mexico, far from their high desert and alpine homeland. Many infants, pregnant women, and elders died on the way to Bosque Redondo. Once there, one-quarter of the Navajo died from starvation and the harsh treatment of the U.S. military. Toward the end of the Fort Sumner imprisonment, food was so scare and the land so infertile that Navajo were forced to eat coffee grinds to survive. In 1868 a treaty was negotiated with Navajo leaders, and the Navajo were finally allowed to return to a portion of their homeland, the present-day Navajo Reservation.

From 1868 to 1922, when oil was discovered in Navajo territory, the Navajo were virtually ignored by the federal government. The land itself had been judged to be worthless, even for Texas longhorn cattle production. The presence of oil, however, led to intense intervention into Navajo affairs. In 1923 the Navajo Business Council was created by the U.S. agent, who needed a centralized authority to grant oil and mineral leases in the name of the entire Navajo Nation. Most Navajo were led by local headmen, who generally did not recognize a central Navajo government and often ignored the Navajo Business Council until its demise in 1936.

The Navajo rejected the Indian Reorganization Act of 1934, federal legislation that sought to structure official tribal governments with constitutions. Instead the federal government allowed the Navajo to hold a constitutional convention, which proposed a government independent from the bureaucratic power of the Office of Indians Affairs, which was renamed the Bureau of Indian Affairs (BIA) in the 1940s. The secretary of the interior rejected the Navajo constitution, which was a bold plan for greater Navajo political freedom. Instead, in 1938 the Department of the Interior created a new Navajo Business Council, originally composed of seventy-four elected Navajo members and generally elected chairman and vice-chairman. This government, known as the Rules of 1938, provides the basis for the present Navajo Tribal Council.

During the late 1930s and 1940s, the Navajo became embroiled in a political and bureaucratic conflict with the BIA and U.S. government over the issues of grazing sheep and cattle on the Navajo Reservation. Most Navajo made their living from livestock, mainly sheep, but Navajo herds were generally small, a few hundred, and designed to supply family food, while some wool and rugs were traded at local trading posts (stores) for necessary manufactured goods. During the 1930s Dust Bowl, government officials decided that the Navajo were raising too many sheep for the amount of grasslands and that the overgrazing would lead to ecological ruin of Navajo lands through erosion. Beginning with a massive stock reduction program, agents of the Agricultural Department slaughtered tens of thousands of Navajo sheep and this intensified Navajo distrust of the federal government for several decades.

The Navajo pastoral economy is gradually being replaced with government-generated jobs, service industry, individually owned business, and the continued development of Navajo natural resources such as oil, gas, coal, and uranium. Much Navajo land was leased by the federal government during the 1920s and 1930s so that the main income generated from the land is from mineral and mining leases and royalties. According to *Tiller's Guide to Indian Country*, approximately 2,600 tribal members work in uranium mining and coal mining, and oil and natural gas generate more than $75 million annually for the Navajo Nation. The Navajo Nation owns and operates a diverse number of businesses including the Navajo Tribal Utility Authority (NTUA), Navajo Forest Project Industries (NFPI), Navajo Indian Irrigation Project (NIIP), and the Navajo Agricultural Products Industries (NAPI). NAPI ships products—primarily potatoes, onions, and alfalfa pellet—to national and international corporations such as Frito-Lay, Campbell's Soup, Eagle Snack Foods, and Bordens.

Despite the Navajo Nation's efforts to develop their economy, the unemployment rate is approximately 59 percent compared to 5 percent for the general U.S. population, and the median income was $11,885 per year in 1997, substantially less than one-half the $30,000 median income of the general U.S. population. Most of those who are unemployed are unskilled and have minimal formal American education. Support services, such as day–care centers, are few. The majority, some 75 percent, of employed Navajo work in the public sector, made possible by U.S. government funding amounting to hundreds of millions of dollars annually. The remaining workers on the reservation are employed in commercial agriculture, mining, forestry, wholesale and retail trade, and construction. Around 5 percent are employed in transportation, communications, and utilities, all of which are Navajo-owned and-operated.

Approximately 25 percent of the Navajo people live away from the Navajo Reservation, and many have migrated to southwestern cities as well as to San Francisco and Los Angeles for jobs. Under the federal government's Indian Relocation Program of the 1950s, most Navajo who relocated chose California, because of the large number already living there, many as workers for the Santa Fe Railroad. Due mainly to economic necessity, migration to and from the Navajo homeland has been constant and continues today. Approximately one-half of the off-reservation Navajo maintain homes both on and off the reservation and often return home for ceremonies, family gatherings, and summer visits.

The influx of federal funds has not increased Navajo incomes even to national poverty levels. Federal funds are generally earmarked to relieve symptoms of poverty, not for capital development. The federal and tribal governments continue to be the primary sources of employment for thousands of people on the reservation.

Since the 1970s there has been a steady increase in economic development activity, with the Navajo Nation taking remarkable initiatives. During the construction of the off-reservation Salt River power plant project at Page, Arizona, Navajo workers experienced blatant racial discrimination in pay and duties. They organized and pressed the Navajo Nation to support their demands, and newly elected Navajo Chairman Peter MacDonald took up the challenge. Trade unions, until then banned on the reservation, were legalized and supported. The actions taken by Navajo workers and the Navajo Nation awakened workers throughout the Southwest, where the combined Mexican and Indian labor force had long been oppressed by ruling Euro-Americans. Both New Mexico and Arizona were traditionally antiunion, with less than 5 percent of their work forces organized into trade unions. The Office of Navajo Labor Relations was established to mandate standards for Navajo workers' wages for jobs on or near the reservation. These standards required major construction projects to hire Navajo on a percentage or quota basis in specific numbers of skilled positions.

In 1971 the Navajo Nation supported the formation of Dine College (DC) at Tsaile, Arizona, on the Navajo Reservation. The locally controlled Dine College was the first of its kind in Indian Country, and many Navajo who otherwise did not want to leave the reservation to take college credit courses enrolled at DC. The college was so successful that within a few years other reservations were starting colleges and were gaining considerable success training reservation people, where U.S. college institutions were showing extremely poor results retaining and graduating Indian college students. Indian-controlled community colleges have been built on about thirty Indian reservations, and many more Indian reservations are contemplating building community colleges for their people and for surrounding non-Indian students. The community college movement became one of the most significant events on many Indian reservations during the 1970s and 1980s. This movement was greatly inspired by the groundbreaking work of the Navajo community and the pioneers who built Dine College.

In November 1982 young activist Peterson Zah won election as Navajo chairman. He was defeated four years later by MacDonald, but won again in 1990. About 35,000 Navajo vote in the Navajo tribal government elections, and over the years the Navajo government has evolved by incorporating both Western and traditional Navajo government institutions. For example, in 1959 the Navajo adopted a court system modeled after the U.S. legal system in order to prevent the states of Arizona and New Mexico from extending their courts onto the Navajo Reservation. The Navajo prefer to manage their own courts and use their own ideas of justice, rather than submit to the U.S. court system. During the 1970s, the Navajo court system gained power and respect, and many local courts, known as Peacemaker Courts, manage disputes in the traditional manner, trying to reconcile contentious parties according to Navajo cultural views of resolving conflict. Until the 1950s the Navajo government suffered from lack of local support, but since then it has tried to directly incorporate local political communities, often called chapters, into the government and electoral process, and in this way gain the support of the Navajo communities, which still tend toward local groupings and local leaders. The Navajo government has made considerable strides in attempting to provide a truly representative government, based to some extent on traditional principles, and has developed the largest tribal government organization in Native North America.

### The Hopi Nation

The Hopi are descendants of the earliest inhabitants of the Southwest and for centuries occupied a large part of present-day northern Arizona. The Hopi elders tell of a time long ago before people were really human beings, when they lived underground; this was the period of the Third World. Before the early beings lived in the Third World, they had to flee two other worlds farther underground because of their immoral behavior and disruption of the social harmony of the First and Second Worlds. For some time these early people lived in peace with all the animals and there were no problems. But then the people began to have disputes. A council was held, with animal representatives participating in the discussions. They agreed that the Third World had become morally corrupted and out of balance, and they had to seek peace by migrating from the underworld to a Fourth World above. The Hopi arrived

Taos Pueblo. (Photo by Manny Pedraza)

in the Fourth World and encountered a frightening yet attractive spirit being, Masau-u, who asked them what they sought. Masau-u told the Hopi that they could live on the land of the Fourth World provided that they followed sacred rules. The Hopi would have to perform rituals to provide water for the desert land, and they would have to accept Masau-u's teachings, abiding by the spirit's social and religious rules. The Hopi agreed and made a covenant to obey Masau-u and serve as caretakers of the land. The Hopi attempt to keep this sacred covenant to this day.

Each Hopi clan retells a variation of the creation story, but they all share the same emergence story and consider the land they occupy as sacred. The Hopi believe they must fulfill particular sacred and ceremonial responsibilities. Creating rain for the dry land is essential and is accomplished through prayers and ceremonies held annually in the Hopi villages.

The Hopi live in northeastern Arizona, where their reservation is entirely surrounded by the large Navajo Reservation. Hopi society is divided into twelve phratries, or collections of clans, with numerous clans within each phratry. Children always belong to the clan of their mother. Like other Pueblo, Hopi honor kachinas, or rain spirits, and clan ancestors. Clans are extremely important for social and religious relations, and each clan has its own special sacred objects and ceremonies. Clan and ceremonial leaders continue to play major roles in Hopi ceremonial and social life. Many Hopi and other Pueblo ceremonies are concerned with creating community harmony and appeasing the kachina spirits to bring rain for the Hopi crops. The Hopi were a horticultural people, who grew several varieties of corn, beans, squash, and other plants. Men hunted animals such as deer and elk, and the women gathered nuts, fruits, and roots.

In the middle and late 1500s, there may have been as many as a dozen Hopi villages along the Colorado River, but they were quickly decimated by early diseases introduced by Europeans, and by 1600, most Hopi retreated to their present villages in northern Arizona. In 1628 the Spanish forcibly established Catholic missions in several Hopi villages. The Hopi helped the Pueblos in the 1680 rebellion, and even after Spanish reconquest, the Hopi strongly resisted Spanish rule and the Catholic religion.

The Hopi now occupy about a dozen villages on the Hopi Reservation. They still maintain many of their ceremonies and beliefs, and many still live in multistoried buildings. Many within the Hopi society continue to uphold the traditional ways and actively resist U.S. cultural influences in religion, education, and government. During the 1930s a small number of Hopi voted to adopt a constitutional government under the provisions of the Indian Reorganization Act (IRA) of 1934. The IRA was designed by the U.S. government to give Indian communities more control over their own affairs, by organizing Western-style governments among them. Many Indian nations, especially among the religiously conservative Pueblo and Hopi, rejected the IRA constitutional governments because they modeled secular Western views of political organization and had little precedent or congruence with Indian political traditions and political governments. The Hopi community became divided between those willing to live under the IRA government and those who wanted to retain Hopi political institutions, which incorporated a considerable degree of traditional Hopi customs and religious orientation.

The conservative Hopi have been some of the most active nationalist Indian groups in the United States. Together with the conservative and nationalist Iroquois people of New York and southern Canada, conservative Hopi leaders have appealed to international forums such as the United Nations in order to gain redress for broken treaty agreements and for recognition of Indian national independence. Not all Hopi share the view that the Hopi Reservation should be recognized as an independent nation within the international community. But the conservative Hopi reflect the active conservatism inherent within tightly interrelated Hopi clan and religious relations, which foster strong attachment to tradition and motivate many Hopi to actively seek preservation of Hopi community and religious institutions.

## The Pueblo Nations of New Mexico

When the Spanish arrived in the 1500s, there were ninety-eight villages, called Pueblos by the Spanish, along the northern Rio Grande and its tributaries; within a few decades, there were only nineteen, all of which exist today. Although all Pueblo peoples have similar economic, governmental, and religious structures, they speak four distinct languages: Zuni, Keres, Tiwa, and Tewa. Language retention is becoming a major concern for many of the Pueblos.

Each Pueblo is autonomous and independent; however, all participate in the All Indian Pueblo Council, which traces its origins to the successful 1680 Pueblo Revolt against the Spanish. The revolt started at Taos Pueblo and moved steadily to the southern Pueblos and the Hopi, driving the Spanish and some Pueblo allies to El Paso in present-day Texas. For about a dozen years, the Pueblo enjoyed autonomy. The Spanish, however, returned to New Mexico by 1695 but thereafter refrained from tampering directly with Pueblo internal affairs, particularly religious ceremonies. Many Puebloans, especially those from Jemez Pueblo, did not want to live under Spanish rule and escaped to live among the Navajo and Apache nations which resisted the Spanish invaders. The remainder of the Pueblo lived under harsh Spanish rule, which demanded Catholic Christian conversion, and forced labor on the ranches of Spanish officers and political land grantees.

Under the rule of independent Mexico from 1821 to 1848, among the Southwest Indians only the Pueblos held full Mexican citizenship. Therefore, when the United States annexed the region, Pueblo people automatically became U.S. citizens, as did the other residents of the area. Not only was citizenship of little use to the Pueblo, but their territories did not fall under the federal government's developing reservation system, which normally put Indian lands under federal protection. Encroachment on Pueblo land, the finest farm

Hilary Clinton and Governor Floyd Tortillno of Acoma Pueblo. (Photo by Carol Lujan)

land in the Southwest, accelerated rapidly. The Pueblo petitioned and then sued for Indian status, which they finally gained in 1916 through a U.S. Supreme Court decision. In the interim, they had lost some of their best lands as well as important religious sites.

Congressional investigation during the 1920s revealed that 12,000 non-Pueblo claimants were living on Pueblo lands. The All Indian Pueblo Council organized delegates from all the Pueblos to regain their lands, which resulted in the 1924 Pueblo Lands Act. Assisting the Pueblo in their fight was John Collier, a young Indian rights activist on the staff of the General Federation of Women's Clubs. President Franklin D. Roosevelt later named Collier as Indian commissioner, a position he held from 1933 to 1945. The Pueblos successfully mounted a campaign among non-Indians for a Native issue and set an important example for other Native peoples across the country. In the 1970s Taos Pueblo was also successful in gaining public support for the return of their sacred Blue Lake.

Pueblo lands are secure, but land in that semiarid region is of no use without water. The most important

contemporary Pueblo Indian struggle is to maintain and to acquire water rights. Water law falls under common law in the Anglo-American legal system, and under federal law devolves to state jurisdiction. Indians fought for and won exemption from state control in the early twentieth century. The Winters Doctrine, arising from a 1909 Supreme Court ruling, defines Indian water rights and is based on the theory that the federal government reserves power over federal lands, which includes the necessary water supply. The Winters Doctrine implies that Indian treaty rights include the right to adequate supplies of water necessary for the Indian reservations to carry on irrigation for agriculture and to meet their population and economic development needs. However, in a court decision in 1973, the Winters Doctrine was declared to be inapplicable to the Pueblo Indians of New Mexico, since the Pueblo were not officially Indians at the time the Winters case was adjudicated.

One of the most significant events in recent Pueblo history is the return of the sacred Blue Lake and about 55,000 surrounding acres to Taos Pueblo in 1975. Taos Pueblo had lost the land to the federal government, but after a thirty-year legal and political struggle, Taos Pueblo regained ownership of Blue Lake, a sacred site in Taos creation history, since it is considered the navel of the universe and the place where the Creator first created people. The people of Taos Pueblo held annual ceremonies at Blue Lake, many of which were crucial to the Taos Pueblo religious cycle, which the Taos people believe ensures the well-being and prosperity of the community. The return of Blue Lake marked one of the few times that the federal government returned a major sacred site and surrounding lands to Indian control. It gave hope that in the future other Indian communities may successfully regain or protect their sacred sites.

During the 1960s and 1970s, Zuni Pueblo became a model for the present-day U.S. government self-determination policy in Indian affairs. Like other Pueblo peoples, the Zuni have a strong tradition of religious community and strong attachments to their social and political freedom. During the 1960s, when federal funds became available through antipoverty programs like the Community Action Programs (CAP), for the first time many Indian communities gained access to significant funds and personnel because of direct federal grants to local tribal governments within the CAP programs. The Zuni, in the late 1960s, seized this opportunity and, armed with a little-used law that required the Bureau of Indian Affairs to contract services to tribal governments, the Zuni tried to gain control over all BIA programs in the Zuni community. The Zuni were able to contract many BIA programs and ran most of them much more effectively and with greater community commitment and participation. The Zuni embarked on this plan as a means to exclude unwanted BIA interference into their government and community affairs. The Zuni came to the attention of President Richard Nixon, and in 1970 he made a speech in which he announced the beginning of the Indian self-determination policy, designed to allow tribal governments and reservation communities greater local control over BIA and federal programs and over local institutions such as schools. President Nixon held up the Zuni as an example to all Indian communities that wished to take a greater role in managing their local affairs.

The nineteen New Mexico Pueblos remain strongly traditional communities that continue to practice and perform the major dances and rituals of their religions. They have consistently rejected U.S. efforts to significantly alter their religious, social, and cultural orders, since they continue to live by many of the religious views and customs of their forefathers. The Pueblo have generated many well-known artists, novelists, poets, scholars, and painters among their people.

## The Pima and Maricopa Nations

The Pima Indians live on the Gila River Reservation and the Salt River Reservation in southern Arizona and speak an Uto-Aztecan language. They refer to themselves as Akimel O'okham or Akieml Au'Authm ("the River People"). They are related to the larger Piman cultural and linguistic group that includes the Tohono O'Odham. Both the Pima Indians and the Tohono O'Odham are believed to be descendants of the ancient Hohokam society located in the same southern Arizona geographical region prior to 300 B.C.E., nearly 2,000 years before the European invasion. The Hohokam society is noted for their extensive irrigation system that included diversion dams and intricate canal systems extending to at least ten miles. During the eighteenth century the Maricopa (Xalchidom Pii-pash) Nation, from the Yuman language group related to the Quechan and Mohave peoples, began to merge with the Pima Nation. The Pima and Maricopa developed an extensive agriculturally based economy and were very successful farmers until the late 1800s when they experienced a severe water shortage brought on by the massive influx of the Euro-American immigrants. The new settlers utilized massive amounts of water and constructed a dam that limited the amount of water available for Pima usage. Consequently, a large number of Pima and Maricopa families moved into the Salt River area creating the Salt River Pima-Maricopa Community. Since the mid–1800s, the Pima and Maricopa have lived on reservations established by an act and/or executive order of the U.S. government. Although the Pima and Maricopa currently share the same land base and government and similar cultural values, they differ linguistically. Today the Maricopa continue to be a distinct and integral part of the Pima nation and take an active role in the tribal government.

The Salt River Pima-Maricopa Indian Community was established by Executive Order on 14 June 1879. Located east of Phoenix, Arizona, and adjacent to several large cities, including Scottsdale, Tempe, and Mesa, it consists of approximately 52,600 acres of trust land comprised mainly of agricultural fields. The Salt River Nation's enrollment now exceeds 6,255 members. Prior to the establishment of gaming, their economy was based primarily on commercial, industrial, and agricultural enterprises. In the late 1990s gaming was approved by the membership and a state compact was agreed upon. Within a short period of time the two casinos located on the Salt River Reservation have successfully increased the revenue for tribal government operations.

The tribal government also owns a number of business enterprises including heavy industries and a tri-city landfill. In addition, they lease property to a number of large and diverse businesses such as Home Depot, Wal-Mart and Toys R Us. Moreover, their two golf courses attract thousands of people throughout the year.

The Gila River Indian Community is also a confederation of the Pima and Maricopa nations. It was established by Executive Order in 1859 and is located approximately ten miles south of the large metropolitan area of Phoenix. The reservation covers over 372,000 acres and consists of desert with mountain ranges and free-standing buttes. The Gila River Nation is governed by a governor, lieutenant governor, and seventeen council members who represent approximately 12,000 enrolled members. Gila River Nation has three industrial parks with over thirty-six operations. The Lone Butte Industrial Park is considered one the most successful Indian industrial parks in the nation. Gila River Nation also continues to maintain a strong agricultural presence. The tribal government established Gila River Farms and a Farm Board in 1968 and within the past thirty years it has developed into a lucrative business. It is comprised of four different ranches that total more than 15,000 acres, and has an approximate $10 million budget. In the early 1990s the tribal government entered into the gaming business and now operates two successful casinos. Currently, they are in the process of building a hotel/golf course resort.

Despite major advances in economic development, the Salt River and Gila River Nations continue to experience difficulties involving health, education, and social welfare. Diabetes affects a major percentage of the adult population and is costly to the well-being of the community. Although the tribal governments maintain their own school systems, the majority of children attend public school. An increasing number of students are graduating from high school. The number of students going to and completing college is also increasing but at a gradual rate. Similar to other Indian nations throughout the United States, these tribal governments are at an important stage of transition. They are moving from a government based on basic survival skills to one based on planning and development for the future.

The Salt River and Gila River population is young, and the majority of members are less than twenty-five years of age. Since the mid–1990s both nations have experienced an increase in gang violence. For example, at least nineteen street gangs were reportedly in existence in Salt River in 1997. Gila River is experiencing similar problems. Their close proximity to a large metropolitan area makes them vulnerable to the expansion of street gangs from cities into the reservation.

These tribal governments are undergoing rapid social change. Although their proximity to large cities offers many economic–related opportunities, it also presents serious challenges to the social and cultural integrity of these nations, particularly as it relates to child and family welfare and cultural preservation.

## The Future

As a result of PL 93–628, the Indian Self Determination and Educational Assistance Act (1975), many American Indian nations are assuming control of federally operated programs such as public safety and education. The southwestern Native nations are aggressively taking control of the operation of public safety and education programs. Many tribal governments have contracted BIA law enforcement and assumed local control of previously federally operated schools. Within the next decade the Navajo Nation expects to assume complete responsibility for the operation of all BIA-funded schools located within their nation. Furthermore, they plan to take control of all federally operated Indian Health Service programs on their reservation. Other tribal governments in the Southwest are taking over the control and operation of programs previously administered by the federal government and have developed innovative and creative programs in reading and science as well as language and cultural preservation. Several Native nations have combined revenues from the federal, state, and tribal governments to enhance their social and educational programs.

The languages and cultures of the Native peoples of the Southwest endure, and their preservation and continuation is extremely important. To assure the continuation of their language, some Native nations are developing language classes and integrating them into their schools' curriculum. For the Native peoples of the Southwest—the Paiute, Ute, Yavapai, Mojave, Quechan, Cocopah, Colorado River, Havasupai, Hualapai, Pascua Yaqui, Tohono O'Odham, Pima, Maricopa, Apache, Navajo, Hopi, and the Pueblos—the Southwest is their ancient homeland. These tribal governments are working hard to ensure that their languages and cultures are maintained into the future and are also availing their children to computers and other technological advances of the twenty-first century. Subsequently young Native people aware of their cultures are completing high school and continuing on to college. Economically, gaming has been an important factor in the economic growth for a few Native nations in the Southwest. However, the majority of Native nations are exploring a diverse number of economic development projects related to tourism and natural resources including establishing their own utility companies as well as expanding agricultural enterprises to enhance and strengthen their governments and to sustain their cultures.

In conclusion, American Indian nations of the Southwest are thriving and are actively involved in the future direction of their nations. They are gaining both economic and political influence at the local, regional, and national levels and are becoming a visible and important force among the general U.S. population. Many southwestern American Indian nations are also concerned about language and cultural loss and are establishing language, culture, and history classes within their schools and/or cultural centers to ensure that their cultures, languages, and histories are sustained well into the future.

*Carol Lujan*
*Arizona State University*

# ◆ NORTHERN PLAINS INDIANS

All contemporary tribal communities in the Plains north of Oklahoma possess both similar and distinctive qualities. A mutual trait is tribalism—loyalty to the group—that endures regardless of a long history of economic and political forces designed to assimilate Plains peoples. Despite attempts by the United States to end tribalism, the Indians' desire to preserve their cultural integrity resulted in the preservation of many aspects of cultural heritage among contemporary northern Plains communities.

Common contemporary images non-Indians have of historic Plains people include horse-mounted warriors, Sun Dance ceremony participants, and large bison-hunting parties. These aspects of Plains cultures were relatively new modes of life for many tribes and were the result of tribal adaptation to the Plains landscape and its inhabitants and to the extension of the colonial sphere of political influence to the Northern Plains.

Many Indian nations identified with the High Plains Culture of horses and bison hunting did not live on the Plains until after 1700. Before European contact, the North American horse was extinct for about 8,000 to 10,000 years. The horses that became part of the wild horses, or the American mustangs, were animals that escaped or were stolen from early Spanish exploring expeditions and settlements.

Prior to the reintroduction of the horse, some Indian nations that lived on the Plains hunted bison on foot and farmed. Other Indian nations, commonly regarded as Plains tribes, lived further east. These soon-to-be-called Plains nations migrated onto the Plains during the early colonial period, often after 1650 when European expansion forced many Indians westward. As a result of European contact, the Iroquois, an upstate New York confederacy, started their own expansionary trade, diplomatic, and military campaigns in the 1600s to control and maintain access to lands with fur-bearing animals, which were necessary for trade with the Europeans.

The Iroquois expansion pushed many Algonkian-speaking nations, such as the Gros Ventre, Chippewa, and Ottawa, to move farther west to the upper Great Lakes country. The Chippewa, for example, during the 1700s, moved into present-day Minnesota. Armed with guns from their European trade allies, they began pushing the eastern Dakota toward the Northern Plains by the latter half of the 1700s. Before moving onto the Plains, many Indian nations, such as the Lakota and Cheyenne, lived by hunting, growing corn, and gathering nondomesticated foods. By the mid–1750s, many Lakota groups had moved from present-day Minnesota onto the Northern Plains, adopted the horse, began hunting bison, incorporated the Sun Dance ceremony, and found themselves in conflicts with resident farming peoples, such as the Mandan, Arikara, and Hidatsa, who were living along the Missouri River in present-day central North Dakota and the Pawnee of Nebraska.

The Cheyenne experience, an Algonkian-speaking nation, illustrated another tribal migration onto the Plains. In the early 1600s, the Cheyenne lived in present-day southern Canada and made their livelihood by hunting, farming, and collecting plants. The Iroquois and European expansion after 1650 pushed the Cheyenne farther west and in the early 1700s French traders reported Cheyenne living in present-day Minnesota. By the late 1700s, the Cheyenne were living in eastern North Dakota, and while still growing corn, they were using the horse to travel and to hunt bison. The Sheyenne River in eastern North Dakota is named after this tribe.

By the middle 1800s, the Cheyenne had moved farther west to the shortgrass prairie and had adopted many traditions associated with Plains cultures, including the Sun Dance—an annual renewal ceremony—military societies for their young men, portable lodges, annual summer gatherings for ceremonial and diplomatic purposes, and collective bison hunting. In the winter, the Cheyenne, as well as other Plains nations like the Omaha, Blackfeet, and Crow, hunted with their kin, and lived in related family groups and endured the cold winter months in their separate Plains territories.

The Plains cultural zenith lasted less than two centuries and does not characterize the way Indians lived for centuries before its emergence in the 1700s or after their confinement on reservations. Nevertheless, the Plains cultures flourished during the 1700s and through the first half of the 1800s. The cultures changed when U.S. authorities gained control over Plains Indians by

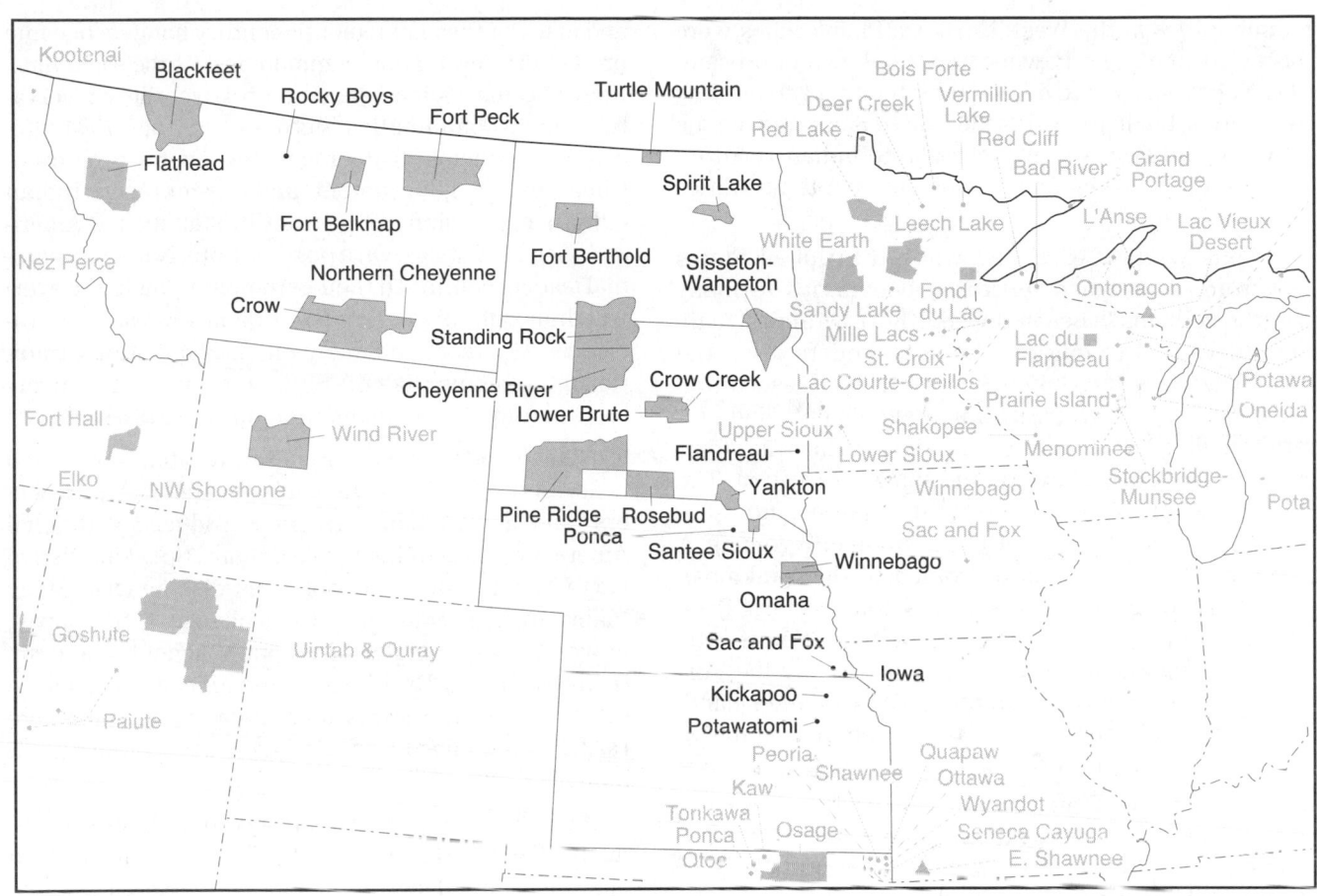

Contemporary Plains Indian tribes. (Courtesy of the UCLA American Indian Studies Center)

confining them on reservations. By the late 1870s, hunting had nearly destroyed the large herds of bison and, without an adequate number of animals and territory, some aspects of the Plains horse culture were no longer possible.

### Historical Precedents

Two centuries ago, French, Scot, English, and Spanish traders moved onto the northern Plains, and their continual presence altered the demographies and material cultures of many Plains tribes. Traders, who wanted to exchange bison hides for guns, pots and pans, cloth, and other goods, preceded the more extensive numbers of white settlers who came to the Northern Plains after the Civil War. Diseases preceded and accompanied the European newcomers and later Americans who brought many epidemics to the Plains nations. Smallpox, cholera, and whooping cough were infections responsible for declines in Plains Indian populations during the eighteenth and nineteenth centuries. In 1837 a smallpox epidemic reduced Mandan numbers and forced them to combine clans and mix family lines; ultimately the Mandan coalesced with the Arikara and Hidatsa and moved to a location near present-day Fort Berthold Reservation in North Dakota. Other Indian nations living on the Plains, such as the Blackfeet and Pawnee, also suffered catastrophic population losses due to disease, though the exact numbers of population decline are difficult to document.

The United States further displaced Plains Indian peoples by moving eastern Indian tribes to lands west of the Mississippi River. In 1830, United States policy encouraged the relocation of Indian nations east of the Mississippi River to new homelands to the west. Eventually, many eastern tribes were moved to present-day Kansas and Oklahoma. In the 1830s, Kickapoo, Potawatomi, and Munsee Delaware tribes migrated West. After signing a series of treaties with the United States government, part of the Winnebago Nation, living on Crow Creek in Dakota Territory, finally settled on the northern section of the Omaha Reservation in northeast Nebraska in 1866. At times, the resident peoples viewed the Indian newcomers as intruders to their lands and hunting territories. Sometimes hostilities ensued as the eastern Indians tried to recreate their communities in the West. Northern Plains tribes were also relocated. The Pawnee and the Ponca of present-day Nebraska tried to defend their hunting and farming territories, but in the 1870s the United States moved the Pawnee and Ponca from Nebraska to Indian Territory in present-day Oklahoma to prevent Lakota hostilities against them.

Plains warfare escalated when the United States government assigned territorial boundaries to many Northern Plains tribes in the 1851 Fort Laramie Treaty and then tried to enforce the new borders. Over the next fifty years, the United States redefined reservation boundaries through treaties and agreements and created smaller and smaller reservations, sometimes forcing several tribes to live on the same reservation. The Shoshoni and Arapaho, separate nations, now cohabitate on the Wind River Reservation in Wyoming. A band of Assiniboine and a branch of the Yanktonai, both Siouan-speaking peoples, inhabit the Fort Peck Reservation; and Assiniboine and Gros Ventre, the latter an Algonkian-speaking people, occupy the Fort Belknap Reservation in Montana. On the other hand, the Lakota split and distinct bands were forced to live on several different reservations.

The Northern Plains nations resented U.S. restrictions on their freedom while the United States tolerated white encroachment on tribal lands. This contradiction frequently led to conflict. The Lakota, Cheyenne, and Blackfeet fought the United States and tried to keep American settlers and miners from staying permanently in their lands. Symbolizing tribal resistance to U.S. policy were the 1864 Sand Creek Battle in Colorado and the 1866 to 1868 Bozeman Trail War in Wyoming Territory. The most familiar conflict was the defeat of U.S. troops led by Colonel George Custer at the 1876 Battle of the Little Big Horn in eastern Montana Territory.

By the end of the Civil War, settlement on a reservation was the only political and economic option available for Plains Indians and they reluctantly began to accept life on U.S.-controlled reservations. After resisting removal to Oklahoma in the late 1870s, the Northern Cheyenne settled on the Tongue River Reservation in eastern Montana Territory in the early 1880s. However, in 1892 Chippewa leader Little Shell and his followers left the Turtle Mountain Reservation in north central North Dakota, because they refused to sign the Ten Cent Treaty, and created a non-federally recognized community that still survives primarily at Great Falls, Montana. In 1916 a group of Plains Chippewa and Cree, both Algonkian-speaking peoples, found a homeland on the Rocky Boy Reservation in Montana.

Eventually, most of the tribal people resided on reservations throughout the northern Plains. The people often built homes near relatives, water, and wood,

and many of these nineteenth-century hamlets became present-day reservation communities. At the same time, Indian agents wielded great control over these reservation Indian communities. Between 1887 and 1934, official U.S. policies discouraged the exercise of traditional Indian government and discouraged Indian cultural expression in favor of Christianity and American social life-styles. On a positive note, Native ceremonial leaders continued their ceremonies out of the ever-watchful sight of government officials, preserving traditions. As a result, on many Plains reservations, traditional ceremonies like the Sun Dance were not actively revived for public consumption until the 1970s.

Schools and mission churches were often constructed near reservation villages, and missionaries, school teachers, and government farmers introduced additional American modes of life to the Indians. Speaking Native languages in federal schools was discouraged. Many Plains Indians continued to challenge U.S. control, however, by keeping children out of schools and practicing tribal rites. Despite initial hostility and resistance to settlement on reservations, today most contemporary Plains Indians consider their reservations their homelands.

Immediately, the reality of reservation poverty forced many Plains Indians to seek clothing from mission charities and federal authorities. Tribal artisans often altered the clothes obtained in this way to suit Plains Indian tastes by adding their own bead designs. Another example of tribal modification is the ribbon shirt. Colored ribbons are sewn on a cowboy shirt in order to make a distinct article of Indian clothing. Quilts followed a similar pattern. Missionaries instructed tribal women to quilt and introduced the eight-point star pattern found on many tribal quilt patterns. Northern Plainswomen are famous for their star quilts. Today, the star quilt has become a distinctive Plains design and the richly designed blankets are purchased by many non-Indians as art pieces. Used as gifts in a giveaway ceremony, the quilts help perpetuate the Plains tradition of public displays of generosity at powwows and at some ceremonies.

### Early Reservation Economic Pursuits

Confinement on reservations limited tribal work opportunities and forced reservation Plains Indians to pursue a narrow range of economic activities. Upstream on the Missouri River, on the Fort Berthold Reservation where the Mandan, Hidatsa, and Arikara settled, residents continued pre-reservation farming by planting crops, but this corresponded with U.S. agrarian reservation policy. Downstream on the Missouri River, the

Omaha and Winnebago also maintained farming pursuits. In North and South Dakota, the tribesmen on the Sisseton Reservation, the Fort Totten Reservation, and the Yankton Reservation developed subsistence agricultural economies. However, they were unable to purchase equipment necessary to farm large operations like their white neighbors because they lacked access to credit and lacked markets for their crops. On the other hand, Indians living on the shortgrass Plains reservations in eastern Montana and western South and North Dakota attempted to farm, but were unable to harvest enough crops for their own subsistence purposes. The semiarid climate of many Northern Plains reservations limited farming success, forcing many reservation Indians to subsist either on government rations or to sell reservation lands and hopefully use land money to survive.

Some Indian agents encouraged cattle ranching as an alternative to agriculture on semiarid reservations. Even after some reservation Indians began stockraising, their ranches remained small because they lacked capital to expand their operations and agents controlled their assets by making decisions. Size, however, did not dictate tribal ranchers' success. By the turn of the century, Blackfeet ranchers registered over 400 cattle brands. Both Blackfeet and Northern Cheyenne ranchers produced quality stock and cattle; Chicago buyers purchased animals from these reservation ranchers.

The Lakota on the Standing Rock Reservation in North Dakota along with the Cheyenne River, Pine Ridge, Lower Brule, Crow Creek, and Rosebud reservations in South Dakota had less success. Unable to stock their ranges with Indian cattle, the Standing Rock, Cheyenne River, and Rosebud peoples leased large portions of their reservations to cattle companies at the turn of the century. A disadvantage to leasing was that the tribes lost short-term control over the land and any profits from cattle operations, despite retaining ownership of the land. Pine Ridge and Rosebud reservations' cattle operations declined further during World War I (1914–1918) when government officials encouraged Indian cattlemen to liquidate their small herds. Without cattle, they were forced either to lease or sell their land.

Despite obstacles and hardships, many Plains Indians considered the early twentieth century cattle operations the zenith of their reservation economic experience because stock provided both a subsistence source and a marketable commodity, enabling them to retain some independence. Many western Plains reservations never recovered from the loss of their early cattle operations, and today only a small percentage of reservation residents manage profitable stock operations. On the Northern Cheyenne Reservation, for example, only 10 percent of the families make a living by cattle

ranching. Even more devastating than the loss of cattle on Northern Plains reservations was land allotment.

## Land Allotment

Beginning with the 1854 Omaha Treaty, land allotment—dividing tribal common lands into small individual tracts—became a standard provision in subsequent Plains treaties and agreements. The General Allotment Act of 1887 established general guidelines for allotting reservation lands and provided a mechanism for granting citizenship to the new land allotees. The legislation authorized the president to order the division of reservation lands into individual tracts. Depending on the reservation and the potential allottee's status, allotting agents issued 40- to 640-acre tracts to individual tribal members in trust, enabling the United States to control the land. After twenty-five years, the allotted land converted to fee simple title (all restrictions against the land ended and the owners could sell whenever they wished or keep the land and pay real estate taxes). American citizenship was intended to be granted to the allotee with the change in land status. Congressmen hoped that the division and privatization of the tribal land base would eliminate Indian reservations and give individual Indians' full status as citizens, and with citizenship, tribesmen could protect their own rights at voting polls and in local courts.

Land allotment failed for many reasons. Dividing semiarid lands into small farming tracts was often ecologically and economically unsound. In addition, reservation Indians lacked access to credit, which was an economic barrier to farm profitability. Land allotment citizenship provisions also stopped short because local communities refused to accept reservation Indians as social and political equals.

Irrigation projects also hastened the sale of allotted land. Limited farming success on the semiarid northern plains encouraged the Office of Indian Affairs (later the Bureau of Indian Affairs, or BIA) to design reservation irrigation projects. At the turn of the century, extensive planning began for large projects on the Blackfeet, Crow, Fort Belknap, and Fort Peck reservations in Montana. Once construction began, those tribes also paid a share of the costs of the irrigation projects through land sales and the tribesmen provided, in many cases, manual labor to construct the projects, which changed the reservation landscape as canals crisscrossed the reservation. To force Indians to use the projects, Congress authorized allottees to take a small irrigable allotment on the project and a larger nonirrigable tract of grazing land. Many reservation Plains Indians sold their irrigated properties because they were unable to build improvements necessary to farm the small tract profitably. The United States also encouraged tribes to sell nonallotted tribal lands to repay the costs of constructing these irrigation projects. This further reduced the reservation resource base. Finally, irrigation projects never recovered operation and maintenance costs from project users. In the end, tribes operated projects for mainly non-Indians who had purchased most of the irrigable allotted lands.

After allotting tribal lands, entire sections of unallotted reservation lands were sold. Homesteaders purchased these nonallotted, surveyed opened tracts. Portions of reservations never opened to homesteading were called closed lands. Outsiders also obtained some of these lands as individual Indians sold allotments when leasing became unprofitable. The Office of Indian Affairs also sold Indian land when the agency declared an Indian allottee or heir incompetent. Now outsiders lived in the midst of the diminished tribal reservation.

Allotment also created heirship lands, which were allotted lands that allottees held when they died without a will. In such cases, the United States granted equal portions of the estate to all heirs. In many cases, when there was a relatively large number of heirs, shares in the deceased's allotted land were very small. Continuing this land division practice beyond the first generation rendered the remaining pieces of individual allotment too small for economic purposes, making the heirs essentially landless. That fact forced the heirs either to sell or lease the land. Today, if heirs lease these fractionalized lands, all receive smaller rent receipts that still decrease as new heirs claim ownership in a piece of small land; and if they sell, the land is lost. Administering heirship lands remains a common problem on Plains reservations, making contemporary resource management decisions difficult.

Allotting land on Plains reservations increased the federal government's role in reservation affairs since more staff were employed to handle additional land-related paperwork. For each allottee, the Indian Service established a government banking system with a separate account known as the Individual Indian Monies (IIM) account where the reservation superintendent deposited monies received from rent and sale of allotted or heirship lands. Consequently, allotees had to trust the BIA to manage their money properly. In the late 1990s, after years of questionable accounting practices, Blackfeet member Elouise C. Cobell filed a class-action lawsuit against the United States for accounting irregularities associated with federal employees' handling of IIM accounts.

## The Reservation New Deal

Land allotment, land sales, and cattle loss reduced the ability of reservation communities to participate in the Plains agricultural markets except as land sellers or lessors. That made any downturn in the local economy particularly hard-felt on reservations. After World War I, Northern Plains communities experienced an agricultural depression that drove lessees off the land and deprived many reservation allottees of unearned income. Hardships escalated and by 1930 the American Red Cross was dispensing assistance to several reservation communities because many tribesmen were suffering and unable to support themselves.

After Franklin D. Roosevelt's inauguration, Congress, seeking to relieve suffering throughout the nation, created a direct work relief program in 1933 known as the Civilian Conservation Corps (CCC) to employ the jobless in land restoration projects. Initially, reservations were excluded from this program, but officials from the Department of the Interior transferred the CCC concept to reservations, where unemployment was higher than among nontribal populations. To direct this effort, Interior officials created the Indian Emergency Conservation Work (IECW) that provided tribesmen temporary employment on reservation irrigation, forestry, and grazing projects. For many reservation Indians, this was the first time they had worked for wages.

Collectively, all New Deal reservation programs were crucial to reduce suffering. The passage of the Social Security Act in 1935 enabled more reservation Indians to obtain additional relief assistance from the federal government. Still, misery was great as nearly 95 percent of the Rosebud Reservation's working population found employment in New Deal direct relief reservation or obtained indirect relief from other programs during the Depression. This also illustrated the extent of tribal dependency on U.S. programs.

Coinciding with reservation work programs, Commissioner of Indian Affairs John Collier advocated the creation of economic corporations to manage tribal resources. Collier's plan became partially embodied in the Indian Reorganization Act (IRA) of 1934, which allowed reservation communities to vote to reorganize their tribal governments along the lines of U.S. municipalities and to create tribal economic corporations.

Although Collier's proposal focused on reservation economic self-sufficiency, his ideas spawned partisan battles as reservation residents discussed the strengths and weaknesses of the IRA.

These disputes contributed to the evolution of contemporary reservation political culture. Despite reasons to support the IRA, many conservative Plains reservation communities opposed this legislation as intruding on the tribe's sovereignty. The Yankton, Standing Rock, Crow, Wind River, and Fort Peck reservation communities rejected the IRA at tribal elections. Other reservations, such as Pine Ridge, approved the IRA by voting to accept the act, then drafted new constitutions, and less frequently approved corporate tribal charters. The IRA was a mixed success on Northern Plains reservations. Those that accepted the IRA often did not create tribal economic corporations.

Overall, Northern Plains tribal support for the IRA decreased by the end of the decade because the act failed to restore reservation self-rule. One reason for this failure was that the Office of Indian Affairs increased the number of Indian Service employees to administer Indian New Deal programs instead of reducing government employees and turning reservation operations over to tribal governments. This trend was especially aggravating to Indians who witnessed funding increases for the Indian Service while they suffered. This disparity created future tribal discontent with the United States and its Indian policies.

## World War II

America's entrance into World War II (1939–1945) ended congressional appropriations for New Deal relief programs. Northern Plains climatic conditions also improved in the early 1940s, advancing agricultural prospects, but most reservation Indian communities did not participate in this returning prosperity. With a diminishing land base, an increasing population, and limited opportunity for employment, most reservation Indians marginally participated in the rural recovery either as field hands in labor-intensive agriculture production or as sellers and lessors of their land.

Since there were few reservation employment alternatives, military service often became an opportunity for young Indian men and many enlisted in the United States armed services. Frequently, Indian soldiers sent money home to relatives who remained on reservations. Others found work in war-related industries such as munitions plants. For example, some Lakota worked at the ammunition ordnance storage facility at Igloo, South Dakota, west of the Pine Ridge Reservation.

### The Postwar Experience

World War II changed Plains reservation life. Many tribal men left the reservations and either went overseas to war or found employment at war industries located off the reservations. After the war, some stayed off the reservation and continued to work in urban communities. On the other hand, those who returned to their reservation homes were often determined to improve their communities' economic, health, and housing conditions. These veterans wanted greater tribal self-rule so tribes would control reservation resources and institutions instead of the United States, and they were determined to protect tribal sovereignty. Wartime experiences coupled with New Deal frustrations made the postwar Northern Plains reservation leaders more vocal than their predecessors in tribal dealings with state, local, and federal authorities.

Tribesmen also demanded equal rights as other citizens. To achieve equality, they requested that Congress repeal discriminatory legislation, especially restrictive liquor laws, which prohibited sale of alcohol to Indians on reservations. In 1952 the reservation alcohol prohibition was lifted, giving tribal people the right to decide whether or not to allow the sale of alcohol on their reservations.

Post–World War II Indian reservation leaders asserted that economic development was a tribal right and prepared reservation economic-planning documents urging greater exploitation of tribal resources and labor to improve tribal economic welfare. Many tribes used recent land claims settlement monies as a foundation for their economic plans, but the Lakota refused to settle for the loss of the Black Hills; therefore they were unable to use that source of money for tribal development. To aid their economic plans, tribal leaders stressed the need to improve educational opportunities for their children, which often required placing their children in public schools.

Despite this postwar planning, Northern Plains reservations remained disadvantaged economically. The Northern Plains peoples were isolated and distant from markets and possessed neither investment income nor access to credit, which made economic improvement difficult. To improve economic conditions, tribal leaders also needed to build reservation infrastructures such as roads, economic development parks, and telephone services that would facilitate economic commerce. Building economic infrastructures, however,

Omaha sacred pole. (Photo by Ilka Hartmann)

was an imposing task because most Plains reservations had few resources and little capital to pay for such improvements.

Reservation people wanted to end that deepening pattern of economic dependency on the United States and local farmers and ranchers. They wanted to develop their own ranching and industrial operations, but many factors worked against them. The inability to find credit and an inadequately divided land base prohibited individuals from beginning ranching operations. In addition, technological evolutions decreased the demand for unskilled manual labor. After World War II, new mechanized combines and other harvesting equipment rapidly spread through the Plains and, for crops like wheat and oats, the new equipment was more efficient and cheaper than previous harvesting methods requiring seasonal labor. Consequently, postwar mechanization took away a major source of temporary farm labor income from many Plains Indian communities, forcing them to slide deeper into poverty.

Unable to increase their participation in the local farm economy, many reservation residents wanted the

opportunity to find wage work. Ideally, tribal leaders wanted labor-intensive industries to locate either on or near reservations. However, industrial leaders were reluctant to establish plants near or on northern Plains reservations because of the distance from investors, suppliers, distributors, and consumers. For Indian communities, reservation-based industries would minimize family disruptions and decrease the necessity of leaving their cultural communities, with its social and ceremonial events, for the oftentimes alien environments of distant cities.

An alternative was to encourage Indian families to resettle in urban centers where jobs could be found. In the early 1950s the United States government sponsored a program to assist rural reservation people to migrate to cities and to find jobs. Blackfeet moved to Seattle and Lakota relocated to Chicago, Dallas, and Oakland. After obtaining employment, frequently in construction, the relocated families were often unable to stay in urban areas because the man's spouse often had not left the reservation and was reluctant to stay in such an environment. This forced families to return home. Many who stayed lost their jobs during the 1957 recession and returned jobless to their depressed reservations. Others, however, remained in urban areas such as Los Angeles, Chicago, Seattle, and Minneapolis, where significant urban Northern Plains Indian communities are present today.

Relocation pulled many Indian people away from the reservation's cultural environment and family activities. In order to maintain reservation ties, many tribal people worked seasonally in urban areas. Other people preferred to find work nearer the reservation. Both situations enabled individuals the time to participate in tribal ceremonies and powwows. The automobile encouraged migration from reservations to cities and enabled many reservation people to work greater distances from their homes while maintaining contact with their rural tribal communities. Many times, Indians seeking off-reservation work selected locales because of their proximity to the reservation or familiarity with the city, or because friends and relatives were already there. The cities, with associated pressures and distractions, strained the ability of many relocatees to preserve their tribal identity because of the need to adjust to the urban environment.

Nearby off-reservation communities provided temporary employment, usually limited to seasonal work. Some Omaha and Winnebago left their reservations and assumed residence in Omaha, Nebraska, and Sioux City, Iowa. Crow moved to Billings, Montana, and Blackfeet found limited employment in Great Falls, Montana. Kansas City, due to its proximity to several reservations, became a common location for Kansas Indians who were looking for work. Rapid City and Sioux Falls, South Dakota, and Bismarck, North Dakota, became Lakota local urban destinations.

Regardless of the destination, relocation changed Plains demography and scattered tribal populations across the country. These migrations made it more difficult to maintain family relations and ceremonial ties. Even short travels off the reservation forced individuals to rely on local and state social services during periods of unemployment. Under these conditions, the emigrants' economic livelihoods did not improve, especially when an entire family depended on intermittent income. Even more important, the limited opportunities available in off-reservation communities made the plight of most reservation Indians more visible, encouraging discrimination.

The departure for urban environments did not improve reservation conditions for those who remained. Throughout the upper Missouri drainage, the U.S. Army Corps of Engineers completed one dam after another in the 1950s and 1960s and changed the living and subsistence patterns of several reservation communities. Tribal communities along the Missouri River lost valuable land that provided many reservation residents with fuel and food to flooding. Fort Berthold, Cheyenne River, Standing Rock, Yankton, Lower Brule, Crow Creek, and Fort Peck reservations lost entire communities, as rising water forced reservation residents either to relocate to new communities (New Town, North Dakota, in the case of the Fort Berthold Reservation) or move to existing communities (Eagle Butte, South Dakota, in the case of the Cheyenne River Sioux Reservation). Construction did not stop with the Missouri River. Tributaries were also dammed, including the Big Horn River on the Crow Reservation. This hydraulic destruction continued the pattern of reservations supplying resources to non-tribal consumers and increased reservation poverty.

Plains reservations did not experience postwar prosperity, but ongoing reservation poverty did exclude them from the 1950s termination legislation designed to turn tribal affairs over to state governments. As a result, Northern Plains state governments often refused to assume responsibilities over Indian people since the gains in tax revenues would have been far outweighed by the costs of social welfare and law and order to support impoverished Indian communities.

## The Contemporary Experience

In the early 1960s, the nation's War on Poverty provided rural Northern Plains reservations with hope for economic progress. Congress extended the Office of Economic Opportunity (OEO) programs to reservations in 1964, enabling tribal governments and reservation organizations to write and administer Indian Community Action Program (ICAP) development grants. This gave tribal groups an opportunity to improve reservation standards of living by building homes, constructing sanitary systems, and enhancing education. Like previous New Deal direct relief programs, the 1960s efforts provided only short-term employment and did not build reservation infrastructures necessary to sustain reservation economies. As a result, government dollars continued to pass from reservations to non-tribal communities.

Despite this fundamental flaw, OEO and its associated programs encouraged reservation communities to take control of even more reservation programs. The Crow tribe initiated a language program for children in the Head Start Program, providing a language foundation that strengthened cultural bonds. Even more important, the 1960s political climate fostered both civil

BIA area directors meeting in Montana. (Photo by Carol Lujan)

rights and greater cultural awareness as well as increased tribal activism. Northern Plains reservations served as focal points for this psychological resurgence and the American Indian Movement (AIM), a Red Power organization, initiated a seventy-three-day siege at Wounded Knee, South Dakota, in early 1973. Wounded Knee was the site of Seventh Cavalry massacre of over two hundred Lakota men, women, and children in 1890, and symbolized ongoing broken American promises to tribal America.

Self-determination—permitting tribes to manage tribal operations—became U.S. policy in 1971 after a speech by President Richard Nixon. Nevertheless over the next two decades, the United States, through the BIA, maintained control over tribal government budgets and law-making procedures, thus making the trend toward tribal government self-determination a hollow victory.

To generate income, some resource tribes began to investigate selling their coal and oil. As energy resources increased in value in the 1970s, companies pursued coal and oil contracts with several Plains reservations. Tribal leaders hoped the international energy crisis would provide jobs and increase tribal government revenues. On the other hand, there was not universal support across reservations on the issue of coal sales because of long-range environmental and cultural effects. In the late 1970s, the Northern Cheyenne voted to reject massive coal sales and potentially millions of dollars of royalty income because strip mining threatened to destroy nearly one-half of the Northern Cheyenne reservation land base.

Different energy programs characterized each reservation, but the desire to control individual reservation energy development remained a common theme. The Crow negotiated coal-mining contracts, the Blackfeet entered into oil exploration contracts, and the Fort Peck leadership opened the reservation to oil exploration.

Erratic energy markets encouraged tribes to pursue more stable economic projects. The Fort Peck (Montana) and Fort Totten (North Dakota) reservations built manufacturing plants that relied on government defense contracts. The Turtle Mountain Reservation,

Boys talking at an Omaha Powwow in Macy, Nebraska, 1989. (Photo by Ilka Hartmann)

North Dakota, also sought contract work with the U.S. Defense Department for manufacturing trailers to haul heavy military equipment. These were only partially successful reservation industries because they employed a small percentage of the people, and the work lasted only until the defense contracts ended and then tribal employees were terminated. Tribal energy programs, political activism, and tribal or federal programs unfortunately did not address major economic problems.

Government funds declined during the administrations of presidents Ronald Reagan and George Bush (1981–1993). Even after decades of economic development plans, Northern Plains reservations remain some of the most impoverished areas in the United States. Regardless of the standard applied, Northern Plains Indians are among the poorest of the poor. For example, real unemployment reached 80 percent on the Northern Cheyenne Reservation. High unemployment creates low reservation standards of living and results in malnutrition, poor health, and substandard housing, which also affects other institutions adversely, such as education.

That reality forced most residents either to seek employment off the reservation or to remain unemployed or underemployed on the reservation. To break that latter trend, many northern Plains reservations decided to capitalize on their sovereignty and initiated high-stakes gambling operations. Though sound in principle, tribal gambling operations encountered many difficulties. The 1988 Indian Gaming Regulatory Act required states to enter into gaming compacts with tribes, and states frequently imposed restrictive rules. Also, the isolation of Plains reservations prohibited gambling operations from growing, and the lack of a work force trained in human service business forced tribes to rely on outside help. Even a successful operation still depends on outsiders to gamble at tribal casinos.

Despite economic difficulties, many Indian reservation communities adopted and modified outside institutions as a means to maintain their identity and traditions. Initially, tribal contact with American schools produced negative experiences, as teachers tried to remove children from their culture, family, and heritage. Instead of fighting the schools, tribal leaders demanded change and assumed greater control over their children's education. In the 1970s reservation parents and leaders insisted that school curricula become more relevant to reservation needs and values. Now, many elementary and secondary reservation schools emphasize the importance of Indian cultures to prepare children to participate in the reservation community.

This trend has been carried into higher education. On the Northern Plains, tribes have been leaders in tribal community education, establishing a large number of tribally controlled community colleges beginning with Sinte Gleska at Rosebud. These institutions satisfy local needs to educate individuals, providing a mechanism for high school dropouts to complete GED requirements and college students with skills essential for employment.

Improving each reservation's education system is essential because residents need specific skills before they can even work for their own tribal governments. For example, tribal governments today administer multimillion-dollar budgets often through 638 contracts that provide funds for a wide array of services from education to economic development. To accomplish these services, tribal leaders require that employees have expertise in accounting, administration, and environmental issues.

Contemporary reservation life is the result of change and continuity reflecting the ability of Northern Plains tribes to accommodate outsiders without surrendering their cultural heritage. As a result, these cultures are renewed when tribal members attend powwows, tribal fairs, Sun Dances, sweat lodge ceremonies, and naming rites. Powwows are held annually in most Plains reservations, and many powwow participants perform traditional and contemporary dances. Traditional giveaway ceremonies are carried out at many Plains powwows that cement ties of friendship with members of tribal communities through public displays of generosity. Since the 1970s, many Plains tribes have revived public enactment of the traditional Sun Dance or adopted new versions of the Sun Dance, as with the Crow, who in the 1940s accepted a Sun Dance ceremony from the Shoshoni on the Wind River Reservation in Wyoming. On the Northern Cheyenne Reservation, each of the four major reservation communities holds a powwow, and a Sun Dance is held in early July at Lame Deer, Montana, where the tribal government is centered. The peyote religion, or Native American Church, finds many converts among the Plains peoples. Urban Indians maintain their cultural ties by either returning to their reservations to take part in the annual ceremonies and powwows or by participating in tribal social activities at urban Indian centers. Many Plains reservation communities strongly support ceremonies and significant

aspects of Plains culture. Despite poverty and isolation, Plains Indian cultures are alive and changing.

*Richmond Clow*
*University of Montana, Missoula*

# ◆ NORTHWEST COAST INDIANS

The cultures of the Northwest Coast have long fascinated scholars because of the region's unique lifestyles, sophisticated art, and flamboyant ceremonies. These cultures underwent dramatic changes beginning in the late eighteenth century when Europeans came into the area. Nevertheless, Northwest Coast Indians persist today as distinct cultures within the ever-expanding Canadian and American societies, largely because of their tenacity, but also because of the leading role they have taken in exerting their aboriginal rights to land and resources. A reliance on two Northwest Coast resources, salmon and cedar, was a characteristic of almost all of the diverse peoples of the area at the time of European contact, and remain so today.

To discuss the nature of the Northwest Coast culture prior to European contact, we have to be largely speculative. Using archaeological, historical, and ethnographic information, it is possible to satisfactorily reconstruct the traditional lifeways of the Northwest Coast people. As today, a great deal of variation was evident among the Northwest Coast tribes. The Indians spoke a variety of languages and represented an assortment of cultural adaptations to the coastal environment. Some groups relied more heavily on salmon than others. Some were whalers or deep-sea fishers. Some lived inland and relied more heavily on the fruits of the forest and on big game. Some traded extensively, while others stayed close to home and let traders come to them. Some warred on their neighbors, while others were warred upon. Despite these differences, the Northwest Coast culture area can be discussed in general terms, as a way of laying a foundation upon which to explore the postcontact history of the various tribes.

## Tribal Distribution

The Northwest Coast culture area is generally considered to be that part of North America that lies along the Pacific Ocean from roughly 42 degrees north latitude (the California-Oregon border) to 60 degrees north latitude. This includes southeast Alaska and the western portions of British Columbia, Washington, and Oregon. To introduce the various Northwest Coast tribes, we will begin at the north end of the culture area and work southward. Present-day place names are used in this discussion. Population estimates are based on the time of first contact with Europeans. There is considerable evidence that the precontact population was much higher. These numbers reflect a population dramatically reduced by introduced diseases.

The Tlingit inhabited the area that is now southeast Alaska, from Yakutat Bay to Portland Canal. The Tlingit fished salmon in kin-owned areas and also depended upon other resources of the sea, especially halibut and seal. Clinging to the mountainous shores and rugged offshore islands, Tlingit villages were usually large in comparison to other Northwest Coast tribes. The total Tlingit population at the time of European contact is estimated to have been 15,000.

Immediately to the south of the Tlingit, the Haida inhabited the southern portion of Prince of Wales Island in southeast Alaska and the Queen Charlotte Islands in British Columbia. Well known along the coast for their woodworking skills, especially large totem poles and huge seaworthy canoes, the several bands of Haida probably numbered about 14,000 when first contacted in the late 1700s.

The Tlingit, the Haida, and a third group, the Tsimshian, are sometimes collectively known as the "northern matrilineal tribes" because of their distinctive form of social organization. The Tsimshian, who include the coastal and southern Tsimshian on the north-central coast of British Columbia, and the Nisga'a and Gitksan inland in the Nass and Skeena River valleys, numbered approximately 14,500 at the time of first contact.

Various bands of Kwakwala speakers lived along the south-central British Columbia coast and adjacent eastern shores of Vancouver Island. These bands can be broadly divided into the northern groups and the southern groups. The northern groups include the Haisla, Haihais, Heiltsuk, and Owekeeno; the southern groups are known collectively as the Kwakiutl, or Kwakwaka'wakw. The Kwakiutl are famous in anthropological literature for their extravagant ceremonies known as "potlatches" (discussed later in this entry) and also for the other types of religious and secular ceremonies that permeated every aspect of their lives. At the time of contact, these groups numbered approximately 7,500 for the northern groups and 19,000 for the southern.

Facing the Pacific Ocean, the west coast of Vancouver Island was home to the Nuu-Chah-Nulth (formerly known as Nootka) and the Ditidaht. They and the Makah (a closely related group who lived across the Strait of Juan de Fuca in present-day Washington State) were famous for their skills as whalers and deep-sea navigators. One of the Nuu-Chah-Nulth bands was host to the first European settlement on the Northwest Coast. The bands totaled about 10,000 at the time of contact.

The Coast Salish, consisting of more than three dozen distinct tribes and bands, resided in southwest mainland British Columbia, southeast Vancouver Island, and much of western Washington. Two linguistically related groups, the Nuxalk (formerly known as the Bella Coola) of the central coast of British Columbia and the Tillamook of the north-central Oregon coast, complete the Salish speakers in the Northwest Coast culture area. The Nuxalk numbered about 3,000, the Tillamook about 4,000. The rest of the Coast Salish, who for linguistic and cultural reasons are perhaps better broken down into four groupings, numbered 4,000 for the Northern Coast Salish, 20,000 for the Central Coast Salish, 12,500 for the Southern Coast Salish, and 12,000 for the Southwestern Coast Salish.

The Chinook inhabited the lower Columbia River from the Cascade Mountains to the Pacific Ocean. The Chinook are, perhaps, the Native group most written about in Northwest Coast history. They are especially renowned in history and legend as traders extraordinaire. Because they controlled the waterways into the interior, the Chinook were masters over trade north and south along the coast and inland to the Columbia Plateau and beyond. In addition to their prowess as traders, the Chinook also realized the potential of the enormous Columbia River salmon runs. Numbering perhaps 10,500 in the mid–1700s, by 1850 the Chinook population had dwindled to just a few hundred.

Numerous bands of linguistically diverse tribes resided along the Oregon Coast and inland in the Willamette River Valley. These groups spoke a number of languages from unrelated linguistic stocks such as Athapascan and Penutian. Culturally, these tribes were transitional between the Northwest Coast and California culture areas and shared many traits in common with both. In all, they numbered as many as 30,000 people when first contacted by Europeans.

### The Annual Cycle of Economic Subsistence

While the most striking thing about the Northwest Coast culture area may be the linguistic and cultural diversity evident from north to south, there are some general characteristics. Let us explore a "yearly round"

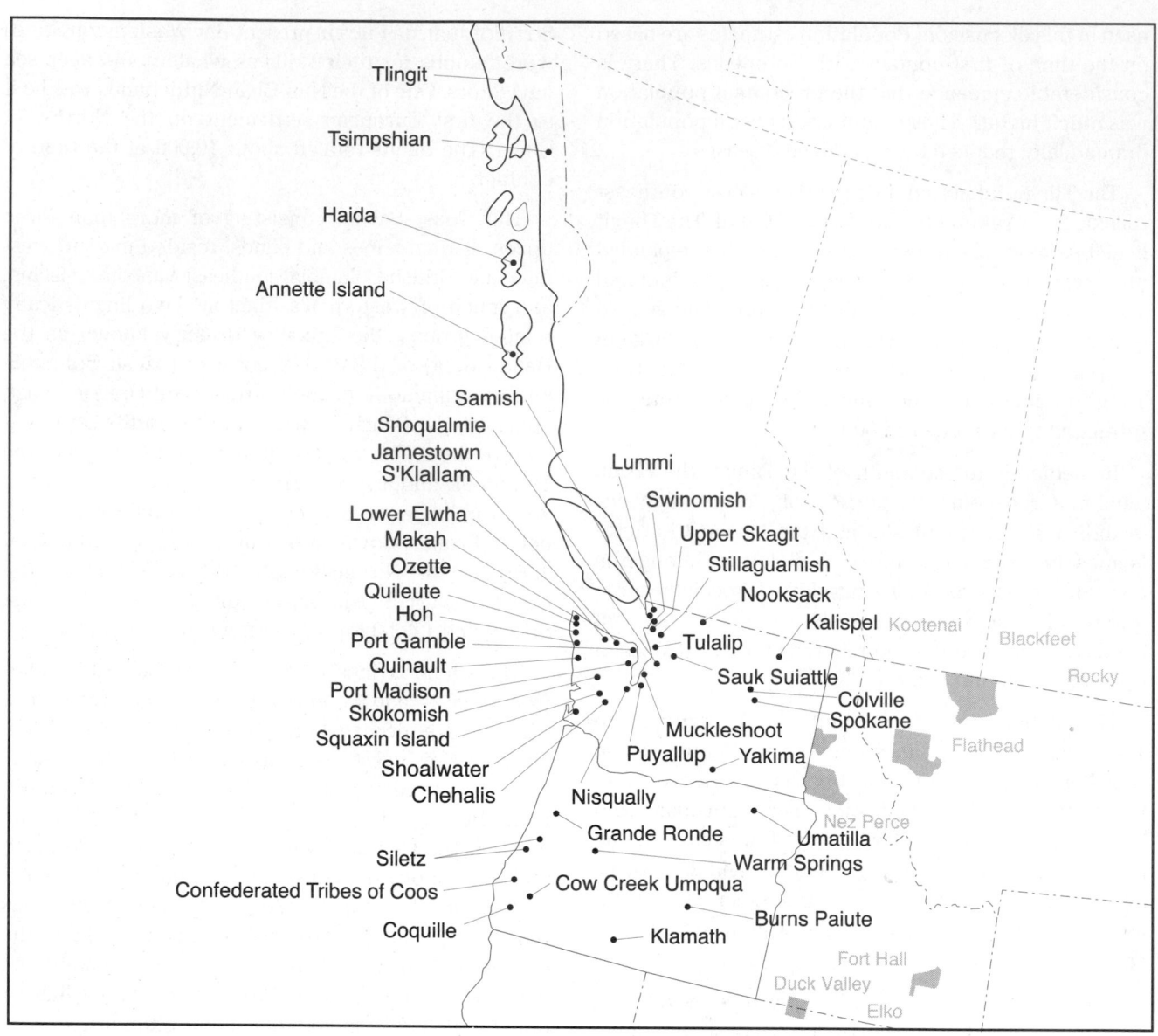

Contemporary Northwest Coast Indian tribes. (Courtesy of the UCLA American Indian Studies Center)

of social and economic activities as a means of identifying some of the culture traits common to the Northwest Coast.

**Housing.** The typical habitation of the Northwest Coast Indians was the longhouse. The structure was large, capable of sheltering several families. Generally, the families that inhabited a longhouse were related to one another in some way: among the northern matrilineal groups, they were related through the female lineage; among the other tribes, the relation was through either the house owner or his spouse.

Inside the longhouse, each family had its own area, usually partitioned off. Central fires burned for heat and light, but each family cooked its own meals and ate

separately. Families could change houses if they wished, or the house might break up in the summer months while individual families pursued subsistence activities. In the winter, the longhouse served as a ceremonial center; the partitions were taken down to make room for dances and for guests.

**Food Resources.** Certainly the most prolific and dependable resource throughout the Northwest Coast was the abundant runs of salmon. Six species of salmon inhabit the Pacific Coast, spending their adult life in the offshore waters and traveling up freshwater streams to spawn. Native people caught some salmon by trolling in the saltwater, but large numbers of fish taken for preservation were captured in or near the freshwater

Chief Highest Peak in a mountain range in New Cold Harbor. (Courtesy of Southwest Museum)

streams with traps, weirs, and nets. Typically, salmon enter freshwater in the spring and subsequent runs may occur throughout the summer and into the fall. Because not every stream supports all six species or their successive runs, some Northwest Coast groups focused their attention on specific runs of fish to take in abundance for drying or smoking as a means of preservation. Preserved salmon provided a dietary staple that was supplemented with other locally available food resources, such as shellfish, plant foods, marine mammals, land mammals, and waterfowl.

Although some salmon fishing took place throughout the year, the bulk of the fish were taken in the spring and fall at specific locations where the family groups tended to resort year after year. Probably the most widely employed fishing device at such locations was the weir, a barricade placed across a stream to divert the runs of fish into a trap. While the men worked the traps, the women cut the fish along the back, removing the bone and internal organs. The filleted fish

were then hung on a rack to be preserved by drying winds, or in the rafters of the longhouse where the slow burning fires would dry them. Some groups preserved as much as five hundred pounds of fish per person through the year and, indeed, to this day, many Native people feel a meal is incomplete without at least a little salmon.

Not all the summer was spent salmon fishing. For many groups shellfish—especially clams, mussels, and oysters—provided important food. Shellfish could be taken anytime of year, although in some areas the flesh might be poisonous in the summer months. Usually the spring tides, when the lowest tides of the year occurred during the daylight hours, were the important shellfish gathering times. As with salmon, shellfish were also dried in abundance, providing not only sustenance, but also an important trade item with groups farther inland.

In late spring, many other types of fish were utilized, depending upon local availability. For example, the Tsimshian harvested tons of a small fish known as *oolichan*, which was rendered into oil. *Oolichan* was an important addition to the diet, as well as a trade item. Other Northwest Coast groups harvested herring (both the fish and the spawn), halibut, rockfish, and other deep-sea fish. Marine mammals—seals, porpoise, and whales—were also harvested. Whales, especially gray whales, were taken during their migratory pass in the spring. The Nuu-Chah-Nulth, Ditidaht, Makah, and Quileute, all expert whalers, hunted these large animals from dugout canoes, using hand-thrown spears. Other Northwest Coast tribes might have used a whale that had beached or drifted ashore, but the Nuu-Chah-Nulth, Ditidaht, Makah, and Quileute pursued the migrating whales far out at sea. Many miles from shore, for days on end, these Native whalers would pursue their quarry in hopes of not only obtaining an important source of food, but also the prestige that came with being a successful whaler.

The land mammals most frequently hunted by the Northwest Coast Indians were deer, elk, bear, and mountain goat. Either solitary hunters would hunt the animals, or groups would drive them into nets or ambushes. Typically, the inland groups were more involved in hunting land mammals. Mountain goats were most particularly hunted for their horns, which could be fashioned into implements, usually spoons, and for their wool, which was spun into yarn and then woven into blankets for ceremonial garb and day-to-day use. In addition to mountain goats, some women kept a type of small dog that could be shorn like a sheep; its woolly fur was then spun into yarn.

The time of gathering plant foods began in the spring, but was more intensive in the late summer and early fall. Starchy tubers, such as camas, wapato, and braken fern roots were taken in abundance, in some cases from kin-controlled and tended plots. Berries and other fruits were also abundant; they were dried in addition to eaten fresh.

**Culture.** Of course, the Northwest Coast people did not simply spend their time in the pursuit of food. Artisans, such as weavers, basket makers, wood carvers, and stone workers spent many hours crafting their handiwork. Winter months were busy with ceremonial activities such as spirit dances, ceremonial performances, the demonstration of inherited privileges like masked dances, and the most famous ceremony of all, the potlatch. Potlatches, the ceremonial distribution of wealth goods, could actually take place any time of year, to commemorate a naming, wedding, house-raising, funeral, or other occasion. Potlatching was a way for an individual to express their social standing in the community, and to reinforce that position through the giving away of wealth and feasting with the guests. Numerous other ceremonies also were held, but certainly the potlatch is the most widely known. Some evidence suggests that potlatching may have increased in the 1800s because of the influx of wealth items through the fur trade and subsequent interactions with Europeans, but that was only one of the dramatic changes to occur during the contact period.

## European Contact

Many of the earliest explorers of northern North America, such as John Cabot, who sailed from England in 1497, were searching for a direct passage from Europe to China by way of an open sea passage across North America. Such an ocean route would have allowed Europeans an efficient means of carrying on trade with the Far Eastern empires. In the end, no such passage existed, but considerable European effort was expended before the nineteenth century in search of the fabled Northwest Passage. In their continuing search for wealth and for the Northwest Passage, Europeans eventually reached the Northwest Coast during the latter part of the eighteenth century. Initially, the Spanish explored northward from their settlements in Mexico. Shortly afterward, the Russians reached southeast Alaska from Siberia. At first, the Europeans found little to compel them to stay. Some shipboard trade took place, but the Northwest Coast was not particularly rich in furs, and the Natives were hard bargainers. Soon, however, sea otter pelts began to bring in phenomenal prices in China, and a lively trade quickly developed.

In 1789 the Spanish established a post at Nootka Sound on Vancouver Island and the struggle for control of trade began. The trade eventually included the Russians, Spanish, British, and Americans. The Native people were unconcerned with European political struggles so long as they gained access to manufactured goods. Such items greatly increased the Natives' efficiency and economic well-being. The initial changes brought by the fur trade were primarily in material goods; little change was evident in social or religious life.

In 1795, the Spanish relinquished claim to the area north of 42 degrees latitude, the Russians held southeast Alaska, and in 1818 the British and Americans agreed to joint occupation of the area in between. In 1811 the establishment of land-based trading operations began with the building of the American Fur Company's post at the mouth of the Columbia River. Lost during the War of 1812, the post eventually fell into the hands of the Hudson's Bay Company, which came to dominate the fur trade of the Northwest. The Hudson's Bay Company expanded operations to Fort Vancouver in 1824, Fort Langley in 1827, Fort Nisqually and Fort McLoughlin in 1833, Cowlitz Station in 1838, Fort Victoria in 1843, and by agreement with the Russians, Fort Stikine and Fort Taku in 1840. The economic control of the Northwest Coast was in the hands of the Hudson's Bay Company until the 1840s, when American settlers began moving into the joint-occupied area. In 1846 the British and Americans negotiated the Treaty of Oregon, establishing the boundary at the forty-ninth parallel between the United States and Canada, and in 1867 Russia sold her claims to Alaska to the United States.

Through the late 1800s, non-Native settlement of the Northwest Coast progressed at a staggering rate. The settlement period was marked by the negotiation of treaties in the United States, by the establishment of reserve communities in British Columbia, and by the contraction of villages into a few Native communities in Alaska. During the same time, the Native population rapidly declined because of European diseases for which the Indians had no resistance. By 1900 non-Natives outnumbered Natives in most areas and the Native societies were quickly engulfed by the growing dominant society.

New religious expressions among the Indians became evident early in the settlement period. Considerable evidence shows that syncretic movements occurred as well as strong efforts to continue the practice of traditional religious expression of shamanism and spirit quests. Christianity attracted many converts as well, especially among those communities in close proximity to non-Native communities. Today in any given Native community, there are a number of Christians, as well as followers of Shakerism, a religious movement stemming from the experience of a Coast Salish prophet in the 1880s. Still other Northwest Coast Indians are practitioners of the traditional forms of spiritualism.

As the non-Native population became more dominant, the Northwest Coast people found it increasingly difficult to continue to fish, hunt, and gather as they had before. Fishing, logging, and farming became the area's principle economic activities. Conflicts over non-Native and Native uses of the land and resources were inevitable. As Native societies became more restricted in their traditional activities, they sought wage labor in nearby non-Native communities, or became entangled in the growing poverty and political domination of the reservation communities. Many Native people chose to leave the reservations during this time, an act encouraged by government policy.

## Contemporary Life

The Northwest Coast culture of the twentieth century is a complex combination of traditional values and of political-economic factors that emerged from interaction with the dominant society. Modern Northwest Coast Natives —now minorities in their own land—are citizens of either Canada or the United States. They also have the rights and privileges that go with being a member of a tribe or band.

While the multifamily longhouses were abandoned in most areas by 1900, the strong kin ties that were a part of the longhouse living situation have endured. Extended family groups depend upon one another in times of need, for assistance in sponsoring feasts or potlatches, and to support one another in the attempt to gain political power. Many Native communities may at first appear indistinguishable from their non-Native neighbors, but behind the familiar housing, clothing, and jobs is an undercurrent of Native life that has persisted and adapted to the modern context.

To understand the changes that have occurred over the past 100 years, we must look at some important events that have had lasting impacts on the Northwest Coast people. Because the Native people have lived under different polities, their situations have been different. Historical changes in the Northwest Coast can best be studied by looking individually at three main areas within the region: Alaska, British Columbia, and Western Washington and Oregon.

**Alaska.**   Until 1867 the Tlingit and some of the Haida lived in an area of North America claimed by Russia. While southeast Alaska was part of Russian America, the impact on the Native people was minimal. Even after the United States acquired Alaska, its isolation meant the Native people were left to themselves. In the 1890s, however, the situation began to change rapidly. With the Alaskan Gold Rush, followed by the influx of settlers, the Native people rapidly found themselves part of a larger political reality. They participated in the growing economy as fishers and loggers, and in other occupations. Many adopted Christianity in the late 1800s and early 1900s. Formal education became a priority for many Tlingit and Haida families.

As interest in Alaska's resources grew, and especially when oil was discovered in the North Slope soon after Alaska's statehood in 1959, it became clear that some settlement had to be reached between the United States government and the Native people. In 1971 the Alaska Native Claims Settlement Act terminated Native title to land in Alaska. In return, Alaska Natives were to select certain lands that they would retain. They received federal funds to establish Native-controlled share holding corporations to be operated as profit-making operations. The Native people of southeast Alaska were formed into one of thirteen corporations that have since become the primary political bodies of the Native people. Although the Native villages have elected their own political bodies and other forms of Native political expression are available, the Native corporations wield the most power and influence.

Since its inception, the Alaska Native Claims Settlement Act has been the primary political influence in Native Alaska. Unencumbered by a reservation system, the Tlingit and Haida have prospered. As they begin to exert their Native rights over land and resources, they will likely continue to be a dominant force in the state of Alaska.

**British Columbia.**   The Native people of British Columbia have had a somewhat different experience. Many of the Native people live in remote areas and have participated in the principle economic activities of the province, especially logging and commercial fishing. Unlike most Native people of Canada, the Natives of British Columbia never signed treaties with the federal government (although the Hudson's Bay Company negotiated a few legally valid treaties with Native people on Vancouver Island). Instead of treaties, British Columbia instituted a system of reserves, setting aside Natives' lands until they became assimilated into the dominant society.

Native policy in Canada primarily stems from the Indian Act, an all-encompassing piece of legislation first passed in 1876 and revised several times since (the last in 1985). With special attention to the Northwest Coast, the Indian Act specifically outlawed the potlatch in 1884. British Columbia officials were incapable of enforcing this policy until the 1920s when concerted efforts were made to abolish the ceremony. While potlatching never completely disappeared, it did go underground for many years. When the potlatch law was abolished in 1951, potlatching was publicly revived.

Beginning in the 1880s, Native leaders in British Columbia sought to affirm Native rights to land and resources. Forming a province-wide organization in 1916, the tribes have actively pursued recognition of their claims. Although seeking reprieve through political channels as early as the 1880s, it was not until recently that the bands began to make some important progress. With the provision in the Canadian Constitution of 1982 that "existing aboriginal and treaty rights of the aboriginal peoples of Canada are. . . recognized and affirmed," the British Columbia Natives finally had a firm commitment on the part of the federal government to support their claims. Nevertheless, the outcomes of land and resource claims have been varied. Perhaps the most famous case was one in which the Gitskan (Tsimshian) were involved. This claim attempted to assert Native sovereignty over a large portion of west-central British Columbia. Simultaneously, a case involving Coast Salish fishing on the Fraser River was decided in favor of the Native claim to aboriginal rights to the resources. As a result of these efforts the federal government enacted two major agreements with the Native peoples of British Columbia. First, in 1992 the Aboriginal Fisheries Strategy was put in place allowing Native peoples to enter into agreements with the federal government to participate in a Native salmon fishery. Second, also in 1992 the Native bands, government of British Columbia, and the federal government of Canada entered into treaty negotiations. Thus far only the Nisga'a have completed the treaty process. There are over eighty other negotiations ongoing.

**Western Washington and Oregon.** The Native people of western Washington and Oregon represent the third set of circumstances of historical change in the Northwest Coast. In the mid–1850s, these tribes entered into treaties with the United States government, forming the basis of interaction for the last 150 years. Most important among the treaty provisions was the establishment of reservations and the protection of certain aboriginal rights, especially fishing. From the treaty era to the present, various federal policies have been enacted which have had lasting impacts on the Native people of the northwest United States. Beginning with assimilationist policy in the late 1800s and continuing into the present era of Self-Determination, the federal policies that have marked the relationship between Native people and the federal government can be used as a means of discussing social changes in this region.

Assimilation refers to the social, cultural, and political incorporation of a person or group into the mainstream national culture and society. From the 1880s to 1934, the U.S. government actively sought to convince Indians to abandon their traditional cultures and join U.S. society and culture. Perhaps the most influential policy of the assimilationist period was the General Allotment Act of 1887. This policy allowed for the allotment of reservation lands. Allotting parcels of land to individuals had two dramatic impacts on the Native people. First, it was designed to instill a Western notion of private property in the form of alienable land. Second, it served to break up the multifamily units and encouraged individual activities, especially farming. The longlasting effect of allotment was that since the land was individually owned, the tribe had no means to keep reservation land in the control of the tribe. Consequently, much land was sold to nontribal members. From the implementation of the General Allotment Act, to the 1930s, the design of federal policy was to break up the tribal units and encourage the assimilation of Native people into the dominant society. This was reinforced by the schooling of children in off-reservation boarding schools that taught them trades and required that they speak English. A famous saying of boarding school administrators succinctly sums up their educational philosophy: "Kill the Indian but save the person." Children from the Northwest Coast went to many different boarding schools, but the most common was Chemawa, near Salem, Oregon.

In 1924 all Native people of the United States were granted citizenship. Instead of marking the desired results of forced assimilation, it marked the end of an era of policy. In the 1930s Congress passed a series of new legislative acts that were designed to strengthen the tribal units and encourage independent tribal economic development. Under the Indian Reorganization Act of 1934 tribes in the Northwest were assisted in developing tribal governments based on a constitution and governed by elected bodies of officials. Rather than encouraging independent development, however, the Indian Reorganization Act actually strengthened the power that the Bureau of Indian Affairs had over the Native people's lives. For example, now the Bureau of Indian Affairs has the power to override decisions made by tribal governments even though tribes are considered sovereigns within the United States. The bold new plans of the federal government during the 1930s were to be short-lived after World War II when the United States began a series of policies designed to terminate the special relationship Native people had with the federal government. Many powers, such as law enforcement, were turned over to the states; individual Indians were encouraged to leave the reservations for urban areas; some tribes were actually terminated—formal ties with the federal government ended and tribal resources divided among the individuals, who collectively ceased being a federally recognized Indian tribe with legal protections for land and tribal rights.

Termination policies were enacted in two important ways. First, the relocation policies, described as "termination by attrition," encouraged reservation residents to move to urban areas where they were to find jobs. However, since the reservation populations were generally undereducated and unskilled, the types of jobs they found were usually menial. Making minimum wage, they were forced to live in the least desirable parts of the cities and as a result urban Indian ghettos were created in cities like Portland and Seattle. Some reservations estimate that as many as one-third of their entire populations were relocated during the 1950s, an action that not only created a drain on the reservation community, but also created an intertribal urban population. Today, approximately 20,000 Native people live in Seattle where they are represented by such groups as the United Indians of All Tribes Foundation.

The second action was the actual termination of some tribes. While many tribes throughout the United States were scheduled for termination, in actuality most were not. Three Oregon tribes were terminated: the Klamath of southeast Oregon and the Siletz and Grande Ronde of the Oregon coast. Siletz and Grande Ronde were the reservation homes of the Oregon coast tribes, and because of their economic success, they were considered likely candidates for termination of their relationship with the federal government. It soon became clear that without their special status as a federally recognized tribe, the Siletz and Grand Ronde had little power to hold their lands together and continue to promote economic well-being. Almost as soon as they were terminated, both tribes sought to be reinstated as federally recognized tribes, an act that was finally granted after nearly thirty years.

### The Future

The prospects for the future are promising. As Native communities in Alaska, British Columbia, Washington, and Oregon begin to assert their sovereignty as a means to develop economically and politically, they will continue to bring about positive change in a culturally sensitive manner. The present era of Self-Determination is marked by Indian tribes successfully exerting their legal rights to land and resources and the strengthening of tribal self-governance to promote development. The Self-Determination policy recognizes tribal interests in regaining greater control over reservation institutions, such as education and local administration, and over tribal economic resources such as land, minerals, and hunting and fishing. Perhaps the most well-known example of this is the 1974 Boldt Decision, the court case *United States v. Washington* brought by the treaty tribes of western Washington. This case determined that Native people retained certain rights to fisheries and other resource gathering activities that included the right to commercial use of the salmon resource. Consequently, the Native people now harvest 50 percent of the commercial salmon resource as well as significant numbers of other fisheries such as herring, halibut, and crab. This treaty-assured right has formed a base upon which other economic activities, such as processing and marketing, have been built. Additionally, Native people operate hatcheries that release millions of salmon into the public waters every year. Exerting aboriginal rights is evident in other actions as well; for example, the Makah Tribe of Washington State has resumed the hunting of gray whales, a right guaranteed by treaty. Gaming, an economic development strategy throughout Indian America, has been an important development in the Northwest.

Although Natives participate in American and Canadian society, this does not mean that they have assimilated or acculturated or any of the other terms that suggest they are no longer Indian. Speaking English, fishing with modern power boats and synthetic nets, or carving a dugout canoe with a chain saw does not mean that the Northwest Coast Natives are any less Indian. Being a Northwest Coast Indian today means participating in the modern political and economic structures of North American society while maintaining a distinct ethnic identity. It is this identity that will strengthen the efforts toward tribal development—a development that will not only lead to the persistence of Native people in the twenty-first century, but will also lead to their prosperity.

*Daniel L. Boxberger*
*Western Washington University*

### ◆ ALASKA NATIVES

### Traditional Life

Alaska is the original home to two major North American language families: Eskimo-Aleut and Na-Dene. Eskimo-speaking groups are divided between Yup'ik and Iñupiat peoples. Iñupiaq, the Inuit language, gradually spread over northern Alaska and Canada, and Greenland. Yup'ik moved south to the Chugach region and Kodiak where individuals speak a local dialect,

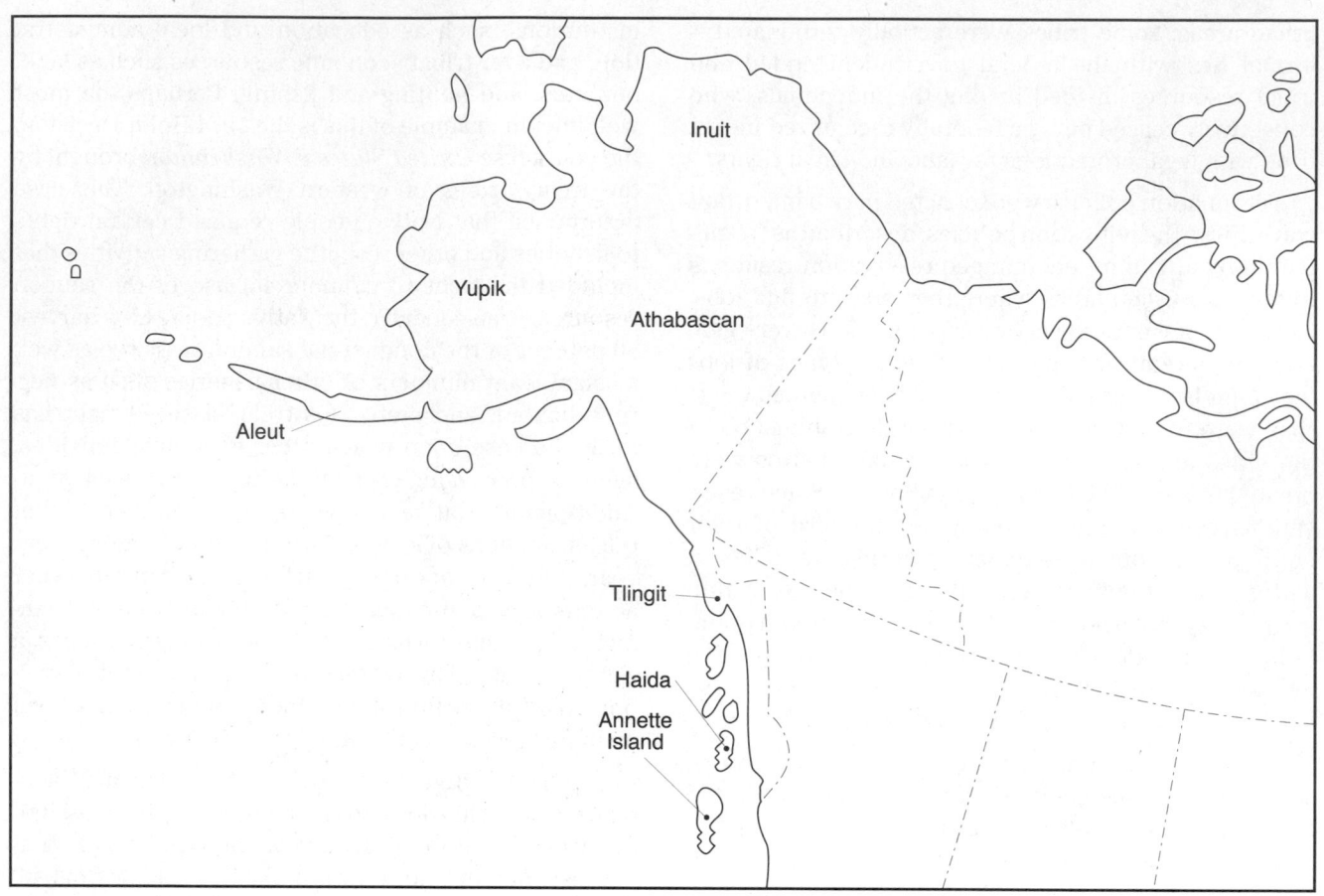

Contemporary Alaska Native tribes. (Courtesy of the UCLA American Indian Studies Center)

Alutiiq (or Sugpiaq). Na-Dene includes thirty Athabascan languages (ten of which were spoken in Alaska), Tlingit, and Eyak. Na-Dene languages extended to western Canada and the southwestern United States. Haidas migrated from the Queen Charlotte Islands to southeastern Alaska a few hundred years ago, and the Tsimshians were settled on Annette Island by an Anglican missionary in 1887. There is little information about the number of indigenous people in Alaska before the Russian voyages in the seventeenth century. Based on archaeological evidence and the records of early explorers, hunters, and missionaries, there may have been 80,000 to 100,000 people living between the western Aleutians and the Canadian border. More than one-third were Yup'ik and Iñupiat, followed by Aleuts, Tlingits, and Athabascans.

The Aleuts occupy the 1,400-mile-long Aleutian Chain, part of the Alaskan Peninsula and the Pribilof Islands in the Bering Sea. An area rich in resources, it supported the densest aboriginal population in Alaska. Most of the estimated 16,000 residents lived in the eastern region. The marine environment provided the Aleut with a wide variety of sea life, including sea urchins, clams,

octopus, fish, sea otters, seals, and whales, which were used for food, clothing, and homes. Birds and their eggs, berries, wild rice, celery, and plant stalks were also part of their diet. The men were skilled open-sea hunters and relied on two-person skin boats (*baidarka*) for hunting seals and whales.

Aleutian villages were situated along the coast, permitting easy access to the sea. They were small, usually supporting 100 to 200 inhabitants. Two to five families lived in semisubterranean houses or *barabaras*. A person's lineage followed the mother's line, and children were disciplined and trained by the mother's family. Men were responsible for hunting and caring for implements and boats. Women tended the home and gathered food along the beaches and shallow intertidal zones. Traditional society was divided between a small group of nobles, commoners, and slaves captured in wars with other villages. Aleut chiefs were the most respected hunters with long experience and exceptional abilities. Chiefs had little power, and decisions required common agreement. Internal conflict was reduced by making war on others for retribution, the taking of slaves, or trading through intermediaries. The

Kwakiutl house. (Courtesy of Southwest Museum)

family served as the basis of village organization, economic exchange, warfare, and occasionally, political authority.

The Eskimo reside in an extensive and diverse environment from the deep fjords and mountain ranges of the south to the windswept mountains of the Alaskan peninsula, to the tundra and relative flat coasts and lowlands of the Arctic province. Yup'ik Eskimo is spoken in southwestern Alaska, and Inuit to the north stretching across northern Canada to Greenland. Subsistence patterns varied from the caribou hunters of interior Alaska, to the Arctic whalers along the coasts, and the fishermen of southwestern Alaska.

Yup'ik and Iñupiat societies were geared toward the continual search for food. They are classified by anthropologists as central-based wanderers who spent part of the year on the move and some time at a settlement, or central base. From twelve to fifty people would travel together. Extended families composed of three to four generations were basic to an individual's life. Families were relatively equal and autonomous; they would often share with others, intermarry, and hunt together. There was considerable conflict, though, between different groups; strangers with no specific reasons for being in an area were in great danger.

Within each family, people were divided by age and gender. At the head was the boss, or *umialik*. Leaders were individuals who displayed exceptional skill or courage, and were able to anticipate future problems. Shamans, or spiritual leaders, were also influential because of their familiarity with the spirit world, their curative powers, and their prescience. Every settlement had a gathering place, or *qargi*, where men, boys, and families would meet for conversation and ritual.

Three major groups occupied southeastern Alaska: the Tlingit, the Haida, and the Tsimshian. Geographically the area is distinct. It is isolated, with high mountains and dense forest to the east and the Pacific Ocean to the west; it is interlaced by fjords and valleys on the mainland and a string of islands off the coast. It is a bountiful environment that nurtured a formal and complex social system.

Societies were divided between two major moieties, the Eagle and the Raven, which had their own rules and corporate functions. Within each moiety were numerous clans. The clan was the fundamental political unit; each had its own territory, history, and particular traits. The clan was responsible for settling feuds, property, and subsistence activities. The most basic unit was the house-group, which was run by a master of the house-group, often a maternal great-uncle. Houses had their own plots, name, and crest, which displayed major cultural figures in the history of the clan and house. Clans and houses had rights to specific areas for fishing, berry picking, and hunting. In practice anyone could use the sites provided they asked for permission. Areas between each territory were open for travel for everyone.

Rank and status, built on the accumulation of wealth, upheld the system of clans and houses. Possession of material goods, including slaves, crests, blankets, totems, a generous disposition, oratorical skill, and past accomplishments, determined the position of individuals, clans, and houses. The potlatch was an integral part of southeastern cultures. It involved a feast, performances, and the distribution of valuable goods. Potlatches were given to honor an individual and they served to strengthen kin relations, to display one's generosity, and to honor the memory of those who had passed away.

The northern Athabascan occupied a vast territory that extended through most of interior Alaska, bordered by the Arctic to the north and the temperate forests to the south. Included in this area were six subgroups: the Ingalik, the Koyukon, Tanana, Tanaina, Ahtna, and Upper Tanana. While each group lacked a formal tribal system, they did occupy an exclusive territory. Within each territory were smaller bands, which followed the seasonal migration of game, and families, who would, for part of the year, live separately in order to fish and hunt. Composed of people related by blood and marriage, bands were responsible for subsistence activities, territorial boundaries, and the settlement of disputes between families.

Men formed hunting partnerships; one killed the animal and the other distributed it. Resources were always shared. Because food was sometimes scarce, mobility and flexibility were imperative. There was little need to accumulate possessions. The Athabascan practiced what is termed strategic hunting, in which fish were led into weirs, caribou were corralled, and waterfowl were taken in their breeding grounds.

Neither primitive nor simple, traditional Native communities in Alaska were extremely well-adapted to the physical environment in which they lived, from the Arctic regions of northern Alaska to the rain forests of the southeast, to the cool and windy climates of the Aleutian chain. The Alaska Natives were also bound by an intricate kinship system that usually specified who could marry and where the couple would live, as well as ownership of fishing and hunting places and leadership. Social and economic relations allowed for popular understanding and local initiative, equity, and community and kinship reciprocity of material goods and services. These relations also delineated the performance of social and religious obligations, such as potlatch exchanges, and other ritual reciprocities, such as performing funeral services for in-laws, as among the Tlingit. There was a precarious balance between the physical environment and the subsistence needs of each community. Natural disasters, population growth, or outside intrusion could easily upset the balance of human and natural environmental relations.

## Russian Colonialism

With the advent of European expansion in the eighteenth century, circumstances in Alaska began to change dramatically. The Russians were first. The voyages of Alexei Chirikof and Vitus Bering in 1741 led to awareness of potential profit from sea otter and seal skins. Siberian fur hunters, the *promishleniki*, soon launched hunting expeditions in the area. An imperial decree was issued in 1766, claiming Russian dominion over the Aleutians, but there was little government regulation of Russian traders and hunters. In response to this anarchy and the competition with other Europeans, the Russian American Company was organized in 1799. The company's charter anticipated the conversion of Natives to Christianity and claimed that the "Islanders" (Aleut) would be treated amicably.

However, the relationship between Russians and Aleut was anything but amicable. Although the exact numbers are not known, it is estimated that 90 percent of the indigenous population was lost to disease or murder. The survivors were in a state of virtual servitude. The Russians used the men as pelagic (open-sea) hunters and, as they moved into eastern Alaska, as warriors. Despite its brutality, Russian commercial expansion in Alaska was limited to the coast. There were occasional forays to the interior, but they were infrequent because of hostile tribes, impassable terrain, and severe temperatures. By 1867, when the United States acquired control of the territory, Russia ruled only a small portion of it.

## American Colonialism

U.S. expansion into Alaska was propelled by an interest in fur and, more important, gold. In 1867 the Treaty of Cession was signed which transferred jurisdiction over Alaska to the United States. Article III was particularly important for Alaska Natives: "The Uncivilized tribes will be subject to such laws and regulations as the United States may, from time to time, adopt in regard to aboriginal tribes in that country." Congress recognized this obligation in 1884 when it passed the first Organic Act, which extended the civil and criminal laws of Oregon to Alaska: "Indians or other persons in said district shall not be disturbed in the possession of any lands actually in their use or occupation or now claimed by them but the terms under which such persons may acquire title to such lands are reserved for future legislation by Congress."

Despite this disclaimer in the Organic Act, land was usually available for the economic interests that needed it. The first fish canneries were built in 1878, and within six years they dotted the southern coast of Alaska. In 1878 the first gold mining camp was established. Gold prospecting and disputes between miners resulted in the territory's first civil government. Legislation in 1891, 1898, and 1900 permitted trade and manufacturing sites, town sites, homesteading, rights of way for a railroad, and timber harvests.

During World War II, national leaders became more aware of the strategic importance of Alaska. This realization, coupled with the influx of money and people, produced a viable effort to achieve admittance into the Union. In his State of the Union message in 1946, President Truman recommended statehood. Owing to partisan opposition and doubts about the financial capability of the territory, recognition was delayed. Finally a compromise was reached, and Alaska and Hawaii were admitted simultaneously. On 3 January 1959, President Eisenhower proclaimed Alaska the forty-ninth state.

## The Land Claims Movement

The Alaska Statehood Act granted the state 104 million acres of land. As public officials began selecting land, imposing rules, and applying laws, Native opposition arose. For example, the Bureau of Land Management, the agency in the Department of the Interior responsible for federal lands, issued a license to the Atomic Energy Commission (AEC), which regulates the use of nuclear materials in the United States, to use 1,600 square miles around Point Hope, an Iñupiat village on the northwestern coast of Alaska, for an experimental nuclear explosion to create a deep water port. However, no one consulted the residents of nearby villages. Another issue was the enforcement of the Migratory Bird Treaty Act between Canada and the United States. The treaty prohibits the hunting of migratory birds between March 10 and September 1. In 1961 the Iñupiat staged a "duck-in" to protest the restrictions. Many were arrested.

In March 1961 the president of the Point Hope Village Council wrote to the Association of American Indian Affairs (AAIA), an organization founded in 1923 to provide legal and technical assistance to Indian tribes, and asked for help. The AAIA and the Indian Rights Association, established in 1882 to protect the rights of American Indians, provided funds for inter-village meetings, where experiences were shared, rights explained, and common solutions proposed. Within six years, twelve regional associations were formed to pursue their respective land claims. Early in 1967 regional leaders formed the Alaska Federation of Natives (AFN) to secure their rights, enlighten the public about their position, preserve their cultural values, and gain an equitable settlement.

The first major bill to settle the claims of Alaska Natives was introduced in June 1967. The key to a congressional decision was oil. In the late 1960s, large quantities of oil were discovered in Prudhoe Bay on the north coast of Alaska. Several large oil companies worked to extract and transport the crude oil to refineries and markets in the lower forty-eight states. Indian land claims, however, prevented construction of the pipeline from Prudhoe Bay to the port at Valdez in southern Alaska. Native villages, in particular Stevens Village, an Athabascan village in the interior, claimed land over the pipeline route, and gained a court injunction against construction until Indian title to the land was clarified. Thereafter the oil companies actively lobbied Congress and President Richard Nixon in order to gain a quick settlement to Native land claims issues in Alaska. By late 1971 an unusual coalition of oil companies, the Alaska Native lobbying organization (AFN), the state of Alaska, and the federal government moved to settle Alaska Native claims through congressional legislation. President Nixon and the U.S. Senate wanted a domestic source of oil that would counter the increase in prices in 1970 and the shortage of fuel and heating oil. The state of Alaska needed the revenue that private development would generate. The oil industry and the House of Representatives wanted a permit to build the Alaska pipeline. Conservationists wanted more parks and wilderness area, and Alaska Natives wanted their land. The Alaska Native Claims Settlement Act (ANCSA) was signed into law on 18 December 1971.

Under terms of the settlement Alaska Natives received $962 million and 44 million acres of land. In exchange, claims over the remaining 335 million acres were extinguished. ANCSA cleared the path for the construction of the Alaska pipeline. It also led to the withdrawal of millions of acres of public lands for national parks and forests, scenic rivers, and wilderness areas. State officials were also permitted to select the remainder of their land under provisions of the statehood act. After all the selections are registered, 12 percent of Alaska will be privately owned by Alaska Natives, 28 percent by the state, and 59 percent by the federal government.

There are two important assumptions of the Settlement Act. First is the expectation that Natives will be assimilated into the American mainstream and away from a communal lifestyle to an economy based on private ownership, individualism, and free enterprise. Twelve regional profit-making corporations were established and given significant responsibilities, including the distribution of money to village corporations and individuals, the control of subsurface resources, the economic development of each region, the promotion of village interests, and the facilitation of inter-village cooperation. Village corporations were also created to use and manage the land and control local development. A second assumption of ANCSA was that the profit corporations and the market system would lead to more employment and educational opportunities, healthier communities, and increasing economic independence for Alaska Natives.

## Social and Economic Profile of Alaska Natives

There are approximately 105,000 Natives in Alaska. Fifty percent are Yu'pik and Iñupiat, more than 33 percent are American Indian (Athabascan, Tlingit, Haida, and Tsimshian, and other Native Americans), and 12 percent are Aleuts. The rate of population growth in rural areas exceeded the overall state average since the last census in 1990. Higher fertility rates explain most of the changes. The largest increases in Native peoples

Chief Shake's house at Wrangell at the turn of the twentieth century. (Courtesy of the National Anthropological Archives, National Museum of Natural History, Smithsonian Insitution, Washington, D.C.)

were in the Arctic, western Alaska, and Yup'ik communities in the southwest. From 1929 to 1990 the Native proportion of the total population steadily dropped from 50.6 percent to 15.6 percent. Beginning in 1991, this downward trend was reversed. By 1998 the percentage of Alaska Natives had climbed to 16.8 percent. The exodus of non-Natives because of base closures, production declines in fishing and timber, and higher Native birthrates explain the change. Alaska Natives are now a majority in most of the state's interior, the northern region, and the southwest, with the exception of Bristol Bay and the western Aleutians.

Alaska Natives are younger than the general population: Their median age is twenty-three, eleven years below the national average. The average Native family is larger and the dependency of children on Native employment is higher than for other Alaskans. In 1997 every one hundred Alaskan workers supported an average of fifty-one persons; for Natives eligible to work, the number of dependents totaled eighty-eight. Alaska Natives continue to move to urban areas. Native residents in Alaska's seven largest cities increased almost 16 percent between 1990 and 1998. Anchorage now has more Alaska Natives than any other area in the state. The populations of regional service centers such as Dillingham, Bethel, Nome, Barrow, and Fort Yukon, as well as small villages, have grown as well.

In the last twenty years, there have been improvements in the lives of Alaska Natives. Through contracts with the Alaska Area Native Health Service and other state and federal agencies, Native associations now administer most health programs. The results have been largely positive. Alaska Natives now live longer and with less fear of epidemic diseases like tuberculosis. Similar changes have occurred in Native education, housing, and employment. Secondary schools now dot the rural landscape, where none existed in the 1960s. The number of high school graduates and those enrolled in college or vocational training has increased. Through the creation of district and regional school boards, Native communities have gained some control over school curriculum and class scheduling. The majority of houses now have indoor plumbing, phones, and sewer and water outlets. Each region has a non-profit housing agency which, through funds from the Department of Housing and Urban Development (HUD), provides low-income housing assistance, builds new houses, and collects rents and mortgage payments. Unemployment has also been reduced in some areas because of the growth of local governments, private construction and organization, and expanding industries in fishing, oil, and gas. The major employer in rural Alaska is government. More than 60 percent of the labor force is employed by either federal, state, or local governments. Most jobs are related to public service and administration.

While ANCSA and subsequent efforts have resulted in a few improvements, fundamental problems remain. The incidence of poverty among Alaska Natives is much higher than for non-Natives. More than 25 percent of the Native population lives below the official poverty level. Unemployment among Natives is twice that of non-Native Alaskans. In the western region of the state, half the Native workforce is without a job. Native family incomes are less then half of the average family income in Alaska. Further, the costs of living in rural areas are much higher than in the cities. An average family in Nome or Kotzebue will spend 62 percent more per week on food or 165 percent more for electricity than a family in Anchorage, the largest city in Alaska. More than 18,000 rural households rely on low-income energy subsidies.

The lack of access to quality health services and preventive care and poor living conditions have led to higher death rates among Alaska Natives from preventable causes, such as infectious and respiratory diseases, congenital problems, and infant mortality. There are other statistics that indicate many Natives have difficult lives, since Alaska Natives die of violent causes, accidents, homicides, suicides, and alcoholism at a much higher rate than in the general population. The Native suicide and homicide rates are four times the U.S. average. Among young males twenty to twenty-four years of age, the suicide rate is twenty times the national average. Death from accidents is five times higher; infant mortality and sudden infant death syndrome are two times higher; and infant spinal disorders are thirty-six times the national rate.

Alaska Natives have addressed these and other problems in three major ways: through the protection of their subsistence lifestyle, through the economic development of their villages and regions, and through the development of their tribal governments.

**Subsistence.**  Traditional subsistence economies in Alaska were small, self-sufficient, and practical household economies. People used what they produced. Alliances for trade did exist. Coastal communities would exchange seal oil for caribou skins for example, but trading relationships were limited. Food and clothing were locally produced and shared between kin and within local camps. People were united through blood and marriage. Kinship was a way of organizing labor, establishing rights, forming groups, and distributing wealth. Aboriginal life was cyclic and inseparable from the patterns and turns of nature. Iñupiat whalers, for example, hunted caribou in the summer for clothing and bedding and snared small animals for food. In the fall they returned to the coast for trade and the gathering of food on the beaches. Later men hunted seals on the open sea, until the ice returned. In midwinter, seals, fish, and bears were hunted on the ice. By April, when the ice melted enough, boat crews were in pursuit of bowhead whales. Near the end of June, when the whales had migrated south, birds and seals were the primary sources of food.

Subsistence, or what many Native groups refer to as their way of life, and what the federal government terms "the customary and traditional uses" of wild resources, is very important to Alaska Natives. The average person in rural Alaska consumes 375 pounds of wild foods a year. In the interior and the arctic the averages are twice as high. The standard harvests in urban areas are about twenty-two pounds a year. Subsistence resources are also used for clothing, transportation, heating, housing, and arts and crafts. Traditional values of sharing, cooperation, and reciprocity also continue. Customary rules guide distribution and consumption of certain subsistence foods. Many Natives consider themselves first and foremost hunters and fishers. There is evidence, too, that subsistence economies are not only resilient, but growing in some villages.

Efforts to protect subsistence have borne some fruit and much rancor. In 1978 the state legislature passed legislation recognizing a subsistence priority in the event of a shortage of fish or game. Native rights to hunt and fish were eliminated by ANCSA, but were partially restored when Congress inserted a rural subsistence preference in the Alaska National Lands Conservation Act (ANILCA) in 1980, which classified all federal lands in Alaska. ANILCA permitted the state to regulate fish and game on national lands as long as Alaska law recognized a rural preference. Subsequently, the state rural priority was challenged in court because it excluded city residents who depend on subsistence and included people in rural Alaska who do not. In 1989 the Alaska Supreme Court agreed and ruled that residency, as a criterion for subsistence, violated state constitutional prohibitions against exclusive or special privileges to hunt and fish and was a denial of equal rights.

Once the subsistence law was overturned, the state was no longer in compliance with the rural preference in ANILCA. Therefore, the national government reluctantly assumed responsibility for management of subsistence resources on federal lands. The regulations they adopted, however, were narrow and limited to game. This led to numerous legal challenges. The most important was a suit filed by upper Ahtna Athabaskan Indians for the protection of subsistence fishing in sections of the Copper River they had used since "time immemorial." ANILCA requires that subsistence fishing and hunting be given a priority over other uses on "public lands." The state claimed that public lands do not include navigable waterways like the Copper River. The Ninth Circuit Court of Appeals disagreed, arguing that the Reserved Water Rights Doctrine gives the United States power reserve waters that fulfill "the purpose of the reservation"—in this case, subsistence fishing. This decision opened the door for federal management of fish and game on both federal and state lands. On 1 October 1999 the Federal Subsistence Board began managing fish and game on federal lands.

In the Circuit Court's *Katie John* decision, the judges called for a legislative, not a judicial, conclusion to the conflict over the management of subsistence. Either the state legislature could propose a constitutional amendment to voters to allow for a rural subsistence preference, or Congress could clarify the meaning of "public lands." Unfortunately, after years of litigation, academic studies, legislative special sessions, and gubernatorial task forces, there is no compromise in sight. Opponents on one side decry any sort of collective solution and fight for individual rights and subsistence protections for only the needy. The governor is against federal control and for a constitutional amendment that recognizes a rural priority. Native delegates to a special convention on subsistence in 1999 called for a declaration of a "subsistence emergency" from the secretary of the interior, the reclassification of ANCSA lands as Indian Country, and increased federal support for tribal governments (to manage subsistence) and tribal laws.

**Economic Development.** Though subsistence remains an integral part of Native life, the equipment used by hunters and fishers, the guns, the boats, snow machines, two-way radios, rifles, and so on is imported. This kind of hunting and fishing is also very expensive. Average expenditures in Arctic Slope coastal villages ranged from $1,900 to $4,800 per year. Ten to 20 percent of the hunters spend more than $10,000 annually. Most individuals, therefore, must find wage employment, at least for part of the year. If work is available, it is often seasonal or part time. The absence of jobs is a serious problem, particularly in rural Alaska. Rates of unemployment in economically peripheral areas like Yukon-Koyukuk and Wade Hampton average less than 27 percent. Even these figures underestimate the difficulty of finding work. The Alaska Department of Labor's official definition of unemployment excludes individuals not actively seeking a job. However, Alaska Natives in most villages do not look for jobs because they do not exist (Alaska Natives Commission 1994).

Although governments are an important part of Alaska's economy, they do not employ many Native people. More than 29 percent of the workforce are public employees; 46 percent work for local governments; 30 percent for the state; and the remainder for the federal government. Governments employ more than 38 percent of the labor force in rural Alaska. In some areas 65 to 70 percent of employees are in public service. The positions are an important source of income. On the Arctic Slope 21 percent of total earnings derive from public employment; in Yukon-Koyukuk the figure is close to 80 percent. Average earnings for the seven Bush Districts (not connected to a highway) was around 50 percent. Only a fraction of public employees is Alaska Natives. Of the 18,000 federal workers less than 6 percent are Alaska Natives. The Bureau of Indian Affairs and the Indian Health Service are the only exception. The state record is even worse. In 1997 only 4.7 percent of Alaska government employees were Alaska Native.

Government spending and subsidies for education, medical services, housing, and utilities are also important to rural communities. There are thirty-seven federal and thirty-eight state economic assistance programs that fund rural initiatives. Federal transfers to Alaska include grants to state and local governments (Medicaid), salaries and wages, direct payments to individuals (social security, food stamps), contracts, and other programs. Federal spending is higher in Alaska ($7,656) than in any other state and second only to the District of Columbia. Alaska state spending represents 41 percent of all economic activity in the interior and 23 percent in the north. Sixty-seven percent of local government revenue in the rural interior is from state aid. In western coastal communities 58 percent of per capita income is from direct government payments (Huskey 1992). The dependence on public funds leave villages vulnerable to changes in popular preferences, legislative priorities, and international financial markets. Thus, while federal spending increased from 1975 to 1999, allocations for Indian programs declined from a high of $7,500 per person in 1976 to slightly more than $4,000 in 1999. In Alaska, urban legislators have, for the last two years, tried to reduce state expenditures for rural education, electrical power, and social services.

The private economy in rural Alaska is weak. Typically villages are connected to the market through the sale of arts and crafts, furs from trapping, commercial fishing, and employment in small businesses. The Alaska economy is built primarily on the exploitation of natural resources, including oil, fish, minerals, and timber. Some Natives find employment in these industries. Commercial fishing in western Alaska (The Community Development Quota for bottom fish) and mining in the northwest Arctic (The Red Dog Mine) are well-known examples. They are also the exception. The most important resource in the state is oil. The center for petroleum production and exploration is the Arctic Slope. Native employees are a rarity. Less than 1 percent of the workforce is Iñupiat. Those who are employed are usually menial laborers. Even the subsidiary service firms owned by the Arctic Slope Regional Corporation, a Native regional corporation, employ mostly non-Natives (96 to 97 percent). One study in Nuiqsut, a North Slope village, claimed that the "Iñupiat fully realize that they are under represented in the oil industry labor force, that the jobs they do hold in the oil industry are different from those held by non-Iñupiat, and that they think that most Iñupiat are hired by the oil companies merely as a 'cost of doing business' and not in any serious attempt to train a skilled Iñupiat labor force." The twelve regional corporations established under the Alaska Native Claims Settlement Act (1971) have become a vital force in Alaska. Their activities encompass oil and gas services, tourism, catering, investments, real estate, timber harvesting, construction, and government contracting. These enterprises could benefit individual Natives through employment and the distribution of dividends. Neither has been realized. Of the more than 13,000 people employed by the regions only 13 percent are Native shareholders. The 180 village corporations offer even fewer opportunities. The Alaska Natives Commission estimates the total number of local part-time, full-time, and seasonal jobs is only 15 percent of what is needed. The regional corporations have barely increased the amount of capital they received from the settlement of land claims. From 1973 to 1993 the "12 regional corporations lost more than two-thirds of their original cash endowment—about $350 million—in direct business operations. Only the sale of $450 million worth of natural resources assets and a special tax preference allowed them to report positive accounting net income. A sample of 18 smaller village

corporations corroborates the results" (Colt 1997). Generally, the impact of dividends on rural incomes has not been large. Between 1995 and 1997 the average annual dividend payment of the ten corporations that represent rural areas in Alaska (excluding Sealaska and Cook Inlet, Incorporated) was $486.

Rates of poverty are higher and incomes lower in Native villages. About 12.5 percent of the state's population is considered poor (U.S. Bureau of Census 1990). In Wade Hampton, where 93 percent of the people are Native, 43 percent are poor; in the Northwest Arctic 22 percent live below the poverty line. There are also intra-regional differences, which follow a distinct pattern. Villages with the least amount of poverty have the largest number of non-Natives. In the Nome area, for example, 13 percent of those who live in the city and 42 percent of the villagers are poor. In the Yukon-Koyukuk district the average rate of poverty in the larger more racially diverse communities of McGrath, Nenana, and Galena is 17.6 percent; the mean rate of poverty in the villages is 51.5 percent. The distribution of income fluctuates widely between residence, heritage, and class. In 1990 the statewide median household income was $41,408 and per capita income was $17,610. Individual Native incomes though were only 45.9 percent of white incomes (Williams 1995). Per capita incomes for whites ($19,903) were more than twice that of Alaska Natives ($9,140). There were considerable differences between regions. Household incomes in Bristol Bay and the North Slope were $51,112 and $50,473 while in Wade Hampton and Yukon Koyukuk they were $20,586 and $23,945. Variations were even greater within regions. In Bethel the median income was $42,232; in Akiak it was $13,751, and in Quinhagak it was $17,500. Per capita incomes varied from $14,413 in Bethel to $4,508 in Kipnuk. The median income is high in Barrow on the North Slope but drops to $33,333 in Wainwright and $37,292 in Anaktuvuk Pass. Per capita incomes range from $10,787 in Nuiqsut to $20,753 in Barrow. Incomes are higher in Bristol Bay because of the fishing industry. Per capita incomes though vary from the predominantly white community of King Salmon ($20,808) to $9,809 where most residents are Native. Disparities are often greater in rural areas because many whites have high-paying professional jobs while Natives are without work or temporarily unemployed. Urban and rural contrasts are also revealing. In Anchorage, Juneau, and Fairbanks the average household and per capita incomes in 1990 were $43,112 and $18,484. The mean figures for the Bush were $25,731 and $10,028 (U.S. Bureau of the Census 1992). Thus in many Alaska villages today incomes are low, costs are high, poverty is widespread, employment is limited, houses are substandard, and public facilities (sewer, water) are inadequate or nonexistent. Such conditions often lead to resignation, despair, suicide, and crime.

## Tribal Sovereignty

The health of Native economies and the vitality of Native governments are, like all economies and polities, inextricably linked. It is the view of many (not all) Native leaders that villages need strong and effective governments to cultivate and protect their way of life. The issue of Native self-government or tribal sovereignty is complicated by private initiative, federal restraint, and state opposition. It is a common misperception that the source of Native dependency is the imposition of paternalistic policies by the U.S. government. In fact, the attack on Native autonomy begins with Russian traders, Boston whalers, and commercial fishers in search of wealth, prelates in search of converts, and settlers in search of land. Russian agents freely appointed and removed Aleut chiefs at will (Case 1984). Reciprocal relations between clan leaders and clans in Southeastern Alaska were undermined by the loss of fishing grounds and outside employment. Shaman powers were weakened by the spread of epidemic disease and contested by Christian missionaries. The Native claims movement completely bypassed village regimes and the final settlement separated ownership and property from public and tribal control. Consequently, a significant impediment to tribal sovereignty is the Native corporation. The divergence of interests between Native corporations and Native tribes was clearly revealed in the battle over the amending ANCSA and transferring private assets to Native organizations in the 1980s.

In the American federal system there is an intrinsic conflict between state and tribal governments. One explanation faults the Constitution for its ambiguity: "Nothing in the U.S. Constitution delineates the scope of tribal-state relations or potential intergovernmental affairs between the governments of states and tribes" (Mason 1998). Consequently, Congress has overlooked treaty obligations, extended state powers over tribal affairs, and abrogated the authority of tribal organizations. The federal courts, more often than not, have been willing accomplices (Wilkins 1997).

A more important source of antagonism between Native peoples and the states lies in the common history of invasion, settlement, and marginalization.

Alaska, like other American territories, was explored and eventually colonized by individuals and enterprises in pursuit of land and wealth. Here the quest was for fur, fish, gold, copper, oil, and gas. The territorial governments of the past, and the state today, have never been neutral participants in negotiations over the development of these resources. The concerns of rural villages are usually sacrificed in the competition for jobs, income, and revenue. The capacity of village governments to respond is limited by law and political circumstances. Governments incorporated under state rules are confined to their charters and state statutes. Alaska Natives are also a minority vulnerable to a majoritarian electoral system and a structure of executive and legislative decision-making that responds best to well-organized and well-financed private interests.

Perhaps a deeper source of the discord and friction lies in the history of relations between Native peoples and states. Through much of Alaska history, territorial and state governments have completely disregarded aboriginal peoples. Tribes were not formally involved in either the statehood or the Native claims movements; movements that led to the formal categorization of all Alaska lands. In 1990 Governor Cowper did issue an administrative order recognizing the existence of tribes, an order that was quickly repealed less than a year later by his successor, Walter Hickel. Ironically, two years before Cowper's order, the state mounted a challenge to tribal authority that would have broad implications for tribal governance. In 1986 the Yukon Flats School District hired a private contractor (the Nesser Construction Company) to build a public school in Venetie. The Village Tribal Government then imposed a gross receipts tax on the contractor for business activities on tribal lands. The state, which was responsible for the taxes, refused to pay. The state attorney general then filed for an injunction in federal district court. The tribe moved to dismiss the complaint, but the motion was denied. In his denial the judge argued that the land conveyed by ANCSA was not Indian Country. Therefore, the tribe did not have the power to tax individuals who were not members of the tribe. Circuit Court of Appeals reversed this decision in 1996. The state then appealed to the Supreme Court. In February 1998 the Court ruled that Congress, in passing the Alaska Native Claims Settlement Act, "sought to end the sort of federal supervision over Indian affairs that had previously marked federal Indian policy." Therefore, Indian Country does not exist in Alaska. The jurisdiction of tribal governments, if it exists at all, extends only to allotment or town site lands.

On the eve of the Supreme Court's decision the governor announced the formation of a Commission on

Tribal judge training at Bethel, Alaska. (Courtesy of Jerry Gardner)

Rural Governance and Empowerment. The commission was directed "to recommend ways the state government should respond to the reality of tribal governance." In June 1999 the commission, in its final report, called for the state of Alaska to: formally recognize tribes; improve relations and communication with tribes; support more flexible decentralized initiatives; strengthen local self-governance and alcohol enforcement; and, finally, resolve the subsistence issue (Commission on Rural Governance 1999). The chairman of the commission warned that if their advice "was ignored, not necessarily in their details, but in the spirit of the kind of diverse Alaska we are seeking to build together, then we will end up having two separate Alaskas" (*Anchorage Daily News* 24 June 1999).

The state did make two concessions. In September the Alaska Supreme Court decided that tribal courts do have jurisdiction in child custody cases. Then in May, Governor Knowles opened a series of tribal-state discussions which he hoped would create "a true tribal consultation process" and "preserve the constitutional rights of every Alaskan, Native and non-Native." A month later the Knowles administration intervened in

two suits to stop the expansion of tribal powers over allotments, town sites, and gaming establishments (*Anchorage Daily News* 21 June 2000). The struggle continues with no plan or policy in sight.

The application of federal laws to Alaska Natives has been unilateral and irregular. Unbeknownst to most Natives the Treaty of Cession declared that the "uncivilized tribes" were "subject to such laws and regulations as the United States may, from time to time, adopt in regard to aboriginal tribes of the country." Two decades later the Bureau of Education began to build schools and underwrite various subsistence and commercial activities. The status of Alaska Natives as Native Americans was not formally acknowledged, however, until the segregation of education in 1905 and the passage of the Native Allotment Act in 1906 (Case 1984). It was not until 1993 that the secretary of the interior formally recognized Native traditional and Indian Reorganization Act councils. According to the secretary these councils "have the same government status as other federally acknowledged Indian tribes by virtue of their status as Indian tribes with a government to government relationship with the United States; are entitled to the same protection, immunities, privileges as other acknowledged tribes; have the right, subject to general principles of Federal Indian law, to exercise the same inherent and delegated authorities available to other tribes; and are subject to the same limitations imposed by law on their tribes" (U.S. Department of the Interior, 21 October 1993).

Tribal governments are important in Alaska. In ninety-four rural villages they are the only government that exists; in other communities tribes provide services along with state municipalities. All Indian Health Services in Alaska are contracted out to Native tribes. There are currently fourteen self-governing compacts that cover 156 rural villages. Tribes manage seven hospitals and twenty-one health centers. Most villages are served by community health aides who work in locally run clinics. Health expenditures for Alaska Natives in 1997 were slightly more than $380 million. Bureau of Indian Affairs funding for tribes in 2000 was more than $24 million. A large percentage of the appropriation goes directly to tribal governments; the remainder is divided between human services, community development, resource management, trust services, and administration. More villages are forming tribal courts. Tribal courts and councils typically deal with children's issues, including custody, traditional adoptions, guardianship, and the enforcement of local ordinances, particularly alcohol-related offenses. The Department of Justice supplies funds for drug courts and tribal police, programs to help abused women, and training for tribal judges.

There is growing support in rural Alaska for expanding the responsibilities of tribal organizations. At an Alaska Conference on Tribes in 1998 delegates from 170 villages approved a Declaration of the Inherent Rights of the First Nations of Alaska, which encompassed the rights to develop and maintain distinctive customs, traditions, and tribal governments; to self-determination; to decide and build meaningful economic and social programs; to own, use, and control community lands; to be informed and to participate in policymaking; and to consent to decisions that affect local residents. At the beginning of 2000 the Alaska Federation of Natives asked Congress for broad authorization to strengthen tribal governments, protect cultural traditions, and to enhance local economic opportunities (*Anchorage Daily News* 5 January 2000).

*David Maas*
*University of Alaska, Anchorage*

## ◆ OKLAHOMA INDIANS

The land that is now encompassed within the state of Oklahoma appears on nineteenth-century maps as "Indian Territory." Even today, Oklahoma is the home of the largest number of Indian tribes and peoples within the United States. At the beginning of the twenty-first century thirty-nine federally recognized Indian Nations continue to exercise their sovereign tribal status within Oklahoma. Ironically, only a few of these tribes occupied any part of the state prior to European contact.

The vast majority of Oklahoma Indian tribes were "resettled" in Oklahoma, most involuntarily, under the nineteenth-century federal Indian removal policy. In the formative years of American Indian policy, settlers and local communities pressured tribal communities to give up their large tribal land holdings. In response, the federal government adopted a policy to compel tribes to exchange their historic homelands for new "permanent" lands on unorganized federal domain in the West, where, theoretically, no conflicts would arise with non-Indians. Under treaty guarantees this new land was to remain forever in the hands of Indian tribes who were promised that non-Indians would not be allowed to settle in their midst. In 1907, in violation of these agreements, Oklahoma was admitted to the Union as the forty-sixth state.

In the late 1820s and throughout the 1830s, the earliest and most dramatic of the Eastern Indian removals to what is now Oklahoma were those of the Five Civilized Tribes (Choctaw, Chickasaw, Creek, Cherokee, and Seminole). These tribes were called "civilized" because some embraced Christianity and all adopted constitutional governments and formed tribal school systems. Driven out of the South on what historians know as the Trail of Tears, tens of thousands perished on forced marches that were often conducted in the dead of winter. As many as one-third of their tribal members, especially the very young and the very old, died before they reached the new Indian Territory. Prior to the American Civil War other tribes, including the Quapaw, Seneca, and Shawnee, were also removed to what is now Oklahoma. Ultimately, at least sixty-five Indian Nations came to be listed historically as having been Oklahoma tribes. These included the Alabama, Anadarko, Apache, Apalachicola, Arapaho, Caddo, Cahakia, Catawba, Cayuga, Cherokee, Cheyenne, Chickasaw, Chippewa, Choctaw, Comanche, Conestoga, Creek, Delaware, Eel River, Erie, Hainai, Hitchiti, Illinois, Iowa, Kaskashia, Kansa, Kichai, Kickapoo, Kiowa, Kiowa-Apache, Koasati, Lipan, Miami, Michigomea, Modoc, Mohawk, Moingwena, Munsee, Natchez, Nez Percé, Osage, Oto and Missouri, Ottawa,

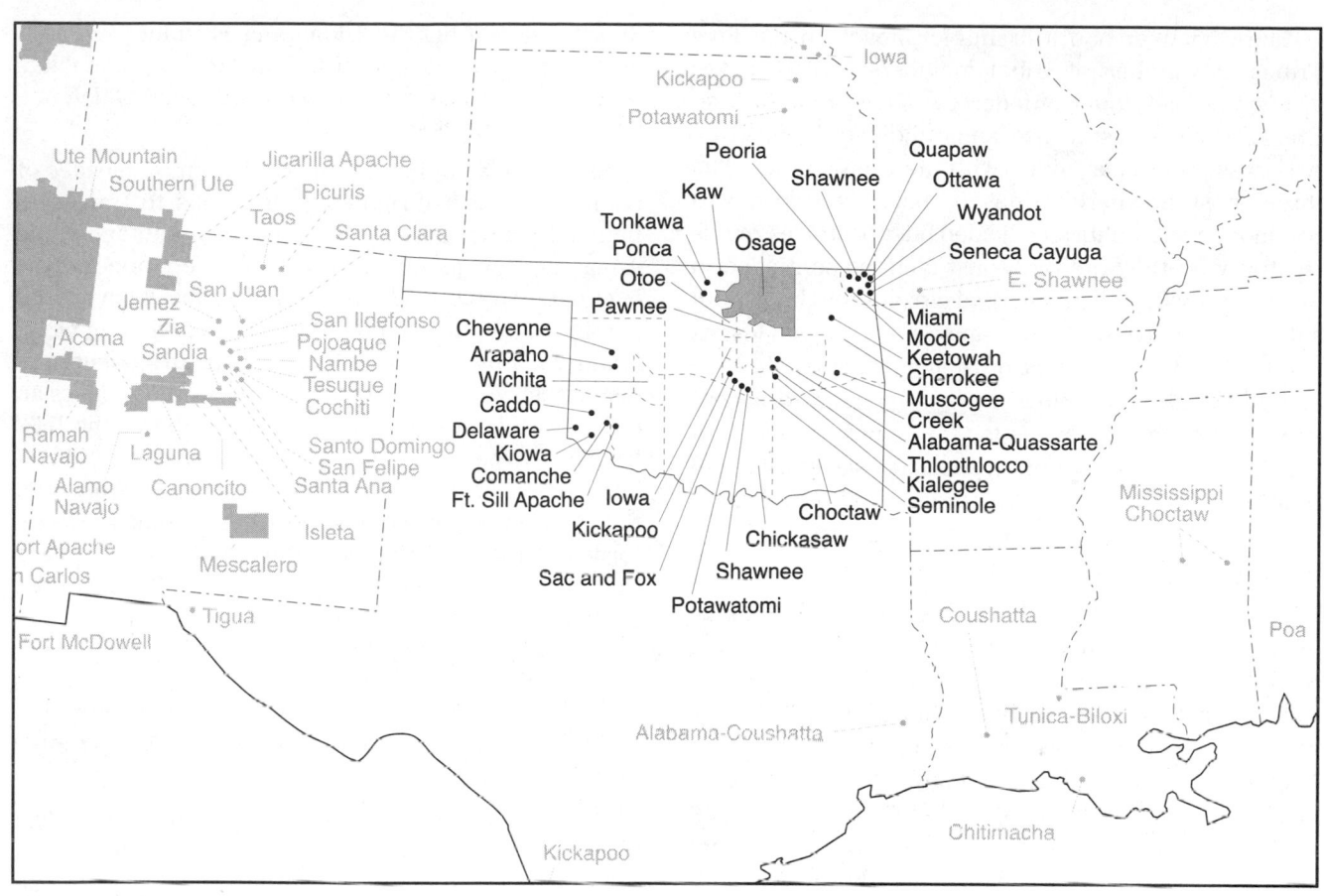

Contemporary Oklahoma Indian tribes. (Courtesy of the UCLA American Indian Studies Center)

Pawnee, Peoria, Piankashaw, Ponca, Potawatomi, Quapaw, Sauk and Fox, Seminole, Seneca, Shawnee, Skidi, Stockbridge, Tamaroa, Tawakoni, Tonkawa, Tuscarora, Tuskegee, Waco, Wea, Wichita, Wyandot, and Yuchi.

During the Andrew Jackson Administration (1829–1837), a companion policy to removal was the proposed establishment of an Indian commonwealth or territory in the removal area (now Oklahoma), to be governed by a confederation of tribes. The Western Territory Bill of 1834 proposed an "Indian Territory" that would be composed of Kansas, Oklahoma, parts of Nebraska, Colorado, and Wyoming. None of these proposals of the 1830s was enacted and the territory set aside for Indians gradually shrank to what is now the state of Oklahoma. Unorganized Indian Territory west of the Mississippi River disappeared as new territorial governments were established and states were admitted to the Union. When Kansas Territory was organized in 1854, the remaining unorganized area reserved for Indian tribes had boundaries almost identical to present-day Oklahoma. By 1868, the land that would later become Oklahoma was the only unorganized territory

left in the lower forty-eight states. It was to this land that the federal government forced many remaining Indian nations. Although no territorial Indian government was ever established, the name *Indian Territory* gradually came into common use as the collective term for the lands of the Five Tribes and the other tribes settled amongst them. From 1865 until Oklahoma's admission to the Union in 1907, Congress frequently used the term *Indian Territory* in statutes and defined the boundaries in laws passed in 1889 and 1890.

Indian tribes in Oklahoma have continuously operated their own sovereign governments from pre-contact times through forced removal and statehood up to the present. After the end of the bloody Trail of Tears, the Five Tribes established comprehensive governments in Indian Territory and exercised self-rule relatively free of federal interference. The Five Tribes achieved a level of literacy and economic prosperity that exceeded many neighboring states. Before the American Civil War, these Indian tribes enjoyed a "golden age" in which tribal Indian traditions and the economic richness of this new land merged to produce a culturally diverse and prosperous Native civilization.

The Civil War had a dramatic impact on the Five Tribes. A number of tribal members owned slaves and supported the Confederacy. The Choctaw and Chickasaw Nations, whose lands adjoined Confederate Arkansas and Texas, sided with the Confederacy. The three most northerly tribes (Creek, Cherokee, and Seminole) were politically divided but nonetheless made treaties with the South. Loyalist factions continued to favor the North, and many tribal citizens fought on both sides. The Cherokee, Creek, and Seminole each lost as much as 20 to 25 percent of their population. In 1866 and 1867, the Five Tribes were compelled to accept new treaties and agreements that ceded western portions of their tribal territories, abolished slavery, granted railroad rights-of-way, and provided for the settlement of other tribes on their former lands and for the eventual allotment of tribal lands.

After the Civil War, other Indians—including many of the powerful Plains tribes such as the Comanche, Kiowa, and Cheyenne—were removed to the western Indian Territory lands yielded by the Five Tribes along with other strong tribal groups such as the Apache. Thousands of U.S. settlers illegally moved into Indian Territory, and many lawless and violent drifters made Indian Territory a notorious haven for bandits and killers. In an effort to maintain law and order for non-Indians in Indian Territory, Congress established a special federal court for Indian Territory over which Isaac C. Parker, known as "the Hanging Judge," presided. In 1889 the famous Oklahoma land run opened the so-called "unassigned lands" in central Indian Territory to U.S. settlers, and in 1890 the Oklahoma Organic Act reduced Indian Territory to its eastern portion, the lands of the Five Tribes and the Quapaw Agency Tribes. During this time an Organic Act created Oklahoma Territory in the western part of Indian Territory and established a U.S. territorial government. The act expressly preserved tribal authority and federal jurisdiction in both Oklahoma and Indian territories. The status of Indian tribes in Oklahoma Territory was thus similar to that of tribes in other organized territories.

During the 1890s, the lands of many Oklahoma tribes were allotted or divided pursuant to the General Allotment Act of 1887. In 1893 the Dawes Commission was established to seek allotment of the lands of the Five Tribes, which were exempted from the General Allotment Act. In 1898 Congress passed the Curtis Act to speed up the allotment process. The act provided for allotment of Five Tribes lands, and other allotment agreements and statutes followed. The Five Tribes Act of 1906 preserved tribal governments and comprehensively addressed allotment and other Indian issues.

Shortly thereafter, the Oklahoma Enabling Act provided for the admission of Indian Territory and Oklahoma Territory as the state of Oklahoma. Oklahoma proclaimed statehood in 1907.

Statehood was the bitter culmination of decades of conflict and of self-righteous programs to transform Indian Territory into a U.S. commonwealth and make American Indians into red farmers. Few non-Indians ever understood the depth of the Indians' agony at the passing of their nationhood. In the *Chronicles of Oklahoma* 26, Edward E. Dale, the dean of Oklahoma's historians, wrote with some surprise of the sadness an Indian woman still felt when she remembered the 1907 festivities to celebrate Oklahoma statehood. This Cherokee woman, married to a non-Indian, refused to attend the statehood ceremonies with her husband. He returned and said to her: "Well, Mary, we no longer live in the Cherokee Nation. All of us are now citizens of the state of Oklahoma." Tears came to her eyes thirty years later as she recalled that day. "It broke my heart. I went to bed and cried all night long. It seemed more than I could bear that the Cherokee Nation, my country and my people's country, was no more" (Dale, Winter 1948–1949, 382).

Since Oklahoma's statehood, the status of Indian tribes in Oklahoma has been similar to that of tribes in other states. The popularly held view that Oklahoma Indians are subject to special regulations generally applies only to narrowly defined property interests of individual members of the Five Tribes and the Osage Tribe. When Congress passed the Indian Reorganization Act of 1934, Oklahoma tribes were excepted from many of its important provisions. Two years later Congress passed the Oklahoma Indian Welfare Act that authorizes tribal organization in a manner similar to the Indian Reorganization Act and extends "any other rights or privileges served to an organized Indian tribe." Like all other Indian tribes, tribes in Oklahoma retain powers of self-government and sovereignty except to the extent that their powers have been limited by treaties, agreements, or federal legislation. Although the land base of Oklahoma tribes has been substantially reduced by the allotment process, their inherent powers are undiminished. Throughout the 1980s and 1990s, there was increasing conflict between state and tribal governments with several Oklahoma Indian cases reaching the United States Supreme Court. As the tribes enter the twenty-first century, a growing number of tribal-state disputes are being resolved by tribal-state compacts and other cooperative agreements, such as joint deputization of state and tribal law enforcement agents.

The time before the American Civil War is remembered as the Golden Age of the Oklahoma Indian. For many Indians this age followed the brutal, nearly genocidal expulsion from their original homelands. Such irony pervades much of Oklahoma's Indian life. The present Indian nature of the state results not from aboriginal Indian choice but from U.S. policy. Most Oklahoma Indians opposed coming to the state. Oklahoma's Indian people are largely descendants of nineteenth-century emigrants who were driven by the U.S. government from almost every other section of the country. More bitterly ironic, Indians found in Oklahoma a quiet haven. Eventually, they came to love this land, and in the end it, too, was taken from them.

Generalizing about the coming of Indians to Oklahoma is not easy. Tribes came at different times and for different purposes. Divisions of the same tribe were often split by migration. Oklahoma was historically a great and open hunting ground through which many Native peoples passed. State boundaries and formal tribal borders were unknown prior to U.S. occupation. Even the rigid recognition of formal tribal units was a political concept borrowed from the European legal tradition. Certainly fee-simple land ownership with its feudal property implications was foreign to the mind of the aboriginal American. Furthermore, in a society where splinter factions were free to move away from the main body of a tribe, portions of groups as large as the Seneca or the Osage or the Cherokee might be settled in several states as well as in Indian Territory. Still other tribes never settled anywhere, in the traditional European sense, but rather ranged from the plains of Texas into the Rocky Mountains and beyond.

Fewer than six of Oklahoma's tribes are indigenous. Only a few of the currently identifiable Oklahoma tribes were within the state when the Europeans arrived. Very early ancestors of the Oklahoma Indians, such as Plainview, Clovis, and Folsom Man, as well as more immediate paleolithic ancestors, had disappeared. The great prehistoric Indian civilizations with their mounds and their monumental art, such as those unearthed at Spiro in the 1930s, were gone when the first European explorers came to Oklahoma. Quapaw and Caddoan ancestors of the Wichita and Caddo by that time had settled on this land with their village farming culture. Tribes like the Osage hunted in these domains, and nomadic bands such as the Plains Apache and the Comanche followed the migratory herds across the state. To appreciate the nature of Indian settlement in the state, we must distinguish among hunting, migration, and permanent residence. Further, we must appreciate the concept of a home base to which roving tribes might return with some regularity.

The major thrust of Indian settlement in Oklahoma resulted from U.S. policy, which consisted of formal negotiations; informal counsel, bribery, and threats;

Kickapoo sweat lodge. (Courtesy of Southwest Museum)

and military force. As early as 1803, Thomas Jefferson had spoken of a permanent Indian area or territory beyond the boundaries of U.S. society. Since before the founding of the nation, Indian tribes had been driven westward by both warfare and treaty negotiations. By various inducements and by the application of brute force more than sixty Indian tribes originally from other states were ultimately removed to and resettled in Oklahoma. Tribes were removed—particularly at the turn of the century for the northern Indians of Ohio, Indiana, Illinois, and New York—without plan or experience. Many once-powerful tribes—such as the Shawnee, Sac and Fox, and Potawatomi—were fragmented, lost, or reduced in station before they arrived in the Indian Territory.

Voluntary migrations and inducements by treaty settled portions of such tribes as the Seneca, Quapaw, Osage, Shawnee, Choctaw, Creek, and Cherokee in Oklahoma before Andrew Jackson's Indian Removal Act was fully implemented in the 1830s. In these earlier removals there seemed to be no system or order. Some tribes were moved several times before they reached Oklahoma. Many tribal groups, sensing the futility of resistance to removal, sought a negotiated compromise that avoided the brutality of a forced military march to their new country. By the early 1830s, there were established tribal governments in Oklahoma of "old settler" or "western" factions of the Choctaw, Creek, and Cherokee, as well as separate political subdivisions of groups like the Osage, whose greatest numbers would not come to Oklahoma until much later. For example, in 1831, the Seneca exchanged land in Ohio's Sandusky Valley for 67,000 acres north of the western Cherokee, while a short time later another group of Seneca and Shawnee received a similar Indian Territory tract. In 1833, a band of Quapaw moved from the Red River to lands north and east of the Cherokee.

The tragedy of the brutal forced migration of almost sixty thousand members of the great southern nations—the Creek, Cherokee, Choctaw, Chickasaw, and Seminole—is known as the Trail of Tears; as many as one-fourth of these Indians died from exposure and exhaustion. The agony of this experience is etched in the consciousness of the Five Civilized Tribes and of non-Indian Oklahomans as well. In turn, other tribes joined these southern tribes in Oklahoma, particularly northern woodland peoples, whose experiences were often as disastrous.

Between the end of the Civil War and the opening of Oklahoma's Unassigned Lands in 1889, the number of Indian tribes permanently living in Oklahoma changed. The many Plains and Woodland tribes that joined the earlier inhabitants brought a diversity of Indian culture not present in any other state. In the northeast corner of the state, the Peoria, Modoc, Ottawa, Shawnee, and Wyandot joined the Seneca and the Quapaw. In the northeastern and central portions of the state were the Osage, Kaw, Pawnee, Tonkawa, Ponca, Oto and Missouri, Sac and Fox, Iowa, Kickapoo, Potawatomi, and Shawnee. Dominating the eastern half of the state and spilling into the west were Cherokee, Creek, Choctaw, Chickasaw, and Seminole. In the western part of the state, around the military outposts of Fort Reno and Fort Sill, the great tribes of the Plains were ultimately located. The Comanche, Kiowa, and Apache lands bordered on Texas. The Wichita and Caddo tribes nestled between this reservation and the reservation lands of the Cheyenne and Arapaho.

Ironically, more has been written and less is known about the history and culture of these Oklahoma tribes than about any other group of Native Americans. As many as 600,000 present-day Oklahomans identify themselves as Indians. Yet within the state of Oklahoma, there remains a widespread perception that Indians and their cultures are vanishing.

The contemporary facts are unmistakable. Oklahoma has more Indians from more varied tribes than any other state in the Union. It has more separate tribal groups historically associated with the state and more

currently recognized tribes than any other state. A higher percentage of its population is Indian, and that population is more widely distributed among the state's counties than in Arizona, New Mexico, or the Dakotas. Indians once owned all the land in the state but now have a greatly reduced land base, the lowest income level, and the highest unemployment rate of any group in the state. Today more Oklahoma Indians are participating in more Indian-sponsored activities than in any period since statehood. The number of Oklahoma Indians is increasing. Indian tribes are again functioning as political and economic units, electing officials, administering programs, and dispensing justice.

The state is truly what Chief Allen Wright's Choctaw name for it, Okla Homma, conveys in a free translation: "Home of the Red People." More than sixty-seven tribes and bands have been located within the state and thirty-nine of them continue to be recognized. A population breakdown suggests that there are 150,000 sociocultural Indians, 300,000 persons recognized by the Bureau of Indian Affairs as legal Indians, and more than 650,000 to 700,000 Oklahomans of Indian descent. Tulsa and Oklahoma City rank second and third behind Los Angeles in Indian population within city boundaries. The sixty-five-mile trade radius of Tulsa constitutes the highest non-reservation concentration of Indians anywhere in the world.

The great diversity of Oklahoma's Indian population is lost in these statistics. Not only the Plains tribes and the Five Civilized Tribes reside in Oklahoma. Among the state's larger tribal groups are peoples as varied as the Ponca, Apache, Comanche, and Choctaw. With urban migration, Indians from at least fifty other non-Oklahoma tribes have recently moved to the state. More and more of Oklahoma's Indians have ancestors from two to four or more tribes. An Osage-Cherokee, a Kiowa-Miami, and a Creek-Omaha are not unusual. The current generation is producing children who are such combinations as Choctaw-Ponca-Cheyenne-Delaware or Cherokee-Osage-Omaha-Creek-Apache.

Even among members of the same tribe there are great cultural and personal differences. Today as many as 10,000 Cherokee speak their Native tongues in a tribe that began adopting European cultural variants in the eighteenth century. While Oklahoma U.S. Senator Robert L. Owen (1907–1925), an enrolled Cherokee, co-authored the Federal Reserve Act of 1913, the Cherokee Keetoowah, an ancient religious society, were reading the ancient wampum belts and feeding the sacred fire with the blood of a white rooster.

Oklahoma has historically been a land of great contrasts between and among Indian people. Contemporary distinctions within the same or among different tribal groups are reflective of similar differences among

Indians even in the age before widespread settlement of non-Indians within the state. Nineteenth century accounts of travelers, Indian tribal documents, missionary diaries, government negotiations, military reports, and trader journals clearly establish that there has never been a single, unified Oklahoma Indian culture. It is as rich and diverse as all of Indian America.

For convenience, Oklahoma's Indian tribes are often grouped into broad categories, such as the Five Civilized Tribes and the Plains Indians, or into semi-geographic, quasi-cultural divisions, such as Hunters of the Plains, Plains Farmers, Woodland Peoples, or Northern and Southern Woodland, Prairie, Plains, and High Plains Indians. Such artificial subdivisions are meaningful only when we remember the broad cross-cultural similarities and the genuinely unique aspects of each tribe. The Choctaw and Seminole, two "civilized" tribes, are in many respects culturally distinct, just as are the Plains groups, such as the Kiowa and the Arapaho. To appreciate these varied cultures and what the Oklahoma Indians lost after the coming of white immigrants, one must understand the nature of Indian life on the prairie and in the woodland before the Civil War and the Treaty of Medicine Lodge. It is the culture of this golden age to which Oklahoma's modern Indians look with nostalgia.

The traditional Indian culture of Plains tribes such as the Cheyenne, Arapaho, Kiowa, and Comanche is familiar to most Americans. Their seemingly free and independent life has come to symbolize Oklahoma's Native peoples. These were hunter cultures, uniquely varied in many respects. Each depended on the existence of open lands that could be freely roamed and an abundant supply of wild game. Plains Indian thought, culture, and organization were complex. A civil, military, and religious structure preserved law and order, provided security, and assured economic and social well-being. It was a life intimately tied to the earth and to the natural cycles of life.

In absolute numbers, the Five Civilized Tribes and the Plains Indians historically constituted the largest blocs of Oklahoma Indians, but there were and still are other important and colorful Oklahoma tribes, such as the Sac and Fox, the Osage, the Potawatomi, the Quapaw, the Delaware, the Kickapoo, the Seneca, and the Shawnee. In addition, surviving portions of such tribes as the Catawba, Natchez, and Biloxi and groups such as the Yuchi and Hitchiti were integrated into Oklahoma Indian governments, particularly those of the Choctaw, Creek, and Cherokee. During his tour of Indian Territory in the 1840s, Major Ethan Allen Hitchcock concluded that "fragments of Indian tribes are scattered in every direction."

The Oklahoma Indian tribes' viewpoints and problems are often lost in their cultural diversity and amidst their internal dissension. Yet even before the opening of Indian lands to non-Indian settlement, these tribes reacted to similar challenges and faced many of the same dangers from their common non-Indian and Indian enemies. As early as 1824, the tribes faced an invasion of commercial hunters and an assault on Native game. General Matthew Arbuckle reported two thousand hunters systematically killing fur-bearing animals in order to sell their peltries.

The United States' challenge to the Indians' way of thinking and living was a challenge to all Indian people. The unity among the Plains, Woodland, and Prairie tribes is not so readily apparent in material life and culture but emerges clearly at philosophical and spiritual levels. The great oneness of Oklahoma Indian tribes is spiritual. Peoples as seemingly diverse as the Cheyenne and the Cherokee reflect Indian attitudes in their perception of the earth, the supernatural, and the association of man's spirit and the spirits of animals.

For example, the Cheyenne Wolf Soldiers, the last of the seven great Cheyenne soldier societies to be organized, served as a defensive and protective association. The Cheyenne soldier-society warrior, draped in the skin of a wolf, sought protective power and acquired strength from the animal. Richard West, the Cheyenne artist, has captured this animal warrior as lawman in his paintings and sculptures of the Wolf Soldier. The Cherokee, too, had many customs and legends about the wolf, which included wolf songs and medicine formulas. Even after the Cherokee had adopted their highly acclaimed constitutional government (1828–1907) and established peace officers or light-horsemen modeled after frontier sheriffs, they turned to the animal powers of the spirit world.

The close of the American Civil War and the 1867 Indian Treaty gathering at Medicine Lodge in Kansas signaled the beginning of the end of the old, free Indian nationhood. New treaties forced upon the Five Civilized Tribes at Fort Smith in 1866 contained provisions that ultimately opened the way for railroads to cross their domains and for the U.S. settler onslaught that followed. The signing of the Treaty of Medicine Lodge with leaders of Plains tribes—including the Kiowa, Cheyenne, Arapaho, and Comanche—foreshadowed the federal government's effort to confine the tribes to reservations and to compel them to follow the "white man's road."

Oklahoma Indians were caught on the crest of one of those great cycles that recur throughout American history. Westward expansion was itself an old story. Many of the Indians removed to Oklahoma, including the Shawnee, Cherokee, Seneca, and Creek, had been

Arapaho family cooking dinner. (Courtesy of Fort Sill Museum)

caught in earlier stages of the cycle. But this expansion was somehow different. It was more determined, better organized, and much faster, more efficient, and more difficult to resist. Powered by technological marvels such as railroads, the steam engine, and the mechanical harvester, the new expansion was also propelled by the go-getter spirit that infused the nation after the war. The military energy of the Union victory survived on the frontier. Americans in congress, boardrooms, taverns, and churches shared a determination to thrust the nation westward. Landless Americans from older sections and newer emigrants who had temporarily settled elsewhere demanded Indian lands. There was no place left to remove the Indian, and there was little sympathy for the preservation of a way of life that left farmlands unturned, coal unmined, and timber uncut.

By 1889, the lives of Oklahoma Indians were changing. The military balance of power rested with the white man. The great romantic, free, nomadic-hunter civilization of the Plains was past or, at least, passing. The Plains Indian wars were coming to an end, with many Oklahoma tribal leaders held captive in distant jails. The brutal massacre known as the Battle of the Washita (1868), in which George Armstrong Custer attacked Black Kettle's peaceful Cheyenne village, demonstrated the growing rift between the Indian "Spartans of the Plains" and U.S. soldiers. The "blue coats" appear more frequently and grow larger and larger in the Indians' ledger-book drawings. Even the golden days of intense tribal creativity were ending for the Five Civilized Tribes, which were now left fiercely struggling to preserve whatever steps toward acculturation they had earlier made.

The year 1889 might appear on an Oklahoma Indian calendar as "the time when white farmers came with wives." Oklahoma Indian tribes were, in a real sense, still sovereign; they were "domestic dependent nations," in the words of U.S. Supreme Court Chief Justice John Marshall. Until that fateful year, although they were subject to many federal regulations, Indians owned all the lands that were to become Oklahoma. Non-Indians within their domain were either government or military officials who relied on Indian sufferance. Illegal intruders were subject to expulsion under existing treaties. These sovereign Indian nations were the only groups in Oklahoma whose political power and landed estate would diminish with the establishment of territorial government that had begun in 1889 and culminated in the admission of Oklahoma to statehood in 1907.

A great drama opened Oklahoma's Indian lands and ended the exclusive Indian possession of these domains. Fifty thousand potential homesteaders vied to stake out claims to ten thousand farms of 160 acres each. It was an epic if condensed enactment of the entire frontier-settlement process. The Oklahoma land rush of 22 April 1889 has been recreated in song and story, in novel and in film, but how the Oklahoma Indian came to that year of 1889 and what happened subsequently has been largely ignored.

Before 1889, when the United States acquired the disputed Unassigned Lands from the Creek and Seminole, Oklahoma was exclusively Indian Country in a legal, political, and social sense. Not so after that eventful year 1889, when the first of a series of runs opened these tribal lands to U.S. settlers. By 1975 the Bureau of Indian Affairs reported that Oklahoma Indian tribal lands encompassed only 65,000 acres and that Indians as private citizens owned only a million acres. The size of tribal acreage grows slowly from year to year but is still a fraction of the once great Indian territories.

The long-range result of federal policy was that by the time of statehood in 1907, many Oklahoma Indians were handed land with a negotiable title. In many cases, this title was a fee-simple absolute title and was subject only to a limitation or restriction by supervision for a term of years in other cases. Most Oklahoma Indians were destined to become landless, because Indian tribes no longer held the land, and title soon passed to non-Indians. Indian land was thus lost, allotted to individuals despite the protests of the vast majority of Indians who wished to retain tribal ownership.

Among the Five Civilized Tribes tribal lands were shifted to individual members with remarkable speed. The Dawes Commission's preparation of the rolls began with the Curtis Act in June 1898 and continued through March 1907, with a few additional names being added in 1914. In all, the commission placed 101,526 persons on the final rolls of the Five Civilized Tribes. Of this number, full bloods constituted 26,794; another 3,534 were enrolled as having three-fourths or more Indian blood; 6,859 were listed as one-half to three-fourths Indian; 40,934 were listed as having less than one-half Indian blood. The commission also prepared a separate roll of 23,405 blacks, known as freedmen. Enrollments and land figures from the Dawes enrollment and allotment follow:

The total Five Tribe's tribal land base was 19,525,966 acres, 15,794,400 acres of which were allotted. The balance of 4 million acres included 309 townsites, which were sold, and segregated coal and timber, as well as other unallotted lands, sold at public auction.

Today, Oklahoma Indians, especially full-blood descendants, suffer from these earlier federal programs to enroll Indians in tribes and to allot to individual Indians their tribally owned domains. When the Dawes Commission rolls were drawn at the turn of the century, many traditionalist Indians like the Crazy Snake Creek and the Keetoowah Cherokee refused to enroll because they believed that the United States was violating its treaty promises. Many were enrolled against their will, but others escaped the roving enrollment parties. Thus Oklahoma's mixed-blood Indians are often federally recognized, while many full-bloods and their descendants are treated as non-Indians. Other full-bloods enrolled themselves as quarter-bloods or eighth-bloods so that they would not have restrictions on their lands and the need for guardians. As a result, in tribes such as the Choctaw, Seminole, Cherokee, Creek, and Chickasaw, whose rolls have been closed by act of Congress, enrollees' descendants are denied educational and other Indian benefits to which, by their correct blood quantum, they are entitled.

But Indians and Indian attitudes were not so easily lost even in the statehood movement. Oklahoma may be the only state in which Indians had a significant and long-lasting impact on the form of state government and on the nature of the constitutional legal system. Many important Oklahoma constitutional provisions, such as prohibition of alien ownership of land and limitation on corporate buying or dealing in real estate, were products of the unique Oklahoma Indian experience. The Five Civilized Tribes and the non-Indians who allied with them to control the Oklahoma Constitutional Convention dominated the attitudes and the development of the new Oklahoma government. Among the reasons for this influence was the experience gained in 1905 at the Sequoyah Constitutional Convention, a meeting called to prepare for the single statehood of the Indian Territory.

Oklahoma Indians have scattered throughout the world. Today, Indians enrolled in Oklahoma tribes exist in very large numbers in other states, especially California, Texas, Kansas, Illinois, New Mexico, and Arizona. Many retain substantial contact with their tribe including voting in tribal elections. Thousands of Oklahoma Indians living outside the state plan their vacations to come home for their tribal celebrations. Whether Comanche, Cheyenne, Kiowa, Shawnee, Ponca, Delaware, Quapaw, Creek, or Seminole, there is a time and a place for renewal, a need to call for strength from the arrows or the wampum. And there is also a time that brings together Indians from many tribes for powwows and gourd dances, rodeos and competitions, visits and quarrels, rekindled romances and revitalized disputes. Oklahoma's Red Earth celebration in June is now the largest Indian celebration in the world.

The summer and the summer dances bring scholars and tourists to see the Indians. But Oklahoma Indianness is hidden and confusing. Much of the Oklahoma Indian way is lost to the outsider because the Indian world has both a public and a private aspect and may, on the same occasion, involve both. An Indian legend shared by many Oklahoma tribes maintains that certain Indians can become transparent, turn into leaves on trees, or become small enough to ride on a bird's wing. Oklahoma Indians have been remarkably successful in doing just that. Indians have succeeded in hiding many aspects of their culture or camouflaging things Indian so that the Indianness is kept from the eye of the tourist or even the scholar. The outsider looking for a buffalo misses the deer, the raven, or the bright summer sun itself, which are all very much a part of Oklahoma Indian life.

Much of the Indianness of Oklahoma is hidden because the Oklahoma Indian does not conform to non-Indian understandings of what is and is not Indian. A Boy Scout hobbyist in feathers and headdress is by definition Indian to students of the frontier myths, while a full-blood worshiper who wears blue jeans, a white shirt, and a Stetson hat and holds up the corporate seal of the Keetoowah is not Indian in the eyes of most U.S. moviegoers.

Furthermore, Oklahoma has few of the great geographic mountain and desert movie-set vistas that proclaim Indianness. There is no Oklahoma Monument Valley. No Oklahoma tribes have, like the Pueblo, drawn a whole school of painters and poets to record and romanticize their cultural ceremonies, crafts, and majestic landscapes. There are no Indian entrepreneurs who merchandise Oklahoma's Indian arts and crafts around a natural attraction such as the Grand Canyon. For this most Oklahoma Indians are grateful.

Non-Indians imagine war bonnets and buffalo when they think of Indians, but many of Oklahoma's Indian people have Woodland or Prairie heritages. They are the descendants of the front-line Indian soldiers of the seventeenth, eighteenth, and early nineteenth centuries. Their brave leaders were the Tecumsehs, the Osceolas, and the Little Turtles (see their biographies), the great warriors of the Seneca, Shawnee, Miami, Creek, Delaware, and Seminole. These tribes fought the bloody pitched colonial and national battles of the eastern forests and the upland rivers. These tribes learned early the lessons of adaptation and acculturation that allowed them to adopt some U.S. cultural forms while retaining Indian substance. That these

tribes survived is a testimony to their ingenuity. They saw that change was, paradoxically, their only hope of survival as an Indian people. Their lifeways, the summer rituals, and the reunions are no less Indian because they celebrate the fire or the green corn and not the buffalo.

Oklahoma Indians have historically loved to perform, play, and dance for themselves or crowds, to "play Indian" or just to play. Colonial Indians traveling to Europe, Geronimo at the St. Louis World's Fair, the professional Indian dance troupe, the Osage ballerinas, Indians in Pawnee Bill's and the 101 Ranch shows all share the same tradition. Modern Indian teams and professional athletes reflect and continue the legacy of the great Indian professional football teams, Oklahoma's long list of Indian athletes, the successful Plains Indian baseball teams, and the most famous of all twentieth century sports figures, Jim Thorpe (see his biography). No competitive sport in the world can be as exciting as a Sunday afternoon stickball game back in the Oklahoma hills, and no group of actors can be as proud or arrogant as a group of Oklahoma Indians dressed by a Hollywood director in make-believe Indian costumes. If one sees only the outward performance of the dances and the dancers and of the Indians at play, one misses the spirit of the real world of Oklahoma's Indian people.

To Oklahoma Indians, the seasons still matter. To a people who are a part of the cycles of life of this planet, who live outside the artificial atmosphere of central heating and cooling and beyond the control of packaged good and preplanned public entertainment, the seasons are a measure of life. To Oklahoma Indians, the summer celebrations bring more than oppressive heat and fresh tomatoes; they bring to life a world of family, tribe, politics, tradition, and ceremony. In its way this world is as Indian, as real for this modern Oklahoma Indian as the world of his ancestors ever could be. As one young Indian explained, "Being an Indian doesn't depend upon how you dress or whether you have an old Ford or a young pony. Indians in bright cars and neat suits are still of the eagle race and as the people of the eagle race we are still a proud people who have kept alive a great spirit" (Gregory and Strickland, 1974, 29).

The crucible of Oklahoma, the sharing of similar historical experiences and government policies, has helped to produce this spirit and contribute to the uniqueness of Oklahoma Indian culture. A great many factors have contributed to the evolution of this modern Oklahoma Indianness. For example, since most Oklahoma Indian tribes, as immigrant Indians, were separated from their historic homelands, the strong and ancient geographic-cultural ties that non-literate as well as literate peoples associate with landmarks do not exist within the state. For a relatively long period of time prior to the Civil War, many Oklahoma Indian tribes adapted themselves and their culture to their new location with neither the pressure of geographic-cultural ties nor the presence of many external non-Indian pressures. Dating from the first half of the nineteenth century, there is a history of tribal coopera-tion and intertribal meetings among the Indian groups in Oklahoma. Stimulated in part by the federal govern-ment's decisions to treat removed and reservation peo-ples alike and in part by a sense of common problems, these conferences reduced tribal hostility and stimu-lated united action.

The opening of Indian Territory to U.S. settlers and the general policy to end common ownership of Indian lands by allotting tribally held lands to individual Indi-ans came at approximately the same time in Oklahoma history. They created a varied series of clashes and conflicts. The present-day absence of a large body of tribally owned land and the earlier federal failure to retain traditional reservations no doubt created a vastly different Oklahoma Indian community, as did the ag-gressive manner in which the Dawes Commission dis-tributed Indian farmlands and township lots which were subsequently sold with government approval. Towns with sizable non-Indian population pockets there-fore existed amidst Indian lands almost from the mo-ment of settlement. The percentage of land in Indian hands was quickly reduced. Over the last quarter of a century, Oklahoma tribes have worked hard to repurchase portions of this land, placing it in trust for the benefit of tribal members.

Yet another crucial factor was the fact that a number of Indian tribes, as well as the state of Oklahoma, shared the assumption that statehood in 1907 changed forever the nature and purpose of tribal government. Following statehood the nation tended to legislate for the Indians of Oklahoma, particularly the Five Civilized Tribes, as separate legislative units not to be treated as the Indian tribes of other states. Added to this was the presence of a great body of mixed-blood Indian leaders who moved easily into the process of creating state governmental structures and who represented the in-terests of the entire state from positions of national or state leadership. Further, full-blood tribal leaders often chose not to move into Oklahoma state government, retreating and withdrawing from the state political arena.

Much of Oklahoma Indian life has been culturally bifurcated. Since statehood, tribes have treated their recognized civil and traditional religious groups as separate tribal bodies, creating uniquely Indian relig-ious and cultural pockets that are hidden within seem-ingly acculturated Native populations. Other issues, divisive in many non-Oklahoma tribes, such as the role of women, have had little disruptive effect in Okla-homa, perhaps because those issues have few historic roots in this population. Oklahoma Indian women, many of whom are from matrilineal groups, exert a major and even dominant influence in many tribes and in most Indian families. Furthermore, Oklahoma Indian tribes have never developed a rigidly defined concept of "Indianness" and have encouraged the development of divergent cultural strains. There is little historical evidence of tribal division based on degree of Indian blood, which indicates a strong degree of cultural confidence, a kind of Native sureness that Oklahoma tribes define as Indian pride and some non-Oklahoma Indians regard as arrogance. Voluntary separation and cultural segregation that is geographically intensified by traditional Indian settlement patterns combine to eliminate factional conflict. Finally, the size of the Indian population that is not physically identifiable as Indian but is of Indian descent in proportion to the size of the non-Indian population of the state creates a kind of "Indian culturality" that exists in no other state and that, at least in the abstract, defines "being Indian" as socially desirable. Although in many parts of the state there is a long history of hostility toward and discrimi-nation against Native people.

This particular set of cultural and historical circum-stances occurred nowhere else in the Indian Country of the West. None of these factors, alone, produced Okla-homa's unique Indian culture. Other factors, no doubt, contributed significantly to the development of Okla-homa Indian culture and values. Taken together, these attitudes and events helped shape the diverse tribal cultures of the immigrant Native American groups who are Oklahoma's Indians.

Today Oklahoma tribes seem to be undergoing a revived interest in the old ways and an increased pride in Indianness. Numbers of modern Indians from all tribes choose to deny, to ignore, or to forget all that appears to be Native. Others retreat completely into the distant Indian hills, into an Indian world of the mind, to hide from the threat of the non-Indian world.

Within the individual Indian's life, there are many distinctly personal values and attitudes that are influ-enced by an Indian heritage. Among Indians of the same generation and of the same tribe, there is no static view of Indianness. The world of the Oklahoma Indian is dynamic, varied, and diverse. And yet in some ways, Oklahoma Indian culture is becoming increasingly pan-Indian in the sense that many tribes share such events as powwows, gourd dances, and urban planning semi-nars. Oklahoma Indian life remains family-oriented, and the tribe is still important. The life of the Indian is more than dances at Anadarko, more than church-sponsored wild-onion dinners or public ceremonials.

Events such as the birthday of Grandmother Anquoe or Mrs. Adair are at the heart of the real Indian world. Much of this personal Indian world remains hidden from non-Indian Oklahomans.

That the contemporary Indian lives in two worlds has generated the misperception of a kind of Native American cultural schizophrenia. Oklahoma Indians, like Oklahoma non-Indians, live in a world that balances elements of diverse cultural traditions. The Indian brings a unique perspective to problem resolution. Two or more cultural currents may coexist so that the Indian must play many roles. Some of these roles are entirely consistent; others are hopelessly discordant. "Indian life does not fall into rigid categories," as one Oklahoma anthropologist, Carol Rachlin, notes. "It is, rather, a complex of interlocking circles, each exerting pressures and controls upon the others. An individual functions in different capacities in these circles or groups" (Rachlin, 1968, 107).

The varied life of the real Oklahoma Indian exposes the bankruptcy of the stereotypic image of the Indian. The Indian lawyer in a three-piece suit can easily transform himself into a feathered championship fancy dancer. An elected county law-enforcement official returns to his office the morning after attending a peyote meeting. A nurse leaves the hospital and goes to have tobacco "treated." The computer worker has her house smoked with cedar. A man of 1/256 Indian blood sits in a French restaurant in Tulsa expounding on tribal genealogy, while the almost full-blood descendant of a great chieftain of the same tribe tells her high school history teacher not to tell her classmates that she is Indian. A gentle, hard-working full-blood is pulled from his job and charged with harboring an Indian felon because, as a religious leader, he has followed the traditional Indian legal ways of his people. A nationally honored scholar-author consults his medicine doctor when a witch is haunting him. An internationally famous Indian artist tours China and Russia to renew her art. Such is the world of the Oklahoma Indian.

The spirit of a civilization conveys more about the meaning of people's lives than do artifacts or documents. To understand cultural spirit is difficult, especially if one was not born into that culture. Attempting to capture the spirit of Christianity, an old Kiowa man went to a missionary service, contributed when the collection plate was passed, and settled down for the sermon. This Kiowa, Old Mokeen, who had already given what he thought to be generous, rose when the request for more funds came, squared his shoulders, and spoke to the missionary in broken English: "Whatza matter this Jesus—why he all time broke?"

The corn road, the buffalo road, and the peyote road are different from one another, but the spirit with

Dwight White Buffalo, a member of the Cheyenne Tribe of Oklahoma, is a champion southern men's traditional dancer with the American Indian Dance Theater. (Photo by Don Perdue. Courtesy of Hanay Geiogamah)

which one follows the road, not the road itself, is the essence of Indianness. This Indian spirit, an Indian way of seeing and of being, makes a quarter-blood Chickasaw or an eighth-blood Comanche an Indian. "I believe that there is such a thing as Indian sensibility," T. C. Cannon, a Caddo-Kiowa, once explained. "This has to do with the idea of a collective history. It's reflected in your upbringing and the remarks that you hear every day from birth and the kind of behavior and emotion you see around you."

*Rennard Strickland*
*University of Oregon*

## ♦ INDIANS OF THE PLATEAU, GREAT BASIN, AND ROCKY MOUNTAINS

Numerous Indian communities continue to live in their ancestral homes on the Columbia Plateau of

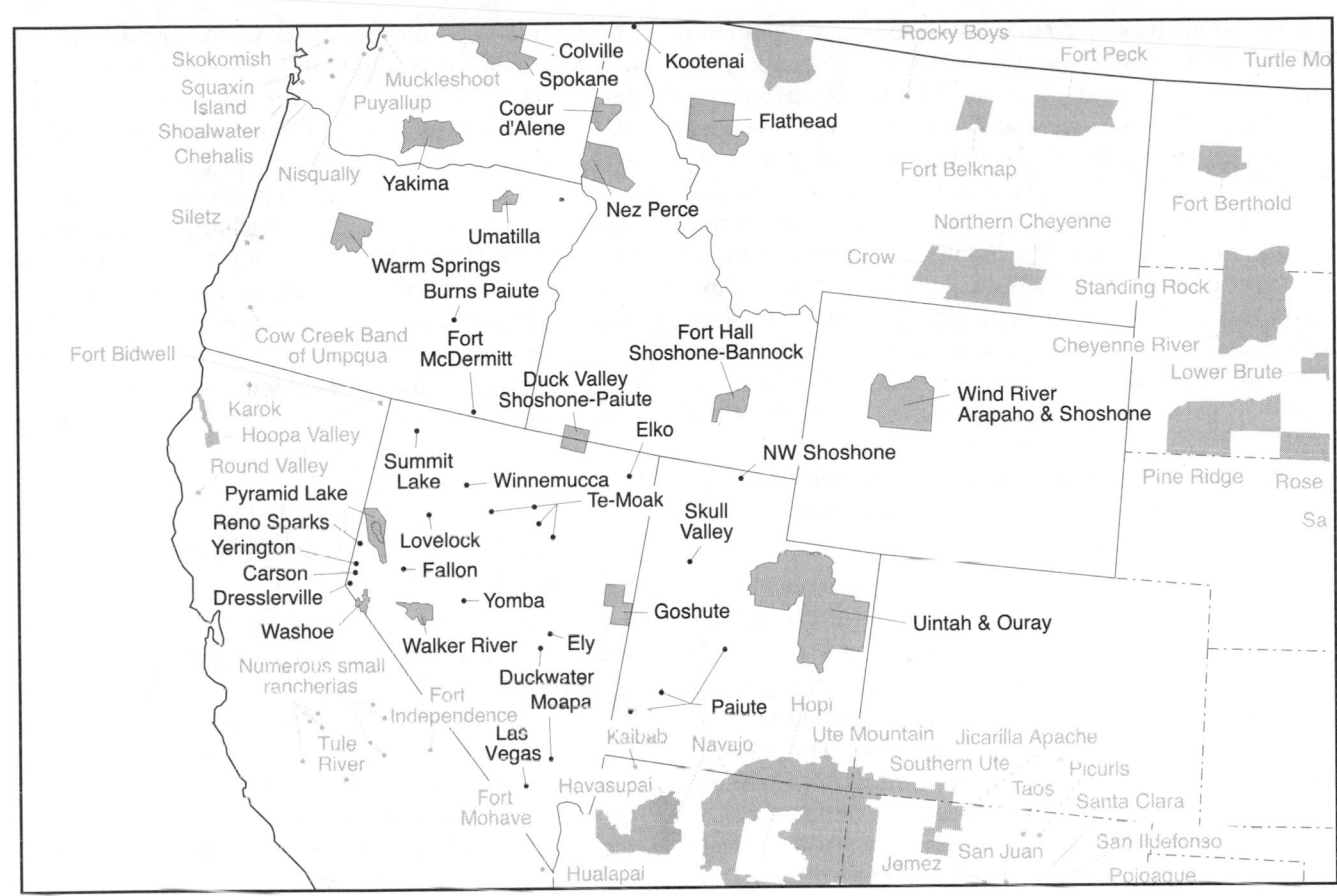

Contemporary Rocky Mountain Indian tribes. (Courtesy of the UCLA American Indian Studies Center)

eastern Oregon and Washington state; in the Great Basin of Nevada, western Colorado, southeastern Idaho, and eastern California; and in the Rocky Mountains of northeastern Colorado, Wyoming, and western Montana. Plateau Indians once enjoyed a rich environment oriented toward the region's rivers where they traditionally fished for salmon. They gathered a variety of roots, berries, and game. The plateau and mountain tribes lived on the edge of evergreen forests and high prairies and respected their environment. The Great Basin peoples, largely Paiute, Bannock, and Shoshoni, lived in the high deserts and intermountain regions. East of the Plateau tribes, the Bitterroot and Rocky Mountains rise majestically. Large portions of Washington, Oregon, Montana, and Idaho contain high deserts and plateaus where a host of Native Americans lived on roots, berries, fish, and game. Similarly, the Paiute and Shoshoni of the Great Basin lived in small bands that hunted for food and gathered roots and berries.

In the plateau and mountain regions, Indian nations shared many similar cultural traditions. Indian elders among the Flathead, Spokane, Wishram, Yakama, Nez Percé, Cayuse, Okanogan, and others say that the Creator placed them on the plateau, basin and in the mountains at the beginning of time. Moreover, they argue that their history began when the earth was young, when plant and animal people interacted closely with the first humans. All the area's tribes enjoy a rich oral tradition telling of their origins, and tribal elders consider the stories to be both literature and history. These stories form the basis of Native American cultural history.

One story recalls a time when five North Wind Brothers moved into the region and locked the plateaus and mountains in freezing cold. Coyote—the culture hero of many western Native peoples whose actions often were the cause of both positive and negative events—became a follower of the North Wind. Many of the plants and animals chose sides as either followers of the North Wind Brothers or antagonists against them. In particular, the North Wind Brothers encountered the Salmon People, large, edible fish who lay their eggs upstream in rivers that run to the ocean. In the stories of the Native peoples, animals often communicate with humans, animals, and other beings. Salmon

Chief and his tribe lived in the Pacific Ocean, but in the spring of the year, they traveled up the rivers flowing into the Pacific. When Salmon Chief led his people up the Columbia River, they were met by thick sheets of ice that prevented their travel to their spawning grounds. The North Wind Brothers stood fast against Salmon Chief, so the leader challenged the brothers to a wrestling match on the ice. The Salmon Chief beat three of the brothers but lost to the fourth. The North Wind Brothers and their followers fell upon Salmon Chief and all his people, killing them in an attempt to destroy the entire tribe. They even cut open the wife of Salmon Chief, who carried numerous eggs. The North Wind Brothers smashed every egg, except one that fell between two deep and tightly wedged rocks. Believing that the egg would dry up, the North Wind Brothers left the area.

The Creator watched the struggle between the Wind and Salmon and took pity on the Salmon People. He sent a strong rain to wash the blood from the earth, and from the bosom of the rocks he washed the tiny salmon egg into the river. The Creator fertilized and nurtured the egg until a small smolt was born. The salmon returned to the ocean where his grandmother cared for him and trained him to meet the future challenge of the North Wind Brothers. When Young Chinook Salmon was of age, he traveled upriver to meet the forces that had killed his mother and father. He met the five North Wind Brothers on the ice, and one by one he defeated them. However, Young Chinook Salmon did not kill the younger sister of the North Wind Brothers, and every winter she returns to bring a mild version of the cold.

Like the battle between the salmon and wind, the Indians of the plateau and mountains have long been engaged in a struggle for survival against European traders and settlers who moved into the region and nearly destroyed the original inhabitants. In the nineteenth century, many Indian communities suffered near-death experiences, but like the small egg that survived, so did these Native people. In the first decade of the 1800s, Indians living in present-day Oregon, Washington, Idaho, and Montana met Meriwether Lewis and William Clark, who led a U.S. expedition from 1803 to 1806 to explore the Louisiana Purchase, land west of the Mississippi River bought from France in 1803. Regional tribes share a common experience through their relations with Lewis and Clark.

When the explorers reached the Great Falls (near present-day Great Falls, Montana) of the Missouri River, they needed horses and information in order to cross the Rocky Mountains. With a small party, Lewis set out on foot to find the Shoshoni Indians. After some time, the men met several Shoshoni women to whom they gave gifts. The women belonged to the Lemhi Band of

Shoshoni led by Chief Kameawaite. After much effort, Lewis convinced Kameawaite to supply horses and guides to lead the explorers over the Rocky Mountains. When the Shoshoni and explorers returned to Great Falls, Kameawaite willingly helped Lewis and Clark, because they had returned his long-lost sister, Sacajewea. She and her husband, Touissant Charbonneau, served as guides for the Lewis and Clark expedition to Great Falls. Some years earlier, enemies of the Shoshoni had stolen Sacajewea who was sold into slavery and eventually bought by Charbonneau. Kameawaite contributed significantly to the safe journey of the famous explorers. The Shoshoni chief led the expedition through most of present-day Montana and showed them the way into the country of the Flathead Indians, located in present-day western Montana. In like fashion, the Flathead guided Lewis and Clark westward across the panhandle of present-day Idaho.

In October 1805, the Lewis and Clark expedition entered Nez Percé lands. The Nez Percé provided the explorers with kindness, food, and canoes to take them to the Pacific Ocean. With the aid of Nez Percé scouts, the explorers traveled quickly by canoe to the homelands of the Palouse Indians, safely reaching the Palouse village of Quosispah. Several Indians greeted Lewis and Clark at this village, and they celebrated the arrival of the *Suyapo*, Crowned Heads or Crowned Hats, by singing long into the night. Palouse, Yakama, Wanapum, Wishram, Walla Walla, Cayuse, Umatilla, and a host of other tribes sent representatives to meet the U.S. explorers. The Indians and explorers traded goods, and Lewis and Clark honored some of the chiefs with special medals bearing the words *peace* and *friendship*. Relations between the two peoples were friendly, and the explorers soon continued their trip down the Columbia River, past the villages of the Skin, Wishram, Tenino, Wasco, Clackamus, Cathlapotle, Wahkiakum, and Cathlamet.

The explorers spent a rainy winter among the Clatsop Indians living south of the Columbia River before returning to the United States, which claimed the entire Northwest, including the plateau, Great Basin, and mountains. The United States encouraged citizens to relocate to the region. Lewis and Clark reported the many wondrous things they had seen, including vast numbers of fur-bearing animals. By 1810, British traders traveled through the Northwest in quest of a river route from the interior of Canada to the Pacific Ocean. Soon, three major fur-trading companies, the Northwest Company, the American Fur Company, and Hudson's Bay Company, set up trading posts or factories in the Northwest.

Fort Astoria in Oregon along the Columbia River served as a key trading center for the Americans, but the British purchased the post in 1813 and renamed it Fort George. In 1824 the Hudson's Bay Company opened Fort Vancouver in present-day Washington, and they operated factories or posts on the plateau. While the company worked with Shoshoni, Paiute, and Bannock to procure furs, they depended on plateau tribes for horses. Fort Nez Percé, Fort Okanogan, Fort Colville, and Fort Spokane, all named after Plateau tribes, traded with Indians and supplied the Hudson's Bay Company with furs and horses. The British company enjoyed a prosperous Indian trade on the Plateau and intermountain areas until the 1850s, when they had depleted the number of fur-bearing animals and when the United States took firm control of the region.

Traders and trappers became the first to occupy Indian lands in the region. A few tried to convert Indians to Christianity, but the major thrust of the mission system on the plateau began in the 1830s. The Presbyterian missionary couples of Marcus and Narcissa Whitman and Henry and Eliza Spalding established the first missions in the Northwest among the Cayuse and Nez Percé. Catholic missionaries followed these early Presbyterian ministers, establishing missions among the Flathead, Sanpoil, Nespelem, Colville, Yakama, Umatilla, and others. Some Indians gravitated toward Christianity while others held fast to their own traditional religions. Controversy over whether to adopt Christianity split many plateau and mountain Indian communities into pro- and anti-Christian factions.

Between 1836 and 1843 the Presbyterian Whitmans and Spaldings worked diligently among the Indians with mixed results. In 1843 a significant event altered the course of events: Joe Meek, William Craig, and other former fur trappers opened a wagon road, later called the Oregon Trail, from Idaho across the Blue Mountains of Oregon, into the Grande Ronde River Valley of Oregon, and along the Columbia River. Soon many settlers used the Oregon Trail to travel to the Pacific coast. The newcomers established territorial governments in the present-day states of Oregon and Washington and assumed political power over indigenous peoples. Tensions mounted as disease, introduced by the newcomers, spread among the Indians and threatened their physical survival. In the interior, measles ravaged the Cayuse, and they blamed Whitman for the epidemic. A few Cayuse murdered the doctor, his wife, and eleven others. Oregon Volunteers engaged the Cayuse but eventually fought the Palouse after the volunteers tried stealing about 400 Indian horses. The conflict was settled after a few Cayuse surrendered and whites hanged them.

Of equal importance, after Maidu Indians discovered gold in 1848 along the American River in northern California, miners invaded California, killing Indians with guns and microorganisms. The California mining frontier moved northward into the lands of the Modoc, Klamath, and Chetco. Gold was soon discovered on the plateau and mountains, and Indians resisted the invasion of their homelands by miners who had little or no regard for the Indians' rights. Miners extended their diggings north into Oregon and Washington and east into Idaho and Montana. The United States soon gave more attention to the area, and in 1853 the country created two separate territories there. Oregon Territory included lands in present-day Oregon, Idaho, and Wyoming. Washington Territory included lands in present-day Washington, Idaho, and Montana. With the new government came American Indian policy bent on liquidating Indian title to land, confining Indians to smaller parcels of land called reservations, and establishing military and civil power over the tribes.

In 1854 Governor Isaac I. Stevens made a whirlwind tour of the coastal tribes of Washington Territory, coercing some into ceding their lands to the government. He made treaties at Medicine Creek, Point Elliott, and Point No Point. The Indians of Puget Sound secured for themselves only a small portion of their lands and fell victim to the power of the Bureau of Indian Affairs. Stevens had a more difficult time with Plateau Indians. In May 1855, Stevens made three treaties with the inland tribes, creating the Yakama, Nez Percé, and Umatilla reservations. Although he did not negotiate treaties with the Salish-speaking Indians of the Plateau, he concluded a treaty with some Flathead, which forced the Kutenai, Kalispel, and Flathead to move onto a reservation.

Oregon Superintendent of Indian Affairs Joel Palmer helped Stevens with the Walla Walla Council before concluding treaties with the Tenino, Wasco, Wishram, and other people living along the Columbia River. He created the Warm Springs Reservation of Oregon south of the Columbia River, where he expected the tribes to live in peace with the Paiute of Oregon. Palmer negotiated treaties with several different tribes in Oregon, but over time, the U.S. government took nearly all Indian land in the territory, leaving Native Americans with virtually no land base. As a result of territorial government, the United States and its citizens took control of the plateau and mountain Indians, but not without a fight.

Shortly after the Walla Walla Council of 1855, white miners discovered gold north of the Spokane River in Oregon Territory. Miners invaded the inland Northwest, and some stole and murdered a few Indians, which led to retaliation by Yakama warriors who executed several miners. War resulted after two Yakama murdered Indian agent Andrew Jackson Bolon. Between 1855 and 1858, the Indians of the Columbia Plateau fought a series of fights with volunteer and U.S. troops.

After some initial successes, the Yakama retreated north. Volunteer troops from Oregon and Washington invaded the lands of the Walla Walla, Umatilla, Cayuse, and Palouse Indians living near the Snake River in present-day Oregon. Few of these people had been involved in the conflict in Yakama Country, but the volunteer soldiers sought to punish all Indians. The Plateau Indian War concluded at the Battle of Four Lake and Spokane Plain when the combined forces of Yakama, Palouse, Spokane, Flathead, Okanogan, and others suffered a loss at the hands of the U.S. military led by Colonel George Wright. Several tribes chose not to enter a war with the United States, but all felt the power of the federal government and the settlers who stole their land.

Contact with settlers came relatively late for the Great Basin peoples, such as the numerous autonomous bands of Paiute. But in the 1850s, many Great Basin Indians went to work for white ranchers and farmers. Many worked for wages as cowboys, freighters, and wranglers, while others earned money planting, cultivating, and harvesting hay and grains. Ranchers and farmers hired Indian workers, since farm and ranch hands were quite scarce in the Great Basin region.

The rapidly changing political and economic situation of the Great Basin region helped spark two social movements, often called the 1870 Ghost Dance and 1890 Ghost Dance. The 1870 movement was started by the Paiute mystic, Wodziwob, whose teachings spread primarily among northern and western California Indians. At this time California Indians were under great distress from disease, poverty, political subordination, and aggressive miners who wanted Indians out of the mining fields. Many California Indians adopted the Ghost Dance-associated hand game, a gambling game with ritual singing and betting in which one team tries to hide bones and the other tries to guess who has the bones. The 1890 Ghost Dance is better known and was initiated by Wovoka. The second Ghost Dance drew upon the early teachings of Wodziwob and emphasized the return of game and relatives who had died since European contact. Many Indians had died of diseases, and game, especially buffalo on the Plains and salmon in the Northwest, was noticeably declining. Many Indian nations in the West were gravely concerned that changing conditions threatened their entire way of life. The Ghost Dance incorporated many Paiute traditions, such as a Round Dance. Performed to gain communication with or honor dead ancestors, the Round Dance became a central feature of the Ghost Dance, which in 1888 to 1890 spread rapidly among many western Indian tribes, especially the Plains nations.

The Ghost Dance was performed to achieve successful transition to the next world after death, and in some versions, the dance helped facilitate a great worldly change in which many dead ancestors would return to live on earth and the game would be replenished. These events would restore the Indian nations to their former, more prosperous condition, before the intrusion of U.S. settlers and government. The Ghost Dance movement declined after the 1890 massacre of Sioux at Wounded Knee in South Dakota. Units of the Seventh Cavalry killed at least two hundred Sioux, mostly women and children. After the Wounded Knee tragedy, the U.S. government officially discouraged the Ghost Dance, and because the Ghost Dance predictions of a cataclysmic worldly reorganization did not come to pass, the movement declined, leaving only a few Ghost Dance spiritual leaders sprinkled among some of the Plains nations. Wovoka encouraged the Great Basin and other Indian people to keep the moral teachings he received in a vision from the Great Spirit by loving one another and living in peace with everyone. As late as the 1920s, Wovoka told other Indians—he usually avoided discussions with non-Indians—that he had visited with God who informed him that a new world was coming for Indians.

The Nez Percé of present-day Idaho lived peacefully with the United States until 1860, when traders found gold on their lands. Gold miners quickly moved into the Nez Percé country, and the Bureau of Indian Affairs responded by shrinking the Nez Percé Reservation to one-tenth of its original size. All the Nez Percé chiefs refused to sign the treaty of 1863, except Chief Lawyer who had no authority to sell Nez Percé lands. Still, he signed the "Thief Treaty," which resulted in war. In 1876 General Oliver O. Howard demanded that the non-treaty Nez Percé move onto the reservation in present-day western Idaho. When the people had to choose between accepting peace or going to war, they chose the peaceful path and moved onto the reservation.

War eventually erupted when three young men killed several settlers. After fighting began, Chief Looking Glass led the Nez Percé out of Idaho into Montana and south toward the Crow Indians. When the Crow refused to help, the Nez Percé turned north toward Canada. U.S. forces led by Colonel Nelson A. Miles intercepted the Nez Percé near the Bear Paw Mountains of Montana, and he accepted the surrender of Chief Joseph, a central Nez Percé leader. Rather than return the Nez Percé to Idaho in accordance with the surrender agreement, General William Tecumseh Sherman forced the men, women, and children to Fort Leavenworth, Kansas, and into Indian Territory, present-day Oklahoma. The Nez Percé and their Palouse allies remained in Indian Territory until 1885 when the government permitted them to return to the Northwest. Some Nez Percé returned to Lapwai, Idaho, but the government forced others, including Joseph, to live on the Colville Reservation in central Washington.

Shoshoni, Bannock, and Paiute people also made a stand against the United States. Originally, the United States established the Fort Hall Reservation in present-day eastern Idaho for the Boise-Bruneau Band of Shoshoni, but soon the government forced the Bannock to Fort Hall as well. Many Bannocks decided to go to the reservation and receive rations. The government, however, did not fulfill its promises of food, and many Shoshoni and Bannock starved. When the Bannock, Paiute, and Shoshoni living on the Fort Hall Reservation tried to continue their seasonal economic migrations for hunting buffalo and gathering roots and berries, the Bureau of Indian Affairs and Christian missionaries demanded their return to the reservation. Discontent spread at Fort Hall, and on 30 May 1878 a few Indians stole some cattle and killed two cowboys, an event that sparked a series of battles. By June 1878 the skirmishes escalated into a significant military conflict. Numbering only 700 people, the Bannock and Paiute joined forces in southeastern Oregon where they fought the Battle of Camp Curry. After the battle, the Bannock and Paiute moved north toward the Umatilla Reservation in present-day Oregon. U.S. forces subdued the Shoshoni and Bannock and returned them to the Fort Hall Reservation.

During the 1880s, reformers of American Indian policies determined that the trouble with Indians was that they held the reservation communally, not individually. In an attempt to help Indians, liberal reformers decided to break up the reservation into individual lots so that Indians would have private lands and would want to work their own ranch or farm. U.S. policymakers reasoned that this land policy, called allotment, would enable Indians to become "civilized," because they would have a direct stake in their own economic livelihood. Most reformers, however, knew little about Indian cultures or economic practices, such as their methods of hunting, fishing, and gathering. Few if any Indians on the Plateau, Rocky Mountain, or Great Basin regions farmed, and it took years for them to alter their cultures to accommodate U.S. reformers. Many Indians refused to give up their traditional economic practices in order to adopt farming. Life on the reservation was hard and people became dependent on government rations. Most reservations could not adequately support the small Indian populations that lived on the reservation.

In 1887 Congress passed the General Allotment Act, which called for the division of reservations into individual parcels of 160, 80, or 40 acres. Each Indian received an allotment, and the government sold the excess land to non-Indian settlers. After twenty-five

John Harmelt (Wenatchi) was a chief when the United States forced the people from the Wenatchi fisheries in 1893. He was forced from his home in 1902. (Courtesy of Robert H. Ruby)

years, Indian allotees could sell their individual allotments.

The government began allotting the Yakama Reservation in Washington state in the 1890s and continued the process until 1914. Conservative Indians, particularly elders and worshipers of the Washani religion, opposed allotment. Some Yakama agreed to take allotments, although many felt it contrary to tribal tradition. Between 1890 and 1914, the United States made 4,506 allotments on the Yakama Reservation, totaling 440,000 acres. Because many conservative Yakama resisted allotments, 798,000 acres of reservation land was not allotted and remained in tribal hands. The government also allotted land on the Spokane Reservation in Washington when Congress passed a resolution directing the secretary of the interior to allot these lands on 19 June 1902. The Indians had little choice in the matter, because the United States forced 651 members of the tribe to accept allotments totaling 64,750 acres. The government sold the remainder of the Spokane Reservation to non-Indian timber, agricultural, and ranching interests.

Like many Indians, the Coeur d'Alene people of Idaho lost a huge portion of their original domain. On 8 November 1873 the president created the Coeur d'Alene Reservation with 598,000 acres. However, in agreeing to the executive order creating the reservation, the Coeur d'Alene lost 184,960 acres of their homeland in eastern Washington and western Idaho. When the government allotted reservation lands from 1905 to 1909 over the objections of Coeur d'Alene Chief Peter Moctelme, the Coeur d'Alene and Spokane were left with only 51,040 acres of their traditional lands.

A similar situation occurred on the Flathead Reservation of Montana, where the Pend d'Oreille (also known as Upper Kalispel), Kutenai, and Flathead lived. Originally, these Indians controlled 1,242,969 acres of land. Between 1904 and 1908, the government allotted eighty acres to individuals interested in farm lands and 160 acres to Indians wishing to ranch. A total of 2,378 Indians received allotments on the Flathead Reservation. At the same time, the U.S. government sold 404,047 acres of former Indian lands to U.S. settlers, and the state of Montana took another 60,843 acres for school purposes. The United States kept 1,757 acres of Indian lands for itself, thus assuming control over most of the original lands of the Flathead people. On 2 May 1910, the government opened the remainder of the reservation land for settlement and development by non-Indians.

During the late-nineteenth and early-twentieth centuries, Native Americans lost more than their estates. They also lost elements of their culture, language, and families through the efforts of the Bureau of Indian Affairs to "civilize" them. Indian reformers often wanted Indians to leave their Native cultures behind, a notion that the reformers considered backward. U.S. policymakers believed that the best road for Indians to travel was to adopt U.S. culture, and argued that education was the most effective way to "civilize" Native Americans. Government-run schools emerged on several reservations, and U.S. teachers tried to discourage Indian students from practicing Indian languages, cultures, traditions, and religions. Churches established mission schools on some reservations, but by the late-nineteenth century, the Bureau of Indian Affairs controlled most reservation educational institutions.

Through the Indian agents and the superintendents of Indian schools, the Bureau of Indian Affairs operated most reservation schools. Although both boys and girls attended these schools, the administrators and teachers focused their attention primarily on boys, mirroring the gender bias prevalent in U.S. society. Teachers taught Indian children to speak, read, and write English, and they punished children when they spoke Indian languages. While Indian students learned the subjects that were taught in most U.S. elementary schools at the time, the schools' major emphasis was on vocational training. Teachers trained girls to be waitresses, maids, and housekeepers, and Indian boys studied printing, masonry, and carpentry. Many Indian boys and girls were sent on outings in nearby towns and homes where they learned from on-the-job training but earned little or no money. Most reservations had elementary schools, but the Bureau of Indian Affairs sent older children—Shoshoni, Bannock, Nez Percé, Nespelem, Paiute, Okanogan, and others—to Carlisle Indian Industrial School in Pennsylvania, Haskell Institute in Kansas, Sherman Institute in California, or to one of the other boarding schools. Some Indian boarding schools continue to function today, although the attitudes and curriculum of the boarding schools no longer directly discourage the expression of Indian cultures as they did in the early twentieth century.

While forced education dramatically altered Indian cultures of the Columbia Plateau, Great Basin, and Rocky Mountains, other factors, such as disease, also influenced the lives of these Indians. While smallpox, measles, and venereal diseases ravaged the tribes in the nineteenth century, tuberculosis, pneumonia, and influenza killed thousands of Indians in the twentieth century. Between 1888 and 1930, among the Indians of the Confederated Yakama Nation, more deaths occurred during a child's first year of life than in any other age category. Infant mortality most often resulted from the above-mentioned diseases. Each tribe had its traditional Native doctors—men and women who knew the area's healing herbs, medical techniques, prayers, and songs—but they were often unable to fight the newly introduced diseases. Some Indians were treated by government doctors, but many were not. The Native American population in the region suffered severely from disease until the 1950s, when the government created the Indian Health Service.

During the 1930s, Congress passed the Indian Reorganization Act, which allowed tribes to reassert themselves in a new way. Indians who accepted the Indian Reorganization Act could place their allotments in a trust so the lands could not be sold. The tribes could also reorganize into new political entities with tribal laws and constitutions. Some of the tribes in the plateau and mountains accepted the Indian Reorganization Act, while others did not. The Confederated Salish and Kutenai Tribes of the Flathead Reservation, the

Students and their instructor at Wyoming Indian High School play the traditional hoop game during Heritage Day activities. (Photo by Sara Wiles)

Confederated Tribes of the Umatilla Indian Reservation, the Confederated Tribes of the Warm Springs Reservation, and others voted to accept the Indian Reorganization Act. Regardless, all the Plateau and Rocky Mountain tribes and many of the Great Basin tribes created tribal governments that helped guide them through the twentieth century. Certainly most tribes took advantage of the Indian Claims Commission established in 1946.

Prior to establishment of the Indian Claims Commission, the United States forced Indian tribes to take their cases directly to Congress, a branch of government not known for its expediency when it came to settling Indian land claims. For years the tribes had taken their problems involving land, water, and resources to Congress without result. The Indians Claims Commission offered tribes a mechanism through which they could sue the federal government for treaty violations involving a host of issues.

In every case settled by the Indian Claims Commission the tribes received a monetary compensation rather than any returned land. Some Native Americans objected to this arrangement, but it was the only one used by the commission. For example, in settling claims of the numerous bands of Shoshoni and Bannock people, the Claims Commission separated the 1957 Shoshoni-Bannock claim into several parts, a part of which dealt with the Northern, Northwestern, and Western bands of Shoshoni. The case took so long that the U.S. Court of Claims made the determination of the case after the Claims Commission expired in 1978. On 8 October 1982, one section of the Shoshoni claim, which dealt with federal mismanagement of timber and grazing resources, was settled in favor of the Shoshoni bands, who were awarded $1.6 million.

In July 1951 the Nez Percé tribe of Idaho and the Nez Percé living on the Colville Reservation filed petitions with the Indian Claims Commission regarding compensation for the theft of their original homelands, particularly those in northeastern Oregon and western Idaho. The Claims Commission combined the petitions of the two groups into one claim on 27 February 1953. Finally,

Smohalla (Wanapum) was leader of the Washeni, who taught the people the Washat or Washasha. The Wanapum Prophet influenced Indians throughout the Northwest. (Courtesy of the Smithsonian Institution)

in 1971 the commission awarded the Nez Percé $3.5 million. The Nez Percé received approximately 50 cents per acre stolen.

During the 1950s, the federal government sought to dissolve or terminate the reservation system and end its treaty and legal relationship with various tribes in the United States. Most notable was the government's attempt to terminate the Confederated Tribes of the Colville Reservation in Washington State. Colville tribal members living off the reservation generally favored termination because it would bring them a cash settlement. However, tribal members living on the reservation generally opposed termination, because it abrogated treaty rights and threatened to disperse Indian cultures and communities. The leaders of the Confederated Tribes struggled over the issue of termination during the 1950s and 1960s. The most vocal opponent of termination was Lucy Covington, a member of a prominent political family on the reservation. Covington stood nearly single-handedly against proponents of termination, and she never surrendered her position.

As a result of her efforts, the tribe never agreed to termination, and it has been solidly opposed to the concept ever since.

Since the threat of termination receded in the 1960s, many tribes have made significant strides in health, education, and economic development. Each year the Colville Tribe sponsors workshops on cultural revitalization, and they encourage their young people to participate in their annual Powwow and Circle Celebration held in Nespelem, Washington. The tribe owns a sawmill, a package log cabin sales business, a trading post, and a casino. Several young people attend colleges and universities in their region, and many students have returned to their reservation to contribute their expertise to developing the reservation economy and community. A similar situation has occurred on the Flathead Reservation where the Kutenai, Kalispel, and Flathead have initiated a cultural heritage project to preserve their languages, oral histories, and songs. The Flathead Tribe maintains a business relationship with Montana Power Company, which operates Kerr Dam on the reservation and a resort at Blue Bay along the shores of Flathead Lake.

The Shoshoni and Bannock people from the Fort Hall Reservation are often employed in ranching, farming, and small businesses. The tribe owns its own agricultural enterprise and construction business, particularly a 20,000–acre irrigation project that brings water to Indians and non-Indians alike. The people at Fort Hall enjoy their own health center, adult education program, and youth recreation program. The tribe places special emphasis on the health of its members, and in the spring of 2000 the tribe demanded that government and corporate research be conducted on the health effects of phosphate plants in the area which many Indians and non-Indians believe contribute to the high rate of asthma, upper respiratory infection, and heart disease in the area. Tribal officials believe that there may be a link to toxic chemicals in the air and illnesses among the Shoshoni-Bannock people at Fort Hall.

Concerns regarding the state of the environment are found among many tribes of the Plateau, Great Basin, and Rocky Mountains, including the Arapaho of Wind River. For years they have expressed concern about the effects of mining, ranching, and logging in Wyoming. In 2000 their interest in the environment led the people to work with federal officials to rebuild and maintain the Washakie Dam on the South Fork of the Little Wind River. The earthen dam was built for flood control, and in recent years the Arapaho have formed a compact with federal officials to ensure that the environment surrounding the dam is protected. Arapaho people have also sought economic development that does not harm the environment, and in 2000 they applied for a federal license to operate a wireless communication system for telephones, internet access, and cable television. During the last decade, Arapahos have also made headway in addressing an epidemic of suicides among young people who experienced extreme depression and ended their lives. In 2000 the Northern Cheyenne of Montana received a grant for $817,000 to address alcohol, drug, and tobacco abuse—social, cultural, and health issues that often lead to suicide. Unfortunately, many tribes live under a cloud of potential suicides, but all the tribes have responded through their own agency, attempting to work cooperatively to end teenage suicide and alcohol and drug abuse.

People on many reservations have addressed suicide by offering youth programs that emphasize the positive and lasting contributions of traditional culture, using modern educational systems to carry this message to young people. The Nez Percé of Idaho have used similar methods and have recently initiated a program supported by gaming money to build a cultural-environmental school serving approximately 320 students, from kindergarten to eighth grade. The school will take advantage of open spaces near Kamiah, Idaho, and will focus on the importance of the natural environment in the traditional and contemporary lives of Nez Percé people. Returning to the natural environment is now being experienced by Chief Joseph's band of Nez Percé in the Wallowa Valley of Oregon. Excluded from the region for years, Nez Percé have returned to the Wallowa and purchased acreage, living in a positive association with many non-Natives who welcomed the people home. Many tribes of the Plateau, Great Basin, and Rocky Mountains have encouraged their children to succeed in non-Native educational systems, and many tribes now offer tribal scholarships that have been endowed in recent years by gaming funds. This has been the case on the Coeur d'Alene, Colville, Warm Springs, Fort Hall, Spokane, Kalispel, Nez Percé, and other regional reservations.

The Warm Springs of Oregon, Yakama of Washington, Nez Percé of Idaho, and Umatilla of Oregon have been very active in educational funding and economic development. Wendell Jim of Warm Springs and his colleagues in the Educational Office have initiated several educational projects to bridge the gap between elders and young people. Some elders on the reservation practice the Washat or Seven Drums Religion as well as the Feather Religion. Many elders lived a traditional life during the twentieth century, and the tribe has preserved their stories by conducting numerous oral histories. These interviews have enriched the education of young people who also benefit from educational and language programs. The tribe launched a language program to ensure that young people will learn Sahaptin and Paiute spoken by many on the reservation. Federal grants have supported some of these cultural programs, but the Warm Springs Tribe has used its own funds to enrich cultural and educational programs that influence the health of the people, particularly young people.

Several tribes have benefited in this way from gaming funds, but the Warm Springs people have also used money from their own Warm Springs Forest Products Industry, wild horse herd, salmon hatchery, sawmill, plywood plant, and resort-convention center at *Kah-Nee-Ta* to benefit education and health programs. The people at Warm Springs have also been leaders in generating electricity, providing power that the tribe sells to the Pacific Power and Light Company. In 1982 the tribe was the first in the nation to open its own hydroelectric plant, the Pelton Reregulating Dam. The tribe hopes to do far more in terms of economic development, and in the spring of 2000 their hopes hinged on the purchase of thirty acres near the Cascade Locks on the Columbia River, land the tribe once "owned" before 1855 when the United States took it through a treaty. Like so many tribes, the Warm Springs people use gaming revenue for education, preservation, law enforcement, courts, housing, health, education, roads, future economic development, and infrastructure development.

Yakama people have also exerted their economic, political, and cultural sovereignty. The fourteen tribes and bands represented by the Confederated Tribes maintains its own forest products industry, annually cutting about 150 million board feet of lumber. They manage 2.7 million acres of range land and 150,000 acres of farm land. Yakama people control their own water through the Wapato Project, and they have successful small businesses, a banking system, and a fishing enterprise. Through the Yakama Tribal Housing Authority, the people have executed major housing projects that have significantly benefited the tribe. In 1980 the tribe opened its extensive tribal culture center. Beautifully designed in the shape of a large longhouse, the cultural center contains a library, archive-special collection, museum, gift shop, theater, and offices. Yakama people emphasize education, offering tribal scholarships and summer educational programs to prepare young people to succeed in college. In addition, the tribe enjoys its own community college on the reservation, serving thousands of students of varying ages. Each year the tribe sponsors several powwows, basketball tournaments, and first foods celebrations that educate and preserve the rich past of the people.

Many tribes of the Plateau, Great Basin, and Rocky Mountains offer classes teaching tribal languages. Since the 1970s, language preservation has been a major priority among tribes, but so has the protection of the environment. Paiutes at Pyramid Lake, Nevada, have protested the dumping of waste water filled with cyanide and other toxins into the desert, poisons that affect the earth, water, and air of the region. The Paiutes and their neighbors at the Reno-Sparks, Nevada Indian Colony have opposed a Chicago-based firm interested in mining kitty litter near their homes because of dust, traffic, and destruction of the landscape. For years development on and near the Colville Reservation of Washington has destroyed the natural environment. With the use of gaming funds and grants, the Colville Confederated tribe has initiated a comprehensive plan to protect natural resources and restore the natural environment. The Colville plan is exemplary because the tribe is listening and learning from elders who remember the reservation before it suffered so much development.

All the tribes living on the Plateau, Great Basin, and Rocky Mountains have taken a special interest in repatriating cultural resources and cultural patrimony (remains and grave goods) taken by archaeologists and placed within museum collections. For the tribes, repatriation is a spiritual issue involving the respect for human rights and dignity. For scientists, the loss of human remains involves ownership and scholarly advancement. In 1990 Congress passed the Native American Graves Protection and Repatriation Act requiring museums receiving federal dollars and holding Native remains and patrimony to create an inventory of their collections so that they could work with culturally affiliated tribes to repatriate the cultural resources. In 2000 the Arapaho and Cheyenne worked closely and cooperatively with the Smithsonian to repatriate cultural items, but the relationship between Indians and non-Native institutions is not always positive.

In 1996 archaeologists working near McNary Dam found Kennewick Man. R. Ervin Taylor radiocarbon-dated the remains at circa 9000 and 4500 B.P., and the Corps of Engineers determined that the Umatilla Confederated Tribe was the culturally affiliated group. The Corps decided to turn the remains over to the Umatillas for reburial but archaeologists filed lawsuits to prevent the action. Archaeologists claim the remains, saying that they will reveal secrets about the past, and many do not want the bones reburied. Most Indian tribes favor repatriation and reburial, although the Colvilles support study of the remains before reburial. It was the hope of Colvilles and others that in the future, archaeologists would work more closely with the tribes during excavations, which are commonly done by some scholars. Tribes look forward to the day when they can work in greater partnership with archaeologists, but this will require mutual respect and trust among all parties. Ultimately, the government ordered the remains of Kennewick man to be returned to the Umatillas who will determine the fate of the remains.

The division between Native and non-Native peoples so prevalent in repatriation issues is also found in cases involving Indian rights. Nez Percé in Idaho have spent years fighting for their water rights to the Snake River, while at the same time challenging the Corps of Engineers and their operation of several dams on the Snake River. The tribe contends that the dams violate the Clean Water Act and that the dams pollute the water

Chelan leaders Nespelem George, Long Jim, and an unidentified man ride in a parade. (Courtesy of Robert H. Ruby)

and warm it, harming the aquatic culture of the river. At the beginning of the twenty-first century, the case is in litigation with no end in sight. Like many tribes, the Nez Percé continue their ancient concern for salmon and other fish. In April 2000 the Colville Confederated Tribes began a new restoration project to protect salmon and increase the number of fish. The Colville have done this in partnership with Portland General Electric. Partnering with companies and governments is developing among many tribes, including the people on the Umatilla Reservation who worked with the Bureau of Reclamation in 1996 to begin the Umatilla Basin Project. The group recently celebrated the fourth annual Salmon Celebration, commemorating the joint initiative. The Umatilla now enjoy a magnificent culture center that showcases the culture of Umatilla, Cayuse, Walla Walla, and other Plateau Indian peoples.

The cooperation between private industry and governments to preserve salmon runs is a new development. In the recent past the tribes have been at odds

with others about preserving fish and taking fish. During the twentieth century, many Native Americans in Washington, Oregon, and Idaho protested the destruction of the salmon, particularly after state and federal government built dams on Northwestern rivers. Oral traditions affirmed the human obligation to protect fish and eat them in communion each year so that the salmon would return. After the people signed treaties with the United States, they had traditional and constitutional rights to take fish in common with non-Natives at all usual and accustomed areas on and off the reservation. Governments and non-Natives tried to block Indian fishing rights, and tribes spent the twentieth century fighting for their rights through protests such as fish-ins. In 1974 the tribes won the Boldt Decision, which acknowledged Indians' rights to fish in common with non-Indians and granted the tribe the right to one-half of the harvestable fish catch. The Supreme Court upheld the Boldt Decision, but the tribes continue to fight opposition of governments, state law enforcement, and recreational fishing organizations.

In the 1980s, David Sohappy, an elder of mixed Yakama and Wenatchi blood, insisted on his right to fish, and law enforcement officials arrested him. In federal court, the government convicted Sohappy, sending him to prison in Washington and California. Ultimately the government released him from prison, and Sohappy continued his fishing, asserting his rights until his death. In 1992 Washington elected a governor who openly favored Indian fishing rights, but not all politicians or citizens joined him in his position. U.S. Senator Slade Gorton from Washington has consistently opposed Indian fishing rights, and in the spring of 2000 Republicans in the state suggested that the National Republican platform should firmly oppose Indian rights. In spite of such opposition, Indians throughout the Northwest and the country continue to support their traditional legal and treaty rights to fish as their ancestors before them.

At the dawning of the twenty-first century, many tribes are creating partnerships with government and industry in an attempt to continue the Native circle. The Indians of the Plateau, Great Basin, and Rocky Mountains are a diverse people who share many things in common. All enjoy a long history of growth and development before the arrival of Lewis and Clark, and all celebrate their survival under the worst of circumstances after non-Indians invaded their homelands. All the tribes have been forced to contend with the United States government as well as hostile state and local governments that championed "citizens," not Native Americans. Even after 1920 when Indians became citizens of the United States, many non-Indians discriminated against the tribes. Undaunted, the tribes have fought for their lives, cultures, languages, resources, and rights. The people continue this struggle today and look forward to the centuries ahead when they will have greater sovereignty over their lives and people. Native people of the Plateau, Great Basin, and Rockies have a spirit about them that links their past to the present and will help determine their future.

*Clifford E. Trafzer*
*University of California, Riverside*

## ◆ CALIFORNIA INDIANS

Without exception, the Native peoples of California believe they originated in North America. Despite unproved theories of a Siberian origin and migration favored by non-Indian academics, traditional origin stories tell of a creator or creators whose wondrous powers brought forth the physical universe and all plant and animal life. The members of each group saw themselves as the center of that creation and viewed their neighbors as less favored. This cultural centrism created the belief that tribal territories were sacred and intimately connected the divine intentions of the Creator. Consequently, land, place, and sacred sites all had a tie to the Creator and to sacred things that were the major events and symbols in Indian histories.

At the time of first contact with Europeans (1542), the population of California Indians was between 310,000 and 340,000. These astounding numbers made it the most densely populated area in what is now the United States. The mild climate and abundance of wild foods proved more than adequate sustenance for such a population. Social organization among this population varied. The San Joaquin Valley Yokut and the Yuman along the Colorado River are examples of large tribes sharing a common language and possessing a well-defined territory and a degree of political unity. More common was the organization of populations that were essentially village-centered, sometimes called *tribelets*. These groups, too, possessed well-defined territories. Villages ranged in size from 100 to 500 persons, with several villages displaying allegiance to a large central village where the headman or chief resided. Although neither type of social organization permitted chiefs more than limited ceremonial authority, they were most often wise and influential individuals who could galvanize community action, supported by various types of councils made up of lineage elders. While female chiefs were not unknown, the majority were men whose

Kwakiutl house. (Courtesy of Southwest Museum)

succession to office was hereditary. Other authority figures included a shaman, a combination physician, psychologist, herbalist, and spiritual leader; and family lineage heads. Social and economic stratification existed to a varying degree throughout aboriginal California, but it was most pronounced in northwestern California, which in many ways resembled the hierarchical and ordered societies of the Pacific Northwest area.

Because of the varied ecological zones found throughout the state, several regional economic adaptive strategies shaped the economy and food quest. Northern coastal tribes fished, hunted sea mammals, and collected tidelands resources. Riverine and lakeshore dwelling groups hunted, trapped, and fished. Central valley, Plains, and foothill tribes hunted and gathered wild foodstuffs. The greatest variety of regional lifeways and economic activities were found in southern California. The Channel Islands, off the coast of present-day Los Angeles, and adjacent coast were rich in sea-associated resources. Inland groups hunted and collected, while tribes living along the Colorado River and a few neighboring groups practiced the only agriculture found in aboriginal California.

Native Californian worldview centered typically around seeking balance between physical and spiritual well-being of the extended family and tribe. Such balance in both spheres is best understood in terms of reciprocity. For instance, individuals and villages made offerings to the creator and earth spirits and in return expected a favorable relationship between themselves and the natural elements, such as access to game animals, wild foods, favorable winds, sufficient rain, fertility, and the like. Similarly, reciprocity formed the basis for economic relationships among individuals, extended families, and neighboring villages. Each group's territory and its resources were jealously guarded. Trespassing and poaching were serious offenses and were the principal causes of intergroup conflicts that periodically erupted.

### European Contact

The arrival of Europeans in California illustrates the profoundly different worldviews that clashed as various European empires scrambled to exploit the resources and peoples of the Americas. The story of one of the earliest European encounters illustrates this point well. In 1579 the English explorer Francis Drake anchored somewhere off the Marin or Sonoma County coast, in present-day northern California. The astounded Coast Miwok peoples exhibited behavior that seemed both incredible and incomprehensible to the English sailors.

English understandings of that encounter included a number of erroneous assumptions. Records of the Drake expedition refer to the headman of the local Indians as a "king," implying a European-like, highly centralized office of authority that could control both subjects' land and lives. In fact, no such offices of authority existed anywhere in Native California societies. The English also claim this "king" gladly surrendered all "his" territory and sovereignty to an unknown ruler half a world away. Finally, the English concluded the Coast Miwok regarded them as "gods."

The Coast Miwok, on the other hand, viewed all material objects of the pale strangers who arrived on their shores with fear and refused to accept the newcomers' gifts. At the same time, they offered gifts of baskets, food, and other ritual objects. While the men showed considerable awe and reverence toward the strangers, the Native women's behavior bewildered the sailors. Females tore at their cheeks and upper chests, crying and shrieking and throwing themselves on the rocky landscape while walking among the young Englishmen. Following a five-week stay, the newcomers departed, still baffled by the odd reception offered them by the otherwise hospitable Natives.

The mystery of the Indians' peculiar behavior was solved when anthropological data provided by Native traditionalists revealed elements of Coast Miwok culture that provided a reasonable explanation. The Coast Miwok Indians believed the land of the dead lay to the west; in fact, the path to that place passed directly beyond Drake's encampment. The women were exhibiting mourning behavior. The young English sailors had sparse beards (like Native men) and were furthermore deeply tanned from years of open ocean sailing. The English gifts were refused because of strict sanctions about bringing back anything from the land of the dead. Clearly, the Coast Miwok believed they had been visited by long departed ancestors.

### Spanish Colonization

Permanent colonization created a catastrophe of indescribable proportions for the Indians of California. Spanish colonization began in earnest in 1769 with the establishment of a mission in the Native village of Cosoy, later called San Diego by the newcomers. The Spanish institutions of colonization were the military presidios (forts) to protect the Franciscan missionaries and later the Hispanic colonists who established pueblos (civilian towns).

It was the missions, however, that had the greatest impact on the Native population. The Spanish empire's plan was to reduce the numerous free and independent Native hunting-and-collecting villages and societies into a mass of peon laborers. To accomplish this goal, the padres created a chain of twenty-three missions, with two missions on the Colorado River in the extreme southeastern tip of the state and a string along the coast from San Diego to Sonoma in the north. These institutions were much more than churches. When fully functional, they resembled Caribbean plantations. Under Spanish law, once baptized, the neophytes, as the Indians were called, were compelled to move from their Native villages into designated areas adjacent to the mission. Between 1769 and 1836, about 80,000 California Indians were baptized and subjected to the mission labor and evangelization programs of the Spanish Empire.

At the missions, the Indians could be more closely controlled. At the age of five or six, the neophyte children were removed from their families and locked in dorm-like barracks under the vigilance of colonists,

Hupa dwelling. (Courtesy of the Southwest Museum)

which served the dual purpose of indoctrinating the children and ensuring that their parents would not attempt to oppose colonial authority. Indian girls were locked up when not laboring or attending religious services, were freed only after marriage, and, if widowed, were again confined in the female barracks until remarriage or death. Adults were compelled to labor without pay. The soldiers and padres instituted floggings, incarceration, and various labor punishments to compel Native acquiescence to Spanish authority. Neither women nor children were exempt from beatings and other forms of compulsion. One Costanoan Indian neophyte named Lorenzo Asisara reported, "We were always trembling with fear of the lash."

The missions were only supposed to exist for ten years, a time limit the Spanish Crown deemed sufficient to convert the Indians into a disciplined and subservient labor force for a small elite of Spanish males. The sincerity of "religious conversions" under such circumstances is doubtful. Despite these harsh measures, considerable resistance erupted among the "converts."

Three types of resistance developed against the nightmare that Native groups found themselves caught up in. The first and most prevalent form of resistance was passive. Many mission Indians either refused to learn Spanish or feigned ignorance of commands given in that language. Slow and poorly performed labor was widely reported and can be seen today in the construction and work of the old missions. Native laborers covertly drew traditional Indian symbols on fired floor tiles and other surfaces throughout the mission's buildings. Both infanticide and abortions were practiced by Native women unwilling to give birth to children conceived through sexual assaults by the soldiers or to supply a new generation of laborers for the colonists. A fascinating aspect of passive resistance was the periodic outbreak of covert Native religious activities to reverse baptisms or offer solace to the terrified masses of neophytes.

Simply running away from the Franciscan labor mills seemed to be the simplest solution, once the unsavory and oppressive nature of mission life was revealed. But Spanish law and Franciscan practice permitted the soldiers to pursue runaway Indians. The padres kept detailed records of baptized Indians for each village, and squads of soldiers stationed at each mission routinely patrolled the surrounding territories. Furthermore, Native traditions forbade anyone not belonging to a village from demanding refuge there. Non-Christian villages soon learned that if they did offer refuge to runaways, they risked military assaults and hostage-taking. Worse still, the fugitives infected non-Christian village populations with the new diseases contracted at the missions. Murderous waves of epidemic diseases and the general poor health of the neophyte population kept many from even attempting the physical rigors of flight. Nevertheless, many escapes were reported. Thousands of Indian neophytes fled. However, only about 10 percent, or about 8,000 people, permanently escaped the missions.

Overt resistance to Spanish domination took several forms. A type of guerrilla warfare became prevalent before 1820. Charismatic and talented ex-neophytes like the Coast Miwok Pomponio and the Northern Valley Yokut Estanislao organized stock-raiding attacks against mission, presidio, and civilian herds of cattle, horses, and sheep.

Individuals and groups of mission Indians sometimes poisoned the padres. Four padres were poisoned at Mission San Miguel, one of whom died in 1801. In 1811 a San Diego neophyte killed a padre with poison. The next year, Indians at Mission Santa Cruz smothered and castrated a padre there for making an especially terrifying new torture instrument and being unwise enough to announce he would employ it the next Sunday. In 1836 southern California Cahuilla Indians kidnapped the padre at Mission San Gabriel and horsewhipped him as so many of their tribesmen had been whipped.

Mission Indian insurrections were spectacular, and several occurred. The earliest revolt occurred at Mission San Diego in October 1775, when 1,000 Kumeyaay warriors sacked and burned the mission and killed the padre. In 1781 the Quechan Indians living along the banks of the Colorado River utterly destroyed two missions established in their territory just the previous year. In that rebellion, they killed fifty-five colonists, including four padres, thirty-one soldiers, and twenty civilians. That military action denied access to the only known overland route to California from Mexico for the remainder of the Spanish era.

In 1785 San Gabriel Mission neophytes, organized by a female shaman called Toypurina, were thwarted in their attempt to destroy the mission and kill the padres. At her trial, the defiant holy woman declared, "I hate the padres and all of you for living here on my native soil. . . for trespassing upon the lands of my forefathers and despoiling our tribal domains."

That sentiment provoked the last large-scale revolt by mission Indians. The Chumash Indians of the Santa Barbara coast had endured nearly three decades of colonization when, in 1824, neophytes from missions Santa Barbara, San Ynez, and La Purisima rose en masse to protect their lives and regain their lost freedom and sovereignty. A pitched battle ensued at Mission Santa Barbara, and then the Indians fled. Santa Ynez neophytes also abandoned their mission and joined the others from Santa Barbara at Mission La Purisima, which they took over for longer than a month. Although most were eventually persuaded to surrender after a siege and full-scale assault by presidio troops using cannons, a significant number of them absolutely refused to return to the missions and instead sought refuge in the interior, where they issued this defiant message to colonial authorities who pleaded with them to return: "We shall maintain ourselves with what God will provide for us in the open country. Moreover, we are soldiers, stone-masons, carpenters, etc., and we will provide for ourselves by our work."

Despite their defiant sentiments, it was the introduced diseases that ultimately destroyed the majority of Native peoples in contact with the colonists. Native Americans had no immunities to even the most common European childhood diseases. A series of murderous epidemics swept through the mission Indian populations from 1777 to 1833. Thousands of Indian men, women, and children succumbed to the previously unknown diseases. When the missions finally collapsed in 1836, about 100,000 Indians had died.

The independence movement that created the Mexican Republic (1820) forbade the Franciscan padres from compelling labor from the Indians. Between 1834 and 1836 the Mexican government allowed Indians to leave the missions, but corrupt officials conspired to prevent a distribution of developed lands to surviving ex-mission Indians. Those tribesmen whose native territories now included missions, presidios, and pueblos were nearly universally deprived of their lands and forced deeply into debt peonage, which resulted in further powerlessness. Many ex-neophytes fled into the interior or to their former tribal domains. But the landscape had changed profoundly. The horses, mules, sheep, pigs, and goats introduced into the California biosphere ravaged the delicate Native grasses and continued to multiply in alarming numbers. Mission agricultural practices began to systematically squeeze out Native vegetation. The California Indians were less able to live off the land than before Spanish colonization.

Some tribes and village populations had virtually disappeared from the face of the earth. So many lineages had been destroyed that the previous forms of aboriginal leadership hardly existed. Out of this political vacuum evolved new leaders, who assumed much more authority than had been previously allowed any single individual in aboriginal society. Some assumed the Spanish title of *alcalde*, or captain, and adapted aboriginal life to include the hunting and capturing of half-wild horses and mules, which provided food and valued trade items. Patterning their tactics on the mission Indian stock raiders of the recent past, a widespread and lucrative stock-raiding complex emerged in post-mission California. Among these new leaders was an ex-neophyte Plains Miwok called Yozcolo, who terrorized the Hispanic military and civilian populations around southern San Francisco Bay until he was killed in battle near Los Gatos in 1839.

In southern California, Cahuilla, Mohave, and Gabrielino tribesmen joined forces with American mountain men in a decade-long series of raids that devastated the Californios' livestock. One spectacular raid in 1840 involved the theft of more than 3,000 horses from ranches as far north as San Luis Obispo to San Juan Capistrano in the south. The Californios pursuing the stolen horses suffered the indignity of having their mounts stolen while resting. Having no choice, they walked across the desert till they were picked up by another group of ranchers.

The Swiss immigrant Johann August Sutter established a fortress deep in the interior of the Sacramento Valley after promising Mexican authorities to stem the tide of stock-raiding that seriously threatened Mexican authority. Like other colonists of the period, he established a private army of Indians to protect his fort and enslave free Indians.

Despite a steady decline in the Native population throughout this period, the constant onslaught of stock raids began to push back interior Mexican outposts. After 1840, numerous interior ranches were abandoned under threat from the now well-mounted and armed groups of "horse thief Indians." Even Sutter began futile efforts to sell his fortress to the Mexican government after costly campaigns with interior Miwok warriors. But the Mexican government had, by 1845, lost control of the actions of its own citizens. The authority of the Mexican Republic was about to collapse. Meanwhile, both disease and violence had taken grim toll of Native lives. By 1845, little over 150,000 California Indians survived the Mexican Republic's occupation of their territories.

The Bear Flag Revolt and the Mexican War (1846 to 1848) brought momentous changes for the Native peoples of California. The majority of Indians who were involved in that conflict allied themselves with the Americans. Company H of the California Battalion was made up of central Valley Miwok and Yokut warriors.

In Southern California loyalties were split. Some, like the mountain Cahuilla chief Juan Antonio, fought for the Mexican Republic, while others participated on the U.S. side in the Battle for Los Angeles in 1847. However the new U.S. occupation brought yet more death and labor exploitation to Native groups, whatever their loyalties.

Shortly after the Treaty of Guadelupe Hidalgo ended the Mexican-American War in 1848, a flood of gold miners descended upon California. Most of the Sierra Nevada and foothill tribesmen had been only indirectly affected by Hispanic colonization efforts, which were concentrated along the coast, but now they would bear the brunt of an incredibly violent horde of immigrants. Early in the Gold Rush, a few Indians were employed by miners or mined gold on their own. Soon Indians found themselves hunted like wild game.

Worse still was a series of state laws passed in the mid-1850s that virtually enslaved Indians and institutionalized the legal kidnapping of Indian children for labor and sexual exploitation, despite the fact that California entered the Union as a "free state" in 1851. At the same time, the federal government was negotiating treaties with California Indians in 1851 and 1852. These treaties promised California Indians 7.5 million acres of land in exchange for surrendering the remainder of the state. A deluge of protests from non-Indian Californians fearing that the treaty lands might contain gold was sufficient to assure the treaties' defeat in the U.S. Senate, which must ratify all treaties. Afterward, the bewildered and now hunted Indians were subjected to the earliest form of reservation life. The federal government began establishing reservations in the state in 1851. They were located on military reserves, where supposedly the Native population might be protected by the army from U.S. citizens.

The early government reserves in reality served fewer than 2,000 Indians at any given time. The vast majority of California Indians survived the best they could, withdrawing into remote and marginal areas and attempting to avoid contact with U.S. settlers, but violence against them continued, ranging from casual homicide of individuals to vigilante raids and the occasional army massacre.

Protesting the taxation of their small cattle herd, the Kupa Indians of southern California fought a war against the citizens of San Diego in 1851. The Hupa Indians to the north successfully fought vigilante and militia campaigns until 1864, when they were granted a reservation of their own, now the largest in the state. The last and largest war against California Indians was fought against the Modoc Indians of northeastern California. Under the leadership of Captain Jack (see his biography), fifty Modoc warriors and their families held off an army of

Miwok dwelling. (Courtesy of the Southwest Museum)

over 3,000 for nearly a year. In the end, Jack and three others surrendered and were hanged by orders of a paramilitary court. Captain Jack and Schochin John were decapitated following their deaths, and their heads were sent to Washington, D.C. and eventually wound up in the Smithsonian Institution.

By 1870 a new religious movement, called the Ghost Dance, swept west from Nevada, predicting the end of the world and promising the return of dead relatives and the game animals. Desperate Natives who had experienced first-hand appalling widespread death, violence, and now real starvation, found the doctrines especially appealing. The movement lasted about two years and revitalized the Kuksu and Hesi ceremonies among the Pomo, Patwin, and neighboring groups. It also developed a new class of spiritual leaders called dreamer doctors. Finally, the Ghost Dance prophecy of the end of the world proved true, for the Indian world was gone.

It is no coincidence that the Ghost Dance swept through California when it did. Just prior to that event, the federal government had inaugurated a new policy to reform the widespread corruption in the Office of Indian Affairs (renamed the Bureau of Indian Affairs, or BIA, in the late 1940s). Part of that plan, called President Ulysses S. Grant's Peace Policy of 1869, called for the introduction of educational programs for Indian children. However, that policy once more unleashed hordes of missionaries upon the Indians to "save" them. Native ceremonies were outlawed on many reservations in a misguided effort to make Indians adopt U.S. culture and lifeways.

The federal campaign to educate Indian children was launched aggressively in 1879. Off-reservation boarding schools took Indian children to schools thousands of miles from their homes and subjected them to military-type discipline. Native languages were forbidden, corporal punishment was used freely, and starchy foods dominated their diets. The dormitories echoed with children's homesick and lonely cries. The legacy of these social engineering policies was the creation of several generations of Indians who, abducted from their tribes, returned home virtually strangers, unable to communicate with their elders and ignorant of the skills and knowledge to continue practicing their culture. Even more evil was the resulting lack of parenting skills in the generations of Indian mothers and fathers. Preventing such practical skills from developing is an effective element in the plan to destroy a people.

The next approach to assimilating Natives was to divide tribal lands on reservations into tiny private parcels. This federal program, called the Dawes Allotment Act of 1887, was intended to introduce the Indians to private ownership of property. If an Indian moved onto his allotment, cut his hair, surrendered his children to the boarding schools, severed his tribal ties, and did exactly as told by the Indian agent for twenty years, he could receive title to his allotment, pay taxes on his land, and become a citizen of the United States. However, like other tribal peoples, California Indians considered this act yet another attack on their religious beliefs about the earth and the tribe's relationship to it. In practice, it proved to be a tool to deprive Indians of their remaining lands, and, almost everywhere, Indians opposed the Dawes Act. Nevertheless, the Office of Indian Affairs missionaries and so-called reformers were unrelenting in these efforts and countless others to make the Indians into what they considered acceptable people.

By 1900 fewer than 18,000 California Indians survived after 130 years of colonization and foreign domination. This staggering population decline left the Indians dazed, reeling, and deeply demoralized. Hunger, destitution, homelessness, unemployment, and discrimination were widespread, yet a number of Native leaders worked diligently for their communities.

Following in the path of the activist Indian Rights Association of Philadelphia, a group of southern California citizens organized the Sequoya League. They assisted the Kupa Indians, who had lost a bid in the Supreme Court to keep their ancestral home, now called Warner's Hot Springs in the mountainous interior of San Diego County. Through their efforts, Kupa leaders reluctantly selected a new home nearby at a place called Pala. Similar groups in northern California helped secure small homesite reservations, called rancherias, for homeless Pomo Indians at Manchester near Point Arena in Mendocino County and another at Chico for Wintun Indians.

One of the choice ironies of the boarding school experience was the unexpected development of a pan-tribal consciousness that emerged among Indian youth, which gave birth to pan-Indian reform groups. The first reform group to actually include California Indians was the Mission Indian Federation (MIF), founded in 1919. The MIF relentlessly attacked incompetent Indian administration officials and policies. Even urban Indians in Los Angeles had an active chapter. The group worked for more autonomy for tribal governments, full civil rights for Indians, protection of Indian water rights, opposition to the Dawes Act, and the elimination of the Bureau of Indian Affairs. In 1921 fifty-seven MIF leaders were arrested for conspiracy against the government for their opposition to allotment. Eventually all charges were dropped.

The first all-Indian reform group, formed in Northern California by Stephen Knight and other Pomo Indians, was the California Indian Brotherhood. That group sought rancherias for homeless Indians and integration of Indian children into public schools with free lunches and clothing assistance. This far-sighted group even sought opportunities for college education for Indian youth.

The problems confronting twentieth-century California Indian survivors had many similarities, with some variation from community to community. One issue united them, however, like no other—the enduring sense of injustice regarding the unratified federal treaties of 1851 and 1852. There was little incentive for the treaties to be honored, since Indians had no voting rights and no way to pressure elected officials. But Native peoples never forgot those solemn promises and were determined to seek redress. Virtually all reform groups as well as individual tribes sought some kind of solution for more than a half a century. Eventually, two settlements were reached. The first in 1944 eventually paid $150 to every California Indian who could prove biological legacy to an Indian alive in 1850. A second effort through the Indian Claims Commission (a federal entity established on the basis of the pioneering claims of the California Indians) resulted in payment of only 47¢ an acre in compensation for lands outside treaty areas. Despite protests, the government per capita payments to individuals resulted in less than $800 per person paid in 1968. Few desperately poor Indians could turn down even that meager amount. However, a small number of Indians refused to cash those checks in hopes of yet a new settlement.

Education remains another important contemporary issue. Federal off-reservation boarding schools were supplemented by reservation boarding schools and day schools before 1900. These schools at least allowed families to remain in contact, but chronic illness and lack of clothing, food, and even shoes caused considerable absenteeism, which eventually closed many of them. By 1917, the public schools began to experience increased enrollment of Indian children. When Congress gave U.S. citizenship to all Indians in 1924, a gradual transfer of Indian students to public schools followed. But academic success did not. Racial

Spring Rancheria (Cahuilla). (Courtesy of H. Vincent Moses, Ph.D., curator of history, Riverside Municipal Museum)

and cultural prejudices in textbooks and among teachers led to isolation, shame, and feelings of low self esteem for Indian children and set them up for failure. The classrooms became battlegrounds where Indian children had to endure the negative experience or fight back. The latter course ensured a perpetual cycle of academic failure, condemning generations of Indian children to economic hardship and unemployment.

One important focus of reform efforts was health access. While seven Indian hospitals had been established at boarding schools and other sites by 1930, local hospitals often refused to treat the Native population, claiming that was the federal government's responsibility. A growing chorus of criticism prompted the establishment of a separate division of health within the Bureau of Indian Affairs in 1924. Public health nurses were then allowed to provide services to Indians. However, services were still denied to unrecognized and homeless Indians, leaving as many as one-third of the Indian population without medical care. A new wave of indignation was forcefully expressed in a federal hearing conducted in 1929, but ironically this hearing only confirmed a 1912 survey that the health of the Indian population was dismal. Ultimately, the loss of their land base and food resources crippled their ability to rebound.

Approximately thirty reservations had been established by 1900. The critical needs of northern California Indians for lands were addressed in a series of congressional acts to provide homesites for landless Indians. By 1930 an additional thirty-six parcels of federal trust properties called rancherias were established. They had the same status as reservations but were substantially smaller, and they lacked developed water sources. Indians have been critical of the Bureau of Indian Affairs for failing to protect water rights, a problem that has plagued reservation leaders to this day. Allotment, or forced division of Indian trust lands into individual parcels, was pursued by the BIA despite the fact that these parcels were often of very small size. Considerable evidence points to the common practice of manipulating tribal leaders through assignment of choice reservation lands to Indians willing to cooperate with government interests. Numerous abuses and a national scandal concerning loss of millions of acres of allotted lands finally prompted Congress to act. The new Roosevelt administration's Indian Reorganization Act of

Sensioni Cibimoat, basket maker from Warmer's Ranch, 1903. (Courtesy of Security Pacific Collection, Los Angeles Public Library)

1934 ended allotment and permitted formation of tribal governments. Despite this progress, however, tribal governments effectively remained under economic control of the Bureau of Indian Affairs.

## Termination

The end of the Second World War (1945) heralded an era of anticommunist xenophobia that ultimately stalled the slow but steady reform in the Bureau of Indian Affairs. The Hoover Commission study of 1948 recommended severing all federal relations with Indian tribes and peoples, including federal assistance to Indian peoples, whose poverty the government had engineered in the first place. That policy would be called Termination. The program called for an end to all health, education, and welfare assistance provided by the federal government and envisioned a division of tribal lands to individuals. In reality, it was a resurrection of the discredited Dawes Allotment Act of 1887.

California Indians were an early target; after allotment Indian land would eventually be subject to state property taxation. Until then, immunity from state taxation allowed poverty-stricken Indians to retain their lands. Taxing them would bring about the final dispossession of the land through tax defaults. Furthermore,

Barona baseball team, 1935. (Courtesy of Barona Cultural Center Museum)

dispossession would bring disintegration to Native California's tribes, communities, and cultures—and the so-called Indian problem would finally be solved, at least as far as the government was concerned. By 1952 Congress had enthusiastically embraced termination. The BIA sold over 1,200 allotments. In the following year, California came under Public Law 280, an act that would further termination goals by turning over civil and criminal jurisdiction from federal authorities to state and local authorities. At first, state and local governments were enthusiastic, envisioning an expanded tax base. However, after several years of study, it became apparent that the burden of services it would have to assume would far outweigh any tax revenues.

Consequently, their enthusiasm began to cool rapidly, though not before Congress passed the Rancheria Act of 1958. This act provided for reservation and rancheria members to decide whether to accept or reject termination. Federal authorities descended upon the isolated and powerless rancheria residents with exaggerated promises of new housing, road and domestic water system improvements, and even college scholarships for Native children. Oblivious to the looming threat of tax defaults, the BIA eventually convinced thirty-six of the most isolated and least sophisticated California Indian groups into committing tribal and cultural suicide by accepting termination. Sure enough, by 1970, 5,000 acres of tribal lands were lost to tax defaults and forced sales. The stunned and reeling tribesmen lost their recognition as Indians, and cultural and social decay of Indian community institutions accelerated.

## Cultural Revitalization

The modern era of California Indian affairs can be divided into civil rights and cultural survival. The national sweep of the civil rights era from the mid-1960s to the present afforded new opportunities for national attention to the cause of the American Indians. On college campuses, racial minorities and their supporters demanded the hiring of minority faculty and staff, along with aggressive recruiting of minority students. The first college to establish a Native American studies program was San Francisco State University. The program's faculty, staff, and students were largely made up of non-California Indians relocated to the San Francisco Bay Area from other states, under part of a national termination program. Followed shortly by the University of California, Berkeley, and the University of California, Los Angeles (UCLA), these programs provided a multidisciplinary approach to the study of American Indians in the past and present.

Most importantly, the new Native studies programs addressed the future of American Indians and tribalism. The idea of actually controlling the future and shaping federal Indian policy made for an intoxicating euphoria that provided a kind of self-assurance not witnessed among Native leaders since the Indian wars of the last century. It furthermore produced a new generation of leaders, pressing legal and other avenues toward creating self-sufficient and responsible Native communities, new scholars contributing to the academic study of the American Indians, and numerous public school teachers in classrooms throughout the state. Both UCLA and UC Berkeley have developed important scholarly journals, the *American Indian Quarterly* and the *American Indian Culture and Research Journal*.

More access to health and legal services also emerged during this period. The California Rural Indian Health Board was established in 1968 to fund several demonstrations projects in fifteen rural and reservation communities, restoring services that in many cases had been denied California Indians since 1956. Legal assistance on issues of land, water, and civil rights became available as part of the U.S. government's War on Poverty programs of the 1970s. California Indian Legal Services strengthened tribal ability to oppose still-archaic BIA policies. They continue to provide important leverage in fighting for civil rights of Indian individuals and tribes.

This era also gave rise to a succession of land occupations by Native peoples in California, setting a national trend. In fall 1969 fewer than 100 Indian college students from UCLA, UC Berkeley, and San Francisco State landed on Alcatraz Island to reclaim that abandoned federal prison as Indian land, causing a media sensation around the world. The Native Americans cleverly pointed out the island was just like reservations: no water, no electricity, no jobs! They also pointed out that it was isolated from the wealth that surrounds it. At last, Native peoples had discovered a vehicle that would focus attention on the current conditions of America's aboriginal people. Following the Alcatraz occupation, other land occupations occurred, such as the protest attempted by the Pit River Indians at a public utility campground in Shasta County in 1971. The Pomo Indian occupation of an abandoned national defense radio listening station in rural Sonoma County resulted in the establishment of Ya-Ka-Ama (our land), an educational and Native plant center. A similar occupation near the University of California at Davis resulted in the establishment of a fully accredited American Indian junior college called Deganaweda-Quetzelquatl University.

Unprecedented population growth in California during the 1970s and 1980s resulted in the construction of millions of new homes and businesses, unearthing thousands of California Indian burials and occupation sites. Traditionalists were dismayed that archaeologists intended to add the findings to existing inventories of skeletons and objects found in Indian burials, long neglected and seldom studied, gathering dust in warehouses, archaeology labs, and campus basements. Anthropologists' standard defense was that they were the Indians' best friends and so much valuable information could be gained from the "data," as they euphemistically referred to the remains of Native ancestors. The Indians demanded to know why these human remains continue to be removed from the ground and why it only happens to Indians.

About this time, it was discovered that the skull of nationally known Modoc war leader (1872) Captain Jack was part of the physical anthropology collection of the Smithsonian Institution in Washington, D.C. Outrage over this case and thousands of other lesser known Indian skeletons and burial goods led to a national program of repatriation of the thousands and thousands of Indian skeletons to their tribes of origin. In 1978 Governor Edmund G. Brown, Jr. created the Native American Heritage Commission (NAHC), which had the responsibility of mitigating human remains issues associated with construction. The NAHC attempted to compel universities and other state agencies holding human remains to submit plans for the

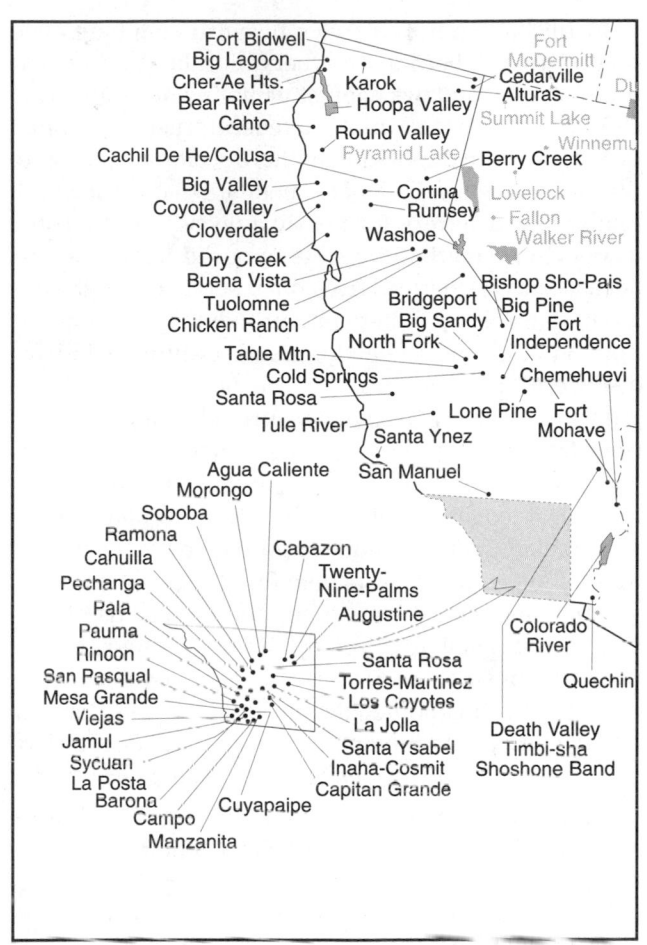

Map of Contemporary California Indian tribes. (Courtesy of the UCLA American Indian Studies Center)

ultimate disposition of the remains and associated burial goods. The NAHC has become an effective clearing house for these matters. Recent federal laws of 1990 mandate that federally funded museums inventory their American Indian human skeleton collections and develop a plan for repatriation to appropriate tribes. While a few archaeologists have argued against this policy, most agree that little new scientific information has been developed from collections that have already been in their possession for as long as a century. Native peoples often counter, if these human remains indeed possess such valuable data, why, then, are they not being systematically studied? For traditional peoples, it is a simple matter of dignity and the respect all citizens expect of their government and its laws.

In 1999 the brain of Ishi, the last Yahi Indian, was "discovered" at the Smithsonian Institution where it had been apparently "given" by University of California Berkeley professor of anthropology Alfred L. Kroeber. Ishi was the last member of his tribe, which had been

exterminated most violently between 1865 and 1871. Ishi lived a life of concealment until he was captured in Oroville in 1911. He was taken to the University of California by anthropologists to study. There he was made a janitor and, at the behest of medical doctors, "entertained" tuberculosis patients and other seriously sick people at the university's medical school next door. Recent efforts by a group of California Indians called the Butte County Native American Cultural Committee petitioned the Smithsonian and the cemetery that held Ishi's ashes to repatriate them. The reuniting of Ishi's preserved brain and ashes occurred in September 2000. His remains were buried in secret and without publicity in his rugged wilderness homeland.

Finally, the appalling loss of California Indian languages was documented in Professor Leanne Hinton's provocative 1998 study entitled *Flutes of Fire*. Since that time several language renewal programs have blossomed. One of the more recent organizations is the Advocates for Indigenous California Languages. They have developed programs statewide to save languages that are in danger of disappearing in the next few years. They have recently received private foundation support and are now funded by the California Council for the Humanities.

### Tribal Recognition

In retrospect, it seems miraculous that Native cultures in California survived at all; yet they have not only survived, but also have undergone a renaissance. Indian education centers throughout the state have developed Native language, culture, and dance classes. The first tribally controlled museum was established by Cahuilla traditionalists on the Morongo Indian Reservation in 1964. The Malki Museum also developed an impressive publication program, including the scholarly quarterly *The Journal of California Anthropology*. Several other reservation communities have followed suit.

In 1987 an entirely unique publication, called *News From Native California*, appeared. The widely read quarterly covers history, ethnography, current events, legislation, and the arts. Another event unique to California is the annual California Indian Conference, established in 1984. This event brings together scholars, Native traditionalists, and experts at state and federal levels to share their research and interests in the past, present, and future of California Indians. Usually, it is hosted at a major college; in 1992 it was held at Sonoma State University and in 2000 it was held at Chaffey College.

Recently, California Indian artists, both traditional and contemporary, have established a national reputation in the larger Indian art world. While late nineteenth- and early twentieth-century California Indian basketmakers have long been acknowledged as the finest in the world, a well-documented decline in the number of practitioners occurred over the last sixty years. With recent new interest in that important Native art form, a new generation of Native basketmakers now holds annual gatherings, notably at Ya-Ka-Ama, and promises to preserve and extend the artistic boundaries of their art. More contemporary California Indian artists such as Jean LaMarr, Frank La Pena, Harry Fonseca, L. Frank Manriquez, James Luna, and Kathleen Smith, among others are considered on the cutting edge of the modern Indian art world.

Despite the declaration by anthropologists, historians, and other writers that several California Indian tribes and cultures are extinct, it is well known among Native peoples that many of these groups are not, in fact, gone. Some have never been recognized by the government, like the Gabrielino and Juaneno of southern California. Others, like the Guidiville band of Pomo Indians, were terminated in 1966 and are seeking reinstatement or recognition. These disenfranchised groups have organized themselves and are currently aggressively pursuing their cause in the U.S. Congress.

### Tribal Gaming

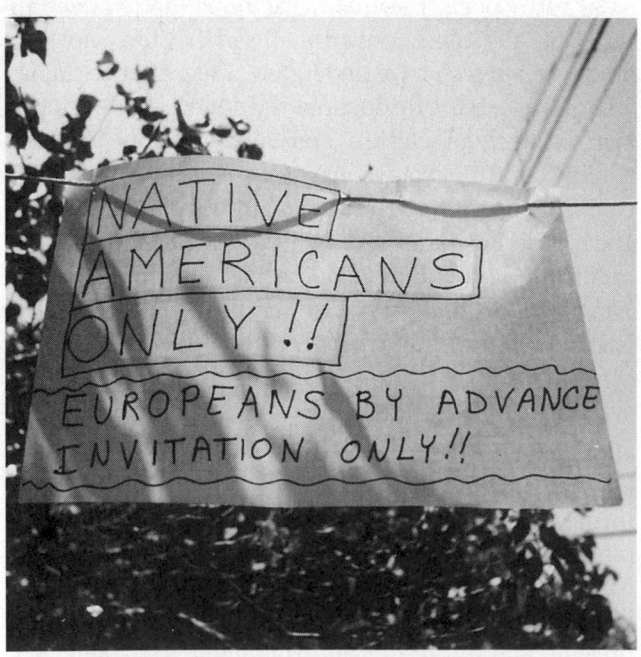

Los Angeles-area Natives celebrate Columbus Day. (Photo by Mary G. Wentz)

In 1986 a handful of tribes began Indian bingo and other forms of betting on reservation lands. This was legal because all laws against gambling are state laws. Only a few state laws apply to federal trust lands. State officials were in opposition to this development despite the fact the state had been benefiting from a multimillion dollar lottery for nearly a decade. Some tribal leaders believed that the state opposed Indian gaming because income derived from on–reservation businesses are not taxable by either state or federal governments. For the first time since statehood, California Indians discovered a reservation source of income. Gaming grew rapidly and literally transformed gaming reservations from pockets of hardcore poverty and unemployment into thriving robust communities. Among the 106 federally recognized tribes 42 have gaming facilities. By 1996 Indian casino revenues approached an estimated $1.4 billion annually. Also benefiting were nearby non-Indian communities who generated thousands of jobs and an additional $237 million of taxable income from vendors, construction projects, and employment taxes. Despite these phenomenal gains it would take decades of such prosperity to wipe out more than a century of federal neglect and orchestrated dependency.

Critics led by Nevada casino owners and California state politicians soon attacked. State officials felt powerless and Nevada interests were stung by the perceived loss of income from California gamblers. These forces combined in an attempt to shut down California Indian gaming. Governor Pete Wilson refused to negotiate compacts with gaming tribes as federal Indian gaming laws required. An impasse resulted in 1997, and the next year the tribes organized the California Self Reliance Initiative to mandate the governor cooperate with gaming tribes in developing compacts. The result was a statewide initiative Proposition 5. Thanks to a hugely successful campaign, voters overwhelmingly passed the law. Not to be defeated by the will of the people, Nevada gambling interests and frustrated California politicians challenged the constitutionality of the new law and tied it up in the courts. A second more carefully constructed initiative was placed on the ballot in the year 2000 and it again was passed by a voter margin of two to one in favor of Proposition 1A. That same election saw the removal of Governor Wilson, and the installment of a new administration willing to work with gaming tribes. Some tribes are now investing in diversified businesses outside of gaming.

At present the casino tribes fund a state bureaucracy that will help regulate Indian gaming. Under the new law non-gaming tribes will share a percentage of gaming profits. The generosity of the gaming tribes has already been demonstrated. Tribal gaming profits provided many services for non-gaming tribes including developing infrastructure for several remote and isolated reservations and rancherias. Gaming tribes have created scholarships and donated large sums of money to education projects. For the first time in nearly two centuries California Indians can look into the future and see an end to the extreme poverty and powerlessness and despair their ancestors endured.

At present, about 201,000 California Indians live in the state. Perhaps as many as 60,000 live on reservations and rancherias. The remainder live in nearby towns and cities. And while about two-thirds have some degree of non-Indian blood in their racial make-up, most proudly claim their heritage.

*Edward Castillo*
*Sonoma (California) State University*

## ◆ ABORIGINAL PEOPLES IN CANADA

Canadian aboriginal peoples, around 3 percent of today's population, were crucial partners of the French and English in founding what has become Canada. The political tension between the English and French continues to be a key Canadian dynamic, although English Canada is now multicultural Canada, and aboriginal peoples have inserted themselves into the debate surrounding modern Canadian identity. The role of aboriginal peoples was acknowledged in the Canadian Constitution Act of 1982, which states that "the existing aboriginal and treaty rights of the aboriginal peoples of Canada are hereby recognized and affirmed" (Section 35.1) and that "in this Act, 'aboriginal peoples of Canada' includes the Indian, Inuit and Métis peoples of Canada" (Section 35.2). However, in the twenty years since these provisions were given constitutional recognition, no meeting of the minds has been reached—politically, judicially, or publicly—about what they mean in practice.

The constitutional recognition of aboriginal peoples and their rights occurred only after a protracted struggle on the part of aboriginal leaders to convince federal and provincial governments of the legitimacy of their claims. While Section 35 signifies a landmark achievement for Canadian Indians, Inuit, and Métis, it is only one step in their quest for a greater degree of control over their future. A snapshot album of Canadian aboriginal communities in the year 2000 reveals grounds for hope, discouragement, and general uncertainty over aboriginal participation in mainstream Canadian culture and society. Still, one immediately visible break from the past has been the migration of aboriginal individuals away from isolated reserves and into Canadian cities and towns; approximately half the aboriginal population of Canada now lives in urban areas.

Another visible demographic is the youth of this population—one-third are under the age of fifteen—with a population growth rate unmatched by other segments of Canadian society. Attention paid to aboriginal issues within the mainstream population has also increased, resulting from the publicity generated by a series of controversies over the relationship between aboriginal Canada and the rest of the country: competing natural resource claims, calls for separate justice systems, revelation of residential school abuses, and resolution of long-standing land claims. Meanwhile, with less attention, aboriginal communities and organizations have assumed responsibility for their children's education, developed homegrown mechanisms to demand accountability from their leaders, and fostered a loosely confederated aboriginal financial sector. Canada's historical effort to assimilate aboriginal peoples was abandoned some time ago, and today aboriginal communities are taking different paths on their journey into the future.

### Aboriginal Peoples: A Profile

Although Indians, Métis, and Inuit are collectively recognized as aboriginal peoples, their varied legal status and socioeconomic circumstances result in different capacities to pursue their respective agendas. Indians in Canada have traditionally been subdivided into three groups: status, treaty, and non-status. A status Indian is a person registered or entitled to be registered as an Indian for purposes of the Indian Act, which was first passed in 1876 and which sets forth a governing regime for Canadian Indian bands. Status Indians are members of the 633 bands across Canada. Bands are legal-administrative bodies that correspond generally to traditional tribal and kinship groups. Unlike the practice in the United States, different tribes in Canada were not placed together on the same reserve and groups of Indians were not relocated far from their ancestral homelands. Most bands are located south of the sixtieth parallel on reserves within the provinces. The Department of Indian Affairs estimates that there are 620,000 status Indians in Canada (1996).

Treaty Indians are those persons who are registered members of, or can prove descent from, a band that signed a treaty. Most status Indians are treaty Indians, except those living in areas not covered by treaties, such as most of the province of British Columbia.

Non-status Indians are those persons of Indian ancestry and cultural affiliation who have lost their right to be registered under the Indian Act. The most common reason for loss of status was marriage between a registered Indian woman and a non-Indian. Loss of status has also occurred in other ways, such as voluntary renunciation, compulsory enfranchisement to non-Indian status, and failure of government officials to include some Indian families in the registry. Indians who served in the military during the world wars, for example, usually became enfranchised, losing their status as Indians. Non-status Indians do not have a distinct constitutional standing but are grouped with the Métis for jurisdictional and public policy purposes. The situation for many non-status Indians changed in 1985, when the federal government amended the Indian Act with Bill C-31 to restore registered Indian status to those women and their children who had lost it through marriage. Aboriginal women's groups welcomed this change. However, the response of Indian communities to Bill C-31 was not uniformly favorable; many Indian bands saw the bill as an unwarranted intrusion on their right to control band membership and doubted their capacity to provide housing and other services to returning members. The reinstatement process was largely completed by 1991, adding approximately 92,000 Indians to the registry.

The Inuit are those aboriginal people who inhabit Canada's northernmost regions, including the Mackenzie Delta, the Northwest Territories, the northern coasts of Hudson Bay, the Arctic Islands, Labrador, and parts of northern Quebec. The Inuit were classified with registered Indians for program and jurisdictional purposes in 1939 by a decision of the Supreme Court of Canada. They are the smallest group of Canadian aboriginal people, numbering around 41,000 as of 1996, and are by far the dominant population in the new territory of Nunavut.

The Métis are people of mixed Indian and non-Indian ancestry; to the Métis National Council, they are more specifically the descendants of the Métis community that developed on the prairies in the 1800s and of individuals who received land grants and/or scrip (a certificate for the value of a parcel of land) under the Manitoba Act of 1870 or the Dominion Lands Act of 1879. The 1996 census set Canada's Métis population at 210,000, but Métis spokesmen suggest the number is larger. Approximately two-thirds of the Métis live in the provinces of Manitoba, Saskatchewan, and Alberta and in the Northwest Territories; the remainder are scattered throughout the rest of the country.

Finally, although aboriginal peoples remain widely distributed throughout rural Canada, recent decades have witnessed a growing migration of aboriginal people to urban areas. In western urban centers such as Vancouver, Edmonton, Calgary, Regina, Saskatoon, and Winnipeg, aboriginal people comprise a significant portion of the population. In these and other cities the Native Friendship Center is a key liaison agency connecting individual aboriginal people to urban services, including housing, employment, cultural programs, court workers, counselors, and elders. The relationship between urban aboriginals and their communities of origin is sometimes problematic. Few non-urban reserves have a presence in the city, although tribal councils—political confederations of reserves—sometimes do. One flash point is voting rights for urban band members in on-reserve band elections. The policy of many reserves to deny absent members voting rights has been struck down by Canadian courts. Still, many urban aboriginal people participate neither in their own community politics nor in the municipal politics of the city or town where they are located and are left without a political voice.

## The Indians

When Europeans first reached the Canadian east coast, every part of Canada was occupied by diverse Indian societies well established in their respective territories. On the Atlantic were the Beothuk, Mi'kmaq, and Malecite, whose economy centered on tidal and river fishing. Around the Great Lakes were farmers—including the Huron and Iroquois—who lived in villages and grew crops such as corn and tobacco. On the prairies the Assiniboine, Plains Cree, Blackfoot, Sarcee, Saulteaux, and Gros Ventre followed the buffalo. On the coastal mountains, seashore, and islands of British Columbia, salmon was the main source of food for the many different peoples who lived there. Stretching across the country throughout the northern forests were the Montagnais, Naskapi, Abenaki, Ottawa, Algonquin, Ojibwa, and Cree, nomadic peoples who hunted and fished. North of the tree line were the seafaring Inuit. Some of the regions were populated by linguistically homogeneous cultures; in others, such as British Columbia, a wide variety of languages were spoken within a small geographic area.

Today the Assembly of First Nations (AFN), formerly the National Indian Brotherhood, represents all but the Inuit at the national level. Twentieth-century Indian political activity in Canada began locally and regionally, national organizing of Indians being forbidden by the 1927 Indian Act. Even today regional influences are apparent in the operation of the AFN, which is composed of the 633 band chiefs from across the country. One important issue dividing AFN members is the difference between treaty and non-treaty regions of the country. Descendants of treaty signatories are in a position to make claims which other Indians cannot, and there have been times when one entire treaty group has pulled its support from the AFN for internal strategic reasons. As demographic shifts have seen increasing numbers of Indians migrating into Canadian cities, the assembly's position has also been challenged by urban-based organizations such as the Congress of Aboriginal Peoples. A final destabilizing force is the fact that Canadian Indian bands vary considerably in their appetite for political militancy. The AFN National Chief sets the tone for relationships with Ottawa (the national capital) during his or her three-year term—conciliation or confrontation—and maintaining solidarity among this diverse constituency can be a challenge. Elected in July 2000, the current National Chief, Matthew Coon Come of Quebec, came to office with a high-profile past of political activism and a pledge to carry Canadian aboriginal demands to an international audience.

**Indian-Government Relationships.** Modern-day Canada was established by the British North America Act of 1867. Prior to that point, relationships between Indians and Europeans involved the French and British Crowns, which began negotiating Indian treaties as early as the 1600s. These early agreements were "peace and friendship" treaties involving military matters. Later treaties, however, involved the surrender by Indians of large tracts of land. This policy was articulated in the Royal Proclamation of 1763, which was issued by King George III after the end of the war between England and France over their North American acquisitions. The main purpose of the proclamation was to establish governments for the territories that England acquired from France; however, the last five paragraphs made reference to Indians, reserving certain areas of the continent for them and providing an elaborate mechanism by which Indian land could be surrendered to the Crown.

The Robinson-Huron and Robinson-Superior treaties, concluded in 1850 in Ontario, established the model for the later land surrender treaties numbered one to eleven. The final treaty, Number 11, was signed in 1921. Upon the surrender of land, Indian reserves were established according to a formula, which since Treaty Number 3 has been one "section" (640 acres) of land for every family of five. The numbered treaties also typically contained a guarantee of Indian hunting rights on surrendered, unoccupied Crown land; made provisions for education and agricultural development on the reserves; and included a system of annuities. What the various signatories to the treaties understood themselves to be agreeing to at the time has since become a

matter for debate. Some Indian leaders argue that their people have been duped and cheated during the treaty-making process and that more lands, rights, and benefits are due. On the other hand, the idea that contemporary relations between Indian peoples and the Canadian government should be bound by these historical documents is also under attack.

The treaty relationship between Indian peoples and the Canadian state is paralleled by another legal relationship. Section 91(24) of the British North America Act established a federal trust or fiduciary duty toward Indian peoples and lands. Like treaty obligations, this is subject to considerable debate. Put simply, the duty suggests that the federal government is obliged to see that the best interests of Indians are served where the management and protection of Indian proprietary interests are involved. The obligations thus created have experienced an uneven history of compliance on the part of the federal government and have become the subject of much-watched court cases, considering, for example, the federal obligation to manage Indian oil and gas royalties effectively or to ensure that Indian real estate revenues reflect fair market value.

**Governing Indian Communities.** To fulfill its responsibilities to Indians under Section 91(24), the federal government created a separate legal regime for them by passing the Indian Act, 1876. This act underwent major revisions in 1951 and 1985. The Indian Act had two major objectives: to establish a regime for administering the affairs of Indians and to create the conditions for their assimilation into the dominant Euro-Canadian society. The Indian Act established a system of Indian reserves, termed *reservations* in the United States, which included a system of Indian governments. Importantly, the Indian Act did not, and still does not, recognize Canadian Indians as retaining any right to self-government, inherent, constitutional, or otherwise. In setting up the reserve system, the act did several things. First, it defined legally who is entitled to be a status Indian. Second, it established a system for the management of Indian lands and monies. Third, it created legal units known as band governments to administer reserve communities and endowed band governments with a number of powers that would ordinarily be exercised by Canadian municipal governments. Fourth, it created a national bureaucracy through which the Department of Indian Affairs provides a complex of services that other Canadians receive from provincial governments, such as health care, education, and law enforcement.

A significant effect of the Indian Act was the imposition on Indian bands of a chief and council elective system that in structure and underlying principle resembles a non-Indian municipal government. With the

Haida village of Skidgate. (Courtesy of Canadian Museum of Civilization)

exception of a few Indian bands, most notably the Mohawk, who fought vigorously to retain their traditional governing methods, the band council elective system is widely established within Indian communities across Canada. However, by the year 2000 the shortcomings of this system became manifestly, and painfully, apparent, particularly with respect to the financial management regimes the system has produced. Grassroots aboriginal organizations have sprung up across the country to call individual Indian leaders to account for the millions of dollars that pass through their hands, while the members of some bands live in poverty and squalor. Various mainstream factions have turned their attention to the issue, too, with forensic audits, criminal charges, and third-party management resulting in some cases. Still others point the finger at the Department of Indian Affairs for failing in its responsibilities to Indian peoples.

The colonial nature of the Indian Act, which established these band governments, remains essentially unchanged today. Ultimate authority over the management of Indian lands and finances remains with the minister of Indian Affairs, should his or her office choose to exercise it. For some years the federal government has been devolving authority to Indian bands over individual programs such as housing, health, schools, and child welfare; still, the Indian Act remains a thorn in the side of many Indian bands. Other options are open for individual bands, however, and some have chosen and negotiated a future unencumbered by the act.

**The Provinces.** As the Canadian federal state has evolved since 1867, the ten Canadian provinces have become more powerful economically and politically—although not uniformly so—and their jurisdiction over various aspects of Canadian life has increased. This jurisdictional expansion, notably over natural resources, affects aboriginal peoples. The jurisdiction of the provinces over Indians is tied to Section 91(24) of the Canadian Constitution and the Indian Act's Section 88, which subjects Indians to all provincially enacted laws that apply generally to provincial citizens. Indians are therefore considered provincial citizens for purposes of these laws. Only in instances where such laws conflict with provisions of the Indian Act, or if they touch rights under treaty, or if they are discriminatory in respect to treatment of Indians, are such laws of general application superseded. Over time, the interpretation of Section 88 by Canadian courts has seen an expansion of provincial authority over Indians. The courts have supported the view that unless there is clear evidence of a conflict that could interfere with federal activity or the application of federal laws, provincial laws of general application apply to Indians even on reserves, unless the laws impair Indianness, as defined by law, custom, or tradition.

Since the 1950s, provincial jurisdiction over Indians and Indian lands has also been expanded by a number of tripartite administrative agreements. In several provinces, for example, the federal and provincial governments have negotiated tripartite agreements that extend provincial power over the administration of justice to Indian reserves, thus allowing the creation of reserve police forces under the provisions of provincial police acts. Indian gaming is another area where provinces and Indian bands meet face to face, as the bands assert an aboriginal right to open a casino or two without provincial sanction and the provinces (eager to claim the revenues as their own) move to shut them down or to negotiate revenue-sharing agreements similar to those in the United States. Natural resource development is also an area where Indian bands and provinces meet at the regulatory table.

The federal responsibility for social services to Indians is based in Section 91(24). Even though this grant of authority is permissive and not mandatory with respect to providing services to Indians, the federal government has traditionally assumed responsibility for Indians living on reserves. On the other hand, it has taken the position that Indians living off the reserves fall under the general social responsibility mandate of the provinces, as do Métis and non-status Indians. For the most part, provinces have accepted social responsibility for Indians living off-reserve. The provinces have, however, consistently refused to extend their social responsibility mandate to Indians living on reserves.

**Jurisdiction over Land.**  A final aspect of Indian-government relationships involves jurisdiction over land. Outside the Yukon, Nunavut, and Northwest Territories, the federal government owns very little land in Canada. Section 109 of the Constitution Act as well as a number of federal-provincial agreements such as the Natural Resources Transfer Act of 1930 gives the provinces control over nearly all Crown lands within their boundaries. Consequently, treaty and land claims by Indian bands or other aboriginal entities for lands outside existing reserves or for aboriginal title (traditional occupancy) claims are laid against the provinces (except in the territories). The historical record of the provinces in accommodating Indian land claims has been mixed. In some instances, land transfer has taken place only after major confrontations. One contentious land claim was that of the Kanesatake Mohawk, who in 1990 forced action on a land claim at Oka, in southern Quebec, by setting up blockades to prevent the development of a golf course on land that the Kanesatake claimed as their own. After the failure of Quebec provincial police to remove the barricades, during which one provincial police officer was killed, the Canadian army was called in to end the seventy-eight-day standoff. To defuse the situation, the federal government purchased the disputed land at Oka and offered it to the Kanesatake as a part of a negotiated settlement package that included economic development and other benefits, a land transfer which finally took place in June 2000. Other land disputes provoking well-publicized confrontations have taken place at Gustafsen Lake, British Columbia and Ipperwash Provincial Park, Ontario (both in 1995).

Most parts of Canada outside the territories are covered by treaty, and land claims settlements tend to follow the formula established in the numbered treaties. The province of British Columbia and the North are the exceptions and at the turn of the twenty-first century British Columbia is the site of several intense controversies over land. Aboriginal land claims cover more than 100 percent of the province's land mass, as some claims overlap. The Canadian jurisprudence outlining the nature of aboriginal title (on which comprehensive land claims are based) comes out of a dispute in this province. In *Delgamuukw v. the Queen* (the Gitksan-Wet'suwet'en claim), a 1997 Supreme Court of Canada decision defined aboriginal title over traditional aboriginal lands as arising out of continuous and exclusive occupancy over the land in question dating from a period before the assertion of Canadian sovereignty.

Only in 1994 did British Columbia first acknowledge that aboriginal title might still exist within its boundaries, and the province opened up a claims negotiation process with its 100,000 First Nations residents. However, after six years and millions of dollars spent the treaty process came to a halt in 2000 when the first and only agreement reached—with the Sechelt Band near Vancouver—was rejected by the membership. The uncertainty which continues to exist over land title in British Columbia is acknowledged to be casting a pall over resource development—a key to the provincial economy. Resource companies who want to harvest trees or drill for oil or mine for gold are being met by First Nations representatives armed with a copy of the Delgamuukw decision and the prospect of lengthy litigation. Canadian courts have repeatedly advised government and aboriginal leaders alike that negotiation is preferable to litigation over land claims, and the collapse of the British Columbia treaty process raises troublesome prospects for everyone.

One region in which negotiation of land claims has prevailed is the North—although even there the sheer length of the process has resulted in "claims fatigue syndrome" on the part of many participants. Still, the main Inuit claims were resolved in 1975, 1984, and 1991. In Yukon, land claims and self-government agreements began to be negotiated with the fourteen First Nations in the mid-1990s. In the Northwest Territories, the Dene Nation and the Métis Association of the Northwest Territories agreed in 1981 to negotiate a joint land claim, and an agreement in principle was reached in 1988. The deal fell apart in 1991 when some of the Dene chiefs balked at the principle that some aboriginal rights would be "extinguished" upon signing. The federal government then agreed to negotiate five separate regional claims, which have been settled with the Gwich'in (1992) and Sahtu (1993). The future of the Northwest Territories will be challenging for all residents. Resource companies are eyeing the Western Arctic's diamonds and other minerals, and a major find of natural gas has been made in the southern Mackenzie Valley. Yet alongside this economic potential the territorial government, which has selected three aboriginal premiers in a row, no longer represents an aboriginal majority, faces economic cutbacks from the federal government, and has all the problems of a young, growing population.

### The Inuit

The Inuit of Canada live in the far north of the country above the tree line in small communities on the Mackenzie Delta, where they are known as the Inuvialuit, along the coasts of the Northwest Territories and the new territory of Nunavut, on the shores of Hudson's Bay, in Labrador, northern Quebec, and scattered across the Arctic Islands. According to the land bridge theory they were the last of the aboriginal peoples to migrate from Siberia to Alaska, their ancestors arriving in Canada around 10,000 B.C.E. The Inuit were once known to outsiders as Eskimos, which comes from a Cree word meaning "raw meat eaters."

The Inuit of Canada share one culture and one language, although there are different dialects of Inuktitut. Their settlement pattern along coastlines reflects a historical lifestyle tied to marine harvesting. They hunted seal, whale, and walrus in the waters of the north but would also travel inland for caribou, fish, and waterfowl. Most lived in small groups of related families, sometimes coming together at fishing or sealing camps. Sharing the results of their hunt was a key aspect of Inuit culture; some communities had formal distribution systems for sharing out the catch. Life in the Arctic was difficult—starvation was always a possibility—but for thousands of years the Inuit survived in this region.

Although Inuit in the eastern Arctic may have encountered the Norse explorers who reached Canada in the tenth century, sustained contact between Inuit and Europeans did not take place until the nineteenth century. American and Scottish whalers sailed north in pursuit of the bowhead whale, which they hunted to near extinction. The whalers hired Inuit to act as guides and crew, and some of them took Inuit wives. The trading posts established by the Hudson's Bay Company were another means of contact between Inuit and Europeans, and over the next century many Inuit forsook their traditional hunting pursuits in favor of fur trapping. They came to rely on European trade goods for survival, and when the fur trade collapsed in the 1940s, the effect on the Inuit was devastating. Hunger and disease afflicted their communities.

The Canadian government did not turn its attention to the plight of the Inuit until the 1950s. Relief supplies were sent to the starving communities, and the Inuit were encouraged to settle permanently around the Hudson Bay trading posts. During this decade, the federal government also relocated a group of Inuit from northern Quebec to two different locations in the High Arctic as an assertion of territorial sovereignty in the north, among other motives. Because of their remoteness from centers of government, Inuit legal status in Canada was ambiguous for a number of years and they were first brought into a direct relationship with the federal government in 1939. In that year, the Supreme Court of Canada decided in *Re Eskimos* that the Inuit come within the term *Indians* in Section 91(24) of the British North America Act. The Indian Act itself excludes Inuit from the operations of the Department of Indian Affairs, but as a result of *Re Eskimos*, the federal government's power to make laws affecting Indians and their lands also includes the Inuit. Today the Inuit are involved with several levels of government. In the Northwest Territories, Inuit and other Canadians are governed by the territorial government, which was moved from Ottawa to Yellowknife in 1967. In northern Quebec, the signing of the James Bay and Northern

Copper Inuit couple, c. 1916. (Courtesy of Canadian Museum of Civilization)

Quebec Agreement in 1975 established a regional government for Inuit in that area. And the province of Newfoundland and the federal government have negotiated a cost-sharing arrangement for provision of government services to the Inuit of Labrador, for whom the provincial government retains primary administrative responsibility.

In the eastern Arctic in the new Territory of Nunavut, the Inuit may find a degree of self-determination. They live in the only part of Canada where aboriginal inhabitants are in the majority, and they successfully sought a public, regional government in the north rather than an ethnically based one. The Inuit political aspirations that gave birth to Nunavut were intimately tied to their

pursuit of land claims. Unlike Indian groups that entered into treaties, the Inuit's claims to aboriginal rights were not dealt with (and were not made) before the modern era. In 1973, the federal government agreed to enter land claims negotiations with the Inuit, and the Inuit Tapirisat (Brotherhood) of Canada submitted its claim on behalf of the Inuit of Nunavut to the federal government in 1976, proposing the creation of a new territory.

The Inuit of northern Quebec had been involved in the first modern land claims agreement to be reached in Canada, along with the James Bay Cree. That agreement, signed in 1975, guaranteed the aboriginal signatories exclusive hunting and fishing rights over parts of northern Quebec; "ownership" of other parcels similar to Indian "ownership" of reserve lands; the Kativik regional government for the Inuit of the area; education and language rights in Inuktitut; and a cash and royalties settlement, which for the Inuit amounted to $90 million. In return, the Inuit and Cree relinquished any further claim to lands covered by the agreement. A second land claim was settled in 1984 with the 2,500 Inuvialuit of the western Arctic, who obtained 242,000 square kilometers of land and a cash settlement of $45 million. But the largest Inuit land claim involved the division of the Northwest Territories between Denedah, Athapascan land in the west, and Nunavut, Inuit land in the east; the claim was settled in 1991, and it involved a payment of $580 million and 350,000 square kilometers of land. Community ratification took place a year later, and in the process, the Inuit agreed to the extinguishment of their aboriginal rights claim to the rest of their traditional lands.

Other groups besides the Inuit had an interest in the development of Nunavut, and their viewpoints were far from uniform. In a 1992 territorial plebiscite, 54 percent of Northwest Territories voters approved the western boundary for the new territory, with an overwhelming endorsement on the part of the Inuit. However, there was opposition to the creation of Nunavut from the Dene Indians, with whom the Inuit have had long-standing border disputes. The Assembly of First Nations criticized the deal for giving up too much in the way of aboriginal rights. Non-Native northerners, who traditionally formed political coalitions with the Inuit and the Inuvialuit, were concerned about the makeup of future governments in the western remainder of the Northwest Territories.

On 1 April 1999 the Northwest Territories were divided in two. Canada's third territory, Nunavut—meaning "Our Land"—was born, comprising all areas north of the tree line in the eastern Arctic. The population—25,000 in 1996—is 85 percent Inuit: a young, relatively poor population whose language of Inuktitut is one of the only Canadian aboriginal languages not considered threatened. In a referendum, Nunavut residents narrowly rejected a proposal (supported by their political leadership) for a gender-balanced legislature—election of a man and a woman from each electoral district. Other innovations, however, were adopted. Inuktitut was selected as the working language of government. A decentralized model for government departments was also adopted—a financial challenge in the eastern Arctic where distances are long, roads between communities non-existent, and airfares high. Finally, the Nunavut Implementation Commission set a target of government staffing by the Inuit equal to the Inuit percentage of territorial population, another challenging goal that the commission hopes will be implemented by 2009.

The Inuit economy has undergone an enormous change in the last forty years, from a hunting and trapping base to diversification involving tourism, arts and crafts, and development of both renewable and non-renewable resources. Government, however, is still the biggest employer in the North, and accounts for 95 percent of the income flowing into what is Canada's poorest region. The outlook for mining and oil and gas exploration is not bright at present, and the tourism sector is underdeveloped. The unemployment rate among the Inuit is very high, the population is young, and educational attainment is low. All the statistics point to an impending crisis.

Many Inuit communities rely on traditional hunting, fishing, and sealing activities as a food supply and a source of cash income. However, the variant of environmental activism known as the animal rights movement has posed a serious threat to survival of northern aboriginal communities. In the late 1960s, a highly emotional campaign was organized against a non-Inuit commercial kill of newly born harp seals in the waters of Atlantic Canada. The campaign developed into an attack on seal hunting in general, and it had a devastating effect on the Arctic Inuit and their traditional hunt for mature ringed seals. By 1982 the European Community had boycotted all seal product imports, a serious blow to the Inuit economy. Many Inuit were forced to leave the land for an uncertain future in communities with little wage employment. Loss of economic self-sufficiency and social alienation have resulted in an escalation of health and social problems.

Canada's small Inuit population faces challenges on many fronts. Protection of Inuit culture is a priority, and there have been positive developments, notably in education. Inuktitut instruction has been introduced into elementary schools, and textbooks have been written in both Inuktitut and English. Nunavut has attracted the attention of the Bill and Melinda Gates Library Foundation, which proposes to link the small communities with each other and with the outside world via the Internet—a proposition for which the physical infrastructure does not yet exist. A Native press has developed, and the Inuit Broadcasting Corporation provides programming in Inuktitut. Canadian Inuit also participate in the Inuit Circumpolar Conference (ICC), which represents 130,000 Canadian, Alaska, Soviet, and Greenland Inuit on international issues affecting the Arctic. The ICC, a non-governmental member of the United Nations, meets every three years to discuss issues such as traditional ecological knowledge, sustainable development, and Arctic whaling; at the 1997 meeting future land use in Nunavut was on the agenda.

## The Métis

Canada's Métis have been called "the forgotten people," and it was considered a major victory for them to have been included as an aboriginal people in Canada's 1982 Constitution. The word "Métis" means "mixed" in French and describes someone of mixed Indian and European ancestry. The original Métis were the children of marriages between Indian women and the European men who participated in the Canadian fur trade. On the prairies, French fur traders took Cree wives and in the north, English and Scottish traders married Dene women. In contemporary times, the term Métis is used more broadly to refer to people of mixed Indian-European ancestry anywhere in Canada, regardless of where their ancestors lived. Two-thirds of the self-identified Métis are still concentrated in the prairie provinces of Alberta, Saskatchewan, and Manitoba. Another significant group of Métis live in the Northwest Territories and have allied themselves with the Dene Nation for the purpose of pursuing land claims.

European fur traders derived many benefits from association with Indian women and their families. Natives' familiarity with forests and waterways, their technological skills, and the indigenous social and political network that facilitated commercial trade all aided these European men in adjusting to the land. The children of these unions, in turn, were often incorporated into the business, acting as interpreters and middlemen. The Métis participated in the Plains economy as hunters, trappers, traders, carters, and small farmers, developing a distinctive culture combining European and Indian traditions. But over time, the Euro-Canadian influence over the Métis homeland expanded, the Métis way of life was threatened, and a sense of Métis nationalism developed. In 1811, the Hudson's Bay Company made a large land grant in the Red River Valley of Manitoba for the purpose of establishing a new colony with an agricultural economy. Over the next half-century, homesteaders from eastern Canada settled along the Red and Assiniboine rivers, arousing Métis antipathy.

In 1869, the Hudson's Bay Company sold the Métis homeland to Canada, a deal opposed by the Métis. A political challenge to the new governor of the territory, the Red River Resistance, was led by Louis Riel, Jr., the son of a prominent Métis. Riel and his followers established a provisional government, asserting their right to do so under the Law of Nations. They arrested several men for resisting Métis law and caused an uproar by executing an easterner named Thomas Scott. Negotiations with the government of Canada ensued, and in the Manitoba Act of 1870 many Métis demands were met, including allotments of land to individual Métis and their children. But conflict continued between the Métis and the incoming settlers. The Plains economy was shifting further to the west along with the buffalo herds and many Métis chose to follow, but Canadian settlers were not far behind. In 1884, the Métis of Saskatchewan, finding the government of Canada unresponsive to their complaints, sent for Louis Riel, then living in Montana. Riel returned to petition Ottawa for land title for the Métis and provincial status for Saskatchewan, Assiniboine, and Alberta. The response was unsatisfactory, and Riel again set up a defiant provisional government. A series of armed conflicts followed, after which Riel was captured, put on trial, and hanged for treason in November 1885.

In the years following the Riel Rebellion, called by the Métis "The War of Resistance at Batoche," the Canadian government made some efforts to deal with the grievances that led to conflict. Manitoba Métis were given 1.4 million acres of land to extinguish their "Indian title" in that province. Both land parcels and scrip were distributed to the Métis. Many chose to sell both land and scrip to head west. By the twentieth century, large numbers of Métis had become impoverished and marginalized.

There is much contemporary debate about Canada's treatment of Louis Riel. To some he is a martyr. As the centenary of his death approached, a call was made for his posthumous pardon. A decade later a Private Member's Bill was twice introduced to Parliament that would have exonerated him. The Métis National Council, however, rejected the bill as isolating Riel from his people by not recognizing the Métis rights he fought for. To others Riel is a more ambivalent figure, whose mental illness and religious mysticism are more interesting than his political activism. In any event, the life and person of Riel continue to fascinate Canadians, a favored subject for artists and writers as well as historians.

The demands that Riel made on behalf of the Métis have met with few substantive answers. Prior to 1982 the Métis had argued that they were entitled to aboriginal rights. Today, despite Constitutional recognition, Métis spokespersons continue the battle for equal recognition with Inuit and Indians as one of Canada's three aboriginal peoples. Various political organizations, at the provincial, territorial, and federal levels, carry on the struggle for Métis rights and jostle with other aboriginal groups for position and resources in Canadian society. The first Métis political organization was established in Saskatchewan in 1937, but it was not until the 1960s that provincial Métis organizations sprang up in Manitoba, Alberta, and British Columbia. In 1971 the Western Métis formed a new organization, the Native Council of Canada (NCC), to represent both Métis and non-status Indians and promote their social, economic, and political aspirations. The NCC took a pan-Canadian approach, defining a Métis as anyone of mixed European and Indian blood. However, in the 1980s, the council faced a challenge from the Prairie Métis, who define "the Métis" as a particular national group that arose in the Red River homeland during the development of the fur trade. The Métis National Council (MNC) was established in 1983 by those Prairie Métis who felt the NCC was not adequately pressing for establishment of a Métis land base. Later the NCC itself metamorphosed into the Congress of Aboriginal Peoples and came to focus on urban aboriginal issues; their current mandate is to represent off-reserve Indians and Métis peoples outside the Prairies.

Métis politics are also carried on vigorously at the provincial level, often through federations of Métis locals. Relations between the Métis and the provincial governments vary considerably. Alberta was the first province to recognize a distinct responsibility to its Métis population. The Métis Betterment Act was passed in 1938 after an investigation into the socioeconomic problems of the Métis. In 1938 and 1939, Alberta established twelve Métis settlements in the northern part of the province, some of which are larger than most Indian reserves; however, four of these communities were displaced when oil and gas were discovered. By 1960 there were only eight settlements left. In the following two decades, the Métis sought not only protection for these remaining lands but also compensation for oil and gas taken from their territory. An agreement was reached in 1990, which saw 500,000 hectares and $310 million transferred to 5,000 of Alberta's Métis. Today the settlements, still eight in number, are governed by elected councils with quasi-municipal powers over such areas as policing, housing, and land use. Métis who live outside the settlements are considered ordinary citizens by the government of Alberta.

Alberta's relationship with the Métis is an exception. In Saskatchewan, Métis farms, with very small land bases, have been established, but special recognition of the Métis has been unusual elsewhere. In some cases, the Métis are pursuing their aspirations through the courts. The most important lawsuit is in Manitoba, where in 1992 the Manitoba Métis Federation filed suit for compensation for the 1.4 million acres granted to individual Métis by the 1870 Manitoba Act but largely lost to their descendants. The issues in this case involve detailed historical research into Métis disposition of land and scrip from 1870 until the early twentieth century.

Other court cases have involved Métis hunting and fishing rights. Métis individuals make the argument, with some success, that like the Indian and Inuit they had a historical lifestyle on the land, necessitating like access to game and fish. The bottom line is the claim that the Métis are equally aboriginal with the Indian and Inuit and that Section 35 of the Constitution equally protects their aboriginal rights. The 1996 Report of the Royal Commission on Aboriginal Peoples, commissioned by the federal Progressive Conservative government in the aftermath of the Oka conflict, recognized the Métis as an aboriginal people and recommended that Canadian governments negotiate self-government with them and provide them with a land base. However, since available Crown land in the areas where most Métis live is provincial—and since the provinces have not accorded Métis special status—it is difficult to envision Métis landlessness being ameliorated any time soon.

Despite their constitutional recognition and the Royal Commission recommendations, the relationship between national Métis organizations and other aboriginal groups has been problematic. The Métis complain that governments do not treat the Métis the same way they do the Indians and Inuit and argue that this is unjust. "Equality for aboriginal peoples" is a Métis battle cry. The Métis national agenda is largely driven by a desire for a concrete land base, rather than for further constitutional amendment; this occasionally puts them at odds with Indian and Inuit organizations, whose assets and aspirations are different. Unlike the Inuit and Indians, the Métis have always been under provincial rather than federal jurisdiction; the "constitutionalization" of their status has not changed that fact. Legally, and despite the Constitution Act of 1982, the Métis claim for aboriginal status has had little practical impact.

### The Changing Status of Canada's Aboriginal Peoples

The modern era of aboriginal politics in Canada can be dated from the release of the 1969 White Paper on Indian Policy by the federal government. The main thrust of the White Paper was a proposal to eliminate the special legal status of Canadian Indians and Inuit, who would then be provided government services through mainstream institutions, primarily provincial ones. Canadian Indians took immediate exception to this proposal and countered with their own Red Paper arguing in favor of special legal status on the grounds of aboriginal and treaty rights. However, the White Paper was more than a policy vehicle. It was a statement of philosophy expressing the liberal individualistic vision of the state, in which the legal equality of individuals takes precedence over special benefits and status for groups. Specific questions of aboriginal rights in Canada have been entangled with a broader and ongoing conflict: a vision of Canada as a liberal individualistic state versus a vision of Canada as a collection of historical communities. The Trudeau government, which produced the White Paper, was strongly committed to the former concept, and the only grounds it acknowledged as justifying special treatment for Indians were social and economic disadvantage.

Although the White Paper was ultimately rejected, the initiative had some important consequences. First, it accelerated a trend started earlier to bring aboriginal people into a consultative role with respect to government policy. A significant outcome of this was the establishment of a program under the jurisdiction of the secretary of state to provide core funding to political associations representing various aboriginal groups. During the 1970s and 1980s the number of government departments involved in the funding of aboriginal political associations increased as well as the mandated purposes for which the funding could be used. Aboriginal people were given federal money to research land and treaty claims, to prepare constitutional proposals, and to provide limited delivery of social services. Second, the White Paper provided a focal point around which aboriginal peoples across Canada could unite and rally in opposition to what they believed to be detrimental government policies. An extended period of political activism followed, and the National Indian Brotherhood (NIB), renamed the Assembly of First Nations in 1981, assumed a position of leadership. Aboriginal organizations demonstrated in the streets, lobbied in the Cabinet, and sued in the law courts, seeking to shake off the bureaucratic yoke of Indian Affairs and acquire greater control over their own communities.

## Aboriginal Peoples and the Constitution

By the 1980s, aboriginal aspirations had become entangled with Canadian constitutional politics. In the face of a growing separatist movement in Quebec, the Liberal government of Prime Minister Pierre Trudeau, the top official of Canada, took control of the national agenda with a project for renovating federalism, adopting the Constitution, and entrenching a Charter of Rights and Freedoms much like the U.S. Bill of Rights.

During the national debate, the leaders of the NIB came to realize that Canadian constitutional renewal was both a threat to their exclusive relationship with the federal government and an opportunity for wider assertion of their claims. When the Constitution was adopted in 1982, the "existing aboriginal and treaty rights of the aboriginal peoples of Canada" were recognized and affirmed, and a series of First Ministers' Conferences was scheduled to work towards definition of those rights. These conferences were held in 1983, 1984, 1985, and 1987, attended by the eleven First Ministers, representatives of the four main aboriginal organizations, and government leaders from the Yukon and Northwest Territories. The agenda for discussion was extensive. Aboriginal title over land; hunting, fishing, and trapping rights; preservation of aboriginal languages and cultures; delivery of government services; aboriginal sovereignty; equality of aboriginal women and men; and constitutional entrenchment of a Charter of Aboriginal Rights were all issues on the table. Over the five-year period, however, discussion came to focus on one main issue: aboriginal self-government.

The aboriginal groups sought constitutional entrenchment of a right to self-government. However, such an amendment was met with considerable resistance by Canadian governments, especially by provincial premiers in provinces with large numbers of aboriginal communities. British Columbia, for example, accounted for 1,629 of Canada's 2,281 Indian reserves. Would the province be forced to negotiate a self-government agreement with every one of them? The provincial premiers wanted a clear definition of self-government prior to constitutional entrenchment, no agreement could be reached with the aboriginal organizations, and the conferences ended in failure and bitterness.

The reluctance of the federal and provincial governments in Canada to legitimize aboriginal claims to self-government was additionally illustrated by the 1987 Constitutional Accord, more commonly known as the Meech Lake Accord, because it was signed in Meech Lake, Quebec. The accord, which was reached without participation by aboriginal peoples, formally recognized Quebec as "a distinct society" with unique linguistic and cultural rights, but gave aboriginal peoples only token recognition in a clause stating that their rights would not be affected. Aboriginal leaders reacted quickly, arguing that the sole recognition of Quebec as a "distinct society" denied that aboriginal peoples also comprise "distinct societies" within Canada.

Despite vociferous opposition to the Meech Lake Accord by aboriginal leaders, only three provinces—Manitoba, New Brunswick, and Newfoundland—responded to their concerns. None of the provincial proposals, however, came close to what aboriginal peoples were demanding as their proper place in the Canadian federal system. By 1990 these three provinces had yet to ratify the Meech Accord, and constitutional melodrama ensued. Indian leaders in Manitoba supported Elijah Harper, the lone Indian member of the Manitoba Legislative Assembly, in his efforts to prevent the Manitoba legislature from ratifying the Meech Lake Accord. By utilizing the procedural rules for considering constitutional amendments, and with the support of mainstream opponents of Meech, Harper was able to block the agreement from being approved before the deadline—leaving aboriginal people in the constitutional position they occupied in 1982 and which they occupy to this day.

Another attempted round of constitutional tinkering by First Ministers (the Prime Minister and the Premiers) resulted in the 1992 Charlottetown Accord, named for the location of the First Ministers' meetings in Charlottetown, Prince Edward Island. The overall focus of this accord, like that at Meech, was getting a constitutional deal with Quebec so Canadian politicians could focus on the economy. But the Charlottetown Accord also incorporated in modified form a number of the constitutional positions on aboriginal peoples put forth previously by the federal government and supported by aboriginal leaders. Most importantly, the accord would have recognized an inherent right of self-government for aboriginal peoples and that aboriginal governments would constitute a "third order of government" within Canada. Significantly, the accord proposed that all aboriginal peoples be brought under Section 91(24) of the Constitution. This provision implied access for the Métis to programs and funding available to status Indians and Inuit, an astonishing reversal of the federal government's position for over a century. Equally astonishing was the fact that Indian and Inuit leaders participating in the constitutional discussions also agreed. In October 1992, however, the Charlottetown Accord was decisively rejected by the Canadian electorate, and because the accord was voted on as a total package, the aboriginal right to self-government once again failed to achieve constitutional status.

Aboriginal constitutional aspirations are thus in limbo, and the general "constitution fatigue" of the Canadian public does not suggest that much appetite exists for a new round of constitutional talks—with or without aboriginal participation. But the decade-long aboriginal involvement in constitutional negotiations has had two interesting results. First, in the absence of constitutional involvement, the importance of the national aboriginal organizations such as the Assembly of First Nations and the Congress of Aboriginal Peoples has diminished. While constitutional talks were underway, large sums of money flowed to these organizations for the specific purpose of hiring their own lawyers, conducting their own hearings, and formulating their own proposals. Those monies are gone, and the organizations have had to cut back. Moreover, the publicity attendant on high-profile constitutional events, the regular television appearance of aboriginal leaders talking one–on–one with premiers and prime ministers, is likewise gone. Only the AFN has much of a national profile.

Second, the continuing debate about the relationship of Quebec to the Canadian federation has been changed forever by the insertion into the debate of the First Nations peoples of Quebec—in particular the Cree and Inuit of northern Quebec. Those groups argue that if Quebec has the right to separate from the rest of Canada, they have the right to separate from Quebec, either remaining Canadian citizens or initiating some independent form of governance over their lands. Those lands, and the rich hydroelectric resources they contain, are the most important issue. While Quebec separatists assert that the borders of modern-day Quebec (which includes Cree and Inuit territory) are inviolable, Cree and Inuit point out that their peoples lived there for thousands of years before French Quebeckers ever came on the scene and they themselves have a prior claim. The most recent referendum held in Quebec (1995) saw Quebec voters reject the separation option by a narrow margin; that same year Quebec Inuit and Cree held their own referendums and voted nearly 100 percent in favor of remaining with Canada. This quintessential Canadian debate has continued unabated, and unresolved, into the twenty-first century, made more complex by the fact that Quebec First Nations are now a permanent part of the equation.

**Community-Based Self-Government.** During the 1980s and 1990s, federal policy in the area of aboriginal self-government was designed to allow a greater degree of self-administration so that aboriginal communities could begin their own process of political, social, and economic development. This policy involved a recognition on the part of the federal government that, given the stalled constitutional negotiations on aboriginal rights, something must be done to accommodate the increasing demands of aboriginal leaders for self-government. The government's actions also responded to a 1983 report of a Special Committee on Indian Self-Government of the Canadian Parliament that delivered a scathing indictment of the restrictive nature of the Indian Act as well as other governmental policies toward Indians. In all cases the federal government has insisted its policies will not prejudice any constitutional negotiations regarding aboriginal self-government or other negotiations involving land claims and treaty rights.

In the case of status Indians, the most significant of the federal policies has been the "community-based self-government" approach, which allows for structural change to band or tribal political institutions and a greater degree of self-administration of programs in the areas of education, health, child welfare, justice, and environment, among others. Since some of these matters touch upon provincial jurisdiction, the provinces must be involved in negotiations between the federal government and bands or tribal groups where provincial interests are involved. Once negotiations for an individual band community have been finalized, Parliament passes a special act removing the band or tribal group from the Indian Act regarding the negotiated points of agreement.

The major precedent for community-based self-government involves the Sechelt Band in lower mainland British Columbia. The Sechelt Act (1986), passed by the British Columbia Legislature and the Canadian Parliament, is an individualized piece of legislation designed to meet the specific needs of the Sechelt Indians in the areas of taxation and control over lands and resources. Despite their disappointment over the failure of the constitutional process, a large number of bands and tribal groups are now involved at some stage in the community self-government negotiations process. A number of Indian bands and groups, including the Gitksan and Wet'suwet'en in British Columbia, the Alexander and Sawridge bands in Alberta, the Kahnawake Mohawk in Quebec, and the United Indian Councils of the Mississauga and Chippewa Indians in Ontario, have signed framework agreements, the final step in negotiations before the agreements go before Parliament. Other Indian bands have sought and accepted devolution of responsibility for individual government programs.

The interest expressed by many Indian communities in community-based self-government reflects a pragmatic recognition that this approach presents them not only with an opportunity to acquire a degree of autonomy not possible under the Indian Act, but also a chance to restore some of their traditional governing practices. Moreover, given the uncertainty about the future of constitutionally based Indian government, many Indian leaders believe that it is better to move ahead on a modest scale than to wait for something that may never be realized. While the community-based approach does provide them with a broader scope for action than the authority given to Indian governments under the Indian Act, it still involves devolution of authority from other levels of government and therefore does not alter the basic positions of the federal government and the provinces with respect to jurisdiction and responsibility over Indians. This approach certainly fits the present mode of Canadian federalism. It remains a long way, however, from meeting the aspirations of Indian peoples for recognition of inherent right to self-government.

The most high profile aboriginal government in Canada belongs to the Nisga'a of British Columbia, a model that received final approval in the year 2000. The Nisga'a agreement grants to approximately 4,000 Nisga'a members $190 million and 1,900 square kilometers of land. The deal removes their four communities along the Nass River from Indian Act jurisdiction but leaves them bound by general Canadian law including the Charter of Rights and Freedoms and the Criminal Code of Canada. Nisga'a aboriginal rights under Section 35 of the Constitution are modified into treaty rights. Prominent among the features of the agreement are the removal of individual Nisga'a's tax exemptions under the Indian Act, and simultaneously the new capacity of the Nisga'a government to tax both their own members and non-Nisga'a citizens occupying Nisga'a land. The new Nisga'a government has received considerable publicity, both positive and negative. Supporters hail the deal as achieving justice for the Nisga'a and providing them the basis for an improved standard of living based on their own natural resources. Critics consider this ethnically based government undemocratic, question the amount of money the arrangement is going to cost taxpayers, and argue that the Nisga'a Act has amended the Canadian Constitution without proper procedures. In any event, the Nisga'a arrangement is a *sui generis* one unlikely to be replicable for many other aboriginal groups, even those who are traveling the community-based self-government route.

The possibility of this kind of community-based self-government for the Métis runs into two obstacles: with the exception of those living in the territories, they remain under provincial jurisdiction and, apart from some of the Métis living in Alberta, they lack a coherent land base. As for the Inuit, their quest for self-government has been linked to land claims settlements and public government. Both matters are resolved in the formal sense, with the exception of the Inuit of Labrador who are still dealing on a number of issues with the government of Newfoundland.

**Land Claims.**  Land claims have held a dominant position on the political agenda of aboriginal peoples for the last several decades, and for any particular aboriginal group, absent some kind of arguable land claim their political aspirations have not gone very far. Land, of course, not only holds a unique status within aboriginal culture, but is also a key bargaining chip with wider Canadian society. Comprehensive land claims policy acknowledges that aboriginal peoples have inherent interests in certain lands based upon traditional occupation; claims can be made when it can be shown that aboriginal interests have not been extinguished. Modern comprehensive claims policy emerged from a decision of the Canadian Supreme Court in the *Calder* case of 1973, which involved a land claim based upon aboriginal title by the Nisga'a of British Columbia. Since 1974 both structures and processes have existed for dealing with aboriginal land claims, but despite the millions of dollars given to aboriginal political associations for land claims research, as well as to various lawyers and government bureaucrats involved, the record of satisfying land claims is poor. This record is the product of a number of factors.

First, non-Indian stakeholders—the provinces and private landowners and corporations—have been reluctant to recognize aboriginal claims where land and other proprietary interests are involved. For example, in the case of natural resources, revenue from royalties can comprise a substantial proportion of government income. Second, the federal government itself, due to a lack of both financial and administrative resources, has limited the number of claims it can handle at any one point in time, creating a backlog in the claims process. Third, there have been a number of disagreements between aboriginal peoples themselves over particular claims. Examples include disagreement between the Inuit and Dene over the appropriate boundaries for territorial divisions; disputes between the Nisga'a and their neighbors over which ancestral land is whose; and divisions between regional and national political associations about the acceptability of proposed claim settlement packages, particularly with respect to extinguishment of rights. Finally, land claims negotiations are no longer conducted in obscurity. The amount of money involved has come to the attention of the general public in Canada, and both the overall claims process and the individual settlements are coming under widespread scrutiny.

Outside of Canada's North, settlements have been few in number. Comprehensive claims, those in non-treaty areas of the country, are in various stages of negotiation. But several hundred specific claims, those that claim violations of treaty obligations, remain to be resolved. In 2000 it was estimated that some 450 specific claims are backlogged in a bureaucratic system which settles around ten claims a year. As early as 1993, the governing Liberal Party promised aboriginal peoples an independent claims agency to speed up the process; this was also a recommendation of the 1996 Royal Commission. An Independent Claims Body to address the specific claims, proposed by the Liberal Government, was expected to come before Parliament in Fall 2000, and seeing this new agency ushered into reality is a priority for the Assembly of First Nations.

## Coming to Terms with the Past and Moving Toward the Future

According to the 1996 Royal Commission Report on Aboriginal Peoples, the core problem facing aboriginal peoples and communities is a fractured historical relationship between Canadian Natives and the Canadian state. The Royal Commission produced a six–volume report—taking five years to complete and costing $58 million—and multiple recommendations, very few of which have been acted on. But the commission's identification of history, or rather the difficulty for contemporary parties in coming to terms with the past, seems on point. The legal regime that governs aboriginal relations—the Royal Proclamation of 1763, the various treaties, the original Indian Act—were drafted in an historical era when the geopolitical realities for aboriginal peoples—and others—were different from what they are today.

One example is land, not just aboriginal claims for land and their resolution, but disputes about the value of what has long been designated aboriginal land and what the Canadian and aboriginal governments' responsibilities are in this area. Should aboriginal communities be able to convert their collective land ownership into "fee simple" ownership, allowing reserve lands to be bought and sold on the market? The historical intent of the involved parties seems to have been perpetual collective ownership, yet many bands, including the Sechelt, have challenged that interpretation. And what about the lands and resources managed on behalf of bands by government bureaucrats? In earlier decades Indian lands were leased at what are now well-below market terms. What, then, when the leases run out? In downtown Vancouver in 1998, the Musqueam Band raised rents from $400 a year to $28,000 for long-term, non-aboriginal tenants, arguing that they were simply bringing their rents up to current value in the hot Vancouver real estate market and that Indian lands should not, in the twenty-first century, be tied to some archaic financial formula. Multiple lawsuits have been filed in the case.

Another example is treaty rights. What do eighteenth- or nineteenth-century treaty terms mean today? Of particular interest on both Canadian coasts is fishing rights. A 1999 Supreme Court of Canada decision found that a Mi'kmaq, Donald Marshall, convicted of fishing out of season, had, according to a 1767 treaty, the contemporary right to earn a "moderate livelihood" from fishing beyond the normal commercial season. Aboriginal people across the country seized the opportunity to experiment with commercial harvest not only of fish and shellfish but also of resources such as timber. The Canadian Supreme Court quickly issued a rare clarification of their decision limiting its scope, but the notion that Indian bands have "commercial" treaty rights may not be so quickly quashed. Indian fishermen confront non-aboriginal ones over the Maritime lobster harvest, similar groups in British Columbia are jousting over the salmon catch, and both non-status Indians and Métis are starting to get in on the action. In the background, concerns over species conservation are starting to rise.

A third area in which historical intent and contemporary reality combine to create a dilemma is culture, in particular the century-long policy of the Canadian government to assimilate Indian children into Canadian society through a nation-wide system of residential schools run by the United, Presbyterian, Anglican, and Roman Catholic churches. Here, too, Canadian courts are involved and as of the year 2000 some 5,800 lawsuits had been filed against the individual churches and the federal government. It was only in the 1990s that widespread criticism of this historical educational regime began, and charges of physical and sexual abuse on the part of school custodians emerged. Those specific accusations have been augmented by broader-based claims involving loss of language and culture, shoddy academic standards, loss and hardship for family members of the students, and increasingly, collective claims on the grounds of cultural genocide.

Three of the churches involved have made formal apologies for these past actions, although not with the uniform support of parishioners. Ottawa has also issued an apology and made available to aboriginal communities a $350 million "healing fund" for treatment and counseling of former residential school students. Former AFN National Chief Phil Fontaine of Manitoba (1997–2000), himself a residential school survivor, was widely credited with negotiating the apology and healing fund. Fontaine's term in office, characterized by cooperation and conciliation, stands in marked contrast to those of his predecessor, Ovide Mercredi, and his successor, Matthew Coon Come. Meanwhile, the churches are paying thousands of dollars in legal fees, over and above their potential liability in settlement monies. The national organizations of the United and Anglican Churches as well as some Catholic dioceses claim to be threatened with bankruptcy and are looking to the federal government to share the load.

Yet alongside the accusations, disputes, and confrontations, aboriginal peoples in Canada are also carving out a new existence within a multicultural society not just for their historical role in the founding of the nation but also for their contemporary accomplishments. June 21, the first day of summer, is now National Aboriginal Day and is celebrated across the country. Standard cable television packages carry the new Aboriginal Peoples Television Network (APTN). Every year a well-funded gala hosts the National Aboriginal Peoples Achievements Awards to honor prominent artists, athletes, professionals, business persons, politicians, youths, and elders. Record numbers of aboriginal students graduate high school, attend college and university, and move on to graduate school. In the 1997 Canadian general elections, nine aboriginal candidates ran for office and three were elected to Parliament: one Indian, one Inuit, and one Métis. Despite discomfort about the past, and uncertainty about some of its unresolved wounds, in contemporary times a vibrant aboriginal presence is apparent in Canadian culture, society, and identity.

*Kate Chiste*

# Federally Recognized U.S. Indian Communities

Five hundred and fifty nine Native communities are officially recognized by the U.S. government through treaty, congressional act, or executive order. These communities are entitled to U.S. legal protections of tribal self-government and rights to tribally owned land. At least 200 non-recognized Indian communities have not signed treaties or have not had regular legal relations with the U.S. government. Other Indian communities, mostly in the eastern states, are not recognized by the federal government but are recognized by state governments. State-recognized tribes have legal protections and legal status within their home states but not with the U.S. government.

## ◆ ALABAMA

**POARCH CREEK INDIANS**
(aka CREEK NATION EAST OF THE MISSISSIPPI)
5811 Jack Springs Rd.
Atmore, AL 36502
(334) 368–9136

## ◆ ALASKA

**AFOGNAK VILLAGE**
215 Mission Road, Suite 212
Kodiak, Alaska 99615
(907) 486–6014

**AGDAAGUX OF KING COVE**
P.O. Box 18
King Cove, Alaska 99612
(907) 497–2312

**AKHIOK NATIVE VILLAGE**
P.O. Box 5050
Akhiok, AK 99615
(907) 836–2229

**AKIACHAK NATIVE COMMUNITY**
P.O. Box 70
Akiachak, AK 99551–0070
(907) 825–4626

**AKIAK NATIVE COMMUNITY**
P.O. Box 52127
Akiak, AK 99552
(907) 765–7112

**AKUTAN NATIVE VILLAGE**
P.O. Box 89
Akutan, AK 99553–0089
(907) 698–2300

**ALAKANUK NATIVE VILLAGE**
P.O. Box 149
Alakanuk, AK 99554–0149
(907) 238–3419

**ALATNA VILLAGE COUNCIL**
P.O. Box 70
Alatna, AK 99720
(907) 968–2304

**ALEKNAGIK NATIVE VILLAGE**
P.O. Box 115
Aleknagik, AK 99555
(907) 842–2623

ALGAACIQ NATIVE VILLAGE
200 Paukan Avenue
St. Mary's, AK 99658
(907) 438–2932

ALLAKAKET VILLAGE
P.O. Box 50
Allakaket, AK 99720
(907) 968–2237

AMBLER NATIVE VILLAGE
P.O. Box 47
Ambler, AK 99786
(907) 445–2180

ANAKTUVUK PASS VILLAGE COUNCIL
P.O. Box 21065
Anaktuvuk Pass, AK 99721
(907) 661–2535

ANDREAFSKI NATIVE VILLAGE
P.O. Box 88
Westdahl St.
St. Mary's, AK 99658–0088
(907) 438–2312

ANGOON COMMUNITY ASSOCIATION
P.O. Box 188
Angoon, AK 99820
(907) 788–3411

ANIAK VILLAGE
P.O. Box 176
Aniak, AK 99557
(907) 675–4349

ANVIK VILLAGE
P.O. Box 10
Anvik, AK 99558
(907) 663–6322

ARCTIC VILLAGE
P.O. Box 22059
Arctic Village, AK 99722
(907) 587–5990

ASA' CARSAMUIT TRIBE OF MOUNTAIN
    VILLAGE
P.O. Box 32249
Mountain Village, AK 99632
(907) 591–2929

ATKA NATIVE VILLAGE
Atka IRA Council
P.O. Box 47030
Atka, AK 99547
(907) 839–2229

ATMAUTLUAK VILLAGE
P.O. Box 6568
Atmautluak, AK 99559
(907) 553–5610

ATQASUK VILLAGE
P.O. Box 91108
Atqasuk, AK 99791
(907) 633–2535

BARROW INUPIAT NATIVE VILLAGE
P.O. Box 1139
Barrow, AK 99723
(907) 852–4411

BEAVER VILLAGE
P.O. Box 24029
Beaver, AK 99724
(907) 628–6126

BELKOFSKI NATIVE VILLAGE
P.O. Box 57
King Cove, AK 99612
(907) 497–2304

BILL MOORE'S SLOUGH NATIVE VILLAGE
General Delivery
Kotlik, AK 99620
(907) 899–4712

BIRCH CREEK VILLAGE
P.O. Box BC
Fort Yukon, AK 99740
(907) 221–2211

BREVIG MISSION NATIVE VILLAGE
P.O. Box 85063
Brevig Mission, AK 99785
(907) 642–4301

BUCKLAND NATIVE VILLAGE
P.O. Box 67
Buckland, AK 99727
(907) 494–2171

CANTWELL NATIVE VILLAGE
P.O. Box 94
Cantwell, AK 99788
(907) 768–2591

CHALKYITSIK VILLAGE
P.O. Box 57
Chalkyitsik, AK 99788
(907) 848–8117

CHEFORNAK VILLAGE
P.O. Box 110
Chefornak, AK 99561–0110
(907) 867–8850

CHENEGA NATIVE VILLAGE
P.O. Box 8079
Chenega Bay, AK 99562–8079
(907) 573–5132

CHEVAK NATIVE VILLAGE
P.O. Box 140
Chevak, AK 99563
(907) 858–7428

CHICKALOON NATIVE VILLAGE
P.O. Box 1105
Chickaloon, AK 99674–1105
(907) 745–0707

CHIGNIK LAGOON NATIVE VILLAGE
P.O. Box 57
Chignik Lagoon, AK 99565
(907) 840–2281

CHIGNIK LAKE VILLAGE
P.O. Box 33
Chignik Lake, AK 99548
(907) 845–2122

CHIGNIK NATIVE VILLAGE
Post Office Box 11
Chignik, AK 99564
(907) 749–2285

CHILKAT INDIAN VILLAGE OF KLUKWAN
P.O. Box 210
Haines, AK 99827–0210
(907) 767–5505

CHILKOOT INDIAN ASSOCIATION
P.O. Box 490
Haines, AK 99827
(907) 766–2323

CHINIK ESKIMO COMMUNITY
(a.k.a. GOLOVIN VILLAGE)
P.O. Box 62020
Golovin, AK 99762
(907) 779–2214

CHISTOCHINA NATIVE VILLAGE
P.O. Box 241
Gakona, AK 99586
(907) 822–3503

CHITINA NATIVE VILLAGE
P.O. Box 31
Chitina, AK 99566
(907) 823–2215

CHUATHBALUK NATIVE VILLAGE
P.O. Box CHU
Chuathbaluk, AK 99557–8999
(907) 467–4313

CHULOONAWICK VILLAGE
General Delivery
Chuloonawick, AK 99581
(907) 949–1147

CIRCLE VILLAGE
P.O. Box 89
Circle, AK 99733
(907) 733–5498

CLARK'S POINT VILLAGE
P.O. Box 90
Clark's Point, AK 99569–0090
(907) 236–1427

COUNCIL NATIVE VILLAGE
P.O. Box 2050
Nome, AK 99762
(907) 443–7649

CRAIG COMMUNITY ASSOCIATION
P.O. Box 828
Craig, AK 99921
(907) 826–3996

CROOKED CREEK VILLAGE
P.O. Box 69
Crooked Creek, AK 99575
(907) 432–2201

DEERING NATIVE VILLAGE
P.O. Box 36089
Deering, AK 99736
(907) 363–2138

DILLINGHAM NATIVE VILLAGE
P.O. Box 216
Dillingham, AK 00576
(907) 842–2384

DIOMEDE NATIVE VILLAGE
(a.k.a. Inalik)
P.O. Box 7079
Diomede, AK 99762
(907) 686–2175

DOT LAKE VILLAGE
P.O. Box 2275
Dot Lake, AK 99762
(907) 882–2695

DOUGLAS INDIAN ASSOCIATION
P.O. Box 240541
Juneau, AK 99824
(907) 364–2916

EAGLE VILLAGE
P.O. Box 19
Eagle, AK 99738
(907) 547–2271

EEK NATIVE VILLAGE
P.O. Box 87
Eek, AK 99578
(907) 536–5128

EGEGIK VILLAGE
P.O. Box 29
Egegik, AK 99579
(907) 233–2211

EKLUTNA NATIVE VILLAGE
26339 Eklutna Village Road
Chugiak, AK 99567–6330
(907) 688–6020

EKUK NATIVE VILLAGE
General Delivery
Ekuk, AK 99576
(907) 842–5937

EKWOK VILLAGE
100 Main Street
P.O. Box 70
Ekwok, AK 99580
(907) 464–3336

ELIM NATIVE VILLAGE
P.O. Box 70
Elim, AK 99739–0070
(907) 890–3737

EMMONAK VILLAGE
P.O. Box 126
Emmonak, AK 99581
(907) 949–1720

EVAK NATIVE VILLAGE
P.O. Box 1388
Cordova, AK 99574–1388
(907) 424–7738

EVANSVILLE VILLAGE
(a.k.a. BETTLES FIELD)
P.O. Box 26087
Bettles, AK 99726
(907) 692–5005

FALSE PASS NATIVE VILLAGE
P.O. Box 29
False Pass, AK 99583
(907) 548–2227

FORT YUKON NATIVE VILLAGE
P.O. Box 169
Fort Yukon, AK 99740
(907) 662–2581

GAKONA NATIVE VILLAGE
P.O. Box 303
Copper Center, AK 99573
(907) 822–4086

GALENA VILLAGE
P.O. Box 244
Galena, AK 99741
(907) 656–1711

GAMBELL NATIVE VILLAGE
P.O. Box 90
Gambell, AK 99742
(907) 985–5346

GEORGETOWN NATIVE VILLAGE
1400 Virginia Court
Anchorage, AK 99501
(907) 274–2194

GOODNEWS BAY NATIVE VILLAGE
P.O. Box 03
Goodnews Bay, AK 99587
(907) 967–8929

GRAYLING VILLAGE
(a.k.a. HOLIKACHUK)
General Delivery
Grayling, AK 99590
(907) 453–5116

GULKANA VILLAGE
P.O. Box 254
Gakona, AK 99586
(907) 822–5213

HAMILTON NATIVE VILLAGE
P.O. Box 20248
Kotlik, AK 99620
(907) 899–4252

HEALY LAKE VILLAGE
P.O. Box 60300
Fairbanks, AK 99706–0300
(907) 876–5018

HOLY CROSS VILLAGE
P.O. Box 89
Holy Cross, AK 99602
(907) 476–7124

HOONAH INDIAN ASSOCIATION
P.O. Box 602
Hoonah, AK 99829–062
(907) 945–3545

HOOPER BAY NATIVE VILLAGE
P.O. Box 41
Hooper Bay, AK 99604
(907) 758–4915

HUGHES VILLAGE
P.O. Box 45029
Hughes, AK 99745
(907) 889–2239

HUSLIA VILLAGE
P.O. Box 70
Huslia, AK 99746
(907) 829–2294

HYDABURG COOPERATIVE ASSOCIATION
P.O. Box 305
Hydaburg, AK 99922
(907) 285–3666

IGIUGIG VILLAGE
P.O. Box 4008
Igiugig, AK 99613
(907) 533–3211

ILIAMNA VILLAGE
P.O. Box 286
Iliamna, AK 99606
(907) 571–1246

INUPIAT COMMUNITY OF ARCTIC SLOPE
P.O. Box 934
Barrow, AK 99723

IQURMUIT TRIBE (RUSSIAN MISSION)
P.O. Box 9
Russian Mission, AK 99657
(907) 584–5511

IVANOFF BAY VILLAGE
100 Olga Kalmakoff Street
Fire Hall Building
P.O. Box KIB
Ivanoff Bay, AK 99695–0050
(907) 669–2200

KAKE ORGANIZED VILLAGE
P.O. Box 316
Kake, AK 99830–0316
(907) 785–6471

KAKTOVIK VILLAGE
P.O. Box 8
Kaktovik, AK 99747
(907) 640–6120

KALSKAG VILLAGE
P.O. Box 50
Kalskag, AK 99607
(907) 471–2248

KALTAG NATIVE VILLAGE
P.O. Box 9
Kaltag, AK 99748
(907) 534–2230

KANATAK VILLAGE
C/O Becharof Corp.
1577 C. St. Plaza, Suite 304
Anchorage, AK 99501
(907) 263–9820

KARLUK NATIVE VILLAGE
P.O. Box 22
Karluk, AK 99608
(907) 241–2218

KASAAN ORGANIZED VILLAGE
P.O. Box KXA—Kasaan
Ketchikan, AK 99950–0340
(907) 561–2230

KASIGLUK NATIVE VILLAGE
P.O. Box 19
Kasigluk, AK 99609
(907) 477–6405

KENAITZE INDIAN TRIBE
P.O. Box 988
Kenai, AK 99611
(907) 283–3633

KETCHIKAN INDIAN CORPORATION
429 Deermount Avenue
Ketchikan, AK 99901
(907) 225–5158

KIANA NATIVE VILLAGE
P.O. Box 69
Kiana, AK 99749
(907) 475–2109

KING ISLAND NATIVE COMMUNITY
P.O. Box 992
Nome, AK 99762
(907) 443–5494

KIPNUK NATIVE VILLAGE
P.O. Box 57
Kipnuk, AK 99614
(907) 896–5515

KIVALINA NATIVE VILLAGE
P.O. Box 50051
Kivalina, AK 99750
(907) 645–2153

KLAWOCK COOPERATIVE ASSOCIATION
403 Bayview Blvd.
P.O. Box 430
Klawock, AK 99925–0430
(907) 755–2265

KLUTI-KAAH NATIVE VILLAGE
(a.k.a. COPPER CENTER)
P.O. Box 68
Copper Center, AK 99573
(907) 822–5541

KNIK VILLAGE
P.O. Box 871565
Wasilla, AK 99687–1565
(907) 373–7991

KOBUK NATIVE VILLAGE
P.O. Box 39
Kobuk, AK 99751
(907) 948–2203

KOKHANOK VILLAGE
P.O. Box 1007
Kokhanok, AK 99606
(907) 282–2202

KOLIGANEK VILLAGE
P.O. Box 5057
Koliganek, AK 99576
(907) 596–3434

KONGIGANAK VILLAGE
P.O. Box 5069
Kongiganak, AK 99559 5069
(907) 557–5226

KOTLIK VILLAGE
P.O. Box 20096
Kotlik, AK 99620
(907) 899–4326

KOTZEBUE NATIVE VILLAGE
P.O. Box 296
Kotzebue, AK 99752
(907) 442–3467

KOYUK NATIVE VILLAGE
P.O. Box 53030
Koyuk, AK 99753
(907) 963–3651

KOYUKUK NATIVE VILLAGE
P.O. Box 49
Koyukuk, AK 99754
(907) 927–2214

KWETHLUK ORGANIZED VILLAGE
P.O. Box 129
Kwethluck, AK 99621–0129
(907) 757–6714

KWIGILLINGOK NATIVE VILLAGE
P.O. Box 49
Kwigillingok, AK 99622
(907) 588–8114

KWINHAGAK NATIVE VILLAGE
(a.k.a. QUINHAGAK)
P.O. Box 149
Quinhagak, AK 99655
(907) 556–8165

LARSEN BAY NATIVE VILLAGE
P.O. Box 35
Larsen Bay, AK 99624
(907) 847–2207

LEVELOCK VILLAGE
P.O. Box 70
Levelock, AK 99625
(907) 287–3030

LIME VILLAGE
General Delivery
Lime Village, AK 99627
(907) 526–5128

LOUDON VILLAGE COUNCIL
P.O. Box 244
Galena, AK 99741
(907) 656–1711

LOWER KALSKAG VILLAGE
P.O. Box 27
Lower Kalskag, AK 99626
(907) 471–2307

MANLEY HOT SPRINGS VILLAGE
P.O. Box 23
Manley Hot Springs, AK 99756
(907 672–3178

MANOKOTAK VILLAGE
P.O. Box 169
Manokotak, AK 99628
(907) 289–2067

MARSHALL NATIVE VILLAGE
(a.k.a. FORTUNA LEDGE)
P.O. Box 10
Fortuna Ledge, AK 99585
(907) 679–6215

MARY'S IGLOO VILLAGE
P.O. Box 630
Teller, AK 99778
(907) 642–3731

MCGRATH NATIVE VILLAGE
P.O. Box 134
McGrath, AK 99627
(907) 524–3024

MEKORYUK, ISLAND OF NUNIVAK, NATIVE
VILLAGE
P.O. Box 66
Mekoryuk, AK 99630
(907) 827–8828

MENTASTA LAKE VILLAGE
P.O. Box 6019
Mentasta Lake, AK 99780–6019
(907) 291–2319

MINTO NATIVE VILLAGE
P.O. Box 58026
Minto, AK 99758–0026
(907) 798–7112

NAKNEK NATIVE VILLAGE
P.O. Box 106
Naknek, AK 99633
(907) 246–4210

NANWALEK VILLAGE
(a.k.a. ENGLISH BAY)
P.O. Box 8028
Nanwalek, AK 99603
(907) 281–2274

NAPAIMUTE NATIVE VILLAGE
P.O. Box 96
Aniak, AK 99557

NAPAKIAK NATIVE VILLAGE
Pouch 2
Napakiak, AK 99634
(907) 589–2135

NAPASKIAK NATIVE VILLAGE
P.O. Box 6009
Napaskiak, AK 99559
(907) 737–7626

NELSON LAGOON VILLAGE
P.O. Box 13
Nelson Lagoon, AK 99571
(907) 989–2204

NENANA NATIVE ASSOCIATION
307.8 Mile Parks Highway
P.O. Box 356
Nenana, AK 99760
(907) 832–5461

NEW STUYAHOK VILLAGE
P.O. Box 49
New Stuyahok, AK 99636
(907) 693–3173

NEWHALEN VILLAGE
P.O. Box 206, TLF
Newhalen, AK 99606
(907) 571–1410

NEWTOK VILLAGE
P.O. Box 5545
Newtok, AK 99559
(907) 237–2314

NIGHTMUTE NATIVE VILLAGE
P.O. Box 90021
Nightmute, AK 99690
(907) 647–6215

NIKOLAI VILLAGE
P.O. Box 9105
Nikolai, AK 99691
(907) 293–2311

NIKOLSKI NATIVE VILLAGE
P.O. Box 109
Nikolski, AK 99638
(907) 576–2225

NINILCHIK VILLAGE
P.O. Box 39070
Ninilchik, AK 99639
(907) 567–3313

NOATAK NATIVE VILLAGE
P.O. Box 89
Noatak, AK 99761
(907) 485–2173

NOME ESKIMO COMMUNITY
P.O. Box 1090
Nome, AK 99762
(907) 443–2372

NONDALTON VILLAGE
P.O. Box 49
Nondalton, AK 99640
(907) 294–2220

NOORVICK NATIVE COMMUNITY
P.O. Box 71
Noorvick, AK 99763
(907) 636–2144

NORTHWAY VILLAGE
P.O. Box 516
Northway, AK 99764
(907) 778–2271

NUIQSUT NATIVE VILLAGE
General Delivery
Nuiqsut, AK 99723
(907) 480–6714

NULATO VILLAGE
P.O. Box 65049
Nulato, AK 99765
(907) 898–2339

NUNAPITCHUK NATIVE VILLAGE
(with KASIGLUCK, a.k.a. AKOLMUIT)
P.O. Box 130
Nunapitchuk, AK 99641

OHOGAMIUT VILLAGE
General Delivery
Fortuna Lodge, AK 99585
(907) 679–6740

OLD HARBOR VILLAGE
P.O. Box 62
Old Harbor, AK 99643
(907) 286–2215

ORUTSARARMUIT NATIVE COUNCIL
835 Ridgecrest Drive
P.O. Box 927
Bethel, AK 99559
(907) 543–2608

OSCARVILLE TRADITIONAL VILLAGE
P.O. Box 6129
Napaskiak, AK 99559
(907) 737–7099

OUZINKIE NATIVE VILLAGE
P.O. Box 130
Ouzinkie, AK 99644
(907) 680–2259

PIAMIUT NATIVE VILLAGE
General Delivery
Hooper Bay, AK 99604

**PEDRO BAY VILLAGE**
P.O. Box 47020
Pedro Bay, AK 99647
(907) 850–2225

**PERRYVILLE NATIVE VILLAGE**
P.O. Box 101
Perryville, AK 99648–0101
(907) 853–2203

**PETERSBURG INDIAN ASSOCIATION**
P.O. Box 1418
Petersburg, AK 99833
(907) 772–3636

**PIAMIUT NATIVE VILLAGE**
General Delivery
Hooper Bay, AK 99604

**PILOT POINT NATIVE VILLAGE**
P.O. Box 449
Pilot Point, AK 99649
(907) 797–2208

**PILOT STATION TRADITIONAL VILLAGE**
P.O. Box 5119
Pilot Station, AK 99650
(907) 549–3373

**PITKA'S POINT NATIVE VILLAGE**
P.O. Box 127
Pitka's Point, AK 99658
(907) 438–2833

**PLATINUM TRADITIONAL VILLAGE**
P.O. Box 8
Platinum, AK 99651
(907) 979–8177

**POINT HOPE NATIVE VILLAGE**
P.O. Box 109
Point Hope, AK 99766
(907) 368–2330

**POINT LAY NATIVE VILLAGE**
P.O. Box 101
Point Lay, AK 99759
(907) 833–2428

**PORT GRAHAM VILLAGE**
P.O. Box 5510
Port Graham, AK 99603
(907) 284–2227

**PORT HEIDEN NATIVE VILLAGE**
P.O. Box 49007
Port Heiden, AK 99549
(907) 837–2296

**PORT LIONS NATIVE VILLAGE**
P.O. Box 69
Port Lions, AK 99550
(907) 454–2234

**PORTAGE CREEK VILLAGE**
P.O. Box 330
Portage Creek, AK 99576
(907) 842–5218

**QAGUN TAYAGUNGIN TRIBE OF SAND POINT**
Box 447
Sand Point, AK 99661
(907) 383–3525

**QAWALANGIN TRIBE OF UNALASKA**
205 West Broadway
P.O. Box 334
Unalaska, AK 99685
(907) 581–2920

**RAMPART VILLAGE**
P.O. Box 67029
Rampart, AK 99767
(907) 358–3312

**RED DEVIL VILLAGE**
P.O. Box 61
Red Devil, AK 99656
(907) 447–3225

**RUBY NATIVE VILLAGE**
P.O. Box 210
Ruby, AK 99768
(907) 468–4479

**SALAMANTOFF VILLAGE**
P.O. Box 2682
Kenai, AK 99611
(907) 283–7864

**SAVOONGA NATIVE VILLAGE**
P.O. Box 120
Savoonga, AK 99769
(907) 984–6414

**SAXMAN ORGANIZED VILLAGE**
Rte. 2, Box 2-Saxman
Ketchikan, AK 99901
(907) 247–2502

**SCAMMON BAY NATIVE VILLAGE**
P.O. Box 126
Scammon Bay, AK 99662
(907) 558–5425

**SELAWIK NATIVE VILLAGE**
P.O. Box 59
Selawik, AK 99770
(907) 484–2165

**SELDOVIA NATIVE VILLAGE**
P.O. Drawer L
Seldovia, AK 99663
(907) 234–7898

**SHAGELUK NATIVE VILLAGE**
General Delivery
Shageluk, AK 99665
(907) 473–8239

**SHAKTOOLIK NATIVE VILLAGE**
P.O. Box 100
Shaktoolik, AK 99771–0100
(907) 955–3701

**SHELDON'S POINT NATIVE VILLAGE**
P.O. Box 27
Sheldon's Point, AK 99666–0027
(907) 498–4182

**SHISHMAREF NATIVE VILLAGE**
P.O. Box 72110
Shishmaref, AK 99772
(907) 649–3821

**SHOONAQ' TRIBE OF KODIAK**
P.O. Box 1974
Kodiak, AK 99615
(907) 486–4449

**SHUNGNAK NATIVE VILLAGE**
P.O. Box 63
Shungnak, AK 99773
(907) 437–2170

**SITKA TRIBE OF ALASKA**
456 Katlian Street
Sitka, AK 99835–7505
(907) 747–3207

**SKAGWAY VILLAGE COUNCIL**
P.O. Box 149
Skagway, AK 99840

**SLEETMUTE VILLAGE**
P.O. Box 34
Sleetmute, AK 99668
(907) 449–4205

**SOLOMON VILLAGE**
P.O. Box 2053
Nome, AK 99762
(907) 443–4985

**SOUTH NAKNEK VILLAGE**
P.O. Box 70106
South Naknek, AK 99670
(907) 246–6565

**ST. GEORGE ISLAND VILLAGE**
P.O. Box 940
St. George, AK 99591
(907) 859–2205

**ST. MICHAEL NATIVE VILLAGE**
P.O. Box 59058
St. Michael, AK 99659
(907) 923–2304

**ST. PAUL ISLAND ALEUT COMMUNITY**
P.O. Box 86
St. Paul Island, AK 99660
(907) 546–2211

**STEBBINS COMMUNITY ASSOCIATION**
P.O. Box 71002
Stebbins, AK 99761
(907) 934–3561

**STEVENS NATIVE VILLAGE**
P.O. Box 13
Stevens Village, AK 99774
(907) 478–7228

**STONEY RIVER VILLAGE**
General Delivery
Stoney River, AK 99557
(907) 537–3314

**TAKOTNA VILLAGE**
General Delivery
Takotna, AK 99675
(907) 298–2212

TANACROSS NATIVE VILLAGE
General Delivery
Tanacross, AK 99776

TANANA VILLAGE
P.O. Box 77093
Tanana, AK 99777
(907) 366–7160

TATITLEK NATIVE VILLAGE
P.O. Box 87
Tatitlek, AK 99677
(907) 325–2311

TAZLINA NATIVE VILLAGE
P.O. Box 188
Glenallen, AK 99588
(907) 822–5865

TELIDA NATIVE VILLAGE
P.O. Box TLF
McGrath, AK 99627
(907) 843–8115

TELLER NATIVE VILLAGE
P.O. Box 567
Teller, AK 99778
(907) 642–3381

TETLIN NATIVE VILLAGE
P.O. Box TTL
Tetlin, AK 99779
(907) 324–2130

CENTRAL COUNCIL OF TLINGIT & HAIDA
    INDIAN TRIBES OF ALASKA
320 W. Willoughby Ave., Suite 300
Juneau, AK 99801
(907) 463–7100

TOGIAK TRADITIONAL VILLAGE
P.O. Box 310
Togiak, AK 99678
(907) 493–5003

TULUKSAK NATIVE COMMUNITY
P.O. Box 95
Tuluksak, AK 99679–0095
(907) 695–6420

TUNTUTULIAK NATIVE VILLAGE
General Delivery
Tuntutuliak, AK 99680
(907) 256–2128

TUNUNAK NATIVE VILLAGE
P.O. Box 77
Tununak, AK 99681
(907) 652–6527

TWIN HILLS VILLAGE
P.O. Box TWA
Twin Hills, AK 99576–8996
(907) 525–4821

TYONEK NATIVE VILLAGE
P.O. Box 82009
Tyonek, AK 99682–0009
(907) 583–2271

UGASHIK VILLAGE
206 East Fireweed Lane
Suite #204
Anchorage, AK 99503
(907) 338–7611

UMKUMIUT NATIVE VILLAGE
General Delivery
Nightmute, AK 99690
(907) 647–6213

UNALAKLEET NATIVE VILLAGE
P.O. Box 270
Unalakleet, AK 99684
(907) 624–3622

UNGA TRIBAL COUNCIL
P.O. Box 508
Sand Point, AK 99661
(907) 383–5215

VENETIE NATIVE VILLAGE
P.O. Box 81080
Venetie, AK 99781–0080
(907) 849–8165

WAINWRIGHT VILLAGE
P.O. Box 184
Wainwright, AK 99782
(907) 763–2726

WALES NATIVE VILLAGE
P.O. Box 549
Wales, AK 99783
(907) 664–3062

WHITE MOUNTAIN NATIVE VILLAGE
P.O. Box 84082
White Mountain, AK 99784
(907) 638–3651

WRANGELL COOPERATIVE ASSOCIATION
P.O. Box 1198
Wrangell, AK 99929
(907) 874–3482

YAKUTAT TLINGIT NATIVE VILLAGE
P.O. Box 418
Yakutat, AK 99689
(907) 784–3238

## ◆ ARIZONA

AK CHIN INDIAN COMMUNITY (Tohono
　O'odham-Akima-O'odham)
Rte. 2, Box 27
Maricopa, AZ 85239
(602) 568–2227

COCOPAH TRIBAL OFFICE
County 15 and Ave G
Somerton, AZ 85344
(520) 627–2102

COLORADO RIVER INDIAN TRIBES (Hopi,
　Chemehuevi, Mohave, Navajo)
Route 1, Box 23–B
Parker, AZ 85344
(520) 669–9211

FORT MCDOWELL MOHAVE-APACHE INDIAN
　COMMUNITY
P.O. Box 17779
Fountain Hills, AZ 85269
(602) 990–0995

FORT MOJAVE INDIAN TRIBE (see
　CALIFORNIA)
(Located in Arizona, California, and Nevada).

GILA RIVER PIMA-MARICOPA INDIAN
　COMMUNITY
P.O. Box 97
Sacaton, AZ 85247
(602) 562–3311 or 963–4323

HAVASUPAI TRIBE
P.O. Box 10
Supai, AZ 86435
(520) 448–2731

HOPI TRIBE
P.O. Box 123
Kykotsmovi, AZ 86039
(520) 734–2441

HUALAPAI TRIBE
P.O. Box 179
Peach Springs, AZ 86434
(520) 769–2216

KAIBAB BAND OF THE PAIUTE INDIANS
HC65 Box 2
Fredonia, AZ 86022
(520) 643–7245
(Located in Arizona and Utah).

NAVAJO NATION
P.O. Box 9000
Window Rock, AZ 86515
(520) 871–6352
(Located in Arizona, New Mexico, and Utah).

PASCUA-YAQUI INDIAN COMMUNITY
7474 S. Camino De Oeste
Tucson, AZ 85746
(520) 883–2838/5000

QUECHAN INDIAN TRIBE
P.O. Box 11352
Yuma, AZ 85366
(619) 572–0487
(Located in Arizona and California).

SALT RIVER PIMA-MARICOPA INDIAN
　COMMUNITY
Rte. 1, Box 216
Scottsdale, AZ 85256
(620) 847–8015

SAN CARLOS APACHE TRIBE
P.O. Box 0
San Carlos, AZ 85550
(520) 475–2361

SAN JUAN SOUTHERN PAIUTE TRIBE
P.O. Box 2656
Tuba City, AZ 86045
(602) 283–4583, -4587

TOHONO O'ODHAM NATION (Papago)
P.O. Box 837
Sells, AZ 85634
(602) 383–2221

TONTO APACHE TRIBAL COUNCIL
Tonto Reservation #30
Payson, AZ 85541
(520) 474–5000

WHITE MOUNTAIN APACHE TRIBE
P.O. Box 700
Whiteriver, AZ 85941
(520) 338–4346

YAVAPAI-APACHE TRIBE
P.O. Box 1188
Camp Verde, AZ 86322
(520) 567–3649

YAVAPAI–PRESCOTT INDIAN TRIBE
530 E. Merritt St.
Prescott, AZ 86301–2038
(520) 445–8790

## ♦ CALIFORNIA

AGUA CALIENTE TRIBE (Cahuilla)
960 E. Tahquitz Canyon Way, #106
Palm Springs, CA 92262
(760) 325–5673

ALTURAS RANCHERIA (Pit River)
P.O. Box 1035
Alturas, CA 96101
(916) 233–5571

AUGUSTINE RESERVATION (Cahuilla)
Thermal, CA 92274

BERRY CREEK RANCHERIA (Tyme Maidu)
5 Tyme Way
Oroville, CA 95966
(530) 534–3859

BIG BEND RANCHERIA (Pit River)
P.O. Drawer 1570
Burney, CA 96013
(530) 335–5421

BIG LAGOON RANCHERIA (Tolowa, Yurok)
P.O. Box 3060
Trinidad, CA 95570
(707) 826–2079

BIG PINE PAIUTE TRIBE OF THE
    OWENS VALLEY
Box 700, 841 S. Main St.
Big Pine, CA 93513
(760) 938–2003

BIG PINE RESERVATION
P.O. Box 700
Big Pine, CA 93513
(610) 938–2003

BIG SANDY RANCHERIA (Western Mono)
Box 337, 7302 Rancheria Lane
Auberry, CA 93602
(559) 855–4003

BIG VALLEY RANCHERIA (Pomo)
2726 Mission Rancheria Rd.
Lakeport, CA 95453–0955
(707) 263–3924

BISHOP RESERVATION (Paiute, Shoshone)
50 Tu Su Lane
Bishop, CA 93514
(760) 873–3585

BLUE LAKE RANCHERIA (Yurok,
    Tolowa, Wiyot)
P.O. Box 428
Blue Lake, CA 95525
(707) 668–5101

BRIDGEPORT INDIAN COLONY (Paiute)
P.O. Box 37
Bridgeport, CA 93517
(760) 932–7083

BUENA VISTA RANCHERIA (Me-Wuk)
4650 Coalmine Road
Ione, CA 95640
(209) 274–6512

CABAZON BAND OF MISSION INDIANS
    (Cahuilla)
84–245 Indio Springs Drive
Indio, CA 92203
(760) 342–2593

CAHUILLA RESERVATION
P.O. Box 391760
Anza, CA 92539
(714) 763–5549

CALAVERAS COUNTY BAND OF MIWOK
    INDIANS
579 Ball Mountain Rd.
West Point, CA 95255

CAMPO BAND OF MISSION INDIANS
    (Diegueño)
36190 Church Rd., Suite 1
Campo, CA 91906
(619) 478–9046

CAPITAN GRANDE RESERVATION (Diegueño)
Lakeside, CA 92040

CEDARVILLE RANCHERIA (Northern Paiute)
200 South Howard St.
Alturas, CA 96101
(530) 233–3969

CHEMEHUEVI INDIAN TRIBE
P.O. Box 1976
Havasu Lake, CA 92363
(760) 858–4219
(Located in California and Arizona).

CHICKEN RANCH RANCHERIA (Me-Wuk)
P.O. Box 1159
Jamestown, CA 95327
(209) 984–4806

CLOVERDALE RANCHERIA (Pomo)
555 S. Cloverdale Blvd., #1
Cloverdale, CA 95425
(707) 894–5775

COLD SPRINGS RANCHERIA (Mono)
(aka SYCAMORE VALLEY)
P.O. Box 209
Tollhouse, CA 93667
(559) 855–5043

COLORADO RIVER INDIAN TRIBES
(see Arizona)

COLUSA INDIAN COMMUNITY (Cachil Dehe
   Band of Wintun Indians)
3730 Highway 45
Colusa, CA 95932
(530) 458–8231

CORTINA RANCHERIA (Wintun)
P.O. Box 7470
Citrus Heights, CA 95621
(916) 374–0836

COYOTE VALLEY TRIBAL COUNCIL (Pomo)
7751 North State St.
Redwood Valley, CA 95470–0039
(707) 485–8724

CUYAPAIPE BAND OF MISSION INDIANS
   (Diegueño)
4054 Willows Rd.
P.O. Box 2250
Alpine Valley, CA 91901
(619) 478–5289

DRY CREEK RANCHERIA (Pomo)
P.O. Box 607
Geyserville, CA 95441
(707) 857–3045

ELK VALLEY RANCHERIA (Tolowa)
P.O. Box 1042
Crescent City, CA 95531
(707) 464–4680

FORT BIDWELL INDIAN TRIBE (Paiute)
P.O. Box 129
Fort Bidwell, CA 96112
(530) 279–6310 or 2233

FORT INDEPENDENCE PAIUTE INDIAN
   TRIBE
P.O. Box 67
Fort Independence, CA 93526
(760) 878–2126

FORT MOJAVE INDIAN TRIBE
500 Merriman Ave.
Needles, CA 92363
(760) 629–4591

GREENVILLE RANCHERIA (Maidu)
P.O. Box 100
Red Bluff, CA 96003
(530) 528–9000

GRINDSTONE RANCHERIA (Muimok,
   Nomelaki, Wintun-Wailaki)
P.O. Box 63
Elk Creek, CA 95939
(530) 968–5365

GUIDIVILLE RANCHERIA
P.O. Box 339
Talmage, CA 95481
(707) 462–3682

HOOPA VALLEY TRIBE
P.O. Box 1348
Hoopa, CA 95546
(530) 625–4211

HOPLAND BAND OF POMO INDIANS
P.O. Box 610
Hopland, CA 95449
(707) 744–1647

INAJA & COSMIT RESERVATION (Diegueño)
P.O. Box 186
Santa Ysabella, CA 92070

JACKSON RANCHERIA (Me-Wuk)
P.O. Box 1090
Jackson, CA 95642
(209) 223–1935

JAMUL INDIAN VILLAGE (Diegueño)
P.O. Box 612
Jamul, CA 91935
(619) 669–4785

KARUK TRIBE OF CALIFORNIA
P.O. Box 1016
Happy Camp, CA 96039
(530) 493–5305

LA JOLLA BAND OF MISSION INDIANS
    (Luiseño)
2200 Highway 76
Pauma Valley, CA 92061
(760) 742–3771/72

LA POSTA BAND OF DIEGUEÑO MISSION
    INDIANS
P.O. Box 1048
Boulevard, CA 91905
(619) 478–2113

LONE PINE RESERVATION (Paiute, Shoshone)
101 S. Main St.
Lone Pine, CA 93545
(619) 876–5414

LOOKOUT RANCHERIA (Pit River)
37014 Mainstreet
Burney, CA 96013
(530) 335–5421
(see CALIFORNIA: PIT RIVER TRIBE)

LOS COYOTES RESERVATION (Cahuilla)
P.O. Box 189
Warner Springs, CA 92086
(760) 782–0711

LYTTON RANCHERIA
P.O. Box 519
Crescent City, CA 95531
(707) 575–5917

MANZANITA BAND OF DIEGUEÑO MISSION
    INDIANS
P.O. Box 1302
Boulevard, CA 91905
(619) 776–4930

MESA GRANDE BAND OF DIEGUEÑO
    MISSION INDIANS
P.O. Box 270
Santa Ysabel, CA 92070
(760) 782–3818

MIDDLETOWN RANCHERIA OF POMO
    INDIANS
P.O. Box 1035
Middletown, CA 95461
(707) 987–3670

MONTGOMERY CREEK RANCHERIA (Pit
    River)
37014 Main St.
Burney, CA 96013
(530) 335–5421
(see CALIFORNIA: PIT RIVER TRIBE)

MOORETOWN RANCHERIA (Concow, Maidu)
#1 Alverda Dr.
Oroville, CA 95966
(530) 533–3625

MORONGO RESERVATION (Cahuilla)
11581 Potrero Rd.
Banning, CA 92220
(909) 849–4697

NORTH FORK BAND OF MONO INDIANS
133 Sierra
Clovis, CA 93612
(559) 299–3729

PALA BAND OF MISSION INDIANS (Pomo)
P.O. Box 50
Pala, CA 92059
(760) 742–3784/5

PAUMA AND YUIMA RESERVATION (Luiseño)
P.O. Box 369
Pauma Valley, CA 92061
(619) 742–1289

PECHANGA RESERVATION (Luiseño)
P.O. Box 1477
Temecula, CA 92593
(909) 676–2768

PICAYUNE RANCHERIA
P.O. Box 269
Coarsegold, CA 93614
(209) 683–6633

PINOLEVILLE RANCHERIA (Pomo)
367 North State St., Suite 204
Ukiah, CA 95482
(707) 463–1454

PIT RIVER TRIBE OF CALIFORNIA
(aka AJUMAWI–ATSUGEWI NATION)
37014 Mainstreet
Burney, CA 96013
(530) 335–5421

POTTER VALLEY RANCHERIA (Pomo)
417D Talmage Rd.
Ukiah, CA 95482
(707) 468–7494 or 7495

QUARTZ VALLEY INDIAN COMMUNITY
　(Karuk, Shasta, Upper Klamath)
P.O. Box 24
Fort Jones, CA 96032
(530) 468–5907

RAMONA BAND RESERVATION (Cahuilla)
P.O. Box 391372
Anza, CA 92539
(909) 763–4105

REDDING RANCHERIA (Pit River,
　Wintun, Yana)
2000 Rancheria Rd.
Redding, CA 96001–5528
(530) 225–8979

REDWOOD VALLEY RANCHERIA (Pomo)
3250 Road 1
Redwood Valley, CA 95470
(707) 485–0361

RESIGHINI RANCHERIA (Yurok)
P.O. Box 529
Klamath, CA 95548
(707) 482–2431

RINCON BAND OF MISSION INDIANS
　(Luiseño)
P.O. Box 68
Valley Center, CA 92082
(760) 749–1051

ROARING CREEK RANCHERIA (Pit River)
(see Pit River Reservation)

ROBINSON RANCHERIA OF POMO INDIANS
1545 E. Hwy 20
Nice, CA 95454
(707) 275–0527

ROUND VALLEY INDIAN RESERVATION
P.O. Box 448
Covelo, CA 95428
(707) 983–6126

SAN MANUEL RESERVATION (Serrano)
P.O. Box 266
Patten, CA 92369
(909) 864–8933

SAN PASQUAL RESERVATION (Diegueño)
P.O. Box 365
Valley Center, CA 92082
(760) 749–3200

SANTA ROSA INDIAN COMMUNITY
　(Tache, Yokut)
P.O. Box 8
Lemoore, CA 93245
(559) 924–1278

SANTA ROSA RESERVATION (Cahuilla)
P.O. Box 390611
Anza, CA 92539
(909) 763–5140

SANTA YNEZ BAND OF MISSION INDIANS
　(Chumash)
P.O. Box 517
Santa Ynez, CA 93460
(805) 688–7997

SANTA YSABEL BAND OF MISSION INDIANS
　(Diegueño)
P.O. Box 130
Santa Ysabel, CA 92070
(760) 765–0845

SCOTTS VALLEY BAND OF POMO
149 N. Main, #200
Lakeport, CA 92070
(707) 263–4771

SHEEP RANCH RANCHERIA (Miwok)
8 School St.
Sheep Ranch, CA 95250
(209) 728–8625

SHERWOOD VALLEY RANCHERIA (Pomo)
190 Sherwood Hill Dr.
Willits, CA 95490
(707) 459–9690

SHINGLE SPRINGS RANCHERIA (Miwok)
P.O. Box 1340
Shingle Springs, CA 95682
(530) 676–8010

SMITH RIVER RANCHERIA (Tolowa)
(aka ELK VALLEY)
250 N. Indian Rd.
Smith River, CA 95567
(707) 487–9255

SOBOBA BAND OF MISSION INDIANS
    (Luiseño)
P.O. Box 487
San Jacinto, CA 92581
(909) 654–2765

STEWARTS POINT RANCHERIA (Kashia
    Pomo)
1420 Guerneville Rd., Suite #3
Santa Rosa, CA 95403
(707) 591–0580

SUSANVILLE RANCHERIA (Maidu, Paiute, Pit
    River, Washoe)
P.O. Box U
Susanville, CA 96130
(530) 257–6264

SYCUAN BAND OF MISSION INDIANS
    (Diegueño)
5459 Dehesa Rd.
El Cajon, CA 92019
(619) 445–2613,

TABLE BLUFF RESERVATION (Wiyot)
1000 Wiyot Dr.
Loleta, CA 95551
(707) 733–5055

TABLE MOUNTAIN RANCHERIA (Yokut)
P.O. Box 243
Friant, CA 93626
(559) 822–2587

TIMBI-SHA SHOSHONE BAND
P.O. Box 206
Death Valley, CA 92328
(760) 786–2374

TORRES–MARTINEZ RESERVATION (Cahuilla)
66–725 Martinez Rd.
Thermal, CA 92274
(619) 397–0300

TULE RIVER RESERVATION (Yokut)
P.O. Box 589
Porterville, CA 93258
(559) 781–4271

TUOLUMNE BAND OF MEWUK INDIANS
Box 699
Tuolumne, CA 95379
(209) 928–3475

TWENTY–NINE PALMS RESERVATION
    (Chemehuevi, Luiseño)
46–200 Harrison St.
Coachella, CA 92236
(760) 775–5566

UPPER LAKE RANCHERIA (Pomo)
P.O. Box 516
Upper Lake, CA 95485
(707) 275–0737

UTU UTU GWAITA PAIUTE TRIBE BENTON
    PAIUTE RESERVATION
Star Rte. 4, Box 56–A
Benton, CA 93512
(760) 933–2321

WINNEMUCCA COLONY (Paiute)
(see NEVADA: WINNEMUCCA INDIAN COLONY).

WINTUN TRIBE-RUMSEY RANCHERIA
P.O. Box 18
Brooks, CA 95606
(530) 796–3400

WOODFORDS WASHOE COMMUNITY
    (Washoe)
96 Washoe Blvd.
Markleeville, CA 96120
(916) 694–2170
(see NEVADA: WASHOE TRIBE).

XL RANCH (Pit River)
P.O. Drawer 1570
Burney, CA 96013
(916) 335–5421
(see CALIFORNIA: PIT RIVER TRIBE).

YUROK RESERVATION
Yurok Tribal Council
1034 Sixth St.
Eureka, CA 95501
(707) 444–0433

◆ **COLORADO**

SOUTHERN UTE TRIBE
P.O. Box 737
Ignacio, CO 81137
(970) 563–0100

UTE MOUNTAIN RESERVATION
P.O. Box 248
Towaoc, CO 81334
(970) 565–3751
(Located in Colorado, New Mexico, and Utah).

◆ **CONNECTICUT**

MASHANTUCKET PEQUOT TRIBE
P.O. Box 3060
2 Matt's Path
Mashantucket, CT 06339
(860) 396–6500

THE MOHEGAN TRIBE OF INDIANS OF THE
    STATE OF CONNECTICUT
5 Crowhill Rd.
Uncasville, CT 06382
(860) 204–6100

◆ **FLORIDA**

MICCOSUKEE TRIBE OF INDIANS OF
    FLORIDA (Creek)
P.O. Box 440021, Tamiami Station
Miami, FL 33144
(305) 223–8380/8383

SEMINOLE NATION OF FLORIDA
6300 Stirling Rd.
Hollywood, FL 33024
(305) 584–0400

◆ **IDAHO**

COEUR D'ALENE TRIBAL COUNCIL
850 A Street, P.O. Box 408
Plummer, ID 83851
(208) 686–1800

DUCK VALLEY SHOSHONE PAIUTE TRIBES
(see NEVADA)

KOOTENAI TRIBE OF IDAHO
P.O. Box 1269
Bonners Ferry, ID 83805
(208) 267–3519

NEZ PERCÉ TRIBE OF IDAHO
P.O. Box 305
Lapwai, ID 83540
(208) 843–2253

NORTHWESTERN BAND OF SHOSHONI
    NATION
427 N. Main, Suite 101
Pocatello, ID 83204
(208) 478–5712

SHOSHONE-BANNOCK TRIBES
Fort Hall Tribal Office
P.O. Box 306
Fort Hall, ID 83203
(208) 238–3700

SUMMIT LAKE RESERVATION (Paiute)
(see NEVADA)

◆ **IOWA**

OMAHA TRIBE
(see NEBRASKA)

SAC AND FOX TRIBE
349 Meskwaki Rd.
Tama, IA 52339
(515) 484–4679

WINNEBAGO TRIBE
(see NEBRASKA)

◆ **KANSAS**

IOWA TRIBE OF KANSAS & NEBRASKA
2310 330th St.
White Cloud, KS 66094
(785) 595–3258

KICKAPOO OF KANSAS
P.O. Box 271
Horton, KS 66439
(785) 486–2131

POTAWATOMI TRIBE
16281 Q Road
Mayetta, KS 66509
(785) 966–2255/2771

SAC AND FOX NATION OF MISSOURI
305 N. Main St.
Reserve, KS 66434
(785) 742–7471
(Located in Kansas and Nebraska).

## ◆ LOUISIANA

CHITIMACHA TRIBE
P.O. Box 661
Charenton, LA 70523
(337) 923–7215

COUSHATTA TRIBE OF LOUISIANA
P.O. Box 818
Elton, LA 70532
(337) 584–2261

JENA BAND OF CHOCTAWS
P.O. Box 14
Jena, LA 71342
(318) 992–2717

TUNICA–BILOXI TRIBE
151 Malacon Dr. P.O. Box 331
Marksville, LA 71351
(318) 253–9767

## ◆ MAINE

AROOSTOOK MICMAC COUNCIL, INC.
P.O. Box 772
Presque Isle, ME 04769
(207) 764–1972

HOULTON BAND OF MALISEET COUNCIL
P.O. Box 748, Bell Rd.
Houlton, ME 04730
(207) 532–4273

PASSAMAQUODDY TRIBE
P.O. Box 301
Princeton, ME 04667
(207) 796–2301

PENOBSCOT NATION
Community Building
6 River Road
Indian Island, ME 04468
(207) 827–7776

PLEASANT POINT PASSAMAQUODDY TRIBE
P.O. Box 343
Perry, ME 04667
(207) 853–2600

## ◆ MASSACHUSETTS

WAMPANOAG TRIBAL COUNCIL OF
   GAY HEAD
(aka AQUINNAH)
20 Blackbrook Rd.
Aquinnah, MA 02535
(508) 645–9265

## ◆ MICHIGAN

BAY MILLS INDIAN COMMUNITY
12140 W. Lakeshore Dr.
Brimley, MI 49715
(906) 248–3241

GRAND TRAVERSE BAND (Chippewa, Ottawa)
Peshabestown Community Center
2605 N. W. Bayshore Dr.
Peshabestown, MI 49682
(231) 271–7128

HANNAHVILLE COMMUNITY OF MICHIGAN
   (Potawatomi)
Hannahville Rte. 1, Road N14911
Wilson, MI 49896
(906) 466–2342

HURON POTAWATOMI INC.
(aka Nottawaseppi Band of Huron Potawatomis)
2221 1–1/2 Mile Road
Fulton, MI 49052
(616) 729–5151

KEWEENAW BAY INDIAN COMMUNITY
   (Chippewa)
Keweenaw Bay Tribal Center
107 Beartown Rd.
Baraga, MI 49908
(906) 353–6623

LAC VIEUX DESERT BAND OF LAKE
   SUPERIOR CHIPPEWA
P.O. Box 249 Choate Rd.
Watersmeet, MI 49969
(906) 358–4577

LITTLE RIVER BAND OF OTTAWA INDIANS
1762 U.S. 31 South
Manistee, MI 49660
(231) 723–8288

LITTLE TRAVERSE BAY BANDS OF ODAWA
  INDIANS
P.O. Box 246, 915 Emmett St.
Petoskey, MI 49770
(231) 348–3410

SAGINAW CHIPPEWA TRIBE
7070 E. Broadway Rd.
Mt. Pleasant, MI 48858
(517) 775–4000

SAULT STE. MARIE TRIBE
523 Ashmun St.
Sault Ste. Marie, MI 49783
(906) 635–6050

#### ◆ MINNESOTA

MINNESOTA MDEWAKANTON SIOUX
39527 Reservation Highway 1
P.O. Box 308
Morton, MN 56270

MINNESOTA CHIPPEWA TRIBE

Six Chippewa reservations in Minnesota are organized as components of one entity under the Indian Reorganization Act of 1934. Each Minnesota Chippewa reservation elects a Business Committee. The six Chairs and Secretary–Treasurers of the Business Committees form a Tribal Executive Committee. The six components are:

BOIS FORTE BAND OF CHIPPEWA
P.O. Box 16
Nett Lake, MN 55772
(218) 757–3261

FOND DU LAC CHIPPEWA
1720 Big Lake Rd.
Cloquet, MN 55720
(218) 879–4593/1251

GRAND PORTAGE TRIBAL OFFICE
P.O. Box 428
Grand Portage, MN 55605
(218) 475–2277/9

MILLE LACS BAND OF OJIBWA
HCR 67 Box 194
Onamia, MN 56359
(612) 532–4181

MINNESOTA CHIPPEWA TRIBE
Leech Lake Reservation Business Committee
6530 US 2 Northwest
Cass Lake, MN 56633
(218) 335–8200

WHITE EARTH TRIBAL COUNCIL
Highway 224
P.O. Box 418
White Earth, MN 56591
(218) 983–3285

PRAIRIE ISLAND INDIAN COMMUNITY
5636 Sturgeon Lake Rd.
Welch, MN 55089
(651) 385–2554

RED LAKE BAND OF CHIPPEWA INDIANS
P.O. Box 550
Red Lake, MN 56671
(218) 679–3341

SHAKOPEE MDEWAKANTON SIOUX
  COMMUNITY
2330 Sioux Trail N.W.
Prior Lake, MN 55372
(612) 445–8900

UPPER SIOUX COMMUNITY OF MINNESOTA
P.O. Box 147
Granite Falls, MN 56241
(612) 564–2360, -2550

#### ◆ MISSISSIPPI

MISSISSIPPI BAND OF CHOCTAW INDIANS
P.O. Box 6010–Choctaw Branch
Philadelphia, MS 39350
(601) 656–5251

#### ◆ MISSOURI

EASTERN SHAWNEE RESERVATION
P.O. Box 350
Seneca, MO 64865
(918) 666–2435

#### ◆ MONTANA

BLACKFEET NATION
P.O. Box 850
Browning, MT 59417
(406) 338–7276

THE CHIPPEWA-CREE INDIANS OF THE
  ROCKY BOY'S RESERVATION
P.O. Box 544, RR 1
Box Elder, MT 59521
(406) 395–4478

CROW TRIBE OF INDIANS
P.O. Box 159
Crow Agency, MT 59022
(406) 638–2601

CONFEDERATED SALISH & KOOTENAI
  TRIBES
P.O. Box 278
Pablo, MT 59855
(406) 675–2700 or (800) 634–0690

FORT BELKNAP COMMUNITY COUNCIL
  (Assiniboine, Gros Ventre)
RR 1, Box 66
Fort Belknap Agency
Harlem, MT 59526
(406) 353–2205

FORT PECK ASSINIBOINE AND SIOUX
  TRIBES
P.O. Box 1027
Poplar, MT 59255
(406) 768–5155

NORTHERN CHEYENNE TRIBE
P.O. Box 128
Lame Deer, MT 59043
(406) 477–6284, -8338

◆ NEBRASKA

IOWA TRIBE OF KANSAS & NEBRASKA
(see KANSAS)

OMAHA TRIBE OF NEBRASKA
P.O. Box 368
Macy, NE 68039
(402) 837–5391
(Located in Nebraska and Iowa.)

PINE RIDGE RESERVATION
(see SOUTH DAKOTA: OGLALA SIOUX TRIBE)

PONCA TRIBE OF NEBRASKA
P.O. Box 288
Niobrara, NE 68760
(402) 857–3391

SAC AND FOX TRIBE OF MISSOURI
(see KANSAS)

SANTEE SIOUX TRIBE
425 Frazier Ave North, Suite 2
Niobrara, NE 68760
(402) 857–2302

WINNEBAGO TRIBE OF NEBRASKA
Hwy 75, P.O. Box 687
Winnebago, NE 68071
(402) 878–2272

◆ NEVADA

BATTLE MOUNTAIN COLONY (Western
  Shoshone Te-Moak)
37 Mountain View Dr., #C
Battle Mountain, NV 89820
(775) 635–2004

CARSON INDIAN COMMUNITY COUNCIL
  (Washoe)
2900 S. Curry St.
Carson City, NV 89703
(772) 883–6459

DRESSLERVILLE INDIAN COLONY (Washoe)
1585 Watasheamu Rd.
Gardnerville, NV 89410
(775) 883–1446

DUCK VALLEY SHOSHONE PAIUTE TRIBES
P.O. Box 219
Owyhee, NV 89832
(775) 757–3161, -3211

DUCKWATER SHOSHONE TRIBE
P.O. Box 140068
Duckwater, NV 89314
(775) 863–0227

ELKO INDIAN COLONY (Western
  Shoshone Te-Moak)
511 Sunset St.
Elko, NV 89801
(775) 738–8889

ELY INDIAN COLONY (Shoshone)
16 Shoshone Circle
Ely, NV 89301
(775) 289–3013

FALLON PAIUTE-SHOSHONE TRIBE
8955 Mission Rd.
Fallon, NV 89406
(775) 423–6075

FORT MCDERMITT PAIUTE-SHOSHONE
  TRIBE
P.O. Box 457
McDermitt, NV 89421
(775) 532–8259
(Located in Nevada and Oregon).

FORT MOJAVE RESERVATION
(see ARIZONA)

CONFEDERATED TRIBES OF THE GOSHUTE
  RESERVATION
(see UTAH)

LAS VEGAS PAIUTE TRIBE
No. 1 Paiute Dr.
Las Vegas, NV 89106
(702) 386–3926

LOVELOCK PAIUTE TRIBE
P.O. Box 878
Lovelock, NV 89419
(775) 273–7861

MOAPA BAND OF PAIUTE INDIANS
P.O. Box 340
Moapa, NV 89025
(702) 865–2787

PYRAMID LAKE PAIUTE TRIBE
P.O. Box 256
Nixon, NV 89424
(775) 574–1000

RENO–SPARKS COLONY (Paiute, Washoe)
98 Colony Rd.
Reno, NV 89502
(775) 329–2936

SOUTH FORK BAND COLONY (Western
  Shoshone Te-Moak)
P.O. Box B–13
Lee, NV 89829
(775) 744–4273

STEWART COMMUNITY COUNCIL (Washoe)
5258 Snyder Ave.
Carson City, NV 89701
(775) 883–7794

SUMMIT LAKE PAIUTE TRIBE
655 Anderson St.
Winnemucca, NV 89445
(775) 623–5151

WALKER RIVER PAIUTE TRIBE
P.O. Box 220
Schurz, NV 89427
(775) 773–2306

WASHOE TRIBE OF NEVADA & CALIFORNIA
919 Highway 395 South
Gardnerville, NV 89410
(775) 265–4191/883–1446

WELLS BAND COLONY (Western Shoshone)
P.O. Box 809
Wells, NV 89835
(775) 752–3045

WINNEMUCCA INDIAN COLONY (Paiute,
  Shoshone)
P.O. Box 1370
Winnemucca, NV 89445
(775) 623–6918
(See CALIFORNIA).

YERINGTON PAIUTE TRIBE
171 Campbell Lane
Yerington, NV 89447
(775) 463–3301/883–3895

YOMBA SHOSHONE TRIBE
HC 61, Box 6275
Austin, NV 89310
(775) 964–2463, -2248

#### ◆ NEW MEXICO

ACOMA PUEBLO (Keresan)
P.O. Box 309
Acomita, NM 87034
(505) 552–6604

COCHITI PUEBLO (Keresan)
P.O. Box 70
Cochiti, NM 87072
(505) 465–2244

ISLETA PUEBLO
P.O. Box 1270
Isleta, NM 87022
(505) 869–3111/6333

JEMEZ PUEBLO
P.O. Box 100
Jemez Pueblo, NM 87024
(505) 834–7359

JICARILLA APACHE TRIBE
P.O. Box 507
Dulce, NM 87528
(505) 759–3242

LAGUNA PUEBLO
P.O. Box 194
Laguna, NM 87026
(505) 552–6654

MESCALERO APACHE TRIBE
P.O. Box 176
Mescalero, NM 88340
(505) 671–4494

NAMBE PUEBLO (Tano-Tewa)
Box 117–BB
Santa Fe, NM 87501
(505) 455–2036

PICURIS PUEBLO (Tewa)
P.O. Box 127
Penasco, NM 87553
(505) 587–2519

POJOAQUE PUEBLO (Tano-Tewa)
#39 Camino, Del Rincon, Suite #6
Santa Fe, NM 87501
(505) 455–2278

SANDIA PUEBLO (Tano-Tigua)
P.O. Box 6008
Bernalillo, NM 87004
(505) 867–3317

SAN FELIPE PUEBLO (Keresan)
P.O. Box 4339
San Felipe Pueblo, NM 87001
(505) 867–3381

SAN ILDEFONSO PUEBLO (Tewa)
Rte. 5, Box 315–A
Santa Fe, NM 87501
(505) 455–2273

SAN JUAN PUEBLO (Tano-Tewa)
P.O. Box 1099
San Juan Pueblo, NM 87566
(505) 852–4400/4213

SANTA ANA PUEBLO (Keresan)
2 Dove Rd.
Bernalillo, NM 87004
(505) 867–3301

SANTA CLARA PUEBLO (Tano-Tewa)
P.O. Box 580
Española, NM 87532
(505) 753–7326

SANTO DOMINGO PUEBLO (Keresan)
P.O. Box 99
Santo Domingo, NM 87052
(505) 465–2214

TAOS PUEBLO (Tano-Tewa)
P.O. Box 1846
Taos, NM 87571
(505) 758–8626

TESUQUE PUEBLO (Tano-Tewa)
Rte. 5, P.O. Box 360-T
Santa Fe, NM 87501
(505) 983–2667

UTE MOUNTAIN RESERVATION
(see COLORADO)

ZIA PUEBLO (Keresan)
135 Capital Square Dr.
Zia Pueblo, NM 87053
(505) 867–3304

ZUNI PUEBLO
P.O. Box 339
Zuni, NM 87327
(505) 782–4481

## ◆ NEW YORK

CAYUGA NATION RESERVATION
P.O. Box 11
Versailles, NY 14168
(716) 532–4847

ONEIDA NATION
Gene S See St., Ames Plaza
Oneida, NY 13421
(315) 361–6300

ONONDAGA NATION
P.O. Box 152
Nedrow, NY 13120

SENECA NATION
P.O. Box 231
Salamanco, NY 14779
(716) 945–1790

ST. REGIS MOHAWK TRIBE
412 State Rte. 37
Community Bldg.
Hogansburg, NY 13655
(518) 358–2272

TONAWANDA BAND OF SENECA
7027 Meadville Rd.
Basom, NY 14013
(716) 542–4244

TUSCARORA NATION
2006 Mountain Hope Rd.
Lewiston, NY 14092
(716) 622–7061, 297–3995

### ♦ NORTH CAROLINA

EASTERN CHEROKEE TRIBE
P.O. Box 455
Cherokee, NC 28719
(828) 497–2771 or 492–4771

### ♦ NORTH DAKOTA

THREE AFFILIATED TRIBES (Arikara, Gros
   Ventre, Mandan)
Tribal Business Office
8 C 3 Box 2
New Town, ND 58763
(701) 627–4781

STANDING ROCK RESERVATION (Teton,
   Yankton Sioux)
P.O. Box E
Fort Yates, ND 58538
(701) 854–3433
(Located in North Dakota and South Dakota).

TURTLE MOUNTAIN BAND OF CHIPPEWA
   INDIANS
P.O. Box 900
Belcourt, ND 58316
(701) 477–0470

### ♦ OKLAHOMA

Most Oklahoma tribes have land reserves called
Federal Trust Areas, but no reservations. Many organized their tribal governments under the Oklahoma Indian Welfare Act of 1936 (OIWA). See Oklahoma Indians in Chapter Three.

ABSENTEE–SHAWNEE TRIBE
2025 S. Gordon Cooper Dr.
Shawnee, OK 74801
(405) 275–4030

ALABAMA–QUASSARTE TRIBAL TOWN
323 W. Broadway, Suite 300
Muskogee, OK 74401
(918) 683–2388

APACHE TRIBE OF OKLAHOMA
P.O. Box 1220
Anadarko, OK 73005
(405) 247–9493

CADDO TRIBE OF OKLAHOMA
P.O. Box 487
Binger, OK 73009
(405) 656–2344

CHEROKEE NATION OF OKLAHOMA
P.O. Box 948
Tahlequah, OK 74465
(918) 456–0671

CHEYENNE–ARAPAHO TRIBES
P.O. Box 38
Concho, OK 73022
(405) 262–0345

CHICKASAW NATION
520 East Arlington
P.O. Box 1548
Ada, OK 74821
(580) 436–2603

CHOCTAW NATION OF OKLAHOMA
16th & Locust Streets
Drawer 1210
Durant, OK 74702
(580) 924–8280

CITIZEN BAND OF POTAWATOMI
1601 South Gordon Cooper Dr.
Shawnee, OK 74801
(405) 275–3121

COMANCHE TRIBE
P.O. Box 908
Lawton, OK 73502
(580) 492–3751

DELAWARE NATION, OKLAHOMA
P.O. Box 825
Anadarko, OK 73005
(405) 247–2448

EASTERN SHAWNEE TRIBE OF OKLAHOMA
(see MISSOURI: EASTERN SHAWNEE
    RESERVATION)

FORT SILL APACHE TRIBE OF OKLAHOMA
Rte. 2, P.O. Box 121
Apache, OK 73006
(580) 588–2314

IOWA TRIBE OF OKLAHOMA
Route 1, P.O. Box 721
Perkins, OK 74059
(405) 547–2402

KAW NATION
P.O. Box 50
Kaw City, OK 74641
(580) 269–2552

KIALEGEE TRIBAL TOWN (Creek)
108 N. Main, P.O. Box 332
Wetumka, OK 74883
(405) 452–3262

KICKAPOO TRIBE OF OKLAHOMA
P.O. Box 70
McLoud, OK 74851
(405) 964–2075

KIOWA TRIBE OF OKLAHOMA
P.O. Box 369
Carnegie, OK 73015
(580) 654–2300

MIAMI TRIBE OF OKLAHOMA
P.O. Box 1326
Miami, OK 74355
(918) 542–1445 or 542–2890

MODOC TRIBE OF OKLAHOMA
515 G St. Southeast
Miami, OK 74355
(918) 542–1190

MUSCOGEE CREEK NATION
P.O. Box 580
Okmulgee, OK 74447
(918) 756–8700

OSAGE NATION
c/o Osage Agency
P.O. Box 779
Pawhuska, OK 74056
(918) 287–1085

OTOE–MISSOURIA TRIBE OF OKLAHOMA
8151 Hwy 177
Red Rock, OK 74651
(580) 723–4466

OTTAWA TRIBE OF OKLAHOMA
P.O. Box 110
Miami, OK 74355
(918) 540–1536

PAWNEE INDIAN TRIBE OF OKLAHOMA
P.O. Box 470
Pawnee, OK 74058
(918) 762–3621

PEORIA TRIBE OF OKLAHOMA
P.O. Box 1527
Miami, OK 74355
(918) 540–2535

PONCA TRIBE
20 White Eagle Dr.
Ponca City, OK 74601
(580) 762–8104

QUAPAW TRIBE OF OKLAHOMA
P.O. Box 765
Quapaw, OK 74363
(918) 542–1853

SAC AND FOX NATION
Rte. 2, P.O. Box 246
Stroud, OK 74079
(918) 968–3526

SEMINOLE NATION OF OKLAHOMA
P.O. Box 1498
Wewoka, OK 74884
(405) 257–6287

SENECA–CAYUGA TRIBE OF OKLAHOMA
(aka SUSQUEHANNOCK NATION)
P.O. Box 1283
Miami, OK 74355
(918) 542–6609

THLOPTHLOCCO TRIBAL TOWN (Creek)
P.O. Box 188
Okemah, OK 74859
(918) 623–2620

TONKAWA TRIBE OF OKLAHOMA
P.O. Box 70
Tonkawa, OK 74653
(580) 628–2561

UNITED KEETOOWAH BAND OF CHEROKEE
    INDIANS
P.O. Box 746
Tahlequah, OK 74465
(918) 456–5491

WICHITA AND AFFILIATED TRIBES
P.O. Box 729
Anadarko, OK 73005
(405) 247–2425

WYANDOTTE TRIBE OF OKLAHOMA
P.O. Box 250
Wyandotte, OK 74370
(918) 678–2297/8

♦ **OREGON**

BURNS-PAIUTE GENERAL COUNCIL
HC71, 100 Pasigo St.
Burns, OR 97720
(541) 573–2088

CONFEDERATED TRIBES OF COOS, LOWER
    UMPQUA, AND SIUSLAW INDIANS
1245 Fulton Ave
Coos Bay, OR 97420
(541) 888–9577

COQUILLE INDIAN TRIBE
P.O. Box 783
North Bend, OR 97549
(541) 756–0904

COW CREEK BAND OF UMPQUA INDIANS
2371 Northeast Stevens, Suite 100
Roseburg, OR 97470
(541) 672–9405n

FORT MCDERMITT PAIUTE-SHOSHONE
    TRIBE
(see NEVADA)

CONFEDERATED TRIBES OF GRANDE
    RONDE
9615 Grand Ronde Rd.
Grande Ronde, OR 97347
(503) 879–5211

KLAMATH TRIBE
P.O. Box 436
Chiloquin, OR 97624
(541) 783–2219

CONFEDERATED TRIBES OF SILETZ
    INDIANS
P.O. Box 549
Siletz, OR 97380
(541) 444–2532

CONFEDERATED TRIBES OF THE UMATILLA
    RESERVATION
P.O. Box 638
Pendleton, OR 97801
(503) 276 3165

CONFEDERATED TRIBES OF THE WARM
    SPRINGS RESERVATION
1233 Veteran St.
P.O. Box C
Warm Springs, OR 97761
(541) 553–1161

♦ **RHODE ISLAND**

NARRAGANSETT INDIAN TRIBE
P.O. Box 268
Charlestown, RI 02813
(401) 364–1100

♦ **SOUTH CAROLINA**

CATAWBA TRIBE
P.O. Box 188
Catawba, SC 29704
(803) 366–4792

♦ **SOUTH DAKOTA**

CHEYENNE RIVER SIOUX TRIBE
P.O. Box 590
Eagle Butte, SD 57625
(605) 964–4155

CROW CREEK SIOUX TRIBE
P.O. Box 658
Fort Thompson, SD 57339
(605) 245–2222

FLANDREAU SANTEE SIOUX TRIBE
P.O. Box 283
Flandreau, SD 57028
(605) 997–3891

LOWER BRULE SIOUX TRIBE
P.O. Box 187
Lower Brule, SD 57548
(605) 473–5561/2

OGLALA SIOUX TRIBE
Pine Ridge Reservation
P.O. Box 51
Pine Ridge, SD 57770
(605) 867–5821

ROSEBUD SIOUX TRIBE
P.O. Box 430
Rosebud, SD 57570
(605) 747–2381

SISSETON–WAHPETON SIOUX TRIBE
P.O. Box 509
Agency Village, SD 57262
(605) 698–3911

STANDING ROCK RESERVATION
(see NORTH DAKOTA)

YANKTON SIOUX TRIBE
P.O. Box 248
Marty, SD 57361
(605) 384–3641

#### ◆ TEXAS

ALABAMA–COUSHATTA TRIBE
Rte. 3, P.O. Box 640
Livingston, TX 77351
(936) 563–4391 or (800) 444–3507

KICKAPOO TRADITIONAL TRIBE OF TEXAS
P.O. Box 972
Eagle Pass, TX 78853
(512) 773–2105
(see KANSAS, OKLAHOMA)

YSLETA DEL SUR PUEBLO (Tigua)
P.O. Box 17579
El Paso, TX 79917
(915) 859–7913

#### ◆ UTAH

CONFEDERATED TRIBES OF THE GOSHUTE
RESERVATION
P.O. Box 6104
Ibapah, UT 84034
(435) 234–1136
(Located in Utah and Nevada).

PAIUTE INDIAN TRIBE OF UTAH
440 N. Paiute Dr.
Cedar City, UT 84720
(435) 586–1112

SKULL VALLEY BAND OF GOSHUTE INDIANS
c/o Uintah and Ouray Agency
P.O. Box 130
Fort Duchesne, UT 84026
(435) 722–2406

UINTAH AND OURAY UTE TRIBE
P.O. Box 190
Fort Duschesne, UT 84026
(435) 722–5141

UTE MOUNTAIN TRIBE
(see COLORADO)

WASHAKIE RESERVATION
(see IDAHO: NORTHWESTERN BAND OF
SHOSHONI)

#### ◆ WASHINGTON

CONFEDERATED TRIBES OF THE CHEHALIS
RESERVATION
P.O. Box 536
Oakville, WA 98568
(360) 273–5911

COLVILLE CONFEDERATED TRIBES
P.O. Box 150
Nespelem, WA 99155
(509) 634–4711

HOH TRIBAL BUSINESS COUNCIL
2464 Lower Hoh Rd.
Forks, WA 98331–9304
(360) 374–6582

JAMESTOWN S'KLALLAM TRIBE
1033 Old Blyn Hwy
Sequim, WA 98382
(360) 683-1109

KALISPEL TRIBE OF INDIANS
P.O. Box 39
Usk, WA 99180-0039
(509) 445-1147

LOWER ELWHA TRIBAL COMMUNITY
    COUNCIL
2851 Lower Elwha Rd.
Port Angeles, WA 98363-9518
(360) 452-8471

LUMMI INDIAN NATION (Lummi, Nooksack)
2616 Kwina Rd.
Bellingham, WA 98226
(360) 384-1489

MAKAH TRIBAL COUNCIL
P.O. Box 115
Neah Bay, WA 98357
(360) 645-2201

MUCKLESHOOT INDIAN TRIBE
39015 172nd Avenue, S.E.
Auburn, WA 98092
(253) 939-3311

NISQUALLY INDIAN COMMUNITY COUNCIL
4820 She-Nah-Num Drive, S.E.
Olympia, WA 98513
(360) 456-5221

NOOKSACK TRIBAL COUNCIL
P.O. Box 157
Deming, WA 98244
(360) 592-5176

PORT GAMBLE S-KLALLAM TRIBE
31912 Little Boston Rd., NE
Kingston, WA 98346-0999
(360) 297-2646

PUYALLUP TRIBAL COUNCIL
2002 E. 28th St.
Tacoma, WA 98404-4996
(253) 597-6200

QUILEUTE TRIBAL COUNCIL
P.O. Box 279
La Push, WA 98350-0279
(360) 374-6163

QUINAULT INDIAN NATION
P.O. Box 189
Taholah, WA 98587-0189
(360) 276-8211

SAMISH TRIBE OF INDIANS
P.O. Box 217
Anacortes, WA 98221
(360) 293-6404

SAUK-SUIATTLE TRIBAL COUNCIL
5318 Chief Brown Lane
Darrington, WA 98241
(360) 436-0131

SHOALWATER BAY TRIBE (Chehalis, Chinook,
    Quinault)
P.O. Box 130
Tokeland, WA 98590
(360) 267-6766

SKOKOMISH TRIBAL COUNCIL
N. 80 Tribal Center Rd.
Shelton, WA 98584-9748
(360) 426-4232

SNOQUALMIE INDIAN TRIBE
P.O. Box 670
Fall Ciry, WA 98024
(425) 333-6551

SPOKANE TRIBE
P.O. Box 100
Wellpinit, WA 99040
(509) 258-4581

SQUAXIN ISLAND TRIBE
70 Southeast Squaxin Lane
Shelton, WA 98584
(360) 426-9781

STILLAGUAMISH TRIBE
3439 Stoluckquamish Lane
Arlington, WA 98223-9056
(360) 652-7362

SUQUAMISH TRIBE
Port Madison Reservation
P.O. Box 498
Suquamish, WA 98392
(360) 598-3311

SWINOMISH INDIAN TRIBAL COMMUNITY
P.O. Box 817
La Conner, WA 98257
(360) 466–3163

TULALIP TRIBE (Samish, Skagit, Snohomish)
6700 Totem Beach Rd.
Marysville, WA 98271
(360) 651–4000

UPPER SKAGIT INDIAN TRIBE
25944 Community Plaza
Sedro-Wooley, WA 98284
(360) 856–5501

### ♦ WISCONSIN

BAD RIVER BAND OF LAKE SUPERIOR
   CHIPPEWA INDIANS
P.O. Box 39
Odana, WI 54861
(715) 682–7111

FOREST COUNTY POTAWATOMI
   COMMUNITY OF WISCONSIN
P.O. Box 340
Crandon, WI 54520
(715) 478–2903

HO-CHUNK NATION OF WISCONSIN (formerly
   WINNEBAGO)
P.O. Box 667
Black River Falls, WI 54615
(715) 284–9343

LAC COURTE OREILLES OJIBWA TRIBE
13394 West Prepania
Hayward, WI 54843
(715) 634–8934

LAC DU FLAMBEAU BAND OF LAKE
   SUPERIOR CHIPPEWA INDIANS
P.O. Box 67
Lac du Flambeau, WI 54538
(715) 588–3303

MENOMINEE TRIBE OF WISCONSIN
P.O. Box 910
Keshena, WI 54135
(715) 799–5100

ONEIDA TRIBE
N-72 N.Seminary
Oneida, WI 54155
(920) 869–2214

RED CLIFF TRIBE (Lake Superior Chippewa)
P.O. Box 529
Bayfield, WI 54814
(715) 779–3701

SOKAOGON CHIPPEWA COMMUNITY
Mole Lake Band
Rte. 1, P.O. Box 625
Crandon, WI 54520
(715) 478–2604

ST. CROIX CHIPPEWA INDIANS OF
   WISCONSIN
P.O. Box 287
Hertel, WI 54845
(715) 349–2195

STOCKBRIDGE MUNSEE COMMUNITY
8476 MohHeConNuck Rd.
Bowler, WI 54416
(715) 793–4111

### ♦ WYOMING

ARAPAHO BUSINESS COUNCIL
P.O. Box 217
Fort Washakie, WY 82514
(307) 332–6120

SHOSHONE BUSINESS COUNCIL
P.O. Box 538
Fort Washakie, WY 82514
(307) 332–3532

# Canadian Indian Bands

Canadian natives are grouped into 633 different bands and live on 2,281 reserves. As in the United States, there are native communities in Canada that are not officially recognized as native communities by the Canadian government. Unfortunately, very little information is available on these communities. Thus, the following list is selective, providing a sampling of the most accessible Canadian reserve communities.

## ◆ ALBERTA

**ALEXANDER (Cree)**
P.O. Box 3419
Morinville, AB T8R IF3
(780) 939–5887

**ALEXIS (Dakota)**
Box 7
Glenevis, AB T0E 0X0
(780) 967–2225

**ATHABASCA CHIPEWYAN**
P.O. Box 366
Fort Chipewyan, AB T0P 1B0
(780) 697–3730

**BEAVER LAKE (Cree)**
P.O. Box 960
Lac La Biche, AB T0A 2C0
(780) 623–4549

**BIGSTONE CREE**
Box 960
Wabasca, AB T0G 2K0
(780) 891–3836

**BLOOD (Blackfoot)**
P.O. Box 60
Standoff, AB T0L 1Y0
(403) 737–3753

**BOYER RIVER (Beaver)**
P.O. Box 270
High Level, AB T0H 1Z0
(780) 927–3697

**COLD LAKE FIRST NATIONS (Cree, Chipewyan)**
P.O. Box 1769
Cold Lake, AB T9M 1P2
(780) 594–7183

**CHIPEWYAN PRAIRIE FIRST NATION**
General Delivery
Chard, AB T0P 1G0
(780) 559–2259

**CREE FIRST NATION**
P.O. Box 90
Fort Chipewyan, AB T0P 1B0
(780) 697–3740

**DENE THA' FIRST NATION (Slave)**
P.O. Box 120
Chateh, AB T0H 0S0
(780) 321–3842

**DRIFTPILE (Cree)**
Box 30
Driftpile, AB T0G 0V0
(780) 355–3868

**DUNCAN'S (Cree)**
P.O. Box 148
Brownvale, AB T0H 0L0
(780) 597–3777

**ENOCH (Cree)**
Box 29
Enoch, AB T7X 3Y3
(780) 470–4505

ERMINESKIN (Cree)
P.O. Box 219
Hobbema, AB T0C 1N0
(780) 585–3741

FORT MCKAY (Chipewyan)
P.O. Box 5360
Fort McMurray, AB T9H 3G4
(780) 828–4220

FORT MCMURRAY (Cree, Chipewyan)
P.O. Box 6130, Clearwater Station
Fort McMurray, AB T9H 4W1
(780) 334–2293

FROG LAKE (Cree)
General Delivery
Frog Lake, AB T0A 1M0
(780) 943–3737

HEART LAKE (Cree)
P.O. Box 447
Lac La Biche, AB T0A 2C0
(780) 623–2130

HORSE LAKE (Beaver)
P.O. Box 303
Hythe, AB T0H 2C0
(780) 356–2248

KAPAE'NO FIRST NATION
Box 10
Gruard, AB T0G 1C0
(780) 751–3800

KEHEWIN (Cree)
P.O. Box 6218
Bonnyville, AB T9N 2GA
(780) 826–3333

LITTLE RED RIVER CREE NATION
P.O. Box 1165
High Level, AB T0H 1Z0
(780) 759–3912/3950

LOON RIVER CREE
Box 189
Red Earth Creek, AB T0G 1X0
(780) 649–3883

LOUIS BULL (Cree)
P.O. Box 130
Hobbema, AB T0C 1N0
(780) 585–3978

LUBICON LAKE (Cree)
P.O. Box 6731
Peace River, AB T8S 1S5
(780) 629–3945

MIKISEW CREE FIRST NATION
P.O. Box 90
Fort Chipewyan, AB T0P 1B0
(780) 697–3740

MONTANA (Cree)
P.O. Box 70
Hobbema, AB T0C 1N0
(780) 585–3744

O'CHIESE (Cree)
P.O. Box 1570
Rocky Mountain House, AB T0M 1T0
(403) 989–3943

PAUL (Cree, Dakota)
P.O. Box 89
Duffield, AB T0E 0N0
(780) 892–2691

PEIGAN FIRST NATION (Blackfoot)
P.O. Box 70
Brocket, AB T0K 0H0
(403) 965–3940

SADDLE LAKE FIRST NATION (Cree)
P.O. Box 100
Saddle Lake, AB T0A 3T0
(780) 726–3829

SADDLE LAKE (GOODFISH LAKE GROUP)
Box 271
Goodfish Lake, AB T0A 1R0
(780) 428–9501

SAMSON (Cree)
P.O. Box 159
Hobbema, AB T0C 1N0
(403) 421–4926

SAWRIDGE (Cree)
P.O. Box 326
Slave Lake, AB T0H 3N0
(780) 849–4311

SIKSIKA NATION
P.O. Box 1100
Siksika, AB T0J 3W0
(403) 264–7250

STONEY (BEARSPAW GROUP) (Dakota)
P.O. Box 40
Morley, AB T0L 1N0
(403) 881–3770

STONEY (CHINIKI GROUP) (Dakota)
P.O. Box 40
Morley, AB T0L 1N0
(403) 881–3770

STONEY (GOOD STONEY) (Dakota)
(WESLEY GROUP)
P.O. Box 40
Morely, AB T0L 1N0
(403) 881–3770

STURGEON LAKE (Cree)
P.O. Box 757
Valleyview, AB T0H 3N0
(780) 524–3307

SUCKER CREEK (Cree)
P.O. Box 65
Enilda, AB T0G 0W0
(780) 523–4426

SUNCHILD CREE
P.O. Box 747
Rocky Mountain House, AB T0M 1T0
(403) 989–3740

SWAN RIVER (Cree)
P.O. Box 270
Kinuso, AB T0G 1K0
(780) 775–3536

TALLCREE
P.O. Box 100
Fort Vermillion, AB T0H 1N0
(780) 927–3727

TSUU T'INA NATION (Sarcee)
9911 Chula Blvd.
Tsuu T'ina, AB T2W 6H6
(403) 281–4455

WHITEFISH LAKE #429 (Cree)
General Delivery
Atikameg, AB T0G 0C0
(403) 767–3914

WOODLAND CREE
General Delivery
Cadotte Lake, AB T0H 0N0
(780) 629–3803

## ◆ BRITISH COLUMBIA

ADAMS LAKE (Shuswap)
P.O. Box 588
Chase, BC V0E 1M0
(250) 679–8841

AHOUSAHT (Nootka)
General Delivery
Ahousaht, BC V0R 1A0
(250) 670–9563

AITCHELITZ (Cowichan)
8150 Aitken Rd.
Sardis, BC V2R 4H5
(604) 792–3104

ALEXANDRIA (Chilcotin)
51 D. S. Fourth Ave
Williams Lake, BC V2J 1J6
(250) 993–4324

ALEXIS CREEK (Chilcotin)
P.O. Box 69
Chilanko Forks, BC V0L 1H0
(250) 481–3335

ALKALI LAKE (Shuswap)
P.O. Box 4479
Williams Lake, BC V2G 2V5
(250) 440–5611

ANAHAM (Chilcotin)
P.O. Box 168
Alexis Creek, BC V0L 1A0
(250) 394–4212/13

ANDERSON LAKE (Lillooet)
P.O. Box 88
D'Arcy, BC V0N 1L0
(604) 452–3221

ASHCROFT (Shuswap)
P.O. Box 440
Ashcroft, BC V0K 1A0
(250) 453–9154

BEECHER BAY (Songish)
4901 East Sooke Rd.
Sooke, BC V0S 1N0
(250) 478–3535

BELLA COOLA
P.O. Box 65
Bella Coola, BC V1C 1C0
(604) 799–5613/5959

BLUEBERRY RIVER (Beaver)
10071 100th Ave
Fort St. John, BC Z1J 1Y7
(250) 630–2584

BONAPARTE (Shuswap)
P.O. Box 669
Cache Creek, BC V0K 1H0
(250) 457–9624

BOOTHROYD (Ntlakyapamuk)
P.O. Box 295
Boston Bar, BC V0K 1C0
(604) 867–9211

BOSTON BAR (Ntlakyapamuk)
SS 1
Boston Bar, BC V0K 1C0
(604) 867–8844

BRIDGE RIVER (Lillooet)
P.O. Box 190
Lillooet, BC V0K 1V0
(250) 256–7423

BURNS LAKE (Carrier)
P.O. Box 9000
Burns Lake, BC V0J 1E0
(250) 692–7717

BURRARD (Squamish)
3082 Ghum-lye Drive
North Vancouver, BC V7H 2V6
(604) 929–3454/5

CAMPBELL RIVER (Kwakiutl)
1400 Weiwaikum Rd.
Campbell River, BC V9W 5W8
(250) 286–6949

CANIM LAKE (Shuswap)
P.O. Box 1030
100 Mile House, BC V0K 2E0
(250) 397–2227

CANOE CREEK (Shuswap)
General Delivery
Dog Creek, BC V0L 1J0
(250) 440–5645

CAPE MUDGE (Kwakiutl)
P.O. Box 220
Quathiaski Cove, BC V0P 1N0
(250) 285–3316

CAYOOSE CREEK (Lillooet)
P.O. Box 484
Lillooet, BC V0K 1V0
(250) 256–4136

CHAWATHIL (Cowichan)
(aka HOPE)
P.O. Box 1659
Hope, BC V0X 1L0
(604) 869–9994

CHEAM (Cowichan)
52203 Mathela
Rosedale, BC V0X 1X0
(604) 794–7924

CHEHALIS (Cowichan)
RR 1, Comp 66 Chehalis Rd.
Agassiz, BC V0M 1A0
(604) 796–2116

CHEMAINUS (Cowichan)
12611 Trans-Canada Hwy.
Ladysmith, BC V9G 1M5
(250) 245–7155

CHESLATTA (Carrier)
P.O. Box 909
Burns Lake, BC V0J 1E0
(250) 694–3334

COLDWATER (Ntlakyapamuk)
P.O. Bag 4600
Merritt, BC V1K 1B8
(250) 378–6174

COLUMBIA LAKE (Kootenay)
P.O. Box 130
Windermere, BC V0B 2L0
(250) 342–6301

COMOX
3320 Comox Rd.
Courtenay, BC V9N 3P8
(250) 339–7122/4545

COOK'S FERRY (Ntlakyapamuk)
Box 130
Spences Bridge, BC V0K 2L0
(250) 458–2224/5

COWICHAN
5760 Allan
Duncan, BC V9L 5J1
(250) 748–3196

COWICHAN LAKE (Nootka)
C/O 470 Ker Ave.
Victoria, BC V9A 2B7
(250) 749–3301

DEASE RIVER FIRST NATION (Kasha, Tahltan)
(formerly LIARD)
Box 79
Good Hope Lake, BC V0C 1E0
(604) 239–3000

DITIDAHT (Nootka)
(aka NITINAHT)
P.O. Box 340
Port Albernie, BC V9Y 7M8
(250) 745–3333

DOIG RIVER (Beaver)
Box 56
Rose Prairie, BC V0C 2H0
(250) 827–3776

DOUGLAS FIRST NATION (Lillooet)
7311 Unit C James St.
Mission, BC V2V 3V5
(604) 820–3082

EHATTESAHT (Nootka)
P.O. Box 59
Zeballos, BC V0P 2A0
(250) 761–4155

ESKETEMC
P.O. Box 4479
Williams Lake, BC V2G 2V5
(250) 440–5611

ESQUIMALT (Songish)
1000 Thomas Rd.
Victoria, BC V9A 7K7
(250) 381–7861

FORT NELSON (Slave)
RR 1, 293 Alaska Hwy.
Fort Nelson, BC V0C 1R0
(250) 774–7257

FORT WARE (Sekani)
622 A. 4th Ave.
Prince George, BC V2L 3H1
(250) 563–4161

FOUNTAIN (Lillooet)
P.O. Box 1330
Lillooet, BC V0K 1V0
(250) 256–4227

GITANMAAX (Gitksan)
P.O. Box 440
Hazelton, BC V0J 1Y0
(250) 842–5297

GITANYOW (Gitksan)
(aka KITWANCOOL)
P.O. Box 340
Kitwanga, BC V0J 2A0
(250) 849–5222

GITLAKDAMIX (Niska)
4518 Tait Ave.
New Aiyansh, BC V0J 1A0
(250) 633–2215

GITSEGUKLA (Gitksan)
36 Cascade Ave., RR 1
South Hazelton, BC V0J 2R0
(250) 849–5490

GITWANGAK (Gitksan)
P.O. Box 400
Kitwanga, BC V0J 2A0
(250) 849–5591

GITWINKSIHLKW (Niska)
(aka CANYON CITY)
P.O. Box 1
Gitwinksihlkw, BC V0J 3T0
(250) 633–2294/5

GLEN VOWELL (Gitksan)
P.O. Box 157
Hazelton, BC V0J 1Y0
(250) 842–5241

GWA'SALA–'NAKWAXDA'W
(aka TSULQUATE)
P.O. Box 998
Port Hardy, BC V0N 2P0
(250) 949–8343

GWAWAENUK TRIBE
Box 344
Port McNeil, BC V0N 2R0
(250) 949–8732

HAGWILGET (Gitksan)
P.O. Box 460
New Hazelton, BC V0J 2J0
(250) 842–6258

HALALT (Cowichan)
RR 1
Chemainus, BC V0R 1K0
(250) 246–4736/7

HALFWAY RIVER (Beaver)
P.O. Box 59
Wonowon, BC V0C 2N0
(250) 772–5058

HARTLEY BAY (Tsimshian)
General Delivery
Hartley Bay, BC V0V 1A0
(250) 841–2500

HEILTSUK
P.O. Box 880
Waglisla, BC V0T 1Z0
(250) 957–2381

HESQUIAHT (Nootka)
P.O. Box 2000
Tofino, BC V0R 2Z0
Fax: (250) 724–8570

HIGH BAR (Shuswap)
c/o Fraser Canyon Indian Admn.
P.O. Box 458
Clinton, BC V0K 1K0
(250) 459–2117

HOMALCO (Comox)
1218 Bute Cres
Campbell River, BC V9H 1G5
(250) 923–4979

HUPACASATH FIRST NATION
P.O. Box 211
Port Alberni, BC V9Y 7M7
(250) 724–4041

HUU-AY-AHT FIRST NATION
P.O. Box 70
Bamfield, BC V0R 1B0
(250) 728–3414

INGENIKA (Sekani)
111839 1st Ave
Prince George, BC V2L 2Y8
(250) 562–8882

ISKUT (Tahltan)
Box 30
Iskut, BC V0J 1K0
(250) 234–3331

KAMLOOPS (Shuswap)
100–315 Yellowhead Hwy.
Kamloops, BC V2H 1H1
(250) 828–9700

KANAKA (Ntlakyapamuk)
Box 210
Lytton, BC V0K 1Z0
(250) 455–2279

KATZIE (Cowichan)
10946 Katzie Rd.
Pitt Meadows, BC V3Y 2G6
(604) 465–8961/4841

KA:'YU:'K'T'H'/CHE:K:TLES7ET'H' FIRST
   NATIONS
General Delivery
Kyuquot, BC V0P 1J0
(250) 332–5259

KINCOLITH (Niska)
General Delivery
Kincolith, BC V0V 1B0
(250) 326–4212

KISPIOX (Gitksan)
Box 25, RR 1
Kispiox, BC V0J 1Y0
(250) 842–5248/9

KITAMAAT (Haisla)
Haisla, Box 1101
Kitamaat Village, BC V0T 2B0
(250) 639–9361/2036

KITASOO (Tsimshian)
General Delivery
Klemtu, BC V0T 1L0
(250) 839–1255

KITKATLA (Tsimshian)
General Delivery
Kitkatla, BC V0V 1C0
(250) 848–2214

KITSELAS (Tsimshian)
4562 Queensway
Terrace, BC V8G 3X6
(250) 635–5084

KITSUMKALUM (Tsimshian)
House of Sim–Oi–Ghets
Box 544
Terrace, BC V8G 4B5
(250) 635–6177/8

KLAHOOSE (Comox)
Box 9 Squirrel Cove
Mansons Landing, BC V0P 1K0
(250) 935–6536

KLUSKUS (Carrier)
P.O. Box 4639
Quesnel, BC V2J 3J8
(250) 992–8186

KWADACHA
622 A 4th Avenue
Prince George, BC V2L 3H1
(250) 563–4161

KWAKIUTL
Box 1440
Port Hardy, BC V0N 2P0
(250) 949–6012

KWANTLEN FIRST NATION
92 Gabriel Lake, Box 108
Fort Langley, BC V1M 2R4
(604) 888–2488

KWAW–KWAW–A–PILT (Cowichan)
Box 412
Chilliwack, BC V2P 6H7
(604) 858–0662

KWIAKAH (Kwakiutl)
1440 North Island Hwy.
Campbell River, BC V9W 2E3
(604) 286–1295

KWICKSUTAINEUK–AH–KWAW–AH–MISH
    (Kwakiutl)
General Delivery
Simoon Sound, BC V0P 1S0
(250) 974–8099

KWIKWETLAM FIRST NATION
65 Colony Farm Rd.
Coquitlam, BC V3C 3V4
(604) 540–0680

KYUQUOT (Nootka)
General Delivery
Kyuquot, BC V0P 1J0
(250) 332–5259

LAKAHAHMEN (Cowichan)
41290 Lougheed Hwy.
Deroche, BC V0M 1G0
(604) 826–7976

LAKALZAP (Niska)
P.O. Box 200
Greenville, BC V0J 1X0
(250) 621–3212/3

LAKE BABINE (Carrier)
P.O. Box 879
Burns Lake, BC V0J 1E0
(250) 692–4700

LAKE COWICHAN
92 Gabriel Lane
Fort Langley, BC V1M 2R4
(604) 888–2488/4546

LAX–KW'ALAAMS
206 Shashaak St.
Port Simpson, BC V0V 1H0
(250) 625–3293

LHEIDLI T'ENNEH
1041 Whenun Road
Prince George, BC V2K 5G5
(250) 963–8451

LITTLE SHUSWAP
P.O. Box 1100
Chase, BC V0E 1M0
(250) 679–3203

LOWER KOOTENAY
42 Center Rd., RR 2
Creston, BC V0B 1G2
(250) 428–4428

LOWER NICOLA (Ntlakyapamuk)
#73 Shulus Hwy 8
Merritt, BC V1K 1N2
(250) 378–5157

LOWER SIMILKAMEEN (Okanagan)
P.O. Box 100
Keremeos, BC V0X 1N0
(250) 499–5528

LYACKSON (Cowichan)
RR 1, 9137 Chemainus Rd.
Chemainus, BC V0R 1K0
(250) 246–5019

LYTTON (Ntlakyapamuk)
P.O. Box 20
Lytton, BC V0K 1Z0
(250) 455–2304

MALAHAT (Cowichan)
P.O. Box 111
Mill Bay, BC V0R 2P0
(250) 743–3231

MAMALELEQALA-QWE-QWA-SOT-ENOX
    (Kwakiutl)
(aka MAMALILLIKULLA)
1441 A. Old Island Hwy
Campbell River, BC V9W 2E4
(250) 287–2955

MASSET (Haida)
P.O. Box 189
Masset, BC V0T 1M0
(250) 626–3337

MATSQUI (Cowichan)
31989 Harris Rd.
P.O. Box 10
Abbottsford, BC V0X 3R2
(604) 826–6145

MCLEOD LAKE (Sekani)
General Delivery
McLeod Lake, BC V0J 2G0
(250) 750–4415

METLAKATLA (Tsimshian)
P.O. Box 459
Prince Rupert, BC V8J 3R1
(250) 628–3234

MORICETOWN (Carrier)
RR 1, Site 15, Box 1
Moricetown, BC V0J 2N0
(250) 847–2133

MOUNT CURRIE (Lillooet)
(aka PEMBERTON)
P.O. Box 602
Mount Currie, BC V0N 2K0
(604) 894–6115

MOWACHAHT/MUCHALAHT (Nootka)
P.O. Box 459
Gold River, BC V0P 1G0
(250) 283–2015

MUSQUEAM (Cowichan)
6735 Salish Dr.
Vancouver, BC V6N 4C4
(604) 263–3261

NADLEH WHUTEN (Carrier)
(aka FRASER LAKE)
P.O. Box 36
Fort Fraser, BC V0J 1N0
(250) 690–7211

NAK'AZDLI (Carrier)
(aka NECOSLIE)
P.O. Box 1329
Fort St. James, BC V0J 1P0
(250) 996–7171

NAMGIS FIRST NATION
P.O. Box 210
Alert Bay, BC V0N 1A0
(250) 974–5556

NANAIMO FIRST NATION (Cowichan)
668 Center St.
Nanaimo, BC V9R 4T4
(250) 740–2300

NANOOSE FIRST NATION (Cowichan)
209 Mallard Way
Lantzville, BC V0R 2H0
(250) 390–3661

NAZKO (Carrier)
3574 Hilborn Rd.
Quesnel, BC V2J 3P7
(250) 992–9085

NEE–TAHI–BUHN
RR 2 Site 7 Comp 28
Burns Lake, BC V0J 1E0
(250) 694–3492

NESKONLITH (Shuswap)
P.O. Box 608
Chase, BC V0E 1M0
(250) 679–3295

NICOMEN (Ntlakyapamuk)
P.O. Box 328
Lytton, BC V0K 1Z0
(250) 455–2279

NIMPKISH (Kwakiutl)
P.O. Box 210
Alert Bay, BC V0N 1A0
(250) 974–5556

NISGA'S VILLAGE OF GINGOLX
1304 Broad St.
Kincolith, BC V0V 1B0
(250) 326–4212

NISGA'S VILLAGE OF GITWINKSIHLKW
P.O. Box 1
Gitwinksihlkw, BC V0J 3T0
(250) 633–2294

NISGA'S VILLAGE OF LAXGALT'SAP
P.O. Box 200
Greenville, BC V0J 1X0
(250) 621–3213

NISGA'S VILLAGE OF NEW AIYANSH
Box 233
New Aiyansh, BC V0J 1A0
(250) 633–2215

NOOAITCH (Ntlakyapamuck)
18 Shacklly Rd.
Merritt, BC V1K 1NR
(604) 378–6141

NORTH THOMPSON (Shuswap)
P.O. Box 220
Barriere, BC V0E 1E0
(250) 672–9995

NUCHATLAHT (Nootka)
P.O. Box 40
Zeballos, BC V09 2A0
(250) 724–8609

NUXALK NATION
P.O. Box 65
Bella Coola, BC V0T 1C0
(250) 799–5613

OHIAHT (Nootka)
974 Poplar Way
Qualicum Beach, BC V9K 5X9
(250) 752–3994

OKANAGAN
RR 7
Vernon, BC V1T 7Z3
(250) 542–4328

OLD MASSETT VILLAGE COUNCIL
P.O. Box 189
Old Massett, BC V0T 1M0
(250) 626–3337

OPETCHESAHT (Nootka)
P.O. Box 211
Port Alberni, BC V9Y 7M7
(250) 724–4041

OREGON JACK CREEK (Ntlakyapamuck)
P.O. Box 940
Ashcroft, BC V0K 1A0
(250) 453–9098

OSOYOOS (Okanagan)
Site 25, Comp. 1, RR 3
Oliver, BC V0H 1T0
(250) 498 4906/3444

OWEEKENO (Heiltsuk)
P.O. Box 3500
Oweekeno Village Rivers Inlet
Port Hardy, BC V0N 2P0
(250) 949–8625

PACHEEDAHT (Nootka)
350 Kalaid St.
Port Renfrew, BC V0S 1K0
(250) 647 5521

PAUQUACHIN (Songish)
8960 W. Saanich Rd.
Brentwood Bay, BC V8L 5W4
(250) 656–0191

PAVILION (Shuswap)
P.O. Box 609
Cache Creek, BC V0K 1H0
(250) 256–4204

PENELAKUT (Cowichan)
P.O. Box 360
Chemainus, BC V0R 1K0
(250) 246–2321

PENTICTON (Okanagan)
RR 2, Site 80, Comp. 19
Penticton, BC V2A 6J7
(250) 493–0048

PETERS (Cowichan)
Comp. 11, RR 2, Peters Rd.
Hope, BC V0X 1L0
(604) 794–7059

POPKUM (Cowichan)
c/o Sto:Lo Nation
Bldg 1–7201 Veddeer Rd
Chilliwack, BC V2R 4G5
Fax: (604) 824–5226

PROPHET RIVER (Slave)
P.O. Box 3250
Fort Nelson, BC V0C 1R0
(250) 773–6555

QUALICUM FIRST NATION (Puntlatch)
5850 River Rd
Qualicum Beach, BC V9K 1Z5
(250) 757–9337

QUATSINO (Kwatkiutl)
P.O. Box 100
Coal Harbour, BC V0N 1K0
(250) 949–6245

RED BLUFF (Carrier)
(aka QUESNEL)
1515 Arbutus Rd., Box 4693
Quesnel, BC V2J 3J9
(250) 747–2900

SAMAHQUAM (Lillooet)
P.O. Box 456
Mount Currie, BC V0N 2K0
(600) 700–3374

SAULTEAUX (Ojibway)
P.O. Box 330
Moberly Lake, BC V0C 1X0
(250) 788–3955

SCOWLITZ (Cowichan)
P.O. Box 76
Lake Errock, BC V0M 1N0
(604) 826–5813

SEABIRD ISLAND (Cowichan)
P.O. Box 650
Agassiz, BC V0M 1A0
(604) 796–2177

SECHELT
P.O. Box 740
Sechelt, BC V0N 3A0
(604) 688–3017

SEMIAHMOO FIRST NATION
16049 Beach Rd
Surrey, BC V4B 3C5
(604) 536–3101/6116

SETON LAKE (Lillooet)
Site 3, P.O. Box 76
Shalalth, BC V0N 3C0
(250) 259–8227/28

SHACKAN (Ntlayapamuk)
37 Chuluf
Merritt, BC V1K 1M9
(250) 378–5410

SHESHAHT (Nootka)
P.O. Box 1218
Port Alberni, BC V9Y 7M1
(250) 724–1225

SHUSWAP
P.O. Box 790
Invermere, BC V0A 1K0
(250) 342–6361

SHXW'OW'HAMEL FIRST NATION
RR 2, Site 22 Comp 4
Hope, BC V0X 1L0
(604) 869–2627

SISKA (Ntlayapamuk)
P.O. Box 358
Lytton, BC V0K 1Z0
(250) 455–2219

SKAWAHLOOK (Cowichan)
Box 388
Agassiz, BC V0M 1X0
(604) 796–9533

SKEETCHESTN (Shuswap)
P.O. Box 178
Savona, BC V0K 2J0
(250) 373–2493

SKIDEGATE (Haida)
P.O. Box 1301, RR 1
Skidegate, BC V0T 1S1
(250) 559–4496

**SKIN TYEE**
P.O. Box 17
Southbank, BC V0J 2P0
(250) 694–3517

**SKOOKUMCHUCK (Lillooet)**
P.O. Box 190
Pemberton, BC V0M 2L0

**SKOWKALE (Cowichan)**
P.O. Box 2159
Sardis, BC V2R 1A7
(604) 792–0730

**SKUPPAH (Ntlakyapamuk)**
P.O. Box 116
Lytton, BC V0K 1Z0
(250) 455–2279

**SKWAH (Cowichan)**
P.O. Box 178
Chilliwack, BC V2P 6H7
(604) 792–9204/5

**SKWAY (Cowichan)**
P.O. Box 364
Chilliwack, BC V2P 6J4
(604) 792–9316

**SLIAMMON (Comox)**
RR 2, Sliammon Rd.
Powell River, BC V8A 4Z3
(604) 483–9646

**SNUNEYMUXW FIRST NATION**
668 Centre St.
Nanaimo, BC V9R 4Z4
(250) 753–3481

**SODA CREEK (Shuswap)**
RR 4, Site 12, Comp. 62
Williams Lake, BC V2G 4M8
(250) 299–2323

**SONGHEES (Songish)**
1500 D–Admirals Rd.
Victoria, BC V9A 2R1
(250) 386–1043

**SOOKE (Songish)**
2154 Lazzar Rd., Box 307
Sooke, BC V0S 1N0
(250) 642–3957

**SOOWAHLIE (Cowichan)**
4071 Soowahlie Rd
Cultus Lake, BC V2R 4Y2
(604) 858–4603

**SPALLUMCHEEN (Shuswap)**
P.O. Box 3010
Enderby, BC V0E 1V0
(250) 838–6496

**SPUZZUM (Ntlakyapamuk)**
Site 3, C-11, RR 1
Yale, BC V0K 2S0
(604) 863–2395

**SQUAMISH**
P.O. Box 86131
North Vancouver, BC V7L 4J5
(604) 980–4553

**SQUIALA (Cowichan)**
8528 Afahwell
Chilliwack, BC V2P 7Z9
(604) 792–8300

**STELLAQUO (Carrier)**
P.O. Box 760
Fraser Lake, BC V0J 1S0
(250) 699–8747

**STELLAT'EN FIRST NATION**
P.O. Box 760
Fraser Lake, BC V0J 1S0
(250) 699–8747

**ST. MARY'S (Kootenay)**
7470 Mission Rd.
Cranbrook, BC V1C 7E5
(250) 426–5717

**STONE (Chilcotin)**
Box 158
Hanceville, BC V0L 1K0
(250) 394–4295/6

**SAIK'UZ FIRST NATION (Carrier)**
RR 1, Site 12, Comp. 26
Vanderhoof, BC V0J 3A0
(250) 567–9293

**SUMAS FIRST NATION (Cowichan)**
3092 Sumas Mountain Rd., RR 4
Abbotsford, BC V3G 2J2
(604) 852–4040

TAHLTAN
P.O. Box 46
Telegraph Creek, BC V0J 2W0
(250) 235–3241

TAKLA LAKE (Carrier)
Suite 345, 1460–6th Avenue
Prince George, BC V2L 3N2
(250) 564–9321

TAKU RIVER TLINGITS FIRST NATION
P.O. Box 132
Atlin, BC V0W 1A0
(250) 651–7615

TANAKTEUK (Kwakiutl)
P.O. Box 327
Alert Bay, BC V0N 1A0
(604) 974–5489

T'IT'Q'ET
P.O. Box 615
Lillooet, BC V0K 1V0
(250) 256–4118

TLA–O–QUI–AHT FIRST NATIONS (Nootka)
(aka CLAYOQUOT)
P.O. Box 18
Tofino, BC V0R 2Z0
(250) 725–3233

TLATLASIKWALA (Kwakiutl)
(aka NUWITTI)
c/o Whe–La–La–U Area Council
P.O. Box 150
Alert Bay, BC V0N 1A0
(250) 974–5501

TL'AZT'EN NATIONS (Carrier)
(formerly STUART–TREMBLEUR LAKE)
P.O. Box 670
Fort St. James, BC V0J 1P0
(250) 648–3212

TL'ETINQOX-T'IN GOVERNMENT OFFICE
P.O. Box 168
Alexis Creek, BC V0L 1A0
(250) 394–4212

TLOWITSIS–MUMTAGILIA
c/o Whe–La–La–U Area Council
P.O. Box 150
Alert Bay, BC V0N 1A0
(250) 974–5501

TOBACCO PLAINS (Kootenay)
P.O. Box 76
Grasmere, BC V0B 1R0
(250) 887–3461

TOOSEY (Chilcotin)
P.O. Box 80
Riske Creek, BC V0L 1T0
(250) 659–5655

TOQUAHT (Nootka)
P.O. Box 759
Ucluelet, BC V0R 3A0
(250) 726–4230

TSARTLIP (Songish)
P.O. Box 70
Brentwood Bay, BC V8M 1R3
(250) 652–3988

TSAWATAINEUK (Kwakiutl)
General Delivery
Kingcome Inlet, BC V0N 2B0
(250) 974–3013

TSAWOUT (Songish)
Box 121
Saanichton, BC V8M 2C3
(250) 652–9101

TSAWWASSEN (Cowichan)
131 N. Tsawwassen Dr.
Delta, BC V4M 4G2
(604) 943–2112

TSAY KEH DENE
#11–1839 First Ave
Prince George, BC V2L 2T8
(250) 562–8882

TSESHAHT
P.O. Box 1218
Port Alberni, BC V9Y 7M1
(250) 724–1225

TSEYCUM (Songish)
1210 Totem Ln.
North Saanich, BC V8L 5F4
(250) 656–0858

T'SOU-KE FIRST NATION
Box 307, 2154 Lazzar Rd
Sooke, BC V0S 1N0
(250) 642–3957

**TZEACHTEN FIRST NATION** (Cowichan)
45855 Promontory Rd.
Chilliwack, BC V2R 4E2
(604) 858–3888

**UCHUCKLESAHT** (Nootka)
P.O. Box 1118
Port Alberni, BC V9Y 7L9
(250) 724–1832

**UCLUELET** (Nootka)
P.O. Box 699
Ucluelet, BC V0R 3A0
(250) 726–7342

**ULKATCHO BAND** (Carrier)
P.O. Box 3430
Anahim Lake, BC V0L 1C0
(250) 742–3260/34/24

**UNION BAR** (Cowichan)
P.O. Box 788
Hope, BC V0X 1L0
(604) 869–9466

**UPPER NICOLA** (Ntlakyapamuk)
P.O. Box 3700
Merritt, BC V1K 1B8
(250) 350–3342/43

**UPPER SIMILKAMEEN** (Okanagan)
P.O. Box 310
Keremeos, BC V0X 1N0
(250) 499–2221

**WEST MOBERLY** (Beaver)
Box 90
Moberly Lake, BC V0C 1X0
(250) 788–3663

**WESTBANK** (Okanagan)
310–515 Hwy. 97 So.
Kelowna, BC V1Z 3J2
(250) 769–4999

**WET'SUWET'EN FIRST NATION**
P.O. Box 760
Burns Lake, BC V0J 1E0
(250) 698–7309

**WHISPERING PINES** (Shuswap)
(aka CLINTON)
RR 1, Site 8, Comp. 4
Kamloops, BC V2B 8P6
(250) 579–5772

**WILLIAMS LAKE** (Shuswap)
RR 3, Box 4, Sugarcane
Williams Lake, BC V2G 1M3
(250) 296–3507/4212

**XENI GWET'IN FIRST NATIONS
   GOVERNMENT**
General Delivery
Nemiah Valley, BC V0L 1X0
(250) 394–4286

**YAKWEAKWIOOSE** (Cowichan)
7176 Chilliwack River Rd., RR 2
Sardis, BC V2R 1B1
(604) 824–5226

**YALE FIRST NATION** (Cowichan)
P.O. Box 1869
Hope, BC V0X 1L0
(604) 863–2443

**YEKOOCHE**
Operations Office
P.O. Box 1239
Fort St. James, BC V0J 1P0
(250) 648–3267

#### ◆ MANITOBA

**BARREN LANDS** (Chipewyan)
General Delivery
Brochet, MB R0B 0B0
(204) 323–2300

**BERENS RIVER** (Ojibway)
Box 131
Berens River, MB R0B 0A0
(204) 382–2161

**BIRDTAIL SIOUX**
P.O. Box 22
Beulah, MB R0M 0B0
(204) 568–4540

**BLOODVEIN** (Cree)
General Delivery
Bloodvein, MB R0C 0J0
(204) 395–2148

**BROKENHEAD OJIBWAY NATION**
General Delivery
Scanterbury, MB R0E 1W0
(204) 766–2494

BUFFALO POINT FIRST NATION (Ojibway)
P.O. Box 1037
Buffalo Point, MB R0A 2W0
(204) 437–2133

CANUPAWAKPA DAKOTA FIRST NATION
   (formerly OAK LAKE SIOUX)
P.O. Box 146
Pipestone, MB R0M 1T0
(204) 854–2261

CHEMAWAWIN (Cree)
Box 9
Easterville, MB R0C 0V0
(204) 329–2161

CRANE RIVER BAND (Ojibway)
General Delivery
Crane River, MB R0L 0M0
(204) 732–2490

CROSS LAKE (Cree)
P.O. Box 10
Cross Lake, MB R0B 0J0
(204) 676–2218/2166

DAKOTA PLAINS
General Delivery
Edwin, MB R0H 0G0
(204) 252–2288

DAKOTA TIPI
2020 Dakota Drive
Dakota Tipi, MB R1N 3X6
(204) 857–4381

DAUPHIN RIVER (Ojibway)
General Delivery
Gypsumville, MB R0C 1J0
(204) 659–5370

EBB AND FLOW (Ojibway)
General Delivery
Ebb and Flow, MB R0L 0R0
(204) 448–2134

FAIRFORD
General Delivery
Fairford, MB R0C 0X0
(204) 659–5705

FISHER RIVER (Cree, Ojibway)
Box 367
Koostatak, MB R0C 1S0
(204) 645–2171

FORT ALEXANDER
P.O. Box 3
Fort Alexander, MB R0E 0P0
(204) 367–2287

FOX LAKE (Cree)
P.O. Box 369
Gilliam, MB R0B 0L0
(204) 486–2463

GAMBLERS (Ojibway)
P.O. Box 250
Binscarth, MB R0J 0G0
(204) 532–2464

GARDEN HILL FIRST NATION (Cree)
General Delivery
Island Lake, MB R0B 0T0
(204) 456–2085

GOD'S LAKE (Cree)
Box 258
God's Lake Narrows, MB R0B 0M0
(204) 335–2130

GOD'S RIVER (Cree)
General Delivery
God's River, MB R0B 0N0
(204) 366–2011

GRAND RAPIDS FIRST NATION (Cree)
P.O. Box 500
Grand Rapids, MB R0C 1E0
(204) 639–2219

HOLLOW WATER (Ojibway)
General Delivery
Wanipigow, MB R0E 2E0
(204) 363–7278

KEESEEKOOWENIN FIRST NATION (Ojibway)
P.O. Box 100
Elphinstone, MB R0J 0N0
(204) 625–2004

KINONJEOSHTEGON FIRST NATION
Box 359
Hodgson, MB R0C 1N0
(204) 394–2255

LAKE MANITOBA (Ojibway)
General Delivery
Vogar, MB R0C 3C0
(204) 768–3492

LAKE ST. MARTIN (Ojibway)
P.O. Box 69
Gypsumville, MB R0C 1J0
(204) 659–4539

LITTLE BLACK RIVER (Ojibway)
General Delivery
O'Hanley, MB R0E 1K0
(204) 367–4411

LITTLE GRAND RAPIDS (Ojibway)
General Delivery
Little Grand Rapids, MB R0B 0V0
(204) 397–2264/42

LITTLE SASKATCHEWAN (Ojibway)
General Delivery
Gypsumville, MB R0C 1J0
(204) 659–4584

LONG PLAIN (Ojibway)
Box 430
Portage La Prairie, MB R1N 3B7
(204) 252–2731

MANTO SIPI CREE NATION
General Delivery
God's River, MB R0B 0N0

MARCEL COLOMB FIRST NATION
P.O. Box 1150
Lynn Lake, MB R0B 0W0
(204) 356–2439

MATHIAS COLOMB (Cree)
General Delivery
Pukatawagan, MB R0B 1G0
(204) 553–2090

MOOSE LAKE (Cree)
General Delivery
Moose Lake, MB R0B 0Y0
(204) 678–2113

MOSAKAHIKEN CREE NATION
General Delivery
Moose Lake, MB R0B 0Y0
(204) 678–2113

NELSON HOUSE (Cree)
General Delivery
Nelson House, MB R0B 1A0
(204) 484–2332

NORTHLANDS (Dene)
General Delivery
Lac Brochet, MB R0B 2E0
(204) 337–2001

NORWAY HOUSE (Cree)
Box 250
Norway House, MB R0B 1B0
(204) 359–6721

O-CHI-CHAK-KO-SIPI FIRST NATION
General Delivery
Crane River, MB R0L 0M0
(204) 732–2490

OPASKWAYAK CREE NATION
P.O. Box 1000
Otinaka Mall
The Pas, MB R9A 1L1
(204) 623–5483

OXFORD HOUSE (Cree)
General Delivery
Oxford House, MB R0B 1C0
(204) 538–2156

PAUINGASSI (Ojibway)
General Delivery
Pauingassi, MB R0B 2G0
(204) 397–2371

PEGUIS BAND OFFICE (Cree, Ojibway)
Box 10
Peguis, MB R0C 3J0
(204) 645–2359

PINAYMOOTANG FIRST NATION
General Delivery
Fairford, MB R0C 0X0
(204) 659–5705

PINE CREEK (Ojibway)
P.O. Box 70
Camperville, MB R0L 0J0
(204) 524–2478

POPLAR RIVER FIRST NATION (Cree,
   Ojibway)
General Delivery
Negginan, MB R0B 0Z0
(204) 244–2267

**RED SUCKER LAKE** (Cree)
General Delivery
Red Sucker Lake, MB R0B 1H0
(204) 469–5041

**ROLLING RIVER** (Ojibway)
P.O. Box 145
Erickson, MB R0J 0P0
(204) 636–2211

**ROSEAU RIVER** (Ojibway)
P.O. Box 30
Ginew, MB R0A 2R0
(204) 427–2312

**SANDY BAY** (Ojibway)
Box 109
Marius, MB R0H 0T0
(204) 843–2462

**SAPOTAWEYAK CREE NATION**
General Delivery
Via Pelican Rapids, MB R0L 1L0
(204) 587–2012

**SAYISI DENE FIRST NATION** (Chipewyan)
General Delivery
Tadoule Lake, MB R0B 2C0
(204) 684–2022

**SHAMATTAWA** (Cree)
Box 150
Shamattawa, MB R0B 1K0
(204) 565–2340

**SHOAL RIVER** (Ojibway)
General Delivery
Pelican Rapids, MB R0L 1L0
(204) 587–2012

**SIOUX VALLEY**
P.O. Box 38
Griswold, MB R0M 0S0
(204) 855–2671

**SKOWNAN FIRST NATION**
General Delivery
Skownan, MB R0L 1Y0
(204) 628–3373

**SPLIT LAKE CREE FIRST NATION**
General Delivery
Split Lake, MB R0B 1P0
(204) 342–2045

**ST. THERESA POINT** (Cree)
General Delivery
St. Theresa Point, MB R0B 1J0
(204) 462–2106

**SWAN LAKE** (Ojibway)
P.O. Box 368
Swan Lake, MB R0G 2S0
(204) 836–2101

**THE PAS** (Cree)
P.O. Box 1000
The Pas, MB R9A 1L1
(204) 627–7100

**VALLEY RIVER** (Ojibway)
General Delivery
Shortdale, MB R0L 1W0
(204) 546–3334

**WAR LAKE** (Cree, Ojibway)
General Delivery
Ilford, MB R0B 0S0
(204) 288–4315/6

**WASAGAMACK** (Cree)
General Delivery
Wasagamack, MB R0B 1Z0
(204) 457–2337/2341

**WATERHEN** (Ojibway)
Box 106
Skownan, MB R0L 1Y0
(204) 628–3373

**WAYWAYSEECAPPO** (Ojibway)
P.O. Box 9
Waywayseecappo, MB R0J 1S0
(204) 859–2879

**WUSKWI SIPIHK FIRST NATION**
P.O. Box 220
Birch River, MB R0L 0E0
(204) 236–4201

**YORK FACTORY** (Cree)
General Delivery
York Landing, MB R0B 2B0
(204) 341–2180

## ◆ NEW BRUNSWICK

**BIG COVE (Micmac)**
RR 1, Site 11, Box 1
Big Cove, NB E0A 2L0
(506) 523–8200

**BUCTOUCHE**
RR 2, Site 1 Box 9
Buctouche Kent Co, NB E0A 1G0
(506) 743–6493

**BURNT CHURCH (Micmac)**
620 Bayview Dr.
Burnt Church First Nation, NB E9G 2A8
(506) 776–1200

**EEL GROUND (Micmac)**
47 Church Rd
Eel Ground, NB E0K 1B0
(506) 627–4600

**EEL RIVER BAR (Micmac)**
11 Main Street, Unit 201
Eel River Bar, NB E8C 1A1
(506) 684–6277

**FORT FOLLY (Micmac)**
P.O. Box 21
Dorchester, NB E0A 1M0
(506) 379 3400

**INDIAN ISLAND (Micmac)**
Box 1, RR 2
Rexton, NB E0A 2L0
(506) 523–4875

**KINGSCLEAR (Malecite)**
77 French Village Rd
Kingsclear First Nation, NB E3E 1K3
(506) 363–3028

**MADAWASKA MALISEET FIRST NATION**
1771 Main St.
Madawaska Maliseet, NB E7C 1W9
(506) 739–9765

**OROMOCTO (Malecite)**
P.O. Box 417
Oromocto, NB E2V 2J2
(506) 357–2083

**PABINEAU (Micmac)**
1290 Pabineau Falls Road
Pabineau First Nation, NB E2A 7M3
(506) 548–9211

**RED BANK (Micmac)**
P.O. Box 293
Red Bank, NB E9E 2P2
(506) 836–2366/6111

**SAINT MARY'S**
35 Dedam St.
Fredericton, NB E3A 2V2
(506) 458–9511

**TOBIQUE (Malecite)**
13156 Rte. 105
Tobique First Nation, NB E7H 5N7
(506) 273–5400

**WOODSTOCK (Malecite)**
3 Wulastook Crt
Woodstock First Nation, NB E7M 4K6
(506) 328–3303

## ◆ NEWFOUNDLAND

**MIAWPUKEK (Inuit)**
P.O. Box 10
Baie d'Espoir
Conne River, NF A0H 1J0
(709) 882–2146

## ◆ NORTHWEST TERRITORY

**ACHO DENE KOE**
General Delivery
Fort Liard, NT X0G 0A0
(867) 770–4141

**AKLAVIK (Loucheux)**
P.O. Box 118
Aklavik, NT X0E 0A0
(867) 978–2340

**BEHDZI AHDA" FIRST NATION**
P.O. Box 53
Colville Lake, NT X0E 0L0
(867) 709–2200

**COLVILLE LAKE (aka FORT GOOD HOPE)**
P.O. Box 80
Fort Good Hope, NT X0E 0H0
(867) 598–2231

**DECHI LAO'TI COUNCIL**
Box 69
Wekweti, NT X0E 1W0
(867) 713–2010

**DEH GOH GOTIE DENE COUNCIL**
General Delivery
Fort Providence, NT X0E 0L0
(867) 699–3401

**DELINE**
P.O. Box 158
Deline, NT X0E 0G0
(867) 589–3151

**DENINOO COMMUNITY COUNCIL**
Box 1899
Fort Resolution, NT X0E 0M0
(867) 394–4335

**DOGRIB RAE**
Box 8
Rae Edzo, NT X0E 0Y0
(867) 392–6581

**FORT GOOD HOPE (Hare)**
P.O. Box 80
Fort Good Hope, NT X0E 0H0
(867) 598–2231

**FORT LIARD (Slave)**
General Delivery
Fort Liard, NT X0G 0A0
(867) 770–4141

**FORT PROVIDENCE (Slave)**
(aka YAHTI DEWE K'O)
General Delivery
Fort Providence, NT X0E 0L0
(867) 699–3401

**FORT SIMPSON (Slave)**
(aka LIIDLI K'OE)
P.O. Box 469
Fort Simpson, NT X0E 0N0
(867) 695–3131/2

**FORT SMITH**
P.O. Box 960
Fort Smith, NT X0E 0P0
(867) 872–2986

**FORT WRIGLEY (Slave)**
(aka PEHDZEH K'I)
General Delivery
Wrigley, NT X0E 1E0
(867) 581–3321/3581

**GAMETI FIRST NATION**
P.O. Box 1
Rae Lakes, NT X0E 1R0
(867) 997–3441

**GWICH GWICH'IN**
P.O. Box 4
Tsiigehtchic, NT X0E 0B0
(867) 953–3201

**INUVIK NATIVE (Inuit)**
P.O. Box 2570
Inuvik, NT X0E 0T0
(867) 777–3344

**JEAN MARIE RIVER FIRST NATION**
General Delivery
Jean Marie River, NT X0E 0N0
(867) 809–2000

**KA'A'GEE TU FIRST NATION**
P.O. Box 4428
Hay River, NT X0E 1G3
(867) 825–2000

**KAKISA LAKE**
(K'AAGEE TU)
Box 4428
Hay River, NT X0E 1G3
(867) 825–2000

**K'ATLODEECHE FIRST NATION**
P.O. Box 3060
Hay River Reserve, NT X0E 1G4
(867) 874–6701

**LIIDLII KUE FIRST NATION**
P.O. Box 469
Fort Simpson, NT X0E 0N0
(867) 695–3131

**LUTSEL K'E DENE COUNCIL (Chipewyan)**
Box 28
Lutsel K'e, NT X0E 1A0
(867) 370–3051

**NAHANNI BUTTE**
(aka NAHZAA DEHE)
General Delivery
Nahanni Butte, NT X0E 0N0
(867) 602–2900

PEHDZEH KI FIRST NATION
General Delivery
Wrigley, NT X0E 1E0
(867) 581–3321

SAMBAA K'E (TROUT LAKE) DENE
　(Chipewyan)
P.O. Box 10
Trout Lake via Fort Simpson, NT X0E 0N0
(867) 206–2800

SMITH LANDING FIRST NATION
P.O. Box 1470
Fort Smith, NT X0E 0P0
(867) 872–4950

TETLIT GWICH'IN
P.O. Box 30
Fort McPherson, NT X0E 0J0
(867) 952–2330

TULITA DENE
P.O. Box 118
Tulita, NT X0E 0K0
(867) 588–3341

WEST POINT FIRST NATION
1–47031 Mackenzie Hwy.
Hay River, NT X0E 0R9
(867) 874–6677

WHA TI FIRST NATION
General Delivery
Wha Ti, NT X0E 1P0
(867) 573–3012

YELLOWKNIVES DENE FIRST NATION
P.O. Box 2514
Yellowknife, NT X1A 2P8
(867) 873–8951

## ◆ NOVA SCOTIA

ACADIA (Micmac)
RR 4, P.O. Box 5914C
Yarmouth, NS B5A 4A8
(902) 742–0257

AFTON (Micmac)
#1 Afton First Nation
Antigonish, NS B0H 1A0
(902) 386–2781/2881

ANNAPOLIS VALLEY (Micmac)
P.O. Box 89
Cambridge Station, NS B0P 1G0
(902) 538–7149

BEAR RIVER (Micmac)
P.O. Box 210
Bear River, NS B0S 1B0
(902) 467–3802

CHAPEL ISLAND (Micmac)
P.O. Box 538
Chapel Island, NS B0E 3B0
(902) 535–3317

ESKASONI (Micmac)
RR2
East Bay, NS B0A 1H0
(902) 379–2800

HORTON
P.O. Box 449
Hansport, NS B0P 1P0
(902) 684–9788

MEMBERTOU (Micmac)
111 Membertou St.
Sydney, NS B1S 2M9
(902) 564–6466

MILLBROOK (Micmac)
P.O. Box 634
Truro, NS B2N 5E5
(902) 897–9199

PICTOU LANDING (Micmac)
RR 2 Site 6 Box 55
Trenton, NS B0K 1X0
(902) 752–4912

SHUBENACADIE (Micmac)
General Delivery
Micmac PO
Hants Co., NS B0N 1W0
(902) 758–2049

WAGMATCOOK (Micmac)
P.O. Box 237
Baddeck, NS B0E 1B0
(902) 295–2598/3222

WHYCOCOMAGH (Micmac)
P.O. Box 149
Whycocomagh Inverness Co., NS B0E 3M0
(902) 756–2337

## ♦ ONTARIO

**AAMJIWNAANG**
978 Tashmoo Ave
Sarnia, ON N7T 7H5

**ALBANY**
P.O. Box 1
Fort Albany, ON P0L 1H0
(705) 278–1044

**ALDERVILLE (Ojibway)**
Box 46
Roseneath, ON K0K 2X0
(905) 352–2011

**ALGONQUIN OF GOLDEN LAKE**
1657 A. Mishomif Inamo
Golden Lake, ON K0J 1X0
(613) 625–2800

**ANISHINABE OF WAUZHUSHK ONIGUM**
P.O. Box 1850
Kenora, ON P9N 3X8
(807) 548–5663

**ANISHNAABEG OF NAONGASHIING**
General Delivery
Morson, ON P0W 1J0
(807) 488–5602

**AROLAND (Ojibway)**
P.O. Box 390
Nakina, ON P0T 2H0
(807) 329–5970/5333

**ATTAWAPISKAT (Cree)**
P.O. Box 248
Attawapiskat, ON P0L 1A0
(705) 997–2166

**BATCHEWANA (Ojibway)**
236 Frontenac St., RR 4
Sault Ste. Marie, ON P6A 5K9
(705) 759–0914

**BEARSKIN LAKE (Cree)**
P.O. Box 25
Bearskin Lake Post Office
Bearskin Lake, ON P0V 1E0
(807) 363–2518/2598

**BEAUSOLEIL (Ojibway)**
Cedar Point Post Office
Christian Island, ON L0K 1C0
(705) 247–2051/2014

**BEAVERHOUSE**
P.O. Box 1022
Kirkland Lake, ON P2N 3L4
(705) 567–2022

**BIG GRASSY (Ojibway)**
General Delivery
Morson, ON P0W 1J0
(807) 488–5614

**BIG ISLAND (Ojibway)**
Morson Post Office
Morson, ON P0W 1J0
(807) 488–5602

**BIG TROUT LAKE (Cree)**
Box 329
Big Trout Lake, ON P0V 1G0
(807) 537–2263/1183

**BIINJITIWAABIK ZAAGING ANISHINAABEK**
General Delivery
MacDiarmid, ON P0T 2B0
(807) 885–3401

**BRUNSWICK HOUSE (Cree, Ojibway)**
P.O. Box 1178
Chapleau, ON P0M 1K0
(705) 864–0174

**CALDWELL (Potawatomi)**
c/o 10297 Talbot Rd
Blenheim, ON N0P 1A0
(519) 676–5499

**CAT LAKE**
2 Back Road West
Cat Lake, ON P0V 1J0
(807) 347–2100

**CHAPLEAU CREE**
P.O. Box 400
Chapleau, ON P0M 1K0
(705) 864–0784

**CHAPLEAU OJIBWAY**
P.O. Box 279
Chapleau, ON P0M 1K0
(705) 864–2910

**CHIPPEWAS OF GEORGINA ISLAND**
RR 2, P.O. Box 13
Sutton West, ON L0E 1R0
(705) 437–1337

CHIPPEWAS OF KETTLE & STONY POINT
RR 2, 53 Indian Lane
Forest, ON N0N 1J0
(519) 786–2125/6

CHIPPEWAS OF MNJIKANING FIRST NATION
5884 Rama Rd., Suite 200
Rama, ON L0K 1T0
(705) 325–3611

CHIPPEWAS OF NAWASH
RR 5
Wiarton, ON N0H 2T0
(519) 534–1689

CHIPPEWAS OF RAMA
5884 Rama Rd, Suite 200
Rama, ON L0K 1T0
(705) 325–3611

CHIPPEWAS OF SARNIA
978 Tashmoo Ave.
Sarnia, ON N7T 7H5
(519) 336–8410

CHIPPEWAS OF SAUGEEN
RR 1
Southampton, ON N0H 2L0
(519) 797–2781

CHIPPEWAS OF THE THAMES
RR 1
Muncey, ON N0L 1Y0
(519) 289–5555

CONSTANCE LAKE (Cree)
Box 4000
Calstock, ON P0L 1B0
(705) 463–4511

COUCHICHING (Ojibway)
RR 2 RMB 2027
Fort Frances, ON P9A 3M3
(807) 274–3228

CURVE LAKE (Ojibway)
Curve Lake Post Office
Curve Lake, ON K0L 1R0
(705) 657–8045

DEER LAKE (Cree)
Box 39
Deer Lake, ON P0V 1N0
(807) 775–2141

DOKIS (Ojibway)
Dokis Bay
Monetville, ON P0M 2K0
(705) 763–2200

EABAMETOONG (Ojibway)
(aka FORT HOPE)
P.O. Box 298
Fort Hope, ON P0T 2H0
(807) 242–7361

EAGLE LAKE No. 27 (Ojibway)
P.O. Box 10
Eagle River, ON P0V 1S0
(807) 755–5526

FLYING POST (Cree, Ojibway)
Box 1027
Nipigon, ON P0T 2J0
(807) 887–3071

FORT SEVERN (Cree)
General Delivery
Fort Severn, ON P0V 1W0
(807) 478–2572

FORT WILLIAM (Ojibway)
90 Anemki Dr., Suite 200
Thunder Bay, ON P7C 4Z2
(807) 623–9543

GARDEN RIVER FIRST NATION (Ojibway)
7 Shingwauk Street, RR 4
Sault Ste. Marie, ON P6A 6Z8
(705) 946–6300

GINOOGAMING (Ojibway)
P.O. Box 89
Longlac, ON P0T 2A0
(807) 876–2242

GRASSY NARROWS (Ojibway)
General Delivery
Grassy Narrows, ON P0X 1B0
(807) 925–2201

GULL BAY (Ojibway)
c/o Gull Bay Post Office
Gull Bay, ON P0T 1P0
(807) 982–0006

HENVEY INLET (Ojibway)
General Delivery
Pickerel, ON P0G 1J0
(705) 857–2331

HIAWATHA FIRST NATION
RR 2
Keene, ON K0L 2G0
(705) 295–4421

HORNEPAYNE
P.O. Box 465, Spruce St.
Hornepayne, ON P0M 1Z0
(807) 868–2039

ISKATEWIZAAGEGAN #39 INDEPENDENT
  FIRST NATION
Kejick PO
Kejick, ON P0X 1E0
(807) 733–2560

KASABONIKA LAKE (Cree)
General Delivery
Kasabonika, ON P0l 1Y0
(807) 535–2547

KEE–WAY–WIN (Cree)
General Delivery
Kee-Way-Win, ON P0V 3G0
(807) 774–1210

KINGFISHER LAKE (Cree)
Kingfisher Lake, ON P0V 1Z0
(807) 536–2067

LAC DES MILLES LACS (Ojibway)
RR 1, Station Main
Pass Lake, ON P0T 2M0
(807) 977–1144

LAC LA CROIX (Ojibway)
P.O. Box 640
Fort Frances, ON P9A 3M9
(807) 485–2431

LAC SEUL (Ojibway)
P.O. Box 100
Hudson, ON P0V 1X0
(807) 582–3503

LAKE NIPIGON OJIBWAY FIRST NATION
P.O. Box 120
Beardmore, ON P0T 2G0
(807) 875–2785

LANSDOWNE HOUSE (Ojibway)
Lansdowne House via Pickle Lake, ON P0T 1Z0
(807) 479–2570/2521

LONG LAKE NO. 58 FIRST NATION (Ojibway)
P.O. Box 609
Longlac, ON P0T 2A0
(807) 876–2292

MAGNETAWAN (Ojibway)
Box 15, RR 1
Britt, ON P0G 1A0
(705) 383–2477

MARTIN FALLS (Ojibway)
Ogoki Post
Via Nakina, ON P0T 2L0
(807) 349–2509

MATACHEWAN (Cree, Ojibway)
P.O. Box 208
Matachewan, ON P0K 1M0
(705) 565–2230

MATTAGAMI (Ojibway)
P.O. Box 99
Gogama, ON P0M 1W0
(705) 894–2072

MCDOWELL LAKE (Cree)
McDowell Lake Band
P.O. Box 740
Red Lake, ON P0V 2M0
(807) 727–1168

M'CHIGEENG FIRST NATION
P.O. Box 2
M'Chigeeng, ON P0P 1G0
(705) 377–5362

MICHIPICOTEN (Ojibway)
RR 1, Site 8 P.O. Box 1
Wawa, ON P0S 1K0
(705) 856–1993

MISHKEEGOGAMANG
Osnaburgh, ON P0V 2H0
(807) 928–2414

MISSANABIE CREE
RR 4, Hwy. 17 East
Bell's Point, Garden River, ON P6A 5K9
(705) 254–2702

MISSISSAUGA (Ojibway)
P.O. Box 1299
Blind River, ON P0R 1B0
(705) 356–1621

MISSISSAUGAS OF NEW CREDIT (Ojibway)
RR 6
Hagersville, ON N0A 1H0
(905) 768–1133

MISSISSAUGAS OF SCUGOG (Ojibway)
22521 Island Rd.
Port Perry, ON L9L 1B6
(905) 985–3337

MOHAWKS OF GIBSON
RR 1
Tyendinaga Mohawk Territory, ON K0K 1X0
(613) 396–3424

MOHAWKS OF THE BAY OF QUINTE
RR 1
Deseronto, ON K0K 1X0
(613) 396–3424

MOOSE CREE FIRST NATION
P.O. Box 190
Moose Factory, ON P0L 1W0
(705) 658–4619

MOOSE DEER POINT (Ojibway)
P.O. Box 119
Mactier, ON P0C 1I0
(705) 375–5209

MORAVIAN OF THE THAMES
RR 3
Thamesville, ON N0P 2K0
(519) 692–3936

MUNSEE–DELAWARE NATION
RR 1
Muncey, ON N0L 1Y0
(519) 289–5396

MUSKRAT DAM (Cree)
Muskrat Dam, ON P0V 3B0
(807) 471–2573

NAICATCHEWENIN (Ojibway)
RR 1 Box 15
Devlin, ON P0W 1C0
(807) 486–3407

NAOTKAMEGWANNING
General Delivery
Pawitik, ON P0X 1L0
(807) 226–5411

NESKANTAGA FIRST NATION
Landsdowne House,
Via Pickle Lake, ON P0T 1Z0
(807) 479–2570

NEW OSNABURGH
Osnaburgh, ON P0V 2H0
(807) 928–2414

NEW POST (Cree)
RR 3 Box 3310
Cochrane, ON P0L 1C0
(705) 272–6315

NEW SLATE FALLS (Cree)
Slate Falls via Sioux Lookout, ON P0V 2P0
(807) #0120
0 – ask for 0920

NIBINAMIK (Ojibway)
(aka SUMMER BEAVER)
Summer Beaver via Pickle Lake, ON P0T 3B0
(807) 593–2131

NICIKOUSEMENECANING (Ojibway)
P.O. Box 68
Fort Francis, ON P9A 3M5
(807) 481–2536

NIPISSING (Ojibway)
RR 1
Sturgeon Falls, ON P0H 2G0
(705) 753–2050

NORTH CARIBOU LAKE
General Delivery
Weagamow Lake, ON P0V 2Y0
(807) 469–5191

NORTH SPIRIT LAKE (Cree)
North Spirit Lake, ON P0V 2G0

NORTHWEST ANGLE NO. 37 (Ojibway)
P.O. Box 267
Sioux Narrows, ON P0X 1N0
(807) 226–5353

OCHIICHAGWE'BABIGO'INING FIRST NATION
P.O. Box 88
Kenora, ON P9N 3W7
(807) 548–5876

**OJIBWAYS OF ONEGAMING**
P.O. Box 160
Nestor Falls, ON P0W 1K0
(807) 484–2162

**OJIBWAYS OF THE PIC RIVER FIRST NATION**
General Delivery
Heron Bay, ON P0T 1R0
(807) 229–1749

**ONEIDAS OF THE THAMES**
RR 2
Southwold, ON N0L 2G0
(519) 652–3244

**PAYS PLAT** (Ojibway)
P.O. Box 849
Schreiber, ON P0T 2S0
(807) 824–2541

**PIC MOBERT** (Ojibway)
General Delivery
Mobert, ON P0M 2J0
(807) 822–2134

**PIKANGIKUM** (Ojibway)
Pikangikum, ON P0V 2L0
(807) 773–5578

**POPLAR HILL** (Ojibway)
General Delivery
Poplar Hill, ON P0V 3E0
(807) 772–8838

**RAINY RIVER** (Ojibway)
P.O. Box 450
Emo, ON P0W 1E0
(807) 482–2479

**RED ROCK**
P.O. Box 1030
Nipigon, ON P0T 2J0
(807) 887–2510

**ROCKY BAY** (Ojibway)
MacDiarmid, ON P0T 2P0
(807) 885–3401

**SACHIGO LAKE** (Cree)
Sachigo Lake, ON P0V 2P0
(807) 595–2577

**SAGAMOK ANISHNAWBEK**
P.O. Box 610
Massey, ON P0P 1P0
(705) 865–2421

**SAND POINT** (Ojibway)
600 Victoria Ave., P.O. Box 27089
Thunder Bay, ON P7C 5Y7
(807) 344–3841

**SANDY LAKE** (Cree)
Sandy Lake, ON P0V 1V0
(807) 774–3421/5121

**SAUGEEN** (Ojibway)
RR 1
Southampton, ON N0H 2L0
(519) 797–2781

**SEINE RIVER** (Ojibway)
P.O. Box 124
Mine Centre, ON P0W 1H0
(807) 599–2224

**SERPENT RIVER** (Ojibway)
48 Village Road
Cutler, ON P0P 1B0
(705) 844–2418

**SHAWANAGA** (Ojibway)
RR 1
Nobel, ON P0G 1G0
(705) 366–2526

**SHEGUIANDAH** (Ojibway, Ottowa)
Sheguiandah, ON P0P 1W0
(705) 368–2781

**SHESHEGWANING** (Ojibway)
Sheshegwaning, ON P0P 1X0
(705) 283–3292

**SHOAL LAKE NO. 40** (Ojibway)
Kejick Post Office
Kejick, ON P0X 1E0
(807) 733–2315

**SIX NATIONS OF THE GRAND RIVER**
P.O. Box 5000
Ohsweken, ON N0A 1M0
(519) 445–2201

**SLATE FALLS NATION**
General Delivery
Slate Falls, ON P0V 3C0

**STANJIKOMING FIRST NATION**
P.O. Box 609
Fort Frances, ON P9A 3M9
(807) 274–2188

**TEME-AUGAMA ANISHNABAI**
Bear Island, ON P0H 1C0
(705) 237–8943

**THESSALON (Ojibway)**
P.O. Box 9, RR 2
Thessalon, ON P0R 1L0
(705) 842–2323

**WABASEEMOONG INDEPENDENT NATIONS**
Whitedog PO
Whitedog, ON P0X 1P0
(807) 927–2068

**WABAUSKANG (Ojibway)**
P.O. Box 418
Ear Falls, ON P0V 1T0
(807) 529–3174

**WABIGOON (Ojibway)**
Site 112 Box 24
Dinorwic, ON P0V 1P0
(807) 938–6684

**WAHGOSHIG (Cree, Ojibway)**
(aka ABITIBI #70)
P.O. Box 629
Matheson, ON P0K 1N0
(705) 567–4801

**WAHNAPITAE (Ojibway)**
P.O. Box 1119
Capreol, ON P0M 1H0
(705) 858–0610

**WAHTA MOHAWK**
P.O. Box 260
Bala, ON P0C 1A0
(705) 762–3343

**WALPOLE ISLAND**
RR 3
Wallaceburg, ON N8A 4K9
(519) 627–1481

**WAPEKEKA (Cree)**
General Delivery
Angling Lake, ON P0V 1B0
(807) 537–2315

**WASAUKSING**
(aka PARRY ISLAND)
P.O. Box 253
Parry Sound, ON P2A 2X4
(705) 746–2531

**WASHAGAMIS BAY (Ojibway)**
P.O. Box 625
Keewatin, ON P0X 1C0
(807) 543–2532

**WAUZHUSHK ONIGUM**
P.O. Box 1850
Kenora, ON P9N 3X7
(807) 548–5663

**WAWAKAPEWIN (Cree)**
c/o Shibogama F.N. Council
P.O. Box 449
Sioux Lookout, ON P8T 1A5
(807) 442–2567

**WEBEQUIE (Ojibway)**
P.O. Box 176
Webequie, ON P0T 3A0
(807) 353–6531

**WEENUSK (Cree, Ojibway)**
P.O. Box 1
Peawanuk, ON P0L 2H0
(705) 473–2554

**WEST BAY (Ojibway)**
P.O. Box 2
West Bay, ON P0P 1G0
(705) 377–5362

**WHITEFISH BAY (Ojibway)**
Pawitik Post Office
Pawitik, ON P0X 1L0
(807) 226–5411

**WHITEFISH LAKE (Ojibway, Ottawa)**
P.O. Box 39
Naughton, ON P0M 2M0
(705) 692–3651

**WHITEFISH RIVER (Ojibway)**
General Delivery
Birch Island, ON P0P 1A0
(705) 285–4335

WHITESAND (Ojibway)
P.O. Box 68
Armstrong, ON P0T 1A0
(807) 583–2177

WIKWEMIKONG UNCEDED (Ojibway, Ottawa)
P.O. Box 112
Wilwemikong, ON P0P 2J0
(705) 859–3122

WUNNUMIN LAKE (Cree)
P.O. Box 105
Wunnumin Lake, ON P0V 2Z0
(807) 442–2559

ZHIIBAAHAASING FIRST NATION
General Delivery
Silverwater, Manitoulin Island, ON P0P 1Y0
(705) 283–3963

### ♦ PRINCE EDWARD ISLAND

ABEGWEIT (Micmac)
P.O. Box 36
Mount Stewart, PE C0A 1T0
(902) 676–2353

LENNOX ISLAND (Micmac)
General Delivery
Lennox Island, PE C0B 1P0
(902) 831–2779

### ♦ QUEBEC

ABENAKIS DE WOLINAK
Conseil de Bande des Abénakis de Wolnick
10120 rue Kolipaio
Wolinak, QC G0X 1B0
(819) 294–6696/6698

ABITIBIWINNI (Algonquin)
45 Street Migwan
Amos, QC J9T 3A3
(819) 732–6591

ATIKAMEKW D'OPITCIWAN
Reserve Indienne d Obedjiwan
Via Roberval, QC G0W 3B0
(819) 974–8837

ATTIKAMEKS DE MANAWAN
135, rue Kicik
Manawan, QC J0K 1M0
(819) 971–8813

ATTIKAMEKS DE WEYMOTACI
Conseil de bande de Wemotaci Case
Postale 221
Wemotaci, QC G0X 3R0
(819) 666–2237

BARRIERE LAKE (Algonquin)
Rapid Lake
Parc de la Vérendrye, QC J0W 2C0
(819) 435–2181

BETSIAMITES
20 Rue Ashini, CP 40
Betsiamites, QC G0H 1B0
(418) 567–2265

CHIBOUGAMAU (Cree)
329 3rd Street
Chibougamau, PQ G8P 1N4
(418) 748–2617

CHISASIBI (Cree)
P.O. Box 150
James Bay, PQ J0M 1E0
(819) 855–2878

CONSEIL DE LA NATION HURONNE-WENDAT
255, Place Chef Michel Laveau
Wendake, PQ G0A 4V0
(418) 843–3767

CONSEIL DES ATTIKAMEKS D'OBEDJIWAN
Conseil de bande d'Obedjiwan Réserve
d'Obedjiwan
Via Roberval, QC G0W 3B0
(819) 974–8837

EAGLE VILLAGE FIRST NATION—KIPAWA
P.O. Box 756
Eagle Village First Nation, Kipawa, QC J0Z 3R0
(819) 627–3455

EASTMAIN (Cree)
P.O. Box 90
Eastmain, QC J0M 1W0
(819) 977–0211/66

GASPE (Micmac)
P.O. Box 69, Fontenelle
Gaspe, PQ G4X 6V2
(418) 368–6005

GRAND LAC VICTORIA (Algonquin)
Grand Lac Victoria via Louvicourt, PQ J0Y 1Y0
(819) 824–1914

INNU TAKUAIKAN UASHAT MAK MANI-
    UTENAM
1089 Dequen, CP 8000
Sept Iles, QC G4R 4LR
(418) 962–0327

KAHNAWAKE (Mohawk)
P.O. Box 720
Kahnawake, QC J0L 1B0
(450) 638–6790; 632–7500

KIPAWA (Algonquin)
Kebaoweck Indian Reserve
P.O. Box 787
Temiscaminque, PQ J0Z 3R0
(819) 627–3455

KITIGAN ZIBI ANISHINABEG (Algonquin)
(aka RIVER DESERT)
P.O. Box 309, 1 Paganakomin-Mikan
Kitigan Zibi Indian Reserve, QC J9E 3C9
(819) 449–5170

LAC SIMON (Algonquin)
1026 Boulevard Cicip
Lac Simon, PQ J0Y 3M0
(819) 736–4501

LISTUGUJ MI'GMAQ FIRST NATION COUNCIL
17 Riverside West Street
P.O. Box 298
Listuguj, QC G0C 2R0

LONG POINT (Algonquin)
P.O. Box 1
Winneway River, PQ J0Z 2J0
(819) 722–2441

MALECITES DE VIGER
3400 Boul. Losch
Suite 39
St. Hubert, PQ J3Y 5T6
(514) 656–9731/34

MICMACS OF GESGAPEGIAG
Maria Indian Reserve
P.O. Box 1280
Maria, QC G0C 1Y0
(418) 759–3441

MISTASSINI (Cree)
Isaac Shecapio Sr. Administration Building
187 Main Street
Mistassini, QC G0W 1C0
(418) 923–3253

MONTAGNAIS DE BETSIAMITES
2, rue Ashini
C.P. 40
Betsiamites, QC G0H 1B0
(418) 567–2265

MONTAGNAIS DE LA ROMAINE
La Romaine, QC G0G 1M0
(418) 229–2110

MONTAGNAIS DE LES ESCOUMINS
27, rue de la Reserve, Box 820
Les Escoumins, QC G0T 1K0
(418) 233–2509

MONTAGNAIS DE MINGAN
8, rue Manitou, Nitassinan C.P. 319
Mingan, QC G0G 1V0
(418) 949–2234/35/2406

MONTAGNAIS DE NATASHQUAN
159A, rue des Montagnais
Natashquan, QC G0G 2E0
(418) 726–3529

MONTAGNAIS DE PAKUA SHIPI
C.P. 178
Pakua Shipi, QC G0G 2R0
(418) 947–2253

MONTAGNAIS DE SCHEFFERVILLE
C.P. 1390
Schefferville, QC G0G 2T0
(418) 585–2601

MONTAGNAIS DU LAC ST–JEAN
Reserve Indienne de Mashteuiatsh
1671, rue Ouiatchouan
Mashteuiatsh, QC G0W 2H0
(418) 275–2473

MONTAGNAIS OF UASHAT MAK MANI-
    UTENAM
1089, rue Dequen
case Postale 8000
Sept–Iles, QC G4R 4L9
(418) 962–0327

NASKAPIS DE QUEBEC
P.O. Box 5111
Kawawachikamach, QC G0G 2Z0
(418) 585–2686

**NEMASKA** (Cree)
Champion Lake
Nemiscau, QC J0Y 3B0
(819) 673–2512

**ODANAK** (Abenakis)
(aka ST–FRANCOIS DU LAC)
102, rue Sibosis
Odanak, QC J0G 1H0
(450) 568–2810/9

**TEMISKAMING** (Algonquin)
P.O. Box 336
Notre-Dame du Nord, QC J0Z 3B0
(819) 723–2335

**WASKAGANISH FIRST NATION** (Cree)
P.O. Box 60
Waskaganish, QC J0M 1R0
(819) 895–8843/8650

**WASWANIPI** (Cree)
Diom Blacksmith Building
Waswanipi, QC J0Y 3C0
(819) 753–2587/2805/2743

**WEMINDJI** (Cree)
(aka OLD FACTORY)
16 Beaver Road, P.O. Box 60
Wemindji, QC J0M 1L0
(819) 978–0264/5

**WHAPMAGOOSTUI** (Cree)
P.O. Box 390
Whapmagoostui, QC J0M 1G0
(819) 929–3384/3518

**WOLF LAKE** (Algonquin)
P.O. Box 998
Temiscaminque, QC J0Z 3R0
(819) 627–3628

♦ **SASKATCHEWAN**

**AHTAHKAKOOP** (Cree)
P.O. Box 220
Shell Lake, SK S0J 2G0
(306) 468–2326

**BEARDY'S AND OKEMASIS** (Cree)
P.O. Box 340
Duck Lake, SK S0K 1J0
(306) 467–4523

**BIG RIVER** (Cree)
P.O. Box 519
Debden, SK S0J 0S0
(306) 724–4700/2161

**BIRCH NARROWS FIRST NATION**
General Delivery
Turnor Lake, SK S0M 3E0
(306) 894–2030

**BLACK LAKE** (Chipewyan)
Box 27
Black Lake, SK S0J 0H0
(306) 284–2044

**BUFFALO RIVER** (Chipewyan)
General Delivery
Dillon, SK S0M 0S0
(306) 282–2033

**CANOE LAKE** (Cree)
General Delivery
Canoe Narrows, SK S0M 0K0
(306) 829–2150

**CARRY THE KETTLE** (Assiniboine, Dakota)
P.O. Box 57
Sintaluta, SK S0G 4N0
(306) 727–2135

**CLEARWATER RIVER DENE**
P.O. Box 389
La Loche, SK S0M 1G0
(306) 822–2021

**COTE** (Ojibway)
P.O. Box 1659
Kamsack, SK S0A 1S0
(306) 542–2694

**COWESSESS** (Cree)
P.O. Box 100
Cowessess, SK S0G 5L0
(306) 696–2520

**CUMBERLAND** (Cree)
P.O. Box 220
Cumberland House, SK S0E 0S0
(306) 888–2226

**DAY STAR** (Cree)
P.O. Box 277
Punnichy, SK S0A 3C0
(306) 835–2834

ENGLISH RIVER (Chipewyan)
General Delivery
Patuanak, SK S0M 2H0
(306) 396–2066

FISHING LAKE (Ojibway)
P.O. Box 508
Wadena, SK S0A 4J0
(306) 338–3838

FLYING DUST (Cree)
8001 Flying Dust Reserve
Meadow Lake, SK S9X 1T8
(306) 236–4437

FOND DU LAC (Chipewyan)
Box 211
Fond du Lac, SK S0J 0W0
(306) 686–2101

GORDON (Cree, Ojibway)
P.O. Box 248
Punnichy, SK S0A 3C0
(306) 835–2232

HATCHET LAKE (Chipewyan)
General Delivery
Wollaston Lake, SK S0J 3C0
(306) 633–2003

ISLAND LAKE (Cree)
P.O. Box 460
Loon Lake, SK S0M 1L0
(306) 837–2188

JAMES SMITH (Cree)
P.O. Box 1059
Melfort, SK S0E 1A0
(306) 864–3636

JOSEPH BIGHEAD (Cree)
P.O. Box 309
Pierceland, SK S0M 2K0
(306) 839–2277

KAHKEWISTAHAW (Cree)
P.O. Box 609
Broadview, SK S0G 0K0
(306) 696–3291/2465/2466

KAWACATOOSE (Cree)
P.O. Box 640
Raymore, SK S0A 3J0
(306) 835–2125

KEESEEKOOSE (Ojibway)
P.O. Box 1120
Kamsack, SK S0A 1S0
(306) 542–2012

KEY (Ojibway)
P.O. Box 70
Norquay, SK S0A 2V0
(306) 594–2020

KINISTIN (Ojibway)
P.O. Box 2590
Tisdale, SK S0E 1T0
(306) 878–8188

LAC LA RONGE (Cree)
P.O. Box 480
La Ronge, SK S0J 1L0
(306) 425–2183

LITTLE BLACK BEAR (Cree)
P.O. Box 40
Goodeve, SK S0A 1C0
(306) 334–2269

LITTLE PINE (Cree)
P.O. Box 70
Paynton, SK S0M 2J0
(306) 398–4942

LUCKY MAN (Cree)
103B Packham Place, Suite 225
Saskatoon, SK S7N 4K4
(306) 374–2828

MAKWA SAHGAIEHCAN (Cree)
P.O. Box 340
Loon Lake, SK S0M 1L0
(306) 837–2150

MISTAWASIS (Cree)
P.O. Box 250
Leask, SK S0J 1M0
(306) 466–4800

MONTREAL LAKE
Box 106
Montreal Lake, SK S0J 1Y0
(306) 663–5349

MOOSOMIN (Cree)
P.O. Box 98
Cochin, SK S0M 0L0
(306) 386–2206

MOSQUITO GRIZZLY BEAR'S HEAD
  (Assiniboine)
P.O. Box 177
Cando, SK S0K 0V0
(306) 937–7707

MUSCOWPETUNG (Cree, Ojibway)
P.O. Box 1310
Fort Qu'Appelle, SK S0G 1S0
(306) 723–4747

MUSKEG LAKE (Cree)
P.O. Box 248
Marcelin, SK S0J 1R0
(306) 466–4959

MUSKODAY FIRST NATION
Box 99
Muskoday, SK S0J 3H0
(306) 764–1282

MUSKOWEKWAN (Ojibway)
P.O. Box 249
Lestock, SK S0A 2G0
(306) 274–2061

NEKANEET (Cree)
P.O. Box 548
Maple Creek, SK S0N 1N0
(306) 662–3660

OCEAN MAN
P.O. Box 157
Stoughton, SK S0G 4T0
(306) 457–2697

OCHAPOWACE (Cree)
P.O. Box 550
Whitewood, SK S0G 5C0
(306) 696–2425

OKANESE (Cree, Ojibway)
P.O. Box 759
Balcarres, SK S0G 0C0
(306) 334–2532

ONE ARROW (Cree)
P.O. Box 147
Bellevue, SK S0K 3Y0
(306) 423–5900

ONION LAKE (Cree)
P.O. Box 100
Onion Lake, SK S0M 2E0
(780) 847–2200

PASQUA (Cree, Ojibway)
P.O. Box 968
Fort Qu'Appelle, SK S0G 1S0
(306) 332–5697

PEEPEEKISIS (Cree)
P.O. Box 518
Balcarres, SK S0G 0C0
(306) 334–2573

PELICAN LAKE (Cree)
P.O. Box 399
Leoville, SK S0J 1N0
(306) 984–2313

PETER BALLANTYNE (Cree)
General Delivery
Pelican Narrows, SK S0P 0E0
(306) 632–2125

PHEASANT RUMP NAKOTA
P.O. Box 238
Kisbey, SK S0C 1L0
(306) 462–2002

PIAPOT (Cree)
General Delivery
Zehner, SK S0G 5K0
(306) 781–4848

POUNDMAKER (Cree)
P.O. Box 220
Paynton, SK S0M 2J0
(306) 398–4971

RED EARTH (Cree)
P.O. Box 109
Red Earth, SK S0E 1K0
(306) 768–3640

RED PHEASANT (Cree)
P.O. Box 70
Cando, SK S0K 0V0
(306) 937–7717

SAKIMAY (Cree)
P.O. Box 339
Grenfell, SK S0G 2B0
(306) 697–2831

SAULTEAUX (Ojibway)
P.O. Box 159
Cochin, SK S0M 0L0
(306) 386–2424

SHOAL LAKE (Cree)
General Delivery
Pakwaw Lake, SK S0E 1G0
(306) 768–3551

STANDING BUFFALO (Dakota)
Box 128
Fort Qu'Appelle, SK S0G 1S0
(306) 332–4685

STAR BLANKET (Cree)
P.O. Box 456
Balcarres, SK S0G 0C0
(306) 334–2206

STURGEON LAKE (Cree)
Box 5, Site 12, RR 1
Shellbrook, SK S0J 2E0
(306) 764–1872

SWEETGRASS (Cree)
P.O. Box 147
Gallivan, SK S0M 0X0
(306) 937–2990

THUNDERCHILD (Cree)
P.O. Box 600
Turtleford, SK S0M 2Y0
(306) 845–3424

WAHPETON (Dakota)
P.O. Box 128
Prince Albert, SK S6V 5R4
(306) 764–6649

WATERHEN LAKE (Cree)
P.O. Box 9
Waterhen Lake, SK S0M 3B0
(306) 236–6717

WHITE BEAR (Cree, Ojibway, Assiniboine)
P.O. Box 700
Carlyle, SK S0C 0R0
(306) 577–2461

WHITECAP DAKOTA/SIOUX FIRST NATION
RR 5, Site 507
P.O. Box 28
Saskatoon, SK S7K 3J8
(306) 477–0908

WITCHEKAN LAKE (Cree)
P.O. Box 879
Spiritwood, SK S0J 2M0
(306) 883–2787

WOOD MOUNTAIN (Dakota)
P.O. Box 104
Wood Mountain, SK S0H 4L0
(306) 266–4422

YELLOW QUILL (Ojibway)
P.O. Box 40
Yellow Quill, SK S0A 3A0
(306) 322–2281

## ◆ YUKON TERRITORY

CARCROSS/TAGISH
P.O. Box 130
Carcross, YT Y0B 1B0
(867) 821–4251

CHAMPAGNE/AISHIHIK (Kutchin, Tlingit)
P.O. Box 5309
Haines Junction, YT Y0B 1L0
(867) 634–2288

KLUANE (Kutchin, Tanana)
Box 20
Burwash Landing, YT Y0B 1V0
(867) 841–4274

KWANLIN DUN (Kutchin)
35 McIntyre Street
Whitehorse, YT Y1A 5A5
(867) 633–7800

LIARD RIVER (Kaska)
P.O. Box 328
Watson Lake, YT Y0A 1C0
(867) 536–2131

LITTLE SALMON/CARMACKS (Kutchin)
P.O. Box 135
Carmacks, YT Y0B 1C0
(867) 863–5576

NACHO NYAK DUN (Kutchin)
P.O. Box 220
Mayo, YT Y0B 1M0
(867) 996–2265

ROSS RIVER DENA COUNCIL (Kaska, Nahani)
General Delivery
Ross River, YT Y0B 1S0
(867) 969–2277

SELKIRK (Kutchin)
Box 40
Pelly Crossing, YT Y0B 1P0
(867) 537–3331

TA'AN KWACH'AN COUNCIL
P.O. Box 32081
Whitehorse, YT Y1A 5P9
(867) 668–3613

TESLIN TLINGIT COUNCIL (Tagish)
Box 133
Teslin, YT Y0A 1B0
(867) 390–2532

TR'ON DEK HWECH'IN
P.O. Box 599
Dawson City, YT Y0B 1G0
(867) 993–5385

VUNTUT GWITCHIN (Loucheux)
General Delivery
Old Crow, YT Y0B 1N0
(867) 966–3213

WHITE RIVER (Kutchin, Tanana)
General Delivery
Beaver Creek, YT Y0B 1A0
(867) 862–7802

## References

### Northeast

American Friends Service Committee. *The Wabanakis of Maine and the Maritimes: A Resource Book About Penobscot, Passamaquoddy, Maliseet, Micmac and Abenaki Indians*. Bath, Me.: Maine Indian Program, 1989.

Brodeur, Paul. *Restitution: The Land Claims of the Mashpee, Passamaquoddy, and Penobscot Indians of New England*. Boston: Northeastern University Press, 1985.

Calloway, Colin, ed. *Dawnland Encounters: Indians and Europeans in Northern New England*. Hanover, N.H.: University Press of New England,1991.

Campisi, Jack. *The Mashpee Indians: Tribe on Trial*. Syracuse, N.Y.: Syracuse University Press, 1991.

Cronon, William. *Changes in the Land: Indians, Colonists, and the Ecology of New England*. New York: Hill and Wang, 1983.

Johansen, Bruce E. *Debating Democracy: Native American Legacy of Freedom*. San Francisco: Clear Light, 1998.

Leland, Charles G. *Algonquin Legends*. New York: Dover, 1992 [1884].

Lyons, Oren, et al. *Exiled in the Land of the Free: Democracy, Indian Nations, and the U.S. Constitution*. San Francisco: Clear Light, 1992.

Morrison, Kenneth M. *The Embattled Northeast: The Elusive Ideal of Alliance in Abenaki-Euramerican Relations*. Berkeley and Los Angeles: University of California Press, 1984.

Satz, Ronald M., et al. *Chippewa Treaty Rights: The Reserved Rights of Wisconsin's Chippewa Indians in Historical Perspective*. Madison, Wis.: Wisconsin Academy of Sciences, Arts and Letters, 1991.

Shattuck, George. *The Oneida Land Claims: A Legal History*. Syracuse, N.Y.: University of Syracuse Press, 1991.

Speck. Frank G. *Penobscot Man: The Life History of a Forest Tribe in Maine*. Philadelphia: University of Pennsylvania Press, 1940.

Trigger, Bruce G., ed. *Northeast*. Vol. 15 of *Handbook of North American Indians*, edited by William C. Sturtevant. Washington, D.C.: Smithsonian Institution, 1978.

*Darrell Ranco*

### Southeast

Alden, John R. *John Stuart and the Southern Colonial Frontier: A Study of Indian Relations, War, Trade, and Land Problems in the Southern Wilderness, 1754–1775*. Ann Arbor: The University of Michigan Press, 1944; New York: Gordian Press, 1966.

Baird, W. David. The *Chickasaw People*. Phoenix, Ariz.: Indian Tribal Series, 1974.

———. *Peter Pitchlynn: Chief of the Choctaws*. Norman: University of Oklahoma Press, 1972.

Bartram, William. *The Travels of William Bartram*. Naturalists ed. Edited by Francis Harper. New Haven: Yale University Press, 1958.

Billie, James. "Fighting Hun Tashuk Teek [Apathy]: The Seminoles v. Florida." *Southern Exposure* 13, no. 6 (1985): 17–20.

Bordewich, Fergus M. "How to Succeed in Business: Follow the Choctaws' Lead." *Smithsonian* 26, no. 12 (1996): 70–81.

Catlin, George. *Letters and Notes on the Manners, Customs, and Conditions of the North American Indians*. 2 vols. New York: Dover Publications, 1973.

Christie, John C., Jr. "The Catawba Indian Land Claim: A Giant Among Indian Land Claims." *American Indian Culture and Research Journal* 24, no. 1 (2000): 173–182.

Clark, Thomas D. and John D. W. Guice. *Frontiers in Conflict: The Old Southwest, 1795–1830*. Albuquerque: University of New Mexico Press, 1989.

Crane, Verner W. *The Southern Frontier: 1670–1732*. Ann Arbor: University of Michigan Press, 1964, 1929.

Debo, Angie. *The Rise and Fall of the Choctaw Republic*. Norman: University of Oklahoma Press, 1934.

———. *The Road to Disappearance: A History of the Creek Indians*. Norman: University of Oklahoma Press, 1941.

———. *And Still the Waters Run*. 1940. Reprint. Norman: University of Oklahoma Press, 1984.

Derks, Scott. "We Can't Turn Back." *Southern Exposure* 13, no. 6 (1985): 67–71.

Duthu, N. Bruce. "The Houma Indians of Louisiana: the Intersection of Law and History in the Federal Acknowledgement Process." *Louisiana History* 38, no. 4 (1997): 409–436.

Duthu, N. Bruce and Hilde Objibway. "Future Light or *Feu Follet* ?: Louisiana Indians and Federal Recognition." *Southern Exposure* 13, no. 6 (1985): 24–32.

Ellsworth, Lucius F. and Jane E. Dysart. "West Florida's Forgotten People: the Creek Indians from 1830 until 1970." *Florida Historical Quarterly* 59, no. 4 (1981): 422–439.

Finger, John R. *Cherokee Americans: The Eastern Band of Cherokees in the Twentieth Century*. Lincoln: University of Nebraska Press, 1991.

———. *The Eastern Band of Cherokees, 1819–1900*. Knoxville: University of Tennessee Press, 1984.

Gaillard, Frye. *As Long As the Waters Flow: Native Americans in the South and East*. Winston-Salem, N.C.: John F. Blair, 1998.

Gibson, Arrell M. *The Chickasaws*. Norman: University of Oklahoma Press, 1971.

Godbold, E. Stanly, Jr., and Mattie U. Russell. *Confederate Colonel and Cherokee Chief: The Life of William Holland Thomas*. Knoxville: University of Tennessee Press, 1990.

Green, Michael D. *The Politics of Indian Removal: Creek Government and Society in Crisis*. Lincoln: University of Nebraska Press, 1982.

Hill, L. Brooks and Philip Lujan. "The Mississippi Choctaws: A Case Study of Intercultural Games." *American Indian Culture and Research Journal* 7 no. 3 (1983): 29–42.

Hudson, Charles M. *The Catawba Nation*. Athens, Ga.: University of Georgia Press, 1970.

———. *The Southeastern Indians*. Knoxville: University of Tennessee Press, 1976.

Jordan, Pat. "In Florida: Filling the Hours with Bingo." *Time* 131, no. 17 (25 April 1988), 13–15.

Kersey, Harry A., Jr. *An Assumption of Sovereignty: Social and Political Transformation Among the Florida Seminoles, 1953–1979*. Lincoln: University of Nebraska Press, 1996.

———. "The Florida Seminole Land Claims Case, 1950–1990." *Florida Historical Quarterly* 72, no. 1 (1993): 35–55.

———. *The Florida Seminoles and the New Deal, 1933–1942*. Boca Raton: Florida Atlantic University Press, 1989.

King, Duane H., ed. *The Cherokee Indian Nation: A Troubled History*. Knoxville: University of Tennessee Press, 1979.

Kniffen, Fred B., Hiram F. Gregory, and George A. Stokes. The *Historic Indian Tribes of Louisiana: From 1542 to the Present*. Baton Rouge: Louisiana State University Press, 1987.

Littlefield, Daniel F., Jr. "The Decline of the Ball Play Among the Civilized Tribes." *Journal of Ethnic Studies* 2, no. 4 (1975): 56–70.

McCulloch, Anne Merline, and David E. Wilkins. "'Constructing' Nations Within States: the Quest for Federal Recognition by the Catawba and Lumbee Tribes." *American Indian Quarterly* 19, no.3 (1995): 361–388.

McKee, Jesse O. *The Choctaw*. New York: Chelsea House, 1989.

McLoughlin, William G. *Champions of the Cherokees: Evan and John B. Jones*. Princeton, N.J.: Princeton University Press, 1990.

Martin, Joel W. *Sacred Revolt: The Muskogees' Struggle for a New World*. Boston: Beacon Press, 1991.

Merrell, James H. *The Indians' New World: Catawbas and Their Neighbors from European Contact through the Era of Removal*. Chapel Hill: Published for the Institute of Early American History and Culture, Williamsburg, Va., by the University of North Carolina Press, 1989.

Miller, Anneta. "Indian Tribes, Incorporated: Native Americans are Beginning to Have Remarkable Success as Small Businessmen." *Newsweek* 112, no. 23 (5 December 1988): 40–41.

Millman, Joel. "Choctaw Chief Leads His Mississippi Tribe Into the Global Market." *Wall Street Journal*. 23 July 1999.

O'Donnell, James H., III. "Alexander McGillivray: Training for Leadership, 1777–1783." *Georgia Historical Quarterly* 49, no. 2 (1965): 172–186.

———. *Southern Indians in the American Revolution*. Knoxville: University of Tennessee Press, 1973.

O'Hare, William P. "America's Minorities—the Demographics of Diversity." *Population Bulletin* 47 no. 4 (1992): 2–47.

Pollard, Kelvin M., and William P. O'Hare. "America's Racial and Ethnic Minorities." *Population Bulletin* 54, no. 3 (1999): 3–48.

Reeves, Carolyn Keller, ed. *The Choctaw Before Removal*. Jackson: University Press of Mississippi, 1985.

Rountree, Helen C. *Pocahontas's People: the Powhatan Indians of Virginia Through Four Centuries*. Norman: University of Oklahoma Press, 1990.

Starna, William A. "The Southeast Syndrome: the Prior Restraint of a Non-Event." *American Indian Quarterly* 15, no. 4 (1991): 493–502.

Steinem, Gloria. "A New Kind of Leader." *Ms. Magazine* 2, no. 3 (1991): 29.

Thornton, Russell. *The Cherokees: A Population History*. Lincoln: University of Nebraska Press, 1990.

U.S. Department of Commerce. Bureau of the Census. *The Statistical Abstract of the United States 1991*. 111th ed. Washington, D.C.: GPO, 1991.

U.S. Department of Commerce. Bureau of the Census. *We, the First Americans*. Washington, D.C.: GPO, 1989.

U.S. National Advisory Council on Indian Education. *Toward the Year 2000: Listening to the Voice of Native America*. Washington, D.C., 1991.

VandeHei, Jim. "Mississippi's Choctaw Find an Unlikely Ally in a GOP Stalwart." *Wall Street Journal* (3 July 2000).

White, Richard. *The Roots of Dependency: Subsistence, Environment, and Social Change Among the Choctaws, Pawnees, and Navajos*. Lincoln: University of Nebraska Press, 1983.

Williams, Walter L., ed. *Southeastern Indians Since the Removal Era*. Athens, Ga.: University of Georgia Press, 1979.

Wood, Peter H., Gregory A. Waselkov, and M. Thomas Hatley, eds. *Powhatan's Mantle: Indians in the Colonial Southeast*. Lincoln: University of Nebraska Press, 1989.

*James O'Donnell III*

## Southwest

Aberle, David Friend. *The Peyote Religion Among the Navaho*. 2d ed. Norman: University of Oklahoma Press, 1991.

Anderson, Duane, ed. *Legacy: Southwest Indian Art at the School of American Research*. Santa Fe, N.Mex.: School of American Research Press, 1999.

Brugge, David M. *The Navajo-Hopi Land Dispute: An American Tragedy*. Albuquerque: University of New Mexico Press, 1994.

Dillingham, Rick. *Fourteen Families in Pueblo Pottery*. Albuquerque: University of New Mexico Press, 1994.

Dobyns, Henry F. *The Pima-Maricopa*. New York: Chelsea House, 1989.

Durrett, Deanne. *Unsung Heroes of World War II: The Story of the Navajo Code Talkers*. New York: Facts on File, 1998.

Eichstaedt, Peter H. *If You Poison Us: Uranium and Native Americans*. Santa Fe, N.M.: Red Crane Books, 1994.

Erickson, Winston P. *Sharing the Desert: The Tohono O'odham In History*. Tucson: University of Arizona Press, 1994.

Fontana, Bernard L. *Of Earth and Little Rain: The Papago Indians*. Flagstaff, Ariz.: Northland Press, 1981.

Gordon-McCutchan, R.C. *The Taos Indians and the Battle for Blue Lake*. Santa Fe, N.Mex.: Red Crane Books, 1995.

Iverson, Peter. *Carlos Montezuma*. Austin, Tex.: Raintree: Steck-Vaugh, 1993.

———. *Carlos Montezuma and the Changing World of American Indians*. Albuquerque: University of New Mexico Press, 1982.

———. *The Navajo Nation*. Albuquerque: University of New Mexico Press, 1983.

Linford, Laurence D. *Navajo Places: History, Legend, Landscape*. Salt Lake City: University of Utah Press, 2000.

Lucas, Phil. *The Native Americans: Natives of the Southwest: White Myths, Native Mythology*. Atlanta, Ga.: Turner Home Entertainment, 1994. Videocassette.

Malinowski, Sharon, ed. *Southwest*. In Vol. 2 of *The Gale Encyclopedia of Native American Tribes*, 51–400. Detroit, Mich.: Gale, 1998.

Ortiz, Alfonso. *The Pueblo*. New York: Chelsea House, 1994.

———, ed. *Southwest*. Vols. 9 and 10 of *Handbook of North American Indians*, edited by William C. Sturtevant. Washington, D.C.: Smithsonian Institution, 1979 and 1983.

Roessel, Ruth., ed. *Navajo Stories of the Long Walk Period*. Tsaile, Ariz.: Navajo Community College Press, 1973.

Roessel, Ruth and Broderick H. Johnson, comps. *Navajo Livestock Reduction: A National Disgrace*. Chinle, Ariz.: Navajo Community College Press, 1974.

Sando, Joe S. *Pueblo Nations: Eight Centuries of Pueblo Indian History*. Santa Fe, N.M.: Clear Light Publishers, 1992.

———. *Pueblo Profiles: Cultural Identity Through Centuries of Change*. Santa Fe, N.Mex.: Clear Light Publishers, 1998.

Shaw, Anna Moore. *A Pima Past*. Tucson, Ariz.: University of Arizona Press, 1974.

Sita, Lisa. *Indians of the Southwest: Traditions, History, Legends, and Life*. Philadelphia: Courage Books, 1997.

Spicer, Edward H. *Cycles of Conquest: The Impact of Spain, Mexico, and the United States on the Indians of the Southwest, 1533–1960*. Tucson: University of Arizona Press, 1962.

Tiller, Veronica E. Velarde. *The Jicarilla Apache Tribe: A History.* Rev. ed. Lincoln: University of Nebraska Press, 1992.

———. *Tiller's Guide to Indian Country: Economic Profiles of American Indian Reservations.* Albuquerque: BowArrow Publishing Co., 1996.

Trimble, Stephen. *The People: Indians of the American Southwest.* Santa Fe, N.M.: SAR Press, School of American Research Press; distributed by University of Washington Press, 1993.

Webb, George. *A Pima Remembers.* Tucson, Ariz.: University of Arizona Press, 1959.

Whiteley, Peter M. *Bacavi: Journey to Reed Springs.* Flagstaff, Ariz.: Northland Press, 1988.

Whiteley, Peter M. *Deliberate Acts: Changing Hopi Culture Through the Oraibi Split.* Tucson: University of Arizona Press, 1988.

*Carol Lujan*

## Plains

Biolsi, Thomas. *Organizing the Lakota: The Political Economy of the New Deal on the Pine Ridge and Rosebud Reservations.* Tucson: University of Arizona Press, 1992.

Brown, Joseph Epes. *Animals of the Soul: Sacred Animals of the Oglala Sioux.* Rockport, Mass.: Element, 1992.

Ewers, John C. *The Blackfeet: Raiders on the Northwest Plains.* Norman: University of Oklahoma Press, 1958.

Fowler, Loretta. *Arapahoe Politics, 1851–1978: Symbols in Crisis of Authority.* Lincoln: University of Nebraska Press, 1982.

———. *Shared Symbols, Contested Meanings: Gros Ventre Culture and History, 1778–1984.* Ithaca: Cornell University Press, 1987.

Grobsmith, Elizabeth S. *Lakota of the Rosebud: A Contemporary Ethnography.* New York: Holt, Rinehart, and Winston, 1981.

Hassrick, Royal B. *The Sioux: Life and Customs of a Warrior Society.* Norman: University of Oklahoma Press, 1964.

Hoxie, Frederick E. *Parading Through History: The Making of the Crow Nation in America, 1805–1935.* Cambridge: University of Cambridge Press, 1995.

Iverson, Peter, ed. *The Plains Indians of the Twentieth Century.* Norman: University of Oklahoma Press, 1985.

Lazarus, Edward. *Black Hills White Justice: the Sioux Nation Versus the United States, 1775 to the Present.* New York: HarperCollins, 1991.

Lewis, Thomas H. *The Medicine Men: Oglala Sioux Ceremony and Healing.* Lincoln: University of Nebraska Press in cooperation with the American Indian Studies Research Institute, Indiana University, 1990.

Llewellyn, Karl N. and E. Adamson Hoebel. *The Cheyenne Way: Conflict and Case Law in Primitive Jurisprudence.* Norman: University of Oklahoma Press, 1941.

Lopach, James J., Margery Hunter Brown, and Richmond L. Clow. *Tribal Government Today: Politics on Montana Indian Reservations.* Rev. ed. Niwot, Colo.: University Press of Colorado, 1998.

McFee, Malcolm. *Modern Blackfeet: Montanans on a Reservation.* New York: Holt, Rinehart and Winston, 1972.

Meyer, Roy W. *The Village Indians of the Upper Missouri: The Mandans, Hidatsas, and Arikaras.* Lincoln: University of Nebraska Press, 1977.

Nurge, Ethel, ed. *The Modern Sioux: Social Systems and Reservation Culture.* Lincoln: University of Nebraska Press, 1970.

Powers, Marla N. *Oglala Woman: Myth, Ritual, and Reality.* Chicago: University of Chicago Press, 1986.

Scherer, Mark R. *Imperfect Victories: The Legal Tenacity of the Omaha Tribe, 1945–1995.* Lincoln: University of Nebraska Press, 1999.

Schusky, Ernest L. *The Forgotten Sioux: An Enthnohistory of the Lower Brule Reservation.* Chicago: Nelson-Hall, 1975.

Schwartz, Warren E. *The Last Contrary: The Story of Wesley Whiteman (Black Bear).* Sioux Falls, S.D.: Center for Western Studies, Augustana College, 1988.

Starita, Joe. *The Dull Knifes of Pine Ridge: A Lakota Odyssey.* New York: Putnam, 1995.

Steltenkamp, Michael F. *Black Elk: Holy Man of the Oglala.* Norman: University of Oklahoma Press, 1993.

Svingen, Orlan J. *The Northern Cheyenne Reservation, 1877–1900.* Niwot, Colo.: University Press of Colorado, 1993.

Wishart, David J. *An Unspeakable Sadness: The Dispossession of the Nebraska Indians.* Lincoln: University of Nebraska Press, 1994.

*Richmond Clow*

## Northwest Coast

Adams, John W. "Recent Ethnology of the Northwest Coast." *Annual Review of Anthropology* 10 (1981): 361–392.

Bierwert, Crisca. *Brushed by Cedar, Living by the River: Coast Salish Figures of Power.* Tucson: University of Arizona Press, 1999.

Boxberger, Daniel L. *To Fish in Common: The Ethnohistory of Lummi Indian Salmon Fishing.* Seattle: University of Washington Press, 2000.

Drucker, Philip. *Cultures of the North Pacific Coast.* San Francisco: Chandler Publishing, 1965.

Gunther, Erna. *Indian Life on the Northwest Coast of North America: As Seen by the Early Explorers and Fur Traders During the Last Decade of the Eighteenth Century.* Chicago: University of Chicago Press, 1972.

Harkin, Michael E. *The Heiltsuks: Dialogues of Culture and History on the Northwest Coast.* Lincoln: University of Nebraska Press in cooperation with the American Indian Studies Research Institute, Indiana University, Bloomington, 1997.

Harmon, Alexandra. *Indians in the Making: Ethnic Relations and Indian Identities Around Puget Sound.* Berkeley and Los Angeles: University of California Press, 1998.

Kan, Sergei. *Memory Eternal: Tlingit Culture and Russian Orthodox Christianity Through Two Centuries.* Seattle: University of Washington Press, 1999.

Miller, Jay. *Tsimshian Culture: A Light Through the Ages.* Lincoln: University of Nebraska Press, 1997.

Stewart, Hilary. *Indian Fishing: Early Methods on the Northwest Coast.* Seattle: University of Washington Press, 1977.

Suttles, Wayne. *Coast Salish Essays.* Vancouver: Talonbooks; Seattle: University of Washington Press, 1987.

———., ed. *Northwest Coast.* Vol. 7 of *Handbook of North American Indians*, edited by William C. Sturtevant. Washington, D.C.: Smithsonian Institution, 1990.

*Daniel Boxberger*

## Alaska

Alaska. Commission on Rural Governance and Empowerment. *Final Report to the Governor.* Anchorage, Alaska: 1999.

Anders, Gary. "The Role of Alaska Native Corporations in the Development of Alaska." *Development and Change* 14, no. 4 (1983): 555–75.

Arnold, Robert D. *Alaska Native Land Claims.* Anchorage, Alaska: Alaska Native Foundation, 1976.

Berger, Thomas, R. *Village Journey: The Report of the Alaska Native Review Commission.* New York: Hill and Wang, 1985.

Case, David. *Alaska Natives and American Laws.* Rev. ed. Fairbanks, Alaska: University of Alaska Press, 1984.

Cornell, Stephen, Jonathan Taylor, Kenneth Grant, The Economics Resource Group, Inc., Victor Fischer, Thomas Morehouse, and The Institute of Social and Economic Research, University of Alaska, Anchorage. *Achieving Native Self-Governance.* Cambridge, Mass.: The Economics Resource Group, 1999.

Gallagher, Hugh Gregory. *Etok: A Study in Eskimo Power.* New York: Putman, 1974.

Huskey, Lee. *The Economy of Village Alaska.* Anchorage, Alaska: Institute of Social and Economic Research, University of Alaska, Anchorage, 1992.

Jorgenson, Joseph G. *Oil Age Eskimos.* Berkeley and Los Angeles: University of California Press, 1990.

Langdon, Steve J., ed. *Contemporary Alaskan Native Economies.* Lanham, Md.: University Press of America, 1986.

Mason, W. Dale. "Tribes and States: A New Era in Intergovernmental Affairs." *Publius: The Journal of Federalism.* 28, no. 1 (1998): 111–130.

Mitchell, Donald, C. *Sold American: The Story of Alaska Natives and Their Land, 1867–1959.* Hanover, N.H.: University Press of New England, 1997.

Price, Robert E. *The Great Father in Alaska: The Case of the Tlingit and Haida Salmon Fishery.* Douglas, Alaska: First Street Press, 1990.

United States. Joint Federal-State Commission on Policies and Program Affecting Alaska Natives. *Alaska Natives Commission Final Report.* 3 vols. Anchorage, Alaska: 1994.

Wilkins, David. *American Indian Sovereignty and the U.S. Supreme Court: The Masking of Justice.* Austin, Tex.: University of Texas Press, 1997.

*David Maas*

## Oklahoma

Bell, Robert E., ed. *Prehistory of Oklahoma.* New York: Academic Press, 1984.

Debo, Angie. *The Five Civilized Tribes of Oklahoma: Report on Social and Economic Conditions.* Philadelphia: Indian Rights Association, 1951.

———. *And Still the Waters Run: The Betrayal of the Five Civilized Tribes.* Princeton: Princeton University Press, 1940.

Foreman, Grant. *The Five Civilized Tribes.* Norman: University of Oklahoma Press, 1934.

———. *Indian Removal: The Emigration of the Five Civilized Tribes of Indians.* Norman: University of Oklahoma Press, 1932.

Green, Donald E., ed. *Rural Oklahoma.* Oklahoma City: Oklahoma Historical Society, 1977.

Howard, James H. and Willie Lena. *Oklahoma Seminoles: Medicines, Magic, and Religion.* Norman: University of Oklahoma Press, 1984.

Jordan, H. Glen and Thomas M. Holm, eds. *Indian Leaders: Oklahoma's First Statesmen.* Oklahoma City: Oklahoma Historical Society, 1979.

Lomawaima, K. Tsianina. *They Called It Prairie Light: The Story of Chilocco Indian School.* Lincoln: University of Nebraska Press, 1994.

McAuliffe, Dennis, Jr. *Bloodland: A Family Story of Oil, Greed and Murder on the Osage Reservation.* San Francisco: Council Oak Books, 1999.

McCoy, Ronald. *Kiowa Memories: Images from Indian Territory, 1880.* Santa Fe, NM: Morning Star Gallery, 1987.

Mankiller, Wilma, and Michael Wallis. *Mankiller: A Chief and Her People.* St. Martin's Griffin ed. New York: St. Martin's Griffin, 2000.

Morgan, Anne H. and Rennard Strickland, eds. *Oklahoma Memories.* Norman: University of Oklahoma Press, 1981.

Morris, John W., ed. *Boundaries of Oklahoma.* Oklahoma City: Oklahoma Historical Society, 1980.

Skolnick, Sharon, and Manny Skolnick. *Where Courage Is Like a Wild Horse: The World of an Indian Orphanage.* Lincoln: University of Nebraska Press, 1997.

Smith, Robert E., ed. *Oklahoma's Forgotten Indians.* Oklahoma City: Oklahoma Historical Society, 1981.

Strickland, Rennard. *The Indians in Oklahoma.* Norman: University of Oklahoma Press, 1980.

———. *Tonto's Revenge: Reflections on American Indian Culture and Policy.* Albuquerque: University of New Mexico Press, 1995.

Warde, Mary Jane. *George Washington Grayson and the Creek Nation, 1843–1920.* Norman: University of Oklahoma Press, 1999.

Wilson, Terry. *The Underground Reservation: Osage Oil.* Lincoln: University of Nebraska Press, 1985.

Wright, Muriel H. *A Guide to the Indian Tribes of Oklahoma.* Norman: University of Oklahoma Press, 1951.

*Rennard Strickland*

## Rocky Mountain

Aoki, Haruo and Deward E. Walker, Jr. *Nez Percé Oral Narrative.* Berkeley and Los Angeles: University of California Press, 1989.

D'Azevedo, Warren L. *Great Basin.* Vol. 11 of *Handbook of North American Indians*, edited by William C. Sturtevant. Washington, D.C.: Smithsonian Institution, 1986.

Fowler, Loretta. *Arapahoe Politics, 1851–1978: Symbols in Crisis of Authority.* Lincoln: University of Nebraska Press, 1982.

Haines, Francis. "The Nez Percé Tribe versus the United States." *Idaho Yesterdays* 8:1 (1964): 18–25.

———. *The Nez Percés: Tribesmen of the Columbia Plateau.* Norman: University of Oklahoma Press, 1955.

Hopkins, Sarah Winnemucca. *Life Among the Piutes: Their Wrongs and Claims.* 1883. Reprint. Reno: University of Nevada Press, 1994.

Josephy, Alvin M., Jr. *The Nez Percé Indians and the Opening of the Northwest.* New Haven: Yale University Press, 1965.

Madsen, Brigham D. *The Bannock of Idaho.* Caldwell, Idaho: Caxton Printers, 1958.

———. *The Northern Shoshoni.* Caldwell, Idaho: Caxton Printers, 1980.

Manring, Benjamin F. *The Conquest of the Coeur D'Alenes, Spokanes and Palouses: The Expeditions of Colonels E. J. Steptoe and George Wright Against the "Northern Indians" in 1858.* Spokane: Inland Print. Co., 1912.

Sapir, Edward. *Southern Paiute and Ute: Linguistics and Ethnography.* Berlin: Mouton de Gruyter, 1992.

Scordato, Ellen. *Sarah Winnemucca: Northern Paiute Writer and Diplomat.* New York: Chelsea House, 1992.

Smet, Pierre-Jean de. *Letters and Sketches: With a Narrative of a Year's Residence Among the Indian Tribes of the Rocky Mountains.* Philadelphia: M. Fithian, 1843.

Teit, James H. *The Salishan Tribes of the Western Plateaus*, edited by Franz Boas. Smithsonian Institution. Bureau of American Ethnology Annual Report v. 45, pt. 1. Washington, D.C.: GPO, 1930.

Trafzer, Clifford E. *Chief Joseph's Allies.* New Castle, Calif.: Sierra Oaks, 1992.

Vogel, Fred W. *The Shoshoni-Crow Sun Dance.* Norman: University of Oklahoma Press, 1984.

Walker, Deward E., Jr. *Conflict and Schism in Nez Percé Acculturation: A Study of Religion and Politics.* Pullman: Washington State University Press, 1968.

———. *Indians of Idaho.* Moscow, Idaho: University Press of Idaho, 1978.

———. *Myths of Idaho Indians.* Moscow, Idaho: University Press of Idaho, 1980.

———, ed. *Plateau.* Vol 12 of *Handbook of North American Indians*, edited by William C. Sturtevant, Washington, D.C.: Smithsonian Institution, 1998.

Weatherford, Mark V. *Bannock-Piute War: The Campaigns and Battles.* Corvalis, Or.: Lehnert Print. Co., 1957.

*Clifford E. Trafzer*

## California

Bean, Lowell John, and Sylvia B. Vane. *California Indians: Primary Resources: A Guide to Manuscripts, Artifacts, Documents, Serials, Music, and

*Illustrations*. Rev. ed. Menlo Park, Calif: Ballena Press, 1990.

Castillo, Edward D., ed. *Native American Perspectives on the Hispanic Colonization of Alta California.* New York: Garland, 1991.

Cook, Sherburne F. *The Conflict Between The California Indian and White Civilization.* Berkeley and Los Angeles: University of California Press, 1976.

Heizer, Robert F. and Albert B. Elsasser. *A Bibliography of California Indians: Archaeology, Ethnography, Indian History.* New York: Garland, 1977.

Heizer, Robert F., ed. *California.* Vol. 8 of *Handbook of North American Indians,* edited by William C. Sturtevant. Washington, D.C.: Smithsonian Institution, 1978.

Hurtado, Albert. *Indian Survival on the California Frontier.* New Haven: Yale University Press, 1988.

Jackson, Robert H., and Edward Castillo. *Indians, Franciscans, and Spanish Colonization: The Impact of the Mission System on California Indians.* Albuquerque: University of New Mexico Press, 1995.

Phillips, George H. *The Enduring Struggle: Indians in California History.* San Francisco: Boyd & Fraser, 1981.

———. *Indians and Indian Agents: The Origins of the Reservation System in California, 1849–1852.* Norman: University of Oklahoma Press, 1997.

———. *Indians and Intruders in Central California, 1769–1849.* Norman: University of Oklahoma Press, 1993.

*News from Native California.* Berkeley, Calif.: Heyday Books, 1987–present.

Trafzer, Clifford E. and and Joel R. Hyer, eds. *Exterminate Them: Written Accounts of the Murder, Rape, and Slavery of Native Americans During the California Gold Rush, 1848–1868.* East Lansing: Michigan State University Press, 1999.

*Edward D. Castillo*

## Canada

Adams, Howard. *Prison of Grass: Canada From a Native Point of View.* Rev. ed. Saskatoon, Sask.: Fifth House, 1989.

Alfred, Gerald R. *Heeding the Voices of Our Ancestors: Kahnawake Mohawk Politics and the Rise of Native Nationalism.* Toronto: Oxford University Press, 1995.

Alia, Valerie. *Un/covering the North: News, Media, and Aboriginal People.* Vancouver: UBC Press, 1999.

Armitage, Andrew. *Comparing the Policy of Aboriginal Assimilation: Australia, Canada, and New Zealand.* Vancouver: UBC Press, 1995.

Asch, Michael, ed. *Aboriginal and Treaty Rights in Canada: Essays on Law, Equity and Respect for Difference.* Vancouver: UBC Press, 1997.

Battiste, Marie and Jean Barman, eds. *First Nations Education in Canada: The Circle Unfolds.* Vancouver: UBC Press, 1995.

Berger, Thomas R. *Northern Frontier: Northern Homeland. The Report of the Mackenzie Valley Pipeline Inquiry.* Rev. ed. Vancouver: Douglas and McIntyre, 1988.

Boldt, Menno. *Surviving as Indians: The Challenge of Self-Government.* Toronto: University of Toronto Press, 1993.

Boldt, Menno, and J. Anthony Long, eds., in association with Leroy Little Bear. *The Quest for Justice: Aboriginal Peoples and Aboriginal Rights.* Toronto: University of Toronto Press, 1985.

Brody, Hugh. *Living Arctic: Hunters of the Canadian North.* Vancouver: Douglas & McIntyre; Seattle: University of Washington Press, 1987.

———. *Maps and Dreams: Indians and the British Columbia Frontier.* Vancouver: Douglas and McIntyre, 1981.

———. *The People's Land: Inuit, Whites and the Eastern Arctic.* Toronto: Douglas and McIntyre, 1991.

Brown, Jennifer S.H. *Strangers in Blood: Fur Trade Company Families in Indian Country.* Vancouver: University of British Columbia Press, 1980.

Cairns, Alan C. *Citizens Plus: Aboriginal Peoples and the Canadian State.* Vancouver: UBC Press, 2000.

Cameron, Kirk and Graham White. *Northern Governments in Transition: Political and Constitutional Development in the Yukon, Nunavut and the Western Northwest Territories.* Montreal: Institute for Research on Public Policy, 1995.

Canada. *Indian Treaties and Surrenders: From 1680 to 1902.* 3 vols. Saskatoon, Sask.: Fifth House Publishers, 1993.

Canada. Royal Commission on Aboriginal Peoples. *Bridging the Cultural Divide: A Report on Aboriginal People and Criminal Justice in Canada.* Ottawa, 1996.

Cardinal, Harold. *The Rebirth of Canada's Indians.* Edmonton, Alta.: Hurtig, 1977.

———. *The Unjust Society: The Tragedy of Canada's Indians.* Edmonton, Alta.: Hurtig, 1969.

Carter, Sarah. *Lost Harvests: Prairie Indian Reserve Farmers and Government Policy.* Montreal: McGill-Queen's University Press, 1990.

Cassidy, Frank, ed. *Aboriginal Title in British Columbia: Delgamuukw v. the Queen.* Lantzville, BC: Oolichan Books and Halifax: Institute for Research on Public Policy, 1992.

Castellano, Marlene Brant, Lynne Davis and Louise Lahache. *Aboriginal Education: Fulfilling the Promise.* Vancouver: UBC Press, 2000.

Chiste, Katherine Beaty, ed. *Aboriginal Small Business and Entrepreneurship in Canada.* North York: Ont.: Captus Press, 1996.

Clark, Bruce A. *Native Liberty, Crown Sovereignty: The Existing Aboriginal Right of Self-Government in Canada.* Montreal: McGill-Queen's University Press, 1990.

Comeau, Pauline and Aldo Santin. *The First Canadians: A Profile of Canada's Native People Today.* Toronto: J. Lorimer, 1990.

*Consolidated Native Law Statutes, Regulations and Treaties 1996.* Scarborough, Ont.: Carswell, 1995.

Dacks, Gurston. *Devolution and Constitutional Development in the Canadian North.* Ottawa: Carleton University Press, 1990.

Daniels, Harry W. *We Are the New Nation: The Métis and National Native Policy.* Ottawa: Native Council of Canada, 1979.

Daugherty, Wayne, and Dennis Madill. *Indian Government Under Indian Act Legislation: 1868–1951.* Ottawa: Department of Indian Affairs and Northern Development, 1980.

Dempsey, Hugh A. *Crowfoot: Chief of the Blackfeet.* Norman: University of Oklahoma Press, 1972.

———. *The Gentle Persuader: A Biography of James Gladstone, Indian Senator.* Saskatoon: Western Producer Prairie Books, 1986.

———. *Indian Tribes of Alberta.* Calgary, Alta.: Glenbow-Alberta Institute, 1978.

———. *Red Crow, Warrior Chief.* Lincoln: University of Nebraska Press, 1980.

Dickerson, Mark. *Whose North?: Political Change, Political Development and Self-Government in the Northwest Territories.* Vancouver: UBC Press, 1992.

Drost, Helmar, Brian Lee Crowley and Richard Schwindt. *Market Solutions for Native Poverty: Social Policy for the Third Solitude.* Toronto: C.D. Howe Institute, 1995.

Duff, Wilson. *The Indian History of British Columbia.* Vol. 1. *The Impact of the White Man.* 2d ed. Victoria, B.C.: Royal British Columbia Museum, 1992.

Dyck, Noel. *What is the Indian "Problem": Tutelage and Resistance in Canadian Indian Administration.* St. John's, Nfld.: Institute of Social and Economic Research, Memorial University of Newfoundland, 1991.

Elias, Peter Douglas. *Development of Aboriginal Peoples' Communities.* North York, Ont.: Captus Press, 1991.

———., ed. *Northern Aboriginal Communities: Economies and Development.* North York, Ont.: Captus University Publications, 1995.

Fisher, Robin. *Contact and Conflict: Indian-European Relations in British Columbia, 1774–1890.* 2d ed. Vancouver: UBC Press, 1993.

Fisher, Robin and Kenneth Coates, eds. *Out of the Background: Readings on Canadian Native History.* Toronto: Copp Clark Pittman, 1988.

Flanagan, Thomas. *First Nations? Second Thoughts.* Montreal: McGill-Queen's University Press, 2000.

———. *Louis 'David' Riel: Prophet of the New World.* Rev. ed. Toronto: University of Toronto Press, 1996.

———. *Métis Lands in Manitoba.* Calgary: University of Calgary Press, 1991.

———. *Riel and the Rebellion: 1885 Reconsidered.* Saskatoon, Sask.: Western Producer Prairie Books, 1983.

Frideres, James S. *Native Peoples in Canada: Contemporary Conflicts.* 3d ed. Scarborough, Ont.: Prentice-Hall Canada, 1988.

Getty, Ian A. L., and Antoine S. Lussier, eds. *As Long as the Sun Shines and Water Flows: A Reader in Canadian Native Studies.* Vancouver: University of British Columbia Press, 1983.

Giraud, Marcel. *The Métis in the Canadian West.* 2 vols. Edmonton, Alta.: University of Alberta Press; Lincoln: University of Nebraska Press, 1986.

Goddard, John. *The Last Stand of the Lubicon Cree.* Vancouver: Douglas and McIntyre, 1991.

Gosse, Richard, James Youngblood Henderson and Roger Carter, comps. *Continuing Poundmaker and Riel's Quest: Presentations Made at a Conference on Aboriginal Peoples and Justice.* Saskatoon, Sask.: Purich Pub. and University of Saskatoon, College of Law, 1994.

Grant, John W. *Moon of Wintertime: Missionaries and the Indians of Canada in Encounter Since 1534.* Toronto: University of Toronto Press, 1984.

Green, Ross Gordon. *Justice in Aboriginal Communities: Sentencing Alternatives.* Saskatoon, Sask.: Purich Pub., 1998.

Haig-Brown, Celia. *Resistance and Renewal: Surviving the Indian Residential School.* Vancouver, B.C.: Tillacum Library, 1991.

Harrison, Julia D. *Métis: People Between Two Worlds.* Vancouver: Glenbow-Alberta Institute in association with Douglas and McIntyre, 1985.

Hawkes, David C., ed. *Aboriginal Peoples and Government Responsibility: Exploring Federal and Provincial Roles.* Ottawa: Carleton University Press, 1989.

Hornung, Rick. *One Nation Under the Gun.* Toronto: Stoddart; New York: Pantheon, 1991.

Humber, Charles J., ed. *Canada's Native Peoples.* Mississauga, Ont.: Heirloom Publishing, 1988.

Hylton, John H., ed. *Aboriginal Self-Government in Canada: Current Trends and Issues.* Saskatoon, Sask.: Purich Pub., 1994.

Imai, Shin, Katherine Logan and Gary Stein. *Aboriginal Law Handbook*. Scarborough, Ont.: Carswell, 1993.

Innis, Harold A. *The Fur Trade in Canada: An Introduction to Canadian Economic History*. Rev. ed. Toronto: University of Toronto Press, 1956.

Isaac, Thomas. *Aboriginal Law: Cases, Materials and Commentary*. Saskatoon, Sask.: Purich Pub., 1999.

Jaenen, Cornelius J. *Friend and Foe: Aspects of French-Amerindian Culture and Contact in the Sixteenth and Seventeenth Centuries*. Toronto: McClelland and Stewart; New York: Columbia University Press, 1976.

Jenness, Diamond. *Indians of Canada*. 7th ed. Toronto: University of Toronto Press, 1977.

Krotz, Larry. *Indian Country: Inside Another Canada*. Toronto: McClelland and Stewart, 1990.

Little Bear, Leroy, Menno Boldt and J. Anthony Long, eds. *Pathways to Self-Determination: Canadian Indians and the Canadian State*. Toronto: University of Toronto Press, 1984.

Long, J. Anthony, Menno Boldt, eds., in association with Leroy Little Bear. *Governments in Conflict? Provinces and Indian Nations in Canada*. Toronto: University of Toronto Press, 1988.

MacEwan, John W.G. *Between the Red and the Rockies*. Toronto: University of Toronto Press, 1952.

MacGregor, Roy. *Chief: The Fearless Vision of Billy Diamond*. Toronto: Penguin Books Canada, 1991.

McMahon, Kevin. *Arctic Twilight*. Toronto: J. Lorimer, 1988.

Manuel, George and Michael Posluns. *The Fourth World: An Indian Reality*. Don Mills, Ont.: Collier-Macmillan Canada; New York: Free Press, 1974.

Miller, Christine and Patricia Chuckryk, eds. *Women of the First Nations: Power, Wisdom, and Strength*. Winnipeg, Man.: University of Manitoba Press, 1996.

Miller, James Rodger. *Shingwauk's Vision: A History of Native Residential Schools*. Toronto: University of Toronto Press, 1996.

———. *Skyscrapers Hide the Heavens: A History of Indian-White Relations in Canada*. Toronto: University of Toronto Press, 1989.

———, ed. *Sweet Promises: A Reader on Indian-White Relations in Canada*. Toronto: University of Toronto Press, 1991.

Milloy, John Sheridan. *A National Crime: The Canadian Government and the Residential School System, 1879 to 1986*. Winnipeg: University of Manitoba Press, 1999.

Morris, Alexander. *The Treaties of Canada with the Indians of Manitoba and the North-West Territories*. Toronto: Belfords, Clarke and Co., 1880; Coles, 1971; Saskatoon, Sask.: Fifth House, 1991.

Morrison, R. Bruce and C. Roderick Wilson, eds. *Native Peoples: The Canadian Experience*. 2d ed. Toronto: McClelland and Stewart, 1995.

Morrow, William G. *Northern Justice: The Memoirs of Justice William G. Morrow*. Toronto: Joint publication of the Osgoode Society for Canadian Legal History and the Legal Archives Society of Alberta; Toronto: University of Toronto Press, 1995.

Newell, Dianne. *Tangled Webs of History: Indians and the Law in Canada's Pacific Coast Fisheries*. Toronto: University of Toronto Press, 1993.

Notzke, Claudia. *Aboriginal Peoples and Natural Resources in Canada*. North York, Ont.: Captus University Publications, 1994.

Peters, Evelyn J. *Aboriginal Self-Government in Urban Areas*. Kingston, Ont.: Institute of Intergovernmental Relations, Queen's University, 1995.

Petrone, Penny, ed. *First People, First Voices*. Toronto: University of Toronto Press, 1983.

———. *Northern Voices: Inuit Writing in English*. Toronto: University of Toronto Press, 1988.

Pocklington, Thomas C. *The Government and Politics of the Alberta Métis Settlements*. Regina: Canadian Plains Research Center, University of Regina, 1991.

Ponting, J. Rick, ed. *Arduous Journey: Canadian Indians and Decolonization*. Toronto: McClelland and Stewart, 1986.

Price, Richard T. *Legacy: Indian Treaty Relationships*. Edmonton: Plains Publishing, 1991.

———, ed. *The Spirit of the Alberta Indian Treaties*. 3d ed. Edmonton, Alta.: University of Alberta Press, 1999.

Raunet, Daniel. *Without Surrender, Without Consent: A History of the Nishga Land Claims*. Vancouver: Douglas and McIntyre, 1984.

Ray, Arthur J. *I Have Lived Here Since The World Began: An Illustrated History of Canada's Native People*. Toronto: Lester Publishing and Key Porter Books, 1996.

Ray, Arthur J. *Indians in the Fur Trade: Their Role as Hunters, Trappers and Middlemen of the Lands Southwest of Hudson Bay, 1660–1870*. Toronto: University of Toronto Press, 1974.

Redbird, Duke. *We Are Métis: A Métis View of the Development of a Native Canadian People*. Willowdale, Ont.: Ontario Métis and Non-Status Indian Association, 1980.

Richardson, Boyce, ed. *Drumbeat: Anger and Renewal in Indian Country*. Toronto: Summerhill Press, 1989.

Ross, Alexander. *The Red River Settlement: Its Rise and Progress, and Present State*. Rutland, Vt.: C.E. Tuttle Co., 1972.

Ross, Rupert. *Dancing With A Ghost: Exploring Indian Reality*. Markham, Ont.: Octopus Books, 1992.

Ross, Rupert. *Returning to the Teachings: Exploring Aboriginal Justice*. Toronto: Penguin Books, 1996.

Rotman, Leonard Ian. *Parallel Paths: Fiduciary Doctrine and the Crown-Native Relationship in Canada*. Toronto: University of Toronto Press, 1996.

Ryan, Joan. *Doing Things the Right Way: Dene Traditional Justice in Lac La Martre, NWT*. Calgary: University of Calgary Press, 1995.

Salisbury, Richard F. *A Homeland for the Cree: Regional Development in James Bay, 1971–1981*. Kingston: McGill-Queen's University Press, 1986.

Sawchuk, Joe. *The Dynamics of Native Politics: The Alberta Métis Experience*. Saskatoon: Purich Pub., 1998.

Schmalz, Peter S. *The Ojibwa of Southern Ontario*. Toronto: University of Toronto Press, 1991.

Smith, Donald B. *Le Sauvage: The Native People in Quebec, Historical Writing on the Heroic Period (1534–1663) of New France*. Ottawa: National Museum of Canada, 1974.

——. *Long Lance: The True Story of an Imposter*. Toronto: Macmillan of Canada; Lincoln: University of Nebraska Press, 1982.

——. *Sacred Feathers: The Reverend Peter Jones and the Mississauga Indians*. Lincoln: University of Nebraska Press, 1987.

Snow, John. *These Mountains Are Our Sacred Places: The Story of the Stoney Indians*. Toronto: Samuel Stevens, 1977.

Tester, Frank James. *Tammarniit (Mistakes): Inuit Relocation in the Eastern Arctic 1939–63*. Vancouver: UBC Press, 1994.

Tennant, Paul. *Aboriginal Peoples and Politics: The Indian Land Question in British Columbia, 1849–1989*. Vancouver: University of British Columbia Press, 1990.

Titley, E. Brian. *A Narrow Vision: Duncan Campbell Scott and the Administration of Indian Affairs in Canada*. Vancouver: University of British Columbia Press, 1986.

Tough, Frank. '*As Their Natural Resources Fail': Native People and the Economic History of Northern Manitoba, 1870–1930*. Vancouver: University of British Columbia Press, 1996.

Trigger, Bruce G. *Natives and Newcomers: Canada's "Heroic Age" Reconsidered*. Kingston: McGill-Queen's University Press, 1985.

Waldram, James B. *As Long as the Rivers Run: Hydroelectric Development and Native Communities in Western Canada*. Winnipeg: University of Manitoba Press, 1993.

*Kate Chiste*

# 4

# *Native North American Languages*

♦ Classification ♦ Phyla and Families ♦ Language Contact
♦ Types of Language Structure ♦ Geographical Areas and Language Areas
♦ Language and Culture ♦ Traditional Literature ♦ Writing Systems
♦ Language Restoration

The term *North American Indian languages* is used here to refer to the Native North American languages of the continental United States and Canada, including Aleut and Eskimo. However, the Inuit (eastern) branch of Eskimo is also the principal language of Greenland (under Danish administration), and several languages of the southwestern United States, such as Pima-Papago (O'odham), are also spoken in northern Mexico. In addition, certain important language groups of the United States, such as the Uto-Aztecan family (to which O'odham belongs) are also represented in Mexico, and southward into Central America as far as El Salvador (for further general information, see Mithun, 1999).

The Native North American languages may have originally numbered as many as 300. However, many have become extinct as a result of contact with European societies and have been replaced by English, French, or Spanish. The study of such languages depends on materials written by missionaries, travelers, educators, anthropologists, and linguists (see Goddard, 1996). Nevertheless, over 100 languages may still be spoken, though some of these may survive mainly in the memories of a few elderly speakers. Still others are spoken by thousands of people and are still learned by children as their first language. Navajo, with around 100,000 speakers, probably leads the list.

Nevertheless, because of the trend toward extinction among American Indian languages, their study is increasingly aimed at three goals: (1) interpreting written data on extinct languages; (2) obtaining data from the last speakers of obsolescent languages; and (3) encouraging the maintenance of languages still spoken by substantial communities. In the history of North American linguistics, the study of Native American languages has played a vital role (see Hymes, 1976b). Indeed, these languages have provided a living laboratory for studying a great variety of linguistic questions. In the following discussion, the present tense refers to extinct and obsolescent languages as well as those which are still viable.

North American Indian languages are as diverse as they are numerous; no single set of characteristics is shared by all of them. They can be grouped into some fifty-seven families, comparable to language families in Europe such as Romance (Italian, Spanish, French) and Germanic (German, Dutch, English). This diversity tends to be concentrated in the western part of the continent: thirty-seven families lie west of the Rockies, with twenty in California alone, so that California shows more linguistic variety than all of Europe. This linguistic diversity of Native North America suggests that the area may well have been populated by several waves of migration from Asia, across the Bering Straits, by peoples of distinct linguistic stocks, many of which may have no modern survivors in Asia.

## ♦ CLASSIFICATION

When a group of languages shows similar vocabulary items, with regular correspondences of sounds, the group is said to have a genetic relationship; that is, the languages are "sister" languages, descended historically from a single origin. Examples in the Romance languages are sets of words like Italian *vacca*, Spanish *vaca*, and French *vache*, or cow, and Italian *bocca*,

Students at the Arapaho Language Immersion Preschool in Ethete, Wyoming, 1997. On the wall behind the students is an Arapaho language sign. (Photo by Sara Wiles)

Spanish *boca*, and French *bouche*, or mouth. These distinguish the Romance family from the Germanic family, which has contrasting sets of words: German *Kuh*, Dutch *koe*, and English *cow*, and German *Mund*, Dutch *mond*, and English *mouth*. Such sets of words also occur among American Indian languages, as with Fox *okimaawa*, Cree *okimaaw*, Menominee *okeemaaw*, and Ojibway *okimaa*, or chief. Such similarities help identify the Algonkian family and assist in reconstructing a proto-language, or prehistoric parent, under such a name as Proto-Algonkian.

Beyond this level of relationship, however, some families show more distant degrees of similarity, indicating shared history at a more remote chronological period. For instance, European language families like Romance and Germanic can be grouped together into Indo-European, which also includes families like Slavic and Indic. In North America, similarities between the Siouan family and the Iroquoian family suggest such a

higher-order grouping, which can be called Macro-Siouan. This type of grouping is often called a *phylum* (plural phyla), referring to a family at a high level of classification. Within a phylum, however, it may also be necessary to recognize some languages that have no close relatives and do not fall into families; these are termed *language isolates* (or simply isolates). Thus the Yuchi language in the southeastern United States may be such an isolate within Macro-Siouan. The classification of languages in these terms helps correlate the history of languages with what archaeology and Native traditions reveal about the history of cultures (see Language and Culture section below). Taken together, these types of evidence aid in the reconstruction of prehistoric homelands, migrations, and culture contacts.

Some other language families, and even language isolates, are not generally recognized as falling into any of the familiar phyla. Such "unclassified" units are the Salishan and Wakashan families of the Pacific Northwest and the Kutenai language isolate of northern Idaho. The possibility remains, of course, that further research will uncover historical links for these languages.

However, at the more remote historical levels, it is not always clear how languages evolve from common origins. An alternative explanation is that prehistoric contact among languages may have resulted in the borrowing of vocabulary, sounds, and grammatical features (see Callaghan and Gamble, 1996). Such phenomena of language contact are discussed in the Language Contact section below.

At present, the classification of Native American language families in terms of phyla is a matter of intense controversy. The only agreement is that the organization into fifty-seven families, as presented by J. W. Powell (1891), is correct. One of the most influential scholars of American Indian linguistics, Edward Sapir (1929), published a classification of these languages into six phyla, and at one time this was widely accepted. In more recent years, however, re-evaluation of Sapir's work has suggested the revised scheme of C. F. Voegelin and F. R. Voegelin (1977), which recognizes six phyla—not identical to Sapir's—as well as several unclassified families and language isolates. Still more recently, opinions have become increasingly divided. Scholars known as "splitters," such as Campbell (1997), have cast doubt on all phylum groupings. By contrast, a "lumper" such as J. H. Greenberg (1987) has proposed that all linguistic families of both North and South America—except for Na-Dené and Eskimo-Aleut in the far north—can be assigned to a single macrophylum that he calls Amerindian.

Various proposals have been made to relate North American Indian languages to language families of

Asia. None of these theories have gained wide acceptance, except for a possible connection between Eskimo-Aleut and some languages of adjacent Siberia. To be sure, Greenberg has suggested connections of his Amerindian to several major language families in Eurasia; however, he has provided little evidence to date.

## ◆ PHYLA AND FAMILIES

The following list of phyla, families, and languages follows the "middle-of-the-road" system of Voegelin and Voegelin (1977), which provides a useful point of reference in terms of its familiarity and use in many reference works.

In some cases, either a phylum or a family must be divided into two or more branches. Sometimes it is not clear whether local speech variants should be called languages of a single family, or dialects of a single language; in such cases, the neutral term "varieties" is used. Where languages have changed location in historic times, both older and newer locations are listed. The names of languages believed to be extinct are followed by an asterisk (*). Some extinct languages on which virtually no information is available are omitted.

Phylum: Eskimo-Aleut
  Family: Aleut, a single language (Aleutian and Pribilof Islands, in Alaska; and Komandorsky Islands, in Siberia)
  Family: Eskimo
    Branch: Yupik, with the following languages:
      Central Siberian Yupik (Chukotski Peninsula; St. Lawrence Island, Alaska)
      Central Alaskan Yupik (southwest Alaska)
      Alutiiq (southwest Alaska)
    Branch: Inuit, a language with many local varieties, including Inupiaq (Alaska), Inuktitut, (eastern Canada), and Kalaallisut (Greenland)

Notes: It has been suggested that Eskimo-Aleut is related to certain native languages of the Chukotski area in Siberia, across the Bering Straits from Alaska. In Canada the label Eskimo is disfavored; the term Inuit is generally used to refer to the people, and Inuktitut to their language. In Greenland, Kalaallisut is an official language along with Danish.

Phylum: Na-Dené
  Family: Tlingit, an isolate (southeast Alaska)
  Family: Haida, an isolate (northwest British Columbia)
  Family: Athabaskan
    Branch: Eyak,* an isolate (southeast Alaska)
    Branch: Northern Athabaskan, including the following languages (grouped geographically):
      Interior Alaska: Tanana, Koyukon, Han, Tutchone, Tanaina, Ingalik, Nabesna, Ahtena
      Alaska and Yukon: Kutchin

Northwest Territories: Dogrib, Bear Lake, Hare, Chipewyan, Slave, Yellowknife, Tahltan, Kaska
Alberta: Beaver, Sarsi
British Columbia: Sekani, Carrier, Chilcotin
    Branch: Pacific Coast Athabaskan, including the following languages (grouped geographically):
      Southwest Oregon: Chasta Costa,* Galice,* Tututni*
      Northwest California: Tolowa, Hupa, Kato,* Wailaki,* Mattole*
    Branch: Southwestern Athabaskan or Apachean (Arizona, New Mexico), including the following varieties:
      Navajo, Western Apache, Chiricahua, Mescalero, Jicarilla, Lipan, Kiowa-Apache

Note: Athabaskan peoples carried out migrations from the sub-Arctic in two southward directions.

Phylum: Macro-Algonkian
  Branch: Algic, with three families:
    Yurok, an isolate (northwest California)
    Wiyot, an isolate (northwest California)
    Algonkian or Algonquian (grouped geographically):
      Central and eastern Canada: Cree, Naskapi, Montagnais
      Northern Great Lakes region: Ojibway (Chippewa), Ottawa, Algonkin, Saulteaux
      Maritime Provinces and New England: Micmac, Malecite, Abnaki, Penobscot, Passamaquoddy (and several extinct languages, such as Massachusett*)
      Central Atlantic coast: Delaware (later moved to Oklahoma and elsewhere)
      Southern Great Lakes region: Menominee, Fox, Sauk, Kickapoo, Potawatomi (partially moved to Oklahoma)
      South Central United States: Shawnee
      Western Great Plains: Blackfoot, Cheyenne, Arapaho, Atsina
  Branch: Gulf, including the following families (all isolates):
    Natchez* (Louisiana)
    Atakapa* (Louisiana, Texas)
    Chitimacha* (Louisiana)
    Tunica* (Louisiana)
    Tonkawa* (east Texas)
    Muskogean, including the following languages:
      Choctaw (Mississippi, Oklahoma)
      Chickasaw (Oklahoma)
      Alabama (Alabama, Texas)
      Koasati (Alabama, Texas)
      Mikasuki (Florida)
      Hitchiti (Florida)

Muskogee or Creek (Georgia, Oklahoma)
Seminole (Georgia, Florida, Oklahoma)

Phylum: Macro-Siouan

Family: Siouan, including the following languages (grouped geographically):

Northern Plains: Crow, Hidatsa, Dakota (Sioux)

Central Plains: Omaha, Osage, Ponca, Kansa, Quapaw

Wisconsin: Winnebago

Ohio Valley: Tutelo,* Ofo,* Biloxi*

Southeastern United States: Catawba*

Family: Iroquoian, including the following languages (grouped geographically):

Northeastern: Seneca, Cayuga, Onondaga, Mohawk, Oneida, Wyandot or Huron (in New York State and adjacent Canada)

Southeastern: Tuscarora (North Carolina, later New York), Cherokee (southern Appalachians, later also Oklahoma)

Family: Caddoan, including the following languages: Caddo, Wichita, Pawnee, Arikara (central Plains)

Family: Yuchi, an isolate (southern Appalachians)

Phylum: Hokan or Hokan-Coahuiltecan, including the following families:

Karuk, an isolate (northwest California)

Chimariko,* an isolate (northwest California)

Shastan, a family with two branches:

Shasta* (north-central California)

Palaihnihan, including Achomawi and Atsugewi (northeastern California)

Yanan, a family including North Yana,* Central Yana,* Southern Yana,* and Yahi* (all in north-central California)

Washo, an isolate (Nevada and east-central California)

Pomoan, a family including Northeast Pomo,* Northern Pomo, Central Pomo, Southwest Pomo or Kashaya, Southeast Pomo, and Southern Pomo (all in north-central California)

Esselen,* an isolate (central California coast)

Salinan, including Miguele-o* and Antoniano* (central California coast)

Chumashan, a family including Obispe-o,* Yneze-o,* Barbare-o,* Venture-o,* and Island Chumash* (all on the southern California coast)

Yuman, a family (languages grouped geographically):

Northwest Arizona: Walapai, Havasupai, Yavapai

Lower Colorado River: Mojave, Yuma, Cocopa

Southern California: Diegue-o

Baja California: Paipai, Kiliwa*

Seri, an isolate (northwestern Sonora, Mexico)

Comecrudan, an extinct family (southern Texas, northwestern Mexico)

Coahuiltecan, an extinct family (southern Texas, northwestern Mexico)

Note: Also hypothesized as belonging to the above phylum are Tequistlatecan, in southern Mexico, and Jicaque, in Honduras.

Phylum: Penutian, including the following families:

Yokutsan, a group of dialects including Chuckchansi, Wikchamni, Yawdanchi, Yawelmani, and Tachi (south-central California)

Miwokan, a family including Sierra Miwok, Plains Miwok, Lake Miwok,* and Coast Miwok* (central California)

Costanoan, a family including Mutsun,* Rumsen,* and Ohlone* (central California coast)

Maiduan, a family including Northeast Maidu, Concow, and Nisenan (north-central California)

Wintun, a family including Wintu, Nomlaki, and Patwin (north-central California)

Klamath-Modoc, an isolate (south-central Oregon)

Takelma,* an isolate (southwest Oregon)

Coos,* an isolate (southwest Oregon)

Yakonan, a family including Alsea,* Siuslaw,* and Lower Umpqua* (west central Oregon)

Kalapuyan,* an extinct family (west-central Oregon)

Molale,* an isolate (north-central Oregon)

Cayuse,* an isolate (northeast Oregon)

Sahaptian, a family including Sahaptin (north-central Oregon) and Nez Percé (west-central Idaho)

Chinookan, a family including several varieties, such as Lower Chinook,* Wishram, and Wasco (northern Oregon, southern Washington)

Tsimshian, an isolate (west-central British Columbia)

Zuni, an isolate (west-central New Mexico)

Phylum: Aztec-Tanoan

Family: Kiowa-Tanoan, including two branches:

Kiowa (Oklahoma)

Tanoan, including three languages: Tiwa, Tewa, Towa (pueblos of New Mexico and Arizona)

Family: Uto-Aztecan, including the following branches:

Numic branch, including the following languages:

Mono (east-central California)

Northern Paiute (northeast Great Basin)

Panamint (east-central California)

Shoshoni (central Great Basin)

Comanche (southern Plains)

Kawaiisu (southeast California)

Ute, including Southern Paiute and Chemehuevi (southern and eastern Great Basin)

Tubatulabal, an isolate (south-central California)

Takic, including the following languages: Serrano, Kitanemuk,* Gabrielino,* Cupe-o, Cahuilla, and Luiseño (all in southern California)

Hopi, an isolate (Arizona)

Sonoran, located in Arizona and northwestern Mexico, including O'odham or Pima-Papago,

Yaqui, and several other languages of northern Mexico, such as Tarahumara

Note: The Uto-Aztecan family includes the Huichol and Cora languages of western Mexico, and the Nahuatl (Aztec) language, spoken not only in central Mexico, but also as far south as El Salvador.

Unclassified family: Salishan or Salish (languages are grouped geographically):
Interior British Columbia: Lillooet, Shuswap, Thompson, Okanagon
Eastern Washington and northern Idaho: Middle Columbia, Wenatchee, Coeur d'Alene, Flathead
Coastal British Columbia: Bella Coola, Comox, Sishistl, Squamish, Halkomelem, Straits Salish
Western Washington: Twana,* Chehalis, Cowlitz, Quinault, Puget Sound Salish
Western Oregon: Tillamook*

Unclassified family: Wakashan (languages are grouped geographically):
West Central British Columbia: Kwakiutl, Bella Bella, Heiltsuk, Kitamat, Haisla
Vancouver Island: Nootka, Nitinat
Northwestern Washington: Makah

Unclassified family: Chemakuan, including two languages:
Chimakum* (northwestern Washington)
Quileute (northwestern Washington)

Unclassified family: Yukian, including two languages:
Yuki* (north-central California)
Wappo* (north-central California)

Unclassified language isolates:
Beothuk* (Newfoundland)
Kutenai (northern Idaho)
Keresan (pueblos of New Mexico)
Karankawa* (southeast Texas)
Timucua* (Florida)

## ◆ LANGUAGE CONTACT

Like all languages of the world, North American Indian languages have always existed in contact with each other, with many degrees of bilingualism or multilingualism determined by socio-cultural factors. The effects of this are shown in various amounts of borrowing between languages, involving not only loan words, but also features of pronunciation, grammar, and semantic organization. Such long-term borrowing can result in a language area—a geographical region in which families of different families or phyla have come to share numerous features on all levels of language

structure. The importance of such areas will be discussed further in the Geographical Areas and Language Areas section below.

In some areas, tribes that lacked a common language but needed to communicate with each other (e.g., for purposes of trade) developed a type of mixed language called a *lingua franca* or *trade language* (see Taylor, 1980). When Europeans arrived on the scene, they often learned to use such trade languages and contributed new vocabulary from European sources. The best known such language is Chinook Jargon, used in the Pacific Northwest. Its bases were in the Chinook language and other native languages such as Nootka and Chehalis, but it acquired many loan words from French and English before its eventual obsolescence. Some examples of French loan words in Chinook Jargon are *kosho*, or pig, from French *cochon* & *lapush*, or mouth, from *la bouche* and *siwash*, or Indian, from *sauvage*. (For typographical reasons, Indian language examples are given here in a practical spelling—e.g., using *sh* as in English *ship*— rather than in the technical phonetic alphabet.) Another such trade language is Mobilian Jargon, used in the southeastern United States and based primarily on Muskogean sources.

A special kind of lingua franca is the Plains Sign Language, a language of gestures used among tribes of the Great Plains, and later by many whites as well (see Mallery, 1881). The tribes of this area spoke many unrelated languages, such as Dakota, a Siouan language, and Cheyenne, of the Algonkian family. But their highly mobile lifestyle made it difficult to cultivate extensive bilingualism in any single spoken language; the need for communication was therefore met by an organized system of gestures.

An unusual result of language contact has occurred in a few areas where an intimate mixture of vocabulary and grammar has given rise to a new language spoken natively by a local community but not clearly classifiable as belonging to the family of either of its parents. The best-known example is Michif, currently spoken by Indians in Canada and North Dakota (see Bakker, 1997). In this language, noun forms are predominantly French, but verb forms are predominantly Algonkian. A sample sentence is *Keeouyashkinastow li feezee avik lee kartoush*, or "He loaded the rifle with cartridges," which begins with an Algonkian verb form, but continues with French *le fusil*, "the rifle," *avec les cartouches*, "with the cartridges."

Another unusual example comes from a mixture of Aleut and Russian, which was formerly spoken on Medny Island in the Komandorsky Islands off the coast of Siberia. In this dialect, Aleut verb stems were combined with Russian endings, as shown in the comparisons given below. (Capital *X* is a 'back velar' fricative; see Sounds in Types of Language Structure below.)

| | Unmixed Aleut | Medny Aleut | Russian |
|---|---|---|---|
| I sit | unguchi-ku-q | unguchi-ju | ja sizh-u |
| you sit | unguchi-ku-Xt | unguchi-ish | ty sid-ish |
| he sits | unguchi-ku-X | unguchi-iton | sid-it |

In addition to the European words that have entered trade languages such as Chinook Jargon, words from English, French, Spanish, and (in Alaska) Russian have frequently been borrowed into native languages. Among the Native peoples, the type and degree of such linguistic borrowing has varied greatly, depending on sociocultural factors. For example, in the southwest, after several centuries of contact with Spanish, Navajo has borrowed almost no Spanish loan words, but the Pueblo languages have borrowed a few more, and O'odham (Pima-Papago) has borrowed a very large number. Sample loan words from Spanish in O'odham are *káwal*, or sheep (from Spanish *cabra*, or goat), *lúulsi*, or candy (from *dulce* ), and *wákial*, or cowboy (from *vaquero* ).

Among the Karuk of northwestern California, a tribe that suffered very harsh treatment at the hands of Anglo-Americans, there are only a few loanwords from English; for example, *ápus*, or apple(s), and a few adaptations based on English; thus pears are called *vírusur*, the native word for bear, because English *pear* and *bear* become merged in Karuk pronunciation. In such languages, which disfavor borrowing, new vocabulary items are frequently formed by new combinations of native materials; thus the Karuk word for hotel is *am-naam*, literally "eating-place."

One other result of language contact, of course, has been word-borrowing in the opposite direction—from Native American languages into European languages (Cutler, 1994). The oldest known loan into English from a North American Indian language is *raccoon*, borrowed from an Algonkian language; the word occurs in a letter written by Captain John Smith from Virginia in 1608. This was quickly followed by many other borrowings from Algonkian, as Europeans made contact with tribes along the Atlantic seacoast. The following examples indicate the major semantic categories of such borrowings, and their earliest dates from which they are known:

Animal names:
 Caribou, 1610
 Opossum, 1610
 Moose, 1613
 Skunk, 1634
 Terrapin, 1672
 Menhaden (fish), 1643
 Woodchuck, 1674
 Muskellunge (fish), 1794
 Quahog (clam), 1799
 Chipmunk, 1841

Plant names:
 Persimmon, 1612
 Hickory, 1629
 Squash, 1643
 Chinquapin (nut), 1676
 Pecan, 1778
 Tamarack, 1805
 Scuppernong (grape), 1825

Prepared foods:
 (Corn)pone, 1612
 Hominy, 1629
 Succotash, 1751
 Pemmican, 1804

Cultural features:
 Totem, 1609
 Moccasin, 1612
 Tomahawk, 1612
 Powwow, 1624
 Wigwam, 1628
 Manitou (a deity), 1671
 Toboggan, 1829

As Europeans moved west across the continent, words were added from other language families, such as *teepee* from Siouan. In a more recent period, words such as the following have been borrowed from Native languages of the far west:

Potlatch (a type of native celebration), from Chinook Jargon

Hooch (illegal liquor), from a Tlingit place name in Alaska

Abalone (a shellfish), from Costanoan of central California

Chuckwalla (a kind of lizard), from Cahuilla of southern California

Hogan (a Native house), from Navajo

Kiva (a Pueblo ceremonial chamber), from Hopi

Kachina (a Pueblo deity), probably from Hopi or Keresan

In addition to such borrowings, English took many words from Spanish that had originated in Indian languages of Latin America. Examples are *maize, potato,* and *barbecue* from languages of the West Indies; and *tomato, chile,* and *coyote* from the language of the Aztecs in Mexico.

Still more numerous are borrowed place names (see Stewart, 1970). One of the earliest is *Massachusetts,*

*Word or idea expressed by sign: To cut, with an ax.*

### DESCRIPTION

With the right hand flattened, palm upward, move it downward to the left side repeatedly from different elevations, ending each stroke at the same point.

### CONCEPTION OR ORIGIN

From the act of felling a tree.

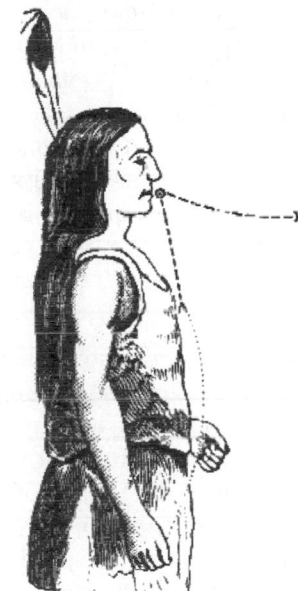

*Word or idea expressed by sign: A lie.*

### DESCRIPTION

Touch the left breast over the heart, and pass the hand forward from the mouth, the two first fingers only being extended and slightly separated (with thumb resting on third finger).

### CONCEPTION OR ORIGIN

Double-tongued.

Examples of Plains sign language. (Public Domain)

originating as the plural of the name of an Algonkian tribe. Many other place names of the northeastern and central parts of the continent are also from Algonkian: *Connecticut, Ottawa, Manhattan, Potomac, Allegheny, Illinois, Michigan, Wisconsin, Chicago, Mississippi* (literally "big-river"), *Manitoba,* and *Saskatchewan*. In the Great Lakes area and in the Southeast, names of Iroquoian origin are common, such as *Ticonderoga, Conestoga, Niagara, Chautauqua, Ohio, Kentucky,* and *Tennessee*. The Midwest has many Siouan place names, including *Iowa, Missouri, Arkansas, Kansas, Nebraska, Minnesota,* and *Dakota*. In the Southeast, many names are from Muskogean sources, such as *Alabama, Appalachia,* and *Oklahoma*. The diverse languages of the far west have also contributed many place names to English, such as *Arizona* and *Tucson,* both from O'odham; *Utah,* from the Ute language (Uto-Aztecan family); *Seattle,* taken from the name of a

Salishan chief in the Puget Sound area; and *Alaska*, from the Aleut language. The name of the western state of *Wyoming*, however, is not from a western American Indian language: it was transferred from a place name in Pennsylvania, which in turn was borrowed from an eastern Algonkian language.

The Native place names of North America have had a certain attraction for the white population, and it has been argued that even more such names should be used. The poet Walt Whitman was so much in favor of Indian names that he proposed substituting them for all others: "California," he wrote, "is sown thick with the names of all the little and big saints. Chase them away and substitute aboriginal names. . . The name of *Niagara* should be substituted for the *St. Lawrence.* . . . " Whitman had a point about the place names of California, but many Native place names are in use there, such as *Shasta* and *Yosemite.* The name *Sequoia*, given to one of California's most famous trees and national parks, is not local: it was borrowed from the name of *Sequoyah*, the Indian inventor of the Cherokee writing system. On the other hand, the name *Pasadena* is not Spanish, as one might guess. Invented during a period when it was popular to apply Indian place names, regardless of their authenticity, the word is in fact a garbled version of a phrase taken from Chippewa (Ojibway), an eastern Algonkian language. And the Pasadena that is a suburb of Houston, Texas, is named after the city in California!

## ◆ TYPES OF LANGUAGE STRUCTURE

Some false stereotypes about Native American languages have long been in circulation: that they spoke only in guttural grunts; that they spoke languages with rudimentary vocabulary, or with "no grammar"; or that they communicated solely by gestures. (As previously explained, the Plains Sign Language was only a supplement to spoken languages such as Dakota or Cheyenne.) In fact, members of each tribe spoke a language with thousands of vocabulary items and with elaborate grammatical structures. These are not "primitive" languages; they draw upon the same linguistic resources as the languages of Europe and display both the regularities and the typical complexities of languages all over the world (see Boas, 1911). For sketches of several Native American structures, see Goddard (1996:325–720).

To be sure, no writing systems were used in North America until the nineteenth century (though writing was developed by the Maya in Mexico and Central America). So the Native North Americans lacked the notion of "standard language" that often accompanies a written tradition; and of course they had no grammars in the sense of books that codified their languages. But they did not lack literary traditions: huge bodies of myth, legend, and song were composed orally and transmitted by memory from one generation to the next—just as the *Iliad* and the *Odyssey* were transmitted in ancient Greece before the invention of the Greek alphabet (see the Traditional Literature section below).

### Sounds

In their systems of pronunciation, American Indian languages show as much diversity as in other parts of language structure. A linguist will generally begin the study of a Native American language by transcribing it in terms of phonetic symbols. As work progresses, it is possible to simplify the phonetic transcription by reducing it to the phonemes of the language, the basic sounds that contrast with one another. Some languages have very few such contrasting sounds; for example, Wichita, a Caddoan language of the southern Great Plains, has only ten consonant phonemes; in contrast, English has twenty-one. Languages of the Pacific Northwest are famous for having large numbers of consonants; Nootka has thirty-seven. Certain languages of the Northwest, such as Bella Coola (Salishan, British Columbia), are also famous for words containing long sequences of consonants—*qnqnklxitXw*, or "lower it!"—and even some with no vowels at all—*sk'lxlxc*, or "I'm getting cold."

Many Indian languages display contrasts of sound that are unfamiliar in European languages. In English, consonants may be voiced (pronounced with vibration of the vocal cords), or voiceless (without such vibration); they may be stops—produced by shutting off the air momentarily—or fricatives—letting the air pass through with audible noise; and they may be produced in several parts of the mouth. Indian languages use these mechanisms and several others also.

A common sound is the glottal stop—an interruption of the breath caused by closing the vocal cords momentarily, as in the middle of English exclamations like *Oh-oh!* Transcribed with an apostrophe, the glottal stop is frequent in many Native American languages, such as in Yurok (northwestern California), which has many words like *'o'rowi'*, or dove. This phenomenon is partly responsible for the stereotypes of American Indian languages as guttural.

Especially in western North America, a common phenomenon is the use of consonants with glottalization—as a consonant is produced in the mouth. There is also closure and reopening of the vocal cords,

## PHONETIC KEY

### Consonants

|  | Labials | Dentals | Palatal Sibilants | Alveolar Sibilants | Laterals | Gutturals | Labialized Gutturals | Velars | Labialized Velars | Glottals | Laryngealized Glottals |
|---|---|---|---|---|---|---|---|---|---|---|---|
| **Voiceless Stops and Affricates** | | | | | | | | | | | |
| Simple | p | t | č | c | ƛ | k | kʷ | q | qʷ | ʔ | ! |
| Glottalized | p̓ | t̓ | č̓ | c̓ | ƛ̓ | k̓ | k̓ʷ | q̓ | q̓ʷ | | |
| Spirants | | | š | s | ł | x | xʷ | x̣ | x̣ʷ | h | ḥ |
| **Voiced Continuants Nasals** | | | | | | | | | | | |
| Simple | m | n | | | | | | | | | |
| Glottalized | m̓ | n̓ | | | | | | | | | |
| **Semivowels** | | | | | | | | | | | |
| Simple | w | y | | | | | | | | | |
| Glottalized | w̓ | ẏ | | | | | | | | | |

### Vowels

|  | Front | | Back | Back Rounded | |
|---|---|---|---|---|---|
| **High** | i | i· | | o | o· |
| **Mid-wide** | e | e· | | ɔ | ɔ· |
| **Low** | | | a   a· | | |

Phonetic table for Nootka. (Courtesy of Yale University)

producing a popping or cracking sound. This feature is also usually transcribed with an apostrophe; for instance, in Hupa, an Athabaskan language of northwestern California, it distinguishes words like *t'eew*, or raw, from *teew*, or underwater.

Another common characteristic in languages of western North America is the expansion in number of consonants by using a larger variety of tongue positions than in most European languages. Many languages distinguish velar consonants, made with the rear part of the tongue (like English *k* ) from uvular consonants, produced even farther back in the mouth (written with *q*, as in Arabic *Iraq* ). Some languages, especially in the Pacific Northwest, even differentiate a front-velar *ky*, a plain-velar *k*, and a backed *q*. In addition, labiovelars, that is velars with simultaneous lip-rounding, are common. Thus, whereas English has only the velar stops *g* and *k* (and the combinations *kw*, *gw* ), Tlingit has twenty-one velar phonemes: *g*, *k*, uvular *G*, *q*, glottalized *k'*, *q'*, labiovelar *gw*, *kw*, *k'w*, *Gw*, *qw*, *q'w*, with the corresponding fricatives *gh*, *x*, uvular *X*, glottalized *x'*, *X'*, and labiovelar *xw*, *Xw*, *x'w*, *X'w*.

In some Indian languages, as in English, stressed syllables are significant in distinguishing the meaning of words. In others, musical pitch plays a role, as it does in Chinese. For example, in Navajo, high pitch can be written with an acute accent, as in *tsé*, or stone, and low pitch with a grave accent, as in *hài*, or winter. Then there are contrasting words like *bíní'*, or his nostril; *bìnì'*, or his face; and *bìní'*, or his waist.

Native American languages, like most languages of the world, have changes of sound associated with distinctions of grammar; compare English *f* versus *v* in *half, halves, to halve*. In some languages, such changes of sound give a diminutive meaning, referring to "smallness." So Luiseño, in southern California, changes *r* to *d* when it adds a suffix referring to small things: *ngarúngru-sh*, or a pot, becomes *ngadúngdu-mal*, or a little pot. Other languages show vowel harmony, a process in which vowels change to resemble vowels in nearby grammatical elements. The Yurok language, for example, has an unusual vowel that can be written *r*, similar to the vowel in English *bird* & when this occurs in a suffix, vowels of the preceding stem change to agree with it, so that *lo'oge*, or black, plus the suffix *-'r'y* gives *lr'rgr-'r'y*, or black animal.

In several Native American languages, linguists have reported systematic differences of pronunciation depending on whether the people speaking and spoken to are men or women. A famous example is in the Yana language of northern California, in which "men's speech" was used only among men; in contrast, "women's speech" was used both among women and between the sexes. The linguistic differences had to do with how words were pronounced in isolation or at the ends of sentences; thus, in men's speech, the word *deer* was pronounced *pana*, but in women's speech it had a shorter pronunciation, as *pah*. Similarly, in men's speech, *Dance!* was *puri'i'*, but in women's speech it was *puri'*.

## Grammar

The concept of grammatical structure refers both to the traditional category of morphology—the ways that words are made up of stems, prefixes, and suffixes; and syntax—the way that words are combined into sentences. Many Native American languages are termed polysynthetic; that is, they put great emphasis on morphology, combining large numbers of elements to express within a single word what European languages may express by an entire sentence. Here is an example from Wichita (Caddoan; see Rood, 1992:113):

*kiyaakiriwaac'arasarikita'ahiiriks*
He carried the big pile of meat up into the top of the tree.

This is composed of the following elements:

*kiya-* information is from hearsay
*a-* 3d person singular subject

*ki-* past tense
*riwaac-* big
*'aras-* meat
*a-* object is plural, i.e., in pieces
*ri-* action is performed on an object
*kita-* goal of action is up above (e.g., in a tree)
*-'a-* come (verb root)
*-hiiriks* action is repeated (here, piece by piece)

Some languages favor incorporation, the compounding of a noun with a verb. This happens rarely in English, as in *to baby-sit;* but it occurs in the Wichita example above (to meat-carry); and it is common in Iroquoian, as in Mohawk *ke-weNna-weieNhoN*, literally "I-language-understand." (The capital *N* is used in this article to represent nasalization of a preceding vowel.)

Some other widespread grammatical characteristics are the following:

(a) In verbs, the person and number of the suffix are often marked by prefixes; for example, Karuk has *ni-áhoo*, or I walk, but *nu-áhoo*, or we walk. Sometimes the prefix indicates the object of the verb as well as the subject, as in Karuk *ní-mah*, or I see him, *ná-mah*, he sees me.

(b) Tense of verbs and related features are usually marked by suffixes, as in many languages of the world; but in some areas, as in the Athabaskan languages, prefixes are used. So, in Chipewyan (Northwest Territories), *hE-tsagh* means "he is crying" (*E* is the vowel of English *met*), *ghiN-tsagh* is "he cried," and *ghwa-tsagh* is "he will cry."

(c) In noun forms, the concept of possession is often expressed by prefixes indicating the person and number of the possessor. Thus Karuk has *ávaha*, or food, *nani-ávaha*, or my food, *mu-ávaha*, or his food, etc. When the possessor is a noun, as in "man's food," the language uses a construction like *ávansa mu-ávaha*, literally man his-food. Many languages have "inalienable" nouns, which cannot occur except in such possessed forms. These generally refer to such things as kin or body parts; to illustrate, Luiseño has *no-ý '*, my mother, *o-y '*, your mother, etc., but no word for mother by itself. The closest one could come would be *a-y '*, or someone's mother.

(d) Nouns in many languages take case suffixes (like those of Latin or Slavic languages) to indicate that they are the subject or object of a sentence, or in some other relationship such as location or direction. Thus a Luiseño noun stem like *kii-* ' house' has the subject form *kíi-cha*, the object form *kíi-sh*, and other forms like *kíi-k '* to the house,' *kíi-ngay* 'from the house,' *kíi-nga* 'in the house,' and *kíi-tal* ' by means of the house'.

(e) In many languages, first person plural pronouns show a distinction between an inclusive form (*we* meaning you and I) and an exclusive form (*we* meaning I and someone else other than you). For example, in Cree, inclusive *ni-nikamo-naw* means "we sing (including you)," but exclusive *ni-nikamo-naan* means "we sing (I and my friends, but not you)."

(f) The process of reduplication, the repetition of all or part of a stem, is used in many Uto-Aztecan languages to indicate the plural of nouns, such as O'odham *gogs*, or dog, *go-gogs*, or dogs. Such reduplication is used in many other languages to indicate repeated or habitual action of verbs, as with Karuk *imyah*, to breathe, *imyáh-yah*, to pant.

(g) In many languages, verb stems are distinguished on the basis of the number, shape, or other physical characteristics of the associated noun. Thus Karuk has *ikpuh*, or one swims, *ithpuh*, or two swim, and *ihtak*, or several swim. In Navajo, in order to refer to the motion of an object, one uses the verb stem *'áN* for round objects, *táN* for long objects, *tíN* for living things, *lá* for ropelike objects, etc.

(h) Verb forms often specify the location or direction of an action by using prefixes or suffixes. Thus, in Karuk, from the verb stem *path*, or throw, we have *páath-roov*, throw upriver, *páath-raa*, throw uphill, *paath-rípaa*, throw across-river, and as many as thirty-eight similar forms. Some languages also specify the instrument of an action, generally by prefixation, as with Pomo *phi-de-*, to move by batting with a stick, *phu-de-*, to move by blowing, and *pha-de-*, to move by pushing with the end of a stick.

(i) Some languages have constructions called evidentials, indicating the source or validity of the information reported. Thus Hopi distinguishes *wari*, he ran, runs, is running, as a reported event, from *wari-kngwe*, he runs (e.g., on the track team), a statement of general truth, and from *wari-kni*, he will run, an anticipated event. In other languages, verb forms consistently distinguish hearsay from eye-witness reports. In fact, the Wintu language of north central California has four contrasting evidential suffixes: (1) non-visual sensory, as in *-nthere*, meaning "it sounds or feels so to me"; (2) hearsay, as in *-kele*, meaning "I heard it said" (used in stories, gossip, or any other second-hand report); (3) inferential, as in *-re*, meaning "it must logically be true"; and (4) experiential, as in *-'el*, meaning "I judge from experience that it is true."

(j) Some American Indian languages, notably in the Pacific Northwest, have numeral classifiers—a type of grammatical element that is required in counting objects, and that differentiates the form or shape of the objects counted. Such elements also occur in Chinese, Japanese, and other languages of East Asia, and in many American Indian languages of Mexico. Thus, in Yurok, the number two is pronounced *ni'iyelh* when counting human beings, but *nr'r'r'y* for animals, *no'oh* for round objects (like stones), *nr'rpi'* for tools, *na'a'r* for trees, *na'ak'wo'n* for smaller plants, *na'a'n* for body parts, *na'ak'* for long flexible objects (like ropes), *no'ok's* for flat objects, *na'a'li* for houses, and *na'ey* for boats. Such differences apply to all numbers through ten.

(k) A striking feature of syntax found in some Native American languages is the ergative construction, a pattern in which the direct objects of certain verb forms are treated grammatically as if they were the subjects of those verbs. Thus, in Yupik Eskimo, an intransitive verb (one that takes a subject but no direct object) occurs with its subject in the "absolutive" case:

*Arna-q yurartuq* The woman is dancing.
woman-abs. is-dancing

But with a transitive verb (one that may take both a subject and a direct object), the absolutive case is used not for the subject, but for the object. With such verbs, the subject is in the "relative" case:

*Arna-m neraa neqa* The woman is eating the fish.
woman-rel. is-eating fish-abs.

## Vocabulary

Words in Native American languages, like those of other languages, are composed both of simple stems and of derived constructions. The derivational processes commonly include prefixation, suffixation, and compounding. A few languages use internal sound change, as when English derives the noun *song* from the verb *sing* and thus Yurok has *pontet*, or ashes, *prncrc*, or dust, *prncrh*, or to be gray. Some languages also acquire new vocabulary items by borrowing, as mentioned above.

In Native American languages, like other languages of the world, the meaning of a word cannot always be guessed from a knowledge of its historical origin or from knowing the meaning of its parts. For instance, in the early nineteenth century, Karuk borrowed the name of a Canadian trapper, Jean-Baptiste McKay, in the form *mákay*, to refer to white people in general. It was then combined with *váas*, or deerskin blanket, to give the new word *makáy-vaas*, used to mean "cloth" (literally, "white-man's blanket"). This in turn was compounded with *yukúku*, or moccasin, to give still another new word, *makayvas-yukúku*, or tennis shoes (literally "cloth shoes").

In the area of vocabulary, American Indian languages are especially likely to present surprises to the outsider. Where European languages label things by different terms, an Indian language may use a single term—or vice versa. Thus, where the English language distinguishes among *airplane, aviator,* and *flying insect,* Hopi calls them all *masa'ytaka,* literally "flyer." Conversely, where English has only the single term *water,* Hopi differentiates *paahe,* water in nature, from *keeyi,* water in a container.

Again, natural phenomena may be classified by different languages on the basis of totally different criteria. In talking about directions in space, European languages use words like *north, south, east,* and *west,* which are basically defined in terms of the rising and setting sun; and many Native American languages have terms corresponding to these. But Karuk and Yurok, along with other languages of northwestern California, use terms defined not in relation to the sun, but rather in relation to the Klamath River, which follows a winding course through their territory. So the principal directional terms of Karuk are *káruk,* upriver (borrowed by whites as the name for the tribe); *yúruk,* downriver; *máruk,* away from the river, uphill; and *sáruk,* toward the river, downhill—supplemented by *ithyáruk,* across-river.

Another semantic area in which languages may differ greatly is in their kinship terms. For example, where English has the single term *uncle,* the Seneca language (Iroquoian) makes a distinction: my father's brother is simply called *ha'nih,* literally "my father," while my mother's brother is called by a separate term, *hakhno'seNh.* But this latter term also refers to my mother's nephew or niece, whom in English I would call my cousin.

Another area that shows many differences among languages is that of counting. Of course English and many European languages have a counting system based on the number ten and its variant forms, so that *thir-teen* was originally "three (plus) ten," while *thir-ty* was "three (times) ten"; this clearly reflects that a person's ten fingers represented a historically important aid to counting. In Native American Indian languages, the numbers five (the fingers of one hand) and twenty (the fingers plus the toes) are also sometimes used as basic units. For example, in the old counting system of Luiseño in southern California, six was called, literally, "five adding one"; ten was "both my hands finished"; fifteen was "both my hands finished and one of my feet"; and twenty was "my other foot finished also." In a few languages, the number four rather than five is used as a basis for counting: Thus Ventureño, a Chumashan language of Southern California, had *pakeet,* one, *eshkm ,* two, *maség,* three, *skumú,* four, followed

by *iti-pakés,* five, literally "one more (than four)"; *yeti-shkom,* six, literally "two more"; *iti-maség,* seven, literally "three more." The numbers for eight, nine, and ten are unitary words, but twelve is *maség skumú,* literally "three fours," while thirteen is *maség skúmu kampakeet,* "three fours plus-one." The next unitary number is sixteen, the square of four, and after that one starts adding again: seventeen is literally "sixteen plus one." Continuing with this strategy of multiplying fours, one logically arrives at numbers such as thirty-two, which is literally "two sixteens." The use of four as a base may go back to counting one's fingers without the thumbs, or to a system of counting the slots *between* one's fingers and thumbs.

It should be noted that many Native American societies have no ethnic name for their own tribe or their own language: they simply call themselves "the people," and their language is called "the language of the people" or "our language." This is in general true among the Athabaskan peoples: thus, in Navajo, *diné* means "person, people, human being(s)," but also "Navajo"; and *diné bi-zaad,* literally "person his-tongue," means "the Navajo language." Other tribes, however, do have names for their own groups; for example, the Hopi in fact call themselves *hopi.*

In any part of the world, the number of words that people use in a particular semantic area depends on the importance of that area to them. For example, one might expect the Inuit (Eskimo) to distinguish several types of snow, and in fact they do. But the exotic qualities of Native American semantic systems need not be exaggerated. Many writers have repeated the claim that the Inuit language has a hundred distinct words for snow. This has been shown to be false. In fact, Boas (1911) reported that Inuit has four words in this semantic area, referring to falling snow, snow on the ground, and two types of drifting snow. This was exaggerated by various writers and journalists. Of course one might equally well say that English has at least four words in the same area: besides the word *snow,* we have terms like *slush, sleet,* and *blizzard.* After all, snow is also important in many parts of the English-speaking world.

## ◆ GEOGRAPHICAL AREAS AND LANGUAGE AREAS

As an alternative to the classification of languages given in the Phyla and Families section above, it is useful to consider Native American languages in terms of the geographical areas in which they are found, understanding these areas in terms not only of physical habitat and shared cultural patterns, but also in terms of the distribution of features of language structure, such as those described in the Types of Language Structure section above (see Sherzer, 1976; Bright and Sherzer, 1976). Eleven such areas, listed and described below, may be distinguished. Some of these prove to be quite close-knit linguistically, reflecting a long history of language contact and structural borrowing; others show much greater diversity of linguistic structure, reflecting situations in which language contact was less important, or had a shorter history.

### The Arctic Area

Constituting the northern edge of the continent, the Arctic area is occupied by two language families, Aleut and Eskimo, comprising the Eskimo-Aleut phylum. The two families are clearly related, but there was relatively little language contact between communities in former times, so that similarities between language can be explained mainly in terms of their common origin.

### The Western Subarctic

In the Yukon and the western part of the Northwest Territories, the Western Subartic is monopolized by languages of the Athabaskan family; thus the genetic similarities among languages far outweigh those possibly due to contact.

### The Eastern Subarctic

Extending from the Northwest Territories through northern Ontario and Quebec, the Eastern Subarctic is occupied entirely by Algonkian languages; once again, the genetic relationship is predominant.

### The Northwest Coast

Extending from southeastern Alaska to southwestern Oregon, the Northwest Coast presents a very different picture. There is a high degree of genetic diversity: the genetic groups represented include Tlingit, Haida, and Athabaskan (the hypothesized Na-Dené phylum); Tsimshian, Chinookan, and several Oregon languages that have been assigned to the Penutian phylum (also represented in the Plateau and California areas); and three families found only in the Pacific Northwest—Salishan, Wakashan, and Chimakuan. Nevertheless, this area is the most striking example in North America of structural similarities that cut across genetic boundaries. Some features that especially characterize the Northwest Coast (as discussed in the Types of Language Structure section above) are complex consonant systems (including glottalized consonants), the use of numeral classifiers, and reduplication in verbs. The spread of such areal features was probably associated with high population density, along with widespread trade and intermarriage among tribes.

### The Plateau Area

Occupying eastern British Columbia, Washington, and Oregon, as well as Idaho, the Plateau area contains languages of the Penutian phylum, the Salishan family, and the Kutenai isolate. It resembles the Northwest Coast area in combining genetic diversity with borrowed structural features. Characteristic traits of the area include elaborate consonant systems (though not quite as complex as those on the Northwest Coast) and the use of sound changes to mark diminutive meaning. Communicative factors seem similar to those in the neighboring Northwest Coast area, though with less intensity.

### The California Area

With boundaries roughly identical to the state, the California area is genetically one of the most diverse on the continent: languages of this area belong to the Hokan and Penutian phyla, each containing several distinct families, and to the Athabaskan, Algic, Yukian, and Uto-Aztecan families. In terms of structural features, the area is also varied; no single features are found throughout the entire area. Nevertheless, there is evidence for a complex history of structural borrowing among adjacent families, and for relatively recent intrusions by the Athabaskan family from the north and Uto-Aztecan from the east. Rather than being regarded as a single language area, California may be considered a set of sub-areas, partly interlocking and partly discontinuous.

### The Southwest Area

Roughly including Arizona and New Mexico, the Southwest area is also highly diverse, containing languages of the Kiowa-Tanoan and Uto-Aztecan families (grouped into the Aztec-Tanoan phylum) as well as the Athabaskan and Keresan families and the isolated Zuni language. As has been noted above, the Athabaskan languages are relatively recent arrivals, and as such have quite different structural features from their neighbors. However, even among the non-Athabaskan languages there is little structural uniformity. As for California, a description in terms of sub-areas may be preferable. The limited amount of structural borrowing is apparently related to an attitude reported in the Pueblo communities, where languages of outsiders are traditionally viewed with mistrust.

## The Great Basin

Nevada, Utah, and parts of adjacent states make up the Great Basin, which is occupied entirely by Uto-Aztecan languages except for the presence of Washo, a supposed Hokan language, on the western edge. Like the Subarctic, this is an area with low population density, limited language contact, and little evidence for borrowed linguistic structure.

## The Plains Area

Occupying the Great Plains region of both Canada and the United States, the Plains is an area of genetic diversity. It contains languages of the Algonkian, Athabaskan, Caddoan, Kiowa-Tanoan, Siouan, and Uto-Aztecan families, most of which are also found outside the Plains. Structural similiarities of Plains languages tend to be with their genetic relatives in other areas, rather than with their geographical neighbors. Thus Blackfoot, Arapaho, and Cheyenne, the Algonkian languages of the Plains, are much more like their Algonkian sister languages in the eastern United States than they are like the nearby Siouan languages. This may be because many Plains languages moved into their historic locations only in relatively recent centuries, especially after horses had been introduced to America by the Spanish. Also, as noted above, the use of Plains Sign Language made communication possible even in the absence of much bilingualism.

## The Northeast Area

Reaching from the Great Lakes region eastward to New England and the Maritime Provinces of Canada, the Northeast is occupied predominantly by the Algonkian and Iroquoian families. There is little areal influence cutting across genetic boundaries; the region is definable as a unit on geographical and cultural grounds, but not linguistically. Low population density may have discouraged language contact and bilingualism in this area.

## The Southeast Area

Occupying the southeastern region of the United States, the Southeast contains languages of the Gulf, Iroquoian, and Siouan families, plus the isolated Yuchi language. Areal traits are not strongly marked.

## Classes of Geographic Areas

It seems possible to distinguish four classes among geographical areas:

1. Genetically uniform areas with sparse population—the Arctic, the Western and Eastern Subarctic, and the Great Basin. Structural borrowing across genetic lines has been largely irrelevant.
2. One genetically diverse area, the Plains, where structural borrowing has conspicuously not occurred, primarily because the historical distribution of tribes is relatively recent.
3. Genetically diverse areas—California, the Southwest, the Northeast, and the Southeast—where structural borrowing has been local rather than sweeping.
4. Finally, two genetically diverse areas—the Northwest and the Plateau—where structural borrowing has been at its maximum. Causal factors seem to include high population density, and cultural attitudes that encourage intimate contacts between tribes.

As noted above, cases of mutual assimilation, such as those found among the Northwest languages, create serious problems for attempts at genetic classification. It may not be possible to decide whether the similarities between the Salishan and Wakashan families, for instance, are the result of common origin, or result from prolonged contact and borrowing within the Northwest Coast language area. It may be best to say simply that the two families must have a great deal of shared history; once that is granted, particular similarities may be examined to determine whether they are more likely to result from common origin or from borrowing.

## ◆ LANGUAGE AND CULTURE

The striking differences that the semantic organization of American Indian languages show from those of European languages, both in grammar and vocabulary, have led many people to think about the degree to which differences in language are correlated with differences in culture, patterns of habitual thought, and world view (the unconscious philosophical outlook held by the members of a society). It is clear that differences in language may be correlated with nonlinguistic differences: that the Karuk use directional terms like "upriver, downriver" results from the fact that the Klamath River is the basis of their habitat. A much more difficult question is whether the language structures people learn as children may, in some ways, provide them with "ready-made" habits of thought, and so in part determine the way they view the world.

The most famous discussion of this problem is that by B. L. Whorf (1939), based on material from Hopi.

Young girls learn how to string beads at the 1988 Arapaho Language and Culture Camp sponsored by the Northern Arapaho tribe and the Wyoming Council for the Humanities. (Photo by Sara Wiles)

Whorf points out that Hopi words referring to units of time (e.g., "day") are different from other nouns in that they have no plural form; in addition, they cannot be counted with the cardinal numerals (one, two, etc.) but only with the ordinals (first, second, etc.). Comparing English and Hopi, Whorf remarks that English speakers say "ten days," as if the days were a collection of separate units (like ten apples), whereas the Hopi speaker means "ten days" to be a cycle, or ten recurrences of the same unit of time. Whorf advances the idea that Hopi speakers think about time differently from English speakers, a contention he supports by pointing to a nonlinguistic aspect of Hopi life: their ceremonial cycle, which involves repeated preparation for future events (such as planting or harvesting). Whorf reasons that the Hopi view each day as a recurrence, rather than something new, so that it is reasonable for them to believe that the daily repetition of ceremonial acts will have a cumulative effect on the future. As Whorf points out, the Hopi attitude seems just the opposite of English-speakers' idea that "Tomorrow is another day."

Such ideas remain controversial; however, the study of the interaction of Native American languages and cultures continues to provide a rich laboratory for study. An interesting problem is found in northwestern California, where several small tribes share most features of culture, but use languages of very diverse types. The languages concerned are Karuk, classified as Hokan; Yurok and Wiyot of the Macro-Algonkian phylum; and Hupa and Tolowa of the Athabaskan family. Whorf might suggest that the differences among these languages would have led to greater diversity in their cultures—or, failing that, the languages might have grown more similar to each other. In fact, it seems that something of a compromise has taken place: linguistic diversity and cultural uniformity have made modest accommodations to each other. An example may be found in the systems that the Yurok and the Tolowa use for semantic groupings of animals. The Yurok language has more generic terms, like *hoore'mos*, or animal, and *nunepuy*, or fish, as well as specific words like *puuk*, deer, and *regork*, trout. This seems consistent with a relatively high degree of complexity in Yurok culture generally, especially with its emphasis on ranks and hierarchies. By contrast, Tolowa has only the specific terms for animal species, and this may be correlated with the relatively lower emphasis on hierarchy that characterizes Tolowa culture.

A different kind of relationship between language and culture is of more interest from the viewpoint of North American prehistory: the fact that language retains traces of changes in culture. Thus the historical study of Native American languages, along with archaeological findings and knowledge of Native historical traditions, helps reconstruct remote past cultures and migrations (see Foster, 1996). Edward Sapir (1936) held that the original homeland of a group of languages is likely to be found in the area of greatest linguistic diversity, noting that there are many more different Indo-European languages and dialects now spoken in Europe than in continents more recently colonized by Europeans, such as North America, South America, or Australia. To take an American Indian example, Sapir pointed out that the Athabaskan languages spoken in Alaska and Canada are much more diverse than the Pacific Coast or Southwestern families of Athabaskan, suggesting that the original center of Athabaskan migration was in the sub-Arctic. To confirm this, Sapir reconstructed parts of prehistoric Athabaskan vocabulary, showing, for instance, how a word meaning *horn* or *spoon* came to mean *spoon* or *gourd*, as the ancestors of the Navajo migrated from the far north (where spoons are made of deerhorn) to the Southwest (where they are made of gourds).

For an excellent recent survey of the relationship of American Indian languages to their cultural and social contexts, see Silver and Miller (1997).

## ♦ TRADITIONAL LITERATURE

Verbal art has always been highly cultivated among Native Americans, though until recent times it was limited to the oral medium. The repeated recitation of myths, legends, and ceremonial formulas by elders, along with the performance of songs, constituted the educational system of the tribe. These practices made it possible for younger people to learn the religion, morals, history, aesthetic values, humor, and music of their ancestors. In modern terms, the traditional literature has provided rich resources for American Indian storytellers and poets expressing their own experience in English or, in some cases, in Native American languages.

*Ethnopoetics* refers to the study of traditional literature in which linguists and anthropologists try to understand how the Native languages—the words, sounds,

the grammatical constructions, pauses, tone of voice— are used to create artistic effect. It has been pointed out that many traditional Native American narratives are not simply prose texts, but that they are organized in terms of lines: sequences somehow parallel in structure (see Hymes, 1976a).

In traditional European literature, poems are organized in lines that often show parallelisms of rhyme or meter, as well as other types. Though the oral literature of the American Indian does not generally use rhyme or meter, it uses many other types of parallelism. The following short myth, from the Karuk of northwestern California, illustrates both the grammatical and literary structures of such texts. The protagonist is Coyote, the divine trickster who stars in hundreds of traditional narratives told by the tribes of western North America. The story consists of two parallel acts, each with two parallel scenes. In Act 1, Scene 1, an aspect of the primeval world is presented; in Act 1, Scene 2, Coyote tampers with it, so that male humans will have to work harder. In Act 2, Scene 1, another aspect of the world is presented; and in Act 2, Scene 2, Coyote again interferes, this time to put a heavier burden on female humans.

*Coyote Lays Down the Law*

Act 1, Scene 1:
*Kun-piip,*
they-say

**It was said,**
*Xâatik ápap yúruk u-vuu-núp-ahi-ti,*
let one-side downriver it-flow-down-condition-durative
**"Let the river flow DOWN-stream on one side,**
*káru ápap káruk u-vuu-nôovu-ti.*
and one-side upriver it-flow-up-durative
**and UP-stream on the other side.**
*Xâatik vaa u-kupi-ti.*
let thus it-do-durative
**Let it be so."**
*Kári xás chémi.*
and so all-right
**And so it was agreed.**
*Vaa uum vúra pa-yúruk tá-kun-víit-rup,*
thus they just when-downstream already-they-paddle-down
**Whenever they traveled downstream,**
*t-u-thívruuh-rup yúruk.*
already-it-float-down downstream
**the boat would drift DOWN-stream.**
*Ithyáruk kúna ú-p-viit-roov-eesh,*
across-river but they-again-paddle-upriver-future
**But they would travel back upriver on the OTHER side,**

*u-thívruuh-roov-eesh káru,*
they-float-upriver-future also

**they'd drift UP-stream too,**

*káruk u-vuu-nôov-ahi-ti pa-íshaha.*
upriver it-flow-up-condition-durative the-water

**it was flowing upriver, that water was.**

Act 1, Scene 2:
*Kári xás pihnêefich u-piip, pûuhara,*
and then coyote he-say no

**And then Coyote said, "No,**

*xáyfaat vaa u-kupi-ti.*
don't that it-do-durative

**let it not be that way,**

*koovúra yúruk kám-vuu-nup-ahi-ti.*
all downriver let-flow-down-condition-durative

**let it all flow DOWN-river.**

*Vaa uum vûra káan ifmaará-piit kam-íktaat-roovu-ti,*
thus they just there husband-new let-push-upriver-durative

**Let the young husbands PUSH their way up there,**

*pa-káruk u-víit-roovu-ti.*
when-upstream they-paddle-up-durative

**when they travel UP-stream."**

Act 2, Scene 1:
*Kári xás kúna kun-piip,*
and then but they-say

**But then it was said,**

*asiktávaan pa-mukun-átimnam máruk tá-kun-sá-naa-n,*
woman when-their-packbasket uphill already-they-carry-up-pl.

**"When women carry their packbaskets uphill,**

*púyava máruk xás áhup sú' tá-kun-máhyaan,*
so uphill then wood inside already-they-put

**then uphill they put wood into them,**

*túr tá-kun-íkyav.*
basketload already-they-make

**they make basketloads.**

*Kári xás tá-kun-pá-vyiih-ship pa-asiktávaan-sa.*
and then already-they-back-go-start the-woman-plural

**And then the women start back home.**

*Kári xás vaa vúra káan tá-kun-íitshur pa-mukún-tur.*
and then thus just there already-they-leave the-their-basketload

**And they just leave them there, those basketloads."**

*Xás kun-piip,*
then they-say

**And they said,**

*vaa vúra kun-írunaa-ti-heesh pa-tur.*
thus just they-walk-durative-future the-basketload

**"They'll just WALK home, those basketloads will."**

Act 2, Scene 2:
*Kári xás pihnêefich u-piip, xáyfaat, pûuhara.*
and then coyote he-say don't no

**And then Coyote said, "No, don't!**

*Vúra uum yarará-piit vúra kám-tuun-ti.*
just they wife-new just let-carry-durative

**Let the young wives just CARRY the loads."**

*Kári xás vaa u-kupí-ti payêem,*
and so thus it-do-durative now

**So that's the way it is nowadays,**

*tá-pu-áhoo-tih-ara pa-tur.*
already-not-walk-durative-negative the-basketload

**now they can't walk any more, those basketloads.**

## ◆ WRITING SYSTEMS

Before the arrival of Europeans, some American Indian peoples kept records by means of *pictographs*—simplified pictures drawn on skin or on wood—as a way of recording their history. These records are not the same as written language, however, since people cannot read them in a uniform and unambiguous way. Of the writing systems that have been developed for Native American peoples, most have been invented and introduced by Europeans—sometimes by missionaries, sometimes by linguists and educators.

Several types of writing have been introduced at various times and places (see Walker, 1996). Early in the settlement of New England the European alphabet was adapted to write the Massachusett language. In the nineteenth century a hieroglyphic system was developed for the Micmac language in Nova Scotia by Jesuit priest Father Chrestien Le Clercq; but this proved difficult to learn, and in recent years the Micmac have used an alphabetic system. Among the Cree people of Canada a syllabary was introduced, in which each symbol stands for a combination of consonant plus vowel. In this system, if a given symbol is rotated 90°, 180°, or 270°, the value of the consonant remains the same, but the vowel changes from *e* to *i*, to *o*, and to *a*, respectively. A modification of this system was adopted by the Inuit people of Baffin Island and continues to be widely used in the Canadian North.

The most famous of North American writing systems, however, is that invented for Cherokee in the nineteenth century by Sequoyah, who knew no English but had seen materials written in English. Deciding that his language should have its own writing system, he succeeded in inventing one: not an alphabet, but a syllabary, in which each symbol indicates a combination of consonant plus vowel. Sequoyah borrowed the

# Cherokee Alphabet

| | | | | | |
|---|---|---|---|---|---|
| **D** a | **R** e | **T** i | **ᵭ** o | **O** u | **i** v |
| **S** ga **O** ka | **ᵽ** ge | **y** gi | **A** go | **J** gu | **E** gv |
| **ᵬ** ha | **ᵱ** he | **ᵴ** hi | **F** ho | **Γ** hu | **ᵬ** hv |
| **W** la | **ᵭ** le | **ᵱ** li | **G** lo | **M** lu | **ᵬ** lv |
| **ᵴ** ma | **ᵭ** me | **H** mi | **ᵴ** mo | **y** mu | |
| **ᵬ** na **ᵼ** hna **G** nah | **ᴧ** ne | **ᵶ** ni | **Z** no | **ᵬ** nu | **ᵬ** nv |
| **ᵵ** qua | **ᵶ** que | **ᵽ** qui | **ᵛ** quo | **ᵶ** quu | **ᵬ** quv |
| **U** sa **ᵬ** s | **4** se | **ᵬ** si | **ᵼ** so | **ᵬ** su | **R** sv |
| **ᵬ** da **W** ta | **ᵴ** de **ᵵ** te | **ᵴ** di **ᵵ** ti | **V** do | **S** du | **ᵬ** dv |
| **ᵬ** dla **ᵬ** tla | **L** tle | **C** tli | **ᵵ** tlo | **ᵱ** tlu | **P** tlv |
| **G** tsa | **V** tse | **ᵬ** tsi | **K** tso | **J** tsu | **ᵬ** tsv |
| **G** wa | **ᵬ** we | **O** wi | **ᵬ** wo | **ᵬ** wu | **6** wv |
| **ᵬ** ya | **ᵬ** ye | **ᵬ** yi | **ᵬ** yo | **G** yu | **B** yv |

## Sounds Represented by Vowels

a, as <u>a</u> in <u>father</u>, or short as <u>a</u> in <u>rival</u>

e, as <u>a</u> in <u>hate</u>, or short as <u>e</u> in <u>met</u>

i, as <u>i</u> in <u>pique</u>, or short as <u>i</u> in <u>pit</u>

o, as <u>o</u> in <u>note</u>, approaching <u>aw</u> in <u>law</u>

u, as <u>oo</u> in <u>fool</u>, or short as <u>u</u> in <u>pull</u>

v, as <u>u</u> in <u>but</u>, nasalized

## Consonant Sounds

<u>g</u> nearly as in English, but approaching to <u>k</u>.   <u>d</u> nearly as in English but approaching to <u>t</u>. <u>h k l m n q s t w y</u> as in English.  Syllables beginning with <u>g</u> except **S** (ga) have sometimes the power of <u>k</u>.  **A** (go), **S** (du), **ᵭ** (dv) are sometimes sounded <u>to</u>, <u>tu</u>, <u>tv</u> and syllables written with tl except **ᵬ** (tla) sometimes vary to dl.

Cherokee syllabary (mistakenly called an "alphabet"). From *Beginning Cherokee*, (1977) by Ruth Bradley Holmes and Betty Sharp Smith. (Courtesy of University of Oklahoma Press)

| Syllabary | ᏔᎵᏏ ᏣᎳᎩ ᎠᏔᎳᏘ |
|---|---|
| Pronunciation | Ta?-li:'-ne Tsa-la-gi' Go-hwe-lv:'-i |
| Translation: | Second Cherokee Lesson |

Example of Cherokee in Sequoyah's syllabary, in phonetic transcription and translation. From *Beginning Cherokee,* by Ruth Bradley Holmes and Betty Sharp Smith. (Courtesy of University of Oklahoma Press)

shapes of some letters in the English alphabet but with no regard to their sounds. In fact, the Cherokee letters *D*, *R*, and *T* are pronounced *a*, *e*, and *i*, respectively.

In most other languages, alphabetic writing systems have been used, adapted from European alphabets when necessary by using additional letters and accent marks. In the nineteenth century the Russian alphabet was adapted to write Aleut; elsewhere, the Roman alphabet was generally used.

However, some Native Americans distrust the use of writing systems for their languages and prefer to emphasize the continuance of the oral medium. In 1991, the president of the 28,000-member Oglala Sioux tribe announced that Lakota was the language of tribal business on the Pine Ridge Reservation; nevertheless, he stated that he does not approve of writing the language. "Writing it is bad," he said, "because you have a tendency to lose some of the spirituality when it's down in black and white." In spite of such feelings, the development of literacy in traditional languages may make it possible for tribal people to transmit and elaborate their literary tradition—not only in the oral medium, and not only in English translation—but also in writing systems adapted to their individual tribes and developed with their active cooperation.

## ◆ LANGUAGE RESTORATION

Since their first contact with Europeans, Native Americans have been under pressure to learn European languages; this pressure has been applied by administrators and educators, as well as by the European-dominated society in general. However, in the early to middle nineteenth century bilingualism was common in many Native communities. Especially in the eastern and central parts of the continent, many people used English or French to deal with Whites, but some schools, churches, newspapers, and government services used Indian languages to communicate with Natives. This situation changed during the late nineteenth and early twentieth centuries, especially in the United States, when the government began to stamp out the use of Native languages. Many individuals were forcibly removed from their homes and taken to boarding schools, where they were punished for speaking anything but English. After the Indian Reorganization Act of 1934 there was some reversal in official attitudes, and attempts began to be made to revive literacy in Native languages. But by this time, many Indian parents had come to believe that assimilation to Anglo-American language and culture offered the only hope for their children. The result was the obsolescence and extinction of many languages. Today it is common to find languages that are only remembered by a few elders. Since the Native language is the principal medium for teaching traditional culture, the loss of languages has been accompanied by the loss of much cultural knowledge.

Since the 1970s, various efforts have been made in Native American communities to preserve and restore traditional languages, sometimes through the teaching of literacy in those languages (see McCarty et al., 1999). In some groups children are growing up as active bilinguals; examples can be found among the Inuit and Cree in Canada, Athabaskan groups in both Canada and Alaska, the Sioux reservations in South Dakota, the Cherokee in North Carolina and Oklahoma, some Pueblos in New Mexico, and the Navajo in New Mexico and Arizona. However, each succeeding generation tends to be less fluent in Native languages than the one before it. It has been estimated that by the mid-twenty-first century not more than a dozen Native American languages will still be actively spoken. Nevertheless, studying extinct and living Native languages broadens understanding of the resources offered by human language, and provides insight into the past history of the North American continent.

*William Bright*
*University of Colorado*

The Inuit people of the Arctic try to preserve their language by providing material in Inuit for their young people. (Courtesy of Inuit Broadcasting Corporation)

### References

Bakker, Peter. *A Language of Our Own: The Genesis of Michif, the Mixed Cree-French Language of the Canadian Métis.* Rev. ed. New York: Oxford University Press, 1997.

Boas, Franz. Introduction to *Handbook of American Indian Languages, Part I.* Smithsonian Institution, Bureau of American Ethnology, Bulletin 40. Washington, D.C.: GPO, 1911; Washington, D.C.: Georgetown University Press, 1964; Lincoln: University of Nebraska Press, 1966.

Bright, William, and Joel Sherzer. "A Real Features in North American Indian Languages." In *Variation and Change in Language: Essays*, selected and introduced by Anwar S. Dil, 228–268. Stanford, Calif.: Stanford University Press, 1976.

Callaghan, Catherine A., and Geoffrey Gamble. "Borrowing." In *Languages*, edited by Ives Goddard. Vol. 17 of *Handbook of North American Indians*, edited by William C. Sturtevant, 111–116. Washington, D.C.: Smithsonian Institution, 1996.

Campbell, Lyle. *American Indian Languages: The Historical Linguistics of Native America*. New York: Oxford University Press, 1997.

Cutler, Charles L. *O Brave New Words!: Native American Loanwords in Current English*. Norman: University of Oklahoma Press.

Foster, Michael K. "Language and the Culture History of North America." In *Languages*, edited by Ives Goddard. Vol. 17 of *Handbook of North American Indians*, edited by William C. Sturtevant, 64–110. Washington, D.C.: Smithsonian Institution, 1996.

Goddard, Ives. "The Description of the Native Languages of North America Before Boas." In *Languages*, edited by Ives Goddard. Vol. 17 of *Handbook of North American Indians*, edited by William C. Sturtevant, 17–42. Washington, D.C.: Smithsonian Institution, 1996.

Goddard, Ives, ed. *Languages*. Vol. 17 of *Handbook of North American Indians*, edited by William C. Sturtevant. Washington, D.C.: Smithsonian Institution, 1996.

Greenberg, Joseph H. *Language in the Americas*. Stanford, Calif.: Stanford University Press, 1987.

Haas, Mary R. "Prehistory and Diffusion." In *The Prehistory of Languages*, 78–97. The Hague: Mouton, 1969.

Hymes, Dell. "The Americanist Tradition." In *American Indian Languages and American Linguistics*, edited by Wallace L. Chafe, 11–33. Lisse, The Netherlands: Peter de Ridder Press, 1976.

———. "Louis Simpson's 'The Deserted Boy'." In *"In Vain I Tried to Tell You": Essays in Native American Ethnopoetics*, 142–183. Philadelphia: University of Pennsylvania Press, 1981.

Mallery, Garrick. "Sign Language among North American Indians, Compared with that Among Other Peoples and Deaf-Mutes." *Annual Report*. Smithsonian Institution, Bureau of American Ethnology, 263–552. Washington, D.C.: GPO, 1881.

McCarty, Teresa L., Lucille J. Watahomigie, and Akira Y. Yamamoto, eds. "Reversing Language Shift in Indigenous America: Collaborations and Views From the Field." *Practicing Anthropology* 21, no. 2 (1999): 2–47.

Mithun, Marianne. *The Languages of Native North America*. Cambridge, UK; New York: Cambridge University Press, 1999.

Powell, John Wesley. "Indian Linguistic Families of America North of Mexico." *Annual Report*. Smithsonian Institution, Bureau of American Ethnology. Washington, D.C.: GPO, 1891; Lincoln: University of Nebraska Press, 1966.

Rood, David S. "North American Languages." In Vol. 3 of *International Encyclopedia of Linguistics*, edited by William Bright, 110–115. New York: Oxford University Press, 1992.

Sapir, Edward. "Central and North American Languages." In *Encyclopaedia Britannica* 14th ed., 1929; In *The Collected Works of Edward Sapir*, Vol. 5. *American Indian Languages*, edited by William Bright, 95–104. Berlin and New York: Mouton de Gruyter, 1990.

———. "Internal Linguistic Evidence Suggestive of the Northern Origin of the Navajo." In *Selected Writings of Edward Sapir in Language, Culture, and Peronality*, edited by David G. Mandelbaum, 213–224. Berkeley: University of California Press, 1949.

Sherzer, Joel. *An Areal-Typological Study of American Indian Languages North of Mexico*. Amsterdam: North-Holland; New York: American Elsevier, 1976.

Silver, Shirley, and Wick R. Miller. *American Indian Languages: Cultural and Social Contexts*. Tucson: University of Arizona Press, 1997.

Stewart, George R. *American Place-Names*. New York: Oxford University Press, 1970.

Taylor, Allan R. "Indian Lingua Francas." In *Language in the USA*, edited by Charles A. Ferguson and Shirley B. Heath, 175–199. New York: Cambridge University Press, 1980.

Voegelin, Charles F., and Florence M. Voegelin. *Classification and Index of the World's Languages*. New York: Elsevier, 1977.

Walker, Willard. "Native Writing Systems." In *Language*, edited by Ives Goddard. Vol. 17 of *Handbook of North American Indians*, edited by William C. Sturtevant, 158–184. Washington, D.C.: Smithsonian Institution, 1996.

Whorf, Benjamin Lee. "The Relation of Habitual Thought and Behavior to Language." In *Language, Culture, and Personality: Essays in Memory of Edward Sapir*, edited by Leslie Spier, 75–93. Menasha, Wis.: Sapir Memorial Publication Fund, 1939; In *Language, Thought, and Reality: Selected Writings of Benjamin Lee Whorf*, edited by John B. Carroll, 134–159. New York: Wiley, 1956.

*William Bright*

# 5

# Law and Legislation

## ♦ OVERVIEW: U.S. LAW AND LEGAL ISSUES

When Europeans first ventured to the Americas, they encountered peoples with their own systems of law. Although Native American legal systems varied widely from group to group, each provided rules for the allocation of political authority, for property rights, and for the conduct of everyday life. These legal regimes ranged from the hierarchical (structured by class or rank), community-centered law of the southwestern Pueblo or Northwest Coast groups to the more libertarian (valuing individual consent and personal freedom), clan-based law of the southeastern Cherokee. For example, most Pueblo rest considerable authority in the heads of religious societies and in the individual of the highest sacred standing; Northwest Coast groups such as the Kwakiutl and Salish accorded prestige and influence to wealthy kinship groups, but only on the condition that these groups generously share their wealth with others. In contrast, the southeastern Cherokee made group decisions only after listening to every member who wished to speak, and never permitted a representative body to force an individual to act contrary to her or his personal judgment. Some Indian governing structures, like the Iroquois Confederacy, were complex and subtle schemes for joining warring tribes together in peace for their mutual benefit, relying heavily on discussion and the creation of consensus as the basis for collective action.

Despite their differences, however, Indian legal systems shared certain common features. Typically, law was transmitted orally rather than in writing, although wampum belts (beads of polished shells strung in strands, belts, or sashes used as ceremonial pledges) memorialized some of the eastern Indians' tribal law. Furthermore, the law was usually entwined with religious beliefs and practices, and was not embodied in separate, exclusively legal institutions. Additionally, tribal law was primarily concerned with restoring harmony in the community, rather than with punishing the guilty or strictly computing compensation for past wrongs. In these respects, the indigenous law of the Americas differed sharply from European law. As a consequence, it was difficult for European explorers to understand and recognize tribal legal systems.

### The Doctrine of Discovery and the Acquisition of Indian Lands

European international law of the sixteenth century dictated that Native peoples were entitled to sovereignty and property rights, even though they were not Christian. Wars of conquest could be fought with the Indians only if the Indians refused Europeans the right to trade and to preach Christianity. Aside from a "just" war, Europeans were only allowed to acquire Natives' lands if the Indians agreed to sell it to them. A complementary "doctrine of discovery" gave the exclusive right of negotiating for the purchase of such land and of establishing settlements to the first European power claiming a particular territory. Until purchase or a "just" war of conquest occurred, the law acknowledged that the Indians retained a "right of occupancy" or "aboriginal title" to the land.

Although excuses for "just" wars were easy to concoct, European powers often purchased land from the Indians. They did so because the Indians were capable of waging prolonged, costly wars and often allied with competing European nations. In the English colonies, settlers intent on land speculation and easy wealth challenged the king's authority to control land purchases from the Indians. Claiming independent authority to deal with the Indians, they often used force and fraud to secure land, thereby complicating the process of land transfer and precipitating Indian wars. Conflict between colonists and the king over the management of Indian affairs contributed significantly to the colonists' desire for independence from England.

Once the colonists gained independence, individual states competed with the new national government for authority to deal with the Indians. Vague and confusing language in the Articles of Confederation (the constitution, later found to be inadequate and thus replaced in 1789 by the current Constitution, that the original thirteen colonies adopted in 1776) left it unclear where ultimate power lay. As a result, both states and the federal government entered into treaty negotiations with the Indians.

Eventually, the Constitution of 1789 clarified that the federal government had supreme authority over Indian affairs. In carrying out this power, the United States continued the European practice of purchasing lands from the Indians. It bought over 20 million square miles from the Indians during the late-eighteenth century and through much of the nineteenth century, largely through treaties negotiated with tribal groups. The coercive circumstances under which many of these treaties were negotiated raise troubling questions about the fairness and consensual nature of the transactions; yet no judicial or political body of that time was prepared to look beyond the high-minded legal talk of "consent."

### Treaty-Making between the United States and the Indians

Between the founding of the nation and 1871, when Congress banned further Indian treaties, the United States entered into hundreds of agreements, most of them embodying the following terms:

1. a cession (giving up) of Indian land, in exchange for a reservation or grant of land set aside for the Indians' permanent and exclusive use and occupancy;
2. acknowledgement that the tribe retains the right of self-government, but that the tribe has also come under the "protection" of the United States;
3. provision for water, hunting, fishing, and gathering rights for the Indians in lands set aside for

them, and sometimes hunting-and-fishing rights in ceded territory as well;
4. assertion of federal control over matters involving non-Indians in areas reserved for the Indians, including trade and crimes between Indians and non-Indians, with such control to supersede state authority; and
5. provision of needed supplies and services by the United States.

Congress eventually abandoned treaty-making with Indian tribes because the House of Representatives did not like the fact that it was excluded from the treaty-making process. Under the United States Constitution, treaties are signed by the president and ratified by a two-thirds vote of the Senate. After 1871 Congress dealt with Indian affairs through legislation, in which both houses of Congress participate. This change of method did not alter the legal status of Indian nations.

Some Indian tribes have never entered into treaties with the United States, either because the Senate refused to ratify treaties that were negotiated or because the tribes' first contact with the United States occurred late in the nineteenth century. Nevertheless, the terms of Indian treaties have served as the model for federal law applicable to all tribes, perhaps because the treaties represent a form of consent to limited tribal incorporation within the American political system. Absent such consent of the governed, American political theory views governmental power as unjust and illegitimate. The treaties are thus a means to justify the authority of the federal government over Indian lands and people.

### Indian Policy of the New American Government

The earliest Indian policy of the American government, embodied in legislation known as the Trade and Intercourse Acts (first adopted in 1790 and reenacted with amendments many times thereafter), sought to preserve peace between Indians and land-hungry settlers by ruling out most contact between the two groups. Among other things, the acts restricted non-Indian entry into Indian lands, regulated trade with the Indians, limited the introduction of alcoholic beverages into Indian Country, and punished interracial crimes involving Indians and non-Indians. One of the most important features of the Trade and Intercourse Acts was the prohibition on transfer of Indian lands without federal approval. Some states, notably New York and Georgia, resisted this policy, and continued to make their own Indian treaties. Land transfers resulting from these agreements have been the source of many modern Indian land claims cases, such as the successful suit

Cherokee delegation to Washington, D.C., in 1866. (Photo by Alexander Gardner. Courtesy of Archives and Manuscripts Division of the Oklahoma Historical Society)

brought by the Oneida of New York. In that litigation, the Oneida challenged treaties with the state of New York that date back to 1793, claiming that the transfer of land to the state was invalid because the federal government never gave its consent. The United States Supreme Court agreed, and found that the passage of time had not weakened the Oneida claims, in part because the state of New York and the United States had done their best to discourage and prevent claims in the past.

The federal policy of physically separating Indians and non-Indians, as embodied in the Trade and Intercourse Acts, began to weaken in the early decades of the nineteenth century, as settler pressure for westward expansion swelled. The crisis was most acute in the lands of the Cherokee, where gold was discovered in the late 1820s. In 1829 Georgia enacted laws purporting to extend its authority onto Cherokee lands and to abolish the Cherokee government. Throughout the 1820s the Cherokee adopted a constitution and tribal laws modeled on the U.S. system, and abolished traditional legal regimes such as the blood feud, which entailed retaliation for the death of a clan member by killing a member of the killer's clan. Treaties with the United States promised the Cherokee a permanent homeland and self-government on that part of their ancestral territory that was located in Georgia. Nevertheless, neither Congress nor the president was willing to challenge Georgia's actions on behalf of the Cherokee. Faced with the prospect of losing their rights, the Cherokee Nation sued in federal court. Chief Justice John Marshall issued decisions in two Cherokee cases (*Cherokee Nation v. Georgia* and *Worcester v. Georgia*) that acknowledged the sovereign powers of Indian tribes and the absence of state authority in areas set aside as tribal homelands. These opinions could not, however, protect the Cherokee against the rising tide of American settlers when the president of the United States and the Congress were unwilling to stand behind treaty promises.

Through a series of laws and coerced treaties in the 1830s to the 1850s, the federal government demanded the "removal" of the Cherokee as well as other eastern and midwestern tribal groups to an area west of the Mississippi River that was established for Indian settlement, known as Indian Territory. As a result, most of the Cherokee were forced to leave their ancient homelands to move to the Indian Territory. Thousands of Cherokee lost their lives in what has become known as the Trail of Tears. In many of these treaties, the United States promised the tribes that the land set aside for them in the Indian Territory would never become part of a state or territory without their consent, and would never be subject to state law. Several times during the first half of the nineteenth century, Congress actually came close to establishing the Indian Territory as an American state exclusively for Indian people, but the legislation never passed both houses of Congress, partly because some Indian groups opposed the idea. By the end of the nineteenth century, the government broke its promise to keep Indian Territory separate from the states when the Indian Territory was reorganized first as part of the Territory of Oklahoma and later as part of the state of Oklahoma. Some of the eastern Indians who hid or refused to move at the time of removal later had their remaining lands declared reservations; thus there are now federally recognized Cherokee and Choctaw tribes both in Oklahoma and on the East Coast.

## Tribal Governments Undermined by the Reservation System and Allotment

Through the second half of the nineteenth century, as pressure from non-Indians made even the existence of Indian Territory politically unfeasible, the federal government embarked on a policy of concentrating Indians on reservation lands where they could become "civilized" and assimilated. The Office of Indian Affairs was established to act as administrator of these new reservations; initially part of the War Department, the office came under the Department of the Interior after 1849.

In the course of administering reservation life, this Office of Indian Affairs came to dominate, weaken, and drive underground tribal government and legal systems. With tribal economies disrupted by the move to reservations, much of the Indian administration's power came from its control over the necessities of life, such as food and shelter. The Office of Indian Affairs established Courts of Indian Offenses and Indian Police, staffed with handpicked Indians, to replace traditional sources of law and authority. The judges and police thus enforced a Code of Indian Offenses, drafted by the Indian Affairs administrators, that prohibited many traditional cultural and religious practices, including the Ghost Dance (part of a largely religious movement), the destruction of an individual's personal property at death, Indian games of chance, and polygamy. Agents of the Office of Indian Affairs on each reservation (called superintendents) also designated tribal leaders who were willing to sign leases of tribal land and otherwise cooperate in pursuing the assimilationist goals of federal policy. Many traditional tribal functions, such as the allocation of land-use rights and the organization of agriculture, were taken over by the superintendents.

The weakening of tribal government and legal systems accelerated in the last decades of the nineteenth century, when Congress enacted laws requiring the allotment (division) of communally held lands on many reservations into individually owned parcels, thereby eliminating a defining element of tribal life. The parcels were to be held in trust (protected from being taxed or sold) by the federal government for a brief period of time, after which they were to be freely owned by the individual Indian. The stated federal purpose of imposing allotment was to transform Indians into individualist farmers. Allotment diminished tribal powers by withdrawing lands from tribal control and reducing the total acreage under Indian ownership. The federal government sold off "excess" lands that it did not deem necessary for allotment, and the parcels allocated to individual Indians often found their way into non-Indian hands, either through fraud or tax sales. Eighty-six million acres, over 60 percent of the Indians' land base, was lost during the allotment era (approximately 1886 to 1934). Another legacy of allotment is the fact that some modern reservations have large numbers of non-Indian residents, living on once-allotted land that they now own. These non-Indian residents often wish

Five Sauk and Fox and three Kansas flank the U.S. commissioner of Indian Affairs. (Courtesy of National Anthropological Archives, Smithsonian Institution)

to be free from tribal authority, even though they are living within the boundaries of an Indian reservation.

Congress formally abandoned the policy of allotment in 1934 and extended the trust period for existing allotments indefinitely. Thus, many previously established allotments remain held in trust by the federal government. Through inheritance, many of these allotments are now owned by hundreds of people, which makes it extremely difficult to use the allotments efficiently. Congress has attempted to find some way to return these allotments to tribal ownership. The United States Supreme Court has refused to allow such transfers, however, unless the United States or the tribes compensate all the allotment owners for their fractions of ownership rights.

Allotment laws frequently abrogated treaty promises to the Indians. But when tribes challenged these laws in the U.S. Supreme Court, they lost on the grounds that the United States was free to act as it thought was best for the Indians, even though that meant violating treaty promises. The U.S. Supreme Court has said that

Congress may abrogate Indian treaties just as it may abrogate treaties with foreign countries, even though Indian tribes are not in the same position as foreign countries. For example, Indian tribes are unable to appeal to international bodies or to military force if the United States unilaterally abandons a treaty promise. Nevertheless, there are some constraints on Congress when it contemplates violating an Indian treaty. If the treaty has created property rights (including rights to hunt and fish), the Supreme Court has said that Congress must compensate the tribe for any rights it loses when the treaty is abrogated. The Sioux claim against their loss of the Black Hills, part of their ancestral lands, is based on this principle. To the disappointment of many Sioux, however, this principle provides only monetary compensation, not a return of land. Some groups of Sioux have refused to accept the money, insisting that they are entitled to reclaim their ancestral lands in accordance with their treaty rights. Evolving international human-rights standards support return of land rather than compensation when indigenous peoples have been deprived of their lands.

### Tribal Legal Systems Continue to Function Today

Despite the often undermining influence of federal law, derivations of the earliest encountered Native American legal systems continue to function today in land set aside under federal protection for the residence of tribal Indians and in other areas collectively described as Indian Country. Indian legal regimes have been transformed after years of contact with non-Indian law and culture, so that the formal institutions more closely resemble U.S. courts, legislative bodies, and regulatory apparatus; the formal rules of everyday conduct, too, codified in ordinances, more closely parallel U.S. norms. On some reservations, for example, there are tribal environmental protection agencies that regulate pollution, and tribal taxing authorities that levy and collect taxes.

Much of this transformation of tribal governments has occurred as a result of the Indian Reorganization Act of 1934, a federal statute that offered tribes some freedom from federal bureaucratic control if they would organize themselves under constitutions modeled after the U.S. Constitution. The Indian Reorganization Act provided that tribal members could take a vote on whether to accept its terms, and about three-fourths of the tribes that held referenda agreed to develop tribal constitutions under the act. The federal rules setting forth who could vote and how many votes were needed to accept the act did not always produce results that reflected the general wishes of tribal communities. Specifically, anyone who failed to vote was counted as a yes vote, even though the traditions of many tribes dictate that opposition to a measure should be expressed by nonparticipation. Nonetheless, constitutions stimulated by the Indian Reorganization Act continue to prevail on many reservations. Some Indian nations, such as the Navajo, preferred to develop their governing systems independent of the act; since federal law does not require that Indian nations even have constitutions, tribes that operate outside the terms of the Indian Reorganization Act are at no formal disadvantage.

The protection of individual rights found in amendments to the U.S. Constitution do not apply to modern tribal governments, because those constitutional provisions control only activities of the federal government and of the states. However, a federal statute enacted in 1968, known as the Indian Civil Rights Act, limits the punishments that tribal courts may impose, and requires that tribal legal institutions comply with some, but not all of the provisions of the Bill of Rights in the U.S. Constitution. For example, the federal constitutional prohibition against the establishment of religion and the federal requirement that criminal defendants be provided with free counsel do not apply to Indian tribes through the Indian Civil Rights Act. The reason for these and other exceptions was Congress's desire to preserve distinctive features of tribal culture and to protect tribes against financially burdensome requirements that they could not reasonably fulfill. Furthermore, even when the Indian Civil Rights Act does incorporate provisions of the Bill of Rights, those requirements are interpreted, wherever possible, to accommodate the special features of tribal cultures. Thus, for example, the requirement of equal protection of the laws in the Indian Civil Rights Act uses the same language as a comparable requirement in the Fourteenth Amendment to the U.S. Constitution. Equality, however, does not necessarily mean the same thing for the tribes as its does for federal or state governments. One example of this is a tribe's decision over whether an Indian tribe may exclude non-Indians from juries or from voting in tribal elections or not.

Out of respect for tribal sovereignty, Congress generally provided that when an individual wants to challenge tribal actions as contrary to the terms of the Indian Civil Rights Act, she or he must do so in tribal court. There is no recourse to a federal court to enforce the Indian Civil Rights Act unless the individual is in a position to bring a petition for a writ of habeas corpus (a claim that she or he is being held in custody in violation of law). Normally this writ is only available to criminal defendants who have been convicted in tribal courts and who claim that their convictions were obtained without adherence to the Indian Civil Rights Act (for example, if evidence was improperly seized or if the criminal statute used as the basis for conviction violated the right to free speech).

Some tribes have protection for individual rights built into their own constitutions and fundamental laws. The Navajo, for example, have their own requirement that individuals be afforded due process of law if the government is acting to deprive them of life, liberty, or property. Thus, an individual who is unhappy with the actions of the tribal government can appeal to tribal law as well as to the Indian Civil Rights Act for redress. The Indian Civil Rights Act has been controversial among Indian people because it can be used to erode distinctive tribal cultures and legal systems, especially when those systems reflect values favoring informality, communal belonging and responsibility, and decision-making by consensus (universal agreement) rather than majority rule. As tribal governments have become more like the non-Indian U.S. government, however, it is possible that a corresponding need for the protection of individual rights has arisen.

Federal measures such as the Indian Reorganization Act and the Indian Civil Rights Act have put great pressure on tribal governments to conform to U.S. institutions. Nonetheless, tribal legal systems still have many distinctive features. First, informal traditional institutions and norms persist amidst the more formal legal systems. In some tribes, for example, religious leaders oversee dispute resolution despite the existence of tribal courts, and clan-based local groups control policy-making despite the existence of a centralized tribal council. Second, the values and principles that are reflected even in formal tribal law often differ from those embodied in U.S. law. Navajo inheritance law, for example, recognizes oral wills and prefers individuals who have cared for the deceased in his or her final years; U.S. law does not. Sometimes these specifically tribal rules of law are embodied in codes adopted by the Tribal Council (the legislative branch), and sometimes they are established by tribal judges through a process of common law (case-by-case) development. Tribes use different means of identifying and incorporating traditional legal norms. For example, some refer matters to a panel of elders, and others have the disputing parties bring forth expert witnesses, usually knowledgeable elders, to explain what tribal tradition prescribes in a particular case. Third, several Indian nations have established a dual court system, which includes both an Anglo-American-style adversarial process and a more traditional peacemaking process. The peacemaking process, which operates only if the parties so choose, takes a more holistic and future-oriented approach to resolving problems. The peacemaker is normally a respected community member who may know the individuals involved, and the participants in the process include family members and anyone else who may be affected by the problem. Everyone is heard until there is a solution that enables harmony and balance to be restored to the community. Some distinctive qualities of Indian justice, such as the emphasis on restitution to victims in criminal cases and special sensitivity to the interests of grandparents in child custody disputes, are finding a receptive audience among non-Indians today.

Thus, despite European and American claims to conquest and dominion over Indian lands and peoples, Native American law and government have not been extinguished. Tribal legal institutions perform important functions of defining tribal membership and office-holding requirements, regulating the use of tribal resources, establishing rules for everyday conduct, and resolving disputes. However, because of their different traditions and values, lack of resources, and straddling of American and Indian forms, tribal governments need not and do not always behave like their non-Indian counterparts.

## The Federal Government Often Supports Tribal Sovereignty and Law

Contemporary federal court decisions, statutes, and presidential statements often provide strong support for tribal self-government. According to U.S. judicial doctrine, for example, tribal legal regimes survive as manifestations of indigenous sovereign powers, rather than as creations of federal law. In keeping with this notion, the Bill of Rights of the Constitution does not apply to actions of tribal governments because the first ten amendments to the Constitution bind only the federal government and its agencies, not independent sovereigns such as Indian nations. Furthermore, a criminal defendant can be convicted for the same crime in federal and tribal court without being placed in double jeopardy, because the protection against double jeopardy in the U.S. Constitution does not apply to situations where a person is convicted for the same crime by two separate sovereigns. Indian nations are able to invoke the doctrine of sovereign immunity (protection against lawsuits) for their activities both on and off reservations, an indication of their distinct governmental status.

If Indian tribes are not federal agencies, however, neither are they mere voluntary associations, like private clubs, whose powers are limited to admitting and excluding members. Instead, they are governing bodies with the power to direct and coerce individuals engaged in activities within their territory, more like cities and states. The U.S. Supreme Court has affirmed, for example, that tribes may impose taxes on activities by Indians and non-Indians alike in Indian Country. The federal government has relied upon Indian nations, just as it has relied upon states, to establish and enforce environmental standards within their territory, so long as they meet minimum federal requirements.

Notwithstanding this recognition of Indian tribes as governments, the Supreme Court has also tried to place some limits on tribes' sovereign powers, particularly where non-Indians or Indians who are members of other tribes are involved. Claiming that the incorporation of tribes into the United States necessarily reduces the scope of tribal powers, the Supreme Court has stated that tribal sovereignty does not include the power to engage in foreign relations, to wage war, to alienate (transfer an ownership interest in) tribal land, or to impose criminal punishments on non-members of the tribe (*Oliphant v. Suquamish Tribe* ). The Court has also restricted the power of tribes to regulate the activities of non-members on land that is owned by non-members but is located within the reservation, at least if those activities have no substantial bearing on the health or well-being of tribal members (*Montana v.*

*United States*). These determinations by the Supreme Court are judge-made law, drawing on the history and practices of federal Indian law, but are not directly tied to language of the U.S. Constitution or specific federal statutes. Consequently, the Court ordinarily acknowledges in its decisions limiting tribal powers that Congress can reactivate those powers by enacting legislation that offers a contrary interpretation of the history and practice.

In order to make tribal sovereignty more meaningful, the U.S. Supreme Court has had to reject efforts by states and local governments to regulate activities in Indian Country. Like any other government, a tribe must be free to make choices about matters such as environmental quality, family life, and economic organization without outside interference. The Supreme Court has been emphatic that states lack authority over Indians on reservations, but it has been less clear about state authority over non-Indians. Particularly in situations where non-Indians engage in activity on non-Indian-owned land, the federal government has diminished tribal authority; where the tribe has not attempted to regulate the activity at issue, where tribal interests will not be seriously compromised, and where the activity jeopardizes off-reservation interests, the Supreme Court has been inclined to permit state power over non-Indians on reservations. For example, the Court has upheld state sales taxes on non-Indian purchasers of cigarettes that are sold by tribal smoke shops on reservations, even though tribal members who purchase the same cigarettes cannot be taxed by the state (*Washington v. Confederated Tribes of the Colville Reservation*). The Court has also affirmed state power to zone parts of reservations that are owned by non-Indians and that have been opened to the public (*Brendale v. Yakima Tribe*). In recent cases, the federal courts have determined that state highways within reservations and other rights-of-way provided for railroads and utilities should be treated the same as non-Indian-owned lands, precluding Indian nations from imposing utility taxes and remedying harm caused by dangerous driving or railway accidents. The Supreme Court has not, however, allowed states to tax non-Indians engaged in federally supported transactions with tribes, to regulate non-Indian hunting and fishing on tribal lands where the tribe has imposed its own regulations, or to regulate certain gambling on Indian lands, at least where the revenue from gambling funds important tribal functions, and where the state does not totally prohibit that type of gambling off the reservation.

By making the issue of tribal versus state authority on reservations turn, in part, on questions of who owns the land and who is being regulated, the Supreme Court has made it difficult to govern Indian Country. Many tribes complain that unless they have complete control over the territory of their reservations, they cannot effectively regulate air-and-water pollution, raise revenue through taxes, guide economic development, or provide for child welfare. Furthermore, uncertainty concerning which government has jurisdiction has led to costly litigation. Increasingly, states and tribes have found it in their mutual interest to negotiate and agree about the allocation of power to regulate reservation activities. Furthermore, because Congress has the power to override Supreme Court decisions determining state and tribal authority over Indians or non-Indians in Indian Country, states and tribes sometimes appeal to Congress to make an allocation. Congress took such action in 1988, when it enacted the Indian Gaming Regulatory Act. This statute established a complex scheme of tribal and state jurisdiction over different types of gambling on reservations.

In recent decades, Congress, like the Supreme Court, has often recognized and supported tribal sovereignty. Since the 1960s, self-determination for Indian tribes has been the official federal policy, reflected in numerous pieces of congressional legislation. In 1975, for example, Congress enacted the Indian Self-Determination and Education Assistance Act. This statute authorizes federal agencies providing services to Indians to contract with tribes so that the tribes can deliver the services themselves. The purpose of this statute was to liberate Indian tribes from some of the bureaucratic control exercised by the Bureau of Indian Affairs. Another Congressional affirmation of tribal sovereignty is the Indian Child Welfare Act of 1978. This statute requires that cases involving foster care and adoptive placement of Indian children be heard in tribal rather than state courts when the children are living or have their permanent home on a reservation. Even in some cases where the Indian children live off-reservation, the Indian Child Welfare Act requires that the cases be transferred from state to tribal court. This act affirms both the value of tribal courts and the importance to Indian tribes of controlling the fate of their children when those children must be separated from their parents. Support for tribal sovereignty is also apparent in various federal environmental laws, such as the Clean Air Act and the Clean Water Act, that accord tribes the same status as states in implementing their regulatory schemes. Finally, Congress reinforced tribal sovereignty in 1991 when it adopted a statute affirming tribal criminal jurisdiction over non-member Indians, overriding an earlier ruling to the contrary by the United States Supreme Court.

Statements of the president of the United States, particularly since the 1970s, have declared support for tribal sovereignty as well. The most memorable phrase from these presidential statements recognizes a "government-to-government" relationship between the United States and the Indian tribes. This language cautions the other branches of government that Indian tribes should be treated with the respect due other governmental entities.

## U.S. Government Retains Its Jurisdiction over Indian Tribes

The U.S. Congress asserts the right to define and limit—indeed to abolish—tribal law and government. It rests this power on Article I of the Constitution, which authorizes Congress to regulate commerce "with the Indian tribes," to enter into treaties, make war, and exercise power over federal lands. Congress and the Supreme Court sometimes justify federal power by invoking the existence of a federal guardianship toward the Indians, which resulted from the weakening of tribal governments by historic U.S. policy. Many Indian groups and modern legal scholars do not accept the federal government's understanding of the scope of Congressional power over Indian affairs. Adopting a narrow interpretation of the Indian Commerce Clause, they would limit that federal power to the regulation of trade and commerce between Indians and non-Indians, excluding all internal tribal matters. Whatever the source and scope of Congress's power, however, all agree that it excludes overlapping state authority in Indian Country. The Supreme Court has acknowledged state authority over Indian affairs only in isolated instances involving non-Indians and where the exercise of state power would not thwart tribal self-government.

Exercising its powers, Congress has enacted criminal laws that apply to Indian/non-Indian crimes and specified major crimes in Indian Country, has made certain state laws applicable in Indian Country in some states, has restricted the sale or lease of tribally owned lands, has regulated trading and the sale of liquor in Indian Country, has required that tribal governments afford individuals some of the civil rights enumerated in the Bill of Rights, and has even terminated the legal status of some tribes. Most of Congress's laws affecting Indians can be found in Title 25 of the United States Code, which compiles all Congressional enactments relating to Indians. These statutes indicate the range of Indian groups to which they apply by the way they define the term *tribe*. Some definitions—such as in the portion of the Non-Intercourse Act prohibiting transfers of Indian land without federal permission—are quite broad. Others are narrower, limiting the application of federal law to tribes that have been officially recognized by the Department of the Interior as generally entitled to federal benefits.

Because of its power of judicial review, the U.S. Supreme Court can set limits on Congressional power respecting tribal law and government. It has largely declined to do so. In the nineteenth century, the Court described congressional power as all-encompassing, or plenary, and dismissed challenges to particular federal actions as entailing political questions unsuitable for judicial resolution. On these bases, the Court rejected Indian suits protesting the forcible break-up of communal tribal lands in violation of specific treaty promises.

Modern Supreme Court doctrine acknowledges more room for judicial intervention. First, any federal action that might impair Indian rights must be interpreted in the manner most favorable to the Indians. This rule of statutory interpretation prevents Congress from diminishing Indian self-government or treaty rights unless it is quite explicit about its intent to do so. Thus, for example, certain federal criminal laws that prohibit the killing of wildlife are not applied to Indians with treaty rights to hunt those particular animals or to use them for ritual purposes, because the laws do not contain language that denies the Indians' rights. Second, federal law that operates to deny Indians their property must be accompanied by the payment of just compensation in accordance with the Fifth Amendment to the Constitution, at least if that property has been recognized by the federal government through treaty or statute. Third, congressional action regarding Indians and tribes can be challenged under the due process clause of the Fifth Amendment if it does not rationally further the federal government's fiduciary relationship (a relationship founded in trust) toward the Indians.

Although the Supreme Court has never actually used the trust responsibility language to reject an act of Congress, it has invoked the same principle to invalidate actions by federal administrative agencies that adversely affect Indian interests. If, for example, the federal agencies that must approve leases of Indian lands and minerals do not carefully oversee compliance with the lease provisions by the lessees, or the federal agencies responsible for investing Indian trust funds do not invest the funds prudently, Indian tribes may sue the federal government for breach of trust. Recent federal litigation has brought to light a long history of mismanagement of Indian trust funds by the federal government, especially those funds maintained for individual allotment holders whose property is held in trust by the federal government. The Bureau of Indian Affairs and the United States Treasury Department failed to maintain adequate records, lost records, failed to invest prudently, and deprived beneficiaries of interest payments to which they were entitled. Billions of dollars may be owed to the Indians for whom these trust accounts have been maintained.

## Indian Treaty and Property Rights Today

Under U.S. law, most Indian tribal title to real property (land and things more or less permanently attached to land) is beneficial; that is, the right to possession and use are subject to an underlying claim of the United States. The United States claims ownership as a trustee for the tribe, which means that the land may not be leased, mortgaged, or transferred without federal as well as tribal approval.

Indian tribes' beneficial title may be either *recognized* or *unrecognized*. The important distinction between these two types of Indian holdings becomes apparent when actions of the federal government attempt to deprive Indians of their lands. At various times in U.S. history, for example, the federal government has flooded ancestral Indian lands in connection with reclamation projects and has declared that Indian lands would become part of national forests. In cases where Indian title to the land is recognized, the Supreme Court has said that the tribe must receive just compensation for its loss under the terms of the Fifth Amendment to the U.S. Constitution. If the title is unrecognized, however, no compensation is constitutionally required, although the federal government has sometimes voluntarily undertaken to provide partial compensation. The Indian Claims Commission, first established in 1946, has been the primary vehicle for assessing and distributing such payments.

Indian title is deemed recognized if the land has been acknowledged in a treaty or acquired for tribal use under the terms of a federal statute. Such land need not have been the tribe's ancestral land. Ancestral lands that have never been confirmed or reserved by treaty or statute are held under unrecognized or aboriginal title. To preserve their rights to such land, Indians must occupy and use it continuously. Another type of Indian land held under unrecognized title is land that was set aside for Indian use by federal Executive Order rather than by treaty or statute.

Although tribes hold reservation property in common for their members, they typically also have their own system for allocating property rights in the communal holdings. These systems usually allocate rights to use property to individuals, families, or clans based on traditional occupation for household, grazing, or farming purposes.

Many Indian reservations were carved out of arid and inhospitable parts of the country. In establishing these reservations, the federal government reserved not only land, but also water associated with the land; the government reserved water to the extent necessary to fulfill the purposes of the reservation, which might include agriculture, livestock raising, domestic use, and fishing.

The existence of these federally reserved water rights has sparked conflict between Indians and non-Indians in parts of the country where water is scarce. Often Indian tribes lack sufficient funds to put their water to use for irrigation, industrial, or other purposes. However, according to the Supreme Court, these rights do not lapse because of nonuse. In arid parts of the United States, non-Indian water-users have tried to gain rights to the Indians' unused water by diverting it for their own purposes. These non-Indian water-users have followed state law that establishes rights to water based on priority of use. The Supreme Court has held, however, that such non-Indian use does not create water rights if a reservation was established before the non-Indians began using the water. Confronted with these decisions, Indians and non-Indians alike have seen the need to quantify the amount of water actually reserved for the Indians. Resolving this sort of dispute through litigation consumes enormous quantities of time and money. Such litigation normally takes place in state court as part of a comprehensive proceeding designed to establish the rights of all water-users, not just the Indians. Negotiations among the disputing parties are often a more attractive alternative, sometimes leading to agreements in which the Indians give up some potential water rights in exchange for funds that enable them to use the remaining water. Increasingly, Indian tribes are adopting water codes that set forth the rules and procedures for securing use of reserved Indian water rights.

Whether or not they contain express guarantees, treaties protect the Indians' right to hunt, fish, and gather on the reservation to the extent that such activities were practiced prior to contact. Some treaty rights also protect the right to carry on these activities off the reservation, sharing the resources with non-Indians. These protections encompass the right to modernize traditional practices with appropriate technology. For decades, non-Indians ignored these treaties, destroying Indian fisheries and taking animals reserved for the tribes. In modern times, it has taken litigation and agreements to protect Indian rights, often over the angry protest of non-Indian recreational hunters and fishers.

Today, tribes typically establish their own rules and licensing systems for hunting and fishing on their reservations, applicable to non-Indians and Indians alike. States sometimes attempt to regulate on-reservation hunting and fishing by non-Indians. The Supreme Court, however, has strictly limited state authority in this area, except in cases where non-Indians want to hunt and fish on reservation land owned by non-Indians.

What has made the issue of Indian hunting and fishing most controversial is the existence of certain treaties that establish Indian rights to hunt and fish off the reservation as well. The most contested language in these treaties promises that Indians may fish in specified off-reservation areas in common with all other citizens. Angry disputes have erupted between Indians and non-Indians as states have become concerned about the interests of recreational hunters and fishers, as well as about the preservation of certain species. In the state of Washington, where this conflict became most intense in the 1970s, courts eventually divided fishing rights equally among the tribes involved and all other fishers. While non-Indians initially bitterly resisted this arrangement, the state and the tribes eventually worked out a system of shared management of the fishery, which involved licensing their respective constituencies and species conservation and enhancement.

Indian tribes have recently beseeched the U.S. legal system to redress another painful loss: the taking of Indian skeletal remains, funeral objects, sacred objects, and objects central to tribal culture by non-Indian museums, scholars, and collectors. Through court cases and legislative lobbying, tribes have demanded the return of these items for reburial or other appropriate disposition, a process usually called *repatriation*. Some states have agreed to this process, and the federal government has passed legislation, entitled the Native American Graves and Repatriation Act of 1990, requiring all federally-funded museums to inventory and return the remains and objects in their possession, assuming they can determine the tribe with which these items are culturally affiliated.

## Indians' Rights under the U.S. Constitution

Tribal Indians were excluded from voting and taxation under the original terms of the U.S. Constitution. The new U.S. government viewed Indians as citizens of foreign sovereigns, not of the United States; in any event, the new government deemed Indians unsuitable for membership in a "civilized" nation. By the end of the nineteenth century, as treaty-making with Indian tribes ceased and the United States sought to assimilate Indian people through allotment and other means, non-Indian groups began to promote the idea of citizenship for Indians. Finally, in 1924, Congress enacted a law granting both state and federal citizenship to all Indians.

As citizens and as persons, Indians are entitled to the same rights under the U.S. Constitution as anyone else. These rights supplement the rights that Indians enjoy under federal statutes and treaties specifically directed at Indian tribes and people. The constitutional provisions that tribal Indians most frequently invoke are the right to free exercise of religion, found in the First Amendment, and the right to equal protection of the laws found in both the Fifth Amendment (where it applies to the federal government) and in the Fourteenth Amendment (where it applies to the states). Because Indian people most often need protection against measures that threaten their survival as a distinctive group, even these rights are not always helpful. The Bill of Rights tends to emphasize protecting the individual against the group, rather than protecting the group against extinction. Nonetheless, there are situations where the Constitution is the only recourse available to Indian people because treaty rights and tribal sovereignty do not apply as sources of protection.

The federal constitutional guarantee of freedom of religion becomes important for Indian people when they seek to practice traditional Indian religions outside Indian Country. For example, some ancestral Indian lands that are sacred to Indian religions are now federal property not located on any reservation due to historic treaty grants or federal seizure. Indians have claimed special rights of access to those lands in order to practice their religion. What is more, some traditional Indian religious practices, such as ingestion of the hallucinogenic drug peyote, are unlawful under the laws of certain states. Indians have claimed exemptions from those laws under the free exercise clause of the Constitution in order to practice their religion. Finally, Indians in non-Indian prisons have claimed that they are entitled to engage in traditional religious practices, such as maintaining their hair long and seeking purification in sweat lodges, the same way that Western religious practitioners are entitled to worship in prison chapels.

In 1988 and 1990 the U.S. Supreme Court decided two cases, *Lyng v. Northwest Indian Cemetery Association* and *Employment Division, Department of Human Resources of Oregon v. Smith*, that rejected Indians' claims of religious freedom. *Lyng* upheld the United States' right to build a logging road through a federally owned wilderness area that was the heart of the traditional religions of the Yurok, Karuk, and Tolowa Indians. Traditional practitioners believed that only by spending time at that site in total silence could they receive their spiritual power. Yet the Supreme Court decided that it would be too burdensome to make the United States reroute the road—even if rerouting the road would not be costly—despite the disastrous effect that disturbing the wilderness would have on the Indian religions.

In *Smith*, the Supreme Court allowed Oregon to enforce its drug laws against an Indian peyotist, even if it meant preventing the Indian from practicing his religion. For almost one thousand years, Indians in the southwestern United States have eaten the bitter, consciousness-altering plant called peyote as a part of prescribed rituals in order to achieve spiritual power, revelation of the supernatural world, personal redemption, and communal solidarity. Over the past one hundred years, Indians from many different tribes have adopted this religion. Most of these Indians belong to the Native American Church, which was formed in the early decades of the twentieth century to protect Indian peyotists from attacks by state, federal, and tribal governments. Departing from earlier decisions addressed to the free exercise of religion, the Court held that states need not have a compelling reason to prohibit activities essential to religious practice, such as the use of peyote. So long as the state prohibitions are established for purposes unrelated to religion, the fact that they have the incidental effect of preventing religious practice does not render them invalid.

These two Supreme Court decisions do not require the suppression of Indian religions, they merely permit it, at least insofar as the suppression occurs as a consequence of some independent government policy. If states and the federal government can be convinced to do so, they may structure their laws and policies to accommodate traditional Indian religious practices. A 1978 federal statute, the American Indian Religious Freedom Act, requires federal agencies to assess and minimize the effects that planning or regulating activities will have on Indian religion. However, that law does not enable Indians to sue when federal agencies disregard Indian religious practices and when agencies pursue their plans despite their adverse affect on Indian religion. On the other hand, Congress amended the American Indian Religious Freedom Act in 1994 to prohibit states and the federal government from banning Indian ceremonial use of peyote, thereby overturning the result in the *Smith* case. And a 1996 Presidential executive order directs all federal agencies to "accommodate access to and ceremonial use of Indian sacred sites by Indian religious practitioners" and to "avoid adversely affecting the physical integrity of such sacred sites," whenever legally allowable.

In cases where the federal government or the states single out Indian people for adverse treatment, individuals may find recourse through provisions in the Fifth and Fourteenth Amendments guaranteeing persons equal protection under the laws. Until quite recently, states regularly denied tribal Indians the right to vote, to run for public office, to serve on juries, or to receive government benefits such as welfare and education. To justify this discrimination, states argued that tribal property was exempt from state taxation, and tribal property was exempt from state taxation, and that Indians' loyalty to their tribes and special relationship to the federal government precluded state citizenship. Modern courts uniformly reject these arguments (noting, for example, that Indians pay many state taxes when they venture off their reservations), and insist that states treat their Indian citizens the same way they treat all others. Thus, for example, while tribes may provide separate schools for members living on the reservation, children of tribal Indians cannot be excluded from state-supported public schools.

Separate treatment of Indians and non-Indians by the federal government presents more complex issues than state discrimination. Because the Constitution authorizes Congress to legislate specially for Indians, and the federal government has a special trust responsibility toward Indian people, many federal benefits and restrictions are directed solely at Indians. The Supreme Court has upheld special treatment of Indians by the federal government, such as the provision pertaining to the Bureau of Indian Affairs for Indian preference in hiring and promotion (*Morton v. Mancari*). According to the Court, such distinctions are political rather than racial, and satisfy constitutional requirements of equal protection so long as they tend to further the federal government's trust responsibility to Indian people. Whether this line of decisions will survive current attacks on affirmative action is unknown.

## Special Issues in Alaska and Hawaii

When the United States purchased Alaska from the Russians in 1867, no treaties were made with the hundreds of groups of American Indians, Aleuts, and Inuits, and no means was provided for resolving Native land, hunting, or fishing claims. During the 1930s, Congress passed legislation inviting Alaska Natives to organize along the lines of the Indian Reorganization Act, and more than seventy-five groups did so. In addition, many reservations were created. Nonetheless, title to land remained uncertain; after Alaska achieved statehood in 1959, the state argued that Native villages did not qualify as federally recognized tribes. Discovery of large oil deposits in Alaska during the 1960s precipitated an urgent need to resolve Native land claims, resulting in the Alaska Native Claims Settlement Act of 1971 (ANCSA). Departing dramatically from conventional Indian policy, this act rejected a reservation system and put in its place a system of Native-run, state-organized, for-profit corporations that received Native lands and sums of money. For an initial period, the shares in these corporations were nontransferable and exempt from state and local taxes. But the villages were free to sell the land, develop it, or transfer it to the village itself.

Despite the boast of ANCSA supporters that the legislation liberated Natives from the heavy bureaucratic hand of the Bureau of Indian Affairs, the act soon drew widespread criticism from Natives themselves. Most troubling for them was the prospect of losing control of their land, their sources of subsistence from the land, and their sovereign powers to determine their own way of life. In 1987 Congress acted to extend indefinitely the restrictions against sale of shares in Native corporations. Furthermore, in 1994 Congress affirmed that Alaska Native villages are federally recognized tribes, just like those elsewhere within the United States. A serious question remained, however, about the territorial basis for Alaska Native governing powers. In the absence of formal reservations or lands held in trust for the benefit of the villages, the United States Supreme Court held that ANCSA had the effect of eliminating Indian Country. It will be difficult for Alaska Native villages to sustain their sovereign powers over many criminal and civil matters under these circumstances, although disputes over domestic relations and membership are likely to remain within tribal authority regardless of the existence of a reservation or comparable territorial base. Subsistence hunting and fishing are also matters of great concern to Alaska Natives in the wake of ANCSA, particularly regarding lands not owned by regional or village corporations. In the Alaska National Interest Lands Conservation Act, Congress sought to protect subsistence rights of Natives and rural residents to public lands in Alaska. Difficulty in securing appropriate cooperation from state government has hindered the implementation of this act.

Unlike Alaska Natives, Native Hawaiians were united under a single monarch in the period preceding European contact. American settlers to Hawaii in the nineteenth century eventually overthrew the monarchy and seized royal lands, ousting the Native people from their settlements. However, no reservations were established, and the Native Hawaiians have never been formally recognized as a tribe. On the one-hundred-year anniversary of the overthrow and seizure, President Clinton issued a formal apology to Native Hawaiians, but offered no specific plan for redress.

Over that one-hundred-year period, Congress had adopted some measures designed to ameliorate the conditions of Native Hawaiians. In 1920 the Hawaiian Homes Commission Act set aside some of the former royal lands for long-term, low-cost leases to Native Hawaiians. When Hawaii joined the Union as a state, it was required to incorporate the terms of this Act into its Constitution. Later, in the 1970s, Hawaii created the Office of Hawaiian Affairs, which was charged with administering funds and programs for the benefit of Native Hawaiians. Only Native Hawaiians were permitted to vote for the trustees of this office. In the 2000 case of *Rice v. Cayetano*, the United States Supreme Court held that this voting arrangement violated the Fifteenth Amendment to the United States Constitution, which prohibits restricting the right to vote based on race or ancestry. Hawaii had argued that the voting system was constitutional because it recognized a political group and its descendants, much as Congress has been allowed to enact special laws benefiting Indians. To support their argument, they pointed out that Congress has extended many benefits designed for Indian tribal members to Native Hawaiians. Non-Native Hawaiians, in response, argued that Native Hawaiians were not equivalent to mainland Indian groups, because they were not organized into federally recognized tribes. The Supreme Court avoided this question by emphasizing the special character of voting restrictions, and stressing that the election was being held by the state, not by an Indian nation. *Rice v. Cayetano* has stimulated even greater interest among Native Hawaiians in exploring options such as more complete self-determination and tribalization.

## International Law Addresses the Rights of Tribal Indians as Indigenous Peoples

Tribal groups have won important legal victories in the courts and in Congress over the past twenty-five years, in disputes over subjects as varied as water rights and the right to conduct bingo games on reservations. Nevertheless, because federal Indian law allows Congress almost complete, unrestrained discretion over Indian affairs and the Supreme Court has not been fully attuned to the requirements of tribal sovereignty, some Indian advocates have turned to the international arena in order to present their grievances over the taking of tribal lands, unfair mineral leases, and restrictions on tribal religious practices. Another reason they have turned to international law is because it offers the possibility of more secure grounding for Indian autonomy than do the discretion of Congress and the reasoning of the U.S. Supreme Court.

A growing body of international law is beginning to recognize that Native Americans are entitled to group rights such as cultural and religious preservation, economic self-determination, and internal self government. International organizations addressing these issues include the Working Group on Indigenous Populations of the United Nations Subcommission on the Prevention of Discrimination and Protection of Minorities, the International Labour Organization, and the Inter-American Commission on Human Rights of the Organization of American States. By the very process of drafting, circulating, and presenting statements of indigenous rights to be adopted by nations and international bodies, these organizations may shape worldwide opinion in favor of such rights.

The existence of culturally separate, semi-autonomous Indian groups operating under federal protection and receiving special federal benefits is anomalous in the United States, with its commitments to egalitarianism and the melting pot ideology. Indeed, contemporary non-Indian hunters and fishers have advocated repealing all Indian treaties on the grounds that the reservation system and its associated special Indian rights are discriminatory and segregationist. Modern justifications for continued federal protection of tribal law and sovereignty rest on the lack of Indian consent to U.S. government, the promises contained in a century of treaties, the inescapable link between tribal self-government and the preservation of Indian culture, and concern for the sensibilities of the international community. Modern support for tribal self-government is also fueled by a discomfort concerning the original rationalizations for U.S. dominion over Indian peoples. Although the early European explorers could neither understand nor appreciate tribal legal systems, contemporary federal Indian law leaves room for their survival and continued development.

*Carole Goldberg*
*University of California, Los Angeles*

## ♦ THE LEGAL SIGNIFICANCE OF U.S. INDIAN TREATIES

After visiting the United States nearly 150 years ago, the famous French political writer, Alexis de Tocqueville, observed that no other European nation had settled the New World with such "chaste affection for legal formalities." Where Spain had failed to conquer the Indians of Central and South America with war, cruelty, and slavery, Americans had succeeded in overcoming most Indian resistance "quietly, legally and philanthropically." "It is impossible," he concluded with a touch of irony, "to destroy men with more regard to the laws of humanity."[1]

Treaties are central to the paradox of U.S. Indian law. Settlers acquired most of the contiguous forty-eight states under treaties and agreements made with the original inhabitants. American Indians today regard their treaties as the foundation of their most precious rights. Yet the fact remains that few treaties were truly fair, and many were exacted from Indian nations at gunpoint. Although the federal courts have generally resolved any ambiguities in these treaties in Indians' favor, they have always upheld the authority of Congress to abolish, or abrogate, Indian treaties completely, subject to a requirement of compensation for eliminating treaty-based property rights. Indeed, the real significance of Indian treaties lies in their symbolism of Indian nationhood or tribal sovereignty, rather than in what they actually state. Additionally, the earliest treaties, negotiated more or less between equals, suggest the outlines of a truly consensual relationship among peoples, an essential requirement of governmental legitimacy under basic American political theory.

### The Origins of Treaty Law

The practice of making written treaties is at least as old as the Roman Empire. After conquering, or threatening to invade, Rome made treaties with surrounding kingdoms to bring them within the empire under Roman law through agreed-upon terms. Few territories outside of Italy and Spain were ever fully absorbed into Roman society. A far larger portion of the Empire consisted of tutelary nations, which enjoyed Roman protection and paid Roman taxes but lacked citizenship and retained their own rulers and local laws. Most of the traditional rules or maxims of international law relating to treaties are still expressed in Latin. The most basic principle was *pacta sunt servanda*, literally, "treaties are respected." Once made, a treaty was presumed to continue in force forever.

After the merger of the church with the Roman state, canon law, or law made by the Holy See (the Catholic pope), developed on Roman foundations. Like the Roman Empire, Catholic Europe had many separate nations, and local rulers were tied together by their respect for a single man (the emperor or pope) and a single system of basic laws. Relations among the Catholic princes were governed by treaties, and these treaties were enforced by the church. When treaties were broken, the Holy See could authorize a war, or excommunicate the offenders. Treaties among medieval Catholic princes were not then very much different from ordinary business contracts, since both could be enforced under laws shared by all Christian nations and peoples.

All of this changed in the fifteenth century due to events within and around Christian Europe. The Protestant Reformation brought Catholic unity and papal authority to a bloody end. New nations were born and demanded complete independence from the Holy See. Constantinople fell and the Balkans were occupied by the Ottoman Empire, forcing Christian nations to abandon their dream of "liberating" the East. The rise of

Muslim power in the Mediterranean, together with Europeans' discovery of the indigenous peoples of the Americas, meant that European princes had to find ways of conducting diplomacy and making treaties with non-Christian governments. Relations among Europeans, and the growing web of relationships between Europeans and other peoples could no longer be governed by shared religious and legal traditions.

By the end of the seventeenth century, European legal scholars had begun devising a new system of rules regarding diplomacy, war, and treaties, based on early Roman principles and the evolving practices of European nations. This new international legal order accepted the independence and equality of sovereign states, and relied upon reason rather than the existence of an emperor or a shared religion, to enforce treaties. Scholars argued that it was in all nations' self-interest to agree on standardized rules of behavior, and to honor their treaty obligations to one another. While this thus termed Law of Nations began in Europe and reflected European thinking, European colonialism brought it to every other part of the world. Since European powers dominated both the League of Nations and, until the 1960s, the United Nations, the Law of Nations has become the basis for all modern international law.

When Europeans began their exploration and colonization of North America in the 1600s, international law was no longer based upon Christian morality or imperial power, but on the principle of contract. All nations were presumed to be legally equal, with equal capacity to enter into treaties with one another. As equals, moreover, sovereign nations were only legally bound by their own agreements, and treaties were to be interpreted and applied solely according to the intentions of the parties. No nation had the right to impose its will on others. Needless to say, this idealized world existed only in the minds of European legal scholars. In reality, then as now, nations differed enormously in their military and economic power. Powerful states were generally able to win concessions from weaker ones, whether by war or by treaty. Treaty-making made nations equal in law, but not in fact.

## European Law and Indian Law

Long before the Europeans arrived, indigenous North Americans had their own ways of making treaties among themselves. Some features of indigenous diplomacy were shared by all tribes, although there were many local variations. Treaty-making generally involved exchanges of symbolic gifts, which were meant to remind the parties about their agreement. Furs and wampum were often used for this purpose in the Eastern Woodlands, and special designs in Algonkian and Iroquoian wampum belts evolved specific meanings, like the written words in a European treaty. Exchanges of gifts went along with the exchange of promises, usually marked by a religious ceremony designed to impress upon all the participants the seriousness of their undertakings. The calumet or pipe ceremony among the tribes of the Ohio and Missouri rivers is a familiar example. The great feasts, or potlatches, of the Pacific Northwest also served to ratify treaties among the chiefs of different clans, villages, and nations. Ceremonial formalities were also part of European diplomacy.

Unlike Europeans, however, indigenous Americans did not generally fill their treaties with military and commercial details and did not use them to buy and sell land. Tribal treaties created family relationships or kinship. Tribes agreed to treat each other as if they were members of the same family: as brothers and sisters, parents and children, and cousins. In this way, the specific responsibilities of each tribe were clear to everyone, without having to be spelled out. Family relationships were shared and understood by all indigenous cultures. Moreover, relationships under treaties, like ordinary family relationships, were the responsibility of every individual, not only of tribal leaders. If two tribes agreed to an uncle-nephew relationship, every member of one tribe was obliged to act as an uncle to every member of the other. Thus indigenous diplomacy joined peoples, rather than governments.

Although tribal treaties concerned kinship rather than business matters, they sometimes had considerable economic value. While land could not be sold, it could be shared with relatives. Joining together as a treaty family allowed tribes to share resources. Allied tribes on the Great Plains freely crisscrossed one another's territories in pursuit of game, often camping and hunting together in the summer. In the Pacific Northwest, related tribes fished together, and formed huge trade networks extending from Alaska to California. Among the Eastern Woodlands peoples there were many regional confederacies, such as the Wabanaki of Maine and Atlantic Canada, and the Chippewa of Lake Superior. Each nation or tribe within a confederacy kept its own distinct territory and government, while sharing some of its hunting and fishing with the others.

Indigenous nations met frequently to retell the history and meaning of their treaties, to resolve disputes, and to reaffirm their past commitments. For indigenous Americans, then, a treaty was not a single document but a continuing, living relationship, which was explained, renewed, and strengthened over the years through periodic meetings and reconciliations. The treaty itself was a simple idea, which could be summarized in a single symbol or word, while its full meaning could evolve and change from generation to generation.

## Treaties and European Colonization

Four European colonial powers were competing for mastery of North America in the seventeenth and eighteenth centuries: Britain, France, Spain, and the Netherlands. Diplomacy with indigenous nations was more practical and profitable than war. European settlers were vastly outnumbered, their towns and forts did not extend far inland, and it was costly to ship large armies across the Atlantic Ocean. Great tribal confederacies controlled the Great Lakes, the Ohio Valley, and the Mississippi River. Any attempt to dislodge them would have been a military expense, and other European states threatened to intervene. As long as there was a balance of power among rival European empires, and tribal confederacies held a numerical and strategic advantage, it made more sense for Europeans to establish their territorial claims by making alliances with the tribes than to do so by conquest.

The idea of making treaties with Indian tribes dates to the sixteenth century. The theologian Francisco de Vitoria helped convince the King of Spain that the governments and rulers of the Indians, although they were not Christian, were entitled to respect. Like other nations, the Indians were the true owners of their lands, and could only be removed by their agreement, or as the result of a "just" war. Colonial authorities in Mexico received instructions to this effect, but to little avail. Spain already enjoyed complete military control of central Mexico, had little interest in the northern deserts and plains (which would become part of the United States three centuries later), and as yet had no military rivals, either European or Indian, for control of Florida or California. Diplomacy was considered unnecessary.

This situation had changed completely by the 1620s, after France had established trading posts on the St. Lawrence and Mississippi rivers, and Britain and the Netherlands had begun to colonize the Atlantic seaboard. The great tribal confederacies mobilized to prevent further European encroachments, while European colonies began to threaten each other. European nations tried to minimize conflicts among themselves by agreeing that the first to discover a new territory would have the exclusive right to make treaties with the Indians. This became known as the Doctrine of Preemption. In practice, however, it was difficult to prove who had first discovered a particular part of the continent. Instead, Europeans relied on their treaties to prove their priority in time and rights. This led to a race to contact tribes in order to establish diplomatic relations with them.

European rivalries gradually evolved into a system of spheres of influence. Each European nation tried to build a competing network of indigenous allies surrounding its own colonies. France was concerned, above all, with the fur trade, and quickly secured alliances with the tribes of Acadia (Nova Scotia), the Great Lakes, and the Mississippi River. Britain's colonies were farther south in agricultural areas, along the Atlantic seaboard where there were many small populous farming tribes. Even Spain began to make treaties with tribes along the Gulf Coast, to block the expansion of British and French colonies. French treaties focused on the right to travel and trade freely in Indian Territory. Dutch and British treaties included purchases of land for colonists and agreements to settle disputes according to European laws.

France was far more successful, at first, in expanding its sphere of influence westward. Indian tribes valued French trade and did not believe that France wanted their land. Over the years, peaceful trade also facilitated intermarriage and tribes' adoption of Catholicism, so that ties of blood and shared religion strengthened the French cause. However, the key to the balance of power in North America was to be found in the great tribal confederacies, especially the Haudenosaunee (Iroquois), which was careful to make treaties with all the rival European powers, favoring none. Their neutrality provided a temporary barrier between the British and French colonies. Britain resolved completely to remove France from the continent, however, and succeeded in 1759 after sixty years of intermittent fighting. These so-called French and Indian Wars were wars between the French and British alliances, with tribal allies fighting on both sides.

Following the final French defeat at Montreal, Britain made peace treaties with the former tribal allies of France, and consolidated its own alliance system into a single "great covenant chain." Sir William Johnson, British superintendent of Indian affairs, was a great admirer of the Haudenosaunee, involving them as go-betweens in expanding the British alliance system. Johnson adopted Haudenosaunee forms of diplomacy, exchanging medals and wampum with the Indians, who came to regard the British King as the "father" of the allied tribes. Treaties were renewed every few years, in accordance with Indian practices. By the 1770s Johnson had succeeded in linking nearly half the continent under British rule, as British subjects, but with their own autonomous tribal governments. There was one fundamental problem, however. The alliance depended on preventing any further settlements on tribal lands. As provided by a Proclamation of King George III in 1763, no lands were to be obtained from these "connected and protected" tribes except with their consent through treaty. British Americans did not accept this restriction on their westward expansion, and it was one of the grievances against the king they listed in the Declaration of Independence.

The Revolutionary War split the British covenant chain in half. Indian tribes fought on both sides of the conflict, and some, like the Haudenosaunee, suffered bitter internal division between pro-American and pro-British parties. For nearly a year preceding the Declaration of Independence, American agents arranged meetings with tribal leaders hoping to win them over to the Revolutionary cause. At first, most tribes shared the view that the war was no business of theirs, and tried to remain neutral. Britain reminded tribes that they had signed treaties of alliance, and were obliged to protect the Crown. American forces attacked the tribes they believed to be pro-British. Neutrality was soon impossible.

Although the North American treaty alliance system collapsed with the outbreak of war between Britain and America, Britain continued its policy of indigenous diplomacy in Canada, the Indian subcontinent, and Africa. Most of India was colonized under treaties with Native rulers that placed them under British protection, and brought them within the British legal system without completely abolishing their local institutions and laws. Having acquired Zimbabwe and Tanzania by treaty, Britain had a firm basis to challenge French and German claims to these territories. In Afghanistan, Britain maintained close diplomatic ties with tribal leaders, blocking Russian claims. As the global system of European colonialism expanded in the nineteenth century, indigenous treaties were often the basis on which European rivalries were settled, and on which European powers relied to recruit local armies.

European nations usually respected these treaties only as long as their colonies were small and weak, or as long as they needed them to prove their territorial claims. In the 1850s, for example, Britain began to seize control of much of southern India, in violation of its local treaties, which British courts claimed to have no power to enforce. In Zimbabwe, British officials divided and sold tribal lands, successfully arguing that British law automatically replaces indigenous laws in the British colonies. The legal significance of treaties in Britain's African and Asian colonies is no longer an issue, of course, because they have all reestablished themselves as independent countries. It continues to be an issue, however, in the United States, Canada, and New Zealand, where, since colonists have become a numerical and political majority, the surviving indigenous nations use treaties to assert their distinct identity.

## Periods of Federal Treaty-Making (1776–1871)

From 1776 to 1871, the United States made more than four hundred treaties with Indian tribes, and nearly all of them were ratified by the Senate in the same manner as treaties with foreign nations. American expansion encountered varying levels of resistance, from guerrilla warfare in the swamps of Florida to great cavalry battles on the Plains in the 1860s. In some instances, the government simply used treaties to create the appearance of legality for what was actually a confiscation of land at gunpoint. In other parts of the country, treaties were part of a long process of diplomacy, accommodation, and confrontation that lasted for decades and left the tribes in possession of much of their land and dignity. Some treaties were very strong, others weak, and each must be understood in the context of the time and circumstances in which it was made.

Until the 1820s, the United States was preoccupied with securing its borders with Indian tribes. This was not motivated by Christian morality as much as by the need to legitimize the new American state in the eyes of European powers; to establish superior American claims to the Great Lakes, the Mississippi valley, and Florida, which were also claimed by Britain, France, and Spain; and to create peaceful conditions for the development of its existing settlements still east of the Appalachian mountains.

During the Revolutionary War, the new American government negotiated treaties of alliance with the Wabanaki Confederacy and with the tribes of the Ohio River valley. Once peace had been restored by the Treaty of Paris in 1783, American diplomats entered into alliances with the Haudenosaunee and with the southern confederacy of Cherokee, Creek, Choctaw, and Chickasaw, hoping to secure a safe, pro-American frontier. In the treaties of this period, tribes simply accepted United States "protection" and authority to regulate Indian trade. In other words, they agreed to be included in a new American sphere of influence. Apart from trade issues, however, they gave up none of their right to self-government, as the U.S. Supreme Court concluded in its famous 1832 decision *Worcester v. Georgia.*

The Haudenosaunee and Ohio valley nations also continued to renew their treaties with Britain, however. As far as they were concerned, everything west of the Appalachians was still Indian Country; the United States-Canadian border did not extend into that region. American settlements west of the Appalachians led to a great uprising under Tecumseh, which coincided with the War of 1812. Once again, tribes fought on both sides, and their future was a major issue at the peace negotiations. The Treaty of Ghent (1814) made it clear that the United States-Canadian border did indeed divide Indian Country, and that only the United States could make treaties with the tribes south of that line.

The Treaty of Ghent secured the northern border of the United States, while the United States purchase of Florida and Louisiana eliminated competition for tribal alliances with France and Spain as far west as the Mississippi. American diplomacy shifted from securing peace to acquiring lands for settlement, chiefly from tribes already under U.S. protection, between the Appalachian crest and the Mississippi. At first, tribes attempted to keep some of their main villages and farmland, selling only small parcels on the fringes of their territories. Beginning in the 1830s, however, the United States aimed for their complete "removal." To acquire lands for the relocation of eastern nations such as the Cherokee and Delaware, the United States made treaties with tribes west of the Mississippi, such as the Osage and Comanche. Treaties with the eastern tribes worked out the details of their move, which included the sale of their homelands to help pay for expenses, and for the development of new schools, farms, and roads in the West. Needless to say, many eastern tribes resisted, and those who left their homes did so only to avoid war.

American leaders still believed that the Plains were economically worthless, and did not hesitate to promise the removed tribes that they would enjoy security and self-government in their new western homes forever. The United States even pledged that this Indian Territory would remain exclusively Indian and would never be included within any state. At the same time, these removal treaties involved the United States more directly in internal tribal affairs than ever before. After arranging for the sale of the tribes' homelands, federal officials spent the proceeds on education, health, and social programs, as specified by each treaty. The federal government became a banker for removed tribes under these treaties. In legal terms, it became a trustee, managing tribal funds and property.

By the 1840s, American settlements had begun on the Pacific Coast and on the edges of the Great Plains. Mexico had won its independence from Spain, and was viewed as the main obstacle to American expansion. In the Mexican War, the United States seized all Mexican territory north of the Rio Grande, and quickly made treaties with the largest nomadic Indian tribes of the

Southwest—the Navajo, Apache, and Ute[2]—to secure the new international border. In the ten years following the Mexican War, the United States made treaties for the first time with the tribes of the West Coast, from California to Washington, although the Senate never ratified California treaties and some Oregon treaties. The Puget Sound (Washington State) treaties were particularly important for U.S. policy, because they helped settle the western border between the United States and British North America (Canada), a border so hotly disputed that it almost led to a third British-American war in 1854. Small and chiefly dependent on fishing, West Coast tribes generally agreed to cede most of their lands in exchange for the protection of their fishing rights.

Indian treaties made after the Mexican War contained some crucial new provisions reflecting the growing military power and expansionism of Euro-Americans. Instead of merely accepting U.S. "protection," the Southwest and West Coast tribes agreed to submit to federal laws or regulations concerning Indians. Never before had the United States tried to extend its legislative power to Indians inside Indian Territory. In a growing number of treaties in the 1850s, moreover, some tribes agreed that the president could take land for roads and railroads, and divide the remaining Indian land into individual family farms called allotments. Any land left over was to be sold to pay for farming equipment, schools, and hospitals, which would be managed by the Office of Indian Affairs.

Some tribal leaders believed that individualizing land ownership would give Indians stronger legal rights to keep their lands. Others simply felt they had no choice but to accept these new conditions. Allotment was carried out chiefly in Iowa, Kansas, Nebraska, and other valuable farming areas on the fringes of the Great Plains, where settlers created the greatest pressure. Most tribes of the desert and West Coast were not allotted, although their treaties authorized allotment. These tribes had little good farmland, and settlers in their regions were more interested in mining, logging, and fishing.

By 1860, then, the United States employed treaties to establish total social programs under federal administration, which were aimed at "civilizing" Indians and assimilating them into the general population. Tribal territories became reservations, and tribal laws were subject to federal laws. But these treaty provisions did not apply everywhere. An exception to this trend was Indian Territory (Oklahoma), where removal treaties expressly guaranteed the right of tribes to complete self-government. These tribes observed the changes surrounding them—particularly the growing tide of settlers in Texas, Colorado, and New Mexico—with

Treaty signing by William T. Sherman and the Sioux at Fort Laramie, Wyoming, 1868. (Photo by Alexander Gardner. Courtesy of National Archives)

alarm. When the first shots of the Civil War were fired at Fort Sumter, most tribes in Indian Territory shifted their allegiances to the South. Treaties with the Confederated States of America, concluded in 1861, guaranteed the permanent independence of the Indian nations were the South to win the war. As in the Revolution and the War of 1812, Indian tribes fought on both sides to fulfill their treaty obligations.

As a result of the Union's victory in 1865, Oklahoma tribes, like the South itself, were forced to sign surrenders and to undergo federally supervised Reconstruction of their economies and political systems. Former slaves became tribal members under many of these treaties, and had the right to take shares of tribal lands and funds. On the whole, the United States renewed its old treaty commitments to tribal self-government in Indian Territory, but subjected the tribal councils to special federal governors or Indian agents, or to a federal veto over their laws. This made tribes such as the Cherokee and Chickasaw more like present-day Puerto Rico or the Virgin Islands: partly self-governing, but still within the U.S. political system.

The Sioux of Minnesota and Dakota, together with allied tribes as far south as Colorado, also launched an offensive against encroaching settlements in 1864 and 1865. Although the Minnesota Sioux fared badly, and their leaders were hanged by President Abraham Lincoln, the Plains War continued until 1868. Anxious to acquire additional lands on the Plains for the resettlement of Civil War veterans and for the post-war flood of European immigrants, the United States made more treaties and purchased more Indian land in the period between 1865 and 1868 than it previously had during any comparable period. At the same time, U.S. negotiators were forced to give the main Plains tribes stronger assurances of the finality and permanence of their new reservation borders. In particular, the United States agreed that no more Indian land could be sold or opened for settlement, except with the approval of three-fourths of the adult men of the tribe. Tribal leaders hoped this would prevent the United States from trying to make future treaties with a handful of friendly individuals who did not represent the whole tribe.

Charles A. Bates, allotment officer on the Pine Ridge Reservation, with American Horse and an interpreter, 1907. On many reservations, allotment violated treaty provisions made a generation earlier. (Courtesy of the Denver Public Library, Western History Collection)

At the end of the treaty era, Indian tribes still controlled one-tenth of the contiguous forty-eight states, or about one-fourth of the land between the Mississippi River and the Rocky Mountains. Immigration from Europe accelerated, however, reaching its peak in the 1880s. Indian Territory, and the large Plains reservations, posed barriers to further settlement, but were protected by strong treaties under which the United States had promised to provide the tribes with substantial financial aid for their development. Further allotment was impossible under the final round of Plains treaties, and tribes were unwilling to part with any more of their reservations. Concerned by the increasing costs and difficulties of negotiating for more Indian land, Congress ordered the president to stop making Indian treaties in 1871.

This did not stop the president from making agreements with the tribes for their land, usually at the request of Congress. Agreements made after 1871 were essentially the same as treaties, except they did not imply that Indian tribes were independent nations.

Often, they were made with tribal leaders chosen by the United States, in violation of the tribes' own political processes, or in violation of the tribes' earlier treaties. The 1874 agreement for the purchase of the gold-rich Black Hills of South Dakota is a typical example. The 1874 agreement was negotiated with a few individual Sioux, although the 1868 Sioux treaty required the approval of three-fourths of the men of the tribe. Congress then passed a law ruling that the agreement overrode the treaty. The Sioux went to war over this—the war in which Custer fell—but the United States had the military power to wear down Sioux resistance and hold onto the Black Hills.

At the same time, the United States began to build railways through tribal lands in violation of treaties, and to establish federally controlled Indian courts and police on the reservations in order to enforce federal laws. Many of these laws were designed to destroy Indian culture rather than to protect Indians from settlers; one such example is a provision prohibiting any kind of traditional religious ceremonies. In 1887

Congress passed the General Allotment Act, which authorized allotments and the sale of "surplus" lands on those reservations where the tribes had not already agreed to this by treaty. A separate law, the Curtis Act, provided for the allotment of Indian Territory as well. The Oklahoma tribes vigorously opposed this as a violation of their treaties, and they brought their objections to the United States Supreme Court. In two crucial decisions, *Cherokee Nation v. Hitchcock* (1902) and *Lone Wolf v. Hitchcock* (1903), the Supreme Court held that Congress has the power to modify or terminate Indian treaties without the Indians' consent.

These decisions opened the way for Congress to treat all Indians the same, regardless of the treaties they had signed. Throughout the nineteenth century, Congress appropriated funds for Indian schools, hospitals, and other programs treaty-by-treaty. Treaties determined how much federal aid each tribe received and how it was used. In 1921 the Snyder Act abolished this practice. All services and programs were combined into a single annual appropriation, broken down by objects (such as health care) rather than by treaties. As a result, Indian tribes with weak treaties got more than they had bargained for, and tribes with strong treaties got less. More importantly, tribes could no longer use their treaties to demand any services at all. The Snyder Act and subsequent federal laws left Indian social programs to the discretion of Congress. After purchasing most of the country by treaty, the United States was no longer willing to pay the agreed price.

In the final days of World War II, in fact, Congress decided that it was time to wind up the Indian business. Many believed that Indians stayed on reservations only because they expected to be repaid someday for all of their broken treaties. This led Congress to establish the Indian Claims Commission in 1946, and to charge it with resolving claims of treaty violations as well as tribes' loss of aboriginal lands regardless of treaty guarantees. Although the commission was supposed to complete its work in ten years, it was still not finished when Congress decided to reassign its cases to the U.S. Court of Claims in 1978. The commission was not given the power to enforce Indian treaties, only to decide how much compensation each tribe should receive for broken promises. The commission adopted a general rule of taking the value of the land or money promised to tribes a century ago, and adding interest. For example, if the United States had promised to set aside a reservation in 1868, and the land could have been sold for $1,000 in 1868, the tribe was awarded $1,000, plus interest equivalent to 1868 rates. Land values were artificially low in the nineteenth century, however, since Indian tribes were being forced to give up so much of it, creating a temporary market surplus. Thus

tracts worth billions today, like the Black Hills, were valued at 1 percent of their current price; with interest, this figure increased to about 10 percent. If tribal land had been taken without a treaty, moreover, the commission did not add the interest. Furthermore, the commission was authorized to subtract from each award the value of goods and rations that had been gratuitously supplied to that tribe.

Congress viewed the Indian Claims Commission process as a means of closing the books on tribal claims, in anticipation of complete assimilation of tribal members. To resist that process, and to uphold the sacred significance of treaty lands, some tribes, especially among the Sioux, have refused to accept awards under the act. They have persisted in claiming that the only proper resolution of their claims of treaty violations is the return of their lands.

Echoing the message of the Indian Claims Commission, Congress initiated a policy of tribal termination during the 1950s. In House Concurrent Resolution 108 (1953), Congress declared its goal of terminating federal responsibilities for Indians as quickly as possible and of making Indians ordinary citizens of the United States. This termination program was very selective, targeting tribes that were relatively prosperous and well-educated, such as the Menominee of Wisconsin and Klamath of Oregon, and some that were small and less well-organized, such as the Rancherias of northern California. Congress assumed that termination not only ended tribes' eligibility for special Indian social programs, but also abolished (or abrogated) their treaties. A 1968 Supreme Court decision involving the Menominee disagreed. Indian treaties continue in effect unless expressly abrogated by Congress, the Court explained. Since Congress had not specifically mentioned the Menominee treaty in its legislation terminating the tribe, Menominee treaty rights, such as hunting-and-fishing rights, could still be exercised by the members of the tribe. This decision paved the way for federal court decisions in the 1970s, reaffirming Indian treaty rights that both Congress and the United States had believed to be extinct.

The decade from 1968 to 1978 was critical for the development of Indian treaty law. President Richard Nixon declared an end to the termination policy of House Concurrent Resolution 108, and made a clear commitment to restoring and strengthening tribal self government. Federal courts in Oregon and Washington handed Northwest tribes stunning victories in treaty fishing-rights disputes. Despite years of violence and efforts to overturn these decisions legislatively, both the Supreme Court and Congress eventually upheld them. On the other hand, in 1978 the Bureau of Indian Affairs adopted rules for deciding which tribes are "recognized as eligible to receive federal services," and treaties were not mentioned as having any role in these decisions.[3] The decade ended as it began, with a surprise decision by the Supreme Court. In *Oliphant v. Suquamish Indian Tribe*, the Court held that tribal rights may be lost by implication, even rights that were never given up by treaty or taken away by Congress.

As the 1970s ended, then, there were signs of greater respect for Indian treaty rights, although Congress, the president, and the courts reserved their power to disregard treaties. The fishing-rights cases had demonstrated that at least some provisions in treaties could still have considerable economic significance. At the same time, the major Indian policy issues of the 1970s and 1980s—education, health, better resource management, and stronger tribal governments—were being addressed through a growing number of federal aid programs, rather than through the enforcement of treaties.

## Contemporary Legal Status of Treaties

The legal status of Indian treaties has changed many times in the course of United States history, and may change again. Supreme Court decisions in the 1970s, 1980s, and 1990s agreed on some basic rules, however, which will form the basis for the further development of Indian treaty law in the twenty-first century. All these rules reflect two fundamental related principles: the plenary power of Congress over Indian affairs under Article I of the Constitution, and federal trust responsibility for the Indian tribes that have been taken under its protection.

Article I, section 8 of the Constitution provides that Congress alone has authority to "regulate trade with the Indian tribes." Since the 1830s, the Supreme Court has interpreted the word *trade* broadly to include all the aspects of federal-tribal relations that have evolved since the Constitution was first adopted in 1789. Originally, this simply meant that states could not question federal Indian laws, policy, or treaties. By the 1890s, the Supreme Court was arguing that Indian tribes themselves could not challenge federal Indian policy, even when it involved modifying or ignoring their treaties. There are at least some limitations on what Congress can do, however, according to cases decided by the Supreme Court between 1974 and 1980. Congress cannot, in its exercise of plenary power over Indian tribes, violate the Bill of Rights, and it cannot take away Indians' property without paying just compensation under the Fifth Amendment.

In the context of Indian treaties, this means that while Congress has the constitutional power to modify or abrogate an Indian treaty, it must pay for any property that is lost by the tribe as a result of this action. Moreover, only Congress can modify an Indian treaty; states cannot. The states must respect Indian treaty rights unless and until Congress says otherwise.

The second fundamental principle of federal Indian law is related closely to the first. Trust responsibility means that Congress and the president, in exercising plenary power, must always consider the best interests of the Indians. At first, this concept had no real legal force. In the 1930s, however, the Supreme Court began ordering the government to pay compensation to tribes for mismanaging their natural resources and financial investments. Although federal officials continue to enjoy a great deal of discretion in handling Indian property, they can be taken to court for the worst cases of mismanagement and waste, such as cutting down forests without replanting, or leasing range land below its market value. The Supreme Court has also applied the trust responsibility principle to the way it interprets federal laws. Since Congress is presumed to be acting in the best interest of the tribes, any doubt as to the meaning of an act of Congress that affects Indian rights is resolved in favor of the Indians. In several cases decided in the 1970s, for instance, it was unclear whether Congress, in allowing non-Indians to settle on certain Indian reservations nearly a century ago, intended to abolish those reservations. Since the legislation was unclear, the Supreme Court held that Congress had not intended to abolish those reservations.

This principle has a very special application to Indian treaties. Indian treaties must be interpreted liberally in favor of the tribes and in the manner in which the tribes themselves would have understood them. Any evidence indicating how the tribes interpreted the agreement governs how the treaty is to be interpreted today. If the intentions of the United States and the tribes can no longer be determined, the courts must give the tribes the benefit of the doubt. While the courts cannot ignore what is written down, they are supposed to interpret what is there from the Indian viewpoint. This leaves room to improve on treaties that were forced on tribes, or were written by non-Indian lawyers to award tribes less than they thought they had bargained for. It recognizes the fact that most tribes were at a great disadvantage in terms of power and knowledge when they negotiated their treaties. Then, once a treaty has been interpreted liberally in favor of the tribe, any subsequent federal act that might adversely affect those treaty rights is interpreted, where ambiguities exist, so as to uphold the treaty rights. Thus, for example, in

The beginning of the Long Walk for Survival. (Photo by Ilka Hartmann)

*Minnesota v. Mille Lacs Band of Chippewa Indians* (1999), the United States Supreme Court used these canons of construction to uphold Chippewa treaty rights to hunt, fish, and gather on lands that had been ceded in an 1837 treaty in exchange for such guarantees.

With respect to treaties, federal Indian law differs from international law. Under international law, a treaty can never be terminated by one side or the other because of a change of one side's policies or interests; it can only be modified by the agreement of both parties. An international treaty is like a business contract: if one party defaults, the other party has the right to enforce the contract or to obtain compensation. As we have seen, the courts have determined that Congress has the power unilaterally to break Indian treaties and that compensation is the only remedy for broken treaties. The courts will not put an abrogated treaty back into force.

On the other hand, international law presumes that the parties to a treaty are equal. The intentions of both parties must be considered when interpreting the treaty and where there is doubt as to the meaning of the

written words the interests of both sides must be balanced. In this respect, federal Indian law is more favorable to tribes than international law. Indian nations that have relatively strong treaties, such as the Haudenosaunee, have nevertheless tried to bring their treaty claims to the International Court of Justice at the Hague; thus far, the World Court has refused to examine these cases. In 1988, however, the United Nations Commission on Human Rights approved an official study of treaties with indigenous peoples, and U.S. tribes are currently participating in the research.

Thirty years ago, the Supreme Court upheld construction of a dam, which flooded the Tuscarora Indian Reservation. Justice Hugo Black filed a dissenting opinion. "Some things are worth more than money and the costs of a new enterprise," he wrote. "Great nations, like great men, should keep their word."[4] In the arena of world politics today, trust is a valuable asset; without it, governments have only military power to defend their interests. The United Nations may never involve itself in the enforcement of Indian treaties, but the United States cannot maintain the trust of other nations if it insists on the right to continue to break its treaties with the original inhabitants of its soil.

## The Future of Indian Treaties

On 21 October 1988 Congress adopted House Concurrent Resolution 331, expressly reaffirming the government-to-government relationship between the United States and Indian tribes, as well as the so-called trust responsibility of the United States to provide the tribes with legal protection and economic assistance. Congress also acknowledged "the need to exercise the utmost good faith in upholding its treaties with the various tribes, as the tribes understood them to be."[5] While congressional resolutions are not legally binding, they reflect policy trends on Capitol Hill. For the time being, at least, Congress is not likely to try to modify or terminate any Indian treaties.

If all Indian treaties were someday fully enforced, and Congress gave up its power to modify or abolish them, how far would this go in achieving tribes' contemporary goals? To begin with, many tribes have no treaties, or have signed treaties that were never ratified, particularly in the Southwest and California. While treaties dealt with the ownership of land and the use of fish and wildlife, very few contained specific commitments to provide the social benefits that today comprise such a large part of federal-tribal relations. The treaties that do refer to schools, physicians, and farm implements generally leave the amount and kinds of aid to the discretion of the president.

More importantly, few tribes outside Oklahoma have treaties that contain explicit guarantees or arrangements for self-government, other than the usual promises to extradite fugitives. Indeed, many treaties conflict with modern-day claims of tribal sovereignty, because they recognize the authority of Congress to impose laws on Indians without their consent. The existence of Indian treaties undoubtedly has great symbolic importance in the continuing debate over the scope of Indian self-government, since they are evidence that tribes were once recognized as completely independent nations. However, in themselves, treaties do not contain concrete solutions.

*Russel Lawrence Barsh*
*University of Lethbridge*

*Carole Goldberg*
*UCLA School of Law*

## Notes

1. Alexis de Tocqueville, *Democracy in America* (New York: Harper & Row, 1966).

2. No treaties were made with farming peoples, such as the Pueblo, Hopi, and Zuni, because they were already Mexican citizens and lived on Spanish land grants. Their legal rights as Mexicans were preserved by Article 9 of the Treaty of Guadalupe Hidalgo (1848) with Mexico.

3. The rules were amended in 1994, presumably to expedite and clarify the recognition process. The new rules do not refer to treaties either.

4. *Federal Power Commission v. Tuscarora Indian Nation*, United States Supreme Court Reports, volume 362 (1960), 142.

5. United States Statutes at Large, vol. 102, 4932.

## ◆ LIST OF SIGNIFICANT U.S. TREATIES AND CASE LAW

**Papal Bull Sublimis Deus of Pope Paul III (1537).** Reflecting arguments first expressed by the Spanish theologian Francisco de Vitoria in 1532, the Pope affirmed that, "the Indians and all other people who may later be discovered by Christians, are by no means to be deprived of their liberty or the possession of their property, even though they be outside the faith of Jesus Christ; and that they may and should, freely and legitimately, enjoy their liberty and the possession of their property; nor should they be in any way enslaved; should the contrary happen, it shall be null and void and of no effect." This led Spain's King Charles V to decree the Laws of the Indies (1542), which declared the Indians "free persons and vassals of the Crown," and forbade slavery or confiscation.

**Francisco de Vitoria's De Indis et De Iure Belli Relectiones (1557).** In this culmination of his legal work, Vitoria rejected arguments that the Indians could be destroyed lawfully because they were pagans. He concluded instead that "the aborigines are the true owners" of the New World, so that European nations could acquire legal rights to land only by purchase under a treaty, not by discovery or conquest. Rights arise from peoples' common humanity, Vitoria argued, rather than from their religion, race, or nationality. In taking this view, he foresaw the idea of human rights in modern-day international law. As a more practical matter, he persuaded European powers to base their claims in the Americas on their ability to make treaties with Indian tribes.

**Instructions by the Virginia Company to the Colony at Jamestown, May 1609. Susan Myra**

**Kingsbury, ed., *The Records of the Virginia Company of London* volume 3 (Washington, D.C.: U.S. Government Printing Office, 1933), 18–20.** The settlers were urged to protect themselves by making treaties of alliance with neighboring Indian tribes against Powhatan, the chief of the tribe nearest to the colony. The tribes were "to acknowledge no other Lord but Kinge James" and in order to "free them all from the Tirrany of Powhaton." Moreover, they were instructed, "Yf you make freindship with any of these nations, as you must doe, Choose to doe it with those that are farthest from you and enemies vnto those amonge whom you dwell for you shall haue least occasion to haue differences with them, and by that meanes a suerer league of Amity." Treaties were also seen as a means of gradually assimilating the Indians, for, "If you intreate well and educate those w[hi]ch are younge and to succeede in the gouvernement in yor Manners and Religion, their people will easily obey you and become in time Civill and Christian."

**Concordat of 1610 between the Holy See and the Mikmaq (Micmac) Nation. David J. Bushnell, "Native Cemeteries and Forms of Burial," Bureau of American Ethnology Bulletin No. 71 (1920).** This may be the earliest surviving wampum treaty. According to Mikmaq oral tradition, it records an agreement made with the Holy See, following the 1610 baptism of Grand Chief Membretou, for establishing churches and missions in what is now Atlantic Canada. The belt shows a priest and a Mikmaq holding hands, with the symbols of the Vatican (crossed keys) on one side, and the symbols of the tribal authorities (pipe and arrow) on the other. It is currently in the Vatican Museum of Ethnology in Rome.

**Certain Propositions exchanged between the Colony of Rhode Island and the Narragansetts, 7 July 1640. John Russell Bartlett, ed., *Records of the Colony of Rhode Island and Providence Plantations*, volume 1 (Providence: State Printer, 1856), 107–108.** Most of the lands of the Colony were obtained by deeds from local tribes. In addition, this earliest recorded treaty established rules for settling disputes between the two cultures. Indians agreed not to burn the woods or set traps near English farms, and not to "idle" near English houses. For minor offenses against Englishmen, Indians would be fined under English law, but for serious matters, including crimes committed by any of the chiefs of any tribe, the Narragansetts' Grand Chief Miantonomi was to be summoned to witness the trial. Many early treaties followed this pattern, subjecting Indians to English law only when they visited English settlements.

**Treaty conference between France, the Hurons, Algonquins, and the Five Nations at Trois Rivieres,**

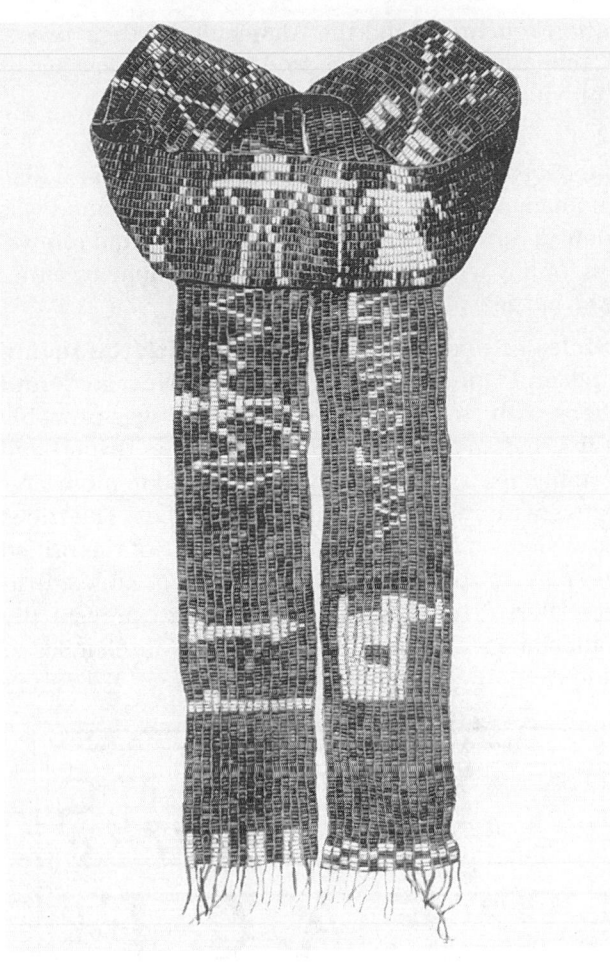

Wampum in the collection of the Vatican in Rome, recording a 1610 agreement with the Micmaq (Micmac) made in present-day Nova Scotia.

**1645. Ruben Gold Thwaites, ed., *The Jesuit Relations and Allied Documents*, volume 27 (Cleveland: Burrows, 1898), 253–269.** This important conference ended years of conflict in New France and helped establish the military and diplomatic supremacy of the Five Nations. In the course of an elaborate "condolence" ceremony, putting an end to the war and all former bad feelings, the speaker for the Five Nations gave a "wampum" belt "to bind us all very closely together."

He took hold of a Frenchman, placed his arm within his, and with his other arm he clasped that of an Algonquin. Having thus joined himself to them, "Here," he said, "is the knot that binds us inseparably; nothing can part us. Even if the lightning were to fall upon us, it could not separate us; for, if it cuts off the arms that hold you to us, we will at once seize each other by the other arm." And thereupon he turned around, and caught the Frenchman and the Algonquin by their two other arms, holding them so closely that he seemed unwilling ever to leave them.

*Condolence* was a device unique to traditional Indian diplomacy, in which a former treaty or alliance was renewed through a ceremony of apologies and forgiveness for any wrongs that may have been done by either of the parties.

**Articles of peace of 29 May 1677, with the Indian Kings and Queens of the Pamunkey, Nottoway and others. King's Printer (1677).** This was probably the first Indian treaty to be printed in Great Britain, and it establishes a pattern that was followed in most later treaties with relatively weak coastal tribes. The tribes acknowledged themselves to be subjects of the British Crown, and promised that they would not molest British settlers. The king in turn agreed to prevent the establishment of any settlements within three miles of the Indian towns, to ensure that the Tribes would be "secured and defended in their persons, goods and properties against all hurts and injuries of the English," and lastly to prevent any interference with their fishing and gathering of wild foods.

**William Penn's 15 July 1682 treaty with the Delawares at the Treaty Elm, Shakamaxon.** *The Papers of William Penn*, **volume 2 (Philadelphia: University of Pennsylvania Press, 1982), 454.** This famous Indian treaty, the first of several made by Penn in 1682 and 1683 on the west bank of the Delaware River, was the subject of a romantic painting by Benjamin West and the source of the folklore of Penn's generosity to the Indians. No text of the treaty survives, but Penn's descendants identified a wampum belt record of its terms of friendship. Penn's notes contain a reference to at least one agreement with the tribes on a topic other than real estate: "we have agreed, that in all differences between them & us, six of them & six of our people shall determin[e] it." Penn added "lett them have Justice & you win them."

**Treaty of Albany with the Five Nations, 2 August 1684. Peter Wraxall,** *An Abridgment of the Indian Affairs* **(New York: Benjamin Blom, 1968).** At this treaty conference, the British governors of New York and Virginia hoped to secure an alliance against France. In exchange, the Five Nations insisted on British recognition of their "conquests" along the Susquehanna River, and better terms of trade for furs. "When the English first came to New York to Virginia & Maryland, they were but a small People & we a large Nation; & we finding they were good People gave them Land & dealt Civilly by them," tribal spokesmen explained. "Now that you are grown Numerous & we decreased, you must protect us from the French, w[hi]ch if you don't we shall loose all our Hunting & Bevers: the French want all the Bevers & are Angry that we bring any to the English." They also emphasized, "that we are a Free People & unite our Selves to the English, and it is therefore in our Power to dispose of our Land to whom we think proper." To serve as a token of their decision to "submit" to the British Crown, they sent the king a pair of deerskins, "that He may write & put a great Red Seal thereto." The Five Nations nonetheless continued to maintain diplomatic ties with France until the final defeat of French forces at Montreal sixty years later.

**John Bulkley's Inquiry in the Right of the Aboriginal Natives to the Lands in America (1724). Collections of the Massachusetts Historical Society, First Series, volume 4 (1795), 159–181.** This influential little tract, published in colonial Connecticut, presented European settlers' view that purchasing land by treaty was unnecessary. Indians could only justly claim the lands they actually cultivated, he argued, so

Title page of the 1677 articles of peace with the Pamunkey and Nottaway of the eastern shore of Virginia, one of the first Indian treaties to be printed in English.

the "darling principle of many, viz, that native right is the only valuable title to any lands in the country, is absurd and foolish." Thus "supposing the English to be the first (of civilized nations) in the discovery of the country, they had (the royal allowance and favour concurring) an undoubted right to enter upon and impropriate all such parts of it as lay waste and unimproved by the natives, and this without any consideration or allowance made to them for it." As the Crown made fewer treaties and colonists found it difficult to acquire more lands, these arguments were repeated more frequently. The Crown's refusal to open Indian lands for settlement was one of the grievances listed in the Declaration of Independence.

**Treaty of Boston of 15 December 1725, with the Wabanaki Confederacy. W.D. Hamilton and W.A. Spray, eds., *Source Materials Relating to the New Brunswick Indian* (Fredericton, N.B.: Hamray, 1977), 24–25.** In this important treaty, the allied tribes of Maine, Nova Scotia, and New Brunswick acknowledged Britain to be the "rightful possessor" of New England under the Treaty of Utrecht between Britain and France, and promised to "submit" to the British Crown "in as ample a manner as we have formerly done" to the king of France. The tribes also agreed "not to molest" any settlements lawfully made in their territories, to pay for any injuries done to settlers, and to take any grievances they might have against the English to the English courts. Thus the tribes became British subjects while preserving their own laws and government within their territories. This treaty was renewed at Annapolis Royale in Nova Scotia in 1726 and again in 1752 as part of a treaty between Great Britain and the Mikmaq, shortly after the fall of New France.

**Oglethorpe's Treaty of 21 May 1733, with the Yamacraw Creeks. Charles C. Jones, *History of Georgia*, volume 1 (Boston: Houghton, Mifflin, 1883), 141–143.** A comprehensive treaty of trade and alliance, by which the Creek agreed to place themselves under the Crown and live at peace with the settlers, while reserving their own separate lands and government. Englishmen harming the Creek were to be punished under English laws; likewise, any Creek guilty of injuring or robbing the English were to be extradited and tried by the English courts. The Creek also agreed that, "though this land belongs to us," the English could settle upon "all those lands which our nation hath not occasion to use; provided always, that they, upon settling every new town, shall set out for the use of ourselves and the people of our nations such lands as shall be agreed upon." Freedom of trade was guaranteed, and the prices of many goods were fixed by a schedule annexed to the treaty. The Creek also agreed

to break off diplomatic relations with the French and Spanish. Tomochichi, principal chief of the Creeks, went in person to London to meet George II and witness the ratification of the treaty.

**The Governor and Company of Connecticut and Moheagan Indians, by Their Guardians, 1743 (London: J. & W. Richardson, 1769).** This was the first formal legal proceeding to consider the nature of Indian rights. Connecticut argued that since the Mohegan (Moheagan) Indians lived inside the boundaries granted to the colony by the king, tribal land could be settled without a treaty. A special royal commission of inquiry, established at Mohegan request, concluded that "the Indians, though living amongst the king's subjects in these countries, are a separate and distinct people from them, they are treated with as such, they have a policy of their own, they make peace and war with any nation of Indians when they think fit, without control from the English." This decision was affirmed by the Privy Council in London, and the colony was ordered to return some lands to the tribe, but this order was never carried out: the Revolutionary War had already begun.

**Royal Proclamation of 7 October 1763. Wilbur R. Jacobs, ed., *The Appalachian Indian Frontier; the Edmond Atkins Report and Plan of 1755* (Lincoln: University of Nebraska Press, 1967).** Inspired by Edmond Atkins' report on the state of Indian affairs in the British settlements, King George III proclaimed it to be "just and reasonable, and essential to our Interest, and the security of our Colonies, that the several Nations or Tribes of Indians with whom We are connected, and who live under our protection, should not be molested or disturbed in the Possession of such Parts of Our Dominions and Territories as, not having been ceded or purchased by Us, are reserved to them or any of them, as their Hunting Grounds." The King strictly forbade any further settlements, except on lands purchased from the Indians under treaties. This resulted in a boundary, roughly along the crest of the Appalachian Mountains, between British colonies and Indian territory.

**Treaty Conference with the Six Nations held at Fort Stanwix, October and November 1768. E.B. O'Callaghan, ed., *Documents Relative to the Colonial History of the State of New York*, volume 8 (1857), 111.** The original purpose of this meeting was to fix the Proclamation line between the British colonies and the various Indian nations west of the Appalachians. Various tribes continued to arrive at different stages of the two-month-long negotiations, supervised by Sir William Johnson, Crown Superintendent of Indian Affairs. Following the Six Nations' own diplomatic protocols, the conference began with a formal "condolence" ceremony, and gifts were exchanged for each request made and promise given. A major problem was the Six Nations' demand that Britain recognize their rights to "conquered" territories as far south as Georgia. Renewing their alliance with Britain, the Six Nation's speaker presented a wampum belt to Sir William and explained:

> We remember that on our first meeting with you, when you came with your ship we kindly received you, entertained you, entered into an alliance with you, though we were then great & numerous and your people inconsiderable and week and we know that we entered into a Covenant Chain with you and fastened your ship therewith, but being apprehensive the Bark would break and your ship be lost we made one of iron, and held it fast that it should not slip from us, but perceiving the former chain was liable to rust; We made a silver chain to guard against it; Then, Brother, you arose, renewed that chain which began to look dull, and have for many years taken care of our affairs by the command of the Great King, & you by your labors have polished that chain so that it has looked bright and is become known to all Nations, for all which we shall ever regard you and we are thankful to you in that you have taken such care of these great affairs of which we are allways mindfull, and we do now on our parts renew and strengthen the Covenant Chain by which we will abide as long as you shall preserve it strong & bright on your part.

**The Albany Conference with the Six Nations, August 1775. Collections of the Massachusetts Historical Society, Third Series, volume 5 (1836), 75–97.** Within a year of the first shots fired at Lexington and Concord, the Continental Congress created three departments of Indian affairs, and instructed them to secure the support, or at least the neutrality of the powerful tribal confederacies located on the colonies' fragile frontiers. On 15 August 1775 American representatives met at Albany with the Six Nations, where they were told, "This is the determination of the Six Nations, not to take any part, but as it is a family affair to sit still and see you fight it out, for we bear as much affection for the King of England's subjects on the other side of the water, as we do for you, born upon this island." The Americans were also warned to keep their war out of Indian territory: "You have just now made a good path; do not so soon defile it with blood." To this they willingly agreed, promising "whatever may happen between us and our enemies, we never will injure or disturb the peace of the Six Nations." However, General Sullivan did take the war into Six Nations

country in 1779, and four of the Six Nations ultimately fought on the British side, led by Mohawk Joseph Brant. In 1784 the Treaty of Fort Stanwix Peace restored peace.

**Treaty of Watertown of 17 July 1776, between the Wabanaki Confederacy and the United States of America. W. D. Hamilton and W. A. Spray, eds., *Source Materials Relating to the New Brunswick Indian* (Fredericton, N.B.: Hamray, 1977), 40–50.** The first treaty ever made that refers to "the United States of America." The first copies of the Declaration of Independence reached Watertown (near Boston) while this treaty was being negotiated, and it was read to the assembled Americans and Indians. "We like it well" an Indian spokesman declared. The treaty itself declares the two nations to be "Friends & Brothers united and allied together for their mutual defense safety and Happiness," and arranges for 600 Wabanaki troops to fight under General Washington's command. In addition, each agreed to pay restitution for any injuries committed by its citizens against the other, and to maintain a trading house at Machias (now in Maine).

**Malecite Declaration of War against Great Britain, 18 August 1778. W. D. Hamilton and W. A. Spray, eds., *Source Materials Relating to the New Brunswick Indian* (Fredericton, N.B.: Hamray, 1977), 50–51.** True to their undertakings at Watertown, the Malecite declared war on their former allies, the British, in 1778. "You know we are Amaricans, that this is our Native Country," they wrote. "You Know the King of England and his Evil Councilors has been Trying to Take away the Lands & Libertys of our Country, but God the King in Heaven-Our King fights for us & Says Amarica shall be free. Amarica is our friends, our Brothers & Countrymen, what they do we do, what they say, we say, for we are all one and the same family." After demanding the withdrawal of all British troops from Malecite territory, this letter ends, "Adieu for Ever." It was not to be. The 1783 Treaty of Paris drew the boundary between British North America and the United States just south of Malecite territory, forcing the Malecite to renew their old alliances with the British Crown.

**Proclamation of 22 September 1783, of the Continental Congress, under the Articles of Confederation. Journals of the Continental Congress, volume 25, 602.** As the Revolutionary War came to an end, Congress believed it was "essential to the welfare and interest of the United States" to keep a "friendship with the Indians." To prevent conflicts, Congress forbade "all persons from making settlements on lands inhabited or claimed by Indians, without the limits [outside the boundaries] of any particular State, and

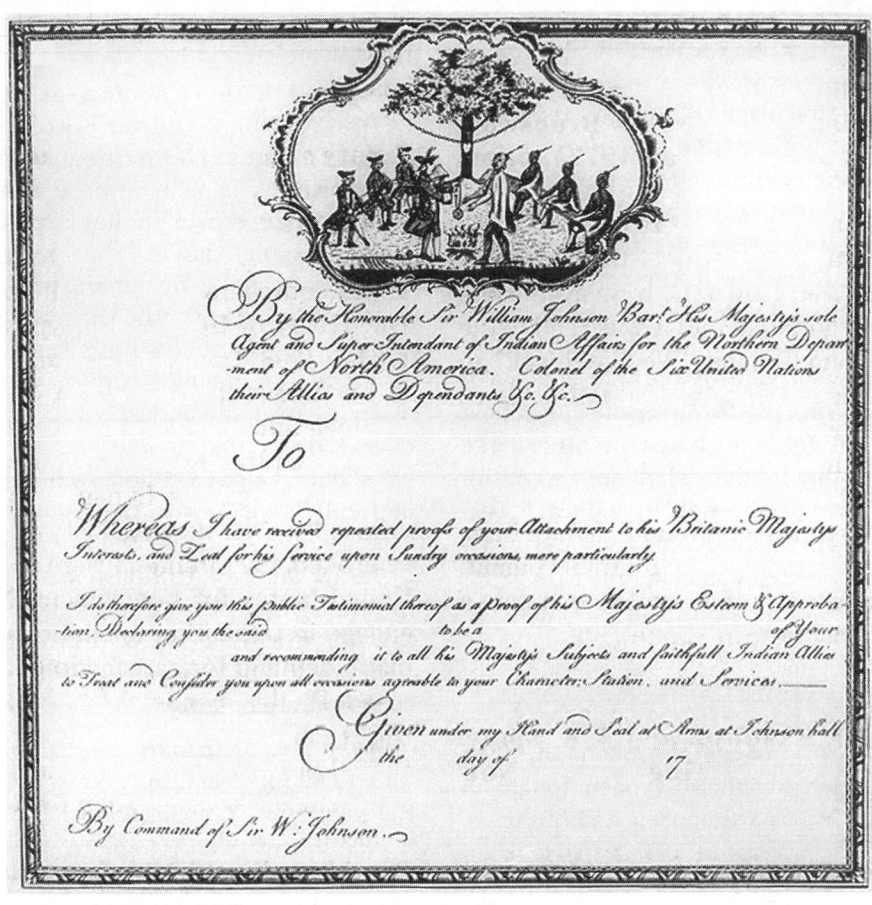

Exchanges of gifts such as furs, skins, and medals marked each stage of negotiations under Six Nations' diplomatic protocols, as depicted in this 1770 engraving. In the background are two symbols of unity: the Covenant Chain and the great Tree of Peace. (Courtesy of the John Carter Brown Library at Brown University)

from purchasing or receiving any gift or cession of such lands or claims without the express authority and directions of the United States in Congress assembled." Like the 1763 Proclamation, this was designed to centralize control of land purchases.

**Treaty of Hopewell of 28 November 1785, with the Cherokee. 7 United States Statutes at Large 13.[1]** Within a year of its treaty of peace with Great Britain, the new government set out to restore peace with the Tribal confederacies that still controlled its frontiers. The Treaty of Hopewell is typical of the period from 1784 to 1798. The Cherokee acknowledged themselves to be "under the protection of the United States of America and of no other sovereign whatsoever," and agreed that the United States would henceforth "regulate trade with the Indians." In case of any serious crimes by Cherokee against whites, or whites against Cherokee, the offenders were to be surrendered to the United States for punishment. Neither nation would engage in retaliation for injuries except after a diplomatic demand for satisfaction had been made and

refused. By this means, the Cherokee and other eastern tribes came under the exclusive "protection" of the United States, without surrendering their right to govern themselves within their own boundaries.

**President Washington's message to Congress on the subject of Indian treaties, 17 September 1789. Annals of Congress, volume 1, 80.** Soon after the adoption of the Constitution, doubts arose as to whether Indian treaties required Senate ratification. "It is said to be the general understanding and practice of nations, as a check on the mistakes and indiscretions of ministers or commissioners, not to consider any treaty negotiated and signed by such officers, as final and conclusive, until ratified by the Sovereign or Government from whom they derive their powers," the president wrote. "This practice has been adopted by the United States respecting their treaties with European nations, and I am inclined to think it would be advisable to observe it in the conduct of our treaties with the Indians." After a lengthy inquiry, the Senate ultimately agreed with the president.

**The Treaty of Amity, Commerce, and Navigation between Great Britain and the United States, 19 November 1794 (Jay Treaty). 8 United States Statutes at Large 118.** Most tribes did not yet recognize the new international border, nor did they see any reason to respect it; they continued to conduct diplomacy with both the United States and Great Britain. This treaty not only restored trade between the former British colonies and British North America (now Canada), but also guaranteed Indians' freedom of movement between the two countries: "nor shall the Indians passing or repassing with their own proper goods and effects of whatever nature, pay for the same any impost or duty whatever. But goods in bales, or other large packages, unusual among Indians, shall not be considered as goods belonging bona fide to Indians." This provision was included in U.S. customs laws until 1897, and in 1928 Congress enacted legislation to exempt Canadian Indians from the provisions of U.S. immigration laws.

**The Treaty of Ghent (United States, Great Britain), 24 December 1814. 8 United States Statutes at Large 218.** The Treaty of Ghent brought an end to the War of 1812, which had largely been fought in Indian territory, with tribes participating on both sides. Discussion of the future status of Indian tribes occupied British and American negotiators for nearly two months. The Americans insisted that the tribes, as "subjects" of the United States, were no longer of any concern of the King, while Great Britain accused the United States of contemplating the removal and "extinction of those nations." The Americans argued that their practice of acquiring Indian land only by treaty demonstrated their "humane" policy, but British negotiators said this merely showed that the United States recognized the tribes as sovereign nations. In the end, the British and Americans simply agreed to restore the rights of the tribes on each side of the international border as they existed before the war. By backing down, Great Britain had accepted the Americans' contention that Indian tribes within the boundaries of the United States could make treaties and sell their land only to the United States (the principle of "preemption").

**Treaty of Spring Wells of 8 September 1815. 7 United States Statutes at Large 131.** In this treaty and nineteen other treaties concluded with Indian Tribes of the Great Lakes and Ohio Valley, the United States complied with its obligations under the Treaty of Ghent to restore the prewar rights and status of those tribes that had fought on the British side in the War of 1812. Omitted from this general amnesty were the British-allied Red Stick segment of the Creek who had surrendered to General Andrew Jackson and had been forced to sign a humiliating treaty acknowledging their "conquest."

**Treaty with the Choctaw at Treaty Ground, 18 October 1820. 7 United States Statutes at Large 210.** This was the first treaty to refer to "civilizing" the Indians as its main purpose, and it anticipated both the "Indian removal" policy and the individual allotment of Indian lands. The treaty specified that all Choctaw "who live by hunting and will not work" were to be removed west, and their lands sold by the president to finance a school fund. The U.S. Indian agent was to pay for organizing a corps of Indian police, and, "in order to promote industry and sobriety amongst all classes of the Red people," was empowered to confiscate liquor. Once the Choctaw had become "so civilized and enlightened as to be made citizens," the United States would subdivide their remaining lands into family farms, and would abolish the boundary line separating them from neighboring settlements. Thus the Choctaw territory was viewed, for the first time, as a temporary, federally administered enclave, rather than as a separate country.

***Johnson v. M'Intosh*, 21 United States Reports 523 (1823).[2]** The first Supreme Court decision on the nature of tribes' rights to land, *Johnson* actually involved a dispute between two whites: one had obtained a deed from the Indians, while the other had obtained a patent from the United States after the Indians had ceded the area by treaty. Chief Justice John Marshall based the Court's decision on the traditional understanding, among European nations, that the discoverer of a territory has the exclusive right to purchase it from the native inhabitants ("preemption"). "However extravagant the pretension of converting the discovery of an inhabited country into conquest may appear," Marshall argued, it had become "indispensible" to the system of laws and government adopted by the United States. Since it limited tribes' ability to sell land to whomever they wished, their "rights to complete sovereignty were necessarily diminished. Marshall carefully added, however, that the United States had "in no instance, entirely disregarded" tribal sovereignty, and had left tribes free to manage their internal affairs among themselves.

**Treaty with the Ponca at White Paint Creek, 9 June 1825. 7 United States Statutes at Large 247.** By the 1820s, American settlements had reached the Mississippi, and the United States negotiated a series of fourteen treaties with Plains Indian tribes, with whom it had few previous diplomatic dealings. Their main object was to secure peace on the frontier, not to acquire the land, which was still regarded as having little value. The Ponca treaty is typical. The Ponca "admitted that they reside within the territorial limits of the United States, acknowledge their supremacy, and claim their protection." The tribe also recognized the United States' authority to regulate trade with them, and promised to return stolen property and "deliver up" Indians who may have committed crimes against whites. The United States, in turn, promised to punish any whites who injured, robbed, or murdered Indians.

***Worcester v. Georgia*, 31 United States Reports 515 (1832).** This was the third of a series of cases challenging the invasion and annexation of Cherokee territory by the state of Georgia in 1828. In the first (*Tassels*), a Cherokee appealed his conviction for murder in a Georgia court; the state executed him before the Supreme Court could review the case. In the second, the Cherokee government-in-exile applied directly to the Supreme Court for an injunction against Georgia, but the Court refused on the grounds that, under Article III of the Constitution, only states and "foreign" nations could take their complaints directly to the Supreme Court. The Cherokee, the Supreme Court ruled, were a "domestic" rather than "foreign" nation. The third case involved Samuel Worcester, a missionary sentenced to hard labor by a Georgia court because he had refused to leave Cherokee territory when ordered to do so by state officials. The Supreme Court finally agreed with Worcester that Georgia had no lawful authority within the borders of the Cherokee Nation. Chief Justice Marshall wrote that the Cherokee had not given up their "right of self-government" when, in the 1794 Treaty of Hopewell, they had accepted the "protection" of the United States. "So long as their actual independence was untouched," they had been willing to accept this exclusive political relationship with the federal government; the federal government had acquired no more power over the Cherokees than what they had freely and explicitly given away by treaty. The treaty relationship "was that of a nation claiming and receiving the protection of one more powerful, not that of individuals abandoning their national character, and submitting as subjects to the laws of a master." Since Indian negotiators were not lawyers, moreover, the words in treaties should be interpreted as the Indians themselves understood them.

**Treaty of New Echota with the Cherokees, 29 December 1835. 7 United States Statutes at Large 478.** Despite the *Worcester* decision, the Cherokee were forced to move to the west side of the Mississippi River where, in the words of this treaty, "they can establish and enjoy a government of their choice and perpetuate such a state of society as may be most consonant with their views, habits and conditions." The tribe's original homeland was sold to pay for the cost of removal, and also to establish a trust fund for agriculture and education administered by the president. In exchange, the United States sold the tribe a tract of land

in what became known as the Indian Territory (now Oklahoma), promising that it would "in no future time without their consent, be included within the territorial limits or jurisdiction of any State or Territory." The United States also promised to "secure to the Cherokee Nation the right to make and carry into effect all such laws as they may deem necessary," provided they were consistent with the U.S. Constitution, and applied only to Indians. The Cherokee were also promised a non-voting "delegate" in the House of Representatives. Negotiated by one Cherokee political party, and viewed as a violation of the Cherokee Constitution by the other, this treaty led to civil war within the Cherokee Nation and the assassination of several Cherokee leaders. In 1846, a further treaty with the Cherokee purported to end this civil war, but private revenge continued for many years. In the meantime the United States forced thirty similar "removal" treaties on Indian tribes.

**Treaty of Guadalupe Hidalgo (United States, Mexico), 2 February 1848. 9 United States Statutes at Large 922.** At the conclusion of the Mexican War, the United States demanded nearly half of Mexico's territory as compensation, including Arizona, New Mexico, Nevada, Texas, and California. This vast region contained a number of Mexican and Indian towns (pueblos), Spanish or Mexican land grants, and Article IX of the 1848 peace treaty guaranteed their rights to "the free enjoyment of their liberty and property, and the free exercise of their religion without restriction." Most of the region outside of California was occupied by hunting and herding tribes such as the Navajo and Apache, however, and in Article XI of the treaty, the United States promised Mexico that it would keep these tribes peaceful and prevent them from making raids into Mexico's remaining territory. Article IX was the basis for claims under the 1924 Pueblo Lands Act, a forerunner of the 1946 Indian Claims Commission Act. The Treaty guaranteed respect for property rights established under Mexican law, which opened the possibility that even tribes without Mexican land grants, such as those in California, might be able to assert traditional use rights under Mexican law. However, the United States made it extremely difficult for tribes and others to assert such rights, and they never received recognition under United States law.

**Treaty with the Navajo at Cheille, 9 September 1849. 9 United States Statutes at Large 974.** Under Article XI of the Treaty of Guadalupe Hidalgo, the United States launched a campaign to subdue the Southwest tribes, by treaty or war. This 1849 treaty with the Navajo, and a similar one made the same year with the Ute, differs from earlier Indian treaties in that the United States obtained authority not only to regulate Indian trade and protect the tribe from settlers, but also to "pass and execute in their territory such laws as may be conducive to the prosperity and happiness of [the] Indians" generally. Such broad legislative powers over tribes' internal affairs had never before been asserted by the federal government. Similar provisions were included in treaties with the Comanche, Kiowa, and Apache, as well as with many tribes of the Great Plains and the Pacific Northwest, in the 1850s.

**Treaty of Fort Laramie, 17 September 1851. 11 United States Statutes at Large 749.** The first great treaty conference on the Great Plains, involving representatives of the Sioux, Crow, Cheyenne and Arapaho, Assiniboine, Gros Ventre, and Arikara, its main purpose was to secure peace among the tribes themselves, and to protect the wagon roads taking settlers across the prairies. The United States pledged to protect the tribes from "depredations" by American citizens, and to pay compensation for any damage done by them. The United States also promised the tribes annual distributions of goods ("annuities"), excluding deductions for any injuries done to whites. The federal government also interfered with tribal government for the first time, requiring each tribe to select "principals or head chiefs through whom all national business will hereafter be conducted."

**Unratified Treaties with California Indians, 1852.** In 1850 the federal government sent special commissioners to deal with Indians throughout California. By 1852 the commissioners had signed eighteen treaties with California tribes, setting aside nearly eight million acres of land. Because of pressure from gold-seekers and non-Indian settlers, the Senate declined to ratify the treaties. The Indians were not informed, however, that the treaties were invalid and they had no title to their land. Several decades passed before the unratified treaties were brought to light.

**Treaty with the Omaha at Washington City, 16 March 1854. 11 United States Statutes at Large 749.** This treaty introduced three new provisions, afterwards included in nearly every treaty made outside the Indian Territory. The most important was an agreement that "the President may, from time to time, in his discretion," survey parts of the tribe's territory and "allot" the parcels to individual Indians. Allotted lands could not be taxed or sold until Congress agreed to remove these restrictions. A second provision gave the president complete control over spending the money paid to the tribe for land sold to the United States, including power to withhold payments from individual Indians caught drinking liquor: in practical effect, land payments became a social program under federal government control. Lastly, the United States would have the right to build roads in Indian country without the tribe's consent, just as the federal government has the right to build roads over land owned by its own citizens. These provisions foreshadowed the eventual dismemberment of the reservation, its settlement by whites, and the assimilation of the Indians, a policy that was finally applied to all tribes, regardless of their treaties, by the General Allotment Act in 1887.

**Treaty with the Duwamish and Allied Tribes, at Point Elliott, 22 January 1855. 12 United States Statutes at Large 927.** In two years (1854–1855), Territorial Governor Isaac Stevens made treaties with most tribes of Washington and northwestern Oregon on terms similar to the 1854 Omaha treaty. There were some important differences, as indicated by this 1855 treaty with twenty-two small tribes in Puget Sound near present-day Seattle (named for one of the signers, Duwamish chief Sealth). Since these tribes relied mostly on fishing for their livelihood, they sold nearly all their lands, but reserved the "right of taking fish at usual and accustomed grounds and stations" throughout the area. On its part, the United States was anxious to concentrate all the Pacific Northwest tribes on one or two reservations. Instead of referring to the reservations as the Indians' "permanent homes," as had previous Indian treaties, the Stevens treaties state that they were for the Indians' "present use and occupation," and the "President may hereafter, when in his opinion the interests of the Territory shall require and the welfare of the said Indians be promoted," move them to any "other suitable place within said Territory as he may deem fit." The United States attempted, with the aid of the gunboat *Massachusetts*, to move all these tribes to one place, which proved an impossible task; the government set aside several more small reservations for them between the 1870s and 1930s.

**21 August 1861 address of John Ross, Principal Chief of the Cherokee Nation, requesting authority to negotiate with the Confederate States.** *The Papers of Chief John Ross*, volume 2 (Norman: University of Oklahoma Press, 1985), 479–481. With war among the states inevitable, Ross called for neutrality. "While ready and willing to defend our firesides, let us not make war wantonly against the authority of the United or Confederate States, but avoid a conflict with either, and remain strictly on our own soil." At the same time, believing that "the permanent disruption of the United States into two governments is now probable," he asked for authority to enter into "an alliance with the Confederate States upon terms honorable and advantageous to the Cherokee Nation." Only this, he argued, would ensure the future of the Cherokee people. "When your nationality ceases here, it will live nowhere else. When these homes are lost, you will find no others like them." Most other tribes in the Indian Territory had already signed treaties with the

Confederacy when Ross spoke, and the Cherokee Nation followed them, on 7 October 1861. General Stand Watie led Indian Territory forces until September 1865, when he became the last Confederate general to surrender.

**Treaty with the Choctaw and Chickasaw made at Washington City, 28 April 1866. 14 United States Statutes at Large 769; Annual Report of the Commissioner of Indian Affairs for 1865. The Chickasaw Freedmen, 193 United States Reports 115 (1904).** A peace commission sent to the Indian Territory in 1865 enraged tribal leaders by arguing that, "by their own acts, by making treaties with the enemies of the United States [they] had forfeited all right to annuities, lands, and protection by the United States." One year later, less confiscatory treaties were concluded with all the tribes in the Indian Territory, of which this one is typical. Slavery among the tribes was abolished, and they agreed to give freedmen equal legal rights of tribal citizenship. Additional tribal lands were sold, and the proceeds used to settle freedmen on their own farms. Land tenure was individualized, but in other respects the tribes were allowed to keep their own laws and representative forms of government. A federal "governor" was appointed to oversee these Reconstruction measures. In 1904 the Supreme Court upheld the constitutionality of selling tribal land for the benefit of freed slaves.

**Treaty of Fort Laramie of 29 April 1868. 15 United States Statutes at Large 635.** With the end of the Civil War, veterans and ruined farmers rushed to settle the Plains. Forty treaties—more than 10 percent of all the Indian treaties ever made by the United States—were signed within three years of the Confederate surrender at Appomattox, and were chiefly concerned with acquiring land for settlement. The second Fort Laramie treaty brought an end to a bitter war, ranging from the Indian Territory to Montana, between the United States and the Sioux Nation, in which the Sioux had largely prevailed, and its terms were somewhat more favorable to the Indians than other treaties of this period. The United States pledged to protect the tribes' "absolute and undisturbed use and occupation" of their reservations, to remove any settlers, and to punish any whites causing injuries to Indians, and provided extensive agricultural and educational aid "to insure the civilization of the Indians." Indians could obtain individual allotments of land, if they wished, but the reservations as a whole were never to be sold or subdivided without the approval of "three-fourths of the adult male Indians." The United States violated this provision six years later, in an 1874 "agreement" with certain Sioux chiefs opening the gold-rich Black Hills for miners, leading to the war in which George Armstrong Custer fell.

**Annual Report of the Commissioner of Indian Affairs for 1869.** In this report to Congress, the commissioner of Indian Affairs strongly argued, for the first time, that no further treaties be made with Indian Tribes, a recommendation Congress adopted two years later. He argued:

> A treaty involves the idea of a compact between two or more sovereign powers, each possessing sufficient authority and force to compel a compliance with the obligations incurred. The Indian tribes of the United States are not sovereign nations, capable of making treaties, as none of them have an organized government of such inherent strength as would secure a faithful obedience of its people in the observance of compacts of this character.... But, because treaties have been made with them, generally for the extinguishment of their supposed absolute title to the land inhabited by them, they have become falsely impressed with the notion of national independence. It is time that this idea should be dispelled, and the government cease this cruel farce of thus dealing with its helpless and ignorant wards.

**End of Treaty-Making, Appropriations Act of 3 March 1871, 16 Statutes at Large 544, 566.** This measure grew out of a long-standing dispute between the Senate and the House of Representatives over control of Indian affairs. Because only the Senate has the power to ratify treaties, treaty relations gave the Senate a preeminent role. Yet the House was required to appropriate funds to fulfill treaty obligations. This Appropriations Act declared:

> [N]o Indian nation or tribe within the territory of the United States shall be acknowledged or recognized as an independent nation, tribe, or power with whom the United States may contract by treaty: *Provided further,* That nothing herein contained shall be construed to invalidate or impair the obligation of any treaty heretofore lawfully made and ratified with any such Indian nation or tribe.

Following passage of this act, agreements continued to be made with Indian tribes. Confirmation of such agreements, however, was henceforth by congressional act, voted upon by both houses.

***United States* ex rel. *Standing Bear v. Crook*, 25 Federal Cases 695 (Circuit Court of Nebraska 1879).**[3] Standing Bear and other Ponca Indians left their reservation in the Indian Territory without the consent of the federal Indian agent, as required by federal regulations. Seized in Nebraska by the army, they sued the commanding officer, General Crook, arguing that he had no constitutional right to prevent their freedom of movement. Stating that no other case had ever "appealed so strongly to my sympathy," the federal judge ruled that "an Indian is a 'person' within the meaning of the laws of the United States," and therefore has the same rights, as an individual, to personal freedom and legal protection. This was the first case to recognize Indians' individual civil rights.

**Ex parte *Crow Dog*, 109 United States Reports 556 (1883).** When the famous Sioux chief Spotted Tail was murdered by a fellow Sioux, Crow Dog, tribal leaders ordered the murderer to compensate the victim's family. Not satisfied with this, federal authorities brought murder charges against Crow Dog in Dakota Territory; he was convicted and sentenced to death. Overturning the conviction, the Supreme Court explained that Congress had never passed any law extending the federal criminal code to reservation Indians, even though the Sioux had agreed to be subject to any laws Congress might impose on them. Congress had the power to impose criminal laws on Indians, the Court reasoned, but had never clearly done so.

**Elk v. Wilkins, 112 United States Reports 94 (1884).** Although John Elk had left his reservation and had begun farming in a white community near Omaha, he was denied the right to vote because of his Indian ancestry. Elk challenged this as a violation of the "Equal Protection Clause" of the Fourteenth Amendment, but the Supreme Court disagreed, saying that "Indians born within the territorial limits of the United States, members of, and owing immediate allegiance to, one of the Indian tribes (an alien, though dependent, power)," are no more entitled to citizenship than the children of foreign visitors. Unlike *Standing Bear, Elk* denied that Indians are "persons" within the meaning of the Constitution, and treated them as foreigners.

**United States v. Kagama, 118 United States Reports 375 (1886).** In response to the Supreme Court's decision in *Crow Dog*, Congress enacted the "Major Crimes Act," imposing certain federal criminal laws on all reservation Indians, regardless of the terms of their treaties. Two California Hoopa Indians charged with murder challenged the act's constitutionality and lost. "The power of the General Government over these remnants of a race once powerful, now weak and diminished in numbers, is necessary to their protection, as well as the safety of those among whom they dwell," the Supreme Court reasoned. "It must exist in that government, because it has never existed anywhere else, because the theatre of its exercise is within the geographical limits of the United States, because it

has never been denied, and because it alone can enforce its laws on all the tribes." In other words, policy may justify overlooking treaty stipulations. Although the Hoopa Valley Tribe did not have a treaty with the United States that had been ratified by the Senate, the Major Crimes Act was applied to treaty tribes as well.

**Talton v. Mayes, 163 United States Reports 376 (1896).** The defendant challenged his conviction in a Cherokee court, citing failure to comply with the Fifth Amendment to the United States Constitution, which requires indictment by a grand jury. The United States Supreme Court found the Fifth Amendment inapplicable to a Cherokee proceeding, because that amendment only binds the federal government. "[T]he existence of the right in Congress to regulate the manner in which the local powers of the Cherokee nation shall be exercised does not render such local powers Federal powers arising from and created by the Constitution of the United States…. [T]he powers of local self government enjoyed by the Cherokee nation existed prior to the Constitution." Although the Bill of Rights does not bind Indian nations and their court systems directly, Congress later adopted the Indian Civil Rights Act of 1968, which applies some provisions of the Bill of Rights to tribal governments as a matter of federal statutory law.

**Lone Wolf v. Hitchcock, 187 United States Reports 553 (1903).** The most forceful of a series of Supreme Court rulings upholding the constitutionality of the allotment of Indian reservation lands in violation of treaty stipulations. Under the Treaty of Medicine Lodge (1867), no part of the Kiowa-Comanche Reservation could be sold to the United States without the approval of three-fourths of the adult male Indians. Congress allotted the reservation and sold off the "surplus" without obtaining this approval. Upholding this action, the Supreme Court explained: "The power exists to abrogate the provisions of an Indian treaty, though presumably such power will be exercised only when circumstances arise which will not only justify the government in disregarding the stipulations of the treaty, but may demand, in the interest of the country and the Indians themselves, that it should do so." The judges described this as "plenary authority over the tribal relations of the Indians," the exercise of which is not reviewable by the courts.

**Winters v. United States, 207 United States Reports 564 (1908).** An 1888 agreement between the United States and the Gros Ventre and Assiniboine tribes provided for cessions of land and creation of a reservation that included part of the Milk River. Subsequently, upstream non-Indian farmers began to use the river's flow for irrigation. When the tribes later tried to irrigate the reservation lands, there was insufficient water left for them to do so. Under ordinary principles of western water law, the first to use water has a prior right. In this case, the Supreme Court adopted a different allocation system, holding that water for irrigation had been reserved for the tribes at the time the reservation was created. It was not necessary for the tribes to actually use the water in order to establish their rights. Although the reservation of water rights was not mentioned in the 1888 agreement, the Court held that "[b]y a rule of interpretation of agreements and treaties with the Indians, ambiguities occurring will be resolved from the standpoint of the Indians."

**Convention concerning Pacific fur seals (United States, Great Britain, Japan, Russia) made at Washington, D.C., 7 July 1911. 37 United States Statutes at Large 1542.**  The first modern international treaty to recognize the rights of Indians and other indigenous peoples to hunt and fish for subsistence. The convention was aimed at reducing commercial sealing in the Bering Sea and Gulf of Alaska, but provided that its restrictions "shall not apply to Indians, Ainos, Aleuts or other aborigines dwelling on the coast of the waters mentioned. . . who carry on pelagic sealing in canoes. . . provided that such aborigines are not in the employment of other persons or under contract to deliver the skins to any person." This provision remained in force until 1986, when, under pressure from animal-rights groups, the United States allowed the 1911 convention to lapse.

**Declaration of Allegiance to the Government of the United States by the North American Indian, 1913. Joseph K. Dixon, *The Vanishing Race; The Last Great Indian Council* (New York: Doubleday, 1913).**  This remarkable document, which many tribal leaders believed was a treaty, was in actuality a publicity stunt by Rodman Wanamaker and a group of East Coast businessmen who had managed to obtain the blessing of President Taft for a signing ceremony at Fort Wadsworth in New York City. As Taft and the chiefs signed, new "Buffalo"-style nickels were distributed to the audience. "Though a conquered race," it reads, in a tone befitting the era of America's Big Stick policy abroad, "with our right hands extended in brotherly love and our left hands holding the Pipe of Peace, we hereby bury all past ill feelings and proclaim abroad to all the Nations of the world our firm allegiance to this Nation and to the Stars and Stripes." Later the same year, the new president, Woodrow Wilson, gave Wanamaker's associate Dixon permission to bring this document (and souvenir American flags) to every Indian reservation in the United States. By Christmas, it had been signed by more than 900 Indians from 189

Tribes, encouraging Wanamaker and other "reformers" to begin the campaign for Indian citizenship.

***United States v. Sandoval*, 231 United States Reports 28 (1913).**  The same year as the "Declaration of Allegiance," ironically, the Supreme Court upheld Congress' power to impose "Indian" status on the Pueblo of New Mexico, who had been regarded as citizens since 1877. The Court was particularly impressed by the fact that the Pueblo held secret dances in their kivas from which whites were excluded; this was proof of their savagery. "Of course," the Court observed, "it would be unconstitutional for Congress to subject anyone to federal supervision by "arbitrarily calling them an Indian tribe." However, with respect to "distinctly Indian communities the questions whether, to what extent, and for what time they shall be recognized and dealt with as dependent tribes requiring the guardianship and protection of the United States are to be determined by Congress, not by the courts."

***United States v. Nice*, 241 United States Reports 591 (1916).**  Like *Sandoval*, this case illustrates the extent to which federal management of Indians' daily lives had become institutionalized, and, to a growing extent, inescapable. Overruling its own 1905 decision in the case of *In re Heff*, the Supreme Court held that becoming a citizen—for example, by obtaining an individual allotment of land under the 1887 General Allotment Act—did not necessarily exempt an Indian from the supervisory control of the Bureau of Indian Affairs. Citizenship and guardianship are not necessarily incompatible, the Court reasoned, and it is for Congress to decide when, if ever, Indians would be fully emancipated. Interestingly, *Nice* involved special federal laws making it illegal for Indians to drink liquor. Prohibition would soon extend this social experiment, unsuccessfully, to the rest of the population.

***United States v. Creek Nation*, 295 United States Reports 103 (1935).**  When the federal government surveyed the lands it had promised to the Creek Nation in the Indian Territory, it made an error and omitted 5,000 acres. When the Creek demanded compensation for this lost land a century later, government lawyers argued that the Creek either should have corrected the survey or should have complained earlier. The Supreme Court disagreed. "The tribe was a dependent Indian community under the guardianship of the United States" at the time, and as such it was entitled "to rely on the United States, its guardian, for needed protection of its interests." While the United States had broad powers and wide discretion in managing Indian tribes' affairs, it remained "subject to limitations inhering in such a guardianship," including an obligation of care in handling Indian property. In *Seminole Nation v. United*

*States*, 316 United States Reports 286 (1942), the Supreme Court referred to this as a "moral obligation of the highest responsibility and trust." Ever since, it has been called "trust responsibility."

### Felix Cohen's Handbook of Federal Indian Law (1941).

This legal treatise, originally written by one of the lawyers for the Department of the Interior as a government manual, has greatly influenced all subsequent thinking about tribal rights. Summarizing past court decisions, federal legislation, and administrative practice, Cohen concluded that Indian tribes retain all their original powers of self-government, except those that have been expressly given up by a treaty, or expressly taken away by an act of Congress. This became known as the principle of "residual Tribal sovereignty" and was quoted with Biblical regularity by judges until 1978, when the Supreme Court established a different rule in the *Oliphant* case.

### Tee-Hit-Ton Indians v. United States, 348 United States Reports 272 (1955).

This case resulted in a crucial decision on the nature of aboriginal Indian land rights which had catastrophic results for Native Alaskans. The United States made no treaties with Alaskan Indians, Aleuts, or Inuit, and Congress had set aside only one small reservation, at Metlakatla. In this case the Tee-Hit-Ton, a Tlingit clan, demanded compensation under the Fifth Amendment for lands settled without their consent. Absent recognition by a treaty or Congress, the Supreme Court concluded, aboriginal title "is not a property right but amounts to a right of occupancy which the sovereign grants and protects against intrusion by third parties but which may be terminated and such lands fully disposed of without any legally enforceable obligation to compensate the Indians." This means that tribes are entitled to protection of their lands from everyone in the world *except* the federal government. Native Alaskans did not give up their struggle for land rights as a result of this case, but could no longer insist on getting full compensation. The 1971 Alaska Native Claims Settlement Act paid them at a rate of less than $5 per acre.

### Williams v. Lee, 358 United States Reports 217 (1958).

Under the 1934 Indian Reorganization Act, new tribal governments and tribal courts were established on many Indian reservations. Until this decision, however, it was unclear just how much state law applied to Indian reservations. A great deal had changed since *Worcester*, and it was no longer realistic, state governments argued, to treat tribes as if they were totally separate from the states surrounding them. In this case, involving a tribe that had not organized under the 1934 act, the Supreme Court held that tribal courts have exclusive jurisdiction over the collection of debts from reservation Indians. The Court did not base this on any specific treaty language or federal laws, but on its belief that it is federal policy "to encourage tribal governments and courts to become stronger and more highly organized." In light of this policy, state governments may not act in any way that "infringed on the right of reservation Indians to make their own laws and be ruled by them." This "infringement test" continues to be used to determine the scope of state powers within Indian Country, although the Supreme Court also assesses state power based on whether federal law preempts that exercise of such power.

### Menominee Tribe of Indians v. United States, 391 United States Reports 404 (1968).

Beginning in 1953, Congress began a program of "terminating" the federal protection of selected tribes, and distributing their property per capita. Advocates of termination expected Indians to welcome this "emancipation from Federal supervision." On the contrary, most tribes fought bitterly against termination. In this case, the Supreme Court accepted the power of Congress to terminate the Menominee Tribe in 1954, but gave the 1954 legislation a narrow interpretation. Treaty rights persist unless expressly legislated away, the Court observed. Hunting and fishing rights reserved by the Menominee in their 1854 treaty had not been mentioned specifically by Congress in 1954, and therefore had not been affected. The Menominee continued to fight for restoration of those tribal rights that were expressly extinguished by Congress in 1954, and finally succeeded in obtaining Congressional "restoration" of their legal status in 1973. Nearly all other "terminated" tribes have either won legislative restoration since 1973 or have been "unterminated" through litigation that challenged the federal government's failure to keep promises it had made as a condition of termination.

### President Nixon's Special Message to Congress on Indian Affairs, 8 July 1970. Public Papers of the Presidents of the United States: Richard Nixon, 1970, 564.

With this influential statement, President Nixon formally brought the "termination" policy to an end and introduced the notion of "self-determination," which he defined as intended "to strengthen the Indian's sense of autonomy without threatening his sense of community." Trusteeship, protection, and Indian services moreover should not be seen acts of generosity. "The special relationship between Indians and the Federal government is the result instead of solemn obligations which have been entered into by the United States Government" in exchange for land. "To terminate this relationship would be no more appropriate than to terminate the citizenship rights of any other American."

### Morton v. Mancari, 417 United States Reports 535 (1974).

In the backlash against affirmative action

policies in the 1970s, preferential employment of Indians by the Bureau of Indian Affairs (BIA) was challenged as discriminatory. The Supreme Court decided that separate federal Indian laws have been based on the "historical relationships" between the United States and tribal governments, not the race of individuals. Hence seeking Indians to work in the BIA "does not constitute 'racial discrimination.' Indeed, it is not even a 'racial' preference. Rather, it is an employment criterion reasonably designed to further the cause of Indian self-government and to make the BIA more responsive to the needs of its constituent groups. It is directed to participation by the governed in the governing agency." The Court also clarified that federal "plenary power" over Indians was subject to constitutional restraints found in the Bill of Rights, and that the exercise of such power would be upheld only if it was rationally related to the fulfillment of the federal government's trust responsibility to Indian nations.

***United States v. Washington*, 384 Federal Supplement 312 (Western District of Washington 1974). Also see 443 United States Reports 658 (1979).[4]** This was the first of a series of federal court rulings on Indian treaty fishing rights in Washington State, later upheld by the Supreme Court. The 1854 and 1855 treaties had not been a grant of rights to the Indians, "but a grant of rights from them," and their terms should be "carried out, as far as possible, in accordance with the meaning they were understood to have by the tribal representatives at the councils, and in a spirit which generously recognizes the full obligation of this nation to protect the interests of a dependent people." Much had changed over the years, including the lifestyles of the Indians, but "the mere passage of time has not eroded, and cannot erode, the rights guaranteed by solemn treaties that both sides pledged on their honor to uphold." The practical effect of the Court's decision was to give the tribes an opportunity, by adjusting fishing regulations, to catch up to half the salmon and steelhead in state waters, and to manage the activities of their own fishermen under their own tribal laws.

**Final Report of the American Indian Policy Review Commission (1977).** Composed of three Senators, three Representatives and five Native Americans, the commission was created by Congress in 1975 to prepare a thorough evaluation of current Indian policy. With one Representative dissenting, the commission concluded that "Indian tribes are sovereign political bodies, having the power to determine their own membership and power to enact laws and enforce them within the boundaries of their reservations," and that "the relationship which exists between the tribes and the United States is premised on a special trust that

A man demonstrates at a San Francisco rally against the extradition of Dennis Banks, 1976. (Photo by Ilka Hartmann)

must govern the conduct of a stronger toward the weaker."

***Oliphant v. Suquamish Indian Tribe*, 435 United States Reports 191 (1978).** Oliphant, a non-Indian, was arrested for reckless driving by the Suquamish tribal police. His argument that Indian tribes do not have criminal jurisdiction over non-Indians was upheld by the Supreme Court in an opinion that undermined traditional principles of federal Indian law. The Court conceded that the tribes had neither given up this power by treaty, nor been dispossessed of this power explicitly by an act of Congress. It ruled, however, that Indian tribes only "possess those aspects of sovereignty not withdrawn by treaty or statute, *or by implication as a necessary result of their dependent status.*" Indian rights "must be read in light of the common notions of the day"—that is, of the nineteenth century—and it was clear that U.S. citizens had never expected someday to be tried by Indian courts. Hence "by submitting to the overriding sovereignty of the United States" in their treaties, "Indian tribes therefore necessarily give up their power to try non-Indian citizens of the United States except in a manner acceptable to Congress." In a companion case, *United States v.*

*Wheeler*, 435 United States Reports 313 (1978), the Supreme Court reaffirmed the "sovereign power of a tribe to punish its *members* for tribal offenses."

***Santa Clara Pueblo v. Martinez*, 436 United States Reports 439 (1978).** This case unsuccessfully challenged the pueblo's decision to deny membership to the child of a woman who married outside the community. The Supreme Court held that, "as separate sovereigns pre-existing the Constitution, tribes have historically been regarded as unconstrained by those constitutional provisions framed specifically as limitations on federal or state authority," such as the Equal Protection Clause of the Fourteenth Amendment. Although "Congress has plenary authority to limit, modify or eliminate the powers of local self-government which the tribes otherwise possess," it had not explicitly done so when it enacted the 1968 Indian Civil Rights Act (ICRA). ICRA directed Indian tribes to respect individual rights, but did not explicitly strip the tribes of the common-law immunity from lawsuits traditionally enjoyed by all governments. As a result, ICRA could only be used in federal court to challenge tribal actions involving detention or imprisonment.

***United States v. Sioux Nation*, 448 United States Reports 371 (1980).** In this decision, the Supreme Court finally reversed its ruling in *Lone Wolf* that the manner in which the federal government manages tribal property is not reviewable by the courts. This case began in 1877, when Congress ratified an "agreement" with the Sioux to sell the Black Hills, in violation of the provisions of the 1868 Fort Laramie Treaty. After several unsuccessful attempts to get this legislation repealed, the Sioux went to the newly-created Indian Claims Commission in 1951. The United States argued that the 1868 Sioux Reservation had not been "property," in the meaning of the Fifth Amendment, and could be disposed of however Congress wished. The Court disagreed: Indian treaties create "vested property rights" under the Constitution, and, as such, can only be taken away for a legitimate public purpose. Since the Black Hills had been sold, not for the benefit of the Sioux, but for the profit of U.S. citizens, the United States would have to pay the value of the land in 1877, plus interest. The Sioux tribes did not accept this decision, however, and demanded the return of the land in another lawsuit. This legislation was unsuccessful, but since then Congress has considered legislation to return parts of the Black Hills to the Sioux.

***Montana v. United States*, 450 United States Reports 544 (1981).** The Crow Tribe prohibited hunting and fishing by non-members throughout the reservation, including on a navigable river. The Supreme Court held that the bed of the river belonged to the state rather than the tribe, relying on a general principle that the federal government normally holds the beds of navigable rivers in trust for states absent a clear provision to the contrary. According to the Court, an 1851 treaty between the United States and the Crow did not clearly reserve this riverbed for the Crow along with the rest of tribal lands, suggesting that the principles favoring treaty interpretation to benefit tribes could be superceded by other competing principles favoring states. Having found that the riverbed belonged to the state, the Court then ruled against tribal regulating of hunting and fishing on the river. Extending the decision in *Oliphant* and relying on findings by the trial court, the Court declared, "[s]ince regulation of hunting and fishing by nonmembers of a tribe on lands no longer owned by the tribe bears no clear relationship to tribal self-government or internal relations, the general principles of retained inherent sovereignty did not authorize the Crow Tribe to adopt [its prohibition]." The Court allowed, however, that tribes could regulate non-Indian activity on non-Indian owned land when the nonmembers "enter consensual relationships with the tribe or its members," or when "that conduct threatens or has some direct effect on the political integrity, the economic security, or the health or welfare of the tribe." This decision spawned a number of court holdings excluding tribal jurisdiction over parts of reservations that fell into non-Indian ownership as a result of allotment, making the exercise of tribal sovereignty far more difficult.

**President Reagan's statement on Indian policy, 24 January 1983. Public Papers of the Presidents of the United States: Ronald Reagan, 1983, volume 1, 96.** Emphasizing that "the Constitution, treaties, laws, and court decisions have consistently recognized a unique political relationship between Indian tribes and the United States," the president stated his commitment to deal with Indian tribes on a "government-to-government" basis. His support of tribal sovereignty was consistent with his conservative political philosophy: "Tribal governments, like State and local governments, are more aware of the needs and desires of their citizens than is the Federal Government and should, therefore, have the primary responsibility for meeting those needs." Shifting costs and accountability for Indian programs to the tribes became, in fact, the hallmark of Reagan-Bush Indian policy.

***County of Oneida v. Oneida Indian Nation*, 470 United States Reports 226 (1985).** Refusing to view the passage of nearly 200 years as an obstacle, the Supreme Court invalidated a 1795 agreement between the Oneida and the state of New York for the conveyance of Oneida lands. New York had failed to secure federal approval for the transaction, in violation of the Trade and Intercourse Act of 1793, 1 Statutes at Large

329. This agreement was one of many made in violation of the act in the nation's early years, and the *Oneida* decision precipitated huge land claims suits by a number of Eastern tribes. Many of these suits have been settled through Congressional payments and the conveyance of some state lands to the tribes.

**Treaty of 28 January 1985 (Canada, United States) concerning Pacific salmon. Public Law 99–5 of 15 March 1985 (99 Stat. 7).** This treaty establishes a special international commission to manage American and Canadian harvests of salmon, from California to Alaska. It specifically protects the treaty fishing rights of Pacific Northwest Indian Tribes and guaranteed the tribes themselves voting representation on the commission and two of its three regional management councils. Like the Jay Treaty, it illustrates the need to take account of Indian treaties in treaties made with other countries. It also marks the first time the United States has involved the tribes directly in the negotiation and implementation of a "foreign" treaty.

*California v. Cabazon Band of Mission Indians*, **480 United States Reports 202 (1987).** California attempted to enforce its laws prohibiting high stakes bingo games against Indian nations. A federal law passed in 1953, known as Public Law 280, had given criminal jurisdiction and civil court jurisdiction to California and several other states. In response to challenges brought by the Cabazon and Morongo tribes, the United States Supreme Court rejected state jurisdiction over the tribal bingo enterprises. The Court found that Public Law 280 did not give the states authority to "regulate," only the authority to bring criminal prosecutions and to open their civil courts to private lawsuits against Indians. And even though the overwhelming majority of the bingo customers were non-Indian, the Court refused to allow state jurisdiction under general principles of federal Indian law, using an analysis that weighed the relative strength of tribal, federal, and state interests. According to the Court, the tribal and federal interests supporting tribal economic development sharply outweighed any state anti-gambling interests, especially since the state already allowed many forms of gambling, including a state lottery, horseracing, card clubs, and even low-stakes bingo games run by charities. The *Cabazon* case alarmed state officials, leading to Congress's enactment of the Indian Gaming Regulatory Act of 1988, which required tribal-state compacts before Indian nations could carry out casino-style gambling.

*Lyng v. Northwest Indian Cemetery Protective Association*, **485 United States Reports 439 (1988).** Three northern California tribes invoked the First Amendment to prevent the United States Forest Service from constructing a road through a national forest. The tribes argued that the road would disrupt their most central religious practices, and consequently the federal government should be required to choose an available alternate route. Rejecting this claim, the Supreme Court stated, "Even if we assume [that the road] will virtually destroy the Indians' ability to practice their religion, the Constitution simply does not provide a principle that could justify upholding [the tribes'] claims…. [A] law forbidding the Indian respondents from visiting [the area] would raise a different set of constitutional questions. Whatever rights the Indians may have to the use of the area, however, those rights do not divest the Government of its right to use what is, after all, its land." The Court failed to note that this land had been part of the traditional territory of the tribes involved, and that the United States had acquired ownership by passing a forfeiture law in 1851. Indian sacred sites have since received somewhat greater protection through a Presidential Executive Order issued in 1996.

*Brendale v. Confederated Tribes and Bands of the Yakima Indian Nation*, **492 United States Reports 408 (1989).** This case challenged the authority of the Yakima Indian Nation to enforce its land use (zoning) regulations on two plots of land that were within the reservation but were owned by non-Indians. In a particularly confusing opinion, four Supreme Court Justices concluded that tribes do not have any inherent regulatory powers over privately owned land. Three other justices, arguing that "tribes may regulate the on-reservation conduct of non-Indians whenever a significant tribal interest is threatened or directly affected," concluded that tribes have the right to zone lands regardless of ownership. Two remaining justices observed that one of the parcels in question was located in a part of the reservation that is "predominantly owned and populated by nonmembers, who represent 80 percent of the population yet lack a voice in tribal governance." In their view, tribes can regulate land-use in predominantly Indian parts of a reservation, but not in predominantly non-Indian communities. As a result of *Brendale* and the 1978 *Oliphant* decision, tribes have lost a great deal of control over the non-Indians in their territories, and now look to Congress to return, legislatively, the government authority the Supreme Court has taken away from them. Congress has done so partially through the enactment of environmental laws which provide tribes with the opportunity to implement tribal regulations throughout the reservation, so long as they meet or exceed federal standards.

**Centennial Accord of 4 August 1989, between the Federally Recognized Indian Tribes in Washington State and the State of Washington. Copies available from the Governor's Office of Indian Affairs, Olympia, WA.** This agreement marks the beginning of a new approach to relations between state and tribal governments, based on negotiated cooperation, rather than confrontation and litigation. The state and tribes agree to develop a "government-to-government relationship," to meet annually to discuss more specific goals and strategies, and to work together to "improve the services delivered to people," Indian and non-Indian, in Washington. Further agreements have been made to share responsibility for the protection of Indian children, and the conservation of natural resources. One example is the TFW, or Timber-Fish-Wildlife process, through which tribal and state agencies are coordinating management of watersheds used by both Indians and non-Indians.

***Kiowa Tribe of Oklahoma v. Manufacturing Technologies, Inc.*, 523 United States Reports 751 (1998).** The Supreme Court affirmed that Indian nations are governments, entitled to immunity from suit regardless whether the litigation involves on-reservation or off-reservation activity by the tribe. Thus, for example, unless the tribe waives (foregoes) its immunity, an Indian nation cannot be sued by a state in order to collect taxes on sales to non-Indians at a tribal smokeshop, and non-Indian customers of a tribal business cannot sue to collect for personal injuries or breach of contract. Widespread attacks on tribal sovereign immunity have taken place both in the courts and in Congress; but the Supreme Court has deferred to Congress's judgment, and bills to end immunity have not passed in the Congress to date.

***Alaska v. Native Village of Venetie*, 522 United States Reports 520 (1998).** The Supreme Court severely limited the governing powers of Alaska Native villages by its determination that the Alaska Native Claims Settlement Act of 1971 had abolished nearly all "Indian country" in Alaska. Under federal Indian law, "Indian country" is the territory within which most tribal jurisdiction operates and within which other special jurisdictional rules apply. The Alaska Native Claims Settlement Act had eliminated all but one reservation in Alaska, in exchange for large land and monetary settlements provided to Native corporations. Some villages, such as Venetie, had transferred their lands from their corporation to the tribal government. However, the Supreme Court found that because the village lands were held in ordinary fee title, rather than in trust by the federal government, the land could not be deemed "Indian country" under the applicable federal statute, 18 United States Code 1151.

***Cobell v. Babbitt*, 91 Federal Supplement2d 1 (District of Columbia 1999).** Individual Indians who are the beneficiaries of trust funds as a result of holding interests in allotted lands brought a class action suit against the secretary of Interior and secretary of the Treasury for trust mismanagement. They alleged the federal government was not maintaining proper records, not collecting money owed to them by lessees and others, not investing their moneys properly, and not making required payments. Indians living in deep poverty were being denied billions of dollars in funds that would allow them a decent standard of living. Although Congress and the Bureau of Indian Affairs had attempted to address the situation, no real progress had been made. Accordingly, the federal district court found a breach of trust. It also found the secretary of Interior in contempt for failing to produce requested records and for destroying some essential records. According to the Court, "The United States' mismanagement of the IIM [Individual Indian Money] trust is far more inexcusable than garden-variety trust mismanagement of a typical donative trust. For the beneficiaries of this trust did not voluntarily choose to have their lands taken from them; they did not willingly relinquish pervasive control of their money to the United States. The United States imposed this trust on the Indian people…. [T]he purpose of the IIM trust was to deprive plaintiffs' ancestors of their native lands and rid the nation of their tribal identity."

***Rice v. Cayetano*, (98–818) 146 F.3d 1075 (2000).** Invoking the Fifteenth Amendment, prohibiting discrimination in voting, the Supreme Court invalidated a Hawaiian statute that allowed only Native Hawaiians to vote for trustees of a state entity that administered a fund and allocated benefits for Native Hawaiians. The fund included one-fifth of the income from lands formerly held by the Hawaiian monarchy, which had been seized by the United States and transferred to the state of Hawaii upon statehood. The state of Hawaii argued that this classification should be treated the same as one singling out tribal members, and upheld as a political rather than a racial classification on the reasoning of *Morton v. Mancari* (1974), *supra*. The non-Native Hawaiians responded that Native Hawaiians should not be subject to the same legal standard because they are not organized into federally recognized political units such as tribes. The Court chose to "stay far off that difficult terrain," determining instead that even if it were appropriate to treat Native Hawaiians the same as tribal Indians, "the elections for OHA trustee are elections of the State, not of a separate quasi-sovereign, and they are elections to which the Fifteenth Amendment applies. To extend *Mancari* to this context would be to permit a State, by racial classification, to fence out whole classes of its citizens from decisionmaking in critical state affairs. The Fifteenth Amendment forbids this result."

*Russel Lawrence Barsh*
*University of Lethbridge*

*Carole Goldberg*
*UCLA School of Law*

### Notes

1. The United States Statutes at Large (frequently cited as "Stat." or "Stat.L." with the volume number preceding, and page number following) is the official annual publication of new laws and resolutions adopted by Congress. Until the 1920s, new treaties were also printed annually in this series. Compiled and revised federal laws can be found in the United States Code ("U.S.C."), organized by subject rather than date.

2. The United States Reports (referred to by lawyers simply as "U.S." with the volume number preceding, and page number following the cite) is the official chronological publication of new decisions by the U.S. Supreme Court. There are also two privately printed series of Supreme Court decisions, the Supreme Court Reporter ("S.Ct.") and the Lawyer's Edition ("L.Ed."), which use different volume and page numbering.

3. Federal Cases (usually abbreviated as "Fed." with the volume number preceding, and page number following) was the official publication of Federal court decisions in the nineteenth century. It has since been replaced by the Federal Supplement ("F.Supp.") for decisions of trial courts ("district courts"), and the Federal Reporter ("F." and "F.2d") for decisions made by federal courts of appeal.

4. The Federal Supplement ("F.Supp." with the volume number preceding, and page number following) is the official publication of decisions by Federal district courts. See note 3.

### ◆ U.S. INDIAN LEGISLATION

Before the formation of the United States, Indian nations had their own laws and governments. Generally agreed-on rules, languages, and customs regulated trade and diplomatic relations among Indian nations. Most Indian laws were closely related to religious laws, and often Indian laws were believed to have been decreed by the Great Spirit, or Creator, at the time of creation. Among the Cherokee, the Great Spirit created seven clans and installed priestly rulers over the nation. Their laws, government, and major ceremonies of the Cheyenne were handed down to them from the Creator through the Prophet Sweet Medicine. Through spokespersons, Hiawatha and Deganawidah, the Creator bestowed the Great Law, or constitution, to the Iroquois Confederacy, consisting of the Seneca, Cayuga, Onondaga, Oneida, and Mohawk nations. Law in most Indian nations has a sacred quality, and regulates much of everyday social, ceremonial, and political life.

In contrast, European and U.S. law tend to regulate activities of the state and restrain economic and political competition, while separating most laws from religious matters and obligations. From the earliest colonial days, Europeans tried to impose their laws on Native peoples. In general, Indian nations usually prefer to live under their own legal and religious laws, rather than adopt the statutes of the United States or European nations. Legislation, passed by the United States Congress, did not seriously affect American Indians until the early nineteenth century when the military strength of Indians declined. After the 1870s, Native American nations could not successfully resist the U.S. Army, leaving their people subjected to the power of their conquerors. As a result, the federal government formed policies, by means of congressional legislation, aimed at reducing Indians to submission and directing Native Americans toward civilization, which was understood to consist of Christianity, farming, and U.S. citizenship. Ultimately, this Americanization of Indian people called for their assimilation into mainstream U.S. society. Assimilation implicitly required that Indians deny their own laws, religions, and customs, and accept U.S. citizenship, culture, and lifestyle.

### Outside the Law

In 1778, during the American Revolution, the Continental Congress made its first treaty with the Delaware Indians. The early U.S. federal government, especially after adopting the Constitution of 1787–89, established control over treaty and commercial relations with the Indian nations. During the colonial period, each colony had its own Indian policy and made its own treaties. Having numerous Indian policies and treaties led to chaotic relations with Indian nations. The federal government wished to centralize the management of Indian affairs and to hold primacy in buying the extensive lands the Indians still held at the end of the seventeenth century. After some protest, the states ultimately agreed to delegate Indian affairs to the federal government. In return, the federal government guaranteed the borders of the eastern states and promised to remove the Indian nations peacefully.

The newly established U.S. government attempted to restrain the Indian nations. The Northwest Ordinance of 1787 and Article 1 of the U.S. Constitution attempted to establish firm relations with the Indian tribes. The first Trade and Intercourse Act of 1790 exemplified this trend by attempting to regulate commercial relations with the tribes. Early U.S. laws affecting Indians generally sought to establish direct legal, political, and trade relations between the federal government and the Indian nations.

During these years, President Thomas Jefferson (1798–1806) advocated democracy for all people and believed that American Indians could be "civilized" to help tame the frontier. However, after the Louisiana Purchase in 1803, which gained extensive territories west of the Mississippi River, President Jefferson suggested that Indians be peacefully removed west of the Mississippi River to make way for U.S. settlers in the East. Congress began a new trend in Indian law with legislation passed in 1819 to "civilize" the tribal nations. This legislation called for missionaries to work among the Indians in order to convert them to Christianity and train them to take up agriculture. U.S. policy makers reasoned that if the Indians adopted farming, they would not need the large tracts of hunting and fur-bearing territories that supported the fur trade and Indian subsistence economies. During the 1820s, however, sectional attitudes of the South and the West challenged Jeffersonian policies; this was especially true following the 1828 election of Andrew Jackson, a frontier Democrat. Jackson, a southern state rights advocate, would not compromise state rights interests in favor of federal interests to preserve Indian constitutional relations and treaty rights.

The crowning legislative achievement of Jacksonian Indian policy appeared in the Indian Removal Act of 1830. The Removal Act authorized and funded the removal of most Indian nations from the eastern United States and resettled most of them in the present-day states of Kansas and Oklahoma. By 1860 most eastern Indian nations, except some in the original thirteen colonies, were induced or forced to migrate west of the Mississippi River.

Indians remained legally outside U.S. constitutional powers due to their status as semi-independent foreign nations. In 1832, U.S. Supreme Court Justice John Marshall in *Worcester v. Georgia* partially preserved Indian national sovereignty. The *Worcester* case set the stage for preserving Indian national rights to self-government, although the increasing military and economic power of the United States rendered Indian military resistance increasingly hopeless. In *Worcester*, the Supreme Court upheld federal supremacy over state laws in Indian affairs. The Court ruled that the state of Georgia could not extend its laws over the Cherokee Nation and that Georgia could not abolish the functioning of the Cherokee government. According to the Constitution, only the federal government could make treaties with Indians, buy land from Indians, or regulate Indian affairs. The *Worcester* ruling preserved Indian nations from state laws and reinforced the direct legal and political relationship between Indian nations and the federal government. In a previous case, *Cherokee Nation v. Georgia* (1831), the Supreme Court held that Indian nations were not foreign nations, but were like "domestic dependent nations." The two Cherokee cases establish the modern doctrine that Indian nations retain inherent rights to self-government, or sovereignty, provided that Congress has not taken away those rights by legislation, or that the Indian nations have not explicitly given such rights away in treaties or other agreements.

## Undermining Tribal Sovereignty

Sovereignty, the right to exercise laws over a particular territory and community, was the major feature of the legal status of Indians as tribes and individuals. The United States' practice of making treaties with Indian nations substantiated Indian sovereignty. During the early 1800s, the United States made more treaties than laws. The outbreak of the U.S. Civil War in the 1860s weakened the federal government and, during the post-war Reconstruction at the end of 1870s, the federal government turned its troops on the tribal nations of the West. The United States perceived most independent Indian nations as a threat, and gave little consideration to the fact that the Native peoples were fighting to defend their families, communities, and homelands.

Federal actions exerted greater control and domination over Indian nations, and Indian military resistance declined. In 1871, Congress enacted an appropriations law that contained a section that abruptly halted the treaty making process. Afterwards, the federal government could not, by law, negotiate any more treaties with Indians as sovereign nations. The act, however, did not abolish any of the 371 ratified U.S. treaties with Indians, although the federal government continued to negotiate agreements with Indians. The agreements and treaties total 389.

After the 1870s, Congress passed laws that decreased Indian sovereignty and increasingly placed Indians under U.S. control. By the 1880s, most Indian nations, by then powerless, were placed on reservations under the administration of the Office of Indian Affairs. Originally founded in 1824, the Indian Office was placed within the War Department, where it remained until 1849 when it was transferred to the Department of Interior. The Office of Indian Affairs presumed to know the most about the tribes and their conditions, and submitted drafts of bills to congressmen to consider for law.

Sergeants Red Tomahawk and Eagle Man, members of the Standing Rock Agency police. (Courtesy of the Denver Public Library, Western History Collection)

## The Forced Assimilation Period

As the Indian population fell further under the control of the United States, Congress entertained bills to coincide with federal policy designed to handle Indian affairs. The defeat of the tribal powers and the resulting impoverishment of Indian living conditions enabled the federal government to force the Indian nations to change their way of life. Nevertheless, most Indians did not accept U.S. citizenship or culture, and preferred to retain their Indian identity and culture. Following the Act of 1871, the second most powerful legislation to affect the tribes was the General Allotment Act of 1887, often known as the Dawes Act. The act divided tribal lands on reservations (exempting a small number of tribes) in an attempt to "civilize" Indians and assimilate them into the nation's mainstream society. Surplus lands were sold to U.S. settlers. Between 1887 and 1934, over 90 million acres of Indian land were transferred to non-Indian ownership.

Congress began to pass laws on an individual basis that placed Indian people under the jurisdiction of the United States. The Major Crimes Act of 1885 specified certain major criminal acts, such as murder and other felonies, that enabled federal officials to arrest Native Americans to face charges in federal court. The Major Crimes Act emerged from an incident involving the murder of a Sioux Indian leader who had just signed a treaty favorable to the United States. A Sioux Indian named Crow Dog killed the treaty-making Sioux leader because he believed that the leader had compromised Sioux national interests by signing the treaty. U.S. officials attempted to bring Crow Dog to trial, but because Crow Dog was not a U.S. citizen and because he had murdered another Indian of his own nation, the courts ruled that the United States had no jurisdiction in the case and therefore could not try Crow Dog. The Congress passed the Major Crimes Act to extend U.S. legal jurisdiction over Indian Country in cases of major criminal acts. The act, however, directly challenged Indian national rights to use their own legal institutions and rules to manage criminal cases. The Major Crimes Act of 1885 was amended twice and the list of major crimes was increased to ten, and then to fourteen. The acts further encroached on Indian rights of self-government by abolishing Indian legal institutions and subordinating Indians to federal courts.

After passage of the Major Crimes Acts, Congress continued to pass laws that usurped tribal sovereignty. The federal view depicted Indian nations as powerless to help their own people. Law and order on the frontier and control of Indian actions seemed to take precedence in Congress. Legislation that regulated individual Indians sought to place them under the same laws as all people in the United States, disregarding the right to self-government inherent in treaty agreements.

The turn of the twentieth century marked the beginning of an era in which Congress created policies for American Indians that would exchange their tribal membership for U.S. citizenship. In 1901 and 1902, Congress passed laws to allot tribal lands in Oklahoma to members of the Five Civilized Tribes: the Cherokee, Choctaw, Chickasaw, Creek, and Seminole. Five years later, however, Congress passed the Burke Act, which amended the Dawes Act and established a twenty-five year "trust" period. The Burke Act sought to protect some Native American groups from fraud and dispossession of their allotted lands. At the same time, the Burke Act placed American citizenship for Indians into abeyance. The passage of the Lacey Act of 1908 allowed the Five Civilized Tribes to sell their allotments, which they had been forced to accept under the Curtis Act of 1898. Many Cherokee, Creek, Seminole, Chickasaw, and Choctaw lost their lands to fraud, taxes, and bankruptcy.

The federal effort to assimilate Native Americans and make them citizens of the country continued in spite of the interruption of World War I. For those Indians who served the United States in the armed services and were honorably discharged, a 1919 act made them U.S. citizens. In 1924, Congress passed the General Citizenship Act to make the remaining Indian population U.S. citizens, whether they consented or not. The Indian citizenship legislation, however, did not change any treaty rights of the Indian people. Indians retained inherent rights to self-government as expressed in treaties and other agreements.

Congress exercised full plenary power over Native Americans as citizens of the United States, as the government policy stressed individualization and assimilation at the cost of the preservation of Indian culture and self-government. The government suppressed traditional Indian governments and actively discouraged Indian community and culture. The Snyder Act, passed three years earlier, attempted to improve the general livelihood of the Indian population by authorizing educational and social welfare programs. Reservation Indians, however, remained impoverished, attesting to the failure of the land allotment policy to prepare Indians for assimilation.

## The Indian New Deal

In 1928, a task force led by Lewis Meriam submitted a report known as the "Problem of Indian Administration," which strongly recommended an end to land allotment. The next year, the Great Depression shocked the nation with the crash of the stock market on Wall Street. A broken national economy enabled the democrats to elect Franklin Delano Roosevelt, who charged ahead with his experimental New Deal programs, which included major changes in the administration of Indian affairs. John Collier, appointed commissioner of Indian Affairs in 1932, championed Indian concerns and set out to push legislation under the New Deal to alleviate Indian suffering. Having learned firsthand about Indian tribes and the strength of their communalism, Collier convinced Congress to pass the controversial Wheeler-Howard Bill, later known as the Indian Reorganization Act of 1934. Two major groups that had been excluded—the Indians of Oklahoma and Alaska Natives—were subject to similar laws passed in 1936, the Oklahoma Indian Welfare Act and the Alaska Native Reorganization Act.

Under the staunch control of Commissioner Collier, the Indian New Deal persuaded Congress to pass the Johnson-O'Malley Act of 1934 to offer general federal assistance to some Indian students in order to attend public schools. The Indian Arts and Crafts Board Act of 1935 promoted the production and showing of Indian arts and crafts. After fifty years of major Indian land losses and encroachments on Indian national sovereignty, the thrust of federal Indian policy shifted to a return to self-government. Congress sought to compensate Indian tribes for land losses with the passage of the Indian Claims Commission Act of 1946, which allowed Indian tribes to present land claims before a federal review commission. With the passage of the act the tribes held hope that some compensation for lands lost and treaties broken would come.

## Termination Legislation

During the 1950s, the population of many reservation communities decreased, as many Indians, financially assisted by the Bureau of Indian Affair's relocation program, migrated to live and work in cities. The urban migration reflected an increase in job opportunities for Indian people due to work in war industries and military service during World War II. Congress shifted the direction of federal Indian policy due to changing attitudes about Indians inspired by their loyal and patriotic performance in the Second World War. The federal view again favored Indian assimilation into mainstream U.S. middle class society. To help this process and decentralize the bureaucracy created during the Collier years, Congress passed Public Law 280 during its eighty-third session, placing Indian Country in five states (California, Nebraska, Minnesota, Oregon, and Wisconsin) under state criminal and civil jurisdiction; a sixth state, Alaska, was later added. Enabling state governments to increase control over criminal and civil cases on Indian reservations was seen as a step toward ending federal and Indian government relations.

Even more dangerous congressional policies concerning Indian self-government came in 1953, when the House passed Concurrent Resolution 108 (HCR 108). The resolution outlined congressional intent to terminate the special federal trust relationship between the United States and Indian tribes. In 1954 legislation passed by the eighty-third Congress mandated the termination of the Menominee of Wisconsin. From 1954 to the mid–1960s, Congress terminated more than one hundred Indian tribes, communities, bands, and allotments. As a part of this decade to "get out of the Indian business," Congress also passed two important laws. One law transferred Indian health care to the Public Health Service, while another law encouraged Indians to apply to state social service programs and to attend public schools as full U.S. citizens.

During the Eisenhower Administration (1952–60), with Indian affairs under the supervision of Commissioner of Indian Affairs Glenn L. Emmons, the federal government attempted to industrialize Indian reservations in order to build viable market economies. Commissioner Emmons, Secretary of Interior Douglas McKay, and Congress worked toward a federal "withdrawal" of trust responsibilities in order to implant a laissez-faire system of capitalism in Indian Country. During the late 1950s, Emmons's efforts created dialogue with several companies concerning building satellite factories near reservations; results were minimal.

In the early 1960s, President John F. Kennedy's administration (1960–63) worked to end the termination policy and began efforts to stimulate economic development on Indian reservations. American Indian communities were included in President Lyndon Johnson's Great Society programs, which were aimed at helping the poor areas of the country. Congress passed the Economic Opportunity Act which provided a means for Indians to participate in and control their own programs for economic development. During the mid-1960s, Congress passed specific laws aimed at individual tribes in order to help their economies, primarily by developing their lands and natural resources. The emergence of pro-Indian legislation forced Congress to authorize additional monies to fund the administration of the Bureau of Indian Affairs.

In 1968, in his "Forgotten American" speech, President Johnson urged Congress to help American Indians both on the tribal and individual levels. Congress responded by passing the Indian Civil Rights Act, defining the government's powers of governance over tribal members and outlining the rights of individual Indians. The Johnson Administration favored such economic assistance to free American Indians from their poor economic and educational conditions. Included in the "Supplemental Appropriation Act, 1969," Congress appropriated $100,000 to establish a National Council on Indian Opportunity to improve Indian health, education, urban development, and welfare. As a continued effort to help the tribes rebuild their economies, Congress passed the Indian Financing Act in 1974 to assist the economic development of Indians and their organizations.

## Claims Cases and Land Returns

The Indian Claims Commission, implemented in 1946, requested that Congress authorize judgment payments to certain tribes as the result of successful land claims filed against the United States. Burdened with many tribal land claims against the United States, the Claims Commission itself required funding appropriations from Congress to carry on its business. While ensuing amendments extended the commission's life to 1978, the opportunity to file land claims ended in 1976 when Congress passed a law dissolving the Claims Commission on 31 December 1978. Starting in 1979, the U.S. Court of Claims heard all awaiting Indian land claim cases; the work of settling Indian land claims, however, was not concluded by the end of the twentieth century.

During the 1960s and 1970s, civil rights unrest and the controversy surrounding the Vietnam War produced great changes in the federal government and in U.S. society. The emergence of Red Power and the founding of the American Indian Movement (AIM) with supportive protests and militant demonstrations influenced the passage of pro-Indian legislation, such as previously unheard-of land returns to Native peoples. In 1970, Congress passed a law returning 48,000 acres in New Mexico, including Blue Lake, to the Taos Pueblo community. The next year, Congress passed the Alaska Natives Settlement Act of 1971, authorizing the return of 44 million acres and $962.5 million in compensation to Alaska Natives for releasing land claims for the rest of Alaska. Through legislation, land returns that benefited the Yakima of Washington State, and the Havasupai of Arizona followed. During the 1970s, court cases appealing to the Trade and Intercourse Act of 1790 resulted in land returns to the Narragansett of Massachusetts and the Penobscot and Passamaquoddy in the famed Maine Indians settlement case (see the northeast section of chapter 3).

## Restoration of Federal Tribal Recognition

During the Nixon Administration (1968–74), some tribes that had been terminated during the 1950s petitioned to restore federal recognition. The Menominee of Wisconsin started the movement and through their protest efforts, DRUMS (Determination of Rights and Unity for Menominee Shareholders) succeeded in pressuring federal officials and the U.S. Congress to pass legislation in 1973, calling for restoration of federal trust status. Two years later, Congress restored the Siletz; other tribes, such as the Klamath of Oregon, another large reservation community, followed, although not all terminated Indian groups had received restored status by 1992.

In the 1980s and 1990s, unrecognized tribes pushed for federal restoration of their federal tribal status

American Indian court judges at training sessions. (Courtesy of Jerry Gardner)

Six-sided courthouse on the Menominee Reservation in Keshena, central Wisconsin. (Courtesy of the UCLA American Indian Studies Center)

to establish their eligibility to apply for federal assistance available to Indian tribes. More than 150 non-recognized Indian communities have petitioned the government for federal recognition under the Federal Acknowledgment Project (FAP) developed by the BIA in 1978.

### Education and Vocation

Financing education has been a major form of federal assistance to the tribal nations and American Indians. Treaty provisions frequently include early efforts to educate Indian people in the American system of learning. Congress passed the Snyder Act of 1921 to encourage American Indians to enter into academic and vocational training. The Indian Reorganization Act of 1934, and other Indian New Deal legislation continued to emphasize education until World War II interrupted most activities. In 1956, during the postwar recovery of the Eisenhower years, Congress passed PL 959 to provide vocational opportunities and training to relocated urban Indians.

Federal studies—the Kennedy Report and the Josephy Report—surveyed Indian educational progress and called for additional legislation to promote educational progress among Indian students. Congress responded to the reports by passing the Education Assistance Act in 1972. In 1975, Congress passed an amended bill called the Indian Self-Determination and Education Assistance Act, which enabled Indian communities to gain greater control over local reservation schools. Three years later, another law empowered Indian communities with substantial control over the development of educational programs.

The limited number of Indians graduating from high school and college inspired Congress to consider legislation to allow tribal communities to exercise full autonomy concerning education on their reservations. In 1978, Congress passed the Tribally Controlled Community College Act, since many Indian youths felt culturally alienated in mainstream public and private college institutions. Currently thirty-one tribally controlled colleges throughout Indian Country offer culturally sensitive curricula based on the needs of their tribal youths.

Tribal drug court training session in Bethel, Alaska, 1999. (Courtesy of Jerry Gardner)

One urban Indian college, Native American Educational Services (NAES) College, is located in Chicago.

## Self-Determination

The failure of the termination policy, coupled with mounting Indian protests, called for a new federal Indian policy. A new Indian leadership of angry youth and emerging urban Indian communities convinced the federal government that after more than two hundred years of paternalistic practices, American Indians could run their own affairs. The Indian Self-Determination and Education Assistance Act of 1975 established the current federal Indian policy with ensuing legislation and federal programs to assist tribal governments and Indian communities and organizations to contract and administer federal services to Indian communities. The act is intended to give Indian communities greater control over services and programs that affect their lives and communities.

Under the rubric of self-determination, Congress has passed the Indian Health Care Improvement Act, authorizing seven years of increased appropriations to improve Indian health standards. In April 1978 Congress passed the American Indian Religious Freedom Act to protect and preserve the inherent right of American Indians to express and exercise their traditions and beliefs. In November 1978 Congress passed the Indian Child Welfare Act, which established a protocol for the adoption of Indian orphans. In order that an Indian orphan not be deprived of his or her cultural heritage the order of adoption moves from relatives, to tribal members, to other Indian persons, and, finally, to non-Indians. When placed in non-Indian homes and institutions, many American Indian youths experience confusion over their identity, frequently due to the denial of their Indian heritage.

During the 1980s, Congress passed the Indian Tribal Government Tax Status Act, granting tribes many of the federal tax advantages that states already enjoy. Tribes began assuming more autonomy over their communities and economies. In 1988 Congress passed legislation that officially ended the termination policy. During the same year, Congress passed the Indian Gaming Regulatory Act which placed limitation on bingo and casino operations on reservations. With the trust status still in effect, the federal government remains currently obligated as the guardian of 558 federally recognized tribes.

In the 1990s, the Bill Clinton Administration supported Indian education by holding a meeting of national authorities. The federal government supported Indian struggles for repatriation and the operation of Indian gaming by 212 tribes in twenty-eight states. By 1999, Indian gaming had become an industry yielding $7 billion per year. Most importantly, Indian economic improvement at the tribal level became, with tribal governance, the foreseen key to Indian self-determination, as Native communities brace themselves for the challenges of the future.

*Donald L. Fixico*
*The University of Kansas*

## ◆ LIST OF SIGNIFICANT U.S. LEGISLATION

The following legislation concerning U.S. Indians includes major laws regarding policy and programmatic changes in tribal life. The list excludes resolutions, very specific laws for tribes, and private laws affecting individuals.

**13 July 1787 Northwest Ordinance.** The Continental Congress passed this measure to establish orderly settlement and peace with the Indians in the Ohio Country (Northwest Ordinance).

**17 September 1787 U.S. Commerce with Foreign Nations and Indian Tribes.** The U.S. Constitution included Indians, granting Congress the power "to regulate Commerce with foreign Nations, and among the several States, and with the Indian tribes" (U.S. Constitution, article I, section 8).

**22 July 1790 Trade and Intercourse Act.** An act regulating trade with Indians, "That no sale of lands made by any Indians, or any nation or persons, or to any state, whether having the right of preemption to such lands or not, unless the same shall be made and duly executed at some public treaty, held under the same authority of the United States" (U.S. Statutes at Large, 1:137–38).

**1 March 1793 Trade and Intercourse Act.** An act restricting anyone without a license from having "any interest or concern in any trade with the Indians," and to be subject to a fine, and or imprisonment (U.S. Statutes at Large, 1:329–32).

**2 March 1793 Appropriation Act for Expenses of a Treaty with Northwest Indians.** An act designating a sum not to exceed $100,000 for commissioners to negotiate a treaty with hostile Indian tribes northwest of the Ohio River (U.S. Statutes at Large, 1:333).

**3 March 1795 Trade Act with Indians.** An act stipulating that a sum not more than $50,000 be appropriated for purchasing goods to supply Indians within the United States during 1795 (U.S. Statutes at Large, 1:443).

**18 April 1796 Trading Houses Act.** An act establishing government trading houses with the Indians, under control of the president of the United States. Trade with Indians continued via legislation when an act of 30 April 1802 continued trading houses, but expired; an act of 28 February 1803 continued trading houses for two years; an act of 3 March 1805 added trading houses; an act of 21 April 1806 repealed trading houses; an act of 3 March 1809 reestablished trading houses according to an act of 2 March 1815; an act of 3 March 1817; an act of 15 April 1818; an act of 3 March 1819; an act of 4 March 1820; an act of 3 March 1821; and trading houses were abolished by an act of 6 May 1822 (U.S. Statutes at Large, 1:452–53).

**19 May 1796 Trade and Intercourse Act.** An act restricting trade and intercourse with Indians. This act also established boundaries between the United States and various Indian groups of the Ohio area (U.S. Statutes at Large, 1:469–74).

**19 February 1799 Appropriation Act for Treaties with Indians.** An act appropriating a sum of no more than $25,000 for expenses to negotiate treaties with Indians (U.S. Statutes at Large, 1:618).

**25 February 1799 Appropriation Act for Treaties with Indians.** An act appropriating a sum of $10,000 to defray expenses of treaties with the Six Nations, Creek, Cherokee, and Chickasaw (U.S. Statutes at Large, 1:618–19).

**3 March 1799 Trade and Intercourse Act.** An act regulating trade and intercourse with Indians until 1802 and calling for a penalty to unlicensed persons dealing with Indians. The act also established boundaries in the area of Lake Erie, Tennessee, Alabama, and Florida (U.S. Statutes at Large, 1:743–49).

**17 January 1800 Peace Preservation Act.** This act aimed at the "preservation of peace with the Indian tribes" was passed to prevent European settlers from inciting Indian tribes on the western frontier to attacks against the United States. The penalties for agitating Indian attacks were $2,000 and $1,000, with the possibility of imprisonment (U.S. Statutes at Large, 2:6–7).

**30 March 1802 Trade and Intercourse Act.** An act regulating trade and activities with Indians and to authorize the president to impose measures preventing the vending or distribution of spirituous liquors to any Indian tribe (U.S. Statutes at Large, 2:139–46).

**3 March 1817 Punishment of Crimes and Offenses within Indian Boundaries Act.** An act for the general crimes act stating that Indians and other persons committing crimes within the exclusive jurisdiction of the United States would be tried and punished accordingly (U.S. Statutes at Large, 3:383).

**3 March 1819 Indian Civilization Act.** An act "making provision for the civilization of the Indian tribes adjoining the frontier settlements" to hire instructors and appropriate $10,000 annually for the Civilization Fund, the first federal Indian education program (U.S. Statutes at Large, 3:516–17).

**6 May 1822 Act to Amend Trading Houses Act.** An act to regulate trade and intercourse and to preserve peace with Indian tribes. The act also specified conditions under which licensed Indian traders were to operate (U.S. Statutes at Large, 3:682–83).

**28 May 1830 Indian Removal Act.** An act to exchange lands with the Indians east of the Mississippi River for their removal and lands located west of the same river (U.S. Statutes at Large, 4:411–12).

**9 July 1832 Commissioner of Indian Affairs Act.** An act to establish the position of commissioner of Indian affairs to be under the supervision of the secretary of war, and to be appointed by the president (U.S. Statutes at Large, 4:564).

**30 June 1834 Trade and Intercourse Act.** An act "to regulate trade and intercourse with the Indian tribes, and to preserve peace on the frontiers" (U.S. Statutes at Large, 4:729–35).

**30 June 1834 Department of Indian Affairs Act.** An act providing for the organization of the Department of Indian Affairs (U.S. Statutes at Large, 4:735–38).

**3 March 1847 Trade and Intercourse Act.** An act to regulate trade and intercourse with the tribes and to maintain peace on the frontiers. This act defined the procedures for eliminating the liquor trade among Indians (U.S. Statutes at Large, 9:203–204).

**29 July 1848 Appropriations for Indian Department Act.** An act appropriating various sums to fulfill treaty provisions to Indian tribes who had signed treaties with the United States (U.S. Statutes at Large, 9:252–65).

**3 March 1849 Department of Interior Act.** An act establishing the Department of the Interior and the position of secretary of the interior and placing the commissioner of Indian affairs in this department (U.S. Statutes at Large, 9:395–97).

**30 August 1852 Appropriations for Interior Department Act.** An act appropriating funds to meet expenses for the Department of Interior and to fulfill treaties through 30 June 1853 (U.S. Statutes at Large, 9:395–97).

**13 February 1862 Trade and Intercourse Act.** An act to regulate liquor traffic and to preserve peace with Indians (U.S. Statutes at Large, 12:338–39).

**14 June 1862 Indian Property Protection Act.** An act to protect the allotted property of Indians whose tribe had signed a treaty with the United States and who have adopted the habits of "civilized life" (U.S. Statutes at Large, 12:427–28).

**20 July 1867 Peace Commission Act.** An act for the president to appoint a Peace Commission to meet with hostile Indian tribes (U.S. Statutes at Large, 15:17–18).

**27 July 1868 Supervision and Appellate Act.** An act to transfer all supervisory and appellate powers and duties in regard to Indian affairs to the Department of the Interior (U.S. Statutes at Large, 15:228–31).

**3 March 1871 Indian Appropriations Act.** A section of this act appropriating funding to fulfill treaties with Indians called for the end of the treaty-making process (U.S. Statutes at Large, 16:566).

**3 March 1885 Indian Major Crimes Act.** An act of seven serious crimes authorizing U.S. officials to arrest Indians who have committed one of these crimes on their reservations. Later, the act was amended to ten crimes and then to fourteen (U.S. Statutes at Large, 23:385).

**8 February 1887 General Land Allotment Act.** An act to set up a commission to arrange the survey and allotment of reservations for distribution to individual tribal members (U.S. Statutes at Large, 24:388–91).

**9 August 1888 White Men and Indian Women Marriage Act.** An act to regulate legal effects of marriages between white men and Indian women. The act prohibited white men from intermarrying to obtain tribal rights, except with the Five Civilized Tribes, to protect property; and to allow for newly married Indian women to become U.S. citizens (U.S. Statutes at Large, 25:392).

**4 January 1889 Minnesota Chippewa Allotment Act.** An act authorizing the president to appoint a commission to negotiate with the Chippewa bands in Minnesota, except White Earth and Red Lake reservations, to allot forty-acre parcels to allottees (U.S. Statutes at Large, 25:642).

**1 March 1889 U.S. Court in Indian Territory Act.** An act that established a U.S. court within Indian Territory under the supervision of a judge, for a four-year term, with deputy marshals and a clerk (U.S. Statutes at Large, 25:783–88).

**19 January 1891 Sioux Indian Act.** An act for the secretary of the interior "to divide a portion of the reservation of the Sioux Nation of Indians in Dakota into separate reservations and to secure the relinquishment of the Indian title to the remainder" (U.S. Statutes at Large, 26:720–21).

**16 February 1891 Indian Schools Act.** An act for the construction of suitable school buildings for Indian industrial schools in Wisconsin, Michigan, Minnesota, and other states, to be based on the model of Carlisle Indian Industrial School, and not to cost more than $30,000 each (U.S. Statutes at Large, 26:764).

**28 February 1891 Land Allotment Act.** An act amending the General Land Allotment Act of 1887 to extend the benefits of the previous land and protection of the laws of the United States to Indians on various reservations (U.S. Statutes at Large, 26:794–96).

**3 March 1891 Indian Depredations Act.** An act "providing for the jurisdiction and payment of claims arising from Indian depredations" (U.S. Statutes at Large, 26:851–54).

**13 July 1892 Indian Agent Act.** Congress passed an act making appropriations for the Indian Department and for military officers to act as Indian agents (U.S. Statutes at Large, 27:120–21).

**23 July 1892 Intoxication in Indian Country Act.** An act to amend sections 2139, 2140, and 2141 of the previous statute. "No ardent spirits, ale, beer, wine, or intoxicating liquor or liquors of whatever kind shall be introduced under any pretense, into the Indian country." Violation of this law was punishable by up to two years imprisonment (U.S. Statutes at Large, 27:260–61).

**15 August 1894 Parent Consent for Education Act.** A general appropriation act to supervise Indian affairs, stressing education for Indians and prohibiting "sending children to schools outside the state or territory of their residence without the consent of their parents or natural guardians" U.S. Statutes at Large, 28:308).

**7 June 1897 Education Appropriation Act.** An act for funding which included a declared policy of Congress to make no appropriation whatever for education in any sectarian school in favor of supporting Indian day and industrial schools (U.S. Statutes at Large, 30:79).

**30 June 1897 Indian Liquor Act.** An act prohibiting the sale, gift, barter, exchange, or other disposition of beer, wine, and other liquors to Indians. This act was amended in 1933 to exclude Indian lands outside of reservations (U.S. Statutes at Large, 29:506).

**28 June 1898 Curtis Act.** An act, commonly called the Curtis Act, that extended all provisions of the General Allotment Act to Indian Territory and established that tribal laws were not to be enforced by the United States (U.S. Statutes at Large, 30:497–98, 502).

**1 March 1901 Creek Land Allotment Act.** An act calling for the general land allotment of 160 acres surveyed and distributed to Creek members in Oklahoma and the establishment of town sites in Oklahoma (U.S. Statutes at Large, 31:861–73).

**27 May 1902 General Appropriation Act.** An act to fulfill treaty obligations, civilize Indians, and carry out allotment. The act also supported schools for Indians, expenses for the Indian office, and supplies to the tribes. The act allows the secretary of the interior to permit heirs to sell trust restricted lands instead of dividing them among heirs (U.S. Statutes at Large, 32:245).

**1 July 1902 Cherokee Land Allotment Act.** An act for the allotment of the lands of the Cherokee Nation in Oklahoma, for the disposition of town sites in Oklahoma, including appraisement of natural resources of the lands, and the listing of a roll of Cherokee citizens (U.S. Statutes at Large, 32 pt. 1:716–27).

**1 July 1902 Choctaws and Chickasaws Land Allotment Act.** An act to ratify and confirm an agreement with the Choctaw and Chickasaw tribes to allot their tribal lands in Oklahoma for distribution to individual Choctaw and Chickasaw (U.S. Statutes at Large, 32 pt. 1:641–57).

**11 March 1904 Pipelines Act.** An act stating "the secretary of the interior is hereby authorized and empowered to grant a right of way in the nature of an easement for the construction, operation, and maintenance of pipelines for the conveyance of oil and gas through any Indian reservation, through any lands held by an Indian tribe or nation in the Indian Territory," including allotted land, with compensation paid to the tribe or individual (U.S. Statutes at Large, 33 pt. 1:65).

**23 April 1904 Practice of Medicine and Surgery in Indian Territory Act.** An act stating "no person shall practice medicine and surgery, or either, as a profession in the Indian Territory without first being registered as a physician and surgeon, or either" (U.S. Statutes at Large, 33 pt. 1:299–301).

**28 April 1904 White Earth Reservation Allotment Act.** An act calling for parcels of 160 acres to be allotted to Chippewa living on the White Earth Reservation according to provisions of the General Allotment Act of 1887 (U.S. Statutes at Large, 33 pt. 1:539).

**26 February 1906 Five Civilized Tribes Council Act.** An act to keep the tribal governments of the Cherokee, Creek, Seminole, Chickasaw, and Choctaw in operation in the form of the national councils (U.S. Statutes at Large, 34:137).

**26 April 1906 Final Disposition of Affairs of Five Civilized Tribes Act.** An act to reaffirm tribal membership among the Five Civilized Tribes for school funding, payments to Indians, acknowledgment of lands held in trust, and recognition for the Five Civilized Tribes' governments (U.S. Statutes at Large, 34 pt. 1:137–48).

**8 May 1906 Burke Act.** An act to amend the Dawes Allotment Act, extending the laws of the United States and Territories over the Indians. Following the end of the twenty-five-year trust period, each allottee was to be subject to civil and criminal laws. Citizenship rights were conferred to allottees on issue of fee simple title of property (U.S. Statutes at Large, 24:182–83).

**17 May 1906 Alaska Allotment Act.** An act for the provisions of the Dawes Act to be applied to Alaska with 160 acres of nonmineral land to individual Natives to receive full title to their homesites (U.S. Statutes at Large, 34:197).

**2 March 1907 Tribal Funds Act.** An act to authorize the secretary of the interior "to designate any individual Indian" to be entitled to an allotment or a share of his or her tribal domain (U.S. Statutes at Large, 34 pt. 1:1221–22).

**27 May 1908 Removal of Restrictions from Some Lands of Allottees of Five Civilized Tribes Act.** An act authorizing the secretary of the interior to remove restrictions from Indians of the Five Civilized Tribes who are of less than one-half Indian blood and/or who are intermarried with whites, freedmen, and mixed-blood Indian minors of less than one-half Indian blood (U.S. Statutes at Large, 35 pt. 1:312–16).

**29 May 1908 Allotted Lands Selling Act.** An act to extend the authority of the secretary of the interior to issue patents in fee to purchases of Indian lands. Indian allotments may be sold on petition of allottee and the secretary must ascertain the legal heirs involved (U.S. Statutes at Large, 35 pt. 1:444–58).

**25 June 1910 Restricted Trust Lands Act.** An act amending the sale of trust lands to improve the order of determining heirs of deceased Indians for the sale and leasing of restricted lands. This act was amended 14 February 1913 to regulate Indian allotments disposed by a will (U.S. Statutes at Large, 36 pt. 1:855–63).

**6 June 1912 Classification and Appraisal of Unallotted Indian Lands Act.** An act authorizing the secretary of the interior to classify or reclassify and appraise or reappraise unallotted or unreserved land within any Indian reservation opened to settlement (U.S. Statutes at Large, 37 pt. 1:125).

**14 June 1918 Five Civilized Heirship Act.** An act authorizing jurisdiction of the Probate Court of the State of Oklahoma to settle the estates of deceased members of the Five Civilized Tribes and to partition lands belonging to the full-blood heirs of deceased allottees of the Five Civilized Tribes (U.S. Statutes at Large, 40 pt. 1:606).

**6 November 1919 U.S. Citizenship for Indian Veterans of World War I Act.** An act granting U.S. citizenship to every American Indian who served in the armed services during World War I and was honorably discharged. If desired, the discharged veteran could, by court of "competent" jurisdiction, be granted full individual or tribal property rights (U.S. Statutes at Large, 41:350).

**2 November 1921 Snyder Act.** An act allowing the expenditure of funds for Indians without regard to amount of Indian blood, membership in a federally recognized tribe, or residence (as long as it is in the United States). Funds were designated to support and "civilize," through such means as education; to improve health; to provide industrial acceptance, manufacturing, irrigation systems, and building repair; to provide general administration of Indian property; and to employ professionals to help Indians (U.S. Statutes at Large, 42 pt. 1:208).

**14 February 1923 Land Purchase Act.** An act to amend the General Land Allotment Act of 1887 to include lands purchased for Indians (U.S. Statutes at Large, 42 pt. 1:1246).

**29 May 1924 Indian Oil Leasing Act.** An act to amend the oil leasing act of 1891 by extending the leasing period of unallotted Indian lands involving oil and gas—other than those of the Five Civilized Tribes and the Osage Nation—until such quantities are exhausted (U.S. Statutes at Large, 43 pt. 1:244).

**2 June 1924 General Citizenship Act.** An act stating that all non-citizen Indians born within the territorial limits of the United States are declared citizens of the United States (U.S. Statutes at Large, 43:253).

**7 June 1924 Public Schools Tuition Act.** An act for the secretary of the interior to pay tuition for Indian students in public schools for the fiscal years 1922 and 1923, with remaining funds to go to Indian day and industrial schools (U.S. Statutes at Large, 43 pt. 1:536–37).

**7 June 1924 Pueblo Lands Board Act.** An act to quiet "the title to lands within Pueblo Indian land grants," and to establish a board to hear claims (U.S. Statutes at Large, 43 pt. 1:636–37).

**13 April 1926 Indian Insurance Act.** An act stating that funds of any tribe under U.S. control are to be used to make insurance premium payments for protection against fire, theft, tornado, hail, earthquakes, and other forces of nature (U.S. Statutes at Large, 44 pt. 2:242).

**17 April 1926 Land Lease Act.** An act for the secretary of the interior to lease lands for mining purposes, and any reservation land for an Indian agency or school (U.S. Statutes at Large, 44 pt. 2:300).

**3 June 1926 Northern Cheyenne Allotment Act.** An act to allot in severalty lands of the Northern Cheyenne Reservation in Montana (U.S. Statutes at Large, 44 pt. 2:690).

**3 March 1927 Indian Oil Leasing Act.** An act recognizing Indian title to executive order Indian lands and Indian rights to the proceeds from mineral leases. The act called for the Indians involved to be consulted about the expenditure of tribal funds (U.S. Statutes at Large, 44 pt. 2:1374).

**13 June 1930 Tax of Ceded Indian Irrigated Lands Act.** An act to amend the taxation of lands, homesteads, and desert land entry classified under the Reclamation Act, and to include ceded Indian lands from Indian irrigation (U.S. Statutes at Large, 46 pt. 1:581–82).

**13 June 1930 Interest of Trust Funds Act.** An act to amend "that all funds without account balances exceeding $500 held in trust by the United States and carried in principal accounts. . . shall bear the interest at a rate of 4 per centum per annum" (U.S. Statutes at Large, 46 pt. 1:584).

**February 1931 Indian Highway Act.** An act to amend the Federal Highway Act of 1921 for the secretary of agriculture to cooperate with state highway departments and with the Department of Interior to construct public highways within Indian reservations (U.S. Statutes at Large, 46 pt. 1:1173).

**3 March 1931 Trust of Acquired Lands for Five Civilized Tribes Act.** An act to continue alienation of nontaxable land of a restricted Indian of the Five Civilized Tribes when such land is sold to Oklahoma or any country or municipality at the secretary of the interior's discretion (U.S. Statutes at Large, 46 pt. 1:1471). (Amended 30 June 1932 [U.S. Statutes, 47 pt. 1:474].)

**1 July 1932 Leavitt Act.** An act stating that no assessments for construction costs would be made against Indian-owned lands within federal irrigation projects until Indian title had been extinguished. The secretary of the interior was authorized to adjust or eliminate debts against individual Indians or tribes in consideration of the circumstances (U.S. Statutes, 47 pt. 1:564).

**26 January 1933 Indian Irrigation Act.** An act stating that the secretary of the interior has authority to defer payment of construction charges on irrigation projects under the direction of the commissioner of Indian affairs (U.S. Statutes at Large, 47 pt. 1:776–77).

**27 January 1933 Five Civilized Tribes Restrictions Act.** An act for the secretary of the interior to restrict all funds and securities of Indians who are one-half blood, enrolled or unenrolled, until 26 April 1956. These people are subject until then to the benefit and expenditures of their funds in the best interests of such individuals (U.S. Statutes at Large, 47 pt. 1:777–79).

**25 February 1933 Indian Monies Due Act.** An act to benefit incompetent and minor Indians owed any amounts from accounts in government agencies. Amounts may also be paid to the superintendent or other bonded officers of the Indian service for the beneficiaries or heirs (U.S. Statutes at Large, 47 pt. 1:907).

**4 March 1933 Indian Timber Contracts Act.** An act to modify terms of existing and uncompleted contracts of Indian tribal timber, under the jurisdiction of the secretary of the interior (U.S. Statutes at Large, 47 pt. 1:1568–69).

**31 May 1933 Pueblo Lands Board Appropriation Act.** An act to compensate Pueblo Indian communities, according to the Act of 7 June 1924, and to meet awards made by the Pueblo Lands Board (U.S. Statutes at Large, 48 pt. 1:108–11).

**16 April 1934 Johnson-O'Malley Act.** An act offering general federal assistance to Indians for education, medical attention, relief of distress, and social welfare (U.S. Statutes at Large, 48:596).

**7 May 1934 U.S. Citizenship for Metlakahtla Indians Act.** An act to declare Metlakatla Indians—who migrated from British Columbia, Canada, to Annette Island in southeast Alaska in 1887, and who established a colony known as Metlakatla, Alaska—to be citizens of the United States (U.S. Statutes at Large, 48 pt. 1:667).

**18 June 1934 Indian Reorganization Act.** An act, commonly called the Wheeler-Howard Act, to restore tribal self-government; to start the Indian credit program; to restore lands to tribal ownership; to stop allotment; to allow vocational and trade schooling; and to issue a charter of incorporation (U.S. Statutes at Large, 48 pt. 1:984–88).

**27 August 1935 Indian Arts and Crafts Board Act.** An act to establish an Indian Arts and Crafts Board of five commissioners to promote the economic welfare of Indian tribes and the Indian wards of the government through the development of arts and crafts and the expansion of the market for such products (U.S. Statutes at Large, 49:891–93).

**11 February 1936.** Leasing of Restricted Lands of Five Civilized Tribes, who were one-half or more Indian blood, enrolled or unenrolled, not for periods longer than five years, for farming and grazing (U.S. Statutes at Large, 49 pt. 1:1135).

**1 May 1936 Alaska Native Reorganization Act.** An act extending certain provisions of the Wheeler-Howard Act (PL 383) to the Territory of Alaska to assist Native people (U.S. Statutes at Large, 49 pt. 1:1250–51).

**4 June 1936 State Contracts for Indian Welfare Act.** An act amending the Act of 16 April 1934, authorizing the secretary of the interior to arrange with states and territories for state universities, colleges, or schools, or with any appropriate state or private corporation, agency, or institution, for the education, medical attention, agriculture assistance, and social welfare of Indians (U.S. Statutes at Large, 49 pt. 1:1458–59).

**26 June 1936 Oklahoma Indian Welfare Act.** An act to provide Oklahoma tribe with provisions similar to those of the Indian Reorganization Action of 1934 (U.S. Statutes at Large, 49:1967–68).

**1 September 1937 Alaska Reindeer Act.** An act intended to provide subsistence to Eskimos and other Natives of Alaska by encouraging a self-sustaining economy and developing activity in the reindeer industry (U.S. Statutes at Large, 50:900–902).

**4 April 1938 Federal Indian Irrigation Act.** An act for the secretary of the interior to grant concessions on reservoir sites, reserves for canals or flowage areas, and other lands under his jurisdiction that have been withdrawn or acquired with respect to the San Carlos, Fort Hall, Flathead, and Duck Valley or Western Shoshone irrigation projects (U.S. Statutes at Large, 52:193).

**11 May 1938 Indian Lands Mining Act.** An act establishing that unallotted lands within an Indian reservation, or lands owned by any tribe, group, or lands of Indians under federal jurisdiction, may, with approval of the secretary of the interior, be leased for up to ten years (U.S. Statutes at Large, 52:347–48).

**24 June 1938 Deposit and Investment of Indian Funds Act.** An act authorizing the secretary of the interior to deposit into banks the funds of any Indian or tribe that agrees to pay a high interest rate under the regulations of the member banks of the Federal Reserve System (U.S. Statutes at Large, 52:1037–38).

**24 June 1940 Indian Lumber Products Act.** An act establishing that forest products produced by Indian enterprises from forests on Indian lands may be sold under regulations as prescribed by the secretary of the interior (U.S. Statutes at Large, 54 pt. 1:504).

**28 May 1941 Wind River Indian Lands Act, PL 77–79.** An act authorizing the secretary of the interior to determine and fix permanent boundaries of allotted, tribal, and ceded lands along the Big Wind River in order to establish the boundaries of the Wind River Reservation (U.S. Statutes at Large, 55 pt. 1:207).

**28 May 1941 Santa Ysabel Indian Reservation Land Exchange Act, PL 77–81.** An act authorizing the secretary of the interior to exchange, with the consent of the tribal government and satisfaction of the secretary, approximately one and eight-tenths acres of the reservation for approximately four and three-tenths acres of equal value (U.S. Statutes at Large, 55 pt. 1:208).

**16 August 1941 Rincon Band of Mission Indians Land Act, PL 77–207.** An act describing a small addition of certain public lands as a part of the Rincon Band of Mission Indians of California. The act further establishes that until otherwise directed by Congress, none of said lands shall be allotted in severalty or subject to taxation (U.S. Statutes at Large, 55 pt. 1:622).

**15 November 1941 Criminal Code for Fires on Public Domain or Indian Lands Act, PL 77–293.** An act to amend section 52 of the Criminal Code (Act of 4 March 1909, 35 Stat. 1098, United States Code, title 18 sec. 106) with respect to public domain described and Indian lands, or on certain lands owned or leased by, or under the partial, concurrent, or exclusive jurisdiction of the United States (U.S. Statutes at Large, 55 pt. 1:763–64).

**29 January 1942 Cheyenne-Arapaho Tribes Lands Act, PL 77–419.** An act to set aside certain lands in Oklahoma for the Cheyenne-Arapaho tribes of Indians, and to carry out certain obligations to certain enrolled Indians under agreement with the United States (U.S. Statutes at Large, 56 pt. 1:21–23).

**20 February 1942 Purchase from Indian Service Appropriations for Alaska Native Act, PL 77–457.** An act authorizing the secretary of the interior to make purchases from appropriations for the benefit of Alaska Natives. Purchases may include food, clothing, supplies, and materials for sale to employees of the Department of Interior who are stationed in Alaska, and to Natives of Alaska and Native cooperative associations under his supervision (U.S. Statutes at Large, 56 pt. 1:95).

**24 February 1942 Lands of Klamath and Modoc Tribes and Snake Indians Act, PL 77–465.** An act for the secretary of the interior to receive on behalf of the United States from individual members of the Klamath Tribe of Indians voluntarily executed deeds of fee simple owned land to be held in trust and subject to restrictions for Klamath and Modoc tribes and the Yahooskin Band of Snake Indians (U.S. Statutes at Large, 56 pt. 1:121).

**9 May 1942 Manchester Rancheria Act, PL 77–546.** An act reserving certain public lands in California for the Manchester Band of Pomo Indians of the Manchester Rancheria (U.S. Statutes at Large, 56 pt. 1:273).

**28 October 1942 Electrical Lines Right-of-Way Parker Dam Project Act, PL 77–764.** An act for the acquisition of Indian lands required for the construction, operation, and maintenance of electrical transmission lines of the Parker Dam Project, Arizona-California (U.S. Statutes at Large, 56 pt. 1:1011).

**24 November 1942 Tribal Acquisition of Deceased Members' Land Act, PL 77–774.** An act of trust lands or interest of estates, without heirs, including accumulated revenue to be turned over to the respective tribe (U.S. Statutes at Large, 56 pt. 1:1021–22).

**24 December 1942 Probate of Deceased Indians of Five Civilized Tribes Act, PL 77–833.** An act conferring to the secretary of the interior the authority to determine heirs and to probate estates of deceased restricted Indians of the Five Civilized Tribes, enrolled or unenrolled, when such estates are valued less than $2,500 (U.S. Statutes at Large, 56 pt. 1:1080–81).

**4 March 1944 Additional Land for Havasupai Reservation Act, PL 78–246.** An act adding described land of the Gila and Salt rivers to the Havasupai Reservation, and for the secretary of the interior to exchange lands in Arizona to become a part of the reservation (U.S. Statutes at Large, 58 pt. 1:110–11).

**29 May 1944 Additional Land to Navajo Reservation Act, PL 78–317.** An act for the secretary of the interior to exchange six acres of land within the Navajo Reservation for four and fourteen one-hundredths acres to the satisfaction of the Navajo tribe and secretary of the interior (U.S. Statutes at Large, 58 pt. 1:257).

**13 December 1944 Marriage and Divorce Among Klamath, Modoc and Snake Indians Act, PL 78–477.** An act stating the conditions for marriages involving the Klamath, Modoc, and Yahooskin Band of Snake Indians shall be solemnized according to the laws of the state of Oregon, and establishing that only a state court can decree a divorce (U.S. Statutes at Large, 58 pt. 1:800).

**23 December 1944 Tulalip Tribe Land Sale Act, PL 78–549.** An act authorizing the secretary of the interior with the governing approval of the Tulalip tribe, to sell and convey to purchasers the tidelands with the proceeds to be reinstated in other lands and subject to the act of 18 June 1934 (U.S. Statutes at Large, 58 pt. 1:917).

**30 June 1945 Sioux Claims Awards Act, PL 79–97.** An act for a sum of $101,630 for payment to certain individual Sioux Indians, their heirs, or devises, in full settlement and satisfaction of their claims against the United States for personal property losses as found and determined by the secretary of the interior (U.S. Statutes at Large, 59 pt. 1:265).

**31 May 1946 Devils Lake Indian Reservation Jurisdiction Act, PL 79–394.** An act conferring to the state of North Dakota jurisdiction over offenses committed by or against Indians on the Devils Lake Indian Reservation in North Dakota to the same extent as its courts have jurisdiction generally over offenses committed within said state outside Indian reservations (U.S. Statutes at Large, 60 pt. 1:229).

**24 June 1946 Additional Land for Kiowa, Comanche and Apache Reservation Act, PL 79–435.** An act eliminating Rainy Mountain School Reserve in Oklahoma and vesting it in the United States in trust for the Indians of the Kiowa, Comanche, and Apache Indian Reservation (U.S. Statutes at Large, 60 pt. 1:305).

**28 June 1946 Fort Berthold Indian Awards Act, PL 79–467.** An act authorizing the sum of $400,000 for final settlement of all claims and demands of the Arikara, Gros Ventre, and Mandan of such reservation, based upon an unrestricted treaty of 27 July 1866 (U.S. Statutes at Large, 60 pt. 1:333).

**28 June 1946 Costs Related to Crow Irrigation Project Act, PL 79–468.** An act setting the aggregate costs of all expenditures at $45,000 made for the construction of the Crow irrigation project on the Crow Indian Reservation in Montana with certain exclusions; to be paid from the U.S. Treasury (U.S. Statutes at Large, 60 pt. 1:333–38).

**8 August 1946 Transfer of Power to Commissioner of Indian Affairs Act, PL 79–687.** An act allowing the secretary of the interior, as he deems, to delegate his powers and duties to the commissioner of Indian affairs to handle Indian affairs in order to facilitate and simplify the administration of Indian affairs (U.S. Statutes at Large, pt. 1:939).

**9 August 1946 Leasing of Indian Lands in Washington, PL 79–702.** An act requiring written consent from the Indian individuals, associations of Indians, or Indian tribes to lease Indian lands, including restricted lands, in the state of Washington (U.S. Statutes at Large, 60 pt. 1:962).

**10 August 1946 Recognition of Keetoowah Indians Act, PL 79–715.** An act stating that the Keetoowah Indians of the Cherokee Nation of Oklahoma shall be recognized as a band of Indians residing in Oklahoma according to section 3 of the act of 26 June 1936 (49 Stat. 1967) (U.S. Statutes at Large, 60 pt. 1:976).

**13 August 1946 Indian Claims Commission Act.** An act to end Indian land claims by making monetary compensations recommended by the Indian Claims Commission to last ten years. Congress extended the commission in 1967 and terminated the commission on 30 September 1978 (U.S. Statutes at Large, 60:1049–56).

**19 May 1947 Division of Shoshoni and Arapaho Trust Funds Act, PL 80–74.** An act dividing the trust funds of the Shoshone and Arapaho tribes of the Wind River Reservation on deposit in the Treasury of the United States (U.S. Statutes at Large, 61 pt. 1:102).

**27 May 1947 Memorial Museum on Fort Hall Reservation Act, PL 80–78.** An act authorizing a sum of $150,000 for the purpose of constructing a memorial museum in commemoration of old Fort Hall and a shop for the sale of Indian handicrafts, with the operation by the Shoshone-Bannock tribes of the Ft. Hall Reservation under the supervision, management, and control of the Bureau of Indian Affairs (U.S. Statutes at Large, 61 pt. 1:120).

**24 June 1947 Sale of Timber on Allotment of Northern Cheyenne Reservation, PL 80–230.** An act allowing the timber on the allotments of the Northern Cheyenne Indian Reservation to be sold pursuant to the provisions of section 8 of the Act of 25 June 1910 (36 Stat. 857; 25 USC, sec. 406) (U.S. Statutes at Large, 61 pt. 1:418).

**27 June 1947 Navajo Gas Lands Lease Act, PL 80–124.** An act for the secretary of the interior, acting through the Bureau of Mines and the Navajo tribe, to enter into an agreement dated 1 December 1945 to substitute new leases for former oil and gas leases on the Navajo Reservation in New Mexico (U.S. Statutes at Large, 61 pt. 1:189).

**19 December 1947 Immediate Relief of Navajo and Hopi Act, PL 80–390.** An act authorizing a sum of $2 million to allow the secretary of the interior to provide immediate relief for needy Navajo and Hopi Indians who are on their reservations or allotted holdings (U.S. Statutes at Large, 61 pt. 1:940).

**5 February 1948 Filing of Actions to Quit Land Titles Act, PL 80–406.** An act that any person may file against an Indian or heirs of any Indian, who was or were granted lands according to a treaty between the United States and Delaware Indians, 3 October 1818 (7 Stat. 188), containing a condition that such lands should never be conveyed or transferred without the approbation of the president of the United States (U.S. Statutes at Large, 61 pt. 1:17).

**5 February 1948 Indian Lands Rights-of-Way Act, PL 80–407.** An act allowing the secretary of the interior to grant rights-of-way for all purposes across Indian lands held in trust by the United States, excluding the Pueblo Indians of New Mexico (U.S. Statutes at Large, 62 pt. 1:17–18).

**5 February 1948 Competency of Certain Osages Act, PL 80–408.** An act authorizing the secretary of the interior to issue certificates of competency to each member of the Osage Tribe of less than one-half Indian blood and at least twenty-one years of age. The legal guardian is to assume business supervision if the Osage member is deemed incompetent by law (U.S. Statutes at Large, 62 pt. 1:18–19).

**27 February 1948 Certain Lands Sale of L'Anse Chippewa Act, PL 80–418.** An act allowing the secretary of the interior to sell for the sum of $2,015, to be conveyed to the village of L'Anse, Michigan, certain tribal lands and allotted Indian lands (U.S. Statutes at Large, 62 pt. 1:35).

**11 March 1948 Uintah and Ouray Indian Reservation Boundaries Act, PL 80–440.** An act establishing the exterior boundary of the Uintah and Ouray Reservation in Grand and Uintah counties of Utah, for the benefit of the Ute Indian Tribe of said reservation (U.S. Statutes at Large, 62 pt. 1:72–78).

**29 March 1948 Klamath Welfare Act, PL 80–463.** An act authorizing the secretary of the interior to pay loans; to purchase land; to build homes, including household equipment and furnishings; and to purchase feed, seed, and grain from the capital reserve fund on deposit for the Klamath, Modoc, and Yahooskin Band of Snake Indians (U.S. Statutes at Large, 62 pt. 1:92–93).

**25 May 1948 Costs on Flathead Indian Irrigation Project, PL 80–554.** An act for the United States to reimburse costs for the construction of the irrigation and power systems of the Flathead irrigation project in Montana, according to construction costs under the act of 7 March 1928 and supplemental acts (U.S. Statutes at Large, 62 pt. 1:269–73).

**30 June 1948 Iowa Jurisdiction over Sac and Fox Reservation Act, PL 80–846.** An act conferring to the state of Iowa jurisdiction over the Sac and Fox Reservation in that state (U.S. Statutes at Large, 62 pt. 1:1161).

**1 July 1948 Estate Sale of Crow Tribe Act, PL 80–870.** An act to provide for the sale to the Crow Tribe the interests of the estates of deceased Crow Indian allottees, and to provide for the sale of certain lands to the Board County Commissioners of Comanche County, Oklahoma (U.S. Statutes at Large, 62 pt. 1:1214–15).

**13 August 1949 Certain Pueblo and Carroncito Navajo Lands in Trust Act, PL 81–226.** An act acknowledging the transfer, approved by the president of the United States, from the secretary of agriculture to the secretary of the interior, of certain public domain to become trust lands for Pueblo and Carroncito Navajo Indians (U.S. Statutes at Large, 63 pt. 1:604–605).

**19 August 1949 Klamath County School Facilities Act, PL 81–256.** An act providing funds for cooperation with the school board of Klamath County, Oregon, for the construction, extension, and improvement of public school facilities to be available to all Indian and non-Indian children without discrimination (U.S. Statutes at Large, 63 pt. 1:621–22).

**7 September 1949 Indian Schools in South Dakota Act, PL 81–301.** An act stating that the schools operated and maintained by the Bureau of Indian Affairs on any reservation in South Dakota shall, by a voting majority of the parents of the children, decide on the course of study which is to meet at least the minimum educational requirements prescribed by the department of public instruction of South Dakota (U.S. Statutes at Large, 63 pt. 1:694).

**7 September 1949 Exchange of Navajo Tribal Lands Act, PL 81–302.** An act authorizing the secretary of the interior with the governing body of the Navajo tribe to exchange surface rights of 640 acres in Arizona for land in Utah (U.S. Statutes at Large, 63 pt. 1:695).

**8 September 1949 Competent Crow Tribe Act, PL 81–303.** An act stating that all Crow Indians born to "competent" parents shall automatically become "competent" members of the tribe (U.S. Statutes at Large, 63 pt. 1:695).

**5 October 1949 Agua Caliente Indian Reservation Jurisdiction Act, PL 81–322.** An act stating that all lands on the Agua Caliente Indian Reservation in the state of California, and the Indian residents thereof, shall be subject to the laws, both civil and criminal, of the state of California (U.S. Statutes at Large, 63 pt. 1:705–706).

**10 October 1949 Land Exchange North Carolina Cherokees Act, PL 81–338.** An act for exchange of lands between the North Carolina Cherokee and the State of North Carolina, involving right of way of the Blue Ridge Parkway, Mollie Gap, Wolf Laurel Gap, and Bunches Gap (U.S. Statutes at Large, 63 pt. 1:726–31).

**25 October 1949 Crow Tribe Buffalo Act, PL 81–384.** An act for the secretary of the interior to transfer to the Crow tribe of Montana the title to all the buffalo owned by the United States on the Crow Indian Reservation (U.S. Statutes at Large, 63 pt. 1:904).

**19 April 1950 Rehabilitation of Navajo and Hopi Indians Act, PL 81–474.** An act providing facilities, employment, and services to the Navajo and Hopi to develop their natural resources and help them become self-supporting (U.S. Statutes at Large, 64 pt. 1:44–47).

**15 September 1950 Indian Land Jurisdiction in New York, PL 81–785.** An act conferring to the state of New York jurisdiction in civil actions and proceedings between Indians or among one or more Indians and any other person or persons (U.S. Statutes at Large, 64 pt. 1:845–46).

**30 September 1950 Separate Settlement Contracts for Sioux Act, PL 870.** An act to authorize the chief of engineers, department of the army, with the secretary of the interior to negotiate contracts separating with the Cheyenne River Sioux and Standing Rock Sioux for the Oahe Dam and Reservoir Project (U.S. Statutes at Large, 64 pt. 1:1093–95).

**21 August 1951 Ute Per Capita and Division Act, PL 82–120.** An act for the secretary of the interior to use the tribal fund of the Ute tribes for a per capita payment to the Ute tribe of the Uintah and Ouray reservations, and to divide the tribal funds with Southern Ute (U.S. Statutes at Large, 65:193–95).

**3 April 1952 Transfer of Indian Health Care Act.** An act to authorize the Public Health Service to receive transfer of unused Indian health facilities to states and local governments to provide health needs to non-Indians. The act further authorizes the secretary of the interior to contract with states and territories for health care facilities to meet Indian needs. The transfer was to be effective 1 July 1955, according to statute in U.S. Statutes 68:674–75 (U.S. Statutes at Large, 66:35–36).

**12 June 1952 Hoopa Valley Reservation School Act, PL 82–389.** An act that the secretary of the interior may convey by deed to the state of California or to the Hoopa Unified School District of the state of California not more than forty-five acres of the agency and school reserve on the Hoopa Valley Indian Reservation for use for the construction of a school for both Indian and non-Indian pupils (U.S. Statutes at Large, 66:135).

**3 July 1952 Five Civilized Tribes Contracts Act, PL 82–440.** An act allowing Five Civilized Tribes to make contracts for professional legal services involving the prosecution of claims against the United States with the approval of the secretary of the interior (U.S. Statutes at Large, 66:323).

**18 July 1952 Cession of Rights-of-Way on Wind River Reservation Act, PL 82–591.** An act authorizing the secretary of the interior to reimburse the Shoshone and Arapaho tribes for an amount not to exceed $458,000, to be paid from funds appropriated for the Missouri River Basin project, to convey and relinquish to the United States the property and rights of the tribes' land needed for the construction, operation, and maintenance of the Boysen Unit of the Missouri River Basin Project (U.S. Statutes at Large, 66:780).

**4 June 1953 Indian School Property Act, PL 83–47.** An act authorizing the secretary of the interior to convey to state and local government agencies federal Indian land and school facilities no longer needed, so long as that land be no more than twenty acres (U.S. Statutes at Large, 66:41).

**4 August 1953 Criminal and Civil Jurisdiction Act.** An act, commonly known as Public Law 280 (PL 83–280), granted the states of California, Nebraska, Minnesota, Oregon, and Wisconsin civil and criminal jurisdiction over reservations (U.S. Statutes at Large, 67:588–90).

**15 August 1953 Shoshoni and Arapaho Compensation Act, PL 83–284.** An act authorizing $1,009,500 in compensation to the Shoshone and Arapaho tribes of the Wind River Reservation for the Riverton reclamation project and for a ceded portion of their reservation (U.S. Statutes at Large, 66:592–613).

**15 August 1953 Termination of Certain Federal Restrictions Act, PL 83–281.** An act to repeal the forbidden sale, purchase, or possession by Indians of personal property which may be sold, purchased, or possessed by non-Indians, amending Section 1157 of title 18 of the U.S. codes pertaining to livestock (U.S. Statutes at Large, 67:590).

**17 June 1954 Menominee Termination Act, PL 83–399.** This act ended the federal trust relationship between the Menominee tribe and the United States and promised to provide a per capita payment of $1,500 to members. The act was amended 8 September 1960 to agree upon a plan for trusteeship over tribal properties (PL 86733) (U.S. Statutes at Large, 68:250–52).

**30 June 1954 Fort Peck Reservation Fee Patents Act, PL 83–461.** An act granting oil and gas in lands to the allottee with fee patents and, if deceased, to heirs or devises, with the majority members of Fort Peck voting to accept these conditions (U.S. Statutes at Large, 68 pt. 1:358–59).

**6 July 1954 Lower Brule, Crow Creek Sioux and Yankton Sioux Act, PL 83–478.** An act to authorize the negotiation and ratification of separate contracts with the Lower Brule Sioux and Crow Creek Sioux in South Dakota for lands and rights involving the Fort Randall Dam and Reservoir, Missouri River Development. The act also reestablished the Indians of the Yankton Indian Reservation in South Dakota (U.S. Statutes at Large, 68 pt. 1:452–54).

**5 August 1954 Indian Health Care Transfer Act, PL 83–568.** An act transferring Indian health care supervised by the Bureau of Indian Affairs and the Department of Interior to the Public Health Service, supervised by the secretary of health, education, and welfare (U.S. Statutes at Large, 68:674).

**13 August 1954 Klamath Termination Act, PL 83–587.** An act terminating federal supervision of the property of the Klamath tribe in Oregon and of the individual members thereof (U.S. Statutes at Large, 68 pt. 1:718–28).

**13 August 1954 Western Oregon Indians Termination Act, PL 83–588.** An act terminating federal supervision over the property of certain tribes and bands of Indians in western Oregon and the individuals thereof (U.S. Statutes at Large, 68 pt. 1:724–28).

**23 August 1954 Alabama and Coushatta Termination Act, PL 83–627.** An act terminating federal supervision of the property of the Alabama and Coushatta tribe of Indians of Texas, and of the individual members thereof (U.S. Statutes at Large, 68 pt. 1:768–69).

**24 August 1954 Fee Patent Allotments for Mission Indians Act, PL 83–653.** An act to confirm authority of the secretary of the interior to issue patents in fee to allotments of lands of the Mission Indians in the state of California (U.S. Statutes at Large, 68 pt. 1:791).

**27 August 1954 Ute Tribe Termination Act, PL 83–671.** An act providing for the partition and distribution of the assets of the Ute Indian tribe of the Uintah and Ouray Reservation in Utah between the mixed-blood and full-blood members thereof; for the termination of federal supervision of the property of mixed-blood members; and for a development program for the full-blood members of said tribe (U.S. Statutes at Large, 68 pt. 1:868–78).

**1 September 1954 Certain Utah Indians Termination Act, PL 83–762.** An act to provide for the termination of federal supervision over the property of certain tribes, bands, and colonies of Indians in the state of Utah and the individual members thereof (U.S. Statutes at Large, 68 pt. 1:1099–1104).

**27 May 1955 Papago Minerals Lands Act, PL 84–47.** An act that all tribal lands within the Papago Reservation are hereby withdrawn from all forms of exploration, location, and entry for minerals, and such lands are hereby made a part of the reservation and held in trust by the United States for the tribe (U.S. Statutes at Large, 69:67–68).

**28 June 1955 Yakima Land Lease Act, PL 84–187.** An act for leasing certain lands of the Yakima tribe to the state of Washington for historical and for public park purposes (U.S. Statutes at Large, 69:391–92).

**28 June 1955 Yakima Land Exchange Act, PL 84–188.** An act authorizing the purchase, sale, and exchange of certain lands on the Yakima Indian Reservation with the state of Washington (U.S. Statutes at Large, 69:392–93).

**9 August 1955 Indian Lands Leasing Act, PL 84–255.** An act to lease restricted Indian lands for public, religious, educational, recreational, residential, business, and other purposes for no longer than twenty-five years with the approval of the secretary of the interior (U.S. Statutes at Large, 69:539–40).

**9 August 1955 Pueblo Land Sale to Navajo Tribe Act, PL 84–276.** An act to authorize the Pueblos of San Lorenzo and Pojoaque in New Mexico to sell certain lands to the Navajo tribe (U.S. Statutes at Large, 69:555–56).

**11 August 1955 Five Civilized Tribes Restrictions Extension Act, PL 84–348.** An act for the period of restriction on lands belonging to Indians of the Five Civilized Tribes in Oklahoma to be extended for the lives of the Indians who own said lands (U.S. Statutes at Large, 69:666–68).

**14 August 1955 Colorado River Indian Reservation Lease Act, PL 84–390.** An act to authorize the secretary of the interior to lease any unassigned lands on the Colorado River Indian Reservation (U.S. Statutes at Large, 69:725–26).

**1 August 1956 Wyandotte Termination Act, PL 84–887.** An act to provide for the termination of federal supervision of the property of the Wyandotte tribe of Oklahoma and the individuals thereof (U.S. Statutes at Large, 70:893–97).

**2 August 1956 Peoria Termination Act, PL 84–921.** An act for the termination of federal supervision of the property of the Peoria tribe of Indians in Oklahoma and of the members thereof (U.S. Statutes at Large, 70:937–38).

**3 August 1956 Ottawa Termination Act, PL 84–943.** An act to provide for the termination of federal supervision of the property of the Ottawa tribe of Indians in Oklahoma and of the individual members thereof (U.S. Statutes at Large, 70:963–66).

**3 August 1956 Adult Indian Vocational Training Act, PL 84–959.** An act to provide programs of vocational assistance to adult Indians living on or near Indian reservations. The act was amended 23 December 1963 (PL 88–230) to exact a sum of $12,000 annually (U.S. Statutes at Large, 70:986).

**12 July 1960 Indian Boundary Markers Act, PL 86–634.** An act "to amend title 18 of the United States Code (25 U.S.C. 216) to make it unlawful to destroy, deface, or remove certain boundary markers on Indian reservations, and to trespass on Indian reservations to hunt, fish, or trap" (U.S. Statutes at Large, 74:469).

**4 November 1963 Revolving Loan Fund Act, PL 88–168.** An act "to establish a revolving fund from which the secretary of the interior may make loans to finance the procurement of expert assistance by Indian tribes in cases before the Indian Claims Commission" (U.S. Statutes at Large, 77:301).

**30 April 1964 Indian Timber Act, PL 88–301.** An act "to amend the Act of June 25, 1910 (36 Stat. 857; 25 U.S.C. 406, 407), with respect to the sale of Indian timber." This act gave the secretary of the interior authority to sell timber on unallotted Indian lands on reservations and on allotments held in trust, and specified that the proceeds be distributed to the Indian owners (U.S. Statutes at Large, 78:186–87).

**7 July 1964 Appropriation of Indian Affairs Supervision Act, PL 88–356.** An act concerning appropriations for the Department of the Interior and related agencies for the fiscal year ending 30 June 1965. The act allocated that the Department of the Interior Public Land Management, Bureau of Indian Affairs, receive an estimated $96 million for education and welfare services; $40.3 million for resource management; $900,000 for immediate revolving fund for loans; $52 million for construction, major repairs, and improvement of irrigation and power systems, buildings, and other facilities on reservations; $17 million for road construction; $4.3 million for general administration of the Bureau of Indian Affairs; $88,000 for Menominee School District; and $3 million from tribal funds for benefit of Indians and tribes for education and land improvements (U.S. Statutes at Large, 78:273–76).

**31 August 1964 Kinzua Dam and Seneca Termination Act, PL 88–533.** An act "to authorize payment for certain interests in lands within the Allegany Indian Reservation in New York required by the United States for the Allegheny River (Kinzua Dam) project, to provide for the relocation, rehabilitation, social and economic development of the members of the Seneca Nation" (U.S. Statutes at Large, 78:738–43).

**11 April 1968 American Indian Civil Rights Act, PL 90–284.** An act guaranteeing to reservation residents many of the same civil rights and liberties in relation to the operation of tribal governments that the U.S. Constitution guarantees to all persons in relations to federal and state authorities (U.S. Statutes at Large, 82:77–81).

**21 October 1968 Supplemental Appropriation Act, 1969, PL 90–608.** This major act to fund general assistance programs of the federal government included an appropriation of $100,000 to establish the National Council on Indian Opportunity (U.S. Statutes at Large, 82:1199).

**29 October 1969 Indian Health Care Act, PL 91–98.** An appropriations act, Title 1-Department of the Interior, called "for expenses necessary to enable the Surgeon General to carry out the purposes of the Act of 5 August 1954 (68 Stat. 674), as amended" for Indian health care and its facilities to be administered under Public Health Services (U.S. Statutes at Large, 83:161–62).

**11 April 1970 Tribes and Corporations Loan Act, PL 91–229.** An act "to provide for loans to Indian tribes and tribal corporations." This law enabled the secretary of agriculture to make loans of reasonable amounts from the Farmers Home Administration Direct Loan Account to federally recognized tribes or tribal corporations, according to the Indian Reorganization Act of 1934, to acquire lands or interests within their own reservations (U.S. Statutes at Large, 84:120).

**13 April 1970 Indian Elementary and Secondary Education Act, PL 91–230.** An act extending programs for elementary and secondary education, Title I Amendments to the Elementary and Secondary Education Act of 1965, Part E applied these programs to Indians on reservations, and Title II Amendments to Public Law 815 and 874 of the Eighty-first Congress (Impact Areas Programs), including construction of schools (U.S. Statutes at Large, 84:151–52, 159).

**15 December 1970 Taos Blue Lake Act.** An act amending section four of the Act of 31 May 1933 (48 Stat. 108), restoring Taos Blue Lake, an area of 48,000 acres of land including Blue Lake, to the Taos Pueblo Indians of New Mexico (U.S. Statutes at Large, 84:1437–39).

**15 December 1971 Navajo Community College Act.** An act authorizing Congress to fund $5.5 million for the construction and operation to match other government funding to build a tribal college on the Navajo Reservation (U.S. Statutes at Large, 85:646).

**18 December 1971 Alaska Native Claims Settlement Act, PL 92–203.** This act extinguished the Alaskan Natives' title to nine-tenths of Alaska in return for 44 million acres and almost $1 billion (U.S. Statutes at Large, 85:688–92, 702–703).

**23 June 1972 Indian Educational Amendments Act, PL 92–318.** Under Part D, the Office of Indian Education called for creating a Bureau of Indian Affairs level office of Indian Education with a National Advisory Council designed to improve the quality of public education for Indian students with grants and contracts for teachers for Indian children (U.S. Statutes at Large, 86:334–45).

**22 December 1973 Menominee Restoration Act, PL 93–197.** An act repealing the act terminating federal supervision over the property and members of the Menominee and restoring the terminated Menominee tribe of Wisconsin to federally recognized status (U.S. Statutes at Large, 87:770–73).

**28 December 1973 Comprehensive Employment and Training Act of 1973, PL 93–203.** An act establishing under Title III-Special Federal Responsibilities, Indian Manpower Programs to help the economically disadvantaged and unemployed Indians. This law was later amended with the name of the program changed to Native American Employment and Training Programs on 5 August 1977 (U.S. Statutes at Large, 87:858–59).

**12 April 1974 Indian Financing Act, PL 93–262.** This act was "to provide for financing the economic development of Indians and Indian organizations," involving the federal definition of an "Indian," "tribe," "reservation," "economic enterprise," and other terms. The act was amended 4 October 1984 (PL 98449, U.S. Statutes, 98:1725) (U.S. Statutes at Large, 88:77–83).

**22 December 1974 Navajo and Hopi Settlement Act, PL 93–531.** An act "to provide for the final settlement of the conflicting rights and interests of the Hopi and Navajo Tribes" (U.S. Statutes at Large, 88:1712–23).

**2 January 1975 American Indian Policy Review Commission Act, PL 93–580.** Acting on a Joint Resolution, Congress passed this law to review the federal government's historical and special legal relationship with American Indian people (U.S. Statutes at Large, 88:1910–11).

**4 January 1975 Indian Self-Determination and Education Assistance Act, PL 93–638.** An act expanding tribal control over tribal governments and education. The act also encouraged the development of human resources, reservation programs, and authorized federal funds to build needed public school facilities on or near Indian reservations (U.S. Statutes at Large, 88:2203–2217).

**29 May 1976 Indian Crimes Act of 1976, PL 94–297.** An act that "provide[d] for the definition and punishment of certain crimes in accordance with the Federal laws in force within the special maritime and territorial jurisdiction of the United States; when said crimes are committed by an Indian in order to ensure equal treatment for Indian and non-Indian offenders" (U.S. Statutes at Large, 90:585).

**20 September 1976 Indian Health Care Improvement Act, PL 95–195.** An act authorizing seven years of increased appropriations to improve Indian Health Care (U.S. Statutes at Large, 88:2206–2208).

**8 October 1976 Appropriations for Indian Claims Commission Act, PL 97–164.** This legislation extended an additional amount not to exceed $1,650,000, and for the claims commission to be ended on 30 September 1978 (U.S. Statutes at Large, 90:1991).

**1 August 1977 Health Scholarship Act, PL 95–83.** An act to amend the Public Health Service Act to extend through the fiscal year ending 30 September 1978. Title III-Health Services Extension of the act called for the "Indian Health Scholarship Program," for the secretary of the interior to decide scholarships, to cover all costs, with "Indian preference," for individuals entering professional health fields. The act stipulated that upon graduation the students are obligated, according to a written contract, to serve in health service shortage areas (U.S. Statutes at Large, 91:393).

**18 November 1977 Restoration Act of Confederated Tribes of Siletz Indians of Oregon, PL 95–195.** This act restored the status of "the Confederated Tribes of Siletz Indians of Oregon as a federally recognized sovereign Indian tribe, to restore to the Confederated Tribes of Siletz Indians of Oregon and its members those Federal services and benefits furnished to federally recognized American Indian tribes and their members" (U.S. Statutes at Large, 91:1415).

**13 March 1978 Indian Claims Commission Act, PL 95–243.** An act amending the Indian Claims Commission Act of 1946, affecting the Black Hills. This act adjudged that the Act of 28 February 1877 (19 Stat. 254), effected a taking of the Black Hills portion of the Great Sioux Reservation in violation of the Fifth Amendment, and shall enter judgment accordingly (U.S. Statutes at Large, 92:153).

**15 May 1978 Certain Oklahoma Tribes Restoration Act, PL 95–281.** An act that reinstated the Modoc, Wyandot, Peoria, and Ottawa Indian tribes of Oklahoma as federally supervised and recognized Indian tribes (U.S. Statutes at Large, 92:246–47).

**11 August 1978 American Indian Religious Freedom Act, PL 95–341.** In the form of a joint resolution, Congress recognized its obligation to "protect and preserve for American Indians their inherent right of freedom to believe, express and exercise [their] traditional religions" (U.S. Statutes at Large, 92:469).

**30 September 1978 Rhode Island Indian Claims Settlement Act, PL 95–395.** An act to settle the Narragansett Indian land claims within the state of Rhode Island and Providence Plantations, resulting in a confirmed out-of-court settlement between the state and the tribe, whereby the tribe received $3.5 million to purchase 900 acres for giving up all land claims in the state (U.S. Statutes at Large, 92:813–18).

**17 October 1978 Tribally Controlled Community Colleges Act, PL 95–471.** This act "provid[ed] for grants to tribal controlled community colleges," including any Alaskan Native village or village corporation as designated by the secretary of the interior (U.S. Statutes at Large, 92:1325–31).

**8 November 1978 Indian Child Welfare Act, PL 95–608.** An act establishing standards for the placement of Indian children in foster or adoptive homes, to prevent the breakup of Indian families, with jurisdiction over all cases handled by tribal courts with respective preferences given to relatives, the child's tribe, and Indian families to adopt the children (U.S. Statutes at Large, 92:3069–84).

**31 October 1979 Archaeological Resources Protection Act of 1979, PL 96–95.** An act calling for the protection of important archaeological sites on public lands and on Indian lands and requiring special permits for people wanting to study or excavate them (U.S. Statutes at Large, 93:721–28).

**3 April 1980 Paiute Bands of Utah Restoration Act, PL 96–227.** This act "restored the Shivwits, Kanosh, Koosharem, and Indian Peaks Bands of Paiute Indians of Utah, and with respect to the Cedar City Band of Paiute Indians of Utah, to restore or confirm, the Federal trust relationship, to restore to members of such Bands those Federal services and benefits furnished to American Indian Tribes by reason of such trust relationship" (U.S. Statutes at Large, 94:317–22).

**17 June 1980 Indian and Federal Trade Act, PL 96–277.** An act affecting Indian trade with federal employees. This act repealed and amended certain laws regulating trade between Indians and certain federal employees to protect the interests of Indians (U.S. Statutes at Large, 94:544–46).

**8 July 1980 Navajo-Hopi Relocation Act, PL 96–305.** An act relocating certain Hopi and Navajo under a commission, and purchasing additional lands purchased for the Navajo tribe (U.S. Statutes at Large, 94:929–36).

**4 September 1980 Reservation for Confederated Tribes of Siletz Indians of Oregon Act, PL 96–340.** An act establishing a reservation of 3,063 acres for the Confederated Tribes of Siletz Indians of Oregon, which were terminated in 1954 and restored in 1977 (U.S. Statutes at Large, 94:1072–75).

**26 September 1980 Indian Will Act, PL 96–363.** This act "permit[s] any Indian to transfer by will restricted lands of such Indian to his or her heirs or lineal descendants" by amending the act of 18 June 1934 (48 Stat. 984, 985; 25 U.S.C. 464) (U.S. Statutes at Large, 94:1207).

**10 October 1980 Maine Indian Claims Settlement Act of 1980, PL 96–420.** An act bringing a final settlement to a large land claim filed by the Maine Indians, consisting of the Passamaquoddy tribe, the Penobscot Nation, and the Maliseet tribe. The law ratified all transfers of land and other natural resources by the Indians, thereby extinguishing their claims to the land. Congress established a Maine Indian Claims Settlement Fund of $27 million in trust. An additional $54.5 million enabled the Indians to purchase 300,000 acres, stipulating that the Indians would be under the jurisdiction of Maine (U.S. Statutes at Large, 94:1785–97).

**22 December 1980 Salmon and Steelhead Conservation Act of 1980, PL 96–561.** An act providing for the conservation and enhancement of the salmon and steelhead, primarily affecting the Pacific Northwest and due mainly to the court cases, *U.S. v. Washington* and *Sohappy v. Smith* (U.S. Statutes at Large, 94:3275–3302).

**13 August 1981 Omnibus Budget Reconciliation Act of 1981, PL 97–35.** This lengthy act, under Title IX-Health Services and Facilities, authorized the secretary of health and human services to make community "block grants" to include "the Indian tribe or tribal organization serving the individuals for whom such determination has been made" for a fiscal year. The act, also called the Head Start Act under Subchapter B, Section 635, implemented Head Start programs in Indian communities and aimed to improve impoverished areas such as Indian reservations. Under Title XIX-Small Business, referred to as the Small Business Budget Reconciliation and Loan Consolidation/Improvement Act of 1981, loans over no more than twenty-five years could be made to qualified small business owned by Indian tribes (U.S. Statutes at Large, 95:499, 511, 536, 767).

**22 December 1982 Indian Mineral Development Act of 1982, PL 97–382.** An act to permit Indian tribes to enter into certain agreements for the disposition of tribal mineral resources (U.S. Statutes at Large, 96:1938–40).

**30 December 1982 Indian Claims Limitation Act of 1982, PL 97–394.** As a part of the appropriations act for 1983 fiscal year, "claims that are on either of the two lists published pursuant to the Indian Claims Act of 1982, any right of action shall be barred unless the complaint is filed within one year after the Secretary of the Interior has published in the Federal Register a notice rejecting such claims or three years after the date the Secretary of the Interior has submitted legislation or legislative report to Congress to resolve such claim" (U.S. Statutes at Large, 96:1976–78).

**7 January 1983 Nuclear Waste Policy Act of 1982, PL 97–245.** An act calling for the "development of repositories for the disposal of high-level radioactive waste and spent nuclear fuel, to establish a program of research, development, and demonstration regarding the disposal of high-level radioactive waste and spent nuclear fuel." Section 2 of the act allowed the administrator of the Environmental Protection Agency to authorize such repositories to be located within the boundaries of Indian reservations "upon the petition of the appropriate governmental officials of the tribe" (U.S. Statutes at Large, 96:2201–2202).

**12 January 1983 Federal Oil and Gas Royalty Management Act of 1982, PL 97–451.** Under Title II-States and Indian Tribes, the act authorized the interior secretary to enter into a cooperative agreement or agreements with any state or Indian tribe to share oil and gas royalty management information, and to carry out inspection, auditing, investigation, or enforcement (not including the collection of royalties, civil or criminal penalties, or other payments) in cooperation with the secretary (U.S. Statutes at Large, 96:2457).

**12 January 1983 Indian Land Consolidation Act, PL 97–459.** Title II, Section 201 of this act authorized the purchase, sale, and exchange of lands by Indian tribes and by the Devils Lake Sioux Tribe of the Devils Lake Sioux Reservation of North Dakota. Section 203 empowered "the Secretary to adopt a land consolidation plan providing for the sale or exchange of any tribal lands or interest in lands for the purpose of eliminating undivided fractional interests in Indian trust or restricted lands or consolidating its tribal land holdings" (U.S. Statutes at Large, 96:2517–19).

**14 January 1983 Indian Tribal Governmental Tax Status Act of 1982, PL 97–473.** The Indian Tribal Government Tax Status Act, Title II-Tax Status of Indian Tribal Governments, granted tribes many of the federal tax advantages enjoyed by states, including that of issuing tax-exempt bonds to finance governmental projects (U.S. Statutes at Large, 97:2607–11).

**19 October 1984 Indian Education Amendments of 1984, PL 98–511.** Under Title V, this legislation was enacted to improve contract schools in accordance with Indian self-determination, and to extend other Indian programs (U.S. Statutes at Large, 98:2391–2401).

**15 March 1985 Pacific Salmon Treaty Act of 1985, PL 99–5.** An act to give effect to the treaty signed 28 January 1985 between the United States and Canadian governments concerning Pacific salmon fishing. The law clarified Indian treaties and executive orders with respect to Native fishing rights (U.S. Statutes at Large, 99:7).

**15 August 1985 Indian Education Technical Amendments Act of 1985, PL 99–89.** An act "to amend title XI of the Education Amendments of 1978, relating to Indian education," and to specify school boundaries, the functions of the Bureau of Indian Affairs, and the availability of appropriations (U.S. Statutes at Large, 99:379–83).

**24 March 1986 White Earth Reservation Lands Settlement Act of 1985, PL 99–264.** An act "to settle unresolved claims relating to certain allotted Indian lands on the White Earth Reservation, to remove clouds from the titles to certain lands," regarding checkerboard Chippewa and non-Chippewa land ownership (U.S. Statutes at Large, 100:61).

**27 August 1986 Klamath Restoration Act, PL 99–398.** An act "to provide for the restoration of the Federal trust relationship with, and Federal services and assistance to, the Klamath Tribe of Indians and the individual members thereof consisting of the Klamath and Modoc Tribes and the Yahooskin Band of Snake Indians" (U.S. Statutes at Large, 100:849–52).

**17 October 1986 American Indian, Alaska Native, and Native Hawaiian Culture and Art Development Act, PL 99–498.** An act to develop a corporation to be known as the "Institute of American Indian and Alaska Native Culture and Arts Development," under the direction and control of a Board of Trustees, to acknowledge the contribution of Native art to American society (U.S. Statutes at Large, 100:1600–1611).

**27 October 1986 Indian Civil Rights Act, PL 99–570.** An act (within a larger Anti-Drug Abuse Act) amending the Indian Civil Rights Act of 1986 to allow tribal courts to impose fines of $5,000 and one year in jail for criminal offenses (U.S. Statutes at Large, 100:3207).

**27 October 1986 Indian Alcohol and Substance Abuse Prevention and Treatment Act of 1986, PL 99–570.** Under Part 1, General Provisions of the Anti-Drug Abuse Act, to prevent illegal narcotics in Indian country and to develop programs for the prevention and treatment of alcohol and substance abuse (U.S. Statutes at Large 100:3207).

**3 February 1987 Alaska Native Claims Settlement Amendment Act, PL 100–241.** An act amending the Alaska Native Claims Settlement Act of 1971 to allow each corporation to decide whether it will sell its stock after 1991 (U.S. Statutes at Large, 101:1788).

**18 August 1987 Wampanoag Tribal Council of Gay Head, Inc., Indian Claims Settlement Act of 1987, PL 100–95.** An act "to settle Indian land claims in the town of Gay Head, Massachusetts," with the State of Massachusetts surrendering up to $2,250,000 for land purchase in trust for Wampanoag Tribal Council of Gay Head, Inc. in return for extinguishment of Native land title (U.S. Statutes at Large, 101:704–10).

**5 November 1987 Indian Tribal Judgement Funds Use or Distribution Act, PL 100–153.** An act, also known as Indian Law Technical Amendments of 1987, "to make miscellaneous technical and minor amendments to laws relating to Indians" for clarification (U.S. Statutes at Large, 101:886–89).

**28 April 1988 Repeal of Termination Act PL 100–297.** An act (within the Indian Education Act of 1988) to repeal the termination policy established by House Concurrent Resolution 108 of 1 August 1953 (U.S. Statutes at Large, 102:395–422).

**28 April 1988 Indian Education Act of 1988, PL 100–297.** This Indian Education Act provided financial assistance to local educational agencies for the education of Indian children, special educational training programs for teachers of Indian children, programs for adult Indians, funding for the Office of Indian Education, and support for the National Advisory Council on Indian Education (U.S. Statutes at Large, 102:395–422).

**29 June 1988 Indian Housing Act, PL 100–358.** An act amending the United States Housing Act of 1937 to establish a separate program to provide housing assistance for Indians and Alaska Natives under the supervision of the secretary of housing and urban development (U.S. Statutes at Large, 102:676–81).

**17 October 1988 Indian Gaming Regulatory Act, PL 100–497.** An act designed "to establish federal standards and regulations for the conduct of gaming activities within Indian country. . . as a means of promoting tribal economic development, self-sufficiency, and strong tribal governments"; "to shield it [Indian gaming] from organized crime and other corrupting influences,. . . to assure that gaming is conducted fairly and honestly by both the operator and players," and " to establish a National Indian Gaming Commission" (U.S. Statutes at Large, 102:2467–88).

**31 October 1988 Native Hawaiian Health Care Act of 1988, PL 100–579.** An act to fund, "or enter into a contract with Papa Ola Lokahi for developing a Native Hawaiian comprehensive health care master plan designed to promote comprehensive health promotion and disease prevention services and to maintain and improve the health status of Native Hawaiians" (U.S. Statutes at Large,102:2916–23).

**1 November 1988 Review of Tribal Constitutions Act, PL 100–581.** An act amending the Indian Reorganization Act of 8 June 1934 to establish procedures for review of tribal constitutions and bylaws or amendments (U.S. Statutes at Large, 102:2938–49).

**28 June 1989 Coquille Restoration Act, PL 101–42.** An act "to provide for restoration of the federal trust relationship with, and assistance to, the Coquille Tribe of Indians and individual members consisting of the Coquille Tribe of Indians" (U.S. Statutes at Large, 103:91–94).

**28 November 1989 National Museum of American Indian Act, PL 101–185.** An act to establish a national museum for preserving the heritage of American Indians. The museum is to be located within the Smithsonian Institution (U.S. Statutes at Large, 103:1336–47).

**30 April 1990 Seminole Awards Act, PL 101–277.** An act "to provide for the use and distribution of funds awarded the Seminole Indians" from the Indian Claims Commission (U.S. Statutes at Large, 104 pt. 1:143).

**3 August 1990 American Indian Heritage Month Act, PL 101–343.** An act designating November as National American Indian Heritage Month (U.S. Statutes at Large, 104 pt. 1:473–84).

**18 August 1990 Indian Law Enforcement Reform Act, PL 101–379.** An act to clarify and strengthen the authority of "certain Department of the Interior law enforcement services, activities, and officers in Indian country" (U.S. Statutes at Large, 104:473–83).

**25 September 1990 Tribally Controlled Vocational Institutions Support Act of 1990, PL 101–392.** Part H of the Carl D. Perkins Vocational Education Act "provides grants for the operation and improvement of tribal controlled postsecondary vocational institutions" (U.S. Statutes at Large, 104:799–804).

**4 October 1990 Indian Environmental Regulatory Enhancement Act of 1990, PL 101–408.** An act "to authorize grants to improve the capability of Indian tribal governments to regulate environmental quality" (U.S. Statutes at Large, 104 pt. 1:883–84).

**30 October 1990 Native American Languages Act, PL 101–477.** An act to preserve, protect, and promote the practice and development of Native American languages as deemed also by federal policy (U.S. Statutes at Large, 104 pt. 2:1153–56).

**31 October 1990 Ponca Restoration Act, PL 101–484.** An act "to provide for the restoration of Federal recognition to the Ponca Tribe of Nebraska" (U.S. Statutes at Large, 104 pt. 2:1167–70).

**16 November 1990 Native American Graves Protection and Repatriation Act, PL 101–601.** An act "to provide for the protection of Native American graves," human remains, and sacred objects (U.S. Statutes at Large, 104 pt. 4:3048–58).

**16 November 1990 Fort Hall Indian Water Rights Act of 1990, PL 101–602.** An act describing and quantifying tribal water for Shoshone-Bannock tribes in the state of Idaho (U.S. Statutes at Large, 104 pt. 4:3059).

**16 November 1990 Fallon Paiute Shoshoni Indian Tribe Water Rights Settlement Act of 1990, PL 101–618.** An act appropriating a total sum of $43 million for fiscal years 1993 through 1997 for economic and tribal developments on the reservation in Nevada (U.S. Statutes at Large, 104 pt. 4:3289–3324).

**28 November 1990 National Indian Forest Resources Management Act, PL 101–630.** An act allowing the secretary of the interior to participate in the management of Indian forest lands, to the land owner's benefit, and to be consistent with the trust responsibility of the secretary (U.S. Statutes at Large, 104 pt. 6:4532–44).

**28 November 1990 Indian Child Protection and Family Violence Prevention Act, PL 101–630.** An act to require reports of abused Indian children and to establish a program to treat and prevent Indian child abuse (U.S. Statutes at Large, 104 pt. 6:4544–56).

**29 November 1990 Indian Arts and Crafts Act of 1990, PL 101–644.** An Act "to expand the powers of the Indian Arts and Crafts Board" to prevent criminal and civil violations against American Indian craftsmanship (U.S. Statutes at Large, 104 pt. 6:4662–72).

**28 October 1991 Criminal Jurisdiction Act, PL 102–137.** This act followed the *Duro* decision against *Reina* (58 U.S.L.W. 4643, May 29, 1990) and established that Indian tribes have the power to exercise criminal jurisdiction over Indians (U.S. Statutes at Large, 105 pt. 1:646).

**4 December 1991 Tribal Self-Governance Demonstration Project Act, PL 102–184.** An act amending the Indian Self-Determination and Education Assistance Act to include feasibility consideration of demonstration projects and to increase the number of tribes from twenty to thirty under the classification of tribal self-governance demonstration project (U.S. Statutes at Large, 105 pt. 2:1278).

**19 March 1992 Morris K. Udall Scholarship and Excellence in National Environmental and Native American Public Policy Act, PL 102–259.** An act to establish the Morris K. Udall Scholarship and Excellence in National Environmental Policy Foundation (U.S. Statutes at Large, 106, Pt. 1:78–84

**23 July 1992 Higher Educational Tribal Grant Authorization Act, PL 102–325, Part B.** An act to make grants to Indian tribes in accordance with the requirements of this part to permit those tribes to provide financial assistance to individual Indian students for the cost of attendance at institutions of higher education (U.S. Statutes at Large, Vol. 106, Pt. 1:798–803).

**23 July 1992 Critical Needs for Tribal Development Act, PL 102–325, Part C.** An act stating that an eligible Indian tribe or organization may, in accordance with the requirements of this part, require any applicant for federally funded higher education assistance, as a condition of receipt of such assistance, to enter into a critical area service agreement in accordance with section 1324 (U.S. Statutes at Large, 106, Pt. 1:803–805).

**23 July 1992 Institute of American Indian Native Culture and Arts Development Act, PL 102–325, Part D.** An act to amend the American Indian, Alaska Native, and Native Hawaiian Culture and Art Development Act to create a board to establish, within the institute, departments for the study of culture, arts, research, exchange, and a museum (U.S. Statutes at Large, 106, Pt. 1: 805–809).

**23 July 1992 Tribal Development Student Assistance Revolving Loan Program Act, PL 102–325, Part E.** An act to establish a revolving loan program to be administered by a tribe or tribal organization for the purposes of increasing the number of college graduates available to work in tribal businesses, tribal government, and tribal services such as schools and hospitals; to conduct research in post-secondary education; and to encourage development, through grants in addition to loans, transitional and follow-up services added to encourage persistence in postsecondary education (U.S. Statutes at Large, 106, Pt. 1:809–812).

**11 August 1992 Zuni River Watershed Act, PL 102–338.** An act to formulate a plan for the management of natural and cultural resources on the Zuni Indian Reservation, on the lands of the Ramah Band of the Navajo tribe of Indians, the Navajo Nation, and in other areas within the Zuni River watershed and upstream from the Zuni Indian Reservation (U.S. Statutes at Large, 106, Pt. 1:866–868).

**14 October 1992 Advisory Council on California Indian Policy, PL 102–416.** An act to restore the federal trust relationship of the United Auburn Indian Community, and to establish the Advisory Council on California Indian Policy (U.S. Statutes at Large, 106, Pt. 3:2131–2137).

**23 October 1992 Indian Employment, Training, and Related Services Demonstration Act, PL 102–477.** An act to demonstrate how Indian tribal governments can integrate the employment, training, and related services they provide in order to improve the effectiveness of those services, reduce joblessness in Indian communities, and serve tribally determined goals consistent with the policy of self-determination (U.S. Statutes at Large, 106, Pt. 3:2302–2306).

**23 October 1992 Jicarilla Apache Tribe Water Rights Settlement Act, PL 102–441.** An act for the settlement of the water rights claims of the Jicarilla Apache tribe against the state of New Mexico, the United States, and other parties (U.S. Statutes at Large, 106:2237–2242).

**24 October 1992 Indian Environmental General Assistance Program Act, PL 102–497.** An act to provide general assistance grants to Indian tribal governments and intertribal consortia to build capacity to administer environmental regulatory programs that may be delegated by the Environmental Protection Agency on Indian lands; to provide technical assistance from EPA to tribal governments and intertribal consortia;

and to develop multimedia programs to address environmental issues on Indian lands (U.S. Statutes at Large, 106, Pt. 4:3258–3262).

**26 October 1992 Native American Languages Act, PL 102–524.** An act to amend the Native American Programs Act of 1974 for the secretary of interior to award a grant to any agency or organization that is to assist Native Americans in ensuring the survival and continuing vitality of Native American languages (U.S. Statutes at Large, 106, Pt. 4:3434–3437).

**26 October 1992 Native American Educational Assistance Act, PL 102–524.** An act for the secretary of the interior to enter into an agreement with a nonprofit captioning agency engaged in manufacturing and distributing captioning decoders for the purpose of carrying out a demonstration project to determine the effectiveness of captioned educational materials as an educational tool in schools operated by the Bureau of Indian Affairs (U.S. Statutes at Large, 106, Pt. 4:3437).

**29 October 1992 Indian Health Care Improvement Act, PL 102–571.** An act which amended the previous Indian health care act. The amendment authorized appropriations for Indian health programs and declared health objectives: "The Congress hereby declares that it is the policy of this Nation, in fulfillment of its special responsibilities and legal obligation to the American Indian people, to assure the highest possible health status for Indians and urban Indians and to provide all resources necessary to effect that policy" (U.S. Statutes at Large, 106 pt. 106:4526–4579).

**30 October 1992 Three Affiliated Tribes and Standing Rock Sioux Tribe Equitable Compensation Act, PL 102–575.** An act regarding that Congress declares that the Three Affiliated Tribes are entitled to additional financial compensation for the taking of 156,000 acres of their reservation lands, as the site of the Oahe Dam and Reservoir, and that such amounts should be deposited in the Standing Rock Sioux Tribe Economic Recovery Fund (U.S. Statutes at Large, 106, Pt. 6:4731–4739).

**30 October 1992 San Carlos Apache Tribe Water Rights Settlement Act, PL 102–575.** An act in which Congress declared that the secretary of the interior will authorize the actions and appropriations necessary for the United States to fulfill its legal and trust obligations to the tribe as provided in the agreement's provisions of this law (U.S. Statutes at Large, 106, Pt. 6:4740–4752).

**3 December 1993 Indian Tribal Justice Act, PL 103–176.** An act to assist in the development of tribal judicial systems, and for other purposes (U.S. Statutes at Large, 107, Pt. 3:2004–2010).

**3 December 1993 American Indian Agricultural Resource Management Act, PL 103–177.** An act to improve the management, productivity, and use of Indian agricultural lands and resources (U.S. Statutes at Large, 107, Pt. 3:2011–2023).

**4 May 1994 Alaska Native Art and Culture Development Act, PL 108–239.** An act for the secretary of the interior to make grants for the purpose of supporting programs for Native Hawaiian or Alaska Native culture and arts development to any private, nonprofit organization or institution that primarily serves and represents Native Hawaiians or Alaska Natives (U.S. Statutes at Large, 108, Pt. 1:606–607).

**23 August 1994 Indian Dams Safety Act, PL 103–302.** An act to maintain and include a repair program within the Bureau of Indian Affairs to maintain identified dams on Indian land that if they failed would present a threat to human life (U.S. Statutes at Large, 108, Pt. 2:1560–1563).

**22 October 1994 Indian Lands Open Dump Cleanup Act, PL 103–399.** An act to clean up open dumps on Indians lands (affecting at least 600 open dumps on Indian and Alaska Native lands) (U.S. Statutes at Large, 108, Pt. 5:4164–4168).

**25 October 1994 Indian Self-Determination Contract Reform Act, PL 103–413.** An act to amend the Indian Self-Determination Act to specify the terms of contracts entered into by the United States and Indian tribal organizations under the Indian Self-Determination and Education Assistance Act and to provide for tribal self-governance (U.S. Statutes at Large, 108, Pt. 5:4250–4278).

**11 October 1996 Navajo-Hopi Land Dispute Settlement Act, PL 104–301.** An act to provide for the settlement of the Navajo-Hopi land dispute, and for other purposes (U.S. Statutes at Large, 110, Pt. 5:3649–3655).

**26 October 1996 Native American Housing Assistance and Self-Determination Act, PL 104–330.** An act to provide federal assistance for Indian tribes in a manner that recognizes the right of tribal self-governance, and for other purposes (U.S. Statutes at Large, 110, Pt. 6:4016–4052).

**13 November 1997 Hoopa Valley Reservation South Boundary Act, PL 105–79.** An act to provide for the conveyance of certain land in the Six Rivers National Forest in the state of California for the benefit of the Hoopa Valley tribe (U.S. Statutes at Large, 111, Pt. 2:1527–1528).

**14 November 1997 Miccosukee Settlement Act, PL 105–83.** An act for the secretary of the interior to aid and assist in the fulfillment of the settlement agreement at all times and in a reasonable manner as trustee for the Miccosukee tribe (U.S. Statutes at Large, 111, Pt. 2:1624–1627).

**2 December 1997 Lower Brule Sioux Tribe Infrastructure Development Trust Fund Act, PL 105–132.** An act to provide certain benefits of the Pick-Sloan Missouri River Basin program to the Lower Brule Sioux tribe, and for other purposes (U.S. Statutes at Large, 111, Pt. 3:2563–2567).

**27 July 1998 Fort Berthold Indian Reservation Mineral Leasing Act, PL 105–188.** An act to permit the mineral leasing of Indian land located within the Fort Berthold Indian Reservation in any case in which there is consent from a majority interest in the parcel of land under consideration for lease (U.S. Statutes at Large, 112, Pt. 1:620–621).

**6 October 1998 Sand Creek Massacre National Historic Site Act, PL 105–243.** An act to authorize the secretary of the interior to study the suitability and feasibility of designating the Sand Creek Massacre National Historic Site in the state of Colorado as a unit of the National Park System, and for other purposes (U.S. Statutes at Large, 112, Pt. 2:1579–1580).

**21 October 1998 Indian Tribal Torts Claims and Risk Management Act, PL 105–277.** An act to provide for a study to facilitate relief for a person who is injured as a result of an official action of a tribal government (U.S. Statutes at Large, 112, Pt. 4:335–337).

**27 October 1998 Advisory Council on California Indian Policy Act, PL 105–294.** An act to extend the Advisory Council on California Indian Policy to allow the council to advise Congress on the implementation of the proposals and recommendations to the advisory council (U.S. Statutes at Large, 112, Pt. 5:2818–2819).

**9 December 1999 Chippewa Cree Tribe of the Rocky Boy's Reservation Indian Reserved Water Rights Settlement and Water Supply Enhancement Act, PL 106–163.** An act to provide for the settlement of the water rights claims of the Chippewa Cree tribe of the Rocky Boy's Reservation, and for other purposes (U.S. Statutes at Large, 106 [Pt. was not established and page numbers were not established as of 18 December 2000], unbound copy of legislation, 1778–1791).

**9 December 1999 Fallen Timbers Battlefield and Fort Miamis National Historic Site Act, PL 106–164.** An act to establish the Fallen Timbers Battlefield and Fort Miamis National Historical Site in the state of Ohio (U.S. Statutes at Large, 113, [Pt. was not established as of 18 December 2000], 1792–1794).

**14 March 2000 Indian Tribal Economic Development and Contract Encouragement Act, PL 106–179.** An act to encourage Indian economic development, to provide for the disclosure of Indian tribal sovereignty immunity in contracts involving Indian tribes, and for other purposes (U.S. Statutes at Large, 110, Pt. 1:36–37).

*Donald L. Fixico*
*University of Kansas*

## ◆ AN OVERVIEW OF CANADIAN ABORIGINAL LAW

The foundations of the Canadian legal system today still reflect the imported civil law from France in relation to Quebec and, for the rest of Canada, the common law from Great Britain. Although the aboriginal nations clearly possessed their own legal systems that governed all internal and external matters before contact, and for many generations thereafter, colonization has effectively dislodged these indigenous legal regimes and largely replaced them with what many aboriginal peoples (Indian, Inuit and Métis) see as "foreign" law. The common law informs key legal principles concerning the aboriginal peoples, even in Quebec, but this judge made law is supplemented by legislation, treaties, royal instruments, and the Canadian Constitution.

Since the common law system is also used by the United States, it is not surprising that American case law, with its far greater volume and earlier vintage, has had great influence on the content of Canadian jurisprudence. As a result, the U.S. law entries in this almanac, particularly those referring to the early American court decisions, are of direct relevance to the Canadian situation. United States law is also relevant because the U.S.-Canadian border crosses the traditional territory of the Mi'kmaq, Maliseet, Iroquois, Ojibway, Cree, Blackfeet, Salish, and Tlingit nations, among others.

Among the many Indian nations, as well as the Inuit (or Eskimo in the United States), the core principles of traditional legal systems are similar. The content and form of the legal regimes of the various aboriginal nations unique to Canada are also rather similar. The laws were passed on orally from one generation to the next, and they largely consisted of rules that had developed over a prolonged period of time, rather than frequently changed by the leadership of the day. The laws reflected religious beliefs and moral values that emphasized the autonomy of the individual while placing primary importance on the harmony and well-being of the community as a whole. Aboriginal law concentrates on restoring peace and tranquility, as opposed to emphasizing punishment for criminal behavior and protection of property, as in the United States and Canada.

### The Initial Legal Position

The common law and official government policy of Great Britain was largely shaped by the emerging international law doctrines first enunciated by Spanish theologians and legal thinkers, especially Francisco de Vitoria, in the mid-sixteenth century. After some debate and a period of controversy, international law recognized the people of the so-called "New World" as human beings with souls, entitled to respect and protection from physical violence. International law also recognized them as peoples who constituted sovereign nations.

Furthermore, the specific aboriginal nation that occupied particular territory was viewed as the rightful owner of that soil in accordance with the terms of its own rules or laws. According to those laws, land was usually held with collective or communal title and could not be individually conveyed or sold. This meant that the "discovering" European nation could not claim exclusive title to the "new" lands but merely the right, vis-à-vis other European countries, to enter into treaty relations regarding trade, or to acquire land for settlement from a willing Indian nation. International law concerning conquest did, however, apply such that a victor in war obtained the legal right to seize territory or alter the sovereignty of the vanquished.

In the seventeenth and eighteenth centuries, Great Britain accepted these principles and sought positive relations with the Indian nations through treaties that would promote lucrative trade (particularly in furs), military alliances (first regarding France and later in reference to the United States after the American Revolution), and peace and friendship. Treaties were also used by the Crown for purchasing Indian lands for the use of colonists. However, there was a clash in cultures and expectations. While the Indian nations had a long history of treaties and trade among themselves, there was no precedent in their histories or laws for selling all interests in land. Instead, territory was viewed as either exclusive to a particular nation or shared with neighbors, but never conveyed away except by war. Thus, the desire by Europeans to acquire absolute title free from Indian presence was often not understood by Indian leaders and resulted in treaty agreements in which the Indian nation's intention was merely to share its territory with the newcomers rather than sell it to be cleared and fenced by individual settlers.

Colonists repeatedly violated those British policies that preserved and respected Indian territory. The settler violations brought conflict and frequent complaints from the Indian nations, including litigation, starting in the early 1700s with *Mohican Indians v. Connecticut*. Numerous treaties had to be reaffirmed or renegotiated by the Crown to reassure Indian nations that their territorial integrity would be respected. The Royal Proclamation of 1763, which is still a constitutional enactment of great import in Canada, was issued by King George III to restrain British colonists throughout the Americas because of the "Great Frauds and Abuses" that had been practiced by the settlers. The proclamation made clear that the Indian nations were not to be disturbed in their peaceful possession of their territory or in their internal governmental affairs. If a nation was prepared to sell tracts of land, then the transaction could take place solely at a public meeting and land could only be sold to official Crown representatives. Thus, the Royal Proclamation reconfirmed earlier agreements for protecting Indian land and supported the concept of aboriginal title.

In the aftermath of American independence, thousands of British Loyalists, including many Indian nations, chose to migrate north to what remained of colonial British North America. The dramatic influx of people who required land for settlement compelled the Crown to acquire large tracts of land by negotiated treaties with the First Nations. Treaty making entered a new phase in what is now Canada in which the Crown's major objective was purchase of Indian land rather than the establishment of peaceful trade and political relations. Land cession treaties became the norm and spread across what is now southern Ontario and then westward along Lake Huron and Lake Superior. The treaty-making process continued after Canada became an independent country in 1867. The Canadian government negotiated eleven treaties from 1870 to 1921 that now cover the three prairie provinces (Manitoba, Saskatchewan, and Alberta), northern Ontario, and the Mackenzie Valley region of the Northwest Territories.

### Confederation

In 1867, the British colonies of Nova Scotia, New Brunswick, Quebec, and Ontario created a new country with British consent. In the early 1870s, the colonies of British Columbia and Prince Edward Island joined the original four colonies in the Canadian Confederation while England also conveyed the huge territory between Ontario and British Columbia to the government of Canada. The United Kingdom Parliament passed the British North America Act (now called the Constitution Act, 1867) as the constitutional foundation for Canada. The aboriginal nations were not invited to partake in the constitutional negotiations, and their interests and rights were largely ignored. This act referred to the indigenous peoples only once, in section 91(24), and then only to indicate that the federal parliament—as opposed to the provinces—had the exclusive jurisdiction to enact laws for "Indians, and Lands reserved for the Indians." Since 1868, this provision of the Constitution Act, 1867 has become the basis for all federal legislation concerning the aboriginal peoples of Canada. The implication from the Canadian Constitution was also that the previous role of the Imperial Crown in negotiating treaties and pursuing relations with the Aboriginal nations had devolved upon the national Canadian government.

### The Indian Act

The Parliament of Canada wasted little time in exercising its authority under section 91(24) as it passed its first statute on Indian issues one year after Confederation. In 1869 the Canadian government began subdividing the Indian population into those who legally qualified as Indians under the Indian Act and all other people of Indian ancestry who were excluded. Indian women married to non-aboriginal or ineligible aboriginal men were the first to be excluded. In this provision, as in all others until 1985, the wishes of the people and the citizenship laws of the individual Indian nations were discounted. The consequences of this policy for Indian families and communities have been tragic beyond measure.

The federal government consistently pursued strategies designed to assimilate Indian people into mainstream Canadian society. The Canadian government forcibly took away status from thousands of Indians for such reasons as obtaining a university degree, leaving the reserve for more than five years, and marrying men who were not registered Indians. At the same time, the government outlawed many traditional religious and political practices (the potlatch and the Tamanawas dance, for example), while imposing Christianity. Aboriginal children were sent to residential schools and removed from the influence of their families and communities. Traditional governments were replaced by elected governments, which were largely controlled by agents from the federal government called "Indian agents." Indian movement off reserve was restricted by pass laws. Canadian government restrictions on wildlife harvesting and farm production restrained economic output below levels necessary for community subsistence needs. Furthermore, all government Indian agents were appointed Justices of the Peace, allowing them to enforce Canadian law within reserves regardless of traditional aboriginal laws and justice systems. The net result was the transformation of the once politically and economically self-sufficient Indian nations into poverty-stricken communities with significant social problems.

## Decline of Aboriginal Rights and Autonomy

Although the Indian Act and its regime were frequently opposed by Indian nations, the federal government's authority went unchallenged in the Canadian courts. As a result, the act was regularly amended by Parliament to strengthen the policies of assimilation without consultation or consent from the First Nations people who were most affected. Indian protests were generally ignored and occasionally suppressed by the police. Indian nations were no longer regarded by the Crown as sovereign in their own right, as they had during the active treaty-making era. Instead, they were deemed creations of federal legislation, with limited delegated powers, fully subject to the demands of Parliament. Aboriginal peoples who fell outside the narrow scope of the Indian Act, including all Métis and Inuit peoples as well as many unrecognized Indian communities, were treated in law and under government policy as if they were non-aboriginal Canadians.

The first major Canadian court decision on whether Indian nations owned land—the doctrine of aboriginal title—was not rendered until 1889. This occurred when the Judicial Committee of the Privy Council in England (the final court of appeal for Canada until 1951) decided *St. Catharine's Milling and Lumber Co. v. The Queen*. The matter went to trial while the Métis and the Cree in Saskatchewan were rebelling against the Canadian government. The decision came almost a century after the first American court decisions on Indian land tenure. Unfortunately European settlers' attitudes toward and relations with aboriginal peoples had changed markedly for the worse. Although the leading U.S. Supreme Court decisions of Chief Justice John Marshall, including *Johnson v. M'Intosh*, *Cherokee Nation v. Georgia*, and *Worcester v. Georgia*, were noted and said to be accurate statements of Canadian law, the U.S. court decisions were not fully followed in Canada. The concept of "domestic dependent nations," developed by Marshall in the early U.S. cases to describe Indian national sovereignty, was ignored by the British court in *St. Catharine's Milling*. Likewise, Marshall's view that aboriginal title was "as sacred as the fee simple of the whites" and deserving of complete recognition by the common law, was not properly respected. Instead, the Privy Council described aboriginal title as a mere right to use and enjoy the fruits of the land. Even this limited legal interest, the Privy Council said, was dependent on the Crown's "good will." The court argued that aboriginal title was simply a restriction on the underlying provincial Crown title and was extinguished when surrendered by treaty. Although the federal government was authorized by the Constitution to negotiate such land cession treaties with First Nations, it received no benefit, according to the Court, because the Indian nations had no land title to convey. In effect, the Court ruled that the treaties transferred Crown lands to exclusive provincial control while eliminating the Indian interest in those lands. It should be noted that the Ojibway Nation, which signed the contested treaty (Treaty Number 3), was not party to the litigation.

Subsequent cases in the late 1800s and the first half of the twentieth century also frequently involved disputes between the federal and provincial governments, occasionally with corporations caught in the crossfire. Aboriginal people were absent as parties, witnesses, or even bystanders. The few exceptions involved aboriginal individuals who were charged with violating federal or provincial criminal, wildlife harvesting, or administrative laws.

This situation began to change drastically in the 1950s as governments became more aggressive in enforcing the federal Criminal Code and provincial game and fishing regulations in reserves and remote communities. Many game and fishing laws directly conflicted with aboriginal and treaty rights to harvest wildlife freely at all times of the year on vacant lands. Aboriginal people began to fight game and fishing regulations and called on the courts to give full effect to aboriginal and treaty rights. In a series of decisions, the Canadian courts wrestled with these important issues and developed a number of principles that can be summarized as follows: (1) federal and provincial laws apply to all aboriginal people outside of reserves regardless of any applicable aboriginal rights to the contrary; (2) federal laws override treaty rights where the two conflict; (3) treaty rights prevail over conflicting provincial laws, except where public safety or essential conservation concerns are present; and (4) provincial laws only apply to Indians on reserves, but not to the reserve land itself, and then only to the degree that provisions of the Indian Act allow, subject to conflicting treaties or band by-laws.

## White Paper to Constitutional Change

The passage of the Canadian Bill of Rights in 1960 focused public and governmental attention on the inequalities that existed within the country. Status Indians on reserves were finally granted the right to vote in federal and provincial elections, but the third world living conditions, high unemployment, and poor health of many Indian people became a national disgrace. The federal government committed itself in 1967 to develop a "Just Society" throughout the land and embarked on a major effort to consult with Indian people about how to respond to the crises they faced. In 1969, after a two year effort, the government released its White Paper.

Recommendations contained within proposed to repeal the Indian Act; abolish reserves in exchange for individual ownership by the residents; create municipalities in place of Indian governments; and settle historic grievances for maladministration of reserve lands and treaty claims. With the slate wiped clean for a new beginning, the federal government planned to provide massive funding to build housing and community infrastructure within Indian communities.

The White Paper was received immediately with outrage and opposition from Indian people across the country. Virtually all wished to terminate federal paternalism, remove the legislative restraints of the Indian Act, and settle longstanding treaty and aboriginal title claims. However, no one wished to see government action similar to the U.S. termination policies of the 1950s. Canadian First Nations did not wish to lose their unique legal and political position as the original owners and governors of the land. The government withdrew its proposal and increased spending considerably. In response to treaty claims, the government established a process for the resolution of specific claims.

The federal government continued to view treaties as containing "limited and minimal promises" and considered aboriginal title claims as "so general and undefined that it [was] not realistic to think of them as specific claims capable of remedy." This resistance to appreciating the true reality of Canadian political history, in which treaties played such a vital role, crumbled as a result of a series of major decisions from the Canadian Supreme Court. In January 1973 the Supreme Court delivered a landmark judgment in *Calder v. Attorney General of British Columbia*. Although the Nisga'a Nation did not regain its land because of procedural issues, the Court declared that aboriginal title was still a part of the common law and that it must be given due recognition where it had not been extinguished. The Court agreed that treaties, conquest or legislation could extinguish aboriginal title. However, it split evenly on the questions of how general or explicit legislation needed to be in order to extinguish aboriginal land title, and if a claim for compensation might arise in circumstances where aboriginal title had been validly terminated.

The *Calder* decision was quickly followed by lower courts ruling that aboriginal title still existed in the Northwest Territories and in northern Quebec. In August 1973 the government of Canada proclaimed its willingness to negotiate new treaties or land claims settlements in areas not covered by earlier land surrender treaties. Negotiations commenced shortly afterward between the Quebec government, two of its Crown corporations, the Cree, and the Inuit, culminating in the James Bay and Northern Quebec Agreement in 1975. This agreement provides the eleven thousand Cree and Inuit with $225 million, exclusive use of 5,345 square miles of land, exclusive wildlife harvesting rights over a further 58,530 square miles, and a range of commitments regarding social, economic, health, environmental, and justice concerns, including income guarantees for those who pursue a traditional economy. In return, the Cree and Inuit relinquished aboriginal title to more than 379,400 square miles, an area about the size of France.

In part influenced by these judicial and negotiated victories, Indians pursued numerous other court cases in which aboriginal and treaty rights were asserted, for the most part, in defense of hunting and fishing rights. The results, however, were not satisfying for aboriginal people. The only significant development was in the *Baker Lake* decision in which the court accepted that the Inuit also possess aboriginal title.

## Constitution Act, 1982

In 1982 the Canadian Constitution was extensively revised. It would now contain the Charter of Rights and Freedoms, inspired in part by the American Bill of Rights, and an amending formula that no longer required action by the British Parliament to implement proposed constitutional reforms. Changes were also made to the division of powers between the federal and provincial governments. Finally, a commitment for regional equalization through federal transfer payments was made and several key provisions affecting Aboriginal peoples were added. As a result, the Constitution Act, 1982 contains section 35(1), which states: "The existing aboriginal and treaty rights of the aboriginal peoples of Canada are hereby recognized and affirmed." The term *aboriginal peoples* is defined in section 35(2) and includes Indian, Inuit, and Métis peoples. The charter also includes a clause (section 25) designed to shield "aboriginal, treaty and other rights or freedoms of the aboriginal peoples" from derogation or abrogation by the individual or collective rights guaranteed by the charter.

A provision in section 37 of the act required the Prime Minister of Canada, within one year, to convene a meeting among the provincial premiers (similar to U.S. state governors), representatives of the aboriginal peoples, and the two territorial leaders to seek "to identify and define" aboriginal and treaty rights. This First Ministers' Conference (FMC) was held in early 1983 and resulted in agreement to undertake several constitutional amendments and to meet three more times by 1987 to discuss an agenda of aboriginal issues. By mid–1984 several amendments were proclaimed in force, declaring that the rights contained in modern land claims settlements constituted treaty rights and thereby had constitutional protection under section 25 and were entrenched under section 35. One amendment guaranteed all aboriginal and treaty rights equally to aboriginal women and men. The Constitution was also altered to require a FMC with aboriginal participation to discuss any future constitutional amendments that might expressly affect the existing provisions concerning aboriginal peoples. The FMCs in 1984, 1985, and 1987 concentrated almost exclusively on developing proposed amendments recognizing the right of aboriginal self-government. Sufficient support among first ministers, however, was not forthcoming for any of the proposed amendments favored by the four major national aboriginal organizations. Consequently, the First Ministers' Conferences ended in failure without confirmation of additional amendments in support of aboriginal rights.

### Recent Advances

Despite its inadequacies, the Constitution Act, 1982, as amended in 1984, has had a dramatic effect on the aboriginal legal situation and the political climate in Canada. A number of major gains have occurred over the intervening years, many of which are directly related to the constitutional provisions, while others were no doubt subtly influenced by the presence of these new constitutional standards. In 1984, the Supreme Court of Canada reconfirmed the common law recognition of aboriginal title in *Guerin v. The Queen*. The Court declared that aboriginal title was a critical element of the Crown-aboriginal relationship, which began at the time of contact, and did not require any express acknowledgment by the Crown to exist for a particular group. Instead, the presence of an aboriginal nation in occupation of the land when the Crown arrived was sufficient. The Court also stated that the Crown owed a fiduciary obligation to Indian nations, somewhat akin to the trustee obligations of the U.S. government to protect the land and interests of Indian tribes, because of the Crown's monopoly on the acquisition of land title.

The Supreme Court subsequently ruled that the peace and friendship treaties of the 1700s, in what is now Atlantic Canada, are still binding such that the harvesting guarantees they contain remain effective (*Simon v. The Queen* [1985]). The Court has also developed a series of rules governing the interpretation of treaties, allowing a broad and liberal interpretation,

to reflect how they would have been understood by their Indian signatories. The Court has adopted a similar approach to the interpretation of any legislation that directly refers to Aboriginal peoples (*Nowegijick v. The Queen* [1983]). The Court also developed a broader concept of what constitutes a valid and binding treaty in *Sioui v. The Queen* (1990).

In *Sparrow v. The Queen* (1990), the Supreme Court rendered a decisive ruling on the constitutional recognition of "existing aboriginal and treaty rights." While section 35 did not revive any rights that had been completely extinguished before the new constitutional affirmation took effect, prior regulation or restriction of aboriginal or treaty rights by federal or provincial law did not terminate these rights, but suppressed them. As a result, the "sleeping" aboriginal or treaty rights could be effectively reasserted after 1982, even if they had been restrained for over a century. The Court's judgment reflected a compromise as it also did not guarantee that these rights would now be completely free from all federal or provincial statutory restrictions. Instead, the Court ruled that it was possible to interfere with the exercise of aboriginal or treaty rights, but only if the Crown could meet a rather onerous test in which it carried the burden of proving that it had maintained the high standard of honorable dealing that is expected of the Crown, particularly as it carries a fiduciary obligation. The Crown would also have to show through hard evidence that its laws interfered as little as possible; that there was an essential purpose underlying the law that could only be met through infringing on these unique rights; that the law reflected the priority status of aboriginal peoples in light of their constitutionally recognized rights; that it had consulted with the aboriginal people affected; and that the Crown had engaged in no sharp dealing. The Court also clarified that the Crown's fiduciary obligations were applicable to Indian, Inuit, and Métis peoples and were protected as part of the rights entrenched by section 35. In the 1999 *Marshall* case, the Supreme Court of Canada recognized that the Mi'kmaqs continue to have the right to trade products from hunting and fishing because such rights are contained in their treaties. As a result, many of the federal and provincial restrictions that apply to others who may engage in such activities do not apply. However, the Court stated that such rights are limited to what is required to earn a moderate living.

In 1997 the issue of aboriginal title was revisited in *Delgamuukw v. British Columbia*. Litigation on this issue was initiated in 1984 by fifty-one leaders of the Gitksan and Wet'suwet'en nations claiming title to a large portion of northwest British Columbia (BC). In its decision, the Supreme Court first reaffirmed that the

Founding fathers of the National American Indian Court Judge Association, 1969. (Courtesy of Jerry Gardner)

Crown has underlying title in land and that any aboriginal title is *sui generis* (unique) and is inalienable to anyone but the Crown in right of Canada. The Court then outlined the conditions that must be met before aboriginal title may be recognized. Therefore, according to the Court, aboriginal title will arise if it can be proven that (1) the land was occupied by the group prior to sovereignty (in this case prior to 1846 when the Crown first asserted its sovereignty); (2) there is continuity of occupation; and (3) at the time of Crown sovereignty, occupation was exclusive (unless the presence of others was by trespass or contract). In determining occupation the Court will look at the type of activities that were undertaken by the group on the land, originally and at present. Although the activities do not have to be limited to those historically practiced by the group, the land cannot have been used in a manner that is "irreconcilable with the nature of the group's attachment to that land." The Court also stated that even once title is established, it may still be limited if a valid legislative objective exists allowing such restrictions, and if the fiduciary relationship requirements were met under the *Sparrow* test.

During the 1980s and early 1990s, several immense land claim settlements were negotiated by the aboriginal peoples of the western Arctic, the Mackenzie River delta, the eastern Arctic, and the Yukon. The eight Métis settlements in Alberta have also received from the province fee-simple title to 1.28 million acres of land that comprise their communities along with new provincial legislation delegating powers of local government and more than $300 million for economic development. The Gwich'in settlement in 1992 involved 6,877 square miles of land and other rights, in the Northwest Territories and the Yukon, along with a $75 million transfer. The Sahtu agreement followed and dealt with similar rights to lands in the Northwest Territories. The Sahtu Dene and Métis received a total of almost 16,000 square miles of land and $75 million. The Nunavut land claim of 1993 gave the Inuit control over 135,486 square miles of land and $1.17 billion to be paid over fourteen years. The Yukon First Nations reached an agreement with the federal and territorial governments which became law in 1995 giving these fourteen First Nations control over 16,055 square miles of land. In 1998 the first modern-day treaty in Southern

Canada was signed with the Nisga'a Nation of British Columbia. It resulted in transfer of land title in fee simple to 768 square miles and control over many natural resources as well as the right for self-government and a transfer payment of $253 million. Finally, the Labrador Inuit have reached an Agreement-in-Principle in 1999 concerning a claim to part of the Labrador coastline and interior involving the provision of 30,000 square miles including 6,100 square miles in fee simple and $140 million. Since the 1973 inception of the federal government's specific claims policy, the Specific Claims Branch had settled 172 specific and treaty land entitlement claims by 1997. Between 1993 and 1998 there had been a total of sixty-seven land entitlement claims settled that involved eighty-five First Nations, $342 million and approximately 482,000 hectares of reserve land.

Comprehensive claims based on aboriginal title are currently under negotiation in southern Labrador, Northeastern Quebec, the Ottawa Valley in Ontario, the remainder of the Northwest Territories, and throughout British Columbia. All the foregoing settled comprehensive claims, as well as those under negotiation, involve much more than land and money as they address wildlife harvesting, water rights, subsurface resources, environmental protection, and social issues. To help manage the treaty-making process in BC the British Columbia Treaty Commission was created in 1992 by an agreement between the federal and British Columbia governments as well as First Nations groups (see http://www.bctreaty.net). As of 2000 the commission was handling forty-two sets of negotiations involving fifty-one First Nations that represent 117 bands.

In addition to the land claims mentioned above, many smaller claims regarding treaty breaches and maladministration of reserve lands or funds have also been settled. Nevertheless, more than one thousand such claims are still outstanding and the rate of settlement averages twenty per year. In light of repeated and extensive criticisms of the federal policy, an independent commission was established in 1991 to hear appeals from First Nations and issue recommendations for action to the parties. Agreement was reached in 1992 among the First Nations, the government of Saskatchewan, and the federal government to transfer more than one million acres of land to reserve status that were promised by the treaties negotiated in the late 1800s. Similar treaty land entitlements in Alberta and Manitoba have been settled in recent years.

All these advances do not mean that social or economic conditions have significantly improved for most aboriginal peoples. While the rate of university education has mushroomed and a small percentage have benefited from legal victories or land claims settlements, 75 percent of aboriginal people have been encouraged by government policy or economic circumstances to migrate to urban areas in search of employment, housing, or better opportunities. At the same time, aboriginal peoples have been undergoing a political and cultural revival as they battle for survival as distinct peoples who are the first to protect, enjoy, and govern this land.

In 1996, after substantial consultation on various issues pertaining to First Nations in Canada, the *Report of the Royal Commission on Aboriginal Peoples* (RCAP) was issued (see http://www.inac.gc.ca/ch/rcap/). The commission presented five volumes with 440 recommendations for improving numerous aspects of the circumstances of the aboriginal peoples in Canada. The *Report* criticized the Canadian government's policies of assimilation while calling for action to repair the damage. Essentially, it urged the Canadian government to renew the relationship with the aboriginal people while providing support to the ailing communities. The Canadian government partially responded to the report with "Gathering Strength—Canada's Aboriginal Action Plan," which contained many commitments to address the recommendations of the *Report*.

The negotiations in Canada in 1992 for further constitutional reform in national institutions and the division of powers between federal and provincial governments, although ultimately unsuccessful, also provided an opportunity for aboriginal peoples to seek their proper recognition as the founding peoples. In 1995 the federal government introduced a new process for negotiating self-government agreements with aboriginal groups. As part of its policy, the government recognized self-government as an inherent right contained in section 35 of the *Constitution Act, 1982*. This federal approach also acknowledged the importance of and preference for negotiation as opposed to litigation. In negotiating self-government agreements, the government stated that it is prepared to enter into covenants that will suit the unique needs of particular aboriginal groups but without ending the relationship between the Crown and the aboriginal peoples. Therefore, the self-government structure will have to operate within the existing federal structure of Canada. Aboriginal groups would have their powers confirmed to establish governments with the ability to control law enforcement, taxation, family law, religion, education, aboriginal language and culture, social services, health, natural resources, among other areas. However, they would not have the power to pass laws regarding issues of national scope such as defense or the national economy. In addition, some federal and provincial laws would still apply to enable "harmony among jurisdictions." The First Nations seek to have their inherent right to govern themselves recognized in the highest law of the land and to gain recognition as one of three sovereign orders of Canadian government. Aboriginal people also seek to engage in nation-to-nation negotiations regarding existing treaties so that the true spirit and intent that were present at the time of their original negotiation can be restored and given effect under Canadian law.

Without these changes, Canada will continue to suffer from a clash of values, beliefs, and histories that cause conflict and mistrust. Aboriginal people will likely continue to view themselves as sovereign nations that have not joined or been absorbed into Canada and retain the right to determine their own laws, governments, and destinies. On the other hand, the federal and provincial governments will likely remain firm in the belief that they retain ultimate control subject only to the limitations that are identified in future self-government agreements and the existing constitutional arrangement. Under the latter view, First Nations exist only as creatures of the *Indian Act* with only those powers that are delegated to them by that act, at least until negotiations on new arrangements are successfully concluded. This perception means that the nearly 75 percent of aboriginal people living outside of Indian reserves do not possess local governments or their own service systems unless they are parties to a recent comprehensive claims settlement. The federal position is that the 610 federally recognized Indian bands have only the rights and benefits that are set out under the *Indian Act*, which includes: tax exemption for income derived from or sales that occur on reserves; the ability to enact by-laws on a small range of municipal-type matters; exemption from seizure of land or goods; restraints on land alienation; and special laws for estates, education, health care and other social services. Unlike the United States, there remains no aboriginal-specific legislation to deal with child welfare, religious freedom, or self-determination. Traditional or customary Indian law receives relatively little recognition in Canadian courts, and aboriginal communities have only a minimal role in the justice system with no accepted general authority to create their own courts.

Aboriginal peoples in Canada are in a significantly weaker legal position than U.S. Indian tribes in some ways despite a history of less military conflict, constitutional guarantees, and greater political weight, and the fact that they comprise a five times larger percentage of the Canadian population than do U.S. Indians. On the other hand, aboriginal peoples in Canada are not subject to having their rights unilaterally affected or abolished, as is the case in the United States, through the exercise by Congress of its plenary power over the Indian tribes. The economic, political, and legal advances made over the past thirty years, however, are remarkable and give a strong basis for guarded optimism about the future.

*Bradford W. Morse*
*University of Ottawa*

## ◆ ABORIGINAL RIGHTS AND TREATIES IN CANADA

Aboriginal rights and privileges in Canada are defined and implemented according to three distinct frameworks: (1) treaties between the Crown and various bands and nations; (2) constitutional guarantees culminating in the Constitution Act, 1982; and (3) statutory provisions flowing from parliamentary legislation, such as the successive Indian Acts and agreements signed with the federal and provincial governments. Aboriginal peoples in Canada have never been considered aliens. In colonial times they were allied nations, independent and self-governing under the sovereignty of the French Crown and later the British Crown. At present, treaty rights refer to reserve inhabitants, but at least half the First Nations people live in urban areas where no bands or community organizations with treaty rights exist.

Acadia until 1713 and Canada until 1763 were French colonies. Native rights, as observed under the French régime, were continued by the British Crown in the Royal Proclamation of 1763. Great Britain handed over responsibility for Indian affairs to the several British North American colonies in 1860. When Nova Scotia, New Brunswick, and the United Canadas (Quebec and Ontario) joined in a federal union in 1867, "Indians, and Lands reserved for Indians" were assigned to the federal government in Ottawa. Indian treaties, therefore, given this political evolution over several centuries, could be negotiated by the Crown in the right of France, Great Britain, the distinct colonies, or the Dominion of Canada. Aboriginal peoples are now commonly called the First Nations.

### French Régime

The French Crown signed no treaties of land surrender with Amerindian peoples in New France as European settlement required no displacement of original inhabitants. In the *pays d'en haut*, the hinterland stretching west from the island of Montreal to the Prairies and Mississippi Basin, French settlement on Native ancestral territories was virtually prohibited. Catholic missions, fur-trading posts, and military garrisons were established with the permission of aboriginal residents in the context of Native hospitality, resource sharing, and trade and war alliances. Likewise, in Acadia (Nova Scotia) there was no displacement of the Mi'kmaq. Cooperation persisted between indigenous inhabitants and colonists through the fur trade, fishing, and resistance to Anglo-American incursions.

Royal instructions to the colonial governor in 1665 stated explicitly that no colonists were to "take the lands on which they [Natives] are living under pretext that it would be better and more suitable if they were [possessed by the] French." Native possessory and territorial rights were acknowledged in the official correspondence by such phrases as "these nations govern themselves" and "they must be deemed free everywhere on their lands." In 1755 a Ministry of War directive reminded serving officers in the colony: "The natives are jealous of their liberty, and one could not without committing an injustice take away from them *the primitive right of property* to the Lands on which Providence has given them birth and located them." The French supported those tribes (such as the Abenakis) that resisted Anglo-American encroachment on their lands. French claims to sovereignty were exercised against European rivals without subjecting First Nations to French laws, taxation, trade restrictions, or military service.

The few treaties the French signed with Native peoples were neither land surrenders nor international treaties between sovereign powers belonging to the "family of nations" as understood in European diplomatic circles. From 1665 to 1667 French officials signed local peace treaties with the League of the Iroquois. The 1701 Treaty of Montreal consisted of a series of peace agreements among the French, the Five Nations Iroquois, Abenaki, Algonkins, Nipissings, and "domiciled" Iroquois of Kanawake and Kanestake. The French were mediators in this general peace and resumption of trade relations which recognized the Five Nations Iroquois as neutral in international conflicts, a status confirmed in the Treaty of Utrecht (1713).

The "domiciled" Huron, Iroquois, Abenaki, and Algonkians were allied to the French as the Seven Fires of Canada, while the tribes of the Great Lakes were united to the French and Seven Fires in the informal Three Fires Confederacy. The property rights and liberty of these allied nations were specifically protected in Article 40 of the Capitulation of Montreal to British forces in September 1760 and Article 4 of the Treaty of Paris (1763) by which Canada became a British colony. It was a well-established principle of international law that the civil rights of subjects acquired by conquest or cession continued in force. In other words, the ancestral rights of Canada's Native peoples were protected

by international treaty in 1763. Not surprisingly, the First Nations were accorded special mention in the subsequent treaties of Paris (1783), Jay (1794), and Ghent (1815).

## British Treaties of Peace and Friendship

British rule in what is now Canada began through the royal charter of the Hudson's Bay Company (1670), Crown colonies in Newfoundland and Vancouver Island, and the cession of the French colonies of Acadia (Nova Scotia) in 1713 and Canada in 1763. In Nova Scotia, the British negotiated a number of "treaties of peace and friendship" with the chiefs of various maritime bands to safeguard incoming settlers and commerce. Among the significant treaties were those agreed to by leaders of small Malecite and Mi'kmaq bands at Casco Bay (1727), Annapolis Royal (1728), Halifax (1749; 1752; 1760; 1779), and Windsor (1779). In return for initial "submission in as simple a manner as was customary prior to this time" to the Crown, the bands were promised "all their lands, liberties and properties" not claimed by settlers as well as "the privilege of fishing, hunting, and fowling as formerly." The 1749 and 1752 treaties were negotiated before the exile of the Acadians, long-time allies of the Mi'kmaq, and the 1760 treaty after the fall of New France in 1760 to obtain assurances of loyalty, as was the case following Mi'kmaq abandonment of an American alliance of 1778. A Mi'kmaq band in the Miramichi region of the colony of New Brunswick adhered to a treaty of friendship in 1794 in which King George III promised "henceforth I will provide for you and for the future generation so long as the sun rises and river flows." By these treaties, most of the maritime band chiefs had recognized a British protectorate without surrendering either lands or other rights. In 1823 these treaties elicited the legal opinion that the Natives were British subjects and were required to obey the laws of the realm. The authority of band leaders to enter into such agreements has been questioned, but recent court cases have upheld colonial treaty terms to the benefit of aboriginal rights to hunt, fish, and use natural resources.

## Treaties of Neutrality

The Seven Fires or Nations of Canada had been important allies of the French in the late seventeenth and early eighteenth centuries. But as New France's defenses began to collapse, these allies sought amicable agreements with the advancing British forces. On 30 August 1760, their delegates concluded a treaty at Oswegatchie or Fort La Galette to the effect they would not assist the French and permit the invaders to descend the St. Lawrence to Montreal, and that if Canada remained in British hands they would enjoy the same privileges as "in the time of the French, but still more and greater," the possession of their lands, their hunting grounds, and the free exercise of the Catholic religion. On 5 September, the Hurons of Lorette signed a separate treaty at Longueuil with Major General James Murray by which they were granted safe passage back to their village, amnesty, the free exercise of their religion and customs, and freedom of trade. These treaties were reconfirmed and ratified by William Johnson, superintendent of the Indian Department, at a special congress at the Kahnawake Reserve on 15 and 16 September 1760. The British were now able to take up the role of apparent protectors of Native lands from Anglo-American intrusion. The Royal Proclamation of 1763 was a two-pronged instrument of Imperial policy: it reserved all lands outside the settled seigneuries as "Indian hunting grounds," and provided for the alienation of any of these lands exclusively to the Crown so as to ensure orderly European settlement as required.

### Hudson's Bay Company Treaties

The London Royal Charter Company founded in 1670, administered all the lands draining into Hudson Bay and granted the Earl of Selkirk permission to bring settlers to the Red River Valley in 1812. To avoid opposition from the Cree and Saulteaux, Selkirk proposed to purchase a block of land in return for "a small annual present, in the nature of a quit rent, or acknowledgment of their right." The Selkirk Treaty was signed on 18 July 1817, granting the local bands 200 pounds of tobacco annually. The implication seemed to be that aboriginal rights were based on common law. When the Canadian government acquired Rupert's Land and the North-West Territories in 1870, the Order-in-Council stipulated that "any claims of Indians to compensation for lands required for purposes of settlement shall be disposed of by the Canadian government in communication with the Imperial government; and the company (HBCo) shall be relieved of all responsibility in respect of them."

On Vancouver Island, Governor James Douglas, acting for the Hudson's Bay Company as well as the Crown colony, entered into six land surrender treaties in April 1850 with the Songhees, two treaties with the Klallam in May 1850, a treaty with the Sooke in May 1850, two treaties with the Saanich in February 1852, and one treaty in 1854 with the Saalequun tribe. Two further purchases were made at Fort Rupert in 1851 and Nanaimo in 1854. These fourteen Fort Victoria Treaties

promised reserve lands for "village sites and enclosed fields," hunting rights "over the unoccupied lands," and fishing rights "as formerly." In return Douglas paid the least acceptable amount "in woolen goods which they prefer to money." This was in line with Colonial Office policy that in all treaties the object should be "the cession of lands possessed by them." In 1965 the Supreme Court ruled these were valid Indian treaties because Governor Douglas was an agent of the British Crown. On the mainland of British Columbia, Douglas asked the various communities to "point out" their habitation and hunting territories, which were defined as reserves, but without any treaty protection, as was the case in Quebec and Newfoundland. Thereafter, the governments of British Columbia long denied any recognition of aboriginal title.

### Upper Canada Treaties of Land Surrender

The Royal Proclamation of 1763 provided a process for the acquisition of Native lands when refugees of the American Revolutionary War poured into Upper Canada (Ontario). Thirty-seven documented treaties were signed between 1781 and 1836. Some, like the Crawford Purchase in the eastern region now subject to an Algonkian claim, have left no trace. Twenty-four treaties of land surrender were signed upon payment of a one-time fixed sum to the Mississaugas and Ojibwa (Chippewa). From the ceded lands two Indian reserves were created for Iroquois Loyalists—the Six Nations Reserve on the Grand River for Joseph Brant's people and the Bay of Quinte Reserve for John Deserontyon's people. Some of the treaties lacked precision, such as the Gunshot Treaty (1787) which defined the ceded tract as running back from designated points on Lake Ontario "as far as a gunshot can be heard on a clear day."

After the war lasting from 1812 to 1814, seven more land cessions were signed in Upper Canada (southern Ontario) before 1830 to make way for immigrants from the British Isles. The Indians were demoralized now by declining numbers and their marginalization in British defense strategy, so they readily signed away valuable lands. They were offered small reserves, fixed annuities, and some farm instructors, blacksmiths, and doctors. A plan unveiled in 1830 to remove all Indians of southern Upper Canada to Manitoulin Island fortunately was shelved. Up to 1829, compensation was paid in goods of the same description as the annual military presents. The annuities were then transformed into credits towards building and equipment on reserves.

In 1850, twice as much land as already ceded in the region was discharged to gain access to forest reserves, mineral deposits, and transportation corridors along the northern shores of Lakes Huron and Superior. When clarification was demanded, William Robinson negotiated two treaties with the Ojibwa whereby they ceded 50,000 square miles of land in return for retention of twenty-one reserves, perpetual annuities, and hunting and fishing rights in the ceded territory except where "sold or leased to individuals, or companies." The Ojibwa could not dispose in any way of any part of their reserves and they were not "at any time [to] hinder or prevent persons from exploring or searching for minerals or other valuable productions" in ceded territory. The appended schedules of reserves stipulated that the lands, whose title remained vested in the Crown, were "held and occupied by the said chiefs and their Tribes in common for the purposes of residence and cultivation." Two further treaties, involving smaller areas—the Saugeen Peninsula in Lake Huron and an eastern portion of Manitoulin Island—were signed in 1854 and 1862 respectively. In 1923 a commission was appointed to negotiate with the Ojibwa of the Georgian Bay-Lake Simcoe region and the Mississauga of the Rice Lake area for further transfer of land. At the present time, a large land claim is in preparation by the Algonkians concerning aboriginal title that has not been extinguished in eastern Ontario.

## Numbered Treaties

The federal government used the constitutional authority defined in the 1867 British North America Act between 1871 and 1921 to negotiate eleven numbered treaties of land surrender for most of the western and northern regions that eventually entered the federal union. Following troubles at Red River concerning provincial status, the Manitoba Act of 1870 set aside 1,400,000 acres for the Métis and their descendants. Treaty Number 1 negotiated at Fort Garry in 1871 set the pattern for cession of all rights and title in return for annuities in perpetuity and reserves for their own use. The federal government was anxious to clear title to western lands in order to open the plains to agricultural settlement.

Among the subsequent treaties, imposed as much as negotiated, several deserve special mention. Treaty Number 3 with the Ojibwa included the Métis in its terms but stipulated that those who received benefits as Indians could not also hold scrip lands under the provisions of the Manitoba Act. The area ceded was crucial to a right-of-way for a transcontinental railway and was of interest to mining and lumbering companies. The chiefs inquired about mineral rights and were told these were held on the reserves by the Crown for their benefit.

Treaty Number 6 of 1876 covering much of what became central Saskatchewan and Alberta, provided for a "medicine chest," which the Indian agents were to keep available to deal with epidemics or "general famine." The Plains Cree in this case faced starvation and were threatened with withdrawal of government food rations if they did not make treaty. Since the nationwide introduction of Medicare in 1984, aboriginal peoples have enjoyed the full range of services both on and off reserves, including optical and dental care, prescription drugs, and transportation to medical care centers. This has been provided by the federal government as a policy decision rather than an aboriginal right.

Treaty Number 7 (1877) in what became southern Alberta, saw the intervention of both missionaries and the North-West Mounted Police in the negotiation process, inasmuch as they had a direct interest in the removal of discontent. The Canadian government had also decided that the sums paid in indemnities and annuities cost less than fighting Plains Indians, if the American examples were relevant.

Treaties Number 1 to 7 included clauses that responded to astute demands made by the chiefs for schools, agricultural supplies and implements, farm instructors, and the prohibition of liquor on reserves. They were also aware that "outside promises," or verbal promises not specifically written into the treaties, had little validity. There is evidence, for example, that Natives were not told clearly that their hunting and fishing rights in treaties 4 and 7, as well as in the four later treaties, were "subject to such regulations as may from time to time be made by the Government of the country acting under the authority of Her Majesty."

Treaties Number 8 to 11 can be characterized as northern resource development treaties. Treaty making was resumed in 1899 after a twenty-two-year hiatus because of an influx of miners into the Yukon and adjacent areas. Treaty Number 11 (1921) followed the discovery of oil in the Mackenzie Valley. Treaty Number 9 (1905) cleared Native title in much of northern Ontario and was negotiated jointly by the federal and Ontario provincial governments because the latter controlled the natural resources within its boundaries. Treaty Number 10, negotiated the following year for northern Saskatchewan was negotiated solely by the federal government because natural resources did not as yet fall within Saskatchewan's jurisdiction.

## Contemporary Agreements

Treaty-making is a continual process in Canada, especially since the federal government launched a comprehensive and specific claims process in 1973.

Comprehensive land claims are negotiated in areas where aboriginal title has not been addressed clearly by treaty or other legal means. Since 1995, an inherent right policy allows simultaneous negotiation for self-government. Since most of the lands and resources subject to comprehensive claim negotiations are under provincial jurisdiction, provincial negotiators participate in the negotiation of agreements with aboriginal groups. Specific claims deal with grievances that First Nations may have about implementation or interpretation of existing treaties. The major recent agreements are discussed below.

**James Bay and Northern Quebec Agreements, 1975, 1978.** When the Quebec government announced a plan in 1971 for a massive hydroelectric development involving diversions of four rivers and dammed reservoirs on La Grande Rivi;re, the Cree and Inuit of the eastern James Bay region through the courts and the media forced the federal and Quebec provincial governments to consider their aboriginal rights. The treaty negotiated in 1975 and implemented in 1990 provided some exclusive hunting, fishing, and trapping territories for each of the Cree and Inuit, $135 million for the Cree and $90 million for the Inuit (both of which have now been paid in full), an income security program for hunters and trappers, self-government under Quebec's Cree-Naskapi Act, and participation in an environmental and social protection regime. In 1978 the Northeastern Quebec Agreement amended the James Bay Agreement to include the Naskapi with comparable benefits.

**Inuvialuit Agreement of Northwest Territories, 1984.** A second comprehensive agreement with the 2,500 Inuvialuit of the Mackenzie Delta and Beaufort Sea area, renowned for its oil and gas reserves, provided for a land base, some of which included mineral rights, wildlife harvesting rights, and participation in environmental management, in addition to substantial allocation of funds to an economic enhancement fund and a social development fund.

**Dene and Métis Agreements, 1992, 1994.** Separate regional settlements with the Gwich'in and Sahtu Dene and the Métis of the Mackenzie Valley in the Northwest Territories (NWT) provided for land reserves with mineral rights, wildlife harvesting rights, and participation in decision-making bodies dealing with renewable resources, land use, environmental assessment, and regulation of land and water use.

**Nunavut Agreement, 1999.** In 1992 the federal government and territorial government of the NWT agreed on the eventual creation of the self-governing Nunavut Territory in the eastern Arctic. The new territory, with a population of just under 20,000 and its capital at Iqaluit, has a highly decentralized government to respond to the specific needs of its twenty-eight Inuit communities.

**Nisga'a Treaty, 2000.** In April 1999 the British Columbia legislature ratified terms of a land settlement with the Nisga'a Tribal Council. The federal parliament passed the necessary legislation a year later providing for ownership and self-government of about 2,000 square kilometers of land in the Nass River Valley and a cash payment of $190 million. It is the first modern-day treaty in British Columbia.

Numerous other claims were being negotiated at the end of the twentieth century, including one involving the Algonquins of Golden Lake who since 1991 have been negotiating a claim to a large area of eastern Ontario encompassing Algonquin Park and the Ottawa Valley.

## Selected Court Decisions

The Supreme Court of Canada has in recent years rendered significant decisions concerning the interpretation of treaties and the application of section 35 of the Constitution Act (1982). Aboriginal rights were ill-served by early court rulings, such as the Imperial Privy Council (London) in *St. Catherine's Milling & Lumber Company v. The Queen* (1889) that ruled on appeal that the tenure of the Indians was "a personal and usufructuary right, dependent upon the good will of the Sovereign," and the *Rex v. Syliboy* (1929) verdict that "treaties are unconstrained acts of independent powers. But the Indians were never regarded as an independent power" because they passed from French to British rule by international treaty along with the colony.

The existence of aboriginal title was recognized in *Calder v. Attorney-General of British Columbia* (1973) because the Nisga'a were settled on ancestral lands when settlers came. A basis for defining an aboriginal right was outlined in a judgment concerning the Caribou Inuit of Baker Lake that had been Hudson's Bay Company territory until transferred to Canada in 1870. In *Hamlet of Baker Lake v. Minister of Indian Affairs* (1980) the essentials were set out clearly: "The elements which the plaintiffs must prove to establish an aboriginal title cognizable at common law are: (1) That they and their ancestors were members of an organized society; (2) That the organized society occupied the specific territory over which they asserted the aboriginal title; (3) That the occupation was to the exclusion of other organized societies; and (4) That the occupation was an established fact at the time sovereignty was asserted by England." Three years later, the Court ruled that "treaties and statutes relating to Indians should be liberally construed and doubtful expressions resolved in favour of the Indians."

There are two techniques for extinguishing aboriginal and treaty rights—unilateral action of the Crown and formal surrender. In the case of *R. v. Sioui* (1990) the court demanded "strict proof" that a treaty provision had been rescinded. In *R. v. Adams* (1996) the court ruled that although Mohawk land had been surrendered the right to fish adjacent to these lands had not been surrendered therewith. In *R. v. Badger* (1996) extrinsic evidence was allowed because "the treaties, as written documents, recorded an agreement that had already been reached orally and they did not always record the full extent of the oral agreement." The court ruled against a narrow technical or contractual interpretation of a treaty, holding that the wording "must be given the sense which it would naturally have held for the parties at the time," as well as being "sensitive to the unique cultural and linguistic differences between the parties."

In *R. v. Van der Peet* (1996) the court distinguished between aboriginal right and aboriginal title. A group could claim an aboriginal right under section 35(1) of the Constitution Act to an activity without at the same time having to establish they had aboriginal title to the land where the activity occurred. This applied especially to bands which varied the location of their settlements in search of food. In 1997, in *Delgamuukw v. British Columbia* (1997) the majority ruled that aboriginal title to land required occupation prior to sovereignty and that "at sovereignty, that occupation must have been exclusive," in the sense that the groups "intended to and attempted to enforce their exclusive occupation" against trespassers.

Following upon the concept of a broad interpretation of historic treaty clauses, the Supreme Court opined in *R. v. Sundown* (1999) that rights were not frozen at the date of signature but a modern exercise should be construed involving "what modern practices are reasonably incidental to the core treaty right in its modern context." Courts are now presented with considerable historical and anthropological evidence. In *R. v. Donald Marshall Jr.* (1999) the Supreme Court ruled that the 1760 treaty provision for a "truckhouse," a trading establishment, should be interpreted as a "treaty right to obtain necessaries through hunting and fishing" commercially as well as for subsistence. Consequently, the Department of Oceans and Fisheries has difficulty imposing its regulations as many Mi'kmaq engage in lobster and crab fishing for commercial purposes. In *R. v. Joshua Bernard* (2000), in which it was argued that trading "to obtain necessaries" included logging, mining, and exploitation of off-shore oil and natural gas deposits, the Supreme Court upheld the conviction for unlawful possession of timber from Crown lands. This case appears to place limits on the "broad interpretation" of treaty and constitutional rights when it affects the common good and public interest.

*Cornelius J. Jaenen*
*University of Ottawa*

## ◆ LIST OF SIGNIFICANT CANADIAN DOCUMENTS

**Articles of Capitulation of Montreal, September 1760.** "Article XL. The Savage or Indian Allies of His Most Christian Majesty, shall be maintained in the Lands they inhabit; if they choose to remain there, they shall not be molested on any pretence whatsoever, for having carried arms, and served His Most Christian Majesty; they shall have, as well as the French, liberty of religion, and shall keep their missionaries. Granted." This clause guaranteed the right to remain unmolested on hunting and fishing grounds as well as traditional village sites and encampments and *réductions*, or reserves. Governor James Murray's royal instructions, dated 7 December 1763, added: "And you are upon no Account to molest or disturb them in the Possession of such parts of the said Province, as they at present occupy or possess; but to use the best means You can for conciliating their Affections, and uniting them to our Government."

**Royal Proclamation of 7 October 1763.** This proclamation issued by George III for the governing of the British North American colonies is often referred to as the "charter of rights" of Indian peoples. It was concerned principally that "the several Nations or Tribes of Indians with whom We are connected, and who live under our protection, should not be molested or disturbed in the Possession of such Parts of Our Dominions and Territories as, not having been ceded to or purchased by Us, are reserved to them or any of them, as their Hunting Grounds." In fixing the bounds of the colonies, the Crown reserved to itself "for the use of the said Indians, all the Lands and Territories not included within the Limits of Our Said Governments" or of the Hudson's Bay Company. Lands could only be alienated to the Crown, never to individuals or companies, by purchase at some public assembly with the Indians concerned. Those who have settled on reserved lands were "forthwith to remove themselves." There were similar limitations on purchase of Indian reserve lands within the colonies. Trade with the Indians was restricted to those who were licensed by the colonial governor. The proclamation was perceived as sound policy for security in dealing with Natives who were "under our Protection" and who retained only parts of

"Our Dominion" as were "reserved to them." The section of the Royal Proclamation dealing with the Indians remains in force today because it has never been repealed by a Canadian statute. It has become the model for the process of surrender of aboriginal title through treaties. Some court decisions have been based on the premise that this proclamation was the basis and source of aboriginal title in Canada.

**Sir Francis Bond Head's Address to the House of Assembly, 1836.** "Over these Lands His Majesty has never exercised his paramount right, except at their request, and for their manifest advantage— within our own communities they have hitherto governed themselves by their own unwritten laws and customs. Their lands and property have never been subject to tax or assessment or themselves liable for personal service. As they are not subject to such liabilities, neither do they yet possess the political privileges of His Majesty's subjects generally." This statement by the lieutenant-governor of Upper Canada indicated a British continuation of traditional French policy before the conquest.

***Connolly v. Woolrich* (Lower Canada, 1867).** This was a case in which the legality of "country marriages" and the inheritance rights of Métis children were upheld in a Lower Canadian (Quebec) court. Judge Monk based his decision on the following grounds: "Neither the French government, nor any of its colonists or their trading associations, ever attempted, during an intercourse of over two hundred years, to subvert or modify the laws and usages of the aboriginal tribes, except where they had established colonies and permanent settlements, and, then only by persuasion." Even in the settled areas of New France, he opined, Indians customs and social organization "were left in full force, and were not even modified in the slightest degree in regard to the civil rights of the natives."

**Treaty Number 8 (1899).** During the negotiations of this northern treaty of surrender the Indian negotiators expressed concern that the agreement would lead to imposition of taxation and enforced military service. The report of the treaty commissioner recorded: "We assured them that the Treaty would not lead to any forced interference with their mode of life, that it did not open the way to imposition of any tax, and that there was no fear of enforced military service." European claims of sovereignty upon "discovery" did not extinguish property right held by Natives at the time of contact.

**The Constitution Act (1982).** There are four provisions in the written portion of the Canadian Constitution that refer to aboriginal and treaty rights:

25. The guarantee in this charter of certain rights and freedoms shall not be construed so as to abrogate or derogate from any aboriginal, treaty or other rights or freedoms that pertain to the aboriginal peoples of Canada including: (a) any rights or freedoms that have been recognized by the Royal Proclamation of October 7, 1763; and (b) any rights or freedoms that may be acquired by the aboriginal peoples of Canada by way of land claim settlement.

35(1). The existing aboriginal and treaty rights of the aboriginal peoples of Canada are hereby recognized and affirmed.

35(2). In this act, 'aboriginal peoples of Canada' include the Indian, Inuit and Métis peoples of Canada.

37(1). A constitutional Conference composed of the Prime Minister of Canada and the first ministers of the provinces shall be convened by the Prime Minister of Canada within one year after this part comes into force.

In this way, "existing rights" became constitutionally entrenched and could not be extinguished or altered thereafter by the federal parliament or provincial legislatures.

*Cornelius J. Jaenen*
*University of Ottawa*

# ◆ LEGISLATION AFFECTING CANADA'S NATIVE PEOPLE

## Pre-Confederation Legislation and Colonial Policy

The history of Canadian-indigenous relations is peppered with a considerable array of legislation about Indians in Canada. As represented through that legislation, however, government policy has remained little changed: assimilation of the indigenous peoples of Canada into white society is still the goal of Crown policy. Originally, the foreign powers who would confederate as Canada sought friendship with indigenous peoples to secure and maintain military alliances and prolific trade relationships. The Royal Proclamation of 1763 reflected this desire. In it, King George III recognized aboriginal people as "nations or tribes" and acknowledged that they continued to possess their traditional lands until such lands were "ceded to or purchased by" the Crown.

Despite the recognition given to indigenous nations in the proclamation, the colonial powers of Northern North America began to legislate for Native peoples. In 1850, an Act for the Better Protection of the Lands and Property of Indians in Lower Canada appointed a commissioner who held lands in trust for Indian people and had the power to do what he wished with the property.

A similar Act for the Better Protection of the Lands and Property of Indians in Upper Canada made it illegal for anyone to purchase, sell, or lease Indian lands without Crown approval. The act also exempted Indians from taxation and prohibited the sale of liquor to Indians. While on the surface they appeared to protect Indian people, these acts, and others like them, were consistent with the government's goal of separating Indians from the negative influences of white society until such time as they were "civilized" or deemed ready to fully assimilate into white society. The 1857 Act to Encourage the Gradual Civilization of the Indian Tribes in the Province, and to Amend the Laws Respecting Indians expressly made assimilation its goal by tying enfranchisement to the level of Western education or "possessing the capability of managing [one's] own affairs."

### Post-Confederation: Paternalism, Absorption, and Cultural Imperialism

**The Constitution Act, 1867.** The colonial policy of assimilation through "civilization" continued after the colonies of Upper Canada (now Ontario), Lower Canada (now Quebec), New Brunswick, and Nova Scotia joined together to confederate as the Dominion of Canada. The Constitution Act, 1867 (formerly the British North America Act) divided the powers of the new state between the provincial governments (Section 92) and the federal government (Section 91) without any recognition of the existing governments of the various nations of indigenous peoples within Canada's claimed borders. This process of exclusion, consistent with pre-confederation legislation about Indian peoples, continues into the twenty-first century where the Crown's vision of self-government consists of authority delegated to Indian bands.

Section 91(24) of the Constitution Act grants the federal government control over "Indians and lands reserved for Indians." This provision has been interpreted as granting the federal government the power and the responsibility to legislate in all aspects of Indian reserve life, from alcohol consumption to governance to schooling for Indian children. The earliest post-confederation acts addressing Indian affairs reflected the perceived scope of the federal government's power over the lives of individual Indians and Indian communities and continued the pre-confederation policy of assimilation and civilization.

An Act Providing for the Organization of the Department of the Secretary of State of Canada, and for the Management of Indian and Ordinance Lands appointed the secretary of State as the superintendent general of Indian affairs and charged him with "the control and management of the lands and property of the Indians in Canada." Ignoring the traditional laws and policies of the indigenous peoples of Canada, an Act for the Gradual Enfranchisement of Indians, the Better Management of Indian Affairs defined what constituted lawful possession of Indian lands and began to legally define the term "Indian". This act, passed in 1869, also introduced the concept of federally recognized local government to the reserves and provided for band elections. It is interesting to note that the form prescribed then remains virtually unchanged to the present day.

**Treaty-Making in the New Dominion.** Section 146 of the Constitution Act, 1867, provided for the admission of Rupert's Land, a vast western track of land, then under the nominal control of the Hudson's Bay Company to the Dominion of Canada. The new federal government quickly negotiated the purchase of this immense territory, which included present day Saskatchewan, Alberta, Manitoba, the Northwest Territory, the Yukon, Nunavut, Northern Quebec, and Western Ontario. Without any consultation with the indigenous peoples occupying these western lands, including the Plains Cree, the Blackfoot Confederacy, and the Métis of the Red River Valley, the federal government proceeded to appoint a governor for the newly named Northwest Territory. Though the Crown immediately began demarcating land for settlers from the east, the resistance to settlement by Louis Riel and the Métis and the other Plains tribes forced the government to rethink its expansion policy. Familiar with the treaties made by pre-confederation colonial governments in the eastern part of what was now Canada (see "Treaties"), the fledgling government of Canada extended the treaty-making process into the Plains through what are known as the "numbered treaties."

The eleven numbered treaties made between 1871 and 1921 are similar to each other. With only slight variation, each treaty seems to take cessions of aboriginal title in return for reserve lands doled out in proportion to population, small annuities, the preservation of hunting, fishing, and trapping rights, and other goods and services.

Today, there is frequently a vast gulf separating Crown and aboriginal understanding of the meaning of the provisions contained in the numbered treaties. The Crown argues that the meaning of the treaties is limited to exactly what is articulated in pen and ink, while most indigenous nations argue that it is the spirit and intent of the treaty that must be honored. Many treaties, for example, make mention of schooling for children and of the gift of a medicine chest for communities. Such provisions have been understood by Native communities to indicate a federal commitment to education and health care. Today, the Crown does provide these services but does not feel bound to do so by the treaties.

Many treaty Indians, or Indians who are members of nations that are parties to a numbered treaty, also understand the numbered treaties as agreements of peace and friendship in which their ancestors agreed to share the land and its resources with the newcomers. The Crown, however, maintains that the nations party to the numbered treaties have entirely given up their aboriginal title to the land.

**The Indian Act, 1876.** First passed while the numbered treaties were still being negotiated, the Indian Act is the most influential piece of Canadian legislation about Indian peoples. The first version of the Indian Act in 1876 was a consolidation of all previous legislation about Indian peoples and, thus, was not original in its policies or intent. The government goal of assimilation and civilization of Indian peoples was evident in the Indian Act's definition of who would be considered "Indian" under Canadian law and in the entrenchment of the Indian agent as a prominent figure in band communities with control of Indian land. Since this first consolidation, the Indian Act has undergone scores of revisions and re-consolidations that continue to this day (see "Corbiere" below).

Thus the impact of the Indian Act is not merely that of a single act passed in 1876. Rather the act and its amendments and related measures, unique in Canadian law, have had the cumulative effect of singling out a segment of society, separating their land and other property from the commercial mainstream and giving the Crown unprecedented invasive power in the day-to-day functioning and governance of Indian community and band life. Pre-confederation definitions of who was and was not an Indian were primarily intended to prevent squatter encroachment on Indian lands and to protect resources belonging to Indian peoples. Soon, however, the definition of Indian, later to be revised into "status" and "non-status," became a tool of exclusion and assimilation. The Indian Act was used to control the lives of Indians, including banning cultural activities such as potlatches and feasts which were seen as uncivilized or contrary to the goals of the government (see An Act to Further Amend the Indian Act, 1880 of 1884). The frequent amendments to the Indian Act responded to the current issues of reserve life or, more frequently, to the most recent concerns of the sitting government. In 1884, the Indian Advancement Act tried to give wider powers over local government to the band councils provided for in the Indian Act, yet it virtually took away those same powers by placing the local Indian agent as chairman of band councils. Following a petition by the Nisga'a Nation of the Nass Valley in British Columbia to the British Privy Council to resolve the Nisga'a's claim to ownership of claimed Crown Land, a 1927 amendment of the Indian

Act made it illegal for Indian bands or individuals to raise or receive funds for the purposes of litigation.

Though some early Indian Act measures, such as the outlaw of the potlatch and the prohibition against fundraising for the prosecution of land claims, were repealed by the middle of the twentieth century, others remained in force until quite recently, while others remain active to this day. When the equal rights provision of the Canada Charter of Rights and Freedoms came into effect in 1985, a measure known as Bill C-31 was also enacted. The bill was intended to amend provisions of the Indian Act that discriminated against women by reinstating women and their children who had previously lost their status due to discriminatory provisions of the act. Bill C-31 has greatly increased the status Indian population and brought new challenges to communities and bands both financially and socially.

From its inception the Indian Act has had a profound effect on Indian communities in Canada. An essential and unavoidable part of Indian life in Canada for generations, the act has shaped not only the perceptions, expectations, and stereotypes of non-indigenous Canada and created the norms and standards of subsequent Crown policy, but it has also played a roll in forging and molding the mentality of Indian peoples themselves.

**Integration and Formal Equality, 1945–1973.** The period beginning with confederation in 1867 to the mid-twentieth century saw little change in Crown Indian policy. The Indian Act still regulated community and band life and its various amendments provided for limited change to accommodate current concerns. The return of many Indian veterans from World War II and the implementation of the Termination Policy in the United States, however, brought about many new Indian Act amendments during the 1950s. A new consolidation of the Indian Act in 1951 repealed the ban on the potlatch and other cultural ceremonies. The ban on fundraising for legal challenges to the Crown was also repealed while a 1960 amendment to the Canada Elections Act allowed Indian people to register as electors in Canada. Yet these measures also included a 1961 amendment to the Indian Act that once again facilitated enfranchisement by allowing an individual to become enfranchised without his or her consent. Thus, even as Indian Act amendments suggested the beginning of a new era of government policy stressing formal equality, if not equality in fact, integration and assimilation were still at the heart of Crown Indian policy.

The 1966 government-sponsored Hawthorne Report made manifest, even as federal policy strived to integrate indigenous peoples, the deplorable condition of life for many Indians in Canadian society. Noting the invasiveness of the oftentimes stifling Indian Act, the

Hawthorne Report recommended an increase in control and authority for Indian bands and a decrease in government intervention, both provincial and federal. Rather than continue its policy of integration and assimilation, the report urged that the government increase the income and life expectancy of individual Indians, who were disproportionately represented in unemployment statistics and whose life expectancy was far lower than the average non-Indian Canadian. The report also advocated "citizen plus" status for Indian people indicating that "in addition to the normal rights and, duties of citizenship, Indians possess certain additional rights as charter members of the Canadian community."

After reviewing the report, the federal government released its response: the White Paper of 1969. Despite extensive consultation with Indian leaders from 1967 and 1968, the response was based on a sweeping conceptualization of equality and called for the total assimilation of Indian peoples. The White Paper's provisions included the abolishment of the Department of Indian Affairs, the end of Indian status, and the repeal of any legislation specific to Indians, including the Indian Act, and the abolishment of all reserves. Describing treaties and land claims as "insignificant," the White Paper called for Canada to relinquish all responsibility for Indian affairs and transfer that responsibility to the provinces. Indian peoples responded violently to the proposals, condemning them through protests and the 1970 Red Paper rebuttal. Indian resistance to the White Paper coupled with favorable court decisions caused the government to formally withdraw the White Paper in 1973 and to rethink its policies. The early 1970s marked the beginning of a new era in Canadian policy, one marked by the language of reconciliation and negotiation.

### Limited Aboriginal Autonomy, 1973 to the Present

**The Courts, *Calder*, and a New Federal Claims Policy.**   Just as protest from indigenous leaders and others forced the federal government to withdraw the White Paper and its proposed overhaul of the relationship between the Crown and the indigenous peoples of Canada, the Crown was also forced to adopt a new policy towards outstanding land claims after the *Calder* decision of 1973. In *Calder v. Attorney General of British Columbia* ([1973] S.C.R. 313), the Nisga'a Tribal Council argued that though the Crown claimed absolute sovereignty to all of Canada, aboriginal title had never been extinguished in the Nass Valley, the Nisga'a's traditional territory in northwestern British Columbia. The Supreme Court of Canada ruled that the concept of

aboriginal title is rooted in the "long-time occupation, possession and use" of traditional territories by indigenous peoples in Canada and that the Nisga'a had held aboriginal title before settlers arrived. The judges split evenly, however, on the question of whether the Nisga'a's title continued to exist; three justices affirmed the continuing existence of aboriginal title in British Columbia while three judges ruled that provincial and federal legislation had effectively abolished aboriginal title. The seventh and final judge dismissed the case on a technicality.

Though the question of the existence of aboriginal title in British Columbia was officially left undecided, the Court's decision in *Calder* rattled federal policymakers. The Crown released a new policy called "In All Fairness: A Native Claims Policy." With the policy, the federal government announced its intention to negotiate with Indian bands through two types of settlements: specific claims (claims dealing with a particular resource or issue) and comprehensive claims (claims encompassing all the outstanding claims of a band or nation). For the Crown, the goal of all negotiations would be to exchange undefined aboriginal rights for a clearly defined package of rights and benefits set out in a settlement agreement. Since the establishment of the land claims policy, twelve comprehensive claims have come into effect.

The *Calder* decision forced the Crown to acknowledge that it could no longer ignore aboriginal title, aboriginal rights, and outstanding aboriginal land claims, issues that indigenous peoples had been advocating in various ways and under various guises since confederation.

**The Constitution Act of 1982 and Section 35.**   The Crown further committed itself to the protection of aboriginal rights in Canada through the Constitution Act 1982, which patriated the Constitution of Canada. Section 35 of the act entrenched the recognition and affirmation of "existing aboriginal and treaty rights" and defined aboriginal peoples as "the Indian, Inuit, and Métis peoples of Canada." Section 35 does not define exactly what rights are included in "existing aboriginal and treaty rights," and in the years following the ratification of the Constitution Act, questions surrounding aboriginal self-government highlighted the section's vagueness: Was a right to self-government protected by Section 35? If such a right was protected, what sort of government it might contain? These questions would help to make aboriginal self-government a key factor in two subsequent efforts to further amend the Constitution of Canada.

The Meech Lake Accord was a set of proposed constitutional amendments agreed to by the first ministers, the premiers of all the provinces, and the prime minister. The amendments were intended to "bring about the full and active participation of Quebec in Canada's constitutional evolution... would recognize the principle of equality of all provinces... [and] would provide new arrangements to foster greater harmony and cooperation between the Government of Canada and the governments of the provinces." Notably absent from the agreement was any mention of aboriginal self-government, an issue that had become increasingly important in the years since the Constitution Act of 1982 and its recognition and affirmation of aboriginal and treaty rights. Protesting against this omission, Aboriginal MLA Elijah Harper of the Manitoba legislature blocked a vote to ratify the accord in the Manitoba legislature. Because official ratification of the Accord required the consent of all provinces before the expiration of a three-year deadline, Harper's actions helped bring about the failure of the Meech Lake Accord.

In August 1992, after negotiations that, unlike the Meech Lake Accord, included representatives from many First Nations, the first ministers reached agreement on another effort to address matters left unresolved by the 1982 Constitution Act. The Charlottetown Accord, as it was called, contained many of the provisions of the Meech Lake Accord, with the addition of a commitment to negotiate the right to self-government of First Nations. Having gained the approval of the provincial premiers, the final acceptance of the accord was put to a national referendum. Ultimately, Canadians rejected the accord by a large majority. The protection offered to self-government by the constitution remains unclear.

**The Courts and Section 35.** Section 35 and the formal recognition of aboriginal rights and title has been the catalyst for a reinvigorated discussion of aboriginal peoples in Canada in the halls of parliament as well as in the courts. Because the Constitution stops short of clearly defining just what aboriginal rights are "recognized and affirmed," and since aboriginal title is left undefined, the courts have been challenged to elaborate and explain the scope and content of the vaguely worded section. In *Guerin v. the Queen* ([1984] 2 S.C.R. 335), the Musqueam Indian Band sued the federal Crown for breach of trust concerning the leasing of reserve land to a golf club in the late 1950s. The Supreme Court of Canada ruled that the federal government had a responsibility to safeguard aboriginal interests—what the court called a "fiduciary responsibility"—which it had breached by leasing band land at lower than market value. Though claims policy is still problematic and there has been no statutory initiative to deal with those problems, the ruling was especially significant because it recognized pre-existing aboriginal rights both on reserves and off reserves.

Reaching the Supreme Court in 1990, the *Sparrow* case (*R v. Sparrow* [1990] 1 S.C.R. 1075) was the first in which the Supreme Court of Canada was called on to interpret what Section 35 actually meant. A member of the Musqueam Indian band appealed his conviction on a charge of violating the Fisheries Act. He argued that the restrictions placed on him by certain provisions of the Fisheries Act were inconsistent with the protections provided by Section 35. The Court overturned Sparrow's conviction and, in doing so, ruled that the Constitution Act provides "a strong measure of protection" for aboriginal rights. The Court also said that any proposed government legislation that infringes on the exercise of aboriginal rights must be constitutionally justified.

In its December 1997 decision in *Delgamuukw v. British Columbia* ([1997] 3 S.C.R. 1010), the Supreme Court of Canada redefined aboriginal title from "the collection of site specific Aboriginal rights dependent on practice, custom, and tradition integral to the First Nations," to a communal right to exclusive use and occupation of land including resources. The Court also expanded the rules of evidence as to the existence of title to give equal weight to oral and written testimony.

Another important Supreme Court case, this one involving the realization of treaty rights, involved Mi'kmaq fishing rights in Nova Scotia (*R. v. Marshall* [1999.] 3 S.C.R 456). On 17 September 1999 the Supreme Court concluded that Marshall, a Mi'kmaq, had treaty rights to harvest and sell or barter his harvest so that he could earn a "moderate livelihood" for himself and his family. Though the 1760 treaty signed between the Mi'kmaq and the Crown did not explicitly spell out the scope of such a right, the Court looked at all the evidence of what both parties originally intended and concluded that the 1760 treaty presumed that the right existed. Important for all treaty First Nations, *Marshall* makes it clear that treaty rights protected by Section 35 may not have been recorded by Crown negotiators in the English printed version of the treaty; the Court will consider treaty documents to be incomplete records of what was actually agreed.

Though the court cases outlined above have not always resulted in direct legislation on the federal or provincial level, they have sparked action as the Crown is forced to respond to the Court's rulings. As mentioned above, the *Calder* decision gave birth to the Crown's comprehensive claim process while the persistent litigation of Indian bands led British Columbia to establish the British Columbia Treaty Process to attempt to resolve the outstanding claims of British Columbia Indian bands.

**Reversing the Damage: Child Welfare.** The devastating effects of federal policy on many Indian communities are still evidenced by the numerous challenges that face today's indigenous communities. As they confront these challenges, some bands have been successful in regaining control over elements of their lives that were taken away through the Indian Act and other government policies. One such area is Indian child welfare.

As discussed above, from its inception in 1876, the Indian Act aimed to "civilize" the indigenous peoples of Canada. An important part of this assimilative process was educating Indian children away from the cultural and traditional influences of their parents and home communities. Supported by the Crown and subsequent amendments to the Indian Act in 1894 and 1920, religious orders operated boarding schools and day schools that forcefully removed children from their parents and their homes. At these residential schools, students were not allowed to speak their own languages or participate in cultural activities or events. Throughout the length of their operation from the end of the nineteenth century to the middle of the twentieth century, parents and band councils alike resisted residential schools and the forced removal of Indian children.

Following World War II and the subsequent reevaluation of Indian policy in Canada, the residential school system was finally ended. The aims of federal Indian child welfare policy, however, would not change, though they would take a new form. Focusing on the physical and material well-being of children without regard for culture or heritage, government agencies removed children from their communities and placed them in foster care or placed them up for adoption to non-Native families. In the early 1980s, sixty of every 1,000 Native children were under the care of the province while eighty of every 1,000 were adopted. The mass adoption of Native children, though at times necessary for the safety of the child, was also a powerful tool of assimilation as Indian children grew up separated from their cultural heritage.

The 1970s saw an increase in interest in the plight of indigenous children, especially after a 1976 Royal Commission on Family and Child Welfare Law made recommendations encouraging the government to try to keep native children in their home communities whenever possible. In 1980, the Spalumcheen Indian Band passed a by-law empowering itself to manage its own child welfare services. The minister of Indian Affairs did not invalidate the by-law, and in subsequent years, Indian bands and the Crown have negotiated over 125 child welfare agreements that have returned control of a nation's most valuable resource, its children, back to Indian communities.

**Indian Affairs at the Beginning of the Twenty-First Century.** As Indian affairs in Canada and Canadian legislation about Indian peoples enters the new century, recent events seem to demarcate policy issues that will punctuate the decades to come. In May 1999, the Supreme Court, in a unanimous decision, ruled that Section 77(1) of the Indian Act, which restricts voting in band council elections to band members living on reserve, was unconstitutional. The *Corbiere* decision (*Canada v. Corbiere* [1999] 2 S.C.R. 203) confirmed that off-reserve Indian band members have the right to vote for chief and council. The ruling came into force on 20 November 2000, eighteen months after the Court's decision, by which time all First Nations in Canada adjusted their election rules and regulations to accommodate the change. In April 1999, the new territory of Nunavut was created. The result of years of negotiations with the Inuit of Northern Canada, Nunavut has a majority Inuit population and possesses self-governing powers and control over resources similar to those of the other territories. Meanwhile, the federal government continues to negotiate land claims and self-governance agreements with the indigenous nations within its borders as those peoples strive to preserve, secure, and restore their communities and cultures.

*Audrey Jane Roy with Taiaiake Alfred*
*University of Victoria*

# ◆ LIST OF CANADIAN LEGISLATION AFFECTING NATIVE PEOPLE

## Legislative Timeline

*The following legislation concerning the indigenous peoples of Canada includes both significant pre-Confederation (pre–1867) colonial acts and post-Confederation acts. Generally, the chronology includes major laws regarding policy and programmatic changes in tribal life and excludes resolutions, very specific laws for tribes, and private laws affecting individuals.*

**1763 The Royal Proclamation of 1763.**  A proclamation by King George III that recognizes aboriginal people as "nations or tribes" and acknowledges that they continue to possess traditional territories until they are "ceded to or purchased by" the Crown (R.S.C. 1985, App. I, No. 1).

**1850 An Act for the Better Protection of the Lands and Property of the Indians of Lower Canada and An Act for the Better Protection of Indians in Upper Canada.**  Acts passed to better protect First Nations in both Lower Canada (now Quebec) and Upper Canada (now Ontario) from settler encroachment. In Lower Canada, all First Nations lands and property were vested in a commissioner of Crown lands. The 93,000 hectares set aside for Indians eventually permitted the creation of nine new reserves. One of the acts passed in Upper Canada made it an offence for anyone to deal with First Nations concerning their lands, or "to enter on, take possession of, or settle on any such lands, by pretext of any right or interest in the same" (S.C. 1850, c. 42/43).

**1857 Act to Encourage the Gradual Civilization of the Indian Tribes in the Province, and to Amend the Laws Respecting Indians.** An Act passed by the colonial government providing for property and monetary inducements to encourage Indians to leave tribal societies and seek enfranchisement, or to give up their status as Indians and become citizens of the colonies. Definitions in the act created a legal distinction between "Indians" and "Canadian Citizens," and articulated the steps an Indian had to take before becoming a "civilized citizen" (S. Prov. C. 1857, 20 Vict., c. 26).

**29 March 1867 The Constitution Act, 1867 (formerly the British North American Act, 1867).** The base document of the Canadian Constitution, this act established the modern nation of Canada by articulating the terms of unification of the original provinces of Upper Canada (Ontario), Lower Canada (Quebec), New Brunswick, and Nova Scotia. Section 91 provided for federal powers while Section 92 laid out the provincial powers. Under Section 91(24), the federal government is given authority "to make laws for the Peace, Order, and good Government of Canada" including laws about "Indians and lands reserved for Indians" (R.S.C. 1985, App. II, No. 5).

**22 May 1868 An Act Providing for the Organization of the Department of the Secretary of State of Canada, and for the Management of Indian and Ordinance Lands.** First federal legislation about Indians after Confederation. Appoints the Secretary of State as the Superintendent General of Indian affairs charged with "the control and management of the lands and property of the Indians in Canada." S.C. 1868, c. 42 (31 Vic).

**31 July 1868 Rupert's Land Act.** An Act accepting surrender of the Hudson's Bay Company lands in the West. Relieved the HBC of any unsettled Indian claims, effectively making claims the responsibility of the Canadian Government. R.S.C. 1985, Appendix ii, No. 9.

**22 June 1869 An Act for the Gradual Enfranchisement of Indians, the Better Management of Indian Affairs, and to Extend the Provisions of the Act 31st Victoria, Chapter 42.** An Act legislating on certain aspects of Indian community life including defining lawful possession of Indians lands, regulating the sale of alcohol to Indians, ruling that women marrying non-Indian men are no longer considered Indians,

allowing for band elections, and encouraging enfranchisement. S.C. 1869, c. 6 (32–33 Vic).

**12 May 1870 Manitoba Act.** Created the Province of Manitoba and established its government. Attempted to extinguish the rights of the Métis people by providing them with land and money. R.S.C. 1985, App.II, No.8.

**3 May 1873 An Act to Provide for the Establishment of "The Department of the Interior".** An Act establishing the Department of the Interior whose minister is responsible for the "control and management of the affairs of the North West Territories" and who shall serve as the Superintendent General of Indian affairs with "control and management of the lands and property of the Indians in Canada." S.C. 1873, c. 4.

**26 May 1874 An Act to Amend Certain Laws Respecting Indians, and to Extend Certain Laws Relating to Matters Connected with Indians to the Province of Manitoba and British Columbia.** An Act amending the 1868 Secretary of State Act and the 1869 Enfranchisement Act and extending the provisions dealing with Indians into British Columbia and the Northwest Territory. S.C. 1874, c. 21.

**12 April 1876 Indian Act, 1876.** An Act to consolidate all previous Indian legislation. The most significant aspects of the Act are that (1) it defined who would be considered 'native' under Canadian law; (2) it gave control of reserve land to an Indian Agent in order to 'protect' it; (3) it gave the federal government unprecedented invasive power into the day-to-day governance of band life and imposed band council governance; and (4) its provisions, most of which still govern the lives of Indians in Canada, attempted to advance Canada's assimilationist policy. R.S.C. 1985, c.I–5.

**15 May 1879 An Act to Amend the "Indian Act, 1876".** An Act to amend certain provisions of the Indian Act including the payment of annuities and the punishment of trespassers onto Indian lands. S.C. 1879, c. 34.

**17 May 1880 Indian Act, 1880.** An Act replacing the Indian Act, 1876, and reconsolidating all amendments. The Act also creates the Department of Indian Affairs headed by the Superintendent-General of the Indian Affairs, a position to be held by the Minister of the Interior, and introduced a new provision denying band governments the power to decide how moneys from the surrender and sale of their lands or other resources would be spent. S.C. 1884, c.27.

**31 July 1880 Adjacent Territories Order (Order of Her Majesty in Council Admitting All British Territories and Possessions in North America and Islands Adjacent Thereto into the Union).** Declared that "all British Territories and Possessions in

North America, not already included within the Dominion of Canada" (except Newfoundland) should be incorporated into the Dominion of Canada. Through this order, "possession" of all lands claimed by Britain but not yet legally obtained through treaty was transferred to Canada. Schedule to the Constitution Act, 1982 (R.S.C. 1985, App. II, No. 44).

**21 March 1881 An Act to Amend "The Indian Act, 1880".** An Act amending the Indian Act and empowering the governor in council to make provisions to regulate or prohibit the sale of produce by Indians and to prohibit the cutting of trees on reserves (S.C. 1881, c. 17).

**17 May 1882 An Act Further to Amend "The Indian Act, 1880".** An Act to amend Indian Act provisions concerning penalties for infractions of the Act and suits between Indians (S.C. 1882, c. 30).

**19 May 1884 An Act Further to Amend "The Indian Act, 1880".** An Act amending the Indian Act, 1880, to outlaw cultural and religious ceremonies such as the potlatch, a practice which is the major social, economic, and political institution of Pacific Northwest coastal peoples (S.C. 1884, c. 27).

**1884 The Indian Advancement Act.** The only major legislative addition was the passage of the Indian Advancement Act in 1884, which was designed for the more "advanced" Indians in Eastern Canada and modeled on town councils (S.C. 1884, c. 28).

**1886 An Act Respecting Indians.** An act replacing the Indian Act, 1880, and reconsolidating all amendments. Enacted simultaneously with the Indian Act amendments is Chapter 44, an amended version of the Indian Advancement Act (S.C. 1886, c. 43).

**23 June 1887 An Act to Amend "The Indian Act, 1886".** An act to amend certain provisions of the Indian Act dealing with prostitution, possession of lumber or tree resources, definition of Indian status, and alcohol (S.C. 1887, c. 33).

**22 May 1888 An Act Further to Amend "The Indian Act".** An act making it illegal, except under "very special circumstances" for a Manitoba Métis to be counted as an Indian under the terms of the Indian Act or to be considered a treaty Indian (S.C. 1888, c. 22 [51 Vic]).

**16 May 1890 An Act to Amend "The Indian Advancement Act".** An act amending the Indian Advancement Act including provisions on band elections (S.C. 1890, c. 30).

**23 April 1894 An Act Further to Amend "The Indian Act".** An act amending the Indian Act including the addition of a provision granting the superintendent general the power to lease reserve land held by physically disabled Indians, widows, or others who could not cultivate their lands. The superintendent general also assumed the power to decide whether non-Indians could reside on or use reserve from band councils. The amendment also allowed the governor general to issue regulations forcing Indian children to attend school (S.C. 1894, c. 32 [5758 Vic]).

**22 July 1895 An Act Further to Amend "The Indian Act".** An act amending the Indian Act in several areas including sale of land and band council governance. The act also extends the powers of Indian agents to include most of the powers of justices of the peace (S.C. 1895, c. 35 [5859 Vic]).

**13 April 1898 An Act Further to Amend "The Indian Act".** An act amending the Indian Act in several areas including sale of land, use of Indian land for logging, and band council governance (S.C. 1898, c. 34 [61 Vic]).

**13 June 1906 The Indian Act.** An act, replacing the Indian Act, 1906, that re-consolidates all previous amendments. The act includes amendments adding responsibility for Inuit affairs to the position of superintendent General of Indian Affairs and empowering the governor in council to make regulations "to secure the compulsory attendance of [Indian] children at school." The act allows that such legislation "may provide for the arrest and conveyance to school, and detention there, of truant children and of children who are prevented by their parents or guardians from attending" (R.S.C. 1906, c. 81).

**4 May 1910 An Act to Amend "The Indian Act".** An Act to amend certain provisions of the Indian Act including requiring the superintendent-general's approval for any agreements dealing with parliamentary gifts or funds to Indians and making it illegal to seize annuity funds or gifts for the repayment of Indian debts (S.C. 1910, c. 28).

**19 May 1911 An Act to Amend "The Indian Act".** An act amending the Indian Act including providing for the removal, with compensation, of Indians from a reserve that "adjoins or is situated wholly or partly with an incorporated town or city having a population of not less than eight thousand" and redefining trespass laws and remedies (S.C. 1911, c. 14).

**12 June 1914 An Act to Amend "The Indian Act".** An act amending Indian Act provisions dealing with schooling and the prohibition against participating in cultural activities (S.C. 1914, c. 35 [4–5 George V]).

**24 May 1918 An Act to Amend "The Indian Act".** An act amending provisions of the Indian Act including the regulations concerning bequest or inheritance of reserve land and empowering the superintendent-general to use band capitol land and assets contrary to the wishes of the band if "such refusal is detrimental to the progress or welfare of the band" (S.C. 1918, c. 26).

**7 July 1919 An Act to Amend "The Indian Act".** An act amending the Indian Act including provisions allowing the federal government to grant mineral leases on un-surrendered reserve land and to acquire reserve land for Indian soldier settlers without the permission of the band council, as consistent with the Soldier Settlement Act, 1919 (S.C. 1919, c. 56).

**1 July 1920 An Act to Amend "The Indian Act".** An act amending the Indian Act including provisions labeling Indian children who did not attend school as delinquents and making their parents subject to penalties, and provisions addressing the status of females marrying non-Indians (S.C. 1920, c. 50).

**1920 Indian Lands, Settlement of Differences.** Passed for British Columbia and Ontario, an act implementing the recommendations of the McKenna-McBride Commission to change and redistribute reserve lands as a "final adjustment of all matters related to Indian Affairs in the province." Allows reductions or "cut-offs" of reserves without consent of aboriginal people, contrary to provisions of the Indian Act (S.C. 1920, c. 51 [B.C.] and S.C. 1924, c. 48 [Ontario]).

**28 June 1922 An Act to Amend "The Indian Act".** An act amending Indian Act provisions including the application of the Soldier Settlement Act (S.C. 1922, c. 26 [12–13 George V]).

**19 July 1924 An Act to Amend "The Indian Act".** An act amending Indian Act provisions concerning inheritance, reserve land leases, and the ability of the governor in counsel to dispense band capitol (S.C. 1924, c. 47 [14–15 George V]).

**1927 The Indian Act, 1927.** An act, replacing the Indian Act, 1906, which re-consolidates and amends all legislation surrounding Indians. The act is amended to make it illegal to "receive, obtain, solicit or request from any Indian any payment or contribution for the purpose of raising a fund or providing money for the prosecution of any claim" without the consent of the superintendent-general of Indian Affairs (s.141) (R.S.C. 1927, c. 98).

**31 March 1927 An Act to Amend "The Indian Act".** An act amending sections of the Indian Act including raising funds for the prosecution of claims and the desecration of Indian graves and art (S.C. 1927, c. 32 [17 George V]).

**10 April 1930 An Act to Amend "The Indian Act".** An act amending Indian Act provisions concerning the mandatory schooling of Indian children. The act also made it illegal for on-reserve Indians to sell cattle, grain, or root crops without the approval of the Indian agent (S.C. 1930, c. 25 [20–21 George V]).

**10 July 1930 Constitution Act, 1930.** An act to amend the constitution containing the Natural Resources Transfer Agreements. These agreements between the federal Crown and the provinces of Alberta, Manitoba, and Saskatchewan transfer rights and interests of certain natural resources and certain legislative authority over to the provinces. The act purports to define or authorize the provinces to define the rights of Indians to hunt, fish, and trap on these lands. The act also obliges these provinces to transfer to the federal government such unoccupied Crown lands as are required to enable the federal government to fulfill its responsibility to set aside reserves under the various treaties (R.S.C. 1985, App. II, No. 26).

**23 May 1933 An Act to Amend "The Indian Act".** An act to amend the Indian Act that empowered the government to order the enfranchisement of qualified First Nations members, even when they had not requested enfranchisement (S.C. 1933, c. 42 [23–24 George V]).

**24 June 1938 An Act to Amend "The Indian Act".** An act amending Indian Act provisions dealing with federally granted leases of reserve lands and loans to Indian bands or individuals (S.C. 1938, c. 31. [2 Geo. VI]).

**14 June 1941 An Act to Amend "The Indian Act".** An act amending Indian Act regulations concerning selling or bartering with or to Indians (S.C. 1940–41, c. 19. [4–5 Geo. VI]).

**20 May 1951 The Indian Act.** An act reconsolidating amendments to the previous Indian Act, 1927. Passed in response to a 1947–1948 Joint Committee of the Senate House of Commons report, the new act of 1951 increased the application of provincial laws to Indians through the introduction of Section 87 (now 88); repealed the provisions of the Indian Act that outlawed the potlatch and prohibited "land claims" fundraising activity; and created the Indian Register, a list of all status Indians maintained by the federal government. The act also names the minister of Citizenship and Immigration as the superintendent-general of Indian Affairs (R.S.C. 1951, c. 29).

**14 May 1953 An Act to Amend "The Indian Act".** An act amending Indian Act provisions including regulations on loans to Indians (S.C. 1953, c. 41).

**14 August 1956 An Act to Amend "The Indian Act".** An act amending Indian Act provisions including the definition of Indian status, the criteria for valid reserve land grants, and the regulations for the removal of materials from reserves (S.C. 1956, c. 40).

**13 August 1958 An Act to Amend "The Indian Act".** An act amending Indian Act provisions defining Indian status (S.C. 1958, c. 19).

**31 March 1960 An Act to Amend "The Indian Act".** An act to amend Indian Act provisions concerning taxation and elections (S.C. 1960, c. 8).

**1960 Canadian Bill of Rights.** Forerunner of the Canadian Charter of Rights and Freedoms that proved unable to protect aboriginal rights (R.S.C. 1985, App. III).

**1960 An Act to Amend the Canada Elections Act.** Allowed Indians registered under the Indian Act to register as electors under the Canadian Elections Act (S.C. 1960, c. 7).

**9 March 1961 An Act to Amend "The Indian Act".** An act to repeal a provision of the Indian Act that allowed for enfranchisement without the agreement of the individual or band (S.C. 1961, c. 9).

**16 June 1966 Government Organization Act.** The federal Department of Indian Affairs and Northern Development (DIAND) is created and given responsibility for Indian affairs in Canada (S.C. 1966, c. 25 [14–15 Elizabeth II]).

**1970 The Indian Act.** An act to reconsolidate legislation surrounding Indian peoples in Canada (R.S.C. 1970, c. 1–6).

**1970 The Indian Economic Development Direct Loan Order.** An order outlining procedures and regulations for loans for Indian Bands (SOR/78–22). Appropriation Act No. 1, 1970.

**8 August 1973 In All Fairness: A Native Claims Policy.** A federal government policy for the settlement of aboriginal claims, "In All Fairness" divides claims into two broad categories: specific claims and comprehensive claims. The government's objective in establishing the policy was to exchange undefined aboriginal rights for a clearly defined package of rights and benefits set out in a settlement agreement. Since the establishment of a federal policy for the settlement of aboriginal land claims in 1973, twelve comprehensive claims agreements have come into effect (Ottawa: Department of Indian Affairs and Northern Development, 1981).

**20 December 1974 Indian Oil and Gas Act.** An act granting federal control over the exploitation of oil and gas in Indian lands including the granting of leases, permits, and licenses and control of any royalties in trust for the Indians (R.S.C., 1985, c. I–7.

**11 November 1975 The James Bay and Northern Quebec Native Claims Settlement Act.** Along with the Northeastern Quebec Agreement signed in 1978 with the Naskapi Indian Band, one of Canada's first modern land claim settlements, the agreement grants the Cree and Inuit of northern Quebec compensation, territory, and hunting and trapping rights (S.C. 1976–1977, c. 32).

**1982 The Indian Act.** New consolidation of the Indian Act (R.S.C. 1982, c. I–6).

**1982 Canada Act.** Last Act of the United Kingdom Parliament containing the English and French versions of the Constitution Act, 1982. From that time on, the United Kingdom Parliament relinquished the power to affect any Canadian laws, including the Constitution (R.S.C. 1985, App. II, No. 44).

**1982 The Constitution Act.** Important modern constitutional document that (1) defines Canada's aboriginal peoples as Indian, Métis, and Inuit; (2) recognizes the aboriginal rights of those peoples; and (3) contains the Canadian Charter of Rights and Freedoms. The specific rights and privileges included in this recognition, however, have yet to be defined (R.S.C. 1985, App. II, No. 44).

**1983 Constitution Amendment Proclamation.** Entrenched the recognition of rights obtained under aboriginal land claims agreements by amending Section 35 of the Constitution Act, 1982. Committed all governments to invite aboriginal and territorial government representatives to conferences on issues related to them (SI/84–102).

**5 June 1984 Western Arctic (Inuvialuit) Claims Settlement Act.** The Inuvialuit become the first aboriginal group from the Northwest Territories to negotiate a comprehensive land claim settlement with the government of Canada (S.C. 1984, c. 24).

**14 June 1984 Cree-Naskapi (of Quebec) Act.** An act fulfilling the Government of Canada's obligations under the James Bay and Northern Quebec Agreement and the Northeastern Quebec Agreement to provide legislation enabling Cree and Naskapi local government control and management of land acquired by the bands, and providing for the protection of certain individual and collective rights (S.C. 1984, c. 18).

**1985 Northwest Territories Act.** An act outlining the powers of the territorial government of the Northwest Territories and describing their powers over the Indians and Inuit therein (R.S.C., 1985, c. N-27).

**28 June 1985 Act to Amend "The Indian Act".** An act, commonly known as Bill C-31, that brought the Indian Act into line with the provisions of the Canadian Charter of Rights and Freedoms by removing discrimination between men and women; restoring status and membership rights; and increasing control of Indian bands over their own affairs. Bill C-31 gave "status" to Indian women (and their minor children) who had married non-Indians (R.S.C. 1985, c. 32 [1ˢᵗ Supp]).

**1985 Department of Indian Affairs and Northern Development Act.** An act establishing the Department of Indian Affairs and Northern Development to be presided over by the minister of Indian Affairs and Northern Development and to be responsible for Indian affairs, Inuit affairs, and the Yukon Territory, the Northwest Territories, and Nunavut and their resources and affairs (R.S.C., 1985 c. I-6).

**17 June 1986 Sechelt Indian Band Self-Government Act.**   An act granting the Sechelt Indian band title to lands in traditional Sechelt territory and providing for limited self-government (S.C. 1986, c. 27).

**28 July 1986 Indian Lands Agreement Act.**   An act allowing the federal government, the province of Ontario and Indian bands to enter into agreements concerning land and natural resources (S.C. 1988, c. 39).

**1 November 1990 Métis Settlements Act.**   An act establishing the only Métis land base (through eight Métis settlements) and the only form of legislated Métis government in Canada (Statutes of Alberta 1990, c.M-14.3, ss.1, 111–129, Sched. 3).

**17 December 1992 Gwich'in Land Claim Settlement Act.**   An act bringing the Gwich'in comprehensive claim, the first negotiated with a Dene/Métis group, into law (S.C. 1992, c. 53).

Canvas tipi at Fort William in Thunder Bay, Ontario. (Courtesy of the UCLA American Indian Studies Center)

**25 May 1993 The Nunavut Land Claims Agreement.**   Enacted through two acts, the Nunavut Land Claims Act (Bill C-133) and the act to create the territory of Nunavut (Bill C-132), this agreement created a new territory with a majority Inuit population from the Northwest Territory. The territory has self-governing powers and control over resources similar to those of the other territories (S.C. 1993, c. 27).

**25 May 1993 Nunavut Land Claims Agreement Act.**   An act enabling the Nunavut Land Claims Agreement including providing for the monetary settlement and establishing the Nunavut Wildlife Management Board (S.C., 1993, c. 28).

**29 May 1993 The Sahtu Dene and Métis Agreement.**   The Sahtu were originally part of a joint Dene/Métis claim but withdrew from joint negotiations in 1990 to negotiate their own agreement (S.C. 1994, c. 27).

**23 June 1994 Sahtu Dene and Métis Land Claim Settlement Act.**   An act affirming a comprehensive claims agreement between Canada and the Dene of Colville Lake, Déline, Fort Good Hope and Fort Norman, and the Métis of Fort Good Hope, Fort Norman, and Norman Wells, as represented by the Sahtu Tribal Council, that "in exchange for the release of certain rights and claims as set out in the agreement, defines the rights that the Sahtu Dene and Métis shall have, and confirms the treaty rights that are unaffected by that release" (C.S.C.1994, c. 27).

**7 July 1994 Yukon First Nations Land Claims Settlement Act and Yukon First Nations Self-Government Act.**   Acts to give effect land claims agreements and self-government agreements, respectively, between Canada, the Yukon Territory, and First Nations in the Yukon Territory entered into after this act comes into force in accordance with the Umbrella Final Agreement agreed to on 29 May 1993. The act also affirmed the separate agreements negotiated by the Champagne and Aishihik First Nations, the First Nation of Nacho Nyak Dun, the Teslin Tlingit Council, and the Vuntut Gwitchin First Nation as part of the umbrella agreement. Importantly, title to land possessed by the First Nations under this agreement is limited to those "rights, titles, obligations, and liabilities" outlined therein (S.C. 1994, c. 34 and c.35).

**15 December 1995 British Columbia Treaty Commission Act.**   An act to establish the British Columbia Treaty Commission, a neutral commission designed to facilitate the negotiation of treaties between the provincial and federal Crowns and the First Nations of that province (S.C. 1995, c. 45).

**1 April 1999 Nunavut Act.**   Enacted in 1993, this act came into force in 1999 and created the territory of

The capital city of Nunavut at night. (Public Domain)

Nunavut. The act defines the powers of the new territory (S.C., 1993, c. 28).

**17 June 1999 First Nations Land Management Act.** An act that allows First Nations to enter into negotiations with the minister to establish a land management regime consistent with the provisions of the act including general rules and procedures pertaining to use and occupancy and revenues from natural resources. Certain lands can be excluded due to environmental conditions or the existence of a conflicting land management regime (C.S.C., 1999, c.24).

**13 April 2000 The Nisga'a Final Agreement Act.** The long-awaited Nisga'a Final Agreement grants the Nisga'a portions of their traditional lands in the Nass Valley, specified hunting and fishing rights and monetary compensation in return for giving up claims to aboriginal title (S.C. 2000).

## Treaties

**1725 to 1779 Maritime Peace and Friendship Treaties.** Treaties between the Mi'kmaq and Maliseet peoples and the British in what was to become Nova Scotia and New Brunswick. The main concerns of the British colonial administration in the period were to establish ongoing peaceful relations, and, in exchange for agreeing to keep the peace and to respect British civil and criminal law, the various nations of Mi'kmaq and Maliseet Indians were promised by the Crown that they could continue to hunt and fish, trade with the British, and continue their customary and religious practices. These treaties did not involve the cession of any land.

**1760 Murray Treaty.** Treaty guaranteeing the Hurons safe passage to their village at Lorette, recognizing their customary and religious practices and protecting trading rights.

**1794 Treaty of Amity, Commerce and Navigation (Jay Treaty) Between His Britannic Majesty and the United States of America.**

**18 July 1817 The Selkirk Treaty.** A treaty between the Crown and the Chippewa or Saulteaux Nation, and the Killistine or Cree Nation, along the Red River and the Assiniboine River in which the Indians convey the shore lands of these rivers to the Crown in return for the unmolested occupation of their other lands "till His Majesty's pleasure shall be known."

**1850 to 1854 Vancouver Island Treaties.** Fourteen land surrender treaties were made between 1850 and 1854 by Governor James Douglas and First Nations living on Vancouver Island in the areas of present-day Victoria, Nanaimo, and Fort Rupert. The total area ceded constituted one-fortieth of the area of Vancouver Island. In return for ceding these lands, the First Nations received lump-sum payments. They retained certain lands for reserves as well as their hunting and fishing rights.

**7 September 1850 Robinson-Superior Treaty.** A treaty between the Crown and the First Nations located around Lake Superior conveying lands to the Crown in exchange for a lump-sum payment and a yearly annuity, protection of hunting and fishing rights in unsold or unleased territory, and particular reserve lands.

**9 September 1850 Robinson-Huron Treaty.** A treaty between the Crown and the Hurons of Upper Canada conveying lands to the Crown in exchange for a lump-sum payment and a yearly annuity, protection of hunting and fishing rights in unsold or unleased territory, and particular reserve lands (Queen's Printer and Controller of Stationary, Ottawa, 1964; Cat. No. Ci 72–1264).

**6 October 1862 Manitoulin Island Treaty of 1862.** A treaty between the Crown and the Indians of the Manitoulin Islands conveying lands to the Crown in exchange for a lump-sum payment and a per-person parcel of land on the island.

**3 August 1871 Treaty Number 1 and Treaty Number 2 between Her Majesty the Queen and the Chippewa and Cree Indians of Manitoba and Country Adjacent (Edmond Cloutier, C.M.G., O.A., D.S.P. Queen's Printer and Controller of Stationery Ottawa, 1957; 92099–1).**

3 October 1873 Treaty Number 3 between Her Majesty the Queen and the Saulteaux Tribe of the Ojibbeway Indians at the Northwest Angle on the Lake of the Woods (Queen's Printer and Controller of Stationery Ottawa, 1966; Cat. No. Ci 72–0366).

20 July 1874 Treaty Number 4 between Her Majesty The Queen and the Cree and Saulteaux Tribes of Indians at the Qu'appelle and Fort Ellice (Queen's Printer and Controller of Stationery, Ottawa, 1966; Cat. No. Ci 72–0466).

20 and 24 September 1875 Treaty Number 5 between Her Majesty The Queen and the Saulteaux and Swampy Cree Tribes of Indians at Beren's River and Norway House (Queen's Printer, Ottawa. 1969; Cat. No.: R33–0557).

23 and 28 August and 9 September 1876 Treaty Number 6 between Her Majesty the Queen and the Plain and Wood Cree Indians and Other Tribes of Indians at Fort Carlton, Fort Pitt And Battle River.   Covers central Alberta.

22 September and 4 December 1877 Treaty and Supplementary Treaty Number 7 between Her Majesty the Queen and the Blackfeet and Other Indian Tribes, at the Blackfoot Crossing of Bow River and Fort Macleod.   Covers Southern Alberta (Queen's Printer and Controller of Stationery, Ottawa, 1966; Cat. No.: Ci 72–0766)

1899 Treaty Number 8.   Treaty between the Queen and "the Cree, Beaver, Chipewyan and other Indians, inhabitants of the territory within." Covers northern Alberta and the MacKenzie Valley.

1905 The James Bay Treaty Number 9.   Made in 1905 and 1906. Adhesions made in 1929.

1906 Treaty Number 10 between the King and "the Chipewyan (sic), Cree and Other Indian Inhabitants of the Territory within the Limits Hereinafter Defined."   Covers northern Saskatchewan (Queen's Printer and Controller of Stationery, Ottawa, 1966; Cat. No.: Ci 72–1066).

27 June 1921 Treaty Number 11 between the King and "the Slave, Dogrib, Loucheux, Hare and other Indians, Inhabitants of the Territory within the Limits Hereinafter Defined."   Covers the MacKenzie Valley (Queen's Printer and Controller of Stationery, Ottawa, 1957).

31 October 1923 Treaty Between His Majesty The King and the Chippewa Indians of Christian Island, Georgina Island and Rama.   One of the Williams Treaties. In exchange for the surrender of their interests in the lands of central southeastern Ontario and their hunting and fishing rights, the aboriginal signatories to the Williams Treaties received a lump-sum cash payment (Queen's Printer and Controller of Stationery, Ottawa, 1967; Cat. No. R33–1467).

15 November 1923 Treaty between His Majesty the King and the Mississauga Indians of Rice Lake, Mud Lake, Scugog Lake, and Alderville.   One of the Williams Treaties: In exchange for the surrender of their interests in the lands of central southeastern Ontario and their hunting and fishing rights, the aboriginal signatories to the Williams Treaties received a lump-sum cash payment (Queen's Printer and Controller of Stationery, Ottawa, 1957; 90200–1).

*Audrey Jane Roy with Taiaiake Alfred*
*University of Victoria*

# U.S. Law and Legal Organizations

## ◆ ALASKA

**ALASKA FEDERATION OF NATIVES**
1577 C Street, Suite 201
Anchorage, AK 99501
(907) 274–3611

**ALASKA INTER-TRIBAL COUNCIL**
431 W. 7th Ave., Suite 201
Anchorage, AK 99501
(907) 563–9334
www.aitc.org

**ALASKA LEGAL SERVICES CORP.**
1016 West Sixth Ave., Suite 200
Anchorage, AK 99501
(907) 276–9431

**NATIVE AMERICAN RIGHTS FUND**
420 L Street, Suite 505
Anchorage, AK 99501
(907) 276–0680
www.narf.org

**SOVEREIGNTY NETWORK**
HC04 Box 9880
Palmer, AK 99645
(907) 745–0505

## ◆ ARIZONA

**BROWN & BAIN**
2901 North Central Ave.
P.O. Box 400
Phoenix, AZ 85012
(602) 351–8000
www.brownbain.com

**DNA-PEOPLE'S LEGAL SERVICES**
P.O. Box 306
Window Rock, AZ 86515
(520) 871–4151

**HOPI LEGAL SERVICES**
P.O. Box 558
Keams Canyon, AZ 86034
(520) 738–2251

## ◆ CALIFORNIA

**AMERICAN INDIAN RESOURCES INSTITUTE**
319 MacArthur Blvd.
Oakland, CA 94610
(510) 834–9333

**CALIFORNIA INDIAN LEGAL SERVICES**
510 16th St., 4th floor
Oakland, CA 94612
(510) 835–0284
www.calindian.org

**CENTER FOR RACE, POVERTY AND THE ENVIRONMENT**
CALIFORNIA RURAL LEGAL ASSISTANCE FOUNDATION
631 Howard Street, Suite 330
San Francisco, CA 94110
(415) 495–8990

**INTERNATIONAL INDIAN TREATY COUNCIL**
710 Clayton St., No. 1
San Francisco, CA 94117
(415) 512–1501

**NATIONAL INDIAN JUSTICE CENTER**
7 Fourth St., Suite 46
Petaluma, CA 94952
(707) 762–8113
www.nijc.indian.com

**TRIBAL LAW AND POLICY INSTITUTE**
8235 Santa Monica Blvd.
West Hollywood, CA 90046
(323) 650–5467
tribal-institute.org/codes/overview.htm

## ◆ COLORADO

**NATIONAL INDIAN LAW LIBRARY**
1522 Broadway
Boulder, CO 80302
(303) 447–8760
www.narf.org

**NATIVE AMERICAN RIGHTS FUND**
1506 Broadway
Boulder, CO 80302
(303) 447–8760
www.narf.org

## ◆ DISTRICT OF COLUMBIA

**GOVERNMENT ACCOUNTABILITY PROJECT**
Mick Harrison
EPA WATCH
810 First St. N.E., Suite 630
Washington, DC 20034
(202) 408–0034

**HOBBS, STRAUS, DEAN & WILDER**
1819 H St. N.W., Suite 800
Washington, DC 20006
(202) 783–5100

**INDIAN LAW RESOURCE CENTER**
601 E. St., S.E.
Washington, DC 20003
(202) 547–2800
www.indian.org

**NATIONAL AMERICAN INDIAN COURT
  CLERKS ASSOCIATION**
1000 Connecticut Ave. N.W., Suite 1206
Washington, DC 20036
(202) 920–8197
tribal-institute.org

**NATIONAL AMERICAN INDIAN COURT
  JUDGES ASSOCIATION**
1000 Connecticut Ave. N.W., Suite 1206
Washington, DC 20036
(415) 647–1755
www.naicja.org

**NATIVE AMERICAN RIGHTS FUND**
1712 N St., N.W.
Washington, DC 20036
(202) 785–4166
www.narf.org

**SONOSKY, CHAMBERS, SACHSE &
  ANDERSON**
1250 I St. N.W., Suite 1000
Washington, DC 20005
(202) 682–0240

## ◆ MINNESOTA

**INDIAN LEGAL ASSISTANCE PROGRAM**
215 North Fourth Ave. W.
Duluth, MN 55806
(218) 727–2881

## ◆ MONTANA

**INDIAN LAW RESOURCE CENTER**
602 North Ewing Street
Helena, MT 59601
(406) 449–2006
www.indian law.org

**UNIVERSITY OF MONTANA SCHOOL OF LAW**
Indian Law Clinic
32 Campus Dr.
Missoula, MT 59812
(406) 243–4311

## ◆ NEW MEXICO

**AMERICAN INDIAN LAW CENTER INC.**
University of New Mexico School of Law
P.O. Box 4456, Station A
1117 Stanford Dr., N.E.
Albuquerque, NM 87131
(505) 277–5462

**AMERICAN INDIAN LAW STUDENTS
  ASSOCIATION**
American Indian Law Center
1117 Stanford Dr., N.E.
Albuquerque, NM 87196
(505) 277–5462

**GOVER, STETSON & WILLIAMS**
2501 Rio Grande Blvd., N.W.
Albuquerque, NM 87104
(505) 842–6961

**COMMUNITY & INDIAN LEGAL SERVICES**
INDIAN PUEBLO LEGAL SERVICES
P.O. Box 817
Bernalillo, NM 87004
(505) 867–3391

NORDHAUS, HALTOM, TAYLOR,
　　TARADASH & FRYE
500 Marquette Ave. N.W., Suite 1050
Albuquerque, NM 87102
(505) 243–4275

#### ◆ NEW YORK

ASSOCIATION ON AMERICAN INDIAN
　　AFFAIRS, INC.
245 Fifth Ave., Suite 1801
New York, NY 10016
(212) 689–8720

NATIONAL LAWYERS GUILD
COMMITTEE ON NATIVE AMERICAN STRUGGLES
55 Avenue of the Americas, Third Floor
New York, NY 10013–1601
(303) 458–5602

#### ◆ OKLAHOMA

AMERICAN INDIAN LAW POLICY CENTER
University of Oklahoma Law Center
300 Timberdell Rd.
Norman, OK 73019–5081
(405) 325–4699
www.law.ou.edu

NATIVE AMERICAN LEGAL RESOURCE
　　CENTER
Oklahoma City University School of Law
2501 North Blackwelder
Oklahoma City, OK 73106
(405) 521–5337

OKLAHOMA INDIAN LEGAL SERVICES
Founders Tower
4200 Permeter Center, Suite 222
Oklahoma City, OK 73112
(405) 943–6457

#### ◆ SOUTH DAKOTA

DAKOTA PLAINS LEGAL SERVICES
106 Second St.
P.O. Box 727
Mission, SD 57555
(605) 856–4444

#### ◆ VIRGINIA

DEPARTMENT OF INTERIOR
BOARD OF INDIAN APPEALS
4015 Wilson Blvd.
Arlington, VA 22203
(703) 235–3816

#### ◆ WASHINGTON

CHESTNUT, VARNELL, BERLEY &
　　SLONIM ARUM
2101 Fourth Ave., Suite 1230
Seattle, WA 98121–2331
(206) 448–1230

COLUMBIA LEGAL SERVICES
Native American Project
101 Yesler Way, Suite 301
Seattle, WA 98104
(206) 464–0838

NORTHWEST INTERTRIBAL COURT SYSTEM
144 Railroad Avenue, #302
Edmonds, WA 98020
(425) 774–5808
firms.findlaw.com/nics/index.htm

PIRTLE, MORISSET, SCHLOSSER & AYER
1115 Norton Bldg.
801 Second Ave.
Seattle, WA 98104
(206) 386–5200

## CANADIAN LEGAL SERVICES

#### ◆ BRITISH COLUMBIA

ASSEMBLY OF FIRST NATIONS
Head Office
Territory of Akwesasne
R.R. #3
Cornwall, ON K6H 5R7
(613) 932–0410
www.afn.ca

UNION OF BRITISH COLUMBIA INDIAN
　　CHIEFS
5th Floor, 342 Water Street
Vancouver, BC V6B 1B6
(604) 684–0231
www.ubcic.bc.ca

## ◆ LABRADOR

**INNU NATION**
P.O. Box 119
Sheshatshiu, Labrador A0P 1M0
(709) 497–8398

**LABRADOR MÉTIS NATION**
P.O. Box 2164 Stn B
Happy Valley-Goose Bay
Labrador, Canada, A0P 1E0
(877) 896–0592
(709) 896–0592

## ◆ MANITOBA

**ASSEMBLY OF MANITOBA CHIEFS**
Winnipeg Manitoba, R3C OM6
(204) 956–0610
www.manItobachief.com.ca

## ◆ NEW BRUNSWICK

**UNION OF NEW BRUNSWICK INDIANS**
385 Wilsey Road
Compartment 44
Fredericton, NB E3B 5N6
(506) 458–9444

## ◆ NOVA SCOTIA

**NATIVE COUNCIL OF NOVA SCOTIA**
P.O. Box 1320
Truro, NS B2N 5N2
(800) 565–4372
(902) 895–1523
ncns.etnet.ns.ca

## ◆ ONTARIO

**ASSEMBLY OF FIRST NATIONS**
1 Nicholas Street, Suite 1002
Ottawa ON K1N 7B7
(613) 241–6789

**CHIEFS OF ONTARIO**
Bloor Street West, Suite 602
Toronto, ON M5S 3A7

**CONGRESS OF ABORIGINAL PEOPLES**
867 St. Laurent Blvd.
Ottawa, Ontario K1K 3B1
(613) 747–6022
www.abo/peoples.org

**INDIGENOUS BAR ASSOCIATION OF CANADA**
408 Queen Street
Ottawa, ON K1R 5A7
(613) 233–8686
www.indigenousbar.ca/

**INDIGENOUS SURVIVAL INTERNATIONAL**
55 Murray Street, 3rd Floor
Ottawa, ON K1N 5M3

**INUIT CIRCUMPOLAR CONFERENCE**
170 Laurier Avenue West, Suite 504
Ottawa, ON K1P 5V5
(613) 563–2642
www.inuitcircumpolar.com

**WORLD COUNCIL OF INDIGENOUS PEOPLES**
100 Argyle Avenue
Ottawa, ON K2P 1B6

## ◆ QUEBEC

**GRAND COUNCIL OF THE CREES**
Cree Regional Authority National Office
2 Lakeshore Road
Nemaska, Quebec J0Y 3B0
(819) 673–2600
www.gcc.com

## ◆ SASKATCHEWAN

**FEDERATION OF SASKATCHEWAN INDIAN NATIONS**
200–103A Packham Ave.
Saskatoon, SK S7N 4K4
(306) 665–1215

**NATIVE LAW CENTRE**
University of Saskatchewan
150 Diefenbaker Centre
Saskatoon, SK S7K 3S9
(306) 966–6189

## References

### U.S. Law and Legal Issues

Barsh, Russel L. and James Y. Henderson, *The Road: Indian Tribes and Political Liberty*. Berkeley: University of California Press, 1980.

Canby, William C., Jr. *Indian Law in a Nutshell.* 3rd ed. St. Paul: West Pub. Co., 1998.

Carrillo, Jo, ed. *Readings in American Indian Law: Recalling the Rhythm of Survival.* Philadelphia: Temple University Press, 1998.

Cohen, Felix S. *Felix S. Cohen's Handbook of Federal Indian Law.* 2d ed. Charlottesville, Va.: Michie: Bobbs-Merrill, 1982.

Deloria, Vine Jr., and Clifford Lytle. *American Indians, American Justice.* Austin: University of Texas Press, 1983.

Getches, David H. *Cases and Materials on Federal Indian Law.* 4th ed. St. Paul, Minn.: West Group, 1998.

Hagan, William. *Indian Police and Judges: Experiments in Acculturation and Control.* New Haven: Yale University Press, 1966.

Pevar, Stephen. *The Rights of Indians and Tribes: The Basic ACLU Guide to Indian and Tribal Rights.* 2d ed. Carbondale, Ill.: Southern Illinois University Press, 1992.

Pommersheim, Frank. *Braid of Feathers: American Indian Law and Contemporary Tribal Life.* Berkeley and Los Angeles: University of California Press, 1995.

Strickland, Rennard. *Fire and the Spirits: Cherokee Law from Clan to Court.* Norman: University of Oklahoma Press, 1975.

Wilkinson, Charles F. *American Indians, Time, and the Law.* New Haven: Yale University Press, 1987.

*Carole Goldberg*

## U.S. Rights and Treaties

American Friends Service Committee. *Uncommon Controversy: Fishing Rights of the Muckleshoot, Puyallup, and Nisqually Indians.* Seattle: University of Washington Press, 1970.

Barsh, Russel L. and James Y. Henderson. *The Road: Indian Tribes and Political Liberty.* Berkeley: University of California Press, 1980.

Calloway, Colin G. *Crown and Calumet: British-Indian Relations, 1793–1815.* Norman: University of Oklahoma Press, 1987.

Deloria, Vine, Jr., and Clifford M. Lytle. *The Nations Within: The Past and Future of American Indian Sovereignty.* New York: Pantheon Books, 1984.

Deloria, Vine, Jr., and David E. Wilkins. *Tribes, Treaties, and Constitutional Tribulations.* Austin: University of Texas Press, 1999.

Jennings, Francis. *The Ambiguous Iroquois Empire: The Covenant Chain Confederation of Indian Tribes with English Colonies from its Beginnings to the Lancaster Treaty of 1744.* New York: Norton, 1984.

———, ed. *The History and Culture of Iroquois Diplomacy: An Interdisciplinary Guide to the Treaties of the Six Nations and Their League.* Syracuse, N.Y.: Syracuse University Press, 1985.

Jones, Dorothy V. *License for Empire: Colonialism by Treaty in Early America.* Chicago: University of Chicago Press, 1982

Jones, Douglas C. *The Treaty of Medicine Lodge: The Story of the Great Treaty Council as Told by Eyewitnesses.* Norman: University of Oklahoma Press, 1966.

Philp, Kenneth R. *John Collier's Crusade for Indian Reform, 1920–1954.* Tucson: University of Arizona Press, 1977.

Prucha, Francis P. *American Indian Policy in the Formative Years: The Indian Trade and Intercourse Acts, 1780–1834.* Cambridge: Harvard University Press, 1962.

———. *American Indian Treaties: The History of a Political Anomaly.* Berkeley and Los Angeles: University of California Press, 1994.

———. *Americanizing the American Indians: Writings by the "Friends of the Indian," 1880–1900.* Cambridge: Harvard University Press, 1973.

Rogin, Michael Paul. *Fathers and Children: Andrew Jackson and the Subjugation of the American Indian.* New York: Knopf, 1975.

Sheehan, Bernard W. *Seeds of Extinction: Jeffersonian Philanthropy and the American Indian.* Chapel Hill: University of North Carolina Press, 1973.

Trafzer, Clifford E., ed. *Indians, Superintendents, and Councils: Northwestern Indian Policy, 1850–1855.* Lanham, Md.: University Press of America, 1986.

Trennert, Robert A. *Alternative to Extinction: Federal Indian Policy and the Beginnings of the Reservation System, 1846–51.* Philadelphia: Temple University Press, 1975.

Williams, Robert A. *The American Indian in Western Legal Thought: The Discourses of Conquest.* New York: Oxford University Press, 1990.

———. *Linking Arms Together: American Indian Treaty Visions of Law and Peace, 1600–1800.* New York: Oxford University Press, 1997.

*Carole Goldberg*

## U.S. Legislation

Bee, Robert L. *The Politics of American Indian Policy.* Cambridge, MA: Schenkman Pub. Co., 1982.

Castile, George and Robert L. Bee, eds. *State and Reservation : New Perspectives on Federal Indian Policy.* Tucson: University of Arizona Press, 1992.

Commission on the Rights, Liberties, and Responsibilities of the American Indian. *The Indian, America's Unfinished Business, A Report.* Compiled by William Brophy, Sophie D. Aberle and others. Norman: University of Oklahoma Press, 1966.

Fixico, Donald L. *Termination and Relocation: Federal Indian Policy, 1945–1960.* Albuquerque: University of New Mexico Press, 1986.

Hoxie, Frederick E. *A Final Promise: The Campaign to Assimilate the Indians, 1880–1920.* Lincoln: University of Nebraska Press, 1984.

Kehoe, Alice B. *North American Indians, A Comprehensive Account.* Englewood Cliffs, N.J.: Prentice Hall, 1981.

*Mending the Circle: A Native American Repatriation Guide: Understanding and Implementing NAGPRA and the Official Smithsonian and Other Repatriation Policies.* New York: American Indian Ritual Object Repatriation Foundation, 1996.

O'Brien, Sharon. *American Indian Tribal Governments.* Norman: University of Oklahoma Press, 1989.

Prucha, Francis P. *The Great Father, The United States Government and the American Indians.* Abridged ed. Lincoln: University of Nebraska Press, 1986.

Rusco, Elmer R. *A Fateful Time: The Background and Legislative History of the Indian Reorganization Act.* Reno, Nev.: University of Nevada Press, 2000.

Trope, Jack F., and Walter R. Echo-Hawk. "The Native American Graves Protection and Repatriation Act: Background and Legislative History." In *Repatriation Reader: Who Owns American Indian Remains?*, 123–168. Lincoln: University of Nebraska Press, 2000.

Tyler, S. Lyman. *A History of Indian Policy.* Washington, D.C.: U.S. Department of Interior, Bureau of Indian Affairs, 1973.

Washburn, Wilcomb E. *The Assault on Indian Tribalism: The General Allotment Law (Dawes Act) of 1887.* Philadelphia: Lippincott, 1975. Reprint. Malabar, Fla.: R.E. Krieger Pub. Co., 1986.

*Donald L. Fixico*

## Canadian Law and Legal Issues

Borrows, John J. and Leonard I. Rotman. *Aboriginal Legal Issues: Cases, Materials and Commentary.* Toronto: Butterworths; Charlottesville, Va.: Michie, 1998.

Canada. Royal Commission on Aboriginal Peoples. *Report of the Royal Commission on Aboriginal Peoples.* Ottawa, 1996.

Imai, Shin. *Aboriginal Law Handbook.* Scarborough, Ont.: Carswell, 1999.

———. *The Annotated Indian Act and Aboriginal Constitutional Provisions.* Scarborough, Ont.: Carswell, 2000.

Morse, Bradford W., ed. *Aboriginal Peoples and the Law: Indian, Métis and Inuit Rights in Canada.* Rev. ed. Ottawa: Carleton University Press, 1989.

Reiter, Robert A. *The Fundamental Principles of Indian Law.* Edmonton, Alta.: First Nations Resource Council, 1990.

Woodward, Jack. *Native Law.* Calgary: Carswell Legal Pub., 1989–. With annual loose-leaf updates.

*Bradford Morse*

## Native Rights and Treaties in Canada

Abel, Karry and Jean Friesen, eds. *Aboriginal Resource Use in Canada: Historical and Legal Aspects.* Winnipeg: University of Manitoba Press, 1991.

Asch, Michael. *Aboriginal and Treaty Rights in Canada: Essays on Law, Equity and Respect for Difference.* Vancouver: University of British Columbia Press, 1997.

Battiste, Marie, ed. *Reclaiming Indigenous Voice and Vision.* Vancouver: University of British Columbia Press, 2000.

Boldt, Menno and J. Anthony Long, eds. *The Quest for Justice: Aboriginal Peoples and Aboriginal Rights.* Toronto: University of Toronto Press, 1985.

Clark, Bruce. *Native Liberty, Crown Sovereignty. The Existing Aboriginal Right to Self-Government in Canada.* Montreal: McGill-Queen's University Press, 1990.

Clayton, Daniel W. *Islands of Truth: The Imperial Fashioning of Vancouver Island.* Vancouver: University of British Columbia Press, 2000.

Dickason, Olive Patricia. *Canada's First Nations: A History of Founding Peoples from Earliest Times.* Norman: University of Oklahoma Press, 1992.

Duff, Wilson. *The Indian History of British Columbia.* New ed. Victoria: Royal British Columbia Museum, 1997.

Fisher, Robin A. *Contact and Conflict: Indian-European Relations in British Columbia, 1774–1890.* Vancouver: University of British Columbia Press, 1977.

Fisher, Robin, and Ken S. Coates, eds. *Out of the Background: Readings on Canadian Native History.* Toronto: Copp Clark, 1996.

Frideres, James S. *Native Peoples in Canada, Contemporary Conflicts.* 3rd ed. Scarborough, Ont.: Prentice-Hall Canada, 1988.

Friesen, John W. *Rediscovering the First Nations of Canada.* Calgary: Detselig Enterprises, 1997.

Getty, Ian A.L. and Antoine S. Lussier, eds. *As Long as the Sun Shines and Water Flows: A Reader in Canadian Native Studies.* Vancouver: University of British Columbia Press, 1983.

Green, L.C. and Olive P. Dickason. *The Law of Nations and the New World.* Edmonton: University of Alberta Press, 1989.

Jaenen, Cornelius J. *The French Relationship with the Native Peoples of New France and Acadia.* Ottawa: Indian and Northern Affairs, 1984.

McNab, David. *Circles of Time: Aboriginal Land Rights and Resistance in Ontario.* Waterloo, Ont.: Wilfrid Laurier University Press, 1999.

Miller, James Rodger. *Skyscrapers Hide the Heavens: A History of Indian-White Relations in Canada.* Toronto: University of Toronto Press, 1989.

———., ed. *Sweet Promises: A Reader on Indian-White Relations in Canada.* Toronto: University of Toronto Press, 1991.

Milloy, John S. *A National Crime: The Canadian Government and the Residential School System, 1879–1986.* Winnipeg: University of Manitoba Press, 1999.

Morris, A. *The Treaties of Canada with the Indians.* Facsim. ed. Toronto: Coles Publishing, 1979.

Morse, Bradford W., ed. *Aboriginal Peoples and the Law: Indian, Métis and Inuit Rights in Canada.* Ottawa: Carleton University Press, 1985.

Muckle, Robert J. *The First Nations of British Columbia: An Anthropological Perspective.* Vancouver: University of British Columbia Press, 1998.

Oakes, Jill, et al., eds. *Sacred Lands: Aboriginal World Views, Claims and Conflicts.* Edmonton: Canadian Circumpolar Institute Press, 1998.

Price, Richard, ed. *The Spirit of the Alberta Indian Treaties.* 3rd ed. Edmonton: University of Alberta Press, 1999.

Purich, Donald. *Our Land: Native Rights in Canada.* Toronto: Lorimer, 1986.

Rogers, Edward S. and Donald Smith. *Aboriginal Ontario: Historical Perspective on the First Nations.* Toronto: Dundurn Press, 1994.

Russell, Daniel. *A People's Dream: Aboriginal Self-Government.* Vancouver: University of British Columbia Press, 2000.

Slattery, Brian. *The Land Rights of Indigenous Canadian Peoples.* Saskatoon: University of Saskatchewan Native Law Centre, 1979.

Tennant, Paul. *Aboriginal Peoples and Politics: The Indian Land Question in British Columbia,* 1849–1989. Vancouver: University of British Columbia Press, 1990.

Upton, L.F.S. *Micmacs and Colonists: Indian-White Relations in the Maritimes, 1713–1867.* Vancouver: University of British Columbia Press, 1979.

Weaver, Sally M. *Making Canadian Indian Policy: The Hidden Agenda, 1968–1970.* Toronto: University of Toronto Press, 1981.

*Cornelius Jaenen*

## Canadian Legislation

Armitage, Andrew. *Comparing the Policy of Aboriginal Assimilation: Australia, Canada, and New Zealand.* Vancouver: University of British Columbia Press, 1995.

Boldt, Menno and Anthony Long, eds. *Governments in Conflict? Provinces and Indian Nations in Canada.* Toronto: University of Toronto Press, 1988.

Canada. Royal Commission on Aboriginal Peoples. *Report of the Royal Commission on Aboriginal Peoples,* 1996.

Canada. Royal Commission on Aboriginal Peoples. *Treaty Making in the Spirit of Co-Existence: An Alternative to Extinguishment,* 1995.

Dickason, Olive Patricia. *Canada's First Nations: A History of Founding Peoples from Earliest Times.* Oklahoma: University of Oklahoma Press, 1992.

Dickason, Olive Patricia and David Alan Long, eds. *Visions of the Heart: Canadian Aboriginal Issues.* Toronto: Harcourt, Brace, 1996.

Macklem, Patrick, et al., eds. *Aboriginal Self-Government: Legal and Constitutional Issues.* Ottawa: Royal Commission on Aboriginal Peoples, 1995.

Miller, James Rodger. *Skyscrapers Hide the Heavens: A History of Indian-White Relations in Canada.* Toronto: University of Toronto Press, 1989.

Opekokew, Delia. *The First Nations: Indian Government and the Canadian Confederation.* Saskatoon, Sask.: Federation of Saskatchewan Indians, 1980.

Treaty Seven Elders and Tribal Council, et al. *The True Spirit and Original Intent of Treaty 7.* Montreal: McGill-Queen's University Press, 1996.

Warry, Wayne. *Unfinished Dreams: Community Healing and the Reality of Aboriginal Self-Government.* Toronto: University of Toronto Press, 1998.

*Audrey Roy and Gerald Alfred*

# 6

# *Administration*

♦ U.S. Federal Administration and Agencies
♦ Canadian Aboriginal-Government Relations  ♦ U.S. Government Agencies
♦ Canadian Government Organizations  ♦ Non-Government Organizations

## ♦ U.S. FEDERAL ADMINISTRATION AND AGENCIES

The large number of federal, state, and local government organizations involved in Indian affairs today reflects an increasingly complex web of interrelationships among Indian tribal governments and federal, state, and local government agencies. Tribal government relations with federal, state, and local governments in the United States are frequently characterized as "government-to-government" relationships, in which tribes are treated as self-determining entities that retain a residual element of their original or inherent sovereignty. This view of tribal governments developed relatively recently; during the entire nineteenth century and first half of the twentieth century, a single federal agency, the Office or Bureau of Indian Affairs, administered Indian affairs. Although other units of the federal government were sometimes involved, the Indian Office's role was, at least in theory, paramount. State and local governments were not deemed to have a role in Indian affairs, and most federal policymakers did not regard tribes as self-determining, sovereign entities. Between 1871—when Congress ended the practice of making treaties with Indian tribes—and 1934—when the passage of the Indian Reorganization Act signaled a new federal policy of strengthening tribal organizations—policymakers viewed the tribal affiliations of Indian people as impediments to achieving the official goal of Indian assimilation.

### Development of an Indian Service

The Constitution empowers Congress to regulate commerce with the Indian tribes in Article I, Section 8. This provision has been interpreted as giving Congress absolute, or plenary power in Indian affairs. Since the early nineteenth century, Congress and the executive branch, subject to judicial interpretations, have administered Indian affairs. In the early years of the republic, the president appointed superintendents of Indian affairs to supervise tribal relations within specific geographic areas, and Indian agents to represent the interests of the United States with specific tribes. Like ambassadors and other diplomatic personnel, these appointments required Senate confirmation. Dealing with the Indian tribes as separate sovereignties or nations, these early agents and superintendents were much like diplomats.

Congress appointed a War Department official to oversee the nation's Indian relations in 1789. In 1806 the secretary of war created a new position, the superintendent of Indian trade, as relations with tribes intensified. The incumbent coordinated all aspects of Indian relations, which included trade, diplomacy, and purchases of land from Indian tribes. In 1819 Congress established an annual appropriation of $10,000 to promote the "civilization," or acculturation, of the American Indians. This appropriation, which continued until 1873, supported Indian schools established by missionary organizations.

**Organization of the Indian Service.** Congress abolished the superintendent of Indian trade position in 1822. Subsequently, the secretary of war directly controlled Indian affairs. In 1824 Secretary of War John C. Calhoun established a Bureau of Indian Affairs in the War Department, placing former Superintendent of Indian Trade Thomas L. McKenney in charge. The agency became known as the Office of Indian Affairs, or simply the Indian Office, a name that persisted until 1947 when the agency adopted its current title, the Bureau of Indian Affairs (BIA). In 1832 Congress created the position of Commissioner of Indian Affairs (CIA) to establish "direction and management" of all Indian affairs. This official assumed charge of the

Indian Office in Washington, D.C. During the next half-century, incumbents of the office would attempt to gain control of Indian affairs in the field. In 1834 Congress organized the Indian Department in the field by establishing a number of agencies and superintendencies. While the commissioner and the Indian Office in Washington were in nominal charge of the work of the agents and superintendents, the president, with the advice and consent of the Senate, appointed the agents and superintendents

The internal structure of the Indian Office, and its relationship with the field service, which consisted of the superintendencies and agencies, was not affected when Congress placed Indian affairs in the newly created Department of the Interior in 1849. The president continued to appoint agents and superintendents, subject to Senate confirmation. These officials in turn had the power to appoint their own subordinates, which amounted to a considerable patronage on the larger reservations. Agents and superintendents also contracted with suppliers of food and industrial and educational materials, sometimes controlling substantial funds with little oversight from the Washington office. By the mid-nineteenth century, the Indian service had become heavily politicized. Patronage, or the provision of public jobs as rewards for political services, provided much of the impetus behind politics in the nineteenth century. The election of Abraham Lincoln in 1860 and the consequent ascendancy of the new Republican Party brought unprecedented demands for patronage appointments in all branches of the federal government, including the Indian service, as a means to reward supporters and establish the party.

**Efforts to Centralize Administration.** During the remainder of the nineteenth century, the commissioner and his Washington, D.C. staff attempted to control activities at the agencies by centralizing administrative control. Indian agents and superintendents, appointed by the president, were generally professional politicians who had their own followers and patrons. Frequent allegations of corruption resulted in the scandals, special investigations, and inspection boards that characterized nineteenth-century Indian affairs.

In an attempt to reform Indian administration, President Ulysses S. Grant, who served from 1869 to 1877, appointed army officers and, later, missionaries, as superintendents and agents. Grant's commissioner of Indian affairs, Ely S. Parker, a member of the Seneca tribe, was the first American Indian to hold the position. Parker, an engineer and former army officer, was a proponent of Indian "civilization" or acculturation. In 1869 Congress created a board of Indian commissioners to supervise accounts and promote Indian assimilation. Superintendencies were phased out during the

1870s and 1880s. Specialized investigators, special agents, and Indian inspectors periodically visited agents, who now reported directly to the commissioner of Indian affairs. By the end of the century, new ideas about civil service reform made it possible for the Washington, D.C. office first to rescind the agent's power to appoint subordinates and later to replace politically appointed agents with agency superintendents appointed under civil service rules.

Federal relations with the Indians of the Great Plains were unsettled from the end of the Civil War to the late 1870s. The expanding U.S. population encroached on Indian lands, as increased railroad construction and settlement diminished game. The Indian service's heavy-handed and insensitive approach inspired frequent military clashes between Indians and settlers, which led to a series of Indian wars and pacification campaigns. Many—particularly Westerners—saw the Indian Office as ineffectual at best, and criminally incompetent and indifferent to the needs of frontier settlers at worst. These critics wanted Indian affairs transferred back to the War Department, contending that the transfer would enable the army to coordinate more effectively with the Indian Office while providing firmer control of Indian affairs. The transfer to the War Department never took place, partly because many reformers believed that administrative reforms could solve the problems of the Indian Office. When armed conflict subsided during the 1880s, public agitation for a transfer of Indian affairs to the War Department diminished.

**Policy Changes in the Nineteenth Century.** Organizational innovation occurred within the context of policy change. The focus of U.S. Indian policy shifted over time. The removal of the Indians from the Eastern United States superseded diplomacy and trade as policy goals during the 1820s and 1830s. In the 1840s and 1850s, policymakers promoted the concentration of the removed tribes on reserved lands west of the Mississippi River. After the Civil War, the "civilization" or forced acculturation of the Indians became a primary goal of the federal government. By the 1880s, most policymakers believed that the education of Indian children and the allotment of Indian lands were the most promising means of assimilating American Indians.

Allotment, which became national policy in 1887, divided tribal lands into tracts of land to be farmed by individual Indian owners. Overriding these specific policy changes were what most nineteenth-century Americans believed to be large-scale and inevitable historical developments: farmers, ranchers, and miners appropriated most of the Indian lands and the Indian population declined. As a result, reformers believed, the Indian population would disappear as a distinct group and European-Americans would settle the North

Opening of the Cherokee Outlet, 16 September 1893. (Courtesy of Archives and Manuscripts Division of the Oklahoma Historical Society)

American continent. The "civilization" of the American Indians, many reformers believed, would integrate American Indian people as farmers and herders into a European-American society whose ascendancy was inevitable.

### The Indian Office in the Early Twentieth Century

During the twentieth century, Indian people neither assimilated nor died out. In spite of widespread poverty and scandalous health conditions, the Indian population, which had been declining during the nineteenth century, increased during the early twentieth century. Indians, however, were not moving to urban areas with the rest of the country. Nor were they successful farmers and ranchers, due in part to a lack of access to capital and in part to the poor condition of reservation lands. Living in rural poverty and dependent on government assistance, the proceeds of leasing reservation land to white farmers and ranchers, and meager wages from migratory agricultural labor, the growing Indian population seemed to personify the failure of nineteenth-century federal Indian policy.

**The 1920s.** To address these altered circumstances, the Snyder Act of 1921 provided permanent funding authorization for "the general support and civilization of the Indians." To carry out these objectives, the act authorized the Indian Office to provide educational, health, and welfare services to Indian people, to irrigate and make other improvements on Indian lands, and to employ personnel to support these objectives. Since the Indian Service had previously provided assistance to tribes under appropriation act authority or under the authority of treaties or agreements with Indian tribes, the Snyder Act signaled a move toward a permanent Indian-federal government relationship. The Indian Citizenship Act of 1924, which granted U.S. citizenship to all American Indians born in the United States, specifically continued all treaty and other specific entitlements.

Reformers attempted to improve the conditions of Indian people by changing the administration of the Indian Service, or by reallocating responsibility for

Indian affairs. During the 1920s, the Indian Office itself attempted to involve state and local governments in the provision of health and educational services to American Indians within their borders, often providing the governments with a federal subsidy. The Johnson-O'Malley Act of 1934 institutionalized these arrangements by permitting the Indian Office to contract with the states to provide education, health, and welfare services to Indians on reservations within their borders. While the act had a broad scope, most Johnson-O'Malley contracting has been for the provision of educational services. States with large numbers of Indian public school students created Indian education divisions in their education departments to manage Johnson-O'Malley contracts.

Problems in Indian administration led to the involvement of other federal agencies in Indian affairs during the 1920s and 1930s. Receiving complaints about the care of inmates at the Canton (South Dakota) Asylum for Insane Indians, an Indian service facility, the Indian Office dispatched a psychiatrist from St. Elizabeth's Hospital, a Public Health Service (PHS) facility in Washington, D.C. Doctor Steven Silk visited Canton in 1928 and 1933, filing inspection reports with the commissioner of Indian affairs after each visit. After Silk's second inspection, the facility was closed and the patients transferred to St. Elizabeth's. During the 1930s, the PHS provided physicians to some reservations. Because of problems in Indian agriculture, the Bureau of Reclamation, an Interior Department agency charged with renewing marginal land, and the Department of Agriculture's Soil Conservation Service began work on some reservations during the 1920s.

The Indian office also had problems with its administrative structure. Administrative authority was concentrated in Washington, leaving little discretion to reservation-level administrators. With over sixty field units to oversee, the Indian Office in Washington, D.C. was often slow to respond. The office's inability to make and act on decisions wasted time as local agency superintendents waited for directives from the nation's capitol. Charles Burke, commissioner of Indian affairs from 1921 to 1928, created some intermediate administrative positions—such as district superintendents and district medical directors—but these posts lacked administrative authority. The Meriam Report of 1928, an exhaustive investigation of Indian administration, recommended against strengthening these intermediate offices in favor of increasing the autonomy of reservation personnel to respond to unique local conditions.

**The Indian New Deal.** More far-reaching changes followed the election of President Franklin D. Roosevelt in 1932. Roosevelt appointed Harold Ickes secretary of the interior and John Collier commissioner of

Indian affairs. Ickes and Collier shared a commitment to reform in Indian affairs. Both had been critics of the Indian Office during the 1920s. Collier's major achievement was the Indian Reorganization Act of 1934. The foundation of the modern tribal government, the act permitted tribes to organize tribal governments and tribal business corporations. It also provided a revolving loan fund and other support services to participating tribes. Collier, an astute promoter and publicist, was able to enlist a number of New Deal agencies to support Indian Service activities. Collier was thus able to secure funds for Indian service activities from the Public Works Administration, a federal agency designed to stimulate the economy through investments in public construction projects; the Emergency Relief Administration, an agency that provided funds for public assistance to the unemployed; and the Civilian Conservation Corps, a program that provided conservation work for unemployed young men. New Deal agencies funded 29 percent of Indian Service expenditures in 1934. During World War II (1939–1945), Collier was able to secure some national defense funds to supplement Indian Office appropriations. The magnitude of these funds, however, did not approach that of the depression-era funds.

## The Modern Bureau of Indian Affairs

**The Termination Era.** John Collier resigned his position as commissioner of Indian affairs in 1945, a few months before the death of President Roosevelt. Having been commissioner of Indian affairs for twelve years—the longest anyone has held the post—Collier left a significant impression on federal government relations with American Indians. After the beginning of World War II, however, Collier's relations with Congress deteriorated. During the war, Congress increased appropriations for health and educational services to individual Indians while cutting appropriations for the tribal development programs that were characteristic of Collier's approach to Indian policy. Congress began to discuss the eventual termination of the special relationship Indians had with the federal government. Following the war, well before it enacted the Termination Resolution in 1953, Congress took steps toward ending the special federal relationship with Indian tribes; this congressional policy was often expressed as "freeing Indians from federal supervision."

In 1946 Congress created the Indian Claims Commission to enable Indian tribes to seek redress for alleged wrongdoing by the United States government. Tribes had previously brought claims before the U.S. Court of Claims, which dismissed most such claims. Between

1881 and 1946, the Court of Claims gave tribes monetary awards in only thirty of 175 cases. In contrast, the Indian Claims Commission completed 546 dockets between 1946 and 1978, granting monetary awards in 342 cases. This more effective mechanism for processing claims encouraged many tribes to seek redress, and attracted attorneys who sought a socially useful and potentially lucrative practice. Thanks to the Indian Claim Commission, the tribal attorney, often retained long term, became an important figure in Indian affairs.

The Indian Office adopted the title Bureau of Indian Affairs in 1947, which it has used ever since. The previous year, Public Law 687, the Indian Delegation Act of 1946, had established the foundation for the area office system by authorizing substantial delegations of formal authority from the secretary of the interior to the commissioner of Indian affairs and from the commissioner to subordinates in the field. In 1946 five field offices were created, at Minneapolis, Minnesota; Billings, Montana; Portland, Oregon; Phoenix, Arizona; and Oklahoma City, Oklahoma. By 1951 there were eleven area offices that had considerable power over reservation administration as a result of authority delegated to them under the authority of Public Law 687.

In 1949 the Commission on Organization of the Executive Branch of the Government, headed by former President Herbert Hoover, recommended the transfer of the Bureau of Indian Affairs' social programs to state governments or to federal agencies serving the general population. This would accomplish the "complete integration of the Indians into the rest of the population," the commissioners believed. Public Law 280, approved in 1953, transferred criminal and civil jurisdiction in Indian country from the federal government to the states of California, Minnesota, Nebraska, Oregon, and Wisconsin, and gave other states the option to assume jurisdiction by legislation. (In 1968 Public Law 280 was amended to require tribal consent to the transfer of jurisdiction.) In 1954 Congress transferred Indian health programs to the U.S. Public Health Service and authorized the PHS to contract with state and local governments or private organizations to provide health care to Indian people.

Following the passage of the Termination Resolution in 1953, Congress terminated the federal relationship with a number of tribes, most notably the Menominee Tribe of Wisconsin and the Klamath Tribe of Oregon. In so doing, Congress ordered the distribution of tribal assets to individual Indians and rescinded special social, health, educational, and land management services that the federal government had provided to members of the terminated tribes. The lands of the terminated tribes became indistinguishable from other lands within the state. Held by individual Indians or business corporations that were created to manage the assets of the former tribe, these lands were subject to land taxes imposed by state and local governments, and were alienable through land sales or by other means.

**The New Frontier and the Great Society.**   Indian opposition to state assumptions of criminal and civil jurisdiction coupled with fears of termination soured relations between many American Indians—particularly tribal government officials—and the federal government. The National Congress of American Indians, organized in 1944, and state federations of Indian tribes, many of them organized in response to state attempts to extend criminal jurisdiction to Indians on reservations, opposed federal termination efforts during the 1950s. Relations did not improve when the federal government acquired Indian lands for flooding with the construction of dams, as happened in North and South Dakota and New York State.

The election of President John F. Kennedy in 1960, however, seemed to herald a new era in Indian affairs. Kennedy appointed a sympathetic commissioner of Indian affairs, anthropologist Philleo Nash. Kennedy's New Frontier promised an administration with a more vigorous domestic agenda. President Lyndon Johnson, who became president after Kennedy's assassination in 1963, pursued the vigorous domestic policy that the Kennedy years had promised. Calling for the development of a Great Society, Johnson declared a War on Poverty and asked Congress to create an Office of Economic Opportunity (OEO) to lead the fight. In response, Congress enacted the Economic Opportunity Act of 1964, which provided funding to local Community Action Programs (CAP) that were to develop and implement programs to serve the poor on the local level. The act authorized Indian tribes to designate themselves as CAP agencies for the purposes of the Economic Opportunity Act. In 1966 President Johnson appointed Robert L. Bennett, a member of the Oneida tribe, commissioner of Indian affairs; he was the second Indian, and the first in the twentieth century, to hold the position.

The OEO leadership opposed the status quo in Indian affairs and elsewhere. Presenting itself as a fresh alternative to the BIA, which it characterized as a tired bureaucracy, the OEO established an Indian desk to process tribal applications for funding, created special technical assistance units to help tribes develop programs, and emphasized the employment of Indian people in key policy making positions. All this was intended to distinguish OEO programs from those of the BIA, and of the PHS, which had become another major agency in Indian affairs since the transfer of health services in 1955.

Some charged that the BIA was a "compromised advocate" for Indian people because it was affiliated with the Department of the Interior. Most Interior Department agencies focused on land use rather than the development of human potential. Further, Western political interests, traditionally opposed to Indian interests, dominated the department. The commissioner of Indian affairs reported to an assistant secretary for public land management, who was preoccupied with resource management questions. However, most tribal governments opposed the proposed transfer of the BIA to the Department of Health, Education, and Welfare in the late 1960s, and the attempt failed. In 1977 the American Indian Policy Review Commission (AIPRC) recommended separating the BIA from the Department of the Interior and making it an independent agency. President James Carter abolished the commissioner position and placed an assistant secretary for Indian affairs in charge of the bureau, giving the agency director more direct access to the secretary of the interior.

As President Johnson's Great Society program developed, the number of federal domestic assistance programs increased. Some were former OEO programs which were transferred to traditional cabinet agencies—such as the neighborhood youth corps program, an employment program for teenagers from poor families, which the Department of Labor took over—while others represented new initiatives—such as Model Cities. Many of these programs designated Indian tribal governments as eligible to receive their assistance, and established "Indian desks" in their headquarters and regional offices to work with Indian applicants. Increased availability of funding for a variety of tribal projects strengthened the tribal governments that had been established by the Indian Reorganization Act. Tribal payrolls grew, and the beginnings of a tribal civil service emerged.

**The Self-Determination Program.** President Richard M. Nixon continued the practice of appointing an American Indian to lead the BIA. Nixon's commissioner of Indian affairs, Louis R. Bruce, a Mohawk-Oglala Sioux, tried to mold the agency into a service organization, responsive to the needs of Indian people. Citing successful tribal administration of OEO and other federal grant-in-aid programs, President Nixon in 1970 called for a policy of tribal "self-determination" to replace the now-discredited termination policy. The self-determination policy, as outlined by Nixon, would enable tribes to contract, at their own option, to provide any service currently being provided by either the BIA or the PHS. Contracting tribes were to receive the same level of funding that the relevant government agency had expended to provide the contracted service. Tribes would have the right of retrocession, which

enabled them to return the administration of a contracted service to the relevant federal agency. In 1975 Congress passed Public Law 93–638, the Indian Self-Determination and Education Assistance Act, Title I of which embodied the self-determination policy as outlined by President Nixon five years earlier.

By permitting tribes to administer services intended to benefit their members, the Indian Self-Determination Act represented a significant conceptual advance in Indian affairs. Congress simplified federal requirements for tribal contracting in 1988 (PL 100–472) and increased tribal participation in the budgeting process in 1994 (PL 103–413). Even as amended, the act was less than completely empowering. In the first place, the power to design programs and devise solutions resided with the federal agency, BIA or PHS. Indian tribes could apply to administer an already existing program, but did not have the power or authority to devise or fund new programs under PL 93–638. Furthermore, the self-determination program provided no budgeting authority: tribes were subject to the mercy of the federal budget cycle. During the 1980s and 1990s, federal budget deficits limited the expansion of funding for self-determination projects. Limited planning funds restricted the tribal role to implementing programs devised by others. In contrast, both the BIA and PHS expanded their planning and monitoring activities after the passage of Public Law 93–638. In both organizations, many of these activities were conducted at area offices rather than at the reservation or headquarters level; the further expansion of the power and authority of the area offices was a major consequence of the self-determination policy.

**New Federal Programs.** Other Indian reform legislation enacted during the 1970s reflected the ideology of self-determination. The Indian Education Act of 1972 provided financial assistance to education agencies in communities with Indian students in their schools. In 1973 the OEO Indian programs merged with a small Office of Indian Affairs in the Department of Health, Education, and Welfare to create the Office of Native American Programs, now the Administration for Native Americans (ANA). The Native American Programs Act of 1974 expanded the program and included Native Hawaiian groups as eligible beneficiaries. The Indian Health Care Improvement Act of 1976 extended the application of Public Law 93–638 to the Indian Health program of PHS.

In 1978 the BIA developed the Federal Acknowledgement Project (FAP), a program intended to determine whether to recognize Indian communities seeking federal recognition. The FAP prescribed specific procedures for unrecognized Indian communities to follow in order to receive recognition. The Indian Child

Welfare and Tribally Controlled Community College Assistance Acts, both also passed in 1978, expanded tribal programs in a variety of directions. The Indian Child Welfare Act gave tribal governments primary jurisdiction in child custody cases involving children of tribal members, and it provided tribes with funds to develop tribal child welfare services. The Tribally Controlled Community College Assistance Act provided funding for reservation higher education.

A conservative mood in the 1980s and 1990s caused policymakers to encourage economic development projects as alternatives to expanded federal funding. President Ronald Reagan affirmed the federal government's self-determination policy in a 1983 statement. He appointed a Presidential Commission on Indian Reservation Economies, which supported increased tribal economic development activity in 1984. Consistent with the President's conservative ideology, the initiative in economic development shifted from the federal government to the tribes. Reductions in federal funding exacerbated the already inadequate accounting capability of the BIA.

**Other Federal Agencies.** Perhaps as important as the changes in the operation of the BIA and PHS were changes in tribal relationships with other federal agencies. While a variety of federal agencies were involved in Indian affairs during the Great Depression, their involvement was limited to transferring funds to the Indian Office, which administered the programs. The involvement of a large number of federal agencies and programs thus did not threaten the domination of the Indian Office in Indian affairs during the 1930s. Beginning with the OEO programs of the 1960s, however, Indian tribes were eligible to apply directly for program grants provided by many federal domestic assistance programs; applications were often routed through special Indian divisions or desks within the headquarters of the agency administering the program. By 1968 significant providers of grant-in-aid programs to Indian tribes included the Department of Labor, a cabinet-level department for employment and labor programs which administered the Neighborhood Youth Corps and other employment programs; the Department of Commerce, a cabinet-level department devoted to the promotion of business, which administered for the Economic Development Administration; and the Office of Education, then an educational assistance agency in the Department of Health, Education and Welfare, now the cabinet-level Department of Education.

Transferring funds from the federal government to state and local governments became a significant element in financing state and local government services during the 1970s. Tribes were frequently designated as eligible grantees for the new grant-in-aid programs. For example, the Comprehensive Employment and Training Act (CETA) of 1973, a program that provided jobs for the unemployed, included Indian tribes, Alaska Native villages, Native Hawaiian groups, and non-reservation Indian groups as eligible grantees. The Department of Labor, which administered CETA, created a Division of Indian and Native American Programs to fund Indian employment and training programs. Initiated in 1972, a general revenue sharing program provided federal funds to state and local governments to be expended for any legitimate governmental purpose: the program designated Indian tribes, together with states, counties, cities, and a variety of other local government entities, as recipient governments for revenue sharing grants. In 1977 Congress created the American Indian Policy Review Commission (AIPRC), composed of congressional and Indian representatives, to advise on needed Indian legislation. The commission recommended "guaranteeing the permanency of tribal governments within the Federal domestic assistance program delivery system." AIPRC viewed access to funds from federal agencies other than the BIA and the PHS as the key to strengthening the autonomy of tribal governments.

By the 1980s the inter-governmental system of funding Indian programs seemed well established. In 1983 President Ronald Reagan transferred White House management of Indian affairs from the Office of Liaison, which managed presidential relations with a variety of interest groups, to the Office of Intergovernmental Affairs, the White House office for relating to states, counties and cities. In doing so, he explicitly defined the relationship between Indian tribes and the federal government as a "government-to-government" relationship. Several new federal grant-in-aid programs became available to Indian tribes during the 1980s. For a variety of reasons, elderly Native Americans were not being helped by Area Agencies on Aging, regional organizations created by the Older Americans Act of 1965 to provide health and social services to older Americans. In response, in 1980 Congress added Title VI, Grants to Indian Tribes, to the Older Americans Act. Title VI provided funds for tribal governments and Alaskan Native villages to provide a variety of special services to older Native Americans. In 1982, Congress replaced CETA with the Job Training Partnership Act (JTPA), a scaled-down employment program with increased participation by private business and industry. The JTPA continued tribal grants, although at a lower level than CETA.

The Reagan administration (1981–1989) cut domestic spending which reduced the funding available for all federal domestic programs, including tribal programs. As a result of a growing federal budget deficit, general revenue sharing, the federal program that provided funds with the fewest strings attached, was eliminated in 1986. The Reagan administration cut BIA expenditures by over 5 percent, Indian Education Act grants by nearly 35 percent, ANA expenditures by 32 percent, and JTPA expenditures by 28 percent. Only PHS expenditures increased during the Reagan administration, by nearly 25 percent.

Financial uncertainty, combined with a complex and varied funding environment, resulted in expanded tribal efforts to acquire funding. The result was a strengthening of tribal government civil service organizations, although not necessarily of the responsiveness or legitimacy of tribal governments. A renewed emphasis on business development resulted in some new projects, such as the development of an automobile parts factory on the Choctaw Reservation in Mississippi. The development of gambling enterprises on reservations, conducted under tribal auspice or provided by nontribal corporations under contract, generated a particularly lucrative source of revenue that in turn strengthened tribal governments and tribal civil service. Issues concerning the responsiveness or legitimacy of tribal government persisted, however. As certain kinds of grants stabilized, national interest groups composed of tribal employees in a specific functional area—such as aging or employment programs—emerged. Frequently, these organizations sought and obtained funding. Groups like the National Indian Council on Aging, composed of tribal Title VI program personnel, had a significant influence on congressional committees and the federal and emerging tribal bureaucracies.

**State Indian Affairs Offices.**   Thirty-nine states have offices or commissions on Indian affairs, which vary from formal commissions with paid staffs to individuals placed in the governor's office or in a legislative staff position. Many states created Indian offices in the 1960s or 1970s to serve as a conduit for federal funds flowing through state government to Indian groups within the state. Some state Indian affairs offices assist tribal economic development programs, assist non-recognized Indian groups to negotiate the federal recognition process, and maintain a liaison with tribes and other Indian groups within the state.

Issues that have affected tribal relations with states in recent decades have been Indian gambling, tribal and state child welfare jurisdiction, and tribal assumptions of governmental authority over non-Indian persons and lands owned by non-Indians within reservation boundaries. Some state Indian commissions have negotiated agreements covering Indian child welfare jurisdiction, and others have negotiated disputes over land use between tribes and local governments. State commissions and offices, however, have been less successful in

negotiating disputes concerning gambling on Indian lands. Many are underfinanced and understaffed, and most, having been established to mediate between federal, state, tribal, and local governments, serve advisory functions and do not have the authority to resolve disputes.

**Tribal Governments.**   Tribal government powers have increased during the past few decades as a result of the self-determination policy, the availability of federal grants-in-aid, and court decisions that have affirmed tribal powers. The Reagan Administration, as noted above, encouraged tribal economic development. However, few anticipated that Indian gaming would be the most significant economic development project of the 1980s. After the Supreme Court ruled in *Seminole Tribe v. Butterworth* (1982) that Indian tribes could create gambling enterprises on reservations, tribes in many areas of the country developed gambling enterprises. In reaction, pressure grew for federal regulation of Indian gambling. In 1988 Reagan signed the Indian Gaming Regulatory Act (PL 100–497), which provided for tribal-state compacts and established a three-person National Indian Gaming Commission to regulate tribal gambling activities.

While some tribes have benefited from the expansion of reservation economic activity, including gaming, tourism, mining, ranching, agriculture, and manufacturing, many have not. The lack of adequate financial support for tribal governments is a major impediment to further growth. Resource constraints at the federal level and a serious need for services and economic development programs at the reservation level combine to make the future of tribal governments uncertain. Strengthening tribal governments remains a major part of the BIA and PHS missions. During the 1990s, several tribes participated in the Rural Empowerment Zone and Enterprise Community Program, the Clinton administration's major anti-poverty initiative.

## Conclusion

It is likely that tribal governments will continue to be funded by a variety of sources in the future. The status of tribes as self-determining entities, independent of the laws of states—except as Congress chooses to assimilate the tribes to state laws—seems secure. Tribal self-determination in the United States, however, is limited. Tribal decisions are subject to review by the BIA, Congress can limit the scope of tribal decision-making power, and Congress appropriates the funds that tribes need to provide programs to Native American people. Without developing independent funding sources, tribes face an insecure future.

BIA staff meeting with the Assistant Secretary of Indian Affairs. (Photo by Carol Lujan)

At the same time, it is unlikely that federal agencies involved in Indian affairs will retreat from the ideology of the self-determination era. Indeed, politicians and federal agency leaders reject the old goals of assimilation and acculturation. In remarks at a ceremony acknowledging the one-hundred-and-seventy-fifth anniversary of the establishment of the Bureau of Indian Affairs in September 2000, Kevin Gover, the assistant secretary of the interior for Indian Affairs, apologized for the BIA's "futile and destructive efforts to annihilate Indian cultures" (see http://www.doi.gov/bia/as-ia/175gover.htm).

Although contemporary policy results in some insecurity for tribes, a complex and diverse funding environment provides incentives for funders to accommodate recipients' needs and desires. For the BIA and PHS, the major federal Indian agencies providing technical assistance, contracting with tribes and monitoring the administration of the contracts are all activities congruent with the structure of the agencies and with contemporary notions about how government should work. These functions will probably dominate the agencies for the foreseeable future. Securing nongovernmental funding through economic development activities seems the most promising strategy for tribes as the United States again enters an era of limited government and individual initiative.

*Paul H. Stuart*
*University of Alabama*

## ◆ CANADIAN ABORIGINAL-GOVERNMENT RELATIONS

Many aboriginal nations began their relationships with European explorers and settlers at the beginning of the seventeenth century in what is now present-day Canada. Initial contact was characterized by cautious respect and friendship. Aboriginal peoples welcomed the newcomers into what was for Europeans a strange and somewhat harsh land. The Europeans needed physical guidance in this new land as well as survival aid—how to adapt to new foods, colder climates, and new methods of travel. They also wished to prosper and profit from lucrative trading opportunities. All of this required positive, peaceful relations with the aboriginal nations they encountered.

The treaty, an agreement between nations, became the primary vehicle to forge the framework of coexistence, with each nation recognizing the sovereignty and vitality of the other. Sharing of ideas and expertise was possible and encouraged, but the origins of the relationship were grounded on mutual respect for their respective autonomy. In treaties such as the Two Row Wampum between the Iroquois Confederacy and the Dutch, later renegotiated with the British in the mid-1600s, the Europeans retained their "ship," a figurative expression for community and territory, within which the Europeans kept their laws, systems of government, customs, and religious beliefs. The Iroquois kept their "great canoe," again figurative language for community or nation, in which they held onto the Great Law, their confederacy system of participatory democracy with full gender equality (which Europeans could not understand as they possessed a monarchy with no rights for women and little for men outside the upper classes), and their religious beliefs, laws, and customs. It was envisioned that each would travel separately down the river of life with all that they needed for their future, but that they were traveling in the same river such that the bounty of the lands and waters were shared and traded peacefully. This arrangement meant that both parties agreed not to interfere in the internal affairs of the other. As settlement by colonists increased, new rules became necessary to deal with lawbreakers. Treaties were negotiated in which both nations agreed to allow hot pursuit into the territory of the other by officials to catch escaping lawbreakers. Other treaties contained terms through which the parties agreed to respect the law of the other when in that party's territory.

### Era of Colonization

Unfortunately, the spirit and intent of the first treaty-making era were broken by the Europeans, particularly by the British, who moved away from the model of allies and partners into becoming a colonizer. The drive to dominate and exploit the land and to relocate tens of thousands of unwanted citizens from England to the "New World" directed British policy toward the acquisition of large land tracts for exclusive use by colonists. At the same time, European attitudes slowly shifted toward notions of superiority and a perceived divine right to dominate all other peoples in the world. Over time, colonial power increased, and Native-European relations shifted from equality of nations and respect for mutual independence to dominance of the law, government, and economy of the European immigrants. The British government began to assert unilaterally the

authority to impose restrictions on the external activities of the aboriginal nations without consultation or consent. This was followed by efforts to interfere in the internal affairs of the sovereign aboriginal nations.

These dramatic changes in colonial policy were also reflected in transformations in diplomatic relations with the aboriginal nations. The initial approach was to authorize the military leadership or the governors of the individual colonies to enter into military alliances and treaties with the Indian nations within their region, so as to promote positive relations for the British in opposition to the French. Numerous treaties were negotiated by generals on behalf of the Crown to gain allies or at least to obtain neutrality from nations formerly or potentially allied with the French. (Such a treaty signed by General Murray with the Huron Nation in 1760 was upheld as still effective under Canadian law by the Supreme Court of Canada in *Regina v. Sioui* in 1990.) Colonial governors along the Atlantic seaboard regularly negotiated treaties to promote trade, secure peace, or purchase land.

On the other hand, express instructions from England to these governors to prevent unauthorized settlement by colonists on Indian lands were frequently violated with impunity by powerful local interests, including by individuals such as George Washington, the first U.S. president. Royal instructions were repeatedly issued to put a stop to such encroachments as they led to protests by and occasional battles with the Indian nations who were the recognized and rightful owners of the lands concerned. The Royal Proclamation of 7 October 1763, was issued by King George III to address the unauthorized settlement of Indian land, as well as to establish new colonial governments over certain former territories of France, which had relinquished all claims in favor of Great Britain under the Treaty of Versailles earlier that year. In order to "Prevent Great Frauds and Abuses" that had been committed against many "Indian Nations or tribes" by settlers, the proclamation outlined several basic initiatives: affirmation of aboriginal title to land; establishment of outer limits to the growth of the colonies beyond which would be Indian territory where the aboriginal peoples would be left "unmolested"; prohibition of the purchase of Indian land by all but the Crown; description of the proper procedure for negotiating treaties; and, appointment of two ambassadors directly from King George III of England to the aboriginal peoples. British territory was divided for this latter purpose, and Sir William Johnson, a close friend of the Iroquois, was assigned responsibility as superintendent general of Indian Affairs for the northern half, which included from New York northwards. Edmond Atkins, a man experienced in the fur trade with the southern Indian nations, was named superintendent of the southern area.

Johnson quickly moved to enhance the friendly relations he enjoyed with some Indian nations. He also responded to Indian complaints about British trade monopoly and military occupation of the French forts in the Great Lakes region, which in 1763 triggered the Indian revolt known as Pontiac's War. At gatherings of many Indian nations in July 1764 at Niagara and on 20 August 1766 at Detroit, Johnson formally read out the Royal Proclamation as a treaty and presented wampum belts (diplomatic tokens made from sea shells) and medals to represent the treaty commitments. Despite continual efforts by Johnson to uphold the promises of the Royal Proclamation, settlers and colonial governments ignored the Crown's protection of Indian land thereby causing considerable conflict between settlers and Indians.

The outbreak of the American Revolution (1776–1783) put on hold actions to implement the Royal Proclamation's promises, but the commitments themselves were regularly renewed so as to obtain the alliance of most Indian nations in fighting against the rebels. The colonists' victory presented immediate and pressing challenges to Indian sovereignty and control over the territory of the Indian nations that lived in eastern North America and within the thirteen original colonies. Most Indian nations opposed expansion by the settlers but none could effectively resist on their own. Demands on the British to continue fighting and honor the treaties of military alliance were turned away. The only alternatives that many Indian nations faced were to seek peace on the best possible terms with the new country, flee westward, or to move northward along with the United Empire Loyalists into what remained of British North America. Many Indians chose to emigrate to present-day Canada.

Great Britain was forced to accommodate the massive immigration of Loyalists and purchased large tracts of land from the Indian nations that had resided there since time immemorial. A colonial government was created for what later became Ontario. These changes compelled the development of a new relationship with both the Indian nations who had always been there and the recent immigrants. A new and larger structure for administering Indian affairs had to be created. Previously, Indian affairs were managed by a single ambassador, but now responsibility for treaty negotiations with aboriginal nations was delegated to the military, which also provided annual presents of goods to allied Indian nations, supervised the lucrative fur trade, and acted upon complaints. As the nineteenth century progressed, the colonial government appointed Indian agents for each local region in order to increase contact between the Crown and the Indians. Many of these early agents were retired military officers and traders who had extensive experience with Indian nations. Soon their sons, many of whom had Indian wives, followed in the footsteps of the fathers and became permanent residents in Indian communities and sometimes landowners of large areas of local property.

## Confederation

After the creation of an independent Canada through confederation in 1867, the new federal government was allocated exclusive authority for "Indians, and Lands reserved for the Indians" under section 91(24) of the Constitution Act of 1867. Legislation was passed the next year by Parliament through which the colonial regime of Indian agents and reserves was renewed under the control of a new federal department. The post of superintendent general of Indian affairs was maintained as the senior federal official, while responsibility for negotiating treaties continued to be assigned to specific individuals. In particular, Alexander Morris, an early superintendent general of Indian Affairs, negotiated a number of treaties dealing with land that extended from western Ontario across Manitoba, Saskatchewan, and Alberta to the Rocky Mountains.

A single statute, the Indian Act, was passed by Parliament in 1876 to consolidate previous laws regarding aboriginal people. Over the years this act was regularly amended and made both more complex and more intrusive into the lives of Indian nations. Traditional governments were displaced by elected ones; sovereignty was ignored in favor of limited and delegated powers requiring federal approval; aboriginal and treaty rights were discounted; the traditional economies, ways of life, and religious beliefs were either outlawed or undermined; all children were removed and sent to residential schools far away; and federal officials were employed as Indian agents with full control over virtually all decisions taken by the Indian reserve governments as well as serving as justices of the peace. Autonomy declined and along with it the size of traditional territory. None of this occurred with the consent of the Indian nations concerned or in keeping with aboriginal and treaty rights. On those rare occasions when federal policy or law coincided with the desires of Indian people or their traditional laws it was by accident rather than by design.

The size of most reserves, created either by the terms of a particular treaty or through unilateral declaration by the Crown, shrank drastically during the nineteenth and most of the twentieth century as federal agents continually prodded Indian communities to surrender land for sale to non-Indians. This tendency did not come to an end until the Indian agent system was abolished by the federal government under pressure from the chiefs and their councils starting in 1965 at Walpole Island First Nation (near Detroit).

The federal government has also exercised total authority in determining which of the aboriginal peoples it would recognize and for what purposes. While many Indian nations were subdivided into bands and located upon reserves, many other Indian communities were simply overlooked. This practice was especially common in remote regions of central and western Canada. The Indian Act was also not extended to the province of Newfoundland after it joined Canada in 1949, and none of Newfoundland's dozen Micmac or Innu communities obtained reserves or had recognized Indian band governments, although one was finally established in 1984.

Since earlier efforts to assimilate aboriginal peoples into Canadian society failed, the federal government established a system to remove aboriginal children from their families through the creation of residential schools. Residential schools services were initially delivered by religious organizations but in 1874 the Canadian government began to share in their administration. To achieve the goal of complete absorption into Canadian society, aboriginal children were isolated from their families, placed in communities other than their own and prohibited from speaking their own language. Instead of achieving integration, the result was a loss of heritage, religious beliefs, and knowledge of their cultures and ways of life. In addition, the infliction of sexual and physical abuse at such schools frequently took place, which has recently been exposed. In 1998 the government acknowledged the social devastation caused by these schools, including the existence of such abuse, as part of "Gathering Strength," a policy that introduced funding and new programs intended to renew the lines of communication with aboriginal people. The Aboriginal Healing Foundation was also established with $350 million in funding to support counseling services for victims of residential schools. By May 2000, 3,431 separate legal actions had been launched involving 6,324 residential school victims against the Canadian government.

## The Métis and the Inuit

The Métis are a post-contact people whose ancestry is derived initially from intermarriage between Indian women and European traders but who developed a unique character setting them apart as an identifiable group from both of their original sources. In eastern Canada they generally lived at the margins of both Indian and Canadian society. In Manitoba, however, they developed a distinct sense of themselves as a people with a right of self-determination. After the Métis declared a provisional government in the Winnipeg region in 1869, the government of Canada was forced to respond. Negotiations ensued resulting in the creation of the new province through the Manitoba Act in 1871. In order to extinguish their "Indian title," the Manitoba Act also promised the Métis that they would keep their current lands as well as acquire more, for a total of at least 1.4 million acres. Due to extensive fraud, little of this land ever ended up in Métis hands for long.

The Métis have become largely landless people across Canada, forced into becoming squatters on road allowances and other unused Crown land, or they have purchased individual holdings. Only eight Métis communities in Alberta have been treated as distinct and somewhat akin to Indian bands with lands set aside for their exclusive use. Even then this positive action emanated from the provincial government, since the federal government has continued to assert that the Métis did not come within the terms of its constitutional authority under subsection 91(24) for "Indians, and Lands reserved for the Indians." The federal government retained this position despite its late nineteenth century policy of either offering the Métis individual land grants called "scrip" or including them within Indian treaties from western Ontario across the Prairies and up into the Northwest Territories.

The Inuit, called Eskimos in Alaska, generally live north of the tree line in the Arctic region from Labrador, across Quebec to the Alaskan border. This distinct population, which shares few attributes in common with their Indian neighbors to the south, has also fallen largely outside of the unique relationship that has been established between the Crown and southern First Nations. Although the Supreme Court declared in 1939 that the Inuit were within exclusive federal jurisdiction under section 91(24) as being "Indians" in constitutional terms, the federal government did not enact special legislation akin to the Indian Act in reference to the Inuit, nor were treaties negotiated between them and the Crown. Canadian courts have subsequently ruled that the Inuit do possess aboriginal title and other aboriginal rights, as a result forcing the federal government to acknowledge their unique legal rights and their claims to their traditional territory.

## Current Governmental Structure

Over the years, responsibility for First Nations affairs has been handled through a variety of bureaucratic structures, at times being demoted to a mere branch in departments with varying other responsibilities from citizenship and immigration (1949–1965) to natural resources (1936–1949, 1965). The Department of Indian Affairs and Northern Development, currently called Indian and Northern Affairs Canada (INAC), was established by an act of Parliament in 1967. Its mandate is twofold: (1) to supervise and promote the economic and political development of the remaining northern territories that have not yet obtained provincehood; and (2) to administer the Indian Act and deliver authorized federal funds and programs to those aboriginal people who qualify to receive them. INAC has interpreted this latter mandate to be primarily limited to bands recognized under the *Indian Act*. Post-secondary education and uninsured health benefits are extended to registered Indians who reside outside of reserves, while the Inuit also receive limited special programs. The Métis and unrecognized Indians, who number approximately half a million people, are ignored by INAC except for those who live in the territories and benefit from programs provided by this department to all northerners. As a result, more than 75 percent of aboriginal people receive few benefits from INAC or under the *Indian Act* and their communities have no recognized aboriginal governments.

INAC is divided internally along the lines of its two major mandates, Northern Affairs and Indian and Inuit Affairs. The Northern Affairs Program is the primary conduit for fostering northern development. This program administers all aspects of government policy associated with the territories. The two territorial governments (the Yukon and Northwest Territories) were increased to three in 1999 as a result of a plebiscite in May 1992 and an agreement between the Inuit and the government of Canada to divide the Northwest Territories into two separate regions, with the eastern territory called Nunavut. These territorial governments are locally elected as responsible governments, but they do not yet have the status of provinces with sovereign powers confirmed by the constitution such that their authority is delegated by Parliament. INAC and its predecessor departments exercised almost full colonial authority from the time this region became part of Canada in 1870 (and concerning the Arctic Islands after they were transferred from Great Britain to Canada in 1881) up until the 1970s. Over the last two decades, INAC's role has changed dramatically with specific authority passing to the two new territorial governments on a subject-by-subject basis in almost all areas within normal provincial jurisdiction.

The far larger role of INAC, in terms of staff, budgetary expenditures, and people affected, relates to Indian and Inuit affairs. This sector is handled administratively by a number of separate branches, each with its own assistant deputy minister, who reports to the Deputy Minister, the senior public servant for INAC, and to the Minister, who is a member of Parliament appointed to this portfolio in cabinet by the Prime Minister. These INAC divisions include: Claims and Indian Government, which deals with aboriginal title or comprehensive land claims, specific claims related to treaties, reserve lands or moneys and Indian self-government; Lands and Trust Services, which relates to the regular management of natural resources on reserve lands, environmental protection, band governance, administration of estates of deceased Indians who resided on reserves, preservation of band moneys raised from leasing or sale of reserve lands, registration of Indians under the act, compliance with treaty obligations, and the Indian Taxation Advisory Board; Policy and Strategic Direction, which covers legislative and other new initiatives, as well as policy research and evaluating existing programs; Socio-Economic Policy and Programs, which sets out the types of programs that will be included in the socio-economic sphere and how these programs will be delivered and funded; and Corporate Services which provides accounting and technical services to the department as a whole.

Beneath this structure in headquarters is a system of regional and district offices across the country. Historically this structure was built from the individual Indian agents assigned to specific reserves, reporting to numerous local offices responsible for a larger area through to regional offices in each province and territory, other than in Atlantic Canada where the four provinces shared one regional office. These regional offices would then report to the national headquarters in Ottawa. After the withdrawal of Indian agents from the individual reserves starting in 1965, INAC increased the importance and number of district offices to carry out much of the former role of the agents but with a philosophy of providing support rather than direct control. This structure has been changed since 1988 with most district offices abolished, and federal officials further pulled back to the regional offices as the First Nations have themselves taken over almost all of the program delivery function and administration from INAC. The latter now views itself more as a provider of technical assistance when requested, a planner of program structures, a source of funds, and the primary negotiating representative for the federal government regarding Indian and Inuit issues. These developments have resulted in a 50 percent reduction in the size of INAC while its budget has more than doubled over the past fifteen years in response to the underdeveloped conditions on most reserves.

The Métis and off-reserve Indians, whether registered under the *Indian Act* or not, are largely ignored by INAC. A federal minister with other cabinet duties has carried the added role since 1985 of serving as an intermediary for this huge population with the rest of the government of Canada. In reality, the Métis and off-reserve Indians receive minimal funding for their political organizations and few programs to address their special needs.

### Role of the Provinces

The initial constitutional theory suggested that in 1867 the federal government was given exclusive authority over First Nations affairs and the provinces had no role to play. Therefore, for many years the federal government alone negotiated treaties and passed special legislation on aboriginal issues. The courts, however, ruled that the provinces held full Crown title whenever aboriginal title was surrendered to the federal government. This left the federal government with many costs and few advantages, and gave the federal government no power to sell aboriginal lands for the benefit of the original owners. In order to encourage First Nations to relinquish their interests in reserve lands, complementary statutes were passed by Parliament and several provinces, and federal-provincial agreements were signed with others, expressly to empower the federal government to take Indian surrenders and sell the land in question to third parties so as to obtain the proceeds for the benefit of the surrendering First Nation.

While provincial governments had little desire to expend money on aboriginal people, they were very desirous of extending their laws to both aboriginal peoples and their lands. Numerous court battles have been fought in this century by provinces seeking to enforce their laws. As opposed to the landmark decision of the U.S. Supreme Court in 1832 in *Worcester v. Georgia*, in which the Court ruled that state law had no force on Indian lands even regarding non-Indians, the Canadian courts have generally upheld provincial laws in reference to all Inuit, Métis, and off-reserve Indians except where aboriginal or treaty rights are in issue. Provincial laws are also applied on Indian reserves when they relate to non-land matters unless they conflict with federal laws, treaties, aboriginal rights, or Indian laws.

Since federal legislation does not provide a comprehensive code of laws on reserves and because Indian sovereignty has not yet been recognized by Canadian courts, provincial statutes frequently are the prevailing law on many subjects. The federal government has entered into agreements with all provincial governments to provide many social and other services under provincial law to First Nations since the 1960s. This has led most provinces over time to begin slowly to contribute some of their own funds to meeting the immense needs of First Nations. Today they are a significant source of financial assistance.

As mentioned earlier, the federal government has denied most responsibility for aboriginal peoples outside of reserves. The provincial governments have consistently complained about this policy and charged that it constitutes an abdication of federal constitutional authority. With the exception of Alberta, the provinces have argued that they lack the constitutional capacity to enact special laws for Métis and non-registered Indians. The courts have also cast doubt on their ability to enact laws that would explicitly refer to on-reserve Indians. As a result, the provinces generally treat aboriginal peoples, except for the reserve communities, the same as other residents with occasional special programs to address economic disadvantages or cultural issues.

The commencement of constitutional negotiations on aboriginal matters in 1982 compelled the provinces to re-evaluate their attitudes and responses toward aboriginal peoples. Over the last twenty years each province has created a department or secretariat mandated to take the lead responsibility in dealing with aboriginal peoples in constitutional talks and in local issues. These agencies are, however, minuscule both in staff size and in budget compared to INAC.

### Aboriginal Organizations

Due in large part to divergent constitutional and governmental treatment and influenced as well by major cultural and historical differences, the aboriginal peoples have organized themselves since 1970 along separate lines. The reserve-based governments have grouped themselves together into tribal councils within their regions and into province-wide bodies consisting solely of the *Indian Act* chiefs. At a national level they are represented politically by the Assembly of First Nations (formerly called the National Indian Brotherhood). The Inuit also have associations in each region across the North and a national body called the Inuit Tapirisat of Canada. The Métis in western Canada have an organization in each of their respective provinces and a federal coordinating body, the Métis National Council. The fourth group, which politically seeks to represent the largest part of the aboriginal population, is the Congress of Aboriginal Peoples (formerly called the Native Council of Canada). Its constituents are the off-reserve Indians across Canada and those Métis living in Quebec, Atlantic Canada and the North. It also has affiliated associations in the provinces and two of three territories.

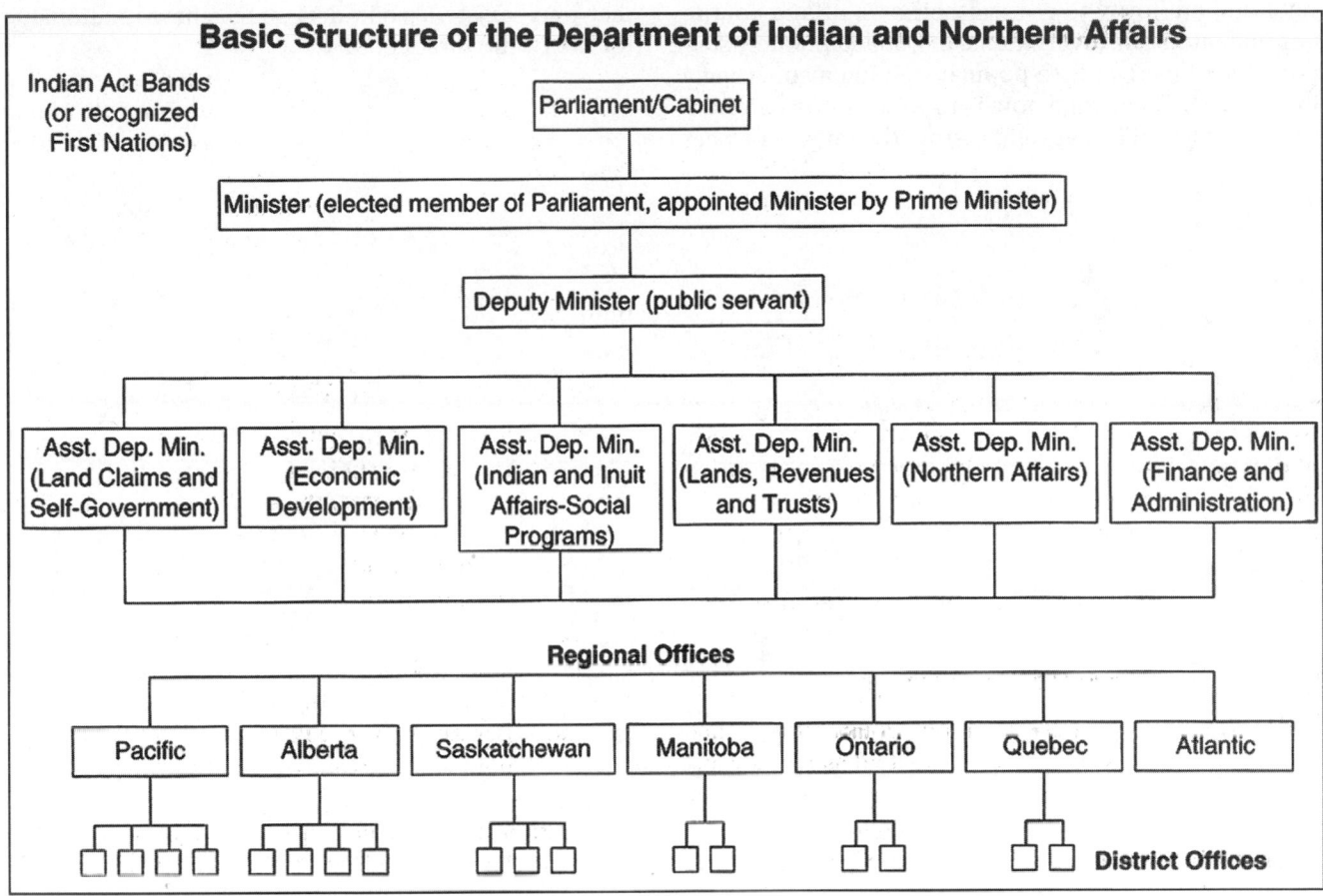

## Basic Structure of the Department of Indian and Northern Affairs

**Indian Act Bands (or recognized First Nations)**

Parliament/Cabinet

Minister (elected member of Parliament, appointed Minister by Prime Minister)

Deputy Minister (public servant)

Asst. Dep. Min. (Land Claims and Self-Government) | Asst. Dep. Min. (Economic Development) | Asst. Dep. Min. (Indian and Inuit Affairs-Social Programs) | Asst. Dep. Min. (Lands, Revenues and Trusts) | Asst. Dep. Min. (Northern Affairs) | Asst. Dep. Min. (Finance and Administration)

**Regional Offices**

Pacific | Alberta | Saskatchewan | Manitoba | Ontario | Quebec | Atlantic

**District Offices**

Department of Indian and Northern Affairs organization chart, 1993. (Courtesy of the UCLA American Indian Studies Center)

In addition to these political organizations, there is also a range of more specifically focused groups including the Native Women's Association of Canada (as well as two Métis and an Inuit women's association), the Aboriginal Youth Council of Canada, the National Association of Friendship Centres (consisting of local aboriginal community service centers in most towns and cities across the country), and a number of profession-specific organizations.

The political associations are primarily responsible for advancing the broad legal and rights agenda. The four national groups have participated in the constitutional negotiations since 1982 and have been in the forefront of attempting to develop a new relationship with both federal and provincial governments. See also the section on Canadian Native activism in chapter 7.

## Conclusion

Canadian courts in recent years have begun to articulate a new relationship between aboriginal peoples and the Crown. A fiduciary obligation has clearly been imposed on the federal government, designed to require it to adhere to a high standard of honorable dealings with Indian, Inuit, and Métis peoples. A similar obligation appears to apply to the provincial governments. The precise scope of this duty, particularly regarding the provinces, is not yet certain, but it obviously means a dramatic alteration in the way governments have developed their policies to advance their own interests, often at the expense of aboriginal peoples. The constitutional recognition and affirmation of aboriginal and treaty rights in 1982 has already led to a significant elevation in the legal status of aboriginal peoples and their unique rights, even to the extent of rendering certain federal and provincial legislation inapplicable when it conflicts with these rights. Efforts at further constitutional change in 1992, which contained formal confirmation of the inherent right to self-government with aboriginal governments as one of three orders of government, was rejected along with the rest of a major overhaul of the Canadian Constitution by the electorate on 26 October 1992. Despite this, the drive by aboriginal peoples to gain further legal respect for their right and authority to govern their own affairs continues unabated. All governments in Canada publicly support this objective, with popular opinion also strongly in favor. The challenge now is to jettison the paternalism of the last 125 years and restore the mutual respect that once existed while designing a new relationship for the twenty-first century.

*Bradford W. Morse*
*University of Ottawa*

# U.S. Government Agencies

## ◆ THE WHITE HOUSE AND CONGRESS

### DEPUTY ASSISTANT TO THE PRESIDENT FOR INTERGOVERNMENTAL AFFAIRS
Old Executive Office Bldg., Room 160
17th and Pennsylvania Ave. N.W.
Washington, DC 20500
(202) 456–2577

### OFFICE OF PUBLIC LIAISONS
SPECIAL ASSISTANTS TO THE PRESIDENT
Old Executive Office Bldg., Room 122
Washington, DC 20500
(202) 456–2930
www.whitehouse.gov

### U.S. HOUSE OF REPRESENTATIVES
COMMITTEE ON INTERIOR AND INSULAR AFFAIRS
1324 Longworth House Office Bldg.
Washington, DC 20515
(202) 225–2761
resourcescommittee.house.gov/
Subcommittees include: Water, Power, and Offshore Energy Resources; Mining and Natural Resources; National Parks and Public Lands; Insular and International Affairs; Energy and the Environment; General Oversight and California Desert Lands.

### U.S. SENATE
COMMITTEE ON INDIAN AFFAIRS
838 Hart Senate Office Bldg., Room SH 838
Washington, DC 20510
(202) 224–2251
indian.senate.gov

## ◆ U.S. DEPARTMENT OF THE INTERIOR

### BUREAU OF INDIAN AFFAIRS (BIA)
Central Office
1849 C St. N.W.
Washington, DC 20245
(202) 208–3711
www.doi.gov/bureau-indian-affairs.html

There are several tiers to the Bureau of Indian Affairs structure: under the national office are area offices that cover the United States; under each area office are separate agencies (with a few field offices, schools, or other designations); under each of those agencies or field offices is one or more Indian communities.

To locate the BIA offices that have jurisdiction over a particular Indian community, first find the community's address in the directory of North American Indian Communities (Chapter 3). Locate the area office for that state, then find the community listed under its respective agency. Occasionally, an Indian community is under the direct jurisdiction of an area office, with no intermediate agency.

Note that some states are under the jurisdiction of two area offices (for example, part of Montana is under Billings, while the rest is under Portland).

### ABERDEEN AREA OFFICE
115 Fourth Ave. S.E.
Aberdeen, SD 57401
(605) 226–7343
www.doi.gov/bia/aberdeen/

AGENCIES:

#### CHEYENNE RIVER AGENCY
P.O. Box 590
Eagle Butte, SD 57625
(605) 964–4155

#### CROW CREEK AGENCY
P.O. Box 139
Fort Thompson, SD 57339
(605) 245–2311

#### FORT BERTHOLD AGENCY
P.O. Box 370
New Town, ND 58763
(701) 627–4707

FORT TOTTEN AGENCY
P.O. Box 270
Fort Totten, ND 58335
(701) 766–4545

LOWER BRULE AGENCY
P.O. Box 190
Lower Brule, SD 57548
(605) 473–5512

PINE RIDGE AGENCY
P.O. Box 1203
Pine Ridge, SD 57770
(605) 867–5121

ROSEBUD AGENCY
P.O. Box 550
Rosebud, SD 57570
(605) 747–2224

SISSETON AGENCY
P.O. Box 688
Agency Village, SD 57262
(605) 698–7676

STANDING ROCK AGENCY
P.O. Box E
Fort Yates, ND 58538
(701) 854–3422

TURTLE MOUNTAIN AGENCY
P.O. Box 60
Belcourt, ND 58316
(701) 477–3191

WINNEBAGO AGENCY
R.R. 1, Box 18
Winnebago, NE 68071
(402) 878–2502

YANKTON AGENCY
P.O. Box 577
Wagner, SD 57380
(605) 384–3651

## SOUTHWESTERN REGIONAL OFFICE
615 First St. N.W., Box 26567
Albuquerque, NM 87125–6567
(505) 346–7590

AGENCIES:

JICARILLA AGENCY
P.O. Box 167
Dulce, NM 87528
(505) 759–3951

LAGUNA AGENCY
P.O. Box 1448
Laguna, NM 87026
(505) 552–6654

MESCALERO AGENCY
P.O. Box 189
Mescalero, NM 88340
(505) 671–4421

BIA NORTHERN PUEBLOS AGENCY
P.O. Box 4269
Espanolia, NM 87533
(505) 753–1406

BIA RAMAH-NAVAJO AGENCY
Ramah, NM 87321
(505) 775–3235

SOUTHERN PUEBLOS AGENCY
P.O. Box 1667
Albuquerque, NM 87103
(505) 766–3021

SOUTHERN UTE AGENCY
P.O. Box 315
Ignacio, CO 81137
(970) 563–4512

UTE MOUNTAIN UTE AGENCY
P.O. Box KK
Towaoc, CO 81334
(303) 565–8471

ZUNI PUEBLO AGENCY
P.O. Box 339
Zuni, NM 87327
(505 782 4481

## SOUTHERN PLAINS REGIONAL OFFICE
WCD Office Complex, Box 368
Anadarko, OK 73005–0368
(405) 247–6673

AGENCIES:

CONCHO FIELD OFFICE
1635 East Hwy. 66
El Reno, OK 73036
(405) 262–7481

HORTON AGENCY
P.O. Box 31
Horton, KS 66439
(785) 486–2161

PAWNEE AGENCY
P.O. Box 440
Pawnee, OK 74058
(918) 762–2585

SHAWNEE FIELD OFFICE
624 West Independence St., Suite 109
Shawnee, OK 74801
(405) 273–0317

## ROCKY MOUNTAIN REGIONAL OFFICE
316 North 26th St.
Billings, MT 59101–1397
(406) 657–6315

AGENCIES:

BLACKFEET AGENCY
P.O. Box 880
Browning, MT 59417
(406) 338–7544

CROW AGENCY
P.O. Box 69
Crow Agency, MT 59022
(406) 638–4433

FORT BELKNAP AGENCY
Rte. 1
P.O. Box 66
Harlem, MT 59526
(406) 353–2205
www.fortbelknap.com

FORT PECK AGENCY
P.O. Box 1027
Poplar, MT 59255
(406) 768–5155

NORTHERN CHEYENNE AGENCY
P.O. Box 40
Cheyenne Ave.
Lame Deer, MT 59043
(406) 477–8242

ROCKY BOY'S AGENCY
R.R. 1 Box 542
Box Elder, MT 59521
(406) 395–4476

WIND RIVER AGENCY
P.O. Box 158
Fort Washake, WY 82514
(307) 332–7812

## EASTERN REGIONAL OFFICE
3701 North Fairfax Dr., Suite 260
Arlington, VA 22203
(703) 235–2571

AGENCIES:

CHEROKEE AGENCY
Cherokee, NC 28719
(828) 497–9131

CHOCTAW AGENCY
421 Powell
Philadelphia, MS 39350
(601) 656–1521

MICCOSUKEE AGENCY
P.O. Box 440021
Tamiami Trail
Maimi, FL 33144
(305) 223–8380
www.miccosukeetribe.com

NEW YORK FIELD OFFICE
FEDERAL BUILDING
100 S. Clinton St.
P.O. Box 7366
Syracuse, NY 13261–7366
(315) 448–0620

SEMINOLE AGENCY
6075 Stirling Rd.
Hollywood, FL 33024
(954) 581–7050

## ALASKAN REGIONAL OFFICE
P.O. Box 25520
Juneau, AK 99802–5520
(907) 586–7177
www.ak.bia.gov/

AGENCIES:

BIA PUBLIC AFFAIRS
P.O. Box 80947
Seattle, WA 98104
(202) 208–3711

FAIRBANKS FIELD OFFICE
Federal Bldg. and Courthouse
101 12th Ave., Rm 166
Fairbanks, AK 99701
(907) 456–0229

WEST CENTRAL ALASKA FIELD OFFICE
3601 C St. Suite 1100
Anchorage, AK 99503–5947
(907) 271–4088

## MID WEST REGIONAL OFFICE
331 Second Ave. S.
Minneapolis, MN 55401–2241
(612) 713–4410

AGENCIES:

GREAT LAKES AGENCY
615 Main St. W., Box 2473
Ashland, WI 54806
(715) 682–4527

MICHIGAN FIELD OFFICE
2901.5 I-75 Business Spur
Sault Ste. Marie, MI 49783
(906) 632–6809

MINNESOTA AGENCY
522 Minnesota Ave Rm 418
Federal Building
Bemidji, MN 56601
(218) 751–2011

RED LAKE AGENCY
SELF GOVERNMENT OFFICE
56671 Hwy 1
Red Lake, MN 56671
(218) 679–3361

EASTERN OKLAHOMA REGIONAL OFFICE
101 North Fifth St.
Muskogee, OK 74401–6206
(918) 687–2296

AGENCIES:

ARDMORE AGENCY
214 Stanley St. S.W.
Ardmore, OK 73402
(405) 226–4821

MIAMI FIELD OFFICE
P.O. Box 391
Miami, OK 74355
(918) 542–3396

OKMULGEE AGENCY
P.O. Box 370
Okmulgee, OK 74447
(918) 756–3950

OSAGE AGENCY
Pawhuska, OK 74056
(918) 287–1032

TAHLEQUAH AGENCY
P.O. Box 948
Tahlequah, OK 74465
(918) 456–0671

TALIHINA AGENCY
P.O. Drawer H
Talihina, OK 74571
(918) 567–2207

WEWOKA AGENCY
P.O. Box 1060
Wewoka, OK 74884
(405) 257–6257

NAVAJO REGIONAL OFFICE
P.O. Box 1060
Gallup, NM 87305
(505) 863–8221

AGENCIES:

CHINLE AGENCY
P.O. Box 7 H
Chinle, AZ 86503
(520) 674–5110

EASTERN NAVAJO AGENCY
P.O. Box 328
Crownpoint, NM 87313
(505) 786–6100

FORT DEFIANCE AGENCY
P.O. Box 619
Fort Defiance, AZ 86504
(520) 729–7224

SHIPROCK AGENCY
P.O. Box 966
Shiprock, NM 87420
(505) 368–4427

WESTERN NAVAJO AGENCY
P.O. Box 127
Tuba City, AZ 86045
(602) 283–4531

WESTERN REGIONAL OFFICE
P.O. Box 10
400 N. 5th St.
Phoenix, AZ 85001–0010
(602) 379–6600
phxao.az.bia.gov

AGENCIES:

COLORADO RIVER AGENCY
Rte. 1, Box 9-C
Parker, AZ 85344
(520) 669–6121

EASTERN NEVADA FIELD OFFICE
1555 Shoshoni Circle Dr.
Elko, NV 89801
(775) 738–0568

FORT APACHE AGENCY
P.O. Box 560
Whiteriver, AZ 85941
(520) 338–5357

FORT YUMA AGENCY
P.O. Box 1591
Yuma, AZ 85364
(520) 782–1202

HOPI AGENCY
P.O. Box 158
Keams Canyon, AZ 86034
(520) 738–2228

PAPAGO AGENCY
P.O. Box 578
Sells, AZ 85634
(520) 383–3250

PIMA AGENCY
P.O. Box 8
Sacaton, AZ 85247
(520)5623985

SALT RIVER AGENCY
2000 E. McDowell Rd
Scottsdale, AZ 85256
(602) 640–2168

SAN CARLOS AGENCY
P.O. Box 209
San Carlos, AZ 85550
(520) 475–2321

U.S. GOVERNMENT
SAN CARLOS IRRIGATION PROJECT
P.O. Box 250
Coolidge, AZ 85228
(520) 723–1179

SOUTHERN PAIUTE FIELD STATION
P.O. Box 720
St. George, UT 84771
(435) 674–9720

TRUXTON CANON AGENCY
P.O. Box 37
Valentine, AZ 86437
(602) 769–2241

UINTAH AND OURAY AGENCY
P.O. Box 130
Fort Duchesne, UT 84026
(435) 722–4300

WESTERN NEVADA AGENCY
1677 Hot Springs Rd.
Carson City, NV 89706
(775) 887–3500

NORTHWEST REGION OFFICE
Federal Building
111th Ave. N.E.
Portland, OR 97232–4169
(503) 231–6702

AGENCIES:

COLVILLE AGENCY
P.O. Box 111
Nespelem, WA 99155
(509) 634–2316

DIVISION OF FLATHEAD IRRIGATION
P.O. Box 666
St. Ignatius, MT 59865
(406) 745–2661

FLATHEAD AGENCY
P.O. Box 40
Pablo, MT 59855
(406) 675–2700

FORT HALL AGENCY
P.O. Box 220
Fort Hall, ID 83203
(208) 238–2301

METLAKATLA FIELD STATION
P.O. Box 450
Metlakatla, AK 99926
(907) 886–3791

NORTHERN IDAHO AGENCY
99 Agency Rd.
Lapwai, ID 83540–0277
(208) 843–2300
www.nezperce.org

OLYMPIC PENINSULA AGENCY
P.O. Box 48
Abordin, WA 98520
(360) 533–9100

PUGET SOUND AGENCY
Federal Building
2707 Colby Ave., Suite 1101
Everett, WA 98201
(425) 258–2651

SILETZ AGENCY
P.O. Box 569
Siletz, OR 97380
(541) 444–2679

SPOKANE AGENCY
P.O. Box 389
Wellpinit, WA 99040
(509) 258–4561

UMATILLA AGENCY
P.O. Box 520
Pendleton, OR 97801
(503) 278–3786

WAPATO IRRIGATION PROJECT
P.O. Box 220
Wapato, WA 98951
(509) 877–3155

WARM SPRINGS AGENCY
P.O. Box 1239
Warm Springs, OR 97761
(503) 553–1161

YAKIMA AGENCY
P.O. Box 632
Toppenish, WA 98948
(509) 865–2255

SACRAMENTO REGIONAL OFFICE
2800 Cottage Way
Sacramento, CA 95825
(916) 978–6002

AGENCIES:

CENTRAL CALIFORNIA AGENCY
1824 Tribute Rd., Suite J
Sacramento, CA 95815 4308
(916) 566–7121

NORTHERN CALIFORNIA AGENCY
1900 Churn RD, Suite 300
Redding, CA 96002–0292
(530) 246–5141

PALM SPRINGS FIELD AGENCY
P.O. Box 2245
650 E. Talcwith Canyon Way, Suite A
Palm Springs, CA 92263
(760) 416–2133

SOUTHERN CALIFORNIA AGENCY
2038 iowa Ave., Suite 101
Riverside, CA 92507
(909) 276–6624

INDIAN ARTS AND CRAFTS BOARD
U.S. Dept. of the Interior, Room 4004
1849 C St., N.W.
Washington, DC 20240
(202) 208–3773
www.iacb.doi.gov

OFFICE OF TRIBAL SERVICES
1849 C St. N.W.
Washington, DC 20240
(202) 208–3463

OFFICE OF TRUST RESPONSIBILITIES
1849 C St. N.W., MS 4513-MIB
Washington, DC 20240
(202) 208–5831
www.doi.gov/bureau-indian-affairs.html

## ◆ ADDITIONAL U.S. GOVERNMENT AGENCIES

Note that most state governments have commissions and offices that address Indian affairs, education,and civil rights. Contact Information/Communications in the appropriate state capital.

ADMINISTRATION FOR NATIVE AMERICANS
370 L'Enfant Promenade Mail Stop 348 F
Washington, DC 20447–0002
(202) 690–7776
www.acf.dhhs.gov/programs/ana/org.htm

ADMINISTRATION ON AGING OFFICE FOR
AMERICAN INDIAN, ALASKAN NATIVE
AND NATIVE HAWAIIAN PROGRAMS
330 Independence Ave.
Washington, DC 20201
(202) 619–0724

DEPARTMENT OF AGRICULTURE
14th & Independence Ave. S.W.
Washington, DC 20250
(202) 720–8732
www.usda.gov

DEPARTMENT OF HEALTH AND HUMAN
SERVICES
Humphrey Bldg.
200 Independence Ave. S.W.
Washington, DC 20201
(202) 619–0257
www.dhhs.gov

DEPARTMENT OF HOUSING AND URBAN
DEVELOPMENT (HUD)
451 Seventh St. S.W.
Washington, DC 20410
(202) 708–1422
www.hud.gov

DEPARTMENT OF JUSTICE
Tenth and Constitution Ave. N.W.
Washington, DC 20530
(202) 514–2000
www.usdoj.gov

**DEPARTMENT OF LABOR**
Division of Indian and Native American Programs
Room 4645
200 Constitution Ave. N. W.
Washington, DC 20210
(202) 219–8502

**DEPARTMENT OF LABOR**
EMPLOYMENT AND TRAINING ADMINISTRATION
Patrick Henry Bldg.
601 D St., N.W., Room 6102
Washington, DC 20213
(202) 219–6666

**DEPARTMENT OF TRANSPORTATION**
FEDERAL HIGHWAY ADMINISTRATION
400 Seventh Street, SW
Washington, DC 20590
(202) 366–0537

**INDIAN ACTIVITIES–OFFICE OF
INTERGOVERNMENTAL AFFAIRS**
14th & Independence Ave. S.W., Room 219-A
Washington, DC 20250
(202) 720–7095

**OFFICE OF NATIVE AMERICAN PROGRAMS**
451 Seventh St. S.W., Room 4126
Washington, DC 20410
(202) 401–7909

**DEPARTMENT OF THE INTERIOR**
INDIAN EDUCATION PROGRAMS
Federal Office Bldg. 6, Room 3530
1849 C St., N.W., MS-3512 MIB
Washington, DC 20240–0001

(202) 208–6123
www.oiep.bia.edu

**INDIAN HEALTH SERVICE**
Park Lawn Bldg., Room 6–05
5600 Fischer's Ln.
Rockville, MD 20853
(301) 443–1083
www.ihs.gov

**LAND AND NATURAL RESOURCES DIVISION**
INDIAN RESOURCES SECTION
P.O. Box 44378
601 Pennsylvania Ave. N.W., Room 6702
Washington, DC 20026–4378
(202) 514–2000

**RURAL DEVELOPMENT**
NATURAL RESOURCES CONSERVATION SERVICE
LIAISON FOR INDIAN ASSISTANCE
South Bldg., Room 6013 South
14th & Independence Ave. S.W.
Washington, DC 20250–2890
(202) 720–2847
www.nhq.nrcs.usda.gov

**OFFICE OF INDIAN HOUSING**
451 Seventh St. S.W., Room 4230
Washington, DC 20410
(202) 708–1015

**PUBLIC AND INDIAN HOUSING**
451 Seventh St. S.W., Room 4100
Washington, DC 20410
(202) 708–0950
www.hud.gov

# Canadian Government Organizations

ABORIGINAL BUSINESS
REGIONAL INDUSTRIAL EXPANSION
235 Queen St., 1st Floor, West Tower
Ottawa, ON K1A 0H5
(613) 954–5430

ABORIGINAL JUSTICE LEARNING NETWORK
St. Andrews Tower, 10th Floor
284 Wellington Street
Ottawa, Ontario K1A 0H8
canada.justice.gc.ca/en/ps/ajln/index.html

ABORIGINAL RELATION HUMAN
    RESOURCES DEVELOPMENT CANADA
140 Promenade du Portage, Phase IV
Hull, Quebec K1A 0J9
(819) 997–8677
www.hrdc-drhc.gc.ca/hrib/aro/common/home.shtml

CANADA MORTGAGE AND HOUSING
    CORPORATION
700 Montreal Rd.
Ottawa, ON K1A 0P7
(613) 748–2000
www.cmhc-schl.gc.ca

CORRECTIONAL SERVICES CANADA (CSC)
Aboriginal Issues Branch
Correctional Operations Programs
340 Laurier Ave. W., 4th Floor, Section 4E
Ottawa, ON K1A 0P9
(613) 995–2555
(613) 992–5891
www.csc-scc.gc.ca/text/prgrm/correctional/
    ab_e.shtml

FEDERAL-PROVINCIAL RELATIONS
    OFFICE (FPRO)
INTER GOVERNMENTAL AFFAIRS SECRETARIAT
Privy Council Office
90 Sparks St., RM 717
Ottawa, ON K1A 0A3
(613) 992–3097

www.pco-bcp.gc.ca

INDUSTRY, SCIENCE AND TECHNOLOGY
    CANADA (ISTC)
ABORIGINAL BUSINESS
235 Queen St., 1st Floor
Ottawa, ON K1A 0H5
(613) 954–4064
www.abc.gc.ca

NATIONAL LIBRARY OF CANADA (NLC)
Native Peoples of Canada
395 Wellington St.
Ottawa, ON K1A 0N4
(613) 995–7969
www.nlc-bnc.ca/caninfo/ep030.htm#305.897

NATURAL RESOURCES CANADA (EMR)
LEGAL SURVEYS
615 Booth St.
Ottawa, ON K1A 0E9
(613) 995–0947
www.nrcan.gc.ca

REVENUE CANADA-TAXATION (RCT)
Technical Interpretations
16th Floor West Tower A
320 Queens St.
Ottawa, ON K1A 0L5
(613) 957–9226

STATUS OF WOMEN CANADA (SWC)
123 Slates St.
Ottawa, ON K1A 1C3
(613) 995–7835 (subject to change)
www.swc-cfc.gc.ca

TREASURY BOARD SECRETARIAT (TB)
EMPLOYMENT EQUITY
140 O'Conners St.
Ottawa, ON K1A 0G5
(613) 995–2855
www.tbs-sct.gc.ca

## ◆ INDIAN AND NORTHERN AFFAIRS OF CANADA

### INDIAN AND NORTHERN AFFAIRS OF CANADA (INAC)
Terrasses de la Chaudiere
10 Wellington St., North Tower
Ottawa, ON K1A 0H4
(819) 997–0380
www.inac.gc.ca

## ◆ REGIONAL INAC OFFICES

### ALBERTA REGION
Indian and Inuit Affairs
9700 Jasper Ave., 6th Floor
Edmonton, AB T5J 4G2
(780) 495–2773

### ATLANTIC REGION
Indian and Inuit Affairs
40 Havelock St.
P.O. Box 160
Amherst, NS B4H 3Z3
(902) 661–6200

### BRITISH COLUMBIA REGION
Indian and Inuit Affairs
1550 Alberni St., Suite 340
Vancouver, BC V6G 3C5
(604) 666–7891

### MANITOBA REGION
Indian and Inuit
275 Portage Ave., Room 1100
Winnipeg, MB R3B 3A3
(204) 983–4928

### NORTHWEST TERRITORIES REGION
Department of Indian Affairs and Northern
  Development (DIAND)
P.O. Box 1500
Yellowknife, NT X1A 2R3
(867) 669–2500

### NUNAVUT
Department of Indian Affairs and Northern
  Development (DIAND)
P.O. Box 2200
Iqaluit, NU X0A 0H0
(867) 979–1605

### ONTARIO REGION
Indian and Inuit Affairs
25 St. Clair Ave. East, 5th Floor
Toronto, ON M4T 1M2
(416) 973–6234

### QUEBEC REGION
Indian and Northern Affairs Canada
320 St. Joseph Street East
P.O. Box 51127, Postal Outlet G. Roy
Quebec, Quebec G1K 8Z7
(418) 648–7551

### SASKATCHEWAN REGION
Indian and Inuit Affairs
2221 Cornwall St.
Regina, SK S4P 4M2
(306) 780–5945

### YUKON REGION
Department of Indian Affairs & Northern
  Development (DIAND)
345–300 Main St.
Whitehorse, Yukon Y1A 2B5
(867) 667–3100

# Non-Government Organizations

Non-government organizations are recognized by the United Nations as international agencies.

## INDIGENOUS SURVIVAL INTERNATIONAL
298 Elgin St., Suite 105
Ottawa, ON K2P 1M3
(613) 230–3616

## INTER-AMERICAN INDIAN INSTITUTE
General Secretariat
Pan American Union
avenida de las fuentes 106
colonia jardines zel pedregal
01900 Mexico D.F.
(525) 595–8410
www.oas.org/EN/PINFO/OAS/olorga7e.htm

## INTERNATIONAL WORK GROUP FOR INDIGENOUS AFFAIRS
Frederiksholms Kanal 4A
DK 1220 Copenhagen
Denmark

## INUIT CIRCUMPOLAR CONFERENCE
3201 C Street, #608
Anchorage, Alaska 99503
(907) 563–6917
www.inusiaat.com/beluga.htm

## References

### U.S. Administration of Indian Affairs

Barsh, Russel L., and Katherine Diaz-Knauf. "The Structure of Federal Aid for Indian Programs in the Decade of Prosperity, 1970–1980." *American Indian Quarterly* 8, no. 1 (1984): 1–35.

Brookings Institution. Institute for Government Research. *The Problem of Indian Administration.* Baltimore, Md.: John Hopkins University, 1928. This work is commonly referred to as the *Merriam Report.*

Cahn, Edgar S., ed. *Our Brother's Keeper: The Indian in White America.* Washington, D.C.: New Community Press, 1969.

Champagne, Duane. "Organizational Change and Conflict: A Case Study of the Bureau of Indian Affairs." *American Indian Culture and Research Journal* 7, no. 3 (1983): 3–28.

Danziger, Edmund J., Jr. "A New Beginning or the Last Hurrah: American Indian Response to Reform Legislation of the 1970s." *American Indian Culture and Research Journal* 7, no. 4 (1984): 69–84

Deloria, Vine, Jr., ed. *American Indian Policy in the Twentieth Century.* Norman: University of Oklahoma Press, 1985.

Dobyns, Henry F. "Therapeutic Experience of Responsible Democracy." In *The American Indian Today*, edited by Stuart Levine and Nancy O. Lurie, 268–291. Baltimore, Md.: Penguin Books, 1968.

Ebbott, Elizabeth. *Indians in Minnesota.* Edited by Judith Rosenblatt. 4th ed. Minneapolis: University of Minnesota Press, 1985.

Fixico, Donald L. *Termination and Relocation: Federal Indian Policy, 1945–1960.* Albuquerque: University of New Mexico Press, 1986.

Fritz, Henry E. "The Last Hurrah of Christian Humanitarian Indian Reform: The Board of Indian Commissioners, 1909–1918."*Western Historical Quarterly* 16, no. 2 (1985): 147–162.

Green, Donald E., and Thomas V. Tonnesen, eds. *American Indians: Social Justice and Public Policy* Milwaukee: Institute on Race and Ethnicity, University of Wisconsin System, 1991.

Gross, Emma R. *Contemporary Federal Policy Toward American Indians.* Westport, Conn.: Greenwood Press, 1989.

Hauptman, Laurence M. *Formulating American Indian Policy in New York State, 1970–1986.* Albany: State University of New York Press, 1988.

Iverson, Peter. "Building Toward Self-Determination: Plains and Southwestern Indians in the 1940s and 1950s." *Western Historical Quaterly* 16, no. 2 (1985): 163–173.

Jorgensen, Joseph G. "Federal Policies, American Indian Polities and the 'New Federalism'." *American Indian Culture and Research Journal* 10, no. 2 (1986): 1–13.

Josephy, Alvin M., Jr., Joane Nagel and Troy Johnson, eds. *Red Power: The American Indians' Fight for Freedom.* 2d ed. Lincoln: University of Nebraska Press, 1999.

Kvasnicka, Robert M. and Herman J. Viola, eds. *The Commissioners of Indian Affairs, 1824–1977.* Lincoln: University of Nebraska Press, 1979.

Levitan, Sar A. *The Great Society's Poor Law: A New Approach to Poverty.* Baltimore, Md.: Johns Hopkins Press, 1969.

Levitan, Sar A., and William B. Johnston. *Indian Giving: Federal Programs for Native Americans.* Baltimore, Md.: Johns Hopkins University Press, 1975.

Lurie, Nancy O. "The Indian Claims Commission." *Annals of the American Academy of Political and Social Science* 436 (1978): 97–110.

Miller, Bruce G. "After the F.A.P.: Tribal Reorganization after Federal Recognition." *Journal of Ethnic Studies* 17, no. 2 (1989): 89–100.

O'Brien, Sharon. *American Indian Tribal Governments.* Norman: University of Oklahoma Press, 1989.

Paredes, J. Anthony, ed. *Indians of the Southeastern United States in the Late 20th Century.* Tuscaloosa: University of Alabama Press, 1992.

Philp, Kenneth R., ed. *Indian Self-Rule: First-Hand Accounts of Indian-White Relations from Roosevelt to Reagan.* Salt Lake City: Howe Brothers, 1986.

———. *Termination Revisited: American Indians on the Trail to Self-Determination, 1933–1953.* Lincoln: University of Nebraska Press, 1999.

Prucha, Francis P. *The Great Father: The United States Government and the American Indians.* 2 vols. Lincoln: University of Nebraska Press, 1984.

Rusco, Elmer R. *A Fateful Time: The Background and Legislative History of the Indian Reorganization Act.* Reno, Nev.: University of Nevada Press, 2000.

Schmeckebier, Laurence F. *The Office of Indian Affairs: Its History, Activities, and Organization.* Baltimore, Md.: Johns Hopkins Press, 1927.

Sorkin, Alan L. *American Indians and Federal Aid.* Washington, D.C.: Brookings Institution, 1971.

Stuart, Paul. "Administrative Reform in Indian Affairs." *Western Historical Quarterly* 16, no. 2 (1985): 133–146.

Stuart, Paul, and Eloise Rathbone-McCuan. "Indian Elderly in the United States." In *North American Elders: United States and Canadian Perspectives,* edited by Eloise Rathbone-McCuan and Betty Havens, 235–253. Westport, Conn.: Greenwood Press, 1988.

Taylor, Theodore W. *American Indian Policy.* Mt. Airy, Md.: Lomond, 1983.

———. *The Bureau of Indian Affairs.* Boulder, Colo.: Westview Press, 1984.

———. *The States and Their Indian Citizens.* Washington, D.C.: U.S. Government Printing Office, 1972.

Tyler, S. Lyman. *A History of Indian Policy.* Washington, D.C.: Bureau of Indian Affairs, GPO, 1973.

U.S. American Indian Policy Review Commission. *Final Report.* 2 vols. Washington, D.C.: GPO, 1977.

*Paul Stuart*

## Canadian Administration of Aboriginal Affairs

Boldt, Menno. *Surviving as Indians: The Challenge of Self-Government.* Toronto: University of Toronto Press, 1993.

Canada. Department of Indian Affairs and Northern Development. Treaties and Historical Research Centre. *The Historical Development of the Indian Act.* 2d ed. Ottawa, 1978.

Canada. Royal Commission on Aboriginal Peoples. *Report of the Royal Commission on Aboriginal Peoples.* Ottawa, 1996.

Frideres, James. *Aboriginal Peoples in Canada: Contemporary Conflicts.* 5th ed. Scarborough, Ont.: Prentice Hall Allyn and Bacon Canada, 1998.

Hawkes, David C., ed. *Aboriginal Peoples and Government Responsibility: Exploring Federal and Provincial Roles.* Ottawa: Carleton University Press, 1989.

Long, J. Anthony, Menno Boldt, and Leroy Little Bear, eds. *Governments in Conflict?: Provinces and Indian Nations in Canada.* Toronto: University of Toronto Press, 1988.

Morse, Bradford and R. Groves. "Canada's Forgotten Peoples: The Aboriginal Rights of Métis and Non-Status Indians." *Law & Anthropology* 2 (1987): 139–167.

Ponting, J. Rick, ed. *Arduous Journey: Canadian Indians and Decolonization.* Toronto: McClelland and Stewart, 1986.

Ponting, J. Rick, and Roger Gibbins. *Out of Irrelevance: A Socio-Political Introduction to Indian Affairs in Canada.* Toronto: Butterworths, 1980.

Weaver, Sally M. *Making Canadian Indian Policy: The Hidden Agenda 1968–70.* Toronto: University of Toronto Press, 1981.

*Bradford Morse*

# *Activism*

◆ U.S. American Indian Activist Movements   ◆ Canadian Native Activist Movements
◆ U.S. Native American Organizations and Political Advocacy Groups
◆ Canadian Native Organizations

## ◆ U.S. AMERICAN INDIAN ACTIVIST MOVEMENTS

Over the generations since the founding of the United States, American Indian people have been engaged in countless and ongoing struggles to survive as distinct political and cultural communities. Native people not only have defended their rights, immunities, and prerogatives as citizens of tribal governments, but they also have pursued equal political and economic rights as U.S. citizens. The fight for sovereign tribal rights and for individual citizenship rights has been fought on many fronts, including the legal, in the courtrooms and chambers of government throughout U.S. history; the military, on eighteenth- and nineteenth-century battlefields; and, more recently, the political, in cities and on reservations. These battles have met with great resistance as U.S. military, legal, and political might were directed against Native efforts to resist mass extermination, defend treaty rights, maintain tribal sovereignty, preserve Native traditions and cultures, and assert collective and individual human rights.

Native nations have a unique, separate legal and political status in U.S. jurisprudence. Indigenous peoples are unlike any other ethnic groups in the United States. American Indian tribes have a special legal relationship with the federal government by virtue of more than 400 treaties and agreements signed between hundreds of Native nations and the U.S. government. As a result of this legal and treaty relationship, American Indian struggles for survival and equality historically have been complex and multi-situated. For instance, many reservation community development projects face regulations and restrictions from outside governments and often must contend with delays resulting from jurisdictional disputes among tribal, local, state, and federal governments. Legal confusion about,

local resistance to, and competition with casino gaming enterprises on reservations necessitated passage of the 1988 federal Indian Gaming Regulatory Act in order to clarify tribal rights to pursue these development projects. Despite this legislation, sovereign reservation communities must still negotiate with state governments to develop gaming enterprises.

Native nations have had to negotiate an uneven and sometimes unpredictable legal terrain in their efforts to protect and nurture sovereign political, economic, and cultural rights. Their strategies for action reflect the diversity of Native individuals, families, and communities as well as the changing U.S. legal landscape. In the late-nineteenth and twentieth centuries, the two major strategies to secure and protect the rights of indigenous people and Native nations have centered on organized political advocacy and protest activism.

### American Indian Political Advocacy Organizations

**Early Indian Rights Organizations.** The importance of law in U.S. society and the complexity of American Indian legal affairs have placed organizations concerned with legal matters in prominent roles in the struggle for Native rights in the United States. Among the earliest organizations dedicated to protect and further the legal rights and interests of American Indian people were the Women's National Indian Association, founded in 1879, and the Indian Rights Association (IRA), founded in 1882. The IRA remains today the oldest still-active organization of its kind in the United States. Founded in Philadelphia by Quakers and other Christian reformers, the IRA's primary goal, as defined by its constitution, is "to secure to the Indians of the United States the political and civil rights already guaranteed to them by treaty and statute of the United

States, and such as their civilization and circumstances may justify." The Indian Rights Association was followed by a number of other early Indian advocacy organizations, such as the Lake Mohonk Conferences of the Friends of the Indian held between 1883 and 1929 near New Paltz, New York, the American Indian Defense Association founded in 1923, and the Council on Indian Affairs formed in 1943.

Indigenous people also formed their own organizations. Perhaps the most prominent of these was the Society of American Indians (SIA), established in April 1911 by Native people, including Christian converts, orphans, and graduates of U.S. Indian schools. SIA founders generally embraced the idea of assimilation as a path to Native progress. Emerging at almost the same time as SIA were a number of urban fraternal organizations such as the Tepee Order of America, the Brotherhood of North American Indians, and the Grand Council Fire of American Indians, as well as assemblies such as the Indian Association of America, the Indian Confederation of America, and the Northwestern Federation of American Indians. Following passage of the Indian Citizenship Act in 1924, Gertrude Simmons Bonnin (Zitkala-sa) organized the National Council of American Indians.

Native advocacy did not only take the form of organizations and associations. Indigenous people authored books, wrote for periodicals and newspapers, spoke during treaty councils, lobbied members of Congress and U.S. presidents, and traveled on national speaking tours in order to challenge dominant political and social Indian policies and practices. Today their words provide a useful study of the evolution of indigenous critical traditions that shaped twentieth-century protest movements.

Native critics and analysts before the two world wars attempted to shape the way non-Indians understood Native people and issues. Charles Alexander Eastman, a Mdewakanton and Wahpeton Sioux and Boston University-trained physician, wrote books and articles in English for U.S. audiences to assert and celebrate what Salish writer, Mourning Dove, called the "ancient way," and to counter the mainstream's assumption that Indian people were savage and backward. Gertrude Simmons Bonnin told *Atlantic Monthly* in 1902 that her traditions were not simply the equal of anything Americans had to offer, but were superior to Euro-American values.

Other, non-English-speaking Natives spoke through translators in order to make their views known. Chief Plenty Coups of the Crow Nation in Montana and Alfred Kiyana of the Mesquakie Settlement in Iowa spoke with historians, anthropologists, and journalists, not as artifacts from a rapidly disappearing past, but as active critics who rejected the idea of American progress and who refused to embrace the identity of the conquerors.

In addition to writing letters and speaking to researchers and writers, indigenous people attempting to inform outsiders about their communities appeared before numerous congressional committees and examiners on behalf of treaty rights and other Native issues. For instance, after he recorded Snohomish elders' memories of U.S. promises and compared them to treaty texts, tribal member Thomas Bishop published his 1915 "An Appeal to the Government to Fulfill Sacred Promises Made 61 Years Ago." The following year Bishop and other Pacific Northwest Natives organized all the Tulalip agency reservations and several off-reservation communities into the Northwestern Federation of American Indians for the purpose of mounting a region-wide campaign to redeem promises made in treaties.

**American Indian Advocacy Groups after World War II.** During and following the Second World War the focus of American Indian political advocacy organizations changed to reflect the interests of a growing urban Indian population and a new emphasis on tribal sovereignty and self-determination, rather than assimilation. One reason for this shift was a series of intertribal contacts facilitated by John Collier, former commissioner of Indian Affairs, as part of the implementation of the Indian Reorganization Act; these meetings allowed members of geographically separated tribal communities to recognize common needs, interests, and goals and to identify similar treaty rights and violations. Another factor contributing to an increased awareness of the importance of tribal sovereignty and self-determination was the Second World War. Veterans from wartime battlefields and Native workers from wartime industries arrived back on reservations with a new view of relationships among indigenous people, Native nations, and U.S. society. This view was based, in part, on what appeared to many Native people to be the U.S. government's and the American people's failure to recognize Indian contributions to the war effort.

Post-war advocacy groups spoke in a strong voice both for Native rights and tribal sovereignty. For instance, the National Congress of American Indians (NCAI) was founded in 1944 by D'Arcy McNickle, Archie Phinney, Charles E. J. Heacock, and other tribal representatives from both cities and reservations with the goal of representing tribal interests, especially before the U.S. Congress. The NCAI's founding members included the young and the old, war veterans, anthropologists, lawyers, business people, elected state and federal officials, tribal leaders, and even a former professional baseball player, George Eastman. Nearly one-half of the founding members served on IRA-chartered tribal councils. At least four had also been founding members of the Society of American Indians, including Henry Standing Bear and Arthur C. Parker.

Another important postwar Native organization was the National Indian Youth Council (NIYC). Established after the 1961 American Indian Chicago Conference, the NIYC's mission was concerned with the rights of Native communities and Native citizens of the United States. Its leaders argued for the pursuit of interests representing "a greater Indian America," and adopted an agenda concerned with issues involving both reservation and urban Indians. While both the NIYC and the NCAI shared goals of defending and representing the interests of indigenous people and Native nations, the newer NIYC was different from the NCAI in two ways: the younger age of its members and its use of new tactics. The NIYC represented a new generation of Native advocates that grew out of a summer program that brought students from around the country to Boulder, Colorado, to learn about the state of Indian affairs and to introduce them to the Southwest Regional Indian Youth Council. Younger Native people like Clyde Warrior, Melvin Thom, and Hank Adams rejected widely held notions that Indian people could not help themselves or that they must change in order to fit into U.S. society. Warrior was the best known early advocate for taking direct protest action. The NIYC also was a pioneer in supporting the pursuit of federal recognition for several unrecognized Native nations whose representatives attended the Chicago conference and several planning sessions that contributed to a new pride, confidence, and direction among the leaders of unrecognized Native communities that, for the first time in Chicago, shared a public stage with tribal chiefs and chairpersons from around the United States.

Although the younger Native leadership challenged politics as usual in Indian Country, these new Indians were also running for and winning elections as tribal officials and national leaders. In 1964, for instance, the National Congress of American Indians selected a thirty-year-old member of the National Indian Youth Council, Vine Deloria, Jr., to be their new executive director. Members and supporters of NIYC and other later organizations such as the American Indian Movement and American Indians United, formed the organizational backbone of what would become the period of greatest Indian activism in the twentieth century, a protest movement that began in the late 1960s that came to be known as the Red Power Movement.

**American Indian Organizational Growth During the 1960s.** Native organizational growth and activist politics on reservations and in cities after 1961 occurred in the larger national context of the U.S. Civil Rights Movement and the anti-colonial struggles taking place around the world. The issues and tactics of Native protests in the 1960s reflected the larger national and international political cultures. Native nationalism, skepticism of established political authorities, and direct-action protests were the hallmarks of the next two decades. The National Indian Youth Council and the American Indian Movement were part of a great organizational proliferation on reservations and in cities. Dozens of American Indian newspapers and periodicals were established during the late 1960s and 1970s, including the American Indian Historical Society's *The Indian Historian* and *Wassaja*, the National Indian Youth Council's *ABC: Americans Before Columbus*, and the influential, *Akwesasne Notes* published by the Mohawk Nation. These periodicals joined the ranks of older, more established newspapers and journals such as the *Navajo Times* and the *Indian Leader*, published by Haskell Indian Junior College (now Haskell Indian Nations University) in Kansas.

In addition to the growth in publications, American Indian history and culture became a topic of serious study during the 1960s, and this new academic focus was reflected in educational institutions. American Indian studies centers were established at a number of universities around the United States, and nearly two dozen reservation community colleges were established in the decade following the 1968 founding of the first tribally controlled institution, Navajo Community College.

Some organizational formation was specifically designed to facilitate Native protest action. For instance, Determination of Rights and Unity for Menominee Shareholders (DRUMS) was founded in the early 1970s by younger Menominees including Ada Deer, Jim White, and Joan Keshena-Harte. Included among DRUMS members also were older, traditional people still living in Menominee County, all of whom opposed both the federal government's plan to terminate Menominee treaty rights and tribally sponsored land sales.

The American Indian Movement (AIM) was another "militant" group started in Minneapolis in 1968 in response to the many unmet social and legal needs of urban Indian people. AIM chapters followed in Cleveland, Milwaukee, Denver, and several other cities and eventually developed into a national organization. Other Native rights organizations emerged after 1961 to broaden the Native organizational landscape, including the National Indian Education Association in 1969, the Native American Rights Fund in 1970, the National Tribal Chairman's Association in 1971, and the Council of Energy Resource Tribes in 1975.

All these regional and national organizations provided lines of communication among diverse and geographically separated American Indian communities and represented Native interests at various levels of the U.S. government. These organizations reflected and clarified the common problems and interests shared by many tribes and by the growing urban Indian population. By 1960, 28 percent of American Indians lived in urban areas. This figure rose to 44 percent in 1970, reached 50 percent in 1980, and by 1990 more than one-half of American Indians lived in cities. The growth of the urban Indian population, particularly during the period from 1960 to 1980, contributed to the emergence of a national Red Power Indian protest movement.

## American Indian Activist Movements

**Early Protest Movements.** American Indian individual resistance and collective action stretches back to the earliest moments of the European invasion. Despite similarities to later protest movements, early Native collective action was unlikely to be characterized as protests by settler populations, but rather, tended to be defined through their eyes as hostility or war. Much Native protest was led by indigenous spiritual leaders. For instance, in 1760 Papoonan, a Munsee Delaware, challenged the greed of English traders and, like other spiritual leaders such as Wangomend, the Assinsink prophet, urged his followers to purify themselves of similar greed by adhering to the ancient customs of their ancestors. Another late-eighteenth-century Delaware spiritual leader, Neolin, preached a rejection of dependence on the British and advocated the avoidance of trade, the return to traditional ceremonial practices, and the gradual abandonment of European-made goods. Visionaries often advocated serious moral and social reform among their followers. They sought Native solutions to the catastrophes of colonialism.

One important type of Native collective action took the form of "revitalization" movements. These were political and spiritual movements that looked toward an end to the destruction resulting from white encroachments on Native land and deterioration of Native economies and societies. Perhaps the best known of many primarily nineteenth-century revitalization movements was the Handsome Lake Movement, which began in 1799, and the two waves of the Ghost Dance Movement, beginning in 1869 and again in 1889. While the Handsome Lake Movement was limited mainly to the Senecas and other Iroquois tribes, the first Ghost Dance Movement involved a number of Great Basin and West Coast tribes, and the second, larger Ghost Dance Movement spread east to include many Plains tribes as well. The Handsome Lake Movement emphasized the importance of maintaining strong traditional families, tribal structures, and land. It permitted some accommodation with U.S. culture and government. The Ghost Dance Movements, on the other hand, took a much more critical stance toward whites, blaming the Europeans and Americans for the miserable state of affairs on Indian reservations and for the destruction of traditional Indian ways of life. Furthermore, Ghost Dance teachings predicted the disappearance of whites and the return to life before the Europeans came.

Unfortunately, the Ghost Dance also differed from the Handsome Lake movement in the response of the U.S. government. The most infamous instance was the massacre of approximately 150 Native men, women, and children by U.S. Seventh Cavalry troops at Wounded Knee, South Dakota, in December 1890. The Ghost Dance indictment of Euro-American rule had been interpreted as a threat by a U.S. military still seeking revenge for the resounding military defeat of George Armstrong Custer and the Seventh Cavalry fourteen years earlier. Upon seeing the carnage at Wounded Knee with his own eyes, Charles Alexander Eastman reported that his faith in Christian love had fallen apart.

**Twentieth-Century American Indian Protest Before Red Power.** Throughout the twentieth century, indigenous people and Native nations organized in defense of treaty rights. Before the Second World War, Native nations also filed land claim lawsuits in federal courts and formed new political pressure groups. The Black Hills Treaty Council first met in 1911 and the All Pueblo Council in 1922 developed separate campaigns to enlist non-Indians in efforts designed to stop squatters and local politicians from robbing additional land. Other regional pressure groups included the Alaska Native Brotherhood and the Alaska Native Sisterhood, founded in 1912 and 1915, respectively, to resist segregation and anti-Indian discrimination in towns across the territory. Redbird Smith joined other Cherokees to establish the Four Mothers Society to resist the expansion of white influence following Oklahoma statehood in 1907.

The Indian Defense League of America (IDLA) was founded by Chief Clinton Rickard of the Tuscarora Nation in 1926, who said that it provided a way for Indians to work together and to speak out independent of non-Natives. The IDLA used collective action to resist the restrictive provisions of the U.S. Immigrant Act of 1924 in the form of refusals to pay customs duties or to possess or surrender passports, resistance against restrictions on their passage across the U.S.-Canadian border, and protests staging reenactments of the earlier treaty negotiations. For other Native nations, the Bureau of Indian Affairs (BIA) was a target of individual and tribal protests. Particularly notable was the Navajo

Tuscarora protest against the New York State Power Authority's condemnation of their lands in order to create a reservoir, 1958. (Courtesy of the Buffalo and Erie County Historical Society)

response to BIA livestock reduction programs during the 1930s and 1940s, which took the form of a prolonged conflict on the reservation, as did the Navajo-Hopi land dispute, whose resolution drags on today.

During the postwar period before 1961, citizens of Native nations often organized against U.S. government public works projects that threatened Indian land holdings and sacred places. Federal water and power projects were among the most common targets of Indian protest. For instance, the various nations of the Iroquois Confederacy resisted several water projects affecting Iroquois land: Seneca legal challenges and protests against the Kinzua Dam project in Pennsylvania during the 1940s and 1950s; Mohawk and Tuscarora legal and activist resistance to the St. Lawrence Seaway project in New York in the 1950s and 1960s; and Tuscarora armed resistance to the seizure of tribal land for a reservoir associated with the Niagara Power Plant project in New York in the 1950s.

**Legal Activism and Direct Action.**  American Indian protest activity often accompanied legal actions. Many twentieth-century Indian Wars have been fought inside closed doors, where the battleground was the courtroom, where the combatants were warriors with attaché cases, and where the weapons of war were the rules and precedents of U.S. law. American Indian attorneys and their legal allies included tribal attorneys who dealt with the day-to-day legal concerns of Native nations. Often, non-violent Indian judicial activism produced "imperfect victories," and only provided partial compensation for centuries of past loss and abuse. For instance, it took twenty-nine years of court battles, known as the Blackbird Bend litigation, for the Omaha tribe to regain in 1966 a small portion of eleven thousand acres that had been a part of its reservation in Nebraska but that ended up on the Iowa side of the Missouri River after a shift in the river's channel.

Many legal battles over indigenous rights took place against a backdrop of Native protests. That backdrop often acquired its symbolic vitality from the ironies and contradictions of Indian-white relations, particularly the tensions between Indian people as tribal citizens of sovereign "dependent" nations on the one hand, and as U.S. citizens (after the 1924 Indian Citizenship Act) on the other.

The use of symbolism in Indian protest was especially characteristic of the Red Power movement after 1969, but could be seen in many earlier protests. For instance, during the 1950s and 1960s Haudenosaunee (the Six Nations or Iroquois) protesters led annual delegations to the United Nations in New York to report U.S. and Canadian violations of various treaties. Delegates wore traditional ceremonial clothing and used their visits, which captured media attention, to spotlight their grievances. For example, two Haudenosaunee delegations arrived at the United Nations in May and September of 1950, at the height of the Cold War between the United States and Soviet Union; the September delegation met with Soviet Foreign Minister, Andrei Y. Vishinski.

Native protest during the 1950s reflected an increasingly sophisticated awareness of how to use the "master's tools" to counter U.S. political hegemony, and protesters increasingly used television media to shape public opinion. For instance, in 1952 a local Iowa television station broadcast an unusual public affairs program, *The Whole Town's Watching*. The program focused viewers' attention on the Sac and Fox Tribe of the Mississippi (the Mesquakie Settlement) in Iowa, one of ten Native nations named in the 1953 House Concurrent Resolution 108, designed to terminate tribal treaty rights. In the broadcast tribal leaders such as George Young Bear outlined for the viewers the problematic nature of Indian citizenship and the failure of the U.S. government to honor treaties and promises.

Indian protesters often drew protest themes and tactics from U.S. popular and political culture. For instance, in December 1960, a group of Utah Utes captured national attention with a strategy that resonated with U.S. domestic history—the Truc Utes seceded from the United States in order to protest the Bureau of Indian Affairs' control over funds paid by the federal government for mineral and land holdings. Still other tribes employed protest tactics from their own cultural repertoire. In September 1953, a group of Cheyennes and Arapahoes protested the draining of water from their hunting and fishing grounds at Canton Lake in Oklahoma by breaking a peace pipe and invoking a curse in a drum-beating ceremony.

The 1960s saw a sharp increase in the use of direct-action protest by American Indians. Again issues tended to center on problems confronting Native nations, and activists tended to be both tribal members living on reservations and urban Indian people acting in solidarity with their reservation sisters and brothers. The most dramatic and widespread of the early- to mid-1960s protests occurred in the Northwest and involved the struggle over fishing rights.

**The Fish-ins of the 1960s.** The term *fish-in* reveals a powerful marriage of protest cultures in the United States: the African American Civil Rights Movement and the beginnings of the Red Power American Indian Movement. The lunch counter desegregation sit-in tactic adopted by members of the civil rights organization, the Student Non-Violent Coordinating Committee found its rhetorical counterpart in the American Indian fish-ins in the Pacific Northwest of the early 1960s. The issues that launched the fish-in movement were different from sit-in opposition to segregation of public space. Fish-in protestors were concerned about intentional legal and law enforcement efforts to restrict Native nations' fishing rights, rights that the tribes asserted, and that the courts later affirmed, were guaranteed by treaty. Fishing-rights activists reflected a broadly shared sense among Native people that the economies and viability of entire indigenous nations were threatened by illegal restrictions on tribal fishing rights.

While tension between Indians and non-Indians over hunting and fishing rights stretched back into U.S. history, the fish-in campaign of the 1960s had its contemporary origins in several Washington State court cases. In 1957, for instance, state supreme court justices split 4–4 over the case of Robert Satiacum, a Puyallup and Yakima who had been arrested for fishing steelhead out of season with fixed gill nets. On the basis of this ambiguous decision, law enforcement efforts to restrict tribal fishing escalated in the 1960s. In 1963,

Washington's high court granted state agencies broader power to regulate fishing, and triumphant state authorities then closed off all of south Puget Sound to off-reservation Native fishing. This action triggered spontaneous protests among Washington's Indian citizens and the fish-in movement was born.

The fish-ins began in 1963 at Frank's Landing down river from the Nisqually Reservation, then expanded across the states of Washington and Oregon. Some Native people fished not only to challenge state regulations but also to defy the wishes and decrees of tribal governments. The movement drew support from groups and individuals outside the region, most notably the National Indian Youth Council and Hank Adams, who had grown up on the Quinault Reservation. The involvement of the NIYC and that organization's recruitment of national entertainment figures, Dick Gregory and Marlon Brando, as sympathizers with the Northwest tribes' cause, brought national media attention to the region.

In 1974, eleven years after spontaneous fish-ins began, U.S. Federal District Court Judge George Boldt ruled in favor of tribal treaty fishing rights. Judge Boldt emphasized that no court decision or act of Congress had annulled what the treaties had preserved for Native nations. Native nations had rights distinct from and superior to the privileges of other state citizens, and that when the tribes agreed to fish "in common with" non-Natives in the 1855 Camp Stevens Treaty, Judge Boldt declared, they did not acquire a right from non-Indians but instead had agreed only to share their own most important resource. Five years later the U.S. Supreme Court affirmed Boldt's decision.

In addition to forcing an eventual legal victory for treaty fishing rights in the Northwest, the fish-in movement provided a training ground for future Red Power activists in other parts of the United States. With the spread of mid-1960s fish-in activism out of the Northwest, the founding of the American Indian Movement in 1968, and the actions of Indian people who occupied Alcatraz Island in 1969, by the end of the decade American Indian protesters became a part of the momentum of the national civil rights mobilization.

**The Occupation of Alcatraz Island, 1969–1971.** In the early morning hours of 20 November 1969, eighty-nine "Indians of All Tribes" landed on Alcatraz Island, former site of the famous U.S. federal penitentiary, in San Francisco Bay. The group claimed the island, by the "right of discovery," and by the terms of an 1868 Sioux treaty that permitted Indians the right to unused federal property on Indian land. In a press statement, Indians of All Tribes set the tone of the occupation:

Tuscarora protesting the construction of a reservoir. (Courtesy of the Buffalo and Erie County Historical Society)

We, the Native Americans, re-claim the land known as Alcatraz Island in the name of all American Indians by right of discovery. . . . We will purchase said Alcatraz for twenty-four dollars in glass beads and red cloth. . . . Our offer of $1.24 per acre is greater than the 47 cents per acre the white men are now paying the California Indians for their land.

During the next nineteen months, the estimated number of Alcatraz occupiers ranged from close to one thousand in June 1970, to fifteen Native people who were removed by federal marshals on 11 June 1971. The Native occupiers and visitors to the island represented many different tribes, including Lakota, Navajo, Cherokee, Mohawk, Puyallup, Yakima, Hoopa, and Omaha. The months of occupation were marked by proclamations, news conferences, powwows, celebrations, skirmishes, and negotiations with federal officials. In the beginning months of the occupation, food and supplies were gathered on the mainland, partly by the San Francisco Indian Center, but over time the occupying force, which generally numbered around one hundred,

had to contend with increasing hardships as federal officials interfered with delivery boats and cut off the supply of water and electricity to the island.

Indians of All Tribes' plans for an American Indian cultural, educational, and spiritual center to be located on Alcatraz Island were never embraced by the federal government, although federal response was not uniformly negative. For instance, on 23 December 1969, House Joint Resolution 1042 was passed directing President Richard Nixon "to initiate immediate negotiations with delegated representatives of. . . the Indian community with the objective of transferring unencumbered title in fee of Alcatraz Island. . . to any. . . designated organization of the American Indian Community."

**Red Power.**   While the negotiations did not result in any plan for the future of Alcatraz Island that was acceptable to the protesters, the occupation itself was a turning point in patterns of American Indian protest. Alcatraz heralded the beginning of the Red Power Movement, a period of greatly increased levels of American Indian activism sited in urban centers as well as on reservations. Red Power activists took their tactical

Waiting for the ferry during the Alcatraz Island occupation. (Photo by Ilka Hartmann)

cue, in part, from the Alcatraz occupation. After federal officials retook the island, Indians of All Tribes moved their protest to an abandoned Nike missile base in the Beverly Hills, overlooking San Francisco Bay. While this occupation lasted only three days, it set in motion a pattern of similar occupations during the next several years, many involving unused or abandoned federal property, at government buildings, or at sites in national parks. Many of these protest events were led by members of the American Indian Movement.

Occupations represented a tactic designed to draw attention to American Indian historical and contemporary grievances: unsettled land claims, poor living conditions on reservations, denial of cultural and social rights, and lack of tribal self-determination. Most occupations were short-lived, lasting only a few days or weeks, such as those that occurred during 1970 and 1971 at Fort Lawton and Fort Lewis in Washington, at Ellis Island in New York, at an unused army communications center in Davis, California, at the Twin Cities Naval Air Station in Minneapolis, at former Nike Missile sites on Lake Michigan near Chicago and at Argonne,

Illinois, and at an abandoned Coast Guard lifeboat station in Milwaukee.

A number of protest camps were also established during the early 1970s, including those in the Paha Sapa (Black Hills), Mount Rushmore, and the Badlands National Monument. During the same years, government buildings also became the sites of protests, including regional Bureau of Indian Affairs offices in Cleveland and Denver, as well as the main headquarters of the BIA in Washington, D.C. Many of these occupations took on a festive air, as celebrations of Indian culture and ethnic renewal, while others represented efforts to provide educational or social services to urban Indians.

As the 1970s proceeded, American Indian protest occupations lasted longer, and some took on a more serious, sometimes violent tone, revealing the depth of grievances and difficulty of solutions to the problems confronting indigenous people and Native nations after nearly five centuries of responding to threats from settler populations. An example was the November 1972 week-long occupation of the Bureau of Indian

Affairs Office in Washington, D.C. The unplanned occupation of BIA headquarters occurred at the end of The Trail of Broken Treaties, a protest event involving caravans that traveled across the United States to convene in Washington, D.C. at a large camp-in, in order to dramatize and present Indian concerns at the national BIA offices in the form of the famous Twenty Points. The first eight points dealt with the restoration of a functioning treaty relationship with the United States, and the remaining points focused on lands, religious freedom, the repeal of oppressive state laws, the rehabilitation of Native prisoners, and program funding. The Twenty Points were never given a real hearing by U.S. officials, and the breakdown of accommodations arrangements resulted in the occupation of BIA offices and the seizure of BIA files by protesters; the protest ended a week later after a series of negotiations with federal officials.

Red Power protest activity shifted after the late-1972 BIA occupation, from mainly symbolic, short-term actions, to longer more violent events often on or near reservations. While these reservation-based protest actions were further dramatizations of long-held grievances against federal, state, and local authorities, they also revealed tensions within Native nations and communities, tensions between urban and reservation Indians as well as tensions reflecting political divisions on reservations. No single event of the Red Power era more clearly illustrated the combination of historical grievances and community tensions than the events on the Pine Ridge Reservation in the spring of 1973, a ten-week long siege that came to be known as Wounded Knee II.

Wounded Knee II involved a dispute within the Oglala Lakota nation over the controversial tribal chairman, Richard Wilson. Wilson was viewed as a corrupt puppet of the BIA by some Oglalas, including those associated with AIM. An effort to impeach Wilson resulted in a division of the Oglala Lakota Nation into opposing camps that eventually armed themselves and entered into a two-and-a-half-month long siege that involved federal law enforcement officials, the BIA, local citizens, nationally prominent entertainment figures, and the national news media.

Just as Red Power tactics in the early 1970s followed the pattern set by the Alcatraz occupation, Wounded Knee II reshaped Red Power protest in the mid-1970s in the direction of longer, reservation-based protest actions. These included a six-month occupation of a former girls' camp in Moss Lake, New York, beginning in 1974, the five-week occupation of a vacant Alexian Brothers novitiate by the Menominee Warrior Society in Wisconsin in 1975, the eight-day takeover of a tribally owned Fairchild Electronics assembly plant on the Navajo Reservation in New Mexico in 1975, and the week-long occupation of a juvenile detention center by members of the Puyallup tribe in Washington State in 1976.

The last major event of the Red Power era occurred in July 1978, as several hundred Natives marched into Washington, D.C. at the end of the Longest Walk, a protest march that had started five months earlier in San Francisco. The Longest Walk was intended to symbolize the forced removal of Native nations from their traditional homelands and to draw attention to the continuing problems in Indian country, both on reservations and in cities. The event also was intended to expose and challenge the backlash movement against Indian treaty rights which was gaining strength. Unlike many events before 1978, the Longest Walk was seen as a peaceful and spiritual event which ended without violence. Red Power had come full circle, from the festive Alcatraz days, through a cycle of violent confrontation, to the spiritual unity which marked the end of the Longest Walk.

**The Legacy of Red Power: Indian Self-Determination.**   The decline of the Red Power movement coincided with a renaissance in federal Indian policy. From 1975 to 1977, the American Indian Policy Review Commission traveled around the United States, holding the first extensive hearings in half a century on the conditions confronting American Indians on reservations and in cities. In the 1970s several pieces of federal legislation were passed denouncing the termination policies of the 1950s and reaffirming Indian tribal self-determination. Among these important legislative acts were the 1971 Alaska Native Claims Settlement Act (ANCSA), which recognized the land rights of Alaska Natives and provided for mineral royalties payments, land payments, and land transfers; the 1974 Indian Financing Act, which established a revolving loan fund to facilitate reservation economic development; the 1975 Indian Self-Determination and Education Assistance Act, which remanded to the tribes many of the decision-making and contracting rights formerly held by the BIA; and the 1978 Rhode Island Indian Claims Settlement Act fashioned after the 1971 ANCSA.

Whether the protest activism beginning with the spontaneous fishing-rights protests in 1963 and ending in 1978 with the Longest Walk was responsible for this new era in federal Indian policy is difficult to determine, since much of this legislation was underway early during the period of protest. However, it is difficult to imagine that U.S. congressional deliberations on these bills occurred without knowledge of what was happening outside the Capitol building—the occupation of Alcatraz Island, the Trail of Broken Treaties, the occupation of BIA headquarters, the sieges at Wounded

Knee and Moss Lake and on the Menominee Reservation, the Longest Walk, and the dozens of collective action events that served as a foil against which federal Indian policy was reviewed and revised.

**American Indian Activism After Red Power.** After 1978, Indian activism shifted from an emphasis on direct action to an approach that balanced protest and legal activism. America's courtrooms today remain contested terrain in American Indian affairs. Native nations and communities demonstrate increasing sophistication when negotiating the legal complexities of Indian resource rights, land claims, and sovereignty issues in U.S. courtrooms and in the arena of public opinion. The law is now more of a double-edged sword that can be wielded *by* Native nations, not only against them. American Indian protest energies are more and more spent in these legal arenas. The numbers of Native attorneys grew dramatically during the Red Power period and legal activism after 1978 focused on several issues: land and environmental issues, self-determination rights, the changing role of Native women, and repatriation of human remains and material culture.

**Land and Environmental Issues.** In 1946, when the U.S. Congress established the Indian Claims Commission (ICC) in order to settle all Native land claims, it expected that the commission would complete its work in ten years. The volume of dockets, about 650, and the time-consuming methods of litigation resulted in repeated extensions of the ICC's tenure until 1978 when all land claims not yet settled were turned over to the U.S. Court of Claims. Although the decisions of the ICC were a disappointment to many Native claimants, the commission served an unintended purpose of mobilizing many formerly quiescent Native communities. As Native kinship nations and communities prepared their ICC cases they organized meetings, researched their histories and genealogies, and consulted with other Native groups. As a result, a number of claimants were able to reestablish and revitalize community life. For instance, the Passamaquoddy of Maine invested a portion of the proceeds from their multi-million dollar settlement in a variety of community enterprises including a housing manufacturing firm and timber mill, as well as in educational programs in Passamaquoddy language and culture.

Many land claims remain unsettled, and with no end to this legal impasse in sight. For instance, for over a century the White Earth Anishinaabeg of northern Minnesota (commonly known as Chippewa or Ojibwa) have fought the state of Minnesota and the U.S. government for control of the White Earth Reservation. In 1983, Mississippi, Pillager, and Pembina band members organized Anishinabe Akeeng, the People's Land Organization, to recover stolen and tax-forfeited land. One

well-known Anishinaabe environmental and Native rights activist and writer, Winona LaDuke, was chosen by the Green Party as their vice-presidential candidate in 1996 and in 2000. LaDuke began her activism with Anishinabe Akeeng. She later helped organize the Indigenous Women's Network in 1985 and the White Earth Land Recovery Project in 1991. The White Earth Land Recovery Project develops alternatives for rebuilding the land base of the White Earth Reservation, encourages a more diverse economic base for the reservation, and educates people about Anishinaabeg history, language, and culture.

Many areas sacred to Native people remain today sites of legal and social conflict as indigenous groups seek to reclaim sacred lands or stop development projects seen as despoiling these religious sites. Blue Lake and the nearly fifty thousand acres of surrounding forests and mountains in New Mexico was one such disputed area. In 1970 Taos Pueblos reclaimed their ancestral sacred lands after a sixty-four-year legal struggle with the U.S. National Park Service. The Black Hills in South Dakota is another contested area still under the jurisdiction of the U.S. government. In 1981 Native protesters and their allies established Yellow Thunder Camp, named in memory of Raymond Yellow Thunder who was brutally murdered in Gordon, Nebraska, in 1972. For eight years, camp leaders resisted pressures to withdraw from the U.S. Forest Service, South Dakota Governor William Janklow, and a federal lawsuit. Although the U.S. government has acknowledged that the Black Hills land was illegally seized, no provision has yet been negotiated for returning the land to its original caretakers, and the Lakota have not accepted the $1.3 million monetary settlement offered by the U.S. government.

In the 1980s American Indian activists also began to focus on the problem of on-reservation hazardous waste disposal. A study of twenty-five reservations found that nearly 1,200 generators or power sites on or near these Indian lands were considered potentially acute health and environmental problems. Six of the reservations had sites that were considered to represent serious dangers to public health. Despite the expressed concerns of Native people, the contamination did not stop.

**The Changing Role of Native Women.** The 1960s and 1970s were a time of social awakening in the United States for both American Indian women and men. Native women were present in large numbers during the 1969 occupation of Alcatraz Island, during the 1972 occupation of the Washington, D.C. office of the Bureau of Indian Affairs, and at Wounded Knee in 1973. In these and other protests, Native women took on both traditional and activist roles: some cooked, some took care

Dennis Banks speaks at a San Francisco rally against his extradition to South Dakota, 1976. (Photo by Ilka Hartmann)

of children, while others marched, petitioned, occupied, and fought alongside their brothers to force the U.S. federal government to acknowledge its treaty obligations, to revoke federal termination and relocation policies, and to open a new era of tribal self-determination and Native rights.

Native women activists were not only part of AIM, but they also established their own organizations. In 1974 Lorelei DeCora Means, a Minneconjou Lakota, Madonna Thunderhawk, and Phyllis Young, both Hunkpapa Lakota, were joined by other American Indian women to form a new group called Women of All Red Nations (WARN). Many of these Native women had been active in AIM, and had developed an awareness of the distinctive gendered experiences of Native men and women at the hands of the U.S. federal government. WARN members argued that the U.S. government's paternalist and colonialist handling of Indian affairs had different consequences for Native women and men. These differences could be seen in both reservation and urban Indian communities. On reservations, Native women and children bore the greater burden of poor nutrition, inadequate health care, and forced or

deceptive sterilization programs, in addition to higher levels of domestic violence resulting from poverty, joblessness, substance abuse, and despair. WARN's response to these problems and abuses was to organize, to participate in protests, to demand an end to police brutality, and to insist on full treaty and civil rights for Native nations.

The 1980s and 1990s was also a time for Native women to take their places alongside their brothers in assuming positions of equality and leadership in Indian self-government and national policy. Native women such as Janet McCloud, LaDonna Harris, Winona LaDuke, Madonna Thunderhawk, LaNada Means Boyer, and Anna Mae Aquash were committed activists during and after the Red Power period of the 1960s and 1970s. It was not until the 1980s, however, that there was a large-scale entry of women into positions of prominence in Indian tribal and federal government. In 1987 Wilma Mankiller became the principal chief of the Cherokee Nation of Oklahoma and in 1993 Ada Deer was sworn in as assistant secretary of Indian Affairs. Even in the face of the contributions of these Native

Singing and drumming on the Long Walk for Survival, California, 1980. (Photo by Ilka Hartmann)

women, there remained pockets of resistance to Indian women as equal participants in the tribal political process. For instance, although Shinnecock women could vote in U.S. and New York State elections following the Indian Citizenship Act of 1924, it took seventy more years until these women were permitted to vote in tribal elections. By the late 1990s, however, Native women were not only voting in tribal elections, they were often running tribal governments. By the turn of the century, women had become heads of governments in forty-four Alaskan Native communities, and women governed seventy-seven Native nations in the lower forty-eight states. In total, nearly one-fifth of Native governments were headed by women.

**Tribal Self-Determination Rights.**   Today U.S. courtrooms remain an important arena where opponents of tribal sovereignty and autonomy continue to challenge tribal self-determination rights. Native efforts to defend existing reservation resources and to return control of stolen and lost energy resources represent another

important set of legal actions since 1978. Millions of dollars obtained from development of energy minerals discovered beneath the lands of several Native nations known as the "energy tribes" have provided these tribes a certain degree of self-determination, but have also resulted in exploitation. Many citizens of Native nations oppose exploitation of their mineral resources despite tremendous economic incentives and pressure from some tribal leaders, from U.S. officials, and from organizations such as the Council of Energy Resource Tribes.

One of the most controversial outgrowths of U.S. legal recognition of tribal sovereignty today involves gaming on Indian reservations. This lucrative source of reservation income often sparks disputes within tribes and between tribes and local and state governments. Similarly controversial is the ambiguous right of tribal governments to tax reservation residents and enterprises. In 1990, for instance, the Devils Lake Sioux Tribe successfully defended itself against attacks from the North Dakota Public Service Commission. Honoring the United States' relationship with the Devils Lake community, the federal court ruled that North Dakota could not regulate tribal utilities used for trust land and tribal enterprises. In May 2000, a federal court in Kansas denied the right of the Prairie Band Potawatomie and Kickapoo nations to collect a tax on fuel sales inside their borders. In addition, matters involving utilities regulation and taxation, battles for control of tribal water rights, mineral and resource development rights, and the right to develop reservation enterprises such as manufacturing, tourism, and recreation, are fought in U.S. courtrooms and on reservations.

Other self-determination campaigns involve the protection of religious rights, the protection of Indian children from adoption by non-Indians, and the continuing struggle to preserve Indian hunting and fishing rights. For instance, a number of Anishinaabeg communities and the state of Wisconsin have clashed several times, as have citizens of the Makah Nation and Washington State, over the matter of treaty hunting and fishing rights. Although the Makah Nation resumed its annual whale hunt in 1999, a federal court reversed an earlier decision the following June, making unclear the future of the whale hunt for Makah people.

**Repatriation of Remains and Artifacts.**   Courtrooms have also been important sites for activists wishing to negotiate the return of ancestral remains. Perhaps most indicative of the shift in acceptable practices among the settler population of the United States was the 1989 decision by the Smithsonian Institution to reverse its historical position regarding the disposition of its Native human and funereal holdings. After many years of negotiation with Native communities and their representatives, Smithsonian administrators began returning the skeletal remains and burial artifacts of hundreds of indigenous ancestors to their modern descendants. Fast on the heels of this decision, the state of New York agreed to return twelve wampum belts, some of which had been in the state's possession since the late 1800s, to the Onondaga Nation, which had been actively seeking their return since the 1950s. In 1990, Zuni people successfully negotiated the return of rare wooden Zuni war gods from museums around the country to their New Mexico homeland for exposure to weather by Zuni spiritual leaders and their rightful decay into dust. These and other successful efforts were accompanied by a lobbying campaign in Washington, D.C., and in 1990 the Native American Graves Protection and Repatriation Act (NAGPRA) was passed. NAGPRA requires U.S. museums and universities to return human remains and other cultural objects to the Native nations and communities from which the remains earlier were taken.

Despite these gains, Native struggles to reclaim ancestral remains continue. For instance, citizens of the Southern Cherokee Nation and the Tennessee River Band of Chickamuga Cherokees today are battling construction crews and the Tennessee Department of Transportation. Road builders recently unearthed burial remains in Tuckaleechee Cove on the Little River at the edge of the Blue Ridge physiographic province along state Highway 73 near Townsend in Blount County. Implementation of NAGPRA also remains controversial and problematic in Texas. During the U.S. settling of Texas, aggressive removal policies and warfare against Native people has left only the Alabama-Coushatta, Kickapoo, and Tigua nations with tiny reservations. Other Native nations were systematically and deliberately destroyed or exiled outside the borders of the state. This history of Indian-white relations in Texas makes it difficult today for even federally recognized tribes to take advantage of NAGPRA. Texas officials and legislators have refused to support the U.S. legislation and have eliminated the Texas Indian Commission. Despite these tremendous obstacles, the Texas Indian Bar Association and others continue to seek justice for indigenous people and Native nations in Texas.

**The Past is Now and in the Future.** The Indian wars continue in the twenty-first century. In 2000, American Indian communities continue to challenge images of Native people created by past and ongoing tourist and sports entertainment industries. Among the central issues for concerned citizens of Native nations

are whether Indian governments will allow their communities to remain "living museums," whether they will be able to control the exploitation of their intellectual and cultural property, and whether outside commercialism can be controlled. Urban Indians and their tribal and non-Indian allies use the strength of numbers and organization to oppose the use of Indian mascots by schools and professional sports teams. For instance, in 1989 Charlene Teters, a Spokane graduate student at the University of Illinois initiated a campaign to retire Chief Illiniwek, the university mascot. These efforts are documented in the film *In Whose Honor*. In Tennessee, the state chapter of the National Coalition for the Preservation of Indigenous Cultures works to eliminate the use of Indian mascots in Tennessee and North Carolina schools. Native and non-Indian organizations that advocate retiring Indian mascots all over the United States and on reservations include the National Congress of American Indians, the National Association for the Advancement of Colored People, the Southern Christian Leadership Conference, the Rainbow Coalition, the Affiliated Tribes of Northwest Indians, the Kansas Association for Native American Education, and the National Coalition on Racism in Sports and Media. Even the state of Georgia House of Representatives is on record opposing Indian school mascots.

Also in 2000, American Indian communities and their allies continue the struggle to restore lost spiritual and material resources and to reinvigorate spiritual traditions. The Newe (or Western Shoshone) of Nevada, for instance, have made fundamental changes in the supervision of and jurisdiction over what they call Newe Sogobia, or Western Shoshone homelands. This transformation is embodied in the Western Shoshone National Council, a collective decision-making body created in 1989 that comprises eighteen separate Newe communities. Assuming hunting and fishing jurisdiction over its collective lands, the Western Shoshone National Council acts for outsiders like a local government. Since 1989 the Western Shoshone National Council has worked to restore, protect, and extend Newe land rights and sovereignty. In 1991 the National Council established the Western Shoshone Defense Project, an advocacy organization that works to prevent the harassment of traditional Newe cattle-grazers by the Nevada Bureau of Land Management. In addition, the Western Shoshone Defense Project manages several other programs. The Mining Action Program works to expose and counter the gold mining industry's destruction of cultural sites and to protect the integrity of lands and waters through public education campaigns. The Outreach and Education Program works within Newe

Grace Thorpe, anti-nuclear activist, and her daughter Dagmar. (Photo by Ilka Hartmann)

communities and with the broader public to share information about Newe cultural, spiritual, environmental, and human rights concerns. Despite two ongoing court cases that challenge the new government, Newes are today in the process of combining recognized and unrecognized elements of their kinship nation into a unified government.

Indigenous people and Native nations not only continue efforts to reclaim stolen lands and reinforce efforts toward restoring self-determination, but they also continue to demand justice for crimes perpetrated against indigenous people. For instance, in response to the brutal murders of Wally Black Elk, Jr. and Ronald Hard Heart near White Clay, Nebraska, on 8 June 1999, Tom Poor Bear and other Oglala Lakotas and their allies organized a "Walk for Justice" from Pine Ridge Reservation south to the location of the murders where they organized Camp Justice. Their ongoing marches, demonstrations, and occupation are reminiscent of Red Power protests. The struggle continues.

*David Anthony Tyeeme Clark and Joane Nagel*
*University of Kansas*

## ◆ CANADIAN NATIVE ACTIVIST MOVEMENTS

On Wednesday, 15 May 2000, in the Nass Valley, British Columbia, home of the Nisga'a Nation, church bells rang as the people celebrated the proclamation by the government of Canada and the province of British Columbia of the first modern treaty with Native people in British Columbia. This concluded a process begun in the late 1800s when the Nisga'a first protested the incursion of non-Native people into their territory. This was followed by a petition to the Privy Council in 1913 urging the authorities in Great Britain to recognize Nisga'a land and leading to fourteen years of intense lobbying and hearings in Ottawa and elsewhere. Other British Columbia tribes joined the Nisga'a as they attempted to achieve justice for their cause. The federal government, urged on by the government of British Columbia, ended all such efforts in 1927 when they made it an offense punishable by fines and/or imprisonment for more than three people to gather together to discuss the Native land issue. The law also outlawed potlatch ceremonies, a major cultural ceremony of the

Native people on the coast of British Columbia. It stopped all public protest on the land question, removed any legal recourse for Native peoples to pursue the issue, set the stage for the removal and destruction of countless First Nations artifacts, and drove all aboriginal cultural ceremonies underground.

As a result of this act, the Native peoples on the Coast of British Columbia, led by the Nisga'a and Haida, formed the first Native organization in the country. The Native Brotherhood of British Columbia stated as its public purpose the furthering of Native commercial fishing. Since this was an acceptable purpose to the non-Native rulers, tribal leaders were able to meet and secretly keep the land question discussions alive among themselves. Today this prestigious organization actively represents First Native people in British Columbia on fishing rights issues and strives to increase Native participation in the commercial fishing industry.

Finally, in 1953 the government of Canada repealed the restrictive law. Within months, Frank Calder, a Nisga'a politician, began to talk to other Nisga'a about the land question, and reconstituted the old Nisga'a land committee as the Nisga'a Tribal Council (see http://www.ntc.bc.ca/). Its purpose was to find a just solution to the long outstanding land question. Frank Calder was the first Native person to attend university in British Columbia. After graduation he worked for the Native Brotherhood and successfully pressured the provincial government to allow Native people to vote in provincial elections. He then ran in the provincial election and was the first person of aboriginal ancestry to be elected to a legislative assembly in the British Commonwealth. Calder convinced the Nisga'a people to raise the funds to go to court. The Nisga'a were allowed to sue the crown—an important accomplishment since up to that point Canadian law did not allow a suit against the crown—and take their case to court in 1958. After losses in the lower courts, the Supreme Court of Canada came down with a split decision. Three judges ruled that aboriginal title had been eliminated by the unilateral acts of the infant government of British Columbia in the 1800s when they passed land acts. Three judges ruled that aboriginal title still existed. The seventh judged ruled against the Nisga'a on the technicality that the crown could not be sued.

In the election of 1968 the Liberal leader and then Prime Minister stated that his party and government would never recognize aboriginal title. On the other hand the party ran on a policy of justice for Native people. But in 1973 the fact that the judges had tied on the substantive issue of the existence of aboriginal title convinced Prime Minister Trudeau and his Minister of Indian Affairs Jean Chretien that aboriginal title might

exist. The federal government changed its mind and established the land claims settlement program. This meant that two-thirds of the landmass of Canada was now up for negotiation.

Since 1974 the dominant issue before the Canadian people has been the struggle to find a just solution to the comprehensive claims process. This was the underlying theme in the efforts of the Dene Nation (known then as the Indian Brotherhood of the Northwest Territories) to protest the building of the Mackenzie River pipeline in the 1970s. It was also a major issue during the years of discussions between governments of Canada and the First Nations over the Canadian constitution. Out of this interface the First Nations peoples federation known as the Assembly of First Nations (AFN) has been a powerful force. Under the Indian Act, all status Indians govern themselves (at the will of the federal government) through their band councils or village governments. These governments each elect representatives to the Assembly of First Nations, which represents about 700,000 of the one million status Indians. The grand chief and their council of chiefs have been the primary advocates to the federal government on all matters of policy. Their concerns have focused on the continued need to establish First Nations rights in all of the areas touched by the treaties and insisting on adequate funding in the areas of housing, social development, and education. Since all the negotiations around land issues and some specific treaty rights are between the government and the particular nation involved, the national chief and the AFN staff spend a lot of time supporting member groups. Their issues range from Native land, fishing, hunting, and treaty rights to all aspects of government policies. Detailed descriptions of their goals can be studied at their website (http://www.afn.ca/).

The Assembly of First Nations and the other national organizations were the key players in the long discussion to embed in the Canadian constitution "the existing aboriginal and treaty right of Indians, Inuit, Métis in Canada." Their success in including that clause in the Constitution means that modern treaties will also be constitutionally protected. This provides a new dimension of certainty for First Nations peoples who enter into a modern treaty. While specific mention of aboriginal self government in the constitution began during these negotiations, the courts have moved in the 1990s to strengthen the idea of aboriginal self-government. The Nisga'a treaty for the first time includes a significant section on self-government. However, that section is being challenged in the courts by the Liberal party of British Columbia and others (see http://www.bcliberals.com/).

Canadian Natives protesting before Parliament for land rights and aboriginal rights within the Canadian Constitution. (Courtesy of CP Pictures Archives)

## Comprehensive Claims Policy

The treaty-making process between Canada and First Nations peoples ended in 1921 without including territory in British Columbia, the Yukon, the Northwest Territories, or Northern Quebec. When the federal government transferred the land tenure of Northern Quebec to the province, a condition of the legislation was that the province had to enter into a treaty with the Native people of that area. At about the same time the *Calder* case was working its way through the courts, the James Bay Cree were successful in achieving an injunction against the province of Quebec which halted the James Bay hydroelectric project. In return for dropping the injunction, the federal government and the province entered into land negotiations with the Cree that led to the James Bay agreement. This was the first modern land claim settlement made in Canada. Despite denials by the government, the terms of this agreement became a model for future settlements. These settlements include control over a portion of the particular nation's traditional territory (between 8 and 15 percent), cash, wildlife and fish management rights, a variety of economic development packages, and other provisions. In return, the First Nation cedes the remainder of its traditional territory to the crown (land title in Canada is held by the provincial crown where there is a legal entity known as a province but by the federal crown in all other jurisdictions). Often the nation retains some specific rights within the territory ceded.

The most recent Supreme Court of Canada decision known as the *Delgamuk* decision (see http://kafka. uvic.ca/~vipirg/SISIS/Clark/97delrul.html) has raised more questions about the nature and existence of aboriginal titles. Study of the AFN site on this matter provides a detailed discussion of possible implications of this development.

Since the provincial government of British Columbia refused to participate in the negotiations until 1992, no progress was made toward a Nisga'a settlement until that time despite the fact that it was the *Calder* case which brought the negotiation process into being. In addition to the James Bay settlement there have been settlements in the Yukon, the Inuvialuit (Inuit) of the Mackenzie River Delta area, the Gwi'chin (the northwest corner of the MacKenzie delta), and the Inuit in the northeast half of the Northwest Territories.

## Specific Claims Policy

The development of the comprehensive claims policy leading to this settlement also triggered a response by the federal government to the charge by treaty Indians that provisions of the treaties had not been kept. These specific issues range from documenting proof that the federal government had actually unilaterally and secretly withdrawn land designated for aboriginal ownership in a particular treaty to calculating the financial worth of gunpowder, which was never delivered annually as promised. The battle for rights on the part of Native people in British Columbia and Northern Canada focused through this century on the long-outstanding land question. The issues for First Nations in the rest of Canada revolved around honoring treaty rights.

**Treaties.**   The treaty-making process in Canada began before Canada became a country in 1867. The Royal Proclamation of 1763 required the expanding British colonial movement to make treaties with Native people as non-Natives moved into areas used and ruled by First Nations. When Canada achieved self-government through confederation the federal government took over the treaty-making process and inherited the treaties made by the British crown. As this process moved westward from Lake Superior, a few more clauses were added to the treaties, which made them distinctive from the very minimal treaties signed in the Maritimes, Southern Quebec, and Ontario. The terms of the treaties have always been understood by First Nations peoples in the context of the verbal promises made during the negotiations by the government representatives. This is a natural assumption on the part of people who lived and trusted oral tradition. And their leaders, when signing, thought they were agreeing to all the oral promises made during the negotiation process. In contrast, it is interesting to note that the Nisga'a treaty is 252 written pages with over 500 pages of appendices. From coast to coast, Native people understood the treaties to be designed to protect them and to help them come to grips with a different way of life as their traditional livelihood of hunting and fishing diminished. They understand to this day that the provision of housing, food, medicine, education, and hunting and fishing rights for sustenance are all rights promised in the treaty in return for the vast amounts of land they ceded to the government. However, the policies of the government of Canada at best were designed to assimilate and control reserve Indians, or at worst, to arrange for Native people to die out through neglect. In order to manage the Native reserve population the government created the Department of Indian Affairs and passed the Indian Act. This act made so-called status Indians wards of the crown and established a system of Indian agents who ran the lives of Native people from coast to coast. Since Native people did not have the right to vote in federal elections, this department ran its affairs as it saw fit with very little supervision from the politicians of the day. Until sometime after the end of the Second World War, the department embarked on a policy of total assimilation using education as its major tool.

Duncan Campbell Scott, deputy minister of Indian affairs from 1913 to 1932 expressed the attitude of the government when he noted that he wanted to get rid of the Indian problem. The objective of the department was to continue until there was not a single Indian in Canada who had not been absorbed into the body politic and there was no Indian question. Education would be the method of achieving this goal. Medical services were minimal as disease ravaged tribe after tribe. Native people travelling in urban areas often found themselves rejected by hospitals because they could only be treated by a federal institution. This terrible situation began to change in the early 1900s because of several events.

The most important event took place in 1959 when the Progressive Conservative government made it possible for Native people to vote in federal elections. For the first time members of Parliament began to pay attention to the activities of the Department of Indian Affairs. It did not take some politicians very long to recognize that the First Nations vote in their riding could make the difference between electoral defeat or victory.

In 1960 a group of concerned church people and others formed what became known as the Indian-Eskimo Association, whose purpose was to provide a public forum for Native people to articulate their concerns and to assist Native voices in such a manner that they would be heard. Further, some Native people began to organize a national organization, which became the National Indian Brotherhood and later the Assembly of First Nations. In Alberta, Saskatchewan, and Manitoba strong provincial Native organizations dominated the struggle around the concerns of treaty Indians. There was such a growing wave of dissent by Indians and whites to government policies that the Liberal government of Lester Pearson began a major consultation with Native people about the Indian Act.

The churches began to examine their policies in relationship to residential schools, and some denominations closed their residential schools during the 1960s. The Anglican church of Canada in its 1967 Synod called for a study of the church's relationship to Native peoples and in 1969 they adopted the recommendations of the resulting Hendry Report. As many federal and provincial politicians throughout the 1960s came to recognize that their continued election could be dependent on the support of Native voters in their riding, they began to pay more attention to the policies of the Department of Indian Affairs. It was against this background that Pierre Elliott Trudeau became leader of the Liberal Party of Canada and fought an election in 1968 in which one of the principles was justice for Native people.

Prime Minister Trudeau decided to implement his justice for Native people's principles by appointing the Honorable Bob Andras minister without portfolio, and Jean Chretien as minister of Indian affairs and northern development. Andras' task was to consult with Native people from coast to coast. Of course, everywhere he went to meet with Indians, senior officials of the Department of Indian Affairs accompanied him and made sure he only talked to people who would support the status quo. However, Native leaders and others arranged private and secret meetings following the public gatherings sponsored by the bureaucracy. At the end of this process it was felt by Native leaders that significant change might happen as it appeared that the government was listening.

In 1969 there was a representative gathering of Native people in Ottawa sponsored by the government, in order to recommend policies as the result of the four to five years of consultations on the Indian Act begun by the previous Liberal government. They deliberated for some days and agreed to recommend policies that urged the government to focus on treaty rights, hunting and fishing rights, and aboriginal land rights. Andras finished his consultation and moved on to another cabinet job, while Chretien came to the gathering to receive their recommendations and announce the government's new policy. The policy was a shock to the assembled gathering and it became known as the 1969 White Paper. It was viewed by almost every Indian present as a policy of assimilation, and they rejected it.

However, the policy caused Indians from coast to coast to unite in common cause as never before. The result was an immense strengthening of the National Indian Brotherhood and its provincial organizations. They began intensive pressure on the government including the recruitment of support from nongovernment public organizations such as the churches, community development groups, organized labor, and many others. In many ways the White Paper was the catalyst for activist Native organizations in Canada. In 1971 this pressure resulted in an about face by the government and the White Paper was discarded. The alliance formed during these years between Native people and nongovernment organizations provided significant political support and weight to Native activism during the next twenty years.

## Native Organizations

As this new century begins Native people in Canada express themselves in active political organizations in a number of ways. In many areas the primary tribal organization consists of the governments of various communities within a distinctive language group and region. For example, the council of the Haida Nation represents all members of the Haida people. In some provinces, status Indians usually belong to a provincial organization. The term *status Indian* is a description of aboriginal ancestry peculiar to Canada. The Canadian government dropped the blood quantum (a definition of *Indian* depending on the percentage of Indian biological inheritance) factor as a definition of Indians and replaced it with a vague description of evidence of living an Indian way of life. This eventually became a definition based on those groups that entered into treaties and therefore were defined as the responsibility of the federal government. The Indian Act in Canada made it possible for people to "sell" their status and become non-Indian. Indeed, for a time this was required of status Indians if they wished to apply for certain kinds of jobs. The Indian Act further confused the issue by defining a non-Native woman who married a status Indian as Indian under the act. However, a Native woman who married a non-Native person became non-Indian. This meant over time that a large number of men and women were defined as non-Native even though they might live very full Native lifestyles. After the failure of the 1969 White Paper, the federal government provided significant funds for provincial Indian organizations and for the national organization. However, they insisted that the membership consist only of status or registered Indians. This led to the formation in most provinces of non-status Indian organizations. They formed the basis of a national nonstatus organization called the Native Council of Canada.

The Native Council of Canada (see http://www.abopeoples.org/affiliates/ncca.html and http://www.unns.bc.ca/) was formed to represent the needs of nonstatus aboriginal people. Their numbers are greater than the registered Indians because of the many people descended from Natives excluded from the treaty-making process. Their interests are different since they have no land base or "band councils" and live largely in urban areas. In the last decade they have taken significant action in urban areas, demanding recognition and some forms of local control. As governments gradually enter into comprehensive modern treaties to settle the long outstanding land questions and rights issues, many urban Aboriginals feel increasingly isolated. One of the major future areas will be the status of urban Native people. The effect of the change in the laws caused by Bill C–51, which makes it possible for many nonstatus people to regain their status, adds another dimension to this scene. In some areas, particularly in British Columbia, many First Nations governments have included all their descendents as eligible for participation in settlements including representation in the evolving tribal governments.

Another major organization concerned with urban Indians has been the development of Indian centers. The National Association of Indian Centres (http://www.unns.bc.ca/) represents agencies existing in most small towns, which have a significant aboriginal population, and in most major cities. These organizations originally were created to pursue cultural goals for urban Indians. However, their staff and boards were immediately overwhelmed with the tremendous needs and suffering of First Nations people in urban areas. They were required to focus on issues such as urban housing, jobs, street issues, and the like. One significant new development is the movement to include more ceremonial and culturally appropriate activities in their work. This is important because many would argue that the root cause of problems for many aboriginal urban people is an identity crisis.

## Métis

In Canadian history there was also a unique development in Manitoba. The provincial government recognized people who were the result of intermarriage between Native and non-Native people, particularly French and Scottish fur traders. This group identified themselves as Métis and in modern times they have formed a national Métis organization. They are fighting in some provinces for land, money, and settlements. In 1983 part of the membership of the Native Council of Canada formed the Métis National Council representing people tracing their ancestry to the Red River Métis, whose descendents now live primarily in Manitoba, Saskatchewan, Alberta, and the Northwest Territories. These people have a distinct culture with their own language. They are descendents of one of the most activist groups in the history of Canada: they have fought to obtain self-determination, land and self-government under the leadership of Louis Riel and Gabriel Dumont. While this effort failed, it continues to be the basis of Métis unity and a model for all aboriginal peoples. Riel's contributions have been recognized by Canadian society and a statue has been erected to honor him. In the last decade the definition of *Métis* has often tended to describe people of mixed-blood and there has been a proliferation of regional Métis organizations in almost every province of Canada.

## Inuit

The fourth significant national organization that has grown up since the White Paper is the Inuit Council of Canada now Nunavit (http://www.unns.bc.ca/), representing the Inuit people of the Northwest Territories and Northern Quebec. This group has been active in seeking a settlement of their land issues. The Nisga'a decision cast doubt on Canada's jurisdiction of the whole of the Northwest Territories. The Inuit in the Eastern Arctic chose a different direction than that followed in the comprehensive land claims negotiations. They have been successful in negotiating a new territory in Canada called Nunavit, the first aboriginal provincial government in Canada.

These organizations continue to be very active in Canada, challenging provincial and federal governments to continue dealing with the issues facing their particular groups. Their success in this has varied from issue to issue and from tribe to tribe. It also varies because of the ideological positions of the leadership of particular Native groups. For example, while there are over forty distinct tribal groups in British Columbia now involved in negotiations with the provincial and federal governments to settle the land question, there are other groups that refuse to negotiate unless the governments recognize the sovereign character of these tribal entities.

While aboriginal identity has become fragmented because the federal government defined Indians in ways convenient for them, there has emerged a collective Native identity that is evident whenever there is a major public crisis. This collective identity works both ways, as non-Natives often treat people who look like or call themselves Native in the same way when a crisis emerges. A major confrontation between the government, police, and Native people in Nova Scotia can cause waves in the day-to-day relationship between non-Natives and aboriginal peoples as far away as British Columbia.

**The Oka Crisis.**    An excellent example of such racial tension was the effect of the armed barricades erected in July 1990 by Mohawks of Kanesetake, Quebec, a community just west of Montreal. This particular Mohawk dispute is two hundred years old. In 1975 the federal government rejected the Mohawk claim under the comprehensive claims policy and in 1977 rejected it again under the terms of the specific claims settlements. The Mohawk have a traditional form of government through their clan chiefs, and like all other Native peoples, an elected form of government imposed by Canada. Over the years a group calling themselves the Warriors have emerged from the traditional side of the Mohawk government. The armed stand-off took place as a protest against the neighboring municipality that planned a golf course on land claimed by the community of Kanesetake. A group of Warriors erected barricades and guarded them with armed and masked Mohawks. In the Quebec provincial police's attempts to take down the barricade, gun shots resulted, and a policeman was killed. The Quebec government called for the army, and the federal government responded with over 2,500 armed soldiers, tanks, and all the firepower of the Canadian armed forces. This event triggered aboriginal supportive blockades on highways, bridges, and railways in Ontario, Quebec, and British Columbia. Moreover, Native people from coast to coast reported individual acts of verbal and physical violence against them by non-Native people.

The overwhelming superior forces of the Canadian Army resulted in the blockade being lifted following a lot of negotiations and a nervous summer for the people involved, not to mention the rest of the country who watched this on television just about every night. The armed protestors were arrested and charged but never convicted. While some aspects of the Mohawk dispute have been addressed, and while local community relationships are returning to some semblance of order, the underlying issues of sovereignty and self government are still unresolved.

## The Royal Commission

A major response to the Oka crisis was the creation by the government of Canada of the Royal Commission on Aboriginal People. In 1996 this commission completed a six-volume, 5,000-page report. The report cost close to $60 million, took four years, held 177 days of hearings and heard 3,500 witnesses. The report lays out a twenty-year plan for Aboriginals at a cost of $38 billion. It covers every aspect of Native life and is available online. First Nations people responded enthusiastically to this report, although the federal government and the provinces have been slow in implementing its recommendations. The Assembly of First Nations held its election in July 2000 and replaced Phil Fontaine with Matthew Coon Come. He ran on a platform of strongly challenging the federal government to take this report seriously and to begin discussions on implementing it.

## Fishing and Hunting Rights

In 1969 the First Nations people gathered in Ottawa told the government that they place high priority on recognition of aboriginal hunting and fishing rights. Since that time there have been a number of court cases affirming First Nations rights to hunt and fish for sustenance as well as for ceremonial and cultural purposes. Further, in British Columbia the *Sparrow* case resulted in a Supreme Court decision stating that such aboriginal rights could not be removed without the consent of the First Nations people. One of the major areas in comprehensive land claims negotiations describes the harvesting of wildlife and fish. For example, in the most recent Nisga'a agreement there is a detailed agreement in the treaty that, among other things, puts a cap on the numbers of fish Nisga'a may harvest in a given season.

While the court cases and political protests around fishing rights have characterized Native relations on the British Columbia coast for the past century, they have quieted down while negotiations are taking place. The opposite is true of the east coast, however. In 1999 the Supreme Court ruled on the terms of an old treaty between the Mi'kmaq and the government. The case is known as the *Marshall* ruling and it upheld Mi'kmaq rights to fish where and when they want. This affects Mi'kmaq in Nova Scotia and New Brunswick. In 1999 Native fishermen immediately began to fish for lobster, and the backlash from local commercial fisherman resulted in the smashing of hundreds of Native traps and a very tense scene in a number of small Atlantic Coast communities. Negotiations between the Department of Fisheries and the Native leadership resulted in agreements with thirty-four Mi'kmaq and Maliseet reserves in Atlantic Canada, but two communities refused to accept this agreement. In the summer of 2000 some Atlantic bands set lobster traps, and fisheries guardians harassed them. The threat of major violence continues to be very real.

## Gender Rights

The status of Native women in Canada has a very confused and discriminatory history. A major factor in this has been the Indian Act whereby Native women lost their status through marriage to non-Indians. Another factor was the confusion created by the conflicting inheritance traditions—that is, many Native cultures traditionally were matriarchal and matrilineal.

Inheritance was through the mother, rather than through the father as it was in Western society. In many communities some families opted for the Western method while other families continued in the traditional model. During the 1980s there was major conflict in the Canadian constitutional discussions. The result of the discussion was that Native people who had lost their status through intermarriage or in other ways could regain their status. Objections to this by many Native (male) leaders were received badly by the general public. However, the underlying reality was that if hundreds of nonstatus people moved back to reserves without significant increases in funding for services by government, there would be disastrous results in those communities. It was in the context of this gender discrimination that the Native Women's Association of Canada and the Inuit Women's Association of Canada were formed. These two organizations work closely together and are very active in asserting gender equality in all aspects of Native life. A major challenge for First Nations peoples in the immediate future will be the way in which aboriginal societies deal with gender discrimination in their own organizations on the one hand and at the same time develop a distinctive understanding of gender equality in the context of many of their traditional values.

## Education

The way in which political leaders at the beginning of the 1900s chose to assimilate Native people was through education. They sent as many young Native people as they could find to residential schools operated by the mainstream churches throughout Canada. While many Native parents chose to send their children to school—not for the purpose of assimilation but for survival—the government forced many others to attend. These schools were not only destructive to Native language and culture, but were also harmful to the students who attended. Canadians are now discovering that many children were sexually abused while attending these residential schools. The result has been hundreds of legal suits against the government of Canada, the churches, and some First Nations band councils. While there are ongoing discussions to discover a better way than litigation to deal with this tragedy, it is expected that this issue will dominate the courts for the next twenty years.

Native people began thirty years ago to take control of their own education. The Rochdale College Institute for Indian Studies, also called the Nishnawbe Institute, was an early expression of a Native–run postsecondary educational institution. However, major movements in the 1970s and 1980s to establish faculties or centers in

post-secondary institutions quickly followed it. One of the policies of the Liberal government after the 1969 White Paper was to provide major funding for status Native students to receive a postsecondary education. In 1965 there were approximately 150 First Nations students in Canada attending postsecondary institutions. In 2000 First Nations students are proportionately up to about 60 percent degree completion with the rest of the population. The most recent movement in postsecondary education has been the development in the 1990s of First Nations–controlled institutions. In order for these institutions to receive accreditation they have had to enter into arrangements with community colleges and universities. Those Native-run educational institutions have formed fledgling provincial and national associations as they struggle with the interface between First Nations values and learning styles and the values and learning styles which characterize Canadian universities and colleges. The institutional power of these mainstream educational institutions is so pervasive that almost all Native-run institutions continue to consider the possibility of separate institutions and the establishment of their own standards and styles of learning. However, the process itself continues to provide a rapid improvement in Native language and cultural courses and materials, which is extremely important given the predictions of some experts that all Native languages might disappear within twenty years.

At the public school level there have also been some significant developments. For example, the Nisga'a established a bilingual and bicultural school district in the 1970s with the Nisga'a language taught from grades one to twelve. Other jurisdictions have included the teaching of tribal languages and cultures in their curriculum. Some universities in Canada have been persuaded to accept knowledge of a First Nations language as a foreign language for entrance purposes.

The interface between Native and non-Native values that is a fundamental reality of all these First Nations postsecondary institutions provides one of the more exciting and positive dimensions for future Native/ white relationships.

## Religion

If you were a student in the middle 1960s and studying Native religious traditions someone might have drawn to your attention a film by the National Film Board of Canada that showed and described what they believed to be the last Sun Dance on the North American continent. One of the contributions of the short-lived Nishnawbe Institute was the creation of the Indian Ecumenical movement. This movement began because some Native leaders believed that tribal life was dependent on religious unity in local communities. Where there was religious strife in a village, whether between Christians and traditionalists, between different Christian denominations, or between feuding traditional factions, the community itself would suffer. Indeed political, cultural, familial, and social life would all be fractured.

The institute raised money from churches to sponsor a conference of First Nation's Christian and traditional leaders. It was felt that Native religious leaders of any stripe, unlike non-Natives, could meet and discuss these matters without falling into religious disputes as the result of their religious differences. Since First Nations peoples do not recognize the Canadian/United States border, religious leaders throughout the continent were invited to meet for ten days each summer from 1969 on. They met first on the Crow reservations in Montana and then at Morley, Alberta.

The assumptions were found to be true. The conference worked, and there was an opening for movement in many local communities toward peaceful coexistence among Christian denominations and between Christians and traditionalists. The movement also brought into the open the continuing existence of strong medicine traditions in many tribes, and it caused a revival of Native religious interest. In some places this has evolved into Christian and traditional coexistence, and in others the incorporation of traditional ceremonies in Christian local rituals. It has led in Roman Catholicism to the pursuit of the establishment of the first Native saint through the Tekiwitha movement. However, in communities where the Christian leadership has maintained a view antagonistic to Native religion and culture, division continues to occur. The successor to the Indian Ecumenical movement is the Centre for Indian Scholars which continues to assert the need for religious unity at the local level, a unity which is inclusive of diversity and respect for the Creator.

*John (Ian) Mackenzie*
*Vancouver School of Theology*

# U.S. Native American Organizations and Political Advocacy Groups

## ◆ ALASKA

**ALASKA FEDERATION OF NATIVES**
1577 C Street, Suite 300
Anchorage, AK 99501
(907) 274–3611

**ALASKA NATIVE BROTHERHOOD CAMP NO 1**
**ALASKAN NATIVE SISTERHOOD CAMP NO 4**
P.O. Box 72
Sitka, AK 99835–0072
(907) 747–3359

**ALASKA NATIVE FOUNDATION**
733 West Fourth Ave., Suite 308
Anchorage, AK 99501
(907) 274–2541

## ◆ ARIZONA

**BLACK MESA INDIGENOUS SUPPORT**
P.O. Box 23501
Flagstaff, AZ 86002
(520) 773–8086

## ◆ CALIFORNIA

**AMERICAN INDIAN LIBERATION CRUSADE, INC.**
4009 S. Halldale Ave.
Los Angeles, CA 90062
(323) 299–1810

**AMERICAN INDIAN MOVEMENT (AIM)**
P.O. Box 6555
Los Angeles, CA 90056
(323) 257–2246

**INTERNATIONAL INDIAN TREATY COUNCIL**
INFORMATION OFFICE
2390 Mission Street, Suite 301
San Francisco, CA 94110
(415) 641–4482

**KUMEYAAY CULTURAL REPATRIATION COMMITTEE**
BARONA CULTURAL CENTER MUSEUM
1095 Barona Rd.
Lakeside, CA 92040
(619) 443–7003 ext. 219

## ◆ COLORADO

**AMERICAN INDIAN ANTI-DEFAMATION COUNCIL**
215 W. Fifth Ave
Denver, CO 80204
(303) 892–7011

**AMERICAN INDIAN COLLEGE FUND**
NATIONAL HEADQUARTERS
8333 Greenwood Blvd.
Denver, CO 80221
(303) 426–8900

COUNCIL OF ENERGY RESOURCE TRIBES
COMPREHENSIVE EDUCATION PROGRAM
1999 Broadway, Suite 2600
Denver, Colorado 80202
(303) 297–2378

NATIONAL TRIBAL JUSTICE RESOURCE
CENTER
1522 Broadway
Boulder, CO 80302
(303) 245–0786

NATIVE AMERICAN FISH AND WILDLIFE
SOCIETY
750 Burbank St.
Boulder, CO 80020
(303) 466–1725

NATIVE AMERICAN RIGHTS FUND
1506 Broadway
Boulder, Colorado 80302
(303) 447–8760

## ◆ CONNECTICUT

SAVE THE CHILDREN FEDERATION
54 Wilton Rd.
Westport, CT 06880
(203) 226–7271

## ◆ DISTRICT OF COLUMBIA

ARROW, INC.
(AMERICANS FOR THE RESTITUTION
AND RIGHTING OF OLD WRONGS)
1000 Connecticut Ave., N.W., Suite 1204
Washington, DC 20036
(202) 296–0685

INDIAN LAW RESOURCE CENTER
Washington Office
601 E. St., S.E.
Washington D.C. 20003
(202) 547–2800

MORNING STAR INSTITUTE
403 10th St., S.E.
Washington, DC 20003
(202) 547–5531

NATIONAL AMERICAN INDIAN COURT
JUDGES ASSOCIATION
1301 Connecticut Ave., N.W., Suite 200
Washington, DC 20036
(509) 422–6267

NATIONAL AMERICAN INDIAN HOUSING
COUNCIL
900 Second St., N.E., Suite 305
Washington, DC 20002
(202) 789–1754

NATIONAL CONGRESS OF AMERICAN
INDIANS
1301 Connecticut Ave., N.W., Suite 200
Washington, DC 20036
(202) 466–7767

NATIONAL COUNCIL ON URBAN
INDIAN HEALTH
501 Capitol Court, N.E., Suite 100
Washington, DC 20002
(202) 659–9159

NATIONAL INDIAN BUSINESS ASSOCIATION
725–2nd Street, N.E.
Washington DC 20002
(202) 547–0680

NATIONAL INDIAN GAMING ASSOCIATION
24 2nd Ave., S.E.
Washington DC 20003
(202) 546–7711

NATIONAL TRIBAL CHAIRMEN'S
ASSOCIATION
818 18th St., N.W., Suite 420
Washington, DC 20006

NATIVE AMERICAN CONSULTANTS
725 Second St., N.E.
Washington, DC 20002
(202) 547–0576

## ◆ FLORIDA

AMERICAN INDIAN CULTURAL SUPPORT
P.O. Box 1783
Lutz, Florida 33548

## ◆ IDAHO

NORTH AMERICAN INDIAN WOMEN'S
　　ASSOCIATION
Rt. 1, Box 139
Lapawi, ID 83540
(208) 843–2678

## ◆ IOWA

INDIAN YOUTH OF AMERICA
P.O. Box 2786
Sioux City, IA 51106
(712) 252–3230

## ◆ KANSAS

INTERNATIONAL OFFICE OF THE LEONARD
　　PELTIER DEFENSE COMMITTEE
P.O. Box 583
Lawrence, KS 66044
(785) 842–5774

## ◆ MASSACHUSETTS

UNITED AMERICAN INDIANS OF NEW
　　ENGLAND
P.O. Box 697501
Quincy, MA 02269
(781) 331–3690

## ◆ MARYLAND

INDIGENOUS PEOPLE'S NETWORK
C/O Daybreak
P.O. Box 98
Highland, MD 20777

LEAGUE OF INDIGENOUS SOVEREIGN
　　NATIONS OF THE WESTERN HEMISPHERE
P.O. Box 131
Accokeek, MD 20607
(301) 490–1879

## ◆ MICHIGAN

MICHIGAN INDIAN CHILD WELFARE
P.O. Box 537, 405 E. Easterday Ave.
Sault Ste. Marie, MI 49783
(906) 632–8062

NORTH AMERICAN INDIAN ASSOCIATION
22720 Plymouth Rd.
Detroit, MI 48239
(313) 535–2966

ORGANIZATION OF NORTH AMERICAN
　　INDIAN STUDENTS
P.O. Box 26, University Center
Northern Michigan University
Marquette, MI 49855
(906) 227–2138

## ◆ MINNESOTA

AMERICAN INDIAN MOVEMENT GRAND
　　GOVERNING COUNCIL
P.O. Box 13521
Minneapolis, MN 55414
(612) 721–3914

INDIGENOUS ENVIRONMENTAL NETWORK
P.O. Box 485
Bemidji, MN 56691
(218) 751–4967

## ◆ MONTANA

INDIAN LAW RESOURCE CENTER
Administrative Office
602 N. Ewing St.
Helena, MT 59601
(406) 449–2006

THE RURAL INSTITUTE ON DISABILITIES
American Indian Disability Legislation
University of Montana
52 Corbin Hall
Missoula, MT 59812
(406) 243–5467

## ◆ NEBRASKA

NATIONAL INDIAN COUNSELORS
　　ASSOCIATION
University of Nebraska
233 Administration M-C-A
Lincoln, NE 68588
(402) 472–2027

## ◆ NEVADA

**WESTERN SHOSHONE DEFENSE PROJECT**
P.O. Box 211106
Crescent Valley, NV 89821
(775) 468–0230

## ◆ NEW MEXICO

**ALLIANCE FOR AMERICAN INDIAN LEADERS**
P.O. Box 20007
Santa Fe, NM 87504

**AMERICAN INDIAN LAW CENTER, INC.**
P.O. Box 4456, Station A
Albuquerque, NM 87196
(505) 277–5462

**AMERICANS FOR INDIAN OPPORTUNITY**
681 Juniper Hill Rd.
Bernalillo, NM 87004
(505) 867–0278

**AMERIND FOUNDATION**
P.O. Box 482
Albuquerque, NM 87103
(505) 837–2290

**CATCHING THE DREAM**
Native American Scholarship Fund, Inc.
8200 Mountain Rd., N.E., #203
Albuquerque, NM 87110
(505) 262–2351

**GATHERING OF NATIONS**
3200 Coors Rd.
Albuquerque, NM 87120
(505) 836–2810

**INSTITUTE FOR NATIVE AMERICAN DEVELOPMENT (NAD)**
NATIVE AMERICAN STUDIES (NAS)
1812 Las Lomas Dr., N.E.
University of New Mexico
Albuquerque, NM 87131
(505) 277–6930

**NATIONAL INDIAN COUNCIL ON AGING**
City Center, Suite 510W
10501 Montgomery Blvd., N.E., Suite 210
Albuquerque, NM 87111
(505) 292–2001

**NATIONAL INDIAN YOUTH COUNCIL**
318 Elm Street, S.E.
Albuquerque, New Mexico 87102
(505) 247–2251

**SOUTHWEST ASSOCIATION ON INDIAN AFFAIRS (SWAIA)**
P.O. Box 31066
Santa Fe, NM 87594
(505) 983–5220

## ◆ NEW YORK

**AMERICAN INDIAN RITUAL OBJECT REPATRIATION FOUNDATION**
461 E. 57th St.
New York, NY 10022
(212) 980–9441

**NORTH AMERICAN INDIAN ASSOCIATION**
22720 Plymouth Rd.
Detroit, MI 48239
(313) 535–2966

**R.A.I.N. (RIGHTS FOR ALL INDIGENOUS NATIONS, INC.)**
R.R. 1, P.O. Box 308 A
Petersburg, NY 12138
(518) 658–3055

## ◆ NORTH DAKOTA

**DAKOTA WOMEN OF ALL RED NATIONS**
(formerly WOMEN OF ALL RED NATIONS)
P.O. Box 69
Fort Yates, ND 58538

## ◆ OKLAHOMA

**AMERICAN INDIAN INSTITUTE**
Public Responsibility and Community Affairs
University of Oklahoma
555 Constitution Ave., Suite 237
Norman, OK 73037
(405) 325–4127

**CHICKASAW FOUNDATION**
P.O. Box 1726
Ada, OK 74821–1726
(580) 421–9030

FOUR TRIBES TRIBAL EMPLOYMENT
   RIGHTS OFFICE
P.O. Box 1193
Anadarko, OK 73005
(405) 247–9711

NATIVE AMERICAN RESEARCH
   INFORMATION SERVICE
American Indian Institute
University of Oklahoma
555 Constitution St., Suite 237
Norman, OK 73072–7820

OKLAHOMA INDIAN AFFAIRS
4545 N. Lincoln, Suite 282
Oklahoma City, OK 73105
(405) 521–3828

UNITED NATIONAL INDIAN TRIBAL
   YOUTH (UNITY)
4010 Lincoln Blvd., Suite 202
P.O. Box 25042
Oklahoma City, OK 73125
(405) 524–3010

#### ◆ OREGON

AFFILIATED TRIBES OF THE NORTHWEST
   INDIANS
222 N.W. Davis, Suite 403
Portland, OR 97232
(503) 241–0070

NATIONAL INDIAN CHILD WELFARE
5100 S.W. Macadam Ave., Suite 300
Portland, OR 97201
(503) 222–4044

ORGANIZATION OF THE FORGOTTEN
   AMERICAN
4509 South 6th St., Rm. 206
Klamath Falls, OR 97603
(541) 882–4441

#### ◆ PENNSYLVANIA

AMERICAN INDIAN ADOPTION RESOURCE
   EXCHANGE
Council of Three Rivers
American Indian Center, Inc.
200 Charles St.
Pittsburgh, PA 15238
(412) 782–4457

INDIAN RIGHTS ASSOCIATION
c/o Janney Montgomery Scott
1801 Market St.
Philadelphia, PA 19103
(215) 665–6000

#### ◆ SOUTH DAKOTA

AMERICAN INDIAN RELIEF COUNCIL
1321 Concord St.
Rapid City SD 57703
(866) 556–2472

ASSOCIATION ON AMERICAN INDIAN
   AFFAIRS, INC.
P.O. Box 268
Tekakwitha Complex Agency, Rd #7
Sisseton, SD 57262
(605) 698–3998

NORTH AMERICAN INDIAN WOMEN'S
   ASSOCIATION
P.O. Box 805
Eagle Butte, SD 57625
(605) 964–2136

WORKING INDIANS CIVIL ASSOCIATION
P.O. Box 537
Pierre, SD 57501

WOUNDED KNEE MEMORIAL ASSOCIATION
Wounded Knee, SD 57794

#### ◆ TENNESSEE

UNITED SOUTH AND EASTERN TRIBES, INC.
711 Stewarts Ferry Pike, Suite 100
Nashville, TN 37214
(615) 872–7900

#### ◆ UTAH

UTAH NAVAJO DEVELOPMENT COUNCIL
P.O. Box 129
Bluff, UT 84512
(435) 672–2381

#### ◆ VIRGINIA

AMERICAN INDIAN HERITAGE FOUNDATION
6051 Arlington Blvd.
Falls Church, VA 22044
(703) 237–7500

AMERICAN INDIAN HIGHER EDUCATION
CONSORTIUM
121 Oronoco St.
Alexandria, VA 22314
(703) 838–0400

THE FALMOUTH INSTITUTE, INC.
3918 Prosperity Ave., Suite 302
Fairfax, VA 22031
(703) 352–2250

NATIONAL INDIAN EDUCATION
ASSOCIATION
700 N Fairfax St., Suite 210
Alexandria, VA 22314
(703) 838–2870

NATIONAL INDIAN RELIEF COUNCIL
National Office
70 Main St., Suite 43
Warrenton, VA. 20186
(800) 370–0872

### ◆ WASHINGTON

AMERICAN INDIAN COUNCIL OF
ARCHITECTS AND ENGINEERS
P.O. Box 477
Grandview WA 98930
(509) 882–1144

CENTER FOR WORLD INDIGENOUS STUDIES
PMB 214
1001 Cooper Point Rd., S.W.
Olympia WA 98502–1107
(360) 754–1990

NATIONAL CENTER FOR AMERICAN INDIAN
ENTERPRISE DEVELOPMENT
Northwest Regional Office
934 N. 143 St.
Seattle, WA 98133
(206) 365–7735

NORTHWEST INDIAN WOMEN'S CIRCLE
8112 112 St. Court
East Puialle, WA 98373
(253) 848–5555

SEATTLE INDIAN SERVICES
606 12th Ave., S.
Seattle WA 98144
(206) 329–6594

UNITED INDIANS OF ALL TRIBES
FOUNDATION
Day Break Star Arts Center
Discovery Park
Box 99100
Seattle, WA 98199
(206) 285–4425

### ◆ WISCONSIN

MIDWEST TREATY NETWORK
731 State Street
Madison, WI 53703
(608) 246–2256

# Canadian Native Organizations

## NATIONAL ORGANIZATIONS & PROVINCIAL/TERRITORIAL ASSOCIATIONS

### ♦ ALBERTA

MÉTIS NATION OF ALBERTA
2003 Suite Basement No 2
909 3rd Ave. N.
Lethbridge, AB T1H 0H5
(403) 328–7828

TREATY 7 TRIBAL COUNCIL HEAD OFFICE
Suite 400, 9911 Chula Blvd.
Tsuutina Nation, AB T2W 6H6
(403) 281–9728

### ♦ BRITISH COLUMBIA

FIRST NATIONS NATIONAL GAMING
    COUNCIL
Suite 50, 666 Burrad St.
Vancouver, BC V6C 3H3
(604) 687–3216

INDIAN HOMEMAKERS ASSOCIATION OF
    BRITISH COLUMBIA
251 E11 Ave.
Vancouver, BC V5T 2C4
(604) 876–0944

MÉTIS PROVINCIAL COUNCIL OF BRITISH
    COLUMBIA
13456–108th Ave.
Surrey, BC V3T 2K1
(604) 581–5863

NATIVE BROTHERHOOD OF BRITISH
    COLUMBIA
Box 45711, 850 W. Hasting St.
Vancouver, BC V5C 1E1
(604) 684–1951

NATIVE FISHING ASSOCIATION
303–100 Park Royal S.
West Vancouver, BC V7T 1A2
(604) 926–8010

NISGA'A LISIMS GOVERNMENT
P.O. Box 231
New Aiyansh. BC V0J 1A0
(250) 633–2601

UNION OF BRITISH COLUMBIA INDIAN
    CHIEFS
5th FL, 342 Water St.
Vancouver, BC V6B 1B6
(604) 684–0231

UNITED NATIVE NATIONS
626 Bute St., 2nd FL
Vancouver, BC V6E 3M1
(604) 688–1821

### ♦ LABRADOR

LABRADOR MÉTIS NATION
P.O. Box 2164
Station B
Goose Bay, LB A0P 1E0
(709) 896–0592

### ♦ MANITOBA

ARCTIC CO-OPERATIVE LIMITED
1645 Inkster Blvd.
Winnipeg MT R2X 2W7
(204) 697–1625

ASSEMBLY OF MANITOBA CHIEFS
200–260 St. Mary Ave.
Winnipeg, MB R3C 0M6
(204) 956–0610

INDIAN COUNCIL OF FIRST NATIONS OF
MANITOBA, INC.
P.O. Box 13, Group 10, R.R. 2
St. Anne, MB R5H 1R2
(204) 422–5193

INDIAN COUNCIL OF FIRST NATIONS OF
MANITOBA, INC.
Mall Box 3848
The Pas, MB R9A 1S4
(204) 623–7227

MANITOBA KEEWATINOWI OKIMAKANAK,
INC.
200–701 Thompson St.
Thompson, MB R8N 2A3
(204) 778–4431

MANITOBA MÉTIS FEDERATION, INC.
150 Henry Ave., 3rd FL
Winnipeg, MB R3B 0J7
(204) 586–8474

NATIONAL NATIVE ALCOHOL AND DRUG
PROGRAMS
20 3rd St., E.
Portage La Prairie, MB R1N 1N4
(204) 857–6178

NATIVE WOMEN TRANSITION CENTER
105 Aikins
Winnipeg MB R2W 4E4
(204) 989–8240

### ♦ NEW BRUNSWICK

ABORIGINAL PEOPLE'S COUNCIL
320 St. Mary's St.
Fredericton, NB E3A 2S4
(506) 458–8422

BIG COVE CHILD AND FAMILY SERVICES
P.O. Box 1078
Rezton, NB E4W 5N6
(506) 523–8224

NEW BRUNSWICK NATIVE INDIAN WOMEN'S
COUNCIL
120 Paul St.
Fredericton, NB E3A 2V8
(506) 458–1114

UNION OF NEW BRUNSWICK INDIANS
385 Wilsey Rd,. Comp 44
Fredericton, NB A3B 5N6
(506) 458–9444

### ♦ NEWFOUNDLAND

FEDERATION OF NEWFOUNDLAND INDIANS
P.O. Box 956
Corner Brook, NF A2H 6J3
(709) 634–0996

LABRADOR INUIT ASSOCIATION
P.O. Box 70
Nain, NF A0P 1L0
(709) 922–2942

OKALAKATIGET SOCIETY
P.O. Box 160
Nain, NF A0P 1L0
(709) 922–2955

### ♦ NORTHWEST TERRITORIES

ARCTIC COOPERATIVE DEVELOPMENT
FUND
321 C. Old Airport Rd.
Yellowknife, NT X1A 3X3
(867) 873–3481

DENE NATION
P.O. Box 2338
Yellowknife, NT X1A 2P7
(867) 873–4081

MÉTIS ASSOCIATION OF THE NORTHWEST
TERRITORIES
P.O. Box 1375, 5125 50th St.
69 Yellowknife, NT X1A 2P1
(867) 873–3505

NATIVE WOMEN'S ASSOCIATION OF
NORTHWEST TERRITORIES
P.O. Box 2321
Yellowknife, NT X1A 2P7
(867) 873–5509

### ♦ NOVA SCOTIA

NATIVE COUNCIL OF NOVA SCOTIA
P.O. Box 1320, Abenaki Rd.
Truro, NS B2N 5N2
(902) 895–1523

NOVA SCOTIA NATIVE WOMEN'S
  ASSOCIATION
P.O. Box 805
Truro, NS B2N 5E8
(902) 893–7402

#### ◆ NUNAVUT

NUNAVUT TUNNGVIK INC.
Box 638
Iqaliuit, Nunavut X0A 0H0
(613) 238–1096

#### ◆ ONTARIO

ABORIGINAL NURSES ASSOCIATION
12 Stirling St., 3rd Floor
Ottawa, ON K1Y 1P8
(613) 724–4677

ABORIGINAL RIGHTS COALITION
153 Laurier Ave. E., 2nd FL
Ottawa, ON K1N 6N8
(613) 235–9956

ASSEMBLY OF FIRST NATIONS
(NATIONAL INDIAN BROTHERHOOD)
1 Nicholas St., Suite 1002
Ottawa, ON K1N 7B7
(613) 241–6789

ASSOCIATION OF IROQUOIS AND ALLIED
  INDIANS
387 Princess Ave.
London, ON N6B 2A7
(519) 434–2761

CANADIAN ABORIGINAL AIDS NETWORK
2–324 Somerset St., W.
Ottawa, ON K2P 0J9
(888) 285–2226

CANADIAN ALLIANCE IN SOLIDARITY FOR
  NATIVE PEOPLE
P.O. Box 574, Station P
Toronto, ON M5S 2T1
(416) 973–6351

CANADIAN COUNCIL FOR ABORIGINAL
  BUSINESS
204A George St., Coach House
Toronto, ON MAR 2N5
(416) 961–8663

CHIEFS OF ONTARIO
344 Bloor St. W., Suite 602
Toronto, ON M5S 3A7
(416) 972–0212

CONGRESS OF ABORIGINAL PEOPLE
867 St. Lauren Blvd.
Ottawa, ON K1A 3B1
(613) 747–6022

CREE-NASKAPI COMMISSION
Capital Square Bldg.
222 Queen St., Suite 305
Ottawa, ON K1A 5V9
(613) 234–4288

FIRST NATION COMMUNICATIONS
Suit 2–203, St. Catherine St.
Ottawa, ON K2P 1C3
(613) 231–3858

GIGNUL NON-PROFIT HOUSING CORP.
396 Maclaren St.
Ottawa, ON K2P 0M8
(613) 232–0016

GRAND COUNCIL OF THE CREES (QUEBEC)
  AUTHORITY
24 Bays Water Ave.
Ottawa, ON K1Y 2E4
(613) 761–1655

GRAND COUNCIL TREATY NO. 3
P.O. Box 1720
Sonora, ON PAN 3X7
(807) 548–4215

INDIGENOUS BAR ASSOCIATION IN CANADA
408 Queen St.
Ottawa, ON K1R 5A7
(613) 233–8586

INTERNATIONAL NETWORK OF INDIGENOUS
PEOPLES ASSOCIATION
54 Lockearnest St.
Hamilton, ON L8R 1W1
(905) 523–7356

INUIT CIRCUMPOLAR CONFERENCE
544–170 Laurier Ave., W.
Ottawa, ON K1P 5V5
(613) 563–2642

INUIT TAPIRISAT OF CANADA
510–170 Laurier Ave., W.
Ottawa, ON K1P 5V5
(613) 238–8181

INUIT WOMEN'S ASSOCIATION
1992 Bank St.
Ottawa, ON K2P 1W8
(613) 238–3977

MÉTIS NATIONAL COUNCIL
Suite 201, 350 Sparks St.
Delta Hotel Office Tower
Ottawa, ON K1R 7S8
(613) 232–3216

MÉTIS NATIONAL COUNCIL OF WOMEN
500–1 Nicholas St.
Ottawa ON
(613) 241–6028

MÉTIS NATION OF ONTARIO
193 Holland Ave.
Ottawa, ON K1Y 0Y3
(613) 798–1488

NATIONAL ABORIGINAL ACHIEVEMENT
FOUNDATION
70 Yorkville Ave., #33A
Toronto ON M5R 1B9
(800) 329–9780

NATIONAL ABORIGINAL FORESTRY
ASSOCIATION
875 Bank St.
Ottawa, ON K1S 3W4
(613) 233–5563

NATIONAL ABORIGINAL NETWORK ON
DISABILITY (NAND)
R.R. 3
Cornwall, ON K6H 5R7
(613) 241–6789 ext. 257

NATIONAL INUIT YOUTH COUNCIL
510–170 Laurier Ave.
Ottawa, ON K1P 5V5
(613) 238–8181

NATIVE CANADIAN CENTRE OF TORONTO
16 Spadina Rd.
Toronto, ON M5R 2S7
(416) 964–9087

NATIVE INDIAN/INUIT PHOTOGRAPHERS
ASSOCIATION
580 Concession St.
Hamilton, ON L8V 1B1
(416) 529–7477

NATIVE WOMEN'S ASSOCIATION OF
CANADA
1292 Wellington
Ottawa, ON K1Y 3A9
(613) 722–3033

ONTARIO NATIVE WOMEN'S ASSOCIATION
101–115 North May St.
Thunder Bay, ON P7B 5Z8
(807) 623–3442

◆ **PRINCE EDWARD ISLAND**

NATIVE COUNCIL OF PRINCE EDWARD
ISLAND
33 Allen St.
Charlottetown, PEI C1A 2V6
(902) 892–5314

◆ **QUEBEC**

ASSEMBLY OF FIRST NATIONS OF QUEBEC
430 Chef Stanislas Koska
Village des Hurons
Wendrake, PQ G0A 4V0
(418) 842–5020

GRAND COUNCIL OF THE CREES OF
QUEBEC
277 Duke St., Suite 100
Montreal, PQ H3C 2M2
(514) 861–5837

KAHNAWAKE YOUTH CENTRE
P.O. Box 907
Kahnawake, PQ J0L 1B0
(450) 632–6601

NATIONAL ASSOCIATION OF CULTURAL
EDUCATION CENTERS
191 Promenade Du Portage # 500
Hull, PQ J8X 2K6
(819) 772–2331

## NATIONAL INDIAN ARTS & CRAFTS CORPORATION

540 Max Gros-Louis
Village Des Hurons
Wendrake, PQ G0A 4V0
(416) 845–2150

## NATIONAL INDIAN & INUIT COMMUNITY HEALTH REPRESENTATIVES ORGANIZATION

P.O. Box 1019
Kahnawake, PQ J0L 1B0
(514) 632–0892

## NATIVE ALLIANCE OF QUEBEC (MÉTIS NON-STATUS)

21 Brodeur St.
Hull, PQ J8Y 2P6
(819) 770–7763

## QUEBEC NATIVE WOMEN'S ASSOCIATION

460 St. Catherine St., W., Suite 610
Montreal, PQ H3B 1A7
(514) 954–9991

## ◆ SASKATCHEWAN

## FEDERATION OF SASKATCHEWAN INDIAN NATIONS

Head Office
Suite 200–103A Packham Ave.
Saskatoon, SK S7N 4K4
(306) 665–1215

## MÉTIS NATION OF SASKATCHEWAN

219 Robin Crescent
Saskatoon, SK S7L 6M8
(306) 343–8285

## NATIONAL ABORIGINAL VETERAN'S ASSOCIATION

32 Moore PL
Saskatoon, SK S7L 3B8
(306) 384–0565

## PRINCE ALBERT GRAND COUNCIL

Opawakoscikn Reserve 291
P.O. Box 2350
Prince Albert, SK S6Y 6Z1
(306) 953–7200

## ◆ YUKON TERRITORY

## COUNCIL FOR YUKON INDIANS

11 Nisutlin Dr.
Whitehorse, YT Y1A 3S4
(867) 667–7631

## YUKON ABORIGINAL WOMEN'S COUNCIL

And ABORIGINAL LABOR FORCE ALLIANCE
103–307 Jarvis St.
Whitehorse, YT Y1A 2H3
(867) 667–6162

## YUKON REPRESENTATIVE

WHITE RIVER FIRST NATIONS
General Delivery
Beaver Creek, YT Y0B 1A0
(403) 862–7802

## References

### U.S. Indian Activism

Ambler, Marjane. *Breaking the Iron Bonds: Indian Control of Energy Development.* Lawrence: University Press of Kansas, 1990.

Blue Cloud, Peter, ed. *Alcatraz is Not an Island.* Berkeley: Wingbow Press, 1972.

Churchill, Ward, and Jim Vander Wall. *Agents of Repression: The FBI's Secret Wars against the Black Panther Party and the American Indian Movement.* Boston: South End Press, 1988.

Cornell, Stephen. *The Return of the Native: American Indian Political Resurgence.* New York: Oxford University Press, 1988.

Cowger, Thomas W. *The National Congress of American Indians: The Founding Years.* Lincoln: University of Nebraska Press, 1999.

Deloria, Vine, Jr. *Behind the Trail of Broken Treaties: An Indian Declaration of Independence.* New York: Dell, 1974.

———. *Custer Died For Your Sins: An Indian Manifesto.* New York: Macmillan, 1969.

———. *We Talk, You Listen: New Tribes, New Turf.* New York: Macmillan, 1970.

Deloria, Vine, Jr., and Raymond J. DeMallie, comps. *Documents of American Indian Diplomacy: Treaties, Agreements, and Conventions, 1775–1979.* Norman: University of Oklahoma Press, 1999.

Fixico, Donald L. *The Invasion of Indian Country in the Twentieth Century: American Capitalism and Tribal Natural Resources.* Niwot, Colo.: University Press of Colorado, 1998.

Fortunate Eagle, Adam. *Alcatraz! Alcatraz!: The Indian Occupation of 1969–1971*. Berkeley, Calif.: Heyday Books, 1992.

Gonzalez, Mario, and Elizabeth Cook-Lynn. *The Politics of Hallowed Ground: Wounded Knee and the Struggle for Indian Sovereignty*. Urbana: University of Illinois Press, 1999.

Johnson, Troy. *The Occupation of Alcatraz Island: Indian Self-Determination and the Rise of Indian Activism*. Urbana: University of Illinois Press, 1996.

Josephy, Alvin M., Jr. *Now That the Buffalo's Gone: A Study of Today's American Indian*. New York: Alfred A. Knopf, 1982.

Josephy, Alvin M., Jr., Joane Nagel, and Troy Johnson, eds. *Red Power: The American Indian's Fight for Freedom*. 2nd ed. Lincoln: University of Nebraska Press, 1999.

Matthiessen, Peter. *In the Spirit of Crazy Horse*. New York: Viking, 1991.

Means, Russell, with Marvin J. Wolf. *Where White Men Fear to Tread: The Autobiography of Russell Means*. New York: St. Martin's Press, 1995.

Nagel, Joane. *American Indian Ethnic Renewal: Red Power and the Resurgence of Identity and Culture*. New York: Oxford University Press, 1996.

Peroff, Nicholas C. *Menominee Drums: Tribal Termination and Restoration, 1954–1974*. Norman: University of Oklahoma Press, 1982.

Smith, Paul Chaat, and Robert Allen Warrior. *Like a Hurricane: The Indian Movement from Alcatraz to Wounded Knee*. New York: Free Press, 1996.

Steiner, Stan. *The New Indians*. New York: Harper and Row, 1968.

Weyler, Rex. *Blood of the Land: The Government and Corporate War Against First Nations*. Rev. ed. Philadelphia: New Society Publishers, 1992.

*Anthony Clark and Joane Nagel*

## Canadian Native Activism

Adams, Howard. *Prison of Grass: Canada From the Native Point of View*. Toronto: New Press, 1975.

Armitage, Andrew. *Comparing the Policy of Aboriginal Assimilation: Australia, Canada and New Zealand*. Vancouver: UBC Press, 1995.

Asch, Michael. *Home and Native Land: Aboriginal Rights and the Canadian Constitution*. Toronto and New York: Methuen, 1984; Vancouver: UBC Press, 1993.

Battiste, Marie and Jean Barman, eds. *First Nations Education in Canada: The Circle Unfolds*. Vancouver: UBC Press, 1995.

Berger, Thomas R. *Fragile Freedoms: Human Rights and Dissent in Canada*. Toronto: Clarke, Irwin, 1981.

——. *Village Journey: The Report of the Alaska Native Review Commission*. New York: Hill and Wang, 1985.

Boldt, Menno, J. Anthony Long, eds., in association with Leroy Little Bear. *The Quest for Justice: Aboriginal Peoples and Aboriginal Rights*. Toronto: University of Toronto Press, 1985.

Brigham, Clarence S., ed. *British Royal Proclamations Relating to America, 1603–1783*. Vol. 12 of *Transactions and Collections of the American Antiquarian Society*. Worchester, Mass.: The Society, 1911.

British Columbia Claims Task Force. *The Report of the British Columbia Claims Task Force*. Vancouver, 1991.

Campbell, Maria. *Halfbreed*. Toronto: McClelland and Stewart, 1973. Reprint. Lincoln: University of Nebraska Press, 1982.

Canada. Royal Commission on Aboriginal Peoples. *Treaty Making in the Spirit of Coexistence: An Alternative to Extinguishment*. Ottawa, 1995.

Cardinal, Harold. "Native Women and the Indian Act." In Elliott, Jean Leonard, ed. *Two Nations, Many Cultures: Ethnic Groups in Canada*, 44–50. Scarborough, Ont.: Prentice-Hall Canada, 1979.

——. *The Rebirth of Canada's Indians*. Edmonton: Hurtig, 1969.

——. *The Unjust Society: The Tragedy of Canada's Indians*. Edmonton: M. G. Hurtig, 1969.

Courchene, Thomas J., and Lisa M. Powell. *A First Nations Province*. Kingston, Ont.: Institute of Intergovernmental Relations, Queen's University, 1992.

Deloria, Vine. *Behind the Trail of Broken Treaties: an Indian Declaration of Independence*. New York: Delacorte Press, 1974.

Dobbin, Murray. *The One-and-a-Half Men: The Story of Jim Brady and Malcolm Norris, Métis Patriots of the Twentieth Century*. Vancouver: New Star, 1981.

Duhaime, Gerard. *The Governing of Nunavik: Who Pays for What?*. Sainte-Foy, Quebec: Groupe D'Etudes Inuit et Circumpolaires, Universite Laval, 1993.

Flanagan, Thomas E. "The History of Métis Aboriginal Rights: Politics, Principle and Policy." *Canadian Journal of Law and Society* 5 (1990): 71–94.

Frideres, James S., with Lilianne Ernestine Krosenbrink-Gelissen. *Aboriginal Peoples in Canada: Contemporary Conflicts* 5th ed. Scarborough, Ont.: Prentice Hall Allyn and Bacon Canada, 1998.

Grant, Agnes. *No End of Grief: Indian Residential Schools in Canada*. Winnipeg, Man.: Pemmican Pubs., 1996.

Harvey, Sioux. "Two Models to Sovereignty: A Comparative History of the Mashantucket Pequot Tribal Nation and the Navaho Nation." *American Indian Culture and Research Journal* 20, no. 1 (1996): 147–194.

Haysom, Veryan. "The Struggle for Recognition: Labrador Inuit Negotiations for Land Rights and Self-government." *Etudes Inuit/Inuit Studies* 16 no. 1–2 (1992): 179–197.

Hermann, John R., and Karen O'Connor. "American Indians and the Berger Court." *Social Science Quarterly* 77, no. 1 (1996): 127–145.

Little Bear, Leroy, Menno Boldt and J. Anthony Long, eds. *Pathways to Self-Determination: Canadian Indians and the Canadian State.* Toronto: University of Toronto Press, 1984.

Mackenzie Valley Pipeline Inquiry. *Northern Frontier, Northern Homeland: The Report of the MacKenzie Valley Pipeline Inquiry.* Vol. 1. Ottawa: Minister of Supply and Services Canada, 1977.

Manuel, George and Michael Posluns. *The Fourth World: An Indian Reality.* Toronto: Collier-McMillan Canada; New York: Free Press, 1974.

McCullum, Hugh, and Karmel McCullum. *This Land is Not for Sale: Canada's Original People and Their Land: A Saga of Neglect, Exploitation and Conflict.* Toronto: Anglican Book Centre, 1975.

Miller, James Rodger. *Shingwauk's Vision: A History of Native Residential Schools.* Toronto: University of Toronto Press, 1996.

————., ed. *Sweet Promises: A Reader on Indian-White Relations in Canada.* Toronto: University of Toronto Press, 1991.

Minore, James Bruce, and M. Hill. "Native Language Broadcasting: An Experiment in Empowerment." In *The Mass Media and Canadian Diversity*, edited by Stephen E. Nancoo and Robert Sterling Nancoo, 162–185. Mississauga, Ont.: Canadian Educators Press, 1997.

Pavlik, Steve, ed. *A Good Cherokee, A Good Anthropologist: Papers in Honor of Robert K. Thomas.* Los Angeles: American Indian Studies Center, University of California, 1998.

Pelletier, Wilfred. *Two Articles.* Toronto: Neewin Pub. Co., 1970.

Ponting, J. Rick, ed. *Arduous Journey: Canadian Indians and Decolonization.* Toronto: McClelland and Stewart, 1986.

Ponting, J. Rick and Roger Gibbins. *Out of Irrelevance: A Socio-Political Introduction to Indian Affairs in Canada.* Toronto: Butterworths, 1980.

Raunet, Daniel. *Without Surrender, Without Consent: A History of the Nishga Land Claims.* Vancouver: Douglas and McIntyre, 1984.

Silman, Janet, ed. *Enough is Enough: Aboriginal Women Speak Out.* Toronto: Women's Press, 1987.

Skea, Warren H. "The Canadian Newspaper Industry's Portrayal of the Oka Crisis." *Native Studies Review* 9, no. 1 (1993–1994): 15–31.

Thomas, Robert K. "Pan-Indianism." In *The American Indian Today*, edited by Stuart Levine and Nancy Oestreich Lurie, 128–140. Baltimore: Penguin Books, 1968.

Tobias, John L. "Protection, Civilization, Assimilation: An Outline History of Canada's Indian Policy." In *As Long as the Sun Shines and Water Flows: A Reader in Canadian Native Studies*, edited by Ian A. L. Getty and Antoine S. Lussier, 39–55. Vancouver: University of British Columbia Press, 1983.

Weaver, Sally M. *Making Canadian Indian Policy: The Hidden Agenda 1968–70.* Toronto: University of Toronto Press, 1981.

Wuttunee, William I. C. *Ruffled Feathers: Indians in Canadian Society.* Calgary, Alta.: Bell Books, 1971.

*Ian Mackenzie*

# 8

# *Environment*

♦ American Indians and Their Environment
♦ Aboriginal Peoples and the Environment in Canada ♦ U.S. Environmental Organizations
♦ Canadian Environmental Organizations

## ♦ AMERICAN INDIANS AND THEIR ENVIRONMENT

The natural world is sacred to many Native Americans. Historically, a direct and abiding understanding of the significance of Nature's cycles—life, death, struggle, and renewal—was integral to the survival of Indian people. Environmental understanding was bound in the cosmologies of each tribe's life, reflecting the elemental expressions of human life on Earth and in the cosmos. The key questions each cosmology addressed included: How should the tribal community ecologically integrate into the place they live? How should direct relationships among the individual, the community, and the natural world be established and maintained? Everywhere they lived, Indian people addressed these questions of survival in diverse yet harmonious ways. They thought of their environments richly and of themselves as deeply related to their world.

*Mitakuye oyasin*, or "We are all related," is the metaphor in Lakota prayer that is echoed in the guiding principles of all Indian people. Guided by this principle, Indian people understood that all entities of their environment—plants, animals, stones, trees, mountains, rivers, stars—embodied relationships that must be honored. Human beings are only one part of a complex natural world and are not superior to its other parts. In each place they lived, Native North American peoples learned the subtle, all-important language of interdependency, and through intimate relationships with various environments over thousands of years, accumulated ecological knowledge. From this orientation they developed responsibilities to the land and all living things, similar to those obligations they felt toward each other. Because they honored all life, Indians lived with as little impact on the natural state of the land as possible. They allowed the land to be, taking from it

only the resources necessary for their survival, always remembering these were given to them. Perpetuation of this sacred and survival-oriented responsibility from one generation to the next was accomplished through myth, ritual, art, and traditional education.

This relationship to the natural world can be called *ensoulment*. The ensoulment of nature, a projection of the human sense of soul with its archetypes into the entities, phenomena, and places in their natural environment, is one of the most ancient foundations of human psychology. The roots of Indian understandings of human meaning were grounded in the same order that they perceived in nature. The people were born of the earth. Nature was a part of them, and they were a part of nature. The land was full of spirit, full of life energy. Every thing—a rock, a tree, a mountain, a bird, an insect—had its own expression of life and way of exuding Spirit.

Over a few generations, physical and psychological traits formed relative to each distinct climate, soil and geography of a place. In the same way that plants and animals of a place develop certain traits through natural selection, the development of mountain people became distinct from that of desert people and from Plains people. Although it is not as apparent now as it was in the past, Native Americans of the Northwest, Southwest, Plains, Great Lakes, and Southeast reflect physical and psychological characteristics that are directly the result of their generations of interaction with the geographies and ecologies of their cultures.

Living in the forests of the Northeast, Indians venerated the trees and integrated that reality into every aspect of their lives. In the Southwest, Pueblo Indians became dry land farmers and venerated the cycles of water, earth, wind, and fire. The fisher and forest people of the Pacific Northwest established intimate

Pueblo Bonito in Chaco Canyon National Park in New Mexico, 2000. (Photo by Gregory A. Cajete)

relationships with the salmon upon which they depended for life, the sea mammals they encountered, and the great rain forests that grew in their land.

People make a place as much as a place makes them. Native people managed their environments in ways that today are termed ecologically viable. Through the practical knowledge gained from long-term experience, they designed their habitats to perpetuate specific, desirable plant and animal life. In the East and Southeast, Indians created a habitat for deer, hare, beaver, turkey, grouse, and quail by burning woodland that grew back as mixed grasslands and young trees. In the prairie areas, fire created additional buffalo habitat. In the Great Basin desert, the Paiute and Shoshoni set fires to encourage the growth of wild plant species and create deer and antelope habitat.

They cultivated, irrigated, and pruned native plants. California Indians practiced selective gathering in their ancestral territories and actually designed the flora and fauna of their region. Their harvesting of wild potatoes, acorns, pine nuts, buckeyes, bunch grass, and other wild staples perpetuated these species and ensured their availability not only for people but also for other animals. The Ojibwa of the Great Lakes area regularly replanted a portion of the wild rice that had been harvested. Plants were also managed for making basketry, clothing, and tools.

The relationship between Indians and their environment was so deep that separation from their home territory by forced relocation in the last century constituted a loss of part of the soul of those Indian communities and for their subsequent generations. Indian people were joined with their land with such intensity that many who were forced to live on reservations suffered a form of soul death. The major expression of this was the loss of a sense of home and a profound homesickness with all its accompanying physical and psychological maladies. The people withered like mountain flowers pulled from their mother soil (Cajete 1994, 74–114).

## The Establishment of Reservations

The restriction of Indian tribes to reservations gave the federal government a powerful role, one that con-

Cliff palace at Mesa Verde National Park in Cortes, Colorado, 2000. (Photo by Gregory A. Cajete)

stantly threatens tribal sovereignty. Many reservations were not established in the original territory of the tribe, making it impossible to maintain the traditional subsistence lifestyle. Some tribes are forced to share reservations with traditional adversaries, disrupting traditional relationships and subsistence patterns. Reservation lands are held "in trust" by the government for the benefit of the resident Indian tribes. "Allotments" of farm land are held "in trust" for an individual Indian or Indian family, but adjoining lands not so allotted were opened to non-Indian settlement, resulting in reservations with both Indian and non-Indian owned lands. Technically, therefore, the land is owned by the government, and tribes or individuals have only the right to use and occupy it.

Because the lands are held by the government and because the government has a "trust responsibility" toward Indians and Indian tribes, the use of the lands is governed by a complex set of federal regulations as well as by tribal law and custom. The "trust responsibility" of the government toward Indians generally means that the government must act in the best interests of the beneficiary, which may be either a tribe or an individual

Indian. But the government has been inclined to act as though it alone knew what constituted the best interests of Indians, and disputes are common.

The government planned that Native Americans would become farmers, but most reservations contained neither good farmland nor traditional subsistence resources. Although the federal government had not intended Indians to acquire rights to valuable land, many reservations were rich in resources undervalued in the nineteenth century, such as timber, coal, gas, oil, and minerals. Over half of all known domestic reserves of uranium and 30 percent of low-sulfur coal on federally controlled lands are found on Indian reservations. Approximately 25 percent of domestic oil reserves are also on Indian reservations. When the treaty makers learned of resources present on proposed reservation lands during the negotiations, the treaties were altered or abrogated. In California, the eighteen treaties negotiated in the early 1850s during the Gold Rush starting in 1849 were never ratified by the United States Senate, primarily out of fear that reservation lands might contain gold. The dispute between the Sioux tribe and the federal government over the gold-filled Black Hills of

South Dakota had a similar basis. It is ironic that lands once deemed useless for any purpose other than Indian reservations would prove rich in nonrenewable resources. As development of these non-subsistence resources required capital and technical expertise, off-reservation companies became involved in the excavation of these resources, a fact at the root of many disputes in the current relationship among Indians, their environment, and the federal government.

## The Role of the Federal Government

Tension between the exercise of tribal sovereignty and the role of the Bureau of Indian Affairs (BIA) often lies in a disagreement about whether an action is in the best interests of a tribe. The current role of the BIA must be understood against this historical backdrop. For example, if a tribe decides to lease lands for oil and gas drilling, the BIA determines whether the lease meets federal regulations. Once a tribal government enters a lease, it is difficult to justify government interference with that decision because a specific lease is not in the best interest of the tribe. However, the BIA can refuse to approve leases based on a number of factors, including a belief that the terms of the lease are unfair to the tribe. It remains in question whether federal regulations reflect the proper factors for deciding whether a lease is in a tribe's best interest. The government has acted in the belief that it has always known what is in the economic and social interests of Indian tribes. Although tribes now typically make independent decisions regarding whether to lease land, it was not uncommon earlier in the century for the BIA to negotiate leases on behalf of tribes with little or no regard to the wishes of the tribes.

In addition to approving the leases for the development of natural resources, the government implements federal environmental laws on reservations. A flaw in the design of the original plan rendered this idea useless. Major environmental laws, such as the Clean Water Act and the Resource Conservation and Recovery Act administered by the United States Environmental Protection Agency (EPA), allow state agencies to assume responsibility from the federal government for administration of the programs within the state. Since 1972, the EPA has provided billions of dollars to states for developing local expertise in environmental regulation. But state governments have no authority to implement these programs on federally owned Indian reservations, and tribal governments were not originally in the statutory programs. Therefore, although Congress intended these environmental laws to cover every square mile of the country, Indian reservations did not fit into the original scheme.

Recently, Congress amended many statutes to allow Indian tribes to play a role similar to states in assuming responsibility for administering these programs on their lands. However, the funding to assist tribes to build their internal agencies, to survey their existing pollution problems, and to implement programs to address decades of neglect are disproportionately low in respect to the size of the problem and number of acres.

The BIA's stewardship left behind a legacy of pollution problems that the federal government could not resolve. Careless and negligent leaseholders polluted land and water and were never held accountable. For example, agricultural leaseholders might leave behind leaking pesticide containers, or gas station leaseholders might leave behind leaking underground storage tanks. Existing waste facilities, such as dumps built by the federal Indian Health Service, do not meet current federal standards and are a major source of pollution on many Indian reservations. The failure of the BIA to address these problems are compounded by the lack of resources available to the tribes to address the problems directly.

## Tribal Management of Renewable Natural Resources Today

As resources became more scarce and the land area open for Native use became more restricted by the federal government, tribal management of cultural and natural resources has become more important to the survival of traditional culture. Today many Indian tribes are taking the lead in managing their natural resources and in regulating the reservation environment. Funding from the Environmental Protection Agency is available for tribes to train members in technical environmental fields, draft tribal codes and regulations, develop enforcement capabilities, and work with other government entities to resolve pollution problems that overlap reservation and state lands. Indian tribes have chosen a variety of methods to manage their remaining lands to better suit the different needs of their communities.

Some tribes are also protecting and rebuilding their natural resources. The Salish Kootenai of the Flathead Reservation in Montana have designated 89,500 acres of the Flathead Reservation as a wilderness area emphasizing protection of grizzly bear habitat. The Confederated Tribes of the Yakima Reservation and the Confederated Tribes of the Warm Springs Reservation have set aside reserves where hunting is forbidden. In Arizona, the Tohono O'Odham and the Pima-Maricopa at Gila River have strong native plant protection programs. The Klamath of Oregon has devoted significant

Hogan left by inhabitants because of stripmining by Peabody Coal Company, which was responsible for the enormous siltation mounds, 1951. (Photo by Ilka Hartmann)

tribal resources to a fishery management program designed to restore the traditional fish species from their current endangered status.

Since many reservation communities are economically distressed, a few tribes have seriously considered commercial proposals to deposit solid and hazardous waste on remote, sparsely populated land. Surrounding non-Indian communities are upset by the possibility of waste disposal on nearby land, since any environmental hazards that might occur will most likely affect the land and environment near the reservation. Local, state, federal, and tribal governments are often locked in conflicting roles when such proposals arise (Crow 1994, 293–602).

## Native Americans and Environmentalists

The relations between Native Americans and environmentalists have been complex and multifaceted. These relations at times have been characterized by collaboration and mutual support; at other times these relationships are fraught with conflict over competing or divergent agendas. This situation arises partly because many aspects of American Indian epistemology as they relate to the environment stand in stark contrast to Euro-American scientific traditions and sociocultural assumptions upon which environmentalists still largely base their thought and practice. In contrast, American Indian traditional knowledge is considered sacred and its transmission is oral; information is neither quantified nor collected for statistical analyses and is couched in fundamentally different philosophical contexts and perceptions of the relationship of humans to nature.

Subsequently, many aspects of American Indian epistemology and education have been considered invalid because its methods, sources, and values are incongruent with Euro-American norms. In its language and implicitly stated position of privilege, science disallows participation of American Indian epistemology in the traditional scientific domain. Therefore, the positive and mutually supportive interaction between Native Americans and environmentalists is contingent upon the ability of environmentalists to become open to a cultural perception that does not separate humans and nature. Indeed, it may be said that environmental science is evolving as the first integrated Western science. With environmentalism's focus on the greater whole of natural systems and on trying to understand the interrelationships among ethics, science, and society, there has evolved a perspective that parallels Native American environmental thought. The challenge of positively developing the relationships of Native Americans and environmentalists is to create methods and processes that promote collaborative learning in which these parallel systems of knowledge can participate equally.

## Native Americans and Hazardous Wastes

The relationship between Native Americans and uranium mining provides a case study that characterizes the adversity and conflicts that often arise around hazardous wastes and Native peoples. Nationwide, uranium is the greatest single source of tribal mineral wealth. According to the Council of Energy Resource Tribes, Indian tribal lands contain almost 80 percent of recoverable uranium in the United States. During the 1970s mining of uranium on tribal lands experienced a boom. By current estimates, about half of the recoverable uranium lies beneath the state of New Mexico and about half of this immense reserve lies beneath the Navajo Reservation (see Grinde and Johansen 1995, 203).

Several mining companies, beginning in the 1940s, began uranium extraction operations on the Navajo Reservation. The remoteness of the area, its sparse population, availability of cheap labor, and lack of regulatory laws made the Navajo Reservation such a prime option for mining companies that by the late 1970s over 700,000 acres in the northeast corner of the reservation were under lease for uranium mining (Grinde and Johansen 1995, 209). Early conditions of uranium mining on the reservation were primitive and hazardous. Little attention was paid to the health and safety of the miners. Health, safety, and pollution regulations were practically nonexistent in those days and the only steady jobs available on the reservation were working in the mines. During the late 1970s the first indications of the long-term health effects of the earlier mining appeared. The inordinate number of deaths of former miners from lung cancer made evident that mining companies "considered miners lives as cheaply as their labor" (Grinde and Johansen 1995, 208).

"The biggest expulsion of radioactive material in the United States occurred on 16 July 1978, at 5 a.m. on the Navajo reservation.... On that morning, more than 1,100 tons of uranium mining wastes-tailings gushed through a mud-packed dam near Church Rock, New Mexico. With the tailings, 100 million gallons of radioactive water gushed through the dam before the crack was repaired" (Grinde and Johansen 1995, 211).

The radioactive water flowed down the Rio Puerco, the major water source for man, animals, and agriculture in the region. Thus, the nuclear mining legacy still blows in the winds, flows in the water, and walks with the Navajo who still live along the Rio Puerco. This example of the nuclear legacy along the Rio Puerco shows the tenuous relationship between Native Americans and hazardous waste that continues to haunt many tribes.

This urgency for mining available sources of uranium will no doubt continue as industrial nations are forced to move away from reliance on fossil fuels because of dwindling supplies, escalating costs, and the accumulating affects of global warming due to carbon dioxide emissions resulting from the burning of fossil fuels. The health and toxic consequences of uranium mining on Native lands will continue to affect Native populations well into the twenty-first century.

## Conclusion

The interplay between government management of natural resources and the priorities of modern tribal governments will continue to present obstacles to environmental balance on reservations, but for American Indians this is not the most important challenge. The real challenge for Indian people and for all people lies in restoring our relationship with our earth. For the first Europeans, America's land was wilderness, an obstacle to be overcome, and then a material object, a commodity to be used for economic gain. Western culture, through its unique play of history, disconnected itself from the natural world in order to conquer, control, and ultimately exploit it for economic gain. In doing so, society became disconnected from the wellspring of the ancient unconscious, primal orientations to spiritual ecology, and a deeply internalized sense of place and the importance of living in harmony with it. Ultimately, there can be no separation between humans and the environment. Native American practices were founded on this undeniable reality and sought to perpetuate a sustainable and mutually reciprocal relationship.

Yet, Native Americans are not entirely free from blame for ecological mistakes. Herd management or animal husbandry by both Native and non-Native farmers has caused overgrazing, soil damage due to concentration of hoof impacts, water contamination, unbalanced predator-prey relationships, and the spread of disease among large, concentrated populations of similar stock. Native Arctic hunters have killed huge numbers of whales and seals, which have not regenerated, to supply demands of world markets. Today fewer and fewer Indians engage the land and its plants and animals in the way their ancestors once did. Yet experience with the land was the cornerstone of traditional education and Indian lifestyle. Traditionally, the connection of Indian people to their land was a symbol of their connection to the spirit of life itself. The loss of such a foundational symbol for Indian tribes led to a tremendous loss of meaning and identity that only recently has begun to be revitalized. Loss of Native homelands took such a toll because inner kinship with the earth is an ancient, natural extension of the human psyche. The disconnection of that kinship can lead to a deep split in the inner and outer consciousness of the individual and the group. It can also create a whole set of social and psychological problems that can only be healed through reestablishment of meaningful ties to the land. Revitalizing ancestral connections with their natural environments can be for American Indians an essential healing and transformational process.

*Gregory Cajete*
*University of New Mexico*

## ◆ ABORIGINAL PEOPLES AND THE ENVIRONMENT IN CANADA

It is widely acknowledged that aboriginal peoples have a close and intimate relationship with the natural world. In the past, the concept "environment" was fully integrated into the daily consciousness of aboriginal people and the decision-making processes of each nation. This often remains the case in contemporary times, particularly in communities that continue to live by their traditional values. The lifeways, cultures, knowledge, and health and well-being of aboriginal peoples are intrinsically linked to the health and integrity of the environment. It is for these reasons that Canada is witnessing a revitalization of traditional aboriginal cultures, an assertion of aboriginal rights, and an increased demand for environmental protection alongside sustainable local economic development by aboriginal peoples.

This section provides a brief overview of aboriginal environmental philosophies. It discusses colonization in relation to the current environmental destruction experienced in contemporary aboriginal communities. Several major environmental issues are examined, including environmental contamination in traditional territories, deforestation, hydroelectric development, and conflict over hunting and fishing rights. The section concludes with a discussion regarding the increased interest in indigenous traditional ecological knowledge and how this is transforming Canadian environmental policy.

### Aboriginal Environmental Philosophies

Although aboriginal peoples in Canada have diverse cultures and live in several unique ecological regions, the foundations of their philosophies and worldviews pertaining to the environment share some common themes. Aboriginal worldviews and knowledge systems are complex and intricate. It takes an entire lifetime of apprenticeship with elders and spiritual leaders to fully understand and appreciate these vast bodies of knowledge. What is presented here is a brief overview of the major elements of aboriginal philosophies regarding the environment, necessary to appreciating the complex issues impacting aboriginal peoples and their territories in Canada.

**Spiritual Foundations.** The connection between aboriginal peoples and their environments is embedded in powerful and real relationships with the spirit world. This is often difficult for non-Native people to understand, yet it remains the foundation of aboriginal worldviews and philosophies. For example, the traditional Mi'kmaq people on the east coast of Canada believe that the original spark of life from the Great Council Fire gave each living thing three components: the body, *ktin*, the lifeforce, *manitu*, and the guardian spirits, *wlwnsaléwimku*, who aid living things on their earth walk (Youngblood Henderson, 1997). For the Anishinaabe (Ojibwa), Cree, Haudenosaunee (Iroquois), Innu, Dene, and the many nations on the Plains and West Coast of Canada, everything alive also houses a spirit. Interactions with the spirit world are important for obtaining knowledge, understanding teachings, and healing. Connections to the spirit world reinforce relationships with all other living things. Ceremonies, prayers, songs, dances, creative works, dreaming, and visions remain prominent ways traditional aboriginal peoples continue to nurture their relationships with the spirit-world.

Living a spiritual life means knowing the teachings of the ancestors and beings of the spirit world and living by this wisdom in daily life. Some aboriginal nations have specific teachings and prophecies outlining their sacred responsibility to protect Mother Earth from destructive forces, while others have teachings that instruct them to make decisions based on time frames and considerations spanning centuries. Regardless of their differences, these nations believe that with

The sweatlodge of Anishinaabe elder Garry Raven of the Hollow Water First Nation. (Courtesy of Steve Daniels)

the gifts of Creation come responsibility to follow the teachings of the elders and ancestors, and to behave as the caretakers of Mother Earth.

**The Natural Law and Reciprocity.** In aboriginal cultures, elders teach their children and youth about following basic teachings in order to live in harmony with oneself, others, and all Creation. These teachings represent the codes of conduct sometimes referred to as the Natural Law. The Natural Law is expressed differently in different cultures through relationships with the natural world, oral traditions, ceremonies, traditional activities, values, ethics, and celebrations. For the Okanagan People in British Columbia, every part of daily life, including gathering food and making clothes, was a spiritual act. Natural resources are regarded as gifts and these gifts are acknowledged through ceremonial processes that were part of the Okanagan daily consciousness (Armstrong 1999). Similarly, the Kwakwaka'wakw People of what is now Vancouver Island also offer acknowledgments to the plants, trees, salmon, and animals for giving up their lives so the people could live (Sewid-Smith and Dick

1998). For the Anishinaabe, this reciprocity is formalized in what is known as *mino bimaatisiiwin*, the good life or continuous rebirth (LaDuke 1999). Like the Kwakwaka'wakw and Okanagan Peoples, Anishinaabe cannot take life without leaving a prayer and an offering, thereby giving the spirit of that life form thanks for giving up its life.

**The Place of Humans in the Environment.** In contrast to western views on the environment, aboriginal peoples believe that humans are an integral part of the environment, dependent upon plants, animals, and spirits in order to survive and prosper. This principle is seen in several different aboriginal cultures. For Anishinaabe, the clans, or animals, hold much power and knowledge regarding the environment. They are viewed as teachers, and the Anishinaabe can learn from them through dreams and ceremonies and by carefully observing their behavior. They also believe that humans are the least important beings in the cosmos, and that hunters must ask animals to give up their spirit in order for humans to survive. It is important to Anishinaabe to acknowledge when they take one of the gifts of creation be it a plant, medicine, or animal by leaving an offering. Anishinaabe environmental ethics teach children that they are to treat the elements of the environment with respect and humility, taking only what they need from the environment, using everything they take, and sharing these gifts with other community members.

**Interconnectedness, Interrelationship, and Balance.** Aboriginal cultures view the sky, sun, moon, earth, plants, and animals as relatives. The Haudenosaunee Thanksgiving Address acknowledges the earth as our mother, the sun as our eldest brother, the moon as a grandmother, and the plants and animals as siblings. It is these relationships that foster and maintain respect for different beings in the natural world, and these interrelationships are expressed in the grammatical structures of aboriginal languages. Balance is seen as the key to maintaining healthy relationships between individuals, communities, nations, and environments. Given that humans are part of the environment, dependent upon their relations for substance and survival, many aboriginal peoples believe that when one of these environmental components becomes sick, human beings will also become ill. Following these traditions means maintaining a delicate balance between social, mental, physical, and spiritual health within oneself, one's community, one's nation, and within the natural environment.

## Colonization, Aboriginal Peoples, and Environmental Destruction

Residential schools designed to assimilate Native children into mainstream society served to disconnect a generation of aboriginal people from the land and their families, cultures, and languages. The restrictive policies of the Indian Act, the legislation the Canadian government uses to control "Indians and lands reserved for Indians" also had a profound effect on the relationship between aboriginal peoples and the land. For nearly sixty years, it was illegal to practice aboriginal spirituality and to perform specific sacred ceremonies. Although these days have passed, aboriginal peoples still have little control over the land and resources in their traditional territories. Many children go to schools with curriculum controlled by provincial governments, and this education is neither culturally based nor linguistically attuned to Native peoples' wishes. As aboriginal peoples continue to resist the forces of colonialism and assimilation they also continue to advocate for control over the decisions that impact their families, communities, nations, and environments.

Early European explorers and settlers viewed Canada as a land with unlimited natural resources. As they focused their efforts on clearing the land, harvesting timber resources, commercial fishing, and trapping animals, their view of mans' domination over the environment was prominent. This clashed with the worldviews of the aboriginal nations. Backed by superior military power and an increasing number of settlers, the Europeans succeeded in making their worldview dominant by building a society and economy based on resource exploitation.

The processes of colonization and colonialism had devastating impacts on both the inner environment of aboriginal peoples and the ecosystems and environments of which they are a part. The Mi'kmaq on the east coast of Canada experienced the destruction of their forests and animals, and an increased pressure on their fish stocks. The Anishinaabe, Haudenosaunee, and Cree of central Canada experienced the creation of large settlements in the southern regions of their territories, causing deforestation, destruction of inland fisheries, and deterioration of animal populations as a result of the fur trade. The Assinibione, Dakota, and Nakota nations and the Blackfoot Confederacy across the prairies experienced the destruction of their culture and way of life with the annihilation of the buffalo. As the colonizers and settlers moved further west and north, these same impacts were felt in the salmon fisheries and forests of interior and coastal nations.

In contemporary times, aboriginal peoples continue to be on the front lines in dealing with environmental crises given their continued dependence upon the natural world for life and sustenance. The Canadian government has legislative responsibility for "Indians and lands reserved for Indians" and is required to protect reserve lands for the benefit of First Nations people. The provincial governments have jurisdiction over most portfolios concerning natural resources and the environment. This creates a difficult bureaucracy for aboriginal nations increasingly governing their land and people, and for grassroots community effecting environmental change. Furthermore, traditional territories are not recognized as aboriginal lands by governments. This reality only adds to an increasingly difficult situation. At the local level, aboriginal communities are dealing with a combination of environmental issues including deforestation, mining, industrial development, water-quality issues, waste management, and industrial pollution, all resulting from the government's refusal to recognize aboriginal jurisdiction over aboriginal lands, the rights aboriginal peoples have to govern themselves, and a denied responsibility to remedy past environmental injustices. Given the seriousness and urgent nature of issues surrounding health, poverty, and housing, it is difficult for community governments to find the resources and energy to funnel into environmental protection and justice.

Aboriginal peoples in Canada are very much in a time of healing from past injustices and they are revitalizing traditional cultural practices. Elders maintain that traditional teachings and values are paramount in building sustainable healthy communities in the future and that they remain relevant for contemporary life. After centuries of mistreatment and injustice, aboriginal peoples are beginning to explore how best to honor their traditions and apply them to contemporary problems. This process holds the most promise for creating innovative environmental solutions for aboriginal communities in the future.

## Industrial Contamination in Aboriginal Territories

Industrial development continues to have major implications for contemporary aboriginal communities. Large-scale mining, logging, and hydroelectric development continue to alienate aboriginal peoples from the land, contaminate rivers and lakes, and destroy sacred sites, traditional economies, and traditional foodways. The sociocultural impacts of these developments are equally damaging to aboriginal communities as members experience a loss of control over their lives, an assault on their traditional roles, and a loss of identity. They are witnessing the destruction of their mother, the earth.

Perhaps the two most well-known examples of the destruction created by environmental contamination in Canada are Grassy Narrows First Nation, an Anishinaabeg community in northwestern Ontario, and Akwesasne, a Mohawk community in southeastern Ontario. Grassy Narrows First Nation began its struggle with environmental contaminants in 1960 when Dryden Pulp and Paper began polluting the Wabigoon River with suspended solids. In 1962 Reed Paper opened a plant that released an estimated twenty pounds of mercury into the river every day. Only a year later, the government relocated the entire community in order to expand hydroelectric development. This expansion resulted in the flooding of their lands including sacred sites (LaDuke 1999). Elders and community members soon began noticing damage in marine life and fish. And since Anishinaabe people, like other aboriginal people in Canada, maintain such an intimate relationship with the environment, it was not long before the contamination reached the people of Grassy Narrows. Finally, in 1975, the Ontario government admitted that 20 to 30 percent of the residents of Grassy Narrows First Nation showed symptoms of mercury poisoning

(LaDuke 1999). This resulted in the closure of the commercial fishery and the virtual destruction of the traditional economy. But the assault on the traditional territory of Grassy Narrows First Nation did not end there. Currently, the Canadian government is studying the possibility of developing a nuclear waste dump site on Grassy Narrows. Extensive clear-cutting by Abitibi Consolidated continues to destroy hunting and trapping areas, sacred sites, berry-picking areas, and medicinal plants.

Despite all these issues, many community leaders, elders, and traditional people remain strong and continue to resist and challenge the environmental injustices taking place on their lands. Community members from Grassy Narrows have worked for justice on these issues for over ten years, generating national and international support for their community's struggle.

Although the culture and ecology are different in the south of Ontario, the Mohawks of Akwesasne report that the impacts of environmental contamination are similar. The people of Akwesasne are part of the Haudenosaunee Nation and they have lived along the shores of *Kaniatarowaneneh*, the St. Lawrence River, for generations. In the early 1900s industrial development began in the region, and now an estimated 25 percent of all North American industry is located on or near the Great Lakes, all of which drain into the St. Lawrence River (LaDuke 1999). Akwesasne is adjacent to three large companies, Reynolds, General Motors, and Domtar, all of which used polychlorinated biphenyls (PCBs), or man-made chemicals that contain 209 different compounds with variable toxicity, until 1978. After PCBs were banned, they ended up in the water, soil, and air surrounding the Mohawk's territory.

Through the persistence of local community activists, General Motors was eventually convicted of unlawful disposal of PCBs. However, levels of PCBs in sediments, fish, and humans are still detected. In 1985 Mohawk women began to organize themselves and created the Mohawk Mothers' Milk Project. Many of the women sampled had elevated levels of PCBs, DDE, a pesticide related to DDT, and Mirex, yet another pesticide (LaDuke 1994). Katsi Cook, a Mohawk midwife commented, "Women are the first environment. We accumulate the toxic chemicals dumped into our waters by various industries" (quoted in LaDuke 1994: 43). The magnitude of the health and sociocultural effects of this contamination are only beginning to be felt in Akwesasne.

Sadly, the situations at Grassy Narrows and Akwesasne are not unique. Walpole Island First Nation is experiencing the impacts of toxic emissions from the chemical valley in southern Ontario in addition to

Pine Falls Pulp and Paper Company in Manitoba. (Courtesy of Steve Daniels)

pollution from pesticides, fertilizers, accidental spills, and municipal sewage (Jacobs 1992). Dene and Métis communities in the Yukon are concerned that their traditional foods are contaminated with toxins left over from the construction of the Alaskan highway and brought to their territories through long-range atmospheric transport. Inuit communities in Nunavut continue to force the governments responsible to clean up contamination left behind by the United States army after the abandonment of Distance Early Warning (DEW) stations decades ago.

### Aboriginal Peoples and Deforestation

It seems sad and rather ironic that most First Nations and Métis communities living in the "productive" forest regions of Canada suffer from extremely high rates of unemployment and poor housing. It is ironic because their traditional territories are located on some of the most lucrative forests in Canada, yet aboriginal communities rarely see the economic benefits of the forest industry. Instead, these communities are only offered a few low-paying seasonal jobs, while they are left to deal with the devastating long-term environmental impacts of clear-cut logging. Many aboriginal people in the boreal forest regions of Canada continue to hunt and trap as part of their traditional economies. Clear-cut logging has devastating impacts on trappers when cut blocks coincide with trap lines or when plant and animal habitat is destroyed in adjacent areas. Once their trap lines are cut, trappers are unable to make a living for several decades. Hunters and trappers report that the destruction of habitat has lead to the reduction of animal populations. Medicine people mourn the loss of medicinal plants and berries. Logging roads increase access to traditional territories for non-Native hunters. Road building, bridge building, and logging all impact fish and their spawning areas. Many aboriginal communities have experienced the destruction of graves and sacred areas as a result of deforestation. The application of pesticides and herbicides in tree plantations is also a concern of the elders as they watch the plants and animals become increasingly scarce and sick.

While some aboriginal communities and organizations see their entry into the forest industry as the

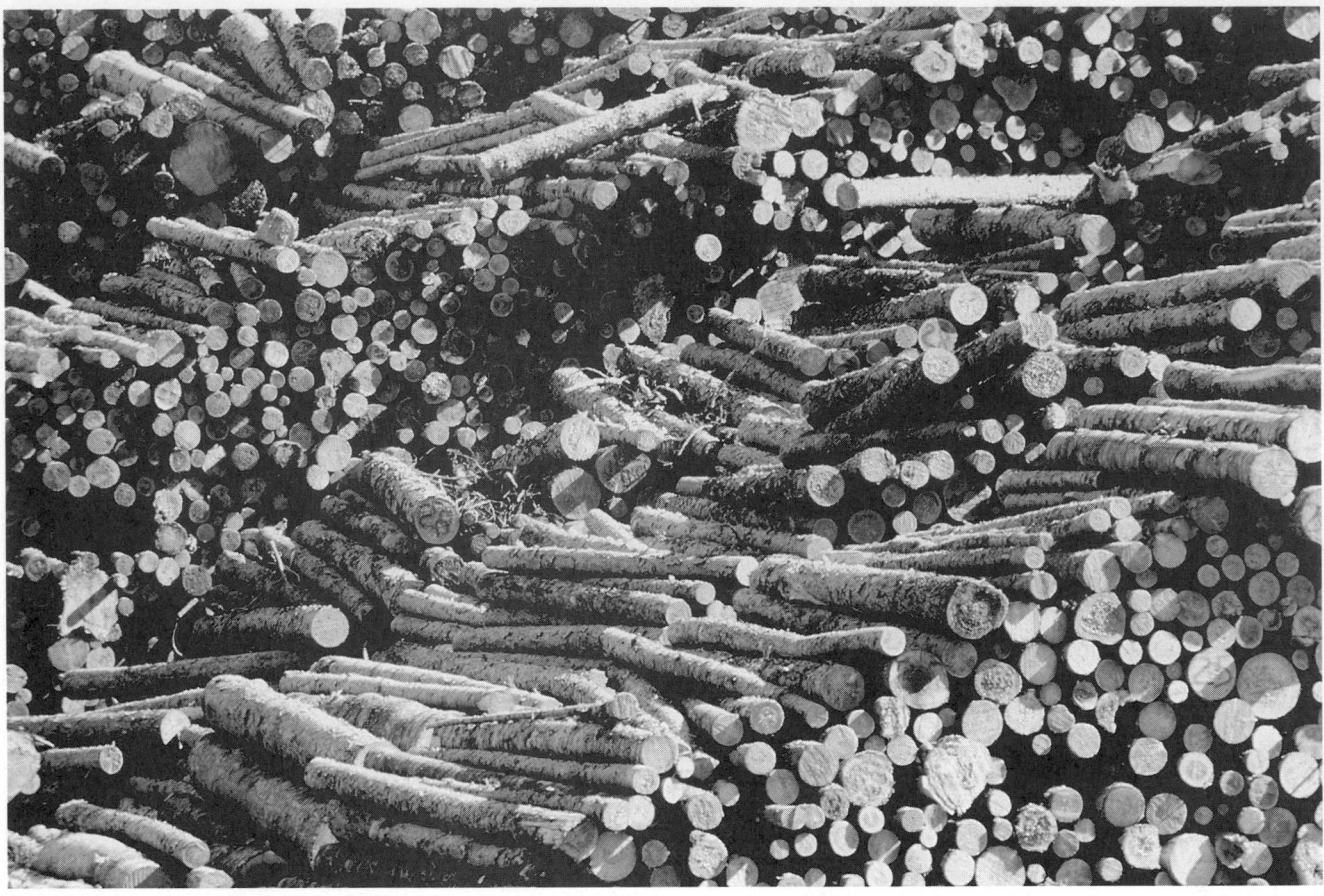

Log pile at the Pine Falls Pulp and Paper Company in Manitoba. (Courtesy of Steve Daniels)

major route to economic development through the equitable sharing of resources and sustainable forest management plans, other communities are looking towards preserving their traditional territories in order to promote traditional economies and alternative economic development plans. Such is the case on the east side of Lake Winnipeg, Manitoba, where several First Nations communities have resisted signing Memorandum Agreements with the local paper company in order to protect their traditional lands.

Alternative economic development plans include developing sustainable local economies using small-scale saw mill operations, the production of value-added forest products, eco-tourism, and non-timber forest products. Still other communities are using their values and ethics to transform conventional forest practices. In central British Columbia, the Gitxsan Nation is using traditional worldviews and values, combined with the technology of geographic information systems (GIS) and global positioning systems (GPS), to develop forestry management plans based on 200 year cycles, rather than the sixty to eighty year cycles used by conventional forest managers (Walsh 1998).

One of the largest environmental victories in Canadian history was led by the members of the Haida Nation on the west coast of Canada. In the face of intensive logging in the area slated to begin in the early 1980s, the council of the Haida Nation created the first two tribal parks in Canada, designating all of Gwaii Haanas (Moresby Island) and Northern Duu Guusd (northwestern Graham Island) permanently protected areas under the Haida Constitution. At the time, pressure from environmental groups, non-Native citizens, and the Haida Nation was mounting over the Western Forest Product's logging in the area and culminated in a political stand-off over Lyell Island in 1985. In response the federal government began negotiations with the Haida to create a federally protected park in the area. In January 1993, the council of the Haida Nation signed the Gwaii Haanas Agreement, creating a National Park Reserve that is co-managed and co-owned by the Haida and the federal government of Canada. The park is managed by a board consisting of two representatives of the Haida Nation and two representatives of the Canadian government. It is managed based on Haida values and knowledge. Members of the Haida Nation provincially owned power companies. In reality, the environmental and cultural impacts of hydroelectric power generation are not felt by urban Canadians. The real impacts are felt by those living close to the land in areas impacted by dam construction, flooding, impoundments, mercury contamination, and power-line construction to deliver energy to the power hungry South.

Excess power is often exported by the provinces of Québec and Manitoba to the northern United States. Two Cree nations in Canada have launched consumer awareness campaigns in the United States in order to bring about national and international attention to the environmental and cultural impacts of hydroelectric development. Cree activism from the James Bay region and campaigning in Canada, the United States, and Europe, along with a damning report by the review bodies conducting environmental and social impact assessment on the Great Whale River Project of Hydro Quebec's environmental impact statement, eventually led to the Quebec government's abandonment of the proposed development. The James Bay Cree are still dealing with the impacts of past hydroelectric development projects and extensive clear-cutting in their traditional land use area. Similarly, the Pimicikamak Cree Nation of Cross Lake in northern Manitoba has resisted accepting a cash settlement, instead lobbying to have the terms of the 1977 Northern Flood Agreement (NFA), a treaty signed between five Cree communities, Manitoba Hydro (the provincial electric utility), the province of Manitoba, and the federal government, honored. The NFA, signed under questionable circumstances after lands had been flooded and the hydroelectric project was already in operation, included promises to replace reserve lands for affected/flooded lands, mitigation of environmental impacts, safe navigation, restitution for damaged property, protection of burial sites, job creation, and comprehensive community development. In exchange for allowing their lands to be flooded, the NFA promises that the Pimicikamak Cree Nation will be treated fairly and equitably, toward the continued viability of the community for the lifetime of the project.

This was considered a progressive response at the time, providing a means to address the property, environmental, and social impacts related to the development without simply paying out lump sums of cash (Hertlein 1999). However, Manitoba Hydro and the provincial and federal governments have not lived up to the terms of the treaty. The leaders of Pimicikamak Cree Nation say about 1.2 million hectares of land have been affected by hydroelectric project, leaving the community to deal with fish contaminated with methyl mercury, constantly changing water levels, the reversal

Clear cut on the east side of Lake Winnipeg, Manitoba, in the traditional territory of Hollow Water First Nation. (Courtesy of Steve Daniels)

maintain rights to freely hunt, fish, gather, and harvest wood within the reserve. The Gwaii Haanas Agreement is a significant milestone for aboriginal peoples in Canada, because Parks Canada no longer has a monopoly over management issues in the Gwaii Haanas National Park Reserve. The agreement acknowledges the continued use of the area by the Haida, without placing them under the authority of the National Parks Act. The Haida's example and experience is of great importance to other aboriginal communities in Canada facing proposed logging and development projects as well as national park initiatives.

## The Impact of Hydroelectric Development

It is rare to find a Métis or First Nation community in northern Québec, Ontario, and Manitoba that has not felt the impacts of hydro dams and flooding. Hydroelectric power is often dubbed a "clean energy" source by

Protesting at the Pine Falls Pulp and Paper Company. (Courtesy of Steve Daniels)

of the seasonal water regime, destruction of moose habitat, changes in caribou migratory patterns, destruction of Cree travel ways, unsafe ice conditions in the winter, destruction of spawning areas, destruction of traditional recreation areas, and the degradation of the traditional economy (Hertlein 1999).

## Conflict Over Aboriginal Rights to Hunt and Fish

Conflicts between Natives and non-Natives over hunting and fishing rights are rooted in non–Native perceptions of aboriginal hunters and fishers as a threat to diminishing resources because they do not have to abide by the same rules as the non-Natives. Some non-Natives do not believe Canada should honor its legally binding treaties with aboriginal peoples. Too often, non-Native anger regarding diminishing animal and fish populations is directed towards aboriginal hunters and fishers instead of governments responsible for past mismanagement and the unsustainable practices of non-Native society.

Aboriginal peoples have rights to hunt, fish, trap, and gather through treaties signed between sovereign

aboriginal nations and the Canadian government, and through constitutionally protected aboriginal rights. Aboriginal rights are a series of undefined rights that stem from the fact that aboriginal nations were self-governing sovereign nations at the time of contact. The federal government has refused to recognize these rights in an operational sense for a number of years. In the last few years, aboriginal peoples have been using the legal system in Canada to force governments to honor these rights.

## Mi'kmaq Treaty Rights, non-Native Lobster Fishers, and Violence in the Maritimes

When the Europeans first came to Canada, they were dependent upon aboriginal nations and their knowledge about the environment for survival. For Europeans that came to the Mi'kmaq Nation, people shared their fishing techniques and catches of lobster with the Europeans. In 1760 a treaty was signed between the two nations in which Mi'kmaq and Maliseet people were given the right to fish, hunt, and gather in order to

Jenpeg Dam impacts the Pimicikamak Cree Nation. (Courtesy of Steve Daniels)

sustain a "moderate livelihood." In subsequent years, the Canadian government refused to uphold the treaty, leaving Mi'kmaq people little opportunity to sustain themselves and their families while non-Native fishers and industrialized logging operations stripped the land of resources and made large profits for non-Native people, governments, and industries.

In 1999 the Supreme Court of Canada upheld the treaty and confirmed the Mi'kmaq and Maliseet peoples' right to fish year-round without the need for a license. The decision sparked non-Native violence and vandalism on Mi'kmaq men and women who attempted to exercise their right to fish in the lucrative lobster fishery. Non-Native fishers with a great financial interest in the fishery were upset that Natives did not have to follow the same rules and regulations as non-Native fishers. Ironically, while stereotypes of Mi'kmaq people destroying the fishery by exercising their treaty rights dominated media reports, the responsibility for overfishing and mismanagement of east coast fisheries lay clearly in the hands of the federal government. Further, the federal government made little effort to prepare non-Native fishers for the entry of Native fishers into

the fishery or for the Supreme Court decision. Negotiations are underway to activate this treaty right and to ensure the sustainable use of the lobster fishery in the territories of the Mi'kmaq and Maliseet peoples. Elders, political leaders, and community members remained strong, maintaining that the ruling also extends to harvesting trees and that it has substantial implications for aboriginal peoples and treaty rights across Canada.

## Environmental Solutions

The Canadian media and to some extent nonaboriginal academics tend to characterize issues over lands and resources in terms of conflict between Natives and Euro-Canadians, the environment and jobs, traditions and modernization. In reality, these issues are far more complex. Many elders and traditional people do not believe that aboriginal communities should or need to abandon their culture, values, and way of life in order to achieve economic development. They recognize that cultures change, and that knowledge will evolve to meet the needs of contemporary aboriginal people.

An eroded island caused by fluctuating water levels on Pimicikamak Cree Nation territory. (Courtesy of Steve Daniels)

They also recognize that the economy and way of life of the dominant society is not sustainable or healthy. Alternative economic development plans rooted in aboriginal values and traditions are those based on the preservation of the environment and the sustainable use of resources. These methods hold the greatest promise for future aboriginal communities. Currently, large multi-national corporations are taking enormous amounts of natural resources out of aboriginal territories, with profits going to a few individuals outside local communities. As aboriginal peoples gain more power in Canada, corporations and governments are increasingly forced to deal with aboriginal concerns regarding the development occurring in their traditional territories. Although a few chiefs and councils may choose to temporarily solve unemployment and financial issues by signing agreements with industry or accepting cash settlements, the majority of aboriginal communities continue to resist such arrangements in favor of long-term sustainable economic development initiatives based on local economies. For aboriginal peoples, these issues are ultimately about justice. They are about governments living up to the spirit and intent of treaties, and to their legal and constitutionally entrenched responsibilities to aboriginal peoples, who possess a desire to build healthy, sustainable communities and nations based on their cultures, values, processes, and knowledge.

Aboriginal peoples want to be self-sufficient. Solutions to these difficult issues will come from within. At the same time, members of the dominant society must take responsibility for past and current injustices. Many aboriginal peoples believe it is possible to live in the modern world while adhering to the ancient values and knowledge that have enabled them to survive and flourish for so many generations. To do this requires aboriginal peoples to have decision-making power over the issues impacting their communities, nations, and traditional territories.

## Indigenous Traditional Ecological Knowledge

It is difficult to engage in a discussion regarding environmental issues and aboriginal peoples in Canada without broaching the concept of Traditional Ecological Knowledge (TEK). Over the past decade, Canadian academics, graduate students, government personnel, and industry have become increasingly interested in indigenous knowledge regarding the environment. Some believe this newfound interest is a result of the perceived environmental crises. As science and technology fail to provide society with solutions to many of the environmental problems they have caused, non-Native people are interested in exploring other philosophies and knowledge systems for answers.

It is interesting to note that the early European explorers and settlers were largely dependent upon indigenous knowledge for their survival. They relied on aboriginal peoples for travel routes, food and food preparation, health care and medicines, recreation, housing, clothing, and technology. As the numbers of Europeans increased, they were able to develop their own infrastructure for survival and their dependence on aboriginal environmental knowledge diminished. With this decrease in dependence came a loss of respect for aboriginal peoples and their knowledge. Indigenous knowledge was ignored, marginalized, and disrespected for the next few centuries. It is with caution then that aboriginal peoples in Canada view this newfound interest in their knowledge.

TEK is now used in research projects, environmental impact assessments, natural resource management, and environmental education in Canada. In some jurisdictions, governments are required by law to include TEK in decision-making. Although this may look like a positive step towards including aboriginal peoples in environmental decision-making, many Native people in Canada are frustrated and suspect that their knowledge is misperceived and wrongly used by government personnel and outside researchers. Often, TEK is documented or written down by outside researchers, with scientists or government personnel deciding how best to fit the knowledge into existing practices. Aboriginal peoples are not afforded the decision-making power in this framework, and this makes it very difficult to bring about positive change in their communities and territories. Further, indigenous peoples worldwide are concerned about the exploitation and appropriation of this knowledge by industry and state government. Aboriginal peoples continue to advocate for themselves, demanding that they be included in a full and meaningful way in environmental decision-making.

The field of TEK is beginning to change in Canada. Aboriginal advocates continue to promote aboriginal perspectives on TEK and models for using it in environmental management. Elders and traditional people continue to use their knowledge in traditional ways, and aboriginal peoples continue to fight for decision-making power in decisions that impact their lives, communities, and traditional territories.

## Aboriginal Peoples in Canada and the Convention on Biological Diversity

In North America, Canada and Mexico are signatories to the United Nations' Convention on Biological Diversity. The convention is an international agreement designed to protect and sustain biological diversity. Article 8j of the convention holds special meaning for indigenous peoples, as it recognizes the importance of indigenous communities in protecting biological diversity. In implementing the convention domestically, Canada has made efforts to include aboriginal peoples in discussions regarding biological diversity in Canada, including species-at-risk legislation for the protection of endangered species and the recent five-year review of the environmental assessment act. Aboriginal peoples have also been a part of international government delegations to the convention. It remains to be seen whether the federal government will include aboriginal knowledge in decision-making regarding the protection of biological diversity, but many aboriginal people continue to advocate for the environment and their people at the international level.

## Returning to the Teachings, Finding Solutions

Aboriginal knowledge, cultures, and way of life, in addition to the health and well-being of individuals, communities, and nations depends upon healthy environments and ecosystems with high integrity. Because of this, aboriginal peoples will continue to advocate for the preservation of local environments, sustainable economic development opportunities, and remediation of past environmental destruction and injustices. Many elders, traditionals, and some non-aboriginal scientists and environmentalists believe that traditional indigenous teachings hold the greatest hope in finding environmental solutions in the future.

*Leanne Simpson*
*University of Manitoba*

# U.S. Environmental Organizations

NATIVE AMERICANS AND THE
ENVIRONMENT
http://conbio.rice.edu/nae/
A comprehensive website containing web addresses
and research material.

## ◆ ALASKA

ESKIMO WALRUS COMMISSION
P.O. Box 948
125 Seppala St.
Anchorage, AK 99762
(907) 443–4452
www.kawerkaincoperated.org

RURAL ALASKA COMMUNITY ACTION
TASK FORCE
P.O. Box 200908
Anchorage, AK 99520–0908
(907) 279–2511
www.ruralalaska.com

## ◆ CALIFORNIA

AMERICAN INDIAN RESOURCES INSTITUTE
319 MacArthur Blvd.
Oakland, CA 94610
(510) 834–9333

INSTITUTE FOR THE STUDY OF NATURAL
SYSTEMS
P.O. Box 2460
Mill Valley, CA 94942–2460
(415) 383–5064

INTERNATIONAL INDIAN TREATY COUNCIL
123 Townsend St., Suite 575
San Francisco, CA 94107
(415) 517–1501

## ◆ COLORADO

COUNCIL OF ENERGY RESOURCE TRIBES
1999 Broadway, Suite 2600
Denver CO 80202
(303) 297–2378

## ◆ CONNECTICUT

CONNECTICUT INDIAN AFFAIRS COUNCIL
Dept. of Environmental Protection
165 Capitol Ave., Room 245
Hartford, CT 96106
(203) 566–5193

## ◆ DISTRICT OF COLUMBIA

U.S. ENVIRONMENTAL PROTECTION
AGENCY
NATIONAL AMERICAN INDIAN
ENVIRONMENTAL OFFICE
1200 Pennsylvania Ave., N.W.
Washington, DC 20460
(202) 260–7939
www.epa.gov

## ◆ MINNESOTA

INDIGENOUS ENVIRONMENTAL NETWORK
P.O. Box 485
Bemidji, MN 56601–0485
(218) 751–4967

INTERNATIONAL INDIAN TREATY COUNCIL
1845 E. Franklin Ave.
Minneapolis, MN 55404
(612) 341–3358

SEVENTH GENERATION FUND
 ENVIRONMENTAL PROGRAM
RR 1
P.O. Box 308
Ponsfurd, MN 56575–0308
(218) 573–3049

#### ◆ MONTANA

INTERTRIBAL AGRICULTURE COUNCIL
100 North 27th, Suite 500
Billings, MT 59101
(406) 259–3525

NATIVE ACTION
P.O. Box 316
Lame Deer, MT 59043–0316
(406) 447–6390

#### ◆ NEW MEXICO

NATIONAL TRIBAL ENVIRONMENTAL
 COUNCIL
1221 Rio Grande Blvd., N.W.
Albuquerque, NM 87104
(505) 242–2175
www.ntec.org

WATER INFORMATION NETWORK
P.O. Box 4524
Albuquerque, NM 87106
(505) 255–4072

#### ◆ NEW YORK

FIRST NATIONS ENVIRONMENTAL
 NETWORK
INDIGENOUS ENVIRONMENTAL NETWORK
Box 672
Hogansburg, NY 13655
Akwesasne Mohawk Territory
(518) 358–2415

#### ◆ NORTH CAROLINA

INDIGENOUS ENVIRONMENTAL NETWORK
ECDL Office
P.O. Box 2259
Cherokee, NC 28719–2259
(704) 497–5203

#### ◆ NEVADA

NEVADA INDIAN ENVIRONMENTAL
 COALITION
1280 Terminal Way, #35
Reno, NV 89502
(702) 323–6432

#### ◆ OKLAHOMA

NATIONAL ENVIRONMENTAL COALITION OF
 NATIVE AMERICANS (NECONA)
2213 W. 6th St.
Prague, OK 74864
(405) 567–4247

NATIVE AMERICANS FOR A CLEAN
 ENVIRONMENT (NACE)
P.O. Box 1671
Tahlequah, OK 74465–1671
(918) 456–4322

#### ◆ OREGON

BUREAU OF INDIAN AFFAIRS
BRANCH OF FORESTRY
P.O. Box 1239
Warm Springs, OR 97761–1239
(541) 553–2416

THE COLUMBIA RIVER INTER-TRIBAL FISH
 COMMISSION
729 NE Oregon St., Suite 200
Portland OR 97232
(503) 238–0667
www.critfc.org

#### ◆ SOUTH DAKOTA

SISSETON-WAHPETON
OFFICE OF ENVIRONMENTAL PROTECTION
R R 2
Sisseton, SD 57262
(605) 698–3911

## ◆ WASHINGTON

CENTER FOR WORLD INDIGENOUS STUDIES
1001 Cooper Point Road, S.W., Suite 140
Olympia, WA 98502–1107
(360) 754–1990
www.cwis.org

NORTHWEST INDIAN FISHERIES
  COMMISSION
6730 Martin Way East
Olympia, WA 98506
(360) 438–1180

## ◆ WISCONSIN

GREAT LAKES INDIAN FISH AND WILDLIFE
  COMMISSION
P.O. Box 9
Odanah, WI 54861
(715) 682–6619
www.glifwc.org

ONEIDA DEPARTMENT OF CONSERVATION
P.O. Box 365
Oneida, WI 54155–0365
(414) 869–2711

# Canadian Environmental Organizations

## ◆ BRITISH COLUMBIA

FIRST NATIONS EMERGENCY SERVICES
    SOCIETY OF BC (FNESS)
1290 Hornby St., Suite 320
Vancouver, BC V6Z 2G4
www.fness.bc.ca

FIRST NATIONS ENVIRONMENTAL
    NETWORK
P.O. Box 394
Tofino, BC V0R 2Z0
(250) 725–2996
www.fnen.org

NATIVE FISHING ASSOCIATION
100 Park Royal St., Suite 303 100
West Vancouver, BC V7P 1A2
(604) 926–8010

## ◆ MANITOBA

CENTRE FOR INDIGENOUS
    ENVIRONMENTAL RESOURCES
245 McDermott Ave., 3rd Floor
Winnipeg, MB R3B 0S6
(204) 956–0660
www.cier.mb.ca

## ◆ NEWFOUNDLAND

INNU NATION ENVIRONMENTAL RIGHTS
Sheshatshiu Box 119
Labrador, NF A0P 1M0
(709) 497–8398
www.innu.ca

## ◆ NORTHWEST TERRITORY

DENE CULTURAL INSTITUTE
HAY RIVER DENE RESERVE
P.O. Box 3054
Hay River, NWT X0E 1G4
(867) 874–8480

## ◆ NOVA SCOTIA

SACRED MOUNTAIN SOCIETY
195 Shore Road
Eskasoni, NS B0A 1J0
(902) 379–2097

## ◆ ONTARIO

FIRST NATIONS ENVIRONMENTAL
    NETWORK
Mississaugas of New Credit First Nation
R. R. # 6
2978 Mississauga Road
Hagersville, ON N0A 1H0
(519) 445–0853

## ◆ QUEBEC

CENTRE FOR INDIGENOUS PEOPLES'
    NUTRITION AND ENVIRONMENT
MACDONALD CAMPUS OF MCGILL UNIVERSITY
21111 Lakeshore Rd.
Ste. Anne de Bellevue, PQ H9X 3V9
(514) 398–7544
http://cine.mcgill.ca

## ◆ SASKATCHEWAN

Indigenous People's Program
University of Saskatchewan
Kirk Hall, Room 134
Saskatoon, SK S7N 5C8
(306) 966–5556

## References

### U.S. Resources and Environment

Anderson, Kat and Gary Paul Nabhan. "Gardners in Eden." *Wilderness* 55, no. 194 (1991): 27–30

Blackburn, Thomas C. and Kat Anderson, eds. *Before the Wilderness: Environmental Management by Native Californians.* Menlo Park, Calif.: Ballena Press, 1993.

Boyd, Robert, ed. *Indians, Fire, and the Land in the Pacific Northwest.* Corvalis, Oreg.: Oregon State University Press, 1999.

Cajete, Gregory A. *Look to the Mountain: An Ecology of Indigenous Education.* Durango, Colo.: Kivaki Press, 1994.

———., ed. *A People's Ecology: Explorations in Sustainable Living* Santa Fe, N.Mex.: Clear Light Publishers, 1999.

Churchill, Ward. *Struggle for the Land: Indigenous Resistance to Genocide, Ecocide, and Expropriation in Contemporary North America.* Monroe, Me.: Common Courage Press, 1993.

Cronon, William. *Changes in the Land: Indians, Colonists, and the Ecology of New England.* New York: Hill and Wang, 1983.

Cronon, William, and Richard White. "Ecological Changes and Indian-White Relations." In *History of Indian White Relations,* edited by Wilcomb E. Washburn, 417–429. Vol. 4 of *Handbook of North American Indians,* edited by William C. Sturtevant, Washington, D.C.: Smithsonian Institution, 1988.

Crow, Margaret. "Environment." In *The Native North American Almanac,* edited by Duane Champagne, 593–602. Detroit: Gale Research, 1994.

Davis, Thomas. *Sustaining the Forest, the People, and the Spirit.* Albany, N.Y.: State University of New York Press, 2000.

Fixico, Donald L. *The Invasion of Indian Country in the Twentieth Century: American Capitalism and Tribal Natural Resources.* Niwot, Colo.: University Press of Colorado, 1998.

Freedman, Milton M.R., Lyudmila Bogoslovskaya, Richard A. Caulfield, Ingmar Edege, Igo I. Krupnik, and Marc G. Stevenson. *Inuit, Whaling, and Sustainability.* Walnut Creek, Calif.: Altamira Press, 1998.

Grinde, Donald A. and Bruce E. Johansen. *Ecocide of Native America.* Santa Fe, N.Mex.: Clear Light, 1995.

Krech, Shepard. *The Ecological Indian: Myth and History.* New York: W.W. Norton, 1999.

LaDuke, Winona. *All Our Relations: Native Struggles for Land and Life.* Cambridge, Mass.: South End Press, 1999.

Lewis, David Rich. "Environmental Issues." In *Native America in the Twentieth Century: An Encyclopedia,* edited by Mary B. Davis, 187–190. New York: Garland, 1994.

———. "Native Americans and the Environment: A Survey of Twentieth-Century Issues." *American Indian Quarterly* 19, no. 3 (1995): 423–450.

Minnis, Paul E., and Wayne J. Elisens. *Biodiversity and Native America.* Norman: University of Oklahoma Press, 2000.

Waller, David. "Friendly Fire: When Environmentalists Dehumanize American Indians." *American Indian Culture and Research Journal* 20, no. 2 (1996): 107–126.

Weaver, Jace, ed. *Defending Mother Earth: Native American Perspectives on Environmental Justice.* Maryknoll, N.Y.: Orbis Books, 1996.

White, Richard. "Native Americans and the Environment." In *Scholars and the Indian Experience: Critical Reviews of Recent Writing in the Social Sciences,* edited by W. R. Swagerty, 179–204. Bloomington: Indiana University Press, 1984.

*Gregory Cajete*

## Canadian Resources and Environment

Alfred, Taiaike. *Peace, Power and Righteousness: An Indigenous Manifesto.* Don Mills, Ont.: Oxford University Press, 1999.

Armstrong, Jeannette. "Keepers of the Earth." In *Ecopsychology: Restoring the Earth, Healing the Mind,* edited by Theodore Roszak, Mary E. Gomes, and Allan D. Kanner, 316–325. San Francisco: Sierra Club Books, 1996.

Ashini, Daniel. "We Have Been Pushed to the Edge of a Cliff." In *Story Earth: Native Voices on the Environment,* compiled by Inter Press Service, 14–18. San Francisco, Calif.: Mercury House, 1993.

Barnaby, Joanne. "Culture and Sovereignty." In *Nation to Nation: Aboriginal Sovereignty and the Future of Canada,* edited by Diane Englestand and John Bird, 39–44. Concord, Ont.: Anansi, 1992.

Barreiro, Jose and Carol Cornelius, eds. *Knowledge of the Elders: The Iroquois Condolence Cane Tradition.* Ithaca, NY: Northeast Indian Quarterly; Cornell University Press, 1991.

Benton-Banai, Edward. *The Mishomis Book: The Voice of the Ojibway.* St. Paul, Minn.: Red School House Publications, 1988.

Blondin, George. *Yamoria, the Law Maker: Stories of the Dene.* Edmonton, Alta.: NeWest Press, 1997.

Canada. Royal Commission on Aboriginal Peoples. *Report of the Royal Commission on Aboriginal Peoples.* Vol. 3, *Gathering Strength.* Ottawa, 1996.

Clarkson, Linda, Vern Morrissette, and Gabriel Regallet. *Our Responsibility to the Seventh Generation: Indigenous Peoples and Sustainable Development.* Winnipeg, Man.: Institute for Sustainable Development, 1992.

Coon-Come, Mathew. "We Reassert Our Right: Native Peoples and Quebec Separatism." *Native Americas* 13, no. 4 (1996): 28–36.

Gawthrop, Daniel. *Vanishing Halo: Saving the Boreal Forest.* Vancouver, B.C.: Greystone Books; Seattle, Wash.: Mountaineers, 1999.

Grenier, Louise. *Working with Indigenous Knowledge: A Guide For Researchers.* Ottawa: International Development Research Centre, 1998.

Gwich'in Renewable Resource Board. *Nánh'Kak Geenjit Gwich'in Ginjik: Gwich'in Words About the Land.* Inuvik, N.T.: Gwich'in Renewable Resource Board, 1997.

Haudenosaunee. "Haudenosaunee Statement of the World, May 1979." *The Indigenous Voice: Visions and Realities.* 2nd ed., edited by Roger Moody, 512–515. Utrecht, Netherlands: International Books, 1993.

Henderson, James Youngblood. *The Mikmaw Concordat.* Halifax, N.S.: Fernwood Publishing, 1997.

Hertlein, Luke M. A. "Lake Winnipeg Regulation Churchill-Nelson River Diversion Project and the Crees of Northern Manitoba." *Indigenous Affairs* no. 3–4 (1999): 120–136. Copenhagen: International Work Group for Indigenous Affairs.

Jacobs, Dean. "Wapole Island in 2005: A View From the Future." In *Nation to Nation: Aboriginal Sovereignty and the Future of Canada,* edited by Diane Englestand and John Bird, 179–185. Concord, Ont.: Anansi, 1992.

Kassi, Norma. "A Legacy of Maldevelopment: Environmental Devastation in the Arctic." In *Defending Mother Earth: Native American Perspectives on Environmental Justice,* edited by Jace Weaver, 73–84. Maryknoll, N.Y.: Orbis Books, 1996.

Knudtson, Peter and David Suzuki. *Wisdom of the Elders.* Toronto: Stoddard Publishing, 1992.

LaDuke, Winona. *All Our Relations: Native Struggles for Land and Life.* Cambridge, Mass: South End Press, 1999.

———. "Breastmilk, PCB's and Motherhood: An Interview with Katsi Cook, Mohawk." *Cultural Survival Quarterly* 17, no. 4 (1994): 43–45.

Martin, Kallen M. "Akwesasne Environments, 1999: Relicensing a Seaway After a Legacy of Destruction." *Native Americas* 16, no. 1 (1999): 24–28.

McGregor, Deborah. "Exploring Aboriginal Environmental Ethics: The Role of Stereotypes." In *Canadian Issues in Environmental Ethics,* edited by Alex Wellington, Allan Greenbaum and Wesley Cragg, 325–329. Toronto: Broadview Press, 1997.

———. "Indigenous Knowledge in Canada: Shifting Paradigms and the Influence of First Nations Advocates." In *Proceedings of the 1999 Sustainable Forest Management Network Conference: Science and Practice: Sustaining the Boreal Forest,* edited by Terrence S. Veeman, 192–198. Edmonton, Alta.: Sustainable Forest Management Network, 1999.

Notzke, Claudia. *Aboriginal Peoples and Natural Resources in Canada.* North York, Ont.: Captus University Publications, 1994.

Paul, Daniel M. *We Were Not the Savages: A Micmac Perspective on the Collision of European and Aboriginal Civilizations.* Halifax, N.S.: Nimbus Publications, 1993.

Richardson, Boyce, ed. *Drumbeat: Anger and Renewal in Indian Country.* Toronto: Summerhill Press; Regina, Sask.: Assembly of First Nations, 1989.

Robinson, Harry. *Nature Power: In the Spirit of the Okanagan Storyteller.* Compiled and edited by Wendy Wickwire. Vancouver, B.C.: Douglas and McIntyre, 1992.

Roche, Judith and Meg McHutchison, eds. *First Fish, First People: Salmon Tales of the North Pacific Rim.* Vancouver: UBC Press; Seattle: University of Washington Press, 1998.

Sewid-Smith, Daisy and Adam Dick. "The Sacred Cedar Tree of the Kakaka'wak People." In *Stars Above, Earth Below: American Indians and Nature,* edited by Marsha C. Bol, 189–211. Niwot, Colo.: Roberts Rinehard Publishers for the Carnegie Museum of Natural History, 1998.

Thorpe, Dagmar, ed. *People of the Seventh Fire.* Ithaca, N.Y.: Akwe:kon Press, 1996.

Wadden, Marie. *Nitassinan: The Innu Struggle to Reclaim Their Homeland.* Vancouver, B.C.: Douglas and McIntyre, 1996.

Walsh, Patricia. "The Power of Maps." *Winds of Change* 13, no. 3 (1998): 28–33.

Wismer, Susan. "The Nasty Game: How Environmental Assessment is Failing Aboriginal Communities in Canada's North." *Alternatives Journal* 22, no. 4 (1996): 10–17.

*Leanne Simpson*

# 9

# Urbanization and Non-Reservation Populations

◆ Non-Reservation Indians in the United States
◆ Urbanization and Canadian Aboriginal Peoples  ◆ U.S. Urban Centers
◆ Canadian Urban Organizations

## ◆ NON-RESERVATION INDIANS IN THE UNITED STATES

Who are the non-reservation Indians in America? There are many ways to examine the detribalization of the Native peoples in this country. It is important to recognize that the Native peoples in this country have survived 500 years of conquest, defeat, genocide and disease. Native peoples were defeated by force of arms, disease and destruction of their life-ways. As one Indian wise man stated, "The White Man never kept his word, except once when he said he wanted our land and he took it." Always the Natives fought for their land; always they were forced off the land. That struggle continues today. Non-reservation Indians are one product of this ongoing conquest for the lands of the New World peoples. Today, three out of every four Indians residing in the United States do not live on reservations. According to the 1990 U.S. Census, among the nearly two million recognized Natives, only 22 percent live on the reservation; 16 percent live in non-reservation states, including Natives such as the Alaskan Aleut, the Oklahoma tribes, the Indians from "non-recognized tribes" (such as the Lumbee), and the "terminated tribes." Preliminary estimates from the U.S. Census Bureau indicated that by 2000 at least 70 percent of Natives would be living in urban areas.

Throughout history many Natives moved to towns to seek a living. The most recent migration of Natives into urban areas began in the 1950s under the Federal Government Relocation Program. These peoples, the "urban Indians," are mostly located in the big cities of the Midwest and the West. The urban Indians are nevertheless *real* Indians, despite the government's attempts to detribalize them. They are the "invisible minority," and are often not recognized in the cities in which they work and live. While they are officially registered with their tribes, many are soon forgotten by

Most urban Indians in the San Francisco Bay area arrived in the city as part of a relocation program. Oakland, California, was another target city for Native American relocation. (Photo by Ilka Hartmann)

657

their reservation tribal governments. On the reservations, there are never enough resources to go around, so when an Indian moves to the city, his/her "share" is distributed on the reservation. Many urban Indians return home to the reservation with valuable skills they learned in the city. Others return lonely and defeated by the stress of city life. About one-third of the urban Indians move between the reservation and the city in search of an escape from the loneliness and the feelings of estrangement that such a marginal existence creates.

Native Americans left their reservation homelands in search of better employment and educational opportunities. Most found life in the cities frightening, and received little institutional support from the Bureau of Indian Affairs (BIA), the agency charged by Congress to help Native Americans. While many relocated Native Americans remain in the city, about one-third return to the reservation, where they find family support and encouragement. Another third move back and forth between the city and the reservation in search of employment and a better way of life.

## Beginnings of the Urban Indian Migration

The number of American Indians residing in the city has rapidly increased in the past forty years. In 1930, less than 10 percent of the Indian population lived in urban areas. By 1970, the number of urban Indians had increased to 45 percent of all Native Americans. In 1990 the percentage of Native urban Indians was almost 66 percent, and by 2000, the number of urban Indians was expected to increase to almost 70 percent. Taking into account the population of Oklahoma Indians and Alaska Natives, who do not reside on reservations, the total percentage of non-reservation Native Americans exceeds 75 percent of the total Indian population in the United States.

## The Beginnings of Urbanization

Native American urbanization is typically viewed as a recent process. However, it is important to understand that long before Europeans arrived in the Western Hemisphere, the Native peoples of the New World developed urban centers of their own. Urban centers in central Mexico, for example, existed several thousand years ago. At the time of European contact, the largest city in the Americas—Tenochtitlan—had a population in excess of 150,000 people.

The indigenous North Americans also built and dwelt in large urban centers (not as large as those in central America, however). Moundville, in present-day Alabama, and Pueblo Bonito, in present-day New Mexico, had several thousand inhabitants. The ancient Indian

city of Cahokia, near present-day St. Louis, Missouri, quite possibly had a population of 40,000 people as late as C.E. 1200. Even after European colonization Native Americans continued to play an important role in the development of cities, particularly in the California mission towns and in the Indian Territory (present-day Oklahoma).

Beginning in the 1950s—as part of the tide of great social change in the post-World War II era—the Bureau of Indian Affairs actively began to relocate American Indians into urban locations such as Minneapolis, Chicago, Seattle, San Francisco, and Los Angeles. Prior to the 1950s most (but certainly not all) Native Americans lived on reservations or in historic Indian areas, such as Oklahoma and Alaska. In the post-war era, however, the federal government embarked on a new policy that was designed to end the so-called "Indian problem" once and for all. That is, the federal government hoped to solve the dilemma of what to do with the American Indians by relocating reservation-based Indians to urban centers, where jobs appeared to be more abundant and where assimilation into mainstream America could be accomplished. Such a policy would permit the federal government to "terminate the tribes" and abolish the reservations.

As a result of the 1953 Termination Policy, which stated that nine groups of Indians should "be freed from federal supervision," several tribes were "terminated." These tribes included the Klamath and later the Menominee tribe, many of whom now fight to be recognized as tribes. Congress also passed Public Law 280, which paved the way for termination acts by allowing states and local government to assume legal authority over tribal members. By 1961, the government began to assess the damage incurred by these policies, and issued this statement: "The experience [of terminating tribes] demonstrates that placing greater emphasis on termination than on development impairs Indian morale and produces a hostile or apathetic response which greatly limits the effectiveness of federal Indian programs." Other tribes, who were not granted treaties when they were defeated, today remain in limbo as "unrecognized tribes." For these Indian people, their struggle continues today.

The recent relocation process began in 1948, when Congress passed into law an act that helped Navajo and Hopi peoples relocate to urban areas in the western states. By 1950, the BIA had established relocation programs in several areas of the United States, all designed to help reservation Indians move to urban areas. The BIA conducted its relocation program in conjunction with federal policy to terminate, or withdraw, all federal responsibilities for American Indians in order to incorporate them into the general populace.

A center for urban Native Americans in Los Angeles, early 1980s. (Courtesy of the UCLA American Indian Studies Center)

By 1952, the BIA had established a national program of "Relocation Assistance" for family heads who would seek employment off-reservation. Four years later, Congress passed another law that encouraged Native Americans to move to urban areas. This law authorized the BIA to provide vocational training for Native Americans between the ages of 18 and 35 and to provide the relocatees with subsistence for six months. In 1962, the "Relocation Assistance" program was renamed the "Employment Assistance" program and was expanded to cities across the United States.

### Urbanization and Social and Cultural Dislocation

Although the BIA has not actively encouraged relocation since the late 1960s, two-thirds of Native Americans today reside in urban centers, many having moved to the city to join friends, or perhaps to seek better employment and educational opportunities. Today there are urban Native Americans who have never seen their reservation, spoken their tribal language, or learned their tribal history and culture. Many Native American leaders see urbanization as the most significant crisis to Indian identity since their initial contact with Europeans five hundred years ago. Today the urbanization process presents a new question: How can Native Americans retain their identity under the pressures of separation, assimilation, and urbanization? Put another way, Will urbanization lead to the disappearance of Native Americans as a distinct people?

Sociologists have observed that the social and cultural disorganization that accompanies the rural to urban transformation has had a greater impact on Native Americans than on other urbanized ethnic groups. Native Americans' cultural shock occurs on two readily identified levels: (1) from the country to the urban setting; and (2) from Indian society to non-Indian society. There is, however, a third level which is often unnoticed and of which most Americans are unaware. American Indian tribes are not the same: there are hundreds of distinct tribes and cultures. Consequently, there is no one language, way of life, culture, or religion. Each tribal group is distinct in its own right.

The urbanization process causes many Native Americans to fear that, with the increasing pressures of urbanization, American Indians will no longer be able to maintain their cultural distinctiveness. There are a number of valid reasons for this concern. As the urban Indian population increases, the rate of natural increase (births) decreases. This decline is typical of non-Indian urbanization as well. Consequently, while Native Americans have typically high birth rates, urbanization tends to reduce this birth rate. With increased urbanization, the Native American birth rate will eventually level off. At that point, the Native American population, no longer increasing, may become a small, stable subpopulation in the United States.

Added to declining birthrate is the high rate of urban Indian intermarriage with non-Indian persons. The intermarriage rate seems to have increased about 20 percent per decade over the past two decades. In 1980, over one-half of all Native Americans were married to non-Indians; today the rate is even higher. If this trend continues there will be even more blending of Indian and non-Indian populations. Eventually, it may be difficult to define Native Americans in purely genetic terms. Based on current trends, by the year 2080, only 8 percent of the Native American population will have more than one-half Indian blood. The number of Native Americans with less than one-quarter Indian blood would correspondingly increase from its current 4 percent to about 60 percent. In order to be legally defined by the BIA as an American Indian, a person must be "registered" as having at least one-fourth Indian blood. No other population on Earth is "registered," "numbered," or classified in this manner.

Finally, urbanization can lessen the importance of tribalism among Native Americans. According to 1970 census figures, 29 percent of urban Indians did not list a tribal affiliation (versus 11 percent for on-reservation persons). The 1980 census showed that nearly one-fourth of all Native Americans did not report a tribal affiliation. An increasing number of Native Americans are also learning English rather than their tribal tongue as a first language. Conversely, the percentage of Native Americans whose tribal language is their first language has decreased significantly over the past 30 years. The changes in tribal identity and in mother tongue may suggest that urbanization tends to decrease tribalism among urban Indians. And as tribalism decreases, the distinctiveness of American Indians may diminish.

On the other hand, not all Native Americans agree that the urbanization process will lead to the complete assimilation of Native Americans into American society. These Native American leaders point to several reasons why the assimilation process has and will continue to fail: (1) Native Americans did not immigrate to the United States and, in fact, still retain a significant land base as their "home"; (2) American cultural values are not seen as superior to Native American cultural values; (3) American society, while advocating assimilation, has not truly sought the incorporation of the Indian people; in fact, people of color are still excluded from the "mainstream" due to American racism; and (4) in American society, many have acknowledged the uniqueness and the value of sacred traditional Indian lifeways, which they wish to strengthen and retain for the benefit of all Americans.

These Native leaders further argue that urban Native Americans maintain their sense of cultural distinctiveness. These leaders argue that in the initial urbanization process, when Native American values are openly questioned and challenged, they become highly cherished. Recognizing the strength of these values, many urban Indians rediscover the importance of these personal and community social underpinnings. In other words, when Native Americans become aware of the fact that their values are considered undesirable, they find themselves clinging more tightly to their values and seeking validation from relatives and other Native Americans. Nonetheless, the tension that a young Indian child faces over conflicting cultural values is great. Consequently, the individual—particularly the child—faces conflicting values and must continually seek out a sense of continuity and harmony from family and friends.

The following is a statement of one anonymous second-generation "urban Indian":

What is an Indian? I don't know. Perhaps that is because I have been raised in white society. My mother was raised on the reservation so perhaps I should know what an Indian is. People say, "It doesn't matter how much Indian you are if you feel Indian." I don't "feel" Indian. I accept my mother as I do myself without pinpointing what is Indian. Perhaps this feeling of Indian is feeling kinship for people with Indian blood. . . . I search for something to validate myself as an Indian. I know Indians are sharing and giving people, they lack materialism—but that's a hard way to live in the city. When I was growing up, I feared being rejected for my dark skin. As a half-breed, I was not fully accepted by either set of relatives.

This young man's remarks illustrate the many psychological problems people experience over their identity in a racist society.

While all Native Americans face cultural traumas, the urban population—because of social conflicts—is especially hard hit. Those new to the urban setting face unaccustomed necessities—such as rent, child care, transportation, and health care—with minimal economic resources. While these services can be found on the reservation, they may be difficult to secure in the city. In many cases, the income level of urban Indian families is insufficient to match their needs. For many, the affluence dreamed of on the reservation remains a dream.

An examination of acculturation in the San Francisco area provides a case study of the urbanization process and helps to identify who is most likely to retain their Indian identity in the urban setting. Using criteria developed to measure Native American identity, Indian researchers in San Francisco developed several models to represent urban Indian families.

The first model, representing approximately one-fourth of the urban Indian population, is the bicultural family model. Families in this model are likely to maintain their tribal language and many of their tribal cultural practices. While these individuals respect their tribal ways, they have also adapted to non-Indian ways. They value education, have steady employment, and are well-informed about both their tribal and the dominant world. They tend to return to their reservations during the summer months so they can maintain their traditions and beliefs. They are also very likely to have made the social and psychological adjustments required by urban life, without having disregarded their sacred tribal ways.

The second model, representing perhaps one-fifth of the urban Indian families, is the traditional family model. These families both know and use their tribal language and culture and maintain close relationships with other Indian families who also live much as they did on the reservation. The women in this model are likely to stay home and are married to Indian men. More than likely, these family heads are graduates of BIA boarding schools or mission schools, and most mothers prefer to send their children back to the reservation to attend school. While many in this model are financially impoverished, they maintain a close, supportive family life. Families in this model are likely to make only a marginal adjustment to urban life and more than likely will return to the reservation if urban life becomes too demanding.

The third model, representing up to 40 percent of the urban Indian population, is the transitional family model. These families tend to let their tribal language, culture and values slip away while adopting mainstream cultural values. Women in these households neither speak their tribal tongue nor teach their children their tribal language. Few of these families send their children back to the reservation for summer instruction. Many of these families are headed by women and a large percentage of these women are married to non-Indians.

Families in this model are becoming assimilated into the lower socioeconomic class in the city. Children of these families are likely to face identity crises and will probably experience lower self-esteem than will children of other family models.

The final model that has been developed, representing about 15 percent of the urban Indian population, is the marginal family model. Families in this model have lost their tribal tongue and do not know their tribal values and culture. Not only are these families likely to have lost all tribal identity, but they also appear to be lost in the dominant ways as well. Consequently, there is a high dropout rate among school-age children, and many of the adults are on public welfare. These families face the greatest social and psychological difficulties and suffer the most from the urbanization process. These are the Indians most apt to fall into the negative stereotype of the "drunken Indian," so often portrayed as the urban Indian.

## Social and Economic Issues

Once in the urban setting, Native Americans experience many social and economic problems, including, but certainly not limited to, unemployment, inadequate

Indian fair in San Francisco. (Photo by Ilka Hartmann)

housing, inadequate education, and lack of health care. Researchers have noted that many policy makers assumed the move from the reservation to the city would force Native Americans to assimilate and that they would disappear as a distinct people. However, as we have seen, such is not the case. Unfortunately, many Indian families have found themselves in the city without basic services, such as health care, and with few economic resources.

The 1980 census indicates that perhaps one out of four urban Indians lives below the federal poverty line (roughly twice the national rate), making it difficult for these families to find adequate food, housing, and medical care. A recent study in Arizona shows that while 30 percent of the urban Indian population lives in what can be described as poverty, only one in ten manages to obtain general assistance. Urban Indians often do not receive public assistance even though they are in great need.

There are many reasons why urban Indians often fail to receive the services they need. Perhaps most important is the general misconception among public agencies that all Native Americans receive assistance from the BIA or the Indian Health Service (IHS); some agencies deny services to urban Indians based on this misconception. Furthermore, public agencies lack knowledge about Native Americans. What is more, Native American access to governmental services is often blurred and restricted because many urban Indians are uninformed about general information regarding rules and personnel. Consequently, many urban Indians fall through the bureaucratic cracks, with state agencies assuming that the federal government has provided needed services.

The ability of urban Indians to secure gainful employment is an important aspect of urbanization. Employment has a direct impact on a family's income level, as well as its health status. Although there are Native Americans employed in professional jobs, most urban Indians tend to be employed in lower income labor and service jobs, which usually do not provide family health insurance. The result is that many of the poorer urban Indians go uninsured and their health care is not provided by the Indian Health Service, which assumes responsibility only for Indians "on or near reservations."

The lack of education is one of the underlying causes of unemployment and underemployment. Indeed, a poor education usually makes it difficult to find employment or, at the least, relegates individuals to lower-paying jobs. Educational level also affects health status, insofar as those who are at an educational disadvantage tend not to receive proper preventative health care. Statistics also indicate that a poor education affects Native American youth at an early age and puts them at an educational and economic disadvantage. The high school dropout rate for urban Indians often exceeds 40 percent and non-Indians are twice as likely to have a college education as are Native Americans. Clearly, educational attainment is of great importance to the economic survival of urban Indians.

As the Native American population migrated to the cities an increasing number of Native Americans found themselves without adequate health services. Some studies have found that urban Indian health conditions are worse than conditions on the reservations. A federal task force on urban Indian health identified many reasons for this disparity, including the difficulty that urban Indians have in proving their eligibility for services, fear of non-Indian institutions, pride, cultural barriers, and the myth of federal services.

Among the greatest urban Indian health concerns are accidents, heart disease, liver disease, cancer, suicide, alcoholism and diabetes. Among children, pneumonia, influenza, pulmonary diseases, and infant mortality are all higher in incidence among urban Indians than in the general population. Many of the health problems of children result from improper prenatal care.

Housing for urban Indians tends to be substandard or incomplete. Many Native Americans reside in low-cost housing or in the equivalent of urban ghettos. Many urban Indian households are crowded, as many families tend to include extended family members and/or friends. A sizable percentage of urban households have neither telephone service nor adequate transportation. Poor housing, limited transportation, low income, high unemployment or underemployment, and low educational attainment combine to relegate many urban Indians to a low quality of life.

## Social and Cultural Life

Twenty-five years ago, as the urban Indian crisis was growing worse, Native Americans began to develop urban Indian programs to meet their unmet needs in the cities. Initially, they established small volunteer clinics, often on a part-time basis, to provide social and economic services as well as community support.

Urban Indians developed programs to maintain and strengthen cultural ties as well as to meet social needs. Most of the initial urban programs were established through tenuous public and private grants. It was not until 1967 that Congress provided any funding for urban Indian programs and for several years the number of urban programs remained small due to a lack of federal financial support. Urban programs that did receive funding were usually underfunded. As a result, urban assistance and services varied greatly from city to city. (See the directory of urban Indian organizations at the end of this chapter.)

Congress has only slowly recognized its obligations to urban Indians, even though no federal legislation ever disqualified urban Indians from receiving services. Although policy makers assumed that the 1921 Snyder Act (the main statutory authority for Indian programs) prevented funding for urban Indian programs, the act makes no such distinction between urban and reservation-based Indians, but instead authorizes funds for "Indians throughout the United States."

It was not until 1976 that Congress enacted legislation affecting urban Indians. This law, entitled the Indian Health Care Improvement Act, set forth an objective of providing adequate urban Indian health care. In passing the law, Congress finally appeared to recognize that it had a responsibility to ensure that all Native Americans were provided with adequate health care. Title V of the act provided a mechanism for the IHS to contract with urban Indian organizations to increase access to existing services funded by other public or private sources. While most funding for urban programs went to community assistance and various non-medical services, the law provided the means whereby urban Indians could receive better health care. By the latter 1980s, $9.6 million was allocated to urban programs, which, in turn, were responsible for more than half a million urban Indians. Despite Congress' recognition that it has a responsibility to urban Indians, it has not provided funding adequate for the proportion of individuals served; the fact that two-thirds of all Native Americans reside in cities brings this point home.

## Legal Status of Urban Indians

Urban Indians are as much "Indian" as are reservation Indians, despite the fact that the federal government has often sought to separate the two groups. As American citizens, Native Americans have the same rights and opportunities as do other Americans. If Native Americans wish to migrate to urban centers, they are free to do so. This does not, however, irreversibly sever an individual from his/her tribe. As citizens of Indian tribes, Native Americans also retain special rights and privileges, even if those rights and privileges are not always recognized.

The heart of the urban funding issue is political recognition. While Congress has recognized its responsibility to reservation-based Indians, there has been a

tendency to avoid acknowledging urban Indians as "real" Indians. Thus, policy makers have often viewed urban Indians as having chosen to leave their tribal community and as having voluntarily severed their special status as American Indians.

The federal trust responsibility, however, makes no distinction between reservation and urban-based Native Americans. The trust responsibility, while originating in the latter eighteenth and early nineteenth centuries, was created to preserve and protect Native Americans and their resources. Since many Native Americans continue to live as tribal members, even if they reside in the city, federal support and recognition is vital. No court or law of Congress has ever stated that the government's responsibility to Native Americans ends when an individual leaves the reservation. Indeed, the Supreme Court ruled that federal services are not limited to reservation Indians.

Native Americans have migrated to the cities for many reasons, some through the relocation program and others seeking greater employment and educational opportunities. While some Native Americans have returned to their reservations, most remain in urban centers. For those who remain, urbanization continues to be a process of struggle, loss, and hope combined with a longing to go and a determination to stay. While Native American migration to the city has resulted in new social adaptations, it has also provided a renewal of the old. And while urbanization has lead to the assimilation of some Native Americans, many more have made the transition into a bicultural world, where both old and new co-exist. Tribalism remains important and urban Indians are increasingly making efforts to reaffirm their Indian identity.

However, the urbanization of the Native peoples has led to many positive things as well. The current American Indian rebirth of spirit has arisen from the political activities of Indians in the city. For example, the historic takeover of Alcatraz in San Francisco was originated by urban Indians. Out of Minneapolis, Minnesota, emerged the politically radical American Indian Movement (AIM). Many tribal leaders on the reservations are themselves former urban Indians who, after becoming leaders in the urban organization, returned to their tribes to continue their leadership careers. Many Native American intellectuals, university professors, artists, and leaders learned their skills as urban Indians. What seems most remarkable is that these successful urban Indians have remained Indian, and continue to serve Indian people, despite the pressure to assimilate. These are the latent results of governmental attempts to "de-Indianize" New World people.

## Federally Unrecognized Native American Indian Tribes, Groups, or Bands

- •Chippewa
- Chippewa
- Mdewakanton
- •Little Shell
- Chippewa
- Brothertown
- Ottawa
- Ottawa & Chippewa
- •Ojibwa
- Ooragak
- Piqua Shawnee
- Ottawa
- Ojibwa
- Chickasaw
- Miami•
- •Shawnee
- Delaware Munsie•
- Wyandot•
- •Cherokee
- •Cherokee
- Wilderness Tribe
- •Cherokee
- Saponi•
- •Chorokees
- Yuchi•
- •Cherokee
- Quachita
- •Cherokees
- •Cherokee
- Caddo Adais•
- Apalachee•
- Choctaw-Apache
- Clifton-Choctaw
- Comanche Penateka
- •Tap Pilam
- Lipan Apache
- Biloxi-Chitimacha
- Point au Chien
- Houma
- Creek
- Eastern Creek
- Mowa Choctaw
- Creek-Euchee
- Apalachicola Creek
- •Oklawaha Yamasee Seminole
- Yamassee Creek
- •Cherokee
- Cherokee
- PeeDee
- PeeDee
- Piedmont
- Tuscarora
- Hattadare
- Indians of Person County
- Coharie
- Lumbee
- Coree
- Waccamaw
- Chicora-Waccamaw
- Chicora
- Santee
- Four Hole Edisto
- Ani-Stohini / Unami
- Occaneechi Saponi
- Eno-Occaneechi
- Meherrins
- Haliwa-Saponi
- Monacan
- Upper Mattaponi
- Mattaponi
- Rappahannock
- Chickahominy
- Shawnee
- Saponi
- Alleghenny
- Piscataway-Conoy
- Accohannock
- Nanticoke
- Nanticoke Lenni-Lenape
- Powhatan Renape
- Ramapough
- Shinnecock
- Montauk
- Montaukett
- Nehantic
- Schaghticoke
- Paugussett
- Eastern Pequot
- Pequot
- Paucatuck
- Pokanoket
- Pokanoket-Wampanoag
- Seaconke Wampanoag
- A Nipmuc
- Mashpee Wampanoag
- Cowasuck Abenaki
- Abenakis
- Mohegan
- Nipmuc
- Mohegan
- Mohegan
- Mohegan
- Poquonnock Pequot
- Pocasset Wampanoag
- Pequot

## Non-Recognized Tribes

Off-reservation American Indians include Native peoples who live as American Indians, although they are not currently officially recognized as "tribes" by the federal government. Some are recognized by the states they live in but are not recognized by the federal government and are therefore not eligible for BIA or IHS services. Approximately 115,000 Indians are members of "non-recognized tribes." Native Americans are victims of their history; non-recognized tribal people are those whom even time forgot. There is no simple explanation as to why some tribes were not recognized. Failure by the federal government to recognize certain Indian tribes has usually been the product of long-forgotten historical accidents, or of the belief that many tribes became extinct.

These are people who have the same rights as other Indian tribes. But they are people who were never powerful militarily and were thus not able to force the United States to deal with them by treaty. Consequently, there was no need to recognize them or to force them to move. Actually, Indian legal rights seem to correspond to the ease with which the United States can abuse Indian communities without fear of retribution. It seems that these unrecognized tribes were so small, so peaceful, or so isolated that they posed no threat to U.S. settlements. In most cases, these people were simply forgotten.

Whereas most tribes gained their recognized status through war and treaty and by lands set aside for them, many, by a historical twist of fate, were denied federal recognition. Many tribes were overlooked and did not negotiate treaties. In California eighteen treaties were negotiated in the early 1850s, but none of them ratified by the U.S. Senate. Treaties must be ratified by the Senate to have force. Over 800 treaties were negotiated by the U.S. government with Indian Nations, but only 371 treaties were ratified by the Senate. In California, there are currently 107 federally recognized tribes, but at least fifty California Native tribes are not recognized. Most California tribes have been recognized by an act of Congress or by executive order from the President of the United States. Other tribes did not negotiate treaties with the United States, or were otherwise overlooked by federal officials. Some few Indian communities do not wish to be recognized by the federal government, believing that their status as an Indian community does not stand on U.S. government recognition. Some disadvantages of nonrecognition are that the nonrecognized Indian communities are not protected by federal laws and trust responsibility, they have no land, they can not protect their sacred sites, and they receive no aid or help from the federal government in compensation for their loss of land. These excluded tribes continue to exist, but have been administratively denied benefits because they were "nonfederally recognized" tribes. In recent years, some nonrecognized but identified Indian groups are receiving belated acknowledgment. These groups have been recognized because they have maintained Indian identities. Most are located east of the Mississippi River but a few are in the West, mainly in California. Many California groups are recognized by the State, but not by the federal agencies.

In 1977, the American Indian Policy Review Commission (AIPRC) identified 133 non-recognized Indian communities in the United States. Of these, 23 were land owners, although the land was not necessarily protected by the federal government. At least 37 communities were found to have formed treaty relationships predating the formation of the United States, and at least 29 communities have treaty rights that were either confirmed by the United States or were negotiated directly between the historic tribe and the United States. In response to the nonrecognized tribes issue, the Bureau of Indian Affairs created the Branch of Acknowledgment and Research (BAR) process. BAR collects, assists, and reviews petitions for recognition. As of April, 2000, more than 200 tribes have petitioned the Bureau of Indian Affairs BAR process. While a handful of tribes have been recognized through the BAR procedure, the process is slow and can take 20 to 25 years. Nonrecognized tribes must collect extensive historical, legal, political and genealogical data to support their petition for recognition. Most nonrecognized tribes are small communities with few resources, and the research demands of BAR puts a great burden upon them. Some research funds are available to nonrecognized communities through the Administration for Native Americans (ANA).

Perhaps the story of Chief Little Shell, a Chippewa leader in present-day northern North Dakota, helps us understand how the accidents of history are closely allied with federal recognition. In the nineteenth century, facing forced removal, Chief Little Shell refused to sign what he believed was an unscrupulous treaty. His descendants have continued to maintain their Indian identity and to protest the injustice of their lack of recognition, but they still lack federal recognition. In recent years the Little Shell band has made considerable progress toward federal recognition. With the help of ANA grants, historians and anthropologists, the Little Shell Band, at this writing, are at the last stages of the BAR recognition process.

Over the period of the conquest, many families and individuals fled white contact when their tribes were conquered, removed, or eliminated. These "runaway" Native-descendants remain Indian, although they are not officially recognized as such. Indians have viewed their lack of recognition as Indians by the federal government in utter disbelief and complete dismay, and feel the classification as "non-federally recognized" is both degrading and wholly unjustifiable.

As the first wave of conquest and destruction moved across this nation, most Native Americans died as the result of disease, starvation, and genocide. Many different invaders—Spanish, Russian, French, English, Dutch, and so on—forged the destruction that decimated the Native peoples of the New World. The Dutch initiated the treaty-making process with the Natives not for the benefit of the Native peoples, but as a mechanism to ward off the threat of competing English colonizers. They then used treaties to protect the trading and colonizing of the New World against other competing European invaders. After the War of Independence, the new U.S. Congress neglected to recognize many existing "treaties" and "agreements" that existed between Native tribes and the British government. The Iroquois, for example, have retained much of their sovereignty due to the failure of the American colonies to recognize English agreements with the tribes.

As a result, Native American peoples may be classified as tribal reservation people, non-recognized tribal people, state- (but not federally-) recognized tribal people, Indians who live off the reservations and individual Indians who "fell through" the treaty process and have no "rights."

### Summary

Today, more than three-fourths of all American Indians reside off the reservation. There are about 560 federally recognized Indian tribes in the United States, but the BIA withholds benefits from at least 200 non-recognized tribes. Urban-dwelling Indians receive very few BIA or IHS services. Despite these legally complex issues, Indians, both within tribes and as individuals, retain their identities and much of their culture. Indian heritage is alive among the 2.4 million survivors of the American Indian holocaust.

*Dorothy Lonewolf Miller*
*Native American Research and Training Center*

*David de Jong*
*Prescott (Arizona) High School*

### ◆ URBANIZATION AND CANADIAN ABORIGINAL PEOPLES

Fewer than half the aboriginal people in Canada live on reserves. Of those living off-reserve, a growing number reside not in the countryside on traditional territories, but in cities and towns. To be Indian (First Nations), Métis, or Inuit in Canada was never a guarantee that one would live in a rural or isolated setting; this is more true now than it ever was.

Aboriginal people choose to live in the cities for many of the same reasons that other people live there. Probably the most important reason is that the cities offer better employment and educational opportunities. The contrast between reserve or community and the city becomes even greater with the passage of time: as the population on many reserves expands there is an ever greater shortage of housing, jobs, and other social amenities. Besides the push of overcrowding and the pull of economic and educational opportunity, people also come to the city to share in the expanded social and cultural options they find there. Finally, it is sometimes desirable simply to get away. Reserves represent home, a cherished safe place to which to retreat; in the worse alternative, they are unhappy places where inhabitants nevertheless incontrovertibly belong.

In the cities there are also an increasing number of aboriginal people who were born there, or who have grown up in communities of aboriginal urban dwellers. Many of the older aboriginal communities were primarily comprised of non-status Indians and Métis, because these people tended to be the first displaced from the countryside. Now, an increasing number of status Indians qualify as urban residents, rather than visitors. Even more recently, Inuit in still small numbers have begun moving to southern cities from the far north; they have also begun moving to the largest centers in the north, where their only economic opportunities are in the wage economy, and where they face many of the same conditions as do aboriginal people in the southern cities.

Considerable numbers of aboriginal people move to the city without necessarily making a decision to leave the reserve or their home community permanently. Especially in western Canada, there is a pattern of frequent moves between the city and the home reserve, as economic or other circumstances dictate. Some aboriginal people "emigrate" to the city virtually permanently, while the majority apparently do not. (All of these generalizations about migration patterns should be accepted with some caution, as statistical data is scarce and spotty, especially for the period prior to the 1991 Canada Census.)

Brooks Hollow Dance in San Francisco, 1972–73. (Photo by Ilka Hartmann)

## A Variety of Settings

Income distribution and work circumstances of the urban population of aboriginal people in Canada is similar to that of recent immigrant groups to Canada—that is, there appears to be a bipolar distribution of wealth. The large majority of urban aboriginal people in Canada are poor and either unemployed or employed in poorly paid, unstable jobs. Many of the poorest households are headed by single-parent families, and many include relations from outside the nuclear family, including siblings, cousins, in-laws, grandparents, and other relatives. Aboriginal people (particularly males) are incarcerated in Canada at many times the rate of non-aboriginal people; for many, the city is a way station on the road to prison, just as it is the place to which they return when they leave jail. But this picture is incomplete: there is also a much smaller, but still substantial white collar and business class of successful aboriginal professionals, business people, and bureaucrats.

Toronto is Canada's largest city, with a metropolitan area population of nearly 3 million; within this large, multi-ethnic urban center live at least 65,000 aboriginal people. Most other Canadian cities have sizable aboriginal populations, though none have as many as Toronto. The smaller prairie cities such as Winnipeg, Calgary, and Regina, however, have a larger proportion of aboriginal people, relative to their size, and therefore this population tends to be much more noticeable than in such polyglot and multicolored larger centers as Toronto, Montreal, and Vancouver.

In all Canadian cities and most towns, there are voluntary and publicly funded organizations with a mandate to serve the urban aboriginal population. Perhaps the best established of these are the Friendship Centres, which exist in a nationwide network in most cities and towns with an aboriginal population of significant size. The Friendship Centres not only provide a social focus and a meeting place, but they also deliver a number of services to women, youth, elders, and the general aboriginal population. The services may include vocational training courses, employment placement assistance, cultural development courses, aboriginal language instruction, crafts courses and marketing, personal counseling and healing circles, and social and fundraising events (see the directory of urban organizations at the end of this chapter).

In addition to the Friendship Centres, some cities now have social service delivery agencies specific to aboriginal peoples. These have proven difficult to establish, despite the clear need for them, because there have been jurisdictional disputes between levels of government in Canada. In a few centers, urban aboriginal people have established "paragovernmental" or political advocacy organizations to represent their interests in negotiations with municipal and provincial as well as federal governments. Most of the urban organizations serve heterogeneous aboriginal populations, rather than specializing in services to particular First Nations.

Underlying the jurisdictional disputes is the reluctance of the federal government (which has by far the most resources) to assume full responsibility for services to all aboriginal people. The federal position is somewhat inconsistent, but generally there has been resistance to recognizing a federal obligation to non-status Indians and Métis. Provincial governments have sometimes filled the gap, but their efforts are hampered by intergovernmental politics. The provinces do not wish to assume what they see to be federal responsibilities. This jurisdictional squabble hampers the ability of cities and smaller municipalities to serve the aboriginal part of their populations, and it leads to serious difficulties for the aboriginal people themselves.

While most aboriginal people live in cities among the general population, there are also a number of urban reserves, where residency and membership are restricted to single First Nations. Located adjacent to or actually within large urban centers, these reserves tend to have a small land base. Examples of urban reserves include the Musqueam Reserve near the city of Vancouver, British Columbia, and the Kahnawake Reserve near Montreal, Quebec. Such reserves are often as prosperous as the surrounding cities, or even more so, as they are able to take advantage of the tax-free status of reserves that is a treaty right in Canada, and of the larger market in their immediate vicinity.

### Special Difficulties in Urban Centers

Many problems of community well-being and service provision arise in the cities. Aboriginal people who come to the city may come with the education and skills to find well-paid employment, or they may come to school in the cities to acquire these skills. Such people form part of the growing aboriginal middle and upper class in Canada. The great majority of urban aboriginal people, however, are very poor. They live in circumstances shared by other poor people in Canada: overcrowded and often temporary accommodation,

discouraging employment prospects, inadequate diets, with the attendant health problems arising from the deprivations and stress of poverty.

Poor urban aboriginal people often have more difficult situations even than the non-aboriginal poor. For example, they may be subject to racism and personal prejudice that may lead to the denial of rental housing and to restricted access to employment. Many may deal simultaneously with loneliness and feelings of isolation from the close community in which they grew up. Additionally, their migration patterns and familial relationships, together with simple overcrowding in housing, often imposes extra financial strain on those people who are able to find work. These income earners may expect and be expected to support a number of unemployed or transient relatives.

A final difficulty is that urban aboriginal people in need may not have access to the same range of services as other people in need in the cities. In addition to resisting responsibility for non-status people, the federal government in Canada has for a long time attempted to deny responsibility for status Indians who do not live on reserves. Urban status people have had and continue to have great difficulty gaining access to the benefits that are their treaty rights, and they may have additional difficulty gaining access to social assistance payments that are available to all poor Canadians.

Until very recently, Canadian provinces and municipalities, which design and deliver most social programs in the country, have been unwilling, on the one hand, to develop special programming to meet the distinct needs of urban aboriginal people, and on the other, to provide services to status Indians whom they have argued are a federal, not a provincial, responsibility. This situation has begun to change. Probably as a result of the legitimacy and power gained through the political and constitutional struggles of aboriginal people, as well as the Canadian population's greater knowledge about the rights of First Nations (another consequence of these struggles), provinces have begun to develop more tailored and sensitive programming, particularly in the areas of education and social services. These initiatives, in turn, have met the newly formed urban aboriginal organizations on their own grounds. Through both developments, the quality of urban aboriginal life is changing, although there is still a long way to go.

### New Political Formations

Technically, there are national aboriginal advocacy organizations whose responsibility it is to represent status and non-status, Métis, and Inuit who live in urban centers. The Assembly of First Nations represents all status Indians in Canada, but has tended over the years to concentrate on the needs of reserve-based populations, and to deal with urban Indian issues from this perspective. The Congress of Aboriginal Peoples (formerly the Native Council of Canada) represents non-status and thus off-reserve Indians. The congress has pursued urban Indian issues in a more focused fashion, although the non-status population does live in diverse circumstances and is not all urban.

There are three organizations of aboriginal women, each of which is interested in the circumstances of women and children living in the cities. Pauktuttit is the Inuit women's organization; the Métis Women's Association represents Métis women; and all aboriginal women, including some members of these first two organizations, are represented by the Native Women's Association of Canada. Though all of these organizations suffer from a shortage of funds, each carries out research and advocacy on behalf of people living in cities.

Each of these organizations face some particular difficulties in representing urban aboriginal people. There are few urban political organizations with which the national organizations can interact in order to maintain contact with the grassroots population. Those that do exist are multinational or multi-tribal, rather than specific to one First Nation or tribal group. The basis of the new urban political organizations in such Canadian cities as Vancouver or Toronto is geographical, and what their members share is their situation in the city. And finally, all of the organizations must address themselves to municipal and provincial governments, as well as the federal government, since it is the first two levels that often have a major influence on their members' well-being.

The multinational character of the urban aboriginal organizations is an interesting development. It suggests that many aboriginal people who move to the city, whether permanently or temporarily, seek a common cause and the company of other aboriginal people, regardless of whether they are members of the same First Nation. Urban aboriginal people in Canada are forming new aboriginal communities, built around co-operative housing developments, the Friendship Centres, and other services and businesses. In short, not all— not even all the successful professionals—are willing to assimilate into the larger, heterogeneous population of Canadian cities and towns. Since the urban aboriginal population is growing, and as the urban people form representative organizations of a character suitable to their circumstances, we may expect that their presence and visibility in Canadian political life will grow.

*Frances Abele*
*Carleton University*

# U.S. Urban Centers

## ◆ ALASKA

LUTHER SOCIAL SERVICES
ASSOCIATION FOR STRANDED RURAL ALASKANS
IN ANCHORAGE (ASRAA)
2606 C St., Suite 2B
Anchorage, AK 99503
(907) 272–0643 ext 23
Fax: (907) 272–5728

RURAL ALASKA COMMUNITY ACTION
PROGRAM, INC.
P.O. Box 200908
731 E. 8th St.
Anchorage, AK 99501
(907) 279–2511

## ◆ ARIZONA

AMERICAN INDIAN ASSOCIATION OF
TUCSON, INC.
P.O. Box 2307
705 N. Main St.
Tucson, AZ 85702
(520) 884–7131

INTERTRIBAL HEALTHCARE CENTER
1230 E. Broadway
Tucson, AZ 85719
(520) 882–0555

NATIVE AMERICANS FOR COMMUNITY
ACTION, INC.
FLAGSTAFF INDIAN CENTER
2717 North Steves Blvd., Suite 11
Flagstaff, AZ 86004
(520) 526–2968

PHOENIX INDIAN CENTER
2601 North Third Street, Suite 100
Phoenix, AZ 85004
(602) 263–1017

TUCSON INDIAN CENTER
P.O. Box 2307
Tucson, AZ 85702
(520) 884–7131

## ◆ ARKANSAS

AMERICAN INDIAN CENTER OF
ARKANSAS, INC.
110 N. University, Suite 143
Little Rock, AR 72207–6344
(501) 666–9032

## ◆ CALIFORNIA

AMERICAN INDIAN AIDS INSTITUTE
333 Valencia, Suite 400
San Francisco, CA 94103

AMERICAN INDIAN CENTER OF CENTRAL
CALIFORNIA
P.O. Box 607, 32980 Auberry Rd.
Auberry, CA 93602–0607
(559) 855–2705

AMERICAN INDIAN CHILD RESOURCE
CENTER
522 Grand Ave
Oakland, CA 94610
(510 )208–1870
www.aicrc.org

CALIFORNIA INDIAN MANPOWER
CONSORTIUM
4153 Northgate Blvd.
Sacramento, CA 95834
(916) 920–0285

FRIENDSHIP HOUSE FOR THE
AMERICAN INDIAN
333 Valencia St., Suite 400
San Francisco, CA 94103
(415) 865–0964

INDIAN ACTION COUNCIL OF
NORTHWESTERN CALIFORNIA
2725 Myrtle Ave.
Eureka, CA 95501
(707) 443–8401

INDIAN HUMAN RESOURCE CENTER, INC.
4040 30th St., Suite A
San Diego, CA 92104
(619) 281–5964
www.americanindiansource.com

INTERTRIBAL FRIENDSHIP HOUSE
523 International Blvd.
Oakland, CA 94606
(510) 452–1235
The oldest urban Indian center in the United States,
started in 1955.

JURUPA MOUNTAIN CULTURAL CENTER
7621 Granite Hill Dr.
Riverside, CA 92509
(909) 685–5818

SOUTHERN CALIFORNIA INDIAN
CENTER, INC.
13252 Garden Grove Blvd., #100
P.O. Box 25550
Garden Grove, CA 92842–2550
(714) 663–1102
www.indiancenter.org

UNITED INDIAN NATIONS, INC.
1320 Webster
Oakland, CA 94612
(510) 763–3410

## ◆ COLORADO

DENVER INDIAN CENTER, INC.
4407 Morrison Rd.
Denver, CO 80219
(303) 936–2688
www.alphacdc.com/dic/

DENVER INDIAN HEALTH AND FAMILY
SERVICES
3749 S. King St.
Denver, CO 80236
(303) 781–4050

## ◆ HAWAII

INTERTRIBAL COUNCIL OF HAWAII
1307 Kalakaua Ave.
Honolulu, HI 96826
(808) 947–3206

## ◆ ILLINOIS

AMERICAN INDIAN CENTER
1630 West Wilson
Chicago, IL 60640
(773) 275–5871
www.aic-chicago.org

NATIVE AMERICAN EDUCATIONAL
SERVICES
2838 W. Peterson
Chicago, IL 60659
(773) 761–5000
http://NAES.indian.com

ST. AUGUSTINE'S AMERICAN INDIAN
CENTER
4512 North Sheridan Rd.
Chicago, IL 60640
(773) 784–1050

## ◆ IOWA

INDIAN YOUTH OF AMERICA
P.O. Box 2786
Sioux City, IA 51106
(712) 252–3230

SIOUX CITY AMERICAN INDIAN CENTER
619 Sixth St.
Sioux City, IA 51102
(712) 255–8957

## ◆ KANSAS

PELATHE COMMUNITY RESOURCE CENTER
P.O. Box 1016
1423 Haskel Ave.
Lawrence, KS 66044
(785) 841–7202
www.pelathe.org

**MID-AMERICAN ALL INDIAN CENTER, INC.**
650 North Seneca
Wichita, KS 67203
(316) 262–5221
http://theindiancenter.com/

#### ◆ MAINE

**WABANAKIE MENTAL HEALTH ASSOCIATION**
02777 State Street, Suite 3B
Bangor, ME 04401
(207) 990–0605

**WILMUSKET (sweet grass)**
132 North Maine
Brewer, ME 04412
(207) 989–4701

#### ◆ MARYLAND

**BALTIMORE AMERICAN INDIAN CENTER, INC.**
113 South Broadway
Baltimore, MD 21231
(410) 675–3535

#### ◆ MASSACHUSETTS

**NORTH AMERICAN INDIAN CENTER**
105 South Huntington Ave.
Jamaica Plain
Boston, MA 02130
(617) 232–0343

#### ◆ MICHIGAN

**GENESEE VALLEY INDIAN ASSOCIATION**
609 W. Court St.
Flint, MI 48503
(810) 239–6621

**INTERTRIBAL COUNCIL**
MICHIGAN INDIAN CHILD WELFARE AGENCY
405 E. Easterday
Sault Ste. Marie, MI 49783
(906) 632–6896
Central administration office for MICWA.

**MICHIGAN DEPARTMENT OF CIVIL RIGHTS**
AMERICAN INDIAN AFFAIR OFFICE
1 Michigan Ave Blvd., Suite 803
Lansing, MI 48913
(517) 241–9377

**MICHIGAN URBAN INDIAN CONSORTIUM (MUIC)**
4990 Northwind Dr., Suite 100
East Lansing, MI 48823
(517) 333–6550

**NORTH AMERICAN INDIAN ASSOCIATION OF DETROIT, INC.**
22720 Plymouth Rd.
Detroit, MI 48239–1327
(313) 535–2966

**NORTH AMERICAN INDIAN CENTER OF GRAND RAPIDS**
215 Straight, N.W.
Grand Rapids, MI 49504
(616) 336–4194

**OFFICE OF URBAN INDIAN AFFAIRS**
2929 Russell St.
Detroit, MI 48207
(313) 396 0416

**SAGINAW INTER-TRIBAL ASSOCIATION, INC.**
3175 Christy Way
Saginaw, MI 48603
(517) 792–4610

**SOUTH EASTERN MICHIGAN INDIANS, INC.**
26641 Lawrence
Centerline, MI 48015
(810) 756–1350

#### ◆ MINNESOTA

**AMERICAN INDIAN FAMILY CENTER**
579 Wells Street
St. Paul, MN 55101
(651) 793–3803

**AMERICAN INDIAN LEARNING RESOURCE CENTER**
106 Pleasant Street, S.E.
125 Fraser Hall
Minneapolis, MN 55455
(612) 624–2555
www.aamd.umn.edu/mad/lrc/ailrc.html

**AMERICAN INDIAN MAGNET SCHOOL**
1075 E. 3rd St.
St. Paul, MN 55106
(651) 293–5938

INDIAN FAMILY SERVICES INC.
1505 Park Street
Minneapolis, MN 555404
(612) 348–5788

INDIAN HEALTH BOARD
1315 East 24th
Minneapolis, MN 55404
(612) 721–9800

UPPER MIDWEST AMERICAN INDIAN
  CENTER
1035 West Broadway
Minneapolis, MN 55411
(612) 522–4436

#### ◆ MISSOURI

HEART OF AMERICA INDIAN CENTER
1340 East Admiral Blvd.
Kansas City, MO 64106
(816) 421–7608

SOUTHWEST MISSOURI INDIAN CENTER
543 S. Scenic Ave.
Springfield, MO 65802
(417) 869–9550

#### ◆ MONTANA

HELENA INDIAN ALLIANCE
Leo Pocha Memorial Health Clinic
436 North Jackson
Helena, MT 59601
(406) 442–9244

INDIAN DEVELOPMENT AND EDUCATION
  ALLIANCE
P.O. Box 726
Miles City, MT 59301
(406) 232–6112

INDIAN FAMILY HEALTH CLINIC
1220 Central Ave., Suite 2B
Great Falls, MT 59401
(406) 268–1510

MONTANA UNITED INDIAN ASSOCIATION
207 N. Broadway
Food Court Level Box 2194
Billings, MT 59101
(800) 654–9085

NORTH AMERICAN INDIAN ALLIANCE
P.O. Box 285
100 East Galena
Butte, MT 59701
(406) 782–0461

#### ◆ NEBRASKA

INDIAN CENTER, INC.
1100 Military Rd.
Lincoln, NE 68508–1089
(402) 438–5231

#### ◆ NEVADA

NEVADA URBAN INDIANS
1190 Bible Way
Reno, NV 89502
(775) 788–7600

#### ◆ NEW MEXICO

ALBUQUERQUE INDIAN CENTER
105 Texas, S.E.
Albuquerque, NM 87108
(505) 268–4418

FARMINGTON INTERTRIBAL INDIAN
  ORGANIZATION
P.O. Box 2322, 100 West Elm St.
Farmington, NM 87499
(505) 327–6296

#### ◆ NEW YORK

AMERICAN INDIAN COMMUNITY HOUSE,
  INC.
708 Broadway, 8th floor.
New York, NY 10003
(212) 598–0100
www.aich.org

NATIVE AMERICAN COMMUNITY SERVICES
1005 Grant St.
Buffalo, NY 14207–2854
(716) 874–4460

NATIVE AMERICAN COMMUNITY SERVICES
P.O. Box 2161
561 Portage Rd.
Niagara Falls, NY 14301
(716) 282–5441

NATIVE AMERICAN CULTURAL CENTER, INC.
1344 University Ave., Suite 230
Rochester, NY 14607
(716) 442–1100

#### ◆ NORTH CAROLINA

CHEROKEE BOYS CLUB
P.O. Box 507
Cherokee, NC 28719
(828) 497–9101

CUMBERLAND COUNTY ASSOCIATION OF INDIAN PEOPLE
200 Indian Dr.
Fayetteville, NC 28301
(910) 483–8442

GUILFORD NATIVE AMERICAN ASSOCIATION
P.O. Box 5623, 400 Prescott
Greensboro, NC 27435
(336) 273–8686

#### ◆ NORTH DAKOTA

UNITED TRIBES TECHNICAL COLLEGE
3315 University Dr.
Bismarck, ND 58504
(701) 255–3285
www.united-tribes.tcc.nd.us

#### ◆ OHIO

NATIVE AMERICAN INDIAN CENTER OF CENTRAL OHIO
756 Parsons Ave.
P.O. Box 07705
Columbus, OH 43207
(614) 443–6120
http://members.tripod.com/ NAICCO

NORTH AMERICAN INDIAN CULTURAL CENTER
MEDICINE WHEEL ASSOCIATION
1062 Triplett Blvd.
Akron, OH 44306
(330) 724–1280

#### ◆ OKLAHOMA

NATIVE AMERICAN CAUCUSES
616 SW 70th St.
Oklahoma City, OK 73139
(405) 634–2005

NATIVE AMERICAN HEADSTART OF TULSA, INC.
1740 West 41st St.
Tulsa, OK 74107
(918) 446–7939

OKLAHOMANS FOR INDIAN OPPORTUNITY
3001 South Berry Rd., Suite B
Norman, OK 73072
(405) 329–3737

#### ◆ OREGON

NATIVE AMERICAN REHABILITATION ASSOCIATION OF THE NORTHWEST
17645 NW St. Helens Hwy
Portland, OR 97231
(503) 621–1069

ORGANIZATION OF THE FORGOTTEN AMERICAN
4509 Six Street, Suite 206
Klamath Falls, OR 97603
(541) 882–4441

#### ◆ PENNSYLVANIA

COUNCIL OF THREE RIVERS AMERICAN INDIAN CENTER, INC.
120 Charles St.
Pittsburgh, PA 15238
(412) 782–4457

UNITED AMERICAN INDIANS OF DELAWARE VALLEY
225 Chestnut
Philadelphia, PA 19106
(215) 574–9020

#### ◆ RHODE ISLAND

RHODE ISLAND INDIAN COUNCIL, INC.
807 Broad Street
Providence, RI 02907
(401) 941–3398

## ◆ SOUTH DAKOTA

AMERICAN INDIAN SERVICE CENTER
P.O. Box 1720
1000 Northwest Ave., Suite 250
Sioux Falls, SD 57104
(605) 334–4060

ST. ISAAC JOGUES
221 Knollwooddog Dr.
P.O. Box 1304
Rapid City, SD 57709
(605) 343–2165

## ◆ TEXAS

AMERICAN INDIAN CENTER OF DALLAS
2219 Euless Blvd.
Euless, TX 76040
(817) 545–9555

DALLAS INTER-TRIBAL CENTER, INC.
209 E. Jefferson Blvd.
Dallas, TX 75203
(214) 941–1050

## ◆ VERMONT

ABENAKI SELF-HELP ASSOCIATION
P.O. Box 276

Swanton, VT 05488
(802) 868–2559

## ◆ WASHINGTON

AMERICAN INDIAN CENTER
East 905 Third Ave.
Spokane, WA 99202–2246
(509) 535–0886

SEATTLE INDIAN CENTER
611 12th Ave. S., Suite 300
Seattle, WA 98144
(206) 329–8700

UNITED INDIANS OF ALL TRIBES
  FOUNDATION
P.O. Box 99100
Seattle, WA 98144
(206) 285–4425

## ◆ WISCONSIN

NATIVE AMERICAN CENTER
University of Wisconsin Stevens Point
206 Student Services Center
Stevens Point, WI 54481
(715) 346–3576

# Canadian Urban Organizations

NATIONAL ASSOCIATION OF
FRIENDSHIP CENTRES
275 Maclaren St.
Ottawa, ON K2P 0O9
(613) 563–4844
www.nafc-aboriginal.com

◆ **ALBERTA**

ALBERTA NATIVE FRIENDSHIP CENTRE
ASSOCIATION
10025 106 St., Suite 1102
Edmonton, AB T5J 1G4
(780) 423–3138

ATHABASCA NATIVE FRIENDSHIP SOCIETY
4919 53rd St.
Athabasca, AB T9S 1L1
(780) 675–3086

BONNYVILLE CANADIAN NATIVE
FRIENDSHIP CENTRE
P.O. Box 5399
Bonnyville, AB T9N 2G5
(780) 826–3374

CALGARY NATIVE FRIENDSHIP CENTRE
SOCIETY
140 Second Ave., S.W.
Calgary, AB T2P 0B9
(403) 777–2263

CANADIAN NATIVE FRIENDSHIP CENTRE
11205 101 St.
Edmonton, AB T5G 2A4
(780) 479–1999

COLD LAKE NATIVE FRIENDSHIP CENTRE
SOCIETY
P.O. Box 1978
Cold Lake, AB T9M 1P4
(780) 594–7526

EDSON FRIENDSHIP CENTRE
P.O. Box 6508
Edson, AB T7E 1T9
(780) 723–5494

GRAND PRAIRIE FRIENDSHIP CENTRE
10507 98th Ave.
Grand Prairie, AB T8V 4L1
(780) 532–5722

HIGH LEVEL NATIVE FRIENDSHIP CENTRE
P.O. Box 1735
High Level, AB T0H 1Z0
(780) 926–3355

HIGH PRAIRIE NATIVE FRIENDSHIP CENTRE
P.O. Box 1448
High Prairie, AB T0G 1E0
(780) 523–4511

LAC LA BICHE CANADIAN NATIVE
FRIENDSHIP CENTRE
P.O. Box 2338
10105 Churchill Dr
Lac La Biche, AB T0A 2C0
(780) 623–3249

MANNIWANIS NATIVE FRIENDSHIP CENTRE
P.O. Box 1358
St. Paul, AB T0A 3A0
(780) 645–4630

NAPI FRIENDSHIP ASSOCIATION
P.O. Box 657
Pincher Creek, AB T0K 1W0
(403) 627–4224
www.nativecenters.org/pinchercreek

NISTAWOYOU ASSOCIATION FRIENDSHIP
CENTRE
8310 Manning Ave.
Fort McMurray, AB T9H 1W1
(780) 743–8555

RED DEER NATIVE FRIENDSHIP SOCIETY
4945 49th St.
Red Deer, AB T4N 1V1
(403) 340–0020

ROCKY NATIVE FRIENDSHIP CENTER
4917 52nd St.
P.O. Box 1927
Rocky Mountain House, AB T0M 1T0
(403) 845–2788

SAGITAWA FRIENDSHIP CENTRE
10108 100th Ave.
Box 5083
Peace River, AB T8S 1R7
(403) 624–2443

SIK-OOK-KOTOK CENTRE
1709 2nd Ave S
Lethbridge, AB T1J 0E8
(403) 328–2414

SLAVE LAKE NATIVE FRIENDSHIP CENTRE
416 Sixth Ave., NE
Slave Lake, AB T0G 2A2
(780) 849–3039

## ◆ BRITISH COLUMBIA

B.C. ASSOCIATION OF ABORIGINAL
  FRIENDSHIP CENTRES
83–2475 Mt. Newton X-road
Saanichton, BC V8M 2B7
(250) 652–0210
Fax: (250) 652–3102
www.bcaafc.com

CARIBOO FRIENDSHIP CENTRE SOCIETY
99 South Third Avenue
Williams Lake, BC V2G 1J1
(250) 398–6831

CONAYT FRIENDSHIP SOCIETY
1999 Garcia St.
Box 1989
Merritt, BC V1K 2B8
(604) 378–5107

DZE L K'ANT FRIENDSHIP CENTRE SOCIETY
P.O. Box 2920
Smithers, BC V0J 2N0
(250) 847–5211

FIRST NATIONS FRIENDSHIP CENTRE
  SOCIETY
2902 29th Ave.
Vernon, BC V1T 1Y7
(250) 542–1247

FORT NELSON ABORIGINAL NATIVE
  FRIENDSHIP SOCIETY
Box 1266
5012 49th Ave.
Fort Nelson, BC V0C 1R0
(250) 774–2993

FORT ST. JOHN FRIENDSHIP SOCIETY
10208 95th Ave.
Fort St. John, BC V1J 1J2
(250) 785–8566

FRIENDSHIP HOUSE ASSOCIATION
744 Fraiser St.
Prince Rupert, BC V8J 1P9
(250) 627–1717

INTERIOR INDIAN FRIENDSHIP SOCIETY
125 Palm St.
Kamloops, BC V2B 8J7
(250) 376–1296

KEEGINAW FRIENDSHIP CENTRE
10208 95th Ave.
Fort St. John, BC V1J 1J2
(250) 785–8566

KERMODE FRIENDSHIP SOCIETY
3313 Kalum St.
Terrace, BC V8G 2N7
(250) 635–4906

KI-LOW-NA FRIENDSHIP SOCIETY
442 Leon Ave.
Kelowna, BC V1Y 6J3
(250) 763–4905

LILLOOET FRIENDSHIP CENTRE
P.O. Box 1270
357 Main St.
Lilloet, BC V0K 1V0
(250) 256–4146

MISSION INDIAN FRIENDSHIP CENTRE
33150A First Ave.
Mission, BC V2V 1G4
(604) 826–1281

NAWICAN FRIENDSHIP CENTRE
1320 102nd Ave.
Dawson Creek, BC V1G 2C6
(250) 782–5202

PORT ALBERNI FRIENDSHIP CENTRE
3555 Fourth Ave.
Port Alberni, BC V9Y 4H3
(250) 723–8281

PRINCE GEORGE NATIVE FRIENDSHIP
CENTRE
1600 3rd Ave.
Prince George, BC V2L 3G6
(250) 564–3568

QUESNEL TILLICUM SOCIETY
319 North Fraser Dr.
Quesnel, BC V2J 1Y9
(250) 992–8347

TANSI FRIENDSHIP CENTRE SOCIETY
P.O. Box 418
Chetwynd, BC V0C 1J0
(250) 788–2996

TILLICUM HAUS SOCIETY
602 Haliburton Ave.
Nanaimo, BC V9R 4W5
(250) 753–8291

VALLEY NATIVE FRIENDSHIP CENTRE
P.O. Box 1015
Duncan, BC V9L 3Y2
(250) 748–2242

VICTORIA NATIVE FRIENDSHIP CENTRE
220 Bay St.
Victoria, BC V9A 3K5
(250) 384–3211

### ◆ MANITOBA

BRANDON FRIENDSHIP CENTRE
836 Lauren St.
Brandon, MB R7A 0T8
(204) 727–1407

DAUPHIN FRIENDSHIP CENTRE
210 First Ave. N.E.
Dauphin, MB R7N 1A7
(204) 638–5707

FLIN FLON INDIAN AND MÉTIS
FRIENDSHIP CENTRE
57 Church St.
Box 188
Flin Flon, MB R8A 1M7
(204) 687–3900
www.mac.mb.ca

INDIAN AND MÉTIS FRIENDSHIP CENTRE
45 Robinson St.
Winnipeg, MB R2W 5H5
(204) 586–8441

KA-WAWIYAK FRIENDSHIP CENTRE
Sagkeeng First Nation
P.O. Box 3
Fort Alexander, MB R0E 0P0
(204) 367–2287

LYNN LAKE FRIENDSHIP CENTRE
Box 460
625 Gordon Ave.
Lynn Lake, MB R0B 0W0
(204) 356–2407

MA-MOW-WE-TAK FRIENDSHIP CENTRE
122 Hemlock Cresante
Thompson, MB R8N 0R6
(204) 778–7337

MANITOBA ASSOCIATION OF
FRIENDSHIP CENTRES
410 181 Higgins Ave
Winnipeg, MB R3B 3G1
(204) 942–6299

THE PAS FRIENDSHIP CENTRE
81 Edwards Ave.
Box 2638
The Pas, MB R9A 1M3
(204) 623–6459

PORTAGE FRIENDSHIP CENTRE
20 3rd NE
Portage La Prairie, MB R1N 1N4
(204) 239–6333

RIVERTON AND DISTRICT FRIENDSHIP
CENTRE
P.O. Box 359
Riverton, MB R0C 2R0
(204) 378–2927

SELKIRK FRIENDSHIP CENTRE
425 Eveline St.
Selkirk, MB R1A 2J5
(204) 482–7525

SWAN RIVER INDIAN AND MÉTIS
    FRIENDSHIP CENTRE
1413 Main St. E.
Box 1448
Swan River, MB R0L 1Z0
(204) 734–9301

### ◆ NEW BRUNSWICK

FREDERICTON NATIVE FRIENDSHIP
    CENTRE
96 Regents Street, 2nd FL
Fredericton, NB E3B 3W4
(506) 459–5283

### ◆ NEWFOUNDLAND

LABRADOR FRIENDSHIP CENTRE
P.O. Box 767, Station B
Happy Valley-Goose Bay, NF A0P 1E0
(709) 896–8302

ST. JOHN'S NATIVE FRIENDSHIP CENTRE
112 Casey Street
P.O. Box 2414, Station C
St. John's, NF A1C 4X7
(709) 726–5902
www.nativefriendship.com

### ◆ NORTHWEST TERRITORIES

DEH CHO SOCIETY
P.O. Box 470
Fort Simpson, NT X0E 0N0
(867) 695–2577

INGAMO HALL FRIENDSHIP CENTRE
P.O. Box 1293
Inuvik, NT X0E 0T0
(403) 979–2166

NORTHWEST TERRITORIES COUNCIL OF
    FRIENDSHIP CENTRES
P.O. Box 2667
Yellowknife, NT X1A 2B2
(403) 920–2288

RAE EDZO FRIENDSHIP CENTRE
P.O. Box 35
Rae, NT X0E 0Y0
(403) 392–6000

SAPPUJJIJIT FRIENDSHIP CENTRE
P.O. Box 58
Rankin Inlet, NT X0C 0G0
(403) 645–2600

SOARING EAGLE FRIENDSHIP CENTRE
P.O. Box 396
Hay River, NT X0E 0R0
(403) 874–6581

TREE OF PEACE FRIENDSHIP CENTRE
P.O. Box 2667
Yellowknife, NT X1A 1H0
(403) 873–2864

UNCLE GABE'S FRIENDSHIP CENTRE
P.O. Box 957
Fort Smith, NT X0E 0P0
(403) 872–3013

ZHAHTI KOE FRIENDSHIP CENTRE
General Delivery
Fort Providence, NT X0E 0L0
(403) 699–3801

### ◆ NOVA SCOTIA

MICMAC NATIVE FRIENDSHIP CENTRE
2158 Gottingen St.
Halifax, NS B3K 3B4
(902) 420–1576

### ◆ ONTARIO

ATIKOKAN NATIVE FRIENDSHIP CENTRE
Box 1510
307 Main St.
Atikokan, ON P0T 1C0
(807) 597–1213

BARRIE NATIVE FRIENDSHIP CENTRE
202 105 Dunlop St. E.
Barrie, ON L4M 1A6
(705) 721–7689

CAN-AM INDIAN FRIENDSHIP CENTRE OF
    WINDSOR
P.O. Box 441, Station A
Windsor, ON N9A 6L7
(519) 258 -8954

DRYDEN NATIVE FRIENDSHIP CENTRE
53 Arthur St.
Dryden, ON P8N 1J7
(807) 223–4180

FORT ERIE NATIVE FRIENDSHIP CENTRE
796 Buffalo Rd.
Fort Erie, ON L2A 5H2
(905) 871–8931

GEEWAEDIN FRIENDSHIP CENTRE, INC.
P.O. Box 241
Kirkland Lake, ON P9N 3X3
(807) 468–5440

GEORGIAN BAY NATIVE FRIENDSHIP
  CENTRE
175 Young St.
Midland, ON L4R 2A7
(705) 526–5589
www.ofifc.org/Centres/Office.asp?FCID=7

HAMILTON REGIONAL INDIAN CENTRE
712 Main St.
Hamilton, ON L8M 1K6
(905) 548–9593
www.hric-hamilton.com

ININEW FRIENDSHIP CENTRE
Box 1499
190 Third Ave.
Cochrane, ON P0L 1C0
(705) 272–4497

INUIT FRIENDSHIP CENTRE
604 Lauren Ave., W.
Ottawa, ON K1R 6L1
(613) 563–3546

KAPUSKASING INDIAN FRIENDSHIP CENTRE
P.O. Box 26
24 Byng St.
Kapuskasing, ON P5N 1E5
(705) 337–1935

MOOSONEE NATIVE FRIENDSHIP CENTRE
P.O. Box 489
Moosonee, ON P0L 1Y0
(705) 336–2808

N'AMERIND FRIENDSHIP CENTRE
260 Colborne St.
London, ON N6B 2S6
(519) 672–0131

NATIONAL ABORIGINAL ACHIEVEMENT
  FOUNDATION
Suite 33A, 70 Yorkville Avenue
Toronto, ON M5R 1B9
(800) 329–9780

NATIVE CANADIAN CENTRE OF TORONTO
16 Spadina Rd.
Toronto, ON M5R 2S7
(416) 964–9087

NE'CHEE FRIENDSHIP CENTRE
P.O. Box 241
Kenora, ON P9N 3X3
(807) 468–5440

NIAGARA REGIONAL NATIVE CENTRE
R.R. 4
Queenston & Taylor Rd.
Niagara-on-the-Lake, ON L0S 1J0
(905) 688–6484

NISHNAWBE-GAMIK FRIENDSHIP CENTRE
Box 1299
52 King St.
Sioux Lookout, ON P8T 1B8
(807) 737–1903

NORTH BAY INDIAN FRIENDSHIP CENTRE
980 Cassells St.
North Bay, ON P1B 4A6
(705) 472–2811
www.nbifc.org

N'SWAKAMOK NATIVE FRIENDSHIP CENTRE
110 Elm St.
Sudbury, ON P3C 1T5
(705) 674–2128

ODAWA NATIVE FRIENDSHIP CENTRE
12 Stirling Ave.
Ottawa, ON K1Y 1P8
(613) 722–3811

ONTARIO FEDERATION OF INDIAN
  FRIENDSHIP CENTERS
207–234 Eglinton Ave., E.
Toronto, ON M4P 1K5
(416) 484–1411

PARRY SOUND FRIENDSHIP CENTRE
13 Bowes St.
Parry Sound, ON P2A 2K7
(705) 746–5970

PINE TREE NATIVE CENTRE OF BRANT
344 Colborne St.
Brantford, ON N3S 3N3
(519) 752–5132

RED LAKE INDIAN FRIENDSHIP CENTRE
P.O. Box 244
Red Lake, ON P0V 2M0
(807) 727–2847

SAULT STE. MARIE INDIAN
    FRIENDSHIP CENTRE
29 Wellington St. E.
Sault Ste. Marie, ON P6A 2K9
(705) 256–5634

THUNDER BAY INDIAN FRIENDSHIP
    CENTRE
401 North Cumberland St.
Thunder Bay, ON P7A 4P7
(807) 345–5840

THUNDERBIRD FRIENDSHIP CENTRE
301 Beamish Ave.,W.
Box 430
Geraldton, ON P0T 1M0
(807) 854–1060

TIMMINS NATIVE FRIENDSHIP CENTRE
170 Second Ave.
Timmins, ON P4N 1G1
(705) 268–6262

UNITED NATIVE FRIENDSHIP CENTRE
P.O. Box 752
Fort Frances, ON P9A 3N1
(807) 274–8541

## ◆ QUEBEC

CENTRE D'AMITI AUTOCHTONE
234, Rue St. Louis
Loretteville, PQ G2B 1L4
(418) 843–5818

CREE INDIAN CENTRE OF CHIBOUGAMAU
95 Jaculet St.
Chibougamau, PQ G8P 2G1
(418) 748–7667

INDIAN FRIENDSHIP CENTRE OF LA TUQUE
315 St. Paul St.
La Tuque, PQ G9X 2Z9
(819) 523–6121

INDIAN FRIENDSHIP CENTRE OF VAL D'OR
1101 Sixth St.
Val d'Or, PQ J9P 3W4
(819) 825–6857

NATIVE FRIENDSHIP CENTRE OF
    MONTREAL
2001 St. Laurent Blvd.
Montreal, PQ H2X 2T3
(514) 499–1854
www.schoolnet.ca/aboriginal/nfcmontreal/

YOUTH COUNCIL
P.O. Box 60
Waskaganish, PQ J0M 1R0
(819) 895–8753

## ◆ SASKATCHEWAN

ABORIGINAL FRIENDSHIP CENTRES OF
    SASKATCHEWAN
4th Avenue South, Room 600
Saskatoon, SK S7K 5M5
(306) 665–1267
www.afcs.com

BATTLEFORDS INDIAN AND MÉTIS
    FRIENDSHIP CENTRE
900 103rd. St.
North Battleford, SK S9A 2Y9
(306) 445–8216

BUFFALO NARROWS FRIENDSHIP CENTRE
P.O. Box 189
Buffalo Narrows, SK S0M 0J0
(306) 235–4633

KIKINAHK FRIENDSHIP CENTRE, INC.
320 Boardman St.
P.O. Box 254
La Ronge, SK S0J 1L0
(306) 425–2051
www.kikinahk.com

LLOYDMINSTER NATIVE FRIENDSHIP
    CENTRE
Box 1364, 4602–49th Ave.
Lloydminster, SK S9V 1K4
(306) 825–6558
www.nativecentres.org/lloydmin.htm

## MOOSE MOUNTAIN FRIENDSHIP CENTRE
318 Railway Ave W
Carlyle, SK S0C 0R0
(306) 453–2425

## NORTHWEST FRIENDSHIP CENTRE
P.O. Box 1780
Meadow Lake, SK S0M 1V0
(306) 236–3766

## PRINCE ALBERT INDIAN AND MÉTIS FRIENDSHIP CENTRE
1409 First Ave. E.
Prince Albert, SK S6V 2B2
(306) 764–3431

## QU'APPELLE VALLEY FRIENDSHIP CENTRE
P.O. Box 240
Fort Qu'Appelle, SK S0G 1S0
(306) 332–5616

## REGINA FRIENDSHIP CENTRE
1440 Scarth St.
Regina, SK S4R 2E9
(306) 525–5459

## SASKATCHEWAN ASSOCIATION OF FRIENDSHIP CENTRES
P.O. Box 240
Fort Qu'Appelle, SK SOG 1S0
(306) 332–5616

## SASKATOON INDIAN AND MÉTIS FRIENDSHIP CENTRE
168 Wall St.
Saskatoon, SK S7K 1N4
(306) 244–0174

## YORKTON FRIENDSHIP CENTRE
108 Dominion Ave.
Yorkton, SK S3N 1S3
(306) 782–2822

## ◆ YUKON TERRITORY

## SKOOKUM JIM FRIENDSHIP CENTRE
3159 Third Ave.
Whitehorse, YT Y1A 1G1
(867) 633–7680
www.skookumjim.com

## References

### Non-Reservation Indians in the U.S.

Fixico, Donald L. *The Urban Indian Experience in America*. Albuquerque: University of New Mexico Press, 2000.

———. *Urban Indians*. New York: Chelsea House, 1991.

Guillemin, Jeanne. *Urban Renegades: The Cultural Strategy of American Indians*. New York: Columbia University Press, 1975.

Lobo, Susan, and Kurt Peters. *American Indians and the Urban Experience*. Walnut Creek, Calif.: Altamira Press, 2000.

Neils, Elaine M. *Reservation to City: Indian Migration and Federal Relocation*. Chicago: Dept. of Geography, University of Chicago, 1971.

Sorkin, Alan L. *The Urban American Indian*. Lexington, Mass.: Lexington Books, 1978.

Stanbury, W. T. *Success and Failure: Indians in Urban Society*. Vancouver: University of British Columbia Press, 1975.

Thornton, Russell, Gary D. Sandefur, and Harold G. Grasmick. *The Urbanization of American Indians: A Critical Bibliography*. Bloomington: Indiana University Press, 1982.

Waddell, Jack O. and O. Michael Watson, eds. *The American Indian in Urban Society*. 1971. Reprint. Lanham, Md. : University Press of America, 1984.

Weibel-Orlando, Joan. *Indian Country, L.A.: Maintaining Ethnic Community in Complex Society*. Rev. ed. Urbana: University of Illinois Press, 1999.

*Dorothy Lonewolf Miller*
*David de Jong*

### Canadian Native Urbanization and Non-Reserve Populations

Canada. Royal Commission on Aboriginal Peoples. *Report of the Royal Commission on Aboriginal Peoples*. Volumes 1 and 4. Ottawa, 1996.

Canada. Statistics Canada. *A Profile of the Aboriginal Population Residing in Selected Off-Reserve Areas, 1986 Census*. Ottawa, 1990.

———. *Projections of Population with Aboriginal Ancestry Canada, Provinces/Regions and Territories, 1991–2016*. Ottawa, 1995.

Chartier, Clem. "Aboriginal Self-Government and the Métis Nation." In *Aboriginal Self-Government in Canada: Current Trends and Issues*, edited by John Hylton, 112–128. Saskatoon, Sask.: Purich Pub., 1999.

Coish, David. *Canada's Off-Reserve Aboriginal Population: A Statistical Overview*. Ottawa: Department of the Secretary of State of Canada, 1991.

Dosman, Edgar J. *Indians: The Urban Dilemma.* Toronto: McClelland and Stewart, 1972.

Dust, Theresa. "The Impact of Aboriginal Land Claims and Self-Government on Canadian Municipalities" *Canadian Public Administration* 40, no. 3 (1997): 481–494.

Graham, Katherine, et al. *Report of the Urban Governance Working Group. Research Report.* Ottawa: Royal Commission on Aboriginal Peoples, 1994.

Graham, Katherine. "Urban Aboriginal Governance in Canada: Paradigms and Prospects." In *Aboriginal Self-Government in Canada: Current Trends and Issues,* edited by John Hylton, 377–391. Saskatoon, Sask.: Purich Pub., 1999.

Larbi, Patrick. *A Portrait of Municipal-Aboriginal Relations in Canada.* Ottawa: Centre for Municipal-Aboriginal Relations, 1998.

Mountjoy, Terry. "Municipal Government Perspectives on Aboriginal Self-Government." In *Aboriginal Self-Government in Canada: Current Trends and Issues.* Saskatoon, edited by John Hylton, 310–328. Sask.: Purich Pub., 1999.

Peters, Evelyn, ed. *Aboriginal Self-Government in Urban Areas.* Kingston, Ont.: Institute of Intergovernmental Relations, Queen's University, 1995.

Ryan, Joan. *Wall of Words: The Betrayal of the Urban Indian.* Toronto: PMA Books, 1978.

*Frances Abele*

# 10

# *Religion*

♦ Native American Religious Life: Creating Through Cosmic Give-and-Take
♦ Traditional Religious Practices Among Contemporary American Indians
♦ Christianity and Native Americans  ♦ Pluralistic Religious Beliefs
♦ Religious Organizations

## ♦ NATIVE AMERICAN RELIGIOUS LIFE: CREATING THROUGH COSMIC GIVE-AND-TAKE

From time immemorial, Native American religiousness has grown out of encounters with spirit, plant, animal, and human "others" who often seemed like dangerous strangers. Grounded in the actual world with its very real threats, neither contemporary nor traditional Native American life can be described by the abstract noun *religion* or the idea of *belief.* Unlike belief, which stresses some other-worldly, mysterious, and unseen reality, the term *worldview* suggests that for Native American peoples "religion" has to do with the ways in which people see the world in the here and now. The adjective *religious* best captures Native American views of reality. Native American respect for what non-Indian people call nature, for example, has always been admired. What has not been appreciated is that Native Americans have always understood that the world is a dangerous place. If respectful trust exists, it has been earned. Disaster, whether personal, social, military, or ecological, may therefore be the result of the people's failings. In this way, Native Americans stress religious responsibility and interdependence with other beings rather than a sense of victimization.

Traditional stories over the centuries have pointed out that the people are threatened, as well as helped, by other beings. American Indians learn hard lessons through the oral tradition and relearn them in ceaseless struggles for intercultural understanding. Navajo mythology recounts the key religious insight: Navajo exist because they have struggled to learn from, rather than about, the many strange people they met along their path. Navajo have learned and are still learning from Protestants, Catholics, Mormons, Peyotists, and from the Lakota of the northern Great Plains. All the while, they have continued to create in their traditional ceremonies that exquisite balance in the world they call *hozho,* a term that expresses beauty, harmony, knowledge, and well-being. Such a condition has always been, in fact, a main objective of Native American ritual life. The people understand that the world itself has always been, and is especially now, threatened. Traditional Hopi call post-contact life *koyanisquatsi* (life out of balance), and so they diligently perform their ritual responsibilities to keep their earthly lives in balance.

Native American religiousness comes from a profound and astute understanding of the relatedness of all beings. The Navajo concept of *hozho,* for example, balances thought and speech, correct understanding and responsible action. In this way, Navajo religious ways exist in the actual, everyday life of the people. The Wabanaki of the Canadian-American Northeast say of their world-transforming culture hero, Gluskap: "He lives here in my story." In this way, the Wabanaki declare their religious life comes into being in the speech of the people. The stories of Gluskap alongside other stories are upheld, brought to life, by their remembrance and retelling, and by the moral guidance and resulting moral conduct engaged in by the listeners. Unlike Christianity, traditional Native American religious world views do not emphasize personal salvation in the next life or in preordained, godly commandments. While the Lakota and many other Plains Indian people evoke the Great Spirit, they also address many other beings as "all my relatives." These beings, understood as kin and addressed as "grandfather" and "grandmother," express a morality of caring relationships with all beings within the cosmos. Indeed, at the heart of Native American languages exists the religious belief that the entire cosmos is composed of powerful beings who either help or hinder human beings.

In all the American languages (more than 250 are still spoken), there is no word, no abstraction, for *religion*. Yet American Indians have always had religious institutions and these institutions are as complex and diverse as the people themselves. For example, shamans, people with special religious gifts, guided the hunting and gathering peoples, while song and dance groups in the larger societies performed ancient rituals celebrating solidarity with the great powers of mythology—Sun, Moon, Stars, the Winds, the Animals, and the Three Sisters (Corn, Bean, and Squash)—and with the ancestors. Both male and female medicine people still guide the people today, as do new kinds of religious practitioners, including Christian priests and ministers and roadmen in the pan-Indian Native American Church. American Indian people cared little for institutional religions constructed on the written word and revelation fixed in dogma; they understand that their religiousness "seeks the path of life."

The religious life of North America has always been poorly understood by Europeans. Writing about his first encounter with indigenous people in 1492, Christopher Columbus told Queen Isabella and King Ferdinand of Spain that the "New World" Natives were "very deficient in everything." It seemed to him that they had no religions, no governments, and no laws. At the same time, however, Columbus assured his monarchs "that in all the world there cannot be a people better or more gentle." Columbus, as did many Europeans after him, wondered how a people could be civilized without organized religion. Columbus thought, as do many still, that those humane qualities associated with religion—ethical behavior, moral leadership, a sense for justice—could not be obtained outside the God-given institutions of European church and state. Columbus did not realize that Native Americans have always located morality in the personal and communal lives of the people.

Traditional Native American religious thought and practice should not be thought of as pure; to the contrary, these traditions have always been muddied with life. These world views evolved over centuries, as Native peoples moved from place to place in North America, discovering new plants and animals and meeting new peoples with different ways of being religious. This process of religious discovery was not always peaceful. When Native Americans intruded on the lands of others, they met resistance. Thus war became part of life's struggle, and so conflict helped shape religious change.

The Peace Council, a religiously guided conference, arose out of the need to end conflict between nations and peoples. The peace councils often opened with smoking the Sacred Pipe with friends or enemies to affirm the relatedness of all living things and to explore and seek understanding of political and cultural differences. Native Americans often celebrated their encounters with European strangers, or early explorers and colonists, with the lighting and sharing of a peace pipe or burning of tobacco. Tobacco was ceremonially burned when the Wampanoag Indians of present-day Massachusetts met with the Pilgrims, and thereafter in countless councils to seek peace. Today the rituals take the form of talking circles, in which urban Indians from many once-hostile tribes seek mutual understanding and support. The act of seeking peace and harmony with the beings of the world and with fellow human beings lays at the heart of Indian religiosity. The long tradition of religiously guided meetings suggests that Native religiousness has always expressed itself in cautious but mutual and respectful conversation with others.

## Native American Mythology

**Stories of the Beginning.** The enduring and dynamic character of Native American mythologies has often been misunderstood. One popular misunderstanding is that because their cultures were based on the spoken word, Native Americans lost their pure, original traditions over the years. Nonetheless, Native American cultures are generally transmitted from generation to generation by the retelling of stories and myths in reenacting rituals and ceremonies. Some North American Indians kept records with religious insights written on wooden sticks or embroidered into wampum belts, but there was no written religious book like the Christian Bible. Instead, all Indian peoples had long traditions of transmitting religious ceremonies and ideas through storytelling and ritual reenactments. The stories and rituals carry the traditions and history of Native American people.

A second and related misinterpretation is that mythology is fictional and therefore an inadequate way of thinking about the world. Mythology is historical because it reflects upon the traditional values of the past in order to make sense of the moral challenge of the present. Mythology makes an unspoken but underlying assumption: the future depends not on what people believe, but on their responsible actions in the here and now. Myth is not narrowly historical in concerning itself actually with what happened where and when. To the contrary, myth addresses urgent issues of personal and social existence and boldly offers Native American peoples basic answers to the basic questions, Why am I

Ceremonies at the death of a chief or a priest. Drawing by Le Moyne; engraving from T. de Bry, *America,* part II, plate XL. (Courtesy of American Heritage Press)

here? and Why are we here? Myths, especially origin myths, answer for a people where they came from, describe the purposes people have on earth, and establish the relations of the individual and the nation to the cosmos. The answers to such questions are given in the details and cosmological meanings of the origin and other myths.

The myth of earth-divers is probably the most widespread way in which Native Americans have dealt with the question of origin. There are many earth-diver stories throughout North America, and often specific details of the stories vary. Nevertheless the central theme of the origin of solid earth (expressing ordering and a haven) emerging within a chaotic and formless cosmos is usually the same. Unlike the all-powerful God of Judeo-Christian religions, these creators needed the cooperation of various birds and animals to form the Earth, or solid ground. Confronted with a preexisting, boundless, and chaotic water world, the creator-transformer sought the assistance of animals or birds, who drove deep into an almost bottomless sea attempting to seize a tiny bit of mud to form the earth

island. These were compassionate, sacrificial acts, because the animal persons often died in their attempts. In the end, one of them succeeds. The creator then expanded the bit of earth into the earth island, where people and animals live. The stories vary about which animal is successful in gaining the bit of earth from under the sea, but that animal is usually highly revered by the people. In an Iroquoian version of earth-diver, Turtle generously offered his back as a foundation to hold up the earth. Similarly, among many Indian cultures, the earth island is considered the turtle's back, who swims in the great sea of water, which embodies chaos and disorder. In Delaware culture, the Turtle clan or social division was considered politically and religiously the most prominent, because the Turtles have the religious responsibility to uphold the society and support the earth island. In all variants of the earth diver stories, cooperation, service, and self-sacrifice bring order into a formerly chaotic cosmos.

In many other stories, great beings, who anthropologists often call culture heroes and who often resemble earth-diver transformers by their actions, wisdom, and sometimes direct law, show people how to act powerfully and responsibly. Like transformers all over the continent, the Wabanaki Gluskap changed the shape of the earth itself. He created the rivers and streams that flow throughout the Northeast by killing a selfish frog who hoarded all the world's water, just as Coyote, the transformer figure of the western Indians, did in California. In the Southeast among the Cherokee a powerful bird formed the landscape by lifting and lowering mountains and valleys with his wings as he inspected the newly formed earth. Gluskap also reduced giant animals like beaver to their present size so that they would live cooperatively with human beings. He created the coming and going of the seasons, thus assuring that the great person Winter interacted reciprocally with Summer.

Besides Gluskap in the Northeast, similar culture hero stories are found throughout North America, although the culture hero's name usually changes from region to region. Similar culture-hero roles are taken up by Raven in the Northwest Coast and Arctic, by Rabbit in the Southeast, and Old Man in the Plains. The actions and deeds of the culture heroes help explain the importance of human responsibility. About each culture hero there are many stories, but invariably they are stories about the culture hero's immoral or irresponsible actions that lead to negative consequences. For example, the cause of death and pain in the world is attributed to the irrational and selfish actions of the culture hero. The lessons taught by the story is that selfish, irresponsible, proud individuals will suffer negative consequences such as illness, death, or other misfortunes. The culture hero stories give an account for the origin of harshness of life—the existence of poverty, suffering, death, the need to labor, the dispersal of the tribes, and the nature of war. Culture heroes also establish safe limits to such negative facts of life. At the same time, the culture hero stories are usually very funny and are told for both moral edification and entertainment. The culture heroes take their misfortunes in stride and thereby provide examples for how individuals are to endure the sufferings of life. Furthermore, the culture heroes are great gift-givers because, in many mythical histories, they form people and instruct them about edible plant and animal foods, and they create the tools—pots, baskets, nets, spears, digging sticks, canoes, and snowshoes—that make human work economically and morally productive. The ritual knowledge and technological gifts of the culture heroes help the people to live either in the desert heat or the Arctic frost. Often, as among the Tlingit of the Northwest Coast, the culture hero—in this case Raven—gives the people their primary ceremonies and their primary social relations. The Tlingit are divided into two moieties,

two social halves, called Raven and Eagle. It was Raven who organized Tlingit society into this two-fold division, which the Tlingit continue to honor.

The emergence tradition is another widespread form of creation history, developed with complexity by the Pueblo, Navajo, and Apache in the Southwest, and by the Creek in the Southeast. Emergence stories have the people climbing out from under the earth, their existence bound up with the character of the world itself. In these accounts, emergence becomes a rich metaphor for moral development or, in the Navajo case, *hozho*—greater harmony, beauty, and order with the beings of the cosmos. Living within the earth, the peoples face serious troubles. Often their world lacks light and warmth. Sometimes the planet is too small, and spinning rapidly makes the people dizzy. Such inhospitable conditions drive the people to seek more suitable living conditions. Traveling upward, some animals flying, others carried by tall plants that reach the vault of the heavens, the people (often animal persons as well as humans) seek their proper, balanced place in the cosmic scheme of things. The people, sometimes animals or insects, are cast out of the lower worlds for their moral indiscretions, and they must find a way to the next world in order to survive and attempt to live more morally ordered lives, or that world will also be destroyed by the cosmic beings whom the people offend.

In the Navajo creation history, humans do not live in the first three worlds that exist beneath the present world. A people of flying insects, Air Spirit People, occupied the First World. Because the Air Spirit People were quarrelsome and committed adultery, they were forced by powerful spirit beings to flee to the next higher world, where they met a people of swallows. By committing adultery with the swallow leader's wife, the Air Spirit People were forced to fly up to the Third World. There they soon committed the same faults with the beings of the third world, where they met the Holy Beings, who are immortal spirits who made the First Man and First Woman. Much of the story of life in the Fourth World revolves around difficulties encountered by the first people over reconciling gender differences and developing harmonious sexual and husband-wife relations. Because Coyote, also created in the Fourth World by the Holy People, kidnapped two children of the water spirit, a great flood forced the people, with the aid two religious leaders, to ride a reed up to the fifth, or present, world. For the Navajo, the Fifth World is not the last possible world. If the people do not maintain moral and harmonious lives in the fifth world—the present world—then this world will also be destroyed, and perhaps only a few lucky survivors will be able to climb to the Sixth World, the next higher world. Navajo emergence mythology emphasizes a search for moral responsibility, seeking a state of being in which humans, plants, animals, sun, and moon exist in a stabilized, moral, and harmonious relationship.

As one result, Navajo understanding of world discovery contrasts dramatically with that of Western Europeans. For European discoverers, the strange, new peoples of the Americas failed to pose new questions about the nature of reality. Judging by their own cultural standards, European discoverers declared that Native Americans were culturally and religiously incomplete. Assured of the godly superiority of their own culture, Europeans have from contact to the present attempted to impose their way of life on Native Americans. To the contrary, Navajo emergence mythology describes a cooperative, open-minded approach to other cultures. People make mistakes towards others, but they can also learn from their errors.

The earth-diver, culture hero, and emergence stories are similar in that they teach all persons, human and otherwise, must share power and responsibility. Otherwise they risk upsetting the ordered relations of the cosmos and thereby will cause disorder, suffering, disease, misfortune, and death among the people. The Winnebago of Wisconsin have another case in point of this cosmic give-and-take. Though most of their story's variations of how the world came to be discuss the origin of the Winnebago clans, a few do focus on the vague figure of Earthmaker. In these stories (here there is the possibility of missionary influence), the Winnebago declare that Earthmaker established a cosmos largely independent of himself, and one in which human beings were an afterthought. As he created the Sun, Moon, Earth, Winds, plants, and animals, he endowed each with particular and exclusive powers, such as the ability to fly for birds and the great strength of the bear. Human beings alone were powerless. To correct his mistake, Earthmaker gave humans beings a special gift of power. He created tobacco and promised that as long as human beings tended the plant with care and offered it to the powerful persons of the cosmos, their needs would be met. It is also telling that Earthmaker gave humans beings the tobacco that he and all spirits greatly desired but lacked. In this way, Earthmaker endowed the Winnebago with tremendous power and an opportunity to express respect toward the great others. As with many other Native American peoples, tobacco and the pipe thus became the way in which the Winnebago obtained religious harmony and order with the beings of the cosmos.

Similarly, New Mexican Zuni mythology describes a time when human beings and the Kachinas, ancestral spirit beings, competed with each other over ownership of the deer and other game animals. After a prolonged battle in which humans and Kachinas found themselves equally powerful, humans decided to use trickery to win the contest. Rather than seek a mutually beneficial sharing of the deer, which the balance of power suggested as the only positive outcome, humans imprisoned all the game in a place that the Kachinas could not find. When the battle continued, humans prevailed. The result was a reciprocal balance that declared the uselessness of conflict: the Kachinas acknowledged human ownership of the deer and, in return, humans recognized that the Kachinas had control of corn and other seeds. Since each group desired the resources of the other, interdependence and reciprocity became a cosmic necessity.

Although Native American mythologies view the cosmos and its formation in very different ways, depending on their ecological setting, they share some common religious insights such as the need to establish constructive relations among themselves and with the great beings of the cosmos, including the plants and animals who sustain life.

**Celebrations of the Life Cycle.**    Throughout North America, Indian peoples express gratitude towards plants who feed, herbs who cure, and deer and bear, who make life possible. They understand that animal bones must be treated with respect and that animal reincarnation, the understanding that the spirits of respectfully treated animals are reborn and replenish the earth, depends on human action. In the Pacific Northwest, for example, the first-catch ceremony celebrates the gift of salmon. Here, the first fish of the year was placed on evergreen bows, themselves expressions of enduring life, and the people thanked the salmon for willfully sacrificing its life so that humans can live. The salmon was then carefully cooked, and each person in the village ate part of this special fish. Finally, the salmon's bones were returned to the water so that they will live again. In the same way, first-fruit ceremonies across the continent acknowledged the cosmic cycle of life. On the eastern seaboard, the widespread Green Corn Ceremony, an annual new year and purification ritual, honors and gives thanks to the corn for its life-giving qualities. In a variety of Iroquois rituals, like Thanks to the Maple and the Strawberry Festival, the people sing and dance to express gratitude to maple trees and strawberries for doing their part to support the lives of humans.

After the 1750s and the development of high Plains horse cultures, human ritual responsibility differed on

R.Holata Outina.

Native leaders often consulted shamans on important issues. Drawing by Le Moyne (1591); engraving from T. de Bry, *America,* part II, plate XI. (Courtesy of American Heritage Press)

the Great Plains. There the well-being of buffalo and horses and the need to achieve success in war were the focus of ceremonial activity. The Plains Pawnee, southwestern Pueblo, and California peoples, among others, keyed ritual performance and human responsibility to seasonal and celestial cycles. All of these ritual performances constitute variants of a single insight, as stated by the Northwest Kwakiutl: Life is about eating and being eaten. Human life plays an essential role in the cosmic cycle of birth, growth, death, and rebirth.

In effect, various North American mythologies teach very similar lessons. The stories explore the meaning of human life in relation to a threatening cosmos. Despite their emphasis on the dangerous nature of existence, the stories also hold out hope. The great others of the beginning teach responsible cooperation. Cosmic councils, in which animals, birds, plants, insects, and other beings come together, identify what would become the heart of Native American religious action: each being has a unique power or ability and the responsibility to contribute and cooperate. Native American mythologies also explore the terrible things that happen when

people—human and otherwise—fail to play their part in this cosmic drama.

## Native American Perspectives and Judeo-Christian Beliefs

The central role that human action takes in Native American cosmic religious life is startling to a Judeo-Christian. For Christians, reality is divided into three spheres that derive from a great chain of being: above all stands an all-powerful God, who is creator of an impersonal, machine-like "universe" which derives from and is focused upon God's being. Directly below God and closely associated with him are angels, who are devoted to his worship. Other angels, associated with rebellious Lucifer, refused such submission. In punishment, God excluded them from his presence, although they remain powerful and destructive. Below this exalted heavenly order stands the realm of "culture" in which humans are the highest beings, served in their turn by a subordinate, exploitable "nature." Judeo-Christian religions are ones in which "higher" beings are superior to lower ones, and therefore religions in which status, power, authority, and grace, or empowerment, comes from higher beings to beings who have a less exalted nature.

Native American religious life, in contrast, strikes a balance. Native piety differs from Christian prayer and worship, and leading a devout life means performing rituals and moral behaviors that created human and world order in the present life. One essential characteristic of Native American piety has to do with acknowledgment. For example, traditional Hopi begin the day by greeting the Sun, the great person whose light and warmth makes life possible. Similarly, in the traditional Southeast, people bathed daily, for bathing was an act that admitted the possibility of both transgression and personal and collective purification. In a related way, Mountain Wolf Woman, a twentieth-century Winnebago, recounts that, after a successful deer hunt, her father directed her and her sister to express thanks by offering tobacco to the thunders, trees, stars, and moon, thus nurturing these beings in return for their gift of meat. Concluding the ritual by fasting, the Winnebago girls experienced humility and gratitude for gifts generously given and gratefully returned.

## Religious Power and Social Life

Just as councils have always been central to the give-and-take of Native American social, economic, and political life, religious ways of life express the collective processes through which the peoples share in creating, maintaining, and transforming relations with others. The relationships of importance include those with one another, with the great persons of the four directions, with the great persons of the above and the below, and with the great persons co-existing with humans on the earthly plane. Native Americans understand these persons and their cosmic domains in various ways. For many, the four directions are fundamental; for others, up-river and down-river describe the central relationships. Whatever the cosmological orientation to the world's persons, Native American ritual action aims for balance, cooperation, and mutual interdependence.

**Importance of Collectivism.** The collective goal of religious action cannot be over-stressed for any of the Native American peoples. Although some interpretations view hunting peoples as religiously individualistic and peoples with permanent settlements and ampler resources as more devoted to communal religious activity, these interpretations miss the mark in several ways. In particular, they reveal a misunderstanding of the diversity of religious outlooks within the various tribal traditions.

In traditional Native American contexts, religious life meant very different things to different people, depending on age, gender, knowledge, and power. Hunting peoples lived in very small kinship groups, and usually only a few persons (male and female) were religious specialists. Only some had the special power to evoke the spirits, foretell the future, find game, and cure. But, far from encouraging individualism, power spread from the few throughout the group: everyone encountered the spirits in dreams, and in everyday work life they contributed their share to make a communal whole. Moreover, religious specialists in hunting societies were no more motivated by self-interest than were their counterparts in larger-scale agricultural or marine-fishing societies.

Indeed, at first glance, important differences do seem obvious between hunting and agricultural societies. In addition to hunting-gathering societies, North America witnessed many large-scale tribal developments apparently associated with technological evolution. In all probability, agriculture—in the milder regions of the Northeast, along the Eastern seaboard, in the Southeast, along rivers on the Great Plains, and even in the desert Southwest—made town life possible. Also striking is the fact that the seagoing, big-canoe cultures of the Pacific Northwest, which won an ample livelihood from fishing and hunting marine mammals, created a complex tribal life, even one divided into upper and lower classes. Similarly, on the Great Plains, a dynamic combination of French guns from the Northeast and horses from the Spanish Southwest apparently helped to create the classic, stereotypical Plains tribes.

Despite these developmental differences and the varying degrees of tribal-wide religious rituals, the scale of these societies did not force them to depart religiously from the rituals of the hunter-gatherers, and they did not separate "religion" from other parts of culture. Tribal rituals —including the Green Corn Ceremony, an annual world renewal ritual of the Huron and Iroquois in the Northeast and the Cherokee, Chickasaw, Choctaw, and Creek in the Southeast; the medicine societies, or ritually exclusive groups of shamans with specialized curing knowledge of the Ojibwa, Odawa, Menominee, and Winnebago of the Eastern Woodlands; the Sun Dance, an annual purification ceremony among the Hidatsa, Cheyenne, Lakota, Crow, and Blackfeet on the Plains; the Kachina rituals, for bringing rain and community well-being of the Southwest Pueblo; the world-renewal rites, ceremonial reenactments of origin histories that ensure the life of the world for another annual or ritual cycle among the Luiseño, Kumeyaay, and Chumash of California; and the winter ceremonials of the Salish, Kwakiutl, Tsimshian, Haida, and Tlingit of the Pacific Northwest—all share an ancient American religious logic. Just as the hunter-gatherers acknowledged life freely given, thus empowering its reincarnation, most major tribal rituals, such as those mentioned above, celebrate human interdependence and reciprocity with the great persons of the cosmos.

Far more important, to say that hunting peoples were religiously individualistic denies their collective orientation. In fact, even small social groups had an intensely religious communalism. Hunting peoples like the Inuit of the Arctic, the Algonquian peoples of the subarctic Northeast, and the hunting and gathering peoples—Ute, Shoshoni, and Paiute of the Southwest and desert areas of the Great Basin and California—all depended on kinship cooperation for their very lives. Hunting and gathering were collective activities conducted by men and women in their respective work groups. These societies were relatively unspecialized in their economic activities, although individuals certainly had special skills in crafting canoes, snowshoes, bows and arrows, spears, nets, pots, and baskets. The telling point is that everyone—religious specialists included—did more or less the same kind of work, usually as part of a group effort.

In both small- and large-scale Native American societies, all contributed to the collective good. Young boys proudly gave their first kill to elders who thanked them for their skill and gift. Similarly, young girls learned from their mothers, aunts, and grandmothers the importance of service. Unmarried men presented their game to headmen, who served as redistributive agents making sure that no one—whether young or old, married or unmarried, healthy or sick—went without food, clothing, or shelter. Selflessness and unvarying attention to others' needs (including the need for courage in defending the people from their enemies) were the hallmarks of "chiefly" status. Individualism did, of course, exist. But self-interest expressed itself in relation to the well-being of the group, since people used laughter, gossip, and social contempt as powerful ways of controlling deviant individualistic behavior that threatened the well-being of the group. When people turned their backs on a wayfaring person, he felt the pain of isolation and soon mended his ways to comply with the general will of the tribal community. Otherwise, Native Americans both respected and valued responsible individuality.

Hunting and gathering peoples thus reveal the religious and cultural challenges all Native American peoples have always faced. They lived in hostile environments peopled by beings who could injure, maim, and kill as easily as they could sustain life. Loners could not survive, and this may be one reason why orphans figure so prominently in Native American stories. Cast adrift from sustaining social contact, orphans were pitied, often treated with contempt, and sometimes cautiously admired. The frequent outcome of orphan stories drives home a collective moral: noticed by benevolent spirits, orphans were given powers—extraordinary knowledge and special skills—withheld from ordinary people. Thus, having been given abilities that people need, orphans become an important part of society, using their power to serve the very people who scorned their social isolation.

**Social Challenges.**   Like the life challenges posed by the environment, the social world within the tribes also posed great moral challenges to both individual and collective well-being. Selfishness, envy, jealousy, lust, anger, hatred, and revenge have always been destructive facts of life. Additionally, in patrilineal societies in which ancestry is descended through fathers, women often came to live with their husbands and their husbands' relatives. As a result, wives were separated from their closest kin, and sometimes lived their lives among a group of strangers. The opposite was often the case in matrilineal groups (among whom identity flowed from maternal kin). In this situation (as among some Apache tribes) a husband found himself put to the moral test by his mother-in-law. Tradition dictated that a husband could not even speak to his mother-in-law, yet she could demand unflinching service from him. Many Apache stories explore the mutual resentment resulting from these traditions. Serious tensions also played themselves out in sibling rivalries. Such contests were particularly true among brothers whose competitive hunting and aggressive warfare created dangerous personalities. Not surprisingly, then, in many tribes purification rituals reoriented warriors to the peaceful values of community life.

The same tension between individualism and collectivism undercut the mythic and religious ideal among American Indian religious specialists. Defined by their unique possession of great power given by the spirits who wished to assist human beings, these specialists could dream the future, call the spirits, destroy enemies, cure disease, find game and even control the weather. Ideally, they carefully held the people's welfare in their hands. They were guardians of traditional knowledge and values, and in their own lives they were to be exemplars of the moral meaning of tradition. Yet they too were men and women, and so subject to every human failing. This truth the people knew all too well, as their emotional reactions declared. The people sought assistance and leadership from their religious specialists, and for those contributions they were grateful. But they also combined respect and admiration with fear. If power could be used to help, it could also serve the religious specialist's own purposes: religious rivalries, duels, love medicine, poisonings, and even witchings were destructive facts of life.

Social struggles within even the smallest Native American group must be understood in a religious context. The struggles represent not the kind of impersonal meaninglessness that has come to characterize so much of contemporary American life (with which present Native Americans also struggle). Rather, Native American religious life reaches for collective order in the face of individualistic chaos. Such a moral challenge derives, in actuality, from the relational laws of the cosmos as declared by mythology. The unvarying need to grapple with such troubles is one major reason why Native Americans' religious life has seemed so perplexing, at least when their differences with mainline Judeo-Christianity have been honestly encountered.

### Native American Religious History: The Colonial Period

With European contact, an era of rapid religious change began. Between 1492 and 1820, significant impact was limited to the English, French, and Spanish/Mexican colonial spheres in the Atlantic coastal lands of the continent, Canada, the Southwest, and California. As part of a larger economic, political, and military colonialism, missionaries single-mindedly stressed the superiority of Christian religion. Destructive as the colonial years were to the American Indian, they were also a time of tremendous creativity, as the tribes applied the lessons of mythology to assess their troubled situations, examine the claims of the missionaries, and work on revitalizing their communities.

**The Northeast.** Missionization in Canada had various outcomes—some people were destroyed, while others adapted. Given the devastating impact of European diseases, intertribal wars, and the loss of lands, it is remarkable that Algonkian-speaking peoples (the Micmac, Wabanaki, Montagnais, and Algonquin) continued to practice important parts of traditional religious life.

The French priests who introduced Catholicism to the Algonkian peoples condemned many traditional Indian practices. While many Indians came to trust Catholicism, it would be incorrect to say that they converted to what they perceived as a superior religion. Rather, in their conversations with French missionaries, the Algonkians rediscovered traditional values; Catholic sacraments were used to preserve several religious functions and to recreate tribal communities at the same time that the sacraments established an important alliance with the French. The fact that the English threatened the Eastern Algonkian (the Wabanaki and Micmac) almost continually between 1675 and 1760, and that the French offered a powerful military alliance, also strengthened the religious relationship.

The Algonkians adapted some Christian rituals to fill their traditional needs. In many instances, for example, baptism was used to cure people afflicted with diseases against which traditional medicine was ineffective. The ritual also was used to maintain contact between the living and the dead. Jesus Christ began to appear in Algonkian dreams as the one who empowered medicine people to predict the future, cure disease, communicate with the dead, and hunt and make war successfully. In all these ways, the French God struck Algonkians as similar to their culture hero. Algonkians noted that when their culture hero withdrew from this world, he promised to return in some future time of need. And up to the present, Algonkians have continued to balance tradition and Christianity in a way that maintains their relationships with the land and the plant and animal persons who still populate it.

For New England Algonkian, change proved much more damaging. Here the impact of disease and territorial displacement was much greater, and intertribal and colonial war also played an important role. After 1640, survivors of once-powerful tribes regrouped in Indian praying towns, which were settlements of remnant Indian communities, adopted Christianity and New England town government, and reconciled themselves to live under colonial law. In the Indian praying towns, English ministers were more critical of traditional life than were the French Catholic priests. Caught between the demanding English and an inability to return to a traditional ecological lifestyle, the praying Indians endured English and Indian attacks during Metacom's (King Philip) War, only to survive thereafter on the margins of English life.

**The Southwest and California.** A fundamental religious conflict emerged in the Spanish Southwest in the early 1600s when the Spanish violently asserted control over the Pueblo peoples of New Mexico and Arizona. Because intolerant Franciscan priests, with military backup, attacked the practice of Pueblo ritual life and used gang labor to create mission centers, the Pueblo remained unimpressed with Catholicism. In addition, the missionaries poorly communicated the abstract character of their new religion. Furthermore, Catholicism simply did not address the Pueblo's urgent religious need to preserve reciprocal relations with ancestral powers who ensured rain and successful crops.

The traditional political independence of each Pueblo made the Spanish conquest easier, but ceaseless oppression eventually united the Pueblo. Under the leadership of San Juan Pueblo's medicine man, Pope, and with the active support of many religious leaders, the

Pueblo tribes drove the Spanish out of the Rio Grande Indian Pueblos in 1680. The Pueblo returned to independent political action but were reconquered by 1696. But times had changed. After 1700 the Spanish became more tolerant, and the Pueblo had learned an important lesson. They practiced Catholicism in public, especially in celebration of their Pueblo's feast day, usually named by the Spanish after a Catholic patron saint, but all the while, traditional religious practice went underground where it remains, largely invisible, to the present day.

Other peoples under Spanish control fared differently. As they had in the Southwest, the Spanish, beginning in 1769, created an immense mission system in California from San Diego to San Francisco. There was some acceptance of Catholicism in these missions, but traditional religious ways survived as well. Among the Gabrielino and Chumash a new religious orientation emerged, called Chingichngish, which asserted the truth of tradition and warned the people that they would die if they accepted baptism. The collapse of the mission system after the Mexican War of Independence in the 1820s created conditions of economic, political, and social marginality, but even in the twentieth century traditional religious practices survive among the former mission Indians of southern California.

The collapse of the mission system in Arizona and northwest Mexico created conditions that encouraged the emergence of Sonoran Catholicism. The missions had less impact on the desert-dwelling Papago (Tohono O'Odham) and Pima. Once free to follow their own interests, these Sonoran peoples continued to maintain positive relations with the patron saints the missionaries had introduced. Some Catholic holidays, like All Souls Day, have developed into community celebrations of solidarity with dead relatives. Likewise, Easter has come to mark the seasonal shift from winter to summer. To this day, Native chapels (independent of the Catholic church) are dispersed throughout the immense Tohono O'Odham Reservation in southern Arizona. At the same time, traditional singers and healers survive, and the culture hero I'itoi is still important to the people.

## Native American Religious History: The American Era

Algonkian, Pueblo, and the peoples of southern California and Sonora all largely maintained ties with their ancestral lands, an important factor in the preservation of traditions. Beginning with the American Revolution, however, many Native American peoples found themselves ecologically displaced. They became either surrounded by American settlers or forcibly removed

to reservations far from original homelands. Native peoples responded to these changes with varying degrees of success. Among the peoples of the Eastern seaboard, the Iroquois-speaking Six Nations Confederacy have been the most successful in religious adaptation. The peoples of the Midwest (the Shawnee, Miami, Fox, Potawatomi, and Illinois, to name a few) and those of the Southeast (the Cherokee, Creek, Choctaw, Chickasaw, and Seminole) struggled through periods of resistance, adaptation, missionization, and removal to Oklahoma reservations in the 1830s. In the process, they lost much, but not all, of their traditional culture.

**The Iroquois and Handsome Lake.** Between the end of the French empire in 1763 and the War of 1812, the Six Nations, or Iroquois Confederacy (before European contact the prophet Deganiwidah abolished the law of revenge between nations and so created the confederacy consisting of the Cayuga, Mohawk, Oneida, Onondaga, and Seneca, and, after 1716, the Tuscarora) experienced severe disruption of their traditional way of life. Iroquois warriors and diplomats once held formidable power, playing an important role during the French and Indians Wars between 1689 and 1763. Acting also as middlemen in the fur trade, the Iroquois were prosperous, especially since Iroquois women were highly successful agriculturalists. As the American colonies began to seek independence, the Iroquois attempted to maintain diplomatic neutrality, but found it impossible. By 1800 the confederacy had disintegrated—the individual nations were confined to separate reservations surrounded by American farms and settlement, traditional male roles no longer existed, and alcohol began to take a harsh toll on the people.

The Iroquois situation can be understood as a breakdown of the give-and-take of life. Although the confederacy had once been a respectful relationship between younger and elder brothers, these relations collapsed. Reciprocity no longer shaped clan, village, national, or confederate life. Women's political influence had been undercut by male warriors and diplomats, then male status disappeared as drinking, vicious politics, and loss of territory replaced hunting, warfare, and diplomacy. The Iroquois disagreed among themselves about whether to accept U.S. economic and political institutions and whether to accept Christianity. As a means to survive under vastly changed political conditions, some, led by the Seneca leader Cornplanter, favored adoption of Christianity and U.S.-style government and agriculture. Others, led by the Seneca conservative Red Jacket argued that if the Iroquois adopted U.S. institutions and Christianity, they would lose their character as a distinct people or culture. In 1794 a smallpox epidemic, compounding an already difficult situation, cut the

U.S. Iroquois population by more than half to some 4,000 people.

In 1799 the prophet Handsome Lake, a former warrior and a chief within the Iroquois Confederacy, arose to reflect upon the people's physical, social, economic, political, and moral condition. Handsome Lake woke from a vision-in-death and, speaking an ancient form of the Iroquois language, called his people to renewal and adaptation. His vision was diagnostic: the people suffered because of their moral failings and, he said, if they did not repent the world itself would end. Handsome Lake particularly condemned the drinking, interpersonal violence, and sexual promiscuity that undercut his people's family life. He stressed traditional values, particularly the close relationship between individual and collective well-being. In this way the prophet affirmed the primary value of kinship. Even while he taught the Iroquois to tolerate American culture, he also urged caution, warning that a capitalistic economy would only further divide the people. He identified sharing as a prime moral directive. To some extent Christianity influenced Handsome Lake (he stressed the ideas of God, sin, repentance, confession, and salvation), but he still emphasized the importance of public rituals, especially those ceremonies that thanked all the powers of the cosmos with whom the people were interdependent. One result of Handsome Lake's religious movement was establishment in the 1830s, some fifteen years after his death, of the Longhouse religion, which professes Handsome Lake's teachings and which survives to this day.

**Tenskwatawa.**  Handsome Lake was neither the first nor the last prophet to urge Native peoples to reform. In the early nineteenth century (1806–1811), Tenskwatawa, the Shawnee prophet and brother to Tecumseh, the great pan-Indian leader, influenced religious, social, and political change among the entire Eastern seaboard. Moved by Tenskwatawa's call to reject American culture, several tribes in the Northeast and a conservative faction among the southeastern Creek went to war against the United States. In these years, religious leaders led resistance to—though sometimes urging compromise with—the growing American presence in their territories. At the same time, the new religious leaders urged their peoples to ritually renew their relations with plant, animal, and cosmic persons on whom their lives depended. The Shawnee prophet taught the tribes to return to the old traditions of economic self-sufficiency, avoid trade with U.S. traders, adopt old-style dress, and throw off political leaders who were willing to sell land to the United States. Tenskwatawa's influence ended after the Battle of Tippecanoe in November 1811, when his power failed against U.S. Army bullets. Thereafter, he had few followers, and his movement was over.

**Religious Change on the Great Plains.**  Europeans had a less direct but still tremendous impact on the Great Plains. Responding to economic, political, military, and technological changes, great migrations of eastern and western peoples converged on the Plains in the eighteenth century, prompting a period of explosive cultural and religious change. The Plains people entered a prolonged period of intertribal warfare as they attempted to establish territories for themselves, yet cultural rebirth also occurred, as the tribes created new or modified religious and political societies, such as soldier societies, tribal councils, religious specialists such as bundle keepers, and rituals like the Sun Dance, to help ensure victory in war, cure horses, and ensure the well-being of the buffalo.

The Cheyenne exemplify the sorts of religious changes that came to affect all Plains tribes as they adapted to a new land with its new beings. Originally living north and east of the Great Plains, the Cheyenne were forced by colonial expansion to migrate west, eventually entering the Plains area. In the neighborhood of the Black Hills, tradition relates, the prophet Sweet Medicine and

Parrot petroglyph near Albuquerque, New Mexico. (Photo by Alexandra Harris)

his wife entered a butte and there met spirits who gave them the great person-bundle, Mahuts—the four Sacred Arrows—considered a living being by the Cheyenne. Sweet Medicine and his wife were also taught the significance of the arrows. Brought to the Cheyenne by Sweet Medicine, Mahuts gave the Cheyenne men power in hunting and war and was an embodiment of a covenant to preserve the Cheyenne people and their way of life. By accepting Mahuts, the Cheyenne agreed to obey the religious laws and perform the annual renewal ceremonies as Sweet Medicine taught them. In this way, the Cheyenne acknowledged the material welfare the arrows brought them through abundant access to game. Among the Cheyenne a particularly virtuous man (as well as his wife and his family) became Mahuts' Keeper with special responsibilities towards both the arrows and the Cheyenne people. The bond between Mahuts and the Cheyenne people was so strong that were a Cheyenne to kill another tribesman, the arrows would be bloodied. In such circumstances, the Cheyenne thought of themselves as powerless until the Keeper called for a ceremony to renew relations between the people and Mahuts. Even at the opening of the twenty-first century, Mahuts continues to play an important role in Cheyenne religious life.

The Cheyenne also adapted religiously in other ways. Sweet Medicine also gave instructions for organizing soldier societies and for creating a council of forty-four chiefs for management of the annual buffalo hunt, the annual summer tribal ceremonies, and national Cheyenne affairs. The leading chief, who was selected by vote each ten years with each new council, stands in the place of the prophet Sweet Medicine, and his place in the council was called the Center of the Cosmos. On the Plains, the Cheyenne met another Algonkian-speaking people, the Suhtai who, in making an alliance with the Cheyenne, brought their great person-bundle, Is'siwun, the Sacred Buffalo Hat. Is'siwun was responsible for world fertility, especially for the reproduction of the buffalo, and she obligated the Cheyenne to perform special rituals, such as the purification rites of the sweat lodge, a cleansing steam bath and the world-renewing powers of the Sun Dance. Like her male counterpart, Mahuts, Is'siwun remains a vital part of Cheyenne life.

**Ghost Dance.** As was true on the Great Plains, religious change was also accelerating in the far west. From California to British Columbia, the tribes experienced sudden and devastating contact with fur traders, missionaries, fishermen, and miners. Also as elsewhere, territorial loss and epidemic sickness caused the tribes to look to religious answers to their crises. Some people sought help in Catholic and Pentecostal forms of Christianity, while many more turned to tradition,

discovering that old stories, foretelling continental devastation, called the people to renewal. Taking various forms, the so-called 1870s Ghost Dances, special songs and dances, sought to reestablish solidarity between the people and their long-dead relatives and, as a result, to recreate the world as it was before white contact. As had happened earlier in the East, prophets reminded the peoples that they had to take moral responsibility for their condition. While these Ghost Dance movements were not always successful, they did lead to several enduring religious adaptations. In California, particularly among the Pomo, the Ghost Dance eventually gave way to the Bole Maru tradition, sometimes called the Dreamers, whose practitioners revealed new rituals, cured disease, and warded off witches. Significantly, the Dreamers democratized access to religious power and so stressed individual responsibility for communal good. As a result, Dreamers condemned drinking, arguing, stealing, and any failure to cooperate religiously. In these ways, the Dreamers have made it possible for the Pomo to preserve their religious and ethnic identity.

By the 1890s Ghost Dance teachings of world renewal and return of dead relatives, given by the Nevada Paiute prophet Wovoka, reached the Great Plains. The Indians there had suffered greatly because the buffalo had been all but eliminated and their people placed on reservations. They hoped that religious resistance would achieve world renewal. The infamous massacre of Lakota at Wounded Knee, South Dakota, where some of the people were practicing the Ghost Dance, marks the general decline of the Ghost Dance Movement. Nevertheless the Ghost Dance persisted in small groups in the Plains area and farther west. Among the Pawnee, the Ghost Dance enabled individuals to communicate with dead medicine men and so to recreate many religious rituals that had been lost. Most important, the Ghost Dance encouraged the people to practice their traditional values in their daily lives by emphasizing traditional cultural understanding about ritual world renewal and the value of ritual to affect world change, even though the United States outlawed many of their religious ceremonies.

**Salish Rituals in the Pacific Northwest.** The Salish of Washington faced cultural annihilation in the 1870s and 1880s, and as was true for the Plains Indians, the Salish intensified religious activity in order to save themselves. While local settlers understood that Indians would act to preserve their way of life, they did not understand Salish rituals. Salish ceremonies were occasions when people danced and sang to acknowledge their interdependence with particular spirit persons who gave them the powers they needed for a successful life. Settlers tended to interpret Salish religious rituals as war dances, because they understood little about Salish culture, and the fact that the rituals were practiced frequently amplified settler anxieties. As a result, in 1871 Salish rituals were outlawed and religious leaders were jailed. These measures were doubly problematic for the Salish. Because their principal ceremonies drew together large numbers of people, they were difficult to perform secretly and, since the rituals were held less frequently after 1871, the need for them increased.

Thus U.S. government policy struck at the center of Salish life. As with many other Native American groups, guardian spirits not only empowered Salish shamans to cure, but also gave most people the craft, hunting, gathering, and fishing skills upon which life depended. Unlike many groups in which guardian spirits were personal and secret (although still used to serve the group), spirits among the Salish required public demonstration of their freely given gifts. The spirits also threatened people when they failed to give public ceremonial witness of the gifts received from friendly helper spirits. Failure to acknowledge the gifts, the Salish understood, led to retribution in the form of some material misfortune at the hands of the formerly allied spirit being.

**Shaker Church.**   In 1882 John Slocum, a Coast Salish Indian man, fell dead, only to revive and reveal a religious vision. He reported that God required the Salish to abandon spirit dancing and shamanism for a new source of power. When Slocum again fell dead, he was revived by his wife Mary, who was possessed by a shaking that many interpreted as the promised gift of power. By 1892 Slocum and his followers, who became known as the Shakers, formed a church that by 1910 was incorporated in the state of Washington.

Although Slocum repudiated much of the past, especially shamanism, and adopted Christian symbols, the Shaker church only gradually shifted allegiance from traditional spirit helpers to the Christian God. In time, an understanding developed that allowed continuity between old and new. Although the Shakers refer to Jesus and God, they vitally depend on the "Spirit of God," the spirit who gives the Salish powers to cure, foretell the future, and counter malicious shamans. Similar to the ancient winter ceremonies, the Shakers publicly witness the abilities they have received and thus address the well-being of the individual. At the same time, the Shaker church celebrates communal solidarity in Sunday gatherings, charismatic meetings often held to cure sickness, weddings, and funerals. Above all, Shakers express in Christian terms the ancient truth of interdependence between humans and the spirits: mutual charity among people makes it possible for the Spirit of God to work effectively among them.

**Peyotism.**   The cultural changes of the late-nineteenth and early-twentieth centuries paved the way for new forms of pan-Indian, as opposed to tribal, religious practices. Increased contact among different tribes, especially in Oklahoma, led to the development of powwows, or festivals of dancing and socializing, which still continue as celebrations of Indian identity all over the continent. Although the American era weakened relations between the tribes and animal persons, a great plant person, Peyote, whose visionary effects and teaching abilities derived from the cactus Lophophora williamsi, emerged on the southern Plains as a new guide to a distinctive religious life. Peyote has a long history among American Indians. Early in the eighteenth century, peyote entered the Southwest from Mexico, with the Mescalero Apache integrating it into their curing rituals. Peyote did not begin to spread northward until the 1880s, when the Plains tribes experienced their greatest despair at reservation life.

Under reservation conditions, and facing religious persecution from the U.S. government, Indian people experienced social alienation, psychological confusion, and a loss of religious confidence. Peyote addressed these problems and helped people reorient their lives. The new religious practice affirmed cultural identity by preserving old world views of worldly interdependence and traditional ritual style, and gave heightened value to being Native American. At the same time, it eased the conflicting demands of traditional religious life and Christianity. Finally, peyote helped the embattled peoples to resist cultural assimilation.

Peyote gave the people ways to reassume religious responsibility: in the church they confessed their failings, achieved purification, cured sickness, recovered from alcoholism, and created powerful bonds of brotherhood—even among tribes which, in the nineteenth century, had been enemies. In many ways, the spread of peyote in the late-nineteenth century was the most significant experiment in Native American religious change.

The early peyote prophets were innovators in drawing together various religious strands to create a new tradition. When mixed-blood John Wilson (Delaware, Caddo, and French) first took peyote at an Oklahoma Ghost Dance in 1890, he received a great vision. Taking pity on him, plant person Peyote showed him the road Jesus took and assured him that if he traveled the same road, he would reach heaven. Hence Wilson added elements of Christianity, such as belief in Jesus as a

Members of the Indian Shaker Church organized by John and Mary Slocum emerge from a holy ceremony. (Courtesy of the University of Oregon Library, Special Collections)

major spirit helper and individual moral responsibility, to traditional peyote religious practice.

The Jesus of Wilson's vision related to Indian peoples differently than he did to Christians. Wilson taught that Christians were given the Bible because they were guilty of killing Jesus; Native Americans had no responsibility for this terrible act and so had a closer relationship to God. He thus taught that while Christians needed the Bible to communicate with God, Indians could learn God's truth directly from the Peyote spirit. Although other prophets insisted that Peyotism and Christianity were the same, over time a consensus emerged that Jesus and Peyote had special concern for Indian people. As did many other peyotists, Wilson declared that Native Americans, unlike Christians, could communicate personally with divinity.

Another prophet, John Rave, had experiences that illustrate the religious quest for meaning that Peyote addresses. Rave had been a restless child and a troubled adolescent. He participated in traditional Winnebago rituals, but they made little impression on

him. Rave eventually left his home and became an alcoholic.

Rave's first experience with peyote, in Oklahoma, had been frightening. He confronted a huge, threatening snake, a powerful and destructive being in Winnebago mythology. As Rave's vision continued, he saw God, and he prayed for mercy and guidance. In time he received assurance and understanding that in all his life he had never known anything that was truly holy.

Rave's experience with peyote was typical. Confused, rootless, unhappy people came to Peyote, and the spirit gave them knowledge and healed them by giving them access to religious life, and by developing an ethic of personal responsibility and morality. According to Rave, peyote could heal because all sickness was merely a symptom of deeper troubles rooted in the soul. As in traditional Indian religious views, peyote, by healing and providing knowledge to the individual spirit, would clear the way for curing illness and other troubles. Rave taught that public confession of sin and trust would achieve redemption and salvation.

Just as Americans suppressed traditional religious practices, they also attacked the use of peyote. Believing that Indian rituals were un-Christian and uncivilized, reservation officials and missionaries spread false rumors that peyote led to wild sexual orgies. Traditionalists in some tribes opposed the new religious practices, and Indian progressives in the pan-Indian Society of American Indians joined forces with non-Indian critics and organized nationally against Peyotism, claiming that it was an excuse to take drugs. They also said that peyote deprived people of real medical care, even though peyotists all opposed alcohol and attempted to lead morally upright lives. As a constructive response to this angry opposition, Oklahoma peyotists incorporated as the Native American Church and began a battle for religious freedom that still continues.

By providing a new moral ethic and religious guidance, peyotists stress that their medicine and ritual often cures the physical, psychological, and religious ills of reservation and urban life. Peyote leaders emphasize the moral unity of all Indian people and have integrated many tribal religious practices into their religious rituals. The Native American Church is a religious institution created by Indians to meet modern Indian needs.

**Reemergence of Traditional Rituals.** As powerful as Peyotism has been in addressing the religious needs of Native American peoples, it has not displaced or replaced traditional religious life. The traditional rituals that went underground in the early-twentieth century began to reemerge in increasingly vigorous forms since the 1930s. The earlier public reintroduction of apparently lost rituals occurred as Native Americans responded to the needs of their men during and after World War II. War ceremonials became vehicles through which Lakota and Navajo, among others, prepared men for service in the armed forces; prayer sustained them during the conflict; and healing ceremonies reintroduced them to community life after their return home. The Native American Church also addressed these needs, but it was far from unique in adding the force of prayer to what many saw as a necessary national war effort. World War II, the Korean War, and the conflict in Vietnam not only provided the focus for a resurgence of traditional and pan-Indian religious practice, but also led many Native Americans to a growing realization that their participation required a prayerful hope for peace for all peoples.

Since the 1960s, then, such forms of participation in national wars brought Native American life into an intensified relationship with U.S. national life. Increasingly, Euro-Americans came to realize that Native Americans possess living rather than dead religious ways of life. As the Civil Rights Movement gained momentum, Native Americans became more outspoken against an oppressive system that continued to attack a traditional life that Indians saw as fundamentally religious and as vital to their distinctive identities. They felt they were oppressed by the trust relationship between the tribes and the United States; that the U.S. government reneged on its promises to protect tribal territories and Indian access to religious sites, and to devise forms of government sensitive to tribalism and to traditional religious leadership. They criticized programs that undermined the religious character of tribal life, including culturally insensitive educational programs, forced relocation to cities, and a variety of other programs designed to detribalize and assimilate the peoples.

The leaders of the American Indian Movement (AIM) have been protesting the woefully inadequate educational, economic, and political situation of all Indians. AIM thus speaks to the full complexity of Native American needs, although not always with the support of traditional leaders. Its agenda expresses the need to strengthen a tribal base that young and old recognize: communal life which is inseparable from constructive association with the spirits; the need to sustain pan-Indian religious forms that speak to urban Indians' situations; and the need for common political action.

AIM is only one voice addressing these concerns. Vine Deloria, Jr., wrote about the unique character of Native American religious life in *God is Red*. In other works—*Custer Died for Your Sins* and *We Talk, You Listen*—Deloria expressed urgent Indian concerns and called for Euro-Americans to recognize a failed pluralism, especially the nation's economic system that has marginalized the tribes and devastated their remaining lands.

### Religiousness and Contemporary Native American Peoples

Unlike Christianity, which concentrates all power in the hands of God who bestows it on human beings as an act of grace, Native American religious world views emphasize the interdependence of all beings. Even the Great Spirit needs humans, just as they need him, because if people live beyond the pale of religious order by not honoring the other beings of the cosmos, they will create disturbances that will cause destruction and chaos. Mother Earth reminds her people that her well-being depends on responsible human action. The Yaqui (Yoeme) people of Arizona, for example, do Jesus's work and think of him as being like their little brother, the Deer. Both Deer and Jesus are perfect innocents who give their lives so that others may live. The Yoeme perform ceremonies in honor of Jesus: at the end of the Easter Ceremony in which they empower Jesus to

Indian medicine conference. (Photo by Ilka Hartmann)

resurrect Himself, they ring the bell of their church to call St. Michael to carry to heaven the flowers that bloom from their ritual labor. Every year, in a ceremony that attracts thousands of people, the Zuni of New Mexico perform Shalako, a ceremony in which the great powers of the cosmos enter the Pueblo and dance with the people. In the Pacific Northwest, the Salish sing and dance the powers given them by their spirit helpers, thereby acknowledging the religious obligations that make life possible.

These are key insights expressed in past and present Native American religious activity. The world is composed of persons, not things. Some persons, including some human beings, are powerful, while some are not. Some persons act in caring, respectful, and nurturing ways; many do not. In brief, all people have responsibility towards others, whether or not they act accordingly. These insights were formed in the mythic period in which Native American cultures came into being, play themselves out in various religious community structures, and are embodied in religious, kinship, political relations, and economic activity. The insights are renewed in ritual performances, great and small. In

all these ways, American Indians create themselves in powerful acts that renew solidarity with all the world's people.

*Kenneth M. Morrison*
*Arizona State University*

## ♦ TRADITIONAL RELIGIOUS PRACTICES AMONG CONTEMPORARY AMERICAN INDIANS

Many people think that the Indians of North America are a vanished race, having disappeared into oblivion some time after the late nineteenth century. In the Western world religion is often associated with specific ceremonies such as church services, marriages, funerals, and prayer before meals and bedtime. However, for Native Americans, religion is more than ceremony. Throughout North America, there are still numerous tribes that live on reservation land and continue to embody and practice traditional Native American religions. While it is true that no one tribe continues to live a religious life as it did prior to contact with European

Ceremony for the Sacred Staff of the Omaha. (Photo by Ilka Hartmann)

Americans, traditional American Indian religion is not dead. Some Native Americans have adopted a form of Christianity and are essentially Christian peoples within the dominant Anglo-American society. Others practice new religions that in some way blend the old ways with the new. Such is the case, for example, in the Peyote Cult or Native American Church.

It is true, however, that a number of Native American peoples in the late twentieth century continue, at some level, to practice the religions of their forebears. Even where it appears that the traditional religious ways of American Indians are a thing of the past, there remains a deep structure of traditional values and perspectives.

Before we examine contemporary examples of traditional Indian religions, it is important to characterize what religion represents to American Indians. Religion is woven into the very fabric of American Indian life such that it is impossible, for the most part, to say where religion ends and secular life begins. Religion relates to that which is experienced as ultimate reality. In other words, what one perceives as essential to everything else is one's religion, and the experience of basic reality for American Indians is refracted through almost every significant aspect of their lives.

Architecture, food production (by way of farming, hunting, and gathering), mining, medicine and healing, family structure, and even eating, sleeping, and sexual activity are all experienced religiously. Each activity carries sacred significance for traditional American Indians. To understand traditional American Indian religion in the modern world is to understand all these aspects of life.

It is important to remember that the twentieth century has seen dramatic changes in all areas of American Indian life in the United States. No Indian people have managed to escape the influence of Western culture. Numerous ceremonies have been lost; others have been shortened in form or are performed less frequently than they once were; still others are performed but have lost their religious significance. For example, among the Eastern Cherokee of North Carolina, the once important new year ritual, the Green Corn Ceremony, is no longer performed in long form. Where it is performed, it may carry a cultural, not religious, meaning. The sacrifice to the Morning Star, a human sacrificial ritual that was performed by the Pawnee of Nebraska, has not been performed since the 1820s or early 1830s.

In some cases it is difficult to state with certainty the continued existence or extinction of certain traditional ceremonies or practices because of the secrecy that often surrounds them. There is a well-known saying among researchers of traditional societies—"those who say do not know; those who know do not say." This principle aptly applies to traditional American Indians, especially concerning religious practices. Many times, talkative and easily accessible Native American consultants are not considered by their own people to be knowledgeable about certain religious matters. On the other hand, the true bearers of sacred wisdom often refuse to talk to outsiders for a variety of reasons. Hence the fact that something is not discussed much, if at all, among outsiders does not mean that it is dead. For example, scholars commonly state that the clans no longer survive among the Eastern Band of Cherokee of North Carolina. Recently, an Eastern Cherokee disclosed to me that some Cherokee still maintain traditional knowledge and practices related to the division of society into seven clans—Wolf, Deer, Bird, Red Paint, Blue Paint, Long Hair, and Wild Potato. However, he refused to discuss the matter in any detail stating that such disclosure to non-members is forbidden. This example demonstrates a fundamental problem in carrying out research related to Native American religions.

Nevertheless, it is clear that traditional American Indian religions have declined and changed since the arrival of Europeans in the New World. The same is true of other aspects of Native American life. House-building has undergone major changes. Very few Plains Indians now make tipis of buffalo skins and very few live in these structures year round. Very few Ojibwa and Winnebago of the Great Lakes live in wigwams. The Cherokee of North Carolina gave up wattle and daub (stick and mud) houses back in the eighteenth century, and in the twentieth century, Cherokee have abandoned the log cabin shelter they borrowed from the Europeans after giving up the wattle and daub house.

Since World War II all American Indians in the United States have subsisted primarily through a cash economy that might be supplemented by more traditional modes of obtaining food, such as hunting, fishing, farming, and gathering wild plants. In the late twentieth century, no Indian group depends primarily upon the traditional ways of gathering food. The traditional patrilineal social structure of U.S. culture has in some way influenced or changed almost every Native American kinship pattern. Nevertheless, traditional Native American religion survives in the late twentieth century in the form of ceremonies, building practices, hunting, farming, fishing, and gathering techniques, kinship patterns, and even in the way in which Native Americans perceive the world itself.

## Sacred Time

In the Western world, time is viewed as historical. That is to say, Americans view time as a linear sequence of novel and separate events unfolding one after the other. In historical time, everything is new and nothing repeats itself. Time marches ever on, and each person is an individual: everything is colored by uniqueness and specificity. Time is very different among traditional American Indians, for whom time is cyclical, so that there is nothing new under the sun. In their view, whatever happens has occurred before and will happen again. This is not to say that American Indians are unaware of historical time. They are aware of singular events and qualities, but they consider that which is unique and novel to be meaningless. What is important is what has happened before. For American Indians, that which is significant occurred in the beginning of time, the time before there was time.

In living their lives, Indians generally do not attempt to do that which has never been done before. They do not seek to break records or to live as no one has ever lived. Rather, they seek to return to the beginning, to reactualize the time of the ancestors, the first people who were created on this earth, and to repeat what those people were taught by the sacred power in the beginning of time. In so doing, American Indians feel that they recapture and relive that time, thus experiencing a sense of eternity in their lives. Asked why he fishes salmon out of the rivers of the Northwest Coast the way he does, a Tlingit is apt to respond, "Because that is the way the ancestors did it." In other words, by fishing as his ancestors first fished, the Tlingit creates timelessness and thus experiences a timeless mode of being. We cannot overestimate the significance of this understanding of time in trying to understand traditional American Indian religious experiences and practices in the late twentieth century. This is especially true where a number of superficial changes have taken place in Native life. An outsider who has observed, for example, the Navajo tribe over the past fifty years might say that he has witnessed a number of changes in their religious life in terms of the form and frequency of their ceremonies. Such an observer might say that the Navajo do not practice the healing ceremonies as frequently or as formally as they did fifty years ago. However, what this observer might not uncover is that the Navajo understanding of cyclical time remains unchanged and that the Navajo understanding of the temporal aspect of life is just as it has always been.

## Sacred Space

Traditional Native American perceptions of space belie the continuity of traditional elements in contemporary Native American religious life. While Westerners perceive space as essentially random—one space has no more sacred significance than another—American Indians do not. Among American Indians, space always has a sacred center. They believe that there is a place in their world where the above, the earth, and the below are joined and are one. The center is the place where all spaces become unified. The center is the "spaceless space," the space that overcomes space. It is the space where American Indians experience complete unity with their world. At the center, American Indians no longer feel separate from the rest of the world. They feel that they are one with the world in which they live. Contemporary American Indians still experience a deep sense of reverence for the center of their world.

Two of the best-known centers are Bear Butte among the Cheyenne and Sioux, and Blue Lake among the Pueblo Indians of New Mexico. These are places to which certain tribes make pilgrimages in order to reexperience their unity with the world, to overcome their feeling of alienation from the rest of the world, and to experience a sense of oneness with everything in life. The Cheyenne and other Plains tribes continue to visit Bear Butte, where individuals fast and meditate in order to acquire a guardian spirit. A guardian spirit is a sacred power, usually manifested by an animal such as hawk, deer, or turtle, who reveals itself to an Indian as a spiritual companion to whom the Indian may turn for help and guidance in significant matters such as hunting, finding lost people, or healing the sick.

The Pueblo Indians of New Mexico say that they emerged to this world through the earth's navel, which is located at Blue Lake. During various important ceremonies that are kept secret from outsiders, the Rio Grande Pueblo tribes visit Blue Lake and deposit prayer offerings at this sacred center in order to renew the world and bring life to the people.

The experience of a sacred center remains fundamental to American Indian perception in the contemporary world and therefore, despite the fact that many surface changes have taken place among American Indians in the twentieth century, their basic understandings of space and time remain traditional and deeply religious.

## Traditional Ceremonies in the Late Twentieth Century

Traditional American Indian religion is alive and well in the late twentieth century. A quick overview of the basic cultural areas of Native North America reveals that American Indians still practice a number of the old ceremonies.

Some of the best-known examples of traditional Indian ceremonies are found among the Pueblo Indians of Arizona and New Mexico. The Hopi, Zuni, and Pueblo Indians of Laguna, Acoma, and the Rio Grande are primarily corn farmers who have performed an extensive ceremonial calendar for hundreds of years. Many of these ceremonies were being performed when the Spanish arrived in the Southwest around 1540, and several are still practiced today.

The Papago still mark the new year by harvesting the fruit of the saguaro cactus. In July, during the Saguaro Harvest Moon, whole families camp out in the desert to gather saguaro fruit. The fruit is raked off the plant with a stick, the meat is dug out, and the pods are dropped on the ground, face up, as a prayer for rain. Later the people drink fermented cactus syrup at the council house as a prayer that the plants will get wet with rain.

The Iroquois federation of tribes, consisting of the Seneca, Mohawk, Onondaga, Oneida, Cayuga, and the Tuscarora, reside in the northeastern woodlands of America. These Indians once lived in longhouses and traditionally practiced important healing rituals during the winter. The Iroquois, now located in upstate New York, still practice these rituals, which involve dancing with wooden or cornhusk masks to drive away evil spirits and to heal illness.

Most Southeastern Indians were forcibly removed west to Oklahoma during the second quarter of the nineteenth century. Among the Eastern Cherokee, however, there are still remnants of some old hunting dances such as the raccoon dance, the opossum dance, and other animal dances that were involved in hunting rituals. At least one observer in the twentieth century witnessed a Booger Man masked curing ritual. The Cherokee have largely adopted Christianity, but a few of the older Cherokees still practice some of the old ways such as Booger Man (false face) curing rites. At Big Cove, traditional rites such as the Green Corn New Year ritual are being revived, although it is not clear whether Indians perform them for religious or cultural reasons, or both. Finally, Eastern Cherokee men continue to play stickball, the forerunner of lacrosse, an activity that carries sacred significance. Prior to the game, the players pray for the agility of the deer, the good vision of the eagle, and the fury of the rattlesnake.

After the game, the stickball players go to the water; that is, they bathe in the river in order to be cleansed and purified.

Small groups of Choctaw, Chickasaw, and Creek Indians also remain in the Southeast. A few of the older Mississippi Choctaw are traditional herbalists who believe that various plants have both medicinal and spiritual powers. Oklahoma holds the largest populations of Cherokee, Creek, Choctaw, and Chickasaw; traditional religious practices, such as the Green Corn Ceremony, continue to thrive side by side with some newer religious ceremonies, possibly because most of the tribal leaders moved west with the others during the nineteenth century.

In the Great Lakes region, the Ojibwa continue to practice their midwinter healing rituals, although the Peyote cult has found its way into Ojibwa life. In the Peyote cult, or Native American Church, Indians eat a cactus that produces sacred visions as they sit around a fire and listen to a drum. The Peyote cult incorporates elements of Christianity with more traditional Indian religious ideas. Nonetheless, the old ways continue among the Ojibwa and do not seem likely to disappear any time soon. Of all the curing rituals, the Midewiwin, or Grand Medicine Society, seems to be the most important. Initiates who have had a supernatural vision are inducted into a curing society and are taught healing practices by an older member. Each initiate is "shot" with a white shell that causes him to go into a trance.

Another Great Lakes tribe, the Winnebago, also continues to perform the traditional Medicine Dance, a four-day ceremony that parallels the Ojibwa's Grand Medicine Society; the vision quest is still very much alive among them as well. In the vision quest, Winnebago go into the woods and fast in order to envision an animal who becomes a guardian spirit, whom they later call upon to help with hunting, curing illness, finding lost children, and other important tasks. Traditional Winnebago also continue to believe in reincarnation and to practice secret rites related to rebirth.

Among the sub-Arctic peoples, those people who live in present-day Canada, the ceremonial complex is quite simple; while elaborate ceremonies are unknown to them, traditional ceremonial activities persist. Shamanism, for example, is still widespread. Shamans are individuals who are able to communicate directly with the spirit world by sending their souls out of their bodies during a trance. Further, hunting people share a ritual taboo concerning menstruating women: everywhere in North America, Indians feel that the blood of the hunt should remain separate from the blood of women, because the hunt takes life while

women give life. The belief that death is a result of witchcraft is still very much alive among such sub-Arctic peoples as the Cree, Yellow Knife, Dogrib, and Beaver.

In the Arctic region, inhabited by the Inuit (Eskimo), traditional rituals persist. For example, Inuit of Alaska perform the bladder ceremony to mark the beginning of a new year. The Alaskan Inuit burn caribou and bird bladders, puncture a seal bladder and replace them into the icehold to return the spirits of the slain animals back to the master of animals to ensure that game will be recreated for a new year.

Among Northwest Coast tribes that live along the Aleutian Islands, South Alaska, and the east coast of British Columbia, Washington, and Oregon, the best-known ceremonies are those surrounding the harvesting of salmon. For example, among the northern tribes such as the Tlingit, Tsimshian, and Haida, each new year is marked by a salmon rite, which involves taking the first salmon from the rivers and addressing it appropriately in order to celebrate the coming of a new year. Among the central Northwest Coast tribes such as the Nootka, Chinook, and Kwakiutl, the potlatch ceremony is most familiar. Occurring at critical junctures or transitions in life such as new year, the building of a new house, marriage, and funerals, it involves giving away or burning surplus material goods, which redistributes wealth and limits the growth of the village. The potlatch also symbolizes the creation of the world by reciting the mythical beginnings of the tribe.

Among the tribes of the Great Basin, primarily tribes that are Paiute or Shoshoni, the ceremonial complex never became very elaborate. The Circle Dance, a simple dance where everyone holds hands, is still performed and seems to be a very old practice. In California, the Hupa continue to speak their native language and perform their most important ceremonies, the Jumping Dance and the White Deerskin Dance. These ceremonies, which last several days, involve the use of elaborate costumes and ritual objects. The Hupa stories of creation are told during these ceremonies and it is understood that the world will be renewed for another year.

Finally, the Plains Indians, such as the Sioux and Crow, continue to perform the Sun Dance, which is undergoing revival. In the Sun Dance, small wooden sticks that are tied to a pole are placed under the skin of a man's chest, and he looks at the sun and blows an eagle bone whistle until he tears himself free. Originally for many Plains tribes a rite of self-sacrifice to show thankfulness to the sacred for some blessing, the Sun Dance today seems to parallel the vision quest as a means of obtaining sacred power. The Plains Indians continue to perform the vision quest for guardian spirits, and they continue to participate in the sweat lodge ritual. The sweat lodge is a conical-shaped structure in which participants pour water onto heated rocks, producing steam that is used to purify their souls and bodies.

## Religion in Traditional Food Production

A number of Native Americans in the twenty-first century continue to obtain food from traditional means. This is significant religiously because traditional food production was fraught with religious meaning for Native Americans. Take, for example, hunting, which was and is a male activity among American Indians. Rarely, if ever, do women take part in hunting animals. Ceremony tends to permeate the hunt. For instance, a few of the old Cherokee of North Carolina recite prayer songs prior to a hunt. On the evening before a hunt a Cherokee may go to a river bank to address a prayer to the two principle guards of the hunters: the river, also known as Long Man, and the fire, known as Ancient Red. The hunter asks that the wind favor him and that he find game at a single bend of the river so he will not have to hunt far. The night before the hunt the hunter rubs ashes on his chest before sleeping, and asks for good dreams to foreshadow a good hunt.

The Cherokee hunter also has specific hunting songs for various animals. Deer continue to provide the food for the Eastern Cherokee, and hunters address prayers to Little Deer to ask for a successful hunt. It is very important that, upon killing a deer, a Cherokee hunter address Little Deer with a prayer for forgiveness, apologizing for having killed one of Little Deer's creatures and promising that all its parts will be carefully used and the remains properly buried. If a hunter does not do this, the Cherokee believe that Little Deer will afflict the hunter with arthritis and disease in revenge for the haughty and disrespectful killing of Little Deer's animals. The feeling that most disease comes from slain animals remains deep-rooted among the Cherokee.

Before a traditional Hopi from Arizona hunts an antelope, mountain sheep, or jackrabbit, he abstains for four days from sexual activity because hunters take life while women give birth, associating them with the creation of life. The rabbit hunt is the most common hunt among the Hopi. Prior to a rabbit hunt, hunters make prayer feathers, symbolic of the breath of the soul of everything. Feathers represent the breath of life. A prayer feather is made for the Mother of All Game Animals, or Chief Animal Spirit, and for Hawk Spirit and Eagle Spirit, because hawk and eagle are great hunters who help the Hopi hunt. A breath prayer road, a feather with a cotton string attached, is made in order that the sun will slow down the rabbits.

Traditionally, Hopi hunters hunted rabbit with throwing sticks, which were modeled after the sparrow hawk's wing. It is said that the Hopi learned to make these throwing sticks by observing the sparrow hawk. Sparrow hawks hunt by diving down onto rabbits, hitting them in the back of the head with their wings, stunning them, and then killing them with their talons. The Hopi throwing stick is marked identically to the sparrow hawk's wing and was traditionally used to hunt rabbit. Today it is used only occasionally for ceremonial hunting when young men are initiated into adult ceremonial societies.

Among other Native American tribes, hunting is accompanied by prayers and ritual activities. However, it would not be right to limit our understanding of the religious nature of Indian hunting to ceremonies that occur alongside the hunt, because hunting is itself a ceremony that carries religious significance. In hunting, an Indian sheds external blood in external space. This is contrasted to the birth-giving powers of women, who create life through the internal blood of their wombs (internal space). Through hunting, men give birth to meat, furs, and skins, thus hunting is understood among Native Americans to be an external, male activity related to the internal life-giving activities of female birth. American Indian male hunters experience symbolically that which women embody simply by being. This accounts for why hunting tribes, such as those in Canada, surround menstruating women with taboo. The blood of hunting is different from the blood of birth, and the two bloods should not be mixed. If a hunter has contact with a woman "on her moon," her life-giving blood may interfere with the blood of the hunt.

Furthermore, the hunt is a male activity that reveals the passive nature of the sacred world. Hunting is an activity in which men impose their wills on the animal world, which is considered to be sacred. In killing an animal, an Indian experiences a sense of shame over having transgressed the sacred world. Thus American Indians throughout Native North America offered prayers of forgiveness to the spirit of animals after a successful hunt.

A Sioux Indian was once recorded giving a prayer of apology to a buffalo for having killed it. He said that he hunted only because his family needed the meat and the skins. When he died, his body would become fertilizer for the earth upon which would grow grasses that would feed descendants of the slain buffalo. While an Indian expresses regret for having killed an animal, he is nevertheless thankful and thanks the chief animal spirit for allowing one of its creatures to be slain. In this sense, Indians are not regretful as much as thankful, believing that it is the will of the Great Spirit that animals sacrifice themselves to the hunter, who then offers prayers of thanksgiving and disposes of the remains of the animal in a ritually proper way to send the spirit of the animal back to the chief animal spirit. The chief animal spirit then recreates animal life. In the Indian view, the hunt embodies religious meaning and is in and of itself a sacred act. In evaluating the religious nature of modern American Indian hunting, it is not enough simply to look at the formal ceremonies that often accompany a hunt. Many Native Americans no longer perform those formal ceremonies, but the hunt persists as the embodiment of a religious ritual; modern-day hunting thus carries traditional religious significance for many American Indians.

## Religion in Daily Activities

For the Hopi of Arizona, farming is a religious activity. While a great deal of ceremony surrounds the farming and harvesting of crops, farming also carries sacred significance at an almost unconscious level, which is simply experienced by performing the activity of planting and harvesting corn.

The Hopi say that they emerged to this world, the Fourth World, from the womb of mother earth. Just before their emergence the Hopi and other peoples were given their choice of foods. The Hopi chose an ear of corn and became farmers, but they did not pick randomly; they chose the short blue ear of corn. Since the short blue corn requires more work for a successful harvest than do other types of corn, the Hopi chose a life of hardship and humility. At the same time, since the short blue corn is the most durable, the Hopi chose a hearty life as well.

The symbolism of blue corn runs throughout Hopi religious life. Indeed blue corn, according to Emory Sekaquaptewa, a Hopi elder, represents the Hopi law. In growing and harvesting the blue corn, the Hopi are following the law, the law laid down in the beginning, in the long ago, when they first chose a hard but meaningful life. By working hard and cultivating blue corn, Hopi people follow the path of the ancestors who lived before them, and they reexperience the primordial era when they first emerged to this world and became Hopi. Therefore, working the corn affords Hopi Indians the experience of the creation of the world. They also experience this reactualization of the creation of the world through other traditional everyday activities such as hunting, gathering, and home-building.

Throughout North America, Indians, in performing everyday work activities, reexperience the beginnings of time and thus transcend their purely historical and temporal situations. When a Makah Indian goes out to hunt the whale in the cold waters of the Pacific Northwest, he feels a unity with his ancestors and returns to the time when the world was first created.

When a Kaska Indian makes fire by striking two stones together he performs religious ritual. First, in striking the rocks together, the Kaska Indian experiences the passivity of rock. He experiences the resistance of rock to human action and will. And yet the rock eventually gives birth to fire; it yields the gift of fire to human beings. In making fire, the Kaska Indian experiences the paradoxical character of human life. Fire is a phenomenon in which the Kaska participate but do not activate. Although the Kaska recognize it as a superior phenomenon, they nevertheless handle it at will. Fire is therefore both an active and passive phenomenon, and creating fire by hand evokes religious significance for American Indians.

Fire is also likened to creation and birth. By striking one stone against another, or in the case of the Hopi, by rotating a firestick in a fireboard, friction generates fire. Just as the friction of male and female sexual activity gives birth to life, so too the friction of firestones or the firestick produces life. Thus production of fire is experienced as an act of creation, and therefore recalls the beginnings of time.

Toolmaking involves religious meaning since, by striking one stone against another, Indians experience the passivity and resistance of stone. Stone strikes Indians as hard, durable, and eternal. Rock resists human autonomy and yet it is eternally fertile: stone is eternally pregnant. Therefore, when a Blackfeet Indian makes arrowheads by striking one stone against a motherstone, it gives birth to chips and flakes or baby stones. Stone is thus eternally fertile for Native Americans. Among the Hopi, stone is known as a female spirit, Hard Substance Woman. Today, traditional tool and firemaking is usually done only during sacred ceremonies; at the turn of the twentieth century tool and firemaking were conducted daily by many tribes.

## The Sacredness of Indian Architecture

While it is true that most Native Americans no longer live in traditional houses, some do, and some traditional houses are maintained for cultural and ceremonial purposes. The Skidi Pawnee of Nebraska, for example, attribute great symbolic significance to the old earth lodge. Like many other major Native American architectural structures, it represents their sacred world. According to Pawnee cosmology, the sky represents

Tirawa, which means "he who lives up there," or "he who lives in the silence of the blue heaven, above the clouds." Tirawa embraces and surrounds the whole universe and can be approached through lesser gods who touch the earth and form a bridge for prayer. Heaven is marked by four quarters: the Evening Star represents the West, the Morning Star represents the East, the Unmovable Star the North, and the Ghost Star the South. These four quarters form a ring that represents the Corona Borealis, a formation of stars in the sky. These four stars represent cosmic pillars that link heaven and earth and encircle the center of the universe.

The traditional earth lodge, which is supported by four posts representing the four directional stars, preserves Pawnee conception of the universe. The ceiling has a ring representing the Corona Borealis, the circular floor of the earth lodge represents earth, and the domed lodge roof symbolizes sky or Tirawa. The earthen altar on the west wall of the earth lodge represents the Garden of the Evening Star; in this altar, corncobs symbolize farming and buffalo skulls symbolize hunting. Each Pawnee child is taught that the lodge is the cosmos. Similarly, the tipi and the sweat lodge of the Plains Indian represent the universe. Among the Navajo, the six-sided hogan symbolizes the entire universe: east, west, north, south, above, and below—and similar cosmic symbolism is found in both the houses and the underground ceremonial chambers of the Pueblo Indians. Throughout Native North America, architecture carries great religious significance.

## Sacred Expression through Art

American Indians of the late twentieth century are perhaps best known by outsiders for their traditional art forms. For example, the Eastern Cherokee are well known for their honeysuckle, white-oak, and river-cane baskets. The Navajo of the Southwest are famous for their blankets and silver jewelry. Pueblo are noted for carving kachina dolls and creating pottery. It is fair to say that there is an increasing market for traditional Native American art objects that are made for sale to outsiders. Marketing art objects, however, is a relatively new development and American Indians continue to use and understand their art in traditional ways.

To understand Native American art, it is important to understand Native American time. All human beings live in the present time, but they differ with respect to reference to the past or future. Western culture, which stresses control, looks to the future as the reference point; when cultures do not emphasize human control over the world, other modes of reality open. Native Americans look at the coherence of life and express its rhythms. Art is not created for art's sake. For Native Americans, human beings are not the locus or center of attention. American Indian art does not show how humans are in control of the world, but how humans enter into the vitalities and rhythms that are life.

Thus, much American Indian art is worked in wood because wood does not last: it cracks, splinters, and turns back to what it once was. Art does not so much emphasize the drama of human existence for American Indians as it illuminates humans' roles in life. For example, Emory Sekaquaptewa notes how kachina dolls, which are given to children, used to be discarded in dumps when no longer useful. Artwork reflects the temporality of human life for Native Americans. The Navajo of Arizona and New Mexico are known for their beautiful sand paintings, but these paintings are not created for aesthetic purpose; they are part of important healing rituals, during which a sick Navajo is made well by securing the blessings of the sacred powers. At the conclusion of the ritual, the sand paintings are destroyed because they are no longer useful in a religious sense.

A further distinguishing point about American Indian art is that it intends to uncover a form already there. In art, as in other activities, American Indians do not force their will onto an object in order to create something. When a Seri from Baja California takes a block of ironwood in order to carve a roadrunner, he sees the roadrunner's form in the wood and then chips away the parts of the wood that do not look like a roadrunner. He deciphers a form that is already present. This activity is religious because the artist receives a revelation from the sacred.

The same can be said of music. Both Hopi and Sioux have said that they compose music by listening to the sounds of nature. By listening especially to wind and water, American Indians decipher musical patterns that already exist and then use their musical instruments to reproduce those sounds. In other words, Indians do not invent music, they uncover it.

## Sacredness of Storytelling

American Indians in the late twentieth century continue to be great storytellers. Many of the important lessons of life are conveyed by elders who sit around a fire at night and relate stories of the ancestors, cultural heroes, and the trickster. The trickster is an animal figure who is universal among Native Americans. In the Northwest Coast area, the trickster is a raven; among the Algonkian-speakers of the Great Lakes region, he is a hare or a raccoon. In the Southwest and Great Basin areas, the trickster is a coyote; in the Plains he is

Iktomi, the spider; and in the Southeast he is a rabbit. American Indian children first learn about time, space, and human reality through the stories of the trickster.

The trickster is best known for the problems he presents for human beings by teaching humans the limits of time and space. Often the trickster teaches American Indians that they must live within the realities of the material world or suffer dire consequences. Sometimes the trickster helps overcome human problems by creating order where there is chaos. For example, the Sioux have a story in which a monster was about to attack and destroy a Sioux camp. The trickster, the spider, discovered the monster's weakness and told it to the Sioux, who were able to kill the monster. In that story, the trickster keeps the Sioux alive.

In the end, the trickster stories signify that the created world is imperfect. The created world is not perfect because creation must not be perfect. Existence is paradoxical: day and night, male and female, up and down, sky and earth. Everything changes to its opposite. The trickster keeps the world going by keeping opposition alive. The world must move to be. Humans live amidst tension and harmony, which means living with paradox.

The Menominee of the Great Lakes region have an excellent example of such a trickster story. Two blind men lived in harmony by a lake. Each day, using a rope, one man guides himself to the water of the lake while the other cooks breakfast. One day, a raccoon decides he will disrupt this orderly existence and steals one-half of the food from each man. Each blind man blames the other for taking part of his share, and as their tempers grow, the raccoon slaps both in the face, provoking a fight. The raccoon then steps in, explaining that he took the food, and he asks the men not to blame each other so quickly. In this story, the trickster introduces tension into an otherwise harmonious situation to demonstrate the paradoxical nature of life.

## American Indian Clowns

Dreams are very important to the Teton Lakota, one of the Sioux tribes that live in South Dakota. Dreams are often experienced as omens and are seen as instructive in some way. Those who share dreams of elk, buffalo, or wolf may join a secret society symbolized by the animal envisioned. Of all the secret societies, the most powerful is made up of those who dream of the Thunderbird, a powerful spirit. Such persons were called Heyoka (fool) and participate in a ceremony called Heyoka Kaga, a Fool Impersonation rite. The Heyoka shows his unworthiness to receive the revelation of the Thunderbird by doing everything backwards: he walks backwards, he weeps at joy, wears

heavy clothing in summer, washes with sand, and dries with water. In acting contrary to others in the tribe, he reveals the impact of the Great Mystery on ordinary life. When a Heyoka performs a ceremony, he announces it by placing an offering to the Thunderbird, usually of tobacco, on tipi poles. The ceremony is generally conducted in the springtime during the first thunderstorms of the year. A crier announces the rite, and all Heyokas are expected to participate. Chosen as leader, a medicine man takes the Heyoka to a ragged tipi in the center of the camp circle. The Heyoka wears ragged clothing and paints his face black and white with lightning streaks symbolic of the Thunderbird, and the village follows, laughing.

The Heyoka tell their dreams and sing songs as a pot of boiling water is hung on a tripod. The medicine man places the Heyoka's offering to Wakan Tanka, the Great Mystery, in a pot. Lone Man, a Sioux elder, explains the symbolism of the boiling pot of water by saying that the water comes from the clouds, the fire is the sun warming the earth, the meat is from animals that are placed on earth for the Sioux. These things, Lone Man explains, teach the people to pray to Wakan Tanka to sustain life.

The Heyoka, after rubbing arms and hands with medicinal herbs, reach into the boiling water to retrieve the meat. They give the meat to the poor people while acting very crazy. For example, Black Elk, a Sioux holy man, tells of acting as though a mud puddle was a river he had to cross. After he took a seven-foot arrow and placed it sideways into the puddle to see how deep it was, he decided the water was too deep to walk, and splashed his face down into the puddle and swam across. Concluding the ceremonies, the Heyokas sing secret power songs. At this point, the Heyoka feels one with the world. The Heyoka exclaims, "A wind wears me. Behold it. Sacred it is."

The Heyoka is different from the medicine man or the lay person in Sioux society. The medicine man renounces society and leads a very moral life. The layperson lives directly within the Sioux society and is more profane than the medicine man. But the Heyoka cannot be said to be either social or moral. Since his life is influenced by the direct experience of the divine through dreams, he lives a life of transcendence which is neither social nor nonsocial but asocial; that is, he lives on another plane of being altogether. Today, only a few traditional Sioux perform the Heyoka rituals infrequently.

The Sioux's neighbors, the Cheyenne, also have clowns who act contrary to the rest of society, and other Indian societies perform clowning ceremonies as well. For example, among the Hopi and other Pueblo Indians, clowns perform various skits and exhibit the human vices of gluttony, selfishness, and ignorance. The crowd that watches these ceremonies laughs at the foolishness of the clowns; they are also laughing at themselves, because the clowns demonstrate life as it is, but should not be, for Pueblo Indians. Therefore, for the Pueblo Indians, clowning reveals the mortal, limited reality of human existence. Among the Pueblo, clowning ceremonies are still performed frequently in the summer months of the year, and are conducted in conjunction with the more solemn dances of the Kachinas, who impersonate various aspects of the spiritual world.

### Conclusion

It is fair to say that American Indians in the late twentieth century continue to embody and practice traditional religion. Even where it seems that the old ways are completely gone, as with tribes that appear to have been completely assimilated into mainstream American culture, aspects of traditional religion persist. For many tribes, elders in centuries past prophesied assimilation into the dominant culture; its occurrence is therefore seen as fulfillment of a religious destiny. In that sense, the loss of traditional religious values and practices is seen as fulfillment of their religious orientation to the world. Furthermore, the names of American Indian tribes suggest that tribal identity affords American Indians a deep rooted sense of religiosity. Many American Indian tribes are known by outsiders by a name that was given to them by either non-Indians or by other tribes. The names by which tribes designate themselves generally mean "the people" or "the human beings." For example, the Nez Percé called themselves Nimapu, which means "Real People," while the Sioux call themselves Ikce Wicasa, meaning "The People." The Seri know themselves as the Comcaac, which also means "The People." American Indian tribes understand themselves as human beings who experience the world in which they live as sacred and as undergirded by some anonymous, autonomous force. The term *Hopi* is translated by Emory Sekaquaptewa as "one who follows the path" and by Peter Nuvamsa, another Hopi elder, as "one who walks in the right direction." American Indians define themselves as people who inhabit a religious world.

Native Americans continue to perform traditional religious practices in the late twentieth century. Among some tribes, such as the Hopi, Sioux, and Navajo, many traditional religious practices remain intact, whereas others retain their traditions in shorter form. Ceremonies, however, do not tell the entire story. Many traditional religious views of the world survive among American Indians, and it is these basic precepts and ideas that

will survive as Indian people enter into the twenty-first century.

*John Loftin*

## ◆ CHRISTIANITY AND NATIVE AMERICANS

The first encounters between Indians and Europeans were marked in some cases by curiosity and welcome, and in others by fear and hostility. These same emotions mark the spiritual encounter with the unknown that is part of the essence of religion. They continued as European missionaries attempted to convert Native peoples to Christianity. Jesuit priests among the Iroquois attempted to discredit Native religious leaders and replace traditional beliefs with Christian ideals. Iroquois people accepted those ideals in varying degrees. In southwestern Pueblos, Catholic priests sometimes used force to coerce Native people into conversion, but they did not destroy beliefs, and figures of Christian saints are carried in feast day ceremonies that incorporate elements of traditional Native ceremonies.

The vast majority of Native Americans in the United States have been exposed in some way to Christianity, and they have absorbed elements of Christian belief, but their responses to and the expressions of Christianity in Native communities are as diverse as the many tribes that have existed in what is now the United States. The differing theologies of Christian missionaries have contributed to this significant diversity. The ceremonial aspects of Catholicism were understandable to Indian people who carried out their own ceremonial cycles, whereas the austere practices of the Puritans were less attractive. The Methodist camp meeting, with preaching, singing, and seizure by religious power, appealed to the Choctaws in the Southeast more than did the strict discipline of Presbyterian theology. These doctrinal differences and the competition among early missionary societies for Indian souls confused Indian people. Red Jacket, a Seneca leader, asked a missionary in 1805, "Brother! You say there is but one way to worship and serve the Great Spirit. If there is but one religion, why do you white people differ so much about it? Why not all agree, as you can all read the book?" (Red Jacket to the missionary, from a pamphlet entitled *Indian Speeches*, delivered by Farmer's Brother and Red Jacket, Two Seneca Chiefs, Canandaigua, New York, 1809).

### Differing Worldviews

There are significant differences between Christian and Indian beliefs that affect intercultural relationships. In the most general terms, Christianity embodies a worldview that differs dramatically from that held by Native American people. Native people lived on and with their lands. As hunters or farmers, they depended upon the cycles of nature for their subsistence, and they valued the repetition of events in the natural world. Their ceremonies presaged and celebrated solstices and other celestial phenomena. The Hopi Soyal ceremony is timed by the winter solstice. The Seneca Midwinter ceremony in upstate New York is determined by the movement of the constellation known as the Pleiades, which appears in the sky from mid-October to mid-May. When they appear at dusk in the night sky, the time for the ceremony is near. The seven stars of the Pleiades are described as young men dancing in the sky above the longhouses. It is interesting to note that in the Christian calendar, Christmas occurs shortly after the winter solstice, and Easter is timed by the first Sunday after the first full moon after the vernal equinox. Christians, however, find their meanings in an allegory of spiritual rebirth rather than in the physical world.

Most important, Indian people believed that they were causal agents in these natural processes. If they did not perform their ceremonies, the moon, sun, and stars might not persist in their patterns. The sun would not turn in its path at the solstice points. Rains would not come. Crops would not grow. Indian beliefs emphasize the repetition of events and the ongoing process of interaction between Indian people and the environment. Ceremonies are times when human beings, through their actions, contribute their energy to make it possible for nature to continue its actions. The songs on the final night of the Mescalero Apache Kinaalda ceremony for pubescent girls literally pull the sun over the horizon at daybreak. The singer is a causal element in the processes of the world. His knowledge of the songs and understanding of the cycles of nature give him power to assure that natural processes continue.

In many Native societies, men established relationships with spiritual forces through visions and dreams. Black Elk, a Lakota (Sioux) holy man born in the 1850s, had a great dream in his youth that gave him power to cure and lead his people into an uncertain future. He also went on a vision quest, fasting and praying in the wilderness of the Black Hills of South Dakota to achieve a personal encounter with a spiritual being. The spirit then became a guardian and protector. Such mystical experiences gave men a sense of personal control over their lives through their relationships with the spirit.

The religions that Europeans brought to Native people were variants of Christianity, but the basic ideals of Christian belief are still in the power of an omniscient, omnipotent, omnipresent, and anthropomorphic God

and in the ultimate sinfulness of God's creatures who chose to disobey His injunction to avoid of the fruit of the Tree of Knowledge. The injunction raises the issue of individual free will and choice to disobey, which leads to the Original Sin of humanity in the Christian sense—disobedience to God's will. Sin invokes sorrow for the loss of Paradise and repentance for disobedience. God, in His ultimate goodness, sends Christ, his son, whose death atones for human sin. The atonement leads to the promise of salvation in Heaven for those who obey God's commandments.

The basic intellectual distinction between Native religions and Christianity can be stated as the distinction between will and law. Native people see nature as a manifestation of spiritual beings who have their own power and individuality. These beings are possessed of their own will and volition. The storm that moves around a community gathering in Kansas responds to the prayer of a spiritual leader who places tobacco on a fence post as an offering of respect and request. The Christian person may pray for God's protection from the power of the storm that threatens harm.

Christian dogma emphasizes the original sin which marks all of humanity until people accept the power of God's ultimate sacrifice of his son Jesus Christ to atone for that sin. Guilt and redemption are essential in Christian belief. Native people understand the failure of human will to do what is in the interest of communal good, and they know that people are not in control of their actions. The distinction between Christian concepts of free will and conscious decision and Native concepts of error, mistake, and lack of control is a key element of the encounter between missionaries and Native people.

Missionaries faced the problems of trying to translate Christian concepts into Indian languages. Although Indian people held the concept of a great creative force in the world—the Manitou of Algonquian speakers, the Wakonda of Siouian speakers, and the Orenda of Iroquoian speakers—these concepts were quite different from the anthropomorphic God of Christianity. Indian languages did not have words that translated into the Christian concepts of sin and guilt. In 1821 Cyrus Byington arrived at the Choctaw mission at Elliot and began learning the Choctaw language. He compiled a dictionary and translated many biblical texts into the Choctaw language. The Choctaw words that he used for sin meant to make a mistake or to be lost in the wilderness, ideas very different from the Christian concept of sin.

Indian beliefs were based on appropriate relationships with spiritual beings and with family. The ethical values of the tribes stressed responsibility to community, and people who acted inappropriately threatened the efficacy of ceremonies. They introduced an element of disrespect for the spirits that could disrupt the relationship between the community and the spirits. To make a mistake in the performance of ceremonies, to be unaware of how to act in a situation—these were the actions that were dangerous in Indian communities, but they did not convey the sense of deliberate disobedience that constituted Christian sin.

Christian religion looks toward an ultimate end of salvation from sin and ultimate bliss in a world beyond this. Indians look toward repetition of events and feel that they are causal agents in renewing this world. Traditional people in the Pueblos in New Mexico attribute the growth of new vegetation in the spring to the cycles of prayers carried out by members of ceremonial societies. Indians believe in their own agency in the repetition of events. This distinction between Native and Christian beliefs is the distinction between the notion of obedience to the will of an all-powerful being and the commitment to and dependence on the will of a community of people and their sense of an ongoing relationship with an environment alive with spiritual power.

## Historical Background

In 1492, when Christopher Columbus sailed in search of new worlds with the support of the Catholic monarchs Ferdinand and Isabella of Spain, Catholicism was still the only religion of the European world. In 1517, Martin Luther nailed his ninety-five theses to the door of the cathedral in Wittemburg, in Germany, challenging the Catholic Church's sale of Indulgences as part of the forgiveness of sins. Two years later, Hernando Cortez sailed to the New World and by 1521 had overthrown the Aztec empire. By the early seventeenth century, Catholics and Protestants in Europe were involved in strong conflicts over religious ideology, and in the early eighteenth century, French, Spanish, English, Dutch, and German rulers fought for colonial control in the Americas.

Indian-Christian interactions are incredibly variable. For instance, French Jesuits encountered Iroquois and Huron people in the Northeast and Spanish Franciscans sought to convert Pueblo and Navajo people in the southwest and in Florida in the seventeenth century, as English Puritans missionized among Indian people on the East Coast. Moravians established missions among the Delaware in what is now Pennsylvania in the eighteenth century. In the nineteenth century American Presbyterians, Congregationalists, Methodists, Catholics, Quakers, Episcopalians, Mennonites, and Baptists

worked with Choctaws, Cherokees, and Chickasaws in the Southeast, Pottawatomies, Osages, Nez Percé and Lakota. The list of tribes and missionaries is much more extensive. Doctrinal and tribal differences make it difficult to discuss the relationships of Indian to Christianity except in the most general terms.

It is true, however, that Christian missionaries became agents of American government policy to assimilate Native people into American society. That they did not succeed in totally destroying Native religions and cultural identity is attributable to the strength of Native worldviews and their traditions of adapting new ideas to their traditional ways of life.

Spain was the first great colonizer of the Americas, and Spanish priests accompanied Hernando de Soto, Francisco Coronado, and Juan Oate in their explorations of the American Southwest. Wherever Spanish explorers found new lands, they were required to read a document called the Requiermiento, promulgated in 1513. It asserted that God had given control of the known world to St. Peter, and from him to the Pope, and from him to the sovereigns of Spain. It embodies the assumption that the Catholic Church had power over all the world. It required the inhabitants of these lands to acknowledge the power of God and the Catholic Church or to be subject to just warfare and enslavement. While Native people died in the silver mines of the Andes mountains in 1550, in Vallodolid, Spain, the priests Juan Sepulveda and Bartolome de Las Cases debated the question, "Is it lawful for the king of Spain to wage war on the Indians before preaching the faith to them in order to subject them to his rule, so that afterwards they may be more easily instructed in the faith?" Even more basic in the debate was whether Natives were even human, whether they had souls capable of an awareness of God's power and ultimate salvation. The Church decided they did, thereby subjecting them to missionaries.

Catholic and Protestant missionaries described their efforts as "reducing" their converts. Native religions were based on a sense of ongoing relationships with spiritual beings, either individual relationships achieved through vision quests or group relationships maintained through ceremonial cycles. Christian dogma, however, demanded complete submission to the will of God. To assume that one was equal to God was the sin of pride. Indians must be taught that they were subservient to God's will, not His equals.

In the Southwest, the Franciscan Alonso de Benavides encountered the Pueblo and Navajo people in 1627. The Jesuit Eusebio Kino penetrated the territory of the upper O'odham (Pima) in 1687. Benavides described the ceremonies of the Natives as idolatry and superstition. They decorated "heaps of small stones" with feathers and believed that the plants near these shrines would relieve "hunger and weariness." Benavides, on the other hand, made a cross and called sick people to come forward to touch it, promising that they would be miraculously cured by the power of the Christian God.

The Franciscans were often incredibly cruel in the name of Christian charity. They pressed Native people into the equivalent of forced servitude to build churches, and they punished traditional religious leaders by whipping. Despite the fact that the priests attempted to treat sickness and tried to protect the Natives from raids by Spanish soldiers, in 1680 a man from San Juan Pueblo, Popé, orchestrated an uprising among the Pueblos. Twenty-one priests and other Spanish mission workers were killed, and those who survived fled the area. For twelve years the Pueblo peoples were free to practice their traditional religions, but in 1692 a Spanish expedition invaded the area to restore political control and reestablish Christian domination.

In the Hopi village of Awatowi, Christian converts within the village refused to participate in the traditional ceremonial cycle necessary to keep the world in process. Their refusal disrupted the cycle that maintained the community and threatened the survival of the people. Leaders of the societies that performed that cycle drove the Christian converts into a kiva (the underground ceremonial chamber), piled burning brush over the entrance, and killed the Christians. This event had profound significance for Indian-Christian relationships. The Hopi valued community harmony and peaceful relations above all. The very term Hopi means "peaceful people." But the disruption of the ceremonial cycle threatened by the withdrawal of the Christian converts threatened the continuation of the Hopi way of life. The Native people of Awatovi were confronted with the choice of violating a basic principle of their culture—peace—or preserving their whole way of life by excising resistance to the ceremonies that sustained their world.

As other European nations joined the explorations and struggled for political control of the Americas, French Jesuits accompanied the voyageurs who explored the Great Lakes region and the lower Mississippi Valley. They mystified Native people with their power to convey messages with writing. The diseases introduced by Europeans to Native people were also mysterious and could not be cured by herbs and ceremonies, and Jesuits thus discredited Native healers and sought to take their places as spiritually powerful people.

The Jesuits were the intellectuals of the Catholic Church. They were trained to be keen observers of human nature, and they made the effort to learn Native languages and to understand Native beliefs, the better to undermine them in the name of Christianity. Their detailed reports to their superiors constitute the earliest ethnographic reports of Indian cultures, as well as providing military intelligence to French colonial governors and generals. They first worked among the Huron, Montaignais, and Algonquian people in Canada. The French Jesuit mission at Sillery became a Christian training ground for young converts. Some Jesuits sacrificed their lives for their faith as they were captured and tortured to death by Iroquois warriors. The torture was not, however, cold-blooded murder but a ritual test of the strength and endurance of a worthy enemy consistent with Iroquois cultural values. The Iroquois people recognized French priests as formidable enemies.

One notable convert, Kateri Tekakwitha, a young Mohawk woman, was educated in the Jesuit mission school at Caughnawaga. Disfigured by smallpox that killed her parents, she was raised near Montreal by relatives who were strongly opposed to the missionaries. She defied her relatives to embrace Christianity and became a model of Christian piety, ultimately beatified by the Catholic Church in 1980 as the final step before sainthood.

The effects of European-introduced diseases reinforced Catholic theology as priests baptized dying Indians to assure that their souls would reach heaven before they had the chance to sin. Although priests attempting to convert adults were assiduous in their instructions and their requirements for conversion, the doctrine of baptism allowed them to claim the infants and those dying from disease. The French Franciscan, Father Louis Hennepin, reported in 1683 that he had baptized Chippewa people who were dying from disease and rejoiced that their souls would go straight to heaven because they would not have the opportunity to sin.

Protestants in New England saw Native people as agents of the Devil. They lived in the woods, which in the Puritan mind was associated with the realm of Satan. Disease, in the mind of John Winthrop, governor of the Plymouth Colony, was the agent through which God cleared the land of its Native inhabitants so that the English, "sons of Adam," could occupy the land.

English colonists came with goals of wealth, ideals of religious freedom, and the object of a harvest of heathen souls for Christianity. The seal of the Massachusetts Bay Colony is emblazoned with an Indian man from whose mouth issues the Macedonian call, "Come Over and Help Us." The Puritan missionary John Eliot preached the gospel beginning in 1646, and the Massachusetts government established "praying towns" for his Christian converts. Fourteen towns were established, with a total population of around 1,100 people. Eliot's rules for the praying Indians, officially promulgated by the colonial government, included prohibitions against "pow-wowing" (an Algonquian term for shamanistic activities), lice-picking, and polygamy.

In the Southeast, Spanish Catholic influence created a number of missions for Indians along the east coast of Florida and North Carolina. The first permanent Spanish establishment at St. Augustine, established in 1565, became the staging ground for efforts to convert the Natives. Although the first Jesuit effort in the 1560s failed, by 1587 Franciscan priests arrived to renew the effort, and beginning in 1595, with reinforcements, the Spanish effort expanded existing missions to the Timucuan people of the Florida coast and the Guale Indians on the barrier islands off the coast of Georgia. A Guale chief rejected a priest's demand that he put aside one of his wives, and he and others killed a number of priests. The uprising did not involve all the Indians, however, and by 1603 the missions had largely recovered their influence. By 1655 the Franciscans claimed 26,000 Indian converts in Florida, but the governor of the province imposed a program of forced labor on them, and a revolt in 1656 undermined the mission effort. In 1675 the Bishop of Cuba confirmed 13,152 Indians.

The Spanish missions were threatened and ultimately destroyed as a result of colonial rivalry. The English established an outpost at Charleston in 1670 and used it as a base to gather Indian allies and to raid Spanish settlements. By 1680 the northernmost mission, Santiago de Ocone on Jekyll Island, had been attacked, and by 1708, James Moore, the British general, and his forces had destroyed the Spanish missions. Despite an appeal by a number of village leaders in 1715, the Franciscans did not have the energy or resources to restore their Indian missions. In 1763, as part of the Treaty of Paris ending the French and Indian War, the Spanish government ceded Florida to the British.

The attachment that Native people felt for the land proved a major problem for missionaries. The job of ministering to their converts would have been much easier had missionaries been able to consolidate them into large settlements, but attempts to move Indian communities usually resulted in Indians' disappearing into the surrounding forests. The apostasy of the Indians was attributable both to their attachment to the homelands and to their exploitation by secular governments and the strictness of Christian discipline as administered by some priests.

In California, the spread of Catholicism was inspired by the threat of Russian colonization on the west coast of North America. Junipero Serra, a Franciscan priest,

led the effort, beginning in 1769, to establish missions to secure Spanish claims to the California coast. Beginning in San Diego, Serra established San Diego de Alcalá on 16 July 1769. The Natives attacked the mission within a month, but they were driven back by Spanish musket fire. Some sought treatment for their wounds at the mission and ceased their resistance, but Serra could not gain any converts. His first attempt to baptize a child failed when the parents snatched the child away and laughed, but by 1773 he recorded eighty-three baptisms, and he established a total of twenty-one missions before his death in 1784.

Other Franciscans took up Serra's work, and by the 1820s there were twenty-one missions along the California coast. Indians in the missions suffered from disease, specifically smallpox and syphilis spread by Spanish soldiers who raped Indian women. They labored to plant crops of wheat and tend herds of cattle that were intended to make the missions self-sufficient but which represented a drastic change from their traditional diets of deer meat and acorn meal. The loss of life among the Indians in the Spanish missions—as much as 90 percent—was tremendous. It was caused by malnutrition, the spread of diseases, the decline in fertility from those causes, and the segregation of men and women in the missions.

As English colonists became Americans and crossed the Allegheny Mountains into Indian lands, Christianity moved with them. With the American victory in the Revolutionary War, the United States government adopted policies to either civilize Indians by making them Christian farmers or segregate them from white society. The seeds of the removal policy were planted by Thomas Jefferson, who in true eighteenth-century Deist tradition, believed that human beings were ultimately perfectable, and that Indians could learn the values of civilized society and become equals with their white counterparts. They could fit Jefferson's model of the yeoman farmer, who was self-sufficient. For those who chose to pursue their traditional ways of hunting and gathering, the western lands that Jefferson acquired with the Louisiana Purchase could become a new home.

The equation of Christianity and salvation was implicit in the Civilization Act of 1819, which appropriated $10,000 for the work of "benevolent societies" that would teach Indians to read, write, and farm. The American Board of Commissioners for Foreign Missions, established in 1810, became a major agent of the civilization policy. Its theology was Presbyterian and Congregationalist. Its missions to the Choctaw, Chickasaw, and Cherokee tribes in the Southeast were supported in part by the Civilization Fund. The American Board favored boarding schools, believing that removing children from their cultural backgrounds would allow the missionaries to replace their culture with a Christian-style life. The missionaries struggled with the question of whether to educate children first so they could read the Bible and be converted, or whether to convert by preaching first so that children could then be educated. Choctaw leaders were more interested in education than conversion, and under their demands, schools established by the American Board became a training ground for young Indians who learned to read, write, and cipher, with a healthy dose of Biblical texts in the curriculum.

The irony of the civilization policy was that while Indians were becoming Christians, white politicians and settlers looked covetously at Indian lands. White Americans often set a poor example of virtue for their Indian neighbors, and missionaries feared that their hard-won converts would be lost. Isaac McCoy, a Baptist minister who established a mission among the Potawatomi in 1822, ultimately proposed that in order to shield Christian Indians from the bad influence of white settlers, a single territory should be set aside for them and they should all be moved there.

McCoy's idea echoed Andrew Jackson's policy to remove Indians from the eastern part of the United States to a territory west of the Mississippi River. Jackson's policy, however, was an expression of American nationalism, the desire for Indian land and a rejection of Indian nations as sovereign governments within U.S. territory. Indian leaders attempted to demonstrate that they were indeed civilized, and Jeremiah Everts, secretary of the American Board of Commissioners, wrote letters protesting the removal policy, but Jackson pushed the Indian Removal Act through Congress, where it passed in the Senate by one vote.

The states of Mississippi, Alabama, and Georgia extended their laws over the Choctaws, Cherokees, Creeks, and Chickasaws. The tribes signed treaties exchanging their eastern lands for land west of the Mississippi River. Missionaries followed their congregations west to the Indian Territory, what is now the state of Oklahoma. After 1830, the territory ultimately became a home or prison for members of sixty-seven tribes.

With the expansion of the United States during the 1840s, Christianity came to western Indians. Pierre De Smet established a Catholic mission in Oregon territory in 1841, while Marcus Whitman, a missionary of the American Board of Commissioners, established one in 1836. Although the Indian tribes in the Oregon Territory seemed receptive to Christianity, conflicts between the denominations confused them. An outbreak of smallpox among the Cayuse led to an attack on the Whitman mission in which Whitman, his wife, and several others were killed.

Beginning in 1851, the United States government established the reservation policy, which attempted to confine all Indians to defined areas. The policy was an effort to put an end to the violent confrontations between Indians and American settlers. Treaties with tribes on the Great Plains continued the idea of the civilization policy, promising schools and farming implements.

The Civil War had a disastrous impact on the Indians of the Indian Territory. It also led to the election of Ulysses S. Grant as president of the United States and a new policy, known as the Peace Policy, toward Indians. Grant sought to assure peaceful relationships with Indians by transferring responsibility for Indian agencies from the Bureau of Indian Affairs to various religious denominations. The process, as with Indian matters in general, became highly politicized, and Indian Christians often found themselves under the control of religious men whose beliefs differed significantly from theirs. On the Pine Ridge Reservation, Catholic converts were subject to Episcopalian control, even though they appealed for a return of the "black robes" who had ministered to them.

The Peace Policy failed to lead to widespread Indian conversions, and ultimately the government pursued a policy of breaking up Indian tribal lands into individual allotments where men would be farmers and women would be housewives. The General Allotment Act of 1887 brought Thomas Jefferson's ideal of the yeoman farmer to fruition. By the late 1800s, Christianity was widespread in Indian communities. Black Elk, an Oglala Lakota (Sioux) spiritual leader, had become a Catholic.

## Indian Responses to Christianity

Indian people adopted a wide range of strategies for dealing with Christianity. In some instances, there was active resistance. A Delaware man, Neolin had a vision in 1763 in which he saw the great deity called the Master of Breath, who instructed him to teach a doctrine of resistance to European settlers. Neolin's doctrine inspired a military rebellion by the Ottawa leader Pontiac against British military posts around the Great Lakes in 1763.

Tenskwatawa, a Shawnee man, fell into a trance during an eclipse of the sun in 1805 and revived to preach a doctrine of resistance to Europeans. His brother, Tecumseh, carried his teachings to tribes up and down the East Coast with the message that the

Log church on the Red Lake Reservation in Pomenah, northern Minnesota. (Courtesy of the UCLA American Indian Studies Center)

tribes must join together to drive White people from Indian lands. Not all tribes joined Tecumseh's proposed alliance, and Tecumseh's death at the Battle of the Thames in 1813 during the War of 1812 destroyed the ideal of a Pan-Indian alliance.

In the Oregon Territory in the 1850s, a Wanapam man named Smohalla had a vision that inspired the Dream Dance. In 1855 federal agents made a series of treaties with Indians in Washington and Oregon that created reservations on which the Indians were to settle and farm. Smohalla's teachings were that Native people should resist farming: "You ask me to plow the land. Should I take a knife and cut the bosom of my mother?" The Dream Dance became a form of passive resistance to the federal policy of making Indians into farmers.

Another strategy was syncretism, in which Native beliefs were blended with Christian beliefs. Handsome Lake, a Seneca man, went into a trance in 1799 and had

a series of visions of the Christian God, punishment of sinners on earth, and George Washington. His descriptions of the messages he received from these visions became the basis for a new religion among the Seneca. It stressed certain Christian values of the subservience of women to men, despite the traditional Seneca values of matrilineal households controlled by women, while it emphasized the importance of the traditional Seneca ceremonial cycle to maintain the world.

Acculturation, or acceptance of Christianity, was most likely to occur where Indians became totally surrounded by Christian influence, as on the east coast of the United States, or in the Spanish-controlled southwest. Ravaged by diseases that traditional practices could not cure, sometimes attacked by neighboring white settlers, they felt that the spirits had deserted them, and Christianity offered a new way to deal with their changed circumstances. Conversion took many forms, however. In some cases there was almost complete acculturation as Native people rejected traditional beliefs. The praying Indians of the New England area adopted Protestant behaviors. In the Southwest, the Pueblo peoples adopted Catholic ceremonialism while maintaining their traditional practices. Black Elk maintained elements of his traditional belief in visions as a source of spiritual power even as he urged his fellow Lakota to accept Catholicism.

The Ghost Dance movements of 1890 demonstrated how Indians sought to reconcile Christianity and their traditional ways, with disastrous results. In 1890 Wovoka, a Paiute man in Nevada, had a vision during an eclipse of the sun. When he revived, he reported a vision of God, who told him that if the Indian people would dance in a certain way and adopt certain beliefs, their dead ancestors would return to life and rejoin them, and the buffalo (which by 1890 were virtually extinct) would return, and Indian life would return to the way it was before the Europeans arrived. The Ghost Dance spread rapidly across the central Plains, as an earlier prophetic vision in 1870 had spread among California Indians. The 1890 Ghost Dance represented an ultimate expression of faith in a supreme being to save Indian cultures from the effects of white society—the impact of diseases and the extinction of the buffalo. Sitting Bull, the Lakota leader who had taken part in the Battle of the Little Big Horn against George Custer's forces in 1876, was an advocate of the Dance. Tribes across the western plains took up the dance. It died, however, with the massacre of some 300 people in Big Foot's band of the Lakota at Wounded Knee Creek in December of 1890. The belief that the painted Ghost Dance shirts inspired by visions in the dance, would protect the Lakota from bullets, died with the adherents under gunfire from the United States army.

The Catholic church at Taos Pueblo. (Courtesy of Manny Pedraza)

A new religion based on the use of peyote, a cactus that affects sensory perception, began among the Mescalero Apache tribe in the Southwest and spread rapidly among Indian tribes throughout the Great Plains during the late 1800s and early 1900s. The peyote religion is based on the spiritual power of the plant that manifested itself in the feelings that it inspired. The ritual of the religion incorporated Christian elements, sometimes equating the peyote with Jesus Christ, the woman who brought water to the participants with the Virgin Mary, and the water bird with the Holy Ghost. The Native American Church was incorporated in 1918 to give First Amendment protection to the use of peyote, which federal agents and Christian ministers considered as pernicious an influence as alcohol in Indian communities. Peyote use was banned in many states.

In contemporary society, many Indian people are Christians. Some attend Christian churches and participate in traditional Indian ceremonies as well. Some find the two antithetical. And some people have adapted Christian religion to suit their own ways of life. The basic question about Indians and Christianity is how,

given the differences between traditional Indian religions and Christian dogma, Indians could experience sincere conversion to Christian religions. Indian people saw the world as full of spirits who manifested themselves in winds, the sun, moon, and stars, and in plants and animals. They established relationships with those beings through dreams and visions, through ceremonies, and those relationships assured the growth of plants and the success of the hunt. To accept Christianity, Indian people had to surrender their sense of personal power for dependence on the power of an omnipotent God. The Christian God laid down rules of behavior and rewarded those who conformed. Native deities responded to those who behaved respectfully and appropriately toward them.

Indian people in contemporary society are members of Christian churches in significant numbers. Depending upon the sources of the statistics used, between 10 and 25 percent of Native Americans consider themselves Christians. Within the Native community, there are approximately 285,000 Catholics, 75,000 Mormons, 35,000 Episcopalians, and 17,500 United Methodists, with the remainder belonging to a number of different denominations. In Canada, 25 percent of the total Native population profess to be Anglican, as do 85 percent of Inuit. The Aleut and Tlingit of Alaska comprise the largest numbers of Native Russian Orthodox church members. Many observers point out that while many Natives are nominally Christian, their faith often is accompanied by strong attachments to traditional ceremonies and worldviews.

The juxtaposition of Christian beliefs and Indian identity is a function of the persistence of Indian communities, inspired by the importance of kinship and physical location for Native people. Although debate continues over whether it is possible to be Indian and Christian at the same time, historical pressures have led to accommodations on both sides. In Indian Baptist churches in Oklahoma, for instance, Christian hymns are often sung in Native languages, despite the fact that Native children in mission schools in the early twentieth century were punished for speaking their own languages. Indian powwows are generally initiated with prayers offered "in Jesus's name."

In the 1970s, the national offices of the Lutheran and Episcopalian churches established formal Indian offices as liaisons with Indian communities, and they contributed funding for Indian activities protesting the effects of past federal and Christian policies. The Indian activism of the 1970s offered serious critiques of the past and current relationships of Indians and Christianity. The most eloquent and intellectual of these came from Robert Thomas, a Cherokee anthropologist, and Vine Deloria, Jr., a Lakota lawyer. Thomas emerged as a leader in the Indian intellectual world in the 1960s through his work with the Carnegie Project on Cherokee language and literacy in the area around Tahlequah, Oklahoma. Characterizing Indian communities as internal colonies, he called for greater Indian self-determination. In 1969, a group known as Indians of All Nations, based in San Francisco, occupied Alcatraz Island and issued a series of demands to the federal government, including funds to establish an Indian university dedicated to the study and preservation of Indian cultural traditions, an indirect repudiation of Christianity.

In 1972, Deloria published *God is Red: A Native View of Religion*. He pointed out crucial differences between Native and Christian worldviews. The Christian view of history is linear, moving toward an ultimate goal, while Native views are based on cycles of human life and natural phenomena. The Christian view separates the sacred from the secular, thereby divorcing religious experience from the day-to-day life of a community, while Native people express their beliefs in their experience with the environment around them.

The Christian view makes time more important than space. This world is not as important as the next. Native views place ultimate value on people's association with a given place, hence the importance of such things as the Black Hills of South Dakota as a center for vision questing. Deloria's book was perceived by many critics as a direct repudiation of Christianity, but he himself characterized it as a call for a reexamination and revitalization of Christian beliefs that would make possible a true American religion, rooted in American soil. The book was not an attempt to alienate Indians from Christianity but to give grounds for a better understanding.

Christian churches have become more sensitive to Native religions. The Oklahoma Indian Mission Conference of the United Methodist Church, whose forerunner was organized in 1844 in Indian Territory, serves twenty eight Native nations: Apache, Arapaho, Caddo, Clallam, Cherokee, Cheyenne, Chickasaw, Choctaw, Comanche, Delaware, Euchee, Iowa, Kickapoo, Kiowa, Missouri, Osage, Oto, Pawnee, Ponca, Potawatomi, Quapaw, Sac and Fox, Seminole, Seneca, Shawnee, Tonkawa, Wichita, and Wyandotte. In 1990 the Indian Missionary Conference had ninety-four churches in Oklahoma, five in Kansas, and two in Texas. Church membership was approximately eight thousand. Over the last four decades a growing number of the churches serve urban areas.

In 1979 David Yanito, a Navajo Episcopal leader, presented a resolution at the Navajo Episcopal Convocation at Oljeto, on the Navajo Reservation in Monument Valley, arguing that while evangelism was good, such efforts must be careful not to destroy traditional Navajo culture through the work of culturally insensitive ministers. Yanito stated that many Navajo people follow the old ways and that the church should incorporate Navajo beliefs and practices into the Christian religion, including prayer early in the morning with white corn pollen, yellow corn pollen during the night, and more prayers spoken in Navajo during the worship services. The Navajo Episcopal Ministers' resolution passed without opposition and now serves as basic policy in the newly created Diocese of the Navajo.

Since the early 1970s, the Anglican church of Canada has implemented the following objectives in regard to its ministry to and among Native peoples. (1) The church must listen to the Native peoples; (2) The church must clarify its basic intentions; (3) The role of the church must be redefined; (4) The church must redeploy its resources; and (5) The church must vitalize its education for ministry.

Acknowledging more than one perspective, the National Conference of Catholic Bishops in 1992 issued a pastoral letter and a separate statement on the Columbus quincentennial in which it apologized for "reflecting the racism of the dominant culture of which we are a part" and pledged to work to ensure American Indian religious freedom and rights in housing and education.

The sensitivity can work against Indian religions, however. The Catholic Church in the early 1970s adopted a doctrine that asserts that Christianity is central to all cultural experiences because culture is based in experiences of nature, and God is the creator of nature. "Inculturation is an ongoing reciprocal process between faith and culture. It is a way of looking at the customs, rites, and rituals of people to discover in them the active and saving presence of God. Through inculturation the Church affirms what is good in a culture; purifies what is false and evil; strengthens what is weak; educates what is ignorant." (*Principles for Inculturation of the Catechism of the Catholic Church* [Washington, D.C.: Department of Education, United States Catholic Conference, 1994], 1.) The Catholic Church still maintains the dominance of a singular God, whose handiwork may be present in all cultures, but whose will is absolute. The church thus subsumes Native cultures rather than giving them validity in their own right.

One result of the activism of the 1970s was the passage of the American Indian Religious Freedom Act in 1978. The act mandated federal agencies to examine their policies and activities to determine whether they infringed on traditional religious practices. The act applied only to federal agencies, and it provided no enforcement mechanisms such as penalties. It was characterized as a law "without teeth." Subsequent attempts to amend the law to provide explicit protection of the use of peyote and exclusive rights to sacred places have failed. One argument maintains that to provide that protection would violate the "establishment of religion" provision of the First Amendment to the Constitution. Despite the act, the National Park Service still permits rock climbing on Devil's Tower in Wyoming, considered a sacred site by the Kiowa and Cheyenne tribes. The Tono O'Odham and Apache people of Arizona continue to protest the building of an array of astronomical telescopes on the peak of Mt. Graham, which they consider a sacred site. The mountain is part of the Coronado National Forest. The National Council of Churches has joined the protests, which appear futile.

While Native religious practices continue under siege by non-Indians, Christian and non-Christian alike, there is a much greater appreciation in the minds of Christian leaders of the power of Native beliefs and how they may be reconciled with Christian beliefs. The question

is still, however, legitimately asked by Indian people: Is it possible to be Indian and Christian at the same time? The answer(s) depend upon the individual, within the context of her or his community and personal experience.

*Clara Sue Kidwell*
*University of Oklahoma*

## ◆ PLURALISTIC RELIGIOUS BELIEFS

Native Americans are very spiritual people. Before European conquest, in fact, spiritual life was the foundation of indigenous society. For the most part, Native American religion had not become institutionalized as it had among the so-called great or world religions, such as Christianity, Judaism, Islam, and Buddhism. Indeed, Indian government and religion were integrated: the political leaders were usually also the spiritual

A skylight at the Marquette Mission and Chippewa Center in St. Ignace, Michigan. (Courtesy of the UCLA American Indian Studies Center)

The Cosmic Tree at the Minneapolis Indian Center in Minnesota. (Courtesy of the UCLA American Indian Studies Center)

leaders. Until the late 1800s, for example, the Cheyenne Nation was governed by a council of forty-four Peace Chiefs comprising four clan chiefs from each of the ten bands and four sacred leaders. These last four leaders presided over the great tribal religious ceremonies— Arrow Renewal, Medicine Hat, Sun Dance, and Massaum or Animal Dance—which integrated the tribe and gave it its collective consciousness or social solidarity.

Traditionalists in the Native American context are those who follow the traditions—the beliefs and rituals— of the old culture. Traditional Indians find it difficult to define or explain religion, because to them spirituality is metaphysical and not material. Navajo Community College, which integrates medicine people and traditional elders into its school curriculum, therefore prefers the term *sacred* to *religion*. Sacred ways and practices are at the heart of life and the essence of cultural survival. The sacred ways of tribal, non-Western peoples the world over do not try to explain or control all the phenomena of the universe. They do not, as organizations, seek to dominate other people's thought, ways of worship, or their societies in the name of religious orthodoxy. This is what makes the sacred

different from schools of philosophical thought and theology, or the denominations of organized religion.

Early French sociologist Emile Durkheim contended that religion embraced more than the ethnocentric "state religion" prevalent in Europe, a property-owning institution with a hierarchical structure of religious specialists who intervene on behalf of the devotees with a supreme being, and who officiate over church dogma. According to Durkheim, the elementary forms of the religious life are found among all peoples, the essence of which is not theological directive but, instead, is its sacred community of believers. The true heart of religion may be defined by Durkheim as a unified system of belief and practices relative to sacred things that unite its devotees into a single moral community called a church.

Furthermore, all peoples, Durkheim notes, divide the world into two separate domains—the sacred and the profane, or secular—but how human beings conceptualize this division, where they make the cutting points, differs from society to society. The sacred can include an object, such as an eagle feather or stone pipe of traditional Indian ceremonies or a crucifix in the Catholic church. It can include a place, such as a Sun Dance enclosure, a Navajo hogan during curing ceremonies, a sacred mountain, like the Papago Indians' Baboquivari Mountain, or a Jewish synagogue. It can include a rite—for instance a Lakota sweat (purification), an Apache woman's "coming out" (puberty) ceremony, or a Protestant baptism. Among all cultures, the dead are consecrated, and burial places are considered sacred ground, no matter what the form of burial or belief in the hereafter. Durkheim rejects the definition of religion as a belief in gods or transcendent spirits or as synonymous with magic. Religious beliefs are determined by the group—the society—and how the sacred and profane are demarcated in practice is called a church. In contrast to non-Native culture, traditional Native Americans live spiritually. Their religion permeates every facet of daily life and is not merely relegated to attending service once a week.

Although all peoples, including non-Western indigenous peoples, practice religion, important differences exist among the religions of Native North America and the Judeo-Christian traditions. Nature has been called the Indians' church, because worship in traditional religions was out-of-doors and believed that all creatures great and small, all things, both animate and inanimate, possess a spiritual life force, sacred power, or *mana*. Vine Deloria, Jr. pointed out that the concept of space—relating land, community, and religion into an integrated whole—is the dimension of traditional Native American religions. Indian spirituality is circular, not linear; it is feeling, not thinking; it is being, not becoming. The Judeo-Christian concept of religion, on the other hand, emphasizes the dimension of time, from creation to apocalypse, a founding or founder, and doctrine.

What, then, has been the ideological impact of the European conquest of North America on the religious life of Native Americans? What has been the result of 500 years of Christianization? In fact, every conceivable religious process has occurred, so that, today, we find significant numbers of Native Americans in each possible category. These include (1) acceptance of Christianity through acculturation; (2) rejection of Christianity through the retention of traditional religious beliefs and practices; (3) reaction to Christianity and Anglo or Canadian domination through the rise of revitalization movements and new religions; (4) the blending or mixture of Christian and traditional Indian religious practices and beliefs, or syncretism; and (5) pluralism, where forms of both Christianity and traditional or new religions are embraced. Few Native Americans today adopt a purely secular world view, one of agnosticism or atheism. The contemporary beliefs of Native Americans in terms of their acculturative, syncretic, and pluralistic practices and associated social movements are examined below.

### Christian Influences

A 1950 survey of Christian missions identified thirty-six Protestant denominations with 39,200 Indian communicants, having increased their Native believers a little over 8 percent since a previous 1921 survey. In addition, Protestant missions claimed influence among 140,000 additional Indians, but this may be an exaggeration. Whereas the majority of Native Americans have been introduced to Christianity, many also participate in one or more traditional ceremonies and practices. Although staff members were predominately non-Indian, these missions claimed 213 Native Americans as having entered the mission field. Today there are probably several hundred ordained Christian ministers of Native American descent. By 1974 the United Presbyterian, Protestant Episcopal, United Methodist, American Baptist, United Church of Christ, and Reformed and Christian Reformed listed 452 Indian parishes with a total staff of 177 missionaries.

Contemporary statistics are difficult to obtain primarily because much religious work falls within standard diocesan categories that contain non-Indians as well. Nevertheless, Catholics have been active in the

Baptism of Paiute Indians. (Courtesy of Anthropological Archives, Smithsonian Institution)

Indian mission field since early colonial times, especially among the Iroquois in the east and among the Pueblo and the Indians in the Southwest and California. Thus they claim a number of Native American communicants today.

Most Christian churches and missions adopt an admittedly assimilationist philosophy: make Indian people into brown-skinned white men. There are exceptions, however, especially in recent years. A 1958 National Council of Churches study found that although 35 percent of Protestants favored outright assimilation for Indian people, 51 percent took a middle ground and said they found "some Native values worth preserving." Thirty-one percent of Catholics favored a blend of cultures. On the other hand, only a small percentage in both groups actually expressed strong sympathy for traditional customs and beliefs. Only 22 · percent of the Protestant mission churches utilize Native leadership in any capacity, compared to one-half of the Catholic missions. The use of Native languages for both

Protestant and Catholic missionaries, except for the Navajo Nation and the Lakota-Dakota (Sioux) reservations, where most Indians still speak or understand the indigenous tongue, was very small. Most denominations, especially the Protestant fundamentalists, believed that traditional Indian beliefs and practices were "almost entirely unreconcilable" with Christianity. Exceptions were the Episcopalians (81 percent), Congregationalists (75 percent), Catholics (74 percent), and Methodists (53 percent), who said that elements of traditional Indian religions were complementary to Christian teachings.

The Catholic position is guided by the 1977 Letter of the U.S. Catholic Bishops on American Indians: "The Gospel must take root and grow within each culture and community. Faith finds expression in and through the particular values, customs, and institutions of the people who hear it. It seeks to take flesh within each culture, within each nation, within each race, while remaining prisoner of none."

Thus St. Stephen's Indian School in Wyoming, a Catholic mission, has celebrated an Indian mass at Christmas, where the priest is dressed in traditional Indian robes and wears a feathered headdress. St. Stephen's was founded in 1884 for Arapaho and Shoshoni Indians. Today it consults with tribal elders, and the pulpit is shaped like a Thunderbird.

Catholic priests on the Lakota-Dakota reservations sometimes incorporate the use of the sacred pipe at mass, and in Oklahoma Catholic Indians have worn traditional regalia for the offertory procession and chant Indian songs. Indian fry bread is consecrated, instead of wafers. Wisconsin Chippewa sing their own hymns at seasonal services. Sage and cedar (traditional Indian purifying herbs) have been used at other services. At San Juan Capistrano Mission in California there are eagle feather blessings. St. Joseph's Church in Los Angeles has held a Native American Mass, and there is also the City of Angels (Los Angeles) Kateri Circle.

There are many Kateri Circles throughout North America, both on reservations and in the cities. Kateri Tekakwitha, a Mohawk Indian woman who converted to Catholicism in the seventeenth century, is the closest thing American Indian Catholics have to a saint. A victim of smallpox, which left her nearly blind, she refused marriage and, despite great hostility, became a devout Christian. She became known for her physical sacrifice and ministrations on behalf of her people. She died on the Mohawk Reserve of Caughnawaga, Canada in 1680. Today, her grave is considered a shrine and visited by Indian pilgrims each year to gain her intercession with the Creator. In 1980, at St. Peter's Basilica in the Vatican, the Beautification of the Blessed Kateri Tekakwitha took place and she became a candidate for sainthood.

The *Peace Pipe Line* is the publication of the Native American United Methodist Church of southern California. The church has sponsored an American Indian festival, a caring center for emergency shelter for Indians, a job board, and the Seventh Generation Walk to promote Indian pride. The term *seventh generation* refers to the traditional Indian concept of planning today in terms of the future generations.

A Native American Awareness Sunday emphasizes what Indian people have added to the life of the church. In 1978 it was the United Methodists who opened their national headquarters in Washington, D.C. to the coordinators of The Longest Walk—the walk from San Francisco across the country to the nation's capital to lobby congressional legislators to protect traditional Indian religious freedom.

The Religious Society of Friends (Quakers) has been active among Native Americans, especially in the last century among the Iroquois and today among the Alabama Choctaw, the Mesquakie of Iowa, and the Oklahoma tribes through the Associated Committee of Friends on Indian Affairs. The American Friends Service Committee (AFSC), a separate Quaker service organization, has for a number of years maintained an Indian program with fieldworkers on Indian reservations and in urban areas. The AFSC, however, does not proselytize. Although influenced by Friends religious ideology, few Indians consider themselves Quakers.

The Charles Cook Theological School in Tempe, Arizona, founded by the Presbyterian Church, is an ecumenically supported institution to educate Native Americans and other indigenous people "to serve God and their people in the context of their own culture." In 1991, for example, a Rosebud Sioux woman trained at Cook Theological School was appointed Episcopal lay pastor for the Gila River Indian Reservation.

In addition to ministering "Christian charity" to the Indians, proselytization remains the central mission of most Christian faiths. The American Ministries International, for example, publishes and distributes scriptures and other Christian literature to Native people in hospitals, schools, correctional institutions, nursing homes, and missions. It also distributes blankets, quilts, baby layettes, and children's clothing.

One of the most active missionary churches among American Indians is the Church of Latter-Day Saints, or Mormons. It is part of Mormon belief that American Indians are descendants of Lamanites—the so-called degenerate progeny of Laman derived from a lost tribe of Israel. The Lamanites produced the prophetic Book of Mormon discovered by Joseph Smith, the founder of the Mormon religion. The church, therefore, conceives as part of its task the re-conversion of the Indians, that they might once again become "a white and delightsome people." The expansion by early Mormon settlers into the lands of the Shoshoni and Ute in the middle of the last century earned them the enmity of these Indian people whom they displaced. Although few Ute have ever converted, Mormonism has made inroads among the Hopi and Dine (Navajo). Again, as with a number of the other Christian faiths, many of the converts claimed by the Mormon church appear to be nominal Christians.

Most Native Americans have contradictory feelings about Christianity. Although a significant number of Native Americans today claim membership, it is even more remarkable, after several hundred years of active missionary and Christianizing work, that so many remain only nominal adherents, and still others actively participate in traditional pre-Christian ceremonies, or are members of syncretic religions like the Native American Church. Christianity, because it was closely identified with the original land dispossession, genocide, and exploitation of the Native peoples, was considered to be the state religion of an oppressive Anglo-American nation. By identifying through the Christian ethic with Anglo-America, Native Americans felt they were weakened ideologically and therefore more easily divided. For example, the terms *Christian* and *pagan* were the oppositional epithets used by the missionaries and the federal government to differentiate the "good" from the "bad" Indians up until the Indian New Deal of the 1930s; that is, those Indians who cooperated with the federal government versus those who opposed it. Sharp religious differences very early divided the Tohono O'Odham (Papago), Apache, Lakota-Dakota, Chippewa, and many other Indian nations and peoples.

This divide-and-conquer strategy, whether always consciously intended by the Christian churches or not, is still operating today. For example, in one small Apache community of only several hundred inhabitants who were studied in the 1960s by the author, there were at least eight competing religious ideologies. The most prominent church in the community was the Lutheran church. It was the official Christian religion in the early reservation days on the Apache reservations in Arizona, so that it became "politically correct" for Apache leaders to be associated with Lutheranism. There was also a small Catholic mission where a priest said Sunday Mass. Traditional curing "sings" by the medicine men were common, although the Mormon church and its "elders" (young men doing two years of missionary service) were also quite active. The Assembly of God church was usually well attended, sometimes by those also attending other Christian churches. The fact that hymns could be sung in the Apache language was especially attractive. The new Miracle Church, which emphasized Pentecostal principles and faith-healing, was Apache led, and it also held services and camp meetings in the Native language. It had split in a factional dispute so that there were actually two functioning Miracle Churches in the community at the time. Finally, there was the Holy Grounds religion. This movement to revitalize Apache culture, combining Catholic, Protestant, and Apache values, had been started by Silas John in the 1920s. Although suppressed by the authorities because of Christian missionaries' influences, it nevertheless survived into the 1960s.

Another kind of factionalism occurred between the established Christian churches, on the one hand, and emergent, Native churches, on the other. In the Southwest, for example, Indians already converted to Presbyterian, Baptist, and Lutheran religions rebelled against being part of a national religious organization and set up their own independent churches. Indian churches grew up from the Baptist congregations on the San Carlos Apache Reservation and from Presbyterian congregations on the Mohave Reservation. They then adopted new names such as Hopi Mission Church, Mohave Mission Church, San Carlos Apache Independent Church, and Pima Independent Church. The Miracle Church was also active on the San Carlos Apache Reservation in the 1960s under an independent Apache lay ministry. A political struggle that manifested itself as a Christian denominational dispute arose in the Navajo Nation in the 1920s and 1930s between two strong Indian leaders. J. C. Morgan, a layworker for the Reformed Church, used anti-Catholicism in his bitter rivalry with Chee Dodge, a Navajo Catholic. Morgan later founded an independent Navajo church and was elected tribal chairman in 1938. Morgan's independent church then affiliated with the Methodists.

There were other changes in evolving Indian Christianity. Often these involved the relationship of form to meaning. The form—for example, hymn singing—might be the same, but the meaning to the Indian converts could be somewhat different than it would be to a non-Indian. One researcher recently examined Iroquois texts of Anglican and Presbyterian Christian hymns used on the Seneca reservations in western New York State. The hymns are actually paraphrases, not literal translations, because Seneca words are much longer than their English equivalents and thus do not fit the meter and length of Christian songs. He found that the source of language in Christian tunes is pre-Christian ritual expression, augmented by special ways to express new Christian ideas. For example, the Seneca expressions for God (there are several, including a female equivalent) are retained. One such term is "Sky Guardian," an archaic Seneca belief. In some cases,

Christian expressions are translated literally into the Seneca language, although they do not make complete sense to the Native speaker unfamiliar with Christian traditions. A few words, such as Jesus, Christ, and place names are taken directly from the Bible.

As with language, a considerable part of hymn theological motifs also reflect pre-Christian cosmology and ceremony, such as the various medicine societies in traditional Seneca culture. At times, sophisticated Christian ideas find their equivalency in like sophisticated Seneca expressions and at other times in the archaic Seneca language. Finally, many Christian ideas have been accepted wholesale with no particular influence by Seneca traditional religious values. In sum, this suggests that there is an Iroquois Christianity apart from non-Indian (mainstream) Christianity, or at least different from the established Protestant denominations, such as the Anglican and Presbyterian, which undertook the task of translating and promoting the hymns.

Historically, Christian influences have played an important role in the Indian community—especially on the reservations—until the termination and relocation period of the 1950s and the rise of the "new" Indian movement of the 1960s. The oldest Presbyterian churches in Idaho and South Dakota are Indian. The First Presbyterian Church of Kamiah on the Nez Percé Reservation was founded in 1891 and had Indian pastors after 1898. The First Presbyterian Church at Flandreau in South Dakota was established in 1869. Both churches functioned as Indian community centers for the next century. Henry Roe Cloud, the pioneer Indian educator, noted that the Christian church was effective in developing some of the first college or seminary-trained Indian leaders. For example, on the Nez Percé Reservation, Catholic laymen organized a council of chiefs in the late-nineteenth century. More recently, in the 1950s, the Presbyterian church at Barrow, Alaska, provided Native community leaders with opportunities for leadership that was unavailable elsewhere, and Episcopal lay leaders exerted similar informal power for the "country" Lakota Sioux on the Pine Ridge Reservation in the 1960s. In the Protestant and Catholic churches, opportunities for leadership, such as they were, in men's, women's, and youth groups represented some areas for Native advancement after traditional forms of worship and religious organization were outlawed. From the late-nineteenth century until 1934, Indians who practiced Native religious ceremonies and customs could be fined and jailed.

Conversion to Christianity among the Native peoples often occurred only after other forms of struggle failed. The Santee Sioux, for example, resisted conversion until after their defeat in the Sioux uprising of 1862. As a "benefit," conversion offered access to non-Indians who could help secure Indian land tenure in some instances. For example, a group of Presbyterian laymen on the Nez Percé Reservation responded to the problem of white encroachment on reservation land by organizing the Nez Percé Indian Home and Farm Association in 1923. Presbyterian laymen founded the Alaska Native Brotherhood in 1912, a pan-Indian, secular organization that pressed for integrated schools, Indian citizenship, and the settlement of Alaska Native land claims.

Alaska was first Christianized by the Russian Orthodox religion, which worked with the Aleut as well as the Tlingit and Haida of the Aleutian Island chain and southeastern Alaska. The Moravians, who had long maintained missions in eastern Canada and Greenland, were persuaded by the missionary Sheldon Jackson in the 1880s to take up mission work among Alaska's Inuit population. They have been especially active among the villages along the Kuskokwim River in the vicinity of Bethel, among the Yupiak. The Catholics, too, have had a firm presence, particularly in education. In the 1970s, for example, young people from St. Mary's Boarding School seemed to be making a better adjustment to college life at the University of Alaska in Fairbanks than Native students from the public schools, and some became leaders in the Alaska Native nationalism that emerged in conjunction with the Native land claims issue of the late 1960s, strongly supporting traditional Native language and culture.

Urbanism increased dramatically in the United States in the 1950s due in large part to the federal policy of reservation termination and urban relocation for the "surplus" reservation populations. The reservation based Christian missions and churches failed to keep pace with this development, but pan-Indian ceremonials such as powwows and the secular social service centers became the new focus of Indian identity and social solidarity in the cities. Kiowa migrants to San Francisco, for example, felt unwelcome at non-Indian Protestant churches, which lacked extensive social interaction with the Kiowa churches of Oklahoma. Some Kiowa attended one of the three inter-tribal Indian Protestant churches in the San Francisco Bay area, but most became increasingly involved in traditional Kiowa religion and culture. Understandably, Indian Christian church attendance is lower in urban areas than it is on many reservations. Non-Indian domination and control of Indian churches, especially in urban areas, undoubtedly explains the decline of the Indian Christian church after the 1960s.

Recent research indicates that although urban Indians now comprise over 60 percent of the contemporary Indian population, urbanism is not a separate entity as such, but is rather an extension of Indian Country generally, with strong ties to reservation culture, including religious traditions. During the late 1960s and early 1970s, urban Indian leadership developed outside the Christian churches in organizations such as the Survival of American Indians, American Indian Youth Council, United Native Americans, and the American Indian Movement. A resurgence in traditional Indian religion has since been noted in the cities, in Indian Country, on the reservations, and in the historic Indian areas of Oklahoma and Alaskan villages.

## New Religions

A frequent response to European conquest and aggression in past centuries was the formation of new religious movements among Native American peoples in both Canada and the United States. In some cases, such as with some of the early prophet movements, both the form and meaning of the new religions were entirely indigenous, but in other instances there was a recombination of Christian and Native spiritual traditions and practices. The latter have been termed *syncretic religions*. In fact, one research has identified three broad religious responses made by indigenous peoples of North America: (1) traditionalism, either retained secretly in the early Indian-non-Indian relations, or else revived at some later point in the contact history when political climate improved; (2) pan-Indianism through intertribal ceremonials; and (3) conversion to Christianity or acculturation. The peyote religion combined all three paths in a spiritual form that did not directly threaten non-Indians. At the same time, it remained distinctly Indian and crosscut different tribal religious traditions.

**Native American Church.** Peyote (*Lophophora williamsii* ) is a small, turnip-shaped cactus grown in the arid Rio Grande Valley of northern Mexico and Texas. Its substance is not addictive and should not be classified as a narcotic. People eat the bitter, dried top, or button, to induce heightened perceptions of sound and color. It enhances concentration and highlights religious truths with vivid imagery during ceremonies.

Spanish chroniclers observed peyote use in the religious ceremonies of northern Mexico in the sixteenth century. Its use in these indigenous community festivals, however, was different from the organized Peyote Church which later developed. Peyote use was first recorded in the United States among the Lipan Apache in the 1870s, who then taught its use to the Kiowa, Comanche, and other Indian tribes. As a religion, it spread through Oklahoma (formerly Indian Territory), the Great Plains, the Great Lakes area, and in various parts of the Northwest during the same fifty years that

Christianity was being spread by paid, federally backed missionaries. In 1918 several peyote groups incorporated under the state laws of Oklahoma as the Native American Church.

Peyotism took hold in the United States when the Native population had reached its lowest point: decimated Indian peoples, hungry and defeated, were confined to reservations as captured nations; indigenous political economy was all but destroyed; individualism and the capitalist ethic conflicted with Indian values and traditions; and Native religions were outlawed. Under these extreme conditions new Indian religions arose, and the Peyote Church offered its adherents a means of religious expression by which they could maintain a positive identity as Indian people, maintain a relationship to the Creator, and obtain personal security (both health and general well-being) in a non-Indian environment. The use of a hallucinogenic substance was common for a number of Indian cultures, in order to achieve a spiritual state of consciousness.

An important figure in the diffusion of the Peyote Church was John Wilson, of mixed Delaware, Caddo, and French parentage. After taking up the peyote religion in 1880, he claimed he had received a number of revelations instructing him in certain ceremonial procedures and preparation of religious paraphernalia, such as the construction of the moon-shaped altar since used in most peyote ceremonies. Wilson's version incorporated a number of Christian elements. Wilson reported being transported, during a peyote-induced out-of-body experience, to the "sky realm," where he learned of events in Christ's life as well as relative positions of spirit-forces, such as the sun, moon, and fire. The Peyote Road, which led from Christ's grave (which he found empty) to the moon, is the road Christ traveled in his ascent into Heaven. To follow the Peyote Road, then, means to follow the way of Christ's teachings and to obtain knowledge by use of peyote.

Wilson also taught specific revealed rituals still in practice today, and he gave a set of moral instructions: abstinence from liquor; restraint in sexual matters; matrimonial fidelity; and prohibitions against angry retorts, falsehoods, vindictiveness, vengeance, and fighting. Witchcraft and malevolent conjuring were also prohibited in the ethics of the Peyote Road. To purge oneself of sins is the function of peyote.

The Christian elements of the peyote religion, or the Native American Church, are obvious. Traditional non-Christian beliefs and practices, however, render it uniquely Indian, for they underlay the religion and make the whole greater than the sum of its parts. The peyote religion incorporates many traditional Native features. Such traditional aspects include communicating with the Creator through spirit forces by means of visions, which lead to power. Curing ceremonies, a central feature of Peyotism using the water drum and eagle fan, were traditional among many Indians, especially on the Plains. Medicine men had many powers, including prophecy, control of weather, locating lost objects, and giving advice on where the enemy could be found. Many Native peoples practiced the vision quest, which involved self-torture for power to protect oneself from the evil powers of others. Traditional ceremonies also used special plants—including tobacco, mescal bean, jimson weed, and peyote—as a means of obtaining visions and, hence, power. Most of these spiritual practices are still used in traditional Indian religions today.

The Native American Church demonstrates its integration of both Christian and traditional Indian religious beliefs and practices in its articles of incorporation:

> The purpose for which this corporation is formed is to foster and promote religious believers in Almighty God and the customs of the several tribes of Indians throughout the United States in the worship of a Heavenly Father and to promote morality, sobriety, industry, charity, and right living and cultivate a spirit of self-respect and brotherly love and union among the members of several tribes of Indians throughout the United States. . . with and through the sacramental use of peyote.

In 1954, the peyote religion became international with the incorporation of the Native American Church of Canada, and by the 1970s there were as many as 250,000 Indian members. It is, without doubt, the largest and fastest-growing Indian religion in North America. Its legal status today, however, remains in doubt. The Comprehensive Drug Abuse Prevention and Control Act, passed in 1970, prohibits peyote use except in an Indian religious ceremony, but permits must be obtained from the U.S. Attorney General's office. Twenty-four states consider its use a misdemeanor, with imprisonment for up to a year in jail and fines from $2,000 to $5,000. Until recently, a number of states, such as Arizona and California, allowed peyote use in ceremonies. In 1990, however, the U.S. Supreme Court struck down federal religious protection for the peyote church in the case of *Employment Division of Oregon v. Smith* and left it up to the various states to decide whether to criminalize peyote use as a religious sacrament by Native Americans. This is one of the main reasons why many Native Americans today say that religious freedom is being denied them and, as a legal precedent, First Amendment rights for all Americans are threatened.

**Early Prophet Movements.**   Prophets and prophecy are an integral part of Native American religions, as with Deganawida and Hiawatha's founding of the League of the Iroquois (Hau-De-No-Sau-Nee, or People of the Longhouse) and its great Binding Law in the fourteenth century at a time of conflict among the Iroquoian nations. A prophet or messiah traditionally arises to give people hope and direction in times of adversity or crisis. In recent decades, Hopi, Iroquois, and other Native religious leaders have been reinterpreting their age-old prophecies to better guide them in their dealings with western society and its institutions, especially in terms of racism and the destruction of the environment. Since Native Americans are deeply spiritual, it was natural for them to draw upon their traditions of prophecy in order to cope with the new problems brought by European conquest, including genocide and the dispossession of their lands. Prophets received their messages from the spirit world and often implored their people to return to the old way of life. Frequently, however, new religious practices and beliefs through songs, dances, ceremonies, and paraphernalia were needed to combat the evils of non-Indian society, such as alcohol, lying, and cheating. The prophecies often included the promise of divine intervention and the restoration of the old order, when Indian peoples would again be sovereign and free of colonial domination. Often they recommended military resistance to U.S. authority, while other prophecies counseled accommodation or non-violence and claimed that ethnic survival would come through new religious practices that promised spiritual intervention.

**Revivalistic Movements.**   In his study of the Seneca Indians and the Handsome Lake religion, Anthony F. C. Wallace coined the term *revitalization* to indicate the attempt on the part of a group of people to re-institute values and social solidarity when faced with cataclysmic changes. Other terms characterizing this phenomenon are *resistance*, *nativistic*, or *millenarian* movements. In the Native American case, many of these movements have been or are prophet-based or prophecy-oriented. The seventeenth-century Pueblo Indian patriot Popé was one of the first messiahs to emerge in response to European Christianization and subjugation. In 1680 Popé led the autonomous Pueblo villages in a war of independence which succeeded in freeing the Indians from Spanish tyranny for fifteen years. After experiencing a heavenly visitation, he prophesied that an Indian millennium was near and that it was the sacred duty of Native people to rise up and fulfill the prophecy.

In the mid-eighteenth century United States, the Delaware Prophet sought to unite the Delaware (Leni-Lenape) people who lost their land and were greatly disrupted by British colonial expansion. Directed by the Great Spirit, he preached that Indians should shed European ways so that the British would mysteriously disappear and the former Indian life be restored. It is believed that Pontiac, the Indian leader who organized the tribes of the Old Northwest against the British at the close of the French and Indian War, drew upon the widespread influence of the Delaware Prophet.

A second Delaware Prophet, the Munsee Prophetess, emerged from the regeneration of the tribes of the Old Northwest (the northeastern United States) in the late-eighteenth century, influencing the Shawnee leader, Tecumseh, to found an all-Indian republic in order to block the westward advance of the United States. Tecumseh was assisted by his brother, Tenskwatawa (the Open Door), a prophet who preached pan-Indian living and what he called "the Way." Creek prophet Josiah Francis rallied a traditionalist segment of Creeks, called the Red Sticks, against American influence in the same conflict and during the War of 1812. Somewhat earlier than the Red Stick Movement, between 1810 and 1813, several prophets emerged among the Cherokee, and several visions were reported that called on the Cherokee to protect their sacred sites and villages and slow down the pace of economic and political change. The Cherokee movement soon died away with the outbreak of the War of 1812 and after several prophetic predictions failed to materialize.

On the other hand, some of the prophetic movements were less militant and sought accommodation with U.S. society. Kickapoo prophet Kenekuk, for example, urged his followers in Illinois to engage in passive resistance. He and his followers ignored government demands to vacate their eastern lands and migrate to Indian Territory in Kansas. Directed by the great Holy Force Above, Kenekuk instructed the Kickapoo people to return to their ancient traditional culture, to live abstemiously, and to worship through meditation and the use of prayer sticks.

**Handsome Lake and the Longhouse Religion.** A religious renaissance occurred on a number of the Iroquois reservations between 1799 and 1815 called Gaiwiio, the Old Way of Handsome Lake, and it survives today among many, if not most, contemporary Iroquois. The American Revolution of 1776 had divided the Iroquois Confederacy and seriously weakened its old unity. Jesuit missionaries had helped to instigate pro-British and other migrations to Canada; the Seneca had half its population decimated through warfare, disease, and alcoholism; and they had lost most of their lands. Depression and suicide were widespread, and charges of witchcraft were on the rise. Many Iroquois men became alcoholics. The Iroquois villages became slums in the wilderness. Although defeated, starving,

and impoverished, they believed the new U.S. government would honor their treaties. But land loss was rapid: the treaty of Fort Stanwix in 1784 had recognized Iroquois land rights to most of central and western New York, but by 1800 only a few small reservation areas remained.

Only two paths seemed open to the dispirited Iroquois: to convert to the ways of the Christians or to preserve Indian ways. Into this cultural abyss came the Philadelphia Quakers, who sent missionaries to the Allegany Seneca to teach literacy, crafts, and technical skills. Cornplanter, the chief warrior of the Seneca, had long advocated that the Indians adopt the economic practices of non-Indians, such as men working in agriculture. The Quakers promoted plow agriculture by men, a gender role reversal for the matrilineal Iroquois where women owned the fields or gardens. In 1799 Cornplanter, his family, and a growing number of others supported the Quaker reforms. Into this situation stepped Handsome Lake, the degenerate brother of Cornplanter, with his drunken fellow warriors. However, through a terrible sickness and near-death state, Handsome Lake had several visions that were recorded by the Quakers and remembered in Iroquois oral tradition.

In the first vision, Handsome Lake received four evil words: whiskey, witchcraft, love magic, and abortion-and-sterility medicine. Persons guilty of any of these wrong-doings should repent and never sin again. Subsequently he had two more visions, and these constitute the Gaiwiio, or Good Word. His teachings from 1799 to 1801 constituted an apocalyptic first gospel, dealing with the immanence of world destruction, a definition of sin, and a prescription for individual salvation. The second is the social gospel and includes the following themes: temperance, peace and unity, land retention, limited acculturation (Western technology and the English language), and a revised domestic morality. Following the social gospel of the code would lead to personal salvation, social betterment, and the postponement of the apocalypse. Although not Christian, the code of Handsome Lake was inspired by Christian teachings, especially those of the Quakers. Christian rituals and symbols were combined with those of traditional Iroquois religion. Impressed by the positive changes among the Iroquois, non-Indians held the prophet in high esteem. Thomas Jefferson described the religion of Handsome Lake as "positive and effective." Handsome Lake also preached against theft, alcoholism, malicious gossip, witchcraft, adultery, wife-beating, and jealousy. Husbands and wives were to love each other and remain faithful, and they were to treat their children with kindness. Compassion should be shown to all those who were suffering. Certain ceremonies were to be conducted in the longhouse (a place of worship), and all were to revere the Great Spirit and all of Creation. Unlike the Native American Church, which is pan-Indian in scope, the longhouse religion is uniquely Iroquois in faith and practice so that its practice today is confined to the Iroquois nations, where perhaps half are followers of the "old way" or Code of Handsome Lake.

## Reservation-Era Religious Movements

Once confined to reservations by the U.S. military at the close of the nineteenth century, Indian peoples in the western United States came to hold the unenviable status of captured nations. All the old tribal institutions—the aboriginal economy, political sovereignty and the system of government, the kinship group and the extended family—were destroyed or else drastically changed. In their place non-Indian authority instituted the 1887 Indian Allotment Act "to break up the tribal mass," the federal boarding school system "to save the man but kill the Indian," and the office of Indian Affairs superintendency. The superintendent or Indian agent was a virtual dictator, and his authority was backed by the Indian police and a code of "Indian crimes." Native Americans, now confined and powerless, were rendered paupers, and the daily roll call and ration system effectively checked organized resistance. There then arose new prophets—Smohalla, Squasachtum, Wodziwob, and Wovoka—and new revitalization movements. The best known of these was the Ghost Dance in the late-nineteenth century.

**Ghost Dance Religious Movement.**   The first phase of the Ghost Dance Movement actually appeared around 1870 among the Northern Paiute soon after the transcontinental Union Pacific Railroad was built. An Indian prophet, Wodziwob (White Hair), had a vision that a big train would bring back the dead ancestors, at which time a cataclysm would engulf U.S. society but miraculously leave its material goods behind for the Indians; then, the Great Spirit would return. This event could be hastened by new songs and religious dancing. After a time, this early Ghost Dance petered out, although many elements were incorporated into the beliefs and practices of California Indians that continue to this day.

In 1889 a new prophet arose among the Paiute: Wovoka. Known also as Jack Wilson, Wovoka was born at Pyramid Lake, Nevada. His father, Tavibo, was a leader of the Paiute community and a "weather doctor," that is, he could control the weather. Wovoka, too, became a weather doctor and led the traditional circle dances. Between dances he preached universal love. Wovoka, "the Cutter," had worked for a non-Indian rancher named Wilson and became familiar with the Christian Bible, learned about Jesus Christ, and watched non-Indian people in their round dances.

On 1 January 1889, a total eclipse of the sun occurred, and Wovoka, while very ill, experienced a powerful vision. When the sun "died" that winter day, he was taken up to Heaven, where God gave him a message of peace and right living. Now a prophet, his preaching influenced even Mormon settlers, who thought for awhile that he might be the messiah prophesied by their founder, Joseph Smith. Using religious paraphernalia from traditional Indian culture, such as red ochre paint and magpie feathers, Wovoka taught a new circle dance "to embrace Our Father, God." The celebrants were to move in harmony sunward, singing Ghost (spirit) songs, and thus live and work in harmony. Although Wovoka himself never left his native land, Paiute believers and visiting delegations of other Indians soon spread the new prophecy. Disappointed in Wodziwob and the first Ghost Dance, the Indians of California and Oregon rejected the new message, as did the Pueblo Indian theocracies and the deeply traditional Navajo. But many other tribes took up the new religion.

Wovoka explained that non-Indians had been sent to punish Indians for their sins but that they could soon expect deliverance. He also promised that their ancestors would return as would the game and the old Indian world, and U.S. settlers would mysteriously be eradicated. Furthermore, until the Indian world regenerated it could be visited through a new religious dance, by wearing spirit regalia, singing Ghost songs, and experiencing self-hypnotic trances. One Kiowa Ghost Song goes as follows:

My father will descend
the earth will tremble
everybody will rise,
stretch out your hands.

A dancer would fall down in a trance, "dying," and then speak of traveling to the moon or the morning star and come back with "star flesh" in his fist that had turned into strange rocks. By these means, one could "visit" the long-dead relatives and see the promised world. Thus the religious celebrants joyously awaited the coming cataclysm that was supposed to occur sometime in 1890.

Among the Lakota Sioux, however, Wovoka's nonviolent message took a militant turn. The Great Sioux Nation had been broken up by white aggression, and the sacred Black Hills were seized for their rich gold deposits in 1877. By 1889 many Sioux were dying of starvation due to a severe drought. They were forced to eat their seed corn and to butcher even their stud bulls.

Food rations promised by Congress were slow in coming, and disease epidemics ravaged the population. Local holymen like Kicking Bear took up the Ghost Dance, which became a form of spiritual resistance to U.S. authority and oppression. It was said that warriors wearing ghost shirts could even turn back soldier's bullets.

Sitting Bull was one of the principal Indian leaders who sympathized with the new religious movement. The Indian agents and local settlers, however, feared an Indian uprising like the one at Little Bighorn in 1876 that resulted in George Custer's defeat, and they set out to suppress the new religion. When Sitting Bull was assassinated by the Indian police, the terrorized followers of the Ghost Dance movement fled south to Pine Ridge Reservation to seek protection from Chief Red Cloud. Just a few miles from Pine Ridge, at Wounded Knee Creek, on 24 December 1890, Custer's old regiment, the Seventh Cavalry, opened fire on the Indians with Hotchkiss (machine) guns. These guns poured two-pound explosive shells at the rate of nearly fifty a minute, mowing down everything alive—warriors, old people, women, children, ponies, and dogs. Chief Big Foot and the elders in the council circle were killed, and the warriors were no match for the army's guns. Of the 370 Indians massacred that day, 250 were women and children. Thus ended the Ghost Dance among the Sioux and with it the twenty-five-year-long Plains Indian war of resistance.

The Ghost Dance nevertheless survived for a number of years among other tribes in both the United States and Canada. The Dakota-speaking Sioux of Saskatchewan Province, Canada, for example, incorporated much of the original Ghost Dance into their New Tidings religion. These Wahpeton Sioux, descendants of refugees from the 1862 Minnesota uprising, created a new form of Ghost Dance that included their traditional Medicine Feast.

Fred Robinson, an Assiniboine, introduced the Ghost Dance to the Dakota at the Round Plain Indian Reserve in Canada about 1900. He had learned it from Wovoka by way of Kicking Bird, a Teton Sioux (Lakota) leader. Believers pray daily and gather as a congregation to pray together and to sing holy songs that remind them of the prophet's journey to God and His promise of eternal life. A communion of meat, corn, berries, and rice with raisins is held. Some people wear Ghost shirts, to protect the wearer from evil temptation. They are to follow the "good Red path" of ochre paint on the earthen altar and the incense rising to Heaven from the sacred pipe and sweetgrass. Medicine bundles, symbolizing the good message of the New Tidings religion, are brought to these prayer meetings and purified in the incense smoke. The New Tidings, the Holy Dance prayer communions, were part of the Round Plain Reserve community for much of the twentieth century.

**Washat or Seven Drums Religion.** Another major religious movement was the Washat religion that originated along the Columbia River in the present-day states of Washington and Oregon. Although influenced by Roman Catholicism, the movement urged Indian people to return to their ancient ways and values. Followers of Washat, called Seven Drums (which are played during service), peacefully resisted government attempts in the late-nineteenth century to herd Indians of the region onto the reservations and to give up their lands and traditional way of life. They chose, instead, to remain on their ancestral lands near the river, to continue to live according to their traditions, to fish, dig roots, pick berries, and maintain their "first foods" and other religious ceremonies. To this day, Washat is practiced along the Columbia River and on the Yakima, Nez Percé, and Warm Springs reservations.

Around 1860, Smohalla, called Preacher, a Wanapum Indian, revitalized the old Washani religion of the Pacific Northwest. He taught that the Indian world invaded by Anglo-American settlers was on a course of self-destruction. It could only be averted by human efforts to restore the original balance of nature and creation. Called the Dreamer religion because of Smohalla's frequent trances and the meditation practiced by his followers, Smohalla prophesied the coming of the millennium and the resurrection of the old Indian world. After this world-cleansing, only the followers of the Seven Drums religion would regain their lands and live as they did before the coming of non-Indians.

Smohalla was adamantly opposed to U.S. government policy to make farmers out of Indian fishermen and hunters. As a result, he was frequently jailed. In 1877, inspired by the teachings of Smohalla, Chief Joseph of the Nez Percé refused a government order to abandon their rich Wallowa homeland and remove to a reservation in Washington under the terms of a bogus treaty. Before being forced to surrender just thirty miles from the Canadian border and freedom in "Mother Canada," he led his people on a 1,300-mile trek in which he continually out-fought and out-foxed the U.S. Army and its best generals.

A basic belief of the Washat religion is that Mother Earth provides all sustenance, the salmon being the foremost. This tradition came in conflict with the dominant society in the post-World War II decades when the Columbia River was dammed, which inundated Indian villages and fishing sites, and depleted salmon runs. Things came to a head in the 1970s and 1980s in the clash over Indian fishing rights in opposition to the interests of commercial and non-Indian sports fishermen on the Columbia River. A number of Indian families still live along the Che Wana (Columbia River), such as Celilo Village and Little White Salmon Indian Settlement, refusing to relocate to nearby reservations. In 1983 David Sohappy, Sr. and thirteen other traditional fishing Indians were convicted of illegally selling fish under the 1981 Lacey Act. Sohappy and the others, all adherents of the old Seven Drums religion and its healing cult, the Feather religion, were sent to federal prison. Sohappy and the others readily admitted to ignoring federal and reservation fishing regulations and welcomed the chance to bring their treaty and religious rights to fish "in their accustomed places" into court. Sohappy, a lineal descendent of the Indian prophet Smohalla, had been instrumental from 1959 to 1974 in getting the courts to issue the Boldt Decision, awarding the Indians 50 percent of the salmon catch. Traditionally the fish are shared by a wide extended family network of poor Indian families. Today there are more than 2,000 of Smohalla's followers living along the river and carrying on the religion.

David Sohappy, Sr. spent two-and-a-half years of a five-year sentence in federal prison. Through the intervention of the Yakima Tribal Court, his courageous attorneys, and the intervention of Senator Daniel Inouye, he was released from prison in 1988. He had suffered three strokes, a series of prison transfers, and separation from his traditional life and spiritual sustenance on the Che Wana. A year later he died.

### Other New Religions

In the 1880s, the Indian Shaker church began among the Coast Salish in the southern Puget Sound area of Washington State, although there is no connection with the Shaker Church of Anglo-America. Both the Indian Shaker church and the Prophet Dance enjoyed increasing influence in the Pacific Northwest in these years and eventually spread to California.

John Slocum, a Nisqually Indian of Mud Bay, and his wife, Mary Johnson Slocum, received their basic inspirations for the Indian Shaker religion in 1882. The church itself was organized as an association in 1892, at Mud Bay, Washington, and incorporated in 1910 in Olympia, the state capital. It is a syncretic religion, incorporating elements of both traditional practices and beliefs and Christian theology. Liturgical aids, such as bells and candles to conduct services, are featured, along with prayers, songs, and dances.

Like other Indian prophets, Slocum "died" and went to Heaven following a serious illness. There he spoke to the angels and received a message from God. The creed is simple, requiring no familiarity with the Bible or Christianity; in fact, Bibles are not to be used or directly quoted in the Shaker church. Healing is the single most important element of the religion. This is accomplished through the Holy Spirit, to restore health and balance. Trembling with power (hence, the word *shaker*) cures diseases and gives a purpose to living. Alcoholics, for example, can recover through the "shake." Among the Tolowa of California, Christianity made little headway because it was perceived as a state religion of an oppressor nation. The Shaker church, on the other hand, provided a midway point in the accommodation process. Christian beliefs have infused old spiritual practices that sometimes appear similar to pentecostal services, but the Indian Shakers maintain their religious independence. On the Warm Springs Reservation in Oregon among the Simnasho, and at Umatilla, Shakers have an obvious presence. The religion is very much alive today.

### Syncretic, Pluralistic, and Other Religious Processes in the Southwest.

E. H. Spicer, social anthropologist and cultural historian, has written extensively on the Indian peoples of the American Southwest and northern Mexico, especially the Yaqui. In *Cycles of Conquest*, he details the religious changes that took place among the various indigenous peoples in the southwestern United States and Sonora, Mexico, as a result of the Spanish conquest and then the Mexican and Anglo-American contact periods. Similar changes have occurred among other Native American groups.

In the Southwest, where one-quarter of all Indian people reside, mostly on reservations, a majority consider themselves Catholic, employing the Spanish word *católico*. These include the Tarahumara (Rarámuri), Yaqui (Yoemen), Mayo, and Opate of Sonora, Mexico, and the lower Pima, many Papago and Gila River Pima (O'Odham), and the Yaqui barrios in the United States. In addition, most Yuma, some Navajo, some Apache, and some Zuni also speak of themselves as Catholic. These Catholic Indians, in particular the Mayo, the Tarahumara, the Yaqui, and the Eastern Pueblo of New Mexico, have developed beliefs and practices so different from mainstream Catholic doctrine and organization that they are held to be syncretic religions, distinctly Indian when observed and practiced by Native Americans.

Spicer described three different types of Catholic syncretism. The Eastern Pueblo added some Catholic elements to their otherwise little-changed traditional religion, which Spicer called *compartmentalization*. The Yoemen, on the other hand, were influenced by the Jesuits in the 1500s and reworked their entire traditional religion until a wholly new religion resulted, which Spicer called *fusion*. And the Papago accepted certain elements of Catholicism without integrating them into their traditional systems of religion, identified as *addition*. Many of these Indian "Catholics" do not accept the European ideas of heaven and hell; many hold little interest in the Virgin Mary or in Jesus; and almost all reject the organized Catholic church. The Tohono O'Odham (Papago), for example, do not allow priests into their village chapels. From a Native American perspective the Pueblo Indian response could be considered pluralism: the practice of more than one religious tradition. In the Pueblo case, the early Franciscan missionaries physically discouraged Native religious practices, which forced Pueblo religion underground. After the Spanish put down a Pueblo revolt under Popé in 1680, they considered the Indians nominally Catholic but allowed them to practice their religious kiva ceremonies. But from the late 1800s until 1934, the Pueblo religion underwent suppression from Anglo-American authorities. Again the Pueblo peoples retrenched through their religious organizations and actions, developing protective and isolationist mechanisms. Thus today they are both Catholic and traditional Indian in their religious observances.

The Yoemen Easter Festival appears to be a complex integration of indigenous ceremonial dance practices with an overlay of Christian liturgy and beliefs. For example, one dancer group, the Pascolas, or "old men of the fiesta," predate Christian influence. To the accompaniment of drum, flute, harp, and violin, they dance wearing sleigh bells around their hips, cocoon rattles on their ankles, and rattles in their hands. The Yaqui Deer Dancer, who performs during Easter and at other ceremonial times of the year, also predates Christian influence.

The next largest Christian faith in the Southwest is Presbyterian. Tohono O'Odham, many Navajo, some Apache, Mohave, Maricopa, and Hopi adhere to this faith's doctrine. Beginning in 1869, under the Grant Administration, it became federal policy to assign the running of Indian reservations to the various Christian missionary groups. The Presbyterians and the Christian Reformed (Lutheran) were the first prominent Protestant churches in the Southwest. The Lutherans took over the education and Christianization of all Apache groups, the Navajo, the Gila Pima and, later, the Zuni. The Presbyterians later took over responsibility for the Gila Pima and shared religious responsibility for the Tohono O'Odham with the Catholics, and then Mohave and the Laguna Pueblo. Next were the Mennonites among the Hopi, the Episcopalians among the Havasupais and later among the Navajo. The American Baptists worked among the Hopi, the Methodists among the Yuma and Navajo, and the Plymouth Brethren among the Walapai, Eastern Pueblo, and Navajo. At the same time, the Franciscan Catholics entered the field among the Navajo, Apache, Gila Pima, and Tohono O'Odham. By 1915, there were eight Christian denominations conducting schools and religious services, and competing for Indian souls.

In 1920 Apache leaders on the San Carlos Reservation petitioned their Bureau of Indian Affairs superintendent to be free of religious persecution at the hands of the two established churches, the Lutheran and the Catholic. They asked for religious freedom and pointed out that their Holy Grounds religion was devoted to the best beliefs and values of both Christian and traditional Apache religions. They also complained that the established Christian sects were not making adequate progress. The Holy Grounds movement grew until 1938 when its founder, Silas John, was sentenced to jail for fifteen years. He had been arrested on the charge of murdering his wife, although many Apache still say he was framed by the government under pressure from the Christian missionaries. In 1954 he was released and then resumed his position as head of this religious movement. The new religion continued to grow until the early 1960s, when it began to be displaced by the independent evangelical Apache church, the Miracle Church.

Finally, on all reservations and in the various Indian communities, whether rural or urban, there are Indian people who have constantly rejected Christian ways and who continue to practice their traditional religions, which in some ways are only slightly modified since European entry into the region several hundred years ago. This has been the case for the majority of Navajo, the Eastern Pueblo generally, and some of the Tohono O'Odham and Seri (Comcáac). Since the 1960s, due to the "new" Indian movement and religious revitalization, there has been a resurgence of traditional religious practices. For example, the International Indian Treaty Council, which supports traditional culture and religion, organized a gathering of Indian nations on the Tohono O'Odham Reservation in 1982, and a Lakota medicine man led a Plains Sun Dance on the Navajo Nation in the early 1980s.

## Religious Revitalization Today

Starting with the decade of the 1980s, a second phase of the "new" Indian movement occurred. While the earlier political organization and militancy of the 1960s and 1970s began with the urban Indians of the cities, the new wave of religious revitalization and cultural renaissance is reservation-based. Today, younger Indian people, both urban and reservation, are orienting themselves to their grandparents' generation; that is to the elders and traditional people.

Nuxalk Nation Blessing. (Photo by Mary G. Wentz)

Native American religion, including modified traditionalism, peyotism, and other syncretic forms, is again the centerpiece of what it means to be Indian for many Native Americans. Medicine men like the late Lakota holy man Henry Crow Dog and other reservation traditionalists have taken American Indian Movement militants under their tutelage. Sweat lodges have been set up in the prisons and the use of sacred pipes and purification ceremonies of the Sun Dance is spreading throughout the United States. The Tipi Religion (or peyote cult of the Native American Church) has become an increasingly important form of therapy and recovery for that part of the Indian population suffering from alcohol and drug addiction. Not only traditional religion, but also Native languages, singing and drumming, long suppressed ritual practices such as piercing as a form of a self-sacrifice in the Sun Dance, storytelling, weaving, and the oral traditions have all seen a revival.

During most of this century, social scientists as well as the federal government promoted the idea that Native American culture was dead or on its way out,

that Indians were "the vanishing Redman." Anthropologists held the belief, which was the basis for their acculturation studies, that the Indians were giving up aboriginal culture and language and would assimilate into the mainstream society. But more recently, Indian scholars such as Vine Deloria, Jr. have taken exception to this view. In *God Is Red* and other works, Deloria compares Native American traditional religious principles to Christianity and underscores the persistence of traditionalism in contemporary Indian culture. More recently, Ake Hulkrantz, a specialist on Indian religion, points out in "Religion" in *Native North America* that the nineteenth-century emergence of Indian revitalization movements should have made it obvious that Indian culture and religion were not dying but, instead, were only changing. In the same work, Amanda Porterfield compares the present-day Indian spirituality movement to the earlier revitalization movements. Religion, language, and culture have seen a new stage of development, if not rebirth, in Native North America today. The evidence is everywhere.

Along the Northwest Coast, the Salish traditional religious dances are being revived, where for many years they were eclipsed by Christian Methodism and the Indian Shaker Church. Among the Eastern Cherokee in North Carolina, there has emerged a Cherokee Christianity, a blend of both traditional and Christian religion. And the Abenaki of Newfoundland today practice a syncretic blend of Catholicism and traditional religion. Traditionalism has gained in prominence. A growing number of Indian people are becoming "sweataholics," participating in the ancient practice of cleansing both body and spirit in a purification sweat lodge. Native Americans, from the Aztecs to the Delaware to the Inuit, observed this rite of purification. Today it is practiced widely on a number of reservations, and it is not uncommon for Indians who live in metropolitan areas to have personal sweat lodges in their own backyards. They invite Indian and even non-Indian friends and relatives to sweats, which often end with the participants sharing a meal and socializing.

Vision quests, the ancient puberty rite for young men, have returned to Indian Country after being almost stamped out by federal authorities in past decades. Women, too, are "going on the hill," or "crying for a dream," as the Lakota call this practice. Not unlike the early Christian prophets, contemporary Indian people believe they can be healed or help heal others through prayer to the Great Spirit, and even obtain spiritual helpers for life's trials and tribulations. By cleansing oneself in an Indian sweat, making tobacco tie offerings, fasting, and "locking" oneself in an altar on a sacred hill, mountain, or in a vision pit, Indians can receive spiritual instruction for walking the "good Red

Road" of Native American culture and values. Furthermore, the traditional, non-commercial Sun Dance religion is thriving among many western tribes in the United States and Canada.

Summertime, especially, is a season of going home to the reservation, visiting Indian Country, seeing one's friends and relatives at the Crow Fair, the Navajo Fair, the powwows, the Sun Dances, and other tribal ceremonies. For the Yoemen of Arizona, in their syncretic Indian Christian religion, Easter is one of the special times in the ceremonial calendar. For the various Pueblo villages along the Rio Grande in New Mexico, and for the western Pueblo, frequent ceremonial occasions include important religious dances and rituals that they have been practicing for thousands of years, even though most Pueblo Indians are nominally Catholic.

One of the lessons that contemporary Native Americans are endeavoring to teach non-Indian America is that the urban versus reservation Indian dichotomy is a false one. One cannot separate urban Indians in terms of values and beliefs from their reservation or rural brothers and sisters. The new revitalization movement makes this clear. For example, on the door of the Intertribal Friendship House, an Indian community center in Oakland, California, one may see the notice "Ceremony Tonight!" A Lakota medicine man from one of the South Dakota reservations may have flown in to administer to Lakota and others in the Oakland-East Bay area. The center's community hall will be darkened with black plastic placed over the windows, tobacco prayer ties will be made, a floor altar constructed, and, drumming and singing, the medicine man will begin to heal and prophesy. The ritual will end with a giveaway of gifts to the attendees by those healed. It is almost the exact ceremony performed back home on the reservation.

Another example is Moyoane, ancestral home of the Piscataway Indians. Located twenty-five miles south of Washington, D.C. on the Potomac River, it lies today within the Piscataway National Park under control of the Alice P. Ferguson Foundation and its colonial farm, the Smithsonian Institution, and the National Park Service. Since 1974 the hundred or so traditional Piscataway living in the area today, survivors of an original population of 12,000, have been waging a ceaseless struggle to regain possession of their sacred burial ground—only twenty-five acres of the 4,200-acre park. Yet they are continually harassed in their attempt to carry on traditional ceremonies at Moyoane and in the exercise of their religious freedom. Living a stone's throw from the nation's capital, they are urban Indians, yet they persist and endure as a traditional people.

The new revitalization movement, too, has sparked political protest for Indian land rights and sovereignty, as in the late 1960s when the Indian, Inuit, and Aleut peoples of Alaska organized the Alaska Federation of Natives to press for their land, and subsistence hunting and fishing rights, and again in 1973 in the occupation protest at Wounded Knee on the Pine Ridge Reservation. In Nevada, led by the Dann sisters, Chief Yowell, and traditional elders, the Western Shoshoni Nation has been waging a long struggle against the U.S. government and its Bureau of Land Management over the issue of Indian land rights and nuclear testing. Under traditional beliefs, Mother Earth cannot be sold. It is therefore maintained that the 1863 Treaty of Ruby Valley did not cede Shoshoni lands to the United States but was, instead, a treaty of peace and friendship. Traditional religious beliefs support the struggle for land and sovereignty, and liberal Catholic and Protestant clergy, ministers and lay leaders, have joined Indian religious leaders in supporting this religious freedom issue on a number of occasions.

In the 1990s important protective legislation was passed by Congress. Notable was the Native American Graves Protection and Repatriation Act (NAGPRA) passed in 1990. This set the stage for procedures and guidelines to eventually return human remains and funerary objects and cultural items in museums to "culturally affiliated" Indian tribes, Alaska Native villages or corporations, and Native Hawaiian organizations. The situation remains complex and problematic, however, because small Native American groups typically lack the written records to establish "cultural affiliation" in courts, and many others are unrecognized by the federal government and are therefore ineligible to apply under NAGPRA.

Unfortunately, an omnibus bill introduced by Senator Daniel K. Inouye of Hawaii in 1994, the Native American Cultural Protection and Free Exercise of Religion Act, failed to pass Congress. This omnibus bill would have given a measure of protection to imprisoned Native people in the exercise of their cultural and religious rights, although it is doubtful it would have protected adherents of the peyote religion. Currently, sweat lodges have been torn down by some prison authorities, and Indian religious ceremonies involving the Pipe religion and the Native American Church have been denied.

Nevertheless, due to the resurgence of Indian traditional culture, over 18,000 Indian human remains held by the national Smithsonian Institution in Washington, D.C. are being returned to their respective tribes for sanctified reburial. Indian remains in the states of Georgia, Alabama, Kentucky, and Kansas have already been removed from public display. Indian leaders and their supporters have long criticized the "specimen collecting complex" of the dominant culture as sacrilegious, racist, and demeaning. One of the most infamous sites, the Dickson Mounds Museum in Illinois, displayed 200 skeletons from a 900-year-old burial mound. It was closed in April 1992 with an Indian sacred pipe ceremony.

Religion, whether pluralistic or syncretic, has now been given a decidedly traditionalist emphasis and has become the foundation of the Native American cultural renaissance, a modern revitalization movement.

*Steve Talbot*
*Oregon State University*

# Religious Organizations

## UNITED STATES

### ♦ ALABAMA

SAINT ANNE'S EPISCOPAL CHURCH
Jack Springs Rd.
Atmore, AL 36502
(334) 368–8606

### ♦ ALASKA

VOICE OF CHRIST MINISTRIES, INC.
P.O. Box 00474
Nenana, AK 99760–0474
(907) 832–5426

### ♦ ARIZONA

AMERICAN INDIAN COLLEGE OF THE
ASSEMBLY OF GOD
10020 North 15th Ave.
Phoenix, AZ 85021
(800) 933–3828

AMERI-TRIBES
P.O. Box 27346
3710 S. Park Ave., Suite 708
Tucson, AZ 85726
(520) 670–9400

CHIEF, INC.
(Christian Hope Indian Eskimo Fellowship, Inc.)
1644 East Campo Bello Dr.
Phoenix, AZ 85022
(602) 482–0828

FLAGSTAFF MISSION TO THE NAVAJO
P.O. Box AA
Flagstaff, AZ 86002
(520) 774–2802

HOLY SPIRIT JEDDITO EPISCOPAL CHURCH
P.O. Box 618
Fort Defiance, AZ 86504

HOPI INDEPENDENT CHURCH
P.O. Box 40
Kykotsmovi Village, AZ 86039
(520) 734–9214

NATIVE AMERICAN BAHA'I INSTITUTE
P.O. Box 3167
Hock, AZ 86506–3167
(520) 587–7599

SOUTHWEST INDIAN MISSIONS
ASSOCIATION
P.O. Box 36535
Phoenix, AZ 85067–6535
(602) 252–2054

UNITED INDIAN MISSIONS, INC.
P.O. Box 3600
2920 North Third St.
Flagstaff, AZ 86003–3600
(520) 774–0651

WORCESTER INDIAN MINISTRIES, INC.
Box 9090
Window Rock, AZ 86515–9090
(520) 371–5749

### ♦ CALIFORNIA

AMERICAN INDIAN LIBERATION
CRUSADE, INC.
4009 South Hallandale Ave.
Los Angeles, CA 90062
(323) 299–1810

# ◆ COLORADO

LIVING WATERS CHURCH
215 W. 5th Ave.
Denver, CO 80204

NAZARENE INDIAN BIBLE COLLEGE
1111 Academy Park Loop
Colorado Springs, CO 80910
(719) 596–5110

# ◆ DISTRICT OF COLUMBIA

BUREAU OF CATHOLIC INDIAN MISSIONS
2021 H St., N.W.
Washington, DC 20006
(202) 331–8542

FRIENDS COMMITTEE ON NATIONAL
  LEGISLATION
245 Second St. N.E.
Washington, DC 20002
(202) 547–6000

# ◆ ILLINOIS

REACHING INDIAN MINISTRIES
  INTERNATIONAL
18 South Schoenbeck Rd., Suite 201
Wheeling, IL 60090–4454
(847) 215–2827

# ◆ KANSAS

MENNONITE INDIAN LEADERS' COUNCIL
c/o Mennonite Church, General Conference
P.O. Box 347
Newton, KS 67114
(316) 283–5100

# ◆ MAINE

NATIVE AMERICAN PROJECT
Saint Luke's Episcopal Church
143 State St.
Portland, ME 04101
(207) 772–5434

# ◆ MINNESOTA

COUNCIL FOR AMERICAN INDIAN
  MINISTRIES (CAIM)/UNITED CHURCH
  OF CHRIST
P.O. Box 412
Excelsior, MN 55331
(952) 474–3532

IMPACT NORTH MINISTRIES
P.O. Box 50
International Fall, MN 56649–0050
(807) 727–2291

# ◆ MISSOURI

ASSEMBLIES OF GOD/DIVISION OF HOME
  MISSIONS
1445 Boonville Ave.
Springfield, MO 65802
(417) 862–2781

# ◆ MONTANA

KATERI INDIAN MINISTRY CENTER
1015 Broadwater Ave., #9
Billings, MT 59102
(406) 256–5142

TEKAKWITHA CONFERENCE NATIONAL
  CENTER (Kateri Circle)
P.O. Box 6768
Great Falls, MT 59406–6768
(406) 727 0147

# ◆ NEW MEXICO

AMERICAN INDIAN BIBLE MISSIONS, INC.
P.O. Box 230, 1275 Hwy. 371
Farmington, NM 87499
(505) 327–9116

BIBLE BAPTIST SHEPHERD
1105 S. Miller
Farmington, NM 87401
(505) 325–1690

NAVAJO MISSIONS, INC.
Box 1230
Farmington, NM 87499–1230
(505) 325–0255

SAINT BONAVENTURE INDIAN MISSION
& SCHOOL
P.O. Box 610
Thoreau, NM 87323–0610
(505) 862–7847

#### ◆ NEW YORK

AMERICAN BIBLE SOCIETY
1865 Broadway
New York, NY 10023
(212) 408–1200

INTERRELIGIOUS FOUNDATION FOR
COMMUNITY ORGANIZATION (IFCO)
Native American Affairs
402 West 145th St.
New York, NY 10031
(212) 926–5757

NATIONAL COUNCIL OF THE CHURCH OF
CHRIST IN THE UNITED STATES OF
AMERICA
Prophetic Justice Unit
475 Riverside Dr.
New York, NY 10115
(212) 870–2511

NATIVE AMERICAN INTERNATIONAL
CAUCUS/UNITED METHODIST CHURCH
475 Riverside Dr.
New York, NY 10115
(212) 678–6161

#### ◆ NORTH DAKOTA

BENEDICTINE OUTREACH TO THE NATIVE
AMERICAN
Queen of Peace Monastery
Box 370
Belcourt, ND 58316
(701) 477–6167

SAINT ANN'S CATHOLIC CHURCH
P.O. Box 2000
Belcourt, ND 58316–2000
(701) 477–5601

#### ◆ OREGON

INTERACT MINISTRIES
31000 S.E. Kelso Rd.
Boring, OR 97009
(800) 258–3464

#### ◆ PENNSYLVANIA

AMERICAN FRIENDS SERVICE COMMITTEE
Native American Affairs
1501 Cherry St.
Philadelphia, PA 19102
(215) 241–7131

INDIAN COMMITTEE OF THE PHILADELPHIA
YEARLY MEETING OF THE RELIGIOUS
SOCIETY OF FRIENDS
1515 Cherry Street
Philadelphia, PA 19102
(215) 241–7210

#### ◆ SOUTH DAKOTA

ROSEBUD EPISCOPAL CHURCH
Mission, SD 57555
(605) 856–4982

SACRED HEART CHURCH
Pine Ridge, SD 57770
(605) 867–5551

#### ◆ TENNESSEE

NATIVE AMERICAN CHURCH, INC.
P.O. Box 53
Strawberry Plains, TN 37871–0053

#### ◆ UTAH

CHURCH OF JESUS CHRIST OF LATTER
DAY SAINTS
INDIAN COMMITTEE
50 East North Temple St.
Salt Lake City, UT 84111
(801) 240–3016

UTE INDIAN BAPTIST CHURCH
White Rocks Rd.
Roosevelt, UT 84066
(435) 722–2389

#### ◆ WASHINGTON

NORTH AMERICAN INDIAN MINISTRIES
(NAIM)
Box 151
Point Roberts, WA 98281
(604) 946–1227

SWINOMISH SPIRITUAL CENTER
St. Paul's Cathedral
1742 Pioneer Parkway
La Conner, WA 98257
(360) 466–5737

### ◆ WISCONSIN

MIDWEST INDIAN MISSION
Box 187
Crandon, WI 54250–1814
(715) 478–2731

### ◆ WYOMING

OUR FATHER'S HOUSE
P.O. Box 8610
Ethete, WY 82520
(307) 332–2660

## CANADA

### ◆ ALBERTA

EDMONTON NATIVE AMERICAN
  HEALING CENTER
111813 123 St., Suite 101
Edmonton, AB T5L 0G7
(780) 482–5522

INTERACT MINISTRIES
202 11th Ave., S.W.
Calgary, AB I2R 0B8
(800) 258–3464

SACRED HEART PARISH
CHURCH OF THE FIRST PEOPLE
10821 96th St.
Edmonton, AB T5H 2J8
(780) 422–3052

### ◆ BRITISH COLUMBIA

NAIM MINISTRIES
P.O. Box 39
Delta, BC V4K 3N5
(604) 946–1227

NATIVE INDIAN NEWSTART CHRISTIAN
  SOCIETY
1600 East Franklin
Vancouver, BC V5L 1P4
(604) 251–9509

TILLICUM NATIVE CENTRE
2422 Main St.
Vancouver, BC V5T 3E2
(604) 873–3767

### ◆ MANITOBA

ALL NATIVE CIRCLE CONFERENCE
UNITED CHURCH OF CANADA
367 Selkirk Ave.
Winnipeg, MB R2W 2M3
(204) 582–5581

ESKIMO MISSIONS, INC.
P.O. Box 159
St. Norbert, MB R3V 1L6
(204) 269–0474

INDIAN LIFE
Box 3765, Redwood Centre
Winnipeg, MB R2W 3R6
(204) 661 9333

INTERTRIBAL CHRISTIAN
  COMMUNICATIONS (CANADA)
P.O. Box 3765, Redwood Centre
Winnipeg, MB R2W 3R6
(204) 661–9333

MENNONITE NATIVE MINISTRIES
Mennonite Church Canada
600 Shaftsbury Blvd.
Winnipeg, MB R3P 0M4
(204) 888–6781

### ◆ NEW BRUNSWICK

NEW LIFE MISSION
155 Lester Ave.
Moncton, NB E1C 4T8
(506) 859–4277

### ◆ ONTARIO

ABORIGINAL RIGHTS COALITION
153 Laurier Ave. 1
Ottawa, ON K1N 6N8
(613) 235–9956

DAYSTAR NATIVE OUTREACH
P.O. Box 193
Manitowaning, ON P0P 1N0
(705) 859–2623

**FRANCIS SANDY THEOLOGICAL CENTRE**

P.O. Box 446

Paris, ON N3L 3T5

(519) 442-7725

**IMPACT NORTH MINISTRIES**

1 Irvining Dr.

Red Lake, ON P0V 2M0

(870) 727-2291

**JEFF SPILLENAAR MINISTRIES**

24 Midland Dr., Unit 703

Kitchener, ON N2A 2A8

(519) 893-5346

**NORTHERN YOUTH PROGRAMS, INC.**

R. R. 3, Suite 306, Box 1

Dryden, ON P8N 3G2

(807) 937-4421

**SHANTYMEN INTERNATIONAL**

2476 Argentina Rd., Suite 213

Mississauga, ON L5N 6M1

(905) 821-6310

**SPIRIT ALIVE**

P.O. Box 280

Deseronto, ON K0K 1X0

(613) 396-1435

## References

**Religion ·**

Aberle, David F. *The Peyote Religion among the Navaho.* 2d ed. Chicago: University of Chicago Press, 1982.

Allen, Paula G. "The Mythopoeic Vision in Native American Literature: The Problem of Myth." *American Indian Culture and Research Journal* 1, no. 1 (1974): 3–11.

Amoss, Pamela T. *Coast Salish Spirit Dancing: The Survival of an Ancestral Religion.* Seattle: University of Washington Press, 1978.

———. "The Fish God Gave Us: The First Salmon Ceremony Revived." *Arctic Anthropologist* 24, no. 1 (1987): 56–66.

———. "The Indian Shaker Church." In *Northwest Coast,* edited by Wayne Suttles. Vol. 7 of *Handbook of North American Indians,* edited by William C. Sturtevant, 633–639. Washington, D.C.: Smithsonian Institution, 1990.

———. "Symbolic Substitution in the Indian Shaker Church." *Ethnohistory* 25, no. 3 (1978): 225–247.

Barnett, Homer G. *Indian Shakers: A Messianic Cult of the Pacific Northwest.* Carbondale: Southern Illinois University Press, 1957.

Basso, Keith H. "Western Apache Witchcraft." *Anthropological Papers of the University of Arizona.* 15. Tucson: University of Arizona Press, 1969.

———. *Wisdom Sits in Places: Landscape and Language Among the Western Apache.* Albuquerque: University of New Mexico Press, 1996.

Bean, Lowell John and Sylvia Brakke Vane. "Cults and their Transformations." In *California,* edited by Robert F. Heizer. Vol. 8 of *Handbook of North American Indians,* edited by William C. Sturtevant, 662–672. Washington, D.C.: Smithsonian Institution, 1978.

Beck, Peggy V. and Anna L. Walters. *The Sacred: Ways of Knowledge, Sources of Life.* Tsaile, Ariz.: Navajo Community College, 1977.

Blowsnake, Sam. *The Autobiography of a Winnebago Indian,* edited and translated by Paul Radin. New York: Dover, 1963.

Bowden, Henry W. *American Indians and Christian Missions: Studies in Cultural Conflict.* Chicago: University of Chicago Press, 1981.

Brown, Joseph Epes. *The Spiritual Legacy of the American Indian.* New York: Crossroad, 1982.

Bunge, Robert. *An American Urphilosophie: An American Philosophy BP (Before Pragmatism).* Landham, Md.: University Press of America, 1984.

Capps, Walter Holden. *Seeing with a Native Eye: Essays on Native American Religion.* New York: Harper & Row, 1976.

Castile, George P. "The 'Half-Catholic' Movement: Edwin and Myron Eells and the Rise of the Indian Shaker Church." *Pacific Northwest Quarterly* 73, no. 4 (1982): 165–174.

Champagne, Duane. "The Delaware Revitalization Movement of the Early 1760s: A Suggested Reinterpretation." *American Indian Quarterly* 12, no. 2 (1988): 107–125.

Clark, LaVerne Harrell. *They Sang for Horses: The Impact of the Horse on Navajo and Apache Folklore.* Tucson: University of Arizona Press, 1966.

Crumrine, N. Ross and Majorie M. Halpin, eds. *The Power of Symbols: Masks and Masquerade in the Americas.* Vancouver: University of British Columbia Press, 1983.

Deloria, Vine, Jr. *Custer Died for Your Sins: An Indian Manifesto.* New York: Macmillan, 1969.

———. *For This Land: Writings on Religion in America.* New York: Routledge, 1999.

———. *God is Red: A Native View of Religion.* 2nd ed. Golden, Colo.: North American Press, 1992.

————. *We Talk, You Listen: New Tribes, New Turf.* New York: Macmillan, 1970.

DeMallie, Raymond J. "The Lakota Ghost Dance: An Ethnohistorical Account." *Pacific Historical Review* 51, no. 4 (1982): 385–405.

————, ed. *The Sixth Grandfather: Black Elk's Teachings Given to John Neihardt.* Lincoln: University of Nebraska Press, 1984.

Dobyns, Henry F. and Robert C. Euler. *The Ghost Dance of 1889 Among the Pai Indians of Northwestern Arizona.* Prescott, Ariz.: Prescott College Press, 1967.

Dooling, D. M. and Paul Jordan-Smith. *I Become Part of It: Sacred Dimensions in Native American Life.* New York: Parabola Books, 1989.

Erdoes, Richard and Alfonso Ortiz, eds. *American Indian Myths and Legends.* New York: Pantheon Books, 1984.

Farella, John R. *The Main Stalk: A Synthesis of Navajo Philosophy.* Tucson: University of Arizona Press, 1984.

Fogelson, Raymond D. and Richard N. Adams, eds. *The Anthropology of Power: Ethnographic Studies from Asia, Oceania, and the New World.* New York: Academic Press, 1977.

Frigot, Arlette. "Hopi Ceremonial Organization." In *Southwest*, edited by Alfonso Ortiz. Vol. 9 of *Handbook of North American Indians*, edited by William C. Sturtevant, 564–576. Washington, D.C.: Smithsonian Institution, 1979.

Frisbie, Charlotte J. *Navajo Medicine Bundles or Jish: Acquisition, Transmission, and Disposition in the Past and Present.* Albuquerque: University of New Mexico Press, 1987.

Geertz, Armin. *The Invention of Prophecy: Continuity and Meaning in Hopi Indian Religion.* Berkeley and Los Angeles: University of California Press, 1994.

Gill, Sam D. *Mother Earth: An American Story.* Chicago: University of Chicago Press, 1987.

————. *Native American Religions: An Introduction.* Belmont, Calif.: Wadsworth Publishing, 1982.

————. *Native American Religious Action: A Performance Approach to Religion.* Columbia: University of South Carolina Press, 1987.

Goldman, Irving. *The Mouth of Heaven: An Introduction to Kwakiutl Religious Thought.* New York: Wiley, 1975.

Grim, John A. *The Shaman: Patterns of Religious Healing Among the Ojibway Indians.* Norman: University of Oklahoma Press, 1983.

Gunther, Erna. "An Analysis of the First Salmon Ceremony." *American Anthropologist* 28, no. 4 (1926): 605–617.

————. "A Further Analysis of the First Salmon Ceremony." *University of Washington Publications in Anthropology.* 2, no. 5 (1928): 129–173.

Hall, Robert L. *An Archaeology of the Soul: North American Indian Belief and Ritual.* Urbana: University of Illinois Press, 1997.

Hallowell, A. Irving. "Ojibwa Ontology, Behavior, and World View." In *Teachings from the American Earth: Indian Religion and Philosophy*, edited by Dennis Tedlock and Barbara Tedlock, 141–178. New York: Liveright, 1975.

Harrod, Howard L. *The Animals Came Dancing: Native American Sacred Ecology and Animal Kinship.* Tucson: University of Arizona Press, 2000.

————. *Becoming and Remaining a People: Native American Religions on the Northern Plains.* Tucson: University of Arizona Press, 1995.

————. *Renewing the World: Plains Indian Religion and Morality.* Tucson: University of Arizona Press, 1987.

Heizer, Robert F. "Mythology: Regional Patterns and History of Research." In *California*, edited by Robert F. Heizer. Vol. 8 of *Handbook of North American Indians*, edited by William C. Sturtevant, 654–657. Washington, D.C.: Smithsonian Institution, 1978.

Hertzberg, Hazel W. *The Search for an American Indian Identity: Modern Pan-Indian Movements.* Syracuse, N.Y.: Syracuse University Press, 1971.

Honigmann, John J. "Expressive Aspects of Subarctic Indian Culture." In *Subactic*, edited by June Helm. Vol. 6 of *Handbook of North American Indians*, edited by William C. Sturtevant, 718–738. Washington, D.C.: Smithsonian Institution, 1981.

Howard, James H., in collaboration with Willie Lena. *Oklahoma Seminoles: Medicines, Magic, and Religion.* Norman: University of Oklahoma Press, 1984.

Hultkrantz, Åke. *Belief and Worship in Native North America.* Edited by Christopher Vecsey. Syracuse, N.Y.: Syracuse University Press, 1981.

————. "Conditions for the Spread of the Peyote Cult in North America." In *New Religions*, edited by Haralds Biezais, 70–83. Uppsala: Scripta Insitui Donneriani Aboensis, 1975; distributed by Almqvist and Wiksell.

————. "Mythology and Religious Concepts." In *Great Basin*, edited by Warren D'Azevedo, 630–640. Vol. 11 of *Handbook of North American Indians*. Washington, D.C.: Smithsonian Institution, 1986.

————. "Myths in Native North American Religions." In *Native Religious Traditions*, edited by Earle H. Waugh and K. Dad Prithipaul, 77–97. Studies in Religion, 8. Waterloo, Ont.: Wilfred Laurier University Press for the Canadian Corporation for Studies in Religion, 1979.

————. *The Study of American Indian Religions*, edited by Christopher Vecsey. New York: Crossroad, 1983.

Hymes, Dell. *"In Vain I Tried to Tell You": Essays in Native American Ethnopoetics*. Philadelphia: University of Pennsylvania Press, 1981.

———. "Mythology." In *Northwest.*, edited by Wayne Suttles. Vol. 7 of *Handbook of North American Indians*, edited by William C. Sturtevant, 593–601. Washington, D.C.: Smithsonian Institution, 1990.

Jorgensen, Joseph G. "Ghost Dance, Bear Dance, and Sun Dance." In *Great Basin*, edited by Warren D'Azevedo. Vol. 11 of *Handbook of North American Indians*, edited by William C. Sturtevant, 660–672. Washington, D.C.: Smithsonian Institution, 1986.

———. *The Sun Dance Religion: Power for the Powerless*. Chicago: University of Chicago Press, 1972.

Kan, Sergei. *Symbolic Immortality: The Tlingit Potlatch of the Nineteenth Century*. Washington, D.C.: Smithsonian Institution, 1989.

Kongas, Elli Kaija. "The Earth Diver." *Ethnohistory* 7, no. 2 (1960): 151–180.

Kroeber, Alfred L. and Edward W. Gifford. *World Renewal: A Cult System of Native Northwest California*. Anthropological Records, vol. 13, no. 1. Berkeley: University of California Press, 1949.

La Barre, Weston. *The Ghost Dance: Origins of Religion*. Garden City, N.Y.: Doubleday, 1970.

Lesser, Alexander. *The Pawnee Ghost Dance Hand Game: Ghost Dance Revival and Ethnic Identity*. Madison: University of Wisconsin Press, 1978.

Lieber, Michael D. "Opposition to Peyotism among the Western Shoshone: The Message of Traditional Belief." *Man* 7, no. 3 (1972): 387–396.

Linton, Ralph. "Nativistic Movements." *American Anthropologist* 45, no. 2 (1943): 230–240. (Reprinted in several editions of *Reader in Comparative Religion*, edited by William A. Lessa and Evon Z. Vogt.)

Loftin, John D. *Religion and Hopi Life in the Twentieth Century*. Bloomington: Indiana University Press, 1991.

Lowie, Robert H. *The Crow Indians*. New York: Holt, Farrar and Rinehart, 1935.

Marriott, Alice L. and Carol K. Rachlin. *American Indian Mythology*. New York: Crowell, 1968.

———. *Peyote*. New York: Crowell, 1971.

Martin, Joel. *Sacred Revolt: The Muskogees' Struggle for a New World*. Boston: Beacon Press, 1991.

McLoughlin, William G. *The Cherokee Ghost Dance: Essays on the Southeastern Indians, 1789–1861*. Macon, Ga.: Mercer, 1984.

Meighan, Clement W. and Francis A. Riddell. *The Maru Cult of the Pomo Indians: A California Ghost Dance Survival*. Southwest Museum Papers, no. 23. Los Angeles: Southwest Museum, 1972.

Merkur, Daniel. *Becoming Half Hidden: Shamanism and Initiation among the Inuit*. Stockholm: Almqvist & Wiksell International, 1985.

Mooney, James. *The Ghost Dance Religion and the Sioux Outbreak of 1890*. Annual Report. Smithsonian Institution Bureau of American Ethnology, vol. 14, pt. 2. Washington, D.C.: GPO, 1896; Chicago: University of Chicago Press, 1965; Lincoln: University of Nebraska Press, 1991.

Morrison, Kenneth M. "Baptism and Alliance: The Symbolic Mediations of Religious Syncretism." *Ethnohistory* 37, no. 4 (1990): 416–437.

———. "The Cosmos as Intersubjective: Native American Other-Than-Human Persons." In *Indigenous Religions: A Companion*, edited by Graham Harvey, 23–36. London: Cassell, 2000.

———. *The Embattled Northeast: The Elusive Ideal of Alliance in Abenaki-Euramerican Relations*. Berkeley and Los Angeles: University of California Press, 1984.

———. "The Mythological Sources of Abenaki Catholicism: A Case Study of the Social History of Power." *Religion: Journal of Religion and Religions* 11, no. 3 (1981): 235–263.

———. "Towards a History of Intimate Encounters: Algonkian Folklore, Jesuit Missionaries, and Kiwakwe, the Cannibal Giant." *American Indian Culture and Research Journal* 3, no. 4 (1979): 51–80.

Moses, L. G. "Jack Wilson and the Indian Service: The Response of the BIA and the Ghost Dance Prophet." *American Indian Quarterly* 5, no. 4 (1979): 295–316.

Moses, L. G., and Margaret C. Szasz. "'My Father, Have Pity on Me!' Indian Revitalization Movements of the Late-Nineteenth Century." *Journal of the West* 23, no. 1 (1984): 5–15.

Mountain Wolf Woman. *Mountain Wolf Woman, Sister of Crashing Thunder: The Autobiography of a Winnebago Indian*, edited Nancy O. Lurie. Ann Arbor: University of Michigan Press, 1961.

Nash, Philleo. "The Place of Religious Revitalization in the Formation of the Intercultural Community on Klamath Reservation." In *Social Anthropology of North American Tribes*, edited by Fred Eggan, 377–442. Enlarged edition. Chicago: University of Chicago Press, 1955.

Ortiz, Alfonso. *The Tewa World: Space, Time, Being and Becoming in a Pueblo Society*. Chicago: University of Chicago Press, 1969.

Overholt, Thomas W. "The Ghost Dance of 1890 and the Nature of the Prophetic Process." *Ethnohistory* 21, no. 1 (1974): 37–63.

Paper, Jordan. *Offering Smoke: The Sacred Pipe and Native American Religion*. Moscow, Idaho: University of Idaho Press, 1988.

Parker, Arthur C. *Seneca Myths and Folk Tales*. Lincoln: University of Nebraska Press, 1989.

Parkhill, Thomas C. *Weaving Ourselves into the Land: Charles Godfrey Leland, "Indians," and the Study of Native American Religions.* Albany: State University Press of New York, 1997.

Pflug, Melissa A. *Ritual and Myth in Odawa Revitalization: Reclaiming a Sovereign Place.* Norman: University of Oklahoma Press, 1998.

Powell, Peter J. *Sweet Medicine: The Continuing Role of the Sacred Arrows, the Sun Dance, and the Sacred Buffalo Hat in Northern Cheyenne History.* 2 vols. Norman: University of Oklahoma Press, 1969.

Powers, William K. *Oglala Religion.* Lincoln: University of Nebraska Press, 1977.

Rachlin, Carol K. "Native American Church in Oklahoma." *Chronicles of Oklahoma* 42, no. 3 (1964): 262–272.

Radin, Paul. *The Trickster: A Study in American Indian Mythology.* New York: Philosophical Library, 1956.

———. *The Winnebago Tribe.* Annual Report. Smithsonian Institution Bureau of American Ethnology, vol. 37. Washington, D.C.: GPO, 1923. Reprint. Lincoln: University of Nebraska Press, 1970.

Reichard, Gladys A. *Navaho Religion: A Study of Symbolism.* 2nd ed. Princeton, N.J.: Princeton University Press, 1974; Tucson: University of Arizona Press, 1983.

Ricketts, Mac Linscott. "The North American Indian Trickster." *History of Religions* 5, no. 2 (1966): 327–350.

Rooth, Anna Birgitta. "The Creation Myths of the North American Indians." *Anthropos* 52, fasc. 3–4 (1957): 497–508.

Ruby, Robert H. and John A. Brown. *Dreamer-Prophets of the Columbia Plateau: Smohalla and Skolaskin.* Norman: University of Oklahoma Press, 1989.

Schwarz, Maureen Trudelle. *Molded in the Image of Changing Woman: Navajo Views of the Human Body and Personhood.* Tucson: University of Arizona Press, 1997.

Shipek, Florence C. "History of Southern California Mission Indians." In *California,* edited by Robert F. Heizer. Vol. 8 of *Handbook of North American Indians,* edited by William C. Sturtevant, 610–618. Washington, D.C.: Smithsonian Institution, 1978.

Slotkin, James S. *The Peyote Religion: A Study in Indian-White Relations.* Glencoe, Ill: Free Press, 1956.

Smith, Theresa S. *The Island of the Anishnaabeg: Thunderers and Water Monsters in the Traditional Ojibwe Life-World.* Moscow, Idaho: University of Idaho Press, 1995.

Speck, Frank G. *Naskapi: The Savage Hunters of the Labrador Peninsula.* New ed. Norman: University of Oklahoma Press, 1977.

Spier, Leslie. *The Sun Dance of the Plains Indians: Its Development and Diffusion.* Anthropological Papers of the American Museum of Natural History, v. 16, pt. 7. New York: The Trustees, 1921.

Steinmetz, Paul B. *Pipe, Bible, and Peyote among the Oglala Lakota: A Study in Religious Identity.* Knoxville: University of Tennessee Press, 1990.

Stewart, Omer C. "The Peyote Religion." In *Great Basin,* edited by Warren D'Azevedo. Vol. 11 of *Handbook of North American Indians,* edited by William C. Sturtevant, 673–681. Washington, DC: Smithsonian Institution, 1986.

———. *Peyote Religion: A History.* Norman: University of Oklahoma Press, 1987.

Tedlock, Dennis. "From Prayer to Reprimand." In *Language in Religious Practice,* edited by William J. Samarin, 72–83. Rowley, Mass.: Newbury House Publishers, 1976.

———. "The Spoken Word and the Work of Interpretation in American Indian Religion." In *Myth, Symbol, and Reality,* edited by Alan M. Olson, 129–144. Notre Dame, Ind.: University of Notre Dame Press, 1980.

———. "Zuni Religion and World View." In *Southwest,* edited by Alfonso Ortiz. Vol. 9 of *Handbook of North American Indians,* edited by William C. Sturtevant, 499–500. Washington, D.C.: Smithsonian Institution, 1979.

Thompson, Stith. *Tales of the North American Indians.* Cambridge: Harvard University Press, 1929.

Tooker, Elisabeth. *The Iroquois Ceremonial of Midwinter.* Syracuse, N.Y.: Syracuse University Press, 1970.

Treat, James, ed. *Native and Christian: Indigenous Voices on Religious Identity in the United States and Canada.* New York: Routledge, 1996.

Underhill, Ruth M. *Red Man's Religion: Beliefs and Practices of the Indians North of Mexico.* Chicago: University of Chicago Press, 1965.

Vecsey, Christopher. *Imagine Ourselves Richly: Mythic Narratives of North American Indians.* New York: Crossroad, 1988.

———. *On the Padres' Trail.* Notre Dame, Ind.: University of Notre Dame Press, 1996.

———. *The Paths of Kateri's Kin.* Notre Dame, Ind.: University of Notre Dame Press, 1997.

———. *Where the Two Roads Meet.* Notre Dame, Ind.: University of Notre Dame Press, 1999.

Viola, Herman J. *After Columbus: The Smithsonian Chronicle of the North American Indians.* Washington, D.C.: Smithsonian Books; New York: Orion Books, 1990.

Voget, Fred W. *The Shoshoni-Crow Sun Dance.* Norman: University of Oklahoma Press, 1984.

Walens, Stanley. *Feasting with Cannibals: An Essay on Kwakiutl Cosmology.* Princeton, N.J.: Princeton University Press, 1981.

Walker, Deward E., Jr. *Conflict and Schism in Nez Percé Acculturation: A Study of Religion and Politics*. Pullman: Washington State University Press, 1968.

———, ed. *Witchcraft and Sorcery of the American Native Peoples*. Moscow, Idaho: University of Idaho Press, 1989.

Wallace, Anthony F. C. *Death and Rebirth of the Seneca*. New York: Knopf, 1970.

———. "The Dekanawidah Myth Analyzed as the Record of a Revitalization Movement." *Ethnohistory* 5, no. 2 (1958): 118–130.

———. "Handsome Lake and the Great Revival in the West." *American Quarterly* 4, no. 2 (1952): 149–165.

———. "Religion as a Revitalization Process." In *Religion: An Anthropological View*, by Anthony F. C. Wallace, 30–38. New York: Random House, 1966.

Weaver, Jace, ed. *Native American Religious Identity: Unforgotten Gods*. Maryknoll, N.Y.: Orbis Books, 1998.

———. *That the People Might Live: Native American Literatures and Native American Community*. New York: Oxford University Press, 1997.

Williamson, Ray A. *Living the Sky: The Cosmos of the American Indian*. Norman: University of Oklahoma Press, 1984.

Witherspoon, Gary. "The Central Concepts of Navajo World View (I)." *Linguistics: An International Review* 119 (1974): 41–59.

———. "The Central Concepts of Navajo World View (II)." *Linguistics: An International Review* 161 (1975): 69–88.

———. *Language and Art in the Navajo Universe*. Ann Arbor: University of Michigan Press, 1977.

Witthoft, John. *Green Corn Ceremonialism in the Eastern Woodlands*. University of Michigan. Museum of Anthropology. Occasional Contributions, no. 13. Ann Arbor: University of Michigan Press, 1949.

Zolbrod, Paul G., trans. *Dine Bahane: The Navajo Creation Story*. Albuquerque: University of New Mexico Press, 1984.

*Kenneth M. Morrison*

## Continuity of Traditional Belief Systems

Beck, Peggy V. and Anna Lee Walters. *The Sacred: Ways of Knowledge, Sources of Life*. Tsaile, Ariz.: Navajo Community College Press, 1977.

Berkhofer, Robert F., Jr. *The White Man's Indian: Images of the American Indian from Columbus to the Present*. New York: Knopf, 1978.

Black Elk. *The Sacred Pipe: Black Elk's Account of the Seven Rites of the Oglala Sioux*. Recorded and edited by Joseph Epes Brown. Norman: University of Oklahoma Press, 1953.

Capps, Walter H., ed. *Seeing with a Native Eye: Essays on Native American Religion*. New York: Harper & Row, 1976.

Deloria, Vine, Jr. *For This Land: Writings on Religion in America*. New York: Routledge, 1999.

———. *God is Red*. New York: Grosset and Dunlap, 1973.

Dockstader, Frederick J. *Indian Art in America: The Arts and Crafts of the North American Indians*. Greenwich, Conn.: New York Graphic Society, 1961.

Fire, John, and Richard Erdoes. *Lame Deer: Seeker of Visions*. New York: Simon and Schuster, 1972.

Gill, Sam D. *Native American Religions: An Introduction*. Belmont, Calif.: Wadsworth, 1982.

Irwin, Lee. *The Dream Seekers: Native American Visionary Traditions of the Great Plains*. Norman: University of Oklahoma Press, 1994.

Jennings, Francis. *The Invasion of America: Indians, Colonialism, and the Cant of Conquest*. Chapel Hill: Published for the Institute of Early American History and Culture by University of North Carolina Press, 1975.

Jones, David. *Sanapia: Comanche Medicine Woman*. New York: Holt, Rinehart and Winston, 1972.

Loftin, John D. *Religion and Hopi Life in the Twentieth Century*. Bloomington, Ind.: Indiana University Press, 1991.

Martin, Calvin, ed. *The American Indian and the Problem of History*. New York: Oxford University Press, 1987.

Martin, Joel. *Native American Religion*. New York: Oxford University Press, 1999.

Spicer, Edward H., ed. *Perspectives in American Indian Culture Change*. Chicago: University of Chicago Press, 1961.

Talayesva, Don. *Sun Chief: The Autobiography of a Hopi Indian*. Edited by Leo W. Simmons. New Haven, Conn.: Yale University Press, 1942.

Tedlock, Dennis and Barbara Tedlock, eds. *Teachings from the American Earth: Indian Religion and Philosophy*. New York: Liveright, 1975.

*John Loftin*

## Christianity and Native Americans

Axtell, James. *The Invasion Within: The Contest of Cultures in Colonial North America*. New York, Oxford: Oxford University Press, 1985.

Beck, Peggy V., and Walters, A. L. *The Sacred: Ways of Knowledge, Sources of Life*. Tsaile, Arizona: Navajo Community College, 1977.

Cogley, Richard W. *John Eliot's Mission to the Indians before King Philip's War*. Cambridge: Harvard University Press, 1999.

Deloria, Vine, Jr. *For This Land: Writings on Religion in America.* New York: Routledge, 1999.

———. *God is Red.* New York: Grosset and Dunlap, 1973.

Gannon, Michael V. *The Cross in the Sand: The Early Catholic Church in Florida 1513–1870.* 2nd ed. Gainesville: University of Florida Press, 1983.

Schultz, Jack M. *The Seminole Baptist Churches of Oklahoma: Maintaining a Traditional Community.* Norman: University of Oklahoma Press, 1999.

Steinmetz, Paul B., S.J. *Pipe, Bible, and Peyote among the Oglala Lakota: A Study in Religious Identity.* Syracuse: Syracuse University Press, 1998.

Treat, James, ed. *Native and Christian: Indigenous Voices on Religious Identity in the United States and Canada.* New York: Routledge, 1996.

Vecsey, Christopher. *On the Padres' Trail.* Notre Dame, Ind.: University of Notre Dame Press, 1996.

———. *The Paths of Kateri's Kin.* Notre Dame, Ind.: University of Notre Dame Press, 1997.

———. *Where the Two Roads Meet.* Notre Dame, Ind.: University of Notre Dame Press, 1999.

*Clara Sue Kidwell*

## Syncretic and Pluralistic Beliefs

Aberle, David F. *The Peyote Religion Among the Navaho.* 2d ed. Chicago: University of Chicago Press, 1982.

Allen, Paula G. *The Sacred Hoop: Recovering the Feminine in American Indian Traditions.* Boston: Beacon Press, 1986.

Anderson, Edward F. *Peyote, the Divine Cactus.* 2nd ed. Tucson: University of Arizona Press, 1996.

Beck, Peggy V. and Anna L. Walters. *The Sacred: Ways of Knowledge, Sources of Life.* Tsaile, Ariz.: Navajo Community College Press, 1977.

Bowden, Henry W. *American Indians and Christian Missions: Studies in Cultural Conflict.* Chicago: University of Chicago Press, 1981.

Champagne, Duane. *American Indian Societies: Some Strategies and Conditions of Political and Cultural Survival.* Cambridge, Mass.: Cultural Survival, 1985.

———. "Social Structure, Revitalization Movements and State Building: Social Change in Four Native American Societies." *American Sociological Review* 48, no. 6 (1983): 754–763.

Deloria, Vine, Jr. *Behind the Trail of Broken Treaties: An Indian Declaration of Independence.* New York: Delacorte, 1974.

———. *God is Red.* 2nd ed. Golden, Colo.: Fulcrum, 1994.

———. "A Simple Question of Humanity: The Moral Dimensions of the Reburial Issue." *NARF Legal Review* 14, no. 4 (1989): 1–12.

DeMallie, Raymond J. and Douglas R. Parks, eds. "The Lakota Ghost Dance: An Ethnohistorical Account." *Pacific Historical Review* 51, no. 4 (1982): 385–405.

Dills, Barbara and Paulette D'Auteuil-Robideau. *In Defense of the Che Wana: Fishing Rights on the Columbia River.* Portland, Oreg.: Columbia River Defense Project, 1987.

Du Bois, Cora. *The Feather Cult of the Middle Columbia.* Menasha, Wis.: George Banta, 1938.

Durkheim, Emile. *The Elementary Forms of Religious Life: A Study in Religious Sociology.* London: G. Allen & Unwin; New York: Macmillan, 1915.

Echo-Hawk, Walter. "Native American Religious Liberty: Five Hundred Years After Columbus." *American Indian Culture and Research Journal* 17, no. 3 (1993): 33–52.

Echo-Hawk, Walter, vol. ed. "Special Edition. Repatriation of American Indian Remains." *American Indian Culture and Research Journal* 16, no. 2 (1992): 1–200.

Erdoes, Richard. *Crying for a Dream: The World through Native American Eyes.* Santa Fe, N.M.: Bear & Co., 1989.

Farb, Peter. "The Hopes of the Oppressed." In *Anthropology 1985/1986,* edited by Elvio Angeloni. Guilford, Conn.: Dushkin Pub. Group, 1986.

Fire, John and Richard Erdoes. *Lame Deer: Seeker of Visions.* New York: Simon and Schuster, 1972.

Gibson, Arrell M. *The American Indian: Prehistory to Present.* Lexington, Mass.: D. C. Heath, 1980.

Gill, Sam D. *Native American Religions, An Introduction.* Belmont, Calif.: Wadsworth, 1982.

———. *Native American Religious Action: A Performance Approach to Religion.* Columbia, S.C.: University of South Carolina Press, 1987.

Graymont, Barbara. *The Iroquois.* New York: Chelsea House, 1988.

Green, Rayna, et al. *American Indian Sacred Objects, Skeletal Remains, Repatriation and Reburial: A Resource Guide.* Washington, D.C.: The American Indian Program, National Museum of American History, Smithsonian Institution, 1994.

Hoebel, E. Adamson. *The Cheyennes: Indians of the Great Plains.* New York: Holt, 1960.

Hinton, Leanne. "Ishi's Brain." *News from Native California* 13, no. 1 (1999): 4–9.

Hultkrantz, Åke. "A Decade of Progress: Works on North American Indian Religions in the 1980s." In *Religion in Native North America,* edited by Christopher Vecsey, 167–201. Moscow: University of Idaho Press, 1990.

———. *The Religions of the American Indians.* Berkeley and Los Angeles: University of California Press, 1979.

Jorgensen, Joseph G. *The Sun Dance Religion: Power for the Powerless.* Chicago: University of Chicago Press, 1972.

Kehoe, Alice B. *The Ghost Dance: Ethnohistory and Revitalization.* New York: Holt, Rinehart, and Winston, 1989.

La Barre, Weston. *The Peyote Cult.* 5th edition, enl. Norman: University of Oklahoma Press, 1989.

Lawson, Paul E. and C. Patrick Morris. "The Native American Church and the New Court: The *Smith* Case and Indian Religious Freedoms." *American Indian Culture and Research Journal* 15, no. 1 (1991): 79–91.

Lobo, Susan and Steve Talbot. *Native American Voices: A Reader.* 2nd edition. Upper Saddle River, NJ: Prentice Hall, 2001.

Martin, Kallen M. "The Beginning of Respect: The U.S. Repatriation Law." *Native Americas* 14, no. 3 (1997): 24–29.

McElwain, Thomas. "'The Rainbow Will Carry Me': The Language of Seneca Christianity as Reflected in Hymns." In *Religion In Native North America,* edited by Christopher Vecsey, 83–103. Moscow: University of Idaho Press, 1990.

Neihardt, John G. *The Sixth Grandfather: Black Elk's Teachings Given to John Neihardt.* Edited by Raymond J. DeMallie. Lincoln: University of Nebraska Press, 1984.

Porterfield, Amanda. "American Indian Spirituality as a Countercultural Movement." In *Religion in Native North America,* edited by Christopher Vecsey, 152–164. Moscow: University of Idaho Press, 1990.

Rice, Julian. *Black Elk's Story: Distinguishing Its Lakota Purpose.* Albuquerque: University of New Mexico Press, 1991.

Ruby, Robert H. *John Slocum and the Indian Shaker Church.* Norman: University of Oklahoma Press, 1996.

Slagle, Al Logan. "Tolowa Indian Shakers and the Role of Prophecy at Smith River, California." In *American Indian Prophets: Religious Leaders and Revitalization Movements,* edited by Clifford Trafzer, 115–136. Sacramento, Calif.: Sierra Oaks Pub., 1986.

Spicer, Edward H. *Cycles of Conquest: The Impact of Spain, Mexico, and the United States on the Indians of the Southwest, 1533–1960.* Tucson: University of Arizona Press, 1962.

———. *A Short History of the Indians of the United States.* New York: Van Nostrand Reinhold, 1969.

Steinmetz, Paul B. *Pipe, Bible, and Peyote Among the Oglala Lakota: A Study in Religious Identity.* 1st Syracuse University Press ed. Syracuse, N.Y.: Syracuse University Press, 1998.

———. "The Sacred Pipe in American Indian Religions." *American Indian Culture and Research Journal* 8, no. 3 (1984): 27–80.

Stewart, Omer C. *Peyote Religion: A History.* Norman: University of Oklahoma Press, 1987.

Stuart, Paul. "The Christian Church and Indian Community Life." *Journal of Ethnic Studies* 9, no. 3 (1981): 47–55.

Talbot, Steve. "Desecration and American Indian Religious Freedom." *Journal of Ethnic Studies* 12, no. 4 (1985): 1–18.

Tedlock, Dennis and Barbara Tedlock. *Teachings from the American Earth: Indian Religion and Philosophy.* New York: Liveright, 1975.

Trafzer, Clifford, ed. *American Indian Prophets: Religious Leaders and Revitalization Movements.* Sacramento, Calif.: Sierra Oaks Pub., 1986.

Trope, Jack F. "Existing Federal Law and the Protection of Sacred Sites: Possibilities and Limitations." In *Cultural Survival Quarterly* 19, no. 4 (1996): 30–39.

Utley, Robert M. *The Last Days of the Sioux Nation.* New Haven: Yale University Press, 1963.

Vecsey, Christopher. "American Indian Environmental Religions." In *American Indian Environments: Ecological Issues in Native American History,* edited by Christopher Vecsey and Robert W. Venables, 1–37. Syracuse, N.Y.: Syracuse University Press, 1980.

———, ed. *Religion in Native North America.* Moscow: University of Idaho Press, 1990.

Wallace, Anthony F. C. *The Death and Rebirth of the Seneca.* New York: Vintage Books, 1972.

Williams, Walter L. *The Spirit and the Flesh: Sexual Diversity in American Indian Culture.* Boston: Beacon Press, 1986.

*Steve Talbot*

# Women and Gender Relations

◆ Women in Traditional Native Societies
◆ Multiple Genders in Historical and Contemporary Native American Communities
◆ Contemporary American Indian Women
◆ Rights and Roles of First Nations Women of Canada

## ◆ WOMEN IN TRADITIONAL NATIVE SOCIETIES

The roles that women fulfilled in Native societies varied widely depending upon the nation's economy, social system, and political structure. However, a number of patterns emerge when different societies are compared. In general, women participated as equal members of their communities in most, if not all, domains of life. They contributed to household subsistence, helped form group consensus when family or community decisions had to be made, and figured prominently in rituals.

Two basic types of economic strategies prevailed in Native America: foraging (hunting and gathering) and horticulture (small-scale farming). Much of the work was assigned according to gender. In foraging societies, women gathered wild plants, fruits, and nuts while men hunted animals and caught fish. Women might also catch birds and fish and might accompany men on hunting expeditions. In most horticultural societies, women were primarily responsible for planting, weeding, and harvesting crops, although men usually cleared new fields and might also help with the harvest. However, men were the farmers in the Puebloan nations of the Southwest, and among the Dine, or Navajo, farming was a cooperative effort of women and men.

Craft-production was often assigned according to gender as well. Women excelled as basket-makers in California and the Great Basin; Inuit women made water-tight sealskin or caribou boots, mittens, and parkas necessary for survival in the Arctic; women in Northwest Pacific Coast societies made baskets, hats, and robes out of cedar bark; Dine women wove woolen blankets; women in the Plains made buffalo-hide tipis; and Puebloan women were skilled potters.

Women usually crafted clothing and household utensils, while men made the tools and weapons necessary for their work.

In addition to direct subsistence work, women were responsible for household tasks. They prepared meals, kept living quarters in good condition, and cared for their children. Men, too, were often involved and affectionate caretakers of children.

Although a division of labor along lines of gender existed, Native economies were characterized by a high degree of role flexibility. Men and women might accompany and aid their spouses whenever necessary and many tasks required joint labor for their completion. For example, Mi'kmaqs in eastern Canada divided some crafts into constituent parts assigned to women and men. Men worked with wood, making frames of canoes and snowshoes and shafts of bows and arrows, while women made the bark coverings of canoes, the sinew webbing on snowshoes, and the quivers of arrows. Southwestern Hopi houses were jointly built. Men cut and assembled sandstone slabs and then women smoothed and plastered the interior walls. Among the Pomoan nations of California, fishing was men's work but women collected shellfish and seaweed. Women gathered plants, seeds, and roots, but men helped collect acorns and insects. Women produced baskets and other items made from fibers, but men made fish-baskets and both women and men made basketry cradles.

Native American social life generally centered on bonds among kin who depended on one another for economic and emotional support and were linked through political and ceremonial networks. Women's roles in kin groups varied depending upon the prevailing system of descent. Some Native nations followed

745

principles of bilateral descent in which a person's maternal and paternal relatives were equally recognized. Others practiced systems of unilineal reckoning in which a person belonged to only his or her mother's or father's family. In matrilineal systems, a child belonged to her or his mother's kin group, while in patrilineal systems children were members of their father's group. In societies following matrilineal descent, women played a significant role as heads of familial lines or clans and as recognized heads-of-households. Women's prominence in matrilineal societies was enhanced by preferences for matrilocal residence, a married couple living with or near the wife's family. This pattern helped strengthen solidarity among women. Bonds between mothers and daughters were especially intense since they not only shared kinship but also worked cooperatively and resided in the same household or compound for most of their lives. For similar reasons, bonds between sisters were also strong. In addition, matrilocal residence provided women with emotional support in the event of conflicts with their husbands. For example, Iroquoian households in the Northeast were composed of an elder couple, their daughters, their daughters' husbands and children, and their unmarried sons. Such extended families, living together in a large house called a longhouse, functioned as a cooperative economic and social unit. The head of a matrilineage collectively controlled and allocated land that she and her daughters farmed. The women produced and distributed the crops. Products of men's labor, including meat and fish, were brought in to their households and then distributed by their mothers or wives. In southwestern Zuni villages, couples also lived with the wife's parents and kin. A group of related nuclear families occupied adjacent rooms in a block of houses. Zuni men did the farming but the land was controlled by their wife's matrilineage. Women were the recognized heads-of-household and prepared and distributed the food that was produced.

In contrast, where families followed patrilineal descent, women tended to be less central to family cohesion and stability. Preferences for patrilocal residence (with or near husband's kin) helped strengthen bonds between men and rendered women somewhat peripheral. However, in many patrilineal societies, a young married couple often began their life together by residing with the wife's family for a period of time, perhaps a year or two or until their first child was born. During this time, the husband helped his wife's father and contributed meat or produce to their household. Although the couple eventually might move to the husband's family's home or village, a transitional period of residence with the wife's kin allowed the woman to establish her marriage within the protective and supportive context of her own relatives.

Patterns of kin affiliation and allegiance in bilateral societies were most variable. Nomadic foraging societies tended to favor establishment of bonds among men since men cooperated together in hunting, trading, and warfare, whereas women's work was less dependent on lifelong ties of cooperation. Among settled, farming peoples with bilateral descent, no single system of affiliation seems to have been preferred.

Although monogamy was the norm for most people, plural marriages were also possible in some Native societies. Polygyny, a marriage between one man and two or more women, was the more common type, although polyandry, or a marriage between one woman and two or more men, was possible as well. Where polygyny occurred, it indicated the wealth and prestige of certain men rather than the subordination of women.

Significant indicators of gender equality are found in attitudes toward women's and men's sexual behaviors, family rights, and sex-preferences for children. In most Native nations, it was traditionally considered normal and natural for people to engage in sexual activity before marriage. Norms for boys and girls were similar. In addition, although adultery was not condoned, the negative repercussions were the same for an errant husband or wife. Their behavior might be criticized and might provide grounds for divorce but severe punishment such as beatings was rare. Wives and husbands had equal rights to seek a divorce from an unhappy marriage. In most societies, violence against women in the form of beatings or rape was rare or even unknown. Finally, where a family's preferences for a son or daughter were stated, the pattern was consistent with the system of kinship descent. Daughters were desired in societies with matrilineal descent while sons were preferred in patrilineal nations. Such preferences therefore centered on the continuity of the kin group rather than on evaluations of the worthiness of girls or boys.

Contrary to generally equal gender relations in Native America, Inuit men did exert some forms of dominance over women. For instance, some violence against women was tolerated: husbands who suspected or imagined that their wives were unfaithful might beat them; women alone might be subjected to abduction or rape. Preference for sons was expressed in some regions, especially in the central Arctic where it was accompanied by female infanticide. Where it occurred, female infanticide led to sex imbalances in the adult population, creating competition among men for wives that in turn motivated husbands to exert greater vigilance and control over their wives out of fear that their wives would desert them for other men. And in some parts of the western Arctic, men might use the sexual services of their wives to cement trading partnerships with other men. Visiting partners were granted the right to have sexual intercourse with each other's wives. It is unclear from the documented evidence whether the women consented freely or were coerced into such relationships.

Inuit gender behavior and attitudes may have resulted from the male monopoly on obtaining resources in a harsh and dangerous environment. Although women's labor was necessary for group survival, especially their work making water-tight clothing and boots, men's hunting and fishing activities contributed the great majority of foods. Men therefore were seen as directly and independently productive, whereas women were economically somewhat peripheral and dependent. Competition for resources in a hazardous setting where success was uncertain led to some degree of fearfulness or suspicion between members of different communities and perhaps among people within a settlement as well. In such a context, men may have translated their centrality to subsistence and survival into personal dominance over women. Still, male dominance was not as intense as in some societies elsewhere in the world. An initial period of residence near the wife's kin in the early years of marriage helped protect a woman's interests. Women were usually supported by their relatives in conflicts with their husbands and could leave an abusive spouse. Elder and accomplished women were respected and their advice was sought after and listened to. Symbols of women's power were transmitted by beliefs in important female spirit beings.

Despite differences in kinship and family composition, a person's individual rights and autonomy were usually respected in Native communities: women and men were considered equally independent and able to make decisions for themselves free from coercion by others. Of course, people did seek counsel from others whom they respected and often followed the advice given but were rarely compelled to do so. Family and community decisions were reached after consultation among the interested people. In informal contexts, women contributed equally to group discussions and decision-making processes. Women of skill, intelligence, and valued personality traits, such as generosity, cooperativeness, and composure, were looked to for advice. Through their wisdom, experience, and example they were able to influence others.

In societies with formalized leadership roles and decision-making bodies, different patterns of women's participation are found. Among the Iroquois, men's and women's functions were clearly demarcated. Women who were heads of clans, or clan mothers, selected the men from their own kin groups to be formally installed as clan leaders, or chiefs. Chiefs never made decisions independent from kin group and community consensus. They received advice from three separate caucuses made up of women, elder men, and young men (active hunters and warriors). If chiefs took actions contrary to their constituents' wishes, they were likely to be demoted or impeached by the clan mothers who had chosen them for office. Therefore, although women did not function as chiefs, they clearly contributed to the formation of group opinion and acted to protect their interests. Elsewhere, although men predominated as community leaders or chiefs in all nations, women might also occupy such roles. In nations of New England and the Southeast, female chiefs served their villages as leaders, advisors, spokespeople, and negotiators. Some figured prominently in the colonial history of the seventeenth and eighteenth centuries. In Pomoan nations in California, some villages had both male and female chiefs. Female chiefs, who were usually sisters or daughters of male chiefs, had somewhat different roles in different communities. In Central Pomo settlements, women and men performed similar functions except that female chiefs did not make public addresses, speaking instead through a male messenger. Coastal Pomo female chiefs prepared foods for communal ceremonials. And among the Kwakwaka'wakw (or Kwakiutls) of coastal British Columbia, inheritance of lineage chieftainships passed from the previous incumbent to the eldest child, whether son or daughter. However, if a woman became a chief, she usually relinquished the position to her eldest child, if a son, when he was of age.

Finally, Native women took an active part in family and community ceremonial life. In each of the Iroquois nations, fifty women and fifty men served as faithkeepers, planning annual calendric rituals of thanksgiving that were tied to the seasonal round of planting and harvesting. Among the Hidatsas and other settled villagers of the eastern Plains, women belonged to a series of four age-grade societies having social and ritual functions. A woman first entered the system in her late teens and then proceeded through the four grades. As a result of membership in and passage through the set of ceremonial societies, women formed close bonds with others outside their own kin group, strengthening solidarity among women. The most prestigious of the associations were the Goose Society for women in their thirties and forties and the White Buffalo Cow Society for elders. Members of the Goose Society performed planting and earth-renewal rites in the spring when the water birds returned to the region after fall and winter migrations. They conducted rites in the summer and fall as well, giving thanks for good crops and successful harvests. Members of the White Buffalo Cow Society held ceremonies during the winter to attract buffalo near the camps so that the animals could be more easily hunted in that difficult season.

Women in nomadic Plains nations also had significant roles in communal rituals. Although Sun Dance procedures and participants varied from nation to nation, women were often in charge of blessing the Sun Dance grounds and of selecting the sacred center pole of the Sun Dance lodge. And among the Kwakwaka'wakw, female shaman performed the Towidi dances, one of the most dramatic dances of the winter ceremonial cycle. The shaman accomplished acts of spirit power such as giving birth to giant animals, producing serpents out of the air, making birds fly around the house, or altering the cycles of the moon.

Girls in many Native nations participated in puberty rituals when they came of age. Apache girls were the center of attention during a complex, four-day ceremony that publicly celebrated their menarche. The rites focused on the girls' physical and social maturity. During the event, the girl was identified with the central Apache deity, Changing Woman, absorbing her powers to heal and bring good fortune. In the Plains, girls (and boys) might go on vision quests when they came of age, seeking spirit powers through direct contact with spirit beings who came to them in intensely personal and powerful visionary experiences. In some nations in the Northeast, California, and the Great Basin, girls at puberty were separated from their households, spending several days in a small hut in the company of female relatives who instructed them in the responsibilities of adult women.

In addition to public roles in community religious events and life-cycle rituals, women functioned as healers, diagnosing and treating illness through their knowledge of the medicinal properties of plants and animal substances and through their ability to employ spirit powers in ritual cures. In some nations, women specialized in certain kinds of treatments while men specialized in others. Inuit women were more likely to treat illness with medicines and songs, whereas men performed shamanic curing rites while in trance. Dine women often functioned as diagnosticians of illness, referring patients to men who conducted ceremonial chants to treat ailments. Dine diagnosticians observed symptoms, took patient histories, and ascertained cause by ritual techniques such as hand-trembling and stargazing. In southwestern Puebloan nations, women and men might join separate medicine societies that practiced medicinal and ritual specialties, each treating different kinds of ailments. And in California and the Great Basin, women were the more frequent sucking doctors, performing dramatic ritual cures by sucking

on patients' painful or swollen areas to draw out illnesses or "pains" and relieve their suffering. In all nations, the role of midwife was a female specialization.

Throughout Native America, balanced symbols of gender were transmitted in beliefs about the creation or transformation of the world in primordial times and in conceptualizations of spirit beings. Although some creation stories emphasize the roles of male or female deities, both female and male deities figure prominently in the belief systems of all Native nations. Female spirits are often credited with gifts of sustenance to the people. Universally among farming peoples, one or more female deities gave corn and other crops to humans. The Puebloan Corn Maidens, the Dine and Apache Changing Woman, and the Iroquoian daughter of Sky-Woman are among the deities responsible for the origin of corn. In nomadic foraging societies, female spirits are also givers of life, knowledge, and sustenance. The Inuit spirit, sometimes known as Sedna, is responsible for providing people with an annual supply of whales, walrus, and seals, while the Lakota White Buffalo Calf Woman gave people the Sacred Pipe and instructed them in performance of their holiest individual and communal rituals.

Symbolism of gender balance and interdependence is most encompassing in Dine belief. Nearly all deities and forces of nature are paired in male-female counterparts: First Man, First Woman, Dawn or Twilight Man, Dawn or Twilight Woman, Pollen Boy, Pollen Girl, and Thought (male) and Speech (female). Red and yellow are female colors whereas blue and white are male colors. South and west are female directions while north and east are male. As symbolic opposite but interdependent forces, femaleness is thought of as active and productive while maleness is thought of as static.

## Transformation of Gender Roles after European Invasions

The basic egalitarianism of most Native nations was undermined by processes unleashed in North America after the arrival of Europeans on the continent in the sixteenth century. European trade, settlement, and the continual appropriation of land and resources had consequences for all aspects of Native life. Women's and men's roles were affected as well. Involvement in trade was the critical factor that began the transformation of work and led to changes in community leadership and the public influence women were able to exert. Interference in Native culture by missionaries and government officials also undermined gender equality by fostering a patriarchal ideology that marginalized women. These processes occurred in different nations at different times due to paths of European invasion but no Native group was left untouched. However, despite the overwhelming nature of Euro-American/Canadian economic, political, and cultural control, some indigenous values regarding gender have survived.

Although trading with other nations for utilitarian and luxury goods was an ancient practice for Native peoples, European trade took on a vastly different character in its seemingly insatiable demand for only a few products, especially animal fur pelts. This overemphasis caused a shift in Native productive strategies. Men's attention increasingly centered on procuring animal skins while women spent more time processing the pelts for market. The specific nature of the shift in focus and activities depended upon the nation's location near commercial routes and their aboriginal subsistence base. People in the Northeast were earliest drawn into European trade networks. For some the focus was relatively brief because French and British merchants soon exhausted beaver supplies in the region and rapidly developed interior routes and sources; for others the effects of trade were more intense. Women were especially marginalized in foraging societies because their aboriginal roles in subsistence production declined in importance as men's work as trappers and traders eclipsed women's labor. In horticultural societies, in contrast, women's crucial, life-sustaining work as farmers and suppliers of essential foodstuffs delayed the deterioration of their status.

In early years of commerce, men and women participated as active traders, exchanging Native products for metal pots, knives, needles, scissors, and other tools and utensils. Women also obtained cloth, clothing, and food. In fact, Europeans who traded with Native peoples of the Canadian Northwest Pacific Coast (such as the Kwakwaka'wakw, Tlingits, and Haidas) complained about the assertiveness of Native women who demanded fair value for their products. And Native men were reportedly reluctant to make final transactions without the approval of their wives, much to the annoyance of the Europeans. However, men came to dominate trade for several reasons. They brought in the animals whose skins were exchanged and they eventually concentrated on trading for goods most valuable to them, including tools and weapons enabling them to hunt and trap more successfully. Women were necessary to the continuation of commerce as well because they tanned or processed the hides or pelts and supplied foods for trade such as corn, pemmican (dried buffalo meat), and cured fish. But their place in trade networks was rendered peripheral because of their rapid exclusion by European practices consistent with a patriarchal ideology. Europeans bypassed female traders and leaders, preferring to deal exclusively with male hunters, trappers, and chiefs.

The complex commercial and cultural processes that led to women's marginalization coalesced in the Plains during the middle of the nineteenth century when trade in buffalo hides and pemmican reached its height. As a result of increasing emphasis on trade and the acquisition of wealth, women in the Lakota, Cheyenne, Blackfoot, and other Plains nations lost rights and status in their communities. Men were the major actors in the expanding trade networks, made possible by the acquisition of horses that allowed hunters to kill more animals and transport the meat and hides to settlements and trading posts. Women contributed significantly to the commerce as well since their labor was required to tan the hides and prepare pemmican, but their participation was directed and controlled by their male kin. In fact, in order to prosper in trade, a man needed the services of several women because the many numbers of buffalo that a man could kill were useless if the hides were not properly prepared. As a result, the incidence of polygyny rose as men sought to gain more female labor through marriage to more than one woman. Successful hunters were able to obtain several wives by giving presents of horses to the fathers of eligible women. The difference in ages of spouses widened because a man usually was well into his twenties or thirties by the time he had amassed enough horses to give to a father-in-law. And fathers were willing to accept the gifts in exchange for daughters in their teens. The age difference between husband and wife contributed to the wife's subordination because seniority itself conferred prestige in Plains cultures. In essence, as commodity production increased, women themselves became commodities in transactions between men. Cultural values that stressed female submissiveness, obedience, and chastity helped legitimate and maintain gender inequality. In this changing context, women's activities were restricted and misbehavior was punished not only with social criticism but also with beatings meted out by fathers or husbands. Increasing emphasis on economic, social, and military bonds among men created or strengthened tendencies toward patrilocal residence after marriage, isolating a young wife from her supportive kin networks. Still, women's autonomy was not totally eliminated. Some women excelled in typically male pursuits as hunters and warriors. And women who conformed to "feminine" cultural norms and who were skilled in "women's work" (especially robe-making and embroidery) were honored in their communities.

Missionary teachings had a profound impact on gender roles and ideologies, helping to suppress women's autonomy, strengthen men's authority over their wives, and rigidify the gender division of labor, although their influence varied considerably and depended on rates of conversion to Christian doctrines. As missionaries' efforts became intertwined with economic and political pressures, however, the social messages they preached filtered into indigenous attitudes and behaviors. For example, French Jesuits working among the Innus (or Montagnais) in eastern Quebec in the early seventeenth century sought to transform Native culture in conformity with European models. They condemned pre-marital or extra-marital sexual activity, especially by women, and criticized the assertive participation of women in household and community decision-making. While these teachings were followed strictly by converts and residents of Jesuit mission villages and ignored by most other Innus, they had a cumulative effect centuries later. Aboriginal attitudes, however, did not fade entirely. Even by the middle of the twentieth century, norms of gender equality and autonomy persisted, especially in households continuing traditional economic pursuits.

Policies of the U.S. and Canadian governments further contributed to undermining women's equality. In the United States, the General Allotment Act of 1887, which mandated the division of communally-owned reservation lands into individual parcels (usually of 160 acres per family), had several consequences. Not only did the act dismantle communal ownership basic to indigenous practice, but it also formally assigned allotments of land to male heads-of-households. Women's collective rights as controllers of land in matrilineal societies and their individual rights as members of families were ignored. When the U.S. government imposed "representative" tribal governments made up of leaders either selected by non-Indian agents or elected by male residents of reservations, men were without exception the only chosen leaders. Suffrage was extended to women at different times on different reservations in accordance with local regulations formulated by each tribe. Some women did not gain the right to vote until the middle of the twentieth century. Since then, women have not only participated in tribal elections, but some have also risen to leadership positions on tribal councils and as principal chiefs.

In Canada, passage of the Act to Encourage the Gradual Civilization of the Indian Tribes in 1857 set up the process of "enfranchisement" through which Indian men could, under certain conditions—men had to be at least twenty-one years of age, literate, and "of good moral character"—be officially "enfranchised." Notwithstanding the positive sound of the word *enfranchise*, "enfranchised" men lost their rights to live on reserves or to be members of Native bands. While the act did no favors for Native men, the fact that it did not

apply to women reveals the government's patriarchal bias. That bias was even more explicit in the 1876 Indian Act that defined *Indian* as a legal status, entitling people to be registered as Indians and enabling them to be members of bands and live on reserves, but restricted "status Indians" to people who were registered on official lists drawn up in 1874, their descendants in the male line, and the wives (whether Indian or not) and children of such persons. Indian women who married non-Indians and the descendants of female Indians whose fathers were not Indian were not considered "Indian" by legal definition. Such individuals were referred to as "non-status Indians." They and their descendants lost membership in bands and lost the right to live on reserves. It was not until a Canadian Supreme Court ruling in 1985 that Indian women married to non-Indians and the descendants of Indian women were given the power to apply for reinstatement as "status Indians." Indian women who marry non-Indians no longer lose their status and rights. The 1876 Indian Act also dismantled communal land ownership by issuing "location tickets" for individual allotments. In keeping with patriarchal practices, such tickets were assigned only to men.

When wage-work became available on reservations and reserves in the middle and late nineteenth century, most jobs were for men in housing and road construction and maintenance and in local policing. The male monopoly of the few existing jobs added to the marginalization of women since only men brought in money that could be used to purchase food, clothing, and equipment. Men's access to wage-earning jobs increased their authority in their families and correspondingly undermined women's status. Women did bring in money, though, mostly through the informal sector, selling baskets, other crafts, and surplus garden products in towns near their reservations.

Conditions that led to loss of equality for women did not occur everywhere with the same intensity. In the Southwest, particularly in matrilineal societies such as Zuni, Hopi, and Dine, women retained much of their aboriginal status well into the twentieth century and, in some cases, until the present day. They remained as the recognized heads of large, extended family households and as heads of lineages. Several factors can explain the stability of women's position in the region. Since southwestern nations were not heavily involved in Euro-American trade until the twentieth century, the kinds of economic and political pressures exerted elsewhere were not as intense. In addition, notions of women's equality were thoroughly interwoven into the fabric of social life, reflected in the composition of households, and the strength of clans and lineages.

Finally, concepts of gender equality permeated indigenous religious and symbolic systems that remained strong despite decades or even centuries of missionary activity in the region.

By the middle of the twentieth century, most Native American households relied on wage-work as their major source of income. Women's labor force participation rates, however, are lower than those of men and in fact are lower than those of women in the general American/Canadian populations. Still, by mid-century, women were becoming more active in their communities as workers and as participants in decision-making bodies.

Despite clear and fundamental changes in women's roles and status, aboriginal supports for gender equality have not been entirely obliterated. Women's centrality to their families as mothers and as wage earners is a significant source of economic and social stability as well as of ideological value. Religious and cultural symbolism that endows female beings with knowledge and power conveys positive images that contribute to forming Native people's attitudes about gender. Finally, Native traditions and a strong pride in heritage help maintain women's rights.

*Nancy Bonvillain*

## ◆ MULTIPLE GENDERS IN HISTORICAL AND CONTEMPORARY NATIVE AMERICAN COMMUNITIES

### Historical Perspective

Gender identities within Native American communities have been changing since precontact and continue today on Native reservations, in rural Native communities, and in urban Native areas. Duties and tasks assigned to girls, boys, women, men, and "others" have varied over the centuries. Some of the so-called traditional assignments are still in place, but gender roles are presented with different meanings and currently have some political implications of cultural resistance. Furthermore, interactions among ethnicity, culture, individual/tribal politics, and sexuality have always played major roles in the way gender identities were and are defined and classified.

Over time, new gender tasks have emerged due to changes within a culture or the introduction of new technologies, which help clarify roles and duties assigned to various individuals. At the same time some tasks were changed, dropped or pushed to the side, simply because of changes taking place within tribal

nations, villages, Pueblos, bands, or groups. This has created sexual politics on Indian reservations, which in some sense spilled over from colonial European-American cultures.

The gender roles of Native people have changed over the years due to the demands on Native societies to change as dictated by colonial governments. In the past Native American men hunted game and women gathered plants for food. Due to the demand of the colonizers for farming through the federal mandate of acculturation and assimilation, men in Native communities began to do less hunting and more farming. Agricultural work demanded different tasks. In many instances, farming required the help of women and children. Former hunters' wives and children began to become an integral part of farming, because it was a multitask occupation and it involved a lot of physical work, which could not be accomplished by only one person.

Deer hunting, for example, could be a single person's task. More importantly, in many tribes, hunting was a ritual. Very few tribes still carry on this practice and belief. Hunting helped men define—if not redefine and clarify their roles as masculine beings. This has changed over the years. Many Native men now hunt in a group of two or more. From observation of different tribal groups of men, they view hunting more as a recreational activity than an act to provide food for their families and relatives. This practice is more common today than in the past and it is less ceremonially focused, except in rite-of-passage cases for adolescent males, who may be expected to bring home a kill as evidence of masculinity, as practiced in Jicarilla Apache culture.

Many of the current accelerated cultural changes in Native American communities occurred due to the arrival of new generations. The process of cultural change took place under the ever-present pressures of acculturation and assimilation into Western cultures, which started in 1492. Prior to that time period, acculturation and assimilation was active through integration with one or more other tribes. Some of the integration of people occurred through tribal intermarriage or merging of two or more tribes for survival. Others occurred through borrowing skills, technology, and so forth from surrounding tribes.

During times of cultural change, people within a specific tribal group had to negotiate and renegotiate how they would maintain their identities, lives, practices, and so forth to continue to exist as a tribe. These practices were not blatantly discussed or planned out, but were part of unconscious acts. They simply reacted and conformed to the changes taking place within their specific cultures. Adopting and adapting is a survival strategy within indigenous nations. The same is true with gender identities.

Native people of the Americas have emerged from their own worlds through legends and creation stories. To tribal peoples, these stories are not myth, but true stories. They are a catalyst on which they base their lives, both morally and ethically. For example, within Navajo traditional culture, how one lives her or his life is based on the basic ground rules set forth in the Navajo creation stories.

There were specific sets of rules set aside for First Man and First Woman. Thereafter, each gender was assigned their particular duties, roles, and tasks that would be their responsibilities and define their spaces within Navajo culture. Sex assignments to men and women were not conducted until the second half of the Third Navajo (Yellow) Underworld. Within the Navajo stories, both genders were created in separate parts of the First Navajo (Black) World. First Man was created in the northeast part of the first underworld and First Woman was created in the southwest portion. Because of the creation of specific gender spaces, today Navajo men and women occupy specific gender spaces within Navajo culture (at ceremonies, within their homes, and so forth).

Gender is a social construction. Gender identities are learned practices, which are provided and presented to children by their parents, relatives, and other adult role models. Children from infancy are taught what specific gender roles they will practice throughout their lives. These learned expectations are then applied to their biological (sex) identity, as ascribed by the dominant society.

Gender identities are superimposed from the beginning of life for all human babies. Human infants are not identified by their biological sexes (female or male), with the exception of documentation on birth certificates, but by their gender (girl or boy). Societal expectation to fit the norm is exerted from the beginning of all human life.

Today, within tribal communities there is an expectation that male infants will grow up to be boys. Later in their lives, they will be adult men. The same is true with female infants; they are expected to become girls, then young women. Gender terms are used quite heavily from the beginning of human life. As a society Native Americans do not use sex (biological) terms as much for human classification.

Biological sex classifications are typically used in determining the sex of nonhuman babies. For example, when a lamb is born within Navajo culture, the owner refers to the new lamb as female or male. There are no Navajo words that classify them differently. Certainly,

there are words that would describe or characterize the newborn lamb as a baby lamb, but that does not contribute to any class of gender or sex identifications of the lamb. It simply classifies the lamb as a part of a species.

Gender diversity, or multiple gendered categories, was a common part of Native communities until prolonged contact with Europeans led to discounting this diversity. At the time of contact, as reported in numerous colonial writings, each gender had a prescribed role within individual tribes in North America. The classic example of genders mentioned, which are repeated throughout various tribal oral traditions, and now in various literary canons, states that men were hunters and practiced religions, women gathered and gave birth to infants, and the cycle continued with each generation. Besides girls, boys, women, and men being in any given Native communities, there were other people who were classified as *berdache* by non-Indians. Anthropologists, historians, sociologists, and their predecessors were not able to classify additional gender identities beyond the terms *man* and *woman* and thereby applied the term berdache (see Roscoe 1991). On the other hand, Native people had and continue to have specific names for people who are neither woman nor man.

### Berdache

Berdache is a term, in general, which means male prostitute. The term arrived with the French fur trappers in present-day eastern Canada in the 1500s. The word also arrived at a similar time when Spaniards moved up from the south to the present-day American Southwest, and while the Dutch were arriving on the upper eastern coastline. The root of the word originated in Persia (see Jacobs et al. 1997; Roscoe 1991; and Williams 1986). It should be noted that berdache is not the term-of-choice in any Native society.

Historically, berdache made up the third gender in a particular tribe. For Navajo, who live in a matrilineal society, a heterosexual woman is the first gender, with the heterosexual man being the second gender. These two genders were common in all tribes, but priority was reversed in patrilineal societies. Men were the first gender in those societies. Navajo third-gender category was designated for people born with both genitals and for specially initiated third-gender beings. This person, in most cases, functioned and carried out duties attributed to women. In some rare cases, the person functioned as a man; however, very little is documented or orally mentioned on this subject in Native communities.

The fourth gender in this matrilineal society, in the past, was a male-bodied woman. As an infant this person was initially born with male sex organ, but later functioned as a woman. In some cases, either this person changed gender identity in childhood or later in life. Some acquired their status through a vision quest or were assigned their duties through spiritual conviction, if not by their tribal religious communities. The fifth gender in a matrilineal society was a female-bodied man; that is, a person who was initially born with female sex organs, but functioned as a man throughout his adult life.

In Western writings about gender, the male-bodied woman and the female-bodied man are both classified as berdache. This was started by the early Western explorers and is erroneous. Such misclassification continues today by Western writers, authors, anthropologists, historians, and so forth. For example, in Will Roscoe's 1991 book entitled *The Zuni Man-Woman*, the author questions tribal elders and they do not understand the term *man-woman*. Some mentioned that such a person might be best called Zuni Male-Woman, since We'wha, the book's subject, was born as a male infant, with male genitalia, and later in life functioned as a woman. Upon her death, she was buried on the male side of the community cemetery plot. The same is true with Sabine Lang's book (1998), which is titled *Men as Women, Women as Men: Changing Gender in Native North American Cultures*. Both book titles create a conflict of gender identities, since one gender cannot be the other, especially within Native North American communities where gender diversity is clearly marked to account for the range of gender possibilities. From a Native perspective, a man cannot be a woman at the same time he is being a man.

Many Indian tribes in the American Southwest had such marked people in their midst right into the early 1900s. Berdache often played major roles within each of their tribes. For example, some acquired children who had become parentless due to tribal warfare. They raised children as though they were their own offspring. Many served as herbalists, expert bead workers, tanners, tipi makers, potters, basket makers, and so forth. In some tribes, berdache went on war parties and raids with their tribal men to serve as health care workers for wounded warriors. In addition, some of their duties entailed spiritual guidance for warriors.

Within some tribes, berdache were key players in negotiation processes with their own and other tribal councils. This might include important intertribal marriages that would have an impact on how two tribes would relate to one another in the future. Some helped settle disputes among tribal members, and facilitated decision-making when the group needed to decide where to move the next season. They were viewed as people with a broader perspective than other men or women, since they were able to see both sides of the world—both feminine and masculine. In some cases, berdache were the only people in a tribe who had the tribal and cultural permission to accumulate material wealth, thereby making them prime candidates to become a second or third wife for a community leader. Their abilities to possess the power of a woman and a man provided them the communal right to acquire material wealth, in addition to cultural knowledge (spirituality). Accumulating wealth was not considered an act of greed, but this practice was not extended to other tribal men or women.

Initially, a berdache was more associated with ceremonial roles. They, at times, were the key role players on how religious activities were carried out and they were keepers of ceremonial, if not specific esoteric tribal cultural knowledge. Their responsibilities were to transmit the knowledge to younger people who were aspiring to become berdache within their specific tribes. Besides functioning in the roles of community religious leaders and negotiators, many of the tasks assigned to berdache of the past were in the realm of traditional/cultural knowledge keepers. Outside of those cultural duties, very little is mentioned about the sex roles of berdache within their communities.

From a Western standpoint, berdache continue to be associated with sexual activity, the norms expected in European-American cultures. Berdache does not equate to Western cultures' gay, lesbian, or other sexual beings and should not even be associated with the concept of homosexuality. The latter Western ideology is more about sexuality and less about gender. The study of berdache is a topic that belongs in gender studies and not in gay and lesbian or sexuality studies. However, it is common for Natives and non-Natives to conflate the two entities (gender and sex).

When it came to sexual activities, berdache in some tribes had limited sexual relationships with men. Within these tribes, men/warriors who were identified as heterosexual maintained their heterosexual status within their communities even when they had sexual relationships with berdache. These heterosexual men were neither viewed nor thought of as becoming homosexuals by their tribal people.

In traditional Native North American cultures, gender identity was more important than sexual identity. Relations between a heterosexual man and a berdache were not homosexual. It was a hetero-gender relationship (see Jacobs et al. 1997). The relationship was viewed and understood as something between a man (gender) and a berdache (gender). It was not between a man and another man. Berdache are of another, third, gender, as defined in traditional Native cultures.

Furthermore, berdache did not have sexual relations with other *berdache*. It would have been considered an incestuous act. In some tribes, this was resolved by death on the part of the aggressor.

Through tribal oral traditions, some stories have been retained about why some of the Native men had sexual relationships with berdache. With current views on sexuality in various cultures, many of these stories are well-guarded by tribal elders and are not readily transmitted outside their circles. The main subject in sexuality, which is part of Native discourse, is the honor of women's reproductive capability.

There was a taboo in Native communities that a man should not have sexual intercourse with his pregnant wife. He could not have a sexual relationship with another woman, because such behavior was considered adulterous and would bring only death or a demotion of their warrior status. In some tribes, the need for sexual outlets was satisfied through relations with a berdache. The man could only have sexual relations with one berdache. After the arrival of the infant, a minor gift might be bestowed on the berdache. This was not considered a payment for services, but an act of reciprocity and appreciation. It was not free-for-all sexual activity, as believed in popular culture or in gay literature, but the relationship was considered a temporary one.

In addition to tribal understanding of sexual relationships, unmarried tribal men (warriors) had limited access to berdache as sexual partners. Upon marriage, a warrior paid honor to the berdache who was available during his time of need. The honor was not only for the sake of understanding and fulfilling the expectation of tribal reciprocity, but also to acknowledge the respect the berdache had within their tribes.

Mostly all the people classified as berdache and those people labeled as "others" went underground within their own tribal nations and circles of friends and family with the arrival of European taboos regarding other genders. They were sheltered and shielded by their tribes, relatives, and family members from hostile outsiders. In some cases, they were concealed from other tribal people or newly Christianized family members. The isolation through extended sheltering and shielding has prevented the berdache from fulfilling their function as role models within their Native communities since the early 1900s.

Some individuals acted out their roles publicly, but the roles within their communities did not fulfill their previous lives' expectations and tribal obligations. Sheltering and shielding has assisted, if not instigated, the disappearance of such important people from Native lives. Still, young children who were living in two worlds—such as the Navajo *nádleeh* and the Lakota *winkte*— during the isolation period were prevented from pursuing their ascribed tribal roles. They were deprived of the acquisition of the skills and traditional cultural knowledge of whom they were and what they were to do and be in their own tribal communities.

## Two-Spirit Identity

In 1987 Native American gays and lesbians rejected the term "berdache" for their community because of its origins as a term for "male prostitute"—a definition still in use in contemporary times. The term "two-spirit" replaced "berdache" in the Native gay and lesbian community, although its members recognize it only as a temporary fix until a more accurate term that reflects the diversity of the community—particularly in relation to the differences between female and male two-spirits—can be agreed upon.

Two-spirits can be found both on reservations and in urban areas; the latter is often the destination for Native Americans questing for their identity, and many Native American homosexuals are drawn to the strong urban gay community. In these places, many Native people are still connected to their tribal cultures, and have emerged to become part of the two-spirit communities. Some two-spirits have returned to their reservation homes with a stronger sense of who they are and with their life's purposes in order. Some tribes even celebrate this renewed identity since it reaffirms the individual's tribal responsibilities. However, the experience of belonging to both the gay and Native communities sometimes results in Native Americans favoring their identity in the gay community over their Native American heritage.

## Gay and Lesbian Identity

Popular culture marginalizes Native Americans either to the reservations of the Southwest or to extinction, and those of us who grew up in urban areas and/or part of a federally recognized tribe find ourselves in the absurd unreality of nonexistence. (Welch 1999, 4)

Marginalization of Native people onto reservations or into unnamed spaces has left many people unsure of their identity. Much of this is attributed to American popular culture and modernity, which surrounds their daily lives. For example, the unsaid messages in presenting gender-specific toys to girls, like Barbie, is that little girls are expected to grow up to act out womanly roles. On the other hand, boys are given toy handguns and firearms, supporting their masculine behavior. If a little girl plays with her brother's toy gun, the parents or other relatives generally object to her preference, since in the minds of the adults such actions are not considered normal. The same is true with a boy who plays with his sister's Barbie doll. A child playing with the opposite sex's toy is ridiculed and discouraged. While "shaming" was a temporary practice that included temporary dismissal from the tribal family circle, they were welcomed back at a later date. Today, there are many Native American gays and lesbians residing in urban America who are disowned by their own families, and do not have any familial relationships since they departed their reservations.

Gender status in contemporary Native America has become confused. Many of the older Native people still believe and hang onto the old values and importance of gender diversity. Each year, these people and their views are becoming smaller in numbers. At the same time, the younger generations have no connection to the values of their elders and have inherited the mindset of European-America, in which multiple genders are taboo and shunned.

Even Native people who categorize themselves as gay or lesbian are struggling with where they belong on their own reservation or in an urban area. Many have found their lives much easier in urban areas than on their own reservations. Since the 1960s, there has been a major movement of Native gays and lesbians into urban areas. In a few cases, some have returned to reservations later in their lives and become role models within their own communities for younger tribal members who identify themselves either as gay or lesbian. The returnees became a resource of information for young Native gays and lesbians. Some are still there, helping clarify what young Native gay and lesbian life is like off the reservation. More importantly, the young Native gays and lesbians are much more informed of the consequences if and when they decide to move away. They are better armed with needed information.

Currently on Native reservations, Pueblos, villages, townsites, colonies, and the like there are mixtures of Native households. Some Native families have gay and/or lesbian members. Others have disowned their children for being gay or for not fitting their defined category of normality, mostly adopted from outside cultures. In some cases, parents see their children as their own creation and pay little attention to how their children live their lives as long as they are healthy,

maintaining their tribal honors, and contributing to tribal societies.

## Conclusion

The important historical role of those once defined as "berdache" no longer exists in Native society, even though the term lives on. Today, many Native Americans in rural and urban areas are reinventing their roles with bits and pieces of information they are able to acquire, although there is little tangible information available on the past lives of these once-honored people. The domination of Western taboos regarding homosexuality and multiple genders erased this unique people group from Native culture.

In spite of the vanishing of the berdache, many members of the Two-Spirit communities have taken on the role the berdache once served as protectors of cultural traditions. The importance placed on "community" in gay and lesbian circles closely resembles that of Native communities, which is threatened by the prevalence of Western individualism. Many two-spirits have returned to their reservations with a renewed sense of the interdependence of all peoples and serve as models of the strength the individual can draw from the community.

*Wesley Thomas*
*Idaho State University*

## ◆ CONTEMPORARY AMERICAN INDIAN WOMEN

"Where are the women?" was a question that the Iroquois, Wyandot, and other First Peoples often asked Europeans when the two groups met centuries ago. The Native Americans were mistrustful about the sincerity of the Europeans who did not include women in the important decisions affecting their communities. The Europeans were amazed and often shocked to see American Indian women serving not only in influential political positions but also as spiritual leaders. More recently, when one looks for information about American Indians, the same question—Where are the women?—might be asked. During the last three decades an avalanche of material on American Indians has flooded the academic and lay markets, yet much of this has inadequately recognized the contemporary contributions of American Indian women who play essential roles in the survival of their communities as nation keepers, the generation builders.

Somà Haaland (Laguna Pueblo) examines a petroglyph in New Mexico. (Photo by Alexandra Harris)

The failure to acknowledge the contributions of Native North American Indian women is not confined to the non-Indian world. For instance, at one of the late 1990s annual meetings of the American Indian Professors Association, during a panel discussion of a new book about the American Indian Movement, one of the panel members asked, "Where are the women?"

The reality is that contemporary American Indian women are everywhere, in education, media, politics, religion, medicine, and business, sometimes serving as publicly recognized leaders but more often remaining unrecognized. Women quietly serve as bridge leaders or cultural mediators facilitating communication and understanding between their tribal worlds and the nontribal worlds, an essential role not often given full recognition by those using Western standards that fail to recognize the traditional nonhierarchical, complementary status of women and men. In addition, many modern American Indian women are bicultural, walking comfortably in two worlds, the indigenous and the Euro-American. While moving successfully between the two cultures, American Indian women have successfully maintained or have recreated the traditional

woman's multiple roles of homemaker, parent/educator, economic provider, and community leader. Few women limit themselves to one or two roles. When examining the lives of American Indian women during the last fifty years, another pattern becomes clear: indigenous women have been leaders in the call for cultural continuity and cultural renaissance.

First Nations women deal everyday with ethnostress, a term coined by Agnes Williams, a Seneca social worker, which is now used by other racial/ethnic groups to describe stress resulting from institutional racism. Situations that may create ethnostress include those related to the structurally influenced social problems that affect every reservation and urban Indian community: unemployment, poverty, religious intolerance, alcoholism, illicit drug abuse, suicide, violence, school dropouts, untimely deaths, discrimination within the multi-jurisdictional criminal and civil justice systems, and environmentally unsound economic development schemes. However, the realities of the strength and adaptive abilities of the majority of contemporary American Indian women's lives negate the negative stereotypes of apathy, alcoholism, and passivity. As will be seen, the women's actions of persistence and courage both illustrate their belief in and support of the growing evidence that American Indians will survive and prosper.

The following discussion of social institutions and First Peoples will identify only a small number of the exemplars amongst the rapidly growing number of remarkable American Indian women who are outstanding role models for their immediate communities and for women everywhere.

## Retention and Restoration of Traditional Family Values and Roles

Contemporary American Indian/Alaska Native women are members of 558 federally recognized nations as well as members of state-recognized tribes or 200 tribal groups awaiting federal recognition. By 1950 the population increase that began to change slightly two decades earlier was still minimal. According to the U.S. Census, 343,410 Native people were living in the United States in 1950 and of that total, 164,586—less than one-half—were women (U.S. Bureau of the Census 1987, 14). Twenty years later, in 1970, a new pattern of major population growth emerged: women now made up 51

Myra Dorothy Brown, known as "Grandma D" by her family, died in July 1991 at the age of 89. (Photo by Sara Wiles)

percent—405,107—of the total indigenous population (U.S. Department of Labor 1975, 45–6). In 1990 American Indian women still outnumbered men; 1 million, or 51 percent, of First Peoples were women.

American Indian women are also living longer. In 1940 American Indians could expect to live to be fifty-one. By the early 1990s women's life expectancy was 75.1 years, outliving their male counterparts by 7.9 years (U.S. Department of Health and Human Services 1997, 20). However, depending on the Indian Health Service (IHS) area within which women live, their life expectancy ranges from sixty-nine to seventy-eight years. Within the majority of the IHS service areas, women have a life expectancy of seventy-four years. Even with these advances, First Nation women's life expectancy is still shorter than that for the total female U.S. population by 3.7 years (U.S. Department of Health and Human Services 1997, 20). Moreover, 49.6 percent of American Indian women, according to the 1990 Census, are younger than twenty-five, whereas only 6.5 percent of American Indian women are over sixty-four (U.S. Department of Health and Human Services 1997, 2).

Demographic data reveal that three American Indian family pattern trends considered to be measures of family stability trends parallel those in the general population. First, for both Indian and non-Indian populations the percentage of children living with two parents has decreased. Second, the percentages of women who have never married or who have divorced have increased. Third, as of 1995 the percentage of American Indian/Alaska Native high school females reporting having sex at least once in their lifetimes—57 percent—did not vary significantly from the sexual patterns of their classmates: Blacks, 67 percent; Hispanics, 53 percent; and whites, 49 percent (National Women's Health Information Center, 27). However, American Indian children are less likely to live with two parents than all U.S. children, and American Indian women are more likely to never marry and are more likely to divorce than are all U.S. women (Sandefur 1996).

Of the people aged twenty-five to thirty-four years who live on the reservation, there are only 94.5 men per one hundred women, thus reducing the marriage pool dramatically. Military involvement, incarceration, accidental death, and urban employment can partially explain the lower number of men remaining on reservations. Also, a number of women choose not to marry or will divorce if potential partners or husbands will not accept the traditional complementary roles of women and men. Traditional women are proud of their independence and ability to be self-sufficient and will not accept physical or emotional abuse.

Amongst First Nation women who have retained traditional ways, the role of mother still holds high status. Mothering should not be misunderstood as limited to a nuclear family household; the extended family still plays an important if not essential part in parenting. Much attention has been given to dysfunctional American Indian families and little formal recognition has been given to the strengths of Indian families that parallel or, given the degree of ethnostress experienced by Indians, far exceed the strengths of families in the general American population.[1] Those strengths include being appreciated by relatives; keeping in touch with relatives; respecting each other; and believing that family members try to look at the bright side, to maintain hope no matter what happens.

Women continue to be tradition keepers through sharing oral history and modeling culturally appropriate roles. Angela Cavender Wilson's article "Grandmother to Granddaughter: Generations of Oral History in a Dakota Family" in *Natives and Academics: Researching and Writing about American Indians* illustrates the use of stories and modeling. Wilson's grandmother's interpretation of what happened to her great-great-great-grandmother during the 1862 Dakota Death March helps clarify the persistence of traditional women's roles:

As I [Angela Wilson] listened to my grandmother telling the last words spoken by her great-great-great-grandmother, and my grandmother's interpretation, "Though she was in pain and dying [facilitated by the inhumane treatment of their captors], she was still concerned about her daughter and little granddaughter who was [*sic*] standing there and witnessed all this," I understood that our most important role as women is making sure our young ones are taken care of so that our future as Dakota people is assured. I learned that sometimes that means self-sacrifice and putting the interests of others above your own. It also was clear through this story and others that although these were and continue to be hard memories to deal with, always there is pride and dignity in the actions of our women. (Mihesuah 1998, 34)

A contemporary exemplar of a First Nation's woman who serves both her family and the larger community is Katsi Cook (Mohawk, Wolf Clan mother), mother of four adult children and one grandchild, a midwife, and a formidable warrior on behalf of her people. In the mid-1980s Katsi Cook helped organize the Akwesasne Mother's Milk Project, which documented the 200 percent increase in toxic PCBs in the breast milk of mothers who ate fish from the St. Laurence River, Great Lakes area, as contrasted to those mothers who were

not from the area. Cook has maintained her optimism through her belief in the Mohawk principles of Kaienarakowa, the Great Law of Peace and the Good Mind, and the hope that comes each time she assisted in the delivery of a new baby.

During the 1970s widespread sterilization abuse occurred in four areas served by the IHS. In 1975 alone, some 25,000 Native American women were permanently sterilized after being coerced, misinformed, or threatened. Despite coerced sterilization, a repeat of similar abuses that occurred during the early 1900s, the fact that new babies are still coming illustrates that nations are not dying. In fact, American Indian/Alaska Native populations are growing three times more rapidly than the white U.S. population. Reasons for this population recovery include high birth rates as well as lower mortality rates, increases in life expectancy, increased disclosure of indigenous identity, and aggressive health care measures largely spearheaded by American Indian women. American Indian/Alaska Native female adolescent childbearing is twice as common as it is among females of all races combined, with 42 percent of all American Indian/Alaska Native mothers being under age twenty when they had their first

Katsi Cook. From *All Our Relations* by Winona LaDuke. (Photo by Susan Alzner)

child. Little ones with low birth weight are at greater risk of morbidity and mortality than bigger infants yet, regardless of ethnostress, Indian mothers are less likely than any racial/ethnic group of mothers to have low-birth-weight babies, 5.9 percent compared to 7.2 percent (U.S. Department of Health and Human Services 1996, 10).

In addition to coerced sterilization, American Indian families have lost great numbers of their children through coerced adoptions and foster home placements. The criteria for foster and adoptive homes have included racial/ethnic and class biases related to the space in a home, the number of rooms, bathroom facilities, the relationship of the caretakers, and family income. Such considerations effectively remove many stable and supportive American Indian families from the pool of prospective foster and adoptee families. Under the bridge leadership of women the Indian Child Welfare Act was passed in 1978 to counteract this trend by setting up special rules and regulations in court proceedings to ensure that Native children were identified and adopted by Indian families. Some of the adopted and foster home children who may have grown up with Indian identity but with no, or very little, cultural knowledge are now returning home.

Yvette Melanson did not know she was American Indian; she grew up believing she was white and Jewish. Taken from her mother against her mother's wishes and placed on the black adoption market, Yvette did not learn she was full-blood Navajo until she was forty-three. In *Looking for Lost Bird* Melanson tells the story of her search to find her identity and the journey to integrate her earlier Jewish cultural socialization with her recently learned Navajo cultural practices and values.

Jane Warren, a nurse's aide and midwife on the Wind River Reservation in Wyoming, was given her grandmother's Cheyenne name when she was young. The name translated to "Singing into the Forest" in English. (Photo by Sara Wiles)

### Health Issues and Health Care Trailblazers

Like family challenges, health issues for American Indian women, overall, are related to institutional racism and poverty. Contrary to the myths about alcoholism, in 1993 the major causes of death for elderly American Indians/Alaska Natives were heart disease, cancer, cerebrovascular disorders, pneumonia and influenza, diabetes mellitus, and accidents. In 1993 approximately five per 100,000 American Indian/Alaska Native women died from firearm related events. The rate of violent crime reported for American Indian women is nearly 50 percent higher than that reported for Black men. In addition, at least 70 percent of the violence against Native peoples is committed by persons of another racial/ethnic group (Greenfeld 1999, NCJ 173386). More than twice as many American Indian/Alaska Native women (twenty-two per 100,000) died in motor-vehicle-related accidents in 1993 as did Black, Hispanic, Asian and Pacific Islander, and white women. Unintentional injuries took the lives of more American Indian/Alaska Native women than did firearm- and motor-vehicle-related deaths and homicides in 1993. The mortality rate for unintentional injuries among American Indian/Alaska Native women was nearly forty-two per 100,000, compared to twenty per 100,000 black women and seventeen per 100,000 white women.

A health issue related to ethnostress, particularly the psychological impact of poverty, racism, sexism, and government-imposed commodity diets high in fat and low in critical vitamins and minerals, is obesity, defined as excess body weight for height. Native American populations are the most likely of all peoples of color to be overweight or obese. Sixty percent of all American Indian women on reservations in 1987 and 63 percent of urban American Indian women were obese. Obesity, of course, is related to diabetes and high cholesterol levels. Smoking is another health issue for American Indian women: 50 percent smoke cigarettes although 54 percent of those living on reservations have never smoked. Much of this smoking is stress related.

Contrary to popular myth, alcohol consumption and reported symptoms of alcoholism among First Nation women has considerable variation among and within American Indian communities. A 1993 national survey challenged the stereotypes of heavy consumption of alcohol or problem drinking, defined as at least sixty drinks in thirty days: among American Indian women problematic drinking was no greater than that of black and white women, 2 to 3 percent of each population. However, alcohol-related deaths among American Indian/Alaska Native women were significantly higher, ranging from twenty-one deaths per 100,000 for those twenty-five to thirty-four years old to sixty-five deaths per 100,000 for those forty-five to fifty-four years old, compared to ten deaths induced by alcohol per 100,000 for white females of all ages.

Parents of American Indian/Alaska Native youth aged twelve to seventeen in 1988 were less likely to rate the health of their adolescents as excellent than the parents of white and Asian and Pacific Islander youth of the same ages. Only one-fourth of American Indian/Alaska Native youths' health was rated as excellent with no limiting conditions.

Barriers to health care include issues of care quality, access to adequate care, lack of trust in non-Native medical care, treatment considered unacceptably rude, and stereotyping and other forms of racism. Thus, one study found that only 66 percent of American Indian/Alaska Native women age sixty and over, as compared to 86 percent among all U.S. women of the same age cohort, had ever had a breast exam. American Indians/Alaska Natives have the lowest cancer survival rates among all the United States racial/ethnic populations. Women have high cervical cancer death rates, although overall their cervical cancer incidence is low. The untimely deaths are often due to late diagnoses and poorer survival rates.

In both reservation and urban settings, poverty, blood quantum criteria, and lack of access to appropriate traditional and Western health services are all factors that have played a critical and often tragic part in the determination of who will receive health care services. Less than one-third of Native peoples can afford private insurance. Although in 1955 the IHS was given the mission of providing comprehensive health services to American Indians and Alaska Native peoples and is now the principal federal health care provider and health advocate for Indian people, health care coverage remains problematic for American Indian women. Urban women may receive routine care at IHS direct care facilities if they meet the blood quantum requirements and if the needed services are available, but these women still are not eligible for more specialized services.

Today more than 62 percent of all IHS employees are of American Indian or Alaska Native descent. Within the last decade major changes to assure that comprehensive, culturally acceptable personal and public health services are available and accessible to First Peoples are being initiated and led by Indian women. One of the women who have been leaders in recognizing and honoring the importance of traditional medical care is Carole Anne Heart (Rosebud/Yankton Sioux), named senior advisor to the director of the Indian Health Service in 1998. Heart, who has a degree in psychology, has been part of the initiative to incorporate traditional medicine with modern Western medicine. Along with Tilly Black Bear, Karen Artichoker, and others, Heart was one of the founding members of the White Buffalo Calf Women's Society, the first organization addressing domestic abuse and internalized oppression in Indian Country, originally formed in South Dakota on the Rosebud Reservation in the 1970s.

Sandra Dodge (Navajo), certified nurse practitioner (CNP) and women's health and public health nurse consultant for the IHS, has been another key woman assuring that the IHS program emphasis on Indian women's health is implemented. Nurses make up a high proportion of professional American Indian women. Most of the nurses have role modeled the path of Suzie Walking Bear Yellowtail (Crow/Sioux), the first American Indian to earn her registered nursing degree. A growing number of the first cohorts of American Indian nurses are now officially retiring yet remain actively involved with the health needs of their extended families and communities. Elaine Vollin (Assiniboine), mother and grandmother, who earned her bachelor of science degree in the early 1950s, retired recently, lives with family in California, but returns to Montana to care for other family members. Nora Hayes (Fort Peck), "auntie" to many children, and other contemporary nurses, many of whom are deeply committed to the American Indian Nurses Association, continue to follow the path of their elders in helping to bring health to Indian communities. In 1987 nurse Loralei DeCora (Winnebago/Miniconjou Sioux) helped found the first entirely community-owned and operated clinic to be established on an Indian reservation. The majority of the National Council of Urban Indian Health (NCUIH) Board of Directors have been women and most of the thirty NCUIH member centers are run by women. Some key NCUIH women are Carole Meyers, Andrea Alexander, Sharon Chahchischilliage, Kay Culbertson, and Barbara Namias.

Trailblazer True Archdale (Assiniboine), traditional crafts artist and musician, also works as a physical fitness trainer in Venice, California, part of the greater Los Angeles area, home to one of the largest American Indian populations in the United States. Before her death in 1997, healer and activist Bonnie Blackfoot (Blackfeet), following the tradition of women warriors, had the courage to step forward to educate others about HIV/AIDS and in doing so has helped people relearn the old ways of dying with dignity.

Medicine women such as Annie Kahn (Navajo), Tu Moonwalker (Apache), and Dhyani Ywahoo, Tsalagi (Cherokee),[2] and others still practice the ancient healing arts. Lori Arviso Alvord, the first Navajo woman surgeon, holds workshops describing the Navajo philosophy of life, Walk in Beauty, which recognizes the whole person and the need to walk in harmony with all of life. Alvord has also written her autobiography *The Scalpel and the Silver Bear*, which describes her journey as she has sought to integrate Western and indigenous approaches to medicine.

Other notable health care activists include Evelyn Lance Blanchard (Laguna), Tessie Naranjo (Santa Clara Pueblo), Cora Nicolasa Solomon (Winnebago), Laura Williams (Juanero/ Gabrieleno), and Rosemary Wood (Osage).

Wilma Goggles raised four daughters. Her Indian name translates as "Singing Star." (Photo by Sara Wiles)

## American Indian Women Changing Education

In the late 1960s the U.S. Senate Special Subcommittee on Indian Education declared the education of indigenous peoples in the United States to be "a national tragedy."[3] The primary recommendation was to involve more American Indians in their own schools. American Indian women have met this call. They were instrumental in the passage of the Indian Education Act of 1972, the Indian Self-Determination and Educational Assistance Act of 1975, and the creation of survival schools in urban areas such as the Red Schoolhouse in St. Paul and on reservations such as Rocky Boys Public School run by Rocky Boy Reservation members in Montana.

Between 1993 and 1994, American Indians earned 0.5 percent of all the bachelor's degrees granted in the United States. American Indian women earned 0.7 percent of all the bachelor's degrees earned (Anderson 1998, 201). Another way to look at the educational accomplishments of American Indian college women during the last several decades is to reflect upon the fact that in 1994 women earned 58 percent of all of the bachelor's degrees earned by American Indians (Anderson 1998, 200).

Of the total number of master's degrees granted in academic year 1993–94—385,419—American Indians earned 1,697 or 0.4 percent of the total. Of the 1,697 masters degrees earned by First Peoples, 1,006—around 60 percent—were earned by American Indian women (Anderson 1998, 198). American Indians were most likely to earn master's degrees in education (605), business management (299), public administration (143), and health professions (137) (Anderson 1998, 198). In academic year 1993–94, of the 43,149 doctoral degrees awarded in the United States, 134 were earned by American Indians—66 by men, 68 by women (Anderson 1998, 199). The First Peoples were most likely to have earned their doctorates in education (42), social sciences and history (12), psychology (11), biological sciences (9), English language (9), literature (9), business management (7), and health professions (7) (Anderson 1998, 199). The majority of women who seek post-secondary and graduate degrees do so to help not only themselves and their families but also their larger communities.

Nii'eiihi', or the Eagle Drum, is the official ceremonial and social drum group of the Arapaho tribe. Its presence is required at any large gathering. Seated at the far left is Helen Cedartree, a noted elder of the tribe. (Photo by Sara Wiles)

Women's leadership and applied professional training often begins while they are students. This was demonstrated as early as 1960 when women helped form the American Indian Club at Montana State College at Bozeman (now Montana State University), one of the first Indian college-student support organizations in the United States. The young women's leadership did not end after they graduated. Thelma Stiffarm (Assiniboine) is now a successful lawyer. Angela Russell (Crow), attorney, went on to become the second American Indian woman to be elected to Montana's state legislature. Marjorie Bear Don't Walk (Flathead), attorney, served as director of the Billings Indian Health Center; chair of the American Indian Health Care Association (now called the National Council of Urban Indian Health or NCUIH); and director of the Flathead Tribal Health Care Program.

A decade later American Indian students at the University of Montana at Missoula joined the Trail of Broken Treaties in 1972. Organized by the American Indian Movement, Native people marched across the country to Washington, D.C., protesting past injustices and proposing a 20-point plan to address Native American concerns. Henrietta Mann (Southern Cheyenne), the new director of the Indian Studies Program, almost lost her position because she allowed independent-study students to join the activists as participant observers. Their journals, photographs, and video tapes are irreplaceable historical documents archived in the university's library.

A number of daughters and granddaughters of the women activists of the 1950s, 1960s, and 1970s have carried on the support of human rights modeled by their mothers and grandmothers. For instance, in the late 1970s Shawn Olson Crawford (Nakota) organized the Fort Peck Reservation Indian students attending the Wolf Point High School to peacefully protest the racist policies of a group calling itself MOD, an acronym for Montanans Opposing Discrimination, a non-Indian group of ranchers and business people unhappy with American Indians seeking fair market value for land rentals and natural resource compensation. More recently, while dealing with the grief and trauma following the murder of her three-year-old daughter Shelena Skye and while completing her bachelor's degree and two master's degrees, Olson Crawford has been a leader in the struggle to end violence against children and women and to empower American Indians. She has served twice as president of the Kyi-yo Club of University of Montana at Missoula, twice as chair of the Missoula Indian Center's Board of Directors, and currently is acting executive director for the Indian Arts Cooperative, which runs the Counting Coup Art Gallery. Under Crawford's leadership, Kyi-yo Club took a stand in 1996 against institutional racism seen through the cancellation of the Twenty-Eighth Annual Conference and Powwow. As a result of the club's action, the university took action to address the many documented incidents of racism committed by faculty and administration as well as by non-Indian students, and the conference was eventually held.

Crawford's sister Nolee Olson Bogdanski (Nakota) has also been a trailblazer for American Indian women. In 1976 during a peaceful American Indian Movement (AIM) visit to the Bureau of Indian Affairs (BIA) building in Washington, D.C. Bogdanski was twelve and her sister Shawn was sixteen when they and the other members in the group were arrested and jailed (Baird-Olson 1994). During the 1980s Bogdanski was the first American Indian woman selected to the University of Montana's dance drill team. After completing the equivalent of a master's degree in merchandising and working as an assistant executive for a well-known department store in New York City, she moved to Portland, Oregon where she has been serving as director of Affiliated Tribes of the Northwest.

There is presently no indication that this quality of leadership amongst bicultural women will not continue. In the fall of 1996, of all the entering college freshmen in the United States, 4.6 percent were American Indian, half of which were women (Anderson 1998). These numbers are significant given the fact that American Indians make up slightly less than one percent of the total U.S. population.

### Professional and Creative Careers

**Educators.**   Of the thirty-two tribal community colleges and one American Indian university, over one-third of the presidents are women. Haskell Indian Nations University is headed by Karen Swisher (Standing Rock Sioux) who was a member of the 1993 task

Mary Wolfrang's name, translated from Arapaho, means "Sweat Lodge." She died in 1992, but her name lives on through her grandchildren. (Photo by Sara Wiles)

force of the World Indigenous Peoples' Conference on Education. Janine Pease Pretty on Top (Crow), president of Little Big Horn College in Crow Agency (Montana), was named 1990 educator of the year by the National Education Association. President Bill Clinton appointed Pretty on Top to the National Advisory Committee of Indian Education in 1994, the same year she was awarded a MacArthur Fellowship. She is also a trustee of the Native American College Fund (Sonneborn 1998).

Many heads of American Indian studies programs are women, such as Loretta Winters (Anishinabe), chair of American Indian studies at California State University at Northridge. The new head of the American Indian Studies Department at the University of Montana (Missoula), the most recently formed of three in the country,[4] is Kate Shanley (Nakota). Pioneering educator Henrietta Mann (Southern Cheyenne), while serving as long-time chair of the program at University

**Figure 11.1
An Abbreviated Roll Call of Notable
Contemporary North American Indian
Women Educators, Administrators, and
Librarians: Public School and Post Secondary**

Joallyn Archambault, Ph.D. (Standing Rock
Sioux)
Ruth Arrington, Ph.D. (Creek)
Carolyn Attneave, Ph.D. (Delaware/Cherokee)
Vivian Ayoungman, Ph.D. (Siksika)
Ruth Bennett, Ph.D. (Shawnee)
Roxann Bighorn (Nakota/Lakota)
May Boyd, M.A. (Lakota/Blackfeet)
Ruth M. Bronson (Cherokee)
Rosemary Ackley Christensen, Ph.D. (Chippewa)
Agnes Dill (Isletta/Lagua)
Joyce Goodstriker (Kainai)
Bette L. Haskins, Ph.D. (Cherokee)
Charlotte W. Heth, Ph.D. (Cherokee)
Gwendolyn A. Hill, M.A. (Chippewa/Cree)
Bernadine Houle-Steinhauer (Cree)
Clara Sue Kidwell (Chippewa/Choctaw)
Anna Lewis (Mohawk/Delaware)
Marigold Linton, Ph.D. (Chahuilla/Cupino)
Henrietta Mann, Ph.D. (Southern Cheyenne)
Cheryl Metoyer-Dusan, Ph.D. (Cherokee)
Marilyn Nichols, M.A. (Lakota)
Mary Nieball, Ph.D. (Apache)
Elizabeth Anne Parent, Ph.D. (Athapascan/Yupik)
Anita Pfeiffer (Navajo)
Rebecca Robbins (Standing Rock Sioux)
Velma S. Salabiye, M.A. (Navajo)
Esther Scalplock (Siksika)
Helen Maynor Scheirbeck, Ph.D. (Lumbee)
Kate Shanley, Ph.D. (Nakota)
Sarah Shillinger, Ph.D. (Mohawk)
Marie Smallface-Marule (Kainai)
Rachael Snow (Nakoda)
Diosa Summers-Fizgerald, M.A. (Mississippi
Choctaw)
Lenore Stiffarm, Ph.D. (Fort Belknap)
Ellen Swaney
Karen Swisher, Ph.D. (Standing Rock Sioux)
Mary Wilson, M.A. (Prairie Band Pottawatomie)
Loretta Winters, Ph.D. (Annisinabe)

Of the full-time 1993 United States instructional post-secondary faculty, 2,000 are American Indian, and 800, almost one-half, of that group are American Indian women (Anderson 1998, 151). Far more women are in the public elementary and secondary schools. Internationally, First Nations women have also acted as educational leaders. Six of the bid committee seeking to host the 2002 World on Education are women: Vivian-Ayoungman (Siksika First Nation, Canada); Marie Smallface-Marule (Kainai First Nation, Canada); Bernadine Houle-Steinhauer (Cree, Canada); Esther Scalplock (Siksika, Canada); Joyce Goodstriker (Kainai, Canada); and Racheal Snow (Nakoda, Canada).

**Writers and Poets.** The literary and artistic voices of First Nation women activists have shaken the world during the last five decades. Recently, Elizabeth Woody's (Warm Springs and Wasco/Navajo) first collection of poetry, *Hand into Stone*, won the 1990 American Book Award. More recently, Joy Harjo (Creek) and Gloria Bird have edited a book of contemporary North American Indian women's poetry and short prose pieces, both fictional and autobiographical. *Reinventing the Enemy's Language* clearly illustrates the long-ranging impact of the reservation system and the more recent

Joy Harjo gives a poetry reading at the University of California, Los Angeles. (Photo by Alexandra Harris)

of Montana at Missoula, helped pave the way for the program to become a department. In recognition of the quality and magnitude of her educational and religious rights contributions, Mann has been honored with an endowed chair position at Montana State University at Bozeman.

effects of social-tinkering policies such as the relocation program. Many notable American Indian women poets also deal with issues of multicultural heritage. At the same time, most of the voices sing of the persistence, strength, and wisdom that only can come with great suffering.

**Artists and Performing Artists.** Not only are women developing a prominent presence in the performing arts, but women such as the Kicking Women Singers also are helping preserve traditional music. Buffy Sainte-Marie (Cree), singer, song writer, and actress, has recently created the Cradleboard Teaching Project website dedicated to creating culturally sensitive Native curriculum that can be used in both reservation and non-reservation schools. Modeling Sainte-Marie's early career, drummer and singer Donna Augustine (Micmac) performs throughout the United States and Canada.

Charlene Teters (Spokane) is not only an artist and senior editor of the *Native News Magazine* but also an activist, lecturer, and a founding board member of the National Coalition on Racism in Sports and the Media. While a graduate student at the University of Illinois at Urbana-Champaign, Teters used her artwork to begin efforts to eliminate the Chief Illiniwek mascot. The award-winning PBS television documentary *In Whose Honor* highlights Charlene Teter's ongoing successes in challenging inappropriate uses of American Indian images. In 1999 the Society of Indian Psychologists (SIP), guided by President Mary Clearing-Sky, passed a statement in support of retiring all American Indian symbols as team mascots.

Adeline DuBoise (Prairie Band Pottawatamie) is a fashion design artist whose shows have been seen across the United States. The fine bead and leatherwork created by Laurie Ashcraft (Little Shell) is widely sought not only in Montana but also nationally. Sisters Vernice and Glenda Moncooyea (Otoe/Ponca) founded the Oklahoma Indian Theater and Dance Company in 1984, which presents yearly theatrical performances across the United States. Elaine A. Ramos (Tlingit), nurse and educator, is the founder of the Raven Dancers. And those who have had the privilege to see ballerinas Moscelyne Larkin (Shawnee/Peoria) and Maria Tallchief (Osage) dance will never forget the brilliance of their performances.

**Journalists.** North American Indian journalist Rose Robinson (Hopi) was a founding member and former executive director of the Native American Journalist Association. Minnie Two Shoes' excellent reporting facilitated her move from the Fort Peck Assiniboine and Sioux tribal newspaper *Wotanin Wowapi* to writing for the national paper *News from Indian Country*.

Patricia Benedict-Phillips (Abenaki) serves as co-editor of the *American Indians for Development Newsletter* and editor of *May Wutche Aque'he: American Indians for Development Journal*.

**Social Scientists and Scientists.** In a June 2000 interview with Vine Deloria, the internationally known American Indian intellectual observed that in addition to poetry American Indians now need to do more scientifically geared writing (Porterfield 2000). He pointed out that not only does the other side of the story of colonialism need to be told, but that it is also "difficult for Indian authors to gain acceptance in the field [of academia] because social science is a closed group. It's a club, a celebrity cult that is based on personality not scholarship. It's time for Indian authors to start earning their spurs." For several decades indigenous women have been demonstrating that they are earning their spurs. Not only are a record number of women completing high school and college degrees including graduate degrees in the sciences, but more and more women are also writing and publishing in a number of academic areas such as education, criminology, and environmental studies. Professor Delores J. Huff (Cherokee) in her recent book *To Live Heroically: Institutional Racism and American Indian Education* examines institutional racism in tribal, mission, and BIA schools and the quality of education for American Indian students.

Professor Luana Ross (Salish) examines colonization and the social construction of deviance in her university courses and in her recent book *Inventing the Savage: The Social Construction of Native American Criminality*. Ross focuses on the intersections of racism, sexism, and the criminal justice system and the implications for Native American women. She adds the heartbreaking yet inspiring narrative of Gloria Wells Norlin (Pembina Chippewa), who has been able to rise above the racism and sexism of the multi-jurisdictional criminal justice system to build a new life for herself and her family.

Speaker, writer, researcher, and activist Winona LaDuke (Anishinaabe, Mississippi Band of Anishinaabeg/Jewish) has drawn national and international attention to the exploitation of natural resources of North America's indigenous peoples and the impact of such exploitation. In 1994 she was named by *Time Magazine* as one of America's fifty most promising leaders under forty years of age; in 1997 with the Indigo Girls, she was named a *Ms. Magazine* Woman of the Year. In 1999 LaDuke's *All Our Relations: Native Struggles for Land and Life* was published and has helped non-Indians and Indians understand that "[i]n the final analysis, the survival of Native America is fundamentally about the collective survival of all human beings" (LaDuke 1999, 5).

Adeline Armour, born in 1919, is shown here with two of her many great–grandchildren in 1990. Adeline's Arapaho name is Tox"uu Niibei, the translation of which is not known. (Photo by Sara Wiles)

Psychiatrist Clare Cifton Brant (Mohawk) has published scholarly works about North American Indian mental issues in Canada. Marigold Linton (Cahuilla-Cupeno), experimental psychologist, has not only published in the areas of long term memory but also is the co-author of the widely used text *The Practical Statistician: A Simplified Handbook of Statistics.* Other Native American women social scientists and scientists include Ella Deloria (Yankton Dakota); Tsianina Lomawaima (Creek); Carol Chiago Lujan (Navajo); Beatrice Medicine (Hunkpapa-Sihasapa Lakota); Henrietta (Whiteman) Mann (Southern Cheyenne); and Loretta Winters (Annisinabe).

**Historians and Cultural Specialists.** American Indian women such as historian Clara Sue Kidwell (Chippewa/Choctaw) are rewriting history, presenting a more balanced view. Olive Patricia Dickason (Métis) has seriously undermined stereotypes in *The Myth of the Savage and the Beginnings of French Colonialism of the Americas.* Ethnohistorian and screenwriter Lee Miller (Eastern Cherokee/Kaw) uses the voices of the First Peoples in her edited book *From the Heart: Voices*

*of the American Indian* to tell the other side of the invasion of the Americas. Twylah Nitsch (Seneca), credited with the preservation and advancement of the Seneca Nation, has published numerous historical pieces on Seneca culture and history. In *The Politics of Hallowed Ground: Wounded Knee and the Struggle for Indian Sovereignty,* Elizabeth Cook-Lynn (Santee/Yankton Sioux) and Mario Gonzales (Oglala Sioux) present another version of what happened in the 1970s' political struggle at Wounded Knee.

Historian and cultural specialist Mardell Plainfeather (Crow) has played a critical role in presenting an accurate picture of what happened at the Battle of the Little Big Horn (Montana), also known as Custer's Last Stand. Charlotte Heth (Cherokee) serves as Oklahoma assistant director of the National Museum of the American Indian. Rayna Green (Cherokee) is currently director of the American Indian Program at the National Museum of the American Indian, Smithsonian Institution.

Biographies and autobiographies are also recreating the past. In *Beyond the Four Corners of the World: A*

> ### Figure 11.2
> ### An Abbreviated Roll Call of Contemporary North American Indian Women Poets and Writers
>
> Paula Gunn Allen (Laguna/Sioux/Scotch and Lebanese American)
> Jeanette Armstrong (Okanagan)
> Kimberly Blaeser, Ph.D. (Anishinaabe/German American)
> Diane Burns (Anishinabe/Chemehuevi)
> Elizabeth Cook-Lynn, M.A. (Crow Creek Sioux)
> Nora Davenhauer (Tlingit)
> Morning Dove (Okanogan)
> Debra Earline (Flathead)
> Louise Erdrich (Anishinaabe/German American)
> Diane Glancy (Cherokee/English and German American)
> Janet Campbell Hale (Coeur d'Alene)
> Joy Harjo, M.F.A. (Creek)
> Linda Hogan (Chickasaw/European American)
> Leanne Howe (Choctaw)
> Beverly Hungry Wolf (Blood Tribe of the Blackfoot)
> Emily Pauline Johnson (Mohawk/European American)
> Maude Kegg (Ojibwe)
> Susan Power (Standing Rock Sioux/European American)
> Wendy Rose (Hopi/Me-wuk)
> Leslie Marmon Silko (Pueblo)
> Virginia Driving Hawk Sneve (Rosebud Dakota)
> Mary Tall Mountain (Athapascan)
> Luci Tapahonso (Navajo)
> Velma Wallis (Athabaskan)
> Roberta Hill Whiteman, Ph.D. (Oneida)

Winona LaDuke. (Photo by Susan Alzner)

*Navajo Woman's Journey*, Emily Benedek presents the story of Ella Bedonie and her family's journey between two worlds: the ancient and the modern. The manuscript of Susan Bordeax Bettelyoan's (Brile Lakota/French American) life history, beginning before the reservation period and ending at the start of the contemporary period, has been edited and published in *With My Own Eyes: A Lakota Woman Tells Her People's History*. Lee Maracle analyzes feminism and sociology from an indigenous perspective in *I Am Woman: A Native Perspective on Sociology and Feminism*.

Even Western philosophy is being challenged by First Nations women. Author and activist Anne Schulherr Waters (Seminole/Choctaw/Chickasaw/Cherokee) is president of the American Indian Philosophy Association and chair of the American Philosophical Association Committee on American Indians in Philosophy.

**Other Professions.**   Engineer Mary Ross (Cherokee) retired from Lockheed in 1973 after pioneering a career in planetary engineering or flyby space vehicles designed to explore the surfaces of Venus and Mars. Award-winning microbiologist Judy Gobert (Salish/Kootnai) is the new chair of the board of directors of American Indian Science and Engineering Society (ASES).

In the world of high technology and mass communications American Indian women are making names for themselves. Filmmaker, writer, and producer Carol Geddes' (Tlingit) first major film, *Doctor, Lawyer, and Indian Chief* (1986), won an award at the 1988 National Educational Film and Video Festival in San Francisco. Communications specialist Gail Guthrie Volaskakis (Ojibwa) addresses mass media stereotypes of Indian women in *Being Native in North America*. Roxann

**Figure 11.3
A Short Roll Call of North American Indian Women
Human Rights Activists: Urban and Reservation**

Dolly Smith Akers (Nakota)
Annie Mae Aquash (Micmac)
LaNada Means Bayer (Shononi/Bannock)
Lisa Bellanger (Ojibwa)
Raymona Bennett (Puyallup)
Gladys Bissonette (Lakota)
Nolee Bogdanski (Nakota)
Myrna Boyd (Nakota/Lakota)
Nellie Cornoyea (Inuvialuit)
Shawn Crawford (Nakota)
Mary Crow Dog (Lakota)
Alice Brown Davis (Seminole)
Ada Deer (Menoninee)
Jan English (Wyandot)
Mary Jane Fate (Athabaskan)
Susan Shown Harjo (Cheyenne/Arapaho)
LaDonna Harris (Comanche)
Debra Harry (Northern Paiute)
Elizabeth Hopps (Mohawk)
Jo Jo Hunt (Lumbee)
Ingrid Washinawatok-El Issa (Menoninee)
Nancy Jemison (Seneca)
Betty Mae Jumper (Seminole)
Cecilia Jumping Bull (Lakota)

Carol Juneau (Flathead)
Rita Keshena (Menominee)
Rosemary Kuptana (Inuit)
Stella Leach (Ogala Sioux/Colville)
Patricia Locke (Sioux/Chippewa)
Wilma Mankiller (Cherokee)
Susan Master (Yurok)
Rosalie McKay-Want (Pomo/Wailaki/Wintun)
Iris McKey (Lakota)
Patti McKey (Lakota)
Theresa McKey (Lakota)
Carol Meyers (Blackfeet)
Minnie Sibbets Olson (Nakota)
Ethel Pearson (Kwawkgewlth)
Helen Peterson (Cheyenne)
Myra Pipe (Lakota)
Viola Marie Robinson (Micmac)
Helen Maynor Scheirbeck (Lumbee)
Tillie Walker (Mandan/Hidatsa)
Della Warrior (Oto)
Laurie Whitright (Lakota)
Agnes Williams (Seneca)
Chris Zane (Wyandot)
Holly Zane (Wyandot)

Bighorn (Lakota/Dakota) teaches computer graphics at Fort Peck Community College in Poplar, Montana.

In keeping with the tradition of women warriors, contemporary women such as Grace Thorpe (Sauk/Fox), Loretta S. Jendritza (Navajo), Marcia Ann Biddleman (Seneca), and Gwen Mail (Lakota) have served honorably in various branches of the United States military.

To end on a recreational, albeit professional, note, by the 1980s and 1990s more women had the leisure and opportunity to pursue athletic careers. In 1995 basketball star Ryneldi Becenti (Navajo) was the first American Indian woman to play professional basketball for a foreign team, the Swiss. In 1996 she became the first Navajo woman to be inducted into the American Indian Athletic Hall of Fame.

### Economic Development and North American Indian Women

The 1969 Special Subcommittee Report on Indian Education noted the "life of poverty and despair to which the First Americans were condemned. At that time the unemployment rate among Indians was nearly 40 percent, more than 10 times the national average" (U.S. Congress 1969, x). By 1990 the rates of unemployment had improved but dismal differences between national and American Indian rates remained. The unemployment rate for American Indian males was 16 percent compared to 6 percent for men of all races; the unemployment rate for all American Indian females was slightly better at 13 percent compared to 6 percent for women of all races (Wilhelmina 1998). Given the lack of employment opportunities other than cottage industries for which the craftswomen have been dismally underpaid on reservations, only 45 percent of the women have been able to find financially meaningful work (Sandefur 1996).

Racism and institutional discrimination have continued to contribute to the poverty in which 27 percent of American Indians/Alaska Natives lived in 1990. According to the 1990 Census, the median household income in 1989 for First Peoples living on the reservation was $19,897 and almost one-third, 31.6 percent, were surviving below the poverty level (U.S. Department of Health and Human Services 1999). One-half of the 26 percent of female-headed American Indian/Alaska Native households had incomes below the poverty level. In the early 1980s Indian women reported incomes that were on average 77 percent of their white sisters. First Nations women who are living in poverty are usually the working poor.

Approximately 50 percent of all American Indian/Alaska Native children under the age of six are estimated to be living in poverty. One-half of all American Indian/Alaska Native adolescents live in poor or near-poor families. Female American Indian/Alaska Native adolescents make up slightly less than one-half of all American Indians/Alaska Natives aged ten to nineteen.

Economic hardships remain but women's conditions are improving more rapidly than men's, and the change is being largely led by women. For instance, Gail Small (Northern Cheyenne) has been another key figure in the fight to empower indigenous peoples. A mother of four, she is a sociologist, a lawyer, a 1997 appointee to the Federal Reserve Board's Consumer Advisory Panel (the first American Indian to have ever served on one of the federal bank's committees), and director of Native Action, a grassroots group dedicated to reservation survival. Like her activist sisters from other nations, Small has taken on formidable adversaries on behalf of her children and her people, the Northern Cheyenne, located on their reservation in Southeastern Montana. Her adversaries are both the BIA and AMAX, a big corporation determined to indiscreetly coal strip the semiarid Northern Cheyenne land. Under Small's leadership, Native Action has been successful in implementing two empowerment strategies for the Northern Cheyenne: economic justice and education. One indicator of the economic success has been the 1997 installation of the first automated bank machine at Lame Deer.

Eloise Cobell (Blackfeet), founder of the Blackfeet Tribal Bank in Montana, spearheaded the lawsuit against the BIA for mismanagement of Indian accounts. Michelle Henderson (Nakota) is the founder and executive director of the National American Indian Business Leaders (AIBL) headquartered in Missoula, Montana. Trudi Lamb (Schaghticoke) and LaFawn Tatoo Copenhager (Nakota) are only two of the many who have achieved environmentally and culturally sound economic development in the forms of business ownership or through other means.

### Sovereignty and American Indian Women as Leaders, Bridge Builders, and Cultural Mediators

In addition to maintaining their traditional roles of mothers, grandmothers, and aunts, as well as trailblazers, cultural mediators, and brokers in health care and Western education, First Nations women have been indispensable in tribal and federal politics both as leaders and bridge builders.[5] Important numbers of women have served both as elected members and chairs of their respective tribal governments, the National Chairman's Association, and other Western organizations. During the last decade, approximately 21 percent, over one-fifth of the chairs, presidents, and governors of Native American communities in the United States and Canada have been women (Furtaw 1993). Circa one-third of the United States American Indian voluntary national organizations are headed by women. A trailblazer in modern politics, Dolly Smith Akers (Assiniboine) was the first American Indian woman to be elected to a state legislature (Montana). Decades before the tribal chair election of Wilma Mankiller (Cherokee), Akers was the first female to be elected chair of the Fort Peck Assiniboine and Sioux Tribal Council.

The American Indian Movement could not have survived without its women. Activist and tribal legal advocate Myrna Boyd (Fort Peck Lakota) was Hank Adam's right-hand advisor during the 1972 Trail of Broken Treaties. Boyd later formed the Walks For Society, the first advocacy group for children on the Fort Peck Assiniboine and Sioux Reservation. Countless women have fought for the release of Leonard Peltier, an Ojibway activist convicted of killing two federal agents in a 1975 shoot-out on the Pine Ridge Reservation in South Dakota. The exclusion of 80 percent of defense testimony during Peltier's trial caused many individuals both inside and outside of the Native American community to regard Peltier as a political prisoner, convicted more for his activities with the American Indian Movement than on the strength of the case against him. As early as 1975 Ethel (Wilson) Pearson (Kwawkgewlth) adopted Peltier in a ceremony in the struggle to free America's internationally known human rights activist.

In May 2000 a Condolence Ceremony of the Longhouse people of the Mohawk Nation was held. A Condolence Ceremony traditionally wiped away the tears and grief of those who had lost love ones to murder during the past year. Over one thousand witnesses and principals from the Eastern and Western Doors of the Confederacy, the Mohawk, Seneca, Onondaga, Oneida, and Cayuga, took part in the ceremony, the first held in over twenty-five years. In keeping with the traditional status of indigenous women, Elizabeth Hopps, clanmother for the Wolf Clan, called forward those chosen to represent her clan. Margaret Laughing was selected to stand as faithkeeper for the Wolf Clan women.

In August of 1999, the three branches of the Wyandot Nations from Kansas, Oklahoma and Canada met for the first time since the dispersion 350 years earlier, largely due to the efforts of women. The ceremonial gathering was held in the Wyandot homeland of the larger Georgian Bay area, Ontario. During the reunion ancestral bones that had been used for scientific research were reburied in a sacred manner.

In the early 1900s the Wyandot Conley sisters took a victorious stand against economic developers seeking to destroy the Huron Cemetery located in the heart of Kansas City. Almost one hundred years later, remembering their ancestors' courage, Jan English (Wyandot), a psychiatric nurse, and her cousins Holly Zane (Wyandot), an attorney, and Chris Zane (Wyandot), an engineer (another set of Wyandot sisters), have served as cultural mediators, resisting once again the destruction of the gravesite.

As in the past when warrior women gave their lives to protect their people, modern heroines have died on behalf of First Peoples. The 1976 murder of AIM activist Annie Mae Aquash (Micmac) has never been solved. While fulfilling the historical role of peacemaker, Ingrid Washinawatok-El Issa (Menominee) gave her life in 1999 negotiating for indigenous rights throughout the world.

### Traditional Spirituality and Christianity

Christianity continues to play an important role in the lives of American Indian women on reservations as well as in urban settings. Small groups of evangelistic and/or fundamentalist church leaders and congregations, albeit often quite vocal and powerful, permit American Indian women to talk about Indian identity but allow little or no engagement in traditional culture, especially traditional spiritual ceremonies. More mainstream Christian congregations with large numbers of American Indians tend to incorporate American Indian symbols and often use indigenous tongues. In all Christian groups women are almost always members or lay leaders rather than ministers or priests. Some women become Catholic nuns as did Gloria Ann Davis (Navajo/Choctaw) in 1952, the first American Indian to enter the Order of the Blessed Sacrament in the Roman Catholic Church.

The Freedom of Religion Act of 1978 officially returned traditional spiritual ceremonies that were up to that time banned and outlawed, a violation of freedom of religious rights strongly supported by certain Christian groups. Almost twenty years later spiritual rights were still being violated so the Freedom of Religion Act of 1994 was passed. Fern Eastman Mathias (Sisseton/Wahpeton Dakota), Elva Stands In Timber (Northern Cheyenne), and Maria Pearson (Yankton Sioux) have been leading activists on behalf of the restoration of not only traditional ceremonies but also repatriation of Indian human remains and sacred objects. Perhaps the best known spiritual rights activist is Henrietta Mann who has received international acclaim for her insightful and poignant critiques of Western stereotypes of the indigenous savage.

A growing body of research demonstrates that women who honor a traditional holistic way of life, respecting mind/body/spirit connections, walk the most balanced paths. These are the contemporary North American women whose hearts and heads are connected and consequently understand the ancient Wyandot and Lakota inclusion of all forms of life: Tsonkwadiyonrat (We are one spirit) and Mitakuye Oyasin (We are all related).

### Conclusion

The preceding discussion of the challenges facing contemporary American Indian women and their accomplishments dispels any lingering myths and replaces the stereotypical image of the pathetic Indian woman with a clear picture of women of remarkable strengths and adaptive abilities, attributes allowing them not only to survive the bitter fruits of internal colonialism but also to do so with style and grace. The following patterns of the accomplishments of contemporary Native North American women are remarkably clear: (1) Native women are everywhere, especially in education, health care, the arts, political activism, economic development, and religious rights; (2) they are leaders in the transculturation process and the renaissance of indigenous cultures throughout the world; (3) they are successfully combining professional and political multiple roles; and (4) they have continued to retain the cultural value of centrality of family and children.

*Karren Baird-Olson*
*California State University, Northridge*

### Notes

1. See Light and Martin 1986; and Baird-Olson 1994.

2. See Perrone 1989.

3. See Thorton 1998.

4. There are three departments in the country that I can determine at this time. The other two are at the University of Minnesota and the University of California, Davis.

5. See Mihesuah 1998.

## ◆ RIGHTS AND ROLES OF FIRST NATIONS WOMEN OF CANADA

In 1989 Jeannette Armstrong of the Okanagan Nation opened the National Symposium on Aboriginal[1] Women of Canada with a moving and heartfelt invocation of the "real power of Aboriginal women":

> In traditional Aboriginal society, it was woman who shaped the thinking of all its members in a loving, nurturing atmosphere within the base family unit.... Traditionally, it was woman who controlled and shaped that societal order to the state of harmony, which in this time of extreme disorder seems nearly impossible.... It was through the attack on the power of Aboriginal women that the disempowerment of our peoples has been achieved, in a dehumanizing process that is one of the cruelest on the face of this earth. (Armstrong 1996, ix–x)

Despite the many cultural, social, political, and spiritual differences among them, Aboriginal women, scholars, and activists share this understanding of women's crucial social and familial roles. They speak of women as keepers of the fire and givers of life, and point to the many ways in which traditional culture symbolized the powers of motherhood. In current times of social disorder and stress mothers are the symbol and power of healing. Standing at the center of their societies, Aboriginal women take on diverse roles and responsibilities as mothers and grandmothers, politicians and community members. Whether they choose to live in large metropolitan areas or to remain within a close family circle in the communities of their birth, women challenge the sociopolitical forces that have suppressed their peoples while they struggle to sustain their cultural integrity.

In order to understand the many dimensions of Aboriginal women's lives we must look at three sociopolitical forces: (1) the ways in which the colonial policies and practices of the Canadian state have oppressed and devalued women; (2) the methods Aboriginal women use to struggle against their oppression; and (3) the many rich and varied contributions women make to their families and communities. This chapter will first address the ways in which the powers of the Canadian state have disrupted the family and community of Aboriginal peoples by the imposition of patriarchal practices and the particular consequences of these for Aboriginal women in their struggles for social justice. It will begin with the ways in which the Canadian state has defined Aboriginal women and has used the Indian Act to limit their social and political rights by privileging male power and identity. Next there will be a discussion of Aboriginal women's struggles against the state and the male privileges that prevail in their home communities. The chapter closes with examples of the roles women play in their home communities as they seek to influence internal and external conditions in order to shape their communities as a reflection and extension of their family relations.

### The Indian Act

The federal government defines the majority of Aboriginal peoples as Indians. Since 1869 it has used patrilineal and patrilocal rules to determine whom it will and will not recognize as Indians. These rules, embedded in the Indian Act, resulted in two social categories: status Indians who, registered by the federal government, have rights stipulated by the Indian Act, and non-status Indians who are denied the rights and protection of federal government fiduciary obligations as set out in federal legislation. In consequence non-status Indians constitute an ethnic and cultural group that, despite having constitutional recognition of Aboriginal origins, are bereft of exercising Aboriginal title or rights to lands and resources. The Canadian government uses the Indian Act to administer status Indians, whom it has organized into bands, and Indian lands, known in Canada as reserves. Although "status Indian" remains a legal term, it is no longer commonly used. *First Nations* has become the accepted term for Indian bands organized and defined by the Indian Act and when used politically it excludes Métis and Inuit peoples and often non-status Indians.[2]

Historically, under the Indian Act regulations men retained Indian status and membership in their band, regardless of the racial or legal status of their wives. They also transferred status to their non-Indian wives and to the children of their interracial marriages. In contrast, Indian women lost status and all entitlements it brought upon marriage to a non-Indian, as defined by the act. Further, any children born to a woman who had had status stripped from her were also denied legal recognition as Indians. Band membership was also constrained by patrilocal regulations. Upon marriage to a man registered in another band, a woman was stripped of membership in her natal community and of all entitlements that she had as a resident member there.

Until 1951, when the act was amended to conform with international law, specifically the United Nations Convention on the Political Rights of Women, Indian women had fewer political rights than men. Unlike men, women over the age of twenty-one were denied the right to vote or hold positions within the Indian Act system of elected band councils. The government also refused women the same property rights as men enjoyed. Whereas men could certify possession of parcels of reserve land for housing, farming, or other purposes, women could not. If their marriages ended women could be forced out of their home. In addition, widows were not guaranteed inheritance rights. Rather they were required to prove themselves to be of "good moral character" in order to hold property. The sexist allocation of rights was even extended off the reserve in some cases. For example in 1926 the provincial government of British Columbia required all trappers to register their traplines and to abide by trapping regulations set by the province. Women were excluded from registering their lands and from trading their furs on the open market as free trappers. Today this means that many women have lost access to traplines, a significant loss, for women traditionally provided for their families from the resources of the traplines (Fiske and Mufford 1998).

Although Indian women had protested the membership regulations of the act for over one hundred years, it was not until the 1970s that Indian women turned to the courts for redress. In 1973 Jeanette Lavell, an Ojibwa woman, lost her court challenge against the marrying out rules, an action that accelerated women's protests nationally and internationally. In the 1960s Mary Two Axe Early, a Mohawk woman, had also been forced from her reserve for marrying a non-Indian. She had formed the National Committee on Indian Rights for Indian Women (IRIW), an association of status and non-status women. For the decade following Lavell's defeat in court, IRIW lobbied the government, took their struggle to national and international forums, held protest marches and annual meetings, and in 1979 went to the United Nations Committee on Human Rights. Finally, in 1981 Sandra Lovelace of the Tobique Maliseet First Nation, New Brunswick, won a partial victory before the United Nations Committee on Human Rights, which ruled that the membership provisions of the act violated the International Convention on Civil and Political Rights because she was forced to live apart from her ethnic community (Silman 1987). Although Canada was embarrassed by this finding, it only made changes to the Indian Act after the Canadian Constitution was repatriated in 1982.

Since 1982 the Canadian Constitution (formerly the British North America Act 1867) has been known as the Constitution Act 1982. The Canadian Charter of Rights and Freedoms, Part 2 of the Constitution Act (sections 15 and 28), protects sexual equality for Canadian women. In order to harmonize the Indian Act with the Constitution the sexist membership regulations were finally

amended, making Indian women among the first women in Canada to benefit from the new equality rights. The amendments became effective in 1985 (when the constitutional equality rights took effect for all Canadian women) under what is popularly known as Bill C-31. The old entitlement regulations were repealed and new provisions added to reinstate women and their children who had lost status. Nonetheless women who intermarried or married out prior to Bill-C 31 remain at a greater legal and political disadvantage than men who did the same, because their children do not have the same rights of registration. Individuals registered under section 6(1) of the amended act, which includes all those having status prior to 1985 or who lost status through any of the old rules of enfranchisement, can intermarry and transfer status to their children, who will be registered under section 6(2). However, individuals registered under 6(2) cannot intermarry and transfer status to their children. This provision, known as the "second generation cut off" rule, threatens population growth of First Nations as increasing numbers are disenfranchised through intermarriage.[3] The second generation rule imposes greater hardship over women than men in another respect: control of reproduction and family unity. The new legislation also demands that in order to register her children under section 6(1), a woman must now prove the father is also registered. For unmarried women, this serious invasion of privacy undermines their security of person.

The new legislation also creates a new distinction between membership in a band and registration of status. The children of reinstated band members may register as status Indians but are not guaranteed band membership, thus leading to family disruption as women return to communities in which their children have no rights or privileges. In order to accommodate First Nations' desires for greater control over their communities, Bill C-31 enables them to enact their own membership codes. Each nation can determine if the children of reinstated members can be registered as members; however, under the policies of the Department of Indian Affairs, these members are not guaranteed the same services as other members. As of 1995, 100,958 women, men and children had their status returned to them and they now make up 16 percent of the total registered population. In consequence, First Nations face immense difficulties in providing housing, health, and education benefits for their new members. In turn new stresses are placed upon women who, having been forced from their natal reserve, find that, upon returning, their community either has insufficient social and capital resources to provide for them in an equitable manner with long-term residents or that services may be denied their children.[4]

## The Canadian Constitution and the Charter of Rights and Freedoms

Issues of women's quest for equality and First Nations struggle for autonomy from colonial legislation makes the Charter of Rights and Freedoms a site of struggle between First Nations women, First Nations governments, and the state as it provides for both Aboriginal rights (Section 35), equality rights (Section 15), and sexual equality (Section 28). These tensions are articulated most clearly in a federal court decision, *Sawridge v. Canada 1995*. Three First Nations of Alberta, Sawridge, Sarcee, and Ermineskin, challenged the right of the federal government to impose membership rules upon First Nations on the grounds that Bill C-31 contravened the inherent right of First Nations to determine their own citizens. The three First Nations argued that under customary laws "women followed men upon marriage" (Isaac 1995, 5). The court ruled against the three First Nations and found that membership rules are a federal jurisdiction and therefore must conform to the Constitution Act 1982, which prohibits sexual discrimination as determinant of rights.

As some women were fighting against the membership rules of the Act, others were challenging the patriarchal regime of reserve property regulations. In the mid–1980s two women who had lost access to marital homes took their cases to the Supreme Court of Canada and lost.[5] The court ruled that provincial laws

Inuit mother and her children. (Photo by Wayne Sturge. Courtesy of Provincial Archives of Newfoundland and Labrador)

regarding marital property rights do not extend to reserve lands because they are a federal jurisdiction. On-reserve women are now the only women in Canada denied marital property rights. This does not mean, of course, that all women residing on reserves find themselves disadvantaged. Some First Nations do grant women equal access to homes and other property. But it does mean that women who do lose homes or other property have no rights of appeal to any other authority. The significance of this for women and communities is profound.

> The significance of matrimonial property for Aboriginal women must be understood in the context of what the reserve represents: it is the home of a distinct cultural and linguistic people. . . . The reserve home is generally not that of a nuclear family—parents, grandparents, brothers, sisters and others in need will all share the home. The home may be the only access a woman and her children may have to their culture, language and family. The economic value of the land is secondary to its value as shelter within a larger homeland—the homeland of her people, her family. (Manitoba 1991, 32–33)

Property rights is one of several issues that has led the Native Women's Association of Canada (NWAC), British Columbia Native Women's Society (BCNWS), and other Aboriginal women's organizations to argue that First Nations governments should be subject to the Charter of Rights and Freedoms. Section 35(1) states that "the existing Aboriginal and treaty rights of the Aboriginal peoples of Canada are hereby recognized and affirmed" and 35(4) guarantees these rights to women and men equally. In 1997 the BCNWS challenged impending legislation that would transfer responsibility for and authority over reserve lands from the federal government to First Nations. The BCNWS argued that women's property rights would not be effectively protected as First Nations governments are not subject to the Canadian Charter of Rights and Freedoms and thus women would have no avenue of appeal if their property rights were violated. They also argued that the government, through the Department of Indian Affairs, was violating its fiduciary obligations to First Nations women by abdicating its control over property management and bylaws. In their defense they appealed to Section 15 of the charter, which provides for individual equality rights, arguing that giving control of land to First Nations governments denied them the same rights as other women of Canada enjoy.

The BCNWS's efforts failed and the respective legislation became effective on 1 January 2000. The First

Nations Land Management Act (FNLMA) transfers the control of day-to-day land management to the First Nations and enables them to create and ratify laws on the use, possession, and occupancy of lands and to regulate division of property upon marriage breakdown. While fourteen of the 634 First Nations are now signatories to the agreement, provision is made for others to opt in at a later date. How this will affect women of participating Nations remains to be seen. First Nations are increasingly privatizing their communal land amongst band members. By means of certificates of possession, for example, individuals can exercise exclusive rights to plots of land within a reserve and hence can benefit personally from economic ventures. Property and real estate held in this manner constitutes an estate and can be willed to specified heirs, thus leaving the land outside communal benefits for generations. Where women do not have access to holding property in their own names they are prevented from establishing small businesses. Privatization, Menno Boldt explains, benefits an "Indian Elite," who wish to sustain the status quo. This explains why First Nations have resisted

> accepting all legitimate descendants (e.g., Indian women and their children whose status was restored under Bill C-31) as equal heirs of the "common wealth." This represents a betrayal of a traditional principle that all band/tribal members are entitled to an equal share in the fruits of the land. . . (Isaac 1995 citing Boldt 1993, 145).

However, we must bear in mind that the electoral system of government provides women an opportunity equal to men's to participate in the administration of their communities. In 1997, eighty-one First Nations women were chiefs of their nations, representing 13 percent of all First Nations. While this number is low, it does not account for the number of women who are elected councilors or who provide leadership through other means, whether as appointed advisors to the elected council or as administrators of social, health, or education programs.

Constitutional reform is a central site of power for all Aboriginal peoples of Canada. However, given that the Constitution defines three distinct sociolegal groups—Indians, Métis, and Inuit—as Aboriginal but excludes Métis, Inuit as well as non-status Indians from the benefits First Nations exercise under the Indian Act or through treaty negotiations, any attempt to address reforms that are meaningful to First Nations women's rights is complicated by the differing impacts such reforms may have on other Aboriginal women and by the political goals of Aboriginal associations privileged

by the state. This was the case in 1992 when the Native Women's Association (along with Women of the Métis Nations) turned to the courts to protest their exclusion from the consultations on proposed constitutional reform. NWAC alleged that exclusion from the constitutional process infringed upon their right to freedom of expression. While lower courts ruled in their favor, NWAC lost before the Supreme Court of Canada in 1994. NWAC's court challenge created tensions in Aboriginal communities, dividing advocates of collective rights from proponents of charter-protected individual rights and male political leaders from women's organizations. Tensions over political agendas and access to government funding also led the AFN to open a Women's Unit to deal with issues raised by NWAC and other women's organizations.

Greater opportunities for women may emerge as a consequence of a recent decision of the Supreme Court of Canada, *Corbiere v. Canada and the Batchewan Band* (20 May 1999). The court found section 77(1) of the Act to violate the charter by denying off-reserve members of First Nations a vote in council elections. The new ruling will affect not only voting rights, but also the delivery of services, issues of governance, funding, and accountability. The ruling will also affect the relations of the AFN with NWAC and other Aboriginal women's organizations and urban social service agencies.[6] This is of particular significance as women outnumber men among off-reserve residents, especially in urban centers, and are now represented at the federal level by women's organizations and the Congress of Aboriginal Peoples, an umbrella association of off-reserve status and non-status Indians.[7]

### The Criminal Justice System

Aboriginal women feel the impact of patriarchy in many ways, but the most damaging has been the legacy of a colonial patriarchy that is marked by contempt for women's well-being. Not only do women confront the ideological and economic violence of colonialism, but they also endure high rates of violence from the men in their communities. It is important to contextualize the dilemma of women within the complex consequences of the cultural violence inherent in colonialism. In order to understand the complexities and contradictions of women's suppressed status, it is important to bear in mind the patriarchal nature of state and law that has been imposed upon, and internalized by, Aboriginal communities in context of the racialization of the first peoples of Canada. As Aboriginal communities and political organizations come to exercise new powers and negotiate new relations with the dominant society they are susceptible to being condemned for patriarchal and sexist actions, actions that not only have marked the treatment of Aboriginal women by the dominant society, but also have been justified by the Canadian state as being in the best interests of Aboriginal communities. In consequence, as Aboriginal women confront violence within their communities they risk having their struggles appropriated and having their peoples as a whole represented in negative, harmful stereotypes. They also risk having the violence of non-Aboriginal against Aboriginal women erased from the public record.

Aboriginal scholars have identified several interrelated causes of the crisis of violence: internalized patriarchy, ideological defamation of Indian womanhood, colonial violence, and impoverishment of their communities. Teressa Nahanee, a Salish legal scholar of southern British Columbia, has labeled the crises "brown patriarchy" while Métis writer Lee Maracle speaks of "lateral violence." Carol LaPrairie, a non-Aboriginal criminologist, argues that colonialism has been harder on men than women. She suggests that while women's traditional roles of nurturing family and community have been marked by cultural continuity, Aboriginal men have lost their traditional roles of provider and protector, which has caused men to lose self-esteem and become violent and cynical. Patricia Monture-Angus places the cause of violence squarely within the violence of colonial relations and the impact of residential schools. As in the United States, children were forcibly removed from their parents and communities to be taken to boarding schools where they lost contact with their families, were punished for speaking their language, and were taught a colonial curriculum that denigrated their peoples. Sexual abuse and physical abuse was rife (at the time of writing 10,000 former students have instigated legal claims for compensation for abuses and loss of culture). Patricia Monture-Angus explains that not only did students learn violence from the school staff, but they also learned to survive, sometimes by "looking the other way." She connects this survival strategy to adult behaviors that discourage community members from confronting violence in their communities (1995, 25).

Speaking on camera before the Manitoba Justice Inquiry and the Royal Commission on Aboriginal Peoples, women described their fear of reprisals for seeking redress from violence through the Canadian criminal justice system. They protested lenient sentencing of Aboriginal sex offenders who are treated sympathetically by judges anxious to respond to cultural differences. They cited instances of judges suggesting that sexual assault was a cultural tradition. They protested sentencing that fails to protect women as a denial of their charter rights to equal benefit of the law on the grounds that when violent offenders are not imprisoned women's lives are endangered.

Women's concern for their safety has brought them into conflict with lawyers and politicians seeking an alternative to incarceration of Aboriginal women and men, who are overrepresented in the prison population. Overrepresentation of Aboriginal men and women in prison has long been a source of concern for Aboriginal peoples who have argued that the adversarial nature of the criminal justice system is in conflict with principles of reconciliation, healing, and community harmony.

Circle sentencing, a new justice measure implemented by a judge in the Yukon ten years ago, is an effort to avoid overreliance on imprisonment in favor of community sentences. In circle sentencing judges are advised by community members as to an appropriate sentence after taking into consideration the views and wishes of the victim, community members, and the offender, who all meet with the judge in a talking circle. When circle sentencing was initiated, it was not intended to be used in cases of sexual violence; however, it is being used in this manner, which concerns many Aboriginal women. Women fear attending the sentencing circles and when they do so they are often silenced by their desire to avoid reprisals. Circle sentencing may be particularly hard on women who have married into a community in which they have few relations to support them or who live in isolated communities that cannot provide social services and healing processes that are necessary to bring about the desired healing and reconciliation.

Like the struggle for reform of the Indian Act, the establishment of Aboriginal forms of justice raises questions regarding whether the charter needs to apply to First Nations governments, and, if so, whether it would afford women the protection they seek. At present it does not seem that the charter has given women the protection from violence that they seek, at least as long as dangerous offenders are not removed from communities, in particular from isolated communities that lack resources to provide for women's safety. Women's claims that lenient sentencing denies them their charter rights to equal benefit of the law have not led to any significant changes in sentencing practices, although these claims are made against federal, provincial, and territorial governments, which are covered by the charter.

The federal government has been slow to respond to Aboriginal women's concerns. In May 2000 Indian Affairs appointed Mavis Ericson, tribal chief of the Carrier Sekani Tribal Council, to conduct a six-month study with a mandate to make recommendations regarding the protection of women's rights "both under the Indian Act and outside of it" according to its recent press release. This new study follows a plethora of government studies over the past two-and-a-half decades investigating women's rights, domestic violence, health, socioeconomic status, and related issues. A small sample includes: the Royal Commission on the Status of Women (1970); Solicitor General (1990; Zambrowksy 1986); Department of Indian Affairs and Northern Development (1996); Manitoba Justice Inquiry (Hamilton and Sinclair 1991); the report of the Royal Commission on Aboriginal Peoples (1996), and its published and unpublished studies and position papers— for example, Manyfingers (1994), Monture (1993), Nahanee (1993), and LaRocque (1993)—Status of Women Canada (Gill 1995; Dion and Kipling 1998); Canadian Panel on Violence against Women (1993); and the British Columbia Ministry of Women's Equality (Frank 1992). These studies complement the multitude of studies conducted by Aboriginal women's associations, including Native Women's Association (1991, 1992a, 1992b, 1997; Sugar and Fox 1990) and the Ontario Native Women's Association (1989).

## Community Life

While the government has resisted responding to social and legal protests against the state, it has responded more positively to individual women's (in particular elders') contributions to culture and community life by awarding community leaders the Order of Canada in recognition of their contributions to culture, politics, community leadership, academic scholarship contributions, and other vital aspects of community and family well-being. These honors speak to the force of women's traditional and innovative community roles and responsibilities, and symbolize the strength of women's achievements in times of cultural turbulence and rapid sociolegal changes. They also recognize the degree to which women "do, despite the influence of patriarchy and paternalism, run First Nations communities. They, for the most part, run the band offices, health programs, education boards, and other community-based organizations" (Turpel-Lafond 1997, 326).

To a large extent, First Nations reserve communities can be accurately described as having a domestic political economy; that is, one that relies less on wage labor and capitalist ventures, and more on government transfer payments, unearned income, and subsistence production. This is particularly true of reserve communities that are located in an economic periphery, distanced from urban centers and isolated from smaller centers of resource harvesting and production. In a domestic economy, women lack access to wage earnings and investment capital. The average on-reserve earnings of First Nations women are the lowest in Canada, moreover their employment rate—38.2 percent according to statistical studies by Indian Affairs—is also the lowest, placing women in a position of multiple jeopardy. "The position of Indian women with respect to labor force participation and income suggests that they are the most severely handicapped in their exchange relations with employers" (Voyageur 1996, 94 citing Gerber 1990).

The domestic economy renders women's subsistence labor highly valuable. Women manage food resources for extended families, often for more than one household, care for dependent and ill relatives as well as for children, and enter into community work that contributes to their families' well-being. Traditional social and economic roles place women in a social position that is in stark contrast to the legal subjugation dictated by the Indian Act. The social, economic, and emotional value of women's work is illustrated by Paul Driben's account, "A Death in the Family." He describes how, in 1983, three traditionally oriented Ojibwa families suffered severe social disruption from the death of female members and in consequence endured staggering economic losses from a lack of subsistence production. When the three women died, their husbands and families no longer functioned effectively; their husbands suffered deep depression and from then on were unable to hunt or sustain close and nurturing relations with their children.

Writing of Cree women at Moosonee and Moose Factory, Ontario, Jennifer Blythe and Peggy Martin McGuire identify similar economic and political strategies to those described by Rosemary Brown of Lubicon Cree women in Alberta. Cree women regard their communities as an extension of their family and kin networks, thus they invest their energies and resources in their communities in ways that strengthen and revitalize their families. The intersection of so-called private and public enhances the social influence and power of women, in particular women who head large extended families and who provide for them through a range of subsistence and emotional labor. Decisions in the extended family are public decisions that direct community life and administrative and political decisions. Cree women struggle against social dislocation and suppression of their social status through balancing traditional roles of nurture with new economic and political strategies.

The intersection of traditional responsibilities and politics merge in the voluntary sector, which offers alternative resources to those allocated by the elected chief and council members who are constricted not only by the mandates of the federal Department of

Indian Affairs but also by electoral politics that shape community relations of power. As women of the Saik'uz Nation of Central British Columbia know, through the voluntary sector, with access to fiscal resources, women can create new social resources: employment, capital development such as public buildings, and alternative positions of influence, esteem, and respect (Fiske 1990; Moran and John 1988; Moran 1990). The social union of family and community allows women to broker power and influence through the establishment of voluntary associations that can sustain political autonomy, at times supporting an elected council, at other times resisting it as women move to provide for their families or to contest outside powers that threaten the resources, land bases, and social equilibrium of their communities.

Cultural renewal and revitalization lie behind women's efforts to redress social crises, such as substance dependency, as was the case at Alkali Lake, a Secwepemc Nation of British Columbia. In 1972 Phyllis Chelsea was shocked into taking action against alcohol; her determined actions, matched by those of her husband Andy, led Alkali Lake to sobriety. Political actions of Chelsea, who received the Order of Canada in 1992, and her husband opened up the possibility for laying charges and seeing convictions against priests who committed sexual abuses at the regional residential school and for dealing with other social issues resultant upon the residential school abuses. As a result, the community has a new school with women teaching language and culture in a continuance of traditional responsibilities of nurture (Furniss 1987).

In addition to being recognized for their cultural work and community leadership in traditional realms women of the First Nations are recognized nationally and internationally for their commitment to their people's land and to political actions necessary to protect their Aboriginal rights and entitlements with respect to traditional territory and resources. In 1986 Canada opened the skies over the Innu of Labrador to NATO for low-flying bomber tests. Faced with a second devastation of their lands (the first had been the damming of Churchill Falls, Patshetshunau, for hydroelectricity) Tshaukuesh mobilized Innu women in protests that attracted international media (Wadden 1991). In a similar move, in 1988 Lubicon Lake Cree women protested exploitation of resources from their lands by multinational corporations (Brown 1996, 160). In 1990 women of the Mohawk Nation, Kanesatake, were joined by Aboriginal women from across Canada as they faced a standoff with the Canadian military regarding the loss of sacred land. As with their other political actions, women undertook these courageous roles as nurturers of their people. Their actions link them to the resistance strategies of First Nations women across Canada who seek social justice for themselves, their families and their communities within a sense of their traditional responsibilities, whether that be as a struggle against the legacy of the Indian Act, a quest for protection of their Charter rights, or a fight for criminal justice.

## Conclusion

The sociolegal position of First Nation women in Canada is complex and multifaceted, being defined by a combination of constitutional rights, federal statutes, and common law, and taking shape in a political economy that has marginalized all Aboriginal peoples but has been particularly damaging to women's economic and social status. In consequence, their political activism and legal struggles reflect not only their subjugation vis-à-vis powers of the state but also their minority position within their communities and the Aboriginal ethnopolitical movement. The diversity of views that arise from Aboriginal women's activism and scholarship underscore this dilemma and define their vulnerable position as a minority within a minority. In these adverse conditions First Nations women across Canada work to revitalize their communities by trying to influence politics and social developments in ways that will strengthen their families and sustain the cultural values that are dear to their ancestors and meaningful to new generations.

*Jo-Anne Fiske*
*University of Northern British Columbia*

## Notes

1. The Canadian Constitution 1982 applies the term *Aboriginal* to the First Peoples of Canada and recognizes three socio-legal categories: Indian, Inuit, and Métis. The manner in which the state has recognized and refused Aboriginal rights to each of these three groups creates very different social and political struggles for them. It is beyond the scope of this chapter to deal with the diverse and complex differences that divide Indian, Inuit, and Métis women. Therefore the focus is on women legally recognized as Indian by the Canadian government. The term *Native* is used less commonly and then usually as synonymous with *Aboriginal* or *indigenous*. In the current political complex, wherein some non-Aboriginal Canadians contest and refute special rights for Aboriginal peoples, the term Native has been appropriated by non-Aboriginal political discourses to signal either a Canadian or regional

identity that erases any distinctive claims of Aboriginal peoples.

2. Tensions between status and non-status Indians arise from the colonial legacy of the Indian Act and continue due to the differential entitlements of Indian bands as opposed to non-status associations and urban communities. It is for this reason that *First Nation* is often applied exclusively to an Indian band.

3. There is an extensive literature on the sex discrimination of the Indian Act. For an overview of the history of the early struggle for equality, see Jamieson 1978. For a discussion of the aftermath of legal and constitutional changes see Jones 1985; Moss 1997; Nahanee 1987; and Silman 1987.

4. An example of this tension is the case of *Courtois and Raphael v. DIANA (1990) CHRRD/363 (CHRT)*. In this case the court found that the Department of Indian and Northern Affairs had failed to intervene when the band council refused a public service to the children of resident mothers due to their status as Bill C-31 registrants. However the Court also ruled that children of parents not ordinarily resident on the reserve could be denied public services.

5. These two cases, *Paul v. Paul 1986* and *Derrickson v. Derrickson 1985*, were heard by the Supreme Court of Canada. For an analysis of these cases see Turpel 1991 and Turpel-Lafond 1997.

6. Other changes are taking place in the relationship between AFN and NWAC. Marilyn Buffalo, former president of NWAC, ran for the position of national chief of AFN. She is the third woman to make an unsuccessful bid for this position.

7. At both the national and international levels First Nations women, along with Métis and Inuit women, seek redress through the membership of several of their organizations in the Indigenous Women's Organization, which represents women of North, Central, and South America.

## References

### Native Women and Traditional Society

Ager, Lynn. "The Economic Role of Women in Alaskan Eskimo Society." In *A World of Women: Anthropological Studies of Women in the Societies of the World*, edited by Erika Bourguignon, 305–317. New York: Praeger, 1980.

Albers, Patricia and Beatrice Medicine. *The Hidden Half: Studies of Plains Indian Women*. Washington, D.C.: University Press of America, 1983.

Bodenhorn, Barbara. "Gendered Spaces, Public Places: Public and Private Revisited on the North Slope of Alaska." In *Landscape: Politics and Perspectives*, edited by Barbara Bender, 169–203. Providence, R.I.: Berg, 1993.

Bonvillain, Nancy. "Gender Relations in Native North America." *American Indian Culture & Research Journal* 13, no. 2 (1989): 1–28.

———. "The Iroquois and the Jesuits: Strategies of Influence and Resistance." *American Indian Culture & Research Journal* 10, no. 1 (1986): 29–42.

Bowers, Alfred. *Hidatsa Social and Ceremonial Organization*. Lincoln: University of Nebraska Press, 1992.

Briggs, Jean. "Eskimo Women: Makers of Men." In *Many Sisters: Women in Cross-Cultural Perspective*, edited by Carolyn J. Matthiasson, 261–304. New York: Free Press, 1974.

Foster, Martha. "Of Baggage and Bondage: Gender and Status Among Hidatsa and Crow Women." *American Indian Culture & Research Journal* 17, no. 2 (1993): 121–152.

Gonzalez, Ellice B. *Changing Economic Roles for Micmac Men and Women: An Ethnohistorical Analysis*. Canadian Ethnology Service, Paper no. 72. Ottawa: National Museum of Canada, 1981.

Green, Rayna. *Native American Women: a Contextual Bibliography*. Bloomington: Indiana University Press, 1984.

Grumet, Robert. "Sunksquaws, Shamans, and Tradeswomen: Middle Atlantic Coastal Algonkian Women During the 17th and 18th Century." In *Women and Colonization: Anthropological Perspectives*, edited by Mona Etienne and Eleanor Leacock, 43–62. New York: Praeger, 1980.

Hamamsy, Laila Shukry. "The Role of Women in a Changing Navajo Society." In *Women and Society: an Anthropological Reader*, edited by Sharon W. Tiffany, 75–92. Boston: Eden Press Women's Publications, 1979.

Jablow, Joseph. *The Cheyenne in Plains Indian Trade Relations 1795–1840*. Seattle: University of Washington Press, 1950.

Klein, Alan. "Plains Economic Analysis: the Marxist Complement." In *Anthropology on the Great Plains*, edited by W. Raymond Wood and Margot Liberty, 129–140. Lincoln: University of Nebraska Press, 1980.

Klein, Laura. "Contending with Colonization: Tlingit Men and Women in Change." In *Women and Colonization: Anthropological Perspectives*, edited by Mona Etienne and Eleanor Leacock, 88–108. New York: Praeger, 1980.

Leacock, Eleanor. "Montagnais Women and the Jesuit Program for Colonization." In *Women and Colonization: Anthropological Perspectives*, edited by Mona

Etienne and Eleanor Leacock, 25–42. New York: Praeger, 1980.

Lewis, Oscar. *The Effects of White Contact Upon Blackfoot Culture with Special Reference to the Role of the Fur Trade.* Seattle: University of Washington Press, 1942.

Peters, Virginia. *Women of the Earth Lodges: Tribal Life on the Plains.* North Haven, Conn.: Archon Books, 1995.

Roessel, Ruth. *Women in Navajo Society.* Rough Rock, Ariz.: Navajo Resource Center, Rough Rock Demonstration School, 1981.

Willoughby, Nona. "Division of Labor Among the Indians of California." In *Reports of the University of California Archaeological Survey,* no. 60, 7–79. Berkeley: University of California Archeological Research Facility, Department of Anthropology, 1963.

*Nancy Bonvillain*

## Multiple Genders in Native Communities

Brown, Lester B., ed. *Two Spirit People: American Indian, Lesbian Women and Gay Men.* New York: Harrington Park Press, 1997.

Jacobs, Sue-Ellen, Wesley Thomas and Sabine Lang. *Two-Spirit People: Native American Gender Identity, Sexuality and Spirituality.* Urbana, Ill.: University of Illinois Press, 1997.

Lang, Sabine. *Men as Women, Women as Men: Changing Gender in Native American Culture.* Austin, Tex.: University of Texas Press, 1998.

Roscoe, Will. *Changing Ones: Third and Fourth Genders in Native North America.* New York: St. Martin's, Press, 1998.

———, ed. *Living the Spirit: A Gay American Indian Anthology.* New York: St. Martin's, 1988.

———. *The Zuni Man-Woman.* Albuquerque: University of New Mexico Press, 1991.

Thomas, Wesley and Sue-Ellen Jacobs. "'…And We Are Still Here': From *Berdache* to Two-Spirit People." *American Indian Culture and Research Journal* 23, no. 2 (1999): 91–107.

Williams, Walter L. *The Spirit and the Flesh: Sexual Diversity in American Indian Culture.* Boston: Beacon Press, 1992, 1986.

*Wesley Thomas*

## Contemporary U.S. Native Women

Albers, Patricia and Beatrice Medicine. *The Hidden Half: Studies of Plains Indian Women.* Washington, D.C.: University Press of America, 1983.

Alkali Lake Indian Band. *The People of Alkali Lake.* Pt. 2 of *The Honour of All.* 3 Documentary Videotapes. Seattle, Wash.: Phil Lucas Productions, 1985–1986.

Alvord, Lori Arviso, M.D. *The Scalpel and the Silver Bear.* New York: Bantam-Doubleday Books, 1993.

Anderson, Charles J., comp. *Fact Book on Higher Education.* New York: American Council on Education; Phoenix, Ariz.: Oryx Press, 1998.

Baird-Olson, Karren. "The Survival Strategies of Plains Indian Women: Coping with Structural and Interpersonal Victimization on a Northwest Reservation." Ph.D. diss., Albuquerque: University of New Mexico, 1994.

Benedek, Emily. *Beyond the Four Corners of the World: A Navajo Woman's Journey.* Norman: University of Oklahoma Press, 1998.

Bernikow, Louise. *The American Women's Almanac: An Inspiring and Irreverent Women's History.* New York: Berkley Books, 1997.

Boyer, Ruth McDonald with Narcissus Duffy Gayton. *Apache Mothers and Daughters: Four Generations of a Family.* Norman: University of Oklahoma Press, 1992.

Champagne, Duane, ed. *Native America: Portrait of the Peoples.* Detroit: Visible Ink Press, 1994.

Conference on the Educational and Occupational Needs of American Indian Women. *Conference on the Educational and Occupational Needs of American Indian Women, October 12 and 13, 1976.* Washington, D.C.: U.S. Department of Education, Office of Educational Research and Improvement, National Institute of Education, 1980.

Cook-Lynn, Elizabeth and Mario Gonzales. *The Politics of Hallowed Ground: Wounded Knee and the Struggle for Indian Sovereignty.* Urbana: University of Illinois Press, 1999.

Coyote, Bertha L. with Virginia Giglio. *Leaving Everything Behind: The Songs and Memories of a Cheyenne Woman.* Norman: University of Oklahoma Press, 1997.

Cradleboard Teaching Project. Available [Online]: http://www.Cradleboard.org [3 September, 2000].

DeFine, Michael Sullivan. "A History of Governmental Coerced Sterilization: The Plight of the Native American Woman." University of Maine School of Law, 1997. Available [Online]: http://www.geocities.com/CapitolHill/9118/mike2.html [3 September, 2000].

Dickason, Olive Patricia. *The Myth of the Savage and the Beginnings of French Colonialism of the Americas.* Calgary: University of Alberta Press, 1984.

Flannery, Regina. *Ellen Smallboy: Glimpses of a Cree Woman's Life.* Toronto, Canada: McGill-Queens University Press, 1995.

Furtaw, Julia C., ed. *Native Americans Information Directory.* Detroit: Gale Research, 1993.

Green, Rayna, ed. *That's What She Said: Contemporary Poetry and Fiction by Native American Indian Women.* Bloomington: Indiana University Press, 1984.

Greenfeld, Lawrence A. and Stephen K. Smith. *American Indians and Crime.* Washington, D.C.: U.S. Department of Justice, Office of Justice Programs, Bureau of Justice Statistics, 1999.

Harjo, Joy and Gloria Bird, eds. *Reinventing the Enemy's Language.* New York: W. W. Norton & Company, 1997.

Huff, Delores J. *To Live Heroically: Institutional Racism and American Indian Education.* Albany: State University of New York Press, 1997.

Klein, Laura F. and Lillian A. Ackerman, eds. *Women and Power in Native North America.* Norman: University of Oklahoma Press, 1995.

LaDuke, Winona. *All Our Relations: Native Struggles for Land and Life.* Cambridge, Mass.: South End Press, 1999.

Lang, Sabine and Sabine Long. *Men as Women, Women as Men: Changing Gender in Native American Cultures.* Austin: University of Texas Press, 1998.

Leigh, Wilhelmina A., and Malinda A. Lindquist. *Women of Color Health Data Book: Adolescents to Seniors.* Bethesda, Md.: Office of Research on Women's Health, Office of the Director, National Institutes of Health, 1998.

Light, Harriett K., and Ruth E. Martin. "American Indian Families." *Journal of American Indian Education* 26, no. 1 (1986): 1–5.

Linton, Marigold. *The Practical Statistician: A Simplified Handbook of Statistics.* Monterey, Calif.: Brooks/ Cole Publishers, 1975.

Mankiller, Wilma and Michael Wallis. *Mankiller: A Chief of Her People.* New York: St. Martin's Griffin, 2000.

Maracle, Lee. *I Am Woman: A Native Perspective on Sociology and Feminism.* 2d ed. Vancouver: British Columbia: Press Gang Publishers, 1996.

Martens, Tony. *Characteristics and Dynamics of Incest and Child Sexual Abuse; with a Native Perspective by Brenda Daily and Maggie Hodgson.* Edmonton, Alta.: Nechi Institute, 1988.

Mihesuah, Devon A. "Commonality of Difference: American Indian Women and History." In *Natives and Academics: Researching and Writing About Native American Indians*, edited by Devon A. Mihesuah, 37–54. Lincoln: University of Nebraska Press, 1998.

———, ed. *Natives and Academics: Researching and Writing About American Indians.* Lincoln: University of Nebraska Press, 1998.

Miller, Lee. *From the Heart: Voices of the American Indian.* New York: Knopf, 1995.

Perrone, Bobbette, H. Henrietta Stockel, and Victoria Krueger. *Medicine Women, Curanderas, and Women Doctors.* Norman: University of Oklahoma Press, 1989.

Powers, Marla. *Oglala Women: Myth, Ritual, and Reality.* Chicago: University of Chicago Press, 1986.

Ross, Luana. *Inventing the Savage: The Social Construction of Native American Criminality.* Austin: University of Texas Press, 1998.

St. Pierre, Mark and Tilda Long Soldier. *Walking in the Sacred Manner: Healers, Dreamers, and Pipe Carrier—Medicine Women of the Plains Indians.* New York: Simon and Schuster, 1995.

Sandefur, Gary D., Ronald R. Rindfuss, and Barney Cohen, eds. *Changing Numbers, Changing Needs: American Indian Demography and Public Health.* Washington, D.C.: National Academy Press, 1996.

Schweitzer, Marjorie M., ed. *American Indian Grandmothers: Traditions and Transitions.* Albuquerque: University of New Mexico Press, 1999.

Shkilnyk, Anastasia M. *A Poison Stronger than Love: The Destruction of an Ojibwa Community.* New Haven: Yale University Press, 1985.

Sonneborn, Liz. *A to Z of Native American Women.* New York, New York: Facts on File, 1998.

Thornton, Russell, ed. *Studying Native America: Problems and Prospects.* Madison: The University of Wisconsin Press, 1998.

U.S. Bureau of the Census. *Historical Statistics of the United States, Colonial Times to 1970.* Washington, D.C.: GPO, 1976.

U.S. Congress. Senate. Special Subcommittee on Indian Education. *Indian Education: A National Tragedy, A National Challenge*, 91st Congress, 1st Session, November 3, 1969. Washington, D.C.: GPO, 1969.

U.S. Department of Health and Human Services. Indian Health Service. Office of Planning, Evaluation, and Legislation. Division of Program Statistics. *Indian Health Focus: Women.* Washington, D.C., 1996.

U.S. Department of Health and Human Services. Public Health Service. Indian Health Service. Office of Planning, Evaluation, and Legislation. Division of Program Statistics. *Regional Differences in Indian Health, 1998–99.* Rockville, Md., 1999.

U.S. Department of Labor. Women's Bureau. *1975 Handbook on Women Workers.* Bulletin 297. Washington, D.C.: GPO, 1975.

Weibel-Orlando, Joan. *Indian Country, L.A.: Maintaining Ethnic Community in Complex Society.* Urbana: University of Illinois Press, 1991.

Weston, Mary Ann. *Native Americans in the News: Images of Indians in the Twentieth Century Press.* Westport, Conn.: Greenwood Press, 1996.

White Plume, Delora. *A Sharing: Traditional Lakota Thought and Philosophy Regarding Domestic Violence.* Pine Ridge, S. Dak.: Sacred Shawl Society, n.d. [1970s].

*Karren Baird-Olsen*

## Gender and Women's Relations in Canada

Armstrong, Jeannette. "Invocation: The Real Power of Aboriginal Women." In *Women of the First Nations: Power, Wisdom, and Strength*, edited by Christine Miller and Patricia Chuchryk, ix–xii. Winnipeg: University of Manitoba Press, 1996.

Bastien, Betty. "Voices through Time." In *Women of the First Nations: Power, Wisdom, and Strength*, edited by Christine Miller and Patricia Chuchryk, 127–128. Winnipeg: University of Manitoba Press, 1996.

Blythe, Jennifer and Peggy Martin McGuire. "The Changing Employment of Cree Women in Moosonee and Moose Factory." In *Women of the First Nations: Power, Wisdom, and Strength*, edited by Christine Miller and Patricia Chuchryk, 131–150. Winnipeg: University of Manitoba Press, 1996.

Brown, Rosemary. "The Exploitation of the Oil and Gas Frontier: Its Impact on Lubicon Lake Cree Women." In *Women of the First Nations: Power, Wisdom, and Strength*, edited by Christine Miller and Patricia Chuchryk, 151–166. Winnipeg: University of Manitoba Press, 1996.

Canada. Department of Indian Affairs and Northern Development. *Aboriginal Women: A Demographic, Social and Economic Profile*. Ottawa, 1996.

Canada. Royal Commission on Aboriginal Peoples. *Perspectives and Realities*. Vol. 4 of *Report of Royal Commission on Aboriginal Peoples*. Ottawa, 1996.

Canada. Royal Commission on the Status of Women in Canada. *Report of the Royal Commission on the Status of Women in Canada*. Ottawa: Information Canada, 1970.

Canadian Corrections Service. Task Force on Federally Sentenced Women. *Creating Choices: The Report of the Task Force on Federally Sentenced Women*. Ottawa: Correctional Service of Canada, 1990.

Canadian Panel on Violence Against Women. *Changing the Landscape: Ending Violence: Achieving Equality*. Ottawa, 1993.

Cruikshank, Julie, in collaboration with Angela Sidney, Kitty Smith, and Annie Ned. *Life Lived Like a Story: Life Stories of Three Yukon Native Elders*. Vancouver: UBC Press; Lincoln: University of Nebraska Press, 1990.

Driben, Paul. "A Death in the Family: The Strategic Importance of Women in Contemporary Northern Ojibwa Society." *Native Studies Review* 6 no. 1 (1990): 83–110.

Fiske, Jo-Anne. "Native Women in Reserve Politics: Strategies and Struggles." *Journal of Legal Pluralism and Unofficial Law* no. 30–31 (1990–1991): 121–137.

Fiske, Jo-Anne and Caroline Mufford. "Hard Times and Everything Like That: Carrier Women's Tales of Life on the Trapline." In *New Faces of the Fur Trade: Selected Papers of the Seventh North American Fur Trade Conference*, edited by Jo-Anne Fiske, Susan Sleeper-Smith and William Wicken, 13–30. East Lansing: Michigan State University Press, 1998.

Frank, Sharlene. *Family Violence in Aboriginal Communities: A First Nations Report*. Victoria, B.C.: Ministry of Women's Equality, 1992.

Furniss, Elizabeth. "A Sobriety Movement Among the Shushwap Indians of Alakali Lake." M.A. thesis, University of British Columbia, 1987.

Gill, Lise. *From the Reserve to the City: Amerindian Women in Quebec Urban Centres*. Ottawa: Status of Women Canada, 1995.

Greschner, Donna. "Aboriginal Women, The Constitution and Criminal Justice." *University of British Columbia Law Review* 26, Special issue (1992): 338–366.

Hungry Wolf, Beverly. "Life in Harmony with Nature." In *Women of the First Nations: Power, Wisdom, and Strength*, edited by Christine Miller and Patricia Chuchryk, 76–81. Winnipeg: University of Manitoba Press, 1996.

Isaac, Thomas. "Case Commentary: Self-Government, Indian Women and their Rights of Reinstatement Under the *Indian Act*: A Comment on *Sawridge Band v. Canada*." *Canadian Native Law Reporter* 4 (1995): 1–13.

Jamieson, Kathleen. *Indian Women and the Law in Canada: Citizens Minus*. Ottawa: Advisory Council on the Status of Women, Indian Rights for Women, 1978.

Jones, Camille. "Towards Equal Rights and Amendment of Section 12(1)(b) of the Indian Act: A Postscript to *Lovelace v. Canada*." *Harvard Women's Law Journal* 8 (1985): 195–213.

Jordan, Elizabeth. "Residual Sex Discrimination in the Indian Act: Constitutional Remedies." *Journal of Law and Social Policy* 11 (1995): 213–240.

LaRocque, Emma. "Re-examining Culturally Appropriate Models In Criminal Justice." *Aboriginal and Treaty Rights in Canada* : Essays on Law, Equity, and Respect for *Difference*, edited by Michael Asch, 75–96. Vancouver: UBC Press, 1997.

———. "Violence in Aboriginal Communities." In *The Path to Healing: Report of the National Round Table on Aboriginal Health and Social Issues*, 72–89. Ottawa: Royal Commission on Aboriginal Peoples, 1993.

Levis, Charlene. "The Silence Speaks Loudly: Considering Whether the Victims' Needs Can Be Met Through Circle Sentencing." M.A. thesis, University of Northern British Columbia, 1998.

Manitoba. Public Inquiry Into the Administration of Justice and Aboriginal People. *The Justice System and Aboriginal People.* Vol. 1 of *Report of the Aboriginal Justice Inquiry of Manitoba.* Winnipeg, Man., 1991.

Manyfingers, B. "Treaty 7 Community Study: Family Violence and Community Stress." Unpublished paper submitted to the Royal Commission on Aboriginal Peoples, 1994.

Maracle, Lee. *I Am Woman: A Native Perspective on Sociology and Feminism.* Vancouver: Press Gang Publishers, 1996.

McConney, Denise S. "Differences for Our Daughters: Racialized Sexism in Art, Mass Media and Law." *Canadian Woman Studies/Les Cahiers de la Femme* 19 no. 1 & 2 (1999): 209–214.

McIvor, Sharon. "Aboriginal Rights as Existing Rights." *Canadian Woman Studies/Les Cahiers de la Femme* 15 no. 2 & 3 (1995): 34–38.

Monture-Angus, Patricia. *Journeying Forward: Dreaming First Nations' Independence.* Halifax: Fernwood, 1998.

———. *Thunder in My Soul: A Mohawk Woman Speaks.* Halifax: Fernwood, 1995.

Monture-Okanee, Patricia. "Reclaiming Justice: Aboriginal Women and Justice Initiatives in the 1990s." In *Aboriginal Peoples and the Justice System: Report of the National Round Table on Aboriginal Justice Issues,* 105–132. Ottawa: Royal Commission on Aboriginal Peoples, 1993.

Moran, Bridget. *Judgement at Stoney Creek.* Vancouver: Tillacum Library, 1990.

———. *Stoney Creek Woman: The Story of Mary John.* Vancouver: Tillacum Library, 1988.

Moss, Wendy. "The Canadian State and Indian Women: The Struggle for Sex Equality Under the *Indian Act.*" In *Women and the Canadian State,* edited by Caroline Andrew and Sanda Rodgers, 79–88. Montreal: McGill-Queens University Press, 1997.

Nahanee, Teressa. "Dancing with a Gorilla: Aboriginal Women, Justice and the Charter." In *Aboriginal Peoples and the Justice System: Report of the National Round Table on Aboriginal Justice Issues,* 359–382. Ottawa: Royal Commission on Aboriginal Peoples, 1993.

———. "Indian Women, Sex Equality and the Charter." In *Women and the Canadian State,* edited by Caroline Andrew and Sandra Rodgers, 89–103. Montreal: McGill-Queen's University Press, 1997.

Native Women's Association of Canada. *An Aboriginal Charter of Rights and Freedoms: A Discussion Paper.* Ottawa: Native Women's Association of Canada, 1992.

———. "Aboriginal Women and the Constitutional Debates: Continuing Discrimination." *Canadian Woman Studies/Les Cahiers de la Femme* 12, no. 3 (1991): 14–17.

———. "Hear Their Stories." In *40 Aboriginal Women Speak.* Ottawa: Native Women's Association of Canada, 1997.

———. *Matriarchy and the Canadian Charter. A Discussion Paper.* Ottawa: Native Women's Association of Canada, 1992.

Nightingale, Margo L. "Judicial Attitudes and Differential Treatment: Native Women in Sexual Assault Cases." *Ottawa Law Review* 23 no. 1 (1991): 71–98.

Ontario Native Women's Association. *Breaking the Silence: Report on Domestic Violence.* Thunder Bay, Ont.: Ontario Native Women's Association, 1989.

Osennontion and Skonaganleh:ra. "Our World." *Canadian Woman Studies/Les Cahiers de la Femme* 10, no. 2 & 3 (1989): 7–20.

Silman, Janet. *Enough is Enough: Aboriginal Women Speak Out.* Toronto: Women's Press, 1987.

Stacey-Moore, Gail. "In Our Own Voice: Aboriginal Women Demand Justice." *Herizons* 6 no. 4 (1993): 21–23.

Stout, Madeleine Dion and Gregory D. Kipling. *Aboriginal Women in Canada: Strategic Research Directions for Policy Development.* Ottawa: Status of Women Canada, 1998.

Sugar, Fran and Lana Fox. "Nistum Peyako Se'ht'wawin Iskwewak: Breaking Chains." *Canadian Journal of Women and the Law* 3, no. 2 (1989): 465–482.

———. *Survey of Federally Sentenced Aboriginal Women in the Community.* Ottawa: Native Women's Association of Canada, 1990.

Turpel, Mary Ellen. "Home/Land." *Canadian Journal of Family Law,* 32, no. 1 (1991): 17–40.

Turpel-Lafond, Mary Ellen. "Patriarchy and Paternalism: The Legacy of the Canadian State for First Nations Women." In *Women and the Canadian State,* edited by Caroline Andrew and Sanda Rodgers, 64–87. Montreal: McGill-Queen's University Press, 1997.

Voyageur, Cora J. "Contemporary Indian Women." In *Visions of the Heart: Canadian Aboriginal Issues,* edited by David Alan Long and Olive Patricia Dickason, 93–117. Toronto: Harcourt Brace & Company Canada, 1996.

Wadden, Marie. *Nitassinan: The Innu Struggle to Reclaim their Homeland.* Vancouver: Douglas and McIntyre, 1991.

York, Geoffrey. *The Dispossessed: Life and Death in Native Canada.* Foreword by Tomson Highway. London: Vintage U.K., 1990.

Zambrowsky, Josh. *Needs Assessment on the Native Women Who Are or May Be in Conflict with the Law in the Region of Montreal.* Ottawa: Solicitor General of Canada, 1986.

*Jo-Anne Fiske*

# 12

# *Arts*

◆ Native Art in North America
◆ Traditional Ceremonies, Rituals, Festivals, Music, and Dance
◆ Contemporary and Pan-Tribal Native North American Music and Dance
◆ Native North American Visual Arts  ◆ Native American Art
◆ Exhibitors of Contemporary Native Arts  ◆ American Indian Cultural Events
◆ American Indian Art Markets and Fairs

## ◆ NATIVE ART IN NORTH AMERICA

The visual arts produced today by artists of Native ancestry throughout Canada and the United States are part of a living cultural tradition with deep roots in the past and much promise for the future. At present, these arts are playing a vital role in the regeneration and flowering of Native communities throughout North America. Artists of Native background today continue to express traditional values and draw upon past images and styles along with modern and post-modern developments to address social, political, spiritual, and environmental issues of relevance both to their Native communities and to the entire human family.

The history of Native art in North America, although undergoing constant transformation, may be divided into Ancient (pre-contact), Colonial (postcontact), and Contemporary (twentieth century), the precise dates of which vary between the sixteenth to the nineteenth centuries from one region of the continent to another. Native art production today falls into at least four major subdivisions, each fulfilling different functions and catering to a different audience: (1) traditional art forms such as sacred drums and ceremonial costumes made for use within Native communities for mainly spiritual purposes and social occasions such as pow-wows and potlatches; (2) tourist or souvenir art forms for sale to non-Natives at such places as airports and Indian arts and craft shops; (3) contemporary Native art with strong traditionalist characteristics for sale in urban art galleries specializing in Indian and Inuit carvings, prints, and various high-quality crafts; and (4) contemporary mainstream or fine art created by artists of Native ancestry trained in major Euro-American art

schools and universities, who perceive themselves primarily as self expressive individualists but work with Native values, beliefs, and concerns uppermost in their practice. These artists address themselves to the world at large in exhibits in major galleries of urban North America. Their works are commissioned or acquired by discriminating patrons, individuals, and provincial, state, and national art institutions.

### Ancient Native Art

Although the beginnings of visual expression in Native North America date from the first appearance of humans on this continent, few of the artworks recovered thus far date much before 3000 B.C.E. This is because most traditional Native art works were made of perishable materials, such as wood, hide, or vegetable and animal fibers that are able to survive in North American sites in only very exceptional climatological circumstances. Best known from the earliest archaeological sites are works in stone, bone, antler, copper, and ceramics, including the smoothly ground and sophisticated Archaic stone carvings of the Eastern Woodlands known as birdstones; animal and human figurines in bone, antler, and shell of many early periods throughout most of North America; and a great variety of carved stone and modeled clay smoking pipes of a more recent era, the latter depicting every variety of creature from frogs and snakes to wolves and bears, as well as humans in a variety of postures.

Another form of visual art, often called rock art, consists of paintings (pictographs) and engravings (petroglyphs) on cliffs, boulders, and bedrock and in rock shelters throughout North America. This form belongs to the most ancient of Native North American traditions. Rock art, however, is extremely difficult both to date and to interpret, owing to the lack of any clear-cut temporal or cultural contexts, and many erroneous opinions abound as to the era of their creation or who the creators actually were.

Rock art imagery continues to be of great importance to many contemporary Native artists. Painters such as the Ojibwa Norval Morrisseau, Chipewayan Jane Ash Poitras, and Cree/Flathead/Shoshone Jaune Quick-to-See Smith, have been much inspired by the images in this ancient pictorial genre. Among the most outstanding of the hundreds if not thousands of rock-art sites in North America are the petroglyphs at Nanaimo on Vancouver Island, British Columbia; Writing-On-Stone Provincial Park in southern Alberta; Petroglyphs Provincial Park near Peterborough, southern Ontario; and the brilliantly hued pictographs in the territory of the Chumash people of southern California. At Writing-On-Stone, for example, hundreds of petroglyphs and some pictographs are carved and painted on sandstone bluffs facing the Sweet Grass Hills of Montana along some twenty miles of the Milk River in southern Alberta. Most distinctive are narrative compositions describing battles and hunting scenes in graphic detail. The Chumash paintings on rocks and in caves in mountainous California, are brilliantly colored mandala-like images of both figurative and abstract circular motifs in pulsating combinations of hues that held a deeply spiritual meaning and were most likely inspired by visions.

Throughout North America, ancient art varies in genre, style, function, imagery, and meaning from one Native group to another. Change accelerated almost everywhere after about 1000 B.C.E. as a result of a number of influential factors, mainly the introduction of agriculture and settled village life in the American Southwest, Southeast, Midwest, and southern Great Lakes area of Canada and the United States.

Particularly noteworthy traditions of ancient Native art include the Dorset culture (800 B.C.E. to C.E. 1000) of the Canadian high Arctic, noted for its abundance of miniature carvings in bone, antler, and ivory. These emphasize plastic, sculptural volumes in which multiple images may coexist in a single work. The visual expressions of the later Thule culture (1000 C.E. onward) of Alaska and northernmost Canada are far more graphic and pictorial, in which everyday hunting scenes and ceremonial dances, among other subjects, are depicted. These Thule pictorial narratives lead directly to the graphic works produced today by contemporary Inuit artists.

On the Northwest Coast, stone and bone carvings of the Marpole culture (500 B.C.E. to 500 C.E.), centered on the Fraser River delta and the Gulf Islands, anticipate Northwest Coast art carving styles in wood of the nineteenth century and give evidence of the great persistence of coastal aesthetic expression that continues well into the twentieth century. It is likely that Northwest Coast art developed out of an ancient North Pacific maritime tradition dating back to about 2000 B.C.E., one showing stylistic and thematic similarities with the Polynesian Islands and with ancient China and Siberia.

In upper New York State and southern Ontario, the Iroquoian peoples between C.E. 900 and 1600 produced pottery decorated with representational and geometric motifs, as well as antler and bone combs and human figurines. Iroquoian stone and clay effigy pipes were produced in great abundance; they depicted the spiritual guardians of their owners and were and still are used in the ritual smoking of tobacco on important occasions.

The entire Eastern Woodlands area before the colonial era is noted for its complex, large-scale ceremonial centers, in which large burial mounds and flat-topped temple mounds, open plazas, and elaborate artworks in exotic materials such as copper and mica, as well as stone, shell, and clay, reveal a more stratified society emerging in the late pre-contact period. A group of recurrent motifs in the so-called Mississippian period, which flourished about 800 C.E., include sun-disks, skulls and bones, elaborately costumed dancing figures, and distinctive ceremonial objects. These motifs comprise an iconographic system known as the Southern Cult or the Southeastern Ceremonial Complex, one that is linked to such important Mississippian-period mound sites as those of Spiro in Oklahoma, Etowah in Georgia, and Moundville in Alabama. Art fulfilled not only utilitarian, spiritual, and social functions in later pre-contact times, but also political and diplomatic ones connected with the emergence of chieftaincies and status groups and with patterns of economic exchange and long-distance trade. Many characteristics of Eastern Woodlands cultural development may have been influenced to some extent by the great civilizations of ancient Mexico, as is also the case for the Pueblo region of the Southwest. In the Four Corners region of New Mexico, Arizona, Utah, and Colorado villagers, such as the Hopi and Zuni, engaged in agriculture and constructed permanent adobe-brick apartment-like dwellings and underground ritual structures known as kivas, the latter with wall-paintings illustrating their supernatural and cosmological belief system. Beautifully painted ceramics are an outstanding art form among the Pueblo, each group producing distinctive designs of their own.

The carving of a Hopi kachina. (Photo by Owen Seumptewa)

Decorative elements of Hopi architecture. (Detail from photo by Owen Seumptewa)

## Native Art in the Colonial Period

The colonial period may date in each region of North America anytime between C.E. 1500 and 1900. It should be noted that history did not begin with the coming of the Europeans with their alphabetical writing systems, as many Euro-Americans believed in the past. Today it is recognized that historical information is also derived from archaeological excavation and from other Native material documents as pictorial records painted, incised, or embroidered on hides, bark, wood, and in such other materials as Iroquoian shell-bead wampum belts, all of which served as memory aids in the narration of oral history. Such oral and pictorial records—considered writings by the Native peoples themselves—are finally being studied as vitally important documents for the recovery of Native art and cultural history.

Very few colonial period artworks remain within their Native communities. Most were "collected" (purchased, stolen, received as gifts, or appropriated) by early explorers, traders, missionaries, travelers, settlers, and various governmental agencies. Thousands upon thousands of such Native North American artworks are stored in art galleries and museums throughout the world, from New York City to St. Petersburg, Russia, mainly in Europe, Great Britain, the United States, and Canada. In some cases, however, Native materials have been returned to their original communities; for example, the Kwakiutl potlatch material—masks and other ceremonial regalia—taken from Alert Bay, British Columbia by the Royal Canadian Mounted Police after the potlatch ban of 1884 by the federal government, has been repatriated to a museum facility in Alert Bay.

What has come to be labeled *tourist, souvenir,* or *airport* art is a category of Native art and craft production that arose to satisfy the Euro-American tourist longing for Indian souvenirs. The sale of traditional Native artworks to colonists and travelers gradually gave way, especially at the beginning of the nineteenth century, to new kinds of objects produced specifically for sale in the marketplace. These included the black argillite stone carvings of the Haida of British Columbia, as well as miniature wooden totem poles and canoes. Bead-worked and embroidered moccasins, pouches, and decorative pincushions and other

Victoriana were popular items for tourists visiting Niagara Falls throughout the nineteenth century. In the American Southwest, Pueblo women produced both traditional and modern styles of pottery for sale, and the Kachina dolls, traditionally made for the education of Hopi and Zuni children, were produced en masse for sale to outsiders. Navajo blankets also became an important commodity in the Southwest, with dealers at trading posts acting as middlemen between the weavers and the tourist trade. Production of Native arts and crafts has also been stimulated and promoted by American and Canadian governmental agencies as make-work projects for the economic improvement of Native communities. This has been the case especially in the Canadian Arctic, where contemporary Inuit sculpture and printmaking have been sponsored by the federal government since the 1950s.

## Contemporary Native Art

Contemporary art by Native North Americans varies widely in form, function, and meaning. These diverse expressions may be located between two poles, depending upon the degree to which they are rooted in either Native or Euro-American aesthetic and cultural traditions. On the one hand, for example, there is the continuing production of traditional art objects made for use within still vital or newly revitalized Native communities. The clearest illustration is that of the Northwest Coast, where the carving of totem poles and masks and the production of dancing blankets and other ceremonial regalia are flourishing once again. Carvers and painters, such as the Haida Bill Reid (1920–1999) and the Kwakiutl artist Tony Hunt (b. 1942), produced art works in the twentieth century that are grounded firmly in the principles of traditional Northwest coastal style for use in ceremonial dances associated with the potlatch as well as for sale on the open market to non-Native collectors. This continuity with tradition among most contemporary Northwest Coast artists had been maintained in the late nineteenth and early twentieth centuries by a handful of such great artists as Charles Edensaw (1839–1920) of the Haida Nation and Willie Seweed (1873–1967) and Mungo Martin (1881–1962) of the Kwakiutl. Once again, totem poles are being carved, painted, and raised in Native villages along the coast, the first in 1969 by Haida Bob Davidson (b.1946) in the village of Masset on the Queen Charlotte Islands. In the Hazelton area of northern British Columbia, too, the 'Ksan community project initiated a program for the revival of traditional arts and ceremonialism

*Southwestern Indian Children,* a watercolor by Earl Sisto for the 1992 UCLA Indian Child Welfare Conference. (Courtesy of the UCLA American Indian Studies Center)

among the Tsimshian, traditionally considered the finest artists on the Northwest Coast.

Artwork produced by Northwest Coast artists for sale to non-Natives, however, may often include traditional items, such as masks, rattles, boxes, and bowls, but more popular are works that cater to Euro-American aesthetic preferences and which are adapted to Western techniques, materials, and functions. Bill Reid, for example, was at first best-known for his small-scale silver and gold jewelry, bracelets, rings, and brooches, which were engraved with Haida mythological images such as Bear, Killer Whale, Raven, and Frog. Most recently, he became internationally recognized for his monumental public sculpture, *The Spirit of Haida Gwaii* (1991), a large mythic canoe commissioned for the Canadian Embassy in Washington, D.C.. This work depicts Reid's personal myth-animals on a canoe voyage, its black patina suggesting argillite, the traditional

Haida stone mined and carved on the Queen Charlotte Islands.

Contemporary artwork produced by Northwest Coast artists is tied more strongly to traditional coastal styles and iconography than many other contemporary Native expressions. While Northwest Coast printmakers and easel painters, such as the Coast Salish/Okanagan Paul Lawrence (b. 1957), may deviate radically from traditional imagery, forms, and compositions, their works are nevertheless created within an established range of visual elements and motifs traceable to the so-called classic style of Northwest Coast art; that is, to that of the Tlingit, Haida, and Tsimshian of the mid-nineteenth century.

Almost equally tied to tradition is the contemporary art of the Inuit of the Canadian Arctic and Alaska, who today produce sculpture, prints, drawings, and wallhangings, all of which have had great success in the marketplace. Contemporary carving began first between 1949 and 1953 when, under the stimulus of the Canadian artist James A. Houston, the Inuit produced soapstone, ivory, and bone carvings for sale in Canada and abroad. Often under the influence of specific guidelines as to subject matter, scale, and style from Houston and other interested parties and agencies, the Inuit produced carvings that departed in certain important respects from ancient and colonial era sculpture. For example, contemporary sculptures were provided with flat bases, giving them a Western, more limited and static perspective than was traditional and most were carved on a much larger scale.

In the late 1950s, too, Houston introduced the Inuit to Western and Japanese techniques of drawing on paper and of various methods of printmaking. In the 1960s and 1970s, Inuit prints—stonecuts, silkscreens, engravings, and etchings—became enormously popular among Euro-American collectors, eventually outstripping sculpture in popularity by the 1980s. Subject matter for both sculpture and prints in contemporary Inuit art is derived for the most part from the traditional hunting, ceremonial, and nomadic lifestyle of the Inuit and from their myths, legends, and shamanic beliefs and practices. More recently, however, the Inuit depict aspects of everyday life in the Arctic; their prints may include airplanes, snowmobiles, Christian iconography, and various Westernized social activities such as fiddleplaying.

In the 1970s and 1980s, Euro-American interest in the creativity of individual Inuit artists overtook interest in the group work of cooperatives. Original drawings, previously stored away, were sought out by dealers and collectors and led to a demand for information on the art and life of such noted artists as Ashoona Pitseolak (1907–1983), Ashevak Kenojuak (b. 1927),

Karoo Ashevak (1940–1974), Jessie Oonark (1906–1985), and Ruth Annaqtuusi Tulurialik (b. 1934).

In spite of all these changes in subject matter, techniques, and materials, and the fact that art is made now for sale to outsiders, contemporary Inuit art maintains fundamental continuities with the past in principles of compositional order. These are continuities that extend as far back in time as that of the ancient cultures of the Old Bering Sea, Dorset, and Thule periods and have to do with how the Inuit perceive and interpret the world around them in terms of space and time, being and becoming. Such sociocultural perceptions and values have survived so long because the Inuit themselves have survived and have adapted their traditions to the realities of the modern world. This remains true for many other Native North American traditions as well.

The aesthetic cultures of the American Southwest have been equally persistent, in spite of massive Western cultural influences. Especially noteworthy are the Navajo and the Hopi, San Ildefonso, and Zuni Pueblo peoples, who continue to produce hand-woven textiles, painted pottery, basketry, and jewelry for sale to collectors, which maintain both ancient and colonial era traditions dating back some 2,000 years. The fame of potters, innovating new techniques and styles within a traditionalist base, such as the Hopi potter Nampeyo (c.1860–1942) and Maria Martinez (d. 1980) of San Ildefonso, has inspired younger Pueblo potters, both men and women, to continue producing pottery to the present day.

The most magnificent expressions of cultural and aesthetic continuity in the Southwest today, however, are the hand-woven blankets still being produced on the Navajo Reservation. The older, more formal geometric patterns persist and outshine the more recent designs in their variety of pattern. The blankets are still crafted on the traditional loom, mainly by women. Both Navajo sacred art and the abstract blanket designs have influenced contemporary Euro-American art. Abstract Expressionist Jackson Pollock, for example, was inspired by the technique of sandpainting, in which a Navajo medicine man distributed colored sands on the ground to make his intricately patterned design for purposes of healing the sick. Pollock's famous action paintings, in which paint is dribbled on canvases spread on the ground, is not the only Navajo influence. Navajo blanket designs, too, were a direct inspiration to Euro-American color-field painters, who did not always acknowledge the creativity of the Navajo women weavers as their source. The instance of the Navajo is but one in an important, unwritten chapter of North American art history; not only was contemporary Native art influenced by Euro-American styles and techniques, but so also were the North American modernists profoundly indebted to traditional Native techniques and styles of painting, sculpture, and even architecture.

In the Southwest, one of the earliest schools of contemporary Native North American painting emerged and persisted between 1910 and 1960. This Southwest Style was associated with the influence of Dorothy Dunn of Santa Fe at the Studio School, founded in 1932. She was a non-Native teacher who played a role in the Southwest akin to that of Houston later in the Canadian Arctic. The Studio style was highly influential and came to be seen as typical of American Indian painting well into the mid-twentieth century until overtaken by modernists and other Native painters who came to reject the rigid Studio formula. Many notable painters came out of the Studio, however, including Gilbert Atoncio of San Ildefonso Pueblo (b. 1930), the Navajo Harrison Begay (b. 1917), and Ciricahuna Apache Allan Houser (b. 1915). In the works of the Southwest school, traditional Southwest ceremonial dances, hunting scenes, and various domestic activities are depicted in a flat, two-dimensional and linear decorative style that favored a pale color scheme and are often reminiscent of European art deco in the 1920s.

On the Plains and Prairies, a similar stylistic mode of expression to that of the Southwest Studio painters is evident in the works of mid-twentieth century Native artists. Such works were encouraged and promoted in the 1940s by the Philbrook Art Center in Tulsa, Oklahoma. Here, too, a non-Native artist and patron, Oscar Jacobson, was involved. The paintings embodied a romanticized nostalgia for past cultural ways and favorite subjects were buffalo hunts and brilliantly colored and costumed warriors engaged in ceremonial dancing. Among the most noted Plains artists working in this manner was Kiowa Stephen Mopope (1898–1974). The flat and decorative style of both the Santa Fe and Oklahoma traditions of contemporary painting extended as far north as the Canadian Prairies, where Blood Indian Gerald Tailfeathers (1925–1975) occasionally painted in the Oklahoma style.

Tradition also informs the work of Ojibwa painter Norval Morrisseau (b. 1932), who began painting in the 1960s and was the inspiration in the 1970s for an entire school of younger artists now known as the Woodlands School or the Legend Painters. Working in a style and with a related system of images and pictorial motifs, these include Roy Thomas (b. 1949), Josh Kakegamic (b. 1952), Saul Williams (b. 1945), and Blake Debassige (b. 1956). Linked with this group, too, is Odawa painter Daphne Odjig (b. 1925), whose style developed independently but along lines similar to that of Morrisseau and his school.

Morrisseau and the entire Woodlands School can be positioned midway along the continuum between Native

Mural wall at the Minneapolis American Indian Center in Minnesota. (Courtesy of the UCLA American Indian Studies Center)

and Euro-American aesthetic traditions in both form and subject matter. Their brilliantly colored and often large canvases are executed in synthetic acrylic paints, a characteristically Euro-American technique of the 1960s and 1970s. Both their subject matter and style are inspired to a large extent by traditional Algonquian pictography as found in the birch-bark pictorial manuscripts used traditionally in rites of the Grand Medicine Society, a group of spiritual leaders and healers, and in the ancient pictographs and petroglyphs of northwestern Ontario. Morrisseau's use of traditionally sacred images was seen as dubious by other Ojibwa, as sacred matters were to be kept from the public eye, reminding us of the similar difficulty Marc Chagall experienced, who had to leave his beloved village in Russia in order to become a painter. In Chagall's case, as a member of an Orthodox Jewish community, it was anathema to even paint images. This matter of sacred versus secular art functions and subject matter is still a very sensitive matter in traditional Native communities. But

Morrisseau's sources of influence also include the stained glass windows of his childhood Catholic church, with their glowing pure-colored images outlined by dark lead. The Ojibwa myths and legends learned at the knee of his maternal grandfather, a practicing shaman, combine with Christian themes and symbols to inform Morrisseau's art.

Contemporary Native artists most akin to twentieth-century Euro-American traditions and artistic practices are the works of a wide and growing network of contemporary artists of Native backgrounds who are neither trained in traditional techniques within their communities of origin nor self-taught, as was Morrisseau and many others. They have studied in the leading art schools of the United States, Canada, and Europe and a considerable number of these people have become teachers in major schools of art. The best known in the United States, so far, include Harry Fonseca (b. 1946), Maidu/Portuguese/Hawaiian; Richard Glazer Danay (b. 1942), Caughnawaga Mohawk; R. C. Gorman (b. 1932), Navajo; Oscar Howe (1915–1984), Yankton Sioux; Peter Jemison (b. 1945), Cattaraugus Seneca; Frank LaPena (b. 1937), Wintu/Nomtipom; George Longfish (b. 1940), Seneca/Tuscarora; George Morrison (b. 1919), Ojibwa; Jaune Quick-to-See-Smith (b. 1940), Cree/Flathead/Shoshone; and Fritz Scholder (b. 1937), Luiseño. In Canada, among the best known to date include Carl Beam (b. 1942), Ojibwa; Bob Boyer (b. 1948), Métis; Robert Houle (b. 1947), Saulteaux/Ojibwa; Alex Janvier (b. 1935), Chipewyan; Gerald McMaster (b. 1953) Plains Cree; Lawrence Paul (b. 1957), Coast Salish/Okanagan; Edward Poitras (b. 1953), Métis; Jane Ash Poitras (b. 1951), Chipewyan/Cree; Joane Cardinal-Schubert (b. 1942), Peigan/German; and Pierre Sioui (b. 1950), Huron.

These are all individualists whose works range in style between realism and abstraction and between modernism and postmodernism in approach. They perceive themselves to be artists first and foremost, and their Native ancestry is a constituent and vital aspect of their identity as individuals. At the same time, they do not negate, but take pride in that identity and see their role as artists in a traditional way, which fulfills not simply a decorative art for art's sake, but often has spiritual healing powers. Their focus is upon making a personal statement through their art about any or all of the social, political, racial, and environmental issues concerning both Native and world societies at large. They are informed at all times in this mission by the spiritual and cultural values of their respective Native backgrounds.

The shift away from Southwest and Plains traditionalism and the beginnings of Western modernist influences in contemporary Native North American painting first began with the work of a mere handful of artists who started working independently in the 1940s, 1950s, and 1960s. Among the most significant of these innovators are Oscar Howe and George Morrison in the United States, and Alex Janvier in Canada. Howe started out as a student of Dorothy Dunn's in 1935, but eventually moved toward a style of painting with abstract Cubist characteristics. Morrison, on the other hand, was trained in an entirely non-Native context at the Minneapolis School of Art in Minnesota, in France, and at the famed Art Students' League in New York City. Morrison was one of the first contemporary artists to consider himself an artist first who happened also to be an Indian. His paintings and sculpture belong within the formal context of American Abstract Expressionism of the 1950s. Unlike their personally expressive aims of communicating psychological states of feeling, however, Morrison's works are aimed at expressing the forces of nature and natural phenomena, such as wind, water, rock, and trees, bringing Native values and perceptions into a Western art context. In Canada, Alex Janvier played a role similar to that of Morrison. He attended the Southern Alberta College of Art in the early 1960s and turned to painting full-time in 1971. His work, too, is entirely abstract, but less geometric and characterized by flowing, curvilinear shapes of varied thickness. Like Morrison, though, Janvier sought to express the forces and shapes of the natural Prairie environment in abstract form.

Another important innovator is Jaune Quick-to-See Smith. She, too, was inspired by the natural landscape, but especially by the sacralized landscape of particular importance to her ancestral heritage. The innumerable pictographs and petroglyphs that marked these sites of special spiritual power throughout Native history were a major source of inspiration. Her manner of juxtaposing these rock art images with abstract forms and shapes, however, is less modernist and more postmodern. Her painting entitled *Osage Orange* (1985), for example, expresses natural forces in terms of angular and zigzag shapes and lines, quite a different concept than either Morrison's or Janvier's. Surrounding the abstractions, representational images borrowed from petroglyphs from sites throughout North America seem to be blasted to the four sides by the powerful shapes and colors at the center.

Modernism was most strongly fostered at the Institute of American Indian Arts in Santa Fe. Founded in 1962 with the support of the Rockefeller Foundation at the same location as Dunn's earlier Studio School, the institute came to play a major role in the training of young Native artists from all parts of North America, Alaska and Canada. Many of the Institute's graduates became well-known as leaders of the contemporary

Native Art movement in the second half of the twentieth century. Fritz Scholder, one of the first teachers at the Institute, exemplifies in the development of his own work, the eventual shift in Native American art from the abstract modernism of figures such as Oscar Howe, George Morrison, and Alex Janvier to the more critical and politically engaged expressions of the current Postmodern era of contemporary Native art. Rather than depictions of traditional subjects and themes, such as ceremonies, dancers, hunting, scenes of everyday Native life, and mythic animals and stories—so characteristic of the early-twentieth-century Southwest school—Postmodern Native artists of the 1970s to the 1990s turned away from nostalgia and romanticism and toward criticism of the past treatment and current impoverished conditions of life for indigenous peoples of North America. For example, in the early 1960s Fritz Scholder was working in a primarily Abstract Expressionist manner—his so-called stripe period—but by 1967 he turned to a representational mode of portraiture, depicting Native individuals. By 1970, Scholder had left the institute in order to devote himself entirely to painting, around which time, too, his work came under the influence of the contemporary British artist, Francis Bacon, whose works Scholder first encountered on exhibit in London's famed Tate Gallery. Bacon's portraits of screaming, blurred faces came to serve for Scholder the epitome of the helpless suffering of Native persons, powerless to do anything but scream in the face of both past and present circumstances. Scholder's work typifies the general shift in contemporary Native art of the 1970s away from the art-for-art's-sake approach of Abstract Expressionism to art with a message and a sociocultural purpose, in short, to what might be described as art as activism.

Bob Boyer is another contemporary Native artist with a message to communicate through his work. He first studied art at the University of Saskatchewan in Regina under a group of Canadian abstractionists—the Regina Five—and in the late 1980s became head of the Indian Art History Department at the Saskatchewan Indian Federated College. His work incorporates traditional Plains' design elements, but he uses them in new ways to make comments upon the history of colonial relationships with and treatment of the indigenous peoples of the Canadian Prairies. Boyer created a series of paintings on ordinary blankets, many with sarcastic titles referencing the colonial era when smallpox-infected blankets were distributed deliberately to spread disease among Native communities.

Robert Houle is similarly inspired by traditional Plains art, particularly by the abstract design elements of the parfleche, the well-known folded-hide carrying case so useful in the nomadic lifestyle of the Plains people. Some of Houle's earlier paintings are extremely close to the abstract parfleche designs, but most are scarcely recognizable as such, for example his series of thirteen *Parfleches for the Last Supper* (1983), which are rendered in a highly abstract manner. These depict the twelve apostles and Jesus Christ, a theme signifying the subject of death and resurrection, not only for Christians, but also for Native peoples. A deeper reading might reference, also, the theme of betrayal, with Judas signifying betrayal of the Native people by the colonial powers of both church and state.

In Canada, the work of Ojibwa Carl Beam is similarly concerned with the plight of Native peoples in history and with Euro-American stereotypical perceptions of Natives and their ways of life. But his work reveals a more global perspective than Scholder's in that his concerns are the fate of humanity throughout the globe, anticipating current concerns for the survival of the planet itself. These include the loss of spiritual values in society at large; the destruction of the natural environment and animal life through pollution, industrialization, and wanton disregard for the fate of Mother Earth; the inhumanity of humans to other humans through assassination, betrayal, and genocide; the threat of over-reliance upon technology and science and their effects upon the dehumanization of humankind; nostalgia for the loss of a more humane and spiritual past; and the place of the self in history and the passage of time. His works juxtapose images derived from photographs and current events from newspapers, with painted representations that include writing and numbers, as well as three-dimensional objects such as feathers and even stuffed birds. A notable recent work consists of a three-year cycle of paintings, prints, sculpture, and installations entitled *The Columbus Project*, completed in 1992. Beam sees himself as somewhat of a modern-day shaman, through his multimedia works that offer insights and solutions to the dilemmas of today's world. He believes, as many other contemporary Native artists do, that the indigenous peoples of North America have much to offer the industrialized Western world, so rapidly heading for environmental and sociocultural disaster.

Much contemporary Native North American art, however, is characterized by the use of humor, for which Native peoples throughout North America have a long history within their cultures, to comment upon the plight of Native peoples in the past and present. Culture theorists who study cartoons and caricature in art and literature have shown that humor is often a more effective means of effecting change than argument, protest, or violence. Humor pokes fun at dominating social and political power structures and helps to subvert their power in the public eye, thereby raising everyone's consciousness to the particular issues concerned. Best known for the use of Native humor in the United States is Harry Fonseca, especially his works of the 1970s and 1980s. The central figure in these works is the traditional figure of Coyote, the trickster, best known among Native cultures of Western North America. Coyote plays a role in traditional lore akin to that of Raven on the Northwest Coast and that of a number of other animal figures throughout North America, all of whom are "tricky" and able to take on many disguises. As the American anthropologist Paul Radin describes the figure in *The Trickster*: "Laughter, humor and irony permeate everything Trickster does" (1956, x). In Fonseca's work, Coyote takes on many disguises, suggestive of the issue of identity, a topic that concerns many Native individuals today. In some works, Coyote wears the clothing of a tourist, complete with Hawaiian shirt, sandals, and a camera, standing in front of Taos Pueblo, one of the most popular tourist spots in the Southwest. In another, Coyote assumes the shape of a female nightclub singer and in the painting *When Coyote Leaves the Reservation* (1980), Coyote wears heavy-metal, black leather garb after leaving the reservation. The fact that Fonseca subtitles the work as *A Portrait of the Artist as a Young Coyote* not only shows the artist as a trickster and transformer, but also points to the underlying issues of identity and rebellion, a concern of many contemporary artists who fight against stereotypes.

Coyote the Trickster plays a more tragic role for Edward Poitras, for whom the figure serves as an icon of confused personal identity. For Poitras, Coyote epitomizes his own dilemma as a Métis, neither white nor full-blooded Indian. A sculpture constructed of bones from the skeletons of seven coyotes was made in 1986, which suggests the lack of unified coherence of the Coyote figure and, in turn, the sense of fragmentation of both personality and culture for many Native individuals. It was most appropriate that Poitras was selected as the first artist of Native ancestry to represent Canada at the prestigious Venice Biennale in 1996, where his Coyote figure took pride of place against a golden background. This was appropriate for both Native Canadians and Euro-Canadians, many of whom are "hyphenated" Canadians for whom identity is a major contemporary dilemma.

In Canada, Gerald McMaster is most noted for using humor to comment on history and identity. His one-man show, *The Cowboy/Indian Show* of 1991, epitomized Native humor at its best. McMaster used both words and images in his Cowboy/Indian series to create paintings in a simple, flat, cartoon-like style that are full of verbal and visual wit. *Trick or Treaty* (1990), for example, works its effect on several levels, all of which require familiarity with Native and Canadian history and culture. The painting depicts a caricatured Sir John A. MacDonald, the first Prime Minister of Canada, whose tenure saw the beginnings of the notorious Indian Act, responsible for the removal of Native children from their homes to be sent to residential schools. The aim was to completely assimilate Native peoples to Euro-Canadian ways, the result of which was their loss of language and many cultural ways as well as the horrendous abuse of so many children. McMaster portrays MacDonald as the evil Joker, with large mouth surrounded by white, as acted by Jack Nicholson in the 1989 Hollywood film, *Batman*. The title, of course, refers to the issue of land claims, when many Native Nations were tricked into signing dubious treaties that are only today being reexamined and renegotiated. At the same time "trick or treat" is a phrase yelled by North American children transformed by alternate costumed identities at Halloween— All Hallows Eve— when ghosts and spirits of the past emerge and prowl the earth. Such layers and networks of meaning are a characteristic of postmodern art, wherein the viewer is invited to "read" and interpret the messages not always explicitly stated.

The aim of this introduction is to show that the history of Native North American art is an ongoing history, that Native art has continued to evolve in relation to changing environmental, historical, cultural, and political circumstances from its beginnings in the mists of antiquity to the present day. And this growth and change will continue today as Native North Americans today move along the path of revitalization. It is also intended to show that influences did not move in only one direction—from Euro-Americans to Natives— but that Native North American cultures have profoundly influenced and contributed to both the arts and culture of the modern West.

*Joan Vastokas*
*Trent University*

# ◆ TRADITIONAL CEREMONIES, RITUALS, FESTIVALS, MUSIC, AND DANCE

Through music, dance, ceremony, rituals, and festivals, Indian peoples of North America distinguish themselves not only from other North Americans, but also from each other. Despite these differences, scholars have tried to find cultural or musical groupings of these events for purposes of study. Because music and religion are abstract and invisible forms, they are not as easy to classify and study as other, visible components of

Wasicun Wakan Sapa (The Black Holy Man) was a Lakota man, probably an escaped slave. Painting by Lolly Vegas (Mato Wambli or Eagle Bear). October, 1999.

culture such as art work, textiles, ceremonial dress, and dance. Even ceremonies that have been described for centuries by European and Euro-American observers may have secret and invisible meanings and may not fit into neat categories when interpreted by the Native performers. The reader will find, when visiting specific events, that the differences are what enliven the activities, not the similarities. For example, Iroquois and Cherokee music and dance share many resemblances, such as counterclockwise motion, small steps, and call-and-response singing, but they do not sound or look alike when heard indoors (in the longhouse of the Iroquois) as opposed to outdoors (at the open-air ceremonial grounds of the Cherokee). Even in using the same tunes, the two groups of singers produce different sound qualities and create different song forms. The same kinds of conclusions can be drawn from dozens of other examples in North America.

Indian music and dance occur everywhere in North America-on large U.S. reservations, like the Navajo; on Canadian reserves; on small California rancherias, like Morongo; in big cities, like Los Angeles; and in rural settings, like the mountains of North Carolina; at specific sacred places, like Canyon de Chelly, Arizona; and at public gatherings, such as fairs and graduation ceremonies. While some Indian music exists without dance, no Indian dance exists without music. The music enables the dance to occur, and the dance makes the music visible. Even the earliest accounts of Indian music and dance from explorers and settlers mention the parallel and interdependent natures of these two art forms. Ordinarily, in ceremonies, music, and dance, women perform lesser roles. In social occasions for music and dance, women are increasingly taking larger roles.

Before the European colonization of America, there is archaeological evidence of music, dance, and ceremony through surviving musical instruments, ceremonial regalia, ritual paraphernalia, and depictions of music and dance in pottery, pictographs, and petroglyphs. After European contact, explorers and settlers give detailed and sometimes sensationalized descriptions of many events, including their ideas of the sounds, colors, and movements.

In Marc Lescarbot's *The History of New France* (1617), a compilation of various explorers' accounts of the Northeast, there is a first attempt to notate Native music. Using a seventeenth-century method, Lescarbot shows tunes that use three- or four-tone scales, have the range of a fourth, and feature a soloist with chorus response. The text includes both translatable words and non-translatable vocables. From earliest times some Indians, such as the Ojibway or Chippewa, have used their own mnemonic writing systems (picture symbols) to record their songs on birch bark or other materials.

Even though some music and dance has always been performed solely for entertainment, religion, life-ways, and world view affects most of the performances. Many Indian ceremonies are practiced to renew the world or keep it in balance. Others, such as those of the Tewa Pueblo Indians, maintain relationships with deities, supernaturals, each other, and strangers through music, dance, and ceremony. These activities range from extremely private and sacred gatherings, restricted to initiated or birth clans, to some that are extremely public and joking in nature and that may be accompanied by carnivals and concession stands. Strangers, and sometimes even other Indian people, are barred from private events, while they are welcomed at the public ones.

After Europeans and later American, Mexican, and Canadian colonists converted many Indians to Christianity (often by coercion), they removed them from their home lands by waging warfare, making treaties, and using other economic and political forces. After some groups of Indians disappeared altogether, other smaller groups, often from necessity, intermarried with neighboring peoples, both Indian and non-Indian, or were adopted by larger tribes. Then the governmental agencies grouped these peoples together arbitrarily, or because of language, cultural similarities, or geographical proximity. Often territorial enemies found themselves living side by side.

Frequently, missionaries were hired to perform what should have been the governmental jobs of supervising the education (including extermination of Native practices, religions, and languages), health, welfare, and Christian life of these Native Americans. After that, many singers, dancers, and traditional religious practitioners could not perform their arts and life-ways in the appropriate places and at the accustomed times, and some of this heritage was lost forever.

Repeatedly, Indian religious practices and ceremonies were forbidden by the churches and colonial governments. After the 1680–96 Pueblo Indian Revolt in New Mexico and Arizona, which forced the Spanish conquerors and missionaries south to El Paso, the Indians achieved some compromises concerning taxation, governance, and some alleviation of religious persecution. Later these Native Americans practiced their religions and dances, to some extent, alongside Catholic rituals. While the U.S. government's ban on Indian religions in the late nineteenth century targeted especially the Sun Dance and Ghost Dance, it also affected all other religions. After prohibiting Northwest Coast Indian potlatches (huge Native giveaway celebrations, such as those held by the Kwakiutl), the Canadian government seized many beautiful sacred and ceremonial objects and much dance regalia, making performances difficult, if not impossible, without these artifacts.

In the 1990s, many Indians living on U.S. reservations, Canadian reserves, and in rural areas carry on the indigenous religions and music that are necessary to Indian life. As long-established activities, they are regionally or tribally specific, and the leaders conduct the events in Native languages following age-old calendars and belief systems. These activities include dances such as the Lakota Sun Dance (a yearly spiritual renewal for the community that sponsors it) and "sings" (gatherings for performing and sharing songs) like those held by the Iroquois singing societies; fiestas (Malki Museum Fiesta, Cahuilla); healing ceremonies (Navajo Enemy Way or "Squaw Dance"); seasonal celebrations (Yuchi Green Corn ceremony); hunting dances (Pueblo game dances); agricultural celebrations (Hopi Bean Dance); Native games (Creek ballgame and dance); courting (Indian flute playing); influencing nature or one's fellows (spiritual songs and prayers); lullabies; and giveaways (Native customs for redistributing wealth). A few other examples of retention include, but are not limited to, the following: southern California (Cahuilla Bird Dance, recounting the creation); Great Basin (Ute Bear Dance, welcoming spring); northwest Alaskan Eskimo (Wolf Dance, honoring the hunter); Northwest Coast (Kwakiutl potlatch, strengthening community ties); Eastern Woodlands (Iroquois Thanksgiving, ending the harvest season); Southeast (Cherokee Stomp Dance, honoring the sacred fire); Plains (Blackfeet Medicine Lodge ceremony, similar to the Sun Dance); Pueblo (San Juan Turtle Dance, celebrating the winter solstice); southern Athapascan (Navajo Kinaalda', recognizing girls' puberty).

Some Indian people are specialists in language, religion, ceremony, and customs. They are necessary members of their tribes and nations and work hard at sharing their knowledge so that their groups can maintain these crucial practices. If young people are willing to learn the oral traditions from the elders and stay with their own people, some of this cultural richness, indigenous to America, will certainly be retained in the future.

## Preservation and Revival

Knowledge of Indian life has always been passed from generation to generation through oral tradition. Starting in the nineteenth century, non-Indian scholars (and a few Indian scholars) of history, folklore, anthropology, linguistics, and music began trying to preserve Indian culture, especially knowledge of ceremonies, music, dance, stories, languages, and customs. They used written, drawn, photographic, and electronic means to achieve their aims. Later in the twentieth century, more Indian people embraced these same media to achieve their own cultural documentation. Some younger Indian leaders have fervently begun recording traditional music and dance and their instructions for performance. They have also recorded stories, sacred narratives, oral histories, and ritual sayings. These efforts culminate in a new trend by Indian people themselves to gather recordings from archives, make recordings of elders, and combine the two to recreate or preserve some partially remembered dance or ceremony. The Federal Cylinder Project at the U.S. Library of Congress and the California Indian Project at the Lowie Museum, Berkeley, have returned many old recordings to these tribal groups.

## Music and Musical Instruments

In Indian music, whether sacred or secular, the voice is the most important instrument. As a result, melody and vocal style become paramount, and texture (layering of parts to create a thick sound) takes the place of harmony in most instances. Performing as a rule in native languages or vocables (non-translatable syllables), the singers utilize solos, responsorial songs (leader and chorus taking turns), unison chorus songs, and multipart songs. Most are accompanied by some sort of rattle or drum, or both rattle and drum.

Members of some Great Lakes and Plains tribes historically played small, shallow drums in unison, keeping time together to accompany their own singing. At the end of the nineteenth century, after many of these groups adopted the large drum, singers began sitting or standing around a single drum, playing together. In the pueblos of the Southwest, several men play large cylindrical or kettle-shaped drums together, each holding his own instrument.

The water drum is unique to North America and is played by only one person at a time. It is made from a small container of wood, pottery, or metal, partially filled with water for tuning, covered with a dampened, soft hide stretched tight, and beaten with a hard stick. It is found among the Eastern Indians (e.g., Iroquois, Cherokee, Creek, and others), the Apache and Navajo,

and members of the Native American church (a Native peyote religion, widespread in North America).

Adding to the texture of the music are various rattles and scrapers. Ordinarily, singers accompany themselves with vessel rattles (globes, cylinders, or irregularly shaped containers enclosing pebbles, fruit seeds, or other noisemakers, fixed with a handle). These may be played by lead or backup singers, dancers, or even by people who are simultaneously dancing and singing. The rattles can be made of carved wood, baskets, gourds, bark, rawhide, moose feet, clay, metal shakers, turtle shells, cow horns, copper, coconut shells, buffalo tails, or other materials.

Other rattles are strung and fastened to sticks, hoops, hides, or textiles and held or attached to the bodies or clothing of dancers. These are made from bird beaks, cocoons, deer hooves, tin cans, turtle shells, petrified wood, sea shells, or metal cones. A few are hollow and may contain pebbles or seeds and then be strung-for example, cocoons, turtle shells, or tin cans. Other instruments such as notched-stick rasps or scrapers, wooden box drums, bullroarers, flutes, whistles, musical bows, fiddles, split-stick clappers, and pairs of clapping sticks are less common.

Simple, short songs with many repetitions and song cycles (several different songs sung in sequence) are the most common musical forms among Native Americans. Vocal style, scales, rhythms, and meters vary according to geographic area, tribe, ceremony, and sometimes even by neighborhood or individual family. Even without knowing a particular song, a knowledgeable listener can usually tell the tribal or regional origin of a song from the vocal style, instrumentation, rhythm, and direction of the melody. Some musical characteristics are true for many but not all tribes: songs are in duple (2/4, 4/4, etc.) meter; scales (number of non-duplicated pitches in an octave) are pentatonic (various 5-tone scales); melodies start high and descend throughout the songs, ending on the lowest or next to lowest pitch (musical tone defined by its frequency, such as A440); songs are vocal with rattle, drum, or other percussive accompaniment.

The most common and easily recognizable form is the Plains Indian powwow, or intertribal song. It features a lead singer (also the lead drummer among several seated around the big drum) who usually starts the song with one phrase, as high as he can (using a letter for each phrase; for simplicity, the first phrase is *A* ). His chorus members (who are both singing and drumming) then answer him, repeating that phrase (*A'*, same as *A* but slightly modified), and all sing the melody together, with the pitch getting lower and lower throughout the middle (*B*, next phrase) and last (*C*, last phrase) sections, resting on the lowest or next to lowest pitch. This last or next to last note is often more than an octave (the distance between two notes whose frequency ratio is 2/1; e.g., A440 and A880) and a half lower than the starting pitch. All singers then repeat the middle (*B'*, slightly modified) and last (*C'*, slightly modified) sections before repeating the whole. This can be shown as *AA'BCB'C' AA'BCB'C'*, etc. Often the *B'C'* section contains words in an Indian language and a change in the drum pattern. Sometimes there is a long pause at the end of the entire rendition, and the singers repeat the *B'C'* section as a "tail," or *coda*, and finish off the dance. The male dancers wear loud ankle bells, and some blow whistles to show their delight with the singers and to ask for another repetition. The "pulsation," or intentional quivering of the voices, enhances the sound and helps to define the style.

Much of the music that is best known by the public belongs to nonprivate ceremonies and social occasions. However, private songs for medicine and curing, prayer, initiation, hunting, trying to control nature, putting children to sleep, telling stories, performing magic, playing games, and courtship are equally important. Many musical, dance-related, and cultural characteristics—such as the words, the number of repetitions, the instrumentation, ceremonial dress, body and face paint, and the way the singers and dancers work together-arise from world view, growing out of long-lasting religious and social customs. Music, dance, religion, and ceremonial life are wholly integrated, and one can hardly exist without the other. For example, if the words to a song mention east, north, west, and south in that order, as they do in some Cherokee songs, the dancers probably start in the east and move counterclockwise throughout the dance. If colors also are mentioned by the Cherokee, they would probably be ordered as red (east), blue (north), black (west), and white (south). Other tribes have different schemes for ordering their worlds and ceremonies. There is no one "Indian Way."

Although the origins of many songs lie in the past, Indian composers and singers continue to play the major roles in creating and passing on the music through oral tradition. Changes do occur, even though many people still cherish the older songs and forms. Some modern instrument makers now use metal bells, tin cans, metal salt shakers, rubber, and plastic materials for musical instruments and dance outfits. Various song makers add English words to Rabbit Dance (a couples, social dance), Forty-nine (a group social dance), and Peyote songs (songs to accompany religious practices of the Native American church). A few American popular melodies have inspired Indian composers, and these words or melodies have found their place in contemporary Indian songs. New songs are composed

every year and spread across the nation during the powwow season (the period of time from Memorial Day to Labor Day in the United States, when most powwows are held).

## Dance

Dance, along with music, is still a major pursuit for many Indian groups still practicing the old religions important to their ways of life. Due to their spiritual and supernatural origins, and because these dances are often tied to seasonal or life-cycle events, they are regionally or tribally specific, the singers usually perform in native languages, and the ceremonies themselves unfold according to local customs. Rather than expressing individual prowess, dancers usually adhere to established patterns and movements.

As with music, there are few solo dances but many group events. Some dances have a leader and chorus; some are unison groups acting together; others are groups with featured soloists; a few offer individual dancers the freedom to "show off." Occasionally, dancers can play a variety of roles in multipart dances. While many dances have vocal and drum accompaniment, often the dancers themselves, activating the rattles and bells that adorn their ceremonial dress, set their own beat.

Indian dancers often use restrained movements, without large motions or leaps. Generally the dancers stay close to the earth, both for religious and practical reasons. Because they must conserve their strength to dance all day or all night to satisfy a particular custom, because of limited space, or because of a large number of participants, they typically take small steps. The torso and head have the most freedom of movement, with little twisting. The feet and legs ordinarily act as a unit when extended, as do the hands and arms. Small movements of the forearms and wrists are limited to times when the dancer shakes an implement, such as a rattle, stick, or branch. Some dances require crouching or bent-over postures; the dancer usually stays in that position for a the length of a musical phrase or section. At times, specific dancers are called on to mimic animals (such as in the Creek Buffalo Dance), or birds (as in the Taos Eagle Dance), or the work of hunting, fishing, planting, harvesting, preparing food, other occupational duties, or warfare.

Dancers often conceive their space in terms of circles, moving either clockwise or counterclockwise, as defined by their cosmology. Other possibilities include lines of people dancing in place, moving forward or backward in unison, or moving into and out of larger dance areas in a procession. As an example, many

Native American dancers are elevating their dancing to higher and higher forms. (Photo by Ilka Hartmann)

Pueblo dances require the dancers to dance, moving forward into the plaza, dance in lines (mostly in place with some turns to right, left, or behind), and then move together to the next dance plaza in what becomes a circling of the village. Often four repetitions of the dances take place in order to cover all four directions in the proper order.

In northern Alaska and Canada, the lines and circles frequently become almost stationary or wind around to use all of the small interior spaces. For the most part, Plains and urban Indian dances, such as powwows, follow clockwise directions. Many Eastern and formerly Eastern tribes dance counterclockwise. A few tribes dance in either or both directions at different seasons or for different ceremonies. Many Navajo social dances allow the dancers to go clockwise during one song and counterclockwise during the next one.

Although some individual expression is allowed in most North American Plains dances, most Pueblo dances require unison action and strict rules of motion, broken up from time to time by the relatively free movements of the ritual clowns (specially initiated members of the Pueblo). One of the most individualistic dances, the Hoop Dance, has been adopted as an exhibition dance by many tribes. It showcases an individual who manipulates at least a dozen large hoops over and around his torso, legs, and arms to create a variety of geometric shapes. Usually, Indian dances mirror each group's norms and types of community interaction: for example, leader and followers, unison action, cooperation of individuals assuming differing roles, and the ideal of several generations working together.

## Games

Almost every game played by North American Indians has music and sometimes dance associated with it. The most popular games are handgames or stickgames. As social and sometimes religious activities, these guessing games are found almost everywhere in North America. Ordinarily, the players sing while hiding an object or the mark on a stick. Their opponents guess the location of the hidden object or mark, and then it is their turn to sing and hide. Each team scores points for fooling its competitors, and the first team to reach a specified point total wins the stakes. Each team has lucky songs and experienced guessers, and the game cannot exist without the music.

Ordinarily, the melodies are simple and easy to sing, with short, repeated phrases, so that the players can concentrate on winning the game. Among the Northwest Coast and northern California tribes (such as the Tolowa), stickgame songs have complicated rhythms and often contain multipart singing. In the Great Basin (Nevada, California east of the Sierras, Utah, Idaho, and parts of Colorado and Wyoming) and Central California-for example, among the Washoe and Pomo-men and women play entirely separate games and have gender-specific songs. Instrumental accompaniment is supplied by drums, sticks, rattles, or clapping sticks.

Eskimos (referring here to the many Arctic peoples called Yupik, Inupiat, Inuit, etc.) have other musical games-the women's throat games (vocal contests between two women at a time) of Baffin Island; the string figure games of northwest Alaska (often accompanied by songs or stories); and the insult-singing contests (to settle differences of opinion) of the Netsilik. The Iroquois in the northeast United States and Canada have a snow snake game played in specially constructed tracks, something like bobsled runs. In the southeastern U.S., the Cherokee, Creek, Choctaw, and Seminole have ballgame songs and dances preceding and following the highly ceremonial stickball game (played with pairs of laced sticks and a small ball, remotely similar to lacrosse). Although some of these songs are similar in style to other southeastern Indian dance music, others resemble curing or hunting songs. Women vocalists are an integral part of the ceremony in these southeastern ballgame songs, singing encouraging words for their own teams and insults against the opposing teams. In the twentieth century these games are sometimes played only for "show" and frequently leave out many of the songs, dances, and ceremonial aspects.

## Arctic and Sub-Arctic

Midwinter gatherings in their large community houses are the most important occasions for music and dance among the Eskimo in Alaska and Canada. At those celebrations, several men gather and sing together in unison while each singer also plays a large frame drum. These round, shallow drums are constructed from the bladders of large sea animals (or sometimes plastic), stretched over driftwood hoops with attached handles. They are played sometimes from above and other times from underneath with long slender sticks hitting either the rim or the drum head. Mostly the male and female dancers act out hunting, fishing, and other daily activities. They often wear gloves or hold decorated dance fans woven from grass and animal hair.

Northern Athapascan and northern Algonkian-speaking tribes have many songs and dances devoted to their traditional occupations of fishing and hunting. For social occasions many of these peoples of the sub-Arctic region play fiddle-guitar music based on European models.

## Northwest Coast and Northern California

Indian music and dance are often part of compelling ritual dramas and ceremonies in the Northwest Coast area of the United States and Canada. These rituals (such as the Kwakiutl potlatch), with their elaborately painted screens, highly decorated ceremonial dress, and multipart singing (accompanied by rattles, drums, and whistles), rival European opera in conception and execution. Often they are held to install a totem pole, a new chief, or to validate other honors and titles of a family or clan. When many Northwest Coast Indians became members of the Russian Orthodox church, they then translated appropriate hymns into their native languages. They also adopted some of the Russian harmonies and incorporated them into a few Native songs, like the Tlingit Death Chant.

In Washington State, an Indian Shaker movement began near the turn of the century. It was not similar to, nor was it affiliated with, the New England Shaker church. Its members concentrated on ritual healing, accompanying the ceremonies with singing and the ringing of bells. The new religion became popular locally and also spread to regions adjacent to Washington and to northwest California.

Until the Gold Rush in the late 1840s, Indians of northwest California saw few non-Indians. Much of their ceremonial life centers around world renewal and

Cheyenne children playing a hand game. (Courtesy of Charlotte Heth)

healing ceremonies like the Hupa White Deerskin Dance and the Yurok Brush Dance. Their ensemble music and dance are characterized by a sobbing, pulsating vocal quality, layers of vocal *ostinatos* (short rhythmic parts repeated over and over) underlying the soloist, and relative lack of instruments. The female dancers move up and down, mostly in place, activating pieces of abalone shell sewn to their dresses to serve as a high, rattling instrumental accompaniment. Meanwhile the men execute varying postures and more vigorous steps. Personal songs exist—such as those for hunting and attracting a lover—and are used primarily to affect nature and one's daily affairs. Organized, ceremonial, team gambling is a popular venue for music. This primarily male activity used to require religious fasting and praying to ensure luck for the game. The singers use rectangular frame drums and deer-hoof rattles strung on a stick.

## Central and Southern California

In central and southern California, the vocal style is somewhat relaxed, rattles of various types serve as primary instruments, and drums are practically nonexistent. Among the Kashaya Pomo of central California, the dreamer-shamans (frequently women) and their helpers (both men and women) sing, dance, and play double whistles and splitstick clappers to accompany healing rituals and ceremonial and social dances.

In southern California, the most common contexts for music and dance are fiestas and funerals. Bird songs commemorating the creation of the world comprise the main repertoire. Here one also finds little influence from outsiders except for the presence of a few Spanish loan words in Diegueo bird songs from the area near the Mexican border.

## Southwest

In the Southwest, Spanish accounts, starting in 1540, and kiva murals from the fourteenth to sixteenth centuries show that masks, decorative textiles, and body painting have always been important arts to Pueblo Indian culture. Prehistoric evidence shows the humpbacked flutist Kokopelli portrayed on many petroglyphs and pieces of ancient pottery throughout the area. Archaeologists have also found prehistoric pottery depicting dance and have unearthed copper bells worn by dancers.

The large Pueblo rawhide, wooden drums, hand-held gourd rattles, and the turtle shell, deer hoof, and marine-shell strung rattles, worn by the dancers, are the most important instruments. The singers rehearse together to create a full, unison, choral sound. Many of the dances involve men singing and dancing simultaneously in lines or moving in a procession. Women participate in the winter, as featured dancers in front of the men, and in the summer, in couples dances and large, group dances.

Most Pueblo ceremonies are seasonal, organized, directed, and regulated by clans and moieties, and feature prescribed roles for ceremonial leaders, singers, dancers, and supporters. Many are called feast days because the members of the Pueblos expect their friends and relatives to visit and accept their hospitality. While some ceremonies are completely closed, others are open to outsiders if they respect the religious aspects of the events, behave with decorum, and do not take pictures or make recordings without permission. Some of the more famous ceremonies are the Zuni Shalako (a masked winter dance), Hopi Snake Dance (a biennial summer dance), San Ildefonso Corn Dance (a harvest dance), and the San Juan Deer Dance (a winter game-hunting dance).

Among the Apache and Navajo (southern Athapascan), curing rituals and girls' puberty ceremonies are the best-known contexts for music and dance. The White Mountain Apache Sunrise Dance (for a girl who is becoming a woman) and the Navajo Enemy Way (sometimes called the Squaw Dance) exemplify these ideals. Each reinforces group beliefs and brings a person into the community or back into the community from outside. Apache and Navajo song style are similar: tense, nasal voices; rhythmic pulsation; clear articulation of words in alternating sections with vocables. Both Apache Crown Dancers and Navajo Yeibichei (Night Chant) dancers wear masks and sing partially in falsetto or in voices imitating the supernaturals.

The hand-held rattle, the voice, and the water drum (an instrument unique to North America) are the most important elements for music-making. The bullroarer (a thin wooden plaque attached to a string and swung in a circle), which survives in popular American culture as a child's toy, is still used today for ritual and ceremonial events in the Southwest. The Navajo use it in the Yeibichei and the Apache in the Mountain Spirit or Crown Dance (a masked dance in which humans impersonate deities of the mountains).

In the desert area and urban sprawl of southern Arizona (Tucson and Phoenix) and in northern Mexico, the Pima and Papago (O'Odham) and the Yaqui continue to carry out traditional ceremonies alongside innovative and hybrid ceremonial forms. An older ceremony, the O'Odham Chelkona, serves as entertainment and is often performed as a contest dance for local powwows, rodeos, and other events. It includes gift-giving, a hopping or skipping dance, feasting, speeches, and games. The Yaqui Deer Dance (a traditional, sacred ceremony) and the Yaqui Pascola (an Easter, Catholic Indian ceremony) exist side by side, reinforcing both the tenacity and the adaptability of these people.

## Plains

The Plains area, stretching from Canada to Texas, is home to many tribes who lived there originally and to some who were moved there in the nineteenth century by their respective governments. As a result of this forced commingling of peoples, some ceremonies and dances spread across tribal boundaries, and new contexts were created for music and dance, most notably the popular, intertribal powwow. Although predecessors of both the Ghost Dance and Sun Dance existed in the mid-nineteenth century, these ceremonies became more widespread and popular at the end of the century. Even in the 1990s, one can find singers and dancers performing these ancient songs and ceremonies.

Before the widespread use of the horse, and before the U.S. Civil War, the smaller, more isolated bands of Plains Indians did not have the large drums that are associated with twentieth-century Indians. For sacred ceremonies, such as opening sacred bundles, they used small, hand-held frame drums, each beaten by a singer. If several men were singing together, each held a drum and played it in unison. The pulsating vocal style (a variation both in pitch and loudness), often loud and somewhat individualistic, is a hallmark of the Plains singer. In addition to drums, rawhide rattles accompanied singing.

The flutes were reserved primarily for love songs. The courting flute deserves special mention as a male instrument. Its music echoes and embellishes well-known melodies, often drawn from love songs, and its influence draws a player's sweetheart to him.

## Eastern

Music of the Eastern Woodlands, the Northeast and Southeast, share many common traits. Many of the dances and songs are responsorial, incorporate shouts and animal cries, are performed by both genders, and circumscribe a counterclockwise dance area. Most feature hand-held rattles and water drums along with strung rattles worn on the dancers' legs. Vocally, the singing tends to be nasal and somewhat high-pitched. Among the Iroquois of the Northeast, many of the ceremonies occur in the longhouses, particularly in midwinter. In the Southeast most occur outdoors with the summer first-fruits or green corn ceremony as the centerpiece.

## Innovations

Although pre-Columbian evidence is difficult to find for stringed instruments, the Apache fiddle (made from a mescal stalk) and musical bows, found in various cultures, are examples of early string instruments. Taking into account the rapid adoption and adaptation of stringed instruments such as guitars, fiddles, and the like, especially in the Mexican and French borderlands, either a few stringed instruments existed in the past, or the novelty was too appealing to resist. In Eskimo, northern Athapascan, Plains, Pueblo, Yaqui, Papago, Métis, Ojibway, Pima, Choctaw, and Cherokee cultures of the twentieth century, fiddle-guitar music and the accompanying dancing is widespread and, in a few cases, overshadows traditional music and dance. For example, the Athapascan Fiddle Festival, held every November in Fairbanks, Alaska, is the premiere Native music and dance event of that area. The Alaskan Kutchin Indians also dance to European fiddle-guitar music imported by Scottish settlers from the Orkney Islands. In addition, Indian fiddlers and guitar players can be found almost everywhere. During the annual Cherokee National Holiday in Tahlequah, Oklahoma, a national Indian fiddler's contest is held.

Early in their careers, missionaries recognized that Indians loved music and began to capitalize on that tendency. Often Indians were lured or forced into the missions to learn and sing the new songs. Then they were proselytized, became Christians, and began translating and composing their own hymns. In California, they became the primary musicians for the Catholic Spanish mission system. In the East, they were both Catholic and Protestant converts. While most sang melodies without harmony, the Cherokees and Tlingits are famous for their improvised harmonies based on the European models. Indian people throughout North America still compose their own hymns and translate others for their own use.

In the 1990s, the Indian churches provide a place for worship, a meeting place for Christians, and a locus for Indian singing. In rural and reservation areas, worshipers attend services held in Native languages with songs in those languages; the ministers are local men with some theological training. In the cities, intertribal groups of Indians come together within specific denominations. Usually conducted in English, these urban services feature songs both in English and in Native languages, and the ministers are usually well-educated Indians.

The "Sings" or "Singings" held at these churches draw Indians from far and wide. Indian choirs, quartets, trios, duets, and soloists travel far to participate in them. Although some groups sing unaccompanied, many use piano, guitar, bass fiddle, organ, or other available Western instruments for accompaniment. In the 1990s, some singers use tape-recorded sound tracks or even synthesizers and electronic keyboards. Many groups harmonize, but in much of the Christian music, early Indian vocal techniques remain. We still hear leader-chorus responsorial patterns, upward-gliding attacks and downward-gliding releases to musical phrases, and generally nasal voice production. The themes of the songs represent basic human needs and communication with God and are not always direct translations of their English counterparts. Just as traditional ceremonies and urban powwows draw Indians together, so do Indian churches, especially through their music. Several choirs and quartets have published commercial recordings.

The renewed interest in Indian flute playing represents another revival and innovation. A first-year recipient of a National Heritage Fellowship from the National Endowment for the Arts, Doc Tate Nevaquaya, a Comanche from Oklahoma, taught several young Indian men through his recordings and personal efforts to play old songs, compose new songs, and adapt Indian vocal melodies and non-Native songs, such as hymns, for the flute. Dick Fools Bull, Sioux, had similar influence on the northern Plains. Among the other Indian flutists who have enjoyed success as concert artists are Kevin Locke (also a National Heritage Fellowship recipient), R. Carlos Nakai (popular also with symphonic and New Age audiences), Edward Wapp, Jr., John Rainer, Jr., Gordon Bird, Fernando Cellicion, Robert Tree Cody, Herman Edwards, Daniel C. Hill, Frank Montano, Cornel Pewewardy, D. M. Rico, Stan Snake, Douglas Spotted Eagle, Robert Two Hawks, Woodrow Haney, and Tom Ware. Nakai also composes and performs in ensembles with synthesizers and other electronic or amplified instruments, carrying the music forward into contemporary life. A few of the other flutists also cross over to contemporary or New Age.

In the 1990s, Indian traditional singers and dancers frequently perform out of context at all kinds of fairs, receptions, national Indian conferences, political rallies, museum and college programs, political demonstrations and the presidential inauguration of 1993, graduation ceremonies, tourist attractions, and in various Indian education programs. Indian traditional music can be studied in schools ranging from preschool to university.

Many Indian people also take their tape recorders to powwows, stomp dances, and other Indian gatherings to record music for pleasure. They may be recording the proceedings to learn the songs or merely for entertainment. This widening influence of Indian music has created an interest among the Indian and non-Indian record-buying public, with at least six commercial record companies now catering to this new market.

Although Indian tribes perform music unique to their own traditions, some tribes have adopted music and accompanying religious ceremonies from others. The most important ceremonies that spread pan-tribally across the West and into the Great Lakes area were the Sun Dance, the Ghost Dance, and the Native American church, or Peyote religion. In each ceremony there is some borrowing along with incorporation of local styles.

Of these three, only the Ghost Dance has almost disappeared, and even it survives in the song repertoire of Shoshoni women on the Wind River Reservation in Wyoming. The Sun Dance, after spreading from its origins in the central Plains north into Canada with the Plains Cree and Plains Ojibwa, south into Indian Territory with the Kiowa, west into Idaho and Utah with the Kutenai, Shoshoni, and Ute, and east into South Dakota and Minnesota with the Santee Dakota, finally began to vanish from the Great Plains by the end of the nineteenth century. Beginning in the 1970s, the Sun Dance has seen a revival on the Plains, in the mountains with the Ute and Shoshoni, and, newly transplanted, in California and other non-traditional sites.

Some modern Sun Dance performances retain the old ways, some revive ceremonies that were temporarily forsaken, and some borrow the ceremony from the Plains to benefit all Indian tribes. The Sun Dance religion requires that candidates for redemption do not withdraw from the world but live here and struggle for the good of all. Proper life requires a good heart, sacrifice for others, and selfless behavior toward family, kin and friends, and the entire Sun Dance community.

These universalist values draw Indians, young and old, from the cities and rural areas to the Sun Dance. Whether sponsored by an ancient tribal group or by a modern organization like the American Indian Movement, the music is so sacred that only the social songs have been released on commercial recordings. The style echoes that of other Plains social dance songs.

The Native American church and its peyote religion and music are also widespread. Urban Indians participate in ceremonies near their cities, while reservation and rural Indians set up teepees in sacred places or in their own yards. Peyote music is so popular that dozens of albums have been released by the two major Indian record companies, Indian House and Canyon. Featured together on these albums are singers from tribes whose indigenous ways contrasted greatly.

Wherever one finds peyote music, the general musical style, as defined by ethnomusicologist David P. McAllester, applies to all areas: peyote music is fast, uses a ceremonial water drum and rattle to accompany the singers, and the melody descends. The speed and driving pulse of the drum characterize the music. The worshipers take turns passing the drum in a clockwise direction around a sacred area upon which fire, sage, a peyote button, water, and cedar have been placed. At special times during the ceremony an eagle-bone whistle is blown outside in the four directions.

The most common pan-tribal music is found at powwows (urban, reservation, and rural). The singers and dancers at powwows often represent many tribes. Sponsored by an organization or club, each powwow group raises money and plans months ahead for this major event. The planners take great care in choosing a good head singer, head man dancer, and head woman dancer. Although the powwow is a gathering that includes activities like feasting, giveaways, arts and crafts sales, raffles, and the crowning of a princess, the emphasis is on singing and dancing. The singers perform Plains Indian music—northern, southern, or often both—with some regionally specific music and dance performed before, after, or as interludes during the powwow.

To open many powwows on the southern Plains and sometimes in the cities, members of a Gourd Dance Society may dance. Representing southern Plains warrior societies, Gourd Dancers, who are members of this honor brotherhood, have prescribed clothing and use special rattles and fans. In contrast to the general powwow fare of War Dances (dances featuring older, traditional clothing and stylized movements), Fancy Dances (dances exhibiting brightly colored clothing and innovative footwork), or Grass Dances (dances based on older northern Plains dances, with modern dress including fringe), the Gourd Dance seems slow and the songs extremely long. The music resembles other southern Plains music but uses a narrower vocal range. The dance is also less vigorous as are most honoring dances.

Frequently, the dancers warm up with Round Dances (slow friendship dances using a side-together step, in a clockwise circle) before the formal opening of a pow-wow (after the Gourd Dance, if it is performed), and Round Dances may be interspersed among War Dances, Grass Dances, Trick Songs (special songs for contests), etc. These social dances, together with the couples dances, such as the Oklahoma Two-Step, Rabbit Dance, Snake Dance, and Owl Dance, offer a chance for audience members to participate freely. At these times, visitors often dance without observing all the formal etiquette and dress requirements for the more serious dances.

Extra or specialty dances include the Navajo Ribbon Dance (a mirror-image dance by one or two sets of partners), the Swan Dance (an imitation of the bird), the Hoop Dance, the Shield Dance (a mock duel by dancers using shield and spears), or one of the pueblo Buffalo Dances (an imitation of male and female buffalos). These dances in a powwow setting are strictly for show, and often the dancers receive payment for demonstrating them. In recent years most powwow clubs have added contests to attract the best dancers and singers to the events they sponsor. The Men's War Dance or Fancy Dance contests offer the top prize money, sometimes one thousand dollars or more.

In the complex social and sometimes religious setting of the powwow, the leaders choose the head singer and head dancers not only for their superior knowledge of song and dance repertoire, but also for their community status and network of family and friends. If these powwow leaders have prestige and command respect, other good singers and dancers will join to show their support. Becoming a head singer requires a strong voice, musical talent, a superior memory, and an ability to guide the group of singers constituting the "drum." A head dancer must know and observe proper etiquette and decorum, must have stamina, must know all genres of powwow dance, be skilled at executing them, and be an easy leader to follow.

The Forty-nine Dances, social dances performed mostly by young people after powwows, may last all night. The dress is casual, and the drum, central to most Plains music, may be replaced by any sonorous surface. Done mostly for fun, the dances and songs may contain words about love, sweethearts, and problems. Changing the words to fit the locale or tribe involved is common; for example, Oklahoma may become New Mexico, or Kiowa may become Pueblo.

These pan-tribal (or pan-Indian) songs contain many vocables (or nonlexical syllables). Because the styles spread across geographical and tribal boundaries, using vocables allows a group of singers from different tribes and language families to sing together with ease. When songs at powwows are language specific, many singers have to drop out unless the members of the group all speak the same Indian language.

Because of Indian migration to cities and towns, and, because of generations of intermarriage with Indians of other tribes and with non-Indians, many young people have never experienced traditional Indian life and have come to rely on powwows, Indian community organizations, and Indian studies programs at schools as sources for reinforcing their "Indianess." Music and dance have contributed greatly to the search for identity by these young Indians. Drums, or groups of Indian men singers, have sprung up in community centers and in schools all across the nation. Although the purpose of these drums is to perform at powwows and other gatherings, the result is a weekly or monthly intertribal gathering of men who practice songs from various tribes in northern or southern Plains style.

In the past, most young women participated only in dancing, doing beadwork, or practicing other Indian crafts, but recently women have taken a visible role in singing and composing, often joining male drums or creating their own.

Intertribal choirs and bands enjoy popularity at Indian schools throughout the country. Depending on local tastes, the choirs may perform Western art or popular music, Christian music, or indigenous Indian music in new choral arrangements. The bands range from marching bands to jazz swing bands with corresponding repertoires. The Navajo Nation Band even marched once in the Pasadena, California, Tournament of Roses parade, performing Navajo social songs on brass instruments.

Louis Ballard, a Quapaw-Cherokee composer, did much to promote Indian choral singing. By traveling throughout the country, to present Indian music workshops, conduct Indian choirs, and produce records and films, Ballard spread his idea of using Indian motifs in traditional Western forms.

A few of the school choirs and bands gaining recognition and producing record albums are Brigham Young University (Provo, Utah), the Institute of American Indian Arts (Santa Fe, New Mexico), Fort Lewis College (Durango, Colorado), Haskell Indian Junior College (Lawrence, Kansas), and Bacone College (Muskogee, Oklahoma).

Professional Indian musicians perform in many styles, including classical, jazz, country, folk/protest, contemporary, rock, rap, and New Age. Some blend Indian tunes with mainstream rhythms, instruments, and styles. Most use some themes, instruments, or melodies from traditional Indian music. Among these are Tom Bee, Robby Bee, Joe Manuel, Sand Creek, Winterhawk, Cody

Bearpaw, Borderline, El Cochise, Eddie and Brian Johnson, Joe Montana and the Roadrunners, Jimi Poyer, Rockin' Rebels, Wingate Valley Boys, Jim Boyd, Arliene Nofchissey Williams, Vincent Craig, Chief Dan George, Burt Lambert and the Northern Express, Frank Montano, Tomas Obomsawin, A. Paul Ortega, Sharon Burch, Jim Pepper, Buddy Red Bow, Joanne Shenandoah, Gene T, Buffy Sainte-Marie, Bruce Hamana, Floyd Westerman, the Fenders, Undecided Takers, the Navajo Sundowners, the Zuni Midnighters, Apache Spirit, Louis Ballard, Brent Michael Davids, XIT, Redbone, Billy Thunderkloud, and John Trudell.

Chicken Scratch (*waila* ), popular dance music of the Indians of southern Arizona, relies heavily on European dance forms such as polkas and schottisches. Similar to Mexican-American Norteo music, employing guitars, concertina, and saxophone, Chicken Scratch finds popularity among the Tohono O'Odham (Papago), Pima, Quechan (Yuma), and Yaqui.

Like other Americans, Indians and Eskimos will sing or dance to almost any variety of music that catches their fancy while reserving their own music for special occasions. Indian musicians have composed music to fit the times while keeping many of their old styles, forms, and contexts to reinforce traditional values. Music pervades Indian life starting from creation stories and ending with death and memorial. American Indian music is important not only because it influences modern American society, but also because it emphasizes the traditions and values of Indian people. This oral tradition has survived solely because the music and dance were too important to be allowed to die.

Indians of North America have been dancing, playing, and singing music, performing speeches and ceremonies, and carving and painting walls, ornaments, and everyday household items that have exhibited group and individual artistry for many centuries. The legacy remains.

*Charlotte Heth*
*University of California, Los Angeles*

# ◆ CONTEMPORARY AND PAN-TRIBAL NATIVE NORTH AMERICAN MUSIC AND DANCE

The creation and performance of music and dance have played an essential part in the lives of North America's indigenous peoples since their earliest times on the continent. European (and later American and Canadian) settlement over a 400-year period had a devastating impact on Indian lifeways. Native music and dance, however, still endure and prosper in old ceremonies and new songs, existing side by side in cultures where continuity, adaptation, and innovation have always been vital elements of life. Today's Indian people are no different from those of the past in this regard. They participate in age-old religious rituals, dance in Pan-Indian powwows, sing Native-language hymns in church, and listen to the latest in Indian country, rock, and hip-hop music, all while living everywhere from reservations and rural areas to inner cities. Contemporary Native American music even includes symphonies, ballets, and operas.

In North America before European contact, hundreds of Indian nations—from small tribes to large city-states—lived in close proximity to each other. Their musical expressions, however, were as varied as the people themselves. Music could be performed by a single man playing a courting flute for his intended bride or by dozens of drummers and pan-pipers accompanying a ritual dance on the central temple-mound at Cahokia, a city located near present day St. Louis. Although many large-scale generalizations can be made about Native American music and dance, Indian groups of the past and present still possess, practice, and perform distinct tribal repertories of songs and dances, enhanced and expanded by occasional exchange with neighboring peoples. Because their spiritual traditions have grown from the life experiences and needs of specific tribal cultures, Native American religions and ceremonies contain a remarkable diversity of beliefs, mirrored by their accompanying music and dance.

## Pan-Tribal Traditions

In addition to the older tribal-specific styles, some types of music and dance are pan-Indian, meaning that they are performed by people from many different tribes together in one setting. Others, such as Indian country, jazz, and rock, are considered hybrid, blended, or syncretic, terms describing new forms of music and dance resulting from contacts between different musical cultures. Still another musical classification is termed *recontextualized performance*, defined as an older form of music that has been reworked to fit into a more contemporary setting.

Music and dance traditions have been shared at mixed tribal gatherings since time immemorial. These kinds of events occurred most often at important annual ceremonials such as harvest or religious ceremonies. Among tribes that usually split into small bands during the winter, seasonal gatherings were social occasions, times to visit with family and friends (perhaps from different tribes), for courtship, and for trading and bartering. Pan-tribal participation was especially common at gambling competitions, today an increasingly popular form of entertainment. As in the past, Indian gambling is accompanied by special power and luck-songs, sung by teams that can range in size from two or three players to fifty. Flute traditions also crossed cultural lines, and have become an important means of intercultural performance, often used in New Age ensembles. Without question, however, the modern powwow is the music and dance tradition that has most broadly crossed Indian cultural lines.

## Powwow Music and Dance

The contemporary pan-Indian powwow has become a major force for music and dance innovation among today's Indian populations. Powwows provide both a gathering place for Indian people to celebrate their culture through music and dance, and a fertile ground for change, as members of diverse tribal groups interact and share music, dance styles, and dance regalia. At every event, scores of traders sell cassettes and videotapes featuring the latest in new songs, regalia, and dance footwork, contributing to an ongoing evolution of styles, especially in urban areas. Because of these trends, a new pan-Indian culture, with regional music and dance layered upon a Plains Indian framework, is shaping an overarching Indian identity for Indians and non-Indians alike. Powwows can be grouped into two broad divisions: competition and traditional, with competition events offering prize moneys in various dance and music categories.

In every region of the United States and Canada, a powwow happens each weekend, drawing dancers from hundreds, even thousands, of miles away, and attracts both Indian and non-Indian spectators and traders. These dances are living events, often central to the lives of their participants, who travel hundreds of miles each week for the chance to "dress to dance."

Within the larger powwow circuit there are two basic types of events: Northern and Southern. The Northern style originates from the northern Great Plains and the Great Lakes regions, and now takes place throughout the northern tier of U.S. states and Canada. Southern powwows sprang from the unique circumstances of Oklahoma, where numerous unrelated tribes were crowded together over a period of fifty years and where the concepts of pan-Indianism or inter-tribalism were born out of necessity. For the most part, the dividing line between Southern and Northern events

is geographic, however, the Wisconsin Ho-Chunk (Winnebago) sing in a Southern style, even though they are surrounded by other tribes such as the Menominee, Potawatomi, and Ojibwa, all of whom sing in the Northern tradition. In many ways, Northern and Southern powwow formats are similar, differing only in the additional Southern dance categories of men's Southern Straight and Women's Southern Cloth.

Historically, events similar to powwows existed in many Indian communities long before the advent of European settlement. For example, the Lakota *wacipi* (dance) was a time when scattered bands of tribal members converged in one location for religious ceremonies, trading, and social interactions including dances. These dances were often the only time that young people from different bands could meet, and young men took great care to look their finest for the female spectators. At times, people would also celebrate successful war parties, horse-stealing ventures, or alliances with dancing sponsored by various warrior societies. One major difference between old-time events and the modern powwow is that powwows are open to any (including non-Indians) who wish to attend, whereas pre-contact events were more exclusive, and included only members of tribes friendly to the those holding the dance.

The musical ancestors to today's powwow repertory are the songs—and especially the song-form—of the Omaha Nation's Heluska War Dance. The Omaha inhabit a mid-Plains region in Iowa and Nebraska, and their singing style and dance regalia greatly influenced the surrounding peoples. As with events, powwow singing is categorized by its practitioners as either Northern or Southern. The Northern-style area includes drums from the Central and Northern Plains, Canada, and the Great Lakes regions, while Southern singing is synonymous with Oklahoma.

Musically, however, all powwow songs share the same basic formal structure. Southern songs have slightly slower tempos, a lower vocal range, three hard (accented) beats between repetitions of each verse, and two additional hard beats in the tail (end) of a song. Northern songs have heavier accent patterns and reoccurring sets of four to five Honor Beats (also hard beats) in the interior of each song.

A third style of singing, Contemporary, is a recent development, describing a move by many younger Northern Drums toward a vocal sound with a higher range, generic delivery, and songs frequently made up entirely of vocables, or syllables without specific meaning. Because Contemporary Drums often replace Native language texts with either vocables or very simple, repetitive words, their songs are more accessible to urban drum groups with multi-tribal memberships. In contrast, Original, equivalent to Traditional, also a Northern style, now signifies reservation drums with members from the same community or geographic area. These singers typically learn their songs from other tribal members, and their music appeals more to an older, more traditional generation of dancers. Powwow musicians currently refer to songs with indigenous language texts as traditional or word songs, and vocable-only songs as straight songs.

The established formal structure of powwow music has remained unchanged for almost half a century. This form, most often termed *incomplete repetition* by scholars (Vennum 1989, 8), has distinct Northern (Original and Contemporary) and Southern variations. In Oklahoma, when the Comanche and Kiowa took up the Omaha Heluska Warrior Society, they referred to its music and dances as O'ho-ma, most likely a mispronunciation of Omaha. Although the Warrior Society was spread from tribe to tribe by the Kiowa and Comanche in the post-reservation era, the geographic distance between tribal groups in Oklahoma was much less than in the North, allowing fewer deviations from the original Heluska style. The Oklahoma Ponca also share the same language and music with the Omaha. Until the 1860s the Ponca were part of the greater Omaha Nation, and have been influential in maintaining Heluska songs in the South. In addition to the tribes mentioned above, the Pawnee and Osage peoples are also known to be accomplished singers.

Powwow songs are in a *repetitive strophic*, or verse, form, which serves as a flexible yet systematic framework for new song creation. Plains powwow songs begin with a solo singer performing an opening phrase, which is then taken up by other members of the group, known as a Drum. Each phrase-grouping ending with a distinctive pattern of vocables, known as a cadence. After the leading phrases, the melody moves into the middle section, which is then repeated (this part is called the end). Diagrammed out, the form looks something like this: A (solo) A¹ (repeat by group) B (middle) C (end). Omaha form, named after its originators, includes three drum accents called honor beats between the middle and end phrase-groupings in the Southern Plains style, and four honor beats within the interior of a B or C phrase grouping in the Northern. In general, Southern singing has slower tempos (with the exception of fancy-dance songs), more fluid vocal lines, and softer dynamic levels, while Northern musicians tend toward faster tempos and more active rhythmic structures. Northern songs also sound louder to the listener, but this is probably because the higher melodies and tighter vocal style of the singers combine for greater sound projection. This high, tight, pulsating voice, often called an Indian throat, is the preferred vocal sound of the North.

Although most of the powwow singers who sit at (play) the drum are men, women are an important part of the musical performance, standing in a half-circle around the men and singing the melody at a higher pitch. Because higher pitches are directional, in order for the special women's part to be heard and not buried in the lower-pitched sounds of the drum and male singing voices, the women must stand while they sing. In some instances, when women do sit at the drum and play, they also sing the men's part at the lower pitch. Although it is not a common practice for women to sit at the drum, in some cases they do, usually at Blackfoot or Cree drums. There is also currently a multi-tribal all-female drum group on the circuit known as the Mankillers, also the name of an prominent Cherokee family.

Many Native American dancers and singers perceive musical structure as cyclic. The melody starts at the higher end of its melodic range and gradually descends to the lower end. This type of melodic construction is called a *terraced melody*, and is common in Native American music. Each cycle through the melody with an internal repeat is called a *round*, *set*, or *pushup*, with four rounds being the normal number of times the song is repeated to make a complete performance. Occasionally at the end of four rounds there is a short pause and a final run-through of the end section called a *tail*. When hard or honor beats are played, they signal to the dancers to raise their fans (Northern) or bow their heads (Southern). Accented beats at the end of the section signal either that the music is speeding up, or that the song is about to end. Loud accents on the drum are one way the musicians communicate to the dancers what is about to happen in the song, and most importantly, how close the song is to its end.

Powwow songs are learned as part of an oral tradition, by either personal composition, being taught by other singers, hearing other Drum groups, or even from cassette tapes. Indian singers do not learn songs by reading notes from a musical score, and other than occasionally writing down song texts, music is not notated in any way. Songs come in a variety of categories defined by whether or not the song has a steady two beat or three-beat pattern, and by its function within the event. Songs organized in steady two-beat patterns are derived from the old Heluska war songs, and are used for general intertribal dancing and competition. Three-beat pattern songs, with the actual drum beats sounding on one and three, are primarily social dance songs in the round-dance and two-step categories, although in the Southern Soldier Dance songs also use this beat pattern. Songs with a series of single accented drumbeats are for Crow-Hop (Northern) or Horse-Stealing (Southern) dances.

Powwow dance styles in urban areas and outside of the Plains regions tend toward the generic, with personal interpretation of the various categories (Traditional, Fancy, Grass, Jingle, and Straight). The spread of competition powwows offering large prize moneys, where different is frequently equated with better, escalates the rate of change in dance and regalia styles, especially at urban events. In this case, the recontextualization of powwows allows older styles, such as Traditional dances, to survive and prosper in the same cultural venue in which male Fancy Dancers perform cartwheels and splits as part of their routines. In recent years Southern powwows have become hosts to sessions of Gourd Dancing, a celebration of the music and dance of the Kiowa Tia-piah Warrior Society (also known as the Gourd Clan), and a strong conservative influence on musical tradition. Although the process of recontextualization may seem threatening to those outside the powwow community, Indians know that the older generations will ensure the preservation of older forms for the young, and continually revitalize the powwow with tradition.

## Flute Performance: Traditional to Contemporary

In contemporary North America, Native flute-playing is widely symbolized by the image of Kokopelli, the hump-backed flute player featured in petroglyphs, who was a symbol of fertility in the Southwest. But in pre-contact times, flutes had a number of associations, including courtship on the Great Plains, health and recovery in curing rituals in the Northeast, and peaceful intent by travelers when approaching a settlement in the Southeast. Flute melodies were most often derived from vocal songs, and performed by the player on the flute in alternation with the sung version. During the post-reservation era from the 1890s though the late 1960s, flute performance traditions (including the art of making flutes) nearly died out, kept alive by only a few elders such as Richard Fool Bull (Lakota). Beginning in the early 1970s, Comanche musician Doc Tate Nevequaya single-handedly revived the Native flute-playing tradition, creating new songs inspired by programmatic influences. Since that time, Native American flutes have gained in popularity with both Indian and non-Indian musicians. Important players and teachers today include Kevin Locke (Lakota), Edward Wapp (Comanche/Sac and Fox), Arnold Richardson (Tuscarora), R. Carlos Nakai (Navajo/Ute), and Mary Youngblood (Lakota).

In Lakota (Northern Plains) society, men played flutes during courtship in an attempt to make women fall in love with them. Lakota courtship was complex. A man not only had to win the heart of a woman, but he also had to convince her parents that he was capable of supporting her. Before a young man could even consider looking at a woman, he had to prove his desirability by earning war honors, killing buffalo or other large, dangerous animals, or stealing horses as a gift for his potential wife's parents. When a young man felt he was finally ready for marriage, he would go *winole* (to seek a woman). His first stop was at the home of the local Elk Dreamer, a man who claimed special medicine, or powers, over women. The Elk Dreamer would give the young man a flute called a Siyotanka—a flute with the open end carved and painted like the head of a waterfowl—and a special love medicine song, with the power to enchant the selected young lady. These love songs, called Wioste Olowan, had both melodic and vocal/textual components. "Inkpataya," an old and well-known flute love song, is translated from the original Lakota text into English as follows:

I am standing where the water begins
I wave a blanket
My goodness, my goodness
Come back over here (translation by Calvin
    Jumping Bull)

Traditional performance practice was for the man to sit outside his intended's lodge in the early evening, playing the song on the flute and then singing the same melody with a text about love. If the song was powerful enough, the young women would fall in love with him. If not, the spurned suitor reconfigured the text into a kind of teasing song, sung from a woman's point of view. The song text in the example above has undergone that transformation, and has entered the larger Lakota musical repertory as a song about a woman of loose morals waving her blanket at men as they pass by, inviting them over for a visit.

## Contemporary and Popular Music

Indians have been participating in popular American musical culture since the years following World War II, which marked the first large-scale Indian participation as equal citizens in the American and Canadian armed forces. Often integrated into units with rural southern white soldiers, Indians learned the basics of country music performance from their white comrades, including how to play guitar, keyboards, and drum-set. After

Ulali at Madison Square Garden, on tour with the Indigo Girls, 1997. (Photo by Susan Alzner)

they mustered-out, Indian veterans took these skills with them back to rural reservations, where country music was the predominant style they heard on the radio. With themes of love and loss to which Natives could easily relate, country music quickly became popular in off-reservation "Indian Bars" (alcohol is illegal on most reservations), and Native musicians formed country bands, such as the Zuni Midnighters, to deal with the demand. Most of these early bands performed covers, or popular songs originally composed and performed by other bands.

From the early 1960s to the present, Native Americans have adapted a number of popular genres to their communities' needs, including folk and protest styles (Buffy St. Marie [Cree] and Floyd Westerman [Dakota]); country (Buddy Red Bow [Lakota] and Bill Miller [Stockbridge/Munsee]); rock (Keith Secola [Ojibwa] and Kashtin [Innu]); jazz and jazz fusion (Jim Pepper [Kaw] and John Trudell [Santee]); and blues (Indigenous [Lakota]). Some musicians, such as the all-female trio Ulali (Tuscarora and Apache/Mexican) and Robbie Roberstson (Mohawk) have broken the mold entirely and created their own unique performance

styles, blending traditional and contemporary sounds. Others such as Wayne Newton (Powhatan) have prospered by catering to the musical tastes of the dominant society.

Oklahoma Cherokee rap artist Litefoot represents the tradition of Native musicians who create music to serve their communities, even though his songs are in a contemporary style. Born near Tulsa, Oklahoma, Litefoot has been rapping since the mid 1980s, and has recently embarked on a series of national tours, performing in venues from inner cities to rural reservations. In addition to his rap performances, Litefoot works as a motivational speaker to Indian youth, and his talks focus on strength and sobriety through Native cultural pride. With major acting roles in *The Indian in the Cupboard* (1995), *Kull the Conqueror* (1997), and *Mortal Combat: Annihilation* (1997), Litefoot used his income to start his own record label, Red Vinyl Records. Taking his responsibilities as a role model and mentor for Native youth seriously, Litefoot assists other Indian rappers, such as Red Vinyl label mate Haida, in building musical careers.

"For My People," a typical Litefoot song, showcases his rapping skills in the African-American West-Coast style. Performed to an underlying Tribalistic Funk beat, Litefoot raps about a variety of subjects, from Indian pride to the day-to-day frustrations of dealing with ethnic stereotypes. Although aimed primarily at an Indian audience, Litefoot's music crosses ethnic boundaries with its smooth style, solid beats, and message of cultural tolerance.

In May 2000, the Grammy Awards added the new category of Native American contemporary pop to their award divisions, giving long overdue recognition to Indian artists (the Canadian Juno awards have had an aboriginal category for over a decade). With the general public's increasing appreciation of Native musical expression, there is hope that opportunities for commercial success will increase, and Native musicians will continue to expand both their performance venues and numbers of recordings.

*Tara Browner*
*University of California, Los Angeles*

# ◆ NATIVE NORTH AMERICAN VISUAL ARTS

In every American Indian society, the visual arts—textiles, architecture, sculpture, pottery, painting, and photography—are inextricably linked with the arts of music, dance, festival, and religious performance. Artistic objects were and still are used for their power in both individual- and group-focused ceremonies. Masks, dance costumes, carved rattles, and other items of ceremonial regalia add to the power and impressiveness of any ceremony in the eyes of both the beholders and the supernaturals. Since the beginning of the twentieth century, some Native artists created paintings and sculptures that are made principally for sale to an international community of art lovers. These arts may draw inspiration from traditional Indian arts as well as from arts of the European tradition.

## Art and Environment

In each region of the North American continent, Native people made art that reflected the environment around them and that best expressed their own unique social structure and worldview. In coastal British Columbia and southern Alaska, Tlingit, Haida, Kwakiutl, and other Northwest Coast peoples have used the wood of the cedar tree in their arts for over one thousand years. The thick trunk can be carved into imposing totem poles. The straight-grained wood of the trunk splits long and true, enabling the architect to fashion planks

as long as forty feet to make the great carved and painted houses so characteristic of this region. Cedar is also easily carved into the masks, dance rattles, great storage boxes and feasting bowls used in extraordinary numbers by all Northwest Coast peoples. The cedar's bark, thin branches, and roots can be pounded to make soft, flexible weaving material for capes, hats, bags, baskets, and mats. The Northwest's rich coastal environment not only provided plenty of cedars, but also afforded an abundance of foodstuffs, including fish, game, and fruit. This abundance allowed people more leisure time to devote to art and other expressive aspects of culture.

In contrast to the large, settled communities of the Pacific Northwest, the small-scale societies that stretched across the mid-section of the United States and the prairies of Canada during the eighteenth and nineteenth centuries were characterized by a high degree of mobility. Sioux, Cheyenne, Kiowa, and other tribes rode their horses over the Plains, following the

The Kwakiutl totem poles at Alert Bay, c. 1910. (Public Domain)

The band Redbone, the only Native American Indian group to have a number–one hit song in the United States ("Come and Get Your Love"), was inducted into the Smithsonian Institute. Its members, from left to right, are Tony Bellamy, Patrick Vegas, Garrett Saracho, and Pete DePoe, (Lolly Vegas not pictured). (Photo by Ron Eyansen. Courtesy of Garrett Saracho)

seasonal migrations of the buffalo herds. For this reason, all their arts had to be small and easily portable. Unlike the great wood houses of the Northwest Coast, Plains peoples lived principally in tepees. Women assembled these structures quickly by setting up long, strong lodge poles and wrapping and anchoring buffalo-hide tepee covers around them. If the band needed to break camp quickly, tepees could be disassembled rapidly.

Small-scale portable arts included many items of personal adornment. Painted shields; hide garments decorated with paint, beads, quills, and hair; soft and sturdy beaded moccasins; and ornate feather and fur headgear were important aspects of Plains arts. As the cedar tree was so fundamental to art and life on the Northwest Coast, the buffalo was the primary artistic material on the Plains. The animal's hide provided skins for tepee covers and clothing, the sinew provided thread to sew these items together, and the horn was used for jewelry and carved utensils.

In the harsh Arctic region of Canada and Alaska, where the only plant materials are tiny flowers and lichen blooming briefly in the summer, life as well as art traditionally depended on the bountiful animal world: caribou, polar bear, salmon, walrus, whale, and seal. Men carved walrus tusks, caribou antlers, and whale bones into fishing and hunting implements, such as harpoon heads, knives, buttons, and toggles that were both practical and beautiful. Women sewed animal skins into fine and warm garments to protect the wearer and to please the spirits of the animals that had sacrificed their lives so humans could eat and stay warm. Especially fine garments were required for the shaman, the spiritual protector of the people, whose role it was to communicate with the spirits of the game animals and of the ancestors.

In the southwestern regions of Arizona and New Mexico, Hopi, Zuni, and other Pueblo people have been sedentary farmers for over 1,500 years. Their relationship with a fixed place on the land is reflected in many of their arts. The unique architectural form of the multistory apartment compounds—some of which have been continuously in use for hundreds of years—allows for a community of people to live together with both privacy and communal space. These housing compounds are made of stone and adobe brick, the interior walls plastered with clay and painted. Clay pottery is made from the "flesh" of mother earth herself, in an unbroken tradition that extends back well over 1,000 years. Clothing was traditionally made from harvested cotton fibers and other plant materials. Shell and turquoise jewelry reflected a trading network that, even 1,000 years ago, extended for hundreds of miles in every direction.

### Art and Power

While modern Western culture customarily characterizes aspects of life as either secular or sacred, there are no such arbitrary divisions in Native American thought. Neither can art be divided easily into religious arts, as something distinct from the arts of daily life. In some arts, the spiritual aspects may be the most obvious, but even arts made for daily use or for outside sale can carry spiritual meaning if they are made in the proper way.

A Zuni altar is a highly sacred construction made up of individual artistic forms: carved and painted figures adorned with feathers, painted pottery bowls for cornmeal, and dry paintings made of sand and crushed minerals. Not only do the individual items have power, but they are also activated as a constellation of sacred forms when the proper ceremonies are performed over them by initiated members of a society. Centuries of custom and ritual dictate how the component parts are to be made and used, and who may be allowed to see them.

A Comanche or Crow shield is a power object as well as a piece of art. A Plains warrior might have a dream or a vision in which a particular animal, insect, or other natural phenomenon appeared to him in a significant fashion. He would then paint his war shield with elements from his vision, and it would bestow upon him power and protection in combat. Each such object is a highly personal and individual work of artistry.

In contrast to these two examples, it might seem that a Navajo rug made for sale would be a completely secular object (see photo on following page). Yet further knowledge of the conditions under which it is produced reveals that, for the Navajo, weaving is a sacred activity. In Navajo creation stories, a sacred ancestor named Spider Woman, who used the materials of the natural world as she wove, wove the universe itself on a giant loom. Lightning, clouds, rainbows, and sunrays were woven together to create the world. Navajo women think about Spider Woman as they combine different products of the natural world (the wool from sheep, the dyes from plants, and their own human creativity) into their weavings. The designs on many Navajo rugs are geometric patterns that are not symbolic but simply demonstrate the weaver's powers of creativity and graphic design. In the example illustrated here, however, the imagery on the rug relates to the sacred arts of medicine and astronomy. It is a design taken from the Navajo art of sand painting, used for physical and spiritual healing. In this design, Mother Earth is depicted by the large figure on the right. Corn, beans, squash, and tobacco (the four most important Native American plants) grow out of her belly. The black figure beside her is Father Sky. In his belly the sun and moon are depicted most prominently, while the background is dotted with constellations, including Orion, the Pleiades, and the Dippers.

An art object may give the viewer only hints of the complex technological, spiritual, and social processes that stand behind it. While anyone may admire the beauty of a Navajo rug or the impressiveness of a Haida totem pole, it is only by learning more about the culture and ideas that stand behind their creation that we can appreciate the true eloquence of these works of art. In many areas of life, art may be used for personal power and prestige or to reveal the power of the entire social group.

In the nineteenth century, a Sioux man would advertise his personal feats of bravery in warfare by painting his exploits on the buffalo robe he wore or on the tepee in which he lived. He owned the rights to these scenes, for they were his own personal history. So, too, he would own the rights to any images he discovered through his dreams and might paint these on his tepee as well. These power symbols could be bought or inherited by others, just like other kinds of property. In similar fashion, a Cheyenne woman who ornamented her own and her family's clothing with carefully sewn designs in dyed porcupine quills owned the rights to these designs. She gained power and prestige through her role as a fine artist, just as a Cheyenne man gained honor through his role as a warrior.

Among the Iroquois of upper New York State and southern Ontario, a man who needed to draw upon the power of the spirit world to aid in healing would dream of a spirit face, and would then carve a mask of this spirit from the trunk of a basswood tree while the tree was still growing. This "False Face" spirit mask would be used in conjunction with tobacco to purge the community of diseases, or to heal a particular individual. To the Iroquois, such masks are more than just inanimate art objects; they are believed to have spiritual power and must be handled respectfully and are ritually offered cornmeal and tobacco.

While artists and art-making can be powerful, myth and folklore sometimes give warnings about abuses of such power, especially if too much attention to making art means that an artist is not leading a balanced life. A Tlingit myth from southern Alaska cautions that cooperation with the human community is the proper model for an artist's life, rather than the Euro-American stereotype of the isolated artist totally devoted to art. According to this myth, in ancient times there was a young Tlingit woman whose most compelling desire was to perfect the art of weaving, an art form not yet commonly practiced on the Northwest Coast. But the demands of her many male admirers made it difficult for her to devote sufficient time to her art. For this reason, she decided to go live in seclusion in the wilderness. She was discovered there by Raven and Marten (two animal heroes in Northwest Coast mythology) who masqueraded as a high-ranking chief and his son in order to get to know her. The chief asked her to marry his son, but she agreed to do so only on the condition that they could remain in isolation in the woods, so that she could continue her weaving undisturbed. Only when the men agreed did she consent to show them her house, which was filled with the most beautiful weavings in the world. While she slept, Raven and Marten stole all her weavings. They flew back to the human communities on the coast and distributed the weavings as gifts to all the women in the communities. From these items, women learned to weave the Chilkat Tlingit blankets that soon became the most valued textiles along the Northwest Coast.

This myth serves as a cautionary tale for those artists whose involvement in their own work leads them to seek isolation from the human community and to withhold knowledge that would be helpful to others. For that lack of moral generosity, the myth says, the artist may lose her art.

### Learning To Be an Artist

Among some tribes, all people may reasonably be considered artistic, and all are responsible for making and ornamenting their own clothing, shelter, and other goods. Even within such societies, however, it is generally recognized that certain people excel at art. If an individual needed a finely made object for a ceremony or gift, he or she might contract with a particularly talented carver or quillworker, for example, in order to ensure a truly fine piece of work. In societies where artistic practice is widespread, children typically learn from their parents or other adult members of the extended family. A young Eskimo boy watched and then ultimately helped his father carve walrus tusks into small amulets. A young Navajo girl helps her mother herd sheep, spin the yarn made from their wool, and finally weave a fine blanket or rug.

In some societies, the making of art is considered a specialty. Like any other specialized profession, one must study hard and apprentice oneself to an expert in order to become an accomplished artist. A young Tlingit or Kwakiutl boy on the Northwest Coast who was interested in being a carver would typically become the apprentice of a master artist. His jobs at first would be menial: keep the fire going, sharpen the master's tools, grind up the mineral pigments to make the paints. As he got older and proved himself worthy of more responsibility, he would be allowed to use the sharp carving tools to remove the bark from a piece of log and rough out the facial features of a mask. The master artist would then perform the fine finishing work, while the boy carefully observed. The more advanced apprentice might work as the "other side man." The master carver would plan out a totem pole design and carve the entire right side of it while the apprentice would follow the carver's example on the left side, striving to replicate his teacher's work with every stroke of the carving tool or every dab of the paint brush.

In societies like those of the Northwest Coast, where art was a specialist's pursuit, elaborate payment schemes and contracts would be worked out between artist and patron. Among the Kwakiutl, for example, a man might host a public feast to announce his intention to commission a new totem pole. The guests at this feast would serve as the witnesses to the oral contract between patron and artist; their participation would ensure that all aspects of the contract would be honored.

Among many Native American societies, people report that one of the principal ways they get ideas for art is through dreams. A Pueblo potter may dream of the complex design she wants to paint on the water jar she has just made—a pattern that incorporates many elements of traditional design, yet is uniquely her own. An Iroquois carver may dream of a particular False Face Spirit, whose facial expression is slightly different from any mask he has carved before. A Sioux beadworker may dream of the ways that the colors of her new beads will fit together into an innovative pattern, or she may dream of the supernatural spirit of Double Woman, who is the patron of Sioux quillworkers and beadworkers. It is said that if a woman dreams of Double Woman, she will be an extraordinary artist.

Most Native American art that was put in museums before the mid-twentieth century was collected anonymously. The collectors and scholars who acquired it did not bother to find out the names of the

Masked dancers participating in a Kwakiutl winter ceremonial. (Courtesy of the National Anthropological Archives, National Museum of Natural History, Smithsonian Institution)

artists who made these works. A visit to most museums gives the false impression that Native American art is anonymous, for few labels bear the names of the makers. Yet, in any tribe, people recognized each other's individual styles and distinctive markings: the particular way one carver might carve the eye socket of a mask, or paint the markings on its face, or the unusual and distinctive way one weaver would finish off the edge of her blanket. It was not necessary to put one's name on the carving or basket for others to recognize or appreciate the achievement when all lived in a small society.

In some regions, early in the twentieth century, artists were encouraged by their non-Native patrons to sign their works, for this had been the custom in Euro-American art since the Renaissance. The famous potter from San Ildefonso Pueblo, Maria Martinez, was urged around 1920 to sign the bottoms of her famous blackware pots, for buyers would pay more money for her signed works (see photo below). Over the next two decades, Maria signed her name to pots made and painted by others, and she polished and signed pots that other

women had formed. To the modern, Western way of thinking, this may seem to be a misrepresentation; within the Pueblo worldview, where community balance and group harmony are valued over individual achievement, this was a mechanism by which other artists could share in the high prices brought by Maria Martinez's overriding fame. This insured that jealousies and unfairness were kept to a minimum.

## Tradition and Innovation

Artists everywhere are curious about the work of other people. They typically draw upon the work of past centuries as they experiment with imagery and motifs. At the same time, new materials and new ways of doing things also stimulate artists to take their work in new directions. Native American artists are no exception.

In ancient times, around AD 1100, Anasazi potters of the present-day U.S. Southwest learned how to manufacture pottery that was beautifully painted and skillfully fired in open-air kilns. The Anasazi potter was not only a master of the elegant vessel form, but she also painted complex abstract designs using only simple decorative motifs like straight lines, zig-zags, cross-hatches, and spirals. In ancient Anasazi pottery there were many regional traditions. Potters learned technical information within their own families, but might draw inspiration for decorative patterns from other pots that were widely traded in the Southwest.

To the south of the Anasazi, the Mimbres people of southwestern New Mexico were also experts at pottery-making and painting. The Mimbres pottery tradition shares some features with Anasazi pottery—both usually used black and white designs. But Mimbres pottery painters were interested in depicting scenes from daily life, from religious stories, and from the animal world. The unique Mimbres pottery-painting tradition died out by AD 1200, as drought set in and Mimbres villages were abandoned. People migrated, new communities were formed, and new artistic traditions established. Mimbres pottery painting was not rediscovered until archaeological excavations brought it to light after 1910. Today twentieth-century descendants of ancient Mimbres and Anasazi potters experiment not only with new ways of doing things, but also with very old methods. Early in the twentieth century, Maria and Julian Martinez incorporated Mimbres serpent and feather designs into their painted pots. Contemporary Pueblo potters at the village of Acoma, too, continue to draw creative inspiration from fine Mimbres designs.

On the Great Plains, in the centuries before the coming of Europeans in the early nineteenth century, artists from Crow, Cheyenne, Sioux, Kiowa, and other tribes experimented with materials and designs in quillwork, hide-painting, and other diverse arts of clothing and personal adornment. Through their trading networks, such goods were exchanged over long distances across the Great Plains. When horses became a fundamental part of Plains culture, these long-distance trading networks grew even more extensive.

While today we think of beadwork as a "traditional" American Indian art, especially on the Great Plains, there was a time when beads were an exciting new material for artists to experiment with. French fur traders brought beads to Western Great Lakes Indians by the early seventeenth century. When the trader François Laroque visited the Crow Indians on the northern Plains in 1805, they were already using blue glass beads obtained from Shoshoni intermediaries, who had, in turn, obtained them from Spanish traders in the Southwest. At that time, beads were such a highly prized commodity that the Crow would trade one horse for only one hundred beads. Later, beads became widespread and inexpensive. Artists quickly recognized the

artistic potential of these wonderful new materials. Strong and durable, with a vivid range of non-fading colors, beads were easy and comparatively quick to work with, compared to the laborious process of quillwork traditionally done by female artists on the Great Plains. At first, beads were used alongside quillwork as an extra form of ornamentation; but by the mid-nineteenth century beads came to replace quillwork in many areas. At the start of the reservation era in 1869, the use of beadwork intensified, becoming a symbol of the ethnicity of the tribes, at a time when Indian cultures were under great pressure to change and assimilate to Euro-American ways. All-over beading of vests, dresses, moccasins, and cradles became common.

When beadwork replaced quillwork as the primary form of female artistry, some of the customs and beliefs associated with quillwork were transferred as well. Among many Plains tribes, quill- and beadworkers were members of professional artistic guilds. It was through such work that women proved their artistry, diligence, and power. George Bird Grinnell, who lived among the Cheyenne in the 1890s, found that for women, good artistry was considered the equivalent of bravery and success in war for men. Grinnell observed that in meetings of the artists' guild, the women would recall and describe their previous fine works in a way similar to men counting coup, or recalling their bravery in war. Counting coup, the ultimate act of courage in war, demands that a man touch his opponent with a coup stick, showing his boldness and finesse. That women's arts demand these traits as well is a persistent idea among some Plains people. Even today, expert Crow beadworker Winona Plenty Hoops of Lodge Grass, Montana says, "A good design is like counting coup."

Just as female artists on the Great Plains embraced new materials like beads and brightly dyed and printed fabrics to use in their art, male artists, too, found new materials of interest. In the eighteenth and nineteenth centuries, men painted on buffalo hides, depicting scenes of their own personal history and war exploits. When they observed visiting Euro-American artists like George Catlin and Karl Bodmer paint highly realistic scenes of Plains life, Native men began to transform their own painting styles, making them more detailed and realistic. They used inks and other materials obtained from these artists and subsequently from traders. As Euro-American hunters ruthlessly slaughtered the great buffalo herds during the second half of the nineteenth century, hides became scarce, and Plains painters turned once again to imported materials to record their autobiographical exploits. Ledger books and muslin cloth became their new canvas. As the end of the century brought even more dramatic lifestyle changes—settlement on reservations, conversion to Christianity, abandonment of some long-held traditions—Plains painters transformed their art of painting from one that recorded ongoing heroic deeds to a form recording the past that was so rapidly slipping from their grasp.

## Native American Art in the Twentieth Century and Beyond

As many other essays in this reference book demonstrate, Native American life of the past century is characterized by great diversity within and among cultures. Some individuals live in a manner that would not be unfamiliar to their ancestors—hunting animals or planting corn, and speaking little English—while others have doctorates in engineering and work in the aerospace industry. Native American artistic traditions of the last few decades are as diverse as their lifestyles and professions. Some artists continue to work in traditions handed down through countless generations. For example, Pueblo women at Hopi, Acoma, Santa Clara, San Ildefonso, and elsewhere continue a pottery-making style and technology that is rooted in Anasazi and Mimbres traditions thousands of years old.

In some communities, artists today are reviving traditions that had languished for decades. When Haida artist Bill Reid erected a totem pole in his ancestral community on the Queen Charlotte Islands in Canada in the 1970s, it was the first pole carved and raised in almost one hundred years. Since then, other Haida artists have turned to carving, printmaking, and the revival of ancestral ceremonial traditions with new commitment and vigor. They want their children to respect and practice the arts that had defined them as Haida since time immemorial.

Yet another way of being a Native American artist in this century is to merge one's own ethnic art tradition with styles and symbols learned through the study of world art history. Many Native artists have earned fine arts degrees in painting, sculpture, and photography from universities. Their work is a dialogue between Native American art and European art histories. T. C. Cannon (1946–1978), whose ancestry included Caddo, Choctaw, Kiowa, and European, lived in Oklahoma and studied both at the Institute of American Indian Art in Santa Fe, New Mexico, and at the San Francisco Art Institute. His self-portraits depict him variously as an artist, a cowboy, an Indian dressed in "traditional" dress, and an art collector. His painting *Collector #5* (1975), while not an exact self-portrait, stands for Cannon as a contemporary artist who draws strength and identity both from his Indian heritage and his love

and knowledge of European art history. This painting turns the customary position of Indian artist and non-Indian patron upside-down. Here it is the Indian man, sitting in a wicker chair atop a Navajo rug, dressed in late nineteenth-century tribal finery, who is the collector and connoisseur of the Van Gogh painting on the wall. Cannon's work displays a motif common in much contemporary Native art: an impulse toward social critique, often done with humor and a sense of irony. Many artists play with this idea of cultural mixing. This may reflect their own ethnically mixed ancestry or simply the mixture of cultures they feel as Native artists making their way through a culture dominated by European-American history and art.

Nora Naranjo-Morse, from Santa Clara Pueblo in New Mexico, merges her family's tradition of pottery-making with her own ironic sense of humor and love of figural sculpture. In *Pearlene Teaching Her Cousins Poker* (1987), Naranjo-Morse takes the Pueblo image of ritual clowns (characterized by their striped bodies), makes them female instead of male, and depicts them playing a game of poker, which they are learning from a book. By making this work of art in clay, Naranjo-Morse identifies with her sisters, mother, and earlier female ancestors, all makers of fine Santa Clara pots. Yet her wit and sense of play links her with the larger community of contemporary Native American artists, whose work speaks across ethnic boundaries to a shared cultural condition.

Jolene Rickard, a Tuscarora (Iroquois) artist from New York State, uses the contemporary mediums of photography, color xerox, and collage, to express her views on contemporary Native art. In *Self Portrait—Three Sisters* (1988), her use of photography links her to experimentation in this artistic medium throughout the world. The subject matter—two ears of corn and her own image—relates to the deeply held belief of Iroquoian people (as well as some other Native Americans) that human beings are related to the corn people. In Iroquois tradition, women in particular are identified with this precious food substance because of a mythical ancestress who caused corn to be planted on the earth and who taught women how to farm. The title of the work also evokes the "three sisters" of Iroquois belief—corn, beans, and squash, the staples of life to many Indian nations.

There has been a tremendous explosion of creativity over the last twenty-five years among Native artists throughout North America. From the Canadian Inuit (Eskimo) printmakers of Cape Dorset and Baker Lake who sell their images of Arctic life worldwide, to the

*Eagle Dancer.* Painting and drawing by Richard Glazer–Danay. (Courtesy of Richard Glazer–Danay)

mask and totem pole carvers among the Haida and Kwakiutl who make works for local Native use as well as for an international art market, to the painters, photographers, and sculptors discussed here, Native art is alive and flourishing. Native American artists, using diverse materials and with many strong and different statements to make about creativity, Native identity and personal artistry, have begun the twenty-first century in a position of power, demonstrating that art continues to be an eloquent statement of indigenous strength.

*Janet Catherine Berlo*
*University of Rochester, New York*

## ♦ NATIVE AMERICAN ART

Native American art today, with all its diverse expressions, remains part and parcel of a uniquely contemporary creativity. All over the country, artists of Native American ancestry are working. Bead-workers tailor and decorate regalia for powwow dancing. Potters update traditional styles for sale in the upscale art markets. Painters and sculptors create challenging, modernist and postmodernist works for exhibition in galleries and museums. The traditions of Native American art stem back thousands of years when ancestors employed visual arts to express religious ideas, to participate in ceremonial and social occasions, or to embellish or decorate objects of day-to-day life. When

*Where the West Ends,* by Jacob Goff. (Courtesy of Jacob Goff)

Europeans arrived on the North American continent, Native artists created art works as objects of exchange to help mediate relations between themselves and the newcomers. The things they made for trade and sale can be understood as acts of self-representation, just as those who collected them saw the objects as souvenirs of cultural encounters. More recently, Native American artists have produced works as profound expressions of cultural survival and resurgence, of social comment, dissent, and protest, and of deeply personal reflections about what it means to be of Native ancestry in the world today.

## Art of Ritual

This year, in late November or December, as they have every year for as long as anyone can remember, six Shalako kachina will step across the shallow Zuni River and enter into Zuni Pueblo at dusk, bringing blessings and word of kachina visitations to come throughout the following year. The Shalako are the courier kachinas, messengers who announce the beginning of the ritual year and the annual cycle of ceremonies that will insure Zuni health and the fertility of their crops. Each Shalako looms over nine feet tall, with a cylindrical, turquoise face framed by a halo crest of large eagle feathers. They are gigantic birds with snapping beaks and ruffles of raven feathers and short wings, the lower body is wrapped with an embroidered robe. Their mysterious warbling resembles birdcalls.

Members of each of the six Zuni kivas, or ceremonial organizations, organize the Shalako event, along with many other kachina performances throughout the year. Kachinas are primordial ancestors of the Zuni who remained in the other world below this terrestrial earth after the Zuni climbed out to emerge on their present homeland. Members of the kiva organizations now impersonate the many different kachina spirits during private and public ceremonies, so that they appear at the Pueblo at an appointed time to dance and bring blessings. The presentation of a kachina performance requires the creation of requisite masks, made of painted leather, as well as countless elements of regalia, such as textile kilts, sashes, and painted moccasins. The dancers are well-rehearsed in their movements and accompanied by singers and attendants. The entire event possesses a strong aesthetic dimension emphasized by the Zuni themselves. Kachina dances are at once religious obligations and artistic expressions of worldview intended to offer wonder and delight to the community.

Zuni kachina performances represent today the kinds of aesthetic and ceremonial traditions that have been practiced in the Americas for untold thousands of years. When Europeans learned of Zuni Kachina performances, they attempted to describe them in terms that made sense within the realm of their own, and very different, kinds of understanding: dance, song, drama, material arts. As a result, many outsiders, drawn to what they considered a "primitive" spectacle, crowded into Zuni to observe kachina dances as spectators. Outsiders collected Zuni masks and other kinds of ritual objects, thinking of them as art appropriate for public display. The experience at Zuni parallels those of other tribes, whose sacred rituals require special kinds of objects that have been collected by anthropologists, collectors, and museums.

Throughout the United States and Canada, factors of enforced assimilation through schools, missionary activities, poverty, and repression have contributed to the loss of ritual objects to museums and collectors. In at least one well-known instance, government agents confiscated ritual objects as a result of laws that made ritual practices a criminal offense. In 1885 the Canadian Indian Act was amended to outlaw a Kwakiutl ceremony known as a potlatch. The Kwakiutl live on the coast of southern British Columbia. In 1922 William Halliday, the government agent for the Kwakiutl community of Alert Bay, raided a potlatch, sent twenty-two participants to jail, and confiscated over 450 ritual objects, including masks, rattles, whistles, and "coppers." Halliday sold these items to museums in Toronto, Ottawa, and New York City.

Many things have changed since then. The anti-potlatch provision was deleted from the 1951 revision of the Canadian Indian Act. The people of Alert Bay have successfully retrieved most of the objects confiscated in 1922. The Zuni and their neighbors the Hopi, who also prepare and perform kachina ceremonies, have enlisted the FBI to help them reclaim masks and other ritual objects they consider stolen from their communities. In 1990 the Native American Grave Protection and Repatriation Act established regulations for the return of religious objects and objects of "cultural patrimony" housed in American museums. Today, there is a more wide spread recognition that some categories of Native arts are intended exclusively for community use and that it is not appropriate for those

outside the community to own them. The people of Zuni Pueblo and many other Native communities welcome visitors to respectfully observe some of their ceremonies, but keep others privately to themselves.

## Ceremonial Arts and the Marketplace

Visual arts and crafts remain a vibrant part of contemporary Native American ceremony and celebration today. Those who participate still turn to talented artists and crafts people to create objects necessary for many different kinds of cultural events. On the other hand, outsider interest in Native American arts and ceremonies has offered economic opportunities in the greater arts market. As a result, many Native artists create things both for use within the community and for sale without. This is possible when such artistic creations are not considered sacred or communal property by members of the community. The practice of making things for sale to outsiders has deep roots in traditional practice and contributes substantially to the survival of traditional crafts techniques and creative skills.

Today, hundreds of powwows (some refer to them as Indian dances) take place all across America. Talented dancers compete for prizes in many different categories: traditional dance, fancy dance, grass dance, and jingle dress dance. Each category of dancing requires special regalia: a dance outfit made of many different component parts. Many participants make their own outfits, honing skills in traditional craft techniques such as glass bead embroidery, silk ribbon applique, and even porcupine quill embroidery for some outfits. The most accomplished practitioners of these techniques may receive commissions from other dancers who recognize their skills. Some of these artists will also make things intended for sale at tribal arts galleries or other venues. For artists from the tribes of the Northern Plains, one of the most prestigious shows is the Northern Plains Tribal Arts, which takes place every September in Sioux Falls, South Dakota. Here, artists compete for prizes awarded in several traditional arts categories: glass bead embroidery, porcupine quill embroidery, textiles, and hide painting.

This kind of recognition and opportunity for skilled artists has a long tradition among the Lakota of North and South Dakota. For those generations that first adjusted to reservation life, after about 1880 or so, the creations of traditional artists were in great demand. Although government officials discouraged traditional ceremonies, they persisted, requiring elaborately decorated regalia in the style of the day. The Lakota considered generosity a central cultural value, as expressed through giveaways, ceremonies conducted when prominent families assembled many different kinds of valuables to distribute to fellow community members during a formal event. Artists were commissioned to create beaded moccasins, quilts, and other items of decorated clothing for distribution during a giveaway. One popular way of doing this was to commission a child's outfit, trousers, and a vest, completely covered with glass bead embroidery. A child of the host family wore the outfit to the giveaway, but then the clothing was presented to one of the guests for special recognition.

During these early years of reservation life among the Lakota, there was not a great deal of opportunity to earn cash, but artists skilled in beadwork discovered there was a market for their creations. Local traders found that it was possible to sell beaded moccasins and other decorated items off the reservation. They purchased items from artists or took them on consignment. Traders published and circulated catalogues and placed advertisements in magazines to establish a modest mail-order business in Lakota arts. Some female artists cut out the middle man and sold their creations directly to railroad passengers on the Great Northern Railway Line that passed close to the Standing Rock reservation, or set up booths at regional fairs.

Lakota commerce in traditional arts did not begin with life on the reservation, however, and predates contact with whites. Early explorers of Lakota territory during the beginning of the 1800s found that there was an active exchange network between many of the Northern Plains tribes, which included trade in decorated shirts made of deer hide, dresses, leggings, moccasins and buffalo robes. Women skilled in the techniques of their manufacture were highly honored within the tribe. Among the neighboring Cheyenne for example, it was customary for women to stand up during formal occasions and be recognized for the numbers of buffalo robes they prepared, just as men could enumerate their accomplishments in battle. Many Plains tribes recognized talent in craft skills as a special, spiritual blessing. Cheyenne women who excelled at porcupine quill embroidery organized themselves into a kind of craft guild with restricted membership. Those who wanted to learn the techniques paid guild members for instruction and admission. Lakota credited the gift of talent to a spiritual being called Double Woman, who exhorted skilled artists to share the products of their abilities with others.

## Traditional Arts and the Marketplace

The ceramic artist Tony Da (b. 1940) of San Ildefonso Pueblo continues his community's tradition of pottery making, but adds contemporary features that stem from his own individuality and creativity. He paints his highly polished vessels of red and black ware with images of Kokopelli, the hunchback flute-player, or the horned serpent, or other ancient symbols. But his art possesses a very contemporary finish, enhanced by his own innovation of turquoise, red coral, and shell inlay. Few of his creations remain in the community. Instead, art collectors compete to acquire his best work from shows, galleries, and fine arts auctions. Tony Da is very much part of the contemporary art world, but he comes to it through a distinguished lineage of artists who helped create the kind of appreciation and collectors' market for Pueblo pottery which he enjoys today. Tony Da's father, Popovi Da (1921–1971) was also a well-known potter, and his grandparents were Maria Martinez (1887–1980) and Julian Martinez (1885–1943), who pioneered the collectors' market for Pueblo pottery during the early decades of the twentieth century.

Historical records show that Pueblo communities have been making pottery for sale to their neighbors since at least as early as the seventeenth century. Archaeologists have determined that trade in pottery is an ancient practice in the Southwest. Outside markets for Pueblo-made pottery expanded appreciably with the arrival of the Santa Fe Railroad in the early 1880s. The tracks ran close to Laguna Pueblo, where trains would stop briefly to allow passengers to buy Laguna pottery and take photographs. Thomas Keams, a trader who had established a post near the Hopi Mesas, organized pottery production at First Mesa during the 1880s to provide saleable items for railroad tourists. Many of the Rio Grande Pueblos are located close to Santa Fe and potters from San Ildefonso, Tesuque, Santo Domingo, and other communities brought pots they had made by wagon to traders located in Santa Fe, where visitors could buy them. These traders stocked shops at the large hotels built by the Fred Harvey Company, the first opening in Albuquerque in 1902, with others following in Sante Fe; Las Vegas, New Mexico; Lamy; and the Grand Canyon.

Julian and Maria Martinez from San Ildefonso worked diligently and creatively to fill the tourist demand for Pueblo pottery. Although traditionally pottery had been constructed and painted by women, Julian and Maria Martinez split the labor, with Maria making the pots and Julian painting them. It had not been the practice in the past to decorate pottery elaborately at San Ildefonso, but Julian and Maria Martinez, along with their contemporaries (some of whom also worked as couples) developed new decorative styles and techniques calculated to appeal to tourists. It had been the custom during the 1800s to paint pottery with a white or red background slip and add decorations with black, organic-based paint. The tourist market encouraged the development of a "polychrome" ware, creating colorful patterns with white, black, and red all together. By 1919 Julian and Maria Martinez had developed a technique to decorate pottery with a matte black background slip contrasting with highly polished black designs, so-called black-on-black pottery. They also began to sign their distinctive creations and gained recognition as individual artists. Maria and Julian Martinez's artistic success established the possibility for a kind of transgenerational family business. After Julian's death in 1943, Maria collaborated with her son, Popovi Da, and remained active until late in her life. The tradition continues today with grandson Tony Da and other descendents of Maria and Julian.

Many different indigenous arts or crafts traditions, like painted pottery of the Southwest, flourish today as a result of their successful transition to the modern art market. In every case, artists of succeeding generations continued to introduce innovations responsive to the demands of the marketplace.

Just like pottery, baskets made by Native women of California proved popular among collectors. Since ancient times, baskets had been made in this region to fill a broad range of utilitarian purposes: collecting, storage, and food processing. Several tribes made special, highly decorated varieties of baskets that represented wealth for display or exchange. These traditions of object manufacture quickly found their way into economic interactions with whites. Neophytes (Christian converts) among the Chumash and other Southern California tribes made baskets for priests and officials of the early Spanish Missions. Throughout the 1800s talented basket makers of many different California tribes produced "fancy baskets" with elaborate decoration for sale. Some individual basket makers became famous, such as Louisa Keyser (b. 1855) of the Washoe tribe, renamed Dat-so-la-lee by her dealer, and Elizabeth Hickox (b. 1872), of mixed heritage, who was affiliated with the Karuk tribe. Both women innovated basket forms and decoration between 1880 and 1920, which proved to be the highpoint of collector interest. Louisa Keyser invented the form known as the *degikup*, a nearly spherical coiled basket, often of enormous size. Elizabeth Hickox made lidded fancy baskets with shapes derived in part from Victorian teapots. Basket makers today of the Pomo, Karuk, and other California tribes build on the accomplishments of the past with their own mixture of tradition and personal creativity.

Carver and printmaker Robert Davidson (b. 1946), of the Haida tribe, also sees his work as the continuation of a legacy that dates back hundreds of years. Davidson is one of several artists from the Northwest Pacific Coast region who have participated in a revival of traditional arts within the last fifty years or so. Their work builds upon the "form-line" tradition, so-called by art historian Bill Holm, a means of graphic representation that uses a restricted number of forms organized with strict rules of design. For hundreds of years, Northwest Coast artists had employed form-line representations of animals to decorate houses, boxes, dishes, spoons, and garments. Contemporary artists like Robert Davidson, and his predecessor Bill Reid (Haida, b. 1920), studied artifacts in museum collections to learn the vocabulary of form-line style and then adapted it to jewelry, printmaking, and other media.

## Fine Arts

In the fall of 1999, the Eiteljorg Museum of Western and American Indian Art inaugurated a fine arts fellowship program designed to recognize and support contemporary artists of Native American ancestry. The accompanying exhibition and catalogue honored five artists: George Morrison (Chippewa b. 1915), Truman Lowe (Ho-Chunk/Winnebago, b. 1944), Lorenzo Clayton (Navajo, b. 1951), Marianne Nicholson (Kwakwaka'wakw/Kwakiutl, b. 1969) Jaune Quick-to-See Smith (Flathead, b. 1940), and Rick Rivet (Sahtu/Métis, b. 1949). Some visitors who entered the large, impressive installation of paintings and sculpture at the Eiteljorg may have thought the work displayed there reflected more the concerns of very contemporary modern and postmodern art rather than the traditions of Native America. And yet, each artist drew on their very personal and unique experiences of their Native American identity to create the eclectic assortment of work presented in the galleries. These artists, and many others working today, represent the impact of the twentieth century upon Native experience. Today, many artists of Native ancestry see themselves simultaneously as inheritors of cultural tradition and citizens of the larger world.

The kind of creative freedom and familiarity with the most advanced thinking about contemporary art enjoyed by Native artists today is the result of a long struggle between generations of pioneer artists against American attitudes and institutions with viewpoints that tended to limit what American Indian art could be. The so-called "fine arts" movement of American Indian art has its roots in the early twentieth century Southwest, when a generation of students at the San Ildefonso Day School and the Santa Fe Indian School—among them Fred Kabotie (Hopi, b. 1900), Alphonso Roybal (San Ildefonso, b. 1898), and Tonita Pena (San Ildefonso, b. 1893)—began to produce watercolor paintings illustrating traditional Pueblo dances and ceremonies. Local anthropologists, intellectuals, and white artists promoted the work of these artists in critical writings and

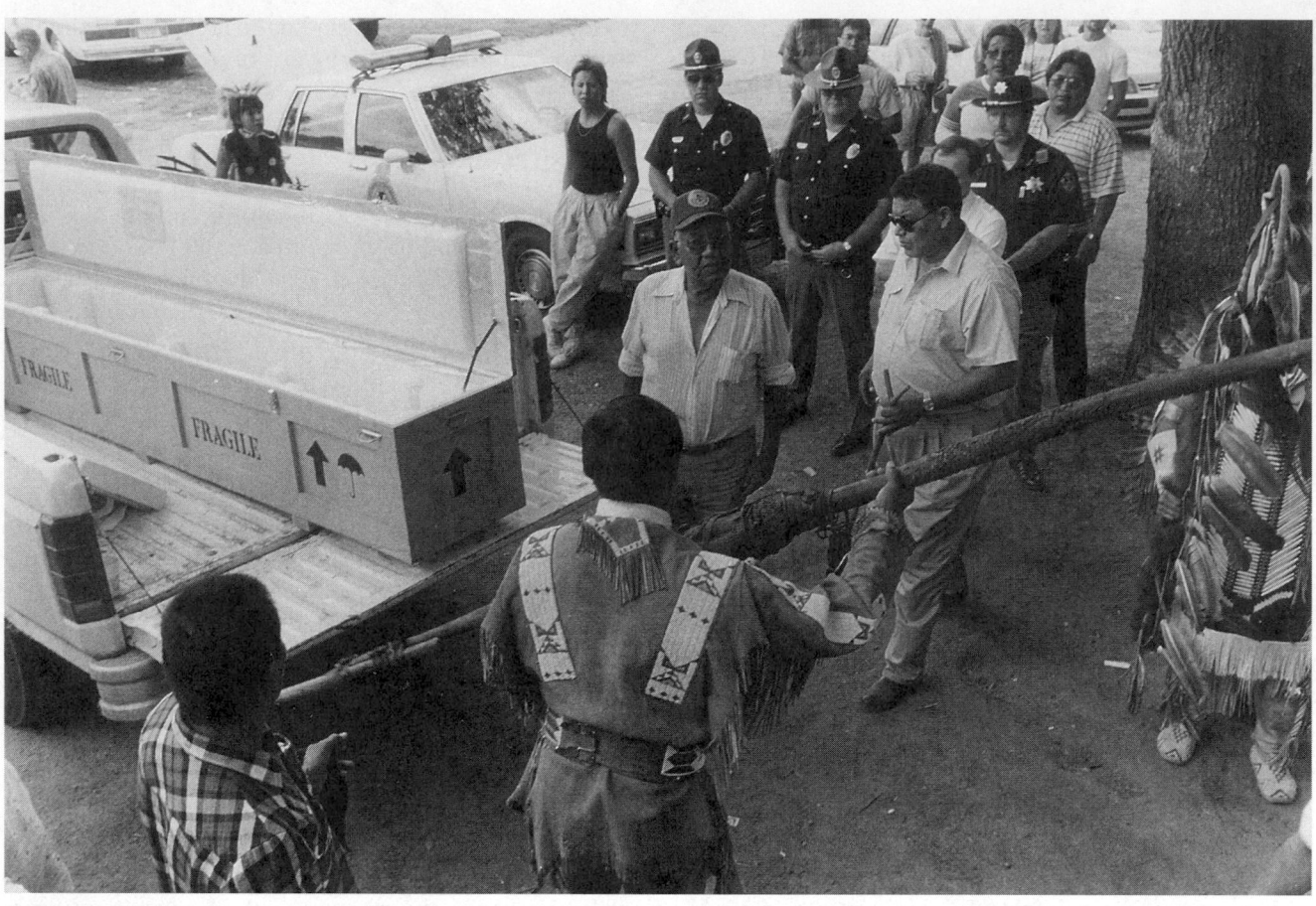

In Macy, Nebraska, the Sacred Staff of the Omaha is returned to the tribe in 1989 after 100 years in the Peabody Museum Collection at Harvard University. (Photo by Ilka Hartmann)

artistic exhibitions in New York, Chicago, Washington, D.C., and elsewhere during the 1920s. Their success, and the idea that art production could contribute substantially to reservation economies, led to the creation in 1934 of the Studio School, an art school affiliated with the Santa Fe Indian School. Here, under the tutelage of Dorothy Dunn, a white artist, an important generation of Native artists received formal arts training.

Probably the most prominent artist to emerge from the program was Alan Houser (Chiricahua Apache, 1914–1994). Trained initially as a water colorist, Houser favored sculpture later in his career. He is best known today for his monumental and ennobling marbles and bronzes of the traditional Apache. Houser was a worldly man, however, who achieved impressive expressive effects through his exploration of abstractions based on the human form. In 1992 he was the first Native American recipient of the prestigious National Medal of Arts

The Studio School was the first art school dedicated to the arts instruction of Native Americans, but it promoted only a very narrow style of art as appropriately Native American. Based loosely on traditional Plains Indian painting, the studio style limited artists to pictorial renderings of Indian subjects (dances, ceremonies, mythology). Some studio-trained artists like Oscar Howe (Yankton Sioux, b. 1915) chaffed under these restrictions. Howe's painting employed the modern art vocabulary of cubism to represent Sioux dances and myths. Nevertheless, in a rather notorious episode, the Philbrook Museum of Art in Tulsa, Oklahoma, rejected Howe's work from the first of their series of juried shows of Native American art beginning in 1946 because it did not conform to the then accepted perimeters for American Indian painting. This slight was rectified the next year, however, and the Philbrook organized a solo show of his work in 1956.

George Morrison (Chippewa, b. 1919), from the very beginning of his career as an artist, eschewed that narrow sense of being that an artist of Native ancestry could be by moving to New York City in 1943 to join the vibrant, post-war art scene of New York. Morrison's nonrepresentational paintings derive from surrealist techniques of automatism and New York abstract expressionism, but are always rooted in his experiences and perceptions of the land, particularly where land meets water. The paintings of his "Red Rock" series are intimate, jewel-like meditations on the landscapes of his tribal homeland, the Grand Portage Reservation on Minnesota's north shore of Lake Superior.

The limitations of the studio style were painfully obvious in the early 1960s, resulting in the creation of a new arts program in 1962 at the Santa Fe Indian School called the Institute for American Indian Art, which is still active today. Under the directorship of Lloyd Kiva New (Cherokee, b. 1916), the program combined fine arts with decorative and applied arts, including design. Fritz Scholder (Luiseño, b. 1937) was recruited to lead the painting program and proved very influential. He, and his best known student, T. C. Cannon (Caddo, Choctaw, Kiowa, b. 1946), challenged the idealized and cartoon-like images associated with the studio style with large, freely painted canvasses drawing from pop art, historical photographs, and the ironies of modern life for their images of Indians. Cannon died tragically in a motorcycle accident in 1979.

By the early 1970s, several artists of Native ancestry had earned master of fine arts degrees (MFAs) at prestigious university programs, some becoming university faculty themselves. Abstract painter George Longfish (Seneca, b. 1942) earned his MFA from The Art Institute of Chicago in 1972 and is now an esteemed professor of fine art at the University of California, Davis. Kay WalkingStick (Cherokee, b. 1935) completed her MFA at the Pratt Institute, Brooklyn, in 1975, and has had a distinguished career as an associate professor of painting at Cornell University. These artists, and others, show at mainstream art galleries in major U.S. cities. Their works are featured in the collections of prominent museums.

Some may ask what distinguishes the work of these very contemporary Native American artists from that of artists of European descent? Theories of contemporary art practice stress the creative act of the individual, but recognize that individual sensibility is shaped by experience: personal, collective, and cultural. As writer and critic Charlotte Townsend-Gault argues, Native American art today is more of a situation than a style. Artists of Native American descent working today are acutely aware of the *situation* of being a Native person, how tribal, family, and personal histories brought them to the present moment. Contemporary art practice allows the individual artist to explore a great range of issues and concerns, but only demands that the artist to be true to him- or herself. Art produced by Native artists today is perhaps the richest and most multilayered expression of the contemporary Native experience, with all its complexities, ironies, and resources.

*David Penney*
*Detroit Institute of Arts*

# Exhibitors of Contemporary Native Arts

The focus of this directory is on tribally owned and operated non-profit cooperatives, and enterprises. For a complete listing of contemporary native art organizations and businesses, including for-profit Indian art galleries, and arts and crafts stores, see *Indian, Eskimo, Aleut Owned and Operated Arts and Crafts Businesses: Source Directory*, published by the Indian Arts and Crafts Board, Room 4004, U.S. Department of the Interior, Washington D.C. 20240 (202) 2083773.

See also Tribal Museums directory in Chapter 1 and Arts directory in this chapter. Also note there are arts and crafts shops at the major historical monuments and landmarks in Chapter 1.

## ◆ ALASKA

CHILKAT VALLEY ARTS
209 Willard St
P.O. Box 145
Haines, AK 99827
(907) 766–2990

INUCRAFT
P.O. Box 549
Kotzebue, AK 99752
(907) 442–2800

NANA MUSEUM OF THE ARCTIC
   CRAFT SHOP
P.O. Box 49
Kotzebue, AK 99752
(907) 442–3304
(907) 442–3747

ST LAWRENCE ISLAND
Original Ivory Cooperative, Ltd
P.O. Box 189
Gambell, AK 99742
(907) 985–5112

YUGTARVIK REGIONAL MUSEUM SHOP
P.O. Box 388
Bethel, AK 99559
(907) 543–2098

YUP'IK GIFT SHOP
P.O. Box 219
Bethel, AK 99559
(907) 543–1819
(nonprofit organization)

## ◆ ARIZONA

COLORADO RIVER INDIAN TRIBES MUSEUM
Rte. 1, Box 23 B
Parker, AZ 85344
(520) 669–1335

GILA RIVER ARTS AND CRAFTS CENTER
P.O. Box 457
Sacaton, AZ 85247
(602) 562–3411

HATATHLI GALLERY
Navajo Community College Development Foundation
Tsaile, AZ 86556
(520) 724–6650

HEARD MUSEUM STORE
22 E Monta Vista
Phoenix, Az 85004
(620) 252–8344

HONANI CRAFTS-GALLERY
P.O. Box 221
Second Mesa, AZ 86043
(520) 737–2238

HOPI ARTS AND CRAFTS-SILVERCRAFT
   COOPERATIVE GUILD
P.O. Box 37
Second Mesa, AZ 86043
(520) 734–2463

NAVAJO ARTS AND CRAFTS ENTERPRISE
P.O. Box 160
Window Rock, AZ 86515
(520) 871–4090/5

NAVAJO ARTS AND CRAFTS ENTERPRISE
P.O. Box 464
Cameron, AZ 86020
(520) 679–2244

NAVAJO ARTS AND CRAFTS ENTERPRISE
P.O. Box 608
Chinle, AZ 86503
(520) 674–5338

NAVAJO ARTS AND CRAFTS ENTERPRISE
Hwys 160 & 163
Kayenta, AZ 86033
(520) 697–8611

#### ◆ CALIFORNIA

AMERICAN INDIAN CONTEMPORARY ARTS
　GALLERY
23 Grant Ave, 6th flr,
San Francisco, CA 94108
(415) 989–7003

AMERICAN INDIAN FILM INSTITUTE
333 Valencia Suite 322
San Fransico CA 94103
(415) 554–0525
www.aifisf.com

EASTERN SIERRA TRADING COMPANY
P.O. Box 731
Bridgeport, CA 93517
(619) 932–7231

INDIAN ARTS GIFT SHOP (NCIDC)
241 F St
Eureka, CA 95501
(707) 445–8451

INTERTRIBAL FRIENDSHIP HOUSE GIFT
　SHOP
523 East 14th St
Oakland, CA 94606
(510) 452–1235

#### ◆ COLORADO

SOUTHERN UTE MUSEUM STORE
P.O. Box 737
Ignacio, CO 81137
(970) 563–4649

#### ◆ DISTRICT OF COLUMBIA

THE INDIAN CRAFT SHOP
1849 C St. NW Rm. 1023
Washington, DC 20204
(202) 208–4056

#### ◆ FLORIDA

MICCOSUKEE GIFT SHOP & CULTURAL
　CENTER
P.O. Box 440021
Tamaimi Station
Miami, FL 33144
(305) 223–8380

#### ◆ GEORGIA

SOUTHWWEST INDIAN ARTISANS
P.O. Box 941759
Atlanta, GA 31141
(770) 840–8111

TEKAKWITHA
P.O.BOX 338
Helena GA 30545
(404) 878–2938

#### ◆ IDAHO

MARSH'S TRADING POST
1105 36th St, N
Lewiston, ID 83501
(208) 743–5778

TRADING POST CLOTHES HORSE
Box 868
Fort Hall, ID 83203
(208) 237–8433

WHITE EAGLE'S NEZ PERCE INDIAN ARTS
P.O. Box 4
Orofino, ID 83544
(208) 476–7753

## ◆ ILLINOIS

BEAR PAWS INC.
217 Ferry St.
Rockton, IL 61072
(815) 624–7427

## ◆ KANSAS

AMERICAN INDIAN ART CENTER
206 S Buckeye Ave
Abilene, KS 67410
(913) 263–0090

INDIAN MUSEUM GIFT SHOP
Mid-America All-Indian Center
650 North Seneca
Wichita, KS 67203
(316) 262–5221, ext. 41

## ◆ LOUISIANA

BAYOU INDIAN ENTERPRISES
P.O. Box 668
Elton, LA 70532
(337) 584–2653

## ◆ MAINE

MAINE INDIAN BASKETMAKERS ALLIANCE
P.O. Box 3253
Old Town, ME 04468
(207) 859–9722
miba@mint.net

## ◆ MASSACHUSETTS

MOWHAWK TRADING POST
874 Mowhawk TrailRt. 2
Shelburn, MA 01370
(413) 625–2412

## ◆ MICHIGAN

INDIAN ARTS & CRAFTS STORE
Native American Arts And Crafts Council
Goose Creek Rd.
Grayling, MI 49738
(517) 348–3190

INDIAN HILLS TRADING COMPANY & INDIAN
ART GALLERY
1581 Harbor Rd.
Petoskey, MI 49770
(616) 347–3789

SWEETGRASS ARTS & CRAFTS
206 Greenough St.
Sault Ste. Marie, MI 49783
(906) 635–6050

## ◆ MINNESOTA

IKWE MARKETING
Rte. 1
Osage, MN 56570
(218) 573–3411
(218) 573–3049

MANITOK FOOD & GIFTS/KENOO FINE
HANDCRAFTS
Hwy 59, P.O. Box 97
Callaway, MN 56521
(800) 726–1863

PIPESTONE INDIAN SHRINE ASSOCTION
c/o Pipestone National Monument
P.O. Box 727
Pipestone, MN 56164
(507) 825–5463

## ◆ MISSISSIPPI

CHOCTAW MUSEUM OF THE SOUTHERN
INDIAN GIFT SHOP
P.O. Box 6010
Philadelphia, MS 39350
(601) 650–1685

## ◆ MONTANA

COUP MARKS
P.O. Box 532
Ronan, MT 59864
(406) 246–3216

FLATHEAD INDIAN MUSEUM TRADING POST
& ART GALLERY
P.O. Box 464
St. Ignatius, MT 59865
(406) 745–2951

FORT BELKNAP VENTURES, INC
RR 1, Box 66
Harlem, MT 59526
(406) 353–2205, ext 403

NORTHERN PLAINS INDIAN CRAFTS
  ASSOCIATION
P.O. Box E,
Browning, MT 59417
(406) 338–5661

PLAINS GALLERY
P.O. Box 126 apt. 28
Lame Deer, MT 59043
(800) 249–2296

#### ◆ NEVADA

MOAPA TRIBAL ENTERPRISES
P.O. Box 340
Moapa, NV 89025–0340
(702) 864–2600

STEWART INDIAN MUSEUM TRADING POST
5366 Snyder Ave
Carson City, NV 89701
(702) 882–1808

THE TEPEE
2500 E 2nd St, Suite #38
Reno, NV 89595
(702) 322–5599

WINTER MOON TRADING COMPANY
P.O. Box 189
Schurz, NV 89427
(702) 773–2088

#### ◆ NEW MEXICO

BIEN MUR INDIAN MARKETING CENTER
P.O. Box 91148
Albuquerque, NM 87199
(800) 365–5400

CROWNPOINT RUG WEAVERS' ASSOCIATION
P.O. Box 1630
Crownpoint, NM 87313
(505) 786–5302

INDIAN PUEBLO CULTURAL CENTER
2401 12th St, NW
Albuquerque, NM 87104
(505) 843–7270
(800) 766–4405

INSTITUTE OF AMERICAN INDIAN ARTS
  MUSEUM SHOP
P.O. Box 20007
Santa Fe, NM 87504
(505) 988–6281

JICARILLA ARTS AND CRAFTS SHOP/
  MUSEUM
P.O. Box 507
Dulce, NM 87528
(505) 759–3242 ext 274

NAVAJO ARTS & CRAFTS ENTERPRISE
P.O. Box 1505
Magdalena, NM 87825
(505) 854–2987

NAVAJO ARTS & CRAFTS ENTERPRISE
1512 E Hwy 66
Gallup, NM 87301
(800) 790–6223

NAVAJO GALLERY
P.O. Box 1756
Leboux St.
Taos, NM 87571
(505) 758–3250
www.rcgomangallcry.com

OKE OWEENGE ARTS AND CRAFTS
P.O. Box 1095
San Juan Pueblo, NM 87566
(505) 852–2372

PORTAL PROGRAM OF THE PALACE OF THE
  GOVERNORS
P.O. Box 2087
Santa Fe, NM 87504–2087
(505) 827–6474

PUEBLO OF ZUNI ARTS AND CRAFTS
P.O. Box 425 Hwy 53
Zuni, NM 87327
(505) 782–5531

TAMAYA COOP ASSOCIATION
Santa Ana Pueblo
Star Rte., Box 37
Bernalillo, NM 87004
(505) 867–3301

ZUNI CRAFTSMEN COOPERATIVE
ASSOCIATION
P.O. Box 426 Zuni Pebulo
Zuni, NM 87327
(505) 782–4425

### ◆ NEW YORK

AMERICAN INDIAN COMMUNITY HOUSE
GALLERY
708 Broadway 2nd Fl
New York, NY 10003
(212) 598–0100

MOHAWK IMPRESSIONS
Box 20 Mohawk Nation
Hogansburg, NY 13655
(518) 358–2467

NATIVE AMERICAN CENTER FOR THE
LIVING ARTS, INC.
25 Rainbow Mall
Niagara Falls, NY 14303
(716) 2842427

NATIVE PEOPLES ARTS AND CRAFTS SHOP
North American Indian Club of Syracuse and
Vicinity, Inc.
P.O. Box 851
210 Fabius St.
Syracuse, NY 13201
(315) 4757425

SENECA-IROQUOIS NATIONAL MUSEUM
GIFT SHOP
794–814 Broad Street
Salamanca, NY 14779
(716) 945–1738

SIX NATIONS INDIAN MUSEUM SHOP
HCR 1, Box 10
Onchiota, NY 12968
(518) 891–2299

SWEETGRASS GIFT SHOP
Akwesasne Museum
Rt 37 RR1 Box 14C
Hogansburg, NY 13655–9705
(518) 358–2461

### ◆ NORTH CAROLINA

HALIWASAPOṈI TRIBAL POTTERY AND ARTS
Box 99 Hwy 561
Hollister, NC 27844
(919) 586–4017

QUALLA ARTS AND CRAFTS MUTUAL, INC
P.O. Box 310
Cherokee, NC 28719
(704) 497–3103

### ◆ NORTH DAKOTA

GREAT PLAINS NATIVE ARTS CO-OP
c/o NDIAA
401 N. Main St.
Mandan, ND 58554–3164
(701) 221–5328

THREE AFFILIATED TRIBES MUSEUM, ARTS
& CRAFTS DIVISION
P.O. Box 147
New Town, ND 58763
(701) 627–4477

### ◆ OKLAHOMA

ADAWA TRIBAL GIFT SHOP
P.O.B ox 110
Miami, OK 74355
(918) 549–1536

BAH-KHO-JE ART GALLERY
103 S. 2nd Street
Guthrie, OK 73044
(405) 282–7282

CHEROKEE NATION GIFT SHOPS
P.O. Box 948
Tahlequah, OK 74464
(800) 256–2123

CHEROKEE NATIONAL MUSEUM GIFT SHOP
P.O. Box 515 TSA-LA-GI
Tahlequah, OK 74464
(918) 456–6007

CHOCTAW INDIAN TRADING POST, INC.
1500 N. Portland Ave
Oklahoma City, OK 73107
(405) 947–2490

FIVE CIVILIZED TRIBES MUSEUM
TRADING POST
Agency Hill, Honor Heights Dr.
Muskogee, OK 74401
(918) 683–1701

OKLAHOMA INDIAN ARTS AND CRAFTS
COOPERATIVE
P.O. Box 966
Anadarko, OK 73005
(405) 247–3486

WEWOKA TRADING POST
C.R. Anthony Indian Arts and Crafts Center
Seminole Indian Museum
Box 1532
524 South Wewoka Ave.
Wewoka, OK 74884
(405) 257–5580

#### ◆ OREGON

WIND SONG GALLERY
7 SE Court
Pendleton, OR 97801
(541) 276–7993

#### ◆ PENNSYLVANIA

TURTLE ISLAND TREASURES
Lenni Lenape Historical Society
Museum Of Indian Culture
R.D. 2, Fish Hatchery Rd.
Allentown, PA 18103
(610) 797–2121
www.lenape.org

#### ◆ RHODE ISLAND

DOVE TRADING POST
390 Summit Road
Arcadia Village
Exeter, RI 02822–1808
(401) 539–2786

#### ◆ SOUTH DAKOTA

OYATE KIN CULTURAL COOPERATIVE
c/o Wesley Hare, Jr.
Marty, SD 57361
No telephone

ST. JOSEPH'S LAKOTA DEVELOPMENT
COUNCIL
St. Joseph's Indian School
Chamberlain, SD 57326
(605) 734–6021 ext. 307

#### ◆ TENNESSEE

EAGLE FEATURE
144 E. Main St.
Jonesbrough. TN 37559
(423)(753–2095

#### ◆ TEXAS

THUR-SHAN ARTS AND CRAFTS CENTER
305 Yaya Lane
El Paso, TX 79907
(915) 859–5287

TRIBAL ENTERPRISE
Alabama-Coushatta Indian Reservation
Rte 3, Box 640
Livingston, TX 77351
(409) 563–4391
(800) 392–4794

#### ◆ WASHINGTON

MAKAH CULTURAL RESEARCH CENTER
P.O. Box 160
Neah Bay, WA 98357
(360) 645–2711

POTLATCII GIFTS
Northwind Trading Company
P.O. Box 217
Anacortes, WA 98221
(206) 293–6404

SACRED CIRCLE GALLERY OF AMERICAN
INDIAN ART
Daybreak Star Arts Center
Discovery Park
Box 999100
Scattle, WA 08100
(206) 285–4425

SUQUAMISH MUSEUM
Box 498 Hwy305
Port Madison Reservation
Suquamish, WA 98392
(206) 598–3311

## ◆ WISCONSIN

**BUFFALO ART CENTER**
Box 51 Hwy13
Bayfield, WI 54814
(715) 779–5858

**HOCAK WAZIJACI LANGUAGE & CULTURE
    PROGRAM**
P.O. Box 390
N 4845 Hwy 58
Mauston, WI 53948–0390
(608) 847–5694
(800) 492–5745

**ONEIDA NATION MUSEUM SHOP**
P.O. Box 365
Oneida, WI 54155–0365

(414) 869–2768

**WA SWA GON ARTS AND CRAFTS**
P.O. Box 477 Hwy. 47
Lac du Flambeau, WI 54538
(715) 588–7636

**WINNEBAGO PUBLIC INDIAN MUSEUM**
P.O. Box 441
Wisconsin Dells, WI 53965
(608) 254–2268

## ◆ WYOMING

**LA RAY TURQUOISE CO**
P.O. Box 83
Cody, WY 82414
(307) 587–9564

# American Indian Cultural Events

This is a partial list of cultural events and gatherings (primarily pow wows, ceremonials, and feast days) throughout the United States and Canada. While many of these events include art markets and fairs, an additional listing of those events follows this one.

The anticipated months or dates for the events and entrance fees may change from year to year. Contact tribal offices, American Indian cultural centers or clubs, university American Indian studies programs, national parks, rodeo associations, museums, travel/visitor's bureaus, and BIA offices for more complete or current information. Inquiries into certified Indian artists' and artisans' arts and crafts and dress, photo taking, and conduct while attending cultural events should be directed to the sponsoring organization. Respect and cooperation are appreciated at all events.

The events are listed alphabetically by state according to title. Addresses listed indicate the location or mailing address. For additional listings you can contact the following organizations:

EIGHT NORTHERN INDIAN PUEBLOS
  COUNCIL
P.O. Box 969
San Juan Pueblo, NM 87566
(505) 852–4265

HOPI TRIBAL COMPLEX
P.O. Box 123
Kykotsmovi, AZ 86039
(520) 734–2441

INDIAN PUEBLO CULTURAL CENTER
2401 12th St. N.W.
Albuquerque, NM 80104
(505) 843–7270

NEWS FROM INDIAN COUNTRY (A monthly
  periodical)
7831 N Grinston Ave.
Hayward WI 54843
(715) 634–5226

OKLAHOMA INDIAN TIMES
12833 E. 41 St.
Tulsa, OK 74146
(918) 438–6548

## UNITED STATES

### ◆ ALABAMA

CREEK INDIAN THANKSGIVING DAY
  HOMECOMING AND POW WOW (November)
5811 Jacksprings Rd
Atmore, AL 36502
(334) 368–9136

### ◆ ALASKA

WORLD ESKIMO AND INDIAN OLYMPIC
  GAMES (July/August)
Parry Gymnasium, University of Alaska
Fairbanks Convention and Visitors Bureau
P.O. Box 2433
Fairbanks, AK 99707
(907) 452–6646

### ◆ ARIZONA

MUSTERING DAY (Labor Day September)
MUL-CHU-THA FAIR (February)
RUSSEL MOORE MUSIC FESTIVAL (October)
Gilas River Indian Community
P.O. Box 97
Facaton, AZ 85247
(520) 562–6000

NAVAJO NATION FAIR (September)
Window Rock Fair Grounds
P.O. Box 2370
Window Rock, AZ 86515
(520) 871–6703 or 6478

O'ODHAM TASH INDIAN DAYS (February)
Tohono O'odham Nation Public Relations Office
P.O. Box 837
Sells, AZ 85634
(520) 383–2028

TEWANIMA FOOT RACE (September)
Hopi Public Relations
P.O. Box 123
Kykotsmovi, AZ 86039
(520) 734–2441

WHITE MOUNTAIN APACHE TRIBAL FAIR
    AND RODEO (September)
Fort Apache Reservation
P.O. Box 700
White River, AZ 85941
(520) 338–4346 ext. 316 or ext. 323

## ◆ CALIFORNIA

AMERICAN INDIAN LEADERS OF TODAY
    AND TOMORROW CONFERENCE (Fall)
AMERICAN INDIAN STUDENT COUNCIL ANNUAL
    POW WOW (Spring)
CSULB American Indian Student Council
c/o American Indian Studies Department
F03 Building, Room 310
1250 Bellflower Blvd.
Long Beach, CA 90840
(562) 985–5293

ANNUAL UCLA CONTEST POW WOW (May)
University of California, Los Angeles
3220 Campbell Hall Box 951548
405 Hilgard Ave.
Los Angeles, CA 90024–1548
(310) 206–7513 or (310) 825–7315

CHUMASH INTERTRIBAL POW WOW
    (October)
Santa Ynez Reservation
P.O. Box 517
Santa Ynez, CA 93460
(805) 688–7997

DQU DEED DAY POW WOW (April)
GRADUATION POW WOW (May)
AMERICAN INDIAN DAY POW WOW (September)
VETERAN'S DAY POWWOW (November)
D-Q University
Pow Wow Committee
P.O. Box 409
33250 County Rd 31
Davis, CA 95616
(530) 758–0470

THE FALL GATHERING (October)
AGABE HARVEST & ROAST (April)
MALKI MUSEUM FIESTA AND POW WOW (May)
P.O. Box 578
Banning, CA 92220
(909) 649–7289

GATHERING SOCIAL POW WOW (November)
MEDICINE WAYS CONFERENCE (May)
MEDICINE WAYS ANNUAL POW WOW (May)
University of California, Riverside
Native American Programs
224 Costo Hall
Riverside, CA 92521
(909) 787–4143

INDIAN INTERTRIBAL AGENCY COMMITTEE
    POW WOW (June)
Indian Intertribal Agency Committee
Bishop, CA 93515
(760) 873–6394

SCIC, INC. ANNUAL POW WOW (August)
CHILDREN'S CHRISTMAS PARTY/POW WOW/TOY
    DRIVE/BOUTIQUE (December)
Southern California Indian Center, Inc.
10175 Slater St.
Fountain Valley, CA 92708
(714) 663–1102

STANFORD UNIVERSITY POWWOW (May)
Stanford American Indian Organization
P.O. Box 20090
Stanford, CA 94309
(650) 725–6944

## ◆ COLORADO

DENVER POW WOW (March)
Denver Coliseum
P.O. Box 19178
Denver, CO 80219
(303) 640–2637

OYATE/AISES SPRING POW WOW (Spring)
University of Colorado
OYATE/AISES
Campus Box 207
Boulder, CO 80302
(303) 492–8874

SOUTHERN UTE BEAR DANCE (May)
SOUTHERN UTE TRIBAL FAIR AND POW WOW
   (September)
Southern Ute Tribal Council Public Affairs
   Committee
P.O. Box 737
Ignacio, CO 81137
(970) 563–0100

### ◆ CONNECTICUT

ANNUAL FEAST OF GREEN CORN
   AND DANCE
Mashantucket Pequot Reservation
Cultural Resource Centre
Schemitzun Committee
P.O. Box 3161
Mashantucket, CT 06339
(860) 396–6531

BLACK ROCK NATIVE AMERICAN
   COMMUNITY POW WOW (September)
Black Rock State Park
Black Rock Pow Wow Committee
123 Wayland Ave.
Waterberry, CT 06708
(203) 754–0039

### ◆ DELAWARE

NANTICOKE INDIAN POW WOW (September,
   weekend after Labor Day)
Nanticoke Indian Association
Rt. 4 Box 107 A
Millsboro, DE 19966
(302) 945–3400

### ◆ FLORIDA

SEMINOLE INDIAN TRIBAL FAIR (February)
Seminole Okalee Indian Village
Seminole Tribal Fair Committee
6300 Sterling Rd. Suite 325.
Hollywood, FL 33024
(954) 966–6300

### ◆ IDAHO

CHIEF JOSEPH AND WARRIORS MEMORIAL
   POWWOW (June)
P.O. Box 35
Lapwai, ID 83540
(208) 843–5901

SHOSHONI-BANNOCK INDIAN FESTIVAL AND
   RODEO (August)
Shoshone-Bannock Tribes
Pow Wow Grounds
P.O. Box 306
Fort Hall, ID 83203
(208) 478–3804

### ◆ ILLINOIS

ANNUAL CHICAGO AIC POW WOW
   (November second week)
Chicago American Indian Centre
1630 West Wilson
Chicago, IL 60640
(773) 275–5871

### ◆ INDIANA

POKAGON BAND OF POTAWATOMI INDIAN
   NATION, INC.
KIE BOON MIENKAA FESTIVAL AND POW WOW
   (September)
RED ROAD POW WOW (March)
Pokagon Band Of Potawatomi Indian Nation
901 Spruce St.
Dowagiac, MI 49047
(888) 330–1234

### ◆ IOWA

MESKWAKIE PROCLAMATION DAY POW
   WOW (July 13)
MESKWAKIE VETERAN'S DAY POW WOW
   (November 11)
MESKWAKIE INTERTRIBAL CONTEST POWWOW
   (September)
MESKWAKIE TRADITIONAL INDIAN POW WOW
   (2nd Weekend In August)
Meskwakie Pow Wow Association
Sac and Fox Reservation
349 Meskwaki Rd.
Tama, IA 52339
(515) 484–4678

## ◆ KANSAS

### ANNUAL INDIAN ARTS SHOW (September)
University of Kansas
Museum of Anthropology Spooner Hall
1340 Jayhawk Blvd.
Lawrence, KS 66045
(785) 864–4245

### COMMENCEMENT POW WOW (Second weekend in May)
HASKELL INDIAN NATION UNIVERSITY
Attn: Pow Wow Committee or Art Committee
155 Indian Ave.
Lawrence, KS 66046
(785) 749–8446

### KICKAPOO NATIONS POW WOW (third weekend in July)
Kickapoo Pow Wow Committee
P.O. Box 271
Horton, KS 66349
(785) 486–2131

### MID AMERICA INDIAN POW WOW (July)
Wichita Chamber of Commerce
650 N. Senica
Wichita, KS 67203
(316) 262–5221

## ◆ KENTUCKY

### TRAIL OF TEARS INTERTRIBAL POW WOW (September weekend after labor day)
Trail of Tears Commission
P.O. Box 4027
Hopkinsville, KY 42240
(270) 886–8033

## ◆ MAINE

### CEREMONIAL DAY (August)
Pleasant Point Passamaquoddy
P.O. Box 343
Perry, ME 04667
(207) 853–2600

## ◆ MARYLAND

### BALTIMORE AMERICAN INDIAN CENTER POW WOW (August)
Pow Wow Committee
113 S. Broadway
Baltimore, MD 21231
(410) 675–3535

### MARYLAND INDIAN HERITAGE FESTIVAL AND POW WOW
(1st wk in June & 3rd wk Sept.)
Maryland Indian Heritage Society
16816 Country Lane
Waldorf, MD 20601
(301) 372–1932

## ◆ MICHIGAN

### FIRST PEOPLES POW WOW (May/June)
26641 Lawrence
Center Line, MI 48015
(810) 756–1350

### NEW YEARS EVE POW WOW (January)
### SAULT TRIBES POW WOW (4th of July weekend)
Sault Ste. Marie Tribe of Chippewa
531 Ashmun St.
Sault Ste. Marie, MI 49783
(906) 635–6050

## ◆ MINNESOTA

### MEMORIAL DAY POW WOW (May)
Minnesota Chippewa Tribal Office
Rte. 3, Box 100
Cass Lake, MN 56633
(218) 335–8289

### VETERANS POW WOW (Second weekend in July)
### MISHKAWSIN POW WOW (First weekend of August)
Little Black Bear Elementary School
Atten: John Henry MacMillian
Pow Wow Committee
105 University Rd.
Cloquet, MN 55720
(218) 878–7551

## ◆ MISSISSIPPI

CHOCTAW INDIAN FAIR (July)
Choctaw Tribal Office Public Information
　Department
P.O. Box 6010
Philadelphia, MS 39350
(601) 656–1537

## ◆ MONTANA

CROW INDIAN FAIR (August)
Crow Tribal Council
P.O. Box 159
Crow Agency, MT 59022
(406) 638–2601

NORTH AMERICAN INDIAN DAYS
　CELEBRATION (July)
P.O. Box 850
Browning, MT 59417
(406) 338–7521

NORTHERN CHEYENNE POW WOW (July)
Northern Cheyenne Tribal Council
P.O. Box 128
Lame Deer, MT 59043
(406) 477–6210

ROCKY BOY POW WOW (August)
Chippewa Cree Tribe
Rocky Boys Agency
Rocky Boy Route, Box 544
Havre, MT 59501
(406) 395–4478/4207

## ◆ NEBRASKA

OMAHA TRIBAL POW WOW (August)
Omaha Reservation
P.O. Box 368
Macy, NE 68039
(402) 837–5391

WINNEBAGO POW WOW (July last full
　weekend)
Attn: Pow Wow Committee
687 Winnebago Tribal Council
Winnebago, NE 68071
(402) 878–2272

## ◆ NEVADA

SHOSHONI-PAIUTE ANNUAL POW WOW
　(4th of July)
VETERAN'S DAY POW WOW (November
　Veteran's Day)
Shoshoni-Paiute Tribal Council (tribal secretary)
P.O. Box 219
Owyhee, NV 89832–0219
(775) 757–3161

SNOW MOUNTAIN POW WOW (May)
Las Vegas Paiute Tribe
Pow Wow Committee
1 Paiute Dr.
Las Vegas, NV 89106
(702) 386–3926

## ◆ NEW MEXICO

ANNUAL TRADITIONAL CHRISTMAS DANCES
　(December)
SANTO DOMINGO PUEBLO FEAST DAY (August 4)
Santo Domingo Pueblo Community Centre
P.O. Box 99
Santo Domingo Pueblo, NM 87052
(505) 465–2214

GALLUP INTERTRIBAL CEREMONIAL
　(August)
Red Rock State Park, Gallup
Intertribal Ceremonial
226 West Coal
Gallup, NM 87301
(505) 863–3896

GATHERING OF NATIONS POW WOW (April)
P.O. Box 75102
Albuquerque, NM 87194
(505) 836–2810

INSTITUTE OF AMERICAN INDIAN ARTS
　STUDENT POW WOW (April)
ALL NA A EVENT GRADUATION CLASS (May)
HIGH SCHOOL COMPETITION (October)
Institute of American Indian Arts
Pow Wow Club
83 Avannopo
Santa Fe, NM 87504

LITTLE BEAVER ROUNDUP (3rd
   weekend July)
Jicarilla Apache Tribe Public Relations Office
Attn: Little Beaver Committee
P.O. Box 507
Dulce, NM 87528
(505) 759–3242 ext. 277

#### ◆ NEW YORK

IROQUOIS INDIAN FESTIVAL (September)
Schoharie Museum of the Iroquois
P.O. Box 7, Caverns Rd.
Howes Cave, NY 12092
(518) 296–8949

SENECA NATION INDIAN FALL FESTIVAL
   (September)
Saylor Complex,
Cattaraugus Reservation
1490 Rte. 438
Irving, NY 14081
(716) 532–4900

SHINNECOCK INDIAN POW WOW (Labor Day
   weekend, September)
Shinnecock Pow Wow Committee
Shinnecock Indian Reservation
P.O. Box 5006
Rte. 25 Old Montauk Hwy.
Southampton, NY 11969
(631) 283–6143

#### ◆ NORTH CAROLINA

CHEROKEE POW WOW (July 4th weekend)
Eastern Band of Cherokee Indians
Ceremonial Grounds
P.O. Box 455
Cherokee, NC 28719
(828) 497–7000

HALIWA-SAPONI POW WOW (third weekend
   in April)
Haliwa-Saponi Tribal Office
P.O. Box 99
Hollister, NC 27844
(252) 586–4017

#### ◆ NORTH DAKOTA

INDIAN ART EXPO AND MARKET
UNITED TRIBES INTERNATIONAL
   CHAMPIONSHIP POW WOW
(Begins the first Thursday after Labor Day in
   September)
United Tribes Technical College
Pow Wow Committee
3315 University Dr.
Bismarck, ND 58504
(701) 255–3285, ext. 346

MANDAREE CELEBRATION AND POW
   WOW (July)
Three Affiliated Tribes
Fort Berthold Reservation
P.O. Box 220
Mandaree, ND 58757
(701) 627–4781

STANDING ROCK POW WOW (first
   weekend August)
Standing Rock Sioux Tribe
Fort Yates Local District
Cave Fort Yates Pow Wow Committee
P.O. Box D
Fort Yates, ND 58538
(701) 854–7201

#### ◆ OHIO

INDIAN MOUND FESTIVAL (first weekend
   October)
The Lions Club
P.O. Box 2
The Plains, OH 45780
(740) 593–1689

MIAMI VALLEY COUNCIL FOR NATIVE
   AMERICANS POW WOW (June/March)
Miami Valley Council For Native Americans
P.O. Box 637
Dayton, OH 45401–0637
(937) 275–8599

#### ◆ OKLAHOMA

ANNUAL PONCA POW WOW (August)
Ponca Tribe of Oklahoma
Atten: Kinsel Lead
20 White Eagle Rd
Ponca City, OK 74601
(580) 762–8104

CHEROKEE NATIONAL HOLIDAY (September)
Cherokee Nation of Oklahoma
P.O. Box 948
Tahlequah, OK 74465
(918) 456–0671

CHOCTAW NATION LABOR DAY FESTIVAL
(September)
Choctaw Nation of Oklahoma
Special Projects Committee
Drawer 1210
Durant, OK 74702
(580) 924–8280

PAWNEE INDIAN HOMECOMING (4th of July
weekend)
Pawnee Tribal Council
P.O. Box 675
Pawnee, OK 74058

RED EARTH NATIVE AMERICAN CULTURAL
FESTIVAL (second weekend in June)
Myriad Convention Center
2100 Northeast 52nd
Oklahoma City, OK 73111
(580) 427–5228

#### ◆ OREGON

CHRISTMAS WINTER HOLIDAY POW WOW
(December)
NA CULTURAL AWARENESS WEEK (includes
Salmon-bake and Pow Wow, May)
United Indian Students in Higher Education
Native Studies Department
P.O.751
Portland State University
Portland, OR 97207
(503) 725–5671

PI-UM-SHA POW WOW AND TREATY
DAYS (June)
Confederated Tribes Of Warm Springs
Public Relations Department
P.O. Box C
Warm Springs, OR 97761
(541) 553–1161

#### ◆ PENNSYLVANIA

COUNCIL OF THREE RIVERS AMERICAN
INDIAN CENTRE
CARIGIE MUSEUM INDIAN POW WOW (May 3rd
weekends in)
COUNCIL OF THREE RIVERS Annual POW WOW
(September)
Council Of Three Rivers American Indian Centre
Pow wow committee Tomi Simms
120 Charles St.
Dorseyville, PA 15238–1027
(412) 782–4457

MOUNTAIN SPRINGS POW WOW AND
FESTIVAL (Second weekend in August )
Mountain Springs Camping Resort
P.O. Box 365
3450 Mountain Rd.
Shartlesville, PA 19554
(610) 488–6859

#### ◆ RHODE ISLAND

ANNUAL NARRAGANSETT COMPLETION
POWWOW & HEALTH FAIR (second
weekend in July)
NARRAGANSETT TRADITION GATHERING POW
WOW (Second Sunday August)
NARRAGANSETT GREAT SWAMP PILGRIMAGE
(last weekend in September)
NARRAGANSETT INDIAN FALL FESTIVAL (1st
Sunday in October)
Narragansett Tribal Council
Narragansett Pow wow Committee
Charlestown, RI 02813
(401) 364–1100

TRUDAU MEMORIAL CENTRE ANNUAL POW
WOW FOR CHARITY
Trudau Memorial Centre
3445 Post Rd.
Warwick, RI 02886
(401) 739–2992

#### ◆ SOUTH DAKOTA

ANNUAL ANTELOPE FAIR & WACIPI
Pow wow Grounds
US Highway 18
Mission, SD 57570

ANNUAL CORN CREEK TRADITIONAL
   WACIPI
Corn Creek Community
Highway 63, 6 miles North of Norris
Norris, SD 57560

BLACK HILLS POW WOW AND ARTS
   EXP.O.(July-October)
Black Hills Pow Wow Committee
P.O. Box 8131
Rapid City, SD 57709
(605) 341–0925

CHEYENNE RIVER SIOUX FAIR AND RODEO
(CHERRY CREEK POW WOW; September)
Cheyenne River Sioux Tribe
Pow Wow Committee
P.O. Box 590
Eagle Butte, SD 57625
(605) 964–6685

FOUNDER'S DAY CONTEST POW WOW (First
   weekend Of February)
Sinte Gleska University
Special Activities Coordinator
Heather Bernadette
P.O. Box 490
Rosebud, SD 57570
(605) 747–2263

FOURTH OF JULY POW WOW (July)
Glacial Lakes Association
P.O. Box 1113
Watertown, SD 57201
(605) 886–5814

HONORING ALL YOUTH POW WOW
Bishop Hare Complex Arbor
Mission, SD 57570
(605) 856–4982

OGLALA NATION POW WOW AND RODEO
   (August)
Pine Ridge Reservation
Pow Wow Committee
P.O. Box H
Pine Ridge, SD 57770
(605) 867–6074

VETERAN'S DAY POW WOWS (Several are
   scheduled for Veteran's Day weekend in
   the area)
NEW YEAR'S EVE TRADITIONAL POW WOW
ANNUAL ROSEBUD SIOUX FAIR AND ALL INDIAN
   RODEO (August)
Rosebud Tribal Office of Tourism
P.O. Box 1192
Mission, SD 57555
(605) 856–2538

◆ **TENNESSEE**

FALL FESTIVAL AND POW WOW (October)
Native American Indian Association of Tennessee
211 Union St., Suite 932
Nashville, TN 37271
(615) 726–0806

◆ **TEXAS**

AMERICAN INDIAN VETERAN'S OF NORTH
   TEXAS SOCIETY POW WOW (Monthly)
American Indian Veteran's Of North Texas Society
P.O. Box 4387
Azle, TX 75208
(214) 333–3908

NATIONAL CHAMPIONSHIP POW WOW
   (September)
Traders Village
2602 Mayfield Rd.
Grand Prairie, TX 75051
(972) 647–2331

TIGUA SAINT ANTHONY'S DAY
   CEREMONY (June)
Ysleta Del Sur Pueblo
Tigua Indian Reservation
119 S. Old Pueblo Rd
El Paso, TX 79917
(915) 856–8888

◆ **UTAH**

NORTHERN UTE POW WOW AND
   RODEO (July)
UTE TRIBAL BEAR DANCE (April)
Uintah and Ouray Tribal Council
P.O. Box 190
Fort Duchesne, UT 84026
(435) 722–5141

## ◆ WASHINGTON

CHIEF SEATTLE DAYS (August)
Suquamish Tribe
Port Madison Reservation
P.O. Box 498
Suquamish, WA 98392
(360) 598–3311

GAULT POW WOW (November 4, January 2,
    February 6, March 3)
Gault Middle School
Tucoma School District Rm. 318
Indian Education Program
601 S. 8th St.
Tacoma, WA 98405
(253) 571–1138

LUMMI STOMISH WATER FESTIVAL (June)
Near Gooseberry Point
Lummi Indian Business Council
2616 Kwina Rd.
Bellingham, WA 98226–9298
(360) 758–2101

MAKAH INDIAN DAYS (August)
Makah Tribal Council
P.O. Box 115
Neah Bay, WA 98357
(360) 645–2201

NATIONAL INDIAN DAY CELEBRATION &
    POW WOW(September, third weekend)
YAKAMA NATION TREATY DAY
    COMMEMORATION OF 1855 (June)
Yakama Nation Tourism Office
P.O. Box 151
Toppenish, WA 94948
(509) 865–5121

NORTHWEST INDIAN YOUTH CONFERENCE
    POW WOW (Spring)
NorthWest Planning Committee
102 Prefontaine Place S.
Seattle, WA 98104
(509) 634–2782

SEAFAIR INDIAN DAY POW WOW (July, third
    weekend)
Daybreak Star Cultural Arts Centre
P.O. Box 99100
Seattle, WA 98199
(206) 285–4425

SPOKANE FALLS NORTHWEST INDIAN
    ENCAMPMENT (August)
905 East Third Ave.
Spokane, WA 99202
(509) 535–0886

## ◆ WISCONSIN

HONOR THE EARTH TRADITIONAL POW
    WOW (July)
Attn.: Earth Traditional Commission
8575 N. Round Lake School Rd.
Hayward, WI 54843
(715) 634–8924

MENOMINEE NATION CONTEST POW WOW
    (August, first weekend)
Menominee Indian tribe of Wisconsin
P.O. Box 910
Keshena, WI 54135
(715) 799–3341

ONEIDA POW WOW (July 4th)
P.O. Box 365
Oneida, WI 54155–0365
(920) 869–2214

## ◆ WYOMING

CHEYENNE FRONTIER DAYS (July/August)
Frontier Park
P.O. Box 2477
Cheyenne, WY 82003
(800) 227–6336

ETHETE POW WOW AND RODEO (July)
Northern Arapaho Business Council
P.O. Box 396
Fort Washakie, WY 82514
(307) 332–6120

SHOSHONI INDIAN FAIR (August last weekend
    of August )
Shoshoni Tribal Business Council Office
P.O. Box 538
Fort Washakie, WY 82514
(307) 332–3532

# CANADA

## ◆ ALBERTA

CALGARY NATIVE FRIENDSHIP SOCIETY
POW WOW (May)
3333–34 Avenue NE
Calgary, AB T2E 2J8
(403) 777–2263

ERMINESKIN INDIAN DAYS (August)
P.O. Box 219
Hobbema, AB T0C 1N0
(780) 585–3741

## ◆ BRITISH COLUMBIA

FIRST PEOPLES CULTURAL FESTIVAL
(August)
1607 E Hastings St.
Vancouver, BC V5L 1S7
(604) 251–4844

KAMLOOPS POW WOW (August)
100–315 Yellowhead Hwy.
Kamloops, BC V2H 1H1
(250) 828–9700

MINI POWWOW (July, 2nd wknd)
St. Mary's Campus
33150A 1st Avenue, Lougheed Hwy.
Mission, BC V2V 1G4
(604) 826–1281

SEABIRD ISLAND FESTIVAL (May)
P.O. Box 650
Agassiz, BC V0M 1S2
(604) 796–2177

## ◆ MANITOBA

OPASQUIA INDIAN DAYS (August)
The Pas Indian Reserve
Box 1000
The Pas, MB R9A 1L1
(204) 627–7100

## ◆ ONTARIO

WIKWEMIKONG INDIAN POW WOW (August)
Unceded Indian Reserve
P.O. Box 112
Wikwemikong, ON P0P 2J0
(705) 859–3122

## ◆ SASKATCHEWAN

SAKIMAY ANNUAL POW WOW (June/July)
Sakimay Band Office
P.O. Box 339
Grenfell, SK S0G 2B0
(306) 697–2831
(888) 725–4629

# American Indian Art Markets and Fairs

## UNITED STATES

### ◆ ARIZONA

ARIZONA STATE FAIR (October)
P.O. Box 6728
Phoenix, AZ 85005
(602) 252–6771

FESTIVAL OF NATIVE AMERICAN ARTS
(June-August)
Coconino Center for the Arts
P.O. Box 296
Flagstaff, AZ 86002
(520) 779–2300

HEARD MUSEUM INDIAN MARKET (March)
Heard Museum
2301 N. Central Ave
Phoenix, AZ 85004
(602) 252–8848

HOPI AND NAVAJO SHOWS (July-August)
ZUNI EXHIBITION (September)
Museum of Northern Arizona
3101 N. Fort Valley Rd.
Flagstaff, AZ 86001
(520) 774–5211

O'ODHAM-TASH INDIAN DAYS (February)
P.O. Box 11165
Casa Grande, AZ 85236–1165
(520) 836–4723

PUEBLO GRANDE MUSEUM ART AND CRAFT
SHOW (December, second full weekend)
4619 East Washington St.
Phoenix, AZ 85034
(602) 495–0901

WHITE MOUNTAIN NATIVE AMERICAN
FESTIVAL AND INDIAN MARKET (July, last
weekend)
Pinetop Chamber of Commerce
P.O. Box 4220
Pinetop, AZ 85935
(520) 367–4290

### ◆ CALIFORNIA

AGUA CALIENTE CULTURAL MUSEUM
HERITAGE FIESTA (Spring)
Agua Caliente Tribal Council
960 East Tahquitz Canyon Way, No. 106
Palm Springs, CA 92262
(760) 778–1079

AMERICAN INDIAN FILM FESTIVAL
(November)
333 Valencia St.
San Francisco, CA 94103
(415) 554–0525

ANNUAL CALIFORNIA INDIAN MARKET (May
and September, first weekend)
San Juan Indian Council
Mission San Juan Bautista
San Juan Bautista, CA 95045
(831) 623–2379

CALIFORNIA INDIAN DAYS (September)
California Indian Manpower
4153 North Gate Blvd.
Sacramento, CA 95834
(916) 920–0285

### ◆ FLORIDA

MICCOSUKEE INDIAN FAIR (December-
January)
Miccosukee Cultural Center
P.O. Box 440021

Miami, FL 33144
(305) 223–8380

#### ◆ NEVADA

STEWART MUSEUM ARTS AND CRAFTS FAIR
AND POW-WOW (June, third weekend)
STEWART MUSEUM CHRISTMAS INDIAN ARTS
AND CRAFTS BOUTIQUE (November)
5366 Snyder Ave.
Carson City, NV 89701
(775) 882–6929

#### ◆ NEW MEXICO

CREATIVITY IS OUR TRADITION EXHIBITION
(On-going)
STUDENT SALES (December-January)
Institute of American Indian Arts
108 Cathedral Pl.
Santa Fe, NM 87501
(505) 983–8900

EIGHT NORTHERN PUEBLOS INDIAN ARTS
AND CRAFTS (July)
P.O. Box 969
San Juan Pueblo, NM 87566
(505) 852–4265

GALLUP CEREMONIAL (August)
Red Rock State Park at Gallup
Gallup, NM 87301
(505) 863–3896

INTERTRIBAL INDIAN CEREMONIAL (August)
Red Rock State Park at Gallup
P.O. Box 1
Church Rock, NM 87311
(505) 863–3896

NATIVE AMERICAN MUSIC FESTIVAL
(August)
P.O. Box 1265
Zuni, NM 87327
(505) 782–2217

NEW MEXICO STATE FAIR (September)
State Fairgrounds
P.O. Box 8546
Albuquerque, NM 87198
(505) 265–1791

SANTA FE INDIAN MARKET (August)
Southwest Association of Indian Affairs
P.O. Box 969
Santa Fe, NM 87504
(505) 983–5220

#### ◆ NORTH CAROLINA

KITUWAH AMERICAN INDIAN EXPOSITION
(September)
P.O. Box 2854
Ashville, NC 28802
(828) 254–0072

#### ◆ OKLAHOMA

AMERICAN INDIAN EXPOSITION (August)
P.O. Box 1583
Anadarko, OK 73005
(405) 247–2733

FOUR CHANGING EXHIBITS
THROUGHOUT THE YEAR
Southern Plains Indian Museum
P.O. Box 749
Anadarko, OK 73005
(405) 247–6221

#### ◆ PENNSYLVANIA

A TIME OF THANKSGIVING (October, second
Sunday)
CORN PLANTING CEREMONY ( May, first Saturday
and Sunday)
ROASTING EAR OF CORN FOOD FESTIVAL
(August, second Sunday)
Museum of Indian Culture
2825 Fish Hatchery Rd.
Allentown, PA 18103
(610) 797–2121

#### ◆ SOUTH DAKOTA

ARTISTS OF THE PLAINS ART SHOW AND
SALE (February)
Augustana College
Center for Western Studies
Box 727, Augustana College
Sioux FallS, SD 57197
(605) 274–4007

## ◆ TEXAS

### AMERICAN INDIAN ART FESTIVAL AND MARKET (October)

American Indian Arts Council, Inc.
725 Preston Forest Shopping Center, Suite B
Dallas, TX 75230
(214) 891–9640

## ◆ WASHINGTON

### INDIAN ART MARKET (October-April, second weekend)

Cultural Arts
P.O. Box 99100
Seattle, WA 98199
(206) 285–4425

### NATIVE AMERICAN ART FAIR (April)

Suquamish Museum
P.O. Box 498
Suquamish, WA 98392
(360) 394–5275

### SPEELYI MI INDIAN ART AND CRAFT FAIR (March)

Yakima Nation Cultural Center
P.O. Box 151
Toppenish, WA 98948
(509) 865–2800

## References

### Native Art in North America

Archuleta, Margaret and Rennard Strickland, eds. *Shared Visions: Native American Painters and Sculptors in the Twentieth Century*. Phoenix, Ariz.: Heard Museum, 1991.

Beam, Carl. *Carl Beam, The Columbus Project, Phase 1*. Peterborough, Ont.: Artspace and Art Gallery of Peterborough, 1989.

Berlo, Janet C. and Ruth B. Phillips. *Native North American Art*. Oxford and New York: Oxford University Press, 1998.

Blodgett, Jean. *Kenojuak*. Toronto: Firefly Books, 1985.

Blodgett, Jean, and Marie Bouchard. *Jessie Oonark: A Retrospective*. Winnipeg: Winnipeg Art Gallery, 1987.

Brody, J. J. *Indian Painters & White Patrons*. Albuquerque: University of New Mexico Press, 1971.

Brodzky, Anne Trueblood, Rose Danesewich, and Nick Johnson, eds. *Stones, Bones, and Skin: Ritual and Shamanic Art*. Toronto: Society for Art Publications, 1977.

Brose, David S., James A. Brown and David W. Penney. *Ancient Art of the American Woodlands*. New York: Abrams, 1985.

Cinader, Bernhard. *Contemporary Indian Art: The Trail from the Past to the Future*. Peterborough, Ont.: MacKenzie Gallery, Trent University, 1977.

Coe, Ralph. *Lost and Found Traditions: Native American Art 1965–1985*. Seattle: University of Washington Press; New York: American Federation of the Arts, 1986.

Conn, Richard. *Native American Art in the Denver Art Museum*. Seattle: Denver Art Museum, distributed by University of Washington Press, 1979.

Gordon, Allan M. "Confluences." In *Confluences of Tradition and Change: 24 American Indian Artists*, 4–7. Davis, Calif.: Richard L. Nelson Gallery, University of California, 1981.

Grant, Campbell. *Rock Art of the American Indian*. New York: Crowell, 1967.

———. *The Rock Paintings of the Chumash: A Study of a California Indian Culture*. Berkeley and Los Angeles: University of California Press, 1966.

Hall, Edwin S., Jr., Margaret B. Blackman, and Vincent Rickard. *Northwest Coast Indian Graphics: An Introduction to Silk Screen Prints*. Vancouver: Douglas and McIntyre, 1981.

Hill, Tom, and Karen Duffek. *Beyond History*. Vancouver: Vancouver Art Gallery, 1989.

Houle, Robert. "The Emergence of a New Aesthetic Tradition." In *New Work by a New Generation*, 2–5. Regina: Norman Mackenzie Art Gallery, 1982.

Houston, James. *Eskimo Prints*. Don Mills, Ont.: Longman Canada, 1971.

Jackson, Marion and David F. Pelly. *The Vital Vision: Drawings by Ruth Annaqtuusi Tulurialik*. Windsor, Ont.: Art Gallery of Windsor, 1986.

Jensen, Doreen and Polly Sargent. *Robes of Power: Totem Poles on Cloth*. Vancouver: University of British Columbia Press, 1986.

Lippard, Lucy R. *Mixed Blessings: New Art in a Multicultural America*. New York: Pantheon Books, 1990.

MacNair, Peter L., Alan L. Hoover, and Kevin Neary. *The Legacy: Traditions and Innovation in Northwest Coast Indian Art*. Vancouver: Douglas and McIntyre, 1984.

Mainprize, Garry. *Stardusters: New Works*. Thunder Bay, Ont.: Thunder Bay Art Gallery, 1986.

Martijn, Charles. "Canadian Eskimo Carving in Historical Perspective." In *Eskimo of the Canadian Arctic*, edited by Victor F. Valentine and Frank G. Vallee, 67–75. Toronto: McClelland and Stewart, 1968.

McLuhan, Elizabeth. *Altered Egos: The Multimedia Work of Carl Beam*. Thunder Bay, Ont.: Thunder Bay

National Exhibition Centre and Centre for Indian Art, 1984.

McLuhan, Elizabeth, and Tom Hill. *Norval Morrisseau and the Emergence of the Image Makers*. Toronto: Methuen, 1984.

McMaster, Gerald and Lee-Ann Martin, eds. *Indigena: Contemporary Native Perspectives*. Vancouver: Douglas and McIntyre, 1992.

Nemiroff, Diana, Robert Houle, and Charlotte Townsend-Gault. *Land, Spirit, Power: First Nations at the National Gallery of Canada*. Ottawa: National Gallery of Canada, 1992.

Pollock, Jack and Lister Sinclair. *The Art of Norval Morrisseau*. Toronto: Methuen, 1979.

Rushing, W. Jackson, III, ed. *Native American Art in the Twentieth Century*. London and New York: Routledge, 1999.

Ryan, Allan J. *The Trickster Shift: Humour and Irony in Contemporary Native Art*. Vancouver: University of British Columbia Press, 1999.

Shadbolt, Doris. *Bill Reid*. Rev. ed. Vancouver: Douglas and McIntyre 1998.

Swinton, George. *Eskimo Sculpture*. Rev. and updated. Toronto: McClelland and Stewart, 1992.

Vastokas, Joan M. "Bill Reid and the Native Renaissance." *Arts Canada* 32, no. 2 (1975): 12–21.

———. "Continuities in Eskimo Graphic Style." *Arts Canada* 28, no. 6 (1971/72): 69–83.

———. "Native Art as Art History: Meaning and Time from Unwritten Sources." *Journal of Canadian Studies* 21, no. 4 (1986/87): 7–36.

Wade, Edwin L., ed. *The Arts of the North American Indian: Native Traditions in Evolution*. New York: Hudson Hills Press, 1986.

Wade, Edwin L., and Rennard Strickland. *Magic Images: Contemporary Native American Art*. Tulsa: Philbrook Art Center; Norman: University of Oklahoma Press, 1981.

*Joan Vastokas*

## Traditional Ceremonies, Rituals, Festivals, Music, and Dance

Black Bear, Ben, Sr. and R. D. Theisz. *Songs and Dances of the Lakota*. Rosebud, S.D.: Sinte Gleska College, 1976.

Collaer, Paul. *Music of the Americas: An Illustrated Music Ethnology of the Eskimo and American Indian Peoples*. New York: Praeger, 1973.

Frisbie, Charlotte J., ed. *Southwestern Indian Ritual Drama*. Albuquerque: University of New Mexico Press, 1980.

Frisbie, Charlotte J., and David P. McAllester, eds. *Navajo Blessingway Singer: The Autobiography of Frank Mitchell, 1881–1967*. Tucson: University of Arizona Press, 1978.

Heth, Charlotte, ed. *Native American Dance: Ceremonies and Social Traditions*. Washington, D.C.: National Museum of the American Indian, Smithsonian Institution with Starwood Publishing, 1992.

Hudson, Charles. *The Southeastern Indians*. Knoxville: University of Tennessee Press, 1976.

Keeling, Richard. *Cry for Luck: Sacred Song and Speech Among the Yurok, Hupa, and Karok Indians of Northwestern California*. Berkeley and Los Angeles: University of California Press, 1993.

———. *North American Indian Music: A Guide to Published Sources and Selected Recordings*. New York: Garland Pub., 1997.

———., ed. *Women in North American Indian Music: Six Essays*. Bloomington, Ind.: Society for Ethnomusicology, 1989.

Kurath, Gertrude P. *Dance and Song Rituals of the Six Nations Reserve, Ontario*. Ottawa: Queen's Printer, 1968.

Kurath, Gertrude, and Antonio Garcia. *Music and Dance of the Tewa Pueblos*. Santa Fe: Museum of New Mexico, 1970.

Marr, Helen H. *Voices of the Ancestors: Music in the Life of the Northwest Coast Indians*. Greenwich, Conn.: Bruce Museum, 1986.

McAllester, David P. *Peyote Music*. Viking Fund Publications in Anthropology, no. 13. New York: Johnson Reprint Corp., 1964.

Nettl, Bruno. *Blackfoot Musical Thought: Comparative Perspectives*. Kent, Ohio: Kent State University Press, 1989.

Nettl, Bruno, Charlotte Heth, and Gertrude P. Kurath. "American Indians." In *The New Grove Dictionary of American Music*. Vol. 2, 460–479. London: Macmillan Press, 1986.

Ortiz, Alfonso. *The Tewa World: Space, Time, Being and Becoming in a Pueblo Society*. Chicago: University of Chicago Press, 1969.

Smyth, Willie, ed. *Songs of Indian Territory: Native American Music Traditions of Oklahoma*. Oklahoma City: Center of the American Indian, 1989.

Speck, Frank G., Leonard Broom, and Will W. Long. *Cherokee Dance and Drama*. Berkeley: University of California Press, 1951; Norman: University of Oklahoma Press, 1983.

Sweet, Jill D. *Dances of the Tewa Pueblo Indians: Expressions of New Life*. Santa Fe, N.Mex.: School of American Research, 1985.

Vennum, Thomas, Jr. *The Ojibwa Dance Drum: Its History and Construction*. Washington, D.C.: Smithsonian Institution Press, 1982.

*Charlotte Heth*

## Contemporary Sacred and Secular Forms of Traditional Ceremonies, Rituals and Festivals

Black Bear, Ben Sr., and R.D. Theisz. *Songs and Dances of the Lakota*. Aberdeen, South Dakota: North Plains Press, 1976.

Hatton, Orin. "In the Tradition: Grass Dance Musical Style and Female Pow-wow Singers." *Ethnomusicology* 30, no. 2 (1986): 197–219.

Heth, Charlotte, ed. *Native American Dance: Ceremonies and Social Traditions*. Washington, D.C.: Smithsonian, 1992.

Howard, James. "Pan-Indianism in Native American Music and Dance." *Ethnomusicology* 28, no. 1 (1983): 71–82.

Isaacs, Tony. "Oklahoma Singing." *American Indian Hobbyist* 5 no. 9 (1959):106–110.

Lassiter, Luke E. *The Power of Kiowa Song: A Collaborative Ethnography*. Tucson: University of Arizona Press, 1998.

Mishler, Craig. *The Crooked Stovepipe: Athapaskan Fiddle Music and Square Dancing in Northeast Alaska and Northwest Canada*. Chicago and Urbana: University of Illinois Press, 1993.

Powers, William. "The Art of Courtship Among the Oglala." *American Indian Art Magazine* 5, no.2 (1980): 40–47.

———. *War Dance: Plains Indian Musical Performance*. Tucson: University of Arizona Press, 1990.

Sakolsky, Ron. "Boyz from the Rez: An Interview with Robby Bee." In *Sounding Off!: Music as Subversion/Resistance/Revolution*, edited by Ron Sakolsky and Fred Wei-han Ho, 163–169. New York: Autonomedia, 1995.

Simonelli, Rich. "Native Flutist R. Carlos Nakai," In *Winds of Change* 7, no. 4 (1992): 16–26.

Smyth, Willie, ed. *The Songs of Indian Territory*. Oklahoma City: The Center for the American Indian, 1989.

Vander, Judith. *Shoshone Ghost Dance Religion: Poetry Songs and Great Basin Context*. Urbana: University of Illinois Press, 1997.

———. *Songprints: The Musical Experience of Five Shoshone Women*. Urbana: University of Illinois Press, 1988.

Vennum, Thomas, Jr. *Ojibway Music From Minnesota: A Century of Song for Voice and Drum*. St. Paul: Minnesota Historical Society, 1989.

Wapp, Edward, Jr. "The American Indian Courting Flute: Revitalization and Change." In *Sharing a Heritage*, edited by Charlotte Heth, 49–59. Los Angeles: University of California, Los Angeles American Indian Studies Center, 1984.

Whidden, Lynn. "'How Can You Dance To Beethoven?': Native People and Country Music." In *Canadian University Music Review* 5 (1984): 87–103.

Young Bear, Severt and R. D. Theisz. *Standing in the Light: A Lakota Way of Seeing*. Lincoln: University of Nebraska Press, 1994.

Young, Gloria Alese. "Powwow Power: Perspectives on Historic and Contemporary Intertribalism." Ph.D. diss., Department of Anthropology, Indiana University, 1981.

*Tara Browner*

## A Selected Discography

*American Indians Play Chicken Scratch*. Canyon C6120, 1974.

Boley, Raymond. *Crow Celebration: Ten Great Drums at Crow Fair*. Canyon 6089, 1971.

Boulton, Laura. *The Eskimos of Hudson Bay and Alaska*. Folkways FE 4444, 1954.

*Comanche Peyote Songs*. Indian House IH 2401–2402, 1969.

Halpern, Ida. *Indian Music of the Pacific Northwest Coast*. Folkways FE 4523, 1967.

Heth, Charlotte. *Oku Shareh: Turtle Dance Songs of San Juan Pueblo*. New World Records, NW 301, notes by Alfonso Ortiz,1979; re-issued on CD as 80301–2, 1992.

———. *Powwow Songs: Music of the Plains Indians*. New World Records NW 343, 1986; re-issued on CD as 80343–2, 1991.

———. *Songs and Dances of the Eastern Indians from Medicine Spring and Allegany*. New World Records, NW 337, 1985; re-issued on cassette as NW337–4.

———. *Songs of Earth, Water, Fire, and Sky: Music of the American Indian*. New World Records NW 246, 1976, re-issued on CD as 80246–2, 1991.

———. *Songs of Love, Luck, Animals, and Magic: Music of the Yurok and Tolowa Indians*. New World Records NW 297, 1977, re-issued on CD as 80297–2, 1992.

Isaacs, Tony. *Cloud Dance Songs of San Juan Pueblo*. Indian House IH 1102, 1972.

———. *Handgame of the Kiowa, Kiowa Apache and Comanche*. 2 vols. Indian House IH 2501–2502, 1969, 1974.

———. *Pueblo Songs of the Southwest*. Indian House IH 9502, 1970.

———. *Songs of the Muskogee Creek*. 2 vols. Indian House IH 3001, 3002, 1970.

———. *Songs of the Sioux: Ironwood Singers Live at Rosebud Fair*. Indian House IH 4321, 1980.

———. *Stomp Dance*. 4 vols. Indian House IH 3003, 3004, 3005, 3006; 1978, 1992.

Merriam, Alan P. and Barbara W. *Songs and Dances of the Flathead Indians*. Ethnic Folkways Library LP P445, 1953.

Mishler, Craig. *Music of the Alaskan Kutchin Indians.* Folkways FE 4070, 1974.

Nevaquaya, Doc Tate. *Comanche Flute Music.* Folkways Records FE 4328, 1979.

Rhodes, Willard. *Apache.* Library of Congress AFS L42, 1954, re-issued on cassette, 1989.

Riemer, Mary Frances. *Seneca Social Dance Music.* Folkways FE 4072, 1980.

*Sioux Favorites.* Canyon Records 6059, 1968?

Smyth, Willie, ed. *Songs of Indian Territory: Native American Music Traditions of Oklahoma.* Oklahoma City: Center of the American Indian, cassette, 1989.

*Songs from the Blood Reserve. Kai-Spai Singers.* Canyon Records 6133, 1975.

Spittal, William Guy. *Iroquois Social Dance Songs.* Iroqraft Q.C. 727, 728, 729, 1969.

Vennum, Thomas. *Honor the Earth Powwow: Songs of the Great Lakes Indians.* Rykodisc RCD 10199, 1991.

*Charlotte Heth*

## Native American Visual Arts

Archuleta, Margaret and Rennard Strickland. *Shared Visions: Native American Painters and Sculpture in the Twentieth Century.* Phoenix: Heard Museum, 1991.

Coe, Ralph T. *Lost and Found Traditions: Native American Art 1965–1985.* Seattle: University of Washington Press and New York: American Federation of Arts, 1986.

Furst, Peter T. and Jill L. Furst. *North American Indian Art.* New York: Rizzoli, 1982.

Harrison, Julia et al. *The Spirit Sings: Artistic Traditions of Canada's First Peoples,* Toronto: McClelland and Stewart and Calgary: Glenbow Museum, 1987.

Jonaitis, Aldona, ed. *Chiefly Feasts: The Enduring Kwakiutl Potlatch.* Seattle: University of Washington Press and New York: American Museum of Natural History, 1991.

Nabokov, Peter and Robert Easton. *Native American Architecture.* New York: Oxford University Press, 1989.

Wade, Edwin L., ed. *The Arts of the North American Indian: Native Traditions in Evolution.* New York: Hudson Hills Press and Tulsa: Philbrook Art Center, 1986.

Wade, Edwin L., and Rennard Strickland. *Magic Images: Contemporary Native American Art.* Tulsa: Philbrook Art Center; Norman: University of Oklahoma Press, 1981.

*Janet Berlo*

## Native American Arts and Visual Culture

Bad Heart Bull, Amos. *A Pictographic History of the Oglala Sioux.* Text by Helen H. Blish. Lincoln: University of Nebraska Press, 1967.

Barbeau, Marius. *Totem Poles of the Gitskan, Upper Skeena River, British Columbia.* National Museum of Canada Bulletin no. 61. Ottawa: F. A. Acland, 1929.

Berlo, Janet Catherine. *Plains Indian Drawings, 1865–1935: Pages From a Visual History.* New York: Harry N. Abrams in association with the American Federation of Arts and the Drawing Center, 1996.

Breeskin, Adelyn D., and Rudy H. Tuck. *Scholder/Indians.* Flagstaff, Ariz.: Northland Press, 1972.

Bunzel, Ruth L. *The Pueblo Potter: A Study of Creative Imagination in Primitive Art.* New York: Columbia University Press, 1929.

Coe, Ralph T. *Lost and Found Traditions: Native American Art 1965–1985.* Seattle: University of Washington Press; New York: American Federation of Arts, 1986.

Conn, Richard. *Native American Art in the Denver Art Museum.* Denver: Denver Art Museum; Seattle: distributed by the University of Washington Press, 1979.

Douglas, Frederic H. and Rene d'Harnoncourt. *Indian Art of the United States.* New York: Museum of Modern Art, 1941.

Feest, Christian F. *Native Arts of North America.* London: Thames and Hudson; New York: Oxford University Press, 1980.

Harrison, Julia, et al. *The Spirit Sings: Artistic Traditions of Canada's First Peoples,* Toronto: McClelland and Stewart; Calgary, Alta.: Glenbow Museum, 1987.

Horse Capture, George P. *Powwow.* Cody, Wyo.: Buffalo Bill Historical Center, 1989.

Jacka, Jerry D., Lois E. Jacka, and Clara Lee Tanner. *Beyond Tradition: Contemporary Indian Art and Its Evolution.* Flagstaff, Ariz.: Northland Pub., 1988.

Penney, David W. *Art of the American Indian Frontier: The Chandler-Pohrt Collection.* Detroit: Detroit Institute of Arts; Seattle: University of Washington Press, 1992.

———. *Native American Art Masterpieces.* New York: Hugh Lauter Levin Associates, Inc., 1996.

Penney, David W., and George C. Longfish. *Native American Art.* New York: Hugh Lauter Levin Associates, Inc., 1994.

Phillips, Ruth B. "Glimpses of Eden: Iconographic Themes in Huron Pictorial Art." *European Review of Native American Studies* 5, no. 2 (1991): 19–28.

Seymour, Tryntje V. N. *When the Rainbow Touches Down.* Phoenix, Ariz.: Heard Museum: dist. by University of Washington Press, 1988.

Wade, Edwin L., ed. *The Arts of the North American Indian: Native Traditions in Evolution.* New York: Hudson Hills Press; Tulsa: Philbrook Art Center, 1986.

Wyckoff, Lydia J. *Visions and Voices : Native American Painting From the Philbrook Museum of Art.* Tulsa: Philbrook Museum of Art; Albuquerque, N.Mex.: Distributed by the University of New Mexico Press, 1996.

*David Penney*

# Literature

## ◆ LITERATURE

Out of their long tenure on the North American continent, American Indians have developed rich and varied literatures, reflecting the diversity of hundreds of indigenous American cultural traditions and languages. With the arrival of Europeans came many new languages and cultures to which Native peoples have been forced to adapt. Thus, what we refer to as "American Indian literature" reflects a wide range of linguistic and cultural experiences.

Major themes in American Indian literature include the place-centered tribal worldview, reverence for the power of the word, kinship ties (to living and dead relatives, to supernatural beings, to celestial bodies, to animals and other spirits in nature), and belief in the importance of renewal of the world through rituals associated with seasonal cycles. Contact with Europeans has led to changes in traditional themes related to warfare and cultural continuance, particularly since the nineteenth century. American Indian resistance has been evident not only in writings in English, French, and Spanish, but also in oral literatures. Such traditions form the basis for writings from tribal cultures, even when the written content is not explicitly about traditional life.

Today, American Indian writers produce works in the English language that can be counted among the most innovative and engaging in contemporary fiction, poetry, drama, and the nonfiction essay. Meanwhile, oral traditions continue to enrich the lives of the people as they have for countless generations, especially as traditional religious ceremonies are being revitalized.

Whether writing from specific tribal traditions or from a pan-Indian point of view (a view that sees indigenous Americans' experiences as a shared experience), American Indian literary artists present unique and imaginative new perspectives on what it means to be an American Indian today and often attempt to recover a history that has been ignored, distorted, or dismissed. Diversity among American tribal cultures and their particular histories becomes all the more apparent as new Native writers emerge.

### Oral Literature

Oral literature exists always and everywhere in human communities. In contemporary American Indian settings and communities, storytelling plays an essential role in the revitalization and preservation of culture. To understand the place of oral literatures within the body of works referred to as American Indian literature, we must recognize that oral literature is a continual aspect of all peoples' lives and that the weaving together of oral literary expressions with writing reveals the unique features and values of many cultures across time.

Oral literature can be defined as that body of literary works, with relatively standard features, that a people have disseminated and preserved for many generations through oral performance. Myths, legends, ritual dramas, prayers, chants, songs, speeches, anecdotes, and even jokes and gossip may all be considered forms of oral literature. While the oral literature studied in classrooms may appear on the page to resemble poems or stories from European and American literary traditions, the reader should nonetheless keep in mind that specific languages, audiences, and settings figure significantly in the shape and content of oral literatures. For example, while a written American Indian myth may seem sparse in its language and focused primarily on plot development, even perhaps resembling a Greek myth, that same story, when told by a Native speaker to a Native (tribal) audience, comes to life through their shared history; that is, the shared knowledge of the characters, tribal customs, and geographical region, as well as family and personal histories. The body language of the storyteller also adds enlivening dimensions to a story that writing cannot capture. The pieces that find their way into print, however, are generally representative of crafted oral works that have enjoyed a long life among a people.

The Gabrieleno petroglyphs were found in San Gabriel Canyon in Southern California. Early American Indians often recorded histories and stories on rocks and cliffs at sacred sites. (Courtesy of the Los Angeles Public Library)

Creation myths form the cornerstone of American Indian cultures' worldview—perhaps of every culture's worldview. A simple definition of myth is "sacred story," and even though the content of myth is fantastic—that is, beyond the realm of fact as we know it—people who hold their myths sacred see a deep, holistic truth in them. Readers outside the cultures being studied see through the windows of myths, as it were, into the culture, glimpsing the life of a people, but by no means seeing it all. On the North American continent, there are at least three common types of creation myths (with variations among different groups). The first is the Earth-Diver Myth, in which the world is covered by water, as after a great flood, often referred to as a deluge. In nearly every form of this myth, a woman falls from the sky, and, in order to create a place for her to land, an animal dives down below the surface of the water. Usually the fourth animal to do so succeeds in retrieving mud or earth to begin the habitable world, after three companions before him fail. The second type is the Emergence Myth, in which humans, animals, and plants who live in a cave below the world as we

know it, emerge by climbing a reed, tree, or root into the sun. The third type is the Two Creators myth, in which two godlike beings (sometimes brothers, sisters, or other relatives) create the world in their efforts to compete with one another. Because creation myths occur as an integral part of a set of stories, which folklorists call "cycles," they are best understood in relation to other stories of that culture. Myths are always geographically situated; they help explain a people's history on a particular landscape, and they illustrate the intricately balanced relationship between the natural environment and its human inhabitants.

Other forms of oral literature related to storytelling include legends, trickster tales, and specialized types of stories (such as coup stories). Most tribes have their own literary terms for their various types of literature. Legends, as opposed to myths, arise from events within historical memory. Over time the story of the event takes on symbolic significance and may be exaggerated in dimensions related to time, place, or factual detail. For example, legendary American folk hero Daniel Boone supposedly could kill a bear with his bare hands.

Among Blackfoot people, Calf Shirt was nearly impossible to kill and was himself the reincarnation of Low Horn, another important figure in Blackfoot history who performed many brave deeds in war.

A common Native American mythic figure, Trickster, often referred to as the trickster/transformer, takes the shape of Coyote in the Southwest, Ikhtomi (Spider) in the High Plains, Hare in the Great Lakes and the Southeast, Raven in the Northwest, and Blue Jay or Wolverine in Canada. Depending on the tribal tradition, stories about such characters may be used to teach proper behavior to children, to instruct and inspire adults, to entertain through humor, to offer a culture hero who saves the people or otherwise makes the world better by his brave (or even unintentional) acts, or to tell of how the universe came to be as we know it. When Plains warriors would tell of their brave deeds in battle through their coup stories, they too played the part of culture heroes, but on a smaller scale than legendary or mythic figures. The other warriors who witnessed the event also had to be there to swear to the truth of the teller's version of what happened. Other types of specialized stories might include stories related to how a person acquired his or her name.

Another category of recorded oral literature arises from the practice of Native religions, the verbal parts of rituals performed for specific purposes, such as preparing for spring planting or fall harvesting. Early anthologies of American Indian lore, such as George Cronyn's *The Path on the Rainbow* (1918), were intended both to enlighten the public regarding the rich literary materials of Native cultures and to further the preservation of Native cultural materials. Toward the end of the nineteenth century and into the early twentieth century, there was much concern among ethnologists and others that American Indian cultures were dying out and that there would be no record of Native cultural practices if great efforts weren't made to record them. Before the 1960s, anthologies designed for a popular audience were frequently compiled from those ethnographic materials. Taken out of context, however, the pieces often raise more questions than they answer. In other words, the meanings a non-Native person may derive from reading them may be entirely different from what a Native from the particular culture that engendered the piece would find in them.

An important consideration in reading oral literatures relates to whether or not the particular American Indian tribe would prefer that such specific knowledge of their ceremonies remain only within their tribe. Back when much of the ethnographic material was first collected, individuals may have revealed sacred tribal information without realizing that it would be published, or may have had it stolen from them by people who claimed they would not publish it. Some tribal groups, nonetheless, believe it is proper to share some of their ceremonies and rituals with non-Native and other tribal audiences. The Iroquois, for instance, have published their Ritual of Condolence, a rite conducted after the death of a high chief to install a new chief to take his place in the council of forty-nine chiefs. The new chief embodies the spirit of the chief who has died, who in his time was believed to embody the spirit of the chief before him, all the way back to the original council chief. Perhaps they chose to publish the rite because it is a public ceremony.

Songs and chants accompany virtually all Native ceremonies. Some are generations old, but others are composed for the occasion, often continuing to be part of the ceremony in the future or simply remaining with the individual involved in the particular ceremony, as in the instance of naming or perhaps healing. Songs created for social occasions, often called "forty-nines," may be in English, a Native language, or both. Among Lakota people, a young man composed flute songs, usually with the help of a medicine man, to court a young woman whom he desired to marry. The young man would sit on a hill behind her tipi and play the song, which might contain words she had spoken. If she wanted nothing to do with him, she would ignore him and his song. If she was interested in him, she might go out with an older female relative to listen to the song. Some cultures regard flute playing to a beloved as a form of love medicine, casting a spell on the person for whom the song was composed. While composing songs and chants continues to be an important aspect of American tribal peoples, flute courting songs are part of a custom that has fallen into disuse, for obvious reasons.

Perhaps the most widely known form of American Indian oral literature is oratory, and a prominent orator was Chief Seattle, after whom the city in Washington State is named; he was known by his own people, the Suquamish, as Chief Sealth, and he lived between approximately 1786 and 1866. Chief Seattle's speech, frequently quoted for its environmental message that all people, plants, and animals are interrelated, has been the subject of much controversy. Questions persist about the reliability of the earliest existing draft of his speech (1887), written down twenty years after his death, and about details added later as the speech became popular through film and printed media. Rudolph Kaiser, in an article that appears in *Recovering the Word*, details the history of Chief Sealth's speech and the implications of such expropriations for Native peoples. Other famous American Indian speeches raise similar questions; however, there can be no doubt that

Stories and legends were often reenacted through dances. Here the American Indian Dance Theatre performs an Eagle Dance. (Courtesy of Hanay Geiogamah)

before earliest contact with Europeans, Native Americans prided themselves on their public speaking abilities, as they do today. In 1772, Samson Occom (Mohegan, 1723–1792) published his *Sermon Preached at the Execution of Moses Paul*, the first example of a literate American Indian (i.e., someone who could read and write English) who controlled the publication as well as the public presentation of his speech. The sermon, in some ways an indictment of non-Natives for supplying alcohol to American Indians, was popular in its day, going through multiple printings. Peter Nabokov's *Native American Testimony: A Chronicle of Indian-White Relations from Prophecy to the Present, 1492–1992* contains many other fine examples of American Indian oratory, as well as excerpts from autobiographies.

## Life Histories and Autobiographies

Early writers such as Samson Occom, William Apes (Pequot, b. 1798), David Cusick (Tuscarora, d. ca. 1840), George Copway (Ojibway, 1818–1869), Peter

Jones (Ojibway, 1802–1856), and others provided a body of work that contains both literature (oral and autobiographical) and literary and historical scholarship. While many early writings were not intended merely to tell a life history, the personal histories contained in those works legitimate and enliven the whole. Since the writings—the sermons, speeches, other types of oral literature, histories, and memoirs—of other Americans (John Smith, Cotton Mather, Henry David Thoreau, and Ralph Waldo Emerson) who are important to the founding of the United States are studied as literature, so too should early American Indian writers be regarded as contributing essential voices to the canon of American literature. Often the subjects they choose to focus on serve the dual purpose of preserving cultural and political histories specific to their tribal nations.

Similarly, Native American autobiography originates because of the need for an individual to set a record straight, as in the case of Sarah Winnemucca Hopkins (Paiute), or to preserve information "for those who come after," as in the case of Black Elk (Lakota). "For

Northwest Coast dancers embodied spiritual beings and reenacted creation histories and traditional stories. (Courtesy of Hanay Geiogamah)

those who come after" is an autobiographical phrase Arnold Krupat borrows for his study of American Indian autobiography, since it so aptly captures the spirit of American Indian autobiographers. American Indian autobiography is a unique literary form in that over 80 percent of what is usually referred to as American Indian and Alaska Native autobiography has been collected and edited by non-Native people, according to H. David Brumble. A lack of Native literary figures is one of the reasons why American Indians are less inclined than their non-Indian counterparts to write autobiographies, but there are other reasons as well. The way tribal people define themselves tends to be in relationship to their communities as a whole, rather than as individuals within nuclear family structures or as individuals opposing themselves to their own societies. That does not mean that American Indians have no stories about themselves to share with one another. Rather, historically they have not had the need to tell personal stories for broad dissemination to outsiders,

particularly in the form in which autobiography has evolved in the Western writing tradition. Tribal people, among whom each person—even in his or her private life—is quite well known by the group, would find it odd to hear the tale of a person's psychological struggles in the shaping of his or her personality. Hence, until quite recently, American Indian autobiography has been written mostly for non-Native audiences or for generations of tribal people to come.

*A Son of the Forest* (1829) by William Apes (also spelled Apess) is the earliest known autobiography in English by a Native person. Apes converted to Methodism after many sad years of abuse by his parents, grandparents, and foster parents, and writes about the abuses he and other American Indian peoples have suffered at the hands of Europeans as well as about his own faith in Christianity. Thus, his narrative compares to conversion narratives of the time, but differs in important ways. Another autobiographer, George Copway had already become well known as a lecturer before he published *Life, History, and Travels of Kah-ge-ga-gah-bowh* (1847), a popular book republished six times in its first year. Like Apes before him and Charles Eastman (Dakota, 1858–1939) after him, Copway explained that he believed Christianity offered hope to American Indians.

The first autobiography by an American Indian woman, *Life Among the Piutes*, also arose from its author's popularity as a lecturer. Sarah Winnemucca Hopkins (Paiute, ca. 1844–1891) was an advocate for her people, the Paiute, who were badly mistreated by their Indian agents and by neighboring U.S. settlers. She speaks out strongly and forthrightly both about the virtues of her people's ways and about the need for government reform to protect the Paiute and other tribes from exploitation and abuse. Her stories of her early years are engaging and endearing, and her dramatic stories of Native women's courage are inspiring. Throughout most of her life, Sarah Winnemucca acted as a liaison between her people and non-Native officials.

Charles Eastman wrote two autobiographies, *Indian Boyhood* (1902) and *From Deep Woods to Civilization* (1916), as well as many books on Dakota culture. In his autobiographies, he chronicles his years before contact with non-Indians at age fifteen through his eastern education and his many professional jobs—as a medical doctor on two reservations, as a Young Men's Christian Association (YMCA) and Boy Scout leader and organizer, as a public lecturer and writer, and as a government records clerk. His presence as the Pine Ridge Reservation physician at the time of the Wounded Knee Massacre (1890) makes his narrative particularly valuable as a historical record. Throughout his life he worked to further the causes of American

Indians, including over twenty years spent lobbying to reinstate his people's (the Santee Sioux's) treaty rights, which were taken from them after the Sioux Uprising of 1862.

Luther Standing Bear (Lakota, ca. 1868–1939) began writing, with the editorial help of E. A. Brininstool, after Standing Bear had spent time traveling with Buffalo Bill's Wild West Show, acting in movies, lecturing, and engaging in activities associated with American Indian political causes. He wrote three books with autobiographical content, the most famous of which is *Land of the Spotted Eagle* (1933). Standing Bear's children's book, *My Indian Boyhood* (1931) and Eastman's book with a similar name were both preceded by Francis LaFlesche's (Omaha, 1857–1932) account of his years in a Presbyterian boarding school, *The Middle Five* (1900). Although the boarding school experience often traumatized American Indian youth, in the most extreme cases to the point of suicide, the story told in *The Middle Five* is heartwarming as well as tragic. The experience of the young people there differs from that of other Native children elsewhere in two important ways: because the school was close to the Omaha camps, the children were able to see their loved ones more frequently; and the philosophy of the teachers seems less oppressive and punishing than that of educators of other Christian denominations. Several studies of the boarding school experience have been published in recent years, most notable among them are Tsinaina Lomowaima's *They Call it Prairie Light* and Brenda Child's *Boarding School Seasons: American Indian Families, 1900–1940.*

Within the special subcategory of American Indian autobiography, as-told-to narratives attract the largest mainstream reading audience. Whether these can rightly be called autobiography or should instead be referred to as life histories depends on the extent of the editorial assistance or intrusion. Whichever they are, they differ from biographies in that the person whose life is being presented participates substantially in their production. *Black Hawk, an Autobiography* (1833), the great war chief's popular story recorded and translated by Antoine Le Claire and edited by John B. Patterson, was the first as-told-to autobiography published. Black Hawk wanted his side of the story of the Black Hawk War (1832) to be known, since all the newspaper accounts ignored the injustices done to his Sauk people. Since then, a large number of as-told-to autobiographies, too numerous to name, have been published. Some of the best-known, with the recorder/editor identified in brackets, include: Blowsnake [Paul Radin], *Crashing Thunder* (Winnebago); Mountain Wolf Woman [Nancy O. Lurie], *Mountain Wolf Woman* (Winnebago); Don Talayesva [Leo Simmons], *Sun Chief* (Hopi); Maria

Chona [Ruth Underhill], *Papago Woman* & John Stands In Timber [Margot Liberty], *Cheyenne Memories* (1967); and Nicholas Black Elk [John Neihardt], *Black Elk Speaks*. Collaborators frequently add their own sense of narrative structure, particularly regarding the ordering of events, to conform to Western notions that an autobiography should begin with childhood events. Some editors/collaborators, however, regard the way the Native person orders his or her own narrative to be essential to the whole of the story. In Julie Cruikshank's introduction to her collaboration with three Alaska Native women, *Life Lived Like a Story* (1990), she claims that landscape and kinship do more than add background to the women's narratives, those things actually determine how those narratives are shaped.

In the tradition of nature writing, John Joseph Mathews (Osage, ca. 1894–1979) wrote *Talking to the Moon* (1945), a contemplation of nature, Osage history, and the struggles of humankind in general. Two decades later, N. Scott Momaday's *Way to Rainy Mountain* (1969) appeared; it also relies on nature as teacher and guide. His text contains drawings by his father, depicting aspects of Momaday's three-sided view of his journey to Rainy Mountain—the mythical, historical, and personal. Leslie Silko's *Storyteller* (1981) also combines several kinds of writing, and contained within her work are photographs, many of which are taken by her father, showing the southwestern landscape of her stories and of her family.

Two recent autobiographies represent a marked departure from previous forms: Gerald Vizenor's *Interior Landscapes* (1990) and Ray A. Young Bear's *Black Eagle Child: The Facepaint Narratives* (1992). Both are highly metaphorized versions of the authors' lives. *Remnants of the First Earth*, a second autobiographical text by Young Bear, depicts a surreal world full of poignantly drawn characters who all, in one way or another, struggle with who they are and who they want to become. Despite the appearance of innovative and imaginative autobiographies by literary American Indians, as-told-to narratives continue to be produced. *Lakota Woman*, by Mary Crow Dog with Richard Erdoes, is the story of a young woman who chronicles her participation in the AIM (American Indian Movement) activism of the 1970s, her life as the wife of a medicine man, and her growing awareness of her place as a mixed-blood in the Indian world.

## Fiction and Poetry

During the nineteenth century and early twentieth century, Indian writers of fiction and poetry were more rare than Indian collectors of their peoples' histories and oral literatures and autobiographers of all types.

Bernd C. Peyer's recent collection of early short stories by North American Indians, *The Singing Spirit* (1989), however, attests to the fact that Native American intellectuals, most of them born in the 1870s, were writing and publishing fiction; these authors include Gertrude Bonnin, Francis and Suzette LaFlesche, William Jones, Alexander Posey, Charles Eastman, Pauline Johnson, John Joseph Mathews, D'Arcy McNickle, and others.

The first American Indian novel, *Life and Adventures of Joaquin Murieta*, was written in 1854 by John Rollin Ridge (1827–1867), a Cherokee who had relocated to California after the removal of his tribe to Oklahoma in the 1830s and the murder of his father and brother because they favored removal. He became a newspaperman and eventually owned his own paper. The novel's hero, an outlaw with a heart, avenges the downtrodden and the wronged as he goes from one wild adventure to another.

Although not much in the way of long fiction appears until after the turn of the century, Alexander Posey (Creek, 1873–1907) wrote satirical pieces called collectively the *Fus Fixico Letters*. In the "letters," which appeared in local as well as regional newspapers, he creates conversations wherein local dialect characters make fun of politics, politicians, and the government. After his death, his widow published a collection of his poetry, one of the earliest by an American Indian poet.

With the rise of the novel form among American Indian writers comes the theme of mixed-blood ancestry and the dilemma of being caught between two worlds, by virtue of having parents who are from different cultures. In the 1920s, Mourning Dove (Christine Quintasket, Colville, 1888–1936) takes up that theme in her novel, *Cogewea, the Halfblood* (1927), the first published by an American Indian woman. It is about a young woman trying to decide between two suitors, one half-Indian and one non-Indian. In finally choosing the man with Indian heritage, she affirms her cultural values and sheds some of her girlish ways. Three other American Indian authors of the early decades of the twentieth century produced novels with mixed-blood or mixed-influence themes: John Milton Oskison (1874–1947), John Joseph Mathews, and D'Arcy McNickle (Cree/Salish, 1904–1977). Variations on that theme would continue well into the 1970s, but as a greater number of writers enter the scene, both subject matter and aesthetics expand.

In 1959, a new phase in American Indian writing was ushered in by the republication of *Black Elk Speaks*. Although an as-told-to autobiography, the text merits discussion under the fiction category both because it is an unusual collaboration and because it spurred a renaissance in Native writing. As John G. Neihardt's study of the life of Nick Black Elk, it is an expression of Neihardt's poetic and visionary aesthetic and, most importantly, a partial, though powerful, record of the Oglala (Sioux) medicine man's vision. As such, many have said that *Black Elk Speaks* ranks among the holy books of the world. Carl Jung, a famous psychologist, intrigued by what he saw as its thematic similarity to other religious autobiographies, figured in the revived interest in the book and its subsequent republication in 1959. It became what Vine Deloria Jr. terms a "veritable Indian Bible" to youth of the 1960s and 1970s. Despite its somewhat fatalistic tone, *Black Elk Speaks* has moved Indians and non-Indians alike beyond fixed or static ideas of American Indians as defeated and has shown the beauty and value in traditional Native religious ways.

In the early 1970s, American Indian writers began producing fiction and poetry as never before and in a manner that suggests the emergence of a writing community. The literary renaissance, spurred by works like *Black Elk Speaks* and *Bury My Heart at Wounded Knee* by Dee Brown (1972), found its first voice in N. Scott Momaday. His book *House Made of Dawn* (1968), winner of the 1969 Pulitzer Prize for literature, along with Vine Deloria's *Custer Died for Your Sins* (1969), coincided with the Indian occupation of Alcatraz Island in California, which caused a tremendous stir in the public imagination. The continued presence of Indians in America was beginning to be felt, and American Indian college students particularly began writing and publishing as never before.

James Welch (Blackfeet, b. 1940) took his place among the writers of that generation, when his first novel *Winter in the Blood* (1974) was reviewed on the front page of the *New York Times Book Review*, prompting the republication of his first book of poetry, *Riding the Earthboy 40* (1971, 1976). Themes of alienation and loss dominate both works, as well as his second novel, *The Death of Jim Loney* (1979).

Many writers took up those themes as well as others and chose poetry as the medium of expression. Duane Niatum (Clallam, b. 1938), with two books of poems already to his credit at the time, edited the much-celebrated *Carriers of the Dream Wheel*, a collection of poetry by American Indians, in 1975. Four years later Geary Hobson's *The Remembered Earth* (1979), a collection that takes its title from Momaday's *The Way to Rainy Mountain*, was published. Niatum's and Hobson's collections became popular classroom texts.

Leslie Silko's *Laguna Woman* (1974) and *Ceremony* (1977) affirm both cultural continuities and change, as do Simon Ortiz's early works: *Going for the Rain* (1976), *A Good Journey* (1977), and *Howbah Indians* (1978). Both authors come from the Southwest, and in their works they evoke the long history American

Indians have had with both Spanish and English colonizers in that part of the country. Along with the themes of alienation and loss comes the theme of healing, and Silko's *Ceremony* depicts the struggles of its mixed-blood protagonist, Tayo, in his attempts to find healing after World War II. Like Momaday's Abel in *House Made of Dawn* and Welch's nameless narrator in *Winter in the Blood*, Tayo must also come to terms with conflicts arising from the colonization of his people, the Laguna. Silko's novel *Almanac of the Dead* (1991) was published to great acclaim. Momaday and Welch have also continued their writings with *Ancient Child* (1989) and *The Indian Lawyer* (1990), respectively.

Louise Erdrich, an Ojibway (b. 1954) from North Dakota, achieved what many writers hope for: her first novel, *Love Medicine* (1984), became a best-seller. Set mostly on the Turtle Mountain Chippewa Reservation, the novel is a weaving of a number of first-person voices and perspectives as well as that of an omniscient narrator. Erdrich's other novels, *Beet Queen* (1986) and *Tracks* (1988), are also set in North Dakota, where she grew up. She claims that her fictional works are produced in collaboration with her recently deceased husband, Michael Dorris (Modoc, 1945–1997), author of the novel *A Yellow Raft in Blue Water* (1987) and *The Broken Cord* (1989), his personal story as an adoptive parent struggling to raise a fetal alcohol syndrome child. Erdrich also has two books of poetry to her credit.

Paula Gunn Allen (Laguna/Lakota/Lebanese, b. 1939) and Wendy Rose (Hopi/Miwok, b. 1948) both began writing poetry in the 1970s. Allen has gone on to write in many forms—as a literary critic (*The Sacred Hoop*, 1986), editor (*Studies in American Indian Literature*, 1983, and *Spider Woman's Granddaughters*, 1989), and novelist (*Woman Who Owned the Shadows*, 1983). Allen's voice in contemporary American Indian literature and literary studies is a unique and essential one, as suggested by the subtitle of *The Sacred Hoop: Recovering the Feminine in American Indian Traditions*— her work often focuses on the concerns of women. Autobiographical pieces by both Allen and Rose appear in *I Tell You Now* (1987), edited by Brian Swann and Arnold Krupat.

Among that generation of writers, Joy Harjo (Creek, b. 1951) and Ray A. Young Bear (Mesquakie, b. 1950) have distinguished themselves as important voices in mainstream American poetry, as well as American Indian poetry. It is important to make that distinction clear, because all too often the talent of Native writers is not recognized by audiences outside ethnic studies circles. Although Harjo's first book of poetry (*What Moon Drove Me to This* ) was not published until 1979, her presence on the writing scene was felt long before that. Women's themes, particularly related to suffering,

are central to her work, thus the moon figures as a symbol throughout this collection. Horses become a metaphor for human energy and struggle in *She Had Some Horses* (1983). Harjo's latest work, *In Mad Love and War* (1990), contains mostly prose poems (poems in paragraph form), and is perhaps her strongest work to date. Ray A. Young Bear's poetry reflects his bilingual language use and his belief in the importance of cultural sovereignty, Native control of cultural development, transformation, and preservation. *Winter of the Salamander* (1980) and *The Invisible Musician* reflect his Mesquakie heritage both in theme and symbolism and in the syntax of his aesthetic.

The phases of writing since the Native renaissance began have become an interweaving of past re-envisioning and recovering by remembering the past. This is the past left out of history books and American literature written by James Fenimore Cooper, who wrote the Leatherstocking Tales series that featured several Indian personalities, and Henry Wadsworth Longfellow, who wrote a long poem about the mythical Indian figure Hiawatha. James Welch's third novel, *Fools Crow* (1986) and Simon Ortiz's *From Sand Creek* (1981) engage a re-memory to recapture some of the more traumatic events in Indian history, such as in Ortiz's case the 1864 Sand Creek Massacre of Cheyenne Indians in Colorado. Linda Hogan (Choctaw, b. 1947), who began as a poet of the stature of Young Bear and Harjo, has also written short fiction and a novel of historical recovery, *Mean Spirit* (1990). Set among the Osage in Oklahoma in the 1920s, the novel depicts the traumatic and unjust circumstances of Osage people when oil was discovered on their land. In many details, the work is historically accurate.

Hogan, like Beth Brant (author of *Mohawk Trail* [1985], *Food and Spirits* [1991], and editor of *A Gathering of Spirit* [1984]), also treats the role of women in Native communities. Both present female characters and relationships between women in realistic and unique ways. With these works come a reassertion of the woman's place in Native communities, as well as an assertion of feminist ideals and issues, conjoined but not necessarily in harmony with mainstream feminist thought and goals.

Of all contemporary writers, none is more prolific or diversified than Gerald Vizenor (Ojibway, b. 1934), who has written at least twenty books. Formerly a journalist, Vizenor writes about a range of topics from tribal history to contemporary legal struggles and other issues, such as tribal gambling. His poetry reflects the time he has spent in Japan, since he often utilizes the Japanese haiku form. Vizenor is perhaps best known for his novels. In his more recent work, he continues themes started in his first novel, *Darkness in Saint*

*Louis Bearheart* (1978). The work develops a world in which contemporary tricksters attempt to find a tribal way to live in the postmodern, postindustrial world. Vizenor has also edited a collection of essays on American Indian literature, with contemporary, postmodern theoretical approaches.

New Native American writers emerge and new literary works surface every day. With each new wave of Native American literary creativity, a measure of cultural sovereignty is achieved for American indigenous peoples. New writers like Luci Tapahonso, Nia Francisco, Irvin Morris, and Rex Lee Jim, all Navajo, write bilingual or "code-switching" works, and incorporate Native song into their works. Playwrights like Hanay Geiogamah (Kiowa/Delaware, b. 1945) and William S. Yellow Robe Jr. (Nakota, b. 1957) produce plays that are gaining international recognition. Two American Indian women writers, Joy Harjo and Gloria Bird, turned their talents to editing with their text, *Reinventing the Enemy's Language: Contemporary Native Women's Writings of North America.*

Sherman Alexie (Spokane, b. 1966), a young writer who rose suddenly to national recognition less than a decade ago, has surely become one of the most celebrated American Indians of all time. With twelve books to his credit—poetry and fiction—Alexie promises to become one of the most prolific American Indian in history. In addition, his first collection of stories, *The Lone Ranger and Tonto Fistfight in Heaven,* was made into the widely acclaimed movie, *Smoke Signals,* for which Alexie wrote the screenplay. Like his predecessor, Thomas King, whose novel *Medicine River* became a made-for-television movie of the same name, Alexie turned his story more in the direction of comedy for the film version.

As a newly recognized field within American literature, Native American literature is destined to grow and to change the ways not only Native America, but also mainstream America sees itself. New themes develop with each new face on the scene, deepening and enriching the corpus of what we call Native American literature.

*Kathryn W. Shanley*
*University of Montana*

## References

Alexie, Sherman. *The Lone Ranger and Tonto Fistfight in Heaven.* New York: Atlantic Monthly Press, 1993.

Allen, Paula Gunn. *The Sacred Hoop: Recovering the Feminine in American Indian Traditions.* Boston: Beacon Press, 1986.

———. *The Woman Who Owned the Shadows.* San Francisco: Spinsters Ink, 1983.

———, ed. *Spider Woman's Granddaughters: Traditional Tales and Contemporary Writing by Native American Women.* Boston: Beacon Press, 1989.

———, ed. *Studies in American Indian Literature: Critical Essays and Course Designs.* New York: Modern Language Association of America, 1983.

Apes, William. *A Son of the Forest: The Experience of William Apes, a Native of the Forest: Comprising a Notice of the Pequod Tribe of Indians.* New York: Author, 1829.

Black Elk. *Black Elk Speaks: Being the Life Story of a Holy Man of the Oglala: As Told through John G. Neihardt.* New York: Pocket Books, 1972; Lincoln: University of Nebraska Press, 1979.

Black Hawk. *Black Hawk, an Autobiography.* 1834. Reprint, edited by Donald Jackson. Urbana: University of Illinois Press, 1955, 1964.

Brant, Beth. *Food & Spirits: Stories.* Ithaca, N.Y.: Firebrand Books, 1991.

———. *Mohawk Trail.* Ithaca, N.Y.: Firebrand Books, 1985.

———, ed. *A Gathering of Spirit: A Collection by North American Indian Women.* Ithaca, N.Y.: Firebrand Books, 1988.

Brumble, H. David. *American Indian Autobiography.* Berkeley and Los Angeles: University of California Press, 1988.

Child, Brenda J. *Boarding School Seasons: American Indian Families, 1900–1940.* Lincoln: University of Nebraska Press, 1988.

Copway, George. *The Life, History, and Travels of Kah-ge-ga-gah-bowh.* Albany: Printed by Weed and Parsons, 1847.

Cronyn, George W., ed. *The Path on the Rainbow: An Anthology of Songs and Chants from the Indians of North America.* 1918. Reprint, *American Indian Poetry: An Anthology of Songs and Chants.* New York: Fawcett Columbine, 1991.

Crow Dog, Mary and Richard Erdoes. *Lakota Woman.* New York: Grove Weidenfeld, 1990.

Cruikshank, Julie, et al. *Life Lived Like a Story: Stories of Three Yukon Native Elders.* Lincoln: University of Nebraska Press, 1990.

Day, A. Grove. *The Sky Clears: The Poetry of the American Indians.* 1951. Reprint, Lincoln: University of Nebraska Press, 1964.

Dorris, Michael. *The Broken Cord.* New York: Harper & Row, 1989.

———. *A Yellow Raft in Blue Water.* New York: H. Holt, 1987.

Eastman, Charles A. *From the Deep Woods to Civilization: Chapters in the Autobiography of an Indian.* 1916. Reprint. Lincoln: University of Nebraska Press, 1977.

———. 1902. Reprint. *Indian Boyhood*. New York: Dover, 1971.

Erdrich, Louise. *Beet Queen*. New York: Holt, 1986.

———. *Love Medicine*. New York: Holt, Rinehart, and Winston, 1984; Bantam, 1985; new and expanded version, New York: H. Holt, 1993; HarperPerennial, 1993.

———. *Tracks*. New York: Henry Holt, 1988.

Harjo, Joy, and Gloria Bird, eds. *Reinventing the Enemy's Language: Contemporary Native Women's Writings of North America*. New York: W. W. Norton & Company, 1997.

Hobson, Geary, ed. *The Remembered Earth: An Anthology of Contemporary Native American Literature*. Albuquerque: University of New Mexico Press, 1981.

Hogan, Linda. *Mean Spirit*. New York: Atheneum, 1990.

Hopkins, Sarah Winnemucca. *Life Among the Piutes: Their Wrongs and Claims*. Edited by Mrs. Horace Mann. 1883. Reprint. Bishop: Chalfant, 1969; Reno: University of Nevada Press, 1994.

Kaiser, Rudolph. "Chief Seattle's Speech(es): American Origins and European Reception." In *Recovering the Word: Essays on Native American Literature*, edited by Brian Swann and Arnold Krupat, 497–536. Berkeley and Los Angeles: University of California Press, 1987.

King, Thomas. *Medicine River*. Toronto: Penguin Books, 1989.

Lomawaima, K. Tsianina. *They Called it Prairie Light: The Story of Chilocco Indian School*. Lincoln: University of Nebraska Press, 1994.

Mathews, John J. *Talking to the Moon*. 1945. Reprint. Norman: University of Oklahoma Press, 1981.

McNickle, D'Arcy. *The Surrounded*. 1936. Reprint. Albuquerque: University of New Mexico Press, 1978.

Momaday, N. Scott. *The Ancient Child: A Novel*. New York: Doubleday, 1989.

———. *House Made of Dawn*. New York: Harper & Row, 1968.

———. *The Way to Rainy Mountain*. Albuquerque: University of New Mexico Press, 1969.

Mountain Wolf Woman. *Mountain Wolf Woman: Sister of Crashing Thunder, the Autobiography of a Winnebago Indian*, edited by Nancy O. Lurie. Ann Arbor: University of Michigan Press, 1961.

Mourning Dove. *Cogewea, the Half-Blood: A Depiction of the Great Montana Cattle Range*. 1927. Reprint. Lincoln: University of Nebraska Press, 1981.

Nabokov, Peter, ed. *Native American Testimony: A Chronicle of Indian-White Relations from Prophecy to the Present, 1492–2000*. Rev. ed. New York: Penguin, 1999.

Niatum, Duane, ed. *Carriers of the Dream Wheel: Contemporary Native American Poetry*. New York: Harper & Row, 1975.

Occom, Samson. *Sermon Preached at the Execution of Moses Paul: An Indian who was Executed at New Haven on the 2d of September 1772*. Bennington: William Watson, 1772.

Ortiz, Simon J. *From Sand Creek*. Reprint. 1984. Tucson: University of Arizona Press, 1999.

———. *Going for the Rain*. New York: Harper, 1976.

———. *A Good Journey*. Berkeley, Calif.: Turtle Island, 1977.

———. *The Howbah Indians*, Tucson: Blue Moon Press, 1978.

Peyer, Bernd, ed. *The Singing Spirit: Early Short Stories by North American Indians*. Tucson: University of Arizona Press, 1989.

Posey, Alexander. *The Poems of Alexander Lawrence Posey*, collected and arranged by Mrs. Minnie H. Posey. Topeka: Crane Printers, 1910.

Ridge, John R. *The Life and Adventures of Joaquin Murieta, the Celebrated California Bandit*. 1954. Reprint. Norman: University of Oklahoma Press, 1977.

Silko, Leslie M. *Almanac of the Dead*. New York: Simon & Schuster, 1991.

———. *Ceremony*. New York: Viking, 1977.

———. *Laguna Woman*. Greenfield Center, N.Y.: Greenfield Review Press, 1974.

———. *Storyteller*. New York: Seaver Books, 1981.

Standing Bear, Luther. 1933. Reprint. *Land of the Spotted Eagle*. Lincoln: University of Nebraska Press, 1978.

———. *My Indian Boyhood, by Luther Standing Bear, Who Was the Boy Ota K'te (Plenty Kill)*. 1931. Reprint. Lincoln: University of Nebraska Press, 1988.

Swann, Brian, and Arnold Krupat, eds. *I Tell You Now: Autobiographical Essays by Native American Writers*. Lincoln: University of Nebraska Press, 1987.

Talayesva, Don C. *Sun Chief: The Autobiography of a Hopi Indian*, edited by Leo W. Simmons. New Haven: Yale University Press, 1942.

Tapahonso, Luci. *A Breeze Swept Through*. Albuquerque, N.Mex.: West End Press, 1987.

Underhill, Ruth. *Papago Woman*. 1936. Reprint. New York: Holt, Rinehart and Winston, 1979.

Vizenor, Gerald. *Interior Landscapes: Autobiographical Myths and Metaphors*. Minneapolis: University of Minnesota Press, 1990.

———, ed. *Narrative Chance: Postmodern Discourse on Native American Literatures*. Albuquerque: University of New Mexico Press, 1989; Norman: University of Oklahoma Press, 1993.

Welch, James. *The Death of Jim Loney*. 1979.

———. *Fools Crow*. New York: Viking, 1986.

———. *Riding the Earthboy 40*. New York: World Pub. Co., 1971.

———. *Winter in the Blood*. New York: Harper & Row, 1974.

Young Bear, Ray A. *Black Eagle Child: The Facepaint Narratives*. Iowa City, Iowa: University of Iowa Press, 1992.

———. *The Invisible Musician*. Duluth, Minn.: Holy Cow! Press, 1990.

———. *Remnants of the First Earth*. New York: Grove Press, 1996.

———. *Winter of the Salamander: The Keeper of Importance*. San Francisco: Harper & Row, 1980.

*Kathryn W. Shanley*

# *Media*

◆ American Indian Tribes in the Media Age ◆ Natives in Film
◆ Recent Events in Native Theater ◆ The Status of Native Journalism in North America
◆ Native Radio ◆ U.S. and Canadian Native Press
◆ Native American Radio, Television, and Theater Organizations
◆ Native American Films and Video

## ◆ AMERICAN INDIAN TRIBES IN THE MEDIA AGE

Since the relatively short time span between the mid-1960s and the present, American Indian tribes have entered what Marshal McLuhan and other American cultural sages have called the Media Age. No single event or happening, as an expression of the period would have labeled it, occurred to mark this cultural process; Indian Americans have always moved slowly and cautiously toward change. The national culture itself was in the midst of a radical makeover, and ethnicity as a human and economic reality for millions of citizens was claiming a large share of the nation's attention via television, the printed press, radio, and films.

American Indians quickly became aware that the tumult and creative excitement generated by the civil rights movements were opening up opportunities in ways that could not even have been imagined in the late 1950s and early 1960s. Here was a challenge to advance an agenda of grievances, demands, and moralistic concerns that had solidified over centuries, when American Indians were at the bottom of the ethnic ladder in the American melting pot. But to effect true, meaningful change, new skills needed to be learned and adapted, old concepts and attitudes discarded, and organized, unified campaigns involving many tribes and tribal groups needed fielding. The images of the Indians—both in their own views and in the minds of non-Indians—would need revision, makeover, and retooling. The non-Indian public would no longer easily envision a party of braves sending smoke signals to convey a coded message from a perch on a far mesa to another on a distant horizon. The much-misrepresented system of sign language, which for centuries served as a *lingua*

*franca* for the millions of Native peoples in North America, would become a quaint relic of the past. Native peoples now communicated and expressed art through many contemporary media, such as satellite dishes, weekly and monthly newspapers, journals and magazines, radio, video cameras, Indian actors reading scripts written by Indian writers, and Indian writers writing poems, journalism, and plays and novels about Indian life.

For tribal peoples the primary means of communication from time immemorial was always oral and intensely focussed in a personal mode. Nevertheless, American Indians are engaging in a complex transformative process, which is developing everything from professional associations for journalists and writers, to an American Indian theater movement, as well as a filmmaking community and plans for a satellite television network to link tribal groups from the top of Alaska to kindred people and communities in all parts of the lower forty-eight states and Canada. Whether this fundamental change in communication modes and systems will prove a positive, beneficial advancement for Indian people and their traditional cultures and belief systems is a question that will not be answered completely any time in the near future. Already this revolution is redefining the identity and role of American Indian communicators and artists, and a productive track record from it has been solidly set in place and is growing. Some major milestones are presented here.

In the 1970s, a group of American Indian journalists in Washington, D.C., established the American Indian Press Association, which sought to establish a pan-tribally representative news bureau to gather and disseminate political, economic, and cultural information

Female members of the American Indian Dance Theatre company perform the Women's Fancy Shawl Dance. (Courtesy of Hanay Geiogamah)

to dozens of reservation and community newspapers and publications across Indian Country. The creative and entrepreneurial energy generated by the press association encouraged many tribal communities and groups to sponsor news publications for their constituents, many for the first time ever, and helped to firmly implant the concept and practice of freedom of information across Indian America. The press association's successor organization, the Native American Journalists' Association, in 1993 boasted a professional staff of eight American Indians at its Boulder, Colorado, offices and represents over 150 newspapers, magazines, and other publications, which serve an estimated readership of nearly one million.

Also in the 1970s, the American Indian Theatre Ensemble, later the Native American Theatre Ensemble, was founded in New York City. The ensemble was the first professional acting company of American Indian performing artists. This group provided impetus and encouragement for the subsequent development of more than a dozen Indian theaters across the United States: the Red Earth Performing Arts Company in

Seattle, Washington; the A-Tu-Mai Community Theater on the Southern Ute Indian Reservation in Colorado; the Navajoland Outdoor Theater in Window Rock, Arizona; Spiderwoman Theatre in New York; and the American Indian Theatre Company of Oklahoma, in Tulsa, among others. More than one hundred original plays, musicals, revues, and assorted theater works have been produced by these groups, and a new generation of trained, experienced actors, writers, directors, producers, and technicians has emerged from this movement.

In the early 1980s, in Lincoln, Nebraska, Indian filmmakers created the Native American Public Broadcasting Consortium (NAPBC) to support and encourage Native work in television, video, and motion pictures. The 1993 catalog of NAPBC lists over 250 entries of original works that its members and contributors have produced for tribal educational, cultural, and arts development programs around the country. NAPBC has also strongly supported American Indian television programming on numerous public television stations across the country and has addressed tribal economic and cultural concerns in all aspects of its agenda.

In 1983, the American Indian Registry for the Performing Arts was established in Los Angeles. The registry serves as an advocate for, and promoter of, American Indian actors, directors, producers, and technical personnel, who are entering mainstream professions in film and television. In the registry's nearly ten years of struggle and survival in Hollywood, it has played a major part in changing the long-stereotyped and abused image of the American Indian in numerous feature films and television series. In late 1992, American Indian creative talent was poised to write, produce, and direct the first movies and television productions about American Indians.

As an outgrowth of the work related to the Native American Public Broadcasting Consortium, in 1990, about seventy-five Native video artists, filmmakers, directors, writers, and producers founded the American Indian Producers Group, which actively pursues an agenda of self-sufficiency and determination within the media industry. The group proclaims its goal as:

> commitment to quality and culturally appropriate productions involving Native Americans. Our Native American vision, as film and television producers, is to empower ourselves to produce our stories. We will enable our future generations to continue this work from the culture of our people. We say our people deserve their inherent right to dignified and respectful presentation.

Indian communicators/artists in the past—storytellers, musical composers, poets, oral historians, and performing artists—lived significantly different lives from their counterparts in contemporary times. There was, in times past, very little "art for art's sake" in tribal societies. Just about everything had a specific purpose, and the communicators were not set apart from the rest of the tribe in any special sense, nor did they want to be. Their unquestioned place was with their people. It was from the people and from their practical needs that the communicators drew their inspiration.

Richard La Course, a Yakima tribal journalist-historian and founder of the American Indian Press Association in Washington, D.C., in the early 1970s, has been a defining presence in introducing the Media Age into Indian Country. He has chronicled the changes and challenges he has experienced. In 1972, La Course said:

> In more secure times than these, everything the Indian individual needed to know for self-definition and for tribal definition was made available with the luxury and times of years. For children,

winters were for stories. For all, summer was for dances, and feasts were held in the early fall. In the different tribal orders of time, the pace of growth and the pace of understanding was assured.

But in many tribal sectors today, these classic lines of Indian communications have suffered from intermittent and contradictory federal policies of suppression of the ceremonies, the enforced separation of parents and children, the continuing loss of the ability on the part of many to converse in their original tribal languages, and the overweening presence of the majority American culture and its alternate system of knowledge.

Much of the knowledge, the definition of Indian life borne in the life of one's own grandfather and grandmother, is vanishing with time and death. It is timely and mandatory to seek avenues not to replace those traditional modes of communication but rather to restore and enhance them toward a truly Indian future.

La Course's basic identification of artist and tribe still holds true today in some cases, but it is no longer so simple or easy for the communicators to fulfill their role in the vanguard of much that keeps the tribal spirits vibrant, strong, and constantly renewed. Ironically, at the dawn of the twenty-first century, it appears that now, more than ever, Indian people need the age-old elements of life that bind them together, unify their style into a living force, and give them strength and pride as a people.

In 1993, the nearly two million Americans who identified themselves as Native Americans and who were registered members of one of the 427 tribes were seeking ways to strengthen their tribal identities and sovereignty. They were searching for strategies to protect their land base and to develop tribal economies and business plans that will provide housing, education, and health programs. They were keenly aware of the fragilities of their natural resources and traditional and spiritual heritages.

As emerging nations with their variously complex agendas for development, the tribes find themselves long on ambition, creative energy, and determination, and short on resources, especially investment capital. Tribal members must be informed, educated, and culturally stimulated, and the world outside the tribal communities must be dealt with similarly. Many tribal leaders share a strong belief in the potential power of the media as an effective tool that, if used cautiously, can contribute significantly to finding answers and achieving goals. The avenues that La Course spoke of in

Morgan Tsosee, a member of the Comanche tribe of Oklahoma, is a champion Southern Men's Traditional dancer with the American Indian Dance Theatre. (Courtesy of Hanay Geiogamah)

1972 are now clearly visible in the myriad new technologies abundantly and even cheaply available, but incorporating them into a balanced, creative process that respects old traditions while making new ones is the far more difficult half of the challenge.

It is in the areas of film, video, and television that much of the creative ferment of the 1990s is centered, and a number of Native American and Alaska Native creative artists have entered these fields of work. A critical review of Indian-produced works in film and video suggests that immediate tribal and family concerns have been the primary focus of much of their output as they sought to explore means of preserving cultural traditions and values as well as problems arising from struggles to retain cultural integrity in the face of strong demands for acceptance of Western culture and general rejection of Native culture by non-Indians.

Artists such as Victor Masayesva (Hopi), Bob Hicks (Creek-Seminole), Phil Lucas (Choctaw), Chris Spotted Eagle (Houma), and Sandra Osawa (Makah) have produced films and documentaries that present positive, culturally sensitive images of American Indians and Alaska Natives. They have shown impressive skills in writing, producing, and distributing a wide variety of video works, documentaries, and short films produced primarily for Native Americans.

Phil Lucas, whose body of creative work has been primarily for television, sees the present explosion in technological advances as a crucial time of opportunity when Native people must take control of their image in the media by applying their creative gifts and energies. "We must be working to replace the outdated, stereotyped images of ourselves with truth, knowledge, understanding and appreciation for the differences in our respective cultures. And as we work for these goals, we must ply our trade in whatever manner and with whatever means we are able to draw unto ourselves."

Bob Hicks, whose award-winning short film *Return of the Country* (1982) is a satirical comedy about identity reversal, offers a pragmatic view of what strategies contemporary Indian communicators should follow:

We need to develop a strong, durable support base to provide funding, housing for production activities and advocacy to sustain us in our work. We need to get the tribes more involved, and we need to help the tribal leaders develop clearer understandings of the importance of this kind of work and what good it can do. If we want to create change, we have to empower ourselves to do so. The people, the tribes, will be our most important sources of strength.

Talent has always been abundant among Indian people, and it is certain that more talent will emerge in such projects as tribal theaters, music and dance workshops, creative writing projects, film programs, and cultural study groups. To nurture this new generation of communicators/artists, a complex support network must be established by all the tribes, which will assure the development of this vital resource. Public and private arts funding for American Indian communicators in terms of money per capita is far below what has been disbursed for non-Indian arts projects. It is imperative that the tribes find ways to allocate their own resources and funds to support their creative members. With tribal support of their communicators/artists will come an expansion of the professional expertise base. Actors, directors, designers, writers, technical personnel, administrators, managers, and producers are all in positions which, when employed, generate both income and tax revenues, as well as prestige for the tribe.

In recent years, American Indian tribes have grown more confident and more experienced in meeting the challenges of a new world. They have grown more sophisticated in their appreciation and respect for their creative, artistic members. As the national American Indian community as a whole grows steadily stronger, so does the need for artistic innovation and sources for new traditions. The new responsibilities that the Media Age bestows on Indian communicators are cogently described by Richard La Course:

Indian communicators, like their non-Indian counterparts, must be busy transcribing the first rough draft of the contemporary history of Indian people, and they must take this moment in Indian history with the utmost seriousness. From within the perspective of Indian concerns, they must have the willingness and the responsibility to hold up a mirror to their times, and to the occasionally troubled and murky matters of tribal times in flux. Indian communicators at this point in history,

must, as in the past, become the reflective, self-aware and trained eyes and ears of our Indian tribal societies. And they must participate in the strengthening of the tribe and the community through their commitment to handing on, and handing down, the tribal realities of the present and the past.

Indian people have endured in large part because of their extraordinary ability to acquire, to adapt, and to be innovative and creative when circumstances require them to be. As they proceed into the Media Age and learn to utilize its technologies for their varied needs and purposes, the American Indian cultural presence and heritage will likely grow stronger, richer, and more resilient.

*Hanay Geiogamah*
*University of California, Los Angeles*

## ◆ NATIVES IN FILM

Since the inception of the film industry over 100 years ago, Native people have been portrayed as stereotypes—stereotypes that affected how Native people see themselves and how others see who Natives are. This is changing as Native people make their own film and television, from documentary, to animation, to feature films. This section provides an overview of the history and effect of the media's portrayal of Native people, how Natives are changing that portrayal, and how Natives are changing the media.

Imagine a movie being filmed in the very beginnings of the twentieth century, when silent films were first made. It had been barely thirty years since the Battle of Little Big Horn in 1876 and only a handful of years since the signing of Treaty Eight in 1899, in Northern Alberta.

Early films portraying Native Americans included *Leather Stocking* (1908), directed by D. W. Griffith and based on stories by James Fenimore Cooper; and *The Battle of Elderbush Gulch* (1914), another film by D. W. Griffith, or *The Redman and the Child* (1908). Actors and extras were hired from a pool of unemployed people. Those who portrayed Indians were Italians, Russians, Irish, and other nationalities. Their faces were painted and their costumes made up in a costume department by a non-Native seamstress. While D. W. Griffith and Tom Ince would sometimes hire Indians as advisors and actors on their films, it is fair to say most

Members of the cast of the all–Native American dancers and musicians with the American Indian Dance Theatre. From left to right is Chester Mahooty, an elder of the Zuni tribe of New Mexico; Morgan Tsosee, a member of the Comanche tribe of Oklahoma; and Ramona Roach, a member of the Navajo tribe of New Mexico. (Courtesy of Hanay Geiogamah)

of these films were written and directed by people who had never met an Indian.

The story lines of these films varied from the standard stories of righteous settlers killing or being killed by the "Red Man," to a few more complex narratives. In *The Squaw Man* (1914), for example, the troubles of an Indian woman who marries a white man are depicted, and in *Red Eagle's Love Affair* (1910) and *Braveheart* (1925), Native people educated in a non-Native way face rejection from both their own people and non-Native society.

Often, the stories were drawn from the pulp fiction of their time, racy dime novels and serialized magazine articles. This pulp fiction reflected the prevailing attitudes toward Native Americans as a vanishing race,

subdued by the newcomers who now claimed the land as their own. Some stories lamented the passing of Native people; others told torrid tales of the "savage"; still others proposed solutions to the supposed Indian problem. Whatever the case, the stories were ficticious—made up by non-Indian people who objectified Native people to serve their own prejudices, ideologies, or versions of history.

On another front, documentary film left its mark on how Native people were perceived. In *Nanook of the North* (1922) Robert Flaherty showed the real Inuit people of the North, starring Allariallak, from Nunavut, in northern Canada. It was later revealed that the director set up many of the scenes in the film, as did Edward Curtis' *In the Land of War Canoe* (1914), which was meant to show the people of the Northwest Coast. Both drew on the reality of the people's lives but were filtered through the filmmakers' romantic notions of Native people as disappearing societies.

Whether classic films like *Stagecoach* (1939) or the somewhat more sympathetic film *Cheyenne Autumn* (1964), both by John Ford, Hollywood adhered to the belief in Manifest Destiny, the inevitable and almost God-ordained right of the newcomers to the land Native people had governed and protected since time immemorial.

A pervasive voice of Manifest Destiny was found in the B Westerns, serialized low-budget cowboy movies often shown during a double bill or a matinee. These films, such as *The Last of the Mohicans* (1932), or the first *The Lone Ranger* (1938)—with Thunder Cloud as the first Tonto—were quickly made and relied on simplistic good guy/bad guy plots. The Indians were usually the bad guys.

While these films were being pumped out, actors made careers out of fighting Indians, especially John Wayne, or being Indians, like Jeff Chandler in *Broken Arrow* or Anthony Quinn, Chuck Connors, or Charles Bronson. Some films were even meant to be funny, like *Paleface* with Bob Hope, or *Out West*, with the Three Stooges.

Still, Indian people tried to make a difference in Hollywood. In fact, Native people participated from the early days of American filmmaking. Notable among them was James Young Deer, a Winnebago director who married actress Winona Red Wing, also Winnebago. James Young Deer's films, such as *White Fawn's Devotion* (1910) and *Yacqui Girl* (1912), were as successful as other films of their day. Young Deer later became the head of Pathe Studios, a major studio in Los Angeles at

Plains Indians with roles in Hollywood movies take a break on a rollercoaster ride in Long Beach, California, 1930s. (Courtesy of the Los Angeles Public Library)

the time. However, after returning from making documentary films during World War I, Young Deer found himself relegated to making B Westerns.

Chief Nipo Strongheart, from the Yakima Nation, came to Hollywood at Cecil B. DeMille's invitation to collaborate on the script for *Braveheart* and stayed in Hollywood, serving as a technical advisor for many decades. Like many Native people of the time, Strongheart was fluent in eight Native languages and many dialects.

Another actor and opera singer from the Yakima Nation was Chief Yowtatchie, also known as Daniel Simmons. His screen career spanned four decades and

over fifty films, starting with *Warpaint* in 1926. Minnie Provost, also known as Minnie Ha Ha, was a larger-than-life character who played mother roles in such films as *Squaw Man* and *Paleface* (1921). John Big Tree, from the Onondaga Nation, worked with John Ford in such films as *The Iron Horse* (1924) and *Stagecoach*.

Wil Rogers, the humorist and actor from the Cherokee Nation, was sometimes cast to play white characters. He also directed and produced a number of low-budget films in his own series called *Ropin' Fool*.

Even later, actors such as Jay Silverheels, the second Tonto in the *Lone Ranger* series, tried to make a difference with his respectful portrayal of an otherwise stoic Indian stereotype. Still, despite the efforts of these and other actors and writers, Hollywood dominated the world of popular film with consequences for Native people. Chief Leonard George, the son of the late Chief Dan George, says there are three oppressors of Native people: "The church, the government, and Hollywood." Just as there were efforts to assimilate Native people through mission schools and government policies intended to erode Native economic, political, and cultural sovereignty, so did these films perpetuate the concept of assimilation and the end of Native culture.

People know films are not real but they want films to reflect what they believe about themselves. In other words, movies manufacture myths and reflect the myths of the audience. American and Canadian people are not comfortable facing the legacy of their history on this land, Turtle Island, for it is a history of cultural genocide. It is easier to imagine Native people as stereotypes, perpetuating the idea that Turtle Island belongs to the newcomers.

Urban Indian picketing the Warner Brothers movie studio during the making of *They Died With Their Boots On.* (Courtesy of the Los Angeles Public Library/Carole Cole)

Chief Leonard George and others are realistic about the role of film and media, however. Chief Leonard George, an actor in his own right (Lester Fallsapart, the traffic reporter, in the recent film *Smoke Signals*) is active in changing Hollywood's effect on Native people, working on a more cultural level and supporting the development of Native filmmaking. Other Native people feel the same way, from actors, to directors and writers. One of those people was Chief Dan George, who started acting in Canadian television in the 1960s. Born in 1899 in the Tsliel-Waututh Nation, Chief Dan George influenced how Native people are seen on screen, starting with his breakthrough role as Ol' Lodgeskins in *Little Big Man* (1970). Directed by Arthur Penn, *Little Big Man* was an epic retelling of American history told through the life of a white man, played by Dustin Hoffman, who was raised by his adopted grandfather, Ol' Lodgeskins—Chief Dan George.

Chief Dan George brought humor, humanity, and skilled acting to all his roles. He was the first American Indian nominated for an Academy Award and a Golden Globe as best supporting actor for *Little Big Man.* George would act in over eleven films, including *The Outlaw Josey Wales* (1976), and many television programs, such as *Marcus Welby, MD* and *Kung Fu.*

Wil Sampson is another significant actor. In *One Flew Over the Cuckoo's Nest* (1975), Sampson played Chief Bromden, the only character strong enough to withstand the oppression of a mental institution. Sampson brought strength and conviction to his other films, including *The Outlaw Josey Wales.*

Following George and Sampson were the talented actors Tantoo Cardinal, Graham Greene, Gary Farmer, August Schellenberg, Gordon Tootoosis, Floyd Westerman, and Wes Studi. Their work elevated the portrayal of Native people in cinema to a new level. Tantoo Cardinal, whose body of work since the 1970s includes *Smoke Signals* (1998), has performed alongside such stars as Margo Kidder and Brad Pitt. Gary Farmer was in two Jim Jarmusch films, notably *Dead Man* (1996) with Johnny Depp. Graham Greene is increasingly cast in roles not specifically related to Native life, such as Joe in *Die Hard: With a Vengeance* (1995). Greene was also nominated for a best supporting actor Academy Award for his role in *Dances with Wolves* (1990). August Schellenberg is known for his role in the three *Free Willy* features. Gordon Tootoosis, popular in the CBC series *North of Sixty*, played the Cree leader Big Bear in the *Big Bear* miniseries also on CBC. Floyd Red Crow Westerman, also a recording artist, acts in diverse productions, including the *X-Files*. Wes Studi was the title character in *Geronimo*

(1993), but he is often cast in nontraditional roles like the Sphinx in the unconventional comedy *Mystery Men* (1999).

Adding to the impressive work of those actors is a new generation of actors from Sheila Tousey to Michael Horse, and from Michael Greyeyes to Litefoot. Tousey starred in *Thunderheart* (1992), with Graham Greene and Val Kilmer, and has since starred in *Grand Avenue* (1996), the story of a contemporary Native California family written by Greg Sarris, and even *Ravenous* (1999), a vampire film. Also a dancer with the American Indian Dance Theatre, Tousey's acting also takes her to the stage, where she appeared in national productions of the work of notable playwright Sam Sheppard. Litefoot was the principal in *The Indian in the Cupboard* (1995). He uses acting and rap performance to encourage Native youth. Michael Greyeyes, in both *Crazy Horse* (1997) and *Searching for Little Bird* (2000), trained as a ballet dancer with the National Ballet of Canada, and Michael Horse, seen in the CBC series *North of Sixty*, is also a renowned artist.

Still, many roles available to Native actors since the 1970s were often historical and limited in complexity. While Indians were cast to play Indians, and while the films took a more enlightened view of Native American humanity, the writers and directors were non-Native. And though *Dances with Wolves* created a stir with respect to revisiting American history, its real focus was the role of the white man—played by Kevin Costner.

In the late 1990s, change was precipitated by an ambitious film called *Smoke Signals* (1998). Directed by Chris Eyre and based on a story by Sherman Alexie, who also co-produced and co-wrote the film, *Smoke Signals* is a commercial feature film aimed at a general audience. Starring Evan Adams, Irene Bedard, and Adam Beach, *Smoke Signals* shows young Native people as they struggle with family and growing up. Cody Lightening and Simon Baker III represented a younger generation of Native actors. Under the skilled directing of Eyre, Evan Adams stands out for his role as Thomas Builds-the-Fire. Adams won recognition as the most promising newcomer at the Independent Spirit Awards in Los Angeles for his role in *Smoke Signals*.

Greg Sarris undertook a similar groundbreaking production, adapting his book *Grand Avenue* (1996) to television. An HBO miniseries, *Grand Avenue* is the story of modern Pomo Indians in San Jose, California, revealing the reality of urban Native life. The families struggle with poverty, but will not give up who they are as a people. Another writer turned producer, Hanay Geiogamah, worked as a producer on a number

of Turner Broadcasting historic dramas, including *Crazy Horse*.

In the late 1990s, three other feature films were directed by Native directors, including Ian Skorodin's *Tushka* (1998), about the abuses of the FBI toward Native political action; Valerie Red Horse's *Naturally Native* (1998), about Native women making money; and Shirley Cheechoo's *Backroads* (1999), about a woman fighting back against white oppressors.

Native directing is not limited to feature film. In fact, Alanis Obomsawin and Gil Cardinal are accomplished directors with decades of experience. Obomsawin, an Abenaki storyteller, started as an adviser to the National Film Board of Canada (NFB) in the 1970s, and has since made numerous award-winning films for the NFB. Her earliest films, like *Mother of Many Children* (1977), brought her unique voice to the documentary form. *Kanehsatake—240 Years of Resistance* (1993), is her epic telling of the events in 1990 at Kanehsatake, when Mohawks protected their traditional burial site from

Writer, composer, and actor Garrett Saracho in the movie *How the West Was Won!* (Courtesy of Garrett Saracho)

becoming a golf course only to be surrounded by the full force of the Canadian army. *Kanehsatake* has won awards throughout the world.

Gil Cardinal started as a cameraman at a television station and went on to create powerful documentaries like *Foster Child* (1987), about his own search for his biological family. *Big Bear* (1999), the story of the Cree Chief who, with his people, resisted confinement to a reservation, was brought to Canadian television by Cardinal.

Bob Hicks' uncommon voice is seen in films like *Return of the Country* (1982), in which a Bureau of Caucasian Affairs is established which forces white kids to give up their culture. With the writer Gerald Vizenor, Hicks also made *Harold of Orange* (1984), starring comedian Charlie Hill as the trickster who reveals the depth of racism in American society.

Another longstanding director is Sandra Sunrising Osawa. Her documentary work spans twenty years, and ranges from *The Black Hills Are Not For Sale* (1980) to *Pepper's Powwow* (1996), about the jazz musician Joe Pepper.

Victor Masayesva Jr. deconstructs the western narrative traditions of documentary, ethnography, and fiction to assert his way of understanding and expressing narrative in work like *Ritual Clowns* (1989) and in *Imagining Indians* (1993), where he deals with the stereotypes of Native people in film.

George Burdeau, producing and directing since the 1980s, continues to work in the style of well-crafted and meaningful public broadcasting documentaries, such as *Backbone of the World* (1997), about Burdeau's Blackfeet Nation. Phil Lucas, who made the important *Honor of All* (1987) about one community's journey to sobriety, is another performer-turned-filmmaker.

Carol Geddes, Dan Jones, Duke Redbird, Willie Dunn, Chris Spotted Eagle, Dan Brown, Diane Reyna, Beverly Singer, Doug Cuthand, Fidel Moreno, Dean Bear Claw, and Greg Coyes are significant filmmakers who started work as early as the 1960s. They continue to contribute important work in content and in remaking the cinematic language into the language of their own storytelling. The subject of their work ranges from role models to sovereignty, from women's wellness to spirituality, and from Native education to Native histories.

A film from the first wave of Native directors is *Navajo Talking Picture* (1987) by Arlene Bowman. Made as her master's thesis film at UCLA, Bowman tries to film her grandmother, who is not interested. The difficulty is that Bowman only speaks English and her grandmother only speaks Diné. The film focuses on Bowman's attempts to understand her grandmother's resistance. It many ways, the film signals the end of ethnographic film as Bowman's grandmother refuses to be objectified. The film is starkly honest. Bowman does not play up being Indian in order to satisfy the audience's need for easy resolutions to the difficult reality of the government policies that broke up extended families and the continuum of traditional languages.

Since the 1990s, another wave of directors, who are also experienced community activists, are making films and video. Some were raised in the city, others on the trap line. Some went to film school, others are self-taught or moved from one medium to another. Like the artists and storytellers of their people, their voices reflect their way of seeing the world.

In fact, a few directors, like Marjorie Beaucage and Ava Hamilton, started as community activists and combine their political work with personal stories of resistance and recovery. Their works employ aesthetic innovation, but the emphasis is on the strength of the speakers and their stories.

Some directors' works are linked to the political governance of their lands. Here, works like *T'lina: The Rendering of Wealth* (1999) by Barb Cranmer, clearly document issues of political import to Native peoples. Loretta Todd is a director and writer who merges a solid foundation in filmmaking with community work and aesthetic and narrative innovation. From her first major documentary film *The Learning Path* (1991) to her later works, such as *Forgotten Warriors* (1996) and *Today is a Good Day: Remembering Chief Dan George* (1998), Todd is known for her poetic, elegiac images that underscore her powerful storytelling. Todd also works in drama, including short dramas such as *Day-Glo Warrior* (1992) and *The Circle* (1993), as well as forthcoming dramatic projects. Her community work contributed to the creation of the Aboriginal Arts Program at the Banff Centre for the Arts, in Banff, Alberta.

Other directors see themselves as artists, like Zach Kunuk, Zach Longboy, Thirza Cuthand, and Shelly Niro. Kunuk makes beautiful dramatic videos of life in Nunavut, like *Qaggiq* (1989), or his series *Nunavut* about Inuit people's lives in 1945. Zach Longboy is a performance artist who produces low-tech masterpieces, such as *The Stone Show* (1999) or *Water into Fire* (1994). Shelly Niro is known for her sense of humor in her film *Honey Moccasin* (1997), and brings her artwork into film. Thirza Cuthand does not flinch at exploring her sexuality in such films as *Baby Dyke Theory* (1998).

A number of Native cinematographers followed Gil Cardinal's route into directing. James Fornier made

Thomas Berryagka creating a film on Alcatraz and the Bay Area Indians. (Photo by Ilka Hartmann)

*Alcatraz is Not an Island* (1999) and Rene Sioui tells the history of his Huron people in *Kanata: Legacy of the Children of Astansic* (1999).

Another important trend in Native media are Native journalists moving from journalism to producing, like Jeff Bear and Jim Compton. With over twenty years experience as a journalist, Bear created the award-winning current affairs program *First Story* for the Baton network in Canada.

In order for Native Indian filmmaking to flourish, there is also a need for organizations to support Native work. Often it is easier for non-Native people to make Native subject stories than it is for Native directors, writers, and producers to do so. This is sometimes called *appropriation*, and as well-meaning as these non-Native projects may be, they are still telling a Native story from a non-Native point of view. Systemic racism—systems that perpetuate the status quo without even being aware of discrimination—has resulted in financial and organizational structures not easily accessible to Native people. Using their own sense of innovation and optimism, Native producers, directors,

and writers created many strategies to counter such difficulties.

Michael Smith has tirelessly showcased Native American films and videos since 1979 at the Native American Film Festival in San Francisco. Frank Blythe and his staff and board of the Native Public Broadcast Consortium help many Native filmmakers, providing production funds and broadcasting on PBS stations. In Canada, George Henry, Rosemary Kuptana, and Abraham Tagalik were instrumental, along with their northern broadcasters, in creating the Aboriginal Peoples Television Network (APTN), the first all-Native broadcast systems in North America. APTN went on air 1 September 1999 in Canada, showcasing Native television, from drama to documentary to children's programming and current affairs.

In the 1980s and 1990s, organizations like the Native Producers' Association and First Americans in the Arts (FAITA) sprang up to promote the interests of Native filmmakers, writers, and actors. FAITA sponsors an awards ceremony each year in Los Angeles honoring

A scene from *Naturally Native,* featuring (from left to right) Irene Bedard, Valerie Red–Horse, Floyd Westerman, and Kimberly Norris–Guerrero. (Courtesy of Valerie Red–Horse)

and celebrating the work of Native actors and performers and sponsoring scholarships. In Canada, there are a number of organizations that showcase Native work and promote training, like the Centre for Aboriginal Media in Toronto and ImaginaNative in Vancouver.

Non-Native organizations are also part of the landscape of Native media. The NFB in Canada assists Native directors, following the lobby efforts of Wil and Maria Campbell. The Sundance Institute and Film Festival develops Native directors and writers through screenings and workshops. Heather Rae was the first Native person hired to coordinate Sundance's Native programs. The Museum of the American Indian holds regular screenings and a biannual festival.

Overall, there is no single way to make a Native film and no one Native filmmaker who represents all the others. Each filmmaker, videomaker, animator, writer, or artist brings his or her distinct voice to the work. Some favor close-ups while others like the camera to stay back. Some like to use fast editing while others like the image to be uninterrupted by cutting. Some use

drama in documentary; others use documentary in drama. Some like to construct an image using lighting and art direction; others are only concerned with the moment in which they film. Some use no narration, preferring to let the people tell their stories; others like to participate in the storytelling themselves, becoming narrators. Though Native people share a colonial history, they each have distinct tribal languages, histories, and traditions that influence how they see the world and how they tell stories.

If there is a constant in the work of Native directors, writers, animators, and artists, it is humor. Humor does not mask the pain and struggle of Native people's history and lives today, but it does put things in perspective and gives Natives a common point of understanding and speaking across cultures to non-Native audiences. Another constant is a political awareness and analysis of the legacy of colonial and imperial forces upon Native lives. These films document the struggles, trials, and triumphs of Native people. They are sometimes a call to defend the land, the elders, the unborn generations, and they are sometimes a call to look deep within to understand the philosophies of those who went before.

In the future, more accessible digital technology will see a new wave of Native directors, writers and producers, and the many voices across Indian Country will continue to do what they have always done—tell stories.

*Loretta Todd*

## ◆ RECENT EVENTS IN NATIVE THEATER

During the last half of the twentieth century Native theater has seemed, at times, more elusive than a Broadway hit. There was a Catch-22 regarding plays, playwrights, and performers. There were few Native plays, because there were few Native performers; there were few Native performers because there were few roles. It has taken many years to address this inequity because of the established avenues for development and production. During the 1990s there was growing interest in the plays of Native people and an increasing demand, by both theater artists and audiences, for the production of Native plays. While Native theater's power and potential has yet to be fully realized, this interest and demand has sparked production, publication, and scholarly debate throughout North America.

At the core of Native theater is an emerging body of Native plays by Native playwrights. What is significant about this body of work is that these plays are being produced for a variety of audiences and production has led to publication. This is a recent development in Native theater. In the past, Native writers often worked in isolation, sending their scripts to literary departments of professional theater companies or publishers in the hope of development, production, or publication. Unfortunately many of these scripts languished unproduced and unpublished—that is, until Native playwrights and performers sought alternative methods of access and production.

A look at the growing list of Native theater productions in grassroots venues, significant community theaters, regional theaters, off-Broadway theaters and in North American academic and training institutions demonstrates the power and scope of Native theater. Venues for Native theater range from vibrant theater in Native communities like the West Bay Reserve of Manitoulin Island and its De-Ba-Jeh-Mu-Jig Drama Company, to the American Indian Community House in New York City, to prominent Native theater companies in metropolitan centers like Native Earth Performing Arts in Toronto. Still other theater companies like the American Indian Dance Theatre and Native Voices present shows in various venues internationally.

Productions beyond the established playhouses on Broadway and in LORT (League of Regional Theatre) companies have encouraged young Native theater artists and aided established artists with alternative venues to showcase their talent. From the increasing production opportunities, a growing number of experienced Native artists and craftspeople are joining the ranks of professional actors, directors, producers, and theater administrators. The productions of Native plays in the 1990s has encouraged mainstream theater companies like the Mark Taper Forum in Los Angeles, The Denver Center, and the Public Theatre in New York City to develop respectful processes to facilitate successful collaborations with Native theater artists.

Access and education will be key to the evolution of Native theater in the next millennium. As it continues to grow so does the need for a new generation of trained theater artists to fill the growing number of positions surrounding these productions. The artists and collaborators working in Native theater need to create meaningful networks for artists, producers, and presenters to support new work. With the improved financial status of Native tribes, Native people need to begin to support their own artists so they can continue to create stories and performances that celebrate, remember, and lead generations to come.

### What is Native Theater?

Does the race or nation of the playwright, actors, director, producers, designers, or production company define whether the play is Native? In the article "Receiving Aboriginality: Tomson Highway and the Crisis of Cultural Authenticity" Alan Filewood states that essentialism in the works of Native writers suggests that ethnicity is more about power than biology (*Theatre Journal*). While Filewood's conclusions about aboriginality are not ultimately satisfying, his work is a good place to begin a discussion about Native theater. His point that Native people are often not in power in mainstream theater is well taken.

Rob Appleford, in his article "The Desire To Crunch Bone: Daniel David Moses and the 'True Real Indian,'" quotes Moses. The playwright from the Delaware Nation states that the idea of something authentically Native is absurd (*Canadian Theatre Review*). Native people recognize that there are many authentic Native voices and points of view within the Native community. Rather than finding the one Native voice that speaks for all Native people, this generation of Native theater artists tests boundaries to tell stories in many different ways. They are making their voices heard and creating wonderful forms of theater. In "Native American Theater

Members of the American Indian Theatre Ensemble performing in New York, 1973. (Courtesy of Hanay Geiogamah)

and the Theater that Will Come," Native writer/scholar Diane Glancy writes that central to Native theater is its reciprocity. She argues that the goal of this style of theater is to loose what she terms *theirstory* by presenting pieces of *yourstory*. Below is a partial list of some of the important events in Native theater during the 1990s in the United States and Canada.

In New York City, The American Indian Community House (AICH) has been at the center of developing and producing Native theater artists and shows for over three decades. Founded in 1969 to locate urban Native Americans in New York, they have supported, produced, and presented many important Native theater events. They produced the critically acclaimed First Nations play, *The Ecstasy of Rita Joe* by George Ryga, with an all-Native cast. AICH's production of Tomson Highway's *The Rez Sisters*, a powerfully comic depiction of seven Native women trying to beat the odds of life and chance through "the biggest Bingo in the world" was the American debut for Highway and a successful collaborative venture between Spiderwoman, Coatlicue Theatre Company, and New York Theatre Workshop.

The productions of *Skin, Stone, Positive* directed by Muriel Miguel, *Grandma* and *Grandpa* by Hanay Geiogamah, and Muriel Miguel's one-person show *Hot and Soft* attest to AICH's commitment to honor Native American theater artists. Their successful production of the Native opera entitled *The Gleaners* demonstrates a commitment to challenging existing forms. They teamed up with Coatlicue Theatre Company to present *1992: Blood Speaks*, which deals with the themes of tradition, religion, colonialization, and genocide. In 1994 they produced Coatlicue's multimedia theater piece *Open Wounds on Tlalteuctli*. The play, which examines the abuse of women and the earth, was remounted at the Museum of Natural History. AICH also has a rich history of presenting performance-art pieces like Murielle Borst's comic and probing view of the challenges of being an urban Indian woman focusing on issues of abuse and identity in *More than Feathers and Beads*.

Two of the most often produced companies at the American Indian Community House have been the work of Colorado Sisters, Elvira and Hortensia Colorado, and Spiderwoman, created by Muriel and Gloria

The American Indian Theatre Ensemble performing their rendition of Buffalo Bill's "Wild West Show," from *Fog Horn* by Hanay Geiogamah. (Courtesy of Hanay Geiogamah)

Miguel and Lisa Mayo. Both companies are internationally respected and often cited in anthologies of contemporary Native theater. The director of theater for the American Indian Community House is Jim Cyrus.

De-Ba-Jeh-Mu-Jig Drama Company, created in 1984 by playwright/performer Shirley Cheechoo, is a major professional theater company located within a Native community. Created as a summer theater company on the West Bay Reserve of Manitoulin Island, it helped launch the careers of two of Canada's most-produced Native playwrights, Tomson Highway and Drew Hayden Taylor. De-Baj nurtured the careers of countless other playwrights, designers, and theater technicians as well as many of Canada's best-known Native performers. Some of the most famous performers in Native theater, film, and television developed their skills there, including Herbie Barnes, Gloria Eshkibok, Gary Farmer, Jonathan Fisher, and Alanis King-Odjig. De-Baj continues to be a prominent theater for developing theater artists and one of Canada's best known companies. It is currently under the artistic direction of Audry Diebassige and Ron Berti.

Canada's premier professional Native theater company is Native Earth Performing Arts in Toronto. Most of their productions have been at the Native Canadian Center Theatre, a community center in urban Toronto, with co-productions with Theatre Passe-Muraille, the Factory Theatre, and Cahoots Theatre Projects. Native Earth has mounted many notable productions including *The Rez Sisters* and the hard-hitting drama *Dry Lips Oughta Move to Kapuskasing*, both by Tomson Highway. The plays won the Dora Mavor Moore Award for Best New Play and the Floyd S. Chalmers Award for Best Canadian Play. *Dry Lips* was remounted in 1991 at the Royal George Theatre in Toronto, where it was a critical and financial success despite its brutal themes of alcoholism and rape.

Other important productions from Native Earth include *Almighty Voice and His Wife* and *Coyote City* by poet and playwright Daniel David Moses; *Dinky* by Columpa C. Bobb; and *No Totem for My Story*, the tender and terrifying tale of a brother and sister lost in an urban wilderness, by Joseph A. Dandurand. Another favorite playwright for Native Earth is the wonderfully witty and comic Drew Hayden Taylor. Taylor, a beloved newspaper columnist and essayist, has had many successful productions of his plays at Native Earth including *Someday*, a poignant and telling story of a family torn apart during the "scoop up" period in Canada's history when Indian children were taken from their communities and placed with well-meaning white families; *Toronto at Dreamers Rock*, a clever coming together of past, present, and future that examines cultural identity and community; and *Only Drunks and Children Tell the Truth*, which revisits the question of identity and family when the daughter from *Someday* is confronted with the death of her birth mother. The play won a Dora Mavor Moore Award for Best New Play in 1996.

In addition to producing plays, Native Earth hosts the annual Weesageechuck Begins to Dance Festival of New Plays. Many new playwrights, performers, and directors have begun their careers at Weesageechuck. Seasoned veterans as well as emerging Native playwrights workshop their newest plays there. The festival/workshop usually features six new theater pieces at various stages of development. From the festival, the company traditionally chooses their next season. Recent festivals have also included modern and traditional dance. Throughout the decade Native Earth grew under the artistic direction and creative energies of Tomson Highway and Drew Hayden Taylor. It continues to thrive with artistic director Alanis King.

In the Twin Cities, St. Paul and Minneapolis, Minnesota, several theaters presented Native theater in the 1990s. *Bring the Children Home*, Marcie Rendon's touching children's play exploring the journey of a young urban Native boy who discovers his identity through his past, was produced at the Child's Play Theatre in 1996 and in 1998. The Great American History Theatre in St. Paul presented Rendon's *Song Catcher*. Through the McKnight National Residency Program, The Minneapolis Playwrights' Center hosted Marie Clements, Randy Reinholz, and Jean Bruce Scott for a workshop and public reading of *Now look what you made me do* in 1995. The script, a disturbing look at the cycle of abuse told through segmented episodic vignettes, flashbacks, choral readings, movement, and music, went on to critical acclaim and publication. That same year the Cricket Theatre produced *Sacred Journey*, a one-man show written by a non-Native from a story told by a Native homeless person; and The Illusion Theatre produced Jim Northrup's one-man tour de force, *The Rez Road Follies*, an insightful vision of reservation life. Both shows were critical and financial successes and demonstrated the viability of Native theater despite their decidedly different approaches. Throughout the decade Sharon Day worked in the Minneapolis/St. Paul region with Native teenagers to create theater pieces about the issues in their lives. These shows toured reservations and conventions throughout the region. The issues in the plays ranged from coyote stories to stories dealing with AIDS. Spiderwoman had residencies several times for extended periods in Minnesota over the past decade and was in residence with Sharon Day's group over the years.

Another grassroots movement in Native theater is Native Voices. In 1994 their first Festival of Native Plays was produced in Normal, Illinois. The festival presented public staged readings of Drew Hayden Taylor's comic look at the powwow circuit and patrimony in *The Baby Blues*, Marie Clement's brooding *Now look what you made me do*, Joseph A. Dandurand's *No Totem for My Story*, William S. Yellow Robe Jr.'s *The Independence of Eddie Rose*, and Bruce King's *Evening at the Warbonnet*. In 1995, Native Voices: Back to Normal featured the Main Stage production of Clement's *Now look what you made me do* in addition to public staged readings of Tomson Highway's musical extravaganza, *Rose*, Taylor's *Only Drunks and Children Tell The Truth*, Joseph A. Dandurand's *Please Do Not Touch the Indians*, and Bill Lang's lighthearted comedy, *Sitting Bull's Laundry*.

The following year Native Voices teamed up with Red Path Theatre in Chicago for Gerald Vizenor's *Ishi and the Wood Ducks* for the 1996 Third World Conference. In 1996 Native Voices and Centre Stage of Pennsylvania mounted the critically acclaimed production of Taylor's *The Baby Blues*. Later that year, Native Voices in New York presented public staged readings of Judy Lee Oliva's historical musical, *Te Ata*, Marie Clement's one-woman show, *Urban Tattoo*, and Vicki Ramirez's *Smoke* at the American Indian Community House. In San Diego, Native Voices presented Taylor's *Pranks* as a public staged reading at the 1998 Theatre of the World Festival and produced *Urban Tattoo* for the 1999 Theatre of the World Festival before opening in Los Angeles at the Autry Museum of Western Heritage. In 1999 and 2000 Native Voices toured the production to Calgary; Oxford, Ohio; Amherst, Massachusetts; and Toronto for the Aboriginal Voices Festival.

Some professional non-Native theater organizations have ventured into the arena of producing Native theater. The Denver Center produced *Black Elk Speaks* in 1994. The show is an adaptation of a story told by Black Elk. The Mark Taper Forum remounted the show in Los Angeles in January 1995. While the show was successful on many levels, a criticism from the Native theater community was that it was based on the interpretation of many artists outside the Native theater community. In an effort to address this criticism, the Taper held a Native Play Reading Series in February 1995. The plays, presented as staged readings for a public audience, were written, directed, and performed by Native theater artists. The series included Roxy Gordon and Leanne Howe's raucous attack on Native stereotypes in *Indian Radio Days*, Drew Hayden Taylor's *The Baby Blues*, and Joseph A. Dandurand's *No Totem for My Story* and *Where Two Rivers Meet*.

If Native theater has been somewhat absent from Broadway, it has been the subject of numerous articles and papers for the last three decades. Periodicals that regularly contain information about Native theater include *TDR: The Drama Review, Theatre Journal, Canadian Theatre Journal, Aboriginal Voices, The University of Oklahoma Press, The Native Playwrights' Newsletter* and *Indian Country Today*. The Association for Theatre in Higher Education (ATHE) included panels on the development and production of Native theater at their annual national conferences throughout the decade.

In the early 1990s the Drama Bookshop in New York City only carried a few plays by Native Americans. The plays most often suggested were *The Rez Sisters* by Tomson Highway and the plays in *New Native American Drama: Three Plays* by Hanay Geiogamah. By the end of the 1990s publications about Native theater expanded to reflect the cultural and geographic diversity of Native people. There were well over one hundred published plays by Native authors with new publications reflecting the impact of regional and community productions of Native theater. *Stories of Our Way: An Anthology of American Indian Plays* and its critical companion *American Indian Theater in Performance: A Reader*, both edited by Hanay Geiogamah and Jaye T. Darby, are the first publications of their kind to chronicle the growing number of Native theater productions and the body of scholarship about Native theater during the past decade. Additional resources for Native plays include Diane Glancy's *War Cries: A Collection of Plays & Contemporary Plays by Women of Color*, edited by Kathy Perkins and Roberta Uno; and *Seventh Generation: An Anthology of Native American Plays*, edited by Mimi Gisolfi D'Aponte.

Addressing a very specific need within the Native theater community is the Native American Women Playwrights Archive (NAWPA) housed in the King Library at Miami University in Oxford, Ohio. A collection of original materials by Native women playwrights of the Americas, NAWPA is an invaluable resource for Native theater artists and scholars creating a network for producing organizations and playwrights. According to William Wortman, director of NAWPA, their goal is "to identify playwrights, collect and preserve their work, try to make it widely known, and encourage

performances and continued creativity. Plays in manuscript, disk, videotape, or other format are cataloged, given appropriate preservation treatment, and made available to anyone who wishes to read them in the library."

## Who Works in Native Theater?

There are many compelling reasons for artists to be involved with Native theater. The plays are exciting, innovative, and culturally rich. Often it is the desire for cultural identity that drives artists to work in Native theater. They want to work on theater that has personal and cultural significance. In the *Canadian Theatre Review*, performance artist James Luna states that Indian artists often feel compelled to live up to stereotypes of "being an Indian" in their chosen art form. Native theater artists create from a deeply personal need to communicate their vision of the world. Beyond the individual artist, theater is a collaborative venture. It relies on the skills of many craftsmen, artists, and business people for a successful venture. If the past decade is any indication, Native theater is thriving because Native theater artists have discovered ways of working for themselves. The tenacity and ingenuity of these artists and their collaborations have defined Native theater and compelled many experts in the field of theater and entertainment to learn from their work.

Academic and training institutions and independent development opportunities have played an important role in the progress and visibility of Native playwrights, Native theater artists, and Native theater growth. They have provided the long-needed access and education for Native theater artists to hone their craft. While these institutions are vital to the growth of Native theater, more support, facilities, and funding are needed to keep them alive.

A Native institution with a history of developing Native theater artists is The Institute of American Indian Arts in Santa Fe, New Mexico (IAIA). Since its inception in 1962, the institute has educated over 3,200 students. In 1964 it established a rigorous training program for Native theater and dance. The Institute of American Indian Arts has recently moved to a new campus, still in Santa Fe. While their theater program is currently on hiatus, Native theater artists anticipate a new theater program at IAIA in the future.

One of the major theater training institutions for Native theater artists in Canada is The Centre for Indigenous Theatre and the Indigenous Theatre School in Toronto. The center started as a summer training program over twenty-five years ago based on the belief that aboriginal actors, directors, and playwrights will

Poster advertising performances by the American Indian Theatre Ensemble. (Courtesy of Hanay Geiogamah)

flourish with an active aboriginal theater school available to them. With the aim of expanding into the next century and offering students a more comprehensive program, the Centre for Indigenous Theatre created the Indigenous Theatre School full-time program. These two programs have trained hundreds of Native theater artists and they produce several plays each year. Many of the artists listed in this article have participated as students or instructors at these two institutions. The current artistic director for the center is the award-winning Native performer and director Carol Greyeyes.

The Haskell Indian Nations University in Lawrence, Kansas, has been the home of Thunderbird Theatre Company since 1974. Pat Melody has been there from beginning. Thunderbird Theatre Company is a student organization that produces theater on the Haskell campus and tours productions throughout the Midwest. While they have produced many titles, including five from Shakespeare and currently *Children of the Sun* by N. Scott Momaday, the show entitled *Songs of Life* has always been a part of the company. Dianne Reyner describes *Songs of Life* as a set of stories and songs told by elders that have been passed on orally

from one generation of students to the next. Dianne Reyner is posting a comprehensive list of current Native plays. A link for the list can be found on the Haskell Indian Nations homepage.

Cultural museums also play an important role in the development and presentation of Native theater. The Mashantucket Pequot Museum and Research Center is a new tribally owned and operated state-of-the-art complex. It is located in Mashantucket, Connecticut, and opened in August 1998. Elizabeth Theobald, noted Native theater director, is the head of public programs for the museum. While much of the focus of the museum is in education, they have also presented plays including Drew Hayden Taylor's *Toronto at Dreamers Rock* and Theobald's adaptation of Joseph Bruchac's *Circle of Thanks*, and have co-hosted an arts conference with Yale University.

The Autry Museum of Western Heritage in Los Angeles and Native Voices Theatre Company created a Native Theater Initiative after their successful co-production of *Urban Tattoo* by Marie Clements. The project begins in 2000 with five play readings each year in the museum's 215-seat Wells Fargo Theater. During the second and third years of the program, a new play will be mounted for full production. The project's artistic director is Randy Reinholz and the executive director is Jean Bruce Scott. The primary thrust of the work at Native Voices is to aid the development, production, and publication of Native playwrights.

A new opportunity and natural career path for playwrights was presented in 1998 when the Native Screenwriter's Workshop, a joint initiative between UCLA American Indian Studies Center and The Sundance Institute, was launched in Los Angeles. The workshop invites Native writers from a variety of fields to apply and to undergo a week of intensive seminars and writing workshops providing an opportunity for Native playwrights, poets, novelists, and screenwriters to develop and write feature-film scripts. The participants revise and develop their own scripts, critique produced movies and attend seminars that cover practical aspects of the feature-film business. Well-known directors, producers, and film-industry professionals are invited to the seminars to provide the participants with first-hand knowledge and experience.

None of these organizations would have any Native theater to present without the individual efforts of theater artists, ensembles, performance collectives, and grassroots organizations. These artists have created a variety of methods to present Native theater. Often large institutions have changed or modified their original mandates to facilitate the work of these individuals and ensembles. Compelling work in Native theater has come from collaborations between these prolific Native theater artists and established institutions, theaters, and museums.

While Native theater is created in a number of different ways, it often begins with a script. There is an old saying in theater that if it ain't on the page, it ain't on the stage. There are many accomplished and treasured writers in various communities. They are the storytellers of this generation of Native theater. They continue to illuminate and explore issues of cultural identity, traditional values, teaching and spirituality, community, urban isolation, colonization, religion, incest, rape, alcoholism, and growing concerns about health issues. Some of the Native playwrights who have shaped the past decade of Native theater and who will shape the next decade are: Marie Clements, Hanay Geiogamah, Diane Glancy, Tomson Highway, Leanne Howe, Margo Kane, Bruce King, Bill Lang, Monique Mojica, Daniel David Moses, Judy Lee Oliva, Drew Hayden Taylor, and William S. Yellowrobe Jr. These writers have been produced and published throughout North America.

Another popular form of creating Native theater is ensemble collaboration. One of the characteristics that these ensembles have in common is that they are groups of artists and friends that want to create stories and performances that are not usually available in local theaters, community centers, universities, or on Broadway. Leann Howe once described New York theater as regional theater, catering to a specific region and audience. Native theater ensembles create productions that are more relevant to their regional communities. In addition to creating new performances, the ensembles regularly work with the next generation of Native theater artists in significant Indian communities. Some of the ensembles and theater companies that have made significant contributions to Native theater over the past decade are the American Indian Dance Theatre, The Colorado Sisters, Native Earth Performing Arts, Native Voices, Red Path Theatre, Spiderwoman, Tulsa Indian Actors' Workshop, Turtle Gals in Toronto, and Wagon Burners.

Whether the plays are scripted or created by ensembles, Native performers are vital to the growth of Native theater. Actors often bring personal experiences to a role when creating a character. Some have first-hand experience while others do research into the imaginary world of the play. In both cases, Native performers are an integral part of the success of Native theater. Many of the growing list of professional Native performers started in the theater and have gained further recognition for their television and film roles (Gary Farmer in *Pow Wow Highway* and *Dead Man*; Graham Greene in *Dances with Wolves*, *Thunder Heart* and *The Green Mile*; Sheila Tousey in *Thunder Heart*; and Monique Mojica in *Smoke Signals*). Many other familiar Native performers got their start and continue to hone their craft in theater. Some of the best known actors include Herbie Barnes, Irene Bedard, Columpa C. Bobb, Jack Burning, Loren Cardinal, Tantoo Cardinal, Shirley Cheechoo, Marie Clements, Charlie Hill, Michael Horse, Kenneth Martines, David Medina, Billy Merasty, and Jennifer Podemski. Their success and visibility will hopefully continue to bring new interest to Native theater as they transport audiences into the worlds they inhabit as characters on the stage and screen.

In addition to actors who play parts in other writers' plays, many new Native theater artists work as performance artists. Typically a performance artist creates theater using many different artistic media, including but not limited to music, dance, video, visual art works, and poetry. Often their work has strong political overtones. A few of the Native performers who have made their mark as performance artists are Murial Borst, Margo Cane, and Marie Clements, all strong female performers and playwrights; James Luna, a provocative visual/performance artist from California; and the wonderful story teller and writer, Jim Northrup.

The work these artists create and present continually challenge the traditional boundaries of theater as well as Native culture and provoke a lively debate about the essence of theater.

Leading much of this work are the producers and directors of Native theater. They are often in the line of fire as they champion playwrights, set a course, raise money, and gather the artistic personnel to produce Native theater. While the growth of Native theater over the past decade has contributed to the number of Native theater artists involved there is still a great need for inclusion and training of new Native theater artists. Some of the leading producers and directors in the United States include Hanay Geiogamah, Randy Reinholz, and Elizabeth Theobald. In Canada the list includes Tomson Highway, Pamela Matthews, and Drew Hayden Taylor.

In tandem with Native theater productions there is an emerging body of scholarship addressing the issues surrounding the development of Native theater. There is a longstanding and continuing debate over what Native theater is or should be. Scholars who made a significant contribution to Native theater over the past decade are Jaye T. Darby, Mimi Gisolfi D'Aponte, Hanay Geiogamah, Diane Glancy, Ann Haugo, David Krasner, Bill Lang, Judy Lee Oliva, Kathy Perkins, Jean Bruce Scott, Roberta Uno, Gerald Vizenor, and William A. Wortman.

Some of the honored leaders in the Native theater community are Elvira Colorado, Hortensia Colorado, Hanay Geiogamah, Tomson Highway, Margo Kane, Lee Maracle, Lisa Mayo, Gloria Miguel, Muriel Miguel, and Gerald Vizenor. These leaders mentor a new generation of theater artists and continue to delight audiences around the world.

If access and education are the key to the future of Native theater, then it is up to established Native theater artists to create access and provide education to future generations of Native theater artists. One of the important projects for the future of Native theater is Project HOOP (Honoring Our Origins and People through Native Theater, Education, and Community Development). The forces behind the project are Hanay Geiogamah, Jaye T. Darby, and Duane Champagne. Project HOOP is a collaborative initiative working to establish academic and artistic programs in Native theater in tribally controlled colleges and communities. The project hopes to develop community-based theater based on Native perspectives, traditions, spirituality, history, culture, language, community, and land. This project represents one of the brightest hopes for Native theater as it continues and expands a longstanding mandate for training Native theater artists. There are many possible outcomes for this project, including a

proliferation in community-based theater performances by, for, and about Native people; more touring and regional professional Native theater companies and performances for ethnically diverse audiences; and a recognizable change in the number of professionals in theater, film, and television whose roots lie in Native theater that is written, directed, designed, produced, and performed by Native people.

While the future of Native theater is at an important crossroads, given the long history of Native theater and the momentum of the 1990s, there is a renewed opportunity to celebrate Native theater artists and the work they create.

*Randy Reinholz*
*San Diego State University*

## ◆ THE STATUS OF NATIVE JOURNALISM IN NORTH AMERICA

Freedom of the press is not an absolute right in Indian Country.

The founders of the United States acknowledged a free press as an essential element in a democratic state through the enactment of the First Amendment to the Constitution, which states that Congress is prohibited from enacting any law qualifying a free press. The authors of the Constitution were aware of the power an open media had in fermenting the American Revolution, convincing them of the significance of free speech and free press to democracy.

Native nations then, as now, were perceived as entities outside the protection of the Constitution and its Bill of Rights. As quasi-sovereign entities, Native nations retained the right to administer their internal affairs in accordance with their own rules and procedures, providing such regulations were not expressly alienated by a specific act of Congress.

The U.S. Supreme Court has held that Native nations are not independent states in the same manner as Canada or Mexico, but have powers akin to those of a state. While Native law enforcement officials may not arrest non-Natives for criminal acts committed within their respective jurisdictions, they may elect to deny their own members the protection of the Bill of Rights.

Native governments have a fairly free hand in passing rules that qualify freedom of speech or the press and may, if challenged, evoke sovereign immunity as a defense. The U.S. courts will generally not hear an appeal from plaintiffs involved in an action against a Native administrative agency unless the petitioner has exhausted all their local remedies first. This means those individuals and/or groups with a complaint have to go through Native courts before moving to U.S. federal courts, which are generally reluctant to become involved in Indian affairs. Unfortunately for many plaintiffs, Native courts are not immune to the powerful political pressures that can be brought to bear upon them by Native executives, since most indigenous nations do not have constitutions clearly acknowledging the independence of the judiciary. The challenge for aboriginal journalists working for publications located on Indian territory is to continue their work despite the considerable authority their respective Native governments have not only to shut them down but also to severely limit their ability to appeal to the courts.

Another major factor in qualifying a free press on Indian territory is the overall poverty in many Native communities, as well as a rather narrow advertising base in and around most reservations. Almost all Native publications are regional in scope and rely heavily on Native funds or local advertising dollars for their financial survival. Articles that might be critical of an institution, business, or politically connected individual may well be met with the withdrawal of financial support from a Native government or business, a boycott of the publication, or, in extreme cases, the dismissal of the publication's staff.

Aboriginal journalists receive their formal training in colleges and universities. Such classes may include the principles and ethics of journalism, training they apply to their writing throughout their careers. Objectivity in researching and reporting is deemed as important as the story itself, with a stress on securing hard facts and firm attributes. Such lessons may well prove to be difficult to apply within a Native community that has a long history of mistrust when it comes to the media.

All writers, regardless of their background, bring personal experiences and perspectives that deeply affect not only the content of their articles, but also the manner and style in which the stories are presented. Aboriginal writers have a unique advantage over their non-Native counterparts in that they are better informed as to Native-centered subject matter and have easier access to primary sources. But there is an important qualifier: Native writers may have deep familial connections within the community and may well risk this relationship if a story is perceived to have brought shame to a fellow nation member or has held a local official up to criticism or ridicule. Aboriginal journalists must then strive to fulfill their professional obligations while providing essential information to their respective nations. Native journalists must disseminate information anticipating resistance from local officials and scolding from those who would have their names excluded from the public police blotter or criminal court.

The key to survival for an aboriginal journalist working on the local level is to convince the community that the art of communication is one that is historically and culturally rooted in Native life, albeit in a new technological format. It is also important to emphasize the services that a local publication is best able to provide, such as communal profiles, civic notices, employment opportunities, school events, obituaries, and the opportunity for community members to voice their concerns in a public forum, all of which were at one time made known through information exchange methods ranging from runners, who traveled over time-worn trails among the nations carrying important news, to public assemblies where people gathered to exchange ideas or listen to reports from their leaders.

As Native communities grew in size, the need for an expanded news dissemination service was apparent. The Cherokee Nation initiated a formal indigenous news outlet with the founding of the *Cherokee Phoenix* at its capital of New Echota (west of Atlanta, Georgia) in 1828. The *Phoenix* was remarkable in that it used as type the Cherokee syllabary invented by Sequoyah just a few years before. The *Phoenix* proved to be the ideal method for spreading the use of the syllabary, but it was a cause for concern to non-Indians who coveted Cherokee lands and opposed any attempt by the Natives to protect and preserve their status as independent nations. The *Phoenix* was destroyed by a white mob as the Cherokee were driven west to Oklahoma, where they then began a second newspaper called the *Cherokee Advocate*. At least two other Oklahoma Native nations, the Choctaws and Chickasaws, followed the Cherokee example and began their own newspapers.

The nineteenth century was, however, not an ideal time for such endeavors. Native people were being systematically stripped of their ancestral lands while they suffered through massive epidemics, forcible removals, and military assaults. Native children were literally taken from their mothers' arms to be shipped to distant residential schools where every attempt was made to convert them into complacent U.S. citizens. But at institutions such as Carlisle in eastern Pennsylvania they were able to make use of the school's printing press, hence the popularity of typesetting as an occupation.

In the twentieth century, a distinctly Native press was slow to develop. The oppressive tactics of the U.S. federal government meant that few Native people had the resources to sustain news journals. The residential school experience did have one legacy that would prove an important resource in the growth of a Native media: pan-Indianism. Native students were brought together in a common environment from many nations. Such shared experiences eventually gave impetus to the idea that Native people were better served if they acted in concert. From this sprouted news journals such as *Wassaja*, the *First American*, and the *American Indian Magazine*, most of which were advocates for gradual integration of Native nations into the American mainstream.

In the years after World War II the move toward a collective Native identity picked up steam. There was no denying the enormous impact Hollywood films had on the way in which Native people were portrayed, an image that consumed Aboriginals. The Termination Era of the Eisenhower years saw tens of thousands of Natives leave their reservation homes for economic and educational opportunities in the country's cities. Aboriginal leaders watched as African Americans pressed for their civil rights and took a lesson from the boycotts and sit-ins of the 1950s and 1960s. A new generation of Native leaders prepared to take the stage, and they were far less willing to bend to the federal government's will. The strategy of an aggressive definition of indigenous rights was taught by citizens of the Haudenosaunee (Six Nations Iroquois) Confederacy, who advocated the rejection of U.S. citizenship and jurisdiction while pressing for an expansion of aboriginal rights as secured by treaty.

The Mohawk Nation, a member of the Haudenosaunee Confederacy, saw the need for the development of an information service that was distinctly Native in design and content. In December 1968 the Nation's Council of Chiefs authorized the creation of *Akwesasne Notes*, a news journal, which, for the first time, gave Native people an opportunity to express not only their concerns but also their desire to achieve cultural and political autonomy. *Akwesasne Notes* became the standard bearer for Native activism in North America and among indigenous people around the world. It gave form to the concept of aboriginalism, a term meant to describe the common experiences of native societies as they struggled to maintain their indigenous identities, despite the forces of colonialism and a capitalistic, materialistic economy. *Notes* was followed by the creation of the American Indian Press Association, under the guidance of Richard LaCourse, the legendary Yakama journalist who has inspired many aboriginal writers to consider the media as a career.

The Mohawks of eastern North America elected to expand from newspapers as represented by *Akwesasne Notes* into radio, magazines, books, and television. The advocates of these new ideas argued that there was a pressing need to take charge of the methods of the external world, in much the same way that the Iroquois of former times sent diplomats and peace missions to Native nations throughout the east and continental Midwest. Communications became not only

a vital part of the Mohawk plan for survival, but also served as a significant economic stimulus as the goods and services of the Mohawk worker found new markets off the reservation. The Mohawk Nation experience stands as a compelling example of the challenges and perils contemporary aboriginal journalists face at this time.

In 1982 a group of Mohawks formed the Akwesasne Communications Society with the intent of using a radio broadcasting facility to change the manner in which Natives were perceived in southern Canada and the northeastern United States. Located along the St. Lawrence River some 100 kilometers southwest of Montreal, Akwesasne was in an ideal place to construct a radio broadcasting unit. Subsequently, a studio facility and tower were built astride the international boundary, which dissects the reservation into Canadian and American halves. The design was intentional; it was meant to make the bold statement that the Mohawks would not be separated by an imaginary line they had no hand in making, nor would they have their concerns filtered through non-Native radio news. On 1 October 1984 Radio CKON went on the air exclusively licensed by the Mohawk Nation Council of Chiefs as a deliberate act of Native sovereignty. CKON remains the only indigenous radio station in North America without a Federal Communications Commission or a Canadian Radio and Television Commission permit.

Other Iroquois communities replicated Akwesasne. Kahnasetake (Oka), Tyendinaga (Deseronto), and Oshweken soon cranked up their own radio stations, and the Mohawk community of Kahnawake actually began broadcasting a few years before CKON aired. Yet as the Mohawks moved toward an expansion of their media outlets, they experienced a number of setbacks, particularly at Akwesasne. The political divisions of the community, created and sustained by government officials in Washington, Albany, and Ottawa, made the implementation of singular economic and social development policies very difficult. Unification efforts made significant progress only to be derailed by internal elements apprehensive that a single Mohawk governing agency would curtail the controversial and lucrative smuggling and gambling activities on the reservation.

Akwesasne was served by the international journal *Akwesasne Notes*, a local newspaper called *Indian Time*, and Radio CKON. Despite these information outlets there was considerable opposition to a free media within the community. The smuggling and gambling cartel saw the Mohawk media as an adversary since both radio and newspapers reported extensively on the issues. Resistance to the media came initially in the form of advertising withdrawal, denial of distribution outlets, and exclusion of reporters from certain businesses. The pro-gambling advocates opposed Mohawk unity since traditional law prohibited gambling. They financed their own publication, which quickly degenerated into a means to attack their opponents using defamation and smear tactics.

Attempts to maintain a so-called objective perspective became impossible since any report on smuggling arrests or secretive gambling deals was seen as a threat. Editorials decrying those illegal activities, a requisite part of any newspaper, drew the wrath of the cartel in the form of threats. The simple act of publishing became an act of defiance against those who feared an open press. The radio tower of CKON was destroyed, and the offices of *Notes* and *Indian Time* were torched soon after. As tensions mounted, the need for a third party peacekeeping element became critical. Yet despite the appeals of the Mohawk Nation for assistance, they were left to their own devices. A second act of arson occurred, but the blaze was contained before causing too much damage to the Akwesasne Communications Center, the building that housed the radio station and *Notes*.

In the spring of 1990, the growing crisis led to a state of civil war, with Mohawks battling other Mohawks on U.S. and Canadian sides of the reservation. On 1 May 1990 two Mohawk men died, finally compelling the external police agencies to intervene. Blood was spilled, however, and despite the best efforts of the Mohawk media to reconstruct a sense of common purpose, the opportunity for true unification had passed. Commercial gambling was stopped for almost a decade after the fighting ended, but smuggling activities exploded as the Mohawk governing councils backed away from any action which might provoke confrontation.

The Mohawk media was also subdued. Aggressive reporting was curtailed, editorial writing subdued, and Radio CKON suspended its hard news broadcasts. It was obvious to the Mohawk Nation that a free press had to be defended using effective courts supported in turn by a respected police service. Akwesasne had neither.

The Mohawk tribulations, while extreme, were not exceptional among Native people. Native politicians and governments moved aggressively against their own journalists and broadcasters in other nations. Karen Michel of the Ho Chunk Nation, Tom Arviso of the *Navajo Times*, Dan Agent of the *Cherokee* (Oklahoma) *Advocate*, and Paul DeMain of *News From Indian Country*, among many others, have weathered similar storms as they struggled to keep a free and open press operating on Native territory. Each one of them was criticized, bullied, and sometimes fired for having the courage to stand their ground when it came to the people's right to know.

As it stands, there are few, if any, "freedom of speech" or "freedom of the press" provisions in Native nation constitutions, a fact of grave concern to organizations such as the Native American Journalists Association (NAJA), which was formed in 1984 and is now the primary advocacy group for aboriginal reporters across the continent. NAJA is an aggressive defender of freedom of the press with its annual conferences serving as a critical means to exchange information and develop strategies to enhance the aboriginal media.

There are many aboriginal journalists working in a variety of news outlet formats ranging from bimonthly publications such as *News From Indian Country* to the national radio talk show *Native America Calling*. They also edit magazines ranging from *Native Peoples* to *Aboriginal Voices*, or they contribute to large, non-Native newspapers, including the *Dallas Morning News*, the *New York Times*, and the *Seattle Times*. Each one expands the perimeters of knowledge and awareness about indigenous issues in a manner that would have pleased the news carriers of the past.

*Doug George-Kanentiio*
*Oneida Iroquois Territory*

## ◆ NATIVE RADIO

Indian radio has been a part of my life since I was a child. I grew up in the San Francisco Bay area, a child of the 1950s Relocation Program, which took Indian families from their reservation—in my case an Oklahoma Indian town—and delivered them to a large urban city. The result of this program, or so the government thought, would be Native assimilation into America's "melting pot." What the government did not realize, however, is that urban Indians are still Indians. The interstates, bus stations, and train stations became our private highways shuttling us between our cousins back home and our new Indian communities in the cities. Every year my family would drive from Oakland, California back to the Creek Nation. As a little girl I remember long, hot drives across the desert, the car draped with a burlap water bag and uncomfortable and scratchy horsehair seats. In the 1960s, as my parents drove Route 66 on our way back home to Oklahoma, across Arizona and New Mexico, they would search the radio dial for the occasional Navajo radio program. A Navajo voice would come through the airwaves delivering content and commercials in that language. Even though we were not Navajo and did not understand the show, it was important to my parents to hear a Native language spoken on the air. Language preservation is one of the reasons behind the Native-radio-station movement across the country; cultural preservation is another.

## Broadcasting Our Survival

If the bow and arrow are the most well known tools used by Native people then broadcasting must be one of their best-kept secrets. What do these two have in common? Not much, other than they are both tools used for survival. One of the reasons Native people survive is their ability to adapt to various environments, no matter how harsh or unusual. Over the centuries they have encountered many cultures and with each meeting Native people took advantage of any situation by adopting new tools. One of the newest survival tools being used is radio and telecommunication satellites. By becoming broadcasters they aim to keep their cultures and traditions strong. When it comes to the Communications Era, Indians are riding in the FM lane and cruising the information superhighways.

Indians, Aleuts, Inuits, Yupiks, and other indigenous societies from the tip of Alaska to Tierra del Fuego have adopted the airwaves as one of the newest tools for cultural survival. Today there are thirty Native-owned public radio stations in the lower forty-eight states and Alaska. This section focuses on the emergence of the tribally or community-controlled public radio stations that began broadcasting in the late 1970s.

## Let's Talk: Native Radio's Beginnings

Did you ever think about how Native peoples spread the word about powwows and ceremonies? Or how they shared music and stories? How did they trade or barter? And how did they call the warriors to arrive in time for the Battle of the Little Big Horn or the Pueblo Revolt? When Native Americans wanted to do something as simple as talking to their relatives over long distances there was only one way—travel. In many cultures, runners carried information from community to community. In California, musicians and traders played a very important role since they not only entertained people but also brought news about births and marriages.

The need to communicate is nothing new. Whether sharing one-on-one conversations, or sharing information with a lot of people over great distances, talking has always been important to all people, and Native Americans have a strong history of oral traditions, keeping people connected from one generation to the next. It is no surprise, then, that the airwaves are part of Native cultural evolution. Technology delivered the tools that Indians are using to preserve their language and carry on traditions for the future generations. But how did it begin to be so?

## Public Radio Moves to the Rez

In the late 1970s, at around the same time that Indian activism took root on reservations and in urban centers across America, government programs designed to make it easier for women and minorities to own their own broadcasting systems in the form of public radio, public television, and production studios, evolved. A program known as the National Telecommunications Infrastructure Administration (NTIA), a part of the Department of Commerce, was formed. One of NTIA's other goals was to expand the public broadcasting signal throughout the United States. A program known as the Public Telecommunications and Facilities Program (PTFP) began offering grants to minority- and women-owned entities to build public broadcasting stations or productions centers. Production centers and low-power television systems were encouraged in rural communities across the United States. In 1980 the PTFP was well underway, but the survival rate of many projects was dismally low, largely due to a lack of funding.

Nevertheless, it was during the late 1970s and early 1980s that Native radio began to emerge across the country, in particular in the Southwest, Alaska, and the Northern Plains. Indian tribes and school boards embraced the idea of having a voice for their own community. For Native Americans this was the beginning of the era that turned Indians from passive consumers of technology to service providers. Native radio stations began to fill the educational frequencies at the lower end of the radio dial, frequencies from 88.1 to 91.9 FM. Navajo, Lakota, Dakota, Zuni, Ojibway, Apache, Hoopa, Inuit, Yupik, and Athabascan are some of the indigenous peoples who jumped on the PTFP wagon and now have their own public radio stations.

## Call Letters: What's In a Name?

In the recent movie *Smoke Signals* there was a parody of a Native radio station supposedly broadcasting during the reservation's "morning drive time." The television series *Northern Exposure* also used community radio in an amusing way. In reality today's Native radio stations have formats that are somewhere in the middle, blending local programs with news, music, public affairs, along with nationally distributed programs such as those from National Public Radio. From the tip of Barrow, Alaska, to the deserts of the Southwest, Indians share messages from one community to the next, broadcasting in English and Native languages. Native radio stations share stories, offer local Indian news, and rock the reservation with country, reggae, or forty-nine music (tunes that accompany post-powwow gatherings).

With recent internet technologies, people can hear Native radio on the World Wide Web. The Internet has expanded the signal for tribal radio, and the voices of Indian people can now be downloaded every day and at any time.

All radio and television stations have call letters. Radio and television stations east of the Mississippi have call numbers which begin with a W, while stations west of the Mississippi begin with the letter K. Often these calls letters brand a station or identify a city. The Southern Ute Tribe in Ignacio, Colorado, has a radio station known as KSUT. The Zuni used a greeting or *keshay* for their KSHI. In South Dakota, the Lakota nations radio choose an indigenous synonym for the word *cool* for the name of KILI. The Confederated Tribes of the Fort Berthold Reservation in North Dakota are the Mandan, Hidatsa, and Arikara, so their station is KMHA. WOJB in Hayward, Wisconsin, refers to the Lac Courtes Oreilles Ojibway Tribe.

WOJB is a 100,000-watt FM flagship station. It serves not only the Lac Courtes Oreilles Ojibway Tribe, but also all surrounding communities. Their eclectic sound includes local talk shows, music, and standard public radio fare. They broadcast mainly in English, although they incorporate their language when it makes sense. WOJB has been on the air since 1981.

One of the first stations on the air was located in Ramah, New Mexico, on the edges of the Navajo Reservation, just thirty miles north of Zuni Pueblo. The Ramah School Board opened their station about twenty-seven years ago when a soft Navajo voice proudly announced, "You're listening to KTDB, the voice of the Ramah Navajo community school district." Those simple words were part of a revolution that continues expanding across Native America. KTDB's first studios were in trailers at the bottom of a hill. Today, they have moved into several buildings high atop Pine Hill, New Mexico. Most of KTDB's programming is done in Navajo, but it also includes NPR's *Morning Edition* (ME) and *All Things Considered* (ATC). In the afternoon *ATC* is broadcast twice, once in English followed by a live version with simultaneous translation into Navajo. The rest of the day, KTDB plays music and local public affairs spots. When the occasional Native radio series comes along they always find a spot for it. There are five Navajo stations on the air now including KTNN, the "Voice of the Navajo Nation," which is an AM station owned by the Navajo Tribe. It is a commercial radio station and since it is a clear channel it can be heard for hundreds of miles around the reservation, and if the atmospheric conditions are right it can be heard in Northern California (AM signals bounce off the atmosphere and can travel hundreds of miles). The other Navajo stations are KABR, serving the Alamo Band of

Navajo on the "little rez" in south central New Mexico; KGHR, a high school station in Tuba City; and KRMH, or Red Mesa High, in the four corners area. The emergence of Native radio in the United States has been overlooked but is far from silent.

From these humble beginnings the voices of Native people have spread across Indian Country. From the prairies of North Dakota to the redwood forests of California and Oregon and throughout the Southwest, Indians began doing for themselves what had not been done before. They began to broadcast news, sports, music, and, most importantly, culture and language.

It is important to note that as early as the 1930s occasional Indian programs existed on commercial radio stations adjacent to reservations. With the advent of educational radio stations in the 1960s, a few individual Native programs could be heard but these were often in urban areas. For the most part, however, Indian people in the United States had no affiliated presence in radio until the late 1980s.

### Don't Touch That Dial: The Era of National Native Programming Dawns

Indian radio tries to do the same thing as its mainstream counterparts: deliver news, local information, music, and whatever else it takes to keep people listening. Unlike the larger public radio system, however, there are no signature programs, but the debut of the AIROS (American Indian Radio on Satellite) is an attempt to remedy that situation.

In 1994 a new way of distributing Indian programs debuted providing Native programs with the opportunity to be heard by all public stations. AIROS, which is a project of the Native American Public Telecommunications, uses channels provided by the Public Radio Satellite System (PRSS) to provide Native programming. *Native America Calling*, hosted by Harlan Makasoto, is a daily one-hour talk show offering the general public insights into Indian issues from politics to culture. *NAC* also goes out over the satellite and Internet. AIROS offers programs from the Smithsonian Institute's National Museum of the American Indian or NMAI, which contributes shows such as *Coyote Bites Back* and *Frank Day: Memory and Imagination*. Another NMAI offering is *Living Voices*, a series of short programs focusing on interesting and outstanding Native people who might otherwise be known only to their communities. Individual producers offer individual interviews, such as Suzanne Aikman's program *Alter-Native*. Documentary programs for 1999 and 2000 include the thirteen-part series *The California Indian Radio Project*, produced by the Northern California

Cultural Communications, based on the Hoopa Reservation in Northern California.

The largest number of Native-run programs center around the music scene. These include *Earthsongs*, produced by Alaska's Native-owned Koahnic Corporation; *Native Sounds, Native Voices* produced by AIROS; *Oyate Ta Olowon*, produced by Milt and Jamie Lee's Oyate Productions at their South Dakota studio; and *Different Drums*, hosted by Alaskan producer Tricia King. In addition to musical shows, the first Indian comedy show, starring Oneida comedian Charlie Hill, premiered in 2001. See http://www.airos.org to hear the latest offerings.

Although Indian Radio and AIROS are producing wonderful programming, both have been criticized for various reasons. Indian radio is still in the early stages, and the future may see new coalitions of producers and stations rising to meet the needs of Native America's youth. The 1990 Census showed that 50 percent of the Native population is under eighteen years, and that another 50 percent no longer live on reservations. How will Native radio meet the needs of the youth and those living in urban areas? That is Native radio's next challenge. What technologies will arrive that will bring Native radio to all homes that want to hear it, Indian or non-Indian? One of the potential solutions is literally up in the air. Will the promise of satellite radio stations—due to premiere in luxury autos later this year—be the answer? For now, the internet offers one solution. Don't touch that dial, just stay tuned to Indian radio, and hear what the future brings.

*Peggy Berryhill*
*Native Media Resource Center (NMRC)*

# U.S. and Canadian Native Press

**NEWSPAPERS: TRIBAL, CONFEDERATION, NATIVE NATION**

Tribal, confederation, and Native nation newspapers primarily publish news (political, social, educational, economic, health, sports) of and for their respective tribal communities and some national Indian news.

## UNITED STATES

### ◆ ALASKA

THE CHICKALOON NEWS
P.O. Box 1105
Chickaloon, AK 99674
(907) 745–0707

### ◆ ARIZONA

AK-CHIN O'ODHAM RUNNER
42507 W. Peters & Nall Rd.
Maricopa, AZ 85239
(520) 568–3665
Ak-Chin Indian Community; monthly

ATLATL
Native Arts Update
402 W. Roosevelt
Phoenix, AZ 85003
(602) 253–2731

AU-AUTHM ACTION NEWS
10005 E. Osborn Rd.
Scottsdale, AZ 85226

FORT APACHE SCOUT
P.O. Box 890
Whiteriver, AZ 85941
(520) 338–4813
White Mountain Apache; biweekly

HOPI TUTU-VEH-NI
Office of Public Relations
P.O. Box 123
Kykotsmovi, AZ 86039
(520) 734–2441
Hopi; biweekly

NAVAJO-HOPI OBSERVER
2608 N. Steves Blvd.
Flagstaff, AZ 86004
(602) 526–3881

NAVAJO TIMES
P.O. Box 310
Window Rock, AZ 86515
(520) 871–6641
Navajo; weekly

### ◆ CALIFORNIA

INDIAN HISTORIAN
1493 Masonic Ave.
San Francisco, CA 94117
(415) 626–5235

INDIAN LAW REPORTER
American Indian Lawyer Training Program
319 MacArthur Blvd.
Oakland, CA 94610
(510) 834–9333

NEWS FROM NATIVE CALIFORNIA
P.O. Box 9145
Berkeley, CA 94709
(510) 549–3564

WESTERN TRIBAL NEWS
36208 Church Road
Campo, CA 91906
(619) 478–2268

## ◆ COLORADO

AMERICAN INDIAN COMMUNITY MENTAL
  HEALTH NEWSLETTER
P.O. BOX 365
Greeley, CO 80631
(303) 692–0054

## ◆ DISTRICT OF COLUMBIA

INDIAN REPORTER
Friends Commission on National Legislation
245 Second St., NE
Washington, DC 20002
(202) 547–6000

SENTINEL
National Congress of the American Indian
900 Pennsylvania Ave. SE
Washington, DC 20003
(202) 546–9404

## ◆ FLORIDA

NATIVE PLAYWRIGHTS NEWSLETTER
Paul Rathbun, Director of Theater
Bravard Community College
1519 Clearlake Road
Cocoa, FL 32922

SEMINOLE TRIBE OF FLORIDA
6300 Stirling Road
Hollywood, Florida 33024
(800) 683–7800

## ◆ IDAHO

COEUR D'ALENE COUNCIL FIRES
Tribal Headquarters
850 A St., P.O. Box 408
Plummer, ID 83851
(208) 686–1800
Coeur d'Alene; monthly

SHO-BAN NEWS
P.O. Box 900
Fort Hall, ID 83203
(208) 478–3888
Shoshone-Bannock, Idaho; weekly

## ◆ IOWA

INDIAN YOUTH OF AMERICA NEWSLETTER
P.O. Box 2786,
Sioux City, IA 51106

## ◆ INDIANA

INDIAN AWARENESS CENTER NEWSLETTER
Fulton County Historical Society
37 E. 375 N.
Rochester, IN 46975
(219) 223–4436

## ◆ MARYLAND

DAYBREAK
P.O. Box 315
Highland, MD 20777–0098

NATIVE AMERICAN NEWS (NAN)
951 Pershing Drive
Silver Spring, MD 20910
(301) 587–1081

THE NATIVE EXPERIENCE
7406 Waldran Avenue
Temple Hills, MD 20748

## ◆ MICHIGAN

ANISHNABEG MOM-WEH NEWSLETTER
220 N. 30th St.
Escanaba, MI 49829
(906) 786–0055

BAY MILLS NEWS
Route 1
Brimley, MI 49715
(906) 248–3241

COUNCIL DRUM NEWS
Grand Rapids, MI
(616) 458–4078

INDIAN WORLD
Detroit, MI
(313) 535–9728

INTERNATIONAL NATIVE NEWS
(I.N.N.)
219 Manchester W.
Battle Creek, MI 49017–2221

KO-BUN-DA
Dowagiac, MI
(616) 782–6323

NATIVE SUN
Detroit, MI
(313) 535–2966

ODAWA TRAILS NEWSLETTER
Petoskey, MI
(616) 348–3410

TRIBAL OBSERVER
Saginaw Chippewa Indian Tribe
7070 East Broadway Road
Mt. Pleasant, MI 48858
(517) 772–5700 ext. 301

WIN AWENEN NISITOTUNG
Sault Ste. Marie Tribe of Chippewa Indians
206 Grennough Street
Sault Ste. Marie, MI 49783
(906) 635–4768

#### ◆ MINNESOTA

THE NATIVE AMERICAN PRESS
Ojibwe News
1819 Bemidji Ave.
Bemidji, MN 56601

#### ◆ MISSISSIPPI

CHOCTAW COMMUNITY NEWS
Communications Program
P.O. Box 6010
Philadelphia, MO 39350
(601) 656–1992
Mississippi Band of Choctaw; monthly

#### ◆ MONTANA

CHAR-KOOSTA NEWS
P.O. Box 98
51396 Highway 93 N.
Pablo, MT 59855
(406) 675–3000
Flathead (Salish and Kootenai); weekly

CROSS AND FEATHER NEWS
Tekakwitha National Center
1800 9th Ave., South, No. 20
P.O. Box 6768
Great Falls, MT 59406
(406) 727–0147

SPIRIT TALK PRESS
The Blackfoot Nation
Postal Drawer V
Browning, MT 59417
(406) 338–2882

WOTANI-WOWAPI
Fort Peck Assiniboine and Sioux Tribes
Box 1027
Poplar, MT 59225
(406) 768–5155

#### ◆ NEW MEXICO

AMERICAN INDIAN LAW CENTER
   NEWSLETTER
1117 Stanford NE
P.O. Box 4456, Station A
Albuquerque, NM 87196
(505) 277–5462

ELDER VOICES
National Indian Council on Aging
6400 Uptown Blvd. NE, Ste. 510-W
Albuquerque, NM 87110
(505) 888–3302

INDIAN ARTS AND CRAFTS ASSOCIATION
   NEWSLETTER
122 La Veta Dr., NE
Albuquerque, NM 87108
(505) 265–9149

JICARILLA CHIEFTAIN
P.O. Box 507
Dulce, NM 87528–0507
(505) 759–3242

MOUNTAIN LIGHT NEWS & VIEWS FROM
   THE SOUTHWEST
Southwest Learning Centers of Santa Fe
P.O. Box 8627
Santa Fe, NM 87504

## ◆ NEW YORK

AMERICAN INDIAN NEWS
Thunderbird American Indian Dancers
215 W. 23rd St.
New York, NY 10011
(212) 741–9221

INDIAN AFFAIRS
Association on American Indian Affairs
95 Madison Ave.
New York, NY 10016
(212) 689–8720

INDIAN TIME
P.O. Box 868
Mohawk Nation
Akwesasne, NY 13655
(518) 358–9531
Canadian Office
P.O. Box 30
St. Regis, PQ H0M 1A0
(613) 575–2063
Akwesasne/Six Nations; weekly

## ◆ NORTH CAROLINA

CHEROKEE ONE FEATHER
P.O. Box 501
Cherokee, NC 28719
(704) 497–5513
Eastern Band of Cherokee; weekly

## ◆ NORTH DAKOTA

MANDAN HIDATSA ARIKARA TIMES
Fort Berthold Communications Enterprise
HCR3, P.O. Box 1
New Town, ND 58763
(701) 627–4307
Mandan, Hidatsa, Arikara; weekly

## ◆ OKLAHOMA

AMERICAN INDIAN LIBRARIES NEWSLETTER
American Indian Library Association (AILA)
University of Oklahoma
401 W. Brooks
Norman, OK 73019

BISHINIK
Choctaw Nation of Oklahoma
P.O. drawer 1210
Durant, OK 74702–1210
(580) 924–8280

CHEROKEE ADVOCATE
P.O. Box 948
Tahlequah, OK 74465
(918) 456–0671
Cherokee Nation of Oklahoma; monthly

THE CHEROKEE OBSERVER
P.O. Box 1301
Jay, OK 74346–1301
(918) 253–8752

CHICKASAW TIMES
107 S. Constomnstant
Ada, OK 74820
(580) 436–2603
Chickasaw Nation; monthly

HOW-NI-KAN
1601 S. Gordon Cooper Dr.
Shawnee, OK 74801
(405) 275–3121
Citizen Band Potawatomi; monthly

MUSCOGEE NATION NEWS
P.O. Box 580
Okmulgee, OK 74447
(918) 756–8700
Muscogee (Creek) Nation; monthly

SAC AND FOX NEWS
Rte. 2, P.O. Box 246
Stroud, OK 74079
(918) 968–3526
Sac and Fox; monthly

THE UNITED KEETOOWAH BAND
    CHEROKEE NEWS
P.O. Box 746
Tahlequah, OK 74465–0746

## ◆ OREGON

THE NATIVE AMERICAN CONNECTION
    NEWSLETTER
P.O. Box 869-M
Oakridge, OR 97463

## ◆ PENNSYLVANIA

MINA-WIHE NATIVE AMERICAN
    NEWSLETTER
P.O. Box 59072
Pittsburgh, PA 15210

## ◆ SOUTH DAKOTA

**EAGLE'S VOICE**
Sinte Gleska College
Box 8
Mission, SD 57555
(605) 856–2321

**INDIAN COUNTRY TODAY**
1920 Lombardy Dr.
Rapids City, SD 57709
(605) 341–0011

**SICANGU SUN-TIMES**
P.O. Box 750
Rosebud, SD 57570–0750

**UNIVERSITY OF SOUTH DAKOTA BULLETIN**
Institute of American Indian Studies
Dakota Hall, Room 12
414 E. Clark St.
Vermillion, SD 57069
(605) 677–5209

**WICOZANNI WOWAPI GOOD HEALTH
  NEWSLETTER**
Native American Women's Health Education
  Resource Center
P.O. Box 572
Lake Andes, SD 57356
(605) 487–7072

## ◆ VIRGINIA

**AMERICA'S EAGLE**
P.O. Box 292
Mount Vernon, VA 22121
(703) 550–2375

**MOCCASIN TELEGRAPH**
2951 Ellenwood Drive
Fairfax, VA 22031–2038

**PATHFINDER NEWSLETTER**
American Indian Heritage Foundation
6051 Arlington Blvd.
Falls Church, VA 22044
(703) 237–7500

## ◆ WASHINGTON

**RAWHIDE PRESS**
Indian Tribes Of Spokane
Box 373
Wellprint, WA 99040
(509) 258–4581

**TRIBAL TRIBUNE**
P.O. Box 150
Nespelem, WA 99155
(509) 634–2200
Colville Confederated Tribes; monthly

**YAKIMA NATION REVIEW**
P.O. Box 151
Toppenish, WA 98948
(509) 865–5121

## ◆ WISCONSIN

**HO-CHAK WOR AK**
Wisconsin Winnebago Business Committee
P.O. Box 667
Black River Falls, WI 54615
(715) 284–9343
Wisconsin Winnebago; monthly

**INDIAN COUNTRY COMMUNICATIONS**
Route 2
Box 2900-A
Hayward, WI 54843
(715) 634–5226

**LAC DU FLAMBEAU NEWS**
P.O. Box 67
Lac du Flambeau, WI 54538

**MASINAIGAN**
Great Lakes Indian Fish & Wildlife Commission
P.O. Box 9
Odanah, WI 54861

**MOHICAN NEWS**
N8476 Moh He Con Nuck Road
Bowler, WI 54416

**NEWS FROM INDIAN COUNTRY**
Rte. 2, Box 2900 A
Hayward, WI 54843
(715) 634–5226

NEWS FROM THE SLOUGHS
Bad River's Monthly Newspaper
P.O. Box 51
Odahnah, WI 54861

SHENANDOAH NEWSLETTER
736 West Oklahoma St.
Appleton, WI 54914
Newsletter for Native-Nation Peoples to help them
understand their national/sovereign rights.

### ◆ WYOMING

AMERICAN INDIAN NEWS
P.O. Box 217
Fort Washakie, WY 82514

## CANADA

### ◆ BRITISH COLUMBIA

THE NUNATSIAQ NEWS
Box 8
Iqaluit, NT X0A 0H0
(819) 979–5357

WIKWEMIKONG NEWS
General Delivery
Wikwemikong, ON P0P 2J0

### NEWSPAPERS: STATE, PROVINCIAL, REGIONAL, CORPORATION

State, provincial, regional, and corporation newspapers primarily publish news of and for their respective constituencies and some national news.

## UNITED STATES

### ◆ ALASKA

THE COUNCIL
Tanana Chief Conference
122 First Ave., Suite 600
Fairbanks, AK 99701
(907) 452–8251
Alaska Natives; monthly

### ◆ MINNESOTA

DE BAH JI MON
Leech Lake Band of Ojibwe
6530 Hwy 2, NW
Cass Lake, MN 56633

### ◆ WISCONSIN

NEWS FROM INDIAN COUNTRY
Indian Country Communications
3831 N. Brinston Ave.
Hayward, WI 54843
(715) 634–5226
Great Lakes Region; semi-monthly

## CANADA

### ◆ ALBERTA

ALBERTA SWEETGRASS
15001–112 Avenue
Edmonton, AB T5M 2V6
(403) 455–2945

BLOOD TRIBE NEWS
TREATY SEVEN NEWS
P.O. Box 410
Standoff, AB T0L 1Y0
(403) 737–2121

### ◆ BRITISH COLUMBIA

HA-SHILTH-SA
P.O. Box 1383
Port Alberni, BC V9Y 7M2
(250) 724–5757
Nuu-cha-nulth Tribes; monthly

### ◆ SASKATCHEWAN

SASKATCHEWAN SAGE
15001–112 Avenue
Edmonton, AB T5M 2V6
(800) 661–5469
Monthly

## NEWSPAPERS: NATIONAL

### AKWESASNE NOTES
Mohawk Nation
P.O. Box 30
St. Regis, PQ H0M 1A0
(613) 575–2063
Occasional

### AKWESASNE NOTES
Kahniakehaka Nation Territory
P.O. Box 196
Rooseveltown, NY 13683–0196
(518) 358–9531 or 9535

### WIND SPEAKER
Aboriginal Multi-Media Society of Alberta
15001 112 Ave.
Edmonton, AB T5M 2V6
(780) 455–2700
Monthly

## NEWSPAPERS: URBAN

### THE CIRCLE
Minnesota American Indian Center
1530 East Franklin Ave.
Minneapolis, MN 55404
(612) 879–1790
Monthly

## MAGAZINES

### ABORIGINAL VOICES INCORPORATED
116 Spadina Avenue, Suite 201
Toronto, ON M5V 2K6
(416) 703–4577

### AMERICAN INDIAN ART MAGAZINE
7314 East Osborne Dr.
Scottsdale, AZ 85251
(602) 994–5445
Quarterly

### AMERICAN INDIAN BASKETRY
Institute for the Study of Traditional American
   Indian Art
P.O. Box 66124
Portland, OR
(503) 233–8131

### GREAT PROMISE CHILDREN'S MAGAZINE
1103 Hatteras
Austin, TX 78753

### INDIAN ARTIST MAGAZINE
544 South Guadalupe St.
Santa Fe, NM 87501
(800) 757–5278

### INDIAN GAMING MAGAZINE
The Public Gaming Research Institute Inc.
15825 Shady Grove Road
Suite 130
Rockville, MD 20850
(301) 330–7600

### INDIGENOUS WOMAN
Indigenous Woman's Network
P.O. Box 174
Lake Elmo, MN 55042

### NATIVE AMERICAS MAGAZINE
c/o Akwe kon (all of us) Press
300 Caldwell Hall
Cornell University
Ithaca, NY 14853
(607) 255–4308

### NATIVE NATIONS
Solidarity Foundation
P.O. Box 1201
Radio City Station, NY 10101–1201
(212) 765–9510
Bimonthly

### NATIVE PEOPLES MAGAZINE
Media Concepts Group, Inc.
P.O. Box 36820
Phoenix, AZ 85067–6820
(602) 252–2236
Quarterly

### NEWS FROM NATIVE CALIFORNIA
P.O. Box 9145
Berkeley, CA 94709
(510) 549–2802
State; quarterly

### TRIBAL COLLEGE
Chronicle of Higher Education Journal
American Indian Higher Education Council
P.O. Box 898
Chestertown, MD 21620
(410) 778–5628

### WAR DRUM STUDIOS
Native American Comic Books
1413 E. Adelaid, #B
Tucson, AZ 85719

WHISPERING WIND MAGAZINE
8009 Wales St.
Dept. 16
New Orleans, LA 70126–1952
(504) 246–3742

## ACADEMIC JOURNALS: UNITED STATES

### ABYA YALA NEWS JOURNAL
Of the South and Meso-American Indian Rights
  Center (SAIIC)
P.O. Box 28703
Oakland, CA 94604
(510) 834–4263

### AKWE: KON PRESS
American Indian Program
Cornell University
300 Caldwell Hall
Ithaca, NY 14853
(607) 255–4308
Quarterly

### AMERICAN INDIAN AND ALASKA NATIVE MENTAL HEALTH RESEARCH JOURNAL
National Center for American Indian and Alaska
  Native Mental Health Research
University of Colorado Health Sciences Center
4455 East Twelfth Avenue A011–13
Denver, CO 80220
(303) 372–3226
Three issues per year and one monograph

### AMERICAN INDIAN CULTURE AND RESEARCH JOURNAL
UCLA, American Indian Studies Centre Publications
3220 Campbell Hall, Box 951548
Los Angeles, CA 90095–1548
(310) 206–7508
Quarterly

### AMERICAN INDIAN LAW REVIEW
College of Law
University of Oklahoma
300 Timberdale Rd., Room 335
Norman, OK 73019
(405) 325–2840
Biannual

### AMERICAN INDIAN QUARTERLY
University of Nebraska Press
P.O. Box 880484
Lincoln, NE 68588–0484
(800) 755–1105

### THE FOUR DIRECTIONS
American Indian Literary Quarterly
Snowbird Publishing Co.
P.O. Box 729
Tellico Plains, TN 37385

### INDIGENOUS NATIONS JOURNAL
215 Fraser Hall
University of Kansas
Lawrence, KS 66045
(785) 864–2660

### JOURNAL OF ALASKA NATIVE ARTS
Institute of Alaska Native Arts
P.O. Box 80583
Fairbanks, AK 99708
(907) 437–7725
Quarterly

### JOURNAL OF AMERICAN INDIAN EDUCATION
Center for Indian Education
Arizona State University
College of Education
Farmer 415
Tempe, AZ 85287
(602) 965–6292
Triannual

### NATIVE AMERICAN RIGHTS FUND
LEGAL REVIEW
1506 Broadway
Boulder, CO 80302
(303) 447–8760
Quarterly

### NORTHEAST INDIAN QUARTERLY
American Indian Program at Cornell University
400 Caldwell Hall
Ithaca, NY 14853
(602) 255–6587

### STUDIES IN AMERICAN INDIAN LITERATURE
University of Richmond
Box 112
Richmond, VA 23173
Quarterly

### TURTLE QUARTERLY
Native American Center for the Living Arts
25 Rainbow Mall
Niagara Falls, NY 14303
Quarterly

WICAZO SA REVIEW
University of Minnesota Press
111 Third Avenue South, Suite 290
Minneapolis, MN 55401–2520
Quarterly

WIND RIVER JOURNAL
P.O. Box 10
Lander, WY 82520
(307) 332–2323
Shoshoni, Northern Arapaho

WINDS OF CHANGE
AISES Publishing, Inc.
1630 30th St., Suite 301
Boulder, CO 80301
Quarterly

## ACADEMIC JOURNALS: CANADA

ABSTRACTS OF NATIVE STUDIES
Bear Publishing
Department of Native Studies
Brandon University
1229 Lorne Ave.
Brandon, MB R7A 6A9
(204) 727–9640
Irregular

ARCTIC
Membership Services
Arctic Institute of North America
The University of Calgary
2500 University Drive N.W.
Calgary, AB T2N 1N4
(403) 220–7518

AYAANGWAAMIZIN: THE INTERNATIONAL
JOURNAL OF INDIGENOUS PHILOSOPHY
Lakehead University Northern and Regional Studies
    Committee
955 Oliver Road
Thunder Bay, ON P7B 5E1
(807) 343–8589
Semi-annual

CANADIAN JOURNAL OF NATIVE
    EDUCATION
Department of Educational Policy Studies
7–104 Education Centre North
University of Alberta
Edmonton, AB T6G 2G5
(403) 492–7625

CANADIAN JOURNAL OF NATIVE
    EDUCATION
First Nations House of Learning
University of British Columbia
1985 West Mall
Vancouver, BC V6T 1Z2
(604) 822–8940
Published twice yearly

THE CANADIAN JOURNAL OF NATIVE
    STUDIES
Publications Office
Department of Native Studies
Brandon University
Brandon, MB R7A 6A9
(204) 727–9640

CANADIAN NATIVE LAW REPORTER
Native Law Centre
University of Saskatchewan
101 Diefenbaker Place
Saskatoon, SK S7N 5B8
(306) 966–6189
Quarterly

EN'OWKIN JOURNAL OF FIRST NORTH
    AMERICAN PEOPLE
Theytus Books LTD
P.O. Box 20040
Penticton, BC V2A 5P9
Annual

ÉTUDES INUIT STUDIES
Études/Inuit/Studies
Pavillon Lemieux
Université Laval
Québec, Canada, G1K 7P4
(418) 656–2353
Twice yearly

FIRST NATIONS FREE PRESS LTD.
363 Sioux Road
Sherwood Park, AB T8A 4W7
(403) 449–1803
Published monthly

FIRST NATIONS GAZETTE
Native Law Centre
University of Saskatchewan
101 Diefenbaker Centre
Saskatoon, SK S7N 5B8
(306) 966–6189
Semi-annual

INUIT ART QUARTERLY
Inuit Art Foundation
2081 Merivale Rd.
Nepean, ON K2G 1G9
(613) 224–8189
Quarterly

JOURNAL OF ABORIGINAL ECONOMIC
    DEVELOPMENT
Cando, Suite 240
10036 Jasper Ave.
Edmonton, AB T5J 2W2
(403) 990–0303

THE JOURNAL OF INDIGENOUS STUDIES
Gabriel Dumont Institute of Native Studies and
    Applied Research
2nd Floor, 505–23rd Street East
Saskatoon, SK S7K 4K7
(306) 934–5073
Biannual

NATIVE SOCIAL WORK JOURNAL
Native Human Services Programme
University of Sudbury, Room #256
Laurentian University, Ramsey Lake Road
Sudbury, ON P3E 2C6
(705) 675–1151 ext. 5049
Annual

NATIVE STUDIES REVIEW
Native Studies Review
Native Studies Department

104 McLean Hall
University of Saskatchewan
Saskatoon, SK S7N 0W0
(306) 277–6178
Quarterly

NATIVE YOUTH NEWS
90 Sioux Road
Sherwood Park, AB T8A 3X5
(403) 449–1803
Monthly

SASKATCHEWAN HISTORY
Saskatchewan Archives Board
University of Saskatchewan
3 Campus Drive
Saskatoon, SK S7N 5A4
(306) 933–5832
Twice a year

SASKATCHEWAN INDIAN
Federation of Saskatchewan
Indian Nations
904–606 Spadina Crescent East
Saskatoon, SK S7K 0C4
(306) 667–1876
Quarterly

RECHERCHES AMERINDIENNES AU QUEBEC
6742 Rue Saint-Denis Dr.
Montreal, PQ H2S 2S2
(514) 277–6178

# Radio, Television, and Theater Organizations

## RADIO AND TELEVISION

## UNITED STATES

### ◆ ALASKA

ASRC COMMUNICATIONS, INC.
P.O. Box 129
Barrow, AK 99723
(907) 852–8633

KBBI
3913 Kachemak Way
Homer, AK 99603
(907) 235–7721

KBRW
P.O. Box 109
Barrow, AK 99723
(907) 852–6811

KCUK
Kashunanuit School
985 KSD Way
Chevak, AK 99563
(907) 858–7014

KDLG
675 Seward St.
P.O. 670
Dillingham, AK 99576
(907) 842–5281

KDLL
P.O. Box 2111
Kenai, AK 99611
(907) 283–8433

KIYU
P.O. Box 165
Galena, AK 99741
(907) 656–1488

KNBA
Distributed by Public Radio International
The Native American Calling, Wellness Edition
Distributed By AIROS
Koahinc Broadcasting Corporation
719 E. 11th Ave.
Anchorage, AK 99501
(907) 258–8890

KNSA
P.O. Box 178,
Unalakleet, AK 99684
(907) 624–3101

KOTZ
P.O. Box 78
Kotzebue, AK 99752
(907) 442–3435

KRBD
123 Stedman St.
Ketchikan, AK 99901
(907) 225–9655

KSKO
P.O. Box 70
McGrath, AK 99627
(907) 524–3001

KUHB
930 Tolstoi St.
St. Paul, AK 99660
(907) 546–2254

KYUK RADIO/ALASKA 1 TV
Pouch 468
640 Radio Street
Bethel, AK 99559
(907) 543–3131

#### ◆ ARIZONA

KGHR
P.O. Box 160
Tuba City, AZ 86045
(520) 283–6271 Ext. 188

KNNB
P.O. Box 310
Whiteriver, AZ 85941
(520) 338–5229

KRMH
Red Mesa Unified School District
HC61, 1000 Box 40
Teecnospos, AZ 86514
(520) 656–3511

KTNN/KWRK NAVAJO NATION RADIO
Box 2569
Window Rock Shopping Center
Window Rock, AZ 86515

NAVAJO NATION TELEVISION 5
P.O. Box 2310
Window Rock, AZ 86515
(520) 871–6655

#### ◆ CALIFORNIA

THE AMERICAN INDIAN HOUR
American Indian All Tribes Church
4009 South Halldale Ave.
Los Angeles, CA 90062
(323) 299–1810

KIDE
P.O. 1220
Hoopa, CA 95546
(530) 625–4245

NATIVE AMERICAN MEDIA
    ENTERPRISES, INC.
1015 Gayley, Suite 1024
Los Angeles, CA 90024
(310) 475–6845

NATIVE MEDIA RESOURCE CENTER
Peggy Berryhill
P.O. Box 1524
Bodega Bay, CA 94923
(707) 875–9835

#### ◆ COLORADO

KSUT
P.O. Box 737
Ignacio, CO 81137
(970) 563–0255

#### ◆ DISTRICT OF COLUMBIA

CENTER FOR PUBLIC BROADCASTING
Richard H. Madden
Andy Bruno
Radio Activities
401 9th St., NW
Washington DC 20004
(202) 879–9733

NATIONAL MUSEUM OF THE
    AMERICAN INDIAN
Caleb Strickland
Smithsonian Institute
Community Programs Office
470 L'Enfant Plaza, Suite 7103
Washington, DC 20560–0934
(202) 287–2020 ext. 152

NATIONAL PUBLIC RADIO (NPR)
635 Massachusetts Ave., N.W.
Washington DC 20001–3753
(202) 513–2000

O'NEAL-HOBBS ASSOCIATES
Loretta Hobbs
73 P St., N.W.
Washington, DC 20001
(202) 667–2777

KGLP
200 College Rd.
Gallup, NM 87301
(505) 863–7625

KSHI
P.O. Box 339
Zuni, NM 87327
(505) 782–4811

KTDB
P.O. Box 40
Pinehill, NM 87357
(505) 775–3215

## ◆ NEW YORK

CKON
P.O. Box 140
Rooseveltown, NY 13683
(518) 358–3426

## ◆ NORTH CAROLINA

WYRU
P.O. Box 0711
Red Springs, NC 28377
(910) 843–5946

## ◆ NORTH DAKOTA

KABU
7889 Hwy 57
St. Michjals, ND 58370
(701) 766–1995

KEYA
P.O. Box 190
Belcourt, ND 58316
(701) 477–5686

KMHA
HCR3, P.O. Box 1
New Town, ND 58763
(701) 627–3333

## ◆ OREGON

KWSO
P.O. Box 489
Warm Springs, OR 97761
(541) 553–1968

## ◆ SOUTH DAKOTA

KILI
P.O. Box 150
Porcupine, SD 57772
(605) 867–5002

KINI
P.O. Box 419
St. Francis, SD 57572
(605) 747–2291

KLND
HC 61, Box 1
McLaughlin, SD 57642
(605) 823–4661

## ◆ UTAH

KRCL
2308 500 W #105
Salt Lake City, UT 84101
(801) 363–3398

## ◆ WISCONSIN

WOJB
13386 W. Trepania Rd.
Hayward, WI 54843
(715) 634–2100

# CANADA

## ◆ ALBERTA

BLACKFOOT RADIO NETWORK
Indian News Media
P.O. Box 120
Standoff, AB T0L 1Y0
(780) 653–3301

CFWE 89.9 FM
Aboriginal Multi-Media Society Of Alberta
P.O. Box 2250
Lac La Biche, AB T0A 2C0
(780) 623–3333
(Native Perspective)

CFWE RADIO (NATIVE PERSPECTIVE)
Aboriginal Multi-Media Society Of Alberta (Ammsa)
15001 112th Ave.
Edmonton, AB T5M 2V6
(780) 455–2700

GREAT PLAINS PRODUCTIC
202–101359 82nd Ave.
Edmonton, AB T2E 1X1
(780) 439–1260

## ◆ BRITISH COLUMBIA

CANADIAN RADIO AND
  TELECOMMUNICATION CC
580 Hornby Street, Suite 530
Vancouver, BC V6C 3B6
(604) 666–2111

THE NATIVE VOICE
Box 45, Suite 71, 850 West Hastings
Vancouver, BC V6C 1E1
(604) 684–1951

NORTHERN NATIVE BROADCA
4562 B Queensway Dr.
Terrace, BC V8G 3X6
(250) 638–8137

## ◆ MANITOBA

CANADIAN RADIO AND
  TELECOMMUNICATION COMM
275 Portage Avenue, Suite 1810
Winnipeg, MB R3B 2B3
(204) 983–6306

NATIVE COMMUNICATIONS INC.
76 Severn Crescent
Thompson, MB R8N 1M6
(204) 778–8343

## ◆ NEW BRUNSWICK

MALISEET RADIO TOBIQUE FIRST
P.O. Box 3240
Perth Andover, NB E7H 5K3
(506) 273–4307

## ◆ NEWFOUNDLAND

OKALAKATIGET SOCIETY
P.O. Box 160
Nain, NF A0P 1L0
(709) 922–2955

## ◆ NORTHWEST TERRITORIES

### NATIVE COMMUNICATIONS SOCIETY OF THE WESTERN NORTHWEST TERRITORY
P.O. Box 1919
Yellowknife, NT X1A 2P4
(867) 920–2277

## ◆ NOVA SCOTIA

### CANADIAN RADIO AND TELECOMMUNICATION COMMISSION
Bank of Commerce Building
1809 Barrington Street, Suite 1007
Halifax, NS B3J 3K8
(902) 426–7997

## ◆ ONTARIO

### CANADIAN RADIO AND TELECOMMUNICATION COMMISSION
55 St. Clair Avenue, East Suite 624
Toronto, ON
(416) 952–9096

### CFBU
500 Glenridge Ave.
St. Catharines, ON L2S 3A1
(905) 688–5550 ext.103

### INUIT BROADCASTING CORPORATION (IBC)
301–331 Cooper St.
Ottawa, ON K2P 0G5
(613) 235–1892

### WAWATAY NATIVE COMMUNICATIONS SOCIETY
P.O. Box 1180, 16 Fifth Ave.
Sioux Lookout, ON P8P 1B7
(807) 737–2951

## ◆ QUEBEC

### CANADIAN RADIO AND TELECOMMUNICATION COMMISSION
Central Office
1 Pomanade Du Portage
Les Terrasses De La Chaudiere
Hull, QC K1A 0N2
(819) 997–0313

### CANADIAN RADIO AND TELECOMMUNICATION COMMISSION
405 de Maisonneuve Boulevard, East Suite B2300
Montreal, QC H2L 4J5
(514) 283–6607

### SOCIETE DE COMMUNICATIONS ATIKAMEKW MONTAGNAIS (SOCAM)
50 boul Bastien
Village des hurons (Wendake), QC G0A 4V0
(418) 843–3873

### TAQRAMIUT NIPINGAT, INC. (TNI)
185 ave. Dorval, Suite 501
Dorval, QC H9S 5J9
(514) 631–1394

## ◆ SASKATCHEWAN

### CANADIAN RADIO AND TELECOMMUNICATION COMMISSION
Cornwall Professional Bld.
2125 11th Avenue, Suite 103
Regina, SK
(306) 780–3422

## NATIVE AMERICAN THEATER ORGANIZATIONS

# UNITED STATES

For the most current information on theaters across North America, contact:

### ASSOCIATION FOR NATIVE DEVELOPMENT IN THE PERFORMING AND VISUAL ARTS
204 9 St. Joseph St.
Toronto, ON M4Y 1J6
(416) 972–0871

## ◆ ARIZONA

### ATLATL
49 E. Thomas Rd.
Phoenix, AZ 85012
(602) 277–3711

## ◆ CALIFORNIA

### AMERICAN INDIAN REGISTRY
1717 N Highland Ave., Suite 614
Hollywood, CA 90028
(323) 269–7014

NATIVE AMERICAN THEATRE ENSEMBLE
c/o Native American Media Enterprises, Inc.
1762 Corning St.
Los Angeles, CA 90035
(310) 841–0836

◆ **MINNESOTA**

OGITCHIDAG GIKINOOAMAAGAD PLAYERS
Indigenous Peoples Task Force
1433 E. Franklin Ave., Suite 1
Minneapolis, MN 55404
(612) 870–1723

◆ **NEW MEXICO**

INTER-TRIBAL INDIAN CEREMONIAL
    ASSOCIATION
226 West Coal
Gallup, NM 87301
(505) 863–3896

◆ **NEW YORK**

AMERICAN INDIAN COMMUNITY HOUSE
    THEATRE
Performing Arts Department
708 Broadway
New York, NY 10003
(212) 598–0100

AMERICAN INDIAN DANCE THEATRE
223 East 61st St.
New York, NY 10021
(212) 308–9555

OFF THE BEATEN PATH
c/o American Indian Community House Theatre
708 Broadway
New York, NY 10003
(212) 598–0100

SPIDERWOMAN THEATER
c/o American Indian Community House Theatre
708 Broadway
New York, NY 10003
(212) 598–0100

THUNDERBIRD AMERICAN INDIAN
    DANCERS
c/o American Indian Community House Theatre
708 Broadway
New York, NY 10003
(212) 598–0100

◆ **OKLAHOMA**

AMERICAN INDIAN THEATER COMPANY
P.O. Box 701926
Tulsa, OK 74170
(918) 838–3875

◆ **VIRGINIA**

CHICKAHOMINY RED MEN DANCERS
8836 Seddergh Dr.
New Kent, VA 23124
(804) 932–4406

# CANADA

◆ **ALBERTA**

FOUR WINDS THEATRE
P.O. Box 912
Hobbema, AB T0C 1N0
(780) 585–3904

◆ **BRITISH COLUMBIA**

LE-LA-LA DANCERS SOCIETY
4036 Trafalgar Crescent
Victoria, BC V8Z 3Y6
(250) 727–7958

RAVEN'S CRY THEATRE
P.O. Box 2264
Sechelt, BC V0N 3A0
(604) 885–4597

SEN'KLIP NATIVE THEATRE COMPANY
2902 29th Avenue
Vernon, BC V1T 1Y7
(250) 549–2921

SPIRIT SONG
454-C West Broadway
Vancouver, BC V5Y 1R3
(604) 877–1338

◆ **ONTARIO**

CENTER OF INDIGENOUS THEATRE SCHOOL
401 Richmond St. West
Toronto, ON M5V 1X3
(416) 506–9436

DEBAJEHMUJIG THEATRE GROUP
8 Debajehmujig Lane
Wikwemikong, ON P0P 2J0
(705) 859–2317

NATIVE EARTH PERFORMING ARTS INC.
720 Bathurst
Toronto, ON M5S 2R4
(416) 531–1402/4525

◆ **QUEBEC**

ONDINNOK INC.
705 1030 St. Alexandre
Montreal, QC H2Z 1E3
(519) 875–7175

◆ **SASKATCHEWAN**

SASKATCHEWAN NATIVE THEATRE
919 Broadway Ave.
Saskatoon, SK S7N 1B8
(306) 244–7779

# Native American Films and Video

## 500 NATIONS
Produced by Jim Wilson, Ralph Tornberg, Lisa
   Sonne, Jack Leustig, Roberta Grossman, Bernd
   Eichinger, and Kevin Costner; directed by
   Jack Leustig
1995

Eight-part documentary examining the history of indigenous people from North and Central America, pre-contact to the end of the nineteenth century. Featuring the voices of Eric Schweig, Gordon Tootoosis, Wes Studi, Gary Farmer, Tom Jackson, Tantoo Cardinal, Michael Horse, and Floyd Red Crow Westerman.

## ABNAKI: THE NATIVE PEOPLE OF MAINE
Produced, directed, and written by Jay Kent
1982

Shot near Passamaquoddy Bay in southeast Maine, this film provides short vignettes of contemporary Indian life which includes storytelling and discussion of the loss or preservation of the native language. Indian people express concern that their ways of life are sustained in the face of the white economy and land claims suits. Tribal members participated as production crew and advisors in the making of this film.

## ABORIGINAL RIGHTS: I CAN GET IT FOR YOU
   WHOLESALE
Produced by TV Ontario
1976

Discusses Native values on Indian ownership of land versus the European approach to land ownership. Includes historical photographs and on-site footage which traces the history of aboriginal rights in North America from Mexico to Canada, from Spanish conquest to modern times.

## ALCATRAZ IS NOT AN ISLAND
Directed by Jim Fortier
1999

An excellent documentary, memorializing the 1969–1971 occupation of Alcatraz by Indians of All Tribes, looks back at the policies and programs that led to the occupation. Includes interviews with the people who made the occupation the beginning of a new era of Indian self-determination and political activism. Featuring Millie Ketcheshawno, Adam Fortunate Eagle, Wilma Mankiller, John Trudell, and LaNada Means Boyer.

## ALLAN HOUSER
Produced and directed by Phil Lucas
1998

A brilliant introduction and beautiful tribute to the man and world-class, innovative art of Warm Springs Chiricahua Apache artist Allan Houser.

## AMERICAN COWBOYS
Directed by Cedric and Tania Wildbill
1999

Inspiring documentary telling the stories of two legendary rodeo cowboys, George Fletcher and Jackson Sundown, the first African American and the first Native American to compete in the World Title at the Pendleton Round-Up. The film uses accounts from historians, relatives, and tribal members to reveal the pride, frustration, and ultimate recognition experienced by two of the greatest cowboys ever.

## AMERICAN INDIAN ARTISTS, PART 1
Produced by KAET-TV, Arizona
1976

Six-part series profiles seven contemporary Native American artists who successfully fuse tradition with personal innovation.

## AMERICAN INDIAN ARTISTS, PART 2
Produced by Native American Public Broadcasting
   Consortium
1984

Three-program series continues the American Indian Artist Series, Part 1.

## AMERICAN INDIAN DANCE THEATRE: DANCES FOR THE NEW GENERATIONS
Directed by Hanay Geiogamah and Phil Lucas
1993

1993 Emmy Award nominee presenting the numerous forms of dance within Native American communities. Various dances from cultures across Native America illustrate the persistence and celebration of contemporary Native American heritage.

## THE AMERICAN INDIAN SERIES
Produced by University of California Extension
    Media Center; directed by Samuel A. Barrett
1961–1965

A series of fifteen films documenting the responses of Native people who were asked to reenact the skills and practices of their tribe; many offer oral traditions as a way of preserving their culture. Many of these films focus upon the California Indians, especially the Kashia Pomo and their traditions of basketry and dream dances.

## ANCIENT SPIRIT, LIVING WORD: THE ORAL TRADITION
Directed by Daniel Salazar
1983

A presentation of the traditional knowledge of Native Americans which spans centuries. Features oral tradition that has been passed by word of mouth from generation to generation and provides a link to the past and a key to the future.

## . . . AND WOMAN WOVE IT IN A BASKET. . .
Directed by Bushra Azzouz
1990

A rich account of Native life experienced and articulated by a Native woman basket weaver and daughter of a fishing family. Builds on the reflexive voice of the filmmaker/observer, and the mythic voice of Klickitat legend.

## ANGOON—ONE HUNDRED YEARS LATER
Produced, directed, and written by Laurence Goldin
1983

Explores the destruction of the Tlingit Indian village on Angoon, Alaska, by U.S. naval forces on 26 October 1882. A testimonial to the Tlingit culture that survived the attack. Explores the attack on Angoon through the pageantry and oratory of commemorative ceremonies held a century later.

## ANNIE MAE, BRAVE HEARTED WOMAN
Produced, written, and directed by Lan Brooke Ritz
1976

Addresses the issue of the unsolved murder of Annie Mae Aquash, an activist in many struggles for Indian rights, including Wounded Knee II. Demonstrated how and why Native Americans have acted to defend their rights and why the federal system is considered the primary abuser.

## APACHE MOUNTAIN SPIRITS
Produced by John H. Crouch; directed by
    Bob Graham
1985

Modern-day story interwoven with ancient Apache mythology follows a contemporary Apache Indian youth beaconed by the Gaan, Apache Mountain Spirits.

## THE ART OF BEING INDIAN: FILMED ASPECTS OF THE CULTURE OF THE SIOUX
Produced by South Dakota ETV
1976

Early cultural history of the Sioux illustrated with paintings and sketches by George Catlin, Seth Eastman, and Karl Bodner. Includes photographs by Edward Curtis, Stanley Morrow, and the St. Francis Mission, as well as contemporary paintings by Sioux artist Bob Penn.

## AS LONG AS THE GRASS SHALL GROW
Produced and written by Lynn Brown
1978

A series of eight programs designed for preschool age children that combine elements of Seneca life to teach children simple concepts and skills, such as how to count to ten in Seneca, while helping them build positive self-images. Teacher's materials are included with the film. Includes storytelling, how to make simple shapes, and identification of colors.

## BACKBONE OF THE WORLD: THE BLACKFEET
Produced by Pamela Roberts; directed by
    George Burdeau
1997

Documentary focusing on the modern existence and contemporary realities of the Blackfeet people, whose members live in both the United States and Canada.

## BACKROADS
Produced by Christine Walker and Phyllis Ellis;
    directed and written by Shirley Cheechoo
2000

Intriguing drama about a Native American woman accused of murder and the complex relationships that develop between family members and the reservation.

THE BALLAD OF CROWFOOT
Produced by Barrie Howells; directed by
    Willie Dunn
1968

Provides a history of the Canadian West by an Indian film crew that wished to reflect the traditions and problems of their people. Utilizes archival illustrations and photographs combined with song to retell the Canadian West history from an Indian point of view.

BEFORE THE WHITE MAN CAME
Produced and directed by John E. Maple
1920

An all-Indian cast presents life as lived in the days before the arrival of white people. Filmed on location in the Big Horn Mountains of Montana and Wyoming, the film incorporates authentic rites and ceremonies of the Crow people.

BLACK COAL, RED POWER
Produced by Shelly Grossman
1972

Provides an overview of the effects of strip mining on grazing lands and corn fields of the Hopi and Navajo people. Indian people present their viewpoints regarding the dislocation of some Navajo people in 1981 and the excessive energy needs of non-Indian cities in the Southwest, which are at the root of the rapid escalation of energy development on Indian land.

BLACK ROBE
Produced by Robert Lantos, Stephane Reichel, and
    Sue Millikan; directed by Bruce Beresford
1991

The tragic story about a seventeenth-century Jesuit priest and his attempts to "Christianize" New France. The priest is assigned to a dangerous journey to a remote mission outpost, and he and his Algonquian companions are captured and tortured by their Iroquois rivals. The picture's cinematography of the stark Quebec scenery earned much praise, and the performances by Canadian Indians August Schellenberg and Tantoo Cardinal were equally commendable.

THE BLACK HILLS ARE NOT FOR SALE
Produced by Sandra Osawa
1980

Provides historical background on the Fort Laramie Treaty of 1868 that guaranteed Sioux ownership of their traditional lands in the Black Hills. Sioux people explain why the Black Hills are not for sale and why they refuse to accept a cash settlement awarded by the U.S. Court of Claims in 1978 for the illegal taking of the Black Hills. Russell Means explains that the Black Hills are sacred lands, the spiritual center of the universe for the Lakota Nation, and sacred to several other tribes as well.

BONNIE LOOKSAWAY'S IRON ART WAGON
Directed by Wes Studi; written by Bruce King
1997

An interesting short-film presenting contemporary Native American life through the view of a young Native American woman, who hits the road on a weekend trip and films the adventure. Conflict emerges once her car breaks down, and a handsome stranger steals her possessions. The film presents a lively cast of characters featuring the acting of Valentina Lopez Firewalks and Wes Studi.

BORDERS
Produced by Duncan Lamb; directed by Gil Cardinal;
    written by Thomas King
1995

An amusing and appropriate short-film centering on a woman and her son who leave their reserve to visit the woman's daughter in the United States. The trip hits an obstacle once they reach the U.S.-Canadian border, and the woman declares her citizenship as Blackfoot—not Canadian, not American, just Blackfoot. An original and timely work. The cast includes Wendy Walker, Jeremy Owen, and Tina Louise Bomberry.

BOX OF TREASURES
Produced by the U'mista Cultural Society and Chuck
    Olin Associates
1983

Following the 1884 prohibition of the traditional potlatch ceremony, Kwakiutl artifacts were confiscated by the Royal Canadian Mounted Police and eventually sold or displayed in museums. This film documents the Kwakiutl Indians' efforts to reclaim these articles.

THE BROKEN CHAIN
Produced by Robert Sertner, Cleve Landsberg, Frank
    von Zerneck, and Randy Sutter; directed by
    Lamont Johnson; written by Earl Wallace
1993

The story of Joseph Brant's political alliances and military activities during the Revolutionary War that led to the break up of the Iroquois Confederacy. The cast includes Eric Schweig, Wes Studi, and Buffy Sainte-Marie.

## BROKEN JOURNEY
Produced and directed by Gary Robinson, Creek
    Nation Communications
1989

Life stories of Native American men and women who have been incarcerated because of alcohol-related problems. The film is intended for a young Native American audience and takes a serious look at the disease of alcoholism, which is portrayed as a deadly killer.

## BROKEN RAINBOW
Produced by Maria Florio and Victoria Mudd;
    directed by Victoria Mudd; narrated by
    Martin Sheen
1986

Addresses the relocation of traditional Navajo from their homes in Big Mountain, Arizona. Provides a sympathetic view of the Navajo perspective on the history of the lands in dispute and clarifies the issue of relocation while protesting the policy decisions leading to it. Also provides the viewer with an introduction to the federal government's interference and power over Indian issues. *Broken Rainbow* won the Academy Award for best documentary in 1985.

## BROKEN TREATY AT BATTLE MOUNTAIN
Produced and directed by Joel L. Freedman;
    narrated by Robert Redford
1974

Documents the struggle of the Western Shoshone to keep their twenty-four million acres of Nevada land, which was guaranteed by an 1883 treaty with the U.S. government. Includes interviews with traditional Shoshone, who discuss the spiritual importance of their land and their relationship to its natural resources. Explains what being a traditional Shoshone means through medicine practice, herb gathering, dance, and prayer

## CANADA'S ORIGINAL PEOPLES: THEN AND NOW
Produced by TV Ontario
1977

Two-part program contrasts the life of Native Canadians before the arrival of Europeans with contemporary Native life in Canada.

## A CANOE FOR THE MAKING
Produced by Bonita Siegel and Roxana Spicer;
    directed by George Bloomfield
Written by Duke Redbird
1995

A clever short-film representing contemporary cultural persistence. An elder, upon learning his granddaughter is being physically abused by her husband, tricks his grandson-in-law into coming to an isolated island in northern Ontario. They must build a canoe to return home and, in the process, the elder helps the young man begin healing his marriage and himself.

## THE CHACO LEGACY
Produced and directed by Graham Chedd
1980

An archaeological film discusses the pueblos that developed between fourteen hundred and one thousand years ago in Chaco Canyon, New Mexico. Various archaeological sites, particularly Pueblo Bonito, are examined. Looks at the interconnection of pueblos, communications among pueblos, how and why such a large society developed in a fragile desert environment, and, lastly, how we can account for its abrupt demise.

## CHEROKEE
Produced by Brenda Horsfield
1976

Cherokee history is reviewed with particular attention to their removal to Oklahoma from the east. The Cherokee community is seeking economic self-support by attracting tourists to a reconstructed seventeenth-century village and a pageant, "Unto These Hills."

## CHILDREN OF THE LONG-BEAKED BIRD
Directed by Peter Davis
1976

A young Crow Indian boy tries to erase stereotypes of Indians made infamous by Hollywood westerns. Provides a review of Native American life and history as well as contemporary events such as an all-Indian rodeo and a ride in a pickup to the Sacred Mountains of the Crow people.

## CIVILIZED TRIBES
Produced by Brenda Horsfield
1976

Provides a short glimpse of contemporary life of two of the five "civilized tribes" who were marched to Indian Territory, west of the Mississippi, because of the

1830 Indian Removal Act. Seminole and Choctaw Indian people discuss their living conditions, tourism as a source of income, and competition with white developers for remaining lands. Provides an overview of the conditions facing Indians on reservations in the southeastern United States and reflects on possible reactions to the development of tourism and dependence on federal agencies.

## CLASH OF CULTURES
Directed by Scott Nielson and Dick Blofson
1978

Four Lakota elders draw upon oral tradition to explain the cultural attitudes of the Indians and the clash of attitudes of white settlers, missionaries, and teachers with whom the Lakota were forced to come into contact on the Great Plains in the nineteenth century. Includes historical photos and informative interviews.

## CLEARCUT
Produced by Stephen J. Roth and Ian McDougall;
    directed by Richard Bugajski
1991

Presents the story of a naive young lawyer who defends an Indian land claim and becomes involved in a bizarre kidnapping ritual. Graham Greene plays the Indian whose anger explodes into rage as he cruelly mutilates his victim, a wealthy capitalist land developer. The Canadian film challenges the idea of Indians as victims and questions the conflict between Native rights and encroaching land developers.

## CONTRARY WARRIORS: A STORY OF THE
    CROW TRIBE
Produced and directed by Connie Poten, Pam
    Roberts, and Beth Ferris
1985

A depiction of the Crow tribe's century-long struggles with the U.S. government to retain their culture and reclaim land in southeastern Montana. The title refers to Crow warriors who showed contempt for their enemies by riding backwards into battle.

## CORN IS LIFE
Produced by Therese Burson and Donald Coughlin;
    directed by Donald Coughlin
1982

The documentary shows the importance of corn in Hopi life as an essential food and a holy substance central to religious life. Portrays traditional ways of preparing corn seed and planting, cultivating, and harvesting the crop. Demonstrates how older generations pass on knowledge to the young, and stresses the value Hopi place on cooperative work. Shows Hopi women grinding corn, then baking piki bread on a hot, polished stone.

## COYOTE MOUNTAIN
Produced by Craig Rosen and Jeffrey Mueller;
    directed and written by Jeffrey Mueller
1990

Friendship between a non-Indian girl and a traditional Navajo boy leads to greater intercultural understanding. The girl follows the boy to his hogan, where she meets his grandfather (a medicine man) and learns something about Navajo culture. All Indian roles are acted by Native people.

## COYOTE TALES
Produced by Kent Tibbitts; directed by Don Mose
1972

Five animated films in the Navajo language developed as Navajo language and culture-based curriculum models for Navajo schools. Told for amusement and instruction, the stories demonstrate how Coyote makes trouble for others but gets what he deserves in the end.

## CRAZY HORSE
Produced by Hanay Geiogamah and Salli Newman;
    directed by John Irving
1996

Examines the life of Oglala-Lakota leader Crazy Horse. The cast includes Michael Greyeyes, Irene Bedard, Lorne Cardinal, Wes Studi, August Schellenberg, Steve Reevis, and Gordon Tootoosis.

## CROOKED BEAK OF HEAVEN
Produced by BBC-Tribal Eye Series; written and
    narrated by David Attenborough
1976

Focuses on the potlatch ceremony of the Pacific Northwest as celebrated by the Gitskan, Haida, and Kwakiutl peoples. Provides an understanding of the ceremonial potlatch, a major feast at which gifts were given to every guest. Features the dance of the supernatural cannibal bird, the "crooked beak of heaven." A well-made, culturally sensitive television documentary.

## CROW DOG
Produced by Mike Cuesta and David Baxter;
    narrated by Rip Torn
1978

A profile of Leonard Crow Dog, one of the leaders of the seventy-one-day occupation of Wounded Knee, South Dakota, by members of the American Indian Movement in 1973. Presents current events from Crow Dog's perspective, viewing the racism of the Sioux's white neighbors and the manner in which the Bureau of

Indian Affairs seems bent on destroying Indian identity through assimilation. Provides an excellent view of a contemporary Indian activist who draws upon traditional beliefs and strengths to support a revival of Indian religion, culture, and language.

## THE CROW-MAPUCHE CONNECTION
Produced by Susan Stewart; directed by Arvo Iho
1991

This collaboration between Crow artist Susan Stewart and the Soviet director Arvo Iho presents an insightful concept of art and international solidarity for Native people.

## DANCE ME OUTSIDE
Directed by Bruce McDonald and David Webb;
　produced by Norman Jewison; written by John
　Frizzell and Bruce McDonald
1994

A highly entertaining drama, set in a present-day Northern Ontario reserve, with plot twists about pranks, adventures, and plans to avenge the murder of a Native woman. The cast includes Ryan Black, Adam Beach, Jennifer Podemski, Sandrine Holt, Gloria May Eshkibok, Lisa Lacroix, and Micheal Greyeyes.

## DANCES WITH WOLVES
Produced by Jim Wilson and Kevin Costner; directed
　by Kevin Costner
1990

The story that brought back the Indian-as-subject to Hollywood films. A sympathetic account of Sioux history as seen from the Indian perspective. The supporting cast features acclaimed performances by Graham Greene, Rodney Grant, and Floyd Red Crow Westerman.

## DANCING TO GIVE THANKS
Produced and directed by Mike Ferrell
1990

Omaha Indian tribe gives thanks to nature by having a ceremonial celebration, He-De-Wa-Chi or Festival of Joy. This video takes the viewer into the midst of the festival to learn how the event began, with participants—both young and old—being interviewed. Includes both traditional and fancy dancing by dancers wearing traditional regalia.

## DEAD MAN
Written and directed by Jim Jarnusch
1995

An original story of two men's comical and violent adventures taking place in many Indian contexts and with much Indian humor. A great performance by Gary Farmer, the Iroquois actor who plays a supporting role to Johnny Depp.

## DINEH: THE PEOPLE
Produced by Jonathan Reinis and Stephen Hornick
1975

Focuses on the impending relocation of Navajos from a joint-use land area surrounding the Hopi Reservation, located in the midst of the Navajo Reservation. Portrays the cultural and economic conditions under which the Navajo attempt to survive while trying to preserve their traditional way of life. Examines a broad range of reservation concerns, including unemployment, malnutrition, alcoholism, and health care issues.

## DISTANT VOICES. . . THUNDER WORDS
Produced by Nebraska Educational Television,
　Instructional Television Unit
1990

This program explores the influence of oral tradition on contemporary Native American literature, examining the role it plays in the development of cultures and societies.

## DOCTOR, LAWYER, INDIAN CHIEF
Directed by Carol Geddes
1986

Profiles the lives and achievements of several Canadian Indian women who are accomplished leaders in various professional fields. They discuss the importance of Native culture and spirituality to their life and work as well as the personal strength they have obtained from their own traditional values.

## THE DRUM IS THE HEART
Produced by Randy Croce
1982

Based on the theme that the values of the Blackfoot Nation are expressed in their modern-day celebrations. Features photographs of ceremonial costumes, tipi interiors, paintings of tipi covers, and interactions between people of all ages. A Blackfoot tribal historian speaks of the pride engendered by powwows and the continuity and contemporary relevance of Indian traditions.

## THE EAGLE AND THE CONDOR
Produced by KBYU-TV, Utah
1975

Indian students from North and South America discuss cultural differences and similarities.

## EARLY AMERICANS
Produced by Douglas Gordon; directed by
　Alan Penny
1976

Provides an overview of the early history of the North American Indian utilizing contemporary evidence.

Discusses the early migration theory of the Bering Land Bridge created during the Paleolithic period. Early North American sites discussed include Llano, Bat Cave, and Cahokia, and a variety of mound-builder sites. Utilizes dioramas, animated maps, and filmed views of archaeological digs.

## EARTHSHAPERS
Produced by Filmedia Ltd.
1975

Focuses on the Woodland Native people of the eastern United States and the mounds that they have created. Constructed in patterns of the eagle, bear, and deer, these mounds represent their spirituality and respect for all living creatures. Provides a window into the past as well as a vision into the future.

## EMERGENCE
Produced and directed by Barbara Wilk
1981

The story of the events that led to the entrance of the Dineh, the Navajo people, onto the surface of the earth out of a series of underworlds. Sacred colors, cardinal directions, the sacred mountains, and the four sacred plants are discussed. Traditional chants, which are versions of those sang in the original Dineh creation stories, are heard in the film.

## ESKIMO, FIGHT FOR LIFE
Produced by Educational Development Center with the National Film Board of Canada
1970

Presents the delicate balance between society and nature and the careful division of tasks among the different members of a group of Netsilik Inuit people camped together during the winter seal-hunting season. Shows how the Inuit adapt the materials from nature that permit their survival in an extreme environment. Provides a reenactment of the old Inuit lifestyle typical of the early twentieth century, showing men, women, and children at their daily activities: hunting seal, interacting, working skins, maintaining the fire for cooking and heating the igloo, and enjoying games.

## EXCAVATION OF MOUND 7
Produced by Division of Audiovisual Arts, National Park Service
1964

Concentrates on the evacuation of the Mound 7, the last and deepest site in Gran Quivira, New Mexico.

## EYES OF THE SPIRIT
Produced by Corey Flintoff; directed by Alexie Isaac
1984

Documents the creation of three traditional wooden masks designed by master carvers of the Yup'ik, the Eskimos of southwestern Alaska. Includes the performance of dances, songs, and stories that culminate in the return of masked dancing after more than fifty years' absence.

## FOLLOW ME HOME
Produced by Bonnie Duran, Eduardo Duran, Jennifer Newell-Easton, Alan Renshaw, Gary Rhine, Irene Romero, Peter Bratt, and Benjamin Bratt; written and directed by Peter Bratt
1997

Engaging, energetic film telling the story of four young artists traveling to Washington, D.C., to paint a mural on the White House. Solid cast includes Steve Reevis, Benjamin Bratt, and Jesse Borrego.

## FOREST SPIRITS—A SERIES
Produced by Northeast Wisconsin In-School Telecommunications, University of Wisconsin—Green Bay
1975–76

Seven half-hour programs focus on the Oneida and Menominee tribes and their heritage, education, relationship to the land, and dreams for the future.

## FORGOTTEN FRONTIER
Produced by KAET-TV, Arizona
1976

Program documents the architectural, political, social, and religious history of the Spanish mission settlements of southern Arizona. Maintains that Jesuit and Franciscan priests created a cultural climate for conversion rather than baptism by force.

## FOSTER CHILD
Directed by Gil Cardinal
1987

Traces the search for family and identity by Gil Cardinal, a young Métis filmmaker. "Métis" is a term used in Canada to refer to people whose ancestry is a mixture of Indian and non-Indian.

## FOUR CORNERS OF EARTH
Produced by Bureau of Florida Folklife and WFSU-TV
1985

Explores the roles and culture of Seminole women where traditional values keep pace with the forces of today's technology.

## FOUR DIRECTIONS: A CALL TO CONSCIOUSNESS
Produced by Veteran's Peace Action Teams
Year Unknown

Dineh elders at Big Mountain in northeastern Arizona tell their story of forced relocation by the U.S. government.

## GANNAGARO
Produced by Alexandra J. Lewis-Lorentz for WXXI-TV, New York
1986

Pieces together life in a seventeenth-century Seneca village based on the excavation of the Gannagaro site. Weaves together footage from the excavation and examines museum archives and collections. Describes an archaeological dig.

## GERONIMO
Produced by Hanay Geiogamah, Norman Jewison, and Chris Cook; directed by Roger Young.
1993

Tells the life of Chiricahua Apache leader Geronimo (Goyathlay). The notable cast includes Joseph Runningfox, Kimberly Norris, Michael Greyeyes, Jimmy Herman, and August Schellenberg.

## GERONIMO: AN AMERICAN LEGEND
Produced by Neil Canton, Walter Hill, and Michael S. Glick; directed by Walter Hill
1993

Focuses on the final attempts to capture Chiricahua Apache leader Geronimo (Goyathlay). Noteworthy performances by Wes Studi, Steve Reevis, Rodney Grant, and Carlos Palomino.

## THE GIFT OF SANTA FE
Produced by Marguerite J. Moritz
1989

Explores the Santa Fe Indian Market, the largest and most prestigious international juried competition of Native American artists in the world. Provides a glimpse of Native American pottery, jewelry, carvings, weavings, and paintings of the highest quality.

## THE GOOD MIND
Produced by Robert Stiles and the United Methodist Communications
1983

Explores the similarities between Christian and Native American beliefs as well as the practices of traditional Native American tribes.

## GRAND AVENUE
Produced by Robert Redford, Paul Aaron, Rachel Pfeffer, Tony To, and Greg Sarris; directed by Daniel Sackheim; written by Greg Sarris
1996

Based on an important novel written by Pomo/Miwok writer and scholar Greg Sarris, this two-part Home Box Office (HBO) miniseries is a refreshing drama unfolding the lives of three Native American families living in Santa Rosa, California. Presents modern, diverse images of Native Americans, illustrating the numerous challenges and realities that exist within contemporary Native American communities, and provides an excellent example of cultural persistence. Brilliant performances by Shelia Tousey, Tantoo Cardinal, Irene Bedard, Diane Debassige, Deeny Dakota, A. Martinez, August Schellenberg, and Cody Lightning.

## THE GREAT SPIRIT WITHIN THE HOLE
Produced and directed by Chris Spotted Eagle; narrated by Will Sampson, Jr.
1983

Documents how spiritual practices and beliefs have altered the lives of Native American prison inmates. The film advocates the reform of inmate religious practices and shows the tragedy of American Indians living in a society that does not comprehend their cultures or their values.

## HAROLD OF ORANGE
Produced by Dianne Brennan; directed by Richard Weise; written by Gerald Vizenor
1983

A comedy that confronts with ironic humor the relationship between reservation communities and the powerful bureaucracies upon which they rely. Harold and his "Warriors of Orange" present a fund-raising proposal to a philanthropic organization and escort its members on a fact-finding mission to a museum and a naming ceremony.

## HAUDENOSAUNEE: WAY OF THE LONG HOUSE
Produced and directed by Robert Stiles and John Akin
1982

Explains the principles and concepts that underlie traditional Haudenosaunee culture and lifeways. The matrilineal organization of family, clan, and society are explained, as is the people's spiritual relationship to the land and the natural world. Concludes by presenting a confrontation between Mohawk traditionalists and opportunists within their community.

## HEALTH CARE CRISIS AT ROSEBUD
Produced by South Dakota ETV
1973

Explores and offers some possible solutions to a serious shortage of physicians on the Rosebud Reservation in 1973. Focuses on health care problems faced by Native Americans and presents viable solutions.

## HERMAN RED ELK: A SIOUX INDIAN ARTIST
Produced by David Allen Silvian
1975

Herman Red Elk, a Yankton Sioux artist from Ft. Peck Agency, Montana, who is best known for his skin painting, speaks of his lifelong interest in art and of the influences of his grandfather's teachings. Red Elk views his style as ranging from realistic to abstract, while he still maintains the old traditions.

## HISATSINOM—THE ANCIENT ONES
Produced by Tim Radford
1976

Provides a glimpse into the spirit power of the Anasazi people of the Colorado and San Juan River valleys. Documents the paths of The Ancient Ones from their creation into the fourth world, with story, song, dance, and ceremony.

## HOHOKAM: AT PEACE WITH THE LAND
Directed by Bill Land
1976

Provides an archaeological overview of the history of the Hohokam people of the southwestern desert of North America. Discusses the introduction of ingenious irrigation works by the Hohokam people in their attempt to control the desert environment for agriculture and speculates on the possibility of contacts with Meso-America.

## HOME OF THE BRAVE
Produced and directed by Helena Solberg Ladd
1985

Examines Indian leadership today and Native Americans' increasing political awareness. The common history and philosophy of Indians in North and South America are emphasized along with the importance of indigenous people working for their rights. Concludes with an international conference on racism in Geneva, Switzerland, attended by Native leaders.

## HONEY MOCCASIN
Produced and directed by Shelley Niro
1998

Humorous story exposing rivalry between friends searching for stolen pow-wow outfits. Showcases an interesting character named Honey Moccasin and features a talented cast, including Tantoo Cardinal, Billy Merasty, Bernelda Wheeler, and Florene Belmore.

## THE HONOUR OF ALL—A SERIES
Produced by Phil Lucas
1987

Exciting three-part series tells the dynamic and inspiring story of Alkali Lake. A powerful educational package for use by those interested in achieving goals of sobriety.

## HOPI: SONGS OF THE FOURTH WORLD
Directed by Pat Ferrero
1983

A complex portrait of the Hopi cultural ideal, the Hopi Way, as it is seen through the eyes of many different community members. The world view and cultural practices of the Hopi are conveyed through interviews and filmed sequences of people taking part in the tasks of everyday life.

## HUCHOOSEDAH: TRADITIONS OF THE HEART
Produced and directed by Katie Jennings
1995

A documentary profiling the efforts of 77-year-old Upper Skagit elder, Vi Hilbert, to preserve Lushootseed as a living language.

## HUTEETL: KOYUKON MEMORIAL POTLATCH
Directed by Curt Madions
1983

Presents the final death rites for an Alaskan Native couple who died in 1981. A memorial potlatch, in the Koyukon tradition, signaling the end of mourning and the resting of the deceased spirits from a year of wandering was celebrated just over one year following the deaths. More than two hundred people joined with the one hundred residents of Hughess, Alaska, for the five days of celebrating.

## I AM DIFFERENT FROM MY BROTHER: DAKOTA NAME-GIVING
Produced by Native American Public Broadcasting Consortium
1981

Docudrama depicts the name-giving ceremony of three young Flandreau Dakota Sioux Indian children. Emphasizes the meaning and importance of being given their Indian names, and what it means to be "Indian."

## I'D RATHER BE POWWOWING
Produced by George P. Horse Capture; directed by
　　Larry Littlebird
1983

The documentary presents a portrait of an Indian whose suburban life is balanced by a strong traditional tie to his Native American heritage. Follows Al Chandler, a Gros Ventre Indian, on his journey to the Rocky Boy Reservation in Montana to take part in a weekend powwow.

## I WILL FIGHT NO MORE FOREVER
Produced by Stan Margulies; directed by Richard
　　T. Effron
1976

Educational video demonstrates how the greed for gold and land resulted in the war between the Nez Percé, led by the peace chief, Joseph, and the U.S. Army, led by Colonel Gibbons. The film presents the motives of both the Nez Percé and the ten separate commands of U.S. Cavalry that pursued them as they attempted to flee the United States for safety in Canada.

## IMAGES OF INDIANS
Produced by Robert Hagopian and Phil Lucas;
　　narrated by Will Sampson
1980

Five-part series examines Hollywood films as a source of Native American stereotypes that pervade popular culture and investigates the effect of the Hollywood image on the Indian's own self-image.

## IN THE HEART OF BIG MOUNTAIN
Produced by Sandra Sunrising Osawa
1988

Provides a background and brief history of the land dispute between the Navajos of the Big Mountain area and the Hopi of Arizona. Navajo elder Katherine Smith speaks of her connection to the land where her ancestors are buried and the importance of Big Mountain as a spiritual center.

## IN THE WHITE MAN'S IMAGE
Produced by Native American Public Broadcasting
　　Consortium
1991

The documentary explores the experiment of the federal government to turn American Indians away from Native cultures and religions and to assimilate them into the white culture during the late nineteenth and early twentieth centuries. Focuses on Captain Richard Pratt's experiment of teaching Indians to read and write English and putting them in uniforms and drilling them like soldiers. "Kill the Indian and save the man" was Pratt's motto. Native Americans who attended government boarding schools help tell the story of the experiment gone bad and its consequences for Native Americans.

## IN WHOSE HONOR?
Produced and directed by Jay Rosenstein
1997

A critical look at the time-honored tradition of using American Indians as mascots and nicknames by professional, collegiate, and high school teams. Follows the story of graduate student Charlene Teters as she challenges the University of Illinois to abolish the use of Chief Illiniwek as a team mascot. A powerful film which includes a passionate backlash by University of Illinois administrators, trustees, fans, and Illinois state legislators.

## INCIDENT AT OGLALA
Produced by Arthur Chobanian; directed by Michael
　　Apted; narrated and executive produced by
　　Robert Redford
1991

A documentary of the events leading up to the 26 June 1975, shoot-out on the Pine Ridge Indian Reservation in South Dakota that left two Federal Bureau of Investigation (FBI) agents and one American Indian dead. The subsequent prosecution of the American Indian Movement is chronicled.

## INCIDENT AT RESTIGOUCHE
Directed by Alanis Obomsawin
1984

Documents the arrest and trial of several Micmac Indians for salmon fishing in Restigouche, Quebec. The provincial government not only suppressed the Micmac claim to sovereignty but urged its police to use excessive force against Indian protestors. A courageous film that confronts traditional racism and reveals the gap between French Canadian and Indian societies.

## INDIAN ARTS AT THE PHOENIX HEARD
　　MUSEUM—A SERIES
Produced by Jack Peterson; directed by Dick
　　Peterson
1975

Six-part series incorporates the extensive collection of Southwest Native American artifacts of the Heard Museum. Explores Native American art, basketry, painting, pottery, textiles, silversmithing, and Kachina doll sculpting. Provides discussion regarding the understanding of the artisans' particular cultural art form and the influences from within a culture and between cultures.

## INDIAN CAMP
Produced, directed, and screenplayed by
  Brian Edgar
1990

Based upon a short story by Ernest Hemingway, Indian Camp reveals the cultural barrier between Indian and white societies as seen through the eyes of a young boy. The performance by Indian actors in pain is disturbingly realistic.

## INDIAN LEGENDS OF CANADA
Produced by Via le Monde; directed by Daniel
  Bertolino
1981–83

Thirteen-part series recounts the legends of Indian people in eastern and northern Canada. The legends are enacted by largely non-professional Native casts from Ontario and Quebec. Special care is given to authentic clothing, housing, culture, and traditions of the Native people.

## ISHI, THE LAST YAHI
Produced and directed by Jed Riffe and Pamela
  Roberts
1992

A documentary on the life of Ishi, the last of the Yahi Indians of northern California, offers a unique view of California Indian life and features Ishi's voice, preserved in wax recordings.

## IT CAN'T RAIN ALL THE TIME
Produced by The American Indian Community
  House, Inc.; directed by Lance Richmond
1995

The suicide and substance abuse rates for Native American teens are the highest among all racial/ethnic groups in the United States. This short-film addresses the issues surrounding youth suicide and substance abuse. Irene Bedard provides an inspiring performance.

## ITAM HAKIM, HOPIIT
Produced, directed, and photographed by Victor
  Masayesva, Jr.
1984

A skillful vision of the Hopi world as seen from within the culture. Hopi independent filmmaker Victor Masayesva, Jr., and an all-Hopi crew present the life story of one of the last members of the tribe's storytelling clan. The oral history account (which includes the Hopi-speaking voice played simultaneously with English translation) covers various epochs in Hopi history. The visual imaging combined with a multi-level sound track is powerful.

## JOURNEY TO THE SKY: A HISTORY OF THE
##   ALABAMA COUSHATTA INDIANS
Directed, written, and photographed by Paul Yeager
1982

Chronicles the passage of hunting and gathering cultures that once flourished in the southeastern United States. The film follows, through use of a folktale, the Alabama Coushatta in their futile struggle to preserve their lifeways after their first contacts with Europeans and through their migration west.

## KEEP YOUR HEART STRONG
Produced by Deb Wallwork, Prairie Public
  Television
1986

The documentary gives an inside view of contemporary Native American culture through the powwow. Features interviews with Indian historians and elders who provide insight into the arts of dance and song-making as well as the relevance of traditional values to contemporary Indian life.

## LACROSSE: THE CREATOR'S GAME
Produced by Scott Calbeck and Kem Murch;
  directed by Kem Murch
1994

Documentary examining the origin, history, and present status of North America's oldest team sport.

## THE LAKOTA: ONE NATION ON THE PLAINS
Directed by Frank Cantor; narrated by N.
  Scott Momaday
1978

Provides a Lakota understanding of the history of the Great Plains. The film, narrated by N. Scott Momaday, utilizes traditional Lakota beliefs to show that all things come together in a sacred circle that forms a natural order of harmony. Utilizes imaginative photographic presentation of art and artifacts.

## LAKOTA WOMAN: SIEGE AT WOUNDED KNEE
Produced by Hanay Geiogamah and Lois Bonfiglio;
  directed by Frank Pierson
1994

Based on the best-selling autobiography co-authored by Mary Crow Dog and Richard Erdoes, the film chronicles the 1973 occupation of Wounded Knee through the eyes of Mary Crow Dog. Talented cast includes Irene Bedard, Pato Hoffman, Michael Horse, Tantoo Cardinal, August Schellenberg, Joseph Running Fox, Tim Sampson, and Floyd Red Crow Westerman.

## THE LAST OF HIS TRIBE
Produced by John Levoff and Robert Lovenheim;
    directed by Harry Hook
1992

Based upon *Ishi: In Two Worlds* by Theodora Kroeber, this made-for-television production recounts the life of the California Yahi Indian and his relationship with anthropologist Alfred Kroeber. Often labeled as "the last wild Indian to survive in North America," Ishi spent his last years at the University of California Museum in Berkeley, working closely with the staff and teaching them about Native culture. Graham Greene is featured in the title role.

## THE LAST OF THE MOHICANS
Produced by Michael Mann and Hunt Lowry;
    directed by Michael Mann
1992

This most recent remake of James Fenimore Cooper's tale of Hawkeye and his Indian companions, set during the eighteenth-century French and Indian Wars, contains some well-staged battle sequences. Supporting roles are played by Indian actors Wes Studi, Eric Schweig, and Russell Means.

## LAXWESA WA: STRENGTH OF THE RIVER
Produced by Cari Green and Barb Cranmer; directed
    by Barb Cranmer
1995

The traditions of three native communities living on the west coast of Canada are portrayed with dramatic effect.

## THE LEARNING PATH
Directed by Loretta Todd
1991

Recounts the experiences of three remarkable Native women who are leading educators in Canada. Their experiences teaching young Native children at residential schools in Edmonton motivated them to preserve their language and culture.

## LEGACY IN LIMBO
Produced by WXXI-TV, New York
1990

Discusses the vast collection of Native American artifacts held by the Museum of the American Indian in New York City. Emphasizes that only a small portion of the more than one million artifacts are on display. Discusses the threats, debates, and lawsuits that have resulted from attempts to move the museum to a more suitable location, as well as the fact that while the legal system moves slowly, the legacy of many Indian cultures hangs in the balance.

## LENAPE: THE ORIGINAL PEOPLE
Produced, directed, and written by Thomas Agnello
1986

Presents a brief history of the Delaware, or Lenape, Indian people who lived originally in parts of New Jersey, Pennsylvania, and Delaware. Focuses on two tribal elders who retained the language and knowledge of traditional customs and beliefs. Describes the Big House Ceremony, which was last held in 1924. Scenes of a 1983 reunion of Lenape people are included.

## LIVE AND REMEMBER
Directed by Henry Smith
1987

Filmed on the Rosebud Sioux Reservation, this documentary presents Lakota Sioux oral tradition, song, and dance; and discusses Lakota medicine, the spirit world, and perceptions of bicultural lifestyle. Discussions with Lakota elders, medicine men, and traditional dancers are included.

## THE LONG WALK
Produced by KQED-TV, San Francisco
1970

Explores the contemporary life of the Navajo people and describes their history. A Navajo woman recounts the Long Walk of the Navajo, when the tribe was driven from their homeland and onto the Bosque Redondo, the most inhospitable land in the Southwest. The film demonstrates how strong the Navajo way of life remains and points to a hopeful future.

## LOYALTIES
Produced by William Johnston, Anne Wheeler, and
    Ronald Lillie; directed by Anne Wheeler
1985

A wealthy British doctor and his family move to a northern Canadian community and hire a Métis woman as their housekeeper. The doctor is distant toward his own wife, but unleashes his hostility when he rapes the Métis woman's adolescent daughter. A disturbing film that depicts how women are often trapped by their own emotions. Cree-Métis actress Tantoo Cardinal gives an unforgettable performance as the Indian woman.

## MAKING A NOISE: A NATIVE AMERICAN MUSICAL JOURNEY WITH ROBBIE ROBERTSON

Produced by Dana Heinz Perry

1998

Robbie Robertson, Mohawk musician, returns to the Six Nations Reserve with personal explorations of his musical past and present.

## MAN OF LIGHTNING

Produced by Gary Moss for Georgia State University

1982

Action-packed tale of a young man's struggle to adulthood is based on two Cherokee Indian legends. Portrays the world of the Cherokee in the years before European contact and highlights the demanding morality and complex spirit world of the Cherokee.

## A MATTER OF RESPECT

Produced and directed by Ellen Frankenstein

1992

Portrays a diverse group of people, each expressing their own sense of what it is to be Tlingit in today's world.

## MEDICINE RIVER

Directed by Stuart Margolin; written by
    Thomas King

1992

Based on the skillful novel written by Cherokee/Greek writer Thomas King. A hilarious movie that presents a contemporary image of a Native community. A Native photojournalist flies to Medicine River following his mother's death. Through a series of amusing misadventures, he recognizes the importance of community. Superb performances by Graham Greene, Sheila Tousey, Tom Jackson, Michael C. Lawrenchuk, Ben Cardinal, Tina Louise Bomberry, Byron Chief Moon, Jimmy Herman, and Maggie Black Kettle.

## MENOMINEE

Produced by Educational Communications,
    University of Wisconsin-Green Bay

1974

Filmed in 1974, this work was produced while legislation was pending in the U.S. Congress to restore the Menominee's tribal status. Three weeks following the first telecast of *Menominee*, federally recognized tribal status was restored. Examines the historical development of the many social and political problems faced by the Menominee Indians, including absence of industry, need for welfare support, and conflict within school systems, following the termination of tribal status by the federal government.

## MINORITIES IN AGRICULTURE: THE WINNEBAGO

Produced by Ralph A. Swain, Briar Cliff College

1984

The documentary highlights economic development programs of the Winnebago tribe of Nebraska. The tribe's canning center, grocery store, farm operation, and corn harvest are all described through interviews with the Winnebago tribal chairperson and others.

## MORE THAN BOWS AND ARROWS

Directed by Roy Williams; narrated by N.
    Scott Momaday

1978

Demonstrates the impact of Native American culture on American society. The film opens with footage of the Kwakiutl shot in 1912 by Edward Curtis, accompanied by rock music by Tom Bee. Focuses on, among other things, Indian democratic tradition, with examples of the Iroquois Confederacy and the Navajo tribe, and architectural developments from the Anasazi dwelling of Mesa Verde to the mound builder societies of the southeastern United States. Produced by a Native American-owned company that utilized Indian experts as consultants in the making of the film.

## MOTHER CORN

Produced by Brian Capener

1977

Examines the historical significance of various types of corn among the Hopi and Pueblo cultures and traces the symbolism of corn across generations to today's modern uses. Explores the relationship of corn to the rain dances, kivas, and Kachina dolls.

## THE MYSTERY OF THE ANASAZI

Produced by WGBH-TV, Boston; directed by
    Russ Morash

1976

Discusses archaeological efforts to discover who the Anasazi, "the ancient ones," were. Located near the point where Colorado, Utah, Arizona, and New Mexico meet, the Anasazi became agriculturalists and constructed an extensive dwelling system seen today at Mesa Verde, Colorado; Chaco Canyon, New Mexico; and Canyon de Chelly, Arizona. The film stresses many questions that remain unanswered; for instance, Why did the Anasazi abruptly abandon their cliff dwellings and become mesa top dwellers some seven hundred years ago?

## MYTHS AND THE MOUNDBUILDERS

Produced, directed, and written by Graham Chedd

1981

Reconstructs the history of ideas surrounding the tens of thousands of earthen mounds that dotted the central United States in the nineteenth century. Debunks earlier theories that the mounds were engineering feats created by a mysterious, lost race. The film points out that the mounds were actually built by the ancestors of the numerous Native American groups that still inhabit the central states. Discusses the two major mound-building groups: the Hopewell and the Mississippian cultures.

## NATIONAL MUSEUM OF THE AMERICAN INDIAN
Produced by Dan Jones; Directed by Lisa Donner
1993

An overview and introduction to the origins and plans for the creation and building of the National Museum of the American Indian.

## NATIONS WITHIN A NATION
Produced by Department of Sociology, Oklahoma
　　State University
1988

Examines the historical, legal, and social background of Native American tribal sovereignty. Examples of tribal governments in operation are drawn from Taos Pueblo, the Mescalero Apache tribe, the Creek Nation, and the Sac and Fox tribe.

## NATIVE AMERICAN IMAGES
Produced by Carol Patton Cornsilk/Southwest Texas
　　Public Broadcasting Council
1984

Profiles the lives, philosophies, and works of three contemporary artists—two Native American and one non-Native American living in Austin, Texas.

## NATIVE VETERANS: A WARRIOR'S STORY
Produced and directed by Joe Beardy
1997

Resourceful documentary profiling the contributions Native Canadians made in World War I, World War II, and the Korean War.

## NATURALLY NATIVE
Produced by Valerie Red-Horse, Dawn Jackson, and
　　Yvonne Russo; directed by Valerie Red-Horse and
　　Jennifer Farmer; written by Valerie Red-Horse
1998

The first film written, directed, produced, and acted by Native American women. Also, the first mainstream dramatic work to be funded entirely by an American Indian Nation (Mashantucket Pequot Tribe of Connecticut). A unique story following the lives of three sisters and their efforts to establish their own Native cosmetics business. The film examines each sister's own issues and the challenges they face at home and in the corporate world. Impressive performances by Kimberly Norris-Guerrero, Irene Bedard and Valerie Red-Horse.

## NAVAJO
Produced by KBYU-TV, Utah
1979

Two young Navajos learn about their matriarchal society, the history of the Navajo Nation, and the Navajo desire to live in peace and harmony with the earth. Suggests that educational and technological changes are partly responsible for the erosion of traditional Navajo culture.

## NAVAJO CODE TALKERS
Produced by Tom McCarthy and KENW-TV
1981

Documents the vital role a small group of Navajo marines played in the South Pacific during World War II, when they confused Japanese code breakers by creating an unbreakable Navajo code. Archival footage of Navajo life in the 1940s and from World War II add considerable reality to the film.

## THE NEW PEQUOT: A TRIBAL PORTRAIT
Produced by Connecticut Public Television
1990

Explores the history and future of the Mashantucket Pequot Indians. The documentary tells a dramatic story of how the tribe has overcome many obstacles, including the dissolving of the tribe by the Treaty of Hatford, signed in 1638. A history that looks at the troubled but rich heritage of one of the most powerful Indian tribes in America and at the amazing twentieth-century resurgence of the tribe.

## NEZ PERCÉ—PORTRAIT OF A PEOPLE
Produced by Phil Lucas
1978

Provides a fascinating and accurate history of the Nez Percé Indians, with archival photos, personal stories, and breath-taking scenery. Begins with the peaceful interaction with white expeditioners, Lewis and Clark, and includes the eventual takeover of more than 90 percent of Nez Percé lands by non-Indians.

## NI'BTHASKA OF THE UMONHON—A SERIES
Produced by Chet Kincaid/Nebraska Educational
　　Television Network for the Nebraska Department
　　of Education-ITV Services
1987

Three-part series follows a thirteen-year-old Omaha boy through a first summer of manhood. Provides a historically accurate presentation of Native American life and culture in the 1800s.

## NO ADDRESS
Directed by Alanis Obomsawin
1988

The documentary examines problems of the Native Canadian people who came to Montreal in search of a better life. Without money or work, these people quickly join the city's growing homeless population and become more and more separated from their traditional values. Discusses their hardships and shows how organizations have helped them survive.

## ON THE PATH TO SELF-RELIANCE
Produced by Peter J. Barton
1982

This documentary of the Seminole tribe of Florida utilizes interviews with tribal employees to describe the Seminole's thriving cattle operation and agriculture and aquaculture programs. Demonstrating that the Seminole tribe is realizing their goal of self-sufficiency, the film points out that the proceeds from bingo have been used to pay back federal monies and that the tribe is exploring new avenues of industrial development.

## OUR PAST IS OUR FUTURE
Directed by Daniel Jumper
1999

An important documentary presenting the historical and cultural significance of Susie Jim Billie, a Seminole elder. She plays a vital role in the continued existence of the Seminole Tribe of Florida by helping her people retain their cultural identity.

## OUR SACRED LAND
Produced and directed by Chris Spotted Eagle
1984

Provides an overview of the importance of sacred sites to the preservation of Native American religions. Shows how strongly sacred places and practices continue to be valued by Native people. Focuses on the continuing struggle of the Sioux to regain title to the Black Hills of South Dakota, which were guaranteed them by the 1868 treaty of Fort Laramie. Examines the reasons why many Sioux people have refused to accept the $105 million awarded by the U.S. Supreme Court for the illegal taking of the lands.

## PAHA SAPA: THE STRUGGLE FOR THE BLACK HILLS
Produced by Mel Lawrence and George Amiotte; directed by Mel Lawrence; written by Cree McCree, George Amiotte, Rubie Sooktis, and Mel Lawrence
1993

Documentary examining the illegal appropriation of the Black Hills by the United States government and the present struggle of Lakota and Cheyenne people to regain their sacred land.

## PEOPLE OF THE FIRST LIGHT—A SERIES
Produced by Glenn Suprenard; directed by Russell M. Peters
1979

Seven-part series demonstrates how Native Americans in southern New England have maintained their cultural identity with dance and art and a strong sense of family and community. Shows how tribal history and tradition are integrated into the daily activities of present-day Native American people.

## THE PEYOTE ROAD
Produced and directed by Gary Rhine and Fidel Moreno
1992

The documentary addresses the 1991 U.S. Supreme Court Smith case, which raised concerns throughout the religious community about the "free exercise" clause of the U.S. Constitution. The court denied Native Americans protection under the First Amendment regarding religious liberty for the sacramental use of peyote under certain circumstances.

## THE PLACE OF THE FALLING WATERS
Produced by Frank Tyro and Daniel Hurt; directed by Roy Big Crane and Thompson Smith
1992

Focuses on the complex and volatile relationship between the Confederated Salish, and Kootenai tribes arising from a major hydroelectric dam situated on the Flathead Indian Reservation.

## POWER
Produced by Glen Salzman; directed by Magnus Isacsson
1996

A sharp documentary focusing on the Cree of northern Quebec and their battle with the Quebec government and its state-owned power utility, Hydro-Quebec. A compelling account of Cree's efforts to stop the second phase of the massive James Bay hydroelectric project on the Great Whale River.

## POWWOW HIGHWAY
Produced by Jan Wieringa; directed by Jonathan Wacks
1988

The adventures of two American Indian buddies who travel across the country to bail a sister out of jail.

As the lively pair journey through the country's reservations and stop at powwows and sacred sites, one teaches the other the importance of cultural identity. The film features Gary Farmer in the lead role, with appearances by Graham Greene and John Trudell.

## PUEBLO PEOPLES: FIRST CONTACT
Directed and co-produced by George Burdeau
1990

Portrays the first encounter between Pueblo Indians of the southwest and the Spanish explorers who were searching for the Seven Cities of Gold. Opens with the Zuni account of the tribal past and features a strong Native American point of view.

## THE REAL PEOPLE—A SERIES
Produced by KSPS-TV, Spokane
1976

Nine-part series made by and about American Indian cultures of the northwest Plateau highlights important aspects of past and current life, both on and off reservation, and provides an important Indian point-of-view.

## RETURN OF THE SACRED POLE
Directed by Michael Marrell
1990

The documentary tells the story of how the Sacred Pole of the Omaha tribe of Nebraska was ultimately reclaimed by the tribe. The pole had been confiscated in 1888 and placed in the Peabody Museum, thus depriving the tribe of its central element of tribal identity.

## RICHARD CARDINAL: CRY FROM A DIARY OF A MÉTIS CHILD
Directed and written by Alanis Obomsawin
1986

Based upon the tragic case of a young Métis boy, this film recreates his life of passing from one foster home to another. The boy's suicide ultimately exposed the flaws in Canada's child welfare system and brought about a successful campaign to reform existing legislation.

## THE RIDE TO WOUNDED KNEE
Directed by Robert Clapsaddle
1992

Starting with the killing of Sitting Bull in December 1890, this film tells the true story about the path of his followers as they flee the U.S. Cavalry and eventually end up at Wounded Knee Creek, where three hundred men, women, and children are massacred by General George Armstrong Custer's old regiment, the Seventh Cavalry.

## RIVER PEOPLE: BEHIND THE CASE OF DAVID SOHAPPY
Produced by Filmmakers Library
1990

Unfolds the events behind the 1982 arrest of David Sohappy and his son, both of whom are detained for illegally catching and selling 344 salmon out of season. Explores the historic conflict over the resources of the Columbia River and the political controversy over fishing rights and religious freedom.

## ROCKIN' WARRIORS
Directed by Andy Bausch
1997

Energetic documentary profiling Native American rock 'n' roll as a form of indigenous cultural expression and an exploding music phenomenon in Europe.

Shot on location in Arizona, Germany, and New Mexico. Includes profiles, interviews, and performances by Joy Harjo & Poetic Justice, Ulalli, John Trudell, Keith Secola, Buffy Sainte-Marie, and Robert Mirabal.

## SEEKING THE FIRST AMERICANS
Directed by Graham Chedd
1980

Archaeological documentary attempts to determine when the earliest American Indians lived on this continent. Sites discussed include Lewisville, Texas, which, it is argued, may be forty five thousand years old. The earliest generally accepted date, however, is around 25,000 B.C.E., when the first identifiable culture, Clovis, is found in various sites. Includes a demonstration of how meat was obtained by preparing a buffalo using stone tools typical of the earliest period and a discussion of plants that the earliest Native Americans might have eaten.

## SILENT TEARS
Produced and directed by Shirley Cheechoo
1997

Based on the true story of one Cree family's attempts to overcome the harsh realities of life on a northern trapline. This short-film illustrates the strength of famliy and cultural tenacity.

## SILENT TONGUE
Directed and written by Sam Shepard
1992

A husband's continual state of mourning prevents his wife from entering the next world, holding the woman as a spiritual prisoner between the worlds of the living and the dead. Gripping performances by Sheila Tousey, Tantoo Cardinal, and Jeri Arredondo.

THE SHADOW CATCHER
Directed by Teri C. McLuhan
1975

Film biography of the life and work of Edward S. Curtis, noted photographer, ethnologist, and filmmaker. Not only a portrayal of Curtis and his studies, but a document of Indian people commenting on his work.

SMOKE SIGNALS
Produced by Larry Estes, Roger Baerwolf, Chris
    Eyre, and Sherman Alexie; directed by Chris Eyre;
    written by Sherman Alexie
1998

Based on the short story, "This Is What It Means To Say Phoenix, Arizona," by Sherman Alexie, the film follows two Native American men, Victor and Thomas, on a road trip to claim the remains of Victor's father. The story is filled with contemporary pan-Indian themes (identity, activism, and humor). A strong cast featuring Adam Beach, Evan Adams, Tantoo Cardinal, Gary Farmer, Irene Bedard, Monique Mojica, John Trudell, Chief Leonard George, Cody Lightning, and Simon Baker.

SPIRIT RIDER
Produced by Wayne Aaron and Derek Mazur;
    directed by Michael Scott
1993

Stimulating drama about a 16 year-old Ojibway, raised in numerous foster homes, then unwillingly returned to his reserve by the band council as part of a repatriation program. His grandfather begins to help the young man establish his place in the community, via horse racing, which provides the young man with a sense of belonging. The film features a notable cast including Gordon Tootoosis, Herbie Barnes, Michelle St. John, Graham Greene, Tom Jackson, Tantoo Cardinal, and Adam Beach.

STARTING FIRE WITH GUNPOWDER
Directed by David Poisey and William Hansen
1991

Chronicles the origins and achievements of the Inuit Broadcasting Corporation, located in the Canadian Arctic. The corporation produces its own documentary, drama, and children's shows entirely in the Inuit language and thereby keeps the culture alive. By controlling their own media, the region's Native people have created a modern Inuit nation.

THE STORY OF SIWASH ROCK
Directed by Annie Frazier-Henry
1999

A Coast Salish rite-of-passage ritual is compellingly described. It is said that Siwash Rock (Vancouver) symbolizes the most sacred of a man's vows, "cleanliness of fatherhood." While trying to balance urban existence with cultural persistence, a young man experiences a spiritual awakening. A wonderful short-film that incorporates the Coast Salish oral tradition in a modern form of cultural expression. A talented cast featuring Chief Simon Baker, Dakota House, Vania Stager, Nathan Smith, and Morgan Rose.

THE STRANGE CASE OF BUNNY WEEQUOD
Directed by Steve Van Denzen; written by Drew
    Hayden Taylor
1999

A delightful short-film with the entire dialogue spoken in Ojibway. The ancient tradition of offering tobacco as thanks for fishing has been neglected, creating chaos for humans, Little People, and the fish that inhabit the lake. Bunny Weequod must reestablish the reciprocal relationship with the environment and restore the harmony of the lake. Remarkable performances by Kateri Walker, Lorne Cardinal, and Bernelda Wheeler.

THE SUN DAGGER
Produced by Anna Sofaer; directed by Albert Ihde
1982

Provides an overview of Anna Sofaer's 1977 discovery of a dagger of light that pierces an ancient spiral rock carving at Chaco Canyon, New Mexico. Sofaer was convinced that she had discovered something significant, and after careful study found that the dagger marks solstices, equinoxes, and the nineteen-year lunar cycle. The importance of Sofaer's discovery has been acknowledged by the scientific community.

SUPER CHIEF
Directed by Nick Kurzon
1999

Home Box Office documentary highlighting politics, money, and corruption on the White Earth Reservation.

SURVIVING COLUMBUS
Produced by Edmund Ladd; directed by
    Diane Reyna
1992

A documentary using interviews with Pueblo elders, scholars, and leaders. A Pueblo perspective of the Columbus Quincentenary is elaborated with history and cultural materials.

TALES OF WESAKECHAW—A SERIES
Produced by Marla Dufour
1984

Thirteen-part series of short programs based on Canadian Cree legends utilize a storyteller and a shadow puppet to tell thirteen stories first told to Indian people.

Presents values and lessons that remain true to the present time.

## TECUMSEH: THE LAST WARRIOR
Produced by Hanay Geiogamah and Dan Blatt;
   directed by Larry Ellikan
1995

Profiles the life of Tecumseh and his efforts to establish a pan-Indian confederacy. Commendable performances by Jesse Borrego, Jeri Arredondo, Tantoo Cardinal, Lorne Cardinal, Jimmy Herman, and August Schellenburg.

## THEY NEVER ASKED OUR FATHERS
Produced by Corey Flintoff; directed by John A.
   McDonald
1982

Provides a historic overview of the interaction between the Yup'ik Eskimos, the Russians, and later the United States government as the two countries lay claims to the traditional homeland of the Yup'ik. Although the Yup'ik were never conquered nor sold their lands, this film depicts how they were robbed of their land by a process they barely recognized. Utilizes historic photographs, documents, interviews with Eskimo elders, and scenes of island life in the Bering Sea to demonstrate the negative impact of contact with non-Indian people.

## THUNDER IN THEIR HEARTS
Produced and directed by Robert Yuhas
1992

Weaves together clips from the film *Thunderheart* and the feature length documentary *Incident at Oglala*. Includes interviews with Val Kilmer, Graham Greene, Sheila Tousey, and Indian activist John Trudell.

## THUNDERHEART
Produced by Robert DeNiro, Jane Rosenthal, and
   John Fusco; directed by Michael Apted
1992

The story of a young Federal Bureau of Investigation (FBI) agent who is part Indian who is sent to South Dakota's Pine Ridge Reservation to investigate the murder of an Oglala Sioux. As he begins to uncover the crime, he comes to know the Indian people and discover his true identity. Set during the volatile 1970s when the Pine Ridge Reservation was torn with factionalism, the film features Indian actors Graham Greene, Sheila Tousey, and John Trudell in supporting roles.

## TO PROTECT MOTHER EARTH: BROKEN TREATY II
Directed by Joel L. Freedman; narrated by
   Robert Redford
1989

Further explores the current battle between the Western Shoshone of Nevada and the U.S. government over Indian land the government insists on reclaiming, first explored in *Broken Treaty at Battle Mountain* (1974). Focuses on the efforts of two Shoshone sisters, Carrie and Mary Dann, to fight eviction from a longtime family-owned ranch.

## TODAY IS A GOOD DAY: REMEMBERING CHIEF DAN GEORGE
Produced and directed by Loretta Todd
1998

A sensational documentary combining family stories, film clips, and re-creations to tell the story of an unassuming Native man who became an actor in his sixties and advanced the images of Native people represented in film. Profiles his life, his career, and his family. Interviews with Dustin Hoffman and Arthur Penn illustrate how Chief Dan George positively influenced the portrayal of Native people onscreen.

## TOMORROW'S YESTERDAY
Produced by KBYU-TV
1971

Provides an overview of the challenges faced by the Pueblo people to adapt to the challenges of modern civilization while maintaining their cultural identity. Depicting Pueblo life as being as colorful and beautiful as the corn they grow, this program shows Native Americans as they were historically, how they are today, and how they hope to be in the future by adapting to the challenges they now face.

## THE TREATY OF 1868 SERIES
Produced by NETCHE (Nebraska)
1987

Two-part video series examines the roots of the dispute over who really owns the Black Hills of western South Dakota. Looks to the Treaty of 1868 to present facts and beliefs that have fueled a century of debate over the taking of the Black Hills. To the Lakota Sioux, it is sacred ground, illegally taken by the U.S. government; to the U.S. government, it is a land fairly claimed and settled. Interviews with Russell Means of the American Indian Movement; Joe Assman, a white resident being sued for his land; Bill Welch, a Black Hills hotel owner; Bill Elison and Ramon Ropbideaus, attorneys; Matthew King, a spiritual leader; and James Hansen, a historian, are provided.

THE TRIAL OF STANDING BEAR
Produced by Marshall Jamison and Gene Bunge
1988

Documents the story of Ponca Chief Standing Bear who was arrested while attempting to return the body of his son for burial in Ponca traditional homelands in northern Nebraska. In 1877, the U.S. government had forcibly moved members of the Ponca Indian Nation from their ancestral home to Indian Territory, in what is now Oklahoma. Standing Bear was fulfilling a promise made to his dying son that he would be buried in the land where he was born. The trial of Standing Bear was the basis for the 1879 legal case that established for the first time that "an Indian is a person within the meaning of the law."

TRIBAL BUSINESS IN THE GLOBAL
   MARKETPLACE
Produced and written by Carol Rand; directed by
   Thomas Hudson
1992

Video provides an introduction into the success of the Montana Indian Manufacturer's Network, a foundation formed by seven tribally owned firms of the Chippewa, Cree, Assiniboine, Sioux, Blackfeet, Cheyenne, and Crow Indians, to create jobs in economically depressed areas.

TRANSITIONS: DESTRUCTION OF A
   MOTHER TONGUE
Produced by Daniel Hart; directed by Darrell Kipp
   and Joe Fisher
1992

Explores the relationship between language, thought, and culture and the impact of language disappearance in Native communities.

TUSHKA
Produced by Ian Skorodin and Orvel Baldridge;
   directed and written by Ian Skorodin
1996

Choctaw filmmaker Ian Skorodin delivers an intriguing, fictionalized drama mirroring the counterintelligence activities of the Federal Bureau of Investigation (FBI) in Native American communities during the 1970s. The cast features Bobby Eades, Orvel Baldridge, and Robert J. Conley.

TWO DECADES OF INUPIAT SELF-
   DETERMINATION
Produced and directed by Beth Rose
1992

Video tells how the Inupiat people fought for, and won, the battle over rights to their land in Alaska's North Slope following the discovery of oil at Prudhoe Bay.

WALKING WITH GRANDFATHER—A SERIES
Produced and directed by Phil Lucas
1988

Six-part series draws on the rich oral traditions of North American Indian people of several tribes. They present, in a sensitive manner, basic human values like kindness, generosity, courage, and love. These stories help people learn a great deal about themselves, the world around them, and the beliefs and values of their own and other cultures.

THE WAR AGAINST THE INDIANS
Produced and directed by Harry Rasky
1992

The documentary accurately portrays centuries of conflict between the Indian and European invaders; the latter are portrayed as largely deceitful. The movie, based on primary historical data, is a tribute to the Canadian Indian people who have argued for the true presentation of the relationship between the Indians and the Europeans.

WARRIOR CHIEFS IN A NEW AGE
Produced by Daniel Hart; directed by Dean Curtis
   Bear Claw
1991

An introduction to Native spirituality, this video presents the lives of two Crow chiefs whose dreams and visions foretold both tragedy and the Native people's power to heal and restore themselves.

WARRIOR'S SONG
Produced by George Amiotte; directed by Vladan
   Mijailovic
1996

Four Native veterans share post traumatic experiences and the techniques they implemented into their healing process.

WE ARE ONE
Produced by Chet Kincade/Nebraska Educational
   Television Network
1986

Eight-part teacher's guide discusses the life and culture of a Native American family in early nineteenth-century Nebraska. Designed to develop the richness and complexity of Native American culture by focusing on the daily rituals and rites of passage of a thirteen-year-old boy and his younger sister.

## WHERE THE RIVERS FLOW NORTH
Directed by Jay Craven
1992

Set in 1927, this compelling drama unfolds in Vermont, where a log-driver must decide whether to sell his land to a power company. Cree-Métis actress Tantoo Cardinal turns in a strong performance in a supporting role.

## WHITE MAN'S WAY
Produced by Christine Lesiak/Nebraska Educational
　　Television Network
1986

Depicts life in the U.S. Indian School in Genoa, Nebraska, which was built as an experiment to transform the American Indian "from savagery into civilization." Provides an informative look into the efforts to force Indian children to learn the white man's language, traditions, and lifestyles while being forbidden to practice their own.

## WINDS OF CHANGE
Executive produced by Carol Cotter
1990

Two-part series presents important and contested issues such as tribal sovereignty, land rights, encroachment of mining interests, and the struggle to sustain traditional cultural values in late twentieth-century America.

## WIPING THE TEARS OF SEVEN GENERATIONS
Produced and directed by Gary Rhine and
　　Fidel Moreno
1991

Multi-award-winning documentary that has been described as "the true story of the Wounded Knee Massacre" recounts the tragic event of 1890 as seen from the Lakota perspective. Interviews with tribal members are combined with footage from the 1990 Bigfoot Memorial ride.

## THE WITNESS
Produced by George Burdeau, Hanay Geiogamah,
　　and Keith Merrill; directed by George Burdeau
　　and Keith Merrill
1997

A historically documented story dramatizing the 1637 massacre of the Pequot Nation owing to misunderstandings and accumulated tensions with colonists.

## WOMEN IN THE SHADOWS
Produced and written by Christine Welch; directed
　　by Norma Bailey
1992

The film portrays a search for Native ancestors by a Métis mother and her daughter. Takes the women "out of the shadows" of history and gives them back their voices.

## WOONSPE (EDUCATION AND THE SIOUX)
Produced by South Dakota ETV
1974

Addresses the problems faced by those involved in Native American education. Examines the four school systems available to Native Americans: Bureau of Indian Affairs (BIA) boarding schools, public schools, tribal contract schools, and mission schools.

## YOU ARE ON INDIAN LAND
Directed by Mort Ransen
1969

Documentary focuses on the Mohawk Indian protest against violations of the Jay Treaty of 1794, which guaranteed duty-free passage across the international borders between Canada and the United States.

## References

### Overview of Native Media Arts

Bahti, Tom, and Mark Bahti. *Southwestern Indian Ceremonials*. Rev. ed. Las Vegas: K.C. Publications, 1997.

Bataille, Gretchen M. and Charles L. P. Silet, eds. *The Pretend Indians: Images of Native Americans in the Movies*. Ames: Iowa State University Press, 1980.

Friar, Ralph E. and Natasha A. Friar. *The Only Good Indian: The Hollywood Gospel*. New York: Drama Book Specialists, 1972.

Geiogamah, Hanay, ed. *The Entertainment Industry Guide to American Indian Productions*. Los Angeles: American Indian Registry for the Performing Arts, 1987.

Katz, Jane, ed. *This Song Remembers: Self-Portraits of Native Americans in the Arts*. Boston: Houghton Mifflin, 1980.

Lincoln, Kenneth. *Native American Renaissance*. Berkeley and Los Angeles: University of California Press, 1983.

Schirer, Thomas E., ed. *Contemporary Native American Cultural Issue: Proceedings from the Native American Studies Conference at Lake Superior State*

University, October 16–17, 1987. Sault Ste. Marie: Lake Superior State University, 1988.

Seller, Maxine S., ed. *Ethnic Theatre in the United States*. Westport: Conn.: Greenwood Press, 1983.

Speck, Frank G. and Leonard Broom. *Cherokee Dance and Drama*. Berkeley and Los Angeles: University of California Press, 1951; Norman: University of Oklahoma Press, 1983.

Weatherford, Elizabeth and Emelia Seubert, eds. *Native Americans on Film and Video*. New York: Museum of the American Indian/Heye Foundation, 1981.

Weatherford, Elizabeth and Emelia Seubert, eds. *Native Americans on Film and Video, Volume II*. New York: Museum of the American Indian/Heye Foundation, 1988.

## Indians in Film

Bataille, Gretchen M., and Charles L.P. Silet. *Images of American Indians on Film: An Annotated Bibliography*. New York: Garland, 1985.

———, eds. *The Pretend Indians: Images of Native Americans in the Movies*. Ames: Iowa State University Press, 1980.

Brathovde, Jennifer, comp. *American Indians on Film and Video: Documentaries in the Library of Congress*. Washington, D.C.: Library of Congress, 1992.

Churchill, Ward. *Fantasies of the Master Race: Literature, Cinema and the Colonization of American Indians*. San Francisco, Calif.: City Lights Books, 1998.

Friar, Ralph E., and Natasha A. Friar. *The Only Good Indian: The Hollywood Gospel*. New York: Drama Book Specialists, 1972.

Hilger, Michael. *The American Indian in Film*. Metuchen, N.J.: Scarecrow Press, 1986.

———. *From Savage to Nobleman: Images of Native Americans in Film*. Lanham, Md.: Scarecrow Press, 1995.

Kilpatrick, Jacquelyn. *Celluloid Indians: Native Americans and Film*. Lincoln: University of Nebraska Press, 1999.

Lund, Karen C., comp. *American Indians in Silent Film: Motion Pictures in the Library of Congress*. Washington, D.C.: Library of Congress, 1992.

O'Connor, John E. *The Hollywood Indian: Stereotypes of Native Americans in Films*. Trenton, N.J.: New Jersey State Museum, 1980.

Rollins, Peter C., and John E. O'Connor, eds. *Hollywood's Indian: The Portrayal of the Native American in Film*. Lexington: University Press of Kentucky, 1998.

Weatherford, Elizabeth, and Emelia Seubert, eds. *Native Americans on Film and Video*. 2 vols. New York: Museum of the American Indian/Heye Foundation, 1981–1988.

## Native Theater

Appleford, Rob. "The Desire to Crunch Bone: Daniel David Moses and the 'True Real Indian'." *Canadian Theatre Review*. 77 (1993): 21–26.

Clements, Marie. *Age of Iron*. Excerpt in *Taking the Stage: Selections from Plays by Canadian Women*, edited by Cynthia Zimmerman, 231–233. Toronto: Playwrights Canada Press, 1994.

———. *Now look what you made me do*. In *Prerogatives: Contemporary Plays for Women*, 9–41. Winnipeg, Man.: Blizzard Publishing, 1998.

———. *The Unnatural and Accidental Woman*. *Canadian Theatre Review*. 101 (2000): 53–88.

Colorado, Elvira, and Hortensia Colorado. *1992: Blood Speaks*. In *Contemporary Plays by Women of Color*, edited by Kathy A. Perkins and Roberta Uno, 79–89. New York: Routledge, 1996.

D'Aponte, Mimi Gisolfi, ed. *Seventh Generation: An Anthology of Native American Plays*. New York: Theatre Communications Group, 1999.

Dutka, Elaine. "Stage is Set for Complete Tales of the West." *Los Angeles Times*. *Calendar*, June 2, 2000, 2.

Filewood, Alan. "Receiving Aboriginality: Tomson Highway and the Crisis of Cultural Authenticity." *Theatre Journal* 46, no. 3 (October 1994): 363–373.

Geiogamah, Hanay. *Grandma*. In *Stories Our Way: An Anthology of American Indian Plays*, edited by Hanay Geiogamah and Jaye T. Darby, 333–338. Los Angeles, California: UCLA American Indian Studies Center, 1999.

———. *Grandpa*. In *Stories Our Way: An Anthology of American Indian Plays*, edited by Hanay Geiogamah and Jaye T. Darby, 317–331. Los Angeles, California: UCLA American Indian Studies Center, 1999.

———. *New Native American Drama: Three Plays*. Norman: University of Oklahoma Press, 1980.

Geiogamah, Hanay, and Jaye T. Darby, eds. *American Indian Theater in Performance: A Reader*. Los Angeles: UCLA American Indian Studies Center, 2000.

———. *Stories of Our Way: An Anthology of American Indian Plays*. Los Angeles: UCLA American Indian Studies Center, 1999.

Glancy, Diane. "Native American Theater and the Theater That Will Come." In *American Indian Theater in Performance: A Reader*, 359–361. Los Angeles: UCLA American Indian Studies Center, 2000.

———. *War Cries*. Duluth, Minn.: Holy Cow! Press, 1997.

Highway, Tomson. *Dry Lips Oughta Move to Kapuskasing: A Play*. Saskatoon, Sask.: Fifth House, 1989.

———. *The Rez Sisters: A Play in Two Acts.* Saskatoon, Sask.: Fifth House, 1988.

King, Bruce. *Evening at the Warbonnet.* In *Stories of Our Way: An Anthology of American Indian Plays,* edited by Hanay Geiogamah and Jaye T. Darby, 355–440. Los Angeles: UCLA American Indian Studies Center, 1999.

Luna, James. "Allow Me to Introduce Myself: The Performance Art of James Luna." *Canadian Theatre Review* 68 (1991): 46–47.

Moses, Daniel David. *Almighty Voice and His Wife: A Play in Two Acts.* Stratford, Canada: Williams-Wallace Publishers, 1992.

Northrup, Jim. *Walking the Rez Road.* Stillwater, Minn.: Voyageur Press, 1993.

Perkins, Kathy A., and Roberta Uno, eds. *Contemporary Plays by Women of Color.* New York: Routledge, 1996.

Ryga, George. *The Ecstasy of Rita Joe and Other Plays.* Toronto: New Press, 1971.

Spiderwoman Theater. *Winnetou's Snake Oil Show from Wigwam City. Canadian Theatre Review* 68 (1991): 54–63.

Taylor, Drew Hayden. *The Baby Blues.* Burnaby, B.C.: Talonbooks, 1999.

———. *Only Drunks and Children Tell the Truth.* Burnaby, B.C.: Talonbooks, 1998.

———. *Someday: A Play.* Saskatoon, Sask.: Fifth House, 1993.

———. *Toronto at Dreamers Rock; and Education is Our Right: Two One Act Plays.* Saskatoon, Sask.: Fifth House, 1990.

Yellow Robe, William S., Jr. *The Independence of Eddie Rose.* In *Seventh Generation: An Anthology of Native Plays,* edited by Mimi Gisolfi D'Aponte, 39–100. New York: Theatre Communications Group, 1999.

———. *Where the Pavement Ends: Five Native American Plays.* Norman: University of Oklahoma Press, 2000.

*Randy Reinholz*

## Native Journalism

Alia, Valerie. *Un/Covering the North: News, Media and Aboriginal People.* Vancouver: UBC Press, 1999.

Danky, James P. ed., and Maureen E. Hady, comp. *Native American Periodicals and Newspapers, 1828–1982: Bibliography, Publishing Record, and Holdings.* Westport, Conn.: Greenwood Press, 1984.

Danky, James P., Maureen E. Hady, and Richard Joseph Morris, eds. *Native American Press in Wisconsin and the Nation: Proceedings of the Conference on the Native American Press in Wisconsin and the Nation, April 22–23, 1982.* Madison, Wis.: University of Wisconsin Library School, 1982.

Littlefield, Daniel F., and James W. Parins. *American Indian and Alaska Native Newspapers and Periodicals.* 3 vols. Westport, Conn.: Greenwood Press, 1984–1986.

Murphy, James E., and Sharon M. Murphy. *Let My People Know: American Indian Journalism, 1828–1978.* Norman: University of Oklahoma Press, 1981.

Raudsepp, Enn. "Emergent Media: The Native Press in Canada." In *The Mass Media and Canadian Diversity,* edited by Stephen E. Nancoo and Robert Sterling Nancoo, 187–206. Mississauga, Ont.: Canadian Educator's Press, 1996.

*Douglas George-Kanatiio*

## Native Radio

Keith, Michael C. *Signals in the Air: Native Broadcasting in America.* Westport, Conn.: Praeger, 1995.

Minore, J. B., and M. E. Hill. "Native Language Broadcasting: An Experiment in Empowerment." In *The Mass Media and Canadian Diversity,* edited by Stephen E. Nancoo and Robert Sterling Nancoo, 162–186. Mississauga, Ont.: Canadian Educator's Press, 1996.

*Peggy Berryhill*

# Health

◆ Health: Traditional Indian Health Practices and Cultural Views
◆ Contemporary U.S. Indian Health Care   ◆ Canadian Native Health
◆ U.S. Indian Health Organizations   ◆ Canadian Indian Health Organizations

## ◆ HEALTH: TRADITIONAL INDIAN HEALTH PRACTICES AND CULTURAL VIEWS

The beneficial effects of Western medicine have long been promoted as the reason why colonized populations should adopt it in place of their traditional healing practices. Historians, however, have recently challenged this assumption by suggesting that Western colonialists and imperialists were primarily the agents of disease rather than of health. Colonists introduced diseases and altered the environment with large-scale imported crops and animals that have contributed to the health problems of the colonized populations. Moreover, the colonizers also introduced a form of medical care that took no account of the indigenous groups' existing culture and its indigenous medical systems, and, in fact, dismissed them entirely.

This chapter provides an overview of the impact of Western medicine on the role and services of indigenous healers as well as their various ceremonial healing practices. The chapter also includes a discussion of federal government and missionary impact on the indigenous health systems and the new health problems that were foreign to the health beliefs and practices of various tribal groups. There is also some discussion of contributions made by indigenous groups to the national formulary.

### Health Systems and the Role of Culture

The health care system developed and maintained by a particular society reflects the ways in which it organizes to care for its sick, and the way treatments are utilized is based on commonly held ideas about health and illness. The sociocultural theories underlying diagnosis and treatment encompass what is thought to have caused an illness and what are the appropriate interventions to prevent or heal it. For example, most modern societies have developed and adopted a theory that attributes many illnesses to bacteria or viruses. Within this model are also fairly rigid ideas about the types of interventions necessary to treat the illness as well as expectations about the most appropriate agency or person to turn to for treatment. In this model, treatment of illness, especially major illness, is carried out by a physician who is expected to utilize scientific means in diagnosis and treatment.

Health care in most societies is also easily identifiable through its social institutions for dealing with illnesses; that is, the places where diagnosis and treatments are performed. During times of illness, patients and their families interact with health care providers within these institutions where diagnosis, treatment, and recuperation take place. In general, the health-care-seeking behavior of patients using these institutions often indicates that they have faith in the providers and share with them ideas about the cause of illness, the symptoms, the diagnostic process, the treatment, and most of the time, the prognosis.

If an illness cannot be cured or successfully treated by providers or institutions of the modern health system, patients and their families may seek alternative resources. Thus faith healing, bio-feedback, meditation, and other alternative forms of treatment may be utilized, and in most cases, the practitioners who provide this alternative care are not part of the formalized medical institutions. Not everyone in every society, however, accepts either their own or other alternative resources in times of illnesses. The religion of a subgroup of a society may teach that the only acceptable treatment of any illness is prayer, and therefore the appropriate healers are religious leaders. For example, members of the Church of Christian Scientists largely hold to the belief that faith and prayer, not medication or surgery, are critical elements in healing. This group therefore has developed its own health care resources, using prayer as the central therapeutic intervention for all illnesses.

Illness is a sociocultural construct, and therefore it is viewed differently by different cultural groups. However, in most cultures illness is defined as the inability of a person to perform his or her normal role in society because of the incapacitating nature of the illness, although this person is also expected to seek a relief or cure. While society generally accepts and excuses members from work or other engagements during times of illness, it does so only if the individual actively seeks treatment. A sick person is expected not only to seek appropriate relief, but also to comply with the treatment recommendations. Any abuse of the sick role (such as feigning illness) is neither condoned nor supported.

An important aspect of the sociocultural understanding about wellness and unwellness is that the society provides culturally relevant diagnoses and links these diagnoses to causes familiar to that society. Such a diagnosis includes a framework for acceptable interventions. Within this framework there are a number of ways to explain why or how an illness occurred, ideas that are important to planning treatment and in predicting the outcome or prognosis.

A culture's health care resources and beliefs about causes of illnesses may not readily be visible to others because these health beliefs may be so integrated into the religion of the culture that it is difficult to notice that healing is one of the primary responsibilities of the religion. Thus religious practices may represent an integral part of that culture's health care system. This is often the case, for example, with many American Indian and Alaska Natives.

As one of the many minority populations conquered and colonized by Europeans and forced eventually to assimilate into majority culture, American Indians and Alaska Natives today are subjected to health policies and practices based on Western cultural values and models. Despite the improvement in the health care delivery system for the U.S. population, access to quality health care is far from adequate for American Indians and Alaska Natives because of poverty, isolation, misunderstanding between federal and state governments of jurisdictional responsibilities, and a variety of other governmental policies. The situation is further aggravated by the fact that access to health care in this country is greatly influenced by the race, language, and socioeconomic circumstances of an individual.

Although a segment of the U.S. population wants health care to be a civil (or government-mandated) right and therefore accessible to all, the political powers in this country view health care as a commodity to be purchased. There is also strong political and economic opposition to the popular opinion of others who think the federal government should finance a greater portion of the health care cost. The inconsistency between popular expectations and the country's socioeconomic reality has resulted in a health care system that is inadequate and largely unavailable to the poor or the near poor in the United States. A majority of the American Indians and Alaska Natives, for example, are among those in the lower socioeconomic strata of U.S. society, experience greater rates of poor health, and are more likely to have little or limited access to health care resources. Although it is not clear how inaccessibility to modern health care influences the use of their indigenous traditional tribal healers, many American Indians and Alaska Natives do use this resource. It is also not uncommon to find tribal members who live in the cities or away from the rural reservations traveling back to the reservation to participate in healing ceremonies. Sometimes the indigenous healers are also asked to come to urban areas to assist patients who are unable to travel.

## Native American Cultural Views

In 1854, the great American Indian orator and leader, Chief Seathl, summarized a basic belief held by many American Indians and Alaska Natives about the concept of harmony and the place of humans within the universe:

> The deer, the horse, the great eagle, these are our brothers. The earth is our mother. All things are connected like the blood which unites one family. Whatever befalls the earth, befalls the sons of the earth. Man does not weave the web of life. He is merely a strand in it. Whatever he does to the web, he does to himself.

The notion of such interrelatedness between people and their environment and the inclusion of various deities or the Great Spirit (called grandfather in some tribes) is a part of the common thread found in concepts of wellness and well-being held by many American Indians and Alaska Natives despite the heterogeneity of culture, language, and traditions. Although there are variations on the theme of interrelatedness and its symbolic meaning, notions of interrelatedness and harmony are aptly illustrated in dances and healing ceremonies held to reaffirm the harmony, or balance, of one's life with the universe. When these relationships are not in balance, then it is thought that the individual may be vulnerable to illness or misfortune. Appropriate ceremonies to reestablish harmony, therefore, play a key role in various healing ceremonies offered during times of illnesses.

### Harmony and Health

The concept of harmony and balance within the context of health is expressed in a number of ways, including by the use of symbols presented in a theoretical framework that emphasizes wholeness; for example, a circle of life as opposed to linear progression may be used to describe the aging process. Among Native Americans, it is often emphasized that the circle is more appropriate because it has no beginning or end. And as in a circle, the life cycle does not end at death because the spiritual being continues even after the physical body becomes dust.

A Native patient is attended to by a medicine man and a drummer in a Plains tipi medicine lodge. From "Life of an Indian," in the 20 June 1868 *Harper's Illustrated Weekly*. (From *American Indian Medicine* by Virgil J. Vogel. Copyright 1970 by the University of Oklahoma Press)

As with the concept of the yin and yang in various Asian cultures, and the notions of hot and cold found in other cultures, balance or harmony is central to the concept of health, illness, and healing or treatment of illnesses in Native American cultures. Balance and unbalance, therefore are underlying principles in health and illness. Balance is also symbolic in the reference to the four sacred cardinal directions, the four winds, the four worlds, and the four elements in the medicine wheel. Each direction, wind, or element in the medicine wheel balances one another. Sometimes, the various elements are referred to as fire, wind, water, and earth. At another level, these four elements may be viewed as sources of strength that symbolize the innate qualities of a person's being—physical, mental, emotional, and spiritual. In order to maintain health, these elements must be in balance within as well as without. For example, a pregnant woman is often told to avoid unpleasant experiences in order to keep her unborn child healthy in mind and spirit.

As a rule, most traditional Indian ideals of maintaining health are dictated by the cultural rules of behavior. In fact, most tribal taboos and other rules are observed or stressed to prevent illness or misfortune. When illness does occur, indigenous healers are called upon to treat and help correct the imbalance. These healers are also called upon to provide personal or group protection; to bless happy occasions such as weddings, the birth of a child, and a new home; to offer thanks for a successful hunt or a bountiful harvest; or to ensure success on an expedition, a hunt, or in a new occupation. Healers in most American Indian and Alaska Native communities are therefore important resources in diagnosis as well as in treating both illness and misfortune faced by individuals, families, or the entire community.

Some of the annual ceremonies that help ensure the safety and health of the communities are conducted seasonally and may include the participation of all members of the tribe. These ceremonies may bless the planting, hunting, or fishing; others may involve prayer for rain or for bountiful crops. In other instances, special ceremonies may be conducted to mark the initiation of new clan members or puberty rites for young men or women in order to prepare them to assume the role of adults. Other ceremonies, such as a give-away, or potlatch, may be held to fulfill a vow, to celebrate achievements, or to give thanks. Some large public ceremonies may also be given to introduce a new healer to the community, albeit this type of celebration is rare now.

As in many cultures, American Indians and Alaska Natives are also very pragmatic about dealing with some of life's problems, including minor illnesses. For example, when faced with a non-life-threatening health problem and before calling on physicians or their own traditional healers, most will likely have tried various home remedies. Sometimes this may entail a prayer to call on the help of the appropriate guardian spirit or an ancestral totem, a helping spirit that may be represented in the spirit of a special animal or bird. If these interventions do not bring relief, then the patient is most likely to go to the physician or an indigenous healer. And as a rule, most know which resource is most appropriate.

## Healers and Healing

Although most tribes have different names for their traditional healers, words such as *medicine man, medicine woman, shaman, Native practitioner*, and *traditional healer* are some of the terms borrowed from non-Indians that are used by Indians to describe indigenous healers. For example, the word *shaman* was borrowed from the Siberian Tungusic word, *saman*, which translates as a "spiritual medicine man." Today,

A medicine man attends to a patient with his mortar and pestle—used for mixing medicines—and a gourd rattle. From *Schoolcraft's History, Condition, and Respect of the Indian Tribes.* (From *American Indian Medicine* by Virgil J. Vogel. Copyright 1970 by the University of Oklahoma Press)

the term *shaman* is usually reserved for identifying healers whose primary practice of healing is treating illnesses attributed to supernatural causes by the use of a self-induced trance. Medicine men or medicine women, on the other hand, are those healers who utilize both herbal or other ceremonial interventions to treat illnesses caused by natural or supernatural causes. Natural illnesses are those caused by explainable sources, such as a cut or an infection. Supernatural causes are those attributed to invisible forces, such as witchcraft or taboo-violation. As a rule, most Native practitioners are specialists who limit their practice or specialty to a specific form of intervention, much as do other members of the indigenous tribal healing systems, including herbalists or diagnosticians.

When treating an ill patient, most healers perform these services in the patient's home, in the presence of family members and sometimes other invited guests. The healing ceremonies, however, are generally private, involving only the patient and his or her family. Depending on the tribe, the type of illness, and the type of intervention or treatment, some healing ceremonies may require a few minutes, while others may require days or a series of different ceremonies over a period of one or two years. In some instances, the preparation for a ceremony such as a Sun Dance may take months. Depending on the nature of the rituals or healing ceremonies, there may be more than one healer or one patient involved. The ceremony may also require singers, dancers, drummers, persons to prepare ceremonial objects, persons to serve as mentors, and elders who help prepare the patient or the dancers.

With few exceptions, most healers are also generally acknowledged as the community's spiritual or religious leaders. Religion is the basis of their practice, and it is with this knowledge that they are able to call upon the power of the spiritual forces to help guide a patient to access the healing power. The role of many traditional healers varies from tribe to tribe, but most also play a key role in governing of the community. Among the Pueblo tribes of the Southwest, for example, the religious leader/healer nominates or names the person to serve as governor for the village. Such a nomination from a spiritual leader is considered appropriate and is most likely to place political leadership in the hands of an individual who is highly respected and who subscribes to the traditional teachings of the culture.

Today, in addition to their responsibilities as healers and religious leaders, healers are often sought to provide consultation on a variety of cultural issues and public health matters confronting tribal communities. In some communities, for example, some healers have concentrated their efforts in working with mental health programs or working within tribal education systems to help teach cultural content in the schools.

A career of a healer in most tribes does not ensure wealth. In most cases, healers charge little or no fee for their services. Because healers are an important resource to the community, some tribal groups require members of the tribe to provide food and other necessities for the healer so that the healer can devote full time to overseeing the health of the community, including training new initiates, teaching the various ceremonial dances, songs, and/or supervising restoration or creation of ceremonial objects to be used in ceremonial activities.

While ministering to the sick is often considered a curative role, most healers in Indian communities view their role as that of a facilitator or a catalyst. For example, in various healing ceremonies, they not only help set the stage for the healing process, but through prayers and songs they also evoke the assistance of the appropriate spiritual forces to help heal the patient or help empower the patient so that he or she can engage the help directly. Among the Navajo, preparations toward this end may include replication of specific deities in a sand painting in order to transfer the power of deities to the patient when he or she sits on the painting during parts of the ceremony. In order to appease the helping spirit, considerable attention is paid to the accuracy with which the ceremony is performed.

During healing ceremonies in other tribes, the traditional healer or other participants in the ceremony may impersonate various spiritual deities called upon in the healing ceremony. The impersonation may include masks worn by dancers or the use of certain sound instruments, such as drums or rattles as well as special songs to invite, accompany, or thank the deities. Similarly, sage, feathers, water, or steam may be used to help purify the environment to welcome the healing spirit and prepare the patient for the arrival of the deities. The preparation also helps prepare the patient mentally for the rest of the healing ceremony. To some extent, preparation such as this can be comparable to what might take place before a patient is examined by a physician, i.e., the nurse taking the patient's temperature, blood pressure, and weight, and/or conducting an interview with the patient in preparation for the physician.

In some healing ceremonies, the healer may be assisted by a cadre of helpers, including dancers, singers, drummers, and the like. Other helpers may concern themselves with the preparation of the site for the ceremonial healing. Many healing ceremonies require specific settings, and some may only be conducted during certain seasons or only during the night.

In addition to healers, other specialists or practitioners may also occupy a place within the network that makes up the tribal healing systems. Some may assist the healer, but others may practice independently and are utilized for their expertise in treating wounds, assisting with birthing, prescribing herbal therapy, or making diagnoses. Although the introduction of modern medicine has all but replaced the functions of some of these various specialists, in some tribes diagnosticians, herbalists, and birth attendants are still active.

Due to the lack of mental health resources in most tribal communities, traditional healers play a strong role in this area. While trauma, infections, birthing, and treatment of some physical health problems are viewed as best treated by physicians and other modern Western health care providers, other illnesses such as recurring bad dreams may readily call for the intervention of a traditional healer. Today, the use of traditional healers or the frequency of their use for a variety of health problems is largely determined by the patient's degree of acculturation or assimilation as well as how well the presenting health problem can be treated by modern medicine. Where modern medicine cannot offer a cure, the patient's use of traditional healers or other alternative therapies is more likely.

The complexity of the traditional healing system also varies from tribe to tribe. In some, the traditional healing system may consist of a highly organized social structure with full-time healers who continually preside over and coordinate a variety of ceremonial and other religious activities for the tribe. In other tribes, a healer may be a part-time solo practitioner, without a cadre of helpers, whose practice focuses primarily on the individual patients and not the entire community. Such a healer may also be employed in other occupations.

Depending on the tribe or culture, the healers may also treat a number of patients at one time. For example, during a Sun Dance, there may be as many as a dozen key participants in the piercing ceremony. Among the Pueblo in the Southwest, all but a few participate in the group's major ceremonies, and children as young as three years of age are encouraged to practice and participate in the ceremonial dances.

## Natural Causes of Unwellness

Illnesses and misfortune in many tribal communities can be attributed to numerous causes, some occurring accidentally, others caused intentionally. The causalities can range from taboo-violation to supernatural intervention that may have occurred as a result of witchcraft or sorcery. For example, in one tribe, a condition such as epilepsy may be thought to be a consequence of exhaustion or the result of unsanctioned behavior such as incest. In another, the same condition may be attributed to supernatural causes such as soul possession completed by witchcraft. The explanations for illness and misfortune, therefore, generally fall within the realm of either natural or supernatural causes.

Natural causes are usually known or easily explained. For example, injuries suffered when an individual falls off a horse are easily understood and are attributed to the accident. It is also understood that this accident happened without negative intention or witchcraft. Those who develop diarrhea as a result of eating something that disagreed with their digestive system is another example of a condition attributed to natural causes. And as would be expected, appropriate treatments for conditions attributed to natural causes are also well-established. Causes of other more traumatic or devastating forms of illness or disabling conditions may not be as easy to explain or treat. For example, certain traumas or long-term disabilities resulting from an accident may be viewed as caused by natural causes; sometimes, however, the inexplicable consequences of an accident may be interpreted as caused by witchcraft. The focus, in this case, turns to finding the answer to why the consequences occurred and to search for the answer. Thus the services of a traditional diagnostician or healer may be sought. To find the answer to the question, "Why?" is important because it helps prevent future mishaps and further complications.

Illnesses or conditions attributed to a breech of cultural taboos may also have natural as well as supernatural causes. For example, a cleft palate may be thought to be caused by parental disregard for tribal rules, such as marriage between close kin. The congenital defect, in this case, may be thought to be punishment for ignoring this taboo. While the cleft palate can be surgically repaired, the traditional practices encourage interventions or ceremonies to help address and repair why the condition occurred.

## Supernatural Causes of Unwellness

Within the supernatural explanations, illnesses or misfortunes are frequently linked to negative willful intention of those who want to do harm to others, causing illness or misfortune. Sometimes, misfortune may not be the cause of witchcraft but may be viewed as punishment. For example, a severe drought or devastation resulting from a communicable disease epidemic may be attributed to the wrath of angry deities who are punishing the peoples for their failure to observe certain prescribed customs or practices.

At the level of the individual patient, various agents may also be identified as creating illness, some caused by witchcraft, such as object intrusion (lodging a foreign object in the body of an unsuspecting victim) in order to cause illness or death. Diagnosticians or healers are called upon for diagnosis and, when applicable, removal of the foreign object.

Another form of witchcraft might be soul loss, a condition in which the patient suddenly becomes unconscious or exhibits incoherent behavior that is deemed unusual. The purpose of the intervention to treat this condition is to coax the soul to return. Sometimes, soul loss may be attributed to influences of other spirits, usually those of departed ancestors who wish the patient to join them.

The opposite of soul loss is soul possession, a condition in which the mental or spiritual part of the person is possessed by another spirit. This diagnosis may be applied to seizure disorders or violent outbursts, and the treatment for these conditions may require ceremonial rituals of exorcism.

Illnesses and misfortune may also be linked to spells, another form of witchcraft. Spells to do harm may intentionally be placed on a victim's article of clothing, hair, nail parings, or the like. The intervention is focused on retrieving or removing the harmful intentions associated with these items. Such action is said to either break the spell or nullify the harmful intention.

The role of the supernatural in the cause of illness, death, or other misfortune is viewed as unnatural, and to counter the power of these harmful intentions, more powerful and benevolent forces are called upon because the harmful intention places the individual and/or a close family member in a vulnerable position. In other words, the individual or the family is out of harmony.

## Plant and Animal Spirits

It is believed by many tribes that within the context of one's relationship with the world that nature, plants, animals, birds, and sacred places all have importance. Many tribes view certain animals, such as eagles, bears, deer, buffalo, whales, and ravens as powerful allies whose spirits or totems may serve as an important source of protection or assistance. Other forms of plant and animal life may be central to many of the sacred ceremonies as well as to daily survival. Because of this, a number of key food resources, i.e., staple food sources such as corn, rice, salmon, whale, and acorn, are emphasized in a number of ceremonial activities. Ceremonies or other elaborate rituals are performed to honor or give thanks to the Creator for providing the food source. Rituals of thanks are also performed giving thanks to the food source itself. For example, a buffalo dance is performed to honor and give thanks to the

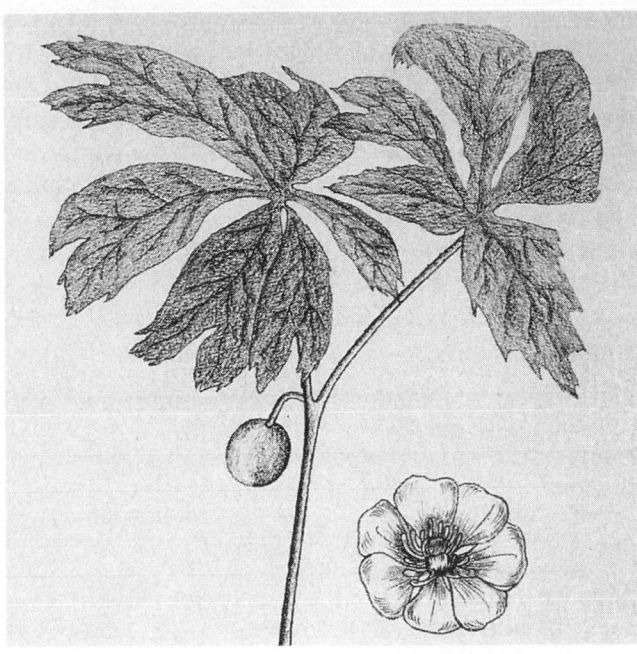

Drawing of a May Apple tree. (From *American Indian Medicine* by Virgil J. Vogel. Copyright 1970 by the University of Oklahoma Press)

buffalo. The dancers doing the honor not only wear buffalo headdresses but also imitate the animal in their dance steps. The spirit of these animals is also called upon during times of illness or misfortune.

Similarly the spirit of certain plants is also important in diagnosis or healing. Some tribes, for example, rely on the use of Indian tobacco to diagnose or purify a patient or a place of healing by the ritual of smudging. Prior to European contact, tobacco was essentially used as medicine, prayer offering, and an expression of good will. The smoke from the tobacco is said to travel upward, carrying the message of the people to the Great Spirit. Among some tribes, tobacco was also given to a healer upon request for help. In addition to tobacco, other plants such as sage, cedar, sweet grass, and sweet pine are also utilized in healing and purification. Roots, leaves, flowers, or the fruit of these and other plants are still used as herbal teas or as medicine.

## Modern and Traditional Ways

The initial introduction of European-style medicine to most Indian tribes came from interactions with traders, missionaries, and army physicians. The latter were asked to prevent smallpox outbreaks among the military personnel by vaccinating tribal groups living near military outposts. In fact, smallpox was one of the first health problems for which the federal government

allocated funds. The funds paid for the smallpox vaccine and provided salary for individuals asked to do the vaccinations. As increasing numbers of missionaries immigrated into tribal communities, many of them also handed out government relief rations and dispensed a collection of generic medicines for minor ailments. Over time, some missions established small hospitals or dispensaries on Indian reservations. These facilities and resources were later augmented by a number of other small health facilities built by the federal government. Thus physicians, nurses, and hospitals gradually became a familiar sight on Indian reservations.

The presence of most federally supported health care providers on Indian reservations, however, was either the result of treaty obligations or served the purpose of stemming the waves of communicable diseases that threatened the general population. Tribes that were able to negotiate with the federal government often asked for medical supplies or services of a physician. In signing the treaty, services such as medical care were promised to the specific tribe in payment for ceding all or most of their land to the government. Once the land was obtained by the government, it became available to be purchased by European immigrants. In a short time, most of the tribes in the eastern United States were displaced or removed. As the ancestral land-base of American Indians diminished, some were forced to relocate to lands set aside by the federal government. These lands became federal Indian reservations. The tribes did not willingly give up their land, and most resisted removal. Events that followed in the wake of forced removal are well-documented for some tribes. For example, the "Trail of Tears" documents the hardships that accompanied the removal of Cherokees to "Oklahoma from Georgia" While a majority of the tribes have been placed on federal reservations, a few of the tribes live on land set aside for them by state governments. A number of tribes, however, were left landless.

As tribes resettled reservations, malnutrition and other health problems became rampant. To help with these problems, a number of physicians were contracted by the federal government during the nineteenth century to provide health care to Indians, especially to Indian children placed in government boarding schools in which mortality rates were high. By the late 1800s and early 1900s, contracted physicians were also assigned to visit reservations during times of epidemics. Among the communicable diseases that attracted such federal attention were tuberculosis and trachoma. These epidemics continued to take a toll on the Indian communities, a toll that began with the European contact and resulted in periodic waves of smallpox, diphtheria, typhoid, and other communicable disease epidemics that severely depopulated the American Indian and Alaska Native population.

The epidemics not only depopulated the Native populations, but also severely crippled the existing indigenous health care system. Many elders, healers, and keepers of special knowledge on healing methods died during these epidemics. More died when tribes were relocated. Once a tribe was resettled in unfamiliar territory, access was no longer possible to familiar places where herbs were gathered as well as other products used in healing. Utilization of healers and treatment by healers from other tribes became increasingly necessary.

The ravages left by waves of epidemics and the forced removal left many tribal members wary of government programs. Although hospitals, physicians, and other health care providers became increasingly visible on reservations, many tribal members were reluctant to utilize them. Hospitals, in particular, were feared because they had become the place of death. This association occurred because most Indian patients utilized other resources or avoided going to the physician until their illness or disease was terminal.

Even when Western medicine became more acceptable, new problems emerged. For example, treatment of tuberculosis posed new problems. The acceptance of the diagnosis was especially difficult for Indian patients because the idea of an invisible microorganism responsible for the disease was not readily understood. An etiology targeting a bacteria that was invisible to the naked eye was not a part of traditional beliefs regarding disease or illness causalities. Even more baffling was the treatment for tuberculosis. Prolonged isolation and bed rest were not interventions used by tribal healers. The treatment was further complicated by the fact that most patients had to be hospitalized miles away from their families, and the family and the patients resisted such long separation.

Although practitioners of modern Western medicine and practitioners of traditional tribal healing shared common concerns about their patients, the treatment methods and the understanding of disease causality differed greatly and sometimes posed conflicts for the patients as well as for the healers. Many physicians discouraged the treatment of tuberculosis by indigenous tribal healers and for hospitalization of these patients. Some of the conflict that arose between the physician and their patients over the use of indigenous healers is perhaps best understood when one compares the two systems. The following comparison builds on the work initiated by J. T. Garrett, a Cherokee health professional. As would be expected, many traditional tribal healers did not believe tuberculosis occurred as a result of a single cause, such as invisible bacteria. There was also disagreement as to how best to treat the patient. Traditional healers believed that successful treatment required the presence of both the family and a familiar environment, not isolation in an unfamiliar setting such as a sanatorium.

| Indian Medicine | Modern Western Medicine |
| --- | --- |
| Wellness-centered | Illness-centered |
| Patient treated in family or community setting | Patient treated alone and isolated from family/community |
| Focuses on why illness occurred | Focuses on how illness occurred |
| Includes natural and supernatural causes | Emphasizes natural causes |
| Accepts multiple causalities | Usually links an illness to a single cause |
| Treatment approach is primarily holistic | Treatment approach is primarily physiological |
| Treatment is personal and reciprocally oriented | Treatment is often impersonal and compliance-oriented |

## On Keeping Healthy

Tribal rules of behaviors or taboos serve as lynchpins for health promotion and wellness among many tribal groups. Elaborate rules and taboos existed and were taught to every child as ways to keep from harming themselves. When such violation occurred, it was necessary to find ways to restore harmony. For example, there are strict rules on moderation, respecting animal and plant life, and dictating ways of conduct, among many others. These rules create a way of life that many elderly tribal members now say has been forgotten or replaced with values learned from majority culture.

Because traditional tribal focus was on illness prevention and wellness, the concern during times of illness was why an illness occurred. Was it because a taboo was violated? Was it the result of intentional harm? In modern Western medicine, the concern is how an illness occurred. In both instances, however, appropriate interventions are determined by the diagnosis and symptoms. In traditional Indian medicine, the etiology may be linked to multiple causes, including supernatural causes. Recurring unpleasant or violent dreams, for example, may be an important indicator of unwellness in a number of tribal groups. Among the

Cherokee, for example, a healer may inquire about dreams when called upon to diagnose an illness. Symptoms such as these are considered important because the healing approach utilized by most tribal healers is holistic: the interventions treat the whole person—physical, spiritual, emotional, and mental well-being—and this treatment is almost always provided in the presence of the patient's family or community.

Moreover, the indigenous healer-patient relationship is often based on reciprocity and/or kinship. The patient and healer may be related; if not, they still are likely to know each other. They will share the same values, traditions, language, and culture. In modern Western medicine, the physician and the patient often do not share a similar culture, life experiences, and/or social position. They will, in most cases, not know each other outside the patient-physician encounters. Also in modern Western medicine, physician-patient encounters involve some element of professional detachment.

## Treatment Modalities

Native knowledge of the human anatomy and physiology was based on observation and experience with processing game animals as well as whales, fish, etc. Names given to various animal body parts were similar to those used for human anatomy and physiology. The

Drawing of a Flowering Dogwood, a fever–reducing agent used by Native Americans. (From *American Indian Medicine* by Virgil J. Vogel. Copyright 1970 by the University of Oklahoma Press)

inner workings of microorganisms, cells, or enzymes that help transform food into energy, however, remained a mystery and was thought to be knowledge known to only spiritual deities or to the Creator. Development of various treatment modalities, however, was based on trial and error. Once a method was discovered to be effective, it became incorporated into the practice of healers or as home remedies used by everyone. For example, once a plant was found to be useful, it became incorporated into the indigenous medical formulary. Because knowledge of plants was limited to certain geographic regions, the types of plants utilized varied from tribe to tribe as well as from region to region.

Some treatment modalities, however, were common across different groups and different regions. Phlebotomy or bloodletting, for example, was used by various tribes, often to cure persistent headaches, fever, swelling, or edema. Boils, tumors, or abscesses were also frequently treated with herbal poultices after the infected area was incised, drained, and cleaned.

Even before European contact, certain herbal antiseptics were known and used in treating skin or wound infections. Hot herbal baths were also used by many tribes in dressing and caring for wounds and infections. To relieve pain or to speed up tissue healing, cautery and moxa by localized burning (using certain reeds or woods) were also used by a number of tribes. Herbal enemas were also utilized to treat various ailments such as constipation and diarrhea. Bladders made from skins of small animals or hollowed bones or reeds were used as enema instruments.

Various heat treatments were also used by tribes. Sweat baths and herbal mixtures were common as were the use of herbal fumigants, the latter burned or poured over heated stones or coals. Smoke treatment was used for various complaints, including insomnia, migraine headaches, head colds, and respiratory disorders. Treatment of fevers often called for rest, use of sweat baths, special liquid diets, or an application of special anti-fever herbal medicines. In some tribes, ritual herbal baths might also be prescribed for treating fever or skin conditions. Hot mud baths mixed with herbs were sometimes used in addition to some other procedures to treat arthritic pain or muscle aches. Mineral springs or natural hot springs were also utilized for treating arthritis and muscle aches.

Massages using herbal oils or ointments were also used. Such massages followed a ritual sweat bath; massages were used to apply pressure to affected areas. Bone setting also included massages before the bones were placed in a splint. Splints were fashioned from wet raw hide that was shaped when wet and kept its shape when it dried. Crutches, stretchers, and arm slings were also fashioned out of available resources when needed.

Diet therapy was also used frequently in treatment of some illnesses. Soft or special liquid diets were used to treat abdominal pain, diarrhea, postpartum healing, and other internal disorders. Diet therapy or special teas were also prescribed to help cleanse the internal body and to rid the body of substances considered toxic or harmful. Certain foods were also considered to have therapeutic qualities that were helpful in restoring physical strength. The latter were frequently prescribed for patients recuperating from a serious injury or illness.

Some forms of public health prevention were also practiced. For example, clothing, bedding, and personal property of the sick or the deceased were burned, and the living area or lodge was abandoned or purposefully burned. In some cases, climatic change may also have been prescribed, especially in cases of prolonged depression.

Today, the use of herbs in treatment of various illnesses continues to be an important part of the healing practices of many tribal communities. As a rule, most of these herbal medicines are valued for both their biological qualities as well as for their healing spirit. During the harvesting of these various herbal plants, the healing spirit of the plant is called upon with special songs and prayers, and the harvester asks permission of the plant to be harvested and used as medicine. Some of the more common herbs are kept by families to have available as home remedies. For example, depending on the geographic region of the country, sassafras, fern, goldenrod, or prickly pear teas may be prepared in various strengths for use as diuretics.

Peyote, an alkaloid plant containing mescaline, is another example of a plant used extensively in the Southwest today. Its use, like a number of other plants, is both medicinal and religious. Peyote is taken as a sacrament by members of the Native American Church (NAC) during NAC meetings or services, and is utilized in healing or to assist in guiding or educating the person taking the peyote. Some of those who have partaken of the peyote frequently recall various lessons they have learned from the visions they have experienced. Sometimes peyote is used this way to help identify the cause of a person's illness or to help determine the best way to treat the illness. Peyote, however, is used primarily to help individuals who are ill and troubled or depressed.

Because the NAC stresses moral values that emphasize the care of the family, the Protestant work ethic, and abstinence from alcohol, it is frequently utilized to help those having problems with alcohol abuse or addiction. In their ceremonies, the practitioners, or Roadmen, blend teachings from Christianity with traditional religious practices. Some songs sung during an NAC ceremony, for example, may contain gospel messages although the songs are sung in the tribal language. The all-night ceremony includes an altar and, in addition to taking peyote during the ceremony, the participants also share sage, cedar, tobacco, water, and a selection of special foods served toward the end of the ceremony. For some patients, the therapeutic aspect of the ceremony is helpful because it includes full disclosure (confession) of wrongdoing, and the patient is able to ask for assistance from those present.

The NAC ceremony is therefore used for a broad range of events, including blessing births, marriages, graduations, and the like. This ceremony may also be used to ensure a successful outcome when a patient faces major events, such as a delicate surgical procedure. NAC practitioners also treat illnesses attributed to supernatural causes.

## Contribution to Modern Medicine

American Indians and Alaska Natives have contributed significantly to the development of many modern pharmaceutical drugs utilized by modern Western medicine. Their knowledge and use of various herbal medicines have introduced a number of important drugs that have become a part of the general formulary. For example, in the1970s historian Virgil Vogel identified at least 170 botanical drugs in the *Pharmacopoeia of the United States* and in the *National Formulary* that were previously discovered and used by Indian tribes in the pre–European contact period. Some of these well-known drugs include digitalis, quinine, belladonna, cocaine from coca leaves, curare, and ipecac. Today, as the international search intensifies to find a cure for AIDS, cancer, and other diseases, researchers have once again turned to indigenous groups for possible leads on plants or herbs that could provide a cure.

## Euro-American Views of Indian Healing Practices

Because traditional indigenous healers held powerful positions in most tribal societies, they were subjected to unusual oppression by the federal government until the mid-1950s. The healers were perceived as threats to efforts being made by missionaries and government agents to assimilate the tribes. This was particularly important because a critical part of the assimilation process was the promotion of Western medicine. It was assumed that the use of traditional healers by tribal members deterred assimilation, and various efforts therefore were made to discredit or destroy these healers. Some missionary physicians were especially harsh in dismissing the value of the indigenous healers, sometimes attacking their healing skills. Patients who displayed visible evidence of having been treated by indigenous healers were frequently turned away from clinics because missionary physicians refused to treat them. Many of the popular healing ceremonies were subjected to ridicule and condemnation. In fact, missionary groups, in cooperation with other leaders, lobbied effectively to have the federal government outlaw certain ceremonies, such as the Sun Dance. The tribes, however, were not ready to forgo these practices. As a result, these ceremonies went underground until the federal ban was lifted.

In addition to ceremonies, objects used during healing ceremonies were also condemned. As recently as 1976, new converts to a Christian church in one Navajo community were asked to bring their traditional ceremonial bundles to be burned as the ultimate evidence of their sincere conversion to the Christian faith. Upon learning this, the Navajo tribal government not only expelled the minister from the reservation but also passed a law prohibiting desecration of sacred ceremonial objects. Such laws can be passed because most religious groups and their missions seek permission from the respective tribes to be allowed to have a mission or church on the reservation.

Efforts to incorporate or acknowledge the value of traditional healing practices were strongly discouraged or disallowed in hospitals staffed by missionary physicians and nurses. Traditional healers were not allowed to see patients in the hospital, and any request to allow this was rejected on the grounds that it would mean glorification of paganism. Practitioners of modern Western medicine who tolerated or attended healing ceremonies were labeled atheists and shunned by others. One physician on the Navajo Reservation in the early twentieth century accused one traditional healer of perpetuating superstition and failing to recognize the limits of his healing skills. Others accused the traditional healers of preying on the ignorance of the poor even though most of the healers did not charge for their services. While these allegations were often unfounded, rumors such as these added to the criticism of indigenous healers and also served to widen the gap between traditional healers and modern Western providers.

Traditional healers, however, continued to be important to many tribal members and were utilized despite rumors and governmental policies that aimed to discredit them. It was, however, other policies that contributed significantly to the decrease of their numbers and their range of influence. Mandatory education, for example, eliminated the chance for many young people to learn to be healers by taking away the time they needed to serve as an apprentice to a healer. As a result, when the number of traditional healers started to decline there were few to take their place. Today, most traditional healers find that their diminishing numbers have made it difficult for them to meet the overwhelming demands for their services.

## Renaissance in the Use of Traditional Healers

The need for traditional healers, in particular, has been greatly influenced by the policies that now allow tribal communities to assume or take over management of formerly federally operated health facilities and health programs in their communities. This change has meant increased attention to incorporating the services of traditional tribal healers. The need for the services of these traditional tribal healers has been specifically noted for helping patients cope with a variety of new health problems. Diabetes, cancer, heart disease, alcoholism, and other forms of chronic health problems are examples of some of the new health problems facing tribal communities. Although these health problems are essentially new to the practice of indigenous healers, they are still able to utilize their

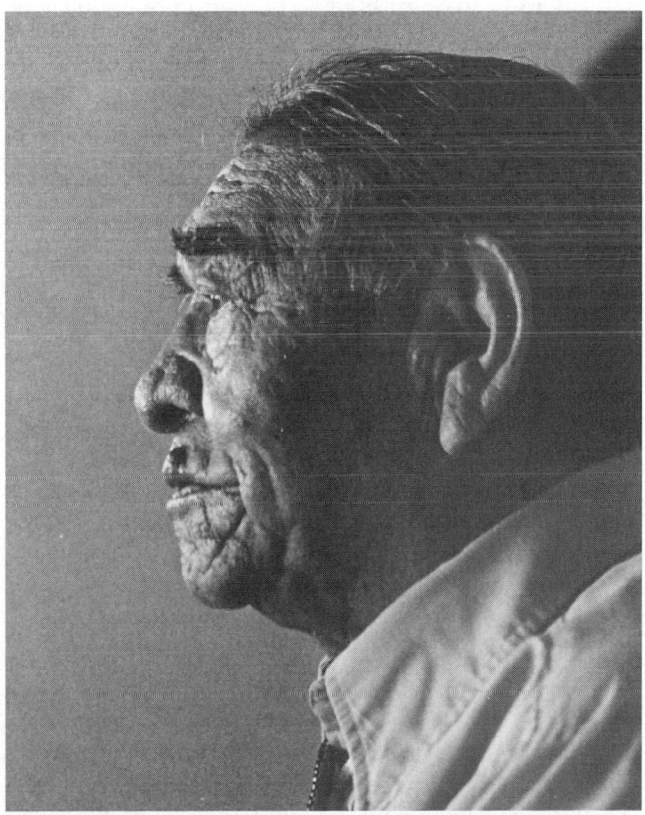

Ben Friday, Sr., was a tribal council member, noted elder, and healer when he died at age ninety in 1994. His Arapaho name translated in English to White Bear. (Photo by Sara Wiles)

other skills to help their patients, especially in helping them adjust to health problems that are chronic and incurable.

For most Indian communities, the renaissance of traditional medicine has been welcomed, but as mentioned earlier, some tribal communities have no healers left. The ravages of communicable diseases, forced removal and relocation, introduction of Christianity, and federal policies banning certain ceremonial activities have all contributed to the decline and decimation of traditional healers. The healers who are still practicing also find that the demand for their services has also increased as a result of the passage of the American Indian Religious Freedom Act (Public Law 95–341) in 1978. The passage of this law formally gives tribes the right to practice their religions. The religious leaders for most tribes are the traditional healers. The exact words of the legislation states that "henceforth it shall be the policy of the United States to protect and preserve for American Indians their inherent right of freedom to believe, express, and exercise [their] traditional religions."

This new law also allows some tribes to regain access to their ancestral sacred sites on federal lands and the right to possess objects used in religious ceremonies such as eagle feathers. The congressional hearings on the bill document extensive testimonies and statements made by tribal members, identifying sacred sites that have been destroyed by deliberate or accidental flooding of burial sites or the building of recreational facilities on sacred grounds that have served as sites of worship for their tribes. Despite the passage of this act and recent efforts to re-authorize the legislation, access to some sacred sites remains a problem. The possession of eagle feathers and the use of peyote also remains a problem.

The passage of another law also has helped the traditional healers repatriate a number of sacred objects used in various religious or healing ceremonies. These objects were illegally taken, sold, or traded by non-Indian collectors or museums. The Native American Graves Protection and Repatriation Act (NAGPRA) has made it possible for tribes to reclaim these sacred objects as well as the remains of their ancestors from various museums. The implementation of NAGPRA, however, has in some instances been met with severe objections from scholars who advocate for keeping the human remains for scientific research. When the research issue has not been a major problem, tribes and scholars have been able to negotiate agreements favorable to both sides.

Although there has been progress in a number of areas, the right of tribal members to use peyote in healing and in the Native American Church prayer meetings continues to be questioned by the courts and by various state governments. This is because peyote is one of the substances subject to control under the Federal Comprehensive Drug Abuse Prevention and Control Act. Approximately nine states with sizable Indian populations, however, exempt peyote from their lists of illegal substances and recognize its importance in the religious and healing practices of Native groups within their state boundaries. These states allow members of the Native American Church the "non-drug use of peyote in religious ceremonies." Although some states have granted permission, courts elsewhere have not. The legal battle in some of these other states continues.

Similarly, the legal debates surrounding the rights of Native Americans to possess bald eagle feathers and/or the right to hunt animals protected by the Endangered Species Act continue. Whale hunting for subsistence, for example, is permitted for a number of arctic Native groups like the Inuit and Inupiat, but the number of whales allowed is limited by the United States and the International Whaling Commission. Without this allowance, however, food shortage would be severe in many villages.

## Traditional and Modern Medicine

In most Indian communities, patients generally utilize a variety of health resources—government hospitals, physicians in private practice, health resources operated by missionary groups, faith healers, other alternative practitioners, and traditional healers who may or may not be members of the patient's tribe. Patients who utilize both modern Western medicine and traditional healers do not see a conflict between the two, and, depending on the symptoms and the perceived cause of the illness, they will select and utilize whichever is deemed most appropriate.

Despite the utilization and access to a variety of health care resources, the health picture of the majority of Native Americans has continued to lag behind that of the rest of society. The leading causes of death and morbidity have begun to mirror those of the majority society, as evidenced by the shift from high rates of death due to infectious disease to death rates that are attributed to problems such as heart disease, cancer, complications associated with other chronic diseases, and accidents. Most of these health problems are now the result of unhealthy lifestyles rather than infectious diseases. Health promotion and disease prevention are now among the desired health programs in tribal communities, including teaching young children about healthy eating, increasing physical activity, and conveying messages about the importance of positive self esteem (mental health). Culturally relevant health education and the inclusion of traditional values or teachings of traditional healers are also an important part of the health agenda promoted by the tribes. Scholarships for promising students interested in a health career are among these priorities. Each year the number of Native Americans completing medical school and returning to work in tribal communities increases. The inclusion of more Native American health professionals in the modern Western health care delivery system has also helped increase the number of providers who are culturally sensitive and are able to provide services that recognize the importance of culture in providing health care. The traditional healers themselves are also becoming more vocal about health issues, some organizing themselves to consult on issues of health, religion, and cultural knowledge.

*Jennie Joe*
*University of Arizona*

## ◆ CONTEMPORARY U.S. INDIAN HEALTH CARE

The delivery of health care services to American Indians is unique because of its history and structure. Since early Western contact with Native peoples, medical care was provided to tribes as independent nations. When reservations were developed, the Department of Interior administered needed care to Indians to halt the spread of epidemics. Today approximately one-half of all Indians receive their health care from the federal Indian Health Service (IHS). What began as a government-to-government relationship has evolved into a federally supported health care system unlike any other in the United States.

Since the beginning of the twentieth century, improved living conditions and access to federally sponsored health care services have been instrumental in the survival of First Americans. This survival, in the face of evolving cultures, changing lifestyles, and an adapting health care delivery system is a study in perseverance and fortitude. That American Indians endured through numerous disastrous epidemics and the impact of rapid social and cultural change, and continue to maintain their cultural heritage is a tribute to their strength and will to survive.

### Health Status of the First Americans

Those physicians, traders, and explorers who made early contact with North American Indians noted the extraordinarily good health of the Natives. They were clean, good-looking, without apparent illness, and peaceful. In a letter to the queen of Spain, Christopher Columbus called Indians a race of hardy people.

With the invading Europeans came the epidemic of diseases that killed millions of Indians, in some instances eliminating entire tribes. Indian people were ill-prepared to fight off the illness and disease brought by early settlers. They had never experienced skin eruptions caused from smallpox or the rash from measles. They had no knowledge of tuberculosis or typhoid. Indian people lived in small communities with clean water, sanitation, and healthy food. They did not have the diseases that were widespread in European countries. Unlike the Europeans who had built up immunity through prior exposure, Indians did not have a natural immunity. Therefore, when they came in contact with the early explorers, they were more likely to come down with various European diseases, and to die more rapidly from these illnesses.

Smallpox had a particularly disastrous effect. It was responsible for more deaths than all Indian wars combined. In one Pueblo of New Mexico, five thousand Natives died after contracting the disease in 1780 and 1781. Up to 90 percent of many East Coast tribal members died of smallpox and several tribes were wiped out entirely. There was no treatment for this viral disease. When the Europeans caught smallpox, they got sick and a small percentage died; for Indians, smallpox was a death sentence.

Euro-Americans used diseases such as smallpox as weapons against Indians. For instance, smallpox became such a well-known killer that written records at Indian trading posts document soldiers distributing smallpox-infected blankets to Indian communities. Men, women, and children alike died in mass numbers.

Tuberculosis (TB), a bacterial disease that affects the lungs and other organs, became so widespread that special hospitals had to be built to house and care for those Indians who contracted it. Infected children and other family members were taken from their homes and placed in these hospitals in an effort to halt the disease. Tuberculosis is more easily spread in close living quarters; hence, the problem was exacerbated when Indians were forced to live on restricted lands and in inadequate housing. It was not until penicillin came into general use during the 1940s that tuberculosis was brought under control. By then TB had taken a severe toll on the Indian community.

Once Indians were placed on restricted Indian lands and later reservations, close living quarters, inadequate nutrition, contaminated water, poor housing, and harsh weather conditions all contributed to the spread of infectious diseases. From an estimated population of 2 million during the fourteenth century, the Native population of North America fell to 250,000 in 1890. Native Americans were almost eliminated because of epidemic disease, famine, warfare, and hardship. Newborn infants died before they reached the age of one. Many adults never reached old age. Traditional ways of life were completely disrupted. Indian people were more easily controlled because their communities were virtually wiped out; they were leaderless, sick, and in many instances removed from their ancestral lands. Their numbers were reduced almost to extinction.

Several events saved American Indians from extinction. First, missionaries alerted the non-Indian population to the poor living conditions and near extermination of Indian people. Second, in 1849 the federal government moved Indian affairs from the War Department to the newly created Office of Indian Affairs. Attention was given to the poor water and sanitation conditions on reservations. Physicians and nurses began providing needed health care services. Since the turn of the century, improved living conditions and access to health care services have supported an increase in the Native population, estimated at 2.3 million for the mid-1990s.

## Changing Lifestyles

Five hundred years ago, Native peoples roamed the vast country of North America. Their subsistence way of life, which depended on nature and the land, was physically and spiritually healthy. Some tribes took up farming and grew corn and squash; others were hunters and gatherers. Game animals were stalked, and physical exercise was a way of life. Conditions such as heart disease, diabetes, high blood pressure, and obesity were unknown.

Today, most Indians no longer fish, stalk game, or live a subsistence lifestyle. They cannot hunt the buffalo because the buffalo is gone, exterminated by the encroachment of European civilization. Salmon fishing in the North has been restricted due to the barriers placed by the dams. Cities have been erected over traditional sites. Herbs and healing medicines have been plowed under or paved over to build highways.

Many American Indians purchase their food at convenience stores or eat federally sponsored surplus foods with high fat and sugar contents. Daily exercise is becoming a thing of the past. Traditional foods are saved for special ceremonies. Nutritionally sound foods are being replaced by junk food.

This change in diet did not come about overnight. Federal policies meant to be helpful resulted in the adaptation of less healthy lifestyles. Western food,

culture, and way of life were recommended as more desirable by the United States government. Treaties, for example, frequently included funds for the purpose of overcoming Indian poverty and starvation and "promoting Indian civilization." In an attempt to Westernize the Native tribes, Congress developed several programs designed to make Indians more acceptable to the dominant society and less Indian or uncivilized. Congress even established a Civilization Fund in 1802 to assist in this effort. In the government's eyes, to be civilized meant acquiring a Western education and owning land.

This assimilationist policy was implemented through several federal initiatives and laws, and continues even today. The first approach to promoting the "civilization" of Indians occurred in the late 1700s and took the form of missionaries. Indians were confined to designated land areas west of the Mississippi River. At many of these sites, they were unable to hunt and fish as they had for centuries. Missionaries were sent to "[teach] them to read and write, to plough and to sew, in order to raise their own bread and meat, with certainty, as the white people do." The ways of the dominant culture were seen as healthier and more proper. The old ways were to be a thing of the past and Indians were to be remade in the image of Western society.

Education and religious teaching became one of the more direct avenues of assimilation. In 1819 Congress established several Indian schools run by missionaries who were not only active in the initial education of tribes, but also worked to convert Indians to Christianity. These missionary schools blossomed into the infamous off-reservation boarding schools of the late 1800s and early 1900s. The schools were (and several still are) located in such states as Oregon, Nevada, California, Arizona, Kansas, Nebraska, and Oklahoma. The policy of these boarding schools promoted integration into the larger society. Children were often forcibly removed from their homes and boarded at schools many hundred miles away. The schools' curriculum emphasized Anglo teaching and values. Indian children were punished if they spoke their Native tongue, performed certain ceremonies, or practiced their traditional religion. Many children did not see their parents for ten to fifteen years, for students did not return home for summer vacations, but returned only after they graduated from high school.

Educating the Indians was only half of the civilization formula, the other half being ownership of real estate. In 1830 the Indian Removal Act created restricted territories for Indians with the intent of isolating this population from the encroachment of Western civilization. Next, the federal government determined that isolation on tribally controlled lands was not the best policy. How could Indians become civilized if they were not allowed to own land? The passage of the Dawes Act in 1887 provided real estate to Indians by dividing reservation lands into allotments (usually between eighty and 160 acres) for individual adult male Indians. After each eligible tribal member was allocated his tract, the remaining tribal lands were declared surplus and put up for sale by the government. This opened Indian land to non-Indian settlement and reduced Indian landholdings from 156 million acres to about 78 million acres by 1900. The federal government wished to thus eliminate reservations. It also aimed at breaking down Indian culture. With the allotment of land the ancient Indian system of common ownership of land was destroyed; the Indian identified less with his tribe and the importance of the tribal government declined.

When significant assimilation did not occur, the Office of Indian Affairs, now called the Bureau of Indian Affairs, began a relocation program in the late 1940s in which several thousand Indians were sent to large metropolitan areas. This mass relocation program was initiated not only to facilitate employment and assimilation of Indians into mainstream America, but also to relieve Congress of its so-called Indian Problem. Termination became an important feature of federal-Indian policy during the 1950s and continues to be seen in some current policies. This federal policy encouraged relocation of thousands of reservation Indians into urban areas, transferred major jurisdiction over Indians from the federal government to states, and terminated the federal relationship with specific tribes. Although the impact of relocation policy was successful to some degree in accomplishing assimilation, it was largely unsuccessful because it created a new breed of Indians commonly referred to as "urban" Indians. This special population, with ill-defined health and social service benefits, still held on to many Indian values and traditional ways, and returned to their homelands often.

These attempts at assimilation fell far short of their goal. For instance, American Indians were the last to obtain citizenship status in the United States. In 1924, four years after suffrage was granted to women in the United States, Congress awarded the same rights of citizenship to Indians. American Indians were finally allowed to vote, but only after serving in World War I. Two states, however, denied Indians the right to vote because they were "confused" over Indian ward status. Following court action in 1948, Arizona and New Mexico finally extended the right of citizenship to Indians.

Although largely unfruitful, these policies and practices had the effect of changing Indians' lifestyles and health status. Many Indians became adept at migrating between reservation and urban areas, maintaining contact with their cultural heritage and identity, and avoiding full assimilation. However, after sustained contact with the dominant culture, American Indians tended to adopt Western behaviors and lifestyles that were often unhealthy.

Those Indians who resided on restricted lands, or reservations, soon faced added health problems. In the late nineteenth and early twentieth century, gold, timber, and water were mined, harvested, and harnessed in the West. Many Indian reservations were found to be rich in these resources and other materials sought by non-Indians. Little thought was given to environmental damage, which resulted in a new threat to Indian health. Arsenic used in mining camps contaminated the water. Logging disrupted the game and damaged the land. Dams erected over rivers changed the course of water to downstream sites and halted the annual migration of salmon. More recently, uranium mining on the Navajo Reservation has left many Indians with new diseases: cancer and radiation poisoning.

For Natives in urban areas, stress caused by unemployment and relocation created new problems. Family members were too far away to visit, and thus the support of the extended family was unavailable. The Indian Health Service clinic was also located on the reservation. Bad habits picked up in new neighborhoods contributed to poor health. Cigarette smoking, poor nutrition, and dysfunctional families added to the stress.

Changes were also rapidly taking place in rural Indian communities. Differences between the living conditions on and off reservations have narrowed rapidly in recent years. For example, federally sponsored houses are becoming a more common sight on reservations than *wickiups* or *hogans*. Some reservation areas have small convenience stores. Development of reservation resources has brought environmental concerns, which mirror those of the United States as a whole. For instance, trace metal content in Hopi teeth is similar to that found in California suburban residents, showing contamination from heavy metals. Reservations on federal lands are often near toxic waste dumps. Contaminated water supplies, soil, and air pollution are now more commonplace at reservation sites. It is not surprising, then, that there is an increase in cancer and other health problems related to the environmental damage of Indian lands.

## Population Trends

The U.S. Bureau of the Census reports that 2.3 million Indians, Eskimos, and Aleuts reside in the United States, representing .09 percent of the U.S.

population (Russell 1996). The Indian population is a mixture of heterogeneous cultural groups living on some 250 reservations and in some major metropolitan areas. The degree of Indian blood in these self-identified Indians is not known. Many tribes have a tribal-specific blood quantum requirement for membership; other tribes have a simple descendant requirement.

There are more than five hundred federally recognized tribes that live for the most part on federal Indian reservations and in small rural communities. Approximately one-half of the American Indian population lives in the West, with the remainder residing primarily in the South (27 percent), Midwest (18 percent), and East (6 percent) (U.S. Bureau of the Census 1990). The 1990 census identified 278 reservations and 217 Alaska Native villages. The Alaska Natives, a term embracing people of the Athapascan, Tsimshian, Tlingit, and Haida tribes and the Eskimo and Aleut peoples, live throughout Alaska, predominantly in remote, isolated villages.

According to the 1990 U.S. Census, the state of Oklahoma has the largest concentration of American Indians (252,420), followed by California (242,164), Arizona (203,527), and New Mexico (134,355). The Cherokee Nation of Oklahoma is the largest nation, followed by the Navajo and the Sioux.

As a whole, American Indian groups have large young populations. The median age for Indians was 24.2 years, compared to 32.9 years for other U.S. races. Thirty-four percent of the Indian population are younger than fifteen years old; only 23 percent of the general population are younger than fifteen years. Elder Indians are in the minority, with only 6 percent over age sixty-five. For the U.S. All Races population, 11 percent are over 64 years of age. With the life expectancy of Indians somewhat lower than the general population, the elder Indian is a rarity. Those who survive to old age often succumb to heart disease or cancer. The unemployment rate for American Indians residing on reservations is estimated to be 55 percent. Although not all tribes have such extreme unemployment rates, it is not unusual for many large tribes to report unemployment rates of 50 to 75 percent.

As a group, American Indians are poorer than the general population, with approximately 28 percent living below poverty level, compared to 12 percent for the United States as a whole. The median household income for the Native household in 1989 was $19,897, which was two-thirds the national median income of $30,056. The Navajo Reservation has the lowest median household income at $8,412 and the Native Alaska area the highest at $15,750. Fifty-five percent of Indians graduate from high school and 7 percent graduate from college as compared to 66.5 percent (high school graduates) and 16.2 percent (college graduates) for U.S. All Races. Data from the 1990 census show that 32 percent of Indian adults had less than a ninth-grade education. In the Indian foster care system, 45 percent of the school-age children are in special education or individual education programs.

Currently, more than three-quarters of Indians live off reservation. Large urban areas such as Los Angeles, San Francisco, Oklahoma City, Chicago, and Seattle have become home to a great number of Indians. The changes in lifestyle of Indians have resulted in a whole host of health problems requiring a new approach for prevention and treatment.

## General Health Considerations

Over the last century the health conditions of American Indians have undergone great changes. In the earlier years, they were victimized by repeated and severe epidemics of disease such as influenza, measles, whooping cough, and diphtheria. Tuberculosis, though its course was more indolent, became the greatest killer of them all. Accidents were and still are a major cause of death and crippling disabilities. *Otitis media*, an infection of the inner ear often causing crippling hearing loss, became especially prominent in the 1950s and 1960s.

Once the infectious diseases were brought under control by a combination of immunizations, new drugs, surgery, and higher standards of living, other patterns of disease evolved, especially behavioral-based conditions in response to the effects of rapid cultural change. Mental disorders, alcoholism, and suicide have become widespread in the past two decades. Other diseases related to lifestyle changes such as hypertension, stroke, diabetes, cancer, and coronary heart disease are now found with frequency. All these trends demonstrate that the health conditions of American Indians and Alaska Natives are heading toward the pattern found in the rest of American society.

The health needs of American Indians in the United States are currently at a critical stage in reservation areas and urban and rural communities. The Indian Health Service reports that Indian deaths due to alcoholism are more than four times greater than those reported for the general population, and death from accidents are double. Death from diabetes is one-and-a-half times greater than for the general population. The American Indian five-year survival rate for all cancers is the poorest recorded for all ethnic groups; in other words, once Indians get cancer, they are less likely to survive for five years as compared to the general population. To address these needs, it is important to emphasize the role of changing lifestyles, environment,

Open–air terrace at the Red Lake Hospital on the Red Lake Reservation in northern Minnesota. (Courtesy of Sara Loe)

and the impact of Western medicine on health and well-being.

American Indians and Alaska Natives continue to lag behind the U.S. general population. Today's Indians are among the poorest, least educated, and most neglected of minority groups in the United States. Identified problems include a pattern of poverty, social problems, and diseases unparalleled among major ethnic groups.

The Indian Health Service reports that during the period between 1989 and 1991, the Indian age-adjusted mortality rate (adjusting for age differences in the two populations, the mortality rate compares the number of deaths per 100,000 population) for the following causes were considerably higher than for all other U.S. races:

(1) tuberculosis, 440 percent greater (or four times greater); (2) alcoholism, 430 percent greater (or four times greater); (3) diabetes mellitus, 155 percent greater (or one-and-a-half times greater); (4) accidents, 165 percent greater (or two times as high); (5) homicide, 50 percent greater; (6) pneumonia and influenza, 46 percent greater; and (7) suicide, 43 percent greater.

Heart disease continues to rate as the leading cause of death. The IHS reported that diseases of the heart accounted for 21.9 percent of all Native deaths among the IHS service population. During this same period (1991–1993), the IHS age-adjusted mortality for diseases of the heart was 132.4/100,000 as compared to 144.3/100,000 for the U.S All Races rate. Three IHS

## Table 15.1
## Mortality (per 100,000 population by IHS areas and for the United States, 1991–1993)

|  | Heart Disease | Cancer | Diabetes Mellitus |
|---|---|---|---|
| Aberdeen | 230/100,000 | 179/100,000 | 54/100,000 |
| Alaska | 135 | 151 | 17 |
| Albuquerque | 84 | 83 | 41 |
| Bemidji | 229 | 171 | 46 |
| Billings | 172 | 160 | 50 |
| California* | 92 | 55 | 15 |
| Nashville | 142 | 95 | 34 |
| Navajo | 108 | 81 | 31 |
| Oklahoma* | 126 | 79 | 22 |
| Phoenix | 134 | 78 | 63 |
| Portland* | 136 | 118 | 24 |
| Tucson | 107 | 81 | 56 |
| 9 IHS Areas | 143 | 113 | 41 |
| U.S.: | | | |
| All races | 144 | 133 | 12 |

*These three IHS areas may be underreported, thus accounting for the low mortality rates.

areas—Billings, Bemidji, and Aberdeen—exceeded the U.S. mortality rate.

Cancer is the second leading cause of death for American Indians. For Alaska Natives, cancer is the leading cause of death. Aberdeen, Billings, and Bemidji report extremely high cancer-incidence rates, exceeding the U.S. rates. Cancers of the nasopharynx, stomach, liver, gallbladder, cervix, and kidney are reported to be higher than U.S. Whites. The increase in cancer incidences is attributable to behavioral issues. Lung cancer, caused by smoking, showed the greatest increase among both men and women and is responsible for 25 percent of all cancer deaths. Cervical cancer is associated with sexually transmitted diseases (STDs) and liver cancer is associated with heavy-drinking behavior. Five cancers (lung, colon/rectum, stomach, nasopharynx, and breast) account for 57 percent of all cancers among American Indians and Alaska Natives.

Colon cancer incidence rates in Indian men and women have increased significantly since the early 1970s. Cancer of the colon/rectum was the most frequently diagnosed malignancy in this population between 1989 and 1993, which is 1.5 times higher than the Surveillance, Epidemiology, and End Results (SEER) rates for 1989 to 1992. It is not clear why Indian men and women report higher colorectal cancer incidence rates.

Diabetes mellitus, specifically Type II diabetes, is extremely high among Native populations. The Pima of Arizona are reported to have a prevalence rate of more than 50 percent. The Sioux of North and South Dakota report diabetes prevalence 60 percent higher than that of the general population. Diabetes is the seventh leading cause of death among American Indians, the death rate being three times that of the general population. Indian deaths due to kidney failure were reported to be more than two-and-a-half times higher than the national average.

Although accidents are reported to be the second leading cause of Indian deaths (heart disease is number one), they are the leading cause of death among Indian youth. Their national accidental death rate is reported to be almost three times higher than the national average. For the one-to-four-year age group, the accidental death rate is four times the national average. For the five-to-fourteen-year age group, the rate is almost twice the national average.

Between 1980 and 1982, the liver disease and cirrhosis death rate for Indians was four times that of the total population. IHS has determined that 75 percent of all accidental deaths among American Indians are alcohol-related. Alcoholism is believed to be the number one problem facing American Indians and contributes to many Indian deaths and illnesses (such as accidents, suicide, homicide, diabetes, birth defects, and pneumonia). Alcohol abuse has also been implicated in one-half of adult crime on Indian reservations.

The Centers for Disease Control (CDC) reported 458 cases of Acquired Immune Deficiency Syndrome (AIDS) among American Indians and Alaska Natives between 1981 and 1992. Proportionally, American Indians represent less than one percent of the total number of persons reported with AIDS in the United States. Approximately 55 percent of AIDS cases were reported among homosexual/bisexual males and 19 percent were among intravenous drug users. Indian males had greater incidence of the disease. Three-hundred-seventy-four males had AIDS, compared to sixty-one females and thirteen children. The high rates of sexually transmitted disease and teen pregnancy indicate potential for heterosexual transmission of AIDS. For example, the Centers for Disease Control (CDC) in Atlanta, Georgia, reports that in 1985 the incidence of syphilis among Indians was three times greater than among the general population.

## Causes and Contributors

Health status is a function of a variety of factors such as behavior (reckless driving, or drinking and eating habits), environment (housing, clothing, sanitation, and poverty), heredity, and health services. Of these, the availability of health services that protect, prevent, treat, and control illness and disease is an essential factor contributing to good health. Many of the identified health problems among Indians are known to be a result of behavior, environment, or poverty, and many of these health problems could and should be prevented. Many, however, are directly attributed to under-utilization of health services, especially involving certain diseases that may lead to disability or death if left unattended. For instance, if such illnesses as influenza, upper respiratory infection, diarrhea, and *otitis media* were treated before they became serious, disabilities such as hearing loss and deaths due to severe respiratory and digestive problems could be curtailed.

Prevention, an area frequently overlooked by service providers, must take higher priority if the health problems of American Indians are to be overcome. Problems such as obesity, diabetes, high blood pressure, and pneumonia are highly treatable or controllable conditions. Other serious problems such as accidents, violence, and suicide continue to frustrate providers as they are rooted in behavior patterns and not as easily treated. Many share a common cause: alcoholism. Heavy drinking is the cause of fetal alcohol syndrome (FAS) and fetal alcohol effect (FAE), a disability condition in infants. Alcohol abuse also contributes significantly to accident-related injuries and disabilities, and is a major factor in suicide, homicide, and behavior-related disorders.

## The Indian Health Service

The delivery of health care services to American Indians is unique among other health programs for civilians in the United States. Military doctors affiliated with the Department of War first provided health care in the 1800s to Indians living near military operations. The first federal hospital built for Indians was constructed in Oklahoma in the 1800s and a concentrated movement was underway to establish hospitals and infirmaries on every reservation and at every boarding school. Support for the building of these Indian hospitals and infirmaries arose from (1) the isolation of Indian land and communities; (2) the lack of nearby medical facilities to serve these areas; and (3) the poor home conditions, which made prescribing a course of treatment outside the hospital difficult and in many cases dangerous to the patient.

In the late 1800s, the Office of Indian Administration moved from the War Department to the newly created Office of Indian Affairs. Indian health care again changed hands in the early 1950s, when responsibility for Indian health care was transferred from the Department of Interior to the Department of Health, Education, and Welfare's Public Health Service (PHS). At the time, both medical facilities and personnel were inadequate to meet the Indians' health needs. The initial program priorities for the new PHS Division of Indian Health were (1) to assemble a competent health staff; (2) establish adequate facilities where services could be provided; (3) institute extensive curative treatment for the many Indians who were seriously ill; and (4) develop a full-scale prevention program that would reduce the excessive amounts of illness and early deaths, especially for preventable diseases.

Today, Indian Health Service operates a delivery system designed to provide a broad spectrum of preventive, curative, rehabilitative, and environmental services. This system integrates health services delivered directly through IHS facilities and staff on one hand, with those purchased by IHS through contractual agreements on the other, taking into account other health resources to which American Indians have access. Tribes are also actively involved in program implementation.

Indian Health Service has twelve administrative area offices throughout the United States that are primarily responsible for providing health care to approximately 1.16 million Indians residing in those areas. Each of these areas is in states with large Indian populations or reservations. The twelve IHS Area Offices are: Aberdeen, Alaska, Albuquerque, Bemidji, Billings, California, Nashville, Navajo, Oklahoma, Phoenix, Portland, and Tucson. Each area office is split into smaller sections called Service Unit Areas, which provide varying services depending on population size and budget allocation.

As of 1 October 1990, the area offices consisted of 136 service units, fifty-eight of which were operated by tribes. The IHS operates forty-three hospitals, sixty-six health centers, four school health centers, and fifty-one health stations, while tribes operate seven hospitals, eighty-nine health centers, three school health centers, sixty-four health stations, 173 Alaska village clinics, and six facilities providing community services.

Since 1955 the Indian Health Service has assumed more responsibilities and has expanded its staff from a small corps of health professionals to more than 9,000 skilled men and women. The number of physicians has risen from 125 to 770, dentists from 40 to 250, and registered nurses from 780 to 2,000. Originally, its staff consisted of clinical physicians and nurses, dentists, pharmacists, and sanitary engineers. The program has added field health physicians, registered medical-records administrators, public health nurses, registered dietitians, therapists, public health nutritionists, community health representative aides, practical nurses, dental assistants, maternal and child health specialists, environmental sanitarians, and auxiliaries in a number of categories. Indian Health Service now has a system of fifty hospitals and 450 outpatient facilities located throughout the United States. Seven of these hospitals and 320 of the outpatient facilities are tribally administered.

The IHS Service Unit provides health care through two methods of delivery: direct services and contract services. Direct services are those provided by the IHS staff in IHS outpatient facilities located on or near reservations. In general, health care services are provided to all residents and other Indians who come to the clinic. Care is often provided to non-Indian family members such as spouses. When need for services is beyond the capability of the IHS clinics (such as some dental, inpatient care, artificial arms and legs, and eyeglasses) or in the event of the unavailability of an IHS clinic (and upon the availability of funds), care is provided through contracts with local providers, which form the Contract Health Service (CHS) system. Because IHS considers itself a residual, or last, resource, patients seeking to use contract services must first exhaust other resources such as Medicare, Medicaid, state health programs, and insurance coverage before the IHS considers them eligible for contract services.

Due to a limited budget and inflationary pressures, IHS has established a policy of setting priorities on eligibility and care. For example, for diagnosis and treatment of a suspicious breast lump, a woman usually is referred from an IHS clinic to another hospital or physician who can handle such cases, since most Indian clinics do not have the radiology equipment to conduct mammographies. Referral is often made to a physician, clinic, or hospital with which the IHS has an established contract. To be eligible for care at a contract location, the individual must (a) be of Indian descent; (b) be a member of a federally recognized Indian tribe; (c) not be excluded from service by other provisions of law; and (d) meet special conditions of eligibility. Others, such as spouses, dependents of an eligible Indian living in the same household, and students who are away for educational purposes, are also provided health care services.

Because the contract health care system does not have enough funds to provide payment for all needed services, the IHS has established priorities for care. The first priority is for life-threatening situations; the second priority is threats to loss of limbs; and third priority are conditions that can wait for up to thirty days. Individuals not ill enough to meet these criteria may have to wait until the condition worsens before they become eligible for treatment. Therefore, an easily treatable inexpensive condition may become a difficult, expensive, and life-threatening condition before treatment is obtainable.

Over the years, the Indian Health Service has developed into a complex structure addressing the prevention, treatment, and control of disease. Changing demographics and diseases have made this task very difficult. Originally, Indian health care concentrated on treatment of acute infections such as smallpox and measles. The current trend toward social problems, chronic disease, and accidental deaths are a different set of problems requiring different solutions. The current IHS system is challenged in its struggle to meet the health demands of the Indian population.

**Legislative Overview of the Indian Health Service.** In order to comprehend fully the relationship between the federal government, American Indians, and Alaska Natives in regard to the provision of health care services, it is necessary to have an understanding of the legislation that has shaped the Indian Health Service through the years.

The Snyder Act of 1921 was the first formal legislative authority allowing health services to be provided to American Indians. For years, the U.S. government provided physicians, nurses, and other health services to Indian communities without such authority. To remedy this, the Snyder Act authorized Congress to continue to appropriate money "for benefit, care, and assistance of the Indians throughout the United States... for the relief of distress and conservation of health... and for the employment of physicians" (23 U.S.C. 13).

In 1955 a congressional act transferred the responsibility of American Indian medical and health-related services from the Bureau of Indian Affairs to the Department of Health, Education, and Welfare (since renamed the Department of Health and Human Services). In 1957 the Indian Facilities Act authorized funds for the construction of community hospitals if such construction would promote a more effective way of providing hospital facilities for Indians. The authority was further expanded in 1959 under the Indian Sanitation and Facilities Act, which authorized the construction and/or maintenance of sanitation facilities for Indian homes, communities, and lands.

The Indian Self-Determination and Education Assistance Act and the Indian Health Care Improvement Act were enacted in 1975 and 1976, respectively. These pieces of legislation have provided a new dimension of flexibility and opportunity to Indian people. The Indian Self-Determination Act (P.L. 93–638) directed Indian Health Service to enter into contracts with tribal organizations in order to carry out any or all of the Indian Health Service functions, authorities, and responsibilities. It also increased funding for Indian higher education. Essentially, tribes can manage and operate all or part of the clinic, hospital, or outreach efforts in their communities, if they so desire.

The Indian Health Care Improvement Act (P.L. 94–437) complemented the earlier legislation and further demonstrated the federal government's commitment to fulfilling its special responsibility and legal obligation to American Indians and Alaska Natives. The purpose of Public Law 94–437 was to raise the health status of Indians and Alaska Natives to a level equal to that of the general U.S. population. This was to be accomplished through a budgetary increase allowing the Indian Health Service to expand health services. In addition, the IHS was able to build and renovate medical facilities, and step up the construction of safe drinking water and sanitary disposal facilities. This law also developed programs designed to increase the number of Indian professionals and to improve health care access for Indians living in urban areas.

As indicated above, special legislation has been enacted to improve the health status of American Indians largely through increased health care services. However, since the recipients of these services are largely American Indians residing on or near reservations, many Indians, such as those living in urban areas and those belonging to federally non-recognized tribes, find themselves ineligible for the Indian Health Service program.

The need to provide health care services to the growing urban Indian population has been partially addressed by Title V of the Indian Health Care Improvement Act (1976) and Title V of the Indian Health Care Amendment (1980). This legislation authorized resources for establishing programs in urban and off-reservation areas to make health care services more available and accessible to the medically underserved urban and rural areas. As a result, the Indian Health Service is currently contracting with urban Indian health organizations in various U.S. cities. These programs are engaged in a wide variety of activities, ranging from outreach and referral services to comprehensive health care services. However, the health needs of urban and rural off-reservation Indians are still largely unmet, and the need for expanded medical services continues to exist.

## Urban and Rural/Reservation Health Care Systems

By virtue of a change in residence, from reservation to non-reservation, the health care eligibility status of the American Indian changes. As a reservation-based Indian, health care services are all but guaranteed. When ill, the reservation Indian need only go to the local Indian Health Service clinic to see a doctor. If the service is unavailable at the clinic, the patient is referred to outside physicians or hospitals. And although IHS operates under a restricted budget, the cost of care is not generally passed on to Indian clients or their families. Indeed, they may never see a medical bill. The structure of the Indian Health Service system virtually ensures the protection of the reservation Indian from the cradle to the grave.

Once relocated to the urban areas, regardless of the reason, access to the federal Indian Health Service system becomes restrictive. Urban Indians are generally not eligible for care under the auspices of IHS. Urban Indians have banded together in metropolitan areas creating a clinic funded from a hodgepodge of sources: city, county, state, and various federal resources. Specialty care through the contract health service system is not available unless the patient is eligible on the reservation. When it comes to health care services, urban Indians are left to fend for themselves with only a small amount of funding from the Indian Health Service.

Urban Indians have a special need for health care services. Once in large metropolitan areas, they are unprepared to deal with new pressures of urban living. Generally, the smog and noise levels are very high; the cost of living in a city is very high. Stress, a major contributor to poor health, can be found everywhere in the city. Poor habits and influences such as cigarette smoking and crime are evident. Supportive family members generally reside in remote locations on reservations; Indian families in urban areas often find themselves isolated without needed support.

Urban Indian programs have always been viewed as separate activities from the IHS reservation-oriented direct services system. The Indian Health Service only began to fund urban Indian programs in 1972, primarily for community outreach efforts. These urban clinics rely heavily for their operating expenses on income derived from patient payment.

## Barriers to Health Care

In seeking needed medical attention through either the Indian Health Service or other sources, American Indians may face many barriers, including financial problems, poor facilities (or none at all), geographic location, and IHS eligibility restrictions, which limit the accessibility and availability of needed health care.

Because of high unemployment rates, many Indians cannot afford to purchase health care outside the Indian Health Service. Medicaid (or Medi-Cal in California) and Medicare coverage to the medically indigent does not necessarily increase access to care. Increasingly, service vendors will not accept publicly insured individuals as patients due to low reimbursement rates.

A waiting area at the Red Lake Hospital on the Red Lake Reservation in northern Minnesota. (Courtesy of Duane Champagne)

Not all Indian reservations or communities have medical clinics or hospitals, and those that do often have small and outdated facilities. The general lack of facilities severely limits the delivery of needed health care services to Indians.

Many Indian communities are located on isolated reservations with access only by primitive roads. As a rule, rural Indians have to travel considerable distances in order to receive health care. Since many Indians do not own reliable automobiles, such factors as distance, highway conditions, transportation, and cost of travel become major barriers to care. Harsh climate conditions add to the difficulty.

When health services are unavailable to Indian people, either because of the lack of facilities or need for specialized care, the IHS is allowed to purchase these services through contracts with physicians, hospitals, and other providers. The IHS Contract Health Service (CHS) program is a substitute for outpatient and inpatient care that would otherwise be provided at an Indian clinic or hospital. However, the priorities and policies established by the CHS seriously limit the care, so that services which would ordinarily be available to Indians at an IHS facility are not available through the CHS program.

Finally, diversity oftentimes becomes a health care issue. There are more than 500 tribes with many languages, customs, and beliefs. Although regional similarities may occur, there are striking differences among tribal groups. Cultural competency is a must in the delivery of health care services.

## The Future of Indian Health Care

With an obsolete health care system, many Indian people wonder how they can reorganize the program to be more responsive to their needs. It is not simple to design a health care system that can effectively treat the chronic and behavioral health conditions now so evident among the Indian population. How does one change a community's lifestyle? Alcoholism, stress, unemployment, and poor eating habits are difficult to address. The answer may lie in the Indian community itself. A combination of culture-sensitive, community-wide efforts initiated and controlled by Indian people may begin the process of healing. Indian people have had the strength to survive for five hundred years under the most difficult of conditions. This strength is needed to ensure the survival of Indians into the next century.

The medical system can assist in reversing destructive trends by becoming more culturally aware of the people it serves and emphasizing preventive measures that involve the patient, the community, and the tribe. The question now becomes how to deliver culturally appropriate health care services within the American Indian and Alaska Native population that are preventive, effective, and include their involvement. Only then will behavior-based problems begin to be addressed.

*Felicia Schanche Hodge*
*University of California, San Francisco*
*University of Minnesota*

## ◆ CANADIAN NATIVE HEALTH

### Historical Perspective

Early explorers and settlers often commented on the fitness and health of the approximately one million Indian people living in present-day Canada at the time of European contact. Written accounts from that time indicate that Indian healers had developed a sophisticated ethnobotany and were well-versed in the use of herbs for pain relief, circulatory stimulation, purging body fluids, purging stomach gases and for laxative effects, for healing, and for other desired immune-producing and health improvement effects to keep their people in a state of good health.

According to Canadian Métis historian Olive Dickason, more than 500 drugs used in the medical pharmacopoeia today were originally used by American Indians.

In 1535, Huron Indian healers cured French explorer Jacques Cartier's men of scurvy, a condition caused by a lack of vitamin C which causes bleeding and swollen gums; if untreated, scurvy can lead to death. The Huron healers used a tonic made from spruce buds, which are rich in vitamin C, thus anticipating the discovery of vitamins.

Healers knew how to recognize fractures and immobilize them, and they had simple techniques for treating hemorrhage and asphyxia. They used mouth-to-mouth resuscitation, which they called "putting the spirit back." They were experts in psychosomatic medicine through the use of the sweat lodge, in which steam rising from water poured on hot rocks purges the body physically, and ceremonies, which are conducted by a healer in order to purge the mind spiritually. Some contemporary doctors credit the success of some Indian healing ceremonies and medicinal treatments to the effects of psychosomatic treatment, by which the very act of the ritual or sweatbath makes the patient feel better because their health concerns were being given attention. In current biomedical terminology this is also known as the placebo effect. An example is the common practice of doctors prescribing antibiotics for the common cold. Although antibiotics have no effect, patients believe they do and thus feel better.

The first Arctic people had a system of ritual procedures known as Shamanism. In Inuit culture the landscape, though sparsely populated, was overrun by spirits. Many were benign, but others were malevolent and brought peril, hardship and sickness. Inuit tried to protect themselves through offerings, amulet wearing, and careful observance of taboos. If, in spite of precautions, an illness resulted, a shaman was consulted.

By conducting confessionals, the shaman discovered the broken taboo or misused observance that had caused the anger of the spirits. With his spiritual allies he would attempt to remedy the illness. Much of what the shaman did through the confessional, incantation, song, and dance was psychotherapeutic; however, they also conducted clinical work, such as wound cleaning, bone setting, and amputating.

Osteological (bone) analyses have demonstrated that the aboriginal people in Canada were not disease-free prior to European contact. Excavations over several decades in the 40,000-square-mile area which was occupied by the southern Ontario Iroquois when Europeans first arrived in the early 1600s, have yielded some of the most extensively studied skeletal remains in Canada. These bone analyses and archeological records indicate that as the Iroquois started to cultivate maize (corn) the incidence of infectious disease increased because of the higher population densities and the accumulation of human and animal waste associated with settlements. These findings are borne out by a large anthropological literature equating agricultural societies with a higher rate of infections.

However few researchers would argue that from the seventeenth century on smallpox, measles, influenza, dysentery, diphtheria, typhus, yellow fever, whooping cough, tuberculosis, syphilis, and unidentifiable fevers brought by the Europeans ravaged the aboriginal population. Many of these epidemics were believed to be "virgin soil epidemics," characterized by unusually high mortality rates in all groups (not only the very young and the very old). Hundreds of thousands of people in all age groups died. Estimates of the pre-contact aboriginal Canadian population range from 220,000 to 2 million with the figure of 500,000 now widely accepted. By 1871 the number had declined to 102,000 due to the effects of disease.

In 1604 the beaver-pelt hat became fashionable in Europe. To get the beaver pelts necessary for the production of the hats the "Company of Adventurers Trading into Hudson's Bay" or the Hudson's Bay Company (HBC) was formed under a charter granted by King Charles II of England. The HBC formed a network of trading posts along the coasts of Hudson's Bay and James Bay. Although the HBC was granted a monopoly, many other rival companies established competing operations. Aboriginal peoples became involved in the fur trade to get goods from Europe such as guns, knives, and pots that improved their lives. They brought their furs to the trading posts in exchange for these goods.

The trading posts were also a significant factor in spreading diseases. Permanent and semi-permanent settlements sprang up around them. Living conditions were often unsanitary and crowded. Contagious diseases thrived. Trappers coming from the wilderness with their furs came into contact with numerous diseases, often for the first time. If they did not die in the periodic epidemics which swept through the trading posts, they carried back the diseases to their own communities, acting as agents of dispersal for the diseases which in turn spread across the continent. Some historians consider the trading posts as significant in the post-contact disease history among aboriginal peoples as the diseases themselves.

With their populations declining from disease and with the collapse of the fur trade after 1821 due to the depletion of beaver, aboriginal people were faced with starvation and poverty. Their traditional economies had collapsed as their dependence on Europeans grew. Their sources of food and clothing from the land dwindled with the slaughter and disappearance of the bison as European people migrated westward. These factors further accelerated the downward spiral in the health status of aboriginal people.

The treaties with the British Crown signed in the eighteenth and nineteenth centuries were attempts to ensure the survival of aboriginal people in the face of increasing disease, poverty, and encroaching European settlement. The effect, however, was worse, as once mobile people were settled on plots of land called *reserves* where resources and economic opportunities were limited. Hunters and trappers were expected to become agricultural laborers.

After the Constitution Act of 1867, which formed the new Canadian nation, the federal government adopted a policy of assimilation designed to make Canada into one community which was to be Christian in religion and European in culture. Out of this desire came two decisions which would have tragic results for aboriginal communities and a serious impact on their health. The control of aboriginal education was given to the churches, which developed church-run residential schools. Ostensibly, the goal of the schools was to provide language education and technical and trades skills so that Indian children could adapt to the changing economic realities of the country. But their real purpose was to assimilate children into the prevalent culture.

Children were forcibly removed from their tribes and spent up to ten months a year under the care of missionaries. The conditions of the schools were appalling due to the low government grants given to the churches. They were overcrowded, food was scarce, and ventilation was poor. Often the schools were sealed shut in order to preserve heat. Contagious diseases, especially tuberculosis, were rampant. In 1907 a report by Peter Bryce revealed a death toll of 24 percent from tuberculosis among 1,537 children in his survey of fifteen schools. Such rates varied, with the highest being 47 percent at the Old Sun School on the Blackfoot Reserve in Alberta.

When the schools closed in the 1960s, stories of the children being subjected to physical and sexual abuse began to emerge. In 1998 the Government of Canada issued a formal apology for the residential school system and set up a $350 million healing fund and offered counseling. Those aboriginal children that survived were robbed of their cultural identity. The residential school system left a generation of people who had no stable family life or positive family role models and relationships. The results can be seen in the statistics on family violence and social and emotional ill health that contribute to the high rates of accidents, injuries, and suicides among aboriginal communities today.

If the residential schools were the agents of "civilization" and deculturalization, the attack on traditional culture and healing were attempts to assist the civilization and assimilation goals of the government's Indian policy by abolishing what a British Columbia official referred to as the evil that lay "like a huge incubus upon all philanthropic, administrative or missionary effort for the improvement of Indians." In 1884, for example, amendments to the Indian Act prohibited the potlatch ceremony, which involved a complex give-away ceremony, feasting, and dancing and was used to mark important events, naming ceremonies, and other social and political events. Other traditional sacred healing methods were ridiculed as witchcraft. Many healers were harassed and prosecuted. The result of these policies left aboriginal people stripped of self-respect.

## Traditional Health and Healing

Our traditional spiritual beliefs are not a religion. Ours is a holistic spiritual way of life. The spiritual way of life is our traditions, beliefs and governments.

*—Dennis Thorne (Tungán Aikala)*
*Edmonton, Alberta, 11 June 1992*

Healing means mending bodies and souls. It also means rekindling the flames that strengthen our Native spirituality. It means physical, mental, psychological and emotional well being. This is known in Native healing circles as the holistic approach to healing.

*—Elder Byron Stiles*
*Orillia, Ontario, 13 May 1993*

The World Health Organization defines traditional medicine as "the sum of all the knowledge and practices whether explicable or not, used in diagnosis, prevention and elimination of physical, mental and social imbalance and relying on practical experience and observation handed down from generation to generation whether verbally or in writing." Traditional aboriginal people believe that healing is also a spiritual process, and that the Creator preordained the nature of the relationship between the natural world, the animal world, and human beings. Therefore good health is achieved by following the Creator's teachings and living in harmony with the Creator and creation. In the Royal Commission on Aboriginal Peoples Report (see glossary) a braid of sweetgrass is used as a metaphor: "Like the three strands of sweetgrass, the mind, body and spirit are intertwined and each must be healthy and in balance. If one strand is weak, the braid is undone." Europeans had great difficulty understanding aboriginal concepts of healing and medicine. Traditional healers treat the whole person—not merely the symptoms of

the disease. An unhealthy individual is seen to be out of balance spiritually as well as clinically or biologically. To restore a person's health the treatment must address the body, spirit, and mind.

Traditionally the healer served a religious function as well as a medical one. Healers administered herbal medicines to cure disease and conducted ceremonies for the individual and the community or both. Ceremonies such as the sweatlodge are ways of maintaining a connection with the Creator. Traditional herbal medicines are also seen as a gift of the Creator and therefore powerful.

Holism is a fundamental value in traditional healing, and medicine is symbolized in many Canadian aboriginal communities by the Medicine Wheel, which embodies four elements of whole health: spiritual health, mental health, physical health, and emotional health.

Aboriginal peoples in Canada differ substantially linguistically and culturally. As a result approaches to healing especially in regard to specific ceremonies and practices also differ. However, it is generally accepted that the goal of traditional healing is to restore harmony to individuals and communities.

## Current Status of Traditional Healing

The 1996 *Report of the Royal Commission on Aboriginal Peoples* recorded broad-based support among the aboriginal and non-aboriginal Canadians who testified before the commission. The commissioners concluded that values and practices utilized or adapted from traditional healing practices could lead to significant improvements in the health status of Canadian aboriginals. They pinpointed the following areas in which significant contributions could be made.

**Non-Physical Determinants of Health.**  Traditional healers can provide insight and help address mental, spiritual, and emotional components of aboriginal ill-health, especially self-destructive, violent, and abusive behavior including substance abuse; assist in chronic illness and pain management; advise and assist in palliative care; and assist in the preparation for death and grief counseling.

**Health Promotion.**  The values and teachings of traditional medicine can contribute to health promotion and disease prevention by suggesting culturally appropriate approaches to health education.

**Support for Increased Personal Responsibility.** Following the precepts of traditional teachings will bring about self-empowerment including greater responsibility for one's own health.

**Treatment.** At a time when there is a great interest worldwide in alternative treatments, traditional herbal remedies which many aboriginal people use are being validated by non-aboriginal practitioners and users. There is also interest in investigating traditional remedies from a scientific and pharmacological perspective.

**Health and Social Services Reorientation.** Utilizing traditional practices and healing policies in the provisions of health and social services will make them more receptive to aboriginal people. Healers can bridge the gap between aboriginal clients and the mainstream service facilities and providers. The cost of biomedical services would also be reduced, as potential problems could be resolved before they reached the critical stage.

The World Health Organization Declaration of 1978 in Alma-Ata in the former Soviet Union suggested that traditional healers could complement the work of primary health caregivers such as physicians, nurses, and community health workers. In Canada the 1989 Health Transfer Forum included intense discussion as to how to incorporate traditional medicine into the Health Transfer Initiative. It was agreed that communities should have the right to consult traditional healers. However it was also felt that local elders should advise as to the appropriateness of including traditional healing in any formal way in the government transfer initiative. Opponents felt strongly that traditional healers should not be subject to government evaluation.

The Canadian health care system in the past has not supported medical pluralism, which would include alternate medical practitioners. As mentioned previously, traditional Indian healing practices were forcefully suppressed along with language and culture as part of the governmental effort to assimilate Indian people. However, as the idea of culturally appropriate health care evolved in the 1970s and 1980s, a more tolerant view toward traditional healers emerged.

A resurgence and revitalization of traditional medicines is taking place on Canadian reserves. In northern Manitoba, federal First Nations and Inuit health nurses routinely refer patients to healers. The Health Canada First Nations and Inuit Health Branch provides transportation subsidies to patients who wish to consult healers. Both Kateri Hospital Centre on the Kahnawake Reserve in Quebec and Anishnawbe Health, an inner-city health center in Toronto, utilize traditional healers. Faculties of Medicine have exposed their students to the holistic concepts of traditional healers. The University of Toronto held a workshop on traditional healing in 1990; the University of Alberta held a Traditional Healing Day for their medical school in 1991; and the Alberta Medical Association held a traditional workshop for practicing physicians in 2000.

The Kenora Native Healers Program in Ontario is a good example of collaboration between traditional Indian healers and physicians. This program was established in 1978 when a group of Indian people interested in promoting sobriety and traditional cultural values requested that a traditional healer be added to the staff of the Lake of Woods Hospital. The hospital board agreed and with funding from the Ontario Ministry of Health hired a coordinator. In the 1980s visiting healers from Alberta, Arizona, Minnesota, and Wisconsin instructed local healers in appropriate practices. By the mid-eighties, there was an effective process in place whereby physicians routinely were referring patients to healers. Although there is no unified policy with regard to integrating traditional medicine into the Canadian health care system, it has become evident that the cooperation of healers and physicians can provide significant benefits to the improvement of First Nations and Inuit health.

## Current Status of First Nations and Inuit People in Canada

According to the 1996 *Royal Commission on Aboriginal Peoples Report*, aboriginal people in Canada endure ill health, insufficient and unsafe housing, polluted water supplies, inadequate education, and poverty and family breakdown at levels usually associated with impoverished developing countries. The persistence of such social conditions in this country—which has been judged by the United Nations for the past four years to be the best place to live according to the quality of life—constitutes an embarrassment to Canadians, an assault on the self-esteem of aboriginal people, and a challenge to policymakers.

**Demographics.** The size, age, structure, and geographical distribution of a population have an impact on its health status and needs. According to the 1996 Census, 799,010 people identified themselves as aboriginal, representing close to 3 percent of the Canadian population. About two-thirds were North American Indians, one-quarter was Métis, and one in twenty was Inuit. The gender distribution in the aboriginal population was very similar to the national distribution, with the proportion of men and women almost the same.

However, the age distribution in the aboriginal population is very different from the general Canadian population. In 1996 the average age of the aboriginal population in Canada was 25.5 years, ten years younger than the average of 35.4 years in the general population. A

**Table 15.3**
**Traditional Indian Medicines**

| Plant | Symptom | Used | Prepared |
|---|---|---|---|
| Black Spruce | Cough | Chewed | Soft white inner bark |
| Spruce Pitch (soft) | Infected wound | Poultice | Applied directly |
| Spruce Gum (hard) | Chest infection | Drink | Boiled, mixed |
| Wild Rhubarb | Infected wound, blood poisoning | Poultice | White inner part chewed or pounded root |
| Wild Rhubarb | Arthritis | Drink | Boiled as tea |
| Hudson's Bay Tea, Labrador Tea | Constipation | Drink as a laxative & tonic | Dried & boiled |
| Strawberry Leaf, Raspberry Leaf | Safe pregnancy & easy delivery | Drink | Dried & boiled |
| Strawberry Root | Diarrhea | Drink | Boiled |
| Spruce Needles | Eye infection | Eye wash | Needles boiled |
| Spruce Needles | | Drink as spring tonic | Needles boiled |
| Willow Leaves | Bee & insect stings | Poultice | Chewed & applied |
| Fireweed | Swelling | Poultice | Large infusion steamed |
| Tamarack Bark (winter) | Stomach trouble | Drink | Beaten & Hudson's Bay tea added |
| Tamarack Bark (summer) | Bad cold, stomach trouble | Drink | Beaten & Hudson's Bay tea added |
| Balsam Bark | Colds, sore throat | Drink | Boiled |
| Lichen (brown high country) | Ulcers | Chewed | Often mixed with other herbs |
| Devil's Club | Aching muscles | Drink | Boiled |
| Bear Root (Cow Parsnip) | Diarrhea | Eaten | Bark & inner bark chewed or prepared as tea |
| Sage | Colds | Inhaled | Boiled |
| Stoneberry | Diarrhea | Eaten | |
| Soapberry Bush | Constipation | Drink | Bark scraped from shrub & boiled as tea |
| Soapberry Bush | Gallstone | Drink | Early leaves, twigs, boiled as tea or berries pureed |
| Soapberries | Gall bladder disease | Eaten | |
| Cranberry | Greasy stomach | Eaten after a fatty meal prevent indigestion | |
| Limestone | | Drink as soup | Used as cooking rocks |
| Marrow Bone, Fishbone, Boiled Gristle | | Chewed for calcium | Boiled to soften |

This list of Indian herbs still used today by traditional Indian people is submitted courtesy of First Nations and Inuit Health, Alberta Region, Health and Welfare Canada.

little over one-third (35 percent) of aboriginal people were younger than fifteen years of age, compared to approximately 21 percent for the general population.

In 1996, the largest proportions of aboriginal people lived in Ontario (17.7 percent), British Columbia (17.5 percent) and Manitoba (16.1 percent) while the fewest lived in the Yukon (0.8 prcent) and in Prince Edward Island (0.1 percent). Ontario had the largest proportion of North American Indians (21.4 percent), Alberta had the largest Métis population (24.1 percent), and the

Northwest Territories had the largest Inuit population (59.9 percent). However, the concentration of aboriginal people was the highest in the Northwest Territories, with almost two-thirds of the total population being Aboriginal. The Yukon, Manitoba, and Saskatchewan had concentrations of 20.1 percent, 11.7 percent, and 11.4 percent, respectively. In contrast, Native people accounted for less than 1 percent of the Prince Edward Island population.

Although 30 percent of the total aboriginal population lived in Canada's twenty-five census metropolitan areas, only 6 percent of Inuit people resided in those areas. In 1997, there were 623 registry groups or bands in Canada. The average number of people in a band was 1,006, with a range of less than one hundred people to more than 2,000 members, with a few numbering between five and ten thousand. In 1996, almost one-half (46.6 percent) the total number of persons registered under the Indian Act lived on a reserve. The proportions of registered Indians living on reserve ranged from close to three-quarters (73 percent) in Nova Scotia to 2 percent in the Northwest Territories (NWT). There is only one reserve in the NWT.

In 1996, 17.7 percent of registered Indian people who lived on reserves lived in a special access zone, which means they had no year-round road access to the nearest service center where supplies, material, and equipment, skilled and semi-skilled labor, financial institutions, health and hospital services, and other provincial and federal services were available. Two percent lived in a remote area (more than 350 kilometers from the nearest service center with year-round road access).

The fertility rate among the aboriginal population is about 69 percent higher than the rate for the general Canadian population. In 1996, there were 491 children less than five years of age for every 1,000 aboriginal women of child-bearing age, compared to 290 children per 1,000 women in the total population. This partially accounts for the higher population growth rate in aboriginal people than in the general Canadian population.

In 1985, Bill C-31 restored Indian status to those who had lost their registered Indian status based on gender and marital status. This act has played a significant role in the aboriginal population growth. In fact, 19,199 additions were made to the Indian Register in 1987 and Bill C-31 registrants accounted for more than 17 percent of the total registered Indian population in 1996. The on-reserve status Indian population is growing at a rate of 2.1 percent a year while the off-reserve status population is growing by 2.9 percent annually, about two times the national rate. The status Indian population is projected to grow by 20 percent between 1998 and 2008, compared to 10 percent for the overall Canadian population.

### Health Status

**Mortality.** The death rate among Canada's First Nations population fell by 21 percent between 1979 and 1993. The largest improvement was in infant (under one year of age) mortality. However, because death rates have fallen in the total Canadian population as well, the gap between First Nations and Canadian populations has stayed the same. Improvements have also been seen in other leading causes of death including injury and poisoning, and diseases of the circulatory, respiratory, and digestive systems, but these rates also remain substantially above Canadian rates. For aboriginal Canadians the benchmark of Canadian health status has not been reached. This fact highlights that the improvements to date in health status have not yet made a significant impact on the quality and length of the lives of many aboriginal Canadians.

In 1996 and 1997, First Nations and Inuit people from eastern Canada, the Prairies, and the western provinces had mortality rates that were up to almost 1.5 times higher than the 1996 rate for the general population. Although only crude rates are available from the Atlantic provinces and Quebec, aboriginal people from these locations had a mortality pattern similar to the total population, with diseases of the circulatory system being the main cause of death, followed by cancer and injuries and poisonings.

In contrast, the leading cause of death in Native people from the Prairies and British Columbia was injuries and poisonings, followed by diseases of the circulatory system and cancer. However, First Nations and Inuit people were about 6.5 times more likely than the total Canadian population to die of injuries and poisonings. The mortality rate attributed to injuries and poisonings was higher in men in both populations. This includes both intentional and non-intentional injuries such as suicide, homicide, and accidents.

**Infant Mortality.** Data from Eastern and Central Canada, the Prairies, and British Columbia indicate that from 1995 to 1997 the infant mortality rate in First Nations was up to 3.5 times higher than the 1996 national rate. The 1997 neonatal death rate was up to two times higher, while the post-neonatal mortality rate was up to almost five times higher in the First Nations than in the general Canadian population in 1995.

**Potential Years of Life Lost.** Data from the Prairies and British Columbia indicate that in 1997, injuries and poisonings were the leading causes of potential years of life lost (PYLL), almost one-half the total PYLL. Premature deaths due to injuries and poisonings in those provinces were almost seven times higher than for other causes. In contrast, the main cause of PYLL in the general Canadian population in 1995 was cancer, although injuries were the principal causes of premature mortality in men and the second leading causes of PYLL in women, along with cardiovascular diseases.

**Life Expectancy.** Life expectancy in the registered Indian population increased approximately ten years between 1975 and 1995. This may be partly due to a decrease in the infant mortality rate and to the influx of Bill-C31 registrants who tended to be relatively young. In 1995, the life expectancy at birth was 69.1 years for men and 76.2 years for women, about a seven-year difference between the sexes. In that same year, the life expectancy in the general Canadian population was 75.4 years for men and 81.3 years for women, a difference of about six years between the sexes.

Men in the general Canadian population were expected to live 6.3 years more than registered Indian men. Canadian women in the general population were expected to live 5.1 years more than registered Indian women. Although the gap between the genders has been slowly narrowing in the general Canadian population since the early 1970s, it increased slightly in the registered Indian population between 1975 and 1980, after which it has remained stable. It is interesting to note that in 1995 the life expectancy of status Indian women exceeded that of non-aboriginal Canadian men. Although death rates among First Nations people have decreased, the Canadian population as a whole has experienced a similar downward trend. Because of this, the overall gap in death rates between First Nations and the Canadian population has persisted.

**Suicide.** Data from eastern Canada, the Prairies, and British Columbia show that First Nations and Inuit people had a suicide rate in 1997 that was almost three times higher than the 1996 rate for the total Canadian population. The 1996 crude suicide rate among the Northwest Territories Inuit was about six times higher than the national average. Young men were the most common population group to commit suicide. Alcohol intoxication appeared in 33 percent of suicides in the Northwest Territories.

Suicide ranks as one of the largest among all the disparities among First Nations and Canadians with respect to mortality. The gap is especially wide between ages fifteen and twenty-four, where rates among First Nations people are from five to eight times the national average.

**Chronic Diseases.** In 1997, the prevalence of self-reported chronic diseases in First Nations and Labrador Inuit people was higher than in the general Canadian population. This applied to all age groups and both genders. Heart disease, high blood pressure, and diabetes are considered relatively new illnesses in aboriginal communities. Although the self-reported prevalence of cancer was relatively low (1.5 percent in men and 2.8 percent in women) compared to other chronic conditions, there has been an apparent increase in cancer in aboriginal people over the years, although the cause is unknown.

The incidence of cancer in women and the young age at which cancer deaths occur has meant that this disease is responsible for the third highest potential years of life lost for aboriginal Canadian women.

**Diabetes.** Diabetes is of special concern to the First Nations population, where it tends to be predominantly of the non-insulin-dependent type. The age at onset is younger and complications, such as end stage renal disease and cardiovascular risks, are more frequent and appear to develop faster in Native people. The Sandy Lake First Nation community in northwestern Ontario has a diabetes rate of 26 percent, the third highest rate in the world and four to five times the national average. A genetic predisposition to fat storage combined with a less active lifestyle and a high-fat diet have been found to play a role in the onset of diabetes in the Ojibwa and Cree living in that small community. Because of the higher rate of diabetes the federal government has funded the Aboriginal Diabetes Initiative to address care and treatment, health promotion, prevention, and lifestyle change.

**Tuberculosis.** Between 1991 and 1996, the incidence of tuberculosis in First Nations and Inuit communities decreased from 58.1 per 100,000 with an average annual decline of 7 percent. The current incidence of tuberculosis among First Nations persons on reserve is on par with rates seen among the foreign-born in Canada and are eighteen times higher than Canadian-born aboriginal populations. Rates were similar between men and women and higher rates were seen among the very young (up to four years old) and the elderly (sixty-five and higher). Among Medical Services Branch, Health Canada regions in 1996, tuberculosis rates were highest in Saskatchewan at 105 per 100,000.

## Socioeconomic Environment

The socioeconomic environment of a population, as expressed by education, employment, and income is a strong predictor of health status and is a major health determinant.

**Education.** In 1996, 54 percent of the aboriginal population aged fifteen and over did not have a high school diploma, compared to 35 percent of the non-aboriginal population. Only 4.5 percent of aboriginal people had a university degree or certificate, compared to 16 percent of non-aboriginal people. However, there was some improvement in the educational attainment of aboriginal people between 1981 and 1996. The proportion of aboriginal people in their twenties with a post-secondary degree or diploma climbed from 19 percent to 23 percent, while those with a university degree or certificate increased from 3 percent to 4 percent.

**Unemployment and Social Assistance.** The unemployment rate on First Nations reserves was about 29 percent in 1997 and 1998, almost three times the official national rate of 10 percent. In 1997, dependency on social assistance on reserve was 46 percent, four times the Canadian rate. In the previous fiscal year, the average number of recipients of social assistance per month in the on-reserve registered Indian population was 68,790, or about one in five people. In 1997, the estimated number of recipients of provincial and municipal social assistance in the general Canadian population was 2,774,900 or about one in ten Canadians.

**Income.** In 1993, the average employment income of aboriginal people was $17,382, about 1.5 times lower than the national average of $26,474.

The average earnings of the on-reserve First Nations population was $14,055, 24 percent lower than of aboriginal people who lived off reserve. In that same year, 44 percent of the aboriginal population was below Statistics Canada's low income cutoffs, compared to 20 percent of the total Canadian population. The rate of aboriginal children who lived in low-income families was more than twice the national rate, which may be partly explained by the larger number of single-parent families in the aboriginal population.

**Single-parent Families.** In 1996, almost one-third (32 percent) of aboriginal children under the age of fifteen lived in a single-parent family, twice the rate of the general Canadian population. This increased their vulnerability to poverty since one-parent families had average family incomes that were one-half of all families in 1995.

**Housing.** Housing and infrastructure are inferior in First Nations communities. A variety of health problems are associated with poor housing conditions, lack of central heating, inadequate water, and crowding that are often seen in these communities. These health problems include infectious diseases, for example, tuberculosis and HIV, non-infectious respiratory diseases such as asthma, chronic conditions such as diabetes and obesity, and mental health conditions related to interpersonal conflicts.

The post-neonatal death rate, a recognized indicator of socioeconomic conditions on health in the first years of life, although almost halved in the past fifteen years, is still three times the Canadian rate in aboriginal communities.

**Environmental Contaminants.** Environmental contaminants such as polychlorinated biphenyls (PCBs) and mercury can pose health risks to children (especially to the developing fetus and newborn infants), such as developmental problems and toxic effects on the immune system. First Nations and Inuit people are more at risk of exposure to environmental contaminants due to their traditional diet of fish and marine mammals, for contaminants tend to accumulate in such animals. Moreover, the levels of methylmercury in the water systems have increased because of hydroelectric reservoirs, mining operations, and the pulp and paper industry.

## Personal Health Practices

Lifestyle, composed of knowledge, beliefs, attitudes, and behaviors can affect an individual's risk of developing chronic health problems.

**Smoking.** In 1997, 62 percent of First Nations and Labrador Inuit individuals fifteen years of age or older smoked, a rate that is little more than twice as high as the general Canadian population (29 percent). First Nations and Labrador Inuit started to smoke as early as six to eight years of age, with a rapid increase at ages eleven and twelve and a peak at age sixteen. First Nations and Inuit smokers were more likely to suffer from a chronic condition. Furthermore, smoking rates were negatively associated with educational attainment.

**Smoking During Pregnancy.** A recent study of Saskatoon pregnant women found that health risk behaviors during early pregnancy were more prevalent among women with an aboriginal or Métis background. Alcohol intake, tobacco use, psychoactive drug experimentation, and caffeine usage were also more frequent in women with lower education and income levels, those not living with a partner, those who had previous births, and in some cases, younger women. An earlier study found that smoking, caffeine intake, and binge drinking were the most prevalent in Inuit and Indian pregnant women, compared to white women and those of mixed racial heritage. Moreover, smoking was significantly associated with low birth weight and a shorter body length of the newborn.

**Alcohol, Substance, and Solvent Abuse.**  Alcohol and substance abuse is considered a major problem in aboriginal communities. In 1996 and 1997, 46 percent of people in detoxification and treatment facilities in the Regina, Saskatchewan Health District were of First Nations or Métis descent. Information derived from addiction treatment centers, alcohol-related hospitalizations, and death due to violent causes (such as suicide) indicate that alcohol is the abused drug of choice and that the negative consequences of alcohol and substance abuse are more severe in indigenous Canadians. Aboriginal youth are at two to six times higher risk for every alcohol-related problem than their non-aboriginal counterparts in the Canadian population. A report by the Canadian Centre on Substance Abuse and the Addiction Research Foundation of Ontario suggest that aboriginal men may be more apt to abuse alcohol while women tend to abuse drugs alone. Binge drinking seems to be a pattern among Native people, which has particular implications during pregnancy.

In 1996, aboriginal people fifteen years of age or older living in the Northwest Territories were almost three times more likely than non-aboriginal residents to have used marijuana or hashish in the past year and three-and-a-half times more likely to have used LSD, speed, cocaine, crack, or heroin. The situation in the First Nations and Inuit population does not appear to be improving. More than one-half of the First Nations and Inuit Regional Health Survey (FNIRHS) respondents perceived no progress in the reduction of alcohol and drug abuse between 1995 and 1997.

The use of solvents and non-beverage alcohol among Native children seems to be widespread. One in five aboriginal youths have used solvents and one-third of users are under the age of fifteen. Over one-half began to use solvents before reaching eleven years of age. According to the 1996 Northwest Territories Alcohol and Drug Survey, aboriginal people aged fifteen or over were about eleven times more likely to have ever sniffed solvents or aerosols than non-aboriginal respondents and almost twenty-four times more likely than the rest of Canada.

**Alcohol-Related Birth Defects.**  The incidence of Fetal Alcohol Syndrome (FAS) appears to be much higher in some aboriginal communities than in other parts of Canada. A recent study of a First Nations reserve in Manitoba found that one in ten children was the victim of FAS or FAE (Fetal Alcohol Effects), or roughly one hundred cases per 1,000 births on the reserve. In contrast, the rate of FAS in western countries is about 0.33 cases per 1,000 births. Alcohol intake, especially binge drinking, during pregnancy seems to be more common in aboriginal women. Furthermore, a study that found a higher frequency of alcohol use and abuse in Inuit and Indian pregnant women also found a significant association between alcohol intake, especially binge drinking, and a lower head circumference.

**HIV/AIDS.**  While the trends in the reported number of AIDS cases has shown a decline in the general Canadian population since 1994, the annual number of aboriginal AIDS cases has risen dramatically. By the end of 1997, the prevalence of AIDS was estimated at 33.2 per 100,000 aboriginal people, almost eleven times higher than the national rate in 1996 (3.1 per 100,000 population). In fact, the proportion of AIDS cases attributed to aboriginal people has risen from 2 percent of all cases in Canada in 1989 to over 10 percent in 1996 and 1997.

The age at diagnosis was lower in aboriginal people than in the non-aboriginal population, with 29.8 percent of aboriginal individuals diagnosed before the age of thirty, compared to 18.6 percent of individuals from the general population. Aboriginal women were more than twice as likely to have AIDS than non-aboriginal women (15.9 percent versus 7.0 percent of total cases, respectively). Aboriginal AIDS cases were more often attributed to injection drug use than were non-aboriginal cases (19.0 percent versus 3.2 percent for men, 50.0 percent versus 17.4 percent for women). Aboriginal people are over-represented in groups at risk for HIV infection, such as injection drug users, prison inmates, and sex trade workers.

## Health Services

Accessibility, satisfaction, utilization, and expenditures are important components of health services, which provide treatment for illness and care of the sick.

**Unmet Health Care Needs.**  Almost one-half of First Nations and Labrador Inuit respondents of the FNIRHS thought that their health services were not at the same level as the rest of Canada. Although the great majority thought that a return to traditional ways was a good idea to promote community wellness, over one-third perceived no progress in at least four of the traditional items specifically measured in the survey.

**Physician Utilization.**  Data from the Prairies indicate that the main reasons First Nations people consulted a physician in 1996 and 1997 were related to diseases of the respiratory system, followed by injuries and poisonings and diabetes and its complications. Respiratory system ailments were the leading reasons for the use of medical services in all age groups, except in those aged sixty-five and over for whom diseases of the circulatory system were the principal reason for physician consultation. Disorders of the nervous system were also common reasons for the use of medical services in children up to age of fourteen. This may reflect the relatively high prevalence of ear problems and the effects of exposure to alcohol and environmental contaminants during pregnancy.

**Hospitalization Rates.** Data from the Prairies indicate that First Nations had a hospitalization rate that was about two-and-a-half times higher than the general Canadian population in 1996 and 1997. Diseases of the respiratory system were the leading causes of hospitalization in First Nations patients, followed by injuries and poisonings and diseases of the digestive system. In contrast, the principal causes of hospitalization in the general Canadian population were related to diseases of the circulatory system. The second and third main causes were diseases of the digestive system and the respiratory system, respectively. Injuries and poisonings represented the fourth leading causes of hospitalization in Canadian male patients.

Despite improvements in many areas, aboriginal people in Canada continue to have a poorer health status than the Canadian population. Aboriginal people die earlier than their fellow Canadians and continue to bear a disproportionate share of the burden of physical and mental illness. This discrepancy in health is in part due to the widespread inequities that the aboriginal population faces in the opportunities for health, notably in socioeconomic conditions.

Improving the health of Canada's Native people will depend on improving their economic and social conditions as well as assisting them to identify and address their health needs in a manner that takes into account and respects their cultural and traditional beliefs and values. Programs and services must be designed and developed that are reflective of these needs and offer culturally appropriate interventions. Aboriginal communities need to be empowered to identify and address their own needs through such means as the training of more aboriginal health workers and increased funding and technical support.

Suicide rates, the bellwether of community wellness, remain unacceptably high and send a powerful signal about the devastating effects of poverty, the history of oppression, and the limitations of the Canadian health care system in addressing the health needs of Canada's aboriginal population.

The bench mark of Canadian health status has not been reached and this means that improvements to date are only a beginning in achieving a significant breakthrough in the physical, mental and spiritual health status of Canada's aboriginal population.

## Historic and Contemporary Role of the Canadian Health System

**The Fur Traders and Whalers.** The Europeans brought their own medical system to Canada as well as their own diseases. However, prior to the formation of Canada in 1867 these services were poorly organized and relatively unsophisticated. Aboriginal people continued to consult their own healers. With the growth of the settlements around the trading posts, missionaries and traders also provided rudimentary medical care to the inhabitants of these settlements. Although some of the aid provided had a humanitarian impulse, the underlying reason was self-interest, as disease victims could neither trap nor hunt and were a drain on the company's accounts not only through the loss of furs but also because they became dependent on the company for subsistence.

The whalers in the northern Arctic were provided with a ship's physician and a medical chest for their health needs. However, in their case, the Inuit (Eskimo) became the healers as the crews suffered from nutritional diseases like scurvy, frostbite, and exposure due to the cold. The Inuit taught the physicians and the crews how to survive in the Arctic climate and how to prevent scurvy by eating fresh meat.

By and large the Hudson's Bay Company did the best they could to keep their suppliers healthy. An example is the case of William Todd, the "most famous surgeon in the western interior of Canada before 1850." He vaccinated the Indian trappers with a new cowpox vaccine that had been sent to Canada by the Hudson's Bay Company and trained an Indian to inoculate his own family and others in his camp. Todd, however, was also a trader for the Hudson's Bay Company. His medical successes did not outweigh his mediocre record as a trader and he was let go.

Another example is Alexander MacKenzie, an explorer who worked for the Northwest Company. Although his descriptions of aboriginal medical practices are unflattering, when European practices failed he was willing to call in healers and somewhat grudgingly give them credit for their success, even if he did not agree with their methods. It could be said that this was the first example of western and traditional medical practices working together to heal a patient.

The Hudson's Bay Company provided medical care and food to the Indians prior to confederation as a means of retaining a healthy and productive workforce of hunters and trappers. But with the decline of the fur trade they attempted to move these responsibilities to the federal government. The government, however, was unwilling to assume the financial burden of providing medical care and relief to the Indians and responded by involving the missionary societies in providing these services.

**Missionaries.**  The missionaries were among the first to have contact with the aboriginal people of Canada. Initially they provided medical services in hopes of converting people to Christianity. Their interest in the spirit as well as the body and their ability to provide medicines gained them the initial respect of the aboriginal population, but increasingly they became regarded with suspicion and fear as their spiritual practices came into conflict with those of the traditional healers.

The missionaries founded the first hospitals in Canada. In 1639 the first one was established in Quebec, followed by a hospital in Montreal in 1644. In Labrador in the seventeenth and eighteenth century the missions that were established provided medical care and in 1897 a temporary hospital was established in Hopedale. Although their main interest was in saving souls their contribution to the medical field was significant. In remote areas, these missionaries may have helped save some aboriginal tribes from extinction during epidemics.

However, this survival came at a price for Inuit people. A decisive clash occurred between missionaries and the Inuk shaman (traditional healer). The shaman was besieged on two fronts. He was challenged as a spiritual authority and as a healer by Christian, western medicine. When shamans either went underground or converted to Christianity, the Inuit lost the most important bearers of the traditions that made their culture. Gradually specialists from the south began to perform the functions that had given the shaman prestige and authority. Shamanism disappeared, surfacing only in carvings and drawings.

**Northwest Mounted Police.**  The 1867 British North America Act, which is the foundation of modern-day Canadian government, defined the responsibility of the federal government for "Indians and lands reserved for Indians." However, medical services continued to be provided by traders and missionaries and after 1873 the newly formed Northwest Mounted Police.

This force was formed in part to combat the American "whisky trade," which was exacting an immense toll on Natives, especially among the Southern Plains Indians. Aboriginal people in Canada at the time of contact did not have a history of alcohol usage. The French fur traders brought alcohol to the eastern seaboard and introduced it as a gift and an item of trade as early as the 1670s. By the mid-eighteenth century all the rival trading companies were giving lavish gifts of alcohol to trappers as an inducement for their furs and

loyalty. In 1753 in York Factory, 864 gallons of rum and brandy were traded.

The use of alcohol and its concomitant public health and social problems were initially limited to the trading posts and decreased when the Hudson's Bay Company discontinued its policy of providing liquor in 1825. However the access to alcohol was not completely severed and many Indian leaders welcomed the Northwest Mounted Police in their efforts to control the trade.

In the following years police surgeons provided medical services to aboriginal peoples, especially in the North. This was part of their job as agents of the federal government. However there was no organized system of services and the quality and extent of medical care was dependent on the individual who administered it. The police, because of their involvement in controlling the whisky trade, were often callous to the plight of their patients who were not seen as victims of poverty and ill health but as lazy and shiftless.

**Federal Health Services.**  In 1880 the first Department of Indian Affairs was established. All responsibilities for aboriginal people were officially handed over to Indian agents. These individuals had already been working since confederation to carry out the government assimilation policy. Their role in providing medical services for which the department had made no budgetary provision was limited to providing famine relief. It was not until 1904 that Peter H. Bryce was appointed the first superintendent of medical services. Bryce was charged with providing health services to Canada's aboriginal peoples.

Bryce was a persistent advocate for improving the health services provided to aboriginal people. A former public health official in the province of Ontario, he was concerned with conditions on reserves, especially the spread of tuberculosis. His first request was to Parliament to fund preventive programs in reserve communities. This request was turned down as too expensive, as the Department of Indian Affairs was more concerned with budgetary restraint than providing medical services.

Bryce then decided to bring public attention to the problem and in 1907 he released a report entitled *The Story of a National Crime: An Appeal for Justice for the Indians of Canada*. This report revealed the appalling conditions in the residential schools and identified them as breeding grounds for tuberculosis, which was threatening not only aboriginal people but also the surrounding non-aboriginal communities.

The reaction to the report criticizing a mainstay of the government's assimilation policy was met with denial and defensiveness by both the churches that ran the schools and the government that funded them. His efforts to remove Indian health from the Department of

Indian Affairs to the Department of Health was also unsuccessful, and Indian Health remained in the Department of Indian Affairs for another twenty-five years.

Although the majority of Bryce's efforts were unsuccessful, he did succeed in laying the foundation for some current health services delivery practices, such as the physicians services being supplemented by community nurses in nursing stations and translating health education circulars into aboriginal languages. He was also the first to fill the vacuum of physician services by contracting with local doctors. Bryce's criticisms of the Indian health system alienated the government and when he retired his position was not filled until 1927 when a medical doctor, Colonel E. L. Stone, took his place and a formal medical branch was created within the Department of Indian Affairs. Some progress occurred during Stone's tenure. He developed public health regulations for communicable diseases, but he was continually hampered by lack of funds. In 1934 the per capita expenditure for health care for the Canadian public was $31.00. For aboriginal people it was $9.60. In 1936 the Department of Indian Affairs was absorbed into the Department of Mines and Resources where it remained until 1944 when the Department of Health and Welfare was established.

Health care has always been considered a treaty right by Indian people based on the eleven numbered treaties made between the tribes and the Canadian government between 1871 and 1921. The claim to a treaty right to health care is based mainly on the Medicine Chest Clause of Treaty 6 (1876) and the verbal agreements made when negotiating Treaty 8 (1899). The Medicine Chest Clause stipulated that "the Medicine Chest shall be kept at the house of each Indian agent for the use and benefit of the Indians."

Two cases were decided on this issue in the Canadian courts. In *Dreaver v. R.* (1935), the judge concluded that the medicine chest was interpreted as meaning that "all medicines, drugs or medical supplies which might be required by the Indians. . . were to be supplied to them free of charge." In *R. v. Johnston* (1966), the judge concluded that "the Indians are entitled to receive all medical services including medicine, drugs, medical supplies and hospital care free of charge." This liberal interpretation, however, was overturned by a higher court. In 1966, the Saskatchewan Court of Appeal ruled that "the Medicine Chest" meant only its literal meaning and did not include a comprehensive range of medical services. In practice, the federal government provides a comprehensive range of services, but the issue of treaty right to health care remains contentious and is the subject of ongoing research and debate.

As described by P. E. Moore in 1946, there were twenty-seven physicians employed full-time and 700 doctors employed part-time by the department. Sixteen hospitals in addition to the hundreds of small tuberculosis sanitoria, which were established by 1935, were servicing aboriginal patients. Traditional healing was still seen as detrimental and a hindrance in providing medical services. Racial segregation was also practiced with non-aboriginal patients refusing to share wards with aboriginal patients.

Many aboriginal patients were forcibly evacuated to southern hospitals for treatment. This was especially true of the Inuit. The handling of Inuit patients was inhumane and has left a legacy of bitterness which still persists today. Those suspected of the disease were simply taken to medical ships and given x-rays. When these turned out positive, they were refused permission to go back to shore. When the ship left they were taken south without any effort to inform their families.

In the hospitals where they were strictly confined and socially isolated they became lonely and depressed, which hampered their recovery. Many died in isolation and their families were informed years later or, due to mix-ups with their Inukitut names that were incomprehensible to staff, never informed at all. Children were routinely deposited in settlements hundreds of miles from their homes. Some never returned and those who did not succumb to the disease were adopted out to white families in the south. According to a current report: "The Inuit people were treated like cattle. To the bulk of the federal staff in Ottawa they were just numbers."

By 1956, National Health and Welfare was operating eighteen hospitals, thirty-three nursing stations, fifty-two health centers containing dispensaries, and thirteen other health centers employing physicians and nurses. The number of contract physicians had expanded to almost 1,300 persons who provided full- or part-time services and the budget of the department exceeded $17 million.

In 1962 the Indian Health Services was eliminated and a new department, the Medical Services Branch, was formed which took over the medical care of all aboriginal people. A regional administrative structure was developed across Canada. Hospitals and sanatoria were closed as the need for them decreased and nursing stations and health centers took over as the primary providers of federal health services to aboriginal patients. In 1971 universal medical care was introduced in Canada and clinical services directed specifically at aboriginal people ceased to be provided by the federal government except in northern and remote areas.

## Contemporary Health Services Delivery

In Canada there is no equivalent to the U.S. Indian Health Services to provide medical services to aboriginal people. Since 1971 there has been universal health insurance in Canada which covers medical fees and hospital stays for all of its citizens. Moreover medical care is the constitutional responsibility of the provinces. The role of the federal government is limited to administering transfer payments to the provinces to cover the cost of all medical services.

There remain, however, a few groups to whom the federal government provides some direct services. One of these groups consists of First Nations (status Indians) and Inuit people. These services have been provided by the government's Health Canada, Medical Services Branch (MSB), since its inception.

On 1 July 2000 MSB became the First Nations and Inuit Health Branch (FNIHB). FNIHB is a highly decentralized, client-oriented organization responsible for several programs with an annual budget of $1 billion as of 2000. The delivery of health services and the management of Indian and northern health are conducted through regional offices, zone offices, and a network of hospitals, nursing stations, health centers, and various other health facilities, many of which are situated in remote and isolated regions. Regions generally correspond to provincial and territorial boundaries, except for Atlantic Region, which includes all the Atlantic provinces.

The mission of FNIHB is to establish a "renewed relationship with First Nations that is based on the transfer of direct health services and a refocused federal role, and that seeks to improve the health status of First Nations and Inuit." The organization's vision is that First Nations and Inuit people will have autonomy and control of their programs and resources within a time-frame to be determined in consultation with First Nations and Inuit people. The mandate of FNIHB with respect to First Nations and Inuit people is to assist First Nations and Inuit communities in addressing health inequalities and threats, and to attain a level of health comparable to that of Canadians living in other locations. The current priorities of the branch are to manage the cost-effective delivery of health services within the fiscal limits of the First Nations and Inuit Health budget. The total FNIHB budget includes resources for all First Nation health programs, accounting for nearly one billion dollars in department expenditure.

The activities of the First Nations and Inuit Health Programs (FNIHP) directorate are guided by both the branch vision, which is to "ensure that First Nations and Inuit have autonomy and control of their health programs and resources within a time-frame to be determined in consultation with them" and by the vision of the Department which is "to help the people of Canada maintain and improve their health." The director provides health professional and program expertise to advance the policy and program directions of branch and department. FNIHP carries out its mandate by (1) conducting health and program surveillance activities to identify trends and emerging issues to facilitate program design, implementation, and evaluation; (2) supporting regions and other directorates, the department, and national First Nation and Inuit organizations in the coordination of health programs to enable effective program development, delivery and evaluation; and (3) planning for and implementing the transfer of programs and functions managed nationally to First Nation and Inuit organizations and/or regions to improve the responsiveness of programs to the changing needs of First Nation and Inuit people. The work of FNIHP is guided by the following principles:

- activities will support knowledge and capacity building among First Nations and Inuit;
- work will be carried out in partnership with First Nations, Inuit, regions, and other stakeholders; and
- First Nations and Inuit control and ownership of health programs and resources will be facilitated and encouraged.

The Health Programs Support Division supports the branch vision and strategic direction through transfer of responsibility and resources to Medical Services Branch regions and/or national aboriginal organizations and supports the delivery of health programs to First Nations and Inuit communities.

The Research and Development Environmental Contaminants Division manages the headquarters (Ottawa) components of the First Nations Environmental Health Program, supports regions in the delivery of the national program, and facilitates the transfer of the Environmental Health Program to First Nations and Inuit control.

The Health Programs Analysis Division supports the branch's vision and strategic direction by developing, analyzing, and disseminating information on health status, programs, and current and emerging health issues and by providing health professional advice. This mandate is carried out by advancing evidence-based decision making through the analysis of First Nation and Inuit population health information, the provision of health professional support and expertise, and the coordination of national communicable disease strategies.

The Non-Insured Health Benefits Program (NIHB) provides a range of health related goods and services to eligible beneficiaries who are status Indians, recognized Inuit, and recognized Innu people in Canada. The NIHB offers specific health-related benefits not provided by other agencies such as the provincial and territorial health plans or other third-party plans. These benefits include vision and dental care, medical transportation, drugs, medical supplies and equipment, and mental health counseling.

The NIHB directorate has three functional divisions. The first, the Program Policy Division, recommends courses of action to guide the development and delivery of the NIHB Program. The focus is on operational policy, bringing together the input of operational and professional expertise from various disciplines and professions. The second, the Program Analysis and Planning Division, provides research, analysis, and advice in support of policy recommendations and strategies for program management and provides planning mechanisms and information to provide accountability to central agencies. The third, the Operational Support Division, coordinates and resolves operational issues which relate to regional delivery of the program; develops and facilitates strategies with the regions for operational manager of the program; and develops, maintains, and manages the national applications required to administer the management of the NIHB program.

## Northern Secretariat

Between 1982 and 1988, Health Canada, Medical Services Branch (MSB), transferred responsibility and resources for health programs, services, and related assets to the government of the Northwest Territories. Since then, any new health programs approved for First Nations and Inuit in the Northwest Territories (NWT) have been handled by MSB, now the FNIHB, in a variety of approaches. With the 1997 transfer of universal health programs to the Yukon territorial government and the signing of the Yukon Self Government Agreements, FNIHB is being challenged to meet the demands of providing First Nations specific programs to Yukon First Nations. The creation of Nunavut Territory, which took effect 1 April 1999, has placed many new demands on Health Canada to ensure that the necessary support to the Nunavut Department of Health and Social Services is provided in a timely fashion, while ensuring the ongoing provision of First Nations and Inuit programs and services.

**Organizational Responsibility.** In order to provide a coordinated, cohesive, and equitable approach to

FNIHB program delivery issue for First Nations and Inuit living in Yukon, the NWT and Nunavut, Health Canada's Medical Services Branch has developed a new organizational structure called the Northern Secretariat. In addition to First Nations and Inuit health programs, the secretariat will also provide the required coordination and support to current and future self-government negotiations in Yukon and NWT.

The Northern Secretariat has become the primary point of contact for territorial governments and other interested parties for issues related to North of Sixty federal health programming, and ensures the necessary internal linkages are made. It will be responsible for strategic and operational policy approaches, negotiation, direction, and oversight of all current and future FNIHB program funding for health programs for the Inuit and First Nations of Yukon, the NWT and Nunavut Territories. In addition, the secretariat will be responsible for overall coordination within FNIHB on North Sixty issues and the lead for Health Canada on Nunavut Department of Health implementation. The Northern Secretariat is headed by a director reporting to the director general of FNIHB and is based in Ottawa to support relationships with other branches of Health Canada and other government departments.

## Community Involvement in Health Care

In September 1978, at an international conference in Alma Ata, in the former Soviet Union, the World Health Organization promulgated a declaration on primary health care, which received the support of delegates from all 134 attending countries including Canada. It defined health as a state of complete physical, mental, and social well-being and not only as the absence of disease. Article III states "primary health care ... requires and promotes maximum community and individual self-reliance and participation in the planning, organization, operation and control of primary health care." It had become obvious both to the Canadian government and to Indian community leaders that the problems of Indian health could not be ameliorated simply by changes or improvements in the conventional diagnosis and treatment of disease or by increasing delivery of health care services. Any improvement would have to come through addressing the underlying socioeconomic, environmental, and cultural causes of Indian ill-health.

On 9 September 1979, the Canadian federal government adopted a new Indian health policy directed at achieving an increasingly improved level of health in Indian communities, generated and maintained by these communities themselves. This policy recognized that the strengthening of social, economic, cultural, and spiritual development in Indian communities was the foundation for improvement in Indian health. Implicit in this is the recognition that although the process is founded on participation at the community level it has an impact at the regional and national level as well.

In the ten years after 1978, both the federal government and Indian nations issued a series of policy statements and took steps to implement the Health Program Transfer Initiative. The intent of this initiative was to transfer the design and management of community health programs to Native control at a pace determined by the Native communities themselves.

The reaction to the transfer program has been mixed. Some bands have seen it as an opportunity for greater control over their health services. Others fear it is an attempt on the part of the Canadian government to withdraw essential services guaranteed by treaty right. To date Health Canada has signed 170 transfer and integrated agreements covering 282 of the 631 First Nations and Inuit communities in the country.

## Community-Based Programs

Indian and Inuit peoples in Canada, with the support of the Canadian federal government, are making a transition from an institution-centered health care system to a community-centered program providing culturally appropriate health care. The system not only addresses the symptoms of disease, but also alleviates the underlying problems of housing, sanitation, and employment. The examples that follow illustrate initiatives that have been undertaken in the past decade at the national, regional, and local levels.

**Health Care and Self-Government: The James Bay Cree.**   In 1984, the Canadian government passed the Indian Self-Government Act, which enables Indian nations to formulate their own constitutions and negotiate recognition through the Department of Indian and Northern Affairs. Control over health services, however, is complicated by the fact that in Canada health care comes under, and is therefore circumscribed by, provincial government jurisdiction.

An example of an Indian health authority that has successfully managed to institute such intersectoral collaboration is the Cree Regional Board of Health and Social Services established under the James Bay and Northern Quebec Agreement of 1975, which led to the emergence of a "homeland for the Cree." This board is controlled by the Cree and has established several

innovative programs including a culturally appropriate nursing program, a first-aid program for Cree living in isolated conditions, and a Cree Methylmercury Surveillance Program. The board has also created the positions of a public health officer, a public safety officer, and a local environmental administrator. By the mid-1980s, its per capita health expenditure was $2,000.

**Regional Initiatives.**   Throughout the 1980s, a number of health authorities whose formal jurisdiction encompassed more than one community were also founded outside the framework of self-government. One example is the Alberta Indian Health Care Commission funded by Medical Services Branch and based in Edmonton. Its board of directors includes representatives from all three Alberta treaty areas. Its mandate is to promote Indian health care concerns throughout the province and to involve Indian people in health care delivery and training. The commission meets with chiefs and councils, provides community health liaison workers in the three treaty areas, and attends community health committee workshops. It has created a unique urban community health representative program in order to improve the delivery of health services to urban Indians who do not fall under federal government jurisdiction and therefore are not provided with free health care services. The commission works with a number of agencies, among them the Assembly of First Nations, the Indian Association of Alberta, the secretary of state, and the municipal governments of Calgary and Edmonton.

Other examples of regional health authorities are the Labrador Inuit Health Commission, which provides a similar service to the Inuit people of Labrador and Newfoundland, and the North Saskatchewan Community Health Development Process. The latter developed out of a grass-roots movement of Cree, Dene, and Chippewyan Indian and Métis communities in response to multiple medical and social problems and the high turnover of physicians—thirty-six came and left in one thirty-two month period. The resultant "health care dialogue action circles" were highly successful, initiating among other things a Youth Activity Committee, which raised enough money to build a recreational center; a New Generation Against Alcohol and Drug Abuse support group; and a working relationship with the University of Saskatchewan Northern Medical Services Program to solve the problem of the lack of primary health care workers.

**Local Initiatives.**   There are also a number of Indian health authorities having jurisdiction in only one community. An example is the Blood Tribe Board of Health in southern Alberta. It delivers health services to the seven-thousand-member Blood Tribe of the Blackfoot

Nation on the largest reserve in Canada. It is federally incorporated and is accountable to the band council, which has both appointed members from the council and elected members. In its efforts to identify and resolve community health care needs, it works with a number of Native and non-Native organizations.

There are many other small rural and urban projects, programs, and groups that have developed in response to the movement to increase community involvement in health. The Kateri Memorial Hospital Center located on the Kahnawake Mohawk Reserve just outside Montreal, Quebec, was founded in 1955 when a local woman obtained Mohawk council and Quebec government funding to revive a bankrupt local hospital formerly operated by a religious order. With Medical Services Branch and McGill University support, a medical clinic was established in the 1960s, and in 1984 a new forty-three-bed hospital building was opened, funded by the Quebec government. Kateri is an example of local, federal, and provincial government cooperation resulting in a local community health center offering a broad range of treatment, prevention, and social services. As a result, staff turnover is low, generating continuity of care that has earned the trust of the community.

One of the many innovative programs at Kateri is the diabetic education program initiated in 1984. Diabetes is one of the new chronic diseases to affect Indian people, and this program aims to help patients understand and manage their own disease. The key features of this program are the use of educators with an understanding of culture and tradition who provide individualized and appropriate teaching to diabetic patients and the involvement of the larger community through two annual Diabetic Awareness Days and to the community by workshops and local radio.

Anishnawbe Health in Toronto, Canada's largest city with over forty thousand off-reserve Indian people, is an urban inner-city center. The people it services have all the multiple health problems of reserve-based Indian people aggravated by the stress of adapting to urban living, with the concomitant problems of unfamiliar health services and communication problems. The center has its roots in a Native nutrition outreach project initiated by a physician and dietitian in 1975. Another venture in collaboration, this modern, culturally appropriate, multi-service urban health center opened in 1990. It promotes the use of traditional holistic methods in health assessment and treatment. Its client workshops include medicine wheel ceremonials by traditional healers, as well as medical treatment, addiction counseling, and crisis intervention by Indian and non-Indian health professionals sensitive to Native health conditions and needs.

**Health Career Development Programs.**  Two Royal Commissions (1980, 1981) concluded that improvements in aboriginal health status would only come about once significant numbers of aboriginal health care providers were trained. A 1983 study identified only 200 aboriginal health professionals out of 325,000 surveyed. Of these, sixteen were physicians. By 1993 these figures exhibited minimal growth. According to the Canadian Medical Association there were then some fifty aboriginal physicians. The ratio of aboriginal physicians to the total aboriginal population is approximately 1:33,000.

Similar under-representation is evident in other health and social services professions. According to the Native Nurses Association, there are approximately 500 aboriginal nurses, a figure which has not changed significantly in the past few years. Figures for other health professionals are not available. Yet a cadre of trained professionals in all these areas is crucial to the theory and practice of community control in the planning, implementation, and utilization of health care activities and the delivery of culturally appropriate programs. Based on the data accumulated by the Royal Commission on Aboriginal Peoples, the 1996 report recommended that 10,000 aboriginal health professionals be trained in the next ten years in order to meet current and future needs.

In response to this need and with the assistance of the Indian and Inuit Nurses of Canada (an organization founded in 1974, which represents the largest group of Indian health professionals numbering approximately four hundred), Medical Services Branch of Health and Welfare Canada established the Indian and Inuit Health Careers Program (IIHCP) in 1984. Its mandate was "to encourage and support Indian participation in educational opportunities and provide a learning environment designed to overcome many of the social and cultural barriers that currently inhibit the Native student's educational achievement."

Components included college scholarships, career-related employment, and professional development assistance for students. The IIHCP also funded programs in recognized post-secondary educational institutions that help students gain access to and succeed in professional health faculties, as well as local and community-based programs. The IIHC Program was discontinued in 1996 as part of the Transfer Initiative and all moneys distributed regionally to individual Bands and communities.

**Professional Training Programs.**  The first program for training aboriginal physicians and other health professionals originated at the University of Manitoba in 1979. The Special Premedical Studies and Professional

Health Program was modeled on the highly successful University of North Dakota Indians into Medicine Program. It is restricted to residents of Manitoba and provides academic, financial, and personal support. From 1988 to 1989 it was funded by a cost-sharing arrangement between the federal and provincial governments and all aboriginal students were fully funded through their pre-medical and medical school years.

The federal government withdrew its support in 1989 and students are no longer fully funded through the program, although financial assistance is available. The program has graduated some twenty-plus physicians and a number of allied health professionals. Students normally enter the Special Premedical Studies Program and continue in their Faculties of choice through the Professional Health Program.

Other universities such as the University of Alberta, the University of Toronto, and the University of Saskatchewan have addressed the challenge of attracting more aboriginal students into health sciences faculties by providing special access through additional or in quota aboriginal positions in their professional health sciences faculties. The Medical Faculties at the University of Alberta and Toronto offer up to five positions and the University of Saskatchewan offers three.

The University of Toronto has had difficulty attracting aboriginal applicants because of the expense of living in Canada's largest city. Aboriginal students also have to compete with other "federally funded applicants" usually from the armed forces. The University of Saskatchewan has enjoyed considerable success but because it is a comparatively recent program established in the mid-1990s, its numbers are still relatively small.

The Office of the Aboriginal Health Care Careers Program (AHCCP) in the Faculty of Medicine and Dentistry at the University of Alberta was established in 1988 with funding from the federal IIHC. Staffed by a coordinator, the mandate of the office is to recruit aboriginal students into medicine and other professional health sciences faculties, assist them in the admissions process, and provide services to help them graduate successfully. Policy and direction is provided by the chair of the AHCC committee who is the only First Nations professor of medicine in a Canadian medical faculty. The committee membership also includes community health careers advisors, elders, and aboriginal medical students. Since its inception the AHCC has featured an aggressive national recruitment strategy. Students and graduates have come from across Canada and represent the Abenaki, Blackfoot, Cree, Delaware, Inuit, Iroquois, Métis, Micmac, Mohawk, Odawa, and Saulteaux nations.

The faculty has graduated twenty physicians in the past twelve years, the largest number of graduates in the shortest period of time in any Canadian medical faculty. Graduates have gone on to honors in various fields. Both the chair of the AHCC committee, Malcolm King, and Lindsay Crowshoe, a 1995 Blackfoot graduate, have won prestigious medical awards from the National Aboriginal Achievement Foundation. Others like Danika Edmunds, one of two Inuit physicians in Canada, have gone on to public health studies at Harvard, where she received a master's degree and was also offered a post-degree fellowship. With few exceptions, graduates have elected to work in the area of aboriginal health, whether as full-time clinicians in aboriginal communities and inner city clinics or by devoting time to shorter placements in remote areas. The University of Alberta program is the most successful in Canada. In the 1999–2000 academic year the total enrollment of eighty-two aboriginal health sciences students and eighty-eight graduates from professional health sciences faculties was the highest in Canada. Other universities such as the University of British Columbia do not offer special positions but give special consideration to aboriginal applicants.

On the post-graduate level, the Department of Family Medicine at Queen's University offers an optional, flexible third year of training for family physicians interested in working in Indian and Inuit communities to provide more culturally sensitive care. It is a unique program offering residents the opportunity to explore the historical roots of health issues facing Native communities as well as to participate in the delivery of care in different communities.

In late 1990, thirty-five physicians of Canadian Indian ancestry, increasingly concerned with the low number of their peers and the lack of input from Canadian Indian and Inuit health professionals into the federal governments' health transfer process, met and founded the Native Physicians Association in Canada. One of the association's first initiatives was to negotiate successfully with the Canadian Medical Association for a scholarship program for Indian and Inuit medical students. By the late 1990s, however, the association had disbanded. Efforts to revive it on a regional basis are underway.

**Paraprofessional Training Programs.** Before the establishment of the IIHC, Health and Welfare Canada through MSB had already become involved in the training of health care personnel. As the department responsible for staffing reserve-based health centers, it always had difficulties recruiting and retaining professionals for remote areas. Consequently, the Community Health Representative Program (CHR) in the early 1960s, the

School of Dental Therapy in 1972, and the Nechi Institute on Alcohol and Drug Education in 1974 were established. A Health Development Administrative Certificate Program was established in 1988 in cooperation with the Yellowhead Tribal Council and Athabasca University in Alberta.

The common characteristic of these programs is that they provide Native-based training and field work and are specifically designed to involve Native people in primary care and health care delivery services in Native communities. The strength of these programs rests in their ability to extend primary health care and health care delivery services to Native communities while controlling costs. Their weakness relates to the relatively low quality of care and the fact that the training of individuals in these programs is not nationally recognized and they are not licensed to work outside Native communities.

The Community Health Representative role encompasses a broad spectrum of activities including emergency first-aid, health education, medical history taking, and health promotion. Since the inception of the program, training programs have evolved and now aim to produce health workers who are able to interpret and help identify physical and mental problems in both individuals and the community at large. Training takes place within or in conjunction with educational institutions such as the Alberta Vocational Center, Arctic College in the Northwest Territories, and Confederation College in Thunder Bay, Ontario. This move to accreditation is helping resolve the role conflict that CHRs formerly experienced due to difficulties in finding acceptance from health care professionals.

The School of Dental Therapy was established at Fort Smith in the Northwest Territories and relocated to Prince Albert, Saskatchewan, in the mid-1980s. It was designed to provide dental care to small, isolated communities lacking professional services. Trainees are taught to chart dental conditions, take x-rays and give local anesthetic, clean and fill teeth, administer fluoride, perform simple extractions, and conduct preventative programs in schools. This program has become a model in the field and has been used successfully in Africa and other developing nations. Students from Africa have graduated from the program.

Similarly, the Nechi Institute was formed in 1974 by Native alcohol counselors who believed that Indian people could most effectively combat their problems in alcoholism and mental health themselves. By the early 1980s, with joint funding from MSB and the Alberta Alcohol and Drug Abuse Commission, it emerged as a model counselor training program. Housed in a $6.5 million building near Edmonton—the only one which combines a Native treatment center and Native training center on the North American continent—it has trained some 1,500 Native counselors in the past ten years. Directed by a Native board and fully staffed by Indian people, it currently trains the staff of thirteen treatment centers, detoxification centers, and halfway houses, and conducts twenty-nine rural and urban Indian training programs.

## Organization for the Advancement of Aboriginal Peoples' Health

Established in March 2000, the Organization for the Advancement of Aboriginal Peoples' Health (formerly called Aboriginal Health Institute) is a national non-profit organization created to provide a bridge between the Canadian health system and aboriginal health and healing. The organization is dedicated to improving the physical, social, mental, emotional, and spiritual health of aboriginal peoples. A fundamental belief of the organization is that the advancement and sharing of knowledge in the field of aboriginal health are key to empowering aboriginal peoples.

The organization's goal is to improve and promote the health of aboriginal peoples and communities, facilitate and promote research, foster the employment of aboriginal people in the delivery of health care services, and affirm, recognize, and promote aboriginal traditional healing practices.

The Assembly of First Nations (the national aboriginal political association whose membership is comprised of the chiefs of all Indian bands who are recognized by the Canadian government) worked for two years in the design and creation of an aboriginal Health Institute, as promised by the federal government. The Inuit Tapirisat of Canada, Métis National Council and Native Women's Association of Canada, and other national aboriginal political organizations have also signed as members of the newly incorporated Organization for the Advancement of Aboriginal Peoples Health.

Consultations on the proposed activities and function of such an organization took place in 1998–1999 fiscal year. A design framework was developed for a structure composed of a secretariat and three centers, one each for First Nations, Métis, and Inuit. This proposal was approved by the federal government in June 1999. In August, an implementation committee, consisting of the five national aboriginal organizations as voting members, with Health Canada as chair, and three non-voting members from the aboriginal health field, worked together to draft bylaws for incorporation as a nonprofit organization. The implementation committee also assisted with the development of a treasury board submission and negotiated a funding agreement with the federal government before 31 March 2000.

In February 2000, the federal treasury board approved a budget of $4 million for the 1999–2000 fiscal year and an additional $5 million over each of the next four years. The funding is in the form of a grant, and allows for surpluses and carry-over of funds.

### Canadian Institutes for Health Research

In June 2000 the federal government also instituted the Canadian Institute for Health Research (CIHR) based on the National Institute of Health in the United States. As part of this new initiative the CIHR included an Aboriginal Health Institute whose function is to address the research challenges of diseases that disproportionately affect aboriginal populations as well as investigate traditional remedies and train a new cadre of aboriginal health researchers.

### Conclusion

The 1979 Indian Health Policy instituted a new era in the delivery of health care to Indian nations in Canada by recognizing that the increased involvement of Indian and Inuit people in the health care system was a fundamental prerequisite to improving their health status. It recognized that Indian health problems relate to poverty, oppression, and racism and that Indian people must empower themselves in order to obtain better health and social services, better employment opportunities, more adequate housing, water supply and sewage disposal systems, and recreational facilities. It recognized that a regeneration of Indian religion, heritage, and cultural values was taking place and that out of this was emerging a desire on the part of Indian leaders and communities for greater self-determination. The Indian Health Policy of 1979 initiated a process by which partnership was to be established between the Canadian government and Indian communities in the planning, implementation, and utilization of health care. The changes brought about by this policy, of which selected examples have been provided in this chapter, are of too-recent origin to make a difference to the bleak statistics presented above. But the fact that empowerment has become a key concept in both Canadian health promotion and Native health philosophy offers hope.

*Anne-Marie Hodes*
*University of Alberta*

# U. S. Indian Health Organizations

## U. S. DEPARTMENT OF INDIAN HEALTH SERVICES

U.S. DEPARTMENT OF HEALTH AND HUMAN SERVICES

INDIAN HEALTH SERVICE
Headquarters East
Parklawn Building
5600 Fishers Lane
Rockville, Maryland 20857
(301) 443–1247

Twinbrook Metro Plaza (Tmp)
12300 Twinbrook Parkway
Rockville, Maryland 20852
(301) 443–1083

INDIAN HEALTH SERVICE
HEADQUARTERS WEST
ALBUQUERQUE–HEADQUARTERS WEST
5300 Homestead Road, NE
Albuquerque, NM 87110
(505) 248–4101

CLINICAL SUPPORT CENTER
Wesley J. Picciotti, Director
1616 East Indian School Road
Aztec Square, Suite 375
Phoenix, AZ 85016
(602) 640–2140

OFFICE OF PROGRAM SUPPORT
Thomas J. Ambrose, Director
(602) 640–2140
Office of Continuing Education
E. Y. Hooper, Director
(602) 640–2140

DHHS HOTLINE NUMBER: 1 (800) 447–8477
OFFICE OF THE INSPECTOR GENERAL
    (OIG) HOTLINE
P.O. Box 23489
Washington D.C. 20007
(800) 447–8477

IHS HOTLINE NUMBER: (301) 443–0658
Indian Health Service (IHS)
5600 Fishers Lane
Parklawn Building, Room 6–48
Rockville, Maryland 20857
To report allegations of fraud, waste, abuse, and/or
    mismanagement by IHS employees. (Not an
    information number.)

## INDIAN HEALTH SERVICE AREA OFFICES AND SERVICE UNITS

### ABERDEEN AREA REGION I

### IOWA, NEBRASKA, NORTH DAKOTA, SOUTH DAKOTA

ABERDEEN AREA INDIAN HEALTH SERVICE
(Iowa, Nebraska, North Dakota, South Dakota)
Federal Building
Office of Professional Services
115 4th Avenue Southeast
Aberdeen, SD 57401
(605) 226–7531

### SERVICE UNITS

### ◆ NEBRASKA

CARL T. CURTIS HEALTH CENTER
Macy, NE 68039
(402) 837–5381

OMAHA-WINNEBAGO SERVICE UNIT
WINNEBAGO PHS INDIAN HOSPITAL
Winnebago, NE 68071
(402) 878–2231

#### ◆ NORTH DAKOTA

FORT BERTHOLD SERVICE UNIT
FORT BERTHOLD PHS INDIAN HEALTH CENTER
P.O. Box 400
New Town, ND 58763
(701) 627–4701

FORT TOTTEN SERVICE UNIT
FORT TOTTEN PHS INDIAN HEALTH CENTER
P.O. Box 200
Fort Totten, ND 58335
(701) 766–1600

STANDING ROCK SERVICE UNIT
FORT YATES PHS INDIAN HOSPITAL
P.O. Box J
Fort Yates, ND 58538
(701) 854–3831

TURTLE MOUNTAIN SERVICE UNIT
BELCOURT PHS INDIAN HOSPITAL
P.O. Box 160
Belcourt, ND 58316
(701) 477–6112

TRENTON-WILLISTON INDIAN SERVICE
   AREA
P.O. Box 210
Trenton, ND 58853
(701) 774–0461

#### ◆ SOUTH DAKOTA

CHEYENNE RIVER SERVICE UNIT
EAGLE BUTTE PHS INDIAN HOSPITAL
P.O. Box 1012
Eagle Butte, SD 57625
(605) 964–7724

CROW CREEK SERVICE UNIT
FORT THOMPSON PHS INDIAN HEALTH CENTER
P.O. Box 200
Fort Thompson, SD 57339
(605) 245–2285

KYLE PHS HEALTH CENTER
P.O. Box 540
Kyle, SD 57752
(605) 455–2451

LOWER BRULE SERVICE UNIT
P.O. Box 248
Lower Brule, SD 57548
(605) 473–5544

MCLAUGHLIN PHS INDIAN HEALTH CENTER
P.O. Box 879
McLaughlin, SD 57642
(605) 823–4459

PINE RIDGE SERVICE UNIT
PINE RIDGE PHS INDIAN HOSPITAL
Pine Ridge, SD 57770
(605) 867–5131

RAPID CITY SERVICE UNIT
RAPID CITY PHS INDIAN HEALTH HOSPITAL
3200 Canyon Lake Drive
Rapid City, SD 57702
(605) 355–2500

ROSEBUD SERVICE UNIT
ROSEBUD PHS INDIAN HOSPITAL
Rosebud, SD 57570
(605) 747–2231

SISSETON-WAHPETON SERVICE UNIT
SISSETON PHS INDIAN HOSPITAL
P.O. Box 189
Sisseton, SD 57262
(605) 698–7606

WANBLEE PHS HEALTH CENTER
Wanblee Health Center
SD 57577
(605) 462–6155

YANKTON-WAGNER SERVICE UNIT
WAGNER PHS INDIAN HOSPITAL
110 Washington Street
Wagner, SD 57380
(605) 384–3621

YOUTH REGIONAL TREATMENT CENTER
P.O. Box #68
Mobridge, SD 57401
(605) 845–7181

**REGION II**

**ALASKA**

ALASKA AREA NATIVE HEALTH SERVICE
4141 Ambassador Drive
Anchorage, AK 99508–5928
(907) 729–3686

## SERVICE UNITS

ALASKA NATIVE MEDICAL CENTER
4315 Diplomacy Drive
Anchorage, AK 99508
(907) 729–1994

ALASKA NATIVE TRIBAL HEALTH
    CONSORTIUM
4141 Ambassador Drive
Anchorage, AK 99508–5928
(907) 729–1900

ALEUTIAN/PRIBILOF ISLANDS ASSOCIATION
201 E. Third Ave.
Anchorage, AK 99503
(907) 276–2700

ANNETTE ISLAND SERVICE UNIT
METLAKATLA INDIAN COMMUNITY
P.O. Box 439
Metlakatla, AK 99926
(907) 886–6601

BARROW SERVICE UNIT
ARCTIC SLOPE NATIVE ASSOCIATION
P.O. Box 1232
Barrow, AK 99723–1232
(907) 852–2762

BRISTOL BAY AREA SERVICE UNIT
BRISTOL BAY AREA HEALTH CORPORATION
P.O. Box 130
Dillingham, AK 99576
(907) 842–5201

CHUGACHMIUT
4201 Tudor Centre, Suite 210
Anchorage, AK 99508
(907) 562–4155

COOK INLET TRIBAL COUNCIL, INC.
670 W. Fireweed Lane, Suite 200
Anchorage, AK 99503
(907) 265–5900

EASTERN ALEUTIAN TRIBES
1600 "A" Street, Suite 104
Anchorage, AK 99501–5146
(907) 277–1440

INTERIOR ALASKA SERVICE UNIT
TANANA CHIEFS CONFERENCE, INC.
122 First Avenue, Suite 600
Fairbanks, AK 99701–4897
(907) 452–8251

KOTZEBUE SERVICE UNIT
MANIILAQ ASSOCIATION
P.O. Box 256
Kotzebue, AK 99752
(907) 442–3311

NORTH SLOPE BOROUGH
Dept. of Health & Social Services
P.O. Box 69
Barrow, AK 99723
(907) 852–0260

NORTON SOUND HEALTH CORPORATION
P.O. Box 966
Nome, AK 99762
(907) 443–3311

SEARHC HEALTH CENTER
201 Deermount Street
Ketchikan, AK 99901
(907) 225–4156

SOUTHEAST ALASKA REGIONAL HEALTH
    CORPORATION
3245 Hospital Drive
Juneau, AK 99801
(907) 463–4000

SOUTHEASTERN ALASKA REGIONAL
    HEALTH CONSORTIUM
Mt. Edgecumbe Hospital
222 Tongass Drive
Sitka, AK 99835
(907) 966–2411

VALDEZ NATIVE TRIBE
P.O. Box 1108
Valdez, AK 99686
(907) 835–4951

YUKON-KUSKOKWIM DELTA SERVICE UNIT
YUKON-KUSKOKWIM HEALTH CORPORATION
P.O. Box 528
Bethel, AK 99559
(907) 543–6000

YUKON-KUSKOKWIM DELTA REGIONAL
  HOSPITAL
Pouch 3000
Bethel, AK 99559
(907) 543–6300

## REGION III

### COLORADO, NEW MEXICO, TEXAS

ALBUQUERQUE AREA INDIAN HEALTH
  SERVICE
5300 Homestead Road, NE
Albuquerque, NM 87110
(505) 248–4102

## SERVICE UNITS

### ◆ COLORADO

IGNACIO PHS INDIAN HEALTH CENTER
P.O. Box 889.
Ignacio, CO 81137
(970) 563–4581

SOUTHERN COLORADO UTE SERVICE UNIT
P.O. Box 778
Ignacio, CO 81137
(970) 563–9447

TOWAOC PHS INDIAN HEALTH CENTER
General Delivery
Towaoc, CO 81334
(970) 565–4441

### ◆ NEW MEXICO

ACOMITA-CANONCITO LAGUNA SERVICE
  UNIT
PHS Indian Hospital
P.O. Box 130
San Fidel, NM 87049
(505) 552–6634

ALAMO NAVAJO HEALTH STATION
P.O. Box 907
Magdalena, NM 87825
(505) 854–2626

ALBUQUERQUE SERVICE UNIT
ALBUQUERQUE PHS INDIAN HOSPITAL
801 Vassar Drive, N.E.
Albuquerque, NM 87106
(505) 248–4000

JICARILLA SERVICE UNIT
JICARILLA PHS INDIAN HEALTH CENTER
P.O. Box 187
Dulce, NM 87528
(505) 759–3291

MESCALERO SERVICE UNIT
MESCALERO PHS INDIAN HOSPITAL
P.O. Box 210
Mescalero, NM 88340
(505) 671–4441

NEW SUNRISE REGIONAL TREATMENT
  CENTER
P.O. Box 219
San Fidel, NM 87049
(505) 552–6091

PINE HILL INDIAN HEALTH CENTER
P.O. Box 310
Pine Hill, NM 87357
(505) 775–3271

SANTA CLARA PHS INDIAN HEALTH CENTER
RR1, Box 446
Espanola, NM 87532–9614
(505) 753–9421

SANTA FE SERVICE UNIT
SANTA FE PHS INDIAN HOSPITAL
1700 Cerrillos Road
Santa Fe, NM 87501
(505) 988–9821

SOUTHWESTERN INDIAN POLYTECHNIC
INSTITUTE DENTAL CENTER
P.O. Box 25927
Albuquerque, NM 87125
(505) 897–5306

TAOS PHS INDIAN HEALTH CENTER
P.O. Box 1956
Taos, NM 87571
(505) 758–4224

ZUNI SERVICE UNIT
ZUNI PHS INDIAN HOSPITAL
P.O. Box 467
Zuni, NM 87327
(505) 782–4431

#### ◆ TEXAS

YSLETA DEL SUR SERVICE UNIT
119 South Old Pueblo Road
P.O. Box 17579
El Paso, TX 79907
(915) 859–7913

### REGION IV

### MICHIGAN, MINNESOTA, WISCONSIN

BEMIDJI AREA INDIAN HEALTH SERVICE
522 Minnesota Ave., N.W., Room 119
Bemidji, MN 56601
(218) 759–3412

## FIELD OFFICES

ASHLAND FIELD OFFICE
2800 Lake Shore Drive East
Ashland, WI 54806

FIELD HEALTH OFFICE/MITC
3601 Mackinaw Trail
Sault Ste. Marie, MI 49783
(906) 635–408

RHINELANDER FIELD OFFICE
P.O. Box 537
Rhinelander, WI 54501
(715) 362–5145

## SERVICE UNITS

#### ◆ MICHIGAN

BAY MILLS INDIAN COMMUNITY
12099 W. Lakeshore Drive
Brimley, MI 49715
(906) 248–3204

EASTERN MICHIGAN SERVICE UNIT
HURON POTAWATOMI BAND
2221 1–1/2 Mile Road
Fulton, MI 49052
(616) 729–5151

GRAND TRAVERSE OTTAWA/CHIPPEWA
2605 N.W. Bayshore Drive
Suttons Bay, MI 49682
(616) 271–5256

HANNAHVILLE INDIAN COMMUNITY
N14911 Hannahville B1. Road
Wilson, MI 49896–9728
(906) 466–2782

KEWEENAW BAY INDIAN COMMUNITY
102 Superior Avenue
Baraga, MI 49908
(906) 353–8666 ext. 10

LAC VIEUX DESERT BAND
E-23560 Choate Road
Watersmeet, MI 49969
(906) 358–4588

NIMKEE MEMORIAL WELLNESS CENTER
2591 S. Leaton Road
Mt. Pleasant, MI 48858
(517) 775–4600

SAULT STE. MARIE HEALTH & HUMAN
  SERVICES
2684 Ashmun Street
Sault Ste. Marie, MI 49783
(906) 632–5200

#### ◆ MINNESOTA

BOIS FORTE TRIBAL CLINIC
P.O. Box 16
Nett Lake, MN 55772
(218) 757–3295

GREATER LEECH LAKE SERVICE UNIT
PHS INDIAN HOSPITAL
R.R. 3, Box 211
Cass Lake, MN 56633
(218) 335–2293

MILLE LACS SERVICE UNIT
Mille Lacs Band
HCR 67, Box 241
Onamia, MN 56359
(320) 532–4163

MIN-NO-AYA-WIN CLINIC
927 Trettel Lane
Cloquet, MN 55720
(218) 879–1227

RED LAKE HEALTH SERVICE
Red Lake, MN 56671
(218) 679–3316

RED LAKE SERVICE UNIT
PHS INDIAN HOSPITAL
Red Lake, MN
(218) 679–3912

WHITE EARTH SERVICE UNIT
PHS INDIAN HEALTH CENTER
White Earth, MN 56591
(218) 983–4300

### ♦ WISCONSIN

BAD RIVER HEALTH SERVICES
P.O. Box 39
Odanah, WI 54861
(715) 682–7137

CENTRAL WISCONSIN SERVICE UNIT
HO CHUNK NATION HEALTH DEPARTMENT
P.O. Box 636, 25 N. 2nd
Black River Falls, WI 54615
(715) 284–7548 or 7830

LAC COURTE OREILLES TRIBAL CLINIC
Route 2, Box 2750
Hayward, WI 54843
(715) 634–4153 or 4795

MENOMINEE TRIBAL CLINIC
P.O. Box 970
Keshena, WI 54135
(715) 799–5482

ONEIDA COMMUNITY HEALTH CENTER
P.O. Box 365
Oneida, WI 54155
(920) 869–2711

PETER CHRISTENSEN HEALTH CENTER
450 Old Abe Road
Lac du Flambeau, WI 54538
(715) 588–3371

RED CLIFF HEALTH SERVICES
P.O. Box 529
Bayfield, WI 54814
(715) 779–3707

ST. CROIX HEALTH SERVICES
P.O. Box 287
Hertel, WI 54845
(715) 349–2195

STOCKBRIDGE-MUNSEE HEALTH CENTER
P.O. Box 86-N8705
Moh He Con Nuk Road
Bowler, WI 54416
(715) 793–4144

### REGION V

### MONTANA, WYOMING

BILLINGS AREA INDIAN HEALTH SERVICE
2900 4th Avenue North
Billings, MT 59101
(406) 247–7107

## SERVICE UNITS

### ♦ MONTANA

BLACKFEET SERVICE UNIT
BROWNING PHS INDIAN HOSPITAL
Browning, MT 59417
(406) 338–6154

CROW AGENCY UNIT
CROW AGENCY PHS INDIAN HOSPITAL
Crow Agency, MT 59022
(406) 638–3461

FLATHEAD TRIBAL HEALTH & HUMAN
    SERVICES
P.O. Box 280, Mission Drive
St. Ignatius, MT 59865
(406) 745–2411 or 745–3525

FORT BELKNAP SERVICE UNIT
HARLEM PHS INDIAN HOSPITAL
Harlem, MT 59526
(406) 353–3192

FORT PECK SERVICE UNIT
POPLAR PHS INDIAN HEALTH CENTER
Poplar, MT 59255
(406) 768–3491

LODGE GRASS PHS INDIAN HEALTH
    CENTER
Lodge Grass, MT 59050
(406) 639–2317

NORTHERN CHEYENNE SERVICE UNIT
LAME DEER PHS INDIAN HEALTH CENTER
Lame Deer, MT 59043
(406) 477–4400

ROCKY BOY SERVICE UNIT
Rocky Boy Route–Box 664 Planning
Box Elder, MT 59521
(406) 395–4982

WOLF POINT PHS INDIAN HEALTH CENTER
Wolf Point, MT 59201
(406) 653–1641

◆ **WYOMING**

ARAPAHOE PHS INDIAN HEALTH CENTER
Arapahoe, WY 82510 Clinical Coordinator
(307) 856–9281

WIND RIVER SERVICE UNIT
FORT WASHAKIE PHS INDIAN HEALTH CENTER
Ft. Washakie, WY 82514
(307) 332–9416

**REGION VI**

**CALIFORNIA**

CALIFORNIA AREA INDIAN HEALTH
    SERVICE OFFICE
650 Capitol Mall
Sacramento, CA 95814
Office of Area Director (OAD) and
Office of Management Support (OMS)
(916) 930–3927

## SERVICE UNITS

CALIFORNIA AREA RURAL HEALTH SYSTEM
CHAPA-DE INDIAN HEALTH PROGRAM, INC.
11670 Atwood Road
Auburn, CA 95603
(530) 887–2800

CONSOLIDATED TRIBAL HEALTH
    PROJECT, INC.
P.O. Box 319
Calpella, CA 95418
(707) 485–5115

INDIAN HEALTH COUNCIL, INC.
P.O. Box 406
Pauma Valley, CA 92061
(760) 749–1410

LAKE COUNTY TRIBAL HEALTH
    CONSORTIUM
925 Bevins Court
Lakeport, CA 95453
(707) 263–8382

LASSEN INDIAN HEALTH CENTER
745 Joaquin Street
Susanville, CA 96130
(530) 257–2542

MODOC COUNTY INDIAN HEALTH
    PROJECT, INC.
P.O. Box 251
Alturas, CA 96101
(530) 233–4591

NORTHERN VALLEY INDIAN HEALTH
207 North Butte Street
Willows, CA 95988
(530) 934–9293

PIT RIVER HEALTH SERVICES
36977 Park Avenue
Burney, CA 96013
(530) 335–5091

RIVERSIDE/SAN BERNARDINO COUNTY
INDIAN HEALTH, INC.
11555 1/2 Potrero Road
Banning, CA 92220
(909) 849–4761

ROUND VALLEY INDIAN HEALTH
    CENTER, INC.
P.O. BOX 247
Covelo, CA 95428
(707) 983–6404

SANTA YNEZ INDIAN HEALTH
P.O. BOX 539
Santa Ynez, CA 93460
(805) 688–7070

SONOMA COUNTY INDIAN HEALTH
P.O. BOX 7308
Santa Rosa, CA 95407–0308
(707) 544–4056

SOUTHERN INDIAN HEALTH COUNCIL, INC.
4058 Willows Road
Alpine, CA 91903–2128
(619) 445–11881

TOIYABE INDIAN HEALTH PROJECT
52 Tu Su Lane
Bishop, CA 93514
(760) 873–8464

TULE RIVER INDIAN HEALTH CENTER, INC.
P.O. Box 768
Porterville, CA 93258
(209) 784–2316

TUOLUMNE RURAL INDIAN HEALTH
PROJECT
19590 Me Wu Street
Tuolumne, CA 95379
(209) 928–4277

UNITED INDIAN HEALTH SERVICES, INC.
P.O. Box 420
Trinidad, CA 95570–0420
(707) 677–3693

WARNER MT. INDIAN HEALTH PROJECT
P.O. Box 126
Ft. Bidwell, CA 96112
(530) 279–6194

## CALIFORNIA AREA URBAN HEALTH PROGRAMS

AMERICAN INDIAN HEALTH SERVICES
CORP.
4141 State Street, B-6
Santa Barbara, Ca. 93110
(805) 681–7356

BAKERSFIELD EDUCATION CENTER FOR
NATIVE AMERICANS
1830 Truxton Ave, Ste 100
Bakersfield, CA 93301
(661) 859–2940

FRESNO INDIAN HEALTH ASSOCIATION, INC.
3720 North First Street
Fresno, CA 93726
(559) 222–9865

FRIENDSHIP HOUSE ASSOCIATION OF
AMERICAN INDIANS, INC.
333 Valencia Street, Suite 400
San Francisco, CA 94103–3547
(415) 865–0964

INDIAN HEALTH CENTER OF SANTA CLARA
VALLEY, INC.
1333 Meridian Avenue
San Jose, CA 95125
(408) 445–2400

SACRAMENTO URBAN INDIAN HEALTH
PROJECT, INC.
2020 "J" Street
Sacramento, CA 95814–3120
(916) 441–0918

SAN DIEGO AMERICAN HEALTH
CENTER, INC.
2630 First Avenue
San Diego, CA 92103
(619) 234–0572

UNITED AMERICAN INDIAN
INVOLVEMENT, INC.
1125 West 6th St., Suite 400
Los Angeles, Ca. 90017
(213) 202–3970

URBAN INDIAN HEALTH BOARD
3124 International Boulevard
Oakland, CA 94601
(510) 261–0524

## REGION VII

### MISSISSIPPI, NORTH CAROLINA, AND EASTERN STATES

NASHVILLE AREA INDIAN HEALTH SERVICE
711 Stewarts Ferry Pike
Nashville, TN 37214–2634
(615) 736–2400

## SERVICE UNITS

### ♦ ALABAMA

POARCH BAND OF CREEK INDIANS
5811 Jack Springs Road
Atmore, AL 36502
(334) 368–9136

### ♦ CONNECTICUT

MASHANTUCKET PEQUOT INDIANS
75 Route 2
Mashantucket, CT 06339
(860) 889–8248

MOHEGAN TRIBE OF INDIANS
67 Sandy Desert Road
Uncasville, CT 06382
(860) 204–6192

#### ◆ FLORIDA

MICCOUSUKEE CORPORATION
US 41 Tamiami Trail
Miami, FL 33199
(305) 223–8380

SEMINOLE TRIBE OF FLORIDA
3006 Josie Billie Avenue
Hollywood, FL 33024
(954) 962–2009

#### ◆ LOUISIANA

CHITIMACHA TRIBE OF LOUISIANA
105 Houma Drive
Charenton, LA 70523
(318) 923–9955

COUSHATTA TRIBE OF LOUISIANA
Powell Road
P.O. Box 519
Elton, LA 70532
(318) 584–2208

JENA BAND OF CHOCTAW
Cowart Street
P.O. Box 14
Jena, LA 71342
(318) 992–2717

TUNICA-BILOXI TRIBE
Highway One South
Marksville, LA 71351
(318) 253–6100

#### ◆ MASSACHUSETTS

NORTH AMERICAN INDIAN CENTER
105 South Huntington Avenue
Jamaica Plains, MA 02130
(617) 232–0343

TECUMSEH HOUSE
107 Fisher Avenue
Roxbury, MA 02120
(617) 731–3366

WAMPANOAG TRIBE OF GAY HEAD
20 Black Brook Road
Aquinnah, MA 02535
(508) 645–9265

#### ◆ MAINE

AROOSTOOK BAND OF MICMAC
10 Edgemont Drive
Presque Isle, ME 04769
(207) 764–7219

HOULTON BAND OF MALISEET
RR #3 Box 460 Acting
Houlton, ME 04730
(207) 532–2240

PASSAMAQUODDY INDIAN TOWNSHIP
1 Newell Drive Box 97
Princeton, ME 04668
(207) 796–2322

PASSAMAQUODDY PLEASANT POINT
P.O. Box 351—Route 190
Perry, ME 04468
(207) 853–0711

PENOBSCOT INDIAN NATION
5 River Road
Old Town, ME 04468
(207) 827–6101

#### ◆ MARYLAND

BALTIMORE AMERICAN INDIAN CENTER
113 South Broadway
Baltimore, MD 21231
(410) 563–4600

#### ◆ MISSISSIPPI

MISSISSIPPI BAND OF CHOCTAW INDIANS
Route 7 Box R-50
Philadelphia, MS 39350
(601) 656–2211

#### ◆ RHODE ISLAND

NARRAGANSETT INDIAN TRIBE
4375 B South County Trail Route 2 Acting
Charlestown, RI 02813
(401) 364–1268

## ◆ NEW YORK

**AMERICAN INDIAN COMMUNITY HOUSE**
708 Broadway Street, 8th Floor
New York, NY 10003
(212) 598–0100

**ONEIDA INDIAN NATION**
2 Territory Road
Oneida, NY 13421
(315) 363–4640

**SENECA NATION OF INDIANS**
Lionel R. John Health Center
987 RC Hoag Drive
Salamanca, NY 14779
(716) 945–5894

**ST. REGIS MOHAWK TRIBE**
Rt. 37 Box 8A
Hogansburg, NY 13655
(518) 358–3141

## ◆ NORTH CAROLINA

**CHEROKEE SERVICE UNIT**
PHS INDIAN HOSPITAL
Cherokee, NC 28719
(828) 497–9163

**EASTERN BAND OF CHEROKEE INDIAN**
P.O. Box 666
Cherokee, NC 28719
(828) 497–9485

**NASHVILLE AREA OFFICE LOCATED AT CHEROKEE, NORTH CAROLINA**
UNITY REGIONAL YOUTH TREATMENT CENTER
P.O. Box C-201
441 N. Sequoyah
Cherokee, NC 28719
(828) 497–3958

## ◆ SOUTH CAROLINA

**CATAWBA INDIAN NATION**
3596 Passmore Drive
Catawba, SC 29704
(803) 366–4792

**REGION VIII**

**ARIZONA, NEW MEXICO, UTAH**

**NAVAJO AREA INDIAN HEALTH SERVICE**
P.O. Box 9020
Window Rock, AZ 86515–9020
(520) 871–5811

## SERVICE UNITS

## ◆ ARIZONA

**CHINLE SERVICE UNIT**
CHINLE COMPREHENSIVE HEALTH CARE
    FACILITY
P.O. Drawer PH
Off Highway 191
Chinle, AZ 86503
(520) 674–7001

**FORT DEFIANCE SERVICE UNIT**
FORT DEFIANCE PHS INDIAN HOSPITAL
P.O. Box 649
Ft. Defiance, AZ 86504
(520) 729–5741

**INSCRIPTION HOUSE HEALTH CENTER**
P.O. Box 7397
Tonalea, AZ 86044
(520) 672–2611

**KAYENTA SERVICE UNIT**
KAYENTA PHS INDIAN HEALTH CENTER
P.O. Box 368
Kayenta, AZ 86033
(520) 697–4000

**TSAILE PHS INDIAN HEALTH CENTER**
Tsaile, AZ 86556
(520) 724–3391

**TUBA CITY SERVICE UNIT**
TUBA CITY INDIAN MEDICAL CENTER
P.O. Box 600
Tuba City, AZ 86045
(520) 283–2501

**WINSLOW SERVICE UNIT**
WINSLOW PHS INDIAN HEALTH CENTER
P.O. Drawer 40
Winslow, AZ 86047
(520) 289–4646

## ◆ NEW MEXICO

**CROWNPOINT SERVICE UNIT**
CROWNPOINT COMPREHENSIVE HEALTH CARE
FACILITY
P.O. Box 358
Crownpoint, NM 87313
(505) 786–5291

**DZILTH-NA-O-DITH-HLE**
PHS INDIAN HEALTH CENTER
6 Road 7586
Bloomfield, NM 87413
(505) 632–1801

**GALLUP SERVICE UNIT**
GALLUP INDIAN MEDICAL CENTER
P.O. Box 1337
Gallup, NM 87305
(505) 722–1000

**SHIPROCK SERVICE UNIT**
NORTHERN NAVAJO MEDICAL CENTER
P.O. Box 160
Shiprock, NM 87420
(505) 368–6001

**TOHATCHI PHS INDIAN HEALTH CENTER**
P.O. Box 142
Tohatchi, NM 87325
(505) 733–8100

## REGION IX

### KANSAS, OKLAHOMA, TEXAS

OKLAHOMA CITY AREA INDIAN HEALTH
SERVICE (Kansas, Oklahoma)
Five Corporate Plaza
3625 NW 56th Street
Oklahoma City, OK 73112
(405) 951–3768

## SERVICE UNITS

## ◆ KANSAS

**HASKELL SERVICE UNIT**
PHS INDIAN HEALTH CENTER
2415 Massachusetts Avenue
Lawrence, KS 66044–4808
(785) 843–3750

**HOLTON SERVICE UNIT**
PHS INDIAN HEALTH CENTER
100 West 6th Street
Holton, KS 66436
(785) 364–2177

**HUNTER HEALTH CENTER**
2318 E. Central
Wichita, KS 67214
(316) 262–2415

**KICKAPOO HEALTH CENTER—KICKAPOO
TRIBE OF KANSAS**
Route 1, Box 221 C
Horton, KS 66439
(785) 486–2154

## ◆ OKLAHOMA

**ADA SERVICE UNIT**
CARL ALBERT INDIAN HOSPITAL
1001 N. Country Club Drive
Ada, OK 74820
(580) 436–3980

**ARDMORE CHICKASAW HEALTH CLINIC**
2510 Chickasaw Blvd.
Ardmore, OK 73401
(580) 226–8181

**BLACK HAWK HEALTH CENTER—SAC AND
FOX NATION OF OKLAHOMA**
Route 2, Box 247
Stroud, OK 74079
(918) 968–9531

**BROKEN BOW**
CHOCTAW NATION HEALTH CENTER
205 E. 3rd
Broken Bow, OK 74728
(580) 584–2740

**CARNEGIE INDIAN HEALTH CENTER**
P.O. Box 1120
Carnegie, OK 73015
(580) 654–1100

**CLAREMORE SERVICE UNIT**
CLAREMORE INDIAN HOSPITAL
West Will Rogers & Moore
Claremore, OK 74017
(918) 342–6200

CLINTON SERVICE UNIT
PHS INDIAN HOSPITAL
Route 1, Box 3060 ll
Clinton, OK 73601–9303
(580) 323–2884

CREEK NATION COMMUNITY HOSPITAL
CREEK NATION OF OKLAHOMA
P.O. Box 228
Okemah, OK 74859
(918) 623–1424

CREEK NATION DENTAL CLINIC
700 N. Mission
P.O. Box 10
Okmulgee, OK 74447
(918) 756–2860

EL RENO PHS INDIAN HEALTH CLINIC
1631A E. Highway 66
El Reno, OK 73036
(405) 262–7631

EUFAULA HEALTH CENTER—CREEK
    NATION OF OKLAHOMA
800 Forrest Avenue
Eufaula, OK 74432
(918) 689–2547

HUGO HEALTH CENTER
P.O. Box 340 R
Hugo, OK 74743
(580) 326–7561

LAWTON SERVICE UNIT
PHS INDIAN HEALTH HOSPITAL
1515 Lawrie Tatum Road
Lawton, OK 73501
(580) 353–0350

MCALESTER HEALTH CENTER
903 E. Monroe
McAlester, OK 74501
(918) 423–8440

MIAMI PHS INDIAN HEALTH CENTER
P.O. Box 1498
Miami, OK 74355
(918) 542–1655

NOWATA INDIAN HEALTH CLINIC
CHEROKEE NATION OF OKLAHOMA
304 East Cherokee
Nowata, OK 74048
(918) 273–0192

OKEMAH INDIAN HEALTH CENTER
P.O. Box 429
Okemah, OK 74859
(918) 623–0555 or (918) 623–1424

OKMULGEE HEALTH CENTER
1313 East 20th
Okmulgee, OK 74447
(918) 756–2717

PAWHUSKA PHS INDIAN HEALTH CENTER
715 Grandview
Pawhuska, OK 74056
(918) 287–4491

PAWNEE SERVICE UNIT
PHS INDIAN HEALTH CENTER
Rural Route 2, Box 1
Pawnee, OK 74058–9247
(918) 762–2517

PHS INDIAN HEALTH CENTER
P.O. Box 828
Anadarko, OK 73005
(405) 247–2458

SALINA COMMUNITY CLINIC
P.O. Box 936
Salina, OK 74365
(918) 434–5397

SALLISAW—REDBIRD SMITH HEALTH
    CENTER
301 JT Stitkes Avenue
Sallisaw, OK 74955
(918) 775–9159

SAM HIDER JAY COMMUNITY CLINIC
P.O. Box 350
Jay, OK 74346
(918) 253–4271

SAPULPA HEALTH CENTER
CREEK NATION OF OKLAHOMA
1125 East Cleveland
Sapulpa, OK 74066
(918) 224–9310

SHAWNEE SERVICE UNIT
KICKAPOO HEALTH CENTER
P.O. Box 1059
McLoud, OK 74851
(405) 964–2081

TAHLEQUAH SERVICE UNIT
W.W. HASTINGS INDIAN HOSPITAL
100 S. Bliss Service
Tahlequah, OK 74464
(918) 458–3100

TALIHINA
CHOCTAW NATION HEALTH SERVICES
    AUTHORITY
Route 2, Box 1725
Talihina, OK 74571
(918) 567–2211

TISHOMINGO CHICKASAW HEALTH CENTER
815 E. 6th Street
Tishomingo, OK 73460
(580) 371–2392

WATONGA PHS INDIAN HEALTH CENTER
Rt. 1, Box 34-A
Watonga, OK 73772
(580) 623–4991

WEWOKA SERVICE UNIT
PHS INDIAN HEALTH CENTER
P.O. Box 1475
Wewoka, OK 74884
(405) 257–6281

WHITE EAGLE PHS INDIAN HEALTH CENTER
P.O. Box 2071
Ponca City, OK 74602
(580) 765–2501

WILMA P. MANKILLER HEALTH CENTER
CHEROKEE NATION HEALTH CENTER
Highway 51 East
Route 1, Box 93
Stilwell, OK 74960
(918) 696–8800

## URBAN HEALTH CENTERS

ABSENTEE SHAWNEE HEALTH CLINIC
15702 E. Highway 9
Norman, OK 73071
(405) 447–0300

BEARSKIN HEALTH CENTER
P.O. Box 30
Wyandotte, OK 74370
(918) 678–2232 or 2282

CHICKASAW/DURANT HEALTH CENTER
1702 W. Elm
Durant, OK 74701
(580) 920–2100

CHOCTAW/RUEBEN WHITE HEALTH CLINIC
109 Kerr Avenue
Poteau, OK 74953
(918) 649–1100

CITIZEN POTAWATOMI NATION HEALTH
    CLINIC
2307 S. Gordon Cooper Drive l
Shawnee, OK 74801
(405) 273–5236

DIABETES TREATMENT CENTER
400 S.W. O Street
Antlers, OK 74523
(580) 298–0210

INDIAN HEALTH CARE RESOURCE CENTER
    OF TULSA INC.
915 S. Cincinnati
Tulsa, OK 74119
(918) 582–7225

MUSKOGEE INDIAN HEALTH CENTER
212 South 38th
Muskogee, OK 74401
(918) 687–0102

OKLAHOMA CITY INDIAN CLINIC
Central Oklahoma American
Indian Health Council, Inc.
4913 W. Reno
Oklahoma City, OK 73127
(405) 948–4900

## ◆ TEXAS

EAGLE PASS HEALTH CENTER
P.O. Box 972
Eagle Pass, TX 78853
(210) 757–0322

KICKAPOO TRIBE OF TEXAS INDIAN
    HEALTH SERVICE
HCI, Box 9700
Eagle Pass, TX 78852
(830) 757–0322

**REGION X**

**ARIZONA, NEVADA, UTAH**

**PHOENIX AREA INDIAN HEALTH SERVICE**
Two Renaissance Square
40 North Central Avenue
Phoenix, AZ 85004
(602) 364–5039

## SERVICE UNITS

#### ◆ ARIZONA

**CENTER FOR NATIVE AMERICAN HEALTH**
P.O. Box 245037
Tucson, AZ 85724
(520) 626–7909

**COLORADO RIVER SERVICE UNIT**
HAVASUPAI INDIAN HEALTH STATION
Supai, AZ 86435
(520) 448–2641

**DESERT VISIONS YOUTH WELLNESS**
CENTER/RTC
P.O. Box 458
198 South Skill Center Road
Sacaton, AZ 85247
(602) 379–3000
Local: (520) 562–3801

**FORT MCDOWELL INDIAN COMMUNITY**
WASSAJA MEMORIAL HEALTH CENTER
P.O. Box 17779
Fountain Hills, AZ 85269
(480) 850–8420

**FORT YUMA SERVICE UNIT**
Fort Yuma PHS Indian Hospital
P.O. Box 1368
Yuma, AZ 85364
(760) 572–0217

**GILA CROSSING HEALTH CENTER**
P.O. Box 380
LaVeen, AZ 85339
(520) 550–3827

**GILA RIVER HEALTHCARE CORPORATION**
HuHuKam Memorial Hospital
P.O. Box 38
Sacaton, AZ 85247
(520) 562–3321

**KEAMS CANYON SERVICE UNIT**
KEAMS CANYON PHS INDIAN HOSPITAL
P.O. Box 98
Keams Canyon, AZ 86034
(520) 738–2211

**PARKER PHS INDIAN HOSPITAL**
Route 1, P.O. Box 12
Parker, AZ 85344
(520) 669–2137

**PEACH SPRINGS PHS INDIAN HEALTH**
CENTER
P.O. Box 190
Peach Springs, AZ 86434
(520) 769–2204

**PHOENIX INDIAN MEDICAL CENTER**
4212 N. 16th Street
Phoenix, AZ 85016
(602) 263–1200

**PHOENIX SERVICE UNIT**
AK CHIN CLINIC
45203 West Farrel Road
Maricopa, AZ 85238
(520) 568–3881

**SAN CARLOS PHS INDIAN HOSPITAL**
P.O. Box 208
San Carlos, AZ 85550
(520) 475–2371

**SAN CARLOS SERVICE UNIT**
BYLAS HEALTH CENTER
P.O. Box 208
San Carlos, AZ 85550
(520) 485–2686

**SCOTTSDALE SALT RIVER CLINIC**
Route 1, Box 215
Scottsdale, AZ 85256
(602) 379–4281

**SECOND MESA PHS INDIAN HEALTH**
CENTER
P.O. Box 98
Keams Canyon, AZ 86034
(520) 734–2496

**WHITERIVER PHS INDIAN HOSPITAL**
P.O. Box 860
Whiteriver, AZ 85941
(520) 338–4911

WHITERIVER SERVICE UNIT
CIBECUE PHS INDIAN HEALTH CENTER
Cibecue, AZ 85941
(520) 332–2560

#### ◆ NEVADA

ELKO SERVICE UNIT
LAS VEGAS PAIUTE HEALTH & HUMAN SERVICES
Number Six Paiute Drive
Las Vegas, NV 89106

MCDERMITT TRIBAL HEALTH CENTER
P.O. Box 315
McDermitt, NV 89421
(775) 532–8259

MOAPA HEALTH CLINIC
P.O. Box 819
Moapa, NV 89025
(702) 865–2700

NEWE MEDICAL CLINIC
400 "A" Newe View
Ely, NV 89301
(775) 289–2134

OWYHEE TRIBAL HOSPITAL
P.O. Box 130
Owyhee, NV 89832
(775) 757–2415

PYRAMID LAKE HEALTH DEPARTMENT
P.O. Box 227
Nixon, NV 89424
(775) 574–1018

RENO/SPARKS HEALTH & HUMAN
SERVICES CENTER
34 Reservation Road
Reno, NV 89502
(775) 329–5162

SCHURZ INDIAN HEALTH CENTER
Drawer A
Schurz, NV 89427
(775) 773–2345

SCHURZ SERVICE UNIT
FALLON PAIUTE SHOSHONE TRIBAL HEALTH
STATION
P.O. Box 1980
Fallon, NV 89407
(775) 423–3634

SOUTHERN BANDS CLINIC
515 Shoshone Circle
Elko, NV 89801
(775) 738–2252

WALKER RIVER PAIUTE TRIBAL
HEALTH CENTER
P.O. Drawer "C"
Schurz, NV 89427
(775) 773–2005

WASHOE TRIBAL HEALTH CENTER
950 Hwy. 395 S.
Gardnerville, NV 89410
(775) 883–4137/265–4215

YERINGTON PAIUTE TRIBAL HEALTH CLINIC
171 Campbell Lane
Yerington, NV 89447
(702) 463–3335

#### ◆ NEW MEXICO

ORYX PROGRAM
5300 Homestead Rd
Albuquerque, NM 87110
(505) 248–4152

#### ◆ UTAH

UINTAH AND OURAY SERVICE UNIT
FORT DUCHESNE PHS INDIAN HEALTH CENTER
P.O. Box 160
Ft. Duchesne, UT 84026
(435) 722–5122

**REGION XI**

**IDAHO, OREGON, WASHINGTON**

PORTLAND AREA INDIAN HEALTH SERVICE
1220 S.W. Third Avenue-Room 476
Portland, OR 97204–2892
(503) 326–2020

### SERVICE UNITS

#### ◆ IDAHO

FORT HALL SERVICE UNIT
NOT-TSOO GAH-NEE INDIAN HEALTH CENTER
P.O. Box 717
Fort Hall, ID 83203
(208) 238–2400

## ◆ OREGON

**WARM SPRINGS SERVICE UNIT**
WARM SPRINGS PHS INDIAN HEALTH CENTER
P.O. Box 1209
Warm Springs, OR 97761
(541) 553–1196

**WESTERN OREGON SERVICE UNIT**
CHEMAWA INDIAN HEALTH CENTER
3750 Chemawa Rd, NE
Salem, OR 97305
(503) 399–5931

## ◆ WASHINGTON

**COLVILLE SERVICE UNIT**
COLVILLE PHS INDIAN HEALTH CENTER
P.O. Box 71-Agency Campus Service Unit
Nespelem, WA 99155
(509) 634–4771

**NEAH BAY SERVICE UNIT**
SOPHIE TRETTEVICK INDIAN HEALTH CENTER
P.O. Box 410
Neah Bay, WA 98357
(360) 645–2233

**WELLPINIT SERVICE UNIT**
DAVID C. WYNECOOP MEMORIAL CLINIC
P.O. Box 357
Wellpinit, WA 99040
(509) 258–4517

**YAKAMA SERVICE UNIT**
YAKAMA PHS INDIAN HEALTH CENTER
401 Buster Road
Toppenish, WA 98948
(509 865–2102

### REGION XII

### SOUTHERN ARIZONA

TUCSON AREA INDIAN HEALTH SERVICE
   (ARIZONA)
7900 S. J. Stock Road
Tucson, AZ 85746–7012
(520) 295–2405

## SERVICE UNITS

SANTA ROSA PHS INDIAN HEALTH CENTER
Star Route, Box 71
Sells, AZ 85634
(520) 361–2261

SAN XAVIER PHS INDIAN HEALTH CENTER
7900 S. J. Stock Road
Tucson, AZ 85746
(520) 295–2480

**SELLS SERVICE UNIT**
SELLS PHS INDIAN HOSPITAL
P.O. Box 548
Sells, AZ 85634
(520) 383–7251

# NONGOVERNMENTAL ORGANIZATIONS AND ASSOCIATIONS CONCERNED WITH INDIAN HEALTH

## ◆ ALASKA

CROSS ROADS MEDICAL CENTER
P.O. Box 5
Glennallen, AK 99588
(907) 822–3203

## ◆ ARIZONA

NAVAJO NATION DIVISION OF HEALTH
P.O. Box 1390
Window Rock, AZ 86515–1390
(520) 871–6350 ext. 6350

OFFICE OF DENE CULTURE LANGUAGE
   AND COMMUNITY SERVICES
Division Of Dine Education
P.O. Box 670
Window Rock, AZ 86515
(520) 871–7660

## ◆ CALIFORNIA

CENTER FOR AMERICAN INDIAN RESEARCH
   AND EDUCATION
University Of Missota
1918 University Avenue, Suite 3A
Berkeley, CA 94704–1024
(510) 843–8661

FRESNO INDIAN HEALTH ASSOCIATION, INC.
3720 North first St., No. 108
Fresno, CA 93726
(559) 291–3475

MASTERS OF PUBLIC HEALTH PROGRAM
  FOR NATIVE AMERICANS
School of Public Health
American Indian Graduate Program
316 Sprawl Hall
University of California-Berkeley
Berkeley, CA 94720
(510) 642–3228

NATIVE AMERICAN HEALTH CENTER
3124 International Blvd.
Oakland, CA 94601
(510) 535–4460

NATIVE AMERICAN HEALTH CENTER
56 Julian Ave.
San Francisco, CA 94103
(415) 621–8051

SACRAMENTO URBAN INDIAN HEALTH
  PROJECT
2020 J St.
Sacramento, CA 95814
(916) 441–0918

SAN DIEGO AMERICAN INDIAN
  HEALTH CENTER
2630 First Ave.
San Diego, CA 92103
(619) 234–2158

#### ◆ COLORADO

DENVER INDIAN HEALTH AND FAMILY
  SERVICES
3749 King St.
Denver, CO 80236
(303) 781–4050

EAGLE LODGE, INC.
Behavioral Health Center
1264 Race St.
Denver, CO 80206
(303) 393–7773

NATIONAL CENTER FOR AMERICAN INDIAN
  AND ALASKA NATIVE MENTAL HEALTH
  RESEARCH
UCHSC
4455 East 12 Ave., Box A011–13
Denver, CO 80220
(303) 315–9232

NATION INDIAN HEALTH BOARD
1385 S. Colorado Blvd., Suite A707
Denver, CO 80222
(303) 759–3075

#### ◆ ILLINOIS

AMERICAN ACADEMY OF PEDIATRICS
  COMMITTEE ON INDIAN HEALTH
141 NW Point Blvd.
Elk Grove Village, IL 60007
(800) 433–9016

AMERICAN INDIAN HEALTH SERVICE
838 West Irving Park Rd.
Chicago, IL 60640
(773) 883–9100

#### ◆ IOWA

NATIVE AMERICAN ALCOHOLISM
  TREATMENT PROGRAM
P.O. Box 773
Sergeant Bluff, IA 51054
(712) 277–9416

#### ◆ KANSAS

WICHITA INDIAN HEALTH CENTER
2318 East Central
Wichita, KS 67214
(316) 262–2415

#### ◆ MARYLAND

CENTER FOR AMERICAN INDIAN HEALTH
Johns Hopkins University
School of Hygiene and Public Health
621 North Washington St.
Baltimore, Maryland 21205
(410) 955–6931

## ◆ MICHIGAN

**AMERICAN INDIAN SERVICES, INC.**
Mental Health Clinic
1110 S. Field Rd.
Lincoln Park, MI 48146
(313) 388–4100

**DETROIT AMERICAN INDIAN HEALTH
   CENTER**
810 Dearborn
480 Longdale St.
Detroit, MI 48121
(313) 846–3718

## ◆ MINNESOTA

**CENTER OF AMERICAN INDIAN AND
   MINORITY HEALTH**
University of Minnesota, Duluth
School of Medicine
10 University Dr. Rm 182 Med. Bld.
Duluth, MN 55812–2487
(218) 726–7235

**INDIAN HEALTH BOARD OF MINNEAPOLIS**
1315 East 24th St.
Minneapolis, MN 55404
(612) 721–9800

## ◆ MONTANA

**BLACKFEET TRIBAL HEALTH PROGRAM**
P.O. Box 866
Browning, MT 59417
(406) 338–6157

**NORTH AMERICAN INDIAN ALLIANCE**
100 East Galena St.
Butte, MT 59701
(406) 782–0461

## ◆ NEBRASKA

**INTERTRIBAL TREATMENT CENTER**
2301 South 15th St.
Omaha, NE 68108
(402) 346–0902

## ◆ NEW MEXICO

**SIPI TWELVE FEATURES LODGE**
Alcoholism Treatment Program
P.O. Box 10146
Albuquerque, NM 87184
(505) 897–5366

## ◆ NORTH DAKOTA

**INDIANS INTO MEDICINE PROGRAM**
University of North Dakota
School of Medicine and Health Sciences
P.O. Box 9037
501 North Columbia Rd.
Grand Forks, ND 58202–9037
(701) 777–3037

## ◆ OKLAHOMA

**ASSOCIATION OF AMERICAN INDIAN
   PHYSICIANS**
1225 Sovern Rd Suite 103
Oklahoma City, OK 73108
(405) 946–7072

**INDIAN HEALTH CARE RESOURCE CENTER**
550 S. Peoria Ave.
Tulsa, OK 74120–3820
(918) 588–1000

**OKLAHOMA CITY INDIAN CLINIC**
4913 W. Reno
Oklahoma City, OK 73127
(405) 948–4900

## ◆ OREGON

**NATIVE AMERICAN REHABILITATION
   ASSOCIATION OF THE NORTHWEST**
17645 N. W. St., Helens Hwy
Portland, OR 97231
(503) 621–1069

## ◆ SOUTH DAKOTA

**HOPE LODGE**
P.O. Box 9750
Rapid City, SD 57709–9750
(605) 342–8925

SOUTH DAKOTA URBAN INDIAN
    HEALTH, INC.
122 East Dakota Ave
Pierre, SD 57501
(605) 224–8841

♦ **UTAH**

INDIAN ALCOHOLISM COUNSELING AND RE-
    COVERY HOUSE PROGRAM
375 South 300 West
Salt Lake City, UT 84101
(801) 328–8516

♦ **WASHINGTON**

SEATTLE INDIAN HEALTH BOARD
P.O. Box 3364
Seattle, WA 98114
(206) 324–9360
www.sihb.org

SPOKANE URBAN INDIAN HEALTH
    SERVICES
East 905 Third Ave.
Spokane, WA 99202
(509) 489–9147

THUNDERBIRD TREATMENT CENTER
9236 Renton Ave. S.
Seattle, WA 98118
(206) 722–7152

♦ **WISCONSIN**

AMERICAN INDIAN COUNCIL ON
    ALCOHOLISM
2240 West National Ave.
Milwaukee, WI 53204
(414) 671–2200

GERALD L. IGNACE HEALTH CENTER, INC.
1711 S. 11th St.
Milwaukee, WI 53204
(414) 383–9526

GREAT LAKE INTER-TRIBAL COUNCIL, INC.
2932 Hwy 47 North
Lac du Flambeau, WI 54538
(715) 588–3324

UNITED AMERINDIAN HEALTH CENTER
407 Dousman
Green Bay, WI 54303
(920) 436–6630

# *Canadian Indian Health Organizations*

## HEALTH AND WELFARE CANADA
Medical Services Branch
Indian and Northern Health Services
Jeanne Mance Bldg., 11th Floor
Ottawa, ON K1A 0L3
(613) 952–9616

## ◆ REGIONAL MEDICAL SERVICES BRANCHS

### ALBERTA REGION
Medical Services Branch
Health Canada
Suite 730, Canada Place
9700 Jasper Avenue
Edmonton, AB T5J 4C3
(780) 495–2703

### ATLANTIC REGION
Medical Services Branch
Health Canada
Suite 634, Ralston Bldg., 6th floor
1557 Hollis Street
Halifax, NS B3J 1V6
(902) 426–6637

### CANADIAN CENTRE ON SUBSTANCE ABUSE
75 Albert Street, Suite 300
Ottawa, ON Canada K1P 5E7
(613) 235–4048

### MANITOBA REGION
Medical Services Branch
Health Canada
Suite 300, 391 York Avenue
Winnipeg, MB R3C 4W1
(204) 983–4171

### NORTHERN SECRETARIAT REGION
Medical Services Branch
Health Canada
Postal Locator: 1921B
Ottawa, ON K1A 0L3
(613) 957–3406

### ONTARIO REGION
Medical Services Branch
Health Canada
1547 Merivale Road, 3rd floor
Nepean, Ontario K1A 0L3
(613) 952–0087

### PACIFIC REGION
Medical Services Branch
Health Canada
Suite 540, Federal Bldg.
757 West Hastings St.
Vancouver, B. C. V6C 3E6
(604) 666–2083

### QUEBEC REGION
Medical Services Branch
Health Canada
Suite 202, 2nd floor, East Tower
Guy Favreau Complex
200 Rene Levesque Blvd.,
Montreal, PQ H2Z 1X4
(514) 283–2856

### SASKATCHEWAN REGION
Medical Services Branch
Health Canada
18th Floor-1920 Broad Street
Regina, SK S4P 3V2
(306) 80–5449

### CANADIAN NONGOVERNMENTAL ORGANIZATIONS AND ASSOCIATIONS CONCERNED WITH INDIAN HEALTH
There are over Five Hundred listing throughout the provinces of Canada regarding health care for Aborigi-

nal Peoples Inquires about health care issues such as Aboriginal Headstart, Aboriginal Health Institute, Alcohol and Drug Abuse, Brighter Futures/Building Healthy Communities, Dental Health and the Dental Therapy Training Program, Health Careers, Healing and Wellness, Home Care, Nursing in First Nations Communities, Nursing Training and Support, Pregnancy and Child Development, Solvent Abuse, Tobacco Reduction, Women's Health at your nearest Health Canada, Regional Medical Services Branch for a specific type of health care service provider in your area or a complete listing of Aboriginal Health Care Service Providers and Organizations throughout Canada.

For nongovernmental First Nations Tribal Health Care Service Providers Organization and Associations in your area please contact your local First Nations Friendship Center or Tribe of Affiliation.

## References

### Traditional Medicine

Adair, John and Kurt W. Deuschle. *The Peoples Health: Medicine and Anthropology in a Navajo Community.* New York: Appleton-Century Crofts, 1970.

Arnold, David, ed. *Imperial Medicine and Indigenous Societies.* Manchester: Manchester University Press; distributed exclusively in the USA and Canada by St. Martin's Press, 1988.

Bahr, Donald M., et al. *Piman Shamanism and Staying Sickness.* Tucson: University of Arizona Press, 1974.

Bergman, Robert L. "The Peyote Religion and Healing." In *Religious Systems and Psychotherapy,* edited by Richard H. Cox. 296–306. Springfield, Ill.: Charles C. Thomas, 1973.

Bonvillain, Nancy. *Native American Medicine.* Philadelphia: Chelsea House, 1997.

Camazine, Scott M. "Traditional and Western Health Care among the Zuni Indians of New Mexico." *Social Science and Medicine* 14B, no. 1 (1980): 73–80.

Coulehan, John L. "Navajo Indian Medicine: Implications for Healing." *Journal of Family Practice* 10, no. 1 (1980): 55–61.

Cunningham, Andrew and Bridie Andrews. Introduction. In *Western Medicine as Contested Knowledge,* edited by Andrew Cunningham and Bridie Andrews, 1–23. Manchester: University of Manchester Press, 1997.

Elferink, Jan G. R. "The Significance of the Pre-Columbian Pharmaceutical Knowledge for European Medicine in the XVIth Century." *Pharmaceutica Acta Helvetiae* 54, nos. 9–10 (1979): 299–302.

Ferro, Marc. *Colonization: A Global History.* London: Routledge, 1997.

Fuchs, Michael and Rashid Bashshur. "Use of Traditional Medicine among Urban Native Americans." *Medical Care* 13, no. 11 (1975): 915–927.

Howard, R. Palmer. "Cherokee History to 1840: A Medical View." *Journal of the Oklahoma State Medical Association* 63, no. 2 (1970): 71–82.

Issacs, Hope L. "Iroquois Herbalism: the Past 100 Years." *International Journal of Social Psychiatry* 22, no. 4 (1976–1977): 272–281.

Long, Walker. A., M.D. "Lessons from the Traditional American Indian Medicine Man." *Pharos* 47, no.1 (1984): 7–10.

Luckert, Karl W. *Coyoteway: A Navajo Holyway Healing Ceremonial.* Tucson: University of Arizona Press, 1979.

———. "Traditional Navaho Theories of Disease and Healing." *Arizona Medicine* 29, no. 7 (1972): 571–573.

MacLeod, Roy, and Milton Lewis. *Disease, Medicine, and Empire: Perspectives on Western Medicine and the Experience of European Expansion.* London: Routledge, 1988.

Martin, Morgan. "Native American Medicine: Thoughts for Posttraditional Healers." *Journal of the American Medical Association* 245, no. 2 (1981): 141–143.

Romm, Sharon. "Native American Treatment of Burns." *Plastic Reconstructive Surgery* 69, no. 5 (1982): 883–892.

Spicer, Edward H., ed. *Ethnic Medicine in the Southwest.* Tucson: University of Arizona Press, 1977.

Straight, William M. "Disease and Medicine among the Pre-Seminole Indians of Florida." *Journal of the Florida Medical Association* 71:7 (1984): 479–490.

Vogel, Virgil. *American Indian Medicine.* Norman: University of Oklahoma Press, 1970.

Waddell, Jack O. and Michael W. Everett, eds. *Drinking Behavior Among Southwestern Indians: An Anthropological Perspective.* Tucson: University of Arizona Press, 1980.

*Jennie Joe*

### U.S. Indian Health

Ablon, Joan. "American Indian Relocation: Problems of Dependency and Management in the City." *Phylon* 26, no. 4 (1965): 362–371.

———. "Relocated American Indians in the San Francisco Bay Area: Social Interaction and Indian Identity." *Human Organization* 23, no. 4 (1964): 296–304.

———. "Retention of Cultural Values and Differential Urban Adaptation: Samoans and American Indians in a West Coast City." *Social Forces* 49, no. 3 (1971): 385–393.

Abramowitz, Joseph. "Planning for the Indian Health Service." *Journal of Public Health Dentistry* 31, no. 2 (1971): 70–78.

Adair, John, and Kurt Deuschle. *The People's Health: Medicine and Anthropology in a Navajo Community.* New York: Appleton-Century Crofts, 1970.

———. "Some Problems of the Physicians on the Navajo Reservation." *Human Organization* 16, no. 4 (1958): 19–23.

Adams, Morton S. and Jerry D. Niswander. "Health of the American Indian: Congenital Defects." *Eugenics Quarterly* 15, no. 4 (1968): 227–234.

Albrecht, C. Earl. "Reflections on the Past: The Development of Eskimo Health Care." *Alaska Medicine* 19, no. 6 (1977): 72–74.

Arnold, Robert D., et al. *Alaska Native Land Claims.* Anchorage: Alaska Native Foundation, 1976.

Bashshur, Rashid, William Steeler, and Tim Murphy. "On Changing Indian Eligibility for Health Care." *American Journal of Public Health* 77, no. 6 (1987): 690–693.

Bryant, John. "Community Health Workers: The Interface Between Communities and Health Care Systems." *WHO Chronicle* 32, no. 4 (1978): 144–148.

Cohen, Felix. *Handbook of Federal Indian Law.* Albuquerque: University of New Mexico Press, 1971.

Dobyns, Henry. "The Indian Reorganization Act and Federal Withdrawal." *Human Organization* 7, no. 2 (1948): 35–44.

Fry, Alan. *How a People Die: A Novel* Toronto: Doubleday Canada; Garden City, N.Y.: Doubleday, 1970.

Getches, David H., Charles F. Wilkinson and Robert A. Williams. *Cases and Materials on Federal Indian Law.* St. Paul, Minn: West Pub. Group, 1998.

Gray, Sharon A. *Health of Native People of North America: a Bibliography and Guide to Resources.* Lanham, Md.: Scarecrow Press, 1996.

Hamer, John and Jack Steinbring, eds. *Alcohol and Native Peoples of North.* Washington, D.C.: University Press of America, 1980.

Herrick, James W. "Powerful Medicinal Plants in Traditional Iroquois Culture." *New York State Journal of Medicine* 78, no. 6 (1978): 979–987.

Hodge, Felicia. "Disabled American Indians: A Special Population Requiring Special Considerations." *American Indian Culture and Research Journal* 13, no. 3–4 (1989): 83–104.

Hodge, Felicia Schanche. *The Health Status of American Indians in California.* Woodland Hills, Calif.: The California Endowment & California HealthCare Foundation, 1997.

Hrdlicka, Ales. "Disease, Medicine, and Surgery Among the American Aborigines." *Journal of the American Medical Association* 99:20 (1932): 1661–1666.

Isaacs, Hope L. "Toward Improved Health Care for Native Americans: Comparative Perspective on American Indian Medicine Concepts." *New York State Journal of Medicine* 78, no. 5 (1978): 824–829.

LaFromboise, Teresa. "American Indian Mental Health Policy." *American Psychologist* 43, no. 5 (1988): 388–397.

Leighton, Alexander. "The Mental Health of the American Indian." *American Journal of Psychiatry* 125, no. 2 (1968): 217–218.

Manson, Spero M., ed. *New Directions in Prevention Among American Indian and Alaskan Native Communities.* Portland: Oregon Health Sciences University, 1982.

May, Philip. "Alcohol Abuse and Alcoholism Among American Indians: An Overview." In *Alcoholism in Minority Populations,* edited by Thomas D. Watts and Roosevelt Wright, Jr., 95–119. Springfield, Ill.: Charles C. Thomas, 1989.

McNickle, D'Arcy. *The Indian Tribes of the United States: Ethnic and Tribal Survival.* New York: Oxford University Press, 1962.

Primeaux, Martha. "American Indian Health Care Practices: A Cross-Cultural Perspective." *Nursing Clinics of North America* 12, no. 1 (1977): 55–65.

Rymer, Sheila. "New Approaches to Health Problems of the Indian People." *Canadian Medical Association Journal* 101, no. 10 (1969): 614–615.

Schmeckebier, Laurence F. *The Office of Indian Affairs: Its History, Activities and Organization.* Baltimore, Md.: Johns Hopkins Press, 1927.

Sclar, Lee J. "Participation of Off-Reservation Indian Programs of the Bureau of Indian Affairs and the Indian Health Service." *Montana Law Review* 33 no. 2 (1972): 191–232.

Sievers, Maurice L. and Jeffrey R. Fisher. "Diseases of North American Indians." In *Biocultural Aspects of Disease,* edited by Henry Rothschild, 191–253. New York: Academic Press, 1981.

Slagle, A. Logan and Joan Weibel-Orlando. "The Indian Shaker Church and Alcoholics Anonymous: Revitalistic Curing Cults." *Human Organization* 45, no. 4 (1986): 310–319.

Staub, Henry P. "American Indians: New Opportunity for Health Care." *New York State Journal of Medicine* 78, no. 7 (1978): 1137–1141.

Trafzer, Clifford E. and Diane Weiner, eds. *Medicine Ways: Disease, Health, and Survival Among Native Americans.* Walnut Creek, Calif.: AltaMira Press, 2001.

U.S. Congress. Office of Technology Assessment. *Indian Health Care.* Washington, D.C.: GPO, 1986.

U.S. Department of Health and Human Services. Public Health Service. Indian Health Service. *A Comprehensive Health Care Program for American Indian and Alaska Natives.* Washington, D.C., 1992.

U.S. Department of Health and Human Services. Public Health Service. Indian Health Service. Office of Planning, Evaluation, and Legislation. Division of Program Statistics. *Regional Differences in Indian Health, 1996.* Rockville, Md., 1997.

U.S. Department of Health and Human Services. Public Health Service. Indian Health Service. *Trends in Indian Health, 1996.* Rockville Md., 1997.

U.S. Indian Health Service. *Illness Among Indians and Alaskan Natives 1970 to 1978.* Washington: U.S. Department of Health, Education, and Welfare, 1979.

Waddell, Jack O. and O. Michael Watson. *The American Indian in Urban Society.* Boston: Little, Brown, 1971.

Wassen, S. Henry. "On Concepts of Disease Among Amerindian Tribal Groups." *Journal of Ethnopharmacology* 1, no. 3 (1979): 285–293.

West, Kelly M. "Diabetes in American Indians and Other Native Populations of the New World." *Diabetes* 23, no. 10 (1974): 841–855.

*Felicia Hodge*

## Canadian Native Health

Berger, Thomas R. *A Long and Terrible Shadow: White Values, Native Rights in the Americas 1492–1992.* Vancouver: Douglas & McIntyre, 1991.

Canada. Minister of Indian Affairs and Northern Development. *Gathering Strength: Canada's Aboriginal Action Plan.* Ottawa, 1998.

———. *Gathering Strength: Canada's Aboriginal Action Plan, A Progress Report.* [Online]. Available: http://www.ainc-inac.gc.ca/gs/index_e.html [2001 January 29].

Canada. Royal Commission on Aboriginal Peoples. *The Path to Healing: Report of the National Round Table on Aboriginal Health and Social Issues.* Ottawa: Royal Commission on Aboriginal Peoples, 1993.

Canadian Medical Association. *Bridging the Gap: Promoting Health and Healing for Aboriginal Peoples in Canada.* Submission to the Royal Commission on Aboriginal Peoples. Ottawa: Canadian Medical Association, 1994.

Culhane Speck, Dara. *An Error in Judgement: The Politics of Medical Care in an Indian/White Community.* Vancouver, B.C.: Talonbooks, 1987.

Dickason, Olive Patricia. *Canada's First Nations: A History of the Founding Peoples from Earliest Times.* Toronto: McClelland and Stewart; Norman: University of Oklahoma Press, 1992.

Fortuine, Robert, et al. *The Health of the Inuit of North America: A Bibliography From the Earliest Times Through 1990.* Anchorage: University of Alaska Anchorage, 1993.

Graham-Cumming George. "Health of the Original Canadians, 1867–1967." *Medical Services Journal, Canada* 23 no. 2 (1967): 115–166.

Hodes, Anne-Marie. "The Plain Need for Natives." *Iatros, Medical Students Association and Medical Alumni Association, University of Alberta* 11, no. 1 (1997): 13–15.

Jilek, Wolfgang G. *Indian Healing: Shamanic Ceremonialism in the Pacific Northwest Today.* Surrey, B.C.: Hancock House, 1982.

Kuhnlein, Harriet V., and Nancy J. Turner. *Traditional Plant Foods of Canadian Indigenous Peoples: Nutrition, Botany and Use.* Philadelphia: Gordon and Breach, 1991.

Lavallee, Claudette, and Elizabeth Robinson. *The Health of the Eastern James Bay Cree: Annotated Bibliography.* Montreal: Northern Quebec Module, Montreal General Hospital, 1993.

Le Clercq, Chrestien. *New Relation of Gaspesia: With the Customs and Religion of the Gaspesian Indians.* Translated and edited by William F. Ganong. Toronto: Champlain Society, 1920. Reprint. New York: Greenwood Press, 1968.

Lemchuk-Favel, Laurel. *Trends in First Nations Mortality 1979–1993.* Ottawa: Health Canada, 1996.

MacMillan, Harriet L., MacMillan, Angus B., Offord, David R., and Dingle, Jennifer L. "Aboriginal Health." *CMAJ: Canadian Medical Association Journal.* 155, no. 11 (1996): 1569–1578.

Martens, Tony., Brenda Daily, and Maggie Hodgson. *The Spirit Weeps: Characteristics and Dynamics of Incest and Child Sexual Abuse.* Edmonton, Alta.: Nechi Institute, 1988.

McCardle, Bennett. *Bibliography of the History of Canadian Indian and Inuit Health.* Edmonton, Alta.: Treaty and Aboriginal Rights Research of the Indian Association of Alberta, 1981.

Meiklejohn, Christopher. *The Native Peoples of Canada: An Annotated Bibliography of Population Biology, Health, and Illness.* Ottawa: National Museums of Canada, 1986.

Ponting, J. Rick, ed. *Arduous Journey: Canadian Indians and Decolonization.* Toronto: McClelland and Stewart, 1989.

Sproat, Bonnie, and Joan Feather. *Northern Saskatchewan Health Research Bibliography.* 2nd ed. Saskatoon, Sask.: Northern Medical Services, Dept. of Family Medicine, University of Saskatchewan, 1990.

Statistics Canada. *Aboriginal Data: Age and Sex.* Ottawa, 1993

———. *Language, Tradition, Health, Lifestyle and Social Issues.* 1991 Aboriginal Peoples Survey. Ottawa, 1993.

———. *Persons Registered Under the Indian Act, Living On and Off Reserve, 1996 Census* [Online]. Available: http://www.statcan.ca/english/Pgdb/People/Population/demo37.htm [2001 January 29].

———. *Schooling, Work, and Related Activities, Income, Expenses, and Mobility.* Ottawa: 1993.

———. Total Population by Aboriginal Group, 1996 Census, Census Metropolitan Areas [Online]. Available: http://www.statcan.ca/english/Pgdb/People/Population/demo39b.htm [2001 January 29].

Waldram, James B., Ann D. Herring, and T. Kue Young. *Aboriginal Health in Canada: Historical, Cultural, and Epidemiological Perspectives.* Toronto: University of Toronto Press, 1995.

Weatherford, Jack. *Native Roots: How the Indians Enriched America.* New York: Crown, 1991.

York, Geoffrey. *The Dispossessed: Life and Death in Native Canada.* Toronto: Lester & Orpen Dennys Pub., 1989.

Young, David, Grant Ingram, and Lise Swartz. *Cry of the Eagle: Encounters with a Cree Healer.* Toronto: University of Toronto Press, 1989.

Young, David E., Leonard L. Smith. *The Involvement of Canadian Native Communities in Their Health Care Programs: A Review of the Literature Since the 1970's.* Edmonton: Canadian Circumpolar Institute, University of Alberta, 1992.

Young, T. Kue. *Health Care and Cultural Change: The Indian Experience in the Central Subarctic.* Toronto: University of Toronto Press, 1988.

*Ann-Marie Hodes*

# 16

# *Education*

- ◆ Primary and Secondary U.S. Native Education ◆ U.S. Indian Higher Education
- ◆ Canadian Native Education ◆ Indian Education Offices and Organizations
- ◆ Canadian Education Organizations ◆ Research Centers and Organizations

## ◆ PRIMARY AND SECONDARY U.S. NATIVE EDUCATION

From its beginnings, formal education for American Indians and Alaska Natives developed differently than it did for other people of the United States. Provisions for educational services and facilities were included in 120 of the nearly 400 treaties between Indian nations and the federal government, which over a period of ninety-three years (1778–1871), exchanged almost one billion acres of Indian land for services (such as health and education), protection against invasion, and self-government in perpetuity, or "as long as the grass grows and the rivers flow." This unique relationship between Indian nations and the federal government created a federal educational system administered by the Bureau of Indian Affairs (BIA). For more than one hundred years, the system was operated by the federal government with little or no local control; in contrast, public education was based on local control with very little assistance from the federal government.

Indian education has been the subject of many research projects and several national studies (see, for example, the Meriam Report, the National Study of American Indian Education, the Kennedy Report, and the American Indian Policy Review Commission, discussed later in this section). One criticism was constant in all reports: Indian parents were not given the opportunity to be involved in the governance of their children's education. In the 1970s, the need for local participation was finally recognized and provided for in several pieces of legislation. Education had come nearly full circle. For the first time since the arrival of explorers in search of the New World, Indian people had the opportunity to participate in determining the direction of their children's education. Throughout the 1980s, 1990s, and into 2000, Indian voices remained strong as Indian leaders and educators continued to assertively raise educational concerns to the federal government in local, regional, and national forums. In addition, educational researchers played a more significant role in the struggle to provide quality education for American Indian and Alaska Native students. The diversity of languages and cultures still found among many tribes are evidence of Indian people's perseverance.

### Informal Education Before Columbus and the Colonists

Every human society has a process for socializing youth and transmitting its culture. This process of education prepares young people for adult participation in their particular culture or society. Prior to white contact, the Native American educational process was one of active participation within a profoundly spiritual and philosophical atmosphere. There was no formal structure, as it is known today, to the education process. Young people learned by watching and doing; the teachers were parents and older siblings, relatives, and elders. The tribal language, customs, values, traditions, and ethics provided the curriculum. Approaches to learning were developed from socialization and child-rearing practices based on the values Indian groups revered. Each person was expected to perpetuate what he or she learned from childhood to adulthood; all that was learned was relevant to Indian life. Informal Native education was interrupted with the arrival of "New World" explorers and colonial settlers.

### Formal Education: Religious, Federal, and Indian

Formal education for Indians after white contact can be roughly divided into three eras of control: religious, federal, and Indian. Although there is some overlap, each era occupies a distinct place in the history of Indian education

**The Religious Influence.**  Beginning with the first school established by the Jesuits in Havana, Cuba, in 1568 for the Indians of Florida, formal education for Indian people has a history reflecting the philosophy and attitudes of the time. Education was viewed by early explorers and colonists as a means of "civilizing" the Indians and acculturating them to the way of life brought from Europe. The European powers, especially England, France, and Spain, each had similar goals of civilizing and Christianizing the Indians to ensure economic gain and political supremacy. Each country's methods were different, however.

For the French and Spanish, who sought to convert the Indians to Catholicism through Jesuit and Franciscan missionaries, education meant teaching about religion or providing religious training or both. Spanish influence is still evident in the Southwest, while the French influence is evident in the Northeast and the Mississippi Valley.

The English Protestant religious groups probably had the most profound influence on early federal Indian policy. Education in the English colonies was a cooperative venture between church and state; the missionaries, who were preachers and teachers, were supported by the colonial governments. Reading, writing, arithmetic, and catechism formed the basic curriculum, along with instruction in the industrial arts; all subjects were intended to teach the ways of civilized life. During the colonial period, two people were key in determining the future educational programs for Indians: the Puritan missionary John Eliot and Eleazer Wheelock, headmaster of the Moors Charity School. Their shared goal to convert and civilize Indians differed in their approaches.

Eliot learned the Algonkian dialect and was able to preach sermons directly to the Indians to convince them to submit their children to a Puritan education. Once convinced, Indian converts requested their own schools, governments, and pseudo-English way of life. Land was purchased and "praying towns" were established in which Indian converts could live together. In these Indian praying towns, attempts to educate and Christianize the Indians were quite successful.

Wheelock's philosophy was to remove Indian youth from the influence of family and tribe and board them at schools and homes where they could be exposed to "civilized life." Ideally, they would then return to their communities and continue to convert and civilize their own people. His school, Moors Charity School (which later became Dartmouth College), accommodated this philosophy. Wheelock, as the first president of Dartmouth College, supported the enrollment of Indian students during the early years of the college's existence. In 1775 the Continental Congress approved $500 to educate Indians at Dartmouth.

The work of Eliot and Wheelock exemplified the efforts of private agencies and government to subsidize missionaries who could go among the Indian people to preach and teach, Christianize and civilize. The education policies of the new federation emerged from Wheelock's philosophy that the most effective way to create change among Indian cultures was to remove the youth from the influence of their people.

**The Federal Role.**  Assimilation has been the dominant and consistent theme in federal educational policy throughout U.S. history. In each of the policy periods of federal-Indian history (treaty-making, removal, reform, termination), including the current period of self-determination, education was and is viewed as one answer to the "Indian problem." Central to educational goals was an ideology of acculturation and assimilation accomplished through isolation and removal to federal boarding schools. The first such school was established in 1860 on the Yakima (Yakama) Indian Reservation in Washington. Five years later, boarding schools away from Indian communities were recommended as a way of providing agricultural and industrial training for Indian students. The first off-reservation boarding school was established in 1879 in Carlisle, Pennsylvania; however, Indian students had also been attending Hampton Normal and Industrial Institute in Hampton, Virginia.

From an early appropriation of $15,000 approved by Congress in 1802 to the operating of more than one hundred schools on and off reservations in 1892, a federal education system evolved that suppressed Native languages and cultures and supported assimilation into the mainstream of European America. Indians did not complacently accept these efforts to be civilized and Christianized through a federal school system. However, resistance only brought regulations regarding attendance of Indian children at the schools that were established for them. The withholding of rations, upon which Indian people placed on reservations had come to depend, was one method of enforcement applied to parents of Indian children for their resistance.

**Indian Schools.**  In the late eighteenth century, the Cherokee, Chickasaw, Choctaw, Creek, and Seminole nations responded to federal efforts of assimilation by developing their own schools and other institutions. With a syllabary that presented the Cherokee language in print, Cherokee people boasted a literacy rate exceeding that of frontier settlers near them. The accomplishments of these five tribes earned them "civilized" status, according to the vernacular of the time. After their forced removal, known as the Trail of Tears, from their homelands in the East and Southeast to Indian Territory (now Oklahoma) to the west, the so-called Five Civilized Tribes continued to adopt and adapt the economic, political, and educational systems of the dominant European-American society. The institutions they established were examples of direct control by Indian nations. These institutions, however, were terminated in the early 1900s when the state of Oklahoma was created.

In 1906 Congress abolished the Oklahoma Cherokee school system, thereby relegating the impressive literacy rate once enjoyed by a majority of Cherokees to a status that needed federal assistance to meet the special educational, cultural, and language needs of current-day Cherokees. The Indian-controlled community school systems established later in the twentieth century had a prototype in those of the Five Civilized Tribes.

### Evolution of an Indian School System

The Indian School System, as it came to be known, was derived from several types of schools: off- and on-reservation boarding schools, training or industrial schools, day schools (operated by the government and/or religious societies), and other schools such as those operated by the Five Civilized Tribes.

**Mission Schools.** During the assimilation policy period in Indian history (1887–1934), several types of schools served Indian students. From the late 1500s to the 1800s, mission schools, operated by missionary societies with subsidies from the federal government, were the primary source of formal education and were the forerunners of federal and public schools. Mission schools continued to exist even after the federal and public schools enrolled a majority of Indian children. The philosophical base of mission schools was viewed as compatible with the "naturally devout" nature of Indian people, and the education provided in these schools was considered superior to that of other schools. Although some of the schools were located far away from the students' homes, many were attached to missions located near Indian lands.

**Off-Reservation Boarding Schools.** Off-reservation boarding schools, which focused on agricultural and industrial training, were established in the 1700s and 1800s. Many students experienced loneliness and longed to return home. However, many of them adjusted to the new life and did not return to their homeland until they had finished their schooling; some students never returned to the reservation. In this respect, the philosophy of assimilation through education far removed from the culture was successful; nonetheless, some

criticisms could not be ignored. This type of education was very expensive. In addition, the assimilation policy presented an either/or situation: students either assimilated completely or "returned to the blanket," or returned to their reservation, and did not influence others to assimilate. The widespread conversion that was expected did not occur.

**On-Reservation Boarding Schools and Day Schools.** Later in the 1800s, the philosophy of removing Indian children from the reservation to schools such as Carlisle was modified, and boarding schools on the reservation were established. These schools were less expensive to operate than off-reservation schools. While Indian parents strongly opposed the off-reservation education policy, they did not oppose education itself; therefore, boarding schools located closer to their homes were somewhat more agreeable than those farther away. Even so, Indian parents were still expected to give up their children for years at a time in order for them to receive an education at the on-reservation boarding school.

Day schools were located in the communities of the children and families they served. The mission schools were the first day schools. Because their children were closer to home, Indian parents were more likely to support this type of formal education. The main objective of day schools, as was true for the boarding schools, was to encourage Indian youth to adopt civilized ways.

In his annual report of 1855, the superintendent of Indian schools remarked that the Indian school system had not been thoughtfully planned and enacted, but instead evolved gradually. He maintained that a system such as this lacked uniformity in administration, management, operation, and quality of instruction among schools. A uniform course of study was the perceived solution to this problem, and by 1916 a standard curriculum had been introduced into all federal Indian schools.

The goal of the federal Indian school system had always been to promote integration of Indian people into mainstream European-American society. Removal of Indian people to reservations defeated this purpose. Indian youth educated in boarding schools returned to home communities segregated from European-American settlement. Therefore the schools' curriculum was not effective in exchanging Indian lifeways for a "more civilized way of life."

**Public Schools.** During the early 1900s, the assimilationists believed that public schools would be best for Indian children. Tuition was offered to public schools to educate some Indian children. The philosophy was to Americanize the Indians by educating them in public schools to become self-reliant, self-supporting citizens. This philosophy coincided with the allotment policy in Indian history. The Allotment Act (Dawes Severalty Act of 1887), which allotted reservation land to individual Indians, also opened up the reservations; "surplus," or non-allotted, land was sold to non-Indians. On some reservations where farm and ranch land was desirable, public schools were needed for the children of the many non-Indian settlers; therefore, public schools were established.

By 1920 more Indian students were in public schools than in federal schools, necessitating legislation to provide school funds in lieu of taxes not generated on the tax-free lands from which the Indian students came. The Johnson-O'Malley Act (JOMA) of 1934 and Public Laws 815 and 874, or the Impact Aid Laws, in 1950 were two such pieces of legislation. JOMA allowed the federal government to sign contracts with states (rather than with the thousands of individual school districts, as was necessary before this act) for Indian students' education in public schools. The Impact Aid Laws were intended to lessen the burden of federal activities and to compensate school districts (in lieu of local taxes) by providing funds for general operating expenses (P.L. 874) and school construction (P.L. 815). These laws were originally intended for areas in which there were military installations, but they were amended to include Indians living on reservation lands.

Both Johnson-O'Malley and P.L. 874 have caused controversy over the years in regard to the basis for funding and the administration of the funds. In the case of JOMA, the funds often boosted general school operation, and non-Indian students benefited from the increased funding more than the Indian students for whom it was intended. In the later reform era, JOMA and Impact Aid were targets for the self-determination, or local reservation control, efforts of Indian and non-Indian reformers; many changes have occurred as a result.

## The Reform Era

In addition to the self-determination policy reform period, two eras in the history of Indian education, occurring in the 1920s and the 1960s, drew national attention to Indian education reform. Each era produced a significant policy study (The Meriam Report and the Kennedy Report, respectively).

During the 1920s, mismanagement in the Bureau of Indian Affairs prompted a 1928 study by the Brookings Institution under the direction of Lewis Meriam, a Brookings Institute staff member trained in economics and law. *The Problem of Indian Administration*, more commonly referred to as the Meriam Report, pinpointed problems throughout the BIA. W. Carson Ryan, an advocate of an educational movement known as progressive education, was responsible for the education section of the report. Young Indians' boarding-school existence received the most scrutiny and criticism. The health and nutrition needs and general welfare conditions of boarding school children were said to be deplorable, causing widespread illness. The curriculum of study was also severely attacked in the report, especially the Uniform Course of Study, which dictated that all children study the same things at the same time throughout the school year. Other areas of criticism included low teacher salaries, the emphasis on vocational training often inappropriate for the job market, and the assimilationist approach the BIA had taken for the previous fifty years. Another fifty years would pass before the recommendations from the Meriam Report would be revisited.

Although the reform movement gained momentum in the 1920s, the 1930s transformed the rhetoric into action. The Education Division of the BIA gained new prominence under a reorganization that occurred in 1931. Headed by W. Carson Ryan, the Education Division's work was a proving ground for the basic tenets of progressive education and served as a model of school change, especially in the areas of rural education, with the emphasis Ryan placed on the community school concept. The Uniform Course of Study was gradually replaced with courses relevant to the cultures and heritage from which the children came, and programs were established to have Indian people come into the schools to teach classes. Ryan also sought to decentralize Indian education by encouraging schools to consider state curriculum standards and requirements, thereby paving the way for states to eventually assume the responsibility for educating Indian children.

In the short time that Ryan was in office, he was able to put the reform wheels into motion. Under the Roosevelt administration, new Commissioner of Indian Affairs John Collier provided the forceful leadership necessary to orchestrate New Deal innovations in Indian education. Reform was reflected in the curriculum, as well as in the printing of bilingual books and the training of teachers and aides to promote bilingual education. Community day schools became centers of community activity and some boarding schools were

Two boys at Riverside High School, a contemporary boarding school. (Photo by Carol Lujan)

closed. In spite of the progress of the 1930s, some aspects of reform promoted by Ryan and his successor Willard Beatty fared better than others. For example, cross-cultural education was more easily carried out in the community day schools than in boarding schools. Restricted by conservative attitudes toward change, many people were not ready to accept the progressive notions proposed by Ryan and Beatty. In addition, insufficient budgets and, the most powerful force of all, World War II stifled reform.

In the 1940s, war efforts took precedence over reforms in Indian education. The attention reform received in the 1920s and 1930s would not resurface until the 1960s, when the nation's collective conscience was awakened by the concern for civil rights and ethnic awareness. The rise of Indian leadership was stimulated by the national emergence of leadership among other ethnic minorities and served to promote the growing sense of Indian self-determination.

Self-determination was further promoted in the mid-1960s by several programs sponsored by the Office of Economic Opportunity (OEO) under the Department of Health, Education, and Welfare. Indian tribal groups were given more responsibility in planning and directing community action projects. As their confidence grew, Native Americans began to play a greater role in governing these programs, which included education and economic development.

At this time, the White House Task Force on Indian Affairs, which held hearings and conducted interviews with Indian representatives, was established. The report they produced stressed economic development and an improved educational system. In a 1968 message to Congress, President Lyndon B. Johnson stressed the importance of Indian involvement in their own affairs and directed the BIA to establish advisory boards at all BIA schools. The BIA also began to contract with Indian groups to operate their own schools. Two notable examples were Rough Rock Demonstration School (Arizona) and Ramah High School (New Mexico), both on the Navajo Reservation. Ramah High School had the distinction of being the first Indian-controlled high school since the closing of the Cherokee and Choctaw school systems in the early 1900s.

Morning Rae Ferris presents her paper on the theme of respect. (Photo by Mike McClure)

Schools in urban communities, such as the Red School House in St. Paul and the Heart of the Earth Survival School in Minneapolis, emerged as a response to the growing number of educators and parents who were dissatisfied with the school experience. Tribal culture, history, and language were given prominent status in the curricula of these and other schools located in urban areas where Indian people relocated during the termination period of the 1950s, when the federal government moved to dissolve Indian reservations.

The policy of Indian self-determination was strengthened by several studies. In 1969, another significant study of Indian policy, which reiterated some of the critical concerns of the Meriam Report of more than forty years before, was initiated. *Indian Education: A National Tragedy—A National Challenge,* or the Kennedy Report, was a study conducted by the Senate Special Committee on Indian Education headed by Senator Robert Kennedy. After Robert Kennedy's untimely death, Senator Edward Kennedy took leadership of the study. The Kennedy Report pointed out the

inequities in education for Indian students and concluded that federal policy had been one of "coercive assimilation," with "disastrous effects" on the education of Indian children. High absenteeism and dropout rates, negative self-image, low achievement, and academic failure were cited as effects of schooling that failed to understand or adapt to cultural differences. Inclusion of Indian history, culture, and language as part of the curriculum and greater involvement of Indian parents in the education of their children were among the many recommendations.

The U.S. Office of Education (USOE) was also interested in the education of Indian people. It sponsored a comprehensive national study of Indian education, lasting from 1967 to 1971. *The National Study of American Indian Education: The Education of Indian Children and Youth,* directed by Robert J. Havighurst and Estelle Fuchs, produced volumes of data that examined the education and lives of Indian children in the various types of schools they attended across the nation. The study was significant because it examined the contexts in which education took place and chronicled the perceptions of Indian people regarding the education of their children. In their 1972 book *To Live on This Earth: American Indian Education*, Estelle Fuchs and Robert J. Havighurst present much of the research from the national study as well as the work of anthropologists and educators who studied Indian education for the years before their study. The study and the book that followed served as a reminder that collecting and analyzing data on all Indians on a national scale was a responsibility not allocated to any one agency. For the first time, data were gathered that presented a cross-section of Indian education: rural and urban as well as public, private, and BIA-funded.

## Significant Legislation

Within ten years of the completion of the Kennedy Report and the publication of *To Live on This Earth*, three of the most significant pieces of legislation on Indian education were enacted. The Indian Education Act of 1972 (Public Law 92–318) was concerned with Indian children in public schools. The Indian Self-Determination and Education Assistance Act of 1975 (Public Law 93–638) provided a means thorough which Indian groups could contract services previously provided by the Bureau of Indian Affairs. Title XI of the Education Amendments of 1978 (Public Law 95–561) reorganized BIA education, creating an Office of Indian Education Programs (OIEP) and providing for more local control by school boards in BIA schools. All of these laws strengthened the voice of Indian people concerning the education of their children and reinforced the reform efforts of the 1960s.

Perhaps the most influential study during this period was the 1976 report on Indian education conducted by Task Force Five of the American Indian Policy Review Commission (AIPRC). Chaired by Helen Scheirbeck, Task Force Five had the responsibility of reviewing governmental policies and practices, as well as the needs and concerns of Indian people. Its goal was to present a statement of the federal role in Indian education as carried out by both the BIA and the United States. The AIPRC concluded that little had changed in Indian education since the last major policy review in 1928 (the Meriam Report), and that Congress should declare a policy of support and financing for Indian community control of all aspects of Indian education. The 1976 reports of the AIPRC greatly influenced the Title XI legislation of 1978 in terms of program funding for both the BIA and the USOE and provided for more local control and involvement of Indian people in all aspects of their education.

Indian education also benefited from other legislation during the New Frontier and Great Society programs of the Kennedy and Johnson administrations. Head Start and Follow Through programs in reservation and urban communities provided Indian preschool children with supplemental assistance that followed them through third grade. The Elementary and Secondary Education Act (ESEA) of 1965 also served Indian children in need of extra basic skills assistance in reading and math. In later amendments, ESEA authorized programs that encouraged the development of culturally relevant and bilingual curriculum materials.

In 1988 the Augustus F. Hawkins–Robert T. Stafford Elementary and Secondary School Improvement Amendments of 1988 (Public Law 100–297), or the Indian Education Amendments, were enacted. This law revised the statutory framework under which federally funded Indian education is administered, consolidating and clarifying laws governing the operation of BIA-funded schools and the Indian Education programs operated by the Department of Education. It also authorized the White House Conference on Indian Education to explore the establishment of an independent Board of Indian Education with responsibility for all federal Indian education programs and to develop recommendations for improvements in Indian education.

## Voices of the People

Over the past three decades, the voices of Indian people have echoed consistent rhetoric, some of it going back as far as seventy years: Indian people want the opportunity to determine all aspects of their children's education.

In 1976, the *Report on Indian Education* expressed the concerns heard from Indian people by Task Force Five of the American Indian Policy Review Commission. In 1987, *And Justice for All* summarized the concerns of Indian people and other ethnic groups from regional hearings conducted by the Office of Human and Civil Rights, National Education Association.

In 1989, *Our Voices, Our Vision: American Indians Speak Out for Educational Excellence* was published by the Educational Equality Project of the College Board and the American Indian Science and Engineering Society (AISES). The report, a result of the National Dialogue Project on American Indian Education, presented the concerns of 150 Indian leaders, school administrators, teachers, parents, and students from eighty-seven tribes. These individuals participated in seven

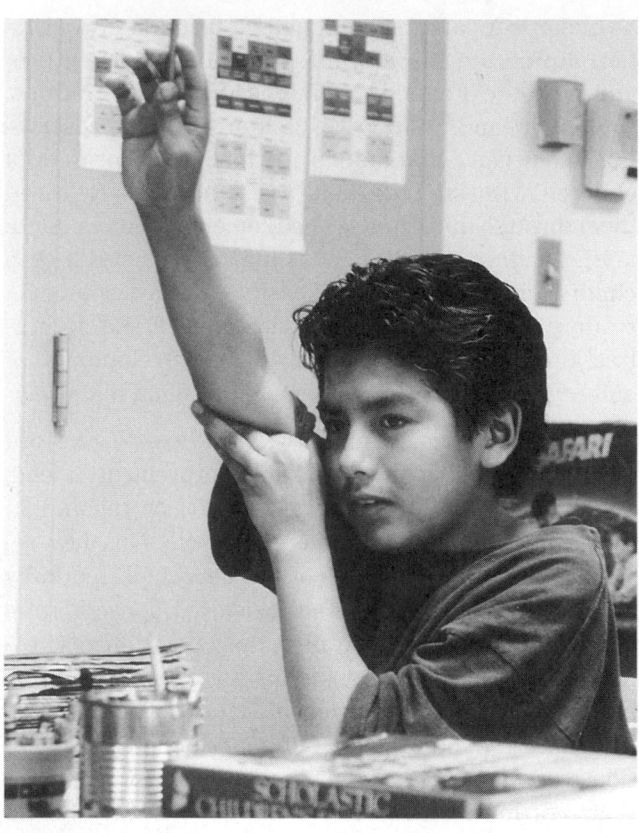

A student raises his hand at the Gila River Day School. (Photo by Carol Lujan)

regional dialogues to discuss the lack of attention given to Indian students in school reform reports. These dialogues clearly indicated that Indian people want their children not only to value their culture and traditions, but also to possess basic academic competencies and subject matter knowledge when they complete their formal education. The reconciliation of spiritual values and formal education was a critical issue in these dialogues.

In 1990 OIEP conducted regional mini-summits to solicit input on four proposed initiatives and to define the most pressing issues in Indian education according to tribes, school board members, and educators. The four initiatives included parent and community involvement, early childhood development, higher expectations in Indian schools, and effective evaluation of schools, students, and teachers.

In late 1990 and 1991, in response to a mandate from former Secretary of Education Lauro Cavazos, hearings sponsored by the Department of Education were held across the country to determine the status of Indian education. This led to the establishment of the Indian Nations at Risk Task Force, chaired by William

G. Demmert, Jr. and Terrel H. Bell. The task force was charged with the responsibility of studying the status of Indian education and issuing a report and recommendations to improve the quality of education in order to improve academic performance.

The White House Conference on Indian Education was authorized by Public Law 100–297, the Indian Education Amendments of 1988. The purpose of the conference was to explore the feasibility of a national independent board of Indian education and to further define issues and set goals for Indian education. Before the January 1992 conference, meetings were held in every state that has a considerable Indian population. Each state prepared a statement to be presented by delegates at the conference consisting of the most important issues facing Indian education. Coincidentally, 1992 was declared the "the year of the American Indian" by Congress and the president. The issues that emerged from the above hearings, dialogues, and meetings are summarized below in the section titled "Indians' Definition of Indian Education Issues."

After more than one hundred years of educational suppression, Indian people have had the opportunity, from the late 1970s until today, to voice their opinions on the status of Indian education. Even though the same concerns have been voiced in the documents described above, there has been little reconciliation of the issues. Nonetheless, Indian education leaders remain optimistic in comparing more than 100 years of non-Indian control to less than thirty years of Indian control. In the years of non-Indian control of Indian education, the reports declaimed the failure of Indian education. Since the 1970s and the emergence of Indian self-determination, there has been remarkable progress. The momentum continues to be evident in Indian-led events such as the Indian Nations at Risk Task Force and the White House Conference on Indian Education.

## Curriculum

Indian education leaders do find some consensus on the issue of integrating language and culture into the curriculum. Except for the serious attention given to language and culture as viable curricular components during the reform era of the 1930s, the curriculum in BIA schools and other schools attended by Indian students were not distinctly different from those of any other schools in the nation until the 1960s. When Indian community-controlled schools began to emerge and grow in number, changes occurred in the instructional programs as well as in the governance and administration of the schools. Bilingual education and cultural studies became an integral part of the curriculum in many schools. Again, the notable example was Rough Rock Demonstration School, the first school contracted to the control of the local community. The Navajo language was the primary language of instruction with special time devoted to English. Considerable importance was placed on instruction in Navajo culture and history as well. Rock Point Community School in Arizona is another contemporary example of a successful Navajo bilingual school. Rock Point High School students participate in a Navajo Research Class, researching issues and reporting results in Navajo or English. The reports are published in their bilingual newspaper.

Across the United States, nearly 100 bilingual programs are operating in schools with considerable numbers of Indian students. This growth is largely attributable to a concern that many indigenous languages are dying. The number of fluent speakers of some languages is in a steady decline, and bilingual programs are viewed as one method for halting the decline. Proponents also believe that bilingual education for Indian students is superior to English-only programs of instruction and recent research seems to support this belief. However, in some communities there is a consensus that language and culture are the responsibility of the home and community and should not be taught in the school; in these communities bilingual programs are not welcome.

The Native American Languages Act was signed into law by President George Bush in 1990 (Native Americans are defined as American Indians, Alaska Natives, Native Hawaiians, and Pacific Islanders). The measure declares that the policy of the United States is "to preserve, protect, and promote the rights and freedom of Native Americans to use, practice, and develop Native American languages." It encourages the use of Native American languages in schools run by the BIA and in public schools enrolling Indians or other Native groups.

While curriculum in Indian schools has been and continues to be a prominent concern, hiring practices of teachers and administrators in Indian schools is just as important as what is taught. According to a recent study using the Schools and Staffing Survey (SASS) data, D. Michael Pavel (Skokomish) found that 47 percent of those principals working in BIA and tribal schools identified themselves as American Indian or Alaska Native. This percentage was compared to high Native student enrollment (HIE) in public schools, which revealed that only 13 percent of all principals were identified as American Indian or Alaska Native. Thirty-eight percent of the teachers who worked in BIA and tribal schools identified themselves as American Indian or Alaska Native and only 15 percent of the teachers in HIE schools were American Indian or Alaska Native.

The voices of Indian people, while not always unanimous, agree that language and culture are important and can be integrated into the curriculum so that their children can experience the positive self-esteem this inclusion generates. In addition, with an increased number of Native teachers and administrators serving in Indian schools, Indian children can experience a quality education equal to or better than that of other children in the United States. Furthermore, Indian people want respectful acknowledgement of their identity as the indigenous people of this country. Actualizing hopes for improved schools and curriculum is possible with the commitment of effective Native teachers and administrators.

## The K–12 Education of Indians Today

Two federal agencies are responsible for the education of Indian students: the Department of the Interior through the BIA Office of Indian Education Programs, and the Department of Education through the Office of Indian Education in the Office of Elementary and Secondary Education. At a local level, tribes and school districts share this responsibility through tribally controlled schools, BIA schools, and public schools.

The Office of Indian Education in the Office of Elementary and Secondary Education, Department of Education, was created by the Indian Education Act of 1972 and signed into law as Title IV of Public Law 92–318 on 23 June 1972. Education amendments in 1974 and 1978 authorized funding of special programs to provide educational opportunities for Indian children and adults, and to address the culturally related academic needs of Indian children. The Office of Indian Education was re-authorized under Title V, Part C of the Augustus F. Hawkins–Robert T. Stafford Elementary and Secondary School Improvement Amendments of 1988 (Public Law 100–297), entitled the Indian Education Amendments of 1988. The Office of Indian Education provides supplemental funding to public and BIA-funded schools based on formulae and/or a competitive basis.

Zia Day School, Zia, New Mexico. (Photo by Carol Lujan)

The Bureau of Indian Affairs funds 185 elementary and secondary schools, 116 of which are operated by Indian tribes and tribal organizations under contracts or grants authorized by Public Law 93–638 and Public Law 100–297. The schools, and several dormitories that house students attending public schools, are located on sixty-three reservations in twenty-three states. There are also five off-reservation boarding schools in five states. Approximately six thousand teachers, administrators, counselors, and support personnel serve more than 55,000 students in BIA schools and/or dormitories. A directory of BIA-funded schools is available from the Bureau of Indian Affairs, Office of Indian Education Programs in Washington, D.C.

Only an estimated 7 percent of approximately 600,000 Indian students in the United States attend schools funded by the Bureau of Indian Affairs. Approximately 5 percent attend private or parochial schools. The majority of Indian students attend public schools. According to the National Center for Education Statistics, 1,260 public schools have an American Indian and/or Alaska Native student enrollment of at least 25 percent. Another 78,625 public schools have enrollments of American Indian and/or Alaska Native students that number less than 25 percent. The total population of American Indian/Alaska Native students represents about one percent of the total K–12 population in the United States.

## Current Issues and Trends

In 1930, Rosa M. Hill, a Mohawk woman, reportedly said, "Going to school and getting an education are two different things and they do not always happen at the same time." This statement reflects a realization recognized in the issues and trends of recent years. Indian students have been going to school, but they have not been getting an education commensurate with the time spent doing so.

Despite national reform efforts from the 1970s until today, Indian students continue to rank among the lowest of all demographic groups in terms of academic achievement and the highest of all groups for dropout rates. Research data on these problems appear throughout the literature on Indian education issues. These issues involve a multitude of complex, sociocultural cause-and-effect relationships that are not easily sorted out and resolved. However, the process to better understand them has been more clearly defined by Indian people themselves from an insider's point of view. The dropout issue is one example.

## Dropouts

A comprehensive review of the literature on K–12 dropouts was conducted for the National Education Association by the Center for Indian Education at Arizona State University. A small number of studies reviewed in the *American Indian/Alaska Native Dropout Study 1991* reveals some significant reasons for leaving school before twelfth-grade completion, as reported by both Indian students who left school and those who remained. Paramount among these were boredom with school, questions related to the relevance of schooling, and the quality of interpersonal interactions that occur among students, their peers, and school personnel. The dropout rates reported in several studies reflect dissatisfaction with the schooling experience by a large percentage of Indian adolescent and pre-adolescent youth. Dropout rates range from a low of 24.4 to a high of 42.5 percent. In some communities the dropout rate is near 100 percent.

Indian education leaders recognize a need to develop more comprehensive databases in several areas concerning the underachievement of Indian students in order to generate a more accurate knowledge base.

## Alternative Schools Attended by Indian Students

**Magnet Schools.**   The magnet school concept is a current trend in many metropolitan areas. It is intended to focus attention on specific curricular areas, such as math, science, or the performing arts, capitalize on the students' strengths, and enhance their developmental growth. In response to a belief that public schooling is not meeting the cultural and linguistic needs of American Indian and Alaska Native students, the magnet school concept has been explored for these students. Two Native American magnet schools have been developed in recent years within the public school systems of Buffalo, New York, and St. Paul, Minnesota. Both the Native American Magnet School in Buffalo and the

Mounds Park All Nations School in St. Paul provide evidence that the concept is working. Their success provides encouragement for other school districts to adopt this model of school enhancement.

**Charter Schools.**   Charter schools are a fairly recent development in educational alternatives to public schooling. Although these schools operate as public schools they are free from many of the state regulations by which traditional public schools must abide. Some Indian communities have applied to their state to operate charter schools that are developed to address the unique educational needs of their Native children. Grey Hills Academy High School located on the Navajo Reservation in Tuba City, Arizona, was granted a charter in 1996. This school serves a large English as a Second Language Navajo student population and is open to non-Indian students. One of the celebrated strengths of Grey Hills is its use of technology in meeting the needs of both students and community. In partnership with the National Association of Laboratory Schools, Northern Arizona University, and two community colleges, Grey Hills Academy High is just one example of many successful charter schools currently serving Indian students.

**Preparatory Schools.**   While college preparatory schools have been an option for Indian students to attend throughout history, only recently have preparatory schools been developed exclusively for Native students. Two such schools are Native American Preparatory School located in Rowe, New Mexico, and Navajo Preparatory School in Farmington, New Mexico.

## Indians' Definition of Indian Education Issues

The issues that have concerned Indian people for five generations of formal education have been defined by the Indian Nations at Risk Task Force, the White House Conference on Indian Education, and a National American Indian/Alaska Native Education Summit. The culmination of efforts on behalf of several organizations resulted in Executive Order 13096 of 6 August 1998, American Indian Alaska Native Education.

**Indian Nations at Risk Task Force.**   The final report of the Indian Nations at Risk Task Force (INARTF) to the U.S. Department of Education in October 1991 was titled *Indian Nations at Risk: An Educational Strategy for Action*. It included ten national educational goals for American Indians and Alaska Natives. Using the president's six national educational goals as a foundation, the task force established a set of goals to guide the improvement of all federal, tribal, private, and public schools that serve American Indians and Alaska Natives and their communities. The goals are stated in Figure 16–1. The Task Force identified four important reasons why Indian nations are at risk:

1. Schools have failed to educate large numbers of Indian students and adults;
2. The language and cultural bases of the American Native are rapidly eroding;
3. The diminished lands and natural resources of the American Native are constantly under siege; and
4. Indian self-determination and governance rights are challenged by the changing policies of the administration, Congress, and the justice system.

The task force expressed a strong belief that a well-educated American Indian and Alaska Native citizenry and language and cultural renewal projects will strengthen both self-determination and economic well-being and will allow Native Americans to contribute to a stronger American presence in global affairs.

The Task Force report recommended five major research-based strategies for addressing educational needs, based on testimony from Indian people across the United States. The strategies are reported in Figure 16–2.

The report concludes that the responsibility for improvement is not situated in any one agency or entity, but is shared by all those involved in the education of Native American students: public, tribal, and federal school personnel and government officials; parents and students; and community members.

**The White House Conference on Indian Education.** With the theme "Honoring Tradition, Inspiring Change," this conference of nearly 1,000 participants, including 234 official delegates, tribal leaders, educators, parents, congressional representatives, and other observers, focused attention on the positive reform of Indian education. Led by co-chairs Lionel Bordeaux, a tribal college president, and Nora Garcia, a tribal leader, the conference delegates drafted more than 100 resolutions in eleven areas formulated by the conference advisory committee. The eleven topics included establishment of an independent board of Indian education; well-being of Indian communities and delivery of services; literacy, student achievement, and high school graduation; safe, alcohol- and drug-free schools; exceptional education; readiness for school; Native language and culture curriculum; structure for schools; higher

education; preparation of Native and non-Native school personnel; and adult education and lifelong learning involving parental, community, and tribal partnerships. Among the several themes emerging from the conference were greater tribal and community involvement, the preservation of language and culture, and increased funding through new and existing legislation.

The conference was successful in unifying the voices of Indian people regarding education from birth to adulthood. The words of Navajo Nation President Peterson Zah succinctly described the conference's success: "We came here hoping to gain one voice, one drum beat and to sing one song. I think we've accomplished that."

In this major convocation, the issues in Indian education were defined by Indian people, and recommended action plans were developed and presented in formal resolutions. The White House Conference on Indian Education (WHCIE), with information from the Indian Nations at Risk hearings and other forums, such as the National Dialogue Project on American Indian Education, represents the embodiment of self-determination in education.

**National American Indian/Alaska Native Education Summit.** The education summit, sponsored by the National Indian Education Association (NIEA), the National Advisory Council on Indian Education (NACIE), and the Native American Rights Fund (NARF), was organized to make sure that the issues raised by INARTF, WHCIE, and other national, regional, and local forums, were kept at the forefront of the conscience of the federal government. Out of this educational summit, concerns and policy recommendations were formulated. Known as the *Red Book*, a draft policy statement about the goals of quality Indian education defined by Indians was the result of the education summit. The *Red Book* presented for consideration a draft of reform recommendations and goals. It served as a synergistic catalyst for the development of a comprehensive federal Indian education policy.

**Executive Order 13096 of 6 August 1998.** President William J. Clinton signed the historic Executive Order 13096 (figure 16–3). This order came from the highest position of government and was the culmination of the work of NIEA, NACIE, NARF, the National Congress of American Indians, and work by Native leaders and educators. The order called for a comprehensive approach to the education of American Indian and Alaska Native students at all levels (pre-kindergarten to adult and higher education). Most importantly, the order recognized the unique status and needs of

---

### Figure 16.1
### National Education Goals for American Indians and Alaska Natives

*Goal 1: Readiness for School*
By the year 2000, all native children will have access to early childhood education programs that provide the language, social, physical, spiritual, and cultural foundations they need to succeed in school and to reach their full potential as adults.

*Goal 2: Native Languages and Cultures*
By the year 2000, all schools will offer native students the opportunity to maintain and develop their tribal languages and will create a multi-cultural environment that enhances the many cultures represented in the school.

*Goal 3: Literacy*
By the year 2000, all native children in school will be literate in the language skills appropriate for their individual levels of development. They will be competent in their English, oral, reading, listening, and writing skills.

*Goal 4: Student Academic Achievement*
By the year 2000, every native student will demonstrate mastery of English, mathematics, science, history, geography, and other challenging academic skills necessary for an educated citizenry.

*Goal 5: High School Graduation*
By the year 2000, all native students capable of completing high school will graduate. They will demonstrate civic, social, creative, and critical thinking necessary for ethical, moral, and responsible citizenship in modern tribal, national, and world societies.

*Goal 6: High Quality Native and Non-Native School Personnel*
By the year 2000, the numbers of native educators will double, and the colleges and universities that train the nation's teachers will develop a curriculum that prepares teachers to work effectively with the variety of cultures, including the native cultures, that are served by schools.

*Goal 7: Safe and Alcohol-Free and Drug-Free Schools*
By the year 2000, every school responsible for educating native students will be free of alcohol and drugs and will provide safe facilities and an environment conducive to learning.

*Goal 8: Adult Education and Lifelong Learning*
By the year 2000, every native adult will have the opportunity to be literate and to obtain the necessary academic, vocational, and technical skills and knowledge needed to gain meaningful employment and to exercise the rights and responsibilities of tribal and national citizenship.

*Goals 9: Restructuring Schools*
By the year 2000, schools serving native children will be restructured to effectively meet the academic, cultural, spiritual, and social needs of students for developing strong, healthy, self-sufficient communities.

*Goal 10: Parental, Community, and Tribal Partnerships*
By the year 2000, every school responsible for educating native students will provide opportunities for native parents and tribal leaders to help plan and evaluate the governance, operation, and performance of their educational programs.

---

*Source: U.S. Department of Education,* Indian Nations at Risk: An Educational Strategy for Action, Final Report of the Indian Nations at Risk Task Force *(October 1991).*

---

Indian students across the United States and Alaska. In keeping with the theme of Indian self determination, the order called for a comprehensive federal Indian education policy based on Indian-initiated goals. In addition, the order charged that the U.S. Department of Education conduct research and establish baseline data with Indian constituencies on the current and continued status of American Indian and Alaska Native

---

**Figure 16.2**
**A Strategic Framework for Improving Schools**

The Task Force recommends five major strategies for implementing its recommendations:

1. Develop comprehensive education plans that bring together federal, state, local, and tribal resources to achieve the native education goals. These plans should draw on the most promising research and effective practices identified over the past twenty years.

2. Develop partnerships among schools and parents, tribes, universities, business and industry, and health and social services agencies. These partners must play an active role in developing local program plans.

3. Emphasize four national priorities that will significantly improve academic performance and promote self-sufficiency among American Indians and Alaska Natives.

   · Developing parent-based, early childhood education programs that are culturally, linguistically, and developmentally appropriate.

   · Establishing the promotion of student's tribal language and culture as a responsibility of the school.

   · Training native teachers to increase the numbers of Indian educators and other professionals and to improve the quality of instruction.

   · Strengthening tribal and Bureau of Indian Affairs colleges as a means to enhance communities and prepare students for higher levels of success when they move on to four-year colleges and universities.

4. Create mechanisms that will hold local, tribal, state, and national officials accountable for achieving the goals.

5. Foster understanding of the relationships between tribes and all levels of government.

---

*Source: U.S. Department of Education,* Indian Nations at Risk: An Educational Strategy for Action, Final Report of the Indian Nations at Risk Task Force *(October 1991).*

---

education.

**American Indian and Alaska Native Education Research Agenda Conference.** As a result of Executive Order 13096, the Office of Educational Research and Improvement in collaboration with the Office of Indian Education and NACIE planned a national conference that examined the state of Indian educational research. The conference brought together Native educators and researchers to discuss several themes: academic achievement, assessment, and retention of American Indians and Alaska Native students, the role of Native culture and language in the development of educational strategies, and Indian identification.

Native educators and researchers discussed the current state of Indian education and with much patience urged each other to continue thinking beyond identification of issues, to push forward and take action in implementing ideas and monitoring follow-through with the research agenda.

Sitting Bull's advice from more than 100 years ago has finally been taken seriously. He advised that we put our heads together to see what we can do for our children. In all the conferences in recent years educators have been putting their heads together and have designed strategies to improve education for this country's American Indian and Alaska Native students.

*Karen Swisher*
*Haskell Indian Nations University*

*Tarajean Yazzie*
*Harvard Graduate School of Education*

## ◆ U.S. INDIAN HIGHER EDUCATION

Until recently, the history of higher education for Indians in the United States has been one of unrelenting failure. Early colonial efforts at Dartmouth College, which began as Moor's Indian Charity School and

Native American students listen to a story read to them by their teacher. (Photo by Carol Lujan)

became Wheelock's Seminary, and the more limited efforts of an Indian college at Harvard University and the College of William and Mary, were followed later by less ambitious, federally supported vocational education, church-mission schools, then by federal day and boarding schools, with little public support for an Indian presence in education beyond high school. Church and federal authorities shared the belief that Indians did not need college or university education; rather, Indians were thought to require vocational education controlled not by Indians but by missionaries. Later efforts at Indian higher education included Bacone College in Oklahoma (1880) and Fort Lewis College in Colorado (1911), both of which identified Indians as part of their educational mission but remained small, rural academies.

During the New Deal of the 1930s, the historic federal-church stranglehold on Indian higher education began to erode. The Indian Reorganization Act (IRA), or Wheeler-Howard Act of 1934, authorized federal support for higher education for Indians. Also passed in 1934 were the Johnson O'Malley Act and federal impact legislation (PL 815 and PL 874), which made federal funds available to public schools that enrolled Indian children from federal trust areas such as Indian reservations. By 1912 there were more Indians in public schools than in federal or mission schools, and the state influence on Indian education continued to grow.

In 1935 Bureau of Indian Affairs (BIA) Commissioner John Collier reported that only 515 Indian students, or less than one half of one percent of the Indian population, were attending colleges and universities. However, in 1954 the Arizona State Indian Education Center was founded at Arizona State University, providing specialized curriculum for non-Indians and Indians who might someday teach on or near an Indian reservation. Later, similar teacher-training programs were founded in South Dakota, Minnesota, and Oklahoma. Still, change was slow. Two-year junior college level courses were available only at three BIA technical institutes: Haskell Institute in Kansas, Chilocco Indian School in Oklahoma, and the Institute of American Indian Arts in New Mexico. In 1963 the first college preparatory program for Indians began at Haskell Institute, which became a federally sponsored Indian junior college two years later. Beyond these few federal and

**Figure 16.3**
**Executive Order 13096 of 6 August 1998:**
**American Indian and Alaska Native Education**

By the authority vested in me as President by the Constitution and the laws of the United States of America, in affirmation of the unique political and legal relationship of the Federal Government with tribal governments, and in recognition of the unique educational and culturally related academic needs of American Indian and Alaska Native students, it is hereby ordered as follows:

## SECTION 1: GOALS

The Federal Government has a special, historic responsibility for the education of American Indian and Alaska Native students. Improving educational achievement and academic progress for American Indian and Alaska Native students is vital to the national goal of preparing every student for responsible citizenship, continued learning, and productive employment. The Federal Government is committed to improving the academic performance and reducing the dropout rate of American Indian and Alaska Native students. To help fulfill this commitment in a manner consistent with tribal traditions and cultures, Federal agencies need to focus special attention on six goals: (1) improving reading and mathematics; (2) increasing high school completion and postsecondary attendance rate; (3) reducing the influence of long-standing factors that impeded educational performance, such as poverty and substance abuse; (4) creating strong, safe, and drug-free school environments; (5) improving science education; and (6) expanding the use of educational technology.

## SECTION 2: STRATEGY

In order to meet the six goals of this order, a comprehensive Federal response is needed to address the fragmentation of government services available to American Indian and Alaska Native students and the complexity of intergovernmental relationships affecting the education of those students. The purpose of the Federal activities described in this order is to develop a long-term, comprehensive Federal Indian education policy that will accomplish those goals.

(a) *Interagency Task Force.* There is established an Interagency Task Force on American Indian and Alaska Native Education (Task Force) to oversee the planning and implementation of this order. The Task Force shall confer with the National Advisory Council on Indian Education (NACIE) in carrying out activities under this order. The Task Force shall consult with representatives of American Indian and Alaska Native tribes and organizations, including the National Congress of American Indians (NCAI), to gather advice on implementation of the activities called for in this order.

(b) *Composition of the Task Force.*

(1) The membership of the Task Force shall include representatives of the Departments of the Treasury, Defense, Justice, the Interior, Agriculture, Commerce, Labor, Health and Human Services, Housing and Urban Development, Transportation, Energy, and Education, as well as the Environmental Protection Agency, the Corporation for National and Community Service, and the National Science Foundation. With agreement of the Secretaries of Education and the Interior, other agencies may participate in the activities of the Task Force.

(2) Within 30 days of the date of this order, the head of each participating agency shall designate a senior official who is responsible for management or program administration to serve as a member of the Task Force. The official shall report directly to the agency head on the agency's activities under this order.

(3) The Assistant Secretary for Elementary and Secondary Education of the Department of Education and the Assistant Secretary for Indian Affairs of the Department of the Interior shall co-chair the Task Force.

**Figure 16.3 (continued)**

(c) *Interagency plan*. The Task Force shall, within 90 days of the date of this order, develop a Federal interagency plan with recommendations identifying initiatives, strategies, and ideas for future action supportive of the goals of this order.

(d) *Agency participation*. To the extent consistent with law and agency priorities, each participating agency shall adopt and implement strategies to maximize the availability of the agency's education-related programs, activities, resources, information, and technical assistance to American Indian and Alaska Native students. In keeping with the spirit of the Executive Memorandum of April 29, 1994, on Government-to-Government Relations with Native American Tribal Governments and Executive Order 13084 of May 14, 1998, each participating agency shall consult with tribal governments on their education-related needs and priorities, and on how the agency can better accomplish the goals of this order. Within 6 months, each participating agency shall report to the Task Force regarding the strategies it has developed to ensure such consultation.

(e) *Interagency resource guide*. The Force shall identify, within participating Federal agencies, all education-related programs and resources that support the goals of this order. Within 12 months, the Task Force, in conjunction with the Department of Education, shall develop, publish, and widely distribute a guide that describes those programs and resources and how American Indians and Alaska Natives can benefit from them.

(f) *Research*. The Secretary of Education, through the Office of Educational Research and Improvement and the Office of Indian Education, and in consultation with NACIE and participating agencies, shall develop and implement a comprehensive Federal research agenda to:

(1) establish baseline data on academic achievement and retention of American Indian and Alaska Native students in order to monitor improvements.

(2) evaluate promising practices used with those students; and

(3) evaluate the role of native language and culture in the development of educational strategies. Within 1 year, the Secretary of Education shall submit the research agenda, including proposed timelines, to the Task Force.

(g) *Comprehensive Federal Indian education policy*.

(1) The Task Force shall, within 2 years of the date of this order, develop a comprehensive Federal Indian education policy to support the accomplishment of the goals of this order. The policy shall be designed to:

(A) improve Federal interagency cooperation;

(B) promote intergovernmental collaboration; and

(C) assist tribal governments in meeting the unique educational needs of their children, including the need to preserve, revitalize, and use native languages and cultural traditions.

(2) In developing the policy, the Task Force shall consider ideas in the Comprehensive Federal Indian Education Policy Statement proposal developed by the NIEA and the NCAI.

(3) The Task Force shall develop recommendations to implement the policy, including ideas for the future interagency action.

(4) As appropriate, participating agencies may develop memoranda of agreement with one another to enable and enhance the ability of tribes and schools to provide, and to coordinate the delivery of Federal, tribal, State, and local resources and services, including social and health-related services, to meet the educational needs of American Indian and Alaska Native students.

h) *Reports*. The Task Force co-chairs shall submit the comprehensive Federal Indian education policy, and the report annually on the agencies' activities, accomplishments, and progress toward meeting the goals of this order, to the Director of the Office of Management and Budget.

**Figure 16.3 (continued)**

## SECTION 3: REGIONAL PARTNERSHIP FORUMS

The Departments of Education and the Interior in collaboration with the Task Force and Federal, tribal, State, and local government representatives, shall jointly convene, within 18 months, a series of regional forums to identify promising practices and approaches on how to share information, provide assistance to schools, develop partnerships, and coordinate intergovernmental strategies supportive of accomplishing the goals of this order. The Departments of Education and the Interior shall submit a report on the forums to the Task Force, which may include recommendations relating to intergovernmental relations.

## SECTION 4: SCHOOL PILOT SITES

The Department of Education and the Interior shall identify a reasonable number of schools funded by the Bureau of Indian Affairs (BIA) and public schools that can serve as a model for schools with American Indian and Alaska Native students, and provide them with comprehensive technical assistance in support of the goals of this order. A special team of technical assistance providers, including Federal staff, shall provide assistance in these schools. Special attention shall be given, where appropriate, to assistance in implementing comprehensive school reform demonstration programs that meet the criteria for those programs established by the Department of Labor, Health and Human Services, and Education, and Related Agencies Appropriations Act, 1998 (Public Law 105-78), and to providing comprehensive service delivery that connects and uses diverse Federal agency practices of the school pilot sites to other local educational agencies. The team shall report to the Task Force on its accomplishments and its recommendations for improving technical support to local educational agencies and schools funded by the BIA.

## SECTION 5: ADMINISTRATION

The Department of Education shall provide appropriate administrative services and staff support to the Task Force. With the consent of the Department of Education, other participating agencies may provide administrative support to the Task Force, consistent with their statutory authority, and may detail agency employees to the Department of Education, to the extent permitted by law.

## SECTION 6: TERMINATION

The Task Force established under section 2 of this order shall terminate not later than 5 years from the date of this order.

## SECTION 7: GENERAL PROVISIONS

This order is intended only to improve the internal management of the executive branch and is not intended to, and does not, create any right or benefit, substantive or procedural, enforceable at law or equity by a party against the United States, its agencies or instrumentalities, its officers or employees, or any other person. This order is not intended to preclude, supercede, replace, or otherwise dilute any other Executive order relating to American Indian and Alaska Native education.

WILLIAM J. CLINTON

THE WHITE HOUSE,
August 6, 1998.

A student studies at Shiprock Alternative High School. (Photo by Carol Lujan)

state endeavors, there was little in the way of a national— or state—directed effort to increase Indian student enrollment in institutions of higher education.

Federal and state indifference to the postsecondary educational needs of U.S. Indians continued unchallenged through the late 1950s and early 1960s, despite widely publicized but largely unexplained low levels of Indian educational achievement. In 1961 only 623 Indian students received BIA assistance to further their education beyond high school. By 1964 the number of Indian students receiving BIA assistance had increased to 1,327, out of a total of 5,900, in postsecondary institutions. Federal appropriations for Indian student scholarships increased in 1963 and 1964, but the percentage of Indian enrollment in U.S. public and private colleges and universities remained far below that of other Americans. The extent to which the educational needs of Indians were being neglected is illustrated by the fact that in 1968 only 181 American Indians received four-year-college degrees.

Until the late 1960s, higher education leaders apparently did not view Indians as potential college students. This may have been because Indians were not a significant community population, lacking numbers and therefore political power. Or it may have been due to a belief that so few Indians were desirous of postsecondary education that the limited opportunities available to them were adequate. Higher education leaders evidently shared the federal government's view that Indians would eventually assimilate, and that what could be done to further this national policy objective was already being done by the imposition of an Americanizing curriculum in reservation day schools, federal boarding schools, and church and state public schools.

Thus, in the national view no major federal or state postsecondary program or policy changes were needed to address the educational needs of Indian people. This out-of-sight-out-of-mind view of Indians by America's college and university leaders did not change until the late 1960s, when Indians and other minorities took to the streets to mobilize political pressure.

## Indian Self-Determination in Higher Education

In 1965 Title III of the Higher Education Act was passed, containing limited provisions for postsecondary assistance to Indians. As Indians made efforts to implement changes in higher education, the manifold failures of American higher education toward Indians and other racial and ethnic minorities became more evident. With the publication in 1969 of the Senate report on Indian education, *Indian Education: A National Tragedy—A National Challenge,* American educators could no longer ignore what the Senate report identified as "the low quality of virtually every aspect of schooling available to Indian children." But still no specific legislation emerged to comprehensively address the postsecondary educational needs of Indian people.

However, in 1968 President Lyndon B. Johnson began to articulate a new national Indian policy promoting community-based self-determination. President Richard M. Nixon continued the policy, and in 1972 the Indian Education Act, the first comprehensive legislation on Indian education since the 1930s, was passed. Two years later the 1974 Educational Amendments to the Indian Education Act were passed, which included several provisions for teacher training and graduate or professional school fellowships for Indian students. In 1975 the Indian Self-Determination and Educational

Two Native students prepare for graduation. (Photo by Mike McClure)

Assistance Act (PL 93–638) was passed and set in motion specific federal guidelines for a greater and even more self-determining Indian voice in federal and state education programs. For the first time, Indian tribes could move outside BIA control and contract directly for education and other services.

Although few specific features of these policy statements were directed toward higher education, Indian leadership and teachers nevertheless welcomed this dramatic shift in federal policy. They saw it as a movement away from the use of education to force assimilation, and as a historic opportunity for members of the Indian community to become active participants in the nation's colleges and universities. Throughout the late

1960s and into the 1970s, Indian college enrollments across the nation increased dramatically, by nearly 500 percent. Four factors accounted for this historic increase: an 80 percent increase in the number of young Indians relative to the total Indian population: an increase in the availability of federal and state scholarships; positive changes in BIA policies; and the federal War on Poverty programs, particularly programs of the Office of Economic Opportunity (OEO), which began in 1964.

As the number of Indians on U.S. college and university campuses grew, Indians began to demand the same kind of control over their college education as the control over education that was emerging on Indian reservations. This meant the hiring of Indian faculty and administrators, the development of culturally relevant curriculum, and the initiation of programs that supported a positive and nonstereotypic view of Indian people and cultures.

Educational leadership did not initially respond to the growing demands from Indian students, parents, tribal leaders, and activists. Indian students wanted a curriculum more relevant to their culture, so that they could assume more effective leadership roles when they returned to their reservations or urban communities. In addition, Indian tribal leaders wanted colleges and universities to train Indian business managers, lawyers, doctors, nurses, engineers, and other professionals to help tribes reassert control over their increasingly valuable reservation lands and natural resources. It was obvious to tribal leaders that without college-educated Indians, the policy of Indian self-determination would fail, destroying what remained of Indian cultures, reservation lands, and other natural resources.

During the same time, members of other ethnic groups were demanding similar changes. College and university administrators and faculty were unwilling at first to make these changes. It took public confrontations in the streets, classrooms, and administrative offices to move the nation's academic hierarchy toward some form of accommodation with its increasingly diverse, multiethnic student body, which included Indians. One focus of the confrontation was Indian activists' demand for the creation of Native American studies (NAS) programs on college and university campuses. These programs are also called Indian studies and American Indian studies.

## The Emergence of Native American Studies Programs

The emergence of NAS programs, centers, and departments on U.S. university and college campuses began during the race- and ethnic-related political and social movements of the 1960s and 1970s. Like the Black Power and Chicano movements, the Red Power movement (primarily the American Indian Movement and National Indian Youth Council) demanded greater access to the institutions of national power, including colleges and universities. Indian leaders hoped that NAS programs would provide that access, permitting the hiring of Indian scholars to provide academic programs directed toward the needs of on-campus Indians

and the Indian community, including reservations. NAS programs were intended to consolidate an Indian voice within America's colleges and universities. Indian activists believed that Indian scholars could revise the stereotype of noble and/or ignorant savage, counterpoint to European expansion and the ordained triumph of Manifest Destiny. One important educational task of NAS programs was the re-integration of Indians into national consciousness on the Indians' own terms. In general, however, support for NAS programs in U.S. colleges and universities was reluctant and limited.

Nevertheless, a few NAS programs did emerge, and Indian enrollment in America's colleges and universities increased. By 1976 more than 76,000 Indians were enrolled in accredited colleges and universities. By 1982 this number had risen to 87,700. However, because of budget cuts and changes in federal program rules and regulations by the Reagan administration, Indian enrollment dropped in 1984 to 82,672. Significantly, 60 percent of these Indian students attended two-year colleges, compared to 36 percent for the non-Indian population. To understand the dramatic difference between the number of Indians attending two-year institutions and the much smaller enrollment at four-year colleges and universities, one must examine NAS programs and the emergence of the tribally controlled colleges.

## A Search for Academic Identity and Credibility

Since their emergence in the late 1960s NAS programs have struggled for academic credibility and acceptance by the non-Indian community of scholars. This struggle is not unique to NAS; other ethnic programs such as African-American studies and Chicano studies have also found formidable administrative and faculty barriers to their development. Indian scholars have tried with limited success to demonstrate a parallel academic need and mission between NAS programs and American Studies, European Studies, Asian Studies, and other, more traditional and widely accepted, ethnic-based academic programs. Most colleges and universities are reluctant to provide sufficient funds for what they perceive to be a political issue rather than an educational one. At many institutions, NAS is not considered an academic subject because it lacks exclusive content and/or some integrating theory or method. However, with the growing integration of all knowledge, exclusivity in content, methods, or theory is a test few academic disciplines can meet.

What, then, is Native American studies? It is not anthropology, archeology, history, comparative sociology, or political science, although it certainly makes

Haskell Indian Nation University, 1999. (Photo by Carol Lujan)

use of the methods and theories of these better-known disciplines. What sets NAS apart from other disciplines is the special relationship it attempts to promote between Native peoples and higher education. Unlike academic disciplines that teach and study Indian peoples and cultures as part of a larger academic mission, NAS is actively committed to the preservation and survival of these peoples and cultures. NAS's definitive commitment, exercised through the preservation and development of academic teaching, research, and service efforts, is not so different from the mission of most colleges and universities, which exist on behalf of the state, church, or nation at large. The mission of NAS is on behalf of all Indian people.

NAS programs vary greatly in size, academic content, and viability because of budgets, institutional support, and the quality of program leadership. Given the location of Indian activism, it is not surprising that some of the earliest NAS programs emerged at the University of California's Berkeley, Davis, and Los Angeles campuses, and at the universities of Washington, Minnesota, Illinois, Chicago, Oregon, and New

Mexico. Smaller programs at public institutions near large and active Indian reservation populations operate in Montana, South Dakota, Oklahoma, Arizona, and Wisconsin. A few Ivy League schools, particularly Dartmouth, Harvard, and Cornell, also initiated NAS programs.

To assess the national growth and direction of NAS programs, a national survey was conducted in 1985 by the American Indian Studies Center at UCLA. The survey found 107 NAS programs on university and college campuses throughout the United States. Nine programs (Pembroke State, Dakota Wesleyan, University of North Dakota, Dartmouth, University of Alaska, University of Washington, San Diego State, Bemidji State, and the University of Minnesota) had departmental status. Eighteen programs provided a major in NAS; forty offered a minor. Only six of the 107 programs offered a graduate degree in NAS. Most of the programs were found to be small, primarily advisory, with one or two survey courses on Indian culture and history, and perhaps one or two selected courses on local Indian culture(s). The courses most widely taught included

The logo of the UCLA American Indian Studies Center.
(Courtesy of the UCLA American Indian Studies Center)

Native American arts, religions, literature, history and culture, policy and law, and education.

In the late 1990s most American Indian studies programs continued as interdisciplinary programs with few, if any, permanent staff. In the United States and Canada, there are thirty programs with majors, about fifty with minors, at least twenty with Native American studies concentrations, fourteen with master's degrees of various kinds, and two doctoral programs dedicated to American Indian studies. The most optimistic change from the 1980s was the two new doctoral programs at the University of California at Davis and at the University of Arizona in Tucson. Similarly, the University of Trent in Ontario, Canada, offers a doctoral degree in Native studies with emphasis on traditional knowledge. Otherwise most Indian studies programs offered minors or several courses for general students, usually with few if any faculty trained directly in American Indian studies. Many programs focused on student support for American Indian students, but few institutions were willing to allocate funds or develop initiatives to create a major national or international department in Indian studies. Few NAS programs have secure state funding similar to that of other departments or programs. Instead, a number of programs are maintained on a year-to-year basis, often through grant writing or by other sources of external funding secured by faculty and staff. Montana State University, Penn State, and a few other universities have been able to maintain Title

IV graduate fellowships in education for qualified Indian students, but many of those grants were discontinued in the early 1990s.

Despite the lack of stable institutional support, a few NAS programs have developed undergraduate and graduate research and teaching liaisons with other academic departments. These liaisons increase Indian access to scientific, business, or other professional degree programs that have traditionally been viewed as outside the educational interests of academically talented Indian students. At Montana State University, for example, the American Indian Research Opportunities (AIRO) Program provides academically talented Indian students from both tribal colleges and campuses with opportunities to work in major research labs in the health-related sciences. The Montana State University NAS program provides an on-campus site for the development of a number of undergraduate and graduate fellowship and scholarship programs for Indian students. These programs have graduated one of the largest number of Indian BAs, MAs, and Ph.D.s in the country. The key to this nationally successful NAS program has been the supportive collaboration among Indian leadership on campus, NAS faculty, tribes, tribal colleges, and the university's president, William Tietz, who insisted that faculty from all the academic programs participate in the development and implementation of educational programs that would benefit Indian students and the state's Indian tribes and tribal colleges.

In contrast to the structure at Montana State, the American Indian Studies Center program at UCLA has been put together from a cross-listing of faculty and courses from several academic departments, with only a few permanent faculty members actually assigned to the Indian studies program. Similar interdepartmental structures have emerged across the country as administrators move to reduce budgets through the consolidation of ethnic studies programs. Despite high course enrollments and community need, the original vision of an identifiable and self-determining NAS department actively serving the Indian reservation community from a college or university campus has been limited or abandoned by most NAS programs as they are merged into the frail and usually underfunded catch-all structure of most generalized ethnic studies programs.

Securing funding for NAS research is unusually difficult. Since NAS is not yet nationally recognized as an academic discipline and has no doctorate-granting programs or discipline-based professional association, access to research funds from federal, state, or private foundations is problematic. To receive research funding, each faculty member from an NAS program either must explain in extensive detail how his or her research relates to nationally recognized disciplines or must devote a large part of the research proposal identifying NAS and specifying what Indian-centered research can contribute to scholarly pursuits. In either instance, a special burden is imposed on researchers who work in NAS.

Despite these obstacles, NAS programs continue to promote an active Indian perspective in many U.S. colleges and universities. One of their most important roles is to continue to provide a link between higher education and Indian communities. Certainly, the greatest boost to Indian higher education, and to NAS programs, has been the emergence of tribal colleges.

A number of journals provide the discipline with an academic voice. At UCLA, the *American Indian Culture and Research Journal* (AICRJ) is now past its twenty-fourth year and has an international following. AICRJ provides peer-reviewed scholarly articles on all aspects of NAS, including current Indian issues, and includes reviews of recent books, journals, and other publications pertinent to NAS. In a somewhat different vein, *The American Indian Quarterly*, edited at Northern Arizona University and published by the University Press of Kansas, tends to be more literary and less historical in focus. It offers book reviews and a wide range of articles on Indian literature and religion. The *Wicazo Sa Review*, published by the University of Minnesota Press, again gives its focus to Indian literature but has also devoted itself to major current issues, such as human rights and indigenous peoples. The *Indigenous Nations Studies Journal*, edited at the new (1997) Indigenous Studies Program at the University of Kansas, published its first issue in spring 2000 and promises to develop an international perspective. All NAS journals have increasingly stronger and longer records of publication, and, as the field continues to expand, will provide source material for NAS as an academic discipline with its own intellectual and community-based concerns. New efforts continue to emerge, especially with the recent growth of Indian literature in American studies and literature departments.

## The Tribally Controlled College Movement

In 1968 the Navajo tribe created the first tribally controlled college in the United States. Over the next decade, fourteen new tribal colleges were created on Indian reservations in Montana (4), North Dakota (4), South Dakota (3), Michigan (1), Washington (1), and California (1). Due in part to their success, the Tribally Controlled Community College Assistance Act (PL 95–471) of 1978 was passed, providing limited federal support for other tribes wishing to start a tribal college. This initially modest investment in self-determination in Indian higher education has now developed into a pan-tribal movement, with thirty-three tribally controlled colleges located on Indian reservations in thirteen states. Most tribal colleges are physically and culturally unique, but all share one important historic feature. All are chartered by the local Indian tribe(s) and not by the state or federal government. They are independent institutions of higher education whose common mission is to serve the educational needs of the local tribe(s), operating within specific tribal cultural norms. Administrative guidelines, programs of study, board actions, and instructional methods must not violate tribal cultural beliefs.

Tribal colleges vary in size, facilities, course offerings, and degrees and certificates offered. Some colleges exist in trailers or abandoned buildings, while others have substantial and modern campuses. These differences reflect the availability of local funding and the size of the student body. In the thirty years since the first tribal college was opened, a few tribal colleges have pushed forward and now provide campus facilities comparable to many non-Indian community colleges. Libraries, student unions, recreational and sports facilities, modern laboratories, and new classrooms are increasingly available.

Initially, the Tribally Controlled College Assistance Act authorized funding for thirteen tribal colleges. The act provides grants for the general operating budget of eligible institutions and includes sections on technical assistance, feasibility determinations, and a college facilities study. To qualify for funding, a tribal college must meet three criteria: a majority of the board of trustees must be Indian; a majority of the student enrollment must be Indian; and the college must be working toward the goal of serving Indian students. From 1978 to 1997, fifteen new tribal colleges came into existence.

The growing list of tribal colleges is evidence that something remarkable is happening in Indian higher education. For the first time, Indians have control over the college education of their tribal members. An institution chartered by the tribes and controlled by Indians is now in place on reservations to shape the direction of Indian life. But this success has required a near-heroic effort on the part of those Indians and non-Indians who brought about the tribal college movement.

---

**Figure 16.4**
**Recommendations for Further Information**

1. Beverly Slapin and Doris Seale, eds., *Through Indian Eyes: The Native Experience in Books for Children* (Philadelphia: New Society Publishers, 1992).

2. Karen Gayton Swisher and AnCita Benally, eds., *Native North American Firsts* (Detroit: Gale Research, 1998).

3. *Native Education Directory Organizations and Resources for Educators of Native Americans and various Digests published by ERIC Clearinghouse on Rural Education and Small Schools* (Charleston, WV: Appalachia Educational Laboratory).

4. *American Indian Digest, Facts About Today's American Indians* (Phoenix: Russell Publications, 1993).

5. The following web sites contain information useful to classroom teachers:

   · *Techniques for Evaluating American Indian Web Sites* at http://www.u.arizona.edu/~ecubbins/webcrit.html

   · *Selective Bibliography and Guide for "I" is not for Indian: The Portrayal of Native Americans in Books for Young People* at http://www1.pitt.edu/!limitten/ailabib.htm

   · American Indian Library Association at http://www1.pitt.edu/~lmitten/aila.html

   · http://www.kidsource.com/kidsource/content3/unbiased.teaching.k12.2.html

   · http://www.unr.edu/nnap/NT/i8_9.htm

---

*Source: Frances V. Rains and Karen Gayton Swisher, "American Indians and Alaska Natives in the Elementary School Curriculum" Social Education 63:1 (1999): 46–50.*

---

Most tribal colleges place extraordinary emphasis on student retention and success. Tribal college faculty and administration carefully track student academic progress and attendance. When problems occur, the student is contacted by an instructor, a counselor, or even the college president. Sometimes it is as simple as car failure, but sometimes the problem is more serious, such as an undiagnosed learning disability or a family crisis. Whatever the problem, tribal college faculty, staff, and administration become actively involved in the solution. This means that college personnel, administrators, faculty, and staff mobilize academic and personal counselors, tutors, study groups, and a variety of other student support functions to provide every opportunity for the student's personal and academic success. In Indian Country, academic success and personal success are inseparable. What happens at home and in the community eventually appears in the classroom—unemployment, family issues, or achievements. This unified personal-academic perspective is promoted throughout the campus. To reduce initial anxiety about the college, formal procedures such as registration, financial aid, and testing are approached in a personal and nonthreatening manner, creating an open and friendly atmosphere that reflects the informal social patterns of the Indian community itself. To be effective, the tribal colleges have come to reflect the character of the communities they serve. These proactive student support strategies have proven to be highly successful. AIHEC colleges reported an average 15 percent Indian student dropout rate for the 1999–2000 academic year. In contrast, the most recent U.S. Department of Education statistics (1997–1998) listed a 65 percent Indian student dropout rate for all U.S. colleges and universities. Perhaps public and private colleges and universities have something to learn from tribal colleges about how to retain Indian students.

These special efforts are necessary for a variety of reasons. Because of the long history of educational failure on Indian reservations, it is not obvious to many potential students, young or adult, that attending college will have a positive impact on their lives. Many tribal colleges have found that all too frequently they must undo years, even generations, of hostility toward schools, hostility that manifests itself as complex personal and communal attitudes associated with widespread patterns of failure. These patterns have made Indians reluctant to accept the challenge of higher education.

## Table 16.5
## Tribal Colleges of the American Indian Higher Education Consortium by Location and Year Established

| Institution | Location | Year |
|---|---|---|
| Dine College | AZ | 1968 |
| United Tribes Technical College | ND | 1969 |
| Haskell Indian Nations University | KS | 1970* |
| Sinte Gleska University | SD | 1970 |
| D-Q University | CA | 1971 |
| Oglala Lakota College | SD | 1971 |
| Southwestern Indian Polytechnic | NM | 1971* |
| Turtle Mountain Community College | ND | 1972 |
| Fort Berthold Community College | ND | 1973 |
| Northwest Indian College | WA | 1973 |
| Si Tanka College | SD | 1973 |
| Sitting Bull College | ND | 1973 |
| Blackfeet Community College | MT | 1974 |
| Cankdeska Cikana Community College | ND | 1974 |
| Dull Knife Memorial College | MT | 1975 |
| Keweenaw Bay Ojibwa College | MI | 1975 |
| Salish Kootenai College | MT | 1976 |
| Fort Peck Community College | MT | 1978 |
| Crownpoint Institute of Technology | NM | 1979 |
| Nebraska Indian Community College | NE | 1979 |
| Sisseton Wahpeton Community College | SD | 1979 |
| Little Big Horn College | MT | 1980 |
| Lac Courte Oreilles Ojibwa College | WI | 1982 |
| Fort Belknap College | MT | 1983 |
| Bay Mills Community College | MI | 1984 |
| Stone Child College | MT | 1984 |
| Red Crow Community College | AB (Canada) | 1986 |
| Fond du Lac Tribal Community College | MN | 1987 |
| Institute of American Indian Arts | NM | 1988** |
| Leech Lake Tribal College | MN | 1990 |
| College of the Menominee Nation | WI | 1993 |
| Little Priest Tribal College | NE | 1996 |
| White Earth Tribal College | MN | 1997 |

Data Source: American Indian Higher Education Consortium, June 2000.
* Federally Chartered
** Congressionally Chartered

Out of necessity, the tribal colleges have set themselves the task of preparing Indians to think of themselves as capable learners before they become active students. To accomplish this, most of the colleges include a variety of non-credit work and learning skills courses, along with personal speaking and social interaction classes to enhance the confidence of potential students, many of whom are beyond traditional college age or are single parents. The result of these extra efforts is a remarkable record of student retention and eventual academic achievement by once-isolated Indian youth and elders. Without such support and monitoring systems, the colleges would lose many of the most needy students. The effective intervention systems developed by the tribal colleges allow them to work successfully with both prepared and

**Map of AIHEC Tribal Colleges**

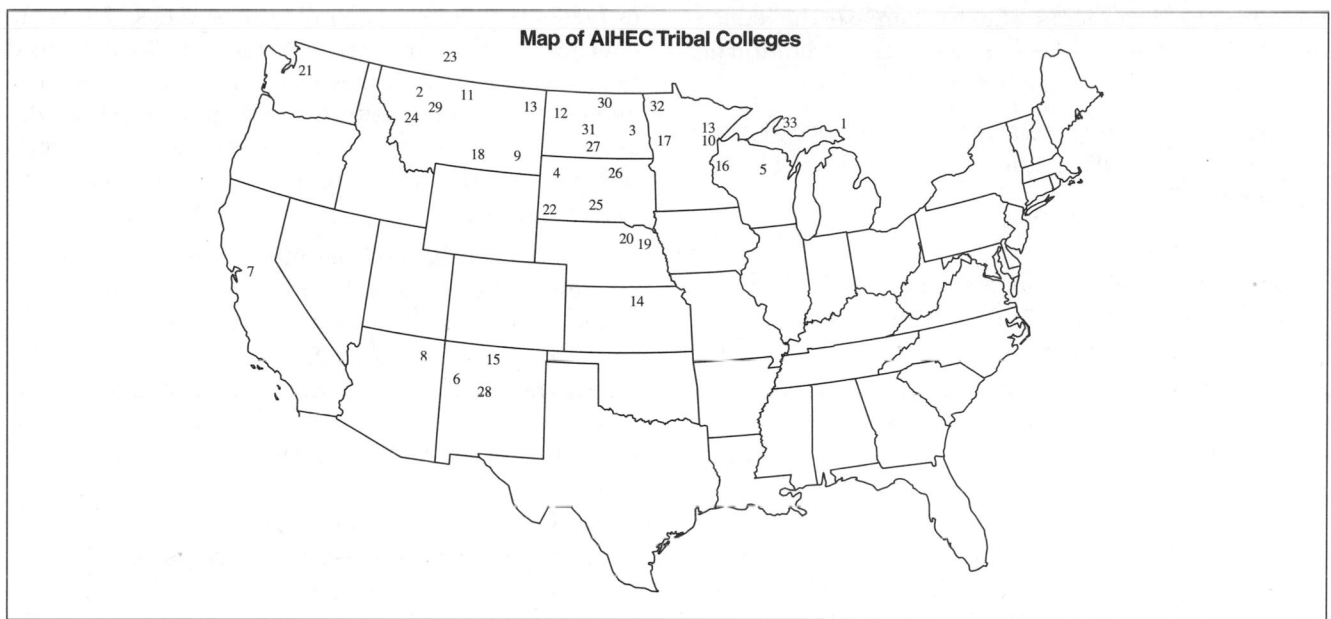

## Tribally Controlled Community Colleges

1. Bay Mills Community College, Brimley, Michigan
2. Blackfeet Community College, Browning, Montana
3. Cankdeska Cikana Community College, Fort Totten, North Dakota
4. Si Tanka College, Eagle Butte, South Dakota
5. College of Menominee Nation, Keshena, Wisconsin
6. Crownpoint Institute of Technology, Crownpoint, New Mexico
7. D-Q University, Davis, California
8. Dine College (formerly Navajo Community College), Tsaile, Arizona
9. Dull Knife Memorial College, Lame Deer, Montana
10. Fond du Lac Tribal and Community College, Cloquet, Minnesota
11. Fort Belknap College, Harlem, Montana
12. Fort Berthold Community College, New Town, North Dakota
13. Fort Peck Community College, Poplar, Montana
14. Haskell Indian Nations University, Lawrence, Kansas
15. Institute of American Indian Arts, Santa Fe, New Mexico
16. Lac Courte Oreilles Ojibwa Community College, Hayward, Wisconsin

17. Leech Lake Tribal College, Cass Lake, Minnesota
18. Little Big Horn College, Crow Agency, Montana
19. Little Priest Tribal College, Winnebago, Nebraska
20. Nebraska Indian Community College, Niobrara, Nebraska
21. Northwest Indian College, Bellingham, Washington
22. Oglala Lakota College, Kyle, South Dakota
23. Red Crow Community College, Cardston, Alberta, Canada
24. Salish Kottenai College, Pablo, Montana
25. Sinte Gleska University, Rosebud, South Dakota
26. Sisseton Wahpeton Community College, Sisseton, South Dakota
27. Sitting Bull College, Fort Yates, North Dakota
28. Southwestern Indian Polytechnic Institute, Albuquerque, New Mexico
29. Stone Child College, Box Elder, Montana
30. Turtle Mountain Community College, Belcourt, North Dakota
31. United Tribes Technical College, Bismarck, North Dakota
32. White Earth Tribal and Community College, Mahnomen, Minnesota
33. Keweenaw Bay Ojibwa Community College, Baraga, Michigan

underprepared students and to increase the educational role of the college beyond that traditionally associated with American higher education.

One long-time tribal college president refers to extra efforts to keep Indian students enrolled as "fan belt scholarships":

> Many times Indian students need money for car repairs, or to attend a funeral on another reservation, or they can't pay their rent and are about to be evicted. We try to figure out how to get them some money to overcome problems that would cause them to drop out of college. Our flexibility in dealing with individual student problems is the key to keeping them enrolled. We can't solve every problem, but we've managed to help hundreds of students stay in college with something as simple as $10 to replace a broken fan belt on a car.

Two institutions—Oglala Lakota College and Sinte Gleska University—offer master's degrees. Six tribal institutions—Haskell, Oglala Lakota, Salish Kootenai, Sinte Gleska, Sitting Bull, and Turtle Mountain—have bachelor degree programs of study (N=51). Every tribal college offers associate degrees (N=486), while twenty-seven provide one- or two-year vocational certificates (N=187). A few colleges have short term diploma, apprentice, and competency training (N=8).

The tribal colleges also offer a wide range of vocational and academic courses, many in response to specific tribal economic needs. Most offer courses in the sciences, math, humanities, social sciences, and various training programs for special careers or to meet local employment demands, such as forestry, carpentry, welding, mechanics, secretarial studies, computers, basic management, electronics, tourism, agriculture, and other curriculum or certification programs, including predental. Because of the cultural and economic importance of fishing to its tribe, one tribal college began as the Lummi College of Aquaculture. It has since broadened its curriculum and is now the Northwest Indian College in the state of Washington. Salish Kootenai College operates a tribal greenhouse and laboratory to preserve native plant species on the reservation. Several of the colleges manage buffalo herds because of the importance of the buffalo to tribal culture.

The tribal colleges have made every effort to supply whatever the local Indian communities need in the way

of higher education. According to surveys, the tribal colleges have contributed substantially to improved Indian employment figures. One survey identified an 85 percent employment rate for its tribal college graduates. Such results are especially remarkable in reservation communities with chronic 40 to 85 percent unemployment rates.

Most of the tribal colleges offer bachelor and associate degrees in business, liberal studies, Native American studies, computer science, agriculture/natural resources, and education. These degree offerings are directly related to specific tribal needs: economic progress (business and computer), student transfer to four-year colleges (liberal studies), strengthening culture (Native American studies), fishing, farming, ranching (agriculture/natural resources), and improving schools (education). Vocational certificate areas are also tied to tribal needs with the most common areas being business, computer science, construction trades, health/social science, and education.

While tribal colleges try to meet the needs of their communities with a variety of academic and outreach programs, they also focus on strengthening the quality of instruction and support services. Tribal college emphasis on improving quality has helped thirty of the thirty-three AIHEC-member institutions earn full accreditation with their respective regional accreditation association.

The success of tribal colleges rests on an Indian cultural foundation. All tribal colleges integrate local culture into the curriculum, including courses in Indian language, religion, music, Indian kinship and social systems, arts, history, and Indian or tribally related sciences such as local ecology and ethnobotany. Most tribal colleges provide NAS degrees and certificate programs in these areas. Tribal colleges also work with tribal elders and cultural leaders to write and record cultural traditions, ensuring that the tribal culture is extended into the college's educational world and that tribal traditions and educational practices go hand-in-hand. Tribal colleges sponsor handgame tournaments, giveaways, powwows, and other local traditions to reach out and participate in the reservation communities. One need only attend a tribal college graduation to see how much Indian culture and higher education have become intertwined into a remarkable success story.

The active involvement of college personnel with the reservation community is another notable aspect of tribal colleges. College faculty conduct economic, educational, and scientific research to benefit the reservation community. College personnel write grants to fund tribal projects, assist in their implementation, and often provide technical assistance to evaluate the effectiveness of existing tribal programs. Many tribal college employees serve on tribal and other community committees, using their special training and experience to assist tribes in meeting community program goals. As one former director of student services at a tribal college describes it:

> It was the busiest time of my life. We helped each other write reports, grants, curriculum and a new catalog. I remember being there before 8 a.m. and staying until 6 p.m. I drove home, made a sandwich and was back at 7:30 p.m. I would work until 10 or 11 p.m. and I was never alone. The hard work was okay; we felt that we were accomplishing something. The worst part was having to deal with all the visitors. We had auditors, grant program evaluators, the BIA feasibility team, the accreditation team visit, consultants helping us with a dozen projects, and representatives from the BIA, commissioner of higher education and other colleges and universities on campus. Some days the visitors outnumbered the employees.

Such special efforts have allowed the tribal colleges to achieve remarkable successes. One survey of tribal college graduates found that Indian students who attended a tribal college directly from high school were eight times more likely to graduate from a non-Indian four-year college or university than Indian students who went directly from high school to an off-reservation four-year college. Such findings give clear evidence that academic preparation in one's own community, nurtured by one's own culture and language, is an important element in the educational success of Indians.

The accomplishments of the tribal college movement are even more remarkable given the constant struggle they face to find sufficient funding to carry out their difficult educational mission. Much of the tribal college movement's struggle for survival can be traced to the politics of funding surrounding the Tribally Controlled Community College Assistance Act of 1978 (TCCCAA) and its later revisions. Since the passage of the act, tribal colleges have never received full funding at the level authorized by Congress. Instead, the Reagan and Bush administrations and Congress have given the tribal colleges promises and underfunding.

Congress never appropriated enough money to meet the authorized level of funding per Indian student.

During the Reagan Administration (1981–1989), funding per Indian student dropped from $2,831 to $1,927. Adjusting for inflation using 1981 dollars, funding support per Indian student decreased 45 percent from 1981 to 1999. In 1981 Congress appropriated 77 percent of the authorized funding level. By 1999, in spite of growing enrollment and facilities needs of tribal colleges, Congress appropriated only 49 percent of the authorized funding level.

Most of the tribal colleges do not receive state support for non-Indian students, and the Tribally Controlled Community College Assistance Act only provides support to students who are enrolled members of an Indian tribe. Thus, at many tribal colleges, TCCCAA funds subsidize the education of non-Indian students.

While education costs soared across the nation during this same period, the level of funding for tribal college students was 50 percent below that provided to full-time students at the nation's community colleges—despite the special cultural and economic needs associated with any effort to start a college in a rural, chronically unemployed area. Yet tribal colleges continued to serve Indian reservation communities.

The Carnegie Foundation for the Advancement of Teaching offered ten recommendations to the federal government and the nation in a 1990 study of the tribal college movement entitled *Tribal Colleges—Shaping the Future of Native America*. The report's recommendations were as follows:

1. Full funding of colleges as authorized by Congress, with appropriations keeping pace with the growth of enrollment;
2. Improvement of facilities through government and foundation funding;
3. Strengthening of ties with non-Indian institutions of higher education;
4. Increase in the number of programs linking colleges and communities;
5. Expansion of the role of tribal colleges in preserving languages, histories, and the cultures of tribes;
6. State funding support for tribal colleges;
7. Creation of faculty development programs at tribal colleges;
8. Strengthening of the Tribal College Institute's ability to develop administrative leadership at tribal colleges;
9. Funding support for a Washington, D.C.-based office of the American Indian Higher Education Consortium; and
10. Funding support for the tribal college endowment.

Since 1990, limited progress has been made on the Carnegie recommendations. Most tribal colleges are still underfunded, lack modern facilities, struggle with relationships with non-Indian colleges, and lack state support for students.

Successes include (1) a growing number of social, cultural, political, and economic programs linking tribal colleges to reservation communities; (2) increased tribal college leadership in the practice and preservation of language, culture, and history; (3) initial efforts in faculty development programs; (4) government recognition of tribal colleges as land grant institutions; (5) the creation of the American Indian College Fund; (6) efforts to work together with indigenous people throughout the world; and (6) the establishment of the national office of the American Indian Higher Education Consortium in Alexandria, Virginia.

In 1997 the Carnegie Foundation commissioned a second study—*Native American Colleges*— which offered a second set of recommendations for improvement. The new recommendations are as follows:

First, we once again urgently recommend that the federal government adequately support tribal colleges by providing the full funding authorized by Congress for the Tribally Controlled Community College Assistance Act. Specifically, we recommend that the $5,820 authorized per student be appropriated and that, from this point on, federal appropriations keep pace with the growth of Indian student enrollment.

Second, we strongly urge full appropriation of Land Grant funds. In addition, we call on state Land Grant colleges to support the work of tribal colleges.

Third, we still urge that tribal college facilities— including libraries, science laboratories, classrooms, and residence halls—be significantly improved through federal government appropriations. We also propose that foundations, corporations, as well as state and federal government agencies, help improve facilities at tribal colleges.

Fourth, we urge the connections between tribal colleges and non-Indian higher education institutions grow even stronger. We recommend that mainstream colleges and universities continue to work with tribal colleges, joining in partnerships that benefit both institutions.

Fifth, we recommend that tribal colleges continue to expand their important work in preserving the arts, philosophy, science, and religious studies of their tribes. Specifically, we urge foundations and government agencies to fund programs that allow colleges to study and teach this essential knowledge.

Sixth, we recommend that tribal colleges enrich their curricula—and build even stronger collaboration with non-Indian institutions—through the expanded use of distance learning technology. We urge foundations and government agencies to support this initiative by providing essential "seed" money for the development of a telecommunications infrastructure and funding for the development of general education courses.

Seventh, we repeat the need for a comprehensive program of faculty development at tribal colleges.

Eighth, we urge continued support of the American Indian Higher Education Consortium. Specifically, we urge increased funding for data collection and technical support to member colleges.

Ninth, we call on foundations, corporations, the federal government, and individuals to continue their support of the American Indian College Fund.

Tenth, we encourage continued funding of the journal *Tribal College*.

### Tribal College and Tribal Community

The emergence of institutions of higher education, even those chartered by the local tribe, raise important issues regarding the complex relationship between such institutions and the communities they are intended to serve. All colleges and universities promote change. What is not clear to some tribal members is how "tradition-as-culture" and "change-as-progress" can coexist.

Despite what appears to be an obvious conflict, Indian educators, tribal leaders, and non-Indian colleagues have brought higher education onto the reservation and into Indian communities. Certainly, this change will bring other changes, but at least Indians themselves will have some say as to which changes, and when and how they might eventually fit into the culture of the local tribe(s). Indians' control over their own institutions of higher education removes a historic barrier to Indian self-determination and development.

## American Indian Higher Education Consortium

To retain Indian-controlled support of the tribal college movement, leadership from the tribal colleges have organized themselves into a consortium, the American Indian Higher Education Consortium (AIHEC). AIHEC represents thirty-three colleges in the United States and Canada that share the institutional mission to serve Indian students. The organization began in 1972 with the goal of helping tribal colleges survive. The six original members selected five purposes for the consortium:

1. To promote, foster, encourage, and implement programs for the improvement of Native and/or tribally controlled postsecondary and higher education for American Indian, Inuit, and Alaska Natives.
2. To promote methods for the training of administrative, teaching, and staff positions for postsecondary and higher education institutions, to establish information centers for advice and information, to facilitate and encourage the seeking out of funds for implementing AIHEC programs from government and private sources, and to foster the development of any and all other programs, centers, plans, and ideas which have as their goal the improvement of the American Indian, Inuit, and Alaska Native higher education.
3. To initiate and carry through, either singly or in cooperation with others, programs under federal or state laws that have as their goal the development, training, and education of persons who are dedicated to the purposes of AIHEC.
4. To promote and encourage the development of language, culture, and traditions of the American Indian, Inuit, and Alaska Natives.
5. To plan, develop, and implement programs that are consistent with the inherent rights of tribal sovereignty and self-determination.

Because of the extensive political and legislative processes associated with the implementation of the Tribally Controlled Community College Assistance Act of 1978, the presidents of the various colleges have used AIHEC effectively to represent the tribal college movement and to promote higher education among the various member colleges. Since its inception in 1972, AIHEC has successfully worked to promote national recognition of the tribal college movement. It has sponsored annual conventions where college administration, faculty, staff, and students from the colleges meet to participate in training workshops, seminars, and intercollegiate academic and sports events. AIHEC also sponsors *Tribal College: Journal of the American Higher Education Consortium*, which focuses on Indian higher education issues and provides a forum for tribal educational leaders to express Indian perspectives on research, government policies, history, and the future. In addition, AIHEC has created and oversees the American Indian College Fund to promote personal, corporate, and foundation gift-giving to support the tribal college movement. Through the activities of AIHEC, tribal college leadership has been able to create a national organizational basis for higher education on America's Indian reservations. And probably most importantly, AIHEC provides opportunities for Indian educators to assume significant leadership roles and for future tribal leaders to deal with the political issues of American Indian higher education at the state and federal levels.

## Toward the Future

Last year more than 30,000 Indian students enrolled in tribal colleges. The American Indian Higher Education Consortium describes the average tribal college student as Indian, female, low-income, twenty-nine years old, single head-of-household, the first generation of her family to attend college, grateful for the opportunity to attend college on the reservation, satisfied with academic and support services, comfortable within the social and cultural context of a tribal college, and hopeful for a better future for her family. Each year tribal colleges provide the gift of hope to thousands of new Indian students. In spite of poor facilities, underpaid faculty, economically depressed communities, and one-half the budget of public community colleges, tribal colleges manage to offer Indian students hope for a better future through a college education. The Carnegie Foundation wrote:

We find the evidence of the success of these Indian higher education institutions is clear. Tribal

A graduate carries a sacred Navajo basket during a Dine College graduation, 1998. (Photo by John Running. Courtesy of the American Indian College Fund)

colleges are continuing to quietly serve their communities by reclaiming and passing on Indian culture, and by creating opportunity and renewing hope. We are convinced that, with ongoing support, they will continue to enrich the lives of students and tribal societies, and indeed will enrich the whole nation.

*C. Patrick Morris*
*Salish Kootenai College*

*Gerald Slater*
*Salish Kootenai College*

*Brigid O'Donnell*
*University of Connecticut*

*Michael O'Donnell*
*Salish Kootenai College*

## ◆ CANADIAN NATIVE EDUCATION

More than fifty Indian tribes are scattered from coast to coast in Canada, each possessing distinct languages, institutions, and customs. The Iroquois lived in the fertile area around Lake Ontario and the St. Lawrence River and were characterized by an agricultural economy, permanent villages, elaborate government structures, a formal religion, clans, and rich traditions expressed in music, dances, and festivals. The Indian tribes of the Canadian prairies, such as the Saulteaux, Plains Cree, Sioux, and Blackfoot, followed the buffalo herds, dispersing into small bands during the winter and reuniting in spring to discuss the affairs of the tribe and to celebrate great ceremonies like the Sun Dance. Each of the Canadian tribes developed its own distinctive culture based on the ecological circumstances in which they lived.

Despite the widely divergent ways of life, a common thread runs through each of the cultures' spiritual worldview. It is a distinctive attitude toward the world and the individual's place within it. Traditional Indian society was based on the knowledge that all things in life are related in a sacred manner and are governed by natural laws set down at the time of creation. The land is therefore held to be a sacred gift from the Creator. As one Indian elder put it "the land doesn't belong to the people, the people belong to the land." In their relationship to the land, people accommodate themselves to it in an attitude of respect and stewardship. To do otherwise would be to violate a fundamental law of the universe.

Proper conduct was determined by natural laws, which obliterated the distinction between the sacred and secular. Each had as its source the activities that resulted as humans and nature interacted with each other. Through this reciprocal relationship humans are provided with the sustenance, both physical and spiritual, necessary to live. Thus, human law was a reflection of natural law, and all of the structures, customs, and tribal ways of life grew out of this central understanding.

### Education in Traditional Indian Society

This worldview had important implications for the education of the young in traditional Indian societies. Before the Europeans came to North America, education in Indian communities was carried out on an informal basis through the experiences of daily life. Traditional education sought to socialize the individual into the group, the extended family, clan, community, and tribe. The teachings included sacred and secular aspects of Indian life. In traditional teachings, all creatures on the earth, including human beings, were given

**Table 16.6**
**Degree and Certificate Programs of Study at**
**United States Tribal Colleges: 1999–2000**

| Institution | MA | BA | AA | VC | O* | T |
|---|---|---|---|---|---|---|
| Bay Mills Community College | 0 | 0 | 11 | 9 | 2 | 22 |
| Blackfeet Community College | 0 | 0 | 15 | 8 | 0 | 23 |
| Cankdeska Cikana Community College | 0 | 0 | 11 | 5 | 0 | 16 |
| College of the Menominee Nation | 0 | 0 | 12 | 3 | 2 | 17 |
| Crownpoint Institute of Technology | 0 | 0 | 6 | 13 | 0 | 19 |
| Dine College | 0 | 0 | 21 | 3 | 0 | 24 |
| D-Q University | 0 | 0 | 14 | 26 | 0 | 40 |
| Dull Knife Memorial College | 0 | 0 | 3 | 12 | 0 | 5 |
| Fond du Lac Tribal Community College | 0 | 0 | 44 | 8 | 0 | 52 |
| Fort Belknap College | 0 | 0 | 9 | 2 | 0 | 11 |
| Fort Berthold Community College | 0 | 0 | 21 | 10 | 0 | 31 |
| Fort Peck Community College | 0 | 0 | 22 | 3 | 0 | 25 |
| Haskell Indian Nations University | 0 | 4 | 13 | 0 | 0 | 17 |
| Institute of American Indian Arts | 0 | 0 | 4 | 0 | 0 | 4 |
| Keweenaw Bay Obijwa College | 0 | 0 | 6 | 0 | 0 | 6 |
| Lac Courte Oreilles Ojibwa College | 0 | 0 | 12 | 7 | 0 | 19 |
| Leech Lake Tribal College | 0 | 0 | 31 | 0 | 0 | 31 |
| Little Big Horn College | 0 | 0 | 9 | 4 | 0 | 13 |
| Little Priest Tribal College | 0 | 0 | 13 | 1 | 2 | 16 |
| Nebraska Indian Community College | 0 | 0 | 7 | 2 | 0 | 9 |
| Northwest Indian College | 0 | 0 | 19 | 10 | 2 | 31 |
| Oglala Lakota College | 1 | 12 | 17 | 6 | 0 | 36 |
| Salish Kootenai College | 0 | 4 | 14 | 7 | 0 | 25 |
| Sinte Gleska University | 1 | 25 | 29 | 8 | 0 | 63 |
| Si Tanka College | 0 | 0 | 9 | 6 | 0 | 15 |
| Sisseton Wahpeton Community College | 0 | 0 | 13 | 4 | 0 | 17 |
| Sitting Bull College | 0 | 4 | 20 | 6 | 0 | 30 |
| Southwestern Indian Polytechnic | 0 | 0 | 16 | 13 | 0 | 29 |
| Stone Child College | 0 | 0 | 12 | 4 | 0 | 16 |
| Turtle Mountain Community College | 0 | 2 | 31 | 7 | 0 | 40 |
| United Tribes Technical College | 0 | 0 | 16 | 7 | 0 | 23 |
| White Earth Tribal College | 0 | 0 | 6 | 3 | 0 | 9 |

Source: American Indian Higher Education Consortium, June 2000.
*Other includes diploma, apprentice, and competency awards
MA=MASTER'S DEGREE
BA=BACHELOR'S DEGREE
AA=ASSOCIATE of ARTS DEGREE
VC=VOCATIONAL CERTIFICATION
O=OTHER
T=TECHNICAL TRAINING

a purpose or, put another way, duties and responsibilities, at the time of creation. The goal of education was, therefore, to produce an individual who would have, as the Plains Cree put it, *minaatsiwin,* "a good way of life." To attain this good life, children were taught about the sacred teachings of the tribe including the oneness of all things, that all things on the earth are alive and have a spirit, and that all elements of the natural world are related. They were taught to know their place in the world and that everything in the natural world is a gift from the Creator and must be treated with respect.

These teachings shaped an individual's behavior. For example, when using a plant, children were taught to pray to ask permission to use the plant, to inform the spirit what the plant would be used for, and to give an offering, such as tobacco, in return for using the plant. If members of the tribe behaved in a proper manner, the spirits would react favorably and provide resources for the people to live.

Education took many forms, including instruction by family members or elders in practical skills like hunting and fishing. Education stressed values such as caring, honesty, proper conduct, respect for the wisdom of elders, the importance of helping others, self reliance, individual responsibility, and obligations to the community. Tribal history and values were passed on through the telling of myths (narrative tales concerned with the Creator, spirits, and the nature and meaning of the universe and humans), legends (folk tales that deal with the experiences of individuals or happenings in the past), and stories. Tribal teachings were reinforced through ceremonies and festivals. The Iroquois, for example, recognized the integral relationship between the peoples' way of life and the land through four festivals each year celebrating the cultivation of the soil, ripening of wild fruits and berries, the harvest, and the passing of the seasons. Festivals were marked by prayers of gratitude, great speeches, feasting, songs, dances, and games.

Another important aspect of traditional education was the marking of important events in the life cycle. Thus, shortly after birth, a child received a name, bestowed at a ceremony by a person, often an elder with supernatural power, who prayed to the spirits on behalf of the child. The name given at the ceremony was considered sacred. It linked the child to a source of spiritual power and provided a clue about future skills or roles that he or she would play in the tribe. The child was held by members who committed themselves to be concerned with the child's welfare throughout his or her life.

During adolescence, children often received encouragement to continue their spiritual development by seeking an elder to supervise a "vision quest." This entailed going to a secluded place and fasting for four days. It was believed that when the body was deprived of food and water, the life-giving forces of physical life, the spiritual consciousness would prevail. If the child was fortunate, he or she would receive a message from the spirits that would give direction to his or her life. At the end of the fast, a feast would be held, at which time an elder might interpret the meaning of the experience.

Various family members played significant roles in the education of children. For example, uncles might be responsible for taking nephews on their first hunting experience. They would teach the child the skills required to hunt animals in an appropriate way, including both the physical and spiritual aspects of the hunt. Among the Cree of James Bay the goose hunt was an important educational event for children. They would be taught such skills as how to construct a blind, make decoys out of natural materials, and call the geese. The killing of the first goose was an important occasion in the child's life and was marked by a feast and ceremony of thanksgiving. The head of the goose was decorated and given to the child.

Education for Indian youth was an all-encompassing experience that occurred in a family environment, an atmosphere of warmth and affection. Children learned to assume adult roles as members of the tribe and to take their place in the community.

## Indian Education and the Arrival of the French

The education of Indian youth changed dramatically as European settlers began to control increasing amounts of territory in Canada. The first permanent settlement was established by the French in 1608 at Quebec on the shores of the St. Lawrence River. They called the area New France. This area was the territory of the Iroquois, Montagnais, Algonkian, and Huron Indians. The policy of the French was to "civilize" the Indians into European ways. They regarded the Indians as a primitive people with no religion or culture and were determined to convert them to Christianity and "make productive French citizens of them." The vehicle to carry out this policy was European education carried out by priests ("blackrobes" as the Indians called them). Four methods of education were attempted. First, the priests traveled to Indian villages, learned their languages, and attempted to convert them to Christianity and teach them European manners. This method failed because the Indians, who believed that they already possessed a satisfying religion and way of life, could simply ignore the priests and carry out their daily life.

A second attempt at education involved taking Indian youth who seemed to possess potential leadership skills to France to be educated. The French thought that when the educated Indians returned to New France, they would serve as role models for other Indians who would then want to become educated and enjoy the benefits of civilized society. The experiment was disastrous because the change in lifestyle was too drastic for the students. They could not cope with life in France, which was foreign to them. They also did not fit into the Indian way of life when they returned, as they had not learned the skills to make a living hunting and trapping in the bush and no longer knew how to behave in Indian communities. They were marginal to both societies and often ended up coping with their intolerable situation by escaping into alcohol addiction.

The third method of educating Indian youth involved sending them to Roman Catholic seminaries. Indian youth were sent to these boarding schools to learn catechism, reading, and writing. By removing the students from their homes and controlling their learning environment, the French believed that the students would have no choice but to learn French values and customs. But before long, the Indian children found the regimen of studies too exacting, the curriculum irrelevant, and the discipline and separation from their families unbearable. Most students ran away and parents, recognizing the detrimental effects of the schools, refused to send them back.

The fourth attempt to educate Indian children involved establishing settlements, called reserves (a tract of land set aside for Indians), near towns where Indians would live permanently. It was thought they would assume aspects of French society, such as practicing agriculture, and eventually become integrated into the French way of life. Each reserve would have a school, a parish church, and a hospital and would be administered by missionaries. From an educational point of view, the reserve was an attempt at total education-acculturation (the process whereby one group, usually a minority, learns the culture of another group and thereby loses its previous culture) of the children and the adults. The goal of integrating the Indians into French society did not occur. Children were not interested in school, and adults did not learn agricultural practices or manual trades or to speak French. Reserves, instead of integrating Indians into life in New France, became institutions of segregation where Indian identity was retained.

Eventually, educators recognized that Indian culture was not easily eradicated, that traditional beliefs and customs were strongly established and could continue to be practiced. Indians were a proud and independent people who believed that they possessed a satisfying way of life that suited the environment in which they lived. Adopting French education involved giving up significant aspects of their old way of life and sacred teachings without offering an opportunity to participate equally in French society. The authoritarian nature of the schools and harsh discipline were foreign to the children and contrasted greatly with their traditional methods of education. The curriculum, with its emphasis on reading and writing, seemed of little use to people whose basis of life was hunting and trapping. Education, for Indians, was not a matter of formal instruction in a building, but a natural part of growing up and learning to assume one's place in the family, clan, community, and tribe. Thus, while Indians adopted some practices of the new society, the majority continued to practice their culture.

## Indian Education under the British and Canadians

When the British assumed control of Canada in 1763, they developed an "Indian policy" similar to the French plan "to protect and civilize" Indians. Their method was to protect them from the "corrupting forces" of British society, particularly alcohol, and to civilize them to become "productive British subjects." As settlement pushed farther and farther west into Indian territory, conflicts between settlers and Indians became increasingly frequent, and the British recognized that something had to be done to prevent further hostilities. They recognized that Indians had aboriginal rights (an inherent right possessed by an aboriginal individual or group by virtue of living in the territory from time immemorial) to the land that had to be extinguished (the act of giving up claims to land in exchange for compensation such as money, parcels of land, and goods and services) before settlement could proceed. The British, and later the Canadian government, took their lead from the French and Americans and signed treaties with the Indians. In the treaties, the Indians agreed to give up title to the land in exchange for the establishment of reserves with land set aside for each family, free education and medical care, farm implements and livestock, and a small amount of money.

Canada currently has 573 reserves scattered through the country. The federal government also established a government department, the Department of Indian and Northern Affairs, to assume control over Indian issues. Initially, education was carried out by missionaries who set up day schools on the reserve. Attendance was voluntary, and consequently the school had little effect in acculturating Indians to the Canadian way of life. Some Indian families requested schools to be established on their reserves in order to become acquainted with aspects of the dominant society. But this knowledge could be acquired without losing contact with their own culture.

## Residential Schools

By the mid-nineteenth century, the Canadian government recognized that Indians were not becoming "civilized" or assimilated. The government decided a new approach was needed to assimilate Indian youth into Canadian society. They adopted the American

An Inuit teacher employs visual aides to teach his students the Inuit language. (Public Domain)

practice of educating Indians in boarding or residential schools run by religious officials.

In these schools, attendance was compulsory (sometimes forcibly removing children from their homes), and all aspects of life, from speaking English to behavior, were carefully regulated. Curriculum was to be limited to basic academic subjects combined with half-day practical training in agriculture, crafts, and household duties, in order to prepare pupils for their expected future roles on the lower fringes of the dominant society. With some exceptions, residential schools were regarded as a negative experience for most of the students who attended them. The children were forbidden to speak their Indian languages or to see their parents for the ten-month school term. Discipline was usually strict and physical conditions harsh. Many students attended a residential school from the age of six until sixteen. As a result, many Indians who attended these schools lost their ability to speak their Indian language and emerged from the schools confused about

their identity as Indian people because it had been devalued by teachers. At the same time, few Indians attained sufficient academic education or learned enough skills to become fully functioning members of Canadian society. In addition, discrimination and negative stereotypes frequently prevented Indians from attaining jobs.

On a more positive side, some Indians who returned home to their reserves with basic literacy and some familiarity with the dominant society attempted to become knowledgeable about their own culture. Many of them became leaders in their communities; others attempted to move between the two cultures and enter the paid labor market.

By 1900, 3,285 Indian children, between six and fifteen years old (out of approximately 20,000) were enrolled in twenty-two industrial schools and thirty-nine boarding schools, and another 6,349 in 226 day schools. By the turn of the century, Indians were no longer a priority to the government. They had become dependent on the government, dominated in most aspects of their lives by the Indian Act (an act of Parliament passed in 1879 that regulated Indian life). The reserves, which were governed by an all-powerful Indian agent, had segregated Indians away from non-Indian settlements and were becoming increasingly irrelevant to the country.

This situation came to be reflected in the government's education policy. The government began to cut back on funds available to schools. The curriculum was simplified, and emphasis was placed on giving students minimal skills necessary to return to the reserve. The new policy, which remained in place until mid-century, ensured that the formal education of Indian children would remain minimal. In 1930, three-quarters of Indian pupils across Canada were in grades 1 to 3, receiving only a very basic literacy education. Only three in every hundred went past grade 6.

By the 1960s there was general recognition that the residential school system was a failure and it was phased out by the government. Generations of aboriginal people had suffered cultural loss, abuse, and identity confusion as a result of their experiences in residential schools. The Canadian government, through the minister of Indian Affairs and Northern Development, issued an official apology to the aboriginal people who endured the negative results of residential schools and established a $350 million fund to establish programs to help heal individuals who had undergone abuse. A number of healing programs have been established to assist people in coping with the effects of the experience.

## Indian Responses

Despite their powerless position, Indian leaders made numerous attempts to protest the poor quality education Indian children were receiving. A chief from Saskatchewan wrote to the governor general requesting that residential schools be replaced by local day schools as promised by treaties in order to keep children from being "torn from their mother's arms or homes." In 1923, the Reverend Ahenakew, a Cree graduate of the University of Saskatchewan, urged the government to put more money into education of Indians and complained that the residential schools took away an individual's initiative. Little changed, however. By 1950, only one-third of Indian pupils went beyond grade three, compared with almost two-thirds of children in provincial public schools across Canada.

## Government Recognition of Failure

After World War II, the Canadian government, like the French some three hundred years before, had to admit that its efforts at educating Indian children had been a failure. Indians had proved unwilling to give up their culture. They had not become assimilated. A parliamentary committee recommended that young Indian children be educated with non-Indian children in public schools. The policy changed from assimilation to one of integration of Indians into the dominant society. By 1960, almost 25 percent of the 38,000 young Indians in school were attending public schools; the total proportion of Indian pupils beyond grade six doubled over the decade to almost 20 percent. The residential schools were closed. By 1980, almost 60 percent of Indian students were enrolled in provincial public schools. An additional 32 percent were attending federal day schools, which provide an educational experience similar to that of provincial educational systems.

The new policy of integrating Indian students into the public school system proved problematic. Many Indian leaders regard the policy as simply a more subtle form of assimilation. Studies have consistently demonstrated that in the 1970s and 1980s, the dropout rate of Indian students attending provincial and federal non-Indian schools was between 60 and 80 percent. These rates are substantially higher than those of non-Indian students in Canada (approximately 30 percent). A number of factors contribute to this problem. Indian students often fail to graduate from high school because of their lack of motivation to attend school, which results from lack of family encouragement, a lack of interest and concern in education, a low self-concept, a failure to see any relevance of courses for their lives outside of school, and negative public comment resulting from an ignorance of Indian life or stereotyping.

Indian students' and parents' lack of interest in education is caused by the failure of students to enjoy or relate to the content of school curricula, which in turn is the result of an inadequate education system. There are few Indian teachers to act as role models for students, and a lack of teachers competent in instructing students of different cultural backgrounds and learning styles. Differences in teaching and learning styles between Indians and non-Indians may contribute to a lack of effective communication and learning. Traditionally, Indian children learned through silent listening and observing, through a hands-on approach with minimum verbal instructions, performing the skill at some later time when they feel that they have completely mastered it. Children are not tested or expected to perform before the instructor.

Another factor in the low achievement of Indian students is the lack of cultural curriculum in terms of Indian language, reserve history and contemporary situation, and general Indian studies in most public schools. In addition, Indians are often portrayed in textbooks as important only by association with Europeans such as contributors to the fur trade as opposed to being important in their own right. Often Indian art such as totem poles or visible aspects of material cultural such as canoes and snowshoes are emphasized in school curriculum without placing the objects into the larger cultural context which give them meaning. This can lead to stereotyping of Indian culture, giving students the impression that Indian culture is something from the past. It also implies that Indian students cannot meet themselves in the curriculum they are studying, which may lead to a feeling of lack of relevance of the curriculum or, worse, an impression that Indian life and culture are not worth studying. This reinforces feelings of low self-worth and contributes to high Indian student dropout rates.

Often, poor school community communication contributes to high dropout rates. Factors that contribute to this include cultural differences, geographic distances, and the "psychological distance" of the reserve for many non-Indian educators. Many non-Indian teachers do not visit the reserve and may be ignorant of its history and the way of life of its people. Also, lack of participation in extracurricular activities may be a problem. Living a long distance from the school and the inability of parents to afford athletic equipment or the cost of travel may serve to limit an Indian student's range of peer contacts and interest in school, which may increase the likelihood of dropping out.

It would appear, therefore, that Indian youth may face serious problems when they attend off-reserve public schools. The problems stem from a situation in many Indian communities where social problems exist. Education is often not encouraged, and schools that are not conducive to successful academic achievement by Indian students.

### Indian Self-Determination

For more than three centuries, the responsibility for education of Indian people has rested with the dominant society. The prevailing goals have been the eradication of Indian cultures and assimilation into the larger Canadian society. In the 1960s, a major shift in the balance of the relationship began, at first because of a recognition of past failures and a willingness to be more tolerant of diversity by members of the dominant society, and then increasingly as a consequence of a movement toward Indian self-determination (Indians exercising their right to govern and to make decisions affecting their own lives and affairs on their own lands). Indian political organizations, such as the National Indian Brotherhood, founded in 1968, were established to work toward solving problems facing Indian people within the context of Indian culture and under the control of Indian people.

But before Indians were able to work toward self-determination, the Canadian government attempted once more to implement assimilation. This came in the form of the Indian Policy or White Paper introduced in Parliament in 1969. It recommended that "all bases of discrimination be removed" by providing all services, including education, through the same service agencies as for all other Canadians. The reserve system and the Department of Indian Affairs would be abolished, and Indians would lose the special status they possessed as a result of their aboriginal and treaty rights.

Indian responses to the White Paper were overwhelmingly negative. Indian political organizations presented counterproposals that asserted their right to self-government and control over their own institutions, including education. They also insisted that aboriginal and treaty rights continue to be recognized and that the historical responsibility of the federal government for Indian affairs continue. As a result of this political pressure, the government withdrew the White Paper.

### Indian Control of Indian Education

In 1972, a new era in Indian education in Canada began with the publication of the National Indian Brotherhood's policy paper entitled "Indian Control of Indian Education." The policy had as its central thrust two educational principles "parental responsibility and local control of education." The document reaffirmed the federal government's treaty commitment to provide education to Indian people, and made clear that "only Indian people can develop a suitable philosophy of education based on Indian values adapted to modern living." The policy stressed that Indian children must be given a strong sense of identity, with confidence in their own personal worth and ability and that Indian bands must exercise full responsibility for educating Indian children. The government accepted the policy in principle in 1973.

Since that time, much has happened. By the mid-1980s, 450 of Canada's 577 Indian bands were administering all or part of the educational system within their communities, with 429 band schools operating by 1996. These schools were educating more than one-half of the children living on reserves, and 75 percent of students were remaining until grade twelve. By 2000 virtually all bands managed their education in terms of operating band schools (especially primary schools), hiring teachers, approving curriculum, and administering funding to post-secondary students from their communities. Indian cultural-survival schools have been established in most provinces. Indian curriculum has been developed in almost every locale. Indian teacher education programs, as well as specialized professional programs in law, health, business, social work, and Indian and Native studies have grown up in universities and colleges throughout the country. Despite the successes, a great deal remains to be done. Differences exist between the government and Indian people over such issues as authority, jurisdiction, and financial control of education.

There have also been major changes in the way public schools treat Indian material in the curriculum. Provincial ministries of education have recognized that, in a multicultural society, there must be recognition given to the country's first peoples. The curriculum has thus been changed to a point where Indians are studied extensively in several grades. For example, in 2000 the Ontario Ministry of Education published a series of curriculum guides for Native studies and Native languages as courses in the intermediate and senior divisions (grades seven to twelve). The aims of Native Studies curriculum is to assist students to recognize and understand the diversity of perceptions, needs, values, cultures, lifestyles, and aspirations that characterize Native peoples in Canada; acquire knowledge about aboriginal rights, claims, and treaties and their meaning for Native people and for Canada as a whole; recognize and understand the effects of the dominant culture on Native peoples; develop an appreciation of Native cultures and of their contributions to Canada, to

North American society, and to the global community; identify and eliminate prejudice; and develop an understanding of historical and systemic barriers to Native peoples' full participation in Canadian society.

The curriculum included courses entitled "English: Contemporary Aboriginal Voices," "Current Aboriginal Issues in Canada," "Aboriginal Beliefs, Values and Aspirations in Contemporary Society" and courses in Ojibwa and Iroquoian languages. A limitation of the curriculum, however, is implementation. There is no detailed content in the curriculum guidelines such as units or lesson plans so that a teacher will have to undertake substantial research to develop a curriculum that can be taught in the classroom. There is no plan in place to operationalize the curriculum and the subjects are strictly optional for students. Thus, the offering of the courses in schools has been minimal. Similar initiatives are occurring in ministries of education across Canada. In some provinces Native studies is now a teachable subject; that is, students are able to take Native studies courses at the university level and count them for credit as subjects they can later teach. It is hoped that these initiatives will meet the dual purpose of making non-Indian children more aware of and sensitive to the aspirations of Indian people and make the public education system more relevant for Indian children.

## Indian Cultural Revitalization

Indian leaders recognize that past government assimilationist policies have eroded much of traditional Indian culture. On the other hand, ironically, the policies in some ways assisted in the preservation of Indian culture. In order for assimilation to occur, there must be continuous, direct contact between members of the minority group and the dominant society. The practice of isolating Indians on reserves, educating their children apart from the dominant society, and restricting access to the larger society actually contributed to the maintenance of a distinct cultural identity. Indian leaders are now looking to an Indian-controlled education system to play a major role in the revitalization of Indian culture by ensuring the transmission of Indian values, identity, language, and traditions. Recognizing that education is a key element in the socialization of Indian children as individuals and as members of a group, Indian people place priority on achieving congruence between home and school. The movement toward taking control of education should, therefore, be seen as part of a larger revitalization of aboriginal societies currently occurring across Canada.

Today's Indian cultures are not traditional aboriginal cultures. At the same time, continuity with the past and a sense of distinctive identity have not disappeared. In the revitalization, Canada's aboriginal peoples are not returning to a previous era; rather, they are reaffirming their identity by selecting aspects of the old ways and blending them with the new. Elements of traditional culture such as sun dances, sweatlodge ceremonies, vision quests, potlatches, and spiritual healing rituals are being revived. The wisdom of Indian elders who have kept alive traditional teachings is being recognized and respected. In many Indian communities, people are emerging with bicultural identities, with an identity firmly anchored in the cultural world of their people and a consciousness of the skills necessary to succeed in the dominant society. This process is neither new nor unusual when people from different cultures meet in a multicultural society. The same process of cultural nationalism has occurred and continues to occur as the many racial and ethnic groups in Canada vie for what they consider to be their rightful place in the Canadian Confederation. Each group is faced with the tasks of attaining an adequate standard of living for its members and of participating in the general civic life of the larger society, while at the same time protecting and valuing its own heritage, institutions, values, and worldview. Indian people, as the original inhabitants of the country, have a particularly strong claim to protect their culture within Canadian society.

This revitalization has helped define an emerging philosophy of Indian education as similarly bicultural, blending the old and new into a unique synthesis encompassing all aspects of a child's development. In some Indian schools the intellectual, physical, and spiritual aspects of the child are viewed holistically, without the separation between secular and sacred knowledge that characterizes schooling in the dominant society. Many elements of traditional Indian teaching have been incorporated into this perspective.

Indian culture and language are central to the curriculum. Respect toward others, particularly elders, is encouraged, as is respect for the environment. While a trained teacher is responsible for teaching specific knowledge, including acquisition of Indian languages, great emphasis is placed on learning through guided experience. Rituals and ceremonies become important learning events. So does storytelling, the use of oral history to pass on a wide range of teachings from traditional myths to history to moral behavior to games and dances. Learning also emerges out of everyday activities, including the way people act toward one another both in school and within the family and community. It is through such means that values like respect, honesty, and sharing are learned, an individual acquires an Indian identity, and comes to understand his or her place in the community.

## Indian Cultural Survival and Language Immersion Schools

Perhaps the best expressions of the cultural revitalization as it relates to education are the Indian cultural-survival schools and Indian language-immersion schools located on reserves and in cities across Canada. These schools grew out of the dissatisfaction of parents with the education—especially the high dropout rates and lack of Indian-specific curriculum— that their children were receiving in provincial public schools. The overarching purpose of the schools is to promote and preserve Indian language, values, and history in order to survive as a distinct people within the larger Canadian society. The cultural-survival schools at Akwesasne and Kahnawake have as their main goal the survival of the Mohawk Nation in terms of "sovereignty, self-sufficiency, and survival." The Akwesasne Freedom School desires "to facilitate learning so that the students will have a good self-concept as Indians, promote self-reliance, promote respect for the skills of living in harmony with others and the environment and master the academic and/or vocational skills necessary in a dualistic society."

The curriculum in these schools is divided between conventional academic subjects and Indian culture, typically about half and half. Often schools integrate Indian materials into the academic curriculum, including Indian-oriented novels, drama, and poetry in English literature or topics such as treaties, the reserve system, Indian politics, and contemporary issues in history or social studies. In science courses, the emphasis is often on ecology, including the relationship between people and the environment as viewed from the traditional Indian perspective.

One of the most exciting developments in Indian education has been the growth of curricula from an insider's (or Indian) perspective. Many Indian educators have begun to produce curriculum materials for use in both Indian and public schools. A good example is *The Mishomis Book: The Voice of the Ojibway*, by Edward Benton-Banai, an Ojibwa from Minnesota. The book takes the perspective of a *mishomis* (grandfather) and *nokomis* (grandmother) to tell Ojibwa oral history and teachings. The book, written at the intermediate and senior levels, uses a storytelling mode to describe such topics as the Ojibwa creation story; the origins and meaning of sacred ceremonies like the *Midewiwin*, pipe, and sweatlodge; the nature of the clan system; legends and history. Ojibwa words are used throughout to convey a sense of authenticity. Increasingly, curriculum materials written from an Indian perspective are being used in classrooms in all grades

to portray a more accurate and sensitive picture of Indian people and their way of life.

An important way survival schools impart culture to their students is through enrichment or extracurricular activities such as Indian films, guest speakers, elders' programs, field trips, ceremonies, social and cultural events, survival and cultural camps, and agricultural and economic projects. Several schools include a cultural survival camp as a major part of their curricula. The staff and students go to a reserve for a week to live with elders in a traditional way. Elders teach students traditional skills, tell stories and legends, and perform spiritual rituals such as sweatlodges and pipe ceremonies. In addition, students learn traditional values such as sharing, cooperation, self-reliance, respect, and responsibility through the day-to-day running of the camp.

Another example of a cultural event in the school is circle time. Some cultural survival schools hold a sweetgrass ceremony (a ceremony in which braided sweetgrass is burnt and participants smudge themselves with the smoke) and pray each morning with the entire school. Prayers are said, announcements are made, and issues dealt with in a traditional Indian talking circle before students go to classes. Other examples of cultural events are feasts, festivals, athletic events, powwows, Indian awareness days, and the celebration of Indian holidays. Elders who are recognized for their wisdom and knowledge of traditional culture often serve as teachers.

Similarly, Indian language-immersion schools teach entirely in an Indian language in the early grades, gradually introducing English in the later grades. The schools grew out of a recognition that if a major initiative to teach children fluency in Indian languages was not undertaken, the languages would be lost. A major limitation of immersion schools is the lack of curriculum materials available in the Indian language. Initiatives are being undertaken to produce such materials. The language and cultural components of the schools are directly linked to the central goal of providing an educational setting that will develop in students an increased self-esteem and a stronger Indian identity. The idea is that if children are taught to understand and value their language and culture, they will value themselves as human beings, and Indian culture will be strengthened.

## Implementation of Indian Control of Indian Education

The most important phenomenon related to Indian education in recent years has been Indians taking control of their education systems in the reserves. The number of reserve-controlled schools has increased from fifty-three in 1975 to 300 in 1989 to 429 in 1996. Most of these schools were federal government day schools. Indian control of education is also reflected in enrollment trends. In 1975, only 4 percent of Indian children attended reserve-controlled schools compared to nearly 40 percent in 1989 and more than 50 percent in 1996. The proportion of children enrolled in federal schools dropped from 41 percent in 1975 to 13 percent in 1989. The proportion of students attending provincial schools fell slightly from 53 percent in 1975 to 47 percent in 1989. The increased involvement in education by Indian communities seems to be reflected in two important educational statistics: lower dropout rates and higher post-secondary enrollments. The number of Indian students who are remaining in school to their final year of high school has steadily increased. In 1960, only 3 percent of students were in their last year of high school compared to 15 percent in 1970, 20 percent in 1980, 42 percent in 1989, and 75 percent in 1996.

An example of a reserve tribe that has taken control of its educational system is the Nisga Indians of Northern British Columbia. In 1973, parents and community leaders articulated the need for a more appropriate high school education for their children based on the ideas of bicultural, bilingual education; direct community involvement in education; and the need to keep Nisga students at home rather than traveling off the reserve to school. In 1974, the British Columbia Ministry of Education agreed to create a separate Indian school district controlled by the Nisga, which would emphasize a bicultural, bilingual curriculum paralleling the basic core curriculum of the province, and to build a new high school on the reserve. The school district is administered by a school board elected by the reserve and is responsible for administrative matters, including finances and personnel, as well as curriculum. The enrollment in the new school was 95 percent Indian. In 1975, most of the grade seven-through-twelve students were three to four years behind in reading, English, math, and science. There was a dropout rate of 90 percent in the secondary school years. Four years after the new school district was in operation, the dropout rate had dropped to approximately 20 percent and the age-grade retardation had narrowed to close to a year.

Many other Indian reserves across Canada have taken control of their education systems. The official policy of the Department of Indian Affairs (the federal government department responsible for Indian affairs) is to "devolve" their responsibility for education to Indian reserves. Financial arrangements are in place whereby reserves receive capital and operating grants on a per student basis to build and administer the schools. Financing is also available for other educational services such as curriculum development, special education, transportation, and Indian language teacher training from both federal and provincial governments. In addition, several Indian teacher training programs have been established in faculties of education in universities throughout Canada, and most provincial ministries of education contain an Indian education department to provide a variety of educational services to Indian communities.

Despite the successes, much remains to be done before Indian communities across Canada have control of a quality educational system for their children. A major educational study, titled *Education and Tradition in 1989*, carried out by the largest national Indian organization, the Assembly of First Nations, reported that a number of issues remain to be resolved as Indian reserves attempt to assume control of their education including: resistance by the federal government to transferring jurisdiction for education to the reserves; inadequate funding from the government to support school administration and educational programs; a lack of qualified people in communities to carry out the transition to local control; a lack of coordination among federal, provincial, and reserve educational agencies to organize a coherent educational system; a shortage of trained Indian teachers; a high rate of turnover of teachers, particularly in isolated communities; a lack of parental involvement in the schools; a shortage of appropriate Indian language and cultural curriculum materials; and inadequate financing of specialized educational programs such as counseling, career planning, vocational training, preschool programs, special education, tutoring, second language programs, language resource centers, and continuing education. Similar conclusions were articulated in 1996 by the Royal Commission on Aboriginal Peoples (a five-year comprehensive commission funded by the federal government to examine issues facing aboriginal peoples in Canada) in Volume 3, Gathering Strength, a study of aboriginal education. The commission made forty-four recommendations as to how to address educational issues. The recommendations included: additional federal government support for aboriginal control over education; the establishment of early childhood education initiatives; increased aboriginal involvement in provincial school systems; increased funding for post-secondary education; more support for teacher education programs; the establishment of new aboriginal language education initiatives; and the establishment of an Aboriginal People's International University. Federal government response to the recommendations have been, to a large degree, disappointing. Many have not been implemented. A notable exception has been the inauguration of an Aboriginal Head Start Program for aboriginal children both on and off reserves.

Numerous models now exist of Indian communities taking control of schools on their reserves. For some (especially smaller reserves), it entails simply taking administrative control of the school and educational services and utilizing the existing provincial curriculum, adding Indian language instruction. For others, it involves integrating Indian cultural material into existing academic subjects such as history, social studies, art, home economics, physical education, environmental studies, and English literature, as well as teaching Indian languages. Curriculum resources now exist that pertain to almost every aspect of Indian life for all grade levels, and, as discussed earlier, Indian material has been added to the curriculum in most grades in the public education system across Canada.

Control of the education system by Indian people has had five broad goals: local jurisdiction, whereby reserve authorities have jurisdiction over education policies, management, curriculum, and program quality and delivery of services; parental and community participation, actively involving parents in such activities as determining the goals of the education program and being involved in classroom and school activities; preparation for total living, ensuring that Indian students are given the opportunity to learn at all levels of education including vocational, academic, professional, and life skills to function effectively in both Indian and non-Indian societies; preservation of language and culture, whereby Indian languages and cultural studies are an integral part of the school curriculum to reinforce students' cultural identity and language; and values education of Indian children, including instruction in the values held in esteem by Indian communities and families so that education is an extension of the culture and the instruction by the family.

Evidence from research demonstrates that Indian communities that have taken control of their education systems have been, by and large, successful in meeting these goals. For example, at the Mi'kmaq School on a reserve in Nova Scotia, testing demonstrated that students' scores in math and reading had risen, attitudes toward school and work had improved, and school attendance had improved significantly since the community took control of the school. Similarly, students' scores on the Canadian Test of Basic Skills improved by 100 percent during the first two years of local jurisdiction over education at the West Bay Reserve in Ontario.

The Alexander Reserve in Alberta reported that assuming control of the education system in their community resulted in bolstering the confidence of community members and improving community cohesion. They also reported that elders and parents regularly participated in school activities. The school's attendance rate increased to 95 percent after only one year of operation. Other communities describe the benefits of training local community teachers to teach in their schools and act as positive role models for students. Local people have also been utilized as resources in the classroom, been trained as teachers' aides and language instructors, and assisted with the locally developed curriculum, thereby increasing the relevance of the school experience for students.

Perhaps the most challenging task of Indian education is, on the one hand, to provide students with sufficient knowledge and skills to be able to succeed in attaining a living in the larger society, while, at the same time, giving students the understandings and values of their tribal culture and language to become functioning members of their community and preserve their traditional way of life. Indian parents clearly want a quality education for their children, that is, one that will prepare them academically and vocationally for post-secondary education and for jobs in the larger society. But if students receive this type of education exclusively, there is a danger that the reserve may lose its potential leaders and best skilled people who, because of an emphasis on the values, skills, and way of life of the dominant society, may take jobs off the reserve and eventually lose contact with the community. Parents, therefore, recognize that for their children to maintain a strong sense of Indian identity and high self-esteem and for their culture to survive, the educational system must include Indian language and culture.

The answer for many Indian communities has been the development of the "bilingual/bicultural" curriculum discussed above. The degree to which Indian communities implement this varies significantly from adopting the provincial curriculum in its entirety with little or no cultural material, to cultural survival and immersion schools with a strong emphasis on culture and language. The majority of Indian schools in Canada, however, adopt some form of bicultural/bilingual education. Research has demonstrated that a balanced educational experience based on both Indian cultural values and mainstream academic and technical skills is possible; in fact, the former can enhance the individual's capacity to deal with and master the latter. With a solid grounding in one's own culture and a positive identity, students achieve greater success in all areas of education.

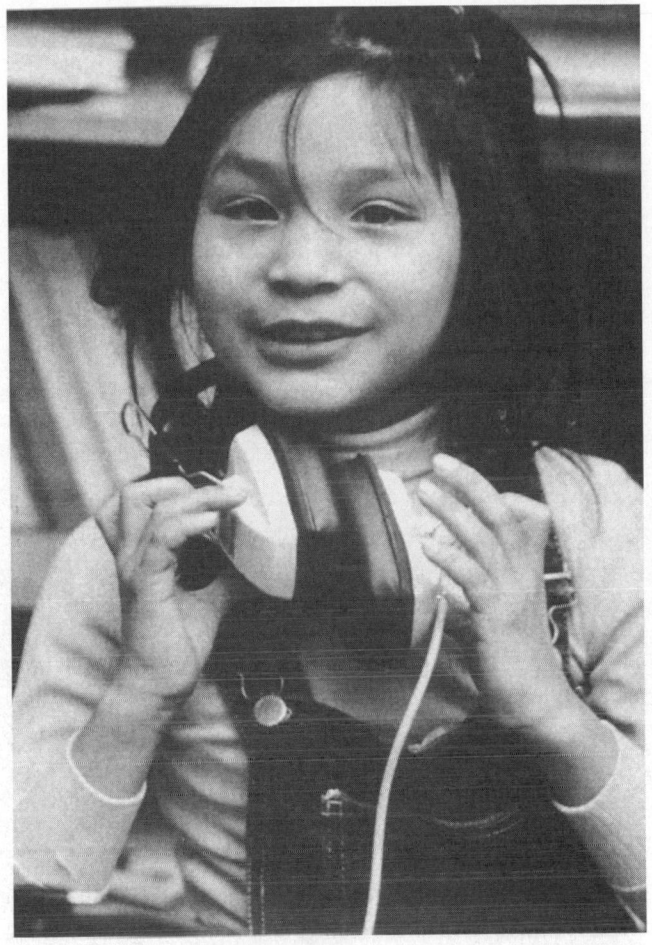

A young girl participates in a language-immersion class intended to preserve Native languages. (Public Domain)

## Indian Post-Secondary Education

The growth in Indian education at the elementary and secondary grades has been paralleled at the post-secondary level. Post-secondary enrollments have increased dramatically with sixty Indian students going to university in 1960, 432 in 1970, 4,455 in 1980, 5,800 in 1985, 18,535 in 1989, and 23,000 in 1996. In 1996, about 40,000 Indian students were enrolled in both colleges and universities in Canada.

The most significant development in university and college education for Indian students has been the establishment of Native, Indian, or First Nations studies programs. The first Native studies department was established at Trent University in Peterborough, Ontario, in 1969. The department started off as a small undergraduate program offering three courses to a small number of students. It currently includes thirty courses as an undergraduate major, an honors program, an affirmative action diploma program (whereby Indian students with less than the regular university admission requirements are accepted into the department and take a combination of academic skill development and regular university courses), and a master's degree in Canadian studies and Native studies. Courses offered by the department include: Indian language courses in Ojibwa and Mohawk; culture courses, such as Indian identity development and culture and community; contemporary issues courses including politics, urbanization, and the north; professionally oriented courses in education, social services, and law; and skill-oriented courses in community development, cross-cultural communication, community-based research methods, oral history methods, and program planning. The department strives to provide an educational experience that, as much as possible, reflects the situation in Indian communities. A number of courses, therefore, include practicum field placements in Indian organizations and communities to provide students with a hands-on experience in an Indian milieu. The department also offers an opportunity to work with international indigenous people through the Thailand Year Abroad Program. The department also offers courses off campus in Indian communities. There are a number of extracurricular events sponsored by the department including cultural ceremonies, field trips to Indian events, and an annual Powwow and Elders Conference. The department is governed by the Aboriginal Educational Council composed of representatives from Indian organizations and communities as well as academics from the university.

In an effort to respond to Indian vocational needs, the department initiated three professional programs: the Native Management and Economic Development Program with the Administrative Studies Program at Trent, the Native Teachers Education Program in conjunction with the Faculty of Education at Queen's University in Kingston and, in 2000, the Indigenous Environmental Studies Program in partnership with the Environmental Studies Program. Approximately two hundred aboriginal students are enrolled in courses in the department with a total of more than nine hundred course enrollments.

In 1998 the department received accreditation to offer the first Native studies doctorate program in Canada, and only the second in North America. It is a culturally based program which includes courses in indigenous knowledge, theory and research methods, social and cultural issues, history and politics, and a practicum field placement in an aboriginal community. The program is overseen by a Native studies graduate council composed of members of the aboriginal community and academics.

Similar Native, Indian, or First Nation studies programs have been established in universities and colleges throughout Canada. In the mid-1970s, an Indian-controlled college, the Saskatchewan Indian Federated College, was founded. Affiliated with the University of Regina, it offers degree programs in Indian studies, social work, fine art, Indian languages, and business administration. Professional schools in universities have also developed Indian programs, including law schools at the universities of Ottawa and British Columbia; education faculties at Brandon, Saskatchewan, Queen's, Simon Fraser, Victoria, and British Columbia universities; social work at the Saskatchewan Indian Federated College and Dalhousie and Laurentian universities; management and administration at Trent and Lethbridge universities and the Saskatchewan Indian Federated College; nursing and health careers at Lakehead and Toronto universities; environmental studies at Trent and York University; and public administration at the University of Victoria.

Native/Indian/First Nation studies has advanced as a distinctive academic discipline with a characteristic research methodology and academic journals. Community-based, applied, or participatory research tends to be the prevailing methodology utilized by Native studies researchers. It differs from conventional social science research in that the people under study are participants in the research in terms of helping to define the nature of the problem to be researched, participating in the data collection, learning research skills, and utilizing the research results. It also recognizes the validity of the indigenous knowledge, particularly the traditional cultural knowledge, of people in the community and aims to be of use in addressing issues the people face. There are two main academic journals in Native/Indian studies: the *Canadian Journal of Native Studies* and the *Native Studies Review*. In addition, there are specialized professional journals such as the *Journal of Native Education* and the *Native Law Reporter*.

Virtually all the academic programs in colleges and universities include Indian faculty. At the same time, it is often difficult to recruit qualified Indian university or college teachers, because many who graduate with a degree prefer to take occupations in professional fields, particularly education and law, or wish to pursue careers in Indian communities and organizations where they feel that they can make a more direct contribution to Indian issues. Thus, most Indian post-secondary students tend not to go beyond an undergraduate degree, and those who do are predisposed to go on for a professional rather than academic graduate degree. The situation may change as an increasing number of Indian students attend universities and colleges.

Perhaps no other area of Indian life has undergone as much change as education. From three hundred years of attempts by outsiders to assimilate them into a foreign culture, to the major struggle to take control of the education of their children, Indian people have recognized the importance of education for their survival as a distinct group within Canadian society. Indian control over Indian education is, therefore, intricately linked to the broader movement toward self-government. Only when a group has control of its institutions, particularly education as the institution responsible for the socialization of the next generation, can it be said that they have achieved true self-determination. A great deal remains to be done. The challenge facing Indian educators today is to develop a bicultural/bilingual educational system that is responsive to the academic and vocational needs of the larger society, while, at the same time, providing students with the understanding and values of their tribal culture and language to become functioning members of their community and preserve their traditional way of life.

*Don McCaskill*
*Trent University*

# Indian Education Offices and Organizations

## UNITED STATES

### ◆ ARIZONA

CENTER FOR INDIAN EDUCATION
P.O. Box 871311
Arizona State University
Tempe, AZ 85287–1311
(480) 965–6292

### ◆ DISTRICT OF COLUMBIA

NATIONAL INDIAN EDUCATION
    ASSOCIATION (NIEA)
700 N. Fairfax St., Suite 210
Alexandria, VA 22314
(703) 838–2870

U.S. DEPARTMENT OF EDUCATION
OFFICE OF INDIAN EDUCATION
400 Maryland Ave., S.W.
Washington, DC 20202
(202) 260–3774

U.S. DEPARTMENT OF THE INTERIOR
BIA OFFICE OF INDIAN EDUCATION
Central Office
Federal Office Bldg. 6, Room 3530
1849 C St. N.W., MS-3512 MIB
Washington, DC 20240–0001
(202) 208–6123
Scholarship Information
(202) 208–6156

U.S. DEPARTMENT OF THE INTERIOR
BIA OFFICE OF INDIAN EDUCATION
Division of School Program Support & Improvement
Family And Child Education (FACE) Coordinator
P.O. Box 1088
500 Gold Ave., S.W., Rm. 7202
Albuquerque, NM 87103
(505) 248–7525

U.S. DEPARTMENT OF THE INTERIOR
BIA OFFICE OF INDIAN EDUCATION
Division of School Services
201 3rd St., N.W., Suite 510
Albuquerque, NM 87102
(505) 346–6544

### ◆ NEW MEXICO

AMERICAN INDIAN GRADUATE CENTER
AMERICAN INDIAN SCHOLARSHIPS
4520 Montgomery Blvd. N.E., Suite 1-B
Albuquerque, NM 87109
(505) 881–4584

CATCHING THE DREAM
Native American Scholarship Fund, Inc.
8200 Mountain Rd., N.E., #203
Albuquerque, NM 87110
(505) 262 2351

INDIAN EDUCATION PROGRAM
3315 Louisiana Ave.
Albuquerque, NM 87110
(505) 880–3995

INSTITUTE FOR NATIVE AMERICAN
    DEVELOPMENT (NAD)
NATIVE AMERICAN STUDIES (NAS)
1812 Las Lomas Dr., N.E.
University of New Mexico
Albuquerque, NM 87131
(505) 277–6930

### ◆ OKLAHOMA

AMERICAN INDIAN RESEARCH AND
    DEVELOPMENT, INC.
2233 W. Lindsey, Suite 118
Norman, OK 73069
(405) 364–0656

## ◆ OREGON

NORTHWEST REGIONAL EDUCATIONAL
   LABORATORY
COMPREHENSIVE CENTER
101 Southwest Main St., Suite 500
Portland, OR 97204–3297
(503) 275–9500

## ◆ VIRGINIA

HIGHER EDUCATION PUBLICATIONS
NEA Publishing
6400 Arlington Blvd., Suite 648
Falls Church, VA 22042

# Tribally Controlled Community Colleges

The following institutions are members of the American Indian Higher Education Consortium (AIHEC).

## UNITED STATES

## ◆ ARIZONA

DINE COLLEGE
(formerly Navajo Community College)
P.O. Box 126
Tsaile, AZ 86556
(520) 724–6669

## ◆ CALIFORNIA

D-Q DEGANAWIDA QUETZECOATL
   UNIVERSITY
P.O. Box 409
Davis, CA 95617
(530) 758–0470

## ◆ MICHIGAN

BAY MILLS COMMUNITY COLLEGE
12214 West Lake Shore Drive
Rte. 1, Box 315A
Brimley, MI 49715
(906) 248–3354

## ◆ MINNESOTA

FOND DU LAC COMMUNITY COLLEGE
2101 14th St.
Cloquet, MN 55720–2964
(218) 879–0800

LEECH LAKE TRIBAL COLLEGE
Route 3, Box 100
Cass Lake, MN 56633
(218) 335–2828

## ◆ MONTANA

BLACKFEET COMMUNITY COLLEGE
P.O. Box 819
Browning, MT 59417
(406) 338–5441

DULL KNIFE MEMORIAL COLLEGE
P.O. Box 98
Lame Deer, MT 59043
(406) 477–6215

FORT BELKNAP COLLEGE
P.O. Box 159
Harlem, MT 59526
(406) 353–2607

FORT PECK COMMUNITY COLLEGE
P.O. Box 398
Poplar, MT 59255
(406) 768–5551

LITTLE BIG HORN COLLEGE
P.O. Box 370
Crow Agency, MT 59022
(406) 638–2228
(406) 638–3100

SALISH KOOTENAI COLLEGE
P.O. Box 117
Pablo, MT 59855
(406) 675–4800

STONE CHILD COMMUNITY COLLEGE
Rocky Boy Route 1082
Box Elder, MT 59521
(406) 395–4313

## ◆ NEBRASKA

LITTLE PRIEST TRIBAL COLLEGE
P.O. Box 270
Winnebago, NE 68071
(402) 878–2380

NEBRASKA INDIAN COMMUNITY COLLEGE
P.O. Box 752
Winnebago, NE 68071
(402) 878–2414

## ◆ NORTH DAKOTA

CANKDESKA CIKANA COMMUNITY COLLEGE
P.O. Box 269
Fort Totten, ND 58335
(701) 766–4415

FORT BERTHOLD COMMUNITY COLLEGE
P.O. Box 490
New Town, ND 58763
(701) 627–3665

SITTING BULL COLLEGE
1341 92nd Street
Fort Yates, ND 58538
(701) 854–3861

TURTLE MOUNTAIN COLLEGE
P.O. Box 340
Belcourt, ND 58316
(701) 477–5605

## ◆ SOUTH DAKOTA

OGLALA LAKOTA COLLEGE
P.O. Box 490
Kyle, SD 57752
(605) 455–2321

SINTE GLESKA COLLEGE
P.O. Box 490
Rosebud, SD 57570
(605) 747–2263

SISSETON-WAHPETON COMMUNITY
    COLLEGE
Old Agency Village, P.O. Box 689
Sisseton, SD 57262
(605) 698–3966

SI TANKA COLLEGE
(Formerly Cheyenne River Community College)
P.O. Box 220
Eagle Butte, SD 57625
(605) 964–6044

## ◆ WASHINGTON

NORTHWEST INDIAN COLLEGE
2522 Kwina Rd.
Bellingham, WA 98226
(360) 676–2772

## ◆ WISCONSIN

COLLEGE OF MENOMINEE NATION
P.O. Box 1179
Keshena, WI 54135
(715) 799–4921

LAC COURTE OREILLES OJIBWA COLLEGE
R.R. 1 (2), Box 2357
Hayward, WI 54843
(715) 634–4790

# American Indian Higher Education Consortium (AIHEC)

These educational institutions are also members of the American Indian Higher Education Consortium (AIHEC).

## ◆ NEW MEXICO

CROWNPOINT INSTITUTE OF TECHNOLOGY
P.O. Box 849
Crownpoint, NM 87313
(505) 786–4100

## ◆ NORTH DAKOTA

UNITED TRIBES TECHNICAL COLLEGE
3315 University Drive
Bismarck, ND 58504
(701) 255–3285

# CANADA

## ◆ ALBERTA

RED CROW COMMUNITY COLLEGE
P.O. Box 1258
Cardston, AB T0K 0K0
(403) 737–2400

## ◆ SASKATCHEWAN

SASKATCHEWAN INDIAN FEDERATED
    COLLEGE
118 College W.
University of Regina
Regina, SK S4S 0A2
(306) 584–8333

# Additional Colleges and American Indian Studies Programs

In addition to the following list of formal studies and certificate programs, many colleges and universities have courses in aspects of Native American cultures, usually taught through departments of anthropology, history, sociology, and literature. American Indian studies courses are also taught within more broadly based ethnic studies programs and centers. The list is organized alphabetically by state.

## ◆ ALASKA

UNIVERSITY OF ALASKA
508 Gruening
Alaskan Native Studies Department
P.O. Box 756300
Fairbanks, AK 99775
(907) 474–7181

## ◆ ARIZONA

AMERICAN INDIAN BIBLE COLLEGE
10020 North 15th Ave.
Phoenix, AZ 85021
(602) 944–3335

ARIZONA STATE UNIVERSITY
American Indian Institute
P.O. Box 879909
Tempe, AZ 85287–2402
(480) 965–8044

NORTHERN ARIZONA UNIVERSITY
American Indian Studies Department
P.O. Box 5653
Flagstaff, AZ 86011
(520) 523–9011

UNIVERSITY OF ARIZONA
American Indian Studies Department
430 Harvill Bldg.
1103 E. Second St.
Tucson, AZ 85721
(520) 621–7108

## ◆ CALIFORNIA

CALIFORNIA STATE UNIVERSITY–LONG
    BEACH
American Indian Studies Department
1250 Bellflower Blvd.
Long Beach, CA 90840
(562) 985–4644 or 5293

CALIFORNIA STATE UNIVERSITY–
    NORTHRIDGE
American Indian Studies Program
Anthropology Department
18111 Nordhoff St.
Northridge, CA 91330
(818) 677–3920

HUMBOLT STATE UNIVERSITY
Center for Indian Community Development
1 Harpst St.
Arcata, CA 95521
(707) 826–3711

PALOMAR COLLEGE
American Indian Studies Department
1140 West Mission
San Marcos, CA 92069
(760) 744–1150 ext. 2425

SAN DIEGO STATE UNIVERSITY
American Indian Studies Department
5500 Campanille Dr.
San Diego, CA 92182–8134
(619) 594–6991

SAN FRANCISCO STATE UNIVERSITY
American Indian Studies Department
1600 Holloway Ave.
San Francisco, CA 94132
(415) 338–1054

SONOMA STATE UNIVERSITY
Native America Studies Program
1801 East Cotati Ave.
Rohnert Park, CA 94928
(707) 664–2458

UNIVERSITY OF CALIFORNIA–LOS ANGELES
American Indian Studies Center
3220 Campbell Hall, Box 951548
Los Angeles, CA 90024–1548
(310) 825–7315

UNIVERSITY OF CALIFORNIA–BERKELEY
Native American Studies Program
506 Barrows Hall #2570
Berkeley, CA 94720–2570
(510) 643–0796

UNIVERSITY OF CALIFORNIA–DAVIS
Native American Studies Department
2401 Hart Hall
One Shields Avenue
Davis, CA 95616
(916) 752–3237

### ◆ COLORADO

NATIVE AMERICAN MULTICULTURAL
    EDUCATIONAL SCHOOL INC.
3600 Morrison Rd.
Denver, CO 80219
(303) 934–8086

### ◆ DISTRICT OF COLUMBIA

WINS
American University
Tenley Campus
4400 Massachusetts Avenue, N.W.
Washington, DC 20016–8083
(202) 895–4967

### ◆ ILLINOIS

NATIVE AMERICAN EDUCATIONAL
    SERVICES (NAES) COLLEGE
2838 West Peterson Ave.
Chicago, IL 60659
(773) 761–5000

### ◆ IOWA

MORNINGSIDE COLLEGE
Indian Studies Department
1501 Morningside Ave.
Sioux City, IA 51106
(712) 274–5000

### ◆ MICHIGAN

KEWEENAW BAY OJIBWA COMMUNITY
    COLLEGE
107 Bear Town Road
Baraga, MI 49908
(906) 353–816

### ◆ MINNESOTA

AUGSBURG COLLEGE
American Indian Support Program
2211 Riverside Ave.
Minneapolis, MN 55455
(612) 330–1000

BEMIDJI STATE UNIVERSITY
American Indian Studies Resource Center
1500 Birchmont Dr., N.E. 321
Bemidji, MN 56601–2699
(218) 755–3977

COLLEGE OF ST. SCHOLASTICA
Indian Studies Department
1200 Kenwood Ave.
Duluth, MN 55811
(218) 723–6170

MINNEAPOLIS COMMUNITY COLLEGE
Department of Social Sciences and American Indians
1501 Hennepin Ave.
Minneapolis, MN 55403
(612) 341–7064

MOORHEAD STATE UNIVERSITY
American Indian Studies
P.O. Box 111
326 MacLean Hall
Moorhead, MN 56563
(218) 236–2196

UNIVERSITY OF MINNESOTA
American Indian Studies Department
2 Scott Hall, 72 Pleasant St., S.E.
Minneapolis, MN 55455
(612) 624–1338

UNIVERSITY OF MINNESOTA–DULUTH
Department of American Indian Studies
116 Cina Hall
10 University Dr.
Duluth, MN 55812
(218) 726–8771

WHITE EARTH TRIBAL AND COMMUNITY
  COLLEGE
210 Main Street South
P.O. Box 478
Mahnomen, MN 56557
(218) 935–0417

#### ◆ MONTANA

MONTANA STATE UNIVERSITY
Center for Native American Studies
P.O. Box 172340
2–179 Wilson Hall
Bozeman, MT 59717–2340
(406) 994–3881

#### ◆ NEBRASKA

NEBRASKA INDIAN COMMUNITY COLLEGE
P.O. Box 428
College Hill
Macy, NE 68039
(402) 837–5078

NEBRASKA INDIAN COMMUNITY COLLEGE
Santee Campus
426 Frazier Ave. Suite 1
Niobrara, NE 68760
(402) 857–2434

#### ◆ NEW HAMPSHIRE

DARTMOUTH COLLEGE
Native American Program
Sherman House
37 N. Main St.
Hanover, NH 03755
(603) 646–3530

#### ◆ NEW MEXICO

UNIVERSITY OF NEW MEXICO
Native American Studies Department
Mesa Vista Hall, Rm. 3080
Albuquerque, NM 87131
(505) 277–3917

#### ◆ NEW YORK

CORNELL UNIVERSITY
American Indian Program
300 Caldwell Hall
Ithaca, NY 14853
(607) 255–6587

#### ◆ NORTH CAROLINA

NORTH CAROLINA STATE UNIVERSITY–
  PEMBROKE
American Indian Studies
P.O. Box 1510
Pembroke, NC 28372
(910) 521–6266

#### ◆ NORTH DAKOTA

UNIVERSITY OF NORTH DAKOTA
American Indian Studies Dept.
P.O. Box 7103
Grand Forks, ND 58202
(701) 777–4314

#### ◆ OKLAHOMA

BACONE COLLEGE
A.A. in American Indian Studies
2299 Old Bacone Rd.
Muskogee, OK 74403
(918) 683–4581

#### ◆ SOUTH DAKOTA

UNIVERSITY OF SOUTH DAKOTA
Institute of American Indian Studies
414 E. Clark St.
Vermillion, SD 57069
(605) 677–5209

♦ **UTAH**

**BRIGHAM YOUNG UNIVERSITY**
Native American Educational Outreach Program
342 Harman Bldg.
Provo, UT 84602
(801) 378–7090

♦ **WASHINGTON**

**EVERGREEN STATE COLLEGE**
Native American Studies Program
Olympia, WA 98505
(206) 866–6000

**UNIVERSITY OF WASHINGTON**
American Indian Studies Center
Padelford Hall
Rm. C514, Box 354305
Seattle, WA 98195
(206) 543–9082

♦ **WISCONSIN**

**NORTHLAND COLLEGE**
Director of Native American Studies Department
Ashland, WI 54806
(715) 682–1204

**UNIVERSITY OF WISCONSIN**
American Indian Studies Program
317 Ingraham Hall
1155 Observatory Dr.
Madison, WI 53706
(608) 263–5501

**UNIVERSITY OF WISCONSIN**
Native American Studies Program
College of Letters & Sciences
P.O. Box 413
Milwaukee, WI 53201
(414) 229–6520

## Government-Operated Schools

Many Indian day schools are operated by local Indian communities and by the Bureau of Indian Affairs. Reservation day schools are not listed below because of space limitations. To contact a reservation day school, call the education department of the appropriate Bureau of Indian Affairs area office. The list of area offices is given first, followed by boarding schools operated largely through BIA funding, in alphabetical order according to state.

## BUREAU OF INDIAN AFFAIRS-EDUCATION: AREA OFFICES

**ALASKAN REGIONAL OFFICE**
P.O. Box 25520
Juneau, AK 99802–5520
(907) 586–7177

**EASTERN OKLAHOMA REGIONAL OFFICE**
101 N. 5th St.
Muskogee, OK 74401
(918) 687–2296

**EASTERN REGIONAL OFFICE**
3701 North Fairfax Dr., MS 260 VASQ
Arlington, VA 22203
(703) 235–2571

**GREAT PLAINS REGIONAL OFFICE**
115 Fourth Ave. S.E.
Aberdeen, SD 57401–4381
(605) 226–7343

**MIDWEST REGIONAL OFFICE**
Henry Wipple Federal Building
1 Federal Dr., Rm. 550
Ft. Snelling, MN 55111
(612) 713–4400

**NAVAJO AREA REGIONAL OFFICE**
P.O. Box 1060
Gallup, NM 87305
(505) 863–8314

**NORTHWEST REGIONAL OFFICE**
The Federal Building
911 11th Ave., N.E.
Portland, OR 97232–4169
(503) 230–5682

**PACIFIC AREA REGIONAL OFFICE**
2800 Cottage Way
Sacramento, CA 95825
(916) 978–6000

**ROCKY MOUNTAINS REGIONAL OFFICE**
316 North 26th St.
Billings, MT 59101–1397
(406) 247–7943

SOUTHERN PLAINS REGIONAL OFFICE
W. C. D. Office Complex
P.O. Box 368
Anadarko, OK 73108
(405) 247–6673 ext. 314

SOUTHWEST REGIONAL OFFICE
P.O. Box 26567
Albuquerque, NM 87102
(505) 346–7517

WESTERN REGIONAL OFFICE
P.O. Box 10
Phoenix, AZ 85001
(602) 379–6600

# BIA-Funded Boarding Schools

## ◆ ALASKA

MT. EDGECUMBE HIGH SCHOOL
1330 Seward
Sitka, AK 99835
(907) 966–2201
Grades 9–12

## ◆ ARIZONA

CHINLE BOARDING SCHOOL
P.O. Box 70
Many Farms, AZ 86538
(520) 781–6222
Grades K-8

DENNEHOTSO BOARDING SCHOOL
P.O. Box 2570
Dennehotso, AZ 86535
(520) 658–3201
Grades K-8

DILCON BOARDING SCHOOL
Star Route 87
HC 63 Box G
Winslow, AZ 86047
(602) 657–3211
Grades K-8

FLAGSTAFF DORMITORY
901 N. Kinlani Rd.
Flagstaff, AZ 86001
(520) 774–5270
Grades 9–12

GREASEWOOD TOYEI CONSOLIDATED
    BOARDING SCHOOL
HC 58, Box 60
Ganado, AZ 86505–9706
(602) 654–3331
Grades K-8

GREYHILLS HIGH SCHOOL
P.O. Box 160
Tuba City, AZ 86045
(520) 283–6271
Grades 9–12

HOLBROOK DORMITORY
1100 W. Buffalo St.
Holbrook, AZ 86025
(520) 524–6222
Grades 9–12

HUNTERS POINT BOARDING SCHOOL
Rt. 12, P.O. Box Drawer 99
St. Michaels, AZ 86511–0099
(602) 871–4439
Grades K-5

KAIBETO BOARDING SCHOOL
East Hwy 160
P.O. Box 1420
Kaibeto, AZ 86053
(520) 673–3418
Grades K-8

KAYENTA BOARDING SCHOOL
P.O. Box 188
Kayenta, AZ 86033
(520) 697–3439
Grades K-8

KEAMS CANYON BOARDING SCHOOL
P.O. Box 397
Keams Canyon, AZ 86034
(520) 738–2385
Grades K-6

KINLICHEE BOARDING SCHOOL
OFFICE OF INDIAN EDUCATION PROGRAM
P.O. Box 800
Ganado, AZ 86505
(520) 755–3439
Grades K-6

LEUPP SCHOOLS, INC.
Hwy 99, HC 61 Box D
Winslow, AZ 86047
(602) 686–6211
Grades K-12

LUKACHUKAI BOARDING SCHOOL
Navajo Rt. 12
Lukachukai, AZ 86507
(520) 787–2301
Grades K-8

MANY FARMS HIGH SCHOOL
P.O. Box 307
Many Farms, AZ 86532
(602) 781–6226
Grades 9–12

NAA TSIS ' ANA COMMUNITY SCHOOL
P.O. Box 10010
Tonalea, AZ 86044
(520) 672–2335
Grades K-8

NAZLINI BIA BOARDING SCHOOL
Navajo Rt. 27
Ganado, AZ 86505
(520) 755–6125
Grades K-6

PINON DORMITORY
P.O. Box 159
Pinon, AZ 86510
(520) 725–3250 or (520) 725  3235
Grades 1–5

ROCKY RIDGE BOARDING SCHOOL
Dinnebito Rd.
P.O. Box 299
Kykotsmovi, AZ 86039
(520) 725–3650
Grades K-8

ROUGH ROCK DEMONSTRATION SCHOOL
R.R. DS, Box 217
Chinle, AZ 86503
(520) 728–3500
Grades K-12

SANTA ROSA BOARDING SCHOOL
Hwy 15
HC 02, Box 400
Sells, AZ 85634
(602) 361–2331
Grades K-8

SANTA ROSA RANCH SCHOOL
HC 02, No. 7570
Sells, AZ 85634–7570
(520) 383–2359
Grades K-8

SEBA DALKAI BOARDING SCHOOL
HC 63, Box H
Winslow, AZ 86047–9423
(520) 657–3208
Grades K-6

SHONTO BOARDING SCHOOL
P.O. Box 7900
Shonto, AZ 86054
(602) 672–2652
Grades K-8

THEODORE ROOSEVELT SCHOOL
101 Thomas Rd.
P.O. Box 567
Fort Apache, AZ 85926
(520) 338–4464
Grades 6–8

TIIS NAZBAS COMMUNITY SCHOOL
Hwy 160, P.O. Box 102
Teecnospos, AZ 86514
(602) 656–3252
Grades K-8

TUBA CITY BOARDING SCHOOL
306 Main St.
P.O. Box 187
Tuba City, AZ 86045
(520) 283–2330
Grades K-8

♦ **CALIFORNIA**

SHERMAN INDIAN HIGH SCHOOL
9010 Magnolia Ave.
Riverside, CA 92503
(909) 276–6332 ext. 207
Grades 9–12

♦ **MINNESOTA**

AMERICAN INDIAN MAGNET SCHOOL
St. Paul Public Schools
1075 East Third St.
St. Paul, MN 55106
(651) 293–5938

CIRCLE OF LIFE SURVIVAL SCHOOL
Country Road 21
P.O. Box 447
White Earth, MN 56591
(218) 983–4180
Grades K-12

#### ◆ MISSISSIPPI

CHOCTAW CENTRAL HIGH SCHOOL
Rte. 7, Box 72
Philadelphia, MS 39350
(601) 656–8938
Grades 7–12

#### ◆ MONTANA

BLACKFEET DORMITORY
Blackfeet Agency
P.O. Box 880
Browning, MT 59417
(406) 338–7441
Grades 1–12

#### ◆ NEW MEXICO

AZTEC DORMITORY
1600 Lydia Rippey Rd.
Aztec, NM 87410
(505) 334–6565
Grades 9–12

CHI-CH'IL-TAH JONES RANCH
    COMMUNITY SCHOOL
P.O. Box 278
Vanderwagen, NM 87326
(505) 778–5574
Grades K-8

CRYSTAL BOARDING SCHOOL
Hwy 134
Navajo, NM 87328
(505) 777–2385
Grades K-6

DLO'AY AZHI COMMUNITY SCHOOL
Sunrise Dr.
P.O. Box 789
Thoreau, NM 87323
(505) 862–7525
Grades K-6

DZILTH-NA-O-DITH-HLE COMMUNITY
    SCHOOL
P.O. Box 5003
Bloomfield, NM 87413
(505) 632–1697
Grades 9–12 (K-8 day school)

HUERFANO DORMITORY
P.O. Box 639
Bloomfield, NM 87413
(505) 325–3411
Grades 1–12 (K day school)

JICARILLA DORMITORY
Emperor Dr. 258
P.O. Box 1009
Dulce, NM 87528
(505) 759–3101
Grades 1–12

LAKE VALLEY NAVAJO SCHOOL
P.O. Box 748
Crownpoint, NM 87313
(505) 786–5392
Grades K-8

MARIANO LAKE COMMUNITY SCHOOL
Navajo Rt. 49
P.O. Box 498
Crownpoint, NM 87313
(505) 786–5265
Grades K-5

NAVAJO PREPARATORY SCHOOL
1200 West Apache
Farmington, NM 87401
(505) 326–6571
Grades 9–12

NENAHNEZAD BOARDING SCHOOL
Country Rd. 6675
P.O. Box 337
Fruitland, NM 87416
(505) 598–6922
Grades K-6

PINE HILL SCHOOL
Route 125
P.O. Box 220
Pine Hill, NM 87357
(505) 775–3242
Grades K-12

SANTA FE INDIAN SCHOOL
1501 Cerrilos Rd.
P.O. Box 5340
Santa Fe, NM 87502
(505) 989–6310
Grades 7–12

SHIPROCK ALTERNATIVE SCHOOLS, INC.
P.O. Box 1809
Shiprock, NM 87420
(505) 368–2070

SKY CITY COMMUNITY SCHOOL
100 Skyline Rd.
P.O. Box 349
Acoma, NM 87034
(505) 552–6671
Grades K-8

TOADLENA BOARDING SCHOOL
P.O. Box 9857
Newcomb, NM 87455
(505) 789–3205
Grades K-8

TO'HAJIILEE-HE (CANONCITO)
P.O. Box 438 Star Route
Laguna, NM 87026
(505) 831–6426
Grades K-12

TSE'II'AHI' COMMUNITY SCHOOL
Navajo Rt. 9, P.O. Box 828
Crownpoint, NM 87313
(505) 786–5389
Grades K-3

WINGATE ELEMENTARY SCHOOL
P.O. Box 1
Fort Wingate, NM 87316
(505) 488–6470
Grades 1–8

WINGATE HIGH SCHOOL
P.O. Box 2
Fort Wingate, NM 87316
(505) 488–6400
Grades 9–12

### ◆ NEW YORK

NATIVE AMERICAN MAGNET SCHOOL
97 West Delavan Ave.
Buffalo, NY 14213
(716) 888–7038

### ◆ NORTH DAKOTA

CIRCLE OF NATIONS SCHOOL
832 Eighth St., N.
Wahpeton, ND 58075
(701) 642–3796
Grades 4–8

### ◆ OKLAHOMA

CARTER SEMINARY
2400 Chickasaw Blvd.
Ardmore, OK 73401
(580) 223–8547
Grades 1–12

EUFAULA DORMITORY
Swadley Dr.
Eufaula, OK 74432
(918) 689–2522
Grades 1–12

JONES ACADEMY
HCR 74 Box 102–5
Rte. 1
Hartshorne, OK 74547
(918) 297–2518
Grades 1–12

RIVERSIDE INDIAN SCHOOL
Rte. 1
Anadarko, OK 73005
(405) 247–6670
Grades 4–12

SEQUOYAH HIGH SCHOOL
Hwy 62 South
P.O. Box 948
Tahlequah, OK 74465
(918) 456–0631
Grades 9–12

### ◆ OREGON

CHEMAWA INDIAN SCHOOL
3700 Chemawa Rd. N.E.
Salem, OR 97305–1199
(503) 399–5721, ext. 222
Grades 9–12

## ◆ SOUTH DAKOTA

CHEYENNE-EAGLE BUTTE SCHOOL
E Street School Administration Building
P.O. Box 672
Eagle Butte, SD 57625
(605) 964–8777
Grades K-12

FLANDREAU INDIAN SCHOOL
1000 North Crescent
Flandreau, SD 57028
(605) 997–2724
Grades 9–12

MARTY INDIAN SCHOOL
P.O. Box 187
Marty, SD 57361
(605) 384–5431
Grades K-12

PIERRE INDIAN LEARNING CENTER
3001 E. Sully Ave.
HC 31, Box 148
Pierre, SD 57501
(605) 224–8661
Grades 1–8

RED CLOUD INDIAN SCHOOL
Holy Rosary Mission
100 Mission Dr.
Pine Ridge, SD 57770
(605) 867–5491
Grades K-12

ROSEBUD DORMITORIES
P.O. Box 69
Mission, SD 57555
(605) 856–4486
Grades 1–12

ST. FRANCIS INDIAN SCHOOL
HCR 59 Box 1A
P.O. Box 379
St. Francis, SD 57572
(605) 747–2299
Grades K-12

## ◆ UTAH

ANETH COMMUNITY SCHOOL
Hwy 262, Drawer 600
Montezuma Creek, UT 84534
(435) 651–3271
Grades K-6

RICHFIELD DORMITORY
765 W. First Ave.
P.O. Box 638
Richfield, UT 84701
(435) 896–5101
Grades 9–12

## ◆ WASHINGTON

PASCHAL SHERMAN INDIAN SCHOOL
25 Omak Lake Rd.
Omak, WA 98841
(509) 422–7583
Grades Pre-K–8

# BIA-Operated Post-Secondary Schools

## ◆ KANSAS

HASKELL INDIAN NATIONS UNIVERSITY
155 Indian Avenue
Box 5030
Lawrence, KS 66046–4800
(785) 749–8497

## ◆ NEW MEXICO

INSTITUTE OF AMERICAN INDIAN ARTS
83 Avan Nu Po Rd.
Santa Fe, NM 87505
(800) 804–6422

SOUTHWEST INDIAN POLYTECHNIC
  INSTITUTE
9169 Coors Rd.
P.O. Box 10146
Albuquerque, NM 87184
(505) 897–5347

# Canadian Education Organizations

**FIRST NATIONS EDUCATION COUNCIL**
240, Place Sondakwa
Wendake, PQ G0A 4V0
(418) 842–7672

**FIRST NATIONS EDUCATION STEERING
   COMMITTEE**
Suite 707–100 Park Royal South
West Vancouver, BC V7T 1A2
(604) 925–6087

**FIRST NATIONS SCHOOLS ASSOCIATION**
Suite 707–100 Park Royal South
West Vancouver, BC V7T 1A2
(604) 925–6087

## Congress of Aboriginal Peoples Chiefs Council on Education

### ◆ ALBERTA

Chief Archie Cyprien
Athabascan Chipewyan First Nation
P.O. Box 366
Fort Chipewyan, AB T0P 1B0
(780) 697–3730

### ◆ BRITISH COLUMBIA

Chief Nathan Matthew
North Thompson First Nation
P.O. Box 612
Barriere, BC V0E 1E0
(250) 672–5652

### ◆ MANITOBA

Chief David Crate
Fisher River First Nation
General Delivery
Koostatak, MB R0C 1S0
(204) 645–2171

### ◆ NEW BRUNSWICK

Chief Everett Martin
Eel River Bar First Nation
P.O. Box 1444, R.R. #1
Dalhousie, NB E0K 1B0
(506) 684–6277

### ◆ NORTHWEST TERRITORIES

Mr. Bill Erasmus, AFN Regional Chief
Denendeh National Office
P.O. Box 2338, 4701 Franklin Avenue
Yellowknife, NWT X1A 2P7
(867) 873–3310

### ◆ NOVA SCOTIA

Chief Morley Googoo
Waycobah First Nation
P.O. Box 149
Whycocomagh, NS B0E 3M0
(902) 756–2337 or 2440

### ◆ ONTARIO

Grand Chief Larry Sault
Association of Iroquois and Allied Indians
387 Princess Street
London, ON N6B 2A7
(519) 434–2761

## ◆ QUEBEC

Chief John Martin
Micmacs of Gesgapegiag
P.O. Box 1280
Maria, PQ G0C 1Y0
(418) 759–3441

## ◆ SASKATCHEWAN

Chief Ken Thomas
FSIN–c/o Irene Oakes
Regal Plaza
Suite A, 1680 Albert Street
Regina, SK S4P 2S6
(306) 721–3600

Chief Perry Bellegarde
200–103A Packham Ave.
Saskatoon, SK S4N 5W5
(306) 665–1215

Grand Chief Vernon Roote
Interim Ontario Alternate
Union of Ontario Indians
Nipissing First Nations
P.O. Box 711
North Bay, ON P1B 8J8
(705) 497–9127

## Primary and Secondary

The Department of Indian Affairs and Northern Development (DIAND) operates schools on reserves and Crown lands and enters into agreements with provincial governments, school boards, and religious or charitable organizations for the education of registered Indian children, from ages six to seventeen inclusive, living on reserves or Crown lands.

Under departmental funding arrangements, Indian band councils or local education authorities may opt to administer all or parts of their education programs. Band school programs are characterized by the greater use of community resources in the delivery of programs, including the participation of Indian elders and the teaching of traditional skills. Band schools offer provincial-type programs, enriched with culturally relevant courses designed to meet the special needs of Indian students from kindergarten to high school completion.

## FIRST NATIONS ADULT AND HIGHER EDUCATION CONSORTIUM

BLUE QUILLS FIRST NATIONS COLLEGE
P.O. Box 279
St. Paul, AB T0A 3A0
(780) 645–4455

FIRST NATIONS ADULT AND HIGHER
EDUCATION CONSORTIUM
Suite 310, 6940 Fisher Rd., S.E.
Calgary, AB T2H 0W3
(403) 258–1775

MASKWACHEES CULTURAL COLLEGE
P.O. Box 360
Hobbema, AB T0C 1N0
(780) 585–3925

NAKODA FIRST NATION
NAKODA EDUCATION
P.O. Box 238
Morley, AB T0L 1N0
(403) 881–3591

OLD SUN COMMUNITY COLLEGE
P.O. Box 1250
Siksika, AB T0J 3W0
(403) 734–3862

PIIKANI POST SECONDARY ADULT AND
CAREER EDUCATION CENTRE
P.O. Box 130
Brocket, AB T0K 0H0
(403) 965–3910

RED CROW COMMUNITY COLLEGE
P.O. Box 1258
Cardston, AB T0K 0K0
(403) 737–2400

TSUU T'INA ADULT LEARNING CENTRE
250–9911 Chula Blvd.
Tsuu T'ina, AB T2W 6H6
(403) 238–6101

YELLOWHEAD TRIBAL COUNCIL EDUCATION
304–17304 105 Ave.
Edmonton, AB T5S 1G4
(780) 484–0303

# First Nations Post Secondary Schools with Aboriginal Studies Departments & Programs

DIAND's Indian Studies Support Program (ISSP) contributes funding to Indian educational organizations, Indian post-secondary institutions, and other post-secondary institutions for the development and delivery of special programs for treaty and status Indian students.

## ◆ ATLANTIC REGION

LETHBRIDGE COMMUNITY COLLEGE
3000 College Dr. S.
Lethbridge, Alta T1K 1L6
(403) 320-6444

## ◆ ALBERTA

GRANT MACEWAN COMMUNITY COLLEGE
Native Communications Department
P.O. Box 1796
10645 156th St.
Edmonton, AB T5P 2P2
(403) 483-2348

UNIVERSITY OF ALBERTA

School of Native Studies
11023 90th Avenue
Edmonton, AB T6G 1A6
(403) 492-2991

INDIGENOUS LAW PROGRAM
Faculty of Law
Fourth Floor, Law Center
Edmonton, AB T6G 2H5
(403) 492-7749

NATIVE HEALTH CARE CAREER PROGRAM
Anne-Marie Hodes, Coordinator
Faculty of Medicine
2J2.11 W.C. MacKenzie Sciences Center
Edmonton, AB T6G 2R7
(403) 492-6350

UNIVERSITY OF CALGARY
Native Studies Department
Calgary, AB T2N 1N4
(403) 220-6516

UNIVERSITY OF LETHBRIDGE
Department of Native American Studies
4401 University Drive
Lethbridge, AB T1K 3M4
(403) 329-2635

## ◆ BRITISH COLUMBIA

UNIVERSITY OF BRITISH COLUMBIA
First Nations House of Learning
The Longhouse
1985 West Mall
Vancouver, BC V6T 1Z2
(604) 822-8940

UNIVERSITY OF NORTHERN BRITISH COLUMBIA
First Nations Studies Program
3333 University Way
Prince George, BC V2N 4Z9
(250) 960-5595

UNIVERSITY OF VICTORIA
P.O. Box 1700
Victoria, BC V8W 2Y2
(604) 721-7424

## ◆ MANITOBA

BRANDON UNIVERSITY
Brandon University Northern Teachers Education Program (BUNTEP)
270 18th St.
Brandon, MB R3H 0J9
(204) 727-7315

YELLOWQUILL COLLEGE
831 Portage Avenue
Winnipeg, MB R3G 0N6
(204) 953-2800

## ◆ NEW BRUNSWICK

UNIVERSITY OF NEW BRUNSWICK
Micmac-Maliseet Institute
Faculty of Education
Marshall d'Avray Hall, Room 343
(506) 453-4840

## ◆ NORTHWEST TERRITORY

### ARCTIC COLLEGE
Nunatta Campus
P.O. Box 600
Iqaluit, NT X0A 0H0
(819) 979–1700

## ◆ NOVA SCOTIA

### UNIVERSITY COLLEGE OF CAPE BRETON
School of Community Studies
Department of Culture, Heritage & Leisure Studies
P.O. Box 5300
Sydney, NS B1P 6T2
(902) 539–5300

## ◆ ONTARIO

### ALGOMA UNIVERSITY
Anishinaabe Language program
1520 Queen Street East
Sault Ste. Marie, ON P6A 2G4
(705) 949–2301, ext. 215

### ANISHINABEK EDUCATIONAL INSTITUTE

P.O. Box 711
North Bay, ON P1B 8J8
(800) 334–3330

Thunder Bay Campus
RR #4, Site 6, Box 37
Fort William, ON P7C 4Z2
(807) 623–8887

Munsee-Delaware Campus
RR #1 Munsee-Delaware Nation
Muncey, ON M0L 1Y0
(800) 441–5904

### LAKEHEAD UNIVERSITY
Native Language Instructors Program
Thunder Bay, ON P7B 5E1
(807) 343–8054

### LAURENTIAN UNIVERSITY
Native Studies Department
University of Sudbury (federated with Laurentian)
Ramsey Lake Road
Sudbury, ON P3E 2C6
(705) 673–5661

### NATIVE TRAINING CENTER
269–201 Main St. W.
North Bay, ON P1B 2T8
(800) 267–2577

### NIPISSING UNIVERSITY
Faculty of Education
P.O. Box 5002
100 College Dr.
North Bay, ON P1B 8L7
(705) 474–3461, ext. 4522

### TRENT UNIVERSITY
Native Studies Department
Otonabee College
Peterborough, ON K9L 1Z8
(705) 748–1466

### UNIVERSITY OF TORONTO
Aboriginal Studies Program
Toronto, ON M5A 1A1
(416) 978–1290

## ◆ QUEBEC

### MCGILL UNIVERSITY
Office of First Nations and Inuit Education
3700 McTavish
Montreal, QB H3A 1Y2
(514) 398–4533

## ◆ SASKATCHEWAN

### SASKATCHEWAN INDIAN FEDERATED COLLEGE

National School of Dental Therapy
710–15th Avenue East
Prince Albert, SK S6V 7A4
(306) 763–8800

Northern Campus
P.O. Box 3003
1500–10th Avenue East
Prince Albert, SK S6V 6G1
(306) 763–0066

Regina Campus
College West 118
University of Regina
Regina, SK S4S 0A2
(306) 779–6200

Saskatoon Campus
710 Duke Street
Saskatoon, SK S7N 0P8
(306) 931–1800

## SASKATCHEWAN INDIAN INSTITUTE OF TECHNOLOGIES

Asimakaniseekan Askiy Reserve
100–103A Packham Avenue
Saskatoon, SK S7N 4K4
(306) 244–4444 in Saskatoon
(800) 667–9704

## UNIVERSITY OF SASKATCHEWAN

Department of Native Studies
104 McLean Hall
106 Wiggins Road
Saskatoon, SK S7N 5E6
(306) 966–6208

## ◆ YUKON

## MALASPINA UNIVERSITY-COLLEGE

For Arts One–First Nations
Nanaimo Campus
(250) 753–3245, local 2758

Cowichan Campus
(250) 748–2591, local 3528

## YUKON COLLEGE CAMPUS

Carcross Campus
Box 142
Carcross, YT Y0B 1B0
(867) 821–4296

Carmacks Campus
First Nations Administration Bldg.
Box 103
Carmacks, YT Y0B 1C0
(867) 863–5806

Dawson City Campus
Old Parks Administration Bldg.
Box 313
Dawson City, YT Y0B 1G0
(867) 993–5231

Faro Campus
Downtown Solar Complex
Box 59
Faro, YT Y0B 1K0
(867) 994–2832

Haines Junction Campus
Commissioner James Smith Administration
    Building
Box 5531
Haines Junction, YT Y0B 1L0
(867) 634–2688

Mayo Campus
J. V. Clark School
Box 250
Mayo, YT Y0B 1M0
(867) 996–2831

Old Crow
Box 96
Old Crow, YT Y0B 1N0
(867) 966–3065

Pelly Crossing Campus
Yukon College Campus Bldg.
Box 50
Pelly Crossing, YT Y0B 1P0
(867) 537–3131

Ross River Campus
The Blue Building
Box 102
Ross River, YT Y0B 1S0
(867) 969–2514

Teslin Campus
Teslin Tlingit Council Administration Building
Box 61
Teslin, YT Y0A 1B0
(867) 390–2650

Watson Lake Campus
College Annex, Watson Lake Secondary School
Robert Campbell Highway
Watson Lake, YT Y0A 1C0
(867) 536–2478

Yukon Native Teacher Education Program
Yukon College
Box 2799 (Courier address: 500 College Drive)
Whitehorse, YT Y1A 5K4
(867) 668–8781

## Cultural/Educational Centres and Institutes

NATIONAL COMMITTEE OF INDIAN
    CULTURAL EDUCATIONAL CENTRES
    (NAITC)
R.R. 3
Cornwall Island, ON K6H 5R7
(613) 932–9452

## ◆ ALBERTA

**BEAVER LAKE CULTURAL PROGRAM**
Bag 5000
Lac La Biche, AB T0A 2C0
(403) 623–4548

**FROG LAKE INDIAN BAND**
Frog Lake, AB T0A 1M0
(403) 943–3980

**KEHEWIN COMMUNITY EDUCATION CENTRE**
Box 6759
Bonnyville, AB T9N 2H2
(403) 826–6200

**NINASTAKO CULTURAL CENTRE**
Box 232
Standoff, AB T0l 1Y0
(403) 737–3774

**OLDMAN RIVER CULTURAL CENTRE**
P.O. Box 70
Brocket, AB T0K 0H0
(403) 965–3939

**SADDLE LAKE CULTURAL EDUCATION PROGRAM**
Box 102
Saddle Lake, AB T0A 3T0
(403) 726–3829

**SIKSIKA NATION CULTURAL EDUCATION CENTRE**
Box 1730
Siksika, AB T0J 3W0
(403) 734–5100

**STONEY NATION EDUCATION PROGRAM**
P.O. Box 120
Morley, AB T0l 1N0
(403) 881–3770

**SUU T'INA CULTURAL PROGRAM**
Box 135
3700 Anderson Rd. SW
Calgary, AB T2W 1N0
(403) 238–2677

## ◆ BRITISH COLUMBIA

**CANOE CREEK CULTURAL CENTRE**
Canoe Creek Indian Band
General Delivery
Dog Creek, BC V0L 1J0
(250) 440–5645

**COQUALEETZA CULTURAL EDUCATION CENTRE**
7201 Vedder Road, Building 21
P.O. Box 2370
Sardis, BC V2R 1A7
(604) 858–9431

**COWICHAN TRIBES**
5762 Allenby Road
Duncan, BC V9L 5J1
(250) 715–1022

**EN'OWKIN CENTRE**
Okanagan Indian Educational
Resources Society
257 Brunswick Street
Penticton, BC V2A 5P9
(250) 493–7181

**HEILTSUK CULTURAL EDUCATION CENTRE**
Box 880
Waglisla, BC V0T 1Z0
(250) 957–2626

**LAKE BABINE BAND EDUCATION AUTHORITY**
P.O. Box 879
Burns Lake, BC V0J 1E0
(250) 692–7555

**MOUNT CURRIE BAND XIT'OLACW COMMUNITY SCHOOL**
P.O. Box 193
Mount Currie, BC V0N 2K0
(604) 894–5424

**NUXALK CULTURAL CENTRE**
P.O. Box 65
Bella Coola, BC V0T 1C0
(250) 799–5613

**SAANICH NATIVE HERITAGE SOCIETY**
7449 West Saanich Road
P.O. Box 28
Brentwood Bay, BC V8M 1R3
(250) 652–5980

SECWEPEMC CULTURAL EDUCATION
SOCIETY
345 Yellowhead Highway
Kamloops, BC V2H 1H1
(250) 828–9779

SLIAMMON CULTURAL CENTER
R.R. #2, Sliammon Road
Powell River, BC V8A 4Z3
(604) 483–3996

STO:LO NATION CULTURAL PROGRAM
Sto:Lo Nation
Building #1–7201
Vedder Road
Chilliwack, BC V2R 4G5
(604) 824–5226

STONEY CREEK ELDERS CULTURAL
SOCIETY
Site 12, Comp. 15, R.R. 1
Vanderhoof, BC V0J 3A0
(250) 567–4916

T'LISALAGI'LAKW SCHOOL NAMGIS
FIRST NATION
P.O. Box 50
Alert Bay, BC V0N 1A0
(250) 974–5591

U'MISTA CULTURAL CENTRE
Box 253
Alert Bay, BC V0N 1A0
(604) 974–5403

◆ **MANITOBA**

BROKENHEAD OJIBWAY NATION
CULTURAL CENTRE
General Delivery
Scanterbury, MB R0E 1W0
(204) 766–2494

CROSS LAKE CULTURAL EDUCATION
PROGRAM
P.O. Box 10
Cross Lake, MB R0B 0J0
(204) 676–2218

DAKOTA OJIBWAY TRIBAL COUNCIL
300–340 Assiniboine Avenue
Winnipeg, MB R3C 1Y0
(204) 988–5383

INTERLAKE RESERVES TRIBAL COUNCIL
Pineimuta Place, General Delivery
Fairford, MB R0C 0X0
(204) 659–4465

KEESEEKOOWENIN CULTURAL PROGRAM
Keeseekoowenin First Nation
P.O. Box 100
Elphinstone, MB R0J 0N0
(204) 625–2004

MANITOBA INDIAN CULTURAL
EDUCATION CENTRE
119 Sutherland Avenue
Winnipeg, MB R2W 3C9
(204) 942–0228

NORWAY HOUSE FIRST NATION EDUCATION
AUTHORITY
Education Authority
P.O. Box 250
Norway House, MB R0B 1B0
(204) 359–6296

PEGUIS CULTURAL CENTRE
Box 10
Peguis, MB R0C 3J0
(204) 645–2359

ROLLING RIVER CULTURAL EDUCATION
PROGRAM
P.O. Box 145
Erickson, MB R0J 0P0
(204) 636–2211

SAGKEENG CULTURAL CENTRE INC.
Box 749
Pine Falls, MB R0E 1M0
(204) 367–2129

WEST REGION TRIBAL COUNCIL CULTURAL
EDUCATION PROGRAM
21–4th Avenue, NW
Dauphin, MB R7N 1H9
(204) 638–8225

◆ **NEW BRUNSWICK**

BIG COVE BAND COUNCIL
Site 11, Box 1
Big Cove, NB E0A 2L0
(506) 523–8200

BUCTOUCHE MICMAC BAND
R.R. #2, Box 9, Suite 1
Buctouche, NB E0E 1G0
(506) 743–6493

EEL GROUND INDIAN BAND
47 Church Road
Newcastle, NB E1V 4E6
(506) 627–4600

EEL RIVER BAR FIRST NATION
P.O. Box 896
Dalhousie, NB E0K 1B0
(506) 684–9916

FORT FOLLY CULTURAL EDUCATION
  CENTRE
P.O. Box 21
Dorchester, NB E0A 1M0
(506) 379–6224

KINGSCLEAR FIRST NATION
77 French Village
Fredericton, NB E3E 1K3
(506) 363–4010

METEPENAGIAG EDUCATION PROGRAM
P.O. Box 120
Red Bank, NB E0C 1W0
(506) 836–7669

OROMOCTO NATION
P.O. Box 417, R.R.#1
Oromocto, NB E2V 2J2
(506) 357–2083

PABINEAU INDIAN BAND
Box L, R.R. #5, Site 26
Bathurst, NB E2A 3Y8
(506) 548–9211

ST. MARY'S INDIAN BAND
35 Deadham Street
Fredericton, NB E3A 2V2
(506) 458–9511

TOBIQUE INDIAN BAND
P.O. Box 840
Perth, NB E0J 1V0
(506) 273–5400

◆ **NORTHWEST TERRITORIES**

DENE CULTURAL INSTITUTE
P.O. Box 3054
Hay River, NT X0E 1G4
(867) 874–8480

◆ **NOVA SCOTIA**

MICMAC ASSOCIATION FOR CULTURAL
  STUDIES
111 Membentoust
P.O. Box 961
Sydney, NS B1P 6J4
(902) 567–1752

WAGMATCOOK CULTURAL PROGRAM
Wagmatcook First Nation
P.O. Box 237
Baddeck, NS B0E 1B0
(902) 295–2598

◆ **ONTARIO**

BATCHEWANA FIRST NATION
Rankin Reserve
236 Frontenac Street, R.R. #4
Sault St. Marie, ON P6A 5K9
(705) 759–0914

LAKE OF THE WOODS OJIBWAY
  CULTURAL CENTRE
P.O. Box 159
Airport Road
Kenora, ON P9N 3X3
(807) 548–5744

NATIVE NORTH AMERICAN TRAVELING
  COLLEGE
R.R.# 3
Cornwall Island, ON K6H 5R7
(613) 932–9452

OJIBWAY & CREE CULTURAL CENTRE
210 Spruce Street, Suite 304
Timmins, ON P4N 2C7
(705) 267–7911

OJIBWE CULTURAL FOUNDATION
P.O. Box 278
West Bay Indian Reserve
Manitoulin, ON P0P 1G0
(705) 377–4902

ONYOTA'A:KA LANGUAGE AND
  CULTURAL CENTRE
R.R. #2
Southwold, ON N0L 2G0

WIKWEMIKONG INTERPRETIVE/HERITAGE
  CENTER
Wikwemikong Unceded Territory
P.O. Box 112
Wikwemikong, ON P0P 2J0

WOODLAND CULTURAL CENTRE
P.O. Box 1506
Brantford, ON N3T 5V6
(519) 759–2653

### ◆ PRINCE EDWARDS ISLAND

LENNOX ISLAND CULTURAL PROGRAM
Box 134, Lennox Island
Prince Edward Island C0B 1B0
(902) 831–2779

### ◆ QUEBEC

ALGONQUIN NATION PROGRAMS AND
  SERVICES SECRETARIAT
Box 367
Notre Dame Du Nord, PQ J0Z 3B0
(819) 723–2019

CENTRE CULTUREL AMIKWAN
Conseil De Bande Du Lac Simon
1011 Rue Amik-Awiche
Lac Simon, PQ J0Y 3M0
(819) 736–4501

CENTRE CULTUREL DE WANASKOADEMEK
102 Rue Waban-Aki
Odanak, PQ J0G 1H0
(514) 568–2810

CONSEIL DE LA NATION ALGONQUINE
  ANISHNABEG
314 Hill Street
Maniwaki, PQ J9E 2G7
(819) 449–1225

CONSEIL DE LA NATION ATIKAMEKW
317, St. Joseph
C.P. 848
La Tuque, PQ G9X 3P6
(819) 523–6153

CONSEIL DE LA NATION HURONNE-WENDAT
225 Place Chef Michel Laveau
Village Des Hurons, PQ G0A 4V0
(418) 843–3767

CONSEIL DES MONTAGNAIS
Du Lac St. Jean
Conseil Des Montagnais Du
Lac St. Jean
Siege Sociale
1671 Oulatchouan
Mashteuiatsh, PQ G0W 2H0

INSTITUT CULTUREL ET EDUCATIF
  MONTAGNAIS
100 Boul. Laure, Bureau 305.2
Uashat (Sept-Iles), PQ G0A 4V0
(418) 968–4424

JAMES BAY CREE CULTURAL CENTRE
Box 291
Chisasibi, PQ J0M 1M0
(418) 745–3931

KANEHSATAKE CULTURAL CENTRE
681 "C" Ste. Philomene
Kanehsatake, PQ J0N 1E0
(514) 479–1783

KANIEN'KEHAKA
RAOTITIOHKWA
KANATAKTA
Box 1988 (969)
Kahnawake, PQ J0L 1B0
(514) 638–0880

KITIGAN ZIBI EDUCATION COUNCIL
41 Kikinamage Mikan
Maniwaki, PQ J9E 3B1
(819) 449–1798

LISTUGUJ ARTS AND CULTURAL CENTRE
EDUCATION & CULTURAL DIRECTORATE
  EDUCATION COMPLEX
17 Riverside West
Listuguj, PQ G0C 2R0
(418) 788–2248

MICMACS OF GESGAPEGIAG BAND
P.O. Box 1280
Maria, PQ G0C 1Y0
(418) 759–3422

## ◆ SASKATCHEWAN

SASKATCHEWAN INDIAN CULTURAL
  CENTRE
205–103b Packham Ave.
Saskatoon, SK S7K 4K4
(306) 244–1146

## ◆ YUKON

CHAMPAGNE/AISHIHIK FIRST NATIONS
Box 5309

Haines Junction, YT Y0B 1L0
(867) 634–2288

TESLIN TLINGIT COUNCIL
P.O. Box 133
Teslin, YK Y0A 1B0
(867) 390–2532

YUKON INDIAN CULTURAL EDUCATION
  SOCIETY
11 Nisutlin Drive
Whitehorse, YK Y1A 3S5
(403) 667–4616

# Research Centers and Organizations

ALASKA NATIVE LANGUAGE CENTER
(ANLC)
University of Alaska, Fairbanks
Box 757680
Fairbanks, AK 99775–7680
(908) 474–7874

AMERICAN INDIAN CULTURE
RESEARCH CENTER
P.O. Box 98, Blue Cloud Abbey
Marvin, SD 57251–0098
(605) 432–5528

AMERICAN INDIAN INSTITUTE
University of Oklahoma
College of Continuing Education
555 Constitution Ave., Ste. 237
Norman, OK 73072–7820
(405) 325–4127
(800) 522–0772, ext. 4127

AMERICAN INDIAN LAW CENTER
P.O. Box 4456, Station A
Albuquerque, NM 87196
(505) 277–5462

AMERICAN INDIAN RESEARCH &
DEVELOPMENT, INC.
2424 Springer Dr., Ste. 200
Norman, OK 73069
(405) 364–0656

AMERICAN INDIAN RESEARCH
OPPORTUNITY
Montana State University
312 Roberts Hall
P.O. Box 173925
207 Culbertson Hall
Bozeman, MT 59717–3925
(406) 994–5847

AMERICAN INDIAN STUDIES RESEARCH
INSTITUTE
Indiana University
422 North Indiana Ave.
Bloomington, IN 47408
(812) 855–4086

THE AMERIND FOUNDATION, INC.
P.O. Box 400
Dragoon, AZ 85609
(520) 586–3666

ARROW, INC.
1000 Connecticut Ave., N.W., Ste. 1204
Washington, DC 20036
(202) 296–0685

CENTER FOR AMERICAN INDIAN RESEARCH
AND EDUCATION (CAIRE)
1918 University Ave., Ste. 3A
Berkeley, CA 94704–1024
(510) 843–8661

CENTER FOR INDIGENOUS STUDIES IN THE
AMERICAS (CISA)
1121 North 2nd St.
Phoenix, AZ 85004
(602) 253–4938

CENTER FOR WORLD INDIGENOUS
STUDIES (CWIS)
1001 Cooper Point Road SW
Suite 140–214
Olympia, WA 98502
(888) 286–2947

FIRST NATIONS DEVELOPMENT INSTITUTE
The Stores Bldg.
11917 Main St.
Fredericksburg, VA 22408
(540) 371–5615

FOUR WORLDS INTERNATIONAL INSTITUTE
FOR HUMAN AND COMMUNITY
DEVELOPMENT
1224 Lakemount Blvd.
Lethbridge, AB T1K 3K1
(403) 320–7144

INTERCULTURAL DEVELOPMENT RESEARCH
ASSOCIATION (IDRA)
5835 Callaghan Rd., Ste. 350
San Antonio, TX 78228–1190
(210) 684–8180

LABRIOLA NATIONAL AMERICAN INDIAN
DATA CENTER
Arizona State University
P.O. Box 871006
Tempe, AZ 85287–1006
(480) 965–6490

NATIONAL CENTER FOR AMERICAN INDIAN
ENTERPRISE DEVELOPMENT
953 E. Juanita Ave.
Mesa, AZ 85204
(480) 545–1298

NATIVE AMERICAN DEVELOPMENT
CORPORATION (NADC)
1000 Connecticut Ave., N.W., Ste. 1204
Washington, DC 20036
(202) 296–0685

NATIVE AMERICAN RESEARCH AND
TRAINING CENTER
University of Arizona
Department of Family and Community Medicine
1642 East Helen St.
Tucson, AZ 85719
(520) 621–5075

NATIVE AMERICAN RESEARCH
INFORMATION SERVICE (NARIS)
University of Oklahoma College of Continuing
Education
555 E. Constitution St., Bldg. 4, Ste. 237
Norman, OK 73072–7820
(800) 522–0772, ext. 4127

NATIVE AMERICAN TECHNOLOGIES,
INC. (NATEC)
3918 Prosperity Ave., Ste. 205
Fairfax, VA 22031
(800) 223–8624

ORBIS ASSOCIATES
1411 K St., N.W., Ste. 700
Washington, DC 20005–3404
(202) 628–4444

ROGER LANG CLEARINGHOUSE FOR
CIRCUMPOLAR EDUCATION
Education and Resources Group, Inc. (ERG)
162 Shawmut St.
Chelsea, MA 02150–3228
(800) 766–7653

## References

### Primary and Secondary U.S. Native Education

Adams, David Wallace. *Education for Extinction: American Indian and the Boarding School Experience, 1875–1928.* Lawrence, Kan: University Press of Kansas, 1995.

Adams, Evelyn C. *American Indian Education: Government Schools and Economic Progress.* New York: Kings Crown Press, 1946.

American Indian Policy Review Commission. Task Force Five. *Report on Indian Education: Final Report to the American Indian Policy Review Commission.* Washington, D.C.: GPO, 1976.

Beatty, Willard W., and Associates. *Education for Cultural Change.* Washington, D.C.: U.S. Department of Interior, Bureau of Indian Affairs, 1953.

Berry, Brewton. *The Education of American Indians: A Survey of the Literature.* Washington, D.C.: GPO, 1969.

Brookings Institution. Institute for Government Research. *The Problem of Indian Administration.* Baltimore, Md.: John Hopkins University, 1928. This work is commonly referred to as the *Merriam Report.*

California Department of Education. *The American Indian: Yesterday, Today, and Tomorrow: A Handbook for Educators.* Rev. ed. Sacramento: California Department of Education, 1991.

Center for Indian Education. ERIC Clearinghouse on Rural Education and Small Schools. *Trends in American Indian Education: A Synthesis and Bibliography of Selected ERIC Sources.* Tempe, Ariz.: Arizona State University; Las Cruces, N.M.: New Mexico State University, 1984.

Child, Brenda J. *Boarding School Seasons: American Indian Families, 1900–1940.* Lincoln: University of Nebraska Press, 1998.

Cleary, Linda Miller and Thomas D. Peacock. *Collected Wisdom: American Indian Education.* Boston: Allyn and Bacon, 1998.

Clinton, William J. "Executive Order 13096 of August 6, 1998: American Indian and Alaska Native Education." *Federal Register* 63 (August 6, 1998): 154.

Coombs, L. Madison. *The Indian Child Goes to School: A Study of Interracial Differences.* Lawrence, Kan.: U.S. Department of Interior, Bureau of Indian Affairs, 1958.

Costo, Rupert and Jeanette Henry. *Indian Treaties: Two Centuries of Dishonor.* San Francisco: Indian Historian Press, 1977.

Educational Equality Project. College Board. *Our Voices, Our Vision: American Indians Speak Out for Educational Excellence.* New York: Educational Equality Project, College Board; Boulder, Colo.: American Indian Science and Engineering Society, 1989.

Forbes, Jack D., ed. *California Indian Education: Report of the First All-Indian Statewide Conference on California Indian Education.* Modesto, Calif.: Ad Hoc Committee on California Indian Education, 1967.

Forbes, Jack D. *A Model for Improvement of Indian Education: The California Indian Education Association.* Berkeley: Ad Hoc Committee on California Indian Education, 1969.

Fuchs, Estelle and Robert J. Havighurst. *To Live on This Earth: American Indian Education.* Garden City, N.Y.: Doubleday, 1973.

Gilliland, Hap, et al. *Teaching the Native American.* Dubuque, Iowa: Kendall/Hunt, 1988.

Havighurst, Robert J. "Indian Education: Accomplishments of the Last Decade." *Phi Delta Kappan* 62, no. 5 (1981): 329–331.

Havighurst, Robert J. and Bernice L. Neugarten. *American Indian and White Children: A Sociopsychological Investigation.* Chicago: University of Chicago Press, 1955.

Henry, Jeanette and Rupert Costo, eds. *Textbooks and the American Indian.* San Francisco: Indian Historian Press, 1970.

Hirschfelder, Arlene. *Happily May I Walk: American Indians and Alaska Natives Today.* New York: Scribner's, 1986.

Indian Nations at Risk Task Force. *Indian Nations at Risk: An Educational Strategy for Action: Final Report.* Washington, D.C.: U.S. Department of Education, 1991.

McBeth, Sally J. "The Primer and the Hoe." *Natural History.* 93, no. 8 (1984): 4–12.

McDonald, Dennis, et al. "Stuck in the Horizon: A Special Report on the Education of Native Americans" *Education Week* Special issue, (August 2, 1989).

McKinley, Francis, Stephen Bayne and Glen Nimnicht. *Who Should Control Indian Education?* Berkeley: Far West Laboratory for Educational Research and Development, 1970.

Mihesuah, Devon A. *Cultivating the Rosebuds: The Education of Women at the Cherokee Female Seminary, 1851–1909.* Urbana, Ill.: University of Illinois Press, 1993.

O'Brien, Elaine M. "The Demise of Native American Education, Part I." *Black Issues in Higher Education* 7:1 (1990): 15–22.

———. "The Demise of Native American Education, Part II: A Foot in Each World: American Indians Striving to Succeed in Higher Education." *Black Issues in Higher Education* 7:2 (1990): 27–31.

———. "The Demise of Native American Education, Part III: Tribal Colleges Thrive Amid Hardship: Building Nations and Preserving Cultural Heritage." *Black Issues in Higher Education* 7:3 (1990): 34–36.

Rains, Frances V., and Karen Gayton Swisher. "Authentic Voices: Advice for Incorporating American Indians and Alaska Natives in the Elementary School Curriculum." *Social Education* 63, no. 1, (1999): 46–50.

Reyhner, Jon, ed. *Teaching the Indian Child: A Bilingual/Multicultural Approach.* Billings, Mont.: Eastern Montana College, 1986.

Reyhner, Jon, and Jeanne Eder. *A History of Indian Education.* Billings, Mont.: Eastern Montana College, 1989.

Swisher, Karen Gayton and John W. Tippeconnic, III, eds. *Next Steps: Research and Practice to Advance Indian Education.* Charleston, W.Va.: ERIC Clearinghouse on Rural Education and Small Schools, 1998.

Szasz, Margaret C. *Education and the American Indian: The Road to Self-Determination Since 1928.* 3rd ed., rev. and enl. Albuquerque: University of New Mexico Press, 1999.

———. *Indian Education in the American Colonies, 1607–1783.* Albuquerque: University of New Mexico Press, 1988.

———. "Listening to the Native Voice: American Indian Schooling in the Twentieth Century." *Montana* 39, no. 3 (1989): 42–53.

Thompson, Thomas, ed. *The Schooling of Native America.* Washington, D.C.: American Association of College for Teacher Education, 1978.

Thompson, Hildegard and Associates. *Education for Cross-Cultural Enrichment: Selected Articles from Indian Education, 1952–1964.* Washington, D.C.: U.S. Department of Interior, Bureau of Indian Affairs, 1964.

Tippeconnic, John, W., III. "American Indians: Education, Demographics, and the 1990s." In *U.S. Race Relations in the 1980s and 1990s: Challenges and Alternatives*, edited by Gail E. Thomas, 249–257. New York: Hemisphere Pub., 1990.

———. "Training of Teachers of American Indian Students." *Peabody Journal of Education* 61 no. 1 (1983): 6–15.

U.S. Department of the Interior. Bureau of Indian Affairs. *American Indians Today: Answers to Your Questions.* 3rd ed. Washington, DC: U.S. Department of the Interior, 1991.

U.S. National Advisory Council on Indian Education. *Toward the Year 2000: Listening to the Voice of Native America: 17th Annual Report to the U.S. Congress.* Washington, D.C.: GPO, 1990.

U.S. National Center for Education Statistics. *Characteristics of American Indian and Alaska Native Education: Results From the 1990–91 and 1993–94 Schools and Staffing Survey.* Washington, DC: GPO, 1997.

Wax, Rosalie H. and Robert K. Thomas. "American Indians and White People." *Phylon* 22 no. 5 (1961): 305–317.

*Karen Swisher and Tarajean Yazzie*

## U.S. Indian Higher Education

American Council on Education, Office of Minorities in Higher Education. *Minorities in Higher Education: 1999–2000, Seventeenth Annual Status Report.* Washington, D.C., 2000.

American Indian Higher Education Consortium and The Institute for Higher Education Policy. *Tribal College Contributions to Local Economic Development.* Washington, D.C., 2000.

———. *Tribal Colleges: An Introduction.* Washington, D.C., 1999.

American Indian Higher Education Consortium, The Institute for Higher Education Policy, and the Sallie Mae Education Institute. *Creating Role Models for Change: A Survey of Tribal College Graduates.* Washington, D.C.: 2000.

*American Indian Issues in Higher Education.* Los Angeles: American Indian Studies Center, UCLA, 1981.

Boyer, Paul. *Native American Colleges: Progress and Prospects.* Princeton, N.J.: Carnegie Foundation for the Advancement of Teaching, 1997.

Carnegie Foundation for the Advancement of Teaching. *Tribal Colleges: Shaping the Future of Native America.* Princeton, N.J., 1989.

Churchill, Ward. "White Studies or Isolation: An Alternative Model for Native American Studies Programs." In *American Indian Issues in Higher Education,* 19–33. Los Angeles: American Indian Studies Center, UCLA, 1981.

Fries, Judith E. *The American Indian in Higher Education, 1975–76 to 1984–85.* Washington, D.C.: Center for Education Statistics, Office of Educational Research and Improvement, U.S. Department of Education, 1987.

Fuchs, Estelle and Robert J. Havighurst. *To Live on This Earth: American Indian Education.* Garden City, N.Y.: Doubleday, 1972.

Garrod, Andrew, and Colleen Larimore. *First Person, First Peoples: Native American College Graduates Tell Their Life Stories.* Ithaca, N.Y.: Cornell University Press, 1997.

Justiz, Manuel, et al. *A Directory of Hispanic and American Indian Higher Education Programs.* Albuquerque, N.Mex.: College of Education, University of New Mexico, 1980.

Locke, Patricia. *A Survey of College and University Programs for American Indians.* Boulder, Colo.: Western Interstate Commission for Higher Education, 1978.

*Multicultural Education and the American Indian.* Los Angeles: American Indian Studies Center, UCLA, 1979.

Native American Information Center. *Indian College Programs.* Muskogee, Okla.: Bacone College, 1981.

Ortiz, Roxanne D., ed. *Final Report from the Round Table of Native American Studies Directors in Forming the Native American Studies Association.* Albuquerque, N.Mex.: College of Education, University of New Mexico, 1980.

Stein, Wayne J. *Tribally Controlled Colleges: Making Good Medicine.* New York : Peter Lang, 1992.

Thornton, Russell. "American Indian Studies as an Academic Discipline." *American Indian Culture and Research Journal.* 2, no. 3–4 (1978): 10–19.

U.S. American Indian Policy Review Commission. Task Force Five. *Report on Indian Education: Final Report to the American Indian Policy Review Commission.* Washington, D.C.: GPO, 1976.

U.S. Department of Education, National Center for Educational Statistics. *The Condition of Education.* Washington, D.C.: GPO, 1999.

U.S. Department of Education, National Center for Educational Statistics. *Digest of Educational Statistics 1998.* Washington, D.C.: GPO, 1999.

*Patrick Morris*
*Gerald Slater*
*Brigid O'Donnell*
*Michael O'Donnell*

## Canadian Native Education

Assembly of First Nations. *Tradition and Education: Toward a Vision of Our Future.* 3 vols. Ottawa, 1988.

Barman, Jean, Yvonne Hebert, and Don McCaskill, eds. *Indian Education in Canada.* 2 vols. Vancouver: University of British Columbia Press, 1986–1987.

Battiste, Marie, and Jean Barman, eds. *First Nations Education in Canada: The Circle Unfolds.* Vancouver: UBC Press, 1995.

Benton-Banai, Edward. *The Mishomis Book: The Voice of the Ojibway.* St. Paul: Red School House, 1988.

Canada. Ontario Ministry of Education. *Native Studies: Intermediate Division: Curriculum Guideline.* Toronto, 1991.

Canada. Ontario Ministry of Education. *People of Native Ancestry: Curriculum Guideline for the Senior Division.* Toronto, 1981.

Haig-Brown, Celia. *Resistance and Renewal: Surviving the Indian Residential School.* Vancouver: Tillacum Library, 1988.

Johnston, Basil H. *Indian School Days.* Toronto: Key Porter Books, 1988; Norman: University of Oklahoma Press, 1989.

Kehoe, John W. *A Handbook for Enhancing the Multicultural Climate of the School.* Vancouver, B.C.: Western Education Development Group, Faculty of Education, University of British Columbia, 1984.

LaRoque, Emma. *Defeathering the Indian.* Agincourt, Alta.: Book Society of Canada, 1975.

MacKay, Ronald and Lawrence Myles. *Native Student Dropouts In Ontario Schools.* Toronto: Ontario Ministry of Education, 1989.

McCue, H. A., ed. *Selected Papers from the First Mokakit Conference, July 25–27, 1984.* Vancouver: Mokakit Indian Education Research Association, Faculty of Education, University of British Columbia, 1986.

Miller, James Rodger. *Shingwauk's Vision: A History of Native Residential Schools.* Toronto: University of Toronto Press, 1996.

National Indian Brotherhood. *Indian Control of Indian Education: Policy Paper.* Ottawa, 1972.

Verrall, Catherine and Patricia McDowell, compilers. *Resource Reading List 1990: Annotated Bibliography of Resources By and About Native People.* Toronto: Canadian Alliance In Solidarity With the Native People, 1990.

*Donald McCaskill*

# 17

# *Economy*

♦ U.S. Indian Business and Enterprise  ♦ Modern Tribal Economic Development
♦ American Indian Labor
♦ An Overview of U.S. Government Assistance and Restitution to American Indians
♦ Aboriginal Economic and Business Activity in Canada
♦ Government Assistance and Restitution for Natives in Canada
♦ An Overview of Economic Development History on Canadian Native Reserves
♦ Economic Organizations  ♦ Native Owned Businesses
♦ Indian Gaming Casinos & Organizations

## ♦ U.S. INDIAN BUSINESS AND ENTERPRISE

In the five hundred years since the first contact between old and new worlds, the characteristics of world and local markets have changed. These changes help in understanding the changing conditions of Indian business. When the two worlds first met, their technologies were at similar levels, but had different capabilities and products. Europeans had long-distance transport capability over the world's oceans; Indians had long-distance transportation networks over land, based on the river network. Indians had advanced agricultural crops, such as corn, cotton, and potatoes. Gold, silver, and fur-bearing animals also existed in the new world. Europe could offer useful animal power, in horses, oxen, and cattle, as well as metal tools. Consequently, very productive trade could start immediately, as each side acquired the new products available from the other. The influx of gold and silver to Europe drove an expanding mercantile economy based on trade by merchants and large trading companies, within controls by governments of the time.

This mercantilist trading period lasted from 1500 to 1750, characterized by relative equality on the two sides. The Indian side diminished for a noneconomic reason—the loss of population due to disease. The European side grew because of its agricultural revolution, which during the 1700s consisted of rapid increases in agricultural productivity as potatoes were introduced to cold parts of Europe, and cropping patterns changed.

Partly as a consequence of the capital provided by the agricultural revolution and partly due to technological and organizational developments, the industrial revolution began in England in the middle of the eighteenth century. By 1750 England had discovered the usefulness of factory organization, had a productive agriculture, and had a trade network with the New World that could provide raw materials. England learned how to harness coal in the production of energy for factory production. It began to move toward less governmental control of trade.

The resulting industrial revolution changed the characteristics of the world market. Newly industrializing countries began rapid expansion of their market needs. Political power, armies, and navies were put to work securing sources of supply for the growing industrial center. In North America, conversion of land from its uses in the mercantile economy (food, furs, and forage) to commercial agriculture fueled a rapid growth in the geographic area of the United States. In the South, additional land was needed for cotton starting in the early 1800s for sale to English textile mills. In the North, timber could be used for building cities, and agriculture could produce food for those cities.

Until 1750 Indians retreated gradually from the Atlantic Coast. Even as late as 1800, Indians were holding their own militarily and economically with the European merchants. The industrial revolution created a juggernaut, however, that overwhelmed Indians over the course of the nineteenth century. In 1870 the United States had completed a rail network; Indian businesses were precarious. Indians lacked the political power to retain ownership of valuable resources and without a resource base their businesses shrank or failed to grow.

The expansion of the American economy continued in the twentieth century, with rapid growth having only one major setback, the Great Depression of the 1930s. World War II restarted the economic engine, which did not falter again until the mid-1970s, when the golden age of capitalism ended. In the 1970s, during the time of the two OPEC (an international alliance of oil-producing nations) oil embargoes, the rate of increase in worker productivity in the United States slowed suddenly and mysteriously. The price of energy rose for a time, which added to the difficulties. The economies of Asia, Africa, and Latin America became more important. Because the U.S. government overspent, the United States became a debtor nation as debt to foreign nations rose higher than the value of U.S. credit to foreign nations. The collapse of the Soviet Union in 1989, however, was followed by a revitalization of the American economy even as other regions of the world, including the former Soviet Union, continued to have economic difficulties. At the start of the new millienium, emerging ecological problems such as global warming present new difficulties to capitalism.

As the general American economy weakened, some American Indians began to develop businesses of their own within the newly changed system. The change in capitalism coincided with a political change, the acceptance of Indian self-government. By the late 1980s, as Indians began to assert greater control over their tribal governments, they began to control the economies on their reservations. The weakened U.S. capitalist market began to show niches into which Indian enterprise could squeeze. Indians began to hold onto their marketable natural resources (land, oil, minerals), and in some cases reclaim them, thus strengthening resource-based business. Tribes near large population-centers developed gaming enterprises in spite of opposition from state governments. Widespread economic growth on Indian reservations, however, has not occurred, because substantial barriers remain for non-gaming tribes. A major obstacle is U.S. government trust responsibility and regulatory control over Indian land and resources, which has resulted from two centuries of sustained subordination to industrial capitalist forces.

### The Consequences of Contact

American Indians had markets, meaning they traded goods, before contact with Europeans. Particular types of sea shells, called wampum, were used as money. Goods produced in one part of the continent have been found in homesites and old cities far from the place of production, such as Cahokia, a large city near present-day St. Louis, and many cities in what is now Mexico. In such trades, one type of good, such as pottery, was exchanged directly for another, such as leather. Trading also occurred in which money, in the form of processed strings of sea shells, would be obtained by selling one good and later used to purchase another.

When two different economies begin to trade with one another, both can benefit considerably. Trade with Europe opened up new possibilities for Indians. They could sell goods to be transported to Europe, and they could purchase useful European goods, particularly metal ones. A consequence of the opening of trade between Europe and the Native Americas was an increase in the income levels of both Europeans and Native Americans. The improved position of American Indians, however, was masked by the rapid depopulation that occurred as a result of disease. American Indians were unable to withstand large-scale epidemics of smallpox and other communicable diseases brought over by Europeans. Between 1500 and 1800, the Native population fell from more than 5 million to less than 1 million people. This freed a great deal of land for use by European colonists, whose population increased to 5 million.

### American Indians and the Mercantile Economy

Throughout the sixteenth century, Europe's economy grew as its merchants increased their levels of trading. The largest part of this pattern in North America was the sale of fur. Beaver was especially valuable, and both the French and English sought to purchase cured and processed beaver pelts from Indians.

During the entire mercantile era, three different ways of managing natural resources coexisted: community property, private property, and open-access. Indians conceived of a hunting area as the property of a whole community, which set up rules that limited the amount of harvest. Usually someone in a community who understood the resource advised everyone on its use. Lands between Indian community-controlled land were open-access areas. Europeans saw resources in one of two ways: either as private property, owned by an individual, or as open-access, in which anyone could take food without concern for resource limitations or traditional Indian hunting areas. The difficulty for Indians was to maintain their community control of hunting areas in the face of the open-access desires of Europeans. During the mercantile era, Indians were able to maintain their control to a great degree. Europeans, familiar only with the concepts of private property and open-access, failed to understand the management methods of the Native peoples. Because the words *enterprise* and *corporation* assume well-defined businesses based on private property, one must recognize that Indian business activity during this period was not organized as enterprises or corporations.

The nature of economic activity differed with the complexity of the Indian communities. Indian "enterprise" was connected to the family, clan, or town structure of each Indian nation. When families controlled territory, "business" was conducted by the family. When a town controlled a territory, business was conducted by the leadership of the town.

In the southeastern part of what became the United States, Indian tribes such as the Cherokee, Choctaw, Chickasaw, and Creek lived in towns. The chiefs of these towns collected a share of products from the members of the town and could use the corn, squash, and other products collected both to care for people who needed food and to trade for needed goods from Europe. They could buy from whichever European colony offered the best trade values, often alternating between trading with the French and English. Indians traded corn and deerskins, purchasing muskets, pots, axes, and blankets. By serving as economic intermediaries, chiefs maintained their political positions as well. They could distribute the European goods to the members of their towns. Indian society was based on giving and receiving gifts, with the leaders being those who gave the most.

Another example of community resource management was the hunting areas of the Cree east of James Bay in Canada. These were organized into family hunting areas, with a "boss" responsible for allocating harvest in each area. When beaver were valuable, the authority of the bosses increased. A non-family member could harvest for food, but the hide belonged to the family or group that controlled the area. At various trading posts, the hides were traded with Europeans for manufactured goods.

In the Pacific Northwest, land and resources were partitioned into areas controlled by "houses." The heads of these houses, the titleholders, regulated salmon harvest as well as other harvesting activities on the lands controlled by his or her house. Title-holding lineages maintained their resource management rights by hosting periodic feasts or potlatches in which they distributed significant amounts of goods to other titleholders. Prestige, power, and access to resources depended upon the ability to share the product of the land with other houses.

European and American approaches to resource-based business differed also in the methods used to distribute the product of hunts. Indians gave each other gifts. A successful hunter was obligated to share his good fortune with his community. Leaders in villages or towns were expected to give more gifts than other people. In the Pacific Northwest, the practice of gift-giving was conducted through potlatches. Indian gift-giving was not a one-way affair, however; the person receiving gifts became obligated to give gifts in return. In the European approach, individuals owned what they harvested. They sold, rather than gave away, surplus. Prestige and power came from owning and holding much property, not from giving it away.

In exchanging goods, both cultures came to understand the ways in which the other side traded. Europeans gave gifts in return for beaver, the amount of gifts being determined by prices set in the European market. Indians understood the effect of prices; if the French were giving fewer gifts for beaver pelts than the English, Indians would take their beaver pelts to the English.

During the mercantile era, Indians did not have to cede control of resources to Europeans. They harvested in their traditional hunting areas and traded furs, hides, and other products of the land for the clothing, guns, and tools available from Europe. Despite disease, Indian populations were equal to European populations. In particular areas of the continent, hunting by Europeans in Indian areas did lead to excessive harvests by both Indians and non-Indians. Some Indians also hunted in other Indians' areas without control. When no one had clear control of an area, its resources were in danger of overuse.

The distinctive feature of market organization in the mercantile era (1600–1750) is that Indian governments retained considerable power over large areas of North America. The European methods of organizing land use and trade, through private property and selling goods for prices determined by markets also under government control, were limited to coastal areas controlled by the colonial government. Indian methods of using land through community control were strong in other areas, where trade involved exchange of gifts. The area between was mixed, with both approaches compromising with each other, or simply competing for resources in an open-access manner.

## American Indians and the Industrial Revolution

The relatively even balance of power between non-Indian colonies and confederations of Indians, such as the Iroquois in New York or the Cherokee and Choctaw in the American South, began to change in the middle of the eighteenth century. Indian business remained based on agriculture and the products of wild lands, forest, and prairies. Non-Indian business increasingly began to

*How They Till the Soil and Plant* (1591). Drawing by Le Moyne from an engraving by Theodore de Bry, *America* part II, plate XXIII. (Public Domain)

be based on a growing industrial sector. The English used cotton and wool to weave new, cheaper, and better cloth. Textile mills were established in America as well. As the mills' ability to purchase cotton increased, plantation owners in the South began to expand their operations.

The Cherokee in Georgia managed to stay in their homeland for many decades after the Industrial Revolution. They developed plantations, selling cotton also. They built a strong economy on their own lands, which made neighbors envious. Non-Indians developed a pattern of using military force to remove Indians, enabling them to take over Indian enterprises and land. This happened throughout the South. The policy of removal, formally adopted by the United States in 1830, allowed forceful removal of Indians from the entire Eastern United States to areas across the Mississippi River, in present-day Oklahoma and Kansas.

By 1850 Indians in different parts of North America had different types of market relationships with non-Indians. In the West and Pacific Northwest, the pattern of trade that had existed during the mercantile era continued. Indians sold food, furs, and deerskins for manufactured goods. But population pressure from the expanding United States had forced many Indian nations onto lands west of the Mississippi River. They had to turn to agriculture and developed large herds of cattle and horses. Indian enterprise consisted of family activities confined to these new lands.

Later in the nineteenth century, non-Indians entered lands controlled by Indians; common pool management changed from community property to an open-access system. Indians had been able to protect resource stocks against extinction by limiting harvests. Where anyone, Indian or non-Indian, could harvest buffalo, for instance, large herds were wiped out, and by 1890 the American bison narrowly escaped extinction.

The industrial era right after the Civil War coincided with the establishment of many reservations, exclusively for Indian occupancy. They offered the possibility of development of Indian enterprise, based on indigenous organizational principles. The process of reservation development ended abruptly in the late 1880s. Congress passed the General Allotment Act, which authorized the division of reservation lands among the Indians living on the reservation and supposedly imposed ownership of private property as a way to manage land. The amount of land given to each Indian was small, between forty and 160 acres. Many families found that their parcels of land were not contiguous. In addition, Indians did not have the funds to purchase the cattle or farm equipment needed.

Non-Indians moved onto the reservations, and they had advantages in the industrial economy. They had access to equipment and money for economic investment. The court system was on their side. Non-Indians usually controlled the stores on reservations. As a result, non-Indians established farms more easily than Indians. This was a period in which Indian enterprise had great difficulty. Individual Indians found working as laborers in non-Indian businesses easier than operating their own firms.

Patterns established during this period on agricultural reservations remained in place at the end of the twentieth century. Lands were allotted to individuals during the period from 1887 to 1934. On reservations such as the Umatilla Reservation in Oregon, the Crow Reservation in Montana, and many Sioux reservations, the result was severely checker-boarded land, because it had been divided among several joint owners, the descendants of an original allottee. Since the joint Indian owners owned such small portions of land, the Bureau of Indian Affairs (BIA) leased many of these individual allotments in large groups to non-Indian ranchers and farmers, who thereby gain actual control over much of the best grazing and agricultural land on the reservations.

In the Pacific Northwest, Indians who had lived by harvesting salmon found that very few salmon were surviving long enough to reach the fishing sites they traditionally used. Non-Indians, using boats, harvested at sea and caught the fish first. By mid-century, Indians were pushed out of the fishery, and states justified limiting Indian river-mouth harvesting by appeals to conservation.

A few tribal enterprises, such as the Menominee lumber mill in Wisconsin, managed to survive the allotment era; but these are special cases, dependent on favorable political circumstances. Because of support from a senator and because they had forested lands, the federal government did not force the Menominee to divide up the land. This is in contrast to the Quinault Reservation in Washington, where pressure from some Indians assigned to the reservation, not Quinaults, forced division of the forested lands among everyone. The consequence was massive clear-cuts of timber,

encouraged by the Bureau of Indian Affairs, and little development of Indian enterprise based on the forest.

In summary, the expansion of the industrial revolution throughout North America from 1750 to 1930 caused massive declines in Indian land ownership and business activity. Indians were denied an opportunity to participate in the expanding industrial economy because non-Indians obtained ownership of the most productive lands. Even after enormous Indian land cessions occurred, with reservations remaining, the reservation lands were often entered and partially conveyed to non-Indians. Commercial agriculture on irrigated lands was primarily non-Indian. Indians were left on the margins, as ranchers, laborers on commercial farms, and workers in non-Indian enterprises.

Although formal transfers of land to non-Indians decreased dramatically in the 1930s, because of the Indian Reorganization Act of 1934 (IRA), other forms of transfer grew in importance. Energy companies leased Indian land for oil and gas, and timber companies purchased Indian timber. Commercially valuable locations were leased with fifty- and one hunded-year leases at low rental rates. The federal government inundated tribal lands with water from reservoirs behind federally owned dams. While title to land remained held in trust for Indians, Indians had little control over the land and its resources.

## American Indian Enterprise in the Post-Golden Age Era

During difficult times for the dominant capitalist economy, such as in the 1930s and from the mid 1970s to the mid 1990s, Indian enterprise was able to advance. When the general economy shrinks, pressure at the edges is reduced. Even though marketing products is difficult when the general economy is weak, the reduction of competition from non-Indians opens opportunities for Indians. Indian enterprise survives if it can become well-established in niches in the world economy. These niches are created by resource endowment, Indian skills, or jurisdictional openings. Examples of resource endowments are tribal timber stands and the presence of oil and gas reserves under reservation lands such as the Osage Reservation in Oklahoma. Indian skills support jewelry production in the Southwest. Smoke shops, which sell cigarettes without state tax, bingo halls, and casinos can operate because of jurisdictional openings that restrict application of state law to reservation governments and communities.

In 1987 the U.S. Census Bureau estimated that approximately 60,000 Indian firms existed throughout the United States. In 1992 the number of American Indian firms had risen to 103,386. The Census Bureau found an

A Navajo shepherd makes his living raising sheep, which are used to make the world-famous Navajo rugs. (Photo by Sara Wiles)

additional 2,738 Aleut-managed firms and 4,493 firms run by Inuit. In its economic censuses, the Census Bureau defines *firm* narrowly: nonagricultural business activities operated by individuals who declared business income on their federal tax form. All Indians are subject to federal income tax if they earn enough income. To become a potential respondent to the bureau's survey, individuals had to have enough income to require submission of the income tax form and had to be identifiable as Indian in some way. The survey form was sent to 21,380 American Indians and Alaska Natives. The Census Bureau estimated that an additional 31,600 nonagricultural firms were not identified. Agricultural firms were counted in the census of agriculture, which reported 7,134 Indian-owned farms and ranches in 1987, and 8,346 such farms in 1992. These numbers are included in the totals above.

The census definition of *firm* excludes corporations, including tribal corporations, as well as enterprise operated directly by tribal governments. A tribal corporation is not operated directly by a tribal government, since it has a board of directors between the

manager and the tribal council. Nonprofit corporations, such as the intertribal organizations concerned with assisting tribal enterprise, were also not counted. The Council of Energy Tribes (CERT), for instance, would not have been counted in this survey. CERT assists tribal groups that have mineral or energy resource endowments to manage and market their holdings. Economic activity organized in traditionally Indian ways, such as through family hunting activities, would be counted only if an Indian head of household sold products and reported them as sales receipts on a federal tax form.

In spite of these omissions, the 1987 survey provided information about Indian economic activity. (In 1992 Indians and Alaskan Native data by industry was combined with data on Asian and Pacific Islanders.) The 60,114 individually owned and operated firms were primarily in agriculture, forestry and fisheries, construction, retail trade, and services. These businesses consist of farmers, ranchers, logging truck operators, salmon fishers, carpenters, electricians, owners of small retail shops, accountants, and other enterprises typical of single-owner firms in a capitalist economy. The ranchers, farmers, and loggers are primarily located on reservations. Those with more mobile jobs, such as long-haul truckers, construction workers, and providers of services could be anywhere, on or off reservations. Because these firms are so diverse and are everywhere, specific information on them is difficult to obtain and hard to summarize. About 9,000 of the 21,000 firms surveyed had one or more employees other than the owner of the firm, indicating that most Indian firms are small.

How have Indians managed to create more than 100,000 firms by 1992? Many of the on-reservation firms were developed during the industrial era. Indians retained control of range land and timber land. As a result, individuals established ranches, and a great many Indians own herds of cattle. Some individuals worked as loggers, selling their harvesting and transport services to non-Indian firms that purchased timber sale contracts for tribally owned timber. Work maintaining the productivity of the forest—thinning, planting, controlled burning—could be done with subcontracts to the federal government under buy-Indian regulations, which mandate that government contracts for work on or near Indian reservations be awarded to Indian firms or laborers.

On allotted reservations, where small parcels of land are jointly owned by many individuals, few Indians were able to succeed as farmers. Although some Indian farmers had equipment and land needed to operate at a large enough scale to do well, the general pattern remained—the legacy of allotment was that non-Indian farming operations dominated use of productive land, even if it was Indian owned.

Another area that developed for Indians was manufacture of jewelry. On the Zuni and Hopi reservations particularly, distinctive styles developed that generated a large market. As a result, individual artisans pursued jewelry making. Other artistic pursuits, such as pottery, painting, and beadwork, also provided ways to earn a living.

A new development in recent times is tribal self-determination, where tribal governments increasingly make decisions without interference from the BIA. This opportunity creates ways for tribal government to encourage development of private and tribal enterprises. To do so, an Indian tribe must overcome a substantial number of barriers inherited from earlier periods. The administration of Indian affairs was purposely set up in ways that removed Indian control over their own resources and territory. In order to develop economically, a tribe needs to restructure its polity and economy in ways that benefit Indians rather than non-Indians. This is a long and hard struggle, not made

easier by the high levels of unemployment, extensive poverty, and dependence on U.S. government sources for support and survival.

If it wishes to support business, a tribe must reorient its government toward support of economic enterprise. The key general principle is to provide a climate of relative certainty and stability. If a tribal court system will enforce contracts made by Indians, then an Indian can promise to repay a loan and be believed. If a non-Indian bank takes an Indian entrepreneur into tribal court, and the Indian in fact does owe the bank money, the tribal court makes him pay. When that happens, banks are willing to support individual Indians who are able to make money in business. This has happened on some reservations. Among the Confederated Salish and Kootenai Tribes of the Flathead Indian Reservation in western Montana, the tribal council respects an independent judiciary, where court decisions are not unduly pressured by private or government intervention. A great deal of economic development on the Flathead Reservation occurs as private enterprise by tribal members. There are smoke shops, retail stores, construction companies, logging operations, restaurants, ranches, and farms. The private sector is probably stronger than the public sector, which consists of about three tribal enterprises.

In the Southwest, tribes needed to obtain control of water and to regain control of land leased to non-Indians. In the Pacific Northwest, Indians needed to regain the right to fish. Tribes owning oil, gas, and minerals needed to obtain better prices for their resources or better enforcement of leases already made by the federal government. The Passamaquoddy and Penobscot in Maine succeeded in regaining title to 300,000 acres of land in Maine as well as $80.6 million to offset claims to additional land.

The immediate consequence of tribal success in the legal area is an increase in opportunity for Indian enterprise. Tribes that had lost their right to fish were able to develop new fishing enterprises. In Washington State, under the Boldt decision, the federal courts upheld Indian treaty rights to half of all salmon entering Washington state rivers. In the Southwest, tribes who won water rights were able to develop agricultural activities. The Navajo set up the Navajo Agricultural Products Enterprise, a large-scale, irrigated farming operation south of Farmington, New Mexico. It is the largest of the tribal farming enterprises. Others exist in Arizona, with the AkChin enterprise on the AkChin Reservation particularly well known. These farms use as much equipment and advanced technology as any industrial farming operation in the United States.

The development of separate jurisdictional space on reservations allowed the development of two special kinds of businesses: smoke shops and gambling enterprises. Both businesses present economic opportunity because they are not subject to state law on the reservation. The U.S. Constitution and many legal decisions uphold direct federal and Indian government relations, while excluding state jurisdiction over Indian affairs. For cigarette sales, individual Indians set up retail stores selling cigarettes without charging state taxes, thus having lower prices and higher volume sales. States objected and took the cases to court. The result of the cases was that tribal governments had to intervene and regulate cigarette sales in order to protect the rights of individual reservation entrepreneurs. As a result in the 1970s many Indians were able to get started in retail sales. Many smoke shops have grown into full-service convenience stores, selling food and gasoline, renting video-tapes, and offering gambling machines to the general public. Battles between states and tribes over cigarette sales continue, however, because states think up new ways to attempt to tax the cigarettes.

Another continuing battle occurs over gambling. The same jurisdictional void that allows cigarette sales also provides a space for tribes to engage in gambling. The first establishments were large bingo halls. The Seminole tribe of Florida, located near Miami, set up a bingo operation that drew huge crowds. Other tribes near large population centers rapidly followed. The courts left the operations open and established the rule that a tribe could do anything that a state permitted, even if the state limited the activity severely. Many states allowed charitable organizations to use bingo as money-raising programs. Indians expanded the bingo games to enormous sizes. State opposition created federal legislation, which required that states and tribes write compacts to regulate gambling on reservations. The principle that a tribe could engage in any type of gambling that was allowed under state law remained in the legislation.

The data from the survey by the Bureau of the Census found substantial numbers of Indian firms in the categories that include smoke shops: food stores (895) and miscellaneous retail stores (5,350). These counts exclude tribal enterprise. All tribes that are running gambling operations should be added to the 1,476 private Indian firms providing amusement and recreation services.

The Nez Percé tribe in Idaho obtained the right to purchase timber from their own lands, enabling them to resell the timber for higher prices than the Bureau of Indian Affairs was receiving, by shipping logs to Japan. Other tribes, such as the White Mountain Apache Tribe and the Confederated Tribes of the Warm Springs Reservation, owned lumber mills that cut tribal timber.

A visitor to the Navajo Reservation would see all types of Indian enterprise. Individual Indians make jewelry and sell the jewelry in roadside stands. They have sheep herds and continue to make wool rugs. The tribe once operated a lumber mill, and at the end of the twentieth century operated an electric utility, a large farming operation, and many small enterprises. Individuals had smoke shops near the borders. The old pattern, in which non-Indians operated the retail shops and the trading posts, was superseded by large retail outlets. On the Navajo Reservation, these are in some cases operated by outside companies. But individual Indians are also operating retail stores.

The White Mountain Apache Reservation in Arizona has a ski resort, a lumber mill, a casino, a construction company, many retail outlets, and a tribal herd of cattle. The White Mountain Apache, much more than many other tribes, have organized their economy with tribal enterprise.

Alaska presents some major differences from the rest of the United States. The relationship between tribal governments and enterprise are different because of the Alaska Native Claims Settlement Act (ANCSA) of 1971. This act settled Alaska Native land claims, left Alaska Natives with 44 million acres, and created thirteen regional for-profit corporations and about two hundred village corporations. Unlike in the rest of the United States, Alaska Natives have been forced to organize their economic enterprises as profit-making corporations. The Census Bureau survey identified four thousand American Indian and Alaska Native firms in Alaska in 1987. Because of the definitions used in the census survey, none of the thirteen regional or more than two hundred village corporations created by ANCSA should have been counted in the survey. Even if they were, there is considerable business enterprise in Alaska by Natives that is outside of the corporations set up by the ANCSA.

Between 1971 and 1989, the regional corporations did not have good profit records. Considerable debate has occurred about the causes of the poor performance; and the debate is nearly unresolvable with the information presently available. On one hand, the corporations were not set up like normal corporations in the capitalist world, because shares could not be sold. Supporters of capitalism point to this flaw as a complete explanation for the poor performance. On the other hand, the corporations also did not have clear title to their land for many years. Even after obtaining title, subsurface and surface rights are held by regional and village corporations, respectively. They do not have shareholders experienced in methods of corporate governance. Corporate structures cost at least

$100,000 a year to administer. The corporations have been involved in many legal battles concerning the authority of other federal agencies, such as the Securities and Exchange Commission, to regulate their behavior. Village corporations are more concerned with preserving subsistence rights, while regional corporations are profit oriented. This creates disagreement between long-term goals of sustainable resource management and short-term goals for profits. The complexity of circumstances surrounding Alaska Native corporations makes it difficult to determine which are the true causes of poor performance.

Starting in 1992, the Northern Pacific Fisheries Council allocated a portion of the fish harvested from the Bering Sea to Alaska Native communities. The communities formed six Community Development Corporations, which were financed with quotas from the fishery; hence the program was called the Community Development Quota program (CDQ). Building on lessons learned from the failures and problems with Alaska Native Corporations under the settlement act, the new corporations utilized village governing structures instead of creating entirely new entities. The State of Alaska provided initial financial and management oversight, creating incentives for good management. The CDQ program created considerable community participation in economic development and benefited Alaskan Natives living on the Bering Sea.

### Conclusion

Historic and contemporary individual and tribal entrepreneurs on Indian reservations are inseparable from political events and political development. In the mercantile era, tribal political power protected traditional economic organization. The struggle over Indian property dates from the expansion of capitalism to reservations. Often legal rights were retained by Indians, in the process of ceding actual control over resources. This political history then colors all development activities. Tribes are fighting to regain control of reservation resources and to maintain or expand their powers to regulate economic activity on reservations.

When a tribe makes progress toward regaining control over reservation resources, it then can create a framework of relative security regarding government policy in order to allow economic development to occur. A stable judicial system can support development of individual Indian businesses. Clear divisions of power between council, judiciary, and chairman within a tribal government can support tribal enterprise. Because many tribes place maintenance of political

autonomy and cultural distinctiveness equal in importance to economic development, some types of economic activity are limited, especially if outside interests are involved.

At the end of the twentieth century, the weakening of capitalism as a political force on reservations has allowed tribes to establish institutions that combine capitalist ideas with traditional Indian ones. While the hybrid institutions are not a return to pre-1750 patterns, they are distinctly Indian in their formulation.

*Ronald L. Trosper*
*Northern Arizona University*

### ◆ MODERN TRIBAL ECONOMIC DEVELOPMENT

Within the United States a large number of distinct cultures are present among the aboriginal population. However, these populations face severe social and economic problems due to past treatment by the federal government. As a result, many of the distinct values and traditional practices of Native American tribes are threatened. But hope is available and cultural, social, and economic progress is being made. As such, a manifest imperative in Indian Country is maintaining the cultures and strengthening sovereign powers. One of the methods of achieving this goal is developing tribal resources within a cultural context. Modern tribal governments face the challenges of moving their communities from the status quo of high unemployment rates, low educational achievement levels, and serious social problems.

Many scholars maintain that economic development is a means to the end of sustaining tribal character, and as such it is vital to formulate all development plans with an understanding of how they impact the overall societal makeup. Only when the individual tribe has control of its resources and sustains its identity as a distinct civilization does economic development make sense; otherwise, the tribe must choose between cultural integrity and economic development. A common misconception involves the seeming conflict between maintaining a tribe's cultural heritage and increased economic activity on the reservation. However, it has been shown that developing the economy increases the potential for strengthening and developing the tribal culture.

The economy is the production mechanism of society. Economic activity is not the end result of anything; rather it is the engine that drives society to higher culture levels. The quest is to design an economic structure that allows the rest of society to maintain its cultural integrity and develop new and improved methods of living. In many cases, the cultural issues outweigh economic activity.

Tribes are interested in developing their economies as a means to self-determination. In other words, developing natural and human resources can strengthen their culture. Clearly, conflicts between culture and economic activity can arise, but this is the common vision only because past development strategies have either been conducted by outside interests for the benefit of outsiders, or the strategies were designed with the goal of assimilating the tribes into the mainstream capitalist styled economy. What is necessary is a rethinking of the potential gains from activities designed by and for Native Americans, while reducing the negative aspects of those activities. These gains include increasing opportunities for and interest by tribal members in their traditions, heritage, language, and identity. Reducing the negative aspects includes designing environmentally sound and culturally sensitive activities. This combination of more positive and fewer negative conditions aims the community toward cultural development as a result of the economic development. This is the first step in achieving healthy communities.

Cultural development involves an ever-evolving system of cultural subsystems, including the spiritual, economic, familial, and ceremonial, among others. This dynamic collection of subsystems and the compatibility among the various sectors defines not only the society as a whole, but also the individuals within that society. This social compatibility paradigm dictates that these subsystems are always changing to bring about a compatible equilibrium. Understating the situation on many Native American reservations, the current cultural system has spiraled downward due to federal policies and governance. The main reason for the current situation is the fact that these societies have undergone drastic changes in several vital subsystems. Most importantly, the federal interference in these communities essentially destroyed many economic and political subsystems. Instead of progressive change being determined within the existing culture, the changes came about as imposed changes by outsiders. One current challenge is to reinvigorate the economic subsystem to help elevate the culture systems of indigenous communities.

Economic development is the engine for overall social development. As Native America integrates into the global economy, decisions have to be made regarding economic activity such that a cohesive structure develops within a cultural context. Using these terms,

we can think of culture as holding together the communities on reservations. The shared property and common experiences provide the feeling of connectedness. Tribal governments are in positions to either better improve the overall community, or cause increased isolation among their members. The social difficulties together with continued isolation extend the problems facing tribal governments. Alternatively, activities that increase the feelings of community, specifically economic ones improve the overall social structure.

## The Economic Development Process

It is very important to understand that economic development—the development of jobs and incomes—is a complex process. Instead of looking at a single project at a time, an overall plan of action must be viewed to understand how the different pieces fit together. The development process can be thought of as a cycle of four stages. Although it is not necessary that all four stages occur for any one community, the stages do tend to lead from one to the next. It is also important to recognize that once set into action, the different stages can—and usually do—occur simultaneously in different directions. For simplicity, these four stages can be termed *import earning, import-replacing, development of new and better products,* and *export generation.*

The first stage of the cycle of growth involves an initial export industry earning imports. At first glance it might be said that an economy facing an excess of a 50 percent unemployment rate and the concomitant dire poverty does not have many such export industries; however, reservation economies clearly have the ability to import products. Tribes do earn revenues from extractive enterprises such as mines, forestry projects, and water sales. Other tribal and private enterprises provide some degree of earnings. A variety of federal, state, and tribal government activities provide additional employment. Besides these salaries, royalties, and profits earned from tribal activities, other major sources of funds are transfer payments and trust account earnings. Recently, many tribes have begun to earn imports with the profits from their gaming facilities. In a few cases, these profits are substantial. Therefore most tribes do satisfy the requirement of earning imports. Moreover, residents typically purchase private imports from the border towns on day trips. Thus, the first stage of the cycle is initially satisfied.

The second stage, and one of primary importance in the current context, is the development of import-replacing industries within the local economy. In this stage the reservation economy begins to produce locally hitherto imported products. The import-replacing phase allows for a drastic reduction of the leakages to

An Anishinabe man and woman gather wild rice from a canoe in Minnesota. (Courtesy of the Minnesota Historical Society)

border communities. In terms of reservation economies, this primarily means an increase in retail and service activity. An extension of this idea is the advent of actually producing some of the products previously imported.

Two of the best examples of this import-replacement can be seen within the economies of the Hualapai and Navajo nations. Both of these First Nations have made specific efforts at developing the retail sectors within their communities. So now instead of driving many miles to border towns, residents can shop at local stores for groceries and other such items. Another example is Cochiti Pueblo where they opened a laundromat in the early 1990s. This new facility was soon overwhelmed with business.

Another important avenue for import-replacing is the local provision of services such as plumbing, electrical, and construction. Some reservations are developing their own road divisions for paving and repairing road systems. Other examples include hair care, accounting and tax services and all the other types of services available in non-reservation communities.

The import replacement phase expands the understanding that trade patterns should follow well-known economic fundamentals. Reducing transport distances, and developing new and improved technology—not to mention lowered wage rates on the reservation—may well allow a tribe to import-replace some previously imported products at a cost savings. The problem is to properly identify those products that can be successfully produced by the tribe, which of course is the question any development plan must answer. Regional science analysis has produced various techniques to help determine the sectors and industries potentially ripe for expansion, but these problems are beyond the scope of the current discussion. Clearly, the activities to be import-replaced are reservation specific, but once the products and services are identified and the tribe begins to domestically produce the product, it is then possible that the direction of the trade actually reverses through the process, which is the next stage in the cycle.

The third stage involves developing new and innovative products and production techniques during the import-replacing phase. For example, modern Navajo arts and crafts industries include world-renowned techniques for weaving and silversmithing. Techniques for dying, spinning, and weaving wool have progressed from rudimentary ones to advanced techniques allowing for intricate designs and patterns. Originally, Navajos developed these industries for domestic consumption of blankets and jewelry; however, these industries are now significant sources of income for individual artisans and the tribally managed Navajo Arts and Crafts Enterprise.

The fourth stage encompasses developing these new techniques and products into new export industries, which provide increased or substitute import earning income. At this stage, the process cycles: new import-replacing takes place, which develops new products, which cultivates a new phase of exports. Thus a cycle of vigorous growth is obtained.

A community can become involved with the development process by engaging in a series of strategies that lead to a more prosperous future. In order for the process to be successful all that is necessary is for a community to be a cohesive entity as a central identity. Nowhere is this identity more pronounced than on and near reservations. Political borders are unimportant in the development process, except for defining sovereignty, and legal and tax systems and their impacts. What makes a reservation and the border towns a cohesive whole is the cultural and economic linkages existing within a definable region with a definable population. The development cycle begins with no other precondition other than an initial earning of imports, which currently occurs within reservation economies.

Growth and development are a process, and not a static burst of energy. Explosive episodes in Indian Country will start small and grow over time. The initial episode will likely evolve over the next fifteen to twenty years. This follows 100 to 500 years of stagnation and deterioration during the periods of colonization and federal oversight.

Growth occurs from the import-replacing and export development process due to five interwoven considerations. First, as import-replacing occurs an increased number and diversity of employment opportunities develop. Second, as employment earnings increase and the multiplier effect obtains, the region has enlarged import markets providing imports of new and different kinds. Third, as activity and employment increases, jobs and activity spread throughout the community, thereby increasing economic activity in the surrounding areas. Fourth, as the process continues there will be new uses for existing technology and new technological developments as entrepreneurial activity occurs. And last, as the process proceeds and new businesses are opened, there will be an increase in the capital stock of the community. These five forces of growth lead to increased economic activity and employment, and lead towards the development of the cycling of growth: new exports earning increased and new imports.

## Constraints on Growth

While it is difficult to generalize across such a wide range of different cultures and events, it does seem evident that the policies of the federal government toward Native Americans have not reflected a sincere concern for Indian communities or their economic interests. On the contrary, federal government regulations and management have inhibited Indian use of human and natural resources for economic growth.

It is possible to identify the several important factors constraining reservation development: (1) fluctuating federal policies, such as containment of most Indian people on reservations, the division of tribal communal lands into small private allotments (the General Allotment Act of 1887 and others), reconstitution of tribes by the Indian Reorganization Act of 1934, termination of reservations during the 1950s, and self-determination, have led to fragmented resources and populations; (2) loss of self-sufficiency and imposed dependency on the federal government through Indian wardship to the Bureau of Indian Affairs (BIA) led to mismanagement of resources and loss of local control; (3) lost self-esteem through cultural genocide brought about by European-based education in schools and the conversion of many Indians to Christianity and other non-Indian worldviews led to cultural incoherence; (4) low expectations based on a history of U.S. interference under laws created to divest Indians of their land and resources further reduced the economic and social assets of the communities; (5) lack of access to capital for investing in productive economic ventures limits potential development; (6) disrupted political institutions that breed nepotism and politicize economic management cause instability and limit long-term planning; (7) subjugated and impoverished reservation communities that do not foster success, social acceptance, and cultural identity among school age populations reduce educational achievement; and (8) bureaucratic and political stultification of initiative resulted in generations of frustrated and restrained tribal leaders.

School board members tour the construction site of a new school building on the Wind River Reservation. (Photo by Mike McClure)

### Current Economic Activities

Although much of Indian history is a tragic tale recounting suffering, changes are taking place that suggest that the cycles of poverty and despair can be broken. The Indian Self-Determination and Education Assistance Act (P.L. 93–638) passed in 1975 has empowered tribal governments to contract for the provision of services that were formerly provided by the BIA. This change combined with the growing levels of professional expertise in all areas of tribal program administration is bringing about major changes in the intention and outcomes of economic development efforts. In other words, tribal leaders are now making their own decisions based on their own ideals instead of federal bureaucrats making decisions for questionable, at best, reasons.

Indian reservations face the major task of using their existing natural and human resource base to create jobs, provide higher standards of living, and improve social welfare for their tribal members. Apart from vigorously import-replacing retail and service sectors, reservation economic development efforts at increasing exports fall into the areas of energy and mining, agriculture and livestock raising, forestry, gaming, cultural tourism, arts and crafts, and manufacturing and assembly. As these sectors increase, additional import-replacement can take place in terms of retail and various services in the cycle of vigorous growth.

**Energy and Mining.**  In 1973 OPEC, an international cartel of oil-producing states, imposed an oil embargo on most Western nations and created a crisis that called attention to the strategic importance of Indian-owned energy resources. Over 200 billion tons of coal, 4.2 billion barrels of oil, and 17.5 trillion cubic feet of natural gas are located on Indian reservations in the West.

These energy resources are significant sources of tribal income for the forty-two members of the Council of Energy Resource Tribes (CERT), an organization of energy resource-rich Indian tribes. CERT monitors and negotiates resource contracts for the sale of oil, coal, gas and minerals found on reservation lands. CERT was organized because BIA leasing policies caused much controversy when the BIA often sold Indian coal, oil, and other natural resources at less than fair market value.

On the Navajo and Hopi reservations, for example, coal companies were granted fifty-year leases at prices of less than 50 cents per ton at a time when the market price was over $70 per ton. Recently, a stunning legal decision was reached regarding the negotiations for this coal. A federal judge determined that the Interior Department is not bound by federal law to uphold the best interests of the Navajo Nation regarding the lease negotiations. Although it was clear that the negotiations between the Interior Department and Peabody Coal Company clearly harmed the Navajo Nation, no remedy is forthcoming.

Royalties that should have been paid to the tribes on the basis of the resource's market value have been underreported or stolen. The Wind River Reservation in Wyoming lost over $750,000 in oil royalties during a nine-year period. Related to this is the fact that energy-resource royalties have not been as beneficial as hoped in terms of improving employment opportunities for tribal members. In part, this is due to the nature of jobs in the oil drilling and coal mining industries, which require fairly high skill levels. Most reservation Indians do not have training in the right skills for employment in these industries. Furthermore, many high-paying jobs are controlled by unions which promote the interests of their members over opportunities to hire local qualified residents.

More recently, tribal self-governance has resulted in several leases being re-negotiated in favor of the tribes. The development of these exports and the improved incomes allows Indian tribes to earn imports.

**Farming and Ranching.**   Several Indian tribes, such as the Cherokee, Creek, and Hopi, have long traditions as farmers. Organized around common land use, families and clans worked together and shared the produce. Between 1887 and 1934 the allotment of reservation land to individual Indians destroyed traditional tribal obligations and ownership and led to a widespread pattern of fractionated reservation land ownership. The Indian Reorganization Act of 1934 prohibited further allotment and alienation of Indian lands.

The general patterns of land ownership on reservations vary. For example, there is "fee simple" land that belongs to individuals; "trust land" that belongs to the tribe but is held in trust by the BIA; and land that belongs to individuals that is BIA-regulated. Of the more than 54 million acres of Indian land, 42.1 million acres, or 77 percent, is tribally owned, and 10.6 million (20 percent) is owned by individuals under BIA trust relations.

Because of the complications arising from the inheritance of allotted lands, parcels of land that could be commercially valuable are often broken up into small disconnected tracts. Such disparate land holdings and the fact that trust land cannot be used as collateral to back up a loan, make it difficult for Indian landowners to get loans for investing in farm equipment, seeds, and fertilizer. Moreover, because of low investment levels, average productivity is much lower than comparable nonreservation farmland. In 1983 Congress enacted the Indian Land Consolidation Act to help reduce the fractionalization of Indian land ownership. Under this law, tribes can establish inheritance codes to govern the disposition of real property. Over time this power may help improve and consolidate Indian land.

Tribes like the Mille Lacs Band of Chippewa in Minnesota are trying to overcome the land fractionation problem by starting a Land Purchase Trust Fund to restore their 61,000-acre reservation. Some of this land was lost to competing claims by non-Indian farmers and timber companies, who purchased fee simple allotted lands from Indian owners, removing it from control and ownership by the Mille Lacs Band.

Leasing trust lands is a strategy used to induce non-Indians to invest and generate income for reservation job creation. About 7 million acres of Indian trust land is leased to non-Indian farmers and ranchers. Another 8 million acres are under mineral leases to large non-Indian companies. The leasing of Indian land resulted in about $68 million in 1984. Of this, $16.8 million was generated by business leases, while $48.4 million was gained from agricultural leases. Oil, gas, coal, and other mineral leases produced over $230 million. While an important source of revenue, the leasing strategy often focuses too narrowly on income generation while ignoring the economic, social, and environmental impacts on the reservation community.

Today, tribal leaders on reservations are starting to recognize the importance of economic development projects that preserve the integrity of their traditional cultures. For example, five Indian Pueblos in New Mexico established a confederation to grow and sell their traditional foodstuff, blue corn. The organization contracts with individual farmers and processes the corn into consumer products, which it sells at fairs and through organic-gardening magazines. In light of this, activities that complement cultural practices such as cattle and sheep ranching, fishing, and truck farming offer jobs and ways to increase the incomes of Indian families. Some tribes also have been managing buffalo, elk, and other game herds for both traditional uses and the sale of hunting licenses.

The lack of available capital funding can be clearly seen by comparing farms and ranches on Indian lands with those on neighboring non-Indian lands. For example, driving along Highway 2 in Montana shows very capital intensive farming and ranching where many of the fields have various watering systems. Then a sign announces that you have entered the Fort Belknap Indian Community and the watering systems are not present and the apparent quality of the fields distinctly lessens.

However as tribal governments gain control of their resources, more capital funding is becoming available. For example, the Colorado River Indian Tribes run and operate a system of farms that produce a variety of crops. This profitable enterprise earns the tribes substantial imports.

**Forestry.** American Indians own about 54 million acres, or about 2 percent of the total land area in the country. Of this, about 5.3 million acres contain commercially valuable timber resources. This translates into approximately 40 billion board feet, or 1.5 percent of the country's total supply.

Forestry contributes substantial revenues for many reservations. Tribes engaged in forestry operations are largely harvesters of raw timber, which is sent to mills outside the reservations. Some reservations such as the Warm Springs and White Mountain Apache operate their own mills. The forestry industry, however, is subject to major cycles of fluctuating demand and profit, which contributes to the difficulty of creating a long-term stable economy around this enterprise.

Since timber-harvesting activities were historically supervised by the BIA there is considerable bureaucratic red tape and opportunity for mismanagement. A government audit of the Red Lake Chippewa of Minnesota discovered that the BIA had misplaced as much as $500,000 per year. In other instances, BIA timber sale accounts have not been balanced in over seventy years. Forestry is a good example of how BIA over-regulation of Indian resources often interferes with reservation economic growth.

As with the Peabody Coal Company case, federal officials have been found to ignore the best interests of the tribes for which they are responsible for. In a classic case, the Quinault tribe sued because the BIA was selling timber for as low as $16 per thousand board feet when the market price exceeded $1,000. And as with the Peabody Coal case, the BIA indicated that managing the resources in the best interest of the Quinault tribe was not mandated by federal law.

More recently, more tribes are taking control of their own resources under the auspice of PL 638. A study in the early 1990s showed very clear evidence of BIA

mismanagement. Comparing seventy-five forests being harvested with either BIA management or self-management, it was found that Indian managed forests were far more productive and profitable than BIA managed forests. One startling result, although not that surprising after all, was that adding a highly skilled BIA employee actually *reduced* the productivity of the timber enterprise. As seen with other types of economic activity, tribal management is far more successful than having the federal government managing resources.

**Gaming.** The issue of Indian gaming is particularly important today. As late as 1979 there were no significant bingo or gaming establishments on Indian reservations. By 1999 gaming income to Indian reservations was estimated at about $8.6 billion, or about 10 percent of all national gaming revenues. Gaming has become a leading source of income for some Indian tribes. Of 558 federally recognized tribes, 198 are engaged in gaming with 326 gaming operations. The Indian gaming industry employs roughly 200,000 people of which 75 percent are non-Indians: many gaming tribes are net importers of employment. A 1997 study showed that in Minnesota, gaming generated over $180 million in payroll and

The casino on the Vermilion Reservation in northern Minnesota. (Courtesy of the UCLA American Indian Studies Center)

over $50 million in taxes. Indian gaming has become a major new export industry for several tribes.

Although only a small number of tribes have successful gaming operations, the new export industry is allowing for increased import earning. Several of the successful tribes are using the increased availability of funds to begin a round of import-replacement and development of alternative enterprises by diversifying their economic systems. Thus, for a few tribes, gaming operations are leading toward more successful community structures. The diversification and import-replacing involves several types of activities.

For example, some have used gaming as a means of generating income to support the elderly and sick, and to pay for health care, sanitation, and housing improvements. Some tribes have bought back ancient land, restored sacred and religious sites, worked to preserve traditional culture, created scholarship funds, and created numerous jobs. A good example of community benefits gained from bingo income is the Sycuan Indian community of Southern California. Most of the Sycuan gaming revenues go directly to financing health care, housing, and general assistance to Sycuan community members. In 1997 Caifornia gaming resulted in a $50 million reduction in AFDC payments with a reduction of $21 million to tribal members. As one tribal leader indicated, tribes are becoming taxpayers instead of tax users.

The success of the gaming facilities is allowing tribes to diversify in much the same way that Las Vegas has diversified. The completion of golf courses, resort hotels and entertainment facilities complements the gaming operations. These expanded facilities offer more employment and income potentials.

**Cultural Tourism.** Another export sector earning imports for tribes is the increasing market for cultural tourism. The idea of marketing selected aspects of Indian culture and traditions for the tourist trade can be an important business activity if properly managed. As long as the activities are self-determined by the tribes themselves with regard to sacred sites and cultural rituals, substantial economic activity can be garnered by developing tourism.

Some tribes have been successful, such as the Eastern Cherokee of North Carolina, who annually produce a pageant play, *Onto these Hills*, which portrays Cherokee life during forced removal to the West in the late 1830s. This also helps communicate Cherokee history and culture to large non-Indian audiences. Powwows and ceremonies performed before public audiences have been favorite tourist attractions for many years. Several Pueblo villages have long traditions of opening some ceremonies to public attendance. Major powwows, like the Crow Fair held near the Custer Battle Ground in southeastern Montana, are open to the public and are well attended by Indians and non-Indians alike. Another example is the new hotel operated by the Hualapai Nation. Combining the hotel operations with their river trips through the Grand Canyon and a visitation site on the rim of the Grand Canyon provides this tribe with substantial revenue. Many tribes use tourism revenues to finance tribal museums, art galleries, and annual powwows.

An important aspect of these cultural tourism activities is the increased demand for tribal members who can provide these services. As a result, there is increasing interest in traditional cultural activities and languages. In addition, the increased income among tribal members is allowing for the rejuvenation of traditional ceremonies and activities.

**Arts and Crafts.** Various types of Indian arts and crafts, such as jewelry, pottery, and woven textiles have become familiar to most Americans. In many instances the sale of these items plays an important role in supplementing limited household income, but only rarely have Indian arts and craft productions become more than small-scale industries.

There is often controversy within reservation communities over whether Indian artisans should make objects for sale to non-Indians, especially if the objects have had traditional sacred or ceremonial significance. Many items produced by Indian artists are not produced for sale, but for specific religious or ceremonial purposes. After the ceremony, the objects were usually destroyed, having served their purpose. For example, among the Hopi of Arizona, representations of ceremonial and ancestral rain spirits called kachinas are painted on the walls of kivas, circular ceremonial rooms below ground. The paintings of the Kachina spirits are made for one ceremony only and then are destroyed. They are not saved for posterity or for artistic display.

Among the Navajo of the Southwest, paintings made from different colored sands have special sacred or purification powers. The sand paintings often depict Navajo sacred beings or represent the order and balance of the universe. Sand paintings are used in curing ceremonies, where they help an Indian doctor restore harmony and balance to a patient, who sits within the sand painting. After the curing ceremony, the sand paintings are destroyed, and each new ceremony demands fresh sand paintings. Many sand paintings, however, are visually attractive, and upon seeing them, tourists have offered to buy them. Needing money, some Navajo started selling sand paintings but included small mistakes in the paintings so they would not desecrate the sacred power of the healing ceremonies. To those who objected to selling sand paintings to tourists, the sellers argued they were not selling sacred powers because they "broke" the painting's power by leaving deliberate mistakes in them, thereby preserving sacred knowledge and powers.

While there are development opportunities for the promotion of Indian arts and crafts, any tribally owned enterprise or cooperative seeking to capitalize on the growing demand faces tremendous competition from the existing brokers and from Indian art copies imported from foreign countries. Many reservations and co-operative enterprises between tribes have been successful in developing marketing enterprises. One example is the Navajo Arts and Crafts Enterprise. This vertical diversification essentially import-replaces the marketing aspect of the industry and provides employment and income for individuals not directly producing the artwork.

In addition to artifacts, several Native American artists are reaching levels of international success in literature and music. Sherman Alexie is a well-known writer and Joanne Shenandoah is a well-known musician. The popularity of these artists then stimulates further demand for cultural tourism and arts and crafts.

**Manufacturing and Assembly.** Developing Indian reservations is frequently understood in terms of creating jobs. The federal government has attempted to induce private companies to expand manufacturing facilities to impoverished reservations. As a result, thousands of new jobs have been created in industries that manufacture consumer goods, electronic components, clothing, and the like.

It is very important that many tribes are exploring alternative economic development approaches. Often the capital for economic development comes from land claims suits against the federal government, mineral royalties, or large federal grants. After receiving $81.5 million to settle disputed land claims, the Passamaquoddy and Penobscot Indians in Maine invested in several commercial enterprises to promote tribal economic development. Dozens of other tribes have followed suit and aggressively pursued manufacturing opportunities. The Blackfeet tribe of Montana founded the Blackfeet Indian Writing Company, which makes pens, pencils, and markers. The company has generated millions of dollars in sales and provided badly needed jobs on the Blackfeet reservation, where unemployment ranged between 55 and 65 percent.

Many tribal governments see light industry as a means to providing long-term jobs and economic growth on Indian reservations. A few reservations, such as the Turtle Mountain and Devils Lake reservations of North Dakota and the Mississippi Choctaw near Philadelphia, Mississippi, have had significant success at managing electronic assembly plants, building military equipment, or manufacturing greeting cards. Indian reservation manufacturing and entrepreneurship is only a beginning, but light manufacturing may hold the greatest promise for ameliorating the deep economic poverty of many Indian reservations.

Another example is Apache Manufacturing. This tribal enterprise on the Whiteriver Apache Reservation produced various parts on a contract for McDonnell-Douglas. Following several attempts at manufacturing difference items, the manager approached McDonnell-Douglas, a major aircraft company recently bought by the Boeing aircraft company, and negotiated from the perspective that if McDonnell-Douglas was producing the Apache Helicopter, a highly successful military attack gunship, then they should at least buy some inputs from Apaches.

## Conclusion

Even today, historical aspects of colonialism shape the progress of Indian economic development. The trust relationship designed to help prevent the continuing exploitation of Indians and further loss of their lands tends to inhibit reservation economic development. Several layers of BIA bureaucracy must approve tribal business decisions, which adds to the cost of doing business. Resource-owning tribes are saddled with unprofitable long-term leases negotiated by the BIA. Indian lands cannot be sold or encumbered without express congressional authorization, which inhibits chances for raising working capital for business investment. Non-Indian businesses are often reluctant about locating on Indian reservations, and tribal councils may lack the business experience to oversee tribal business operations.

Another significant problem is the lack of economic linkages that sustain the benefits of economic development projects. Because there are few reservation businesses, Indians usually drive many miles to buy needed goods and services. Without a local economic base, most local income and revenues accruing to Indian communities are passed on to non-Indian businesses without much impact within the reservation economy. In order to capture income and employment enhancing effects, known as "multipliers," Indians must spend more income with businesses that hire Indian employees and invest in Indian communities.

As more and more tribes begin the process of self-determined economic activities the population is becoming more and more self-sufficient. The process of economic development via the cycle of vigorous growth is leading Indian nations to greater success. Import-replacing retail and service sectors allows the multiplier effect to reverberate the importance of incomes and employment. Vertically diversifying existing enterprises, such as mills for processing timber, is another example of import-replacement. Developing new products for export, such as cultural tourism, earns more imports and leads to further income and employment. When these activities are designed and managed by the indigenous populations, then not only do they tend to be more productive, they avoid conflicts between traditional cultures and resource management.

Over time, with complementary improvements in education and health care and increased political stability, more tribal communities are demonstrating economic successes. The history of American Indians demonstrates that the most important factor is that they do it on their own terms.

*Dean Howard Smith*
*Northern Arizona Unversity*

# ◆ AMERICAN INDIAN LABOR

## Historical Background

**Before Columbus.** Not much is known about how the Natives of North America labored before Europeans arrived. There was probably a great deal of variety in their work and in the way they organized their labor. It certainly required complex division of labor to sustain the large complex societies that once occupied the Southwest and the Mississippi River valley. Certain types of work were probably assigned by gender and others by social position such as family or clan memberships. Presumably, these societies were organized hierarchically, so that the most unpleasant and disagreeable tasks were delegated to those in the lowest social positions. Some of these societies might have taken slaves from enemy villages who were then employed to perform the most undesirable labor.

Much of North America also was inhabited by small, nomadic hunting-and-gathering societies. Although these societies had simpler divisions of labor, gender and social position were probably still important for allocating work duties. These people probably spent most if not all their working lives in activities related to providing adequate food, shelter, and clothing for survival. Unlike larger complex societies, small populations cannot ordinarily produce economic surpluses large enough to allow some members to engage full-time in practicing art, medicine, or religion. Nor do they have the means to encourage long distance trade with other communities.

**The Arrival of Capitalism.** Although none of this may sound very surprising, and may even mirror societies in parts of the world today, capitalism as a system of economic organization was unknown in the western hemisphere; the arrival of the Europeans changed this. Capitalism introduced new ways of organizing economic production and conducting trade. In particular, capitalism is an economic system designed to maximize personal wealth by maximizing business profits. Profits are greatest when it is possible to exploit labor through low wages and to gain advantage over trading partners such as suppliers, customers, and competitors.

We do not know much about indigenous economies before 1492, but it is quite possible that in many Native societies, economic production was not aimed exclusively at personal gain. If anything, economic production promoted the well-being of the village or community. Similarly, personal wealth was not a measure of personal status as it is in capitalist societies. In fact, it is possible that some societies regarded personal wealth as a reflection of individual greed and that social status was acquired through demonstrations of generosity. Even today in American Indian communities—in potlatches or giveaways, ceremonies in which one person or family presents gifts to others at the ceremony—personal status is enhanced by giving away material goods, not by acquiring them.

The expansion of capitalism into the New World together with the introduction of novelties from the Old World—such as horses, guns, and metal goods—completely reshaped the way Native North Americans sustained themselves. American Indians' incorporation into the expanding world market first changed their work ways by introducing new tools and techniques. Guns, metal knives, traps, and other implements made Indian hunters more efficient, allowing them to kill game more easily and possibly more quickly. Metal pots, needles, and other domestic goods also changed women's work.

The introduction of trade initiated a subtler, more profound change in the nature of work among American Indians. Archaeological evidence indicates that trade and exchange had been prevalent among American Indian societies for thousands of years. However, because trade and exchange in these societies were not guided exclusively by the desire for personal gain, trade with Euro-Americans brought a new cultural ethos to the work of American Indians. As American Indians worked and produced goods for trade with Euro-Americans, new motives and rationales gradually leeched into older cultural beliefs about the meaning and importance of work, creating conflicts that are still visible today.

The incorporation of American Indians into the world economy also changed their work by fostering new markets for Native goods and by creating flourishing trade networks. The Spanish, French, and English, among others, launched far flung trading operations that were driven by the heavy demand in Europe for fur and other animal skins. Deerskin, for example, was highly valued for making breeches.

The establishment of the fur trade in the sixteenth and seventeenth centuries depended heavily on the labor of American Indians. Indian hunters, using guns, traps, and knives manufactured in Europe, exploited animal populations for the enrichment of the fur companies. It is important to remember, however, that the Indians were not employees of the fur companies. Nonetheless, it was not unusual for traders to extend credit and manage these accounts in ways that kept Indian hunters perpetually in debt. Traders frequently held a near monopoly over manufactured goods which allowed them to dictate trade terms: they set high prices for manufactured goods and low prices for furs. Fraud and usury were also commonly employed to keep Indian hunters in debt. In many ways, these practices made the relationship between fur traders and Indian hunters resemble an employer-employee relationship.

The fur trade had an impact on other aspects of the working lives of American Indians. For example, in some tribes, it accentuated the division of labor between men and women. During the mid-seventeenth century, in the Southeast, there was a thriving trade for deerskins. As a result, the Indian men in this region devoted most of their energies to deer hunting and other activities related to this trade. While women helped process the skins, they also took over responsibility for tending the home and garden, assuming duties that had previously been performed by the men who were now occupied with hunting.

The fur trade was an important source of work for American Indians; while it was important as a first experience in providing labor for a capitalist economy, the fur trade was relatively short lived. The fur trade declined because animal resources dwindled and because the demand for furs in Europe declined. The demise of colonialism in the Americas, marked by the emergence of the United States as a political sovereign, signaled a new era in the economic role of American Indians. While the fur trade did not entirely disappear, U.S. citizens increasingly took over. The American Fur Company was a major corporation in the nineteenth century. In the first century of the U.S. republic, however, Indian labor did not have a place.

**The Expanding American Economy.**  Until the late nineteenth century, the United States economy was decidedly agrarian. Economic expansion meant clearing additional land for agricultural production. Consistent with this policy, the nation adopted a political ideology known as Manifest Destiny that called for populating the country with settlers from coast to coast. European immigration to the United States exploded in this century and many immigrants migrated West in search of agricultural land. The immigrant farmers' desire for land ultimately required that the people living on the land be removed and resettled. Ironically, some Indians, such as those living in the Southeast, were already farmers, but this made no difference to the immigrant settlers. At this time, the idea that American Indians could have a productive economic role was considered ridiculous by the dominant society.

The removal and resettlement of American Indians to reservations and places in Oklahoma was complete by the late nineteenth century, and it was devastating to these people who had once been self-sufficient and self-governing. Hunting and fishing no longer provided a comfortable living, and many traditional agricultural practices were either not viable or were discouraged by federal Indian agents. Reservation settlement created the abject poverty that persists today.

The late nineteenth century was also a time when the United States was quickly becoming an urban industrial society. Reformers concerned about past treatment of Indians believed that it was time to "civilize" them by encouraging and often forcing them to give up their traditional tribal culture. For nearly forty years, from the early 1890s to 1934, the federal government tried to accomplish this by forcing Indians to adopt Euro-American farming practices. Such efforts generally failed, and Indian men, accustomed to hunting or fishing, rejected farming. A few Indians took up farming or ranching like their non-Indian neighbors, and, like their neighbors, were often economic failures.

**Entering the Work Force.**  By the early twentieth century, American Indians began increasingly to look outside the reservation for employment. Because they often had few skills, they often settled for unskilled labor such as farm work, clearing brush, or digging ditches. The Navajo, for example, sometimes provided unskilled labor for the Southern Pacific Railroad. A very small number of American Indians obtained an education, and a handful went on to become noted doctors, lawyers, and writers, such as Charles Eastman (Ohiyesa) or Carlos Montezuma.

By 1930 American Indians had in large measure adopted modern occupations. In the 1930 Census, more than 80 percent of the men over the age of eighteen were counted as "gainful workers," most of whom (63 percent) were agricultural workers. In the early 1930s, the federal government reconsidered its efforts to "civilize" American Indians and turned its attention to helping Indians find work in the midst of the Great Depression. The Indian New Deal (legislation enacted during the Roosevelt Administration in the early 1930s to promote tribal government and economic recovery programs for reservations) was enacted through a series of laws, the first of which passed in 1933. Among its many provisions, the Indian New Deal established programs aimed at providing jobs and income to desperately needy reservations. For example, federal projects employed many Indians to prevent soil erosion, for flood control, and for road and bridge construction.

The Indian New Deal was important through the 1930s, but the coming of World War II curtailed many of its programs, and it was not reinstated after the war. Reservations languished in intense poverty and unemployment while the rest of the nation prospered in the postwar years. In the early 1950s, federal officials proposed eliminating reservations to move Indians to cities where they might find work. In 1951 the federal government established the Direct Employment Assistance program to encourage reservation Indians to move to preselected urban areas such as Los Angeles. This, together with subsequent programs, came to be known as Relocation. Federal relocation programs moved thousands of American Indians—often long distances from their former homes—to cities such as Los Angeles and Seattle.

The relocation programs were not very successful in helping Indians find work. The American Indians who benefited most from relocation were those with the education, job skills, and desire to compete in urban labor markets. However, many relocated Indians had a limited education and few skills. These Indians benefited little from relocation as they went from being unemployed on the reservation to being unemployed in the city.

**Jobs and Reservation Development.** The federal government abandoned relocation programs in the late 1960s and have since implemented efforts to revitalize reservation economies. Through job training, the government has attempted to help American Indians qualify for semi-skilled and skilled jobs. Roads, sewage systems, and industrial parks were built to attract new businesses to reservations. Tribal governments also vastly increased in size as tribes became more involved in governing their own reservations. Efforts to attract business to reservations and to provide education and job training were at best a mixed success. American Indians are better educated today than twenty years ago, but relatively few industries have located permanently on reservations.

In the absence of private industry, the largest single sources of reservation employment have without question been tied to the growth in tribal government and related services. This has made American Indian reservations extremely vulnerable to changing federal policies that affect local government spending. Predictably, massive cutbacks in federal spending in the early 1980s produced massive increases in unemployment on reservations across the country.

Since the early 1980s, the federal government has focused on helping private enterprise develop on reservations. While some reservations have successfully promoted private development, the outlook for many others is not good. Due to a lack of resources, capital, or location, reservations are not often fertile grounds to nurture new business. One possible exception has been the advent of reservation gambling.

Reservation gambling, sometimes described as Indian bingo, has generated tremendous sums of money for some, but not all reservations. Reservation gambling initially began on a few reservations as high stakes bingo, with prizes exceeding $100,000 (the Florida Seminole tribe were the first to adopt reservation gambling). Bingo operations soon spread to reservations across the country as tribes searched for ways to provide jobs and income. These establishments soon moved beyond bingo to include other types of gambling such as blackjack, roulette, and slot machines.

Although not universally successful, reservation gambling has been an important source of tribal revenue and employment. However, most jobs directly related to gaming are low-wage service positions such as cashier, attendant, and waitress. While gambling creates employment in spin-off industries such as restaurants and motels, these are not highly desirable jobs in terms of wages and fringe benefits. At this time, it is unclear whether gambling and related developments will act as an economic panacea to provide workers with desperately needed employment and a decent standard of living.

## American Indians in the Labor Force

Information about the experience of American Indians in the labor force is scarce, and up-to-date information becomes available only once every ten years: the only good source of statistical information about American Indians is the U.S. Census, which is conducted once every decade. As of this writing, information from the most recent census, taken in 2000, is not yet available. We must therefore rely on data from 1990; these data, however, should be adequate since economic conditions for American Indians have scarcely changed in the past forty years, and since there is little to suggest

The Pacific Auto Mechanic Center in California's Bay Area trains Indian people in the skills and trade of auto mechanics. (Photo by Ilka Hartmann)

that conditions in the early 2000s will differ much from those of the early 1990s.

**Labor-Force Participation.** One of the most common ways of describing the status of any group in the labor market is in terms of labor-force participation rates. To participate in the labor force one must be employed or be actively seeking employment. Persons outside the labor force are either not able to work or have abandoned hope of finding employment and have become discouraged workers. Because American Indians face many obstacles to becoming employed, such as their geographic location, they experience relatively high rates of unemployment and low rates of labor-force participation. It should be noted that this is in terms of the percentage of the labor force without employment; unemployed persons who have given up their search for work are not counted in this statistic because they are not considered part of the labor force. In 1990 for example, about 15 percent of American Indian men were unemployed. In the same year, only about 5 percent of white men were jobless. Similarly, in

1990, about 31 percent of adult American Indian men were not part of the labor force, while this figure was 25 percent for white men.

These figures clearly indicate that American Indians are more jobless than whites. However, these numbers gloss over another important element in labor-force participation for employed American Indians, including time at work and recent episodes of unemployment. Many American Indians who are employed do not necessarily have a full-time job, or a job that consistently provides them with full-time work. Other American Indians, although considered employed, do not work during much of the year because they are employed in seasonal industries such as construction or tourism.

From the standpoint of employment, most American Indians are not employed in year-round jobs. In fact, 50 percent of American Indians who worked in 1989 worked less than fifty weeks. This is very different from the experience of non-Hispanic white workers, of whom only 35 percent spent less than fifty weeks on a job.

Navajo woman teacher at a school for auto mechanics, 1972. (Photo by Ilka Hartmann)

Likewise, the time spent at work is very different for Indians than for whites. Full-time employment for American Indians, defined as working thirty-five hours or more a week, tends to be sporadic. In 1979, only 47 percent of American Indians who found full-time work reported working for the entire year. On the other hand, 65 percent of white workers held full-time, full-year jobs.

**Worker Characteristics and Labor-Force Participation.** Gross statistics on unemployment or hours worked obscure a much more complicated situation. Of course, American Indians are not all alike and some spend more time working than others. Opportunities to secure full-time, full-year work depend heavily on the personal qualifications of workers, and on-the-job supply in the local labor market.

Gender, age, education, and family circumstances each have an important role in helping or hindering American Indian's participation in the labor force, just as it plays a role in the employment of most workers, regardless of race. Gender plays a very important role because, not surprisingly, employment opportunities for women differed markedly from those for men. The subject of American Indian women in the work force merits a more detailed discussion, which will follow shortly.

Age also affects access to employment. Older American Indians sometimes have obsolete job skills or physical infirmities that limit their employability, while younger American Indians often lack the work experience desired by employers. American Indians who are at the prime working age, between twenty-five and fifty-four years old, are most often employed, least often outside of the labor force, and are less likely to be unemployed than older or younger American Indians. For example, about 73 percent of Indian men aged twenty-five to fifty-four were employed in 1989, compared to approximately 54 percent of Indian men over age fifty-five.

Education is another obvious prerequisite for labor-force participation. Employers understandably desire employees who are capable of reading and performing basic math, and who can follow instructions. Unfortunately, many American Indians are severely handicapped by their lack of schooling. The educational deficit among American Indians often begins at the high school level. American Indian youths leave school before graduating at much higher rates than other youths. In 1990, 19 percent of American Indians ages sixteen to nineteen had dropped out of school, compared to 10 percent of white youths. The employment prospects for these youths are bleak: only 36 percent of American Indian dropouts have any type of employment. Predictably, American Indians have a lower rate of high school completion than whites: 56 percent of American Indians finish high school compared to 69 percent of white students. Of the American Indians who successfully finish high school, relatively few attend college.

It is clear that well-educated American Indians have considerably more success in the job market than their poorly educated brethren. In 1990, for example, college-educated American Indian men had average earnings exceeding $30,000, while Indian men who had dropped out of high school had average earnings of less than $15,000. It is clear that American Indians benefit economically from continued education.

A stable family environment also is a powerful incentive to Indian men to stay in the labor force. Married American Indian men have higher employment rates and lower unemployment than single or divorced men. For the same reasons, married American Indian women tend not to work, especially if there are children at home. Family disruptions such as death or divorce also work against labor-force participation; men have less incentive to stay at work, while women have more incentive to find work, especially if they must support their children.

**Local Economies and American Indian Labor-Force Participation.** The role of personal characteristics in shaping labor-force participation is certainly important. The cure for unemployment among American

## Table 17.1
### Percent Distribution of Time at Work and Unemployment in 1989 for
### American Indians and Alaska Natives Aged Sixteen and Over*

| Residence and Gender | Worked 26 Weeks or Less | Worked 35 Hours or Less | Unemployed |
|---|---|---|---|
| Metropolitan | | | |
| Male | 21.0 | 15.4 | 11.9 |
| Female | 25.7 | 28.0 | 10.8 |
| Non-Metropolitan | | | |
| Male | 32.1 | 15.1 | 20.3 |
| Female | 34.0 | 28.4 | 16.3 |

*1 percent of persons did not work 35 or more hours per week for a period of 6 months or more.
Source: 1990 Census of Population, Social and Economic Characteristics, United States.

Indians does not merely entail measures such as providing job experience for younger workers, encouraging them to stay in school and go on to college, and promoting family stability. If there are no jobs available in the local economy, no amount of education will help secure employment. In fact, some experts contend that American Indian youths drop out of school because they see no opportunity for work in their community, and no reason for staying in school. There is no question that for many American Indians, especially those living in rural reservation areas, opportunities are limited.

For reasons explained here and elsewhere in this volume, American Indian reservations often present few economic opportunities and extreme economic hardship. On many large reservations, unemployment rates hovered around 20 to 30 percent while unemployment in the rest of the nation settled at 6 to 7 percent. Some of these reservations are severely distressed: the Pine Ridge Reservation in South Dakota, for example, had an unemployment rate of 33 percent in 1980.

For American Indians who have some job skills or a good education, urban areas offer more opportunities. Urban Indians typically have higher rates of labor-force participation and lower unemployment rates than reservation Indians. American Indians living in cities had an unemployment rate of approximately 11 percent in 1990; this figure is lower than that of many reservations, but is still about six points higher than white unemployment rates. While urban areas may provide better opportunities for a select number of American Indians, moving to these locations often entails other costs in terms of leaving behind family, friends, and a familiar culture.

The labor markets in which American Indians seek employment vary regionally. Since some regions of the United States are economically healthier than others,

American Indians seeking work in these areas are more likely to find employment than those who seek work in regions with weak economies. Until very recently, the West, especially the so-called Sunbelt, has been the most economically vigorous region in the United States. Predictably, American Indians living in this region find more employment than those living in other areas of the United States, especially those living in the hard hit Northeast Rust Belt region. American Indian employment rates also reflect declines in the U.S. agricultural economy. Relatively few Indians work in agriculture, but the economic depression of regions that depend on agriculture ultimately translates to a decrease in the number of jobs available to American Indian workers.

### American Indians at Work

**Occupations.**   We can view the work performed by American Indians from several perspectives. We can simply group together the kinds of jobs or occupations filled by American Indians; jobs that entail similar activities are grouped together into distinct categories such as manual or nonmanual occupations, for example. We can also look at American Indian workers in relation to the places where they work; that is, whether they work on farms, in offices, or in manufacturing plants. A third perspective can focus on ownership to consider whether American Indians are self-employed, employed by privately owned businesses, or employed by a government agency. Each of these perspectives provides a unique picture of American Indians at work.

The occupations of American Indians vary considerably depending on gender, job location, and education. About 69 percent of American Indian men, for example, are in employed manual occupations. This partially

## Table 17.2
## Percent Distribution of the Labor-Force Participation of American Indians
## Aged Sixteen and Over Residing on the Sixteen Largest Reservations in 1990

| | 1980 | | 1990 | |
|---|---|---|---|---|
| Reservation | In Labor Force % | Unemployment Rate % | In Labor Force % | Unemployment Rate % |
| Navajo (AZ, UT, NM) | 58.3 | 23.7 | 43.7 | 29.5 |
| Pine Ridge (SD) | 61.8 | 35.8 | 48.1 | 32.7 |
| Gila River (AZ) | 61.5 | 29.5 | 44.7 | 30.6 |
| Papago (AZ) | 58.6 | 20.4 | 36.1 | 23.4 |
| Fort Apache (AZ) | 64.1 | 20.3 | 54.9 | 35.3 |
| Hopi (AZ) | 54.7 | 20.5 | 48.0 | 26.8 |
| Zuni Pueblo (NM) | 79.7 | 23.2 | 64.4 | 13.8 |
| San Carlos (AZ) | 59.1 | 21.1 | 59.1 | 21.1 |
| Rosebud (SD) | 65.0 | 28.7 | 50.6 | 29.5 |
| Blackfeet (MT) | 72.2 | 37.0 | 56.2 | 31.1 |
| Yakima (WA) | 70.1 | 32.5 | 49.8 | 24.5 |
| Eastern Cherokee (NC) | 73.7 | 21.1 | 66.2 | 17.7 |
| Standing Rock (ND, SD) | 65.8 | 36.0 | 50.2 | 33.1 |
| Osage (OK) | 65.9 | 14.2 | 56.9 | 10.2 |
| Fort Peck (MT) | 75.7 | 39.3 | 57.6 | 29.7 |
| Wind River (WY) | 68.2 | 30.2 | 50.5 | 32.4 |

Sources: "American Indians, Eskimos, and Aleuts on Identified Reservations and in the Historic Areas of Oklahoma," *1980 Census of Population, Subject Report*; and "Social and Economic Characteristics, American Indian and Alaska Native Areas," *1990 Census of Population, Subject Report.*

accounts for the frequent disruptions of work that trouble many American Indians. Manual occupations are subject to disruptions of work due to weather, seasonal variations in production schedules, and economic downturns. On the other hand 61 percent of American Indian women work in nonmanual occupations. These women primarily hold lower-status white collar positions such as teachers, secretaries, and nurses; few are doctors, lawyers, or executives.

The socioeconomic disadvantages that hinder the competitiveness of Indian workers are also reflected in their occupational status. In 1990 27 percent of white men were employed in high-status professional and technical occupations while only 15 percent of American Indian men held such jobs. The gap in the occupational status between American Indian women and white women is nearly as large as it is for men. Significantly, American Indian women are substantially more concentrated in so-called service occupations than either white women or American Indian men. Approximately one-fourth of Indian women are employed in occupations such as motel maid or waitress.

The occupations of American Indians also vary according to whether they are employed in urban labor markets or in rural reservation areas; the differences are predictable. American Indians who work in an urban labor market are much more likely to hold a white collar job—in an office or a similar setting—than their counterparts in rural areas. This reflects the fact that there are many more white collar jobs for both men and women in urban areas. On the other hand, jobs as fishermen, farm workers, and loggers are more common in rural areas; rural American Indians are naturally more apt to be employed in these and related occupations than are American Indians in urban areas.

Although many American Indians continue to practice their traditional tribal culture, relatively few are able to sustain themselves in an exclusively traditional manner. Hunting, fishing, and gardening are important, especially for reservation Indians. However, American Indians living on reservations and in urban areas rely on a cash economy for certain goods and services. Most find that this work for income is not closely related to traditional tribal activities. American Indians who earn their living as hunting and fishing guides, trappers, or artisans who make pottery, jewelry, or rugs are uncommon exceptions.

**Industries.**   Because certain kinds of industries (defines here as groups of firms that produce similar goods or services) tend to employ certain kinds of occupations, patterns of industrial employment closely parallel occupational patterns. For example, American Indians are more often employed in extractive industries such as agriculture, forestry, or mining than either whites or African Americans. Not surprisingly, Indian men living in rural areas are most likely to be employed in these industries. Construction companies are also an important source of employment, although this is true primarily for American Indian men and not for Indian women. The overwhelming majority of American Indians, especially men, tend to be concentrated either in service or manufacturing jobs.

American Indian women, on the other hand, are not concentrated in manufacturing or in other industries that typically demand arduous physical labor. In 1990 nearly one-half (45 percent) of all employed Indian women worked in the so-called service sector of the economy, in establishments that provide social services, health care, and education. In this respect, American Indian women are not very different from other women insofar as they often find themselves working in places with large concentrations of female workers. They often work in companies that have many so called female jobs such as secretaries, clerk-typists, nurses, physician's assistants, teachers, and teacher's aides.

**Public Sector Employment.**   Due to the lack of job opportunities for American Indians, especially for those living on reservations, American Indians depend heavily on the federal and tribal governments for employment. The federal government, by virtue of its legal and treaty obligations, exercises a substantial role in day-to-day reservation affairs. The Bureau of Indian Affairs and the Indian Health Service employ many workers in jobs ranging from law enforcement, road construction, and logging, to health care, law, and real estate. Similarly, tribal governments increasingly have assumed a greater role in managing community affairs, employing a variety of workers, especially in tribal enterprises such as tourist developments or manufacturing establishments.

American Indians depend substantially on public sector employment. While it is true that a higher percentage of American Indians are hired by private sector employers than by the federal or tribal governments (more than two-thirds of Indian workers were employed in the private sector in 1980), a lower percentage of American Indians—compared to both whites and African Americans—are employed in the private

sector. In 1990 approximately 14 percent of the American Indian work force held jobs in federal and state government, compared to only 7.5 percent of the white labor force. Most of these jobs held by American Indian workers were probably with agencies such as the Indian Health Service or the Bureau of Indian Affairs (BIA). Similarly, in 1990 about 9 percent of the Indian work force were employed by local governments. With respect to reservations, the term *local government* means tribal government. It is also interesting to note that between 1980 and 1990 the percentage of American Indians working in local government decreased from 12 percent to 9 percent, reflecting the cutbacks in tribal government that took place during the 1980s and job growth in other sectors of the economy.

American Indians' heavy dependence on public sector employment reflects the scarcity of employment available to them, especially to those living on reservations. There are relatively few opportunities for productive employment in the private sector. In fact, in many of these areas, jobs with the BIA or with the tribe may be the best employment available. While such jobs may be desirable in terms of wages and working conditions, they are often highly insecure. These jobs are often created by soft money, that is, funds that have been appropriated for various kinds of social programs.

These programs appear and disappear, depending on the political agenda set by the federal government. Workers in such programs are seldom covered by civil service rules and find themselves jobless when federal support for a program or project is reduced or eliminated. American Indians' dependence on public sector employment also makes them vulnerable to changes in the national political climate that are reflected in terms of support for public policy initiatives. In the early 1980s, in the wake of massive federal budget reductions, unemployment skyrocketed on many reservations.

Tribal leaders are acutely aware that their communities' dependency on public sector employment makes them vulnerable to shifting political fortunes in Washington, D.C. Many tribes promote economic development in order to lessen this dependence. For the foreseeable future, however, jobs with federal agencies and tribal government will continue to be a major source of employment, especially for skilled and professional workers.

## American Indian Women in the Work Force

Like other women, American Indian women face certain obstacles in the labor market that men do not. American Indian women participate in the labor market under somewhat different circumstances from other

**Table 17.3**
**Percent Distribution of Blacks, Whites, and American Indians Aged Sixteen and Over**
**Employed in Manual and Non-Manual Occupations, 1980–1990**

|  | 1980 | | 1990 | |
|---|---|---|---|---|
|  | Males | Females | Males | Females |
| **Blacks** | | | | |
| Manual | 73.1 | 48.3 | 66.5 | 39.9 |
| Non-Manual | 26.9 | 51.7 | 33.5 | 60.1 |
| **Whites** | | | | |
| Manual | 55.5 | 30.3 | 51.1 | 26.0 |
| Non-Manual | 44.5 | 69.7 | 48.9 | 74.0 |
| **American Indians** | | | | |
| Manual | 72.1 | 43.6 | 69.1 | 38.7 |
| Non-Manual | 27.9 | 56.4 | 30.9 | 61.3 |

Sources: 1980 Census of Population, General Social and Economic Characteristics, United States Summary; 1990 Census of Population, Social and Economic Characteristics, United States.

women. Indian women also live in remote areas, may have fewer opportunities, and may face special problems finding work because the few existing jobs may be in industries—such as logging or fishing—that are traditionally dominated by men. Furthermore, by virtue of tribal culture, American Indian women may also have special obligations to their families and community that may limit their ability to work outside the home.

Nonetheless, the constraints that limit the labor-force participation of American Indian women are similar to those that hinder women of other races. Family obligations, especially child-rearing duties, often determine whether Indian women join the labor force. In 1990 46 percent of American Indian women with children under age six were not active in the labor force. However, as children spend more time at school, the reduction in child care duties allows many of these women to resume their jobs or to enter the labor force. Only 31 percent, approximately, of women with children ages six to seventeen are not participating in the work force. Predictably, women with no children have the highest rates of labor-force participation.

The fact that Indian women often have large families further limits their participation in the labor force. American Indian women tend to have more children than either white or African-American women and hence are burdened with more child care responsibilities. This may explain, in part, why the labor-force participation rates of American Indian women are lower than the rates for either whites or African Americans.

Finally, the relationship between child-bearing and labor-force participation is further complicated by the fact that less-educated Indian women tend to have more children and lower rates of labor-force participation. Without question, poorly educated Indian women have a difficult time finding work. It is not clear, however, whether these women abandoned their education to have children or whether a low level of education somehow contributes to their having larger families. Both explanations probably have some merit.

Providing economic support is another important element determining the labor-force participation of American Indian women, especially in cases where the woman's partner is absent or unable to find work. For most American Indian women, the decision to work is a complex calculation that takes into account the need to provide child care, the presence of a husband or partner, and the opportunities available in the local job market. We know little about how Indian women prioritize and sort through these competing contingencies.

We might expect American Indian women with young children to stay home to provide child care regardless of whether they live with the children's father. If the father is present, we might assume that he will support the family, or, if he is unemployed, that welfare assistance will allow the mother to remain at home. However, research indicates that women with young children under age six who are married and living with their husbands are only slightly less likely to be active in the

## Table 17.4
## Percent Distribution of Class of Worker
## of Employed Blacks, Whites, and American Indians, 1980–1990

| Class | Blacks | | Whites | | American Indians | |
|---|---|---|---|---|---|---|
| | 1980 | 1990 | 1980 | 1990 | 1980 | 1990 |
| Private Wage and Salary Worker | 70.2 | 73.2 | 76.0 | 77.6 | 66.3 | 71.1 |
| Federal and State Government Worker | 14.2 | 13.0 | 7.7 | 7.5 | 16.9 | 13.6 |
| Local Government Worker | 13.1 | 10.8 | 8.2 | 6.8 | 11.6 | 9.1 |
| Self-employed Worker | 2.4 | 2.8 | 7.5 | 7.6 | 4.8 | 5.8 |
| Unpaid Family Worker | 0.1 | 0.2 | 0.6 | 0.5 | 0.4 | 0.4 |

Sources: 1980 Census of Population, General Social and Economic Characteristics, United States Summary; 1990 Census of Population, Social and Economic Characteristics, United States.

labor force than are women with young children who are unmarried or living alone.

Whether her husband is employed and whether her husband's earnings meet household needs also affect an American Indian woman's decision to work. We might consider the labor-force participation of American Indian women to be compensatory: that is, Indian women work when their husbands are unemployed or do not earn enough to meet household needs. On the other hand, men and women often marry spouses who have similar backgrounds and characteristics. Consequently, Indian women with unemployed or poorly paid husbands face similar, if not more difficult, hardships than their spouses.

One study suggests that the labor-force participation of American Indian women does not compensate for the disadvantages faced by their husbands. On the contrary, American Indian women who are married to poorly educated and unemployed men tend to be poorly educated and either unemployed, or simply not active in the labor force. By the same token, relatively well-educated American Indian women often have relatively well-educated husbands, both of whom are considerably more successful in finding well-paid employment than are couples with less education. Contrary to popular wisdom, opposites do not attract; the result is that husbands and wives do not compensate but compound whatever advantages or disadvantages each has in the labor market.

## Concluding Observations

American Indians' current position in the U.S. labor market reflects a complex mix of long-term historical processes with recent developments in the United States and international economy. American Indians have

always—even prior to the arrival of Europeans—worked, in the broadest sense of the word. While all societies require some division of labor, the complexity of this division, and the norms for allocating its products can vary enormously. The norms by which American Indians govern the distribution of economic resources were unquestionably very different from those common among sixteenth-century Europeans.

The arrival of Europeans introduced mercantile capitalism to the New World, and with this system came a new set of conditions, expectations, and norms governing economic transactions. Today we take the terms of this system for granted in our everyday lives; for the indigenous cultures of North America, however, a market economy organized by capitalist principles was an entirely alien system. Such elements of capitalistic trade as credit, interest rates, and profits were utterly foreign. And although Natives who dealt regularly with the mercantile traders soon learned about these concepts, they did not readily accept them. Capitalism as a system designed to maximize personal material gain has never meshed well with traditional tribal cultures that value communal well-being above personal avarice.

The emergence of large-scale industrial capitalism in the nineteenth century, characterized by large-scale factory production, confronted Native cultures with yet another alien element. The organization of large-scale factories requires a submissive work force comprised of workers who are willing to accept industrial discipline, and who will order their lives around the passage of time on a clock. Traditional tribal cultures do not measure time by the clock and are often highly egalitarian, and this did not mesh well with industrial capitalism. These are among the many reasons why the expansion of capitalism in the United States depended on the exploitation of Indian lands, while it did not depend on

**Table 17.5**
**Percent Distribution of Employed Blacks, Whites, and American Indians**
**and Alaska Natives in Selected Occupations, 1990**

| Occupation | Blacks | | Whites | | American Indians | |
|---|---|---|---|---|---|---|
| | Males | Females | Males | Females | Males | Females |
| Managerial and Professional | 14.5 | 21.3 | 26.8 | 29.3 | 15.4 | 21.7 |
| Technical, Sales, and Administrative Support | 19.0 | 38.7 | 22.1 | 44.7 | 15.6 | 39.6 |
| Service | 18.8 | 25.1 | 8.8 | 15.4 | 14.2 | 23.4 |
| Farming, Forestry, and Fishing | 2.7 | 0.3 | 3.8 | 0.9 | 5.3 | 1.1 |
| Precision Production, Craft, and Repair | 14.6 | 2.4 | 19.5 | 2.2 | 22.9 | 3.1 |
| Operators, Fabricators, and Laborers | 30.4 | 12.1 | 18.9 | 7.5 | 26.7 | 11.1 |

Source: 1990 Census of Population, Social and Economic Characteristics, United States.

the exploitation of Indian labor. American Indians were considered to be unfit for work because they were economically self-sufficient, especially before they were moved to reservations; they were seldom inclined to submit to the kinds of industrial exploitation that European and Chinese immigrants suffered. As a matter of deliberate policy, the federal government sought to isolate American Indians from the mainstream of the U.S. economy; in retrospect, they were highly successful.

Today, despite periodic attempts to resettle American Indians away from reservations, many continue to live in Indian Country, often in places that are extremely remote and isolated. After generations of living at the margins of the U.S. economy, it should be no surprise that American Indians face some of the greatest economic hardships known in American society. And relocation should not be seen as a simple way to ease these hardships. Without the resources to compete successfully in a modern urban labor market, American Indians have few prospects for success. The marginal areas where many American Indians live often lack the resources required to succeed in the labor market. Lack of education is often a serious impediment to Indians who seek work. On the other hand, it is difficult to encourage American Indian youth to pursue an education when the lack of employment opportunities offers little incentive to stay in school.

American Indians who find employment still face a number of hurdles, at least by the standards of mainstream American society. American Indian men are typically employed in blue collar jobs that entail physical labor in difficult working conditions, and they often work in industries, such as construction, that are plagued

by mandatory stretches of unemployment. Compared to men, relatively few American Indian women are employed in blue collar jobs, but many hold menial jobs as service workers. Better qualified Indian women often find jobs in low status white collar jobs such as teachers, nurses' aides, or social service workers, but relatively few attain professional and technical occupations.

The experience of American Indians in the labor market has improved over the past several decades, but much improvement is still needed. American Indians continue to need more vital resources such as education and training to help them to compete in the labor market. At the same time, job opportunities must be created in the places where American Indians live. Unless these objectives are addressed American Indians' traditional role as the nation's poorest of the poor will continue indefinitely.

*C. Matthew Snipp*
*Stanford University*

### ◆ AN OVERVIEW OF U.S. GOVERNMENT ASSISTANCE AND RESTITUTION TO AMERICAN INDIANS

This section examines the relationship between U.S. government assistance and restitution programs to American Indians and American social welfare policies and programs. The roots of federal assistance and restitution programs arose from the appropriation of Indian lands by the European colonists and frontier settlers. Contact between the indigenous people of this

Three affiliated tribes participate in a giveaway in North Dakota, 1989. (Photo by Ilka Hartmann)

continent and non-Indians resulted in dramatic social and cultural changes associated with the loss of the traditional land base. Guarantees of services were proffered to American Indians in recognition that the blatant takeover of Indian lands required some level of compensation. The final annexation of land was accomplished with the establishment of the reservation system and the passage of the General Allotment Act. This section will discuss the current demographic and socioeconomic status of American Indians and the subsequent need for services; issues associated with the Temporary Assistance to Needy Families program; and the range of assistance programs currently available to American Indians.

### Consequences of Contact

Worse and worse have become reservation conditions under a system that was bad from the beginning. Such a deplorable state of affairs could only continue to exist because of several reasons, mainly, because of slight public concern for the Indian; because the declaration of President Coolidge on June 5, 1924, presumably made the Indian a citizen of the United States; and because the mass of people think and say, 'The Government takes care of the Indian.'

—*Luther Standing Bear, 1933*

Although American Indians experience similar problems to those confronted by other minority groups in the United States, the American Indian experience cannot be compared with the experiences of any other ethnic or racial minority in the United States. Every aspect of American Indian life—all resources, opportunities, and struggles—are influenced by the special political and legal relationships that exist between Indian tribes as sovereign nations and the federal and state governments. Contemporary American Indian life is affected by the social, historical, political, and cultural conditions that are the result of contact between American Indians and Euro-Americans.

*Bringing in Wild Animals, Fish, and Other Stores* (1591). Drawing by Le Moyne, from an engraving by Theodore de Bry, *America,* part II, plate XXIII. (Public Domain)

Five hundred years ago, European explorers and settlers discovered and began to explore a world that was new to them. This so-called New World was inhabited by various groups of people, indigenous tribes and nations, whose lives were shaped by cultural, social, spiritual, and political systems that differed radically from those of the Europeans. Every part of the continent was populated. The ecological environment and physical geography offered the natural resources necessary for the construction of life and influenced culturally based behaviors and practices. For example, the buffalo influenced the construction of life for the Plains tribes and the salmon, whale, and other marine life influenced life for the coastal tribes of the Northwest. Cultural, social, spiritual, and political life was organized with reference to the natural resources and the ecological environment that was home to a given Indian community. In the Southwest, Navajo were hunters and gatherers and Pueblo were farmers, because the physical and biological geography predisposed different sociocultural structures that would support group survival. Despite the diversity of physical environments

and culturally based practices that reflected the interactions between the people and the place where they resided, there were similarities across these indigenous tribes who populated the New World. Typically, the social structures and lifestyles of each group developed in ways that recognized balance, harmony, and mutuality with the environment. Similarities are evident in the fundamental belief systems, in the history and consequences of contact with non-Indians and in the processes of accommodation and survival. For example, most indigenous people believed that humans are composed of spirit, mind, and body; that plants, animals, and nature have equal status to humans in the natural world; that a Creator exists who is the giver and sustainer of life; that spirit-helpers exist who model appropriate behavior and provide support and guidance; that each individual is responsible for his or her own behavior; and that harmony, balance, and reciprocity are necessary for supporting life.

There existed a family and a collective orientation that can be found in the origin stories, tribal histories, and rituals of American Indians. The legacy of contact is visible in the social and cultural shifts that occurred as a result of the many losses and challenges experienced as Native people interacted with non-Indians. Yet many American Indian communities managed to resist, accommodate, and survive despite the brutal consequences of contact with non-Indians. These similarities across groups that lived in a large and diverse geographical territory, allow discussion of issues that are the consequence of contact with non-Indians from a broader intertribal or pan-Indian perspective.

As the American frontier experience and sensibility evolved, it became important for the dominant society to minimize the numbers of American Indians and groups whose lives and communities were destroyed and disrupted as a result of contact with non-Indians. It became equally important to judge, dehumanize, and render insignificant the lifestyles and social and cultural structures of American Indians and declare American Indians savage, lazy, and ignorant. These ideas were necessary in order for non-Indians to justify and rationalize the elimination of native opposition to the annexation and the take-over of life sustaining resources, the imposition of different lifestyles and social structures, the removal of Indians from traditional lands, and the eventual confinement of American Indians on reservations in the 1800s.

The expropriation of Indian territories began with the colonists and settlers who obtained land by force, fraud, and treaty. Subsequently, the governments of France, England, and the United States appropriated land through treaties. Through the treaty mechanism, a legal, formal, and binding agreement entered into between two nations, American Indians ceded land in exchange for money and services. As the nineteenth century unfolded, non-Indians promoted the policy of removal, which allowed the exploitation of native resources.

The Indian Removal Act of 1830 provided for "an exchange of lands with any of the Indians residing in any of the states and territories and for their removal west of the river Mississippi." By 1850 much of the American Indian territory east of the Mississippi River was no longer inhabited by Native people. The infamous Trail of Tears, which can rightfully be described as one of the most shameful events in American history, is the most renowned example of the removal policy. The Cherokee who survived this death march were relocated in what is now the state of Oklahoma and what was then territory occupied by other indigenous groups.

The General Allotment Act (Dawes Act of 1887) represented another intrusion into the social, political, and cultural fabric of Native life. The traditional land base that had been historically held in common by the group was redistributed in forty, eighty, and 160 acre shares. American Indians who accepted shares were required to use the land for agricultural purposes. The General Allotment Act was proclaimed a mechanism for introducing American Indians to the American farming lifestyle. This legislation also introduced the system of blood quantum, land trusts, and federal recognition of individual Indians. It was an overt effort to expropriate the traditional land base and exploit natural resources. It resulted in the separation of American Indians from their land and traditional way of life and resulted in the loss of approximately two-thirds of the traditional land holdings to the federal government. The establishment of reservations by the federal government completed the seizure of the traditional American Indian land base and the disruption of traditional life.

The history of Native and non-Native interactions can be summarized as a history of contact, conflict, anguish, accommodation, and adjustment. Contemporary issues confronting American Indians on and off the reservation are the consequences of this history. Disease, death, dependence, and sociocultural disorganization are the consequences of contact, conquest, removal, and reservation policies. Disease has decimated American Indian communities for centuries. Dependence was fostered when tribes were disenfranchised from life-sustaining land bases and when the practice of life-affirming spiritual and cultural rituals was forbidden. Disorganization was promoted when traditional political and cultural structures were changed as a result of the removal and reservation policies. The current assistance initiatives and the contemporary issues confronting Indian Country must be understood as consequences of this history of Native and non-Native interaction.

Treaties forced upon and entered into by Indian nations ratified the dual policies of removal and reservation and offered guarantees for assistance and restitution via the provision of multiple services. Treaties were the end result of contact, force, brutality, and military conquest. The sovereign nation status of American Indian groups is recognized in treaties, and treaties mandate that the government of the United States provide assistance and restitution to American Indian nations. Therefore, the first forms of assistance and restitution can be understood as examples of foreign policy rather than social welfare policy. Contemporary programs providing services to American Indian communities and individuals must be understood as examples of the historical guarantees that were originally set forth in the various treaties that exist between American Indian sovereign nations and the United States government. This concept was operationalized in the Snyder Act of 1921, which guaranteed health, welfare, and education services to every American Indian on and off the reservation.

## American Social Welfare Policy

Many of the services mandated by treaty and the Snyder Act are now included in the national social welfare policy debates that are defined by federal legislation and implemented under state jurisdiction. The American social welfare system developed independent of the treaty obligations that offer guarantees of the social welfare services to American Indians. For example, treaties in the eighteenth century typically mandate peace, education, health, family, and community support services in exchange for land, and the federal government provided these services. However, the English Poor Law traditions and values, which made available local resources to the needy only when the family could not meet its care-giving responsibilities, influenced American social welfare policies.

In the English Poor Law tradition, government overseers were required to collect taxes from property owners and to distribute relief to the impoverished. The laws required that able-bodied recipients work in exchange for assistance. The provision of assistance was based on the overseer's assessment of need and the assessment of the personal responsibility/culpability for the needy condition. Assistance was discretionary; individuals might be provided with direct relief or assigned to work for another or placed in a workhouse or almshouse. In the latter half of the nineteenth century, attention was focused on the mentally ill, on physically abused children, and on freed slaves and veterans. This resulted in the development of federal legislation and services and led to the development of the formal American social welfare system. This system evolved at a rather slow pace through the beginning of the twentieth century. Most assistance came from private sources that were dependent upon the goodwill of individual citizens. By the end of the century, private charities were the main source of assistance and the main mechanism for the delivery of social welfare. The Great Depression, however, promoted the dramatic growth of the social welfare system.

Historically, social welfare policies that influence the design and delivery of health, educational, nutritional, and social services in the United States reflect traditions associated with the English Poor Laws. There are two philosophical perspectives that influence social welfare in the United States: the *residual* and the *institutional* approaches. Most social welfare interventions reflect the residual perspective. The residual concept of social welfare is based on the idea that individual and family needs should be met in the marketplace and that social welfare is required only during times of market disruption. In theory, social welfare services are withdrawn because they are no longer needed, when the marketplace is stabilized and restored to healthy functioning. Therefore, various forms of government assistance can be made available to individuals and families during periods of economic recession or depression. Eligibility for services is generally determined by individuals offering proof that there is a need that cannot be met by the family. The philosophical values that support this orientation assume that everyone in society has equal access to the resources and opportunities needed to interact with the market place and that chronic dependence on social welfare services is indicative of individual failure to exercise proper moral or personal choice.

The institutional concept of social welfare is based on the idea that social welfare is a legitimate function of modern society. It is assumed that there are naturally occurring conditions that will limit the individual or the family from meeting all needs. Philosophically, social welfare is perceived to be a necessary, permanent, and desirable part of the social structure. Currently, in most western European countries, the institutional model dominates. The American social welfare philosophy has been described as reluctant, because of its failure to provide universal access for the range of social services that are required to maintain a healthy society. Unfortunately, there are multiple barriers that undermine access to the marketplace. Therefore, there is a great burden that is placed on those sectors of the population that lack sufficient discretionary income to purchase the social welfare services required for survival. The reluctance of the American social welfare system to policies from the institutional perspective mirrors the reluctance of the federal government to assume responsibility for the multiple hazards that undermine contemporary American Indian life. These hazards are the direct and lingering result of contact and the loss of the traditional land bases that sustained life. Further, there is reluctance to focus on restitution in lieu of assistance to American Indian communities.

Federal legislation defines the parameters of social welfare policies. Assistance and restitution services for American Indians are influenced by social welfare policies, despite the fact that the promises for these services originally reflected foreign policy to the extent that they operationalized provisions of treaties. Therefore, the federal government is involved in the management of two parallel systems of assistance. One system, directed toward American Indians, mandated by treaties and typically managed by the Bureau of Indian Affairs or other federal departments, is driven by the

A group of Lakota children at a Catholic Indian Mission boarding school, circa 1940. (Photo by Rita Ledesma)

legal obligations incurred as a result of the appropriation of land to provide assistance and restitution. The other system, directed primarily toward all citizens, is driven by the traditions of the English Poor Laws, the general reluctance of the federal government to step into the private family arena, and a preference for intervening only when the family, the marketplace, or local institutions cannot effectively manage the caregiving needs of the citizenry. Each system of care is influenced by the values articulated in the English Poor Laws and the dominant society.

Boundaries between the two systems have blurred over the years for three reasons. American Indians are eligible for services that are available to all citizens. Each system responds to similar needs and issues, and the same federal departments administer services directed specifically toward American Indians. Finally, the values associated with the English traditions have influenced the evolution and development of social welfare policies within the United States. This has resulted in tension and contradiction between the federal government's obligation to American Indian peoples and the American social welfare traditions that

favor the most minimal levels of assistance. These include a preference for the pull-yourself-up-by-your-bootstraps mentality, minimal encroachment into the marketplace and family life, and the provision of services on a temporary basis. The subtext of federal assistance initiatives to American Indians also has been historically influenced by the belief that assistance initiatives can be used to create fundamental change in the structure and fabric of American Indian societies. For example, as early as 1790 the federal government allocated at least $10,000 to a Civilization Fund that supported economic development and education among Indians in order to promote the transformation of Indians into farmers and citizens.

This orientation of American social welfare policies fails to account for federal policies that have consistently eroded and stressed the fabric of American Indian life and the federal obligation to provide assistance and restitution for the loss of land. Equally important, the residual approach that characterizes American social welfare policies does not adequately address issues of restitution. The residual approach is directed toward the provision of temporary assistance to those who demonstrate that they meet specific eligibility criteria. With regard to American Indians, social welfare policies reflect the need to minimize the magnitude of the disruptions to American Indian societies as a result of the removal, reservation, and relocation policies. There is also a preference within the residual approach for attributing the cause of the current distress confronting American Indians solely to personal deficits. The social and economic status of American Indians and contemporary social welfare policy debates illustrate these issues.

## Contemporary Social and Economic Issues

Multiple problems have resulted from the losses incurred by American Indians as a result of contact with non-Indians, despite the federal guarantees to provide assistance and restitution. These problems include substandard housing, low educational attainment, poverty, substance abuse, toxic and hazardous environments, compromised health status, high mortality rates, interpersonal violence, despair, and depression. Current federal social welfare assistance programs direct interventions at these problems.

The concentration of American Indians in the western United States reflects the conquest of Indian nations, the decimation of the indigenous population, and the federal policies of removal and relocation. The increasing urbanization of the population reflects the relocation policies of the 1950s and the search for employment and educational opportunities in environments. Although American Indians are mobile, moving on and off the reservation, the distribution of the population has remained and is projected to remain, relatively stable. This means that solutions to the current social problems that are fueled by environmental conditions are not likely to be solved with geographic cures. Assistance and intervention initiatives for American Indians must acknowledge the physical geography, environmental conditions, and cultural considerations in the design and implementation of social welfare policy. For example, the current welfare-to-work policies mandate that recipients work in exchange for receiving unearned income benefits. This mandate assumes that the environment has jobs available for welfare recipients and the jobs sites are accessible. For the welfare recipient who lives in one of the districts on Pine Ridge Reservation, this assumes that there is a local job available and that transportation to the job is accessible. Both assumptions may be incorrect, not only on Pine Ridge, but also on other reservations. On many reservations, employment opportunities are extremely limited and public transportation is almost nonexistent. The relative stability of the residential

patterns of American Indians indicates that urban Indians are at risk of being disconnected from reservation-based assistance programs, such as those provided by the Bureau of Indian Affairs (BIA) and the Indian Health Service (IHS).

Although there are more than 500 recognized tribes, 50 percent of the American Indian population identifies with one of the eight largest tribes. These are the Cherokee, Navajo, Chippewa, Sioux, Choctaw, Pueblo, Apache, and Iroquois. Membership in a large tribe does not offer protections or access to the social and economic benefits that are associated with American life in this new century.

For example, Pine Ridge reservation, home to the Lakota, is located in Shannon County, which has long been the poorest county in the United States. One-half of American Indian homes on the Navajo Reservation and trust lands lack complete plumbing. Nationally, about 20 percent of American Indian homes lack complete plumbing, and approximately 18 percent of American Indian homes on the reservation and 3 percent of American homes off the reservation lack complete kitchen facilities (a sink with piped water, a cook stove, and a refrigerator). Although telephones are considered as common as air to the average American adolescent, 53 percent of American Indian homes do not have a telephone. The telephone is such a staple of American life that it is difficult to conceptualize the multiple ways that access to a telephone can constrain daily life—from calling 9-1-1 in an emergency, to following up on a job interview, to crossing the digital divide.

These material deficits that characterize American Indian life reflect the deep poverty that impacts Indian Country and the residual approach to social welfare to the degree that the accouterments of modern industrial life—telephones and indoor plumbing—are expected to be purchased in the market place. These deficits symbolize the failure of this approach to adequately support federal obligations to American Indians for assistance and restitution.

Educational attainment is consistently associated with economic opportunity and personal independence. The federal government and its agents have a long history as providers of educational services to Indian children. The earliest boarding schools and federal educational initiatives were quite harsh and dedicated to separating Indian children from their families, communities, and cultures by educating the Indian out of Native children. Current Population Survey data provides the following information about the educational attainment of American Indians between the ages of twenty-five and forty-four years: 18 percent have less

Children from the Campos family around 1940 at Holy Rosary Boarding School, Rosebud Reservation in South Dakota, circa 1940. (Photo by Rita Ledesma)

than a high school education; 41 percent have a high school education; 26 percent have some college education; and 15 percent have a bachelor's degree or higher.

With regard to American Indians and poverty the same data indicated that: 25 percent live in poverty; 13 percent live in extreme poverty (below 50 percent of the official poverty threshold); and 50 percent received some form of welfare (Temporary Assistance to Needy Families, Supplemental Security Income, Medicaid, food stamps, free or reduced school lunches and housing, or rent subsidies). Further, 88 percent of the poor American Indian population received some form of welfare assistance. Thus, American Indians are well represented as consumers of federal assistance/social welfare programs that are designed to support all citizens.

The poverty and educational status of American Indians is associated with federal policies that have unfolded in the last two centuries; however, current social welfare assistance programs do not in any way acknowledge this. Thus, the root causes of the problems that plague American Indians are not addressed in

the contemporary social welfare arena, even as sanctions and limitations are developed for those sectors of the community who continue to need assistance. For example, the assistance program for poor families, Temporary Assistance for Needy Families (TANF), has mandated strict work requirements, established time limits for services, and instituted sanctions for failures to adhere to program requirements. In California, for example, parenting minors must be enrolled and making satisfactory progress in order to continue to receive benefits. Nationally, aid is limited to not more that five years in a lifetime. Welfare reform, as demonstrated in the TANF initiative, illustrates the residual approach and assumes that the root causes of poverty resides within the individual. Clearly, welfare reform is potentially devastating to American Indian children and families for these reasons.

Poverty is overcome when structural and institutional changes support individual growth and development. Economic development is one mechanism for promoting the structural changes to eradicate poverty

Los Angeles urban Indians drum to prevent the closing of a drug rehabilitation center. (Photo by Mary G. Wentz)

and its consequences in the American Indian community. However, in Indian Country economic development is chronically underdeveloped. Gambling operations have constituted the major form of economic growth since the passage of the 1988 Indian Gaming Regulatory Act. Gambling represents an indigenous response to the pervasive problems that have become entrenched across generations. It also reflects the absence of federal leadership in fostering assistance and restitution initiatives that honor historical obligations. For a small number of gaming tribes, gambling operations have been the engine driving economic success, but it is not a panacea. The Navajo have consistently opposed gambling on religious/ceremonial grounds, and many reservations are located too far away from the large population centers needed to generate and sustain profitability.

Other tribes have explored different routes to economic development. The Havasupai have focused on tourism to promote economic development. The Oneida of Wisconsin and the Mississippi Band of Choctaw Indians have promoted the development of factories. The work ethic and commitment to care for their own

families is as strong in American Indian communities as it is in other communities. Tribal governments must continue to look to federal sources of support in order to address the educational, health and social services needs of their constituents. Major funding for these programs comes from federal sources. The income support assistance programs are developed and funded in the social welfare arena, while health, education and social services are typically housed within the BIA and IHS, whose budgets are annually the subject to debate and cutback. The rate of Indian poverty, the absence of economic development in reservation communities, the residual orientation in social welfare, and the long history of federal ambivalence with regard to providing assistance and restitution undermine the lives and opportunities of many American Indians.

## Assistance and Restitution Programs

The Bureau of Indian Affairs was the first major provider of assistance to American Indians. Originally housed in the War Department, its mission was to direct and manage all Indian affairs. It established a system of boarding schools, provided subsistence services and managed land issues as determined necessary by a network of agents, supervisors, and the Indian commissioner.

On the national level, many states in 1911 began to provide Mothers' Pensions to widows with children. This was the first indicator that federal and local governments were willing to assume responsibility for citizens and insure a minimum standard of living. Although there was always opposition to these programs from social conservatives, the Great Depression forced a reevaluation of the government's role as a provider of assistance, because so many citizens were poor and unemployed. The Social Security Act of 1935 marks the entry of the federal government as a central provider of assistance. The Social Security Act included economic assistance programs, federal and state unemployment insurance, a national system for retirement benefits, and social services. The economic assistance programs included Aid to Families with Dependent Children, Aid to the Blind, Aid to the Permanently and Totally Disabled, and Old Age Assistance.

The 1928 Meriam Report documented the plight of American Indians and the crisis conditions on reservations, resulting in a reorganization of the Office of Indian Affairs. The Great Depression had a critical impact on reservations. However, tribes had to fight throughout the 1940s to receive the benefits of these programs. Arizona and New Mexico were the last states to accord the rights enjoyed by other citizens to Indians, including access to federal and state economic assistance programs. The terrible impact of the Depression on reservations was buffered temporarily with the creation of public works jobs. Beginning in the 1940s, the BIA instituted a cash assistance program to offset the extreme poverty on reservations. The first assistance was provided in the form of vouchers that could be exchanged for food at trading posts. By the late 1940s the administration of general assistance programs was placed in Bureau agency offices on or near the reservation. The BIA general assistance program can include families who do not meet the eligibility criteria for state administered programs.

In the 1960s poverty was rediscovered as an issue that continued to affect non-Indians and a War on Poverty was declared. The Economic Opportunity Act of 1964 (EOA) established a number of initiatives designed to give people the opportunities and assistance necessary for overcoming poverty. These initiatives included the Head Start program, which gave economically disadvantaged children educational opportunities, and Community Action Programs, which were designed to give local communities the opportunity to identify needs and develop solutions. Indian tribes, like

states and cities could apply to administer programs funded by the EOA, thus, tribes could exercise more control over these social welfare initiatives as compared to those that were under federal jurisdiction. Health care and social services amendments were added to the Social Security Act during this period, which included Medicaid for the elderly and the impoverished. The federal government committed to funding up to 75 percent of these services. However, as costs escalated in the 1970s, new amendments were passed that placed spending caps on states and that stipulated eligibility for services. These limitations continued into the 1980s when huge cuts in social welfare programs and block grant funding were instituted. These changes were driven by the desire to limit federal spending and the affirmation of the residual approach to social welfare.

Independent of the national assistance program available to all citizens, the last fifty years have seen the birth of three changes with regard to the provision of assistance to Indians only. The Bureau of Indian Affairs was reorganized in the late 1940s and given oversight responsibility for implementing federal policies and programs, all federal lands and all Indian affairs. The Indian Health Service was established in 1955 as a part of the Public Health Service, and charged with the responsibility for the health of all Indian people. The passage of the Indian Self Determination and Education Assistance Act of 1975, Public Law 638, encouraged tribal administration of programs previously administered by the BIA. There was some opposition to this act as it could be used to terminate a tribe's special trust status and thus, the authority of treaty agreements. Tribes could hardly be self-supporting without adequate federal funding for contracts. Since the 1950s, administration of the primary federal programs developed for tribes and Indians living off the reservation have been divided between two federal agencies: the Department of the Interior and the Department of Health and Human Services. As noted, tribal members are also eligible for services available to all citizens. Therefore, American Indians may interact with assistance programs administered by the federal, state, BIA and IHS agencies. There are also special programs for Indian people in all twelve cabinet level departments, as well as hundreds of local and privately funded programs. The complexity associated with accessing all these programs is staggering. Another issue continues to surface that makes this complexity even more challenging.

The federal government continues to confront contradictions in the efforts to devise programs that adhere to the American social welfare value orientations and treaty obligations. Many of the programs offered to Indian communities that fall under the mantle of the

Social Security Act and the poverty initiatives of the 1960s are neither supportive of nor compatible with tribal ways and environmental conditions. Programs may conflict with community values or contain provisions that are unrealizable in the local community. The preceding discussion on Temporary Assistance to Needy Families illustrates this, as program directives assume that jobs are locally available and that a community infrastructure exists (plumbing, utilities, transportation, child care) to support work. One outcome of this contradiction is that programs cannot achieve intended results. Although the federal government had invested heavily in assistance programs the lack of attention to the root causes that drive the need for assistance programs and the lack or attention to cultural and environmental considerations consistently undermine efforts. The income assistance program designed for needy families illustrate these issues.

## Temporary Assistance to Needy Families

Passage of the *Personal Responsibility and Work Opportunity Reconciliation Act of 1996 (PL 104–193)*, commonly known as welfare reform, solidified the residual approach to income assistance for poor children and their families and marks a retreat from the federal responsibility to insure a minimum standard of living for all families. A year after passage of the welfare reform legislation, Congress amended the law by establishing *Welfare to Work* legislation. These laws create significant change in the provision of welfare assistance to needy individuals, children, and families. Aid to Families with Dependent Children (AFDC) has been dismantled and transformed into the Temporary Assistance for Needy Families program (TANF). TANF is now funded via discretionary block grants to the states and mandates strict work participation requirements for all participants. All welfare-related assistance programs and service—Food Stamps, Medicaid, Medicare, child care, and children's programs—are impacted as state and local governments are now charged with responsibility for program implementations and given spending authority. In the process, the residual approach that promotes temporary assistance, minimal intrusion from the federal government, and personal responsibility is affirmed as the federal government shed much of its fiscal and jurisdictional responsibilities for income assistance to poor children and families. Vocational training, job search activities, and employment are mandatory for recipients of Temporary Aid to Needy Families.

As noted earlier in this discussion, Indian Country is significantly impacted by poverty and its consequences. As such, the potential impact of welfare reform is especially hazardous to the health and well being of Indian communities. The contradictions associated with American social welfare policy and American Indians are glaringly apparent. There are few provisions within the welfare reform legislation that address the unique status or issues of Indians in American society. Tribal governments now have less standing, rights, and privileges in the design and implementation of welfare reform programs than do states. The long-standing problems of tribal and reservation economic development significantly undermine the capacity of Indian recipients to meet eligibility criteria and the mandatory requirements; therefore, they are at great risk of being sanctioned for non-compliance. Tribes are able to operate their own tribal TANF programs, and many are doing so. However, the resources available to the states for implementation are not available to tribal governments. Therefore, tribes are burdened in the earliest stages of development because they lack the resources needed to develop and sustain TANF programs. States have partnered with the federal government for many years to provide income assistance programs. Because tribes have not been provided with the support required for a fair and equal collaboration with federal government, their TANF initiatives will likely be plagued with special problems in the initial phases of implementation. It appears that it will be extremely difficult for tribes to mount locally controlled TANF programs without state fiscal support. Yet states are not required to match tribal resources; therefore, there is little motivation for them to do so. As tribes are offered the opportunity to develop tribal TANF initiatives, they must be prepared to assume the costs for enormously expensive welfare programs and to provide comprehensive services to a historically needy population. TANF recipients are required to meet strict work requirements and eligibility for assistance is limited to a period of not more that two consecutive years and not more than five years in a lifetime. These provisions clearly reiterate the residual approach to social welfare, and the assumption that poverty is a personal choice, that jobs are available and that infrastructure supports exist to promote and enhance employability. A special provision is provided for Indians who reside on reservations where the unemployment rate is at least 50 percent in a designated reporting period. However, unemployment rates fluctuate over time and an unemployment rate of 48 percent does not eliminate work requirements, so this provision does not offer significant relief. As noted previously, there is a significant relationship between economic development and poverty. The chronic absence of economic development fuels chronic poverty. True welfare reform on reservations requires jobs and economic development. True welfare reform on and off the reservation would acknowledge the unique legal relationships that exist between Indians and the federal government and recognize that the root causes of poverty must be addressed.

## Federal Programs for American Indians

There are eleven cabinet-level federal departments, the BIA under the Department of the Interior, and a number of independent federal agencies that provide programs designed to serve Indian tribes and/or off-reservation Indian people. The BIA has five major divisions—Office of Administration, Office of Indian Education Programs, Office of Tribal Services, Office of Trust and Economic Development, and Area Offices—and each has a number of subdivisions and programs. Information about some of these programs is provided. Readers can access more detailed and specific information about these programs via the Internet and in federal documents and reports on federal assistance programs written for the Senate Committee on Indian Affairs. Since both houses of Congress are responsible for Indian policy and for funding and overseeing programs for Indians, special committees are appointed to carry out these responsibilities, such as the Senate Committee on Indian Affairs. Committee staff persons become knowledgeable about Indian programs, and the committee holds special hearings to acquire information needed by members of Congress and the general public.

*The Department of Agriculture* administers programs designed to enhance utilization of natural resources (soil conservation, for example) and technical assistance programs designed to aid persons engaged in farming and forestry, in addition to the food programs described in the preceding section.

*The Department of Commerce* administers programs to stimulate economic development and alleviate unemployment, such as loans and technical assistance to develop small businesses to determine feasibility of a proposed enterprise. The Minority Business Development Agency provides financial assistance for business development to American Indian businesses, business owners, and tribes. The department administers special programs related to the fishing industry. Indian tribes, like states, can apply for grant monies for the construction of public facilities to encourage long-term economic growth in communities where economic growth is seen to be lagging behind.

*The Department of Defense* sponsors a program to recruit American Indians into the National Guard. The Air Force's Affirmative Employment American Indian/ Alaskan Native Special Emphasis Program assesses barriers in the recruitment process and in the work place to American Indian participation. The Defense Department shares the cost of running Procurement Technical Assistance programs to tribally based businesses to increase tribal opportunities to obtain Defense Department contracts. The Army's Corps of Engineers may assist in assessing the feasibility of developing tribal land areas for income producing recreational purposes.

*The Department of Education* has many programs related to American Indians. Central goals are to establish and enrich Indian-controlled schools and projects that meet the educational and cultural needs of Indian children. Formula grants are available to tribes, local educational agencies, and tribal schools to provide financial assistance in the development, establishment, and operation of elementary and secondary school programs that meet the culturally related academic needs of Indian children. Resources also are available to develop adult education programs to increase basic academic skills of American Indian adults; increase the number of adults who earn a high school equivalency diploma; and support the heritage of American Indian adults. All these funds are allocated using a competitive, grant proposal process. In addition, the department provides technical assistance and training to education agencies, parent committees, and tribes and Indian organizations in the design, management, implementation, and evaluation of education programs in which more than 5,000 Indian children are enrolled. Fellowships are available to Indian persons admitted to undergraduate or graduate programs in engineering, business administration, natural resources, and related fields and to Indian students in graduate programs in medicine, psychology, law, education, and related fields.

*The Department of Energy* offers a state formula grant program for energy-efficient homes to low-income homeowners, especially the aged and handicapped, and offers programs designed to conserve energy. The department assists minority financial institutions, such as banks, by providing long-term capital to increase the funds available for loans and investments in minority communities.

*The Department of Housing and Urban Development* provides funds for housing construction in Indian communities. Most of these funds are used to subsidize privately owned family homes.

*The Department of Health and Human Services* is the key department of the executive branch of the U.S. government responsible for income support and social service programs. Its diverse programs are administered by a number of subdivisions within the department. The Administration for Children, Youth, and Families administers several programs for which tribes

The American Indian clubhouse in downtown Los Angeles serves Native students in an after–school program. (Photo by Mary G. Wentz)

may apply, two of which are the Head Start program, which provides health, educational, nutritional, and social services to economically disadvantaged preschool-aged children and their families, and the Child Welfare Services program, which establishes and strengthens the child welfare services provided by state and local public welfare agencies to enable children to remain in their own homes or, when that is not possible, to provide alternate permanent homes. Funds are available to Indian tribal organizations to provide child welfare services.

The Administration for Native Americans (ANA) places a priority on funding innovative projects that will, in the administration's opinion, have the greatest impact on promoting economic, political, and social self-sufficiency for Native peoples to increase their independence from U.S. programs. ANA-funded projects assist tribal governments to exercise control over their resources; to foster development of stable, diversified local economies to increase jobs, promote economic well-being, and reduce dependency on public

funds and social services; and to foster social development to support access to, control of, and coordination of services and programs that safeguard the health and well-being of people.

The Office of Policy, Planning, and Legislation funds small grants to prevent family violence and alleviate its effects.

The Indian Health Service of the Public Health Service was established in 1955 to improve the health of American Indians and Alaska Natives by providing a full range of curative, preventive, and rehabilitative health services. In addition, IHS is supposed to build the capacity of tribes to manage their own health programs. Tribes may contract with IHS to provide direct services to tribal members. Funds are available for recruitment and scholarship support to increase the number of Indian health care professionals.

The Office of Community Services of the Family Support Administration can fund tribes to assist low-income families to meet their costs of home energy. This program office also can award block grants to tribes to ameliorate poverty by providing a number of services to low-income members, including employment, education, improved use of their available income, housing, emergency assistance, removal of obstacles to self-sufficiency, community participation, better use of other programs related to decreasing poverty, improved coordination of service delivery, and increased use of private sector resources to fight poverty.

*The Department of the Interior* houses the Bureau of Indian Affairs (BIA), the major agency responsible for Indian programs. The BIA serves as the intermediary between tribes and the federal government. Most of the BIA's attention is focused on land and resource management. However, within the several divisions some attention is given to social welfare issues. Authorized by the Snyder Act of 1921, the Division of Education provides financial aid to enable Indians to attend college and to enable adults to increase their basic skills and to obtain a high school equivalency degree.

The BIA Division of Self-Determination Services, Office of Tribal Services, can provide grants to the governing bodies of federally recognized tribes to improve tribal governing capacities, prepare for contracting of bureau programs, enable tribes to provide direction to the bureau and to other federal programs intended to serve Indian people. These are called self-determination grants, and Public Law 93–638, the Self-Determination and Education Assistance Act of 1975 authorizes them. Provided in the form of project grants, and thus competitive, projects must be designed to improve a tribe's capacity to enter into contracts, including the purchase of third party technical assistance, the acquisition of land, and the designing, monitoring, and evaluation of federal programs serving Indian tribes. The funds requested for 1991 were less than one-third the funding request for 1990 (one-third of $13.5 million). Again, resources available for these programs are decreasing. The number of programs alone, without assessing the amount of funds available, does not tell us the value of the support to American Indians.

The BIA initiated cash General Assistance Program on reservations in the early 1940s. In addition, the BIA administers social service programs for families and children and awards funds competitively through a grant application process for tribal Indian child welfare service programs. The BIA has a guaranteed loan program designed to increase the number of lending institutions that will loan money to Indian organizations and individuals residing on or near a federally recognized reservation and to Indian-run business ventures.

*The Department of Justice*, Civil Rights Division, enforces the civil rights of American Indians defined in federal statute, the Constitution, and civil rights acts. The latter includes protection of equal rights to federal programs. Also, funds are available to improve reporting of child abuse and services to victims.

*The Department of Labor* administers Indian training and employment efforts.

*The Department of Transportation* provides assistance toward increasing Native employment opportunities in transportation linked projects and toward assuring Indian access to Department of Transportation contracts.

*The Department of Veteran Affairs* offers assistance toward Indians receiving earned benefits.

The massive number of programs can be deceptive if the actual program size and available funding for each program are not assessed. For example, substandard housing, family violence, and substance abuse prevention continue to impact Indian communities. On paper there is a program through the Department of Health and Human Services, Office of Policy, Planning and Legislation, yet 85 percent of the available funds are designated for states, thus monies for tribes to address this critical issue are very limited. Assistance initiatives to American Indians must address the multitude of issues that erode the fabric of American Indian communities and that support comprehensive, coordinated and well-funded service delivery systems.

Indian families consistently receive less support than non-Indian families. For example, state support for day care for low-income families commonly is not available to the same extent to families living on reservations. Since states will only reimburse state-licensed day care providers if such providers are not accessible to Indian families, the families cannot receive subsidized day care services. A number of tribes continue to have the lowest per capita income levels in the United States, with large numbers of families falling well below national poverty levels. Overall the average income for Indian families is lower than the incomes of other families, including minority of color populations such as African American families; the unemployment rates are higher; and the employment resources, housing, sanitation, and life expectancy rates are all lower.

Government agencies provide subsistence-level public assistance to tribal communities, but the federal government has historically been unwilling to launch the major economic development programs that could lead to economic independence and that would compensate for the social and economic disorganization and dependence that is a consequence of the contact between Indians and non-Indians. Economic assistance and restitution initiatives to American Indians must address the root causes of the poverty in Indian Country and all the social, cultural, material, and psychological consequences. Assistance initiatives must be connected with restitution and disconnected from the residual philosophies that characterize American social welfare policies.

*Rita Ledesma*
*California State University, Los Angeles*

# ◆ ABORIGINAL ECONOMIC ACTIVITY IN CANADA

Aboriginal economic activity has been important to the early survival of European settlers and the development of Canada throughout its history as a country. Trade with aboriginal peoples sustained many of the early settlers. In later years, aboriginal labor helped build the railway, harvest crops, bring in the hay, herd cows, pick fruit, can salmon, transport furs along waterways, and guide settlers through unknown territory, among myriad other activities. Yet, by any statistical standard one wishes to apply, aboriginal peoples have come to occupy the lowest rung on the economic ladder in Canada. Through several decades of the welfare state and various state initiatives to address the economic problems of aboriginal peoples, levels of income, labor force participation, and education remain stubbornly and significantly below that of the general population.

Aboriginal peoples have been seen as a people somehow ill suited to commercial or capitalist activity and hence unable to participate effectively in a capitalist economy. The communal nature of aboriginal culture, the absence of institutions of private property, and the lack of a profit motive, the argument runs, has rendered aboriginal peoples unable to compete in a competitive marketplace and limited the community's ability to adjust to rapidly changing times.

A quick historical profile of indigenous economic activity reveals that these generalizations are not supportable. Long before Europeans arrived in North America, aboriginal people maintained extensive and productive trade networks, exchanging surplus products, securing supplies of necessary items, and distributing new materials and products. Trade in North America was not, therefore, a European innovation or import.

The Royal Commission on Aboriginal Peoples (1996) describes aboriginal economic history in four periods which correspond roughly to the development of the relationship between aboriginal peoples and Canadians.

## The Pre-Contact Period (Before 1500)

Prior to the arrival of Europeans, most aboriginal peoples in Canada were hunters, fishers, and gatherers. Those who lived near the Pacific, Arctic, and Atlantic oceans had an economy that involved sea harvesting; those on the St. Lawrence valley and Great Lakes engaged in agriculture.

Aboriginal peoples were thinly scattered with two principal concentrations: the Pacific Northwest and the Lower Great Lakes Regions. For the most part, economic activity varied according to the seasons and the availability of fish, wildlife, and vegetation. The emphasis was on living in balance with nature rather than on accumulating economic surpluses or wealth. For most this meant paying close attention to the food needs of the group, the ability of the land or sea to sustain future inhabitants.

Robin Riddington, an anthropologist at the University of British Columbia, theorizes that the technology used as the basis of aboriginal economies was based upon knowledge rather than tools. More than material technology, he argues, it was intimate knowledge of the ecosystem, developed over thousands of years, and aboriginal ingenuity that enabled aboriginal peoples to survive in the harsh northern environment.

Extensive trade networks were used for the movement of goods and technology across the country: fish from the Northwest Coast were transported to the interior; obsidian (a volcanic rock used in tools), originating in British Columbia, was found in the western plains; abalone from California was found in the interior.

Aboriginal economic activity was undertaken for a number of reasons: profit or material gain, prestige, to build or maintain alliances, or cement agreements. In some aboriginal societies, particularly those of the Pacific the accumulation of wealth was accompanied by ceremonies for giving it away: the potlatch. Prestige and status accrued to those who were most generous.

## The Fur Trade (1500–1814)

In this period, aboriginal peoples and Europeans regarded each other as distinct and autonomous, left to govern their own internal affairs but cooperating in areas of mutual interest and occasionally and increasingly linked in various trading relationships and other forms of nation-to-nation alliances.

In the initial period of contact, aboriginal peoples were able to continue their traditional patterns of economic activity. In the early 1500s, Mi'kmaq began to trade furs for European goods: knives, iron goods, foodstuffs, and clothing. Across the continent, aboriginal peoples' early encounters with Europeans were primarily as potential trading partners and occasionally as suppliers of local goods, contractors (trappers) who harvested local wildlife in exchange for European goods, and middlemen between aboriginal suppliers and European trading companies. The fur trade began to expand; Maliseet, Montagnais, Iroquois, Cree, and Ojibwa, among others were actively engaged in the trade as either trappers or middlemen.

Aboriginal people initially adapted well to the demands of the fur trade, which built upon and supported traditional lifestyles rather than displacing them. Aboriginal peoples were also important players in the economies of the time. They were excellent harvesters and negotiators, seeking the best deals for their furs, and they were adept at playing off the English and French, or one boat against another, to get the best prices. The Hudson Bay Company had to develop a standard of exchange for furs and European goods to counter aboriginal negotiating prowess.

Métis people were also important actors in the fur trade. The Métis lived in and around trading posts; some worked as independent laborers, as freighters on boat brigades, or in clerical or supervisory jots at trading posts. The merger of the North West Company and the Hudon's Bay Company in 1821 reduced labor requirements somewhat, but many Métis people were still employed in the fur trade and in new opportunity areas of buffalo hunting and exporting of buffalo hides and furs to the United States. The continuing arrival of European settlers and the growth of towns and villages led to the emergence of a small Métis merchant class and Métis skilled craftsmen who built churches, housing, and commercial establishments and manufactured carts.

The fur trade also had negative consequences, including the depletion of fur-bearing animals as new technologies permitted greater harvests and European market demands rose; conflict among aboriginal groups as they pushed into new territories in search of resources; exposure to the boom and bust cycle for staple production and its resultant unemployment, first in the fur trade but then in other areas such as whaling, forest production, fishing, sealing, and mineral mining; and exposure to contagious disease which devastated aboriginal populations and caused much social, economic, and cultural disruption.

## The Settler Period (1814–1930)

In this period, non-aboriginal society was for the most part no longer willing to respect the distinctiveness of aboriginal communities. Non-aboriginal society made repeated attempts to recast aboriginal peoples and their institutions to conform to the expectations of mainstream Canada. Aboriginal peoples remained determined to maintain their distinctiveness and conduct their relations in line with their original and agreed upon understandings as outlined in treaties and other agreements.

As Europeans created new and permanent communities, they came to see aboriginal peoples as a hindrance to the development of Canada's lands, waters, and other natural resources. Aboriginal peoples were pushed to the margins and the alienation of aboriginal peoples from their lands and resources began. In many cases, Europeans simply assumed that they had title to these new lands and resources (or were given title by those whom they assumed had the authority to grant it). In some cases, Europeans recognized that some form of negotiation and compensation was necessary. This recognition lead to and informed a period of treaty making which transferred large amounts of land and resources from aboriginal peoples to Canada. In some cases, particularly in British Columbia, no treaties were offered and there is no agreement on the sharing of lands and resources. The Canadian government has established a treaty claims process aimed at rectifying problems with treaties (through specific claims) and at dealing with areas and aboriginal peoples who did not sign treaties.

The decline of the fur trade and the continued development of the settler economy led to extreme disruption of aboriginal economies to the point where aboriginal peoples experienced severe economic deprivation. For example, Métis people on the prairies saw their overland hauling routes undermined by railroads and steamboats; the decline of the buffalo damaged both Indian and Métis livelihoods; and all experienced the depletion of forbearing animals in the woodland areas of the Great Lakes and the overfishing of lakes and streams.

The new government of Canada in 1867, through the Constitution Act, assumed the exclusive responsibility for Indians and lands reserved for Indians. The Gradual Enfranchisement Act of 1869 replaced traditional Indian governments with elected chiefs and councilors whose decisions required the approval of a federally appointed Indian agent acting on behalf of a minister of the Crown. The transfer of control from Indian people to the government of Canada caused enormous disruptions in the socioeconomic development of communities which last into today. Laws which restricted mobility, the ownership of property, and the extension of credit, among others, impeded economic development.

In the late nineteenth and early twentieth century, Canada made significant attempts to persuade Indian people to become farmers. The goal was to have Indian and Métis people settle down and adopt a European way of life. For the most part these efforts were unsuccessful; government policies did not permit sufficient resources, either land, equipment, or seed, while drought, overproduction of land, and low prices hindered success. More often than not, non-Indian farmers persuaded the government to sell productive Indian lands to them, place restrictions on the sale of Indian produce, and limit Indian use of new technologies.

As Canada industrialized, aboriginal people began to participate in the market economy, mostly on the margins and in manual occupations. Aboriginal peoples again began to develop a measure of self-sufficiency, although at low levels of income. They participated in the new industries springing up, worked their own farms or as hired hands on others, constructed houses, and established businesses in such areas as crafts.

Rolf Knight, in his book *Indians at Work: An Informal History of Native Labor in British Columbia, 1858–1930* (1978), documents the various ways in which aboriginal peoples in British Columbia participated in logging, transportation, construction, long shoring, commercial fishing, and canning, among other industries since the arrival of Europeans; Fred Wein in *Rebuilding the Economic Base of Indian Communities: The Micmac in Nova Scotia* (1986) documents the participation of Mikm'aq people in the Atlantic economy in road construction, ship loading, pip prop cutting for coal mines, and arts and crafts production. Many traveled to Maine for seasonal harvesting of blueberries and potatoes; when unable to find employment locally, they took up jobs in the emerging manufacturing industries of New England.

There is some evidence that aboriginal peoples were successfully making a transition from a traditional to a modern economy, albeit this transition has been difficult and uneven.

## The Period of Dependence (1930–)

Aboriginal participation in the settler economy was tenuous, marginal, and vulnerable. The great depression of the 1930s led to a large decline in aboriginal participation in the labor force as businesses and jobs disappeared. Aboriginal peoples, as a result of their vulnerable position, were often the first to lose their jobs or businesses. Labor force participation increased temporarily as a result of labor shortages during the Second World War, but the end of the war and the return of soldiers displaced these peoples again. Indian people increasingly turned to governments to assist in dealing with the effects of economic distress and to take advantage of economic opportunity.

Aboriginal people were viewed as existing outside local society and, therefore, also beyond the responsibility of the federal government. Local municipalities and provinces did not seem to take any responsibility for assisting local Indian populations, particularly those living on reserves. Local services were not available, banks were reluctant to do business with people on reserves without federal guarantees on loans, and businesses saw the reserve community primarily as a market for their goods and services, not thinking of a reciprocal obligation to provide employment or other types of community support.

In an effort to address problems of Indian poverty and unemployment, the federal government began to act to try to improve the situation. It began to relocate and consolidate reserves in order to create larger communities and to locate near more suitable land or natural resources. This approach did not work: it ignored the social effects of relocation, and the jobs created were often short-term and only available at the start of the relocation. Once the work of building and housing the members was over, the jobs disappeared.

The government also put into place an extensive welfare system. Starting in the 1960s, this was supplemented by on-reserve job creation programs. While these programs were helpful in dealing with the immediate problem of poverty and unemployment, they did not address the problem of building an economic base for the community. They were developed with little aboriginal involvement and often worked against local economic recovery. As the aboriginal population grew, the demand for jobs increased. With the rate of job creation much below the demand, the demand for social assistance increased. Over time, communities unable to meet the demand for jobs from their members grew to depend significantly on social assistance funding.

At the same time, private sector companies engaged in a series of actions that hampered the development of aboriginal economies. In the northern areas, major resource companies established operations in areas where aboriginal peoples were trying to continue to live a traditional lifestyle. Mining, forestry, oil, and gas projects were highly disruptive of aboriginal land use and harvesting patterns. In this period of expanding government, federal and provincial governments adopted whole new regimes of regulations with a wide variety of objectives: to preserve fish and game, to register tramlines, and to control access to Crown lands. They ignored aboriginal and treaty rights or interpreted them very narrowly. Starting in the 1970s, courts began to interpret these rights more broadly.

The period of dependence started in the 1930s and continues for the most part to the present. It has a number of roots, including the disruption of traditional ways of making a living; dispossession from a rich land and resource base; laws, regulations, and government policies that blocked the rebuilding of economies; failure of an education system to provide an appropriate education for aboriginal children; shifts in the mainstream economy as labor-saving technology replaced people and required more highly educated people to operate it; lack of capital to purchase this technology for their own enterprises; and the general racism exhibited toward aboriginal peoples.

## Displacement Over Time

As the Canadian industrial economy continued to evolve, aboriginal people generally discovered that there was little room for them within the mainstream. Deeply entrenched patterns of racial discrimination limited the options of many otherwise qualified people. The arrival of Oriental workers on the west coast, for example, led to the displacement of substantial numbers of aboriginal workers from the fishing fleets and canneries. Few aboriginal people found work in the industrial plants and factories or in the growing number of mining and lumber operations springing up across the country. It is misleading to suggest, however, that aboriginal people did not adjust to the changing economic order, although the opportunity to do so was often circumscribed by non-Native assumptions and actions.

The economic situation of aboriginal peoples reflects a complex mix of Native choice, discrimination, and a poor fit between aboriginal skills and the changing needs of the national economy. Where possible, aboriginal people tended to preserve the harvesting option as long as they could, even if this meant only casual and seasonal involvement with the wage economy. Over time the very skills that made aboriginal people so economically important during the early days of the fur trade, commercial fishery, Arctic whaling, and other sectors were devalued by the advent of new technology or the decline of the industry. Without adequate education and still wishing to retain a substantial connection to the land, aboriginal people found themselves trapped on the outside of the evolving market economy. When groups made concerted efforts to join the new order, however, as in the case of the Plains Indians who took up commercial agriculture in the late nineteenth century, they often found that government policy and non-Native discrimination stood in their way.

A fundamental transition had occurred. In the first period of contact, aboriginal skills and knowledge had been highly valued and were essential to the success of non-Native economic development. By the late nineteenth century, reliance on aboriginal peoples had declined precipitously, and by the middle of the next century aboriginal people had been rendered essentially irrelevant to the Canadian economy. Aboriginal people attempted to adapt to the new realities but found that the newcomers had erected substantial barriers to full participation. Aboriginal peoples suffered from discrimination, which denied them access to employment and other economic opportunities. A flawed missionary-based education system was coupled with the self-serving belief that aboriginal peoples should be kept separate from non-Native peoples until they were "ready" for full integration. Not surprisingly, a variety of social and cultural difficulties accompanied the loss of autonomy and economic freedom that accompanied the loss of aboriginal lands, access to resources, and commercial opportunities. By the 1950s, when the Canadian government decided that it had an obligation to take substantial measures to address the economic gap between aboriginal and non-aboriginal peoples, the First Nations found themselves on the margins of the Canadian economy.

## Renewal

Since the 1960s there have been consistent and continual efforts to try to improve the economic circumstances of aboriginal peoples. The federal government has been a key actor in this effort. Over the forty-year period starting in the 1960s, there has been a consistent evolution of the approach to aboriginal economic development. The primary focus of the early efforts was business development. In order to facilitate the start up of businesses, the federal government established the Indian Revolving Loan Fund in 1960. It provided loans and assistance (business advice and training, and small equity contributions to Indian individuals who wished to start small businesses). In the mid-1960s, this focused approach on individuals was broadened to include communities and, in 1963, the Community Development Program was established. This program increased the scope of the development effort by including social development as part of a comprehensive approach.

The Hawthrone Report (1966) recommended "that economic development should be based on a comprehensive program on many fronts besides the purely economic." This thinking was to form the basis of economic development policy for the 1970s and 1980s.

These two decades saw the development of an increasing broader set of economic development programs. These programs, NEED (Native Economic and Employment Development) and NEDP (Native Economic Development Program) in the early 1980s and CAEDS (Canadian Aboriginal Economic Development Strategy) in the late 1980s, were comprehensive and broad on a number of fronts.

First, the scope of assistance has increased from direct loans and equity contributions to include loan guarantees, provision of management and technical assistance directly by the federal government and then by nongovernmental organizations such as CESO (Canadian Executive Services Overseas now Canadian Executive Services Organization), FBDB (Federal Business Development Bank), Frontiers Foundation, and many others. Second, the number of target groups has increased from exclusively Indians on-reserve, to Inuit, Métis, and off-reserve Indian people, women, and youth. Third, the scope of program objectives has widened. The objectives were initially focused narrowly on small business development through the Indian revolving loan fund, then included community development through the community development program; economic sector development through support and assistance to arts and crafts, agriculture, fishing, and forestry; institutional development through the NEED and CAEDS program; and human resource development through the NEED, ICHRS (Indian Community Human Resource Strategy), and CAEDS programs. Fourth, the number of government departments involved has also increased. There has been a shift from the single-agency approach centered on INAC (Indian and Northern Affairs Canada) in the 1960s to a multi-department approach of the 1990s, which now includes Human Resources Canada, Aboriginal Business Canada, and Health Canada. In addition, there is now a more coordinated approach among the various federal departments involved. Fifth, the degree of participation and control by aboriginal people has also increased. In the 1960s and early 1970s, the federal government retained control over all aspects of economic development: planning, setting priorities, and developing and approving projects. Since then, aboriginal peoples and their institutions have assumed larger and larger roles in all of these processes. Finally, significant growth in the institutional capacity of aboriginal communities has furthered their socioeconomic development.

Aboriginal people have demonstrated a remarkable consistency in their preferred approach to economic development. This approach was set out in the *Wahbung: Our Tomorrows*, a report prepared by the Manitoba Indian Brotherhood in response to the White Paper[1] of 1969. This report called for development to proceed, not in bits and pieces, but according to a comprehensive plan. This plan consisted of three essential elements: (1) a plan to help individuals and communities recover from the pathological consequences of poverty and powerlessness; (2) a plan for the protection of Indian interests in lands and resources; and (3) a concerted effort toward human resource and cultural development. The report argued that any change that was to be beneficial would have to directed and evaluated by Indian people themselves, who could take individual and communal interests into consideration better than the federal government. It also argued that Canadian governments would have to relinquish some powers to Indian people to enable self-government and that Indian people would also have to link Canadian and local cultures.

*Wahbung*, while it may have been a reaction against government policy, was a positive statement of principle and value by aboriginal leaders. It outlined a vision of how they wanted the future to unfold. It was an act of a human agency. This act had an enormous effect. Over the next thirty years, aboriginal leaders were to advocate for these principles in almost all areas.

The Royal Commission on Aboriginal Peoples (1991–1996) undertook significant research into aboriginal economies and their future development. This effort was one of the first in contemporary times to examine in great detail what had gone wrong in Native economic development and how to rectify it. The research was one of the first efforts to focus on a distinct entity called an *aboriginal economy*. In this sense, it represented a shift in thinking about aboriginal peoples, causing a shift in public policy away from a project-oriented approach to a community-development approach based on long term agreements for resources and assistance.

Aboriginal leaders and Canadian policymakers have started to think about something called an *aboriginal economy* or *aboriginal economies* and to explore the nature and functioning of that economy and the appropriate micro economic policies to develop it. There is now an understanding that these economies are enormously varied across a number of different spectra, from predominately traditional economies to modern market economies. Each has varying levels of natural and human resources, varying economic, social and political goals, and differing institutional capacities to facilitate, encourage, advocate, assist in and direct the development of local economies.

## The Report of the Royal Commission on Aboriginal Peoples and Economic Development (1996)

The commission concluded, on the basis of its hearings, community visits, and research during the 1991–1996 period that current conditions and approaches to economic development would bring little improvement in the conditions and prospects for aboriginal peoples. Achieving a more self-reliant economic base for aboriginal peoples would require significant, even radical, departures from business as usual.

While the current situation was bleak, the commission found that the situation was not static and that there were some promising new directions. Over the past two decades, several major comprehensive claims agreements have been signed. These provide access to new human, financial, and natural resources for economic development. There has been much growth in the number of aboriginal businesses, especially those started by women. There have been significant improvements in the institutional base to support economic development as evidenced by the emergence of personnel and organizations specializing in economic development and providing capital, education, and training programs.

The commission also found a realistic appreciation of the challenges that lie ahead as well as a spirit of determination to regain stewardship of aboriginal economies and to develop them in accordance with the values and priorities of particular nations and communities. Strategies for change, the commission argues, must be rooted in an understanding of the forces that have created economic marginalization in the first place. Factors essential for economic development, such as the economic provisions in historical treaties, the freedom for aboriginal peoples to manage their own economies, and a fair share of the land and resource base that sustained aboriginal economies in the past were ignored and now needed to be addressed.

The problem of economic development is often defined as an individual based problem (i.e., aboriginal individuals do not have access to opportunities for employment or business development in the larger Canadian society). This approach ignores the collectivity in aboriginal society. It overlooks the fact that economic development is the product of interaction of many factors: health, education, self-worth, functioning communities, stable environments, and the like. While economic development must support individuals, it must also support collectives. Some of the most important steps that need to be taken involve this collectivity, for example regaining control over decisions affecting the economy, and regaining greater ownership and control over economic development.

Economic development is also a process that can be supported or frustrated. The role of aboriginal and non-aboriginal governments should be to support the process, help create the conditions under which economic development can thrive, and remove the obstacles that stand in its way.

Aboriginal economies are diverse, ranging from comprehensive claims regions such as the Inuvialuit regions of the western Arctic, Nunavut, and James Bay; Métis settlements in northern Alberta; reserves such as Six Nations which have a dynamic small business sector; and rural and urban communities where a self-sustaining economic base is far from being achieved or where traditional pursuits such as hunting, fishing, or trapping are interwoven into the wage economy. This means that a policy developed and issued in Ottawa to be applied uniformly across the diversity of economies would not be helpful to aboriginal peoples.

**Aboriginal Economic Goals.** The commission also reported on the economic goals that aboriginal people want to achieve. These include:

1. Respect for the treaties, the comprehensive claims, and other agreements made with the Crown and to remedy past injustices concerning land and resources, including securing a land base for all aboriginal people, including Métis;
2. Jobs that provide a decent income that do not necessarily require moving from aboriginal communities and that provide meaning to people's lives, contributing to the development of self-esteem and aboriginal identity. Aboriginal economies should provide choices for people rather than dictating directions;
3. Economies capable of supporting those who wish to continue traditional pursuits while enabling those who wish to participate in a wage and market economy to do so;
4. Economies that are largely self-reliant and sustaining, not in the sense of being independent from trade networks and other economic systems, but in the sense of being in a position to give and receive fair value in economic exchanges;
5. Economies providing not only the basis for survival but also an opportunity to prosper and help build a sense of accomplishment and self-worth for the individual and the collective;
6. Choices about the nature of this economy, its structure, and processes made to the largest extent possible by aboriginal peoples and their institutions;

7. Economic development that will contribute to the development of aboriginal peoples as distinct peoples within Canada and to permit them to exercise, in a significant and substantial manner, governance in their communities and stewardship of lands and resources. In short, economic development is expected to enable aboriginal peoples to govern themselves; and

8. Economies structured in accordance with aboriginal values, principles, and customs, contributing to the development and affirmation of aboriginal culture and identity.

In the view of aboriginal peoples, the commission notes, economic development is more than just individuals striving to maximize incomes and prestige. It is about maintaining and developing culture and identity; supporting self-governing institutions, and sustaining traditional ways of making a living. It is about giving people choice in their lives and maintaining appropriate forms of relationships with their own and other societies.

**The Commission's Critical Issues.** The commission highlights three critical economic issues facing aboriginal peoples: (1) the need to develop stronger, more self-reliant aboriginal economies to accompany and sustain self-government; (2) the need to eliminate the sharp inequalities in employment and incomes that separate aboriginal people from Canadian standards; and (3) the need to come to grips with the rapid increase in the aboriginal population, which will need 300,000 new jobs by the year 2016.

The commission sees the economic development as a process with three principal participants: aboriginal individuals, communities, and nations. It sees governments, both aboriginal and non-aboriginal, as facilitators of the process of change. They can set the stage for economic development, remove barriers, create opportunities and provide support. In some cases, they may also own and manage business ventures on behalf of their communities.

The commission underlines the importance of understanding the goals that aboriginal peoples are trying to achieve and using this understanding as the basis for action by non-aboriginal and aboriginal governments.

**The Call for a New Relationship.** The economic development recommendations of the Royal Commission on Aboriginal Peoples (RCAP) are made within the context of its call for a new relationship between Canada and aboriginal peoples. This new relationship, in the commission's view, should be a nation-to-nation one, based upon the restoration of aboriginal nations.

The sixty or so aboriginal nations would have governments with a wide range of powers and authorities and constitutionally situated as a third-order of government. One of the powers of these new governments would be over the development of its economy.

The commission concludes that the transformation of aboriginal economies from dependence on government transfers to interdependence and self-reliance is fundamental to the development of self-government. Aboriginal nations and communities must be able to generate sufficient wealth to provide an acceptable quality of life for their members. They also state that this type of transformation will require a concerted, comprehensive effort over an extended period of time. It will take a deliberate commitment of time and resources by Canada and aboriginal peoples. Given the diversity of aboriginal economies across the country, no single approach to their development is possible. Each must be allowed, encouraged, and supported to find and follow their own path.

**Key Issues.** The commission has identified six key issues which it felt it was necessary to address in order to support economic development. These issues are:

1. The restoration of fair shares in the lands and resources of Canada through the recognition of aboriginal rights and treaty provisions and the negotiation of new or renewed treaties;

2. The development of effective institutions of governance and economic development whereby aboriginal peoples regain control of key decisions concerning economic strategy;

3. The creation and management of enterprises that can harvest resources and manufacture the resources and services that generate income and wealth;

4. The mastery of professional and technical skills necessary to work in modern economy and influence the way business is conducted;

5. A concerted national effort in job creation and training to achieve aboriginal employment rates similar to those of other Canadians; and

6. New approaches to the use of social assistance for aboriginal communities which link income supplements to productive activity.

The commission makes fifty-two recommendations regarding aboriginal economic development in the areas outlined above. While the government has not yet responded to all of them, it is important to understand that what was proposed is consistent with aboriginal thinking on these issues over the last three decades and lays a foundation for future economic development efforts.

The fundamental view of the commission is that aboriginal economic development is a process that needs to be under the control and guidance of aboriginal peoples and their institutions of governance for it to be successful. The economic goals which aboriginal peoples pursue are broad and not narrowly focused on income or the creation of individual wealth. Economic development is expected to further the movement toward self-government.

In the commission's view, there are a number of critical but highly interrelated tasks which need to be undertaken. The high level of interrelatedness of the tasks themselves, the links between aboriginal economies and the mainstream economies, and the enormity of the development task indicate the need for a concerted and coordinated long-term development effort.

## Aboriginal Business Development in Canada

One of the areas in economic development that tends to be ignored is the area of business development. Relatively little attention is paid to the nature and extent of business development within aboriginal communities. The popular conception is that aboriginal economies consist mainly of occasional wage work, employment in government and administrative service, and reliance on transfer payments. However, contrary to this conception, aboriginal businesses are becoming important elements in the economic realm of aboriginal peoples in Canada and an important part of the economic development strategies of aboriginal communities.

The 1991 Aboriginal Peoples' Survey indicated that 25,275 aboriginal people in Canada reported current business ownership and/or income from self-employment. Another 12,575 reported prior business ownership. The 1996 Aboriginal Business Survey reported that 20,000 aboriginal people were self-employed. The growth in self-employment from the period 1991 to 1996 was 2.5 times that of the Canadian national increase in self-employment. Aboriginal entrepreneurs are active in every sector of the economy, from the old economy to the new economy. Fifty percent of aboriginal businesses are located in urban centers. The same 1996 investigation of aboriginal businesses found that the vast majority of these enterprises were profitable, contributed about 5,000 new jobs in aboriginal communities and provided many other spin-off benefits. This is still a far cry from the 300,000 new jobs needed by the year 2016 to accommodate the growth in the aboriginal labor force population.

Business activity by Indians was limited by the legal restrictions under which Canadian Indians[2] live. Under the terms of the Indian Act, first passed in 1867, status Indians living on an Indian reserve were prevented from owning reserve land as a private holding, taking out a mortgage, securing a bank loan, or otherwise taking the steps necessary to establish a business. These limitations, coupled with government paternalism and non-aboriginal discrimination, prevented many aboriginal people from participating fully in the commercial arena. A few who wished to capitalize on commercial opportunities were forced to seek enfranchisement, which required surrendering their Indian status in order to be freed from the restrictions. While some of these constraints remain in place—reserve lands, for example, are held in trust by the federal government and hence cannot be used as collateral for loans (although there have been changes to the Indian Act that permit First Nations to designate lands for development and create a separate legal regime for them)—the post–Second World War period saw significant barriers lifted to aboriginal business prospects.

Since the 1950s, aboriginal people have been aided by a variety of government support programs to start small businesses. The initiatives started in a limited fashion, through the provision of small loans to purchase trucks for wood-cutting or other such ventures. By the 1960s, full-fledged national programs were in place, providing development capital, formal advice and oversight, and ongoing government support for aboriginal peoples (individuals and communities) interested in starting a business as well as special programs in sectors such as agriculture, mining, forestry, and arts and crafts. Programs like the Indian Business Development Fund provided financial support for Indian-owned businesses. Application and approval procedures were often cumbersome and the success rate (defined in terms of long-term, profitable operations) was quite low. These early business development programs evolved into larger economic development programs NEED, NEDP, ICHRS, and CAEDS, in which business development become a part of a larger more comprehensive development strategy.

Government support efforts were also supplemented by other efforts both within and outside aboriginal communities. Aboriginal organizations made similar efforts to assist individuals wishing to establish commercial ventures. There were efforts in the 1970s to establish a national Indian Business Association whose goal was to assist business startup and to advocate on behalf of aboriginal businesses. Business advice was provided through organizations like CESO which established the Canadian Native Business Program and recruited retired business people to provide management and technical advice to aboriginal businesses. Universities across the country, through their business schools, provided expertise through the Indian Business Assistance Program (later the Indian Management Assistance Program). Local community economic development organizations also provided support in the form of training, advice, and small loans. A group of Canadian business leaders formed the Canada Council for Aboriginal Business to provide advice and support for aboriginal entrepreneurs and to encourage Canadian businesses to assist in establishing aboriginal businesses.

Aboriginal peoples over the past two decades have challenged the popular conception that engaging in business activity is not part of aboriginal culture and that individuals would not be supported if they started businesses or that collectively owned enterprises would not work and could not be profitable. There is now a small but solid foundation of aboriginal businesses, both individually and collectively owned. There is a great determination to move away from the culture of dependency that has characterized many aboriginal communities over the past half century. Aboriginal businesses are now seen as much a part of the movement towards self government as is the reestablishment of aboriginal governments.

Aboriginal Entrepreneurs in Canada, a 1999 study by Aboriginal Business Canada reported that an active business sector of privately owned Native-run businesses is emerging. Although this sector is relatively small in the overall context of Canadian business, it is growing. This report found that aboriginal businesses parallel other Canadian business: they are relatively small (54 percent have no full-time employees versus 60 percent of Canadian businesses that have no employees; 46 percent versus 40 percent have at least one full-time employee); more and more aboriginal women are establishing their own businesses; the majority (62 percent) of aboriginal businesses are profitable, but their profitability is less (approximately two-thirds that of Canadian businesses) and aboriginal businesses tend to be concentrated in recreational/personal services, construction, and transportation industries. Only a few are in the new economy. The survey indicated a high level of awareness among aboriginal entrepreneurs of the skills and knowledge necessary to survive in businesses as well as a desire to constantly improve their own skill levels.

There are still many problems facing aboriginal businesses, particularly those located in areas where markets are small or financing is not readily available, or where there are insufficient numbers of educated and

trained people to fill managerial and technical positions. The small size of many businesses means that they are more vulnerable to changes in economic and market conditions. The high demand by communities for employment places great pressure on aboriginal businesses for rapid growth. Racism against aboriginal peoples continues to be a factor in many places. Government assistance programs tend to ignore aboriginal peoples living off reserve or Métis people, focusing primarily on status Indians. All pose challenges that need to be addressed if the aboriginal business sector is to continue to grow. Yet it is a tribute to the perseverance and ingenuity of aboriginal people coupled with the assistance of the Canadian state and some members of the private sector that they have been able to create this small but central business community after Natives peoples' forced exclusion from the Canadian economy.

*David Newhouse*
*Trent University*

### Notes

1. In 1969, the government of Canada introduced for discussion a policy paper entitled "Statement of Indian Policy of the Government of Canada." It proposed, among other measures, the repeal of the Indian Act, the termination of Indian status, the dissolution of Indian reserves, and the shift of responsibilities for Indians to provinces. Governments release policy statements for discussion in what are termed *white papers*. The government policy paper became know as The White Paper, an ironic title given its Anglo- centric perspective.

2. The Indian Act creates a category of person called Status Indian; that is, a person registered in the official Indian registry maintained by the Indian Registrar. There are non-status Indians, i.e. people who are Indians but not entitled to be officially registered. The government of Canada limits its legal obligations only to those 400,000-plus status Indians and then mainly to those 225,000-plus living on Indian reserves.

### ◆ GOVERNMENT ASSISTANCE AND RESTITUTION FOR NATIVES IN CANADA

Canada covers the northern part of North America except for Alaska. As a former colony of Great Britain, Canada is now an independent country, although it is a member of the British Commonwealth. Canada became a country in 1867. It is now a federation of ten provinces and three territories and is bordered by the Atlantic Ocean on the east, the Pacific Ocean to the west and the Arctic Ocean to the north. The geography of Canada is very diverse and most of the population lives within a couple hundred miles of the Canada-United States border. In 1982 the Constitution Act transferred constitutional power from the British Parliament to the Canadian government. The population of Canada in 2000 was estimated to be 31,281,092. It covers 3,851,781 square miles. The federal and provincial governments are responsible for social services to Native people as outlined in the British North American Act (1867), the Canadian Constitution (1982) and the Indian Act (1876).

The number of Native people in Canada ranges from 2 to 3 percent of the total population, depending on what definition of *Indian* is used. By some estimates, the total Native population (status and non-status and Inuit) is over 1 million. The term *Indian* means different things, depending on who is doing the defining. The three groups of Indian in Canada are status Indian, non-status Indian, and Treaty Indian. The Inuit are the original inhabitants of northern Canada who reside north of the sixtieth parallel as well as in northern Labrador and Quebec. They are generally considered to be status Indians. On the other hand, the Métis are people of mixed Native and European ancestry. They have a unique culture based on their ancestral origins. The recognition and status of Métis people across Canada varies from province to province. All groups are collectively referred to as *aboriginal* or *Native* people. Detailed information about the Métis and non-status Indians is unavailable because of problems of definition and the failure to collect this information; however, population estimates for these people range between 500,000 and 1 million. In addition, 25,000 Inuit live in Canada's northern regions.

Almost two-thirds of status Indians live on reserves, which are often referred to as First Nations. Reserves are assigned to different bands and the average population of reserves is 450. Reserves are located in all provinces and territories in Canada, with the exception of Newfoundland. Most status Indians live in areas that are remote from urban centers and the non-Indian world.

## History

Sadly, our history with respect to the treatment of Aboriginal people is not something in which we can take pride. Attitudes of racial and cultural superiority led to a suppression of Aboriginal culture and values. As a country, we are burdened by past actions that resulted in weakening the identity of Aboriginal peoples, suppressing their languages and cultures, and outlawing spiritual practice. . . . The Government of Canada formally expresses to all Aboriginal people in Canada our profound regret for past actions of the federal government which have contributed to these difficult pages in the history of our relationship together.

*—excerpt from the Statement of Reconciliation*

Before the arrival of the Europeans, many unique cultures of aboriginal peoples existed in what is now Canada. They consisted of many different peoples, with unique languages and cultures. These peoples shared a deep spiritual connection to the land as well as the shared goal of living in harmony with nature.

In 1534 Jacques Cartier claimed Canada on behalf of France. In 1604 Samuel de Champlain established a French settlement. Champlain was followed by French settlers who were enticed by the seemingly limitless supply of fish and furs. In 1670 the English established the Hudson's Bay Company to compete with the French for the fur trade. Conflict erupted between the French and the English over the land and abundant resources. The fur trade and pressure for Native-European alliances aggravated the existing animosity and conflicts between certain tribes. In 1763 the English won a battle against France, gaining control over Canada.

By the end of the eighteenth century and the beginning of the nineteenth century, the population of settlers increased significantly. Between 1763 and 1800 many treaties of land surrender were signed with the Indians of Upper Canada (now Ontario). The underlying motive of the government was to give land to the settlers. At the same time, the fur trade also wiped out fur-bearing animals in eastern Canada, causing a movement West, where the buffalo soon also faced decimation.

Native people were forced off their land and the agricultural needs of the settlers interfered with the traditional use of the land. More treaties were signed with various tribes from Ontario to Alberta. In 1871 British Columbia entered the Confederation on the condition that a railway be built. The railroad brought an influx of settlers and the government took more land from the Native people. Between 1871 and 1921 the Numbered Treaties were signed.

The fate of the northern Inuit shares a similar history. Canada's north, which is the homeland of the

Inuit, is unique. Before the arrival of the white man, Inuit lived a subsistence existence by harvesting fish, plants, and wildlife. Their survival depended on sharing. Throughout recent Canadian history, the traditional lifestyle of the Inuit has been eroded by the economic and political development of the north.

The Hudson's Bay Company established a monopoly over all the lands draining into Hudson Bay, subordinated the Native people, and produced a continuous supply of resources to the southern part of the country. The Northwest Mounted Police entered the northern lands and enforced southern laws. The new ways hurt traditional Inuit culture. Mining also brought settlement to the north. Furthermore, the north played a strategic military role in World War II. When vanishing wildlife threatened the survival of many Inuit, the federal government attempted to relocate them and in the process created dependency on the federal government. To this day, the main industry of the north is its primary industries. In many northern regions, government provision of housing, education, health, defense, law enforcement, and public works continues to be a significant chunk of the northern economy.

Canada became a country in 1867. This era is known as Confederation. The pre-Confederation period was dominated by military and missionary activities directed toward Native peoples. The missionaries believed they were morally superior and used this belief to convert Native people to Christianity and to impose their European cultural traditions.

In 1850 the first statutory definition of who was considered Indian was enacted. The concept of enfranchisement was first introduced in 1857 whereby an aboriginal *man* with the correct qualifications could relinquish his heritage and become a full citizen. Responsibility for assimilation moved to the civilian sector, where the imposition of European ways and confinement of Native people to rural communities were attempted. Following the Indian Act of 1867, the government started the Indian Register, which is the official record identifying all status Indians in Canada. Later legislation redefined who is and is not an Indian.

The Canadian government policy toward its Native peoples has been protection, civilization, and assimilation. It must be remembered that degradation is the other side of assimilation because the underlying belief of assimilation is that certain cultures are inferior. The outgrowth of these activities was that the Indian assumed special status in the political and social fabric of Canada. This unique status became enshrined in the constitutional structure of Canada in 1867, when the federal government assumed exclusive jurisdiction over Indians and Indian land.

Recently, the federal government has started to change its approach to Native peoples. Two incidents sparked this shift: disclosures of residential school abuse and the Oka Crisis. Residential schools started out of the missionary zeal of various Christian churches. They were located in almost every province and territory. At its apex, there were approximately one hundred such schools in operation. The federal government operated most residential schools in conjunction with various churches until 1969, when the government assumed full responsibility. Most schools were closed by the mid-1970s, with only seven remaining open through the 1980s. The last school closed in the 1980s.

In recent years, former students have come forward with tragic stories of physical and sexual abuse at residential schools. Many continue to struggle with the aftermath of this abuse. Currently as many as twenty lawsuits are being filed every week against the government and churches, and they now number about six thousand.

In 1998 the government of Canada released Canada's Aboriginal Action Plan, calling for a renewed partnership with Native people. The government signaled its intentions to rectify past mistakes and injustices, and move toward reconciliation and support healing. As part of this initiative, the federal government committed $350 million to support a community-based strategy for healing arising from the legacy of physical and sexual abuse at residential schools. This money is known as the Healing Fund. The government also renewed its commitment to Native self-government.

## Legislation

The rights of Native peoples in Canada are legislated primarily by the Indian Act (1876) and three other pieces of legislation: the British North America Act (BNA 1867), the Canadian Constitution (1982), and the Canadian Charter of Rights and Freedoms (1984). The Indian Act, discussed in more detail in the next section, provides the legal definition of *Indian* in Canada, outlines Native rights, and details the responsibility of the federal government toward them. The British North America Act determined that "Indians and lands reserved for Indians fell under the jurisdiction of the Canadian Parliament," thereby assigning fiduciary responsibility for the Native people to the Canadian government. This responsibility has been the foundation of the development of social programs for Native people in Canada. Finally the Charter of Rights and Freedoms is a document that supersedes any other Canadian legislation that denies equality because of race, national origin, color, religion, or sex. Ultimately, it is the Indian Act that defines Native rights in a practical way and is the main legislation that affects Native people in Canada. The Indian Act has also been the primary instrument through which the federal government has oppressed Native people in the past.

The implementation of Canada's public policy concerning Native people primarily resides within one government department. While most federal departments play a role in assisting and supporting Native peoples, implementation of policy is the responsibility of the Department of Indian Affairs and Northern Development (DIAND). DIAND, in its current form, was created in 1966 to focus specifically on the delivery of programs and services to the Indian and Inuit peoples. Now its role is intended to be advisory. It also provides basic services in the form of funding and supporting various programs for status Indians.

The federal and provincial governments disagree about their respective roles and obligations toward Native people. While the federal government has exclusive legislative responsibility for Native people, some social services available to other Canadians fall within provincial mandates. Moreover, Native people are subject to the same laws and benefits as other Canadians.

Typically, the provinces are responsible for education, health, and social services and under usual arrangements, the federal government transfers funds to the provinces for these services. Both levels of government share the cost of these provincially mandated services. Because of the legislation giving the federal government exclusive jurisdiction over Native people, it carries the brunt of the cost. Fund transfer is based on the status Indian composition of a provincial population. To date, the provinces have refused to provide social services on reserves. In this vacuum, DIAND bears the complete financial burden for on-reserve services in all provinces.

## Treaties

Some restitution is made to Native people according to the conditions of treaties, especially the more recent ones. A treaty is a signed agreement between the Crown and a specified group or groups of Native people. Treaties are legal documents outlining promises, obligations, and benefits of the parties to the treaty. Approximately seventy historic treaties have been made to date in Canada, with new treaties being negotiated yearly. The interpretation of historic treaties have assumed greater importance because they are protected in the Constitution Act of 1982. Current questions about the meaning of older treaties often

pertain to the definition and extent of promised benefits. Promised benefits typically concern fishing, hunting and trapping rights, educational and health services, taxation exemption, mandatory military service, eligibility for treaty annuities and portability of treaty rights. Every treaty is unique, as are the promised benefits. Historically, the government and Native people have had different intentions and viewpoints when signing treaties. Today, some suggest that the former treaty process was fraudulent and exploitive of Native people.

## The Indian Act

The first Indian Act was passed in 1876 as a consolidation of existing legislation with some new sections. For example, it brought forward the idea of enfranchisement from the Act to Encourage Civilization of Indian Tribes (1857). Enfranchisement was a mechanism through which Native men could renounce Indian status and become part of the dominant society. It also defined "Indianess" by introducing the designation of "status" and "non-status" Indians. Since then, the Indian Act has been amended many times, often becoming more restrictive. The main advantages of Indian status fall into the areas of education, health care, tax benefits and housing. To this day, the word *status* separates those who were entitled to reside on Indian lands and qualify for federal government programs from those who could not.

Historically, the Indian Act has been a racist and oppressive piece of legislation. Native women lost Indian status when they married a non-Indian. By comparison, Native men kept their status when they married a non-Native and their non-Native spouses acquired Indian status. Moreover, earlier versions of the act defined a person as "someone other than an Indian." Only by voluntarily enfranchisement could an Indian become a person. Finally, Native peoples were denied the right to vote well into the twentieth century.

The definition of who could legally be called Indian continues to create tension and conflict. Some people are denied the benefits derived from Indian status because they do not qualify for status although they have similar Native ancestry as those who do have status. Non-status Indians generally include Indian peoples and their descendants who lost their rights to be registered as defined by the Indian Act. They are therefore excluded from claiming rights and services. Those opposed to the special status claim that the Indian Act violates normative standards of equality. These critics are usually non-aboriginal. The federal government argues that its major aim is to preserve Native culture and to provide Indians with additional rights and safe-guards guaranteed by the Canadian Constitution as well as various treaties. Among the many complaints about the Indian Act is the argument that it still assigns too much power and authority to the government. This government control prevents Native communities from developing their lands and resources in their own ways.

With the implementation of Bill C-31 in 1985, Native women who lost their status by marrying a non-Indian could apply to have their status restored, as could their children. The bill also abolished enfranchisement. Finally bands could set their own criteria for membership so long as the criteria does not conflict with the rights of existing First Nations members or with the rights of those who had their status restored under Bill C-31. One criticism of Bill C-31 is that it is infused with a European value-base that encourages a legislated notion of "Indianess."

Today all matters impacting status and membership fall under the Indian Act. The act continues to define who is Indian. It also endorses the maintenance of the Indian Registry (which is the list of status Indians), and band lists of First Nations members who have not yet passed their own membership codes.

While the Indian Act was apparently designed both to protect Native peoples and, earlier, to facilitate assimilation, it has not weathered the storms of time well. The Indian Act is blamed for the creation of structural inequality, poverty, massive social problems, and lack of achievement among Native people. It has also undermined the freedom and morale of Native people across Canada. On one hand, it accorded Indians special status, legally and constitutionally; on the other, it denied them equality in other realms of Canadian life (Berger 1981).

## Department of Indian and Northern Affairs

In 1966 the Department of Indian Affairs and Northern Development (DIAND) was created to deliver programs and services to the status Indians and Inuit peoples. The minister of Indian affairs and northern development is responsible for Indian and Inuit affairs. DIAND supports band and tribal councils and helps them offer on-reserve programs. It also fulfills legislative and treaty obligations. Money is transferred by means of funding agreements with reserves. Much criticism has been leveled at this department, in part because of the historical connection to colonial domination and assimilation as well as the fact that it has such a wide mandate, which makes it an easy target.

The amount of funding transferred to bands is based on a formula that uses band membership numbers,

location, on-reserve population size, type, and value of programs and services delivered by the band, and the number of band employees who administer services. After a century of discriminatory and oppressive policies, DIAND is changing its role from that of a direct service provider to that of program funding and facilitation. The welfare of status Indians is its primary mandate and as such is shifting its policy toward giving decision-making power to the people.

## Demographics and Social Problems

Whatever the social or economic indicator you wish to choose, the situation of the Indian people in Canada constitutes an inexcusable embarrassment to all Canadians.

—*David Ahenakew, national chief of the Assembly of First Nations, 1983*

In 1996 and 1997 DIAND administered 2,406 reserves for 608 bands across Canada, covering 2.6 million hectares of land. The largest concentration of Native peoples is in the North, accounting for 62 percent of the population of the Northwest Territories and 20 percent in the Yukon. In addition, it is estimated that 85 percent of the new territory of Nunavut is Native or Inuit. The greatest numbers of Native people live in Ontario, whereas in Alberta the Métis population is largest.

Native people experience high rates of problems that social programs are designed to address. For example, social programs are designed to ameliorate problems such as poverty, unemployment, child abuse, crime, illiteracy, and inadequate housing. As discussed below, the standard of living of many Native people in Canada is well below the living conditions of most other Canadians. Economic impoverishment and personal and structural social dependency contribute to high rates of social problems among Canada's Native peoples.

The Native population is growing faster than the general Canadian population. Between 1986 and 1991, the aboriginal population increased by 43 percent, a figure that includes an estimated 80,000 people who gained Indian status from Bill C-31. The non-status Indian population is also experiencing rapid growth. This growth compares to the much smaller increase of 7 percent for the non-Native population.[1]

The number of children in Native communities is large—almost twice that of the general population. Almost one-half of the Native population is younger than fifteen years, and two-thirds are younger than twenty-five. Because of this, the aboriginal population, on average, is ten years younger than the general population.[2] Much concern has been focused on the young people who are the hope for the future in many Native communities, which are in crisis. They experience disproportionate rates of suicide and substance abuse. In addition, proportionally more Native young people are in care, fewer complete secondary school, and they have the highest suicide rates in the country.

Many have compared the living conditions of Native peoples in Canada to those of Third World countries. In comparison to other groups in Canada, Native people experience greater difficulty in terms of employment, housing, health, education, and poverty. In addition, houses on reserves are overcrowded and substandard, and incomes and employment rates fall short of national standards. Equally troublesome, a disproportionate number of Native people face incarceration and Native people are overrepresented in federal and provincial prisons, a trend most evident in Western Canada.

Between 1986 and 1991 movement between reserves and urban centers increased. Information about mobility is important because census data on mobility is used to set transfer payments from the federal government to the provinces. Mobility is particularly high for young people between the ages of fifteen and twenty-four, leading to decreasing numbers of on-reserve status Indians.[3] This mobility sometimes results in cultural conflicts, gaps in services, and a variety of social problems. The situation is further complicated by distrust of service providers in urban centers because most are non-Native professionals. This cultural insensitivity has been a major flaw of urban services. While greater appreciation for culturally sensitive services is starting to develop, there is much work to be done.

## Federal Programs and Services

The BNA Act of 1867 outlined the responsibilities of the provincial and federal governments. Provinces assume the primary responsibility for health, welfare, and education and offer these services to their provincial citizens. However, under the Indian Act, the responsibility for status Indians resides with the federal government. While the federal government contends that Indian people are subject to the same laws as the general population unless they conflict with treaties or the Indian Act, provinces have refused to provide provincially mandated services to status Indians on reserves. The provinces argue that the welfare of status Indians is the responsibility of the federal government. In response, the federal government claims that because it already transfers money to the provinces for status Indians, the provinces should shoulder their

responsibilities. The outcome of this disagreement is that the Department of Indian and Northern Development still shoulders the bulk of the responsibility for providing support and administering services to status Indians. Status Indians are eligible for the benefits provided through the social service division of DIAND in addition to the social welfare benefits available to all Canadians.

DIAND transfers funds through different funding arrangements with bands. Comprehensive Funding Arrangements (CFA) involve the basic transfer of money from DIAND to Native bands for programs and services. Alternative Funding Arrangements (AFA) expand the authority of band councils to develop programs. There are fewer conditions attached to Alternative Funding Arrangements and bands can keep carryover to finance other programs. Bands with a successful history of administering programs and have the administrative structure in place and mechanisms for accountability are eligible for Alternative Funding Arrangements. CFAs cover a one-year period while AFAs last for five years and are subject to audit. Over one-half of the bands currently receive AFA funding.

In light of provincial reluctance to provide services for status Indians, the federal government is obligated to fill this void. It provides a range of direct services discussed later in this chapter. The paternalistic and bureaucratic approach is starting to change in recent years as federal policy is starting to value client involvement and self-determination.

As citizens of Canada, all Native people benefit from the same general federal programs available to everyone, regardless of status. The major programs available to all Canadians are discussed below. They include Old Age Security, Guaranteed Income Supplement, Employment Insurance, Workers Compensation, Canada Pension, and Health Care. In addition to these widely available programs, there are specific programs arising out of Canada's constitutional and statutory obligations to status Indians and Inuit. Some programs in this latter category are also available to status Indians living off-reserve. These two types of social programs are discussed separately.

## Programs Available to all Canadians

Under the Canada Assistance Plan (CAP 1966), the federal government shares the cost of provincial welfare programs and social services with the provinces. Because of the expense of these programs, the federal government is trying to find ways to slash costs, but it is encountering resistance from the provinces as well as the Canadian population. CAP assists provinces to provide comprehensive social programs. As mentioned before, however, the provinces do not provide these services to status Indians who live on reserves.

Employment Insurance (EI) is a federal social program designed to assist individuals who are unable to work due to illness, pregnancy, or loss of a job for other reasons. The benefits are tied into the labor force; that is, only those individuals who have worked for a specified number of weeks prior to losing their job are entitled to collect Employment Insurance. In addition, the amount and length of eligible EI benefits is based on how much a worker has contributed to the plan. Recipients are also required to register for work or attend an approved course for upgrading while collecting benefits.

Canadians are very proud of their health care system, which is a universal program. Individuals can receive most health care services at no cost to the individual. Instead, they pay a small monthly premium to the province for individual or family coverage, and in return, the cost of health services, including hospitalization, is covered. Individuals are free to select the doctor of their choice. Individuals who are unable to pay the monthly premium can apply for a subsidy from the province. Health care is legislated by the Canada Health Act, which is federal legislation. The federal government transfers money to the provinces for part of the cost of health care, under the condition that the provinces meet the stipulations of the federal policies. For example, no province can set up a private health care system. The federal government enacts the national policies for health care while the provinces are responsible for implementing them. Through this system, all Canadians have equal access to health care. Some provinces also cover other services, such as optometrists, chiropractors, home care, and prescription drugs. Health care, together with the Canada Assistance Plan, can also cover glasses, prostheses, dental care, and prescriptions for qualifying individuals. Health care spending by the government is very costly, and governments are trying to find better ways to provide quality health care services.

All people over the age of sixty-five receive Old Age Security (OAS). Individuals must live in Canada for ten years prior to receiving OAS. For those seniors who have little or no other income besides OAS, they are eligible for the Guaranteed Income Supplement (GIS). The spouse of an individual who receives OAS is also entitled to receive the Spouse's Allowance provided their combined income is less than a specified amount determined by the government.

The Canada Pension Plan (CPP) covers individuals who are over the age of sixty-five or disabled and who paid into the plan while working. CPP also pays benefits to widows and survivors. Finally, the Child Tax Credit Benefit Program assists families with low and middle incomes with children under the age of eighteen.

## Services for Status Indians

In addition to the social programs discussed above, the federal government also funds programs and services specifically for status Indians who live on reserves. It funds the delivery of a broad spectrum of services including Social Assistance and is responsible for ensuring that basic services are provided to communities it serves. Other programs available to status Indians include (1) exemption from income tax earned on reserves; (2) partial exemption from federal and provincial sales tax; (3) medical benefits not covered by the universal medical insurance of provinces, including dental care; (4) subsidized on-reserve housing; (5) post-secondary education support and scholarships; (6) elementary and secondary school education; (7) housing; (8) community infrastructure support; and (9) band administration costs.

Many reserves are starting to administer the programs themselves, according to their unique priorities and policies. A few programs are offered to status Indians who do not live on a reserve. These include assistance for post-secondary education and some non-insured health benefits. While the federal government provides some services directly to Natives who do not live on reserves, its view is that provincial governments should provide the same basic services to this group that are provided to other provincial residents. However, provinces typically consider status Indians a federal responsibility regardless of where they live. Although the provinces, in practice, will usually provide needed services, certain services such as welfare and childcare are only available after a specified residency off-reserve.

**Education: Elementary, Secondary and Post-Secondary.** Elementary and secondary educational programs are available to status Indian children living on reserves. Three different educational systems may exist: band-operated schools, provincially administered schools off reserves, and federal schools operated by DIAND. The federal government is responsible for a full range of elementary and secondary educational services for school-aged Native students. Additional educational services include the provision of teachers, school supplies, administrative and paraprofessional support, and curriculum development. Education services to Native children in the territories (Yukon, Northwest Territory and Nunavut) are provided by the respective territorial governments. In addition, post-secondary funding is available from DIAND for eligible status Indians and Inuit regardless of where they live in Canada. Full-time post-secondary students receive financial assistance for tuition, travel, living expenses, and books. Currently DIAND sponsors more than 15,000 students in post-secondary education programs across Canada.

While the retention of Native children in secondary schools is increasing, the school completion rate is still well below the national rate. Nevertheless the educational attainment of Native people is increasing. For example, the number of Native people with less than grade nine education decreased to 18 percent in 1991 from 26 percent five years earlier. The proportion of Native people with some secondary schooling also increased in 1991 to 43 percent from 34 percent during the same period. This compares favorably with the non-aboriginal rate, which rose to 39 percent from 27 percent.[4] The failure of school systems to provide culturally appropriate and language-specific education is cited as a major reason for the poor educational attainment of Native people. In addition, the high rate of social problems on reserves also interferes with the education of young Native people.

**Health.** The federal government funds a range of health services to status Indians beyond what the provincial health systems offer. Federally funded health services include community health services, environmental health and surveillance, non-insured health benefits, the National Native Alcohol and Drug Abuse Program (NNADAP), hospital services, and capital construction. NNADAP was created as a community-based program for alcohol treatment facilities. Responsibility for delivery of these special health services resides in Health and Welfare Canada, Medical Services Branch (MSB). Bands and tribal councils can apply to Medical Services Branch for financial resources to assess community health care needs, prepare a health development plan, and develop a health management structure, in preparation for self-government of health services.

Medical Services Branch also delivers Public Health services, including health education, nutrition, mental health, dental services, medical and dental advice and assistance, counseling, and federal hospital or alcohol treatment services. The federal government also pays hospital insurance premiums. Through the Medical Services Branch, the federal government also provides treatment and public health services in remote areas. MSB may also assist with certain non-insured health benefits such as prescription drugs, dental services, glasses and medical transportation not covered by provincial health insurance plans. Most of the conflict surrounds the non-insured services.

The federal government is trying to pass the responsibility for health services directly to the bands. Criticism of health services provided to status Indians has partially focused the failure to consult communities as well as insufficient funding. With the shift to self-government, some also fear that the hidden agenda of the federal government is to eliminate the parts of Indian health care services unavailable to non-Native Canadians. Others suspect that the federal government is intending to withdraw special health services because they are a provincial responsibility. A final concern is that a condition of health care transfer to the bands is a "no enrichment" clause. This means that health services cannot be enhanced once they are in band control. However, this is a problem because the present services are underfunded. In addition, because transfer payments are based on the number of registered band members living on the reserve, it can exclude band members who are mobile and live off the reserve. Another potential problem is that band health by-laws must align with provincial health care policies, producing potential conflict between the band and the province.

Nevertheless, the federal government has committed to a long-term goal of a "more integrated, culturally relevant community health care program and improved health conditions for Indian people." The transfer process seems to have increased community interest in community health issues, but it has not been without controversy. Some Native leaders suspect that the ultimate aim of the government is to reduce spending on health and social services, abdicate legal and fiduciary responsibility for the delivery of health care services to Native people, and deny treaty rights. The long history of injustice at the hands of the government makes their suspicion easy to understand.

The previous approach to the provision of health care services to Native peoples has been a dismal failure and the health of Canadian Native peoples remains a concern. Their health status is affected by poor living conditions such as housing, economic impoverishment, availability of safe drinking water, and nutrition. Obviously, improved health status of Canada's Native peoples will only be improved through a holistic approach to health. Currently, life expectancy remains below the national average, mainly because of high infant and youth mortality. Substance abuse is also a significant health problem and over half of all of illnesses and deaths may be alcohol-related. Stories of the horrific health problems of Native people abound, involving alcohol and drug abuse, gas sniffing, infectious diseases, and mental health problems such as depression, stress, and high suicide rates. Deaths by suicide, homicide, and accident accounted for over one-third of the deaths of Native people. In response, Native communities are demanding involvement in the planning and delivery of health and mental health services. They would like to blend traditional methods of healing with Western medicine, and many bands have started along this path. Ultimately, the effectiveness of the health transfer policies will only be revealed by the next generation.

**Social Assistance.** The social services division of DIAND is obligated to guarantee that services offered to Native people are equivalent to provincial services available to non-Indians. As with other social services and programs, it is seeking the participation of Native peoples in the design and implementation of social assistance programs. An important part of this process has been the transfer of financial responsibility for the implementation and operation of programs to band councils. This objective seems to be working since most bands now administer the delivery of social assistance. The federal government would also like social services to be provided by other government and private agencies. This point remains contentious in federal-provincial relationships.

Social assistance provides money to single persons or heads of families to meet basic needs, for food, clothing, and shelter. Another category of social assistance targets disabled individuals who are unable to work. The amount paid for social assistance depends on the rate set by each province. The cost of social assistance to status Indians is rising significantly. For example, federal expenditures almost tripled between 1981 and 1994. During the same period, the number of recipients rose from 39,000 to almost 68,000.[5] Social assistance comprises 10 percent of the DIAND budget. Because the amount of social assistance paid is determined through specified provincial eligibility criteria and benefit rates in each of the provinces, the federal government is unable to control the costs of social assistance paid to status Indians. In addition, because of the socioeconomic conditions on reserves, the amount paid for social assistance is only expected to rise.

Transfer of responsibility is also occurring in direct services. DIAND has implemented a program providing basic material needs to status Indians. In recent years, this has been expanded to include day-care services and institutional and special care for the aged, the physically infirm, and the mentally handicapped. Again, where possible, responsibility for these services has entailed training Native peoples to plan and operate them. As the trend away from the reserves continues, DIAND is striving to ensure that services are available in urban centers. A function of these urban services is helping needy Indians connect with existing provincial, municipal, and voluntary services.

The government relationship with Native peoples has created a situation whereby Native peoples are one of the most economically disadvantaged groups in Canada. While the situation is improving slightly, much progress remains to be made. For example, while the average individual income for non-Native people increased by 7 percent between 1986 and 1991, it rose by almost one-third for Native people over the same time.[6] This increase did little to rectify the gap in income between non-Native and Native peoples, whose income remains significantly lower than other groups. Many still live in such dire poverty that the Human Rights Commission urged that poverty be acknowledged as a human rights issue.

Approximately 40 percent of status Indians currently receive government transfer payments. The average income for off-reserve status Indians, Inuit, and Métis in 1991 was $12,000, while the income of on-reserve status Indians plummeted to $9,000. In addition, the unemployment rate for aboriginal people is about double that of non-aboriginal people. While unemployment rates are decreasing, the rates are still distressing and unacceptable. For example, the unemployment rate for off-reserve status Indians was 25 percent in 1991 and 31 percent for on-reserve status Indians. Unemployment has produced reliance upon social assistance and this reliance is increasing. DIAND provided approximately $60 million in 1993 for social assistance for aboriginal people (Frideres 1998).

As with other social problems, poverty, unemployment, and dependence on social assistance cannot be addressed in a piecemeal fashion. Unemployment is related to education, gender, age, experience, language, and area of residence as well as institutional discrimination. These factors—considered alongside national unemployment rates, poverty, and long-term reliance on social assistance—depict a bleak life for many Native people.

**Housing.** Because of restrictions imposed by the Indian Act, most people who live on reserves cannot obtain conventional mortgages to purchase or build houses. The restrictions in the Indian Act make it impossible for bands or individuals to use their land as collateral. They are consequently unable to obtain mortgages without a government guarantee of repayment in case of default. Therefore, government assistance is required to build and maintain adequate housing because of the limited economic opportunities on many reserves.

While the federal government is not bound by legislation or treaties to provide housing, it continues to do so out of historical obligation (Frideres 1998). Consistent with the shift in government policy in other social programs, Indians and bands are encouraged to take control of the administration of the housing program. The long-term objective is to have housing meet national building standards. In addition, housing programs must now include local involvement, cost effectiveness, and linkages between home construction and community economic development and employment. Canada Mortgage and Housing Corporation (CMHC) in partnership agreements under the National Housing Act with government and nonprofit corporations builds social housing across Canada. CMHC contributes up to 90 percent of the capital cost and 50 percent of continued operations costs for new construction and rehabilitation projects.

Three basic programs are included in this agreement. The On-Reserve Rental Housing Program provides First Nations with suitable, affordable rental housing in First Nations communities. CMHC provides interest-free repayable loans for proposal development for rental housing projects. It also ensures loans by approved lenders for housing projects and annually subsidizes the project's operating costs for the duration of the loan. The Emergency Repair Program assists homeowners who live in rural areas to implement emergency repairs to make their homes safe and covers the cost of materials and labor. The Homeowner Residential Rehabilitation Assistance Program Helps Native homeowners living in substandard housing by allowing them to repair their homes and upgrade them to a minimum level of health and safety.

Similar to other initiatives, the federal government is shifting the emphasis for the housing program to First Nations control, using local resources for on-reserve home building. Under this policy, communities can also build expertise through on-the-job formal training. A five year and $160 million commitment on the part of the federal government, combined with $300 million in ongoing annual housing support, are helping reserves develop the skills and organizational ability to address the conditions of housing.[7] CMHC and DIAND also fund training, management, and technical expertise to help communities administer their own housing programs. Today most bands deliver their own housing programs. Programs are accountable to band councils and new houses must meet the residential standards of the national building code.

DIAND can approve housing proposals submitted by bands for housing development. The policy enables First Nations to develop community housing programs, create jobs, and improve housing conditions in a single initiative. The funding is split between DIAND and Canada Mortgage Housing Corporation. This new policy links housing to other community assets and needs such as training and and social assistance.

The rapid birth rate of First Nations peoples is creating pressure for affordable and appropriate housing on reserves across Canada. Chronic housing shortages have led to overcrowding, which exacerbates and contributes to social, familial, and health problems. Houses on reserves have short life spans because of overcrowding and poor construction. Consequently, many of the new houses being built are replacing dilapidated houses instead of freeing up new houses to accommodate the population growth. By one estimate, over one-half of the houses on reserves are substandard.

While housing conditions on reserves are notoriously poor, they are improving. On average, 90 percent of houses have central electricity and 75 percent have running water. By 1990 86 percent had an adequate water supply and 77 percent had adequate sewage disposal. (Frieders 1998, 171). Houses on reserves are relatively new with 93 percent built between 1961 and 1991. Two decades ago, only one-half of the houses on reserves were considered adequate. While the number of houses increased between 1989 and 1996, still only one-half were considered adequate. In the same period, many other houses on reserves were renovated.[8] However, housing shortages continue on reserves where lack of affordable housing remains a problem. The percentage of dwellings on reserves with more than one person per room (an indicator of overcrowding) is decreasing but there is room for improvement. The situation is complicated by the fact that many reserves are remote, making housing costs higher than for urban centers. In addition, Crown ownership of reserve lands makes it difficult for Native people to finance housing and mortgages. Those who live in northern regions also have the added burden of threatening weather conditions that require extra housing costs.

**Tax Benefits.**    Canadians pay some of the highest taxes in the industrialized world. However, under the Indian Act, status Indians do not pay any federal and provincial taxes on personal and real property on a reserve. Income is considered personal property. Status Indians who earn income and live on reserves do not have to pay taxes. In addition, for the purposes of taxation, post-secondary scholarships provided by DIAND for status Indians are considered to be "situated on a reserve." Payment of the Goods and Services Tax (a federal tax on purchases) depends on where the goods and services are consumed or purchased.

**Community Infrastructure Support.**    DIAND provides financial assistance for infrastructure support on reserves. This assistance pertains to building, operating, and maintaining community facilities and schools.

Money is also allocated to address problems with water, sanitation, electrical, and road systems, fire protection facilities, and flood and erosion control.

**Law Enforcement.** Policing on reserves is provided by the provincial police forces. The Royal Canadian Mounted Police (RCMP) are responsible for rural areas where there is no provincial force. DIAND assists the Royal Canadian Mounted Police (RCMP) for a RCMP Special Constable Program on reserves. Constables are accountable to local RCMP detachments. Special constables offer police enforcement under the jurisdiction of the Indian Act and other federal statutes. Other funded policing arrangements include the Ontario Indian Constable Program, which is co-funded under a federal-provincial agreement with the solicitor general in Ontario.

In other law enforcement initiatives, the federal solicitor general funds programs to improve Native policy and programs through research, pilot projects, and information. Two final initiatives are available. The Native Law Students Program helps Native people enter the legal profession and the Native Court Workers Program provides paralegal support to Native defendants.

**Culture.** Together with the secretary of state, DIAND funds support Native culture and educational activities. This initiative covers friendship centers, the development of Native political lobby associations, the promotion of traditional and contemporary art forms, language maintenance and revitalization, and the adaptation of modern communication tools for Native use. There is now a high quality aboriginal television station that is available across the country.

**Small Business Loan Program.** The Small Business Loan Program helps Native entrepreneurs involved in a variety of businesses. Federal funds offer loans, loan guarantees and financial planning services, investment banking facilities and management services. These funds are used to promote businesses. The Indian Economic Development Guarantee Order guarantees bank loans for Native businesses.

The oil and gas deposits on Alberta Reserve have created a situation where massive royalty payments accrue to the affected bands. Thus, there are isolated pockets of some very wealthy Native bands, such as the Samson band (Hobbema) and the Ermineskin and Louis Bull bands from the same reserves. The Inuvialuit of the western Arctic has also settled on a range of benefits and rights in recognition of the non-fulfillment of the original treaty.

**Child Welfare.** Child welfare falls under provincial jurisdiction and until recently Native people were subjected to culturally insensitive child welfare practices.

In earlier years Native children were taken from their families and placed for adoption with white families, even to families outside of Canada. This loss of Native children has been the source of much grief for Indian bands. Many bands have made valiant efforts to repatriate these children, which means returning these children to their home reserves.

Now in some provinces, there are branches of the Child Welfare Department specifically targeting Native child welfare services. Native overrepresentation in child welfare is particularly evident in western Canada where Native children comprise more than one-fifth of the children in substitute care. In the western provinces, the ratio of Native children in care to the provincial total is particularly high, and at times accounted for as many as one-half of the children in care.

The implementation of new child welfare agreements with bands is the first step in the restoration of Native control over their child welfare services. Previously, child welfare services were carried out within the context of colonization. These efforts devalued or ignored Native culture and aimed to assimilate Native children into the dominant culture. Newly designed child welfare agreements challenge the colonization philosophy of the past. To Native peoples, gaining control over their own child welfare services is as significant as other rights including health, education, land claims, and economic development. To date, most Native child welfare services follow a delegated authority model whereby Native agencies administer provincial child welfare legislation and procedures with the provincial government retaining ultimate authority. These Native child welfare agencies have executive rather than legislative authority. The Blood band in Alberta is in the process of developing their own legislation, which may serve as a prototype for other bands across the country.

## Services for Inuit

Although the federal government delivers some services directly to Inuit in the north, most programs are delivered by the respective territorial governments. Territorial governments receive approximately 80 percent of revenues in transfer payments from the federal government. Similar agreements have been made between the Inuit and the government of Quebec. The federal government contributes a share of the funding for these services. In Labrador, the Newfoundland provincial government exercises primary responsibility for administering services to Inuit, again under a cost-sharing agreement with the federal government.

### Programs for Aboriginal People Provided by Other Federal Departments

The list of programs specifically targeting Native peoples in Canada is extensive. At least eleven federal departments have Native-specific programs designed to preserve, maintain, and enhance the cultural heritage of Native peoples across Canada. Examples of these programs include the Northern Native Broadcast Access Program, the Aboriginal Friendship Centre Program, and Spiritual Services for Federal Inmates. Human Resources Development Canada works with Native people to help them assume control of the employment services and skills development.

**Self-Government and Land Claims.** Native peoples in Canada have fought for self-government and economic independence for many years. In particular, they are eager to control their own destiny and make decisions about the preservation of their unique cultures. A number of highly organized Native political organizations in Canada have been at the forefront of this struggle. Land claims and accompanying benefits is an important form of government assistance and restitution to Native peoples. Natives are struggling to reclaim the land and resources promised to them by previous Canadian governments. The federal government has failed to recognize or honor these aspirations until recent years. The federal government was criticized recently by the Canadian Human Rights Commission, which called for an independent and evenhanded system of dealing with Native land claims.

There are two types of land claims in Canada: comprehensive and specific. Comprehensive land claims acknowledge that there are continuing unresolved Native rights to their lands. Comprehensive claims occur where Native title has not yet been assigned through a treaty or legal settlement. They are comprehensive because of their wide scope, which typically includes land title, fishing, and trapping rights and financial compensation. Specific claims deal with existing treaties that have not been honored, and with how their lands and other assets under the Indian Act are administered. A particular problem with past settlements is that many echoed the belief that assimilation was a desirable inevitable—a prevailing government attitude toward the indigenous peoples of Canada.

There is now a glimmer of hope in the form of a shift in government thinking. The previous way in which the federal government has dealt with Native peoples has been a dismal failure. This is especially evident because of the high rate of social problems among Canada's Native peoples. Recently, a process was started whereby the federal government, in partnership with First Nations communities, would strive for self-government, which refers to governments designed, established, and administered by Native peoples. This seems to be the wave of the future. Each agreement will be unique in terms of the special historical, cultural, political, and economic circumstances of each community. Areas of self-government will typically fall into the areas of health care, child welfare, education, housing, and economic development. Negotiations in this new process would ideally include provincial and territorial governments, but the extent of provincial involvement remains to be seen. The right to self-government is protected through the constitution as well as through changes in existing treaties or as part of land claim settlements.

There is reason to be optimistic. The federal government has publicly recognized the importance and necessity of Native self-government and has vowed that it will not end its fiduciary relationship with Native peoples. Ideally, self-government should be a shared financial responsibility between federal, provincial, and territorial governments.

### Conclusion

Government assistance and restitution attempts have failed Native people in Canada in the past. Earlier attempts have been blamed for fostering dependency of Native people on the government. The historical impact of colonization as well as racist and assimilationist policies reinforces the need for special social and economic rights for Canada's Native peoples. The political ideology of assimilation reflected in the attempts of missionaries and early settlers to "civilize" Native people has been evident throughout Canadian history. Nevertheless, Native people in Canada have held onto their proud heritage and have refused to relinquish their claim to sovereignty and their unique rights and benefits, despite a hostile and oppressive environment making it difficult to do so.

Their battle is for the preservation of separate and distinct Native cultures. However, efforts for self-government, sovereignty, and cultural continuity have been eroded by lack of control over the political and social institutions that affect them. This is very evident in the social services that affect them. Increasingly, Native peoples are questioning the value and effectiveness of these social programs and institutions.

The political activism of Native peoples combined with distrust of government around such issues as land claims, aboriginal rights, and the legal status and definition of the word *Indian* has been the impetus for greater self-government. Native peoples have shown increasing interest in assuming control of the formal social services now provided by the established health and welfare system. Out of this has evolved a commitment to the development of services designed by and administered for Native peoples.

The present situation dictates that social policies concerning Native people be designed and administered by Native people themselves. Moreover, these policies demand recognition of their unique position in the Canadian social fabric. Social policies must move beyond the present obstacles to offer services that support the right to Native self-determination through self-government. In this shift, the government cannot withhold needed financial resources to help make their dream come true.

After centuries of domination and discrimination, the dominant society is starting to become sensitive to Native peoples and their issues. However, there is more work to be done. Indian activism will continue to confront the status quo. Goals for the future include strengthening and affirming the identity of Native peoples and redressing historical wrongs.

Despite some progress, many problems continue as a result of the legacy of Native people's treatment in Canada. Native people remain over-represented in most social problems and they still carry the wounds of culturally insensitive and blatantly discriminatory social programs. Discriminatory attitudes and actions negate the basic premise of cultural and human respect and serve to credit the negative stereotyping that still exists.

The Native peoples of Canada have a strong and proud heritage. They also have the strength and resources to overcome historical injustices done to their culture and well being, but they need support from the dominant society to improve their situation. At the very least, their aspirations should not be thwarted. Canada owes them the best it has to offer.

*Heather Coleman*
*University of Calgary*

*Don Collins*
*University of Calgary*

### Notes

1. Statistics obtained from "Indian and Northern Affairs Canada," <http://www.inac.gc.ca/stats/facts/1995/howdo.html>, 1995.

2. "1996 Census: Aboriginal Data," <http://www.statscan.ca/Daily/English/980113/d980113.html>, 1995.

3. "Indian and Northern Affairs Canada," <http://www.inac.gc.ca/stats/facts/1995/abocon.html>, 1995.

4. Ibid.

5. Ibid.

6. Ibid.

7. "Housing," <http://www.inac.gc.ca/index>.

8. Ibid.

## ◆ AN OVERVIEW OF ECONOMIC DEVELOPMENT HISTORY ON CANADIAN NATIVE RESERVES

The historical evolution of the economic development of Indian communities has gone through profound changes since the arrival of Christopher Columbus five hundred years ago. This section will examine how the indigenous peoples of Canada have adjusted, adapted, accommodated to, and resisted the various social, political, cultural, and economic institutions introduced by the waves of European newcomers settling in their respective homelands. Many indigenous populations declined drastically from the ravages of diseases and dislocation due to warfare. Many indigenous institutions were altered or replaced by European models and, over time, Native societies became powerless and unable to control their fate. Nevertheless, the Native people of Canada remain undefeated and continue to resist assimilation into mainstream Canadian society.

This overview will examine the primary political events that have shaped the institutions and circumstances of Canada's First Nations, the original peoples in the North American continent, in their dealings with the British Crown and Canada's federal government. A political transition occurred from 1850 to the early twentieth century when twelve numbered and several other treaties were signed covering most territory within central and western Canada. Upon conclusion of the treaty-making process, Indian nations unwittingly came under the paternalistic guidance of the Indian Act, first enacted in 1876. It defined Canadian Indian rights and status under the bureaucratic management of the Department of Indian Affairs established in 1880. These factors remain the determinant forces in Indian policy to the present day.

### The Newcomers' Legacy

Canadian Indians signed a series of "peace and friendship" treaties with the European newcomers starting with the French in the early sixteenth century during the settlement of New France. After decades of warfare, the French were displaced by the British after the conquest of 1760. Subsequently, the British government granted the Royal Proclamation of 1763, the fundamental document setting out Indian political and land rights, in order to effect a lasting peace with the Indian First Nations. The unique constitutional status of Canada's aboriginal peoples has its beginnings in the Royal Proclamation whereby the British Crown, the British head of state, officially recognized the Indian peoples' interest in the land of this "Great Island" (which the English named British North America). It was soon apparent that the Indian nations had little input into defining British-Indian affairs as European settlement proceeded westward into Indian territory. The aboriginal peoples were treated as subjects of the colonizing state, but they remained sovereign allies economically and militarily until the early eighteenth century.

During the seventeenth and eighteenth centuries, the focus of both the French and British colonial governments was regulation of the fur trade commerce. The Indian nations controlled access to the resources of the country including furs, timber, fish, and agricultural goods. In turn, the indigenous population became conspicuous consumers of European goods and developed a growing dependency on modern technology and manufactured goods, such as guns and metal utensils. Inevitably the Indian nations and the colonizers clashed over land use and the exploitation of the natural resources.

The progressing commercial trade was paralleled by a growing European military presence as the newcomers' settlements expanded into the interior of North America. The Indian nations were either potential allies or enemies, because global politics did not recognize neutrality, and the First Nation confederations welcomed alliance with the technologically powerful newcomers in their struggles with other confederacies. Numerous peace and friendship treaties were signed to ensure the protection of commerce and the vulnerable European settlements. The newcomers' population remained relatively small and largely dependent on the indigenous people, and the colonial governments reaffirmed the friendship agreements through a system of presents or annuities. Thus treaty payments and promises regarding the sharing of resources became the foundation of colonial Indian policy during the eighteenth and nineteenth centuries.

The economics of the New World trade, based on the transatlantic shipment of fish, timber, and furs to the European mercantile nations, became bound up with the imposition of European values and standards—whether religious conversion to Christianity, formal education, or social-political institutions. The Native people were expected to become "civilized" according to European standards. Conflicts arose over land use and ownership, and these remained the root of much misunderstanding when treaties were signed. The British Crown interpreted the treaties as land "surrenders" and "extinguishment" of aboriginal title and certain rights. Indian First Nations invariably regarded a treaty as a promise to keep the peace and to share the bountiful resources from the land. A land sale or exchange or proprietary ownership was contrary to the philosophy and attitudes of most indigenous peoples about their relationship with Mother Earth; land was not a possession that could be sold. Natural resources were provided for all people to share for their survival.

## Traditional Indian Economies

Indian nations across Canada at the time of first prolonged contact with European explorers in the sixteenth century enjoyed a diversity of economics. The sea coast peoples living in British Columbia along the Pacific Ocean coast, the northern Arctic Ocean peoples, and the Atlantic east coast maritime nations utilized the rich marine life and fisheries in their resource-based economies. The rich plant life of the sea, shorelines, and forest supplied all the necessary raw material for food, clothing, transportation, fuel, and shelter. Life was generally easier than in the harsher and less-productive regions of the interior plains. Complex and sophisticated social, economic, religious, and political institutions developed to suit their respective environments during the centuries before European contact.

We may generalize to describe pre-contact economic development as seasonal resource management revolving around hunting, trading, fishing, and gathering. The use of natural resources, however, varied from culture to culture. The Woodlands people, in the large forested lands of central Canada used the canoe for transportation and raised crops. The Plains people of the great western prairie lands traveled on foot and used dog travois until their culture was radically transformed by the introduction of the horse onto the prairies in the early eighteenth century. Indigenous technology included the spear, hook, bow and arrow, snare, deadfall, buffalo jumps, and pounds. Shelter was easily constructed out of tree materials or hides. Social groupings varied from the large one-house villages of the Eastern Iroquois to small wandering bands of less than one hundred members characteristic of the plains buffalo hunting camps.

The great Iroquois Confederacy, composed of the Cayuga, Mohawk, Oneida, Onondaga, Seneca, and later the Tuscarora, developed a horticultural economy in southeastern Ontario and upstate New York based on corn, squash, beans, and tobacco. Their sedentary lifestyle was augmented by trading surplus food to neighboring tribes whose lifestyle was centered around a hunting and trapping economy. There was an overlap of seasonal activities revolving around fishing, hunting, preparing fields, planting, harvesting, trading, gathering wild crops and firewood, socializing, making new articles, and conducting special ceremonies throughout the year.

The hunting and gathering economies characterized the traditional way of life for the large number of tribes living in the forest belts, parkland and the prairies covering much of Canada. All enjoyed their own language, customs, ceremonies, songs and institutions. The largest group was the Algonkian-speakers, the dominant Indian language group, represented by the Mi'kmaq (Micmac) and Maliseet of the Maritimes, the Innu (Montagnais) and Cree-Naskapi of Quebec, and the large Plains bands of the Cree, Blood, Peigan, and Siksika (Blackfeet) of the prairies.

Within the span of a few generations after the arrival of European traders and settlers in North America, modern warfare, epidemics, alcohol, and the depletion of fur animals and game had reduced most First Nations to considerable dependence on the European way of life. The coexistence that characterized initial contact gradually gave way to a growing reliance on imported manufactured goods. The local economy became enmeshed in a continent-wide trading system. A growing number of Indian communities began to rise near trading posts and the rapidly expanding European settlements. The traditional gathering, fishing, hunting, and local subsistence lifestyle was gradually replaced by working for wages, barter, and demand for goods and services found only in urban settlements.

European settlements expanded across British North America, starting on the East Coast in the 1600s and extending across the North American continent over the next two hundred years. The newcomers came to exploit the natural resources including the fisheries, timber, and the fur trade. This exploitation-settlement pattern started an unstoppable chain of events. To the Indian Nations, the European settler was a visitor to an already occupied homeland. The normal procedure was to establish a "peace and friendship" treaty to allow mutual sharing of the land and its resources. The subsequent cross-cultural contact in time significantly altered the Indian way of life, customs, and institutions.

The main focus of contact in much of Canada, notably around the Great Lakes and across the prairies and the wooded north, was the fur trade industry. Formally initiated by a royal charter granted by the king of England in 1670, the Hudson's Bay Company promptly precipitated a new economic relationship based on a barter exchange system, which eventually altered Indian social structures and living patterns and gradually created a dependence on new manufactured products imported from Europe. The Hudson's Bay Company dominated the fur trade in western Canada until the late eighteenth century when rival independent traders formed the North West Company from the 1790s until 1821, when the two companies merged as the reorganized Hudson's Bay Company.

The Native peoples accepted what the newcomers had to offer, and, with acceptance, their traditional way of life changed. Equipment such as guns and metal traps, and new transportation methods made it possible to kill more animals for food and for trading of the skins. This included beaver and fur-bearing animals in the eastern and northern forests, sea otter on the West Coast, and buffalo on the great plains. Indian families from the Mi'kmaq (Micmac), Iroquois, Ojibwa (Chippewa), and Cree nations gained wealth as "middlemen" in the new trade economy. Members of these tribes closest to the trading centers served as distributors for the trader and the trappers living in the interior forests. Some tribes, such as the Ojibwa, Cree, and Athabaskan people of Northwest Canada, exploited the new technology of metal traps, metal tools, and guns. The more efficient traps were a better guarantee against starvation; furs were exchanged for food and luxuries; and weapons were more effective and increased security. The value of furs was based on the value of a prime beaver pelt (known as a made beaver), and credits from the trade of pelts were used to purchase trade goods from the distributors or the trading factor employed by the Hudson's Bay Company. The most discernible impact of the fur trade on indigenous societies was in their material culture and social organizations. The rifle replaced spears and arrows; metal utensils displaced bone, wooden, stone, and leather tools; manufactured goods dominated hand-produced products.

Among the Indians of the Northwest Pacific, potlatch ceremonies grew bigger and more elaborate as a result of the influx of new goods as hosting clans distributed or destroyed personal possessions to enhance their status. The potlatch ceremonies helped to define the economic and social status of families and might be held to validate an inherited position or the adoption of a name or ceremonial title. On the prairies, a hunter had the means and reason to kill many more buffalo and attain more new possessions to fill his larger tipi. Families would settle near the forts and towns to obtain more easily European tools, clothing, food, and resources. Many became entrapped in a new economy as dependent consumers rather than as self-sufficient suppliers of trade goods.

The fierce commercial competition for furs lasted for two centuries until the union of the Hudson's Bay Company and the North West Trading Company in 1821. When beaver became scarce due to overtrapping, a band of families either moved into new trapping territory or became impoverished dependents residing near the forts.

Increased contact between the various Indian nations brought further change in territorial boundaries and intertribal trade patterns. The Mi'kmaq (Micmac) expanded throughout the Atlantic maritime provinces and New England states and were key allies in the British-French battle for domination in North America. The Six Nations Iroquois Confederacy displaced the Huron, one of the greatest Iroquois tribes known for their farm villages, as the dominant people around the Great Lakes of Ontario. In the Hudson's Bay Company territory of western Canada, the Cree Nation emerged as dominant traders with their new wealth of guns, metal tools, and highly valued trade wares. The Cree tribes along the prairie waterways spread north into the lands of the Chipewyan, the Slave, and the Beaver people who shared the great forest lands of the Northwest Territories. The horse-oriented buffalo hunt of the Plains Cree culture flourished until the buffalo herds, once numbering in the tens of millions, were reduced to a few hundred by the 1880s.

In the Canadian West, the economic cycles of the fur economy changed the tribal system, and the family-based band system broke down for many people. The trade in alcohol led to social disintegration for families tied to the traditional economy. The struggle for power and wealth was irrevocably imbalanced by the spread of new diseases from Europe, which killed thousands of Natives. Measles, smallpox, influenza, fevers, and venereal disease swept across North America carried by traders, explorers, and intertribal contact. It is speculated that up to half (sometimes entire bands) of the original peoples on the prairies were killed by the epidemics of the 1780s and 1830s. The leadership, ceremonial practices, and oral history lost in these epidemics could never be regained. The loss of confidence in Native healers and spiritual powers further encouraged acceptance of the Christian teachings and some acceptance of schools.

The fur trade posts became centers of social and commercial activity. As Indian families accepted more European customs and adopted more manufactured goods, the indigenous economy was no longer self-sufficient (producing for immediate family or tribal needs), but eventually became bound to the ever-demanding European trading market.

An elaborate trade ritual reaffirmed the basis of peace and friendship between the cultures. The trade ceremony would begin with a presentation to the head man of a gift of tea, tobacco, or alcohol, or colorful cloth or ribbon for the women and candy for the children. Then followed a lengthy discussion and haggling, often extending over several days, over the comparative value of furs and trade goods. After business was completed, there was an exchange of parting presents to re-confirm the bonds of friendship. A spirit of cooperation and mutual exploitation characterized the Hudson's Bay Company's relationship with its indigenous partners. The trade ritual was also a political ceremony to cement the company-Indian alliance. These early ceremonies and protocol rituals were later adopted during the treaty negotiations of the nineteenth century.

By the mid-nineteenth century, with the fur trade era in rapid decline, a new economy based on agricultural settlement and ranching began to shape the Canadian West. This period of European-Native coexistence was characterized by rapid cultural adjustment among all tribes and by the corresponding destabilization of the traditional indigenous economy based on hunting of game and trading of furs. By the end of that century, there was little game left to hunt and few fur animals to trap. The once-populous beaver, muskrat, otter, and forest fur-bearing animals had been reduced to dangerously low levels. The large game such as bison, moose, elk, and deer were in rapid decline from overhunting and loss of habitat to agriculture and forest fires. For Canada's indigenous peoples, the consequences were catastrophic. Their traditional food supplies were severely reduced or totally gone, notably the buffalo. Disease had killed tens of thousands of Natives and alcohol threatened many others. Economic trade evolved into political-social colonization. The political-economic consequences are still felt today.

Whereas during the fur trade era, the Indian people had some measure of control and the reciprocal trade patterns created an interdependency among the participants, during the post-1870s settlement period, the newcomers completely disrupted the traditional way of life. Settlers, ranchers, and urban residents did not depend on mutual cooperation and did not respect the original inhabitants. Indeed, Native society was typified as a hindrance to "progress," and Native people were viewed as the government's "problem." Euro-Canadian culture not only began to dominate, but a new economy and lifestyle were also forced on the Natives by the actions of missionaries and by the surrounding communities of farmers, ranchers, and townspeople. Nation-to-nation relations originally founded on coexistence and sharing of resources was gradually replaced in the nineteenth century by Euro-Canadian dominance based on paternalism, assimilation, and subjugation.

## The Treaties and Economic Self-Determination

The legal, political, social, and economic basis of Indian First Nation government relations are governed by the Canadian Constitution and by a variety of legislative acts passed by the Canadian Parliament and by provincial legislatures. The First Nations of central Canada began negotiating modern treaties in 1850, starting with the Robinson-Superior and Robinson-Huron treaties covering the north shore of the Great Lakes of Ontario. Subsequently, Treaties 1 to 11 were signed between 1871 and 1923 covering mostly western Canada. It is important to understand the terms and conditions, as well as the spirit and intent, of these modern numbered treaties to appreciate the socioeconomic and political evolution of First Nation governments over the past two centuries.

Treaties between the Crown and the First Nations confirmed their separate status, and the documents set out certain obligations for their future benefit now commonly referred to as "treaty rights." Throughout the treaty process, the First Nations were dealt with on a nation-to-nation basis, which is recognized today in constitutional law and in government-to-government protocol. This bilateral relationship was assured when the Canadian Parliament was given the power by the 1867 Constitution Act (formerly the British North America Act) for "Indians and Lands reserved for the Indians" under section 91(24), which Parliament has interpreted as its authority to make laws for Canadian registered or "status" Indians, who were defined by the act. Most First Nations assert that they never surrendered their sovereignty and that they enjoy an inherent (inalienable) right to self-determination. The right to self-government is now widely accepted in Canada, a reversal of events starting over 125 years ago.

Soon after the first numbered treaties were negotiated in the 1870s the traditional economy of Indian nations was wiped out when the great bison herds were completely decimated by the early 1880s. Indian treaty negotiators focused on securing the economic future of their people. The first request was a guarantee to continue their traditional hunting and trapping economy, but government commissioners insisted these rights be made subject to the queen's regulations. The establishment of Indian reserves, lands set aside for Indian occupation, was not intended to maintain the traditional way of life in the new economic order, but

rather to assist Native people toward assimilation into Canadian society. Treaty negotiations often covered the terms and conditions whereby an Indian agricultural economy could be encouraged, including the provision of plows, agricultural implements, seeds, and stock to build up community herds as Natives settled on reserve lands. The stated object of the government's policy was to prepare the Indian people for a new way of life centered on the industrial arts and agriculture. To facilitate this goal Parliament passed the 1876 Indian Act, which enforced regulations for protecting Native people from exploitation by the white majority and for managing the affairs of Indians until they became "civilized." The end result, however, was economic dependency and underdevelopment. Indian reserve economies did not flourish and social assistance became a prevalent means of subsistence. Native reserves became pockets of poverty surrounded by expansive and wealthy non-Native communities.

In part, the treaties were economic agreements to share the land and its resources, and in return, the federal government agreed to provide compensation in various ways. The government did operate a number of demonstration farms to serve as models for training. However, as the official government authority, the local Indian agent controlled all commercial activities and business conducted on the reserve. Later the "pass system," requiring a letter of permission to cross the reserve's border, was instituted to control Native movement off the reserve. Government policy was directed toward breaking down the Indian culture through education and encouraging integration and eventual assimilation into Canadian society.

## Early Economic Programs

Among the severe limitations on Indian economic development are the various sections of the Indian Act dealing with management of reserve lands, Indian monies, and tribal governments operating through an elective band council system. In addition, hundreds of federal statutes, federal provincial agreements, administrative rules and regulations, and by-laws must be considered in land transactions, economic development loan funds, taxation, and financial management. Today, there are numerous publications dealing with the legal complexities of operating business enterprises on Indian reserves.

The powers of Indian band councils, which are reserve governments specified in the Indian Act, are not clearly identified, and the role of local government has shifted dramatically over the past century. From the 1870s to the 1920s, the Canadian government extended control over every aspect of life on Indian reserves. Some First Nations, such as the Iroquois on the Six Nations Reserve in Brantford, Ontario, and the Kahnawake in the province of Quebec, retain much of their traditional form of governance and leadership. But on most Indian reserves, the Indian agent dominated political and economic decision making. Official policies for assimilating Native peoples were supported by a combination of power groups within Canadian society, especially the Christian denominations. The denominational churches sought to convert the band members, and Roman Catholic, Anglican, and Methodist-United Church mission societies also operated day schools and boarding or industrial schools. The Christian boarding schools combined year-round residence facilities with practical training in agriculture, carpentry, and manual work taught half the day and the traditional subjects (reading, writing, and arithmetic) taught in the second half.

After World War I, national and provincial Native organizations were formed across Canada, such as the League of Indian Nations. Native leaders began to question the Canadian government's unilateral management of Native political, economic, and cultural affairs. Year after year, resolutions were passed at annual assemblies calling for changes to the Indian Act and demanding recognition of aboriginal and treaty rights. With Indians stereotyped as a dying race until the 1930s, the poor quality of life evident on Indian reserves could not be dismissed or corrected with paternalistic policies. The high unemployment, short life expectancy, high infant mortality, systemic poverty, shoddy housing, inadequate community services and facilities, and open discrimination became controversial issues in the public press and legislative debates. There were calls for legal inquiries, royal commissions, and just treatment of Canada's Native peoples.

From 1946 to 1948, the joint Senate and House parliamentary committees held hearings and recommended massive revision of the Indian Act. The revised act passed in 1951 removed over fifty sections, including the most blatant discriminatory policies such as the pass system, prohibition on religious ceremonies, and restrictions on property ownership. Still the government and the minister of Indian affairs retained final authority on all land matters and severely limited the powers of local Native government. Indeed the basic policy of controlling Indian socioeconomic development and integrating people into Euro-Canadian institutions remained unchanged. During the 1960s, the Black Power movement gained momentum in the United States, and a corresponding Red Power movement

raised the political profile of Native issues all across North America. A push for radical change gained momentum during the activist 1960s decade, and there was renewed pressure to radically amend the Indian Act and to realign the long-entrenched policies of the Department of Indian Affairs headquartered in Ottawa. Residential boarding schools were closed, and education evolved toward local community control. Churches became more supportive of Indian issues, and support groups such as the Indian-Eskimo Association allied with provincial Native organizations and militant Red Power groups such as AIM (American Indian Movement).

When problems reach crisis proportions, the government's response is invariably to set up an inquiry. The federal government commissioned a broadly mandated but detailed "Survey of the Contemporary Indians of Canada: Economic, Political, Educational Needs and Policies," commonly known as the Hawthorn Report, after its chairman, Harry Hawthorn, an anthropologist. Through intensive interviews with local community leaders and by compiling massive statistics, the report presented an embarrassing indictment of the social and economic conditions of Canada's first citizens. Nothing had changed since reserves were established—low life expectancy (although populations were rising), poor education and health services, inferior housing, high unemployment coupled with demoralizing welfare, high levels of incarceration often rooted in alcohol abuse, inadequate capital funds, and endemic discrimination at every level of interaction with Canadian society and institutions continued. Few Indians could get business or personal loans, credit was limited, and the right to vote in federal elections came only in 1960 with passage of the Canadian Bill of Rights. The Hawthorn Report noted the dismal failure of government efforts to achieve assimilation and suggested many innovative changes in policies and programs. Perhaps the most controversial recommendation was to extend provincial services to Indians contrary to the historically based bilateral treaty relationship between federal and Indian governments.

## Recent Strategies for Socioeconomic Development

During the 1960s, the Indian leadership in bands, councils, and provincial organizations demanded greater control over their own affairs. They wanted to develop their own programs, administer their own monies, control their internal affairs, and plan their own future. The major hindrance was the Indian Act, but there was no consensus on how to amend or abolish the archaic piece of legislation. Many community members were under the misunderstanding that the act was the basis of their rights. A growing number called on the Canadian government to honor the spirit and intent of the modern treaties rather than following its legal obligations limited to the strict written terms with the narrowest of responsibility. Gaining confidence and organizational lobbying skills from the social action movement of the 1960s, a new generation of Indian leaders gained the public's attention, and the government was forced to pay attention.

The most popular concept for promoting development in rural and remote communities took the form of community development. The provinces of Ontario, Manitoba, and Alberta were the first to experiment with this new grassroots approach to self-help change. Community members were encouraged to define their own problems and solutions for attaining their own goals. The next phase involved finding the resources necessary to implement long-term development. The federal administration yielded to the mounting pressure and introduced its own community development program in 1963, and coincidentally in the late 1960s, the provinces began to withdraw support or transfer resources to local Native organizations. A new spirit, pride, and vitality was evident in Native communities. They challenged government goals and methods and, typically, the government was unprepared to meet the heightened expectations and limited its commitment to the community development process. The century-old policy of assimilation and paternalism was finally under severe attack for its ineffective and antiquated approach in dealing with the clearly identified social and economic problems endemic to Canada's Indian communities.

As an alternative, the Department of Indian Affairs established a number of regional advisory boards to discuss revision of the Indian Act. A consultation process commenced with the National Indian Advisory Board comprised of prominent Indian leaders from across Canada, which expanded its mandate to investigate budgeting, program evaluations, and administration policy. This new assertiveness was paralleled by a rise in power of provincial Indian political organizations such as the Indian Association of Alberta led by Harold Cardinal, the Federation of Saskatchewan Indians led by Walter Deiter, the Manitoba Indian Brotherhood led by Dave Courchene, the powerful Union of Ontario Chiefs, and the long-established Indian Brotherhoods in British Columbia, the North West Territories, and the Maritimes. One manifestation of the increased sophistication of Indian political organization and communication was the revival of a national body, the National Indian Brotherhood (NIB). During the 1980s, the NIB fostered the growth of Indian leadership and gained momentum and credibility under its

president, George Manual, from the Shuswap Nation of British Columbia. In 1981, the NIB reorganized itself as the Assembly of First Nations (AFN).

The electrifying selection of Pierre Elliott Trudeau as the Liberal Party leader in 1968 heralded a new era of hope for aboriginal peoples who were initially attracted to his vision of a "just society." The 1969 White Paper entitled "Statement of the Government of Canada on Indian Policy," has become a landmark in Native resistance to Indian affairs policy makers. The underlying assumption remained: the bureaucratic solution to economic advancement was assimilation into mainstream society. The federal government proposed to eliminate the special status (or rights) of Indians; it projected the disappearance of reserves; and it planned to transfer responsibility for Indians to the provinces albeit under cost-sharing programs. The Indian Act and the Department of Indian Affairs would be terminated, and special legislative, administrative, and judicial rights would give way to equality within modern Canadian society. Indians were to receive the same services as other Canadians through the provincial or municipal delivery systems. The long-honored trust responsibility of the federal government, whereby the minister of Indian Affairs is ultimately responsible to Parliament, was to be abrogated, and management of Indian lands transferred to local control. The Liberal government's policy reflected its ideological emphasis on individual equality and opportunity, but this threatened the collective communal survival of distinct Indian societies in Canada. The historic and cultural uniqueness of the aboriginal peoples, their special constitutional status, their belief in treaty rights, the sovereignty of Indian lands, and the validity of outstanding aboriginal land claims and inherent rights were arbitrarily rejected by the policy makers in Ottawa. The reaction to this bureaucratic reformulation of old assimilationist goals was fast and furious from the "New Indians" of the Red Power movement.

The government White Paper galvanized the local, provincial, and national Native organizations into a united rejection of the proposed changes to federal Indian policy. Under the leadership of the charismatic Cree leader from the Sucker Creek reserve in Alberta, Harold Cardinal, the chiefs of the forty-four Indian bands in Alberta presented their own vision for future development in a counter-publication called the "Red Paper" (1971). Similarly, the Manitoba Indian Brotherhood responded with "Wahbung: Our Tomorrows" (1971), and the Council for Yukon Indians published their terms and conditions for a comprehensive land claim, called "Together Today for our Children Tomorrow" (1973). These and other position papers stressed the cultural and spiritual heritage of their peoples and called for a new relationship based on their special status as "Citizens Plus," as the Alberta Red Paper was retitled.

Indian communities required money and resources to implement self-government. Existing support programs for office administration, health services, recreation, and most importantly social welfare funds could be redirected toward education and training programs. Community infrastructures—roads, utilities, housing, power, heat, recreation, schools, and administration buildings—would require long-term planning and training programs. Nevertheless, it was generally acknowledged that the key to success was the special relationship with the land, their cultural identity, as reflected in the Yukon Indian vision published in their land claim statement in 1973: "Without land Indian people have no soul—no life—no identity—no Purpose. Control of our land is necessary for our Cultural and Economic Survival." During the first half of the twentieth century, surplus or underdeveloped reserve land was "surrendered" to government officials. Some reserves in western Canada lost as much as one-third of their most productive farmland. The Canadian government is currently undertaking to return much of this land where available or providing cash compensation to Indian bands.

During the 1960s, the main source of funds for local economic development was the Indian Revolving Fund, created by the Department of Indian Affairs to provide start-up capital on reserves, which was limited in scope to small business. The 1970s may best be characterized as the experimental decade to jumpstart economic development in Indian communities across Canada. Although the controversial White Paper of 1969 was withdrawn, the White Paper's economic plan was instituted in 1971 through the Indian Economic Development Fund, which in the 1970s made available over $100 million for economic investment on Indian reserves. About $70 million was dispensed by direct loans through the Department of Indian Affairs and Northern Development (DIAND), the national office for administering Canadian Indian affairs; about $30 million was distributed by financial institutions in the form of guaranteed loans; and approximately $10 million was made available in outright grants. Hundreds of projects were funded through the Canadian employment programs and the Department of Regional Economic Expansion with priority given to small independent business ventures such as retail stores, gas stations, handicraft shops, and service outlets.

Unfortunately, the centralized bureaucratic administrators selected economic development projects that had little relevance to the social, cultural, or political needs of the indigenous communities. Red tape and endless reporting requirements, progress reports, and financial statements thwarted local control. But as young leaders gained experience, local communities benefited from a variety of federal development programs, such as LIP (Local Initiative Program), LEAP (Local Employment Assistance Program), cultural/education centers, and other federally funded enterprises. Hundreds of communities gained short-term economic benefits while funds lasted. Some large industrial schemes were dismal failures but the debate continues whether the lessons learned were worth the investment. Many training programs were targeted for Natives but the results were variable. In terms of community self-esteem, adoption of planning procedures, and political awareness, some short-term benefits accrued to the reserve economies. Yet the social problems associated with poverty, unemployment, under-education, and self-identity are still major hurdles to community development. To the Indian leadership, economic development in the 1970s was tied to the government's policy of assimilation and therefore was viewed as a threat to Indian culture and traditional lifestyle. The federal government's economic development plans, policies, and programs have not been seen as effective in solving the root problems of underdevelopment and poverty on Indian reserves.

The late 1970s witnessed a series of independent national studies, inquiries, and reports on the future direction of Indian self-determination, most critical of the federal government's progress. The governments' limited economic approach to development problems continued to ignore the social, cultural, educational, and political realities on Indian reserves. Its shortcomings were critically analyzed by the National Indian Brotherhood (NIB) in 1973 at a federal-provincial economic conference when the NIB released its "Statement on Economic Development of Indian Communities." In 1976 and 1977, the NIB released "A Strategy for the Socioeconomic Development of Indian people." Both NIB reports criticized the lack of an overall socioeconomic development program that was integrated, well-coordinated, and meaningful to local communities. The Indian Economic Development Fund was criticized as another experiment in problem solving conceived, designed, and managed by government bureaucrats. The government, the reports said, denigrated the viability of an Indian economy and failed to link economic development with community development. The National Indian Brotherhood suggested that a more realistic approach was to encourage the planning process at the community level, which would incorporate the social, cultural, education, and political factors into long-range goals. Local community leaders argued that they had to have control over decision making in consultation with the elders and band members if real community development was to succeed. New policies for self-government and community-based planning were the only realistic alternative to the existing program structures based on federal-Native power relationships. There was a sense of optimism that the federal government was finally willing to listen to its critics and commissioned reviews of its failed policies.

At the national level, the National Indian Brotherhood called for the economic emancipation of Indian communities so that local control could be a reality. The brotherhood proposed transfer and equalization payments to Indian governments similar to that given to provincial governments. This implied political autonomy and the establishment of new institutions better suited to reflect each First Nation's culture, tradition, capitalization, and resource base. Although new fiscal arrangements would need to be negotiated, much of the planning and infrastructure could be assumed through the settlement of land claims, honoring treaty rights, and recognizing the inherent rights of Indian First Nations. Flexibility would be essential to meet the differing economic, cultural, and political evolution of almost six hundred Indian bands occupying over two thousand reserves scattered across Canada. The NIB recommendation reinforced local Native government and traditional economic relations. The strategy report made sixty-eight recommendations, of which the primary starting point was transfer of all authority and decision-making powers to local band governments. DIAND would be merely the financial conduit and fulfill the trust responsibility of the federal government.

Unfortunately, the growing entrenchment of the federal agencies shelved many of the ideas, theories, and approaches discussed among the Indian organizations and its leadership during the 1970s. The federal government's attention was focused on negotiating the massive comprehensive land claim known as the James Bay and Northern Quebec Agreements, signed in 1975. This coincided with the public hearings into the Mackenzie Valley gas pipeline chaired by one of Canada's most noted jurists, Mr. Justice Thomas Berger. He was appointed by the federal government to undertake a comprehensive analysis of the environmental and socioeconomic impacts of a proposed oil and natural gas pipeline extending twenty-six hundred miles from the Beaufort Sea in the Canadian Arctic southward along the Mackenzie River valley of the Northwest Territories to link up with the existing pipelines in Alberta that served markets in the United States. During nineteen months of hearings, listening to over a thousand witnesses including professionals but also people from

twenty-six Dene communities, Judge Berger was told that the Dene feared that their survival as a race was at stake. The environment would be damaged, but the influx of southern construction workers would irrevocably alter Dene aspirations for self-determination as eloquently articulated in the famous Dene Declaration of July 1975. In their statement of rights the Dene people declared: "What we seek then is independence and self determination within the country of Canada (as a distinct people and as a nation). This is what we mean when we call for a just land settlement for the Dene Nation."

The Dene people challenged the Canadian government and the Canadian people to recognize their unique culture and the right to self-determination as a nation within Canada. The federal minister swiftly rejected the declaration as a separatist statement prompted by radical back-room academic advisors. Nevertheless, Justice Berger recommended a ten-year moratorium on development, and land claim settlement negotiations continue into the 1990s in northern Canada.

In the 1970s, the Liberal government under Prime Minister Pierre Elliot Trudeau responded to Native issues by sponsoring community and regional studies. The government provided funding for housing, community services and infrastructure, career training, natural resource development, band government, cultural education centers, health and welfare programs, and capital investment programs.

During the 1970s to mid-1980s, the Indian Economic Development Fund provided $150 million to Indian business, comprising about half of the total funding for economic development. This averaged out to about $40,000 per band annually and was not adequate to meet the growing demand from bands and individuals. During the 1980s the federal government shifted its priority to funding regional and tribal programs, and it created a new all-Native advisory board called the Native Economic Development Program (NEDP). A fund of $345 million was allocated over a four-year period commencing in April 1984 with the specific task "to assist the development of economic self-reliance among Canada's Aboriginal people." The programs were open to all status and non-status Indian, Métis, and Inuit. The NEDP called for creation of: (1) Native-operated financial and economic institutions organized to fund Native entrepreneurial business; (2) community-based economic development to enhance Native economic self-reliance; (3) special projects for marketing research and analysis, and sponsoring special studies on Native business issues; and (4) greater Native accessibility to other federal agencies and federal departments.

NEDP funds proved difficult to obtain. The full amount available was never committed, and many projects simply died from neglect. The bands were rewarded with attractive grants and government loan guarantees, only if the band councils persevered and completed the research on market feasibility, raised enough equity investment, justified the social and economic costs and benefits, and provided land and economic infrastructure such as roads, water, and electricity.

In 1989, the NEDP was replaced by the Canadian Aboriginal Economic Development Strategy (CAEDS). As in previous federally sponsored programs of the 1970s, the economic development approach was encouraged through entrepreneurship and individual enterprise rather than community-based employment strategies. Increasingly DIAND wanted to concentrate on community-based economic development and focus on employment-intensive major resource projects, maximizing the use of traditional resources. The objective of CAEDS is to mobilize the resources of several government departments within a single economic development proposal. The Department of Employment and Immigration funds job training and skill development, while the Department of Industry, Science and Technology provides technical assistance to Native-owned businesses, joint ventures, and financial institutions.

The promotion of the entrepreneurial spirit and work ethic among the Native business community is best represented by the Canadian Council for Native Business (CCNB) established by business leaders in 1984 (in 1993 the organization changed its name to the Canadian Council for Aboriginal Business [CCAB]). The organization encourages the involvement and participation of aboriginal people in the mainstream workforce by offering business education internships for Natives to work in large corporate offices. CCNB-CCAB business members also provide business development advice to prospective Native entrepreneurs with the hope that they will succeed in developing the economic self-sufficiency of Canada's First Nations. Corporate employers are assisted in recruiting post-secondary students, and the private sector is encouraged to develop joint venture partnerships with Native corporations in order to share their business, financial, and management expertise while perhaps gaining some beneficial tax exemptions by operating on Indian lands.

The CCNB-CCAB has a high profile with federal government departments including DIAND, Employment and Immigration Canada, the CAEDS, and the Aboriginal Workforce Participation Initiative (AWPI). The government wants Canadian corporations to open their doors to the ninety-two thousand Native graduates with post-secondary (university/college) education and over thirty thousand graduates from job skills training programs each year. The federal government has promised to improve the socioeconomic conditions among Native communities and it has targeted business and natural resource ventures. These are the most promising areas for aboriginal peoples to gain "the skills and experience needed to become full participants in the Canadian economy." The CCNB-CCAB has hosted several high-profile networking conferences to bridge the gap between job opportunities and the growing Native business community and Native professionals. The organization publishes a newsletter called *Contact* with the objective of sharing "information and experiences about Aboriginal employment and develop more effective hiring, promotional and retention strategies."

Numerous Native communities and entrepreneurs are utilizing the CAEDS program to gain valuable skill development and managerial experience within the private sector and the Canadian public service. While demonstrating some success in the 1980s, the number of Native workers in the public service continued to decline in the 1990s, perhaps as a reflection of disillusionment with the federal government's objective of integrating Native graduates into mainstream society. The trend toward favoring business enterprise and entrepreneurship is welcomed by some Indian communities but feared by others as part of a suspected "hidden agenda" to undermine traditional aboriginal culture. The paternalistic approach of earlier government objectives has practically disappeared, and options to Native communities and individuals are expanding as self-confidence and experience grows. Economic self-reliance and the desire to control their own destiny are seen as the fundamental basis for political self-determination in the 1990s.

One of the provincial organizations most active in promoting Native economic well being is the Federation of Saskatchewan Indian Nations (FSIN). FSIN utilizes a series of boards to plan for the future. An indication of future directions is suggested by the responsibility given to the Economic Development Board, which includes the Saskatchewan Indian Resource Council; the Northern Economic Council; the Economic Action Resource Management Program; the Institute for Management, Energy, and Business; small businesses; and trade and commerce.

Federal and Native organizations typically enter into a long-term (usually three to five year) economic development framework agreement, which may be part of a comprehensive socioeconomic package called an Alternate Funding Arrangement (AFA). Indian governments are assured of their base funding for business management training and entrepreneurship and once into the agreement, they can shift funds among their programs and projects. Thus long-range planning and funding contributions provide a basis for stability and predictability in expenditures with the realistic prospect of reducing unemployment and achieving self-sufficiency.

## Modern Land Claim (Comprehensive) Settlements

Comprehensive land claims negotiations covering northern Canada across British Columbia, Yukon, North West Territories, and the Arctic have focused on four major aboriginal organizations: the Council of Yukon Indians (CYI), the Dene/Métis groups of the Mackenzie River Valley; the Committee for Original Peoples' Entitlement (COPE), representing the Beaufort Sea area; and the Tungavik Federation of Nunavut (TFN) in the central and eastern Arctic covering the new territory of Nunavut, which means "Our Land" in the Inuktitut language. Not unexpectedly, since the discovery of massive gas pools in the Beaufort Sea, a settlement was reached with COPE in 1984 and was quickly implemented. The same year, the CYI reached an agreement in principle on its land claims, but not all bands are ready for ratification. Economic development was interconnected with political self-determination and cultural identity. Access to lands and natural resources to meet present and future needs was written into the comprehensive land claims settlement negotiated by the Council of Yukon Indians (CYI) in 1991 and 1992.

In 1982, a territory-wide plebiscite approved (by 56 percent of the territory's voters) the division of the vast North West Territories into two jurisdictions: the Western Arctic dominated by the Dene and Métis with a large non-Native population centered in Yellowknife, and the eastern Arctic, homeland to twenty thousand Inuit, in Nunavut. The Dene, Métis, and Inuit agreed to negotiate a political boundary based on their respective but overlapping land claims areas. The idea of division was widely discussed during the Berger Inquiry into the Mackenzie Valley gas pipeline in the mid-1970s by the Inuit, who combined political issues of self-determination with the federal government's comprehensive land claims policy.

In 1988, the Dene/Métis land claim was tentatively settled with the federal government. Two years later when debated at their chiefs assembly representing twelve thousand people throughout the Mackenzie Valley, the Dene leadership rejected a clause that referred to the "extinguishment" of their aboriginal rights. Moreover, the proposed settlement made the Dene relinquish rights to 225 square miles of land in Nunavut territory where they hunted caribou and other wildlife. A fierce debate arose over the urgency to gain a measure of political and economic control over their own affairs

rather than deferring to the federal or territorial governments.

The federal government proceeded to negotiate separate comprehensive land claims agreements with the Gwich'in Indians from the North West Territories and the Inuit. Native leaders, who were forced to agree with one group against the other, voiced objections to Ottawa's "divide-and-conquer" tactics. The Gwich'in Nation of two thousand members retained title to 9,200 square miles in the Yukon and North West Territories as well as receiving $75 million in compensation over fifteen years. In return they relinquished their claim (and perhaps rights) to 18,500 square miles of traditional lands rich in natural resources already under development by international corporations.

In December 1991, the Inuit of the Arctic signed a self-government agreement with the federal government returning ownership of over 140,000 square miles, while conceding their claim to 640,000 square miles in return for $1.1 billion dollars paid over fourteen years.

Subsequently, several Dene bands from northern Saskatchewan filed a statement of claim in the Federal Court of Canada seeking affirmation of their historical presence in 9,600 square miles of land included in the Nunavut territory. Their forefathers served as middlemen traders with the Hudson's Bay Company and regularly trapped fur, and hunted caribou and other game animals in the Nunavut Territory. The ongoing debate may be settled in court if the political impasse is not resolved between the Inuit and Dene.

Political control and self-determination will inevitably be a key determinant in the scope, direction, and intensity of economic development in Canada's newest northern territories. They also will be vital factors in their preparation toward provincehood within confederation in the twenty-first century.

## Statutory Limitations on Indian Business

Under the terms of the Canadian Constitution, section 91(24), the treaties, and the Indian Act, the federal government holds "lands reserved for Indians" in a trust relationship. The legal title is vested in Her Majesty the Crown and reserve lands are not legally "Indian property" but remain under the guardianship of the federal government. Reserve land is managed for "the use and benefit of a band" in a communal sense. Reserve land can only be leased or sold after a "surrender" is agreed to by a vote or referendum of eligible voters, and approved by the minister of Indian affairs.

Band-controlled businesses or band members wanting to start a business have to carefully define their type of proprietorship. Some reserves, mainly in eastern

Canada, do issue a "certificate of possession" through the Department of Indian Affairs, but any business operation that is legally incorporated or has non-Indian investment will require a surrender, permit, or lease, and the entrepreneurs will lose their tax-exemption privileges. Reserve property cannot be seized or mortgaged; consequently, capital investment or loans are practically impossible to arrange. This places another limit on the ability of reserve-based enterprises to borrow or attract capital investment.

Even after many of the most blatant discriminatory aspects of Indian policy were removed in 1951 when the Indian Act was revised, federal economic development schemes have been short-term, stop-gap measures entangled in bureaucratic red tape. Special loan funds for Indians date back to 1938, but the current regulations were adopted in the early 1970s. The Department of Indian Affairs has adopted two approaches to encourage reserve business development. Direct loans may be granted by the department to start a business and to purchase assets. Alternatively the government may guarantee a loan from a bank or financial institution. The usual procedures and criteria are applied, such as developing a business plan, in order to assure an enterprise's viability, profitability, and ability to ensure repayment of any loans.

Requests for government loans or grants from band councils, individuals, or Native groups may take months or even years to go through the bureaucratic approval process. Once a band council resolution detailing the economic request is passed, it goes to the departments' district office or to the regional office and finally to headquarters to await the minister's signature. At each level of bureaucracy, the request is analyzed and questions are raised requiring answers from the band council or the local-regional office. At headquarters other federal departments may be involved in the decision making, such as the Justice Department, Treasury Board, and Canada Employment, and secretary of state and cabinet approval may be required for politically sensitive projects or programs.

## Economic Self-Determination for Aboriginal People

The urgency of change is apparent in light of the poverty, unemployment, and social-economic conditions on most Indian reserves. Many economic programs are available, but often times information on policy shifts is not effectively communicated to band leaders and members. All too often, economic change has been imposed on local reserve communities. Urbanization, assimilation pressures, and political developments off the reserves may give rise to conflicts, loss of

values and culture, depression, social problems, frustration, and lack of hope. The interface of Indian government with the federal and provincial governments is extremely complex. Band governments must deal with several departments managing hundreds of services and programs. Band councils must serve and be accountable to their community members, but must also prepare, negotiate, and account for their annual operations with the government. This dual accountability may be streamlined in the future as self-government is implemented to reflect local needs, priorities, culture, and economic base for the community and individual enterprises.

Across Canada, there are close to four hundred thousand status Indians in about six hundred bands living on about twenty-five hundred reserves and "Crown Land" settlements. Generally, the reserves are small, scattered in rural lands, and lack the administrative infrastructure or resources to economically sustain their rapidly growing population. About one hundred bands are described as resource producing (with oil and gas production or timber and mining), and several large prosperous reserves are located adjacent to metropolitan centers, such as Vancouver, Calgary, Saskatoon, Brantford, Montreal, Quebec City, Fredericton, and Sydney.

A common analytical approach sees post-treaty economic developments as the fault of "colonial exploitation" and "underdevelopment," where Indian reserves have become pockets of poverty and unemployment. The land base of First Nations has been severely limited, and the indigenous people increasingly have been denied access to natural resources. We have seen how the Indian Act and legislation has limited the powers of band councils and in fact has served to entrench the Department of Indian Affairs' control over every aspect of an individual's life and band administration. Combined with the paternalistic nature of the Indian Act, the creation of Indian reserves has kept Indian people from participating in the political and economic processes of the dominant Canadian society and from significantly improving their socioeconomic position.

Indian communities are largely dependent on government transfer payments—social welfare programs—or they find their traditional economies replaced by a system based upon wage labor and market competition. The depletion of natural resources, the static land base, increase in population, and lack of jobs, housing, and work opportunities have prompted an ever-increasing migration from reserves to urban centers. The demands of urban living based on a wage economy and resulting different lifestyle have had profound effects on traditional Indian culture, values, and expectations.

Acculturation pressures have forced the Native population to move from a relatively independent subsistence economy to involvement in an economic market place requiring formal education, technical training, and structured work styles.

When taking note of the socioeconomic and cultural environment on an Indian reserve, an individual entrepreneur or tribal corporation (small business) is faced with a number of institutional constraints unique to Canadian Indians. The legal aspects of economic development on Indian reserves are key determinant factors as to what can be done and how it can be achieved.

There are also numerous factors within a reserve community external to the economic environment that will help or hinder change. Some of these include (1) political and legal frameworks (government policy and laws, financial regulations); economic marketplaces (markets, supply and demand, operational costs, capitalization, competition, availability of resources); financial institutions (access to loans); sociocultural constraints (cultural attitudes, collective versus individual values, spiritual values); education (level of education and dropout rate); and physical limitations (community infrastructure for communications, housing, roads, services, and available natural resources)

The fundamental goal is to create jobs on the reserve for band members and coincidentally to take control of economic development in order to assure control over decision-making (whether planning, hiring and firing, creating income, or assuming self-determination). Resource-rich bands have demonstrated initiative and diversification during the 1980s. In 1984, production of oil and gas on Indian land amounted to $346 million, but by 1991 the economic returns had declined to $56 million, according to Indian Oil and Gas Canada (IOGC). Much of the investment activity in the oil and gas industry is centered on Indian reserves in the province of Alberta and some in the province of Saskatchewan. Bands have established development trust funds to enter into joint ventures with established oil companies and thereby gain technical and managerial expertise and provide employment opportunities. The enticement for non-Native corporations are enhanced tax exemptions and a positive corporate image.

In the spring of 1992, the newly formed Canadian Indian Energy Corporation (IEC) hosted the All Chiefs Oil and Gas Conference in Calgary, Alberta, to promote a closer working relationship between Indian nations and the major oil and gas companies. A Memorandum of Understanding and Statement of Principles was signed by IEC chair Joe Dion and Canadian Petroleum Association president Ian Smyth to ensure joint planning and joint ventures and cooperation in developing

employment, investment, training and business opportunities. The conference theme, "Working with Industry," highlighted the importance of economic development to coordinate the human, financial, and productive resources of the IEC First Nations. The IEC will focus on resource control and management while serving as a business advisory body to new locally controlled entrepreneurial ventures.

On less affluent reserves, economic development is motivated by the need to earn an income and is often centered around traditional work (producing handicrafts) or a family project. Community development is similarly motivated by the desire to create employment and is more likely to follow a business plan with well-defined goals and detailed accounting projections provided by outside advisors/consultants.

Community development is not gauged by economic factors alone. Projects are commonly judged according to whether the community or individual will retain its special character and resist assimilation into Canadian culture; whether the project will further self-esteem, affirm their pride, protect land ownership, enhance community values, and respect the sacredness of the land and environment are all considerations.

To some, dealing with bureaucratic red tape and an endless line of civil servants at local, regional, and national offices is simply another hurdle in creating employment on the reserve. DIAND support ranges from seed money for market studies, subsidizing construction costs or purchase of fixed assets, providing loan guarantees or lines of credit, offering work capital, and providing wage subsidies or technical assistance through advisors. These incentives are offset by the administrative delay in the approval process, unrealistic financing structures relating to cash flow, and the threat of termination of tax exemptions.

In recent years, many aboriginal communities have initiated change; they are preparing long-range plans, setting down goals and objectives, and forming a vision for the future. In the past, the most contentious issue has been over control and political change and pressure for change is increasing as the twenty-first century approaches. Political self-determination will depend on economic self-reliance, and the political-economic framework must reflect the cultural values of each indigenous society. Canada's aboriginal peoples have gained recognition in the Constitution for "the inherent right to self-government" as a "third order government" equal in stature to the federal and provincial governments within Canada. This fundamental human right, the inherent right to aboriginal self-government, means that aboriginal communities will have control within their own reserve lands or settlement areas. Aboriginal governments will be jurisdictionally autonomous over all economic, social, political, and cultural aspects of their lives. Ultimately, if properly implemented, the exercise of self-government will empower each aboriginal community to practice its traditional form of government outside the current limitations imposed by the Indian Act. Many of the current restraints are under review by government-sponsored committees, involving subjects such as lands management, Indian monies, taxation, and financing of Indian government, in order to resolve or remove the various alien rules and regulations imposed by Parliament. Now, instead of being necessarily reactive to government proposals or resistant to unexpected change, aboriginal peoples can take the initiative in planning and decision making.

## Entering the Twenty-First Century

If the 1980s were dominated by constitutional First Minister's Conferences and comprehensive land claims negotiations, the 1990s have been marked by unprecedented growth in economic development opportunities for Canada's First Nations as they continued their strident advancement towards self determination and laid the foundations for political, economic, and professional growth. More than ever, economic power has reinforced political power and influence. The expansive growth of self-government since the 1970s has been the key catalyst at the local, regional, and national levels, which has made economic development a priority on many fronts. As their economies grow due to land claim settlements, Supreme Court of Canada decisions, and entrepreneurial expansion, First Nations have seen corresponding rise in their political strength and influence on decision making at the corporate levels to complement their legal and political gains.

Some of the systemic impediments to establishing and sustaining the economic viability of First Nations communities have been successfully challenged. There is a growing recognition that First Nations must have access to financial capital and better education and training. First Nations must also benefit from natural resource development in order to rebuild their communities and sustain self governance, preferably without taxation revenue. Formerly denied access to off-reserve lands and to traditional sources of food, clothing, housing, jobs, and training, Native peoples today have unlimited opportunities.

For example, since 1985 there have been about fifty Supreme Court of Canada decisions involving First Nations rights. The *Guerin* decision of 1985 ruled that the federal government of Canada did owe a fiduciary trust to Indian bands to ensure that they received equitable economic compensation for surrendered lands. The landmark decision in *Regina v. Apsassin* (1995

Blueberry River Indian Band) resulted in a $147 million settlement involving compensation for oil and gas mineral rights located under allegedly surrendered reserve lands.

Other far-reaching judgments made by the Supreme Court of Canada in November 1997 known as *Delgamuukw/Gisdayway* and in the 1999 *Donald Marshall* decision have confirmed that First Nations all across Canada do have aboriginal jurisdiction over traditional lands and natural resources such as forestry, fisheries, and the right to a reasonable level of livelihood utilizing the natural resources in their traditional territories. The courts at all levels continue to grapple with the reality of post-contact aboriginal economies and what aboriginal and treaty rights are essential for making a livelihood. Nevertheless, the federal Crown continues to ignore aboriginal history and pursues legal challenges in a seemingly endless series of litigation aimed at denying First Nations commercial access to wildlife, fisheries, forestry, and natural resources.

In an attempt to avoid costly litigation, the federal government originally adopted a policy on specific claims in 1973 as an alternative dispute resolution mechanism. Research monies were increased in 1990 following the "Oka Crisis" which has resulted in the submission of 1,014 submitted specific claims of which over 500 remain unsettled or ignored. The economic spin-off of the settlements is estimated in the hundreds of millions of dollars and one study estimated the total cost might reach $5 billion. In the past decade there have been about fifty Treaty Land Entitlement agreements implemented in the prairie treaty areas of Alberta, Saskatchewan, and Manitoba, which has pumped millions of dollars into the economy. While it is the Canadian society that benefits the greatest from these kind of settlements, the addition of Indian reserve lands and cash settlements put into trust agreements has begun to provide a sound economic foundation for the beneficiary First Nations. Similar economic results will eventually flow from the Treaty Process in British Columbia and the Comprehensive Land Settlements covering northern Canada. The economic impact of all these land claim settlements will be critical to the self-determination and self-reliance of Canada's aboriginal peoples in the future.

A major undertaking of the federal government arising out of the failed attempts at constitutional reform in the 1990 Meech Lake Accord and the 1992 Charlottetown Accord, was the appointment of the Royal Commission on Aboriginal Peoples (or RCAP). After five years of hearings, interviews and round table consultations at an expenditure of about $60 million, the Royal Commission released its five-volume report in November 1996. The reports not only create a historical baseline for the treaties, Indian Act, residential schools, governance, lands and resources, economic development, social policy, health, housing, education, and a constitutional framework, but it also made 440 recommendations to lay the foundation of a renewed relationship between Canada and the First Nations peoples.

The general recommendations call for a spirit of reconciliation and reinforce the need for mutual respect and recognition of wrongdoing. But some of the recommendations are dramatic and call for the complete overhaul of existing policies and structures. The Commission's recommendations span all levels of aboriginal life as it currently exists in Canada, ranging from the formation of an Aboriginal Parliament to detailed recommendations on revamping child care, social policy, membership codes, and policies affecting elders, women, and youth. Many proposals are innovative and creative, calling for the acknowledgment of past injustices, treaty obligations, oral testimony, and the importance of financial resources. In some respects, however, the proposals would reinforce the status quo by encouraging a top-down approach to programming and continue to include health and education within the mainstream systems. Many critics resent the amalgamation of combining all aboriginal groups (Indian, Métis, and Inuit) under one policy while conspicuously avoiding contentious political hot issues such as international status, sovereignty, and fiscal resourcing for First Nations governance.

Release of the long awaited RCAP in November 1996 prompted both First Nations and the Department of Indian Affairs to commence a lengthy process of technical analysis, consultation meetings, and months of silence interspersed with calls for extreme caution and further study and analysis of the 440 recommendations. The recommendations on Economic Development are covered in Volume 2, "Restructuring the Relationships" which emphasizes that there must be "mutual and shared responsibility" for resource development based upon "co-jurisdiction and co-management arrangements" to attain the predicted 300,000 additional jobs needed over the next twenty years to attain a comparable employment level with mainstream Canadians. The Commission made fifty-two recommendations (out of 440 in total) on how to begin restructuring the employment, programming, training, social development, and social assistance programs which have historically fostered dependence on governmental institutions and were premised on a colonial mentality. The RCAP report discusses the transformation of economic development programs by developing a diverse strategy that responds to local community needs, goals and priorities developed cooperatively based upon capacity building, financing, and self-reliance, and grounded in long term economic development agreements. To achieve these changes, First Nations governments, businesses, and entrepreneurs need less bureaucratic access to business advice, trade promotion opportunities, government support programs designed to support self development initiatives, and business financing. In fact, resource management and fiscal arrangements for economic development continue to be an important part in ongoing treaty and land claim settlements.

In summary, RCAP concludes that aboriginal economies require access to land and resources based on historic and modern treaties; that each community is unique and diverse; that economic participation must be enhanced, facilitated, and self-empowering; that plans be made to motivate young people through training and promoting new approaches to commercial activity; and that the development of economies must cross several sectors such as health, education, governance, and social services in an integrated holistic manner. Finally, the commission recommends the creation of economic institutions which reflect aboriginal values and be accountable primarily to its membership without political interference; the establishment of capital corporations to serve aboriginal people with loan guarantees and limited subsidies; the inauguration of a national development bank to provide financing and technical assistance, raise capital investments, and create leadership opportunities; and the creation of a special employment and training initiative to provide training, identify employment sectors, and place permanent employment in collaboration with government agencies, private sector corporations, and employment service agencies.

Despite the initial public fanfare upon the release of the long delayed and anxiously anticipated RCAP in five volumes, and hundreds of commissioned background research reports (available on CD-ROM), it took the federal government a further two years of "analysis" to prepare its official response to a selection of the 440 RCAP recommendations.

Meanwhile there was a parallel analysis being undertaken by Native organizations and groups which were questioning the non-critical emphasis on healing, reconciliation, new partnership, and strengthening self-governance themes which were prominently featured in a national program entitled "Gathering Strength: Canada's Aboriginal Action Plan" launched in January 1998 by then Indian Affairs Minister Jane Stewart along with a statement of apology and reconciliation. The "Gathering Strength" program focuses on four core areas of community development: a healing and reconciliation strategy; social development; fiscal relations; and economic development.

The plan generally adopted the principles set out in RCAP of mutual respect, recognition of rights, and political responsibility combined with accountability and sharing. The key objectives were to review the Canada-First Nations partnerships, strengthen community-based governance, develop a new fiscal model, and provide support for strong communities and economies.

At the same time the government established a healing foundation with a grant of $350 million to support healing initiatives such as counseling, spiritual guidance, workshops, and other processes to begin addressing the detrimental legacy of physical, cultural, and emotional abuse suffered at residential schools and government-sponsored institutions.

In July 2000, federal ministers Robert Nault and Ralph Goodale issued "A Progress Report" on the initial two years of the program which lauded the "Gathering Strength" action plan. The report concluded that (1) aboriginal peoples and governments should work together to build jobs, growth, stability, and standard-of-life improvements for all Native people and (2) strong aboriginal communities depend on partnership, good governance, and a new fiscal relationship. The 2000 progress report identified several achievements in strengthening communities and economic development opportunities, including:

- completion of 100 professional development projects to strengthen skills of native administrators;
- settlement of sixteen specific claims and implementation of the precedent setting Nishga'a Final Agreement in northern British Columbia;
- completion of income security reform projects involving more than 350 First Nations (out of 610 communities); and
- participation of more than eighty First Nations in community-based housing initiatives.

The progress report concludes that the government is successful in promoting self-sufficiency and the quality of life. The vision captured in Gathering Strength is fairly straightforward. They plan:

- a new partnership among aboriginal people and other Canadians that reflects mutual interdependence and enables people to work together to build a better future;
- financially viable aboriginal governments able to generate their own revenues and able to operate with secure, predictable government transfers;
- aboriginal governments reflective of their communities' needs and values; and

- a quality of life for aboriginal people like other Canadians.

In hindsight, the obstacles and barriers to participating and implementing economic development programs in First Nation communities are thoroughly identified now in academic publications, government studies, and in the 1996 RCAP study.

There are numerous conferences and workshops held by government agencies and Native organizations and business agencies on every aspect of economic development. Typically the conference/workshop themes include: economic self-reliance; Native business opportunities in the new reality; financing First Nations; investing in self-reliance; First Nations tourism and resort development; financing the aboriginal economy in the twenty-first century; manufacturing on aboriginal lands; the future of aboriginal gaming in Canada; creatively developing aboriginal lands; and Native women's business issues.

The significant advances and strength of economic development activity in the 1990s culminated in May 2000 with an announcement by the Canadian government to triple its economic development funds to $75 million for that fiscal year with the promise of an additional $100 million for 2001. Promoted as " building on the significant success of Gathering Strength—Canada's Aboriginal Action Plan." the infusion of funds especially for economic growth very much reflects Indian Affairs Minister Robert Nault's belief in the restorative value of economic projects to lay the foundations for community self-sufficiency into the next century.

Aside from government policies, there is a demonstrable growth in professional organizations such as the Council for the Advancement of Native Development Officers (CANDO). Under their first president, Charles Sampson, they began publishing in 1993 an educational journal called *Mawio'mi Journal* to share information among economic development officers. Then in 1995 the organization established the Economic Developer Recognition Award to promote awareness of entrepreneurs and organizations in the field of aboriginal economic development. Another professional magazine entitled *First Nations Business—Canada's Aboriginal Business Magazine* was started in 1996 to feature individual and business profiles, interviews, financial markets, policy analyses, and general business advice on "exciting developments in the world of business development in Aboriginal Canada."

This growth in professionalism is also reflected in the formation of national and provincial organizations such as the Alberta Indian Economic Development Officers Network (AIEDON) established in 1997. The

AIEDON officers adopted as their mission statement: "Achieving self-sufficiency for grassroots First Nations peoples and First Nations through a collective economic development voice." The organization's goals and objectives emphasize networking and maximizing their access to programs, services, and institutions.

## Conclusion

Economic development combined with self-reliance and self-governance is clearly one of the essential building blocks to the renewal of First Nations' communities. Many social, political, and economic problems will continue to challenge First Nations leaders, such as inadequate housing, under capitalization, restricted access to financing, lack of training programs, high suicide rates, health problems, racism, bureaucracy, and political disempowerment. But there are also new community based programs, healing foundations, more post-secondary graduates, professional networking, support for individual entrepreneurs and businesses, and greater economic opportunities through land claims settlements than ever before at the turn of the new millennium. Despite a century of many frustrations, disappointments, and incredible hurdles, many of Canada's First Nations are well positioned to enter the twenty-first century ready for the political and economic challenges they face to become truly self-reliant and self-governing.

*Ian Getty*
*The Stoney Tribal Administration*

# Economic Organizations

## UNITED STATES

ALASKA NATIVE INC.
2600 Cordova Street, Suite 211
Anchorage, AK 99503
(907) 263–7013

ALASKA VILLAGE ELECTRIC
COOPERATIVE, INC.
4831 Eagle St.
Anchorage, AK 99503–7431
(907) 561–1818

ALASKA VILLAGE INITIATIVE
1577 C St. Plaza, Suite 304
Anchorage, AK 99501
(907) 274–5400

AMERICANS FOR INDIAN OPPORTUNITY
681 Juniper Hill Rd.
Bernalillo, NM 87004
(505) 867–0278

ARIZONA NATIVE AMERICAN ECONOMIC
COALITION
P.O. Box 22247
Flagstaff, AZ 86002–2247
(520) 523–7320

BERING SEA FISHERMEN'S ASSOCIATION
725 Christensen Dr.
Anchorage, AK 99501
(907) 279–6519

COUNCIL OF ENERGY RESOURCE
TRIBES (CERT)
695 S. Colorado Blvd., Suite 10
Denver, CO 80246
(303) 282–7576

FIRST NATIONS DEVELOPMENT INSTITUTE
11917 Main St.
Fredericksburg, VA 22408
(540) 371–5615

LAKOTA FUND
P.O. Box 340
Kyle, SD 57752
(605) 455–2500

NATIONAL AMERICAN INDIAN CATTLEMAN'S
ASSOCIATION
1541 Foster Rd.
Toppenish, WA 98948
(509) 854–1329

NATIONAL CENTER FOR AMERICAN INDIAN
ENTERPRISE DEVELOPMENT
Head Quarters
953 East Juanita
Mesa, AZ 85204
(480) 545–1298

NATIVE AMERICAN FINANCE OFFICERS
ASSOCIATION
Marlene Lynch
P.O. Box 170
Fort Defiance, AZ 86504
(520) 729–6211

NEW MEXICO INDIAN BUSINESS
DEVELOPMENT CENTER
123 Fourth St. Southwest, P.O. Box 400
Albuquerque, NM 87103
(505) 889–9092

NORTHWEST REGIONAL OFFICE
934 N 143 St.
Seattle, WA 98133
(206) 365–7735

PACIFIC REGIONAL
Pacific Regional
11138 Valley Mall, Suite 200
El Monte, CA 91731
(626) 442–3701

THE PUEBLO OF SANTA ANA
2 Dove Road
Bernalillo, NM 87004
(505) 867–3301

UIDA CONSULTING GROUP
430 Commeres Park Dr., SE
4th FL 424
Marietta, GA 30063
(770) 494–0117

UPPER TANANA DEVELOPMENT
  CORPORATION
P.O. Box 459
Tok, AK 99780
(907) 883–5158

WORLD VISION INTERNATIONAL
800 West Chestnut Ave
Monrovia, CA 91016
(818) 303–8811

# CANADA

## ABORIGINAL BUSINESS CANADA OFFICES

To obtain more information about how ABORIGINAL BUSINESS CANADA can work with Aboriginal firms, please contact the office nearest you.

### ◆ HEAD OFFICE

ABORIGINAL BUSINESS CANADA
Industry Canada
1st Floor West
235 Queen Street
Ottawa, ON K1A 0H5
(613) 954–4064

### ◆ ALBERTA & NORTHWEST TERRITORY

ABORIGINAL BUSINESS CANADA
Industry Canada
Canada Place Room 725
9700 Jasper Avenue
Edmonton, AB T5J 4C3
(780) 495–2954

### ◆ ATLANTIC

ABORIGINAL BUSINESS CANADA
Industry Canada
1505 Barrington Street
Maritime Centre, Suite 1605
P.O. Box 940, Station M
Halifax, NS B3J 3K5
(902) 426–2018

### ◆ BRITISH COLUMBIA & YUKON TERRITORY

ABORIGINAL BUSINESS CANADA
Industry Canada
300 West Georgia Street, 21st Floor
Vancouver, BC V6B 6E2
(604) 666–3871

### ◆ MANITOBA

ABORIGINAL BUSINESS CANADA
Industry Canada
4th Floor, 400 St. Mary Avenue
Winnipeg, MB R3C 4K5
(204) 983–7316

### ◆ ONTARIO

ABORIGINAL BUSINESS CANADA
Industry Canada
3rd Floor, 151 Yonge Street
Toronto, ON M5C 2W7
(416) 973–8800

ABORIGINAL BUSINESS CANADA
Industry Canada
c/o Indian and Northern Affairs Office
1760 Regent Street South
Sudbury, ON P3E 3Z8
(705) 522–5100

### ◆ QUEBEC & NUNAVUT

**ABORIGINAL BUSINESS CANADA**
Industry Canada
5 Place Ville-Marie, 8th Floor
P.O. Box 289
Montreal, QC H3B 2G2
(514) 283–1828

### ◆ SASKATCHEWAN

**ABORIGINAL BUSINESS CANADA**
Industry Canada
7th Floor
123–2nd Avenue South
Saskatoon, SK S7K 7E6
(306) 975–4329

## External Delivery Organizations

A number of Aboriginal business organizations across the country also deliver program services. For a list of these organizations, please call your nearest Aboriginal Business Canada office.

## ABORIGINAL CAPITAL CORPORATIONS

Aboriginal Capital Corporations (ACCS) are Aboriginal-owned and controlled business lending organizations. A listing of the ACCs throughout Canada can be found below.

### ◆ ALBERTA & NORTHWEST TERRITORY

**ALBERTA INDIAN INVESTMENT CORPORATION**
Box 180
Enoch, AB T7X 3Y3
(780) 470–3600

**APEETOGOSAN (Métis) DEVELOPMENT INC.**
12527–129th Street
Edmonton, AB T5L 1H7
(780) 452–7951

**INDIAN AGRI-BUSINESS CORPORATION**
210–2720-12th St. N.E.
Calgary, AB T2E 7N4
(403) 291–5151

**NORTHWEST TERRITORY COOPERATIVE**
Business Development Fund
321-C Old Airport Road
Yellowknife, NT X1A 3T3
(867) 873–3481

**NWT METIS-DENE DEVELOPMENT FUND**
P.O. Box 1805
5125–50th Street
Yellowknife, NT X1A 2P4
(867) 873–9341

**SETTLEMENT INVESTMENT CORPORATION**
10339–124th Street, Suite 777
Edmonton, AB T5N 3W1
(780) 488–5656

### ◆ ATLANTIC

**ULNOOWEG DEVELOPMENT GROUP INC.**
139 Esplanade Street
P.O. Box 1259
Truro, NS B2N 5N2
(902) 893–7379
(888) 766–2376

### ◆ BRITISH COLUMBIA & YUKON

**ALL NATIONS TRUST COMPANY**
Suite 208 West
345 Yellowhead Highway
Kamloops, BC V2H 1H1
(250) 828–9770

**BELLA BELLA COMMUNITY DEVELOPMENT SOCIETY**
P.O. Box 880
Waglisia, BC V0T 1Z0
(250) 957–2381

**DANA NAYE VENTURES**
409 Black Street
Whitehorse, YK Y1A 2N2
(867) 668–6925
(800) 661–0448

FIRST NATIONS AGRICULTURAL LENDING
ASSOCIATION
Suite 200–345 Yellowhead Highway
Kamloops, BC V2H 1H1
(250) 828–9751

NATIVE FISHING ASSOCIATION
Suite 102–1500 Howe Street
Vancouver, BC V6Z 2N1
(604) 684–0699

NUU-CHAH-NULTH ECONOMIC
DEVELOPMENT CORPORATION
7563 Pacific Rim Highway
PO. Box 1384
Port Alberni, BC V9Y 7M2
(250) 724–3131

TALE'AWTXW ABORIGINAL CAPITOL
CORPORATION
Units 29 & 30
6014 Vedder Road
Chilliwack, BC V2R 5M4
(250) 824–2088

TALE'AWTXW ABORIGINAL CAPITOL
CORPORATION
(Branch Office)
R.R. #1, Trans Canada Highway
Ladysmith, BC V0R 2E0
(250) 245–9903

TRIBAL RESOURCES INVESTMENT
CORPORATION
217–3rd Avenue West
Prince Rupert, BC V8J 1L2
(250) 624–3535

## ◆ QUEBEC & NUNAVUT

CORPORATION DE DEVELOPMENT
ECONOMIQUE MONTAGNAIS
1005, boul. Laure, suite 110
Sept-;les, QC G4R 4S6
(418) 968–1246
(800) 463–2216

KAHNAWAKE LOAN GUARANTEE FUND INC.
P.O. Box 1110
Kahnawake, QC J0L 1B0
(450) 638–4280

NUNAVIK INVESTMENT CORPORATION
C.P. 239
Kuujjuaq, QC J0M 1C0
(819) 964–2035

SOCIETE DE CREDIT COMMERCIAL
AUTOCHTONE
Native Commercial
Credit Corporation
265–201, Place Chef Michel Laveau
Wendake, QC G0A 4V0
(418) 842–0972
(800) 241–0972

## ◆ MANITOBA

ANISHINABE MAZASKA CAPITOL
CORPORATION
300–208 Edmonton Street
Winnipeg, MB R3C 1R7
(204) 957–0045

LOUIS RIEL CAPITAL CORPORATION
24–1635 Burrows Avenue
Winnipeg, MB R2X 3B5
(204) 586–8474 ext. 275

TRIBAL WI-CHI-WAY WIN CAPITAL
CORPORATION
203–400 St. Mary Avenue
Winnipeg, MB R3C 4K5
(204) 988–1888

## ◆ ONTARIO

INDIAN AGRICULTURAL PROGRAM OF
ONTARIO
P.O. Box 100
220 North Street
Stirling, ON K0K 3E0
(613) 395–5505

NISHNAWBE-ASKI DEVELOPMENT FUND
P.O. Box 20119, Green Acres
Thunder Bay, ON P7E 6P2
(807) 623–5397

OHWISTHA CAPITAL CORPORATION
P.O. Box 1394
Cornwall, ON K6H 5V4
(613) 933–6500

OMAA DEVELOPMENT CORPORATION
452 Albert Street East
2nd Floor-Walrus Building #1
Sault Ste. Marie, ON P6A 2J8
(705) 949–8220

TECUMSEH DEVELOPMENT CORPORATION
R.R. #1
Muncey, ON N0L 1Y0
(519) 289–2122

TWO RIVERS COMMUNITY
  DEVELOPMENT CENTRE
P.O. Box 225
Ohsweken, ON N0A 1M0
(519) 445–4567

#### ◆ SASKATCHEWAN

SASKATCHEWAN INDIAN EQUITY FUND
224B-4th Avenue South
Saskatoon, SK S7K 5M5
(306) 955–4550

SASKATCHEWAN INDIAN LOAN COMPANY
224B-4th Avenue South
Saskatoon, SK S7K 5M5
(306) 955–8699

SASKNATIVE ECONOMIC DEVELOPMENT
  CORPORATION
#108–219 Robin Crescent
Saskatoon, SK S7L 6M8
(306) 477–4350

# Native Owned Businesses

## ◆ ALASKA

**AHTNA, INC.**
Glennallen Office
P.O. Box 649
Glennallen, AK 99588
(907) 822–3476

**ALEUT CORPORATION**
4000 Old Seward Hwy., Suite 300
Anchorage, AK 99503
(907) 561–4300
www.aleutcorp.com

**BERING STRAITS NATIVE CORP.**
P.O. Box 1008
Nome, AK 99762
(907) 443–5252

**BRISTOL BAY NATIVE CORP.**
P.O. Box 100220
800 Cordova St., Suite 200
Anchorage, AK 99510–6299
(907) 278–3602
www.bbnc.net

**CALISTA CORP.**
301 Calista Court, Suite A
Anchorage, AK 99518
(907) 279–5516
www.calistacorp.com

**CHUGACH ALASKA CORP.**
560 E. 34th Ave., Suite 200
Anchorage, AK 99503
(907) 563–8866

**COOK INLET REGION, INC.**
203 W. 15th Ave., Suite 102
Anchorage, AK 99501
(907) 274–8638

**DOYON, LTD.**
1 Doyon Place, Suite 300
Fairbanks, AK 99701
(907) 452–4755
www.doyon.com

**KONIAG, INC.**
4300 B St., Suite 407
Anchorage, AK 99503
(907) 561–2668
www.koniag.com

**NANA REGIONAL CORPORATION**
P.O. Box 49
Kotzebue, AK 99752
(907) 442–3301
www.nana.com

**SEALASKA CORP.**
One Sealaska Plaza, Suite 400
Juneau, AK 99801
(907) 586–1512
www.sealaska.com

## ◆ ARIZONA

**FORT APACHE TIMBER COMPANY (FATCO)**
P.O. Box 1090
1 Fatco Rd.
Whiteriver, AZ 85941
(520) 338–4931

## ◆ MINNESOTA

**NATIVE TOURS & TRAVEL**
6875 Highway 65, NE
Minneapolis, MN 55432
(763) 571–8184
www.nativetours.com,

◆ **MISSISSIPPI**

CHAHTA Development Company (CHOCTAW)
201 James Billy Rd.
Philadelphia, MS 39350
(601) 656–7350

CHAHTA Enterprise Plant I & II (CHOCTAW)
390 Industrial Rd.
Philadelphia, MS 39350
(601) 656–7350

CHOCTAW ELECTRONICS
404 Industrial Rd.
Philadelphia, MS 39350
(601) 656–3650

CHOCTAW MANUFACTURING ENTERPRISE
Rte. 7, Box 3-D
Carthage, MS 39051
(601) 267–5681

◆ **MONTANA**

A & S TRIBAL INDUSTRIES
P.O. Box 308
Industrial Park
Poplar, MT 59255
(406) 768–5151

BLACKFEET NATIONAL BANK
P.O. Box 730
Browning, MT 59417
(406) 338–7000

WEST ELECTRONICS
P.O. Box 577
Industrial Park
Poplar, MT 59255
(406) 768–5511

◆ **NEW MEXICO**

LAGUNA INDUSTRIES, INC.
P.O. Box 1001
Laguna, NM 87026
(505) 552–6041

NAVAJO AGRICULTURAL PRODUCTS
  INDUSTRIES (NAPI)
P.O. Drawer 1318
Farmington, NM 87499
(505) 327–5251

2-D
P.O. Box 1669
Crownpoint, New Mexico 87313
(505) 208–5973

◆ **OKLAHOMA**

FIRST OKLAHOMA BANK OF SHAWNEE
130 East MacArthur
Shawnee, OK 74801
(405) 275–8830

◆ **OREGON**

KAH-NEE-TA RESORT
Box Office K
Warm Springs, OR 97761
(541) 553–1112

WARM SPRINGS FOREST PRODUCTS
  INDUSTRIES
P.O. Box 810
Warm Springs, OR 97761
(541) 553–1131

◆ **NORTH DAKOTA**

FORT BERTHOLD DEVELOPMENT
  CORPORATION
THREE AFFILIATED TRIBES
Box 867
New Town, ND 58763
(701) 627–4828

MANDAREE ELECTRONICS
  CORPORATION (MEC)
1 Community Center Rd.
P.O. Box 425
Mandaree, ND 58757
(701) 759–3399

TURTLE MOUNTAIN MANUFACTURING
Highway 5 W.
Belcourt, ND 58316
(701) 477–6404

UNIBAND CORPORATION
P.O. Box 1059
Belcourt, ND 58316
(701) 477–6445
www.uniband.com

♦ **WASHINGTON**

KALISPEL CASE LINE
P.O. Box 267
Cusick, WA 99119
(509) 445–1121

SPOKANE TRIBAL WOOD PRODUCTS
P.O. Box 100

Wellpinit, WA 99040
(509) 258–7431

♦ **WISCONSIN**

MENOMINEE TRIBAL ENTERPRISES (M.T.E.)
P.O. BOX 10
Neopit, WI 54150
(715) 756–2311

# Indian Gaming Casinos & Organizations

## ♦ UNITED STATES

**INSTITUTE FOR THE STUDY OF GAMBLING AND COMMERCIAL GAMING**
College of Business Administration
Reno, NV 89557–0208
(775) 784–1442

**NATIONAL INDIAN GAMING ASSOCIATION**
224 Second Street, SE
Washington, DC 20003
(202) 546–7711
1–800–286–6442

**NORTH AMERICAN GAMING REGULATORS ASSOCIATION**
P.O. Box 21886
Lincoln, NE 68542–1886
(402) 474–4261

## NATIONAL INDIAN GAMING COMMISSION & REGIONAL OFFICES

**NATIONAL INDIAN GAMING COMMISSION**
NATIONAL HEADQUARTERS
1441 L Street NW, 9th Floor
Washington, DC 20005
(202) 632–7003

**REGION 1**
Solomon Building, Suite 212
620 Main Street
Portland, OR 97205
(503) 326–5095

**REGION 2**
501 I Street, Suite 12400
Sacramento, CA 95814
(916) 930–2230

**REGION 3**
One Columbus Plaza Suite 880
Phoenix, AZ 58012
(602) 604–2951

**REGION 4**
190 E. 5th St., Suite 170
St. Paul, MN 55101
(651) 290–4004

**REGION 5**
224 South Boulder
Tulsa, OK 74103
(918) 581–7924

## STATE GAMING ORGANIZATIONS

### ♦ ARIZONA

**ARIZONA DEPARTMENT OF GAMING**
202 E. Earl, Suite 200
Phoenix, AZ 85012
(602) 604–1801

### ♦ COLORADO

**CENTRAL CITY–BLACK HAWK OFFICE**
142 Lawrence Street (location address)
P.O. Box 721
Central City, CO 80427–0721
(303) 582–0529

**COLORADO DIVISION OF GAMING**
Lakewood (Headquarters) Office
1881 Pierce Street, Suite 112
Lakewood, CO 80214–1496
(303) 205–1355

**CRIPPLE CREEK OFFICE**
433 E. Carr Avenue (location address)
P.O. Box 1209 (mailing address)
Cripple Creek, CO 80813–1209
(719) 689–3362

## ◆ CALIFORNIA

CALIFORNIA COUNCIL ON PROBLEM
   GAMBLING
121 S. Palm Canyon Drive, Suite 225
Palm Springs, CA 92262
(760) 320–0234
Helpline: (800) GAMBLER

CALIFORNIA NATIONS INDIAN GAMING
   ASSOCIATION
1130 K Street, Suite 150
Sacramento, CA 95814
(916) 448–8706

# U.S. INDIAN GAMING CASINOS & BINGO HALLS

## ◆ ALABAMA

CREEK INDIAN BINGO PALACE
Poarch Band of Creek Indians
5811 Jack Springs Road
Atmore, AL 36502
(334) 368–9136

## ◆ ALASKA

KLAWOCK COOPERATIVE ASSOCIATION
P.O. Box 430
Klawock, AK 99925
(907) 755–2265

METLAKATLA INDIAN COMMUNITY
P.O. Box 8
Metlakatla, AK 99926
(907) 886–4441

## ◆ ARIZONA

APACHE GOLD CASINO
San Carlos Apache Tribe
P.O. Box 1210
San Carlos, AZ 85550
(520) 475–2361

BLUEWATER CASINO
Colorado River Indian Tribes
Route 1, Box 23-B
Parker, AZ 85344
(520) 669–9211

BUCKY'S CASINO
Yavapai-Prescott Indian Tribe
530 East Merritt St.
Prescott, AZ 86301
(602) 445–8790

CASINO IN THE SUN
Pascua Yaqui Tribe of Arizona
7474 S. Camino De Oeste
Tucson, AZ 85746
(520) 883–2838

CLIFF CASTLE CASINO
Yavapai Apache Tribe
P.O. Box 1188
Camp Verde, AZ 86322
(602) 567–3649

COCOPAH CASINO
Cocopah Indian Tribe
15136 South Ave. B
Somerton, AZ 85350
(602) 627–2102

FORT MCDOWELL CASINO
Fort McDowell Mohave-Apache Indian Community
P.O. Box 17779
Fountain Hills, AZ 85269
(602) 837–5121

GILA RIVER CASINO
Gila River Indian Community
P.O. Box 97
Sacaton, AZ 85247
(602) 963–4323

HARRAH'S PHOENIX AK-CHIN
Ak Chin Indian Community
42507 W. Peters & Nall Rd.
Maricopa, AZ 85239
(520) 568–2227

HONDAH RESORT, CASINO, AND
   CONFERENCE CENTER
White Mountain Apache Tribe
P.O. Box 700
Whiteriver, AZ 85941
(602) 338–4346

MAZATZAL CASINO
Tonto Apache Tribe
Tonto Apache Reservation #30
Payson, AZ 85541
(602) 474–5000

QUECHAN INDIAN TRIBE
P.O. Box 11352
Yuma, AZ 85366
(760) 572–0213

SALT RIVER PIMA-MARICOPA INDIAN
    COMMUNITY
10005 Osborn Road
Scottsdale, AZ 85256
(602) 850–8000

TOHONO O'ODHAM NATION
P.O. Box 837
Sells, AZ 85364
(602) 383–2221

### ◆ CALIFORNIA

AUBERRY BIG SANDY RANCHERIA
P.O. Box 337
Auberry, CA 93602
(209) 855–4003

BARONA CASINO
Barona Band of Mission Indians
1095 Barona Road
Lakeside, CA 92040
(619) 443–6612

BIG PINE PAIUTE TRIBE OF THE
    OWENS VALLEY
545 Butcher Lane
Big Pine, CA 93513
(619) 938–3359

BLACK BART CASINO
Sherwood Valley Rancheria
190 Sherwood Hill Drive
Willits, CA 95490
(707) 459–9690

CAHTO TRIBE OF THE LAYTONVILLE
    RANCHERIA
P.O. Box 1239
Laytonville, CA 95454
(707) 984–6197

CAHUILLA BAND OF MISSION INDIANS
P.O. Box 391760
Anza, CA 92539
(909) 763–5549

CASINO MORONGO
Morongo Band of Mission Indians
11581 Potrero Road
Banning, CA 92220
(909) 849–4697

CHERAE HEIGHTS BINGO AND CASINO
Trinidad Rancheria
P.O. Box 630
27 Scenic Drive
Trinidad, CA 95570
(707) 677–0211

CHICKEN RANCH BAND OF ME-WUK
    INDIANS
P.O. Box 1159
Jamestown, CA 95327
(209) 984–4806

CHUMASH CASINO
Santa Ynez Band of Mission Indians
P.O. Box 517
Santa Ynez, CA 93460
(805) 688–7997

COAST INDIAN COMMUNITY OF THE
    RESIGHINI RANCHERIA
P.O. Box 529
Klamath, CA 95548
(707) 482–2431

COLUSA CASINO
Colusa Band of Wintun Indians
50 Wintun Road #D
Colusa, CA 95932
(916) 458–8231

EAGLE MOUNTAIN CASINO
Tule River Tribe of the Tule River Indian
    Reservation
P.O. Box 589
Porterville, CA 93258
(209) 781–4271

ELK VALLEY CASINO
Elk Valley Rancheria
440 Mathews Street, P.O. Box 1042
Crescent City, CA 95531
(707) 464–1020

FANTASY SPRINGS CASINO
Cabazon Band of Mission Indians
84–245 Indio Spring Drive
Indio, CA 92201
(619) 342–5000

FEATHER FALLS CASINO
Mooretown Rancheria
#1 Alverda Drive
Oroville, CA 95966
(916) 533–3625

FORT MOJAVE TRIBAL COUNCIL
500 Merriman Avenue
Needles, CA 92363
(760) 326–4591

GOLD COUNTRY CASINO
Tyme Maidu Tribe of the Berry Creek Rancheria
5 Tyme Way
Oroville, CA 95966
(916) 534–3859

GOLDEN BEARS CASINO
Resighini Rancheria
158 E. Klamath Beach Road
Klamath, CA 95548
(707) 482–5501

HAVASU LANDING RESORT AND CASINO
Chemehuevi Indian Tribe
P.O. Box 1976
Havasu Lake, CA 92363
(619) 858–4219

HOOPA VALLEY TRIBE
P.O. Box 1348
Hoopa, CA 95546
(916) 625–4211

HOPLAND CASINO
Hopland Band of Pomo Indians
P.O. Box 610
Hopland, CA 95449
(707) 744–1647

JACKSON RANCHERIA CASINO
Jackson Rancheria Band of Miwuk Indians
P.O. Box 429
Jackson, CA 95642
(209) 223–1935

KONOCTI VISTA CASINO AND BINGO
Big Valley Rancheria of Pomo Indians
P.O. Box 955
Lakeport, CA 95453
(707) 262–0629

LUCKY SEVEN CASINO
Smith River Rancheria
250 North Indian Road
Smith River, CA 95567
(707) 487–9255

MONO WIND CASINO
Big Sandy Rancheria Band of Western Mono Indians
P.O. Box 337
Auberry, CA 93602
(559) 855–2703

NORTHERN LIGHTS CASINO
SYCUAN CASINO:
Sycuan Band of Mission Indians
5459 Dehesa Road
El Cajon, CA 92019
(619) 445–6002

PAIUTE PALACE CASINO
Bishop Paiute Tribe
P.O. Box 548
Paiute Professional Bldg.
Bishop, CA 93515
(760) 873–3584

PALACE BINGO INDIAN GAMING CENTER
Santa Rosa Band of Tachi Indians
17255 Jersey Ave.
Lemoore, CA 93245
(800) 942–6886

PECHANGA CASINO
Pechanga Indian Nation
P.O. Box 1477
Temecula, CA 92593
(909) 694–3333

PIT RIVER CASINO
Pit River Tribe
20265 Tamarack Avenue
Burney, CA 96013
(916) 335–2334

RINCON RIVER OATS CASINO
Rincon Indian Reservation
33750 Valley Center Rd.
Valley Center, CA 92082
(619) 749–2100

ROBINSON RANCHERIA CASINO
Robinson Rancheria of Pomo Indians
1545 E. Highway 20
Nice, CA 95464
(707) 275–9000

RUMSEY INDIAN RANCHERIA
P.O. Box 18
Brooks, CA 95606
(916) 796–3400

SAN MANUEL CASINO
San Manuel Band of Mission Indians
5795 Victoria Ave.
Highland, CA 92346
(909) 864–5050

SHINGLE SPRINGS RANCHERIA
P.O. Box 1340
Shingle Springs, CA 95682
(530) 676–8010

SHODAKI COYOTE VALLEY CASINO
Coyote Valley Band of Pomo Indians
P.O. Box 320
Calpella, CA 95418
(707) 485–8723

SOBOBA CASINO
Soboba Band of Mission Indians
P.O. Box 817, 23333 Soboba Rd.
San Jacinto, CA 92581
(909) 654–2883

SPA HOTEL AND CASINO
Agua Caliente Band of Cahuilla Indians
600 E. Tahquitz Way
Palm Springs, CA 92262
(760) 325–3400

SPOTLIGHT 29 CASINO
Twenty Nine Palms Band of Mission Indians
46–200 Harrison Street
Coachela, CA 92236
(760) 775–5566

SUSANVILLE INDIAN RANCHERIA
745 Joaquin Street
Susanville, CA 96130
(559) 257–6264

TABLE MOUNTAIN CASINO AND BINGO
Table Mountain Rancheria
8184 Table Mountain Road
Friant, CA 93626
(800) 541–3637

TWIN PINE CASINO
Lake Miwok Indian Nation of the Middletown
　　Rancheria
P.O. Box 1035
Middletown, CA 95461
(707) 987–0197

VIEJAS CASINO
Viejas Band of Mission Indians
5000 Willows Road
Alpine, CA 91901
(619) 445–5400

WINRIVER CASINO BINGO
Redding Rancheria
2100 Redding Rancheria Road
Redding, CA 96001
(916) 243–3377

### ◆ COLORADO

SKY UTE CASINO AND LODGE
Southern Ute Indian Tribe
P.O. Box 737
Ignacio, CO 81137
(970) 569–3000

UTE MOUNTAIN CASINO
Ute Mountain Ute Tribe
P.O. Box V
Cortez, CO 81321
(970) 565–8800

### ◆ CONNECTICUT

FOXWOODS CASINO
Mashantucket Pequot Tribe
P.O. Box 410, Route 2
Ledyard, CT 06339
(800) PLAY-BIG

MOHEGAN SUN
Mohegan Tribe of Indians of Connecticut
1 Mohegan Sun Blvd.
Uncasville, CT 06382
(860) 204–8000

## ◆ FLORIDA

**MICCOUSUKEE TRIBAL INDIANS OF FLORIDA**
500 SW 177 Avenue
Miami, FL 33194
(305) 222–4600

**SEMINOLE TRIBE OF FLORIDA**
506 S. First Street
Immokalee, FL 34142
(941) 658–1313

## ◆ IDAHO

**CLEARWATER RIVER CASINO**
It'se Ye-Ye Casino
Nez Percé Tribe
7463 N. And S. Highway
Lewiston, ID 83501
(208) 746–0723

**COEUR D'ALENE TRIBAL BINGO AND CASINO**
Coeur d'Alene Tribe
P.O. Box 236, U.S. Highway 95
Worley, ID 83876–0236
(208) 686–5048

**KOOTENAI RIVER INN**
Kootenai Tribe of Idaho
River Plaza, 7160 Plaza St.
Bonner's Ferry, ID 83805
(800) 346–5668

**SHOSHONE BANNOCK CASINO**
Shoshone-Bannock Tribes
P.O. Box 868
Fort Hall, ID 83203
(208) 237–8765

## ◆ IOWA

**CASINOMAHA**
Omaha Tribe of Nebraska
P.O. Box 89
Inawa, IA 51040
(800) 858-UBET

**MESKWAKI BINGO AND CASINO HOTEL**
Sac & Fox Tribe of Mississippi in Iowa
1504 305 Street
Tama, IA 52339
(515) 484–2108

**WINNAVEGAS CASINO AND BINGO**
Winnebago Tribe of Nebraska
1500 330 St.
Sloan, IA 51055
(800) 468–9466

## ◆ KANSAS

**GOLDEN EAGLE CASINO**
Kickapoo Nation in Kansas
1121 Goldfinch
Horton, KS 66439
(785) 486–6601

**IOWA TRIBE PARTY GAMES**
Iowa Tribe of Kansas and Nebraska
Route 1, Box 58A
White Cloud, KS 66094
(913) 595–6640

**PRAIRIE BAND CASINO**
Prairie Band Potawatomi
12305 150 Rd.
Mayetta, KS 66509
(913) 966–7777

**SAC AND FOX NATION OF MISSOURI**
P.O. Box 105-A
Powhatan, KS 66527
(913) 742–7438

## ◆ LOUISIANA

**CYPRESS BAYOU CASINO**
Chitimacha Tribe of Louisiana
832 Martin Luther King Road
Charenton, LA 70523
(800) 284–4386

**GRAND CASINO AVOYELLES**
Tunica-Biloxi Indian Tribe of Louisiana
711 Grand Blvd.
Marksville, LA 71350
(318) 253–1946

GRAND CASINO COUSHATTA
Coushatta Tribe of Louisiana
P.O. Box 1510, 777 Coushatta Dr.
Kinder, LA 70648
(800) 584–7263


♦ **MICHIGAN**

BIG BUCKS BINGO AND OJIBWA CASINO
Keweenaw Bay Indian Community
797 Michigan Ave.
Baraga, MI 49908
(906) 353–6333


BINGO PALACE
EAGLE'S VIEW CASINO
LEELANAU SANDS CASINO
TURTLE CREEK CASINO
Grand Traverse Band of Ottawa and Chippewa
   Indians
2649 N. West Bayshore Drive
Suttons Bay, MI 49682
(616) 271–7333


CHIP IN'S ISLAND RESORT AND CASINO
Hannahville Indian Community
P.O. Box 351-W399 Hwy 2 and 41
Harris, MI 49845–0351
(906) 466–2941


KEWADIN CASINO, HOTELS, AND
   CONVENTION CENTER
Sault Ste. Marie Tribe of Chippewa Indians
2186 Shunk Road
Sault Ste. Marie, MI 49873
(800)KEWADIN


KING'S CLUB CASINO
BAY MILLS CASINO
Bay Mills Indian Community
12140 W. Lakeshore Dr.
Brimley, MI 49715
(906) 248–3715


LAC VIEUX DESERT CASINO
Lac Vieux Desert Band of Lake Superior Chippewa
   Indians
P.O. Box 129 N45
Watersmeet, MI 49969
(906) 358–4226


LITTLE RIVER BAND OF OTTAWA INDIANS
P.O. Box 214
Manistee, MI 49660
(231) 723–1535


SOARING EAGLE CASINO AND RESORT
Saginaw Chippewa Indian Tribe
6800 Soaring Eagle Blvd.
Mt. Pleasant, MI 48858
(517) 775–5777


VICTORIES CASINO ENTERTAINMENT
   CENTER
Little Traverse Band of Odawa Indians
101 Greenwood
Petoskey, MI 49770
(231) 439–6807


♦ **MINNESOTA**

BLACK BEAR CASINO AND HOTEL
FOND-DU-LUTH CASINO
Fond du Lac Band of Lake Superior Chippewa
1785 Hwy. 210; Box 777
Carlton, MN 55718
(218) 878–2327


FIREFLY CREEK CASINO
Upper Sioux Community
P.O. Box 96
Granite Falls, MN 56241
(320) 564–2121


FORTUNE BAY RESORT CASINO
Bois Forte Band of Chippewas
1430 Bois Forte Road
Tower, MN 55790
(218) 753–6400


GRAND CASINO HINCKLEY
Mille Lacs Band of Chippewa Indians
777 Lady Luck Dr., Rt. 3, Box 15
Hinckley, MN 55037
(800) 472–6321


GRAND CASINO MILLE LACS
Mille Lacs Band of Ojibwe
777 Grand Ave., HCR 67
(HWY 169 W Shore of Mille Lacs Lake)
Onamia, MN 56359
(800) 626–5825

GRAND PORTAGE CASINO
Grand Portage Band of Chippewa Indians
70 Casino Drive
Grand Portage, MN 55605
(218) 475–2401

JACKPOT JUNCTION CASINO HOTEL
Lower Sioux Indian Community
39375 Co., Hwy 24, P.O. Box 420
Morton, MN 56270
(507) 644–3000

LAKE OF THE WOODS CASINO AND BINGO
RIVER ROAD CASINO
RED LAKE CASINO AND BINGO
Red Lake Band of Chippewa Indians
1012 E. Lake Street
Warroad, MN 56763
(218) 386–3381

LITTLE SIX CASINO AND MYSTIC
    LAKE CASINO
Shakopee Mdewakanton Sioux Community
Country Road 83
Prior Lake, MN 55372
(612) 445–8982

NORTHERN LIGHTS CASINO
PALACE BINGO CASINO HOTEL
Leech Lake Band of Chippewa Indians
HCR73 Box 1003
Walker, MN 5663–3484
(218) 547–2744

SHOOTING STAR CASINO
White Earth Band of Chippewa Indians
P.O. Box 418
Mahnomen, MN 56557
(218) 935–2711

TREASURE ISLAND RESORT AND CASINO
Prairie Island Indian Community
5734 Sturgeon Lake Road
Red Wing, MN 55066
(651) 388–6300

## ◆ MISSISSIPPI

SILVER STAR RESORT AND CASINO
Mississippi Band of Choctaw Indians
P.O. Box 6048, Highway 16 West
Philadelphia, MS 39350
(800) 557–0711

## ◆ MISSOURI

BORDER TOWN BINGO
Eastern Shawnee Tribe of Oklahoma
P.O. Box 350
Seneca, MO 64865
(918) 666–8702

## ◆ MONTANA

BLACKFEET TRIBAL BINGO
Blackfeet Tribe of Indians
P.O. Box 850
Browning, MT 59417
(406) 338–5751

CHARGING HORSE CASINO AND BINGO
Northern Cheyenne Tribe
P.O. Box 128
Lame Deer, MT 59043
(406) 477–6677

FT. BELKNAP CASINO
Gros Ventre and Assiniboine Tribes
Ft. Belknap
Rt. 2, Box 66
Ft. Belknap, MT 59526
(800) 343–6107

FOUR C'S CASINO
Chippewa Cree Tribe of the Rocky Boy's
    Reservation
Rocky Boy Route, Box 544 RR1
Box Elder, MT 59521
(406) 395–4863

KWATAQNUK RESORT AND CASINO
Confederated Salish & Kootenai Tribes of the
    Flathead Nation
303 US Hwy 93 East
Polson, MT 59860
(406) 883–3636

LITTLE BIG HORN CASINO
Crow Indian Tribe
Box 1–580
Crow Agency, MT 59022
(406) 638–4444

SILVER WOLF CASINO
Assiniboine & Sioux Tribes of the Fort Peck
    Reservation
P.O. Box 726, Hwy 13 W
Wolf Point, MT 59201
(406) 653–3476

## ◆ NEBRASKA

OMAHA TRIBE OF NEBRASKA
P.O. Box 368
Macy, NE 68039
(402) 837–5391

ROSEBUD CASINO
Rosebud Sioux Tribe
HC 14 Box 135
Valentine, NE 69201
(605) 378–3800

SANTEE SIOUX TRIBE OF NEBRASKA
Route 2, Box 163
Niobrara, NE 68760
(402) 857–2393

## ◆ NEVADA

AVI RESORT AND CASINO
Ft. Mohave Indian Tribe
10000 Aha Macav Parkway
Box 77011
Laughlin, NV 89028–7011
(702) 535–5555

MOAPA BAND TRIBAL ENTERPRISE CASINO
Moapa Band of Paiutes
Moapa Indian Reservation, Box 340
Moapa, NV 89025
(702) 864–2601

SMOKE MOUNTAIN SMOKE SHOP
Las Vegas Paiute Tribe
11515 Nu-Way Kaiv Blvd.
Las Vegas, NV 89124
(702) 645–2957

## ◆ NEW MEXICO

APACHE NUGGET CASINO
Jicarilla Apache Tribe
Narrow Gage Rd.
Dulce, NM 87528
(505) 759–3777

CASINO APACHE
Mescalero Apache Tribe
P.O. Box 205
Mescalero, NM 88340
(505) 630–4100

CITIES OF GOLD CASINO
Pueblo of Pojoaque
10 B Cities of Gold Road
Santa Fe, NM 87501
(505) 455–3313

ISLETA GAMING PALACE
Pueblo of Isleta
11000 Broadway, SE
Albuquerque, NM 87105
(505) 869–2614

OH KAY CASINO
Pueblo of San Juan
P.O. Box 1270
San Juan Pueblo, NM 87566
(505) 747–1668

PUEBLO OF SANDIA
Box 10188
Albuquerque, NM 87184
(505) 897–2173

PUEBLO OF TESUQUE
Route 5 Box 360-T
Santa Fe, NM 87501
(505) 983–2667

SANDIA CASINO
SANTA ANA STAR CASINO
Pueblo of Santa Ana
54 Jemez Canyon Dam Road
Bernalillo, NM 87004
(505) 867–0000

SAN FELIPE CASINO HOLLYWOOD
Pueblo of San Felipe
25 Hogan Rd., P.O. Box 4152
San Felipe, NM 87001
(505) 867–6700

SKY CITY CASINO
Pueblo of Acoma
P.O. Box 519
San Fidel, NM 87049
(505) 552–6017

TAOS MOUNTAIN CASINO
Pueblo of Taos
P.O. Box 777
Taos, NM 87571
(505) 737–0777

## ◆ NEW YORK

AKWESASNE MOHAWK CASINO
MOHAWK BINGO PALACE
St. Regis Mohawk Tribe
Akwesasne Community Building
Rt. 37, Box 670
Hogansburg, NY 13655
(518) 358–2222

SENECA NATION OF INDIANS
P.O. Box 231
Salamanca, NY 14779
(716) 945–1790

TURNING STONE CASINO
Oneida Nation of New York
P.O. Box 126, Patrick Road
Vernon, NY 13478
(315) 361–7711

## ◆ NORTH CAROLINA

HARRAH'S CHEROKEE CASINO
Eastern Band of Cherokee Indians
P.O. Box 455
Cherokee, NC 28719
(828) 497–7777

## ◆ NORTH DAKOTA

4 BEARS CASINO AND LODGE
Three Affiliated Tribes of the Fort Berthold
    Reservation
Mandan, Hidatsa & Arikara Nation
P.O. Box HC 3, Box 2
New Town, ND 58763
(701) 627–4018

PRAIRIE KNIGHTS CASINO AND LODGE
Standing Rock Sioux Tribe
7932 Hwy 24
Fort Yates, ND 58538
(701) 854–7777

SPIRIT LAKE CASINO AND RESORT
Spirit Lake Sioux Nation
7889 Highway 57
St. Michael, ND 58370–9000
(701) 766–4747

TURTLE MOUNTAIN CHIPPEWA CASINO
Turtle Mountain Band of Chippewa Indians
P.O. Box 1449, Hwy 5 West
Belcourt, ND 58316
(701) 477–3281

## ◆ OKLAHOMA

CHEROKEE CASINO
Cherokee Nation of Oklahoma
P.O. Box 948
Tahlequah, OK 74465
(918) 456–0671

CHICKASAW GAMING CENTER
Chickasaw Nation of Oklahoma
1500 North Country Club Rd.
Ada, OK 74820
(405) 436–3740

CHOCTAW GAMING CENTER
Choctaw Nation of Oklahoma
3735 Choctaw Rd., P.O. Box 1909
Durant, OK 74702
(580) 920–0160

CIMARRON BINGO CASINO
Iowa Tribe of Oklahoma
W. Freeman Ave.
Perkins, OK 74059
(405) 547–5352

CITIZEN BAND POTAWATOMI INDIANS OF
    OKLAHOMA
1601 S. Gordon Cooper Dr.
Shawnee, OK 74801
(405) 273–2242

COMANCHE RED RIVER CASINO
Comanche Indian Tribe
P.O. Box 231
Randlett, OK 73501
(580) 281–3580

DELAWARE TRIBAL GAMES
Delaware Tribe of Western Oklahoma
P.O. Box 806
Anadarko, OK 73005
(405) 247–6979

FOX FIRE BINGO
Sac & Fox Nation of Oklahoma
Route 2 Box 246
Stroud, OK 74079
(918) 968–3526

KAW NATION BINGO
Kaw Nation of Oklahoma
Drawer 271
Kaw City, OK 74641
(405) 269–2552

KEETOOWAH BINGO
United Keetoowah Band of Cherokee Indians
2450 S. Muskogee
Tahlequah, OK 74464
(918) 456–6131

KICKAPOO TRIBE OF OKLAHOMA
P.O. Box 70
McLoud, OK 74851
(405) 964–2075

KIOWA TRIBE OF OKLAHOMA
P.O. Box 369
Carnegie, OK 73015
(580) 654–2300

LUCKY STAR BINGO
Cheyenne and Arapaho Tribes of Oklahoma
7777 N Hwy 81
Concho, OK 73022
(405) 262–0345

MIAMI TRIBE ENTERTAINMENT
Miami Tribe of Oklahoma
202 South Eight Tribes Trail
P.O. Box 1326
Miami, OK 74355
(918) 542–1445

MODOC TRIBE OF OKLAHOMA
517 G Southeast
Miami, OK 74354
(918) 542–1190

MUSCOGEE (CREEK) NATION
121 W. Lincoln
Bristow, OK 74010
(918) 367–9168

NAISHA GAMES
Apache Tribe of Oklahoma
P.O. Box 768
Anadarko, OK 73005
(405) 247–3260

OTOE BINGO
Otoe Missouria Tribe of Oklahoma
Box 2585
Red Rock, OK 74076
(405) 723–4444

PONCA TRIBAL BINGO
Ponca Tribe of Oklahoma
20 White Eagle Drive
Ponca City, OK 74601
(580) 762–8104

SEMINOLE NATION BINGO
Seminole Nation of Oklahoma
P.O. Box 1484
Seminole, OK 74868
(405) 382–7922

SENECA-CAYUGA TRIBE OF OKLAHOMA
Rt. 4, Box 374 S. 50
Grove, OK 74344
(918) 542–6609

THLOPTHLOCCO TRIBAL TOWN
Box 188
Okemah, OK 74859
(918) 623–0072

THUNDER BIRD ENTERTAINMENT CENTER
Absentee-Shawnee Tribe of Oklahoma
2025 S. Gordon Cooper Drive
Shawnee, OK 74801
(405) 360–9270

TONKAWA TRIBAL BINGO
Tonkawa Tribe of Oklahoma
P.O. Box 70
Tonkawa, OK 74653
(405) 628–2561

♦ **OREGON**

CHINOOK WINDS CASINO &
   CONVENTION CENTER
Confederated Tribes of the Siletz Indians of Oregon
1777 NW 44th Street
Lincoln City, OR 97367
(541) 996–5825

CONFEDERATED TRIBES OF THE GRAND
    RONDE INDIAN COMMUNITY
9615 Grand Ronde Road
Grand Ronde, OR 97347
(503) 879–2350

INDIAN HEAD CASINO AT KAH-NEE-T
    RESORT
Confederated Tribes of the Warm Springs
    Reservation of OR
P.O. Box 1240
Warm Springs, OR 97761
(541) 553–6122

KLAMOYA CASINO
Klamath Tribes
P.O. Box 490
34333 Hwy. 97 N.
Chiloquin, OR 97624
(541) 783–7529

THE MILL CASINO
Coquille Indian Tribe
3201 N. Tremont
North Bend, OR 97459
(541) 756–8800

THE OLD CAMP CASINO
Burns Paiute Tribe
2205 W. Monroe Street
Burns, OR 97720
(541) 573–1500

SEVEN FEATHERS HOTEL AND CASINO
Cow Creek Band of Umpqua Indians
146 Chief Miwaleta Lane
Canyonville, OR 97417
(541) 839–1111

WILDHORSE CASINO RESORT
Confederated Tribes of the Umatilla Indian
    Reservation
72777 Highway 331
Pendleton, OR 97801
(541) 278–2274

### ◆ SOUTH DAKOTA

CHEYENNE RIVER SIOUX TRIBE
P.O. Box 590
Eagle Butte, SD 57625
(605) 964–4155

DAKOTA SIOUX CASINO
Sisseton-Wahpeton Sioux Tribe
I-29 & E. Hwy. 10 Exit 232
Sisseton, SD 57262
(605) 698–4273

FORT RANDALL CASINO AND HOTEL
Yankton Sioux Tribe
West Hwy. 46, Box 756
Wagner, SD 57380–0756
(605) 487–7871

GRAND RIVER CASINO
Standing Rock Sioux Tribe
W. Hwy. 12
Mobridge, SD 57601
(800) 475–3321

LODE STAR CASINO
Crow Creek Sioux Tribe
P.O. Box 140
Fort Thompson, SD 57339
(605) 245–6000

LOWER BRUTE CASINO
Lower Brule Sioux Tribe
P.O. Box 204
Lower Brule, SD 57548
(605) 473–5577

PRAIRIE WIND CASINO
Oglala Sioux Tribe
HC 49, Box 10
Pine Ridge, SD 57770
(605) 535–6300

ROSEBUD CASINO
Rosebud Sioux Tribe
P.O. Box 430
Rosebud, SD 57570
(605) 747–2381

ROYAL RIVER CASINO, BINGO, AND MOTEL
Flandreau Santee Sioux Tribe
607 S. Veterans St.
P.O. Box 326
Flandreau, SD 57028
(605) 997–3746

### ◆ TEXAS

KICKAPOO TRADITIONAL TRIBE OF TEXAS
P.O. Box 972
Eagle Pass, TX 78853
(210) 773–2105

**SPEAKING ROCK CASINO**
Ysleta Del Sur Pueblo Indian Tribe
119 S. Old Pueblo Road
P.O. Box 17579-Ysleta Station
El Paso, TX 79917
(915) 860–7777

♦ **WASHINGTON**

**EMERALD QUEEN RIVERBOAT**
Puyallup Tribe of Indians
2002 East 28th Street
Tacoma, WA 98404
(253) 597–6200

**HARRAH'S SKAGIT VALLEY CASINO**
Upper Skagit Indian Tribe
590 Dark Lane
Bow, WA 98232
(360) 724–7777

**LITTLE CREEK CASINO**
Squaxin Island Tribe
West 91, Hwy. 108
Shelton, WA 98584
(360) 427–7711

**LUCKY EAGLE CASINO AND BINGO**
Confederated Tribes of the Chehalis Reservation
12888 188th Street, SW
Rochester, WA 98579
(360) 273–2000

**MAKAH TRIBAL BINGO**
Makah Indian Tribe of the Makah Indian Reservation
P.O. Box 115
Neah Bay, WA 98357
(360) 645–2264

**MILL BAY CASINO**
Confederated Tribes of the Colville Reservation
455 Wapato Lake Rd.
Manson, WA 98831
(509) 687–2102

**MUCKLESHOOT CASINO**
Muckleshoot Indian Tribe
2402 Auburn Way S.
Auburn, WA 98002
(206) 804–4444

**NISQUALLY INDIAN TRIBE**
12819 Yelm Highway SE
Olympia, WA 98513
(360) 412–5000

**NOOKSACK RIVER CASINO**
Nooksack Indian Tribe
5048 Mt. Baker Hwy
Deming, WA 98244
(360) 592–5472

**PORT GAMBLE S'KLALLAM TRIBE**
31912 Little Boston Road NE
Kingston, WA 98346
(206) 297–2646

**SEVEN CEDARS CASINO**
Jamestown S'Klallam Tribe
270756 Hwy 101
Sequim, WA 98382
(360) 683–7777

**SHOALWATER BAY CASINO**
Shoalwater Bay Indian Tribe
4112 State Hwy 105 (P.O. Box 560)
Tokeland, WA 98590
(360) 267–2048

**SUQUAMISH CLEARWATER CASINO**
Suquamish Tribe
15347 Suquamish Way, NE
Suquamish, WA 98392
(360) 598–6889

**SWINOMISH CASINO**
Swinomish Indian Tribal Community
P.O. Box 817
LaConner, WA 98257
(360) 466–3163

**TULALIP CASINO BINGO**
Tulalip Tribes of Washington
6410 33rd Ave, NE
Marysville, WA 98271
(360) 651–1111

**TWO RIVERS CASINO**
Spokane Tribe of Indians
61–828 B. Hwy 25, S.
Davenport, WA 99122
(509) 722–4000

YAKAMA LEGENDS CASINO
Confederated Tribes and Bands of the Yakama
    Indian Nation
580 Fort Road
Toppenish, WA 98948
(509) 865–8800

#### ♦ WISCONSIN

BAD RIVER CASINO
Bad River Band of Lake Superior Tribe of Chippewa
    Indians
P.O. Box 8, Hwy 2
Odanah, WI 54861
(715) 682–7121

GRINDSTONE CREEK CASINO
Lac Courte Oreilles Band of Lake Superior
    Chippewas
13767 West County Road B
Hayward, WI 54843
(715) 634–2430

HO-CHUNCK CASINO
Ho-Chunk Nation
S 3214 A Highway 12
Baraboo, WI 53913
(608) 356–6210

HOLE IN THE WALL CASINO
St. Croix Chippewa Indians of Wisconsin
Hwy 35 and 77
Danbury, WI 54830
(800) BET-U-WIN

ISLE VISTA CASINO
Red Cliff Band of Lake Superior Chippewas
P.O. Box 1167-Lucky Hwy. 13 N.
Bayfield, WI 54814
(715) 779–3712

LAKE OF THE TORCHES RESORT CASINO &
    CONVENTION CENTER
Lac du Flambeau Band of Lake Superior Chippewa
    Indians
P.O. Box 550—510 Old Abe Rd.
Lac du Flambeau, WI 54538
(715) 588–7070

MENOMINEE CASINO
Menominee Indian Tribe of Wisconsin
P.O. Box 910
Keshena, WI 54135
(715) 799–5114

MOHICAN NORTH STAR CASINO AND BINGO
Stockbridge-Munsee Community
W 12180A Country Road A
Bowler, WI 54416
(715) 787–3110

MOLE LAKE CASINOS AND BINGO
Sokaogon Chippewa Community
Route 1, Box 277
Crandon, WI 54520
(715) 478–5290

ONEIDA BINGO/CASINO
Oneida Tribe of Indians of Wisconsin
2020/2100 Airport Drive
Green Bay, WI 54313
(920) 494–4500

POTAWATOMI BINGO AND CASINO
Forest County Potawatomi Community
1721 W. Canal Street
Milwaukee, WI 53233
(414) 645–6866

#### ♦ WYOMING

WIND RIVER INDIAN RESERVATION CASINO
10369 Highway 789 S.
Riverton, WY 82501
(307) 332–6120

## CANADA

### GAMING REGULATORY AGENCIES

ALBERTA GAMING AND LIQUOR
    COMMISSION
50 Corriveau Avenue
St. Albert, AB T8N 3T5
(403) 447–8818

ALCOHOL AND GAMING COMMISSION
    OF ONTARIO
20 Dundas Street West, 7th floor
Toronto, ON M5G 2N6
(416) 326–0381

BRITISH COLUMBIA GAMING COMMISSION
P.O. Box 9310, Stn Provincial Government
844 Courtney Street
Victoria, BC V8W 9N1
(250) 387–5311

## BRITISH COLUMBIA: REGIONAL OFFICES

Lower Mainland
300–601 West Broadway
Vancouver, BC V5Z 4C2
(604) 660–6970

Northern British Columbia
1044 Fifth Avenue
Prince George, BC V2L 3H9
(250) 565–6997

Southern Interior
108–347 Leon Avenue
Kelowna, BC V1Y 8C7
(250) 861–7363

Vancouver Island
204–2100 LaBieux Rd.
Nanaimo, BC V9T 6E9
(250) 751–7009

## CANADIAN CENTRE ON SUBSTANCE ABUSE

75 Albert Street, Suite 300
Ottawa, ON K1P 5E7
(613) 235–4048

## CASINO REGINA, SASKATCHEWAN GAMING CORPORATION

1880 Saskatchewan Drive, 3rd Floor
Regina, SK S4P 0B2
(306) 787–1592

## GAMING POLICY SECRETARIAT

Province of British Columbia
P.O. Box 9311
506 Government Street
Victoria, BC V8W 9N1
(250) 953–4482

## MANITOBA GAMING CONTROL COMMISSION

215 Gary Street, Suite 800
Winnipeg, MB R3C 3P3
(204) 954–9400

## RÉGIE DES ALCOOLS, DES COURSES ET DES JEUX

Minist;re de la sécurité publique
1 rue Notre-Dame Est
Montréal, QC H2Y 1B6
(514) 864–2088

## SASKATCHEWAN LIQUOR AND GAMING AUTHORITY

North Canadian Oils Building
P.O. Box 5054
2500 Victoria Avenue
Regina, SK S4P 3M3
(306) 787–1762

# CASINOS

## ♦ ALBERTA

ARKAY CASINO
Elbow River Inn
1919 McCloud Trails SE
Calgary, AB T2G 4S1
(403) 266–4355

BACCARAT CASINOS
10128 104 Avenue
Edmonton, AB T5J 4Y8
(780) 413–3178

CASH CASINO PALACE
4040 Blackfoot Trails SE
Calgary, AB T2G 4E6
(403) 287–1635

CASII CASINO–RED DEER
6350 67th St.
Red Deer, AB T4P 3L9
(403) 346–3339

CASINO ABS
1251 3rd Avenue South
Lethbridge, AB T1K 0K1
(403) 381–9467

CASINO ABS–CITY CENTRE
12464 153rd St.
Edmonton, AB T5V 1S5
(780) 424–9467

EDMONTON'S KLONDIKE DAYS
Box 1480
Edmonton, AB T5J 2N5
(780) 471–7210

GOLD DUST CASINO
24 Boudreau Rd.
St. Albert, AB T8N 6K3
(780) 460–8092

**MEDICINE HAT LODGE-HOTEL & CASINO**
1051 Ross Glen Drive SE
Medicine Hat, AB T1B 3T8
(403) 529–2222

**PALACE CASINO**
170th St., Suite 2710–8882
Edmonton, AB T5T 4J2
(780) 444–2112

**WINNERS CIRCLE CASINO**
9725 Hardin St.
Fort Mcmurray, AB T9H 4G9
(780) 790–9739

### ◆ BRITISH COLUMBIA

**BILLY BARKER CASINO AND HOTEL**
308 Maclean Street
Quesnel, BC V2J 2N9
(250) 992–7763

**BINGO NETWORK GAMING INTERNATIONAL**
535 Thurlow, Suite 510
Vancouver, BC V6E 3L2
(604) 681–3864

**CASINO HOLLYWOOD**
494 George St.
Prince George, BC V2L 1R6
(250) 561–2421

**GRAND CASINO**
206–5050 Kingsway
Burnaby, BC VH5 4H2
(604) 437–1696

**GREAT CANADIAN CASINO**
Attn: Marketing
350–13775 Commerce Parkway
Richmond, BC V6V 2V4
(604) 303–1000

**GREAT CANADIAN CASINO**
620 Terminal Ave
Nanaimo, BC V9R 5E6
(250) 753–3033

**GREAT CANADIAN CASINO**
709 West Broadway
Vancouver, BC V5Z 1G5
(604) 872–5543

**GREAT CANADIAN CASINO MAYFAIR**
3075 Douglas St.
Victoria, BC V8T 4N3
(250) 380–3998

**KAMLOOPS CASINO**
540 Victoria St.
Kamloops, BC U2C 2B2
(250) 372–3336

**KELOWNA CASINO**
Landmark Square
1007–1708 Dolphin Ave.
Kelowna, BC V1Y 9S4
(250) 860–9467

**ROYAL DIAMOND CASINO**
Plaza of Nations
B106–750 Pacific Boulevard South
Vancouver, BC V6B 5E7
(604) 685–2340

### ◆ MANITOBA

**CLUB REGENT CASINO**
1415 Regent Ave., West
Winnipeg, MB R2C 3B2
(204) 957–2700

**CRYSTAL CASINO**
Hotel Fort Garry
222 Broadway
Winnipeg, MB R3C 0R3
(204) 942–8251
(800) 665–8088

**MCPHILIPS STREET STATION CASINO**
484 McPhilips Street
Winnipeg, MB R2X 2H2
(204) 957–3900

### ◆ NOVA SCOTIA

**SHERATON CASINO NOVA SCOTIA**
1983 Upper Water Street
Halifax, NS B3J 3Y5
(902) 425–7777

**SYDNEY'S CASINO NOVA SCOTIA**
525 George Street
Sydney, NS B1P 1K5
(902) 563–7777

## ◆ ONTARIO

### CASINO NIAGARA
P.O. Box 300
5705 Falls Avenue
Niagara Falls, ON L2E 6T3
(888) 946–3255

### CASINO WINDSOR
377 Riverside Drive West
Windsor, ON N9A 7H7
(519) 258–7878

### GOLDEN EAGLE CHARITABLE CASINO
P.O. Box 2860
Kenora, ON P9N 3X8
(807) 548–1332

### GREAT BLUE HERON CHARITABLE CASINO
21777 Island Rd.
Port Perry, ON L9L 1B6
(905) 985–4888

### ONTARIO LOTTERY AND GAMING CORPORATION
70 Foster Dr., Suite 800
Saulte St. Marie, ON P6A 6V2
(416) 326–0076

## ◆ QUEBEC

### CASINO DE HULL
1, boulevard Casino
Hull, PQ J8Y 6W3
(819) 772–2100

## ◆ SASKATCHEWAN

### BEAR CLAW CASINO & LODGE
White Bear First Nation
P.O. Box 1210
Carlyle, SK S0C 0R0
(306) 577–4577

### EMERALD CASINO
P.O. Box 6010
Saskatoon, SK S7K 4E4
(306) 683–8848

### GOLD EAGLE CASINO
11902 Railway Avenue
North Battleford, SK S9A 3K7
(306) 446–3833

### LLOYDMINSTER EXHIBITION ASSOC.
Box 690
Lloydminster, SK S9V 0Y7
(306) 825–5571

### NORTHERN LIGHTS CASINO
44 Marquis Rd West
Prince Albert, SK S6V 7Y5
(306) 764–4777

### PAINTED HAND CASINO
30 Third Avenue North
Yorkton, SK S3N 1B9
(306) 786–6777

### SWIFT CURRENT
Swift Current Exhibition Assoc.
Box 146
Swift Current, SK S9H 3V5
(306) 773–2944

## References

### U. S. Indians and the Economy

Anders, Gary. "Social and Economic Consequences of Federal Indian Policy: A Case Study of the Alaska Natives." *Economic Development and Cultural Change* 37, no. 2 (1989): 285–303.

Anderson, Terry L., ed. *Property Rights and Indian Economies.* Lanham, Md.: Rowman & Littlefield, 1992.

Barrington, Linda, ed. *The Other Side of the Frontier: Economic Explorations into Native American History.* Boulder, Colo.: Westview Press, 1999.

Carlson, Leonard A. *Indians, Bureaucrats, and Land: The Dawes Act and the Decline of Indian Farming.* Westport, Conn.: Greenwood Press, 1981.

Cohen, Fay G. *Treaties on Trial: The Continuing Controversy over Northwest Indian Fishing Rights.* Seattle: University of Washington Press, 1986.

Committee to Review the Community Development Quota Program. *The Community Development Quota Program in Alaska.* Washington, D.C.: National Academy Press, 1999.

Cornell, Stephen and Joseph Kalt. "Pathways from Poverty: Economic Development and Institution-Building on American Indian Reservations." *American Indian Culture and Research Journal* 14, no. 1 (1990): 89–125.

Gerdes, Karen, Maria Napoli, Clinton M. Pattea, and Elizabeth A. Segal. "The Impact of Indian Gaming on Economic Development." *Pressing Issues of Inequality and American Indian Communities,* edited by Elizabeth A. Segal, and Keith M. Kilty, 17–30. New York: Haworth Press, 1998.

Hosmer, Brian C. *American Indians in the Marketplace: Persistence and Innovation Among the Menominees and Metlakatlans, 1870–1920.* Lawrence, Kan.: University Press of Kansas, 1999.

———. "Creating Indian Entrepreneurs: Menominees, Neopit Mills, and Timber Exploitation, 1890–1915." *American Indian Culture and Research Journal* 15, no. 1 (1991): 1–28.

Huff, Delores J. "The Tribal Ethic, The Protestant Ethic, and American Indian Economic Development." In *American Indian Policy and Cultural Values: Conflict and Accomodation,* edited by Jennie R. Joe, 75–89. Los Angeles: American Indian Studies Center, UCLA, 1986.

Karpoff, Jonathan M. and Edward M. Rice. "Structure and Performance of Alaska Native Corporations." *Contemporary Policy Issues* 10 no. 3 (1992): 71–84.

Marglin, Stephen A., and Juliet B. Schor, eds. *The Golden Age of Capitalism: Reinterpreting the Postwar Experience.* Oxford: Clarendon Press; New York: Oxford University Press, 1990.

McCool, Daniel. *Command of the Waters: Iron Triangles, Federal Water Development, and Indian Water.* Berkeley and Los Angeles: University of California Press, 1987.

Miner, H. Craig. *The Corporation and the Indian: Tribal Sovereignty and Industrial Development in Indian Territory, 1865–1907.* Columbia, Mo.: University of Missouri Press, 1976.

Oberg, Kalervo. *The Social Economy of the Tlingit Indians.* Vancouver: J.J. Douglas, 1973.

Trosper, Ronald L. "That Other Discipline: Economics and American Indian History." In *New Directions in American Indian History,* edited by Colin G. Calloway, 199–222. Norman: University of Oklahoma Press, 1981.

Van Hoak, Stephen P. "Untangling the Roots of Dependency: Choctaw Economics, 1700–1860." *American Indian Quarterly* 23, no. 3 & 4 (1999): 113–128.

Vinje, David L. "Cultural Values and Economic Development on Reservations." In *American Indian Policy in the Twentieth Century,* edited by Vine Deloria, Jr., 155–175. Norman: University of Oklahoma Press, 1985.

Weatherford, Jack. *Indian Givers: How the Indians of the Americas Transformed the World.* New York: Crown, 1988.

———. *Native Roots: How the Indians Enriched America.* New York: Crown, 1991.

White, Richard. *The Middle Ground: Indians, Empires, and Republics in the Great Lakes Region, 1650–1815.* Cambridge: Cambridge University Press, 1991.

———. *The Roots of Dependency: Subsistence, Environment, and Social Change among the Choctaws, Pawnees, and Navajos.* Lincoln: University of Nebraska Press, 1983.

White, Robert H. *Tribal Assets: The Rebirth of Native America.* New York: H. Holt, 1990.

*Ronald L. Trosper*

## U.S. Reservation Economic Development

Anderson, Joseph and Smith, Dean Howard; "Managing Tribal Assets: Developing Long Term Strategic Plans." *American Indian Culture and Research Journal* 22, no. 2 (1999): 139–156.

Barsh, Russell L. "Indian Resources and the National Economy: Business Cycles and Policy Cycles." In *Native Americans and Public Policy,* edited by Fremont J. Lyden and Lyman H. Legters, 193–222. Pittsburgh: University of Pittsburgh Press, 1992.

Cornell, Stephen and Joseph P. Kalt. "Pathways from Poverty: Economic Development and Institution-Building on American Indian Reservations." *American Indian Culture and Research Journal* 14, no. 3 (1990): 89–125.

———. "Reloading the Dice: Improving the Chances for Economic Development on American Indian Reservations." Cambridge: Harvard Project on American Indian Economic Development, John F. Kennedy School of Government, 1992.

———. *What Can Tribes Do? Strategies and Institutions in American Indian Economic Development.* Los Angeles: American Indian Studies Center, UCLA, 1992.

———. "Where's the Glue? Institutional Bases of American Indian Economic Development." Cambridge: Harvard Project on American Indian Economic Development, John F. Kennedy School of Government, 1991.

Guyette, Susan. *Planning for Balanced Development: A Guide for Native American and Rural Communities.* Santa Fe, N.M.: Clear Light Publishers, 1996.

Hurt, R. Douglas. *Indian Agriculture in America: Prehistory to the Present.* Lawrence: University Press of Kansas, 1987.

Jacobs, Jane. *Cities and the Wealth of Nations: Principles of Economic Life.* New York: Random House, 1984.

———. *The Nature of Economies.* New York: Modern Library, 2000.

———. *Systems of Survival: A Dialogue on the Moral Foundations of Commerce and Politics.* New York: Vintage Books, 1992.

Kalt, Joseph. "The Redefinition of Property Rights in American Indian Reservations: A Comparative Analysis of Native American Economic Development." Cambridge: Harvard Project on American Indian Economic Development, John F. Kennedy School of Government, 1987.

Krepps, Matthew B. "Can Tribes Manage Their Own Resources? A Study of American Indian Forestry and the 638 Program." Cambridge: Harvard Project on American Indian Economic Development, John F. Kennedy School of Government, 1991.

Langdon, Steve J., ed. *Contemporary Alaskan Native Economies.* Lanham, Md.: University Press of America, 1986.

Legters, Lyman H. *American Indian Policy: Self-Governance and Economic Development.* Westport, Conn.: Greenwood Press, 1994.

Miner, H. Craig. *The Corporation and the Indian: Tribal Sovereignty and Industrial Civilization in Indian Territory, 1865–1907.* Columbia: University of Missouri Press, 1976.

Ortiz, Roxanne D., ed. *Economic Development in American Indian Reservations.* Albuquerque: Native American Studies, University of New Mexico, 1979.

Reno, Philip. *Mother Earth, Father Sky, and Economic Development: Navajo Resources and their Use.* Albuquerque: University of New Mexico Press, 1981.

Smith, Dean Howard. "Apache Manufacturing Company: A Teaching Case Study in Tribal Management." Teaching Case C-8. Cambridge: Harvard Project on American Indian Economic Development, 1996.

———. "The Issue of Compatibility Between Cultural Integrity, and Economic Development Among Native American Tribes." *American Indian Culture and Research Journal* 18, no. 3 (1994): 177–206.

———. *Modern Tribal Development: Paths to Self-Sufficiency and Cultural Integrity in Indian Country.* Walnut Creek, Calif.: Altamira Press, 2000.

———. "Native American Economic Development: A Modern Approach." *Review of Regional Studies* 24, no. 1 (1994): 87–102.

Smith, Dean Howard, and Jon Ozmun. "Fort Belknap's Community Development Plan: A Teaching Case Study in Tribal Management." Teaching Case C-5. Cambridge: Harvard Project on American Indian Economic Development, John F. Kennedy School of Government, 1994.

Stanley, Sam, ed. *American Indian Economic Development.* The Hague: Mouton: Chicago: distributed by Aldine, 1978.

Trosper, Ronald L. "Multicriterion Decision Making in a Tribal Context." In *Native Americans and Public Policy,* edited by Fremont J. Lyden and Lyman H. Legters, 223–242. Pittsburgh: University of Pittsburgh Press, 1992.

Wilkinson, Charles F. *Fire on the Plateau: Conflict and Endurance in the American Southwest.* Washington: Island Press/Shearwater Books, 1999.

*Dean Howard Smith*

## U.S. Indian Labor

Ambler, Marjane. *Breaking the Iron Bonds: Indian Control of Energy Development.* Lawrence, Kan.: University Press of Kansas, 1990.

Driver, Harold E. *Indians of North America.* 2d ed. Chicago: University of Chicago Press, 1969.

Fixico, Donald L. *Termination and Relocation: Federal Indian Policy, 1945–1960.* Albuquerque: University of New Mexico Press, 1986.

Gundlach, James H. and Alden E. Roberts. "Native American Indian Migration and Relocation: Success or Failure." *Pacific Sociological Review* 21, no. 1 (1978): 117–128.

Gwartney, James D. and James E. Long. "The Relative Earnings of Blacks and Other Minorities." *Industrial and Labor Relations Review* 31, no. 3 (1978): 336–346.

Hackenberg, Robert A. and C. Roderick Wilson. "Reluctant Emigrants: The Role of Migration in Papago Indian Adaptation." *Human Organization* 31, no. 2 (1972): 171–186.

Jacobsen, Cardell K. "Internal Colonialism and Native Americans: Indian Labor in the United States from 1871 to World War II." *Social Science Quarterly* 65, no. 1 (1984): 158–171.

Sandefur, Gary D., Ronald R. Rindfus, and Barney Cohen (eds.). *Changing Numbers, Changing Needs: American Indian Demography and Public Health.* Washington, D.C.: National Academy Press, 1996.

Snipp, C. Matthew. *American Indians: The First of This Land.* New York: Russell Sage, 1989.

———. "A Portrait of American Indian Women and Their Labor Force Experience." In *The American Woman, 1990–91: A Status Report,* edited by Sara E. Rix. New York: Norton, 1990.

Snipp, C. Matthew, and Isik Aytac. "The Labor Force Participation of American Indian Women." In *Research in Human Capital and Development,* edited by Ismail Sirageldin, vol. 6, 189–211. Greenwich: JAI Press, 1990.

Snipp, C. Matthew, and Gary D. Sandefur. "Earnings of American Indians and Alaska Natives: The Effects of Residence and Migration." *Social Forces* 66, no. 4 (1988): 994–1008.

*C. Matthew Snipp*

## U.S. Assistance and Restitution

Blanchard, Evelyn Lance. "The Growth and Development of American Indian and Alaska Native Children." In *The Psychosocial Development of Minority Group Children* edited by Gloria Johnson Powell, 115–130. New York: Brunner/Mazel, 1983.

Brookings Institution. Institute for Government Research. *The Problem of Indian Administration.* Baltimore, Md.: John Hopkins University, 1928. This work is commonly referred to as the *Merriam Report.*

Cooper, Mary H. "Native Americans Future: Do U.S. Policies Block Opportunities for Progress?" *CQ Researcher* 6, no. 26 (1996): 601–624.

Chambers Donald E. *Social Policy and Social Programs: A Method for the Practical Public Policy Analyst.* 3rd ed. Boston: Allyn and Bacon, 2000.

Jansson, Bruce S. *The Reluctant Welfare State: American Social Welfare Policies—Past, Present, and Future.* Pacific Grove, Calif.: Brooks/Cole, 1997.

Johnson, Troy R. "The State and the American Indian: Who Gets the Child?" *Wicazo Sa Review* 14, no. 1 (1999): 197–214.

Kopp, Judy. "Crosscultural Contacts: Changes in the Diet and Nutrition of the Navajo Indians." *American Indian Culture and Research Journal* 10:4 (1986): 1–30.

Kunitz, Stephen J. *Disease Change and the Role of Medicine: The Navajo Experience.* Berkeley: University of California Press, 1983.

Philp, Kenneth R., ed. *Indian Self-Rule: First-Hand Accounts of Indian-White Relations from Roosevelt to Reagan.* Logan, Utah: Utah State University Press, 1995.

Pollard, Kelvin M. and William P. O'Hare. "America's Racial and Ethnic Minorities." *Population Bulletin* 54, no. 3 (1999).

Rosaldo, Renato. *Culture and Truth: The Remaking of Social Analysis.* Boston: Beacon Press, 1989.

Sandefur, Gary D., Ronald R. Rindfuss, and Barney Cohen, eds. *Changing Numbers, Changing Needs: American Indian Demography and Public Health.* Washington, D.C.: National Academy Press, 1996.

Standing Bear, Luther. *Land of the Spotted Eagle.* Lincoln: University of Nebraska Press, 1933.

———. *My Indian Boyhood.* Lincoln: University of Nebraska Press, 1931.

Stewart, Paul H. "Government Agencies." In *Native America in the Twentieth Century: An Encyclopedia*, edited by Mary B. Davis, 210–214. New York: Garland, 1994.

———. *The Indian Office: Growth and Development of an American Institution, 1865–1900.* Ann Arbor, Mich.: UMI Research Press, 1979.

Stiffarm, Lenore and Phil Lane. "The Demography of Native North America: A Question of American Indian Survival." In *The State of Native America: Genocide, Colonization and Resistance*, edited by M. Annette Jaimes, 23–53. Boston: South End Press, 1992.

U.S. American Indian Policy Review Commission. *Final Report: Submitted to Congress May 17, 1977.* 2 vols. Washington, D.C.: GPO, 1977.

U.S. General Accounting Office. *Food Assistance Programs: Nutritional Adequacy of Primary Food Programs on Four Indian Reservations. Report to Congressional Requesters.* Washington, D.C., 1989.

Walke, Roger. *Federal Programs of Assistance to Native Americans: A Report Prepared for the Senate Select Committee on Indian Affairs of the United States Senate.* Washington, D.C.: GPO, 1991.

*Rita Ledesma*

## Canadian Native Economic Development

Barrington, Linda, ed. *The Other Side of the Frontier: Economic Explorations into Native American History.* Boulder, Colo.: Westview Press, 1999.

Canada. Royal Commission on Aboriginal Peoples. *Report of the Royal Commission on Aboriginal Peoples.* Ottawa, 1996.

Carter, Sarah. *Lost Harvests: Prairie Indian Reserve Farmers and Government Policy.* Montreal: McGill-Queen's University Press, 1990.

Elias, Peter Douglas. *Development of Aboriginal People's Communities.* North York, Ont.: Captus Press, 1991.

Evans, Simon M., Sarah Carter and Bill Yeo, eds. *Cowboys, Ranchers and the Cattle Business: Cross-border Perspectives on Ranching History.* Calgary: University of Calgary Press; Boulder, Colo.: University Press of Colorado, 2000.

Cornell, Stephen and Joseph P. Kalt. *What Can Tribes Do? Strategies and Institutions in American Indian Economic Development.* Los Angeles: American Indian Studies Center, UCLA, 1992.

Knight, Rolf. *Indians at Work: An Informal History of Native Labour in British Columbia, 1848–1930.* Vancouver: New Star Books, 1996.

Littlefield, Alice, and Martha C. Knack, eds. *Native Americans and Wage Labor Ethnohistorical Perspectives.* Norman: University of Oklahoma Press, 1996.

Notzke, Claudia. *Aboriginal Peoples and Natural Resources in Canada.* North York, Ont.: Captus University Publications, 1994.

Savoie, Donald J. *Aboriginal Economic Development in New Brunswick.* Moncton, N.B. : Canadian Institute for Research on Regional Development, 2000.

Sloan, Pamela and Roger Hill. *Corporate Aboriginal Relations: Best Practice Case Studies*. Toronto: Hill Sloan Associates Inc., 1995.

Tough, Frank. *'As Their Natural Resources Fail': Native Peoples and the Economic History of Northern Manitoba, 1870–1930*. Vancouver, B.C.: UBC Press, 1996.

Wien, Fred C. *Rebuilding the Economic Base of Indian Communities: The Micmac in Nova Scotia*. Montreal, Quebec: The Institute for Research on Public Policy, 1986.

Wuttunee, Wanda A. *In Business for Ourselves: Northern Entrepreneurs: Fifteen Case Studies of Successful Small Northern Businesses*. Montreal: McGill-Queen's University Press, 1992.

*David Newhouse*

## Overview of Government Assistance and Restitution

Bartlett, Richard. *The Indian Act of Canada*. 2nd ed. Saskatoon: University of Saskatchewan, Native Law Centre, 1988.

Berger, Thomas R. *Fragile Freedoms: Human Rights and Dissent in Canada*. Toronto: Clarke, Irwin, 1981.

Canada. *The Annotated Indian Act, Including Related Treaties, Statutes and Regulations*. Scarborough, Ont.: Carswell, 1988.

Canada. Department of Indian Affairs and Northern Development. *Basic Departmental Data*. Ottawa, 1997.

———. *Federal programs for Status Indians, Métis, Non-Status, and Inuit: Major National Programs*. Ottawa, 1980.

———. *Growth in Federal Expenditures on Aboriginal Peoples*. Ottawa, 1993.

Getty, Ian & Lussier, Antoine, eds. *As Long as the Sun Shines and Water Flows: A Reader in Canadian Native Studies*. Vancouver: University of British Columbia Press, 1983.

Fleras, Augie, and Elliott, Jean. *The "Nations Within": Aboriginal-State Relations in Canada, the United States, and New Zealand*. Toronto: Oxford University Press, 1992.

Frideres, James. *Native People in Canada: Contemporary Conflicts*. 5th ed. Prentice Hall: Scarborough, Ont., 1998.

Howlett, Michael. "Policy Paradigms and Policy Changes: Lessons From the Old and New Canadian Policies Towards Aboriginal Peoples." *Policy Studies Journal*, 22, no. 4 (1994): 631–649.

Hylton, John (ed.). *Aboriginal Self-Government in Canada: Current Trends and Issues*. Saskatoon, Sask.: Purich Publishing, 1994.

Johnston, Patrick. *Native Children and the Child Welfare System*. Toronto: Canadian Council on Social Development in association with James Lorimer, 1983.

Long, J. Anthony and Menno Boldt, eds. *Governments in Conflict?: Provinces and Indian Nations in Canada*. Toronto: University of Toronto Press, 1988.

McKenzie, Brad. "Social Work Practice with Native People." In *An Introduction to Social Work Practice in Canada*, edited by Shankar Yelaja, 272–288. Scarborough, Ont.: Prentice-Hall, 1985.

Miller, James Rodger. *Skyscrapers Hide the Heavens: A History of Indian-White Relations in Canada*. Toronto: University of Toronto Press, 1989.

Morrison, Bruce and Roderick Wilson, eds. *Native Peoples: The Canadian Experience*. Toronto: McClelland and Stewart, 1995.

Patterson, E. Palmer. "Native Peoples and Social Policy." *Canadian Social Policy*. rev. ed., edited by Shankar A. Yelaja, 175–194. Waterloo, Ont.: Wilfred Laurier University Press, 1987.

Turner, Joanne C. and Francis J. Turner, eds. *Canadian Social Welfare*. 3rd ed. Scarborough, Ont.: Allyn and Bacon, 1995.

*Heather Coleman*

## Canadian Native Economic Development on Reserves

Boldt, Menno, J. Anthony Long, and Leroy Little Bear, eds. *The Quest for Justice: Aboriginal Peoples and Aboriginal Rights*. Toronto: University of Toronto Press, 1985.

Canada. Royal Commission on Aboriginal Peoples. *Report of the Royal Commission on Aboriginal Peoples*. Ottawa, 1996.

Cardinal, Harold. *The Rebirth of Canada's Indians*. Edmonton: Hurtig, 1977.

———. *The Unjust Society: The Tragedy of Canada's Indians*. Edmonton: Hurtig, 1969.

Cassidy, Frank, ed. *Aboriginal Self-Determination*. Lantzville: Oolichan Books, 1991.

Elias, Peter D. *Development of Aboriginal People's Communities*. North York, ON: Captus Press, 1991.

Frideres, James S. *Native Peoples in Canada: Contemporary Conflicts*. 3rd edition. Scarborough: Prentice-Hall Canada, 1988.

Hawthorn, Harry B. *A Survey of the Contemporary Indians of Canada: A Report on Economic, Political, Educational Needs and Policies*. 2 vols. Ottawa: Queen's Printer, 1966–67.

Kariya, Paul, ed. *Native Socio-Economic Development in Canada: Adaptation, Accessibility and Opportunity*. Institute of Urban Studies, Native Issues 1. Winnipeg: University of Winnipeg, 1989.

National Round Table on Aboriginal Economic Development and Resources. *Sharing the Harvest: The Road to Self-Reliance.* Ottawa: Royal Commission on Aboriginal Peoples, 1993.

Native Investment & Trade Association. [Online] Available: http://www.native-invest-trade.com/ [2001 January 28].

Ponting, J. Rick, ed. *Arduous Journey: Canadian Indians and Decolonization.* Toronto: McClelland and Stewart, 1986.

*Ian Getty*

# Prominent Native North Americans

**Abby Abinanti (1947–)**
*Yurok attorney and activist*

Abby Abinanti is president of the Tribal Law and Policy Institute. She is also a California juvenile dependency judge. Born in San Francisco, California, Abinanti received her law degree from the University of New Mexico in 1973. She later became a specialist in education, tribal development, and social services. She has developed model tribal court systems and codes, trained Indian Child Welfare Act workers, and taught seminars at the National American Indian Court Judges Association.

Since 1977 Abinanti has been active in the national Women and the Law Conferences and has become a strong advocate for women's rights in the areas of educational equity, child abuse, day care, affirmative action, and ratification of the Equal Rights Amendment (ERA). She has previously served as the chair of the California Indian Legal Services board of directors and as trustee of the Humboldt County Law Library. Her publications include *The Indian Child Welfare Act: Strategies for Implementation* (1981) and *Three Optional Tribal Court Structures* (1981).

**Abraham (d. 1780)**
*Mohawk tribal leader*

Abraham was the son of Old Abraham and adopted brother and successor to Hendrick, a prominent Mohawk leader. In 1755, when Hendrick was killed in the Battle of Lake George, Abraham became a Mohawk chief. Like Hendrick, Abraham was a renowned orator and diplomat. He served as spokesman for the Iroquois League, an alliance of six Iroquoian speaking nations including the Mohawk, at the Albany Conference of 1754, where colonial leaders gathered to discuss a possible union. During these negotiations Abraham met with Benjamin Franklin and William Johnson. In 1775 the colonists turned to Abraham once again. In that year treaty commissioners from the Continental Congress met with the sachems of the Iroquois League, to acquaint them with what he termed the "United Colonies dwelling upon this Island." The commissioners, according to protocol, selected Abraham as the representative speaker for the Iroquois. Late in the summer of 1775, the colonists appealed to Abraham and his people to remain neutral during the American Revolution. Abraham conveyed to the colonists that his people would remain neutral during the conflict. Later, however, under the leadership of Mohawk Joseph Brant, who had strong personal and political ties to the British, some Mohawk villages gave their support to the British in the American Revolution.

**George Abrams (1939–)**
*Seneca anthropologist, author, and arts administrator*

George Abrams is an anthropologist who specializes in the Seneca and other Iroquoian peoples. He is a member of the Seneca tribe, which originally occupied an extensive territory in eastern Canada (from Lake Ontario southward) and the United States. He is a member of the Blue Heron clan.

Abrams was born on the Allegany Indian Reservation near Salamanca, New York, on 4 May 1939. He received his bachelor's degree in anthropology from the State University of New York at Buffalo in 1967 and obtained his master's degree from the University of Arizona in 1967 and studied in the university's doctoral program from 1968 to 1971. His general interests include Native American ethnology, Indian education, applied anthropology, ethnohistory, and museum science. He has published several works, including "The Cornplanter Cemetery," published in *Pennsylvania Archeologist* (1965); "Moving the Fire: A Case of Iroquois Ritual Innovation," published in *Iroquois Culture, History, and Prehistory* (1967); "Red Jacket," published in the *World Book Encyclopedia* (1976); and *The Seneca* (1976).

From 1990 until 1992, he served as special assistant to the director of the National Museum of the American Indian in New York City. He has won many academic awards and has served as a member of several advisory boards and committees, both at the national and state levels. For over ten years, Abrams was chairman of the American Indian Museums Association. Since early 1998, he is director of the Yager Museum, Hartwick College, in Oneonta, New York.

### Andrew Acoya (1943–)
*Laguna Pueblo architect and urban planner*

Andrew Acoya is a facilities planner for the Bureau of Indian Affairs in Albuquerque, New Mexico. He is registered as an architect in the state of New Mexico and is a member of the American Institute of Architects.

Born at Fort Wingate, New Mexico, on 24 June 1943, Acoya obtained his bachelor's degree in Architecture at the University of New Mexico (1968) and earned a master's degree in Architecture at the Massachusetts Institute of Technology (MIT) in 1970. He is said to be the first full-blooded Native American to graduate from the MIT School of Architecture. He was awarded scholarships and awards from the Laguna Pueblo tribe, the Bureau of Indian Affairs, the John Hay Whitney Foundation, and the Massachusetts Institute of Technology.

Acoya completed his master's thesis at MIT with a study entitled "Community Planning for the Acoma Tribe of New Mexico," which examines the relevance of Pueblo village life as form givers in the planning of new Pueblo communities.

He has held the positions of professor of architecture at the University of New Mexico and director of planning for the All Indian Pueblo Council. He assisted in the design of the Pueblo Indian Cultural Center in Albuquerque, New Mexico and the San Juan Pueblo Arts and Crafts Cooperative Building, and influenced a decision to provide space for Native healing ceremonies in a new hospital designed for the Laguna Pueblo

and Acoma Pueblo tribes. He lives in Corrales, New Mexico, with his wife, Maria, of San Felipe Pueblo, and their son, Andrew.

### Clarence Acoya (1930–)
*Laguna Pueblo business administrator*

Clarence Acoya, a business administrator and member of Laguna Pueblo, was born in Albuquerque on 20 October 1930. Acoya attended Albuquerque Indian School, Bacone College, the University of New Mexico, and Yale University. On completing his education, he served in the United States Marine Corps (1951–1954) and later went on to hold a number of important positions as a planner and administrator. He has served as executive director for the New Mexico Commission on Indian Affairs, treasurer for the Pueblo of Laguna, director of Ford Foundation projects for the National Congress of American Indians, and administrative assistant to the mayor of Tucson, Arizona.

Acoya has also been a member of various advisory boards, such as the National Indian Training and Research Center in Washington, D.C. He is a member of the National Congress of American Indians and was president of the American Athletic Hall of Fame.

### Evan Tselsa Adams (contemporary)
*Coast Salish actor and writer*

Born to the Sliammon Band (located near Powell River, British Columbia) of the Coast Salish people, Evan Adams has become a well-known actor and writer in recent years. Reared on the Sliammon Reserve, Adams graduated from St. Michael's University School and Lester B. Pearson College of the Pacific, which are both located in Victoria.

Adams began his acting career early, at age nineteen, when he performed a cameo role in *Toby McTeague*, a movie about a dog sled race. Adams stars in the Emmy-winning television movie *Lost in Barrens* and its sequel *The Curse of the Viking Grave*.

Most recently, Evan Adams starred in the popular movie *Smoke Signals*, which was based on a short story by Sherman Alexie and directed by Chris Eyre. Adams plays Thomas Builds-the-Fire in the film and won an award for Best Debut Performance at the Independent Spirit Awards in Los Angeles.

Architect Andrew Acoya.

## Hank Adams (1944– )
*Assiniboine/Sioux activist*

Hank Adams was born on the Fort Peck Indian Reservation in Montana at a place known as Wolf Point, commonly referred to as Poverty Flats. He graduated from Moclips High School in 1961, where he was student-body president, editor of the school newspaper and annual, and a starting football and basketball player. Following graduation he developed an interest in politics and moved to California where he was a staunch supporter of President John F. Kennedy and a campaign worker for the president's brother, Robert F. Kennedy, in the 1968 Democratic primary.

In 1964 Adams played a behind-the-scenes role when actor Marlon Brando and one thousand Indians marched on the Washington State capitol in Olympia to protest state policies toward Indian fishing rights. Indians reserved the right to take fish in "the usual and accustomed places" in numerous treaties negotiated in the 1850s. State officials, commercial, and sports fisherman tried to restrict the amount, time, and places where Indian people could fish, thus prompting the treaty/fishing-rights battles.

Adams began his activist career in April 1964 when he refused induction into the U.S. Army until Indian treaty rights were recognized. His attempt failed and he ultimately served in the U.S. Army.

In 1968 Adams became the director of the Survival of American Indians Association, a group of 150 to 200 active members primarily dedicated to the Indian treaty/fishing rights battle. Late in 1968, he actively campaigned against state regulation of Indian net fishing on the Nisqually River near Franks Landing, Washington. For this and his role in the fishing-rights battles, Adams was regularly arrested and jailed from 1968 to 1971. In January 1971, on the banks of the Puyallup River near Tacoma, Washington, Adams was shot in the stomach by an unknown assailant. He and a companion, Michael Hunt, had set a fish trap about midnight and remained to watch it. That section of the Puyallup River had been the scene of recent altercations as Indian people claimed fishing rights guaranteed by treaties despite state laws to the contrary. Adams recovered from the gunshot

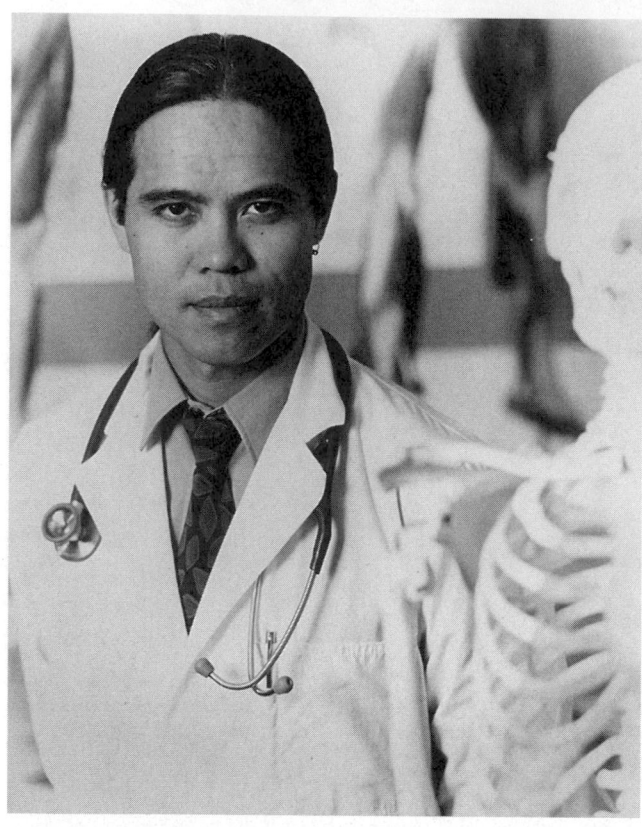

Evan Tselsa Adams.

wound and continued to fight for Indian fishing rights in the state of Washington into the mid-1970s.

## Margaret B. Adams (1936–)
*Navajo anthropologist and museum director*

Margaret Adams is a retired anthropologist of Navajo descent, formerly associated with several museums in the Monterey, California area. Born in Toronto, Ontario, Canada, on 29 April 1936, Adams attended college in California at Monterey Peninsula College and San Jose State University, from which she received her bachelor's in 1971. She completed her master's degree at the University of Utah in 1973. She then returned to Monterey and became chief of the museum branch at Fort Ord Military Complex and head curator of the Fort Ord and Presidio of Monterey Museums, a position she held from 1974 until 1988.

Adams has been a strong advocate of higher education for Native Americans throughout her career, serving on the Indians in Science Panel of the American Association for the Advancement of Science from 1972 until 1985. Adams is involved in protecting Native

American burial and ceremonial sites and in conducting research on Native American diet and food preparation methods. She is a member of the National Indian Education Association, the California Indian Education Association, the American Anthropological Association, and the American Association of Museums.

## Rebecca Adamson (1949–)
*Cherokee economist*

Rebecca Adamson has been active in many Native American concerns, particularly education and economic development. From 1972 to 1976, Adamson was a member of the board of directors of the Coalition of Indian-Controlled School Boards in Denver, Colorado, and her efforts were directed toward synthesizing and facilitating policy reform issues at the national level. In 1982 she founded and became president of First Nations Development Institute in Falmouth, Virginia, whose purpose is to promote economic development and the founding of commercial enterprises on reservation lands. She has always worked directly with grassroots tribal communities, advocating local tribal issues on a national level.

Rebecca Adamson, president of First Nations Development Institute.

In 1986 Adamson served as an advisor to the United Nations (UN) on rural development during the United Nations Decade of Women. In 1988 and 1989, she was advisor for the UN's International Labor Organization for International Indigenous Rights. She has served on the board of directors of several organizations, including the National Center for Enterprise Development, the Calvert Social Investment Fund, and the Council on Foundations.

Her interests in economic development of Indian communities led her in 1992 to become an advisor for the Catholic Conference's Campaign for Human Development on strategic planning for economic development. She has served on the President's Council on Sustainable Development/Sustainable Communities Task Force. She was awarded the 1996 Robert W. Scrivner Award from the Council on Foundations for creative and innovative grantmaking and the National Center for American Indian Enterprise Development's 1996 Jay Silverheels Award. In addition, she was named by *Ms. Magazine* as one of their seven Women of the Year (1997), and in 1998 she was named as one of the top ten Social Entrepreneurs of the Year by *Who Cares* magazine.

Adamson holds a Master's of Science in Economic Development from New Hampshire College in Manchester, New Hampshire, where she teaches a graduate course on indigenous economics within the Community Economic Development Program. She also writes a monthly column for *Indian Country Today* devoted to alternative economic development and other issues.

### Edward Ahenakew (1885–1961)
*Plains Cree minister and author*

Edward Ahenakew was one of the first people to collect and transcribe Cree legends. Born at Sandy Lake in Saskatchewan, Canada, in June 1885, he was named after Edward Matheson, an Anglican missionary who had taught at Sandy Lake. Ahenakew attended the missionary school until he reached the age of eleven, when he was sent to boarding school at Prince Albert, Saskatchewan. Upon graduation, Ahenakew returned to Sandy Lake, where he taught at local mission schools until his acceptance as a ministry candidate at Wycliffe College in Toronto. Throughout his years studying, Ahenakew returned to Saskatchewan during the summers to work in the Diocese of Saskatchewan. He completed his religious studies at the University of Saskatoon in 1912.

Following his ordination, Ahenakew traveled to a mission at Onion Lake, Saskatchewan, to assist Matheson's brother, the Reverend John Matheson, who had fallen ill. Ahenakew proved a vital assistant and friend to John Matheson and remained close to his family after Matheson's death in 1916. In the winter of 1918, a flu epidemic swept the reserves, and Ahenakew resolved to study medicine to help his people. Soon after beginning his new studies, however, Ahenakew himself fell very ill, partly because he had so little money to spend for food.

Ahenakew eventually recovered, but was unable to return to medical school. Instead, he set out to collect and transcribe Cree legends and stories, which were published in 1925 as *Cree Trickster Tales*. Ahenakew also helped to publish a Cree-English dictionary and edited a monthly journal in Cree syllabics. Another collection of Ahenakew's writings, *Voices of the Plains Cree*, was published posthumously in 1974. At the age of seventy-six, Ahenakew died while traveling to Dauphin, Manitoba, to help establish a summer school.

### Freda Ahenakew (1932–)
*Cree scholar*

Freda Ahenakew is a renowned scholar of Cree language and literature, known for her careful transcription and translation of Cree stories and biographies. She was born in 1932 and raised on the Ahtahkakoop Reserve at Sandy Lake in central Saskatchewan. After raising twelve children of her own, Freda Ahenakew became a Cree language teacher. Her formal education includes a bachelor's of education degree from the University of Saskatchewan (1979), and a master's degree in Cree linguistics from the University of Manitoba (1984). She has taught at the Saskatchewan Indian Cultural College (1976–1981) with the Lac La Ronge Band (1979–1980) and the Saskatoon survival school (1980–1981). From 1983 to 1985, she was assistant professor of Native studies at the University of Saskatchewan and later served as associate professor of Native studies at the University of Manitoba and was head of the department from 1990 to 1995.

In addition to technical studies, an introductory book (*Cree Language Studies: A Cree Approach* [1987]), and a series of illustrated children's books, Ahenakew has published several volumes of Cree texts, including *Stories of the House People*, told by Peter Vandall and Joe Duquette (1987). In recent years, Ahenakew has devoted most of her time and energy to the careful transcription, analysis, and translation of traditional stories and autobiographical accounts of Cree people, especially Cree women. She has been preparing such stories and accounts for publication in Cree with English translation. In 1992 Freda Ahenakew received the Citizen of the Year Award from the Federation of

Saskatchewan Indian Nations, a province-wide organization of aboriginal nations aimed at the advancement of aboriginal rights. For her work in education, Ahenahew was appointed in 1998 to the Order of Canada, which recognizes outstanding achievement and service in various fields of human endeavor.

## Martha Aiken (1926–)
*Inupiaq educator and translator*

Martha Aiken is an educator and bilingual curriculum developer of Inupiaq descent. Born at Barrow, Alaska, on 12 July 1926, Martha Aiken is the author of seventeen bilingual books for the North Slope Borough School District in Barrow. She has also translated eighty hymns of the Presbyterian Church and was a major contributor to an Inupiaq dictionary. In the course of this work she also designed and developed an IBM typing element for the Inupiaq language.

Aiken has been a member of the board of the Arctic Slope Regional Corporation and has also served on the Alaska State Committee on Services to the Elderly. She testified at recent hearings on sea mammal hunting, mainly to offer a woman's perspective on these Native traditions. She also volunteered as a cultural consultant for KBRW Broadcasting Company in Barrow. Aiken is active in the movement to preserve Inupiaq language among children and educators and makes public lectures encouraging cultural and linguistic retention.

## Sherman Alexie (1966–)
*Spokane-Coeur d'Alene poet, novelist, and screenwriter*

Sherman Alexie grew up in Wellpinit, Washington, on the Spokane Indian Reservation. Winner of a 1991 Washington State Arts Commission poetry fellowship and a 1992 National Endowment for the Arts poetry fellowship, Alexie has published more than two hundred poems, stories, and translations in publications such as *Another Chicago Magazine, Beloit Poetry Journal, Black Bear Review, Caliban, Journal of Ethnic Studies, New York Quarterly, Red Dirt, Slipstream, ZYZZYVA,* and others.

His first book of poetry and short stories, *The Business of Fancydancing*, was published by Hanging Loose Press in January 1992 and quickly earned a favorable front-page review from *The New York Times Book Review*. This first poetry book was the result of poems and stories written in Alexie's first creative writing workshop at Washington State University in Pullman. Alexie soon published a second collection, *I Would Steal Horses*, which was the winner of Slipstream's

Writer Sherman Alexie.

fifth annual Chapbook Contest in March 1992. In January 1993 he published a third poetry book, *Old Shirts & New Skins* with the UCLA American Indian Studies Center. In 1994, his first collection of short stories, *The Lone Ranger and Tonto Fistfight in Heaven*, was published and received a citation for the PEN/Hemingway Award for Best First Fiction.

In 1995 Alexie won the Before Columbus Foundation's American Book Award and the Murray Morgan Prize for his first novel, *Reservation Blues*. His second novel, *Indian Killer*, published in 1996, was named one of *People Magazine*'s Best of Pages and a *New York Times* Notable Book.

In 1997 Alexie and Chris Eyre, a Cheyenne/Arapaho filmmaker, agreed to collaborate on a film project based on Alexie's short story, "This is What it Means to Say Phoenix, Arizona." Produced by Shadow Catcher Entertainment and released as *Smoke Signals*, the film premiered at the Sundance Film Festival in January 1998, where it won the Audience Award and the Filmmakers Trophy, and was distributed nationwide by Miramax Films.

In June of 1998, he competed in his first World Heavyweight Poetry Bout competition. He went on to win the title the next two years in a row, becoming the first poet to hold the title for three consecutive years. He is the current reigning World Heavyweight Poetry Bout Champion.

Alexie has been widely acknowledged as one of the top writers for the twenty-first century. He resides with his wife and son in Seattle, Washington, and has published fourteen books to date, including his most recent collection of short stories, *The Toughest Indian in the World*, and his newly released poetry collection, *One Stick Song*.

## Paula Gunn Allen (1939–)
*Laguna Pueblo and Sioux novelist, poet, and professor emerita*

Paula Gunn Allen is a distinguished literary figure of mixed ancestry. She was born in Cubero, New Mexico, in 1939. Her father is a Lebanese-American and a former lieutenant-governor of New Mexico, and her mother is Laguna Pueblo on one side and Sioux-Scottish on the other. Thus, she grew up in a multicultural household where Spanish, German, Laguna, English, and Arabic were all spoken and understood. This mixture of ancestry—with all its blessings and difficulties—has been a primary fact of life for Allen and a theme that figures in various writings such as her novel *The Woman Who Owned the Shadows* (1983).

As a scholar and literary critic, Allen has worked to encourage the publication of Native American literature and to educate others about its themes, contexts, and structures. Her book *The Sacred Hoop: Recovering the Feminine in American Indian Traditions* (1986) analyzes the fiction of several Indian writers and has done much to improve understanding of this new literature. She has also introduced the reading public to emergent Native American writers in anthologies such as the award-winning collection *Spider Woman's Granddaughters: Traditional Tales and Contemporary Writing by Native American Women* (1989). These are only a few titles to her credit, as Allen has been an extremely prolific critic and has also published several volumes of poetry.

Allen has won several awards, including fellowships from the National Endowment for the Arts (1978) and the American Indian Studies Program at UCLA (1981), and has also been appointed an associate fellow at the Stanford Humanities Institute. She has served on the faculties at San Francisco State University, the University of New Mexico, the University of California, Berkeley, and the University of California, Los Angeles, until her retirement in 1999.

The mother of three children, Allen is also a dedicated feminist who has stated that her convictions can be traced back to the woman-centered structures of traditional Pueblo society. She has been active consistently in American feminist movements and in antiwar and antinuclear organizations. She is the sister of the Laguna Pueblo writer Carol Lee Sanchez and cousin of the novelist Leslie Marmon Silko. Her most recent publications include *Off the Reservation: Reflections on Boundary-Busting, Border-Crossing Loose Canons* (1998) and *Outfoxing Coyote: Poems*, edited by Allen and Carolyn Dunn (2000).

## Thomas Almojuela (1943–)
*Squamish army officer*

Thomas Almojuela is a retired United States Army Lieutenant Colonel and a member of the Squamish tribe. Born in Seattle, Washington, on 24 April 1943, Almojuela was the first Native American from the Pacific Northwest to graduate from the United States Military Academy at West Point. After attending Olympic College in Washington State, he came to the academy as a congressional appointee and went on to become a member of the dean's honor list at West Point. In addition to these academic honors, Almojuela was also an outstanding athlete who lettered in four sports and was an all-state basketball player two years in a row while attending high school in the Seattle area.

Before his service in Vietnam, Captain Almojuela commanded a tank company in Germany. In Vietnam, he flew the AH1G Cobra gunship and was also in ground combat. His military honors include the Silver Star, two Distinguished Flying Crosses, the Bronze Star, the Air Medal with thirty-three oak clusters, the Army Commendation Medal, the National Defense Medal, the Vietnamese Campaign Medal, and the Combat Infantryman's Badge. He retired in 1992 and is now living in Chile.

## Lori Arviso Alvord (1958–)
*Navajo surgeon*

Lori Arviso Alvord, M.D., is the first Navajo female surgeon. She currently holds the positions of associate dean for student and minority affairs and assistant professor of surgery at Dartmouth Medical School. She is also a practicing general surgeon.

Widely regarded for combining modern medicine with the traditions of her Navajo heritage, Alvord graduated cum laude from Dartmouth and Stanford Medical School (1985), and she trained in surgery at Stanford University Hospital, serving as chief resident in 1990 and 1991. When her training was complete, she worked for the Indian Health Service as general surgeon at the

Gallup Indian Medical Center in Gallup, New Mexico, from 1991 to 1997.

She has served on numerous committees and panels, including the National Committee on Foreign Medical Education and Accreditation, U.S. Department of Education (2000–2001); the Office of Research on Women's Health (ORWH) (1997); the working group for the conference "Beyond Hunt Valley: Research on Women's Health for the Twenty-first Century"; the National Institute of Health (NIH) Task Force on Recruitment and Retention of Women in Clinical Trials, Office of Research on Women's Health (1993); and the NIH Concept Review Panel for the Community Randomized Trial Component of the Women's Health Initiative (1992).

In 1999 Alvord delivered the convocation keynote address at Dartmouth College. She also co-authored a book, with Elizabeth Cohen Van Pelt, entitled *The Scalpel and the Silver Bear: The First Navajo Woman Surgeon Combines Western Medicine and Traditional Healing*, which was published in 1999. Alvord is married to Jonathan Alvord and has two children, Kodiak (Kodi) and Kaitlyn (Katie-bear).

## American Horse (1840–1876)
*Oglala Sioux tribal leader*

In the 1860s and 1870s, American Horse was a Sioux leader in Red Cloud's War, which was fought for control of the Bozeman Trail, a major passage through the present states of Wyoming and Montana. He was a cousin of Red Cloud, another major Sioux leader and, until his death, remained a militant opponent to U.S. settlement of the western Plains.

In the mid-1860s, U.S. settlers and military attempted to build a string of forts along the Bozeman Trail. Settlers and miners had traveled the important passageway illegally since its discovery by John Bozeman in 1863. Much of the trail crossed land that was reserved by treaty for the Sioux and Cheyenne, and from 1866 to 1888 the Sioux and Cheyenne tried to maintain control of the region. American Horse, the son of Smoke, participated in many of the skirmishes and battles of Red Cloud's War.

Despite the temporary land concessions made to Red Cloud in the Fort Laramie Treaty of 1868 and the momentary peace that agreement procured, American Horse remained contentious and militant. In 1870 he accompanied Red Cloud to Washington, D.C., for a meeting with government officials, but diplomatic relations were short-lived. In 1874, after discovery of gold in the Black Hills, an area sacred to the Sioux and located in present-day South Dakota, U.S. miners and speculators streamed into the area. In 1876 American Horse once again took up arms in the fight for the Black Hills and was present at the Battle of the Little Bighorn in 1876.

In September 1876 American Horse took a band of Oglala and Minniconjous southward to present-day South Dakota. Their encampment was attacked by General George Crook. The ensuing Battle of Slim Buttes resulted in the capture of American Horse. Alerted to American Horse's capture, the prominent Sioux leaders Sitting Bull and Gall gathered a rescue party to secure American Horse's release. Although he had been badly wounded from a shot to the abdomen, American Horse refused help from army surgeons. His rescuers were unable to come to his aid or negotiate his release, and American Horse died.

The capture and death of American Horse was one in a series of defeats for the Sioux after the Battle of the Little Bighorn and foreshadowed the Sioux surrender in 1877.

## Jack Iyerak Anawak (1950–)
*Inuit minister and member of Parliament*

The Honorable Jack Anawak is a member of Parliament for Rankin Inlet North and minister of Community Government and Transportation of Nunavut. Born in 1950 in a tent on the Arctic Circle near Repulse Bay to Donat and Margaret Anawak, Jack Anawak was later adopted by Lionel Angotingoar and Phillipa Piova. Raised on the land, Anawak acquired all the traditional Inuit survival skills before attending school in Chesterfield Inlet and Churchill, Northwest Territories. He went on to undertake business management certificate coursework from the Western Canada Co-op College in Saskatoon, Saskatchewan.

After completing his studies, Anawak combined a successful business career with public service. During the 1970s and 1980s, he held a number of high-profile positions in the business community in the Northwest Territories, including the executive director of the Keewatin Chamber of Commerce in Rankin Inlet and the chief executive officer of the hamlet of Repulse Bay. For four years in the 1980s, Anawak was the president and owner of Kivalliq Consulting, Management, and Training Services, Ltd., in Rankin Inlet. Anawak also served as mayor of the hamlet of Rankin Inlet in 1985 and 1986, sitting on numerous committees, including the Repulse Bay Education Committee. He sat on the boards of several organizations devoted to northern economic development, including the Federal Native Economic Development Board. In November 1988, Anawak was elected to the Canadian House of Commons in Ottawa and was appointed in 1989 the official opposition critic for northern affairs. Anawak was still a member of the House of Commons in April 1997, when he accepted the position of interim commissioner to oversee the creation of a territorial government for Nunavut. His term as interim commissioner expired when Nunavut gained territorial status in April 1999.

## Owanah Anderson (1926–)
*Choctaw administrator and author*

Born in Choctaw County, Oklahoma, on 18 February 1926, Owanah Anderson has been an important advocate for advancing the status of American Indian women, especially in the areas of business and media. She was a member of President Carter's Advisory Committee on Women from 1978 to 1981 and chaired the National Committee on Indian Work of the Episcopal Church in 1979 and 1980. She has also served on the Health, Education, and Welfare Advisory Committee on Rights and Responsibilities of Women.

Anderson founded the Ohoyo Resource Center in 1979. Ohoyo means "woman" in Choctaw, and this organization is a women's employment network service, which, among others things, produces national

Owanah Anderson.

directories of Native American women with professional skills in various areas. She also served as project director with National Women's Program Development, Incorporated, in Wichita Falls, Texas. She is chair and interim volunteer executive director of the Indigenous Theological Training Institute of North America, Incorporated.

Anderson was a recipient of the Ann Roe Howard Award from the Graduate School of Education at Harvard University (1981). She has authored *Resource Guide of American Indian and Alaska Native Women* (1980) and *400 Years: Anglican/Episcopal Mission Among American Indians* (1997). She retired in 1998.

## Mary Ann Martin Andreas (1945–)
*Cahuilla/Serrano political leader and activist*

Having been elected tribal chair of the Morongo Band of Mission Indians four times, Mary Ann Andreas has become an effective leader on both state and federal fronts in the battle to protect tribal sovereignty and American Indian interests.

Born Mary Ann Eileen Martin in Soboba, California, to John Martin and Marjorie Saubel in 1945, Andreas grew up on the Morongo Reservation, located at the foot of the San Gorgonio Mountains, just west of Palm Springs. Formerly named the Malki Reservation, Morongo was named after Andreas' great-grandfather, Captain John Morongo, a tribal leader who was fluent in five languages. She is a member of the Coyote Clan.

In 1963 Andreas graduated from high school in Banning, California, and soon after moved to the San Francisco Bay Area under the federal government's relocation program. She stayed in northern California for eight years, during which time she attended Heald Business College.

When she returned home, she became involved in tribal politics. She became active, participating in the housing commission, the scholarship commission, and the enrollment committee, just to name a few. Soon she was elected chair, and the tribe has experienced great economic success since her election.

As chairwoman, Andreas worked closely with her tribal council to oversee the growth of Casino Morongo, one of the most successful gaming operations in California. What started as a modest bingo hall in 1983 now hosts more than 3,000 guests each day and is the largest employer in the region.

During Andreas' tenure as chairwoman, welfare and unemployment have been eliminated on her reservation. She also uses her status to speak out on the importance of her people's traditions and cultural beliefs. While some Cahuilla and Serrano words and concepts are no longer known, Andreas believes that the tribe must cling to their traditions harder than ever. She focuses on children's cultural development and teaches the importance of understanding both tribal and non-Indian worlds.

She also became a media spokeswoman for Proposition 5, the ballot measure overwhelmingly passed by California in a landslide victory in 1998. Featured in the campaign's television commercials, she works countless hours educating state, national, and international reporters and helped to organize grassroots get-out-the-vote efforts.

To reinforce the importance of tribal self-government, Andreas and her council issued the Morongo Sovereignty Bar, a unique chocolate bar with a label explaining the importance of Indian self-sufficiency. The bars are passed out to legislators as well as to children across the country as a teaching tool. Other tribes from throughout the United States write to the Morongo tribe to request donations of the Sovereignty Bar for educational and political events.

In more than two decades as a tribal leader Andreas has received many awards and honors. In 1998 she received the California National Indian Gaming Association Award for Tribal Leader of the Year, and in 2000 Andreas was named California's Woman of the Year by the state's lieutenant governor. She also recently became the first member of her tribe to attend Harvard University where she completed a special studies program for senior executives in local and state governments.

## Anne (Queen Anne) (d. 1725)
*Powhatan tribal leader*

As a Powhatan leader, Anne was a forceful defender of her people's rights. Anne's husband Totopotomoi had allied himself with Virginia colonists to fight an alliance of inland tribes. Upon his death in battle about 1655, Anne assumed leadership of her husband's band. She and her people lived at the junction of the Pamunkey and Mattapony rivers in present-day Virginia. This land was under the jurisdiction of the Powhatan Confederacy, a large Indian confederacy whose power had significantly declined by the 1670s.

Anne played a pivotal role in the Virginia Colony's internal dispute known as Bacon's Rebellion, after Nathaniel Bacon who, in the mid-1670s, tried to overthrow the Virginia colonial government. In 1675, the governor of the colony, William Berkeley, came to Anne for military assistance. With her son at her side, Anne addressed the Virginia legislators and responded to their request for aid. She chastised the surprised body for neglecting her people after her own husband had given his life in defense of the colony. Only after the colony promised to redress these grievances did Anne offer the services of her warriors. After the rebellion, the Virginia government proclaimed her "Queen of Pamunkey." She remained a forceful advocate for her people in negotiations with the Virginia colonists during her rule. In 1715 Anne again addressed the Virginia legislature and outlined the interests of her people within the Virginia Colony.

## Will Antell (1935–)
*Chippewa trustee and educator*

Will Antell is currently a trustee for the Minnesota State colleges and universities, the fifth largest higher education system in the United States. The board has policy responsibility for system planning, academic programs, fiscal management, personnel, admissions requirements, tuition and fees, and rules and regulations.

Born on the White Earth Reservation in Minnesota on 2 October 1935, Antell attended Bemidji State College in Minnesota, where he received a bachelor's of science degree, Mankato State College in Minnesota, where he received a master's of science, Northern

Will Antell.

Michigan University, and St. Cloud State University of Minnesota, where he received his doctorate in education in 1973.

Early in his career, Antell was a teacher of social sciences at the high school level and a human relations consultant for the state of Minnesota. He has also taught courses on Native American culture and history and he recently retired from the Minnesota Department of Children and Families.

Besides his activities as a professional consultant in the field of education, Antell has served on numerous boards and commissions relating to Indian affairs and has been a lecturer at the Harvard Graduate School of Education, St. Mary's University (Halifax, Nova Scotia), and Wisconsin State University. He also has several publications to his credit, including *American Indian Leadership Training Programs* (1974) and *Culture, Psychological Characteristics, and Socio-Economic Status in Educational Program Development for Native Americans* (1974).

He is the owner of Antell Companies, a consulting firm and insurance agency specializing in service to the American Indian community.

### Paul Apodaca (1951–)
*Navajo scholar and artist*

Paul Apodaca was born in Los Angeles, California, of Navajo, Mexican Indian (Mixton), and Spanish descent. Apodaca is currently associated with Chapman University as a professor of American studies in the Social Sciences Division. He has taught for Cal State Fullerton (CSUF), University of California, Irvine (UCI), and is a visiting professor at the University of California, Los Angeles (UCLA). For seventeen years, Apodaca served with the Bowers Museum, the largest museum in Orange County, California, as an exhibiting artist, artist-in-residence, curator of the Native American art, folk art, and California history collections, and contributing writer and illustrator for Bowers Museum Press publications including *Images of Power*. He is a member of the Autry Museum of Western Heritage Native Voices Advisory Board and a consultant for the Smithsonian Institution National Museum of the American Indian. The state of California hired Apodaca to design state-funded arts programs and to develop a new administrative plan for the California State Indian Museum.

Apodaca works with many arts and academic agencies and funders including the California Arts Council (CAC), the California Council for the Humanities (CCH), the Arizona Commission on the Arts, the Los Angeles Cultural Affairs Department, the Corporation for Public Broadcasting, the National Endowment for the

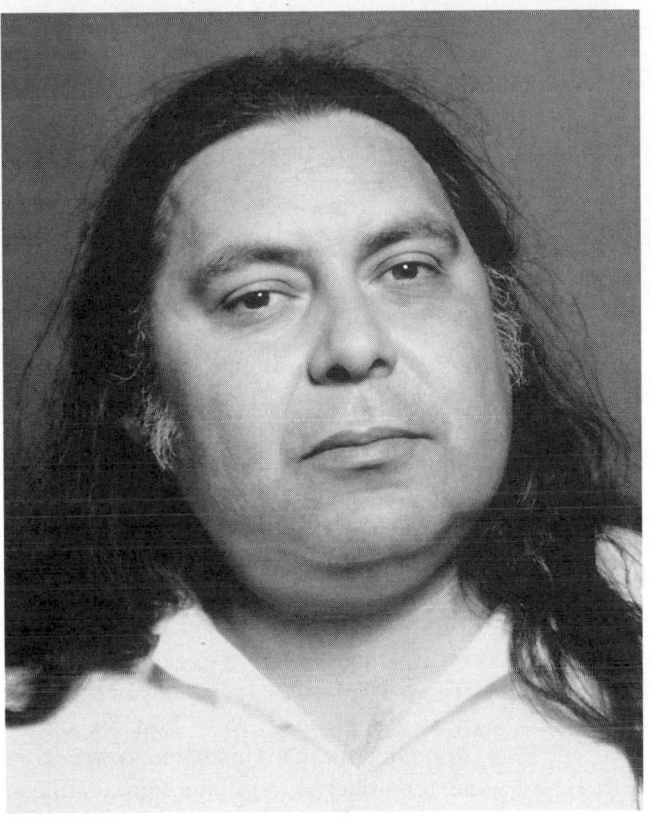

Paul Apodaca.

Humanities (NEH), and the Fulbright Senior Scholar Program. His work includes consultations for Knott's Berry Farm in Buena Park, California, the Disney Imagineering Group, and Universal Pictures. In 1990, Apodaca worked as committee member and consultant for the Los Angeles Festival as well as master of ceremonies for the Pacific Rim arts and culture event. He is the book review editor for *News From Native California*, teacher-consultant for the Scott-Foresman textbook, *California—Our State, Its History*, and the editor of the *Journal of California and Great Basin Anthropology*. He writes articles and museum exhibition reviews for the *Journal of American Anthropology* and the *Chronicle of Higher Education*.

Throughout his career, Apodaca has been honored with numerous awards and grants including the Smithsonian Institution Minority Museum Professional Fellowship, the Orange County Human Rights Award, and the Daughters of the American Revolution Mary Smith Lockwood Medal for Education. He was part of a team that won the Academy Award for the 1985 feature documentary, *Broken Rainbow* which helped stop the forced relocation of Navajo and Hopi families. The California State Legislature adopted an 8,000-year-old stone carving of a bear found in San Diego County as an official state symbol, recognizing California's indigenous population in response to efforts made by Apodaca, Jon Erickson of UCI, and Henry Koerper of Cypress College.

Apodaca received a master's degree in American Indian studies and a doctorate in folklore and mythology from UCLA. Chancellor Charles Young presented Apodaca with the UCLA Alumni Outstanding Graduate Student Medal in 1995.

### Raymond "Ray" Duran Apodaca (1946–)
*Ysleta del Sur Pueblo Tribe of Texas administrator*

Raymond Apodaca is currently employed as Temporary Assistance to Needy Families' tribal team leader and executive officer for the Division of Tribal Services, Administration for Children and Families, U.S. Department of Health and Human Services. He also serves on the board of directors for the Indian Law Resource Center. He once served as executive director of the Texas Indian Commission, an agency of the state of Texas. Born at Las Cruces, New Mexico, on 15 October 1946, Apodaca obtained his bachelor's degree (1969) and a master's degree in public administration (1976) from New Mexico State University. In the period after graduating and before returning to the university for advanced studies, he served in the United States Air Force from 1969 to 1972.

Apodaca's interests include history, government, theology, and education, and he is the author of *Directory of Information on Health Careers for American Indians* (1977). Apodaca has been an active member of several advisory boards, committees, and other organizations over the years, including the National Indian Education Association, the National Congress of American Indians, the North American Indian Museums Association, and the Texas State Committee on the Protection of Human Remains and Sacred Objects. He was the national president of the Governors' Interstate Indian Council in 1985 and 1986.

### Anna Mae Aquash (1945–1976)
*Micmac activist*

Anna Mae Aquash, nee Pictou, a Micmac Indian from Nova Scotia, Canada, was active in the American Indian Movement (AIM), an organization aimed at advancing the rights of Indian people in North America. Originally formed in 1968 to address the problems of Indian people living in urban areas, the organization quickly expanded to address issues surrounding housing, education, and treaty rights. In the early 1970s, AIM became involved in events on the Pine Ridge Reservation in South Dakota, home to approximately 14,000 Oglala Sioux and mixed-blood Indians. Charges of corruption had been leveled against the Pine Ridge Tribal Council, and AIM members, together with members of the reservation committed to the impeachment of the tribal chairman Richard Wilson, occupied the town of Wounded Knee, located within the Pine Ridge Reservation. Wounded Knee is identified in American Indian history as the 1890 site at which an estimated three hundred Indian men, women, and children were massacred by federal cavalry as they were surrendering their arms. Although the 1973 siege resulted in a negotiated settlement, AIM's occupation of the town also ended in tragedy. Two Indians were killed by government fire.

Anna Mae Aquash was born and raised by her mother, Mary Ellen Pictou, on a Micmac Reserve five miles outside the town of Shubenacadie, Nova Scotia. The Micmac people traditionally have occupied lands located in eastern Canada. After attending school in Nova Scotia, Aquash left her reserve and lived in Boston for several years, where she had two children, became involved in political causes aimed at improving the life of urban Indians, and worked at a low-income day care center. In Boston, she met Nogeeshik Aquash, a Chippewa artist from Ontario, and in 1973, they traveled to Wounded Knee to show solidarity with AIM. They married in Wounded Knee in April 1973 in a traditional Sioux ceremony. Their marriage lasted little more than a year, and Anna Mae became increasingly involved in AIM's activities.

In 1975 the Pine Ridge Reservation again was the site of a confrontation between AIM and federal authorities. Two FBI agents were killed. Anna Mae was found dead five months later, her body abandoned in a field on the Pine Ridge Reservation. According to autopsy reports, she died from a bullet wound to the head. This homicide has not been solved.

### Dave Leon Archambault (contemporary)
*Standing Rock Sioux educational administrator*

Dave Archambault is the former president of Standing Rock College in Fort Yates, North Dakota. He obtained his bachelor's degree in secondary education from Black Hills State College in South Dakota (1976) and went on to complete the master's program in educational administration at Pennsylvania State University in 1982. Archambault's major interest is educational reform, and his master's research focused on ways of changing kindergarten through twelfth-grade curricula to better meet the needs of Indian learners.

On completing his graduate studies, he became a principal at Little Wound School in Kyle, South Dakota, and served in this capacity for eight years. He later became acting recreation director at United Tribes Technical College in Bismarck, North Dakota.

Archambault has been active in many public service boards and organizations, including the American Indian Higher Education Consortium and the North Dakota Humanities Council. He has also won several awards, particularly in the area of athletics; he was named South Dakota Cross Country Coach of the Year (1980), South Dakota Indian Educator of the Year (1982), and National Indian Basketball Coach of the Year (1980).

### Joallyn Archambault (1942–)
*Standing Rock Sioux anthropologist, administrator, and artist*

Joallyn Archambault is director of the American Indian Program, an outreach program to Indian communities established by the National Museum of Natural History, Smithsonian Institution, Washington, D.C.

Born in Claremore, Oklahoma, on 13 February 1942, Archambault received her bachelor's (1970), master's (1971), and doctoral (1984) degrees at the University of California, Berkeley, in anthropology.

Her primary scholarly interests are in the areas of art and material culture, modern social movements, political systems, ethnic relations, and patronage systems. Her dissertation was entitled "The Gallup Ceremonial: A Study of Patronage within a Contemporary Context of Indian-White Relations."

Archambault held several teaching positions early in her career, serving on the faculties at the University of California, Berkeley (1976–1979); California College of Arts and Crafts (1979–1983); California State University, Hayward, and the University of Wisconsin at Milwaukee (1983–1986). She was a research associate for the Center of Race, Crime, and Social Policy at Cornell University (1980–1982) and a field ethnographer for the Sonoma State Foundation in Rohnert Park, California (1983–1984). Archambault became director of American Indian Programs at the Smithsonian Institution in 1986.

She has given many conference papers and organized conference sessions on a wide variety of topics. Most recently, she won a Smithsonian Scholarly Studies Fellowship and an America in Berlin fellowship, which allowed her to conduct research on early Plains ethnographic collections in German museums.

As program director, she has organized numerous outreach activities that served tribal priorities and hosted many individual Indian researchers at the National Museum of Natural History. She organized the first professional organization for American Indian anthropologists and the Ella Deloria Award for Indian graduate students of anthropology.

Besides her academic accomplishments, Archambault received many awards as an artist and her work is part of the permanent collections at the Navajo Tribal Museum, the Indian Arts and Crafts Board, the Red Cloud Cultural Center, the Gilcrease Museum, and other private collections.

### Annette Arkeketa (1958–)
*Otoe-Missouria/Creek poet, playwright, journalist, and scriptwriter*

Annette Arkeketa is currently working on her master's in interdisciplinary studies at Texas A;M University. Arkeketa is a poet and playwright whose work is widely anthologized. She is the author of a book of poems, *The Terms of a Sister*, published in 1997. She received the Wordcraft Circle Award for Playwright of the Year (1998) for her play *HOKTI*, which has been performed by the Tulsa Indian Actors' Workshop in Tulsa, Oklahoma, and at Haskell Indian Nations University. Arkeketa has taught playwriting at Cornell University, Truman State University, Kansas University, and

Writer Annette Arkeketa.

Red Mesa High School. She participates in numerous community activities: she is a board member for the Native American arts organization ATLATL, a caucus member for Wordcraft Circle of Native Writers and Storytellers, president of the Literary Guild at Texas A;M, and a member of Sigma Tau Delta. In 2000 she was presented with a Wordcraft Circle Award for *Mentor of the Year.*

Arkeketa is daughter to Benjamin Arkeketa (Buffalo Clan) and Mary E. Freeman-Arkeketa (Tiger Clan). She is married with three children and one granddaughter.

## Ruth Arrington (1924–)
*Creek scholar and administrator*

Ruth Arrington has been a major influence in advancing cultural awareness and educational importance among young Indian people. She was professor of speech and coordinator of Indian studies at Northeastern Oklahoma State University in Tahlequah, Oklahoma, until her retirement in 1988.

Born in Tulsa, Oklahoma, on 15 October 1924, Arrington received her doctorate in speech from Louisiana State University in 1971. She produced and directed an influential film entitled *The American Indian and His Government* and has also published numerous professional articles and reviews. Arrington was named Outstanding Oklahoma Woman of the Year by the Oklahoma Federation of Indian Women in 1972, and served as a member of the Oklahoma Indian Affairs Commission from 1982 until 1987.

## John H. Artichoker (1930–)
*Winnebago and Oglala Sioux educator and administrator*

John H. Artichoker is an educator and administrator who dedicated his career to helping young Indian people complete their college education. He was born in Pine Ridge, South Dakota, on 17 January 1930. Artichoker received his bachelor's and master's degrees in education from the University of South Dakota.

His first professional position was as director of Indian education for the state of South Dakota and he later served as tribal affairs chairman for the Bureau of Indian Affairs and the United States Public Health Service. He served as superintendent of the Northern Cheyenne Agency in Montana and of the Colorado Indian Agency, in both cases bringing extensive development programs to rural Indian communities.

Over the years, Artichoker has conducted much research on the special problems of Native American college students, and the results appear in his publication *The Sioux Indian Goes to College* (1959).

## Atironta (seventeenth century)
*Huron tribal leader*

Three chiefs of the Ahrendarrhonon (Rock) Nation—one of five nations that comprised the Huron confederacy (the others being the Attignawantan [Bear], Attigneenongnahac [Cord], Tahontaenrat [Deer], and the Ataronchronon [Beyond the Silted Lake] Nations)—bore the name Atironta in the seventeenth century, following the Huron custom of resurrecting the name of a deceased chief. The first was a chief of a village near what has become Hawkstone, Ontario. The village is said to have consisted of over two hundred longhouses. According to many scholars, Atironta had been the first Indian chief to make contact with Samuel de Champlain, a French voyager and administrator known in Quebec as the Father of New France. When Champlain sailed up the St. Lawrence River into what is now the Province of Quebec in 1611, he reportedly was met by Atironta and a party of Huron at the Lachine Rapids just west of Montreal and presented with strings of beads from each of the Huron tribes and a beaver pelt from each of the chiefs in the confederacy. Relations between the French and the Huron, which developed into a historic alliance for war and trade, thereafter became the special responsibility of Atironta.

In 1615 Atironta participated in a war party of Huron and Algonkian led by Champlain in an attack on an Iroquois village south of Lake Ontario. On the return journey, Atironta shared a cabin and provisions with Champlain. The next summer, Champlain brought Atironta to Quebec City, where he was entertained and referred to as the "host" of the French people.

## Carolyn L. Attneave (1920–1992)
*Delaware and Cherokee psychologist*

Carolyn Attneave was a professor of psychology and a noted authority on the cross-cultural adaptation of mental health services for Native Americans of the United States and Canada.

Born in El Paso, Texas, on 2 July 1920, Attneave obtained her doctorate in psychology from Stanford University in 1952. Over the years, she worked as a consultant to numerous tribal and urban mental health programs. She was the president of the American Indian Psychologists from 1978 to 1980 and was also an expert witness in federal and state legislative hearings on Indian child custody cases. She was a professor of psychology and adjunct professor of psychiatry and behavioral sciences at the University of Seattle.

Attneave advocated women's rights and educational equity. During World War II, while serving as a naval officer, she developed curricula and training programs for women. She later served on the National Advisory Council on Women's Educational Programs (1980–1981) and was also a campus ombudsman for sexual harassment cases (1978–1981). She produced numerous publications, including the *Bibliography of North American Indians in Mental Health* (1982).

### Awashonks (ca. 1670s)
*Wampanoag tribal leader*

In 1675, when the so-called King Philip's War broke out between New England colonists and the Wampanoag Confederacy, an alliance of Algonkian-speaking nations living in present-day New England, Awashonks was the leader of the Saconnet Indian Band of the Wampanoag Confederacy living near present-day Little Comptom, Rhode Island. It is believed that Awashonks's husband, Tolony, died before the outbreak of the war, and the Saconnet chose Awashonks to succeed her husband as leader.

It appears that Awashonks was initially undecided about which side to support during the war. The Wampanoag Confederacy was led by Metacom, whom the colonists called King Philip. A number of Awashonks's warriors joined King Philip's forces early in the conflict. It is believed, however, that Awashonks was persuaded to side with the colonists after a meeting with Benjamin Church, a colonial militia officer who led the British forces in the conflict against Metacom. Awashonks lent more than her moral support. A number of Saconnet warriors, including Awashonks's son Peter, joined with the colonists. The colonial recruitment of Indian groups, including warriors, during the war was a significant factor in King Philip's eventual defeat. During the war, Awashonks took her people to a safe haven in Sandwich, Massachusetts. After the conflict, and Metacom's defeat, Awashonks remained an ally of Church. According to colonial records she met often with Church and the two became friends.

### Elgin Bad Wound (1946–)
*Oglala Sioux educator*

Elgin Bad Wound, whose Sioux name is Tasunke Kokipapi, is an educator and former president of Oglala Lakota College. Born on the Pine Ridge Reservation in South Dakota on 19 April 1946, Elgin Bad Wound was raised in his tribal community and graduated first in his class from Pine Ridge High School in 1965. He joined the army and served in Vietnam from 1969 until 1971. On returning home, Bad Wound went to work as an adult education instructor at Oglala Lakota College on the Pine Ridge Reservation from 1972 to 1975. Deciding then on a career in education, he obtained his bachelor's degree in secondary education from Black Hills State University (1977) and a master's degree in higher education from the University of Colorado (1978). He then returned home and took over the leadership of Oglala Lakota College, serving as the vice-president from 1978 to 1979 and as president from 1979 until 1986.

At that point Bad Wound returned to school again and completed the doctoral program in higher education at Pennsylvania State University (1990). While he was still a graduate student, he worked on a Ford Foundation research project to examine the factors contributing to the success of Native American students in transferring from local, tribally controlled colleges to major colleges and universities. He became a member of Phi Delta Kappa (PDK), a professional education fraternity, and was one of two winners of the 1988 Kozak Memorial Fellowship, an award presented each year to PDK graduate students demonstrating the highest potential for research, teaching, and public service. He published *Teaching to Empower: Tribal Colleges Must Promote Leadership and Self-Determination in Their Reservations* in 1990.

Since returning to the Pine Ridge area, Bad Wound has been even more actively involved in a variety of other community service programs. He has received awards and recognition for his distinguished scholarship and dedicated public service.

### Louis W. Ballard (Honganozhe) (1931–)
*Quapaw and Cherokee composer and educator*

Louis Ballard is the first person to hold the position of Distinguished Professor of Music at William Jewell College in Liberty, Missouri. As the preeminent Native American composer of classical music, Ballard's innovative music curriculum guides and cultural resources are widely used in public schools, colleges, and universities. He earned his bachelor of arts, bachelor of music education, and master of music degrees from the University of Tulsa and studied privately with Darius Milhaud and Mario Castel-Nuovo Tedesco in Hollywood. He received numerous awards for his musical contributions and an honorary doctorate from the College of Santa Fe.

As a contemporary and classical composer, Ballard expanded the percussion and orchestral vocabulary of western music while introducing and integrating new

Composer and flutist Louis Ballard.

idioms of Native American expression to the concert hall. He collected Indian songs from various tribes in continental North America, and was inspired to create his own original style for piano preludes, chamber music, symphonic, and other classical forms. He wrote the first American Indian ballet (*Koshare* ), which premiered in Barcelona, Spain, in 1966 and was first presented in the United States in 1967. His ballet *The Four Moons* also premiered in 1967, and in 1969 he won the Marion Nevins MacDowell Award for the chamber ensemble composition, *Ritmo Indio*.

He was honored as the first American composer to present a concert of his own music in the new Beethoven-House Chamber Music Hall adjoining Beethoven's birthplace in Bonn, Germany. Ballard is also an educator and has written classroom materials aimed at helping all singers and students reinforce musical skills through mastery of tribal songs. He is perhaps the first composer to develop a philosophy of ethnic music education. He was the first dean of the music department at the Institute of American Indian Arts in Santa

Fe, New Mexico. In his own words, "It is not enough to acknowledge that American Indian music is different from other music and that the Indian, somehow, 'marches to a different drum,' as a way of paying obeisance to the unique culture of our Native American people. What is needed in America is an awakening and re-orienting of our total spiritual and cultural perspective to embrace, understand, and learn from the aboriginal American what it is that motivates his musical and artistic impulses."

### Dennis J. Banks (Nowacumig) (1932–)
*Anishinaabe activist*

Dennis Banks was born on the Leech Lake Indian Reservation in northern Minnesota. In 1968 he founded the American Indian Movement (AIM), which was established to protect the traditional ways of Indian people and to engage in legal cases protecting treaty rights of Natives, such as treaty and aboriginal rights to hunt and fish, trap, and gather wild rice.

AIM has been quite successful in bringing Native American issues to the public. Among other activities, AIM members participated in the occupation of Alcatraz Island, where demands were made that all federal surplus property be returned to Indian control. In 1972 AIM organized and led the Trail of Broken Treaties Caravan across the United States to Washington, D.C., calling attention to the plight of Native Americans. The refusal of congressional leaders to meet with the Trail of Broken Treaties delegation led to the 1972 takeover of the Bureau of Indian Affairs offices in the nation's capital.

Under the leadership of Banks, AIM led a protest in Custer, South Dakota, in 1973 against the judicial process that found a non-Indian innocent of murdering an Indian. As a result of his involvement in the 71-day occupation of Wounded Knee, South Dakota, in 1973, and his activities at Custer, Banks and 300 others were arrested. Banks was acquitted of charges stemming from his participation in the Wounded Knee takeover, but was convicted of riot and assault stemming from the confrontation at Custer. Refusing to serve time in prison, Banks went underground but later received amnesty from Governor Jerry Brown of California.

Between 1976 and 1983, Banks earned an associate of arts degree at the University of California, Davis, and taught at D-Q University (an Indian-controlled institution), where he became the first American Indian university chancellor. In the spring of 1979, he taught at Stanford University in Palo Alto, California.

After Governor Brown left office, Banks received sanctuary on the Onondaga Reservation in upstate New

York in 1984. While living there, Banks organized the Great Jim Thorpe Run from New York City to Los Angeles. This spiritual run ended in Los Angeles, where the Jim Thorpe Memorial Games were held and where the gold medals that Thorpe had previously won in the 1912 Olympic games were restored to the Thorpe family.

In 1985 Banks left the Onondaga Reservation to surrender to law enforcement officials in South Dakota, and served eighteen months in prison. When released, he worked as a drug and alcohol counselor on the Pine Ridge Reservation in South Dakota. Banks was active in passing laws in Kentucky and Indiana against desecration of Indian graves and human remains. He organized reburial ceremonies for over 1,200 Indian grave sites that were disturbed by grave-robbers in Uniontown, Kentucky.

In 1988 Banks organized and led a spiritual run called the Sacred Run from New York to San Francisco, and then across Japan from Hiroshima to Hakkaido. Also in 1988, his autobiography *Sacred Soul* was published in Japan, and won the 1988 Non-fiction Book of the Year Award. In 1994, in order to bring attention to Native issues, Banks led the four-month Walk for Justice from Alcatraz Island in San Francisco to Washington, D.C.

Bank's autobiography, *The Longest Walk* was published in 1997. He played roles in several movies, including *War Party*, *The Last of the Mohicans*, and *Thunderheart*. Banks stays involved in American Indian issues, lecturing, teaching, and sharing his experiences.

## Thomas Banyacya Sr. (1910–1999)
*Hopi tribal and spiritual leader*

Thomas Banyacya Sr. was a Hopi elder and traditionalist who spoke out against the relocation of the Navajo and other possible effects of U.S. Public Law 93531, which mandated that the Navajo be relocated, ostensibly so that the land could be returned to the Hopi. The Hopi are a Pueblo tribe whose Native territory is located in northeastern Arizona.

Born in the village of New Oraibi around 1910, Banyacya was one of four young men chosen by Hopi elders in 1948 to be their "ears and tongue"; that is, they were selected as interpreters to tell the outside world of certain direful warnings contained in the ancient Hopi prophecies. According to Banyacya, the depredations of the Americans and their ultimate self-destruction were all revealed ages ago in certain traditional Hopi prophecies. The prophecies mentioned a "gourdful of ashes" (the atomic bomb), predicting the world would end in a global explosion or "purification" unless human beings changed their destructive ways and prayed to the Great Spirit.

Banyacya was the last surviving member of the group, and in recent years he became recognized as a major spokesman for the traditionalist viewpoint on controversial issues, such as the future of a huge expanse of land in the area of Black Mesa in northeast Arizona.

The Hopi-Navajo Land Dispute involves an area of 1.8 million acres of high desert plateau where Navajo herders have lived on little-used Hopi land for generations. In 1972, the Congress passed Public Law 93531, which involved the forced removal of more than ten thousand Navajo and the erection of a barbed wire fence 285 miles long.

When the Navajo protested during the 1970s, many others joined them, including Hopi traditionalists such as Thomas Banyacya and his son, Thomas Banyacya Jr. The Banyacyas and others believe that the government is mainly interested in clearing the land so that puppet tribal councils can be established and mining companies can gain access to the area's immense deposits of coal, uranium, and oil shale.

## Barboncito (1820–1871)
*Navajo tribal leader*

In the 1860s, under government orders the U.S. military with the government's backing tried to resettle or exterminate the Navajo. Barboncito, along with Delgadito (his brother) and Manuelito, led the Navajo resistance from 1863 to 1866.

Barboncito was born at Canyon de Chelly in present-day Arizona. He was both a military and religious Navajo leader. In 1846, Barboncito signed a treaty pledging friendship with the United States. Peace would soon become impossible. In the early 1860s the U.S. military waged an ongoing mixed campaign of warfare and negotiation to halt Apache and Navajo raids on U.S. settlements in the Southwest. The raids were a response to settler encroachment on Indian land. One important area of contention was the grazing lands around Fort Defiance located in present-day eastern Arizona. In 1860, after soldiers shot a number of Navajo horses, Barboncito and Manuelito led Navajo warriors in retaliation against the soldiers at Fort Defiance. After nearly taking the fort, the Indians were pushed back into their mountain strongholds. Stalemated, U.S. military leaders and Indians agreed to a short-lived peace council.

In early 1862, Barboncito made peace overtures, but these efforts were short-lived. That year, the military chose a barren parcel of land located in present-day eastern New Mexico, called Bosque Redondo, as a Navajo relocation site. The relocation plans pushed Barboncito into open warfare with the United States. In 1864 at Canyon de Chelly, Barboncito was taken prisoner by soldiers commanded by Colonel Kit Carson. He was taken to the relocation camp at Bosque Redondo, where living conditions could barely sustain survival. In 1865, Barboncito rejoined Manuelito after escaping with about five hundred followers. He later surrendered and in 1868, Barboncito signed a treaty that established the Navajo Reservation in present-day New Mexico and Arizona. The Navajo leader died three years later.

## Jim Barnes (1933–)
*Choctaw poet, translator, and university professor*

Jim Barnes is a poet and translator of Choctaw descent. Born near the San Bois Mountains in eastern Oklahoma in 1933, Barnes migrated to Oregon in 1951 and worked as a lumberjack there until 1960. He then returned to Oklahoma and entered Southeastern Oklahoma State University, where he majored in English, French, and drama, receiving his bachelor's in 1964. He

Jim Barnes.

later earned his master's degree and a doctorate in comparative literature from the University of Arkansas.

Barnes began writing fiction and poetry in the 1950s and began publishing in the 1960s. Professor Barnes has published numerous books of poetry, criticism, fiction, and translations (from German and French). His poems have also appeared in numerous anthologies, most notably *Carriers of the Dream Wheel: Contemporary Native American Poetry* (1975) and *Heartland II: Poets of the Midwest* (1975). Barnes continues to be a prolific writer. He wrote an autobiography entitled *On Native Ground: Memoirs and Impression,* and published *Paris: Poems* in 1998.

In 1978, he was awarded a fellowship for poetry by the National Endowment for the Arts, and in 1980 the Translation Center at Columbia University awarded him a prize for his translation of a volume of poetry by the German Dagmar Nick. He has won an Oklahoma Book Award and an American Book Award. He is currently editor of *The Chariton Review* and professor of comparative literature at Northeast Missouri State University.

## Irene Bedard (1967–)
*Inupiat/Cree Actress*

Born in Anchorage, Alaska, Bedard became interested in acting young in life. Convincing the neighborhood children to perform the Beatles' *Yellow Submarine* and other such skits, Bedard heard her calling early. Since then the actress has performed in many highly regarded films including *Smoke Signals* and *Grand Avenue.*

Bedard grew up visiting and participating in potlatches and powwows as a youngster. Her father was politically active during Bedard's youth, and her family insured that she was knowledgeable about her heritage. After studying at a Pennsylvania College for a few years, where she majored in physics and philosophy, Bedard transferred to the University of the Arts in Philadelphia. She changed her major to theater and graduated.

Although she thought she would work in theater her entire life, she was introduced to television and film when Disney offered her a role in its 1994 movie *Squanto: A Warrior's Tale.* Bedard played Squanto's wife in the movie opposite Adam Beach. The same year she also starred in *Lakota Woman: Siege at Wounded Knee,* a Turner Network Television (TNT) movie based on the autobiography of Mary Crow Dog, which chronicles one woman's journey through the 1973 occupation of Wounded Knee.

While on location in Nova Scotia filming *Squanto*, Bedard and her husband Dennis Wilson were married on the movie's set. Her husband grew up in Ohio, but spent part of his childhood in the Southern California area. He is a musician and the couple moved to Ojai when they returned from the shoot.

Since her debut on-screen acting performances, Bedard has been busy working on several film and television projects. Among these projects are *Pocahontas* (1995), for which she performed the voice for the film's title character (she also provided the voice for the movie's sequel); *Grand Avenue* (1996), a HBO movie based on the book by Greg Sarris; *Smoke Signals* (1998), based on a short story by author Sherman Alexie; *Naturally Native* (1998), a movie describing the trials of three California Indian women searching for their identity; and *Tortilla Heaven* (2000), a film based on a New Mexican myth.

Bedard still dabbles in theater performance and founded her own theater company, Chukalukoli Theater Ensemble. In fact, she has written a play for the group entitled *Point Hope*. In addition, Bedard formed a production company titled The Half Moon. Among other projects, the company is involved with film score production.

Bedard has received numerous awards for her performances. She accepted the American Indian Film Festival's Best Supporting Actress Award for her role as Suzy Song in *Smoke Signals*. In addition, she received a Golden Globe nomination, a First Americans in the Arts Award for Best Actress, and the Cowboy Hall of Fame Award for Best Actress for her role as Mary Crow Dog. In 1995 she was named one of *People Magazine*'s Fifty Most Beautiful People.

### Tom Bee (1947–)
*Santee Sioux (Dakota) performing artist, songwriter, music producer, and record company executive*

Born at Gallup, New Mexico, on 8 November 1947, Tom Bee is best known as founder and featured artist of the Native American popular music group XIT, which first appeared in 1970. During the early years of the group, Bee's composition "We've Got Blue Skies" was recorded by Michael Jackson and the Jackson Five. Soon after, XIT was signed by Motown Records. While under contract with Motown, the group released two widely acclaimed albums entitled *Plight of the Redman* and *Silent Warrior*, and their single "Reservation of Education" was among the five best-selling records in France in 1973.

Tom Bee, president of the Soar Corporation.

The political overtones of XIT's music has kept them from achieving superstar status in the United States, but the group has developed a cult status in America and Europe that has allowed their music to survive for the last twenty years.

In 1989, Bee founded a Native American recording company called SOAR (Sound of America Records). The first two releases by SOAR featured the music of XIT, but Bee's company soon expanded to include various other traditional and contemporary forms of music. SOAR now has over 300 quality titles including flute music, powwow music, peyote songs, Navajo music, and round dance songs, as well as their familiar rock-and-roll.

### Fred Begay (1932–)
*Navajo experimental physicist*

Fred Begay is a nuclear physicist and currently is senior staff physicist at the Los Alamos National Laboratory with research interests in the controlled thermonuclear fusion problem and related phenomena, assistant for science and technology to the president and vice-president of the Navajo government, and president of the Seaborg Hall of Science. The Seaborg Hall of

Physicist Fred Begay.

Science, named after the late Nobel chemistry laureate Glenn T. Seaborg, is an independent nonprofit education and research institution dedicated to provide public services to the Navajo community in science and technology matters. The volunteer core members include Navajo professionals who have established distinguished careers in science, engineering, and medicine. Begay is a member of the American Physical Society, the American Association of Physics Teachers, and the American Nuclear Society.

Born on the Ute Mountain Indian Reservation in Towaoc, Colorado, in 1932, Begay attended the Bureau of Indian Affairs-managed Vocational Indian Schools at Ignacio from 1942 to 1946, where his training was in farming. As a non-commissioned officer Begay served in the U.S. Air Force (1951–1955) and was assigned to an air-rescue squadron in Korea during the Korean Conflict.

Without the benefit of a solid pre-college science and mathematics background, Begay attended the University of New Mexico (1955–1956; 1959–1963) and was awarded a bachelor's of science degree in physics and mathematics (1961), a master's of science degree in physics (1963), and a doctorate degree in nuclear physics (1972). Begay was invited to join a NASA-funded space physics research team at the University of New Mexico to conduct fundamental studies on the origin of high energy gamma rays and solar neutrons.

Since 1971 Begay has been employed at the Los Alamos National Laboratory where he has participated in numerous controlled thermonuclear fusion programs. He has held research and teaching appointments at Stanford University and University of Maryland. Begay has published numerous articles on the progress of the controlled thermonuclear fusion problem and related fundamental problems.

Begay has provided expert advice in science and technology issues as the chairman to the Navajo Nation's Environmental Protection Commission (1974–1976), as principal investigator for the NSF-funded Navajo Research Committee at Navajo Community College (1972–1976), as an advisor to the Board of Science and Technology for International Development, U.S. National Academy of Sciences (1979–1981), as a member of the National Research Council (1979–present), and as an advisor for the Center for Research on Education in Science, Mathematics, Engineering, and Technology, Arizona State University (2000–present).

Begay's life as a physicist and as a Navajo has been documented in various televisions films and documentaries, including *Nation within a Nation* (1972); *In Our Native Land* (1973); *The Long Walk of Fred Young-Begay* (1978); and *Dancing with Photons* (1997). In addition, numerous articles have been published on the physicist in newspapers, magazines, and textbooks, including a feature piece in *National Geographic* (1987).

Because of his groundbreaking work in science, and his contributions to science education and public service, Begay has received various awards, including the Ely Parker Award from the American Indian Society for Engineering and Science (1992); the Lifetime Achievement Award from the National Science Foundation (1994); and the Distinguished Scientist Award from the Society for the Advancement of Chicanos and Native Americans in Science (1999). In addition, Begay has received awards from the Department of Energy and the Navajo government for his work.

Begay is involved with efforts to improve public literacy regarding science and technology. He supports the work of the Los Alamos National Laboratory's Community Relations Office, whose primary objective is improve the quality of Navajo human resources who can improve the quality of the Navajo human and natural environment. Navajo socioeconomic indicators show that the Navajo exist in a human and natural environment which is similar to that of a Third World country. Begay has given numerous lectures on the Navajo and modern perspectives of nature.

## Notah Ryan Begay III (1972–)
*Navajo professional golfer*

Notah Begay is expanding the range of sports icons for Native Americans in the twenty-first century. Born in Albuquerque, New Mexico, he began playing golf at the age of six. Because his family was impoverished, Begay saved spare change to purchase golf balls. His hard work paid off, and he is now a rising star on the Professional Golf Association Tour.

A three-time All-American selection at Stanford University, Begay was a member of the school's 1994 NCAA championship team, and a member of the 1995 United States Walker Cup team, winner of fifteen major junior and amateur titles. He holds the record for lowest eighteen-hole score in NCAA championship history with sixty-two in the second round of the 1994 tournament.

In 2000, Begay won multiple titles for the second straight year, posting back-to-back victories at the St. Jude Classic and Greater Hartford Open. He also went 3–2 for the victorious United States Presidents Cup team.

John Kim Bell, president of the National Aboriginal Achievement Foundation.

## John Kim Bell (1953–)
*Mohawk symphony conductor and composer*

John Kim Bell has been making music and history ever since he was a child. Born on the Kahnawake Mohawk Reserve in Quebec, Bell studied since he was eight and was conducting Broadway musicals for such luminaries as Gene Kelly and Vincent Price in New York City at the young age of eighteen, becoming the youngest professional conductor in the United States. Bell completed his musical training at Ohio State University and later at the Academia Musicale Chigiana in Sienna, Italy. In 1980, after conducting numerous Broadway musicals, Bell was appointed apprentice conductor with the Toronto Symphony, becoming the first American Indian to become a symphony conductor.

In 1984, the Canadian Broadcasting Corporation produced a documentary profile of Bell, which sparked a large response from the Native community. Bell received a number of requests seeking information and assistance about musical training for aboriginal youth. In response to these requests and because of his ongoing concern about the many difficulties facing Native

youth, Bell created the Canadian Native Arts Foundation (CNAF). CNAF is a privately and publicly sponsored national charity that provides scholarships for Native youth so they may be trained in the arts. Between 1988 and 1992, CNAF has awarded approximately $1 million in scholarships to Native youth across Canada. The CNAF raises funds for scholarships through the production of concerts and events. The most ambitious production recently undertaken by CNAF was the staging of the first Native ballet produced by John Kim Bell, entitled *In The Land of The Spirits*. Bell also co-wrote the ballet's orchestral score. The ballet was premiered at the National Arts Centre in Ottawa, Canada's capital, and was a huge artistic and financial success.

CNAF has now awarded over $10 million in scholarships to more than 1,000 recipients and operates a national series of career fairs targeting aboriginal youth. In 1993, Bell established the National Aboriginal Achievement Awards, an awards system celebrating career achievement in the aboriginal community. Bell is an officer of the Order of Canada and he has received four honorary doctorates. He also serves on the boards of the Canadian Broadcasting Corporation, the Canada Millennium Scholarship Foundation, the Aboriginal

Human Resource Development Council of Canada, and the Toronto 2008 Olympic Bid Committee.

## Clyde Bellecourt (1939–)
*Ojibwa activist*

Born on the White Earth Reservation in Minnesota in 1939, Clyde Bellecourt is a founder and director of the American Indian Movement. He was one of the leaders during the 1973 occupation of Wounded Knee. Clyde has been an active participant in the Sun Dance since the early 1970s, and he played a role in organizing the Big Mountain movement that brought attention to the situation of displaced Navajo who were forced by government policy to move from the Hopi-Navajo joint use land in the 1970s. He also played a key role in organizing the Legal Rights Center and the International Indian Treaty Council. He is also directing the Peacemaker Center for Indian Youth and working with the National Coalition on Racism in Sports and the Media. He is also founder and currently chairman of American Indian OIC, an innovative job program that has assisted the transition of over 14,000 people from welfare to full-time employment.

## Patricia Benedict-Phillips (1956–)
*Abenaki editor and administrator*

Patricia Benedict-Phillips was born in Waterbury, Connecticut. She earned an associate degree in drug and alcohol rehabilitation counseling from Mattatuck Community College in Waterbury. She served as executive director for six years at American Indians for Development, a social service agency. She was also a member of the Energy Assistance Program policy-making board in Meriden, the American Indian Committee in New Haven, chair of Eagle Wing Press Pow-wow Committee, as well as board member of the Eagle Wing Press. In addition, she was co-editor of American Indians for Development Newsletter, and editor of *May Wutche Aque'ne: American Indians for Development Journal*. She was appointed by the governor of Connecticut to the Connecticut Legislative Task Force on Indian Affairs where she served three years. She also helped incorporate the New England Indian Task Force and was chair of the Waterbury Title IV Indian Education program. She lives in Waterbury, Connecticut.

## Ramona Bennett (1938–)
*Puyallup administrator and activist*

Ramona Bennett served as the principal administrator for the Puyallup tribe for eleven years, controlling a maximum budget of $9 million annually. From 1971 until 1978 she was the elected chair of the Puyallup Tribal Council. The Puyallup are a Northwest Coast tribe whose original territory was located along the Puyallup River and Commencement Bay in northwestern Washington.

Born in Seattle, Washington, on 28 April 1948, Bennett received her bachelor's degree from Evergreen State College in Washington State and went on to obtain a master's degree in education from the University of Puget Sound.

Besides her tribal activities Bennett is a well-known spokeswoman for Indian rights at the national level, particularly in the areas of fishing rights, Indian child welfare, and Indian health and education. She is an officer of the Survival of American Indians Association, a Native American advocate group, and is a board member of the National Coalition to Support Indian Treaties. As an activist for Indian rights she has often been profiled in the broadcast media and in national publications such as *Redbook, The Socialist Worker's Forum, National Geographic,* and the *New York Times*. Bennett remains active in local tribal issues.

## Robert L. Bennett (1912–)
*Oneida commissioner of Indian affairs*

Robert L. Bennett is a distinguished administrator and legal professional. He is a member of the Oneida Nation, an Iroquoian tribe whose territory is located mainly in New York, though some Oneida also live in Wisconsin and Ontario, Canada.

Born at Oneida, Wisconsin, on 16 November 1912, Bennett attended Haskell Institute in Kansas and went on to obtain his degree in law from Southeastern University School of Law in Washington, D.C. in 1941. He then served as a Bureau of Indian Affairs administrative assistant on the Navajo Reservation and remained there until serving as a marine during World War II. Following the war he worked at the Veteran's Administration, and in this capacity he helped literally hundreds of Indian veterans obtain an education under the GI Bill.

Bennett later returned to the Bureau of Indian Affairs and served in a variety of positions before his appointment as commissioner of Indian affairs in 1966. In the early 1960s, he served as an area director in Juneau, Alaska, and while working there successfully blocked the state of Alaska from selecting certain lands prior to settling the land claims of Alaska Native peoples. Bennett became known as an extremely vigorous commissioner; he traveled all over the United States helping tribes establish and direct their own social programs and fighting against the movement to exclude tribes from federal assistance.

He retired as commissioner in 1969, and then served as director of the American Indian Law Center at the University of New Mexico until 1975. Bennett has since worked as a legal consultant for various tribal groups and as a lecturer in seminars on American Indian affairs for legal professionals and administrators. He is retired and lives in Albuquerque.

## Ruth Bennett (1942–)
*Shawnee educator*

Ruth Bennett, a Shawnee, is a bilingual education specialist. Born on 12 December 1942, she graduated from Indiana University in 1964 and obtained a master's degree in English at the University of Washington in 1968. She later received a Standard Secondary Teaching Credential from California State University, San Francisco (1973), and finally went on to complete a Ph.D. program in education at the University of California, Berkeley (1980). She also conducted post-doctorate research at the Universidad de Yucatan in Mexico (1994).

Bennett held various teaching positions in the San Francisco Bay Area during the early years of her career, but gradually her work became focused on the tribes of northwestern California. In 1978, she started working with bilingual education programs at the Center of Community Development at Humboldt State University in Arcata, California. In 1980, Bennett became director of a Title VII Bilingual Education Program offering a bilingual teaching credential in Yurok, Hupa, Karok, and Tolowa. Since 1993, she has been an ethnographic researcher, and has served as a Hupa language consultant for the Hoopa Valley Tribe.

Bennett has been involved in creating innovative curriculum materials for many years and has published many articles and books, including *Four Hupa Songs by Alice Pratt* (1994), *Dundi Ne:sing? Dixwe:di 'Unt'e:n? (Who is It? What are You Doing?)* (1997), "It Really Works," (1998) and "Does Writing Have a Place in Preserving an Oral Language?" (1999).

## William Beynon (1888–1958)
*Tsimshian cultural researcher*

William Beynon conducted important cultural research on his own Tsimshian culture and that of other neighboring tribes, for which he has gone almost unrecognized. Born in Victoria, British Columbia, in 1888, Beynon was the son of a Welsh steamer captain and a Tsimshian woman from Port Simpson. The Tsimshian are a Northwest Coast tribe located along the Nass and Skeena rivers and adjacent coastal areas in western British Columbia (Canada) and also on Metlakatla Island in Alaska.

Far from having a traditional upbringing, he was raised in the city of Victoria and was the only one of six brothers to learn the Tsimshian language from his mother. As a young man, he worked for the Canadian Public Railroad and the Department of Public Works. But in 1913, he went to his mother's home of Port Simpson and developed a strong interest in his Indian heritage. For the rest of his life, when not working in the fishing or canning industries, he devoted himself to cultural research and served as a collector and interpreter of ethnographic data for several well-known anthropologists.

Beynon started working for ethnomusicologist Marius Barbeau in 1914, collecting song-texts, speeches, narratives, and other types of information from elderly Tsimshian speakers and translating the texts into English. For the most part this was done quite independently, as Beynon would write the material in field notebooks and mail these to Barbeau in Ottawa. Over the years between then and his death in 1958, Beynon also worked in a similar fashion for the linguist Edward Sapir and for cultural anthropologists Franz Boas and Philip Drucker.

Beynon's actual contributions to anthropology have been badly slighted, as he is usually identified in the literature only as an "informant and interpreter." He published only one short article under his own name ("The Tsimshians of Metlakatla, Alaska," *American Anthropologist*, 1941), but several hundred pages of his unpublished texts and fieldnotes are among the holdings at the Canadian Centre for Folk Culture Studies (National Museum of Man, Ottawa) and other archives. Perhaps the most important manuscript is a 544-page typescript entitled "Ethnographic and Folkloristic Texts of the Tsimshian," which is part of the Boas Collection at the American Philosophical Society in Philadelphia. This contains rare and important texts that are different from those published in Boas's classic study *Tsimshian Mythology* (1916).

## Big Bear (1825?–1888)
*Cree tribal leader*

Big Bear (Mistahimaskwa) was born near Fort Carlton, Saskatchewan, and became head man and chief of approximately sixty-five Cree lodges. Concerned about the disappearance of the buffalo and the effects of European settlement on traditional Indian life, Big Bear fought for better treaty terms for his people until he died in 1888. He refused to sign his consent to Treaty Six, one of several treaties that Canada entered into with First Nations, because in his view it did not provide his people with sufficient compensation and protection against further settlement and development. Big Bear constantly spoke out against the relocation of First Nations onto reserves and the turn toward agriculture by Indian people. He maintained this view until the buffalo were gone and starvation took hold in his community.

Big Bear also strove to unite the Northern Cree people, and he once succeeded in attracting more than two thousand Indians to join him in his thirst dance at the Poundmaker Reserve near Battleford, Saskatchewan. Late in life, Big Bear began to lose the support of many of his followers who became more militant. Led by Little Bad Man (Ayimisis) and Wandering Spirit (Kapapamahchakwew), the militants killed several white settlers when they became involved in what is known as the second Northwest Rebellion. The rebellion was led by Louis Riel, leader of the Métis people, who sought to establish a provisional government in Saskatchewan against the wishes of Canadian authorities. They were captured shortly thereafter, and Big Bear subsequently surrendered. Big Bear was tried for treason-felony, found guilty, and imprisoned for three years in Stony Mountain Penitentiary. Big Bear became ill in prison and was released after serving two years of his sentence. He died within a year of his release.

### Samuel Billison (1925–)
*Navajo WWII code talker and education administrator*

Samuel Billison is a WWII code talker and veteran, a delegate to the Navajo tribal council, and the first Navajo to receive a doctorate degree in education.

Born at Ganado, Arizona, on 14 March 1925, Billison was raised on the reservation by parents who had no formal education. His grandfather, Hosteen Gani, was a medicine man. He studied at Albuquerque Indian School, Bacone College, East Central State College, and completed the master's program at the University of Oklahoma. He served as a high school principal in Oklahoma and in Texas, and returned to the Navajo Reservation where he held various administrative positions including director of public services for the Navajo tribe before he pursued a doctoral degree in education at the University of Arizona.

Billison had a distinguished military career. He served in the U.S. Marines during World War II as a Code Talker and participated in the landing on Iwo Jima. The code talkers were specially trained Navajo Marines who translated radio communications into unbreakable codes using the Navajo language during World War II.

As one of approximately 150 surviving Navajo code talkers, Billison supplied his voice for the Navajo Code Talker G.I. Joe, an action figure created by the Hasbro Toy Company. The toy, which went on sale in January 2000, speaks seven Navajo phrases and comes with a short history of the Navajo code talkers.

### Black Hawk (1767–1838)
*Sac (Sauk) tribal leader*

During his lifetime Black Hawk resisted the expansion of U.S. settlement into his homeland, located near the Rock River in present-day Illinois. As a young man, Black Hawk showed interest in forming a confederation of Indian tribes to protest the many dubious treaties that were the basis of U.S. settlement in the region. In 1832, he fought a series of ill-fated engagements with U.S. forces, known as Black Hawk's War.

In 1829, when Black Hawk and his followers returned to their homeland in the Rock River country from a hunting trip, they found it occupied by white squatters. Some settlers had even moved into Indian dwellings. For the next few years Black Hawk and his people lived an uneasy coexistence with the U.S. intruders. In June 1831, the U.S. Army tried to dislodge Black Hawk from his village. Black Hawk and his people escaped by crossing the Mississippi River.

Black Hawk and about two thousand followers remained on the western side of the Mississippi River until 5 April 1832. As he crossed the Mississippi, U.S. Army troops were hurriedly deployed to meet him. On May 14, the two forces met and Black Hawk's men won the first battle with U.S. forces.

For the next few months, Black Hawk and his followers moved northward into Wisconsin. Meanwhile, the U.S. troops were put under the command of General Winfield Scott who organized a large army in Chicago. Two U.S. military forces caught up with Black Hawk and his followers after months of traveling and subsistence living. On 21 July 1832, at the battle of Wisconsin Heights, a number of Black Hawk's people were killed. Black Hawk hoped to escape via the Mississippi. His path was blocked on 1 August 1832, by the cannon-laden steamship *Warrior*. With reinforcements of thirteen hundred U.S. regular troops, on August 3 the U.S. forces attacked and killed about three hundred of Black Hawk's people. Black Hawk and a few followers escaped to northern Wisconsin.

On August 27, Black Hawk and about fifty companions were persuaded to surrender. Black Hawk was imprisoned at Fort Monroe, Virginia. In 1833, the defeated leader was taken to Washington, D.C., where he met President Jackson. In the ensuing years, Black Hawk became something of a media celebrity. Many authors vied to write his biography, which he dictated in 1833. In 1837, Charles Bird King painted his now-famous portrait of Black Hawk. Black Hawk died in 1838 in a land that was not his own and among people he barely knew.

## Black Kettle (1803–1868)
*Southern Cheyenne tribal leader*

Black Kettle was a Cheyenne tribal peace leader whose band was attacked in the infamous Sand Creek Massacre during the Cheyenne and Arapaho War of 1864 and 1865. During his youth, Black Kettle was actively engaged as a warrior against the Ute and Delaware, who were enemies of his tribe. He, however, advocated good relations with the Americans and ratified a treaty maintaining peace in Colorado and along the Santa Fe Trail. After traveling to Washington, D.C., in 1863, he met with President Abraham Lincoln.

Events such as the rapid settlement of Kansas and Nebraska territories after 1854 and the Colorado gold rush of 1859 promoted uneasiness between Indians and Americans, and reprisals on each side were not uncommon. Black Kettle and other Cheyenne and Arapaho chiefs met with the governor of Colorado near Denver and were assured that if each band would camp near army installations and regularly report to military officers, they would be safe from attack. Black Kettle moved his people to Sand Creek near Fort Lyon in present-day Colorado and informed the garrison of their peaceful presence.

On the morning of 29 November 1864, the Third Colorado Volunteers, under the command of Colonel John Chivington, took up position around Black Kettle's encampment. Over his tipi, he raised the American flag and a white truce flag. Nevertheless, Chivington's troops, many of whom were drunk, swept into camp, slaughtering and sexually mutilating the fleeing Indians. Black Kettle managed to escape, but about two hundred others, mostly women and children were killed.

The news of the slaughter caused a wave of condemnation. Chivington was brought before the Committee on the Conduct of the War, and was condemned, denounced, and forced to resign from the military. Meanwhile, the Cheyenne sought swift and destructive retribution; travel across the Great Plains to Denver was completely halted.

Despite this, Black Kettle still encouraged his people to remain at peace. He signed a treaty at the Medicine Lodge council in 1867 that granted reservations to the Southern Cheyenne, the Southern Arapaho, the Comanche, and the Kiowa within Indian Territory (Oklahoma). Black Kettle led his followers to the Washita River and traveled to Fort Cobb to assure the garrison there that he wanted nothing but peace. Nevertheless, U.S. officials refused to issue guns and ammunition to Southern Cheyenne men for fear that they would raid settlers or other Indian tribes. Consequently, about two hundred Cheyenne raided several settlements in Kansas and caused U.S. troops to enter the field. Major General Philip Sheridan organized three columns of troops in an offensive aimed against the recently relocated Plains Indians.

Lieutenant Colonel George Armstrong Custer learned about the presence of Black Kettle's encampment on the Washita from Osage scouts. Disregarding the fact that the camp was on the reservation and had been guaranteed safety, he and the Seventh Cavalry attacked at dawn on 27 November 1868. Black Kettle rode out with his wife in a blinding snowstorm hoping to prevent the attack by parleying with the soldiers. Both were shot dead on sight and their bodies trampled by the advancing columns. The regimental band played "Garry Owen" as Custer and his men killed another hundred Cheyenne, mostly women and children.

## Ethel Blondin-Andrew (1951–)
*Dene secretary of state and member of Parliament*

The Honorable Ethel Blondin-Andrew was born in the northern community of Fort Norman, in the Northwest Territories, Canada. She is a member of the Dene Nation, which includes a number of different peoples who live in the Northwest Territories. In accordance with the custom of her people, Blondin-Andrew was adopted by her aunt and uncle at the age of three months and spent her early childhood living in various hunting-and-trapping communities with her extended family. As a child, she attended residential school in Inuvik, Northwest Territories and later attended a school designed to promote leadership among Native and northern Canadian youth. Blondin-Andrew received a bachelor's of education degree from the University of Alberta in Edmonton, Alberta.

From 1974 to 1984 she taught in the remote Northwest Territories communities of Tuktoyaktuk, Fort Franklin, Providence, and Yellowknife. During this time, she was the recipient of an award from a private foundation for her work in developing a Dene teaching program. In the mid-1980s, her focus shifted first to public service and then to elected office. From 1984 to 1986, she was first manager and then acting director of the Public Service Commission of Canada, the commission representing federal public servants in Ottawa, the nation's capital. Returning to the Northwest Territories, Blondin-Andrew was appointed assistant deputy minister of culture and communications in Yellowknife.

She was first elected to the Canadian Parliament in 1988, and quickly became a strong voice for aboriginal people by serving on committees relevant to indigenous affairs. In 1993, she was appointed secretary of state, training and youth. She was reappointed in 1997 to the position. Her efforts led to the creation of Youth Service Canada and Youth Employment Strategy. She is married and has three children.

### George Blue Spruce Jr. (1931–)
*Laguna/San Juan Pueblo dentist and health worker*

George Blue Spruce Jr., is a retired public health administrator who works to increase the number of Indians in the medical profession. Born at Santa Fe, New Mexico, on 16 January 1931, Blue Spruce received a degree in dentistry from Creighton University in Omaha, Nebraska, in 1956. Upon graduation he went into private practice but soon went to work for the U.S. Public Health Service as dental officer on the reservation in Taos, New Mexico.

He later returned to school, earning a master's degree in public health from the University of California, Berkeley (1967), and then served as a public health officer in several agencies connected with the Department of Health, Education, and Welfare (HEW). He was appointed director of the Phoenix Area Indian Health Service, a division of the Department of Health and Human Services.

Over the years, Blue Spruce has received numerous honors and has written influential articles on the need for Indian medical professionals. Besides these activities, he is also an avid tennis player; he was captain of his college team and winner of the men's singles competition at the Second Annual National Indian Championships in 1977. In the early 1990s, Blue Spruce was director of Phoenix Area Indian Health Service and a member of national dental, health, and educational

organizations. He publishes in the newsletter of the Association of American Indian Physicians.

### Frank M. Blythe (1940–)
*Cherokee motion picture and television producer*

Frank Blythe is a founding member and executive director of Native American Public Telecommunications, Inc. (NAPT). Born at Pipestone, Minnesota, on 7 November 1940, Blythe received his bachelor's degree in radio and television management at Arizona State University (1962). He is also NAPT director for American Indian radio on Satellite Network, co-director for the American Indian Higher Education Consortium's Distance Education Network, and director of Vision Maker Video. NAPT maintains a media library through which Native American programs are made available for public television, Indian organizations, and other educational users. The organization also provides grants for the creation of new programs concerning Native American subjects and themes.

Among Blythe's own production credits are *I am Different from My Brother*, *American Indian Artists II*, and *Native American Calling*. Blythe served as the operations manager for KAET-TV in Phoenix from 1971 to 1977. He has been a member of several advisory boards, including the National Association of Education Broadcasters, the Nebraska Committee for the Humanities, and the Nebraska Arts Council.

### Jarrett Blythe (1886–1977)
*Eastern Cherokee tribal leader*

Jarrett Blythe was principal chief of the Eastern Cherokee for twenty-four years over several terms. The Cherokee are a southeastern tribe, most of whom who relocated to Oklahoma during the 1830s.

Born in Cherokee, North Carolina, on 30 May 1886, Blythe was descended from a group of Cherokee who defied the government's order to relocate in Oklahoma Territory and instead took refuge in the Smoky Mountains. Finding it difficult and expensive to enforce their original order, the government finally allowed them to remain and establish a reservation there.

Blythe went to school on the reservation, then attended Hampton Institute in Virginia and Haskell Institute in Lawrence, Kansas. On completing his education, he spent four years working on a government reclamation project in Montana. Then, feeling a "hang for home," he returned to the reservation in Cherokee, North Carolina, and never left again.

Blythe was elected tribal chief in 1931 and served four consecutive terms; he was elected again in 1955 and in 1963, holding the office for a total of twenty-four years. Each of his administrations produced major economic results: most importantly, he initiated a loan fund for tribal members wishing to go into business for themselves, and he helped to arrange for the purchase of land to build a high school. He also made valuable gifts of land to young couples, which became known as Jarrett Blythe Homesteads.

In the area of cultural activities, Blythe founded the Cherokee Historical Association and also helped initiate performances of the historical drama *Unto These Hills*, which relates the story of the Cherokee removal.

### Gertrude Simmons Bonnin (Zitkala-Sa) (1876–1938)
*Sioux author and activist*

Gertrude Simmons Bonnin, also known as Zitkala-Sa, or Red Bird, was born at the Yankton Sioux Agency in South Dakota on 22 February 1876, the third child of Ellen Simmons, a full-blood Sioux. Sioux agency land allotment applications indicate that her father was white. She was reared as Sioux until she was eight years old, at which time she left the reservation to attend a Quaker missionary school for Indians, White's Indiana Manual Labor Institute in Wabash, Indiana. She received her high school diploma and at the age of nineteen went on to Earlham College in Richmond, Indiana, where she received recognition and prizes for her oratorical skills. Following graduation Bonnin taught for two years at Carlisle Indian School in Carlisle, Pennsylvania. She then left to study at the Boston Conservatory of Music. In 1900, she accompanied the Carlisle Indian Band to the Paris Exposition where she performed as a violin soloist. During this period she also wrote three autobiographical essays, which were published in the *Atlantic Monthly* and two stories based on Indian legends for *Harper's Monthly*. Her book *Old Indian Legends* was published in 1901.

She returned to Sioux country and in 1902 married Raymond Talesfase Bonnin, a Sioux employee of the Indian Service. In 1902, they transferred to the Uintah and Ouray Reservation in Utah, where she was employed as a clerk and briefly as a teacher. She organized a brass band among the children of the reservation and undertook home demonstration work among the women. During this period, she also became a correspondent of the Society of American Indians, entering into what would become a life work in Indian reform. The society, organized at Ohio State University in 1911, was the first Indian reform organization to be managed exclusively by Indians and to require that active members be

of Indian blood. Its aims included not only governmental reforms, but also the employment of Indians in the Indian Service, the opening of the Court of Claims to all equitable claims of Indian tribes against the United States, and also the preservation of the accurate Indian history and its records. Essentially, the society's aims were assimilationist: citizenship for all Indians, abolition of the office of Indian affairs (after 1930s called the Bureau of Indian Affairs), and termination of communal property holdings.

Bonnin was elected secretary of the society in 1916 and moved to Washington, D.C., which remained her home until her death in 1938. She carried on the society's correspondence with the Office of Indian Affairs, lectured from coast to coast as its representative, and acted as editor of its periodical, the *American Indian Magazine*. After the demise of the society in 1929, Bonnin organized the National Council of American Indians. She remained its president until her death, lobbying in Washington on behalf of Indian legislation.

Bonnin's activities as author slackened after she abandoned the editorship of the *American Indian Magazine*. Her second book, *American Indian Stories* (1921), reprinted stories written at the beginning of the century. She retained her interest in music, and one of her last undertakings was the composition, with William F. Hanson, of an Indian opera, *Sun Dance*. She died in Washington, D.C., in 1938, at the age of sixty-one.

### Lionel Bordeaux (1950–)
*Sioux educator and administrator*

Lionel Bordeaux is president of Sinte Gleska College in South Dakota. Born on the Rosebud Sioux Reservation in South Dakota on 9 February 1940, Bordeaux graduated from St. Francis Indian Mission High School in St. Francis, Minnesota (1958), then received a bachelor's degree from Black Hills State College (1964). From 1964 until 1972, he worked for the Bureau of Indian Affairs in various Indian communities as a teacher, counselor, or educational specialist. During these years he also continued his own education, completing a master's degree at the University of South Dakota and becoming a doctoral candidate in educational administration at the University of Minnesota in Minneapolis.

In 1973 he became president of Sinte Gleska College, where he helped develop the first fully accredited bachelor's and master's degree programs at a reservation-based college. He also provided leadership for congressional passage of important legislation relating to the authorization of tribal colleges. Besides these activities as an educator, Bordeaux has played a major role in tribal leadership, serving as a councilman in the

Rosebud Sioux tribal government for eight years, co-chair of the White House Conference on Indian Education, chair of the Rosebud Sioux Tribal Education Committee, and chairman of the United Sioux Tribal Education Board.

## Mary Bosomworth (Coosaponakeesa) (1700–1763)
*Creek tribal leader*

As a young girl, Mary Bosomworth was taken from Creek country to South Carolina, where she was educated and baptized into the Church of England. Her father was English and her mother Creek. As a young woman, she returned to her tribe and married John Musgrove, a trader who lived and worked among the Creek. In 1733, Bosomworth was hired by the governor of Georgia to act as interpreter between the colonial government and the Creek. During this time she became an influential figure among the Creek and rallied their support behind the British against Spanish influence in the Southeast. The Spanish colony in Florida had tried to win the political, military, and trade alliance of the Creek as a means of opposing the expansion of the English colonies. In 1749 Mary Bosomworth married her third husband (her first two had died), Thomas Bosomworth, who, a few years later, was appointed by the Carolina colonial agent to the Creek. At the same time, Mary Bosomworth proclaimed herself empress of the Creek Nation. As such, Bosomworth and her husband laid claims to a large piece of land in South Carolina and a number of islands off the Georgia coast. The Bosomworths, who had fallen deeply into debt, demanded payment by the colonists for their diplomatic services. After marching on Savannah with a contingent of Creek warriors, they were briefly imprisoned by colonial officials. They continued to press grievances all the way to England, and in 1759 they were granted a small settlement and official title to two islands off the Georgia coast.

## Elias Boudinot (1803–1839)
*Cherokee editor and writer*

Elias Boudinot's Cherokee name was Galgina (Buck). His parents sent him to study in Salem, North Carolina, at a school run by Moravians, an extremely strict German Protestant sect. In 1818, the New Jersey philanthropist, Elias Boudinot, sent Galgina and several other young Cherokee scholars to a mission school in Cornwall, Connecticut. Galgina adopted the name Elias Boudinot in honor of his benefactor. He studied at Cornwall for a few short years, then he and John Ridge,

another Cherokee scholar, met and courted local girls, whom they decided to marry. This caused considerable disturbance within the town and, although the marriages took place, the incident resulted in the closing of the school.

Upon returning to the Cherokee Nation, Boudinot served the Cherokee government as clerk for the national council and in 1828 was appointed editor of the *Cherokee Phoenix*, the new Cherokee national newspaper written in English and Cherokee. Along with Samuel Worcester, Presbyterian missionary to the Cherokee, Boudinot worked on a translation of the Bible into Cherokee, using the Cherokee syllabary created by Sequoyah. In 1835, Boudinot supported the Treaty of New Echota, under which a minority of economically well-off Cherokee agreed to migrate to present-day Oklahoma because they thought it not possible to preserve the Cherokee Nation from U.S. territorial and political threats. Most Cherokee opposed the treaty, and after the U.S. Army forced most of them to migrate during the winter of 1838–1839, in a march called the Trail of Tears, they became embittered against the treaty makers. In the summer of 1839, Elias Boudinot and several other treaty advocates were assassinated.

## Billy Bowlegs (1810–1864)
*Seminole tribal leader*

Billy Bowlegs was the leader of the last group of Seminole Indians to remain in Florida against the will of the United States government. In the Seminole War of 1835–1842, following the death of Seminole leader Osceola and the surrender of other leaders, Bowlegs led two hundred Seminole warriors in an 1839 attack on a government trading post that had been opened on Seminole land, killing most of the garrison. Following the attack, Bowlegs and his band hid in the Florida Everglades for almost a year, hiding during the day and raiding during the night.

Bowlegs was a superior warrior who resisted efforts to remove his tribe. After many battles he finally made peace with the U.S. Army, and on 14 August 1842, Bowlegs surrendered and was allotted a small parcel of land. That same year Bowlegs and other Seminole chiefs visited Washington, D.C., and the U.S. government announced the end of the eight-year Seminole War, the most costly Indian war in U.S. history: 1,500 soldiers killed and $20 million spent.

In 1855, as the result of a party of army engineers and surveyors stealing crops and destroying others belonging to Bowleg's band, violence flared up in what is sometimes referred to as the Third Seminole War. Bowlegs led his warriors in a campaign of guerrilla warfare, attacking settlers, trappers, and traders in the region, then retreating into the wilds. Once again neither army regulars nor volunteers could contain them.

Finally, in 1858, negotiations between the U.S. government and Bowlegs took place and an offer of peace was made. As a result Bowlegs and members of his band agreed to emigrate to Indian Territory, in present-day Oklahoma, which they did in 1859. Bowlegs fought for the North in the Civil War in 1861.

### LaNada Means Boyer (contemporary)
*Shoshone/Bannock activist*

LaNada Means Boyer was one of the original Indians who occupied Alcatraz Island on 20 November 1969. In addition to being an organizer and leader on the island, Boyer traveled throughout the United States giving lectures and raising support for the occupiers on Alcatraz.

Boyer moved to the San Francisco Bay Area as part of the U.S. government relocation program, which was intended to assimilate reservation Indians into urban populations. During the occupation of Alcatraz Island, she commuted daily from the island to the University of California, Berkeley, to continue her studies, and received her B.A. from Berkeley in 1972. She completed her master's degree work in public administration and in 1999 earned a doctorate of arts in political science at Idaho State University.

### Beth Brant (1941–)
*Mohawk writer and poet*

Beth Brant, Degonwadonti, is a widely published writer and poet. Many of her works appear in *Kitchen Talk: An Anthology of Canadian Women's Prose and Poetry* (1992); *Getting Wet* (1992); *An Anthology of Native Canadian Literature in English* (1992); *Talking Leaves* (1991); and *Piece of My Heart* (1991). A variety of magazines and journals have published her stories, and "Turtle Gal" was adapted and aired by the Canadian Broadcasting Corporation in Toronto, Ontario, in 1990. Her publications include *Mohawk Trail* (1985), *A Gathering of Spirit* (1989), *Food and Spirits* (1991), *Writing as Witness* (1995), and *I'll Sing Till the Day I Die* (1996).

Brant was a lecturer at the University of British Columbia in 1989 and 1990 and has contributed to numerous writing workshops, such as the Women of Color Writing Workshop in Vancouver, British Columbia, and the Michigan Festival of Writers in East Lansing, Michigan, both in 1991.

In 1992, she participated in the Festival of North American Native Writers in Norman, Oklahoma, at the International Feminist Book Fair in Amsterdam, Holland, and at the Flight of the Mind Writing Workshop for Women in Eugene, Oregon.

In 1993 Brant was the writer-in-residence at the Kanhiote Library on the Tyendinaga Mohawk Reserve in Canada, and guest lecturer in women's studies and Native studies, at New College, University of Toronto, Ontario. She has received many grants and awards including grants from the Michigan Council for the Arts (1984 and 1986) and the Ontario Arts Council (1989), and in 1991, she received the National Endowment for the Arts Literature Fellowship. In 1992, Brant was awarded the Canada Council Award in Creative Writing.

### Clare Clifton Brant (1941–1995)
*Mohawk psychiatrist*

Clare Clifton Brant was a psychiatrist of Mohawk descent. Born in Belleville, Ontario, on 7 July 1941, Brant received his medical degree at Queen's University in Ontario (1965) and then went on to obtain a degree in psychiatry from the University of Western Ontario (1978). He worked as a psychiatrist in private practice and, earlier in his career, was an assistant professor of psychiatry at the University of Western Ontario.

Brant has many scholarly publications to his credit, including articles entitled "Programming for Native American Mental Health" (1982) and "The Examination of the North American Indian" (1983). He served as chairs of the Native Mental Health Association of Canada and the Native Health Program of the Canadian Psychiatric Association.

### Joseph Brant (Thayendanegea) (1742–1807)
*Mohawk tribal leader*

Joseph Brant (Thayendanegea) was a British Army officer and a Mohawk tribal leader. The Mohawk were the easternmost tribe of the Iroquois Confederacy (a group of six nations), and their native territory is located along the Hudson and Mohawk River Valleys in New York State and Canada.

He was the son of a full-blooded Mohawk chief. After the death of the father, his mother remarried a man named Brant; thus he became known as Joseph Brant among the colonists. His sister Molly married Sir William Johnson, a British official who was superintendent in charge of Indians north of the Ohio from 1755 until 1774, and the young Brant went to live in their home as a child.

He attended a Christian school in Connecticut and mastered spoken and written English. In the early 1760s and 1770s, as a translator and diplomat, he helped the English to negotiate with Iroquois tribes. When the American Revolution broke out, Brant aligned himself with the Loyalist cause and traveled to England in 1775. He was quickly commissioned a colonel in the British army and put his diplomacy skills to work enlisting Iroquois allies for the Loyalist cause.

Brant participated in a number of battles directly, and insisted on using his own military tactics and stratagems. In 1777 and 1778, the persistent raids by Indians and British soldiers against settlements in the Ohio Valley convinced General George Washington, the future U.S. President, to send an army into Iroquois country. The Americans succeeded in destroying a number of Iroquois villages, but Brant did not sanction the subsequent American-Iroquois peace treaty and continued to launch raids against American forces.

In appreciation of his military services the English gave him a retirement pension and a large tract of land along the Grand River in Ontario, Canada. Like many others, Brant was an Indian who lived between two worlds. He is credited with having translated the Bible into the Mohawk language and died near his estate near Brantford, Ontario, on 24 November 1807.

## Mary (Molly) Brant (1736–1796)
*Mohawk tribal leader*

Mary Brant, better known as Molly Brant, was probably born in the Mohawk Valley in New York and was reportedly the daughter of a Mohawk sachem. She was a sister of Joseph Brant, a famous Mohawk leader.

Brant first attracted the attention of Sir William Johnson, one of the wealthiest and most influential men in colonial America, when she displayed her spirit and agility by vaulting to the back of a galloping horse behind a military officer. She became Johnson's consort after his first wife, Catherine Weisenberg, died. Her name first appears in Johnson's papers in 1759 when she bore him the first of nine children. In Johnson's will, he referred to them as his natural children by his housekeeper, terms implying no legal marriage.

Brant became the mistress of the Johnson home at Fort Johnson on the Mohawk River in present-day New York State and in 1763 of the new baronial mansion at Johnstown, New York, where Johnson lived a life of gentlemanly elegance in a frontier setting. Brant presided at Johnson Hall with dignity and charm, entertaining distinguished visitors and, by her influence with Indian leaders, supplementing Johnson's diplomacy in pacifying the Indian nations.

Following Johnson's death in 1774, Brant and her children moved to a farm near Canajoharie, New York, where she engaged in trade. During the Revolutionary War, she and her relatives aided the British. Peter Johnson, a son, was credited with the capture of Ethan Allen during the fighting at Montreal. Joseph Brant, another son, led Iroquois forces against the Americans in the Mohawk Valley and elsewhere. It was Molly Brant who informed the British of the patriot movements before the battle of Oriskany, and Joseph Brant later testified that "she sent ammunition to the Loyalists and fed and assisted such as had taken refuge in the woods." When the American commander, General Nicholas Herkimer, forced Brant to leave her home, she sought refuge with relatives among the Iroquois Nation farther west, where she used her great prestige to keep the Cayuga and Seneca on the British side.

With the coming of peace in 1783, Brant went with other loyalists to Cataraqui (Kingston, Ontario), where she lived for the remainder of her life. A devout Anglican, she died in Kingston, where she was buried in the St. George's Churchyard. Brant contributed in some measure to the great influence exerted by Sir William Johnson over the Indians of the northern colonies; during the Revolution, the force of her personality, buttressed by the dominant role of women in Iroquois society, enabled her to influence the Iroquois toward alliance with the British.

## Lester Jack Briggs, Jr. (1948–)
*Chippewa college administrator*

Lester Jack Briggs, Jr., is president of Fond du Lac Community College. Born at Duluth, Minnesota, on 18 September 1948, Briggs attended Rainy River Community College and Bemidji State College, both in Minnesota, where he completed a bachelor's degree in community service in 1980. He later went on to receive a master's in education administration from the University of Minnesota, Duluth (1990). During these years he also received special training in substance abuse and alcoholism counseling at the University of Minnesota, Duluth, and Rutgers University.

His first professional position was as American Indian student advisor and planning assistant for the Minnesota Higher Education Coordinating Board (1978–1981). He then became regional director for the Services to Indian People Program at Arrowhead Community College in Minnesota (1983–1989). Over the years, Briggs has been involved in many community activities involving education and social welfare, and was named American Indian Administrator of the Year by the Minnesota Education Association in 1986 and 1987.

### Ruth M. Bronson (1897–1982)
*Cherokee educator*

Ruth Bronson was a teacher who devoted her career to helping Indian youth understand and appreciate their heritage. Born in Whitewater, Oklahoma, in 1897, Ruth Bronson began her career as a YMCA playground instructor for Apache children. She studied at the University of Kansas in 1922 and later received an A.B. degree from Mount Holyoke College in South Hadley, Massachusetts. She was employed at the Bureau of Indian Affairs in 1931 and in 1935 taught at Haskell Institute in Kansas.

Bronson served as the director of the Bureau of Indian Affairs scholarship and loan program from 1931 until 1943 and later became the executive secretary of the National Congress of American Indians. In 1957 she took a position as health education specialist for the San Carlos Apache Reservation in Arizona, which she held until her retirement in 1962. After retiring, Bronson worked among the Papago and Yaqui in Arizona as a representative for the Save the Children Foundation, an organization that serves needy children all over the United States. She passed away on 12 June 1982 at the age of eighty-four.

### Louis R. Bruce, Jr. (1906–1989)
*Oglala Sioux and Mohawk commissioner of Indian affairs*

Louis R. Bruce, Jr., is an administrator and businessman of Oglala Sioux descent. Born on the Oglala Sioux Reservation at Pine Ridge, South Dakota, on 30 December 1906, Bruce grew up on the Onandaga Reservation in rural New York where his father served as Methodist pastor. He studied at Cazenovia Seminary, a Methodist school, and later graduated from Syracuse University with a degree in psychology.

During the Great Depression, Bruce proposed a plan to employ Indian youth as counselors and teachers of Indian lore in summer camps for children in New York and other New England states. This program was a huge success, creating jobs for more than six hundred Indian boys. He was soon after appointed New York State director of Indians under the National Youth Administration in 1935.

In the following years, Bruce found success in different types of business and adminstrative positions. He worked as manager of a large dairy farm (480 acres) that he inherited from his wife's father, as an executive for a national advertising firm, as a special assistant commissioner for the Federal Housing Administration, and as public relations director for a chain of supermarkets.

Bruce was appointed commissioner of Indian affairs in August 1969, becoming the third Indian to be chosen for this position. As commissioner he sought to increase the role of Indian people in business and management. Upon receiving an Indian Council Fire Achievement Award, Bruce said: "The way to Indian progress is involvement. . . . I want to see Indians buying cars from Indians on reservations, and buying food in Indian-owned stores, driving on Indian-planned and Indian-built roads, talking on Indian-owned telephone systems, and living in an Indian-managed economy."

### Joseph Bruchac (1942–)
*Abenaki writer and editor*

Joseph Bruchac lives with his wife Carol in the Adirondack foothills where he was raised by his grandparents. Much of Bruchac's writing draws on that land and the Abenaki heritage from the maternal side of his

Joseph Bruchac.

family. Although his Indian heritage is only part of an ethnic background that includes Slovak and English, his Native roots are deepest and he has cultivated them the most.

Born on 16 October 1942, Bruchac received his bachelor's degree in English from Cornell University (1965), then went on to complete a master's in English from Syracuse University in 1966. From 1966 to 1969 he lived and taught in Ghana, West Africa, and on his return to the United States, founded the Greenfield Review Press. From 1972 to 1974, Bruchac completed the doctoral program at Union Institute Graduate School in Yellow Springs, Ohio. His articles, stories, and poems have appeared in more than five hundred publications and have been translated into several different languages. He has authored more than seventy books, including *Keepers of the Earth* (with Michael J. Caduto), *Tell Me a Tale, Dawn Land, The Waters Between,* and *The Heart of a Chief.*

Bruchac has won several awards for his writing over the years, including fellowships from the National Endowment for the Arts (NEA) and the Rockefeller Foundation, a PEN Syndicated Fiction Award, the Cherokee Nation Prose Award, Wordcraft Circle of Native Writers and Storytellers Writer of the Year, and the 1999 Lifetime Achievement Award from the Native Writers Circle of the Americas.

## Leonard Bruguier (Tashunke Hinzi) (1944–)
*Yankton Sioux historian*

Leonard Bruguier is director of the Institute of American Indian Studies and assistant professor of history at the University of South Dakota. Bruguier was born in Wagner, South Dakota. He earned a bachelor's and master's degree in public administration from the University of South Dakota, and a doctorate at Oklahoma State University. Bruguier served in the U.S. Marine Corps in Vietnam from 1963 to 1970. He reached the rank of sergeant and received a Combat Action Ribbon, a Presidential Unit Citation, a Vietnam Service Medal, a Vietnam Campaign Ribbon, an Armed Forces Expeditionary Medal, and a National Defense Medal.

His research interests focus on the Pipe religion and its influence in Indian-U.S. relations. He is also conducting ongoing research into Indian men and women who served in the U.S. Armed Forces and their impact on reservation, government, and social patterns. Bruguier is a member of the Organization of American Historians and the Western Historical Association. He has received a Minority Doctoral Study Grant by the Oklahoma State Regents for Higher Education, a Towsend Memorial Minority Scholarship, and an Archie

B. Gillfillan Award for Creative Writing. His published works include *Remember Your Relatives, Conference on Reburials, The Yankton Sioux,* and *South Dakota Leaders.*

## Louis (Smokey) Bruyere (1948–)
*Ojibwa activist*

Smokey Bruyere was raised in bush camps in northwestern Ontario. He attended school until the age of eighteen and then worked with a mining company for a year and in the lumber industry in the bush camps for more than ten years. During this time, Bruyere helped establish the Ontario Métis and Non-Status Indian Association, an organization geared to the advancement of the Métis people. The Métis are persons of mixed Indian-European heritage who forged a common identity on the plains of Western Canada in the nineteenth century; non-status Indians are aboriginal people not legally recognized by Canadian authorities as Indians. Bruyere served as president of the association for two years and was involved in constitutional reform and dealings with the provincial government of Ontario, trying to secure better housing and employment services for his people.

In 1979, Bruyere turned his attention to the Native Council of Canada, a national organization representing Métis and non-status Indians. He was subsequently elected president of the council in 1981 and served in this capacity until 1988. During this time, aboriginal issues were attracting greater attention on the national stage, and Bruyere and the council advocated stronger constitutional guarantees to protect aboriginal people. He also was at the forefront of a movement to amend federal law so that Indian women no longer were treated as non-Indians by law when they married non-Indian men. In March 1991, Bruyere was hired by the federal Department of Indian and Northern Affairs as a spokesperson for aboriginal trappers. After eight years of negotiation, Bruyere, as an Indian and Northern Affairs Canada (INAC) member of the International Humane Trapping Standards Negotiating Team agreed to scientific standards with the European Union and Russia for the humane trapping and marketing of fur bearing animals. For their work, the negotiating team was presented with an Award of Excellence by the Canadian government in 1999.

Bruyere has long been a domestic and international advocate of aboriginal people. He has traveled with the World Council of Indigenous Peoples to the United States, Central and South America, and Europe, assisted in the drafting of a United Nations Declaration of Indigenous Peoples, and lectured in many universities throughout the world on indigenous peoples and the law.

## Buffalo Hump (1810–1870)
*Comanche tribal leader*

Born in the early 1800s, Buffalo Hump proved himself as a war chief of the Comanche in his many raids into Texas and Mexico for horses and slaves. Buffalo Hump also led Comanche attacks on the neighboring Cheyenne and Arapaho. He is most often remembered for his participation in the attacks following the Council House Affair in 1838. The Texas Rangers, who were pursuing the Comanche and had suffered heavy casualties, seized a number of chiefs who had come to San Antonio to bargain for the release of Texas prisoners held by the Comanche. Thirty-five Comanche were killed during the fight even though the Comanche were negotiating under a flag of truce. In reaction, Buffalo Hump led a war party down from the Comanche lands, north of the Red River along the Guadalupe Valley, all the way through Texas to the Gulf of Mexico, attacking villages and killing settlers as they went. The Texas Rangers ambushed the Indians on their return northward at Plum Creek, near Lockhart, and managed to kill some warriors. The breaking of the truce at the Council House had proved much more costly to Texas than to the Comanche.

Buffalo Hump became principal chief of the Penateka Band of Comanche in 1849, following the cholera epidemic that swept through the Southern Plains. In the late 1850s, Texas Rangers and army regulars launched a coordinated campaign against the Comanche. Buffalo Hump managed to evade the combined force although his band suffered a major defeat at Rush Springs, Oklahoma. Fifty-six warriors and two women died.

In October 1865, Buffalo Hump, with chiefs from other Southern Plains tribes, attended a treaty council with U.S. commissioners along the Little Arkansas River, in present-day Kansas. As a result of the treaty, the Comanche, Kiowa, Kiowa-Apache, Southern Cheyenne, and Southern Arapaho were forced to relinquish claims to territory north of the Arkansas River.

Buffalo Hump's son, who inherited his father's name, carried on the fighting under the new Comanche chief Quanah Parker.

## George Burdeau (1944–)
*Blackfeet producer, director, and screenwriter*

George Burdeau is a screenwriter and director of Blackfeet descent. He was born on 16 November 1944. He received a bachelor's degree in communications from the University of Washington and did graduate work at the Anthropology Film Center in Santa Fe, New Mexico. He also studied at the Institute of American Indian Arts in Santa Fe.

The earliest of his works include various documentaries on Native American subjects that were produced for the Public Broadcasting System (PBS), and since the mid-1980s, Burdeau has become increasingly active as a producer and director for major network television programs. His projects include *Forest Spirits, Surviving Columbus, Colonization of the Pacific*, the Plains Indian segment of *The Native Americans* series for TBS, *The Witness, Cherry Tree*, and *Backbone of the World*. Burdeau is currently a producer/director for the Alaskan Native Heritage Association and a consulting producer for the Pequot Tribe.

## Diane Burns (1957–)
*Anishinaabe (Ojibwa) and Chemehuevi poet*

Diane Burns is a poet of Anishinaabe (Ojibwa) and Chemehuevi descent. She studied at the Institute of American Indian Arts in Santa Fe, New Mexico, where she was awarded the Congressional Medal of Merit for academic and artistic excellence. She also attended Barnard College in New York City.

Her first book of poetry, *Riding the One-Eyed Ford* (1981), was nominated for the William Carlos Williams Award and was named one of the ten best books of the year by the St. Marks Poetry Project. Her poetry has also appeared in magazines and journals such as *The Greenfield Review, Sunbury, White Pine Journal, New York Waterways*, and *Hard Press*.

Burns is also a painter and illustrator and has been a book reviewer for the Council on Inter-Racial Books for Children. She is a member of the Poet's Overland Expeditionary Troop (POET), which performs theatrical presentations of poetry in galleries and schools throughout the United States. Burns also belongs to the Third World Writers Association and the Feminist Writers Guild.

## Barney Furman Bush (1945–)
*Shawnee and Cayuga poet and educator*

Barney Bush, Shawnee and Cayuga, is president of LifeBlood International, a corporation designed to create small businesses, whose profits will endow the new College of the Redwinds, the first indigenous peoples' institution of its kind in the world.

Born in August 1945, he studied graphic arts at the Institute of American Indian Arts in Santa Fe, New Mexico, earning a bachelor's degree in humanities at Fort Lewis College in Durango, Colorado (1972). He later completed a master's degree in English and fine arts at the University of Idaho (1978).

His books of poetry and fiction include *Longhouse of the Blackberry Moon, My Horse and a Jukebox, Petroglyphs, Inherit the Blood, By Due Process,* and *Redemption of the Serpent,* a recently completed novel. His poems are widely published, anthologized, translated into more than a dozen languages, and recorded, including *A Sense of Journey, Left for Dead, Remake of the American Dream, Destinations, Oyate,* and *By Due Process.*

Bush has served as visiting writer/artist in public schools and colleges through the arts councils of a dozen states. He has been awarded grants and fellowships from the National Endowment for the Arts, PEN, the Author's Guild, and the Newberry Library. His work has been used in international films and for public radio and television.

He has taught his artforms, Native American literature, and related subjects at the University of Wisconsin, Brunswick College, the Institute of American Indian Arts, and New Mexico Highlands University. He has three grown sons and is a member of the Four Corners Gourd Dance Society.

## George Bushotter (1864–1892)
*Teton Sioux ethnographer*

George Bushotter lived only twenty-eight years, but during his short lifetime he crossed the boundaries between two worlds and became the first Lakota to write an account of his own people in their own language. Born in Dakota Territory in 1864, he showed many signs throughout his childhood that he would probably become a medicine man. Instead he traveled east, motivated by a curiosity about Americans and a desire to learn more about them. He entered Hampton Institute in Hampton, Virginia, in 1878 and made such excellent progress that he worked as an assistant teacher in 1881.

In 1887, Bushotter began working for the Reverend James Owen Dorsey, a Siouan scholar employed by the Bureau of Ethnology in Washington, D.C. Dorsey worked out a method by which he could work independently, writing a myth or other text phonetically in the Lakota language and then adding free translations and more detailed word-for-word translations in English. In this way, he produced some 258 separate texts and a total of 3,296 pages of Lakota ethnographic material during a period of only ten months. These texts, currently among the holdings of the National Anthropological Archives (Smithsonian Institution), are important not only because they are the earliest cultural documents obtained

from a Lakota Indian, but because Bushotter himself determined the subject matter.

Bushotter suffered periodically from various illnesses after he arrived in the East and passed away on 2 February 1892, in Hedgesville, West Virginia.

## Frank Arthur Calder (1915–)
*Nisga'a tribal leader*

Frank Calder was the first Indian member of a Canadian legislature, serving as a member of the National Assembly of British Columbia for twenty-six years and as a provincial cabinet minister for a short time in the 1970s. His people, the Nisga'a, occupy the Nass River valley and adjacent lands of the British Columbia coastline. Calder was raised by his aunt and uncle, whose own son had died, and in accordance with Nisga'a custom, they adopted him in order to pass family rank onto a son. His adoptive mother, Louisa, was the eldest of six sisters in a leading Nisga'a family. His adoptive father, Arthur Calder, himself played a leading role in the political life of the Nisga'a Nation. Calder attended a Methodist residential school far from home that was established to inculcate Anglo-Canadian values in First Nation children. Much of his tribal cultural learning occurred during summers when, home from school, he went fishing with his father and other elders who instructed him on his future responsibilities as a Nisga'a leader.

Calder has been an important political leader of the Nisga'a Nation. He was the founder and president of the Nisga'a Tribal Council, which united four diverse clans (Eagle, Wolf, Raven, and Killer Whale) located in four communities in northwest British Columbia (Kincolith, Greenville, Canyon City, and Aiyansh). He is also widely known as a result of the landmark Supreme Court of Canada decision in *Calder v. The Queen* (1973), in which the Court held that aboriginal people located in British Columbia possessed special rights to their ancestral lands that survived the establishment of the province. He received a Lifetime Achievement Award by the National Aboriginal Achievement Foundation in 1996.

## Ben Nighthorse Campbell (1933–)
*Northern Cheyenne U.S. senator*

Campbell is the first Native American elected as a United States senator. Born in Auburn, California, he received a bachelor's degree in physical education and fine arts from San Jose State University in 1957 and later attended Meiji University in Tokyo in 1960 as a special research student. Before entering college, Campbell served in the U.S. Air Force from 1951 to 1953, stationed in Korea, attaining the rank of Airman Second Class.

Senator Campbell's athletic career in judo was particularly outstanding, because he took the gold medal at the Pan-American Games in 1963 and won the United States championship in his weight division three times. He was also a member of the United States Olympic team in 1964 and wrote a judo manual, *Judo Drill Training* (1975).

He became the second Native American elected to the Colorado legislature, where he served from 1983 to 1986. His committee assignments included agriculture and natural affairs and business and labor. During this period he was also appointed as an advisor to the Colorado Commission on International Trade and the Arts and Humanities. He was named Outstanding Legislator of 1984 by the Colorado Bankers Association and was voted one of the Ten Best Legislators of 1986 in a survey of state legislators conducted by the Denver Post and News Center 4.

Campbell has always been a man of many talents. Campbell is also a self-employed jewelry designer, rancher, and a trainer of champion quarter horses. He was inducted into the Council of Forty-Four Chiefs by his Northern Cheyenne tribe in Lame Deer, Montana.

Senator Campbell currently belongs to four key Senate committees. He chairs the Indian Affairs Committee and the Treasury and General Government Committee. He is a member of the Interior, Foreign Operations, Transportation and Commerce, Justice, State, and Judiciary subcommittees. He is vice-chairman of the National Parks, Historic Preservation, and Recreation subcommittee. Senator Campbell also serves on the Veterans' Affairs Committee and is co-chairman of the Helsinki Commission.

### Canassatego (d. 1750)
*Onondaga tribal leader*

This Onondaga leader was a strong supporter of the Iroquois League of Nations, the government of the Mohawk, Oneida, Onondaga, Tuscarora, Cayuga, and Seneca of present-day upstate New York. He represented the league in a number of important conferences, alliances, and agreements with English colonists. Canassatego worked to ensure that no treaties were signed by members of the league without full consent of the league's governing body.

In 1742, Canassatego, with translator Conrad Weiser, negotiated an alliance between the Iroquois League and

Pennsylvania officials who were anxious to ally themselves with the Indians in order to prevent French encroachment. During these negotiations, Canassatego demonstrated a keen understanding of republican principles and urged the English colonists to respect the pledges and concepts of the league and its "league of friendship" with the colonists. A few years later in 1750 at Albany, New York, Canassatego also advised the English on issues concerning colonial unity. He recommended that the English colonies form a union like the Iroquois League, since the colonies would be stronger united than when they acted separately.

It is believed that Canassatego was killed by a fellow Iroquois allied with the French. According to English reports from this era, Canassatego was an impressive speaker with a presence that commanded attention from all persons in a room with him. This might explain why, after his death, he was "immortalized" in a British literary work that romanticized the Iroquois leader and built him into a nearly mythical figure. John Shebbeare immortalized Canassatego in his book *Lydia, or, Filial Piety* (1755), which satirized the materialism, impersonality, and inequality of British urban life as compared to the Iroquois political and social views of equality and negotiated political consensus.

### Captain Jack (d. 1873)
*Modoc tribal leader*

Captain Jack was a famous Indian leader in the Modoc War of 1872–1873. The original territory of the Modocs was centered around lower Klamath Lake and Tule Lake in southeastern Oregon and northeastern California. Modern descendants of the tribe also live on reservations in Oklahoma.

Born somewhere along the Lost River in present-day Modoc County, California, the man whom the U.S. settlers would call Captain Jack was originally given the Modoc name Kintpuash. He became the leader of his band when his father died in 1846. Captain Jack was drawn into the Modoc Wars through a complex series of events that began in 1864, when the Modoc signed away much of their indigenous territory and were removed to the Klamath Reservation in Oregon. The living conditions on the reservation were miserable; there was much disease and not enough food to support both the Modoc and the Klamath tribe. The Modoc request for their own reservation in California was rejected.

Captain Jack and the Modoc returned to California anyway, but there were many complaints from white settlers and the federal government ordered troops to the area in 1872. A series of violent incidents ensued;

then Captain Jack and his followers escaped and worked their way south to a volcanic area with lava formations that offered excellent natural fortifications. Another Modoc group joined them so that the rebel group consisted of about two hundred people, eighty of whom were warriors. They ambushed a wagon train on December 22, thus obtaining more ammunition, and in January 1873 they successfully repulsed a force of over three hundred regular soldiers led by Lieutenant Colonel Frank Wheaton.

Shortly thereafter, General Edward Canby planned to lead another attack and gathered a force of about a thousand men. At the same time a peace plan was set in motion. The first negotiation on February 28 produced no results, and at the second meeting Captain Jack produced a hidden revolver and fatally shot General Canby. Modoc warriors Boston Charlie and Schonchin John also fired on the peace commissioners that had been sent by President Grant, and the Modoc retreated to another lava formation to the south. Throughout these months there were scattered conflicts such as the one that took place on 26 April 1873, when the warrior Scarfaced Charlie attacked a patrol of sixty-three soldiers and killed twenty-five, including all five officers.

Despite their successes, however, the Modoc were badly lacking food and water, and their forces became less and less unified. General Jefferson C. Davis finally organized a relentless pursuit of the scattered bands that remained, and Captain Jack and other leaders were finally cornered in a cave and captured on 1 June 1873. Captain Jack was executed by hanging on 3 October 1878, while two other Modoc leaders were sentenced to life imprisonment on Alcatraz, a penal facility on an island in San Francisco Bay. On the night after the hanging, Captain Jack's head was stolen by grave robbers, embalmed, and put on display in a carnival that toured cities in the eastern United States.

The Modoc War was one of the few Indian wars that ever took place in California, as tribes of the California region were not highly organized militarily. Because of this and the relatively late date of the uprising, it had a shocking effect on the public, gaining a great deal of national attention. A more detailed account of the events described here is given in Keith Murray's book *The Modocs and their War* (1969).

### Douglas Joseph Cardinal (1934– )
*Métis architect*

Douglas Cardinal is an internationally renowned architect. Born in Red Deer, Alberta, Douglas Cardinal was the eldest son of a family of eight. His father was half Blackfoot and worked as a provincial wildlife

Douglas J. Cardinal.

warden. The Blackfoot are located on the plains of western Canada. His mother was a nurse. Cardinal enrolled in the University of British Columbia School of Architecture at the age of nineteen, but was asked to withdraw from the program in his second year because his architectural designs were considered too radical. Several years later, he enrolled at the University of Texas and graduated in 1963. He then returned to Red Deer to begin an architecture career that continues today.

Cardinal's first commission was to design the round Guloien House, a private residence, in Sylvan Lake, Alberta. He then designed St. Mary's Church in Red Deer, pioneering the use of computer-enhanced electronic drawing. St. Mary's Church is considered by many to be an architectural triumph, with its circular and semi-enclosed design. In the 1970s, he immersed himself in Native religion and numerous aboriginal causes. In 1983, Cardinal was awarded the commission to design the Canadian Museum of Civilization in Hull, Quebec. With its unique curves, the museum now stands along the banks of the Ottawa River, opposite the Parliament buildings and the Supreme Court of Canada.

His firm, a pioneer and world leader for incorporating computers in architecture, has designed and undertaken many projects, including the design commission for the National Museum of the American Indian, the Edmonton Space Science Center, the Saskatchewan Indian Federated College in Regina, Saskatchewan, and a major hotel complex and Children and Elders' Center for the Oneida Indian Nation of New York.

He is a recipient of the Order of Canada, Canada's highest honor. In 1999 he was awarded the Royal Architectural Institute of Canada Gold Medal, the highest award bestowed in the Canadian profession of architecture.

### Gil Cardinal (1950–)
*Cree/Métis filmmaker*

Gil Cardinal is president and co-founder of Kanata Productions. A skilled director, producer, writer, and editor, Gil Cardinal has been working both in front of and behind the camera for over twenty years. He graduated in 1973 from the Radio and Television Arts Program at the Northern Alberta Institute of Technology in Edmonton, and in 1976 became the director and associate producer of *Come Alive*, a daily, live magazine-format show in Alberta. Cardinal continued to produce and direct a variety of shows, including *Shadow Puppets*, a series of seven programs adapting Cree and Blackfoot legends to electronic animation.

Cardinal began his association with Canada's National Film Board, a federally established organization devoted to the advancement of film, in 1980. His numerous projects include *Children of Alcohol* (1983), a documentary on the effects of parental alcoholism; *Discussions in Bioethics: The Courage of One's Convictions* (1985), an inquiry into medical/legal ethics; and *Fort McPherson* (1986), a look at a community's struggle with alcohol and suicide. *Foster Child* (1987), which traces Cardinal's search for his natural family and features him as a director, associate editor, and subject, has won nine film festival awards since its premier.

Cardinal's varied experience in Canadian media also includes a half-hour television drama, *Bordertown Cafe* (1988), and a one-hour documentary, *Tikinagan* (1991), for Tamarack Productions of Toronto, Ontario. His latest National Film Board documentary, *The Spirit Within* (1990), co-directed with Wil Campbell, focuses on the importance of Indian spirituality for Native inmates in Canada.

He directed numerous episodes of the Gemini award-winning CBC series *North of 60*, and episodes of CBC television's Native anthology series *Four Directions* and *The Rez*. In 1997, Cardinal received a National Aboriginal Achievement Award for his work in film and television.

### Harold Cardinal (1945–)
*Cree tribal leader/scholar*

Harold Cardinal is a political leader and writer, active on the provincial and national level. He was born in High Prairie, Alberta, on 27 January 1945, and raised on the Sucker Creek Reserve in north-central Alberta. Cardinal attended Joussard Indian Residential School and then high school in Edmonton, Alberta. Cardinal interrupted two years of university study at St. Patrick's College in Ottawa, Ontario, where he studied sociology, to work with the Canadian Union of Students as associate secretary for Indian affairs in 1966 and 1967. That same year, Cardinal was elected president of the Canadian Indian Youth Council.

In May 1968, Cardinal returned to Alberta to take up what he thought would be a summer job with the Alberta Native Communications Society. In June 1968,

Harold Cardinal.

he was elected president of the Indian Association of Alberta, with associated membership on the board of the National Indian Brotherhood, a national organization devoted to the advancement of aboriginal rights, and worked with others to develop the Assembly of First Nations.

As president of the Indian Association of Alberta, Cardinal served nine terms in office, initiating a variety of programs to promote Native culture and economic development. He assisted in the drafting of Citizens Plus (1970), an aboriginal response to federal efforts to abolish differential treatment of aboriginal people in Canada. He authored two texts, *The Unjust Society* (1969, 1999) which describes the social and political conditions of First Nations in Canada, and *The Rebirth of Canada's Indians* (1977) affirming the importance of Indian identity and culture. In 1977, Cardinal was appointed regional director general of Indian affairs for a controversial seven-month term, after which he became a consultant to northern Alberta Indian Bands. He worked as the Prairie Treaty Alliance representative in the Constitutional Conferences with the Assembly of First Nations, federal, and provincial governments.

In 1992, Cardinal studied law at the University of Saskatchewan. He obtained his degree in law and earned a master's in law at Harvard University. He was awarded an honorary doctorate of law and an indigenous scholar-in-residence from the University of Alberta. From 1997 to 1999, he worked as a negotiator for the Treaty Eight First Nations of Alberta Bilateral Process. Cardinal is currently working with the Assembly of First Nations on traditional governance and treaty rights while completing his doctorate in law at the University of British Columbia.

### Tantoo Cardinal (1950–)
*Cree/Métis actress*

Born in Fort McMurray and raised in Anzac, a small town 350 miles northeast of Edmonton, Alberta, Tantoo Cardinal is one of Canada's most renowned Native film actresses. Never formally trained as an actress, she began her career in the 1970s with a series of small roles in film, theater, and television. Her first feature film appearance occurred in *Marie Anne* in 1977, produced in Canada by Fraser Films and directed by Martin Walters. In 1985, Cardinal played the lead role in *Loyalties*, a feature film written, directed, and produced by Anne Wheeler, which tells the fictional story of a British man who moves to the Canadian plains to escape his past. For her stirring performance, Cardinal was nominated for the prestigious Canadian film award, the Genie, as best actress, and she received a best actress award at the American Indian Film Festival, as

well as a number of other awards. Her performance served to expand Cardinal's audience beyond the Native community in which she was well known.

She has enjoyed significant success in television, film, and theater. Her credits include *Grand Avenue*, *Where the Rivers Flow North*, *Dances With Wolves*, *Smoke Signals*, *The Education of Little Tree*, *Honey Mocassin*, *The Campbells*, *Street Legal*, and *Wonderworks*, as well as hosting a five-episode public television series *As Long as the Rivers Flow* and a nine-episode series entitled *Native Indians: Images of Reality*.

### Edward D. Castillo (1947–)
*Cahuilla and Luise–o historian, anthropologist, and professor*

Edward Castillo is a university professor specializing in Native American Studies. Born at San Jacinto, California, on 25 August 1947, Castillo graduated from the University of California, Riverside, in 1969 and went on to receive his master's degree and doctorate in anthropology from the University of California, Berkeley (1977). He was a lecturer in Native American Studies at UC Berkeley from 1970 to 1971 and 1973 to 1977,

Ed Castillo.

then became associate professor of Native American Studies and director of the Native American Studies Program at UC Santa Cruz from 1977 until 1982. He was director of a Title IV Program for the Laytonville, California, Unified School District from 1985 until 1988, and since then he has been the director of the Native American Studies Program at Sonoma State University in Rohnert Park, California.

He has numerous publications in anthropology and Native American Studies, but is best known for the chapters entitled "History of the Impact of Euro-American Exploration and Settlement on the Indians of California" and "Recent Secular Movements among California Indians, 1900–1973" in the Smithsonian Institution's *Handbook of North American Indians*, Volume 8: California (1978). He also wrote a book entitled *Native American Perspectives on the Hispanic Colonization of Alta California* (1990).

### John Castillo (1956–)
*Chiricahua Apache social worker and community organizer*

John Castillo is the former executive director of the Southern California Indian Center, Inc. (SCIC), located in Garden Grove, California. Castillo's commitment to work in the Indian community was encouraged by his parents. His father moved to Gardena, California, from Arizona. John, his three sisters, and one brother were born in Southern California. His parents emphasized the importance of working within and for the Native American community because they knew firsthand the needs of reservation and urban Indians.

Castillo attended Orange Coast College for two years and then went on to graduate with a bachelor of arts in ethnic studies from California State University, Fullerton. In 1979, he entered the University of California, Los Angeles (UCLA) in the graduate school of social welfare. In 1981, he graduated with a master's degree in social work with an emphasis on community organization and joined SCIC, becoming executive director in 1989. Castillo has worked in many capacities in the SCIC, including as a classroom trainer and coordinator. He established the SCIC's program sites in Los Angeles and Long Beach, before assuming administrative work in the main office. In October 1985, Castillo was named a Kellog National Fellow, a prestigious award. From 1985 through 1989, he conducted research on the leadership skill, styles, knowledge, and motivations of tribal leaders in the United States and abroad.

Castillo has taught American Indian studies and social work at California State University at Long Beach. He has also served as chair of the Los Angeles City/County Native American Indian Commission, the Los Angeles County Child Welfare Task Force, and the Los Angeles American Indian Mental Health Task Force. He has lectured on American Indian issues for over two hundred television and radio shows, served as guest lecturer on American Indian issues at major universities, and has published articles on job training programs.

Castillo's years of service to the urban Indian community are the result of his early vision and commitment to make a contribution to the community. In recent years he has worked for nonprofit agencies related to Indian affairs.

### Duane Champagne (1951–)
*Turtle Mountain Chippewa sociologist and professor*

Duane Champagne is a sociologist and university professor of Chippewa descent. Most of his writings

Duane Champagne, director of the UCLA American Indian Studies Center.

focus on issues of social, cultural, and political change in American Indian societies as they adapted to European political domination, cultural interpenetration, and economic incorporation.

Champagne received his bachelor's degree in mathematics from North Dakota State University in 1973. After serving a year with Volunteer in Service to America (VISTA), a domestic peace corps program, he finished a master's degree in sociology at North Dakota State University in 1975. In 1982, he received a Ph.D. in sociology from Harvard University. In 1982 and 1983, Champagne received a postdoctoral award from the Rockefeller Foundation and, during this time, completed fieldwork trips to the Tlingit of southeast Alaska and to the Northern Cheyenne in Montana. He taught at the University of Wisconsin, Milwaukee, in 1983 and 1984 and started teaching at the University of California, Los Angeles (UCLA) in 1984, where he became full professor in 1997. In 1986, Champagne became editor of the *American Indian Culture and Research Journal*, and, in 1991, he became director of the UCLA American Indian Studies Center, which carries out research, offers a master's degree program in American Indian studies, and publishes books for academic and Indian audiences.

Champagne has published broadly in both sociology and American Indian studies. He has published two books, *American Indian Societies: Strategies and Conditions of Political and Cultural Survival* (1989), and *Social Order and Political Change: Constitutional Governments among the Cherokee, the Choctaw, the Chickasaw, and the Creek* (1992). In addition, he has published articles in various academic journals, edited many books, and contributed numerous chapters to other books. In 1999 he received Writer of the Year award for anthology/collections from the Wordcraft Circle of Native Writers and Storytellers.

## Paul L. A. H. Chartrand (1943–)
*Métis lawyer and professor*

Paul Chartrand is a private consultant and a commissioner on the Manitoba Aboriginal Justice Implementation Commission. He was born to J. Aime Chartrand and Antoinette Bouvier in the historic Métis fishing village of Saint-Laurent, Manitoba. Until the age of seven, Chartrand lived with his family in a log cabin. His father was a fur trapper, and he would dry muskrat skins on frames in the house. His father also dug seneca root, a medicinal plant. Chartrand himself snared rabbits for food and hunted small game and waterfowl in the nearby marshes. He attended school in the village, where missionary nuns were his teachers.

When he finished grade twelve, Chartrand moved with his family to Winnipeg, and he continued his studies with degrees from the Manitoba Teachers College and the University of Winnipeg, Manitoba. He later studied law at the Queensland University of Technology in Australia, graduating with an honors degree, and at the University of Saskatchewan, where he specialized in Native law and received a master of law degree. In 1991, he was appointed by the Canadian government to serve as a commissioner for the Royal Commission on Aboriginal Peoples, which was established to inquire into and report on a wide range of matters relating to aboriginal peoples in Canada.

He has served as head of the Department of Native Studies at the University of Manitoba and was a founding member of the Aboriginal Healing Foundation. He is a member of the Indigenous Bar Association of Canada, a member of the advisory committee for the Canadian National Judicial Institute, the author of numerous publications in law and policy, and performs consulting work in the area of domestic, comparative, and international law and policy. He lives in Victoria, British Columbia, is married, and has three children.

## Dean Chavers (1941–)
*Lumbee educator*

Dean Chavers, a member of the Lumbee tribe, is an important figure in Native American education. Born in Pembroke, North Carolina, on 4 February 1941, Chavers attended the University of Richmond from 1960 to 1962. He then entered the United States Air Force and served with distinction as a navigator, flying 138 missions during the Vietnam Conflict. He left active duty in 1968 with the rank of captain, having won the Distinguished Flying Cross, the Air Medal, and eight other decorations. He returned to school and received a bachelor's degree in journalism from the University of California, Berkeley (1970), then went on to obtain master's degrees in communications (1973) and anthropology (1975) from Stanford University in Palo Alto, California. He later received his Ph.D. in communications at Stanford, writing a dissertation entitled "Social Structure and the Diffusion of Innovations: A Study of Teachers at Four Indian Boarding High Schools and the Effects of their Interpersonal Communication Behavior on their Adoption of New Ideas in Education" (1976).

Dean Chavers.

Even as a student, Chavers was very productive in communications and education, serving as the managing editor of *Indian Voice* magazine (1972) and as an assistant professor of Native American studies at Hayward State University (1972–74). During this period he was chair of the Higher Education Committee of the California Indian Education Association.

Between 1970 and 1978, Chavers was the president of the Native American Scholarship Fund, an organization which raised more than $300,000 for Indian college students and made 522 grants to Indian students in northern California. He served as president of Bacone College in Muskogee, Oklahoma, from 1978 to 1981, then returned to his work as an educational fundraiser and communications consultant in the position of president of his own company: Dean Chavers and Associates (1981–1988). He resumed his post as president of the Native American Scholarships Fund, now called Catching the Dream, and continues working for this important organization today.

Chavers has won awards and honors throughout his life, including the Virginia State spelling championship as a high school student in 1959. He has published five books, including *How to Write Winning Proposals*

(1983), *Funding Guide for Native Americans* (1983), *Tribal Indian Development Directory* (1985), and *The National Indian Grant Directory* (2000), and more than thirty articles.

### Shirley Cheechoo (contemporary)
*Cree filmmaker*

Shirley Cheechoo, a member of the Cree Nation, James Bay, Quebec, is an award-winning actress, producer, director, and visual artist. She first gained national attention in 1991 with her play, *Path With No Moccasins*. She made her directorial debut with the short film *Silent Tears* (1997), which has won several film festival awards for Best Short Film. It was screened at the 1998 Sundance Film Festival and was awarded the Telefilm Canada/Television Northern Canada Award for Best Canadian Aboriginal Language Television Program.

Cheechoo is the first aboriginal woman to write, produce, direct, and act in a feature length film from Canada. In 1998, she attended the Sundance Institute's filmmaker/screenwriters lab, where she workshopped and filmed scenes of *Backroads*, a 1970s story of three sisters who suffer the consequences of racism and sexism when one of them is accused of murder. The 1999 movie was screened at the 2000 Sundance film festival. Cheechoo has also appeared on several Canadian film and television series and programs, including *The Rez*.

Her latest work is *Tracks in the Snow* (2000), a short film documenting a sixty-two-mile traditional journey into the bush during which Cree students, adults, and elders camped for four days and four nights, teaching the children the traditional way of life.

### Michael Chiago (1946–)
*Tohono O'Odham illustrator and dancer*

Michael Chiago is an illustrator whose art reflects his experiences as a powwow dancer. Born in Kohatk Village on the Tohono O'Odham Reservation in Arizona on 6 April 1946, Chiago started dancing and drawing when he was just a boy. He attended St. John's Academy High School in Laveen, Arizona, then joined the U.S. Marines, and served in Vietnam and Okinawa.

On returning home, Chiago studied commercial art and magazine layout techniques at the Maricopa Technical School. He is best known for a style of painting that he developed by himself. He uses water color and adds a special coating or glaze to certain parts when the painting is finished, thus producing a surface of unusual depth and brilliance.

Chiago's paintings are surrealistic in character, rather than being strictly representational, and they often depict dramatically costumed Indian dancers, drawing on Chiago's personal experiences as a powwow dancer who has toured throughout Arizona, California, Nevada, and the East Coast. Chiago has been recognized as an outstanding dancer since he was a young man, and he often attends powwows to watch and learn from the techniques of other dancers. All these images find a place in his paintings, which are included in the permanent collection at the Heard Museum in Phoenix, Arizona, and are often exhibited throughout Arizona and New Mexico.

## Robert Keams Chiago (1942–)
*Navajo educator*

Robert K. Chiago was born on 22 June 1942 in Arizona. He received a bachelor of arts degree in education from Arizona State University in Tempe in 1965. He served in Vietnam from 1967 to 1968 as an officer in the United States Marine Corps, where he attained the rank of captain. He was company commander of a marine unit near Phu Bai and Hue and served with the First Battalion Ninth Marines at Con Tien. He was logistics officer with Shore Party Battalion in Khe Sahn, Dong Ha, and in other parts of Vietnam.

After the Vietnam War, Chiago received a master's degree in education from Northern Illinois University in 1970 and his first post was as associate director at the American Indian Culture Center at UCLA. In 1971 he was the director of the Ramah Navajo School Board (now called Pine Hills School) in New Mexico and, from 1971 to 1973, he was the director of the Navajo Division of Education in the Navajo Nation (Reservation). From 1973 to 1983, Chiago was the director of Native American Studies, director of the Indian Education Program, and a visiting assistant professor of humanities at the University of Utah, Salt Lake City. He has also served as special assistant to the chairman of the Navajo Tribal Council, and deputy assistant director for intergovernmental operations in the Department of Economic Security of the state of Arizona. From 1988 to 1991, Chiago was the director of the Department of Education of the Salt River Pima-Maricopa Indian Community. During that period, with the aid of grants from the U.S. Department of Education, he established three learning centers in the reservation. In 1991, Chiago was appointed the executive director of NACIE, the National Advisory Council on Indian Education, and managing editor of NACIE's newsletter.

Chiago has published several articles including "A Review of Indian Energy Resources from a Manpower and Educational Perspective" in *Bureau of Indian Affairs Education Research Bulletin* 6, number 1 (1978) and "Making Education Work for the American Indian," published in *Theory into Practice* XX, number 1 (1981).

Chiago has been a delegate to the White House Conference on Indian Education Advisory Committee and is currently working as a BIA line education officer for schools at the Ft. Apache Agency.

## Rosemary Ackley Christensen (1939–)
*Mole Lake and Bad River Wisconsin Ojibwe educator*

Rosemary Ackley Christensen teaches at the University of Wisconsin, Green Bay. Born on the Bad River Reservation in Wisconsin on 16 February 1939, Christensen received her master's degree in education from Harvard University (1971) and obtained her doctorate in education at the University of Minnesota (1999). Her dissertation was entitled "Anishinaabeg Medicine Wheel Leadership: The Work of David Courchene, Jr."

In addition to teaching, Christensen has ample experience as an administrator, curriculum developer, writer, researcher, and Indian education advocate. She is a founding member of the National Indian Education Association (NIEA), and in recent years she worked with the Ojibwa language, writing and producing five units for family use.

## Edward P. Churchill, Sr. (1923–)
*Tlingit fisherman and tribal leader*

Edward P. Churchill, Sr., is a Tlingit fisherman and lobbyist for Alaska Natives and natural resources. The Tlingit are a Northwest Coast tribe occupying the southeastern Alaskan coastline from Yakutat Bay to Cape Fox.

Born at Ketchikan, Alaska, on 1 January 1923, Churchill graduated from Wrangell (Alaska) High School in 1941 and became first mate on a tugboat for the U.S. Corps of Engineers (1942–1944). He served in the U.S. Army from 1944 to 1946 and has mainly worked as a commercial fisherman since then. Since 1988, he has been the chairman of Alaska Aquaculture, a fish hatchery at Burnett Inlet, Alaska, and a member of the Southeast Alaska Native Fisheries and Native Resources Commission.

Churchill has been active as a lobbyist for Alaska Native land claims in Washington, D.C., and is the only

Rosemary Auckley Christensen.

Ward Churchill. (Photo by Leah Renae Kelly)

Indian to have been elected mayor of Wrangell, Alaska. Churchill is a member of the Alaska Native Brotherhood and he has served as secretary and treasurer of the Salmon Bay Protection Association.

### Ward Churchill (1947–)
*Creek/Keetoowah Cherokee Métis activist, academic, and educator*

After reading one of Ward Churchill's many books, including *Fantasies of the Master Race: Literature, Cinema, and the Colonization of American Indians* (1992), *Agents of Repression: The FBI's Secret War Against the Black Panther Party and the American Indian Movement* (1988), and *Indian Are Us? Culture and Genocide in Native North America* (1994), it becomes clear that he holds important opinions not to be ignored. His work in academia and his role as an activist have bestowed upon Churchill a serious reputation for trying to create and inspire change across Native America. Specifically, Churchill's goal is to incite others to question the reality that oppressors create for subaltern peoples and to explore the power that lies in refusing to accept that reality.

The to-be academic was born and raised in and around Urbana, Illinois, to Maralyn Allen and Jack Churchill. His parents divorced early and his mother remarried, eventually providing Churchill with two half-brothers and a half-sister. Churchill graduated from Elmwood Consolidated High School and received his associate's degree from Illinois Central College.

Churchill's experiences in the Vietnam War awoke his radical sentiments. In 1968 Churchill found himself sent on missions into "Indian Country," a phrase used in Vietnam to refer to the Vietcong's territory. He then received an undergraduate degree from Sangaman State University with a major in communications. Churchill continued his education at Sangaman and received a master's degree in cross-cultural communications in 1975.

While focused on academics and activism, Churchill was also an artist. His work, which consisted mostly of painting and printmaking, was exhibited at nationally recognized museums across the United States. The art Churchill created related to his activism and academic work. In 1983, however, he decided to focus solely on these latter aspects of his life, leaving his artwork behind.

Since then Churchill has been actively amassing job titles and positions in activist organizations and academia. He was the co-director of the American Indian Movement of Colorado, the vice-chairperson of the American Anti-Defamation Council, the national spokesperson for the Leonard Peltier Defense Fund, and the associate chair of the Department of Ethnic Studies at the University of Colorado, Boulder. He is the author or editor of approximately seventeen books and is currently a full professor of ethnic studies and joint professor of communications with a specialization in American Indian Studies at the University of Colorado, Boulder.

Churchill does not draw a line between his roles as an activist and academic. Because there is no such thing as objectivity, he argues, there should never be a line between the two professional fields. His objective is to integrate his life and work, something he has done successfully for many years.

The professor is presently working on a retooling of *Indians Are Us?*, which examines the connections between American culture and genocide in Native North America. In addition, he is completing a companion book to *Native North American Studies*, a comprehensive history of FBI repression, and a book to be titled *Diversions of Justice*. He currently lives in Boulder County, Colorado, with his wife, photographer Leah Renae Kelly.

Carter Blue Clark.

### Carter Blue Clark (1946–)
*Muscogee (Creek) historian*

Carter Blue "CB" Clark is interim director of the Native American Legal Resource Center and David Pendleton Professor of American Indian studies at Oklahoma City University. He is a member of the Muscogee (Creek) Nation, a member of the Cedar River/New Tulsa ceremonial town, and a member of Big Cussetah United Methodist Church. He received his bachelor's, master's, and Ph.D. (1976) from the University of Oklahoma at Norman. Clark wrote his dissertation on the history of the Ku Klux Klan in Oklahoma. He has taught history at a variety of colleges and universities, such as the University of California at Los Angeles, San Diego State University, Morningside College, the University of Utah, and the University of Oklahoma, and was professor of ethnic studies, U.S. History, and American Indian studies at California State University at Long Beach from 1984 to 1993, where he also served many years as director of the university's American Indian Studies Program.

He served as president of Oklahoma City University in 1997 and as provost and executive vice-president from 1992 to 1998. Professor Clark is president of the Oklahoma City Muscogee Association, chairman and co-fundraiser for the Tribal Flag Plaza at the Oklahoma State Capital, and fundraiser for the 1996 PBS documentary *Beyond Reservation Road*.

He is the editor of four books and the author of four books, sixty-one book chapters and journal articles, twenty-five book reviews, and twenty-two professional papers or commentaries. Clark published the prize-winning *Lone Wolfe v. Hitchcock: Treaty Rights and the Law at the End of the Nineteenth Century* in 1994.

### Joseph J. Clark (1893–1971)
*Cherokee admiral and businessperson*

Joseph J. Clark was a military man and business executive. Born in Pryor, Oklahoma, on 12 November 1893, Clark graduated from the U.S. Naval Academy at Annapolis, Maryland, in June 1917. He then served in World War I and became an instructor at the Naval Academy after the war, earning the rank of naval aviator in 1925. During the years that followed and throughout World War II, Clark served in several different shore and sea assignments. He received numerous decorations, including the Navy Cross, the Distinguished Service Medal (twice), and the Legion of Merit. His last command was as commander-in-chief of the Seventh Fleet.

Clark retired from the navy in 1953 with the rank of admiral and then pursued a career as a business executive, becoming chairman of the board at Hegeman Harris, Inc., a New York stock investment firm. He died at St. Albans Naval Hospital in New York on 13 July 1971.

## Frank Clarke (1921–)
*Walapai and Mission physician and administrator*

Frank Clarke is a retired physician and hospital administrator. Born at Blythe, California, on 11 November 1921, Clarke first went to school at Sherman Institute, a high school for Indian students in southern California, then studied at Los Angeles City College, and completed his bachelor's degree at UCLA. He later obtained an M.D. in obstetrics from St. Louis University School of Medicine.

Clarke is said to have decided on a career in medicine when he was only ten after recovering from a severe eye condition that nearly caused him to be blind. Unfortunately, his family had no funds to pay for such an education, and he had to work as a field hand and a janitor to get through the early years of college.

Clarke enlisted in the navy and served for twelve years, seeing active duty in the Solomon Islands during World War II. After seven major engagements with the enemy, he was selected for Naval Officer Training and then began his pre-medical education. When the navy college program ended, he went back to school and supported himself by working nights as a laboratory assistant.

He eventually graduated from St. Louis University School of Medicine, and after two years of private practice was named chief of medicine, and chief and president of staff at Memorial Hospital in Exeter, California, the first time that one person had held both positions. Clarke also headed the Department of Obstetrics at the same hospital. He has won numerous honors and awards over the years, and was winner of the Indian Council Fire Achievement Award in 1961.

## Henry Roe Cloud (1884–1950)
*Winnebago educator*

Henry Roe Cloud was best known as an educator, minister, and humanitarian. He was born on 28 December 1884, in Winnebago, Nebraska, and raised in a traditional Winnebago manner, speaking only the Winnebagan language until he was ten years old. Cloud mastered English, Latin, and Greek as well by the time he turned seventeen. When he entered the government school, his name was Anglicized to Henry Cloud, after his grandfather, Yellow Cloud. He entered Yale University when he was sixteen, and earned his bachelor and master of arts degrees in anthropology.

While at Yale, Cloud was adopted by Dr. and Mrs. Walter Roe, whose last name he adopted as his own. In 1910, at Fort Sill, Oklahoma, he helped his foster father obtain the freedom of Apache, Comanche, and Kiowa children who were considered prisoners of war (see the biographies of Geronimo, Naiche, Quanah Parker, and other southern Plains chiefs). Cloud was ordained a Presbyterian minister at Auburn Theological Seminary in 1913 and received a Doctor of Divinity degree in 1932 from Emporia Kansas College.

Cloud served as vice-president of education on the board of the Society of American Indians, an Indian rights organization highly active during the 1920s. He established the American Indian Institute for boys in Wichita, Kansas, and successfully administered it for fifteen years. He turned the school over to the Presbyterian ministries when, in 1931, he accepted an appointment with the U.S. Indian Service and spent two years developing plans for the Indian Reorganization Act, which was passed in 1934 and provided for greater Indian self-government and cultural practice. In 1933, Cloud became superintendent of the famous Indian boarding school, the Haskell Institute in Lawrence, Kansas, and became its supervisor of education three years later. His final Indian Service post was superintendent of the Umatilla Indian Reservation at Pendleton, Oregon.

## Elouise Cobell (1946–)
*Blackfeet businesswoman and political activist*

After leading a class-action suit against the Interior Department and the Bureau of Indian Affairs (BIA) for mismanagement of Indian trust accounts, Elouise Cobell made a name for herself across the United States. Before she gained national attention, however, Cobell was making business news among her people, the Blackfeet, located in northwest Montana, just east of Glacier National Park.

Born at the southern tip of the 1.5-million-acre Blackfeet Reservation, Cobell and her eight brothers and sisters attended a one-room school. The young leader often helped the teacher care for the younger students, and led field trips onto the reservation's prairies, searching for arrowheads. Because of her reservation's lack of modern conveniences, such as running water and telephones, Cobell longed for the comforts of urban life.

Once she was old enough to leave the reservation, Cobell moved to several different cities in the western half of the United States. While she enjoyed the conveniences such a lifestyle offered, she always kept one eye on home.

When her mother died in 1968 while Cobell was pursuing an undergraduate degree in business, she decided to leave college and return home to help her father run their family's ranch, despite a pleading call from the dean of the university.

Because of her training in the business arena, Cobell and her husband, Alvin "Turk" Cobell, and their son, Turk Russell, eventually took over the family ranch's business affairs. The ranch had $18,000 in debts when she took it over, and her research into the ranch's financial affairs led her on a winding and complicated path with no easy answers. She went to the BIA and to several congressional leaders to uncover the details of her family's financial matters. After twenty years of searching, Cobell was left with contradictory information and little explanation from the federal government.

During her search for answers to her family's financial troubles, Cobell served as tribal treasurer for her reservation from 1976 to 1988, responsible for a $20 million budget. During her tenure the savvy businesswoman corrected past budget mismanagement and gained the trust of her tribal constituency. She also was the driving force behind the creation of the first national bank established on a reservation. When the Blackfeet National Bank opened its doors in 1987, the tribe owned 94 percent of the operation. The bank has prompted a substantial growth in business based on the Blackfeet Reservation. Most of these ventures are Indian-owned and operated. Cobell considers her work as the chair of the bank's board the most rewarding of her professional experiences.

While serving as her tribal government's treasurer, Cobell began noticing discrepancies in the BIA's reports to the tribe. When she discovered that other tribal governments were facing similar difficulties, Cobell and other tribal representatives took their complaints to Congress. In 1989, a scandal erupted that has yet to be quelled. Federal auditors calculated discrepancies of $17 million in the BIA's botched records.

Soon after this discovery, Cobell approached the Native American Rights Fund (NARF) about filing a lawsuit. With NARF's support, she and many other Indians from across the country filed a class-action lawsuit against the federal government for their failure to compensate individuals and tribes for money it was

presumably managing for them. *Cobell v. Babbitt* is still in the courts and has yet to be resolved by the U.S. government. The financial scandal, however, is said to be more complex than the savings and loan crisis of the 1980s. It seems that the Individual Indian Monies Trust has so drastically mishandled records over the years, that Cobell and others filing the suit do not know exactly how much money they are due to receive for resources, including oil and timber, that were taken from their land.

Cobell has been recognized as a great economic reformer by the national government as well as Indian Country. In 1992 she was one of fifty women invited to build an economic agenda for President-elect Bill Clinton, and she serves on the board of both the National Rural Development Finance Corporation and Women and Foundations/Corporate Philanthropy. In 1997 Cobell was awarded a MacArthur Foundation Genius Grant.

## Cochise (1812–1874)
*Chiricahua Apache tribal leader*

In 1861, Indians in the Southwest United States began an ongoing war against the U.S. settlers and army in a series of conflicts known as the Apache Wars. From 1863 to 1872, Cochise was the leader of this resistance.

The Apache Wars began when Cochise, falsely accused of abducting a rancher's child, was imprisoned by an American lieutenant. He escaped, but the ensuing years were a cycle of attack and revenge. From his stronghold in the Dragoon Mountains (located in southern Arizona), Cochise and his ally, Mangas Coloradas, led an effective guerrilla campaign against U.S. and Mexican forces. In 1863, the United States military stepped up its campaign to pacify the Apache. Although losses and atrocities occurred on both sides and the Apache were forced to return to their mountain strongholds, no Apache band was ever conquered.

In 1871, Cochise rebuffed efforts to relocate his people to a reservation in New Mexico. A year later, however, the Apache leader agreed to abstain from attacks in exchange for reservation land in eastern Arizona. Consequently, peace did come to the region for the few short years before Cochise's death in 1874.

## Karita Coffey (1947–)
*Comanche ceramics artist and educator*

Karita Coffey is a world-renowned ceramic artist. Born at Lawton, Oklahoma, on 10 August 1947, Coffey received her high school diploma from the Institute of

American Indian Arts in Santa Fe, New Mexico (1965). She then completed her bachelor's degree in art (ceramic design) at the University of Oklahoma (1971) and went on to graduate study in art and education at the same university. She received her teaching certificate in art in 1975 and a master's of education in 1979.

Coffey has exhibited her ceramics throughout the United States and abroad since 1964. Some of her outstanding shows have been at the Edinburgh Festival in Scotland; the Berlin Festival in Germany; the thirty-second Annual American Indian Artists Exhibition at Tulsa, Oklahoma; and an exhibit entitled "American Indian Art Now," at the Wheelwright Museum in Santa Fe, New Mexico. She also had a solo exhibit at the C. N. Gorman Museum at the University of California, Davis. Coffey has been an artist-in-residence for the Oklahoma City Public Schools System and has organized and presented workshops for Indian Education Programs in Oklahoma and at Dartmouth College in Hanover, New Hampshire.

Coffey has received many honors and awards over the years, including a scholarship from Oklahomans for Indian Opportunity (1967) and the Letzeiser Art Award (1971–1972). In 1977 and 1978, she was named a Bilingual/Bicultural Fellow by the Department of Health, Education, and Welfare. She is also included in *Who's Who in American Indian Art* (1973) and the *Dictionary of International Biography* (1973). She currently teaches at the Institute of American Indian Arts.

## Mangas Coloradas (1797–1863)
*Mimbreno Apache tribal leader*

Mangas Coloradas was a member of the Mimbreno Apache, a tribe closely related to the Chiricahua Apache. Coloradas was a leader in the early years of the Apache Wars of the 1860s.

Coloradas fought two enemies during his lifetime. In the 1830s, there was conflict between the Apache and the Mexican government. In 1837, a number of important Mimbreno leaders were massacred by Mexican trappers who were motivated by the Mexican government's bounty on Indian scalps. Following the massacre, Coloradas united a number of tribes in present-day southern Arizona and New Mexico to rid themselves of intruding Mexican miners and trappers.

In 1846, the United States took possession of the New Mexico Territory, and Coloradas's enemy became the United States Army. In the 1850s, American miners began pouring into the region. Coloradas was captured and whipped by a group of miners, then released as a message to other Indians to stay away. Coloradas, who

was probably close to sixty years old at the time of the beating, survived and stepped up his warring against U.S. and Mexican miners. In the early 1860s, when the U.S. cavalry left the southwest region to fight in the Civil War, military protection for settlers and miners was taken on by the governor of California, who dispatched around three thousand troops to the region. In 1862, Coloradas and his Apache ally, Cochise, attacked the California troops in southern Arizona at a place now known as Apache Pass. Coloradas was wounded, but continued to press his attacks. As a result, in 1863, he was invited to a peace parley by U.S. military authorities. The peace parley was a ruse. Coloradas was murdered at Fort McLane, although U.S. authorities reported that he was killed while trying to escape. After his death, Coloradas's son, Mangus, continued his father's war to retain possession of the Apache land.

## Elizabeth Cook-Lynn (1930–)
*Crow Creek Sioux intellectual, writer, and professor*

Elizabeth Cook-Lynn comes from a family of political leaders and scholars. Her father and grandfather served on the Crow Creek Tribal Council for years, and a great-grandfather (Gabriel Renville) was a Native linguist who helped develop early Dakota dictionaries. Cook-Lynn herself was raised on the Crow Creek Reservation and speaks Dakota.

Born on the Crow Creek Reservation in South Dakota, on 17 November 1930, Cook-Lynn received a bachelor's degree in journalism and English from South Dakota State College (1952) and later completed the master's degree in education, psychology, and counseling at the University of South Dakota (1970). She completed additional graduate work in literary criticism at the University of Nebraska, Lincoln, and at Stanford University.

Early in her career, she worked as a journalist and teacher at the secondary level, but since 1970 Cook-Lynn has been on the faculty at Eastern Washington State University and, in 1993 was professor emeritus (retired) of English and American Indian studies. She is a founding editor of *The Wicazo Sa Review*, a journal of Native American studies, and since her retirement from Eastern Washington University, has been a visiting professor and consultant in Native American Studies at University of California-Davis and Arizona State University.

She is considered by many to be a modern American Indian intellectual and author. After the age of forty, her stature as a poet grew with publication of *Then Badger Said This* and *Seek the House of Relatives*. Her short stories have appeared in journals such as *Prairie Schooner, Pembroke Magazine, South Dakota Review, Sun Tracks,* and *The Greenfield Review.* She is the author of three novellas, and her collection of essays, *Why I Can't Read Wallace Stegner and Other Essays* (1996) was awarded the Myers Center Award for the Study of Human Rights in North America in 1997. She has been writer-in-residence at several universities and lives in the Black hills of South Dakota.

## Matthew Coon Come (1956–)
*Cree tribal leader*

Matthew Coon Come is national chief of the Assembly of First Nations, after his recent election in July 2000. A former grand chief of the Council of the Cree of Northern Quebec, he is the principal architect of the effort by the Cree to stop a hydroelectric development in northern Quebec known as James Bay II or the Great Whale project. Coon Come was born in northern Canada, and at the age of six he was forcibly removed by Canadian authorities to attend school. He then went on to study at Trent University, and spent two years studying law at McGill University. During his university studies, Coon Come kept close ties with his people.

From 1981 to 1986, Coon Come served as a board member and an executive committee member of the Grand Council of the Cree, a province-wide organization devoted to advancing the interests of Cree in Quebec. He studied law, political science, economics, and Native studies at Trent and McGill universities.

While at law school in 1987, Coon Come was asked by Cree elders to become grand chief to lead the struggle against the James Bay project, which threatened to flood much of the Cree homeland in northern Quebec. Coon Come accepted and began to chart an extremely successful campaign against hydroelectric development in the area. He quickly organized environmental, human rights, and indigenous communities on the local, national, and international levels to create a strong coalition opposing the project. Primarily targeting New York State as a likely hydroelectric consumer, Coon Come also organized a canoe trip of Cree elders from James Bay, through Lake Erie, and down the Hudson River. Under his leadership the Cree people were able to renegotiate with Quebec the terms under which hydroelectric development would occur in the north.

Coon Come has served as chairman of the James Bay Eeyou Corporation, managing over one hundred million dollars in assets. He was also chairman of James Bay Native Development Cooperation, which under his leadership assisted in starting up fifty-four businesses within the Cree communities. He was a founding director of the First Nations Bank of Canada in 1995.

He was awarded the Goldman Prize, considered the "Nobel Prize of Environmental Awards" (1994). In 1998, Trent University granted him the degree of Doctor of Laws Honoris Causa in further recognition of the significance of his work. He also received the National Aboriginal Achievement Award in 1995. He is married and is the father of five children.

## Nellie Cornoyea (1940–)
*Inuvialuit politician*

Nellie Cornoyea is the chair and chief executive officer of the Inuvialuit Regional Corporation (IRC). The Inuvialuit Regional Corporation is a company set up to administer the Inuvialuit people's 1984 land claim settlement with the Canadian government. Before her election as chair, Cournoyea was premier of the Northwest Territories for four years beginning November 1991. Representing the Western Arctic riding of Nunakput from 1979 to November 1995, Cournoyea held a number of portfolios including Health and Social Services, Renewable Resources, and Culture and Communications.

The second of eleven children, she was born near Aklavik in the Canadian Arctic to Nels Hvatum, a Norwegian, and Maggie, a member of the Inuvialuit who live in the western Canadian Arctic. Cornoyea spent her childhood in the bush, hunting, trapping, and fishing with her family and educating herself through correspondence courses. When she turned eleven, she worked as a volunteer secretary for the local hunters' and trappers' association. At the age of eighteen, she married and had two children. The marriage broke up soon thereafter, and Cornoyea obtained work at a new Canadian Broadcasting Corporation (CBC) station in Inuvik, a town in the far northwestern corner of the Northwest Territories, in order to support her young children. Cornoyea worked for the CBC for more than nine years as an announcer and station manager, persuading many young people to take up radio as a career.

Before her election to the Northwest Territories Legislative Assembly in 1979, she was a founding member for the Committee for Original People's Entitlement (COPE), an organization devoted to the rights of the Inuvialuit of the western Arctic. She was also a land claims officer for the Inuit Tapirisat of Canada, a national agency mandated to promote Inuit culture and identity and to develop Inuit political, economic, and environmental policy. In 1984, the Inuvialuit of the western Arctic signed an agreement with the federal government in which they received title to large areas of land. Cornoyea coordinated aspects of the implementation of the agreement and served on the board of directors of the Inuvialuit Petroleum Corporation, the Inuvialuit Development Corporation, and the Enrollment Authority and Arbitration Board.

She received the Woman of the Year Award from the Northwest Territories Native Women's Association (1982) and, in 1996, she was honored with a National Aboriginal Achievement Award for her contributions and public service.

Cournoyea was the first managing director of the IRC, after being part of the land rights negotiating team. She also held the position of implementation coordinator for the Inuvialuit Final Agreement for several years, and served on the board of directors of the Inuvialuit Petroleum Corporation, the Inuvialuit Development Corporation, and the Enrollment Authority and Arbitration Board. She decided not to run in the 1995 NWT election and returned to the Beaufort-Delta where she was elected chief executive officer and chair of IRC in 1996. She was reelected for a third two-year term in 2000.

## Cornplanter (d. 1836)
*Seneca tribal leader*

Cornplanter was a leading warrior and village leader among the Seneca, one of six nations of the Iroquois Confederacy, who lived in present upstate New York. The Iroquois Confederacy consisted of forty nine chiefs, or sachems, whose families attended the first meeting of the Iroquois Confederacy some few hundred years before Europeans arrived in North America. Cornplanter belonged to the Seneca Turtle clan, whose sachem held the title of Handsome Lake. Cornplanter, however, was not elected sachem. He earned his role as leader largely through military command and personal influence, which attracted friends and relatives to live on his reserved lands, which by 1800 totaled 1,300 acres in northern Pennsylvania.

Cornplanter's father was a trader named John O'Bail, who, during the 1730s, lived among the Seneca and traded manufactured goods for furs and skins. O'Bail chose not to live among the Iroquois and left his Seneca wife and child in care of her clan. Cornplanter grew to be a warrior leader. He fought with the French during the French and Indian War (1755–1759) and with the British during the American Revolutionary War (1775–1783).

After the Revolutionary War, Cornplanter argued that the Iroquois would not survive unless they adopted agriculture and U.S. forms of government. He was opposed by the nationalistic Seneca leader, Red Jacket, who thought the Iroquois would lose their identity if they adopted American life-styles. Between 1799 and 1815, however, Cornplanter's half-brother, Handsome Lake, led a religious and social movement that reorganized much of Iroquois culture. Cornplanter supported this movement, which led to adoption of agriculture, small farms, and new emphases on moral and religious order within Iroquois communities. Late in life, Cornplanter emphasized the need to retain Iroquois culture and ways.

## Jesse Cornplanter (1889–1957)
*Seneca cultural interpreter and author*

Jesse Cornplanter was an interpreter of the cultural traditions of the Seneca, whose native territory is centered south of Lake Ontario in western New York State.

Born in 1889 on the Cattaraugus Seneca Reservation in upstate New York at a place called Newton Longhouse, Cornplanter grew up in a very traditional setting. He learned Seneca as his first language and was an avid player of lacrosse, a Native American goal game in which players use a long-handled stick that has a triangular head with a loose mesh pouch for carrying and catching the ball. He also participated in religious events of the longhouse from his earliest childhood, beginning as a dancer and later becoming a singer in traditional Seneca ceremonies, such as the Great Feather Dance and the Drum Dance.

Although he thought in Seneca, Cornplanter wanted to learn English even as a child. He attended the district school and went as far as the fifth grade, after which he was largely self-taught. He worked as a touring showman during his early twenties, performing in a dramatization of "Song of Hiawatha," a poem by the American poet Henry Wadsworth Longfellow (1802–1887). He later joined the army and served in World War I, receiving the Purple Heart for injuries suffered during combat in France.

Cornplanter was thoroughly imbued with his own traditions and became a major source of current knowledge concerning songs, mythology, crafts, and other aspects of Seneca culture. Despite his limited formal education, he recorded a vast body of cultural information in letters written to anthropologists and others during the years between 1900 and 1957, and to a lesser extent in publications that appeared in his own name. Among his own published works are *Iroquois Indian Games and Dances* (1903) and *Legends of the Long House* (1938), but he also provided information that was presented in the writings of anthropologists such as William Fenton, Harold Conklin, and Frank Speck.

Like William Beynon and George Bushotter, Cornplanter was an intellectual figure who bridged the gap between two worlds and two ways of thinking.

### Robert T. Coulter (1945–)
*Potawatomi lawyer and activist*

Robert T. Coulter, an attorney who focuses on Indian law and international human rights, is currently the executive director of the Indian Law Resource Center in Helena, Montana.

Born in Rapid City, South Dakota, on 19 September 1945, Coulter received his bachelor's degree from Williams College in Williamstown, Massachusetts, (1966) and went on to get a degree in law from Columbia University Law School (1969).

Coulter is the past chairperson of the American Bar Association Committee on Problems of American Indians, Section of Individual Rights and Responsibilities (1982–1984) and was a Ralph E. Shikes Visiting Fellow, Harvard Law School, in 1995. He has published numerous articles, essays, and books, and is also a longstanding member the American Society of International Law.

Robert T. Coulter, executive director of Indian Law Resource Center.

### Bruce Cox (1934–)
*Anishinabe anthropologist and professor emeritus*

Bruce Cox is an environmentally conscious anthropologist and a retired university professor. He was born at Santa Rosa, California, on 29 June 1934. Cox earned his bachelor's degree in anthropology at Reed College in Oregon (1956), obtained a master's degree from the University of Oregon (1959), and a doctorate from the University of California, Berkeley (1968). Over the years, he has taught courses in anthropology at Lewis and Clark College in Idaho (1964–1965), the University of Florida (1966), the University of Alberta (1967–1969), and taught at Carleton University in Ontario, Canada, from 1969 to 1999.

Cox is mainly interested in the cultural ecology of indigenous North American peoples and understanding how these Native beliefs and institutions concerning the environment are disrupted by large-scale energy development projects such as the James Bay hydroelectric plant near Quebec (Ontario, Canada) or the coal strip-mining of Black Mesa in northern Arizona. These issues are discussed in his publications, including *Cultural Ecology of Canadian Native Peoples* (1973), *Native People, Native Lands* (1988), and *A Different Drummer: Readings in Anthropology with a Canadian Perspective* (1989).

### Crazy Horse (1842–1877)
*Oglala-Brule Sioux tribal leader*

Crazy Horse was a war leader of the Oglala subgroup of the Teton Sioux. He was born to the east of the sacred Black Hills near present-day Rapid City. As a boy, he was called Curly. Since his mother was a Brule Sioux, he spent time in the camps of the Oglala and the Brule. By the time he was twelve, he had killed a buffalo and received his own horse. His father, a holy man, changed Curly's name to the same as his own, Crazy Horse, after watching his son's exploits in battle against another tribe. While still a young man, Crazy Horse had a vivid dream of a rider on horseback in a storm, which his father interpreted as a sign of future greatness in battle.

In the 1866 to 1868 war over the Bozeman Trail, Crazy Horse joined the Oglala chief Red Cloud in raids against U.S. settlements and forts in Wyoming. In these forays, Crazy Horse became adept in the art of decoying tactics. With the 1868 treaty at Fort Laramie, the U.S. Army agreed to abandon its posts along the Bozeman Trail. Crazy Horse became war chief of the Oglala and married a Cheyenne woman. He later took a second Oglala wife.

The Black Hills Gold Rush in 1876 brought more conflict to the region when miners and speculators began indiscriminately exploring the Sioux's sacred territory. Crazy Horse's camp became a rallying point for many warriors eager to drive the intruders away. On the upper Rosebud Creek in present-day southern Montana, in the spring of 1876, General George Crook's army of thirteen hundred attacked Crazy Horse's force of twelve hundred. Crazy Horse's feinting and assault techniques baffled Crook, who withdrew after heavy losses. Crazy Horse then moved his camp to the Bighorn River in Montana and joined Sitting Bull and Gall. U.S. Army troops, including a force led by Colonel George Armstrong Custer, set out to find and pacify the Sioux and Cheyenne, who were gathering at the Bighorn River.

On 25 June 1876, the famous Battle of the Little Bighorn commenced. In a masterful series of decoys and feints by the Sioux, aided by poor military judgment by Colonel Custer, Crazy Horse and his predominantly Cheyenne warriors attacked Custer's men from the north and west. Gall, after routing Major Marcus Reno's forces, charged Custer from the south and east. The U.S. troops were surrounded and completely annihilated.

Despite several other brilliant campaigns against U.S. troops, the Sioux were starving and weary of battle. On 6 May 1877, Crazy Horse reluctantly surrendered with eight hundred followers at Fort Robinson in northwestern Nebraska. However, the promises of a reservation for the Sioux were not kept. Crazy Horse was bayoneted at Fort Robinson during an attempt to confine him to a guardhouse on 5 September 1877. According to legend, he is buried in his homeland near Wounded Knee, South Dakota.

### Roland Crowe (1943–)
*Piapot Cree tribal leader*

Roland Crowe is chief of the Piapot First Nation and a senator of the Federation of Saskatchewan Indian Nations (FSIN), an organization devoted to the advancement of aboriginal rights in Canada. He was born and raised on the Piapot Indian Reserve, located approximately twenty-four miles north of Regina, Saskatchewan. His father was a farmer and later a driver training instructor. His mother was a social worker with the Family Service Bureau. The oldest of six children, Crowe worked on the family farm and eventually became a farmer himself.

At the age of fifteen, Crowe worked as a page at the Saskatchewan Legislative Assembly, a job that sparked a deep and abiding interest in politics. Soon after this experience, Crowe worked as a corrections officer at a provincial corrections center. Other jobs early in his life included a stint at the federal Department of Indian Affairs and program director/executive director of the Regina Friendship Center, an institution aimed at providing support to urban Indians.

Crowe entered politics at the band level, serving as band councillor for two years and then, for six years, as chief of the Piapot Indian Reserve until his election as chief of the Federation of Saskatchewan Indian Nations. As chief, Crowe spearheaded the historic 1992 Treaty Land Entitlement Agreement, which resulted in the addition of 1.6 million acres to First Nations' land base and over $550 million for First Nations to carry out land acquisitions. He played a key role in obtaining 1,000 low-income housing units through the creation of off-reserve housing programs and securing 18 million dollars in funding for the training and employment of First Nation people in the Saskatchewan region.

He has counseled a philosophy of non-violent protest by aboriginal people in their dealings with the Canadian state and is committed to the negotiation of aboriginal self-government in Canada. Chief Crowe lives in Regina with his wife Brenda and family.

### Crowfoot (circa 1830–1890)
*Blackfoot Confederacy tribal leader*

Crowfoot (Isapo-Muxika) was born a Blood Indian at Blackfoot Crossing near present-day Calgary, Alberta, but upon his father's death moved with his mother to the Blackfoot lodge of her new husband. Crowfoot was known as Bear Ghost (Kyi-i-staah) among his people during his youth and was only thirteen years old when he participated in the first of nineteen battles as a Blackfoot warrior. He became known to settlers when he rescued a Roman Catholic priest from Cree Indians in 1866. In 1877, Canadian authorities treated Crowfoot as head chief of the Blackfoot Confederacy, which included at the time the Blackfoot, Blood, Peigan, and Sarcee tribes, at the signing of Treaty Seven, one of the several treaties that Canada entered into with First Nations. In the same year, Crowfoot was commended by Queen Victoria of England for refusing to assist Sitting Bull of the Sioux Nation during the wars between the Plains Indians and the American Cavalry. Following the Battle of the Little Bighorn (known as Custer's Last Stand), many Sioux fled to Canada, at which time Crowfoot and Sitting Bull shared tobacco and achieved peace between the two nations.

By the summer of 1879, the Blackfoot faced starvation and were forced to follow the last buffalo herds into Montana. Two years later they crossed back into Canada and faced continued shortages of food. Eventually, the Blackfoot were forced to sell many of their possessions, including their horses, to survive. In 1885, Crowfoot's adoptive son, Poundmaker, led a Cree attack on the town of Battleford on the North Saskatchewan River, as part of a larger rebellion, known as the second Northwest Rebellion of 1885, in which Louis Riel, leader of the Métis people, sought to form a provisional government in Saskatchewan against the wishes of Canadian authorities. Crowfoot kept the Blackfoot out of the rebellion, although he encouraged his people to assist any Cree passing through their territory. Crowfoot lost most of his children to smallpox and tuberculosis.

## Charles Curtis (1860–1936)
*Kaw and Osage politician and vice president of the United States*

Charles Curtis served as vice-president of the United States under Herbert Hoover, as well as many years in Congress. Born near the present-day town of Topeka, Kansas, in 1860, Curtis was only one-eighth Indian but was raised on the Kaw Reservation near Council Grove. He attended the Indian mission school on the reservation, then returned to Topeka when the Kaw were attacked by Cheyenne militants. As a young man, he worked as a jockey during the summer seasons and attended Topeka High School.

Curtis became a lawyer in 1881 and later entered politics as a Republican, serving eight consecutive terms in the U.S. House of Representatives from 1892 until 1906. As a legislator Curtis is best known as sponsor of the Curtis Act of 1898, which called for the dissolution of tribal governments and the institution of civil government throughout Indian Territory (Oklahoma). This was intended to hasten the assimilation of Indian peoples. The act also extended the allotment policy to all of the tribes in Indian Territory, by authorizing the Dawes Commission, a special congressional committee, to extinguish tribal title in Indian Territory and proceed to make allotments of land to Indians as individuals. These efforts toward assimilation and allotment were opposed by many Indian leaders, who felt that the United States had no right to dissolve their tribal governments and did not wish to enter U.S. society.

Curtis was later elected to the Senate and served in that body from 1907 to 1913 and 1915 to 1929. He

campaigned for president and lost, then ran successfully for vice-president on the ticket with Herbert Hoover. They served one term in office, from 1929 until 1933.

## Linwood Little Bear Custalow (1937–)
*Mattaponi tribal leader and physician*

Linwood Little Bear Custalow was born on the Mattaponi Indian Reservation in King William County, Virginia, where he lived until age thirteen. Custalow was sent by the State Board of Virginia to an Indian high school on the Cherokee Reservation in North Carolina. At his request, he was allowed to complete his high school education at Bacone High School in Muskogee, Oklahoma.

He graduated from the University of Richmond with a degree in chemistry to become the first American Indian from a tribe in Virginia to graduate from a Virginia university. He went on to earn a medical degree from the Medical College of Virginia in 1964, becoming the first American Indian to graduate from medical school in Virginia.

In 1969, Custalow set up his own medical practice in Hampton, Virginia. In 1970, he and several American Indian physicians formed the Association of American Indian Physicians, based in Oklahoma City, Oklahoma, where he served as president and remained on the executive board for ten years

Besides his medical career, Custalow is an advocate for Native American issues, with a focus on the Indians from King William County. He was instrumental in organizing the Adams Town urban group of King William County American Indians into a tribe under the name Upper Mattaponi Tribe, using the tribal name at the permission of the Mattaponi tribal chief.

He is a diplomat of the American Board of Otolaryngology and the American Board of Environmental Medicine. He is a fellow of the National Board of Medical Examiners, the American Academy of Otolaryngology-Head and Neck Surgery, and the International College of Surgeons.

Custalow is currently retired from private practice. He is actively assisting the Mattaponi Tribe and is chairman of the finance committee of the Association of American Indian Physicians.

## Datsolalee (Luisa Keyser) (d. 1925)
*Washo basketmaker*

Datsolalee was a Washo woman who became famous for her skills as a basketmaker. The Washo are a

Hokan-speaking tribe occupying the eastern slopes of the Sierra Nevada Mountains in northern California and Nevada.

She was born near Carson City, Nevada, around 1835 and learned the refined art of traditional basketry as a girl. Basketry is particularly developed among the California tribes, and Washo styles are among the more intricate, involved designs with as many as thirty-six stitches per inch. In 1844, Datsolalee was one of the Washo who welcomed John C. Fremont, the famous early explorer of territories west of the Mississippi River, when he arrived in the Carson City area. She later married a Washo man named Assu and had two children by him. Upon Assu's death, she married another Washo man named Charlie Keyser, and thus she also became known by an English name, Louisa Keyser.

Datsolalee's historical importance is owed at least partly to the bravery she showed in a marketing conflict with the Paiute. During the 1850s, this neighboring tribe had defeated the Washo in battle, and they prohibited the Washo from selling baskets to U.S. settlers, in order to increase their own sales. Without this source of income, the Washo suffered extreme poverty. Finally, however, Datsolalee decided to defy the ban, and in 1895 she took several of her finest pieces and sold them to Abram Cohn, a merchant in Carson City. This was the beginning of a long-standing relationship, and over the years Cohn bought some 120 works from Datsolalee, who is said to have produced about 300 baskets in her lifetime.

Datsolalee worked on baskets until she died, even though she had become nearly blind long before then. Her baskets, the largest and most intricate of which took more than a year to produce, became very valuable after her death, and one of them is said to have sold for $10,000 only five years later.

## Nora Dauenhauer (1927–)
*Tlingit author and translator*

Nora Dauenhauer is an author and translator of the language of the Tlingit, a Northwest Coast tribe occupying the southeastern Alaskan coastline. Born in Juneau, Alaska, in 1927, Dauenhauer received her bachelor's degree in anthropology from Alaska Methodist University in Anchorage (1976) and then completed a special research training program for Native Americans sponsored by the Smithsonian Institution in 1977. From 1978 until 1980, she served as a cultural coordinator for the Cook Inlet Native Association, one of the twelve Alaska Native regional associations, and in

1980 and 1981 she conducted a translation project that was supported by the National Endowment for the Humanities.

Though Dauenhauer turned to cross-cultural research relatively late in life, she has spent considerable time since 1977 collecting and translating Tlingit oral traditions. Her translation of Tlingit oratory has been published in the volume *Because We Cherish You* (1981), and she and her husband published language texts entitled *Beginning Tlingit* (1976) and *A Tlingit Spelling Book* (1984). Dauenhauer is also a creative writer whose poems and stories have been published in two anthologies entitled *Earth Power Coming: Short Fiction in Native American Literature* (1983) and *That's What She Said: Contemporary Poetry and Fiction by Native American Women* (1984). Her recent books *The Droning Shaman, Haa Shuka, Our Ancestors*, and *Haa Tuwundaagu Yis, For Healing Our Spirit*. Other writings by Dauenhauer have also appeared in *The Greenfield Review* and *Northward Journal*.

## Alice Brown Davis (1852–1935)
*Seminole tribal leader*

Alice Brown Davis served for many years as an emissary of the Seminole Nation and the U.S. government, and was appointed chief of the Seminole in 1922. Born near Park Hill, in the Cherokee Nation in Indian Territory, present-day Oklahoma, she was the daughter of Dr. John F. Brown, a Scot, and Lucy Redbeard, a Seminole of the Tiger clan. During the Civil War Alice lived at Fort Gibson, and following the war she met and married George Davis. The young couple lived for a time in Okmulgee in the Creek Nation, Indian Territory, but returned to the Seminole Nation, Indian Territory, in 1882, where they established a trading post. Davis gave birth to eleven children and, after being widowed, raised her four sons and seven daughters while running the trading post. In 1903, Davis spent three months at Santa Rosa, Chihuahua State, Mexico, with other Seminole, as delegates to a conference on important tribal affairs. In 1905 she went to Palm Beach, Florida, to act as an interpreter for the U.S. government in a murder trial involving a prominent Seminole Indian.

In 1909, Davis was sent as an emissary from the Indians of her nation to the Seminole still living in the Florida Everglades. She remained with them for many months, living among them, preaching to them, and endeavoring to interest them in the advantages of civilization. As a result of her visit, a more friendly understanding was established, and the Oklahoma Seminole began to receive visits from Seminoles and other tribes from Florida to become better acquainted.

Davis made two trips to Mexico City in 1905 and 1910, trying to gain information regarding a vast tract of land allegedly granted to the Seminole by the Mexican government in exchange for protection from ongoing Indian attacks. The title grant was never proved, however.

In 1922, President Warren G. Harding appointed Davis chief of the Seminole Nation, to succeed her brother, John F. Brown Jr., who had served his people for thirty years. Davis proved to be an excellent choice, because she was a vigorous woman with a clear and intelligent mind, devoted to the interests of the Seminole. On 21 June 1935, the Associated Press announced the death of Chief Davis, a victim of heart disease, at the age of eighty-two years.

### Frank Day (1902–1976)
*Concow Maidu painter and tribal historian*

Frank Day was a self-taught artist whose surreal paintings drew upon Maidu history and mythology. The Concow Maidu are a California tribe whose native territories covered a fairly large area surrounding the modern cities of Chico and Oroville in northern California. Like many other California Indian traditionalists, Frank Day remained outside the mainstream of modern American Indian culture, and there is little published information about his life. His father was a village headman, and Day inherited ceremonial knowledge and responsibilities from him upon his death in 1922. One of Day's own legacies was to help in the founding of a dance group called the Maidu Dancers; he accomplished this by teaching the younger dancers the songs, the meaning of the words in the songs, and the dance steps that should be used.

His paintings are more widely known, but Day probably did not consider himself a "professional" artist in the generally accepted sense of the word. His paintings are powerful, filled with religious significance and imagery derived from a period when the world was being created. The style is without formal training but visionary, and there are about three hundred of his paintings in existence, mainly in private collections.

### Ada E. Deer (1935–)
*Menominee educator and activist*

Ada E. Deer is a Menominee social worker and political organizer who was involved in restoring federal recognition to her tribe in the 1970s. The Menominee

Ada E. Deer.

(whose name means Wild Rice People in Ojibwa) are located along the Menominee River in Wisconsin and Michigan.

Born at Keshena, Wisconsin, on 7 August 1935, Deer received her bachelor's degree in social work from the University of Wisconsin-Madison (1957) and went on to complete her master's degree in social work at Columbia University (1961).

In the 1970s, Deer played a major role in the social and political development of her tribe. During 1972 and 1973, she was vice-president and Washington lobbyist of an organization called National Committee to Save the Menominee People and Forest, Inc. From 1973 until 1976, she was the chair of the Menominee Restoration Committee, and the group was largely responsible for congressional action to restore Menominee to tribal status following the termination of the tribe in 1954. The Menominee were one of the major tribes whose reservation was dissolved by federal policies of the 1950s, and since 1977 several other terminated tribes have been restored to federal recognition, all following the Menominee example.

From 1977 to 1993, Deer was a faculty member in the School of Social Work and Native American Studies at the University of Wisconsin-Madison. She has won many awards and honors over the years, including honorary doctorates from Northland College in Wisconsin and the University of Wisconsin-Madison. Ada E. Deer is the first woman assistant secretary for Indian Affairs in the history of the Department of the Interior. President Clinton announced his intention to nominate Deer on 11 May 1993. She was confirmed by the United States Senate on 16 July 1993. Deer served as assistant secretary until November 1997. She then became the first woman to serve as chairperson of her tribe and is currently director of American Indian studies at the University of Wisconsin-Madison.

## Deganawida (circa 1300)
*Huron spiritual leader*

Deganawida is the founder of the Iroquois Confederacy. Its origin is unknown, but it is generally dated before the landing of Columbus in 1492. In Iroquois history, Deganawida lived in a time when there was little peace among the Iroquois-speaking nations, of which the Huron, Deganawida's tribe then residing in present-day Ontario in southern Canada, is one. These nations were often at war with one another because there was no agreed-upon means of resolving conflict between the various nations. A murder of one man by a man of another nation led to revenge raids and war between the nations.

Deganawida had a vision from the Great Spirit that instructed him to give the Great Law, a set of rules and procedures for working out differences and settling hostilities between nations. Deganawida traveled among the Iroquois Nations in present-day New York and Ohio spreading the message of peace. Most rejected the message, but on his travels he met Hiawatha, a member of the Iroquoian-speaking Mohawk Nation living near present-day Albany, New York. Since Deganawida had a speech impediment, Hiawatha, a powerful orator, became the spokesperson for the message of Deganawida and the Great Spirit. Both Deganawida and Hiawatha traveled among the Iroquois Nations, and after some resistance among the Onondaga, convinced the Seneca, Cayuga, Onondaga, Oneida, and Mohawk to form a confederacy of forty-nine chiefs. Through ceremonies and agreements they settled their disputes peacefully at the annual gatherings of the Confederate Council, which met at Onondaga, near present-day Syracuse, New York. Decisions of the Confederate Council required unanimous consensus among all nations, thereafter called the Five Nations. The elderly clan matrons nominated and deposed the chiefs of their own lineages from office if they did not conform to the will of the lineage. The purpose of the league was to create peace and to spread the Great Law of peace to all nations in the world.

## Joseph B. DeLaCruz (1937–2000)
*Quinault tribal leader*

For twenty-two years Joseph B. DeLaCruz was the president of the Quinault Nation, located in the northwestern part of Washington State. During this time he was involved in domestic-tribal, intertribal, state-wide, regional, national, and international issues. As a tribal leader, he provided policy guidance and instruction on Quinault Business Council directives, and he served as primary representative for the Quinault Nation in government-to-government, corporate, and intertribal relations. Among the activities he promoted to preserve Quinault Nation interests were development of the Quinault Forestry Management Program, the Quinault land restoration, and the Quinault Housing program, as well as two enterprises: the Quinault Seafood Plant and the Quinault Land and Timber Enterprises. In 1992, DeLaCruz supported a tribal ordinance that provided tribal members with a means to secure financing for home construction on reservation land.

From 1977 to 1981, DeLaCruz was president of the National Tribal Chairmen Association, an organization developed as a tribal leaders forum for instituting legislation, and monitoring and evaluating decisions in priority areas in Indian Country such as education, housing, and economic development. From 1977 to 1982, he helped organize the Conference of Tribal Governments, which provided the foundation for the state and tribal relations on a government-to-government basis. From 1985 to 1988, he mediated the negotiation among the United States, Canada, and Indian tribes in the Northwest of the Pacific Salmon Fisheries Treaty, which regulates the fishing in those waters. Beginning in 1985, he was a member of the Northwest Indian Fish Commission that serves as an intergovernmental fisheries management and technical assistance agency for tribes in western Washington. The commission was also a mechanism for developing co-management strategies for state and federal agencies and Indian tribes. DeLaCruz also served two terms as president of the National Congress of American Indians, a major national lobbying organization for Indian issues and legislation.

In 1991 and 1992, DeLaCruz was the commissioner for the National Commission on American Indian, Alaska Native, and Hawaiian Housing. The commission was composed of twelve members and conducted on-site visits to remote Native areas where housing problems still exist. The commission's duty was to submit a report to Congress and to make recommendations for housing and opportunities for development, management, and modernization of housing on reservations.

## Delaware Prophet (circa 1760s)
*Delaware (Lenape) spiritual leader*

During the early 1760s—a time of threatened trade, military, and diplomatic domination by the English—several religious leaders emerged among the Delaware Nation living in the eastern Ohio region. In North America, the French and Indian War had just been concluded in December 1759 when Montreal in New France fell to Indian and English troops. The defeat of the French left many Indians who had fought with the French cause without allies and military support. The British threatened to gain monopoly control over the fur trade, the distribution of guns and manufactured goods, and threatened to establish military control over the Ohio and Great Lakes region by occupying the old French forts at places such as Detroit.

With their economy potentially in crisis, the Delaware responded to the rise of new leaders who attempted to reorganize their society. Although we do not have their names, the strategies of two of them are sufficiently different to distinguish them as a militant prophet and a church-building prophet.

The militant prophet had a vision that he died and visited heaven, where he was given a message for gaining the spiritual and political salvation of the Indian people. He preached that because the Indians gave up the traditions and lifestyle of their forbears and traded and accepted the goods of the Europeans, the path to heaven for the Indians was blocked. Concepts of heaven and the strong emphasis on personal salvation were ideas borrowed, probably indirectly, from the Christian religion. Pontiac, an Ottawa leader, supported the teachings of the militant prophet as a means to form a multi-tribal military alliance that would push the English out of Indian territory in the Great Lakes region. In 1763 Pontiac initiated a coordinated military attack on the British-occupied forts, but he was not able to sustain the fight or evict the English.

The church-building Delaware Prophet, unlike the militant prophet, had a religious message only for the Delaware, not for a multi-tribal coalition. This Delaware Prophet brought together elements of Delaware religion and formed a centralized Delaware national ceremonial and religious order, often called the Bighouse Religion. Previously, the Delaware were formed into about forty small bands, which were severely disrupted during the colonial period. The prophet reorganized the kinship and political organization of Delaware society and instituted a system of three phratries—often called

Turtle, Turkey, and Wolf—and each of which was subdivided into twelve smaller clans or subdivisions. This prophet created a system of chiefs for the Delaware with ceremonies of installation, and one chief, who led the Turtle phratry, was designated principal chief, although he had little authority over the other two major chiefs. The three major divisions were recognized with the Bighouse Religion ceremonies and each had complementary religious and political duties. After 1765, the Delaware prophets appear to disappear from the record.

## Ella Deloria (1888–1971)
*Yankton Sioux ethnologist, linguist, and novelist*

Ella Deloria was an anthropologist whose work focused mainly on the language and culture of her own tribe, the Sioux (also called Dakota).

Deloria was born on the Yankton Sioux Reservation in southwestern South Dakota. She attended All Saints Boarding School in Sioux Falls, and later studied at Oberlin College in Ohio and received her bachelor's degree from Columbia University in 1915. Upon graduation, she returned to teach at All Saints and then in 1919 accepted a job with the YWCA as secretary of health education for Indian schools and reservations. In this position, she traveled widely throughout the western United States and became acquainted with many different Indian tribal groups.

Her career in anthropology began in 1929, when she accepted an offer from Franz Boas to be a linguistic informant and research associate at Columbia University. Because she was a fluent speaker of Dakota (Sioux), she gave instruction on various dialects of the language and also worked on several publications. During this period she wrote *Dakota Texts* (1932) and co-authored *A Dakota Grammar* with Boas in 1941.

After Boas's death in 1942, Deloria began working on her own and produced books that attempted to move beyond the standard anthropological point of view. *Speaking of Indians* (1944) was a non-technical but sophisticated description of Indian (especially Sioux) culture, and the first draft of her novel *Waterlily* was also written during the 1940s, although it remained unpublished until 1988. All the while, she also kept up her purely anthropological studies and became one of the leading authorities on Sioux culture in her lifetime.

## Philip Sam Deloria (contemporary)
*Standing Rock Sioux lawyer*

Philip Sam Deloria is director of the American Indian Law Center, Inc. (AILC) in Albuquerque, New Mexico, and is a member of the Standing Rock Sioux. Deloria is responsible for policy, staff, budget, and management of the law center. One of the most important functions of the AILC is its summer program, which provides a three-month intensive course for Indian students who wish to enter the field of law.

The program provides financial support to Indian law students, as well as educational enrichment in areas of Indian law not covered in the normal curriculum of many law schools. In addition, the law center conducts research, technical assistance, and training with respect to legal issues confronting American Indians, with particular attention paid to tribal government.

The AILC also conducts research on such matters as intergovernmental relationships and the status of tribal government with the federal domestic assistance program delivery system. Deloria received a bachelor of arts degree in philosophy from Yale University in New Haven, Connecticut, and received his law degree from Yale Law School.

He is the former deputy assistant secretary for Indian affairs for the U.S. Department of the Interior, the former secretary general for the World Council for Indigenous Peoples, and originator of the Commission on State-Tribal Relations.

### Vine Deloria, Jr. (1933–)
*Standing Rock Sioux writer, lawyer, and professor*

Through his widely published books *Custer Died for Your Sins* (1969) and *God is Red* (1973), Vine Deloria, Jr., has brought greater understanding of American Indian history and philosophy to a vast global audience. He was born in Martin, South Dakota, to an unusually distinguished family. His grandfather was a Yankton chief. His aunt (Ella Deloria) was a noted scholar of Indian ethnology and linguistics, and his father (Vine Deloria, Sr.) was an Episcopal minister. The younger Vine Deloria graduated from Iowa State University in 1958, then took a master's degree in theology (Lutheran School of Theology, 1963) and later a degree in law (University of Colorado, 1970).

While assuredly influenced by the religious teachings of his father, Deloria became known as a revolutionary thinker who spoke out against the decadence of U.S. culture and insisted that young Native Americans receive traditional teachings before exposing themselves to the philosophies of the dominant Euro-American culture. He has always held that Indian people must remain Indian, rather than assimilating into U.S. society, and that education and ideology—not violence—are the keys to achieving dignity and justice for Native Americans of all tribes.

Deloria served as the executive director of the National Congress of American Indians in Washington, D.C., from 1964 to 1967. He has also provided leadership in other organizations such as the Citizens Crusade Against Poverty, the Council on Indian Affairs, the National Office for the Rights of the Indigent, the Institute for the Development of Indian Law, and the Indian Rights Association. He was a member of several college and university faculties before taking a post as professor of political science at the University of Arizona at Tucson in 1978. In 1990, he moved to the University of Colorado, Boulder, and taught history until his retirement in 2000.

Deloria has received many awards, literary citations, and honorary degrees. Some of his other well-known books include: *We Talk You Listen* (1970), *Behind the Trail of Broken Treaties* (1974), *The Metaphysics of Modern Existence* (1979), *The Nations Within: The Past and Future of American Indian Sovereignty* (1984), *The Aggression of Civilization: Federal Indian Policy Since the 1880s* (1984), *American Indian Policy in the Twentieth Century* (1985), *Red Earth, White Lies* (1995), *Documents of American Indian Diplomacy* (1999), *Spirit and Reason* (1999), *Singing for a Spirit* (1999), and *Tribes, Treaties, and Constitutional Tribulations* (2000).

### Vine Deloria, Sr. (1901–1990)
*Yankton Sioux minister*

Vine Deloria, Sr., was the first American Indian to be named to a national executive post in the Episcopal Church. His father, Philip Deloria, was a full-blood Sioux and served as a missionary priest at Standing Rock Sioux Reservation, converting thousands of Indians to Christianity during his career. He was even honored with a statue in the Episcopal Cathedral in Washington, D.C. As a boy, Deloria attended a military academy, where he rose to the rank of cadet colonel, and then he received a bachelor of arts degree from Bard College in New York. His first job was as a mine worker in Colorado, then later he became an advisor in an Indian school.

Only after this did he decide to join the ministry. He completed the theological course at General Theological Seminary in New York City and was subsequently ordained in his father's church, where he had been baptized and confirmed. He served in the Indian missions for thirty-seven years and for several years as assistant secretary in the Division of Domestic Missions on the national staff of the Episcopal Church in New York City. Before his retirement in 1967, Deloria was made archdeacon of the Niobrara Deaconry, a

Vine Deloria, Jr.

William G. Demmert.

position in which he worked among Indian people all over the state of South Dakota.

## William Demmert (1934–)
*Tlingit and Sioux professor and administrator*

William Demmert is a professor of education at Western Washington University, Bellingham. Born on 9 March 1934, Demmert received his doctorate in education from Harvard University in 1973. His dissertation was entitled "Critical Issues in Indian Education" (1972–1973), and he has published prolifically in the field since then. He is co-author of the report *Characteristics of Successful Leaders* (1986) and has written several articles and essays, including "Education for Marine Resources Management" (1981), "The Process of Education: A Personal Experience" (1983), and "Indian Education Revisited: A Personal Experience."

Demmert served as a dean at the University of Alaska, Juneau, and was a visiting scholar and professor at Stanford University. He has taught at the University of Washington, and directed the American Indian Program at Harvard University early in his career. He also served as the director of Indian education for the U.S. Bureau of Indian Affairs from 1976 to 1978 and was

the first U.S. deputy commissioner of Indian Education at the U.S. Office of Education (1975–1976). In the 1980s he was commissioner of education for the state of Alaska.

The pedagogue was a member of the National Commission on Teaching and America's Future. He continues to be active in educational policy as the chairperson of an international steering committee that focuses on the education of Native peoples in the circumpolar north. He is a member of the Independent Review Panel, a congressionally created group that provides advice to Congress and the secretary of education on all federal programs administered by the U.S. Department of Education.

## Lionel H. deMontigny (1935–)
*Turtle Mountain Chippewa physician*

Lionel deMontigny, is a retired physician and public health specialist who has served several Indian communities through his work in the U.S. Public Health Service.

Born at Belcourt, North Dakota, on 17 October 1935, he received both a bachelor of arts and bachelor of science degree from the University of North Dakota. He then graduated as a medical doctor from the University of Wisconsin Medical School and went on to complete a master's degree in public health from the University of Oklahoma.

DeMontigny joined the U.S. Public Health Service as a field officer in 1962. He was soon appointed to a three-year residency training program in preventive medicine established by the Division of Indian Health in cooperation with the University of Oklahoma School of Medicine and the Oklahoma State Health Department. After this special training, he was appointed deputy director of the Portland (Oregon) area office of the U.S. Public Health Service. While working there deMontigny initiated many tribally operated health programs and encouraged Indian youth to take up careers in medicine.

He has won many awards and honors, including a scholarship from the Division of Indian Health and a fellowship from the John Hay Whitney Foundation. He is a member of the American Public Health Association and the American Medical Association.

### John Deserontyon (circa 1740–1811)
*Mohawk tribal leader*

John Deserontyon, popularly known as Captain John Deserontyon, was an accomplished warrior and chief of the Mohawk Nation. Before the American Revolution, he became chief of the Mohawk village at Fort Hunter in New York State. When the revolution began, Deserontyon, along with many Mohawk, sided with Britain and actively participated in raids and scouting expeditions into American territory to gather intelligence for the British. On one expedition into upper New York State in 1777, he scouted the defenses at Fort Stanwix in Rome, New York, and discovered that the fort was more secure than had been previously thought. When the British subsequently attacked the fort, Deserontyon was part of a force that defeated a group of American militia approaching to offer reinforcements in what has become known as the Battle of Oriskany.

When peace returned it became clear that the Mohawk would not be able to re-occupy ancestral lands in upstate New York. Deserontyon, together with Joseph Brant, another Mohawk chief who had sided with Britain during the revolution, negotiated with the British for a new homeland for their people. Initially, the choice was for lands bordering the Bay of Quinte, on the north shore of Lake Ontario just west of Kingston, Ontario. Brant, however, changed his mind and decided in favor of the valley of the Grand River, north of Lake Erie. Despite British pressure, Deserontyon stuck

with the initial choice, with the result being that two separate Mohawk villages were established. With British assistance, he built a church and school for his people. The town of Deseronto in eastern Ontario is named after Captain John Deserontyon.

### Billy Diamond (1949–)
*Cree tribal leader*

Billy Diamond, a spokesperson for Cree opposition to hydroelectric development that threatened Cree homelands, is the son of Malcolm Diamond, a chief of the Rupert House Cree and a trapper. He was born in a tent on the outskirts of Rupert House, Quebec, on the shore of James Bay. When he was growing up, Billy Diamond lived in the bush, helping his father with his traplines. At the age of eight, he was sent to a residential school run by Canadian authorities. Diamond went on to complete high school, but he decided to forgo university studies at the behest of his father, who urged him to return to Rupert House and work for his people. In 1971, at the young age of twenty-one, Diamond was elected chief of the Rupert House Cree, and he immediately began to develop links with other Cree in the north. In 1974, Diamond became a founding member of the Grand Council of the Cree of Quebec, a province-wide organization devoted to advancing the interests of Cree in Quebec, and he served as grand chief of the council from 1974 to 1984. Diamond galvanized the Cree in opposition to hydroelectric development in James Bay and ultimately negotiated an agreement in the 1970s with the provincial government that gave the Cree greater political control over their homelands. The agreement stands as a model to many other aboriginal communities in Canada that are seeking greater autonomy and control over their identities.

Diamond became chairman of the Cree Regional Authority, which was established in 1975 and administered the implementation of the James Bay Agreement in relation to land development and services affecting the Cree. Diamond has served as chairman of the James Bay Cree School Board, founder and president of Air Creebec, a Cree-owned regional airline, owner of Cree Commercial Construction Company Limited, and Cree Yamaha Motors.

### Olive Patricia Dickason (1920–)
*Métis historian*

Olive Dickason is professor emeritus at the University of Alberta, and adjunct professor at the University of Ottawa. She is the author of several books and

Professor Olive Patricia Dickason.

countless articles on the history of relations between Europeans and the indigenous peoples of North America, including *Canada's First Nations: A History of Founding Peoples* (1992, 1997, 2001), which won the Sir John A. Macdonald Prize from the Canadian Historical Association in 1992.

Born in Winnipeg, Manitoba, to an English father and a Métis mother whose people were buffalo hunters in the Dakotas, Dickason and her family moved one hundred miles north of Winnipeg during the Great Depression of the 1930s, where her father had mining property. Dickason received a high school education by correspondence and then went on to study at Notre Dame College, a collegiate affiliate of the University of Ottawa located at Wilcox, Saskatchewan. After obtaining a bachelor of arts degree in philosophy and French in 1943, Dickason worked for almost thirty years as a journalist for several dailies, including the *Regina Leader-Post*, the *Winnipeg Free Press*, the *Montreal Gazette*, and the *Toronto Globe and Mail*. She also reared three girls.

During this time, Dickason became increasingly aware of her Métis heritage, a subject that was never spoken of when she was growing up. She returned to academic life, this time to study the history of relations between French settlers and indigenous people. She obtained her master of arts degree in 1972 and her doctorate from the University of Ottawa in 1977. Her Ph.D. dissertation, "The Myth of the Savage and the Beginnings of French Colonialism of the Americas," which she researched in Ottawa, Quebec City, England, and France, was subsequently published by the University of Alberta Press in 1984 and became an instant classic.

A prolific and careful scholar, Dickason was named a member of the Order of Canada in 1996, received a lifetime achievement award from the National Aboriginal Achievement Foundation in 1997, and holds eight honorary doctorate degrees. She has presented many papers at conferences in the United States and Canada, and is a member of the Métis Nation of Ontario Cultural Commission and the Women of the Métis Nation of Alberta.

### Henry Chee Dodge (1860–1947)
*Navajo businessperson and tribal leader*

Henry Chee Dodge was a businessman and chairman of the Navajo Tribal Council. The Navajo occupy extensive parts of Arizona and New Mexico (14 million acres) and have the largest population of any tribe in the United States or Canada.

Dodge has been called the Horatio Alger of the Navajo Nation because he grew up during hard times yet succeeded against all odds. When he was only four years old, he and his family were among the thousands of Navajo who were imprisoned and forced to make "the Long Walk" from Canyon de Chelly to Fort Sumter. They were forced to march for three hundred miles at bayonet point, carrying their belongings. Many did not survive the journey, but those who did faced conditions even worse at Fort Sumter, as disease and famine were rampant there. Eventually the government acknowledged their error and allowed the Navajo to return to their own land.

Dodge lived through all of this to become a wealthy and progressive businessman. He graduated from the Indian School at Fort Defiance, Arizona, and went on to become the owner of two ranches with large herds of sheep and cattle. He was the first chairman of the Navajo Tribal Council, and he served in that capacity for eight years. His son, Thomas Dodge, became an attorney and superintendent of the Navajo Nation, while daughter, Annie Dodge Wauneka, was the first woman elected to the Navajo Tribal Council.

## Donnacona (?–circa 1536)
*Iroquois tribal leader*

Donnacona was the headman of the St. Lawrence Iroquoian village of Stadacona near Quebec City between 1534 and 1536, when Jacques Cartier, the first French explorer to the region, voyaged to and from France and North America. Donnacona met Cartier while fishing in the mouth of the St. Lawrence River in what now is the province of Quebec and protested when Cartier raised his cross to claim French sovereignty. Donnacona was seized, but then befriended by Cartier, and he permitted Cartier to take his sons Domagaya and Taignoagy back to France. A year later, they showed Cartier the way to Stadacona.

Donnacona taught Cartier's men how to cure scurvy with a drink rich with vitamin C made from white cedar. He also spoke to Cartier of the Kingdom of Saguenay to the west, said to be rich in gold and silver and inhabited by white men. Some historians have suggested that Donnacona knew of the Spanish in Mexico, but most believe that Donnacona was embellishing facts about copper deposits around Lake Superior and possibly referring to the Huron in what is now the province of Ontario. Cartier reconsidered his plan to find a passage to the Pacific Ocean and instead established a French colony on the St. Lawrence River as a base to explore the interior of the continent. To this end, Cartier lured Donnacona and his sons onto his ship. Although initially resistant, Donnacona agreed to accompany Cartier to France, when he was promised that he would be returned within a year. Upon his arrival in France, Donnacona was presented to France's King Francis I, who was impressed by Donnacona's description of the Kingdom of Saguenay and decided to challenge Spanish claims to North America by establishing a French settlement on the St. Lawrence. Cartier did not live up to his promise that he would return Donnacona to his homeland, and Donnacona died abroad.

## Marie Dorion (1786–1853)
*Iowa guide and interpreter*

Marie Dorion, who was from the Iowa Nation, served as guide and interpreter for several trapping expeditions in the early 1800s. The Iowa were Siouan speakers, who lived in the north central parts of the Mississippi Valley.

Dorion was born along the Red River, in present-day Arkansas. She married Pierre Dorion, a mixed French Canadian and Yankton Sioux. Her husband was a fur trader and worked a route extending from St. Louis in present-day Missouri to Mandan, a town in North Dakota.

In 1811, Marie Dorion accompanied her husband on an expedition led by Wilson Price Hunt. Hunt's reservations about bringing Dorion along were quickly dispelled. Like Sacajewea, who contributed greatly to the success of the Lewis and Clark expedition, Dorion proved to be a valuable guide, interpreter, and diplomat for Hunt's expedition. Dorion lost a child during the trip, but arrived successfully in Astoria, Oregon, in February 1812.

In that same year, Dorion set out on another expedition to the Snake River country in the Pacific Northwest. All members of the party were killed by hostile Indians, except Dorion and her two sons. They endured a harsh winter, and in the spring Dorion led her boys to Walla Walla Indian country in eastern Washington. In the years that followed, Dorion married twice more to trappers, who valued her skills. Her eldest son, Baptiste, became an interpreter for the Hudson's Bay Company, the major fur trading establishment in Canada and the Pacific Northwest. In 1841, she settled in the Willamette Valley, where she lived until her death in 1853.

## Michael Dorris (1945–1997)
*Modoc novelist and scholar*

Michael Dorris was a novelist and anthropologist who taught Native American studies at Dartmouth College in New Hampshire.

Born in Dayton, Washington, on 30 January 1945, Dorris was raised in Washington, Idaho, Kentucky, and Montana. He studied English and classics at Georgetown University, graduating with honors in 1967. He then received a master's degree in anthropology from Yale University in 1970.

After leaving Yale, Dorris held various teaching positions and became a professor of anthropology and Native American studies at Dartmouth in 1972. He produced many scholarly publications in this area, most importantly the books *Native Americans: Five Hundred Years After* (1975) and *A Guide to Research on North American Indians* (1983), co-authored with Arlene Hirschfelder and Mary Lou Byler.

However, Dorris became better known as a novelist. His first novel *A Yellow Raft on Blue Water* was published in 1989, and he wrote a best-selling novel entitled *The Crown of Columbus* (1991) with his wife Louise Erdrich, a well-known fiction writer. Dorris and Erdrich also co-wrote *The Broken Cord: A Family's On-Going Struggle with Fetal Alcohol Syndrome* (1989); this nonfiction book describes the effects of the syndrome on the couple and their adopted son Adam. Other important works by Dorris include *Guests* and *Morning Girl*, children's books, *Paper Trail*, a collection of personal essays, and *Working Men*, a collection of short stories. His writing is praised for its sensitive and intelligent treatment of American Indian issues.

## Lewis Downing (d. 1872)
*Cherokee tribal leader*

Lewis Downing was principal chief of the Cherokee Nation from 1867 until his death in 1872. Downing was a popular Baptist minister whose church in Delaware Town, in present-day northeast Oklahoma, was the center of the Baptist mission to the Cherokee Nation. The Delaware church was the site of large gatherings of Christian Cherokee, most of whom were converts of the Baptist ministers Evan Jones and his son John. Downing was a close religious and political associate of the Joneses. During the Civil War, the Cherokee Nation divided into southern and northern supports. The conservative Cherokee of the National Party, led by Principal Chief John Ross, eventually sided with the North, while the relatively well-to-do Cherokee slave-owners sided with the South. These differences resulted in an internal Cherokee civil war and bloodshed on both sides. During most of the Civil War, Ross resided in the East and left Lewis Downing as acting chief of the loyal Cherokee. In 1866, the Cherokee agreed to a treaty of reconciliation, and he died soon after. Ross's nephew, William P. Ross, served as acting principal chief until an election was held in 1867.

Lewis Downing, the Joneses, many members of the National party, and some selected former slaveowners formed a new party of reconciliation, and Downing won the office of principal chief over the National party candidate. Serving from 1867 to 1872, Downing emphasized postwar reconstruction, national and political unification, prohibition of U.S. railroads over Cherokee Nation land, and strong support for the rights of citizenship for Cherokee freedmen.

After his death, the political coalition that was forged in 1866 won the election for principal chief in 1875 and was named the Downing party. It was composed primarily of conservative small-holding Cherokee, but issues over preservation of Cherokee national government, and the death of Downing and the Joneses, broke the Downing coalition in the late 1870s, and most of the conservative Cherokee returned to the National party, which became the party of the conservative small farmers. The Downing party then became the party of the former slave-owners and businessmen. The Downing party gained control of the Cherokee government in the 1887 election and maintained control until dissolution of the Cherokee constitutional government in 1907.

## Edward P. Dozier (1916–1971)
*Santa Clara Pueblo anthropologist and linguist*

On 23 April 1916, Edward Dozier was born at Santa Clara Pueblo, one of twenty-three villages of Pueblo Indians in New Mexico and Arizona.

He attended off-reservation high schools, and earned his doctorate in anthropology at the University of California at Los Angeles. He served in the air force as a staff sergeant during World War II and was married and had three children.

Dozier earned an international reputation in the field of anthropology. He was a fellow at the Center for Advanced Studies in the Behavioral Sciences at Stanford, California. He held a Senior Postdoctoral Fellowship from the National Science Foundation and was also a Guggenheim fellow. Dozier was a vice-president for the Association on American Indian Affairs (an Indian advocacy organization) and a fellow of the American Association for the Advancement of Science, the American Anthropological Association, and the American Sociological Association.

Dozier's works in linguistics include studies of Native people in the Philippines. His works on the Pueblo are particularly significant and highly reliable, since non-Indian anthropologists have always had difficulty obtaining accurate Pueblo linguistic materials. Dozier was a member of the Linguistic Society of America.

Dozier is perhaps best known for his book *The Pueblo Indians of North America*, which remains a cornerstone in the anthropological field.

## Wayne Ducheneaux (1936–)
*Cheyenne River Sioux tribal leader*

Wayne Ducheneaux is executive director of the Cheyenne River Tribal Housing Authority. In 1968, he began serving the Cheyenne River Sioux Reservation as chairman of the reservation district surrounding Eagle Butte, South Dakota. From 1974 to 1978, he was elected chairman of the Cheyenne River Sioux tribe. During the same years, Ducheneaux was vice-chairman and then chairman of the task force on tribal-state relations of the Indian Affairs Commission, vice-chairman of the United Sioux Tribes, founder and chairman of the American Indian Agriculture Credit Consortium, and a member of the President's Commission on Indian Nutrition. He was also founder and chairman of the NCAI (National Congress of American Indians) Litigation Committee, which monitors Indian legal rights and legal claims.

As a tribal official, Ducheneaux helped make many reservation improvements. Under his administration, a main waterline from Cheyenne River to Eagle Butte was completed, as was a modern underground telephone system; a 1,200-mile rural water distribution system was built, and improvements were made to the existing hospital. Ducheneaux established a tribal computer division, a centralized accounting system, and a centralized records and microfilm system. He also developed a buffalo program on the reservation and a new criminal, juvenile, and civil code for the Cheyenne River Sioux Tribe.

From 1986 to 1990, Ducheneaux was again tribal chairman of the Cheyenne River Sioux, and chairman of the Indian Agriculture Working Group, which evolved into the Indian Agriculture Council. He was also the honorary co-chairman of the Indian AIDS Committee.

Ducheneaux served as president of the National Congress of American Indians from 1989 to 1991, and he was appointed special judge in the Cheyenne River Sioux Tribal Court. During his second term at NCAI, he obtained a resolution declaring war on drug and alcohol abuse. He also instituted alcohol-free Indian fairs, rodeos, and powwows and a drug testing program for law enforcement personnel and tribal council members. He established a legal division, strengthened the tribal court system, and established an investment policy for the tribe.

### Dull Knife (1810–1883)
*Northern Cheyenne tribal leader*

Dull Knife and his warriors were active in the Cheyenne-Arapaho War in Colorado in 1864 and 1865, the Sioux Wars for the Northern Plains in 1866 and 1867 (including the Fetterman Fight), and the War for the Black Hills of 1876 and 1877. Many of his warriors participated in the battle of the Rosebud and the Little Bighorn in June 1876, where Colonel Custer and over two hundred soldiers met their death in present-day southern Montana.

Dull Knife and Little Wolf, another Cheyenne war chief, proved difficult to capture, even during the massive government retaliation for the Little Bighorn defeat. On 25 November 1876, General George Crook attacked Dull Knife's camp in the battle of Dull Knife on the Red Fork of the Powder River in Wyoming. The Indians suffered twenty-five deaths and 173 tipis destroyed, along with food and clothing, plus five hundred ponies captured. In May 1877, Dull Knife and his followers surrendered at Fort Robinson in Nebraska, and were relocated to a reservation in Indian Territory (present-day Oklahoma).

The Northern Cheyenne were not happy living in Indian Territory, far from their traditional lands on the Northern Plains. The government had provided few supplies, little food, and malaria was rampant. Dull Knife and Little Wolf led an escape of nearly three hundred people from the assigned reservation in September 1878. They set out for their Tongue River homeland in northern Wyoming and southern Montana.

In a six-week, 1,500-mile flight, Dull Knife and his followers eluded some ten thousand pursuing soldiers and an additional three thousand civilians until many became too sick or exhausted to continue the flight. Dull Knife's group was captured on 23 October 1878, and taken back to Fort Robinson. Upon learning that they were once again en route to Fort Robinson, Dull Knife led his followers on another breakout on 9 January 1879, in the dead of winter. Only Dull Knife, his wife, son, daughter-in-law, grandchild, and another boy escaped capture and completed the trip to Chief Red Cloud's Pine Ridge Reservation in present-day South Dakota. Dull Knife and his small party were allowed to remain at Pine Ridge until, finally, in 1884, the Northern Cheyenne were officially granted the Tongue River Reservation in Montana. Dull Knife had died the year before, however, and was buried on a high butte near the Rosebud River in present-day South Dakota.

### Gabriel Dumont (circa 1837–1906)
*Métis tribal leader*

Gabriel Dumont was active in the second Northwest Rebellion of 1885, in which Louis Riel, another Métis leader, sought to form a provisional government in Saskatchewan. Dumont could neither read nor write, but he had a great reputation as a guide, hunter, canoeist, and warrior. Dumont first engaged in plains warfare at the age of thirteen, when he took part in the defense of a Métis encampment against a Sioux war party. At the age of twenty-four, with his father, Dumont concluded a treaty between the Sioux and the Métis, which helped bring peace to the Canadian prairie. Dumont also participated in the creation of a treaty between the Blackfoot Nation and the Métis. When he was twenty-five, Dumont was elected permanent chief of his community.

In 1884, Dumont traveled to Montana where Louis Riel was living in exile, and he obtained Riel's agreement to return to Canada to lead resistance to the settlement of what is now known as Saskatchewan. Dumont became the militant leader of approximately three hundred Métis, in what became known as the second Northwest Rebellion. They were victorious in several battles against Canadian authorities, including a violent attack on Frog Lake in what is now Alberta, where nine people were killed. While Riel subsequently surrendered to authorities, Dumont fled to the United

States. Dumont attempted to organize an escape route for Riel, which never came to pass, and Riel was executed in 1885 for treason. Dumont spent several years living with the Métis of Montana before returning to Canada in 1890. In addition to dictating two memoirs of the rebellion, Dumont continued to hunt and trade up until his death in 1906.

## W. Yvon Dumont (1951– )
*Métis tribal leader*

Yvon Dumont is the former president of the Manitoba Métis Federation. He was born at St. Laurent, Manitoba, on 21 January 1951. His father, William Dumont, was a noted political leader with the Manitoba Métis Federation, and drew his son into political life at a young age. At the age of sixteen, Dumont was elected secretary-treasurer of the St. Laurent Local of the Manitoba Métis Federation. Five years later, he was elected vice-president of the Native Council of Canada, a national organization devoted to advancing the rights of Métis and other aboriginal people not accorded Indian status by Canadian authorities.

During this time Dumont maintained his involvement with the Manitoba Métis Federation and was elected president of the federation in 1984, having run on a platform of fiscal responsibility for the federation and a promise to recommence a complicated Métis land claims case, which had been stalled in the courts for some time. Dumont hired a new lawyer, Thomas Berger, a high-profile proponent of Native rights and a former justice of the Supreme Court of British Columbia. Berger had been successful recently in gaining several important procedural victories before the Supreme Court of Canada.

Under Dumont's leadership, the finances of the Manitoba Métis Federation have stabilized and grown, and the federation has been able to participate in the building of new housing projects and related initiatives for its people. Dumont continues to be active in advocating the Métis cause throughout Manitoba and Canada. Dumont is also a governor of the University of Manitoba and has served on the National Board of the Canadian Aboriginal Economic Development Strategy.

## Sophia McGillivray Durant (circa 1760–?)
*Creek interpreter*

Sophia McGillivray was the daughter of Lachlan McGillivray, a Scot, and Sehoy Marchand, the daughter of a Creek woman of the Wind clan, the most powerful family in the Creek Nation. She married Benjamin Durant, of Huguenot ancestry.

While not a chieftain, Durant is described as having "an air of authority about her, equal, if not superior, to that of her brother, Alexander," the famous Creek leader. During the Revolutionary War, Alexander McGillivray became a leader among the Creek in the present-day Alabama. Durant was well acquainted with the Indian language of her people, and when her brother held councils she delivered his ideas and sentiments in a speech, to which the Creek headmen listened with attention. She was accustomed to writing letters for her brother to the Spanish governor and other officials.

In the summer of 1790 while McGillivray was in New York negotiating a treaty of peace with President George Washington, some Creek threatened to attack a U.S. settlement near the Creek country. Durant and a companion mounted horses and rode for four days to prevent the attack. When she arrived at Hickory Ground, her home village and one of the most sacred towns in the Creek Nation, she assembled the Creek chiefs and threatened them with the vengeance of her brother when he returned from the North. Her bravery put a stop to the planned murders, and the leaders were arrested. Two weeks later Durant gave birth to twin daughters.

## Charles A. Eastman (1858–1939)
*Wahpeton (Santee) Sioux physician and author*

Charles Eastman was the first Native American physician to serve on the Pine Ridge Reservation and a prolific author of works about Indian life and culture. Born at Redwood Falls, Minnesota, in 1858, Eastman was raised in a traditional Santee Sioux setting and had little contact with American society until the age of fifteen. His mother died shortly after his birth, and he was raised by his father's extended family. His father was a Sioux warrior named Many Lightnings. Many Lightnings was taken prisoner by the army during the Minnesota Sioux uprising of 1862 and later executed. After that, Eastman was raised by a paternal grandmother and learned much about the old ways and practical things that hunters and warriors had to know.

In 1874, the family moved to Flandreau, South Dakota, and Eastman was enrolled in school, which brought him into contact with U.S. culture for the first time. He would gradually come to know American society remarkably well and became a well-known Native American intellectual. Eastman attended Dartmouth College and Boston University Medical School, receiving a degree in medicine in 1890. He then became a physician at the Pine Ridge Indian Reservation in South Dakota, the first Native American in a position of authority there. During this time he witnessed the Ghost Dance

Movement and was one of the first people to visit Wounded Knee after the massacre of 1890.

Eastman later became a prolific author whose writings dealt with Indian culture and basic philosophical differences between Native beliefs and those of U.S. society. His autobiographical work *Indian Boyhood* (1902) describes his childhood and reflects a concern with youth and the experience of growing up that would last throughout his career; he was later active in the Young Men's Christian Association and was one of the founders of the Boys Scouts of America. His autobiography was followed by a series of novels on Indian life including *Red Hunters and the Animal People* (1904), *Old Indian Days* (1907), *Wigwam Evenings: Sioux Folktales Retold* (1909), and *The Soul of the Indian* (1911).

In later writings, Eastman focused more on the conflicts between Indian and U.S. culture and the historical experiences of Native American people. A second autobiography, *From the Deep Woods to Civilization* (1916) tells of his experiences as an adult Indian person in U.S. society and is strongly critical of its values and the actions of the United States government. Other, related historical subjects are treated in *The Indian Today* (1916) and *Indian Heroes and Great Chieftains* (1918).

Attorney Walter R. Echo-Hawk.

### Walter Echo-Hawk (1948–)
*Pawnee attorney*

Walter Echo-Hawk was born on 23 June 1948, near Pawnee, Oklahoma. He received a political science degree from Oklahoma State University in 1970 and a law degree from the University of New Mexico in 1973. He has been admitted to practice law before the U.S. Supreme Court, the Supreme Court of Colorado, and several courts of appeal.

Echo-Hawk is a senior staff attorney of the Native American Rights Fund (NARF), a national, Indian-interest legal organization headquartered in Boulder, Colorado. His legal experience includes cases involving religious freedom of American Indians, prisoner rights, water rights, treaty rights, and reburial rights. In recent years, Echo-Hawk has been active in issues concerning protection of Native American human remains and Indian graves from desecration and mistreatment. He was involved in precedent-setting Nebraska legislation that directs museums to return human remains and funerary objects to tribes of origin upon request.

In 1989, Echo-Hawk represented a number of Indian tribes in negotiating the Smithsonian Institution reburial agreement, which received national attention and was enacted into law. In 1989 and 1990, he was a national leader in the Indian campaign to obtain passage of the Native American Grave Protection and Repatriation Act, which is considered the most important human rights law for Native people ever passed by Congress. He also represented the Native American Church of North America to secure passage of the 1994 amendments to the American Indian Religious Freedom Act, protecting the religious use of peyote by Indians.

Echo-Hawk is well published in the areas of religious freedom of American Indians, prison law and rights of prisoners, water rights, treaty rights, and issues concerning protection of deceased Native Americans. In 1991, he was awarded the Civil Liberties Award from the American Civil Liberties Union of Oregon "for significant contributions to the cause of individual freedom."

### John E. Echohawk (1945–)
*Pawnee attorney and rights activist*

John Echohawk, executive director of the Native American Rights Fund (NARF), is an attorney who has

John E. Echohawk, executive director of the Native American Rights Fund.

devoted all his attention to Native American legal questions. Born in Albuquerque, New Mexico, on 11 August 1945, Echohawk graduated from the University of New Mexico in 1967, and entered a special pre-law program at the University of New Mexico School of Law that had just been initiated for Native Americans. He then went on to take a degree in law from the University of New Mexico School of Law in 1970.

On graduating, he received the Reginald Heber Smith Community Lawyer Fellowship to work with the California Indian Legal Services program in Berkeley, California. Shortly thereafter he became a cofounder of the Native American Rights Fund (NARF), a national organization centered in Boulder, Colorado, which takes major legal cases for Indian tribes.

Echohawk has been very active in community service over the years and worked to create opportunities for Indian youth. He has served on the board of directors of groups such as the Association on American Indian Affairs, the American Indian Lawyer Training Program, and the National Committee on Responsive Philanthropy. He has received several honors for these activities, receiving the President's Indian Service Award from the National Congress of American Indians and a Distinguished Service Award from the Americans for Indian Opportunity.

## Eda'nsa (c. 1810–1894)
*Haida tribal leader*

Eda'nsa (Melting Ice from a Glacier) was a Haida chief, born on Graham Island of the Queen Charlotte Islands off the coast of mainland British Columbia. Eda'nsa also called himself Captain Douglas, testifying in 1878 that he descended from Haida Chief Blakow-Coneehaw, who had secured a trade alliance and exchanged names with a British captain named William Douglas in 1788. Eda'nsa reportedly had an association with James Douglas, governor of the colony of Vancouver Island from 1851 and governor of British Columbia until 1864.

In 1841, Eda'nsa became Haida Eagle chief of the Sta Stas Shongalth lineage, one of three lineages that vied for control of the Eagle town of Kiusta on Graham Island. Upon becoming chief, Eda'nsa succeeded in asserting his authority over the town. It has been noted that while Eda'nsa sought to be the greatest Haida chief of all, his people were not in unanimous approval of his methods. Eda'nsa became a trader in Indian slaves, acquired by other Natives by barter or raid. White traders were certainly aware of his prominence, and he served as a useful guide through the difficult waters of the Queen Charlotte Islands. It is said that trading boats occasionally encountered raiding parties from the Haida when they were in trouble. In one instance, a neighboring Haida chief raided a vessel being piloted by Eda'nsa, took white men as prisoners, plundered the strong box, and burned the ship. It was believed by the white captain that Eda'nsa had been complicit in the raid and shared in the spoils, but this charge was never proved. Eda'nsa became a Christian in 1884 and continued to seek new trading opportunities in the Queen Charlotte Islands until his death, when his title passed to his nephew Charlie Edenshaw, a renowned Haida artist.

## Charlie Edenshaw (1839–1924)
*Haida artist*

Charlie Edenshaw was a prosperous and renowned Haida artist, member of the Eagle clan, and chief of Yatza village on Graham Island located in the Queen Charlotte Islands of British Columbia. Named Takayren (Noise in the House) at birth, Edenshaw was schooled in Haida tradition by his uncle, Eda'nsa, who himself was a chief of the Sta Stas Eagle clan of Graham Island. It is said that upon reaching adulthood, his mother gave him a small pistol. He promptly held it to his head and pulled the trigger three times. The gun went off on the third try, wounding him slightly in the face. In celebration of his brush with death, he held a potlatch, a Haida traditional ceremony and feast involving the giving of food and goods, in which he demonstrated the episode to others. Charlie Edenshaw also became known among his people as Nngkwigetklas (They Gave Ten Potlatches for Him), perhaps in recognition of his repeated participation in potlatches. Charlie Edenshaw married and had five children. The early death of his only son, Robert (Gyinawen), profoundly affected him, and it is said that he never fully recovered from the loss.

Charlie Edenshaw demonstrated artistic talent at an early age and became a skilled carver of wood and argillite, a type of black slate. His work, noted for its flowing sculptural design, grew in popularity, and he became one of the first professional Haida carvers. Edenshaw was equally talented as a silversmith, goldsmith, and woodcarver. He frequently met with anthropologists and art collectors, and so provided others with insight into Haida culture and art. Many of his carvings, including model totem poles, as well as drawings and sketches, were collected by museums and art patrons. His work dramatically illustrates the intricacy of Northwest Coast art.

### Lloyd Elm (1934–)
*Onondaga educator*

Lloyd Elm was born in 1934 and attended the Haskell Institute in Lawrence, Kansas, where he graduated in 1953. He served in the United States Marine Corps and was released with an honorable discharge in 1958. Elm then attended Syracuse University, where he received a bachelor of arts degree in biology and education in 1964. In 1966 and 1967, he received a National Science Foundation Grant in science education. Elm was employed first in 1970 as a classroom teacher in biology and physics, then as principal of the Onondaga Indian School in Lafayette, New York. From 1976 to 1981, Elm was education programs specialist in the Office of Indian Education at the U.S. Department of Education in Washington, D.C. In 1973 and 1974, he was elected to the board of directors of the National Education Association, and from 1972 to 1978, he served on the board of directors of the National Indian Education Association. In 1976, Elm published, in the special edition of the *New York Conservationist*, an essay entitled "The History of the Ho–Dee–Nau–Sau–Nee, the People of the

Longhouse." During the 1970s, Elm resumed his education, receiving a master's degree in educational administration from Pennsylvania State University in 1979 and a Ph.D. in educational administration from the same university in 1983. He then began serving as principal of the Native American Magnet School Number 19, in Buffalo, New York, the first American Indian magnet school in the country.

From 1987 to 1990, Elm served on the New York State Commission on Education and on the initial Native American Advisory Committee on Native American Education. From 1990 to 1991, he served on the Social Studies Syllabus Review and Development Committee, and in 1992, he was appointed by the New York State Board of Regents to serve on the New York State Curriculum and Assessment Committee for Social Studies.

### Georges Erasmus (1948–)
*Dene tribal leader*

Georges Erasmus has been a central figure in aboriginal politics in Canada since the 1970s. He was born at Fort Rae in the Northwest Territories just after the World War II. His people, the Dene Nation, are Athabaskan Indians in the Northwest Territories. Athabaskan is a Cree term that covers all the indigenous people from the interior of Alaska to the Hudson Bay whose languages are related to one another. In their own languages, these people refer to themselves as Dene or Dinneh.

Erasmus became president of the Dene Nation in 1976, during which time he successfully led efforts to stop the construction of the Mackensie Valley Pipeline, a proposed natural gas pipeline running south from Alaska through the Northwest Territories and British Columbia. In 1985, he was successful in persuading Greenpeace, an international environmental organization, to halt a proposed anti-fur campaign, arguing that it threatened traditional ways of life of his people.

Erasmus served from 1985 to 1991 as the national chief of the Assembly of First Nations, a national organization of First Nations in Canada. In 1991, Erasmus was appointed co-chair of the Royal Commission on Aboriginal Peoples. The commission was established by the federal government to examine and report on a broad range of issues concerning aboriginal peoples in Canada, including government, treaties, economic, social and cultural issues, as well as matters relating to the administration of justice and aboriginal people. Erasmus also serves as board member for many organizations and foundations across Canada dedicated to the advancement of human rights and ecological concerns. He is the co-author of *Drumbeat: Anger and Renewal in Indian Country* (1989). He has received the Order of Canada and honorary doctorate of law degrees from seven universities.

### Louise Erdrich (1954–)
*Turtle Mountain Chippewa novelist, poet, and critic*

The daughter of a German-American father and Chippewa mother, Louise Erdrich was born at Little Falls, Minnesota, in 1954 and raised in Wahpeton, North Dakota. She was among the first group of Native American women to be recruited and accepted to Dartmouth College shortly after they began accepting women, and graduated with a major in English and creative writing in 1976. After graduation, Erdrich returned to North Dakota and conducted poetry workshops throughout the state under the auspices of the Poetry in the Schools Program of the North Dakota Arts Council. She later returned to graduate school and completed a master's degree in creative writing from Johns Hopkins University, after which she moved to Boston and became editor of the Boston Indian Council newspaper.

Erdrich's intricately interwoven novels include *Love Medicine* (1984), *The Beet Queen* (1986), *Tracks* (1988), *The Bingo Palace* (1994), *Tales of a Burning Love* (1996), and *The Antelope Wife* (1998). Erdrich has often collaborated with her late husband, Michael Dorris, and together they co-authored a best-seller entitled *The Crown of Columbus* (1991) and a non-fiction book entitled *The Broken Cord: A Family's On-Going Struggle with Fetal Alcohol Syndrome* (1989), which describes the effects of the syndrome on the couple and their adopted son Adam. Erdrich is a prolific poet, as evidenced by her highly praised works *Jacklight* and *Baptism of Desire: Poems*.

### William R. Ernisse (1949–)
*Seneca corporate executive*

William R. Ernisse is vice-president of sales operations and marketing for the Western Operations of Xerox Corporation. Ernisse's organization is responsible for supporting the achievement of customer satisfaction, revenue, and profits from Illinois to Texas, and from Alaska to California. It represents $3.5 billion in annual revenue.

Ernisse joined Xerox in 1970 as a financial analyst in Rochester, New York. Since then he has held a number

William Ernisse.

of key management positions, including vice-president of worldwide training and vice-president of field operations for Xerox' western area. Most recently, he served as vice-president and general manager of Xerox's Greater Los Angeles Customer Business Unit.

Ernisse is one of the select group in Xerox who has earned the company's top achievement award, the President's Award, for superior performance. In addition, he has won top awards from the American Society of Training Development and the National Society for Performance and Instruction. He has been actively involved with education issues and "stay in school" initiatives for over thirteen years; he most recently served as a business representative with Al Gore's initiative on after-school programs.

Ernisse earned his undergraduate and business degrees from the Rochester Institute of Technology. He has served on the Workforce Los Angeles Steering Committee and is a member of the Los Angeles Public Education Council, and the advisory board of the Los Angeles Business Council. Ernisse has been active in establishing the first business partnership with the Los Angeles Philharmonic. In addition, he is a board member of both the Long Beach Police Athletic League and the United Way, and a board chairman of the Center for the Improvement of Child Caring. He resides with his wife, Margarete in Mission Viejo, California, and has two grown children.

## Pierre Falcon (1793–1876)
*Métis poet*

Pierre Falcon, a well-known poet and troubadour, was born in the Swan River Valley, in what is now east-central Saskatchewan, at a trading post of the Hudson's Bay Company, a British trading company active in the Canadian plains. Falcon's father was French, and his mother was a Missouri River Indian, possibly Mandan or Cree. Thus, Falcon was Métis, a term that refers to persons of mixed Indian-European heritage who forged a common identity on the plains of western Canada in the eighteenth and nineteenth centuries. When Falcon was five, his father took him to Quebec, where he attended school until the age of fifteen, when he obtained work with the North West Company, another trading company active in the plains of Canada. He moved back to the Swan River Valley, where he traded for the company and set up a home.

Falcon's interests soon turned political, in the face of a settlement that threatened Métis landholdings in the nearby Red River Valley. Falcon joined other Métis in a skirmish, the Battle of the Seven Oaks, that resulted in the death of the governor of the territory. In the evening following the battle, Falcon composed the famous song, "Chanson de la Grenouilliére," known to many as the Battle Hymn of the Métis.

Falcon eventually settled at White Horse Plain in the Canadian prairies and embraced agriculture and the annual buffalo hunt. For several years, he served as commander of the Métis buffalo hunt and then as a justice of the peace for White Horse Plain. Falcon authored many poems and songs commemorating the Métis. He died at the age of eighty-three.

## Gary Dale Farmer (1953–)
*Cayuga actor, producer, and activist*

Gary Dale Farmer is an actor and producer involved with Native American projects for film, television, and radio. Born on the Six Nations Reserve in Ontario, Canada, on 12 June 1953, Farmer studied at Genesee Community College and Syracuse University (both in New York State). He also had theater training at various private studios in Toronto, Canada. Farmer's first theatrical role was in Michael Cook's *On the Rim of the Curve*, which was produced during the 1976 Olympics in Montreal.

He co-starred in *Powwow Highway* (1988), which won best film at the American Indian Film Festival and for which he took the best actor award. His performance also won him a nomination for best actor from the Independent Feature Project West in Los Angeles. He appeared in the 1992 film *The Dark Wind*, based on the novel by Tony Hillerman, and co-executive produced by Robert Redford. Other films Farmer has appeared in are *The Believers* (1987), *Police Academy, Dead Man* (1996), and the award-winning *Smoke Signals* (1998).

Farmer has many acting credits in television, theater, and radio dramas, and recently he has also been active as a producer of television and radio programs dealing with Native American subjects. He produced a series of television shows called *Our Native Land* for the Canadian Broadcasting Corporation, and in 1989 he produced and hosted a magazine-style radio program called *Prevailing Winds*. He also produced and hosted a series of eight thirty-minute programs called *Powwow for Multilingual Television* (MTV) in Canada.

Since 1989, Farmer has lectured on Native American issues and other related topics at Dartmouth College, Cornell University, and many other campuses in the United States and Canada. In these talks, he discusses Native media programming, the importance of literacy, protecting the environment, and the need for taking an active role in community affairs. Since then he has played in countless Native theater productions and toured throughout Canada's Northern Native communities. He has published the journal *Aboriginal Voices* since the early 1990s.

## Donald Fixico (1951–)
*Creek/Seminole/Sac and Fox/Shawnee historian and professor*

Donald L. Fixico is professor of history and director of the Indigenous Nations Studies Program (a master's degree program) at the University of Kansas. Born in Shawnee, Oklahoma, Don is a full-blood American Indian of the Sac/Fox, Shawnee, Creek, and Seminole tribes. After earning a doctorate from the University of Oklahoma, he received postdoctoral fellowships at the University of California, Los Angeles' American Indian Studies Center and the D'Arcy McNickle Center for the History of the American Indian at the Newberry Library in Chicago. He has been a visiting lecturer at the University of California, Berkeley and Los Angeles, and visiting professor at San Diego State University and at the University of Michigan, Ann Arbor. He was an exchange professor at the University of Nottingham, England, and a visiting professor in the John F. Kennedy Institute at the Freie University in Berlin, Germany. He has been on the faculty at the University of

Donald Fixico.

imagery invoked by ancient mythologies. At that point, he says, he became drawn to the old myths "like a magnet" and would sit for hours listening to stories told by his uncles and cousins. He states that he did some library research then but found that the writings of anthropologists and scholars lacked the excitement and personal involvement in stories told by his own relatives.

Fonseca is probably best known for paintings and other graphics depicting Coyote, the cunning, reckless, and irresponsible trickster of Maidu mythology. In these works, Coyote is typically rendered in ultramodern clothing or absurd situations that somehow produce satirical images of contemporary American society. One painting from the early 1980s depicts Coyote and his female counterpart, Rose, performing a ballet step in Tchaikovsky's *Swan Lake*.

Fonseca had already mastered formal painting techniques and established a reputation as an artist before becoming involved with Coyote and other subject matter based on Maidu mythology. His career took a major leap when the Coyote paintings first appeared at the Wheelwright Museum in Santa Fe, New Mexico, during the 1970s. Countless delightful manifestations have been produced in the years since then. The artist currently lives in Santa Fe, exploring new images and new techniques in painting and print-making.

Wisconsin-Milwaukee and at Western Michigan University, Kalamazoo.

Fixico has written four books, *Termination and Relocation: Federal Indian Policy, 1945–1960* (1986); *Urban Indians* (1991); *The Invasion of Indian Country in the Twentieth Century: American Capitalism and Tribal Natural Resources* (1998); and *The Urban Indian Experience in America* (2000). He has edited two books: *An Anthology of Western Great Lakes Indian History* (1988) and *Rethinking American Indian History* (1997). He is completing a new book, *The American Indian and History: Native Reality and Indigenous Ethos*. His publications include over forty articles on Indians in the nineteenth and twentieth centuries.

### Harry Fonseca (1946–)
*Maidu artist*

Harry Fonseca grew up in Sacramento, California, and has been creating art for over forty years. He has exhibited nationally and internationally in numerous solo and group shows. While pursuing an art degree at Sacramento State College, Fonseca became interested in Indian and other Native cultures and the power of

### Philip Fontaine (1944– )
*Sagkeeng Ojibway leader*

Philip Fontaine is former national chief of the Assembly of First Nations and former grand chief of the Assembly of Manitoba Chiefs. He is well-known in Canada for his work in advancing the cause of aboriginal rights. He was born at the Fort Alexander Reserve ninety miles north of Winnipeg, Manitoba, in 1944. Fontaine learned English while attending residential school. He went on to complete high school and earn a bachelor's degree in political studies from the University of Manitoba in 1981.

Fontaine served as chief of the Fort Alexander/ Sagkeeng First Nation between 1972 and 1976. During this time, he worked to introduce unique reforms, including one of the first locally controlled First Nation school programs in the country, a locally controlled child welfare agency, and the first alcohol treatment center for aboriginal people in Manitoba. As grand chief of the Assembly of Manitoba Chiefs, Fontaine was one of several aboriginal leaders who fought successfully for the demise of the Meech Lake Accord, a 1990 federal proposal to amend the Canadian Constitution to respond to demands by the province of Quebec for greater autonomy, but which ignored aboriginal concerns. Fontaine was also responsible for organizing a leadership debate on aboriginal issues during Manitoba's provincial election in 1990. In addition, he has been a leader in calling for the public disclosure of, and a federal inquiry into, Native child abuse by residential school authorities. Fontaine has worked to reunite Native children adopted early in life out of their communities with their birth mothers, sought to place authority traditionally exercised by federal authorities over such matters as education and medicine in the hands of First Nations themselves, and has been active in the politics of constitutional reform in Canada.

## Jack D. Forbes (1934–)
*Powhatan and Lenape author and scholar*

Born in Long Beach, California, on 7 January 1934, Jack Forbes once wrote that his heritage is "the long trail of Indians from the east coast, driven little by little towards the west." He graduated from the University of Southern California in 1953 and went on to receive his master's degree (1955) and Ph.D. (1959) in anthropology from the same university. During the 1960s Forbes was an organizer of activist groups such as the Native American Movement, the Coalition of Eastern Native Americans, and the United Native Americans. He was also a founder of D-Q University in Davis, California, and worked as a volunteer instructor there. He became a professor and department chair of Native American studies at the University of California, Davis, in 1969 and continued teaching in that position until his retirement in 1998.

Forbes has guest lectured all over the world and served as a visiting Fullbright professor at the University of Warwick, England, as the Tinbergen Chair at the Erasmus University of Rotterdam, as a visiting scholar at the Institute of Social Anthropology and Linacre College of Oxford University, and as a visiting professor in literature at the University of Essex, England.

Over the years Forbes has published several important books on Indian subjects, including *Warriors of the Colorado: the Yuma of the Quechan Nation and their Neighbors* (1955), *The Indian in America's Past* (1964), *Native Americans of California and Nevada* (1969), and *Native Americans and Nixon: Presidential Politics and Minority Self-Determination* (1981). His novel *Red Blood* was published in 1997. His chapbook *What is Time?* is now in print, along with *Naming Our Land* and *El-Lay Ritos*, two collections of poetry.

## Josiah Francis (Hillis Hayo) (d. 1818)
*Creek and Seminole tribal leader*

Josiah Francis was a leader in the Creek War of 1813 and 1814. He is also known by the name Hillis Hayo or Hillis Hadjo, which is a Muskogean religious title.

In 1811, Francis traveled with Tecumseh, helping him to spread his message of Indian confederation and unity and opposition to U.S. expansion to southeastern Indian nations. Tecumseh was trying to create an alliance of Indian nations that would block further U.S. expansion onto Indian lands. Influenced by Tecumseh, Francis helped organize the Red Stick Creek, mostly the conservative Creek villages in present-day Alabama who opposed U.S.-inspired changes in Creek government, laws, and horticulture. In the Creek War, Francis, with William Weatherford, another upper town Creek leader, led the Red Sticks against U.S. and Indian forces led by General Andrew Jackson. In 1815, Francis traveled to England in search of support for his struggle against the United States. In 1818, he was captured by U.S. forces at St. Marks, a trading post in northern Florida, after General Jackson lured him onto a gunboat flying a British flag. Jackson had Francis executed.

Francis's daughter Milly also gained notoriety during the 1800s due to an alleged incident in which she begged her father to spare the life of a Georgia militia soldier. According to the story, Francis relented and the soldier was spared, but he ordered the soldier to shave his head and join the tribe.

## Lee Francis (contemporary)
*Laguna Pueblo/Anishinabe and Lebanese writer/ editor and administrator*

Lee Francis is associate professor of Native American studies and director of the Native American Studies Department at the University of New Mexico. He is also the national director of Wordcraft Circle of Native Writers and Storytellers.

Francis received his bachelor's degree and master's degree from San Francisco State University and a doctorate from Western Institute for Social Research in Berkeley, California. He has taught in the American studies program at The American University, in Washington, D.C., where he served as director of the Washington Internships for Native Students (WINS) program. He has also served as director of the Pre-Engineering Intensive Learning Academy for Native students at California State University, Long Beach, student affairs officer at the University of California, Santa Barbara, associate director of the Educational

Opportunity Program at San Francisco State University, and is a senior faculty member with Meta-Life Adult Professional Training Institute.

He is a member of the editorial board of Contemporary Native American Communities book series of AltaMira Press and a trustee and secretary of the board of the Laguna Pueblo Educational Foundation. Francis serves on the First Book Award (for Poetry and Prose) Selection Committee for the Native Writers' Circle of the Americas and is a member of the board of directors for the Greenfield Literary Review.

Francis has also held government appointments including Indian youth specialist with the U.S. Department of the Interior's assistant secretary for Indian Affairs Office of Alcohol and Substance Abuse Prevention, legislative assistant to United States Senator Hugh Scott, special assistant to U.S. Senator Pete V. Domenic (R-NM), and staff assistant to the Joint Committee on Congressional Operations of the U.S. Congress.

Francis is also an elected life member of the National Psychiatric Association and an active member in numerous organizations including the National Indian Education Association and the American Indian Philosophy Association.

His literary accomplishments include *Native Time: A Historical Time Line of Native America* (1996), *Reclaiming The Vision—Past, Present and Future: Native Voices for the Eighth Generation* (co-editor, 1996), and *When the Rain Sings: Poems by Young Native Americans* (editor, 1999).

## Milly Francis (circa 1802–1848)
*Creek recipient of Congressional Medal of Honor*

Milly Francis was the daughter of Josiah Francis (Hillis Hadjo), a Creek tribal leader. In 1817, the Creek captured Captain Duncan McKrimmon of the Georgia militia, tied him to a stake, and prepared to shoot him. Milly Francis interceded and saved McKrimmon's life. McKrimmon later proposed marriage. However, Milly declined, stating that "she would have interceded for any white captive."

During the removal of the Creek to Indian Territory beyond the Mississippi River, in present-day Oklahoma, Francis relocated with the transplanted Creek Nation in present-day Muskogee, Oklahoma. Widowed and with eight children, she found it difficult to support her family. Major Ethan Allen Hitchcock reported her case to Washington, and in 1844, Congress voted her a Congressional Medal of honor and an annual pension of $96 for having saved the life of Captain McKrimmon. Four years passed, however before the U.S. agent to the Creek was instructed to notify Francis of the award.

The agent found her "in a most wretched condition," dying of tuberculosis. She died without receiving either the medal or the pension. A granite marker on the campus of Bacone College, a Baptist Indian school near Muskogee, records the main events of her life and her burial "somewhere in this vicinity."

## Billy Frank, Jr. (1931–)
*Nisqually activist*

Billy Frank, Jr., is a grassroots political activist who for the past fifty years has fought for the land and fishing rights of Native Americans in the Pacific Northwest. Frank's own tribe, the Nisqually, live in eastern Washington State. Many Northwest Coast tribes claim the right to fish at their traditional and customary places as negotiated in treaties with the United States in the 1850s. Since then, however, many northwestern states have refused to recognize Indian treaty fishing rights. Over the past three decades Frank participated in Washington State and tribal relations as the state moved from confrontational police tactics, to litigation, and eventually to cooperation on Indian fishing rights issues.

In the 1960s, Frank was jailed frequently for his role in civil acts of disobedience, which included "fishing out of season." He opposed Washington State fishing authorities and a powerful sports fishermen's lobby. Years of resistance finally paid off. Since the 1974 *Boldt* decision that affirmed the treaty fishing rights of tribes, Frank's work has been less controversial. He is widely credited for playing a major role in turning a bitter two-decade battle between Northwest states and Indian tribes from physical and legal confrontation to negotiation.

Currently, Frank is chairman of the Northwest Indian Fisheries Commission. This organization represents twenty western Washington tribes in negotiating fisheries and habitat management plans with state and federal governments, and it makes many decisions that were once made by Frank's opponents in state government. In this role Frank has been a tireless worker on behalf of building salmon and steelhead runs for Indians and non-Indians. Celebrated nationally as a Native American leader, he was awarded the Albert Schweitzer Prize for Humanitarianism at Johns Hopkins University in Baltimore in 1991.

## Gregory W. Frazier (1947–)
*Crow businessperson and author*

Gregory Frazier is a successful business entrepreneur who has used his expertise to help Indians in the

Northwest. Born at Richmond, Indiana, on 5 September 1947, Frazier graduated from Temple University in Philadelphia with a degree in business administration (1972), and then completed an M.B.A. (1978) and Ph.D. (1988) at the University of Puget Sound in Washington State.

Frazier has been an extremely dynamic leader in business and economic development since the early 1970s and now owns and operates several business enterprises. From 1972 until 1974, he was an instructor for the American Indian Management Institute, an educational institution for training Indian people in business; then he served as executive director of the Seattle Indian Center from 1974 to 1977. From 1977 until 1979, he was the executive director of AL-IND-ESK-A, the thirteenth regional corporation, in Seattle, Washington. As part of the Alaska Native Claims Settlement Act of 1971, the U.S. government created thirteen for-profit corporations, twelve in Alaska and one for at-large shareholders consisting of Aleut, Indian, and Eskimo people living in the lower forty-eight states. This thirteenth corporation became known by the acronym AL-IND-ESK-A.

In 1977, Frazier also became president of Absarokee Investments in Seattle and, during the 1980s, started several other private businesses including Alpine Adventure Films and Cablestar Distributing, both of Englewood, Colorado. Besides running these and other business enterprises, Frazier has remained active in organizations such as National Advisory Council on Indian Education and the National Urban Indian Council. He is the author of several books, including *While We're At It, Let's Get You a Job* (1984), *American Indian Index* (1987), and *Smoke Signals* (1989). Frazier is a professional motorcycle road racer and top desert race competitor. One of only seven Americans to complete a global motorcycle tour, Frazier is currently on an unprecedented second tour of the world.

### Robert Lee Freeman (1939–)
*Dakota and Luiseño graphic artist*

Robert Lee Freeman was born at Valley Center on the Rincon Indian Reservation in southern California on 14 January 1939. His mother was a Dakota (Sioux) from the Crow Creek Reservation in South Dakota, and his father a Luiseño who was raised nearby. He began painting in 1961 and received an associate of arts degree from Palomar College in San Marcos, California, in 1976. Freeman works in a variety of styles ranging from cartooning to fine art painting and is adept in a variety of media including oil and watercolor painting,

etching, pen and ink drawing, bronze sculpture, airbrush painting, and lithography. He has applied his diverse abilities as a teacher of Native American art at Grossmont College in San Diego and at Palomar College in San Marcos, California.

Freeman has won more than 150 major Indian art awards and has numerous exhibitions to his credit, including shows at the Department of the Interior (Washington, D.C.), the Heard Museum (Phoenix, Arizona), and the Scottsdale National Indian Art Exhibit. He has a forty-five-foot mural installed at the Los Angeles Public Library.

### Gall (Pizi) (1840–1894)
*Hunkpapa Sioux tribal leader*

In the 1860s and 1870s, Gall was a leader in the wars for the Bozeman Trail and the Black Hills in present-day Wyoming, Montana, and South Dakota. He was one of the principal strategists in the Battle of Little Bighorn, where in June 1876 Colonel George Custer and some two hundred U.S. soldiers were badly defeated. Gall is credited with developing the successful tactics that led to Custer's defeat.

Raised as an orphan until his adoption by Sitting Bull, a major Sioux leader, Gall proved his abilities as a warrior early in life. During the skirmishes for control of the Bozeman Trail in 1866 and 1867, Gall established and honed the guerrilla techniques and decoy tactics he used later in the struggle for control of the Black Hills. During the war for the Black Hills, he was Sitting Bull's chief military strategist. In the now-famous Battle at Little Bighorn, Gall's military prowess gained its greatest notoriety, and his tactics played a major role in the victory.

After the Indian defeats following Little Bighorn, Gall left for Canada with Sitting Bull. In 1881, he returned to the United States with about three hundred people and surrendered at the Poplar Agency in present-day eastern Montana. He was relocated on the Standing Rock Reservation in North Dakota. There, Gall became friends with Indian agent James McLaughlin and adopted a way of life more European than Indian. Gall negotiated a number of treaties that divided Sioux lands, and he did not take a stance in the Ghost Dance Uprising of 1890. His relationship with the U.S. government was not well perceived by other Indians, including those who had fought with him years earlier. In a gesture of rejection by another veteran of the Little Bighorn Battle, Kicking Bear left out Gall's portrait from a famous pictographic version of Custer's defeat.

## Carol Geddes (1945–)
*Tlingit filmmaker and writer*

Born in the small Yukon village of Teslin, Carol Geddes received a B.A. in English and philosophy from Carleton University in Ottawa, Ontario, Canada's capital city. She later did post-graduate work in communications at Concordia University in Montreal, Quebec.

Beginning in 1983, Geddes has devoted herself to filmmaking and occasional writing. In her first documentary, *Place For Our People* (1983), Geddes introduced the successful Montreal Native Friendship Centre and called for the development of similar community institutions across the country. In 1986, Geddes wrote and compiled a report entitled *Community Profiles: The Native Community*, for the National Film Board of Canada, a federally funded organization devoted to the advancement of film. Geddes's report highlighted the needs of First Nations in Canada and evaluated existing films on Native people. From 1986 to 1990, Geddes produced twenty videos, many focusing on the traditions and art of Native people in Canada. Her first major film, *Doctor, Lawyer, and Indian Chief* (1986), documented the lives of five Native women in Canada and won an award at the 1988 National Educational Film and Video Festival in San Francisco. As a writer, Geddes received the *National Magazine*'s Silver Foundation Award in 1991 for her article, "Growing Up Native," which appeared in *Homemaker's* magazine.

In 1990, Geddes was appointed the first producer of the National Film Board's Studio One, located in Edmonton, Alberta, and devoted entirely to the production of indigenous media. Recently, she directed *No Turning Back* (1997), *Forgotten Warriors* (1997), and *Picturing a People: George Johnston, Tlingit Photographer* (1997).

## Hanay Geiogamah (1945–)
*Kiowa/Delaware playwright, director, and scholar*

Hanay Geiogamah is professor of Theatre and American Indian studies at the University of California, Los Angeles. He was artistic director of the Native American Theater Ensemble (NATE) in New York City from 1972 to 1976. He received a bachelor's degree in theater and drama in 1980 from Indiana University in Bloomington, where he worked also as freelance director, producer, and instructor-organizer for American Indian communications and arts projects. From 1980 to 1982, he was the artistic director of Native Americans in Arts in New York City. Then in 1983, he was visiting professor of theater and Native American Studies at Colorado College in Colorado Springs. He also has been artistic director of the Native American Theater Ensemble in Los Angeles and of the American Indian Dance Theater, a national professional dance company.

Geiogamah served as director of communications and then executive director of the American Indian Registry for the Performing Arts in Los Angeles from 1984 to 1988, and in 1989, he worked as technical consultant advisor for *Dark Wind*, a feature film produced by Wildwood Production, whose executive producer was Robert Redford. In the following years, he combined his professional career with teaching experiences, as well as with writing and producing plays. From spring 1988 through January 1989, he conducted tours of the American Indian Dance Theater in the United States and Europe, with a special eight-week engagement at the Casino de Paris Theater in Paris, France. In 1989, Geiogamah co-directed and helped produce the American Indian Dance Theater's Special on *Great Performances, Dance in America Series*, aired nationally on the Public Broadcasting System in 1990. Also in 1990, he wrote a teleplay based on N. Scott Momaday's 1969 book *The Way To Rainy Mountain*.

Geiogamah's plays have been written for productions by American Indian Theaters and performing arts groups. Among them are *Body Indian* (1972), performed both in the United States and in Europe; *Foghorn* (1973), premiere production by the Native American Theater Ensemble in Reichskabarrett, West Berlin, Germany; and *Coon Cons Coyote* (1976). He has received various honors and awards, such as the William Randolph Hearst National Writing Award from the University of Oklahoma in 1967 and the Charles MacMahon Foundation Scholarship in Journalism in 1963, and he was guest speaker at the American Theater Association's Forty-Sixth National Convention in New York City in 1982. From 1972 to 1989, Geiogamah received numerous grants from a variety of institutions to develop and promote NATE, the American Indian Registry for Performing Arts, and for NAPAF, the American Indian Dance Theater/Native American Performing Arts Foundation.

## Alexander General (Deskahe) (1889–1965)
*Cayuga and Oneida tribal leader and activist*

Alexander General was a tribal leader and intellectual figure of Cayuga and Oneida descent. The Cayuga and Oneida are both tribes of the Iroquois Confederacy; the Cayuga were located along the shores of Cayuga Lake in New York State, and the Oneida are also located in New York, though some now also live in Wisconsin and Ontario, Canada.

Born on the Six Nations Reserve in Ontario, Canada, in 1889, General was the youngest of eight children. His family lived in poverty as marginal subsistence farmers, a situation that worsened after the accidental death of his father when General was only ten years old.

After his father's death, General went to work to help support his mother and therefore never went beyond the fourth or fifth grade in school. He later said that he learned more English through working than in school, holding jobs on the railroad and in foundries. Through diligence and good fortune he gradually saved enough money to go into farming with his brother and became a very successful farmer by reservation standards.

Alexander belonged to a chiefly lineage of the Iroquois Confederacy and at the age of eighteen he began memorizing the ritual speeches of the Iroquois longhouse, the meeting place of confederate council. He gradually became known as the major speaker and ritualist of his community, and later, at the age of thirty-six, General was elected by his lineage to represent their views and took the chiefly title Deskahe.

Because of his cultural knowledge and his ability to explain Longhouse ceremonials and religious concepts in an intellectual manner, Deskahe became an important figure in anthropology. Frank Speck's book *The Midwinter Rites of the Cayuga Longhouse* (1949) was written as a collaboration with Deskahe and includes his name on the title page, but Speck was only one of many scholars who worked with this extraordinary leader and ritualist during the years between 1932 and 1959.

Most importantly, Deskahe was a political activist who once even traveled to England (in 1930) to argue that Canada had no jurisdiction over the Iroquois. He felt that tribal sovereignty could only be guaranteed by retaining the hereditary Iroquois council, and he also fought to re-establish the position of traditional Iroquois chiefs and to broaden their authority. He argued to anthropologists, in the news media, and to anyone who would listen, that his people had been robbed of their birthright. He also organized groups such as the Indian Defense League and the Mohawk Workers to help the Iroquois resist Canadian government authority.

## Dan George (1899–1981)
*Squamish actor*

Dan George was an accomplished and acclaimed actor, perhaps best known for his portrayal of a Cheyenne elder named Old Lodge Skins in the film *Little Big Man*. For this role, he was awarded the New York Film Critics Award for best supporting actor in 1970. Popularly referred to as Chief Dan George, he was born on the Burrard Indian Reserve near Vancouver, British Columbia, and began acting late in life. Until the age of sixty, he worked as a longshoreman, logger, and musician. He was chief of the Squamish band of Burrard Inlet, British Columbia, from 1951 to 1963.

Dan George was discovered as an actor in 1959, and he dedicated the rest of his life to improving the image of Indian people in film, theater, and television. He portrayed an Indian elder in Canadian television and theater, including the Canadian Broadcasting Corporation production of *Caribou Country* and the original production of *The Ecstasy of Rita Joe*, a contemporary drama about Indian people. He had roles in at least eight feature films, including *Smith* (1969), *Harry and Tonto* (1974), and *The Outlaw Josey Wales* (1975), as well as his role in *Little Big Man*. He also was the author of two books of prose-poetry, *My Heart Soars* (1974) and *My Spirit Soars* (1982). Dan George refused to endorse Indian political causes, but throughout his career he sought to change dominant images of Indian people in the media. Dan George died in Vancouver at the age of eighty-two.

## Forrest J. Gerard (1925–)
*Blackfeet government administrator and assistant secretary of the interior*

Forrest Gerard is a public health specialist who has served as an official in various government agencies relating to Native American concerns. Born in Browning, Montana, on 15 January 1925, Gerard graduated from Montana State University and had additional training at the National Tuberculosis Association Training Institute and the American Management Association. He then served as executive secretary of the Wyoming Tuberculosis and Health Association and as a staff member of the Montana Tuberculosis Association. For six years he was the tribal relations officer for the Division of Indian Health in the U.S. Public Health Service in Washington, D.C., and then he was chief of the division for four years.

In 1965, Gerard was awarded a fellowship in Congressional Operations, which allowed him a year of intensive study in Washington focusing on the organization of Congress and the legislative process. In 1966 he was appointed legislative liaison officer for the Bureau of Indian Affairs (BIA), a position in which he worked to strengthen the Indian position in government. Later, he became director of the Office of Indian Affairs in the Department of Health, Education, and Welfare.

During the late 1970s, Gerard was appointed assistant secretary of the interior for Indian affairs. This position superseded the old position of commissioner of Indian Affairs. His administration was deeply concerned with the task of implementing the Self Determination and Educational Assistance Act of 1975 (P.L. 93–638).

Gerard opposed the dismantling of the BIA, mandated by P.L. 93–638, and fought many public battles with Senator James Abourezk, who authored the act and tried to manage its implementation.

A member of numerous boards and committees, Gerard has also won many awards and honors for his service to Indian people. He was an air force pilot during World War II and flew thirty-five combat missions.

### Geronimo (Goyathlay) (1825–1909)
*Chiricahua Apache tribal leader*

After the death of Cochise in 1874, the Chiricahua Apache once again entered an era of nearly constant warfare. Into this conflict, a younger generation of Indian leaders rose up to take the place of older Apache leaders such as Cochise and Mangas Coloradas. One of the most feared and respected of these warriors was Goyathlay, who is generally known as Geronimo.

Like many Apache of his generation, Geronimo's early years were drenched in violence and warfare. His own wife and children were killed by Mexican soldiers. From this point onward, his life was filled with a succession of military raids, captures, escapes, and brief attempts to live on Indian reservations.

Although he was pursued relentlessly, Geronimo eluded the larger U.S. forces until 1886, when he was forced to surrender. Newspapers, presidents, and politicians called for Geronimo's execution, but, instead, he was imprisoned.

In 1894, Geronimo and many of his close Apache comrades were moved to Fort Sill, Oklahoma. In 1909, Geronimo died at Fort Sill, still a prisoner of war and, as such, never allowed to return to his homeland.

### Tim Giago (Nanwica Kciji) (1934–)
*Oglala Lakota publisher and author*

Tim Giago is editor and publisher of the *Lakota Nation Journal*. He is also founder and former editor/publisher of *Indian Country Today/Lakota Times*, the largest, independently owned American Indian weekly newspaper. Born on the Pine Ridge Reservation on 12 July 1934, Giago attended San Jose State College and the University of Nevada at Reno. His writing career

Tim Giago.

began in 1979, when he became an Indian affairs columnist for the *Rapid City Journal* in Rapid City, South Dakota. This led to a position as a full-time reporter, and in 1981 Giago created the *Lakota Times/Indian Country Today*, which he sold in 1998.

He is the author of three books *The Aboriginal Sin* (1978), *Notes from Indian Country, Volume I* (1983), and *Notes From Indian Country, Volume II* (1999). In 1984, he founded the Native American Journalists Association and became the first American Indian to serve on the advisory board of the Freedom Forum in Arlington, Virginia.

Giago continues to write a syndicated column about contemporary Indian issues that appears in newspapers nationwide and his work has been featured in *People Magazine*, *New York Times*, and the *Denver Post*. He has appeared on the *Oprah Winfrey Show*, *NBC Nightly News with Tom Brokaw*, and many national radio programs.

He is the recipient of two doctoral degrees and has won many awards, including the Civil Rights and Human Rights Award given by the South Dakota Education Association (1988). In 1982, he was named Print Media Person of the Year at the Native American Media Convention. Giago was the first American Indian to receive a Nieman Fellowship for Journalism at Harvard University. Giago was inducted into the South Dakota Hall of Fame in 1994.

### George A. Gill (1925–)
*Omaha educator*

Born at Sioux City, Iowa, on 25 July 1925, George Gill attended the University of Nebraska and later received his bachelor's and master's degrees in education from Arizona State University. He is the first Indian to receive a master's degree with a specialization in Indian education and was the recipient of numerous awards, including scholarships from the American Indian Foundation, the National Congress of American Indians, the Association on American Indian Affairs, and the American Missionary Association.

Early in his career, Gill served as a teacher in federal Indian schools and in public schools, and he also directed workshops for instructional aides. Later he became a faculty member in the Department of Education and director of the Indian Education Center at the University of Arizona. He has been a director of the Annual Indian Education Conference and has also served as editor of the Journal of Indian Education. In 1960, he was the Arizona Indian delegate to the White House Conference on Children and Youth.

Besides these accomplishments, Gill had a total of twenty-two years and four months in the U.S. Navy (active and inactive), serving in Europe, the Mediterranean, the Pacific, and Korea; he was awarded the Navy Good Conduct and Combat medals.

### James Gladstone (1887–1971)
*Blood senator*

As Canada's first aboriginal senator, James Gladstone was a strong advocate of the rights of First Nations. Also known as Akay-na-muka (Many Guns), he was born at Mountain Hill, Northwest Territories, on 21 May 1887, and was raised on the Blood Reserve in Alberta. In his early twenties, Gladstone worked as a typesetter for the *Calgary Herald* and then as a scout and interpreter for the Royal Northwest Mounted Police on his reserve. During World War I, Gladstone promoted bigger production from the reserves' farms. He excelled at farming his eight hundred acres of land on the Blood Reserve, where he was the first Indian to have electricity and to own a tractor.

Gladstone was one of the initial members of the Indian Association of Alberta, which was formed in 1939, and was its president from 1948 to 1954, and again in 1956. He traveled to Ottawa on a number of occasions to represent aboriginal interests in negotiations with the federal government. Gladstone became Canada's first aboriginal senator when he was appointed to the Senate in 1958. In his first speech as a Canadian senator, Gladstone spoke in Blackfoot, "as a recognition of the first Canadians."

In 1959, Gladstone was named co-chairman of a joint Senate and House of Commons committee to study Canadian Indians. Gladstone was on the committee in 1960 when treaty Indians were given for the first time the right to vote in national elections. In 1969, Gladstone travelled to Japan as a member of the Canadian delegation to the Moral Rearmament Asian Assembly. Gladstone died in Fernie, British Columbia, on 4 September 1971.

### Diane Glancy (1941–)
*Cherokee writer, educator, and dramatist*

Diane Glancy was born in Kansas City, Missouri, in 1941. Her mother was German and English, and her father was Cherokee. She received her B.A. in English

Diane Glancy.

from the University of Missouri in 1964, her M.A. in creative studies from the University of Central Oklahoma in 1983, and her M.F.A from the University of Iowa in 1988.

Glancy was artist-in-residence for the State Arts Council of Oklahoma from 1981 to 1988. She is now a professor at Macalester College in St. Paul, Minnesota, where she teaches Native American literature and creative writing. She was also the Edlestein-Keller Minnesota Writer of Distinction at the University of Minnesota in 1998.

She has published six volumes of poetry. The latest is *The Relief of America*. She has published four collections of short stories and edited three anthologies and a collection of nine plays. Her four novels include *Flutie* and *Pushing the Bear: The 1838 Trail of Tears*.

Among her awards are an American Book Award, the Native American Prose Award, a Minnesota Book Award, a National Endowment for the Arts, a National Endowment for the Humanities, a Minnesota State Arts Fellowship, a Pushcart Prize, and the Emily Dickinson Poetry Prize from the Poetry Society of America.

## Carl Nelson Gorman (1907–1998)
*Navajo artist*

A distinguished artist, Carl Gorman was among the first to employ traditional Navajo motifs in producing modern works of art. He was born on the Navajo Reservation at Chinle, Arizona, on 5 October 1907. A member of the Black Sheep clan, Gorman came from a distinguished family. His parents founded the first Presbyterian mission at Chinle; his father was also a cattleman and Indian trader, while his mother focused on the arts. She was a traditional weaver and translated many religious hymns from English into Navajo. Others in the family were also tribal leaders and well-known silversmiths.

During World War II, Gorman served in the U.S. Marine Corps and became one of the famous Navajo Code Talkers, whose messages in their native language confused the Japanese military in the Pacific campaigns. On leaving the service, Gorman used the GI Bill to support formal art studies at Otis Art Institute in Los Angeles, California, and he worked as a technical illustrator for Douglas Aircraft, established his own silkscreen design company, and taught Indian art at the University of California, Davis.

Gorman's works have appeared in numerous solo and group shows and is represented in many public and private collections. His works include a variety of styles and media. Always an innovator, yet firmly grounded in tradition, this creative figure once even originated a Navajo Gourd Rattle Dance, a new dance based on a combination of traditional elements.

## R. C. Gorman (1932–)
*Navajo artist*

R. C. Gorman is one of the leading contemporary American Indian artists. Born on the reservation at Chinle, Arizona, on 26 July 1932, Gorman is the descendant of distinguished artists and traditionalists on both sides of his family. He was encouraged while still quite young to follow in his father's footsteps, and he once said in an interview that he could remember making his first drawings when he was three years old by tracing designs with his fingers in the sand and mud of the wash at the base of the Canyon de Chelly, a beautiful and famous Navajo landmark.

As a youth he lived in a hogan, or traditional Navajo-style dwelling, and herded sheep with his grandmother, but he soon became exposed to wider influences and developed a cosmopolitan art style of considerable range and depth. After graduating from Ganado Presbyterian High School, he went on to study art at Northern Arizona University at Flagstaff and at San Francisco State University. He later received a grant from the Navajo Tribal Council to study art at Mexico City College. This was the first time the tribe had awarded a grant for study outside the United States.

Gorman has received an extraordinary number of awards and honors and is probably the most heralded of all contemporary Indian artists. In 1973, he was the only living artist to be included in the show "Masterworks of the Museum of the American Indian," held at the Metropolitan Museum in New York, and two of his drawings were selected for the cover of the show's catalog. In 1975, he was honored by being the first artist chosen for a series of solo exhibitions of contemporary Indian art at the Museum of the American Indian in New York.

Over the years, Gorman has published several articles about some of his other interests, which include Mexican art and artists and cave paintings, or petroglyphs.

## Kevin Gover (1955–)
*Pawnee political leader and lawyer*

As the assistant secretary of Indian Affairs, Kevin Gover heads the Bureau of Indian Affairs (BIA), a part of the U.S. government's Interior Department. His appointment by the Clinton Administration came in 1997 after former BIA head Ada Deer resigned. Prior to this appointment, Gover was one of the nation's leading lawyers, focusing on Indian rights.

Born in Lawton, Oklahoma, Gover was one of three children of a white mother, Margaret Lou Richardson, and a Pawnee father, Billy Gover. When he was fifteen, a VISTA (Volunteers in Service to America) worker noticed Gover's potential and arranged for him to attend the prestigious Saint Paul's Preparatory School in Concord, New Hampshire, from which he graduated in 1973. From there, Gover attended Princeton University and graduated in 1978 with a major in public and international affairs.

During his undergraduate work, Gover's family relocated to Albuquerque, New Mexico, and immediately after college, Gover headed to his new home to attend law school at the University of New Mexico. He received his law degree from the university in 1981. It was during this time that Gover married; he and his former wife would have two children by the end of their marriage ten years later.

Soon after law school Gover was hired as a clerk to the late U.S. District Court Judge Juan G. Burciaga, and from 1983 to 1986 he worked for the well-known Washington, D.C.-based law firm of Fried, Frank, Harris, Shriver, and Jacobsen, where he specialized in environmental and natural-resource law, as well as federal Indian law.

Upon his return home to Albuquerque, Gover formed his own law firm in 1986 with Cate Stetson and Susan Williams. The firm specializes in federal Indian, environmental, natural resource, and housing law.

In 1992 Gover stepped back into national governmental affairs as the coordinator for Bill Clinton's campaign through Indian Country. He also attended the 1996 Democratic National Convention in Chicago as the head of a nation-wide voter registration for Native peoples. In the same year, Gover and his law partners contributed $22,000 to the Democratic National Committee and congressional candidates.

In 1999 Gover was the recipient of a Distinguished Alumni Award from the University of New Mexico.

### Cuthbert Grant (1793–1854)
*Métis tribal leader*

Cuthbert Grant was perhaps the first leader of the Métis. Grant played a large role in shaping a sense of Métis nationalism. He worked most of his life as a fur trader first for the North West Company, a group of Montreal traders formed in 1779, and later in life for the company that first capitalized on the fur trade, the Hudson's Bay Company. When he was nineteen years old, he was put in charge of a small outpost in Fort Esperance, on the Qu'Appelle River in what later became Saskatchewan.

Historians claim that Grant was chosen by his superiors to foster a sense of Métis identity partly to solidify the North West Company's trading rights in the region, as it was facing stiff competition from the Hudson's Bay Company. Grant was named "captain of the Métis" by his superior in 1814 and led efforts to persuade, through friendly and unfriendly means, recent settlers who put a strain on the community's resources to return to central Canada. In 1816, Grant also led an attack on the Hudson's Bay Company, resulting in a massacre of approximately twenty people. Although charges were brought against Grant for these and other actions, they were eventually dropped, and after the Hudson's Bay Company and the North West Company merged in 1821, Grant worked for the Hudson's Bay Company in a number of different positions. He briefly served as a special constable at Fort Garry (later known as Winnipeg) and later as warden, justice of the peace, and sheriff. He served as captain of the Métis annual buffalo hunts, and in the 1840s, Grant mediated a temporary truce between the Métis and the Sioux, who had been fighting over territory and buffalo hunting.

### Rayna Diane Green (1942–)
*Cherokee museum administrator and folklorist*

Rayna Green is a museum administrator and folklorist who has made many contributions to our understanding of Native American achievements in the areas of science and technology and has also published books on other aspects of American folklore and on the writing and other accomplishments of Native American women.

Born in Dallas, Texas, on 18 July 1942, Green received her bachelor's degree from Southern Methodist University (1963) and went on to complete her M.A. and Ph.D. in folklore and American studies at Indiana University (1966 and 1974, respectively).

On completing her doctorate she directed a major research program on Native Americans in science under sponsorship of the American Association for the Advancement of Science (1975–1980) and later served as director of a similar program at Dartmouth College (1980–1983). From 1983 to 1985, Green helped plan the American Indian Program at the National Museum of American History, Smithsonian Institution, Washington, D.C., and she has been the director of the program ever since. In previous years she was also a visiting professor at the University of Massachusetts and at Yale University.

Green has published articles in the *Handbook of American Folklore*, the *Handbook of North American Indians*, and various other scholarly volumes and magazines. She has also written or edited her own books including *Native American Women: A Contextual Bibliography* (1982) and *That's What She Said: Contemporary Poetry and Fiction by Native American Women* (1984). Her most recent work is *The British Museum Encyclopedia of Native America (1999)*.

## Graham Greene (1950–)
*Oneida actor*

A film actor who has found success in Canada and the United States, Graham Greene is a full-blood Oneida born on the Six Nations Reserve in southwestern Ontario in 1950. He began his career in television, film, and radio in 1976. Before becoming an actor, Greene worked at a number of different jobs, including stints as a high steel worker, a civil technologist, and a draftsman. He also worked as an audio technician for rock and roll bands and owned his own recording studio in Hamilton, Ontario. Greene also lived for a short time in Britain in the early 1980s, where he performed on stage.

Upon his return to Canada, Greene was cast in the British film, *Revolution*, starring Al Pacino and directed by Hugh Hudson. Greene is perhaps best known for his performance in *Dances with Wolves*, a 1991 film produced and directed by Kevin Costner, which won several Academy Awards, including the award for best picture. Greene has been cast in a number of television series and is known for his work in *The Campbells*, *Spirit Bay*, *Captain Power*, *Running Brave*, *Adderley*, and *Night Heat*. His film roles include *Powwow Highway*, *Clearcut*, *Medicine River*, *Die Hard With a Vengeance*, *The Education of Little Tree*, and *The Green Mile*.

## Hagler (1690–1763)
*Catawba tribal leader*

It is believed that Hagler was born along the Catawba River in northern South Carolina and became principal chief of the Catawba about 1748. By this time the Catawba had been greatly reduced in numbers as the result of warfare with their traditional enemies, the Shawnee, Cherokee, and Iroquois, as well as from European-introduced diseases such as smallpox.

Hagler developed friendly relations with the British colonists, meeting with them on numerous occasions for negotiations, and thus helped ensure his people's survival and maintenance of their traditional ways. In

1751, he attended a peace conference in Albany, New York. In a meeting with North Carolina officials in 1754 and in a letter to the chief justice in 1756, he argued against the sale of liquor to the Catawba. In 1758, during the French and Indian War, Hagler and his warriors sided with the English in an attack on the French garrison at Fort Duquesne (present-day Pittsburgh, Pennsylvania). In 1759, Hagler assisted the English in battle against Cherokee militants. Because of his support, the English built forts along the Catawba River to prevent attacks on the Catawba by other tribes. They also granted a reservation to the Catawba in 1792, near present-day Rock Hill, South Carolina.

Hagler was killed by a party of Shawnee in 1763. In 1826, South Carolina erected a statue of Hagler at Camden, considered to be the first such memorial to an American Indian in the United States.

## Janet Campbell Hale (1947–)
*Coeur d'Alene novelist*

Janet Campbell Hale was born in Los Angeles, California, in 1947 and raised mainly on the Yakima Indian Reservation in Washington State. She returned to California and received her bachelor's degree from the University of California, Berkeley, and her M.A. in English from the University of California, Davis. She attended law school at Berkeley and Gonzaga Law School in Spokane, Washinton.

Hale's first novel *Owl's Song* (1974) focuses on the experiences of an Indian boy who is forced to live with alcoholism and other social problems on the reservation, and then finds himself placed in an urban setting and urban schools that are unprepared to deal with Indian students. Her other major work is entitled *The Jailing of Celia Capture* (1985), which portrays an urban Indian woman trying to cope with alcoholism and to rebuild her life after being separated from her husband and children. She also wrote *Bloodlines: Odyssey of a Native Daughter* (1993) and has a forthcoming volume of short stories entitled *Women on the Run*. She currently lives in Idaho on the Coeur d'Alene reservation.

## Hancock (early 1700s)
*Tuscarora tribal leader*

From 1711 to 1713, the Iroquoian-speaking Tuscarora, living in present-day North and South Carolina, fought a series of battles to protect their lands against English settlers. Hancock, who some colonists called "King Hancock," was a Tuscarora leader in these wars.

The open conflict between the Tuscarora and English settlers began in 1711. Swiss settler Christoph Von Graffenried forced a group of Tuscarora families off their land. When Von Graffenried refused to pay for the land he seized, Tuscarora warriors retaliated with raids against settlements between Pamilic Sound and the Neuse River. A series of attacks and counterattacks ensued. In 1712, leaders in North and South Carolina sent a large military brigade led by Colonel John Barnwell to quell the Tuscarora. The first battle took place in Cotechney, Hancock's home village. After the English attackers were repulsed, a temporary truce was struck between Hancock and Barnwell. North Carolina officials, however, ordered Barnwell back into the field. In the face of another battle, Hancock agreed to a lasting truce, which was quickly violated by Barnwell's men, who captured Tuscarora for slaves. (During the late 1600s and early 1700s, many Indians were sold to work on plantations or shipped for sale in the Caribbean Islands off the southern coast of the present-day United States.)

In 1713, the colonists amassed a final assault on the Tuscarora. Under the command of Colonel James Moore, the colonial army and 1,000 Indian allies defeated Hancock and his followers. Hundreds of Tuscarora were killed, and hundreds more sold into slavery. Many Tuscarora survivors fled northward to the New York colony.

When they arrived in New York, the Tuscarora found that they spoke a language closely related to the Iroquois of the Iroquois Confederacy, composed of the Seneca, Oneida, Mohawk, Cayuga, and Onondaga Nations. The Tuscarora were not allowed to place their leaders among the forty-nine chiefs of the Iroquois confederate council, but Tuscarora interests were represented by the Oneida chiefs. The Tuscarora took up residence near Oneida villages and have ever since maintained close alliance with the Oneida. Before the arrival of the Tuscarora in the 1710s, the Iroquois Confederacy was often called the Five Nations, but after the Tuscarora arrival the confederacy was often referred to as the Six Nations.

### Handsome Lake (d. 1815)
*Seneca spiritual leader*

The name Handsome Lake is the sachem title of the Turtle clan from among the Seneca, the westernmost nation of the Iroquois Confederacy. The Iroquois Confederacy consisted of six nations and forty-nine sachems, or chiefs, chosen from historically privileged families. Handsome Lake obtained his title sometime before 1799 and held it until his death in 1815. A relative within the Turtle clan, reckoned only through the female line, assumed the name and leadership role after his death.

As a young man, Handsome Lake participated in the forest wars of the period: the French and Indian War (1755–1759), Pontiac's War (1763), and the American Revolutionary War (1775–1783). By the late 1790s, the once-powerful Iroquois lost most of their territory and were relegated to small reserves in upstate New York. While the Iroquois were experiencing social and cultural depression resulting from their recent losses, starting in 1799 Handsome Lake reported a series of visions and preached the *Gaiwiio* or "Good Word" to the Iroquois. He quickly obtained many followers and taught that the Iroquois must reorganize central aspects of their economic, social, and religious life. Under Handsome Lake's guidance, many Iroquois communities adopted new moral codes, men took up agriculture and constructed family farms, and many individuals adopted new religious ceremonies and beliefs. Handsome Lake's message combined elements of Quakerism, Catholicism, and traditional Iroquois beliefs. The new religion helped the Iroquois make the transition from a hunter society to a reservation agricultural community. In the 1830s, after his death, Handsome Lake's followers formalized his teachings into a church, known as the Handsome Lake Church; his teachings are still practiced today by many Iroquois.

### Chitto Harjo (1846–1912)
*Creek tribal leader*

Chitto Harjo (Crazy Snake) was born in Indian Territory, in present-day Oklahoma, and was a member of the ancient holy town of Abihka in the Creek Nation. The sacred white towns among the Creek western or upper town villages were always centers of resistance to political and cultural change in Creek society. After Isparhecher, the leader of the conservative Creek, became principal chief in 1895 but failed to prevent the dissolution of the Creek government, Harjo assumed leadership of the Creek conservatives, who did not wish to surrender their government or their land. The Curtis Act of 1898 decreed the allotment of land and the abolishment of the governments in Indian Territory. The Creek government had little choice but to conform to the demands of the stronger U.S. government.

In a last-ditch effort to avoid allotment and abolishment of the Creek government, the conservative Creek elected Harjo leader. Between 1897 and 1901, the conservative Creek, called Snakes, formed a "snake" or underground government. Harjo was declared hereditary chief, and the government was installed at Hickory Ground, a sacred village within the Creek tradition. The Snakes held the position that the Creek Treaty of 1832 guaranteed them the right to maintain their own government. They refused to recognize that the United States had the power to abolish the Creek government. Harjo ran for principal chief in 1903 but lost handily to Pleasant Porter, who was willing to accommodate the U.S. plans for allotting Creek land and dismantling the Creek government. The Snakes under Harjo's leadership continued to disobey the Creek constitution and government, and on several occasions between 1900 and 1912, U.S. troops and marshals were called in to arrest Snake leaders, quell unrest, and break up Snake meetings. In one skirmish, Harjo was wounded and later died from his wounds. Without this strong leader, the Snake movement faded away.

## Joy Harjo (1951–)
*Muscogee poet and educator*

Joy Harjo is associate professor of American Indian studies and English at the University of California, Los Angeles. She was born in Tulsa, Oklahoma, and is an enrolled member of the Muscogee Nation. She is a graduate of the Institute of American Indian Arts in Santa Fe, New Mexico. She received a BA from the University of New Mexico and an MFA in creative

Joy Harjo.

writing from the University of Iowa. She has also completed the filmmaking program at the Anthropology Film Center and a songwriting workshop at Berkelee School of Music in Boston.

She has published six books of poetry, including *The Last Song, What Moon Drove Me to This?, She Had Some Horses, In Mad Love and War, The Woman Who Fell From the Sky*, and her latest, *A Map to the Next World*.

Harjo was the narrator for the *Native Americans* series on the Turner Network and also narrated the Emmy award-winning show, *Navajo Codetalkers* for National Geographic.

Harjo has received several wards for her writing, including the 1998 Lila Wallace–Reader's Digest Award, the 1997 New Mexico Governor's Award for Excellence in the Arts, The Lifetime Achievement Award from the Native Writers' Circle of the Americas, the William Carlos Williams Award from the Poetry Society of America, the poetry award from the Oklahoma Center for the Arts, and the Oklahoma Book Award.

She also performs nationally and internationally alone and with her band, Joy Harjo and Poetic Justice. Their first CD, *Letter from the End of the Twentieth Century*, was released in 1997.

## Suzan Shown Harjo (1945–)
*Cheyenne and Muscogee activist and poet*

Born in El Reno, Oklahoma, Suzan Shown Harjo has worked to reshape federal Indian policy in Washington, D.C. An energetic and effective advocate, she has helped Native peoples recover over one million acres of land and has developed the most important Native cultural laws in the modern era, including the 1996 Executive Order on Indian Sacred Sites, 1990 Native American Graves Protection and Repatriation Act, 1989 National Museum of the American Indian Act, and the 1978 American Indian Religious Freedom Act.

President of the Morning Star Institute in Washington, D.C., since 1984, she is an Artists Council founder and co-chair of Indian Art Northwest (1996–), and a founding trustee of the National Museum of the American Indian (1990–1996). A special assistant in the Carter Administration and principal author of the President's Report to Congress on American Indian Religious Freedom in 1979, she also served as executive director of the National Congress of American Indians (1984–1989).

Harjo has an extensive background in journalism in addition to her accomplishments as a widely-published poet and curator of numerous art shows at the House and Senate Rotundas, Peabody Essex Museum, and Eitlejorg Museum.

## Elijah Harper (1949– )
*Cree provincial legislator*

Elijah Harper is perhaps best known in Canada for his opposition to the Meech Lake Accord, a 1990 federal proposal to amend the Canadian Constitution to respond to demands by the province of Quebec for greater autonomy. Harper became the voice of aboriginal people, who objected to the exclusion of aboriginal concerns from the accord. In June 1990, Harper blocked the accord's passage in the Manitoba legislature. The accord's demise heightened the awareness of political demands by aboriginal people in Canada and led to new talks on constitutional reform that placed aboriginal issues at the top of the agenda.

Harper was born at Red Sucker Lake, Manitoba, and attended residential school. After completing high school, he studied anthropology at the University of Manitoba in Winnipeg from 1970 to 1972. He married Elizabeth Ann Ross in the fall of 1973, and they have four children. During these years, Harper worked in a number of different community development positions and was elected chief of his home community's Red Sucker Lake Band in 1977. He held that post until his election to the Manitoba legislature in 1981, with reelections in 1986, 1988 and 1990. Harper served as legislative assistant to the minister of Northern Affairs between 1981 and 1986 and co-chaired the Native affairs committee of the provincial cabinet. In 1986, Harper was appointed minister responsible for Native affairs and in 1987 became minister of Northern Affairs.

The image of Harper standing in the Manitoba legislature, holding a single eagle feather and depriving the legislature of the necessary unanimous consent to pass the Meech Lake Accord struck a deep chord in the Canadian national psyche. Harper was awarded the 1990 Canadian press newsmaker of the year award and, in 1991, the Stanley Knowles Humanitarian Award.

## LaDonna Harris (1931– )
*Comanche activist*

LaDonna Harris is a Comanche woman who has promoted equal opportunity for Indian people on a national level and has accomplished much in helping to strengthen self-government and economic self-sufficiency among Native Americans throughout the United States. Born in Temple, Oklahoma, on 15 February 1931, Harris was raised in a conservative household and spoke only the Comanche language before attending public school. Her work in the public eye began during the 1960s, when she was thrust onto the national political scene as the wife of Fred Harris, the Democratic Senator from Oklahoma. In 1965 she founded Oklahomans for Indian Opportunity, a nationally known Indian self-help organization, and since then she has been active as chair or board member of groups such as the Women's National Advisory Council on Poverty, the National Rural Housing Conference, the National Association of Mental Health, and the Joint Commission on Mental Health of Children. In 1970, Harris founded and served as president of Americans for Indian Opportunity, a national advocacy group dedicated to helping Indian tribal groups achieve self-determined political, economic, and social goals. In 1980 she became the vice-presidential nominee for the environmentalist Citizen's Party.

A strong activist for world peace, Harris has participated in several international conferences on peace since 1968. She has traveled in the (then) Soviet Union, Mali, Senegal, and various South American countries as a representative of the Inter-American Indigenous Institute, an agency of the Organization of American States. Harris has received many awards, including an honorary doctorate in law from Dartmouth University. LaDonna Harris lives in New Mexico, and currently serves as the president of Americans for Indian Opportunity, which manages many Indian leadership training programs including The American Indian Ambassador Program.

## Ned A. Hatathli (1923–1972)
*Navajo businessperson and educator*

A person of many talents, Ned Hatathli contributed to the welfare of the Navajo people in various ways. Hatathli was born in a Navajo hogan in Coalmine Mesa, Arizona, on 11 October 1923, and was raised in a very traditional setting. He attended a government boarding school in Tuba City, Arizona, and got his first glimpse of the outside world when the school sponsored a field trip to industrial areas in the south. From that point on, he sought further education. He attended Haskell Institute in Lawrence, Kansas; then, after serving two years in the U.S. Navy during World War II, he attended Northern Arizona University and received his bachelor's degree. He later received a doctorate in education from the University of Colorado, Boulder.

Hatathli's service to the Navajo community began as manager of the Navajo Arts and Crafts Guild. He also played a major role as a member of the tribal council in developing the utilization of natural resources—especially coal, uranium, and timber—and is credited with helping to produce major increases in employment on the Navajo Reservation. Hatathli was a founder and the first Indian president of Navajo Community College. He once said that the college "stands for Indians controlling their own destiny"; when asked what made it different from other colleges, he said, "Well, we don't teach that Columbus discovered America."

## Ira Hamilton Hayes (1923–1955)
*Pima World War II hero*

A full-blooded member of the Pima tribe, Ira Hayes was probably the most famous Indian soldier of World War II. Born in Sacaton, Arizona, on 23 January 1923, Hayes joined the marines in 1942 and saw action throughout the Pacific as a paratrooper. In February 1945, he landed as part of the Fifth Marine Division assault troops on Iwo Jima, a barren island considered important as a base for launching air strikes against Japan. There he took part in a forward attack on Mount Suribachi and was one of six marines who raised the United States flag on the summit of the volcanic peak in the midst of heavy enemy fire. An Associated Press photographer captured the moment on film, and it became one of the most inspiring war photographs ever taken. The famous bronze monument commemorating the battle of Iwo Jima in Washington, D.C., is based on this image.

Brought back to the United States with two other survivors of the Mount Suribachi flag-raising, Hayes was feted as a hero and indeed received extra attention because he was an Indian. However, he was confused and disturbed by the unwanted and excessive publicity. He became an alcoholic, was arrested many times, and died of exposure on 24 January 1955. He once said, "Sometimes I wished that guy had never made that picture."

## King Hendrick (1680–1755)
*Mohawk-Mahican tribal leader*

Born among the Mahican, an Algonkian Nation living in present-day eastern Connecticut, Hendrick was adopted by the Mohawk, one of the Five Nations of the Iroquois Confederacy. He was an important leader of his people and liaison to British settlers when he made his famous trip to England in 1710. Though American

Indians had visited England before 1710, the visit of Hendrick and his Iroquois colleagues was the first royal invitation. The event generated a mountain of publicity. The four Mohawk visitors were dined, feted, toured, and gawked at, much like any instant celebrity. Of the four "kings," only Hendrick could be construed in any way as an ambassador of his people. After his return to North America, Hendrick became a spokesman for the Iroquois League and was a key English ally in their battles against the French in New France, present-day Canada. In 1754, Hendrick was invited to the Albany Congress where he consulted with the colonists on their plans for unification. Hendrick also chastised the colonial government for failing to protect the "frontier" against the French and hostile enemies. Perhaps as a result of Hendrick's relationship with colonial leaders, the colonial and later U.S. government in many ways reflected the structure of the Iroquois League. In 1755 Hendrick died of wounds suffered at the battle of Lake George, during the French and Indian War (1756–1763). He had been leading a force of Mohawk warriors with British troops against French forces. Hendrick lived on, however, albeit in a rather fanciful way, in the imagination of English readers. A number of English literary works glorified and extolled Hendrick as an example of the "noble savage," a popular philosophical and literary theme of this era.

## William L. Hensley (1941–)
*Inuit state senator and lawyer*

William L. Hensley is an Alaska state senator whose district covers more than 150,000 square miles and has a population of nearly twenty thousand people, 90 percent of whom are Eskimos like himself. The term *Eskimo* is actually an Algonquian derogation meaning "raw meat eaters," which historically has been used to identify Inuit- and Yupik-speaking peoples living along the Arctic Rim in North America and Asia. Many modern descendants feel that the word Inuit would be more correct, but this term excludes the Yupik-speakers of Alaska.

Born in Kotzebue, Alaska, in 1941, Hensley attended the University of Alaska in 1960 and 1961, then studied at George Washington University in Washington, D.C., and received his bachelor's degree from that school in 1966. He later studied law at the University of Alaska (1966), the University of New Mexico (1967), and the University of California, Los Angeles (1968).

Hensley has been active in land claims implementation and rural economic development since the late 1960s, when he served as chair of the Alaska State Rural

William L. Hensley.

Affairs Commission (1968–1972) and also directed the Land Claims Task Force (1968). In 1966 he wrote a paper "What Rights to Land Have the Alaska Natives: The Primary Issue," where as a graduate student at the University of Alaska he circulated the paper that argued the Alaska Native lands had never been sold. Also in 1966 Hensley wrote letters to all the villages in his home area and helped gather them into a unified organization called the Northwest Alaska Native Association (NANA), composed mainly of Inupiat Villages in the Kotzebue region. He was one of the founding members (1966) and president (1972) of the Alaska Federation of Natives (AFN), a state-wide organization that lobbied in Washington for resolution of Native land claims in Alaska during the 1960s. He played an active part in the passage of the Alaska Native Claims Settlement Act of 1971, which granted Alaska Natives $962 million and 44 million acres of land.

Hensley served in the Alaska House of Representatives from 1966 to 1970 and has been a member of the state senate since 1970. He has been active in many Native organizations over the years, including executive director of the Northwest Alaska Native Association in 1968. He was commissioner with Alaska Department of Commerce and Development from 1995 to 1997

and served on various state boards concerned with economic development and employment training. Since 1997 Hensley has been working for Alyeska Pipeline.

## Lance David Henson (1944–)
*Cheyenne poet and playwright*

To date Lance Henson has seventeen books of poetry published. Of these, half are published in the United States and the others are printed in countries around the world. He has lectured and read in nine countries, and his work has been translated into twenty-five languages. Clearly, this Southern Cheyenne poet and playwright is the one of the foremost Native American writers of the late twentieth century.

Born in Washington, D.C., Henson was reared on a farm by his grandparents and their family on government-allotment land outside Calumet, Oklahoma. The poet has described his childhood as culturally centered and traditional. In fact, he is an active member of the Native American Church and has participated in the Cheyenne Sun Dance on several occasions as both a painter and a dancer. A member of the Cheyenne Dog Soldier Society, Henson served in the U.S. Marine Corps after high school and during the Vietnam War. He is a black belt in karate.

The poet remained in Oklahoma for college, receiving his bachelor's degree in English from Oklahoma College of Liberal Arts (now the University of Science and Arts of Oklahoma) in Chickasha. He then obtained his master's degree in creative writing at the University of Tulsa.

In the early 1970s, Henson published his first book of poetry, *Keeper of Arrows*, with Renaissance Press in Johnstown, Pennsylvania. The work, along with others published in that decade, including *Naming the Dark: Poems for the Cheyenne* (1976) and *Buffalo Marrow on Black* (1979), focus on Cheyenne culture, language, and history. The poems often explore the exploitation of the tribe by the encroaching white population. His more recent works, such as *Another Song for America* (1987), *Teepee* (1987, published in Italy), and *Another Distance: New and Selected Poems* (1991), broaden his subject base by bringing in his travel experiences, recent historical events, environmental issues, and human rights. Many critics contend that his newer poems expound on tribal concepts and culture.

Expanding his literary talents, Henson has become recognized as a playwright in recent years. He co-wrote two plays in the early 1990s: *Winter Man*, with Andy Tierstien, and *Coyote Road*, with Jeff Hooper. The former received a warm reception at the La MaMa Experimental Theatre Company.

For ten years following his education, Henson conducted poetry workshops for the Artist in Residence program of the State Arts Council of Oklahoma. After this, the poet began traveling throughout the United States and Europe. While Henson continues to lecture and read around the globe, he inherited his grandparents' land and considers the home there his base.

## Charlotte W. Heth (1937–)
*Cherokee ethnomusicologist and educator*

A leading figure in research on American Indian music, Charlotte Heth is equally well known for developing innovative programs in Native American studies at the university level. Born 29 October 1937, Heth took her bachelor's and master's degrees at the University of Tulsa in Oklahoma and went on to complete a doctorate in ethno-musicology at the University of California, Los Angeles (1975). She then became a member of the faculty in ethnonomusicology at UCLA for the next thirteen years, also serving as director of the UCLA American Indian Studies Center for much of this time.

Cherokee ethnomusicologist and educator Charlotte W. Heth.

After completing a two-year visiting professorship at Cornell University (1988–1989), Heth returned to UCLA and retired in 1992.

As an ethnomusicologist, Heth is perhaps most important for bringing attention to contemporary developments in American Indian music and underlining the importance and validity of these art forms for contemporary Indian people. This marked a significant departure from earlier research, which mainly sought to characterize Indian music from an anthropological perspective. Her focus on actual Indian singers also led Heth to produce a series of eight videotapes in which Native performers talked about their music and musical techniques in their own terms. Besides these activities she produced six record albums of Native American music for New World Records and has several books and articles on the subject to her credit. Heth was the editor of a collection of essays on Indian music in the series entitled *Selected Reports in Ethnomusicology* at the University of California, Los Angeles, and wrote the introductory article, "Traditional Music of the North American Indians" (1980).

As an educator and administrator, Heth helped develop and implement an interdisciplinary master's degree program in American Indian studies at UCLA and was co-author (with Susan Guyette) of a book-length needs assessment entitled *Issues for the Future of American Indian Higher Education* (1985). She has been the recipient of numerous honors and fellowhips and served on various arts and humanities panels in California, New York, and Washington, D.C.

## John Brinton Napoleon Hewitt (1859–1937)
*Tuscarora anthropologist*

John Hewitt was a noted anthropologist in the late 1800s and into the 1900s. His study and research of Iroquois political and social systems shed light on the nature of the Iroquois Confederacy and drew parallels with the democratic system of the United States.

Hewitt was born in western New York, of a part-Tuscarora mother and a Scottish father. He gave up his first ambition to be a doctor of medicine (like his father) to pursue anthropology. In 1880, he met Erminie A. Smith, who employed him to help her record Iroquois legends. Six years later, when Smith died, Hewitt continued his research and information collecting. By this time, Hewitt was in the employ of the Smithsonian Bureau of Ethnology. Hewitt also interviewed two future principal chiefs of the Creek Nation, Pleasant Porter and Legus Perryman, in the early 1880s. He wrote a manuscript on Creek history and society, which remained unpublished until 1939. The manuscript was edited by the famous anthropologist John Swanton and published as "Notes on the Creek Indians" *Anthropological Papers*, American Bureau of Ethnology, Bulletin 123. Hewitt provided a major source of information about the history and culture of the Creek Nation, who traditionally lived in present-day Georgia and Alabama, but most now live in Oklahoma. Many of Hewitt's ideas can be examined in his published collection of letters to Arthur C. Parker, another famous Iroquois scholar.

### Hiawatha (unknown)
*Iroquois tribal leader*

Aiowantha, who is sometimes called Hiawatha, devoted his life to ending the bloodshed between the Five Nations—the Mohawk, Oneida, Cayuga, Seneca, and Onondaga. In conjunction with Deganawida, he established the Confederation of Five Nations or the League of the Iroquois.

The exact date is unknown but most likely before 1492, Hiawatha, together with the Huron prophet Deganawida, developed plans to end tribal feuding by establishing laws and ceremonies for peacefully settling disputes among the Five Nations. Because Deganawida had a speech impediment, Hiawatha became the principal spokesperson. His early efforts to end the violence plaguing the Iroquois Nations were thwarted by a powerful Onondaga opponent named Tadodaho, who opposed the reform movement and confederation plan. When Hiawatha's message fell upon unreceptive ears among his own people, he left his home to preach his message among the Mohawk, Oneida, and Cayuga who embraced his ideas. Eventually even the Onondaga, and Tadodaho himself, were convinced (Deganawida gave Hiawatha increased legitimacy in the eyes of the Onondaga) of the benefits offered by Hiawatha's plan. The Onondaga were persuaded to join the proposed league, and the Iroquois Confederacy, based on democratic, representative government, came into being. The Founding Fathers of the U.S. Constitution knew about and discussed the example of the Iroquois League. They borrowed a number of political concepts from the confederacy such as political equality, separation of governmental powers, checks and balances on political powers, and emphasis on preserving political freedom.

### Tomson Highway (1951–)
*Cree playwright*

Tomson Highway was born in a tent along his father's trapline in northern Manitoba on 6 December 1951. His first language was Cree; he learned English when he was sent to a boarding school in The Pas, Manitoba, at the age of six. Highway remained at the Catholic-run school until he was fifteen, returning to his family for only two months each year. He went on to high school in Winnipeg, Manitoba, living in white foster homes and graduating in June 1970. At the University of Manitoba and later at the University of Western Ontario, Highway studied music, graduating with a bachelor of music honors in 1975. He then worked for seven years with several Native organizations, helping to develop cultural programs with Native inmates and children.

At the age of thirty, Highway decided to write his first play, hoping to bring life on "the rez" to a mainstream audience. The reaction to *The Rez Sisters* in December 1986 took Highway by surprise. It was a huge success, winning the prestigious Dora Mavor Moore award for best new play in Toronto's 1987–1988 theater season; it was runner-up for the Floyd S. Chalmers award for outstanding Canadian play of 1986. *The Rez Sisters* toured to sold-out audiences across Canada and was one of two plays representing Canada on the main stage of the Edinburgh International Festival, a festival that showcases international drama. Highway's next play, *Dry Lips Oughta Move to Kapuskasing*, won four Dora Mavor Moore awards, including best new play. The University of Toronto produced *Rose*, the third play in the Rez Cycle, in 2000.

Until June 1992, Highway was the artistic director of Native Earth Performing Arts, Inc., Toronto's only professional Native theater company. Highway has written five other plays and continues in his quest to celebrate Canada's Native people through his art. His first novel, *The Kiss of the Fur Queen* (1998), was on the Canadian Best Sellers list for seven weeks.

### Charlie Hill (1951–)
*Oneida-Mohawk-Cree comedian and actor*

After frequent spots on *The Tonight Show* and *Late Night with David Letterman*, as well as several television bit parts, Charlie Hill has become a nationally recognized entertainer and performer. Hill believes that the tragedies of Indian history are made easier through laughter, and he strives to make people laugh with—not at—Indian life.

Born the son of Eileen and Norbert S. Hill, Sr., Hill grew up mostly in Detroit and on the Oneida Indian Reservation in Wisconsin. Throughout his elementary and high school years, Hill's teachers often reprimanded him for entertaining instead of learning. As is his style, Hill took such censure positively, a sign of his eventual break into the comedy scene.

Writer, comedian Charlie Hill.

Hill's first comedy appearance was at Catch a Rising Star in New York City. While he was somewhat comfortable onstage due to his background in theater, Hill feels that stand-up is a performer's greatest challenge, for the only person stand-up comedians have to depend on is themselves. Such challenges did not stop him, however. A few years later in Los Angeles, Hill auditioned at The Comedy Store for Richard Pryor, who gave Hill his first national television appearance. Pryor, in fact, is one of Hill's idols, alongside such comic geniuses as Lenny Bruce and Dick Gregory.

Hill's on-stage performance led to several television and screen roles, including a part on the *Bionic Woman* and on the hit show *Roseanne*. He eventually became a writer for *Roseanne*, writing jokes and creating story lines.

The Native comic emphasizes the importance of traditional comedians in Indian mythology and history. He oftentimes refers to the *heyokas*, traditional Lakota holy men, and other trickster figures who contribute to a powerful history of Indian laughter and humor.

Hill has received the American Indian Entertainer of the Year award four times, and has been voted the number one Indian comedian in America. In the fall of 2000 a documentary on Hill was released on PBS

entitled *On and Off the Rez with Charlie Hill*. In addition the comedian hosts a national comedy series on public television titled *Club Red with Charlie Hill*. He lives in Los Angeles with his wife Lenora and children Nizhone, Nasbah, Nanabah, and Nabahe.

### Gwendolyn A. Hill (1952–)
*Chippewa and Cree educator and administrator*

Born in Fort Belknap, Montana, on 31 October 1952, Gwendolyn Hill received her bachelor's degree in education from Northern Montana College (1976) and later completed a master's degree in public administration at the University of South Dakota (1989). From 1975 to 1980, she was a teacher at Stewart Indian School near Carson City, Nevada. She later became the dean and president of Sisseton-Wahpeton Community College in Sisseton, South Dakota.

Over the years, Hill has helped to promote Indian education nationally and at the local level, working with organizations such as the American Indian Higher Education Consortium, the Native American Student Advisory Council, and the Sisseton (South Dakota) Public Schools Parent Advisory Committee.

### Norbert S. Hill, Jr. (contemporary)
*Oneida educator*

Norbert S. Hill, Jr., is the former executive director of the American Indian Science and Engineering Society (AISES) in Boulder, Colorado, and is the founder of *Winds of Change*, a magazine devoted to developing young scientists and engineers within the Indian community. At the University of Wisconsin-Oshkosh he received a bachelor of science in sociology/anthropology in 1969 and a master of science in guidance and counseling. He is completing his Ph.D. at the University of Colorado on social foundations of education.

For more than fifteen years, Hill has actively developed and administered educational programs for American Indians. He worked as a high school guidance counselor before becoming director of the Indian Education Opportunity Program at the University of Colorado in 1977. Hill created or co-founded many successful projects and was selected as educational policy fellow by the Institute of Educational Leadership in 1980.

He served as executive director of AISES from 1983 to 1998 and transformed it from a professional society to a national resource in Indian education. He has written over a dozen articles and reports in the fields of education and Indian history and demography. Hill's honors include the National Council for Minorities in Engineering's Reginald H. Jones Distinguished Service

Norbert S. Hill, Jr.

Award and the Chancellor's Award from the University of Wisconsin-Oshkosh in 1988.

### Roberta Hill (1947–)
*Oneida poet, short story writer, and educator*

A well-known and highly respected poet, Roberta Hill, formerly published as Roberta Hill Whiteman, is best known for her 1984 poetry collection *Star Quilt*, published by Holy Cow! Press. More recently, however, Hill published Philadelphia Flowers in 1996. Her work has been anthologized in numerous publications, including *Carriers of the Dream Wheel: Contemporary Native American Poetry* edited by Duane Niatum (1975), *Reinventing the Enemy's Language: Contemporary Native Women's Writing of North America* edited by Joy Harjo and Gloria Bird (1997), and *The Third Woman: Minority Women Writers of the United States* edited by Dexter Fisher (1980).

Professor Roberta Hill. (Photo by Timothy Francisco)

A member of the Oneida Nation of Wisconsin, Hill was born in Baraboo, Wisconsin, to parents Eleanor Smith and Charles Allen Hill. Throughout her youth, Hill and her family traveled frequently between Green Bay and Oneida. While her mother died when Hill was young, her father and grandmother played crucial roles in shaping Hill's poetic predilection. Her father was a musician and teacher, and taught Hill the importance of rhythm and language. Her grandmother often told stories, recited poetry, and read aloud to the young girl, who was already avidly writing in journals and experimenting with poetry.

Despite her natural inclination toward creative pursuits, Hill's father wanted her to become a doctor like her grandmother. Initially, Hill majored in pre-med at the University of Wisconsin; later, however, she would shift her focus to creative writing and psychology, graduating with a double major. After college, Hill continued her education, receiving an M.F.A. from the University of Montana in 1973. While in Montana, Hill worked with Richard Hugo, a student of Theodore Roethke, who taught the developing writer to make poetry her life's work.

In addition to Hugo, Hill credits many other poets—especially Native lyricists—with helping her develop a distinct poetic voice. In particular, Hill spoke and worked with Lance Henson, Leslie Marmon Silko, and James Welch throughout her early years. Before her works were published together in *Star Quilt*, her work was published in various literary magazines and anthologies in the mid-1970s. During this period, Hill worked for the Poets-in-the-Schools Program in several states, including Arizona, Wyoming, Oklahoma, South Dakota, and Minnesota. She taught on the Oneida and Rosebud reservations, and at the University of Wisconsin, Eau Claire.

In 1980 Hill married Ernest Whiteman, an Arapaho artist, with whom she had three children, Jacob, Heather, and Melissa. Many of her poems focus on her children, and on her life as a mother and a woman. In addition, her poetry often creates conceits, or elaborate metaphors, between seemingly disparate ideas or images. Her work has been noted for its focus on detail, and for its spiritual Oneida consciousness.

Hill is an advisory board member for the *Wicazo Sa Review* and is currently a professor of American Indian studies and English at the University of Wisconsin, Madison. She is working on a biography of her grandmother, Doctor L. Rosa Minoka-Hill.

### Geary Hobson (1941– )
*Cherokee/Quapaw writer and scholar*

Geary Hobson is associate professor of English at the University of Oklahoma. He was born 12 June 1941, in Chicot County, Arkansas. His mother, Edythe, is Quapaw and his father, Gearld, was Cherokee. Hobson graduated from Desha High School in Rohwer, Arkansas, in 1959. He received a bachelor of arts degree (1968) and master's degree (1969) in English from Arizona State University. In 1986 he completed a Ph.D. in American studies at the University of New Mexico. Before beginning a college teaching career, he worked as a farm laborer, a trapper, a construction worker, and a surveyor's assistant. He also played semi-pro baseball and served in the U.S. Marine Corps.

Hobson has taught at the university level since 1970. He taught English at the University of New Mexico from 1970 to 1976 and served as coordinator for the Native American Studies Program there from 1976 to 1978. Between 1980 and 1982 he taught English at the University of Arkansas at Little Rock and at Central Arkansas University.

He is completing a two-volume work, *Indian Country: Native American Literature Since 1968*, a comprehensive study of Native American writers from the United States and Canada.

Geary Hobson.

Hobson's other writings include an anthology of Native American literature entitled *The Remembered Earth* (1979), a collection of poems, *Deer Hunting and Other Poems* (1990), and a novel, *The Last of the Ofos* (2000). He is perhaps best known for his article "The Rise of the White Shaman as a New Version of Cultural Imperialism," in *Y'Bird* 1 number 1 (1977), which objects to non-Indian poets representing themselves as true Indian writers and visionaries.

### Linda Hogan (1947– )
*Chickasaw writer*

Linda Hogan is a writer, poet, and essayist whose work reflects ideas and images of Chickasaw life. She was born in Denver, Colorado, in 1947, but raised mainly in Oklahoma. She received a master's degree in English and creative writing from the University of Colorado at Boulder.

Hogan's poetry has appeared in several important anthologies devoted to Native American writers, including *Carriers of the Dream Wheel* (1975) and *Harper's Anthology of Twentieth Century Native American Poetry* (1988). Her own poems are featured in the collections *Eclipse* (1983) and *Seeing through the Sun* (1985).

Besides her poetry, Hogan has published a collection of short stories entitled *That Horse* (1985) and the novel *Mean Spirit* (1990), which was a finalist for the Pulitzer Prize for fiction. She received a fellowship for fiction from the National Endowment for the Arts in 1986 and has been poet-in-residence for the Oklahoma and Colorado state art councils. In 1998, she was awarded the Lifetime Achievement Award of the Native Writers' Circle of the Americas, an international Native American writers' organization.

Other works by Hogan include *Red Clay: Poems and Stories* (1991), *The Book of Medicines* (1993), *Dwellings: A Spiritual History of the Living World* (1995), *Solar Storms* (1995), *Power* (1998), and *Intimate Nature: The Bond Between Women and Animals* (1999). She teaches at the University of Colorado, Boulder.

### Hole-In-The-Day (1825–1868)
*Chippewa (Ojibwa) tribal leader*

Hole-In-The-Day was a leader among the Chippewa, who lived near the mouth of the Mississippi River in present-day Minnesota. In 1846, Hole-In-The-Day became chief and continued the efforts of his father (who had the same name) to prevent encroachment by Sioux living west of the Mississippi. Hole-In-The-Day also negotiated a number of important treaties and agreements with the U.S. government.

Hole-In-The-Day and his father fought against the Sioux for land located between Lake Superior and the upper Mississippi River in present-day Minnesota. Armed with European-made guns, the Chippewa pushed the Sioux westward and back across the Mississippi River. Hole-In-The-Day also represented his people in their dealings with the U.S. government, making several trips to Washington, D.C., where he negotiated a number of important agreements with the federal government. During one of these trips, Hole-In-The-Day met and married an American woman. She was one of Hole-In-The-Day's eight wives.

Hole-In-The-Day's relations with the U.S. government jeopardized his standing among his own people. He was accused by tribal leaders of using his influence in Washington for personal aggrandizement. Hole-In-The-Day must have felt besieged from both sides when, in 1862, the U.S. government accused him of planning an uprising among the Chippewa. The accusation was fueled by the general unrest among Indians, such as the 1862 Sioux uprising in western Minnesota, and U.S. officials were fearful that more Indian nations would join in the hostilities. Beginning in 1864, Hole-In-The-Day signed a series of treaties that ceded large amounts of Chippewa land in present-day Minnesota. Consequently, by 1868 most of Hole-In-the-Day's band was settled on the White Earth Reservation, a small plot of land in western Minnesota. In that same year Hole-In-The-Day was murdered, most likely for his role in negotiating treaties with the United States.

### George P. Horse Capture (1937–)
*Gros Ventre museum curator*

George Horse Capture, a museum curator and administrator, is actively engaged in researching Indian art, history, and culture.

Born in Fort Belknap, Montana, on 20 October 1937, Horse Capture graduated from the University of California with a bachelor's degree in anthropology in 1974. He later received a master's degree in history from Montana State University (1979) while working as an assistant professor in the American Indian Studies Department. Horse Capture served as curator of the Plains Indian Museum at the Buffalo Bill Historical Center in Cody, Wyoming, from 1980 until 1990. In 1996,

George P. Horse Capture.

Montana State University awarded him an Honorary Doctorate in Letters.

Besides having curated exhibits on numerous subjects including Wounded Knee, the site of a U.S. Army massacre of Sioux Ghost Dancers in 1890, and the Indian powwow, Horse Capture has been very productive in other areas of Indian culture and history. He edited a book entitled *The Seven Visions of Bull Lodge* (1980) and was winner of the 1983 William E. Cody Motion Picture Award for his film *I'd Rather Be Powwowing*. He is, in fact, an active participant in powwows and has also conducted research on Indian artwork in museums throughout the United States, Canada, and Europe. He recently published a study on a collection of Indian robes at the Musee de l'Homme in Paris that had been obtained by the Jesuit explorer Jacques Marquette during the seventeenth century.

In 1990, the American Association for State and Local History presented Horse Capture with an Award of Merit for historical research in bridging the cultures. Since that year, he has worked for the Fort Belknap tribes and lectured at Harvard, Yale, the Smithsonian Institution, and other organizations across the country. Most important in this regard is his role as an ongoing consultant in the development of the National Museum of the American Indian in Washington, D.C., where he is employed as special assistant, cultural resources, and senior counselor to the director. He now resides in Kensington, Maryland.

## Allan Houser (1914–1994)
*Chiricahua Apache artist and art instructor*

Allan Houser was an internationally recognized sculptor and painter whose works have a serene but powerful quality that reflects Chiricahua Apache culture. Born in Apache, Oklahoma, on 30 June 1914, he attended Santa Fe Indian School in New Mexico and later studied art at Utah State University. A muralist and painter during the late 1930s, Houser had to give up his artwork during a long period when he lived in the Los Angeles area in the 1940s and supported his family by working as a pipefitter and at various construction jobs. During this period he turned to wood carving and got a commission to create a stone monument at Haskell Institute, a junior college for Indian students in Lawrence, Kansas. The resultant work, entitled *Comrade in Mourning*, was a memorial to the Indian casualties of World War II carved from a half-ton block of marble.

In the following year (1949), Houser was awarded a fellowship from the Guggenheim Foundation and from that point his career was established. He later had many solo shows at places such as the Museum of New

Mexico in Santa Fe; the Heard Museum in Phoenix, Arizona; the Southern Plains Museum in Anadarko, Oklahoma; and the Philbrook Center in Tulsa, Oklahoma. He won many prizes during his mid-career, including the Palmes Academique, awarded to Houser by the French government in 1954.

In 1962, Houser became a teacher at the Institute of American Indian Arts in Santa Fe, New Mexico, and he remained on the faculty there until retiring as head of the sculpture department in 1975.

## Ron Houston (1945–)
*Pima-Maricopa educator and administrator*

Ron Houston was born in Los Angeles on 18 January 1945. He received a B.A. in elementary school education in 1967 from Arizona State University in Tempe. In 1970, he earned an M.A. degree in education counseling from Northern Illinois University in De Kalb. His teaching career started in 1967, when he taught third grade at Tuba City Elementary School in Tuba City, Arizona. From 1968 to 1979, Houston was a teacher and counselor at Fremont Junior High School in Mesa, Arizona. During this time, from 1974 to 1976, he was also a community school specialist responsible for identifying the needs of the community and acquiring teachers to teach classes for the Mesa Public Schools. In 1976, he became a counselor at the Mesa Community College, in charge of personal and academic counseling with junior college students; he also taught personal resources development classes.

Houston joined the National Education Association (NEA) in 1979, and since then he has been actively involved in providing technical assistance, training, and information to local and state NEA affiliates and to American Indian members. He was the principal author of the NEA booklet *The Quest for Quality Education*, published in 1982, and coordinated the development of the NEA handbook *American Indian/Alaska Native Education: Quality in Classroom*, for teachers of American Indian and Alaska Native children. From 1989 to 1992, Houston was the vice president of the National Education Association Staff Organization in Washington, D.C.

## Oscar Howe (1915–1983)
*Yankton Sioux graphic artist*

Born at Joe Creek, South Dakota, on the Crow Creek Reservation in 1915, Oscar Howe's Sioux name was Mazuha Koshina (Trader Boy). He graduated from

Pierre Indian School in South Dakota (1933), then studied painting at the U.S. Indian School in Santa Fe, New Mexico (1934–38), and had special training in mural techniques at the Indian Art Center in Fort Sill, Oklahoma. He later received a bachelor's degree (1952) from Dakota Wesleyan University in Mitchell, South Dakota, and a master of fine arts degree from the University of Oklahoma at Norman (1954).

Howe served as an assistant instructor during his years at Dakota Wesleyan and taught art at Pierre High School in South Dakota from 1954 to 1957. He then became a professor of fine arts and artist-in-residence at the University of South Dakota at Vermillion; he remained on the faculty there until well into the 1970s. Howe employed a modern style to depict poignant images of Indian culture in transition and once wrote, "One criterion for my painting is to present the cultural life of the Sioux Indians. It is my greatest hope that my paintings may serve to bring the best things of Indian culture into the modern way of life."

Howe's paintings have been shown in numerous solo shows and group exhibitions. He was named the Artist Laureate of South Dakota by Governor Herseth in 1960 and also received the Waite Phillips Trophy for Outstanding Contributions to American Indian Art from the Philbrook Art Center in Tulsa, Oklahoma, in 1966. He has also created distinguished murals that were commissioned for the Civic Auditorium in Mobridge, South Dakota, (1942) and for the walls of Proviso High School in Hinsdale, Illinois, (1956).

Howe contracted Parkinson's disease while in his sixties and passed away in his sleep on 7 October 1983.

### George Hunt (1854–1933)
*Tlingit cultural interpreter*

George Hunt was an interpreter of the culture of the Tlingit, a tribe located along the southeastern Alaska coastline, and other Northwest Coast tribes. He was born at Fort Rupert, British Columbia, in 1854. His mother was a Tlingit named Mary Ebbets, and his father was British and director of the Hudson Bay Company's trade business with Indians on the coast of British Columbia. Hunt's cultural heritage was yet more complex and enriched by the fact that he was raised among the Kwakiutl Indians (another tribe of the Northwest Coast, located further south), and he married a Kwakiutl woman.

Hunt's career as a guide and cultural interpreter began in 1881, when he was hired by the Norwegian-born Johan Adrian Jacobsen to help collect ethnological artifacts for a museum in Berlin. He later worked for anthropologist Franz Boas, beginning in 1886, and provided Boas with cultural information that was later published in *Kwakiutl Texts* (1905–1906) and *The Ethnology of the Kwakiutl* (1921). In 1897 Hunt served as a guide and interpreter for the Jesup Expedition, a major collaborative research survey that sought to investigate the cultural factors connecting the Northwest Coast Indians and Alaskan Eskimos with the indigenous peoples of northeastern Asia.

Hunt helped to organize the Northwest Coast exhibit at the American Museum of Natural History in New York City in 1903, and he was instrumental in recreating Native ceremonials and other scenes shown in Edward Curtis's film *In the Land of the War Canoes*. He was eventually selected as a chief of the Kwakiutl. Hunt passed away in 1933 at the place where he was born.

### Ishi (d. 1916)
*Yahi/Southern Yana survivor*

In 1911, this middle-aged Yahi from northern California became famous throughout the United States as "the last wild Indian." The Yahi (also called Southern Yana) originally lived along Mill Creek and Deer Creek, two eastern affluents of the Sacramento River in northern California.

In August 1911, Ishi wandered out of the mountains and found himself in the town of Oroville (Butte County). He was the last survivor of a tribe that had gone into seclusion more than forty years before. For much of this time, Ishi had been living in a band that never numbered more than a dozen for most of his adolescent and adult life. His last years before discovery were spent with just three other people: an old man and woman, probably his parents, and a middle-aged woman who was his sister. For the last several months, he had been completely alone, until finally—weaponless, pressed by hunger, and his hair still singed from mourning for his relatives—he gave up a lifetime of hiding and allowed himself to be captured.

Apparently, he expected to be killed but was instead placed in jail for a few days and soon afterwards was taken to the San Francisco Bay area, where he was studied by Alfred Kroeber and other anthropologists at the University of California until his death in 1916. The researchers marveled at the genuineness of his aboriginal condition, which was also sensationalized in the press: here, after all, was a completely unacculturated Indian who spoke no English and still practiced ancient skills such as flint shaping and bow making. A number of publications on Yahi language and culture came about because of Ishi's knowledge, but he is probably best known to most Americans because of Theodora

Kroeber's book *Ishi in Two Worlds* (1960). For most Americans, Ishi is a romantic symbol of the last unspoiled Native, but to many Native Americans in California, he represents a terrible era of genocide and cultural devastation.

## Isparhecher (1829–1902)
*Creek tribal leader*

Isparhecher was born in the upper Creek towns of present-day Alabama. While only a small child of six or seven, he and the Creek were forced to leave their homeland in the U.S. South and migrate to Indian Territory in present-day Oklahoma. During the U.S. Civil War, the Creek Nation was evenly divided between the upper towns (the more conservative villages, who favored Union alliance) and the lower Creek towns, which contained the largest proportion of Creek slaveowners, who favored alliance to the South. Isparhecher at first fought with the Confederates, but later chose to switch sides and fight with the conservative Creek in alliance with the Union Army. He became a leader of the conservative Creek.

After the Civil War, in 1867 the Creek formed a new constitutional government, and Isparhecher was elected to the national council, but instead accepted a position as judge. In the early 1870s, however, he was impeached from the court for alleged misuse of funds. This experience embittered Isparhecher, and he joined the conservative Creek, who met at Nuyuka, a white town of refuge in the traditional Creek Nation. When in the late 1870s, the conservative Creek leader Lochar Harjo died, Isparhecher succeeded to leadership. His leadership inspired the conservatives to more actively pursue the restoration of the traditional Creek government by town chiefs, and inspired them to try to topple the progressive or constitutional party, which supported the new Creek constitutional government.

Throughout the 1870s, 1880s, and 1890s, the conservatives challenged the legitimacy of the Creek constitutional government, which was strongly supported by the U.S. government. The major outbreak occurred in 1882 and 1883, the so-called Green Peach War, in a controversy about the election procedures, which plagued Creek politics until the 1890s. In the Green Peach War, Isparhecher and the conservatives, about a third of the Creek men, were driven out of the Creek country after a series of minor skirmishes. The U.S. Army brought the conservatives back, and they agreed to pledge allegiance to the Creek government. Isparhecher continued to run for the office of Creek principal chief and was elected in 1895, on a campaign to prevent the United States from abolishing the Creek government and allotting its land to individual Creek. During his four-year term, Isparhecher was not able to resist the forced breakup of the Creek government, and after 1899, he retired to his ranch in a state of depression and despair. In 1907, the Creek government was superseded by the state of Oklahoma.

## G. Peter Jemison (1945–)
*Seneca artist and arts administrator*

G. Peter Jemison is director of Ganondagan (Seneca) Historic Site in New York. He is well known for his paintings and drawings and for his active participation in Indian cultural affairs. He was the administrative director for the Seneca Education Program in 1973 and 1974; project director for the North American Indian Culture Center in Buffalo, New York; director of the Seneca Nation Organization for the Visual Arts; and, starting in 1978, gallery coordinator of the Gallery of American Indian Community House in New York.

Jemison was born in 1945 in Silver Creek, New York, and received his bachelor of science degree in art education at the State University of New York's College at Buffalo and attended additional courses at both the University of Siena (Italy) and the State University of New York at Albany. His cultural interests include a wide variety of experiences, from his collection of art by Seneca children to his posts as member of the New York State Iroquois Conference and board member for the America the Beautiful Foundation in New York.

Jemison's activities are focused on preserving Seneca cultural heritage within the contemporary society, as shown by his illustrations for the controversial book about Iroquois contributions to the U.S. Constitution, *The Iroquois and the Founding of the American Nation* (1977). The cultural issues of the Mohawk, Oneida, Onondaga, Tuscarora, Seneca, and Cayuga tribes, which constitute the New York Iroquois, find expression in his works and in his promotion of cultural programs for Iroquois Indians. He is chairman of the Haudenosaunee Standing Committee on the Burial Rules and Regulations.

## E. Pauline Johnson (1861–1913)
*Mohawk poet*

Pauline Johnson was an internationally acclaimed Mohawk poet and performer who lived and worked in the second half of the nineteenth century. A distant relative of Joseph Brant, a Mohawk chief who fought alongside the British during the American Revolution, Pauline Johnson was born to a Mohawk father, George

Johnson, and a non-Native mother, Emily Howells. The Johnsons lived in Chiefswood, across the Grand River from the Six Nations Indian Reserve located near Brantford, in southwestern Ontario. Pauline wrote poetry as soon as she learned to write, and as a young child she was a voracious reader. She was educated mostly at home until she went to college in Brantford, where she performed in plays and pageants and decided to become a poet and performer. During her teens, she wrote many poems and had several minor publishing successes with local and regional magazines.

When her father died in 1885, Pauline moved with her mother to Brantford, where she often attended recitals and theater productions. Johnson's career blossomed when she started to recite her poetry in front of audiences. As a result of her successes, she saved enough money to travel to London, England, where she gave numerous recitals and arranged publication of a book of her poems, entitled *The White Wampum*, released in 1895. Upon her return to Canada, Johnson traveled from Newfoundland to Vancouver, performing and reciting her poetry. She also toured throughout the United States.

Besides being a poet, Johnson was also one of the first Indian women to publish short fiction. Especially interesting is *The Moccasin Maker* (1913), a collection of short stories on diverse subjects but mainly focusing on the lives of Indian and non-Indian women in Canada. Some are love stories, some focus on pioneer women who established homes for their families despite great hardships, and several deal with what would become a dominant theme in American Indian literature of the twentieth century: the mixed-blood's search for his or her proper place in the modern world. One story called "A Red Girl's Reasoning" tells of a mixed-blood woman who remains true to her Indian values even when the decision forces her to leave her husband, who is critical of such ideas. Johnson also was a prolific author of essays and magazine articles. She died in 1913 after a lengthy illness.

## Basil H. Johnston (1929–)
*Ojibwa (Chippewa) author and educator*

Basil Johnston was born 13 July 1929 on the Parry Island Reserve in Ontario, Canada. He graduated from Loyola College in Montreal in 1954 and received a secondary school teaching certificate from the Ontario College of Education in 1962. Johnston started his career as assistant manager and manager of the Toronto Board of Trade from 1957 to 1959, and he taught for the first time at Earl Haig Secondary School from 1962 to 1969. Beginning in 1969, he was a lecturer at the

Ethnology Department at the Royal Ontario Museum, and in 1974, he became an English teacher for the Ojibwa in Toronto.

Johnston has been affiliated with the Canadian Indian Center in Toronto, the Union of Ontario Indians, and the Indian Eskimo Association, for whom he was legal and executive member of the committee from 1965 to 1968. He was also a member of the Indian Hall of Fame from 1968 to 1970 and of the Ontario Geographic Names Board beginning in 1977.

Johnston has written numerous stories and essays, as well as guides to learning the Ojibwa language, including *Ojibwa Language Course Outline* (1979), *Ojibwa Language Lexicon for Beginners and Others* (1979), and *Ojibwa Heritage* (1976). Among his works of fiction are *Moose Meat and Wild Rice* (1978), and numerous short stories that appeared in *The Ontario Indian*, such as "Where's Simon?" (December 1980), "My Rope" (February 1981), and "Batman and Robin" (March 1981). *By Canoe and Moccasins* (Lakefield, ON: Waapoone Publishing and Promotion, 1986) is one of his best-known works of children's literature.

Johnston's non-fiction articles have appeared in various Canadian magazines dealing with educational issues, including "Forget Totem Poles," (March 1975) and "Indian History Must Be Taught" (March 1971), both published in *The Educational Courier*. He has written on racial and interracial issues in "Indian, Métis and Eskimos" in *Read Canadian* (1972), and "Cowboys and Indians" in *The Ontario Indian* (August 1981). Johnston has received many honors and awards, including the Centennial Medal in recognition of work on behalf of the Native community in 1967, the Samuel S. Fells Literary Award for first publication, "Zhowmin and Mandamin" in 1976, and the Order of Ontario in 1989, for services of great distinction and singular excellence, benefiting society in Ontario and elsewhere. His most recent books are *The Bear-Walker and Other Stories* (1995) and *Crazy Dave* (1995).

## Ted Jojola (1951–)
*Isleta Pueblo scholar and author*

Ted Jojola is a professor in the master's program in Community and Regional Planning, School of Architecture and Planning at the University of New Mexico. He was director of Native American studies from 1980 to 1996.

Jojola was born in Isleta Pueblo, New Mexico, in 1951. He received a B.A. in architecture from the University of New Mexico, an M.A. in city planning from the Massachusetts Institute of Technology, and a Ph.D.

in political science from the University of Hawaii in Manoa in 1982. In 1985, he received a Certificate of International Human Rights and Law from the University of Strasbourg in France. Jojola began his career as internal planner at the National Capital Planning Commission in Washington, D.C. in 1973. In 1976 he was legal and historical researcher for the Institute for the Development of Indian Law in Washington. From 1977 to 1982, he was a visiting researcher at the Institute of Philippine Culture in Manila, visiting professor of urban planning at the University of California at Los Angeles, and assistant professor of planning at the University of New Mexico in Albuquerque.

Jojola has conducted research on a variety of topics, such as a preschool computer program in isolated American Indian communities in 1985, a 1990 project for the U.S. Census Bureau on ethnographic undercounts, and research involving the Isleta Pueblo living in New Mexico and Arizona, descendants of the ancient cliff dwellers, in cooperation with the U.S. Department of Health and Human Services in 1989.

Among Jojola's numerous grants and honors are a postdoctoral fellowship at the American Indian Studies Center at UCLA in 1984, and the Atherton Trust, a public grant in Honolulu, in 1976. Jojola has appeared in two editions of *Who's Who in the West* (Marquis, 1985) and *Who's Who Among Young Emerging Leaders* (Marquis 1987). In 1976, he published *Memoirs of an American Indian House: The Impact of a Cross-National Housing Program on Two Reservations*, and in 1988 he was the guest editor of *Wicazo sa Review*, a journal of Indian studies with emphasis on issues, literature, and culture. He was also the series editor of *Public Policy Impact on American Indian Development*, and *Pueblo Style and Regional Architecture* (1989).

## Peter Jones (1802–1856)
*Ojibwa minister, chief, and translator*

Peter Jones was a well-known religious leader and spokesman for Native rights. He was born in Ontario in the Credit River Mississauga settlement near the west end of Lake Ontario on 1 January 1802. His father, Augustus Jones, was a Welsh surveyor and a friend of Joseph Brant, the Mohawk leader. His mother, Tuhbenahneeguay, was the daughter of the Mississauga Ojibwa chief Wahbonosay. Jones's Ojibwa name was Kahkewaquonaby (Sacred Feathers), and he lived traditionally until he was about sixteen. At sixteen, his father had him baptized into the Episcopalian faith and he was given the name Peter. As a young adult, Jones became actively involved in services at the Wesleyan

Methodist Church and became the first Native Methodist missionary to the Ojibwa in 1827.

As a Methodist missionary, Peter Jones visited several bands in western Ontario and, with his brother John, provided the first translations of the Bible from English into Ojibwa. In 1830, Jones was made a deacon of the Methodist church and in 1833 became a minister. He was elected chief of two Ojibwa bands and visited New York, London, and several other large cities on behalf of the Ojibwa. Jones was well known not simply for his religious activities, but as an articulate spokesman for the protection of Native land rights.

Jones married an Englishwoman, with whom he had four sons. One son assumed his father's name and published a local journal, *The Indian*, devoted to Native matters of the day. Jones died near his birthplace, in Brantford, Ontario, on 29 June 1856. His *Life and Journals of Kah-ke-quo-na-by (Rev. Peter Jones) and History of the Ojebway Indians* were both published posthumously. In 1857, a monument dedicated to Jones' memory was erected by the Ojibwa in Brantford.

## Rosalie M. Jones "Daystar" (contemporary)
*Pembina Chippewa artist, choreographer, educator*

Born on the Blackfeet Reservation in Montana, Jones holds a master's degree in dance from the University of Utah (1968) and studied at the Juilliard School in New York City (1969–1970).

She began her artistic career as a solo dancer during the 1970s, touring numerous reservations where she taught and performed dance. In 1980, she founded her own dance company, Daystar: Contemporary Dance Drama of Indian America.

The Daystar Company was the first company of its kind in America. Daystar is credited with pioneering the early development of modern, Native American dance, which fuses traditional Native and Western modern dance and drama techniques.

Some of her significant choreography, deriving from tribal oral traditions, include Wolf (Anishinabe), Tales of Old Man (Blackfeet), Legend of the Black Butterfly (Maidu), and The Gift of the Pipe (Lakota).

She helped revitalize performing arts at the Institute of American Indian Arts in Santa Fe, New Mexico, while serving as chair of performing arts during the early 1990s. She was Distinguished Visiting Artist at American University in Bulgaria, and the Chancellor's Distinguished Visiting Professor in Dance at the University of California, Irvine. As a guest of Roots of Theatre in Helsinki, Finland, during the 2000 Millennium Celebration, she conducted workshops and performances. She was artist-in-residence of the School of

Rosalie M. Jones, artistic director of the Daystar Dance Company.

Arts and Performance at the SUNY College at Brockport, New York, from 1999 to 2001.

## Joseph (1840–1904)
*Nez Percé tribal leader*

Joseph was born in the Wallowa Valley in present-day Oregon. The Nez Percé lived in the area where the present-day states of Washington, Oregon, and Idaho adjoin. The various Indian tribes in this region signed the Isaac Steven's Treaty in 1855 ceding Indian lands in the Washington Territory in exchange for reservation lands, homes, tools, and money. As more settlers and miners arrived into the region, however, the treaty was ignored. Like his father before him, Joseph originally carried out a plan of passive resistance to U.S. land encroachment and to efforts by the U.S. government to relocate his people to the Nez Percé Reservation.

A fragile peace was shattered in 1877, when U.S. settlers began moving into the Wallowa Valley. The government had recently overturned an earlier decision granting this land to the Nez Percé as a reservation, and they were given thirty days to relocate. On June 12, the inevitable fighting erupted when three young Nez Percé killed four settlers who had moved into the Wallowa Valley.

After some initial battles, in which Joseph showed remarkable military skill by defeating superior U.S.

forces, Joseph and the Nez Percé from the Wallowa Valley decided to attempt an escape into Canada. For roughly the next three months they eluded both U.S. troops and enemy Indian bands. In late September the Nez Percé group was only miles from the Canadian border when they found themselves surrounded and outnumbered by forces augmented with howitzer cannons and Gatlin guns, which were early machine guns. On 5 October 1877, Chief Joseph finally surrendered, but not before hundreds of Nez Percé escaped to Canada.

When the long odyssey was finally over, many of the Nez Percé leaders were dead or in Canada. The final surrender agreement was signed by Joseph. Subsequently, the exhausted leader is credited with giving a dramatic, often quoted, speech at the surrender. The actual text of the speech is unknown, and popular interpretations glowed in the hands of embellishing journalists. In the minds of the American public, Joseph became permanently identified with the courageous journey taken by the Nez Percé. According to historical accounts, the campaign of the Nez Percé in 1877 was characterized by restraint and relative non-violence on the part of Joseph and the tribe. Sent to Indian Territory in Oklahoma, the Nez Percé were allowed to return to Idaho in 1883 and 1884. Joseph spent the rest of his life on a number of different Indian reservations, but was allowed only a brief return to his homeland in the Wallowa Valley. He died on the Colville Indian Reservation in the state of Washington.

### Betty Mae Jumper (1923–)
*Seminole tribal leader*

Betty Mae Jumper was born in 1927 in Indiantown, Florida. She was the first Seminole to receive a high school diploma, which she obtained in 1949 from the Cherokee Indian School in Cherokee, North Carolina. Within the Seminole community, she served first as secretary-treasurer for the tribal council, then as vice chairperson until 1967, when she became the first woman elected chair of the tribe, holding the post for four years. Jumper was also director of communications and editor-in-chief of the *Seminole Tribune*, the newspaper of the Seminole tribe in Florida.

In 1968, Jumper joined representatives of three southeastern tribes in signing a Declaration of Unity in Cherokee, North Carolina, which implemented the Inter-Tribal Council of the United Southeastern Tribes. While serving as chair of the Seminole tribe, she was appointed by President Richard Nixon one of eight Indian members of the National Congress on Indian Opportunity.

Jumper did much to improve health, education, and social conditions among the Seminole. In 1984, she published . . . *And With the Wagon Came God's Word*, published by the Seminole Print Shop. After retirement Jumper published *Legends of the Seminoles* (1994). She has been a speaker on the Seminole at schools throughout Florida, and an advisor for the Manpower Development and Training Committee for the state of Florida. She was a member of the Native American Press Association and the Florida Press Association. Jumper was chosen Woman of the Year by the Department of Florida Ladies Auxiliaries of Jewish War Veterans of the United States, for her outstanding contribution in the field of humanities.

She still lives on the Hollywood Reservation, and is the mother of three children, grandmother to ten, and great-grandmother to three.

### Hattie Kauffman (contemporary)
*Nez Percé national news correspondent*

Hattie Kauffman has made her name as the first Native American journalist to report a national broadcast. She received her bachelor of science degree from the University of Minnesota, where she also attended the Graduate School of Journalism under a WCCO-TV Minorities in Broadcasting Scholarship. Kauffman launched her career as a journalist early by broadcasting on-air radio reports while in college.

In November 1999 Kauffman was named national correspondent for CBS News' *The Early Show*. Prior to this appointment, she served as senior consumer correspondent for *This Morning* from 1990 to 1999.

Her particular style of reporting human-interest stories has earned her acclaim throughout her successful career. She also reports on intriguing vacation ideas, as evidenced in her five-part series, "Something Wild," in which Kauffman went rock climbing, white-water rafting, and scuba-diving.

Before working for *This Morning*, Kauffman worked as a reporter for *Good Morning America* from 1987 to 1990. Early in her career she worked for KING-TV in Seattle, during which time she earned four Emmy Awards for her work.

### William W. Keeler (1908–1987)
*Cherokee businessperson and tribal leader*

In 1949, William Keeler was appointed principal chief of the Cherokee Nation in Oklahoma. He served as appointed principal chief until 1971, and between 1971 and 1975 was the first elected principal chief since 1907. Keeler's initial appointment was made under laws that abolished the Cherokee government in 1907. Between 1907 and 1971, the Cherokee principal chief was appointed by the U.S. president and was responsible for administering the Cherokee land estate and attending to associated legal and political issues. It was thought that the Cherokee Nation would ultimately dissolve. In 1971, however, the Cherokee regained the right to elect their own leadership, and the nation continues.

Starting at age sixteen, as a part-time worker, Keeler pursued a corporate business career with Phillips Petroleum Company. In 1951, he was elected to the board of directors. In 1968, he was elected chairman of the board and vice-president of the executive department. Because of his reputation as a strong administrator, government agencies often tapped Keeler for advice on solving problems in the oil and refining industry. Keeler actively contributed his services to many public interest groups, including fraternal, veteran, civic, and business organizations.

During Keeler's administration as principal chief, he gained a reputation as an able administrator and leader. He served on two major government task forces, which investigated and reported on major issues in Indian affairs. One task force reported in 1961 with a critical review of government policies toward Indians during the 1950s, which included termination or the dissolving of tribal reservations and governments. In 1962, Keeler also served on a task force that investigated conditions of Alaska Natives and their land claims. He also helped establish the Cherokee Foundation, which endeavors to promote the welfare and culture of the Cherokee Nation and its members.

## Peter Kelly (1885–1966)
*Haida activist and minister*

Peter Kelly was an Indian activist of Haida descent. The Haida people live in the Queen Charlotte Islands off the coast of mainland British Columbia (BC) and are recognized for their totem poles and huge communal houses made of cedar. Kelly was an ordained Methodist, and later a United Church minister. By the time he was twenty-six, Kelly became involved in various ancestral land claims brought by Indians of BC. In 1916, he organized a conference in Vancouver to address tribal rights to land. Sixteen tribal groups from across the province were represented, and the conference formed itself into the Allied Indian Tribes of British Columbia. Kelly was elected chairman of the executive committee. In 1919, after extensive consultation, the Allied Tribes prepared a statement of Indian rights to ancestral land in British Columbia that many viewed as the authoritative statement of BC Indian claims. It also lobbied the federal and provincial governments extensively on Indian issues. In 1927, Kelly testified before a special parliamentary committee in Ottawa formed to address Indian issues. In calling for the recognition of Indian title to ancestral lands in BC, Kelly stated: "Why not keep unblemished the record of British fair dealing with Native races? Why refuse to recognize the claim of certain tribes of Indians in one corner of the British Dominions, when it has been accorded to others in another part of the same Dominion?" The committee refused to recognize aboriginal title and recommended the prohibition of any transaction designed to assist the bringing of Indian land claims to court. When the committee's recommendation became law in 1927, it was the death knell for the Allied Tribes, and Kelly devoted himself to the ministry. He re-emerged politically in the 1940s when he joined the Native Brotherhood of BC, a province-wide Indian organization formed in the wake of the Allied Tribes' demise.

## Kenekuk (Kickapoo Prophet) (1785–1852)
*Kickapoo tribal and spiritual leader*

Kenekuk was the religious and political leader of a community of Kickapoo, which was later joined by some Potawatomi. The Kickapoo lived in Illinois, while the Potawatomi occupied parts of present-day Michigan, but a small group of them joined Kenekuk and his Kickapoo community when they were removed to Kansas after 1933. Kenekuk was influenced by the Shawnee prophet, who before the War of 1812 advocated strong and overt military resistance to U.S. settlers and territorial expansion. The War of 1812 left the Kickapoo and other northern Great Lakes Indian nations in a state of disarray and destitution. In 1819, the Kickapoo ceded half of the present-day state of Illinois to the U.S. government. Thereafter during the 1820s, some Kickapoo Bands migrated to Texas, while others sought refuge in Mexico.

Kenekuk, like the Shawnee prophet before him, claimed he had a vision, containing a message from the Great Spirit for the Indian people, but for the Kickapoo in particular. Kenekuk's vision differed from the Shawnee prophet's message in that it preached accommodation to U.S. culture and land demands. The Kickapoo prophet worked to create a new moral and religious community for his followers, one that drew on elements of Catholic, Protestant, and traditional Kickapoo religious beliefs. He advocated the taking up of agriculture, the formation of self-sufficient Indian farming communities. He banned alcohol, instructed his followers to maintain friendly relations with U.S. settlers, and developed a self-contained religious moral community, which tried to preserve its land and identity from the onslaught of U.S. settlers and the demands of the U.S. government.

In 1832, Kenekuk's community did not join with Black Hawk in his war to regain parts of Illinois. Nevertheless, he tried hard to avoid the removal of his people from Illinois to present-day Kansas. In 1833, however, he and 350 followers were required to move. In Kansas, Kenekuk continued his preaching, and he attracted some converts from among the Potawatomi. He died in 1852, but his community continues to survive until this day, and the people retain the distinct religious teachings of the Kickapoo prophet.

## William Kennedy (1814–1890)
*Métis explorer*

William Kennedy was the son of a Cree mother and a Scottish father who worked for the Hudson's Bay Company, a trading company active in the Canadian interior. As a result, Kennedy was Métis, a term that refers to persons of mixed Indian-European heritage who forged a common identity on the plains of Western Canada in the nineteenth century. At the age of eleven, William and his brother, George, were sent to Scotland to obtain an elementary education for seven years. Upon his return to Canada, Kennedy began to work for the Hudson's Bay Company, but left, disillusioned with the company's trading practices.

His life changed dramatically in 1851, when he was chosen to lead an expedition to search for Sir John Franklin, an explorer who had gone missing while searching for a Northwest passage between the Hudson Strait and the Pacific Ocean. Kennedy returned to Scotland, where he captained a ship and a crew of seventeen and set sail for the Canadian Arctic. Seventeen months later, Kennedy and his crew returned to Scotland without having located Sir Franklin and his ship; nonetheless Kennedy was able to discover, identify, and map a great deal of territory in the Canadian north.

Kennedy eventually made what was to become the province of Manitoba his home, and he worked diligently to secure the establishment of a direct transportation and mail route between Toronto and Fort Garry in the Canadian plains. He also worked for the extension of Canada westward into the area that has now become Manitoba. Kennedy was unstinting in his support for the betterment of Native people, devoting much time to the education of young people and the establishment of colonies for Native people on productive land.

## Maurice Kenny (1929–)
*Mohawk poet, short story writer, and educator*

Nominated for the Pulitzer Prize in 1982 for *Blackrobe: Isaac Jogues, b. March 11, 1607, d. October 18, 1646*, and in 1987 for *Between Two Rivers: Selected Poems 1956–1984*, Maurice Francis Kenny is one of the leaders of the Native American literary renaissance of the 1970s. His poetry explores the links between the human spirit and the natural world, and many of his poems speak from the perspective of natural objects.

Born to Andrew Anthony Kenny and Doris Marie Parker Herrick Kenny Welch in Watertown, New York, Kenny is of Mohawk and Seneca ancestry. His hometown is set at the foothills of the Adirondacks, and his experiences there shaped his poetic relationship with nature.

In 1956, Kenny graduated with a bachelor's degree in English from Butler University in Indianapolis, Indiana.

Maurice Kenny.

Soon after graduation, Kenny moved back to his home state, where he studied at St. Lawrence University in Canton, and at New York University in New York City. While in the city, Kenny studied with poet Louise Bogan, who helped him hone his technical expertise and his passion for poetry. His first book of poetry, *Dead Letter Sent*, was published by Troubador Press in 1958.

Kenny left New York, going on a long hiatus to Mexico and the Virgin Islands, ending his travels in Chicago where he wrote obituaries for the *Chicago Sun*. While Kenny returned to New York in 1968 a productive writer, most of his work would not be published until the following decade. The poet stayed in New York City, however, until later in life, when he moved back to Adirondack country in New York State.

*I Am the Sun*, a collection of poems, was released in 1973, and in the mid-1970s Kenny established the Strawberry Press, which published poetry and art by Native people. Also during this time Kenny and J. G. Gosciak began co-editing *Contact/II*, an influential magazine dedicated to the contemporary world of poetry. Kenny was also an advisory editor for *S.A.I.L.*, *Akwesasne Notes*, and *Time Capsule*.

The early 1980s brought Kenny wide recognition for his poetic and literary accomplishments. In 1984 *The Mama Poems* won the American Book Award and *Blackrobe* received the National Public Radio Award. The next year, Kenny left Brooklyn to teach at North Country Community College, where he was also poet-in-residence. In 1987 and 1988 Kenny coordinated the Robert Louis Stevenson Annual Writers Conference, and he has lectured and read throughout the country. His most recent books are *On Second Thought: A Compilation* (1995), *Backward to Forward: Prose Pieces* (1997), and *Tortured Skins, and Other Fictions* (2000). He presently lives in Saranac Lake, New York, teaching Native American literature at St. Lawrence University from which he received an honorary doctorate in literature in 1995.

## Kenojuak (1927– )
*Inuit artist*

Kenojuak is probably the best-known Inuit artist in Canada. She was born on Baffin Island, Northwest Territories, north of the province of Quebec in the Canadian Arctic. Cape Dorset, on Baffin Island, was a community well known in artistic circles for soapstone carvings. Kenojuak was the first woman to become involved in a new printmaking shop established at Cape Dorset in the 1950s. The shop experimented with stone-block printing, in which the design is carved on a slab of soapstone, which is then inked, and the paper is pressed onto it to create a print. Kenojuak began to draw and make prints of her drawings at that time. Her drawings were and still are primarily of birds and human beings, and they often involve intertwined figures and fantasies. Strong, colorful, richly composed and designed, Kenojuak's drawings and prints were almost immediately recognized as unique and valuable, and they continue to be sought after by national and international collectors and museums.

Although she is primarily known for her drawings and paintings, Kenojuak also carves and sculpts soapstone and other material. She was acclaimed for a mural that she and her now-deceased husband created for the 1970 World Fair in Osaka, Japan. Kenojuak has traveled widely throughout Canada and Europe and has shown her work in many exhibitions, perhaps the most famous being a thirty-year retrospective of her art at the McMichael Canadian Collection Gallery in Kleinburg, Ontario, just outside of Toronto, in 1986. Kenojuak has been featured in a film about her work produced by the National Film Board of Canada in 1962 and in a limited edition book published in 1981. In 1992 Kenojuak was awarded honorary degrees from Queens University and the University of Toronto. In 1995, she received the Lifetime Aboriginal Achievement Award.

## Keokuk (1783–1848)
*Sac (Sauk) tribal leader*

Keokuk was born around 1783 in the village of Saukenuk in present-day Illinois. He obtained a position of power among his people by demonstrating bravery against the Sioux, although he was not a hereditary chief.

By the early 1800s, the official policy of the U.S. government had become one of forced treaties and acquisition of Indian land. Keokuk, though not recognized as a chief among his own people, was selected by the U.S. government as the official representative of the Sauk because of his refusal to support the British in 1812 and his friendly overtures to the United States. During this era, the government used bribery to bring Keokuk into line with federal land policies. Keokuk signed a number of treaties that included an exchange of Sauk land in the Rock River country for a tract located westward and an annual cash compensation, which was to be administered by Keokuk.

In the 1830s, Keokuk redeemed himself in the eyes of some Sauk by his skillful defense of Sauk land interests

Keokuk.

against Sioux territorial claims in Washington, D.C. In 1845, Keokuk ceded Iowa lands in exchange for a reservation in Kansas. He died three years later, amid reports that followers of Black Hawk had killed him. Though it is believed Keokuk actually died of dysentery, the rumors of murder were not surprising since in the eyes of many, Keokuk, unlike his peer Black Hawk, did not represent his people in the most loyal fashion.

## K. Kirke Kickingbird (1944–)
*Kiowa lawyer*

Kirke Kickingbird is former director of the Native American Legal Resource Center at the Oklahoma City University School of Law, a position he filled since the center opened in July, 1988. He was appointed by Governor Henry Bellmon to serve on the Oklahoma Constitutional Revision Commission (1988–1991) and by Governor David Walters to serve on the governor's Health and Human Services Cabinet Review Team in

1991. Kickingbird was co-curator of "Moving the Fire: The Removal of the Indian Nations to Oklahoma," an International Monetary Fund Visitor's Center Exhibit in Washington, D.C., presented 21 January through 15 April 1993, coinciding with the United Nations resolution to declare 1993 the International Year of the World's Indigenous Peoples. He was appointed on 24 August 1992 by orders of Chief Justice Marian P. Opala to serve as a member of the Oklahoma Supreme Court Committee to recommend standards for granting full faith and credit to the judicial proceedings of the Indian tribes, nations, and bands.

Before joining the faculty at Oklahoma City University Law School, he founded and directed a private nonprofit Indian legal research center (1971–1985), the Institute for the Development of Indian Law, in Washington, D.C., where he worked with tribes throughout the United States and Canada. From 1976 to 1977, he served as general counsel of the U.S. Congress American Indian Policy Review Commission, which made a special two-year study of U.S. Indian policy.

In 1988 and 1989, Kickingbird was a member of the U.S. delegation to the International Labor Organization (ILO) annual conference, a United Nations agency, which revised the only modern treaty addressing the rights of indigenous peoples. In 1980 he lectured at universities in northern Europe as part of a U.S. International Communications Agency program. In 1977, he was member of the U.S. delegation to the United Nations International Conference on Discrimination Against Indigenous Populations in the Americas. The Australian Constitutional Centenary Foundation invited him to present a paper at Canberra, Australia, on 3–4 June 1993 at a conference on the Position of Indigenous Peoples in National Constitutions. The International Conference on the Law of Indigenous Peoples asked him to present a paper in Moscow on September 24–26 on "Indigenous Peoples Rights: Legislation and Implementation in the United States."

His first book on Indian land issues, *100 Million Acres*, was published by Macmillan in 1973. Kickingbird has written numerous books and articles on Indian affairs and Indian law. His latest, *Indians and the U.S. Constitution: A Forgotten Legacy*, won an award in 1988 from the U.S. Commission on the Bicentennial of the Constitution.

Kickingbird was appointed in 1995 by the governor of Oklahoma as special counsel on Indian affairs. Kickingbird is a past chair of the Oklahoma Indian Affairs Commission and Chief Justice of the Supreme Court of the Cheyenne and Arapaho Tribes of Oklahoma. From 1996 to 1999 he was a member of the Board of Governors of the American Bar Association (ABA).

He was the first Native American to serve on the ABA Board of Governors in the history of the association.

## Clara Sue Kidwell (1941–)
*White Earth Chippewa-Choctaw historian and professor*

Clara Sue Kidwell is director of Native American Studies at the University of Oklahoma. She was born on 8 July 1941, in Tahlequah, Oklahoma. She received her diploma from Muskogee Central High School in Muskogee, Oklahoma, in 1959 and continued her academic studies at the University of Oklahoma at Norman where she received both a master of arts (1966) and a Ph.D. (1970) in the history of science.

Since 1966, Kidwell has taught history at various institutions, including Everett Junior College in Everett, Washington, and the Kansas City Art Institute in Kansas City, Missouri. In 1970, she became coordinator of publications at the Experimental Education Unit at the University of Washington, Seattle. From 1970 to 1972, she worked as an instructor in social sciences and chair of the Social Sciences Division at the Haskell Indian Junior College in Lawrence, Kansas. From 1974 to 1993, Kidwell taught in the Native American studies program at the University of California, Berkeley.

Kidwell published her first article, "The Apiarium: An Early Example of Microscopic Study," in *Proceedings of the Oklahoma Academy of Sciences XLVI* in 1966, and since has published twenty four essays and numerous book reviews. In 1980, she authored *The Choctaws: A Critical Bibliography*, a bibliographic guide to the study of the Choctaw. In 1995, she published *Choctaws and Missionaries in Mississippi*.

Her Indian background shapes most of Kidwell's research and studies, which are focused on various aspects of American Indian culture. She is interested in American Indian women's issues, as shown in the essay "The Status of Native American Women in Higher Education" in *Proceedings of a Conference on the Educational and Occupational Needs of Native American Women* (1980), as well as in historical events of the Indians of South America, as seen in "Aztec and European Medicine in the New World, 1521–1600," published in *Anthropology of Medicine* (1982).

Throughout her active academic life, Kidwell has received numerous fellowships: the National Defense Education Act Title IV Fellowship, 1962–1965; the John Hay Whitney Foundation Opportunity Fellowship, 1965–1966; and the Rockefeller Foundation Humanities Fellowship, 1977–1978. More recently, she was awarded the University of California Humanities Fellowship, the Newberry Library Summer Fellowship, and in 1984, the Smithsonian Institution Fellowship.

## Gary Kimble (1943–)
*Gros Ventre lawyer and educator*

Gary Kimble is head of the Native American Program at the Office of Child Support Enforcement in Washington, D.C. He is a member of the Gros Ventre tribe and was raised on the Fort Belknap Reservation in northern Montana, near the Canadian border. Kimble received a bachelor's degree in journalism from the University of Montana in 1966 and a law degree from the same university in 1972. In 1972, he was elected to the Montana House of Representatives and served for three terms, specializing in environmental policy and labor law. During the years 1974 and 1979, he was assistant professor of American Indian studies and Indian law at the University of Montana. In 1979, he was chief counsel for his tribe at the U.S. Senate Select Committee on Indian Affairs in Washington, D.C.

In 1978, Kimble was the first American Indian to run for the U.S. House of Representatives in more than twenty years. In 1980, he was appointed to direct the Columbia River Inter-Tribal Fish Commission in Portland, Oregon, a federal tribal advocacy organization for the inter-tribal fishery in the Columbia River basin. Kimble returned to Montana in 1982 and organized Kimble and Associates, a management and legal consulting firm, in Missoula. His chief clients were the governor's office in Montana, American Training and Technical Assistance in Albuquerque, and numerous tribal governments and groups in Montana and the Northwest.

In 1986, Kimble moved his business to Portland, Oregon, and began teaching federal Indian law at the Northwestern School of Law at Lewis and Clark College. In 1989, he became executive director of the Association on American Indian Affairs in New York and a member of the Aboriginal Public Policy Institute, a northern California organization that provides networking and technical assistance to aboriginal people worldwide. From 1994 to 2000, he served as commissioner of the Administration for Native Americans (Children and Families).

## Thomas King (1943–)
*Cherokee/Greek writer/photographer and scholar*

Thomas King, an award-winning novelist, short story writer, scriptwriter, and photographer of Cherokee and Greek ancestry, is associate professor of English at the

University of Guelph (Canada). He was born in Sacramento, California, in 1943, and obtained his Ph.D. from the University of Utah (1986).

His first novel, *Medicine River* (1990), won several awards, including the runner-up for the 1991 Commonwealth Writers prize. King adapted the novel into a television movie in 1992, which won the Best Film award at the 1993 American Indian Film Festival in San Francisco, California.

He has also written two acclaimed children's books, *A Coyote Columbus Story* (1992) and *Coyote Sings to the Moon* (1998). His highly praised collection of short stories, *One Good Story, That One* (1993), was a Canadian bestseller.

Other works by King include *All My Relations: An Anthology of Contemporary Canadian Native Literature* (ed., 1990), *Green Grass, Running Water* (1993), which won the Canadian Authors Award for fiction, and *Truth and Bright Water* (2000).

King is also creator of CBC Radio One's *Dead Dog Café Comedy Hour*. He is currently working on a photography exhibition and *Warriors*, a television movie.

### Rosemarie Kuptana (contemporary)
*Inuit journalist and tribal leader*

Rosemarie Kuptana was born in Sachs Harbour, a community of just over a hundred Inuit people on Banks Island, in Canada's Northwest Territories. She went to school in Inuvik, a village in the Northwest Territories, and first became involved with Inuit organizations in 1975. In 1979, she joined the northern service branch of the Canadian Broadcasting Corporation (CBC), hosting the morning and noon radio shows on CBC Western Arctic. Her programs focused on the cultural, social, and political issues of the day, including the Inuvialuit land claim, where Inuits sought province-like self-government within the Canadian government, and oil and gas explorations in the Beaufort Sea, located off the north shore of eastern Alaska and the western Northwest Territories.

After a period of work with community organizations in Sachs Harbour, Kuptana joined the Inuit Broadcasting Corporation (IBC). IBC's programs, which are in the Inuit Native language of Inuktitut, are a mixture of current affairs and contemporary and traditional Inuit culture of the Arctic, Alaska, and Northern Canada. She began as assistant production coordinator in

1982 and was promoted to network production coordinator; she was elected IBC president in December 1983. As president from 1983 to 1988, Kuptana supervised IBC's programming and managed a staff of fifty located in six widely dispersed production centers. She initiated many of the IBC's existing systems, such as its administrative policy, training programs for production staff, journalistic policy, as well as a children's educational television programs in Inuktitut language.

In recent years, Kuptana has researched and published a book about child sexual abuse in Inuit communities, promoted Inuit interests at the 1991 Canada-USSR Cooperation Conference held in Moscow and Leningrad, and continued her interests in journalism as vice-chair of Television of Northern Canada.

She also co-chaired the International Arctic Council, a project that would have eight circumpolar governments cooperate on a wide range of issues with special attention to the concerns of circumpolar Native peoples. Kuptana has also served as president and as the Canadian vice-chair of the Inuit Circumpolar Conference (ICC). The ICC is the international political organization representing Inuit from Canada, Alaska, Greenland, and the former Soviet Union.

From April 1991 to June 1996, Kuptana was elected president of the Inuit Tapirisat of Canada, the national political voice of Canadian Inuit. In this capacity Kuptana was engaged in a series of constitutional negotiations involving aboriginal leaders, territorial, provincial, and federal first ministers. In the last round of negotiations she obtained the recognition in principle of the inherent right of aboriginal self-government, as third order of government, by all the Canadian governments. In 1994, she was awarded the National Aboriginal Achievement Award for public service.

### Richard Vance La Course (1938–)
*Yakima journalist*

Richard Vance La Course is a journalist who has worked extensively for the mainstream press and for the American Indian press. He was born in Toppenish, Washington, and studied at Portland State University, Oregon, and the University of Washington, Seattle. From 1969 to 1971, La Course was news editor and correspondent for the *Seattle Post-Intelligencer*. He was managing editor of the *Confederated Umatilla Journal* in Pendleton, Oregon, from 1971 to 1974; and of the *Yakima Nation Review* in Toppenish, Washington, from 1975 to 1978. In 1977, he founded and became managing editor of the *Manatabla Messenger*, published by the Colorado River Tribes in Parker, Arizona.

Since 1983, La Course has managed his own company, La Course Communications Corporation, in Washington, D.C. The corporation is an Indian-owned media firm that provides services in publication research and development, graphic design, publication of directories, market analysis, and specialized mailing lists related to American Indian concerns. La Course hopes eventually to publish a full-size weekly newspaper.

La Course is a co-founder and board member of Native American Press Association and co-founder of the Northwest Indian News Association. He is a member of the Nation Congress of American Indians, a national Indian political interest organization, and Americans for Indian Opportunity. In 1978, La Course was the keynote speaker and honoree at the Second Annual Indian Media Conference and American Indian Film Festival in San Francisco, California. In 1980, he was the recipient of the Indian Media Man of the Year Award at the Nation Indian Media Conference held in Anaheim, California. In 1984, he received a National Recognition Award of Accomplishment given by the Americans for Indian Opportunity, Washington, D.C.

La Course is the author and editor of *The Schooling of Native America: Native American Teachers Corps and Northwest Tribal Profiles.*

Activist Winona LaDuke.

## Winona LaDuke (1959– )
*Ojibwa (Chippewa) Anishinaabe political and environmental activist, journalist, and author*

An enrolled member of the Mississippi band from the White Earth Reservation in Minnesota, Winona LaDuke is one of the most respected women in American Indian politics. Among her many interests, LaDuke is best known for her strong environmental stances and for her work in favor of American Indian land restoration. She protested the uranium mines on the Navajo Reservation, resisted Hydro-Quebec's construction sites built at James Bay, and demonstrated against the toxic waste sites on Native Canadian and Alaskan lands bordering the Arctic Ocean.

The daughter of activists Vincent (Sun Bear), a Chippewa writer, and Betty, a Jewish painter, LaDuke was reared in a politically charged environment. Because of her father's occupation as an extra in Hollywood Westerns, she was born in Los Angeles. When she was five, however, her parents divorced and LaDuke and her mother moved to Ashland, Oregon. LaDuke maintained her Native ties, however, frequenting her father's home on the White Earth Reservation throughout her youth.

LaDuke received her bachelor's degree in economic development from Harvard University in 1982. While there she met Jimmy Durham, a well-known Cherokee activist, who helped her formulate ideas of activism and grassroots organization. When she was just eighteen, LaDuke spoke to the United Nations about environmental exploitation issues occurring throughout Indian Country.

After her undergraduate work, LaDuke moved to the White Earth Reservation and began to protest environmental racism and work for Ojibway land recovery. In the late 1980s, the activist graduated from Antioch University with a master's degree in rural development.

LaDuke received the first Reebok Human Rights Award, which recognizes activists under the age of thirty, in 1989. With the $20,000 grant she received with the award, LaDuke founded the White Earth Land Recovery Project (WELRP), an organization formed to raise funds to regain original White Earth land holdings. If people do not manage their own land, LaDuke argues, they do not control their future. WELRP has regained more than 1,000 acres of land for the White Earth people and LaDuke hopes to bring approximately 30,000 acres of land under Ojibway control by 2010.

In addition to WELRP, LaDuke also co-founded the Indigenous Women's Network (IWN), an organization helping Indian women achieve change in their own communities. In addition, LaDuke and the Indigo Girls, along with other activists, formed Honor the Earth, which has raised over $500,000 for Native environmental issues to date.

LaDuke has testified at many government hearings and has published numerous articles in books, newspapers, journals, and magazines throughout the United States. Some of her numerous articles may be found in *Ecocide of Native American: Environmental Destruction of Indian Lands and Peoples* (1995) edited by Donald A. Grinde and Bruce E. Johansen; *A Gathering of Spirit: A Collection by North American Indian Women* (1988) edited by Beth Brant; the feminist magazine *off our backs* (February 1981); and the politically focused *Utne Reader* (January/February 1990). Her most recent book, *All Our Relations: Native Struggles for Land and Life* (1999), is dedicated to Native environmentalism.

While most of LaDuke's writing is non-fiction, she has published a novel entitled *Last Standing Woman* (1997), a story of three generations of women named Ishkwegaabawiikwe, or Last Standing Woman. Interwoven into this plot is the history of the White Earth Reservation and the Anishinabe community at large from 1860 to the present. The work addresses many of those issues LaDuke considers important in her life, including the social, economic, and racial injustices the Anishinabe faced and continue to face after contact with American colonists.

LaDuke was named one of the fifty most promising future leaders by *Time* in 1995 and ran for vice president of the United States with Ralph Nader for the Green Party in 1996 and 2000. She presently lives on the White Earth Reservation with her two children and continues her work.

### Francis La Flesche (1857–1932)
*Omaha anthropologist*

Francis La Flesche was the first American Indian to become a professional anthropologist. Born on the Omaha Reservation in Nebraska in 1857, La Flesche grew up in a family of distinguished individuals. His father, Joseph La Flesche (Iron Eye), was half-French but became a head chief and a force for change among the Omaha. (Because of his support for adopting Christianity and other European customs, his village became

known as "Place of the Make Believe White Men.") One of Francis's sisters, Susan, became the first Indian physician and an activist for social reform. Another, Susette (Bright Eyes), became well known as a lecturer, writer, and painter.

Francis himself was raised on the Omaha Reservation near Bellevue and learned the traditional customs of his tribe, participating in buffalo hunts and ceremonials. He began lecturing and interpreting for other Native speakers during the late 1870s and became an advisor and interpreter for the Bureau of Indian Affairs in 1881.

While living in Washington, D.C., La Flesche became acquainted with Alice Cunningham Fletcher and together they wrote the classic studies *A Study of Omaha Music* (1893) and *The Omaha Tribe* (1911). La Flesche also wrote an autobiographical book describing his life as a student in a Presbyterian mission school in northeastern Nebraska during the Civil War titled *The Middle Five* (1900). He also wrote *A Dictionary of the Osage Language* (1932).

### Susan La Flesche (1865–1915)
*Omaha physician and tribal leader*

Susan La Flesche has been labeled the first female Indian physician, although this label reflects a rather narrow, Western definition of medicine. In the late 1800s, La Flesche practiced medicine among the Omaha Indians, a Siouan-speaking nation living in Nebraska. She was also a political liaison for her people with the federal government and was active in the temperance movement. She is the sister of Susette La Flesche, a well-known activist.

La Flesche was the daughter of the Omaha chief Joseph La Flesche. Her mother, Mary Gale, was part Iowa, a tribe of Siouan-speaking Indians who were then living in Kansas. As a child, La Flesche studied with Christian missionaries. After attending the Elizabeth Institute for Young Ladies in New Jersey and the Hampton Institute in Virginia, she went on to receive her degree in medicine from the Women's Medical College of Pennsylvania in 1889.

In the years following, La Flesche practiced medicine on the Omaha Reservation, often traveling by buggy or on foot to reach patients unwilling or unable to come to her office. Besides her work doctoring for the Omaha, La Flesche was a temperance speaker and worked for the Women's National Indian Association. She married in 1894 and established a private practice in Bancroft, Nebraska, where she treated both Indian and non-Indian patients. After the death of her husband in 1905, La Flesche worked as a missionary at the

Blackbird Hills Presbyterian Church and continued to practice medicine. In her later years, La Flesche became a political advocate for her people and traveled to Washington, D.C., in 1910 to lobby the federal government for tribal land rights.

### Susette La Flesche (1854–1903)
*Omaha activist*

Susette La Flesche devoted much of her life to working for women's and Indian rights. Her father was Chief Joseph La Flesche, and she was a stepsister of Francis La Flesche, the famous Omaha anthropologist. La Flesche was also known by her translated Omaha name, Bright Eyes (Inshata Theumba).

Like her sister, Susan La Flesche, Susette was educated by Christian missionaries and later studied art at the University of Nebraska. From 1877 to 1879 she was a teacher and conducted a Sunday school for Omaha children. During that time La Flesche became involved in the plight of the Ponca and the controversy over their removal. In 1877, the Ponca were forced by the U.S. government to leave northern Nebraska and move to Indian Territory, present-day Oklahoma, and settle on a 101,000-acre reservation. The Ponca were greatly dissatisfied with the forced removal and petitioned Congress for permission to return to their homeland in Nebraska. They were eventually granted a 10,000-acre reservation in Nebraska, but lost their Oklahoma lands to U.S. settlers. In 1879 and 1880, La Flesche made a speaking tour of the eastern United States, with her brother Francis and Ponca chief Standing Bear on behalf of the Ponca. La Flesche was called "Bright Eyes" on the tour. The purpose of the tour was to publicize the conditions and plight of Standing Bear and his people. La Flesche continued to tour the United States speaking on Indian affairs. In 1881, she met and married philanthropist and journalist Thomas H. Tibbles. Throughout the late 1880s, La Flesche and her husband made numerous public appearances, including trips to England and Scotland, where they made pleas for improving the condition of the Omaha and Ponca. In 1894, La Flesche and her husband were supervising editors of *The Weekly Independent*, a Populist newspaper in Lincoln, Nebraska. With Standing Bear, La Flesche co-authored *Ploughed Under: The Story of an Indian Chief*.

### Moscelyne Larkin (1925–)
*Shawnee/Peoria ballerina*

Moscelyne Larkin is an internationally renowned ballerina of Russian and Shawnee/Peoria descent. Born in Miami, Oklahoma, on 14 January 1925, Larkin first studied ballet with her mother, Eva Matlagova, and later continued her studies in New York City. At the age of fifteen Larkin joined the Original Ballet Russe and became first soloist and then ballerina. She toured South America, the United States, Canada, and Europe as a member of the Original Ballet Russe, and in 1947 London critics described her as "the first ray of sunshine" after World War II.

Larkin then became a protege of Alexandra Danilova in the Ballet Russe de Monte Carlo and toured the world with Danilova's Great Moments of Ballet. In 1956, Larkin and her husband, Roman Jasinski, also an outstanding performer in the Ballet Russe, founded the Tulsa Civic Ballet, which evolved into the Tulsa Ballet Theatre, a nationally acclaimed ballet company of thirty-two dancers, with an extensive national touring schedule.

Larkin and her late husband have received several important awards and honors, including the prestigious *Dance Magazine* Award, which had previously been given to legendary dance artists such as Mikhail Baryshnikov, Rudolph Nureyev, and Fred Astaire. The couple were awarded honorary doctorates of fine arts from the University of Tulsa in 1991. Other honors bestowed on Larkin individually include the Governor's Arts Award, the Harweldin Award, and memberships in the Oklahoma Hall of Fame and the Tulsa County Historical Society Hall of Fame.

### Stella Leach (contemporary)
*Oglala Sioux/Colville activist*

Stella Leach was a central participant in the 1969 Indian occupation of Alcatraz Island in San Francisco Bay. The occupation was an attempt by urban Indians to attract national attention to the failure of U.S. government policy toward American Indians and was a symbolic cry for self-determination following the official government policy of termination of federal responsibility for Indian tribes.

Before the Alcatraz occupation Leach worked in the all-Indian Well Baby Clinic in Oakland, California, a clinic she had helped organize in 1963. In 1969, she took a three month leave of absence and went to join the Indian protesters on Alcatraz Island where she set up a health clinic for the Indian occupiers and their families. Because of her dedication to the occupation and the continuing need for a clinic, she received an additional three-month leave of absence from the Well Baby Clinic. Leach was elected to the Island Council, the elected governing body of Indian occupiers on Alcatraz Island. She was a recognized leader when the negotiations between the Indian occupiers and the federal government reached an impasse in 1970. When questioned about what she would like to see take place on the island she stated "to see the dreams of all of these young people who took this island come true. If a University is what they want then I am all for it. Whatever pleases our young people, because to me this is the greatest thing that has occurred in my generation. To see our Indian youth take their place in society and once again become warriors in our society." Leach's four sons, Mike, Gary, Leo, and David, three of whom were Vietnam veterans, accompanied Stella on the island and served as members of the island's security police.

## Greenwood LeFlore (1800–1865)
*Choctaw tribal leader*

By the middle 1820s, Greenwood LeFlore was one of the biggest owners of black slaves and one of the wealthiest men among the Choctaw. Of the three Choctaw political districts, he resided in the northwestern or Okla Falaya (The Long People) district. In 1826, LeFlore gained enough political support to replace the northwestern district chief, Robert Cole, on the grounds of lack of education and inability to resist U.S. land demands. LeFlore and other young chiefs wrote a constitution and advocated adoption of agriculture, education, and Christianity as ways to strengthen Choctaw resistance to U.S. territorial demands.

In January 1830, two district chiefs resigned and delegated their authority to LeFlore, who became principal chief. They argued that the traditional government of three equal chiefs inhibited government decision making and uniform law enforcement. By 1830, LeFlore was convinced that resistance to U.S. territorial expansion was not possible. He negotiated a treaty to cede Choctaw lands and migrate west, but it failed ratification by the U.S. Senate, which thought the treaty too generous. Meanwhile, Moshulatubee and Nitakechi, traditional leaders in the northeastern and southern districts, challenged LeFlore's authority as principal chief. LeFlore failed to suppress the rebellion and was forced to recognize the two district chiefs. Later in 1830, at the Treaty of Dancing Rabbit Creek, Choctaw leaders agreed to migrate to present-day Oklahoma. The Choctaw reacted by deposing the chiefs, but the United States refused to recognize any chiefs but those who signed the treaty. LeFlore did not migrate west, but remained on his plantation in the state of Mississippi, later serving in the state legislature.

## Left Hand (Nawat) (1840–1890s)
*Southern Arapaho tribal leader*

As one of the principal chiefs of the Southern Cheyenne, Left Hand tread the delicate line between advocating peace and defending against U.S. encroachment. He also represented his people in negotiations with the federal government in the early 1890s.

In 1864, Colonel John Chivington, a U.S. officer commanding some seven hundred soldiers, attacked the Southern Cheyenne and Southern Arapaho in order to open their hunting grounds for U.S. settlers. Left Hand tried to keep his people out of the conflict. He and his warriors were present with the Southern Cheyenne leader Black Kettle at the Battle of Sand Creek in November 1864, when about two hundred Cheyenne men, women, and children were indiscriminately killed by Chivington's troops. The incident was considered one of the most grievous of the Civil War. Left Hand was wounded during the shooting, but he refused to take up arms and return fire against Chivington's forces. His pacifist stance met with skepticism from some of his warriors, and a number of them adopted a more militant posture.

Left Hand became the principal chief of the Southern Arapaho in 1889, upon the death of Little Raven. In 1890, he agreed to allotment of Southern Cheyenne land in present-day Oklahoma, despite opposition from most Southern Cheyenne who preferred traditional sharing and collective ownership of land. Allotment settlements allowed the U.S. government to divide Indian land and distribute them to individual Indians for farms, usually about 160 acres for a head of household. Any surplus land available after allotment usually was sold to U.S. settlers. The allotment of land left most Indians in Oklahoma with a greatly reduced land base.

## David Lester (1941–)
*Creek economic development administrator*

David Lester has been active in government and private organizations that promote economic development in the Indian community. He was born in Claremore, Oklahoma, on 25 September 1941. In 1967 he received a bachelor's degree in political science and public administration from Brigham Young University in Provo, Utah. In Denver, Colorado, Lester became executive director of the Council of Energy Resource Tribes (CERT), a coalition of energy resource-rich Indian tribes that consults with and helps tribes negotiate more favorable contracts for the sale of minerals and energy resources like oil, gas, uranium, and coal. For two years, Lester served as vice-chairman of the

American Indian Scholarships, Inc., in Taos, New Mexico, an organization that provides grants to Indian college and graduate students. For eight years, he was president of the United Indian Development Association in Los Angeles, an organization that seeks to strengthen Indian business enterprise, usually in urban areas. Lester also served as commissioner to the Administration for Native Americans (ANA) at the U.S. Department of Health and Human Services in Washington, D.C. ANA provides federal administrative assistance and funds to tribal governments and urban Indian organizations in order to enhance their greater administrative capacities. Along with his interests in Indian economic development, Lester served as a member of the board of directors for the American Indian National Bank in Washington, a federally funded bank that provides economic development loans to reservation Indian businesses. Since 1992, he has been member of the board of trustees of the Institute of the American Indian Arts in Santa Fe, New Mexico, a member of the board of directors of the National Center for American Indian Enterprise Development in Mesa, Arizona, and also member of the Secretary of Energy's Advisory Board Task Force on Radioactive Waste Management.

Among his community activities, Lester has served as presidential appointee to the National Advisory Council on Minority Enterprise, which advised cabinet-level officials on strategies to stimulate minority business ownership, and he was human relations commissioner and chairman of the Los Angeles American Indian Commission. He is currently a trustee of the Institute of American Indian Arts.

Among Lester's honors and awards are the Americans for Indian Opportunity's Distinguished Services Peace Pipe Award, a proclamation of David Lester Day by the governor of Oklahoma, and the White Buffalo Council of American Indians' National Award for outstanding service to American Indians.

### Jane Lind (contemporary)
*Aleut actress, director, playwright, and choreographer*

Jane Lind was one of seven children born on her father's trapping grounds in Humpback Bay, near the village of Perryville on the Alaska Peninsula. She is of Aleut, Russian, and Swedish descent, and she was raised in the Russian Orthodox Church.

Lind began her professional career while a high school student at the Institute of American Indian Arts in Santa Fe, New Mexico. Her performances there led her to a variety of roles in famous theaters. In the early 1970s, she helped found the Native American Theater

Jane Lind.

Ensemble and performed in various productions, such as Hanay Geiogamah's *Body Indian*, John Vaccaro's *Night Club*, and Andrei Serban's *Fragments of a Greek Trilogy*. After appearing in *The Taming of the Shrew* at the Alaska Repertory Company in 1982, Lind helped teach drama in rural communities in Alaska as a way to help children improve their educational skills and self-esteem.

During the ensuing years, she has sung, acted, and directed in various productions across the United States and Europe, including a stage performance with Robert Redford. In numerous off-Broadway productions, she has played in Peter Brook's *The Birds*, Ellen Stewart's *Another Phaedra Via Hercules*, Dave Hunsaker's *The Summer Face Woman*, and Jack Gelber's *The Independence of Eddi Rose*. Lind has worked also for television productions such as *Footprints in Blood*, *Days Of Our Lives*, and *Ryan's Hope*.

In 1991, Lind appeared in the movie *Salmonberries*, directed by Percy Adlon, which won first place in a Canadian film festival. She played the Eskimo wife opposite Chuck Connors. In 1992, Lind was the female lead and choreographer for Robert Jonanson's production of *Black Elk Speaks*, a new version of Christopher Sergel's play, originally presented at the Folger Theater in Washington, D.C., and based on the book of the same name.

In 1993, she played the role of Many Tears in the mini-series *Return to Lonesome Dove*. In 1994, she won an award for best choreographer for the Denver Center Theater production of *Black Elk Speaks*. The next year, she received the First Americans in the Arts award for best actress for her performance in the production.

She also appeared in the TNT production of *Crazy Horse* (1996). In 1998, she wrote, directed, and choreographed *So They Say* at Seward, Alaska. In 2000, she directed Hanay Geiogamah's play *Grandma* at Sinte Gleska University.

## Marigold Linton (1936–)
*Cahuilla and Cupeno psychologist and educator*

Born on the Morongo Indian Reservation in southern California on 30 September 1936, Marigold Linton received a bachelor's degree in experimental psychology from the University of California, Riverside, in 1958. She then did graduate work at the University of Iowa from 1958 to 1960 and completed her doctorate in experimental psychology at the University of California, Los Angeles, in 1964.

Linton is an internationally recognized expert in the area of long-term memory and has published more than twenty research papers in this area, including "Transformations of Memory in Everyday Life" (1982) and "Memory as Chimera: the Changing Face of Memory" (1990). She is also co-author of a text entitled *The Practical Statistician: A Simplified Handbook of Statistics* (1975), which has sold more than 75,000 copies.

Linton was professor of psychology at San Diego State University (1964–1974) and at the University of Utah (1974–1986). She was director of the Office of Educational Services in the College of Education at Arizona State University (1986–1994) and director of American Indian Programs (1994–1998).

She has been director of American Indian Outreach at the University of Kansas since 1998 and was co-founder of the National Indian Education Association, served on the board of directors of SACNAS (Society for the Advancement of Chicanos and Native Americans in Science).

## Little Crow (1810–1863)
*Santee Sioux tribal leader*

Little Crow was a Santee Sioux and son of a chief of the Kaposia Band of Mdewakanton Santee, who live in western Minnesota. Upon his father's death in 1834,

Little Crow became the fifth hereditary chief to lead his people. He lived at the present site of south St. Paul, Minnesota, and had six wives and twenty-two children during the course of his life. Through much of his chieftaincy, Little Crow maintained good relations with the United States.

In 1851, Little Crow signed the Treaty of Mendota in 1851, which transferred much of the Santee land to the United States in exchange for a reservation on the upper Minnesota River, plus annuities in an annual payment. In 1858, Little Crow was part of a Sioux delegation that traveled to Washington, D.C., for further treaty negotiations with the U.S. government. His participation in the signing of the Treaty of Mendota angered many members of his tribe, and he was not nominated as a tribal representative to the general council.

In August 1862, the Santee Sioux rose up against the settlers of Minnesota when the government annuity, guaranteed by the treaty of 1851, was delayed. The Sioux were hungry and impatient, while U.S. government agents stole and delayed distribution of necessary food to the Santee Sioux. Little Crow opposed the uprising at first, but eventually joined it and led several successful skirmishes. The Santee opened their war with raids on trading posts and settlements. As many as four hundred Minnesotans died the first day. Little Crow led an assault on Fort Ridgely where he lost approximately a hundred warriors before calling off the siege.

After a protracted battle at Birch Coulee, thirteen miles from Fort Ridgely, many of the surviving Santee withdrew to Dakota Territory or Canada, Little Crow among them. He died in July 1863 on a horse-stealing expedition out of Canada to Minnesota, shot by settlers who were paid bounties for Sioux scalps.

## Little Turtle Michikinikwa (1752–1812)
*Miami-Mahican tribal leader*

Little Turtle was the leader of a Miami Band located near present-day Fort Wayne, Indiana. He was principal war chief of his people during the 1780s and 1790s.

After the American Revolution, a number of wars broke out in the Old Northwest between the Indians living in this region and the growing number of white settlers. Between 1783 and 1790 ongoing skirmishes and attacks made the region a flash point for Indian relations. In 1790, President George Washington ordered federal troops into the region to quell the attacks. Their staunchest opponent was Little Turtle, principal war chief of the regional tribes. During his initial encounters with the federal troops, Little Turtle perfected military tactics, making the best use of concealment, and quick, short attacks. The methods were devastatingly effective in two major encounters against Generals Josiah Harmar and Arthur St. Clair. On 3 November 1791, Little Turtle and his forces surprised St. Clair leaving behind over 600 dead, and almost 300 wounded. It was the worst defeat suffered by U.S. forces against Indians.

Washington's response was to field a third army, this time under the leadership of a seasoned revolutionary war veteran, General Anthony Wayne. Wayne planned his attack carefully and cautiously. Little Turtle's warriors, with the encouragement of British officials, were confident of victory. Little Turtle himself, however, counseled peace in the face of Wayne's well-organized campaign. The attack came in an area known as Fallen Timbers. Wayne's forces took so long to get to the battle that many of Little Turtle's troops had left the battle site. Though the Battle of Fallen Timbers was short, with only a few casualties, it was a disheartening defeat for Little Turtle and his followers, who realized that their British supporters were not going to come to their aid. After the battle, Wayne proceeded to destroy Indian villages and farmlands.

The defeat changed Little Turtle's outlook. A year later Wayne dictated the terms of the Treaty of Greenville, in which Little Turtle ceded large sections of Ohio and parts of Indiana. Little Turtle also signed a number of treaties in Fort Wayne in 1803 and 1809, and put his signature on the Treaty of Vincennes in 1805. Little Turtle spent the later part of his life traveling to eastern cities, where he met some of his former adversaries, including George Washington. The former U.S. adversary was granted an annual pension by the government and returned to his homeland on the Maumee River. Even the pleas of Tecumseh to join his cause could not persuade Little Turtle to take up arms again. The former war chief was committed to peace, and encouraged his people to take up farming and abstain from alcohol. He died in 1812 while at Fort Wayne.

## Little Wolf (circa 1820–1904)
*Northern Cheyenne tribal leader*

Little Wolf was a chief of the Cheyenne military society known as the Bowstring Soldiers and, along with Dull Knife, was a war leader of the Northern Cheyenne. Little Wolf established his reputation as a war chief in his battles against the Comanche and Kiowa.

During the 1866–1868 war for the Bozeman Trail, Little Wolf fought alongside the Sioux leaders Crazy Horse and Gall in an attempt to protect Sioux lands in present-day Montana and Wyoming. In May 1868, Little Wolf was one of the signers of the Fort Laramie Treaty, which obligated the U.S. government to vacate the forts along the Bozeman Trail. In July 1868, after the Indians had driven the soldiers from the Powder River country, Little Wolf and his followers occupied Fort Phil Kearny (one of the Bozeman Trail forts in present-day northern Wyoming), abandoning and burning it one month later.

When the Southern Cheyenne surrendered in 1875, however, the government concentrated on uniting the two Indian tribes onto one Indian reservation, primarily because gold was discovered in the Northern Cheyenne area of the Black Hills in present-day South Dakota. Little Wolf was one of the most active war chiefs in the War for the Black Hills of 1876–1877. He was shot seven times during the Battle of Dull Knife (in present day Wyoming) in November 1876 but survived the wounds.

The Northern Cheyenne were not willing to live in Indian Territory (Oklahoma) and repeatedly tried to return to their homeland in present-day Wyoming and Montana. Little Wolf joined Dull Knife, the Cheyenne chief, in the flight of the Northern Cheyenne from their assigned reservation in Indian Territory and proved difficult to capture. Dull Knife surrendered in October 1878, but Little Wolf successfully evaded government troops until March 1879, when he surrendered. The soldiers forced Little Crow and his remaining warriors to march from North Dakota south to Indian Territory. Though Little Wolf and Dull Knife escaped during the forced march, they finally surrendered in 1879.

Little Wolf became an army scout for General Nelson Miles and was allowed to remain in the Tongue River country of Montana. In 1880, he killed a fellow Cheyenne and lost his standing as chief. As was the Cheyenne tradition, he went into voluntary exile until his death in 1904.

## J. Wilton Littlechild (1944–)
*Cree legislator and athlete*

Willie Littlechild was first elected to the Canadian House of Commons in 1988 after a landslide victory in Wetaskiwin, Alberta, a constituency on the outskirts of Edmonton. Littlechild was born on the Ermineskin Indian Reserve in Hobbema, Alberta, where he attended grade school. He then went to St. Anthony's College and subsequently to the University of Alberta, both located in Edmonton. At the University of Alberta, Littlechild obtained bachelor's and master's degrees in physical education before entering law school and graduating with a bachelor of law degree in 1976.

Before his election to the House of Commons, Littlechild ran his own law office and was involved in a number of different business ventures. He also devoted much of his time attempting to foster a sense of physical and mental well-being among his people through sports and physical exercise. He assisted in the organization and development of the Indian Sports Olympics, which helped to create sports and recreation programs on Indian reserves. He has been active in a host of organizations devoted to sports among aboriginal people, including the Native Golf Association, the Indian Hockey Council, the Native Summer Games, the National Indian Activities Association, and the National Indian Sport Council. He has coached basketball, football, hockey, and a swim team. The Willie Littlechild Award, presented by the Indian Association of Alberta in his honor, rewards Native students in Alberta for outstanding contributions to their communities as well as for athletic and academic excellence.

In his elected capacity, Littlechild has sat on a range of parliamentary committees, including aboriginal affairs and justice and the solicitor general committees. Littlechild is married and has three children, all of whom share their father's enthusiasm for athletics.

He has been inducted into three Sports Halls of Fame and the University of Alberta Wall of Honour. He recently became the first two-time F"ete Excellence Laurette winner for sports at the United Nations in Geneva to go with two Tom Longboat Trophies as the most outstanding Indian Athlete of the Year in Canada. In 1999, he received the highest Canadian civilian award, the Order of Canada.

### Kevin Locke (1954–)
*Lakota/Anishinabe musician and dancer*

Kevin Locke is a performer and teacher interested in preserving Indian, especially Lakota, artistic traditions. Born in 1954 on the Standing Rock Reservation in South Dakota, Locke is a member of the Lakota tribe. Fluent in Lakota (a subgroup of the Sioux) languages and a preeminent traditional flute player and hoop dancer, he received master's degrees in educational administration and community education from the University of South Dakota.

Locke is also a popular performer and storyteller, working to ensure that his cultural heritage survives and prospers. He has traveled throughout the world, performing and lecturing in more than seventy countries, his goal being to show people, through the Lakota hoop dance, that humanity can be unified through an appreciation of diversity. Locke uses twenty-eight hoops to tell a story, depicting such things as flowers, butterflies, stars, the sun, and an eagle. The hoops represent

Actor Kevin Locke.

unity, and their colors—black, red, yellow, and white—represent the four directions, the four winds, the four seasons, and the four complexions of people's skin.

In 1982, Locke performed in the play *In Deo* and in *The Night of the First Americans* at the Kennedy Center in Washington, D.C. In his performances, he uses a traditional flute, which for the Lakota/Dakota Nations is the essence of the wind. The flute gives voice to the beauty of the land, and its sound is the sound of the wind rustling grass and leaves. The instrument consists of seven notes; four represent the directions, one represents the heavens, another the earth, and the last one represents the place where the six come together—the heart of the people listening to it.

Locke also organizes children's interactive and participatory workshops involving games, music, dancing, and storytelling, as well as lectures on American Indian issues, value and belief systems, social structure, and education. In the early 1990s, he participated in various festivals and programs such as the Hunter Mountain Festival in Hunter Mountain, New York; the Frontier Folklife Festival in St. Louis, Missouri; and the First Annual Storytelling Festival in Reno, Nevada. In 1992, he was appointed a delegate for Earth Summit 1992, an international environmental conference held in Rio De

Janeiro, Brazil. Locke was a featured performer at the 1996 United Nations Habitat II Conference in Turkey.

In 1990, Locke was awarded a National Heritage Fellowship by the National Endowment for the Arts for his contributions to the preservation of his cultural heritage and for his efforts to make it known and appreciated around the world.

### Arlinda Faye Locklear (1951–)
*Lumbee lawyer*

Arlinda Locklear is an attorney with wide experience in federal Indian law and in complex federal litigation at all levels, including two successful appearances before the United States Supreme Court. Locklear is an enrolled member of the Lumbee tribe of North Carolina, a tribe living mostly in North and South Carolina. In 1973, she received a B.A. degree with high honors in political science from the College of Charleston in South Carolina, and in 1976 a law degree from Duke University School of Law in Durham, North Carolina. In 1990, she was awarded the Doctor of Humane Letters from New York State University.

In 1975 and 1976, Locklear was the winner of the Moot Court Competition at the New York City Bar Association. This competition is a reproduction of a trial based on an actual case, in which students from different law schools confront one another; the most outstanding among them eventually reach the national competition and confront real judges.

Since the beginning of her career, Locklear has worked in the area of federal Indian law. From 1976 to 1987, she was employed as a staff attorney with NARF, the Native American Rights Fund, where she had primary responsibility for major litigation on behalf of tribes located in Arizona, Florida, Nebraska, New York, South Dakota, Wisconsin, and Virginia.

Locklear was the first Indian woman to argue a case before the United States Supreme Court. In 1983, she argued *Solem v. Bartlett*, which challenged the jurisdiction of the state of South Dakota to prosecute a member of the Cheyenne River Sioux tribe for on-reservation conduct. She won the case unanimously. In 1985, she argued her second case in the Supreme Court, *Oneida Indian Nation v. County of Oneida*, in which the Oneida of New York sought to reclaim lands from control of the local county government. In this case, she formulated a theory under federal common law that allows tribes to claim title to their homelands whenever Indian land was taken without the consent of the United States government. Because of her successes in these cases, Locklear is recognized as the leading authority on tribal land claims.

Locklear has published several articles on legal claims: "The Oneida Claims: A Legal Overview," in *Iroquois Land Claims* (Syracuse University Press, 1988); "The Historic Quality of Nation-to-Nation Relationship," in *Northeast Indian Quarterly* (1988); and "The Allotment of the Oneida Reservation and Its Legal Ramifications," in *The Oneida Indian Experience: Two Perspectives* (1988).

### Frederick Olgilve Loft (1862–1934)
*Mohawk activist and soldier*

Fred Loft was known for his vision of a unified organization speaking for Indian people from coast to coast in Canada. Born in Grand River in Mohawk territory in southwestern Ontario, Loft was largely self-educated and served as an officer for the Canadian army during World War I. In addition to enlisting himself (by claiming to be ten years younger than he was at the time), Loft brought with him a number of other Ontario. They were assigned to the forestry corps, and Loft was commissioned lieutenant for the duration of the war. During his months in service in France, Loft met other enlisted Indian men from Canada and discovered that, despite their differences, they shared similar difficulties when dealing with Canadian authorities. Before returning home, he met King George V of England and spent some time talking to him in private.

Loft began to realize his vision of a unified Indian organization as soon as he returned home. He created the League of Indians of Canada and was elected president-chief in 1919. He spent several years writing to Indian people across the country informing them of the aims of the league, which were to protect Indian rights to ancestral lands and to seek a greater voice in governmental decisions. Canadian authorities did not take kindly to Loft's organizational efforts, and they unsuccessfully sought to persuade Loft to renounce his heritage in return for the right to vote and own property. In the early 1920s, Loft traveled to Saskatchewan and Alberta to meet with Plains Indians about the league. His wife of many years, Affa Northcote Gears, fell ill in 1923, and they moved to her hometown of Chicago so she could recuperate. Loft tried to run the league from Chicago, but his advancing years, lack of resources, and continued harassment by Canadian authorities made it almost impossible to continue.

### John Logan (Tachnechdorus) (1725–1780)
*Mingo (Cayuga) tribal leader*

John Logan was a Mingo leader during the Lord Dunmore's War of 1774, when the Mingo and Shawnee

Nations tried to block Virginia settlers from crossing the line set by the Proclamation of 1763, which forbade colonial settlement beyond the crest of the Appalachian mountains. Despite the proclamation, settlers and merchants continued to swarm into the Mississippi and Ohio Valleys. During this era a number of Shawnee and Mingo allies attempted to withstand the onrush. The Mingo were a group of Iroquois who moved to live and trap in the Ohio Valley and left their homeland in present-day upstate New York.

Logan (Tachnechdorus) was the leader of the bands of Iroquois-speaking Mingo who lived near the headwaters of the Ohio River in western Pennsylvania. He was born a Cayuga, an Iroquois nation, near the Susquehanna River. Over the years Tachnechdorus was given the name Mingo or The Great Mingo. Mingo is the tribal name given to Iroquois living in Pennsylvania and Ohio. After moving to the Ohio region, Logan became a strong supporter of peaceful relations with the colonists. However, when members of his family were massacred for no apparent reason by settlers in 1774, Logan adopted a militant stance and began a series of raids against settlers throughout the trans-Appalachian region. His actions were abetted by British allies and the Shawnee leader, Cornstalk. Logan and Cornstalk fought together in what is known as Lord Dunmore's War. After their defeat in 1774, at the Battle of Point Pleasant, Pennsylvania, Logan refused to attend a peace conference at Scioto, Ohio. It is believed (though some doubt its authenticity) that he delivered an eloquent letter much admired at the time and later cited by Thomas Jefferson. Logan continued his attacks during the American War for Independence. He was killed while returning from Detroit in 1780.

### Charles Loloma (1921–1991)
*Hopi artist*

Charles Loloma's jewelry is among the most distinctive in the world. The originality of his designs stems from the combination of non-traditional materials, like gold and diamonds, with typical Indian materials like turquoise. He received great recognition as a potter, silversmith, and designer.

Loloma was born in Hotevilla, Arizona, in 1921. He grew up and was educated on the Hopi Reservation in northern Arizona; he attended the Hopi High School in Oraibi and the Phoenix Indian High School in Phoenix. In 1939, Loloma painted the murals for the Federal Building on Treasure Island in San Francisco Bay, as part of the Golden Gate International Exposition. The following year, he was commissioned by the Indian Arts and Crafts Board to paint the murals for the

Museum of Modern Art in New York. Also in 1940, Loloma was drafted into the army, where he spent four years working as a camouflage expert in the Aleutian Islands off the Alaskan coast. After his discharge, he attended the School for American Craftsman at Alfred University in New York, a well-known center for ceramic arts. This was an unprecedented move on Loloma's part, since ceramics was traditionally a woman's art among the Hopi, but it was also indicative of his future course.

In 1949, Loloma received a Whitney Foundation Fellowship to study the clays of the Hopi area. After that, he and his wife set up a shop in the newly opened Kiva Craft Center in Scottsdale, Arizona, which was intended to become a center for high-quality arts and crafts. From 1954 to 1958, he taught pottery during the summers at Arizona State University, and in 1962 he became head of the plastic arts and sales departments at the newly established Institute of American Indian Arts in Santa Fe, New Mexico.

In 1963, Loloma exhibited his work in a private showing in Paris and then returned to the institute in Santa Fe until 1965, when he moved back to the Hopi Reservation in northern Arizona. By this time, his reputation as a jeweler was well established, and his pieces were winning first prizes in Indian arts competitions. By the mid-1970s, his jewelry was exhibited throughout the country and in Europe. Loloma spent the rest of his years on the Hopi Reservation, where he continued working and teaching his art to several apprentices. He was one of the first prominent Indian craftsmen who worked outside the traditional Indian influence; a variety of influences resulted in his unique personal style, which has been widely imitated among Indian artisans.

### Linda Lomahaftewa (1947–)
*Hopi-Choctaw painter and educator*

Linda Lomahaftewa, a painter whose works highlight the culture of the Plains Indians, is professor of painting and drawing at the Institute of American Indian Arts (IAIA), in Santa Fe, New Mexico. She was born on 3 July 1947 in Phoenix, Arizona. In 1962, she entered IAIA, where, in 1965, she received her diploma in art. She also received a bachelor of fine arts degree and a master of fine arts degree (1971) at the San Francisco Art Institute.

Since 1970, Lomahaftewa has been an art educator, first as a teaching assistant at the San Francisco Art Institute and, from 1971 to 1973, as assistant professor of Native American art at California State College in

Linda Lomahaftewa.

Tsianina Lomawaima.

Sonoma. From 1974 to 1976, she was an instructor of painting and drawing in the Native American Studies Program at the University of California in Berkeley.

During the 1970s, Lomahaftewa's paintings were shown in more than forty exhibitions, including "New Directions," an Institute of American Indian Arts alumni traveling exhibition, and "Contemporary Native American Artists" at the Alternative Center for International Arts in New York City in 1977. In 1977, her works were also presented in the exhibition "Eleven Women Artists" at the Elaine Horwitch Gallery in Santa Fe, New Mexico.

Lomahaftewa's paintings were featured in a solo show in 1978 at the C. N. Gorman Museum at the University of California at Davis. Her work was exhibited in the "Pintura Amerindia Contemporanea" tour, organized by the United States Communication Agency in 1979. In 1980, she exhibited her paintings at the special exhibition organized by the Indian Arts and Crafts Board's Southern Plains Indian Museum and Crafts Center in Anadarko, Oklahoma. Lomahaftewa was listed among other prominent figures of the contemporary Native American artistic scene in two editions of *Who's Who in American Indian Arts*, in 1976 and in 1978.

## K. Tsianina Lomawaima (1955–)
*Creek anthropologist*

K. Tsianina Lomawaima is professor of American Indian studies at the University of Arizona. She received a bachelor's degree in anthropology in 1976 from the University of Arizona, earned a master of arts degree in 1979, and a doctorate in anthropology from Stanford University in 1987. From 1979 to 1980, she was the curriculum developer on the Northern Cheyenne Reservation at Lame Deer Public School in Lame Deer, Montana, and then was a lecturer in Native American studies at the University of California at Berkeley. From 1988 to 1994, Lomawaima taught anthropology and American Indian studies at the University of Washington in Seattle.

Professor Lomawaima's publications appear mainly in the *American Indian Quarterly*, where she has published "Oral Histories from Chilocco Indian Agricultural School, 1920 to 1940" (1987), as well as several book reviews and review essays. Her first book, *They Called It Prairie Light: The Story of Chilocco Indian School* (1993), won the 1993 North American Indian Prose Award, and 1995 Critic's Choice Award of the American Educational Association.

Lomawaima has received numerous fellowships, honors, and grants, such as the Phillips Fund research grant from the American Philosophical Society in 1983, the Summer Research Grant from the College of Arts and Sciences of the University of Washington, Seattle, in 1989, and a Distinguished Teaching Award from the University of Washington in 1991. In 1992 she earned a grant from the Institute for Ethnic Studies for a study entitled "Southwest Pueblos and the Atchinson Topeka and Santa Fe Railway."

## Lone Wolf (Guipago) (1820–1879)
*Kiowa tribal leader*

During the 1860s and 1870s, Lone Wolf became one of his tribe's most respected band chiefs and warriors. He was one of the signers of the Medicine Lodge Treaty of 1867 and later fought a series of military campaigns against U.S. forces.

During the first part of his life, Lone Wolf came to negotiate with U.S. agents in a spirit of peace and hope for close, friendly ties. In 1863, he visited President Abraham Lincoln as part of a delegation of southern Plains Indian leaders. In 1866, he became principal chief of the Kiowa. The election of Lone Wolf was a compromise between the militant Satanta and the pacifist Kicking Bird. As chief, Lone Wolf signed the Medicine Lodge Treaty of 1867, which established the boundaries of the combined Kiowa and Comanche Reservation in present-day Oklahoma. When members of his tribe refused to comply with the treaty, Lone Wolf was taken hostage by U.S. authorities.

Although Lone Wolf traveled to Washington, D.C., in 1872 to negotiate a peace settlement, the death of his son at the hands of federal soldiers in 1873 pushed him into war. For the next two years, he and other tribal leaders of the Southern Plains met federal and state troops in a number of consequential engagements. Lone Wolf participated in the Red River War (1874–1875) fighting alongside Quanah Parker, the Comanche leader. During the middle 1870s, the Kiowa and Comanche feared that the wholesale slaughter of buffalo by U.S. hunters would destroy their economic base and way of life. The Kiowa and Comanche started the Red River War to discourage buffalo hunters from killing the buffalo herds. After the battle at Palo Duro Canyon in September 1874, however, Lone Wolf's supply of horses and tipis was devastated. He was forced to surrender at Fort Sill in the Indian Territory in 1875. Lone Wolf, along with Mamanti, a Kiowa spiritual leader, was sent to Fort Marion in Florida. (The exiles had been handpicked by Kicking Bird, whom U.S. officials had appointed Kiowa chief.) Lone Wolf returned to his homeland in 1878 and died one year later of malaria.

## Buffalo Child Long Lance (Sylvester Long) (1891–1932)
*Catawba/Cherokee actor*

Buffalo Child Long Lance was an author, newspaper reporter, and movie actor of the 1920s and 1930s. He was born Sylvester Long in Winston, North Carolina, in 1891. His father, Joe Long, was part Catawba Indian and part Black. Long Lance attended a school for Blacks until the age of twelve, at which time he joined a Wild West show. At the age of eighteen, he applied for admission to Carlisle Indian School in Pennsylvania, enrolling as a Cherokee.

In 1915, Long Lance was a candidate to West Point, but instead he went north to join the Canadian army, as that country was already at war with Germany. Long Lance served overseas with the Canadian Expeditionary Force and rose to the rank of staff sergeant. He was wounded twice in action. After discharge, he became a reporter for the *Calgary Daily Herald*, traveling across western Canada and writing numerous articles on the Native peoples. During this time, he became a friend of Archdeacon S. H. Middleton, the Anglican missionary on the Blood Reserve in western Canada, who accepted Long Lance completely as a Cherokee Indian and introduced him to many Indian elders. In 1922, Middleton arranged for Long Lance to be inducted as an honorary chief of the Blood tribe. An article in the 14 February 1922 *Calgary Herald* was entitled "Cherokee Given a High Honor by Blood Indians."

In 1928, Long Lance published his autobiography, *Long Lance: The Autobiography of a Blackfoot Indian Chief* (Cosmopolitan Book Corporation of New York). As a result of the ensuing publicity, Long Lance was invited to star in the film, *The Silent Enemy*, which was sponsored by the American Museum of Natural History and released by Paramount Pictures. Following *The Silent Enemy*, Long Lance was invited to star in a talking film dealing with the exploits of an Indian flying ace during the Great War. He died in 1932 in California, while preparing for his Hollywood debut.

## Looking Glass (1823–1877)
*Nez Percé tribal leader*

Looking Glass was the son of Apash Wyakaikt, who was also called Looking Glass because of the small trade mirror he wore as a pendant. The pendant was passed on to Looking Glass the younger. Looking Glass the elder participated with Old Joseph in the Walla Walla Council of 1855 as one of the chiefs who refused to sign the treaty proposed by Governor Isaac Stevens of the Washington Territory.

Looking Glass the younger, leader of the Asotian Band of the Nez Percé, refused to sign a second treaty in 1863 that would have further reduced the tribe's land. While Looking Glass had been appointed Nez Percé tribal war chief in 1848, he hoped to avoid war with the United States. He turned militant on 1 July 1877, when a combined force of army regulars and volunteer militia attacked his camp near the forks of the Clearwater Creek in present-day Idaho.

Looking Glass's band joined with the band of Nez Percé leader Joseph, who had also been attacked on June 17. United, they fought General Oliver Howard at the Battle of the Clearwater on 11 July 1877. The Nez Percé now counted seven hundred among their ranks, but at least five hundred of these were women, children, or men too old to fight. Still, the Nez Percé warriors outfought and outflanked the larger Howard force.

Following the Battle of Clearwater, the majority of the Nez Percé chose to head east through the Bitterroot Mountains to seek a military alliance with the Crow. Looking Glass was given overall command of the journey. To his dismay, he learned that some Crow were scouting for the U.S. Army. Counseling with other leaders, Looking Glass decided to lead his band northward through Montana Territory to Canada. They now planned to seek the assistance of Sitting Bull, the famous Sioux leader, who had escaped across the border that same year. During the next two weeks, the trail- and battle-weary Nez Percé outmaneuvered and outfought the army while they wound their way through the Montana wilderness toward the Canadian border. Finally, army troops led by Colonel Nelson Miles caught up to Looking Glass and the Nez Percé near the Bear Paw Mountains, where they laid siege to the Indian camp. Howard's troops arrived on the scene on October 5, forcing an ultimate surrender by the Nez Percé. Looking Glass, who refused to surrender, was struck by a stray bullet and killed.

## Phil Lucas (contemporary)
*Choctaw producer and director*

Phil Lucas is the owner of Phil Lucas Productions, Inc., an independent film production company that develops projects for motion picture and television productions. In 1970, he received a bachelor's degree in science and visual communication from Western Washington University in Bellingham, Washington. From 1979 to 1981, he was the co-producer, writer, and co-director of a five-part Public Broadcasting Corporation series, *Images of Indians*, which explored the problem of Indian stereotypes as portrayed and perpetuated by Hollywood Western movies. The series won a Special Achievement Award in Documentary Film in 1980 from the American Indian Film Institute and the Prix Italia Award in 1981.

His productions deal with accurate portraits of Indians, as in *Nez Percé: Portrait of People* (1982), a twenty-three-minute color film on the culture and history of the Nez Percé tribe. His commitment to spreading information about issues affecting the Indian community has been strengthened in recent years through the production of documentaries on the AIDS virus, and drug and alcohol prevention, such as *Circle of Warriors* (1989) and *Lookin' Good* (1988). Alcoholism is treated also in *Where We've Been And Where We're Going* (1983), a two-part series produced for the University of Lethbridge in Alberta, Canada. In *I'm Not Afraid of Me* (1990), Lucas presents the story of a Native woman and her daughter, both of whom have AIDS.

His international television credits include two documentary series, *The Native Americans* for TBS in 1994 and *Storytellers of the Pacific* in 1996. Lucas also produced *The Broken Chain*, a 1995 TBS movie about the Iroquois Confederacy. The movie starred Wes Studi, Pierce Brosnan, and Buffy Saint-Marie.

Lucas lives in Issaquah, Washington, with his wife Nancy and five children. He is currently developing a major PBS series about Native Americans in the twenty-first century.

## Phillip Lujan (contemporary)
*Kiowa-Taos Pueblo lawyer*

Phillip Doren Lujan grew up in the Rainy Mountain area of Kiowa country in western Oklahoma. In 1970, Lujan graduated from Washington University with a degree in sociology, and in 1974 he graduated from the New Mexico University School of Law in Albuquerque, New Mexico. After graduation, Lujan worked as a staff attorney for the Native American Legal Defense and Education Fund in Albuquerque, New Mexico, and from 1974 to 1976, he was a staff attorney for the American Indian Law Center at the University of New Mexico Law School. In 1976 and 1977, he was director of the Special Scholarship Program in Law at the New Mexico University Law School.

Lujan has served numerous tribal communities throughout his career as chief prosecutor for the Oklahoma Indian Affairs Commission for the Court of Indian Offenses of Western Oklahoma for the Anadarko (Oklahoma) area (1979–1981), as magistrate for the Court of Indian Offenses at the Concho Agency (1984–1986), and magistrate for the Court of Indian Offenses at the Shawnee Agency (1984–1985).

He has served as chief judge for the Court of Indian Claims for Western Oklahoma (1986–1992), chief judge for the Potowatomi tribe (1986–1993), and was chief judge for the Sac and Fox tribe (1987–1993). He currently balances tribal judicial duties and an associate professorship of communications at the University of Oklahoma.

## Oren Lyons (1930–)
*Onondaga tribal leader and scholar*

Oren Lyons (Joagquisho) is a member of the Onondaga Nation Council of Chiefs of the Six Nations of the Iroquois Confederacy, a traditional Faithkeeper of the Turtle Clan, and professor of Indigenous studies (American studies) at the State University of New York at Buffalo.

Born in 1930 and raised on the Seneca and Onondaga reservations, Chief Lyons attended Syracuse University, earning All-American honors in lacrosse, and obtained a bachelor of fine arts in 1958.

Chief Lyons serves on the executive committee of the Global Forum of Spiritual and Parliamentary Leaders on Human Survival, is a notable member of the Traditional Circle of Indian Elders, and helped establish the United Nations' Working Group on Indigenous Populations.

He has authored numerous books including *Exiled in the Land of the Democracy, Indian Nations, and the U.S. Constitution* & as well as *Voice of Indigenous Peoples* (1992) and *Native People Address the United Nations* (1994).

His honors and awards include the Ellis Island Congressional Medal of Honor, National Audubon Award for the Environment, and the First International Earth Day Award.

## Mark Andrew Macarro (1963–)
*Luiseño tribal leader and gaming spokesperson*

Being chairman of the Pechanga Band of Luiseño Indians' Tribal Council at the turn of the century is not easy. Not only is Mark Macarro asked to make crucial decisions for his Southern California tribe, but he was also the acting spokesman for California Indian gaming rights. Propositions 5 and 1A, the state's Indian casino initiatives, passed in 1998 and 2000, respectively, showing Macarro's well-honed and influential political abilities. These initiatives ensure that California Indian

Mark Macarro.

tribes may operate casinos on their lands without state interference.

Born in Colton, California, located in San Bernadino County, Macarro is one of four children of working-class parents, Martha and Leslie. His father worked as a landscape laborer, a barber, and a correctional peace officer for a state youth authority in Chino, California. In the late 1980s, Leslie was killed while chasing a prisoner who was trying to flee. It is through his father that Macarro traces his indigenous roots.

After graduating from high school in 1981, Macarro attended San Bernadino Valley College and later the University of California, Santa Barbara, from which he graduated with a bachelor's degree in political science. Shortly after graduation, Macarro was accepted into the Naval Aviation Officer Candidate School in Florida. After just a few days in Florida, however, Macarro was physically disqualified from the school because his "butt-to-knee length" was too short. The future tribal leader returned home and taught for a year as a middle- and high-school substitute teacher.

In the mid-1980s, Macarro was hired as the federal grants administrator for the Pechanga Indian Reservation near Temecula, California. Soon after he ran the Soboba tribe's reservation school, and became library and museum manager at the Rincon Indian Reservation in San Diego County.

Then, in 1995, Macarro was chosen to replace a Pechanga tribal chair who had left his post mid-term. The same year Pechanga opened their entertainment center, Macarro was elected tribal chair. During this time, Macarro also married wife Elizabeth in 1991. They have since had two children, David and Rebecca.

In addition to remaining active in the Native political realm, Macarro maintains ties to more traditional practices. Among other activities, he sings Nukwaanish songs in Luiseño at important ceremonial events.

Now that Native gaming rights are ensured in California, Macarro is trying to protect traditional tribal customs during this period of economic growth. Macarro hopes to use gaming at Pechanga to develop other forms of economic development and to enhance tribal institutions that may need improvement.

## Peter MacDonald (1928–)
*Navajo tribal leader and businessperson*

Peter MacDonald is probably best known for his tenacious and imaginative defense of Navajo land and energy resource rights. The Navajo occupy extensive parts of Arizona and New Mexico (14 million acres) and have the largest population of any tribe in the United States or Canada.

He was born on the Navajo Reservation at a place called Teec Nos Pos, and Navajo was his first language. His father died when he was only two, and MacDonald was forced to leave school after the seventh grade to herd sheep and work. Later, during World War II, he served in the marines and became one of the highly esteemed Navajo Code Talkers, whose messages in the Native language confused the Japanese military cryptographers during the Pacific campaigns. On being discharged, MacDonald resumed his education, getting a bachelor's degree from Bacone Junior College in Muskogee, Oklahoma, and earning a degree in electrical engineering from the University of Oklahoma in 1957.

In 1963, MacDonald returned to the Navajo Reservation, first to serve on the New Mexico Economic Development Advisory Board and later to become director of the Office of Navajo Economic Opportunity (ONEO). His aggressive management brought in more than $20 million in federal grants between the years 1965 and 1968. These successes led to his election as tribal chairman in 1970, and during his three terms in office, he fought to renegotiate the leases through which outside industrial interests gained access to minerals on Navajo land and sought a more favorable policy for controlling Colorado River water rights. MacDonald also worked to keep industrial development under tribal control and tried to expand Navajo influence by encouraging the people to participate in elections.

MacDonald has received numerous honorary awards and served on many advisory boards, both in his capacity as a political leader and as an engineer.

Over the years, MacDonald has been an outspoken critic of the Bureau of Indian Affairs. His administrations faced serious issues, such as the land dispute between the Navajo and Hopi, and were subject to charges of fraud and favoritism. But his achievements in energy use management and Navajo self-determination are hard to question.

He is currently in the seventh year of a fourteen-year sentence for conspiracy to overthrow the Navajo Nation government and bribery. He was convicted of profiting from a deal in which real estate agents sold a ranch near Seligman, Arizona, to business associates of his for $26.2 million. The next day, they sold it to the Navajo Nation for $33.4 million, and he was paid a small sum of the profits. MacDonald, now seventy, was pardoned by the Navajo Nation Council in 1995 and is seeking a medical release from prison due to health concerns.

## Edna Ahgeak MacLean (contemporary)
*Iñupiaq administrator and scholar*

Edna Ahgeak MacLean is president of Ilisagvik College, in Barrow, Alaska. She earned her master's in bilingual education from the University of Washington and received her doctorate in education from Stanford University. MacLean also did graduate study in Greenlandic Eskimo at Aarhus University and received her teaching credentials from University of California, Berkeley.

While at the University of Alaska, Fairbanks, MacLean was awarded tenure and promoted to associate professor of Iñupiaq Eskimo. For several years, she was the special assistant for Rural and Alaska Native Education to the State of Alaska Commissioner of Education.

A Native speaker of Iñupiaq, Edna MacLean has developed many documents used extensively as references and guides to the Iñupiaq language and is well-known for her numerous presentations and workshops at conferences and seminars.

MacLean received the Alaska Federation of Natives Higher Education Award (1995), and has been elected as a fellow of the Arctic Institute of North America. In

1999, she received the Educator of the Year Award from the Alaska Native Education Council.

### Wilma P. Mankiller (1945–)
*Cherokee tribal leader*

Chief Wilma Mankiller's roots are planted deep in the rural, Rocky Mountain community in Adair County, Oklahoma. She was born at the Indian hospital in Tahlequah, Oklahoma, and grew up with few amenities. When she was eleven, her family moved to California as part of the Bureau of Indian Affairs Relocation program.

She experienced an awakening, or call to action, during the occupation of Alcatraz Island, and performed volunteer work among Native Americans in California before returning to Oklahoma with her two children.

Her initial work for the Cherokee Nation included the recruitment of young Native Americans for university training in environmental science. In 1979, she earned a bachelor's degree in social work, and then began commuting to the University of Arkansas for graduate study. En route to school, she was in a near fatal head-on automobile collision. She implemented

Wilma Mankiller.

what Cherokees call "being of good mind," in order to recover from her extensive injuries.

As the founding director of the Cherokee Nation Community Development Department (1980–1983), she persistently pursued proposals to improve housing, education, and health care projects for Cherokee people.

In 1983, she was the first woman elected deputy chief of the Cherokee Nation. When the Cherokee principal chief resigned in December 1985, she succeeded him. In the historic 1987 tribal election, Mankiller became the first woman elected principal chief of the Cherokee Nation, with 56 percent of the vote.

She was reelected, in 1991, receiving nearly 83 percent of the vote. During her tenure as principal chief, the annual budget doubled, tribal membership tripled in size, and health services and programs benefiting children were significantly expanded.

Chief Mankiller, who left office in 1995, is the recipient of honorary doctorate degrees from thirteen colleges and universities, and served as a Montgomery Fellow at Dartmouth College during the 1996 winter term. She also co-authored *Mankiller: A Chief and Her People* (1993), authored *Keeping Pace With the Rest of the World* (1997), and co-edited the *Reader's Companion to the History of Women in the United States* (1998).

She has been inducted into the Oklahoma Women's Hall of Fame (1986), the International Women's Forum Hall of Fame (1992), the National Women's Hall of Fame (1993), San Francisco State University Hall of Fame (1995), and the Oklahoma Hall of Fame (1995).

Her honors and awards include *Ms.* Magazine's Woman of the Year (1987); the Henry G. Bennett Distinguished Service Award, Oklahoma State University (1990); The Freedom Forum, Free Speech, Free Spirit Award (1994); The National Education Association Leadership Award (1995); The Chubb Fellowship, Timothy Dwight College, Yale University (1995); Who's Who in America, One of the Fifty Most Important People in the U.S. (1996); The Elizabeth Blackwell Award (1996); the Dorothy Height Lifetime Achievement Award (1997); The Presidential Medal of Freedom (1998); and "One of the 50 Most Influential People of the Century," in the State of Oklahoma (2000).

Chief Mankiller is a trustee for the Freedom Forum, First Amendment Center, and the Ford Foundation. She is on the advisory boards of the Native American Preparatory School and Cornell University Indian Publishing and a board member of the Leadership Academy, University of Maryland, and the Buffalo Trust.

She is married to Charlie L. Soap, has two daughters, three sons, and seven grandchildren. She lives in the Rocky Mountain community of Adair County, Oklahoma, on the Mankiller land allotment.

Henrietta Mann.

## Henrietta Mann (contemporary)
*Cheyenne tribal leader and educator*

Henrietta (Whiteman) Mann, "The Woman Who Comes to Offer Prayer," has made important contributions in promoting understanding of Cheyenne culture.

The great-granddaughter of White Buffalo Woman, a Cheyenne medicine woman, she earned a master of arts degree from Oklahoma State University and a doctoral degree in American Studies from the University of New Mexico in 1982.

Mann is the first individual to occupy the Endowed Chair in Native American Studies at Montana State University, Bozeman. Prior to becoming the Endowed Chair at Montana State, she was on the Native American Studies faculty at the University of Montana, Missoula, for twenty-eight years. She served a two-year Interpersonnel Assignment to Haskell Indian Nations University as visiting professor in Indian Studies and interim dean of instruction.

On both state and national levels, Mann served two terms on the board of the National Indian Education Association and a two-year term as a commissioner for the National Commission on Head Start Fellowships of the Head Start Bureau, Administration on Children,

Youth and families, U.S. Department of Health and Human Services.

Mann serves as secretary of the Native Lands Institute in Albuquerque, New Mexico, and she is on the board of Native Action, a contemporary Cheyenne women's society, located on the Northern Cheyenne Reservation. She is also the secretary for the Montana Advisory Committee for House Bill 412, which is in the process of changing the names of seventy-four Montana sites that have a pejorative Indian word as a name. She is also in her second term as a board member of the Smithsonian's National Museum of the American Indian.

In 1998, the University of Colorado Press published her book, *Cheyenne-Arapaho Education, 1871–1982*. She has been an interviewee, consultant, and technical advisor for television and movie productions, including the American Experience's *In the White Man's Image* & Discovery Channel's *How the West Was Lost* & Home Box Office's *Paha Sapa : The Struggle for the Black Hills* & and PBS's documentary *The West*. She was the Cheyenne consultant and a language coach for the film, *Last of the Dogmen*.

Mann presented a workshop, served as a panelist, and delivered a keynote address at the closing general assembly of the 1999 World Indigenous Peoples' Conference on Education in Hilo, Hawaii. She has lectured extensively throughout the United States, as well as in Mexico, Canada, Germany, Italy, and New Zealand.

## George Manuel (1921–1989)
*Shuswap tribal leader*

George Manuel was born in the Shuswap village of Neskainlith, on the South Thompson River, about thirty miles east of Kamloops, in south-central British Columbia. The Shuswap people are one of four groups that comprise the Interior Salish people, the others being the Lillooet, Thompson, and Okanagan peoples. Salmon fishing is one of the major activities of the Interior Salish, and the Shuswap would spend summers and falls in mobile bands intercepting the spawning runs in numerous canyons that slice through the interior of the province. During the winter, they would form relatively permanent villages, living on stored food and engaging in major social and ceremonial activities. There they would live in pithouses, subterranean structures that protected them from the cold.

During his early years, Manuel was raised more by his grandparents than by his parents. He spent some time in a Kamloops residential school. He fell ill with tuberculosis, however, and was transferred to a hospital for children in Coqualeetza in the Lower Fraser

Valley. There he was able to improve his reading and writing skills. His formal education was never resumed.

Manuel became chief of his people in the late 1940s. He began to organize the Interior Salish people and launched an organization in 1958 called the Aboriginal Native Rights Committee of the Interior Tribes of British Columbia, which in 1960 reconstituted itself as the North American Indian Brotherhood. Manuel was elected president of the brotherhood that year, and shortly thereafter he presented a lengthy brief to a parliamentary committee in Ottawa detailing his people's claims to land.

In 1966, Manuel was hired by the federal government to be a community development worker with the Cowichan Band on southern Vancouver island. His stint there was highly successful, although a subsequent assignment with the Nuu-chah-nulth on the western coast of the island was not, as the Nuu-chah-nulth were resistant to outside advisors. During this time, Manuel remained active in pressing the claims of aboriginal people in British Columbia with federal authorities. He was active in the formation of the Union of British Columbia Indian Chiefs in 1969, a province-wide organization devoted to the advancement of Aboriginal claims, and was elected president of the National Indian Brotherhood in 1970, a national organization of Indian groups. Manuel was also a major figure in the World Council of Indigenous Peoples, an international organization of indigenous peoples.

## Manuelito (1818–1894)
*Navajo tribal leader*

Manuelito was a Navajo leader during the Navajo War of 1863 to 1866. Born in southeastern Utah, he became a powerful warrior in raids against the Mexicans, Hopi, and Zuni, and rose to prominence within his band. Unlike the peaceful Navajo leader, Ganado Mucho, Manuelito carried out a number of attacks and maintained resistance against U.S. Army troops.

Manuelito succeeded Zarcillas Largas as the head of his band in the 1850s when the latter resigned over failure to control his warriors' reprisals against U.S. soldiers. Although a major peace treaty had been ratified in 1849 by both sides, there were continuing clashes and depredations between the United States and the Navajo. The area around Fort Defiance in present-day Arizona was a major point of contention; both sides wanted the pasture land for their livestock to graze on, and both shot or stole the other's horses.

Troops destroyed Manuelito's home, crops, and livestock in 1859. The next year, he and the headman of another band led a contingent of warriors in an attack on the fort and nearly succeeded in capturing it. Colonel E. R. S. Canby (who later campaigned against the Modoc, a California Indian tribe, and was killed by the Modoc leader Captain Jack) pursued Manuelito and his followers into the Chuska Mountains near the present-day Arizona and New Mexico border. In early 1861, both sides met at Fort Fauntleroy, later renamed Fort Wingate in present-day western New Mexico, and at the council agreed to work toward a peaceful resolution. But in September 1861, hostilities again erupted after a horse race at the fort in which the Navajo claimed that Manuelito had been cheated. Artillery was fired into the crowd of Navajo to quell the ensuing riot, and ten Indians were killed. Warfare resumed between both sides.

Troops and Ute scouts and allies under Colonel Kit Carson began a scorched-earth policy culminating in the Navajo War. Carson's orders were clear: kill all hostiles and relocate all prisoners to Bosque Redondo near Fort Sumner in present-day eastern New Mexico. Of all the resistant Navajo bands, Manuelito's held out the longest. Faced with army pursuit and starvation, Manuelito led his remaining warriors back to Fort Fauntleroy and surrendered. He joined other Navajo held in captivity at Bosque Redondo.

Along with headmen of other bands, Manuelito traveled to Washington, D.C., to petition for the return of the Navajo homelands. A peace treaty was ratified by both sides in 1868. Manuelito returned to serve as principal Navajo chief and chief of tribal police. He again traveled to Washington and met President Ulysses Grant before his death at the age of seventy-six.

## Leonard Stephen Marchand (1933–)
*Okanagan Canadian senator*

Len Marchand has been a pioneer in the field of government. He was born in Vernon, British Columbia, on 16 November 1933. He attended residential school and then became the first Native person to graduate from his hometown's high school. Marchand went on to earn a bachelor of science degree in agriculture in 1959 from the University of British Columbia and a master's degree in forestry from the University of Idaho in 1964. During this time, Marchand became active in the North American Indian Brotherhood, a national organization devoted to advancing the rights of aboriginal people in Canada, working to obtain the federal vote, self-government, and improved education for aboriginal people.

In 1965, Marchand was the first Indian appointed as special assistant to a cabinet minister, and in 1968 he was the first Indian to be elected to the Canadian House of Commons. Marchand was reelected in 1972 and again in 1974. In 1977, Marchand was named minister of state for small business and became minister of state for the environment in 1977. Upon the defeat of the Liberal government in 1979, Marchand returned to British Columbia to work for four years as an administrator for the Nicola Valley Indian Bands, an organization representing Indian bands located in the Nicola Valley in south-central British Columbia. At this time, Marchand also became a director of the Western Indian Agricultural Corporation, a company designed to encourage the use of advanced agricultural techniques and production among Native people. Marchand also acted as a consultant on a variety of projects, among which was the Round Lake Treatment Centre, the first Native drug and alcohol treatment center located near Vernon, his place of birth. Marchand was appointed to the Canadian Senate in June 1984 and has remained active on agricultural and aboriginal committees. Marchand resigned from the Canadian Senate in 1998. He has been named honorary chief of the Okanagans, a people who live in south-central British Columbia.

## Marin (d. 1834)
*Miwok tribal leader*

This Coast Miwok chief is known through fairly obscure historical sources. He played an important role in the early history of the San Francisco Bay area. The territory of the Coast Miwok included most of modern Marin County in northern California.

Marin led his people in several successful battles against the Spanish during the years between 1815 and 1824, but despite these victories he was subsequently captured and imprisoned. Later he escaped on a balsa raft and took refuge on a small island in San Francisco Bay. After he was recaptured by the Spaniards, Marin was nearly executed, but priests from the nearby mission at San Rafael intervened on his behalf. He was later converted to Catholicism and lived close to the mission until he died there in 1834. The island where he took refuge, the adjacent peninsula, and county were named after him.

In 2000, the federal recognition status of the Coast Miwok tribe was restored, granting the tribe access to land and tribal benefits.

## Peter Martin (1841–1907)
*Mohawk physician*

Peter Martin, perhaps the first Mohawk licensed by Canadian authorities to practice medicine, was born in 1841 in the Grand River valley in southwestern Ontario.

Mohawks had moved to the Grand River valley after the American Revolution, when they had sided with the British against the American revolutionaries. Peter Martin's Mohawk name was Oronhyatekha (Burning Cloud). He first attended a small school near his home and then was sent to the Wesleyan Academy at Wilbraham, Massachusetts, where, in his final year, he was first in his class. Martin returned to his hometown for a year to teach in a local school and to raise funds for further schooling. He attended Kenyon College at Gambier, Ohio, for three years and then spent one year at the University of Toronto in Ontario, for preparatory courses in medicine.

At the young age of twenty, Martin had the occasion to greet, on behalf of his people, the Prince of Wales, later to be King Edward VII, on a visit by the prince to Canada. Their encounter led to an invitation from the prince to attend Oxford University to study medicine. After three years of study, Martin returned to the University of Toronto for a final year of study necessary to obtain his degree in medicine and to marry Ellen Hill, a Mohawk woman from the Bay of Quinte on Lake Ontario in eastern Ontario.

Martin and his new wife moved a number of times early in their marriage, as Martin practiced medicine in several small towns in southern Ontario, including Frankfort, Stratford, Napanee, and Deseronto, eventually moving to London, Ontario, in 1873. His practice in London was very successful, and he eventually became involved in a number of fraternal organizations, including the Good Templars, the Orange Order, and the Royal Order of Foresters. His wife, Ellen, died in 1901. Peter Martin lived for another six years.

## Phillip Martin (1926–)
*Choctaw political leader and chief of the Mississippi Choctaw Nation*

In Philip Martin's forty-year tenure as Mississippi Choctaw leader, the tribe's economy has brought thousands of jobs to the reservation and to the east-central Mississippi area in which the reservation is located. Born in Tucker, Mississippi, located in the heart of the Mississippi Choctaw Reservation, Martin was the middle of six children. Unlike many living on the reservation at the time, Martin's father was regularly employed by the Bureau of Indian Affairs (BIA) office in Philadelphia, Mississippi, where he acted as both a janitor and as a Choctaw interpreter.

In 1937, when Martin was only eleven, his father died suddenly in a car accident. Immediately following this traumatic loss, a BIA superintendent began coaxing Martin to attend a BIA-run boarding school. The school catered largely to Cherokee students and was located in North Carolina, far away from his family and tribe. Because Martin did not want to leave his home, he told the superintendent that he was not interested in attending school. However, the BIA employee persevered and eventually drove Martin to the boarding school, promising to buy the boy new clothes upon arrival. When the representative did not fulfill his promise, Martin knew that he could not trust any U.S. government official.

Martin stayed at the far-off school for six years, visiting home only once during that time. Before graduation in 1945, the young man left the school to join the Air Force. Like his two brothers, Raymond and Edmund, he planned to become a part of the World War II effort. While Martin arrived in France in January 1946, just after the end of the war, his brother Raymond fought at Normandy Beach in 1944 and was later killed in battle just before the war's close.

After spending several years in Europe, as well as in places such as San Francisco and Okinawa, Martin was discharged from the Air Force in 1955. He moved home to his reservation, bringing with him his new wife, Bonnie Kate Bell. The couple raised two daughters, Debbie and Patricia, who later provided them with six grandchildren and one great-grandchild.

Martin did not expect to stay on his reservation for a long time, for he felt that there were no economic opportunities on or around his people's land. His wife liked living on the reservation, however, and landed a job as a secretary at the BIA agency in Philadelphia, Mississippi. Because of his wife's success, Martin decided to stay with the Choctaws. Bonnie continues to work at the agency today, and has become the education program administrator.

Working odd jobs for six years, Martin was not as lucky as his wife in finding a regularly paying job. He worked as an electrician and a plumber for a time, and eventually was hired by the Meridian-based Naval Air Academy in 1961 to work in the maintenance department.

During the time that Martin was not regularly employed, he attended tribal council meetings with his wife, who was acting as an interpreter for the BIA superintendent, for the meetings were conducted largely in the Choctaw language. Because of his dissatisfaction with the way politics were handled on the reservation, Martin ran for tribal council in 1957 and won. In 1959 he was reelected and was appointed chairman of the tribal council by the other tribal representatives.

While the appointment was an important one, Martin knew that the economic prospects of his people were bleak at best. The tribe had neither money nor governmental space—they were meeting at four-month intervals in a demonstration kitchen at the BIA agency

office. In addition, the councilpersons were paid nothing for their governmental work, and were thus concentrating on their other jobs to pay the bills and feed their families. With such prospects, Martin realized early that the tribe could no longer depend on the federal U.S. government. If they wanted more than the bare essentials, Martin said, the Mississippi Choctaw would have to find their own economic support system.

In order for the tribe to become economically self-sufficient, Martin knew that he and his fellow council members had to develop a reservation-based economy. Because of their large workforce, spacious land-base, and eastern-U.S. location, the Mississippi Choctaw could offer economic opportunity to private companies that were heading overseas to Third World countries to find similar opportunities. In addition, federal Indian reservations are exempt from state and local taxes, making economic development all the more alluring to private enterprise.

Since Chief Martin's appointment, the tribe's economy has boomed. He has restructured the government and drawn many businesses into the area that now employ many tribal members. He has also managed to save enough tribal funds not only to pay government employees, but also to fund many tribal resource efforts, including the Choctaw Housing Authority, the Chata Development Company, which constructs most buildings on the reservation, and the Choctaw Health Center. Choctaw factories today assemble components for clients as various as Ford, Xerox, AT;T, Harley-Davidson, General Motors, and Boeing.

## Massasoit (1580–1661)
*Wampanoag tribal leader*

Massasoit was a principal leader of the Wampanoag people in the early 1600s who encouraged friendship with English settlers. As leader of the Wampanoag, Massasoit exercised control over a number of Indian groups that occupied lands from Narragansett Bay to Cape Cod in present-day Massachusetts. Massasoit negotiated friendly relations with the recently arrived Puritan settlers. As early as 1621, with the aid of Squanto, a Wampanoag who spoke English, Massasoit opened communications with the pilgrims at their Plymouth settlement. He established trading relationships with the settlers, exchanging food for firearms, tools, and other sought-after European products.

Massasoit helped the Puritan settlers in a number of ways including donations of land and advice on farming and hunting. Massasoit also offered the settlers important council on how to protect themselves from other tribes. In 1623, he warned them of an impending attack by hostile Indians. Massasoit's alliance with the settlers created divisions among the region's Indian nations and problems for the Wampanoag who were loyal to Massasoit. Consequently, Massasoit's warriors were forced to wage frequent attacks against hostile Indian groups less inclined to welcome the English settlers.

The Wampanoag chief became close friends with the progressive-minded theologian, Roger Williams, and according to many accounts influenced Williams's relative understanding and favorable view of New England Indians' lives and right to territory. In 1636, when Williams was threatened with imprisonment for heresy by the Massachusetts colonial government, he fled to Massasoit's home. Despite the efforts of Williams to maintain peace, Massasoit eventually came to resent the growing encroachment of English settlers. It would be his son Philip, however, who would turn this resentment into war in 1675 and 1676.

Though the exact details of the event have become clouded in secular mythology, it is believed that Massasoit participated in what has come to be called the first Thanksgiving. Around 1621, Massasoit traveled to Plymouth with a number of followers where they took part in a meal with the colonists. Judging by the inability of the colonists to provide for themselves at this time, it is most likely that Massasoit and his people provided the food for the "historic" meal.

## Susan Masten (1952–)
*Yurok tribal leader*

Susan Masten is president of the National Congress of American Indians and Yurok tribal chairperson. She received a bachelor of science degree in 1975 from Oregon State University. In 1976, she became the secretary of the California Press Women, and is a board member of the American Indian Film Festival, emceeing the annual event in San Francisco, California.

From 1980 to 1981, Masten was the California Indian representative in the Salmon Advisory Subpanel to the Pacific Fishery Management Council, and in 1987 and 1988 her appointment was renewed. In 1988, she chaired the Del Norte County (California) Democratic Central Committee and served as a delegate to the Democratic National Convention in 1980 and 1988. Among her numerous appointments and offices are president of the Humboldt Bay Business and Professional Women in 1988, membership on the national Commission on the Status of Women, and president of the Klamath Chamber of Commerce in Klamath, California. Since 1992, Masten has been one of the organizers of a Yurok women's support group. From 1986 to 1992 she served as co-chair of "To Have A Heart Salmon and Steelhead Fishing Tournament," proceeds from which benefit the American Heart Association.

Prior to her presidency, she served as the first vice-president of the National Congress of American Indians (1994–1996), the Sacramento area vice-president (1992–1994), and the marketing and promotion specialist for United Indian Development Association.

Masten was appointed by the secretary of the interior to serve as a Yurok Transition Team member, to implement the Hoopa-Yurok Settlement Act (1988–1991). She served on the Intertribal Monitoring Association on Indian Trust Funds (1991–1999), became chair of the Klamath River Traditional Indian Fishers Committee, and has won numerous awards, including Outstanding Young Woman of America, Humboldt County's Outstanding Citizen award, and Del Norte County's Young Woman of the Year.

## Matonabbee (1736–1782)
*Chipewyan guide and translator*

Matonabbee lived in the Hudson Bay region of Northern Canada in the mid-1700s and was brought up in both European and Indian cultures. His ability to move easily between the two worlds made him a valuable liaison for European traders and explorers in the region.

Matonabbee was born near Fort Prince of Wales, located at the mouth of the Churchill River. When Matonabbee's father died, Richard Norton, a Hudson Bay Company manager, adopted and educated him. When Norton returned to England, Matonabbee returned to live among the Chipewyan people, Athapascan speakers who lived mainly by hunting large game animals and gathering wild plants. For the next few years Matonabbee learned Chipewyan ways and traveled about much of present-day northern Manitoba, northern Saskatchewan, and the eastern Northwest Territories.

When he was sixteen years old, Matonabbee returned to Fort Prince of Wales and took employment with the British as a hunter. Matonabbee's valuable background was soon noticed by the British, who asked Matonabbee to perform other duties as well, such as negotiating with Indian tribes and translating. While accompanying the British on southern trading trips, Matonabbee learned the Algonkian language of the Cree Indians. Matonabbee's prestige rose among his own people as a result of his growing stature among the British, and he soon became a respected leader.

In the 1760s, Englishman Samuel Hearne made two failed expeditions for the Hudson Bay Company to find the Northwest Passage and copper deposits. Many explorers sought a way across northern Canada because such a route promised efficient shipping and trade routes from Europe to China and Japan. Many sea captains and explorers tried to find a Northwest Passage, but there never was an easy route to find, since the Arctic Ocean freezes over much of the year and blocks any easy shipping lanes. During his second expedition, Hearne and his company were in danger of perishing from hunger, when Matonabbee, whom Hearne had met at Fort Prince of Wales, walked into his camp and helped him return safely to the English settlements. The two became friends, and in 1771 they planned a third expedition to search for the Northwest Passage. Matonabbee provided Hearne with guides for the trip. Chipewyan bands followed the expedition and provided protection from enemies and provided food by hunting. In 1772 the expedition reached the Arctic Ocean, but Hearne was dismayed to find no passage. The return trip was brutal for the expedition and several Chipewyan died from starvation.

## Lisa Mayo (contemporary)
*Kuna/Rappahannock performance artist*

Lisa Mayo, of Kuna and Rappahannock ancestry, was born and raised in Brooklyn, New York. Mayo and her sisters, Muriel and Gloria Miguel, founded the Spiderwoman Theater group in 1975.

Her career activities also include founding Off the Beaten Path, a Native American performing arts group, performing as a member of Masterwork Laboratory Theater of New York and training as a mezzo-soprano at the New York School of Music.

Mayo also received a CAPS Fellowship and a grant from the New York State Council of the Arts for the development of *The Pause That Refreshes*, a work she both created and directed

Mayo and fellow Spiderwoman Theater founder Gloria Miguel also received a Rockefeller grant and funding from the Jerome Foundation to create *Nis Bundor: Daughters from the Stars*.

In 1997, she received an honorary doctorate of fine art from Miami University in Ohio. Mayo has performed worldwide with Spiderwoman Theatre and she currently serves on the board of directors of the Native American Actor's Showcase at the American Indian Community House.

Published plays by the Spiderwoman Theater include *Sun, Moon, and Feather*, in *Contemporary Plays by Women of Color: An Anthology* (1996), and also published in *Stories of Our Way: An Anthology of American Indian Plays* (1999), and *Power Pipes*, in *Seventh Generation: An Anthology of Native American Plays* (1999).

## David P. McAllester (1916– )
*Naragansett ethnomusicologist*

David McAllester has been a prolific scholar and a key figure in the history of research on Native American music. He was born in Everett, Massachusetts, in 1916 and graduated from Harvard University in 1938. During the 1940s he studied under George Herzog at Columbia University. Herzog was best known for comparative studies that attempted to define and classify various forms of ethnic music in "scientific" terms, and McAllester's dissertation, "Peyote Music" (1949) approaches its subject from this viewpoint. While studying at Columbia, however, McAllester was also influenced by Margaret Mead and became increasingly intrigued with the problem of describing Native music as a reflection of the culture from which it springs. He was also influenced in this direction by Robert Linton and Abraham Kardiner, two exponents of the culture and personality school of anthropology.

McAllester is probably best known for his research on Navajo and Apache music, but he has also conducted research on music of the Zuni, Passamaquoddy, Penobscot, Comanche, and Hopi. His mature writing mainly attempts to describe Indian music from a culture-bearer's perspective, and his work has influenced many other ethnomusicologists in this direction. Some of his other important publications include *Enemy Way Music* (1954), *Myth and Prayers of the Great Star Chant* (1956), *Indian Music of the Southwest* (1961), *Reader in Ethnomusicology* (1971), *Navajo Blessing-way Singer* (with Charlotte Frisbie, 1978), and *Hogans: Navajo Houses and House Songs* (with Susan McAllester, 1980). A book dedicated to his work *Essays in Ethnomusicology: Essays in Honor of David P. McAllester* was published in 1986. McAllester is currently emeritus professor of music and anthropology at Wesleyan University.

## Alexander McGillivray (1759–1793)
*Creek tribal leader*

Alexander McGillivray's father was a Scottish trader who married a woman of Creek and French ancestry and who belonged to the prominent Creek Wind clan. McGillivray was born near the upper town village, Little Talisee, which was a "daughter village" or related village to Coosa, a traditional leading white, or peace, village among the upper Creek towns, located in present-day Alabama. He was sent to school in Charleston, in present-day South Carolina, and received additional private tutoring from a relative. The American Revolutionary War disrupted his studies, and he returned to the Creek Nation, where the upper towns generally favored British alliance. In late 1778, the upper town chief, Emisteseguo, also chief of Little Talisee, transferred political leadership to McGillivray, who was then only about eighteen years old. Emisteseguo, who belonged to a lowly ranked clan, feared assassination from pro-American villages and told McGillivray that his membership in the sacred Wind clan would protect him. This plan seemed to work as McGillivray was not troubled with assassination. The choice of McGillivray as upper town principal chief was unusual, since Creek leaders were generally older men who had acquired considerable training in ritual and religious knowledge. McGillivray, however, spoke English and knew colonial institutions, which were great advantages in treaty and diplomatic negotiations.

After the war, McGillivray entered into a business partnership with the British trading firm, Panton, Leslie and Company. He worked a plantation at Hickory Ground, a sacred white village in the upper town region. As chief, McGillivray tried to protect Creek lands from U.S. settlers, and tried to reorganize the Creek national council by replacing the elderly town chiefs with the village head warriors. In 1790, he negotiated a treaty with George Washington in New York City.

### William McIntosh (1775–1825)
*Creek tribal leader*

William McIntosh, a mixed blood, became a successful entrepreneur, owning an inn, two plantations, and slaves. In addition, he rose to political influence as head warrior of Coweta. Coweta was the central red or war village among the Creek lower towns, located in present-day western Georgia. McIntosh came to prominence during the Red Stick War (1813–1814), when mainly upper town Creek villages—those in present-day Alabama—rebelled against U.S. influence over the leaders of the Creek Council. During the war, McIntosh zealously led the lower towns and cooperated with U.S. forces to secure the Red Stick defeat in 1814. In 1814 at Fort Jackson, present-day Jackson, Mississippi, General Andrew Jackson (future U.S. president) demanded 22 million acres of Creek national territory. The Creek, staggered at the demand, thereafter resolved not to cede land again to the United States, and to punish with death any persons who sold land without national council authorization.

Nevertheless, in 1818 and 1821, McIntosh led Creek delegations that ceded more land to the United States. After the second treaty, McIntosh was warned by the council that further unauthorized treaty cessions would result in his trial for treason. In the Treaty of Indian Springs of 1825, McIntosh and a dozen other chiefs ceded the last Creek holdings in western Georgia. For this act, McIntosh was condemned and executed by the Creek council. While McIntosh gained private advantages from the treaty negotiations, he argued that the Creek could not remain in their homeland in present-day Georgia and Alabama because of U.S. settler expansion. Thus, he argued, it was better to sell the land and migrate west of the Mississippi River. Most of the Creek, however, disagreed and preferred to remain in their sacred homeland by resisting land cessions.

### Hilliard McNab (1916–1990)
*Cree elder and tribal leader*

Hilliard McNab, the youngest son of eight children of Samuel and Harriet (Pratt) McNab, was born and raised on the Gordon Indian Reserve, a small community located about seventy-five miles northeast of Regina, Saskatchewan. A prominent member of the Saskatchewan Indian community, McNab was a founding member and then a senator of the organization now known as the Federation of Saskatchewan Indian Nations, a province-wide organization devoted to the advancement of aboriginal rights in Canada.

As a child, McNab attended Gordon's Residential School before working as a farmer on the reserve. His interest in helping his people began early. During the Great Depression, he actively helped people in need on the reserve in innumerable ways. McNab served as chief of the Gordon Reserve for nine consecutive terms. He also served as a member of the Saskatchewan Human Rights Commission from its inception in 1972 until 1982 and as a member of the education council to the provincial Ministry of Education. In 1984, he received the Order of Canada, a medal conferred by the governor general of Canada to select Canadians in recognition of exemplary merit and achievement. McNab's people conferred on him the ceremonial name of Opamihow, meaning "One Flying Above." McNab's legacy to his people was a profound one. Known for his ability to mold consensus while not surrendering principle, McNab was a powerful and persuasive political leader and elder of the Saskatchewan Cree.

### D'Arcy McNickle (1904–1977)
*Cree and Flathead writer and government administrator*

Author of several books, both fiction and non-fiction, D'Arcy McNickle also held several posts at the

Bureau of Indian Affairs and was one of the founders of the National Congress of American Indians. Born in St. Ignatius, Montana, McNickle was a mixed-blood of Cree ancestry on his mother's side and of Scotch ancestry on his father's. As a child, however, he and all his siblings, along with his mother, were adopted into the Flathead tribe.

McNickle was one of the most highly educated Indian people of his generation, having attended the University of Montana, Oxford University in England, and the University of Grenoble in France. He worked as a writer in New York City from 1925 to 1935 and then became involved in the Federal Writers Project in 1935 and 1936. This was one of four programs begun in the United States in 1935 by the Works Progress Administration as a relief to artists impoverished by the Depression. From 1936 until 1952, McNickle worked for the Bureau of Indian Affairs, first as director of tribal relations and later as executive director of American Indian development.

His novel *The Surrounded* (1936) was a masterpiece of Native American literature in its time. It describes the disintegration of a tribe as a result of the loss of Indian lands to the U.S. government and settlers and the destruction of tribal religion and values. Other important books by McNickle include *They Came Here First: The Epic of the American Indian* (1949), *Runner in the Sun: A Story of Indian Maize* (1954), *Indians and Other Americans: Two Ways of Life Meet* (with Harold Fey, 1959), *Indian Tribes of the United States: Ethnic and Cultural Survival* (1962), and *Indian Man: A Life of Oliver La Farge* (1971).

McNickle won several literary awards, including the distinguished Guggenheim Fellowship (1963–1964), and the D'Arcy McNickle Center at the Newberry Library in Chicago has become one of the leading institutions for Native American historiography.

### Russell Means (1940–)
*Oglala-Yankton Sioux activist*

Russell Means led the American Indian Movement (AIM) in a 1973 armed seizure of Wounded Knee, South Dakota, site of the previous massacre of Sioux by Seventh U.S. Cavalry troops on 29 December 1890. AIM held off hundreds of federal agents on the Pine Ridge Reservation for seventy-one days before their surrender.

Means was born at Porcupine, South Dakota, on the Pine Ridge Reservation, but was raised around the Oakland, California, area. His father was part Oglala, part Irish, and his mother was Yankton Sioux. He was a rodeo rider, Indian dancer, ballroom dance instructor, and public accountant before returning to South Dakota

Russell Means.

to work in the Rosebud Agency's tribal office. He moved to Cleveland, Ohio, and became director of the Cleveland Indian Center, which later changed its name to Cleveland AIM.

In February 1972, an Oglala man, Raymond Yellow Thunder, died after being beaten, publicly humiliated, and locked in a car trunk in Gordon, Nebraska. AIM led a caravan of two hundred cars filled with supporters across the state line to demand the arrest of the two brothers who perpetrated the crime. Means and others were successful in dismissing the local Gordon police chief and initiating dialogue regarding racial grievances between Indians and local Nebraskans.

In January 1973, a subsequent altercation between AIM and police at the Custer, South Dakota, courthouse exploded into a riot after Wesley Bad Bull Heart was killed by a South Dakota businessman. Thirty people were arrested, and this incident prompted the Federal Bureau of Investigation (FBI) to assign sixty-five U.S. marshals to Pine Ridge to enforce security, protect mining interests, and conduct surveillance. Fed up with government intervention, Means, along with several hundred people, traveled to the small community of Wounded Knee and demanded recognition as a sovereign nation on 28 February 1973. They were quickly surrounded by the FBI and other government agents. What began as a two-day protest became a prolonged siege. When it was over, two Indians were dead and a federal marshal was permanently paralyzed. Means and Dennis Banks were prominent within the international media as spokesmen for the Sioux. Both were arraigned on ten felony counts in a trial that lasted eight months. The federal judge, Frederick Nichol, finally threw the case out of court on the grounds of prosecutorial misconduct.

In February 1974, in a hotly contested and rigged election, Dick Wilson barely defeated Means as tribal chairman. AIM was pitted against non-AIM factions. Tensions increased dramatically when Wilson's supporters ordered all those who voted for Means off the reservation and terrorized AIM members. Means was shot in the kidney by a Bureau of Indian Affairs officer and, along with six other pending charges against him, arraigned for assault.

Between 1973 and 1980, Means was tried in four separate cases, spent one year in state prison in Sioux Falls, South Dakota, was stabbed there, and survived four other shootings. In April 1981, Means and a caravan of twenty cars journeyed to Victoria Creek Canyon in the Black Hills and established Camp Yellow Thunder, with the intent to build eighty permanent structures. Claims against the U.S. Forest Service were filed for 800 acres of surrounding forest, and the issue became embroiled in legal proceedings.

Means has traveled extensively and adopted many causes, including the investigation of the oppression of the Miskito Indians in Nicaragua. In 1987, he became the first American Indian to run for president of the United States, seeking the nomination of the Libertarian party.

He has appeared in many films and documentaries, including *The Last of the Mohicans* (1992), *Windrunner* (1992), *Natural Born Killers* (1993), *Paha Sapa* (1993), and *Thomas and the Magic Railroad* (2000). He co-authored his autobiography, *Where White Men Fear to Tread*, with Marvin J. Wolf, in 1995. Means lives in Santa Fe, New Mexico.

## Beatrice Medicine (1924–)
*Dakota (Sioux) anthropologist*

Beatrice Medicine is a recognized expert in the field of anthropology. Much of her work has focused on the study of tribal traditions among the Dakota Indians.

Medicine was born and raised on the Standing Rock Sioux Reservation in northern South Dakota. She came from a family that stressed the maintenance of her cultural identity and encouraged her to pursue her interest in researching Native American culture. Medicine has taught at a number of universities, including the University of Washington, Stanford University, Dartmouth College, Michigan State University, and the University of South Dakota, before retiring as professor of anthropology at California State University, Northridge.

In addition to work at the university level, Medicine has been involved in research with aboriginal people in New Zealand, Australia, and Canada. She has also done extensive research work in the field of mental health with a focus on issues facing Native Americans, including alcohol and drug abuse. Medicine has been an advocate for Indian leadership and has worked to establish a network of Indian social service centers in urban areas.

Medicine served as coordinator of research for the Canadian Royal Commission of Aboriginal Affairs. She is a member of the American Anthropological Association, the National Congress of American Indians, North American Indian Women's Association, and a number of other professional research associations.

She has contributed to a number of publications, including *Native American Women: A Perspective* (1978). She has written a number of articles including, "The Role of Elders in Native Education," *Indian Education in Canada II*; "Understanding the Native Community," *Multicultural Education;* and "Contemporary Cultural Revitalization: Bilingual and Bicultural Education," *Wicazo Sa Review*, Spring 1986. She has received numerous awards, including the Distinguished Service Award from the American Anthropological Association.

## Menawa (1765–1865)
*Creek tribal leader*

Menawa, also called Hothlepoya, was war chief of the Upper Towns Creek, who were located in present-day Alabama. Born along the Talapoosa River in Alabama, he established his reputation as a daring warrior through numerous raids for horses on settlements in Tennessee. Menawa joined William Weatherford against troops under Andrew Jackson in the Creek War of 1813–1814.

Menawa earned the title Crazy War Hunter for his exploits in battle, including his bravery at the battle of Horseshoe Bend in 1814. During the battle, Menawa was shot seven times and left for dead. He crawled off to a hidden camp in the swamps where he later recovered and surrendered, losing all his land and possessions to the United States.

Menawa was one of the Creek leaders opposed to removal of the Creek to land west of the Mississippi, and he led a raiding party that killed William McIntosh in 1825. McIntosh had been sentenced to death by the Creek Council after having signed the Treaty of Indian Springs in 1825, ceding twenty-five million acres of Creek land. The selling of land without Creek Council consent was unlawful under Creek law and was punishable by death.

The death of McIntosh did not stop settlers' incursion onto Creek land, however, and Menawa himself was forced to accommodate U.S. territorial demands. He traveled to Washington, D.C., in 1826. In exchange for promises of peace, the Creek were to be allowed to retain their lands in present-day Alabama, but gave up their lands within the charter limits of Georgia. As a show of friendship, Menawa led warriors in support of federal troops early in the Seminole War of 1835–1842. Despite his assistance, and before the Seminole War was over, Menawa was forced to relocate to the Indian Territory (Oklahoma) in 1836.

### Ovide William Mercredi (1945–)
*Cree tribal leader*

Ovide Mercredi, former national chief of the Assembly of First Nations (1991–1997), began his role as a political advocate in the late 1960s when he observed first-hand the social upheaval resulting from a massive hydroelectric development project in his home community of Grand Rapids, Manitoba. He obtained a law degree from the University of Manitoba in 1977 and practiced criminal law in The Pas, Manitoba, for several years. In the 1980s, Mercredi turned his mind to constitutional reform, and ever since he has been actively involved in efforts by first nations to amend the constitution of Canada to recognize aboriginal rights to land and government. Mercredi was one of several aboriginal leaders to speak out against a constitutional reform package known as the Meech Lake Accord. Negotiated with a view to placating nationalistic concerns of the province of Quebec, the accord did not address first nations' concerns. Mercredi provided key advice to Elijah Harper, an elected member of the Manitoba legislature who succeeded in blocking the accord's passage. In 1992, as national chief, Mercredi entered into successful negotiations with the federal government on constitutional reform.

Before his election as national chief, Mercredi represented and served his people in a number of different ways. He represented the Assembly of First Nations in Geneva in 1989 in seeking improvements to the International Convention on the Rights of the Child and acted as the assembly spokesperson for the United Nations Indigenous Peoples Working Group. He served as a

Commissioner for the Manitoba Human Rights Commission. He is the recipient of numerous awards, including Honorary Doctorates of Law from St. Mary's University (1992), Bishop's University (1994), and the University of Lethbridge (1999). He was presented the Thakore Foundation Award (1993) and is a three-time nominee by the Mahatma Gandhi Foundation for World Peace, for the Gandhi Prize.

He is the subject of two Canadian film documentaries, *Our Home and Native Land* and *Half a World Apart and a Lifetime Away*. Mercredi lives with his wife, Shelley, and daughter, Danielle, in Orleans, Ontario.

### Cheryl Metoyer (1947–)
*Cherokee educator and administrator*

Born in Los Angeles, California, in 1947, Cheryl Metoyer received a bachelor's degree in English (1968) and a master's degree in library science (1969) from Immaculate Heart College in Los Angeles, California, and then went on to complete her doctorate in library science at Indiana University (1976). On completing her education, she went on to do important work planning and developing Indian library services both in

Cheryl A. Metoyer.

urban settings and on reservations. She was a Native American delegate to the 1979 White House Conference on Library and Information Science and has also worked for the Bureau of Indian Affairs as a consultant on library, media, and information services.

Metoyer is the director of information resources at the Mashantucket Pequot Museum and Research Center in Mashantucket, Connecticut. Her research areas include the information-seeking behavior of culturally diverse groups and the design and evaluation of information services provided by institutions to American Indians. From 1973 to 1979, she held the Rupert Costo Chair in American Indian history at the University of California, Riverside. Metoyer has published in major research journals. Her book, *Gatekeepers in Ethnolinguistic Communities*, was honored by the Association of College and Research Libraries. Her current research project, based at the UCLA American Indian Studies Center, is the development of a thesaurus of American Indian terminology.

### Gloria Miguel (contemporary)
*Kuna/Rappahannock performance artist*

Miguel, of Kuna and Rappahannock ancestry, was born and raised in Brooklyn, New York. She and her sisters Muriel Miguel and Lisa Mayo founded the Spiderwoman Theater group in 1975. Her activities have also included studying drama at Oberlin College and appearing in numerous film, television and stage productions.

Her stage credits include performing in *Grandma*, a one-woman show written by Kiowa/Delaware playwright and producer Hanay Geiogamah, touring Canada as Peliajia Patchnose in the original Native Earth production of Cree playwright and novelist Tomson Highway's *The Rez Sisters*, and performing in *Bootlegger's Blues*, *Jessica*, and *Son on Ayash* in Canada.

Miguel has also been a visiting professor and drama consultant at Brandon University (Canada), a drama consultant for the Minnesota American Indian Youth AIDS Task Force, performer at the fourth World Women's Conference, in China, and, along with Lisa Mayo, a Rockefeller grant recipient. In 1997, she received an honorary doctorate of fine arts from Miami University (Ohio).

### Muriel Miguel (contemporary)
*Kuna/Rappahannock performance artist*

Muriel Miguel is a founding member and artistic director of Spiderwoman Theatre, the longest-running Native American women's theatre group in North America. Miguel, of Kuna and Rappahannock ancestry, was born and raised in Brooklyn, New York.

During the 1960s, as an original member of Joseph Chaikan's Open Theatre, Miguel performed in shows as Vietrock, Handcuffs and Sidewinder. She also taught drama at Bard College for four years.

She toured Canada, playing the role of Philomena Moosetail in the award-winning work by Cree playwright and novelist Tomson Highway, *The Rez Sisters*. She teaches extensively, having worked at the Centre for Indigenous Theatre in Toronto and the Working Classroom in New Mexico, where she has been instrumental in the training of Native youth in theatre and dance. Muriel developed her latest one-woman show, *Trail of the Otter*, at the Banff Centre for the Arts during the Aboriginal arts program's Winter Village 1996.

In 1997, Muriel was selected for the Bread and Roses International Native Women of Hope poster. Also in 1997, Miguel and her sisters were awarded honorary doctorates in fine arts from Miami University (Ohio), the site of the newly founded Native Women's Playwrights' Archives. Muriel's original dance/theatre work, *Throw Away Kids*, was selected for full production during the 1999 Chinook Winds Aboriginal Dance program and was also performed at the Mashantucket Pequot Museum and Research Centre in Connecticut.

### Devon A. Mihesuah (1957–)
*Choctaw professor and editor*

Devon Mihesuah is the editor-in-chief of the *American Indian Quarterly*, an academically focused journal of American Indian studies. She received her doctorate degree in 1989 from Texas Christian University and holds a doctorate in education.

Mihesuah is the author or editor of various articles and books, most notably *Repatriation: Social and Political Dialogues*, *American Indian: Stereotypes and Realities* (1996), *Cultivating the Rosebuds: The Education of Women at the Cherokee Female Seminary, 1851–1909* (1993), *Natives and Academics: Researching and Writing about American Indians* (1998), *Repatriation Reader: Who Owns American Indian Remains?* (2000), and *The Roads of My Relations: Stories* (2000).

She is a professor of history and applied indigenous studies at Northern Arizona University and has received numerous awards and honors, including the 1989 Phi Alpha Theta and Westerners International Award for Best Dissertation in Western History; the 1992 Northern Arizona University Outstanding Faculty Woman of the Year Award; the 1994 Native American

Students United Award for Outstanding Faculty; the 1995 Critics' Choice Award of the American Educational Studies Association for *Cultivating the Rosebuds* and the 1996 Ford Foundation Postdoctoral Fellowship.

## Billy Mills (1938–)
*Oglala Sioux athlete*

On 14 October 1964, against overwhelming odds, Billy Mills won the 10,000 meter run at the Olympic games in Tokyo, Japan. He set a world record that day, and it was the first time an American had ever won a distance race in the Olympic games. His victory is still hailed as one of the greatest athletic upsets of all time.

The story of Mills's life is an inspiring comeback tale. (The real-life drama of the event was not lost on Hollywood—a movie called *Running Brave* has been made about his boyhood and Olympic victory.) He was born on the Pine Ridge Reservation in South Dakota. He attended government schools through high school and was offered a full athletic scholarship to the University of Kansas when he graduated. Though Mills was a member of his collegiate track team that won the

Olympic gold medalist Billy Mills.

national track championships two years in a row, and was the Big Eight cross-country champion, he did not gain much prominence. In his final year at the university, Mills tried out for the Olympic team, but did not qualify. He quit college track.

Mills graduated and accepted an officer commission in the marine corps. He married his college sweetheart along the way and had no plans to resume running. During this time, a fellow marine officer who knew of Mills's past track victories prodded him into running again. After his victory in the inter-service 10,000-meter run, the marine corps sent Mills to the Olympic trials. He was truly a dark horse in the Olympic competition. Just minutes before the race, the U.S. track coach came into the locker room Mills was sharing with Gerry Lindgren, the star U.S. runner, to discuss the ten runners he believed stood between Lindgren and the gold medal. Mills's name was never mentioned. Moments after Mills won the race, the Japanese Olympic officials had to ask him his name—he was a complete unknown, even to some of the runners.

Mills returned to the United States a hero. He raced again and set another record for the six-mile. He was eliminated from the 1968 Olympic team due to a formality in his application form. Other athletes threatened to protest if officials did not overlook the formality, but Mills was not allowed on the team. Mills put the disappointment behind him. He is now a successful businessman in Sacramento, California, active in Native American social, political, and athletic causes. An empowering public speaker, Mills travels across the United States lecturing to students, corporations, and community organizations

## Lillie Rosa Minoka-Hill (1876–1952)
*Mohawk physician*

Lillie Rosa Minoka was born on the St. Regis Reservation in New York State. Her Mohawk mother died shortly after giving birth to her. She then resided with her Mohawk relatives until she was old enough to attend school, at which time her father, Joshua Allen, a Quaker physician, brought her to Philadelphia. Allen taught her about her tribal heritage and sent her to the Grahame Institute, a boarding school from which she graduated in 1895.

She planned on entering nursing, but her family deemed medical school more appropriate for an educated woman. Before beginning her medical education, her father sent her to study French in Quebec where she lived in a convent and converted to Catholicism. Upon returning to Philadelphia, she entered the Woman's Medical College of Pennsylvania, graduating in 1899.

Following her internship at the Woman's Hospital in Philadelphia, she attended indigent, immigrant women at a dispensary connected with the Woman's Medical College and established a private practice with a fellow graduate student. Later, while working at a government boarding school for Native Americans, she met Charles Hill, an Oneida graduate of Carlisle Institute. They were married in 1905 and moved to the Oneida Reservation in Wisconsin, where Minoka-Hill talked with Oneida medicine men and women, adding their herbal remedies to her medical school knowledge. Neighbors who distrusted the sole physician in Oneida began to seek her services. Local physicians, including her family doctor, encouraged her to treat them, although she did not hold a Wisconsin medical license.

Minoka-Hill had six children in nine years. Charles Hill died in 1916, leaving his wife only a mortgaged farm and a few farm animals. She established a "kitchen-clinic" stocked with herbs and medicines supplied by physicians from nearby Green Bay, Wisconsin, and by her friends. Patients appeared at her door anytime from seven in the morning to ten at night; in exchange for her services, they gave her food or worked on her farm. A dedicated healer, Minoka-Hill traveled long distances to deliver babies or treat patients, many of them suffering from malnutrition and tuberculosis. Encouraged by Green Bay physicians who loaned her the $100 application fee, Minoka-Hill took the two-day examination and received her Wisconsin medical license in 1934, thirty-five years after she had graduated from medical school.

Minoka-Hill practiced medicine on the Oneida Reservation for the remainder of her life. She adjusted her fees for services and medicines to a patient's ability to pay. In 1931 she received fifteen dollars to deliver a baby; two chickens were payment for another, and nine dollars for a third.

Named outstanding American Indian of the Year in 1947 by the Indian Council Fire in Chicago, Minoka-Hill received many other honors as well. The Oneida tribe adopted her with the name You-da-gent (She Who Serves). The State Medical Society of Wisconsin granted her an honorary lifetime membership and also financed a trip to the American Medical Association national convention in 1949 and to her fiftieth college reunion. Minoka-Hill died in 1952 of a heart attack in Fond du Lac, Wisconsin.

## N. Scott Momaday (1934–)
*Kiowa Pulitzer Prize-winning novelist and poet*

N. Scott Momaday, one of the premier writers in the United States, is regents professor of the humanities at the University of Arizona. Born in Lawton, Oklahoma,

he graduated from the University of New Mexico (B.A. 1958) and Stanford University (M.A. 1960, Ph.D. 1963). He has held tenured appointments at the University of California-Santa Barbara, the University of California-Berkeley, and Stanford University, He has been a visiting professor at Columbia and Princeton, and was the first professor to teach American literature at the University of Moscow, in Russia.

Momaday was awarded the 1969 Pulitzer Prize for his first novel, *House Made of Dawn* (1968). He is also the author of several books including *The Way to Rainy Mountain* (1969); *Angle of Geese and Other Poems* (1974); *The Gourd Dancer* (1976); *The Names* (1976), an autobiographical memoir; *The Ancient Child* (1989); *In the Presence of the Sun* (1992); *The Man Made of Words* (1997); *In the Bear's House* (1999); and *Circle of Wonder: A Native American Christmas Story* (1999).

His drawings, prints, and paintings have been exhibited in the United States and other countries. In 1992 and 1993, a one-man, twenty-year retrospective was mounted at the Wheelwright Museum in Santa Fe, New Mexico.

In 1994, his play, *The Indolent Boys*, was given its world premiere at the Syracuse Stage, and, in 1997, *Children of the Sun*, a children's play, opened at the Kennedy Center.

Momaday is a fellow of the American Academy of Arts and Sciences and president of the American Indian Hall of Fame. He sits on the boards of the Grand Canyon Trust, the Wheelwright Museum, First Nations Development Institute, and the School of American Research.

Momaday is founder and chairman of the Buffalo Trust, a nonprofit foundation for the preservation and restoration of Native American culture and heritage. He has lectured and given readings in many countries around the world, and holds twelve honorary degrees from American colleges and universities, including Yale University, the University of Wisconsin, and the University of Massachusetts.

## Carlos Montezuma (1867–1923)
*Yavapai physician and journalist*

Carlos Montezuma was a successful physician who advocated the abolition of the Bureau of Indian Affairs. In 1915, he wrote the pamphlet "Let My People Go," and in 1916, he founded the Indian magazine *Wassaja: Freedom's Signal for the Indian*, which remained in press from 1916 to 1922.

Montezuma was born among the Yavapai Indians in Arizona, but as a boy was captured by the Pima Indians who sold him to Carlos Gentile, a white photographer, who named him Carlos Montezuma. After Gentile's death, Montezuma was shuttled between a number of non-Indian benefactors. In 1884 he graduated from the University of Illinois with a bachelor of science degree, and in 1889 graduated from the Chicago Medical College. After an attempt at private medical practice, Montezuma was appointed physician-surgeon by the Indian Service at the Fort Stevenson Indian School in North Dakota. Montezuma practiced medicine at a number of reservations until his frustration with conditions led him to take a position at Carlisle Indian School in Pennsylvania. In 1896, Montezuma opened a private practice in Chicago, specializing in stomach and intestinal diseases. The practice was successful, and Montezuma turned his attention to activist work on Indian rights.

Montezuma's experiences working in the reservation health system made him an advocate for the abolition of the Bureau of Indian Affairs and the reservation system. His criticisms were acknowledged by government officials. Presidents Theodore Roosevelt and Woodrow Wilson asked him to become the Commissioner of Indian Affairs. Montezuma refused and continued his calls for the abolition of the BIA. He wrote essays against the institutions and people he believed exploited and suppressed Indian people.

For the rest of his life, Montezuma urged citizenship and equal rights for Native Americans, though not at the cost of sublimating cultural identity. Montezuma continually stressed the importance of maintaining "Indianness" in Native American society. He died in 1923 of tuberculosis at the Fort Dowell Reservation in Arizona, where he was born.

## Norval Morrisseau (1932–)
*Ojibwa artist*

Norval Morrisseau is a renowned, self-taught Ojibwa artist, perhaps the first Indian to break through the barriers of the non-indigenous professional art world in Canada. His unique style of painting, which combines European easel painting with the pictography of indigenous rock paintings, has been described as "x-ray art" or "legend art." With his bold and brilliant use of color and lines, he shows simultaneously the interiors and exteriors of figures—animals and humans—often using figures within figures. Morrisseau's style has given rise to a genre called "Woodlands art," which younger artists have embraced with enthusiasm and which has received international acclaim.

Morrisseau, whose Ojibwa name means "Copper Thunderbird," was born at the Sand Point Reserve near Lake Nipigon, Ontario, north of Lake Superior. His Ojibwa heritage was instilled in him at an early age by his maternal grandfather, Moses Nanakonagos. The initial inspiration for his art came from the legends of his people and from Ojibwa images on birch bark scrolls and rock paintings. Early on in his career, he came into conflict with his elders because some of his work broke a taboo against depicting legendary figures outside of Ojibwa spiritual rituals. Morrisseau was first noticed by the broader Canadian art community in 1962, when he displayed his work at the Pollack Gallery in Toronto, Ontario. His work demonstrates a deep commitment to religious and spiritual values, and Morrisseau continues to study Ojibwa shamanistic practices, which he believes assist him in his creative work. In 1978, he was awarded the Order of Canada and elected to the Royal Academy of Arts. He gave a one-man show at the 1989 Bicentennial of the French Revolution in France. Morrisseau lives in British Columbia.

## Ganado Mucho (1809–1893)
*Navajo-Hopi tribal leader*

Culturally and linguistically similar to the Apache, their Athapaskan neighbors, the Navajo often raided other tribes throughout the Southwest for horses, livestock, and possessions. During the eighteenth and nineteenth centuries, the Navajo acquired large amounts of land for their increasing herds of sheep and cattle. Ganado Mucho was the son of a Navajo mother and Hopi father. He grew up to be a successful rancher, band headman, and peacemaker in northeastern Arizona.

Ganado Mucho was a young man when the Navajo carried out particularly vehement strikes on Mexican troops in the 1830s. From 1846 to 1849, United States troops sent five expeditions in attempts to control the marauding Navajo. It seems that Ganado Mucho did not participate in any of this warfare. However, because of his large herds, in the 1850s he was accused of cattle theft, but he successfully denied the charges. In 1858, he signed an agreement with other peaceful Navajo ranchers to report any thefts of livestock and return any livestock found. Mucho became the head of his band, but since the Navajo comprised many small bands, he possessed no authority outside his own local band group, which among the Navajo was usually composed of close relatives and in-laws.

Despite the ratification of a peace treaty between some Navajo bands and the United States, other Navajo bands continued their raids and clashes with U.S. Army troops. These forays led to the outbreak of the Navajo War of 1863. Backed by Ute Indian scouts and allies,

Colonel Kit Carson led U.S. forces through the heart of Navajo country on a search-and-destroy operation. Ganado Mucho and his followers hid from Carson, all the while encouraging peace between both sides. During the war, Mucho lost two daughters and a son to raids by the Ute and Mexicans. His band surrendered, and he led them along with others on the brutal "long walk" from Fort Defiance in Arizona to Fort Sumner at Bosque Redondo in New Mexico.

The Navajo were held as prisoners until a peace treaty was signed by Ganado Mucho and others in 1868. Until his death at age eighty-four, he lived on the Navajo Reservation, rebuilt his ranch, and continued to work for peace between the United States and the Navajo.

### James Murie (1862–1921)
*Pawnee ethnographer*

James Murie was born in Grand Island, present-day Nebraska, in 1862. His mother, Anna Murie, was a full-blood Pawnee, a member of the Skiri Band. His father, James Murie, was a Scot who later commanded a battalion of Pawnee scouts.

Murie spent his young life in Nebraska where he lived as a traditional Pawnee. Before leaving Nebraska for Indian Territory (present-day Oklahoma) in 1874, he attended a day school at the agency in Genoa, Nebraska, for four months. After moving to the new Pawnee Reservation in Indian Territory, he attended day school for a year and spent one year at the boarding school at the agency. Murie soon learned English and served as an interpreter for the Indian agent at the reservation.

Murie entered the Hampton Normal and Agricultural Institute in Virginia in October 1879, at age sixteen. School records credit him with one year of prior schooling and the ability to speak some English. Four years later, Murie left, having received a diploma in the Normal (Teaching) Department. He returned home, the first student from an Eastern boarding school to do so.

Murie's anthropological career began in the 1890s when Alice Fletcher came to Pawnee to begin a study of Pawnee ceremonialism. Murie assisted Fletcher as a collaborator in her work and accompanied her to ceremonies and to the homes of informants to whom he introduced her. He also transcribed and translated songs and other textual material, and assisted her in various other ways. Murie continued to work with Fletcher after her return to Washington, D.C. They corresponded extensively over a five-year period from 1898 to 1902, as he answered questions and provided her with additional material. Additionally, he made several trips to Washington on tribal business with older Pawnee, and visited with Fletcher and provided her other information. In 1902 Murie ended his work with Fletcher and began full-time work for George A. Dorsey, curator of anthropology at the Field Museum of Natural History in Chicago. He worked with Dorsey until 1909 during which time he completed extensive, minutely detailed descriptions of three major Pawnee ceremonies.

Beginning in 1912, Murie began working with Clark Wissler, curator of anthropology at the American Museum of Natural History (Washington, D.C.), editing a series of descriptive papers on Pawnee warrior societies, religious and social groups for young men who acted as a police force and assisted the chiefs. Murie sought out Pawnee elders who were knowledgeable about each society and interviewed them, and subsequently wrote out what they had told him. The histories were published in 1914 as *Pawnee Indian Societies*. Murie continued to work with Wissler, and in 1921 the manuscript of "Ceremonies of the Pawnee" was completed. It was never published and remains in the archives of the Bureau of American Ethnology (now the National Anthropological Archives) in Washington, D.C.

Throughout his adult life in Oklahoma Murie was active in both tribal and community affairs. He accompanied Pawnee delegations to Washington on tribal business, and in 1915, he was elected president of the Indian Farmers' Institute in Pawnee.

Murie's unpublished work is extensive and includes the collection of ethnographic notes at the Field Museum and the Smithsonian's "Ceremonies" manuscript. These unpublished notes on Pawnee religion and ethnography constitute a rich source for further work.

### R. Carlos Nakai (1946–)
*Navajo-Ute musician*

R. Carlos Nakai is a composer and musician. His instrument of choice is the Native flute, and in many regards, he has kept its tradition alive by defining both its presence and its haunting sound throughout his recordings. Nakai was born in Flagstaff, Arizona, and raised on the Navajo Reservation.

Nakai began playing trumpet in the 1960s, but switched to Native flute in 1972 after failing to be accepted at the Juilliard School of Music, the prominent New York City music school. He blames this rejection on evidently "being the wrong color."

In 1982, he met the founder of Canyon Records, Ray Boley, and made his first record, *Changes*. Since then, he has released a number of recordings on the Canyon label, including *Winter Dreams* and *Carry the Gift* with guitarist William Eaton; *Spirit Horses*, a concerto for Native American flute and chamber orchestra; and *Natives* and *Migrations* with pianist Peter Kater.

Nakai is a certified secondary teacher in graphic communications, and he worked as a science teacher at several schools on the Navajo Reservation. He has been a folk and visual artist in the artist-in-education program for the Arizona Commission on the Arts. In 1985, he performed at the Magic Flute Festival in St. Paul, Minnesota, with flutists from around the world. He has worked with the San Diego, California, Flute Guild of the National Flute Association in the study of theory and application of flute music in Native culture. In 1994, he was a Grammy Award finalist for "Best Traditional Folk Album." Also in 1994, Nakai released *Island of Bows*, recorded with a Japanese group using traditional Japanese instruments. In 1995, he released an album entitled *Feather, Stone & Light* and in fall 1996, he released a jazz album, *Kokopelli's Cafe*. Nakai has produced twenty-seven commercial albums and has worldwide sales of over 2 million.

## Raymond Nakai (1918–)
*Navajo tribal leader*

Raymond Nakai is a former Navajo tribal chairman (1963–1970), and, under his leadership, the reservation made great strides toward a more technologically progressive community.

Born in Lukachukai, Arizona, and educated at Fort Wingate and Shiprock Indian schools, Nakai served in the navy in the South Pacific during World War II. Returning home, he became a radio announcer and disc jockey. In 1963, he became tribal council chairman and began a series of administrative and cultural programs designed to enhance the quality of life and produce income for the reservation. Traditional crafts such as weaving and silversmithing were fostered by the Arts and Crafts Guild. His administration encouraged the installation of irrigation systems, a hotel-motel-restaurant complex, and Navajo Community College.

However, the Nakai council also promoted the controversial production of uranium, coal, gas, oil, and timber resources on the reservation and allowed many outside plants and factories to be constructed. The industrialization resulted in increased pollution and land erosion, and such labor problems as lack of fair jobs and royalty payments. Navajo women were hired for the factories but had to relocate to dormitories far from their homes for up to two weeks at a time, leaving their husbands to care for the children.

The successes and failures of the Nakai Administration point out valuable lessons to tribal councils interested in developing their ancestral lands. Careful economic policy implementation should produce tribal self-determination without impacting social structures and natural resources.

## Nampeyo (circa 1860–1942)
*Hopi-Tewa potter*

Nampeyo is a world-recognized potter who, besides developing her own style, was instrumental in bringing about a revival of traditional Native American ceramics.

Nampeyo was born at Hano Pueblo in Arizona. In the 1890s, Nampeyo took an interest in pottery and concluded that the ceramic work being done by the artisans of her time was inferior to that of ancient potters. Her husband, who was working with an archaeologist at the time, helped her to find shards of ancient pottery. Using these pieces as a model, Nampeyo developed her own style based on these traditional designs. Nampeyo and her husband often traveled to Chicago to display her work. Nampeyo's beautiful designs evoked images of an era long past, and were quickly embraced by the art world. The Smithsonian Institution purchased her pottery and soon it was sought after by collectors from around the world. For years, her work was sold at the Grand Canyon Lodge of the Fred Harvey Company.

Nampeyo has been credited with bringing about a renaissance of pottery-making among her people. Furthermore, it was her ideas and inspiration that elevated pottery among her people to an art form, as it had been centuries ago.

## Nana (Nanay) (1810–1895)
*Chiricahua Apache tribal leader*

Nanay was the oldest of all the 1880s Apache resistance leaders, including Naiche, Loco, Taza, Chihuahua, Victorio, and Geronimo. Younger than Mangas Coloradas and older than Cochise, he became war leader of the Eastern Chiricahua, or Warm Springs Apache, in present-day Arizona after the death of Victorio in 1880.

The Apache intensely disliked the San Carlos Reservation in present-day Arizona, where they had been forcibly relocated in May 1877. After the murder of a number of soldiers and an Apache medicine man at Cibecue (Arizona), the Warm Springs Apache under Nanay fled the reservation. Nanay was probably in his seventies, half-blind, crippled with rheumatism, and aching from a number of wounds he had suffered during his lifetime. Nevertheless, he led forty Apache over a thousand miles of southern Arizona, New Mexico, and Mexico in raids on settlements and pack trains. They fought and won at least ten separate skirmishes while being pursued by over a thousand soldiers and civilians; they stole two hundred horses and mules along with supplies, and finally retreated to the Sierra Madre mountains with only the loss of several men.

General George Crook set about hiring two hundred Apache scouts from rival White Mountain and Pinal bands to hunt down the Chiricahua. Nanay, with Naiche and Geronimo, surrendered to Crook after the scouts traced them to their Sierra Madre stronghold. He took his followers back to the San Carlos Reservation, while Naiche and Geronimo stayed in Mexico to round up some missing Apache men. Nanay's band was moved by the Indian Service to Turkey Creek in present-day Arizona, a location they found much more to their liking.

However, the Indian Service tried to turn the Apache into farmers, and this plan was met with considerable Apache resistance and resentment. In May 1885, once again Nanay and other Apache leaders fled the reservation. They raided both sides of the U.S.-Mexican border for the next ten months. Crook again tracked them down, and Nanay and Chihuahua agreed to surrender their weapons and return to the reservation. They and their followers were immediately shipped off to Florida on a train. From there, Nanay and many Apache were transported to Mount Vernon Barracks in Alabama, then to Fort Sill in Indian Territory (Oklahoma). Nanay died shortly thereafter.

## Natchez (Naiche) (1857–1921)
*Chiricahua Apache tribal leader*

Naiche was the younger son of the great Chiricahua Apache leader Cochise. When Cochise died and was secretly buried in the Dragoon Mountains of Arizona in 1874, Naiche assumed leadership of the Chiricahua. Never claiming to be equal to his father, Naiche guided the Chiricahua through their transition and surrender to General Oliver O. Howard in 1876.

The Chiricahua were moved north to the San Carlos Reservation in Arizona. In summer 1881, a White Mountain Apache brought news of the first Ghost Dance to the Chiricahua Apache by telling them Cochise and spirits of the great chiefs would reappear soon thereafter. At Cibecue (Arizona) in August, a number of soldiers and the Apache medicine man were murdered. When word of this spread hundreds of U.S. troops poured into Arizona to quell what was perceived to be a Chiricahua uprising. In September 1881 Naiche and his

followers fled the hot, dusty San Carlos Reservation because of the Cibecue incident.

In retaliation for the soldiers' murder, two Apache scouts were sent to Fort Alcatraz in San Francisco Bay and three others were later hanged at Camp Grant, near Bonita, Arizona, the site of the 1871 massacre of nearly one hundred Apache men, women, and children. This incident marked the beginning of four more years of bloody warfare. Naiche and the Chiricahua conducted many raids along both sides of the U.S.-Mexican border.

Naiche and his group surrendered after General Crook and his Indian scouts traced them to their Sierra Madre stronghold. They returned to the San Carlos Reservation, and in May 1884 were removed to Turkey Creek in present-day Arizona. This region was more to the Apache's liking and provided cooler temperatures and more wooded terrain. It was proposed that they be given cattle and sheep to raise, but the Indian Bureau decided that the Apache should become farmers instead. Unhappy with the situation and with additional restrictions imposed upon them, Naiche, Geronimo, Nanay, and their followers again fled the reservation for Mexico in May 1885. They again raided both sides of the border for the next ten months.

Crook again met up with Naiche, Geronimo, and Nanay, and after two days of negotiation, they agreed to surrender and move to the East for a period of not longer than two years. A whisky peddler sneaked into camp that night and sold liquor to the Apache. By morning, Naiche and Geronimo and their followers were again off to the mountains. As a result of this incident, General Nelson A. Miles replaced Crook. Telegraph wires, which could easily be cut down by the Chiricahua, were replaced by the heliograph, which used the sun to send Morse code messages. Five thousand troops, nearly five hundred Apache scouts, and hundreds of Mexican troops chased the small band to no avail, so Miles reduced his forces to a contingent of scouts and sent several of them to contact Naiche and Geronimo. They agreed to surrender for the final time.

By 8 September 1886, Naiche, Geronimo, and their followers were on a train bound for Florida. From there they were transferred to Mount Vernon Barracks in Alabama. The collective group of Apache were still assimilating this move when they were transferred again to Fort Sill, Indian Territory (Oklahoma). Naiche welcomed this move because the terrain was more similar to Arizona. His family built a house, and he became a government scout. However, an attempt was made to seize even this land from them. They appealed and were finally allotted the Mescalero Reservation east of the Rio Grande in central New Mexico. Naiche and his family moved there in April 1913, and he spent the remainder of his days at peace.

## Lloyd Kiva New (1916–)
*Cherokee artist and art educator*

Lloyd Kiva New has established himself as an important artist and designer in leather, fabrics, and fashion. He was born in Fairland, Oklahoma, and educated at Oklahoma State University. Later, he studied at the Art Institute of Chicago, where in 1938, he became the first Native American to obtain a degree in arts education. After moving back to Arizona in 1950, New turned some farmland into "Fifth Avenue," a center of shops that specialized in local and Indian arts and crafts. Using his name, New developed the Kiva Craft Center, which championed handcrafted leathers and Indian and hand-painted fabrics.

In 1959, New received a grant from the Rockefeller Foundation to develop a program in art education for Indian students at the University of Arizona. In 1961, he played a prominent role in the founding of the Institute of American Indian Arts (IAIA) in Santa Fe, New Mexico. New served as art director and, in 1967 he became president.

Lloyd Kiva New has also served on a number of committees, including the Indian Arts and Crafts Board and the National Council of the Museum of the American Indian. In 1990, he was named president emeritus of the IAIA and was honored as a Living Treasure of Santa Fe, New Mexico.

In 2000, he was awarded an honorary doctorate from his alma mater, the School of the Art Institute of Chicago. He continues to be an active contributor to Native American art education and he lives in Santa Fe with his wife, Aysen.

## Duane Niatum (1938–)
*Klallam poet*

Duane Niatum was born in Seattle, Washington, and is a member of the Klallam tribe. As a young man, he changed his name from McGinnes to Niatum—a family name given to him by an older relative. He received his bachelor's degree in English at the University of Washington, his master's degree in Creative Writing from

Duane Niatum.

Johns Hopkins University, and his doctorate in American Cultural Studies from the University of Michigan.

He has published more than 300 poems and his work has appeared in over sixty anthologies and 1,000 American, British, and European magazines. His first book, *After the Death of an Elder Klallam*, was published in 1970 under the name Duane McGinnes. Later works include *Digging out the Roots* (1977) and *Ascending Red Cedar Moon* (1974). A 1981 collection from the University of Washington Press, *Songs for the Harvester of Dreams*, received the National Book Award from the Before Columbus Foundation in 1982. From 1973 to 1974, Niatum was the editor of the Native American authors series at Harper and Row. In 1975, he was the editor of *Carriers of the Dream Wheel*, one of the most widely read books on contemporary Native American poetry. In 1988, he edited a second anthology entitled *Harper's Anthology of Twentieth Century Native American Poetry*. His latest book, *Crooked Beak of Love*, was published in 2000.

Niatum has taught courses in poetry, fiction, and American Indian literature at several schools, including Western Washington University, Pacific Lutheran University, and the University of Washington. He currently lives in Bellingham, Washington.

## Twylah Nitsch (1912–)
*Seneca historian*

Twylah Nitsch is the founder of the Seneca Indian Historical Society. She is credited with the preservation and advancement of the Seneca Nation history and culture.

Nitsch was born on 5 December 1912 in Irving, New York. She received her education at Empire State College and the State University of New York at Buffalo. Nitsch has been a teacher, lecturer, and historian, the focus of her work being the Seneca Nation and its history. She has presented a number of programs and lectures on the knowledge and culture of the Seneca Nation and how this information continues to be relevant to present-day society. Besides lecturing in the United States, Nitsch has presented her program in Scotland, Ireland, England, Italy, Canada, and Mexico.

Nitsch is also the founder, director, and president of the Seneca Indian Historical Society, an organization devoted to the preservation and dissemination of Seneca history and culture. Nitsch's published works include *Entering Into the Silence—the Seneca Way* (1976), *Wisdom of the Senecas* (1979), *Language of the Stones* (1980), *Language of the Trees* (1982), and *Nature Changes and Dances* (1984), all published by the Seneca Indian Historical Society. In 1991 Nitsch published *Creature Totems* and in 1997 she published *Creature Teachers: A Guide to the Spirit Animals of the Native American Tradition.*

## Grayson Noley (1943–)
*Choctaw educator*

Grayson Noley has made important contributions in the field of educational research, school administrator preparation, and Native American education.

Noley was raised in Wilburton, Oklahoma. He received his bachelor's degree in 1969 from Southeastern Oklahoma State University, and his master of education degree and doctorate from Pennsylvania State University in 1975 and 1979, respectively. He served as assistant professor, director of the American Indian Leadership Program, and director of the American Indian Education Policy Center at Pennsylvania State University for nine years. Noley was director of the Cherokee Nation's Education Department for four years. In 1993 he was interim associate dean for personnel

Grayson Noley.

and student services at the Arizona State University College of Educational Leadership. He is currently department chair and associate professor of educational leadership and policy studies in the College of Education at the University of Oklahoma.

He has worked to promote the needs of his community through service on a number of local and national boards and committees including the Graduate Record Examination Board's Minority Graduate Minority Education Committee. He is a member of the American Educational Research Association, the Comparative and International Education Society, and the National Indian Education Association.

Noley is the author of many journal articles and book chapters on the status of American Indian education. His research has focused on teenage alcohol abuse, life in Bureau of Indian Affairs' off-reservation boarding schools, the need for more American Indian school administrators, teachers, and professors, and early-nineteenth century American Indian education policy development. Named as a fellow by the Kellogg Foundation's National Fellowship Program in 1984, Noley also was honored as a distinguished scholar by a standing committee of the American Educational Research Association in 1989.

## John Norquay (1841–1889)
*Métis politician*

John Norquay was a Métis politician who served as the premier of Manitoba from 1878 to 1887. He was born in 1841 to Métis parents, persons of mixed Indian-European heritage. Norquay's mother died when he was only two years old, and he was left in the care of his grandmother. He excelled at school, attending a parish school during his childhood. With the help of a scholarship, he attended St. John's Academy. He then turned to teaching, first at the parish school that he attended as a child and later at a school known as Park's Creek, where he met, courted, and in 1862 married Elizabeth Setter. After the wedding, Norquay took up farming in High Bluff, and for four years he worked the land. His interests quickly turned to political matters, however, and he was elected by acclamation to Manitoba's first legislature in 1870. He quickly moved up through the political ranks, becoming the minister of public works and then minister of agriculture. When the premier of Manitoba resigned in 1878, the lieutenant-governor of the province called upon Norquay to form a new government and serve as premier. During his nine-year tenure, he faced difficult and divisive political issues dealing with French representation in the government, among other matters. His government eventually collapsed on the issue of extending the railway through the province. In an effort to force the hand of the federal government, Norquay proposed the construction of a railway to the United States. His plan backfired, however, and he was forced to resign shortly thereafter. Norquay died soon after leaving office, in 1889.

## nila northSun (1951–)
*Shoshoni and Chippewa poet*

Nila northSun's poetry is considered part of the Native American Renaissance, the title given to American Indian literature that emerged during the Civil Rights period, or the late 1960s and early 1970s. In addition to her own books, including *diet pepsi & nacho cheese* (1977) and *a snake in her mouth* (1997), northSun's writing is anthologized in such works as *Reinventing the Enemy's Language: Contemporary Native Women's Writings of North America* (1997), edited by Joy Harjo; *The Remembered Earth: An Anthology of Contemporary Native American Literature* (1980), edited by Geary Hobson; and the German-published *Turpentine on the Rocks* (1978), edited by Charles Bukowski and Carl Weisner.

Similar to most Native American poetry, northSun's work depends on both traditional poetic forms and specific tribal sources for its inventiveness. In northSun's

nila northSun.

case, her poetry is informed by Shoshoni culture and tradition, as well as by such literary influences as Raymond Carver and Charles Bukowski.

Although she was born in Schurze, Nevada, northSun spent most of her early years in and around San Francisco, a city hosting one of the largest urban Indian populations in the United States. When northSun was a teen, she witnessed the American Indian Movement's 1969 occupation of Alcatraz Island, located off the coast of San Francisco, and the rise of American Indian activism throughout not only the Bay Area, but also the entire United States.

While California was bustling with activity in the late 1960s and early 1970s, northSun did not stay in-state for college. The to-be poet studied at the University of Montana, from which she received her bachelor's degree. It was in Missoula that northSun started delving into poetry. Once she graduated, she and then-husband Kirk Robertson founded Duck Down Press in Fallon, Nevada, part of the Fallon Paiute-Shoshoni Reservation. Her first publication, *diet pepsi & nacho cheese*, was issued in 1977 as a limited edition by their press. In addition, Duck Down Press also published two other chapbooks, or small books containing poetry by northSun: *coffee, dust devils & old radio*, co-authored by Robertson, and *small bones, little eyes*, co-authored by Jim Sagel.

Her most recent book, *a snake in her mouth*, published by West End Press, includes poetry printed in her previous books as well as more recent inventions. NorthSun now writes and works in Fallon. She is the director of a teen crisis center.

## Richard Oakes (1942–1972)
*Mohawk activist*

Richard Oakes was born on the St. Regis Reservation in New York, near the Canadian border. He attended school until he was sixteen years old and quit during the eleventh grade because he felt the U.S. school system "never offered me anything." Oakes then began a brief career in the iron work industry, working both on and off reservation. The early years of his life were spent in New York, Massachusetts, and Rhode Island before he moved to California. During that time, he attended Adirondack Community College in Glen Falls, New York, and Syracuse University. While traveling cross-country to San Francisco, California, Oakes visited several Indian reservations and became aware of their political and economic situations.

Oakes worked at several jobs in San Francisco until he had an opportunity to enroll in San Francisco State College in February 1969. During this time, he married Annie Marufo, a Kashia Pomo Indian from northern California, and adopted her five children.

Oakes was a leader in the November 1969 occupation of Alcatraz Island, an event that became the catalyst for the emerging Indian activism that continued into the 1970s. The occupation of Alcatraz Island was an attempt by urban Indians to attract national attention to the failure of U.S. government policy toward American Indians. The press and many of the Indian occupiers recognized Oakes as the "Indian leader" at Alcatraz. He left Alcatraz Island in January 1970 after his step-daughter, Yvonne Oakes, died from a head injury after falling down a stairwell. After leaving Alcatraz Island, Oakes remained active in Indian social issues and was particularly instrumental in the Pit River Indian movement to regain ancestral lands in northern California.

On 21 September 1972, Oakes was shot and killed by a YMCA camp employee in Sonoma County, California. He had gone to the camp to find a youth who was staying with the Oakes family. The camp employee was charged with involuntary manslaughter, but charges were later dropped on the grounds that Oakes had come "menacingly toward" him.

Richard Oakes still lives in the memory of thousands of Indian people who remember the rise of Indian activism and the effort to regain traditional Indian lands in the Bay Area. Most particularly, Oakes is remembered for his leadership during the Alcatraz Island occupation.

## Alanis Obomsawin (1932–)
*Abenaki writer/director and producer*

Alanis Obomsawin, a successful speaker, teacher, and filmmaker, was born in New Hampshire, and lived on the Odanak reservation northeast of Montreal until the age of nine. In 1970, she appeared in the Canadian film, *Eliza's Horoscope*, before becoming one of the country's leading documentary filmmakers. Her first film, *Christmas at Moose Factory* (1971), reveals Cree lifestyle as seen through the drawings and paintings of its children. Obomsawin's early films celebrate the richness and diversity of Indian culture. *Mother of Many Children* (1977) highlights the language and storytelling of traditional women, and *Amisk* (1977) explores the beauty of Indian dance and music.

Later films reveal Obomsawin's deep commitment to Canada's struggling Native people. *Incident at Restigouche* (1984) documents the brutal Quebec Provincial Police raid on the Restigouche Reserve over fishing rights, and *Richard Cardinal: Cry from a Diary of a Métis Child* (1986) is a heartbreaking story of a young Cree adolescent whose abuse and neglect by the child welfare system leads to his suicide. *Poundmaker's Lodge: A Healing Place* (1987) examines an Indian drug and alcohol center, and *No Address* (1988) focuses on Montreal's homeless aboriginal people. She also released an album in 1988, *Bush Lady*, which featured traditional Abenaki songs and original compositions.

In 1993, she wrote, directed and co-produced *Kanehsatake: 270 Years of Resistance*, a feature-length film documenting the 1990 Mohawk uprising in Kanehsatake and Oka. To date, the film has won eighteen awards and received international recognition.

Obomsawin is the former chair of the board of the directors for the Native Women's Shelter of Montreal, and was once a member of the Canadian Council First Peoples Advisory Board. She is a board member of Studio 1, the Aboriginal Studio, and a former advisor to the New Initiatives in Film, a program for women of color and women of the First Nations.

She has been honored with many awards, including the Order of Canada, the Toronto Women in Film and Television's Outstanding Achievement Award in Direction, the Canadian Native Arts Foundation National Aboriginal Achievement Award, and she was the first non-sociologist/non-anthropologist to earn the Outstanding Contributions Award from the Canadian Sociology and Anthropology Association.

Obomsawin also received a fellowship from the Ontario College of Art, an honorary doctorate of letters from York University, an honorary doctorate of laws degree from Concordia University, an honorary doctorate of law from Queen's University, an honorary doctorate of laws from Trent University, an honorary doctorate of literature from Carleton University, and a Lifetime Achievement Award from the Aboriginal Film Festival and the Taos Talking Picture Film Festival.

Her more recent films are *My Name is Kahentiiosta* (1995), *Spudwrench—Kahnawake Man* (1997), and *Rocks at Whisky Trench* (2000).

## Samson Occum (1723–1792)
*Mohegan minister*

Occum became a Christian convert at the age of eighteen. As a minister and educator he devoted his life to teaching and converting Indians to Christianity. He was the first Indian to preach in England.

Occum was born in New London, Connecticut. He was the first student of Eleazor Wheelock, a Christian missionary who had been teaching Indians since about 1743 in his church-sponsored Indian Charity School. Wheelock's goal was to train his students to become Christian ministers. When Occum finished his studies, he became a school teacher for a short while at which time he married Mary Montauk. In 1759, he was ordained by the Presbyterian Church. Occum's parish was among the Montauk Indians, and among his duties was the recruitment of Indian youths for Wheelock's school.

In 1765, Occum traveled to England as Wheelock's representative. He stayed in England for two years, preaching and fund raising. It was during this trip that Occum obtained the funds to establish a new school for Indian children. While Occum was in England, Wheelock's Indian school was moved to New Hampshire and, in 1769, became Dartmouth College.

When he returned to New England, Occum left Wheelock's organization over differences on the emphasis and focus of their mission. Wheelock was interested mainly in training non-Indian missionaries. Occum wanted to teach and minister to the Indians directly. As a result, Occum became a minister and teacher in an Algonkian-speaking community of Indian people in eastern New York called Brotherton. Brotherton was composed of several Indian tribes that accepted Christianity, and Occum welcomed them all to his church and school. Because of encroachment by New York settlers, Occum spent many of his later years working to relocate his followers further west on Oneida territory in central New York. The Oneida, one nation of the Iroquois Confederacy, welcomed the Brotherton community and allowed them to live on their land. The resettlement to Oneida territory was completed in 1786 with the establishment of a town named New Stockbridge. Occum died six years later.

## Oconostota (1710–1785)
*Cherokee tribal leader*

By the time he was twenty years old, Oconostota had been to England to meet King George II. He and Attakullakulla, also in the delegation, returned to South Carolina and, thirty years later, participated in the 1760 war against King George and his son, George III. Attakullakula was the Cherokee peace chief and Oconostota their war chief. The Cherokee fought on the side of the British during the French and Indian War (1756–60) and assisted in the capture of Fort Duquesne, in present-day Pittsburgh, Pennsylvania.

Peace reigned between British and Cherokee until increasing numbers of colonists began entering Indian territory in the 1750s. In 1759, Oconostota headed a delegation of thirty-two chiefs to discuss peace at Charleston, South Carolina. The Carolina colonists demanded that the warriors, who had earlier killed several Virginia settlers, be turned over to Carolina authorities. The Cherokee delegation refused, and South Carolina governor William Littleton ordered the Cherokee arrested. Attakullakulla, however, negotiated a release that surrendered one man to Carolina authorities and released the rest of the Cherokee delegation. After this incident, however, there was little chance for negotiated peace.

Two armies were necessary to defeat Oconostota and his guerrilla warfare tactics. Fifteen hundred Scottish Highlanders under the command of Colonel Archibald Montgomery were routed by the Cherokee. However, in 1761, an army of Royal Scots, British Light Infantry, and Carolina Rangers led by Colonel James Grant adopted a scorched earth policy. Along with crops, any Cherokee town Grant encountered was burned to the ground. Many villages in the Cherokee country were destroyed.

Oconostota and the Cherokee continued to fight from their mountain retreats, but were finally forced to accept defeat and signed a peace settlement on 22 December 1761. The treaty terms were quite favorable to the colonials, and they gained large portions of Cherokee land in the bargain.

Oconostota sided with the British during the Revolutionary War, during which the Cherokee again saw many of their crops and towns destroyed by colonial troops. Oconostota relinquished his position as war chief to his son Tuksi; he died at the close of the war.

## Daphne Odjig (1910–)
*Odawa artist*

Daphne Odjig, a well-known and influential artist, was born on the Wikwemikong Indian Reserve on Manitoulin Island in Lake Huron, Ontario, in 1910. Her father and grandfather were both artists in their own right, and they encouraged young Odjig to explore artistic activities as she grew up.

Odjig lived, painted, and worked on the reserve until 1938, when she moved to British Columbia. Her move did not signal a change in career, however, as she was subsequently elected to the British Columbia Federation of Artists. Odjig has also lived in Manitoba, where, in 1970, she opened a museum in Winnipeg devoted to indigenous art and formed an association of Native artists, including the renowned Norval Morrisseau. This had a powerful effect on her work, which combines Western techniques and styles with an emphasis on Native modes of artistic statement. Many younger Native artists owe a debt to Odjig's style, which continues to be influential in the Native artistic community.

Odjig has exhibited in Europe, Israel, and Japan, as well as in numerous cities in Canada. The National Arts Centre in Ottawa, Ontario, is home to a magnificent mural by Odjig, entitled *The Indian in Transition*. Odjig has received a number of honorary degrees from universities in Canada, and in 1987, she was made a member of the Order of Canada, an award conferred by the governor general of Canada to select Canadians in recognition of exemplary merit and achievement. In the 1990s she experimented with colored pencil art, and introduced a series of silkscreen prints entitled "Love Suite" in 1992.

## V. Paul Ojibwa (1950–)
*Ojibwa Catholic priest*

V. Paul Ojibwa professed final vows in 1976 and was ordained into the priesthood in 1978 in Richmond, British Columbia. He earned his bachelor of arts degree in psychology at St. Mary's College of California and a pontifical degree in systematic theology from Catholic University of America in 1977, with further study in theology at Fordham and Boston universities and the Jesuit School of Theology (Berkeley). Additional studies included depth psychology and psychotherapy at the Human Relations Institute at Santa Barbara and the C. G. Jung Institute in both San Francisco and New York.

Ojibwa has been involved in parish ministry, diocesan and national leadership in Young Adult Ministry, Campus Ministry, and has been chaplain for the Ports of Los Angeles and Long Beach. He contributed to *The People: Reflections of Native Peoples on the Catholic Experience in North America*, and served as editor for several publications and published articles in professional, religious, and popular media.

Ojibwa is former liaison to the American Indian community for the Archdiocese of Los Angeles, past director of American Indian Ministry for the Archdiocese, and was director of American Indian programs at Loyola-Marymount University in Los Angeles. He is a member of the Urban Ministry Board, National Tekakwitha Conference; former commissioner for the Los Angeles County and City Native American Indian Commission; and was chair of the Gathering Table, an ecumenical collaboration of seven churches with outreach to the Native American community in Southern California. He has also served as chair of the programming committee and American Indian and religious community representative on the community advisory board for Public Broadcasting Service (PBS) affiliate KCET/Channel 28 in Los Angeles.

Since the middle 1990s, Father Ojibwa has worked in Washington D.C. as lobbyist and advisor for the Interfaith Impact For Justice and Peace.

## Old Briton (d. 1752)
*Miami tribal leader*

In the early 1700s, Old Briton was an important trading ally of the British. The Miami leader helped to establish the trading center at Pickawillany, near present-day Piqua, Ohio. Old Briton also repulsed a number of French military attacks to maintain his control of the Miami territory in present-day Indiana.

Old Briton was a member of the Piankashaw band of Miami. He originally lived in what is now northwestern Indiana. Though the Piankashaw had traditionally traded with the French, sometime in the first half of the 1700s, Old Briton began developing a trading relationship with the British. There were two reasons for the change. First, Old Briton had become convinced of the superiority of British trading goods. Secondly, Old Briton hoped to use British influence and resources to gain stature and power among his own people. In 1748, a treaty between Old Briton and the British formalized the trading partnership. To better accommodate his new trading partners, Old Briton moved his people eastward to the village of Pickawillany.

Pickawillany eventually grew into an important trading center for the region's many Indian groups. French power in the region, however, was threatened by Pickawillany. The French made numerous attempts to destroy the trading center. In 1749, a French force was repelled when Old Briton pretended to lead his followers back to Indiana. In 1752, after an unsuccessful French attack, Old Briton executed three French soldiers in a general attempt to organize an uprising of the area tribes. The French, under command of Charles Langlade, responded with a substantial force that included a number of Ottawa, Ojibwa, and Potawatomi warriors. The force attacked Pickawillany while most of its warriors were away on a summer hunt. Old Briton was killed in the attack, while vainly hoping for military support from Pennsylvanian Colony. After Old Briton's death, his followers returned to the Wabash River in present-day Indiana.

## Barney Old Coyote (1923–)
*Crow administrator*

Barney Old Coyote has worked extensively as a government official for the Bureau of Indian Affairs (BIA), a writer, and university professor.

Born in 1923 on the Crow Reservation in Montana, Old Coyote is the great-grandson of Mountain Sheep, a noted Crow chief. He is a highly decorated WWII veteran. An Ace in the Army Air Corps, Old Coyote flew in the lead ship with General Jimmy Doolittle on a mission over France. By speaking in the Crow language, he and his brother were able to safely break air silence to communicate important information to the next wave of American bombers.

Old Coyote has worked with the National Park Service on the Crow Agency, and for the BIA on the Standing Rock Sioux Reservation in Fort Yates, North Dakota, and the Crow Agency in Montana. From 1964 to 1969, Old Coyote was a special assistant to the secretary of the Department of the Interior. In 1970 he became the assistant area director of the BIA area office in Sacramento, California. His duties included administering to the needs and interests of the California Indian tribes. Old Coyote has taught at Montana State University, Bozeman, Montana, and was the director of the American Indian Studies program.

In 1968, Old Coyote received an honorary doctorate of humane letters from Montana State University and a distinguished service award from the U.S. Department of the Interior. He is a past president and past chairman of the board for the National Federation of Federal Employees Credit Union, which provides low cost banking services to federal workers. Old Coyote has also written on a variety of topics, including the education and general participation of American Indians in U.S. society.

## Old Hop (d. 1757–1758)
*Cherokee tribal leader*

During the 1750s, Old Hop was the headman of the village of Chota when the village asserted leadership of the Cherokee Nation over rival villages from other regions. Old Hop was a member of the Wolf clan, the clan from which Chota selected its headman and second leader of the village. As a young man, Old Hop was a warrior, and he was not a member of a hereditary priestly lineage within Cherokee society. He was knowledgeable about Cherokee ceremony and political culture, but he was a relatively secular leader of his village.

During the 1730s and 1740s, colonial officials in Carolina had tried to establish a central authority among the Cherokee by appointing a "Cherokee Emperor." For some years the emperor was located at the village of Tellico, a leading village of the Valley Towns region within the Cherokee Nation. During this time, however, Chota was generally ignored by colonial officials, although it claimed to be "Mother Town of the Nation." During the early 1750s, the leaders of Tellico faltered when an embargo was imposed on the Cherokee Nation by the English colonies for the killing of an English trader during a battle between the Creek and Cherokee. Around the same time the Creek defeated and destroyed several Cherokee villages. The trade embargo and military defeat gave Chota, led by Old Hop, who was by this time an old man with a limp, a chance to assert leadership. Chota gained the allegiance of most Cherokee villages, and after 1752, Chota was delegated the task of managing trade and diplomatic relations with the English and French colonies. From 1752 until Old Hop's death around 1758, Chota consolidated its leadership by holding annual national councils and ceremonies during the late summer and early fall. Chota maintained leadership of the Cherokee Nation until 1788, when U.S. militia overran and destroyed it.

## Old John (1850s)
*Takelma/Tututni tribal leader*

John, or Old John, was a chief of the Takelma and Tututni Indians living in southwestern Oregon and along the California border. These Indian tribes were commonly known as Rogue River Indians because of their repeated attacks on travelers along the Siskiyou Trail. A river in their traditional homeland became known as the Rogue River, and the 1855–1856 hostilities between the Indians and U.S. settlers were called the Rogue River War.

Old John armed his followers by having them prospect for gold in order to trade for guns and ammunition. In the spring of 1853, Rogue River warriors attacked and killed a party of miners at Cow Creek and later ambushed others at Applegate and Galice creeks.

In 1855, with tensions growing between the Takelma/Tututni Indians and the Yakima Indians and U.S. miners east of the Cascade Mountains, the commander of Fort Lane, Andrew Jackson Smith, opened up the fort for the protection of the Native population. En route to the fort, however, Oregon volunteers attacked and killed twenty-three Rogue River women, children, and old men.

In retaliation for the murder of their families, warriors raided a settlement in the Rogue Valley, killing twenty-seven settlers and setting off a renewed cycle of violence. Throughout the winter of 1855–1856, the warring parties attacked and counterattacked. Hostilities continued until the resolution of the war in 1856. General John Wool was dispatched to the Rogue River Valley after completing a campaign against the Yakima. The Rogue River chiefs, Old John, Limpy, and John, sent word to Captain Smith that they were willing to surrender at Big Meadows. Old John made plans, however, for an ambush. The ambush was foiled by advance warning, and the soldiers held out against overwhelming numbers and heavy casualties. The Indians became trapped between two forces in a pincer operation; the army regulars attacked from the rear while militiamen charged from the hilltop.

During the next weeks, many of the Indians warriors surrendered. Old John and the last of the hold-outs eventually surrendered as well. Most were relocated to the Siletz Reservation in present-day Oregon. Old John and his son, Adam, were imprisoned on Alcatraz Island in San Francisco Bay. Released several years later, it is believed that Old John spent his last days alone in the hills overlooking the Rogue River.

### Earl Old Person (1929–)
*Blackfeet tribal leader*

Earl Old Person is chairman of the Blackfeet Tribal Business Council and former president of the National Congress of American Indians (1969–1971). He was born in Browning, Montana, on 13 April 1929, to Juniper and Molly (Bear Medicine) Old Person, who were from prominent families on the Blackfeet Reservation in northern Montana. Old Person was raised on the Blackfeet Reservation in the community of Starr School, where he attended grade school, and later graduated from Browning (Montana) High School.

By the time Old Person was seven, he had started his long career of representing Native Americans, presenting Blackfeet culture in songs and dances at statewide events. In 1954, at the age of twenty-five, he became the youngest member of the Blackfeet Tribal Business Council. He was elected as its chairman ten years later in 1964, and, except for two years, has held that position ever since. Under his guidance, a major recreational complex, an industrial park, a museum and research center, housing developments, and a community center were constructed.

Old Person also served as president of the Affiliated Tribes of the Northwest from 1967 to 1972 and was chosen in 1971 as a member of the board of the National Indian Banking Committee. In 1977, he was appointed task force chairman of the Bureau of Indian Affairs (BIA) Reorganization, which was assigned the task of recommending to the secretary of the interior changes in BIA policy that were in accordance with Indian leaders. He won the prestigious Indian Council Fire Award in 1977 and has traveled extensively and met with many dignitaries and celebrities. In 1986, President Ronald Reagan appointed Old Person to the advisory council to the congressional delegation. In 1990 he was elected vice-president of the National Congress of American Indians (NCAI), a national political interest group that lobbies on behalf of U.S. tribes. His interests have long focused on educational and business opportunities for Indians.

One of the most highly esteemed and honored individuals in the state of Montana as well as the nation, Old Person, through his gentle demeanor and sincere desire to help others, has done much to promote the ideals of Native Americans in this country and further positive relations between Indian communities and U.S. society. His involvement in national, state, and local advisory committees and organizations has been for the betterment of all people in this country.

Chief Old Person is one of the most highly esteemed and honored tribal leaders in Montana and the nation, having met with and been acknowledged by all U.S. Presidents from Eisenhower to Clinton, the English Royal Family and Canadian Prime Ministers. He became chief of the Blackfeet Nation, a lifetime appointment, in 1978. In 1998, the American Civil Liberties Union of Montana honored Chief Earl Old Person with its most prestigious award, The Jeannette Rankin Civil Liberties Award, for his efforts toward advancing civil liberties in the state of Montana.

## Bernard Ominayak (1950–)
*Lubicon Cree tribal leader*

Bernard Ominayak is chief of the Lubicon Lake Nation. The son of a trapper, he was born in a cabin on the eastern shore of Lubicon Lake, 220 miles northwest of Edmonton, Alberta. He spent his early years living on the shores of the lake during the summers, hunting duck and small game with his father and friends, and riding horses in nearby meadows. He spent winters in a cabin on his father's trapline, where he and his family trapped by dog team and snowshoe. At the age of eight, Ominayak was sent to a residential school five miles from home in Little Buffalo, Alberta. His family joined him in Little Buffalo shortly thereafter, when it became apparent that Ominayak was unhappy being far from home. He went on to study at a nearby vocational school and returned to Lubicon Lake to marry and raise a family.

Ominayak was elected a band councilor and subsequently chief of the Lubicon Lake band at the age of twenty-eight. He soon became embroiled in a famous lawsuit against the federal government, stemming from the government's refusal to provide reserve land to the band. Legally, the Lubicon people were squatters on land they viewed as their ancestral homeland, and oil companies began to drill for oil and disturb their traditional lifestyle. Ominayak battled the federal government and several oil companies in the courts and the media for a decade, making appeals to the United Nations, the World Council of Churches, and the World Council of Indigenous Peoples. Eventually he and his people set up a peaceful blockade on their land, leading to twenty-six arrests, but resulting in a settlement in which the Lubicon Lake band obtained certain mineral rights to their homeland.

## Opechancanough (1545–1644)
*Powhatan tribal leader*

As the brother of and advisor to Chief Powhatan, leader of the Powhatan Confederacy then living in present-day Virginia, and later in his role as de-facto leader of the confederacy, Opechancanough remained a fierce opponent to English settlement in Tidewater, Virginia. In 1622 and again in 1644, Opechancanough led the Powhatan Confederacy in war against the Virginia settlers.

More militant than his brother Wahunsonacock (Powhatan), Opechancanough early on recognized the territorial and political dangers that English settlers posed for the Powhatan people. When his brother died in 1618, Opechancanough turned away from appeasement and conciliation. The popularity of tobacco growing in Virginia had intensified English desire for Powhatan land. Opechancanough organized a surprise attack against the settlers. On 22 March 1622, over three hundred men, women, and children were killed in the English settlements. In what would become a common cycle, instead of subduing the settlers, the Powhatan attack provoked an equally violent response from the English colonists. A peace treaty signed in 1632 was broken by a second Powhatan attack on 18 April 1644. Though nearly five hundred colonists were killed, the English settlers responded with counterattacks. During one of these raids Opechancanough was captured and shot. After his death, the political and military power of the Powhatan Confederacy dissipated.

## Opothleyoholo (d. 1862)
*Creek tribal leader*

In the early 1820s, Opothleyoholo was speaker for Tuckabatchee, the leading red town among the Creek upper towns, located in present-day Alabama; the lower towns were located in present-day western Georgia. The Creek were divided into red and white towns; white towns led during times of peace and red towns led during times of war. Between 1810 and 1862, Tuckabatchee, with U.S. political support, led the upper towns. Talisee (present Tulsa), the leading white upper town, led the opposition and favored British alliance between 1790 and 1820. In the Red Stick War or Creek War (1813–1814), most upper town Creek villages rebelled against the U.S.-supported villages, which consisted mostly of lower towns, with some exceptions like Tuckabatchee. The Red Sticks lost the war in 1814.

Opothleyoholo played an increasingly important role in Creek leadership. By the middle 1830s, he was the leading upper town chief. He led delegations to negotiate the treaty of 1826, which ceded most of western Georgia, and the treaty of 1832, which provided the Creek villages with small reservations within the state of Alabama. By 1836, the Creek reservations were overrun by settlers. A brief insurgency by several lower town villages was put down by U.S. and upper town forces. Creek leaders felt compelled to migrate west to present-day Oklahoma. While retaining upper town leadership, Opothleyoholo emphasized retention of Creek culture and political institutions, but favored adoption of agriculture. The U.S. Civil War split the Creek Nation, largely between upper and lower town factions. In 1862, while Opothleyoholo led his people north toward Union alliance and protection, he was killed by Confederate forces.

## A. Paul Ortega (contemporary)
*Mescalero Apache composer*

A. Paul Ortega has been hailed as one of America's most renowned Native American composers and singers. His 1971 album *Two Worlds* is considered to be an important landmark in the development of contemporary Native American music.

Ortega, a member of the Mescalero Apache tribe, lives in Albuquerque, New Mexico. Ortega's music and compositions take many of their themes from traditional American Indian music. *Two Worlds* was considered a milestone in developing and spreading knowledge of this genre; then he released *Three Worlds*, which was received equally well. He has also taught music and the history and use of traditional Native American instruments at the Institute of American Indian Arts in Santa Fe, New Mexico. Ortega is a champion Apache dancer, and practices and teaches traditional Apache medicine ways. He recently released an album with Joanne Shenandoah entitled *Loving Ways*.

## Alfonso Ortiz (1939–1997)
*San Juan Pueblo anthropologist*

Alfonso Ortiz made momentous contributions in the field of anthropology and in public service as an advocate for Native Americans. He authored *The Tewa World: Space, Time, Being, and Becoming in a Pueblo Society* (1969), a classic work in anthropology.

Ortiz was born and grew up at the San Juan Pueblo in New Mexico. He has degrees from the University of New Mexico (A.B. Sociology, 1961) and the University of Chicago (M.A. Anthropology, 1963, Ph.D. Anthropology, 1967). At the time of his death, he was professor of anthropology at the University of New Mexico. He also taught at Claremont College in California, the University of California at Los Angeles, Rutgers University, Princeton University, and Colorado College.

Much of Ortiz's work and writing as a social anthropologist focused on the Southwest Indian tribes. His first book, *The Tewa World*, is considered an exemplar in anthropological writing. He was the editor of volumes 9 and 10 (Southwest Indians) of the *Handbook of North American Indians* (Smithsonian, 1980).

Besides his accomplishments in the academic field, Ortiz is a vigorous advocate for his community. He

founded University of New Mexico's Kiva Club, the first American Indian organization on campus. He also founded and headed the San Juan Indian Youth Council. He was elected to the board of the Association on American Indian Affairs in 1967 and later served as president from 1973–1988.

The Association on American Indian Affairs is credited with contributing to a number of achievements, including the Taos Pueblos community's regaining ownership of their sacred Blue Lake; the Alaska Native Claims Settlement Act of 1971, which secured 44 million acres of land for Alaska Natives; and the American Indian Child Welfare Act of 1978, which helps ensure that orphaned Indian children are placed in Indian foster homes.

Ortiz was also a member of the board of trustees of the National Museum of the American Indian from 1989–1990, and a member of the National Advisory Council on the National Indian Youth Council from 1972 to 1990.

Over his lifetime, he was awarded numerous honors, including the Roy D. Albert Prize from the University of Chicago (1964); a postdoctoral fellowship from the the John Simon Guggenheim Memorial Foundation (1976); and a postdoctoral fellowship from the Center for Advanced Study in Behavioral Sciences in Stanford (1977–1978).

The Department of Anthropology and the Maxwell Museum of Anthropology at the University of New Mexico have recently established the Alfonso Ortiz Center for Intercultural Studies to promote the efforts of current and future community scholars, artists, healers, and writers.

## Simon Ortiz (1941–)
*Acoma Pueblo poet*

Simon Ortiz is one of the most respected and widely read Native American poets. His work is characterized by a strong voice that resounds with and recalls Native American storytelling traditions.

Ortiz was born in Albuquerque, New Mexico, and raised on the Acoma Pueblo reservation located in western New Mexico. He attended the Bureau of Indian Affairs (BIA) school at McCartys on the Acoma Reservation, went to St. Catherine's Indian School, Albuquerque Indian School, and graduated from Grants High School.

Originally going to Fort Lewis College in 1961 with the goal of becoming a chemist, he eventually quit and joined the army, serving for three years. In 1966, he

Singer, songwriter A. Paul Ortega.

enrolled at the University of New Mexico and his poems and short fiction stories were published in a number of small magazines. In 1968, Ortiz received a fellowship to the International Writing Program at the University of Iowa.

Although he never received a college degree, Ortiz began teaching in the 1970s. Over the years, he has taught creative writing and Native American literature at San Diego State University, the Institute of American Indian Arts, Navajo Community College (now known as Dine College), College of Marin, the University of New Mexico, Sinte Gleska College (now Sinte Gleska University), Colorado College, and Lewis and Clark College.

His career has also included work as a journalist, public relations director, and literary editor. He also served as First Lieutenant Governor and Interpreter at Acoma Pueblo in the late 1980s.

In 1969, he received a Discovery Award from the National Endowment for the Arts followed by a fellowship award in 1980. Other awards, prizes, and recognition include the White House Salute to American Poetry

and Poet Honoree (1980), the Pushcart Prize for selected poems (*From Sand Creek*) in 1981, the Humanitarian Award in Literature from the New Mexico Humanities Council (1989), the Lifetime Achievement Award for Literature (1993), the Lila Wallace-Reader's Digest Writer's Award (1997–1999), the Lifetime Achievement Award from Western States Arts Federation (2000), the Lannan Foundation Writing Residency (2000), and the New Mexico Governor's Award for Excellence in the Arts (2000).

Ortiz's work is a reflection of his Native American heritage and oral tradition. He states that the social, political, and cultural movements of the 1960s were major influences on his work. During this era, Ortiz presented a contemporary tribal voice that had been absent in previous works of Native literature.

Published works by Simon Ortiz include *Naked in the Wind* (1971), *Going for the Rain* (1976), *Howbah Indians* (1976), *A Good Journey* (1977, 1985), *Song, Poetry, and Language* (1978), *Fight Back: For the Sake of the People, For the Sake of the Land* (1980), *From Sand Creek* (1981, 2000), *A Poem Is a Journey* (1983),

*Earth Power Coming* (Ed.,1983), *Blue and Red* (1984), *The Importance of Childhood* (1984), *Fightin': New & Collected Stories* (1984), *Willkommen Indianer* (1991), *Woven Stone* (1992), *After and Before the Lightning* (1994), *Speaking for the Generations* (Ed., 1998), *Resistere* (1999), and *Men on the Moon* (2000).

## Sandra Osawa (1942–)
*Makah producer and writer*

Sandra Osawa, a successful, independent television producer and writer, was born in Port Angeles, Washington. In 1975, she became the first Native American to produce an informational series on Native Americans for commercial television. In 1980, she received an Emmy nomination for *I Know Who I Am*, a television program on Native American cultural affairs, made for KSTW-TV in Seattle, Washington.

A majority of Osawa's work explores modern Native American cultural, social, and political issues. She has produced more than forty videos for non-broadcast use and her video work has been featured at domestic and international venues, including the Sundance Film Festival, the Amiens Film Festival, the Vienna Film Festival, the Munich International Film Festival, and the Margaret Mead Film Festival.

She received her bachelor of arts degree from Lewis and Clark University and attended graduate school for one year at UCLA, studying creative writing and filmmaking. Over the years, Osawa has served as co-director for the Washington State Fishing Rights project, director of the Head Start program for the Makah tribe, and taught at the Clyde Warrior Institute.

A member of the Writers Guild of America, her production credits are *Lighting the Seventh Fire, In the Heart of Big Mountain*, and, more recently, *Pepper's Powwow*. Osawa and her husband currently own their own production company, Upstream Productions, in Seattle, Washington.

## Osceola (1803–1842)
*Seminole tribal leader*

In the 1830s, Osceola led a resistance movement to prevent the relocation of his people from their homeland in Florida to Indian reservations west of the Mississippi in present-day Oklahoma.

It is believed that Osceola was born near the Talapoosa River along the border between present-day Georgia and Alabama. As a boy, he and his mother moved to Florida, where they first settled along the Apalachicola River and in 1815 moved to St. Marks, a trading post in northern Florida. During this time, the Seminole Indians were caught up in the general removal of Indians from the Southwest United States that affected, among others, the Cherokee and Creek. When he was still a teenager, Osceola fought in the First Seminole War of 1817–1818. Seven years later, Osceola would fight in a Second Seminole War for his people, but this time in the role of leader.

A number of agreements and laws in the 1820s and 1830s led to the Third Seminole War. In 1823, an agreement at Camp Moultrie, Florida, was signed by a single tribe of Seminole in which they agreed to live on a reservation in exchange for annual payments of food and money. Passed by the U.S. Congress in 1830, the Indian Removal Act authorized the removal of all Indians in Florida within three years. In 1832, a treaty signed by a minority of Seminole at Payne's Landing required them to move to lands west of the Mississippi in exchange for food and money. By 1835, many Seminole had not complied with the removal treaty. Osceola traveled from band to band, urging his people to remain in their homelands. On 28 December 1835, Osceola led a party that ambushed Wiley Thompson, an Indian agent who was working to gain Seminole compliance with the removal treaty. (This marked the beginning of the Third Seminole War, within which fighting continued long after its recorded ending date of 1842.) Three days after the ambush of Thompson, Osceola and his warriors met and defeated General Duncan Clinch and a force of eight hundred troops.

For the next two years, Osceola spearheaded a relocation resistance movement. The Seminole warriors made good use of the Florida Everglades, a swampy region, to wage a successful hit-and-run campaign. Although many of the Indian chiefs fighting with Osceola surrendered during the war, Osceola continued to fight until his capture in 1842 by General T. S. Jesup, who captured him by deceiving him into attending a "peace council." As Osceola met with Jesup's envoy several miles outside of St. Augustine, Florida, troops secretly surrounded the Seminole leader, eventually swooping in to take him and his followers prisoner. The U.S. military often used such deception to capture and control Indian leaders. Osceola died in prison three months after his capture.

The capture of Osceola marked the official end of the Third Seminole War, although many Seminole continued to resist U.S. removal efforts by retreating to the isolated swampy regions of Florida. It is estimated that the war resulted in the deaths of fifteen hundred American troops and cost the U.S. government $20 million. Although many of the Seminole eventually relocated to Indian Territory in present-day Oklahoma, a number remained behind, clinging to their strongholds in the Everglades. To this day, their descendants can be found in southern Florida, where they live on state and federally recognized reservations.

## Ouray (circa 1820–1880)
*Ute tribal leader*

Ouray was born in what became Taos, New Mexico, and became a leader of the Ute, a nomadic tribe living in present-day Colorado. As a young man, Ouray was revered as a cunning and dangerous warrior, but his career shifted as he came to realize that white settlement in his tribe's territory was inevitable. With the growth of the mining frontier in western Colorado, the Ute had been forced by whites to cede more and more of their territory.

In 1863, Ouray helped negotiate a treaty with the federal government at Conejos, Colorado, in which the Ute ceded all lands east of the Continental Divide. In 1867, Ouray assisted Kit Carson, a U.S. Army officer, in suppressing a Ute uprising. In 1868, he accompanied Carson to Washington, D.C., and acted as spokesman for seven bands of Ute. In the subsequent negotiations, the Ute retained sixteen million acres of land.

The growth of the Colorado mining frontier continued, and more miners trespassed on Ute lands. In 1872, Ouray and eight other Ute again visited Washington, D.C., in an attempt to stress conciliation over warfare. As a result, the Ute were pressured into ceding four million acres for an annual payment of $25,000. For his services, Ouray received an additional annuity of $1,000.

Ouray encouraged his fellow tribesmen to increase their efforts at farming in an attempt to protect their claims to land. The Ute did not have a farming tradition, however, and many among them resisted, preferring their ancient hunting and gathering subsistence ways. Nathan Meeker, a new Indian agent who attempted to force farming upon the Ute, was evicted from the reservation. This resulted in a military confrontation that left twenty-three Ute and fourteen U.S. soldiers dead, and forty-three wounded. Ouray secured the release of Meeker's wife and daughter who were captured during the battle.

Ouray traveled to Washington, D.C., again in 1880, where he signed the treaty by which the White River Ute were to be relocated to the Unitah Reservation in Utah. Soon after his return from Washington, Ouray died while on a trip to Ignacio, Colorado, where the Southern Ute Agency had been relocated. He was buried at the Southern Ute Agency; however, his remains were later returned to Montrose, Colorado, for reburial.

Louis Owens.

## Louis Owens (1948–)
*Choctaw/Cherokee/Irish critic, novelist, and educator*

Both novelist and critic, Louis Owens has published extensively on both mainstream American literature as well as Native American writing. His novels, including *Dark River* (1999), *Nightland* (1996), *Bone Game* (1994), *The Sharpest Sight* (1992), and *Wolfsong* (1991), are well-read and widely studied contributions to the American and Native American literary canons.

Born in Lompoc, California, to Hoey Louis and Ida Brown Owens, the young boy of mixed heritage spent his early years between California and Mississippi, his father's homeland. After his father's discharge from the army in the early 1950s, his parents made ends meet working as laborers on California farms and ranches. His family eventually grew to include nine children, with Owens the third oldest. Owens's first job came at nine years old when he was hired to hoe weeds in a bean field.

After graduating from high school Owens worked in a can factory in the San Francisco Bay Area before friends convinced him to enroll in junior college in San Luis Obispo, California. After two years there, where he became editor of the student newspaper, with strong encouragement from his journalism advisor Owens reluctantly applied to the University of California at Santa Barbara (UCSB) as an English major. Shortly after enrolling at UCSB Owens met the Kiowa author N. Scott Momaday, a meeting that spurred Owens's own study of Native American literature outside of the traditional university classroom where, at that time, such literature was seldom included. It was also during his time at UCSB that Owens met his wife Polly, whom he married in 1975. In addition, while at UCSB Owens began a ten-year career as a seasonal worker for the U.S. Forest Service.

After receiving his B.A. and M.A. in English from UCSB, and taking time out from school to work as wilderness ranger and firefighter in Washington and Arizona, Owens returned to school to complete a Ph.D. from the University of California at Davis. Since that time, his impressive and influential work on John Steinbeck's writings, including the 1985 *John Steinbeck's Re-Vision of America* and the 1989 *The Grapes of Wrath: Trouble in the Promised Land*, have become well-known in academia. The first fruits of his long interest in Native American writing appeared also in 1985 with *American Indian Novelists*, a work co-authored with Tom Colonnese. A few years later, his criticism and exploration of American Indian literary efforts resulted in *Other Destinies: Understanding the American Indian Novel* (1992), a book used in many introductory courses across the United States and Canada. In 1998, Owens added *Mixedblood Messages. Literature, Film, Family, Place*, a book combining critical essays and personal narratives in examinations of mixed-blood identity.

Since beginning his career in 1982 at California State University, Northridge, Owens has taught at the University of New Mexico and the University of California at Santa Cruz before joining the University of California at Davis as professor of English and Native American Studies. In 1981 he taught as a Fulbright lecturer at the University of Pisa in Italy, and since that time has received numerous awards including the American Book Award for *Nightland*, France's Roman Noir Prize for *The Sharpest Sight*, and the Writer of the Year Award from the Wordcraft Circle of Native Writers and Storytellers for *Mixedblood Messages*. His work is anthologized in many collections and appears regularly in academic journals and periodicals.

### Bastonnais Pangman (circa 1778–?)
*Métis political leader*

Bastonnais Pangman was one of the first leaders of the Métis, a term that refers to persons of mixed Indian-European heritage who forged a common identity on the plains of western Canada in the eighteenth and nineteenth centuries. His Dutch father, Peter, was well-known in the fur trade, battling established companies for an independent share of the fur business in the Canadian prairies. His mother was Cree. Peter left his Métis family and moved to Montreal when Bastonnais was fifteen. Being a skilled hunter, Bastonnais was sought after by the North West Company to work as a fur trader, but, like his father, he valued his independence. He lived and hunted buffalo on the plains, supplying badly need buffalo meat to the newly founded colony of Selkirk. When leaders of the colony attempted to regulate the free sale and movement of buffalo meat, however, they incurred the wrath of the local Métis people. Matters came to a head in 1814, when one of the first persons to be arrested for violating the regulation was Bastonnais Pangman, who had been so helpful to the settlers in the past. Pangman and others began to lead raids on the settlement in an effort to force settlers to leave the area. One such raid, the Battle at Seven Oaks in 1816, resulted in the death of the governor of the area and twenty of his men. Although there was no evidence to suggest that Pangman was an actual participant in the incident, he was arrested by colonial authorities in 1818. Eventually Pangman was acquitted of all charges brought against him.

### Elizabeth Anne Parent (1941–)
*Athabaskan and Yupik educator*

Elizabeth Parent is professor of American Indian studies at San Francisco State University. Born in Bethel, Alaska, she attended the Harvard Graduate School of Education from 1972 to 1974, where she received a master of education degree and a certificate of advanced study. She received a master's and doctoral degree from Stanford University. She wrote her dissertation on the relations of Moravian missionaries to the Yupik people in the Bethel Alaska area.

She has served on the board of directors of the Eskimo, Indian, and Aleut Publishing Company, as director of the Greater Fairbanks Head Start Association, and on the Fairbanks Native Association Education Committee.

Parent's research interests lie in American Indian education, history, and politics. Her work has also focused on educational psychology, women's issues, and child development. She is a member of the Society for Values in Higher Education, the American Association for Higher Education, and the National Indian Education Association. Parent has been honored with a postdoctoral fellowship from the UCLA American Indian Studies Center, and has been a Ford Fellow (1975) and a Danforth Fellow (1975–1980).

## Arthur C. Parker (1881–1955)
*Seneca scholar and author*

Arthur C. Parker was an acclaimed expert in the field of ethnology. In his later years, Parker devoted himself to the cause of pan-Indianism and was a leader of the Society of American Indians.

Parker was born of mixed ancestry on the Cattaraugus Seneca Reservation. As a young man he studied Iroquois archaeology and folklore. He later did professional work in archaeology for the New York State Museum. He published a number of important works on Iroquois culture such as *The History of the Seneca Indians* (1926), and *Red Jacket, Last of the Seneca* (1952). A selection of Parker's work is reproduced in *Parker on the Iroquois*, edited by William Fenton (1968).

Parker also became an influential figure in the pan-Indian movement, dedicated to unifying all Indian groups. His hope was to instill a race consciousness among all American Indians to preserve their culture and people. Parker was active in the Society of American Indians, a group dedicated to pan-Indianism. He also founded and edited the society's journal, *American Indian Magazine*. In his later years, Parker devoted himself to museums and writing. Parker is the author of over two hundred books, ranging from scientific works to children's books. Parker's great uncle was General Ely S. Parker, commissioner of Indian affairs under President Ulysses S. Grant.

## Ely S. Parker (1828–1895)
*Seneca tribal leader, commissioner of Indian affairs, and engineer*

Ely S. Parker was the first Indian commissioner of Indian affairs. During the Civil War, Parker, a close friend and colleague of General Ulysses S. Grant, served the Union cause and penned the final copy of the Confederate army's surrender terms at the Appomattox Courthouse in 1865.

Ely Parker was educated at Yates Academy in Yates, New York, and Cayuga Academy in Aurora, New York. In 1852, he became a chief among the Seneca Indians and helped the Tonawanda Seneca secure land rights to their reservation in western New York State. Parker hoped to become a lawyer, but because he was an Indian, he was denied entry to the bar. Undaunted, Parker studied engineering at Rensselaer Polytechnic Institute instead.

With the outbreak of the Civil War, Parker tried to serve the Union by enlisting in the Army Corps of Engineers but was refused again because of racial prejudice. He eventually received a commission in May

Ely Samuel Parker, first Indian commissioner of Indian Affairs.

1863 as captain of engineers in the Seventh Corps. This was due in part to his friendship with General Ulysses S. Grant, whom he had met by chance before the war and with whom he later served during the Vicksburg campaign. When Grant became president in 1868, he appointed Parker his commissioner of Indian affairs. It was the first time an Indian had held the post. As commissioner, Parker worked to rid the bureau of corruption and fraud. He was an advocate for western Indian tribes and gained a reputation for fairness and progressive thinking. In 1871, Parker was falsely accused of fraud. Although he was acquitted of all charges, Parker resigned and moved to New York City, where he lived and worked until his death in 1895.

## Quanah Parker (1845–1911)
*Comanche tribal and spiritual leader*

In the decades following the American Civil War, the American military turned its attention to pacifying and destroying American Indian groups, including those in the southern Plains. At the Medicine Lodge Council of 1867, several Comanche leaders agreed to move onto reservations. Indian groups who refused to relocate

Quanah Parker, Comanche tribal and spiritual leader.

became outlaws. One of the most fearless and powerful of these "renegade" groups was led by Quanah Parker.

Parker was the son of Peta Nocona, chief of the Kwahadi band in Texas, a subgroup within the Comanche nation, and Cynthia Parker, a non-Comanche captive. Throughout the 1860s, Parker led numerous attacks against U.S. soldiers. He and his band escaped capture longer than most of the Comanche bands in their final days living freely on the Plains. In the 1870s, however, new high-powered rifles and increasing numbers of U.S. hunters were systematically killing buffalo and destroying the way of life for the Plains Indians. In 1875, after years of battle and their buffalo nearly gone, Parker and his warriors turned themselves in, defeated by hunters with repeating rifles. The Comanche were among the last American Indians to roam freely over the southern Plains.

Parker quickly adapted to reservation life in present-day Oklahoma. In a few short years he became a successful cattle rancher. He counseled his people to adapt to the reservation without surrendering their Comanche customs and heritage. Parker adopted the peyote religion, which offered a modified world view, different in many ways from traditional religions, but offering many Indians a new form of religious belief that provided moral and spiritual support in the reservation setting. Parker helped spread the peyote religion to the Indian peoples of the Plains when they were desperately depressed and disoriented from the early reservation captivity of the 1880s and 1890s.

Parker became an appointed judge and served in the court of Indian affairs from 1886 to 1898. By 1890, he was the chief representative for the Comanche people in the allotment of tribal lands, which divided up tribal domains into small individual plots of 160 acres or less, while government officials made the surplus available to U.S. settlers. Parker also negotiated for the release of Geronimo by offering refuge to Apache warriors on the Comanche Reservation.

### Rain Parrish (1944–)
*Navajo author and museum curator*

Rain Parrish is the author of a number of books on Navajo arts and has served as the former curator of the Wheelwright Museum of the American Indian in Santa Fe, New Mexico.

Parrish was born in Tuba City, Arizona, and received a bachelor's degree in anthropology from the University of Arizona in 1967. In 1979, she became the curator of the Wheelwright Museum of the American Indian where she has applied her extraordinary knowledge of American Indian art. Parrish has done extensive research on Native American art, which she has applied to the exhibits in the museum. Parrish is an artist and jeweler herself. She is the co-owner of Rainon Productions, which produces filmstrips for children on Native American culture. She has also served as Navajo curriculum specialist at Rough Rock School on the Navajo Reservation.

Parrish is the author of the following publications: *The Stylistic Development of Navajo Jewelry* (Minneapolis Institute of the Arts, 1982); *Women Holy People* (Wheelwright Museum, 1983); and *The Pottery of Margaret Tafoya* (Wheelwright Museum, 1984). She is a member of the New Mexico Museum Association and was honored in 1985 as Navajo Woman of the Year in the Arts.

### William Lewis Paul, Sr. (1885–1977)
*Tlingit lawyer and activist*

William Lewis Paul was born in southeast Alaska, and as a young man was sent to the Carlisle Boarding

William Paul, c. 1943. (Photo by William Paul, Jr. Courtesy of Frances Paul DeGermain and Sealaska Heritage)

School in Pennsylvania. He went on to complete a law degree, which he used to campaign against discrimination and to fight for labor rights and Tlingit land rights. The Tlingit are a Northwest Coast people, organized into Raven and Eagle moieties (half divisions), which are further subdivided into clans and houses.

After finishing his education, Paul became an active leader within the Alaska Native Brotherhood (ANB), which was formed in 1912 by one Tsimpshian and eleven Tlingit Indians, as an organization to fight for Tlingit and, more generally, Indian civil rights and economic development. During the 1920s and 1930s, Paul became one of the main leaders of the ANB, and the organization made considerable progress in increasing membership and in pursuing its organizational goals. From 1923 to 1932, Paul edited *The Alaska Fisherman*, a newspaper devoted to Indian issues and especially fishing rights issues. In *The Alaska Fisherman*, Paul criticized non-Indian use of fish nets that took too much fish and threatened to destroy the salmon supplies. He also took on civil rights issues and advocated the boycotting of theaters that forced Natives to sit in special sections of the theater. Paul used his legal background to gain the right of Natives to vote in Alaska Territory elections, for Native children to attend public schools, and to form a union for Alaska Natives who worked in the cannery industry.

Paul was a central figure in the Tlingit and Haida land claim case between 1929 and 1965. The Haida are another Northwest Coast people who live at the southern tip of the Alaska panhandle and are organized by moieties and clans like the Tlingit. In 1929, the ANB initiated a land claim suit against the United States for the loss of most of the land in the panhandle of Alaska, which the U.S. government in 1912 made into the Tongass National Forest. After gaining a waiver from the U.S. government in the 1930s, the Tlingit and Haida were allowed to sue for their lost land. Nevertheless, the Tlingit and Haida claim was not settled until the late 1950s, and in 1965 Tlingit and Haida Indians were paid $7.5 million. Paul devoted much of his time to seeing through the successful resolution of the Tlingit and Haida land claims case.

For his work for and dedication to the Indian community, the Tlingit and Haida people greatly revere Paul's name and memory. His papers (1915–1970) are deposited at the University of Washington archive in Seattle.

### Andrew Paull (1892–1959)
*Squamish activist*

Andrew Paull was born at the Mission Reserve of the Squamish Nation in southwestern British Columbia. He worked as a longshoreman until the age of twenty-one, when he quit his job to become an interpreter for the McKenna-McBride Commission, established by the federal and British Columbia governments to address issues surrounding Indian reserves in the province. Paull interpreted and translated the Salish language, the language of the Squamish people and other aboriginal groups in southwestern British Columbia. His participation brought him prominence and introduced him to many different indigenous peoples of the province.

In June 1916, Paull, with Peter Kelly of the Haida Nation, organized a conference in Vancouver to address tribal rights to land. Sixteen tribal groups from across the province were represented, and the conference formed itself into the Allied Indian Tribes of British Columbia. In 1919, the Allied Tribes, after extensive consultation, prepared a statement of Indian rights to ancestral land in British Columbia that many viewed as the authoritative statement of British Columbia Indian claims. In 1927, Paull advocated the recognition of Indian lands before a special parliamentary committee struck in Ottawa to address Indian issues. The committee refused to recognize aboriginal rights to land and recommended the prohibition of any transaction designed to assist the bringing of Indian land claims to court. When the committee's recommendation became law, the Allied Tribes ceased to exist, and Paull turned to other activities. He became a sportswriter for a Vancouver daily and promoted Indian social events ranging from lacrosse games to beauty pageants. He reentered political life in 1944 when he served as president of the North American Indian Brotherhood for three years before quitting amid charges of financial mismanagement. Paull then spent the next decade as a spokesperson for Salish people in the British Columbia interior.

## Daniel Peaches (1940–)
*Navajo legislator and tribal administrator*

Daniel Peaches is a Navajo tribal administrator in Arizona. He was also elected to the Arizona State Legislature and served there from 1974 to 1985.

Peaches was born 2 September 1940, in Kayenta (Navajo Country), Arizona. In 1967, he received a bachelor's degree from Northern Arizona University and, from 1968 to 1969, studied Indian Law at the University of New Mexico. He also completed an internship at the American University in 1969.

Although the main focus of Peaches's career has been his role as Navajo tribal administrator, he has served the community in a number of ways. He is a member of the board of regents at Northland Pioneer College in Holbrook, Arizona, and is the president of Navajo Community College in Tsaile, Arizona. He is also a member of the Arizona Townhall Council and has served on the National Indian Education Advisory Council.

Peaches served on the Navajo Environmental Protection Commission (1976–1985) and was a member of the Governor's Commission on Arizona Indian Affairs (1974). He has won numerous awards, including an appointment by President Nixon in 1972 to the National Indian Education Advisory Council. From 1974 to 1985, he was an elected member of the Arizona State Legislature from District 3. Peaches has been profiled in *Newsweek* (1981), *Arizona Republic, Sunday* (1982), and *Time* (1984).

In 1998, he was elected to the Navajo Nation Council, the governing body of the Navajo Nation, where he serves on the Ethics and Rules Committee, setting agenda for the quarterly meetings of the council and the annual budget session.

His articles and letters have appeared in the *Navajo Times*, *The Arizona Republic*, the *Boston Globe*, and the *San Francisco Examiner*. Peaches is also a traditional leader and a member of the Navajo Medicine Men Association.

## Ethel (Wilson) Pearson (1912–2000)
*Kwawkgewlth tribal leader*

Ethel (Wilson) Pearson was born in 1912 in Kingcome Inlet on the coast of British Columbia. Her people, the Kwawkgewlth, are known for their potlatch system, a series of ceremonies marking special occasions such as the birth of a new heir or the completion of a carved totem pole. Prominent features of a potlatch ceremony include the distribution of gifts to guests, the giving of speeches in which speakers from the host group recount their history and hereditary rights, and elaborate dances by masked performers re-enacting ancestral encounters with spirits. Pearson was the eldest of seven children and was specifically raised to take her father's place as a leader of her people. According to traditional ways, she was married at fourteen in an arranged marriage to Alfred Coon, a man she did not know. The marriage lasted only a short time, and Pearson married Charlie Wilson and moved to the town of Comox on Vancouver Island, so their children could attend public school. After the death of her husband, Ethel married a non-Native man, Fred Pearson, and lost her Indian status under Canadian law. Loss of status resulted in the forfeiture of special benefits provided by the federal government to Indian people. Pearson, along with countless other aboriginal women, fought for repeal of the law, and eventually it was amended in June 1985.

## Maria Pearson (1932–)
*Yankton Sioux activist*

Maria Pearson has been at the forefront of the movement to protect Indian burials. She has also been active in establishing substance abuse programs for Native Americans in Nebraska.

Pearson was born in Springfield, South Dakota. She went to school at the Marty Indian School in Marty, South Dakota, and attended Iowa Western Community College in Council Bluffs. In her career as a consultant on Indian affairs, Pearson has spearheaded the crusade for the protection of Indian burials and the reburial of remains that have been placed in museums, universities, and private collections. Pearson is credited with a major contribution toward gaining the first significant law passed on the repatriation or restoration of Indian human remains and sacred objects. Pearson's repatriation activities came to fruition in

1989 when the Nebraska legislature passed a major Indian repatriation law.

Pearson has also been an advocate for substance abuse treatment for Indians in Omaha, Nebraska, and founded one of the first programs of this kind in her area. Her efforts led to the funding of national programs for substance abuse on Indian reservations and in other cities through the Indian Health Service. Pearson has been an important advisor to the Iowa government on matters of this nature and has lectured repeatedly both locally and nationally. A number of publications have profiled Pearson and her work, including *Newsweek*, *Time*, and *The Wall Street Journal*.

## Leonard Peltier (1944–)
*Anishinabe-Lakota activist*

Leonard Peltier is considered by many to be a political prisoner serving two consecutive life sentences for the murders of two Federal Bureau of Investigation (FBI) agents.

Born on 12 September 1944, in Grand Forks, North Dakota, Peltier spent a difficult childhood moving with his family from copper mines to logging camps. When his parents separated, he was placed in Wahpeton

Leonard Peltier.

Indian School in North Dakota, where he encountered strict disciplinary treatment. He returned to live with his mother in Grand Forks, but at fourteen, he left home to find work, and by the age of twenty, he was part owner of an auto body shop in Seattle, Washington.

Peltier first became involved with the American Indian Movement (AIM) in 1970 and was soon a member of AIM's inner circle, traveling with Dennis Banks, a major AIM leader, to raise financial support for the group. Peltier participated in many AIM activities, including the takeover of the Bureau of Indian Affairs offices in the early 1970s. In October 1973, Peltier returned to Seattle but spent the next year-and-a-half traveling about the country. In the summer of 1975, he was living on the Pine Ridge Reservation in South Dakota.

There are many conflicting stories regarding the events of 26 June 1975, which ultimately led to Peltier's conviction and jail sentence. Nevertheless, this much is clear: FBI agents Jack Coler and Ronald Williams and Pine Ridge resident Joe Killsright were killed in a shootout near Oglala, South Dakota, on the Pine Ridge Reservation. Leonard Peltier was among a group of Lakota engaged in a shooting exchange with the FBI agents. FBI and Indian police reinforcements soon arrived and returned fire, killing Killsright. Peltier and others hid out in homes of relatives or friends in Pine Ridge; Peltier then slipped into Canada, where he was arrested in early 1976.

In a controversial and disputed trial at Fargo, North Dakota, from which 80 percent of the defense testimony was excluded, Peltier was convicted of the murder of the two FBI agents. Peltier was sentenced to two consecutive life terms in prison and transferred to the high-security penitentiary at Marion, Illinois. After a brief transfer to a prison in California, Peltier was returned to the Marion prison.

He is currently seeking executive clemency from the President of the United States. Among his millions of supporters are Archbishop Desmond Tutu, the Dalai Lama, Amnesty International, the European Parliament, the Italian Parliament, the Belgium Parliament, the Green Party, fifty members of the U.S. Congress, Robert Redford, the National Congress of American Indians, and Reverend Jesse Jackson.

Leonard Peltier has continued to advocate for the human rights of Indigenous peoples and in doing so has won numerous human rights awards. He was recently declared an official Human Rights Defender at the Human Rights Defenders Summit in Paris, which commemorated the fiftieth anniversary of the Universal Declaration of Human Rights. He has also established himself as a talented artist, poet, and author, and he has worked toward establishing access to the practice of traditional Native American religions in prison.

## Macaki Peshewa (1941–)
*Shawnee spiritual leader*

Macaki Peshewa is a roadman or spiritual leader in the Native American Church in Knoxville, Tennessee. He was born in Spartanburg, Tennessee, and received a bachelor of arts degree from Wofford College (1968), a master of science degree from the University of Tennessee (1974), and a doctorate in human development from the Native Americas University (1975).

Peshewa has served as regional coordinator of the Catawba Labor Program, chairman of the Tennessee Indian Council and the Indian Historical Society of the Americas, and founder and chairman of Native Americans in Media Corporation. His archival material was published in *Longest Walk for Survival* (1981), and he produced the film *Amonita Sequoyah* (1982).

Among Peshewa's honors and awards are notary-at-large and a Key-to-the-City Certificate of Appreciation from Knoxville, Tennessee. His interests include memoirs of living elders, existential philosophy, herbal medicine, yoga, and parapsychology.

## Helen Peterson (1915–2000)
*Cheyenne activist*

As a young child, Helen Peterson was enveloped and surrounded with the culture of the Oglala Sioux, although she is a Cheyenne by blood. She began her education intending to be a teacher. While working in the Colorado State College education department, however, Peterson became acquainted with other fields including minority group relations. This would become the focus of much of her life's work.

She served in Nelson Rockefeller's national office of Inter-American Affairs as director of the Rocky Mountain Council on Inter-American Affairs at the University of Denver Social Science Foundation. This provided a springboard for her career in human relations. In 1949, Peterson was sent to the Second Inter-American Indian Conference in Peru, where she presented a resolution on Indian education that was adopted by the body. In 1953, Peterson was appointed executive director of the National Congress of American Indians, a national organization that works on behalf of Indian issues. Under her leadership the congress became involved in international conferences and issues. In 1961, the Chicago Conference of Indians was held at the University of Chicago. This was one of the largest gatherings of Indians activists ever held and resulted in a document outlining Indian issues and the viewpoints of the Congress of American Indians on them.

When her tenure with the National Congress of American Indians was finished, Peterson returned to Colorado and became the director of the Denver Commission on Community Relations and head of the Organization on American Indian Development.

In her work, Peterson remained a staunch advocate of maintaining tribal identity and culture. According to Peterson, an understanding of tribal identities and sovereignty is important for Indian unity and for maintaining an effective relationship with the federal government, which recognizes the tribal governments and laws.

## Philip (Metacom) (1639–1676)
*Wampanoag tribal leader*

From 1675 to 1676, Philip planned and carried out an unsuccessful attempt to oust English settlers from New England. The conflict has come to be known as King Philip's War. It was one of the most destructive Indian wars in New England's history.

Like his father Massasoit, Philip (among the English colonists, he was called King Philip) was the grand sachem of the Wampanoag Confederacy, an alliance of Algonkian-speaking peoples living in present-day New England. Unlike his father, however, Philip found peace with the New England colonists impossible, and he led a revolt against them. The seeds of revolt were laid before Philip became grand sachem. Although Massasoit had worked successfully with the progressive-minded New England minister, Roger Williams, to maintain peaceful relations between Indians and the English, when Philip came to power the mood of his people was more militant. There were several reasons for the change: colonists now outnumbered Indians in the region two to one, and English farms, animals, and villages were overtaking Indian land. Puritans subjected Philip's people to unfair laws, taxes, and jurisdictions. Alcohol and disease were also taking their toll. It was against this back-drop that Philip planned for war against the English.

Fighting erupted in 1675 at the frontier settlement of Swansea on June 16. The conflict quickly escalated across southern New England, involving the colonies of Plymouth, Massachusetts, Connecticut, and, to a limited extent, Rhode Island. Some tribes, including the Narragansett and Nipmuck, supported Philip; others gave valuable assistance to the English. Losses on both sides were brutal. (Puritans recorded with relish the massacre of noncombatants.) Villages, farms, and animals were destroyed. The colonists had underrated

Philip's talents as a military strategist and leader. Wampanoag and Narragansett warriors fought with a deep courage fostered by equal doses of optimism and desperation. Although for the first few months of the war the outcome was in doubt, the English eventually were victorious. On 19 December 1675, a decisive battle in southern Rhode Island resulted in the deaths of as many as six hundred Indians with four hundred captured. In August 1676, Philip was killed after being betrayed by his own warriors. His body was mutilated and displayed publicly.

## Archie Phinney (1903–1949)
*Nez Percé anthropologist and activist*

Archie Phinney was a scholar, anthropologist, and ethnographer. He grew up in a traditional Nez Percé home cherishing Indian customs and was an outstanding student. He won the Idaho State Spelling Tournament at the age of fourteen and was the first Indian to receive his bachelor of arts degree from the University of Kansas (1926). He continued in postgraduate work at George Washington University and New York University, and specialized in the study of Indian reservation life at Columbia University in New York. He was the recipient of an honorary degree from the Academy of Science in Leningrad, a high academic honor from the former Soviet Union, now Russia. He authored two anthropology books and several journal articles. His best known anthropological work is *Nez Percé Texts* (1934), which contained Nez Percé stories and legends, written in the tribe's native tongue.

Phinney worked for the Bureau of Indian Affairs (BIA) as superintendent of the Northern Idaho Agency, a local office within the BIA organization that serves a reservation Indian community. Superintendents are usually the highest administrative officer of the BIA on a reservation, and the BIA offices compose the agency. Phinney was also active in national Indian issues and became a central figure of the National Congress of American Indians, an active organization created in the late 1940s to lobby in Congress and pursue favorable Indian legislation. He received the prestigious Indian Council Fire Award in 1946, three years before his untimely death at the age of forty-six.

## Piapot (circa 1816–1908)
*Cree tribal leader*

Also known as Payepot (One Who Knows the Secrets of the Sioux), Piapot was a respected leader and warrior during a time of many conflicts for the Cree. He was raised by his grandmother after his parents were

killed by a smallpox epidemic introduced by settlers. Piapot and his grandmother were captured by the Sioux and lived among the Sioux people for fourteen years until a Cree raiding party freed them. After his rescue, Piapot became an important source of information to the Cree, due to his knowledge of the ways of the Sioux. Following his selection as chief of his community in Manitoba, Piapot led a number of successful raids against the Sioux and the Blackfoot. In 1870, he took approximately seven hundred warriors into Blackfoot territory and destroyed several lodges. The Blackfoot, with the assistance of their kindred allies, the Peigan, counterattacked, killing at least half of Piapot's warriors. According to historians, the counterattack led to a significant adjustment of power between the Cree and the Blackfoot on the Canadian plains.

Piapot was also known for his resistance to white settlement of the western Plains and, in 1874, he refused to sign a treaty with Canadian authorities that would have resulted in his people moving to a reserve. He reluctantly signed a year later but he continued to resist the containment that its terms imposed. Piapot moved his people westward into Saskatchewan and disrupted the building of the Canadian Pacific Railroad by pulling up surveyor stakes and erecting tipis in the path of crews laying track. The Mounties responded by dismantling the tipis, and Piapot again moved his people to a nearby stretch of barren reserve land. Approximately one quarter of Piapot's people died before they relocated to the more fertile valley near Regina, Saskatchewan. Piapot was eventually "deposed" as chief by white authorities after his people held a forbidden "Sun Dance," an annual tribal renewal ceremony. The Cree remained loyal to Piapot until his death in 1908.

## Anthony R. Pico (1945–)
*Kumeyaay tribal leader and gaming advocate*

As chairman of the Viejas Band of Kumeyaay Indians, Anthony R. Pico is one of California's most outspoken advocates of Native self-sufficiency. His tribe owns and operates the Viejas Casino and Turf Club near San Diego and, according to Pico, the gaming establishment has raised the 270-member band out of economic poverty and into self-determination. Casino profits have brought revitalization in such forms as housing, jobs, loans, and scholarships.

In 1966 Pico was sent to Vietnam with the 101st airborne. He later transferred to the 25th infantry, located in Cu Chi, twenty-five miles north of Saigon. While there, Pico witnessed many men die, and saw his closest friend killed by a grenade. A year later Pico joined the 82nd airborne and was shipped back to the United States.

In the early 1980s Pico ran an adult education program for Viejas and other nearby reservations. Also, in an attempt to better understand his people's past, Pico brought an elder to a recording studio where the man performed bird songs, or ancient Kumeyaay cycle songs. Using the recordings, Pico and two of his cousins learned the songs, began using them in ceremonies, and encouraged others to train to become Bird Singers.

Soon after his teaching experiences, Pico became involved in tribal politics. In 1982 Pico was elected tribal chairperson. For years Pico struggled to find a business to serve as his reservation's economic foundation. Until gaming came along in 1991, however, nothing worked to pull Viejas Reservation out of its economic depression. The Viejas gaming establishment now provides each adult tribal member with a monthly per capita, jobs, health care, and many other government benefits. Children receive their accumulated per capita, held in trust, when they reach eighteen years.

Pico was one of the leaders of the successful and historic Yes on Propositions 5 and 1A campaigns in California (gaming initiatives) and was the driving force behind initiatives ensuring that gaming proceeds be split among all California tribes. Viejas is one of the tribal forerunners in economic diversification projects. The tribe is majority stockholder in a bank that was purchased in 1996. Also that year, the band opened the Viejas Retail Outlet Center, the only one of its kind on an Indian reservation in the United States.

During the Summer Olympics that same year, Chairman Pico was selected as one of 5,500 Community Hero Torchbearers and helped transport the Olympic Flame across the United States. Pico has been honored time and again for his political efforts and successes. In September 1998 he received the prestigious Jay Silverheels Achievement Award from the National Center for American Enterprise Development for outstanding leadership and contributions that improve the quality of life of Native Americans. In 1997 Pico was named the National Indian Gaming Association's Man of the Year and received that organization's 1999 Award for Outstanding Spokesperson for Indian Gaming. Pico was the first Native American named one of San Diego's upcoming leaders in *San Diego Magazine's* 1995 People to Watch Awards, and was one of *East County's Home Town Heroes*, a book published in 1999. Pico was also the first Native American to be honored by the American Jewish Committee, receiving the Humanitarian Award from the San Diego Chapter of the forty-four-chapter national human relations organization. He presently resides on his reservation with his son.

## F. Browning Pipestem (1943–1999)
*Otoe-Missouri/Osage lawyer*

F. Browning Pipestem was a member of the Coordination Council on Resources to Resolve State Tribal Civil Justice Issues of the National Center for State Courts. Since 1972, Browning managed a successful general law practice in Norman, Oklahoma, where he pursued justice, recognition of tribal sovereignty, and confirmation of the rights of Indian tribes and individuals through the judicial and legislative processes. He also served as general counsel and attorney general for several Indian tribes and organizations in Oklahoma and other states, as well as being appellate judge for several tribes.

Pipestem earned his bachelor of arts degree from Northwestern Oklahoma State College and a law degree from the University of Oklahoma School of Law, and he did graduate work in law at George Washington Law School in Washington, D.C. His legal career has paralleled the development of Indian law and jurisprudence in Oklahoma, and his significant cases include *Oklahoma State v. Littlechief, CMG v. Oklahoma State,* and *Ashbrook v. Kiowa Housing Authority.* After *Littlechief,* Pipestem was the first chief magistrate for the Court of Indian Offenses in western Oklahoma since statehood (1907). He has published extensively, including *Court Rules: Court of Indian Offenses, Anadarko Area Office Jurisdiction,* and *The Mythology of the Oklahoma Indian: A Survey of the Legal Status of Indian Tribes in Oklahoma.*

Browning took great pleasure in being a member of the adjunct faculty at the University of Oklahoma School of Law where he taught tribal law. In recent years, the Indian law program at Oklahoma University Law School had become a favorite topic for Browning. He believed that the University of Oklahoma was the logical place for a premier Indian law program and had worked with the law school and the American Indian Alumni Society of the University of Oklahoma.

To honor his legacy, the F. Browning Pipestem Memorial Scholarship Fund has been established at the University of Oklahoma School of Law.

## Peter Pitseolak (1902–1973)
*Inuk photographer*

Peter Pitseolak took up photography in his early thirties when he realized that traditional Inuit life was disappearing due to Southern and European influences. He was born on Nottingham Island in the Northwest Territories in 1902 and became an Inuit camp leader.

His first photograph was of a polar bear, taken on behalf of a non-Native man who lacked the courage to take it himself. Ten years later, Pitseolak was able to obtain a camera from a Catholic missionary while working for fur traders in Cape Dorset, and he quickly became proficient in the medium. He first developed his own photographs in a hunting igloo with the assistance of a flashlight covered with a red cloth. Pitseolak spent the next twenty years photographing Inuit camp and hunting life, and he left more than fifteen hundred negatives of traditional Inuit life for museum and public consumption.

Pitseolak was also well known as a painter of watercolors. In addition, he authored an autobiography of his early life *People from Our Side* (published posthumously in 1975), which he wrote in Inuit syllabics. Another posthumously published book is an account of near death on the Arctic ice, entitled *Peter Pitseolak's Escape From Death* (1977). Pitseolak's photographic legacy is a profound one; many of the activities and scenes he captured on film would have gone unnoticed, forgotten in the march of time, had he not served as a recorder of his people.

### Mardell Plainfeather (1945–)
*Crow historian*

Mardell Plainfeather is a former park ranger and Plains Indian historian. Her research and work at the Little Big Horn Battlefield National Monument have extensively educated the general public about the culture and history of the Plains Indians.

Born in Billings, Montana, she attended Maricopa County Junior College in Phoenix, Arizona, and has a bachelor's degree in history from Rocky Mountain College in Billings, Montana. Plainfeather has worked at the Little Big Horn Battlefield National Monument on the Crow Reservation in eastern Montana. She was also a part-time instructor of U.S. history and Montana state history at the Crow Tribal Junior College and Little Big Horn College on the Crow Agency in Montana. Plainfeather's interests are in the cultural history of the Plains Indians from prehistory to the 1880s. She strives to be sure that history is told correctly and includes the American Indian perspective. Plainfeather is also interested in oral history and the preservation of Native American sacred sites.

She has served on the boards of the Fort Phil Kearny/Bozeman Trail History Association and the Crow Tribal Archives. She is a member of the Little Big Horn Battlefield Historical and Museum Association, the Montana State Oral History Association, and the Montana Committee for the Humanities. In 1982 Plainfeather

received a Performance Achievement Award from Custer Battlefield National Monument, and in 1987 she was honored by the St. Augustine Preservation of Indian Culture in Chicago, Illinois.

Plainfeather is the author of *A Personal Look at Curly after the Little Big Horn* and *The Apsaalooke: Warrior of the Big Horns*. She is currently the extension agent at Little Big Horn College, Crow Agency, Montana, and serves on the board of directors for the International Traditional Games Society.

### Pocahontas (1595–1617)
*Powhatan cultural mediator*

Pocahontas was the daughter of Powhatan and the niece of Opechancanough, both leaders of the Powhatan Confederacy that occupied much of the present-day state of Virginia. She married John Rolfe, an English settler in Virginia. She is credited with helping early English settlers maintain peaceful relations with the Powhatan.

Although the actual events are undocumented, it is widely believed that Pocahontas intervened to prevent the execution of John Smith, the Jamestown (Virginia) leader who was being held captive by Powhatan allies because he was thought to have commanded raids on several Indian villages. Her actions did not guarantee her own safekeeping, however, for in 1612, Pocahontas was abducted by English settlers and held hostage. During this time Pocahontas learned English and converted to Christianity. One year later, she married John Rolfe, one of the colony's leading citizens. The good relations between the English and Indians that followed the marriage allowed Rolfe to learn about tobacco planting, thereby setting the future course of the colony, which excelled in the production and export of tobacco.

In 1616, Pocahontas and her husband made a widely publicized trip to England. For the Virginia colonists, Pocahontas was good publicity. She was offered as proof that the struggling colony could survive and maintain good Indian relations. For Pocahontas, however, the trip proved deadly; she died a year later of a European disease. The life of Pocahontas soon became popularized in fiction, often clouding the historical accuracy of what is actually known about her life.

### Pocatello (1815–1884)
*Shoshone tribal leader*

Born in the early 1800s, Pocatello became headman of the northwestern band of the Shoshone Indians in

1847. This band was blamed for much of the violence along the California Trail, Salt Lake Road, and Oregon Trail as westward expansion and the California gold rush brought more and more settlers onto traditional Shoshone lands in the northwestern corner of present-day Utah.

Pocatello was captured and imprisoned in 1859, but worked to maintain a delicate neutrality among the different Indian bands, Mormons, miners, ranchers, and missionaries who came into the Idaho region. In 1863, he signed the Treaty of Box Elder. From 1867 to 1869, he traveled and hunted with the Washakie's Wild River Shoshone. By 1872, Pocatello's band was forced to relocate to the Fort Hall Indian Reservation in Idaho when the Union Pacific and Central Pacific railroads connected and brought further U.S. settlement into the region.

In order to be allowed to live on an off-reservation farm, Pocatello converted to Mormonism, a religion whose followers had settled at Salt Lake City, Utah. Ultimately, the local inhabitants requested federal troops to force Pocatello and other Shoshone Indians to return to Fort Hall. Pocatello then rejected Mormonism and lived the remainder of his life at Fort Hall. He became known as General Pocatello to distinguish him from other members of his family. The town of Pocatello, Idaho, is named after this Indian leader.

## Pontiac (1720–1769)
### Ottawa tribal leader

It is believed that Pontiac was born along the Maumee River, in present-day northern Ohio. By 1755, he was chief and probably participated in the French and Indian War of 1754–1763 as a French ally. Pontiac had built up a profitable trading partnership with the French, so it was with dismay that he watched the British gradually gain control of French land and trade relationships. Besides the less-favorable trading policies of the British, Pontiac also was apprehensive over the British propensity for settling on Indian lands. For these reasons, in 1763, Pontiac led a military campaign against the British, who were occupying the old French forts such as Detroit in the Great Lakes region.

Pontiac's plan was founded on the belief that he could unite diverse Indian nations against the British and that the French would follow through on their promises of support. Pontiac's efforts to forge an anti-British alliance were fairly successful. The Ottawa leader was a skillful orator, and he spread his message of resistance effectively throughout the Old Northwest tribes of the Great Lakes area. He was aided in this cause by the Delaware prophet, whose anti-British teachings and spiritual visions provided Pontiac's crusade with a spiritual foundation. Though Pontiac and the Delaware Prophet disagreed on the use of guns (Pontiac advocated their use), the two leaders were a potent organizing force that united many diverse Indian nations.

Traders in the region spread the news of Pontiac's alliance and eventually alerted the British, who sent reinforcements into the Detroit region. In April 1763, Pontiac made final plans for a coordinated siege carried out by separate Indian bands throughout the Great Lakes region. On May 5, he visited Fort Detroit probably for reconnaissance purposes. The fort's leader, Major Henry Gladwin, knew of the planned surprise attack and prevented Pontiac from bringing in any large numbers of his warriors. Finally on May 9, Pontiac, under pressure from restless warriors, attacked the fort. Simultaneously, he ordered a siege of the entire region, by alerting his network of sympathetic bands.

Many tribes answered Pontiac's call for attack, including Chippewa, Delaware, Huron, Illinois, Kickapoo, Miami, Potawatomi, Seneca, and Shawnee. In the ensuing attacks, about two thousand settlers were killed and a number of British posts and forts fell. In October 1763, the British government issued a Royal proclamation that forbade English settlement on land west of the Appalachians. Pontiac, meanwhile, persisted in his siege of Fort Detroit. When French support failed to materialize, however, Pontiac's warriors began to question the wisdom of continuing the siege with winter approaching and food supplies dwindling. A letter from a French commander finally persuaded Pontiac to call off the siege. Although he continued to believe in his resistance movement, he signed a peace pact in 1765 and a peace treaty in 1766. He was pardoned by the British and returned to his village on the Maumee River.

Despite the 1763 proclamation forbidding it, English settlers continued to settle on Indian lands west of the Appalachians. However, Pontiac counseled peace. In 1769, the Ottawa leader was killed by an Indian who had probably been paid by the British. The alliances that Pontiac forged among diverse Indian groups set a precedent for future resistance efforts among Indian leaders of this region, who like Pontiac, sought ways to halt settler encroachment on their lands.

## Horace Poolaw (1909–1984)
### Kiowa photographer

Horace Poolaw was one of the most prolific Indian photographers of his generation. His photographs captured the tumultuous period of Kiowa history, including the arrival of U.S. settlers to Oklahoma and the allotment of tribal lands. The Kiowa are a southern Plains Nation who took up the Plains culture of the horse, buffalo hunting, bundles of sacred objects given by the Great Spirit, and annual summer gatherings for ceremonial purposes. In the late 1870s, the U.S. government forced the Kiowa to settle on a reservation in present-day Oklahoma.

Poolaw was born on the Kiowa Indian Agency in Anadarko, Oklahoma. At age seventeen, he was apprenticed to landscape photographer George Long. Under Long's tutelage, and that of his successor, John Coyle, Poolaw learned the art and technique of photography. During the mid-1920s, Poolaw began to develop his own collection of photographs by taking pictures of Kiowa daily life. In 1929, the American Indian exposition opened in Anadarko (where it remains to this day). Poolaw was the official photographer of the exposition. When World War II broke out, Poolaw enlisted and served three years in the army air corps, training soldiers to take aerial photographs. A number of Poolaw's Kiowa contemporaries served with him. After the war, Poolaw returned to Oklahoma, where he raised cattle and farmed, all the while taking many photographs. In 1978, failing eyesight finally forced Poolaw to put down his camera. Poolaw's photographs were printed, cataloged, and exhibited for the first time in 1990. His work is considered one of the best sources of information about Kiowa life in the early twentieth century.

## Popé (d. 1690)
*Tewa Pueblo tribal leader*

Popé was an important spiritual and military leader of his people. In the 1680s, he led a successful rebellion against the Spanish in the upper Rio Grande region by uniting a number of pueblo villages. After the rebellion, for nearly a decade, Popé was a central leader among the temporarily free pueblo villages.

The Spanish founded the colony of New Mexico on Indian land in 1598. The Europeans soon were using their soldiers to collect taxes and promote the Catholic religion among the Indians living in the region. Under the *repartimiento* system, Indians were forced to pay the Spanish taxes in the form of labor, crops, and cloth. Unlike British settlers in the east who chose to drive the Indians from their land, the Spanish conquerors preferred to rule over the Native inhabitants in a feudal economy. The Catholic Church in its zeal to convert Indians called for the expurgation of Indian religious beliefs and rituals. These efforts were enforced by the ever-present Spanish military. The Indians living under Spanish jurisdiction were forced to practice their beliefs in hiding. Among the pueblo villages along the Rio Grande, religious ceremonies took place in semi-subterranean ceremonial chambers known as *kivas*. Many Indians gave lip service to Christian beliefs in public, but clung to their own faith in private.

Popé was an important medicine man of the San Juan Pueblo, who had resisted repeated attempts to convert him. He was captured and flogged by Spanish authorities on at least three occasions. His beatings became a symbol of resistance to his people and enhanced his efforts to gain recruits for a hoped-for uprising. In 1675, Spanish authorities arrested Popé and a number of other Pueblo medicine men. The prisoners were taken to Santa Fe where they were jailed and beaten. An Indian delegation won their release after threatening the Spanish with violence. Upon his release, Popé went to the Taos Pueblo where he began organizing a rebellion and covertly enlisting recruits. He preached that the *kachinas*, or ancestral spirits, had ordered him to restore the traditional way of life for his people. A number of towns pledged allegiance to Popé's cause, and on 10 August 1675, he ordered an attack. Resistance fighters from numerous pueblos in the region moved against the Spanish. After a number of successful smaller engagements, a large Indian force moved on to Santa Fe in present-day New Mexico. A week of fighting and four hundred deaths later, the Spanish retreated south to El Paso, in present-day western Texas. About 250 Indians died in the uprising.

For the next twelve years, the pueblos held control of their homeland. Popé oversaw the destruction of all Spanish property and cultural institutions. Indians who had been baptized by Catholic priests were washed with suds from the Yucca plant to "cleanse" their spirits. Popé chose to live in Santa Fe and used the carriage left behind by the Spanish governor. By the time of his death in 1690, the alliance of the region's Indians had dissolved in the face of drought and attacks by Apache and Ute bands. By 1692, Santa Fe was once again under Spanish control.

## Alexander Posey (1873–1908)
*Creek journalist and poet*

Alexander Posey was a well-known Creek poet and journalist. His skillful satirization of U.S. culture provided his people with an important source of identity during a time when their lands and culture were being stripped from them.

Alexander Posey's father was Scotch-Irish and his mother was Creek. He was raised in Creek culture by his mother near Eufaula, Oklahoma. He mastered English as a teenager while going to Bacone Indian University in Tahlequah, Oklahoma. At the university, Posey learned to set type and began writing.

Some of Posey's most direct work was done in the *Indian Journal*, a Native Oklahoma newspaper, in which he regularly satirized U.S. society. He especially liked to point out American fondness for material possessions, including Indian land. Posey cleverly mixed pidgin English, puns, and inside jokes with a recurring cast of characters who dealt with attempts to change Indian ways through new names, haircuts, and slogans. One of Posey's most beloved characters was Hotgun, a droll, seasoned veteran of the conflict between Indian cultures and U.S. culture. Hotgun's humorous comments helped Indians maintain a sense of belonging and identity. Posey's humor was a much-needed witty tonic for Indians whose way of life and lands were under siege in the late 1900s.

Posey was also directly active in tribal affairs and was superintendent of public instruction of the Creek Nation. In 1905, he helped draft a revised Creek constitution.

## Poundmaker (circa 1842–1886)
*Cree tribal leader*

A trader who met Poundmaker in the 1860s described him as "just an ordinary Indian, [an] ordinary man as other Indians." Poundmaker's life changed several years later, however, when, during a truce between the Cree and the Blackfoot, he was noticed by a wife of the Blackfoot chief Crowfoot. The two were struck by Poundmaker's resemblance to a son who had been killed by Cree warriors before the truce. Crowfoot immediately adopted Poundmaker as his son and gave him a Blackfoot name, Makoyi-koh-kin (Wolf Thin Legs). Poundmaker's stature increased when he returned to his people in central Saskatchewan and was chosen to be one of several spokespersons for the Plains Cree in negotiations over a treaty with Canadian authorities in 1876. During negotiations, Poundmaker pressed for better terms, including education and assistance, stating that once the buffalo were gone, he and his people would have to learn how to farm and survive in a new world. His pleas fell on deaf ears, however, and he eventually signed the treaty and agreed to a reserve for his people in central Saskatchewan.

Poundmaker and his followers participated in the second Northwest Rebellion of 1885, in which Louis Riel, leader of the Métis people, sought to form a provisional government in Saskatchewan against the wishes of Canadian authorities. Poundmaker's followers ransacked the abandoned village of Battleford in what now is central Saskatchewan. A military force of some three hundred men were sent in retaliation. When they attacked Poundmaker's camp, however, they suffered heavy casualties. When he learned of Louis Riel's surrender in 1885, Poundmaker also surrendered to Canadian authorities. He was convicted of treason and after serving a year of his three-year sentence, Poundmaker fell ill and was released. He died four months later.

## Powhatan (1550?–1618)
*Powhatan tribal leader*

In the late 1500s and early 1600s, the Indian chief Wahunsonacock presided over the Powhatan Confederacy, an alliance of Indian tribes and villages stretching from the Potomac River to the Tidewater region of present-day Virginia. The English called Wahunsonacock Powhatan (Falls of the River), after the village where the Indian leader dwelled. (Today this village is Richmond, Virginia.) As ruler of this region, Powhatan played a pivotal role in relations with early English colonists in Virginia. One colonist described Powhatan as regal and majestic: "No king, but a kingly figure." Powhatan's daughter, Pocahontas, married John Rolfe, the Englishman who developed tobacco farming in Virginia. Powhatan's brother, Opechancanough, led the Powhatan uprisings against English settlers in 1622 and 1644.

Powhatan inherited from his father a confederacy of six tribes, but the ambitious leader quickly expanded his domain. Estimates of the Powhatan Confederacy range from 128 to 200 villages consisting of eight to nine thousand inhabitants and encompassing up to thirty different tribes. It is believed that Powhatan built the confederacy using a combination of incentives and coercion.

Communities under Powhatan's jurisdiction received military protection and adhered to the confederacy's well-organized system of hunting and trading boundaries. In return, subjects paid a tax to Powhatan in the form of food, pelts, copper, and pearls. Europeans who visited Powhatan in the 1600s have described a large structure filled with "treasures," probably Powhatan's storehouse and revenue collection center.

Powhatan was an important figure in the opening stages of English efforts to settle in the Tidewater region, in particular the Jamestown expedition of 1607. Setting foot on the shores of Powhatan's domain the

English were unaware that they were trespassing on a land ruled by a shrewd and well-organized head of state. Powhatan, approximately sixty years old at the time, could easily have demolished the faltering community, but instead chose to tolerate the English for a time—one reason being his desire to develop trade with them. Metal tools and weaponry were of special interest to Powhatan. Despite a mutual desire for trade, relations between Powhatan and the Virginia settlers were rocky; attacks and counterattacks were common.

The English government in the early 1600s knew that maintaining friendly relations with the Powhatan people was a key to establishing a foothold in the region. For this reason, Powhatan was courted by several colonial leaders. In 1609, he was offered a crown from the King of England and reluctantly agreed to have it placed ceremoniously on his head. In return, Powhatan sent the King of England his old moccasins and a mantle.

In 1614, a degree of harmony was eventually achieved after the marriage of Pocahontas (who, in 1613, was kidnapped by the Virginia settlers) to John Rolfe, a leading citizen of Jamestown Colony. After the marriage of his daughter, Powhatan negotiated a peace settlement that produced generally friendly relations with the English until a few years after Powhatan's death in 1618.

## Janine Pease Pretty On Top (1949–)
*Crow educator*

Janine Pease Pretty On Top, president of Little Big Horn College, is a noted educator and career services specialist. She was born in Nespelem, Washington, though her tribal affiliation is with the Crow, who have a reservation in southeastern Montana. The educator received her bachelor of arts degree from Central Washington University in Ellensburg, Washington. She has worked as a counselor at Navajo Community College, women's basketball coach at Big Bend Community College, and career services director at Eastern Montana College. During her career in education, she has served on the Washington State Youth Commission (1971) and the Montana State Advisory Committee on Vocational Education (1977), co-chaired the Native American Telecommunication Demonstration (1978), and was chair of the Crow/Shell Scholarship Committee (1981).

Her honors include being nominated for Outstanding Woman of the Year in Washington (1972) and the same award in Montana (1976). Among her interests are women's rights and Native American educational issues.

## Puccaiunla (Hanging Grapes) (circa 1760–1838)
*Chickasaw tribal leader*

Puccaiunla was the wife of Ish-te-ho-to-pah, the last hereditary principal chief of the Chickasaw (1820–1850). In 1856, the Chickasaw adopted a constitutional government, and thereafter until 1906, the U.S. government abolished the Chickasaw government. Although the extent of her authority is not known, it is known that Puccaiunla was deeply loved by her people. It is believed that the wife of the principal chief was without any authority and was regarded only as other Chickasaw women were. Before the Chickasaw removal to Indian Territory in present-day Oklahoma in 1838, however, they donated fifty dollars a year to Puccaiunla, a financial bonanza at that time. The Chickasaws felt grateful to their old leaders for long and faithful service and believed it a duty to keep them from want in their old age. A Chickasaw government bill on the Chickasaw national treasury stated, "Queen Puccaiunla is now very old and very poor. Justice, says the Nation, ought not to let her suffer in her old age; it is therefore determined to give her, out of the National funds, fifty dollars a year during her life, the money to be put in the hands of the agent to be paid out for her support, under his direction, with the advice of the chiefs."

During Chickasaw removal to Indian Territory in the early 1840s, smallpox and lack of provisions interfered with efforts to move the tribe. Puccaiunla was among those who died during the removal period.

## Pushmataha (1764–1824)
*Choctaw tribal leader*

Choctaw legend says that Pushmataha was an orphan, and he himself maintained that he was born of a splinter from an oak tree. Such a story was unusual in Choctaw society where everyone was conscious of their Native iksa (local matrilineal family). At a young age, Pushmataha was recognized as a great warrior and hunter. He participated in many Choctaw hunting forays across the Mississippi River into the Osage and Caddo country, since by the early 1800s, fur-bearing animals suitable for trade were already significantly depleted in Choctaw country. These hunting trips led to war with the Caddo and Osage, who protected their land from the Choctaw intruders.

In 1805, Pushmataha was elected chief of the southern or Six Towns district of the Choctaw Nation. The Choctaw government was divided into three politically independent districts, each with a chief and council. From 1805 to 1824, Pushmataha led the southern district, which was the most conservative district, and, before 1760, allied to the French Louisiana Colony.

In the early 1800s, Pushmataha owned a small farm, had two wives—which was possible under Choctaw custom—and owned several slaves. Pushmataha favored friendly relations with the United States, siding with the United States against the British, and Tecumseh, the Shawnee war leader, and the Red Stick Creek during the War of 1812. For his services, he earned the rank of U.S. brigadier general. The Choctaw, including Pushmataha, signed treaties of land cession in 1805, 1816, and 1820. In 1824, Pushmataha died from an infection while in Washington negotiating yet another treaty. He was buried with full U.S. military honors.

### Al Qoyawayma (1938– )
*Hopi engineer and artist*

Al Qoyawayma, a prominent engineer and noted ceramicist, was one of the founders of the American Indian Science and Engineering Society (AISES) and was its first chairman.

Born in Los Angeles, California, unlike many Hopi who are born on the reservation, he succeeded in maintaining his Hopi roots while prospering in the non-Hopi world.

Qoyawayma earned a bachelor of science degree in mechanical engineering at California Polytechnical State University in San Luis Obispo in 1961 and a master of science degree from the University of California in 1966. He began working in 1961 for Litton Systems, Inc., in the development of high technology systems and products, including inertial guidance systems and airborne star tracking devices, and holds several domestic and foreign patents. In 1971, as a means of providing greater assistance to Arizona Indian tribes, he became manager of environmental services for the Salt River Project in central Arizona. Among other duties, he is in charge of preparing environmental statements, recommending corporate policy, and providing computer and technical support.

Qoyawayma has become famous for his exquisite ceramics. On vacation visits to see and study with his aunt, Polingaysi Qoyawayma, he perfected various pottery techniques and currently turns out approximately thirty individual pieces per year. He uses traditional methods in personally collecting his clays and pigments, and he grinds them by hand. He then applies his engineering talents in molding and stretching the clay into art forms. His work has been displayed at the Smithsonian Institute of Natural History, the American Craft Museum, and the Kennedy Art Center in Washington, D.C.

He was a member of the dean's advisory council at California Polytechnic State University's School of Engineering in San Luis Obispo (1994–1996); a Fulbright Fellow with the Maori and South Pacific Arts/Te Waka Toi (1991); commissioner for the Arizona Commission on the Arts (1991–1992); a member of the board of directors at the Heard Museum in Phoenix (1990–1992); vice-chairman for the board of trustees at the Institute of American Indian Arts in Santa Fe, New Mexico (1988–1994); a member of the board of directors for the National Action Committee on Minorities in Engineering (1984–1986); and co-founder and chairman emeritus of the American Indian Science and Engineering Society (1977–present).

He received the Popovi Da Memorial Award from the Scottsdale National Arts Exhibition in 1976, was awarded an honorary doctorate of humane letters from the University of Colorado in 1986, and accepted the Ely S. Parker Award from the American Indian Science and Engineering Society in 1986. He also holds U.S. and international patents on Inertial Guidance Systems (IMU), 747, F-15, and other commercial and military aircraft and applications.

### Rain-in-the-Face (Iromagaja) (1835–1905)
*Hunkpapa Lakota tribal leader*

Rain-in-the-Face was a leading Sioux war chief who participated in the defense of Sioux land in the 1860s and 1870s. He was one of several Indian chiefs who joined together to defeat Custer's Seventh Cavalry at the Battle of the Little Bighorn in June 1876.

Rain-in-the-Face was born in present-day North Dakota at the forks of the Cheyenne River. It is believed that he received his name from two episodes, one in which blood streamed down his face during a boyhood fight and a second when his warpaint became smeared during a fight with the Gros Ventre. He became a chief through meritorious deeds in battle.

Rain-in-the-Face participated in several important battles during the 1860s and 1870s for control of the Sioux lands. In 1866, he fought alongside fellow Hunkpapa leaders such as Gall, and the Oglala chief, Crazy Horse, during Red Cloud's War to prevent settlement along the Bozeman Trail in present-day Wyoming and Montana. In 1868, he led a raid on Fort Totten in North Dakota. In 1873, Rain-in-the-Face was finally arrested for murder at Fort Abraham Lincoln, near present-day Bismarck, North Dakota, but he escaped to join Sitting Bull in the fight for the Black Hills in 1876. Rain-in-the-Face was a major leader in the defeat of Colonel George Custer and about two hundred men at the 1876 Little Bighorn Battle in southern Montana.

For a time, it was believed that Rain-in-the-Face dealt the fatal blow to Custer, but this has never been substantiated.

In 1880, Rain-in-the-Face surrendered at Fort Keogh, Montana. He spent his remaining years living on the Standing Rock Reservation in North Dakota.

## Ramona (1865–1924)
*Cahuilla (Kawia) basketmaker*

Ramona was a Cahuilla Indian who lived in present-day San Diego County, California. She became something of a celebrity in the late 1880s, due to the fictional story *Ramona* by the famous historical novelist Helen Hunt Jackson.

The central character in the novel is a romantic figure who bears little resemblance to the real-life Ramona. Jackson came to California in 1881 as an investigative reporter for *Century* magazine. While gathering information, she became entranced with the picturesque Roman Catholic past of southern California and wrote a sympathetic portrayal of the context and purposes of Spanish Catholicism and colonization in California. In contrast, *Ramona* was a work of social protest that underscored the plight of California Indians, often called Mission Indians, who were forced to live and work in the Catholic missions. In her investigative reporting, Jackson recorded the grave population decline of California Mission Indians and the role of the Spanish in this decline. Jackson became determined to write a work that would bring the plight of the Mission Indians to the American public's eye. *Ramona* was first serialized in 1884 by *Christian Union* magazine.

The real-life Ramona, a Cahuilla Indian living in present-day Temecula, California, had been married to Juan Diego, who was murdered in dramatic fashion by a local villain named Sam Temple. The novel, which incorporated a fictionalized romance, became an instant success and spawned a movie in the early 1900s, and the real-life Ramona became something of a celebrity, selling baskets and photographs of herself to eager tourists at a souvenir stand. Today, the myth of Ramona continues to live in numerous reenactments and festivals celebrating her life and character.

## Elaine A. Ramos (contemporary)
*Tlingit performing artist, educator, and nurse*

Elaine Ramos is a nurse, educator, and the founder of a traditional Tlingit performing ensemble. She was raised by her parents to speak Tlingit and learned tribal history, legends, and culture.

After graduating from nursing school at Sage Memorial Hospital in Arizona, Ramos worked among the Navajo during a diphtheria outbreak and delivered babies in hogans. She eventually missed her Tlingit homeland and returned to Yakutat, Alaska, one of the northernmost villages of the Tlingit Indians, who live along the southern panhandle of Alaska. The northern Tlingit are well known for their strong sense of preserving traditional Tlingit culture and especially for their keeping of potlatches, a giveaway ceremony of large amounts of goods and money in honor of the clan ancestors. With the nearest hospital three hundred miles away in Juneau, the state capital, Ramos continued with her nursing as the only person in Yakutat with any knowledge of medicine. She also became active in local efforts to consolidate educational services.

Ramos enrolled at Sheldon Jackson College in Sitka, Alaska, in 1966 and was salutatorian of her graduating class. She became an assistant dean of students and was appointed vice-president of the college in 1972. In the late 1960s, she founded the Raven Dancers to promote Tlingit storytelling, singing, and costuming. The ensemble has performed across Alaska and venues in the continental United States. In 1973, Ramos received the prestigious Indian Council Fire Award.

## James Ransom (1958–)
*Mohawk environmentalist*

James Ransom is the first director of the environmental program on the St. Regis Indian Reservation, located on the New York-Canadian border. In this capacity, he is leading a campaign to clean the region of environmental pollutants. The Mohawk are an Iroquoian-speaking people, and one of the nations of the Iroquois Confederacy (see the biographies of Deganawidah and Handsome Lake).

Ransom graduated from Clarkson University in Potsdam, New York, with a civil engineering degree in 1988; in the same year, he became the first director of St. Regis Mohawk Education and Community Fund, a program to clean up the environmental waste choking the St. Regis Indian Reservation. Pollutants are an acute problem in the area, which is a favorite dumping ground for nearby industries. The soil and water near the reservation are saturated with toxic wastes and heavy metals. In 1989, on behalf of his tribe, Ransom sued Reynolds Metals, General Motors Central Foundry Division, and major aluminum manufacturer ALCOA for environmental damage to the St. Lawrence River.

Ransom's environmental advocacy propelled him into an elected position as sub-chief of the St. Regis Mohawk tribe. Ransom's long-term goals include the creation of a consulting group that would seek out other communities and help them deal with environmental issues. Ransom believes the St. Lawrence River region can be restored as a prime fishing and recreational area once the pollution problem is addressed and remedied.

## Red Cloud (1822–1909)
*Oglala Sioux tribal leader*

Red Cloud was a war chief and leader of the Oglala subdivision of the Teton Sioux. He was born in present-day north-central Nebraska near the forks of the Platte River. His father was Lone Man and his mother was Walks as She Thinks. Lone Man died soon after the birth of his son, and Red Cloud was raised by an Oglala headman, Smoke, his mother's uncle. Red Cloud quickly gained a reputation for bravery and cunning in raids against the Pawnee and Crow. When he was about nineteen, Red Cloud shot his uncle's rival, the most powerful Oglala chief, Bull Bear, at Fort Laramie, located in present-day eastern Wyoming. Because of these exploits, he was chosen to be leader of the Iteshicha (Bad Face) band over Man Afraid of His Horses, the hereditary leader.

Tensions dramatically increased between the Plains tribes and the United States with the advent of the Bozeman Trail, which passed through the present-day states of Wyoming and Montana, and its connection to the Oregon Trail, which provided passage to the Northwest Coast. Immigrants, miners, wagon trains, and U.S. troops began entering the area that was a prime resource to the Indians for bison hunting. The Oglala and Hunkpapa Sioux, Northern Cheyenne, and Northern Arapaho were enraged by these transgressions. Revenge for the murders of several hundred Cheyenne people at the 1864 Sand Creek Massacre in present-day Colorado may also have played a role. At Fort Laramie in 1866 Red Cloud, along with Man Afraid of His Horses, refused to sign a non-aggression treaty and declared war on all non-Indians entering the region.

Red Cloud was the architect of a number of attacks against U.S. settlers and miners who were traveling the Bozeman and Oregon trails. The Sioux employed guerrilla-like tactics to harry soldiers and would-be settlers. In December 1866, Captain William Fetterman led a relief party of eighty-one men to their deaths after supposedly boasting, "Give me eighty men and I'll ride through the whole Sioux nation." Subsequent battles, including the Wagon Box Fight and the Hayfield Fight, led the army to evacuate the region in 1868 and then agree in the Treaty of Fort Laramie to relinquish the Bozeman Trail in exchange for the cessation of further

Indian raids. The Sioux celebrated this announcement by burning down every abandoned fort along the trail.

In 1870, Red Cloud traveled to Washington, D.C., to meet with President Ulysses Grant and then went on to New York City, where he gave a public speech. A Sioux agency bearing his name was established in present-day southern South Dakota, and Red Cloud spent the remainder of his life seeking to mediate peaceful relations between the Sioux and the United States. After government officials accused him of secretly aiding the Sioux and Cheyenne bands that defeated Colonel George Custer at the Battle of Little Bighorn in June 1876, the Red Cloud Reservation was renamed Pine Ridge, which name the reservation still bears.

Few on either side trusted Red Cloud's willingness to compromise, although he maintained that he supported peace, even during the Ghost Dance Uprising in 1890, when many Sioux sought religious solutions to reservation poverty and political confinement. During his later years, Red Cloud lost his sight, and he was baptized in the Catholic Church. He died in his home on the Pine Ridge Reservation.

## Red Crow (circa 1830–1900)
*Blood tribal leader*

Also known as Mekaisto, Red Crow was born and raised in what is currently Alberta in the Canadian Plains. Descended from a long line of Blood chiefs, including his father, Black Bear, Red Crow continued the family tradition. The Blood people, together with the Blackfoot and Peigan nations, were part of the powerful Blackfoot Confederacy that lived on the Canadian Plains. Red Crow became a warrior in his teens, and over his lifetime participated in at least thirty-three raids against the Crow, Plains Cree, Nez Percé, Assiniboine, and Shoshoni peoples. He was known for his remarkable ability to remain unscathed and late in life boasted, "I was never struck by an enemy in my life, with bullet, arrow, axe, spear or knife."

Red Crow became leader of his people, the Fish Eaters band, when smallpox claimed the life of his father in 1869. He forged alliances with the Northwest Mounted Police and Plains Indian leaders and became the leading chief of the Blood people. During the 1870s, the buffalo were virtually destroyed by American hunters in Montana Territory, and Red Crow realized that his people would have to change their ways in order to survive. In 1880, he selected a reserve for his people and organized the construction of log shanties. He and his people turned to agriculture and cattle raising. Unlike many other Plains Indian communities, Red

Crow's people did not participate in the 1885 North-west Rebellions, in which Louis Riel, leader of the Métis people, sought to form a provisional government in Saskatchewan against the wishes of Canadian authorities. In fact, Red Crow joined a delegation of Blackfoot chiefs on a tour of eastern Canada provided as a gesture of thanks from Canadian authorities for not participating in the rebellions. After visiting the Mohawk Institute in Brantford, Ontario, a school for Mohawk students, Red Crow became a strong supporter of education and encouraged the schooling provided by various missionaries on the reserve. Red Crow died quietly in 1900 on the banks of the river that ran through his reserve.

### Valerie Red-Horse (contemporary)
*Cherokee-Sioux actor, director, screenwriter, and producer*

With the 1998 release of the movie *Naturally Native*, Valerie Rochelle Littlestar Red-Horse Mohl and her production company, Red-Horse Native Productions, have opened doors for aspiring Native actors, writers, producers, and directors. Not only was the movie the first to be produced by the Mashantucket Pequot Tribal

Valerie Red-Horse.

Nation, but it also starred and employed almost entirely Native Americans. *Naturally Native* explores the lives of three urban Indian women who are searching for their roots. Through this search the women start their own business, making cosmetic products from traditional Native California herbs and plants.

Valerie Red-Horse grew up in Fresno, Califorina, the daughter of an English mother and a Cherokee and Sioux father, Joseph Red-Horse. Her father was seventy when Red-Horse was born and he left when she was three years old. While Red-Horse saw her father only sporadically after that, her mother encouraged her to be proud of her heritage and raised her conscious of her background.

The to-be actress and businesswoman graduated at the top of her high school class and attended the University of California, Los Angeles (UCLA). She graduated cum laude with a major in theater. She later studied at the Lee Strasberg Theater Institute as well.

While in college she met her husband, Curt Mohl, an offensive lineman for the UCLA football team and later an NFL football player. They have worked together on several business projects, including a successful advertising specialty business and the herbal cosmetic line, recently launched on the Internet and inspired by *Naturally Native*. The couple has three children, Courtney, Derek, and Chelsea.

Red-Horse's acting career started slowly. She spent her first twenty years in the business being told she was either too ethnic for mainstream or was not ethnic enough to play Native roles. She did break into the business, however, with lead roles on *Santa Barbara*, *The Dennis Miller Show*, *Anything But Love*, and *Babylon Five*. Fed up with the opportunities provided Native Americans in film and television, Red-Horse started her own production company in the early 1990s to create films that accurately portray the Native experience. Her first screenplay, *Lozen*, based on the life of the Apache woman warrior, was selected for the Sundance Institute's Writer's Lab. In 1995 Red-Horse created the story for the Emmy-award winning CBS Special *My Indian Summer*. The next year she produced an American Film Institute project entitled *Looks Into the Night*, which won Best Live Action Short at the American Indian Film Festival.

In addition to her film-related achievements, Red-Horse organizes and funds Hollywood Access Program for Natives, a nonprofit organization that provides film production internships for students from reservations. In the last three years, the program has sponsored over a dozen students. Red-Horse also heads a liturgical dance company and was the live model promoting the

Pocahontas doll. She is an active member of the Presbyterian Church and is involved with outreach ministries and youth workshops at reservations nationwide.

While an aspiring artist, Red-Horse worked for the investment banking and high-yield bond departments of the highly successful brokerage firm Drexel, Burnham & Lambert. During this time she realized a lack of American Indian presence in the financial industry and vowed to someday change that. In 1998 she formed the first American Indian-owned stock brokerage on Wall Street, Native Nations Securities, Incorporated, and is principal owner. Besides their normal business activities, the brokerage offers a complex training program for Indian youth, providing internships and preparation for their own licensing exams.

In her years of working, Red-Horse has received many awards and honors. She was awarded the Eagle Spirit and Producer of the Year awards by the American Indian Film Festival. In addition, she was a 1997 Girls, Inc. honoree and 1998 Changing Images in America honoree. In 1999 Red-Horse received a Cherokee Medal of Honor. In 2000 Red-Horse received awards from the First Americans in the Arts for outstanding achievement in directing, writing, and producing *Naturally Native*.

Red-Horse Native Productions just signed on to executive produce *Whisper the Wind*, an upcoming studio blockbuster about the Navajo Codetalkers. This feature will be coupled by *True Whispers*, a documentary about the same subject to be directed by Red-Horse. The artist presently lives with her husband and children in the Los Angeles area.

### Red Jacket (1758–1830)
*Seneca tribal leader*

Red Jacket supported the British during the American Revolution (1777–1783) and later became a spokesman for his people in negotiations with the U.S. government. Red Jacket was also a staunch opponent of Christianity and worked to prevent Iroquois conversions to Christianity.

Although Red Jacket eventually allied himself with other Indian nations in support of the British during the American Revolution, he was originally hesitant about the affiliation. This ambivalence perhaps explains why he did little fighting during the conflict. According to a number of accounts, Red Jacket's reluctance to fight was perceived as cowardice by some Iroquois war leaders such as Cornplanter and Joseph Brant.

After the war, Red Jacket became a principal spokesman for the Seneca people. He was present at treaty negotiations in 1794 and 1797 in which major portions of Seneca land in upstate New York were ceded or partitioned into smaller reservations. During this era, Red Jacket also became an outspoken opponent of Christianity and an advocate for preserving traditional Iroquois beliefs. His efforts to protect traditional beliefs culminated in the temporary expulsion of all Christian missionaries from Seneca territory in 1824. Red Jacket and the so-called Pagan Party were undermined in the ensuing years, however, by accusations of witchcraft and Red Jacket's own problems with alcohol. In 1827, Red Jacket was deposed as a Seneca chief. He died three years later, after his own family had converted to Christianity.

Red Jacket is immortalized in a now-famous painting by Charles Bird King. In this historical painting, Red Jacket is depicted with a large, silver medal that was given to him in 1792 by President George Washington during a diplomatic visit to the then-U.S. capital at New York City.

### Kevin Red Star (1942–)
*Crow-Northern Plains artist*

Kevin Red Star is a Crow Indian born on the Crow Reservation in Lodge Grass, Montana. His father had an

Kevin Red Star.

abiding interest in music, and his mother is a skilled craftswoman. In this nurturing environment, Red Star developed an early artistic capability. He studied at the Institute of American Indian Art (IAIA) in Santa Fe, New Mexico, from 1962 to 1964, then at the San Francisco Art Institute, and, later, at Montana State University.

In 1965, Red Star won a scholarship to the San Francisco Art Institute. As a freshman there, he was awarded the governor's trophy and the Al and Helen Baker Award from the Scottsdale National Indian Arts Exhibition. Red Star's first one-person exhibition was in 1971 at the Museum of the Plains Indian in Browning, Montana, where he drew heavily upon his Plains Indian culture, using Crow art and design concepts to inspire his own interpretation of the life force that exists beyond the surface of decorated objects. In 1974, after having worked as an assistant art instructor at his alma mater, Lodge Grass High School, Red Star was invited to return to IAIA to participate in the artist-in-residence program and became the first graduate of IAIA to return as an artist-in-residence. While in Santa Fe, he expanded his art to include lithography, serigraphs, and etchings and was selected as Artist of the Year by *Sante Fean* magazine in 1976 and 1977.

Red Star returned to his own community to teach art and served as Crow tribal art consultant, helping to form the Crow-Cheyenne Fine-Arts Alliance to organize art exhibitions. Redstar has emerged as one of the premier Northern Plains fine artists. His latest works include exciting use of color and refined graphic design. Red Star continues to work daily, primarily in oils. With galleries all over the country, he is free to live where he chooses. Red Star's goal is to move to his native Pryor area to create a studio for monotypes and ceramics and to focus on art and music. Red Star has been recognized as being among the masters of Indian artists.

## William Ronald "Bill" Reid (1920–1998)
*Haida sculptor*

Bill Reid was a renowned Haida sculptor, known around the world for his monumental sculptures of Haida life. He was born in Vancouver, British Columbia, in 1920 to a Haida mother and a Scottish-American father and was unaware of his indigenous background until he was a teenager. It was only in the 1950s, after studying jewelry and engraving in Toronto and working as a broadcaster for the Canadian Broadcasting Company, that Reid began to explore Haida art and sculpture in earnest. He continued with his artistic education, studying at the Central School of Art and Design in London, England. He eventually returned to British Columbia where he quickly became known as an accomplished expert on Haida art, while simultaneously transforming the tradition to include his work. Perhaps his best known piece is a four-and-a-half ton cedar sculpture on display in the University of British Columbia School of Anthropology entitled *Raven and the First Humans*. It depicts an enormous raven perched on top of a half-open seashell from which human beings are peering out at the world. Other noteworthy works include a bronze killer-whale sculpture entitled *The Chief of the Undersea World* on display at the Vancouver Aquarium. Reid is accomplished in a number of media and has illustrated and collaborated on a number of books. He was awarded an honorary doctorate from the University of British Columbia in 1976. Prior to his death in 1998, Reid was involved in efforts to preserve South Moresby Island, located in the Queen Charlotte Islands off the coast of British Columbia, from economic development and the logging industry.

## Ben Reifel (1906–1990)
*Dakota-Brule U.S. congressman*

Ben Reifel's mother was a Sioux, and his father a German-American. As a young man, Reifel had to fight for his education; his father wanted him to remain on the family farm. Reifel left his family and eventually received a high school diploma. He went on to earn a bachelor's degree and a master of science degree from South Dakota State College. He later became one of the first Native Americans to obtain a doctorate degree from Harvard University. Reifel entered public service after active duty in the U.S. Army during World War II where he was commissioned a second lieutenant. After the war Reifel entered the Indian Service where he worked to establish and organize Indian businesses as legislated by the Indian Reorganization Act of 1932. From that post, Reifel was promoted to superintendent of the Pine Ridge Reservation in southern South Dakota. He was the first Sioux Indian to hold that position, the highest Bureau of Indian Affairs administrative post on an Indian reservation.

In 1960, Reifel was elected to the U.S. House of Representatives and was reelected for five consecutive terms in races that demonstrated a growing popularity with voters. As a representative, Reifel served on the Appropriations Committee, Interior and Related Agencies Subcommittee, Legislative Subcommittee, and was a ranking minority member. Reifel's effectiveness as a legislator was certainly aided by his own research and data collection on the land and people living in the Plains area.

Carter Revard.

## Carter Revard (1931–)
*Osage writer*

Carter Revard is a nationally acclaimed writer whose works, drawn from traditional images of Native American culture, is combined with contemporary issues. Osage on his father's side, he was born in Pawhuska, Oklahoma. When he was two, his mother remarried and he grew up with an Osage stepfather, Addison Jump, six brothers and sisters, his Ponca aunt, Jewell McDonald, and her children, in the Buck Creek community.

The Osage people may earlier have been connected with the Cahokia Mound people of the Mississippian culture, who flourished from 800 to 1400 C.E. Before 1835, Osages dominated the Ozark region of Missouri, south of the Missouri River, but then were forced onto a reservation in southern Kansas until 1872, when they moved to present-day northeastern Oklahoma.

After graduating from Buck Creek School, he completed high school in Bartlesville, Oklahoma. He then won a radio-quiz scholarship to the University of Tulsa, graduating in 1952. The same year, he was given his Osage name by tribal elders, and with the help of a Rhodes Scholarship, he took a degree from Oxford University in 1954, and in 1959, a Ph.D. from Yale University.

After teaching at Amherst College until 1961, Revard moved to Washington University, in St. Louis, Missouri, where he taught medieval English and contemporary Native American literature until his retirement in 1997. He has also served as member, secretary, and president of the American Indian Center of Mid-America.

Revard is a Gourd Dancer, a sacred traditional dance among the southern Plains Indians (originating among Kiowa and Comanche people).

Revard's books of poetry and prose include *War Dancers: An Eagle Nation*, which won an Oklahoma Book Award in 1984, and *Winning the Dust Bowl*. Revard's writings have also been published in several anthologies of Native American writing, including *Earth Power Coming, The Remembered Earth, Voices of the Rainbow, Voices of Wahkontah, Native American Literature, Returning the Gift, Norton Anthology of Poetry*, and *Nothing But The Truth: An Anthology of Native American Literatures*.

## Everett B. Rhoades (1931–)
*Kiowa physician*

Everett Rhoades was the first Kiowa to obtain a medical degree and complete medical training. Though his life's work is in medicine, he is also an active member of the Kiowa Tribal Council and an advocate for his people in political and social issues.

Rhoades attended the University of Oklahoma and became chief resident in medicine at the university's medical center. After five years of active duty in the U.S. Air Force, Rhoades accepted an appointment at the University of Oklahoma Medical Center as chief of infectious diseases at the Veterans Administration Hospital and as assistant professor of medicine and microbiology. In 1970, Rhoades went to South Vietnam on a special assignment for the American Medical Association and the Agency for International Development, where he acted as consultant to the University of Saigon Medical School.

Throughout his career, Rhoades has studied Indian health issues, including the rates of infectious diseases and infant mortality among Indian people. In his addresses to Indian groups, Rhoades has been critical of welfare-providing agencies in the Indian community, and he argues that Indian communities must assume responsibility for their health.

Rhoades is a member of the National Congress of American Indians health committee and an advisor on long-range planning for the Indian Health Service. Rhoades is currently clinical professor and associate dean for community affairs in the Department of Medicine at Oklahoma University Health Science Center in Oklahoma City.

### John Rollin Ridge (1827–1867)
*Cherokee journalist and author*

John Rollin Ridge was the son of John Ridge (1803–1839) and the grandson of Major Ridge (1771–1839), both Cherokee leaders who favored Cherokee removal from Georgia in the 1830s. Both Ridges were assassinated in 1839, in part because they led the Treaty Party, a group of economically well-off Cherokee slaveholders, merchants, and plantation owners who agreed to migrate west to present-day Oklahoma by signing the Treaty of New Echota in 1835. Most Cherokee were not in favor of removal to the West, and many conservative Cherokee blamed the elder Ridges and other Treaty Party leaders for the deaths of their relatives during the Trail of Tears (1838–1839), when the U.S. Army forced most Cherokee to migrate from the East to present-day Oklahoma.

John Rollin Ridge grew up in the ensuing internal political disturbances among the Cherokee. In 1849, he killed a member of the conservative anti-Treaty Party and was forced to flee for his life. He traveled to California and worked as a newspaper editor and author. Ridge often wrote in defense of the political rights of the Cherokee, Creek, and Choctaw. Although California Indians of his day were suffering greatly from political oppression and even genocide, Ridge did not take up a consistent defense of the California tribes. In 1854, he published *The Life and Times of Joaquin Murieta, the Celebrated Californian Bandit,* which was a romantic and probably fictitious story about a Spanish-American bandit who raided the American gold fields. The book on Murieta became his most famous work and is well known in Mexican and Chilean literature. Ridge lived a lively but short life, and left a legacy of writings in politics, fiction, and poetry.

### Major Ridge (1771–1839)
*Cherokee tribal leader*

In his younger days, Major Ridge went by his Cherokee name, Nunna Hidihi (He Who Stands on the Mountaintop and Sees Clearly), a name of great respect for a man who showed wisdom and understanding in the Cherokee councils. As a young man, Ridge fought as a warrior in the numerous border wars with U.S. settlers until the peace emerged about 1795. Thereafter, Ridge and a small group of Cherokee leaders decided that agriculture and political change were the only means of ensuring Cherokee national survival from U.S. pressures for land cessions. Between 1797 and 1810, Ridge was a leading advocate for abolishment of the law of blood, the rule that clans exacted a death for a death in cases of murder. During the Creek War of 1813–1814, many Cherokee fought with the U.S. Army and lower town Creek villages. Ridge rose to the rank of major, and thereafter was called Major Ridge.

Between 1810 and 1828, the Cherokee incrementally formed a constitutional government, modeled after the U.S. government. The new Cherokee government instigated strong efforts by surrounding state governments to resettle the Cherokee west of the Mississippi River, because they feared the Cherokee might remain permanently in their eastern homeland. In 1835, Ridge and a minority group of Cherokee planters signed the Treaty of New Echota, thereby agreeing to migrate to present-day Oklahoma. The treaty signers feared that remaining in the east was impossible because American settlers were confiscating Cherokee property and the Cherokee government was outlawed. Many conservative Cherokee considered Major Ridge and the others traitors for signing the treaty and were embittered by the significant loss of life during the ensuing forced removal, the Trail of Tears, during the winter of 1838–1839. Major Ridge and several others were assassinated in 1839.

### Louis David Riel Jr. (1844–1885)
*Métis leader*

Louis Riel was a leader of the Métis people. He led what have become known as the Northwest Rebellions of 1870 and 1885. Riel was born to a French-Ojibwa father, Louis Riel Sr., a political leader in his own right, and a French mother, Julie Lagimodiere, in the Red River Settlement in what is now Manitoba. He began his education in St. Boniface, Manitoba, and went on to study languages, philosophy, mathematics, and the sciences in a Montreal seminary, and then went on to study law.

After traveling throughout the United States, he returned to the Red River in 1868 and became involved in the first Northwest Rebellion, in which he and his followers drove away federal surveyors planning to section off the territory into townships contrary to Métis patterns of landholding that divided the land into strips extending out from the river. A group of Canadians responded with an attempt to organize a militia, but Riel formed his own "Comité National des Métis," peacefully seized Fort Garry in Winnipeg, took numerous prisoners, and declared a provisional government in 1869. After declaring an amnesty of all prisoners, his government re-arrested one William Scott, who had plotted an attack on Fort Garry. Scott was found guilty and sentenced to death. When Riel supported the verdict, sentiment against him in the rest of Canada hardened. Riel fled to the United States shortly after his government reached an agreement with Canada to create the province of Manitoba. Riel was elected twice in absentia to the Canadian Parliament, returning once to claim his seat only to be evicted by a motion of the House of Commons. Shortly thereafter he suffered a nervous breakdown and was admitted for a short time to a mental institution. Released in 1878, Riel moved to Montana where he became an American citizen, married, and worked as a schoolteacher. He returned to Canada to help lead Métis resistance to the settlement of Saskatchewan in 1884, seizing a local church and again establishing a provisional government. He surrendered two months later, and was convicted of treason and executed in Regina, Saskatchewan, in 1885.

## Lynn Riggs (1899–1954)
*Cherokee playwright and poet*

Lynn Riggs was born on 31 August 1899 in Indian Territory, near present-day Claremore, Oklahoma. Following the death of his mother, Rosa Ella Duncan Riggs, when he was two, Riggs lived with his father and stepmother before spending the majority of his youth with his aunt, Mary Riggs Brice.

In 1917, he graduated from Eastern University Preparatory School in Claremore, Oklahoma, and moved to Chicago and later New York, where he worked as a movie extra and began his interest in theatre. He also lived in Tulsa, Oklahoma, and Los Angeles, California, before returning to Oklahoma. Riggs attended the University of Oklahoma from 1920 to 1923, serving as poetry editor of the *University of Oklahoma Magazine*.

He authored more than twenty plays and numerous poems. His first play, *Cukoo*, was produced at the University of Oklahoma, in 1922. His play, *Green Grow the Lilacs*, was produced by the Theatre Guild and, in 1931, was a success in New York. Rodgers and Hammerstein later adapted the play for the classic musical, *Oklahoma!*

Other works by Riggs include *The Cherokee Night, Knives from Syria, Sump'n Like Wings, Big Lake, All the Way Home, Roadside, Out of Dust, A Lantern to See By, Russet Mantle*, and *The Cream in the Well. The Cherokee Night*, which addresses early-twentieth century Cherokee identity, is still considered a groundbreaking play in the field of Native American drama.

He worked as a writer throughout the rest of his life, living mostly in Santa Fe, New Mexico, and New York, and was inducted into the Oklahoma Hall of Fame in 1948.

## Rebecca Robbins (1951–)
*Standing Rock Sioux educator*

Rebecca Robbins is president of Robbins Enterprises, Inc., and a specialist in the field of Native American education. She is also an assessment team member for the Ford Foundation's Rural Community College Initiative, a cluster evaluation team member (ORBIS Associates) for W. K. Kellogg Foundation's Native American Higher Education Initiative, and, in 1999, an evaluation team member for the David and Lucile Packard Foundation's Tribal Scholars Program.

She earned her B.A. in elementary education/library science at Arizona State University (1975), her master of education in educational administration at Pennsylvania State University (1978), and her doctorate in education theory and policy/speech communication at Pennsylvania State University (1983).

She has held academic positions in the Pennsylvania State Native American Graduate Program, was director

Rebecca Robbins.

of the National Indian Education Association (NIEA) education research projects, and taught and served as director of the American Indian Leadership Program at Arizona State University. Robbins served on the ERIC/CRESS All-Indian Task Force from 1976 to 1981, and the ERIC/CRESS National Advisory Board from 1976 to 1980. ERIC/CRESS is an organization that provides a national information service to teachers and researchers about issues in educational research and practice. Robbins has also served as an advisor and participant on many special education commissions and committees for the state of Minnesota and for the federal government, such as the National Conference for Inclusion of Minority Women and the Commission on Status of Women, which meets in Washington, D.C.

In addition to publishing numerous essays and articles, Robbins has edited eight semi-annual issues of the National Education Association's refereed journal of higher education, *Thought and Action*; written and edited forty-six issues of the National Education Association's newsletter, *The NEA Advocate for Higher Education*; and edited five issues of the National Education Association's annual *NEA Almanac of Higher Education*.

## Rose Robinson (1932–1995)
*Hopi journalist*

Rose Robinson made vital contributions in the areas of Indian communications and journalism. A member of the Butterfly Clan, Robinson was born in Winslow, Arizona, and earned degrees from the Haskell Institute and the American University (journalism studies). She was a founding board member and former executive director of the American Indian Press Association, which is currently known as the Native American Journalist Association.

Robinson served as a member of the Indian Arts and Crafts Board of the U.S. Department of the Interior (1963–1968); information officer in the Office of Public Instruction, Bureau of Indian Affairs (1972–1975); assistant director, Bicentennial Program, Bureau of Indian Affairs (1975–1976); vice president and director, American Indian Program, Phelps-Stokes Fund, Washington, D.C. (1976–1986); and director of the Commission for Multicultural Ministries, Native American Program in Chicago (1987).

Robinson has also taken leadership roles with the National Congress of American Indians, the North American Indian Womens' Association, and was the BIA liaison for coordinating the first Indian women's conference in 1970. She also oversaw the publication of periodicals for the Native American-Philanthropic News

Service, which issues publications such as the quarterly magazine *The Exchange, The Roundup*, and *D.C. Directory of Native American Federal and Private Programs.*

She was named Indian Media Woman of the Year in 1981 and served on numerous boards, including the National Indian Lutheran Board, the National Indian Education Association, the American Indian Graduate Program, and the National Committee on Indian Work for the Episcopal Church, U.S.A., and its subcommittee on economics and justice.

## Viola Marie Robinson (1936–)
*Micmaq tribal leader*

Viola Robinson has been a strong advocate for the rights of indigenous peoples, especially non-status Indians. The daughter of Micmaq herbal apothecary Frank Cope, she attended elementary school at the Micmaq Indian Day School on the Micmaq Indian Reserve in Shubenacadie, Nova Scotia. She went on to study at Sacred Heart Academy, a convent in Meteghan near Digby, Nova Scotia. When she was thirteen, Robinson's mother died suddenly, and she went to live with her grandfather. She then studied commercial secretarial courses at the Maritime Business College in Halifax, Nova Scotia—courses that helped her to become self-sufficient in her working life.

Robinson married early, at the age of sixteen, and had four of her six children by the time she was twenty-two years old. Although full Micmaqs, she and her husband were not recognized as "Indians" by the federal law and thus lived off the reserves. In early November 1974, Robinson was visited by a Micmaq woman named Catherine Brown who was organizing a grassroots effort to change the law governing Indian status in Canada. Robinson decided to attend a meeting on the subject convened by a group of similarly situated Indian people, where she spoke out on discrimination that she had faced as a "non-status" Indian. The meeting became the founding meeting of the Non-Status Indian and Métis Association of Nova Scotia, an organization that later changed its name to the Native Council of Nova Scotia. Robinson subsequently served as president of the council for fifteen years. Throughout this period she was synonymous with advocacy for the rights of non-status Indian people in Nova Scotia and across Canada. Over the years, she has initiated countless community-based efforts at improving the social and economic conditions of indigenous people in Canada. In 1991, Robinson was appointed commissioner of the Royal Commission on Aboriginal Peoples, which was established by the Canadian government to inquire into and report on all aspects of the lives of aboriginal peoples. She has also served as president of the Congress of Aboriginal Peoples and president of the Native Council of Canada.

## Howard Rock (1911–1976)
*Inupiat activist and editor*

Howard was born at the Inupiat (Eskimo) village of Point Hope in northeastern Alaska. As a boy he attended Bureau of Indian Affairs boarding schools, often traveling long distances from home. In the mid-1930s, he attended the University of Washington, Seattle. During the 1940s and 1950s, he worked as an artist, producing work with Inuit cultural themes, much of his work was bought by tourists. Rock was not happy with his life or work as an artist. In the early 1960s he returned to Point Hope, in search of some direction to his life within traditional Inuit culture.

In the late 1950s and early 1960s, the U.S. government was planning to use an atomic bomb to create a harbor near Point Hope. This project was billed as a peace time use of atomic energy. The Inuit people in the area, however, hunted sea mammals like whales and seals, which would be exposed to serious radiation from exploding an atomic device. Since Rock had some writing skills, the village elders of Point Hope commandeered him to join in the protest movement called Inupiat Paitot, or The People's Heritage. In order to publicize the issue and to gather Native Alaskan and other supporters, the Inupiat Paitot created a newsletter and Rock became the editor. This newsletter became the means of publicizing Inuit and other Native issues and in 1962, it became the Native newspaper *The Tundra Times*. At first *The Tundra Times* was published at Fairbanks, Alaska, but it soon moved to Anchorage, the largest urban center in Alaska. Rock was the first editor and served from 1962 until his death in 1976.

After successfully preventing the use of atomic explosives at Point Hope, the Alaska Natives were confronted with a series of other issues such as protection of their right to hunt game and the prevention of the Rampart Dam, which threatened to flood large areas of Athabaskan hunting land in central Alaska. Perhaps the most important issue was the claim of the state of Alaska of about ninety million acres of Native land. Between 1961 and 1965, Alaska Natives tried to mobilize and protect their land. Through *The Tundra Times*, Howard Rock wrote editorials, printed articles, actively brought Native issues to the press, and helped Native villages and regional organizations form protests. In 1965, he helped organize the first Alaska Federated Natives (AFN) meeting in Anchorage. The

AFN was a state-wide Native organization that represented the land, political, and social welfare issues of Alaska Natives. From 1965 to 1971, the AFN lobbied Congress for a solution to Native land issues in Alaska, and in 1971 helped gain passage of the Alaska Native Claims Settlement Act (ANCSA), which provided 44 million acres of land and $962.5 million to the Alaska Natives in return for surrendering claims to about 250 million acres.

Rock published articles on Native culture, history, Native land claims, and social and welfare issues, and wrote many commentaries about the events leading up to passage of the ANCSA. *The Tundra Times* became revered as a representative of the Alaska Native communities, and Rock was honored throughout Alaska for his tireless and selfless contributions toward solving Native issues.

## Paul Albert Roessler (1920–)
*Navajo economist*

Paul Roessler in an international economic consultant who has done extensive work for the U.S. government.

He was born in Buckman, New Mexico, earned a bachelor of arts degree in foreign service from Georgetown University, and did post-graduate work at the University of Maryland. During his military service in World War II (1941–1945), Roessler was awarded a Purple Heart with cluster, a Philippine Defense Medal, a Philippine Liberation Medal, and a Philippine Presidential Unit Citation with two clusters. Roessler served in some of the most significant military campaigns against Japan in the Pacific theater.

From 1949 to 1951, he worked as a field representative for the War Claims Commission in Washington, D.C., and from 1951 to 1952 he was a legislative analyst for the Foreign Claims Settlement Commission. He worked in the Foreign Service as Philippine Liaison officer in 1952 and as assistant atomic energy attaché to Japan from 1957 to 1961. From 1963 to 1965, Roessler was the associate program director of the National Science Foundation (NSF) in Washington, D.C. The NSF is a major backer of scientific projects in the United States. Roessler worked for the U.S. Army as an international economist from 1965 to 1975, then he was appointed chief of the Division of Economic Development in the Office of Policy Planning. In 1980, Roessler began working for the Bureau of Indian Affairs (BIA) and also became president of American Economic Consultants, Inc. He is a member of the National Economists Club, the Society of Government Economists, and the American Political Science Association.

## William Rogers (1879–1935)
*Cherokee entertainer*

Will Penn Adair Rogers was a cowboy, writer, actor, entertainer, and unique humorist who became widely famous during the Great Depression of the 1930s for his witty, homespun commentaries. He was born near Oolagah, Indian Territory (now Claremore, Oklahoma) on 4 November 1879 of parents who were prominent mixed-blood Cherokee ranchers.

Rogers grew up in the saddle, enjoying the freedom of roping and riding on the range. He attended four schools on the Cherokee Reservation but was never more than an average student. He was a cowboy in Texas in 1898 and went to Argentina to work as a gaucho at the age of twenty-three. Several months later, he joined his first traveling company in South Africa, Texas Jack's Wild West Show, and toured Australia, New Zealand, and the United States as "The Cherokee Kid." Between his trick riding stunts, he developed the witty, engaging patter with audiences that became the hallmark of his performances.

Rogers's popularity increased when he attracted media attention in the 1920s. He published widely read books, including *The Peace Conference* and *Rogerisms— the Cowboy Philosopher on Prohibition* (1919), *Illiterate Digest* (1924), and the posthumous *Autobiography* (1949). He participated in lecture tours, radio broadcasts, and at least fifteen motion pictures. He wrote nearly three thousand "daily telegrams," over one thousand newspaper articles, fifty-eight magazine pieces, and published hundreds of various other items. He also raised a great deal of money for victims of a hurricane in Florida, floods in Mississippi, a drought in the Southwest, and an earthquake in Nicaragua, among other numerous benefits.

Rogers was killed along with pilot Wiley Post in a plane crash near Point Barrow, Alaska, on 15 August 1935. His family ranch in Oklahoma and his own ranch near Santa Monica, California, were both designated state parks in his honor.

## Roman Nose (1830–1868)
*Southern Cheyenne tribal leader*

Roman Nose was a leader of Indian warriors and a member of the Crooked Lance Society of the Cheyenne Indian tribe. During the wars of the 1860s, he became a prominent warrior and because of his bravery in battle earned the respect of a war chief.

Roman Nose fought in the Battle of the Platte Bridge in July 1865 during the Bozeman Trail dispute in present-day Wyoming and Montana. In 1866, Roman Nose fought alongside the Southern Cheyenne Dog Soldiers military society. In 1867, he was present at the Fort Larned Council with General Winfield Scott Hancock. Roman Nose declared to members of the Dog Soldiers that he intended to kill Hancock, but was prevented from doing so by Tall Bull and Bull Bear.

Roman Nose attended the preliminary meetings preparing for the Medicine Lodge Council of October 1867 but did not partricipate in the council itself or the signing of the Medicine Lodge Treaty. During 1867, he and the Dog Soldiers carried out numerous raids along the Kansas frontier, focusing on wagon trains and railroad work parties. In August 1867, he and his warriors defeated the U.S. Cavalry at the battle of Prairie Dog Creek in Kansas.

Roman Nose was killed in September 1868 in an engagement known by non-Indians as the Battle of Beecher's Island in present-day Kansas and to Indian people as the Fight When Roman Nose Was Killed. Major George Forsyth and his troops had prepared for battle by digging themselves in on Beecher's Island, and during an afternoon charge, Roman Nose was shot. He died later that day. According to Cheyenne tradition, Roman Nose's "medicine" had been broken either when his feathered war bonnet was touched by a woman or when he ate food prepared with metal utensils.

## Juan de Jesus Romero (Deer Bird) (1874–1978)
*Taos tribal and spiritual leader*

If there was one cause in life for which Juan de Jesus Romero fought, it was the return of the sacred Blue Lake (Maxolo) to the Taos Pueblo. He was hereditary *cacique* or headman of Taos Pueblo as well as its spiritual leader.

As early as 1906, Romero began a personal campaign for the return of the ancestral lands surrounding Blue Lake that the U.S. government had expropriated from the Taos Indians. Romero met with little success in this endeavor, but vowed to keep up pressure on the government. The Taos believe that Blue Lake, in present-day eastern New Mexico, is a sacred site where the world was created and, therefore, has great religious and symbolic significance in Taos Pueblo culture. Ceremonies acknowledging the creation of the world and of man were annually celebrated by the Taos community at Blue Lake. Forty-five years passed before the tribe filed a lawsuit against the government for the area including the lake and the land. In 1965, the Taos were awarded cash compensation in lieu of their claims, but this was rejected by them in favor of their original claim.

Romero was adamant that the lake be returned, and he traveled to Washington, D.C., in 1970 to plead his case before President Richard M. Nixon. A motion was put before the U.S. Senate and passed, with seventy senators for and twelve against the return of Blue Lake to the Taos along with 48,000 acres of surrounding land. Nixon signed the bill in 1971, and Blue Lake was again within the Taos domain. For his lifelong efforts in the fight for Blue Lake, Romero won the prestigious Indian Council Fire Award in 1974.

### Wendy Rose (1948–)
*Hopi and Miwok poet*

Wendy Rose is the coordinator of American Indian Studies at Fresno City College, where she is also a full-time instructor. Rose is a poet whose work explores the conditions of Native Americans in modern urban society. Several collections of her poetry are published, and she teaches at the Fresno City College where she is also affiliated with the American Indian Studies Program.

Rose was born in Oakland, California, and descends from Hopi and Miwok parentage. She studied at Contra Costa College and the University of California at Berkeley. Growing up in a large city influenced her later writings, which focus on the experiences of urban Indians in America. Rose also confronts in her writing the "hybrid" nature of her heritage and culture. She states: "The poetry, too, is hybrid—like me, there are elements of Indian-ness, of English-ness, of mythology, and of horse ness." Besides writing and teaching, Rose has been active in a number of Indian organizations, and served as editor for the *American Indian Quarterly*, a scholarly journal in Indian studies.

Published works by Rose include *Hopi Roadrunner Dancing* (1973); *Long Division: A Tribal History* (1976); *Academic Squaw: Reports to the World from the Ivory Tower* (1977); *Builder Kachina: A Home-Going Cycle* (1979); *Lost Copper* (1980); *What Happened When the Hopi Hit New York* (1982); *The Halfbreed Chronicles and Other Poems* (1985); *Going to War With All My Relations* (1993); *Now Poof She Is Gone* (1994); and *Bone Dance: New and Selected Poems, 1965–1992* (1994).

### John Ross (1790–1866)
*Cherokee tribal leader*

John Ross was probably only one-eighth Cherokee and spoke halting Cherokee, yet he led the Cherokee Nation as principal chief from 1828 to 1866. His father was a Scottish trader, who married a part-Cherokee woman. For his early education, Ross's parents hired private teachers, and he later attended school in Kingston, Tennessee. While a young man, Ross became

John Ross.

a successful merchant and plantation-slave owner. He strongly advocated agricultural and political change for the Cherokee as a means to preserve the nation from U.S. demands for cessions of land and for Cherokee migration west of the Mississippi River. In 1811 he was appointed to the standing committee, which met to transact Cherokee government business while the national council, composed of about fifty village headmen, was not in session.

During the 1820s, the Cherokee incrementally adopted a constitutional government and became an agricultural nation. During much of the 1820s, Ross served as secretary to the Cherokee principal chief, Path Killer, who was greatly influential among the conservatives, who constituted a large majority within the nation. Most conservatives preferred to remain in their eastern homeland and declined U.S. pressures to migrate west. After Path Killer's death in 1827 Ross inherited his great influence among the conservatives. In 1828 he served as chairman of the Cherokee Constitutional Convention and was elected principal chief by the Cherokee National Council. Between 1828 and 1866, Ross led the Cherokee conservatives, who formed the National party. The conservative majority consistently reelected Ross as principal chief, and in return he worked to preserve

Cherokee national and territorial independence from U.S. encroachments.

## Mary G. Ross (1908–)
*Cherokee engineer*

Mary Ross is an important aeronautical engineer, philanthropist, and philologist of Cherokee culture and history. She was born in Oklahoma, and her great-great grandfather, John Ross, was principal chief of the Cherokee Nation between 1828 and 1866. Ross graduated from high school at the age of sixteen, received a bachelor of arts degree from Northeastern State Teachers College in Tahlequah, Oklahoma (1928), and a master's degree in mathematics from Colorado State University (1938).

Ross taught science and mathematics for eight years and was girls' advisor at a Pueblo and Navajo coed school becoming a researcher for Lockheed, a large aerospace company, in 1942. At first, she worked under a mathematician solving differential motion equations for fighter and transport aircraft. Supervisors decided that she should become an engineer, and she took further classes in mechanical and aeronautical engineering from UCLA. In 1949, Ross became a registered professional engineer. From then until 1953, she worked on payloads, stress analysis, and computations involving vehicles breaking through the sound barrier.

When the company formed what would be known as the Lockheed Missiles and Space Company, Ross was chosen to be one of the first forty employees and the only female engineer in the group. She worked for five years on feasibility, performance, and evaluation research of defense and ballistic missile systems, and she also studied ocean wave pressure distribution and velocities affecting ships. She became a research specialist in 1958 and focused her attention on satellite orbital calculations and on the Agena rocket series that boosted every Apollo mission and took astronauts to the moon and back. Ross graduated to advanced systems engineer and, among other projects, worked on the Polaris reentry vehicle and engineering systems for manned space flights. She appeared on the television show *What's My Line?* and stumped the panel with her esoteric occupation. Ross retired from Lockheed in 1973, closing out her career in the field of planetary engineering of flyby space vehicles designed to explore the surfaces of Venus and Mars.

Ross's achievements in engineering were exemplary. She was a charter member of the Los Angeles section of the Society of Women Engineers (1953), and served as its national treasurer (1969–1971), national audit committee chairman (1977–1978), and as a member of the Fellowship Selection Committee (1983–1984). *The San Francisco Examiner* nominated her Peninsula Woman of the Year (1961).

Ross is also a respected historian of Cherokee legacy, and her home is filled with a collection of Native American carvings, rugs, and pottery as a remembrance of her heritage. The Mary G. Ross Award is named in her honor, and is given to outstanding Native Americans who make significant contributions to American society. Now retired, Ross promotes educational opportunities for American Indian youth.

## Sacajawea (1784?–1812)
*Shoshone guide*

In the early 1800s, Sacajawea accompanied Meriwether Lewis and William Clark on their historical expedition from St. Louis, Missouri, to the Pacific Ocean. Sacajawea is responsible in large part for the success of the expedition, due to her navigational, diplomatic, and translating skills.

Although Sacajawea's exact date of birth is unknown, the best estimates are 1784 or 1787. She was born among the Lemhi Shoshone who lived in present-day Idaho. When she was only ten years old, a group of Hidatsa Indians kidnapped her during a raid and took her to a village near present-day Mandan, North Dakota. In 1804, she was purchased, or won, by French-Canadian fur trader Toussaint Charbonneau. When Charbonneau was hired by Lewis and Clark in 1804, he insisted that Sacajawea accompany the expedition. Sacajawea herself entertained hopes that she would be reunited with the Shoshone Nation during the trip.

Sacajawea proved to be a valuable liaison for the U.S. explorers, since she spoke a number of languages, including Shoshone and Siouan. Sacajawea translated Shoshone into Hidatsa for her husband, who would then translate again into English for the leaders of the expedition. When language barriers were insurmountable, Sacajawea communicated with others by sign language. During the expedition Sacajawea revealed to Lewis and Clark important passageways through the wilderness. She also provided the expedition with valuable information about edible plants. Besides these duties, Sacajawea performed countless services during the trip, like the time she saved the expedition's records when her boat capsized. One of the most amazing incidents during the trip was the almost miraculous reunion of Sacajawea with her brother Cameahwait in

August 1805. They met at the Three Forks of the Missouri River in present-day Montana. Cameahwait was then chief of his band. He gave the expedition horses and the use of an elderly Shoshone guide. The expedition reached the Pacific Ocean in 1805.

The strength and endurance of this amazing woman cannot be exaggerated. Just two months before the expedition left Mandan in 1805, Sacajawea gave birth to Charbonneau's child. The journals of the trip show there was no hesitation over a teenage Sacajawea carrying an infant on her back at least as far as the Rocky Mountains. Throughout the trip she carried the infant (known as Little Pomp to those on the expedition) in a cradleboard strapped to her back. Sacajawea continued to travel despite a debilitating illness that struck her midway through the trip. Besides her duties as guide and interpreter, Sacajawea was responsible for housekeeping and food preparation. However, Lewis and Clark only paid her husband.

## Buffy Sainte-Marie (1942–)
*Cree singer and composer*

Buffy Sainte-Marie is a well-known folk singer and Academy Award-winning songwriter. Throughout her career as a recording artist, she has remained an advocate for Indian rights.

Sainte-Marie was orphaned as an infant and was raised in Massachusetts by a Micmaq couple. In college, she studied Oriental philosophy. Sainte-Marie has been playing guitar and writing songs since she was sixteen years old. In the 1960s, spurred on by the positive reaction to her singing, Sainte-Marie went to New York City, where she began singing in the numerous folk clubs in the Greenwich Village section of the city. In a short time, she was offered a recording contract with Vanguard Records.

Her song "Up Where We Belong," recorded by Joe Cocker and Jennifer Warnes for the film *An Officer and A Gentleman*, won an Academy Award in 1982.

Over the years, she had numerous hit singles, including "Universal Soldier" and "Until It's Time for You to Go." Her 1993 recording entitled *Confidence and Likely Stories*, marked a departure for the artist. The new songs included lush strings and multi-rhythmic textures that set them apart from her earlier pop and folk recordings.

Sainte-Marie has infused both her recording career and her general life with a sense of purpose relating to Indian culture and concerns, both past and present. She has contributed writings to *The Native Voice*, *Thunderbird, American Indian Horizons*, and *Boston Broadside* in the field of North American Indian music and Indian affairs. Sainte-Marie is the author of *Nokosis and the Magic Hat* (1986), a children's adventure book set on an Indian reservation.

In February 1996, Sainte-Marie released *Up Where We Belong*, a collection of new songs with new recordings of her best songs. She was also awarded the Award for Lifetime Musical Achievement by the First Americans in the Arts. She has taught at York University, Indian Federated College in Saskatchewan, Evergreen State College in Washington State, and the Institute for American Indian Arts in Santa Fe, New Mexico. Buffy Sainte-Marie is president of the Cradleboard Teaching Project, which promotes multicultural education programs to grade schools around North America.

## Velma S. Salabiye (1948–1996)
*Navajo librarian*

Velma (Vee) Salabiye was born, raised, and educated in Arizona. She is originally from Lower Greasewood, Navajo Nation. Her education extended from kindergarten at Bellemont Hogan School, a school especially for children of parents employed at the Navajo Army Depot, to the University of Arizona, Tucson, where she earned a bachelor's degree in elementary education in 1971 and a master's degree in library science in 1974. Having earned provisional certification in special education from Northern Arizona University in 1971, she taught developmentally handicapped and emotionally disturbed Navajo children at St. Michael's School for Special Education. This school was the first of its kind established on an Indian reservation. As a librarian, Salabiye began the first planning and industrial development library for the Navajo Nation in 1975. She was a recipient of a D'Arcy McNickle fellowship from the Newberry Library Center for the History of the American Indian in 1979 and is a founding member of the American Indian Library Association, an affiliate of the American Library Association. She is acknowledged in various scholarly publications.

Salabiye served on the advisory committee for *Native Press Journal* and was an assistant editor for the *American Indian Culture and Research Journal*. Her work as a consultant included a 1991 video *The Land Is for the People*. She also was a book purchasing consultant for the UCLA bookstore. Among her published works are *American Indian Library Resources at UCLA* (1980), "Library and Information Resources" in *A Guide to Library-Based Research* (1981), and "Selection of Materials for Culturally Diverse Communities" in *Developing Library Collections for California's Emerging Majority: A Manual of Resources for Ethnic Collection Development* (1991). The 1993 edition of *Indi'n Humor: Bicultural Play in Native America* by Kenneth Lincoln includes her "Humor and Joking of the American Indian: A Bibliography." Salabiye was also a contributor to the first edition of this volume.

## Lilly Salvador (1944– )
*Acoma Pueblo potter*

Lilly Salvador is a nationally acclaimed potter and founder of the first pottery gallery at the Acoma Pueblo, New Mexico, which she hopes to develop and expand into a major southwestern art center. There are nineteen Pueblo villages in eastern New Mexico, all of which continue to adhere closely to their religious and cultural traditions. Salvador's pottery is displayed in numerous museums throughout the United States.

Salvador was educated at New Mexico State University. She has traveled extensively throughout the Southwest and Northwest regions of the United States to exhibit her traditional handcrafted and hand painted Acoma Pueblo pottery and figurines. Her work is displayed at museums in Boston (Boston Museum of Fine Arts), Phoenix (Heard Museum), San Diego (Museum of Man), Los Angeles (Natural History Museum), and Boulder (Whitehorse Gallery).

Salvador has won numerous awards for her work, including first, second, and third prizes from the Southwest American Indian Arts Association and first prize from the Gallup (New Mexico) Intertribal Indian Ceremonial. She is an active member within the Acoma Pueblo community and is a member of the Southwest American Indian Arts Association, the National Indian Arts and Crafts Association, and the Smithsonian Institution.

## Samoset (1590–1653)
*Pemaquid tribal leader*

Samoset was a sachem of the Pemaquid band of Abnakis, living on Monhegan Island off the coast of present-day Maine. He greeted the Pilgrims, at Plymouth, in present-day Massachusetts, in English (which he had learned from contact with traders) and became an instrumental liaison between the Pilgrims and the Indians.

Samoset and Squanto, the Wampanoag Indian who had been taken to England as a slave arranged a meeting between the colonists and Massasoit, grand sachem of the Wampanoag Confederacy, an alliance of Algonkian-speaking Indians in present-day New England. Squanto, who had returned to North America in 1619, also spoke English, and he and Samoset helped negotiate the first peace treaty with the Wampanoag chief Massasoit in 1621.

In 1625, Samoset signed the first land deed in America, ceding close to twelve thousand acres of Pemaquid lands to John Brown of New Harbor, Maine. In 1653, he sold an additional one-thousand acres to the Englishmen William Parnell, Thomas Way, and William England. Samoset died later that same year.

## Will Sampson (1934–1987)
*Creek actor and artist*

Will Sampson was a widely known American Indian actor when he died in 1987. He received high acclaim for his portrayal of an Indian chief feigning muteness in the film, *One Flew over the Cuckoo's Nest* (1975, directed by Jan Kadar).

Sampson was born and raised in Oklahoma. He came to acting late in life. After stints as a cowboy, forest ranger, and professional artist, he received an opportunity that would change his life. A friend of Sampson who was a rodeo announcer had been asked by a member of producer Michael Douglas's staff to keep his eye out for a "large" Indian. Sampson, who was six feet seven inches tall, was found and subsequently hired for the part in *One Flew over the Cuckoo's Nest*. The film, based on a novel by Ken Kesey, won five Academy Awards and critical praise for Sampson's portrayal of Chief Bromden. Sampson was nominated for an Academy Award as best supporting actor, and his acting career was launched.

Sampson went on to act in a number of films, including *The Outlaw Josey Wales, White Buffalo, Buffalo Bill and the Indians, Old Fish Hawk* (in which he had the title role), *Orca*, and *Fighting Back*. In 1982, he was awarded best narration honors by the Alberta, Canada, film commission for his work on *Spirit of the Hunt*, a major Canadian film. Sampson also joined the American Indian Theater Company of Oklahoma and took on the role of Red Cloud in the production of *Black Elk Speaks*.

Sampson said that he studied acting the way he prepared for his paintings of cowboys, Indians, and western landscapes. "I research thoroughly," said Sampson, who did not accept the *Cuckoo's Nest* role until he had read the book. "I've done paintings of the all the great Indian chiefs and I studied everything about them." His art work has been featured in numerous shows, exhibitions, and galleries.

### Joe S. Sando (1923–)
*Jemez Pueblo educator*

Educator Joe Sando is director of the Institute for Pueblo Indian Studies and Research at the Indian Pueblo Cultural Center, in Albuquerque, New Mexico. He was born at Jemez Pueblo, New Mexico, on 1 August 1923, educated at Santa Fe Indian School, received a bachelor of arts degree from Eastern New Mexico University, and studied audiology as a graduate student at Vanderbilt University.

As a young man, Sando was too small to play football and basketball, games he dearly loved. His English was limited, and this drawback motivated him to devote his life to education. He enlisted in the navy at the onset of World War II (1941–1945) and took part in the invasion of the Gilbert and Marianas islands in the Pacific campaign against the Japanese Empire. He worked as a counselor in government Indian schools before becoming an audiologist and speech pathologist in Albuquerque, New Mexico. While there, he worked with many air force test pilots and future astronauts. He also traveled to New Zealand, in 1969, under an exchange program funded by the Ford Foundation.

Joe Sando inaugurated the first All-Indian Track Meet at Jemez Pueblo. He is former chairman of the All-Indian Pueblo Housing Authority, past chairman of the New Mexico Judicial Council, and once chaired the Educational Committee of the All-Indian Pueblo Council. He has served on the boards of Americans for Indian Opportunity and the Northern New Mexico Economic Development District.

He has taught at the Institute of American Indian Arts, International Universities, and he has lectured in West Germany, Spain, Italy, and Brazil. His publications include *Pueblo Indian Biographies*, *The Pueblo Indians*, and *Popé*.

### Greg Sarris (contemporary)
*Miwok-Pomo-Filipino-Jewish author, professor, and chief of the Coast Miwok Nation*

A full professor of English at the University of California, Los Angeles, Greg Sarris is the author of several fiction and non-fiction books, all pertaining to modern and traditional Native American life. His first novel, *Watermelon Nights*, was published in 1998 and received acclaim across Native and non-Native North America.

Born and raised in Santa Rosa, California, Sarris's father was of Native American and Filipino decent, while his mother was Jewish. Sarris, adopted at birth, was brought up in both white and American Indian households. After attending Santa Rosa Junior College, Sarris matriculated at and graduated from the University of California, Los Angeles. He later received his Ph.D. from Stanford University in 1989.

His first book, *Keeping Slug Woman Alive: A Holistic Approach to American Indian Texts*, was published in 1993 by the University of California Press. The book is a collection of critical essays that deals with cross-cultural interpretation. Mabel McKay, a Cache Creek Pomo medicine woman, helped raise the to-be academic and artist, and in 1994 *Mabel McKay: Weaving the Dream*, the story of McKay's life, was released. Sarris describes the lauded work as a bi-autobiography in that the text also describes Sarris's life and experiences with McKay.

While both the above titles are non-fiction, Sarris has received substantial recognition for his two fictional works. *Grand Avenue*, a collection of short stories, was published in 1994, and was adapted by Sarris for an Home Box Office (HBO) mini-series, for which Sarris was executive producer (along with Robert Redford) and screenwriter. The HBO adaptation received many awards, including Best Picture and Best Screenplay from the First Americans in the Arts and Best Picture from the American Indian Film Festival. His second work of fiction, *Watermelon Nights*, continues the family saga introduced in *Grand Avenue*. In addition to these works, Sarris edited *The Sound of Rattles and Clappers: An Anthology of New California Indian Writing*, released from the University of Arizona Press in 1994. Sarris draws on the stories of his people to inform his work. He is also strongly influenced by American writers such as William Faulkner and Herman Melville.

The writer plans to expand his creative repertoire in the near future. He has been commissioned to write plays, teleplays, and a musical, all due out in the next two years. He just completed a three-hour miniseries for Showtime about a Mexican-American family in Los Angeles to be directed by Alfonso Arau, who directed *Like Water for Chocolate*. Sarris is writing a pilot and three episodes for a weekly one-hour HBO series entitled *Casino*. In addition, he is developing a musical (commissioned by Jeffrey Sellers) called *Homesong*. Other titles to look out for in the next few years include *Land of Dreams* (teleplay), *Laguna Beach Indians* (play), *The Life and Times of Latina Turner* (play), and *Seagulls* (play).

While creative work demands much of Sarris's time, he also is the chief of the Federated Coast Miwok Tribe of northern California. In July 1998 Sarris co-authored and introduced a bill to Congress that would restore his tribe's land to trust status. In 2000 the tribe was recognized by the federal government.

### Sassacus (1560–1637)
*Pequot tribal leader*

In the 1630s, Sassacus was grand sachem of the Pequot Nation, which was located in present-day Connecticut. He led the Pequot against English colonists in the Pequot War that took place in 1636 and 1637.

When English settlers first arrived in New England, the Pequot Indians were consolidating and conquering their weaker Indian neighbors under the strong and ambitious leadership of Sassacus, who became grand sachem in 1632. Under Sassacus's leadership the Pequot domain had grown to include most of present-day Connecticut and Long Island. For a while, Sassacus skillfully played English and Dutch traders against one another, but eventually the Pequot's power became too much of a threat to the growing settler population.

The Pequot Indians living in the Connecticut River Valley were among the first of the New England tribes to resist the growing English presence on their lands. In 1936, English soldiers attacked the Pequot Nation in retaliation for the murders of two traders, John Stone and John Oldham, although it is not clear that the perpetrators were Pequot. For two years after Stone's death in 1633, a precarious peace had been maintained in the area. The death of Oldham, however, in 1636 resulted in a coordinated offensive on the behalf of the settlers against the Pequot. Acting at the behest of Massachusetts Bay officials, Captain John Endecott, with a force of about ninety men, attacked a number of Indian villages on Block Island, which was located off the southern coast of present-day Rhode Island. Although the villages there belonged to the Narragansett Nation, who were not connected with the killings of English traders, this seemed not to matter to the English forces sent there. Endecott then marched to the Connecticut mainland seeking out Pequot to demand reparations. After a minor encounter in which one Indian was killed, Endecott returned to Boston, leaving the Connecticut settlers to contend with the Pequot. Sassacus laid plans for war and attacked several English settlements, including those at Fort Saybrook, located at the mouth of the Connecticut River. In 1637, a retaliatory brigade of English colonists, Narragansett warriors, and seventy Mohegan, another Algonkian nation living in present-day Connecticut, attacked a major Pequot town on the Mystic River. Sassacus and his warriors managed to repel the assault behind their well-fortified palisades until the colonists set the town on fire. It is estimated that six hundred to a thousand Pequot perished in the flames. The Plymouth governor called it a "sweet sacrifice."

Sassacus managed to escape and sought sanctuary among the Mohawk, a trade rival and enemy nation to the Mohegan. Fearful of English reprisals, the Mohawk put Sassacus to death. At the end of the so-called Pequot War, the people of the Pequot Nation dispersed. Many who were captured faced enslavement or subjugation under old enemies, but some migrated to the Ohio valley and joined the Shawnee Nation.

### Satank (Sitting Bear) (1810–1871)
*Kiowa tribal leader*

Satank was born in the Black Hills and became a prominent war chief among the Kiowa and a leader among the Principal Dogs military society. Satank was instrumental in establishing the peace between the Kiowa and Cheyenne, thus producing a formable fighting force against the U.S. settlers on Indian lands in the southern Plains. Though respected by his tribe, his vengeful personality bred fear among even his own people.

In 1867, Satank was one of the principle spokesmen for the Kiowa at the Medicine Lodge Council. This council had been called by advocates of President Ulysses Grant's peace policy and cited the Sand Creek massacre as an example of heavy-handed military tactics. The resulting Medicine Lodge Treaty of 1867 assigned the Kiowa to a combined reservation (with the Arapaho) in Indian Territory in present-day Oklahoma. Raiding for the Kiowa was a way of life, however, and would persist, despite U.S. attempts at acculturation, Christianizing, and pacifying the Indians. Satank continued to lead these raids.

In May 1871, Satank joined Satanta and Kicking Bird, two other Kiowa leaders, in an attack on an army wagon train traveling along the Butterfield Southern Stage Route in Young County, Texas. In the ensuing battle, the Kiowa killed eight of the twelve defenders, routed the rest, and plundered the wagons.

Lured into a council by General William Tecumseh Sherman, Satank and Satanta were later arrested. En route to Fort Richardson, Texas, for trial for the wagon train murders, Satank attempted an escape from the army guards and was shot and killed. He was buried in the Fort Sill military cemetery.

## Satanta (1830–1878)
*Kiowa tribal leader*

In the 1860s and 1870s, the Kiowa Indians waged an ongoing battle to protect their land and way of life from U.S. encroachment. Satanta, also known as White Bear, was a major Kiowa leader in favor of resistance. Besides his prowess as a warrior, Satanta was also a famed orator, attested to by his American-given nickname the Orator of the Plains.

Satanta was born on the northern Plains, but later migrated to the southern Plains with his people. His father, Red Tipi, was keeper of the tribal medicine bundles or Tai-me. Much of Satanta's adult life was spent fighting U.S. settlers and military. He participated in raids along the Santa Fe Trail in the early 1860s, and in 1866 became the leader of the Kiowa who favored military resistance against U.S. military forces. In 1867, he spoke at the Kiowa Medicine Lodge Council, an annual ceremonial gathering, where, because of his eloquent speech, U.S. observers gave him his nickname. At the council, Satanta signed a peace treaty that obligated the Kiowa to resettle on a reservation in present-day Oklahoma. Shortly thereafter, however, he was taken hostage by U.S. officials who used his imprisonment to coerce more Kiowa into resettling on their assigned reservation.

For the next couple of years, Satanta participated in a number of raids in Texas where cattle ranchers and buffalo hunters were steadily pushing Kiowa and Comanche Indians onto reservations. It was one of these raids that eventually led to Satanta's capture. In May 1871, Satanta planned an ambush along the Butterfield Stage Route on the Salt Creek Prairie. After allowing a smaller medical wagon train to pass, Satanta and his warriors attacked and confiscated the contents of a larger train of ten army freight wagons. Unfortunately for Satanta, the train he had allowed to pass was carrying General William Tecumseh Sherman, the famous Civil War general, then commander of the U.S. Army. Sherman took the attack as a sign that a more militant and coordinated offense was needed to subdue the Kiowa and Comanche, who were unwilling to settle permanently onto reservations. A short time later Satanta was lured into a peace council and then arrested and was sentenced to death. Humanitarian groups and Indian leaders protested the harsh sentence. In 1873,

Satanta was paroled on the condition he remain on the Kiowa Reservation.

In 1874, during the Comanche and United States conflict called the Red River War, Satanta presented himself to U.S. officials to prove that he was not taking part in the hostilities. His demonstration of loyalty was rewarded with imprisonment. Four years later, an ill Satanta was informed that he would never be released. He jumped to his death from the second story of a prison hospital.

## Helen Maynor Scheirbeck (1935–)
*Lumbee educator*

Scheirbeck has devoted much of her life to children's welfare, serving on a number of human resource agencies, including the Office of Education and the Department of Health, Education, and Welfare.

Born in Lamberton, North Carolina, she was educated at Berea College in Berea, Kentucky. She went on to receive a doctorate from the Virginia Polytechnic Institute and State University in 1980, for which she wrote her dissertation, "Public Policy and Contemporary Education of the American Indian."

Scheirbeck has served on a number of important government agencies and chaired the Indian Education Task Force of the American Indian Policy Review Commission. Other positions include director of the Congressional Office of Indian Affairs; staff member of the U.S. Office of Education, within the Department of Housing, Education, and Welfare; and member of the U.S. Senate Subcommittee on Constitutional Rights. Scheirbeck also served with the Save the Children Federation in Westport, Connecticut.

Author of such works as *The History of Federal Indian Education Policy*, "Indian Education: Tool for Cultural Politics," "The First Americans," and "A Study of Three Selected Laws and Their Impact on American Indian Education," Scheirbeck has been honored with the John Hay Whitney Foundation Opportunity Award, the Outstanding Lumbee Award, and an Outstanding Indian Award. She currently works in the U.S. Department of Health and Human Services, Head Start Program, American Indian Branch, in Washington, D.C.

## Fritz Scholder (1937–)
*Luiseño artist*

Fritz Scholder is recognized as a leading modern artist in the United States. His work often deals with themes relating to the Native American experience.

Scholder was born in Breckenridge, Minnesota. His grandmother was a member of the Luiseño tribe, although Scholder describes himself as "a non-Indian Indian." He earned his master of fine arts degree from the University of Arizona in 1964. For five years, Scholder was instructor of advanced painting and art history at the Institute of American Indian Arts.

Although Scholder's upbringing was not acutely focused on his Native American heritage, his art awakened in him a desire to explore this background. Scholder's work often combines surrealist pop imagery and Native American mysticism. The artist has frequently addressed issues facing American Indians, including alcoholism, assimilation into mainstream U.S. society, and the degradation of Native American culture. In some ways, Scholder has been controversial. His critics complain that he has not taken Native American problems seriously enough and that his pop art has reduced their culture to kitsch—popularized art with little aesthetic value. Some would like to see Scholder use his high profile as a popular artist to advance Native American causes. Scholder himself prefers to communicate through his work. He states, "I'm not at all militant. I have a way out: I can put something down on canvas or do a lithograph."

In 1980, Scholder made a promise to himself to no longer paint "Indians." The decision was based entirely on artistic grounds. In 1992, he broke that rule, for a lithograph titled *Indian Contemplating Columbus*. The forty-by-sixty-inch work is the largest ever made by Scholder. "I'm very divided about Columbus," Scholder states, "because I grew up thinking of him as a hero. When I was a boy, I didn't think about my being part-Indian. . . . But now, I can understand the other side, and now, after much more reading as an adult, I realize that Columbus's trip was the beginning of the end for many cultures." The lithograph portrays a silhouetted figure sitting in a chair, facing the corner. A brightly colored moccasin on his foot is the only clue that the figure is Indian.

## Bert D. Seabourn (1931–)
*Cherokee-Chickasaw painter*

Bert D. Seabourn is an internationally known painter who has exhibited his works both in the United States and abroad.

Seabourn was born in Iraan, Texas. He earned a master of fine arts degree from Oklahoma City University and also attended Central State University in Edmond, Oklahoma, and the University of Oklahoma. He served in the U.S. Navy from 1951 to 1955.

Seabourn works mainly in watercolor, oil, graphics, acrylics, and drawings, and has also done some sculpture. His works are exhibited at the Heard Museum in Phoenix, Arizona; the Five Civilized Tribes Museum in Muskogee, Oklahoma; the Oklahoma Art Center in Oklahoma City, Oklahoma; Red Cloud Indian School, Pine Ridge, South Dakota; the Vatican Museum of Modern Religious Art, Rome, Italy; and the Inter-Tribal Indian Ceremonial Association, Gallup, New Mexico.

Seabourn has received many honors and awards for his work, including Best of Show award at the Oklahoma Art Guild Annual, Oklahoma City, 1966; Grand Award in acrylics at Five Civilized Tribes Museum, Muskogee, 1973; Best of Show award in watercolors at Red Cloud National Indian Art Exhibition, Pine Ridge, 1974; Governor's Award, presented by Governor George Nigh at Oklahoma state capitol, Oklahoma City, 1981; sculpture commissioned by Southwestern Bell Corporate Headquarters, Oklahoma City, 1986; and Best of Show award for Master Artist Show at Five Civilized Tribes Museum, 1988. Seabourn has also shown his work internationally in such places as Taiwan, Singapore, and Germany. He lives in Oklahoma City, Oklahoma.

## Seattle (Sealth) (1788–1866)
*Duwamish-Suquamish tribal leader*

In the early 1800s, U.S. settlers poured into the Pacific Northwest region, leading to inevitable conflict with the Indians living there. During the first half of the nineteenth century, Sealth, a principal chief of the Duwamish people, encouraged friendship and commerce with the newcomers and avoided being drawn into the ongoing regional conflicts between settlers and Indians that were permeating the Northwest during this time.

Sealth had already witnessed the growing number of U.S. settlers moving into his homeland as a youth. In the 1830s, he was influenced by French missionaries and converted to Catholicism. Throughout the Gold Rush era of the 1850s, he maintained peace, despite the influx of miners and settlers. Sealth fostered trading relationships with the newcomers. By 1855, tensions between settlers and the other Indians in the area were mounting, and the breaking of treaty terms finally led to the Yakima War of 1855–56. Sealth chose not to fight and signed the Fort Elliot Treaty, in which he agreed to relocate his people to a reservation. Chief Sealth and his people remained allied with American forces and withstood an attack by the neighboring Nisqually Indians. He and his people later relocated to the Port Madison Reservation, near present-day Bremerton,

Washington. The city of Seattle, Washington, was named after the Duwamish chief Sealth in 1852.

## Thomas Segundo (1921–1971)
*Papago (Tohono O'Odham) tribal leader*

When he was elected chairman of the Papago (now called Tohono O'Odham) Indian Tribal Council in 1951, Thomas Segundo became the youngest Indian chief in the United States. During his tenure, he was a staunch advocate for his people and strengthened the tribe's economic and political institutions.

Segundo was born on the Papago Reservation in southern Arizona. As a young man, the future tribal chairman left his traditional culture behind and settled in California, earning a living in the shipbuilding industry, eventually being promoted to a supervisory position. Originally, Segundo planned to continue his career in shipbuilding by obtaining a degree in engineering. In 1946, however, he returned for a vacation to his homeland on the Papago Reservation. The poverty and desolation that he found there changed the direction of his life. The Papago asked Segundo to help them improve the economic conditions on the reservation. He never returned to his job in the shipbuilding industry.

Segundo's initial efforts on the reservation were on a small scale, helping the Papago to feed their livestock more economically and developing athletic activities for Papago youth. Segundo was amazed at the range of needs demanding his attention. The Papago took notice of him and persuaded him to run for tribal chairman. He won the 1951 election by a large percentage.

Segundo worked to revive the tribal government. By taxing traders who had previously taken advantage of reservation resources, Segundo dramatically increased tribal revenue. Segundo himself was able to serve as tribal leader full time. Papago who previously had gone to U.S. government officials for help turned to Segundo. He codified Papago laws and organized a large voter registration drive on the reservation. After seven terms as tribal chairman, Segundo went to the University of Chicago for courses in law and social science. He returned to his home with hopes of implementing a long-range development plan, which had a multi-pronged focus. Acknowledging the limited potential of the arid Papago land, Segundo proposed conservation measures to increase range land for cattle ranchers and implemented irrigation programs for farmers. He believed that no matter how productive the reservation land could be made, however, one-third of the Papago people would have to find livelihoods off the reservation. He hoped to provide the training and education

they needed for these careers on the "outside." Segundo also proposed the construction of boarding schools for children and expanded public health facilities. Segundo's plan was the result of a long process of evaluation that included input from the Papago people. As a result, it was endorsed nearly unanimously.

Sadly, Segundo was killed in 1971 in a plane accident. His contributions to the Papago people, however, continue to impact the Papago community.

## Eugene Sekaquaptewa (1925–)
*Hopi educator*

Eugene Sekaquaptewa is best known for his work in the field of education. He was born on 7 July 1925 in Hotevilla, Arizona, on the Hopi Reservation. Hotevilla is the Hopi village where many of the most conservative Hopi people live. Many conservative Hopi try to preserve their ancient customs, religion, and way of government. He received his bachelor of science and master of arts degrees from Arizona State University.

Sekaquaptewa enlisted in the marines during World War II (1941–45), and survived the early morning beach assault of Iwo Jima, a volcanic island in the Pacific Ocean, within air attack distance of the Japanese mainland. He and several other U.S. marines rescued a wounded soldier from enemy fire. Besides Iwo Jima, he took part in the invasion of Saipan, Tinian, and the Marshall Islands, all of strategic significance for the U.S. war effort against Japan. After discharge from the armed forces, he served as a captain in the U.S. Air Force Reserves.

Sekaquaptewa was a Hopi Tribal Council representative, a training specialist for the Arizona State University (ASU) Indian Community Action Project and has taught education courses at ASU. He also taught at the Sherman Institute, an Indian boarding school, and was recreation director on the Navajo Reservation. Sekaquaptewa has written a number of professional papers on Hopi education and curriculum and is the author of *Coyote & the Winnowing Birds: A Traditional Hopi Tale* (1994).

## Sequoyah (1770–1843)
*Cherokee linguist*

Sequoyah is justly celebrated for his development of the Cherokee syllabary, which is a set of symbols for each syllable sound in the language, rather than an alphabet in which symbols represent fewer but shorter sounds. Sequoyah's syllabary served the Cherokee people admirably for many decades and was the genesis of several Cherokee publications.

Sequoyah was born in Taskigi near present-day Vonore, Tennessee. His mother was Cherokee and his father a U.S. trader. Sequoyah's early life was varied. He was a skilled farmer, hunter, and trader. He also served under General Andrew Jackson in the Creek War of 1813–1814.

The Cherokee language is still spoken by approximately ten thousand Cherokee whose families were deported to Oklahoma in the 1830s and the thousand or so who remain in North Carolina. In 1809, while living in present-day Arkansas, Sequoyah began working on a written version of the Cherokee language. He recognized the importance of a written constitution and official records, and this was originally his main purpose in developing a written Cherokee language. At first he developed a pictographic version of the Cherokee language, but soon abandoned this approach in favor of syllabary of eighty-six characters representing the different syllable sounds. It took twelve years for Sequoyah to finish the project. It was a historic achievement in many ways. Despite limited proficiency in English and little in the way of formal education in writing, Sequoyah produced a workable syllabary of Cherokee characters, one of the few people in world history to singlehandedly create an entire syllabary.

Sequoyah's achievement was initially met with some skepticism by his fellow Cherokee, but after a demonstration of how the system could be used to carry messages from an Indian family in Arkansas to relatives living in the east, it was adopted with enthusiasm. The Cherokee Council sanctioned the syllabary, and in a few short months, thousands of Cherokee were reading and writing. Christian missionaries, inspired by the translation of the Bible into Cherokee, helped obtain a printing press with a Cherokee syllabary font. In 1828, the *Cherokee Phoenix*, the first Cherokee newspaper was published in both English and Cherokee. Also in 1828, the Cherokee constitution was ratified and written down. Sequoyah was invited to Washington, D.C., by the U.S. government, and his achievement was celebrated.

In subsequent years, Sequoyah continued to play an active role in politics and linguistics. In the late 1830s, as president of the Western Cherokee he sponsored the Cherokee Act of Union, which united eastern and western parts of the Cherokee nation. Before 1838, some Cherokee had migrated west as part of U.S. removal policies that encouraged eastern Indian tribes to exchange their land for territory in present-day Kansas or Oklahoma. The plan was designed to free more eastern Indian land for U.S. settlement. Most

Cherokee refused to migrate west, but in 1838–39, most were forced on the "Trail of Tears" to migrate west. For several years the late Cherokee arrivals, who were the majority, and the earlier migrants, the "Old Settlers," could not agree on a shared government. The Act of Union in July 1839 helped provide a basis for a united government.

In 1842, Sequoyah set out on an expedition to locate a lost band of Cherokee who had migrated westward during the American Revolution. He hoped to locate them by cross-referencing languages. When he failed to return from the expedition, a fellow Cherokee named Oonoleh went searching for him. Sadly, Sequoyah had died during his quest for the lost band. In perhaps the most eloquent testimony to his lifetime achievement, the news of Sequoyah's death reached his people in the form of a letter written in the syllabary he had created. Sequoyah has been honored in many ways, including the naming of a distinct genus of giant redwood trees, sequoia, found along the northern California coast.

## Bill Shakespeare (1901–1975)
*Northern Arapaho tribal leader*

Bill Shakespeare was born in May 1901 on the Wind River Reservation in Wyoming. His father, War Bonnet, had attended Carlisle Indian Industrial School and was a strong influence on his son; he encouraged Bill to learn both Arapaho and English. As a result, Shakespeare emerged bilingual under the tutelage of his father. He was acknowledged as one of the few Arapaho who spoke "old time" Arapaho and could communicate fluently and eloquently in the Arapaho language.

Shakespeare's early school days were spent at St. Stephen's Indian Mission operated by Jesuits on the Wind River Reservation, attending intermittently from 1908–1917. In October 1917, he enrolled under the name Nestor Whiting at Haskell Institute Boarding School in Lawrence, Kansas, but attended for only two months. Shakespeare next enrolled at Genoa Boarding School in Genoa, Nebraska, in September 1918, where he attended until April 1919, at which time he left to enlist in the army.

Shakespeare returned to the reservation and throughout the next three decades made sporadic attempts to construct a role for himself in the reservation community. On the reservation he was able to use his bilingual skills as interpreter and secretary for tribal meetings. He married and at various times worked as a policeman, government herder, and interpreter. He served on the council of Arapaho leaders and frequently spoke for his tribe in dealings with federal agents, on one occasion writing to the secretary of the interior to request an investigation of financial irregularities on the part of the Indian agent assigned to the Wind River Reservation. Shakespeare was an important intermediary, serving as a communication link between tribe and agent in the days when few Arapaho spoke English.

Shakespeare was a Hollywood actor and a world traveler, and in later years he worked as an informant for anthropologists studying Arapaho language and culture. Toward the end of his life, he spoke on Indian culture and history in many schools around the country.

## Joanne Shenandoah (contemporary)
*Oneida actress, singer, and songwriter*

Joanne Shenandoah is a woman whose art focuses sharply on issues vital to Native Americans. Her music has garnered her an international reputation as an artist with a unique vision that reflects her Oneida roots.

A wolf clan member of the Iroquois Confederacy's Oneida Nation, Shenandoah's musical roots can be traced to her parents. Both lovers of music, they insisted on providing their children (Shenandoah is one of four children) with formal music training. In fact, her father, the late Clifford Shenandoah, was an Onondaga chief and jazz guitarist. Her mother, Maisie, was a singer.

Shenandoah worked as a computer programmer in Washington, D.C. for fourteen years before devoting herself to music full time. She attributes this dramatic career change to her rediscovery of the stories and songs of her people. Since her decision to change her career's direction, she has sung with musical greats such as Willie Nelson, Robbie Robertson, and Neil Young. Her first album was released in 1989.

Many of her songs deal with vital issues in Indian Country, including the desecration of Native American graves and the treatment of American Indian leaders and activists throughout the history of colonization. In fact, she contributed to *In the Spirit of Crazy Horse*, a compilation album dedicated to the plight of activist Leonard Peltier, who was imprisoned for allegedly contributing to the murder of two FBI agents. She has recorded her music for several national and international companies, including NATO Records in France, EYE-Q Records in Germany, and Featherwind Productions, Silver Wave Records, and Canyon Records in the United States.

The singer performs tirelessly throughout the world, especially in the United States, Canada, and Europe. Recently she performed in Capetown, South Africa, at the Parliament on World Religions, and at the White House for First Lady Hillary Clinton and Tipper Gore in 1999. In addition, Shenandoah has composed and contributed to several film soundtracks, including songs from "Naturally Native," "Indian in the Cupboard," and "Dance Me Outside."

The singer's hard work has brought her multiple awards, including several Native American Music Awards, including 1998 and 1999 Best Female Artist of the Year awards. Some of her most popular albums include *Matriarch: Iroquois Women's Songs*, *Once in a Red Moon*, and *All Spirits Sing*, a children's album.

*Peacemaker's Journey*, released in March 2000, is an artistic journey recounting Iroquois history and myth. She lives with her husband, Doug George, and her daughter, Leah, in Oneida, New York.

## Leslie Marmon Silko (1948–)
*Laguna Pueblo novelist and poet*

Leslie Marmon Silko is an acclaimed novelist. She is the author of the highly praised novels *Ceremony* (1977) and *Almanac of the Dead* (1991).

Silko was born in Albuquerque, New Mexico, although she spent her childhood at the Laguna Pueblo in eastern New Mexico, where she was surrounded with the culture and lore of the Laguna and Keres people. It was during these years that she learned about the traditions of Native American storytelling, principally through her grandmother and aunt. Silko received a bachelor's degree in English from the University of New Mexico, at which time she wrote her first short story, "The Man to Send Rain Clouds." Published in 1969, the story, based on an incident that had occurred at Laguna, gained Silko a National Endowment for the Humanities Discovery Grant.

Silko temporarily considered a law degree but, after three semesters, left law school to pursue a career in writing. In 1974, *Laguna Woman*, a book of poetry, was published. In 1977, *Storyteller*, a collection of short stories, and *Ceremony*, a novel, were published. *Ceremony*, the story of an inner journey that takes a young Indian back to his roots, established Silko's reputation as a leading U.S. author. This novel had crossover appeal for the larger audience of serious readers. Largely on the basis of *Ceremony*, Silko received one of twenty-one "genius" fellowships awarded by the MacArthur Foundation, which granted her a five-year annual stipend of $33,600 to pursue her writing.

In 1991, *Almanac of the Dead* was published. The seven-hundred-page novel was called by one reviewer, "the most ambitious literary undertaking of the past quarter century." The novel interweaves an apocalyptic depiction of declining Western society with sacred traditions of the Native American people. Underlying the entire work is the tragedy and anger Silko feels for the violation and humiliation Native Americans have suffered since the 1500s.

Silko believes that "our identity is formed by the stories we hear when we're growing up. Literature helps us locate ourselves in the family, the community and the whole universe." Consequently, Silko's work has the "feel" of traditional Native American storytelling, interweaving tales that she has remembered and imagined. Silko's recent writings include *Yellow Woman and a Beauty of the Spirit* (1996) and *Gardens in the Dunes* (1999).

In addition to writing, Silko has taught at the University of New Mexico, Navajo Community College, and the University of Arizona. In 1994, she was awarded the Lifetime Achievement Award of the Native Writers' Circle of the Americas, an international Native American writers' organization.

## Mary Sillett (1953–)
*Inuit tribal leader*

Mary Sillett was born in the small town of Hopedale, Labrador. Labrador is mainland Newfoundland, on the northeastern border of the province of Quebec. Her parents, Ester and Jerry Sillett, both of Inuit ancestry, raised a large family, of which Mary was the oldest girl. She attended elementary and high school in Labrador, and then went on to receive a bachelor of social work degree from Memorial University in St. John's, Newfoundland, in 1976.

She has been involved with aboriginal issues at the regional, provincial, national, and international levels. Her career began with the Labrador Resources Advisory Council, a body created to advise the province on the impact of economic development on the Inuit.

Sillett has served numerous organizations in many capacities, including executive assistant to the president of the Labrador Inuit Association; a senior policy analyst with the Aboriginal programs of Heritage Canada; the president and executive director of the Inuit Women's Association of Canada; a commissioner on the Royal Commission of Aboriginal Peoples; and the vice-president and president of the Inuit Tapirisat of Canada (the national Inuit political organization). In 1997 Sillette was a member of the jury for the National Aboriginal Achievement Awards (NAAA).

She is currently the district social worker in Hopedale, the mother of two sons, Matthew and Martin Lougheed, and a foster parent and guardian.

## Jay Silverheels (1912–1980)
*Mohawk actor*

Jay Silverheels is probably best known for his role as Tonto, the Lone Ranger's Indian partner, in the popular 1950s television series of the same name.

Silverheels, whose real name was Harold J. Smith, was born in Canada and came to the United States as a member of Canada's national lacrosse team in 1938. A short time later he began acting in films. His first role was as the Indian prince in *The Captain from Castille*. In 1950, he portrayed Geronimo in the movie *Broken Arrow*, which has been hailed as the first film to portray Indians in a sympathetic light. Silverheels gained his greatest notoriety, however, playing Tonto. He was actually the second actor to play the role of the Lone Ranger's sage companion. The popular series ran for eight years. Two film features were also made based on the television series, and Silverheels appeared in both.

In the middle 1960s, Silverheels founded the Indian Actors Workshop in Hollywood. He was the original director of this organization. During the same period, he worked extensively with public service projects focusing on substance abuse and the elderly. In 1979, he became the first Native American awarded a star on Hollywood's "Walk of Fame."

## Konrad Haskan Sioui (1953–)
*Huron tribal leader*

Konrad Sioui is the chief negotiator and political advisor for the Montagnais-Innu Council of Septiles, Quebec, as well as First Nations specialist for the Senate of Canada. He was born in Wendake, a Huron village in the province of Quebec, on 16 April 1953. The fifth of seven children of Georges and Eléonore Sioui, he was raised in traditional ways by the mothers of the Sioui clan and was taught by the elders of his people. He also attended elementary school on the reserve before going on to obtain a bachelor's degree in sociology and a master's degree in administration.

Sioui served two terms as the vice-grand chief of the Huron-Wyandotte First Nation and three terms as the grand chief of the Quebec and Labrador Assembly of First Nations. When the Innu people of Labrador protested low-level flying, Sioui personally took up their cause and joined their fight for government recognition of their rights. He invited the Innu to join the Quebec Assembly of First Nations, creating a new organization in the process. Nationally, he has served as senior analyst and special advisor with the Royal Commission on Aboriginal Peoples. He was also director of international affairs for the Assembly of First Nations, and he has worked with the 1992 Nobel Peace Prize recipient Rigoberta Menchu Tum to foster ties between North and South American First Nations and to improve conditions for aboriginal people in Guatamala and Columbia.

He is perhaps best known for successfully asserting, together with three of his brothers, a treaty entered into by the British Crown and the Huron Nation in 1760 against provincial laws that curtailed the exercise of religious practices of the Huron people. In 1990, the Supreme Court of Canada held that the Huron Nation was entitled to rely on the treaty to engage in a number of protected practices. The Court's ruling supported their claim that Huron people can carry on their traditional activities on Crown Land. In 2000, Sioui received the National Aboriginal Achievement Award for public service.

## Sitting Bull (1831–1890)
*Hunkpapa Sioux tribal leader*

Sitting Bull was a major military, spiritual, and political leader of his people in the 1800s. He was an important figure in the war for the Black Hills from 1876 to 1877 and helped to engineer the Indian victory at Little Bighorn.

Sitting Bull's military and leadership abilities became evident at an early age. At age twenty-two, he was leader of a warrior society known as the "Strong Hearts." It was probably not a coincidence that a warrior society would come into existence in the 1850s. It was during this time that U.S. settlers were sowing the seeds for a larger conflict that would force Sioux warriors like Sitting Bull into a major military confrontation.

The Hunkpapa Sioux were able to avoid the early confrontations in the 1860s. However, when Red Cloud, a major Hunkpapa Sioux leader, negotiated the Fort Laramie Treaty of 1868, Sitting Bull chose not to abide by its territorial provisions, which would have restricted his ability to hunt and travel. Sitting Bull's adherence to traditional ways of life had made him a spiritual as well as military leader among his people. In 1874, gold was discovered in the Black Hills, and the subsequent illegal incursions by U.S. miners created tension with Sitting Bull and the Sioux bands. After a number of limited skirmishes with the U.S. military, matters came to a head in 1876. It was in this year that the U.S. government ordered all hunting bands to report to U.S. government agencies attached to reservations. It was an impossible situation for Sitting Bull who now prepared for all-out battle with U.S. forces. As it turned out, the confrontation would be a historical one.

To enforce the U.S. order to have all Indian bands report to agencies by the January 1876 deadline, a number of military divisions were sent. A three-pronged military attack had been planned by U.S. forces to pin down the Indians in the Bighorn Valley in present-day eastern Montana. Unbeknownst to U.S. forces, one of the largest concentrations of Plains Indians ever assembled had gathered in response to the U.S. presence. Due in large part to Sitting Bull's influence, a village of between twelve and fifteen thousand Indians gathered along the Little Bighorn River. Sitting Bull engaged forces under General George Crook in the Battle of the Rosebud on June 17 and sent the U.S. Army into retreat. Eight days later, the U.S. troops led by Colonel George A. Custer attacked several points along the Indian encampment and were soundly defeated. Custer's forces were annihilated. The Battle of Little Bighorn is recorded as a signal Indian victory.

The Indian successes at Rosebud and at Little Bighorn were the last major Indian victories of the campaign. As was the custom, the large Indian encampment dispersed into small bands, since there was not enough food and grazing land to sustain such a large population for long at one place. The U.S. increased its military presence and forced many of the Sioux into surrender. Instead of capitulation, Sitting Bull and a number of his followers escaped to Canada. The Canadian government, however, offered no refuge, and the emigrant Sioux led by Sitting Bull were near starvation. Sitting Bull and most of his camp surrendered to U.S. authorities on 19 July 1881, at Fort Buford, North Dakota. For nearly two years, Sitting Bull was held prisoner; in 1883, he was allowed to settle on the Standing Rock Reservation, which straddles the border of present-day North and South Dakota.

From 1885 to 1886, Sitting Bull joined William Cody's Wild West Show, a traveling exhibition of "Indian fighters" and "Indian War Chiefs." In 1886, Sitting Bull left the Wild West Show and returned to Standing Rock Reservation.

In his remaining years, he continued to oppose assimilation into U.S. culture and the seemingly inevitable breakup of Sioux land. Sitting Bull was killed by government-paid Indian police in October 1890 over a dispute that erupted during a Ghost Dance ceremony at Standing Rock. Government officials were extremely nervous about Sioux participation in the Ghost Dance, because they thought it might lead to the organization of militant resistance to U.S. authority.

### Allogan Slagle (1951–)
*Cherokee lawyer*

Allogan Slagle has been a professor of Native American studies at Berkeley, California, and an attorney advocating for the rights of Native healers and Indian inmates to practice Indian religion in prisons. He is staff attorney with the Association on American Indian Affairs, a New York-based activist organization working for Indian civil rights and legislation.

Slagle has served as assistant director for advocacy in the Lutheran Office for Governmental Affairs in Washington, D.C.; attorney-trustee member/chair of California Legal Services; and assistant librarian at the University of California Research Library, Serials Department, in Los Angeles. He co-authored *The Good Red Road: Passages into Native America* (1987) with Kenneth Lincoln and has written or reviewed over forty articles. His current activities include acting as a consultant to tribes, scholars, organizations, tribally run schools, and California minority-oriented treatment

Allogan Slagle.

programs. He is a member of the board of directors of Urban Indian Health Clinics.

Much of Slagle's energy since the mid–1980s has focused on providing legal and research assistance to Indian communities seeking recognition from the federal government. As many as 150 Indian communities that usually do not have treaty or administrative relations with the U.S. federal government are seeking to gain federal recognition under a congressional act passed in 1978. Slagle's primary focus has been on the national legislation of the recognition process, and he has been active in preserving the federal recognition status of the Keetoowah Band of Cherokee in Oklahoma and many of the numerous California Indian tribes. Allogan Slagle has represented the United Keetoowah Band (UKB) of Cherokee Canadian District since 1992, and serves as Chair of the Membership Committee, and on the Law Reform Committee and the Gaming Commission. He represented the UKB in their effort to regain federal recognition. His work has been supported by the Association of American Indian Affairs since 1989.

### John Slocum (d. 1896–1898)
*Coast Salish spiritual leader*

John Slocum was a member of the Squaxin Band of Southern Coast Salish Indians and achieved importance as the founder the Indian Shaker Church. Slocum was born near Puget Sound, Washington, during the early 1830s, but there was nothing particularly remarkable about his life until the fall of 1881, when he became sick and apparently died. Friends had been summoned and preparations were being made for the funeral when he suddenly revived. He then announced that he had been to visit the judgment place of God and received instructions about certain ways in which Indian people needed to change their lives if they wanted to achieve salvation. This visionary experience became the basis of Tschaddam or the Indian Shaker Church as it is known in English.

This religion is exclusive to Indians and has no connection to millenarian Shakerism as practiced by ascetic Protestant communities in New England. Indian Shakerism incorporates Christian beliefs concerning God, heaven, hell, and the relationship between sinfulness and damnation, but in this religion these ideas are combined with Native concepts, particularly beliefs relating to sickness as a penalty for spiritual offenses.

The "shake" element developed out of a later incident. About a year after his "resurrection," Slocum became ill again and was expected to die. Faced with the impending catastrophe of his death, his wife Mary became hysterical; she approached his prostrate body praying, sobbing, and trembling uncontrollably. When her convulsion had passed, it was observed that Slocum had recovered slightly. This was attributed to her seizure, which was understood as a manifestation of divine power. Thus, curing through "the shake" and laying on of hands became a basic element in Shaker services which continues to this day.

The Indian Shaker religion still flourishes among coastal Indians of British Columbia, Washington, Oregon, and northwestern California. John Slocum died between 1896 and 1898, and the religion has undergone many changes since its inception in 1881.

## Nelson Small Legs (1932–1993)
*Peigan tribal leader*

Nelson Small Legs, chief of the Peigan Indian Reserve from 1976 to 1991, was known to many Canadians because of his and his people's aggressive stance against the construction of a dam on the Oldman River in Alberta. The Peigan Nation, together with the Blackfoot and Blood Indians, formed part of the once-powerful Blackfoot Confederacy on the North American Plains. Small Legs held a variety of jobs before being elected as chief, including working as a farm laborer and miner in Washington and Idaho during his teens and early twenties. He also worked as a ranch hand for several farmers in the Brocket area of southern Alberta before becoming an operator of heavy oilfield equipment in 1966. After failing health forced him to resign his position on the oilfields, Small Legs took a job with the Native Counselling Services of Alberta.

His work counseling Native people led Small Legs to develop an interest in Native politics. Following his election as chief of the reserve, which is located about ninety-five miles west of Lethbridge, Alberta, Small Legs led his band in 1978 in a three-week blockade of the dam site in disobedience of a court-ordered injunction. He eventually reached a highly publicized settlement worth approximately $3.5 million with the government of Alberta permitting development but granting access rights to the Peigan people. Small Legs, with his wife, Florence, raised a large family of eleven children.

## Redbird Smith (1850–1918)
*Cherokee tribal leader and activist*

Redbird Smith was an advocate for the restoration of cultural traditions among his people and led a resistance movement against policies of the U.S. government to redistribute Indian lands. He and a number of colleagues revived the Keetoowah Society to protect Indian sovereignty.

Redbird Smith was born near Fort Smith, Arkansas. His father was Cherokee and his mother part-Cherokee. By the late 1890s, the U.S. government's land allotment policies were finally reaching the so-called Five Civilized Tribes in present-day Oklahoma. The Choctaw, Chickasaw, Cherokee, Creek, and Seminole were called the Five Civilized Tribes because they had formed constitutional governments, many had accepted Christianity, and they had organized school systems. For most Indians, allotment was tantamount to cultural and political extinction. In 1898, Congress passed the Curtis Act, which abolished most operations of the governments among the Five Civilized Tribes. For land to be allotted, however, the government still sought some degree of Indian acceptance. This approval was usually obtained through rather unscrupulous methods. In response to these events, some members of the Cherokee Nation revived the Nighthawk Keetoowah society, an old religious group with a strong interest in perpetuating Cherokee culture and religion. Redbird Smith was one of the primary leaders in the revival movement.

The Nighthawk Keetoowah was a conservative wing of the original Keetoowah society that had been reorganized in the late 1850s before the U.S. Civil War in order to promote political unity among the Cherokee. Smith and the Nighthawks claimed that their society was a religious organization and refused to recognize the right of the U.S. government to disperse tribal lands. Smith led a passive resistance movement that used civil disobedience tactics to disrupt enrollments for distribution of allotted land, which was usually about 160 acres for a male head of household. In 1902, Smith was arrested by federal marshals and forced to sign the enrollment. Under unrelenting federal pressure, the allotment agreements were eventually signed.

In 1907, the Indian Territory became the state of Oklahoma. Smith himself was elected principal chief of the Cherokee in 1908. His activism did not end, however. In 1912, he co-founded the Four Mothers Society, dedicated to preserving and advocating for the political and legal rights of Indian tribes. The Keetoowah society continues to exist today, including the Nighthawk segment revived by Smith's activities in the mid–1890s.

## H. A. (Butch) Smitheram (1918–1982)
*Okanagan tribal leader*

Butch Smitheram is best known for his political activities with non-status Indians in British Columbia. He was born in Penticton, in the interior of British Columbia. His mother was Okanagan and his father was English; at the time of their marriage, an Indian woman who married a non-Indian man lost her status as Indian under Canadian law. After starting but not finishing high school, Butch Smitheram held a variety of jobs before he began to work for the federal Department of Indian Affairs in 1950. Several years later, he decided to go back to school, passed the provincial high school equivalency examinations, and studied English literature at the University of British Columbia.

Smitheran was a founder of the British Columbia Association of Non-Status Indians, which sought to include not only non-status Indians but Métis in British Columbia, the latter being non-status Indians whose mixed Indian-European origin can be traced to the settlement of the prairies and the Northwest Territories but not to the settlement of British Columbia. Smitheram saw that non-status Indians and the Métis people shared similar disadvantages, which could be overcome through unity and shared purpose. He fought hard for improvements in education, as he believed that the education of the young was critical to improve the conditions of his people: "Children are the wealth of our nation—give them the opportunity and the inspiration and they will build on the foundations that you have laid for them." Smitheram was also instrumental in the establishment of the Native Council of Canada, a national organization of non-status Indians in Canada.

## Smohalla (1815–1907)
*Wanapam spiritual leader*

Smohalla was a member of the Wanapam Indian tribe, which lived along the upper Columbia River in present-day eastern Washington State. He left this area around 1850 after a dispute with a local chief. Smohalla traveled for several years. Despite being influenced by Catholic missionaries, Smohalla became a warrior. He was wounded and left for dead during an encounter with a Salish war party. When he returned to his homeland he claimed to have visited the Spirit World during this near-death ordeal. He brought back a message which, to the Wanapam, had the ring of authenticity due to his death-and-resurrection experience.

Smohalla's preaching was a combination of nativist sentiment, cultural purity, and resistance to the U.S. government and Christianity. His popularity came at a time when the Indian population of the region was declining due to diseases and land losses to U.S. settlers. According to Smohalla, religious truths came to him in dreams, thus the name of his religion: "Dreamer Religion." Among Smohalla's teachings was the repudiation of U.S. culture, including alcohol and agricultural practices. Smohalla has been credited with the oft-mentioned quotation, "You ask me to plow the ground. Shall I take a knife and tear my mother's bosom? You ask me to cut grass and make hay and sell it and be rich like white men. But dare I cut off my mother's hair?" Smohalla also prophesied that Indians would be resurrected and banish whites from their lands. He taught that Indians would be saved though divine intervention, but did not advocate violence. His teachings and sermons were often accompanied by ceremonial music and dance.

Smohalla spread his message throughout the region and had many converts, including Old Joseph, a former Christian. His teachings got him into trouble with U.S. authorities and Smohalla was often jailed. Smohalla's teachings influenced a number of later prophets who also preached a message of resistance and cultural identity.

## Reuben A. Snake Jr. (1937–1993)
*Winnebago tribal and spiritual leader*

Reuben Snake was a founding trustee and the spiritual advisor for the American Indian Ritual Object Repatriation Foundation. He was born in Winnebago, Nebraska, and was educated at the University of Nebraska (1964–1965) and Peru State College (1968–1969).

Snake was a legislative aide to Senator Robert Kerrey of Nebraska and worked with numerous national Native American organizations, serving as national chairman of the American Indian Movement (1972), national president of the National Congress of American Indians (1985–1987), and council to the Americans for Indian Opportunity, Washington, D.C.

He was chairman of the Winnebago Tribal Council from 1975 to 1988, and his other professional posts include college instructor and conflict management specialist. Among his awards are the 1986 Citizenship Award from the Nebraska Indian Commission, 1986 Distinguished Nebraskan, and 1986 Certificate of Recognition by the U.S. Secretary of the Interior.

## David Sohappy, Sr. (1925–1991)
*Yakima fisherman and activist*

After he was laid off from a sawmill in the 1960s, David Sohappy returned to the traditional Indian way of life, settling in a self-made wooden house on the Columbia River. From there he undertook a campaign for Indian treaty fishing rights along the rivers in Washington state. For Sohappy, there was no compromising his belief that Indians have the right to fish when and where they want guaranteed by the Yakima Nation's Treaty of 1855. In a long-standing battle to assert tribal fishing rights, Sohappy was arrested numerous times and had 230 fishing nets confiscated over twenty years because of his insistence on fishing out of season on the Columbia River to assert his tribal right to take fish in the usual and accustomed places and times. The 1968 case *Sohappy v. Washington State* started a series of legal rulings and investigations resulting in the 1974 Boldt Decision by U.S. District Court judge George Boldt, who held that treaties negotiated in the 1850s gave many western Washington State Indian nations the right to catch half the harvestable salmon in Washington waters. The Boldt Decision was considered a great victory for Indian fishing rights and cleared the path for a resurgence of commercial and subsistence fishing activity by the western Washington State Indians.

In 1983, Sohappy was convicted of selling 317 fish out of season to undercover agents taking part in a federal sting operation. When he was sent to prison, he served eighteen months and was released in poor health in 1988. He died at a nursing home in Hood River, Oregon, at the age of sixty-six. He is considered a major figure and activist within the Northwest Coast Indian fishing rights campaign, a major economic issue in the region that continues to require legal and legislative attention.

### Cora Nicolasa Solomon (1933–)
*Winnebago health worker*

Cora Solomon is an important leader in developing health care delivery systems within Native American communities. She is also a community leader of the Winnebago Indians of Nebraska.

She was born in 1933 in Winnebago, Nebraska, and has served as director of the National Community Health Representatives (CHR) Program. The program, which is part of the Indian Health Service (IHS), is a community-based health delivery system using indigenous paraprofessionals.

She has been the director of the Winnebago Tribe of Nebraska Health Department and secretary of the Winnebago Tribal Council. She has also served on the Winnebago public school board and the Nebraska Indian Commission. Solomon is also a member of the Nebraska Indian Inter-Tribal Development Corporation, the Goldenrod Hills Community Action Agency, the Seven States Indian Health Association, and the American Indian Human Resource Center Board, which administers an alcohol abuse program.

Solomon is a member of the National Association of Community Health Representatives and the National Congress of American Indians (NCAI), a major national Indian lobbying organization that looks after Indian interests in Congress. She has received numerous honors and awards, including the Woman Pioneer Award given to her by the governor of Nebraska.

### Towana Spivey (1943–)
*Chickasaw historian, archaeologist, and curator*

Towana Spivey has spent his professional career preserving and interpreting the prehistory/history of the Trans Mississippi West with a particular interest in the Oklahoma area.

Born in Madill, Oklahoma, he is a descendent of several generations of Chickasaw who came to Indian Territory, now Oklahoma, in 1842 from northern Mississippi. He received an undergraduate degree in history/natural science and did graduate work in museum studies and anthropology. A recognized authority in the restoration and interpretation of nineteenth century structures, he has conducted archaeological investigations at nineteenth-century military posts such as Fort Washita, Fort Sill, and Fort Towson.

Towana Spivey.

Spivey has served on advisory committees and boards for the Oklahoma Archaeological Survey, the governor's review committee for the Oklahoma State Preservation Office, Oklahoma's Museum Association, and the Southwestern Oklahoma Historical Society. He worked as historic archaeologist for the Oklahoma Anthropological Society, curator of anthropology at the Museum of the Great Plains, and director/curator of the Fort Sill Museum.

He has authored several books and articles and has served as a primary or featured consultant in at least thirty-five television documentaries. In 1984, he recorded several hours of tape on Native American and frontier history for the *Voice of America*, broadcast in the Soviet Union.

Spivey has regularly been involved with preserving the history, language, and material culture of many Oklahoma tribes, including the Comanche, Kiowa, Chiracahua and Warm Springs Apache, Apache Tribe of Oklahoma and others. He has also testified as an expert witness in state and federal courts on Native American issues.

He was director of the Fort Sill Museum (1982–2000) in Fort Sill, Oklahoma, where he incorporated major cultural programs, designed and implemented Native American sculptures, and utilized bilingual exhibit labels.

Chris Spotted Eagle.

## Chris Spotted Eagle (contemporary)
*Houma film producer and director*

Chris Spotted Eagle is a member of the Muskogean-speaking Houma people, who live in Louisiana. He is an independent film producer and director from Minneapolis, Minnesota. He has worked as a photojournalist, advertising photographer, project manager, and field producer at Twin Cities Public Television, KTCA, in Minneapolis. Spotted Eagle is a veteran of the U.S. Army and Air Force and his interests include cultural work, art, and social activism toward peace and justice.

He has produced such films as *Our Sacred Land* (1984) and *The Great Spirit Within the Hole* (1983), balancing his livelihood with commercial endeavors. His personal work emphasizes the expression of Indian views on land and legal issues that affect Indian peoples in the twentieth century.

Spotted Eagle's major films are designed to give non-Indian audiences access to the thoughts and political positions that American Indians have on land issues and insights to their world views, especially creation histories and views of the sacred found within various Indian nations.

He has served as a staff director for the American Indian Center in Minneapolis and as a board member of numerous civic and community organizations, including the Minnesota Humanities Commission, Minnesota Civil Liberties Union, and the Twin Cities Chapter of the National Lawyers Guild. Spotted Eagle remains active in the Minneapolis Indian community making videos and continues to have a strong interest in Native spiritualism.

## Spotted Tail (1833–1881)
*Brule Sioux tribal leader*

Spotted Tail was born in the 1830s, either along the White River in South Dakota or near Fort Laramie in Wyoming. His adult name, Spotted Tail, is associated with a raccoon and was given to him by a trapper. Spotted Tail and Little Thunder, another Brule chief, sought revenge for the 1854 killing of the Sioux chief

Brave Bear during a battle with army forces near Fort Laramie. In August 1855, at Ash Hollow, Nebraska, troops under William S. Harney overtook the Brule Sioux and on October 18, Spotted Tail and his companions surrendered. Following his release from prison, Spotted Tail took a more diplomatic line with U.S. settlers, though he continued to struggle for Sioux land rights.

Although famed as a warrior, he generally advised peace to his fellow Sioux. During the War for the Bozeman Trail of 1866–1868, under Red Cloud, he counseled accommodation with U.S. intruders. He was one of the signers of the Fort Laramie Treaty of 1868, establishing the Great Sioux Reservation in present-day North and South Dakota.

In 1870, Spotted Tail traveled to Washington, D.C., and met with President Ulysses S. Grant and his Seneca Commissioner of Indian Affairs, Ely Parker. Spotted Tail made subsequent trips to Washington and proved to be a skillful negotiator. In 1873, agencies bearing his name and that of Red Cloud were established in Nebraska. In his largest negotiating role, the government offered the Sioux $6 million for the Black Hills following the discovery of gold; Spotted Tail demanded $60 million, which the U.S. government rejected.

The influx of miners into the Black Hills led to new wars in 1876 and 1877, led by the Sioux leaders Sitting Bull, Crazy Horse, and Gall. Following the Indian victory at Little Bighorn in 1876, Spotted Tail was appointed chief of the Sioux at the Spotted Tail and Red Cloud agencies. After the Little Bighorn battle, Spotted Tail negotiated the surrender of Sioux militants in 1877. Following the surrender, the government relocated the Sioux from the Spotted Tail and Red Cloud agencies into the Great Sioux Reservation. In 1878, the two agencies were renamed the Rosebud and Pine Ridge agencies, respectively.

Though respected by many of his people, some of the Sioux never forgave Spotted Tail for negotiating the surrender of the militants and for the death of Crazy Horse, which soon followed. Spotted Tail was killed by a fellow Sioux, Crow Dog, in 1881 at Rosebud. An ensuing U.S. Supreme Court decision, *Ex Parte Crow Dog*, based on the killing of Spotted Tail by Crow Dog, resulted in a landmark court decision, which stated that federal courts did not have criminal jurisdiction for major crimes in Indian Country. This ruling incensed Congress, which in 1881 passed the Major Crimes Act, giving federal government jurisdiction over major crimes such as murder and kidnapping in Indian Country. The act curtailed the rights of tribal governments to manage crimes among their own people.

## Squanto (Tasquantum) (1580–1622)
*Wampanoag interpreter and cultural mediator*

In 1605, Tasquantum, also known as Squanto, was abducted in present-day Massachusetts by Europeans and sold into slavery in Malaga, an island off the Mediterranean coast of Spain. He eventually escaped to England where he enlisted in the Newfoundland Company. After sailing to America and back again, Squanto finally returned to his homeland in 1619 to find his people wiped out by disease. Squanto took up life with the Pilgrims at Plymouth and provided invaluable instruction on farming, hunting, fishing, and geography. According to one colonial historian: "He directed them how to set their corne, when to take fish, and to procure other commodities, and was also their pilott to bring them to unknowne places for their profitt." It is also believed that Squanto helped the Pilgrims maintain friendly relations with neighboring tribes.

In 1622, Squanto died of disease while helping the Pilgrims negotiate trade agreements with the Narragansett Indians. In recent history the story of Squanto and the Pilgrims has become an oft-repeated, frequently distorted tale for young people as an example of friendly relations between Indians and the early colonists.

## Steven L. A. Stallings (1951–)
*San Lusieno corporate executive*

Steven Stallings, a member of the Rincon Band of San Lusieno Mission Indians, is senior vice-president and director of Native American Banking Services for Wells Fargo.

He was born and raised in San Diego, California, and attended San Diego High School. Raised in a single parent family, he is the oldest of two sisters and four brothers. As a young boy, he began working in his grandfather's small construction company, fueling his interest in business.

As a business school graduate of California State University, Long Beach, and the University of Southern California, he went to work for the United Indian Development Association (UIDA), a California-based business assistance program for American Indians.

He became president, taking the organization to a national-level and changing its name to the National Center for American Indian Enterprise Development (NCAIED), and opened offices in Phoenix, Arizona; Seattle, Washington; and Los Angeles, California. Under Stallings's leadership, it raised over $800 million in capital and sales contracts for tribal and Indian companies.

Steve Stallings.

In 1995, he joined Wells Fargo, where he is responsible for the delivery of commercial credit and treasury management products to Native American communities and enterprises throughout Wells Fargo's twenty-three-state region. In 2000, Stallings was awarded the Annie G. Ross Award, which is presented to an outstanding American Indian whose life and career have made contributions to American society and bring honor to all American people.

Stallings is currently vice-president of Wells Fargo Bank, a board member of the American Indian Graduate Center (a scholarship fund located in Albuquerque, New Mexico), and a member of Atlatl, a national Native American Arts organization. He resides in Chandler, Arizona, with his wife Peggy (Navajo), and his two daughters, Stefanie and Celena.

### Stand Watie (1806–1871)
*Cherokee tribal leader*

Stand Watie was a Cherokee tribal leader and Confederate general. He was a leading member of the Treaty Party favoring Cherokee removal west in the 1830s.

Born near present-day Rome, Georgia, Stand Watie received his education in mission schools, then returned to his homeland to work with his brother, Elias Boudinot, on the *Cherokee Phoenix* newspaper. During this time Stand Watie became a pro-removal supporter and embraced the Treaty of New Echota in 1835, which forced the Cherokee to leave their homeland in present-day western Georgia, eastern Tennessee, western Carolina, and eastern Alabama. Together with his cousins John and Major Ridge, Stand Watie and Boudinot led a pro-removal group known as the "Treaty Party." The inevitable tension with anti-removal forces almost cost Stand Watie his life in 1839 when embittered anti-removal Cherokee killed Boudinot and the two Ridges.

From 1845 to 1861, Stand Watie built and maintained a successful plantation in Indian Territory (present-day Oklahoma) using black slave labor. During this time, Stand Watie served on the Cherokee Council, including stints as speaker of the lower Cherokee legislative house.

When the Civil War broke out in 1861, Stand Watie, now a well-to-do landowner, joined the Confederate forces and organized a cavalry regiment. He was commissioned colonel in the First Cherokee Mounted Rifles in October 1861. Stand Watie had major roles in several battles. In the 1862 Battle of Pea Ridge, Arkansas, Stand Watie's troops captured Union artillery positions that had been a major obstacle to Confederate strategy. As the war progressed, a number of Indian Confederate leaders withdrew from the conflict. Stand Watie, however, continued the fight, and was promoted to brigadier general. Under his command two regiments of Mounted Rifles and three battalions of Cherokee, Seminole, and Osage infantry fought throughout Indian Territory, Arkansas, Missouri, Kansas, and Texas, and won a number of significant battles. It is believed Stand Watie's unit fought more battles west of the Mississippi River than any other Confederate unit.

In 1865, Stand Watie surrendered to Union forces, the last general in the Confederate Army to do so. After the war, he acted in his new capacity as principal chief of the southern Cherokee, rebuilding tribal assets (including his own diminished holdings) during Reconstruction. Stand Watie and his nephew, Elias C. Boudinot, entered the tobacco processing business in 1868. He and his nephew were temporarily arrested over a legal dispute on Cherokee tax exemptions. Subsequently, the U.S. Supreme Court ruled in 1870 that Cherokee enterprises were not exempt from federal tax laws. Stand Watie was married to Betsy Bell, with whom he had five children.

## Standing Bear (Mochunozhi) (1829–1908)
*Ponca tribal leader*

Standing Bear was a Ponca principal chief who won a U.S. federal case to bury his son in the Ponca homelands of Nebraska. Traditional enemies of the Sioux, the Ponca negotiated a treaty in 1858 that established boundaries between the two tribal groups. The treaty was abrogated when the government included Ponca lands within the Great Sioux Reservation in the Fort Laramie Treaty of 1868. In 1876, Congress passed a law to remove the Ponca from their homeland in present-day northern Kansas and forcibly relocate them to Indian Territory (Oklahoma).

One-third of the tribe perished from disease and hunger once they arrived. Two of Standing Bear's children died, and he set out to return his son's body to the old Ponca homeland. Accompanied by thirty warriors, the party set off on the journey. They were spotted by settlers, and, fearing an uprising, General George Crook ordered cavalry officers to arrest them. They were taken to Omaha, where they were interviewed by journalist Thomas H. Tibbles.

After the nature of the Ponca trip was understood, General Crook and others were sympathetic to Standing Bear's mission. However, federal attorneys argued that the Indians were not legally persons under the U.S. Constitution and therefore had no rights. Federal judge Elmer Dundy ruled against the attorneys, and Standing Bear's party was allowed to continue. He buried his son in northeastern Nebraska. Sympathy grew for the Ponca, and Standing Bear went on a lecture tour of the East. Congress formed a commission to study the Ponca case and granted Standing Bear and his party land in Nebraska in 1880. He lived until he was about eighty years old and was buried on the original Ponca homeland (see also the biography of Sarah Winnemucca).

## Dorothy Stanley (1924–1990)
*Miwok basketmaker*

Dorothy Stanley was a basketmaker and cultural spokeswoman among the Northern Miwok, a group of tribes whose native territory was centered in the Sierra Nevada mountains of eastern California.

Born in Los Angeles, California, on 14 July 1924, Stanley was descended from families of hereditary leaders among the Northern Miwok in the areas of West Point and Railroad Flat, California. Her early life was difficult, as she was raised in many different households, often far from home, but she still managed to absorb much traditional Miwok knowledge and passed these teachings on to many other people, both Indian and white, during her lifetime.

Stanley was educated at Stewart Indian School in Stewart, Nevada, and worked at the nearby Wai-Pai-Shone Trading Post until she graduated from Stewart in 1942. Over the following decades, she held many types of jobs in various places in California and Nevada, but finally returned home in the early 1970s. Remembering the teachings she received from her relatives, she then became very active in promoting, defending, and teaching her culture. She worked as a Native American liaison for the Department of the Interior, as tribal chair for the Tuolumne Mewuk Tribal Council, as director of a tribal health project, and as supervisor of the Indian Cultural Program at Yosemite National Park.

A warm and outspoken person, she was known as much for her teaching as for her basketry, which was very fine, and she gave cultural demonstrations of basketmaking and other Native crafts for festivals and classes from Los Angeles to Washington, D.C. Stanley valued the past and fought against the loss of Miwok culture by younger Miwok whom she saw embracing the trappings of pan-Indian culture rather than their own distinctive culture.

## Emmet Starr (1870–1930)
*Cherokee historian*

Emmet Starr was born in the Going Snake District, Cherokee Nation, Indian Territory (present-day Oklahoma), on 12 December 1870. He was educated in the Cherokee Nation public schools, graduated from the Cherokee National Male Seminary in 1888, and received a degree in medicine from Barnes Medical College at St. Louis in 1891.

According to tradition, Starr dreamed of becoming the "Herodotus of the Cherokees." Herodotus is a famous Greek historian who wrote during the fifth century. Starr practiced medicine for five years and began gathering materials for his *History of the Cherokee* about 1891, but in 1896, he began to devote himself full time to studying Cherokee history. In 1899, he issued a prospectus for his book *Gazeteer of the Cherokee Nation, Indian Territory*. The book, however, never appeared. Starr also served one term in the Cherokee National Council as a representative of the Cooweescoowee District and as a delegate to the Indian Territory statehood meeting known as the Sequoyah Convention in 1905. The Sequoyah convention was trying to hold off the U.S. abolition of the Indian Territory governments, but was unsuccessful since by 1907 Oklahoma had become a state.

After Oklahoma statehood, Starr continued the preparation of his Cherokee histories. He published four books: *The History of the Cherokee Indians* (1922), *Early History of the Cherokees* (1917), *Cherokees West* (1910), and *Encyclopedia of Oklahoma* (1912). While working on his histories, Starr was associated with the Cherokee National Seminaries and the Normal School which became Northeastern State University in Tahlequah, Oklahoma. In 1958, a bronze plaque was placed on the wall of the Northeastern State College Library honoring him as a former college librarian.

Undoubtedly, the most popular sections of Starr's *The History of the Cherokee Indians* were the chapters and charts entitled "Old Families and Their Genealogy." Starr's genealogical notes were used as evidence by the Dawes Commission in establishing eligibility for Cherokee settlements and for listing on the official tribal rolls.

Emmet Starr is recognized as a major Cherokee historian. Nevertheless, he died in St. Louis, Missouri, in 1930, suffering a self-imposed exile, convinced that he had failed his people in a mission to "perpetuate the facts relative to the Cherokee tribe."

## Henry Bird Steinhauer (circa 1818–1884)
*Ojibwa missionary*

It is believed that Henry Bird Steinhauer was originally known as Sowengisik (Southern Skies). He was born in 1818 to Ojibwa parents on the Rama Indian settlement at Lake Simcoe just north of Toronto, Ontario. When he was ten years old, he was given the name Henry Bird Steinhauer after an American benefactor who agreed to finance the education of an Indian boy if the child adopted his name. Steinhauer attended school in Ontario from 1829 to 1832 and then attended a seminary in Cazenovia, just east of Syracuse, New York, until 1835.

Steinhauer was sent by the Wesleyan Methodist Church to teach at the Credit River Mission on Lake Ontario in 1835 and later was enrolled at the Upper Canada Academy in Cobourg, Ontario. After interrupting his studies briefly to teach, Steinhauer graduated from the academy at the top of his class. Several years later, he was sent west to northern Ontario and Manitoba to assist in the translation of the Bible and hymns into Cree, as it was thought that his knowledge of Ojibwa would be of assistance since the two languages share the same language group. Steinhauer married in 1846 and eventually was the father to five children. He was ordained in 1855 and immediately sent to Lac La Biche in what is now Alberta. Steinhauer moved his mission several times, eventually settling in an area called Whitefish Lake. Steinhauer is known in later life for a letter written to the Missionary Society of the Wesleyan Methodist Church in Canada in which he stated that "there is always a distrust on the part of a native to the foreigner, from the fact that the native has been so long down-trodden by the white man."

## Ralph Garvin Steinhauer (1905–1987)
*Métis politician*

Ralph Steinhauer, the first Native person to serve as lieutenant-governor of a Canadian province, was born in 1905 in Morley, a small town in east-central Alberta. His great-grandfather, Henry Bird Steinhauer, was a distinguished Ojibwa missionary. Ralph attended the Brandon Indian Residential School. Until the age of twenty-three, he also worked on his father's farm in Saddle Lake during the summer and at a local store during the winter. In 1927, Steinhauer met Isabel Davidson, who had recently moved from the eastern United States to Alberta with her widowed mother. They were married the following year and moved to the Saddle Lake Indian Reserve in east-central Alberta to farm in earnest. The Steinhauer farm grew steadily, and he became an enormously successful farmer, teaching others to use the reserve system to maximize agricultural opportunities.

Steinhauer began to develop an interest in politics, serving as chief of the Saddle Lake Reserve for three years. In 1963, he was nominated by the Liberal party to run for election to the federal House of Commons, although he did not get elected. However, his successes were many. He was a founder of the Indian Association of Alberta, a province-wide organization devoted to the advancement of aboriginal rights. In 1974, Steinhauer was sworn in as the lieutenant-governor of Alberta, a position he held until 1979. In light of his contribution to his community, Steinhauer was named a Companion of the Order of Canada, an award conferred by the governor general of Canada to select Canadians in recognition of exemplary merit and achievement. He also received honorary doctoral degrees from the Universities of Alberta and Calgary.

## Rennard James Strickland (1940– )
*Osage-Cherokee lawyer*

Rennard Strickland is dean and Philip H. Knight Professor of Law at the University of Oregon. He was born in St. Louis, Missouri, and earned a bachelor of

Rennard Strickland.

arts degree from Northeastern State College in 1962 and two law degrees from the University of Virginia, in 1965 and 1970, respectively.

Strickland is the first person to have served as both president of the Association of American Law Schools and chair of the Law School Admission Council. He was also editor-in-chief for the third edition revision of *Cohen's Handbook of Federal Indian Law* for the U.S. Department of the Interior (1975–1982) and was appointed by the Federal District Court for the Northern District of Oklahoma as chair and arbitrator for the Osage Constitutional Commission (1992–1995).

He has been dean of the College of Law at Oklahoma City University (1996–1998), dean of the College of Law at Southern Illinois University (1985–1988), and acting dean at the University of Tulsa (1974–1975). Strickland has also been director of the American Indian Law Center, and professor of law at the University of Oklahoma School of Law (1990–1996) and the University of Wisconsin at Madison (1988–1990). He served as director of the Indian Heritage Association of Muskogee, Oklahoma (1966–1984), and chairman of the Indian Advisory Board of the Philbrook Art Center (1979–1983).

Among Strickland's honors and awards are the Spirit of Excellence Award of the American Bar Association

Commission on Minorities in the Profession (1997), the SALT Award for legal reform from the Society of American Law Teachers (1980), the Sacred Sash of the Creeks for Preservation of Tribal History (1970–1971), Fellow of the Doris Duke Foundation (1970–1973), Award of Merit from the Association for State and Local History (1981), and Distinguished Service Citation from the American Indian Coalition (1985).

He has published numerous books including *Tonto's Revenge* (1998), *Masterworks of American Indian Art* (1983), *The Indians in Oklahoma* (1980), *Fire and Spirit* (1975), and *Cherokee Spirit Tales* (1969).

His interests include law, culture, and ethnohistory of American Indians, contemporary American Indian art and painting, and the development of traditional legal systems among tribes.

### Diosa Summers-Fitzgerald (1945–1992)
*Mississippi Choctaw artist*

Diosa Summers-Fitzgerald was an educator and artist who worked with Native American art forms, and she developed and designed art programs to teach Native American art and traditions.

Born in New York City she earned a bachelor of arts from State University College at Buffalo (1977), and a master of education degree from Harvard University (1983). The focus of her work and studies was Native American art. She was both an artist herself and a teacher of Native American art traditions. In the classroom, Summers-Fitzgerald worked to foster a clearer understanding of the roots of Native American tradition through art.

From 1975 to 1977, Summers-Fitzgerald was the director of education of the History and Continuing Education Department at the State University College of New York College at Buffalo, and an instructor at Haffenreffer Museum of Anthropology in Bristol, Rhode Island, from 1979 to 1980, at which time she was also acting tribal coordinator of the Narragansett Tribal Education Project. From 1982 to 1985, she was artist-in-residence at the Folk Arts Program in Rhode Island State Council on the Arts in Providence, Rhode Island, and also an artist working with the Native American Art Forms Nishnabeykwa Production in Charlestown, Rhode Island. Beginning in 1985, she served as the education director of the Jamaica Arts Center in Jamaica, New York.

Summers-Fitzgerald authored several Indian museum brochures including "Native American Food," "Finger-weaving," "Narrative and Instruction," and "Ash Sapling Basketry."

## Sun Bear (1929–1992)
*Chippewa spiritual leader*

Sun Bear became best known as president of the Bear Tribe Medicine Society in Spokane, Washington, and the editor and publisher of *Many Smokes* magazine.

Born on the White Earth Reservation in eastern Minnesota, Sun Bear was an actor and technical director for *Wagon Train, Bonanza,* and *Wild, Wild West* television shows from 1955 to 1965. He founded the Bear Tribe Medicine Society to spread Native American culture, and he taught, lectured, and toured extensively for the cause. His international tours include Europe, Australia, and India. In the 1980s, his ideas on self-sufficiency and living with the earth were embraced by a number of environmental and holistic living groups.

Sun Bear is a member of the Midiwiwin Society, a Chippewa association of spiritual leaders and healers, and the National Congress of American Indians, a national organization that lobbies in Congress for Indian political interests. Books written by Sun Bear include *At Home in the Wilderness, Buffalo Hearts, Walk in Balance, The Bear Tribe's Self-Reliance Book, The Medicine Wheel Book,* and *Sun Bear: The Path of Power.*

## Sweet Grass (?–1877)
*Cree tribal leader*

Sweet Grass, also known as Wikaskokiseyin, was born in Cree territory to a Crow mother who had been kidnapped during a war between her people and the Cree. As a young man, he was called Le Petit Chef or Apistchikoimas, and was supposedly renamed Sweet Grass when, during his youth, he entered into enemy Blackfoot territory by himself, killed a Blackfoot warrior, and stole more than forty horses. Upon his return home amid cheers of victory, it is said that he held up a fistful of grass dipped in the blood of his victim and thereafter became known as Sweet Grass.

In 1870, Sweet Grass converted to Roman Catholicism and was baptized as Abraham. He had already become the principal chief of many of the Plains Cree, and in the same year he wrote to Canadian authorities protesting the effects of European settlement, hunting, and fishing. In relation to the acquisition by Canada of land that soon became Manitoba, Saskatchewan, and Alberta, Sweet Grass wrote, "We heard our lands were sold and we do not like it; we do not want to sell our lands; it is our property, and no one has a right to sell them." He sought assistance in the form of a treaty: "Our country is getting ruined of the fur-bearing animals, hitherto our sole support, and now we are poor and want help—we want you to pity us. We want cattle,

tools, agricultural implements, and assistance in everything when we come to settle—our country is no longer able to support us." Six years later, Sweet Grass signed a treaty with Canadian authorities on behalf of his people. He died a few months later, but his name is memorialized in the Sweet Grass Reserve established for his people near Battleford in central Saskatchewan.

## Ross O. Swimmer (1943–)
*Cherokee tribal leader*

Ross Swimmer is president of the Cherokee Group, L.L.C., and a former assistant secretary of Indian affairs with the U.S. Department of the Interior. He was born in Oklahoma and received a bachelor of science degree and a law degree from the University of Oklahoma.

Swimmer has been general counsel and principal chief of the Cherokee Nation (1972–1985) and president of the First National Bank of Tahlequah, Oklahoma (1975–1985). He has served as co-chairman of the Presidential Commission on Indian Reservation Economies (1983–1984), executive committee member of the Eastern Oklahoma Boy Scouts of America, former chairman of the Tahlequah Planning and Zoning Commission, and past president of the Cherokee National Historical Society.

From 1986 to 1989, Swimmer was assistant secretary of Indian affairs within the Department of the Interior. This is the highest ranking U.S. government administrative position and oversees the Bureau of Indian Affairs, the major government agency concerned with U.S. Indian issues. Swimmer, appointed by President Ronald Reagan, worked to carry out the business and self-sufficiency goals of the Reagan Administration, promoting economic development and encouraging tribal governments to take more leadership and financial responsibility for their tribal communities.

He returned to Tulsa, Oklahoma, in 1989, and joined the law firm of Hall, Estill, Hardwick, Gable, Golden and Nelson, P.C., to begin the practice of tribal law. The firm has offices in Tulsa, Oklahoma City, Fayetteville, and Washington, D.C.

Swimmer is president of the Simon Estes Educational Foundation, Incirca, a Tulsa-based scholarship granting organization; a member of the Philbrook Museum board of trustees; a trustee for the University of Tulsa; and a board member of the Cowboy Hall of Fame and Western Heritage Center in Oklahoma City, Oklahoma.

Swimmer has been awarded the Distinguished Service Award from the University of Oklahoma, an honorary doctorate from Phillips University, and the Crystal

Crown Award from Birmingham, Alabama, for his work with American Indians.

## Gerald Tailfeathers (1925–1975)
*Blackfoot artist*

Gerald Tailfeathers, one of the first Native Canadian artists to pursue a professional artistic career, was born in 1925 at Stand Off, Alberta. His talent was apparent to others early in his life; in his teens, he received a scholarship from the Anglican Church to study art and was not yet twenty when he had his first exhibition. He trained in art at the School of Fine Arts in Banff, a small resort town in the Rocky Mountains in Alberta, and at the Provincial School of Technology and Art in Calgary, Alberta. Tailfeathers's career began to flourish while he was in his twenties; apart from a stint as a technical draftsman for a petroleum company, he worked as a full-time artist.

Tailfeathers's painting style was pictorial and nostalgic. His paintings often depicted his people, the Blackfoot and Blood Indians, as they lived in the nineteenth century, hunting buffalo, setting up camp, and engaging in ceremonial practices. He was influenced by other Indian painters of his generation, as he traveled often to view the work of others. He spent a summer studying at the Summer Art School in Glacier National Park in Montana, for example, with several portrait painters, including Winold Reiss and Carl Linck from New York. Later in his career, after a visit to the Arizona studio of the sculptor George Phippin, Tailfeathers began to experiment with bronze sculpture depicting life on the Plains.

## Maria Tallchief (1925–)
*Osage ballerina*

Maria Tallchief is a world-renowned ballerina and one of the premiere American ballerinas of all time. She was the first American to dance at the Paris Opera and has danced with the Paris Opera Ballet, the Ballet Russe, and later with the Balanchine Ballet Society (New York City Ballet).

Tallchief was raised in a wealthy family. Her grandfather had helped negotiate the Osage treaty, which created the Osage Reservation in Oklahoma and later yielded a bonanza in oil revenues for some Osage people. Tallchief began dance and music lessons at age four. By age eight, she and her sister had exhausted the training resources in Oklahoma, and the family moved to Beverly Hills, California. By age twelve, Tallchief

was studying under Madame Nijinska (sister of the great Nijinsky) and David Lichine, a student of the renowned Russian ballerina Pavlova. At age fifteen at the Hollywood Bowl, Tallchief danced her first solo performance in a number choreographed by Nijinska. Following high school, it was apparent that ballet would be Tallchief's life. Instead of college, she joined the Ballet Russe, a highly acclaimed Russian ballet troupe. Tallchief was initially treated with skepticism—the Russian troupe was unwilling to recognize the Native American's greatness. When choreographer George Balanchine took control of the company, however, he recognized Tallchief's talent and selected her for the understudy role in The Song of Norway. Under Balanchine, Tallchief's reputation grew, and she was eventually given the title of ballerina. During this time, Tallchief married Balanchine, and when he moved to Paris, she went with him.

As with the Ballet Russe, Tallchief was initially treated with condescension in Paris. Her debut at the Paris Opera was the first ever for any American ballerina, and Tallchief's talent quickly won French audiences over. She later became the first American to dance with the Paris Opera Ballet at the Bolshoi Theatre in Moscow. She quickly became the ranking soloist and, soon after, joined the Balanchine Ballet Society, now the New York City Ballet. At the New York City Ballet, Tallchief became recognized as one of the greatest dancers in the world. When she became the prima ballerina, she was the first American dancer to achieve this title. In 1949, Tallchief danced what was perhaps her greatest role in the Balanchine-choreographed version of *The Firebird*. Balanchine had choreographed the role for Tallchief, and her dazzling blend of physical control and mysticism enchanted audiences.

## Mary TallMountain (1918–1994)
*Athabaskan poet*

Mary TallMountain was a widely respected Athabaskan author and poet. She was born in 1918 in Nulato, a village along the Yukon River in Alaska, of Athabaskan-Russian and Scots-Irish parents. At age six, because her mother was sick with tuberculosis, she was adopted by a non-Indian couple. Although her adoptive parents could teach her little about her culture, she retained vivid memories of her early childhood, and much of her poetry captures a delighted child's view of village life among the Athabaskan of central Alaska.

As an adult, TallMountain moved to San Francisco, where she worked as a legal secretary and began to write poetry, which was featured in dozens of anthologies and periodicals, such as *Earth Power Coming, The*

*Remembered Earth, The Language of Life, The Harper's Anthology of Twentieth Century Native American Poetry, The Alaska Quarterly, Animals Agenda,* and *That's What She Said.* In 1960, she came under the tutelage of Pueblo poet and author Paula Gunn Allen. TallMountain has published several collections of poems, including *The Light on the Tent Wall* (1990), *A Quick Brush of Wings* (1991), and a posthumous collection *Listen To the Night* (1995). The Rasmussen Library at the University of Alaska in Fairbanks houses an archival collection of TallMountain's published and unpublished works.

Mary TallMountain had a close association with the Tenderloin Reflection and Education Center (TREC), a community-based nonprofit spiritual and cultural center in her San Francisco neighborhood. She was a poet-in-residence there in 1991 and 1992 and participated in many of TREC's workshops and performances.

The TallMountain Circle was established as a project of TREC and each year the advisory board selects Mary TallMountain Awards for Creative Writing and Community Service to benefit low-income writers, particularly Native Americans and writers living in San Francisco's Tenderloin District.

## Luci Tapahonso (1951–)
*Navajo poet*

Luci Tapahonso, a member of the Salt Water clan of the Navajo Nation, teaches in the American Indian Studies and English departments at the University of Arizona.

She is the author of collections of poetry, short stories, and children's books, including *Songs of Shiprock Fair* (1999), *Blue Horses Rush In* (1997), *Naanii Dhatall: The Women Are Singing* (1993), *A Breeze Swept Through* (1989), and *Seasonal Woman* (1982).

Tapahonso has also taught at the University of New Mexico and the University of Kansas. Her awards include the New Mexico Eminent Scholar award from the New Mexico Commission of Higher Education (1989), Woman of Distinction from the National Association of Women in Education (1998), and the Mountains and Plains Booksellers Award for her poetry (1998).

She has served on the board of directors at the Phoenix Indian Center, was a member of the New Mexico Arts Commission Literature Panel, steering committee of Returning the Gift Writers Festival, Kansas Arts Commission Literature Panel, Phoenix Arts Commission, Telluride Institute Writers Forum advisory board, and commissioner of the Kansas Arts Commission. She is a member of the Modern Language

Association, Poets and Writers, Inc., Association of American Indian and Alaska Native Professors, and the New Mexico Endowment for the Humanities.

## Drew Hayden Taylor (1962–)
*Ojibwa playwright, scriptwriter, director, short story writer, and journalist*

One of Canada's most prominent writers, Drew Hayden Taylor, an Ojibway from the Curve Lake First Nations, works in a variety of genres to describe and satirize modern Native North American life. Known for his use of humor in depicting Native responses to public opinion and government decisions, Taylor is a frequent columnist for *The Globe and Mail* and *The Toronto Star* and is often featured as a commentator on the Canadian Broadcasting Corporation's *Newsworld.* He is a regular columnist for three Canadian newspapers.

Perhaps best known for his plays, Taylor is one of the former artistic directors of Native Earth Performing Arts, a Toronto-based company that provides a home for Native writers, actors, artists, and technicians. *Someday* (1993), one of his more popular plays, was adapted from one of Taylor's short stories, the only piece of fiction ever printed on the front page of *The Globe and*

Drew Hayden Taylor.

*Mail.* Some of his other plays include *Only Drunks and Children Tell the Truth* (1996), *A Contemporary Gothic Indian Vampire Story* (1992), *The Bootlegger Blues* (1990), and *Toronto at Dreamer's Rock* (1989). Two of his most recent plays, *alterNATIVES, TDR.com* and *400 Kilometres*, are often performed throughout Canada and the United States, and in the fall of 2000 his eleventh book, which contains two one-act plays for youth titled *The Boy in the Treehouse* and *Girl Who Loved Her Horses*, was released. The writer's drama is studied not only throughout North America, but also in countries such as Italy, Germany, and New Zealand.

These plays have brought him substantial literary recognition. He won the Canadian Authors' Association Literary Award for Best Drama and the Floyd S. Chalmers Canadian Play Award in 1992, the Dora Mavor Moore Award for Outstanding New Play in the Small Theatre Division and the University of Alaska Anchorage Native Playwriting Award in 1996, and the James Buller Award for Playwright of the Year in 1997.

Screenwriting and directing are yet other genres in which Taylor explores the issues of Native North American life. His forays into screenwriting include not only scripts for some of Canada's most popular television shows, including *Street Legal* and *North of 60*, but also an independently produced short entitled *The Strange Case of Bunny Weequod*. In August 2000 the National Film Board of Canada launched a documentary Taylor directed on Native humor called *Redskins, Tricksters, and Puppy Stew*. He is also in development with the Canadian Broadcasting Corporation for a Native sketch comedy series. The working show's title is *Seeing Red.*

Taylor has published two books of essays entitled *Funny You Don't Look Like One: Observations of a Blue-Eyed Ojibway* (1998) and *Funny You Don't Look Like One Two: A Second Collection From a Blue-Eyed Ojibway* (1999). He has also released a collection of short stories, *Fearless Warriors* (1998).

### Tecumseh (1768–1813)
*Shawnee tribal leader*

In the early 1800s, Tecumseh and his brother Tenskwatawa organized Indian resistance to U.S. territorial expansion along the Mississippi Valley. Tecumseh was born in a Shawnee settlement known as Old Piqua (near the present-day city of Springfield, Ohio) in the Ohio Valley. Tecumseh, (which means "goes through one place to another"), learned warfare early in life. In his early teens Tecumseh took part in the American Revolution on the side of the British.

After the revolution, the Shawnee regularly took up arms to defend their Ohio land against U.S. settlers. In 1795, many of the Indian leaders living in the Ohio region gathered at Greenville, Ohio, to negotiate sale of land to the United States. When the land exchange was formalized in the Treaty of Greenville, Tecumseh refused to recognize it. Upon hearing of U.S. intentions to buy Indian land, Tecumseh is said to have replied, "Sell the land? Why not sell the air, the clouds, the great sea?" This belief in an Indian land with no tribal borders would become the foundation for Tecumseh's Indian confederation in the years to follow.

Tecumseh soon emerged as a spokesman for the Midwest Indians. He attended councils, studied treaties, and learned all that he could about the historical and legal status of American Indians. It was during this time that Tecumseh conceived a new mission for his life, a destiny linked to the growing restlessness among the Indians of the Old Northwest Territory (present-day Great Lakes area). This restlessness was caused in part by the preachings of a new Indian leader spreading a message of religious rebirth and resistance. Tecumseh knew this emerging leader very well for he was Laulewasika, his younger brother who had changed his name to Tenskwatawa (which means "open door") but was generally known as the Shawnee Prophet.

The two brothers united to forge an intertribal confederacy, which they hoped would contain U.S. territorial expansion into Indian lands. Tecumseh and his brother urged their people to forgo the sale of Indian land, to reject European ways, and to renew Indian traditions. In particular, the brothers warned against the use of alcohol, which was devastating many Indian communities.

Within a few years, the brothers had assembled a growing community of believers in Prophetstown, located at the junction of the Wabash River and Tippecanoe Creek in present-day Indiana. Tensions between the growing Indian community and the U.S. government were high, however, because of Indian resentment over recent treaties ceding about 110 million acres to the United States. At the Battle of Tippecanoe in November 1811, the Prophet and his followers fought U.S. Army units. The Prophet proclaimed that his spiritual power would protect the Indians from army bullets, but when the Indians suffered significant casualties in the battle, the Prophet lost prestige and his followers abandoned him. Many members of Tecumseh's alliance dispersed, and Tenskwatawa himself fled to Canada.

Tecumseh joined the British to fight against the Americans in the War of 1812. He played a decisive role in the British capture of Detroit. In the months to follow, Tecumseh rallied other Indians to the British effort and continued to lead them into battle. On 5 October 1813, however, he was killed at the Battle of the Thames, in southern Ontario.

## Kateri Tekakwitha (1656–1680)
*Mohawk Catholic nun*

Kateri Tekakwitha, whom many Catholics call Lily of the Mohawks, converted to Christianity in the 1670s and became a nun. She was a person of uncommon religious conviction and is currently a candidate for canonization by the Roman Catholic Church.

Tekakwitha was born near present-day Auriesville, New York. Her father was a Mohawk chief and her mother an Algonquin who had been captured by the Mohawk. Tekakwitha's mother was a Christian convert. Her parents died when she was four years old, and she grew up with her uncle in the village of Caughnawaga, near present-day Fonda, New York.

Jesuits visited Tekakwitha's village in the 1670s, and she was baptized at the age of twenty by Jacques de Lamberville, a Jesuit missionary. Her uncle, also a Mohawk chief, opposed her conversion, and her religion caused her ridicule and made her an outcast among her people. In 1677, Tekakwitha fled her village with some visiting Christianized Oneida Indians. She settled near a Christian Mohawk community outside of present-day Montreal. Tekakwitha hoped to establish a convent on Heron Island. Church authorities rejected her plan, but did accept her into an order of nuns. Tekakwitha's religious fervor never wavered, and her almost fanatical devotion and commitment to helping others were well known among her people. Many stories have grown around Tekakwitha, including the account that when she died in 1680, scars from a childhood case of smallpox disappeared.

Tekakwitha became a candidate for sainthood in the Roman Catholic Church in 1884. In 1943, the Church declared her venerable, and in 1980 blessed. These are the first two steps toward sainthood.

## Tenskwatawa (Open Door) (1778–1837)
*Shawnee spiritual leader*

Tenskwatawa, better known as the Shawnee Prophet, was the brother of Tecumseh, the famous Indian leader who tried to rally Indian forces against U.S. expansion before and during the War of 1812. Tenskwatawa was born at Piqua near present-day Springfield, Ohio, of a Shawnee war chief and his Cherokee-Creek wife. As a result of their defeat at the Battle of Fallen Timbers in 1794 and the Treaty of Greenville the next year, the Shawnee were left leaderless and demoralized throughout Tenskwatawa's childhood. He became an alcoholic and lost the sight in his left eye in a hunting accident. In 1806, while living in the Delaware villages in present-day Indiana stretching from Indianapolis to Munsee, Tenskwatawa was influenced by the cultural and ceremonial revival created by the Munsee prophetess, who in 1804 and 1805 reformed the Delaware Big House religion, the main religious ceremony of the Delaware people. Since 1675, many Shawnee had lived with the Algonkian-speaking Delaware, or Lenape, and some groups within both nations became very closely tied. In February 1806, Tenskwatawa had an out-of-body experience and a vision that he died and went to heaven to see the Great Spirit, and brought back a message to the Indian people.

Tenskwatawa began to preach a return to traditional Shawnee customs, condemned intermarriage with Europeans, and rejected contact with them. He promoted claims that he could cure sickness and prevent death. The brothers Tenskwatawa and Tecumseh envisioned a vast Indian confederacy strong enough to keep the colonists from expanding any further west. Tenskwatawa's influence began to grow with other Indians, and he and Tecumseh traveled extensively among tribes from Wisconsin to Florida spreading the message. Indiana governor William Henry Harrison challenged him to "cause the sun to stand still" and "the moon to change its course." Tenskwatawa promptly did as much in accurately predicting the total eclipse of the sun on 16 June 1806. Thousands of Indians quickly became believers and hastened to join the new religion.

Tecumseh and Tenskwatawa founded Prophet's Town along the confluence of the Wabash River and Tippecanoe Creek in Indiana, and many Indians came to live there. Tecumseh began to exert a larger presence than his brother in the organization of the town and its operations. When he left on a trip in 1811, leaving Tenskwatawa in charge, Tecumseh cautioned his brother to avoid any confrontation with Harrison's troops. Perhaps seeking to regain preeminence, Tenskwatawa was drawn into attacking Harrison at the Battle of Tippecanoe in November 1811. During the battle, he stayed at the rear using magic to drive the U.S. soldiers into retreat. Tenskwatawa had no power that day, and the Indians were soundly defeated at Tippecanoe. After the battle, the prophet was left without influence and could no longer command believers.

As a result, upon his return, the enraged Tecumseh broke with his brother. Tenskwatawa fled to Canada, returning fifteen years later in 1826 and eventually settling in Wyandotte County, Kansas. George Catlin painted Tenskwatawa in 1830. The oil-on-canvas portrays a pensive old man wearing a nose ring. Holding his once-powerful firestick wand in his right hand, and in the left, a sacred string of beads given to him during the long-ago vision, his portrait seems to contemplate what once was to be.

## Louis Tewanima (d. 1969)
*Hopi athlete*

Louis Tewanima was teammate of the famous Indian athlete Jim Thorpe, and world-class athlete in his own right. He was born at Shongopovi, Second Mesa, New Mexico, on the Hopi Indian Reservation. The Hopi are a Pueblo people who live in villages and practice elaborate seasonal dances and religious rituals. As a boy, Tewanima would chase jackrabbits. When he arrived at the famous Carlisle School in Pennsylvania, Tewanima weighed only 110 pounds. He approached the legendary coach Glenn "Pop" Warner for a position on the track team, and when Warner saw him run, he compared Tewanima to a deer in flight.

Tewanima established world records in long-distance running. He competed in the 1908 Olympics in the marathon and placed ninth. At one track meet, Tewanima, Jim Thorpe, and Frank Mount Pleasant of Carlisle beat twenty athletes from Lafayette College. Tewanima and Thorpe were selected for the U.S. Olympic team without having to undergo trials, which was a rare honor. They sailed from New York to Stockholm on Flag Day, 14 June 1912; they returned as U.S. heroes. Thorpe had been proclaimed "the greatest athlete in the world" by the king of Sweden. Tewanima won a silver medal in the 10,000-meter race, and his performance set a time record that lasted for fifty-two years until Billy Mills, the Sioux distance runner, surpassed it in the 1964 Tokyo Olympics. Tewanima was the first athlete from Arizona to win a medal in the Olympics.

Tewanima returned home to Second Mesa and decided to do what he enjoyed the best—tending his sheep and raising his crops. Just for fun, to watch the trains go by, he would run to Winslow, Arizona, eighty miles away. In 1954, he went back to New York to be named to the All-Time United States Olympic Track and Field Team. In 1957, he was the first person inducted, to a standing ovation, into the Arizona Sports Hall of Fame at a dinner given in his honor.

Into his nineties, Tewanima remained active and happy. A traditional religious man, he participated in Hopi kiva ceremonies throughout his life.

## Russell Thornton (1942–)
*Cherokee sociologist and author*

Russell Thornton is professor of anthropology at the University of California, Los Angeles. He is a well-known sociologist who graduated from the University of Florida with a doctorate in demography, the study of human population growth and decline. Thornton has become one of the leading experts in the study of Native American demography, with population studies of U.S. Indians in a book named *American Indian Holocaust and Survival: A Population History Since 1492* (1987), and a more specific demographic study of the Cherokee in *The Cherokees: A Population History* (1990). Recently, he edited *Studying Native America: Problems and Prospects* (1998).

In addition, Thornton has published articles and a book on the demographic conditions of Plains Indians during the 1870s and 1890s and their influence on the rise of the first (1870) and second (1890) Ghost Dance Movements. The Ghost Dances were a reaction of the California, Plains, and other Indians to the harsh political and economic conditions of the early reservation period in the latter part of the 1800s. Many Indians sought a spiritual solution to their problems by means of the new Ghost Dance religion, which promised a quick return of dead relatives and ancestors, the return and restoration of the buffalo and other depleted animals, and restoration of the old Indian life, free from the reservations and suppression of the United States.

His book *We Shall Live Again: The 1870 and 1890 Ghost Dance Movements* (1982) provides an argument that the rapid declines in population among the Indians during the latter part of the 1800s helped trigger the eruption of the Ghost Dances and also contributed to the Ghost Dance emphasis on the return of dead relatives. In addition, Thornton co-edited with Mary Grasmick an annotated bibliography on urban Indians entitled *Sociology of American Indians: A Critical Bibliography* (1980). This volume provides a listing of major references on issues of Native American urbanization and urban life. In addition, he is the author of numerous academic and other articles on Indian history, demography, and higher education.

Professor Thornton has taught at numerous universities and colleges, including the University of Minnesota, the University of California at Berkeley, and Dartmouth College.

Professor Thornton has served as chair of the Smithsonian Institution's Native American Repatriation Review Committee and is a member of the Native American Studies Advisory Panel for the Social Science

Research Council and the North American Committee of the Human Genome Diversity Project. He has published articles in the *American Indian Quarterly*, *Ethnohistory*, the *American Sociological Review*, and the *American Journal of Physical Anthropology*.

### Grace F. Thorpe (1921— )
*Sauk and Fox political and environmental activist*

Born in Yale, Oklahoma, Grace F. Thorpe, or No-ten-o-quah (Wind Woman), has dedicated her life to improving the conditions of her people as well as American Indians across the nation. She belongs to the Thunder Clan and received her great-grandmother's name—No-ten-o-quah—through a naming ceremony conducted when she was young. Both she and her father, Jim Thorpe, a renowned football player and the first American Indian Olympic gold medalist, received degrees from the Carlisle Indian School in Pennsylvania and the Haskell Institute in Kansas.

Thorpe's career as an activist began around her fiftieth birthday in the 1960's. Before that time, she served two years in New Guinea as a member of the Women's Army Corps during World War II. After being appointed to General Douglas McArthur's staff in Japan,

Grace Thorpe (No-ten-o-quah or Wind Woman).

Thorpe met and married Fred Seeley. The couple gave birth to a son, Thorpe, and a daughter, Dagmar, but later decided to end their marriage.

Around 1950, after selling the Yellow Pages in New York suburbs, Thorpe sold her house, and moved to Washington, D.C., where she worked for the National Congress of American Indians (NCAI), a pan-Indian lobbying organization, for a year. In 1966, Thorpe helped secure land for an educational institution geared toward the needs of American Indian and Chicano students, D-Q University.

While active in the political realm, Thorpe's career as an activist was earmarked by the American Indian occupation of Alcatraz Island in 1969 and 1970. She and her daughter lived on Alcatraz during the first months of 1970, and Thorpe acted as a liaison between the protesters and the media and various governmental agencies. Through her astute negotiations, Thorpe acquired an emergency generator for the island, which helped to prolong the occupation.

After her experiences at Alcatraz, Thorpe and several other activists began demonstrating to reacquire land for American Indians. In June 1970, for example, Thorpe joined a group of Pit River Indians to combat Pacific Gas and Electric's attempts to destroy a 52,000-acre sacred site in Big Bend, California. Although Thorpe was arrested for trespassing, the demonstration was a success. Her later attempts to bring awareness of and change to Native Americans' lives, however, would employ less direct action and more educational and congressional lobbying efforts.

Through the 1970s, Thorpe earned a bachelor degree from the University of Tennessee and pursued post-graduate training in urban studies at the Massachusetts Institute of Technology. In addition, she worked for the American Indian Policy Review Commission and served as a legislative assistant to the U.S. Senate Subcommittee on Indian Affairs. On a more local level, Thorpe taught a seminar on surplus land acquisitions at D-Q University when it opened its doors in 1971 and helped form Return Surplus Lands to Indian People Committees, organized to facilitate the return of unused government lands to Indians.

Thorpe's Oklahoma retirement through the 1980s did not last when she learned in 1992 that her tribe's government was considering nuclear-waste storage in an effort to develop the tribe's economy. The U.S. Department of Energy (DOE) was offering $100,000 to any entity willing to store such wastes. Because of Thorpe's concerted efforts to educate her people about the ill effects of nuclear power and waste, however, tribal members ultimately rejected DOE's offer. After learning that NCAI was holding seminars to promote nuclear-waste storage, she initiated a campaign to ensure that all Indian reservations are nuclear-free, and now 75 tribal communities are nuclear-free zones. She continues to educate Indian peoples about nuclear hazards, participating in such organizations as the National Environmental Coalition of Native Americans and the Nuclear Information and Research Service, and in 1999, she received the Nuclear Free Future Resistance Award in Los Alamos, New Mexico.

She also organized a successful campaign to have her father, Jim Thorpe, declared ABC's *Wide World of Sports'* Athlete of the Century, which was proclaimed prior to Super Bowl XXXIV, on 30 January 2000. Thorpe lives with her daughter, Dagmar, and granddaughter, Tena, in Prague, Oklahoma.

### James Francis Thorpe (1887–1953)
*Sac and Fox athlete*

King Gustav of Sweden described Jim Thorpe as "the greatest athlete in the world." The young man from Prague, Oklahoma, had just won gold medals in the pentathlon and the decathlon in the 1912 Stockholm Olympics and was on top of the sporting world. Seven months later, however, he was stripped of the medals, and his records were expunged from the official Olympic record book. A newspaper reporter learned that he had played semi-professional baseball for fifteen dollars a week. By the Olympic rules in effect in 1912, acceptance of payment for athletic performance disqualified Thorpe from further amateur sports and from eligibility for participation in the Olympic games.

Jim Thorpe excelled in athletics at Carlisle College in Pennsylvania. He held world records in track and field and was a college All-American in lacrosse, basketball, and football. He was coached in football by the legendary Glenn "Pop" Warner and scored fifty touchdowns in forty-four games. In a memorable game against Harvard, he scored a touchdown and kicked four field goals as Carlisle won by a score of 18–15.

After the Olympics, Thorpe played professional baseball from 1913 to 1919 with a career batting average of .252. He went on to play professional football, became the first president of the American Professional Football Association, an organization that would evolve into the modern National Football League.

He was named to both college and professional football halls of fame. The Associated Press voted him the greatest athlete of the first half of the century in 1950. Also in 1950, a feature film starring Burt Lancaster and directed by Michael Curtiz was made about his life.

Jim Thorpe died three years later on his sixty-fifth birthday at his home in Lomita, California. In 1954, a town in Pennsylvania was renamed in his honor. Many Americans from all walks of life began a campaign to have his Olympic medals restored. A rule was found stating that all complaints against athletes had to be filed within thirty days after the conclusion of events; it was not until seven months had gone by that the grievances against Thorpe had been brought up. Twenty years after his death and seventy years after the Stockholm Olympiad, replicas of his medals were returned to his children Charlotte, Gail, Grace, Carl, Bill, and Jack, during the 1984 Olympics in Los Angeles.

On 30 January 2000, ABC's *Wide World of Sports* proclaimed Thorpe Athlete of the Century. He is still the only athlete in history to win both the pentathlon and decathlon in Olympic competition.

### John W. Tippeconnic III (1943– )
*Comanche-Cherokee educator*

John Tippeconnic is professor of education and director of the American Indian Leadership Program at Pennsylvania State University. He previously served as director of Indian education programs with the Department of Education in Washington, D.C. As director, he

John W. Tippeconnic, III.

supervised most of the national Indian education programs that are not delivered by the education division within the Bureau of Indian Affairs. He is also the former director of the Center for Indian Education at Arizona State University, a major research organization focusing on Indian education issues.

He was born in Oklahoma and received a bachelor of arts degree in secondary education from Oklahoma State University and a doctorate from Pennsylvania State University (1975).

Tippeconnic has been a teacher at the Tuba City Boarding School, vice-president of Navajo Community College, and associate professor at Arizona State. He has published twelve articles including "The Place of Bilingual Education in the Education of American Indians" (1982) and "Public School Administration on Indian Reservations" (1984). In 1999, he co-authored with Karen Gayton Swisher, *Next Steps: Research and Practice to Advance Indian Education.*

He has served on the editorial board of the National Association for Bilingual Education, the advisory board of the Urban Indian Law Project, and as consultant at the Native American Research and Training Center at the University of Arizona. His service includes two terms as president of the National Indian Education Association, chair of the American Education Research Association American Indian Education Special Interest Group, and membership on the National Family Literacy Board.

Tippeconnic has served as a consultant to numerous organizations, such as the Native American Rights Fund, National Science Foundation, and the W. K. Kellogg Foundation. His interests include studies in educational policy, Indian control of education, and leadership.

## Tomochichi (circa 1650–1739)
*Creek tribal leader*

Tomochichi was born in the mid-1600s and lived at the Creek village of Apalachukla, along the Chattahoochee River in present-day Alabama. Tomochichi moved to present-day Georgia in the early 1700s when the new English colony was rapidly being settled with the active assistance of Creek leaders like Tomochichi. The Creek tribe was the most cooperative with the English settlers in the Georgia colony.

In 1733, Tomochichi was visited by a party of English colonists led by James Oglethorpe, the founder of the Georgia colony, at which time he signed a peace treaty on behalf of the Creek Nation. In return for massive land grants, the Creek were accorded privileges, such as protection under English law and liberal trading rights.

Tomochichi was praised for his peacemaking efforts and, in 1734, headed a Creek delegation to England with Oglethorpe, where he and his family were presented to King George II and Queen Caroline. The artist Cornelis Verelst painted a famous portrait of the chief and his nephew, Toonahowi, which is on display at the Smithsonian Institution in Washington, D.C.

Tomochichi's friendship with the English led to a long-term Creek-British trade relationship, and he remained a friend to the English for the remainder of his life.

## John Baptiste Tootoosis, Jr. (1899–1989)
*Cree activist*

The grandson of Poundmaker, the famous Cree chief who fought for better treaty terms from Canadian authorities for his people, John Tootoosis was an important political organizer and leader of the Plains Cree people, a tribe that had moved west from central Canada to the Canadian plains with the expansion of the fur trade in the seventeenth century. He was born on his grandfather's reserve, the Poundmaker Indian Reserve in Saskatchewan, and was one of eleven children. When he was young, Tootoosis tended to his father's sheep. At the urging of Canadian authorities, he was sent by his parents to a residential school. At the age of sixteen, John worked for a farmer in Saskatchewan to contribute to the family expenses. In his late teens, he nearly died of an unknown disease, and while he was ill, he vowed that he would devote his life to his people if he were to recover.

Upon his recovery, Tootoosis was chosen chief of his people at the tender age of twenty, only to be informed by Canadian authorities that Canadian law prohibited the selection of a chief under twenty-one years of age. In the same year, Tootoosis demonstrated his rebellious and proud nature by fencing in land on his reserve to prevent Canadian authorities from leasing it to third parties against his people's will. Tootoosis spoke out often against the failure of Canadian authorities to permit Indian people to participate in decisions that affect their lives. He fought for better health care and educational facilities for his people. Tootoosis was instrumental in organizing Native people throughout the province of Saskatchewan and indeed across the country. He was a founding member of the League of Indians of Canada in 1919, the National American Indian Brotherhood in 1943, and the Union of Saskatchewan Indians in 1946. Later in life, Tootoosis worked as a teacher and an authority on the Cree language.

## Sheila M. Tousey (contemporary)
*Menominee performer*

Born in Keshena, Wisconsin, Tousey was raised on both the Menominee and Stockbridge-Munsee reservations in Wisconsin. She began dancing as a small child but did not perform on stage until she attended the University of New Mexico at Albuquerque. At first, she enrolled in the University of New Mexico's Indian Law Program, because she was interested in a career in Indian law, with specialization in federal contracts and Indian-federal legal relations. Later, Tousey changed her major from pre-law to English and studied theater arts.

After completing her undergraduate degree, Tousey attended the graduate acting program at the New York University (NYU) Tisch School of Arts, where she received a master of fine arts degree in 1989. While at NYU, she performed in numerous plays such as *Yerma, The American Dream, The Bald Soprano, The Normal Heart, Children of the Sun, As You Like It,* and *Endgame.*

In 1989, Tousey began performing with the American Indian Dance Theatre, an internationally acclaimed dance troupe based in New York City. As an actress, she has appeared at the Vortex Theatre in Albuquerque, New Mexico, where she had parts in plays such as *Baby with the Bath Water* and *And a Nightingale Sang.*

She made her motion picture debut in *Thunderheart* (1992), and she soon delivered award-winning performances in *The Silent Tongue* (1993), *Medicine River* (1993), and *Grand Avenue* (1996). Her film credits also include *Slaughter of the Innocents* (1994), *Lord of Illusions* (1995), *Ravenous* (1999), *Wildflowers* (2000), and *Backroads* (2000).

## Toypurina (fl. 1780s)
*Gabrielino tribal leader*

Toypurina was a religious and political leader, who, in the 1780s, led a short-lived rebellion against the Spanish at the San Gabriel Mission near present-day Los Angeles, California.

Like many Indians of this region in the late 1700s, Toypurina's people were struggling with the institutions of Spanish settlement and rule. Many Gabrielino Indians believed that Toypurina had spiritual powers that would help them to overcome their Spanish overlords. In 1785, Toypurina planned an uprising against the San Gabriel Mission. She was aided by her apprentice, Nicolas Jose. Together they convinced the Indians of six villages to unite against the Spanish. The recruits were convinced that Toypurina had slain the inhabitants of the mission with her powers. On October 25,

the war parties moved on the mission. The priests and soldiers in the mission had learned of the uprising, however, and arrested the Indian forces.

During their trial Toypurina and Nicolas Jose spoke out against the Spanish. Toypurina decried the taking of Indian land by the Spanish and the suppression of Indian culture and traditional ceremonies. The accusations fell on unsympathetic ears. Participants in the raid were flogged. Nicolas Jose was imprisoned in the presidio at San Diego. Toypurina was exiled from her people to the San Carlos Mission in present-day Carmel, California.

## Clifford Trafzer (1949–)
*Wyandotte historian*

Clifford Trafzer is a distinguished professor of American Indian history and culture at the University of California, Riverside. He is also director of Native American Studies and Public History, and he serves as curator of history at the Western Center.

He was born in Mansfield, Ohio, was raised in Arizona, received his bachelor and master degrees in history from Northern Arizona University, and earned his doctorate in 1973 from Oklahoma State University.

Trafzer has won the Governor's Book Award for *The Renegade Tribe* (1986), the Penn Oakland Award for *Earth Song, Sky Spirit* (1993), and a Wordcraft Circle of Native American Writers Award for *Death Stalks the Yakima* (1999).

He has published over twenty-five books, including *As Long As the Grass Shall Grow and Rivers Flow* (2000), *Exterminate Them!* (1999), and *Chemehuevi People of the Coachella Valley* (1997). He is completing a biography of Wyandot-Huron elder Eleanore Sioui, a new study of Chemehuevi people, and a book on tuberculosis among southern California Indians.

Trafzer has been a museum curator for the Arizona Historical Society, archivist of Special Collections at Northern Arizona University, and tribal consultant for the Colville Confederated Tribe, Shoalwater Bay Tribe, and Twenty-Nine Palms Band.

## Mark N. Trahant (1957– )
*Shoshone-Bannock publisher, editor, and journalist*

Mark Trahant is chairman and chief executive officer at the Robert C. Maynard Institute for Journalism Education in Oakland, California. A member of the Shoshone-Bannock Tribe of Idaho, Trahant was born in Fort Hall, Idaho. He attended Pasadena City College and Idaho State University.

His successful career includes work as a columnist for the *Seattle Times*, editor and publisher of the *Moscow-Pullman Daily News* in Idaho, and syndicated columnist of "Letter from Moscow."

Trahant was also executive news editor at the *Salt Lake City Tribune* & editor-in-chief for the *Sho-Ban News* & a reporter at the *Arizona Republic* & publisher of the tribal weekly *Navajo Times Today* & and the founder, editor, and publisher of *Navajo Nation Today*.

In 1983, he converted the *Navajo Times* into the *Navajo Times Today*, making it the first daily newspaper published for a Navajo audience. As editor and later as publisher, he raised the daily circulation from 2,000 to nearly 12,000. In 1995, he received the National Press Foundation's Editor of the Year citation.

He also was the national desk reporter for *The Arizona Republic*, where he was a finalist for the Pulitzer Prize in 1989 for co-authoring "Fraud in Indian Country." Trahant is also the recipient of the Elias Boudinot Award for Lifetime Contributions to Journalism, the Paul Tobenkin Memorial Prize from Columbia University, the Heywood Broun Award, and the George Polk Award for National Reporting.

In 1995, Trahant was a visiting professional scholar at the Freedom Forum's First Amendment Center at Vanderbilt University. He is the author of *Pictures of Our Nobler Selves* (1995), a historical survey of American Indian contributions to journalism.

He is a trustee of the Freedom Forum and serves on a number of advisory boards, including the D'Arcy McNickle Center for American Indian History at the Newberry Library in Chicago. Trahant is past president and a current member of the Native American Journalists Association. He is married to LeNora Begay Trahant, and they have two sons, Marvin and Elias.

## John Trudell (1947–)
*Santee Sioux activist and musician*

John Trudell was an active leader in many Native American protests of the 1960s and 1970s.

He participated in the 1969 occupation of Alcatraz Island by Indians of All Tribes, Inc., an organization that symbolized participation of all American Indians. He joined the Alcatraz occupation ten days after the 20 November 1969 landing and remained on the island until U.S. officials removed the last fifteen occupiers on 11 June 1971. The occupation of Alcatraz Island was an attempt by urban Indians to attract national attention to the failure of U.S. government policy toward American Indians. Trudell became the occupation's voice through Radio Free Alcatraz, a radio station set up on the island which broadcast from Berkeley, Los Angeles,

John Trudell.

and New York City, thus bringing the occupation and the concerns of Indian people before a national audience. During the occupation period, Trudell traveled throughout the nation, speaking to Indian and non-Indian groups regarding the occupation and raising support for the return of Alcatraz Island to Indian people. Alcatraz Island, however, later became a national park. The occupation of Alcatraz Island is seen by many as an early catalyst to the rising Red Power movement which continued into the mid-1970s.

Trudell joined the American Indian Movement (AIM) in the spring of 1970 and became a national spokesman for AIM soon thereafter. Although much of its inspiration derived from Indian fishing-rights battles during the 1960s and 1970s in the states of Washington and Oregon, AIM's initial concerns were jobs, housing, education, and the protection of Indians from police abuse and violence. In 1970, AIM started a program to assist juvenile offenders as an alternative to reform school.

Trudell participated in the 1972 Trail of Broken Treaties, a national car-caravan bringing together urban and reservation Indians from across the nation designed to culminate in the presentation of a formal list of demands on the federal government by Indian people. Lack of communication between leaders of the caravan and federal officials resulted in an impasse and a seventy-one hour occupation of the Bureau of Indian Affairs office in Washington, D.C., where thousands of dollars worth of damage to the building and office equipment occurred.

Trudell was elected co-chair of AIM in 1973, and he participated in the 1973 armed seizure of Wounded Knee, a small town in the heart of the Pine Ridge Sioux Reservation in South Dakota. Wounded Knee is the site of the 1890 massacre by the Seventh Cavalry of Sioux Chief Big Foot and two hundred or more Sioux men, women, and children.

In 1976, he coordinated the AIM support for the defense of Leonard Peltier, who was convicted of murdering two FBI agents in June 1975 on the Pine Ridge Reservation. Trudell's wife Tina, her mother, and the three Trudell children were burned to death in a mysterious fire on 11 February 1979, twelve hours after Trudell, during a demonstration in support of Leonard Peltier, burned an upside-down American flag on the steps of the FBI building in Washington, D.C.

Devastated by the loss of his family, Trudell began writing poetry as a form of therapy. In 1981, Trudell published a book of poetry, *Living in Reality*, and soon decided he wanted to combine his poetry with music.

In 1985, he met Jesse Ed Davis, a Kiowa guitarist from Oklahoma. A year later, Davis provided the music on Trudell's debut album, *AKA Grafitti Man*. Released on Trudell's own label, Peace Company, in cassette-only format, the album gained critical attention despite its limited distribution. Trudell and Davis released a second album, *Heart Jump Bouquet*, together and recorded in the Tribal Voice series, *...But This Isn't El Salvador*, in 1987.

Following the death of Davis in 1988, a tour as the opening act for the popular and highly politicized Australian band, Midnight Oil, brought Trudell and the Grafitti Band mainstream exposure. In 1991, Trudell recorded a third album, *Fables and Realities*. In 1992, Trudell produced a third in the Tribal Voice series titled *Child's Voice: Children of the Earth*. The same year, he signed with Rykodisc and with a remake of his original *AKA Grafitti Man*, produced by Jackson Browne, his music reached worldwide distribution. *Johnny Damas and Me*, his second album with Rykodisc, was released in 1994.

Trudell has also appeared in numerous films and documentaries, including *Powwow Highway* (1989), *Incident at Oglala* (1992), *Thunderheart* (1992), *On Deadly Ground* (1994), *Extreme Measures* (1996), *Smoke Signals* (1998), and *Alcatraz Is Not an Island* (2000).

He tours worldwide with his band, lives in Los Angeles, California, and is currently completing *Permanent Paranoia*, an autobiographical play.

### Roger Tsabetsye (1941–)
*Zuni Pueblo artist*

Roger Tsabetsye was born in Zuni, New Mexico. The Zuni Pueblo is one of nineteen villages in eastern New Mexico known for their strong ties to their traditional religion, ceremonies, and culture. Tsabetsye was educated at the Institute of American Indian Arts, the government-operated Indian art school in Santa Fe, New Mexico, and also studied at the School for American Craftsmen, where he majored in silver and metal processing, and the Rochester Institute of Technology.

He is one of the first people, along with Fritz Scholder, the famous California Indian artist, to actively express their combined traditional and modern artistic training gained from the arts program at the Institute of American Indian Arts. Tsabetsye taught art at the institute and helped develop the school's curriculum and philosophy.

Working principally in three different media—painting, ceramics, and silver—Tsabetsye has exhibited at the Heard Museum in Phoenix, the Scottsdale (Arizona) Indian National Art Show, the Museum of Santa Fe, the New York American Indian Art Center, and numerous other exhibitions. His work has received many awards and honors, and in 1968 he was asked by President Lyndon Johnson to create a squash blossom for the president of Costa Rica. During this time, Tsabetsye was an Indian representative at several conferences in Washington, D.C., to help initiate President Johnson's War on Poverty.

Tsabetsye is also the founder and owner of Tsabetsye Enterprises, a company specializing in the merchandising (retail and wholesale) of Zuni jewelry. The company illustrates Tsabetsye's personal philosophy that American Indians should be partners with the rest of U.S. society.

### Richard Van Camp (1971–)
*Dogrib author*

A recipient of the 1997 Canadian Authors Association Air Canada Award for "most promising Canadian author under 30," Richard Van Camp is a member of the Dogrib Nation from Fort Smith, Northwest Territory (NWT), Canada. He is the author of a novel, *The Lesser Blessed*, and two children's books: *A Man Called Raven* and *What's the Most Beautiful Thing You Know About Horses?*, illustrated by Cree artist George Littlechild.

Besides receiving his bachelor of fine arts in creative writing from the University of Victoria and two certificates—one from the En'owkin International School of Writing (Certificate in Native Creative Writing) and the other from Aurora College (Certificate in Native Management Studies)—he has studied land claims in Yellowknife, NWT, Reiki in Bella Bella, British Columbia, and acupuncture in Hangzhou, China.

Van Camp was a script and cultural consultant for CBC Television's *North of 60* television series for four seasons. He has been published in numerous anthologies including *Crisp Blue Edges: Indigenous Creative Non-Fiction, A Shade of Spring, Blue Dawn, Red Earth, Gatherings,* and *Descant* (Summer 1993); *Inner Harbour Review,* and *Whetstone* (Fall 1994); and *Steal My Rage.* He was also commissioned to write a radio drama in 1998 for CBC's Festival of Fiction. "Mermaids" was broadcast nationally several times and was narrated by Cree actor Ben Cardinal. "Mermaids" was later published in the *International Indigenous Anthology: Skins.*

His awards include the 1992 Bessie Silcox Scholarship Award from the Dene National Office; the 1992 En'owkin International School of Writing's William Armstrong Award for Poetry; the 1993 Yellowknife Rotary Club's Donald J. Cardinal Memorial Award; the 1993 NWT Literacy Council's Norman Macpherson Award; the 1995 University of Victoria Scholarship's Millen Undergraduate Award; the 1996 University of Victoria Scholarship's The Hazel Partridge-Smith Bursary in Creative Writing; and the 1999 Canadian Children's Centre's Our Choice Award for *What's The Most Beautiful Thing You Know About Horses?*

Van Camp has toured internationally with visits from coast to coast Canada to Jamaica, Australia, and the United States. *The Lesser Blessed* was recently translated into German by Ravensberger. Van Camp is currently working on a graphic novel titled *Gift.*

### Joseph Vasquez (1917–)
*Sioux-Apache activist*

Joseph Vasquez has been an advocate for Native American causes throughout his life, on both national and local levels. Among his many posts and positions, he has served as a Los Angeles city commissioner (1968–1970) and president and chairman of the Los Angeles Indian Center from 1958 to 1970.

Vasquez was born in Primero, Colorado. He was educated at the U.S. Armed Forces Institute and later attended classes at the University of California, Los Angeles. He served in the U.S. Army Air Corps from 1943 to 1945 as a pilot and flight engineer. From 1947 to 1968, Vasquez worked for Hughes Aircraft as a small business coordinator and minority group representative. From 1970 to 1972, he worked for the National Council on Indian Opportunity in Washington, D.C. From 1972 to 1980, Vasquez worked for U.S. Department of Commerce, Office of Minority Business Enterprise. Vasquez held a number of other positions, including officer of the National Congress of American Indians, a national organization for mobilizing Indian communities on congressional legislative issues. He also founded and promoted the National Business Development Organization for Native Americans. Vasquez has served on advisory committees for the mayor of Los Angeles and the California attorney general's office. Vasquez retired by 1980.

### Pablita Velarde (1918–)
*Santa Clara Pueblo painter*

Pablita Velarde is an acclaimed Native American painter whose works reflect the culture and heritage of her people.

Velarde was born in the Santa Clara Pueblo of New Mexico and educated at the Santa Fe Indian School. Her love for art and talent as an artist has been traced to a childhood eye disease that temporarily restricted her sight. According to one biographer, when Velarde's sight was regained, it gave her a new appreciation of visual perception. Velarde studied art under Dorothy Dunn, a pioneer among Indian artists. In 1938 Velarde built a studio for her work in Santa Clara and began her career in earnest.

One of Velarde's first works is still her most renowned—a series of painted murals containing composite pictures depicting the day-to-day life and culture of the Rio Grande Pueblos. In 1954 she was decorated by the French government in appreciation of her art. During the middle 1950s, Velarde developed a unique painting technique that employs colored rocks that are ground and mixed to create a pliable, textured painting material. With this material, Velarde has produced works that recall the art of her ancestors and that make effective use of traditional designs and pictographs in her work. Another of Velarde's paintings that has received widespread acclaim is *Old Father, the Story Teller* (1960). With a unique and insightful composition, the painting links traditional Native American legends and universal human beliefs. Velarde is also the author and illustrator of *Old Father, the Story Teller* (1989), in which the painting of the same name appears. Her work is shown in the Museum of New York's Hall of Ethnology, the De Young Museum of San Francisco, many southwestern galleries, and held in numerous private collections.

## Wilma Victor (1919–)
*Choctaw educator*

Wilma Victor is a distinguished educator who is now retired. Born in Idabel, Oklahoma, she was educated at Haskell Institute, an Indian boarding school, and at the University of Kansas. She received a bachelor of sciences degree in education from the University of Wisconsin, then earned a master of school administration degree from the University of Oklahoma in 1952 and a doctorate from Utah State University.

Victor grew up listening to tales of the Choctaw Trail of Tears to Indian Territory (present-day Oklahoma), and she decided at an early age to complete school and pursue the field of education. It was rare in those days for an Indian woman to aspire to higher education. After receiving her bachelor's degree, she worked for the Bureau of Indian Affairs (BIA) in Shiprock, New Mexico, on the Navajo Reservation. During World War II, she enlisted in the Women's Army Corps (WACs) from 1943 to 1946. Then Victor resumed work for the BIA, where she steadily rose through the ranks and worked in several important positions, including deputy area director for its Phoenix, Arizona, office, and for the Institute of American Indian Arts in Santa Fe, New Mexico.

Other duties Victor has had include superintendent of the Intermountain School District, director of women's programs for the U.S. Department of the Interior, acting director of Indian Education, and special assistant to Secretary of the Interior Rogers C. B. Morton. Her honors include Indian Council Fire National Achievement Award, the Anadarko Indian Exposition's Indian of the Year Award (1971), Distinguished Alumnus Award from the University of Wisconsin (1972), and Distinguished Service Award from the Department of the Interior (1975), the department housing the BIA which is responsible for managing Indian affairs. Her interests feature women's advocacy issues and Indian self-determination.

## Victorio (Beduiat) (1825–1880)
*Mimbreno Apache tribal leader*

As a young man, Victorio fought with Mangas Coloradas, a leader in the early Apache war of the 1860s. Upon Coloradas's death in 1863, Victorio assumed control of his followers. The fighting group consisting of warriors from many tribes collectively came to be known as Ojo Caliente (Warm Springs), since their agency was located near Ojo Caliente in present-day southwest New Mexico.

Throughout the 1870s, Victorio and his followers alternated between sporadic raiding and confinement to reservation lands. In 1877 Victorio agreed to end the fighting if he and his followers were allowed to settle at Warm Springs. When these negotiations broke down, Victorio and his followers were moved to the San Carlos Reservation in present-day Arizona. They found reservation life unbearable, however, and on 2 September 1877, Victorio and about three hundred followers escaped the reservation. Though the majority of the Apache gave themselves up a month later, Victorio and about eighty warriors remained in mountain hideouts where they continued to wage a war of resistance for several years. His strategically placed encampments forced U.S. soldiers to fight in small numbers, allowing Victorio's forces to make good use of their limited numbers.

In 1879, Victorio tried once again to settle at Warm Springs, then later at the Mescalero Reservation at Tularosa, New Mexico. When U.S. authorities threatened to try him for murder, however, Victorio escaped. Joined by a large force of Mescalero, Victorio continued to wage strikes in Texas, New Mexico, and Arizona. For several months, Victorio confounded U.S. forces by keeping them off balance and forcing them to disperse their troops over wide areas, thereby diminishing their effectiveness. Finally, in October 1880, he was surprised by Mexican forces on the plains of Chihuahua in Mexico. He fought until his ammunition was gone, then killed himself.

## Gerald Robert Vizenor (1934–)
*Chippewa author and teacher*

Gerald Vizenor, professor of American studies at the University of California, Berkeley, is a teacher, novelist, and poet. He was born in Minneapolis, Minnesota, and spent a difficult childhood as a consequence of his family's poverty and his father's death. Both of these elements have been incorporated as metaphors in a number of his works.

Vizenor was educated at New York University, received a bachelor of arts from the University of Minnesota, and later studied at Harvard University. He has been a social worker, civil rights organizer, journalist, and community advocate for tribal people living in urban centers. He organized an Indian Studies program at Bemidji State University in Minnesota, and has previously taught tribal literature at Lake Forest College, the

University of Oklahoma, and the University of California, Santa Cruz.

Vizenor has been recognized as a multifaceted writer, and his published works include novels such as *Darkness in Saint Louis/Bearheart* (1978), *Griever: An American Monkey King in China* (1987), which won the American Book Award, and *The Trickster of Liberty* (1988). He has created volumes of haiku, a Japanese form of writing poetry, some of which are published in *Raising the Moon Vines* and *Seventeen Chirps* (1964) and *Empty Swings* (1967). Narratives and traditional tales and songs are published in *The Everlasting Sky: New Voices from the People Named Chippewa* (1972), *Wordarrows: Indians and Whites in the New Fur Trade* (1978), and *Summer in the Spring* (1981).

His most recent publications include critical studies, *Manifest Manners: Narratives on Post-Indian Survivance* (1999), and *Fugitive Poses: Native American Scenes of Absence and Presence* (1998); novels, *The Heirs of Columbus* (1991), *Dead Voices* (1992), *Hotline Healers: An Almost Browne Novel* (1997), and *Shadow Distance: A Gerald Vizenor Reader* (1994); autobiographical works, *Interior Landscapes: Autobiographical Myths and Metaphors* (1990), and *Post-Indian Conversations* (1999).

## Wabaunsee (1780–1848)
*Potawatomi tribal leader*

Wabaunsee was a renowned Potawatomi war chief who lived on the Kankakee River in present-day Illinois, forty miles southwest of Lake Michigan. During the War of 1812, Wabaunsee fought on the side of the British, helping take Fort Dearborn in present-day Michigan. After the battle, however, he protected U.S. captives from execution.

Wabaunsee participated in the Greenville Council in July 1814, in which he and several other tribes agreed to ally themselves with the United States against Britain. In 1816, he signed the Treaty of Wabash in Indiana, selling tribal lands to the U.S. government. In 1826, Wabaunsee signed the second Treaty of the Wabash, ceding even more Potawatomi lands. This selling of Indian lands led to internal strife among the Potawatomi, and Wabaunsee was attacked and stabbed. Indian agent Thomas Tipton intervened and saved his life.

In 1832, during the Black Hawk War, Wabaunsee joined the Illinois militia and fought against the Sac and Fox. In 1835, he traveled to Washington, D.C., and signed a treaty ceding the remainder of Potawatomi lands in Illinois and Indiana in exchange for territory west of the Mississippi River in present-day Kansas.

Wabaunsee settled on the Missouri River near Council Bluffs, Iowa.

## Walkara (Walker) (1801–1855)
*Ute tribal leader*

Between 1830 and 1855, Walkara was probably the most powerful and renowned Native American leader in the Great Basin area, largely western Nevada. His daring bravery and cunning sagacity earned him nicknames such as Hawk of the Mountains, Iron-Twister, and Napoleon of the Desert. Walkara's sheer prowess, physical strength, and agility allowed him to gain enough influence to eventually surmount tribal feuds between the Ute, Paiute, and Shoshone, and organize a corps of raiders who terrorized an area from the Mexican border almost to Canada and from California to New Mexico.

A fierce opportunist, Walkara at various times collaborated with Indians, mountainmen, and Mormons, a religious sect that settled around Salt Lake in present-day Utah. In the winter of 1839, he and several companions stole more than three thousand horses in a daring night raid on the wealthiest Los Angeles rancheros. This escapade earned him the title Greatest Horse Thief in History. For over a decade, he and his followers raided villages for slaves and demanded goods and supplies from travelers on the Old Spanish Trail, which passed through much of present-day Nevada. He became wealthy, kept a number of wives, and wore both Indian and American finery.

Accepting of the Mormons at first, Walkara even converted to their religion under the persistence of Brigham Young, an early founding leader of Mormonism. However, their ubiquitous population of Ute tribal territories soon frustrated him. Overgrazing of land, coupled with a measles epidemic, and an Indian-Mormon confrontation at Springville, Utah, led him to fight and lose the bitter "Walker War" in 1853. His power all but gone and his land now in the possession of the Mormons, Walkara died two years later. Fifteen horses were killed in his honor at his funeral.

## Kateri Walker (contemporary)
*Ojibwa actress*

Kateri Walker, whose full name is Mary Margaret Kateri Tekakwitha Walker, has acted in many films and plays, including the 1994 and 1995 theater production of *Black Elk Speaks*, the 1998 film *Outside Ozona*, the 1999 Ojibway language film *The Strange Case of Bunny Weequod*, and the HBO television series *Arliss*. While these are some of the actress' personal favorites, she

Kateri Walker.

University of Michigan, where she received her degree in theater and drama.

Walker feels that the performance industry needs more Native voices and perspectives: "Unless we continue to grow as writers, producers, directors, and actors, our concerns will lay dormant. We won't be able to address our concerns regarding ourselves until we tell our stories." She argues that Native actors continue to be cast in a romantic light. Native American performers must take an active role in changing and expanding their career options.

In addition to her acting, Walker is a jingle-dress dancer on the powwow circuit. She also spends a lot of time speaking to people about American Indian issues and cultures. Walker believes that education is the key to understanding and overcoming differences.

The actress has received several awards for her performances. In 1999, she accepted a Horizon Award for Rising Talent at the San Francisco Film Institute's American Indian Motion Picture Awards for her lead roles in *Home*, a film short, and *The Strange Case of Bunny Weequod*. The same year, Walker was presented with the Outstanding Performance by an Actress in Film Award at the First Americans in the Arts, held in Beverly Hills, California, for her role in *Outside Ozona*.

Walker now resides in the Los Angeles area and is a devoted aunt to her fifteen nephews and three nieces.

also appeared in the 1995 film version of Nathaniel Hawthorne's *The Scarlet Letter*, and on the popular soap opera *As the World Turns*.

Walker was born in Michigan, the fifth of six children to Mary Anne Julienne (DeLeary) Walker (Chippewa of the Thames First Nations) and James Raymond Walker (Saginaw Chippewa). Although her early years were spent on the reservation, she attended a government-run Catholic boarding school for Indian children, where she officially performed for the first time. When she was six, Walker and her best friend performed at a school assembly. The nuns, however, did not support their creative efforts and told the girls that acting was an unethical profession not worth pursuing.

When Walker was in second grade, her mother moved the family off the reservation to give them a better life. Despite conflicts with her high school counselor, who told her that her SAT scores were too low and that she had little chance of becoming successful, Walker graduated with honors and entered Michigan Technological University, the only school to which she applied. While there, Walker studied chemical engineering. Before graduation, however, the to-be actress decided to follow her dreams; she transferred to the

## Nancy Ward (circa 1740–1822)
*Cherokee tribal leader*

Nancy Ward was a descendant of Osconostota, the Great Warrior of the Cherokee Nation. While some authorities argue that she was a full-blood, others state that her father was a British officer named Ward. Nancy Ward was of the Wolf clan and was the niece of Old Hop, emperor of the nation in the 1750s, and sister to Attakullaculla, the Wise Councillor of the Cherokee, also active in the 1750s.

Ward received her title Ghighau, "Beloved Woman," from the Cherokee as the result of her bravery during the battle of Taliwa in 1755. While still a teenager, she came to the battlefield at Taliwa (near the present Canton, Georgia) with a five-hundred-man attack party led by Osconostota, the Great Warrior of the Cherokee. Fighting bravely, Ward stood fast in the battle against the Creek, enemies of the Cherokee. As a result of the battle, the Creek abandoned their Georgia and Alabama towns and opened that land to the Cherokee, who gradually occupied the area.

As a reward for her participation in the battle, Ward received a Negro slave and became the first Cherokee slaveholder. She then rejoined her two children at

Chota, the Cherokee capital in present-day Monroe County, Tennessee, and took her place of leadership in the Cherokee Nation. She married Brian Ward, a trader who had fought in the French and Indian War.

In the years following the Battle of Taliwa, Ward intervened on numerous occasions to save the lives of non-Indian captives of the Cherokee, a supreme right available only to the Ghighau (denied even to chiefs), and during the outbreaks of 1780, she helped many colonial prisoners escape, thus earning the respect of the American troops encroaching on Cherokee lands. Ward accompanied Old Tassell, chief of the Cherokee, to Hopewell on the Keowee River in South Carolina for a council with the Americans. Ward spoke for the Cherokee people at the peace conference and, following her speech, gave two strings of wampum, a pipe, and some tobacco to the U.S. commissioners. Following the treaty, Ward and her people entered into a more peaceful era. Her last recorded official act was a warning to the Cherokee people against further treaties and land cessions. The document was a premonition of the treaties that ultimately took Cherokee lands and forced them onto the infamous Trail of Tears and relocation to Indian Territory in present-day Oklahoma.

Ward's counsel, according to her people, bordered on the supreme. A granite statue of Ward now stands in Arnwine Cemetery, Granger County, Tennessee, a lasting tribute to a Beloved Woman.

## Washakie (Gambler's Gourd) (1804–1900)
*Flathead-Shoshone tribal leader*

Few Indians were as helpful to the westward passage of immigrants as Washakie. He was probably born in Montana's Bitterroot Mountains. When his father died, Washakie went to live with his mother's eastern Shoshone family in the Wind River mountain chain of Wyoming. He was evidently a brave fighter as a young man against the Blackfeet and Crow. The Shoshone in this area maintained friendships with mountain men and trappers. During the 1820s through the 1830s, Washakie met and became friends with Jim Bridger, the famous mountain man, and Christopher "Kit" Carson, the U.S. commander who rounded up the Navajo in the 1860s.

Washakie became the principal head of his band in the 1840s. The Shoshone became known for their hospitable relations with the United States. Washakie went as far as providing regular patrols of his men to guard and assist immigrants along that region of the Oregon Trail. During this time, he became friends with Brigham

Young and spent part of one winter at the Mormon leader's home.

Washakie's band settled on the Wind River Reservation in present-day Wyoming. The Treaty of Fort Bridger in 1863 guaranteed safe passage for U.S. travelers in exchange for a twenty-year annuity paid to Washakie. The same year, he signed a second treaty giving the Union Pacific Railroad Company right-of-way to lay track in the region. The Shoshone served as scouts for the military against the Arapaho, Cheyenne, Sioux, and Ute in 1869, when Camp Brown was constructed in present-day Wyoming. In 1876, Washakie and two hundred warriors joined forces too late to help General Crook against the Sioux at the Battle of the Rosebud in southern Montana, but harassed and pursued Crazy Horse's warriors to the Powder River region in present-day eastern Montana.

In honor of his help to the U.S. military, Camp Brown was renamed Fort Washakie in 1878. President Ulysses S. Grant gave him a silver saddle the same year, and President Chester A. Arthur visited him in 1883 on a trip to Yellowstone Park. In 1897 Washakie became a Christian and was baptized as an Episcopalian. He died three years later and was buried with full military honors at the fort bearing his name.

## Lucille J. Watahomigie (1945–)
*Hualapai educator*

Lucille Watahomigie is an educator and has extensive skills in Indian education, health, program development, and employment. She was born in Valentine, Arizona, and received a master of science degree specializing in education from the University of Arizona (1973). Watahomigie is a member of the Hualapai tribe of Arizona, a people who lived near the Grand Canyon and whose economy was based on hunting and gathering in the desert and river terrain.

Watahomigie worked as a curriculum specialist for San Diego State University (1978–1980). She has served as a member of the Hualapai Tribal Council (1978–1981) and as chair of the Hualapai Tribal Education Committee (1980–1981). She has published extensively about Hualapai studies. Her written work includes *Spirit Mountain: An Yuman Anthology of Stories and Songs* (1984), co-edited with Leanne Hinton, an anthropologist, and *Hualapai Reference Grammar* (1982), co-edited with Jorigine Bender and Akira Y. Yomaota. Watahomigie's honors include the Phoenix High School Hall of Fame (1977) and she was designated an Outstanding Young Woman of America (1980). She remains active publishing papers on language and literacy among American Indians and with a focus on the

Hualapai language. In 1998 she published "The Native Language is a Gift: A Hualapai Language Autobiography" in *The International Journal of the Sociology of Language* 132. Among her interests are women's advocacy activities centered on child-care programs.

## Charlie Watt (1944–)
*Inuit senator*

Charlie Watt was born in Fort Chimo, a small settlement destined to become the administrative center of the Inuit community in northern Quebec, as well as its largest population center. Watt learned the Inuit skills necessary to become a respected hunter and fisherman. He entered a training program sponsored by Canadian authorities and later found employment with the federal Department of Indian Affairs and Northern Development. During this period, Watt became increasingly critical of the department's policies regarding the Inuit people, and he concluded that the Inuit needed to organize in order to speak for themselves. He was soon conducting a tour of all the Inuit communities in northern Quebec to promote an Inuit association. His work and travels paid off when, in 1972, he became the founding president of the Northern Quebec Inuit Association.

Charlie Watt soon occupied the national spotlight when Quebec announced plans to construct a massive hydroelectric project, known as James Bay I, in the north of the province. Watt and his association, in alliance with the Cree people, fought the project and later participated in the negotiation of a land claims agreement with the Quebec government. The agreement created numerous Inuit governmental agencies, including the Makivik Corporation, an exclusively Inuit organization mandated to represent and promote Inuit interests. Watt became the founding president of the Makivik Corporation in 1978.

Watt also was one of several aboriginal leaders to negotiate with the federal government in the 1980s on matters relating to constitutional reform and aboriginal people. In recognition of his contribution to Canada, Watt was appointed to the Canadian Senate in 1983. As senator he has been active in many Native and Inuit issues. At a meeting of the Inuit Circumpolar Conference in 1998, Senator Watt proposed formation of an economic union among the Inuit peoples of the circumpolar region, which spans the United States, Canada, Russia, and Greenland. He has consistently promoted economic development for his people, and he has been involved in numerous successful business ventures, including a commercial fishery and the first aboriginal-owned airline in the country. In 1994, he was awarded

the Order of Quebec, and in 1997, he received a National Aboriginal Achievement Award.

## George Watts (1945–)
*Nuu-chah-nulth tribal leader*

George Watts's people, the Nuu-chah-nulth, are located on the western coast of Vancouver Island, British Columbia. They are famed canoe builders, known for carving oceangoing canoes out of huge cedar trees. Watts was born and raised in Port Alberni, British Columbia, in a large family and spent his childhood picking wild berries and vegetables in the mountains. His father worked six days a week and Watts sold fish at a local market to buy clothes for school. He attended elementary and high school in his hometown until 1963, and then moved to Vancouver to attend Vancouver City College and then the University of British Columbia to study chemical engineering and education. During his university years, he worked in a local paper mill to help finance his studies.

Watts has served as president of the Nuu-chah-nulth Tribal Council, formed in 1958 to advance the rights and interests of the Nuu-chah-nulth Nation, comprised of otherwise disparate and dispersed communities. The tribal council has been extraordinarily successful in this regard; it has shaped aboriginal politics in the province and produced aboriginal leaders of significance. For a relatively brief period in the 1970s, Watts also was a member of the executive committee of the Union of British Columbia Indian Chiefs, a province-wide organization devoted to aboriginal rights, at a time when the union placed great emphasis on grassroots organizing and economic and political self-sufficiency for aboriginal people in the province.

In more recent years, Watts was instrumental in directing and organizing a challenge to clear-cut logging on Meares Island, British Columbia, and in 1985, he and his people succeeded in obtaining an injunction against further logging activity. The court's reasons had major, positive ramifications for similar claims made by other aboriginal groups in the province. Watts has participated in a number of federal and provincial committees and boards addressing matters of economic development and education. He is a board member of Forest Renewal, British Columbia, and the owner of a consulting firm. As a chief of the Nuu-chah-nulth Tribal Council, representing twelve First Nations, Watts participated in negotiations for a modern treaty with British Columbia. After six years of negotiation, in December 2000 British Columbia made a formal treaty offer to return land, funds, and economic and cultural rights to the Nuu-chah-nulth Tribal Council. The offer is under negotiation.

### Annie Dodge Wauneka (1910–1997)
*Navajo tribal leader*

Annie Dodge Wauneka, the daughter of Henry Chee Dodge, was a strong advocate for the Navajo people in politics, economics, and health. She was the first woman to be elected to the Navajo Tribal Council and in 1964 was the first Native American to receive the Presidential Medal of Freedom.

Wauneka's passion for Native American advocacy can be traced, in part, to the influence of her father Henry Chee Dodge, who was an important figure in the Navajo community. His ideas and actions became a model for many Navajo in the early twentieth century. Annie Dodge was born in a hogan in Old Sawmill, Arizona, and attended the Albuquerque Indian School. Perhaps her principal education, however, came at the side of her father, as he traveled the Navajo Reservation tending to the needs of his people. The poverty and sickness she witnessed as a young child became the focus of her life's work.

Wauneka concentrated her efforts on reducing death and illness from tuberculosis on the reservation. After studying with the U.S. Public Health Service, she sought to implement a health education program in her own community. Four years after her father's death, Wauneka was elected to the tribal council.

As a member of the tribal council, Wauneka focused on Navajo health issues and was appointed chair of the council's Health and Welfare Committee. In this role she campaigned for and won funds for water sanitation and home improvements. Wauneka also established a radio program that focused on health information and an open discussion of social concerns. Wauneka's efforts paid off; during her years as health director the incidence of tuberculosis among her people was greatly reduced.

Wauneka was equally adamant about obtaining better education for her people. She believed that poor education was a major factor inhibiting a better life for the Navajo. Wauneka was also an outspoken advocate against alcohol abuse and combined her health and education programs with alcohol awareness and treatment.

Wauneka received numerous awards and honors throughout her lifetime, including Arizona's Woman of the Year Achievement Award, given by the Arizona Women's Press Association, the Josephine B. Hughes Memorial Award, and the Indian Achievement Award. She continued to advise the Navajo tribal council and

her people on numerous issues until her death on 10 November 1997, at the age of eighty-seven.

### James Welch (1940–)
*Blackfeet-Gros Ventre novelist*

James Welch is a critically acclaimed novelist whose works have dealt with realistic portrayals of life on and off the Blackfeet Indian Reservation in Montana. He was born in Browning, Montana, and attended the University of Minnesota, Northern Montana College, and received a bachelor of arts degree from the University of Montana. He has been a laborer, forest service employee, firefighter, and counselor for Upward Bound. He served on the literature panel of the National Endowment for the Arts and on the Montana State Board of Pardons. He has taught American Indian literature and creative writing at the University of Washington, Cornell University, and Colorado College.

His novel *Fools Crow* (1986) received an American Book Award, the *Los Angeles Times* Book Prize, and the Pacific Northwest Bookseller's Award. Welch's other novels include *Winter in the Blood* (1975), *The Death of Jim Loney* (1979), *The Indian Lawyer* (1990), and *The Heartsong of Charging Elk* (2000). Other works include a collection of poetry, *Riding the Earthboy 40* (1971), and a non-fiction book with Paul Steckler, *Killing Custer* (1994).

### W. Richard West (1943–)
*Cheyenne/Arapaho museum director and lawyer*

Before becoming director of the Smithsonian Institution's National Museum of the American Indian, W. Richard West was a legal partner in the Washington, D.C., legal office of Fried, Frank, Harris, Shriver, and Jacobson, and later in the Indian-owned Albuquerque office of Gover, Stetson, Williams, and West, P.C. While working in this capacity, West represented numerous Indian people, tribes, and organizations before federal, state, and tribal courts, various executive departments of the federal government, and Congress. He devoted much of his personal time to working with American Indians on cultural, legal, and governmental issues.

As director of the National Museum of the American Indian, West is responsible for guiding the successful opening of the three facilities that will comprise the entire museum's holdings and facilities. He oversaw the completion of the George Gustav Heye Center, the museum's exhibition that opened in October 1994 in New York City. He is presently supervising the overall planning of the museum's Cultural Resource Center in

Painter W. Richard West.

Suitland, Maryland, which will house the museum's 800,000-object collection. The Mall Museum, the last to be added to the National Mall in Washington, D.C., is scheduled to open in 2002.

West is a member of the Ford Foundation, the American Indian Research Institute, the National Trust for Historic Preservation, the Bush Foundation, and the National Support Committee of the Native American Rights Fund. He is the former chair (1998–2000) of the board of directors of the American Association of Museums, the nation's only national membership organization representing all types of museums and museum professionals.

West grew up in Musckogee, Oklahoma, and was born in San Bernardino, California, to Walter Richard West, Sr., and Maribelle McCrea West. He earned a bachelor of arts degree in history from the University of Redlands in California in 1965. He received his master's degree in American history from Harvard University in 1968. West graduated from Stanford University School of Law in 1971, where he was the recipient of the

Hilmer Oehlmann, Jr., Prize for excellence in legal writing.

West is married to Mary Beth Braden West, who is an attorney and an ambassador with the Department of State in Washington, D.C. The couple is rearing two children, Amy and Ben.

## Wetamoo (1650–1676)
*Wampanoag tribal leader*

Wetamoo was a sachem of the Pocasset band of Wampanoag in 1675 when King Philip's War broke out. She provided important military support to Philip during the conflict.

Wetamoo was raised in the area around Tiverton, Rhode Island, not far from the outskirts of Plymouth Colony. Her father was a sachem of the Wampanoag Confederacy, which was an alliance of Algonkian-speaking Indians living in present-day New England. When Wetamoo's second husband died, Wetamoo succeeded him as a sachem of the Pocasset band of Wampanoag, making her a representative in the Wampanoag Confederacy. Wetamoo's third husband was King Philip's brother, Alexander, who died in 1661. Wetamoo and Philip believed that the colonists had poisoned Alexander. Upon Alexander's death, Philip became grand sachem of the Wampanoag Confederacy in 1662.

In 1675, when King Philip's War erupted, Wetamoo was married to Petononowit, who expressed his intention to align himself with the colonists. Wetamoo, however, left him and threw her forces into the fray on Philip's behalf. She provided Philip with valuable military support during the war. One of the war's first major conflicts took place near Wetamoo's village in Pocasset Swamp in July 1675. Wetamoo sent her warriors into the battle. The battle, however, turned out badly for the Wampanoag, and Wetamoo took refuge with the Narragansett leader Canonchet, who refused to turn her over to the English. It is believed that Wetamoo helped construct rafts and canoes that were used during the Great Swamp Battle in December 1675. In 1676, however, English forces surrounded Wetamoo's village. When she tried to escape by canoe, soldiers fired upon her and she drowned.

## Cornelia Wieman (contemporary)
*Six Nations psychiatrist*

Cornelia Wieman, a member of the Little Grand Rapids band in Northern Manitoba, is the first practicing aboriginal female psychiatrist in Canada.

A 1993 graduate of McMaster University, she was elected president of the Resident's

McMaster University in 1996, and she was instrumental in developing the chief resident position in emergency psychiatry at McMaster University. She also was elected the chair of the Native Mental Health Section of the Canadian Psychiatric Association.

During her residency, she played an important role in developing the Six Nations Mental Health Services in Ohsweken, Ontario, and was awarded the Medical Services Branch Indian/Inuit Health Careers Scholarship and the Medical Research Council of Canada Farquharson Scholarship.

In 1998, she was the recipient of a National Aboriginal Achievement Award, presented by the National Aboriginal Achievement Foundation, in recognition of her career achievements as an aboriginal professional. Wieman is currently a psychiatric emergency consultant and the Native students health sciences coordinator at McMaster University.

### Robert A. Williams, Jr. (1955–)
*Lumbee lawyer and educator*

Robert A. Williams, Jr., is the E. Thomas Sullivan Professor of Law and American Indian Studies at the

bert Williams, Jr.

University of Arizona. He is a noted legal scholar and teacher in the fields of federal Indian law and indigenous human rights. He received his education from Loyola College with a bachelor of arts degree (1977) and obtained a law degree from Harvard University (1980).

His teaching posts have included associate professor of law at the University of Wisconsin, visiting professor of law at the University of Washington, and the Bennett Boskey Visiting Lecturer and Professor of Law at Harvard University.

He is director of the Indigenous Peoples Law and Policy Program at the University of Arizona. He is also chief justice of the Court of Appeals of the Pascua Yaqui Indian tribe and serves as legal counsel and advisor to Indian tribes and indigenous peoples organizations in the United States, Canada, Australia, and Latin America.

Williams is the author of *Federal Indian Law: Cases and Materials* (Fourth edition, with D. Getches and C. Wilkinson), *The American Indian in Western Legal Thought: The Discourses of Conquest*, and *Linking Arms Together: American Indian Treaty Visions of Law and Peace, 1600–1800*.

### Susan M. Williams (1955–)
*Sisseton-Wahpeton Sioux lawyer*

Susan M. Williams is a member of the Albuquerque, New Mexico, law firm of Williams, Janov, and Cooney, P.C., which focuses on Indian and environmental law. She was born in Klamath Falls, Oregon, on 8 May 1955, and received her education from Radcliffe College, earning a bachelor of arts degree in 1977 and a law degree from Harvard University in 1981. She was subsequently admitted to the bar in the District of Columbia and in New Mexico in 1988. Admission to the bar means that the person has passed a test that measures knowledge about the law, and passage of the tests grants the individual the right to practice law.

She has served as chairperson of the Navajo Tax Commission (1983), a board member of the Conservation Foundation/World Wildlife Fund (1986), the University of Colorado Natural Resources Law Center (1988), and the Grand Canyon Trust (1999). In 2000 Williams was elected to the board of directors of the Harvard University Alumni Association.

Williams's interests focus specifically on taxation laws as applied to the Navajo, to non-Indian corporations, and to reservation lands in Colorado and New Mexico and water laws. Among her published writings

Susan M. Williams.

are *Mineral Development in Indian Land* (1989), "Multiple Taxation of Mineral Extraction in Indian Country: State and Indian Tribal Jurisdiction," "State and Indian Tribal Taxation on Tribal Reservations: Is It Too Taxing?" (1989), and "Tribal Jurisdiction Over Reservation Water Quality and Quantity" (1998).

## Elvin Willie, Jr. (1953–)
*Pomo/Paiute tribal leader*

Elvin Willie is a public health administrator and a member of the Pomo and Paiute tribes. Born on the Walker River Paiute Reservation in Schurz, Nevada, on 15 September 1953, Willie received a bachelor's degree in political science at the University of California, Berkeley, in 1976, and later returned to complete a master's degree in health policy and administration in 1989.

In the interim he held various positions for the Walker River Paiute tribe. He worked in education in 1976 and 1977, developing an Indian-oriented curriculum and a resource center library for elementary school students; then, from 1977 to 1979, he managed a tribal retail store. From 1979 to 1986, Willie served as the

tribal chairman, supervising a staff of forty persons and managing all phases of tribal government operations.

Since then, Willie has been particularly active in the area of public health as related to rural Indian communities, publishing articles in the *Journal of Rural Community Psychology* (1988) and the *Alcohol Treatment Quarterly* (1989). His article "Suicide Contagion among American Indians" appeared in *Handbook on Suicide among Indians*, edited by Eduardo Duran (1989), a publication of the U.S. Indian Health Service. Willie is currently an officer of the U.S. Indian Health Service and works between the Walker River Paiute Reservation and the agency office in Phoenix, Arizona.

## Bill Wilson (1944–)
*Kwawkgewlth tribal leader*

Bill Wilson is well-known in Canada for advancing the rights of aboriginal people. Born in 1944 to Charles William Wilson and Ethel Johnson, Wilson is a Kwawkgewlth Indian. The Kwawkgewlth live on the northern coast of Vancouver Island and the nearby coast of British Columbia. Wilson began to work for his father when he was twelve at a fish purchasing plant in Comox, British Columbia, on Vancouver Island while attending grade school and high school. Although he wanted to quit school when he turned fifteen, his parents persuaded him to continue, and Wilson went on to obtain a bachelor of arts degree from the University of Victoria on Vancouver Island in 1970 and a bachelor of law from the University of British Columbia in 1973. During his summer vacations and weekends, he worked at numerous jobs, including stints as a taxi driver, fisherman, logger, laborer, pulp-mill worker, bartender, and car salesman.

Wilson became involved at an early age in Indian political activities. At fourteen, he joined the Native Brotherhood of British Columbia, a province-wide organization devoted to advancing the cause of Indian rights. His early involvement with the Native Brotherhood of British Columbia developed into a full-time commitment to aboriginal politics that has spanned more than three decades, during which time he has actively participated in countless aboriginal organizations.

While in law school, Wilson was instrumental in the creation of the Union of British Columbia Indian Chiefs, an organization representing Indian bands across the province. In 1976, Wilson was the founding president of the United Native Nations, an association designed to represent aboriginal people by tribe instead of according to bands defined by Canadian authorities. In 1990 and 1991, Wilson was a vice-chief of the Assembly of First Nations, a national organization representing Indian bands across the country, and in 1991 he became the political secretary of the Assembly of First Nations. As the chairman of the First Nations Congress, Wilson succeeded in commencing negotiations on land claims in the province for the first time with the government of British Columbia.

He was recently elected to the Task Group of the British Columbia First Nations Summit, which represents 90 percent of the aboriginal people in British Columbia. Since 1997 he has been chief negotiator for the Lheidli T'enneh Band within the British Columbia treaty making process. Most British Columbia bands are negotiating modern treaties with the province of British Columbia and the government of Canada. He is now one of the two senior Indian leaders in British Columbia. Wilson has two daughters and a son, and currently lives in Vancouver.

## Winema (1836–1920)
*Modoc cultural mediator*

Winema was a peacemaker and negotiator during the Modoc War of 1872–1873. She was born among the Modoc Indians in northern California, in a village located along the Link River. Among her people she was well respected for her bravery. According to one story, at the age of fourteen, she rallied the warriors of her village to victory during a surprise attack by another California tribe. However, she tested her people's patience a year later when, at age fifteen, she married a Kentucky miner named Frank Riddle. She and her husband settled on a ranch, and Winema became known as Toby Riddle. Initially, Winema's own people refused to sanction the marriage. Eventually, however, she became a valuable interpreter for the Modoc in their negotiations with U.S. settlers. Over time, Winema developed a reputation as a peacemaker and diplomat— two skills that would be sorely needed in the Modoc War.

In the mid-1860s, a group of Modoc Indians who had settled in the Klamath Reservation in Oregon returned to their homelands along the Link River. Foreseeing the likelihood of conflict with the growing settler population, Winema tried to convince some of her relatives to return to Oregon and petition for a separate Modoc Reservation. Captain Jack, a Modoc leader, accused Winema of over-friendliness to settlers. In the years to follow, a number of battles between the Modoc and settlers ensued. Winema and her husband served as negotiators, interpreters, and intermediaries for the opposing sides. In February 1873, a peace council was held on neutral ground. During the parley, Captain Jack and another Modoc killed two U.S. military officers. A third U.S. officer, Alfred Meacham, was saved when Winema threw herself between him and a gun. After the ordeal, Winema nursed the wounded Meacham back to health.

Winema's actions made her a celebrity in the U.S. national media. She was escorted to Washington, D.C., for a special visit with President Ulysses S. Grant. For the next seven years she toured eastern cities with Meacham and family members in dramatic re-enactments of Indian history and issues. Winema spent her remaining years in Oregon. Her son, Jeff Riddle, published *The Indian History of the Modoc War*, which was based largely on Winema's recollections.

## Winnebago Prophet (Wabokieshek) (1794–1841)
*Winnebago spiritual leader*

Wabokieshek (White Cloud) was an important supporter of Black Hawk, the Sac and Fox leader, during the final conflicts for the old Northwest Territory in the 1830s. Due to his prophetic visions, he has also been called the Winnebago Prophet. The Winnebago are a Siouan-speaking people who currently live in Nebraska and Wisconsin.

Wabokieshek was born in the heart of what was to become the final battleground for control of the old Northwest Territory, now known as the Great Lakes region. His homeland was situated near the present-day site of Prophetstown, Indiana, at the junction between the Tippecanoe and Mississippi rivers. Although Wabokieshek had long preached for resistance to U.S. encroachment and culture, he had advocated peace with the United States during the Winnebago uprising of 1827. Five years later, however, he agreed to take up arms in support of Black Hawk in the so-called Black Hawk's War of 1832.

Wabokieshek came to Black Hawk in 1832, when the Sac and Fox leader was gathering forces for his return to Saukenuk, a major Sac village in present-day Illinois. Wabokieshek told Black Hawk of his visions, in which the Great Spirit would help defeat their enemies. He promised that with the aid of certain ceremonies, he could create an army of spirit warriors who would aid Black Hawk in defeating the U.S. Army. Thereafter, the Indians could reclaim their homelands that were occupied by the United States. Prophecies of this sort were not uncommon. Both the Delaware Prophet (1760–1763) and Tenskwatawa, the Shawnee Prophet (1806–1811), had made similar prophecies in their people's conflicts with European colonists and U.S. settlers. Wabokieshek's alliance with Black Hawk resulted in the enlistment of a number of Sac and Winnebago warriors to Black Hawk's cause. Wabokieshek remained with Black Hawk throughout the conflict and was at his side when the Indian leader surrendered at Prairie du Chien in present-day Wisconsin. Wabokieshek was imprisoned with Black Hawk and traveled with him as a kind of war trophy in the eastern United States. After his release, Wabokieshek lived for a number of years in relative obscurity, first with the Sac and later with the Winnebago.

### Sarah Winnemucca (1844–1891)
*Northern Paiute activist and educator*

Sarah Winnemucca was active as a peacemaker, teacher, and defender of her people's rights. She was born near the Humboldt River in western Nevada, the fourth of nine children. When she was ten, she and her family moved to where her grandfather, Truckee, lived near San Jose, California. When she was fourteen, she moved in with the family of a stagecoach agent, Major William Ormsby, where she learned English. She returned to San Jose in 1860 at her grandfather's dying request. Winnemucca was able to study at a convent school only one month before several non-Indian parents objected to the presence of Paiute girls. Thereafter, she found work as a servant and spent much of her salary on books.

The Paiute War began in 1860 and was led by Winnemucca's cousin, Numaga. She and many non-hostile Paiute were moved to a reservation near Reno, Nevada. During the Snake War in 1866, the military requested that she and her brother, Naches, act as intermediaries. Winnemucca became the official interpreter in the military's negotiations with the Paiute and Shoshone. She was convinced that the army could be trusted more than the Indian agents, and she voiced her concerns to U.S. Senator John Jones about mistreatment of Indians by Indian service employees.

Some northern Paiute, including Winnemucca, were relocated to the Malheur Reservation in Oregon in 1872. While there, she met and became friends with reservation agent Samuel Parrish. She assisted with his agricultural program, served as interpreter, and taught school. Agent William Rinehart replaced Parrish, and his failure to pay the Paiute for their agricultural labors led to the Bannock War of 1878. General Oliver Howard used Winnemucca as a peacemaker and interpreter. The Paiute were forced to leave the Malheur Reservation and relocate to the Yakima Reservation in present-day Washington State.

Winnemucca went to San Francisco and Sacramento in 1879; in lectures to sympathetic audiences, she discussed the treatment of Indians by Indian service employees. Despite widespread public support for the Paiute's right to return to Malheur, no funding was raised for the project. Winnemucca commenced a lecture tour of the East in 1883 and 1884 and dressed as an Indian princess to draw crowds. While there, she met with many important sympathizers of Indian rights and published *Life among the Paiutes, Their Wrongs and Claims*. Winnemucca returned to Nevada and founded a school for Indians with the money she had saved and from private donations. The school operated for three years until funding ran out and Sarah's health faltered. She died of tuberculosis at the age of forty-seven.

### Shirley Hill Witt (1940–)
*Mohawk anthropologist*

Shirley Witt is an anthropologist who has done extensive research in the area of civil rights. In 1981, she became the director of the Rocky Mountain Regional Office of the U.S. Commission on Civil Rights. She is also an author and co-editor of numerous publications.

At age twenty-two, Witt had her second child. That same year, she enrolled at the University of Michigan and went on to obtain her doctorate in anthropology from the University of New Mexico. Witt distanced herself from an overly specialized focus early on and developed a multi-disciplinary approach to her work. Her thesis research was on migration into the San Juan pueblo. She went on to teach at the University of North Carolina and Colorado College.

Witt's career led her to an interest in the employment problems of women, including discrimination against women by male department heads. When the U.S. Commission on Civil Rights offered her a job, Witt accepted. The position offered her a chance to apply her anthropological skills to day-to-day problems. Her work entails directing a research unit made up of social scientists, attorneys, and writers who investigate civil rights violations in a six-state region. Her research resulted in written recommendations to the president and Congress. Although Witt's work encompasses the challenges faced by Native Americans, the research addresses all cultural groups in the United States. Since the early 1990s, Witt has been a foreign service officer working for American embassies on overseas assignments. Eventually, she hopes to return to the academic field and participate in a multi-disciplinary program to apply anthropological theory to social problems.

Witt was the co-editor of *The Way: An Anthology of American Indian Language and Literature* (1972) and

*The Tuscaroras* (1972). She has written numerous articles including "Pressure Point in Growing Up Indian" in *The Indian Reader* I, number 2 (Summer/Fall 1986); and "Punto Final," "Seboyeta Chapel," and "La Mujer de Valor" in *That's What She Said: Contemporary Fiction and Poetry of Native American Women*, ed. Rayna Green (1983).

### Laura Waterman Wittstock (1937–)
*Seneca and Stockbridge Munsee journalist and author*

Laura Waterman Wittstock is president of MIGIZI Communications, a nonprofit media corporation located in Minneapolis, Minnesota, that provides information to the Indian public, educates elementary, secondary, and adult students in a communications-related setting, and commits resources to address problems which threaten the stability of the Indian community.

She has made significant contributions in the field of media communications with a focus on issues relating to Native Americans. She has been recognized for her commitment to developing a free tribal press. Wittstock has also helped establish alcoholism abuse and education programs in the Indian community.

Wittstock was born on the Cattaraugus Indian Reservation in New York and was educated at the University of Minnesota. Much of her life's work has been in media communications. In 1975 she was the executive director of the American Indian Press Association. She was also the editor of a monthly report on legislation affecting Native Americans. She has worked abroad with indigenous people and with the International American Treaty Council, a non-government organization working for international recognition of Indian treaty and political rights.

Her recent publications are a children's book, *Ininatig's Gift of Sugar: Traditional Native Sugarmaking* (1993) and *Changing Communities, Changing Foundations: The Story of the Diversity Efforts of Twenty Community Foundations*.

She continues to serve on numerous boards, including the Minneapolis Foundation, Intermedia Arts, the Community Solutions Fund, and the Institute for Research and Education (HealthSystem Minnesota). She is treasurer of the Minnesota Partnership for Action Against Tobacco (MPAAT), and vice-chair of the Minnesota Minority Health Advisory Committee.

Wittstock received the 1992 Minnesota Advocates for Human Rights Award for twenty years of work in free expression and alternative media coverage of American Indians, and she is currently a St. Paul Companies

LIN grant recipient, conducting research on Dakota reconciliation.

### Rosita Worl (contemporary)
*Tlingit tribal leader and educator*

Rosita Worl has made important contributions in developing public awareness of Tlingit culture and Alaska Native subsistence cultures.

A member of the Thunderbird Clan and House Lowered from the Sun of Klukwan, Alaska, and a Child of the Sockeye Clan, Worl earned a master of science degree and a doctoral degree in anthropology from Harvard University in 1998.

Worl holds a joint appointment as assistant professor of anthropology at the University of Alaska Southeast and president of the Sealaska Heritage Foundation. The foundation is dedicated to preserving and maintaining the Tlingit, Haida, and Tsimshian cultures and languages.

Rosita Worl.

In the late 1980s, she was elected to the board of the Sealaska Corporation, which owns the land base of the Southeast Alaska Indians and is the major economic institution in contemporary Tlingit society and in southeast Alaska.

On both state and national levels, Worl serves on the boards of the Alaska Native Heritage Center and the subsistence committee for the Alaska Native Federation of Natives.

She served as the first chair of the Alaska Native Education Association, and, in 1977 she was chairperson of the first Alaska Native Women's Statewide Caucus and Alaska State delegate to the International Women's Year Houston Conference. Worl was also a founding member of the Smithsonian's National Museum of the American Indian and was appointed to President Bill Clinton's Northwest Coast Sustainable Development Commission.

Worl has done extensive research throughout the Alaska and circumpolar Arctic and has served on the National Science Foundation Arctic Program Committee, the National Science Committee overseeing the social scientific studies of the Exxon Valdez oil spill, the Scientific Committee of the Arctic Eskimo Whaling Commission, and the International Whaling Commission (1979).

She has written a number of landmark studies and reports published by foundations, universities, federal organizations, and Alaska Native organizations on bowhead whale and seal hunting, impacts of industrial development on Native communities, repatriation, and Tlingit real and property laws. Worl was elected to the board of directors of Sealaska Corporation (1987–2000), is executive director for the Sealaska Foundation, works with the Alaska Native Federation, and teaches at the University of Alaska-Southeast.

## Wovoka (Jack Wilson) (circa 1856–1932)
*Paiute spiritual leader*

The Ghost Dance religion of 1890 originated with this Paiute visionary and prophet, who grew up in the area of Mason Valley, Nevada, near the present Walker Lake Reservation. His proper name, Wovoka, means "The Cutter" in Paiute. On the death of his father he was taken into the family of a white farmer named David Wilson and was given the name Jack Wilson, by which he was known among local American settlers.

During the late 1880s, Wovoka became ill with a severe fever at a time that happened to coincide with a solar eclipse. In his feverish state, Wovoka received a vision, and an account of this experience as told in Wovoka's own words was documented by James Mooney in his book *The Ghost Dance Religion and the Sioux Outbreak of 1890*: "'When the sun died,' Wovoka said, "I went up to heaven and saw God and all the people who had died a long time ago. God told me to come back and tell my people they must be good and love one another, and not fight, or steal, or lie. He gave me this dance to give to my people.'" This vision became the basis of the Ghost Dance religion, which was based upon the belief that there would be a time when all Indian people—the living and those who had died—would be reunited on an earth that was spiritually regenerated and forever free from death, disease, and all the other miseries that had recently been experienced by Indians. Word of the new religion spread quickly among Indian peoples of the Great Basin and Plains regions, but it is said that Wovoka himself never traveled far from his birthplace. A complex figure, he was revered by Indians while being denounced as an impostor and a lunatic by the local settlers throughout his entire life.

## Allen Wright (Kiliahote) (circa 1825–1885)
*Choctaw principal chief, minister, and translator*

Allen Wright was born along the Yaknukni River in Mississippi, the son of mixed-blood Choctaw parents. Wright was removed to Indian Territory with his father and sister in 1832 during the government relocation era.

Kiliahote received his name, Allen Wright, from a Presbyterian missionary, Cyrus Kingsburn, who took an interest in the boy and provided him with an education at local missionary schools. Wright continued his education in New York, graduating from Union College in 1852 and from Union Theological Seminary in 1855. In 1856, Wright was ordained into the Presbyterian Church after which he began work among the Choctaw. He became involved in tribal affairs and was elected to the Choctaw House of Representatives and the senate, and served as the tribe's treasurer. During the Civil War, Wright served in the Confederacy.

Following the war, Wright was elected principal chief of the Choctaw Nation and served two terms, from 1866 to 1870. Wright is given credit for first suggesting the name Oklahoma, meaning "red people's land" in the Muskogean language, for the new Indian Territory. Following the Removal Act, part of the land which is now Oklahoma was designated Indian Territory comprising the Choctaw and Cherokee Nations, and later the Chickasaw Nation. Following the Civil War, the U.S. government began to consider the idea of merging all the tribal governments in the territory, at which point Wright suggested they rename it Oklahoma. The reorganization did not take place until 1890, in an act that was passed by Congress, and Oklahoma became the official name of the state in 1907.

During the 1870s and 1880s, Wright translated numerous works, including the Chickasaw constitution and codes of law into English. In 1880, his Choctaw dictionary was published.

## Ray A. Young Bear (1950–)
*Mesquakie poet and novelist*

Author of the highly acclaimed works *Winter of the Salamander* (1980), *The Invisible Musician* (1989), *Black Eagle Child: The Facepaint Narratives* (1992), and *Remnants of the First Earth* (1997), Ray A. Young Bear has made a name for himself among Native and non-Native literati. Born in Marshalltown, Iowa, and raised on the Mesquakie Tribal Settlement, Young Bear's first language is Mesquakie. The author draws on the language's complex oratory style to shape his English writing. His maternal grandmother, Ada Kapayou Old Bear, influenced his appreciation of the lyrical, and his wife, Stella L. Young Bear, continues to support his literary endeavors.

Young Bear attended Claremont College, the University of Iowa, Grinnell College, Northern Iowa University, and Iowa State University. The writer began writing poetry in the late 1960s, and his first poem was published in 1968, although his formal introduction as a tribal poet came later when he was published in the *South Dakota Review*. Young Bear performs readings throughout the country and conducts workshops with young poets. He has held visiting faculty positions at several universities, including the University of Iowa and Eastern Washington University.

In 1983 Young Bear and his wife Stella formed the Woodland Song and Dance Troupe, also referred to as Black Eagle Child. The performing arts group brings together Mesquakie artists who perform traditional Mesquakie song and dance styles for Native and non-Native audiences. Young Bear often begins these performances with readings of his own works, as well as Mesquaki songs.

Young Bear's poetry draws extensively from his people's oral tradition. His writing is a reflection of old-time storytelling and events and modern-day speech patterns and actions. When referring to or describing his work, Young Bear often uses the third-person plural (the pronoun we), because his work is the product of many minds and lives. The cover of Young Bear's books are decorated with his wife's elaborate bandolier-style beadwork. He presently lives on his tribe's settlement with his wife and nephew, Jesse.

## James Young Deer (fl. 1900–1920)
*Winnebago actor, producer, and director*

Little is known about the talented Young Deer, who produced, directed, and acted in many notable Indian-themed Western movies during the silent film era, before the 1920s. Born in Dakota City, Nebraska, he performed in circuses and Wild West shows as a child and, about 1900, entered the moving picture industry. Young Deer and his wife, Princess Redwing, performed in Cecil B. DeMille's *The Squaw Man* (1914), served as technical advisors for film pioneer D. W. Griffith, and gained roles in *The Mended Flute* (1909) and *Little Dove's Romance* (1911). Young Deer's expertise behind the camera led to his position as chief of the West Coast division of Pathé Fréres Studios, a French film company in Orange County, California. In 1912, Young Deer produced and directed dozens of short western movies, many of them highly successful and featuring Indian stories such as *The Cheyenne Brave, Red Deer's Devotion, Squaw Man's Revenge,* and *The Yaqui Girl.*

By 1913, however, the Pathé Fréres Company left its Orange County studio location and transferred Young Deer to its studios in France. According to some film historians, while in France, Young Deer directed several films and returned to the United States after World War I. For a short time, Young Deer operated an acting school in Hollywood, California, and then resumed production of low-budget films.

## Peterson Zah (1928–)
*Navajo tribal leader*

Peterson Zah is the former chairman and president of the Navajo Nation, which occupies extensive parts of Arizona and New Mexico (14 million acres) and has the largest population of any tribe in the United States or Canada.

As a youth, teachers at the Phoenix Indian School discouraged Zah from entering college; nevertheless, he attended college on a basketball scholarship and graduated from Arizona State University with a bachelor's degree in education in 1963. On completing his education, Zah returned to Window Rock, Arizona, on the Navajo Reservation, to teach carpentry as part of a pilot program intended to develop employment skills among Navajo adults. He then served as a field coordinator at the Volunteers in Service to America (VISTA) Training Center at Arizona State University. VISTA was a federally sponsored domestic peace corps, and Zah was involved in cultural sensitivity training for VISTA volunteers in preparation for their service on Indian reservations throughout the United States.

In 1967, Zah joined DNA-People's Legal Services, Inc., a nonprofit organization chartered by the state of Arizona to help indigent and other economically disadvantaged Indian people. DNA had nine offices on the Navajo, Hopi, and Apache reservations, and in San Juan County, New Mexico. Zah later became executive director of this organization, a position he held for ten years. In this capacity he supervised thirty-three tribal court advocates, thirty-four attorneys, and a total of 120 employees. Under his direction, DNA lawyers took several landmark cases to the U.S. Supreme Court, winning cases that helped establish the rights of individual Native Americans and the sovereignty of Indian nations.

In 1982, Zah was elected chairman of the Navajo Tribal Council; in this capacity, he presided over the tribal council and served as chief executive officer of the Navajo Nation government. In 1987, he became chief fundraiser for the Navajo Education and Scholarship Foundation, a nonprofit organization that solicited funds from the private sector and provided scholarships to needy and worthy Navajo students. In 1988, he founded Native American Consulting Services, a private firm which provided educational services to school districts on and off the reservation. As sole proprietor of the company, he developed curriculum materials on Navajo culture and history and worked with Congress on efforts to secure funds for new school construction on the Navajo and San Carlos Apache reservations.

Zah was elected president of the Navajo Nation in 1991, a new position created by the Navajo Nation Council in a reorganization of the Navajo Nation governmental structure. As such, Zah became the only Navajo leader to be elected as chairman and president, and the first elected president in the history of the Navajo Nation. In recent years, Zah acts as a special consultant to the president at Arizona State University. He continues to work on national boards, national political issues, and Indian education issues.

## Ofelia Zepeda (1954–)
*Tohono O'odham linguist, poet, and educator*

Ofelia Zepeda's scholarly achievements distinguish her as one of the leading scholars in Native American language study, or linguistics. Her 1983 book *A Papago Grammar*, the first grammar of the Tohono O'odham language, remains one of the most highly regarded books in its field.

The first member of her family to graduate from high school, Zepeda was born in Stanfield, Arizona, a rural community near the Tohono O'odham and Pima reservations. Zepeda, along with her eight siblings and parents, traveled to Mexico during the summers to visit relatives and participate in tribal ceremonies. While Zepeda and her family may have traveled to their homeland during her childhood, her community in Arizona was tight and tribal traditions and history remained distinct, despite the borders separating the Tohono O'odham from their home base.

Zepeda began her higher education at Central Arizona College, but later transferred to the University of Arizona, where she initially studied sociology. After delving into her tribe's language as part of an outside project, however, the academic's focus moved to a more linguistic level. Her passion for scholarship is clear through her quick academic achievements: Zepeda received her bachelor's degree in 1980, her master's degree in 1981, and her doctorate in linguistics in 1984.

In 1986, Zepeda was appointed director of the American Indian Studies Program at the University of Arizona and continues to be associated with the department. She is a professor of linguistics, and the former president of the American Indian Alumni Association.

Zepeda is currently co-director of the American Indian Language Development Institute (AILDI), an internationally recognized summer program sponsored by the University of Arizona for American Indian educators in the fields of language education, promotion, and revitalization. The organization, which emerged when several academics and parents expressed interest in studying aspects of their Native languages, assists educators and practitioners throughout Native America, Canada, and parts of Mexico develop and promote Native-language learning. She often works as a consultant in Native language curriculum development with the Tohono O'odham and other tribes. Zepeda also is an executive board member of the Institute for the Preservation of the Original Languages of the Americas (IPOLA), and is also an executive board member for the National Museum of the American Indian, a branch of the Smithsonian Institute.

In addition to these achievements, Zepeda is currently the series editor of Sun Tracks American Indian Literary series published by the University of Arizona Press. In 1995, she authored a book of poetry entitled *Ocean Power: Poems from the Desert* and co-edited *Home Places: Contemporary Native American Writing* with Larry Evers. Her work has been anthologized in numerous collections.

In 1996, Zepeda accepted the Tanner Award from the University of Arizona's American Indian Alumni Association for her significant contribution to the American Indian community, and in 1997 she received a grant from the Endangered Language Fund in order to continue work on the Tohono O'odham dictionary project. Most recently, Zepeda was awarded a 1999 MacArthur Fellowship for her work as a linguist, poet, editor, and community leader.

# Glossary

## A

**aboriginal**　The first people or native people of an area. The Native Americans are the aboriginal people of North America. Under the Canadian Constitution Act of 1982, an aboriginal person is defined as being an Indian, Inuit, or Métis. Aboriginal is often used interchangeably with the terms *native* and *indigenous*.

**aboriginal rights**　Rights enjoyed by a people by virtue of the fact that their ancestors inhabited an area from time immemorial before the first Europeans came. These rights include ownership of land and resources, cultural rights, and political self-determination. There are widely divergent views on the validity of these rights. On one end of the spectrum, some deny the existence of aboriginal rights; on the other end, some claim that aboriginal rights give natives the inherent right to govern themselves and their lands.

**aboriginal title**　The earliest discussion of aboriginal title in Canada came in a nineteenth-century lawsuit involving Indian lands in Ontario. At that point, aboriginal (then "Indian") title was understood to be of a usufructuary nature, that is, to give Indians a temporary right to use their lands for subsistence purposes. Indian title was not understood to equal "fee simple" ownership. A century later, however, the doctrine of aboriginal title has been expanded to include in practical terms much broader rights. *See* fee-simple ownership *and* usufructuary.

**abrogation**　The termination of an international agreement or treaty, for example, when Congress enacts a law completely abolishing a treaty and breaking all the U.S. promises to an Indian nation.

**acculturation**　The transference of culture from one group to another, usually from a more dominant group to a less dominant one, which thereby loses its previous culture.

**age grades**　A series of social and ceremonial associations based on age. Members enter the first grade at the appropriate age and then proceed through the set.

**agriculturalists**　Indian peoples who depended to a significant extent on crops which they planted themselves.

**Alaska Native Claims Settlement Act (ANCSA)**　A 1971 congressional act that extinguished Alaska Natives' claims to land. In compensation, the Alaska Natives retained 44 million acres and received $962.5 million.

**Algonkians**　A group of Indian peoples who speak an Algonkian language. This is the largest language group in Canada. It includes many peoples with very different cultures, from the Atlantic coast to the western prairies.

**alienate**　Transfer of an ownership interest, for example, when tribal land is sold to nontribal members.

**alkaloid**　Any of a number of colorless, crystalline, bitter organic substances, such as caffeine, morphine, quinine, and strychnine, having alkaline properties and containing nitrogen. Alkaloids are found in plants and, sometimes, in animals and can have a strong toxic effect on the human or animal system.

**allotment**　The policy, peaking in the 1880s and 1890s, of subdividing Indian reservations into individual, privately owned ("patented" or "fee patent") parcels of land. The division of communally held lands on many Indian reservations into individually owned parcels, thereby nearly eliminating communal ownership of land and resources, which was a defining element of tribal life. The allotment policy was ended in 1934, but it left a legacy of "checkerboard" land ownership on reservations, where often, the tribe, non-Indians, and Indian allottees own small and scattered segments of land. *See* General Allotment Act of 1887.

**Amargosa complex**   A series of artifacts linked to the ancient hunting and gathering peoples of the Mohave Desert in the southwest, dated from 1600 B.C.E. to C.E. 1000.

**American Indian Movement (AIM)**   An Indian activist organization originating in Minneapolis, Minnesota, in the 1960s. AIM was originally organized to protect urban Indians from police harassment and to assist Indian children in obtaining culturally sensitive education. In the 1970s, AIM expanded its activities to include more traditional issues, such as assertion of treaty rights, tribal sovereignty, and international recognition of Indian nations.

**Anasazi**   An early pueblo culture that flourished between C.E. 900 and 1200. The present-day Hopi Indians are believed to be descendants of the Anasazi, which in Hopi means *ancient ones*.

**annuities**   In the United States, annuities are annual payments for land in accordance with Indian treaties. Instead of paying for Indian land in one large sum, the U.S. government usually spread the expense by paying smaller sums over a number of years. In Canada, annuities were small annual payments made to bands, which surrendered lands to the Crown, or English monarch, who formally claimed public land in Canada.

**archaeology**   The study of past cultures through an analysis of their physical remains, such as tools or pottery. From such remains, archaeologists piece together an idea of what ancient cultures may have been like.

**Archaic period**   The time between eight thousand and two thousand years ago defined in most areas by cultures dependent on hunting and gathering.

**Articles of Confederation**   The original agreement among the thirteen original U.S. colonies to form a new, independent country. The articles were adopted on November 15, 1777, ratified by the thirteen colonies in 1781, and remained in force until 1789, when the present constitution was ratified.

**artifacts**   Any products of human cultural activity, such as tools, weapons, or artworks, found in archaeological contexts.

**Assembly of First Nations (AFN)**   The successor organization to the National Indian Brotherhood (NIB) as the national political body representing first nations of Canada at the national political level, such as at the First Ministers' Conferences, where the Canadian prime minister and provincial leaders met to discuss provisions of a new Canadian constitution. The chiefs of each Indian first nation represent their bands at the national assemblies of chiefs, which constitutes the AFN.

**assimilation**   The idea that one group of people, usually a minority, are becoming like another and are being absorbed by a majority society. For example, for many years it was believed that U.S. Indians were assimilating into the dominant culture, but that idea no longer holds much credence.

**associated funerary objects**   Objects believed to have been placed with individual human remains at the time of death or later as a part of the death rite or ceremony of a culture and which, along with the human remains, are currently in the possession or control of a federal agency or museum. Items exclusively made for burial purposes or to contain human remains are also considered associated funerary objects.

**Athapaskan**   A group of Indian peoples who speak an Athapaskan language. These languages dominate in northwestern Canada south of the tree line.

# B

**band**   (1) A small, loosely organized social group composed of several families. (2) In Canada, originally a social and economic unit of nomadic hunting peoples, but, since confederation, a community of Indians registered under the Indian Act. Registered Indians are called "status Indians." Each band has its own governing band council, usually consisting of one or more chiefs and several councillors. Today, many bands prefer to be known as First Nations. *See* status Indians.

**band council**   In Canada, the local form of native government consisting of a chief and councillors, who are elected for two- or three-year terms to carry on band business. Community members choose the chief and councillors by election, or sometimes through traditional custom. The actual duties and responsibilities of band councils are specified in the Indian Act. *See* Indian Act.

**band council resolution**   The method by which Canadian band councils pass motions or record decisions. Band council resolutions are statements outlining a decision of the band council. The minister of Indian and Northern Affairs Canada, or senior officials of that department, must approve band council resolutions whenever they involve band lands or monies.

**Berengia**   During the last glacial age, before fifteen thousand years ago, a land mass between Asia and Alaska in the Bering Sea that served as a land bridge for the first migrations to the continents of the western hemisphere.

**bicultural/bilingual education**   An education system that combines the languages, values, and beliefs of two cultures in its curriculum to give students the skills to live and function in both cultures.

**bilateral kinship**   A system of descent and inheritance that recognizes relationship to both a person's mother's and father's kin.

**Bill C-31**   The pre-legislation name of the 1985 *Act to Amend the Indian Act* of the Canadian Parliament that restored legal status to aboriginal women and their children who had lost status through marriage to non-Indians. The bill corrected a section of the Indian Act that revoked status for women married to non-Indians while permitting Indian men to confer Indian status upon non-Indian wives. While aboriginal women's groups welcomed this change, many Indian communities opposed the bill as an intrusion into their jurisdiction over band membership. Bill C-31 enabled people affected by the discriminatory provisions of the old *Indian Act* to apply to have their Indian status restored. Since 1985, over 100,000 individuals have successfully regained their status.

**bill of rights**   A statement of fundamental rights guaranteed to members of a nation. The U.S. Bill of Rights consists of the first ten amendments to the Constitution and were adopted in the late 1780s. Canada adopted its first bill of rights in 1960. The fundamental purpose of the Canadian Bill of Rights was to ensure equality of rights, and, as a consequence, Canada's native people were allowed to vote in Canadian federal elections.

**boarding school**   A school run by the government or a religious or private organization, in which the children live. Boarding schools designed to educate native children took them away from the influence of their family and culture.

**"booming"**   Forceful nineteenth-century advocacy of the desirability of seizing most of the remaining land of Native Americans.

**Bosque Redondo**   The Navajo reservation in present-day eastern New Mexico where for four years (1864–1868), the Navajo were forced to live after being rounded up and concentrated together.

**branch**   In linguistics, a subdivision of a language grouping (either a phylum or a family of languages).

**Branch of Acknowledgement and Research (B.A.R.)**   Established in 1978 by an act of Congress, a Bureau of Indian Affairs department, and at that time called the Federal Acknowledgement Project (F.A.P.), that established procedures to extend federal recognition to previously unrecognized Indian tribes and communities. About 150 Indian communities have applied to the U.S. government for certification as Indian tribes. *See* federal recognition.

**British North America Act (1867)**   The legislation passed by the British Parliament in 1867 that created the country of Canada. The British North America Act was renamed the Constitution Act, 1867. The act outlines in section 91 the areas of federal (Canadian national government) jurisdiction, and sub-section 24 of section 91 gives the Canadian Parliament exclusive powers to pass legislation concerning "Indians, and lands reserved for the Indians."

**Bureau of Indian Affairs (BIA)**   A federal agency charged with the trust responsibility for tribal land, education, and water rights.

# C

**Cadastral**   Mapping property boundaries and other details of realty, as well as of territory, hence reservations, and keeping such records in a cadastre (map office).

**California Missions**   The twenty-one individual Catholic missions founded between 1769 and 1823, containing a church, a dormitory for Native Americans, and successful farm and cattle operations based on forced Indian labor.

**camas**   A plant (Camassia quamash), the bulbs of which were an important source of food for the native people of the Northwest Coast and the Columbia Plateau. The bulbs were gathered in the late summer and baked to prepare for eating or storage.

**Campbell tradition**   Archaeological remains of a group of California cultures dated from 3000 B.C.E. to C.E. 1500 and later. The remains are believed to be ancestral to the present-day Chumash from the Santa Barbara area.

**Canada**  Originally this designation referred only to part of France's possessions in Canada (roughly corresponding to today's southern Quebec). After 1791 it came to refer to the two Canadas, Lower Canada (southern Quebec) and Upper Canada (southern Ontario). With confederation by the British North American Act in 1867, it came to refer to all the provinces and territories collectively.

**Canadian Aboriginal Economic Development Strategy (CAEDS)**  Launched in 1989, a program that seeks to promote economic development among native people. The program coordinates funding services of several federal agencies to focus on aboriginal economic development problems. Participating federal agencies include the Indian and Northern Affairs Canada (INAC), the Department of Employment and Immigration Canada (EIC), and the Department of Industry, Science and Technology. The program emphasizes long-term planning and is geared toward business ventures and entrepreneurship.

**Canadian Charter of Rights and Freedoms**  This section of the Canadian Constitution Act, 1982, combines protection of individual rights, such as freedom of conscience and religion, with group rights involving issues such as language. Judicial decisions involving the charter are having a profound impact on Canadian society. In the 1982 Constitution, aboriginal and treaty rights were not included in the charter itself but in a separate part of the text. A provision of the Canadian charter that differentiates it from the U.S. Bill of Rights allows governments to "opt out" of charter requirements through legislative fiat.

**Canadian test of basic skills**  A test of a student's reading, writing, and mathematical skills commonly used in Canada.

**castor gras**  A French term meaning *greasy beaver*, which referred to beaver pelts that had been used as clothing long enough for the long guard hairs to fall out and for the shorter barbed hairs to absorb body oils and perspiration. Especially during the early fur trade, Europeans sought castor gras because of its value for making felt.

**cautery**  The act of cauterizing, which is to burn with a hot iron or needle, or with a caustic substance, so as to destroy dead or unwanted tissue in order to prevent the spread of infection.

**caveat**  Meaning "caution." A legal action by which a person or party claims ownership of, or interest in, land registered in the name of another party.

**cession**  Giving up of Indian land, often in exchange for a reservation or grant of land set aside for the Indians' permanent and exclusive use and occupancy.

**Charlottetown Accord (1992)**  An attempt at constitutional reform in Canada, named after the Prince Edward Island city where it was reached. It would have entrenched the inherent right to aboriginal self-government in the Constitution, as well as decentralizing many aspects of Canadian government. In the process of drafting this accord, national aboriginal leaders were included as quasi-equal participants for the first time. However, in a national referendum in October 1992, both aboriginal and other Canadians rejected the Charlottetown Accord, and aboriginal political aspirations were again forced to seek out non-constitutional forums.

**chiki**  A Seminole word for their open-sided, thatched-roof shelter, which evolved in Florida from the Creek cabin of their ancestors.

**cimarrone**  A Spanish term for wild or untamed. Cimarrone was applied to the Lower Creek Indians who migrated into Florida in the latter part of the eighteenth century and later became the Seminole Indians.

**circle sentencing**  A way of dealing with community members who have broken the law, that is most frequently practiced in Canada and several communities in Minnesota. Based on traditional practices, the process emphasizes peacemaking, consensus decision making, and taking the interests of the offender, the victim(s), and the community as a whole into account as the offender accepts responsibility for the crime. The participants sit in a circle, speaking in turn as a "talking piece" comes to them, and express themselves concerning the matter at hand and their support for all concerned. Each participant must agree on the outcomes that emerge from the discussion. These outcomes are the sentence.

**"citizens plus"**  In Canada, the concept that Indians are a distinct class of persons with special rights by virtue of their aboriginal title and treaty rights, which non-Indian citizens do not enjoy.

**civil law**  The body of law developed from Roman law that is codified into a single comprehensive body of laws, as opposed to developed from case law or custom. Civil law is the legal system used in most non-English speaking jurisdictions. It is also used in the state of Louisiana and the province of Quebec in Canada. The term "civil law" is also used within the common law system to refer to all non-criminal laws.

**civil service reform**    Late nineteenth-century movement in the United States to reform government service. The policy separated politics from government office holding, which meant in the Indian Service that elected officials were prevented from directly appointing political friends to well-paying positions. Appointment to and retention of government administrative positions became based on competence and the possession of formal qualifications of individual applicants and job holders.

**"civilization" or forced acculturation**    A major U.S. Indian policy from 1887 to 1934 that included pacification of Indians, their conversion to Christianity, and their adoption of a "civilized" occupation such as farming. *See* acculturation *and* assimilation.

**clan**    The basic social and political organization of many, but not all, Indian societies, which consists of a number of related house groups and families. In some cases, persons claim to be related and share a common symbol or totem, often an animal, such as the bear or the turtle.

**Clovis points**    Ancient spearheads made in a style of polished, tapered, and cylindrical shape, which first appeared among North American peoples about 10,000 B.C.E. These peoples practiced a hunting and gathering way of life that depended on many now-extinct species such as woolly mammoth and dire wolf.

**Cochise culture**    The name that refers to groups of hunters and gatherers who lived in present-day southeastern Arizona and southwestern New Mexico from about 13,000 to 500 B.C.E. This cultural period is named in honor of the Apache leader, Cochise, who in the late 1800s resisted U.S. troops in the same area.

**common law**    The body of law that is based on principles developed by judges in case law as opposed to statute. First developed in England, this system of law forms the legal foundation in English speaking jurisdictions including the United States (except Louisiana) and Canada (except Quebec). The term "common law" is also used to refer to the legal principles created within the royal courts of England in contrast to those principles coming from the courts of equity.

**Community Health Representatives (CHR) Program**    A Medical Services Branch (MSB) program to train Indian and Inuit people at the community level in elementary public health, so that they can provide a link between their community and the health facility in that community.

**Compact of 1802**    Agreement between the state of Georgia and the U.S. federal government in which the latter retained rights to negotiate land treaties with Indians in present-day Mississippi, Georgia, and Alabama, while Georgia was restricted to its present-day boundaries and given assurance that the federal government would peaceably remove any Indian nations from within Georgia's chartered limits.

**comprehensive claim**    According to the Canadian government's land-claims policy, an aboriginal claim, based on aboriginal rights, to land not covered by treaty.

**concentration**    A major U.S. government Indian policy of the mid-nineteenth century involving concentration of Indian tribes on reservations west of the Mississippi River. *See* Removal Act.

**Concordat**    In Roman Catholic Church law ("canon law" or sacred law), a treaty made by the Vatican (or "Holy See" or the Pope).

**confederacy**    An alliance of friendship among several tribes or bands in which they agree to regulate some of their activities under common rules and obligations. This could mean the obligation to give military aid if attacked or the right to seek redress for personal or group injuries suffered from other alliance members before the body of the confederacy. The latter was the case within the Iroquois Confederacy of upstate New York.

**consensus**    Universal agreement. Indian political or social decisionmaking usually required that all interested groups agree to a proposition before it was binding. Majority rule was not sufficient for a decision, but rather all groups (bands, clans, lineages, villages, or triblets) had to agree, otherwise each group acted the way it thought proper or best.

**conservatives**    Members of an Indian nation who followed traditional ways of living, often claiming the native American way as preferred. Conservatives often represent a cultural and political segment of an Indian nation and usually live differently. They have political and cultural goals of preserving Indian culture and identity that other members of the nation might be willing to give up.

**constituencies** Groups of individuals, where each group forms a district for purposes of representation.

**constitution** The written form of a country's governing structure, which establishes the basic functions and division of powers between different levels of government, such as federal and provincial governments in Canada, or federal, state, and city governments in the United States. In the United States, the Constitution was adopted in 1789, but since then several amendments or changes have modified the original document. The Canadian constitution is set forth in the Constitution Act 1867, 1930, and 1982. *See* British North America Act.

**Contract Health Service (CHS)** The purchase of health care by the Indian Health Service (IHS) through contractual arrangements with hospitals, private physicians, and clinic groups, and dentists and providers of ancillary health services to supplement and complement other health care resources available to American Indians and Alaska Natives.

**Council on Energy Resource Tribes (CERT)** An organization formed by U.S. Indian tribes who have substantial marketable natural resources on their reservation lands. CERT provides its member tribes with expertise for marketing and managing their resources.

**Crown** The formal head of state, symbolized by the king or queen of England. In Canada, the Crown is divided between the federal government, "the Crown in right of Canada," and the provincial governments, as "the Crown in right of (name of province)."

**crown lands** Land under the sovereign ownership or protection of the Canadian federal government or the provincial governments. The treaties recognized the Indians' right to hunt and fish on "unoccupied Crown lands," which has been greatly diminished by privatization of land, designation of national parks or wilderness parks, or reservation by legislation (i.e., "occupied") by any purpose.

**cultural patrimony** Refers to any object having ongoing historical, traditional, or cultural importance central to the Native American group or culture itself, rather than property owned by an individual Native American. It therefore cannot be alienated, appropriated, or conveyed by any individual regardless of whether the individual is a member of the tribe. Any such object is considered inalienable, not for sale, by such Native American group at the time the object was separated from the group.

**culture** The nonbiological and socially transmitted system of concepts, institutions, behavior, and materials by which a society adapts to its effective natural and human environment.

**culture area** A device anthropologists have used to discuss large numbers of people in a contiguous geographical area. Generally, it is assumed that the various peoples in a culture area are similar in lifeways.

# D

**Dawes Act** *See* General Allotment Act of 1887.

**demography** The statistical study of populations, including migration, birth, death, health, and marriage data.

**dependence** (1) In nineteenth-century international law and federal Indian law, the relationship between a weak country and a strong country that agrees to protect it. In 1831, the Supreme Court labeled Indian tribes as "domestic nations," because the United States had agreed, by treaty, to protect them from others. (2) The situation by which Indians came to depend on trade of animal furs for European manufactured goods, especially metal goods like hoes, guns, and hatchets. Indians stopped producing their own stone tools and came to depend on trade to supply some necessary economic goods.

**diminutive** In linguistics, a grammatical construction conveying a meaning of smallness.

**discouraged workers** Unemployed workers who have abandoned their search for a new job.

**diuretic** An agent that increases the amount of urine.

**domestic dependent nation** The expression was used by U.S. Supreme Court Justice John Marshall in the case *Cherokee Nation v. Georgia* in 1831, which denied the Cherokee Nation, and all Indian nations, status as independent foreign nations. Instead, Justice Marshall described the relation of the Indian governments to the United States as more akin to "domestic dependent nations."

**Dorset culture** An Inuit (Eskimo) cultural tradition dated from 1000 B.C.E. to C.E. 1000. They were adapted to the harsh environments of the Canadian Arctic, relying heavily on fishing and hunting sea mammals.

# E

**Economic Opportunity Act of 1964**   A congressional act that provided funding to local Community Action Programs (C.A.P.) and authorized Indian tribes to designate themselves as C.A.P. agencies for the purposes of the act.

**economy**   The sphere of society in which individuals and the community organize to satisfy subsistence needs with production of food, clothing, shelter, and, in some societies, personal wealth.

**edema**   An abnormal accumulation of fluid in cells, tissues, or cavities of the body, resulting in swelling.

**egalitarianism**   The view that people are equal, especially politically or socially.

**EIR or EIS**   The first is an Environmental Impact Report and the second is an Environmental Impact Statement. The former is usually employed by states and local governments while the latter by the federal government.

**Encinitas tradition**   Archaeological remains of a group of cultures derived from Paleo-Indian ancestors. The Encinitas people depended heavily on fishing and collecting shellfish along the California coast. The Encinitas tradition dates from 5500 to 3000 B.C.E.

**encomienda**   A practice by which the Spanish king rewarded public service with grants of land and rights to demand work from the local population. Encomiendas were granted in the Southwest and throughout Latin and South America. Local Indians were forced to work for the landlords, who in turn tried to convert the Indians to Christianity.

**encroach**   The illegal and sometimes forcible entry of an individual or group on the land or property of another. For example, during much of the 1800s, Indian nations often complained that U.S. settlers established farms on Indian lands without permission and in violation of treaties with the U.S. government.

**enema**   A liquid injected into the colon through the anus, as a purgative or for medicinal purposes.

**enfranchisement**   In Canada's Indian Act, a process by which an aboriginal Canadian gives up legal status as an Indian and assumes all the rights of a citizen of Canada. Until 1960, this was the only procedure for a Canadian Indian to gain the right to vote or to purchase alcohol. Few native people chose enfranchisement because they would lose their treaty rights, they would have to accept their share of band trust funds, and they would surrender all rights to reserve lands or participation in band elections or community affairs.

**Equal Protection Clause**   Part of the Fourteenth Amendment to the U.S. Constitution, adopted in the wake of the Civil War, which requires the equal treatment of all citizens—except "Indians not taxed" (tribal Indians).

**ergative**   In linguistics, a grammatical construction in which the subjects of some verb forms are treated similarly to the objects of other verb forms.

**ethnography**   A descriptive account of a particular culture. Ethnographies generally discuss the economic, political, social, and religious life of a people.

**ethnopoetics**   The study of traditional oral literature, concerned with how linguistic features are used for artistic effect.

**etiology**   The causes of a specific disease.

**evidential**   In linguistics, a construction indicating the source of validity of the information in a sentence.

**exclusive**   In linguistics, referring to a first-person plural pronoun, which excludes the person spoken to, "I and someone else, but not you."

**extended family**   A family unit consisting of three or more generations.

**extinguished**   The act of giving up claims to land in exchange for compensation such as money, parcels of land, and goods and services.

**extradition**   The process by which a person who has escaped from the country where he or she is accused of a crime is demanded by and then returned forcibly to that country to stand trial. Extradition is usually governed by treaties between the countries concerned. There is no general principle in international law that requires governments to return fugitives.

# F

**family**   In linguistics, a group of languages clearly descended from a single "parent" language.

**Federal Acknowledgment Project (F.A.P.)** *See* Branch of Acknowledgment and Research. *See also* federal recognition.

**federal agency** Any department, agency, or instrumentality of the United States.

**federal lands** Any land, other than tribal lands, that are controlled or owned by the United States.

**federal recognition** Acknowledgment by the U.S. government of government-to-government relationships with certain Indian tribes. Federal recognition can be obtained by satisfying the criteria of the Federal Acknowledgment Process administered through the U.S. Department of the Interior, by federal statute enacted by Congress, or by court decree. *See* Federal Acknowledgement Process *and* federally recognized tribes.

**federally recognized tribes** Those Indian tribes with which the U.S. government maintains official relations, as established by treaty, executive order, or act of Congress.

**Federation of Saskatchewan Indian Nations (FSIN)** An association organized along with the Indian Association of Alberta in the 1940s, which has a mandate and objective to serve the political interest of the native bands with federal treaties within the province of Saskatchewan. *See* Indian Association of Alberta.

**fee-simple ownership** A form of individual ownership of property, usually land, where the owner has the sole right to sell the land to any buyers, and no other parties have significant claims to the land.

**fiduciary** A relationship founded in trust and responsibility for looking after the best interests of a group, organization, or committee.

**Fifth Amendment** Part of the Bill of Rights of the U.S. Constitution, which forbids any taking of "private property" without "due process of law" and compensation. Indian treaties and reservation lands are now recognized as being "property" within the meaning of this provision.

**First Ministers' Conference (FMC)** A recently developed Canadian political tradition, the FMC is a gathering of Canada's "first ministers"—the ten provincial premiers and the national prime minister. In the 1990s, leaders of the Canadian territories have been included on occasion along with aboriginal leaders. At first, FMCs were oriented toward specific issues and problems; however, increasingly the FMC is supplanting traditional parliamentary politics as the primary decision-making forum in Canada.

**first nations** A term that came into common usage in the 1970s to replace the word "Indian" which many people found offensive. The term distinguishes and gives recognition to Canada's Indian nations as the original peoples on the North American continent. Although the term First Nation is widely used, no legal definition of it exists. Among its uses, the term "First Nations peoples" refers to the Indian people in Canada, both status and non-status Indians and treaty Indians.

**Five Civilized Tribes** A name given to the Cherokee, Choctaw, Chickasaw, Creek, and Seminole tribes during the second half of the 1900s because they adopted democratic constitutional governments and schools.

**Folsom points** Ancient flaked and grooved pieces of flint that were used as spearheads by paleo-Indians, or Stone Age Indians, before 10,000 B.C.E.

**foraging economy** An economic system based on obtaining foods from naturally occurring sources, hunting, fishing, and gathering plants.

**Formative period** A term used to describe the period of early settlement of Indians into villages. In the Southwest, the settlement of villages, with some dependence on farming, occurred between C.E. 200 and 900.

**freedmen** Former slaves who were freed after the Civil War and by the Thirteenth Amendment to the U.S. Constitution. The Cherokee, Choctaw, Chickasaw, Creek, and Seminole all held slaves and, after the Civil War, in one way or another included their freedmen into their national institutions.

**fricative** In linguistics, a consonant produced by letting the air pass through the mouth with audible noise, as contrasted with a stop, when the air is abruptly held in the mouth.

# G

**General Allotment Act of 1887** A law that applied the principle of allotting in severalty tribal reservation lands to individual resident tribesmen. Generally, a tract of 160 acres for a head of household, 80 acres for single people, and 40 acres per child was received in trust status for a period of twenty-five years; thereafter, the allottee owned the land in fee simple. The General

Allotment Act was designed to divide Indian reservations into small, privately owned plots and release the surplus lands to U.S. settlers. Under the General Allotment Act, between 1887 and 1934, over 90 million acres of Indian land were sold to U.S. citizens. This law is often referred to as the Dawes Act, named for the law's principle author, U.S. Senator Henry Dawes of Massachusetts.

**General Revenue Sharing Program (1972–1986)** A federal program to share federal tax revenues with state and local governments in the United States, including states, counties, cities, towns, and Indian tribes and Alaska Native villages, "which perform substantial governmental functions."

**genetic relationship** In linguistics, the relationship between "sister" languages descended from a single parent language.

**Ghost Dance** Part of a largely religious movement in the 1870s and into the late 1880s and early 1890s. The movement hoped to restore the buffalo herds to the Plains and restore the old Indian Plains life. It was believed that many of the people lost in epidemics and warfare would be returned to life if certain ritual and religious precautions were observed. *See* the biography of Wovoka and information on the Great Basin and Plains in the 1870s to 1890s.

**glottal stop** In linguistics, a consonant produced by closing and opening the vocal cords, interrupting the flow of air.

**glottalization** In linguistics, a closure and re-opening of the vocal cords simultaneously with the production of a sound in the mouth.

**government-to-government relationship** The official relation between the U.S. federal government and the tribal governments of Indian tribes, which is defined by the mention of Indian tribes in the U.S. Constitution and through legal rulings. In this relation, the U.S. government recognizes inherent rights of Indian tribes to self-government and to the ownership of land.

**Great Basin** Elevated region covering a great deal of several western U.S. states (Nevada, eastern California, western Colorado, Utah, eastern Oregon, and western Wyoming), which contains no drainage for water outside the region. Consequently, water must drain toward the center, hence the name Great Basin.

**Great Society** Name given to domestic policy during the administration of President Lyndon B. Johnson (1963–1969), especially anti-poverty and social welfare measures.

# H

**habeas corpus** Literally, from Latin "you have the body." A claim presented to a court stating that a person is being held in custody or jail in violation of law. In Indian country, normally this writ of habeas corpus is available only to criminal defendants who have been convicted in tribal courts and who claim that their convictions were obtained without adherence to the Indian Civil Rights Act (for example, evidence was improperly seized or the criminal statute used as the basis for conviction violated rights of free speech).

**Haudenosaunee** The name of the people often called the Iroquois or Five Nations, or Six Nations after 1717. Literally, it means "The People of the Long House," referring to the extended multifamily houses in which the Iroquois lived.

**Health and Welfare Canada** The department of the Canadian federal government responsible for the health of all Canadians. It is divided into several branches; the Medical Services Branch serves the health needs of Inuit and Indians.

**health status** A measurement of the state of health of a given population, usually reported in numbers per 1,000 population and utilizing such indicators as morbidity, mortality, and infant death rates.

**heathens** Anyone of another religion with different fundamental views of religion. Indians were considered heathens by the early Catholic Spanish explorers and by the Puritans in New England. Indians considered Europeans also to have little understanding of religion or culture. For example, the Choctaw regarded early English traders as untutored and nonspiritual beings because they did not understand Choctaw religious views and did not practice correct religious rituals and social etiquette.

**hierarchical** Structured by class or rank.

**Home Guard Indians** In Canada, bands of Indians who lived near fur trade posts and had a relatively more intense trading relationship with traders than most Indian bands. Home Guard bands and traders exchanged various goods and services, and also tended to develop kinship ties.

**homestead**   With reference to the federal lands (public domain), a homestead is a parcel of land—usually 80 to 160 acres—acquired by an adult who had to develop a portion of the land and build a minimal home on the site. The Homestead Act of 1862 was the initial law that made homesteading possible on public lands.

**hunters**   Indians who depended on hunting, fishing, or gathering, as opposed to farming, for their food. Most aboriginal groups in Canada were hunting peoples.

# I

**IHS Service Population**   Those American Indians, Eskimos, and Aleuts (as identified by the census) who reside in the geographic areas in which the Indian Health Service (IHS) has responsibilities. These areas are the thirty-two reservation states (including California), and the geographic areas are defined as on or near reservations or within a contract health service delivery area (CHSDA).

**Immersion schools**   Canadian schools where the language used is different from the students' first language. For example, Indian children who spoke their native language were often sent to schools where only English was spoken. This was a method of getting them to speak English and learn Canadian culture.

**in situ**   "In place." A term applied to archaeological remains found in their original, undisturbed location or position.

**inalienable**   In linguistics, referring to a noun for which a possessor must always be specified, especially kin terms and body parts.

**inclusive**   In linguistics, referring to a first-person plural pronoun that includes the person spoken to, "I and you."

**incorporation**   In linguistics, refers to the object of a noun being part of a verb form.

**Indian**   (1) In Canada, according to the Indian Act first passed in 1876 and revised in 1985, a term that describes all the Aboriginal people in Canada who are not Inuit or Métis. Indian peoples are one of three groups of people recognized as Aboriginal in the *Constitution Act*, 1982. The act specifies that Aboriginal people in Canada consist of Indians, Inuit and Métis people. In addition, there are three legal definitions that apply to Indians in Canada: status Indians, non-status Indians and treaty Indians. (2) In the United States, any individual who self-identifies as an American Indian or Alaska Native and who is determined by his tribe to be a fully enrolled tribal member.

**Indian Act**   In Canada, the overriding legislation that sets forth the policies of the federal government towards native people. This legislation passed by the Canadian government defines the legal status of Indians. First passed by the Canadian Parliament in 1876, the act was revised in 1951 and subsequently amended in 1985. Essentially, the Indian Act had four major objectives. First, it defined status Indians. Second, it established the reserve system. Third, it created legal entities known as bands with governments to administer reserve communities. And fourth, it created a national administrative structure, now known as Indian and Northern Affairs Canada, to administer the act. Under the Indian Act, the head of this administrative structure holds ministerial and trust responsibility for "status Indians" recognized by the Canadian federal government. The minister's responsibilities include managing certain monies belonging to First Nations and Indian lands, and approving or disallowing First Nations by-laws. *See* band, band council, British North America Act, *and* status Indians.

**Indian agents**   In Canada, government agents appointed to Indian regions to increase contact between the Crown and Indian nations. Their presence marked the replacement of traditional Indian governments by elected governments, largely controlled by these agents.

**Indian and Northern Affairs Canada (INAC)**   The Canadian government department (formerly known as the Department of Indian Affairs and Northern Development) that administers the *Indian Act* and delivers authorized federal funds and programs, often through provincial governments, to those Aboriginal people who qualify to receive them.

**Indian Association of Alberta (IAA).**   Officially incorporated in 1944, IAA serves as an organization representing the political interests of the treaty Indians of the province of Alberta. The IAA promotes unity and spiritual strength of Indian nations in the protection of their lands, rights, and cultures. The organization receives its mandates from the chiefs, councillors, and members of the Alberta first nations, the member native bands of Alberta.

**Indian country**   Land where Indian government and custom rule. In more recent times, Indian country refers to Indian reservations where Indian tribal governments are regulated by federal law and the Bureau of Indian Affairs.

**Indian Delegation Act of 1946 (Public Law 687)** A congressional act that authorized substantial delegations of formal authority from the secretary of the interior to the commissioner of Indian affairs and from the commissioner to his subordinates, the twelve area directors who work on a day-to-day basis with local BIA agency offices and tribal governments on Indian reservations.

**Indian Education Act (1972)** A congressional act that provided education financial assistance to communities with Indian students in their schools.

**Indian Health Care Improvement Act (Public Law 94–437)** Through a program of increased funding levels in the Indian Health Service budget, the act was intended to improve the health status of American Indians and Alaska Natives up to a level equal to the general U.S. population. Funding was directed to urban populations and funds were used to expand health services, and build and renovate medical and sanitation facilities. It also established programs designed to increase the number of Indian health professionals and to improve care access for Indian people living in urban areas.

**Indian Health Service (IHS)** The seventh agency within the U.S. Public Health Service, this federal agency's mission is to upgrade the health status of American Indians to the highest level possible. The IHS is composed of eleven regional administrative units called area offices. Within these units, the IHS operates 45 hospitals, 65 health centers, 6 school health centers, and 201 other treatment programs. In 1987, the state of California was designated an area office, the latest addition to the IHS. There are no IHS facilities in California, only Indian-operated and -managed clinics.

**Indian New Deal** Legislation enacted in the early 1930s during the Roosevelt administration promoting tribal government and economic recovery programs for reservations.

**Indian Removal** The United States government policy, beginning in the 1820s and lasting through the 1850s, of moving all Indian tribes west of the Mississippi River, to make room for U.S. settlement of the lands in the east. By 1860, this policy resulted in the removal of most eastern Indian nations to locations in present-day Kansas and Oklahoma.

**Indian Reorganization Act of 1934 (IRA)** A congressional act providing reservation communities the opportunity to re-organize their tribal governments and adopt a new tribal constitution and tribal charter, and

organize tribal business corporations. It also provided a revolving loan fund and other support services to participating tribes.

**Indian Self-Determination and Education Assistance Act of 1975 (Public Law 93–638)** This act enabled tribes to contract, at their own option, to provide any service currently being provided by either the Bureau of Indian Affairs or the Indian Health Service. If the tribes change their policies about contracting government services, they have the right to return the administration of a contracted service to the relevant federal agency. The Self-Determination Act was designed to give Indian tribes and organizations more direct control over federal programs that operated within reservation communities.

**Indian status** In Canada, an individual's legal status as an Indian, as defined by the *Indian Act*.

**Indian Territory** The area west of the Mississippi River, primarily present-day Kansas and Oklahoma, to which the United States once planned to move all of the eastern Indians. Indian Territory was the home of nearly one-third of all U.S. Indians in 1880. Parts of Indian Territory were opened to U.S. settlers, over Indian objections, in 1889. By 1907, the last remnants of Indian Territory were admitted to the Union as the state of Oklahoma, as non-Indians had become an overwhelming majority of the population.

**Indian tribe** Any tribe, band, nation, or other organized group or community of Indians recognized as being eligible for special programs and services provided by the United States because of its status. *See* federally recognized tribes.

**indigenous** Native to the area.

**industry** A term used in a classification system of economic activity in which firms that produce similar goods or services are grouped together into distinct categories.

**infant death rate** A ratio of infant deaths within the first year of life to the total live births in a particular time period, usually five or ten years.

**injunction** A court order prohibiting a person or legal entity from carrying out a given action, or ordering a person or organization to carry out a specific task. For example, in 1832, the U.S. Supreme Court in the case *Worcester v. Georgia* ruled that the Georgia government had no legal right to abolish the Cherokee government, which had its capital in territory claimed by Georgia. The Court, however, did not issue an injunction to the state of Georgia to prohibit it from extending its laws over the Cherokee nation.

**inpatient**    A patient admitted to a bed in a hospital to have treatment and stay overnight at least one night.

**intransitive**    In linguistics, characterizing verbs that have subjects but not direct objects, opposite of transitive.

**Inuit**    Formerly known as Eskimos, Inuit are members of one of several peoples who traditionally inhabited areas north of the treeline in northern Alaska, northern Canada, and Greenland. They all speak dialects of the same language. In Canada, Inuit have the same legal status as Indians. The word Inuit means *people* in the Inuit language– Inuktitut. The singular of Inuit is Inuk. Forming a majority in the new Canadian territory of Nunavut, they are in effect self-governing since the turn of the twenty-first century.

**Inuk**    The singular of Inuit.

**Iroquoian**    Indian peoples who speak an Iroquoian language, such as the Huron, Mohawk, and Onondaga.

**Iroquoian League**    The Iroquois Confederacy, an alliance of government and cultural and legal unity, which was formed before European colonization by the Mohawk, Cayuga, Onondaga, Oneida, and Seneca nations of present-day upstate New York. Also called the Five Nations and, after being joined by the Tuscarora in the early 1700s, the Six Nations.

**isolate (language isolate)**    A language without close historical relationships to other languages.

## J

**Jim Crow Legislation**    After 1890, laws passed by many southern states designed to segregate the U.S. population by race. Many native people were automatically classified as black.

**Johnson-O'Malley Act of 1934**    Permitted the Indian Office to contract with the states to provide education, health, and welfare services to Indians on reservations within their borders. For example, the act allowed Indian children to attend public schools at the expense of the Indian Office.

**jurisdiction**    The empowerment of a governing body to oversee regulations and laws within an assigned area. The extent of legal power of a government, legislature, or of a court over its people and territory. Jurisdiction is defined in terms of persons, subject matter, and geography. For example, Alabama courts have jurisdiction in cases involving people, property, or activities only in the state of Alabama.

## K

**Kachina**    A deity or group of benevolent spirit beings among the Pueblo.

**kiva**    Among the Pueblo cultures, an underground ceremonial chamber formed in the shape of a circle. A cycle of often-secret annual rituals takes place in the kivas. Leaders gather in the kivas to discuss religious and other important issues concerning the pueblo community.

## L

**labiovelar**    In linguistics, characterizing consonants produced with the rear part of the tongue, with simultaneous rounding of the lips.

**labor force participation**    An individual who is working or looking for work is considered to be participating in the labor force. Anyone who does not have a job and is not looking for work is not in the labor force.

**land cession treaty**    A treaty in which a group of people surrender certain rights to land in exchange for other rights, usually hunting rights or an annual payment.

**land claim, comprehensive**    In the 1970s, the Canadian government agreed to negotiate comprehensive land claims with aboriginal groups whose ancestors had not ceded their land rights by signing a land surrender treaty. Claims negotiations involve a lengthy process, which, when successful, leads to cash settlements, land title, and devolution of authority. When settled, comprehensive claims agreements acquire the constitutional status of treaties.

**land claim, specific**    Specific land claims are made against the Canadian state where it is argued that treaty commitments have not been met. The meaning of treaty rights themselves has expanded considerably over the years, allowing ever more specific claims to be made on treaty grounds. But usually specific land claims refer to as-yet unallocated lands.

**land tenure**   Land tenure has to do with how land is held—by communities, tribes, nations, individuals—and how it functions in terms of utilization, devisement, etc. In Indian affairs, land tenure is basically dichotomous; tribal and individual (allotment), but reservations may include non-Indian allotments, federal public lands, and even state lands.

**language area**   A geographical region in which languages of different families have become similar due to borrowing.

**law**   A measure or set of rules passed by a governing body to regulate the actions of the people in the interest of the majority of the nation.

**legend**   A folktale that deals with the experiences of individuals or happenings of a distant past.

**libertarian**   A person who places great value on individual consent and personal freedom.

**life expectancy**   The average number of years remaining to a person at a particular age, based on a given set of age-specific death rates, generally the mortality (death rate) conditions existing in the period mentioned.

**line**   A unit in the structure of a literary composition, defined in terms of its parallelism of structure with an adjacent line.

**lineage**   A group of people who can trace actual descent from a common ancestor.

**lingua franca (trade language)**   A mixed language used for communication between people of different native languages.

**linguistics**   The study of language. Usually the sounds, structure, and meaning of a language are analyzed and compared with other languages.

**litigation**   The use of courts or a legal process to achieve an end or contest an issue. For example, when in the early 1830s, the state of Georgia extended its laws over the Cherokee nation, the Cherokee appealed to the U.S. Supreme Court to resolve their differences with the Georgians.

**location ticket**   In Canada, the right granted by the government to an Indian to use part of reserve land as if it were private property. Location tickets were part of the Canadian government's attempts to encourage Indians to accept private property rather than hold land in common.

**Long Walk**   The 300-mile forced walk in 1864 from the Navajo's home in the west to an assigned reservation, Bosque Redondo, near Fort Sumner, 180 miles southeast of Santa Fe, New Mexico. During the 1970s and early 1980s, several long walks by Indians traveling across the country were organized to protest treaty and Native issues. Often the long walks started at Alcatraz Island, or on the West coast, and ended in Washington, D.C. In 1972, one such long walk ended in the pillaging of the BIA offices in Washington D.C. Sacred runs continue to be organized.

**longhouse**   In the Northwest Coast, a longhouse is a dwelling in which several nuclear families share the structure. Usually, the families are related to one another. The Iroquois or Six Nations of upstate New York also had a similar tradition of living in longhouses with related extended families.

**loyalists**   An expression used during the Revolutionary War (1775–83) for persons who chose the side of the British and attempted to help the British cause.

# M

**Magna Carta**   An agreement of fundamental rights, also known as the Great Charter of England, signed in 1215 C.E. by King John and his English noblemen. Many of our modern ideas on government and democracy have developed from this fundamental constitutional document, empowering freedom and justice. *See* Proclamation of 1763.

**maize**   Also known as corn, an important crop plant, initially domesticated in Mexico over six thousand years ago.

**Manifest Destiny**   During the 1900s, a broadly held belief among the U.S. population that it was inevitable that the U.S. nation would expand across the North American continent from the Atlantic to the Pacific Ocean. Belief in Manifest Destiny served as a rationalization for the seizure of Indian land, and, in 1846, to justify war with Mexico, which led to the annexation of Texas, New Mexico, Arizona, and California.

**materialism**   The belief that economic well-being or wealth are of central human concern, while spiritual or cultural understandings or comforts are of secondary concern or relatively meaningless.

**Matrilineal descent**   A kinship system in which relationships are traced through women. Children belong to their mother's kin group. Inheritance of names, wealth, or other property transfer through the mother's family and/or clan.

**matrilocal residence**    A pattern of residence where a married couple lives with or near the wife's family.

**Medical Services Branch (MSB)**    The branch of the Department of National Health and Welfare of the Canadian federal government responsible for Indian and Inuit health.

**Medicine Chest Clause**    A clause in Treaty No. 6 (1876) between the Canadian government and the Indian tribes in Northern Alberta on which is based the claim that Indian people in Canada have a perpetual right to free health care provided by the Canadian federal government.

**mega-fauna**    The large animals, such as woolly mammoth, ground sloth, and saber-toothed tiger, which died off about 8,000 B.C.E. after the last glacier receded far north.

**Meriam Report of 1928**    An exhaustive investigation of Indian administration and a major criticism of Indian policies and administration since passage of the General Allotment Act of 1887. The report had a major influence on Indian affairs during the administrations of Presidents Herbert Hoover (1929–1933) and Franklin D. Roosevelt (1933–1945). It helped formulate the policies of the Indian New Deal, which originated with passage of the Indian Reorganization Act of 1934, and allowed Indians greater self-government and the right to retain cultural ceremonies and events. Produced by the Brookings Institution's Institute for Government Research, the actual title of the report is *The Problem of Indian Administration.*

**mescaline**    A white, crystalline alkaloid, psychedelic drug obtained from the cactus *Lophophora williamsi* (peyote).

**metate**    A stone with a slightly hollow center that is used for grinding corn.

**Métis**    French for "mixed-blood." This term has been used in several different ways. Usually it refers to mixed-blood people in western Canada who are conscious of belonging to a distinct community. The Canadian Constitution recognizes Métis as aboriginal peoples. The term is also used to refer to any person of mixed Indian-European descent, and more specifically to a descendant of a native parent, usually Cree or Ojibway, and a non-native parent, usually French, but also some English, who settled in the Red River area of

what is now the province of Manitoba during the days of the fur trade, which lasted from the 1700s to the late 1800s.

**Mississippian period**    The period between C.E. 900 and 1500 when in the eastern United States there arose complex chiefdom societies and maize-farming communities. The Mississippian tradition is associated with the building of flat-topped earthen mounds, which were religious and political centers. Many of the Mississippian towns, sometimes holding as many as thirty thousand people, were fortified with palisades. One of the largest Mississippian societies was located at Cahokia, near present-day St. Louis, Missouri.

**moiety**    A French expression which means divided into two halves. For anthropologists, the term refers to a society divided into two major clusters of clans. For example, among the Tlingit, there are Eagle and Raven moieties, which divide the society into two groups of about twenty-five clans. Among the Tlingit, moiety relations govern marriage rules, since Raven moiety members must marry an Eagle and vice-versa.

**morphology**    In linguistics, the formation of words by combinations of stems, prefixes, and suffixes, as contrasted with syntax.

**mortality**    The proportion of deaths to population.

**moxa**    A soft, downy material, burned on the skin as a cauterizing agent or counter-irritant.

**Muskogean**    A family of related languages spoken by many Indian nations of the southeast including the Choctaw, Chickasaw, Creek, Seminole, and Natchez.

**myth**    A narrative tale concerned with the Creator, spirits, and the nature and meaning of the universe and humans.

# N

**Nation**    A community of people who share the right to political self-rule, and/or who share a common identity, and who usually share a similar culture, the same language, the same economy, and a mutually recognized territory.

**National Indian Brotherhood (NIB)**    Founded in 1968, a Canadian national Indian political organization. The NIB now serves as the legal executive office for the Assembly of First Nations. *See* Assembly of First Nations.

**Native American**     Of or relating to a tribe, people, or culture indigenous to the United States.

**need**     An estimate of the amount of medical care required to provide adequate services to a population in terms of the amount of disease present or preventable, often contrasted to demand.

**New Deal**     Name given to domestic policy during the administration of President Franklin D. Roosevelt (1933–1945).

**New Frontier**     Name given to domestic policy during the administration of President John F. Kennedy (1961–1963).

**non-IHS-service population**     Those Indians who do not reside in the geographic areas in which Indian Health Service has responsibility.

**non-recognized tribe**     Indian communities that do not have official government-to-government relations with the U.S. government because they did not sign a treaty with the United States, lost their recognized status by termination, or have no executive orders or agreements that require the U.S. government to provide services or to protect their land and resources in a trust relationship.

**non-status Indians**     People in Canada who consider themselves to be Indians but whom the Canadian government does not recognize as Indians under the Indian Act because they have failed to establish or have lost or abandoned their Indian status rights.

**non-treaty Indians**     Canadian Indian people whose relationship with the government is not affected by any treaties. Non-treaty Indians can be either status or non-status Indians.

**Northwest Passage**     As late as the 1790s, Europeans believed there was a short ocean passage in the northern latitudes connecting the Atlantic and Pacific Oceans. Many of the earliest European explorations in northern North America were prompted by this myth.

**Northwest Territories (NWT)**     Today this term refers to the western central portion of Canadian territory (capital city, Yellowknife) north of the 60th parallel. The territory of Nunavut was formed in 1999 from the province of Northwest Territories as constituted at that time. Originally (1870), the Northwest Territories referred to most of Canada west of Ontario except

British Columbia, including present-day Alberta and Saskatchewan and most of Manitoba.

**numeral classifier**     In linguistics, a grammatical element used in counting, indicating the form or shape of the objects counted.

**Nunavut**     As of 1 April 1999, a new territory (previously part of the Northwest Territories), which covers the majority of Canada north of the tree line. Inuit are the majority of the region's population. The establishment of Nunavut was part an aboriginal land claim.

# O

**occupation**     A term used in a classification system of economic activity in which jobs that require similar activities are grouped together into distinct categories.

**Oklahoma "Runs"**     Spectacular one-day chances to legally acquire former Indian land in present-day Oklahoma. Most of the "runs" occurred in the 1890s.

**"On or near"**     The federal regulation that Contract Health Service can be provided only to American Indians residing on a reservation or in a county that borders a reservation.

**Oolichan (Eulachon)**     A small fish (*Thaleichthys pacificus*) captured in freshwater streams by the Northwest Coast people. Oolichan were especially important as a source of oil.

**oral history**     A historical research method that investigates the past by speaking to people rather than relying on the written word.

**outpatient**     A patient who receives diagnosis or treatment in a clinic or dispensary connected with a hospital but is not admitted as a bed patient. (Sometimes used as a synonym for ambulatory.)

# P

**Paleo-Arctic tradition**     A term used to describe the tools left behind by the first Native Americans, who lived in the arctic regions of Alaska and Canada. The Paleo-arctic tradition began between 9000 and 8000 B.C.E. and continued as late as 5000 B.C.E.

**paleo-Indians**     The ancestors of contemporary Native Americans and the first people to come to North America over fourteen thousand years ago.

**Paleo-Plateau tradition** A term used to describe the various Archaic period cultures of the Columbia-Fraser Plateau of Washington state and British Columbia. The Paleo-Plateau tradition lasted from 8,000 to 3,000 B.C.E.

**Papal Bull** A decree made by a Catholic Pope. Bulls used to have the force of law within the Roman Catholic Church, but today are considered to be statements of policy only.

**patriarchy** A social system in which men have exclusive control over power and wealth in the society.

**patrilineal descent** A kinship system in which relationships are traced through men. Children belong to their father's kin group.

**patrilocal residence** A pattern of residence where a married couple lives with or near the husband's family.

**patronage** Providing jobs in exchange for political services. For example, before 1890 most jobs with the U.S. Indian administration were jobs gained through patronage relations with congressmen and other high government officials.

**Penner Report** A report prepared in 1983 by a special committee of the House of Commons on Indian self-government in Canada. The report is named after committee chairman, Keith Penner, a member of Parliament for the Liberal party.

**per capita** A Latin term meaning by or for each person, equally to each individual. It is one way used for distributing funds to every adult member of a tribe.

**peyote** A bitter stimulant obtained from the button-like structures of the mescal cactus plant, which some Indian groups use as part of their religious practices. The peyote buttons are taken during ceremonies of the Native American Church, which was officially established in 1918, but began on the Plains as early as the 1860s.

**phoneme** In linguistics, one of the set of contrasting sound units in a language.

**phylum** Plural phyla. In linguistics, a group of language families hypothesized to be descended from a single parent language.

**pictograph** A simplified pictorial representation of an historical occurrence.

**Piedmont** A region in the southeast United States marked by rolling hills and open valleys located between the relatively flat coastal plain and the more rugged Appalachian Mountains.

**Pinto Basin tradition** A term describing a series of archaeological hunting and gathering cultures from the Great Basin, dating over the period of 5000 to 1500 B.C.E.

**plenary power** The exclusive authority of Congress (as opposed to the states of the Union) to make laws concerning Indian tribes. This special power can be traced to Article I, Section 8 (the "Indian Commerce Clause") of the Constitution. Plenary means full or complete.

**policy** A statement that outlines the means and philosophy by which a group or government will try to fulfill one or more of its major goals or interests.

**polyandry** A marriage involving one woman and two or more men.

**polygamy** Having more than one spouse at the same time.

**polygyny** A marriage involving one man and two or more women.

**polysynthetic language** In linguistics, a type of language marked by long word forms with complex morphologies, which may often function as complete sentences.

**potlatch** A feast in recognition of important life events, e.g., birth, death, marriage. The giving of a potlatch conferred value, prestige, and honor to all those involved. During a potlatch, or "giveaway," the hosts gave food, clothes, songs, and culturally significant gifts, such as copper engraved valuables, to the guests. The potlatch ceremony was practiced by tribes in the Pacific Northwest. "Giveaways" are similar events held in other regions of North America.

**poultice** A hot, soft, moist mass, as of flour, herbs, mustard, etc., sometimes spread on cloth, applied to a sore or inflamed part of the body.

**preemption** The power of the federal government to override state law in fields such as Indian affairs. This power comes from Article VI, Section 2 of the U.S. Constitution (the "Supremacy Clause"), which says federal laws and treaties are "the supreme Law of the Land."

**presidio**   Spanish military post in the American Southwest.

**Privy Council (Judicial Committee of the Privy Council)**   In the British Empire, the Privy Council in London was the final court of appeal from the colonial governors and courts. It was a committee of Peers (titled noblemen) chosen by the Crown (the reigning King or Queen). Until 1949, the Privy Council, in London, England, was the highest court of appeal in Canada and was therefore somewhat analogous to the U.S. Supreme Court.

**Proclamation of 1763**   The document signed by King George III issued as a declaration of policy by the British government to address the unauthorized settlement of Indian land. The Proclamation was never fully implemented, in part due to the outbreak of the American Revolution. The commitments contained within were, however, often renewed to obtain alliances with most Indian nations in fighting against the rebels. In areas that later became part of the United States, the policy reserved the land west of the Appalachian Mountains for Indian use, and restricted English settlements to land east of the divide, or central ridge, of the Appalachians. In Canada, the Proclamation provides the basis of English recognition of Indian rights to use and live on their territory, but only at the pleasure of the British Crown, which by this act claimed ownership of all Indian lands. It remains part of the Canadian Constitution.

**proto-language**   The prehistoric parent language from which several historical languages are descended.

**Public Law 280 (1953) 67 Stat. 588**   A congressional act that transferred criminal and civil jurisdiction in Indian country from the federal government to the states of California, Minnesota, Nebraska, Oregon, and Wisconsin (and after 1959 to Alaska). Other states were given the option to assume jurisdiction by legislation. In 1968, P.L. 280 was amended to require tribal consent to the transfer of jurisdiction.

**pueblo**   A Spanish word for the multi-storied stone or adobe Indian villages of the American Southwest. Also a name used for the Indians who inhabited such communal buildings.

## R

**radiocarbon dating**   A technique that measures the natural radioactive content of organic materials, such as charcoal, in order to measure the approximate age of the materials or objects found in archaeological sites.

**rancheria**   A Spanish word applied to the numerous, small Indian reservations of California.

**range condition**   The annual health of browsable vegetation that supports domesticated animals—e.g., cattle, sheep, etc. The determination of a range condition will decide how many head will be permitted to graze given areas in a given year or season.

**ratification**   The confirmation of a treaty by the national legislature—in the United States, by the Senate. In most countries, a treaty must be ratified before it becomes law.

**recognized**   *See* federally recognized, state recognized, *and* nonrecognized tribes.

**recognized & original title**   Recognized title lands refer to those ceded by treaties or statutes and original title lands are those that have had to be reconstructed on the basis of ethnographic and historic research, including information provided by Indian informants.

**red power**   A term applied to an Indian social movement and a series of protest activities during the 1960s and 1970s.

**reduplication**   In linguistics, repetition of part of a stem, often used to indicate plurality or habitual action.

**referenda**   Referring measures passed upon or proposed by the legislature to the voters for approval or rejection. In some states a referenda can be placed on the ballot by petition of registered voters.

**registered Indians**   *See* status Indians.

**relocation**   In 1951, the federal government established the Direct Employment Assistance program to encourage reservation Indians to move to urban areas such as Los Angeles, Chicago, Minneapolis, and Denver. This and subsequent programs came to be known as "relocation" programs.

**Removal Act**   A congressional act passed in 1830 which authorized and funded the peaceful exchange of lands and removal of Indians to Indian Territory, west of the Mississippi River.

**repatriation**   Through court cases and legislative lobbying, tribes have demanded the return of museum-

and university-held skeletal remains of Indians and funerary objects for reburial or other appropriate disposition.

**reservation/rancheria** Lands set aside by U.S. government authority for use and occupation by a group of Indians.

**reservation state** An area within which the Indian Health Service has responsibilities for providing health care to American Indians or Alaska Natives.

**reserve** In Canada, land set aside for specific Indian bands. "Indian reserve lands" as defined by the Indian Act. Essentially the same meaning as the U.S. term "reservation." In Canada, legal title is held in trust by the federal Crown in the right of Canada and may not be leased or sold until "surrendered" to the Crown by a referendum by band members.

**reserved-rights doctrine** A legal theory that Indian communities and governments maintain all rights to self-government, exercise of cultural rights, religious freedom, land, water, and other resources, unless Congress expressly takes those rights away.

**residential schools** Schools administered by the Canadian government and religious organizations that housed and educated many Indian and Inuit children in the 19th and 20th centuries. The use of such schools was intended to achieve the goal of complete assimilation of Indians into Canadian society by way of isolating children from their families and communities. Many instances of physical and sexual abuse took place at such schools and the Canadian government as well as the churches involved are facing lawsuits as a result.

**residual resource** The final or remaining course of action for patients seeking medical care from a provider.

**restitution** Transfer of property or payment of money to prevent an unjust loss from the acts of another.

**retrocession** A bureaucratic procedure of the Bureau of Indian Affairs that allows Indian communities within Public Law 280 states (California, Alaska, Wisconsin, Oregon, Nebraska, and Minnesota) to petition the federal government to bar state government regulation of courts and law enforcement on the reservation.

**revitalization** A social movement carried out by a group, usually in response to major changes in its society, such as pressures to assimilate. Revitalization attempts to create new culture with beliefs, values, and attitudes that blend some aspects of the old culture with the new living conditions.

**Robinson Superior Treaty of 1850** On 7 September 1850, at Sault Ste. Marie, Ontario, the Honorable William B. Robinson of Toronto, Ontario, acting on behalf of the British Crown, met with three chiefs and five principal men representing Michipicoten, Fort William, and Gull River bands of Ojibwa Indians to sign a document referred to as the Robinson Superior Treaty, the first modern Indian treaty in Canada.

According to the treaty, the Ojibwa people surrendered considerable land, and were paid two thousand pounds in English money and allotted three reserves. A similar agreement, referred to as the Robinson Huron Treaty of 1850, removed Indian land claims from the north shore of Lake Huron.

**Rose Spring phase** A term given by archaeologists to a time period (1500 B.C.E. to C.E. 500) when hunter and gatherer cultures occupied the region of the Owens Valley of present-day eastern California.

**Royal Commission on Aboriginal Peoples** This Commission was appointed in 1991 by the federal government of Prime Minister Brian Mulroney "to examine the economic, social and cultural situation of the Aboriginal Peoples of Canada." Seven commissioners visited 96 communities, held 178 days of hearings, heard briefs from 2,067 people and accumulated more than 76,000 pages of testimony. The five-volume report constitutes the most in-depth analysis ever undertaken on Aboriginal people in Canada. Highly controversial due to its recommendations and its cost, the current government has yet to implement any of its proposals.

**royal prerogative** The rights and privileges of a sovereign over subjects independent of both statutes and the courts.

**rural Indian** An Indian residing in a non-urban area, generally on or near a reservation.

# S

**sacred objects** Specific ceremonial objects needed by Native American religious leaders for the practice of traditional Native American religions.

**San Dieguito tradition** A distinctive artifact tradition known from present-day California and Nevada and dating to about 8000 to 6000 B.C.E. The tools of the

San Dieguito people show a heavy reliance on hunting, but with some evidence of gathering of wild plants.

**scrip**   A document given to Métis people during the late nineteenth century in order to extinguish aboriginal title. Scrip could be exchanged for money or land.

**secular**   A word referring to the mundane or ordinary and nonreligious aspects or times of everyday life.

**sedentary**   A term that refers to permanent settlement, where the people usually engage in farming for a livelihood and, for the most part, have abandoned hunting or nomadic herding as the mainstay of their economy.

**self-determination**   Indians exercising their right to govern and make decisions affecting their own lives and affairs on their own land. In international law, the right of every "people" to choose its own form of government and control its own future. Since the 1970s, Congress has used this word to describe programs designed to give Indian tribes greater control over the schools, health facilities, and social services on reservations. *See* Indian Self-Determination and Education Assistance Act.

**seminars**   Roman Catholic schools that teach religion and other subjects.

**settlement acts**   The term refers to laws enacted by Congress that finally end conflict and litigation over designated tribal land claims. Many of these acts carry the term within their title—e.g., The Saddleback Mountain Settlement Act of 1995.

**severance tax**   A tax assessed by a government on mining or petroleum companies when they remove minerals or natural resources from the ground.

**Shaker Religion**   A religious movement that began with the prophet John Slocum, whose death and rebirth in the 1880s started a movement among the native people of Puget Sound. The movement combined many elements of traditional Coast Salish religion with Christianity. It soon spread through the northwest United States.

**shaman/shamanism**   An individual versed in supernatural matters who performed in rituals and was expected to cure the sick, envision the future, and help with hunting and other economic activities. Often, a shaman is a healer who uses spiritual encounters or contacts to enact a cure on the patient. Many shamans deal with ailments that are spiritual rather than physical.

**Siouan**   A large language family that includes Siouan-related languages such as Lakota, Nakota, Dakota, and Crow.

**site**   In archaeology, a location of past cultural activity of defined space with more or less continuous archaeological evidence.

**smallpox**   A highly contagious disease which left survivors with badly scarred skin. Native Americans often died by the thousands because their ancestors had not developed resistance to the infection, which was introduced to North America by Europeans.

**smoke shop**   An Indian-owned store on a reservation that sells cigarettes at a relatively cheap price because state sales tax need not be included.

**Snyder Act of 1921**   Provided permanent funding authorization for "the general support and civilization of the Indians." To carry out these objectives, the act authorized the Indian Office to provide educational, health, and welfare services to Indian people, to irrigate and make other improvements on Indian lands, and to employ personnel to support these objectives. The Snyder Act signaled a change toward a permanent Indian-federal government relationship.

**socialize**   A process by which an individual learns to adjust to the group by acquiring social behaviors of which the group approves.

**Sooner**   Frontiersmen who illegally squatted on Indian land before the U.S. government had extinguished Indian land claims and title.

**sovereignty**   Deriving from *sovereign*, which means a ruler or king. In international law, being completely independent and not subject to any other ruler or government. The inherent right of a nation to exercise complete and absolute governance over its people and its affairs. In U.S. federal Indian law, sovereignty means having a distinct, but not completely independent government.

**specific claim**   According to Canadian government land claims policy since 1973, an aboriginal claim based on rights set out in treaties, Indian acts, or other legislation.

**Spirit Dance**   In the Northwest Coast, a song and dance performed by an individual who has had a guardian spirit encounter. The Spirit Dances are held in the winter months.

**squatter**   A person who occupies land without having title to it.

**state-recognized tribes**   Those Indian communities whose governments and land are officially recognized by their surrounding state government, but are not usually recognized by the federal government as an Indian reservation.

**status Indians**   In Canada, if a person meets the definitional requirements of the Indian Act, they are entitled to be registered on the Indian Register (or Band Membership List) kept by Indian and Northern Affairs Canada in Ottawa. The guidelines for determining status are complex. The criteria is legal rather than based on racial characteristics or blood quantum. All treaty Indians are status Indians, but not all status Indians are treaty Indians. In 1985, Parliament passed an amendment to the Indian Act that allows each native band to adopt its own rules for determining band membership. Many of the new band codes for determining Indian status vary among themselves and with the old rules of the Indian Act.

**statute**   A law enacted by the highest legislature in the nation or state.

**statutory**   Refers to those provisions enacted by law by a legislative body.

**stop**   In linguistics, a consonant produced by shutting off the flow of air momentarily.

**Strait of Georgia tradition**   An archaeological cultural tradition from the western coastal area of Canada believed to be ancestral to the Coast Salish and other present-day Native American groups of the area. The Strait of Georgia tradition dated from 3,000 to 200 B.C.E.

**subsistence**   A term that describes a small and localized economy oriented to the production of goods and services primarily for household use, and bound by rules of kinship, sharing, and reciprocity.

**sui generis**   So unique that it constitutes a class of its own. A term that is used to explain the status of aboriginal title in Canada. It is unique and is therefore inalienable to anyone but the Crown.

**Sun Dance**   An annual world renewal and purification ceremony performed with some variation among many of the northern Plains Indian nations such as the Cheyenne and the Sioux. One striking aspect of the ceremony was the personal sacrifice that some men made by self-torture in order to gain a vision that might provide spiritual insight and knowledge beneficial to the community.

**sweat lodge**   A sacred Indian ceremony involving construction of a lodge made of willow saplings bent to form a dome and covered with animal skins, blankets or canvas tarp. A hole is dug in the middle of the lodge in which hot rocks are placed and water poured over them, often by a medicine man, in a ceremonial way often accompanied by praying and singing. The ceremony can have many purposes including spiritual cleansing and healing.

**sweetgrass ceremony**   A ceremony in which braided sweetgrass is burned and participants "smudge" themselves with the smoke, similar to incense in other religions.

**syllabary**   A type of writing system in which the basic unit represents a sequence of consonant plus vowel, constituting a syllable. In comparison, alphabets have either a consonant, a letter, or a vowel (in English— a, e, i, o, u), which compose the basic unit of the writing system, as in English or Latin. The famous Cherokee writing system invented by Sequoia is a syllabary and not an alphabet.

**syncretic movements**   A religious belief system that combines symbols and beliefs from two or more religions. In native North America, there are many native religions that combine elements of traditional religion with Christianity. Some such Indian religious movements are the Delaware Prophet movement of the early 1760s, the Handsome Lake movement beginning in 1799, the Ghost Dances of the 1870s and early 1890s, the ongoing Shaker movement of the Pacific Northwest, and the Native American Church or Peyote cult.

**syntax**   In linguistics, the combination of words into sentences, as contrasted with morphology, the formation of words by combinations of stems, prefixes, and suffixes.

# T

**termination**   The policy of Congress in the 1950s and 1960s to withdraw federal trust status from Indian bands, communities and tribes. Those tribes that were "terminated" by an act of Congress no longer functioned as governments that made their own laws, but instead were placed under state laws.

**theocracy**    A government or society led by religious leaders.

**Thule tradition**    The archaeological culture, dated from C.E. 100 to 1500 and later, defined as the direct ancestral culture of the present-day Inuit throughout the Arctic. The Thule people were hunters skilled at exploiting sea mammals.

**trade language (lingua franca)**    A mixed language used for communication between people of different native languages.

**traditional ecological knowledge**    The knowledge of Indigenous Peoples including worldviews, values, processes and factual information.

**Trail of Tears**    In the 1830s, a series of forced emigrations by groups of Cherokee, Creek, Seminole, and perhaps some Choctaw, from the Southeast to Indian Territory, present-day Oklahoma, caused by the removal policy.

**transitive**    In linguistics, a characterizing verb that has both subject and direct object, opposite of intransitive.

**treaties**    Agreements negotiated between two parties, which set out the benefits both sides will receive as a result of one side giving up their title to a territory of land. In Canada, commonly referred to as Modern Treaties or Numbered Treaties. After Canada gained its own constitution under confederation in 1867, the new federal government of Canada signed a series of modern treaties numbered 1 through 11 between 1871 and 1921. Also included as "modern " treaties are the Robinson-Superior and Robinson-Huron treaties of 1850 with the Ojibway of Ontario occupying the north shores of Lake Huron and Lake Superior. The government negotiator, the Honorable William B. Robinson of Toronto is recognized for establishing the "treaty method" of obtaining Indian "title surrenders" to land in return for "treaty rights." The Chippewa and Missassauga Agreements of 1923 were the last formally negotiated Indian treaties in Canada. *See* treaty.

**treaty**    (1) In Canada, an agreement between Indian peoples and the Canadian government. Some maintain that these treaties are comparable to treaties between independent nations, while others claim they are merely contracts between the government and some of its subjects. Between 1871 and 1923, the Canadian government made twelve numbered treaties with native bands. Since 1923, the Canadian government has stopped using this term in its agreements with aboriginal peoples. (2) A formal agreement between two or more sovereign nations on issues of war, peace, trade, and other relations. Before 1871, the U.S. government ratified about 270 treaties with Indian nations. After 1871, the U.S. government stopped making treaties with Indians. *See* treaties.

**treaty Indian**    In Canada, descendants of Indians entitled to benefits under the treaties signed by the Crown and specific Indian bands between 1725 and 1921. Those who "took treaty" and surrendered their land rights for specific benefits.

**tribal corporation**    An enterprise owned and operated by a tribe under articles of incorporation, thereby protecting tribal assets not held by the corporation from lawsuits. While providing economic opportunities for tribal members, tribal corporations often employ many non-members as well.

**tribal groups**    A term, especially in British Columbia, for various language and culture groups that reject centralized bureaucracies, whether attached to government or native organizations.

**tribal sovereignty**    The powers of self-government held by Indian communities.

**tribe**    A group of natives sharing a common ancestry, language, culture, and name.

**tripartite**    A term meaning divide into or composed of three parts or parties. A reference to the three distinct governments within Indian Country: federal, tribal, and state.

**trust**    Property that is protected from being taxed or sold by the federal government for a period of time and is held in benefit of a trustee. In U.S. Indian affairs, the government holds trust of Indian lands and resources.

**trust responsibility**    The responsibility of the federal government to protect Indian lives and property; to compensate Indians for any loss due to government mismanagement; and, generally, to act in the best interests of Indians. Originally called "guardianship" and sometimes described by lawyers as a "fiduciary duty."

**trust status**    A legal relationship of an Indian person or tribe with the United States, within which the U.S. government has final and broad authority over the actions of individual Indians or over tribal governments.

# U

**unemployment rate**    A statistic published by the federal Bureau of Labor Statistics. It is the percent of the labor force without employment. Unemployed persons who have given up their search for work are not counted in this statistic because they are not considered part of the labor force.

**unilaterally**    "On its own," often referring to U.S. government policy when it abandoned a treaty promise without agreement or compensation to an Indian nation.

**unilineal descent**    A system of kinship relations and inheritance where descent is traced through only women (matrilineal) or men (patrilineal).

**urban Indian**    An Indian residing in urban metropolitan areas or cities.

**usufructuary**    (1) In Canada, the inherent right to use and enjoy the natural products of lands (e.g., game, fish, plants, fruits) of which the underlying title belongs to another, usually the Crown. (2) A way of using land, common among Indian farmers and hunters, where land belongs to an individual, clan, or village as long as that group has a history of continual usage of the land, hunting area, or fishing site. Usufruct rights are recognized by others and are lost whenever a group discontinues use.

**uvular**    In linguistics, a feature of a consonant sound made with the back of the tongue and the rear of the soft palate or uvula.

# V

**values**    The generally agreed upon goals, purposes, and issues of importance in a community.

**variety**    In linguistics, a local language variant, referring either to languages of the same family or to dialects of the same language.

**velar**    In linguistics, characterizing consonants produced with the rear part of the tongue. *See* labiovelar.

**vision quest**    A sacred Indian ceremony that involves an individual, often a teenage boy, going to a secluded place to fast (go without food or water) for a period of time (usually a few days) to learn about the spiritual side of himself and possibly have a vision of his spiritual helper, a spirit being who will give him guidance and strength.

**voiced**    In linguistics, a sound pronounced with vibration of the vocal cords.

**voiceless**    In linguistics, a sound pronounced without vibration of the vocal cords.

**vowel harmony**    In linguistics, a process in which vowels change to resemble vowels in nearby grammatical environments.

# W

**wampum**    Small, cylindrical, blue and white beads cut from the shell of the quahog, a large Atlantic coast clam. Long strings of wampum were used as trade exchange, while broad, woven "belts" of wampum were used to record treaties among the tribes and, later, with Europeans.

**Wapato**    A plant (Sagittaria latifolia) that grows in shallow lakes and marshy areas. The root was an important source of food for many groups in the Northwest Coast.

**wardship**    According to some legal theories, the relationship between the U.S. government and Indians, where the government has trust responsibility over the affairs and resources of the Indians.

**weir**    A fishing device that operates by blocking off a portion of a stream with a fence-like structure. Migrating fish are then forced to find openings in the weir where the people then capture them.

**Westward movement**    Name given the displacement of Native American peoples by the movement of Americans from the eastern shoreline in the seventeenth century to the West Coast in the nineteenth century.

**Woodland period**    A major time period usually dating from 500 B.C.E. to C.E. 900. During this period, Native American cultures developed complex ceremonial centers that included construction of large mounds. The Woodland period cultures were the first to practice farming in northeastern North America.

**world view**    The unconscious philosophical outlook held by the members of a society.

# General Bibliography

♦ General Studies   ♦ Anthropology   ♦ Architecture   ♦ Art   ♦ Atlases
♦ Autobiography   ♦ Demography   ♦ History   ♦ Image/Stereotype   ♦ Land
♦ Legal Status/Law   ♦ Literature and Poetry   ♦ Oral Tradition   ♦ Policy   ♦ Prehistory
♦ Religion   ♦ Sociology   ♦ Urbanization   ♦ Women   ♦ Canada

## ♦ GENERAL STUDIES

Armstrong, Virginia Irving. *I Have Spoken: American History Through the Voices of the Indians*. Athens, Ohio: Swallow Press, 1971.

Bierhorst, John. *The Mythology of North America*. New York: Morrow, 1985.

Boas, Franz. *Race, Language and Culture*. New York: Macmillan, 1940.

Bowden, Henry Warner. *American Indians and Christian Missions: Studies in Cultural Conflict*. Chicago: University of Chicago Press, 1981.

Boxberger, Daniel L., ed. *Native North Americans: An Ethnohistorical Approach*. Dubuque, Iowa: Kendall/Hunt, 1990.

Champagne, Duane. *American Indian Societies: Some Strategies and Conditions of Political and Cultural Survival*. Cambridge, Mass.: Cultural Survival, 1989.

Davis, Mary B., ed. *Native America in the Twentieth Century: An Encyclopedia*. New York: Garland Pub., 1994.

Edmunds, R. David. *American Indian Leaders: Studies in Diversity*. Lincoln: University of Nebraska Press, 1980.

Feest, Christian F. *Indians and Europe: An Interdisciplinary Collection of Essays*. Lincoln: University of Nebraska Press, 1999.

Hamilton, Charles. *Cry of the Thunderbird: The American Indian's Own Story*. Norman: University of Oklahoma Press, 1972.

Hoxie, Frederick E., ed. *Encyclopedia of North American Indians*. Boston: Houghton Mifflin Company, 1996.

Hoxie, Frederick E., and Harvey Markowitz. *Native Americans: An Annotated Bibliography*. Pasadena, Calif.: Salem Press, 1991.

Leitch, Barbara A. *A Concise Dictionary of Indian Tribes of North America*. Algonac, Mich.: Reference Publications, 1979.

Malinowski, Sharon, ed. *The Gale Encyclopedia of Native American Tribes*. Detroit: Gale, 1998.

Mihesuah, Devon A., ed. *Natives and Academics: Researching and Writing about American Indians*. Lincoln: University of Nebraska Press, 1998.

Moerman, Daniel E. *Native American Ethnobotany*. Portland, Oreg.: Timber Press, 1998.

Swisher, Karen Gayton, and AnCita Benally. *Native North American Firsts*. Detroit: Gale, 1998.

Thornton, Russell, ed. *Studying Native America: Problems and Prospects*. Madison, Wis.: University of Wisconsin Press, 1998.

Weeks, Philip. *The American Indian Experience: A Profile, 1524 to the Present*. Arlington Heights, Ill.: Forum Press, 1988.

White, Phillip M. *American Indian Studies: A Bibliographic Guide.* Englewood, Colo.: Libraries Unlimited, 1995.

## ◆ ANTHROPOLOGY

Bean, Lowell John. *Mukat's People: The Cahuilla Indians of Southern California.* Berkeley and Los Angeles: University of California Press, 1972.

Biolsi, Thomas. *Organizing the Lakota: The Political Economy of the New Deal on the Pine Ridge and Rosebud Reservations.* Tucson: University of Arizona Press, 1992.

Biolsi, Thomas, and Larry J. Zimmerman. *Indians and Anthropologists: Vine Deloria, Jr., and the Critique of Anthropology.* Tucson: University of Arizona Press, 1997.

Deloria, Vine, Jr. *Red Earth, White Lies: Native Americans and the Myth of Scientific Fact.* New York: Scribner, 1995.

―――. *We Talk, You Listen: New Tribes, New Turf.* New York: Macmillan, 1970.

Eggan, Fred. *Social Anthropology of North American Tribes.* 2nd enlarged ed. Chicago: University of Chicago Press, 1970.

Ewers, John Canfield. *Plains Indian History and Culture: Essays on Continuity and Change.* Norman: University of Oklahoma Press, 1997.

Fowler, Loretta. *Shared Symbols, Contested Meanings: Gros Ventre Culture and History, 1778–1984.* Ithaca: Cornell University Press, 1987.

Lowie, Robert. *Indians of the Plains.* 1954. Reprint. Lincoln: University of Nebraska Press, 1982.

Miller, Jay. *Tsimshian Culture: A Light Through the Ages.* Lincoln: University of Nebraska Press, 1997.

Nabokov, Peter, ed. *Native American Testimony: A Chronicle of Indian-White Relations From Prophecy to the Present, 1492–2000.* Rev. ed. New York: Penguin, 1999.

Ortiz, Alfonso. *The Tewa World: Space, Time, Being, and Becoming in a Pueblo Society.* Chicago: University of Chicago Press, 1969.

Parker, Arthur C. *Parker on the Iroquois.* Edited by William N. Fenton. Syracuse, N.Y.: Syracuse University Press, 1968.

Sando, Joe S. *Nee Hemish, a History of Jemez Pueblo.* Albuquerque: University of New Mexico Press, 1982.

―――. *Pueblo Nations: Eight Centuries of Pueblo Indian History.* Santa Fe, N.Mex.: Clear Light, 1992.

Stands In Timber, John. *Cheyenne Memories.* 1967. Reprints. Lincoln: University of Nebraska Press, 1972; New Haven, Conn.: Yale University Press, 1998.

Sturtevant, Willam C., ed. *Handbook of North American Indians.* 11 vols. to date. Washington, D.C.: Smithsonian Institution, 1978–.

Swanton, John R. *The Indian Tribes of North America.* 1952. Reprint. Washington, D.C.: Smithsonian Institution Press, 1968.

―――. *The Indians of the Southeastern United States.* 1946. Reprint. Grosse Pointe, Mich.: Scholarly Press, 1969.

Swindler, Nina, et al., eds. *Native Americans and Archaeologists: Stepping Stones to Common Ground.* Walnut Creek: AltaMira Press, 1997.

Watkins, Joe. *Indigenous Archaeology: American Indian Values and Scientific Practice.* Walnut Creek, Calif.: AltaMira Press, 2001.

## ◆ ARCHITECTURE

Krinsky, Carol H. *Contemporary Native American Architecture: Cultural Regeneration and Creativity.* New York: Oxford University Press, 1997.

Morgan, William N. *Precolumbian Architecture in Eastern North America.* Gainesville, Fla.: University Press of Florida, 1999.

Nabokov, Peter, and Robert Easton. *Native American Architecture.* New York: Oxford University Press, 1989.

## ◆ ART

Berlo, Janet C., ed. *The Early Years of Native American Art History: The Politics of Scholarship and Collecting.* Seattle: University of Washington Press; Vancouver: UBC Press, 1992.

————. *Plains Indian Drawings, 1865–1935: Pages From a Visual History*. New York: Harry N. Abrams in association with the American Federation of Arts and the Drawing Center, 1996.

Berlo, Janet C. and Ruth B. Phillips. *Native North American Art*. Oxford and New York: Oxford University Press, 1998.

Brody, J. J. *Anasazi and Pueblo Painting*. Albuquerque: University of New Mexico Press, 1991.

————. *Indian Painters & White Patrons*. Albuquerque: University of New Mexico Press, 1971.

Dockstader, Frederick J. *Indian Art in America: The Arts and Crafts of the North American Indian*. Greenwich, Conn.: New York Graphic Society, 1966.

Feder, Norman. *Two Hundred Years of North American Indian Art*. New York: Praeger, 1972.

Feest, Christian F. *Native Arts of North America*. London: Thames and Hudson; New York: Oxford University Press, 1980.

Grant, Campbell. *Rock Art of the American Indian*. New York: Crowell, 1967.

Heth, Charlotte, ed. *Native American Dance: Ceremonies and Social Traditions*. Washington, D.C.: Smithsonian, 1992.

Lester, Patrick D. *The Biographical Directory of Native American Painters*. Tulsa, Okla.: SIR Publications; distributed by University of Oklahoma Press, 1995.

Mathews, Zena Pearlstone, and Aldona Jonaitis. *Native North American Art History: Selected Readings*. Palo Alto, Calif.: Peek Publications, 1982.

Matuz, Roger, ed. *St. James Guide to Native North American Artists*. Detroit: St. James Press, 1998.

National Museum of the American Indian. *The Changing Presentation of the American Indian. Museums and Native Cultures*. Washington, D.C.: National Museum of the American Indian; Seattle: University of Washington Press, 2000.

Penney, David W. *Art of the American Indian Frontier: The Chandler-Pohrt Collection*. Detroit: Detroit Institute of Arts; Seattle: University of Washington Press, 1992.

Porter, Frank W., III. *The Art of Native American Basketry: A Living Legacy*. New York: Greenwood Press, 1990.

Rushing, W. Jackson, III, ed. *Native American Art in the Twentieth Century*. London and New York: Routledge, 1999.

Wade, Edwin L., ed. *The Arts of the North American Indian: Native Traditions in Evolution*. New York: Hudson Hills Press; Tulsa: Philbrook Art Center, 1986.

Wyckoff, Lydia J. *Visions and Voices: Native American Painting From the Philbrook Museum of Art*. Tulsa: Philbrook Museum of Art; Albuquerque, N.Mex.: Distributed by the University of New Mexico Press, 1996.

## ◆ ATLASES

Coe, Michael D., Dean Snow, and Elizabeth Benson. *Atlas of Ancient America*. New York: Facts on File, 1986.

Ferguson, Thomas J. *A Zuni Atlas*. Norman: University of Oklahoma Press, 1985.

Goodman, James M. *The Navajo Atlas: Environments, Resources, People, and History of the Dine Bikeyah*. Norman: University of Oklahoma Press, 1982.

Prucha, Francis P. *Atlas of American Indian Affairs*. Lincoln: University of Nebraska Press, 1990.

Sturtevant, William C. *Early Indian Tribes, Culture Areas, and Linguistic Stocks*. Reston, Va.: Dept. of Interior, U.S. Geological Survey, 1991.

Tanner, Helen Hornbeck, et al., eds. *Atlas of Great Lakes Indian History*. Norman: Published for the Newberry Library by the University of Oklahoma Press, 1987.

Waldman, Carl. *Atlas of the North American Indian*. Rev. ed. New York: Facts On File, 2000.

## ◆ AUTOBIOGRAPHY

Allen, Elsie C. *Pomo Basketmaking: A Supreme Art for the Weaver*. Rev. ed. Happy Camp, Calif.: Naturegraph, 1972.

Bennett, Kay. *Kaibah: Recollection of a Navajo Girlhood*. Los Angeles: Westernlore Press, 1964.

Bettelyoun, Susan Bordeaux. *With My Own Eyes: A Lakota Woman Tells Her People's History.* Lincoln: University of Nebraska Press, 1998.

Blackman, Margaret B. *During My Time: Florence Edenshaw Davidson, A Haida Woman.* Seattle: University of Washington Press, 1982.

———. *Sadie Brower Neakok, An Inupiaq Woman.* Seattle: University of Washington Press, 1989.

Blaine, Martha Royce. *Some Things Are Not Forgotten: A Pawnee Family Remembers.* Lincoln: University of Nebraska Press, 1997.

Blowsnake, Sam. *Crashing Thunder: The Autobiography of an American Indian.* 1926. Reprint. Lincoln: University of Nebraska Press, 1983.

Brave Bird, Mary. *Lakota Woman.* New York: Grove Weidenfeld, 1990.

Brumble, H. David. *American Indian Autobiography.* Berkeley and Los Angeles: University of California Press, 1988.

———. *An Annotated Bibliography of American Indian and Eskimo Autobiographies.* Lincoln: University of Nebraska Press, 1981.

Campbell, Maria. *Halfbreed.* 1973. Reprint. Lincoln: University of Nebraska Press, 1982.

Cruikshank, Julie. *Life Lived Like a Story: Life Stories of Three Yukon Native Elders.* Lincoln: University of Nebraska Press, 1990.

Cuero, Delfina. *The Autobiography of Delfina Cuero, a Diegueno Indian.* 1968. Reprints. Banning, Calif: Malki Museum Press, 1970; Menlo Park, Calif.: Ballena Press, 1991.

Dauenhauer, Nora. *Life Woven with Song.* Tucson: University of Arizona Press, 2000.

Eastman, Charles Alexander. *From the Deep Woods to Civilization.* 1916. Reprint. Lincoln: University of Nebraska Press, 1977.

———. *Indian Boyhood.* 1902. Reprint. New York: Dover, 1971.

Fools Crow. *Fools Crow.* Lincoln: University of Nebraska Press, 1990.

Giago, Tim A. *The Aboriginal Sin: Reflections on the Holy Rosary Indian Mission School.* San Francisco: Indian Historian Press, 1978.

Greene, Alma. *Forbidden Voice: Reflections of a Mohawk Indian.* 1971. Reprint. Toronto: Green Dragon Press, 1997.

Hale, Janet Campbell. *Bloodlines: Odyssey of a Native Daughter.* New York: Random House, 1993.

Harris, LaDonna. *LaDonna Harris: A Comanche Life.* Lincoln: University of Nebraska Press, 2000.

Hopkins, Sarah Winnemucca. *Life Among the Piutes: Their Wrongs and Claims.* 1882. Reprint. Reno: University of Nevada Press, 1994.

Horne, Esther Burnett. *Essie's Story: The Life and Legacy of a Shoshone Teacher.* Lincoln: University of Nebraska Press, 1998.

Johnson, Broderick H. *Stories of Traditional Navajo Life and Culture.* Tsaile, Navajo Nation, Ariz.: Navajo Community College Press, 1977.

Kakianak, Nathan. *Eskimo Boyhood: An Autobiography in Psychosocial Perspective.* Lexington: University Press of Kentucky, 1974.

Krupat, Arnold. *For Those Who Come After: A Study of Native American Autobiography.* Berkeley and Los Angeles: University of California Press, 1985.

La Flesche, Francis. *The Middle Five: Indian Schoolboys of the Omaha Tribe.* Madison: University of Wisconsin Press, 1963.

Lame Deer, John (Fire). *Lame Deer, Seeker of Visions.* New York: Simon and Schuster, 1972.

Left Handed. *Left Handed, Son of Old Man Hat: A Navajo Autobiography.* 1938. Reprint. Lincoln: University of Nebraska Press, 1996.

Little Coyote, Bertha. *Leaving Everything Behind: The Songs and Memories of a Cheyenne Woman.* Norman: University of Oklahoma Press, 1997.

Lurie, Nancy Oestreich, ed. *Mountain Wolf Woman, Sister of Crashing Thunder: The Autobiography of a Winnebago Indian.* Ann Arbor: University of Michigan Press, 1966.

Mankiller, Wilma, and Michael Wallis. *Mankiller: A Chief of Her People*. New York: St. Martin's Griffin, 2000.

Mitchell, Frank. *Navajo Blessingway Singer: The Autobiography of Frank Mitchell: 1881–1967*. Tucson: University of Arizona Press, 1978.

Modesto, Ruby, and Guy Mount. *Not for Innocent Ears: Spiritual Traditions of a Desert Cahuilla Medicine Woman*. Angelus Oaks, Calif.: Sweetlight Books, 1980.

Mohatt, Gerald V., and Joseph Eagle Elk. *The Price of a Gift: A Lakota Healer's Story*. Lincoln: University of Nebraska Press, 2000.

Mourning Dove. *Mourning Dove: A Salishan Autobiography*. Lincoln: University of Nebraska Press, 1990.

Scott, Lalla. *Karnee: A Paiute Narrative*. Reno: University of Nevada Press, 1966.

Snell, Alma Hogan. *Grandmother's Grandchild: My Crow Indian Life*. Lincoln: University of Nebraska Press, 2000.

Two Leggings. *Two Leggings: The Making of a Crow Warrior*. 1967. Reprint. Lincoln: University of Nebraska Press, 1982.

Underhill, Ruth Murray. *Papago Woman*. New York: Holt, Rinehart and Winston, 1979.

Waheenee. *Waheenee: An Indian Girl's Story, Told by Herself to Gilbert L. Wilson*. Lincoln: University of Nebraska Press, 1981.

Yava, Albert. *Big Falling Snow: A Tewa-Hopi Indian's Life and Times and the History and Traditions of His People*. New York: Crown Publishers, 1978.

Yellowtail, Thomas. *Yellowtail, Crow Medicine Man and Sun Dance Chief: An Autobiography*. Norman: University of Oklahoma Press, 1991.

Zitkala-Sa. *American Indian Stories*. 1921. Reprint. Lincoln: University of Nebraska Press, 1985.

## ◆ DEMOGRAPHY

Cook, Sherburne F. *The Conflict Between the California Indian and White Civilization*. Berkeley and Los Angeles: University of California Press, 1976.

Crosby, Alfred W., Jr. *The Columbian Exchange: Biological and Cultural Consequences of 1492*. Westport, Conn.: Greenwood Publishing Company, 1972.

Dobyns, Henry F. *Their Number Become Thinned: Native American Population Dynamics in Eastern North America*. Knoxville: University of Tennessee Press in cooperation with the Newberry Library Center for the History of the American Indian, 1983.

Duffy, John. *Epidemics in Colonial America*. Baton Rouge, Louisiana State University Press, 1953.

Reddy, Marlita A., ed. *Statistical Record of Native North Americans*. 2nd ed. Detroit: Gale Research, 1995.

Shoemaker, Nancy. *American Indian Population Recovery in the Twentieth Century*. Albuquerque: University of New Mexico Press, 1999.

Snipp, C. Matthew. *American Indians: The First of This Land*. New York: Russell Sage Foundation, 1989.

Stearn, Esther W. *The Effect of Smallpox on the Destiny of the Amerindian*. Boston: Bruce Humphries, Inc., 1945.

Stuart, Paul. *Nations Within a Nation: Historical Statistics of American Indians*. New York: Greenwood Press, 1987.

Thornton, Russell. *American Indian Holocaust and Survival: A Population History Since 1492*. Norman: University of Oklahoma Press, 1987.

Verano, John, and Douglas H. Ubelaker, eds. *Disease and Demography in the Americas*. Washington: Smithsonian Institution Press, 1992.

## ◆ HISTORY

Calloway, Colin G. *First Peoples: A Documentary Survey of American Indian History*. Boston: Bedford/St. Martin's, 1999.

———., ed. *New Directions in American Indian History*. Norman: University of Oklahoma Press, 1988.

———. *Our Hearts Fell to the Ground: Plains Indian Views of How the West Was Lost*. Boston: Bedford Books of St. Martin's Press, 1996.

Costo, Rupert, and Jeannette Henry Costo. *The Missions of California: A Legacy of Genocide*. San Francisco: Indian Historian Press, American Indian Historical Society, 1987.

Debo, Angie. *A History of the Indians of the United States*. Norman: University of Oklahoma Press, 1970.

Gibson, Arrell M. *The American Indian: Prehistory to the Present*. Lexington, Mass.: D.C. Heath, 1980.

Hoxie, Frederick E., and Peter Iverson. *Indians in American History: An Introduction*. 2nd ed. Wheeling, Ill.: Harlan Davidson, 1998.

Hurt, R. Douglas. *Indian Agriculture in America: Prehistory to the Present*. Lawrence, Kan.: University Press of Kansas, 1987.

Hurtado, Albert L., and Peter Iverson. *Major Problems in American Indian History: Documents and Essays*. Lexington, Mass.: D.C. Heath, 1994.

Josephy, Alvin M., ed. *America in 1492: The World of the Indian Peoples Before the Arrival of Columbus*. New York: Knopf, 1992.

Kehoe, Alice. *North American Indians: A Comparative Account*. 2nd ed. Englewood, N.J.: Prentice Hall, 1992.

Leacock, Eleanore Burke, and Nancy O. Lurie, eds. *North American Indians in Historical Perspective*. Prospect Heights, Ill.: Waveland Press, 1988.

McNickle, D'Arcy. *Native American Tribalism: Indian Survivals and Renewals*. New York: Oxford University Press, 1973.

———. *They Came Here First: The Epic of the American Indian*. Rev. ed. New York: Harper & Row, 1975.

Olson, James S., and Raymond Wilson. *Native Americans in the Twentieth Century*. Provo, Utah: Brigham Young University Press, 1984.

Prucha, Francis Paul. *American Indian Treaties: The History of a Political Anomaly*. Berkeley and Los Angeles: University of California Press, 1994.

Spicer, Edward H. *Cycles of Conquest: The Impact of Spain, Mexico, and the United States on the Indians of the Southwest, 1533–1960*. Tucson: University of Arizona Press, 1962.

Trigger, Bruce G., and Wilcomb E. Washburn, eds. *North America*. Vol. 1 of *The Cambridge History of the Native Peoples of the Americas*. New York: Cambridge University Press, 1996.

Waldman, Carl. *Biographical Dictionary of American Indian History to 1900*. Rev. ed. New York: Facts on File, 2001.

## ◆ IMAGE/STEREOTYPE

Bataille, Gretchen, and Charles L.P. Silet, eds. *The Pretend Indians: Images of Native Americans in the Movies*. Ames: Iowa State University Press, 1980.

Berkhofer, Robert F. *The White Man's Indian: Images of the American Indian from Columbus to the Present*. New York: Knopf, 1978.

Bird, S. Elizabeth. *Dressing in Feathers: The Construction of the Indian in American Popular Culture*. Boulder, Colo.: Westview Press, 1996.

Boehme, Sarah E., et al. *Powerful Images: Portrayals of Native America*. Seattle: Museums West in association with the University of Washington Press, 1998.

Deloria, Philip J. *Playing Indian*. New Haven: Yale University Press, 1998.

Dippie, Brian W. *The Vanishing American: White Attitudes and U.S. Indian Policy*. Lawrence, Kan.: University Press of Kansas, 1991.

Hauptman, Laurence M. *Tribes & Tribulations: Misconceptions About American Indians and Their Histories*. Albuquerque: University of New Mexico Press, 1995.

Hirschfelder, Arlene B., Paulette Fairbanks Molin, and Yvonne Wakim. *American Indian Stereotypes in the World of Children: A Reader and Bibliography*. 2nd ed. Lanham, Md.: Scarecrow Press, 1999.

King, C. Richard, and Charles Fruehling Springwood, eds. *Team Spirits: The Native American Mascots Controversy*. Lincoln: University of Nebraska Press, 2001.

Mihesuah, Devon A. *American Indians: Stereotypes & Realities*. Atlanta, Ga., 1996.

Moses, Lester G. *Wild West Shows and the Images of American Indians, 1883–1933*. Albuquerque: University of New Mexico Press, 1996.

National Museum of the American Indian. *The Changing Presentation of the American Indian: Museums and Native Cultures.* Washington, D.C.: National Museum of the American Indian; Seattle: University of Washington Press, 2000.

Rollins, Peter C., and John E. O'Connor, eds. *Hollywood's Indian: The Portrayal of the Native American in Film.* Lexington: University Press of Kentucky, 1998.

Slapin, Beverly, and Doris Seale, eds. *Through Indian Eyes: The Native Experience in Books for Children.* Los Angeles: American Indian Studies Center, University of California, Los Angeles, 1998.

Spindel, Carol. *Dancing at Halftime: Sports and the Controversy Over American Indian Mascots.* New York: New York University Press, 2000.

Stedman, Raymond W. *Shadows of the Indian: Stereotypes in American Culture.* Norman: University of Oklahoma Press, 1982.

## ◆ LAND

Berger, Thomas R. *Village Journey: The Report of the Alaska Native Review Commission.* Rev. ed. New York: Hill and Wang, 1995.

Clow, Richmond L. and Imre Sutton, eds., *Conservation and the Trustee: Environmental Essays on the Management of Native American Resources.* Boulder: University Press of Colorado, 2001.

Confederation of American Indians, comp. *Indian Reservations: A State and Federal Handbook.* Jefferson, N.C.: McFarland, 1986.

Fixico, Donald L. *The Invasion of Indian Country in the Twentieth Century: American Capitalism and Tribal Natural Resources.* Niwot, Colo.: University Press of Colorado, 1998.

Frantz, Klaus. *Indian Reservations in the United States: Territory, Sovereignty, and Socioeconomic Changes,* Geography Research Paper 242. Chicago: University of Chicago Press, 1999.

Hart, E. Richard. *Zuni and the Courts: A Struggle for Sovereign Land Rights.* Lawrence, Kan.: University Press of Kansas, 1995.

Johansen, Bruce E. *Shapers of the Great Debate on Native Americans—Land, Spirit, and Power: A Biographical Dictionary.* Westport, Conn.: Greenwood Press, 2000.

Kickingbird, Kirke, and Karen Ducheneaux. *One Hundred Million Acres.* New York: Macmillan, 1973.

LaDuke, Winona. *All Our Relations: Native Struggles for Land and Life.* Cambridge, Mass.: South End Press, 1999.

Sutton, Imre, ed. *Irredeemable America: The Indians' Estate and Land Claims.* Albuquerque: University of New Mexico Press, 1985.

Tiller, Veronica E. Velarde, ed. *Tiller's Guide to Indian Country: Economic Profiles of American Indian Reservations.* Albuquerque, N.Mex.: BowArrow Publishing Co., 1996.

Vecsey, Christopher, and William A. Starna. *Iroquois Land Claims.* Syracuse, N.Y.: Syracuse University Press, 1988.

White, Richard. *The Roots of Dependency: Subsistence, Environment, and Social Change Among the Choctaws, Pawnees, and Navajos.* Lincoln: University of Nebraska Press, 1983.

## ◆ LEGAL STATUS/LAW

Burton, Lloyd. *American Indian Water Rights and the Limits of Law.* Lawrence, Kan.: University Press of Kansas, 1991.

Canby, William C., Jr. *Indian Law in a Nutshell.* 3rd ed. St. Paul: West Pub. Co., 1998.

Clark, Blue. *Lone Wolf v. Hitchcock: Treaty Rights and Indian Law at the End of the Nineteenth Century.* Lincoln: University of Nebraska Press, 1994.

Cohen, Felix S. *Felix S. Cohen's Handbook of Federal Indian Law.* 2d ed. Charlottesville, Va.: Michie/Bobbs-Merrill, 1982.

Deloria, Vine. *Tribes, Treaties, and Constitutional Tribulations.* Austin: University of Texas Press, 1999.

Deloria, Vine, and Clifford M. Lytle. *American Indians, American Justice.* Austin: University of Texas Press, 1983.

Deloria, Vine, and Raymond J. DeMaille, comps. *Documents of American Indian Diplomacy: Treaties, Agreements, and Conventions, 1775–1979*. Norman: University of Oklahoma Press, 1999.

Falkowski, James E. *Indian Law/Race Law: A Five-Hundred Year History*. New York: Praeger, 1992.

Getches, David H. *Cases and Materials on Federal Indian Law*. 4th ed. St. Paul, Minn.: West Group, 1998.

Kappler, Charles J., comp. and ed. *Indian Affairs. Law and Treaties*. 7 vols. 1904–1971. Reprint. New York: AMS Press, 1972.

Norgren, Jill. *The Cherokee Cases: The Confrontation of Law and Politics*. New York: McGraw-Hill, 1996.

O'Brien, Sharon. *American Indian Tribal Governments*. Norman: University of Oklahoma Press, 1989.

Pevar, Stephen L. *The Rights of Indians and Tribes: The Basic ACLU Guide to Indian and Tribal Rights*. 2nd ed. Carbondale, Ill.: Southern Illinois University Press, 1992.

Shattuck, Petra T., and Jill Norgren. *Partial Justice: Federal Indian Law in a Liberal Constitutional System*. New York: Berg, 1991.

Wilkinson, Charles F. *American Indians, Time, and the Law: Native Societies in a Modern Constitutional Democracy*. New Haven: Yale University Press, 1987.

## ◆ LITERATURE AND POETRY

Alexie, Sherman. *The Business of Fancydancing: Stories and Poems*. Brooklyn, N.Y.: Hanging Loose Press, 1992.

———. *Indian Killer*. New York: Atlantic Monthly Press, 1996.

———. *The Lone Ranger and Tonto Fistfight in Heaven*. New York: Atlantic Monthly Press, 1993.

———. *Old Shirts & New Skins*. Los Angeles: American Indian Studies Center, University of California, Los Angeles, 1993.

———. *One Stick Song*. Brooklyn: Hanging Loose Press, 2000.

Allen, Paula Gunn. *The Sacred Hoop: Recovering the Feminine in American Indian Traditions*. Boston: Beacon Press, 1986.

———, ed. *Song of the Turtle: American Indian Literature, 1974–1994*. New York: Ballantine Books, 1996.

———, ed. *Spider Woman's Granddaughters: Traditional Tales and Contemporary Writing by Native American Women*. Boston: Beacon Press, 1989.

———, ed. *Studies in American Indian Literature: Critical Essays and Course Designs*. New York: Modern Language Association of America, 1983.

———, ed. *Voice of the Turtle: American Indian Literature, 1900–1970*. New York: Ballantine Books, 1994.

———. *The Woman Who Owned the Shadows*. San Francisco: Spinsters Ink, 1983.

Brant, Beth. *Food & Spirits: Stories*. Ithaca, N.Y.: Firebrand Books, 1991.

———. *Mohawk Trail*. Ithaca, N.Y.: Firebrand Books, 1985.

Bruchac, Joseph. *Survival This Way: Interviews with American Indian Poets*. Tucson: University of Arizona Press, 1987.

Bush, Barney. *Inherit the Blood: Poetry and Fiction*. New York: Thunder's Mouth Press, 1985.

———. *My Horse and a Jukebox*. Los Angeles: American Indian Studies Center, University of California, Los Angeles, 1979.

Conley, Robert J. *Mountain Windsong: A Novel of the Trail of Tears*. Norman: University of Oklahoma Press, 1992.

———. *The Way of the Priests*. New York: Doubleday, 1992.

———. *The Witch of Goingsnake and Other Stories*. Norman: University of Oklahoma Press, 1988.

Cook-Lynn, Elizabeth. *Aurelia: A Crow Creek Trilogy*. Niwot, Colo.: University Press of Colorado, 1999.

———. *I Remember the Fallen Trees: New and Selected Poems*. Cheney, Wash.: Eastern Washington University Press, 1998.

Cronyn, George W., ed. *The Path on the Rainbow: An Anthology of Songs and Chants from the Indians of North America.* 1918. Reprint, *American Indian Poetry: An Anthology of Songs and Chants.* New York: Fawcett Columbine, 1991.

D'Aponte, Mimi. *Seventh Generation: An Anthology of Native American Plays.* New York: Theatre Communications Group, 1999.

Dorris, Michael. *A Yellow Raft in Blue Water.* New York: H. Holt, 1987.

Erdrich, Louise. *Beet Queen.* New York: Holt, 1986.

———. *The Bingo Palace.* New York: Harper-Collins, 1994.

———. *Love Medicine.* New York: Holt, Rinehart, and Winston, 1984; Bantam, 1985; new and expanded version, New York: H. Holt, 1993; HarperPerennial, 1993.

———. *Tracks.* New York: Henry Holt, 1988.

Geiogamah, Hanay, and Jaye T. Darby, eds. *American Indian Theater in Performance: A Reader.* Los Angeles: UCLA American Indian Studies Center, 2000.

———. *Stories of Our Way: An Anthology of American Indian Plays.* Los Angeles: UCLA American Indian Studies Center, 1999.

Glancy, Diane. *Firesticks: A Collection of Stories.* Norman: University of Oklahoma Press, 1993.

———. *Iron Woman: Poems.* Minneapolis, Minn.: New Rivers Press, 1990.

———. *The Voice That Was in Travel: Stories.* Norman: University of Oklahoma Press, 1999.

Hale, Janet Campbell. *The Jailing of Cecelia Capture.* New York: Random House, 1985.

———. *Women on the Run.* Moscow, Idaho: University of Idaho Press, 1999.

Harjo, Joy. *A Map to the Next World: Poetry and Tales.* New York: W.W. Norton & Co., 2000.

———. *In Mad Love and War.* Middletown, Conn.: Wesleyan University Press, 1990.

———. *She Had Some Horses.* New York: Thunder's Mouth Press, 1983.

Harjo, Joy, and Gloria Bird, eds. *Reinventing the Enemy's Language: Contemporary Native Women's Writings of North America.* New York: W. W. Norton & Company, 1997.

Hogan, Linda. *The Book of Medicines: Poems.* Minneapolis: Coffee House Press, 1993.

———. *Mean Spirit.* New York: Atheneum, 1990.

Kabotie, Michael. *Migration Tears: Poems About Transitions.* Los Angeles: American Indian Studies Center, University of California, Los Angeles, 1987.

Lesley, Craig, ed. *Talking Leaves: Contemporary Native American Short Stories.* New York: Laurel, 1991.

Lincoln, Kenneth. *Native American Renaissance.* Berkeley and Los Angeles: University of California Press, 1983.

Mathews, John Joseph. *Sundown.* 1934. Reprint. Norman: University of Oklahoma Press, 1988.

———. *Talking to the Moon.* 1945. Reprint. Norman: University of Oklahoma Press, 1981.

McNickle, D'Arcy. *The Surrounded.* 1936. Reprint. Albuquerque: University of New Mexico Press, 1978.

Momaday, N. Scott. *The Ancient Child: A Novel.* New York: Doubleday, 1989.

———. *House Made of Dawn.* New York: Harper & Row, 1968.

———. *The Way to Rainy Mountain.* Albuquerque: University of New Mexico Press, 1969.

Mourning Dove. *Cogewea, the Half-Blood: A Depiction of the Great Montana Cattle Range.* 1927. Reprint. Lincoln: University of Nebraska Press, 1981.

Niatum, Duane, ed. *Harper's Anthology of 20th Century Native American Poetry.* San Francisco: Harper & Row, 1988.

Ortiz, Simon J. *A Good Journey.* Berkeley, Calif.: Turtle Island, 1977.

———. *From Sand Creek.* Reprint. 1984. Tucson: University of Arizona Press, 1999.

———. *Men on the Moon: Collected Short Stories.* Tucson: University of Arizona Press, 1999.

———. *Woven Stone.* Tucson: University of Arizona Press, 1992.

———, ed. *Speaking for the Generations: Native Writers on Writing.* Tucson: University of Arizona Press, 1998.

Owens, Louis. *Bone Game: A Novel.* Norman: University of Oklahoma Press, 1994.

———. *Other Destinies: Understanding the American Indian Novel.* Norman: University of Oklahoma Press, 1992.

Rainwater, Catherine. *Dreams of Fiery Stars: The Transformations of Native American Fiction.* Philadelphia: University of Pennsylvania Press, 1999.

Rose, Wendy. *Bone Dance: New and Selected Poems, 1965–1993.* Tucson: University of Arizona Press, 1994.

Sarris, Greg. *Grand Avenue.* New York: Penguin, 1995.

———. *Keeping Slug Woman Alive: A Holistic Approach to American Indian Texts.* Berkeley and Los Angeles: University of California Press, 1993.

Silko, Leslie M. *Almanac of the Dead.* New York: Simon & Schuster, 1991.

———. *Ceremony.* New York: Viking, 1977.

———. *Gardens in the Dunes: A Novel.* New York: Simon & Schuster, 1999.

———. *Storyteller.* New York: Seaver Books, 1981.

Spatz, Ronald, ed. *Alaska Native Writers, Storytellers & Orators.* Anchorage: University of Alaska, 1999.

TallMountain, Mary. *The Light on the Tent Wall: A Bridging.* Los Angeles: American Indian Studies Center, University of California, Los Angeles, 1990.

Tapahonso, Luci. *Saanii Dahataal, The Women Are Singing: Poems and Stories.* Tucson: University of Arizona Press, 1993.

Tedlock, Dennis. *The Spoken Word and the Work of Interpretation.* Philadelphia: University of Pennsylvania Press, 1983.

Treuer, David. *Little.* Saint Paul, Minn.: Graywolf Press, 1995.

Vizenor, Gerald R. *The Heirs of Columbus.* Middletown, Conn.: Wesleyan University Press, 1991.

———. *Shadow Distance: A Gerald Vizenor Reader.* Hanover, N.H.: Wesleyan University Press, 1994.

———. *Wordarrows: Indians and Whites in the New Fur Trade.* Minneapolis: University of Minnesota Press, 1978.

Walters, Anna Lee. *Ghost Singer: A Novel.* Flagstaff, Ariz.: Northland Publishing, 1988.

———. *The Sun is Not Merciful: Short Stories.* Ithaca, N.Y.: Firebrand Books, 1985.

Welch, James. *The Death of Jim Loney.* 1979.

———. *Fools Crow.* New York: Viking, 1986.

———. *The Indian Lawyer.* New York: W.W. Norton, 1990.

———. *Riding the Earthboy 40.* New York: World Pub. Co., 1971.

———. *Winter in the Blood.* New York: Harper & Row, 1974.

Witalec, Janet, ed. *Native North American Literature: Biographical and Critical Information on Native Writers and Orators From the United States and Canada From Historical Times to the Present.* New York: Gale Research, 1994.

Young Bear, Ray A. *Black Eagle Child: The Facepaint Narratives.* Iowa City, Iowa: University of Iowa Press, 1992.

♦ ORAL TRADITION

Bullchild, Percy. *The Sun Came Down.* San Francisco: Harper & Row, 1985.

Clements, William M., and Frances M. Malpezzi. *Native American Folklore, 1879–1979: An Annotated Bibliography.* Athens, Ohio: Swallow Press, 1984.

Erdoes, Richard, and Alfonso Ortiz, eds. *American Indian Myths and Legends.* New York: Pantheon Books, 1984.

———. *American Indian Trickster Tales.* New York: Viking, 1998.

Garter Snake. *The Seven Visions of Bull Lodge.* Ann Arbor, Mich.: Bear Claw Press, 1980.

Margolin, Malcom, ed. *The Way We Lived: California Indian Reminiscences, Stories, and Songs.* Berkeley: Heyday Books, 1981.

Norman, Howard A., trans. *The Wishing Bone Cycle: Narrative Poems From the Swampy Cree Indians.* Expanded ed. Santa Barbara, Ca.: Ross-Erikson, 1982.

Quam, Alvina, tr. *The Zunis: Self-Portrayals, By the Zuni People.* Albuquerque: University of New Mexico Press, 1972.

Swann, Brian, ed. *Coming to Light: Contemporary Translations of Native Literatures of North America.* New York: Random House, 1994.

———. *Smoothing the Ground: Essays on Native American Oral Literature.* Berkeley and Los Angeles: University of California Press, 1983.

## ◆ POLICY

Castile, George P. *To Show Heart: Native American Self-Determination and Federal Indian Policy, 1960–1975.* Tucson: University of Arizona Press, 1998.

Castile, George P., and Robert L. Bee. *State and Reservation: New Perspectives on Federal Indian Policy.* Tucson: University of Arizona Press, 1992.

Deloria, Vine, Jr. *Behind the Trail of Broken Treaties: An Indian Declaration of Independence.* New York: Dell, 1974.

Deloria, Vine, Jr., ed. *American Indian Policy in the Twentieth Century.* Norman: University of Oklahoma Press, 1985.

Dippie, Brian W. *The Vanishing American: White Attitudes and U.S. Indian Policy.* Middletown, Conn.: Wesleyan University Press, 1982.

Fixico, Donald L. *The Invasion of Indian Country in the Twentieth Century: American Capitalism and Tribal Natural Resources.* Niwot, Colo.: University Press of Colorado, 1998.

———. *Termination and Relocation: Federal Indian Policy, 1945–1960.* Albuquerque: University of New Mexico Press, 1986.

Green, Donald E., and Thomas V. Tonnesen, eds. *American Indians: Social Justice and Public Policy.* Milwaukee: Institute on Race and Ethnicity, University of Wisconsin System, 1991.

Horsman, Reginald. *Expansion and American Indian Policy, 1783–1812.* East Lansing: Michigan State University Press, 1967.

Joe, Jennie R., ed. *American Indian Policy and Cultural Values: Conflict and Accommodation.* Los Angeles: American Indian Studies Center, University of California, Los Angeles, 1986.

Josephy, Alvin M., Jr., Joane Nagel, and Troy Johnson, eds. *Red Power: The American Indian's Fight for Freedom.* 2nd ed. Lincoln: University of Nebraska Press, 1999.

Legters, Lyman H., and Fremont J. Lyden, eds. *American Indian Policy: Self-Governance and Economic Development.* Westport, Conn.: Greenwood Press, 1994.

McNickle, D'Arcy. *Native American Tribalism: Indian Survivals and Renewals.* New York: Oxford University Press, 1973.

Mihesuah, Devon A. *Repatriation Reader: Who Owns American Indian Remains?* Lincoln: University of Nebraska Press, 2000.

Philp, Kenneth R. *John Collier's Crusade for Indian Reform, 1920–1954.* Tucson: University of Arizona Press, 1977.

———. *Termination Revisited: American Indians on the Trail to Self-Determination, 1933–1953.* Lincoln: University of Nebraska Press, 1999.

Prucha, Francis P. *The Great Father: The United States Government and the American Indians.* 2 vols. Lincoln: University of Nebraska Press, 1984.

Prucha, Francis Paul, ed. *Documents of United States Indian Policy.* 3rd ed. Lincoln: University of Nebraska Press, 2000.

Satz, Ronald N. *American Indian Policy in the Jacksonian Era.* Lincoln: University of Nebraska Press, 1975.

Sheehan, Bernard W. *Seeds of Extinction: Jeffersonian Philanthropy and the American Indian.* Chapel Hill: University of North Carolina Press, 1973.

Snipp, C. Matthew. *Public Policy Impacts on American Indian Economic Development.* Albuquerque: Institute for Native American Development, University of New Mexico, 1988.

Trennert, Robert A. *Alternative to Extinction: Federal Indian Policy and the Beginnings of the Reservation System, 1846–51.* Philadelphia: Temple University Press, 1975.

Washburn, Wilcomb E. *Red Man's Land/White Man's Law: The Past and Present Status of the American Indian.* 2nd ed. Norman: University of Oklahoma Press, 1995.

## ◆ PREHISTORY

Aveni, Anthony F., ed. *Native American Astronomy.* Austin: University of Texas Press, 1977.

Dixon, E. James. *Bones, Boats, & Bison: Archaeology and the First Colonization of Western North America.* Albuquerque: University of New Mexico Press, 1999.

Fagan, Brian M. *Ancient North America: The Archaeology of a Continent.* Rev. and expanded ed. New York, N.Y.: Thames and Hudson, 1995.

Fowler, Melvin L. *The Cahokia Atlas: A Historical Atlas of Cahokia Archaeology.* Rev. ed. Urbana, Ill.: Illinois Transportation Archeological Research Program, University of Illinois, 1997.

Gibbon, Guy. *Archaeology of Prehistoric Native America: An Encyclopedia.* New York: Garland, 1998.

Jennings, Jesse D. *Prehistory of North America.* 3rd ed. Mountain View, Calif.: Mayfield Pub., 1989.

Jennings, Jesse D., ed. *Ancient Native Americans.* San Francisco: W.H. Freeman, 1983.

Shaffer, Lynda. *Native Americans Before 1492: the Moundbuilding Centers of the Eastern Woodlands.* Armonk, N.Y.: M.E. Sharpe, 1992.

Snow, Dean R. *The Archaeology of North America.* New York: Viking Press, 1976.

————. *The Archaeology of North America.* New York: Chelsea House Publishers, 1989.

## ◆ RELIGION

Beck, Peggy V., and Anna L. Walters. *The Sacred: Ways of Knowledge, Sources of Life.* Flagstaff: Northland, 1990.

Black Elk. *Black Elk Speaks: Being the Life Story of a Holy Man of the Oglala Sioux.* 21st-century ed. Lincoln: University of Nebraska Press, 2000.

Bonvillain, Nancy. *Native American Religion.* New York: Chelsea House Publishers, 1996.

Coffer, William E. *Spirits of the Sacred Mountains: Creation Stories of the American Indian.* New York: Van Nostrand Reinhold, 1978.

Deloria, Vine, Jr. *For This Land: Writings on Religion in America.* New York: Routledge, 1999.

————. *God is Red: A Native View of Religion.* 2nd ed. Golden, Colo.: North American Press, 1992.

Gill, Sam D. *Native American Religions: An Introduction.* Belmont, Calif.: Wadsworth Publishing, 1982.

————. *Native American Religious Action: A Performance Approach to Religion.* Columbia: University of South Carolina Press, 1987.

Hall, Robert L. *An Archaeology of the Soul: North American Indian Belief and Ritual.* Urbana: University of Illinois Press, 1997.

Harrod, Howard L. *Becoming and Remaining a People: Native American Religions on the Northern Plains.* Tucson: University of Arizona Press, 1995.

————. *Renewing the World: Plains Indian Religion and Morality.* Tucson: University of Arizona Press, 1987.

Hittman, Michael. *Wovoka and the Ghost Dance.* Expanded ed. Lincoln: University of Nebraska Press, 1997.

Hultkrantz, Ake. *Native Religions of North America: The Power of Visions and Fertility.* San Francisco: Harper & Row, 1987.

Loftin, John D. *Religion and Hopi Life in the Twentieth Century.* Bloomington, Ind.: Indiana University Press, 1991.

McLoughlin, William G. *The Cherokee Ghost Dance: Essays on the Southeastern Indians, 1789–1861.* Macon, Ga.: Mercer, 1984.

Mooney, James. *The Ghost-Dance Religion and the Sioux Outbreak of 1890.* Lincoln: University of Nebraska Press, 1991.

Powers, William K. *Oglala Religion.* Lincoln: University of Nebraska Press, 1977.

Stewart, Omer C. *Peyote Religion: A History.* Norman: University of Oklahoma Press, 1987.

Sullivan, Lawrence E., ed. *Native Religions and Cultures of North America.* New York: Continuum, 2000.

Treat, James, ed. *Native and Christian: Indigenous Voices on Religious Identity in the United States and Canada.* New York: Routledge, 1996.

Vecsey, Christopher. *Handbook of American Indian Religious Freedom.* New York: Crossroad, 1991.

Zolbrod, Paul G., trans. *Dine Bahane: The Navajo Creation Story.* Albuquerque: University of New Mexico Press, 1984.

## ◆ SOCIOLOGY

Champagne, Duane. *American Indian Societies: Some Strategies and Conditions of Political and Cultural Survival.* Cambridge, Mass.: Cultural Survival, 1989.

———. *Social Order and Political Change: Constitutional Governments Among the Cherokee, the Choctaw, the Chickasaw, and the Creek.* Stanford, Calif.: Stanford University Press, 1992.

Faiman-Silva, Sandra L. *Choctaws at the Crossroads: The Political Economy of Class and Culture in the Oklahoma Timber Region.* Lincoln: University of Nebraska Press, 1997.

Fixico, Donald L. *The Urban Indian Experience in America.* Albuquerque: University of New Mexico Press, 2000.

Guillemin, Jeanne. *Urban Renegades: The Cultural Strategy of American Indians.* New York: Columbia University Press, 1975.

Kurkiala, Mikael. *Building the Nation Back Up: The Politics of Identity on the Pine Ridge Indian Reservation.* Uppsala: Uppsala University, Department of Cultural Anthropology, 1997.

Ross, Luana. *Inventing the Savage: The Social Construction of Native American Criminality.* Austin: University of Texas Press, 1998.

Sorkin, Alan L. *The Urban American Indian.* Lexington, Mass.: Lexington Books, 1978.

Thornton, Russell. *We Shall Live Again: the 1870 and 1890 Ghost Dance Movements as Demographic Revitalization.* New York: Cambridge University Press, 1986.

Weibel-Orlando, Joan. *Indian Country, L.A.: Maintaining Ethnic Community in Complex Society.* Rev. ed. Urbana: University of Illinois Press, 1999.

White, Richard. *The Roots of Dependency: Subsistence, Environment, and Social Change Among the Choctaws, Pawnees, and Navajos.* Lincoln: University of Nebraska Press, 1983.

## ◆ URBANIZATION

Danziger, Edmund J. *Survival and Regeneration: Detroit's American Indian Community* Detroit: Wayne State University Press, 1991.

Fixico, Donald L. *The Urban Indian Experience in America.* Albuquerque: University of New Mexico Press, 2000.

Guillemin, Jeanne. *Urban Renegades: The Cultural Strategy of American Indians.* New York: Columbia University Press, 1975.

Lobo, Susan, and Kurt Peters. *American Indians and the Urban Experience.* Walnut Creek, Calif.: Altamira Press, 2000.

Neils, Elaine M. *Reservation to City: Indian Migration and Federal Relocation.* Chicago: Dept. of Geography, University of Chicago, 1971.

Sorkin, Alan L. *The Urban American Indian.* Lexington, Mass.: Lexington Books, 1978.

Stanbury, W. T. *Success and Failure: Indians in Urban Society.* Vancouver: University of British Columbia Press, 1975.

Waddell, Jack O. and O. Michael Watson, eds. *The American Indian in Urban Society.* 1971. Reprint. Lanham, Md.: University Press of America, 1984.

Weibel-Orlando, Joan. *Indian Country, L.A.: Maintaining Ethnic Community in Complex Society.* Rev. ed. Urbana: University of Illinois Press, 1999.

### ◆ WOMEN

Albers, Patricia, and Beatrice Medicine. *The Hidden Half: Studies of Plains Indian Women.* Washington, D.C.: University Press of America, 1983.

Allen, Paula Gunn. *The Sacred Hoop: Recovering the Feminine in American Indian Traditions.* Boston: Beacon Press, 1986.

Alvord, Lori Arviso, M.D. *The Scalpel and the Silver Bear.* New York: Bantam-Doubleday Books, 1993.

Bataille, Gretchen M., ed. *Native American Women: A Biographical Dictionary.* New York: Garland, 1993.

Bataille, Gretchen M., and Kathleen Mullen Sands. *American Indian Women, Telling Their Lives.* Lincoln: University of Nebraska Press, 1984.

Benedek, Emily. *Beyond the Four Corners of the World: A Navajo Woman's Journey.* Norman: University of Oklahoma Press, 1998.

Boyer, Ruth McDonald, with Narcissus Duffy Gayton. *Apache Mothers and Daughters: Four Generations of a Family.* Norman: University of Oklahoma Press, 1992.

Green, Rayna. *Native American Women: A Contextual Bibliography.* Bloomington: Indiana University Press, 1984.

Green, Rayna, ed. *That's What She Said: Contemporary Poetry and Fiction by Native American Women.* Bloomington: Indiana University Press, 1984.

Harjo, Joy, and Gloria Bird, eds. *Reinventing the Enemy's Language: Contemporary Native Women's Writings of North America.* New York: W. W. Norton & Company, 1997.

Klein, Laura F., and Lillian A. Ackerman, eds. *Women and Power in Native North America.* Norman: University of Oklahoma Press, 1995.

Landes, Ruth. *The Ojibwa Woman.* 1938. Reprint. Lincoln: University of Nebraska Press, 1997.

Perdue, Theda. *Cherokee Women: Gender and Culture Change, 1700–1835.* Lincoln: University of Nebraska Press, 1998.

Peters, Virginia. *Women of the Earth Lodges: Tribal Life on the Plains.* Norman, Okla.: University of Oklahoma Press, 2000.

Powers, Marla. *Oglala Women: Myth, Ritual, and Reality.* Chicago: University of Chicago Press, 1986.

Schweitzer, Marjorie M., ed. *American Indian Grandmothers: Traditions and Transitions.* Albuquerque: University of New Mexico Press, 1999.

Shoemaker, Nancy, ed. *Negotiators of Change: Historical Perspectives on Native American Women.* New York: Routledge, 1995.

Sonneborn, Liz. *A to Z of Native American Women.* New York, New York: Facts on File, 1998.

Spittal, W. G., ed. *Iroquois Women: An Anthology.* Ohsweken, Ont.: Iroqrafts, 1990.

### ◆ CANADA

Adams, Howard. *Prison of Grass: Canada From a Native Point of View.* Rev. ed. Saskatoon, Sask.: Fifth House, 1989.

Asch, Michael. *Home and Native Land: Aboriginal Rights and the Canadian Constitution.* Toronto and New York: Methuen, 1984; Vancouver: UBC Press, 1993.

Barron, F. Laurie, and James B. Waldram. *1885 and After: Native Society in Transition.* Regina, Sask.: Canadian Plains Research Center, University of Regina, 1986.

Boldt, Menno, and J. Anthony Long, eds., in association with Leroy Little Bear. *The Quest for Justice: Aboriginal Peoples and Aboriginal Rights.* Toronto: University of Toronto Press, 1985.

Brown, Jennifer S.H. *Strangers in Blood: Fur Trade Company Families in Indian Country.* Vancouver: University of British Columbia Press, 1980.

Cairns, Alan C. *Citizens Plus: Aboriginal Peoples and the Canadian State.* Vancouver: UBC Press, 2000.

Canada. Royal Commission on Aboriginal Peoples. *Report of the Royal Commission on Aboriginal Peoples*. 5 vols. Ottawa, 1996.

Carter, Sarah. *Lost Harvests: Prairie Indian Reserve Farmers and Government Policy*. Montreal: McGill-Queen's University Press, 1990.

Castellano, Marlene Brant, Lynne Davis, and Louise Lahache. *Aboriginal Education: Fulfilling the Promise*. Vancouver: UBC Press, 2000.

Clark, Bruce A. *Native Liberty, Crown Sovereignty: The Existing Aboriginal Right of Self-Government in Canada*. Montreal: McGill-Queen's University Press, 1990.

Coates, Ken S., and Robin Fisher, eds. *Out of the Background: Readings on Canadian Native History*. Toronto: Copp Clark, 1996.

Dewdney, Selwyn H. *They Shared to Survive: The Native Peoples of Canada*. Toronto: Macmillian of Canada, 1975.

Dickason, Olive P. *Canada's First Nations: A History of Founding Peoples From Earliest Times*. Norman: University of Oklahoma Press, 1992.

———. *The Myth of the Savage and the Beginnings of French Colonialism in the Americas*. Edmonton, Alta.: University of Alberta Press, 1984.

Frideres, James S., with Lilianne Ernestine Krosenbrink-Gelissen. *Aboriginal Peoples in Canada: Contemporary Conflicts* 5th ed. Scarborough, Ont.: Prentice Hall Allyn and Bacon Canada, 1998.

Getty, Ian A. L., and Antoine S. Lussier, eds. *As Long as the Sun Shines and Water Flows: A Reader in Canadian Native Studies*. Vancouver: University of British Columbia Press, 1983.

Grant, John W. *Moon of Wintertime: Missionaries and the Indians of Canada in Encounter Since 1534*. Toronto: University of Toronto Press, 1984.

Innis, Harold A. *The Fur Trade in Canada: An Introduction to Canadian Economic History*. Rev. ed. Toronto: University of Toronto Press, 1956.

Isaac, Thomas. *Aboriginal Law: Cases, Materials and Commentary*. Saskatoon, Sask.: Purich Pub., 1999.

Jenness, Diamond. *Indians of Canada*. 7th ed. Toronto: University of Toronto Press, 1977.

King, Thomas, ed. *All My Relations: An Anthology of Contemporary Canadian Native Fiction*. Norman: University of Oklahoma Press, 1992.

Krotz, Larry. *Indian Country: Inside Another Canada*. Toronto: McClelland and Stewart, 1990.

Little Bear, Leroy, Menno Boldt, and J. Anthony Long, eds. *Pathways to Self-Determination: Canadian Indians and the Canadian State*. Toronto: University of Toronto Press, 1984.

Long, J. Anthony, Menno Boldt, eds., in association with Leroy Little Bear. *Governments in Conflict? Provinces and Indian Nations in Canada*. Toronto: University of Toronto Press, 1988.

Lowes, Warren. *Indian Giver: A Legacy of North American Native Peoples*. Penticton, B.C.: Theytus Books, 1986.

Manuel, George, and Michael Posluns. *The Fourth World: An Indian Reality*. Toronto: Collier-McMillan Canada; New York: Free Press, 1974.

McMillan, Alan D. *Native Peoples and Cultures of Canada: An Anthropological Overview*. 2nd ed. Vancouver: Douglas & McIntyre, 1995.

Miller, Christine, and Patricia Chuckryk, eds. *Women of the First Nations: Power, Wisdom, and Strength*. Winnipeg, Man.: University of Manitoba Press, 1996.

Miller, David R., et al. *The First Ones: Readings in Indian/Native Studies*. Craven, Sask.: Saskatchewan Indian Federated College Press, 1992.

Miller, James Rodger. *Shingwauk's Vision: A History of Native Residential Schools*. Toronto: University of Toronto Press, 1996.

———. *Skyscrapers Hide the Heavens: A History of Indian-White Relations in Canada*. Toronto: University of Toronto Press, 1989.

———., ed. *Sweet Promises: A Reader on Indian-White Relations in Canada*. Toronto: University of Toronto Press, 1991.

Morrison, R. Bruce, and C. Roderick Wilson, eds. *Native Peoples: The Canadian Experience*. 2d ed. Toronto: McClelland and Stewart, 1995.

Morrisseau, Norval. *Legends of My People: The Great Ojibway.* New York: McGraw-Hill Ryerson Press, 1965.

Pelletier, Wilfred, and Ted Pool. *No Foreign Land: The Biography of a Northern American Indian.* New York: Pantheon Books, 1974.

Perreault, Jeanne, and Sylvia Vance, eds. *Writing the Circle: Native Women of Western Canada: An Anthology.* Norman: University of Oklahoma Press, 1993.

Peterson, Jacqueline, and Jennifer S. H. Brown, eds. *The New Peoples: Being and Becoming Métis in North America.* Lincoln: University of Nebraska Press, 1985.

Price, John A. *Indians of Canada: Cultural Dynamics.* Scarborough, Ont.: Prentice-Hall of Canada, 1979.

Ponting, J. Rick, and Roger Gibbins. *Out of Irrelevance: A Socio-Political Introduction to Indian Affairs in Canada.* Toronto: Butterworths, 1980.

Purich, Donald. *Our Land: Native Rights in Canada.* Toronto: Lorimer, 1986.

Ray, Arthur J. *I Have Lived Here Since The World Began: An Illustrated History of Canada's Native People.* Toronto: Lester Publishing and Key Porter Books, 1996.

———. *Indians in the Fur Trade: Their Role as Hunters, Trappers and Middlemen of the Lands Southwest of Hudson Bay, 1660–1870.* Toronto: University of Toronto Press, 1974.

Redbird, Duke. *We Are Métis: A Métis View of the Development of a Native Canadian People.* Willowdale, Ont.: Ontario Métis & Non Status Indian Association, 1980.

Russell, Daniel. *A People's Dream: Aboriginal Self-Government.* Vancouver: University of British Columbia Press, 2000.

Smith, Donald B. *Sacred Feathers: The Reverend Peter Jones (Kahkewaquonaby) & the Mississauga Indians.* Lincoln: University of Nebraska Press, 1987.

Tennant, Paul. *Aboriginal Peoples and Politics: The Indian Land Question in British Columbia, 1849–1989.* Vancouver: University of British Columbia Press, 1990.

Trigger, Bruce G. *Natives and Newcomers: Canada's "Heroic Age" Reconsidered.* Kingston: McGill-Queen's University Press, 1985.

Waldram, James B., Ann D. Herring, and T. Kue Young. *Aboriginal Health in Canada: Historical, Cultural, and Epidemiological Perspectives.* Toronto: University of Toronto Press, 1995.

Warry, Wayne. *Unfinished Dreams: Community Healing and the Reality of Aboriginal Self-Government.* Toronto: University of Toronto Press, 1998.

Weaver, Sally M. *Making Canadian Indian Policy: The Hidden Agenda 1968–70.* Toronto: University of Toronto Press, 1981.

# Occupation Index

# Subject Index

Personal names, place names, events, organizations, and various subject areas or keywords contained in *The Native North American Almanac, 2nd ed.* are listed in this index with corresponding page numbers indicating text references. Page numbers appearing in boldface indicate a major biographical profile. Page numbers appearing in italics refer to photographs, illustrations, and maps found throughout the *Almanac*.

# F

# G

# J

# O

# Q

# T